CONGRESSIONAL QUARTERLY'S

Guide to the U.S. Supreme Court

Congressional Quarterly Inc.

Congressional Quarterly Inc., an editorial research service and publishing company, serves clients in the fields of news, education, business and government. It combines specific coverage of Congress, government and politics by Congressional Quarterly with the more general subject range of an affiliated service, Editorial Research Reports.

Congressional Quarterly was founded in 1945 by Henrietta and Nelson Poynter. Its basic periodical publication was and still is the CQ *Weekly Report,* mailed to clients every Saturday. A cumulative index is published quarterly.

The CQ *Almanac,* a compendium of legislation for one session of Congress, is published every spring. *Congress and the Nation* is published every four years as a record of government for one presidential term. Congressional Quarterly also publishes paperback books on public affairs.

CQ Direct Research is a consulting service which performs contract research and maintains a reference library and query desk for the convenience of clients.

Editorial Research Reports covers subjects beyond the specialized scope of Congressional Quarterly. It publishes reference material on foreign affairs, business, education, cultural affairs, national security, science and other topics of news interest. Service to clients includes a 6,000-word report four times a month bound and indexed semi-annually. Editorial Research Reports publishes paperback books in its field of coverage. Founded in 1923, the service merged with Congressional Quarterly in 1956.

Copyright 1979 by Congressional Quarterly Inc.
1414 22nd St. N.W., Washington, D.C. 20037

Library of Congress Cataloging in Publication Data

Congressional Quarterly, Inc.
    Congressional Quarterly's Guide to the U.S. Supreme Court.

    Bibliography: p.
    Includes index.
    1. United States. Supreme Court.
I. Title: Guide to the U.S. Supreme Court.
KF8742.C65 1979   347'.73'26   79-20210
ISBN 0-87187-184-X

Contributors to the
Guide to the U.S. Supreme Court

Editor: Elder Witt

Major Contributors: Martha V. Gottron, W. Allan Wilbur

Associate Editors: DuPre Jones, John L. Moore

Editorial Coordinator: Barbara L. Risk

Contributors: Mary Costello, Suzanne de Lesseps, Michael J. Glennon, Warden Moxley, Barbara L. Risk, Park Teter, Warren Weaver.
Linda Cumbo, Edna Frazier, Robert E. Healy, Mary M. Neumann, Laura B. Weiss.

Subject Index: Sharon C. Leuthy

Case Index: Lynda McNeil

Art and Graphics: Richard A. Pottern (Director), Gwendolyn Hammond.

Proofreaders: Eugene J. Gabler, Sari Horwitz, David Long, Jodean Marks, Evan K. Westwood.

Congressional Quarterly Inc.

Executive Editor: Wayne Kelley
Book Department Editor: Patricia Ann O'Connor
General Manager: Paul Massa
Production Manager: I.D. Fuller
Assistant Production Manager: Maceo Mayo

Introduction

The Founding Fathers, greatly influenced by the writings of Locke and Montesquieu, divided governmental powers into three parts. The judicial branch, headed by the Supreme Court, was placed third, and last. As Hamilton wrote in *The Federalist Papers* (No. 78), "The judiciary, from the nature of its functions, will always be the least dangerous to the political rights of the Constitution." But Hamilton also wrote (*Federalist Papers* No. 22) that "Laws are a dead letter without courts to expound and define their true meaning and operation."

Over the years, the United States Supreme Court has played a pivotal role not only in the interpretation of the laws, but also in the development of the country. In the early days, the decisions of the court did much to unify the nation, to assist in its orderly economic growth and to broaden federal powers. One of the most important early decisions was *Marbury v. Madison* (1803), where the court held that it had the power to pass on the constitutionality of laws enacted by Congress, and to hold a statute to be invalid if, in the opinion of the court, Congress was not authorized to enact it. This decision has been fundamental in making the United States subject to "the rule of law." It is a power rarely given to the courts by the constitutions of other countries, and it is the basis for the special role which the Supreme Court plays in the government of the United States.

Congressional Quarterly's *Guide to the U.S. Supreme Court* helps us to a better understanding of the history of the Supreme Court and the importance of its decisions in shaping our system of government.

The Role of the Court

The Supreme Court has played a key role in defining the powers of government. In some cases, as in *Marbury v. Madison* on judicial review, the result reached by the court is not expressed directly in the Constitution, but is said to be a necessary implication from the governmental structure set up by the Constitution. This is true, for example, of decisions involving separation of powers among the three branches of government. It is also true of certain other questions which have been prominent in recent years, such as the power of the president to "withhold" money appropriated by Congress, or the extent of "executive privilege." On other problems, such as the regulation of interstate commerce, the results reached may turn on the interpretation of the power over commerce expressly granted to Congress by the Constitution and on doctrines which the court has found to be necessarily implied from this grant.

In addition to its role in defining the powers of the government, the Supreme Court has also in this century acted as the conscience of the country. Under the original Constitution, and especially in the amendments, it has been assigned vast responsibilities.

Shortly after the Constitution went into force in 1789, ten amendments were adopted, effective in 1791, and these are known collectively as the Bill of Rights. These include the First Amendment, guaranteeing freedom of speech and of the press; the Fourth Amendment, providing safeguards against unreasonable searches and seizures; the Fifth Amendment, providing that no person shall be deprived of life, liberty, or property without due process of law; and the Sixth Amendment, providing for a speedy and public trial of criminal cases by jury, and that the accused shall have compulsory process for obtaining witnesses and the assistance of counsel for his defense. These amendments applied to the federal government only, but they were supplemented after the Civil War by the Fourteenth Amendment, which provides that no state shall "deprive any person of life, liberty, or property, without due process of law; nor deny to any person within its jurisdiction the equal protection of the law." In recent years, the court has held that this guarantee makes most of the provisions of the original Bill of Rights applicable to the states.

Some of these provisions in the amendments are quite general, and leave considerable room for construction by the Supreme Court. In considering the decisions interpreting them, it is necessary to pay close attention to the facts of the cases in which the questions have arisen, and to consider very carefully the reasoning which the court has adopted in reaching its conclusions.

These aspects of the court's role in American life are important not only to lawyers, but to all students of government and to citizens generally. In the past, Congressional Quarterly has performed an important public service in providing its *Guide to U.S. Elections* and its *Guide to Congress.* Now this *Guide to the U.S. Supreme Court* is being added to the series. This will be a very useful volume for teachers, students, lawyers, journalists, for here can be found much of the material necessary for an understanding of the role of the court and the impact of its decisions over the years.

The work of the court is best comprehended through a careful examination of its decisions. This book will be a great aid in that task. *McCulloch v. Maryland, Gibbons v. Ogden, Dred Scott v. Sandford, The Slaughterhouse Cases, Pollock v. Farmers' Loan & Trust Co., Plessy v. Ferguson, Ashwander v. Tennessee Valley Authority, Brown v. Board of Education of Topeka,* The Pentagon Papers case *(New York Times v. United States), United States v. Nixon,* and many more, are all here, clearly discussed and analyzed in non-technical terms.

The Justices

This volume also provides valuable background material on the operations and traditions of the court, as well as biographical information on the 101 men who have served on the court. To many the Supreme Court is remote and impersonal. No one votes for Supreme Court justices, and they rarely make speeches. They are not seen about the country for they do their work in a marble building in Washington where they are virtually inaccessible. Yet, as Anthony Lewis has written, "The court is the least abstract of institutions. It is nine men, nine very human men, participating in a process that can be impressive or disturbing, grave or funny. And contrary to the general impression, the process is more visible than most of what goes on in government."

The Supreme Court sits and works in its own building in Washington, across the plaza from the Capitol. Over the portal of the building, the legend "Equal Justice Under Law" is carved into the pediment, and in many eyes this is in effect the motto of the court. With minimum aid, the justices "do their own work," and accept direct responsibility for what they do. Despite the pressures of their task, the court is not a bureaucracy, and we may fervently hope that it stays that way.

In the course of history, the court has been thrown into the center of many highly controversial questions and has been the subject of complaint and even of denunciation. As Justice Holmes once said: "We are quiet here, but it is the quiet of a storm center." The court has never shirked its duty, or failed to exercise conscientiously the great powers which have been entrusted to it under the Constitution. It deserves to be understood, and we are all greatly indebted to the publishers of Congressional Quarterly for providing this *Guide to the U.S. Supreme Court* and its work.

Erwin N. Griswold
Washington, D.C.
August 1979

Editor's Note

In his introduction to this volume, Dean Erwin Griswold has highlighted the importance of the U.S. Supreme Court and the need for increased understanding of the court as an institution and as a vital force shaping life in the United States.

This note offers suggestions to readers and users of the *Guide to the U.S. Supreme Court* to facilitate their locating material of interest to them. It also identifies the persons responsible for writing the various portions of the *Guide*.

Research Aids

There are three primary research aids in the *Guide* — the Table of Contents, the Subject Index and the Case Index.

The Summary Table of Contents offers, at a glance, an overall view of the organization of the *Guide*. The Detailed Table of Contents provides a closer look at the organization of each major portion of the volume.

The Subject Index pinpoints references to the particular subjects and persons mentioned throughout the book. The Case Index pinpoints references to the hundreds of Supreme Court cases and decisions described and analyzed in various chapters of the *Guide*.

The Organization of the *Guide*

Part I, Origins and Development of the Court, traces the growth of the Supreme Court from an idea into the world's most powerful judicial institution. It takes the court from its beginnings in the discussions of the Constitutional Convention in 1789 to the decisions of 1979.

Part II, The Court and the Federal System, analyzes the impact which the court's decisions have had upon the U.S. system of government. It consists of four chapters — The Court and the Powers of Congress, The Court and the Powers of the President, The Court and Judicial Power, The Court and the States.

Part III, The Court and the Individual, examines the effect of the court's rulings on the rights and freedoms of the individual. Its five sections include an Introduction; Freedom for Ideas, focusing on the freedoms guaranteed by the First Amendment; The Rights of Political Participation, concerned with the court's rulings defining voting rights and the freedom of political association; Due Process and Individual Rights, which traces the use of the concept of due process to guarantee a widening category of rights to the individual; and Equal Rights, a look at the court's use of the equal protection guarantee to move the nation toward the goal of equal opportunity.

Part IV, Pressures on the Court, analyzes some of the factors influencing the work of the Supreme Court — congressional pressure, presidential pressure, public opinion, and the press.

Part V, The Court At Work, examines the operations of the court, past and present, its traditions, its personnel, and its meeting places through history.

Part VI, Members of the Court, surveys the characteristics of the select group of 101 men who have served the nation as Supreme Court justices. This part also includes brief biographies outlining the personal background and public career of each of these men — from John Jay to John Paul Stevens.

Part VII, Major Decisions of the Court, consists of capsule summaries of the court's major decisions from 1790 to the summer of 1979. These summaries provide the case name, citation, date announced, vote, author of the major opinion, dissenters and a summary statement of the significance of the ruling.

The Appendix includes a variety of documents important to those interested in the history of the court — from the Constitution, through the various major judiciary acts, to the court-packing proposals of 1937, to the present.

In addition, each major chapter is followed by footnotes indicating the Supreme Court cases cited and the sources used throughout the chapter. At the end of each chapter is a selected bibliography.

The Writers

Martha V. Gottron wrote the chapters of the *Guide* on The Court and the Powers of Congress, Freedom for Ideas, Equal Rights, and Congressional Pressure.

W. Allan Wilbur wrote the chapters on The Court and the Powers of the President, The Rights of Political Participation, Due Process and Individual Rights, and Presidential Pressure.

Elder Witt wrote the chapters on Origins and Development of the Court, The Court and Judicial Power, The Court and the States, and the Introduction to The Court and the Individual.

Warren Weaver wrote the chapter on The Court and the Press.

Park Teter wrote the chapter on Public Opinion.

Mary Costello wrote the chapter on The Court At Work.

Warden Moxley wrote the introductory section to Members of the Court, as well as a number of the individual biographies. In addition, biographies were written by Suzanne de Lesseps, Michael Glennon, and Barbara Risk.

The chapter entitled Major Decisions was written by Martha V. Gottron, W. Allan Wilbur and Elder Witt.

Barbara Risk served as editorial coordinator of the *Guide to the U.S. Supreme Court.*

Elder Witt
Editor

Summary Table of Contents

Introduction vii

Editor's Note ix

**Part I. Origins and Development
of the Court** 1

**Part II. The Court and the
Federal System** 59

**Part III. The Court and the
Individual** 369

Part IV. Pressures on the Court 649

Part V. The Court at Work 727

Part VI. Members of the Court 779

Part VII. Major Decisions of the Court 867

Appendix 911

Subject Index 989

Case Index 1009

Table of Contents

Introduction vii
Editor's Note ix

Part I
Origins and Development of the Court

Introduction 5
The Origins of Power 6
A Slow Start: 1790-1800 8
Establishment of Power: 1801-1835 10
State Power and Slavery: 1836-1860 18
War and Recovery: 1861-1872 23
The Balance of Power: 1873-1888 26
The Conservative Court: 1889-1919 31
New Times, Old Court: 1920-1937 38
The Court and Rights of Persons: 1938-1969 45
The Contemporary Court 54

Part II
The Court and the Federal System

The Court and the Powers of Congress

Introduction 65
    The Commerce Power 66
    Fiscal and Monetary Powers 67
    Foreign Affairs 67
    States, Territories and Citizens 67
    Amending Power 68
    Investigations and Internal Affairs 68

Judicial Review and Legislative Power 69

Marbury v. Madison 69
Implied Powers.. 73
Inherent Powers... 74
Delegation of Power 75

The Power to Regulate Commerce 81

Congress, Commerce and the Railroads 87
Congress and Antitrust Law................................. 90
A Federal Police Power..................................... 95
New Deal and the Commerce Power.......................... 97

Fiscal and Monetary Powers................................. 109

Direct Taxes.. 109
Uniformity 112
Taxing as Police Power 112
Federal-State Tax Immunities................................ 116
The Power to Spend 116
Spending for the General Welfare 117
The Currency Powers 118

The Power Over Foreign Affairs 125

The War Power... 125
Raising Armies 128
Wartime Legislation 128
Postwar Legislation... 130
Treaty Powers 130
Other Foreign Policy Powers 131

The Power to Admit States, Govern
Territories and Grant Citizenship 133

New States... 133
The Power to Govern the Territories 135
The Power Over Citizenship and Naturalization 142

The Power to Amend the Constitution 149

The Amending Power 149
Enforcement Power 151
Modern Enforcement 151

Miscellaneous Powers 155

Bankruptcy... 155
Patents and Copyrights 155
Postal Power 155
District of Columbia 156

The Power to Investigate 157

The Contempt Power 158
Judicial Review 159
Witness Rights... 160
The Fifth Amendment 163
Investigating Elections 164

The Power Over Internal Affairs 165
  Qualifications 165
  Power to Punish Members............................ 166
  Congressional Immunity 167
  Elections Regulation................................. 171
  Election Returns 173
  Lobby Regulation 174
  Rules.. 175
Selected Bibliography 176

The Court and the Powers of the President

Introduction 181
The Commander in Chief 185
  President Lincoln and the Civil War.................... 187
  President Wilson and World War 190
  President Roosevelt and Total War.................... 190
  Postwar Powers..................................... 193
  China, Cuba and Vietnam 194
  The Court's Role 196
The Architect of Foreign Policy 199
  The Treaty Power: Its Effect and Its Limits 202
  The Use of Executive Agreements..................... 204
The President as Executive 209
  The Power of Appointment 209
  The Removal Power.................................. 211
  Executive Discretion................................. 216
  Delegation of Power 216
  Executives and Emergencies 217
The Power to Veto and to Pardon 221
  The Veto Power 221
  The Pocket Veto..................................... 222
  The Power to Grant Pardons and Reprieves........... 224
Privilege and Immunity................................. 229
  Executive Immunity 229
  Executive Privilege 230
  Modern Privilege 232
Confrontation: The President v. The Court............. 235
  Jefferson v. Marshall 235
  Jackson, the Court and the Indians 238
  Lincoln v. Taney..................................... 238
  The Court and the Roosevelt Revolution 240
  Truman v. the Court 244
  Nixon, Watergate and the Court...................... 245
Selected Bibliography 250

The Court and Judicial Power

Introduction 255
Federal Jurisdiction 256
  The Constitutional Possibility 256
  The Political Reality 256
  Federal Questions 257
  Admiralty and Maritime Law 257
  A Question of Party 258
  Supreme Court Jurisdiction 260

Federal Judicial Power 267
  Judicial Review 267
  The Power to Issue Writs 271
  The Contempt Power 279

Judicial Restraint 287
  Cases and Controversies 287
  'Standing to Sue' 291
  Political Questions 292
  The Role of Precedent 294
  The Demands of Comity 294
Selected Bibliography 296

The Court and the States

Introduction 299
Judicial Review and the States 303
  Sources of Power 303
  Challenge to Power 305
  Repeal and Resistance 307
  Taxes, Slaves and War 307

The States and the Economy 309
  The Obligation of Contracts 309
  The Control of Commerce 315
  The Police Power 322
  The Taxing of Commerce 328

The State and the Individual 337
  The Constitution 337
  The Civil War Amendments 338
  The Guarantee of Due Process 342
  The Quiet Revolution 343
  The Guarantee of Equal Protection 347

The State as Sovereign 353
  Reserved State Powers 353
  Liability to Lawsuits 354
  Political Powers 356

The Taxing Power.. 357
The Police Power 358
The Judicial Power.. 360
The Power to Govern 363

Interstate Relations.. 365
Selected Bibliography 368

Part III
The Court and the Individual

Introduction 373
A Narrow Base: 1789-1865 373
The Civil War Amendments................................... 375
Broadening Protection: 1925-1938........................... 378
Freedom for Ideas 378
Political Rights.. 380
Equality Before the Law 381
Fundamental Fairness.. 382

Freedom for Ideas

Freedom of Expression 387
The First Amendment 387
Government Restraints 389
The Task of Balancing 390
The Standards 394

Freedom of Speech... 395
Seditious Speech and the Safety of the State 396
Public Speech and Public Safety 406

Freedom of the Press...................................... 423
Prior Restraint: Censorship................................... 424
Subsequent Punishment: Libel................................ 433
Free Press v. Fair Trial....................................... 440
Access and Confidentiality 443

Freedom of Religion 451
Free Exercise of Religion 452
Establishment of Religion 461
Selected Bibliography 471

The Rights of Political Participation

Introduction 475
The Right to Vote 477
The Right and the Power: A Narrow View 477
The Pattern of Exclusion..................................... 479
The Right and the Power: A Broad View 484

The Right to an Equal Vote 489
    Baker v. Carr. 490
    Congressional Districts: Strict Equality 494
    State Legislative Districts: More Leeway 495

Freedom of Political Association 499
    Communism and Cold War 501
    Political Association in the 1970s...................... 516
Selected Bibliography 520

Due Process and Individual Rights

Introduction 523
    Due Process: Early Views 524
    A Fair Trial.. 529

Search and Seizure 539
    The Neutral Magistrate 539
    Probable Cause..................................... 540
    Search with Consent 540
    Property, Papers and Effects.......................... 541
    Arrests and Searches 544
    Automobile Searches................................ 547
    Electronic Eavesdropping 547

Self-Incrimination. 555
    Privilege and Immunity.............................. 555
    The States and Self-Incrimination 557
    Coerced Confessions................................. 558
    Confessions and Counsel 560

The Aid of Legal Counsel 565
    A Fundamental Right................................ 565
    The Federal Rule 566
    The Appointment of Counsel 566
    The 'Adequate Protective Device'...................... 567
    The 'Critical Stage'................................. 568
    'Effective' Aid 569

Double Jeopardy 571
    Dual Sovereigns 571
    Appeal and Retrial.................................. 571
    States and Double Jeopardy.......................... 572
    Appeal and Resentencing............................. 572
    Acquittals and Appeals 573

Cruel and Unusual Punishment 575
    Too Severe A Penalty 575
    Death, Drugs and the States.......................... 575
    Capital Punishment 576
Selected Bibliography 580

Equal Rights

Introduction 583
   The Measure of Discrimination 583
   Traditional Standard 583
   Modern Standard 584
   Suspect Categories 584
   Fundamental Interests 585

Racial Equality 587
   Equal Educational Opportunity 590
   Travel and Public Accommodations 607
   The Right to Fair Housing 613
   Equality of Employment Opportunity 618

Aliens and Equal Protection 625
   Early Victories 625
   Period of Exceptions 625
   A Closer Scrutiny 626
   The Modern Standard 627
   Aliens and the Federal Government 628

Sex Discrimination and Legal Equality 631
   Early Paternalism 631
   Reassessment 632
   The Search for a Standard 632
   Job Discrimination 635
   Pension Contributions 638

Poverty and Equal Protection 641
   Access to Justice 641
   The Right to Travel 642
   Political Rights 643
   Education and Wealth 643
Selected Bibliography 646

Part IV
Pressures on the Court

Congressional Pressure

Introduction 653
Individual Pressures 655
   Selection 655
   Rejections 655
   Controversial Confirmations 657
   Removal from Office 658
   Impeachment 658
   Salaries 663

Institutional and Procedural Pressures 664

  Size of the Court 664

  Extraordinary Majority 665

  Terms 665

  Removal of Jurisdiction 666

  The McCardle Case 667

  Recent Repeal Efforts 669

Reversals of Rulings 672

  Constitutional Amendments 673

  Legislative Reversals 676

  Recent Reversals 677

Selected Bibliography 680

Presidential Pressure

Introduction 683

Politics and Appointments 687

The Court as a Campaign Issue 692

Selected Bibliography 694

Public Opinion

Introduction 695

Foundations of Independence 696

Intangible Influences 697

The Court and Change 697

Race Relations 699

Response to Crisis 701

Selected Bibliography 703

The Court and the Press

Introduction 705

Early Years: 1790-1850 706

Middle Years: 1850-1900 710

20th Century: 1900-1950 714

The Modern Era: 1950-1979 717

Covering the High Court 721

Selected Bibliography 725

Part V
The Court at Work

Operations of the Court 732

  Schedule of the Term 732

  Decision Days 734

  Reviewing Cases 734

Arguments 735
Conferences 739
Opinions 739
Issuing the Opinion 742
Reporting of Decisions 743

Traditions of the Court 744
Secrecy 744
Courtesy 745
Seniority 746
Continuity 746

The Chief Justice 748
First Among Equals 748
Head of the Judicial System 751
Extra-Judicial Roles 751
Perquisites 752

The Justices 753
A Judicial Family 753
Retirement 755
Impeachment Attempts 756
Extra-Judicial Activities 756
Perquisites 758

Supporting Personnel 759
Solicitor General 759
Clerk of the Court 759
Marshal of the Court 761
Reporter of Decisions 762
Supreme Court Bar 763
Press Officer 764
Librarian 764
Law Clerks 765
Messengers 766

Supporting Organizations 767
U.S. Judicial Conference 767
Administrative Office 767
Federal Judicial Center 767
Historical Society 768

Housing the Court 769
Early Days 769
Courtrooms in the Capitol 769
New Court Building 771

Cost of the Court 773
Salaries of the Justices 773
Retirement System 774

Selected Bibliography 776

Part VI
Members of the Court

Overview 783
Biographies 793

Part VII
Major Decisions of the Court

Introduction 871
Decision Summaries 872

Appendix

Declaration of Independence 913
Articles of Confederation 914
The Constitution 918
Acts of Congress Held Unconstitutional 926
Rules of the Supreme Court 932
Supreme Court Nominations 946
Judiciary Act of 1789 949
Circuit Court of Appeals Act of 1891 957
Judiciary Act of 1925 960
Roosevelt's 1937 Court Reform Plan 964
Fortas' Letter Explaining Resignation 983
Glossary of Legal Terms 984

Indexes

Subject Index 989
Case Index 1009

Photographs

Most of the photographs appearing in the *Guide to the U.S. Supreme Court* were obtained from the collection of the Library of Congress, including the photographs of the individual members of the court, the group pictures of the justices, the meeting places of the court and the lithograph on page 869.

The Architect of the Capitol provided the photographs of the aerial view of the court building, page ii; the Supreme Court chamber, page 3; the west front of the Supreme Court, page 61; and the justices' bench, page 781.

The photograph of the facade of the Supreme Court building on page 371 was taken by Dan De Vay; the photograph of the statue in front of the court, page 651, by Laura B. Weiss; and the court building, page 770, by Steven Karafyllakis.

Ankers Capitol Photographers provided the photograph of the court in 1954, page 51; United Press International, the photograph of the Supreme Court building at night, page 729; and Wide World Photos Inc., the Abe Fortas photograph, page 862.

PART I

ORIGINS AND DEVELOPMENT OF THE COURT

Introduction 5

The Origins of Power 6

A Slow Start: 1790-1800 8

Establishment of Power: 1801-1835 10

State Power and Slavery: 1836-1860 18

War and Recovery: 1861-1872 23

The Balance of Power: 1873-1888 26

The Conservative Court: 1889-1919 31

New Times, Old Court: 1920-1937 38

The Court and Rights of Persons: 1938-1969 45

The Contemporary Court 54

View of the Supreme Court Chamber.
Architect of the Capitol Photo No. 35570.

Origins and Development Of the U.S. Supreme Court

"We must never forget that it is a constitution we are expounding," Chief Justice John Marshall admonished his fellow justices in 1819. [1]

To modern ears, Marshall's words may seem a truism, yet they state with clarity the reason that the Supreme Court plays such an important role in shaping life and government in the United States.

The role of the court has been unique, a direct outgrowth of the new meaning that the word "constitution" assumed in the American experiment.

In 1789 every government and every society could be said to have some constitution. The word simply was used to refer to whatever principles and assumptions underlay the existing system.

But in the United States the word was invested with new significance. "A Constitution, in the American sense of the word," Justice Samuel Miller would write a century after its adoption, "is a written instrument by which the fundamental powers of the government are established, limited, and defined, and by which these powers are distributed among several departments, for their more safe and useful exercise for the benefit of the body politic."

Miller continued: In the Constitution of the United States "the people themselves have undertaken to frame an organic law governing the relations of the whole people, as well as of the individual states, to the federal government, and to prescribe in many cases the limits and rules of private and personal rights. It is the fundamental law pursuant to which the government is permanently organized and conducted." [2]

In the United States, then, the Constitution was far more than a passive description of the existing system. It was an active instrument, the charter of a new national system, the source of power and of the limits of power.

But the Constitution of the United States of America was hardly self-enforcing. As Chief Justice Marshall wrote:

> A constitution, to contain an accurate detail of all the subdivisions of which its great powers will admit, and of all the means by which they may be carried into execution, would partake of a prolixity of a legal code. . . . It would probably never be understood by the public. Its nature, therefore, requires, that only its great outlines should be marked, its important objects designated, and the minor ingredients which compose those objects be deduced from the nature of the objects themselves. [3]

The question was obvious. Who would undertake these all-important deductions? Who would enforce the limits the Constitution set upon the powers of Congress, the president, the states? Who would fill in the broad outlines of the powers it granted? Who would ensure its continuing validity as circumstances changed?

The answer was not long — if ever — in doubt. The Supreme Court would serve this function, declared Marshall in the 1803 ruling in *Marbury v. Madison* — and that point has been underscored in almost every ensuing constitutional decision by the court. The "weakest branch" of the new system — six men — would undertake this critical responsibility; the court would become "the particular guardian of the terms of the written constitution." [4]

In the 190 years of its history, the Supreme Court — by virtue of this responsibility — has become the most powerful court the world has ever known.

It can override the will of the majority expressed in an act of Congress. It can forcefully remind a president that in this nation all persons are subject to the rule of law. It can require the redistribution of political power in every state of the Union. And it can persuade the nation's citizens that the fabric of their society must be rewoven into new patterns.

There have been mistakes and contradictions along the way; several constitutional amendments bear witness to the most notable of these. Constitutional development in the United States follows no tidy pattern. The court does not initiate cases, solicit issues, nor arrange the order in which it deals with them. It must take them as they come. And when it decides the cases before it, it often seems tentative and hesitant, zigging and zagging from case to case within a particular issue.

The pattern is not neat, but it is quintessentially human. For all the remoteness of the black-robed justices working in isolation within marble chambers, the court is the most human of government institutions.

Issues come to the court only when individuals disagree upon them. Black and white, merchant and consumer, prisoner and warden, president and pauper — they come before the court to seek resolution of their disputes.

The men before whom their case is made are neither monks nor oracles. They respond to the same concerns and influences as their fellow citizens. They hear the arguments, then they meet, talk, and vote. The court has decided. The justices write, comment, edit. The opinions are signed. The decision is announced. The dispute is resolved — and the role of the court in the continuing development of the American system is once again affirmed.

The court is the nation's balance wheel. As Justice Robert H. Jackson explained in 1954:

> In a society in which rapid changes tend to upset all equilibrium, the court, without exceeding its own limited powers, must strive to maintain the great system of balances upon which our free government is based. Whether these balances and checks are essential to liberty elsewhere in the world is beside the point; they are indispensable to the society we know. Chief of these balances are: first, between the Executive and Congress; second, between the central government and the States; third, between state and state; fourth, between authority, be it state or national, and the liberty of the citizen, or between the rule of the majority and the rights of the individual. [5]

This is the story of the court and those balances.

The Origins of Power

In contrast to Articles I and II of the Constitution, which set out in considerable length and detail the powers and prerogatives of Congress and the executive, Article III is brief, simply sketching the outline of a federal judiciary.

One scholar, Julius Goebel Jr., suggests that "to some delegates, provision for a national judiciary was a matter of theoretical compulsion rather than of practical necessity ... more in deference to the maxim of separation [of powers] than in response to clearly formulated ideas about the role of a national judicial system and its indispensability." [6]

At any rate, with little discussion and less debate, the Constitutional Convention approved language that simply declared in Article III:

> The judicial Power of the United States, shall be vested in one supreme Court, and in such inferior Courts as the Congress may from time to time ordain and establish.

Section 1 of the article goes on to state that the judges of these courts will hold their posts during good behavior, and that their salaries may not be diminished during their terms in office.

Article II already had provided that the members of the Supreme Court would be appointed by the president by and with the advice and consent of the Senate — and that judges, along with all other civil officers of the new national government, "shall be removed from office on Impeachment for, and Conviction of, Treason, Bribery, or other high Crimes and Misdemeanors."

Section 2 of Article III describes the reach of the judicial power. It includes some cases because of their subject — "all Cases, in Law and Equity, arising under this Constitution, the Laws of the United States, and Treaties made, or which shall be made, under their Authority ... all Cases of admiralty and maritime Jurisdiction...." And federal judicial power reaches other cases because of the parties involved — "all Cases affecting Ambassadors, other public Ministers and Consuls; ... Controversies to which the United States shall be a Party; ... Controversies between two or more States...."

The Supreme Court would have original jurisdiction — the power to hear the initial arguments — in cases involving foreign dignitaries and those involving states. In all other types of cases, the Supreme Court's jurisdiction was to be appellate — it would only hear appeals from the rulings of lower courts.

There ended the Constitution's description of the nation's judicial branch. The remaining sections of Article III deal with jury trials, the place of trials, and the crime of treason.

The brevity of the constitutional description left to Congress and the court itself the task of filling in much of the substance and all of the details of the new judicial system. One early observer commented, "the convention has only crayoned in the outlines. It is left to Congress to fill up and colour the canvas." [7]

An Independent Branch

Although the Articles of Confederation had not provided for a system of national courts, the concept of a separate and relatively independent judiciary was generally accepted by the delegates to the Constitutional Convention. At the time of the adoption of Article III by the convention, six of the original 13 states had such judicial branches. [8]

There was some debate in the convention over the need for any inferior federal courts. Some delegates argued that state courts were adequate to handle all judicial business other than that which the Supreme Court would consider. That debate was resolved by leaving the final decision on the creation of lower federal courts to Congress.

There also was disagreement over whether Congress or the president should appoint the members of the Supreme Court — and whether the court should try impeachments. A compromise resulted in giving the President the power to name the court's members with the advice and consent of the Senate — and in granting the Senate the power to try impeachments.

To safeguard the independence of the judges, the "good behavior" and salary provisions were added. Alexander Hamilton wrote in *The Federalist Papers*:

> The standard of good behavior for the continuance in office of the judicial magistracy is certainly one of the most valuable of the modern improvements in the practice of government. In a monarchy it is an excellent barrier to the despotism of the prince; in a republic it is a no less excellent barrier to the encroach-

ments and oppressions of the representative body. And it is the best expedient which can be devised in any government to secure a steady, upright, and impartial administration of the laws. [9]

The provision for impeachment of judges would, on the other hand, wrote Hamilton, ensure the responsible conduct of their duties. [10]

Federal Supremacy

Neither the separateness nor the independence of the Supreme Court is truly unique. The most notable and peculiar of its characteristics is its power to review and nullify state and federal laws that collide with the Constitution.

This role was made necessary by the convention's adoption, in Article VI, of the declaration that:

> This Constitution, and the Laws of the United States which shall be made in Pursuance thereof; and all Treaties made, or which shall be made, under the Authority of the United States, shall be the supreme Law of the Land; and the Judges in every State shall be bound thereby, any Thing in the Constitution or Laws of any State to the Contrary notwithstanding.

Article VI went on to state that all officials of the national and state governments were to take an oath to support the Constitution. Left unsaid — again — was who would enforce the provisions and prescriptions of the Constitution if some officials chose to ignore that oath.

Insofar as the supremacy of federal authority over state actions was concerned, that omission was remedied by the Judiciary Act of 1789, enacted by the First Congress. That statute gave the Supreme Court the power to review, and affirm or reverse, rulings where state courts rejected claims that state laws or actions conflicted with the U.S. Constitution, federal laws or treaties. It also specified that the Supreme Court would consist of a Chief Justice and five associate justices, meeting twice each year, in February and in August.

This provision for judicial review of state rulings was the famous Section 25 of the Judiciary Act, the subject of much criticism and many repeal efforts over the next three decades.

Judicial Review and Acts of Congress

Congress never granted the Supreme Court parallel authority to review acts of Congress for their constitutionality. And the Constitution itself is silent on whether the court can nullify an act of Congress.

In 1803 the court simply claimed this role for itself. Asserting the power for the first time, the court in the case of *Marbury v. Madison* struck down a portion of the same Judiciary Act that had granted it the power to review state court rulings. The offending section, wrote Chief Justice John Marshall, purported to enlarge the original jurisdiction of the court — and that Congress had no power to do.

Marbury v. Madison sparked a long scholarly debate over whether the Supreme Court was undertaking a role the Framers intended it to fill or was usurping more power than it had been intended to possess. Despite its sporadic intensity, the debate is irrelevant. The court's power to review the acts of Congress is firmly established in practice and has never been seriously challenged.

> *". . . Where the will of the legislature . . . stands in opposition to that of the people, declared in the Constitution, the judges ought to be governed by the latter. . . ."*
> —Alexander Hamilton,
> *The Federalist Papers*

Most scholars view this role as envisioned by the members of the Constitutional Convention. They point to various comments during the convention debates — and during the ratification conventions in the states — as indicating that many members of the convention simply assumed that the Supreme Court would exercise this power.

Most enduring of the arguments of this early period are those set out by Alexander Hamilton in *The Federalist Papers*. Hamilton reasoned that this function of the court was essential to the existence of a limited constitutional government. The federal courts, he said, would serve as "bulwarks of a limited Constitution. [11]

After his often-quoted description of the judicial branch as "incontestably . . . beyond comparison the weakest of the three departments of power," Hamilton continued:

> The complete independence of the courts of justice is peculiarly essential in a limited Constitution. By a limited Constitution, I understand one which contains certain specified exceptions to the legislative authority; such, for instance, as that it shall pass no bills of attainder, no *ex post facto* laws, and the like. Limitations of this kind can be preserved in practice no other way than through the medium of courts of justice, whose duty it must be to declare all acts contrary to the manifest tenor of the Constitution void. Without this, all the reservations of particular rights or privileges would amount to nothing. [12]

Hamilton rejected the counter-argument that to allow the court to declare acts of Congress invalid would elevate the "weakest branch" to a position superior to that of Congress:

> . . . every act of a delegated authority, contrary to the tenor of the commission under which it is exercised, is void. No legislative act, therefore, contrary to the Constitution, can be valid. To deny this would be to affirm . . . that the representatives of the people are superior to the people themselves; that men acting by virtue of powers may do not only what their powers do not authorize, but what they forbid. . . .
>
> . . . the courts were designed to be an intermediate body between the people and the legislature in order, among other things, to keep the latter within the limits assigned to their authority. The interpretation of the laws is the proper and peculiar province of the courts. A constitution is, in fact, and must be regarded by the judges as, a fundamental law. It therefore belongs to them to ascertain its meaning as well as the meaning of

any particular act proceeding from the legislative body. If there should happen to be an irreconcilable variance between the two, that which has the superior obligation and validity ought, of course, to be preferred; or, in other words, the Constitution ought to be preferred to the statute, the intention of the people to the intention of their agents.

Nor does this conclusion by any means suppose a superiority of the judicial to the legislative power. It only supposes that the power of the people is superior to both, and that where the will of the legislature, declared in its statutes, stands in opposition to that of the people, declared in the Constitution, the judges ought to be governed by the latter. . . .[13]

A Slow Start: 1790-1800

On Sept. 24, 1789, President George Washington signed the Judiciary Act into law — and sent to the Senate his nominations for the first members of the Supreme Court.

One of the men so honored declined so that he could accept a state position; another accepted but never attended a formal session of the court; and John Jay, the first Chief Justice, would spend much of his tenure abroad, engaged in diplomatic duties, and would resign after six years to become governor of New York.

The First Justices

Washington's original selections — all of whom were active in the founding of the new government — were:

● Chief Justice John Jay, 44, of New York, co-author with Hamilton and James Madison of *The Federalist Papers*.

● John Rutledge of South Carolina, 50, a member of the Constitutional Convention.

● Robert Hanson Harrison of Maryland, 44, who declined the post to accept that of chancellor of Maryland.

● John Blair of Virginia, 57, a member of the Constitutional Convention and a leader in the effort to obtain Virginia's ratification of the new national charter.

● James Wilson of Pennsylvania, 47, signer of the Declaration of Independence, member of the Constitutional Convention, and a leader in obtaining ratification of the new charter by his state.

● William Cushing, of Massachusetts, 57, a state judge and leader of the state ratification effort.

After Hanson's refusal, Washington selected James Iredell of North Carolina, 38, for the fifth associate justice's seat. Iredell had led the initially unsuccessful effort to win North Carolina's vote in favor of the new Constitution.

Confirmation of the first set of nominees came within two days, on Sept. 26. Iredell was nominated early the next year, on Feb. 9, 1790, and confirmed Feb. 10.

The tenure of these original members, with the exception of Cushing, was brief. Jay resigned in 1795. Two other men would follow him as Chief Justice within the court's first decade.

Rutledge resigned in 1791, never having attended a formal session of the full court. Blair, after several years of irregular attendance, resigned because of his poor health in 1796. Wilson died in 1798. Iredell, the only member of the first court to move his family to the new nation's capital, New York, resigned in 1799.[14]

Cushing alone would serve into the 19th century, remaining on the court for 21 years until his death in 1810.

The First Terms

"The status of the federal judiciary in the 1790s," wrote Robert G. McCloskey, "was ambiguous and . . . comparatively minor. . . . The paramount governmental tasks were legislative and executive."[15]

The record of the Supreme Court's first decade bears out that statement.

Only three of the six justices were present for the court's opening session on Feb. 1, 1790. Jay, Wilson and Cushing, wearing robes and, at least in Cushing's case, a wig, met briefly in the Royal Exchange Building in New York.

By Feb. 2 Blair had arrived, making the quorum needed for transaction of business. But there was no business, aside from organizational matters, chief among which was the appointment of a clerk. After several days of admitting attorneys to practice before it, the court adjourned its first term on Feb. 10, 1790.

The second term lasted two days — Aug. 2-3, 1790. Iredell, confirmed in February, was present.

In 1791 the capital and the court moved to Philadelphia where the court shared, with the mayor's court, a room in the new City Hall. No cases were decided by the court in 1791 or 1792.

The court met in Philadelphia until 1800. Three times — in 1793, 1794 and 1797 — the court was forced by epidemics of yellow fever to cancel its August term.[16]

In 1791 Justice Rutledge resigned to take a state judgeship. Two of the men offered his seat declined, preferring to retain their seats in state legislatures.[17] President Washington then selected Thomas Johnson of Maryland, at 59, one of the court's oldest members. Johnson would hold the seat only 14 months.

In 1792 Chief Justice Jay conducted an unsuccessful passive campaign from the bench for the post of governor of New York. At that point he described the post of a Supreme Court justice as "intolerable."[18]

The First Major Decision

On Feb. 18, 1793, the court announced its decision in the case of *Chisholm v. Georgia*, its first major ruling. Within five years, the ruling was overturned by adoption of a constitutional amendment.

Reading the language of Article III literally, the court upheld the right of citizens of one state, South Carolina, to bring original suits in the Supreme Court against another state, Georgia. The vote of the court was 5-1. Iredell dissented. Each of the justices announced his opinion orally.

The states were shocked by the ruling, seeing in it the potential for their economic ruin. Early in 1798 the 11th Amendment was added to the Constitution. It declared that states could not be sued, without their consent, in federal courts by citizens of another state.

Circuit Duty

Despite the lack of many notable decisions by the full Supreme Court during these first years, the justices found themselves kept quite busy — and rather unhappy — due to the demands of their duty as circuit judges. For a full century, the justices worked to convince Congress to abolish this role for them.

The Judiciary Act of 1789 provided no separate set of judges for the federal circuit courts. The act instead provided that that Supreme Court justices would travel throughout the states to hold circuit court where and when necessary.

This aspect of judicial duty, though onerous, served an important function in the new nation. Historian Charles Warren notes that "it was . . . almost entirely through their contact with the judges sitting in the circuit courts that the people of the country became acquainted with this new institution, the federal judiciary." [19]

But the distances the justices were required to travel were long, traveling conditions difficult, and questions were raised about the propriety of the justices participating in cases at the circuit level that were then reviewed by the Supreme Court. As early as 1790 Chief Justice Jay asked Congress and the executive to remove this burden. Congress responded with minor changes in the system in 1793; the quickly repealed Judiciary Act of 1801 abolished this duty temporarily; and until late in the 19th century the requirement that justices fill this function remained on the statute books. [20]

The Court, Congress and the President

During this decade, the court, on two occasions, made clear its character as a purely judicial branch, declining to perform non-judicial functions assigned by Congress or to issue advisory opinions in response to executive queries.

In 1792 Congress imposed upon the circuit courts the duty of ruling upon claims of invalid pensioners. Justices Iredell, Blair and Wilson, sitting as circuit judges, refused to carry out that duty, declaring that Congress had overstepped itself by requiring them to undertake such non-judicial responsibilities. As a result of their protest, Congress amended the pension law. [21]

The following year, President Washington asked the court for advice on certain questions of foreign policy, neutrality and treaty law. The justices politely declined to give such advice, citing "the lines of separation, drawn by the Constitution between the three departments of the government" and "our being Judges of a Court in the last resort." The court thereby established its policy of issuing no advisory opinions. [22]

Early in 1793 Johnson resigned. He was quickly replaced by William Paterson of New Jersey, 44, one of the two key senators responsible for the drafting and enactment of the Judiciary Act of 1789. Paterson would serve until 1806.

During the February 1794 term the court heard the case of *Georgia v. Brailsford,* one of a handful of cases tried before it by a jury. [23] And in the last major case in which John Jay would participate, the court rejected the assertion that a foreign country had the right — independent of any treaty or other legal guarantee — to set up a prize court in the United States to decide the disposition of captured vessels. [24]

Two More Chiefs

In April 1794 Jay accepted an appointment as special ambassador to England; he never returned to his seat on the court. After concluding the treaty with Britain, he resigned in June 1795 to become governor of New York.

John Rutledge of South Carolina, the absentee justice of the court's first terms, was nominated by Washington — at Rutledge's own suggestion — to succeed Jay. Appointed while the Senate was in recess in 1795, Rutledge presided over the court's August 1795 term, but was then refused confirmation by the Senate in December. The Senate acted upon reports of Rutledge's criticism of the Jay Treaty — and on rumors of his mental instability, rumors to which Rutledge gave new credibility by attempting suicide after his rejection by the Senate.

Washington then, early in 1796, named Cushing, the senior justice, to lead the court. Although he was quickly confirmed, Cushing declined the post on the basis that at 64 he was too old. He would serve for 14 more years.

President Washington then offered the post of Chief Justice to Sen. Oliver Ellsworth of Connecticut, who, with Paterson, had drafted the Judiciary Act. Ellsworth, 51, was nominated March 3, 1796, confirmed the following day, and took his seat March 8.

Treaties and Taxes

Without Ellsworth, who was sworn in too late to take part in the decisions, the court during the February 1796 term decided the two most significant cases of the decade. They were the treaty case of *Ware v. Hylton* and the tax case of *Hylton v. United States.*

John Marshall argued *Ware v. Hylton* before the court, apparently his only appearance as an advocate before the tribunal he would lead for more than three decades. He lost the case.

In *Ware v. Hylton,* the court established the supremacy of federal treaty provisions over conflicting state laws. A Virginia law that allowed the confiscation, or payment in depreciated currency, of debts owed by Virginians to British subjects was invalid, held the justices, because it conflicted with provisions of the peace treaty with Britain, which ensured the collection of such debts.

Hylton v. United States brought to the court the first clear challenge to an act of Congress as unconstitutional.

John Jay

Oliver Ellsworth

There was no debate over the court's power to rule on that point. Each of the sitting justices — while on circuit duty — had indicated his belief that federal courts were empowered to resolve such challenges. [25]

Congress had imposed a tax on carriages. The tax was challenged as a direct tax, which the Constitution required be apportioned among the states by population. The definition of "direct tax" was unclear, but the court declared that the carriage tax was not a direct tax and thus was not subject to the apportionment requirement.

In its ruling the court declared that direct taxes were only those on land and on individuals, a definition that would stand for a century, until its repudiation by the court in 1895.

Justice Chase

A new member of the court took part in these two decisions — Samuel Chase of Maryland. Chase, a political maverick, would be the only justice in history to be impeached and tried by the Senate.

Chase was Washington's surprise choice to fill the seat left vacant by the resignation of Justice Blair. A signer of the Declaration of Independence, Chase had opposed ratifi-

---

"It was ... almost entirely through their contact with the judges sitting in the circuit courts that the people of the country became acquainted with this new institution, the federal judiciary."

—Charles Warren
The Supreme Court in United States History

---

cation of the Constitution, arguing that it was an undemocratic document.

Nominated and confirmed in January 1796, he took his seat as the February 1796 term began — and voted with the majority in both the tax and the treaty cases. Chase and Ellsworth were the last of Washington's appointments to the court. With Cushing and Paterson, Chase would serve well into the next century.

The Adams Administration

The major decision of the court during the administration of John Adams came when the court in *Calder v. Bull* declared that the constitutional ban on *ex post facto* laws applied only to criminal, not civil, laws. Few other decisions of lasting significance were announced during the 1797-1801 terms.

With the deaths of Justices Wilson and Iredell, Adams had the opportunity to fill two seats on the court. To succeed Wilson, Adams named Bushrod Washington of Virginia, 36, President Washington's nephew. To succeed Iredell, he chose Alfred Moore, 44, of North Carolina. Washington would serve for more than three decades; Moore resigned in 1804 after barely five years on the bench.

The 1799 and 1800 terms of the court were uneventful. The August 1800 term was the last to be held in Philadelphia. Only three justices attended — Paterson, Moore and Washington. Ellsworth, named ambassador to France in February 1799, was abroad — as he would be for the remainder of his time as Chief Justice. Cushing was ill. Chase was campaigning, unsuccessfully, for the re-election of President Adams.

In the election of 1800 the staunch nationalist position of the court became a campaign issue, coupled with complaints about the ambassadorial service of Chief Justices Jay and Ellsworth, acting as agents of the Federalist administrations.

Notwithstanding such criticism, the court's first decade had been a cautious one. As Julius Goebel Jr. concluded:

Its [the court's] posture toward acts of Congress, except for a few instances of individual critique, was one of respect. There were, indeed, occasions ... that invited inquiry into the constitutional basis for congressional action where less deference would have been appropriate. These opportunities were not seized, nor was there succumbing to the temptation to a loose construction of statutory language sometimes advanced by counsel in argument.

When the Court was constrained to explore the intendment of statutory language, it did so as a court of law in terms familiar to the profession and not by flights of fancy about the "spirit" of the Constitution. . . .

The Supreme Court during its first decade . . . left the formulation of policy to the branches of government where it conceived such belonged. [26]

Establishment of Power: 1801-1835

The year 1801 was a watershed for both the nation and the court. A new president — Thomas Jefferson — and a new Chief Justice — John Marshall — took office. Although Jefferson and Marshall shared the home state of Virginia they were life-long antagonists — a fact that added to the natural tension between executive and judiciary at this point in the life of the young nation.

There was also a new capital in 1801. The seat of the government moved to Washington, D.C. The Capitol was under construction as the home of Congress; a residence was provided for the president, but no place was set aside for the Supreme Court to meet. At the last minute, it was allotted a small committee room in the unfinished Capitol. There it convened for its February 1801 term.

Ellsworth Steps Down

In 1800 Oliver Ellsworth, still in France on diplomatic assignment, resigned as Chief Justice.

President Adams first named former Chief Justice Jay to the seat. Confirmation was immediate; so was Jay's letter declining the honor. Jay noted his failing health and the continuing responsibilities of the justices for holding circuit court. He wrote:

> ...the efforts repeatedly made to place the Judicial Department on a proper footing have proved fruitless. I left the bench perfectly convinced that under a system so defective, it would not obtain the energy, weight and dignity which are essential to its affording due support to the National Government, nor acquire the public confidence and respect which, as the last resort of the justice of the nation, it should possess. [27]

Adams was a lame duck, defeated for re-election in 1800. (The tie in electoral votes between Jefferson and Aaron Burr remained unresolved until February 1801.) But Adams was not about to relinquish this opportunity. On Jan. 20, 1801, he named John Marshall Chief Justice. Marshall was then his secretary of State, after serving for a time on diplomatic assignment and in the House of Representatives.

After a brief delay by Federalist advocates of Justice Paterson's elevation to the chief justiceship, the Senate confirmed Marshall Jan. 27.

The Marshall Era Begins

Chief Justice Marshall was sworn in on Feb. 4, 1801, the second day of the court's first term in Washington. He was 45 years old. He would serve for 34 years, until his death.

On the day set for the opening of the term, Feb. 2, only Justice Cushing was present. By Feb. 4 there were four members present — Cushing, Chase, Washington and Marshall. No cases were reported as decided during the term.

But events outside the court's makeshift chamber were moving quickly with broad implications for the court and its new Chief Justice.

In February the House broke the electoral deadlock between Burr and Jefferson, and chose Jefferson as the new president. He took office March 4, 1801.

Only a few days before Jefferson's selection, Congress enacted the Judiciary Act of 1801. The act eliminated circuit duty for the justices, providing for a separate staff of circuit judges. It shifted the court's schedule, providing for June and December terms, instead of February and August sessions; and it reduced to five the number of seats on the court.

The law was widely viewed as a Federalist plan to allow Adams to name a last group of Federalist judges and to protect the Supreme Court from any immediate change through Jeffersonian appointments. Adams quickly filled the new judgeships with Federalist loyalists, confirming Jefferson's view that the federal judiciary would indeed remain a "strong fortress in the possession of the enemy." [28]

Another late-session law produced the situation that brought the case of *Marbury v. Madison* to the court. This second law created a number of justice-of-the-peace positions for the District of Columbia. On March 2 outgoing

"Let the end be legitimate, let it be within the scope of the Constitution, and all means which are appropriate ... which are not prohibited ... are constitutional."
—Chief Justice Marshall, *McCulloch v. Maryland,* 1819

President Adams appointed men to fill those posts; they were confirmed the following day. Their commissions were made out and signed. But still-acting Secretary of State John Marshall (also by now the sitting Chief Justice) failed to deliver all the commissions to all the nominees before the end of the Adams administration at midnight March 3.

President Jefferson appointed a number of these people to their sought-after posts, but not William Marbury, who came to the Supreme Court late in 1801, asking the justices to order Secretary of State James Madison to deliver him his commission.

Marbury filed an original suit with the court, asking that the justices use the authority granted them by the Judiciary Act of 1789 and issue a writ of *mandamus* to Madison.

Already the court was pursuing a path quite independent of the Jefferson administration. In August the justices declined Jefferson's offer to provide them with his views on the application of a certain law at issue in a case before them. The president's position, the court indicated, was not relevant to their consideration of the matter.

Then, in December, the court backed Jefferson's position in a prize vessel case. But also that month the court agreed to hear Marbury's case, setting arguments for the next term — the June 1802 term.

Jefferson was convinced that the court intended to use the Marbury case as a vehicle for interfering in the operations of the executive branch. That view — and the Jeffersonians' view of the Judiciary Act of 1801 — sparked repeal of that law early in 1802. Circuit court duty was reinstated for the justices, and a single annual term was set for the court, beginning each year in February.

Because the change in schedule was enacted after February 1802, this last provision delayed for 14 months the next term at which the arguments would be heard in *Marbury v. Madison.* The court did not meet from December 1801 until February 1803.

Marshall the Man

Two major decisions were announced in the 1803 term. In both their coupling and their resolution the skilled leadership of John Marshall already was evident.

Marshall's legal training was meager; he had little experience in the practice of law and none as a judge. Before his appointment as Chief Justice, he had been a politician and a diplomat, and it was those skills that characterized his tenure as Chief Justice. For three decades his personality dominated the court and the men who served with him.

More than at any other time in the court's history, the personal characteristics of the Chief Justice were of considerably more importance than his legal talents.

The court operated as a family firm, not a federal institution. The justices, most of whom came to Washington only for a few months each year, leaving their wives and families at home, lived together in a boardinghouse. After their dinners together, they often, over wine, discussed and resolved the cases brought before them. [29]

Marshall's contribution as Chief Justice has been often described. Alexander M. Bickel's words are among the most evocative:

> Congress was created very nearly full blown by the Constitution itself. The vast possibilities of the presidency were relatively easy to perceive and soon, inevitably, materalized. But the institution of the judiciary needed to be summoned up out of the constitutional

---

". . . The institution of the judiciary needed to be summoned up out of the constitutional vapors, shaped and maintained; and the Great Chief Justice, John Marshall — not singlehanded, but first and foremost — was there to do it and did."

—Alexander M. Bickel,
The Least Dangerous Branch

---

vapors, shaped and maintained; and the Great Chief Justice, John Marshall — not singlehanded, but first and foremost — was there to do it and did. [30]

The *Marbury* Ruling

Two years after Marshall assumed his post, the court announced its decision in *Marbury v. Madison.* On Feb. 24, 1803, the court at once claimed, exercised and justified its power to review and nullify acts of Congress it found to conflict with the Constitution.

But in so doing it neatly avoided the expected collision with the Jefferson administration, although it did manage to rebuke Jefferson for not delivering Marbury his delayed commission.

The court held that Marbury was due his commission, that it should be delivered to him, but that the court was powerless to order the delivery. The court lacked that power because it found the section of the Judiciary Act authorizing it to issue such orders to be unconstitutional and void, an impermissible expansion of its original jurisdiction.

This decision, one scholar has explained, "became authority . . . for the proposition — which had already been adopted in a majority of the states and which was destined to form a distinct feature of the whole political system of the United States — that a constitution is a fundamental law, that legislative and executive powers are limited by the terms of this fundamental law, and that the courts as interpreters of the law are expected to preserve and defend constitutions as inviolable acts, to be changed only by the people through the amending process." [31]

Judicial Restraint

During congressional debate over repeal of the 1801 Judiciary Act, the possibility was raised that the court might declare the repeal unconstitutional, an improper effort by Congress to encroach on the independence of the court.

One week after the *Marbury* decision, the court made clear that it would exercise its newly affirmed power with care. The court upheld the Repeal Act of 1802. This ruling, announced March 2, 1803, came in the case of *Stuart v. Laird.* [32]

It would be more than 50 years before the court again declared void an act of Congress.

The Chase Impeachment

The business before the court steadily increased during the first decade of the 19th century, but few of its decisions during that period were of as much significance for the future of the court and the country as some of the extra-judicial matters affecting the court.

Most notable of these was the impeachment, trial and acquittal of Justice Samuel Chase.

Chase, a maverick at the time of his selection to the court, continued, from his seat, to make enemies. He actively campaigned for President Adams in 1800. He strongly supported the hated Sedition Act of 1798 — and presided as the judge in the trials of a number of persons charged with violating it.

After a particularly partisan speech to a grand jury in Baltimore in May 1803, Chase became the object of an impeachment drive. The charges against him involved both his conduct during the Sedition Act trials and this particular charge to the Baltimore grand jury. On March 12, 1804, the House impeached Justice Chase by a vote of 73-32.

His trial in the Senate began early in 1805. Chase, who continued to participate in the court's functions, appeared in the Senate with his attorneys. Presentation of the evidence and arguments consumed a month. On March 1, 1805, he was acquitted. More than a majority of the senators voted to find him guilty on three of the charges against him, but the vote fell short of the two-thirds required for conviction.

The Chase acquittal ended the rumored plans of Republicans to impeach all four remaining Federalist justices — Marshall, Cushing, Paterson and Washington.

Furthermore, wrote historian Charles Warren, the acquittal represented a rejection of the Republican argument that impeachment could be used as "a means of keeping the courts in reasonable harmony with the will of the nation, as expressed through Congress and the executive, and that a judicial decision declaring an Act of Congress unconstitutional would support an impeachment and the removal of a judge. . . ."[33]

Reporting the Decisions

At the end of the 1804 term, William Cranch, then chief justice of the circuit court in the District of Columbia, began publication of Cranch's *Reports* of the decisions of the Supreme Court.

Alexander J. Dallas, a noted attorney in Pennsylvania, had reported some of the court's decisions during its terms in Philadelphia. But after the court moved to Washington, Dallas discontinued this service.

Cranch, who would perform this public service for a dozen years, first published a volume including the decisions from 1801 through 1804. "Up to that time, the opinions in the cases heard . . . [during that period] had been practically unknown to the Bar and to the general public," writes Warren, "with the exception of the *Marbury Case,* a summary of which had been widely published and commented upon in the newspapers." [34]

In his preface to the first volume, Cranch expressed the hope that publication of the court's decisions would eliminate "much of that uncertainty of the law, which is so frequently, and perhaps so justly, the subject of complaint in this country."

Furthermore, wrote Cranch, reporting of the actual decisions of the court should limit judicial discretion:

> . . . Every case decided is a check upon the judge. He cannot decide a similar case differently, without strong reasons, which, for his own justification, he will wish to make public. The avenues to corruption are thus obstructed, and the sources of litigation closed. [35]

New Justices

Early in Marshall's tenure — undoubtedly with the encouragement of Reporter Cranch — the court began to write down its decisions and opinions.

In addition, Chief Justice Marshall exerted all his considerable personal influence to convince his fellow justices to speak with one voice in these decisions. He persuaded them to drop the practice of *seriatim* opinions, under which each justice wrote and read his own views, and to adopt the "opinion of the court" approach, usually allowing him to write that opinion.

Appropriately enough, however, William Johnson, the first Republican justice, who served for most of Marshall's tenure, provided a counterbalance to the Chief Justice's push for judicial unanimity.

Johnson, known as the "father of dissent," was but 32 at the time of his appointment to the Supreme Court, but he nevertheless did not hesitate to voice his disagreement with the Chief Justice and the court.

President Jefferson filled two other seats on the court during his two terms in office. In 1806 Justice Paterson died and Jefferson named H. Brockholst Livingston of New York, 49, John Jay's brother-in-law, as Patterson's successor. Livingston served on the court for 16 years.

In 1807 increases in territorial and judicial business spurred Congress to create a new circuit that took in Kentucky, Tennessee and Ohio, and a seventh seat on the Supreme Court. Jefferson, after polling the members of Congress from those three states, named Thomas Todd, Kentucky's chief justice, to the new seat. Todd, 41, was nominated and confirmed in 1807, seated at the 1808 term, missed the 1809 term, and issued his first opinion — a dissent — in 1810. He served until 1826 but, like Livingston, his judicial career was notable mainly for his steady support of Chief Justice Marshall.

The Burr Trial

In 1807 the Jefferson administration brought former Vice President Aaron Burr to trial for treason. The charge was related to Burr's alleged efforts to encourage an uprising in and a movement for the independence of the western states from the United States. The actions of the Supreme Court and its Chief Justice in this affair further heightened the animosity felt by the president for the court.

Early in 1807 the Supreme Court, affirming its power to issue a writ of *habeas corpus* to challenge the detention of an individual by federal officials, held that there was insufficient evidence for the government to prosecute two of Burr's accomplices for treason. [36]

Jefferson, writes Charles Warren, regarded this ruling as "another deliberate attack by the court upon his executive authority" while the Federalists viewed it as "a noble example of the judicial safeguards to individual liberty." [37]

After the Supreme Court's term ended, Chief Justice Marshall traveled to Richmond to preside personally as circuit judge over the trial of Burr. His rulings that the government's evidence was insufficient to support a charge of treason were seen as directly contributing to Burr's acquittal later in the year. Jefferson, irate at the rulings and the outcome, suggested that the Constitution be amended to provide other means than impeachment for removing justices from the bench. The amendment was not approved.

Jefferson's feelings toward the court were further exacerbated during the national resistance to his administration's Embargo Act imposed during the conflict with Britain. Justice Johnson — one of Jefferson's own choices as a member of the court — declared illegal and void the president's effort to instruct customs officials to detain all vessels thought to be intending to evade the embargo. [38]

Fletcher v. Peck

In 1810 the Supreme Court for the first time exercised its power to strike down a state law as unconstitutional.

In the case of *Fletcher v. Peck*, the court invalidated a law passed by Georgia's legislature in 1796 to repeal a 1795 land grant law obtained through bribery of the members of the 1795 legislature.

The repeal was challenged by the innocent third parties who had acquired land under the 1795 grant and who now found their titles null and void. They argued that the legislative nullification was unconstitutional, a clear violation of the Constitution's language, which forbids states to impair the obligation of contracts.

The case was argued twice — in 1809 and 1810. One of the attorneys for the property owners bringing the challenge was 32-year-old Joseph Story of Massachusetts.

On April 16, 1810, the court — for whom Chief Justice Marshall spoke — held unconstitutional the legislative repeal of the land grant law and the nullification of the titles granted under it.

Story won his case — and the following year he was appointed, at 34, to the Supreme Court.

The Last of the First

In September 1810 Justice Cushing died — the last of the original six justices named to the court in 1790; he had outlived all his original colleagues by a decade or more.

The interest that attended the search for Cushing's successor on the bench provided some indication of the status the court had attained in its first decades. The court was then evenly divided between Federalists (Marshall, Washington, Chase) and Republicans (Johnson, Todd, and Livingston).

President Madison received much advice on the selection of a nominee, including some from his predecessor,

Thomas Jefferson. Notwithstanding all the advice — or perhaps because of it — Madison required four tries to fill Cushing's seat.

His first selection was Levi Lincoln, who had served as attorney general to Jefferson. Lincoln declined; Madison nominated him anyway; the Senate confirmed the nomination and Lincoln again firmly declined, early in 1811.

In February, Madison named Alexander Wolcott, a Republican leader in Connecticut, to the seat. Criticized as unqualified, Wolcott was rejected by the Senate: Only nine votes were cast in favor of his confirmation. Madison subsequently nominated John Quincy Adams, then ambassador to Russia; Adams was confirmed but declined the appointment.

Madison then waited for the better part of 1811 before making another choice. The 1811 term — for which there was neither a quorum of justices present nor any business — passed virtually unnoticed.

At mid-year Justice Chase died, creating a second vacancy. In November President Madison nominated Gabriel Duvall of Maryland, comptroller of the treasury for almost a decade, to fill the Chase seat; he named Story to the Cushing seat. Both were quickly confirmed and would serve long terms — Duvall, 23 years; Story, 34.

In Time of War

For the next several years, the conflict with England — the War of 1812 — was a dominant factor in the work of the court. After the Capitol was burned by the British in August 1814, the court met in temporary quarters for the next four terms, even holding some sessions in a tavern.

The cases before the court largely involved wartime issues — neutral rights, ship seizures, foreign affairs. The court made clear in these rulings that violations of neutral rights were to be resolved diplomatically, not judicially. And it affirmed broad power for the federal government over the person and property of enemies during wartime.

Challenge to Power

One result of *Fletcher v. Peck* was considerable state resistance to the court's exercise of its power to invalidate state actions. States began to question whether in fact Congress could authorize the court to curtail state power in such a final manner.

In 1816 the court itself considered that question. The case presenting it was *Martin v. Hunter's Lessee*, a long-running dispute over the ownership of a large parcel of land

William Johnson   **Thomas Jefferson**

in Virginia. Chief Justice Marshall did not participate in the court's consideration of the matter due to his own ties to the matter.

In 1813 the court had ruled on the substance of the case, deciding in favor of the British claim to the land, rejecting the Virginian's claim. But the Virginia courts refused to obey the decision, ruling that the Supreme Court could not constitutionally tell a state court what to do.

This direct challenge to its authority returned to the court in 1816. On March 20, 1816, it was firmly rebuffed. Justice Story wrote the court's opinion, upholding the power of Congress to grant the Supreme Court appellate jurisdiction over all matters involving federal laws, treaties and the U.S. Constitution — regardless of the court in which such cases had first been heard. This opinion, declared Charles Warren, "has ever since been the keystone of the whole arch of federal judicial power."[39]

In another 1816 ruling, however, the court left the large and controversial area of criminal law almost entirely to state courts. In the case of *United States v. Hudson and Goodwin*, the justices declared that federal courts had no jurisdiction over criminal activity — except for matters which Congress had specifically declared to be federal crimes.

New Questions, New Reporter

Warren describes the end of the 1816 term as the end of an era. With the end of the War of 1812, he writes, the attention of the people turned toward industrial and manufacturing endeavors, transportation, communication and economic change. Questions of war, prize vessels, and embargo acts — which had taken so much of the court's attention during the first years of the century — faded from the docket, to be replaced by questions of contract obligations, commerce regulation, and state powers.

Also at the end of this term, Cranch ended his work as unofficial reporter of the court's work. An official reporter, Henry Wheaton, was appointed; Congress authorized him a salary of $1,000 a year. He would hold that post for 11 years.

The 1819 Term

The term that convened in a new courtroom on Feb. 2, 1819, was one of the most notable in the court's history. The court announced three major constitutional decisions — in the cases of *Dartmouth College v. Woodward, McCulloch v. Maryland* and *Sturges v. Crowninshield*.

The court moved back into permanent quarters for this term; the courtroom under the Senate chamber had been rebuilt. Here the court would meet until the Civil War.

The court announced its decision in the *Dartmouth College* case on the opening day of the term. Argued for three days in the preceding term, the case had drawn little attention in the nation's press. The dispute between a small college in New Hampshire and the state legislature hardly seemed notable. But the issue it presented was of major significance for the nation's economic development: Did the Constitution's contract clause protect private corporate charters — as well as public grants — against impairment by the state?

With only Justice Duvall dissenting, the Supreme Court answered that question with a resounding "yes." Not only did the court protect Dartmouth College from legislative efforts to reshape its structure and purpose, the justices with this decision promised the corporations beginning to form that they too would be secure against this type of interference.

Two weeks later the court seemed to tie the hands of the states even further in economic matters. On Feb. 17 the court held invalid New York's insolvency law — enacted to ease the difficulties of debtors in default. The court held that the New York law violated the ban on state action impairing the obligation of contracts, because it allowed the discharge of debts contracted before its passage.

The day before this ruling the *National Intelligencer* became the first newspaper in the country to begin printing daily announcements of the actions of the Supreme Court. Notwithstanding this new channel of communication of its decisions, the decision in the New York insolvency case, *Sturges v. Crowninshield*, was misreported and misunderstood.

Until a second ruling came in 1827, it generally was thought that the states lacked any power to afford debtors this sort of relief. [40]

McCulloch v. Maryland

After these two rulings were announced, the court moved on to hear arguments — for nine days in late February and early March 1819 — in the case of *McCulloch v. Maryland*.

Daniel Webster, a young member of Congress from Massachusetts who had argued successfully for Dartmouth College, argued for the Bank of the United States in this case. Again, he won.

McCulloch v. Maryland posed two questions to the justices: Did Congress have the power to charter a national bank? Did states have the power to tax the operations of such a bank?

The court announced its decision on Saturday, March 6, affirming the power of Congress and curtailing the power of the states.

Writing for a unanimous court, Chief Justice Marshall declared that Congress had broad power under the "necessary and proper" clause to select the means to implement its powers specifically granted by the Constitution. "Let the end be legitimate, let it be within the scope of the Constitution," wrote Marshall, "and all means which are appropriate . . . which are not prohibited . . . are constitutional."[41]

The bank was a useful fiscal instrument for national economic stability, so Congress might properly decide to incorporate it.

Furthermore, this power could not be hampered by the states — and thus states could not tax the bank, for by taxing it, they could destroy it and frustrate the congressional purpose in chartering the bank. This decision aroused intense opposition, particularly in the South and the West where the bank was hated.

McCulloch v. Maryland, wrote Robert G. McCloskey, "is by almost any reckoning the greatest decision John Marshall ever handed down." In upholding the constitutionality of the bank's incorporation, he continues, Marshall "set down the classic statement of the doctrine of national authority. The argument he advanced was not new; its main outlines had been endlessly debated since the first Congress. . . . But Marshall deserves the credit for stamping it with the die of his memorable rhetoric and converting it from a political theory into the master doctrine of American constitutional law." [42]

Review and Reaction

In 1821 the court for the second time reaffirmed its own power to review the decisions of state courts.

The case of *Cohens v. Virginia* arose from different circumstances than had *Martin v. Hunter's Lessee,* but like the earlier case *Cohens* presented to the court a basic challenge to its power under Section 25 of the Judiciary Act.

With equal firmness, Chief Justice Marshall reiterated the points Justice Story had made in the 1816 ruling. It was the constitutional obligation of the court to review cases in which state courts rejected challenges that state actions were in conflict with the Constitution, U.S. laws or treaties, Marshall declared.

Those who approved the decision considered it "one of the chief bulwarks of American unity." Critics — still led by former President Jefferson — saw it as one more blow to state sovereignty. Jefferson complained that the court was "working like gravity . . . to press us at last into one consolidated mass." [43]

By 1825 the court had nullified as unconstitutional statutes of 10 states. These rulings set off an effort to remove or at least restrict the power of the court to review state court decisions.

Among the measures discussed were repeal of Section 25; a constitutional amendment providing that all cases involving a state would be appealed to the Senate, not the court; statutes requiring that five — or all seven — justices concur in holding a state law invalid.

Jefferson proposed that each justice should be required to issue a separate opinion — as in the pre-Marshall days. He suggested that Congress then denounce the views of those with whom it disagreed — and impeach the justices who did not respond with a change of view. None of these proposals were approved by both chambers of Congress.

Period of Stability

There were no changes in the court's membership from late 1811 until early 1823. Then in March 1823 Justice Livingston died. President Monroe chose Secretary of War Smith Thompson, also of New York and related by marriage to the Livingston clan, to fill the seat. Confirmed late in the year, Thompson took his seat in the February 1824 term. Due to his relationship to the Livingston family — to whom the contested steamboat monopoly involved in the case of *Gibbons v. Ogden* had been granted — Thompson did not participate in that case, the most important one decided by the court in his 20 years of service.

Congress and Commerce

The Constitution granted Congress the power to regulate interstate and foreign commerce. With the exception of an early law providing for the licensing of vessels in the coastal trade, Congress did not exercise this power to any degree in the first years of the nation's existence.

The states, however, passed a variety of laws regulating commerce and transportation within their borders. In the case of *Gibbons v. Ogden*, the court began the long process of defining the reach of federal commerce power and the limits it set to state power.

Gibbons v. Ogden brought before the justices a challenge to New York's grant of a steamboat monopoly to the Fulton-Livingston partnership, giving that company exclusive rights to run steamships on New York waterways. The monopoly provoked considerable interstate animosity threatening to destroy both the national peace and any sort of incipient national commercial network.

The challengers of the monopoly claimed that it interfered with the federal power to regulate interstate commerce because it excluded from New York waterways vessels licensed under the federal coasting law.

The case divided Republican against Federalist in Congress and in the states. It was argued for five days in February 1824. Daniel Webster argued for the challengers.

On March 3, 1824, Chief Justice Marshall, as usual in major cases, delivered the court's opinion. Commerce, the court held, was not merely buying and selling of goods, but included "intercourse" of all sorts. Commerce also included navigation.

Congress had licensed vessels in the coasting trade. The state monopoly conflicted with the free operation of those federally licensed vessels and so must be held invalid.

Gibbons v. Ogden ranks with *McCulloch v. Maryland* as one of the two major rulings of the Marshall era establishing national power and national supremacy. *Gibbons v. Ogden,* furthermore, served as the "emancipation proclamation of American commerce," [44] giving impetus to the development of the port of New York, the railroads and a national system of commerce.

Federal Authority Extended

A few weeks after *Gibbons,* the court approved further extension of federal authority at the expense of state prerogatives — holding in the case of *Osborn v. Bank of the United States* that the bank could sue state officials in federal court even if the state did not consent to the suit. The court went on to declare that a state official who acted in reliance upon an unconstitutional state law — or exceeded his proper authority — was not immune from being sued in federal court for his actions.

In 1825 the court held that if creditors could sue debtors in federal rather than state courts, the federal courts were free to disregard state laws enacted to ease the debtors' plight by, for example, allowing debts paid in depreciated currency. [45]

Also in that term the court for the first time considered a case involving slaves. The court held that slavery was not illegal under international law. [46]

Changes at Court

Congress responded to the court's steadily increasing workload by lengthening its term. Beginning in 1827, the court convened its term on the second Monday in January.

When the 1827 term began, the court had a new member. Justice Todd had died in 1826. President John Quincy Adams named federal Judge Robert Trimble of Kentucky as his successor. Trimble would serve only two terms before his death in 1828.

The 1827 term was a busy one. One historian reports that the court resolved 77 cases during the two-month session, leaving 109 for resolution in the next term. [47]

With the January 1828 term a new reporter took over the function of publishing the court's opinions. Richard Peters Jr. would fill that post for 15 years.

State Powers

Having firmly established federal supremacy and national power in *Marbury, McCulloch* and *Gibbons v. Og-*

den, the court in the 1827 term now upheld the right and power of states to act concurrently with the federal government in some areas.

In the case of *Ogden v. Saunders,* the court clarified the power of states to enact laws to help debtors. By an unusually close vote of 4-3, the justices upheld New York's revised insolvency law, which — as amended after the 1819 ruling in *Sturges v. Crowninshield* — applied only to debts contracted after its passage. For the first and only time in his career, Chief Justice Marshall was on the losing side in a constitutional case. Emphasizing the deference the court owed to the decision of state legislators, Justice Bushrod Washington wrote the majority opinion. Justices Duvall and Story joined Marshall in dissent.

Later in the term, the court upheld a state's power to abolish the penalty of imprisonment for debtors. This did not impair the obligation of a contracted debt, held the court in the case of *Mason v. Haile* but simply modified the remedy for defaulting on that obligation.

Advocates of state powers did lose a major case in the 1827 term, however. *Brown v. Maryland* posed to the justices the question of a state's power to tax persons who sold imported goods in the state. Arguing for the state was Roger B. Taney, who would follow Marshall as Chief Justice. As Marshall had lost the case of *Ware v. Hylton,* so Taney came out on the losing end in this contest.

The court held that a state could not tax persons who sold imported goods, that such a tax interfered with the federal power to regulate imports and impose import duties. So long as imported goods remained in their original package, held the court, they could not be taxed by the state.

Jackson's Justices

In 1828 Justice Trimble, the court's junior member, died. Despite his defeat for re-election that year, President Adams named John J. Crittenden of Kentucky to fill the Trimble seat. The Senate refused to consider the nomination.

Within a week after taking office, President Andrew Jackson named John McLean of Ohio, who had served Adams as postmaster general, to the empty seat.

McLean, a perennial presidential candidate during his 31 years as a justice, had served in the House, run unsuccessfully for the Senate, and had expanded the Post Office into the largest department in the executive branch. As one of the most political men who ever sat on the bench, McLean did not hesitate to use his judicial opinions for political ends. His insistence upon defending the power of Congress to exclude slavery from the territories would precipitate the unfortunate breadth of the Supreme Court's *Dred Scott* decision in 1857 denying that power.

In 1829 Justice Washington died after 32 years on the court. Jackson selected Henry Baldwin of Pennsylvania to the seat. Baldwin, one of the more eccentric men to serve on the court, would hold the seat for 14 years.

Business and Taxes

The 1829 term produced four major rulings on questions of state power. In the case of *Providence Bank v. Billings,* the court held that a state would not be assumed to have granted a corporation a tax exemption unless such a special privilege was explicitly included in the corporation's charter. In the case of *Weston v. City of Charleston,* the court denied cities and states the power to tax U.S. stock, holding such a tax an impermissible interference with the federal borrowing power.

In *Willson v. Blackbird Creek Marsh Co.,* the court upheld some state power to regulate its waterways and navigation thereupon, at least so long as Congress had not exercised its power over those waters.

But in the case of *Craig v. Missouri,* the court held that a state violated the constitutional ban on state bills of credit when it authorized the issuance of state loan certificates.

Another slavery question was before the court in the 1829 term. In *Boyce v. Anderson* the justices held that a slave who drowned in a steamboat accident was a passenger, not freight. The slave owners in the case were disappointed; their recovery would have been greater had the slave been considered cargo.

The Cherokee Crisis

Georgia's effort to bring the Cherokee Indians within its jurisdiction brought the Supreme Court and the state into collision in the last years of the Marshall era.

The Cherokees sought to file an original case in the Supreme Court asking for an order directing Georgia to stop enforcing the stringent new state laws affecting the Indians and their land. While this case was pending before the court late in 1830, the state ignored another court order staying the execution of an Indian convicted of murder under the challenged laws. The state executed the Indian before the court could hear his case.

In January 1831 the House rejected another move for repeal of the statute authorizing the court to review state court rulings. In March the court held that the Cherokees could not bring an original suit because they were not a separate nation in the eyes of the federal law.

But a second case arose quickly. Georgia had convicted and sentenced to hard labor two missionaries who had not complied with state law regarding white persons living in Indian territory. The missionaries took their case to the Supreme Court, arguing that the state lacked the power to impose or enforce such a requirement.

On March 3, 1832, Chief Justice Marshall announced the court's decision, holding the state law was unconstitutional. Federal jurisdiction over Indian matters was exclusive; the state had no power to pass such laws; the missionaries' conviction was reversed and they should be released.

Georgia refused to comply or release the missionaries. President Jackson openly sympathized with the state, allegedly remarking, "Well, John Marshall has made his decision, now let him enforce it."

For months the confrontation persisted. Chief Justice Marshall was most depressed, writing to Justice Story that he doubted that the Union would survive in the face of such rebellion by state authority.

But late in 1832 South Carolina's adoption of a declaration "nullifying" a new tariff law and barring appeals to the Supreme Court from decisions upholding state laws provoked Jackson to label such state resistance treason. He asked Congress to increase the power of federal courts to enforce federal laws in the face of such challenges.

It was abruptly made clear to Georgia officials that their resistance to the Supreme Court's order concerning the missionaries no longer could expect tacit presidential backing. The governor pardoned the missionaries. The case

Daniel Webster　　　　　　**Joseph Story**

ended. In 1833 Congress approved Jackson's request for expanded federal judicial power.

The Bill of Rights

Marshall's last major constitutional opinion came in 1833. In the case of *Barron v. Baltimore,* the court held that the Bill of Rights was intended to limit only federal, not state, action. "It is a striking fact," wrote Charles Warren, "that this last of Marshall's opinions on this branch of law should have been delivered in limitation of the operations of the Constitution whose undue extension he had been so long charged with seeking." [48]

As a result of the decision in *Barron v. Baltimore,* it was a full century before the court addressed itself at length to questions of the rights of individuals rather than of institutions. And this decision made necessary the enactment of the 14th Amendment, which would eventually, in the 20th century, be read to extend the guarantees of the Bill of Rights against state action and thus would serve as the basis for an expansion of federal judicial power comparable to that of the Marshall era.

Three major cases were argued in the early 1830s but carried over to later terms because of the court's inability to resolve the questions they posed. These were the cases of *Charles River Bridge v. Warren Bridge, Briscoe v. Commonwealth Bank of Kentucky* and *New York v. Miln.* The court's pace was slowed: Marshall was nearing 80, Johnson and Duvall were ill and absent much of the time.

End of an Era

An era was coming to a close. In August 1834 Justice Johnson, the independent soul who fathered the court's tradition of dissent, died. To succeed him, Jackson named James M. Wayne of Georgia. Wayne would serve for 33 years, until 1867.

In January 1835 the aged Duvall resigned. Jackson named Roger B. Taney, former attorney general and Treasury secretary, to succeed him.

But Taney had played a key role in Jackson's war on the Bank of the United States, implementing the president's order to remove U.S. funds from the bank. In that post he had won many enemies. Whig opposition to the nomination convinced the Senate, on the last day of its 1835 session, to postpone consideration of the Taney nomination. The vote was 24-21. The Duvall seat remained empty.

Then, on July 6, 1835, Chief Justice John Marshall died. The court's great center chair was vacant.

Eulogies of Marshall were numerous and elaborate. But perhaps the most objective assessment of his accomplishment as Chief Justice came from abroad. After traveling through the United States in the last years of the Marshall era, Alexis de Tocqueville wrote of the Supreme Court:

> The peace, the prosperity, and the very existence of the Union are vested in the hands of the seven Federal judges. Without them the Constitution would be a dead letter: the executive appeals to them for assistance against the encroachments of the legislative power; the legislature demands their protection against the assaults of the executive; they defend the Union from the disobedience of the states, the states from the exaggerated claims of the Union, the public interest against private interests, and the conservative spirit of stability against the fickleness of the democracy. Their power is enormous, but it is the power of public opinion. [49]

No single man had done more than John Marshall to establish that enormous power or to win the essential public respect for and support of the still-young Supreme Court of the United States.

State Power and Slavery: 1836-1860

It is perhaps a mark of how infrequently presidential nominees to the Supreme Court adhere to the views of their patron that the court never has been known by the name of a president, even if he named all or most of its members.

President Washington of course selected the entire original court; it was never referred to as the "Washington Court." The next president to name more than half the tribunal's members was Andrew Jackson. Jackson named six justices in eight years. Of the six, four served for more than a quarter of a century, well into the Civil War.

Jackson's first three nominees were McLean, Baldwin and Wayne. The fourth was Roger B. Taney.

After Jackson's nomination of Taney as an associate justice was postponed by the Senate early in 1835, Chief Justice Marshall's death opened a second vacancy on the court. When Congress convened late in 1835, Jackson sent it a second Taney nomination, this one for the post of Chief Justice.

To fill the vacant seat of an associate justice Jackson chose Philip B. Barbour of Virginia, who had argued the state's case in *Cohens v. Virginia.* Barbour had served several terms in the House, during which he had advocated proposals that required five of seven justices to concur in holding a statute unconstitutional; he also had served as a state and a federal judge. Barbour would have the briefest tenure of all the Jackson appointees. He died in 1841 after five years on the court.

The same political opposition that delayed action on Taney's first nomination to the court delayed confirmation of him as Chief Justice until March 15, 1836. Leaders of the opposition to his selection were two of the foremost Supreme Court advocates of the era, Daniel Webster and Henry Clay. Nevertheless, the Senate at length confirmed Taney's nomination by a vote of 29-15.

While the Senate considered the nomination, the court met without a Chief Justice for its 1836 term. Story, the senior sitting justice, presided.

Taney's First Term

In 1837, Chief Justice Taney's first term, the court finally decided the three major constitutional cases that had been pending throughout the last years of the Marshall era — *Charles River Bridge v. Warren Bridge, New York v. Miln* and *Briscoe v. Commonwealth Bank of Kentucky.*

Many saw the court's rulings in these cases as clear evidence that the Taney court would favor the rights of the states, which the court under Chief Justice Marshall consistently had curtailed.

A more measured assessment of the relationship between the court under Taney and that under Marshall is provided by Carl B. Swisher:

> The work of the 1837 term . . . marked the beginning of a new order. The transition was not a sharp one, and those who saw it as such were mistaken. In spite of the radical doctrines sponsored by some Jacksonians of the time, the Court was careful to adhere to traditional patterns. . . . The change was limited . . . and yet it was there. There was a greater tendency to look to items of local welfare and to emphasize the rights of the states, a greater concern with living democracy in a rapidly changing society. [50]

Contracts

First and most famous of the decisions of this term is that in the *Charles River Bridge* case, first argued before the court in 1831. The issue was the constitutional ban on state action impairing the obligation of contracts.

The Charles River Bridge Co., originally chartered by the state to build a bridge to bear passenger traffic across the Charles River near Boston, challenged a subsequent state act allowing a second bridge to be built across that river. Daniel Webster argued for the original company that implicit in its charter was the exclusive privilege to carry such traffic. After five days of argument in January 1837, the court announced its opinion in February. Chief Justice Taney wrote the court's decision.

The court did not undercut its earlier rulings recognizing and protecting contract obligations, but it ruled against the Charles River Bridge Co. A charter, Taney explained, would not be construed to be more favorable to its corporate recipient — at public expense — than its express terms required. In the absence of an explicit grant of monopoly privilege, the state had not infringed the first charter by granting a second to another company.

Commerce and Credit

A few days after that ruling, the court held that a state might properly require shipowners to report all passengers on ships arriving in its ports. This reporting requirement had been challenged, in the case of *New York v. Miln,* as an infringement of the federal power to regulate foreign commerce. But the court held the requirement a legitimate exercise of the state police power.

The term's third major ruling also worked to give states more room in which to exercise their power. In the case of *Briscoe v. Commonwealth Bank of Kentucky,* like *Miln* first argued in the 1834 term, the court upheld a state law that authorized a state-chartered bank to issue bank notes. Henry Clay had argued for the victorious bank.

This law, like that struck down seven years earlier in *Craig v. Missouri,* had been challenged as infringing the constitutional ban on state bills of credit. But where the Marshall court had struck down the law in *Craig,* the Taney court upheld that in *Briscoe.* Justice Story dissented, as he had in the earlier two decisions, saying that Chief Justice Marshall would have disagreed too.

The Nine-Man Court

On the last day of President Jackson's term in office, Congress expanded the court to nine seats. Jackson immediately nominated John Catron of Tennessee and William Smith of Alabama to fill the two new seats.

Catron, the Tennessee campaign manager for the newly elected president, Martin Van Buren, was confirmed and served until 1865. Smith declined the second seat.

Van Buren then named Alabama senator-elect John McKinley to the seat. He was confirmed and served 15 years, although illness curtailed his participation in the court for half that period.

The Exercise of Power

During Taney's tenure as Chief Justice, the court continued sturdily to assert its own power and that of lower federal courts to resolve the increasingly frequent questions of the allocation of governmental authority. The *Dred Scott* decision provides dramatic example of the extreme to which this point could be carried.

But unlike that ruling, most of the court's pronouncements in this area simply consolidated and reinforced the position the court already had assumed in earlier years.

In 1838 Rhode Island came to the court asking the justices to resolve a boundary dispute with Massachusetts, the first such case to come to the court. Massachusetts moved to dismiss the case, arguing that the court lacked the power to hear it. Over the dissent of the Chief Justice, the court rejected the motion and proceeded with the case, which finally was resolved in favor of Massachusetts in 1846.

The 1838 term also brought the court's decision in the case of *Kendall v. United States,* upholding the power of a federal court to issue an order directing an executive branch official to perform non-discretionary "ministerial" duties — even if the court order was in direct conflict with presidential instructions to the official. Such orders, held the court, did not breach the separation of powers.

Cases and Corporations

The increase in the number of corporate enterprises operating within the United States brought questions of corporate rights and state powers before the court.

In 1839 the court held, on one hand, that states could forbid out-of-state companies to do business in their territory. But in the same case the court effectively moderated that holding by declaring that without clear evidence that a state intended to exercise this power, it would be assumed to consent to the operations of such "foreign" corporations.[51]

Five years later, the court opened the doors of the federal courts to corporate litigation by modifying the strict view of a corporation's "residence" adopted early in the Marshall era. The new rule allowed more cases involving corporations to be heard in federal courts, rather than state courts, on the basis that the corporation and the opposing party were residents of different states.[52]

Slavery and States' Rights

Advocates of state sovereignty tasted defeat in a number of rulings from the Taney court early in the 1840s. In *Holmes v. Jennison,* decided in 1840, the court made clear that the Constitution left states no power to engage in foreign affairs. Two years later the court held that federal courts were not bound by state judges' interpretations of state laws. In another case decided that term, the court held that states could not tax the income of federal officials.

By the 1840s virtually all questions of states' rights seemed to tie back into the increasingly sensitive issue of slavery. The court had carefully avoided addressing this issue in any but peripheral ways, but by 1841, writes Swisher, "the court found itself in the thick of the slavery discussion, from which it did not actually escape until the close of the Civil War period, even though there were intervening years in which no such cases were actually decided." [53]

Thus, even when the issue was commerce in general, with no evident tie to the slavery issue, the court's opinions were closely perused and construed as expanding or curtailing state powers to deal with slavery.

The double-edged nature of the issue — and all judicial efforts to deal with it — were evident in the 1841 and 1842 rulings of the court and their public reception.

In 1841 the court decided the case of *Groves v. Slaughter* on a point other than the slavery questions presented. But Justice McLean's opinion, declaring the right of a state to exclude slavery, was interpreted by some southerners as upholding the right of a state to exclude free blacks as well.

The following year the court decided the case of *Prigg v. Pennsylvania.* It struck down a Pennsylvania law setting

John McLean   Roger B. Taney

up certain procedures for determining whether a black person was in fact the sought-after fugitive before he or she was removed from the state by a pursuer. Federal power over fugitive slaves was exclusive, leaving states no opportunity to pass such laws, held the court. But, wrote Swisher, "while upholding the power of the federal government to provide for the return of fugitive slaves, it nullified the obligations and seemed to nullify the power of the states to aid in the process, [and] it at once gave incentive to abolitionist activities and led the South to demand enactment of a Fugitive Slave Act which could be effectively administered without the aid of the states. Thereby it added to the furor of sectional conflict and the hysteria of competing parties." [54]

Court Vacancies

The court's efforts to deal with the increasingly difficult questions before it were hampered by the illness and disability of some of its members and then by long-vacant seats, the product of political turmoil outside the courtroom.

In this period occurred the longest vacancy in Supreme Court history to date. After the death of Justice Baldwin in April 1844, his seat remained empty for more than two years.

This extented vacancy was in large part the result of the political disaffection that marred the relationship between President John C. Tyler and Congress. Tyler had more nominations to the court rejected than any other president. Of his six nominations, only one was confirmed.

Before Tyler took office, there was another new justice. Justice Barbour died during the 1841 term. The lame-duck president, Van Buren, nominated — and the Senate quickly confirmed — Peter V. Daniel of Virginia, a federal judge, to Barbour's seat. Daniel served until 1860.

Tyler had his first opportunity to name a justice when Justice Smith Thompson died in 1843. He chose Treasury Secretary John Spencer; Spencer was rejected by the Senate in January 1844. Tyler next nominated Reuben Walworth of New York, state chancellor. Before its mid-year adjournment, the Senate tabled that nomination.

In April, Justice Baldwin died. Tyler nominated Philadelphia lawyer James Edward King for that seat. The King nomination was also tabled by the Senate. Both the King and the Walworth nominations finally were withdrawn.

Early in 1845, Tyler, now a lame duck in addition to his other political disabilities, sent two more names to the Senate. To fill the Thompson seat he chose Samuel Nelson, a New York judge. Nelson, a well-respected figure, was quickly confirmed; he would serve on the court for 27 years, until 1872. But Tyler's selection of John M. Read as Baldwin's successor was ignored by the Senate. That seat remained empty for another full year.

Early in the Polk administration, Justice Story died. He had served longer than any other justice to that time — 34 years. Late in 1845 Polk nominated George W. Woodward of Pennsylvania to fill the Baldwin seat — and Sen. Levi Woodbury of New Hampshire to fill Story's chair. Woodbury — Taney's successor as secretary of the Treasury — was quickly confirmed early in 1846; he would serve only six years before his death in 1851. Woodward, his nomination opposed by one of his state's senators, was rejected.

Finally, in August, Polk named Pennsylvania judge Robert C. Grier to the Baldwin seat. He was quickly

confirmed, ending the 28-month vacancy on the court. He served for 24 years, until his resignation in 1870.

For the next five years, the court's membership was complete and stable.

Commerce Confusion

Despite its stability of membership, the court's performance on the interlocking issues of commerce and slavery was confusing, to say the least. In the December 1846 term, the court again upheld the federal fugitive slave law.[55] But in the same term, it backed state power to regulate commerce in intoxicating liquor.

The diversity of reasoning among the justices in these latter cases — known as the *License Cases* — from Massachusetts, Rhode Island and New Hampshire reflected the court's increasing division over the location of the lines dividing state and federal power over commerce. Six justices wrote nine opinions in the *License Cases*.

In early 1849 this uncertainty of opinion flowered into complete confusion with the decision of the court in the *Passenger Cases*. These two cases, from New York and Boston, involved state laws that required masters of vessels to post bonds and to pay a tax for each immigrant landed in the state. The laws were challenged as infringing upon federal power to regulate foreign commerce. They were defended as a proper exercise of the state's police power to protect its public health and welfare.

After hearing each case argued three times, the court found these laws unconstitutional because they conflicted with federal power over foreign commerce. But beyond that point the court splintered, with eight justices writing separate opinions that took seven hours to read from the bench. The justices could not agree on whether the federal power over foreign commerce was exclusive, leaving no room for state regulation, or whether there might be such room if Congress had not exercised its power in a particular area.

There was no opinion of the court in these cases, and Reporter Benjamin C. Howard, exercising considerable wisdom, declined to summarize the ruling beyond the fact that it struck down the challenged laws. For details and reasoning, he simply referred the reader to the "opinions of the judges."

Political Questions

In the 1829 case of *Foster v. Neilson,* the court had refused to resolve an international boundary dispute because it said such a disagreement presented a "political question" that should be resolved by the representative branches of the government.

Twenty years later the court applied this doctrine in the case of *Luther v. Borden* and refused to decide which of two competing factions was the legitimate government of Rhode Island. This too was a political question, held the court, suitable for resolution by Congress, not the court.

Internal Changes

In 1844 Congress responded to the increasing workload of the court by lengthening its terms. Opening day was moved back from January to the first Monday in December.

Other procedural changes during this time reflected the end of the days when the court considered only a few cases and did so at a leisurely pace that allowed time for lengthy arguments and required less record keeping. In 1839 the court required that all motions to it be filed in writing with the clerk. In 1849 the court limited the time for arguments, giving counsel for each side two hours to present his case, but no more, without special leave.

In 1843 Richard Peters, for 15 years the court's reporter, was fired by four of the justices acting in the absence of the Chief Justice and their other colleagues. Peters had fallen out of favor with several of the justices as a result of differences over the inclusion of their opinions in the reports.

Peters was replaced by Benjamin Howard of Maryland, a former member of Congress and a college friend of Justice Wayne. Howard would serve until 1861.

Public Confidence

Despite the personnel changes and philosophical difficulties endured by the court during the 1840s, public confidence in it continued to rise. Charles Warren reports that public esteem for the Supreme Court was at a peak in the last years of that decade. He wrote that "while there were extremists and radicals in both parties who inveighed against it and its decisions, yet the general mass of the public and the Bar had faith in its impartiality and its ability." [56]

The first decisions of the next decade — which would bring a precipitate drop in public respect for the court — appeared to bear out this confidence. The court exercised restraint in dealing with the slavery issue — and appeared to be clarifying its position on commerce matters.

In the December 1850 term the court heard arguments in the case of *Strader v. Graham*.[57] The basic question presented was the same one that would arise in the *Dred Scott* case a few years later: Were slaves owned in Kentucky still slaves after they worked for a time in a free state and returned to Kentucky?

The court held that this matter should be resolved in the courts and under the laws of the state where the slaves were residing. This was not a matter for federal courts to resolve, held the justices.

Cooley, Curtis and Commerce

Late in 1851 Justice Woodbury died. As his successor, President Millard Fillmore chose Benjamin R. Curtis, 41, a noted Boston attorney. Confirmed in December 1851, Curtis would serve only six terms, but in that brief tenure he would leave his mark on history in several notable constitutional opinions.

The first of these rulings came during his first term in the case of *Cooley v. Board of Wardens of the Port of Philadelphia,* which required the justices to decide whether a city could enact ordinances concerning the use of pilots in its harbor. Philadelphia's ordinance regulating this matter was challenged as infringing on the federal power over commerce.

The court upheld the Philadelphia ordinance. Curtis wrote the majority opinion. The court declared that there were two categories of interstate and foreign commerce: one essentially local, which could be regulated locally, at least so long as it was not regulated by Congress; the other essentially national, which needed a uniform rule if it was to be regulated at all, and thus could never be regulated by the states.

In a sense, the Curtis opinion was no more than "an eloquent statement of indefiniteness," wrote Carl B. Swisher a century later, but "with the statement the indefiniteness came to seem in some way manageable, by contrast with the confusion of multiple opinions in the License Cases and the Passenger Cases. The opinion promised to give a more pragmatic, less conceptual and categorical direction to the Court's thinking concerning state regulation of commerce." [58]

The December 1851 term included two other decisions of importance in the area of navigation and commerce. In the case of *Pennsylvania v. Wheeling & Belmont Bridge Co.,* the court held that a bridge built by the state of Virginia across the Ohio River was too low and thus obstructed interstate commerce. The court ordered the bridge torn down. But Congress in 1852 passed a law that declared the bridge did not obstruct interstate commerce, allowing the bridge to stand. This was the first example of Congress overturning the court's decision by legislation.

Also that term, the court responded to the growing network of national commerce and transportation, substantially enlarging the federal government's admiralty jurisdiction to include all the nation's navigable waterways, not just those subject to the ebb and flow of tides.[59]

The Southern Seat

In July 1852 Justice McKinley died. To fill his place, President Fillmore chose Edward Bradford of Louisiana, who failed to win Senate confirmation during that session. Fillmore next named Sen. George E. Badger of North Carolina, whose nomination was effectively killed when the Senate, in an unusual breach of tradition, postponed consideration of it — by a one-vote margin — early in 1853. In the last week of his term, Fillmore sent still a third name to the Senate — that of Louisianan William C. Micou — but the Senate refused to confirm him.

The new president, Franklin Pierce, chose John A. Campbell of Alabama, 41, well known both for his scholarship and for his advocacy before the Supreme Court. Campbell was quickly confirmed and served until the outbreak of the Civil War.

Due Process

In 1856 the court began the long process of finding a definition of due process. In the case of *Murray v. Hoboken Land & Improvement Co.* the court held that the Fifth Amendment guarantee of due process applied to actions of Congress, as well as to executive and court actions.

John A. Campbell   **Benjamin R. Curtis**

And Justice Curtis, writing for the court, defined due process — by indirection — as procedures that did not conflict with specific written provisions of the Constitution or with the established practice in England at the time of the settlement of the New World colonies.

The *Dred Scott* Case

Also in 1856 the court heard arguments in the case of Dred Scott, a Missouri slave who claimed that he was free as a result of a sojourn in Illinois and other territories that were "free states" under the Missouri Compromise of 1820. Scott's case was argued Feb. 11, 1856. In May of that year the court ordered the case argued again. Reargument took place early in the December 1856 term. Justice Curtis' brother was one of the attorneys appearing in the case before the court.

Chief Justice Taney was aging. This factor, along with health and family problems of other members of the court, slowed its operations. Not until February 1857 — a year after the first arguments — was the *Dred Scott* case discussed at conference.

At the conference the court agreed the decision would follow that in *Strader v. Graham* a few years earlier — holding that Scott's status was a matter to be resolved under state law. The majority agreed not to consider the

---

As long as the Constitution endures, "this tribunal must exist with it, deciding in the peaceful forms of judicial proceedings the angry and irritating controversies between sovereignties, which in other countries have been determined by the arbitrament of force."

—Chief Justice Roger B. Taney,
Ableman v. Booth, 1859

---

larger issue — whether Congress had the power to exclude slavery from some territories, as it had done in the now-repealed Missouri Compromise. Justice Nelson was assigned the task of writing this majority opinion.

But Justices McLean and Curtis, both convinced anti-slavery men, dissented, and announced their intention to declare in their opinions that the Missouri Compromise was proper, that Congress indeed did have the power to ban slavery from the territories.

The majority thus was compelled to revise its plan. Nelson's assignment was withdrawn. Chief Justice Taney took upon himself the task of writing the majority's main opinion.

Taney's illness delayed announcement of the decision until March 6, 1857, just after President Buchanan was inaugurated. Each justice wrote a separate opinion in this case; the reading of the opinions in court took two days.

The court declared blacks forever disabled from attaining citizenship, the Missouri Compromise unconstitutional, and Congress powerless to halt the spread of slavery.

The court had overreached its power in setting such limits to the hopes of black men and the powers of Congress. It forced the issue of slavery out of the courtroom and the legislative chambers and onto the battlefield. This was also the first of the "self-inflicted wounds" of the court.

One scholar summarized the weakening impact of this decision upon the court:

During neither the Civil War nor the period of Reconstruction did the Supreme Court play anything like its role of supervision, with the result that during the one period the military powers of the President underwent undue expansion, and during the other, the legislative powers of Congress. The court itself was conscious of its weakness. . . . [A]t no time since Jefferson's first administration has its independence been in greater jeopardy than between 1860 and 1870.[60]

The *Dred Scott* decision was endorsed by southern Democrats and denounced by northern Democrats, dividing the party into warring factions and enabling the Republican Party to win the White House in 1860. Thus, Charles Warren would write, "it may fairly be said that Chief Justice Taney elected Abraham Lincoln to the presidency." [61]

Curtis' Resignation

Another result of the *Dred Scott* decision was Justice Curtis' decision to resign after only six years on the court. His philosophical disagreement with his colleagues and his general lack of confidence in the court, compounded by an acrimonious exchange with Chief Justice Taney over access to the *Dred Scott* opinions, spurred him to leave the bench and return to his more lucrative practice of law. He resigned in September 1857. He would argue more than 50 cases before the court in subsequent years, including the first *Legal Tender Case*, which he lost.

To replace Curtis in the "New England seat" President Buchanan nominated former Attorney General Nathan Clifford. Clifford, considered a party hack by some in the Senate, was confirmed by a three-vote margin, early in 1858. He served until his death in 1881.

Federal Judicial Power

Although Chief Justice Taney's name became almost synonymous with his *Dred Scott* opinion — and the damage it did to the nation and the court — his last major pre-war opinion was both far more eloquent and more enduring in its impact.

Two years after the *Dred Scott* ruling, the court decided the case of *Ableman v. Booth*. In speaking for the court, Chief Justice Taney delivered a ringing reaffirmation of federal judicial power.

The case of *Ableman v. Booth* involved an abolitionist in Wisconsin who was tried and convicted of violating the federal Fugitive Slave Act. Both before his trial and after his conviction, state judges ordered federal officials to release him, using the writ of *habeas corpus* and declaring his detention improper.

Finally the case came before the Supreme Court in January 1859. The state did not send anyone to argue its case. On March 7, 1859, the unanimous Supreme Court declared that state judges lacked the power to so interfere in federal judicial proceedings.

To allow such interference, wrote Chief Justice Taney, "would subvert the very foundations of this Government." As long as the Constitution endured, he continued, "this tribunal must exist with it, deciding in the peaceful forms of judicial proceedings the angry and irritating controversies between sovereignties, which in other countries have been determined by the arbitrament of force."[62]

The Taney Court: A Modern View

The *Dred Scott* decision and the conflict that followed it so colored historians' view of the Taney court that only after a century had passed was an objective assessment of its accomplishments possible.

In the concluding chapter of his history of the Taney era, published in 1974, Carl B. Swisher described the court's decisions and operations during this period:

> By contrast with the work of the same tribunal in various other periods, the essence of its contribution was seldom focused in eloquent philosophical statement from the bench. The Taney Court was peculiarly unphilosophical.... [I]t tended to be assumed that the federal constitutional system was now generally understood so that the earlier forms of judicial explanation were unnecessary. The government was no longer experimental but was a going concern....
>
> The Taney court fell upon evil times not because of Jacksonianism or even because of lack of ability on the part of its members, but because it was caught in the grinding pressures of sectional conflict. A Court committed to application of the law was bound to crash into difficulties when the nation itself divided over whether there was indeed a surviving body of constitutional law binding on all the states and all the people.
>
> ... [I]n this time of civil war the strident ... voice of Mars ... drowned out the voice of the law, with its stress upon reason and rightness rather than ruthless power....[63]

War and Recovery: 1861-1872

The decade of the Civil War saw the Supreme Court sink to its lowest point in public esteem. This, Carl Swisher explains, was "not merely because it had handed down the Dred Scott decision but because the rule of law as interpreted by the judiciary had given way to a rage for unrestricted exercise of power — which seemed to flare with even greater violence once the battlefields were stilled. There could be a restoration of the prestige of the judiciary only with restoration of respect for the rule of law."[64]

During this period, which includes the last years of Chief Justice Roger B. Taney and almost the entire tenure of his successor, Chief Justice Salmon P. Chase, the court as an institution underwent considerable change.

It moved into a new courtroom, was expanded to 10 seats and contracted to eight, gained five new members — including the new Chief Justice — and found itself faced with the most sensitive questions to date concerning the powers of the president.

New Justices

In mid-1860 Justice Daniel died. His seat remained empty well into 1862.

Late in his term, President Buchanan named his former attorney general and secretary of State, Jeremiah S. Black, to fill Daniel's seat. But political opposition within both parties brought the rejection of Black's nomination by a vote of 25-26 in February 1861.

The Civil War broke out in April. That same month two more vacancies occurred. Justice McLean died and Justice Campbell resigned when his home state, Alabama, seceded. The court's other southern members — Wayne and Catron — continued to hold their seats through the war.

President Lincoln thus had three seats to fill. In January 1862 he selected Noah H. Swayne, an Ohio attorney, 57, to fill the McLean seat. Swayne would serve 19 years.

In July 1862 Lincoln filled the empty Daniel seat with Samuel Freeman Miller of Iowa, 46, the only justice trained in medicine as well as law. He would serve for 28 years, until 1890, writing 616 opinions.[65]

To the third seat Lincoln named his close friend and political adviser David Davis of Illinois, 47. Davis would serve 14 years, until he resigned to take a Senate seat.

In March 1863 Congress added a 10th seat to the court, giving Lincoln a fourth appointment. To that new seat he named Stephen J. Field, chief justice of the California Supreme Court, who would serve almost 35 years and be the only justice ever the target of an assassination attempt as a result of his rulings. When Field was appointed he had to travel to Washington by steamship and railroad across Panama — the transcontinental railroad was not completed until 1869.

New Chambers

When the court met for its December 1860 term, it met in a new courtroom. After four decades in the basement room under the Senate chamber, the court moved upstairs. The new wings of the Capitol housing the Senate and House had been completed; the old Senate chamber had been refurbished for the court at a cost of $25,000. The court would meet in this room for the next 75 years, until moving into its own building.

There was a new reporter for the court in 1861. Benjamin C. Howard resigned to run unsuccessfully for governor of Maryland. He was succeeded by Jeremiah Black, Buchanan's unsuccessful nominee for the Daniel seat. Black served for only two years, resigning in 1863 to resume his successful private practice of law full time. He was succeeded in 1864 by John William Wallace of Pennsylvania, who held the post until 1875.

Presidential War Powers

The Civil War began in April 1861. Congress did not meet until mid-summer. In the interim President Lincoln moved to deal with the emergency, calling for troops, imposing a blockade on southern ports, and in some circumstances authorizing military commanders to suspend the privilege of the writ of *habeas corpus.*

These actions marked the most dramatic expansion of executive power in the nation's history to that point and, not surprisingly, some of them were challenged as exceeding the president's constitutional authority.

Chief Justice Taney was among the first to declare Lincoln's actions unconstitutional. In May, the month after war had broken out, a military commander in Baltimore refused to comply with Taney's order — issued as a circuit judge, not a Supreme Court justice — to produce in court one John Merryman, a civilian imprisoned by the Union army for his anti-Union activities.

The commander cited, as grounds for his refusal, Lincoln's instructions allowing him to suspend the privilege of the writ of *habeas corpus,* the instrument used to inquire into the reasons justifying an individual's detention.

Taney responded with an opinion, which he sent to Lincoln himself, declaring that only Congress could suspend this privilege and that Lincoln's actions were thus unconstitutional. If such authority can be "usurped by the military power . . . the people of the United States are no longer living under a government of laws, but every citizen holds his life, liberty, and property at the will and pleasure of the army officer in whose military district he may happen to be found." [66]

Lincoln, undeterred, continued to insist that emergency conditions required the exercise of extraordinary power. Five years later, after both Taney and Lincoln were dead, the Supreme Court in the case of *Ex parte Milligan* would confirm Taney's position.

The *Prize Cases*

The legality of Lincoln's actions blockading southern ports was the major war issue resolved by the court during the war years. And it was decided in the *Prize Cases* in 1863 in favor of presidential power, if only by a vote of 5-4.

Had the vote tipped the other way, all of Lincoln's wartime actions would have been called into question, seriously undermining his ability to lead the nation in the conflict.

The majority upheld the president's power to institute the blockade even before Congress officially had authorized such an action. The vote made clear the importance of Lincoln's appointments to the court. The majority consisted of his first three nominees — Swayne, Miller and Davis — and Wayne and Grier, who wrote the majority opinion. Dissenting were Taney, Nelson, Catron and Clifford.

Having resolved that critical question, the court retreated to a position of restraint in dealing with issues of war. In the December 1863 term, Taney's last, the court held that it lacked jurisdiction to hear a challenge to the use of paper money as legal tender (necessary to finance the war),[67] or over a petition of *habeas corpus* ordering military officials to justify their detention of a civilian.[68] Within six years, the court would reverse both holdings.

The Court in 1865

From left: Court Clerk Daniel W. Middleton, Justices David Davis, Noah H. Swayne, Robert C. Grier, James M. Wayne, Chief Justice Salmon P. Chase, Justices Samuel Nelson, Nathan Clifford, Samuel F. Miller, Stephen J. Field.

A New Chief

In October 1864, as the war neared its end, Chief Justice Taney died. He was 87 years old and had served the nation as its Chief Justice for 28 years.

President Lincoln wished to name a man who would back the administration on the critical issues of emancipation — another exercise of extraordinary presidential powers that lacked any clear base in the Constitution — and legal tender. Congress had passed laws making paper money legal tender in place of gold to enable the Union to finance its war effort.

Lincoln chose Salmon P. Chase, a potential political rival who had, nevertheless, served until mid-1864 as secretary of the Treasury. After his re-election in 1864, Lincoln nominated Chase as Chief Justice. He was quickly confirmed and seated as the court began its December 1864 term. Chase was 56, three years younger than Taney when he had assumed the post, yet he would serve only nine years before his death in 1873.

Military Justice

"Never again would there be a term wherein so few questions of importance were answered as in that of 1864-65," wrote historian Charles Fairman.[69]

But the following term brought before the justices another facet of the problem that had confronted Chief Justice Taney in the *Merryman* case five years earlier: Can a president in wartime replace the nation's civilian courts with courts-martial, to which civilians as well as military men are subject?

In April 1866 the Supreme Court answered this question with an emphatic "no" — just as Taney had. The justices were unanimous in holding that Lincoln had acted illegally when he instituted trial by military commission for civilians in non-war areas where the civil courts continued to function.

The court divided 5-4 on the related issue of whether Congress and the president acting together could replace civilian justice with courts-martial in such areas.

The court's full opinions in this case of *Ex parte Milligan* were not released until December 1866 — eight months later. The majority opinion was written by Lincoln's personal friend, Justice Davis, who warned as Taney had that suspension of constitutional guarantees during wartime would lead to despotism.

These opinions and this ruling provoked violent criticism in Congress. There they were viewed as evidence that the court would — at its first opportunity — hold unconstitutional the military regimes imposed as Congress' effort to reconstruct the defeated South.

Congressional criticism took the forms of proposals for impeachment of the majority justices, "reorganization" of the court through the addition of new seats, curtailment of the court's appellate jurisdiction, and the requirement that the court be unanimous on constitutional rulings.

In fact, the court did undergo some reorganization at this point, due, however, more to the unpopularity of President Johnson than to the court's own rulings.

In May 1865 Justice Catron died after 28 years on the court, the last of which he had spent in virtual exile from his southern home. Johnson's April 1866 nomination of his close friend, Attorney General Henry Stanbery, died after the Senate abolished the vacant seat, and reduced the size of the court to seven by providing that both Catron's seat and the next two becoming vacant would not be filled.

In mid-1867 Justice Wayne — the court's other southern member — died after 32 years on the bench. He was the last of the Jackson justices; his service had spanned the Taney era. His seat was not filled; the court was now eight members.

The *Test Oath Cases*

The apprehensiveness of Reconstruction architects about the court's view of their measures was heightened early in 1867. The court struck down an act of Congress requiring persons wishing to practice law before the federal courts to take a "test oath" affirming their loyalty — past and present — to the Union.

Augustus H. Garland, a noted Supreme Court advocate, later attorney general, who had served in the Confederate government during the war, challenged this test oath requirement. A similar state law also was challenged.

In the cases of *Ex parte Garland* and *Cummings v. Missouri*, the court in 1867 held both state and federal oath requirements unconstitutional. The majority found them a violation of the Constitution's ban on *ex post facto* laws and bills of attainder. The only Lincoln justice voting with the majority was Field; the arguments of his brother, David Dudley Field, who had argued one of the cases before the court, apparently persuaded Justice Field to vote against the test oaths.

A Matter of Jurisdiction

After *Milligan* and the *Test Oath Cases*, however, the Supreme Court showed no stomach for battle with Congress on the overall issue of Reconstruction.

In the 1867 term — only months after deciding the Garland case — the court unanimously refused Mississippi's request that it order President Johnson to stop enforcing the Reconstruction Acts. Such an order, the court held in *Mississippi v. Johnson*, was outside its power and its jurisdiction. Similar reasoning brought rejection of a like request from Georgia the following month.

The following term, however, the application of a southern editor named McCardle to the court for a writ of *habeas corpus* to force military authorities in Mississippi to justify their holding him for trial brought to a peak the concern of Reconstruction advocates in Congress.

McCardle was being held for trial by a military commission on charges that his anti-Reconstruction articles were impeding the process of "reconstructing" the South.

The court heard arguments in the case the first week of March 1868, just as the Senate opened its impeachment trial of President Johnson. Three days after the court had taken the *McCardle* case under advisement, Congress revoked its jurisdiction over such cases. Johnson vetoed the bill. It was immediately repassed over his veto.

The court then considered the new issue — the impact of the repeal of its jurisdiction on the pending case. Later in the spring the court postponed final consideration of the case until the next term.

In May the Senate acquitted President Johnson.

The following April — 1869 — the court dismissed the *McCardle* case. The court held unanimously that when Congress revoked its jurisdiction over a category of cases, it was left powerless to do anything but dismiss all pending cases of that type.

The same day, in the case of *Texas v. White,* the court's majority endorsed the view that as a matter of law the seceding states never had left the union — that states had no power to secede — a moot point in 1869. Justices Swayne, Grier and Miller objected that the majority was endorsing a legal fiction and ignoring political reality.

Gold or Greenbacks?

To finance the war, Congress had passed the Legal Tender Acts, allowing the use of paper money in the payment of debts. These laws — which resulted in drastic change in the nation's economic system — repeatedly were challenged in federal courts.

In the December 1867 term, the Supreme Court heard such a challenge argued in the case of *Hepburn v. Griswold.* The justices ordered a second round of arguments that took place in December 1868; one of the attorneys arguing for the acts was the former justice, Benjamin R. Curtis, who had resumed an active legal practice upon resigning his seat.

Contemporary coverage of the case indicated little expectation that the court would hold the acts unconstitutional. After all, Chief Justice Chase had been Treasury secretary when the challenged laws were approved at the behest of the Lincoln administration.

But even after the second arguments, no decision was announced during the December 1868 term. The justices apparently did not reach a decision until November 1869 — and then their efforts were hampered by the vacillations of the aged Justice Grier, who voted in conference first to uphold the acts, then to strike them down.[70] The final vote in November was 5-3 against the validity of the Legal Tender Acts. The majority consisted of Chase, Nelson, Clifford, Field and Grier.

Congress in 1869 provided that a justice might retire and continue to receive half his salary. In December — before the court announced its decision in *Hepburn v. Griswold* — Justice Grier, 76, was persuaded to retire, effective Feb. 1, 1870.

Six days after his resignation, on Feb. 7, 1870, the court announced that by a 4-3 vote it found the statutes unconstitutional. They were inappropriate means for the exercise of the war powers, held the majority, and, as applied to debts contracted before the passage of the laws, they were a clear impairment of contract obligations. The dissenters were Justices Miller, Swayne and Davis.

Court Packing?

Even as Chase was reading the opinion in *Hepburn v. Griswold,* either the most effective court packing in the nation's history — or at least the best timing of appointments — was under way.

After Grant's election as president in 1868, Congress increased the size of the court to nine, giving Grant a new seat to fill. Grier's decision to retire opened a second vacancy.

Grant first chose Attorney General Ebenezer Hoar of Massachusetts for the new seat. But personal and political opposition developed to block that nomination in the Senate. To smooth the way for Hoar's confirmation, Grant nominated former Secretary of War Edwin M. Stanton — the choice of most members of Congress — for the Grier seat. Stanton was confirmed immediately, but died four days later. Hoar's nomination was rejected in February 1870; the vote was 24-33.

And so on Feb. 7, 1870, Grant sent two more nominations to the Senate — Joseph P. Bradley of New Jersey, 57, a railroad attorney, and Grier's personal choice as his successor; and William Strong of Pennsylvania, a state judge. Bradley and Strong were confirmed and seated in the spring of 1870.

Within weeks of their seating the court announced it would rehear the constitutional challenge to the Legal Tender Acts. The second *Legal Tender Case — Knox v. Lee* — was argued in the December 1870 term.

On May 1, 1871, 15 months after *Hepburn v. Griswold,* the court overruled itself. By a 5-4 vote, the court reversed the 4-3 vote in the earlier case. The five-man majority upheld the Legal Tender Acts as a proper exercise of the power of Congress. Justice Strong, who with Bradley converted the dissenters in *Hepburn* into the majority in *Knox,* wrote the majority opinion. The full opinions were not released until January of the following year.

This abrupt about-face — so clearly the result of a change in the court's membership — damaged the public confidence the court had been slowly regaining after the *Dred Scott* ruling and the war decade. It was, in the words of Charles Evans Hughes, the second of the court's self-inflicted wounds. Hughes declared that "there was no ground for attacking the honesty of the judges or for the suggestion that President Grant had attempted to pack the court." But he added: "Stability in judicial opinions is of no little importance in maintaining respect for the court's work." [71]

The Balance of Power: 1873-1888

The Union had been preserved. Indeed, in *Texas v. White,* a majority of the Supreme Court endorsed the legal fiction that it never had been disrupted. Now — as the critical war issues of the 1860s faded from its docket — the court set about restoring the state-federal balance of power.

Concern for the maintenance of the states as effective functioning units of the federal system was paramount in the minds of the justices. And so, to enhance state power, the court curtailed federal authority.

The court's power of judicial review of acts of Congress was wielded with new vigor. Between *Marbury* in 1803 and the *Slaughterhouse Cases* in 1873, the court held unconstitutional 10 acts of Congress. Six of the 10 were struck down between 1870 and 1873.

Another sign of the court's new sensitivity to the claims of states was its decision in 1871 that, even as the salaries of federal officials were not subject to state taxes, so state officials' salaries were immune from federal taxes.

The 14th Amendment

No better example of the court's view of the proper balance between state and federal power can be found than its rulings interpreting the Civil War Amendments — in particular the 14th Amendment.

In 1865 the addition of the 13th Amendment had formally declared the abolition of slavery. In 1868 the 14th Amendment gave added protection to the rights and liberties of persons threatened by state action. And in 1870 the 15th Amendment guaranteed blacks the right to vote.

Intended as instruments of radical change in the nation's social fabric, these amendments were so narrowly construed by the court in the decades immediately after their adoption that they lay virtually useless for most of the ensuing century.

The effect of these rulings was to preserve state power over the rights of individuals by denying any expansion of federal authority in that area.

The *Slaughterhouse Cases*

The court's first ruling on the scope of the 14th Amendment came in 1873 with the *Slaughterhouse Cases.* It was indicative of the direction in which 14th Amendment protections would first be extended that these cases were brought by butchers seeking to protect their businesses rather than by blacks seeking to assert their newly granted civil rights.

Louisiana had granted one company a monopoly on the slaughtering business in New Orleans. That grant was challenged by other butchers as denying them the right to practice their trade. They argued that this right was protected by the 14th Amendment's guarantee of the privileges and immunities of U.S. citizenship, of equal protection of the laws, and of due process.

The *Slaughterhouse Cases* were first argued in January 1872, just before the court's opinions in the second *Legal Tender Case* were read.[72] But those arguments were before an eight-man court. Justice Nelson, now 80, was absent. The court apparently was evenly divided, and ordered the cases reargued in the following term.

Before the December 1872 term began, Nelson resigned after 27 years of service. President Grant named Ward Hunt, a New York judge — as Nelson had been — to the seat. Hunt was seated in December 1872.

The *Slaughterhouse Cases* were reargued over a three-day period in February 1873. Attorney for the butchers was former Justice John Campbell.

The court announced its decision April 14, 1873. By a vote of 5-4, the court held that Louisiana had not violated the 14th Amendment by its grant of a slaughtering monopoly.

Writing for the court Justice Samuel Miller stated that the amendment did not increase the number of rights an individual possessed, but only extended new protection to those few rights, privileges and immunities that had their source in one's federal, rather than state, citizenship. The right to do business did not derive from one's U.S. citizenship, held the majority.

Any other decision, wrote Miller, would convert the court into "a perpetual censor upon all legislation of the States on the civil rights of their own citizens." [73]

Chief Justice Chase dissented, as did Swayne, Field and Bradley.

The next day, over Chase's lone dissent, the court held that a state did not deny a woman the privileges or immunities of U.S. citizenship when it refused, because of her sex, to license her to practice law in its courts.[74]

The Court in 1876

From left: Justices Joseph P. Bradley, Stephen J. Field, Samuel F. Miller, Nathan Clifford, Chief Justice Morrison R. Waite, Justices Noah H. Swayne, David Davis, William Strong, Ward Hunt.

Chief Justice Waite

Within the month, Chief Justice Chase was dead of a sudden stroke. His seat remained vacant for most of the following year.

President Grant tried unsuccessfully to place two of his personal friends in the seat — naming first Attorney General George Williams of Oregon and then Caleb Cushing, a former attorney general, of Massachusetts. Finally, he chose a little-known Ohio attorney, Morrison R. Waite, 58. Waite, who never had argued a case before the Supreme Court and who had no judicial experience, was quickly confirmed. He was seated in March 1874.

The term in which Waite began his 14 years as Chief Justice was the first to begin in October. Early in 1873 Congress had provided that the court's term would begin the second Monday in October rather than in December as it had since 1844.

Privileges and Immunities

Unlike his predecessor, Chief Justice Waite agreed fully with the court's narrow view of the privileges and immunities of federal citizenship.

In 1875 he wrote the court's opinion as it reinforced its decision in the *Slaughterhouse Cases,* holding that the right to vote was not a privilege or immunity of U.S. citizenship.[75]

The court under Waite was just as reluctant to acknowledge that the Civil War Amendments had expanded federal power to enforce individual rights as it was to admit that the amendments had expanded the list of protected rights.

In 1876 the court struck down several key portions of the laws Congress had enacted to enforce the 15th Amendment's guarantee of the right to vote and the 13th Amendment's abolition of slavery. Again, the new Chief Justice spoke for the court as it declared that Congress overreached

---

"For protection against abuses by Legislatures the people must resort to the polls, not to the courts."

—Chief Justice Morrison R. Waite,
Munn v. Illinois, 1877

---

itself in enacting such a broad statute penalizing persons who employed violence to deny blacks the right to vote. The court reiterated that the right to vote came from the states; only the right to be free of racial discrimination in voting came from the U.S. Constitution. These rulings left Congress virtually powerless to protect the newly enfranchised black.[76]

The Election of 1876

The disputed presidential election of 1876 drew the court into political controversy when five of its members — Bradley, Miller, Strong, Field and Clifford — served on the Electoral Commission that resolved the dispute over electoral votes, and paved the way for the election of Republican Rutherford B. Hayes. Hayes subsequently placed Stan-

ley Matthews — the man who had helped negotiate the compromise which elected him — on the Supreme Court.

State Powers

Not surprisingly, the court of the 1870s, which refused to grant Congress broad power to enforce the civil rights of individuals, was quite willing to allow states to exercise their police power in ever-widening fields.

The rapid growth of large manufacturing and transport companies after the Civil War had prompted their customers to organize and seek state regulation of those businesses to curtail their power over the individual consumer. Among the most successful were farmer groups, including the Grange, which in some states obtained the passage of "Granger laws" setting limits on the rates railroads and grain elevator companies could charge for hauling or storing farm products and other goods.

Despite the failure of the butchers to win 14th Amendment protection of their right to do business in the *Slaughterhouse Cases,* the railroad and grain storage operators mounted a similar challenge to these Granger laws. They argued that the state, in passing these laws, deprived them of their liberty and property without due process of law.

The *Granger Cases*

In a group of cases known as the *Granger Cases* and by the title of one of them — *Munn v. Illinois* — the court in 1877 rejected this challenge to state regulatory laws.

Upholding the laws, Chief Justice Waite explained that in the court's view some private property, by virtue of its use, was so invested with a public interest that states could properly exercise their police power to regulate it. Justices Field and Strong dissented.

The majority also rejected the idea that federal courts should review such laws to determine if the regulations were reasonable. Chief Justice Waite acknowledged that the state might abuse this power to regulate business, but found that insufficient argument "against its existence. For protection against abuses by Legislatures the people must resort to the polls," he concluded, "not to the courts."[77]

Three years later, the court — again with Waite as its spokesman — found in the state police power a substantial qualification of the Constitution's ban on state impairment of contract obligations. In the case of *Stone v. Mississippi,* the court held that a legislature could never contract to place a subject beyond the exercise of this power. It upheld a decision of the Mississippi legislature to ban lotteries, even though this decision nullified the charter of a lottery corporation granted by a previous legislature.

New Justices

A week after the court's decision in *Munn v. Illinois,* Justice Davis resigned to take a Senate seat. As his replacement the new president, Hayes, chose a 44-year-old lawyer, a namesake of the first Chief Justice, John Marshall Harlan.

Harlan would serve well into the 20th century, his 34-year tenure characterized by a long line of opinions dissenting from the court's narrow view of the 14th Amendment.

At the turn of the decade, the court's personnel underwent further change. By 1881 only three of the justices who participated in the 1873 *Slaughterhouse* decision remained on the bench — Miller from the majority and Field and Bradley from the dissent.

By 1880 the court was operating under the handicap of having three members unable to fill their proper roles. Swayne, now 75, had been in failing mental health for three years.[78] Hunt suffered a stroke in 1879 and never returned to the bench. Clifford had been disabled for some time but refused to resign until a Democratic president could choose his successor.

But the first departure from the court of the 1880s was none of these but Justice Strong, who, although in his 70s, still was at the peak of his abilities. President Hayes chose William B. Woods of Georgia as Strong's successor. Woods, a federal circuit judge, was the first southerner named to the court since Justice Campbell was selected in 1852. Although only 56 at the time of his appointment, he served but six years before his death.

In January 1881, shortly after Woods was confirmed, Swayne resigned. To succeed him, Hayes selected Sen. Stanley Matthews, 56, also of Ohio. Matthews had been instrumental in the compromise that placed Hayes in the White House in 1877. Nominated first by Hayes and then by incoming President James J. Garfield, Matthews was confirmed by the narrow margin of one vote, 24-23. He served on the court for seven years, until his death in 1889.

Later in 1881 Justice Clifford died. To replace him President Arthur selected Horace Gray, chief justice of the Massachusetts supreme court. Gray, 53 at the time, served for 20 years.

Finally in 1882, after three years of absence from the bench, Justice Hunt resigned. After Arthur's first choice, Roscoe Conkling, declined, Arthur chose federal Judge Samuel Blatchford of New York to fill the seat. He served for 11 years.

Personal Rights

The 14th Amendment, ratified in 1868, proved a rich source of Supreme Court litigation. In the 15 years between the *Slaughterhouse Cases* — the court's first 14th Amendment ruling — and the end of Chief Justice Waite's term in 1888 — the court decided some 70 cases on the basis of that amendment. In the ensuing 30 years there would be 10 times as many — some 725 14th Amendment cases — decided by the court.[79]

In general, individuals who sought to invoke the protection of the amendment's privileges and immunities, due process or equal protection clauses had little success. The court on the whole was unresponsive to "social" legislation or to claims of individual rights, although there were exceptions.

Racial Equality

In 1878 the Supreme Court struck down a state law that required equal access for black and white passengers to railroads operating in the state. The law was impermissible state interference with interstate commerce, held the court in the case of *Hall v. DeCuir.*

In 1880 the court applied the 14th Amendment to deny states the freedom to restrict jury service to white persons. But three years later, in the *Civil Rights Cases,* the court made clear that it would condone use of the amendment only to reach clearly discriminatory *state* action.

Private Discrimination

In the *Civil Rights Cases,* the court declared Congress powerless to reach acts of *private* discrimination against blacks. With Justice Bradley writing the majority opinion,

the court struck down the far-reaching Civil Rights Act of 1875, enacted to implement the guarantees of the Civil War Amendments.

The court declared that the 14th Amendment did not give Congress the power to regulate matters that traditionally had been left to state control. Congress could act only to correct — not to prevent — discrimination by the state.

In 1884, however, the court upheld the power of Congress to provide for the punishment of persons who beat up a black man to keep him from voting in a federal election.[80]

The Bill of Rights

The same day, however, the court demonstrated its reluctance to use the 14th Amendment to curtail state authority. Joseph Hurtado was convicted of murder under California law that did not provide for a grand jury indictment in serious crimes. Citing the Fifth Amendment guarantee of charge by indictment for serious federal crimes, Hurtado challenged his conviction as a violation of the 14th Amendment's due process guarantee. That guarantee, he argued, applied the indictment provision to the states.

The court rejected Hurtado's argument reaffirming the view — first set out in *Barron v. Baltimore* by Chief Justice Marshall — that the Fifth Amendment applies only against federal, not state, action. The 14th Amendment, held the court, did not extend the right to an indictment to persons charged with state crimes. Justice Harlan dissented from this ruling in *Hurtado v. California.*

In its first major ruling concerning the guarantees of the Fourth and Fifth Amendments against federal authority, however, the court just two years after *Hurtado* read those provisions to give broad protection to the individual.

The court's decision in *Boyd v. United States,* decided in 1886, was a ringing defense of individual privacy against the threat of governmental invasion. Justice Bradley, for the court, declared that "constitutional provisions for the security of person and property should be liberally construed. A close and literal construction deprives them of half their efficacy and leads to gradual depreciation of the right. . . ."[81]

And later that year, in one of the first successful equal protection cases brought by an individual, the court held that the equal protection guarantee extended to all persons, not just citizens, and meant that city officials could not deny all Chinese applicants the right to operate laundries.[82]

Property Rights

In the 1870s — most notably in the *Slaughterhouse* and *Granger* cases — the court steadfastly had rejected the efforts of businessmen to use the 14th Amendment as a shield against government regulation.

But in the 1880s that stance began to weaken.

In 1869 the court had held that corporations were not citizens and so could not invoke the protection of the 14th Amendment's privileges and immunities clause.[83]

But 17 years later, in 1886, Chief Justice Waite simply announced — before the court heard arguments in the case of *Santa Clara County v. Southern Pacific Railway* — that there was no need for the arguing attorneys to discuss whether corporations were persons under the protection of the 14th Amendment's equal protection clause: The court had decided that they were.

That same year the court sharply limited the power of the states to regulate railroad rates. In the case of *Wabash,*

St. Louis and Pacific Railway Co. v. Illinois, the court held that states could not set rates for railroads that formed part of an interstate network. Such regulation infringed the federal power over interstate commerce. This ruling cut back sharply the power that the court had seemed to grant to the states in *Munn v. Illinois,* just nine years earlier.

Yet in other areas the court of the late 1880s continued to back the exercise of the state police power. It upheld state laws regulating intoxicating liquors and colored oleo, refusing to find such laws either violations of the due process guarantee or burdens on interstate commerce.[84]

Changes in the Court

In 1887 Justice Woods died. President Cleveland filled this "southern seat" with Lucius Quintus Cincinnatus Lamar of Mississippi. Lamar, 62, had served both in the House and the Senate and was secretary of Interior at the time of his selection to the court. He was the first Democrat placed on the court in 25 years. Although the Republican-dominated Senate Judiciary Committee opposed confirmation, he was confirmed by a vote of 32-28. He served only five years, until his death in 1893.

In March 1888 Chief Justice Waite, 72, died of pneumonia.

As the new Chief Justice President Cleveland selected Melville W. Fuller, a successful Chicago attorney whose clients included several major railroads. Fuller had argued

a number of cases before the court. He was 55 years old at the time of his selection. Nominated in May 1888, he was

> *"...Constitutional provisions for the security of person and property should be liberally construed. A close and literal construction deprives them of half their efficacy and leads to gradual depreciation of the right...."*
>
> —Justice Joseph Bradley
> *Boyd v. United States,* 1886

confirmed in July by a vote of 41-20. He would lead the court for 22 years, until his death in 1910.

By the end of its first century, the court had become more institutional and less personal in its operations. No longer did the justices live, as well as work, together. That practice had ended soon after the Civil War. And after Reporter Wallace left that post in 1875, the volumes of the court's decisions were no longer cited by the name of the Reporter, but by the impersonal "U.S." designation.

The Court in 1888

From left: Justices Joseph P. Bradley, Stanley Matthews, Samuel F. Miller, Horace Gray, Chief Justice Melville W. Fuller, Justices John Marshall Harlan, Stephen J. Field, Samuel Blatchford, Lucius Q. C. Lamar.

The Conservative Court: 1889-1919

Melville Fuller became Chief Justice of the United States at the end of the court's first century. His tenure would span the transition — chronologically, politically and socially — from the world of the 18th and 19th centuries to that of the 20th century. Vast change would come to the nation during this period, change that would bring new challenges to the Supreme Court. William Swindler describes it:

> The passing of the frontier, the rise of an interstate industrialism, the shift from a rural to an urban distribution of population, the breakdown of 19th century capitalism and the efforts to construct in its stead a twentieth-century capitalism, the breakthrough in science and technology, the change in the society of nations brought about by global wars and the militant dialectic of totalitarianism — the constitutional posture of the American people had to be readjusted in response to each of these.

> Fuller's court stood upon the watershed, with a powerful pull of ideological gravity toward the past. At least three of his colleagues when he came onto the bench dated from the constitutional golden age: Justices Bradley, Field and Miller all had begun their careers under men who in turn had known John Marshall and Joseph Story. From these venerated predecessors, who interpreted the Constitution with reference to a pioneer economy and an *ante-bellum* concept of the Federal function, Fuller and his intimate associates undertook to derive a jurisprudence to apply to issues never imagined by the early Federalist jurists.[85]

Justice Brewer

Within five years of Fuller's assuming the seat of Chief Justice, there were four other new members of the court — all chosen by President Benjamin Harrison and all men of conservative bent.

The first and most notable of Harrison's selections came in 1889. Justice Matthews died in March. As his successor, Harrison chose Federal Circuit Judge David J. Brewer of Kansas, Justice Field's nephew. Brewer, 52, was confirmed late in the year. During his 20 years on the court he would be one of its most articulate members.

Segregation and Substantive Due Process

On March 3, 1890, Justice Brewer delivered his first major opinion for the court.

In the case of *Louisville, New Orleans and Texas Railway Co. v. Mississippi*, the majority upheld a state law requiring railroads to provide separate accommodations for black and white passengers on trips within the state. Justices Harlan and Bradley dissented.

Accepting the state court's finding that the requirement applied only to intrastate trips, the Supreme Court majority held it no burden on interstate commerce.

Although the case rested on a different constitutional basis, it clearly marked the way to the position the court would take six years later in *Plessy v. Ferguson*, accepting the "separate but equal" doctrine as constitutional, and

confirming the segregation of U.S. society into black and white compartments for the next 60 years.

Three weeks later, on March 24, 1890, the court majority for the first time accepted and declared the doctrine of substantive due process, the belief that the due process clause (included in the Fifth and the 14th Amendments) gives federal courts the power to review the substance of legislation, in this case legislation intended to regulate business.

In the case of *Chicago, Milwaukee & St. Paul Railway Co. v. Minnesota*, the court held that Minnesota denied businessmen their right to due process when it set the rates they could charge and did not provide for judicial review of the reasonableness of those rates.

No longer would the court defer to legislative judgment in rate-setting, as it had indicated it would in *Munn v. Illinois*. Now it assumed for itself the power to review the wisdom of these economic decisions.

Justice Brown

This ruling, which extended the protection of the 14th Amendment to business — a view the court had so firmly rejected in the *Slaughterhouse Cases* — came in the last term of Justice Samuel F. Miller, author of the *Slaughterhouse* opinion. In October 1890 Miller died after 28 years on the bench.

Harrison chose federal Judge Henry B. Brown, a Yale classmate of Brewer's, to succeed Miller. Brown, from Michigan, would serve on the court for 15 years.

The Circuit Court of Appeals Act

For the nation's first century, the Supreme Court was essentially the only body to hear appeals from the decisions of other federal courts. As a result of increasing litigation in the federal courts, the Supreme Court's workload mushroomed. From the end of the Civil War until 1891 it was not at all uncommon for a case to wait two or three years after being docketed before it was argued before the court.

The court adopted various changes in its operations to promote more expeditious handling of cases, but all such efforts were negated by the increasing volume of business.

Finally, in 1891, Congress eliminated the justices' obligation to ride circuit. It set up a system of federal appeals courts — between the old district and circuit courts, on the one hand, and the Supreme Court on the other. The decisions of these new circuit courts of appeals were final in many cases; the Supreme Court had complete discretion in deciding whether or not to hear appeals from them. The result, at least for a time, was a reduction in the press of business at the court. *(Box, p. 32)*

Incrimination and Immunity

Early in 1892 the Supreme Court decided the case of *Counselman v. Hitchcock*, one of its rare 19th century rulings concerning the Bill of Rights. And, as in the case of *Boyd v. United States* six years earlier, the court construed those amendments to provide broad protection for individuals against federal authority. The court held the immunity provisions of the Interstate Commerce Act to be constitutionally insufficient. If a witness was to be compelled to testify and provide authorities with evidence against himself, held the unanimous court, the government must promise that it would not use that evidence in any way against him. This was the requirement of the Fifth Amendment guarantee that an individual would not be forced to incriminate himself.

New Justices

Within 10 days of the *Counselman* ruling, Justice Bradley died. As his successor, President Harrison chose George Shiras Jr., a Pennsylvania lawyer whose clients included the great iron and steel companies of Pittsburgh and the Baltimore & Ohio Railroad. Despite opposition to his nomination from the senators from his home state, Shiras was unanimously confirmed. He served on the court for a decade.

In January of the following year, 1893, Justice Lamar died. To succeed him, Harrison chose a friend from his Senate days — Howell E. Jackson of Tennessee, a federal circuit judge. Jackson, however, became ill within a year of his appointment and died after two years on the court, only a few months after the court's landmark income tax ruling of May 1895.

The Hazards of Riding Circuit

The attempted murder of Justice Stephen J. Field — by a litigant unhappy with one of his circuit decisions — may have hastened the passage of the Circuit Court of Appeals Act of 1891, which finally relieved Supreme Court justices of the duty of sitting as circuit judges.

In 1888 Field, sitting as a circuit judge in California, his home state, delivered an opinion that held invalid a purported marriage contract between Sarah Althea Hill and William Sharon. Sharon, a wealthy mine owner and senator from Nevada (R 1875-81), was by the time of the ruling deceased.

Hill, by now the wife of one of Field's former colleagues on the California Supreme Court, David Terry, was incensed at the ruling. As a result of a brawl in the courtroom upon announcement of the ruling, she and Terry were imprisoned for contempt of court.

In 1889 Field returned to California to hold circuit court. Concern for his safety led the attorney general to authorize protection for Field. Thus he was accompanied by David Neagle, an armed federal marshal. As Field and Neagle were traveling by train to Los Angeles where Field was to hold court, the Terrys boarded the train. While Field was eating breakfast, Terry accosted him and struck him. Neagle, thinking that Terry was reaching for a knife with the intent of attacking Field, shot and killed Terry.

Neagle was arrested and charged with murder by state officials. He contested his detention, arguing to the federal courts that the state could not hold him for actions taken in the performance of his duties under federal law.

The case came to the Supreme Court in 1890. Justice Field did not participate in the matter, but the court agreed with Neagle's argument and ordered his release. (*In re Neagle*, 135 U.S. 1, 1890).

In mid-1893 Justice Blatchford died. The seat he had filled had been held by a New Yorker since 1806, but this tradition came to an end in 1894. President Cleveland tried twice, without success, to place another New York attorney in the Blatchford seat. But the opposition of Sen. David Hill of New York blocked both the nominations of William Hornblower and Wheeler Peckham.

Finally in February 1894 Cleveland nominated Sen. Edward D. White of Louisiana, 48, to the seat. He was confirmed the same day. White would serve on the court 27 years. After 17 years as an associate justice, he would become the first sitting justice named Chief Justice, a post in which he would serve for a decade more.

The Protection of Property

The conservative character of the court of the 1890s was demonstrated with stunning force in the term that began October 1894, one of the most notable single terms in court history. With three landmark decisions, the court placed itself firmly on the side of propertied interests, defending them against both federal power and organized labor.

Antitrust Act

On Jan. 21, 1895, the court by a vote of 8-1 held that the Sherman Anti-trust Act could not be used to outlaw manufacturing monopolies — because manufacturing was not commerce and so was not reachable under the federal commerce power, upon which the Sherman Act was based.

Chief Justice Fuller wrote the majority opinion in the case of *United States v. E. C. Knight & Co.*, agreeing with the argument of the attorneys representing the sugar refining monopoly that the United States could not challenge its concentration of power. The monopoly remained intact, and the antitrust law lay virtually useless as a means of controlling concentrated economic power.

Income Tax

On May 20, 1895, the court struck down the act of Congress imposing the nation's first general peacetime tax on personal income. The decision came in the twice-argued case of *Pollock v. Farmers' Loan and Trust Co.*

By a 5-4 vote, the court overturned a century-old precedent and declared the income tax a direct tax, subject to — and, in this case, in conflict with — the constitutional requirement that direct taxes be apportioned among the states according to population.

The ruling, which Justice Brown, one of the four dissenters, described as "nothing less than a surrender of the taxing power to the moneyed class,"[86] resulted in the eventual addition of the 16th Amendment to the Constitution. In 1913 that amendment lifted the apportionment requirement for income taxes.

Again Chief Justice Fuller wrote the majority opinion. Dissenting were Justices Harlan, Brown, Jackson and White.

Strikes and Injunctions

Having fended off assaults upon property from the antitrust and the tax laws, the court was not yet finished. A week after the income tax decision, the court approved the use of federal judicial power to stop strikes.

In the case of *In re Debs*, the unanimous court upheld the contempt conviction of labor leader Eugene V. Debs for disobeying a court order to call off the Pullman strike that had halted rail traffic. Justice Brewer wrote the court's opinion.

As a result of this ruling, such court orders frequently were used by employers against labor unions. In the 37 years between *Debs* and enactment by Congress in 1932 of a statute forbidding this use of injunctions, such orders were sought in more than 120 major labor cases.[87]

In August 1895 Justice Jackson died. President Cleveland in December chose Rufus W. Peckham of New York — brother of his earlier unsuccessful nominee — for the seat. Peckham, 57, and a state judge, was quickly confirmed. During his 13 years on the court, he would serve as the court's spokesman in some of its most notable rulings in defense of property rights.

Separate and Equal

The economic conservatism of the Supreme Court of the 1890s was matched by similar views on social issues. The decision of May 18, 1896, in the case of *Plessy v. Ferguson* made that point clear.

By an 8-1 vote, the court upheld Louisiana law requiring railroads operating in the state to provide separate cars for white and black passengers. This was no violation of the 14th Amendment's equal protection clause, declared Justice Brown for the majority. It was a reasonable exercise of the state police power to preserve the public peace and public order.

Reflecting the court's view of the inadequacy of laws as social instruments, Brown wrote that social equality of the races could not be accomplished by laws that conflicted with general community sentiment.

The government can secure its citizens equal legal rights and equal opportunities, but it can and should go no further. "Legislation is powerless to eradicate racial instincts or to abolish distinctions based upon physical differences, and the attempt to do so can only result in accentuating the difficulties of the present situation. If the civil and political rights of both races be equal one cannot be inferior to the other civilly or politically. If one race be inferior to the other socially, the Constitution of the United States cannot put them upon the same plane." [88]

In lonely if prophetic dissent, Justice Harlan warned that this decision would "in time, prove to be quite as pernicious as the decision made by this tribunal in the *Dred Scott case.*" [89] He continued:

> If evils will result from the commingling of the two races upon public highways established for the benefit of all, they will be infinitely less than those that will surely come from state legislation regulating the enjoyment of civil rights upon the basis of race.[90]

This law, Harlan concluded, "is inconsistent with the personal liberty of citizens, white and black . . . and hostile to both the spirit and letter of the Constitution. . . ." [91]

Justice Field Resigns

Abraham Lincoln had nominated Justice Stephen J. Field of California to the court in 1863. Field was the only person ever to have held the new "western" seat.

In 1897 he was 81 years old; his health was failing and his irritability growing. Justice Harlan was selected by his colleagues to suggest that Field consider retirement. His reminder that Field had made such a suggestion to Justice

Grier 25 years earlier was met with an angry rejoinder. But after 34 years and nine months — the longest service of any man in the court's history — and a record unsurpassed for another 75 years — Field resigned in October 1897.

To succeed him President McKinley named Attorney General Joseph McKenna of California, 55, a political protégé of railroad magnate Leland Stanford, then a U.S. senator. McKenna, a former member of Congress, was

---

"If evils will result from the commingling of the two races upon public highways established for the benefit of all, they will be infinitely less than those that will surely come from state legislation regulating the enjoyment of civil rights upon the basis of race."

—Justice John Marshall Harlan, dissenting, *Plessy v. Ferguson*, 1896

---

confirmed, seated early in 1898, and served on the court well into the next century.

After McKenna filled Field's seat, there was no change in the court's membership for the next four years.

Freedom of Contract

The last major decisions of the 19th century provided the doctrinal foundation for the court's continuing insistence that the 14th Amendment should be used to protect businessmen against governmental interference in their economic decisions, but not to protect individuals against government infringement of their personal rights.

The court's increasing willingness to fend off state regulation of business matters produced a pair of decisions announced March 1, 1897. In *Allgeyer v. Louisiana*, Justice Peckham set out the court's view that the liberty protected by the 14th Amendment included "the right of the citizen . . . to earn his livelihood by any lawful calling; to pursue any lawful avocation, and for that purpose to enter into all contracts which may be proper, necessary and essential" to those ends.[92]

This doctrine of the freedom of contract would provide the court, for 40 years, with one of its most potent weapons against state laws intended to protect the individual worker by setting the maximum hours he might work and the minimum wage he should be paid.

In the second ruling announced that day, in the case of *Chicago, Burlington & Quincy Railway Co. v. Chicago*, the court — in a business context — acknowledged that some of the guarantees of the Bill of Rights might be of such a nature as to be included in the 14th Amendment's guarantee of due process against state action.

With Justice Harlan writing for the court, the justices upheld state police power to require railroads to maintain certain safety measures. In so doing, it stated that due process required the government to compensate the owner of private property for property "taken" for use in the public interest.

Hours, Rates and Wages

Despite its new freedom-of-contract doctrine, the court in 1898 upheld the first state maximum-hour law challenged as violating that freedom. In the case of *Holden v. Hardy,* the justices found that a law limiting the hours persons could spend working in underground mines was a proper exercise of the state's power to protect the health of its citizens.

The following week, the court in *Smyth v. Ames* reaffirmed the power of the judiciary to consider due process challenges to state regulation. When states set the rates that railroads may charge, wrote Justice Harlan for the majority, the rates must be set high enough to ensure the railways a fair return on their investment. And the courts will decide what return is fair.

In 1898 the court also demonstrated its continuing willingness to accept state laws governing the right to vote — even if those laws operated to deny Negroes that right. In the case of *Williams v. Mississippi* the court found no violation of the equal protection guarantee in a state law that required voters to pass a literacy test before being allowed to cast their ballot. Justice McKenna wrote the court's opinion, one of his first.

The Turn of the Century

In the *Slaughterhouse Cases* of 1873 the court had held that the right to do business was not a privilege or immunity of U.S. citizenship protected from state abridgment by the 14th Amendment. In later rulings it held that the right to vote was not such a privilege either.

But were the guarantees of the Bill of Rights — which clearly protected U.S. citizens against federal action — among those privileges and immunities? In one of its first 20th century rulings, the court answered that they were not.

The answer came in 1900 in *Maxwell v. Dow.* Justice Peckham, for the court, rejected the argument that the 14th Amendment required states to provide 12-person juries to try persons accused of crimes. Justice Harlan dissented.

The following year, the court showed equal reluctance to extend constitutional protections to any new groups of persons. In the *Insular Cases* decided in 1901, the court held that it was up to Congress to decide whether the Constitution and its guarantees applied to persons residing in territory newly acquired by the United States.

Justice Holmes

Late in 1902 Justice Gray resigned. As his successor President Theodore Roosevelt chose Oliver Wendell Holmes Jr., 61, chief justice of the Massachusetts Supreme Judicial Court.

Holmes served on the court for more than 29 years, through the terms of three Chief Justices and into a fourth. He was, by all measures, one of the nation's greatest justices. Like Harlan, he often found it necessary to dissent from the rulings of the conservative court of this era; also like Harlan, many of his dissents were later adopted as the views of the modern court.

The following year Justice Shiras resigned. Roosevelt chose Federal Circuit Court of Appeals Judge William R. Day as his successor. Day, 53, a successful railroad lawyer and McKinley's secretary of State before moving to the bench, would serve for 19 years.

The Expanding Federal Commerce Power

The first few years of Holmes' service saw the court give a broader reading to the federal commerce power than it had been willing to give in the last years of the 19th century.

The Court in 1897

From left: Justices Edward D. White, Henry B. Brown, Horace Gray, Stephen J. Field, Chief Justice Melville W. Fuller, Justices John Marshall Harlan, David J. Brewer, George Shiras Jr., Wheeler H. Peckham.

In 1903 the court recognized the existence of the federal police power, upholding in the case of *Champion v. Ames* an act of Congress forbidding the use of the mails for transmitting lottery tickets. But the vote was close — 5-4. Justice Harlan wrote the majority opinion; the dissenters were Chief Justice Fuller, Justices Brewer, Peckham and Shiras.

The following year the court enlarged on that ruling as it upheld a "police" use of the federal tax power to discourage the marketing of colored oleomargarine, holding that it would not inquire into the purposes of such a tax.[93]

In March 1904 the court began to revive the usefulness of the Sherman Anti-trust Act, ruling for the government in *Northern Securities Co. v. United States.*

Four of the justices, for whom Justice Harlan again spoke, read the Sherman Anti-trust Act literally — forbidding all restraints of trade. The four dissenting justices — White, Holmes, Peckham and Chief Justice Fuller — argued that the law forbade only unreasonable restraints of trade. The Harlan group became the majority through the concurrence of Justice Brewer, who found that the securities company was an unreasonable restraint of trade.

In a separate dissenting opinion, Justice Holmes set out one of his most often-quoted epigrams:

> Great cases, like hard cases, make bad law.... For great cases are called great, not by reason of their real importance in shaping the law of the future, but because of some accident of immediate overwhelming interest which appeals to the feelings and distorts the judgment.[94]

Holmes' comment appeared to be aimed directly at the man who had placed him on the bench — Theodore Roosevelt — whose intense interest in the success of the government's trust-busting effort, and this case, was well known. Roosevelt disregarded his nominee's comment and hailed the decision as a reversal of the 1895 holding in the sugar trust case.

In 1905 the court unanimously backed the government's prosecution of the beef trust. Justice Holmes wrote the opinion in the case of *Swift & Co. v. United States,* basing the ruling on a broad concept of commerce as a "current" among the states, a "stream" of which meatpacking was a part — and so was within the reach of the antitrust laws.

Due Process and State Power

Although the court was still willing to support the exercise of the state police power over a variety of subjects, its 1905 decision in the case of *Lochner v. New York* gave notice of its intention to curtail state efforts to interfere with wage and hour bargaining between employer and employee.

In February 1905 the court upheld state power to compel its citizens to be vaccinated against small pox. This, wrote Harlan, was a proper use of the police power.[95]

Six weeks later, in April, however, the court over the dissent of Harlan, Holmes, Day and White, decided in *Lochner* to strike down a New York law setting an eight-hour maximum work day for bakery employees.

Justice Peckham wrote the majority opinion, finding that the state law impermissibly interfered with the freedom of contract, protected by the 14th Amendment's due process clause. "It must . . . be conceded," wrote Peckham, "that there is a limit to the valid exercise of the police power by the state." And that limit was reached when the

state attempted to interfere with the liberty of bakers to contract as to their hours of work: "Clean and wholesome bread does not depend upon whether the baker works but ten hours per day or only sixty hours a week."[96]

Roosevelt's Last Justice

In 1906 Justice Brown resigned. President Roosevelt named his attorney general and close friend, William Moody, 52, as Brown's successor. Only four years later, Moody would retire from the court, an invalid due to acute rheumatism. Congress passed a bill allowing him to retire with special benefits.

Labor and the Court

The 1895 ruling in the case of Eugene V. Debs and the Pullman strike had made clear that the Supreme Court found the arguments and the tactics of the working man's labor movement uncongenial. The decisions of 1908 reaffirmed that point emphatically.

On Jan. 6, 1908, the court struck down an act of Congress enlarging the liability of railroads for injuries to their employees. By a 5-4 vote the court held that the law was invalid because it seemed to apply to intrastate aspects of interstate commerce.[97]

Three weeks later, the court invalidated an 1898 act that outlawed "yellow-dog" contracts, used by railroads to make their employees promise, as a condition of keeping their jobs, not to join labor unions.

Justice Harlan wrote the opinion of the court in the case of *Adair v. United States,* finding that such a federal restriction on the freedom of contract violated the due

---

> *"Great cases, like hard cases, make bad law. . . . For great cases are called great, not by reason of their real importance in shaping the law of the future, but because of some accident of immediate overwhelming interest which appeals to the feelings and distorts the judgment."*
>
> —Justice Oliver Wendell Holmes Jr., dissenting, *Northern Securities Co. v. United States,* 1904

---

process guarantee of the Fifth Amendment, which operates against federal action. Holmes and McKenna dissented.

On Feb. 3, 1908, the court unanimously agreed that the Sherman Anti-trust Act applied to forbid secondary boycotts by labor unions; Chief Justice Fuller wrote the court's opinion in *Loewe v. Lawlor,* the *Danbury Hatters* case.

The 'Brandeis Brief'

This same term did bring one major victory for the workingman — and a key figure in that victory was a Boston lawyer named Louis D. Brandeis.

Oregon law set the maximum hours that women should work in laundries. The law was challenged, on the basis of *Lochner,* as a violation of the liberty of contract and thus of due process. The state engaged Brandeis as its counsel. He submitted a brief full of factual data supporting the argument that long hours of hard labor had a harmful effect upon women, and thus, through mothers, upon their children.

Brandeis won his case. A unanimous court upheld the law, modifying *Lochner* by allowing such interference with the liberty of contract when it could be justified as protecting the public health. Justice Brewer wrote the opinion in the case of *Muller v. Oregon.* And the name "Brandeis brief" came to be used to refer to briefs filled with factual, as well as legal, arguments.

Individual Rights

The court continued to hold its narrow views of the Constitution's protection for individual rights. In May 1908 the court — over the dissent of Justices Day and Harlan — upheld a state law that required Berea College in Kentucky to segregate black and white students in classes.[98]

And in November 1908 the court again declared, as it had in *Maxwell v. Dow,* that the 14th Amendment did not automatically extend the guarantees of the Bill of Rights to state defendants.

In the case of *Twining v. New Jersey,* the court refused to hold unconstitutional a state judge's comments on the failure of a defendant to testify in his own defense. That comment had been challenged as a violation of the Fifth Amendment guarantee against self-incrimination. But the court held that that guarantee did not apply in state trials. Justice Moody wrote the opinion; Justice Harlan dissented alone.

The Taft Justices

On March 4, 1909, William Howard Taft — solicitor general during the Harrison administration — was sworn in as president. During his term he appointed six members of the court; a dozen years later, he himself would become Chief Justice.

In 1909 Justice Peckham died. To succeed him Taft chose Horace H. Lurton, 65, with whom he had served on the court of appeals for the sixth circuit. Lurton had served on that court for 16 years at the time of his selection to the Supreme Court. He would serve there only four years before his death in 1914.

Edward D. White

Oliver Wendell Holmes Jr.

In 1910 Taft placed three more new members on the court — and elevated Justice White to the seat of Chief Justice.

Justice Brewer died in March after 20 years of service. Taft chose Charles Evans Hughes, 48, governor of New York, as his successor. Hughes would serve six years before resigning to run unsuccessfully for president in 1916. He would return to the court in 1930, Taft's successor as Chief Justice.

In July 1910 Chief Justice Fuller died. He had served as Chief Justice for 22 years. Taft broke precedent and named Justice Edward D. White as the court's new chief. White immediately was confirmed and served for more than 10 years in his new seat.

To fill White's now-vacant seat, Taft chose Joseph R. Lamar, 53, a Georgia attorney, whom he had met playing golf in Augusta. Lamar died after only five years on the court.

In November 1910 Justice Moody resigned. Taft named to the seat Willis Van Devanter of Wyoming, 51, a member of the circuit court of appeals for the eighth circuit. Van Devanter would serve for 26 years, Taft's longest serving appointee.

In October 1911 Justice Harlan died after a long and distinguished, if often lonely, career on the court. As his successor, Taft chose Mahlon Pitney of New Jersey, 54, a member of that state's supreme court. Pitney served until 1922.

With Harlan's death, only two members of the court remained from the court of the 1890s — White and McKenna.

The 'Rule of Reason'

For a few years after White replaced Fuller as Chief Justice, the court appeared to relax its conservative stance somewhat.

In Harlan's last term, the court adopted the "rule of reason" for applying the Sherman Anti-trust Act against restraints of trade, the rule that Harlan had so vigorously rejected in the *Northern Securities* case seven years earlier.

In mid-May 1911 the court by an 8-1 vote declared that the antitrust act outlawed only *unreasonable* restraints of trade, not *all* restraints of trade. The majority went on to order the break-up of the Standard Oil trust, which they found to be an unreasonable restraint. Chief Justice White wrote the majority opinion, declaring reasonableness the standard — which the courts would apply. Justice Harlan dissented.[99]

Two weeks later the court ordered the dissolution of the tobacco trust. Again Harlan dissented, arguing that the court was acting as a legislature, rewriting the law by adding the "rule of reason."[100]

Nevertheless, the court continued to use the "rule of reason" as the standard by which the federal antitrust laws would be applied against combinations charged with restraint of trade.

Federal Police Power

The court continued to back the exercise of a federal police power, upholding the Pure Food and Drug Act in 1911, a revised employer's liability act in 1912 and the White Slave Act in 1913.[101]

And other aspects of the federal commerce power were broadly construed. In the *Shreveport Rate* case of 1914, the court held that in some situations the federal commerce power authorized Congress, through the Interstate Commerce Commission, to set rates for railroads operating entirely within a state.

The Income Tax

With the antitrust rulings culminating in the oil and tobacco trust decisions, the court had resuscitated the Sherman Anti-trust Act, which its sugar trust ruling of 1895 had seemed to leave useless.

Congress and the states overrode the second of those landmark 1895 rulings — the income tax decision. In 1913 Congress and the states added to the Constitution the 16th Amendment, which declared that a federal income tax was not subject to the Constitution's apportionment requirement.

Congress quickly enacted a statute taxing incomes of more than $3,000 and $4,000 for single and married persons, respectively.

In the 1916 case of *Brushaber v. Union Pacific Railroad Co.,* the court upheld the act as constitutional. Chief Justice White wrote the opinion for the court, acknowledging that the clear intent of the new amendment was to overturn the court's reasoning in the 1895 *Pollock* case.

Rights and Remedies

In 1914 the court adopted the "exclusionary rule" to enforce the Fourth Amendment promise of personal security against unreasonable searches and seizures by federal agents.

In the case of *Weeks v. United States,* the unanimous court held that persons whose rights were violated by such searches could demand that any evidence so obtained against them be excluded from use in federal courts. Half a century later, when the court applied this rule against state action as well, it would become one of the most controversial of the court's rulings.

In 1915 the court applied the 15th Amendment to strike down Oklahoma's grandfather clause, which made it difficult for blacks to register to vote in the state. This decision in *Guinn v. United States,* however, did not settle the matter. Twenty-four years later, in the case of *Lane v. Wilson,* the court struck down a similarly discriminatory law Oklahoma adopted in place of the grandfather clause.

New Justices

President Woodrow Wilson named three men to the court, one of whom refused to speak to the other two for most of their tenure.

In 1914 Justice Lurton died. To succeed him, Wilson nominated his attorney general, James C. McReynolds, 52, of Tennessee. McReynolds, one of the most conservative men to serve on the court in the 20th century, also was one of the most difficult. He went out of his way to avoid dealing with Justices Louis D. Brandeis and Benjamin Cardozo — both Jewish — and refused to speak to Justice John Clarke, whom he considered unintelligent.[102]

Brandeis was Wilson's second nominee to the court, chosen to fill the seat left vacant by Justice Lamar's death in 1916. The nomination of Brandeis, 59, was opposed by a number of leaders of the American bar, including former President Taft, who considered him a dangerous radical. After five months of hearings, he was confirmed in June 1916 by a vote of 49-22. He served on the court for 23 years.

As soon as Brandeis was confirmed, Justice Hughes resigned to run unsuccessfully against Wilson for the White House. Federal Judge John H. Clarke of Ohio, 58, was Wilson's choice to fill this seat. Clarke resigned after six years on the bench, to work for the United States' entrance into the League of Nations. He lived for 23 more years, dying in 1945.

After Clarke joined the court, there were no other changes in its membership until 1921.

Maximum Hours

By 1917 the court appeared to have silently overruled *Lochner v. New York.* In two decisions early in the year, the court upheld maximum-hour statutes — in *Wilson v. New,* a federal law setting an eight-hour work day on interstate railroads, and in *Bunting v. Oregon,* a state law setting maximum hours for all industrial workers. The law upheld in *Bunting* also set minimum wages for women and children workers; by implication the court sustained those provisions as well.

But the votes were close on both cases. Day, Pitney, Van Devanter and McReynolds dissented from *Wilson. Bunting,* decided by only eight justices, found White, Van Devanter and McReynolds in disagreement with the majority.

Conservatism Confirmed

In the war years the court's liberal interlude came to an end.

In 1918 the court abruptly halted the steady expansion of federal police power since the turn of the century. By a 5-4 vote the court in *Hammer v. Dagenhart* struck down a 1916 act of Congress intended to outlaw child labor by barring from interstate commerce goods produced by child workers.

Justice Day wrote the court's opinion, returning to the distinction between manufacture and commerce set out in the 1895 sugar trust case, and holding that this act of Congress attempted to regulate manufacturing and so overreached its commerce power. Child labor was a subject left to state regulation, Day proclaimed. The court's most senior members, McKenna and Holmes, and its most junior ones, Brandeis and Clarke, dissented.

War and Freedom

World War I saw enactment of the Selective Service Act, providing for a military draft. In June 1917 nine and a half million men were registered for military service.[103] The law immediately was challenged as exceeding federal power and as violating the 13th Amendment, which abolished involuntary servitude.

In January 1918 the court unanimously upheld the law. Chief Justice White wrote the court's opinion in the *Selective Draft Cases.*

Wartime also brought enactment of an espionage act and a sedition act, the most repressive legislation since the Alien and Sedition Acts of 1798. But unlike their predecessors — which never were challenged before the court — the World War I legislation promptly was contested as violating the freedom of speech protected against federal action by the First Amendment.

In 1919 the court unanimously sustained the espionage act in the case of *Schenck v. United States.* Justice Holmes wrote the court's opinion, setting out his famous definition of the "clear and present danger" test for determining when government might permissibly curtail free speech.

The First Amendment, Holmes wrote, would "not protect a man . . . [who] falsely shout[ed] fire in a theater and caus[ed] a panic." The question to be asked, he continued, "is whether the words are used in such circumstances and are of such a nature as to create a clear and present danger that they will bring about the substantive evils that Congress has a right to prevent. It is a question of proximity and degree." [104]

Schenck was quickly followed by several other decisions upholding convictions under these challenged wartime statutes.

The court soon divided over the use of the "clear and present danger" test — but *Schenck* remains notable for its declaration that the First Amendment does not provide an absolute protection for free speech and as the first step in the court's effort to find and define the standards for deciding when government may permissibly curtail free speech.

New Times, Old Court: 1920-1937

In May 1921 Chief Justice White died suddenly. Former President William Howard Taft — who had made no secret of his long-held ambition to be Chief Justice — was chosen by President Harding as the 10th man to hold that post.

Taft was confirmed in June 1921. He would serve for nine years, during which he would play a key role in winning passage of the Judiciary Act of 1925, giving the court more control over its workload, and in initiating work on the court's own building.

Under Taft, the court's conservatism intensified. It revived the *Lochner* doctrine of freedom of contract and used it vigorously to restrain state efforts to regulate economic matters.

And it curtailed federal authority, persisting in the view that Congress could not regulate matters such as agricultural production and manufacturing, and converting the little-invoked 10th Amendment into a potent instrument for protecting state sovereignty and business matters from federal power.

During the Taft era the court accelerated its use of its power of judicial review. While the court had struck down only two acts of Congress in the years between the nation's founding and the Civil War, it struck down 22 federal laws in the period between 1920 and 1932. [105]

Despite such clearly conservative views, it was this same court that set the nation on its course toward the "due process revolution" of the 1960s.

Labor Law

In 1921 the court reaffirmed its willingness to allow management to convert the antitrust laws into a tool for halting labor union efforts to organize and improve the conditions of workers in the United States.

Congress in 1914 responded to some of the court's earlier rulings on this subject by including, in the Clayton Act of that year, a specific exemption for labor unions from the reach of the antitrust laws.

But in the 1921 decisions of *Duplex Printing Press v. Deering* and *American Steel Foundries v. Trades Council* the court interpreted this exemption into uselessness. A decade later Congress finally forbade the use of federal injunctions in labor disputes.

Elections Regulation

The Taft court's narrowing view of federal power moved it to strike down acts of Congress regulating spending in primary elections — and attempting again to outlaw child labor.

In 1921 the court in the case of *Newberry v. United States* held that Congress could regulate spending only in general election campaigns — not primary campaigns — for federal office.

The effect of the decision striking down part of the 1911 Federal Corrupt Practices Act was to leave the subject of primary elections entirely under state control. The successful attorney in this case was former Justice Charles Evans Hughes.

Child Labor

In the 1904 ruling in *McCray v. United States* the court had declared that so long as the subject taxed by Congress was properly within federal power, the justices would not look behind the tax to ascertain its purpose.

Thus, after the court in 1918 struck down Congress' commerce-based effort to outlaw child labor, Congress passed the Child Labor Tax Act — placing a high tax on products made by industries which employed children.

The likelihood that such a tax would be sustained seemed high. In 1919 the court upheld a similar tax measure intended to outlaw narcotics. [106]

But even as the court under Chief Justice Fuller had found the due process clause useful for striking down state efforts to regulate business practices, so the Taft court found the little-used 10th Amendment a handy instrument for curtailing federal regulation.

The 10th Amendment, included in the first set of amendments (Bill of Rights) to the Constitution in 1791, states that "[t]he powers not delegated to the United States by the Constitution, nor prohibited by it to the States, are reserved to the States respectively, or to the people."

In May 1922 the court struck down the 1918 child labor tax law.

Chief Justice Taft wrote the majority opinion in the case of *Bailey v. Drexel Furniture Co.* The court declared that Congress — in using the tax power to ban child labor — was infringing upon the reserved rights of the states to regulate such matters.

The same day the court used the 10th Amendment to invalidate a 1921 law in which Congress had attempted to use the tax power to regulate the commodities futures trade. This too was a matter reserved to state control, wrote Chief Justice Taft.

If this sort of law were upheld, Taft wrote,

all that Congress would need to do hereafter, in seeking to take over to its control any one of the great number of subjects of public interest, jurisdiction of which the states have never parted with and which are reserved to them by the Tenth Amendment, would be to enact a detailed measure of complete regulation of the subject and enforce it by a so-called tax.... To give such magic to the word "tax" would be to break down all constitutional limitation of the powers of Congress and completely wipe out the sovereignty of the states.

(Congress passed a new grain futures regulatory law based on the commerce power; the court upheld it in 1923.) [107]

New Justices

After the close of Taft's first term, three of the justices resigned — Clarke in September 1922, Day in November and Pitney in December.

To fill the empty seats President Harding chose former Utah Sen. George Sutherland, 60; Minnesota corporate attorney Pierce Butler, 56; and federal Judge Edward T. Sanford of Tennessee, 57. Sutherland would serve for 16 years, Butler, 17, and Sanford, eight.

Early in 1925 Justice McKenna — the last of the 19th century justices — resigned after 26 years on the court; he was 82 years old. President Coolidge named Harlan Fiske Stone of New York, his attorney general, to the McKenna seat. Stone, 53 at the time of his appointment and for 15 years a professor of law, would serve for 16 years as an associate justice, becoming Chief Justice in 1941, and holding that post for five years until his death.

After Stone's confirmation, there were no further changes in the court's membership until Taft's death in 1930.

Lochner Revived

The court's rulings upholding state maximum-hour laws for workers were assumed by many to have silently overruled the *Lochner* principle that a state violated the 14th Amendment guarantee of due process when it interfered with this aspect of the liberty of contract.

But in April 1923 *Lochner* was revived with new force by the court's decision in *Adkins v. Children's Hospital.* The court by a vote of 5-3 struck down as invalid the act of Congress providing a minimum-wage law for women workers in the District of Columbia.

With Justice Sutherland writing one of his first and most important opinions, the court held that such a law unconstitutionally infringed on the freedom of the employer and the employee to make whatever contract they wished concerning wages.

Chief Justice Taft, Sanford and Holmes dissented. Brandeis did not participate in the case.

Taxpayers and Defendants

The year 1923 brought several other notable decisions. In *Frothingham v. Mellon* the court held that a federal taxpayer lacked sufficient personal interest in the use of tax monies to justify a federal suit challenging federal taxing and spending programs. For 45 years this decision insulated federal spending from such taxpayer challenges.

And the court began to edge toward the role it would adopt, later in the century, of ensuring that state criminal procedures adhered to fundamental standards of fairness.

In *Moore v. Dempsey* the court upheld federal intervention in a case where persons were convicted of a crime after a trial in a state court dominated by a mob. Through Justice Holmes the majority declared that in such a situation, where "the whole proceeding is a mask — that counsel, judge and jury were swept to the fatal end by an irresistible wave of public passion, and . . . the state courts failed to correct the wrong," the federal courts must act to secure the defendants their constitutional rights to due process and a fair trial. [108]

Due Process and Free Speech

The court's role as balance wheel gives its work a paradoxical character at times. So it was in 1925 when the conservative court of the 1920s provided the spark that would flare into the "due process revolution" of the 1960s.

In the case of *Gitlow v. New York* the court upheld the conviction of Benjamin Gitlow, a left-wing socialist, for violating New York's criminal anarchy law by distributing a pamphlet calling for the overthrow of the government. Gitlow challenged his conviction as a violation of the First Amendment, which, he contended, was extended by the 14th Amendment against state, as well as federal, action.

Although the court upheld Gitlow's conviction, it also accepted his argument. Almost in passing, Justice Sanford stated that the court now assumed "that freedom of speech and of the press . . . are among the fundamental personal rights and 'liberties' protected by the due process clause of the Fourteenth Amendment from impairment by the states." [109]

In the 1930s, this announcement would provide the basis for the court's first decisions striking down state laws as encroaching upon the protected freedoms of the First Amendment.

Federal Law Enforcement

In the 1920s the court upheld as constitutional the practices of federal agents in searching vehicles without search warrants — when they suspected the car had been used in violating a law — and in employing wiretaps to obtain evidence. Neither practice, held the court in the 1925 case of *Carroll v. United States* and the 1928 case of *Olmstead v. United States,* violated the individual's right to be secure from unreasonable search and seizure. *Carroll* remains in effect in the late 1970s; *Olmstead* protected electronic surveillance from constitutional challenge until 1967 when it was overturned.

Individual Rights

In 1927 the court for the first time overturned a state conviction because it did not comport with the due process guarantee of the 14th Amendment.

In the case of *Tumey v. Ohio* the court held that due process required that a person charged with a violation of the law be tried before an impartial judge. Thus it overturned the conviction of a person tried before a city court, whose judge was the mayor, and from which fines were deposited in the city treasury.

The court's definition of the liberty protected by the 14th Amendment was slowly beginning to expand in the area of personal rights, even as it had expanded earlier into the area of property rights.

In 1923 the court struck down a state law that forbade a teacher in the state schools to use any language but English.[110] The right of teachers to teach a foreign language — and of parents to engage teachers to teach their children such a subject — was protected by the 14th Amendment, held the court.

Two years later in the case of *Pierce v. Society of Sisters,* the court invalidated a state law that sought to ban private schools by requiring all children to attend public schools. Again, the court found the freedom of parents to choose private or public education to be within the protected area of personal liberty.

Negro citizens, however, continued to meet with little success in asserting their rights under the 14th Amendment. In 1926 the court in *Corrigan v. Buckley* clung to its 19th-century view that the 14th Amendment did not reach any form of private discrimination, and so could not be used to ban restrictive covenants limiting the sale of real estate to Negroes.

However, when state action was involved, the court was willing to exercise the power of the Civil War Amendments. In 1927 the court in *Nixon v. Herndon,* the first in a long line of "white primary" cases, struck down Texas' efforts to exclude Negroes from participating in the all-important Democratic primary elections.

The States' Police Power

In 1926 the court in *Euclid v. Ambler Realty Co.* firmly established the power of local government to control the use of its land through zoning ordinances. This, proclaimed the court, was a legitimate use of the police power. The following year, in *Buck v. Bell,* the court went even further, approving the use of the police power to sterilize mentally defective state residents.

But when the state asserted its power over economic transactions, it again collided with the court's insistence upon the freedom of contract protected by the due process guarantee.

Adkins in 1923 was followed by a 1924 decision striking down a state law regulating the weight of loaves of bread sold to the public.[111] In 1927 the court held that the resale of theater tickets was a matter outside permissible state regulation, and in 1928 it placed employment agency practices beyond state reach.[112]

The Court in 1925

From left: Justices James C. McReynolds, Edward T. Sanford, Oliver Wendell Holmes Jr., George Sutherland, Chief Justice William Howard Taft, Justices Pierce Butler, Willis Van Devanter, Harlan Fiske Stone, Louis D. Brandeis.

Presidents and Tariffs

Executive power was upheld in two rulings during the 1920s.

In the 1926 case of *Myers v. United States* the court held that Congress could not deny the president the power to remove postmasters without its consent. The power to remove was a necessary corollary of the power to appoint, and was virtually unlimited, held Taft in the majority opinion. Congress could not properly force the president to retain subordinates whom he wished to remove.

Two years later, in the case of *J. W. Hampton Jr. & Co. v. United States,* the court upheld as proper Congress' decision to delegate power to the president to adjust tariff rates in response to competitive conditions.

Hoover and the Court

In February 1930 Chief Justice Taft resigned, a dying man. President Hoover selected Charles Evans Hughes to return to the court as Chief Justice. Hughes, then 67, would serve through the turbulent decade of the New Deal, resigning in 1941.

Taft died March 8, 1930. So — by coincidence — did his colleague Justice Sanford. To replace Sanford Hoover chose federal Judge John J. Parker of North Carolina. But opposition to the nomination from labor and Negro groups resulted in rejection of the nomination by the Senate in May. The vote was 39-41 against confirmation. It was the first rejection of a Supreme Court nominee in the 20th century, the first since Cleveland's New York nominees were blocked in 1894 by Sen. Hill.

Hoover then chose Owen J. Roberts of Pennsylvania to fill the Sanford seat. Roberts, 55, was a Philadelphia lawyer who had served as one of the two government prosecutors in the Teapot Dome scandal. He would serve on the court for 15 years.

In 1931 Justice Holmes was 90, the oldest man to serve on the court in its history. Hughes was the fourth Chief Justice with whom he had served.

Age had slowed his activities, and Chief Justice Hughes — for the court — gently suggested to Holmes that the time for retirement had come. On Jan. 12, 1932, he resigned after 28 years on the court. He died, at 93, in 1935, leaving his estate to the nation; it eventually would be used to fund a history of the court.

To replace Justice Holmes, Hoover selected New York Judge Benjamin Cardozo, 62, who had been almost unanimously proposed as Holmes' successor by leaders all over the nation. Cardozo's selection clearly represented the victory of merit over more mundane geographic or ethnic criteria. At the time, there were two New Yorkers already on the court — Hughes and Stone — and there was already a Jewish justice. Cardozo served only six years before his death in 1938.

After Cardozo took his seat on the court in early 1932, there were no further changes in the court personnel for more than five years.

The State and Free Expression

The first years of the 1930s were quiet ones at the Supreme Court. A nation devastated by the economic crash and resulting depression was preoccupied with survival and had little time for litigation.

In 1931 the court for the first time struck down a state law because it infringed upon the freedoms protected by the First Amendment.

In the case of *Stromberg v. California* the court divided 7-2 to invalidate California's law forbidding citizens to display a red flag as a symbol of opposition to organized government.

Chief Justice Hughes wrote the opinion, declaring that the opportunity for free political discussion was a fundamental principle of the U.S. constitutional system, both in itself and as a means of achieving lawful change and responsive government. Justices Butler and McReynolds dissented.

Two weeks after *Stromberg,* the court struck down yet a second state law on similar grounds. In *Near v. Minnesota* the court by a 5-4 vote found that a state law penalizing newspapers for criticizing public officials violated the guarantee of a free press. Joining Butler and McReynolds in dissent were Sutherland and Van Devanter. Hughes again wrote the majority opinion.

The *Scottsboro* Cases

Twice in the first half of the decade the court considered constitutional questions arising from the case of "the Scottsboro boys" — several young black men arrested in Alabama, away from their homes, and charged with raping two white women.

In 1932 the case of *Powell v. Alabama* came to the court. The issue was the right of these defendants — tried in state court — to have the effective aid of a lawyer in preparing a defense. This right to counsel is guaranteed defendants in federal trials by the Sixth Amendment, but the court had not before read the 14th Amendment guarantee of due process as extending this right to state defendants.

In November 1932 the court by a 7-2 vote held that these black men — represented only at the last minute by a local lawyer — had been denied their constitutional right to due process. In these particular circumstances, wrote Justice Sutherland for the court, the Constitution guaranteed these defendants the effective aid of an attorney. Justices Butler and McReynolds dissented.

Three years later — in the busy term of 1935 — the second *Scottsboro Case* came to the court. In *Norris v. Alabama* the issue was not the right to counsel but the right to trial by a fairly chosen jury.

On April 1, 1935, a unanimous court held that the Scottsboro defendants were denied their 14th Amendment rights when they were indicted and tried by all-white juries, the result of the state's consistent practice of excluding blacks from jury duty. Chief Justice Hughes wrote the court's opinion.

Voting Rights

On the same day that it announced its decision in *Norris v. Alabama,* the court decided *Grovey v. Townsend,* the third of its rulings concerning the persistent effort of the state of Texas to keep Negroes from voting in primary elections, the only significant elections in the Democratic-dominated South.

After the court in *Nixon v. Herndon* (1927) struck down the state law barring Negroes from voting in primary elections, the state delegated to state political parties the task of determining who could vote in its primary. In *Nixon v. Condon,* decided in 1932, the Supreme Court held that this delegation resulted in a denial of equal protection to Negro voters.

The state took no further action, but the Texas Democratic Party barred all Negroes from membership. In

Grovey v. Townsend the court held that the party's exclusion of Negroes was beyond the reach of the 14th Amendment because the party's action was not state action. The court was unanimous; Justice Roberts wrote the opinion.

State Powers

In 1934 the court lifted one long-standing restriction on state power to regulate business — and loosened another. In March of that year the court abandoned the view — first set out in *Munn v. Illinois* 57 years earlier — that states could regulate only businesses "affected with a public interest."

In the case of *Nebbia v. New York*, the court by a vote of 5-4 upheld a New York law setting milk prices, and declared that any business was subject to reasonable regulation. Roberts wrote the court's opinion; McReynolds, Butler, Sutherland and Van Devanter dissented. This decision was followed by rulings overturning the Taft court's decisions nullifying state regulation of bread weights, ticket sales and employment agencies.

Earlier in the term, the court had upheld a state mortgage moratorium law against a challenge that it violated the Constitution's language protecting against state action the obligation of contracts. Again the vote was 5-4; the dissenters were the same as in *Nebbia*. Chief Justice Hughes wrote the opinion, finding the law a reasonable means of responding to the economic emergency of the Depression.[113]

The Court and the New Deal

"The court," wrote Robert H. Jackson in 1941, "is almost never a really contemporary institution. The operation of life tenure in the judicial department, as against elections at short intervals of the Congress, usually keeps the average viewpoint of the two institutions a generation apart. The judiciary is thus the check of a preceding generation on the present one; a check of conservative legal philosophy upon a dynamic people, and nearly always the check of a rejected regime on the one in being."[114]

Never was that point more dramatically made than in the events of 1935, 1936 and 1937. A court made up of men born in the mid-19th century, and appointed to their seats by Presidents Wilson, Harding, Coolidge and Hoover, looked with distaste upon radical legislative measures espoused by President Franklin D. Roosevelt and the Congress elected in the midst of national economic depression.

The 1935 Court

The court that began to consider the major legislation of the New Deal in 1935 was composed of six men in their 70s and three in their 60s. Roberts, at 60, was the court's youngest member. President Roosevelt was only 53.

The court's first ruling on New Deal measures came in the first week of January 1935. In *Panama Refining Co. v.*

The Court in 1932

From left: Justices Louis D. Brandeis, Owen J. Roberts, Willis Van Devanter, Pierce Butler, Chief Justice
Charles Evans Hughes, Justices Harlan Fiske Stone, James C. McReynolds, Benjamin N. Cardozo, George
Sutherland.

Ryan the court struck down part of the National Industrial Recovery Act (NIRA), finding it invalid because in it Congress delegated power to the executive without setting sufficiently specific limits or standards for its use. The vote was 8-1. Chief Justice Hughes wrote the opinion; only Cardozo dissented.

Six weeks later, in mid-February 1935, the court in the three *Gold Clause Cases* upheld the power of Congress to shift the nation away from the use of gold as its standard currency. The vote was 5-4; Hughes wrote the opinion; Sutherland, McReynolds, Butler and Van Devanter dissented. McReynolds, distressed by the rulings, added to his dissenting opinion the extemporaneous lament: "As for the Constitution, it does not seem too much to say that it is gone. Shame and humiliation are upon us now!" [115]

But the *Gold Clause Cases* would be the administration's solitary victory before the court in the October 1934 term.

On May 6, 1935, the dissenters in the gold decision were joined by Justice Roberts to form a majority invalidating an act of Congress setting up a comprehensive retirement system for the railroad industry. The court in *Railroad Retirement Board v. Alton Railway Co.* found the commerce power an insufficient basis for such a system.

The railroad decision was a harbinger of "Black Monday," which came three weeks later, on May 27, when a unanimous court handed President Roosevelt three major defeats. In the case of *Schechter Poultry Corp. v. United States,* the court held invalid key provisions of the NIRA as an excessive delegation of power from Congress to the president.

The court also found the Federal Farm Bankruptcy Act a violation of the due process guarantee and, in a third decision, the justices sharply limited the president's removal power, which it had envisioned as virtually unlimited only nine years earlier. [116]

The 1936 Term

When the court opened its next term, in early October 1935, it met for the first time in its own building. Chief Justice Taft had persuaded Congress to approve the idea in 1929; the cornerstone had been laid by Chief Justice Hughes in October 1932; and the court moved into the handsome marble building across from the Capitol for its 1936 term.

As the court convened, it was clear this would be a crucial term for the New Deal. A number of cases testing the validity of New Deal legislation were pending. And the justices — even before they addressed these cases — were clearly divided. As Arthur M. Schlesinger Jr. described it:

> They were already forming into distinct personal as well as constitutional blocs. The four conservatives used to ride to and from the Court together every day of argument and conference. To offset these riding caucuses, Stone and Cardozo began to go to Brandeis' apartment in the late afternoon on Fridays before conferences. Each group went over cases together and tried to agree on their positions. [117]

Hughes and Roberts were the two "swing men" between these two blocs.

On Jan. 6, 1936, the court struck down the Agricultural Adjustment Act, which adopted crop controls and price subsidies as measures to stabilize the agricultural produce market. By a vote of 6-3 the court held that Congress in this legislation intruded upon areas reserved by the 10th Amendment for state regulation. Justice Roberts wrote the opinion in *United States v. Butler.*

On May 18 the court by the same division struck down the Bituminous Coal Conservation Act with its decision in the case of *Carter v. Carter Coal Co.* The coal act was designed to control working conditions of coal miners and to fix prices for the sale of coal. This act was unconstitutional, held the court; coal mining was not commerce and so was outside the reach of federal authority. The same day, the court by a vote of 5-4 struck down the Municipal Bankruptcy Act. [118]

The administration could claim just one victory in the spring of 1936: the court upheld — as a proper exercise of the commerce power — the creation of the Tennessee Valley Authority. [119]

As the term ended, Justice Stone commented:

> I suppose no intelligent person likes very well the way the New Deal does things, but that ought not to make us forget that ours is a nation which should have the powers ordinarily possessed by governments, and that the framers of the Constitution intended that it should have. . . . We finished the term of Court yesterday, I think in many ways one of the most disastrous in its history. [120]

Due Process and Minimum Wages

In this same term, so devastating in its impact on the effort of federal authority to deal with the nation's economic difficulties, the court once again wielded the due process guarantee to strike down a state minimum-wage law.

In the case of *Morehead v. New York ex rel. Tipaldo* the same conservative majority that struck down the bank-

---

"As for the Constitution, it does not seem too much to say that it is gone. Shame and humiliation are upon us now!"

— Justice James C. McReynolds, dissenting,
The Gold Clause Cases, 1935

---

ruptcy act struck down New York's law setting the minimum wage to be paid women workers. Such a law, wrote Butler for the court, impaired the liberty of contract. Dissenting were Hughes, Stone, Brandeis and Cardozo.

Almost overlooked amid the New Deal controversy, the court in February 1936 took one more step toward imposing constitutional requirements on state criminal procedures. In the case of *Brown v. Mississippi* the unanimous court held that the 14th Amendment guarantee of due process denied states the power to use as evidence against a man a confession wrung from him by torture.

The Power of the President

In December 1936 the court — which held such a dim view of the president's efforts to deal with domestic crises — endorsed virtually unlimited power for the president in the field of foreign affairs.

In the case of *United States v. Curtiss-Wright Export Corp.,* the justices declared the president to be the sole negotiator of U.S. foreign policy. Justice Sutherland, author also of the opinions curtailing the removal power and striking down the coal act, described this aspect of presidential power as "plenary and exclusive."

Packing the Court

Highly frustrated by the court's adamant opposition to his efforts to lead the nation toward economic recovery, President Roosevelt began to look for a way to change the court's views.

His entire first term had passed without a court vacancy, despite the age and length of service of many of the justices. In part this may have been due to the fierce opposition of the conservative justices to Roosevelt's New Deal, but in part it was also due to much more practical considerations.

In 1936 there was no "retirement" system for justices; they could withdraw from full-time active service only by resigning. Upon resignation the largest pension a justice could draw was $10,000. Chief Justice Hughes later would say that he felt that both Van Devanter and Sutherland would have retired early in his term as Chief Justice, had the provisions for retirement income been more accommodating.[121]

'Judicial Reform' Plan

Roosevelt decided to create vacancies by convincing Congress that the court was handicapped by the advanced age of its members. Early in February, just after his inauguration for his second term, Roosevelt sent to Congress a "judicial reform" proposal — quickly labeled his "court-packing plan." The core of the proposal was that Congress should authorize him to appoint an additional member of the Supreme Court for each justice over 70 who did not resign. If approved, this would have enabled Roosevelt immediately to appoint six new justices, and in all likelihood, assured him a majority in favor of the New Deal.

The reaction to the proposal was adverse on all sides. Yet Congress began formal consideration of it. In a move that would prove crucial, Congress immediately separated out and passed a new Supreme Court Retirement Act on March 1. It provided that Supreme Court justices could retire and continue to receive their salary, just as other federal judges already were able to do.

The Senate Judiciary Committee then turned to consideration of the proposal's more controversial items.

The Court's Turnabout

Unknown to any but the justices themselves, however, the court already had begun to abandon its conservative effort to protect business from state and federal regulation. Signalling this change was its decision, reached before the court-packing proposal was made known, to abandon the *Lochner-Adkins* line of reasoning and uphold state minimum-wage laws. Implicit in this reversal was the willingness of a majority of the court to accept government authority to act to protect the general welfare of society — and to withdraw from its own role as the censor of economic legislation.

On March 29, 1937, while the Senate committee was still considering the Roosevelt plan, the court announced its decision in the case of *West Coast Hotel Co. v. Parrish.*

By a 5-4 vote the court upheld Washington State's minimum-wage law, overruling *Adkins* and effectively reversing the previous year's ruling in *Morehead v. New York.* Justice Roberts, who had voted to strike down the New York law, now voted to uphold the Washington law. Chief Justice Hughes wrote the majority opinion; Sutherland, Butler, McReynolds and Van Devanter dissented.

In his opinion, Chief Justice Hughes interred the doctrine of freedom of contract. No such freedom was mentioned in the Constitution, he pointed out. The "liberty" protected by the due process clauses of the Fifth and 14th Amendments, he continued, was not liberty of contract, but instead "liberty in a social organization which requires the protection of the law against the evils which menace the health, safety, morals and welfare of the people." [122] That liberty was protected by the minimum-wage law, which thus was fully constitutional.

The same day the court unanimously upheld two New Deal statutes — a second Federal Farm Bankruptcy Act, virtually identical to the one struck down on Black Monday, and a provision of the Railway Labor Act encouraging collective bargaining.[123]

Two weeks later, on April 12, the court — by the same 5-4 vote as in *Parrish,* upheld the National Labor Relations Act. Writing the majority opinion in the case of *National Labor Relations Board v. Jones & Laughlin Steel Corp.,* Chief Justice Hughes declared that the right to organize for collective bargaining, a fundamental right, was well within the scope of Congress' power over commerce.

On May 18 the Senate Judiciary Committee reported Roosevelt's court-packing bill, recommending against its enactment. Almost simultaneously, Justice Van Devanter, now 78, informed President Roosevelt that he intended to retire at the end of the current term.

Less than a week later, on May 24, the court confirmed the completeness of its turnabout. In the cases of *Steward Machine Co. v. Davis* and *Helvering v. Davis,* the court by votes of 5-4 and 6-3 upheld the unemployment compensation and old-age benefits programs set up by the Social Security Act. The court upheld the first as a proper use of the taxing power and the second as an appropriate means of acting to protect the general welfare. Justice Cardozo wrote the majority opinions in both cases.

Justice Black and the Due Process Revolution

To replace Van Devanter, Roosevelt chose Alabama Sen. Hugo L. Black as his first nominee to the court. Black, 51, was confirmed in August 1937. He would serve on the court until a week before his death in 1971.

In December 1937, soon after Black took his seat, the court announced its decision in the case of *Palko v. Connecticut.* With Cardozo writing for the majority, the court firmly declined to rule that the due process clause of the 14th Amendment automatically extended all the guarantees of the Bill of Rights against state, as well as federal action. Only those rights essential to a scheme of ordered liberty were binding upon the states through the due process guarantee, stated Cardozo. In Black's 34 years on the court, the justices would, one by one, place almost all of the guarantees of the Bill of Rights in this "essential" category.

The Court and the Rights of Persons: 1938-1969

On Oct. 4, 1937, Justice Hugo L. Black took his seat as the Supreme Court's most junior justice. It was the beginning of a new era.

The court-packing bill had been deflated into a judicial procedure reform bill, signed into law in August 1937. The first of the conservative quartet of justices had left the bench, the others would follow shortly. And the court had resigned its role as arbiter of the wisdom of economic legislation, and would now turn its attention to questions of individual rights and liberties.

In the next six years Roosevelt, who had waited five years to place a man of his choice on the court, would name eight justices and elevate a ninth to the position of Chief Justice. The men he would place on the court would, with a few exceptions, be young enough to be the sons of the men they succeeded, and the views of the court would change accordingly. Black, for example, was 51 when he replaced the 78-year-old Van Devanter.

The Roosevelt Justices

A few months after Black was seated, Justice Sutherland retired at 75. To that seat Roosevelt named Solicitor General Stanley F. Reed, 54. Reed served 19 years until retiring in 1957.

In mid-1938 Justice Cardozo died. In his place Roosevelt chose his close friend and adviser, Felix Frankfurter, a professor of law at Harvard. Frankfurter, 56, was seated early in 1939 and served for 23 years on the court.

Soon after Frankfurter took his seat, Justice Brandeis resigned. He was 82 years old and had served on the court 23 years. He was succeeded by a man literally half his age. William O. Douglas, the 41-year-old chairman of the Securities and Exchange Commission would serve on the court for 36-1/2 years — longer than any man in the court's history.

Late in 1939 Justice Butler died at 73. He was replaced by Attorney General Frank Murphy, 50, who served until his death in 1949. When Murphy took his seat in January 1940, Roosevelt nominees composed a majority of the court. Of the four staunch conservatives who had blocked Roosevelt's New Deal plans, only Justice McReynolds remained on the bench.

From Commerce to Civil Rights

The philosophical shift evident in the decisions of 1937 was reinforced by the rulings of the succeeding terms. Not only did the court redirect its efforts away from matters of property rights and toward issues of personal rights, but it also began to evolve different standards for the two types of cases.

The change was illustrated in *United States v. Carolene Products Co.* decided April 25, 1938. Over McReynolds' lone dissent, the court upheld a federal law barring the interstate transportation of certain milk products.

In the majority opinion, Justice Stone tentatively set out a double standard for constitutional cases. When a law was challenged as impinging upon economic rights, he said, the court would presume the law to be valid, unless the challenger could prove otherwise. But if a law was challenged as impinging upon personal liberties protected by the Bill of Rights, the court might be less inclined to assume the law's validity. As Stone worded it, "there may be narrower scope for operation of the presumption of constitutionality when legislation appears on its face to be within a specific prohibition of the Constitution, such as those of the first ten amendments." [124]

The reasoning behind such a double standard, Stone explained, was based upon the relationship of economic rights and personal rights to the political processes. Laws infringing upon the individual rights guaranteed by the Bill of Rights restricted the operation of the very processes that could be expected to produce the repeal of repressive legislation. Laws operating to curtail economic freedom, on the other hand, did not hinder the political processes that therefore could be used to repeal or modify the offending laws.

This new set of standards — plus the extension of the guarantees of the Bill of Rights to the states, begun with *Gitlow* 13 years earlier — provided the doctrinal underpinnings for the civil rights revolution to come. One observer calls the *Carolene Products* standard — set out in a footnote — "the manifesto in a footnote." [125]

The New View of Federal Power

In a steady line of decisions beginning with those announced on March 29, 1937, the court upheld revised versions of virtually all the major New Deal legislation it had struck down in 1935 and 1936. [126]

Abandoning its restrictive view of the relationship between state's rights and federal power, the court overturned its earlier decisions granting the incomes of federal officials immunity from state taxes and granting those of state officials similar immunity from federal taxation. [127]

This line of rulings — in which the court also renounced many of the various doctrines it had invoked to curtail state and federal power over economic matters — culminated on Feb. 3, 1941.

By a unanimous vote the court upheld the Fair Labor Standards Act of 1938, which prohibited child labor, set a maximum 40-hour workweek and a minimum wage of 40 cents an hour for workers in interstate commerce.

This decision, in the case of *United States v. Darby Lumber Co.*, specifically overruled *Hammer v. Dagenhart*, the 1918 ruling placing child labor beyond the reach of the federal commerce power. The court implicitly reaffirmed Hughes' earlier statement discarding the "freedom of contract" doctrine and declared the 10th Amendment of no relevance to questions of federal power. Writing for the court Justice Stone explained that the justices viewed that amendment as "but a truism [stating] that all is retained which has not been surrendered." [128]

With this decision, writes William F. Swindler, the court returned to Marshall's view of the broad commerce power:

... after half a century of backing and filling, the court had come unequivocally to acknowledge that a plenary power over interstate commerce was vested in Congress, and that Congress was the sole judge of the appropriate use of this power. The new constitutionalism, in this, was returning to the concept enunciated by John Marshall a century before, that the commerce power "is complete in itself, may be exercised to its utmost extent, and acknowledges no limitations other than are prescribed in the Constitution." [129]

Later in this same term, in May 1941, the court extended federal power in another direction. In the case of *United States v. Classic,* the court asserted that Congress had the power to regulate primary elections when they were an integral part of the process of selecting members of Congress. This ruling overturned the statement to the contrary in *Newberry v. United States,* decided 20 years earlier.

Rights and Freedom

Already in Black's first term questions of individual freedom and civil rights were beginning to occupy more of the court's attention.

In March 1938 the court unanimously held that the First Amendment guarantee of freedom of religion was abridged when a city required Jehovah's Witnesses to be licensed before they could distribute religious literature on city streets. This decision came in the case of *Lovell v. Griffin.*

In May the court confirmed the broad scope of the Sixth Amendment guarantee — for federal defendants — of the right to counsel. In the case of *Johnson v. Zerbst* the court held that federal courts were constitutionally bound to provide defendants with legal counsel unless they waived that right.

And in December 1938 the court began seriously to test the constitutional validity of the "separate but equal" doctrine, which had made possible the pervasive racial segregation of much of American life.

In the case of *Missouri ex rel. Gaines v. Canada* the court held that the Constitution required a state providing white residents the opportunity for higher education to offer it to blacks as well. This promise of equal protection, wrote Chief Justice Hughes, was not fulfilled by a state's offering to pay the tuition for a black student to attend law school in another state.

The following term, the court decided the case of *Hague v. CIO,* striking down a city ordinance used to prevent union organizers from meeting and discussing labor union membership and related subjects. The First Amend-

The Court in 1940

From left: Justices Owen J. Roberts, William O. Douglas, James C. McReynolds, Stanley F. Reed, Chief Justice Charles Evans Hughes, Justices Felix Frankfurter, Harlan Fiske Stone, Frank Murphy, Hugo L. Black.

ment guarantee of the freedom of speech and assembly forbids such official restriction of these rights, held the court. And in 1940 the court in *Thornhill v. Alabama* extended this rationale to strike down a state law forbidding labor picketing. [130]

Also in 1940 the court in *Cantwell v. Connecticut* held that a state violated the First Amendment when it used a permit system to restrain and a breach-of-the-peace law to punish persons for making provocative statements about religion.

War and Patriotism

The war in Europe encouraged a resurgence of patriotic display in the United States. In 1940 the court's emerging views on state power and religious freedom were tested by the case of *Minersville School District v. Gobitis.* State efforts to inculcate patriotism prevailed, at least temporarily, over religious freedom.

By a vote of 8-1 the court upheld a state's right to require public school students to recite daily the national pledge of allegiance to the flag, even if the recitation conflicted with their religious beliefs. Justice Frankfurter wrote the majority opinion; only Justice Stone dissented.

The Changing of the Guard

Early in 1941 Justice McReynolds, after 26 years on the court, resigned. He was 78 years old, the last of the conservative foursome of the New Deal to leave the bench.

At the end of the 1941 term, Chief Justice Hughes retired, Roosevelt chose Justice Harlan Fiske Stone, a Republican with 16 years service on the court, to move to the center chair. Stone, then 69, served in that post until his death in 1946.

To fill McReynolds' seat, Roosevelt chose South Carolina Sen. James F. Byrnes, 62. Byrnes did not find the post a congenial one and resigned after one term, in October 1942, to take a more active role in the Roosevelt administration's war effort.

As Byrnes' successor Roosevelt chose federal Judge Wiley B. Rutledge, 48. Rutledge took his seat in February 1943 and served until his death six years later.

To fill the seat Stone left vacant upon becoming Chief Justice, Roosevelt in 1941 chose Attorney General Robert H. Jackson, 49, who served for 13 years.

Issues of War

The United States was forcibly brought into World War II early in Stone's first term as Chief Justice. The issues of personal liberty and governmental power raised by the war dominated the work of the court during his tenure in that post.

After his first term, a special session was called in July 1942 so that the court might consider the constitutional challenge brought by Nazi saboteurs, arrested in the United States, to Roosevelt's decision to have them tried by a military commission, not civilian courts. The court in *Ex parte Quirin* upheld the president's actions, as within the scope of the authority delegated to him by Congress.

In three later decisions in 1943 and 1944, the court also upheld against constitutional challenge the actions of the president and Congress restricting the liberty of persons of Japanese descent living on the West Coast through a program of curfews and removal from the coast to inland camps. The court conceded the odious nature of ethnic

distinctions, but found them justified in this particular wartime situation. [131]

In one of these cases, however, *Korematsu v. United States,* the court for the first time declared that "all legal restrictions which curtail the civil rights of a single racial group are immediately suspect . . . the courts must subject them to the most rigid scrutiny." [132] Thus, even in condoning severe infringements of personal liberty and individual rights in the war years, the court laid the foundation for later decisions expanding those rights.

The Flag and the First Amendment

A primary characteristic of the court of the early 1940s — unlike its immediate predecessor — was its experimental approach to constitutional law, its "readiness to change new landmarks as well as old" ones. [133]

This readiness was amply demonstrated in the midwar term that began in October 1942. In that term the court reversed two of its own recent rulings concerning the First Amendment rights of Jehovah's Witnesses, a sect whose particular beliefs and evangelistic fervor brought its members into frequent collision with state and local authority.

In the 1940 *Gobitis* case the court had upheld Pennsylvania's rule that schoolchildren participate in the pledge of allegiance to the U.S. flag each day. In 1942 the court

---

"If there is any fixed star in our constitutional constellation, it is that no official, high or petty, can prescribe what shall be orthodox in politics, nationalism, religion or other matters of opinion or force citizens to confess by word or act their faith therein."

—Justice Robert H. Jackson,
West Virginia Board of Education v. Barnette, 1943

---

had upheld, in the case of *Jones v. Opelika,* a city ordinance requiring street vendors — including Jehovah's Witnesses passing out religious material — to obtain city licenses for their activity. [134] The vote was 5-4. Justice Reed wrote the majority opinion.

But three of the dissenters in *Opelika* — members of the majority in *Gobitis* — announced that they were ready to reverse the flag salute case. This unusual public confession of error came from Justices Black, Murphy and Douglas.

Eleven months later, on May 3, 1943, the court reversed *Jones v. Opelika,* returning to the view set out initially in *Lovell v. Griffin.* By a 5-4 vote the court in the case of *Murdock v. Pennsylvania* struck down licensing requirements similar to those upheld in the *Opelika* case, finding that they burdened the free exercise of religion when they were applied to the Jehovah's Witnesses. Justices Frankfurter, Reed, Roberts and Jackson dissented.

Six weeks after *Murdock* the court reversed its *Gobitis* ruling. The vote in the case of *West Virginia Board of Education v. Barnette* was 6-3. The majority was composed of Stone, the lone dissenter in *Gobitis,* now joined by Black,

Douglas and Murphy, and the two new members of the court — Jackson and Rutledge. Dissenting were Frankfurter, Reed and Roberts.

Justice Jackson eloquently stated the view of the new majority:

> If there is any fixed star in our constitutional constellation, it is that no official, high or petty, can prescribe what shall be orthodox in politics, nationalism, religion, or other matters of opinion or force citizens to confess by word or act their faith therein. [135]

The Right to Counsel, The Right to Vote

In 1941 the court rejected the argument that the 14th Amendment required states to provide all criminal defendants with the aid of an attorney. This ruling in *Betts v. Brady* came over the dissenting votes of Justices Murphy, Black and Douglas; 22 years later, Black would write the opinion overruling it.

In 1944 the court in the case of *Smith v. Allwright* expanded its definition of state action to strike down, once again, Texas' effort to maintain its "white primary." Relying on *United States v. Classic,* the court held that when a primary election is an integral part of the process of electing officials, the action of a political party to exclude Negroes from voting is state action within the reach of the 14th Amendment.

Chief Justice Vinson

In mid-1945 Justice Roberts resigned after 15 years on the court. President Truman selected his friend, Republican Sen. Harold Burton of Ohio, 57, to fill the seat. Burton,

a Republican, served on the court for 13 years.

Despite the addition of Justice Burton to the bench, the court operated for its October 1945 term with only eight members present. Justice Robert H. Jackson was absent for the term, acting as prosecutor at the Nuremberg trials of German war criminals.

On April 22, 1946, the court — over the dissent of Stone, Reed and Frankfurter — overruled several earlier decisions to hold that conscientious objectors were eligible for naturalization as citizens, even if they were unwilling to bear arms in the defense of their adopted country.

As Stone spoke from the bench to register his dissent from this ruling in *Girouard v. United States,* his voice faltered. He then had to be helped from the bench. He died that evening.

"The bench Stone headed was the most frequently divided, the most openly quarrelsome in history," wrote one observer. [136] That point was quickly borne out by events following his death. A long-distance feud erupted between Jackson, still absent in Europe, and Justice Black, now the court's senior member. Many assumed that Truman would elevate Jackson to the post of Chief Justice; rumors flew that two other justices had said they would resign if he were appointed.

Hoping to smooth over the differences, Truman chose Secretary of the Treasury Fred M. Vinson to head the court. Vinson, 56, served for seven years, until his death in 1953.

Civil Rights, 'Political Questions'

After Stone's death, the court — now with only seven participating members — announced its decision to strike down state laws requiring separate seating for black and

The Court in 1941

From left: Justices Stanley F. Reed, James F. Byrnes, Owen J. Roberts, William O. Douglas, Chief Justice Harlan Fiske Stone, Justices Frank Murphy, Hugo L. Black, Robert H. Jackson, Felix Frankfurter.

white passengers on interstate buses. In the case of *Morgan v. Virginia,* the court held that such a rule was a burden on interstate commerce — that the subject of seating on such vehicles was a matter for uniform national regulation. This ruling effectively reversed the court's 1890 decision upholding such requirements.

Also, late in the October 1945 term, the court by a vote of 4-3 in the case of *Colegrove v. Green* declined to enter the "political thicket" of electoral malapportionment.

Freedom and Fairness

Questions of individual freedom came before the court in increasing numbers during the postwar terms. In its first rulings on the application of the First Amendment's establishment clause to state action, the court in 1947 began its long effort to determine when — and in what manner — a state may provide aid to parochial schools or students at such schools without infringing upon the amendment's guarantee.

In 1947 the court reaffirmed its view that the due process clause of the 14th Amendment did not require states to abide by all the provisions of the Bill of Rights. In that same term, however, the court simply assumed that the Eighth Amendment ban on cruel and unusual punishment did apply to state action. [137]

In 1949 the court in the case of *Wolf v. Colorado* declared that the states — like the federal government — were bound by the Fourth Amendment guarantee of security against unreasonable searches and seizures. But the court rendered this declaration of little practical effect by refusing to require state judges to exclude evidence obtained in violation of the guarantee.

Also, in 1948, the court effectively curtailed the use of restrictive covenants to perpetuate housing segregation. In the case of *Shelley v. Kraemer* the court held that although the 14th Amendment did not reach the covenant itself, an agreement between private individuals, it did reach — and forbid — state court action enforcing those agreements.

Justices Clark and Minton

In mid-1949 Justice Murphy died. President Truman selected Attorney General Tom C. Clark to fill the seat. Clark, 49, served on the court for 18 years.

Almost as soon as Clark was confirmed, Justice Rutledge died. Truman named Sherman Minton, 59, a colleague from his days as a senator, to that seat. Minton, who had become a federal judge, served on the court for seven years.

Subversion and Segregation

Cold War issues and the emerging civil rights movement dominated the work of the Supreme Court during most of the 1950s.

The intense national concern over the threat of world communism produced a variety of laws and programs intended to prevent domestic subversion. Many of these anti-subversive efforts were challenged as infringing on freedoms of belief and expression protected by the First Amendment.

In May 1950 the court ruled on the first of these challenges. In *American Communications Association v. Douds* the court upheld the Taft-Hartley Act's requirement that all labor union officers swear they were not members of the Communist Party.

Chief Justice Vinson explained the majority view that Congress, under its commerce power, had the authority to impose such a requirement to avoid politically based strikes impeding the flow of interstate commerce. Justice Black in dissent argued that the commerce clause did not restrict "the right to think."

In 1951 the court in *Dennis v. United States* upheld the Smith Act, which made it unlawful to advocate or teach the violent overthrow of government in the United States or to belong to an organization dedicated to the accomplishment of these ends. The court upheld the convictions of 11 leaders of the U.S. Communist Party under the act. Chief Justice Vinson wrote the opinion; Justices Black and Douglas dissented.

During this term the court also upheld the power of the attorney general to prepare a list of organizations considered subversive — and backed state power to require public employees to take an oath denying membership in the Communist Party. [138]

In a special term called in the summer of 1953, the court considered a stay of execution granted by Justice Douglas for Julius and Ethel Rosenberg, convicted under the Espionage Act of 1917 of passing atomic secrets to the Soviet Union. The court — over the dissents of Black and Douglas — lifted the stay, allowing the Rosenbergs to be executed. [139] Douglas' action in granting the stay sparked the first of two impeachment attempts against him.

The Steel Seizure Case

By 1950 President Truman had named four members of the court, including the Chief Justice. Thus, when he found himself before the court in May 1952, defending his decision to seize the nation's major steel companies to avoid a strike and disruption of steel production during the Korean conflict, he might have expected a favorable decision.

Instead, on June 2, 1952, the court by a vote of 6-3 rebuked Truman, ruling that he had acted illegally and without constitutional authority. In an opinion by Justice Black, the majority upheld a lower court's order blocking the seizure. Justices Burton and Clark voted against Truman; Chief Justice Vinson and Minton voted for him.

The decision in *Youngstown Sheet & Tube Co. v. Sawyer* marked one of the rare instances where the Supreme Court flatly told the president he had overreached the limits of his constitutional power. And it was a mark of the court's power that President Truman, fuming, complied.

Separate But Equal?

In June 1951 the court announced two unanimous decisions that called into further question the continuing validity of the "separate but equal" doctrine it had espoused in *Plessy v. Ferguson,* 55 years earlier.

In *Sweatt v. Painter,* the court ordered the University of Texas law school to admit a Negro student. The court found the educational opportunity provided by a newly created "black" law school in the state was in no way equal to that at the university law school. Thus the state did not fulfill the promise of equal protection under the 14th Amendment by providing a separate black law school, held the court in an opinion written by Chief Justice Vinson.

In *McLaurin v. Oklahoma State Regents,* the court rebuffed the effort of the University of Oklahoma, forced by court order to accept a Negro student, to segregate that student in all phases of campus life.

A year and a half later, in December 1952, the court heard arguments in a group of five cases challenging the segregation of public elementary and secondary schools. The cases are known by the title of one — *Brown v. Board of Education of Topeka.*

In June 1953 the court ordered reargument in the cases in the October 1953 term. Before the reargument took place, however, the court had a new Chief Justice.

Chief Justice Warren

Chief Justice Vinson's last years were difficult ones. The sensitive questions of anti-subversive legislation in the McCarthy era, the face-off with Truman over the steel seizure, the tense special session considering the Rosenberg case, all confirmed Justice Holmes' description of the court as the quiet center of national storms.

Less than three months after the Rosenberg decision, Vinson died, in September 1953.

President Dwight D. Eisenhower then had the task of selecting a new Chief Justice within his first year of taking office. He looked to California, and chose that state's governor — 62-year-old Earl Warren.

Warren, a Republican, had run unsuccessfully for vice president on the Dewey ticket in 1948. As governor during World War II he had supported the relocation of residents of Japanese ancestry. He had just announced that he would not run for a fourth gubernatorial term when Vinson died. Explaining his choice, President Eisenhower said that he had selected Warren for his "integrity, honesty, middle-of-the-road philosophy." [140]

Warren received a recess appointment and began serving as the October 1953 term opened. He was confirmed in March 1954. He served for 16 years, retiring in June 1969.

Brown v. Board of Education

When the *Brown* cases were reargued in December 1953, Warren presided over the court.

When they were decided on May 17, 1954, Warren spoke for the court. With his brief opinion, the unanimous Supreme Court reversed *Plessy v. Ferguson,* decided 58 years earlier when Earl Warren was but five years old.

Concluding this, his first major opinion, Chief Justice Warren said:

> We conclude that in the field of public education the doctrine of "separate but equal" has no place. Separate educational facilities are inherently unequal. [141]

Richard Kluger, 20 years later, assessed the impact of *Brown:*

> Having proclaimed the equality of all men in the preamble to the Declaration of Independence, the nation's founders had then elected, out of deference to the slaveholding South, to omit that definition of equalitarian democracy from the Constitution. It took a terrible civil war to correct that omission. But the Civil War amendments were soon drained of their original intention to lift the black man to meaningful membership in American society. The Court itself would do much to assist in that process, and *Plessy* was its most brutal blow. Congress passed no civil rights laws after the Court-eviscerated one of 1875, and those that remained on the books were largely ignored by the states and unenforced by federal administrations. . . .

It was into this moral void that the Supreme Court under Earl Warren now stepped. Its opinion in *Brown v. Board of Education,* for all its economy, represented nothing short of a reconsecration of American ideals. . . . [142]

In April 1955 rearguments were held on the question of implementing the *Brown* ruling. In May 1955 the second *Brown* ruling set out the standard — the states should proceed to end segregation in public schools with "all deliberate speed." Again the court was unanimous; again, Warren was its spokesman.

Although the court had carefully limited its opinion to the subject of schools, "it became almost immediately clear that *Brown* had in effect wiped out all forms of state-sanctioned segregation." [143]

The impact of *Brown* was so fundamental — and the public reaction to it so broad and deep — that it tends to dominate all descriptions of the court's work during the 1950s. Yet — with the exception of its 1958 ruling in *Cooper*

"We conclude that in the field of public education the doctrine of 'separate but equal' has no place. Separate educational facilities are inherently unequal."

—Chief Justice Earl Warren,
Brown v. Board of Education, 1954

The Warren court's "opinion in Brown v. Board of Education, for all its economy, represented nothing short of a reconsecration of American ideals. . . ."

—Richard Kluger, *Simple Justice*

---

v. Aaron rebuking Arkansas Gov. Orval Faubus for his resistance to desegregation — the court did not hand down another major civil rights decision until the 1960s.

In case after case challenging various forms of segregation, the court did not hear arguments but simply told lower courts to reconsider the facts in light of *Brown.*

Resistance to these rulings was fierce, and was soon felt in Congress. The period from 1954 to 1960, writes William F. Swindler, was one of "tension between the high tribunal and Congress unparalleled even by the early years of the 1930s." But now the roles were reversed: The court was the vanguard of change — and Congress the bulwark of reaction. [144]

Security and Due Process

The tension between Congress and the court created by the school desegregation decision was further heightened by subsequent decisions invalidating federal and state anti-subversive programs — and beginning to impose new due process requirements upon police practices.

In 1956 the court struck down a state sedition law, holding, in *Pennsylvania v. Nelson,* that Congress in passing the Smith Act had pre-empted state power to punish efforts to overthrow the federal government. The same term, the court in *Slochower v. Board of Education* held that a state could not automatically dismiss employees simply because they invoked their Fifth Amendment right to remain silent when questioned by congressional committees.

And in the same term the court applied the equal protection guarantee to require that a state provide an indigent defendant with a free transcript of his trial, so that he might appeal his conviction. In this case of *Griffin v. Illinois,* as in *Slochower,* Burton, Minton, Reed and Justice John Marshall Harlan dissented.

The Eisenhower Justices

Just as the October 1954 term opened, Justice Jackson died. As his second nominee to the court, President Eisenhower chose John Marshall Harlan, grandson and namesake of the famous dissenting justice whose career spanned the turn of the century. Harlan, a distinguished New York attorney, was 55 when he was appointed to the Supreme Court. He was confirmed in March 1955 and served for 16 years.

Two years later, in October 1956, Justice Minton retired. As his successor, Eisenhower named William Joseph Brennan Jr., 50, a judge on the New Jersey Supreme Court. Brennan was the first member of the court born in the 20th century.

Early in 1957 Justice Reed retired after almost two decades on the bench. Eisenhower nominated federal Judge Charles Whittaker, 56, of Kansas. Whittaker would serve only five years before resigning in 1962.

In October 1958 Justice Burton retired, giving Eisenhower his fifth and last vacancy to fill. Eisenhower chose Potter Stewart of Ohio, a 43-year-old federal judge. Seated in the fall of 1958 as a recess appointment (as were Harlan and Brennan), Stewart was confirmed in May 1959.

Cases and Controversy

The criticism already aroused by the court's decisions of the early years under Chief Justice Warren was intensified by several lines of decisions in the late 1950s.

In 1951 the court in *Dennis v. United States* upheld the Smith Act, under which the leaders of the U.S. Communist Party were prosecuted for advocating the violent overthrow of the federal government. On June 17, 1957, the court in the case of *Yates v. United States* set such a strict standard for convictions under the Smith Act that it made successful prosecutions under the law almost impossible. Justice Harlan wrote the court's opinion, making clear that only advocacy of subversive *activity* — not just advocacy of certain *doctrine* — could be penalized without infringing on the First Amendment.

The same day the court in *Watkins v. United States* reversed the contempt citation of a witness who had refused to answer questions from the House Un-American Activities Committee about the Communist Party membership of persons other than himself.

These opinions and two others announced that day led conservative critics to label June 17, 1957, "Red Monday" — as May 27, 1935, had been "Black Monday" to supporters of the New Deal — and March 29, 1937, "White Monday" for the same group. [145]

The Court in 1954

From left: Justices Felix Frankfurter, Tom C. Clark, Hugo L. Black, Robert H. Jackson, Chief Justice Earl Warren, Justices Harold H. Burton, Stanley F. Reed, Sherman Minton, William O. Douglas.

Public and political criticism of the court was intense as a result of these rulings. Legislation was proposed to reverse or circumvent them and to withdraw the court's jurisdiction over all matters of loyalty and subversion. Southerners critical of the desegregation rulings joined others unhappy over the anti-subversive rulings to raise congressional hostility toward the court to a point unprecedented in the 20th century. [146]

A week after "Red Monday" the court in the case of *Mallory v. United States* overturned a young man's conviction for rape because he had been interrogated by federal officers too long without being informed of his rights and held too long between his arrest and arraignment. The court was unanimous in this ruling; the criticism was almost as unified.

The same day, the court in *Roth v. United States* made clear that obscene material did not have First Amendment protection, beginning a long and difficult process of setting a definition of obscene material.

In July 1957 after hearing arguments late in the term, the court cleared the way for Japanese courts to try an American soldier for killing a Japanese woman on an Army rifle range, another ruling that won the court few friends.[147]

In 1958 the court began to give full constitutional recognition to the freedom of association — striking down Alabama's efforts to force the National Association for the Advancement of Colored People (NAACP) to disclose its membership lists. [148]

An unusual special session was called late the summer of 1958 to consider the Little Rock, Ark., desegregation case. The court in *Cooper v. Aaron* unanimously rejected city officials' request for delay in implementing the desegregation plan for the city's schools.

The Reapportionment Revolution

In *Brown v. Board of Education* the Supreme Court set off a long overdue revolution in civil rights.

But after *Brown* the court played only a secondary role in the accelerating civil rights movement. The court left it to Congress to implement, at last, the guarantees of the Civil War Amendments through effective legislation. The court's role was crucial, but secondary. When that legislation was challenged, as it had been in Reconstruction, the court upheld it as constitutional.

But in one area of voting rights, the court did — unexpectedly — take the lead.

In 1946 the court had rebuffed a constitutional challenge to maldistribution of voters among electoral districts, declaring such a matter a political question beyond its purview.

In 1962 the court abandoned that cautious stance, and held that constitutional challenges to such malapportionment of political power were indeed questions the courts might decide.

This ruling was foreshadowed in the 1960 decision in *Gomillion v. Lightfoot*. In that case the court unanimously agreed that a state, in gerrymandering a district to exclude all black voters, had clearly violated the 15th Amendment.

Because such state action violated a specific constitutional guarantee, held the court, it was properly a matter for federal judicial consideration. It was from that ruling only a short step to *Baker v. Carr*, announced March 26, 1962.

Tennessee's failure to redistrict for most of the 20th century had produced electoral districts for the state legislature of grossly unequal population. This maldistribution of electoral power was challenged as violating the 14th Amendment guarantee of equal protection.

Abandoning the "political thicket" view of *Colegrove v. Green*, the majority held that this was clearly a case under the Constitution and thus within the jurisdiction of the federal courts.

New Justices

Later in 1962, Justices Whittaker and Frankfurter retired. President John F. Kennedy named Deputy Attorney General Byron R. White, 44, and Secretary of Labor Arthur Goldberg, 54, to fill the empty seats. White took his seat in April 1962; Goldberg was seated at the beginning of the October 1962 term.

'One Person, One Vote'

In March 1963 the court set out the standard for constitutionally valid reapportionment plans. In the case of *Gray v. Sanders*, Justice Douglas wrote for the court that the promise of political equality, contained in the nation's most basic documents, meant "one person, one vote."

A year later, in February 1964, the court applied that rule to congressional redistricting in the case of *Wesberry v. Sanders*. Four months later in the June 1964 ruling in *Reynolds v. Sims*, the justices held that the same standard applied to the electoral districts for the members of both houses of the states' legislatures.

The result of these rulings, which Warren considered the most important of his tenure, was the redistribution of political power in Congress and every state legislature.

In 1969 the court in *Kirkpatrick v. Preisler* reaffirmed its commitment to this standard, requiring congressional districts within a state to be mathematically equal in population.

State Trials and Due Process

Involving itself in still another area traditionally left to state control, the court in the 1960s accelerated the step-by-step application of due process requirements to state law enforcement and criminal procedures. By 1969 the court had required states to abide by virtually every major provision of the Bill of Rights — until then applicable only to federal action.

The first major ruling in this "due process revolution" came on June 19, 1961. By a 5-4 vote, the court held in *Mapp v. Ohio* that evidence obtained in violation of the Fourth Amendment guarantee of security against unreasonable search and seizure must be excluded from use in state, as well as federal, courts. Justice Clark wrote the opinion; Justices Stewart, Harlan, Frankfurter and Whittaker dissented.

A year later, the court for the first time applied the Eighth Amendment ban on cruel and unusual punishment to strike down a state law. In *Robinson v. California* the court held that a state could not make narcotics addiction a crime.

In 1963 the court declared in *Gideon v. Wainwright* that states must provide legal assistance for all defendants charged with serious crimes. If the defendant is unable to pay his attorney, the state must pay him, wrote Justice Black for the unanimous court, overruling the 1941 court's refusal, in *Betts v. Brady*, to extend this right to state defendants.

On June 15, 1964, the same day that it decided *Reynolds v. Sims,* the court held that states must observe the Fifth Amendment privilege against compelled self-incrimination. The vote in *Malloy v. Hogan* was 5-4; Brennan wrote the opinion; Harlan, Clark, Stewart and White dissented.

A week later, by the same vote, the court held, in the case of *Escobedo v. Illinois,* that a suspect has a right to legal assistance as soon as he is the target of a police investigation.

In April 1965 the court overruled its 1908 decision in *Twining v. New Jersey,* and held that state judges and prosecutors may not comment adversely upon the failure of a defendant to testify in his own defense. Such comment infringes upon the Fifth Amendment right to remain silent rather than incriminate oneself, declared the court in *Griffin v. California.*

The most controversial single Warren court criminal law ruling came the following term, on June 13, 1966.

In the case of *Miranda v. Arizona,* the court held by a vote of 5-4 that police may not interrogate a suspect in custody unless they have informed him of his right to remain silent, of the fact that his words may be used against him, and of his right to have the aid of a lawyer. If the suspect wishes to remain silent — or to contact his attorney — interrogation must cease until he wishes to speak or until his attorney is present. Statements obtained in violation of this rule could not be used in court. Chief Justice Warren wrote the majority opinion; dissenting were Harlan, Clark, Stewart and White.

The next term, as criticism of the court mounted in Congress and in statehouses across the nation, the court extended to state defendants the right to a speedy trial, enlarged the due process guarantees for juvenile defendants, and brought wiretapping and electronic surveillance under the strictures of the Fourth Amendment warrant requirement. [149]

This step-by-step process of applying the Bill of Rights against state, as well as federal, action was completed with the 1968 ruling in *Duncan v. Louisiana,* extending the right to a jury trial to state defendants and the extension of the guarantee against double jeopardy in *Benton v. Maryland,* announced on Warren's last day as Chief Justice.

Loyalty and Freedom

Questions of freedom of belief and association, arising from the anti-subversive measures of the 1950s, were still before the court during the 1960s.

Generally, the court scrutinized these restrictive measures closely, and often it found some constitutional flaw.

In 1961 the court upheld the constitutionality of the Subversive Activities Control Act of 1950, under which the Communist Party was required to register with the Justice Department. But this ruling in the case of *Communist Party v. Subversive Activities Control Board* (SACB) came by a 5-4 vote. Four years later a unanimous court held in *Albertson v. SACB,* that individuals could not be compelled to register under the law without violating the Fifth Amendment protection against self-incrimination.

In 1966 the court closely circumscribed the use of state loyalty oaths and in 1967 it struck down the portion of the Subversive Control Act that made it a criminal offense for a member of a "subversive" group to hold a job in the defense industry. [150]

The Court and Civil Rights

Congress in 1964 reasserted its long-dormant power to implement the promises of the Civil War Amendments through legislation. Passage of the comprehensive 1964 Civil Rights Act was followed in 1965 by the Voting Rights Act, and in 1968 by the Fair Housing Act.

The modern Supreme Court — unlike the court of the 1870s and 1880s — reinforced congressional action, holding that these revolutionary statutes were clearly constitutional.

In late 1964 the court upheld the contested public accommodations provisions of the 1964 Act with its ruling in *Heart of Atlanta Motel v. United States.* Justice Clark wrote the opinion for a unanimous court.

In 1966 the court rebuffed a broad challenge to the Voting Rights Act of 1965 as violating state's rights. In *South Carolina v. Katzenbach* the court, with only Justice Black dissenting in part, upheld the sweeping statute as well within the power of Congress to enforce the 15th Amendment guarantee against racial discrimination in voting.

And a few months after passage of the modern Fair Housing Act, the court in *Jones v. Mayer* reinterpreted the Civil Rights Act of 1866 to prohibit racial discrimination in the sale of real estate.

School Segregation

Throughout the 1960s the court continued to exercise a supervisory role over the desegregation efforts of school systems across the country. In its first major school ruling since 1954, the court in the 1964 case of *Griffin v. County School Board of Prince Edward County* said that a state could not avoid the obligation of desegregating its public schools by closing them down.

Four years later, in *Green v. County School Board of New Kent County,* the court declared that "freedom-of-choice" desegregation plans were acceptable only when they were effective in desegregating a school system. The court made clear that, in its view, there had been entirely too much deliberation and not enough speed in the nation's effort to implement the *Brown* decrees.

Personal Liberty

The court during this decade substantially expanded constitutional protection for matters within the private concerns of individuals.

In 1965 the court in *Griswold v. Connecticut* struck down as unconstitutional a state law that forbade all use of contraceptives, even by married couples. The justices could not agree on the exact constitutional basis for this ruling, but they did agree there were some areas so private that the Constitution protected them from state interference.

Two years later the court, using similar reasoning in the case of *Loving v. Virginia,* held it unconstitutional for a state to forbid a person of one race to marry a member of another race.

School Prayer

The criticism the Warren court engendered by its rulings on security programs, segregation and criminal procedures was further intensified by its interpretation of the First Amendment's "establishment" clause in the so-called "school prayer" decisions.

On the basis of this ban on state action "establishing" religion, the court in 1962 held that a state may not prescribe a prayer or other religious statement for use in public schools. This ruling in *Engel v. Vitale* was followed in 1963 by the holding that a state could not require Bible reading as a daily religious exercise in public schools. [151]

Libel and Symbols

The court also expanded the meaning of other provisions of the First Amendment. In the landmark libel case of *New York Times v. Sullivan,* decided in March 1964, the court enlarged the protection the First Amendment provided the press by stating that public officials and public figures could recover damages for libelous statements made by the news media only if they could prove the statements were published with "actual malice."

And early in 1969 the court held that the First Amendment's protection for symbolic speech guaranteed students the right to engage in peaceful non-disruptive protest of the war in Vietnam through the wearing of black armbands to school. [152]

Federal Courts

Also during the 1960s, in decisions that drew far less public attention, the court made it easier for state prisoners, federal taxpayers and persons threatened by state action to come into federal court for assistance.

On March 18, 1963, the same day that it announced its decisions in *Gray v. Sanders* and *Gideon v. Wainwright*, the court in *Fay v. Noia* relaxed the requirements placed upon state prisoners who wished to challenge their detention in federal courts. Two years later, in *Dombrowski v. Pfister,* the court indicated that federal judges should not hesitate to intervene and halt ongoing state proceedings under a law challenged as violating the First Amendment.

And in 1968 the court in *Flast v. Cohen* substantially modified its 1923 holding that federal taxpayers generally lacked the qualifications to bring lawsuits challenging the use of their tax monies.

Justices Fortas and Marshall

Impatient to place a man of his own choosing on the Supreme Court, President Lyndon B. Johnson in 1965 persuaded Justice Goldberg to leave the court for the post of ambassador to the United Nations.

In the vacated seat Johnson placed Washington attorney Abe Fortas, his close friend and adviser and the successful advocate in the case of *Gideon v. Wainwright.* Fortas, 55, took his place on the bench just before the October 1965 term began.

Two years later, when his son, Ramsey Clark, became attorney general, Justice Tom Clark retired. To fill Clark's seat, Johnson nominated the nation's first black justice, Thurgood Marshall, who had argued the *Brown* cases for the NAACP Legal Defense Fund. Marshall, 59, began his service just before the opening of the October 1967 term.

Warren's Retirement

In 1968 Chief Justice Warren informed President Johnson that he intended to retire as soon as a successor to him was confirmed. Johnson promptly moved to elevate Justice Fortas to the post of Chief Justice.

Johnson was a lame duck; he had announced in March that he would not run for re-election. The Republicans had hopes of winning the White House — and wished to have their candidate, Richard Nixon, select the new Chief Justice. These hopes were given added significance by the fact that the court itself was among the major campaign issues sounded by candidate Nixon. He criticized the court for "coddling criminals" and promised to appoint justices who would turn a more receptive ear to the arguments of policemen and prosecutors.

Charges of cronyism — related to Fortas' continued unofficial role as adviser to Johnson — and conflict of interest further compounded the difficulties of his nomination as Chief Justice. After a filibuster stymied the nomination in October 1968, Johnson withdrew it at Fortas' request. Simultaneously, Johnson withdrew his nomination of federal Judge Homer Thornberry of Texas to succeed Fortas as associate justice.

The following May, Fortas resigned his seat under threat of impeachment, the result of a magazine article charging him with unethical behavior. Fortas asserted his innocence in his letter of resignation, and said he left the court to avoid placing it under unnecessary stress.

The Contemporary Court

On June 23, 1969, Chief Justice Warren retired. With President Richard M. Nixon looking on, Warren E. Burger took his oath of office as the nation's 15th Chief Justice.

Despite the controversy surrounding Fortas — who had resigned only a week before the announcement of Burger's selection — Nixon's nomination of Burger, 61, a conservative court of appeals judge, moved easily through the Senate. Burger, of Minnesota, had caught the new president's attention earlier by voicing concern that the Warren court was ruling too often in favor of criminal defendants without sufficient concern for the societal costs of such rulings.

Haynsworth and Carswell

But Nixon's effort to appoint a second conservative to fill Fortas' seat ran into more difficulty than any nomination in decades. The seat Fortas resigned on May 14, 1969, remained vacant for a year.

In August 1969 Nixon selected Appeals Court Judge Clement F. Haynsworth Jr. of South Carolina. In November the Senate denied Haynsworth confirmation by a vote of 45-55. It was the first time since 1930 that a presidential nominee to the court had been rejected. The rejection came in part because of charges of conflict of interest against

Haynsworth, in part as a liberal backlash to the Fortas resignation.

Early in 1970 Nixon named G. Harrold Carswell of Florida, another appeals court judge, to fill the empty seat. But Carswell too was denied confirmation. In April 1970 the Senate rejected his nomination, 45-51. It had been opposed by a wide variety of groups because of his racial views and his undistinguished career record.

Soon after the Carswell defeat, Nixon selected Harry A. Blackmun, an appeals court judge from Minnesota and a longtime friend of Chief Justice Burger. Blackmun, 61, was quickly confirmed. He took his seat in June 1970.

The Conservative Court

President Nixon had promised to give the court a more conservative character, and some of the rulings of the court in the 1970s did narrow the effect of the landmarks of the Warren era. But none of those landmarks were overturned in the 1970s — and the so-called conservative court itself set out a few surprising decisions, particularly in areas of the law not dealt with by earlier courts.

Burger's first term was relatively uneventful, except for the controversy over efforts to fill the empty Fortas seat.

But Blackmun's first full term — beginning in October 1970 — produced several major rulings. In the case of *Swann v. Charlotte-Mecklenburg County Board of Education* the court unanimously upheld the use of such controversial methods as busing, racial balance ratios and gerrymandered school districts to remedy school segregation. Burger wrote the opinion, which made clear that the court had no intention of retreating from *Brown*.

In *Harris v. New York* the justices modified the *Miranda* decision by allowing some limited in-court use of statements obtained from suspects who were not given their *Miranda* warnings. And in a set of cases known as *Younger v. Harris* the court curtailed the impact of its 1965 ruling allowing federal judges to halt enforcement of state laws challenged as infringing upon First Amendment rights.

But the court in 1970-71 for the first time held invalid a state law discriminating against women, finding it a denial of equal protection. And during this term it declared alienage, like race, always a suspect classification for lawmakers to use. [153]

The most dramatic ruling of the term came on June 30, 1971, when the court resoundingly rejected the Nixon administration's effort to halt publication of newspaper articles based upon the classified "Pentagon Papers." [154]

The Court in 1979

From left: Justices Byron R. White, William H. Rehnquist, William J. Brennan Jr., Harry A. Blackmun, Chief Justice Warren E. Burger, Justices Lewis F. Powell Jr., Potter Stewart, John Paul Stevens, Thurgood Marshall.

New Justices

Just two weeks before the opening of the October 1971 term, Justices Black and Harlan, both in failing health, resigned. Black, 85, had served 34 years; Harlan, 72, had served almost 17 years.

Nixon chose Lewis F. Powell Jr., a former president of the American Bar Association and a successful Virginia attorney, to fill the Black seat. He named William H. Rehnquist of Arizona, an assistant attorney general, to the Harlan seat. Powell, 64, and Rehnquist, 47, were confirmed in December 1971. Not since Warren Harding had one president in his first term placed four men on the court.

The 'Nixon Court'?

But despite the fact that four of its members had now been handpicked by President Nixon for their conservative views, the court's decisions hardly justified the label "the Nixon court."

In the first term in which all four Nixon nominees participated, the court struck down all existing death penalty laws, expanded the right to counsel still further than *Gideon v. Wainwright,* and refused to allow the administration to use electronic surveillance without a warrant in national security cases. [155]

In the growing controversy over a woman's right to have an abortion, President Nixon had expressed his opposition to this right. Yet in January 1973, in the same week as his second inaugural, the Supreme Court by a 7-2 vote upheld this right. Justice Blackmun wrote the court's opinion. Only Justices Rehnquist and White dissented from the court's ruling in *Roe v. Wade* and *Doe v. Bolton.*

In that same term, the court rejected a constitutional challenge to the use of property taxes as the basis for financing public schools, but it extended desegregation requirements to non-southern school systems. [156] The justices formulated a new definition of obscenity, and held that state legislative districts need not always meet the standard of strict equality they had applied in 1969 to congressional districts. [157]

The most stunning blow dealt by the court to President Nixon was a peculiarly personal one. The Watergate scandal had set off full-scale investigations in the Senate — and under the direction of a special prosecutor.

In the course of these investigations, the special prosecutor subpoenaed the president for certain taped recordings of White House conversations that could be used as evidence in the trial of former White House aides charged with obstructing justice.

Nixon refused to comply with the subpoenas, asserting executive privilege — the privilege to refuse with impunity to comply with such a court order to protect the confidentiality of his conferences with his aides.

In June 1974 the case came to the Supreme Court, which heard *United States v. Nixon* argued in a special late-term session in July. On July 24 the court — by a unanimous vote of eight members — informed Nixon he must comply with the subpoena. Only Rehnquist did not participate.

The conservative court reasserted the power claimed by Marshall — to say what the law is — and confronted the president with a flat denial of his claim.

Nixon said he would comply and, as a result of the information disclosed in his compliance, he resigned his office early in August 1974 to avoid impeachment.

Justice Douglas Retires

In 1973 Justice William O. Douglas had surpassed Justice Stephen Field's record to become history's longest serving justice. Disabled by a stroke early in 1975, Douglas retired from the bench in November 1975. He had served on the court 36-1/2 years since his appointment by President Roosevelt in 1939. He retired at the age of 77.

To replace Douglas, President Gerald R. Ford selected John Paul Stevens, 55, a federal appeals court judge from Chicago. Stevens quickly was confirmed and was sworn in as the court's 101st member on Dec. 19, 1975.

Speech, Commerce and Death

Stevens' first term was a busy one. In January 1976 the court held invalid several major portions of the 1974 Federal Election Campaign Act Amendments intended to regulate contributions and spending in federal political campaigns. The court in *Buckley v. Valeo* invalidated the spending limits as diminishing political expression and thus violating the First Amendment. Two years later, in 1978, the court followed up the *Buckley v. Valeo* ruling with a decision denying states the power to restrict corporate spending in behalf of one side of an issue in a referendum. [158]

At the end of the October 1975 term, the court for the first time in almost 40 years held that Congress had exceeded the limits of the power to regulate commerce. The court nullified 1974 amendments to the Fair Labor Standards Act, which extended minimum wage and overtime requirements to the employees of state and local governments. Such matters, wrote Justice Rehnquist in *National League of Cities v. Usery,* were for state, not federal authority, to resolve. The question of the scope of the commerce power closely divided the court, however; the vote was 5-4.

Ten days later the court upheld certain carefully drafted death penalty laws, enacted in the wake of its 1972 ruling striking down all capital punishment statutes, but it declared that states could not make death the mandatory penalty for first-degree murder. [159] On this latter point the court again divided 5-4.

And that same week the court cut back the opportunity of state prisoners to challenge their convictions in federal court, holding that prisoners whose challenge was based on the argument that illegally obtained evidence was used to convict them should be released by federal courts only if the state failed to provide such prisoners an opportunity to air that claim earlier. [160]

'Reverse Discrimination'

The most-publicized decisions of the late 1970s involved the issue of "reverse discrimination" — claims by white men that they were denied fair treatment as a result of the efforts of schools and employers to implement affirmative action programs to remedy past discrimination against women, blacks and other minority group members.

Even as that issue divided the country, it divided the court. In 1978 the court in *University of California Regents v. Bakke* held racial "quotas" invalid but refused to ban consideration of race in university admissions decisions.

The following year the court in *United Steelworkers v. Weber* upheld the right of employers to adopt voluntary affirmative action programs to eliminate clear racial imbalance in certain job areas. The votes in *Bakke* were 5-4; in *Weber,* 5-2.

Footnotes

[1] *McCulloch v. Maryland*, 4 Wheat. 316 at 407 (1819).

[2] Samuel F. Miller, *Lectures on the Constitution of the United States* (New York and Albany: Banks & Brothers, 1891), pp. 71, 73-74.

[3] *McCulloch v. Maryland*, 4 Wheat. 316 at 407 (1819).

[4] Charles Grove Haines, *The American Doctrine of Judicial Supremacy* (Berkeley, Calif.: University of California Press, 1932; reprint ed., New York: Da Capo Press, 1973), p. 23.

[5] Robert H. Jackson, *The Supreme Court in the American System of Government* (Cambridge: Harvard University Press, 1955), p. 61.

[6] Julius Goebel Jr., *History of the Supreme Court of the United States: Vol. 1, Antecedents and Beginnings to 1801* (New York: Macmillan Publishing Co., 1971), p. 206.

[7] Ibid. p. 280.

[8] Charles Warren, *Congress, the Constitution and the Supreme Court* (Boston: Little, Brown & Co., 1925), p. 23.

[9] James Madison, Alexander Hamilton and John Jay, *The Federalist Papers*, with an Introduction by Clinton Rossiter (New York: New American Library, Mentor Books, 1961), No. 78, p. 465.

[10] Ibid., No. 79, p. 474.

[11] Ibid., No. 78, p. 469.

[12] Ibid., p. 466.

[13] Ibid., pp. 467-468.

[14] Goebel, *Antecedents and Beginnings*, p. 554.

[15] Robert G. McCloskey, "James Wilson" in Leon Friedman and Fred L. Israel, eds. *The Justices of the United States Supreme Court, 1789-1969: Their Lives and Major Opinions*, 4 vols. (New York: Chelsea House Publishers in association with R. R. Bowker Co., 1969) I:93.

[16] Charles Warren, *The Supreme Court in United States History*, rev. ed., 2 vols. (Boston: Little, Brown & Co., 1922, 1926), I:102.

[17] Ibid., p. 57.

[18] Ibid., p. 89.

[19] Ibid., p. 58.

[20] Goebel, *Antecedents and Beginnings*, pp. 556-559, 566-569.

[21] Ibid., pp. 560-565; Warren, *Supreme Court in U.S. History*, I: 70-82.

[22] Warren, *Supreme Court in U.S. History*, I:108-111.

[23] Ibid., p. 104, note 2.

[24] *Glass v. The Sloop Betsey*, 3 Dall. 6 (1794).

[25] Goebel, *Antecedents and Beginnings*, pp. 589-592.

[26] Ibid., p. 792.

[27] Warren, *Supreme Court in U.S. History*, I:173.

[28] Ibid., p. 194.

[29] Ibid., p. 791-792.

[30] Alexander M. Bickel, *The Least Dangerous Branch* (Indianapolis: Bobbs-Merrill Co., 1962), p. 1.

[31] Haines, *Judicial Supremacy*, pp. 202-203.

[32] *Stuart v. Laird*, 1 Cr. 299 (1803).

[33] Warren, *Supreme Court in U.S. History*, I:293.

[34] Ibid., p. 288.

[35] William Cranch, Preface to Volume I of *Reports of Cases Argued and Adjudged in the Supreme Court of the United States in August and December Terms, 1801, and February Term, 1803.*

[36] *Ex parte Bollman*, 4 Cr. 75 (1807).

[37] Warren, *Supreme Court in U.S. History*, I:307.

[38] Ibid., p. 326.

[39] Ibid., p. 339.

[40] Ibid., p. 494.

[41] *McCulloch v. Maryland*, 4 Wheat. 316 at 421 (1819).

[42] Robert G. McCloskey, *The American Supreme Court* (Chicago: University of Chicago Press, 1960), pp. 66-67.

[43] Warren, *Supreme Court in U.S. History*, I:550.

[44] Ibid., p. 616.

[45] *Wayman v. Southard*, 10 Wheat. 1 (1825).

[46] *The Antelope*, 10 Wheat. 66 (1825).

[47] Warren, *Supreme Court in U.S. History*, I:699.

[48] Ibid., p. 780-781.

[49] Alexis de Tocqueville, *Democracy in America* (New York: Alfred A. Knopf Inc. and Random House, Vintage Books, 1945) pp. 156-157.

[50] Carl B. Swisher, *History of the Supreme Court of the United States: Vol. V, The Taney Period, 1836-1864* (New York: Macmillan Publishing Co., 1974), p. 97.

[51] *Bank of Augusta v. Earle*, 13 Pet. 519 (1839).

[52] *Louisville Railroad v. Letson*, 2 How. 497 (1844).

[53] Swisher, *The Taney Period*, p. 535.

[54] Ibid., p. 546.

[55] *Jones v. Van Zandt*, 5 How. 215 (1847).

[56] Warren, *Supreme Court in U.S. History*, II: 207.

[57] *Strader v. Graham*, 10 How. 82 (1851).

[58] Swisher, *The Taney Period*, p. 407.

[59] *Propeller Genesee Chief v. Fitzhugh*, 12 How. 443 (1852).

[60] Edward S. Corwin, "The Dred Scott Decision in the Light of Contemporary Legal Doctrine" in the *American Historical Review* (1911), XVII, quoted in Warren, *Supreme Court in U.S. History*, II: 316-317.

[61] Warren, *Supreme Court in U.S. History*, II: 356.

[62] *Ableman v. Booth*, 21 How. 506 at 525, 521 (1859).

[63] Swisher, *The Taney Period*, pp. 973-974.

[64] Ibid., pp. 974-975.

[65] William Gillette, "Samuel Miller" in Friedman and Israel, *The Justices of the Supreme Court*, II:1023.

[66] *Ex parte Merryman*, Federal Cases 9487, p. 152.

[67] *Roosevelt v. Meyer*, 1 Wall. 512 (1863).

[68] *Ex parte Vallandigham*, 1 Wall. 243 (1864).

[69] Charles Fairman, *History of the Supreme Court of the United States: Vol. IV, Reconstruction and Reunion, 1864-1888, Part One* (New York: Macmillan Publishing Co., 1971), p. 32.

[70] Frank Otto Gatell, "Robert C. Grier" in Friedman and Israel, *The Justices of the Supreme Court*, II:883.

[71] Charles Evans Hughes, *The Supreme Court of the United States* (New York: Columbia University Press, 1928), p. 53.

[72] Fairman, *Reconstruction and Reunion*, p. 759.

[73] *The Slaughterhouse Cases*, 16 Wall. 36 at 78 (1873).

[74] *Bradwell v. Illinois*, 16 Wall. 130 (1873).

[75] *Minor v. Happersett*, 21 Wall. 162 (1875).

[76] *United States v. Reese, United States v. Cruikshank*, 92 U.S. 214, 542 (1876).

[77] *Munn v. Illinois*, 94 U.S. 113 at 134 (1877).

[78] William Gillette, "Noah H. Swayne" in Friedman and Israel, *The Justices of the Supreme Court*, II:998.

[79] Warren, *Supreme Court in U.S. History*, II: 599.

[80] *Ex parte Yarbrough*, 110 U.S. 651 (1884).

[81] *Boyd v. United States*, 116 U.S. 616 at 635 (1886).

[82] *Yick Wo v. Hopkins*, 118 U.S. 356 (1886).

[83] *Paul v. Virginia*, 8 Wall. 168 (1869).

[84] *Mugler v. Kansas*, 123 U.S. 623 (1887); *Powell v. Pennsylvania*, 127 U.S. 678 (1888).

[85] William F. Swindler, *Court and Constitution in the 20th Century: The Old Legality, 1889-1932* (Indianapolis: Bobbs-Merrill Co., 1969), pp. 1-2.

[86] *Pollock v. Farmers' Loan and Trust Co.*, 158 U.S. 601 at 695 (1895).

[87] Swindler, *Court and Constitution: 1889-1932*, p. 60.

[88] *Plessy v. Ferguson*, 163 U.S. 537 at 551-552 (1896).

[89] Id. at 559.

[90] Id. at 562.

[91] Id. at 563.

[92] *Allgeyer v. Louisiana*, 165 U.S. 578 at 589 (1897).

[93] *McCray v. United States*, 195 U.S. 27 (1904).

[94] *Northern Securities Co. v. United States*, 193 U.S. 197 at 400 (1904).

[95] *Jacobson v. Massachusetts*, 197 U.S. 11 (1905).

[96] *Lochner v. New York*, 198 U.S. 45 at 57 (1905).

[97] *First Employers' Liability Case*, 207 U.S. 463 (1908).

[98] *Berea College v. Kentucky*, 211 U.S. 45 (1908).

[99] *Standard Oil Co. v. United States*, 221 U.S. 1 (1911).

[100] *United States v. American Tobacco Co.*, 221 U.S. 106 (1911).

[101] *Hipolite Egg Co. v. United States*, 220 U.S. 45 (1911); *Second Employers' Liability Case*, 223 U.S. 1 (1912); *Hoke v. United States*, 227 U.S. 308 (1913).

[102] David Burner, "James C. McReynolds" in Friedman and Israel, III:2023.

[103] Swindler, *Court and Constitution: 1889-1932*, p. 197.

[104] *Schenck v. United States*, 249 U.S. 47 at 52 (1919).

[105] Arthur M. Schlesinger Jr., *The Politics of Upheaval* (Cambridge: Houghton Miffin Co., 1960) p. 455.

[106] *United States v. Doremus*, 249 U.S. 86 (1919).

[107] *Hill v. Wallace*, 259 U.S. 44 at 67-68 (1922); *Chicago Board of Trade v. Olsen*, 262 U.S. 1 (1923).

[108] *Moore v. Dempsey*, 261 U.S. 86 at 91 (1923).

[109] *Gitlow v. New York*, 268 U.S. 652 at 666 (1925).

[110] *Meyer v. Nebraska*, 262 U.S. 390 (1923).

[111] *Burns Baking Co. v. Bryan*, 264 U.S. 504 (1924).

[112] *Tyson & Bro. v. Banton*, 273 U.S. 418 (1927); *Ribnik v. McBride*, 277 U.S. 350 (1928).

[113] *Home Building & Loan Association v. Blaisdell*, 290 U.S. 398 (1934).

[114] Robert H. Jackson, *The Struggle for Judicial Supremacy* (New York: Alfred A. Knopf, 1941), p. 315.

[115] William F. Swindler, *Court and Constitution in the 20th Century: The New Legality, 1932-1968* (Indianapolis: Bobbs-Merrill Co., 1970), p. 37.

[116] *Louisville Joint Stock Land Bank v. Radford*, 295 U.S. 555 (1935); *Humphrey's Executor v. United States*, 295 U.S. 602 (1935).

[117] Schlesinger, *Politics of Upheaval*, p. 468.

[118] *Ashton v. Cameron County District*, 298 U.S. 513 (1936).

[119] *Ashwander v. TVA*, 297 U.S. 288 (1936).

[120] Schlesinger, *Politics of Upheaval*, p. 483.

[121] Swindler, *Court and Constitution: 1932-1968*, p. 5.

[122] *West Coast Hotel Co. v. Parrish*, 300 U.S. 379 at 391 (1937).

[123] *Wright v. Vinton Branch*, 300 U.S. 440 (1937); *Virginia Railway Co. v. System Federation*, 300 U.S. 515 (1937).

[124] *United States v. Carolene Products*, 304 U.S. 144 at 152 (1938).

[125] Leo Pfeffer, *This Honorable Court: A History of the United States Supreme Court* (Boston: Beacon Press, 1965), p. 342.

[126] *NLRB v. Jones & Laughlin Steel Corp.* 301 U.S. 1 (1937); *Steward Machine Co. v. Davis*, 301 U.S. 548 (1937); *Helvering v. Davis*, 301 U.S. 619 (1937); *Alabama Power Co. v. Ickes*, 302 U.S. 464 (1938); *United States v. Bekins*, 304 U.S. 27 (1938); *Mulford v. Smith*, 307 U.S. 38 (1939); *United States v. Rock Royal Cooperative*, 307 U.S. 533 (1939); *Chicot County Drainage District v. Baxter State Bank*, 308 U.S. 371 (1940); *Sunshine Coal Co. v. Adkins*, 310 U.S. 381 (1940).

[127] *Helvering v. Gerhardt*, 304 U.S. 405 (1938); *Graves v. New York ex rel. O'Keefe*, 306 U.S. 466 (1939).

[128] *United States v. Darby Lumber Co.*, 312 U.S. 100 at 124 (1941).

[129] Swindler, *Court and Constitution: 1932-1968*, p. 104.

[130] *Thornhill v. Alabama*, 310 U.S. 88 (1940).

[131] *Hirabayashi v. United States*, 320 U.S. 81 (1943); *Korematsu v. United States*, 323 U.S. 214 (1944); *Ex parte Endo*, 323 U.S. 283 (1944).

[132] *Korematsu v. United States*, 323 U.S. 214 at 216 (1944).

[133] Swindler, *Court and Constitution: 1932-1968*, p. 139.

[134] *Jones v. Opelika*, 316 U.S. 584 (1942).

[135] *West Virginia Board of Education v. Barnette*, 319 U.S. 624 at 642 (1943).

[136] Alpheus T. Mason, *The Supreme Court from Taft to Warren* (Baton Rouge: Louisiana State University, 1958) p. 154.

[137] *Adamson v. California*, 332 U.S. 46 (1947); *Louisiana ex rel. Francis v. Resweber*, 329 U.S. 459 (1947).

[138] *Joint Anti-Fascist Refugee Committee v. McGrath*, 341 U.S. 123 (1951); *Garner v. Board of Public Works*, 341 U.S. 716 (1951).

[139] *Rosenberg v. United States*, 346 U.S. 273 (1953).

[140] Anthony Lewis, "Earl Warren" in Friedman and Israel, IV:2728.

[141] *Brown v. Board of Education*, 347 U.S. 483 at 495 (1954); see also Richard Kluger, *Simple Justice* (New York: Alfred A. Knopf, 1976), p. 707.

[142] Kluger, *Simple Justice*, pp. 709-710.

[143] Ibid., p. 750.

[144] Swindler, *Court and Constitution: 1932-1968*, p. 235.

[145] Ibid., p. 243.

[146] Ibid., p. 246.

[147] *Wilson v. Girard*, 354 U.S. 524 (1957).

[148] *NAACP v. Alabama ex rel. Patterson*, 357 U.S. 449 (1958).

[149] *Klopfer v. North Carolina*, 386 U.S. 213 (1967); *In re Gault*, 387 U.S. 1 (1967); *Katz v. United States*, 389 U.S. 347 (1967).

[150] *Elfbrandt v. Russell*, 384 U.S. 11 (1966); *United States v. Robel*, 389 U.S. 258 (1967).

[151] *Abington School District v. Schempp*, 374 U.S. 203 (1963).

[152] *Tinker v. Des Moines Independent Community School District*, 393 U.S. 503 (1969).

[153] *Reed v. Reed*, 404 U.S. 71 (1971); *Graham v. Richardson*, 403 U.S. 365 (1971).

[154] *New York Times Co. v. United States, United States v. The Washington Post*, 403 U.S. 713 (1971).

[155] *Furman v. Georgia*, 408 U.S. 238 (1972); *Argersinger v. Hamlin*, 407 U.S. 25 (1972); *United States v. U.S. District Court, Eastern Michigan*, 407 U.S. 297 (1972).

[156] *San Antonio Independent School District v. Rodriguez*, 411 U.S. 1 (1973); *Keyes v. Denver School District No. 1*, 413 U.S. 921 (1973).

[157] *Miller v. California*, 413 U.S. 15 (1973); *Mahan v. Howell*, 410 U.S. 135 (1973).

[158] *First National Bank of Boston v. Bellotti*, 435 U.S. 765 (1978).

[159] *Gregg v. Georgia, Proffitt v. Florida, Jurek v. Texas*, 428 U.S. 153, 242, 262 (1976); *Woodson v. North Carolina, Roberts v. Louisiana*, 428 U.S. 380. 325 (1976).

[160] *Stone v. Powell, Wolff v. Rice*, 428 U.S. 465 (1976).

PART II

THE COURT AND THE FEDERAL SYSTEM

The Court and the Powers of Congress............ 65

The Court and the Powers of the President....... 181

The Court and Judicial Power 255

The Court and the States 299

View of the West Front of the Supreme Court.
Architect of the Capitol Photo No. 30405

THE COURT AND THE POWERS OF CONGRESS

Introduction 65

Judicial Review and Legislative
   Power 69

The Power to Regulate Commerce. 81

Fiscal and Monetary Powers. 109

The Power Over Foreign Affairs 125

The Power to Admit States, Govern
   Territories and Grant Citizenship 133

The Power to Amend the Constitution 149

Miscellaneous Powers 155

The Power to Investigate 157

The Power Over Internal Affairs 165

The Court and the Powers of Congress

While the framers of the Constitution recognized that the new government needed an executive to carry out the laws and a judiciary to resolve conflicts in the laws, it was Congress that was the heart of the new democracy. The House of Representatives was the only part of the federal government originally elected by the people; consequently, Congress was the branch of government expected to respond directly to their needs.

It was thus to the national legislature that the framers entrusted most of the power necessary to govern the new nation. To Congress the Constitution granted the power to tax, regulate commerce, declare war, approve treaties, and raise and maintain armies.

The framers also granted Congress some authority over the other two branches. Congress had the power to establish whatever federal judicial system below the Supreme Court seemed desirable and to impeach and convict the president, federal judges and other federal officers for treason, bribery or other high crimes and misdemeanors.

The framers placed specific constitutional limitations on the exercise of power by Congress. The national legislature may not use its power to single out individuals for punishment: it may not pass *ex post facto* laws or bills of attainder. It may not impose a direct tax that is unapportioned or an indirect tax that is not uniform. Perhaps the most important constitutional limits are those added by the First Amendment, prohibiting Congress from interfering with the free exercise of speech, the press, assembly or religion; the Fifth Amendment, prohibiting the taking of life, liberty or property without due process of law, and the 10th Amendment, reserving to the states and the people powers not granted to Congress.

But the framers were silent as to which branch of government would ensure that Congress observed these limits. Was Congress to police itself, or would the judiciary — most particularly, the Supreme Court — have this role?

Writing as Publius in *The Federalist Papers,* Alexander Hamilton contended that this was the role of the courts. "[T]he courts," Hamilton wrote, "were designed to be an intermediate body between the people and the legislature in order, among other things, to keep the latter within the limits assigned to their authority." [1]

Judicial Review

Many constitutional scholars agree that most of the framers intended the Supreme Court to assume this role, determining whether acts of Congress conformed to the Constitution. But the question of whether the court could actually nullify an act of Congress as unconstitutional remained unanswered until the 1803 decision in *Marbury v. Madison.* Holding that Congress had impermissibly enlarged the original jurisdiction of the Supreme Court, Chief Justice John Marshall declared that "a law repugnant to the Constitution is void." In so doing, he firmly asserted the power of the Supreme Court to make such determinations: "It is, emphatically, the province and duty of the judicial department, to say what the law is," Marshall said. [2]

While scholars have questioned Marshall's legal reasoning in *Marbury v. Madison,* the significance of the decision has never been challenged. The nation might not have ceased to function if the Supreme Court had not established its powers to review and declare invalid acts of Congress that conflict with the Constitution. But without the power of judicial review and its implicit check on the exercise of legislative power, wrote historian Charles Warren,

> ... the Nation could never have remained a Federal Republic. Its government would have become a consolidated and centralized autocracy. Congress would have attained supreme, final and unlimited power over the Executive and the Judiciary branches and the States and the individual citizens could have possessed only such powers and rights as Congress chose to leave or grant to them. The hard-fought-for Bill of Rights and the reserved powers of the States guaranteed by the Constitution would have been subject to the unlimited control of the prejudice, whim or passion of the majority as represented in Congress at any given moment. Though such a government might possibly have operated in this country, it would not have been the form of government which the framers of the Constitution intended, but a government with unlimited powers over the States. [3]

Having claimed this right and power, the Marshall court never again exercised it to declare an act of Congress unconstitutional. Rather than confine the exercise of legislative powers by a narrow reading of the language of the Constitution, the Marshall court consistently defined the powers of Congress broadly. Perhaps most important of these decisions was the court's declaration that the clause giving Congress the power to make all laws "necessary and proper" to the exercise of its specific powers gave the legislature the authority to enact any measure that was an appropriate means to a constitutional end.

In 1825 the Marshall court further broadened the scope of congressional power when it recognized that Congress had the authority to delegate at least some legislative responsibilities to other branches of government. In 1828 the court acknowledged that Congress had, in addition to its enumerated powers, powers that were inherent in the fact of national sovereignty.

Even as the Marshall court established the supremacy of the Constitution over acts of Congress, it curtailed enactments of the states that infringed on congressional powers. Nowhere was this point made more forcefully than in the famous steamship monopoly case of *Gibbons v. Ogden* (1824). There the court ruled that a permit issued under federal law took precedence over a monopoly granted by state law. Navigation between two states was interstate commerce, wrote Marshall for the court, and the grant of power to Congress to regulate commerce between the states could not be limited by state action.

The Commerce Power

In the same case, the Marshall court held that the federal power to regulate commerce among the states was not limited to transportation but extended to all commercial intercourse affecting two or more states. The only commerce Congress could not reach, Marshall said, was that which was wholly within one state and which did not affect any other state.

The importance of this broad definition was not fully apparent until the late 19th century when Congress began to regulate first the railroads and then the huge trusts that monopolized many of the nation's major industries. Although some of the railroads and many of the trusts operated within single states, under Marshall's definition Congress could regulate such operations because they affected more than one state. But late in the 19th century a court sympathetic to business interests narrowed Marshall's definition to hold that Congress could only regulate those intrastate matters that *directly* affected interstate commerce. Intrastate matters affecting interstate commerce only indirectly were reserved to the states to regulate. And it was for the court to determine which effects were direct, which indirect.

From these two versions of Marshall's view, the court developed two lines of precedent that it applied in unpredictable and conflicting fashion. Using the narrow view in 1895, for example, the court held that a trust processing 98 percent of all refined sugar in the nation was not in violation of the antitrust law. Sugar refining was manufacturing, the court held, and manufacture was not commerce and did not affect commerce directly. Ten years later the court, taking the broad view, ruled that an intrastate stockyard operation did violate the antitrust act. Even though it was intrastate and processing, the court said the stockyard was an integral part of a stream of interstate commerce.

During this same period, Congress began to use its commerce and tax powers for social as well as economic purposes, developing a federal "police" power used to protect public health and morals. In 1903 the Supreme Court sustained an act of Congress prohibiting the sale and shipment in interstate commerce of lottery tickets. In 1904 it upheld a high tax placed on colored oleo to remove this competition to butter from the market. In subsequent

terms, the court sanctioned other uses of this new federal power. Encouraged, Congress exercised this power to bar from interstate commerce goods made by child labor.

Then, in 1918, the court struck down that law. Returning to its narrow view of commerce, the court found that Congress had attempted to regulate manufacture, not commerce. This was true, but the child labor law was essentially the same sort of social measure as the ban on lottery tickets in interstate commerce. The court distinguished the two cases by saying that lottery tickets were harmful in themselves while goods made by children were not.

Congress responded to this ruling by enacting an extremely high tax on the profits of any company that employed children. The court in 1922 struck down the tax on the ground that it was intended as a penalty, not a revenue-raising device. The court distinguished the child labor tax from the oleo tax by refusing to acknowledge that the oleo tax had any other purpose than to raise revenue.

For the next few years, the two child labor cases stood as anomalies of little value as precedent. The court continued to uphold other congressional uses of the federal police power and even sanctioned wider federal regulation of some intrastate matters.

Only against labor unions did the court maintain a consistently conservative stance, ruling repeatedly that many strikes and boycotts were illegal restraints of trade under the antitrust law and diluting the force of new laws designed to protect the rights of organized workers. By 1930, however, the court appeared to be rethinking its position on labor, upholding a federal statute guaranteeing collective bargaining rights to railway workers.

With the advent of the Great Depression, the president proposed and Congress enacted recovery laws regulating business to an unprecedented degree. When these laws were challenged as unconstitutional, in almost every instance the Supreme Court agreed, ruling that Congress did not have the broad power necessary to cope with the national crisis.

The court struck down a law encouraging adoption of wage and hour standards for coal miners on the ground that mining was an intrastate operation that had no direct effect on interstate commerce. It struck down fair competition codes because they affected some industries that were not in and did not directly affect interstate commerce. The court invalidated a plan to tax food processors and use the revenue to pay benefits to farmers who curtailed production of certain crops as an unconstitutional scheme to regulate agricultural production that was not in interstate commerce. It declared that a federal pension plan for retired railroad workers was outside the reach of the interstate commerce power. In short, a majority of the court in this early New Deal period refused to acknowledge that local economic conditions had any direct bearing on the health of the national economy or that Congress had the authority through its commerce and tax powers to try to improve local conditions.

Apparently responding to the president's "court-packing" threat, the court in 1937 reassessed the scope of the commerce power and returned to Marshall's broad view of its sweep. In quick succession, the court upheld acts of Congress banning unfair labor practices and regulating wages and hours and agricultural production. It approved federal laws establishing the Social Security pension system and the federal/state unemployment compensation system. It even upheld application of agricultural marketing regulations to a farmer who produced wheat not for sale either intrastate or interstate but for his own consumption.

The court, in the words of Justice Benjamin N. Cardozo, finally "confronted ... the indisputable truth that there were ills to be corrected, and ills that had a direct relation to the maintenance of commerce among the states without friction or diversion." [4] And the commerce power was held to be equal to deal with those problems.

With this recognition, the court gave up its effort to judge whether Congress had acted wisely in the exercise of its commerce power and returned to simply deciding whether Congress had acted constitutionally. Unless its choice is clearly arbitrary, the court said, Congress has the power to determine whether an intrastate matter affects interstate commerce to a sufficient degree to require federal regulation.

Only once since 1937 has the court declared an act of Congress an unconstitutional exercise of the commerce power. During the same period, it sustained the commerce power as a tool to reach and prohibit racial discrimination in public places and to guarantee the right to travel within the United States.

By 1979 constitutional issues surrounding the scope of the commerce power appeared largely resolved, giving Congress almost unlimited discretion to regulate commercial intercourse in the United States. "[I]f we moved into an era of novel economic measures or major nationalization programs, the court might reassert its authority," wrote constitutional scholars Alan F. Westin and C. Herman Pritchett, "but the decades since 1937 have been years of consolidation rather than innovation in economic regulation, and the Court's withdrawal from constitutional intervention is therefore not likely to change in the immediate future." [5]

Fiscal and Monetary Powers

The court's exercise of its power to overturn the fiscal and monetary decisions of Congress has proved largely futile. It has sustained most congressional tax, spending and currency laws. But in three major cases the court declared such laws unconstitutional and in all three cases, that decision was overturned.

Those three decisions were handed down between 1870 and 1936, the same period in which the court was delivering its often contradictory opinions on the commerce and federal police powers. All three favored business interests and states' rights at the expense of congressional authority.

In the 1870 Legal Tender Case, the court by a 4-3 vote declared that Congress had unconstitutionally exercised its war powers during the Civil War to substitute paper money for gold and silver as legal tender for the payment of certain debts. Even as the decision was being announced, President Grant named two new justices. Within 15 months, the court by a 5-4 vote overturned its earlier decision. While the decision pleased debtors across the country, the government and many businesses, the quickness of the reversal, the closeness of the vote and Grant's appointment of the new justices aroused much public criticism.

In 1895 the court declared unconstitutional the first general peacetime income tax. It held that a tax on income from real estate was a direct tax. Because the Constitution required that direct taxes be apportioned among the states on the basis of population, and this tax was not, it was unconstitutional. The court then held that this flaw invalidated the entire tax statute. To reach this conclusion, the court overlooked both its earlier declaration that the only direct taxes were head and property taxes and its earlier decision sustaining a wartime income tax. The 1895 deci-

sion was overturned in 1913 with ratification of the 16th Amendment, exempting income taxes from the apportionment requirement.

In 1936 the court ruled for the first time on the scope of Congress' power to spend for the general welfare. It struck down a New Deal effort to raise farm prices by taxing food processors and using the revenue to pay benefits to farmers who reduced their production of certain crops. The court held that the tax-benefit scheme was unconstitutional because it intended to regulate production which was beyond the scope of congressional power. This was one of many New Deal decisions that precipitated the "court-packing" threat; although it was never specifically overruled, its value as a precedent largely vanished when the court in 1937 approved similar tax-benefit plans contained in the federal Social Security Act.

Since 1936, the court has not attempted to limit Congress' power to exercise its fiscal and monetary powers.

Foreign Affairs

Though it played an active role in shaping the commerce and federal police powers, the Supreme Court has assumed a passive stance regarding congressional powers in the field of foreign affairs. Responsibility for exercising many of these powers, including the war powers, is shared by the executive and the legislature. The president as commander in chief conducts war, but the Constitution gives Congress the powers to declare war and raise and maintain armies. The president negotiates treaties; the Senate must ratify them. While the president has great discretion to deal with foreign nations on a wide range of issues, many of his actions must be approved ultimately by Congress, usually through appropriation of funds.

In many instances, the Supreme Court has refused to review a foreign affairs or war powers case by describing it as a political question solvable only by the political branches of government. The court first adopted this stance in the case of *Foster v. Neilson* (1829) which involved an international dispute over title to part of the Louisiana territory. A more recent example was the court's repeated refusal in the late 1960s and early 1970s to hear cases challenging the validity of the Indochina War on the ground that it had not been formally declared by Congress.

In cases the court has agreed to hear, it generally has upheld exercise of the power in question. This has been particularly true of the war powers, where the court has sustained establishment of the draft and large delegations of discretionary power to the executive branch to conduct war. Where the court has felt compelled to declare a wartime statute unconstitutional, it has done so usually on a ground other than the war power and after combat has ceased.

In short, the court for the most part has refused to limit congressional flexibility to exercise its powers over foreign affairs. The court also undoubtedly realizes that a decision contrary to the will of the political branches and the people might go unobeyed. "[F]or better or for worse," observed Prof. Robert G. McCloskey, "the fact remains that [the powers over foreign affairs] are now subject to constitutional limits only ... by legislative and executive self-restraint and by the force of public opinion." [6]

States, Territories and Citizens

The Constitution gives Congress the power to admit new states to the union, govern territories held by the union and make rules for the naturalization of aliens. The Supreme Court has been steadfast in its insistence that new states be admitted on an equal political footing with those already in the union, a precept now clearly established. But questions of citizenship in the United States and territories pose continuing problems for the court.

In what is probably its most infamous opinion, the court declared in the 1857 *Dred Scott* decision that blacks were not and could not become citizens. The Civil War overturned that decision and ratification of the 14th Amendment made citizens of all persons born in the United States and subject to its jurisdiction.

Residents of the territories of the continental United States generally enjoyed the guarantees and protections of the Constitution as those areas were prepared for statehood. But in the 1890s and 1900s the nation acquired several new territories in the Caribbean and the Pacific, and a debate ensued as to whether the Constitution automatically followed the flag into these territories. In a series of decisions known as the Insular Cases, the court adopted a rule still in use in 1979. If Congress formally incorporated the territory into the United States, the rights, responsibilities and protections of the Constitution would devolve on the inhabitants of the territory. If Congress did not incorporate the territory, its residents were not guaranteed the Constitution's protections.

Congressional control over citizenship in the United States is extensive. In addition to setting conditions for naturalization, Congress, with the court's approval, has prohibited several categories of people from entering the country or applying for citizenship. It was Congress that wrote the 14th Amendment, the first definition of citizenship to appear in the Constitution.

Following the dictates of that amendment, the court has sustained the citizenship of any person born in the United States, even if the child's parents were not and could not become citizens. Not fully resolved by the court, however, is the question of whether Congress may revoke the citizenship of a native-born or naturalized citizen against his or her will. The ruling case, decided by a 5-4 vote, holds that Congress may not revoke citizenship. But the closeness of the vote and conflicting precedents leave the question open to further interpretation.

Amending Power

As it does with many foreign policy questions, the court views the adoption of constitutional amendments as political decisions and is reluctant to interfere. Most of the court's decisions in this area have concerned procedural questions of ratification. But it did rule that liquor was proper subject matter for a constitutional amendment and that the amendment extending suffrage to women did not destroy the political autonomy of those few states that refused to ratify it.

Several of the 26 amendments to the Constitution confer political rights and give Congress specific power to enforce those rights. The most significant of these are the Civil War Amendments (13th, 14th and 15th), which extended citizenship and political rights to blacks. To enforce these newly won rights and freedoms, the Reconstruction Congress quickly enacted several civil rights statutes, but the Supreme Court, construing the enforcement power narrowly, struck down almost all of them. In general, the court held that Congress could only act to correct, not prevent, discriminatory action by states. It had no power,

the court said, to reach discriminatory actions by private individuals.

These restrictive rulings, coupled with a waning public concern, meant that blacks remained victims of political and social discrimination in many states of the union for almost a century, until an activist court began to reassess national authority to enforce the rights guaranteed by the three amendments. In the 1950s and 1960s, the court sustained congressional power to prevent state discrimination before it occurred and to reach certain private discrimination, particularly in public places and housing.

Investigations and Internal Affairs

The court has never questioned the right of Congress to investigate its own members for possible misconduct. Nor has it denied the use of such power to examine issues so that Congress might legislate more effectively. In aid of both kinds of investigations, the court has sustained the right of Congress to compel witnesses to testify and to punish for contempt of Congress those who refuse.

The court has even been reluctant to curb the exercise of the investigatory power in order to protect constitutionally guaranteed individual rights. To protect witness rights, the court requires that the investigations serve a valid legislative purpose and that the questions asked of witnesses be pertinent to the investigation. At the same time, the court, in the interests of national security, has upheld investigations that were clearly designed only to focus publicity upon witnesses holding unpopular political beliefs.

The Constitution gives Congress powers over its own internal affairs. By no means insignificant, these powers include judging the qualifications of members, punishing members it finds guilty of misconduct, regulating federal elections and establishing rules of procedure.

Anxious to preserve the separation of powers, Congress has taken few of its internal problems to the court. In only one major case has the court clearly limited Congress' power over its own affairs. In 1969 it held that Congress did not have the authority to add to the Constitution's list of qualifications for membership in the House and Senate.

On the other hand, the court has guarded zealously the institutional integrity of Congress. Nowhere has this been more apparent than in its interpretation of the "speech or debate" clause. The court has extended this constitutional grant of immunity for actions taken during the course of legislating to cover criminal acts and certain actions of employees.

Footnotes

[1] *The Federalist Papers*, with an Introduction by Clinton Rossiter (New York: The New American Library, Mentor, 1961), p. 467.

[2] *Marbury v. Madison*, 1 Cr. 137 at 177 (1803).

[3] Charles Warren, *The Supreme Court in United States History*, rev. ed., 2 vols. (Boston: Little, Brown & Co., 1922, 1926), I:16-17.

[4] *Carter v. Carter Coal Co.*, 298 U.S. 238 at 332 (1936).

[5] C. Herman Pritchett and Alan F. Westin, *The Third Branch of Government: 8 Cases in Constitutional Politics* (New York: Harcourt, Brace & World Inc., 1963), p. 3.

[6] Robert G. McCloskey, *The American Supreme Court*, (Chicago: The University of Chicago Press, 1960), p. 190.

Judicial Review and Legislative Power

Judicial review — the right of the Supreme Court to review acts of Congress to determine whether they are consonant with the Constitution and to strike down those that it finds in conflict — was not expressly granted to the courts by the Constitution. The implicit justification for this authority lies in the supremacy clause (Article VI, Section 2), which states:

This Constitution, and the Laws of the United States which shall be made in Pursuance thereof; and all Treaties made, or which shall be made, under the Authority of the United States, shall be the supreme Law of the Land; and the Judges in every State shall be bound thereby, any Thing in the Constitution or Laws of any State to the Contrary notwithstanding.

Most scholars of constitutional history believe that the framers did not intend to deny the court review power by omitting an express grant from the Constitution. The concept of judicial review was relatively well-recognized in the colonies at the time the Constitution was drawn. The Privy Council in London had reviewed the acts of the colonies for compliance with English law prior to the Revolution. Several state courts had voided state laws considered inconsistent with their state constitutions.

During the Constitutional Convention it was proposed on several occasions that the Supreme Court share the veto power over acts of Congress with the president. These suggestions were voted down, largely on the ground that the court should not be involved in enacting the law it might later be required to enforce, not because a majority was opposed to judicial review.

According to the records of the Constitutional Convention compiled by Max Farrand, only two framers of the Constitution expressed reservations about judicial review, although other scholars have placed the number of persons expressly and implicitly opposed somewhat higher.[1] During the ratification period, James Madison, who would later qualify his endorsement, and Alexander Hamilton supported the concept in *The Federalist Papers*. Future Supreme Court Chief Justices Oliver Ellsworth and John Marshall endorsed the principle at their state ratification conventions. *(Box, p. 70)*

The first Congress, in section 25 of the Judiciary Act of 1789, specifically granted the Supreme Court the right of judicial review over state decisions

. . . where is drawn in question the validity of a treaty or statute of, or an authority exercised under, the United States and the decision is against their validity; or where is drawn in question the validity of a statute of, or an authority exercised under any State, on the ground of their being repugnant to the constitution, treaties, or laws of the United States, and the decision is in favor of their validity, or where is drawn in question the construction of any clause of the constitution, or of a treaty, or statute of, or commission held under the United States, and the decision is against the title, right, privilege, or exemption, specially set up or claimed by either party, under such clause of the said constitution, treaty, statute or commission. . . .

Most of the early Supreme Court justices seemed to believe that they enjoyed a similar power of judicial review over federal statutes. Several of the justices, sitting as circuit court judges, refused to administer a 1792 federal pension law, arguing that the administrative duties it required of them were not judicial and so were in conflict with the constitutional separation of powers.[2]

Sitting as the Supreme Court in 1796, the justices assumed the power of judicial review when they held valid a federal tax on carriages.[3] The ruling, since it upheld the law rather than nullified it, occasioned little comment. A few days later, the court ruled for the first time that a state law was invalid because it was in conflict with a federal treaty.[4]

Thus, by the time John Marshall was appointed Chief Justice in 1801, the court already had exercised the power of judicial review although it had not had occasion to test the extent of its power by declaring an act of Congress unconstitutional. When it did find the opportunity, the occasion arose as much from the politics of the day as from a clearcut reading of the law.

Marbury v. Madison

The decision believed by many the most important in the court's history had its genesis in the aftermath of the bitter presidential election of 1800. In that year Republican Thomas Jefferson defeated Federalist John Adams for the presidency. Unwilling to relinquish the power they had held since the beginning of the Union, the Federalists sought to entrench themselves in the only branch of government still open to them — the judiciary. One of Adams' first acts

'The Proper and Peculiar Province'

Writing in No. 78 of *The Federalist Papers,* Alexander Hamilton made a strong case for the principle of judicial review in the new government. Reminding his readers that the Constitution limited legislative authority, Hamilton wrote:

Limitations . . . can be preserved in no other way than through the medium of courts of justice, whose duty it must be to declare all acts contrary to the manifest tenor of the Constitution void. Without this, all the reservations of particular rights or privileges would amount to nothing. . . .

. . . There is no position which depends on clearer principles than that every act of a delegated authority, contrary to the tenor of the commission under which it is exercised, is void. No legislative act, therefore, contrary to the Constitution, can be valid. To deny this would be to affirm that the deputy is greater than his principal; that the servant is above his master; that the representatives of the people are superior to the people themselves; that men acting by virtue of powers may do not only what their powers do not authorize, but what they forbid.

If it be said that the legislative body are themselves the constitutional judges of their own powers and that the construction they put upon them is conclusive upon the other departments it may be answered that this cannot be the natural presumption where it is not to be collected from any particular provisions in the Constitution. It is not otherwise to be supposed that the Constitution could intend to enable the representatives of the people to substitute their *will* to that of their constituents. It is far more rational to suppose that the courts were designed to be an intermediate body between the people and the legislature in order, among other things, to keep the latter within the limits assigned to their authority. The interpretation of the laws is the proper and peculiar province of the courts. A constitution is, in fact, and must be regarded by the judges as, a fundamental law. It therefore belongs to them to ascertain its meaning as well as the meaning of any particular act proceeding from the legislative body. If there should happen to be an irreconcilable variance between the two, that which has the superior obligation and validity ought, of course, to be preferred; or, in other words, the Constitution ought to be preferred to the statute, the intention of the people to the intention of their agents.

Nor does this conclusion by any means suppose a superiority of the judicial to the legislative power. It only supposes that the power of the people is superior to both, and that where the will of the legislature, declared in its statutes, stands in opposition to that of the people, declared in the Constitution, the judges ought to be governed by the latter rather than the former.

Source: *The Federalist Papers,* with an Introduction by Clinton Rossiter (New York: Mentor, 1961), pp. 466-468.

after the election was to appoint his secretary of state, and committed Federalist, John Marshall as Chief Justice to replace Oliver Ellsworth.

The lame duck Congress speedily confirmed Marshall, who also continued for six weeks to serve as Adams' secretary of state until Adams left office on March 4, 1801. The Congress, at Adams' behest, also approved legislation creating 16 new circuit court judgeships, authorizing Adams to appoint as many justices of the peace for the newly created District of Columbia as he deemed necessary and reducing the number of Supreme Court justices from six to five at the next vacancy. This last was intended to deprive Jefferson of a quick appointment to the bench.

Adams named and Congress confirmed the 16 new circuit court judges and 42 justices of the peace. On March 3, Adams' last night in office, he signed the commissions for the new justices of the peace and had them taken to Marshall who was to attach the Great Seal of the United States and have the commissions delivered to the appointees. Marshall did affix the seal but somehow failed to see that all the commissions were actually delivered.

William Marbury, an aide to the secretary of the Navy, was one of the appointees who did not receive his commission. With three other men in the same position, he asked Jefferson's secretary of state, James Madison, to give him the commission.

When Madison, at Jefferson's direction, refused, Marbury asked the Supreme Court to issue a writ of *mandamus* ordering Madison to give the four men their commissions. In December 1801, Chief Justice Marshall asked Madison to show cause at the next session of the court why he should not comply with the order.

At the same time, the Republicans were talking of repealing the 1801 Act creating the new circuit court judgeships. Congress did this in March 1802, and to forestall a court challenge on the ground that the repeal was invalid since the Constitution stipulated that federal judges are appointed for life or good behavior, Congress also delayed the next meeting of the court until February 1803.

In addition to the antagonism between the two political parties, Marshall and Jefferson shared a mutual dislike, and Marshall did not relish the thought that Jefferson would best him in this contest. Marshall, whose oversight had led to Marbury's suit in the first place, probably would have had to disqualify himself under modern ethical standards. And there also would be some question whether the case was moot by the time the court heard it. But neither factor deterred Marshall from taking it up.

His insistence created an apparent dilemma. If the court ordered delivery of the commission, Madison might refuse to obey the order and the court had no means to enforce compliance. It seemed likely that Madison would refuse; the government did not even argue its viewpoint before the court. And if the court did not issue the writ, it would be surrendering to Jefferson's point of view. Either way, the court would be conceding its lack of power.

Marshall resolved his problem with a remarkable decision that has been called a "masterwork of indirection, a brilliant example of Marshall's capacity to sidestep danger while seeming to court it, to advance in one direction while his opponents are looking in another." [5]

Initially ignoring the question of jurisdiction, Marshall ruled that once the president had signed the commissions and the secretary of state had recorded them, the appointments were complete. He also ruled that a writ of *mandamus* was the proper tool to use to require the secretary of state to deliver the commissions. [6]

Having thus rebuked Madison, and, more importantly, Jefferson by implication, Marshall turned to the question of whether the Supreme Court had the authority to issue the writ — and concluded it did not. Congress, Marshall said, had added unconstitutionally to the court's original jurisdiction when, under the Judiciary Act of 1789, it authorized the court to issue such writs to officers of the federal government.

To justify striking down a section of a federal statute, Marshall drew heavily on Hamilton's reasoning in No. 78 of *The Federalist Papers.* The Chief Justice wrote:

> ... The powers of the legislature are defined and limited; and that those limits may not be mistaken or forgotten, the constitution is written. To what purpose are powers limited, and to what purpose is that limitation committed to writing, if these limits may, at any time, be passed by those intended to be restrained? The distinction between a government with limited and unlimited powers is abolished, if those limits do not confine the persons on whom they are imposed, and if acts prohibited and acts allowed, are of equal obligation. It is a proposition too plain to be contested, that the constitution controls any legislative act repugnant to it.[7]

Having established the Constitution's supremacy over legislative enactments, Marshall turned to the question of whether the judiciary had the authority to determine when acts of Congress conflicted with the Constitution:

> It is, emphatically, the province and duty of the judicial department to say what the law is. Those who apply the rule to particular cases, must of necessity expound and interpret that rule. If two laws conflict with each other, the courts must decide on the operations of each. So, if a law be in opposition to the constitution; if both the law and the constitution apply to a particular case, so that the court must either decide that case, conformable to the law, disregarding the constitution; or conformable to the constitution, disregarding the law; the court must determine which of these conflicting rules governs the case: this is of the very essence of judicial duty. If then the courts are to regard the constitution, and the constitution is superior to any ordinary act of the legislature, the constitution, and not such ordinary act, must govern the case to which they both apply . . . .
> . . . The judicial power of the United States is extended to all cases arising under the constitution. Could it be the intention of those who gave this power, to say, that in using it, the constitution should not be looked into? That a case arising under the constitution should be decided, without examining the instrument under which it arises? This is too extravagant to be maintained.[8]

Thus, while denying the court the power to issue writs of *mandamus* in such cases Marshall asserted for the court the far more significant power of judicial review.

Marshall's claim of authority for the court was not generally viewed by his contemporaries with the same import given by future readers. In fact, Jefferson, who believed that the legislature was the only branch capable of determining the validity of its actions, apparently did not find Marshall's claim of power particularly significant. According to historian Charles Warren, "Jefferson's antagonism to Marshall and the Court at that time was due more

to his resentment at the alleged invasion of his Executive prerogative than to any so-called 'judicial usurpation' of the field of Congressional authority."[9]

Marshall himself appeared willing to sacrifice the court's role as the final authority on the constitutional validity of federal statutes in the face of a later political threat from the Republicans. Attempting to use impeachment to remove Federalist judges from office, the Republican Congress impeached and tried Justice Samuel Chase in 1805. Chase escaped conviction by the Senate, but not before Marshall, plainly concerned about the security of his own position, wrote in a letter to Chase:

> I think the modern doctrine of impeachment should yield to an appellate jurisdiction in the legislature. A reversal of those legal opinions deemed unsound by the legislature would certainly better comport with the mildness of our character than [would] removal of the Judge who has rendered them unknowing of his fault.[10]

The Power Exercised

The next two major rulings striking down acts of Congress both had decidedly negative effects on the court itself. The ill-conceived decision in the 1857 *Dred Scott* case invalidating the already-repealed Missouri Compromise of 1820 was followed in 1870 by the court's holding in *Hepburn v. Griswold* that Congress could not make paper money legal tender for the payment of certain debts. Listed as two of three "self-inflicted wounds" by Charles Evans Hughes (the third was the 1895 invalidation of the federal income tax), the two opinions severely strained public confidence in the court. Both were subsequently reversed — the *Dred Scott* case by the 14th Amendment and the *Legal Tender* case by the court itself. *(Dred Scott case, p. 135. Legal Tender case, p. 119)*

Nonetheless, 54 years passed between the *Marbury* and *Dred Scott* decisions, and in the intervening five and a half decades, the court reviewed and upheld several federal statutes. Each time it did so, it reinforced the power it had claimed in the *Marbury* decision. And each time that the government appeared in court to argue for the federal statute, it again conceded the court's right of review.

As Congress began to exercise its powers more fully in the late 19th century, the number of federal laws the court found unconstitutional increased. In several instances — such as the *Legal Tender* cases and the *Income Tax* case — judicial opinion ran directly contrary to popular opinion and stirred bitter public animosity against the court. Yet the court's authority to review these statutes was never directly assaulted. As two constitutional historians observed:

> . . .It is interesting to note that at no time in our history has the power of judicial review been seriously endangered. Despite attacks on the Court's decisions, on its personnel, and even on the procedures by which review is exercised, no major political party has ever urged the complete abolition of the power of review itself. The resounding defeat in Congress of the so-called 'Court Packing Plan,' suggested by President Franklin D. Roosevelt at the height of his popularity, indicates that popular dissatisfaction with the use of the power of judicial review does not necessarily imply a feeling that the Court should be dominated by the political branches of the government."[11]

The Power Restrained

One major reason why the review power has not been successfully challenged is the court's own recognition of the necessity of imposing some restraints on its exercise. Conse-

---

'Popular Review'

Although the concept of judicial review is well-entrenched in American legal history and practice, arguments against it still recur. One of the earliest and, many agree, one of the most persuasive was written in 1825 by John Gibson, an associate justice of the Pennsylvania Supreme Court. Dissenting from a decision involving the state court's power to invalidate a state statute, Gibson wrote:

In theory, all the organs of the government are of equal capacity; or, if not equal, each must be supposed to have superior capacity only for those things which peculiarly belong to it; and, as legislation peculiarly involves the consideration of those limitations which are put on the law-making power, and the interpretation of the laws when made, involves only the construction of the laws themselves, it follows that the construction of the constitution in this particular belongs to the legislature, which ought therefore to be taken to have superior capacity to judge of the constitutionality of its own acts. But suppose all to be of equal capacity in every respect, why should one exercise a controlling power over the rest? That the judiciary is of superior rank, has never been pretended, although it has been said to be co-ordinate....

The negative which each part of the legislature may exercise, in regard to the acts of the other, was thought sufficient to prevent material infractions of the restraints which were put on the power of the whole; for, had it been intended to interpose the judiciary as an additional barrier, the matter would surely not have been left in doubt. The judges would not have been left to stand on the insecure and ever shifting ground of public opinion as to constructive powers: they would have been placed on the impregnable ground of an express grant....

But do not the judges do a positive act in violation of the constitution, when they give effect to an unconstitutional law? ... The fallacy of the question is, in supposing that the judiciary adopts the Acts of the Legislature as its own; whereas the enactment of a law and the interpretation of it are not concurrent acts, and as the judiciary is not required to concur in the enactment, neither is it in the breach of the Constitution which may be the consequence of the enactment. The fault is imputable to the legislature, and on it the responsibility exclusively rests....

For these reasons, I am of opinion that it rests, ultimately, with the people, in whom full and absolute sovereign power resides, to correct abuses in legislation, by instructing their representatives to repeal the obnoxious act .... (*Eakin v. Raub,* 12 Sergeant and Rawle 330 Pa., 1825.)

---

quently, the court has developed several rules to guide its deliberations.

The first states that the court will not hear a case unless it involves a real controversy between real adversaries.

The court generally refuses to take so-called friendly or collusive suits, although, as with most of these rules of restraint, the rule is often honored in the breach. Major exceptions to this rule were the 1895 *Income Tax* cases in which a stockholder in a bank sought to prevent the bank from paying the income tax. It was clear that neither party wanted to pay the tax and that both wanted to test the constitutionality of the tax law. *(Details p. 109)*

A second rule is that the court will not pass on the constitutionality of a federal statute if it can decide the issue without doing so. A major exception to this rule was the *Dred Scott* case, in which the court invalidated the already-repealed Missouri Compromise in order to make a pronouncement on slavery in the territories when it might have decided the case on much narrower grounds. *(Details, p. 135)*

If there are two reasonable interpretations of a statute, one upholding it and one striking it down, the court will favor the one upholding it. By corollary, if the constitutionality of a statute must be considered, the court will make every effort to find it valid.

A major exception to these two rules was John Marshall's opinion in *Marbury v. Madison.* In this first case asserting the judiciary's right to strike down acts of Congress, Marshall held that in authorizing the court to issue writs of *mandamus* to federal officials, Congress had added impermissibly to the court's original jurisdiction. Most scholars agree that Marshall could have found the statute valid by viewing the power to issue this order to federal officials as incidental to the court's original jurisdiction.

A fifth rule states that if a statute is valid on its face, the court will not look beyond it to examine Congress' motives for enacting it.

Two examples of exceptions to this rule are the opinions striking down congressional attempts to eliminate child labor. In *Hammer v. Dagenhart* (1918), the court said Congress did not design the Child Labor Act of 1916 as a regulation of interstate commerce but to discourage the use of child labor, an impermissible objective.

A subsequent attempt to tax goods manufactured by children was struck down in *Bailey v. Drexel Furniture Co.* (1922) on identical reasoning; the tax was not intended to raise revenue, the court said, but to penalize employers of children.

If the rest of a statute can stand on its own when part of it has been invalidated, the court will strike down only the unconstitutional portion. Major exceptions to this rule of severability were the *Income Tax* cases and *Carter v. Carter Coal Co.* (1936), the case invalidating New Deal legislation regulating coal production. In both cases, the court found one section of the law invalid, and then, without further examination, used that infirmity to strike down the rest of the statute. *(Severability, p. 113, Income Tax cases, p. 109, Carter case, p. 98)*

A sixth rule states that the court will not review cases that present so-called political questions — those that involve matters regarded as within the discretion of the political branches of government. Intervention by the courts in such questions has been considered a violation of the principle of separation of powers.

A major exception to this rule was the court's decision in *Baker v. Carr* (1962), where the court held that federal

courts could review state apportionment plans for violations of federally guaranteed rights. Until that landmark
decision, the federal courts had consistently refused to
review challenges to both federal and state apportionment.
(Details, Baker v. Carr, p. 490)

Constitutional scholar Robert K. Carr wrote that the
primary significance of these rules of judicial restraint

> ...probably lies in the conscious strategic use which
> the Court has made of them. They are often available
> as props to strengthen the particular decision which
> the Court has chosen to render and have frequently
> had no small value in enabling the Court to support
> the view that judicial review is subject to many limita-
> tions which have been self-imposed by the justices.[12]

Carr has also written that the exceptions to the rule
were probably inevitable:

> For the most part these rules are of such a charac-
> ter that they cannot always be followed in an abso-
> lutely consistent manner. At the same time they have
> been followed so often that it would be misleading to
> suggest that they have had no significance at all.[13]
> *(Further discussion of judicial restraint, pp. 287-295)*

Implied Powers

In contrast to the first 17 clauses of Article I, Section 8
of the Constitution, which enumerate the specific powers
granted to Congress, the 18th clause is a general grant to
Congress of the power "To make all laws which shall be
necessary and proper for carrying into Execution the Foregoing Powers, and all other Powers vested by this Constitution in the Government of the United States, or in any
Department or Officer thereof."

A major question posed to the court early in U.S.
history by this sweeping or "elastic" clause was whether it
restricted or enlarged the enumerated powers of Congress.

Thomas Jefferson and Alexander Hamilton in 1791
argued the opposing viewpoints on this question, after
Congress passed legislation establishing the first national
bank. Before deciding whether to sign the bill, President
Washington solicited opinions on its constitutionality,
which he then submitted to Hamilton, chief advocate of the
bank, for rebuttal.

In his opinion, Jefferson viewed the legislation as
invalid because the Constitution did not specifically grant
Congress the power to incorporate a bank. He said that the
phrase "necessary and proper" meant Congress could only
enact those laws that were *indispensable* to carrying out a
delegated power.

Hamilton, on the other side, contended that Congress
had two sorts of implied powers — those derived from the
fact of the national government's sovereignty, such as its
autonomous control over territories, and those derived from
the necessary and proper clause. The criterion for determining if an act of Congress is constitutional, Hamilton said,

> ... is the *end*, to which the measure relates as a *mean*.
> If the *end* be clearly comprehended within any of the
> specified powers, and if the measure have an obvious
> relation to that *end* and is not forbidden by any
> particular provision of the Constitution, it may safely
> be deemed to come within the compass of the national
> authority.[14]

Early Interpretation

The court under the leadership of Chief Justice John
Marshall gave an early indication that it would adopt
Hamilton's broader view. In 1805 the court upheld a federal
statute that gave payment priority to the United States in
cases of bankruptcies. It "would produce endless difficulties if the opinion should be maintained that no law was
authorized which was not indispensably necessary to give
effect to a specified power...," Marshall said. "Congress
must possess the choice of means and must be empowered
to use any means which are in fact conducive to the exercise
of a power granted by the Constitution."[15]

'Not a Splendid Bauble'

Marshall would not fully develop this position until
1819. When he did, it was unanimously supported by the
court.

McCulloch v. Maryland involved the second national
bank.[16] Chartered in 1816, the bank was extremely unpopular, particularly in the western and southern states, many
of which tried to keep the bank from opening branches at
all or, failing that, tried to tax branches out of existence.
One of the latter was Maryland, which imposed a hefty tax
on the notes issued by the bank's Baltimore branch. James
McCulloch, a bank cashier, refused to pay the tax.
McCulloch claimed the state tax was an unconstitutional
infringement on the federally chartered bank, while Maryland contended that Congress had exceeded its powers
when it chartered the bank. The state also claimed that in
any event it had the power to tax the bank within its
borders.

For the court, Marshall first upheld the power of
Congress to incorporate the bank. He noted that the
national government is "one of enumerated powers" but
asserted that "though limited in its powers [it] is supreme
within its sphere of action."[17]

He acknowledged that the power to establish a bank
and create corporations were not among the enumerated
powers. But, he wrote,

> ... there is no phrase in the instrument which, like the
> articles of confederation, excludes incidental or im-
> plied powers; and which requires that everything
> granted shall be expressly and minutely described.
> Even the 10th amendment, which was framed for the
> purpose of quieting the excessive jealousies which had
> been excited, omits the word "expressly," and declares
> only that the powers "not delegated to the United
> States, nor prohibited to the states, are reserved to the
> states or to the people"; thus leaving the question,
> whether the particular power which may become the
> subject of contest has been delegated to the one gov-
> ernment, or prohibited to the other, to depend on a fair
> construction of the whole instrument.[18]

Although the Constitution did not specifically authorize Congress to incorporate banks, Marshall said, it did
grant it "great powers" — to tax, to regulate commerce, to
declare war and to support and maintain armies and
navies. Therefore, he said,

> ...it may with great reason be contended, that a
> government, entrusted with such ample powers, on the
> due execution of which the happiness and prosperity of
> the nation so vitally depends, must also be entrusted
> with ample means for their execution.[19]

Incorporation, Marshall said, was one of these means. "It is never the end for which other powers are exercised, but a means by which other objects are accomplished," he said.[20]

Marshall then turned to the meaning of the word "necessary" as it is used in the Constitution. The attorneys for Maryland had used Jefferson's argument that the word limited Congress to those means indispensable for implementing a delegated power. "Is it true that this is the sense in which the word 'necessary' is always used?" asked Marshall. He continued:

. . .Does it always import an absolute physical necessity, so strong that one thing to which another may be termed necessary, cannot exist without the other? We think it does not. . . . To employ the means necessary to an end, is generally understood as employing any means calculated to produce the end, and not as being confined to those single means, without which the end would be entirely unattainable. . . .

. . . It must have been the intention of those who gave these powers, to insure, so far as human prudence could insure, their beneficial execution. This could not be done by confiding the choice of means to such narrow limits as not to leave it in the power of Congress to adopt any which might be appropriate, and which were conducive to the end. This provision is made in a constitution intended to endure for ages to come, and, consequently, to be adapted to the various *crises* of human affairs. . . . To have declared that the best means shall not be used, but those alone without which the power given would be nugatory, would have been to deprive the legislature of the capacity to avail itself of experience, to exercise its reason, and to accommodate its legislation to circumstances.[21]

Marshall next pointed out that the central government had already relied on the concept of implied powers in its exercise of the delegated powers. The Constitution specifically empowers Congress to punish only a few federal crimes such as counterfeiting currency and crimes committed on the high seas, Marshall said. Yet, he added, no one has questioned the power of Congress to provide punishment for violations of other laws it passes. The Constitution, while it gives Congress authority to establish post roads and post offices, does not specify that the government has the authority to carry the mail, Marshall noted; yet the government assumed that authority.

In conclusion, Marshall wrote:

The result of the most careful and attentive consideration bestowed upon this clause is, that if it does not enlarge, it cannot be construed to restrain the powers of Congress, or to impair the right of the legislature to exercise its best judgment in the selection of measures to carry into execution the constitutional powers of the government. If no other motive for its insertion can be suggested, a sufficient one is found in the desire to remove all doubts respecting the right to legislate on that vast mass of incidental powers which must be involved in the constitution, if that instrument be not a splendid bauble.

We admit, as all must admit, that the powers of the government are limited, and that its limits are not to be transcended. But we think the sound construction of the constitution must allow to the national legislature that discretion, with respect to the means by which the powers it confers are to be carried into

execution, which will enable that body to perform the high duties assigned to it, in the manner most beneficial to the people. Let the end be legitimate, let it be within the scope of the constitution, and all means which are appropriate, which are plainly adapted to that end, which are not prohibited, but consist with the letter and spirit of the constitution, are constitutional.[22]

In the remainder of the opinion, Marshall developed the famous doctrine that since "the power to tax involves the power to destroy," the state tax on the federal bank threatened the supremacy of the federal government. "[T]here is a plain repugnance, in conferring on one government a power to control the constitutional measures of another, which other, with respect to those very measures, is declared to be supreme," Marshall wrote.[23] *(Details, p. 329)*

Constitutional scholar Robert G. McCloskey called *McCulloch v. Maryland* "by almost any reckoning the greatest decision John Marshall ever handed down — the one most important to the future of America, most influential in the court's own doctrinal history, and most revealing of Marshall's unique talent for stately argument."[24]

The opinion forcefully upheld the supremacy of federal law over conflicting state law, reaffirmed the Supreme Court's judicial review powers and espoused a broad construction of the necessary and proper clause in particular and congressional power in general that has been in use ever since. Hardly a bill passed by Congress does not rely to some extent on the necessary and proper clause for its validity. It has been especially significant to congressional control over fiscal affairs and to the establishment of the vast network of regulatory agencies. As Marshall himself pointed out, it is the basis of the federal power to punish violations of the law. It is also the foundation for the doctrine of eminent domain. All of these are powers that have in one way or another touched the life of every citizen of the United States. Marshall's contribution was summarized by Professor R. Kent Newmyer:

As in *Marbury v. Madison*, the genius of the *McCulloch* opinion lay not in its originality but in its timing, practicability, clarity and eloquence. Original it was not . . . . Marshall did not create these nationalist principles. What he did do was seize them at the moment when they were most relevant to American needs and congenial to the American mind, and (aided by the rhetoric of Alexander Hamilton) he translated them gracefully and logically into the law of the Constitution. Basing his interpretation of the law on the needs and spirit of the age, Marshall gave it permanence. Hamilton himself was unable to do as much.[25]

Inherent Powers

In addition to the power implied by the necessary and proper clause, the court has acknowledged that Congress derives some of its authority from the fact of the nation's sovereignty. In his *Commentaries on the Constitution of the United States*, Justice Joseph Story defined this authority as that which results "from the whole mass of the powers of the National Government, and from the nature of political society, [rather] than a consequence or incident of the powers specially enumerated."[26]

Chief Justice John Marshall relied on these inherent powers in 1828 when he declared that the absolute authority conferred on the central government to make war and treaties gave it the power to acquire territory by either war or treaty.[27]

The inherent or resulting powers have also been used to justify federal authority to acquire territory by discovery, to exclude and deport aliens, and to legislate for Indian tribes.[28]

Inherent power has generally been invoked only to rationalize an exercise of power over exernal affairs. As Justice George Sutherland wrote in 1936:

> . . . [S]ince the states severally never possessed international powers, such powers could not have been carved from the mass of state powers but obviously were transmitted to the Unied States from some other source. . . . The powers to declare and wage war, to conclude peace, to make treaties, to maintain diplomatic relations with other sovereignties, if they had never been mentioned in the Constitution would have vested in the federal government as necessary concomitants of nationality.[29]

Delegation of Power

The Latin phrase *"delegata potestas non potest delegari"* summarizes an old legal doctrine — "a power once delegated cannot be redelegated." Some have used this doctrine to contend that because Congress' powers have been delegated to it by the Constitution, it cannot in turn delegate them to anyone else. Practically speaking, however, Congress does delegate its power and has done so almost from the beginning of its history.

While it occasionally pays lip service to the doctrine, the Supreme Court acknowledges that it has little meaning for Congress. "Delegation by Congress has long been recognized as necessary in order that the exertion of legislative power does not become a futility," the court has said.[30]

Filling Up the Details

There are two types of legislative delegation. In the first, Congress sets an objective and authorizes an administrator to promulgate rules and regulations that will achieve the objective. The administrator may have only the broadest standards to guide his regulation-making, or he may be required to incorporate a host of congressionally approved details in regulations.

This type of delegation was first upheld in 1825. Congress had granted authority to the federal courts to set rules of practice so long as they did not conflict with the laws of the United States. The court approved this delegation:

> The difference beween the departments undoubtedly is, that the legislature makes, the executive executes, and the judiciary construes the law; but the maker of the law may commit something to the discretion of the other departments, and the precise boundary of this power is a subject of delicate and difficult inquiry, into which a court will not enter unnecessarily.[31]

Nonetheless, Chief Justice John Marshall felt capable of distinguishing between "those important subjects, which must be entirely regulated by the legislature itself, from those of less interest, in which a general provision may be made, and power given to those who are to act under such general provisions to fill up the details." [32]

Congress and the court have found few subjects to fall into the first part of Marshall's distinction, viewing most as amenable to some delegation.

Thus Congress enacted and the court in 1904 sustained a law that gave the secretary of the treasury authority to appoint a Board of Tea Inspectors to set standards for grading tea. The statute also barred the import of any tea that did not meet the inspection standards. The act was challenged as an unconstitutional delegation of a policy-making function, that is, the establishment of the standards. But the court said no, that Congress had set a "primary standard" that was sufficient.[33]

Justice Edward D. White wrote for the court:

> Congress legislated on the subject as far as was reasonably practicable, and from the necessities of the case was compelled to leave to executive officials the duty of bringing about the result pointed out by the statute. To deny the power of Congress to delegate such a duty would, in effect, amount but to declaring that the plenary power vested in Congress to regulate foreign commerce could not be efficaciously exerted.[34]

In another case, the court upheld congressionally mandated penalties for violations of administrative regulations, while making clear in a subsequent case that the administrative agency could not impose additional punishments.[35]

A major use by Congress of its power to delegate has been in creation of agencies to regulate the nation's transportation and communications systems, trade practices, securities, and interstate power distribution and sales. The authority of Congress to make this delegation of power was first upheld in 1894.[36]

Deciding When To Act

The second type of legislative delegation authorizes an administrator to take a certain course of action if and when he determines that certain conditions exist. This contingency delegation was first upheld by the Supreme Court in 1813 when it sustained the right of Congress to authorize the president to reinstate the Non-Intercourse Act of 1809 under certain conditions. "[W]e can see no sufficient reason, why the legislature should not exercise its discretion in reviving the act. . ., either expressly or conditionally, as their judgment should direct," the court declared.[37]

Expansion of this contingency delegation came in 1892 when the court upheld congressional delegation of authority to the president to prohibit free entry of certain items when he determined that foreign governments were imposing unreasonable duties on U.S. imports. The court held that the president was not making law but finding fact. The president, the court said, was a "mere agent of the lawmaking department to ascertain and declare the event upon which its expressed will was to take effect." [38]

In 1928, the court sustained a delegation of tariff authority to the president. Upholding the Fordney-McComber Act, which authorized the president to raise or lower tariffs by as much as 50 percent to equalize production costs between the United States and competing countries, Chief Justice William Howard Taft offered an oft-quoted "common sense and inherent necessities" doctrine to govern the delegation of powers:

> The well-known maxim *'Delegata potestas non potest delegari,'* applicable to the law of agency in the general and common law, is well understood and has had wider application in the construction of our Federal and State Constitutions than it has in private law.

Specific Constitutional Limits . . .

The Constitution contains in Article I, Section 9, eight specific prohibitions on congressional action.

Taxes

One prohibition that had primary significance in the first century of U.S. history forbids Congress to levy a direct tax unless it is apportioned among the several states on the basis of population. Until 1895 the Supreme Court repeatedly stated that the only direct taxes were capitation taxes and taxes on land. In 1895 the court struck down a general income tax by ruling that a tax based on the income from land was also direct and invalid because it had not been constitutionally apportioned.[1] This decision was overturned in 1913 when the 16th Amendment, which specifically exempted income taxes from the apportionment requirement, was ratified. *(Details p. 111)*

A second tax requirement stipulated that all indirect taxes be uniform throughout the United States. The requirement has presented little difficulty since the court in the early 20th century defined it to mean that indirect taxes must be applied uniformly to the class being taxed.[2] *(Details, p. 112)*

Habeas Corpus

The second clause of Section 9 prohibits the suspension of the privilege of the writ of *habeas corpus* "unless when in Cases of Rebellion or Invasion the public Safety may require it." A protection against illegal imprisonment, a writ of *habeas corpus* is a command to the detaining authority to bring a prisoner before the court and justify his continued detention.

The clause does not state whether it is Congress or the president who has the authority to suspend the writ in emergencies. In the early Civil War years, President Lincoln suspended the privilege on his own authority. His authority to do so was challenged by Chief Justice Roger B. Taney, sitting in the circuit court in Baltimore, in the case of *Ex parte Merryman.*[3] Despite Taney's ruling, Lincoln continued to suspend the writ of *habeas corpus* on his own authority until March 1863 when Congress gave him specific authority to do so.

In three other instances, Congress has asserted its power to suspend the writ — in nine South Carolina counties during a conflict with the Ku Klux Klan in 1871, in the Philippines during the 1905 insurrection and in Hawaii during World War II.

The full Supreme Court has not ruled on the question of the president's authority to suspend the writ in periods of emergency. Clinton Rossiter, noted scholar of the American presidency, has written that the lesson of Lincoln's assertion of this power is that "in a condition of martial necessity," the president does have the power. "The most a court or judge can do is read the President a lecture based on *Ex parte Merryman."*[4] *(Details, p. 189)*

The Supreme Court has determined that when suspension occurs, it is the privilege that is suspended and not the writ itself. The writ may still be issued but the responsibility for complying with it is lifted.[5]

Bills of Attainder

The third clause of prohibition forbids enactment of bills of attainder and *ex post facto* laws. In the case of *Cummings v. Missouri* the Supreme Court defined a bill of attainder as "a legislative act which inflicts punishment without a judicial trial."[6]

Of the 105 acts of Congress declared unconstitutional as of mid-1979, three have been held to be bills of attainder.

The third federal statute struck down by the court, and the first invalidated by a 5-4 vote, was an 1865 law that barred attorneys from practicing before federal courts unless they had sworn an oath that they had remained loyal to the Union throughout the Civil War. Persons taking the oath falsely could be charged with and convicted of perjury.

A. H. Garland of Arkansas had been admitted to practice law before the federal courts during the 1860 Supreme Court term. When Arkansas subsequently seceded from the union, Garland went with the state, becoming first a representative and then a senator in the Confederate Congress. Garland received a full pardon from the president for his service to the Confederacy in 1865. His case, *Ex parte Garland,* came to the court in 1867 when he sought to practice in federal courts without taking the oath.[7]

Justice Stephen J. Field wrote the majority opinion. Because lawyers who had violated the conditions of the oath could not take it without perjuring themselves, he said,

> . . . the act, as against them, operates as a legislative decree of perpetual exclusion. And exclusion from any of the professions or any of the ordinary avocations of life for past conduct can be regarded in no other light than as punishment for such conduct.[8]

The minority claimed that the statute was not a bill of attainder, because it did not specifically name the persons to which it was to apply. *(Details, p. 225)*

Subversive Activities. The court's holdings in *Ex parte Garland* and its sister case, *Cummings v. Missouri,* served as precedent for the next bill of attainder case.

United States v. Lovett (1946) involved three government employees, Lovett, Watson and Dodd.[9] In 1943 Rep. Martin Dies, D Texas (1931-45, 1953-59), chairman of the House Committee on Un-American Activities, listed 39 federal employees, including Lovett, Watson and Dodd, as "irresponsible, unrepresentative, crackpot, radical bureaucrats" who were affiliated with "communist front organizations." Dies urged that Congress refuse to appropriate funds to pay those employees' salaries.

After a special subcommittee of the House Appropriations Committee heard testimony in secret session, it pronounced Lovett, Watson and Dodd guilty of subversive activities and unfit to hold their government positions. Congress then passed a provision barring appropriations to pay the men's salaries. President Roosevelt signed the bill but declared that in his view the provision was an unconstitutional bill of attainder.

. . . On Congressional Powers

A majority of the court agreed. Justice Hugo L. Black wrote that "legislative acts, no matter what their form, that apply either to named individuals or to easily ascertainable members of a group in such a way as to inflict punishment on them without a judicial trial are bills of attainder prohibited by the Constitution." [10]

Black maintained the provision amounted to a "permanent proscription to serve the Government," which he said was punishment "of a most severe type. . . ." [11]

Party Membership. The third case, *United States v. Brown* (1965) concerned a provision of the Labor Management and Reporting Act of 1959 which made it a crime for anyone to serve as an officer or employee of a labor union if he were a member of the Communist Party or had been at any time in the previous five years.[12] Designed to prevent politically motivated strikes, the provision replaced a section of the 1947 Taft-Hartley Act that had required labor unions seeking access to the National Labor Relations Board to file affidavits swearing that none of the union's officers were members of or affiliated with the Communist Party. That requirement had been upheld by the court in *American Communications Association v. Douds* (1950).[13]

The Supreme Court, however, found the successor provision an illegal bill of attainder. "The statute," wrote Chief Justice Earl Warren for the five-justice majority, "designates in no uncertain terms the persons who possess the feared characteristics and therefore cannot hold union office without incurring criminal liability — members of the Communist Party." [14]

Warren distinguished *Brown* from *Douds* by pointing out that the Taft-Hartley provision could be escaped simply by resigning from the Communist Party, while the 1959 act applied to persons who had been members of the party for the last five years. Warren said it did not matter whether the five-year provision was intended as retribution or to prevent *pro forma* resignations from the Communist Party, which would not remove the threat of politically motivated strikes. "It would be archaic to limit the definition of 'punishment' to 'retribution,'" said Warren. "Punishment serves several purposes; retributive, rehabilitative, deterrent — and preventive." [15]

Ex Post Facto Laws

An *ex post facto* law makes an already committed act illegal or makes the punishment greater than it was when the crime was committed. In *Calder v. Bull* (1798), the earliest Supreme Court discussion of *ex post facto* laws, the court held that the constitutional prohibition did not apply to civil statutes but only to criminal laws.[16]

In addition to declaring it a bill of attainder, the court in *Ex parte Garland* also found the loyalty oath requirement an *ex post facto* law on the ground that to prohibit an attorney from practicing before federal courts without taking the oath was to punish him for past acts not defined as illegal at the time they were committed.

In other instances, however, the court has upheld, against charges they were *ex post facto* laws, statutes that denied the right to vote in a territorial election to polygamists, that deported aliens for criminal acts committed prior to the deportation law's enactment and that revoked naturalization papers obtained fraudulently before passage of the law.[17]

Export Duties

The Constitution also prohibits Congress from laying taxes or duties on items exported from any state. Using this prohibition, the court has declared invalid a stamp tax on foreign bills of lading and a tax on charter parties that operated from ports in the United States to foreign ports.[18]

The court, however, has said that the prohibition does not extend to a general property tax that affects goods intended for export so long as the tax is not levied only on goods for export and so long as the goods are not taxed in the course of exportation.[19] The court has also held that a tax on corporate income including income from exportation was not forbidden by the constitutional limitation.[20]

Other Limits

The remaining restrictions on congressional authority are of less legal than historical interest. They have required little judicial interpretation. The first barred Congress from banning the importation of slaves for the first 20 years after the Constitution was ratified.

Other clauses in this category stipulate that Congress shall give no preference to the ports of one state over those of another, that it should not grant titles of nobility and that Congress must appropriate all money before it can be drawn from the Treasury.

---

[1] *Pollock v. Farmers' Loan & Trust Co.,* 157 U.S. 429 (1895), 158 U.S. 601 (1895).

[2] *Knowlton v. Moore,* 178 U.S. 41 (1900).

[3] 17 Fed. Cases 9487 (1861).

[4] Clinton Rossiter, *The Supreme Court and the Commander-in-Chief* (Ithaca, N.Y.: Cornell University Press, 1951), p. 25.

[5] *Ex parte Milligan,* 4 Wall. 2 (1866).

[6] *Cummings v. Missouri,* 4 Wall. 277 (1867).

[7] *Ex parte Garland,* 4 Wall. 333 (1867).

[8] Id. at 377.

[9] *United States v. Lovett,* 328 U.S. 303 (1946).

[10] Id. at 315.

[11] Id. at 315-316.

[12] *United States v. Brown,* 381 U.S. 437 (1965).

[13] *American Communications Association v. Douds,* 339 U.S. 382 (1950).

[14] *United States v. Brown,* 381 U.S. 437 at 450 (1965).

[15] Id. at 458.

[16] *Calder v. Bull,* 3 Dall. 386 (1798).

[17] *Murphy v. Ramsey,* 114 U.S. 15 (1885); *Mahler v. Eby,* 264 U.S. 32 (1924); *Johannessen v. United States,* 225 U.S. 227 (1912).

[18] *Fairbank v. United States,* 181 U.S. 283 (1901); *United States v. Hvoslef,* 237 U.S. 1 (1915).

[19] *Cornell v. Coyne,* 192 U.S. 418 (1904); *Turpin v. Burgess,* 117 U.S. 504 (1886).

[20] *Peck & Co. v. Lowe,* 247 U.S. 165 (1918); *National Paper Co. v. Bowers,* 266 U.S. 373 (1924).

The Federal Constitution and the State Constitutions of this country divide the governmental power into three branches.... [I]n carrying out that constitutional division ... it is a breach of the national fundamental law if Congress gives up its legislative power and transfers it to the President, or to the Judicial branch, or if by law it attempts to invest itself or its members with either executive power or judicial power. This is not to say that the three branches are not co-ordinate parts of one government and that each in the field of its duties may not invoke the action of the other two in so far as the action invoked shall not be an assumption of the constitutional field of action of another branch. In determining what it may do in seeking assistance from another branch, the extent and character of that assistance must be fixed according to common sense and the inherent necessities of the governmental coordination.[39]

Congressional Standards

One of the factors the court has used to judge the validity of a legislative delegation has been the adequacy of the guidelines and standards Congress has set for the administrator to follow. In most cases, the court found the standards sufficient. In some instances, it has upheld a statute delegating power even though the law did not offer any standards at all to guide the administrator.[40]

But a court whose conservative bent clashed with the New Deal philosophy of President Franklin D. Roosevelt seized on the inadequacy of congressional standards to negate two major pieces of New Deal legislation.

'Hot' Oil. The first of these two 1935 cases was *Panama Refining Co. v. Ryan,* which concerned a provision of the National Industrial Recovery Act (NIRA) that authorized the president to prohibit from interstate commerce so-called "hot oil," oil produced in violation of state regulations controlling the amount of production.[41]

The provision was challenged on a number of fronts, and because the court had never before struck down an act of Congress as an invalid delegation of powers, the government gave only 13 pages of its 427-page brief to a refutation of the allegation that the delegation to the president was too broad.[42]

It was thus a surprise when the court struck down the provision on the ground that it transferred too much legislative power to the president. The court said:

Among the numerous and diverse objectives broadly stated [in the act], the President was not required to choose. The President was not required to ascertain and proclaim the conditions prevailing in the industry which made the prohibition necessary. The Congress left the matter to the President without standard or rule, to be dealt with as he pleased. The effort by ingenious and diligent construction to supply a criterion still permits such a breadth of authorized action as essentially to commit to the President the functions of a Legislature rather than those of an executive or administrative officer executing a declared legislative policy.[43]

The only justice to dissent, Benjamin N. Cardozo, found enough "definition of a standard" in the statute's declaration of intent to justify the delegation. "Discretion is not unconfined and vagrant," Cardozo wrote. "It is canalized within banks that keep it from overflowing."[44]

Sick Chickens. But in the next case in which legislative delegation figured, Cardozo, in a concurring opinion, agreed with the court that Congress had left the president "virtually unfettered" in his exercise of the delegated power.[45] The case, *Schechter Poultry Corp. v. United States,* popularly known as the "Sick Chicken" case, challenged the validity of the fair competition codes set for various industries under the NIRA. The statute authorized the president to approve an industry code if he had been asked to do so by at least one association representing the industry. The Schechters had been charged with violating the poultry code; they responded by challenging this delegation of power as too broad. *(Details p. 98)*

Cardozo conceded that in this case the "banks" set up by the NIRA were not high enough, that discretion was "unconfined and vagrant," and that, in short, it was a case of "delegation running riot."[46]

Congress quickly caught on to this test of validity. When it passed the Fair Labor Standards Act in 1938, it added what two commentators referred to as "a rather detailed, though uninstructive, list of factors to guide the administrator's judgement."[47] The court upheld this delegation in *Opp Cotton Mills v. Administrator of Wage and Hours Division* (1941).[48]

Delegations to Private Parties

In the "Sick Chicken" case, the court also struck down the provisions of the NIRA that authorized trade associations to recommend fair competition codes to the president for his approval.

Writing for the court, Chief Justice Charles Evans Hughes posed the question whether Congress had such power. "The answer is obvious," he wrote. "Such a delegation of legislative power is unknown to our law, and is utterly inconsistent with the constitutional duties and prerogatives of Congress."[49]

Unconstitutional delegation of legislative powers to private parties was also one of the reasons the court gave for its decision to strike down the Guffey Coal Act of 1935. That statute had authorized the coal industry to establish mandatory wage and hour regulations for the industry.

In *Carter v. Carter Coal Co.* (1936), the court said:

The power conferred upon the majority [of the coal industry] is, in effect the power to regulate the affairs of an unwilling minority. This is legislative delegation in its most obnoxious form; for it is not even delegation to an official or an official body ... but to private persons whose interests may be and often are adverse to the interests of others in the same business.[50]

The court, however, later upheld a federal law that required two-thirds of tobacco growers to approve the designation of markets to which the growers would be restricted if they wished to sell their tobacco in interstate commerce. The justices said this was not an attempt to delegate powers. Instead, the referendum was simply a condition of the federal regulation.[51]

Prior to the holdings in *Schechter* and *Carter,* the court had sustained federal statutes giving the force of law to local customs regarding miners' claims on public lands and to the determination by the American Railway Association of the standard height of freight car draw bars.[52] The court has not reconciled these seemingly conflicting rulings.

Wartime Delegations

Since its 1827 decision upholding an act of Congress delegating to the president the power to decide when to call out the militia, the Supreme Court has never found it necessary to overturn a wartime delegation of legislative power.[53] This has been true despite the fact that the discretion given by Congress to the president during times of war or other national emergency has been far broader than any peacetime delegation.

That legislative delegations are viewed differently when related to such emergencies was perhaps best stated in *United States v. Curtiss-Wright Corp* (1936). In that case the court upheld a grant of authority to the president allowing him to bar the sale of arms to warring countries in South America if he thought the prohibition might contribute to the restoration of peace.[54] For the court, Justice George Sutherland wrote:

> It is important to bear in mind that we are here not dealing alone with an authority vested in the President by an exertion of legislative power, but with such an authority plus the very delicate, plenary and exclusive power of the President as the sole organ of the federal government in the field of international relations — a power which does not require as a basis for its exercise an act of Congress.... It is quite apparent that if, in the maintenance of our international relations, embarrassment ... is to be avoided and success for our aims achieved, congressional legislation which is to be made effective through negotiation and inquiry within the international field must often accord to the President a

degree of distinction and freedom from statutory restriction which would not be admissable were domestic affairs alone involved. [55] *(For details on specific cases involving wartime delegations, see pp. 129, 190)*

Delegations to States

The court has also upheld congressional delegation of power to the states — generally refusing to call it a delegation. One of the leading cases involved the Federal Assimilative Crimes Act of 1948, which made any crime committed on a federal enclave and not punishable under federal law punishable under state laws in effect at the time.

The court reasoned that since Congress had the power to assimilate state laws on a daily or annual basis, it also had the power to do it on a permanent basis. "Rather than being a delegation by Congress of its legislative authority to the States, it is a deliberate continuing adoption by Congress for federal enclaves of such unpre-empted offenses and punishments as shall have been already put in effect by the respective States for their own government," the court held.[56]

In another case, the court upheld the Webb-Kenyon Act of 1913, which prohibited the shipment of liquor in interstate commerce into any state that was dry. Because the same law allowed states to ban liquor by passing a prohibition law, the federal statute was challenged as an unconstitutional delegation of powers. The court disagreed, declaring it was not a delegation since the act established the precise conditions under which it would take effect.[57] *(Details, p. 325)*

Footnotes

[1] Max Farrand, *The Records of the Federal Convention of 1787*, rev. ed. (New Haven: Yale University Press, 1937), vol. 1, quoted in Library of Congress, Congressional Reference Service, *The Constitution of the United States of America: Analysis and Interpretation*, S. Doc. 92-82, 92nd Cong., 2nd Sess. (Washington, D.C.: Government Printing Office, 1973), p. 670, n. 5. For summary of discussions on the topic, see Raoul Berger, *Congress v. The Supreme Court*, (Cambridge: Harvard University Press, 1969), pp. 37-143.

[2] *Hayburn's Case*, 2 Dall. 409 (1792).

[3] *Hylton v. United States*, 3 Dall. 171 (1796).

[4] *Ware v. Hylton*, 3 Dall. 199 (1796).

[5] Robert G. McCloskey, *The American Supreme Court* (Chicago: University of Chicago Press, 1960), p. 40.

[6] *Marbury v. Madison*, 1 Cr. 137 (1803).

[7] Id. at 176-177.

[8] Id. at 177-179.

[9] Charles Warren, *The Supreme Court in United States History*, rev. ed., 2 vols. (Boston: Little, Brown & Co., 1926), I:232.

[10] Albert J. Beveridge, *Life of Marshall*, 4 vols. (Boston: Houghton-Mifflin Co., 1916-1919), III:177, quoted in Robert H. Jackson, *The Struggle for Judicial Supremacy* (New York: Random House, Vintage Books, 1941), p. 28.

[11] Robert E. Cushman and Robert F. Cushman, *Cases in Constitutional Law*, 3rd ed. (New York: Appleton-Century-Crofts, 1968), p. 23.

[12] Robert K. Carr, *The Supreme Court and Judicial Review* (New York: Farrar & Rinehart Inc., 1942), p. 20.

[13] Ibid.

[14] Alfred H. Kelly and Winfred A. Harbison, *The American Constitution: Its Origins and Development*, 5th ed. (New York: W.W. Norton & Co. Inc., 1976), p. 169.

[15] *United States v. Fisher*, 2 Cr. 358 at 396 (1805).

[16] *McCulloch v. Maryland*, 4 Wheat. 316 (1819).

[17] Id. at 405.

[18] Id. at 406.

[19] Id. at 408.

[20] Id. at 411.

[21] Id. at 413-415.

[22] Id. at 421.

[23] Id. at 431.

[24] McCloskey, *American Supreme Court*, p. 66.

[25] R. Kent Newmyer, *The Supreme Court under Marshall and Taney* (New York: Thomas Y. Crowell Company, 1968), p. 45-46.

[26] Joseph Story, *Commentaries on the Constitution of the United States* (Boston: Hilliard, Gray & Co., 1833; reprint ed., 3 vols. New York: Da Capo Press, 1970), III:124, Section 1251.

[27] *American Insurance Company v. Canter*, 1 Pet. 511 (1828).

[28] *United States v. Jones*, 109 U.S. 513 (1883); *Fong Yue Ting v. United States*, 149 U.S. 698 (1893); *United States v. Kamaga*, 118 U.S. 375 (1886).

[29] *United States v. Curtiss-Wright Corp.*, 299 U.S. 304 at 316, 318, passim (1936).

[30] *Sunshine Anthracite Coal Co. v. Adkins*, 310 U.S. 381 at 398 (1940).

[31] *Wayman v. Southard*, 10 Wheat. 1 at 43 (1825).

[32] Ibid.

[33] *Buttfield v. Stranahan*, 192 U.S. 470 at 496 (1904).

[34] Ibid.

[35] *United States v. Grimaud*, 220 U.S. 506 (1911); L. P. Steuart & Bro. v. Bowles*, 322 U.S. 398 (1944).

[36] *Interstate Commerce Commission v. Brimson*, 154 U.S. 447 (1894).

[37] *The Brig Aurora*, 7 Cr. 382 (1813).

[38] *Field v. Clark*, 143 U.S. 649 (1892).

[39] *J. W. Hampton Jr. & Co. v. United States*, 276 U.S. 394 at 405-406 (1928).

[40] See, for example, *Fahey v. Mallonee*, 332 U.S. 245 (1947); *Arizona v. California*, 373 U.S. 546 at 583 (1963).

[41] *Panama Refining Co. v. Ryan*, 293 U.S. 388 (1935).

[42] C. Herman Pritchett, *The American Constitution* (New York: McGraw-Hill Book Co. Inc., 1959), p. 176.

[43] *Panama Refining Co. v. Ryan,* 293 U.S. 388 at 418 (1935).

[44] Id. at 440.

[45] *Schechter Poultry Corp. v. United States,* 295 U.S. 495 at 542 (1935).

[46] Id. at 551, 533, passim.

[47] Alpheus T. Mason and William M. Beaney, *The Supreme Court in a Free Society* (Englewood Cliffs, N.J.: Prentice-Hall Inc., 1969), p. 33.

[48] *Opp Cotton Mills v. Administrator of Wage and Hours Division,* 312 U.S. 126 (1941).

[49] *Schechter Poultry Corp. v. United States,* 295 U.S. 495 at 537 (1935).

[50] *Carter v. Carter Coal Co.,* 298 U.S. 238 at 311 (1936).

[51] *Currin v. Wallace,* 306 U.S. 1 (1939).

[52] *Jackson v. Roby,* 109 U.S. 440 (1883); *Erhardt v. Boaro,* 113 U.S. 527 (1885); *Butte City Water Co. v. Baker,* 196 U.S. 119 (1905); *St. Louis, Iron Mountain & Southern Railway Co. v. Taylor,* 210 U.S. 281 (1908).

[53] *Martin v. Mott,* 12 Wheat. 19 (1827).

[54] *United States v. Curtiss-Wright Corp.,* 299 U.S. 304 (1936).

[55] Id. at 319-320.

[56] *United States v. Sharpnack,* 355 U.S. 286 at 294 (1958).

[57] *Clark Distilling Co. v. Western Maryland Railway Co.,* 242 U.S. 311 (1917).

The Power to Regulate Commerce

Commerce, wrote Chief Justice John Marshall in the 1824 case of *Gibbons v. Ogden,* is commercial intercourse. Commerce among the several states refers to all commercial intercourse that is not wholly within one state and that does not "extend to or affect other states." The grant of power to Congress to regulate commerce among the states "is complete in itself, may be exercised to its utmost extent, and acknowledges no limitations other than those prescribed by the Constitution." [1]

With this opinion, Marshall laid down the basis for the Supreme Court's subsequent interpretations of the commerce clause. The broad view gives Congress almost unfettered authority to regulate all interstate and any intrastate matter — production, business practices, labor relations — that in any way affects interstate commerce so long as the regulation does not conflict with other constitutional rights or limitations.

But this expansive interpretation did not win the court's full approval until its insistence on a narrower interpretation, more protective of states' rights and business interests, prompted President Franklin D. Roosevelt's court-packing plan which threatened the independent existence of the court itself. From the late 19th century until 1937, the court in several rulings described manufacture and labor relations as intrastate matters without a direct bearing on interstate commerce. Such intrastate matters, the court held, were reserved to the states to regulate and were outside the reach of Congress.

For several decades after *Gibbons v. Ogden,* Congress found little need to exercise the commerce power and most cases before the Supreme Court involved the question of state power to regulate matters in interstate commerce in the absence of federal controls. In 1851 the court adopted the *Cooley* doctrine under which the federal government would regulate those matters of commerce that required a uniform national approach such as immigration. Matters in interstate commerce but of primarily local concern, such as insurance, would be reserved for state regulation. It was up to the court to determine which matters were national and which local in scope.

Not until the 1880s and 1890s did Congress begin actively to regulate interstate commerce. With the Interstate Commerce Act of 1887 and the Sherman Antitrust Act of 1890, Congress was responding to a changing economic scene in which post-Civil War industrial growth produced interstate railroads and large national corporations and trusts. Concentration of major segments of industry and

transportation in a few hands meant less competition and higher prices. The laissez-faire doctrine of little or no government regulation of business, which encouraged this concentration, was becoming less acceptable to farmers, laborers, consumers and small-business men. With the states foreclosed by the Constitution from regulating businesses that spread over more than one state, the farmers and laborers sought relief from Congress.

Many of the members of the Supreme Court that reviewed these first major exercises of the commerce power were disinclined by philosophy to favor government regulation of business. Some of the justices had been corporation and railroad company lawyers before their appointment to the bench. Several of them were part of the majority that construed the 14th Amendment to protect business from state regulation.

But the conservative court did not view all federal regulation as inherently bad or unconstitutional. Thus, in order to uphold federal regulation it approved while striking down that which it disapproved, the court developed two lines of contradictory precedent. As a result, the court found itself at times in the awkward position of declaring that some intrastate commercial operations did not directly affect interstate commerce and so were not subject to federal regulation, while at the same time it asserted that other similar operations did directly affect interstate commerce and could be regulated by Congress.

The Narrow View

In 1895, the same year that it declared a federal income tax unconstitutional and sanctioned the use of federal troops to quell the Pullman strike, the Supreme Court held that a sugar trust, which processed 98 percent of all refined sugar in the country, did not violate the antitrust law because processing was not a part of, and did not directly affect, interstate commerce. In other words, the federal power to regulate commerce did not extend to intrastate manufacture unless that manufacture directly affected interstate commerce.

In this ruling the court adopted a narrow view of Marshall's 1824 statement that the federal legislature could regulate intrastate matters that "extended to or affected" other states. The 1895 court allowed regulation only if that effect was direct.

The court, in arrogating to itself the power to determine what had a direct effect, seemed to some to grant itself the power to legislate by judicial fiat. Such judicial legislation was sharply criticized by Justice Oliver Wendell Holmes Jr., an economic conservative but an even stronger advocate of judicial restraint. "It must be remembered," Holmes told his colleagues in 1904, "that legislators are the ultimate guardians of the liberties and welfare of the people in quite as great a degree as the courts." [2]

The one area in which the court consistently failed to heed Holmes' admonition was labor. In 1908, the court converted the antitrust law into an anti-union weapon when it held that a union-organized secondary boycott was an illegal restraint of interstate trade. Congress subsequently specifically exempted unions from the antitrust act, but the court in 1921 narrowed that exemption by ruling that it applied only to normal union activities. Secondary boycotts still were a restraint of trade in violation of the antitrust act, the court said.

In a second 1908 case the court ruled that Congress had exceeded the scope of its commerce power when it outlawed "yellow dog" contracts, agreements that required, as a condition of employment, that employees not belong to labor unions. Membership in a labor union did not have a direct effect on interstate commerce, the majority declared.

While it sustained federal worker safety laws and even upheld an emergency and temporary minimum wage for railway workers to avert a nationwide strike in 1917, the court generally viewed unions and labor relations as intrastate matters that could not be regulated by Congress. The height of its pre-New Deal efforts to protect business from government-imposed labor regulations came with the 1918 decision of *Hammer v. Dagenhart* in which the court struck down the act of Congress that prohibited the transportation in interstate commerce of any goods made by child laborers. Congress was not regulating transportation, the court said, but manufacture, which its power did not reach.

The Broad View

These restrictions on the exercise of the commerce power, however, were in large part exceptions to the court's fundamentally broad view of that power. For during this same period, the court endorsed innovative uses of the commerce power. Beginning with a 1903 decision upholding a federal ban on interstate sale of lottery tickets, the court, with the notable exception of the child labor case, sanctioned the use of the commerce power as a federal police power to protect the public health and morals. Among the police power statutes sustained were those prohibiting transportation across state lines of impure food and drugs, women for immoral purposes and stolen cars.

In 1905 the court modified its sugar trust decision to hold unanimously that the federal antitrust act did reach a combine of stockyard operators even though the individual stockyards were wholly intrastate. Because the yards received shipments of cattle from out of state for slaughter and sale in other states, the court found that they were part of a stream of interstate commerce subject to federal regulation. Although the court still further modified its antitrust position in 1911, ruling that the antitrust act applied only to unreasonable combinations and restraints of trade, the "stream-of-commerce" doctrine was subsequently applied to other intrastate businesses that were part of a larger interstate enterprise and so held subject to federal regulation. *(Box, p. 94)*

In another extension of federal power over intrastate commerce, the court in 1914 held that the Interstate Commerce Commission could regulate intrastate rail rates in cases where the intrastate regulation was necessary to

achieve effective interstate regulation. To do otherwise, the court said, would make the federal power to regulate subordinate to the state's power to regulate.

By 1930, the court had even begun to retreat from its reluctance to protect organized labor, sustaining in that year Congress' authority to enact a law providing for collective bargaining in the railway industry.

But the court had not specifically overturned any of its restrictive rulings on the federal commerce power and so it had both sets of precedents to draw on in review of New Deal legislation that called for unprecedented federal regulation of the economy. That regulation proved too pervasive for a majority of the court, which struck down as unconstitutional eight of the first 10 statutes enacted to reinvigorate the economy. Among these were three acts based on the commerce clause — a railway workers pension plan, the National Industrial Recovery Act and the Bituminous Coal Conservation Act of 1935. In all three instances, the court held that Congress had unconstitutionally intruded into intrastate matters that it had no authority to regulate.

Irate that the court had blocked most of his economic recovery program, President Roosevelt offered his famous court-packing plan, and the initial likelihood of support by Congress apparently had an impact on the court. By a 5-4 vote, the court in 1937 abandoned its distinction between direct and indirect effects on interstate commerce. In upholding federal regulation of labor-management relations, the court sustained the federal power to regulate intrastate matters, even if their effect on interstate commerce was only indirect.

This decision was followed in 1941 by one upholding a federal minimum wage law. In this case, the court acceded to the congressional opinion that substandard labor conditions unconstitutionally burdened interstate commerce.

These two decisions were capped in 1942 when the court ruled that even a farmer's production of goods for his own consumption — in this case, wheat — directly affected the demand for those goods in interstate commerce and was thus subject to federal regulation.

One commentator summarized this series of decisions:

> The Commerce Clause was now recognized as a grant of authority permitting Congress to allow interstate commerce to take place on whatever terms it may consider in the interest of the national well-being, subject only to other constitutional limitations, such as the Due Process Clause. The constitutional grant of power over commerce was now interpreted as enabling Congress to enact all appropriate laws for the protection and advancement of commerce among the states, whatever measures Congress might reasonably think adopted to that end, without regard for whether particular acts regulated in themselves were interstate or intrastate. No mechanical formula any longer excluded matters which might be called "local" from the application of these principles.[3]

This summary continued through the 1970s to be an accurate description of the court's modern interpretation of the commerce power. Only once between 1937 and 1979 did the court find unconstitutional a congressional exercise of the commerce power.

Early History

The necessity for federal control over interstate and foreign commerce was one of the primary reasons for the calling of the Constitutional Convention in 1787. "Most of our political evils may be traced to our commercial ones," James Madison had written to Thomas Jefferson the previous year.[4]

Under the Articles of Confederation, adopted in 1781 during the Revolutionary War, Congress had power to regulate trade only with the Indians. Control of interstate and foreign commerce was left to the individual states; each state attempted to build its own prosperity at the expense of its neighbors. State legislatures imposed tariffs upon goods coming in from other states as well as from foreign countries. Thus, New York levied duties on firewood from Connecticut and cabbages from New Jersey.

Different currencies in each of the 13 states likewise hampered commercial intercourse. And if a merchant were able to carry on interstate business despite tariff and currency difficulties, he often had trouble collecting his bills. Local courts and juries were less zealous in protecting the rights of distant creditors than those of their neighbors and friends.

This condition was universally recognized as unacceptable. Even those, like Samuel Adams and Patrick Henry, who feared that a federal executive would repeat the tyranny of the English monarch, favored regulation of commerce by Congress. As a result, the inclusion of the congressional power "to regulate Commerce with foreign Nations, and among the several States, and with the Indian Tribes" as clause 3 of Article I, Section 8, occasioned comparatively little discussion at the Philadelphia convention.

It is ironic, therefore, that the commerce clause should have generated more cases, if not more controversy, than any other power the framers granted to Congress.

Gibbons v. Ogden

Not until 1824 did the Supreme Court rule on the scope of the commerce power. The circumstances leading to the court's decision in the case of *Gibbons v. Ogden* involved precisely the sort of commercial warfare that had prompted the drafting of the Constitution in the first place.[5]

New York in 1798 granted to Robert R. Livingston, chancellor of the state, a monopoly over all steamboat operations in New York waters. Taking on the inventor Robert Fulton as a partner, Livingston turned the steamship monopoly into a viable transportation system. So successful were they that in 1811, the pair was granted similar exclusive rights to operate in the waters of the territory of New Orleans. Thus the monopoly controlled transportation on two of the nation's largest waterways and ports.

Attempts to break the monopoly were frequent but unsuccessful. Connecticut, New Jersey and Ohio enacted retaliatory measures closing their waters to ships licensed by the New York monopoly while five other states granted steamship monopolies of their own. The ensuing navigational chaos brought the states to what one attorney would describe as "almost . . . the eve of war."[6]

The case that broke the monopoly involved Aaron Ogden, a former New Jersey Governor (1812-13), who in uneasy partnership with Thomas Gibbons ran a steam-driven ferry between Elizabethtown, N.J., and New York City. Ogden in 1815 had acquired a license from the Livingston-Fulton monopoly while Gibbons held a permit under the federal Coastal Licensing Act of 1793 for his two boats. Despite the partnership, Gibbons ran his boats to

New York in defiance of the monopoly rights that Ogden held and in 1819 Ogden sued for an injunction to stop Gibbons' infringement of his rights to monopoly. New York courts sided with Ogden, ordering Gibbons to halt his ferry service. Gibbons appealed to the Supreme Court, arguing that his federal license took precedence over the state-granted monopoly license and that he should be allowed to continue his ferrying in New York waters.

Public interest in the case ran high during the four years between the time the court said it would take the case and the time it heard arguments. The steamboat monopolies were unpopular with many who were eager for the court to prohibit them. In addition, the case fueled the public debate between the nationalist beliefs of the Federalists and the states' rights beliefs of the Republicans. As historian Charles Warren wrote, the New York monopoly "had been created by Republican legislators, owned by Republican statesmen and defended largely by Republican lawyers. . . ."[7] Those lawyers, some of the ablest in the land, argued their case before Chief Justice John Marshall, a leading exponent of a strong centralized government. It was widely assumed that Marshall would side with Gibbons but whether the remainder of the court would follow Marshall was uncertain.

The Arguments

The questions before the court were: Did Congress have power under the commerce clause to regulate navigation and if so, was that power exclusive? Could federal regulation of commerce leave room for the states to act and still be supreme?

In Gibbons' behalf, Daniel Webster argued "that the power of Congress to regulate commerce was complete and entire, and, to a certain extent, necessarily exclusive."[8] Navigation was one of the areas where federal power precluded all state action, Webster claimed.

But the attorneys for Ogden construed the commerce power narrowly, contending that it applied only to "transportation and sale of commodities," not to navigation, a matter left to the states to regulate.[9]

The Decision

Delivering the court's opinion on March 2, 1824, Chief Justice Marshall refused to construe the federal commerce power narrowly or to omit navigation from its scope:

> The subject to be regulated is commerce; and . . . to ascertain the extent of the power, it becomes necessary to settle the meaning of the word. . . . Commerce undoubtedly is traffic, but it is something more; it is intercourse. It describes the commercial intercourse between nations, and parts of nations, in all its branches, and is regulated by prescribing rules for carrying on that intercourse. The mind can scarcely conceive a system for regulating commerce between nations, which shall exclude all laws concerning navigation. . . . All America understands, and has uniformly understood, the word 'commerce' to comprehend navigation. . . . The power over commerce, including navigation, was one of the primary objects for which the people . . . adopted their government, and must have been contemplated in forming it. . . .[10]

The second question, Marshall said, was to what commerce does the power apply? The first was commerce with foreign nations. The second, he said:

...is to commerce 'among the several states.' The word 'among' means intermingled with. A thing which is among others, is intermingled with them. Commerce among the states cannot stop at the external boundary line of each state, but may be introduced into the interior.[11]

But Marshall did not find that the commerce power foreclosed all state regulation:

> It is not intended to say that these words comprehend that commerce which is completely internal, which is carried on between man and man in a state, or between different parts of the same state, and which does not extend to or affect other states. Such a power would be inconvenient or unnecessary.

> Comprehensive as the word 'among' is, it may very properly be restricted to that commerce which concerns more states than one.... The completely internal commerce of a state, then, may be considered as reserved for the state itself.[12]

With regard to the supremacy of the federal power, Marshall said:

> This power, like all others vested in congress, is complete in itself, may be exercised to its utmost extent, and acknowledges no limitations, other than are prescribed in the constitution.... If, as has always been understood, the sovereignty of congress, though limited to specified objects, is plenary as to those objects, the power over commerce with foreign nations, and among the several states, is vested in congress as absolutely as it would be in a single government, having in its constitution the same restrictions on the exercise of the power as are found in the constitution of the United States.[13]

Marshall did not deal with the question whether states could regulate areas Congress has not regulated. Here, he said, Congress had acted when it passed the coastal licensing act. Nor did he answer the question whether the states could regulate commerce simultaneously with Congress. Marshall did say that in exercising its police powers a state might take actions similar to those Congress adopted in the exercise of its commerce power. But if the state law impeded or conflicted with the federal law, the federal law would take precedence. The Chief Justice then enumerated the ways in which the New York monopoly statute interfered with the federal coastal licensing act and declared the state law granting the monopoly invalid.

Justice William Johnson's concurring opinion argued that the commerce power "must be exclusive; it can reside but in one potentate; and hence, the grant of this power carried with it the whole subject, leaving nothing for the states to act upon."[14]

Reaction. The decision in *Gibbons v. Ogden* was politically popular. But staunch Republicans, including Thomas Jefferson, were appalled. In 1825, Jefferson wrote a friend that he viewed "with the deepest affliction, the rapid strides with which the federal branch of our government is advancing towards the usurpation of all the rights reserved to the states."[15] Also disturbed were slave owners who feared that Congress might exercise the commerce power to wrest control over slavery from the states and then abolish it.

Marshall's opinion settled only one point — where state exercise of its power conflicts with federal exercise of

the commerce power, the state must give way. But in reaching that pronouncement, Marshall laid the groundwork for extending the commerce power to forms of transportation and communications not yet contemplated. By leaving the power to regulate wholly internal commerce to the states only so long as that commerce did not "extend to or affect" other states, he planted the seeds that would eventually allow Congress to regulate manufacture of goods and matters that themselves were not in commerce but were deemed to affect interstate commerce.

Scholars have wondered why Marshall, having gone so far, did not go on to claim exclusivity for the federal commerce power. To do so would have avoided many of the inconsistencies, confusions and contortions that found their way into constitutional law as the court sought to determine what was in or affected interstate commerce and how far Congress could reach to regulate that commerce.

At the least, they have speculated on why the Marshall court did not adopt, as a later court would, Daniel Webster's argument that congressional power over some areas of commerce was exclusive. Professor Felix Frankfurter provided perhaps the best answer when he noted the double-edged potential of Webster's argument: Marshall may have "ignored Webster's formula not because it would have failed to serve in his hands as an instrument for restricting state authority, but because its very flexibility was equally adaptable in hands bent on securing state immunity." Frankfurter also postulated that Marshall did not endorse Webster's theory because it would then be apparent what "large powers of discretion ... judges must exercise" in determining over which subjects Congress had exclusive control.[16]

Commerce and the States

Congress did not make much use of the power claimed for it by Marshall until later in the century. Between 1824, when *Gibbons v. Ogden* was decided, and the 1880s when need for federal regulation of the interstate railroads and interstate corporations became apparent, the court's rulings on the commerce power focused primarily on determining when state actions impinged unconstitutionally on the federal commerce power.

Before Marshall's death in 1835, the court handed down two more major decisions defining the range of state power to affect commerce. In *Brown v. Maryland* (1827), it forbade states to tax imports as long as they remained unopened in their original packages.[17] In *Willson v. Blackbird Creek Marsh Co.* (1829), it held that a state could exercise its police power over matters affecting interstate commerce in the absence of conflicting federal legislation.[18]

The commerce power rulings by the court under Marshall's successor — Roger B. Taney — reflected that court's uncertainty as to the proper line between state regulation and the federal commerce power. At various times, different judges put forth various doctrines. Taney, for instance, maintained that Congress and the states held the commerce power concurrently; Justice John McLean held it exclusive to Congress. Rarely did any one doctrine win a majority. If it did, the majority dissolved when the next case was heard.[19]

The conflict was temporarily resolved in *Cooley v. Port Wardens of Philadelphia* (1852) when the court upheld state regulation of city harbor pilots and adopted the so-called selective exclusiveness doctrine first enunciated by Webster in 1824.[20] In his majority opinion, Justice Benjamin R. Curtis shifted the focus of judicial scrutiny from the power itself to the nature of the subject to be regulated. Some fields of commerce were of necessity national in nature and demanded a uniform regulation provided by Congress, he said. Others demanded local regulation to accommodate local circumstances and needs. This doctrine left it up to the court to determine on a case-by-case basis what matters were reserved to Congress and which were local in nature. *(The states and the commerce power, pp. 315-322)*

Commerce and Navigation

The opinion in the steamboat monopoly case also settled a second issue. The court concluded that navigation was commerce. But immediately the question became one of state power: Was the federal power over navigation exclusive or were there some situations where states could regulate traffic on the waterways?

Five years after deciding *Gibbons v. Ogden* the Marshall Court sustained Delaware's right to build a dam across a small but navigable tidal creek as an exercise of its police power in the absence of conflicting federal legislation.[21] The Chief Justice conveniently ignored the fact that the owner of the ship protesting the dam as an obstruction to interstate commerce was licensed under the same federal coastal licensing act that figured so prominently in Marshall's reasoning in the monopoly case. *(Details of case, p. 83; federal coastal licensing act, box, this page)*

But in the next major navigation case, the court held that Congress could use its commerce power both to override state law and an earlier court decision. In 1852, the court ruled that a bridge on the Ohio River must either be raised so that ships could pass under it or be taken down altogether. The court held that the bridge not only obstructed interstate commerce but violated a congressionally sanctioned compact between Virginia and Kentucky agreeing to keep the river free of such obstructions.[22]

However, Congress immediately passed a law overruling the court by declaring that the bridge was not an obstruction and requiring instead that ships be refitted so they could pass under the bridge. In 1856, the court upheld this act of Congress:

> So far . . . as this bridge created an obstruction to the free navigation of the river, in view of the previous acts of Congress, they are regarded as modified by this subsequent legislation; and although it still may be an obstruction in fact, [the bridge] is not so in the contemplation of law. . . . [Congress] having in the exercise of this power, regulated the navigation consistent with its preservation and continuation, the authority to maintain it would seem to be complete.[23]

In the same period, the court held that navigation on a river wholly in one state and involving commerce that was not connected to interstate or foreign commerce could not be regulated by Congress.[24]

In 1866 the court reaffirmed Congress' complete control over navigable waters "which are accessible from a State other than those in which they lie."[25] In 1871, congressional authority over navigation was further extended to permit federal regulation of a boat that transported goods in interstate commerce even though the boat operated solely on waters entirely within one state. In an opinion that was clearly a forerunner of the "stream of commerce" doctrine, the court said:

The Coastal Licensing Act

In one of the earliest exercises of its commerce power, the First Congress in 1789 enacted a statute "for enrolling or licensing ships or vessels to be employed in the coasting trade and fisheries, and for regulating the same." Partly because the major commercial transportation system in the country for the next 50 years was water-based and partly because Congress seldom exercised its commerce power until late in the 19th century, this federal coastal licensing act played a key role in several major Supreme Court cases interpreting the commerce power. Among them were:

● *Gibbons v. Ogden* (1824) in which the court ruled that Congress' power to regulate navigation between two states pre-empted the state's power to regulate that subject. *(Details, p. 83)*

● *Willson v. Blackbird Creek Marsh Co.* (1829) in which the court held that the states could regulate interstate commerce in the absence of conflicting federal legislation. *(Details, p. 316)*

● *Pennsylvania v. Wheeling and Belmont Bridge Co.* (1851) in which the court held that a bridge that was too low to allow ships to pass under it interfered with Congress' power to regulate commerce through the coastal licensing act. Congress later overturned this decision by declaring the bridge was not an obstruction. *(Details, this page)*

● *Veazie v. Moor* (1852) in which the court held that the federal act did not automatically entitle licensed vessels to operate on wholly intrastate waters.

The 1789 licensing act has been renewed repeatedly but is substantially unchanged in modern times and is still the subject of Supreme Court cases. In the 1977 case of *Douglas v. Seacoast Products, Inc.* (431 U.S. 265), for example, the court ruled that a Virginia law denying certain fishing rights to federally licensed non-citizens must fall as in conflict with the act. In the 1978 case of *Ray v. Atlantic Richfield Co.* (435 U.S. 151), the court struck down a Washington state law requiring state-licensed pilots on tankers entering and leaving Puget Sound. The court said the law was in conflict with federal power to regulate pilots on tankers licensed under the coastal act.

> So far as [the ship] was employed in transporting goods destined for other States, or goods brought from without the limits of Michigan and destined to places within that State, she was engaged in commerce between the States, and however limited that commerce may have been, she was, so far as it went, subject to the legislation of Congress. She was employed as an instrument of that commerce; for whenever a commodity has begun to move as an article of trade from one State to another, commerce in that commodity between the States has commenced.[26] *("Stream of commerce" doctrine, p. 91)*

Hydroelectric Power

Control over the nation's waterways eventually led to disputes over who controlled, and thus benefited from the sale of, the hydroelectric power generated by those waterways. In 1913 the court sustained an act of Congress allowing the federal government to sell excess electricity

Congress and Maritime Law: A Matter of Commerce?

The Constitution gives Congress no express authority over admiralty and maritime matters. The only mention of the subject is in Article III, Section 2, which states that the "judicial Power shall extend . . . to all Cases of admiralty and maritime jurisdiction. . . ." This phrase implies that a body of admiralty and maritime law existed; the question was whether Congress had any power to modify this law.

In the case of *The Lottawanna* (1875), the court, for which Justice Joseph P. Bradley spoke, sought to answer the question. The framers of the Constitution could not have meant to leave changes in this law to the states, he said:

One thing . . . is unquestionable; the Constitution must have referred to a system of law coextensive with, and operating uniformly in, the whole country. It certainly could not have been the intention to place the rules and limits of maritime law under the disposal and regulation of the several states, as that would have defeated the uniformity and consistency at which the Constitution aimed on all subjects of a commercial character affecting the intercourse of the States with each other or with foreign states.[1]

Nor, wrote Bradley, can it be "supposed that the framers . . . contemplate that the law should forever remain unalterable. Congress undoubtedly has authority under the commercial power, if no other, to introduce such changes as are likely to be needed." [2]

But in two cases denying states authority in this field, Bradley declared for the court that Congress' power over maritime law was based not on the commerce clause but on Article III, Section 2, supplemented by the necessary and proper clause. "As the Constitution extends the judicial power of the United States to 'all cases of admiralty and maritime jurisdiction,' and as this jurisdiction is held to be exclusive, the power of legislation on the same subject must necessarily be in the national legislature and not in the state legislatures," Bradley wrote in 1889.[3]

Two years later, he wrote:

. . .It is unnecessary to invoke the power given to Congress to regulate commerce in order to find authority to pass the law in question. The act [being challenged in the case] was passed in amendment of the maritime law of the country, and the power to make such amendments is coextensive with that law. It is not confined to the boundaries or class of subjects which limit and characterize the power to regulate commerce; but, in maritime matters, it extends to all matters and places to which the maritime law extends.[4]

---

[1] *The Lottawanna*, 21 Wall. 558 at 574-75 (1875).
[2] Id. at 577; see, for example, *Providence and New York Steamship Co. v. Hill Manufacturing Co.*, 109 U.S. 578 (1883); *The Robert W. Parsons*, 191 U.S. 17 (1903).

[3] *Butler v. Boston & S. Steamship Co.*, 130 U.S. 527 at 557 (1889).
[4] *In re Garnett*, 141 U.S. 1 at 12 (1891).

---

generated as a result of a plan to improve the navigability of a stream. "If the primary purpose [of the legislation] is legitimate," the court wrote, "we can see no sound objection to leasing any excess of power." [27]

The court in 1931 ruled in *Arizona v. California* that it would not inquire into the motives behind congressional waterways projects, in this case the Boulder Canyon Project Act, so long as the waterway concerned was navigable and the project not unrelated to the control of navigation:

Whether the particular structures proposed are reasonably necessary is not for this court to determine. . . . And the fact that purposes other than navigation will also be served could not invalidate the exercise of the authority conferred even if those other purposes would not alone have justified an exercise of congressional power.[28]

TVA. Congress in 1933 created the Tennessee Valley Authority (TVA), a three-member board authorized to set up a comprehensive development program for the Tennessee Valley that included flood control, power generation and agricultural and industrial development. Although its establishment involved no extension of federal authority over navigation, the TVA represented a major source of government-sponsored competition for the private power companies in the area, and its constitutionality was immediately challenged.

The first case to reach the Supreme Court was *Ashwander v. Tennessee Valley Authority* (1936), in which the stockholders of a power company challenged the validity of a contract between the company and the TVA for the sale of the excess energy generated by a TVA-operated dam.[29] The stockholders hoped the court would declare the act authorizing the TVA unconstitutional, but the court restricted itself to the narrower issue before it, upholding the TVA's authority to make the contract.

Direct challenges to the constitutionality of the TVA by the power companies failed in 1939 when the court ruled that the companies did not have a right to be free from competition and therefore had no standing to bring the challenge.[30]

Non-Navigable Waters

Congressional power over the nation's waterways was made virtually complete in 1940 when the court held that federal authority even extended to some waters that were not at the time navigable. In *United States v. Appalachian Electric Power Co.*, the court said the Federal Power Commission had the authority to regulate dam construction on a portion of Virginia's New River that might be made navigable by the dam. "A waterway, otherwise suitable for navigation, is not barred from that classification merely because artificial aids must make the highway suitable for use before commercial navigation may be undertaken. . . ," the court wrote.[31]

Congress, Commerce and the Railroads

Extension of the federal commerce power over railroads came less directly than the extension of the power over navigation but ultimately it became just as complete.

Like ships, railroads were clearly carriers in interstate commerce. Although privately owned, the rails were public in nature, a fact recognized by the Supreme Court as additional justification for federal regulation. Observing in 1897 that interstate railroads were public corporations organized for public reasons and supported by public grants and the use of public lands, the court said the railroads "primarily owe duties to the public of a higher nature even than that of earning large dividends for their shareholders. The business which the railroads do is of public nature, closely affecting almost all classes in the community. . . ."[32]

Because the first railway lines were operated locally, most early regulation was left to the states. As late as 1877, the court upheld the authority of the states to set rates for hauling freight and passengers within their boundaries.[33] (*Details, p. 318*)

The business panics of the 1870s and 1880s and the westward expansion of the country led to the consolidation of the railroads into vast interstate networks. As a result, regulation by individual states became increasingly less effective even as the public was demanding tougher regulation to end rebate and price-fixing practices that resulted in high prices for both shippers and passengers and favored certain companies and regions over others.

Two major events served to shift the responsibility of regulating the railroads from the states to the federal government. In 1886, the court essentially ended state authority over interstate railroads by holding that the states could not set even intrastate freight rates for goods traveling interstate. Basing its decision in part on the selective exclusiveness doctrine accepted in the 1851 *Cooley* decision, the court found that "this species of regulation is one which must be, if established at all, of a general and national character, and cannot be safely and wisely remitted to local rules and local regulations."[34]

Creation of the ICC

That decision in the case of *Wabash, St. Louis & Pacific Ry. Co. v. Illinois* made it necessary for Congress to provide for federal regulation of interstate railroads. The Interstate Commerce Act of 1887 stipulated that all rates should be reasonable and just, and prohibited rebate and price-fixing practices. To enforce the law, the act set up the Interstate Commerce Commission (ICC) which could issue cease-and-desist orders to halt any railroad found in violation of the act's provisions. The ICC was not given specific power to set rates or adjust those it found to be unreasonable, and it was unclear whether Congress intended the commission to have these powers.

At the time the ICC was created and for several years thereafter, a majority of the members of the Supreme Court adhered for the most part to the principles of economic laissez-faire, opposing most government regulation — federal or state — that would impinge on the free development of business and industry. Moreover, many of the justices had been corporation lawyers before coming to the court; three of them — Chief Justice Melville W. Fuller and Justices Henry B. Brown and George Shiras Jr. — numbered major interstate railroads among their clients. Thus,

it was not surprising that the court viewed the ICC with little pleasure.

In 1894 the court upheld the ICC as an appropriate delegation of congressional powers.[35] But three years later, the court stripped the fledgling commission of its essential regulatory authority, holding that Congress had granted it no rate-fixing powers. "There is nothing in the act fixing rates," said the court, and so "no just rule of construction would tolerate a grant of such power by mere implication."[36] The court majority also thought that the power to establish rates was a legislative function that could not constitutionally be delegated to an executive agency without violating the separation of powers. "The power given [by Congress to the ICC] is partly judicial, partly executive and administrative, but not legislative," the majority wrote.[37]

In another case decided in 1897, the court held that the commission's findings of fact in cases before it were subject to review and reinterpretation by the courts.[38]

These cases left the ICC toothless and the practices that led to its creation resumed with full force. Renewed demands from the public as well as some of the rail companies encouraged Congress to attempt to revive the ICC as an enforcement mechanism. In 1906 it passed the Hepburn Act, which among other things specifically authorized the commission to adjust rates it judged to be unreasonable and unfair.

The court in 1907 indicated that the new powers given to the ICC would pass constitutional muster when it said it would accept the commission's findings of fact as true, confining its review of ICC decisions to constitutional questions.[39]

In 1910, the court upheld the commission's authority to adjust interstate railroad rates. The case arose after the ICC substituted a lower rate schedule for that set by several western lines. The court said that the "commission is the tribunal intrusted with the execution of the interstate commerce laws, and has been given very comprehensive powers in the investigation and determination of the proportion which the rates charged shall bear to the service rendered. . . ."[40]

With the agency's power to adjust rates established, Congress in 1910 gave the ICC authority to set original rates. The railroads challenged the act as an unconstitutional delegation of legislative authority, but the court in 1914 called the contention "without merit." How could it be, the court asked, that the authority to set rates "was validly delegated so long as it was lodged in the carriers but ceased to be susceptible of delegation the instant it was taken from the carriers for the purpose of being lodged in a public administrative body?"[41]

The court had now sanctioned what it had forbidden only 17 years before. As one commentator noted, "the Court, which had long accepted the principle of rate regulation by the states, could find no constitutional reason to refuse to accept the same power when exercised unambiguously by the national government."[42]

Intrastate Rates

With federal control established over interstate rail rates, the next question was whether the federal government could exert any control over intrastate rates, and if so, under what circumstances. The court took the opportunity to address this question in the 1913 *Minnesota Rate Cases.* Justice Charles Evans Hughes wrote for the majority:

> . . .[T]he full control by Congress of the subjects committed to its regulation is not to be denied or thwarted by the commingling of interstate and intrastate operations. This is not to say that the nation may deal with the internal concerns of the State, as such, but that the execution by Congress of its constitutional power to regulate interstate commerce is not limited by the fact that intrastate transactions may have become so interwoven therewith that the effective government of the former incidentally controls the latter.[43]

This statement was extraneous to the case at hand, however, and thus did not have the full force of law. But it was a harbinger of the court's ruling the following year in the *Shreveport Rate Cases.*

The Shreveport Doctrine. The 1914 *Shreveport Rate Cases* concerned a railroad based in Shreveport, La., that carried freight and passengers into East Texas in competition with two Texas-based railroads. The rail rates set by Texas officials for the state lines were substantially lower than those set by the ICC for the interstate Shreveport line, giving the Texas railroads a decisive competitive edge. To equalize the competition, the ICC required the intrastate lines to charge the same rates as the interstate rail company. They protested but the court upheld the ICC order:

> . . .Wherever the interstate and intrastate transactions of carriers are so related that the government of the one involves the control of the other, it is Congress, and not the State, that is entitled to prescribe the final and dominant rule, for otherwise Congress would be denied the exercise of its constitutional authority and the States, and not the Nation, would be supreme in the national field.[44]

In time, the court would expand the so-called Shreveport doctrine beyond transportation to justify congressional intervention in other intrastate matters, such as manufacture, that touched on interstate commerce.

The court endorsed an even greater expansion of federal control over intrastate rail rates in 1922 when it upheld the section of the 1920 Transportation Act that authorized the ICC to set intrastate rates high enough to guarantee the railroads a fair income based on the value of their railway property. The 1920 law had been passed to return the railroads to private control; they had been run by the government during World War I. The court held that a state burdened interstate commerce by lowering its intrastate rates to undercut interstate rates. Lower intrastate rates meant proportionately less income from intrastate companies, which in turn could force interstate rates higher in order to guarantee the congressionally-mandated rate of return. Noting that intrastate systems used the same tracks and equipment as the interstate systems, Chief Justice William Howard Taft wrote: "Congress as the dominant controller of interstate commerce may, therefore, restrain undue limitation of the earning power of the interstate commerce system in doing state work."[45]

On the other hand, the court in 1924 also upheld the profits recapture clause of the 1920 Transportation Act. This provision authorized the federal government to recover half of all railroad profits above 6 percent. The excess profits were put into a fund to compensate those rail lines earning less than a 4-1/2 percent profit. Stressing the public

nature of railroads, a unanimous court declared that a railroad "was not entitled, as a constitutional right, to more than a fair operating income upon the value of its properties."[46] The recapture provisions proved ineffective however, and were repealed in 1933.

Railway Labor

The court's initial antipathy to the organized labor movement displayed itself particularly in railway union cases. In 1895, the court upheld contempt citations against Eugene V. Debs and other leaders of the Pullman strike and sanctioned the use of federal troops to control strike-related violence.

In 1908, the court handed down two major decisions adverse to labor and its unions. The court in the first case, *Loewe v. Lawlor,* held that certain labor practices, such as organized boycotts, were illegal restraints of trade under the Sherman Antitrust Act of 1890. The second case, *Adair v. United States,* struck down a federal law aimed at strengthening the organized railway labor movement. *(Details of In re Debs, p. 217; Loewe v. Lawlor, p. 93)*

'Yellow-dog Contracts.' Aimed at ensuring collective bargaining rights for railway laborers, an 1898 railway labor law contained a provision prohibiting employers from making contracts that required an employee to promise not to join a union as a condition of employment. These so-called "yellow-dog contracts" had been effective in management's fight against the railway brotherhoods and the statute barring them was challenged as exceeding congressional power over interstate commerce and as a violation of the Fifth Amendment, which the court then viewed as guaranteeing freedom of contract.

In 1908 the Supreme Court in *Adair* sustained the challenge, striking down that portion of the law. "In our opinion," said Justice John Marshall Harlan, "the prohibition is an invasion of the personal liberty, as well as of the right of property, guaranteed by that [Fifth] Amendment." As to the commerce clause, Harlan said that there was not a sufficient "connection between interstate commerce and membership in a labor organization" to justify outlawing the yellow-dog contracts.[47]

Justice Oliver Wendell Holmes Jr. disagreed, saying "it hardly would be denied" that some labor relations in the railroad industry were closely enough related to commerce to rationalize federal regulation. He also chastised the majority for interfering with congressional policy: "Where there is, or generally is believed to be, an important ground of public policy for restraint [of the freedom of contract], the Constitution does not forbid it, whether this court agrees or disagrees with the policy pursued."[48]

The following year, the court by a 5-4 vote declared unconstitutional a second effort to regulate labor-management relations in the rail industry.[49] The 1906 Employers' Liability Act made every common carrier liable for the on-the-job deaths of employees. This act modified two common law practices that held the employer not liable if the employee died through negligence on his own part or of a fellow worker.

Declaring the law invalid, the court in 1909 said the statute was an infringement of states' rights since it covered railway employees not directly involved in interstate commerce as well as those who were. Congress shortly thereafter enacted a second liability act that covered only railway workers in interstate commerce. The court upheld the modified law in 1912.[50]

As part of the Transportation Act of 1920, Congress created the Railway Labor Board to review and decide railway labor disputes. But in two subsequent cases, the court held that the board had no power to enforce its decisions.[51]

Congress then in 1926 enacted the Railway Labor Act setting up new procedures for settling railway labor disputes. Among the provisions of the Act was a prohibition against employer interference with the right of employees to select their bargaining representatives.

In 1930, the court upheld an injunction against railway employers who had violated this ban by interfering with the representative selection process. In so doing, it upheld the constitutionality of the 1926 act as a valid means for Congress to avoid interruptions of interstate commerce by resolving disputes before they resulted in strikes. The court also distinguished the case from the 1908 *Adair* ruling, rejecting the railroad company's claim that the statute infringed on the employers' Fifth Amendment freedom of contract:

> The Railway Labor Act of 1926 does not interfere with the normal exercise of the right of the carrier to select its own employees or to discharge them. The statute is not aimed at this right of the employers but at the interference with the right of employees to have representatives of their own choosing. As the carriers subject to the act have no constitutional right to interfere with the freedom of the employees in making their selections, they cannot complain of the statute on constitutional grounds.[52]

Railway Safety

In 1911, the court, which already had approved the use of both the federal tax and commerce powers as police tools to regulate such matters as the color of oleo and the interstate shipment of lottery tickets, upheld the application of this same police power to encourage railway safety, even if that meant federal regulation of intrastate equipment and employees.

In *Southern Railway Co. v. United States,* the court upheld the federal Safety Appliance Act, which required safety couplers on railroad cars used in interstate commerce. In an opinion that foreshadowed its reasoning in the *Minnesota* and *Shreveport* rate cases, the court ruled that this law also applied to intrastate cars since the cars used in interstate and intrastate traffic were so intermingled that to regulate one necessitated regulation of the other.[53] *(Minnesota and Shreveport cases, p. 88)*

In the same year the court upheld as an appropriate use of the federal police power a federal safety measure setting maximum hours that interstate railway employees could work:

> In its power suitably to provide for the safety of employes and travelers, Congress was not limited to the enactment of laws relating to mechanical appliances, but it was also competent to consider, and to endeavor to reduce, the dangers incident to the strain of excessive hours of duty on the part of engineers, conductors, train dispatchers, telegraphers, and other persons embraced within the class defined by the act.[54]

Minimum Wage

In 1917 — just a year before the court would hold that Congress did not have the power to set minimum wages and maximum hours for child laborers — the justices upheld congressional authority to set temporary wage and permanent hour standards for interstate railway employees.[55] The case of *Wilson v. New* arose after unionized rail workers asked for a reduction in their workday from ten to eight hours with no reduction in wages. When their employers refused, the unions threatened a nationwide strike. To avoid the potential economic calamity, President Wilson urged Congress to establish an eight-hour workday for railway employees with no reduction in wages pending a six-to-nine-month commission study.

With U.S. entry into World War I imminent, the court in a 5-4 decision, ruled the emergency legislation constitutional. Congress' power to set an eight-hour workday was "not disputable," the court said, although the question of wages was not so clear-cut. Acknowledging that wage agreements were "primarily private," but emphasizing the public nature of the railways and the failure of the unions and management to settle the dispute, the court concluded that Congress had the authority

> ...to exert the legislative will for the purpose of settling the dispute, and bind both parties to the duty of acceptance and compliance, to the end that no individual dispute or difference might bring ruin to the vast interests concerned in the movement of interstate commerce....[56]

The four dissenters said the act went beyond the power granted by the commerce clause and furthermore was a violation of due process guaranteed by the Fifth Amendment because it took property (wages) from one party (employers) and gave it to another (employees) by legislative proclamation.

Pensions

Among New Deal legislation the court struck down was the Railroad Retirement Pension Act, which set up a comprehensive pension system for railroad workers. A majority of the court in 1935 found that several parts of the pension plan violated the guarantee of due process. It also held that the pension plan was unrelated to interstate commerce. Speaking for the court, Justice Owen J. Roberts wrote:

> ...The theory [behind the legislation] is that one who has an assurance against future dependency will do his work more cheerfully, and therefore more efficiently. The question at once presents itself whether the fostering of a contented mind on the part of any employee by legislation of this type, is in any just sense a regulation of interstate commerce. If that question be answered in the affirmative, obviously there is no limit to the field of so-called regulation.[57]

For the minority, Chief Justice Charles Evans Hughes agreed that parts of the plan were unconstitutional. But he refused to hold that the plan itself was altogether outside the scope of congressional commerce powers. "The fundamental consideration which supports this type of legislation is that industry should take care of its human wastage, whether that is due to accident or age," said Hughes, adding that the "expression of that conviction in law is regulation." [58] Since railroads are interstate carriers and their employees are engaged in interstate commerce, said Hughes, regulation of pension benefits falls under the interstate commerce power.

Federal legislation passed in 1935, 1937 and 1938 set up a railroad employees' pension fund financed by a tax on both employers and employees. The constitutionality of the pension plan was not challenged in the ensuing 40 years.

Other Common Carriers

Having determined that Congress had broad authority to regulate the railroads, the court had little hesitancy in permitting Congress to regulate other common carriers. The *Pipe Line Cases* (1914) upheld Congress' inclusion of oil pipelines under the coverage of the Interstate Commerce Act. The Standard Oil Co., either through complete or almost complete stock ownership of several pipeline companies, had made itself, in the words of Justice Oliver Wendell Holmes Jr., "master of the only practicable oil transportation between the oil fields east of California and the Atlantic Ocean. . . ." Standard Oil required that any oil transported through the pipelines it owned be sold to it. The court, speaking through Holmes, rejected the oil company's contention that it was simply transporting its own oil from well to refinery. Holmes said that the "lines we are

considering are common carriers now in everything but form" and that Congress has the power under the commerce clause to "require those who are common carriers in substance to become so in form." [59]

The court subsequently held that the transmission of electric power from one state to another was interstate commerce and that rate regulation of that power by the original state was an interference with and a burden on interstate commerce. The court also upheld the right of the Federal Power Commission to set the price for natural gas found in one state and sold wholesale to a distributor in another state.[60]

The court furthermore ruled that forms of communication crossing state borders, though intangible, were nonetheless interstate commerce. Thus, in 1878, the court held that Florida's attempt to exclude out-of-state telegraph companies by granting a monopoly to a Florida company was a burden on interstate commerce.[61] In 1933, the court upheld federal regulation of radio transmissions. "No state lines divide the radio waves, and national regulation is not only appropriate but essential to the efficient use of radio facilities," the court said.[62]

Congress and Antitrust Law

Simultaneous with development of the railroads into interstate networks was the growth of combinations or trusts in many areas of business and industry. Designed to circumvent the vicious competition that so often resulted in bankruptcy, the trusts frequently eliminated most competition of any significance and drove the smaller entrepreneur out of the market. By 1901, trusts dominated the steel, oil, sugar, meat packing, leather, electrical goods and tobacco industries.

This threat to the traditional concept of the free enterprise system was not popular, nor were the unsavory methods frequently used by the trusts to gain control and enlarge their hold on the industry involved. Public outcry against the trusts led Congress in 1890 to pass the Sherman Antitrust Act which made illegal "[e]very contract, combination in the form of trust or otherwise, or conspiracy, in restraint of trade or commerce among the several states, or with foreign nations. . . ."

Commerce and Manufacture

Like the Interstate Commerce Act, the Antitrust Act represented a major assumption of power by Congress. Not only the trusts, but economic conservatives in general warned of the day when laissez-faire principles would fall to congressional attempts to control all phases of commercial enterprise, including manufacture and production. The court itself already had spoken to this issue. In *Veazie v. Moor* (1852) it indicated that the federal power over commerce did not extend to manufacturing or production, even if the resulting products were destined to be sold through interstate or foreign commerce:

A pretension as far reaching as this, would extend to contracts between citizen and citizens of the same state, would control the pursuits of the planter, the grazier, the manufacturer, the mechanic, the immense operations of the collieries and mines and furnaces of

the country; for there is not one of these avocations, the results of which may not become the subject of foreign [or interstate] commerce, and be borne either by turnpikes, canals or railroads, from point to point within the several States, towards an ultimate destination. . . .[63]

This viewpoint was given the force of law in the 1888 decision in the case of *Kidd v. Pearson* upholding a state prohibition on producing liquor for interstate shipment. In that case, the court said:

No distinction is more popular to the common mind, or more clearly expressed in economic and political literature, than that between manufactures and commerce. Manufacture is transformation — the fashioning of raw materials into a change of form for use. The functions of commerce are different. The buying and selling and the transportation incident thereto constitute commerce. . . .[64]

The full significance of this holding as a precedent became apparent when the court in 1895 delivered its first antitrust ruling in *United States v. E.C. Knight Co.*[65]

The Sugar Trust Case. Defendants in the suit were the American Sugar Refining Co. and four smaller Philadelphia processors. Through stockholders' agreements, the larger company had purchased stock in the smaller ones and the resulting trust controlled more than 90 percent of all the sugar processed in the United States. The federal government's case, prosecuted less than vigorously by Attorney General Richard Olney, who had opposed passage of the Sherman Act and later worked for its repeal, challenged the sugar combination as an illegal restraint of trade in interstate commerce designed to raise sugar prices.

Relying on the narrow interpretation of commerce expounded in *Veazie v. Moor* and *Kidd v. Pearson*, Chief Justice Melville W. Fuller for the court declared again that manufacture was not part of interstate commerce:

. . .Doubtless, the power to control the manufacture of a given thing involves in a certain sense the control of its disposition, but this is a secondary and not the primary sense; and although the exercise of that power may result in bringing the operation of commerce into play, it does not control it, and affects it only incidentally and indirectly.[66]

The fact that the sugar was manufactured for eventual sale, possibly in another state, also had only an indirect effect on interstate commerce, Fuller said:

. . .The fact that an article is manufactured for export to another state does not of itself make it an article of interstate commerce, and the intent of the manufacture does not determine the time when the article or product passes from the control of the state and belongs to commerce.[67]

This view virtually limited the definition of interstate commerce to transportation. "Slight reflection will show," said Fuller, that if the federal antitrust law covers all manufacturing combinations "whose ultimate result may effect external commerce, comparatively little of business operations and affairs would be left for state control."[68]

The court majority had claimed that the combination in question related solely to the acquisition of refineries in Pennsylvania and to sugar processing in that state and was therefore not in interstate commerce and not touchable by the Sherman Act. The state had authority under its police power to relieve the situation if the monopoly burdened intrastate commerce, the court said.

Fuller's insistence that the states were the proper instruments to deal with manufacturing monopolies ignored the reality that states were incapable of regulating the gigantic trusts. This meant there was no effective mechanism for regulation at either the state or national level, and as Justice John Marshall Harlan wrote in his vigorous dissent, the public was left "entirely at the mercy" of the trusts.[69]

Fuller's rather artificial distinction between the direct and indirect effects of manufacture on interstate commerce was a significant qualification of Marshall's opinion that sanctioned congressional regulation of intrastate matters that "affect" other states. It would provide a handy tool for future courts that wished to thwart congressional regulation of intrastate matters. As Justice Wiley B. Rutledge wrote in 1948: "The *Knight* decision made the [antitrust] statute a dead letter for more than a decade and, had its full force remained unmodified, the Act today would be a weak instrument, as would also the power of Congress, to reach evils in all the vast operations of our gigantic national industrial system antecedent to interstate sale and transportation of manufactured products."[70]

Sherman Act Applied. While the *Knight* ruling seriously limited the scope of the Sherman Act, it did not declare it unconstitutional and the court in 1897 readily applied the law to strike down a combination of railway companies joined together to set freight rates that all the companies would charge. A similar ruling was handed down a year later in a second case.[71]

In 1899 the court sustained for the first time application of the Sherman Antitrust Act to an industrial combine. It held that a regional marketing agreement drawn up by six corporations that made and sold iron pipe interstate was an illegal restraint of trade in violation of the act. Justice Rufus W. Peckham said the situation in this case was

unlike that in the sugar trust case because the pipe combine "was clearly involved in selling as well as manufacturing."[72]

The Holding Company Case

In 1904 the court moved further away from its narrow ruling in the sugar case. A result of President Theodore Roosevelt's trust-busting campaign, the case of *Northern Securities Co. v. United States* involved the government's challenge to a holding company set up by the major stockholders of two competing railroads to buy the controlling interest of the roads.

By a 5-4 vote, the court held that the holding company clearly was intended to eliminate competition between the two rail lines. "This combination is, within the meaning of the act, a 'trust;' but if not, it is a *combination in restraint of interstate and international commerce* and that is enough to bring it under the condemnation of the act," wrote Justice Harlan for the majority.[73]

In an important modification of the holding in the sugar trust case, Harlan declared that the holding company, unlike the sugar company, was really in commerce. The antitrust act, he maintained, applied to "*every* combination or conspiracy which would extinguish competition between otherwise competing railroads engaged in *interstate trade or commerce,* and which would *in that way* restrain *such* trade or commerce. . . ."[74]

Harlan was unimpressed with the defendants' contention that, because the holding company was incorporated by a state, the attempt to enforce the antitrust act was an undue interference with the internal commerce of the state:

. . .An act of Congress constitutionally passed under its power to regulate commerce among the States . . . is binding upon all. . . . Not even a State, still less one of its artificial creatures, can stand in the way of its enforcement. If it were otherwise, the Government and its laws might be prostrated at the feet of local authority.[75]

The four dissenters adhered to the reasoning in the *Knight* case, contending that commerce did not extend to stock transactions or corporations simply because they were indirectly involved with matters in interstate commerce.

The 'Stream of Commerce'

The following year, with its adoption of the "stream of commerce" doctrine the court did away almost entirely with the distinction it had drawn in the sugar case between direct and indirect effects on commerce. *Swift & Co. v. United States* (1905) concerned the "beef trust" — meat packing houses that had made extensive agreements among themselves to control livestock and meat prices in many of the nation's stockyards and slaughtering houses.[76] Swift claimed that its livestock was bought and sold locally and was therefore not in interstate commerce. The unanimous opinion rejecting the claim was written by Justice Oliver Wendell Holmes Jr.

"Although the combination alleged embraces restraint and monopoly of trade within a single State, its effect upon commerce among the States is not accidental, secondary, remote or merely probable," Holmes wrote. He then enunciated what became known as the "stream of commerce" doctrine:

. . .When cattle are sent for sale from a place in one state, with the expectation that they will end their transit, after purchase, in another, and when in effect they do so, with only the interruption necessary to find a purchaser at the stock yards, and when this is a typical constantly recurring course, the current thus existing is a current of commerce among the states, and the purchase of the cattle is a part and incident of such commerce.[77]

This "stream of commerce" doctrine eventually would be used to rationalize federal regulation of actual production. But long before that, the significance of the *Swift* case had been acknowledged. Wrote Chief Justice William Howard Taft in a 1923 decision:

> ...[The *Swift*] case was a milestone in the interpretation of the commerce clause of the Constitution. It recognized the great changes and development in the business of this vast country and drew again the dividing line between interstate and intrastate commerce where the Constitution intended it to be. It refused to permit local incidents of great interstate movement, which, taken alone, were intrastate, to characterize the movement as such. The *Swift* case merely fitted the commerce clause to the real and practical essence of modern business growth.[78]

Beyond Antitrust. The stream of commerce doctrine was reinforced and its scope expanded beyond antitrust matters in 1922 when the Supreme Court upheld federal regulation of business practices that might contribute to an illegal interference with interstate commerce. *Stafford v. Wallace* (1922) concerned the validity of the Packers and Stockyards Act of 1921, which prohibited certain unfair and discriminatory practices believed to lead to restraint of trade.

The court sustained the federal regulation, ruling that packers and stockyards were parts of the stream of interstate commerce. As Chief Justice Taft put it, the stockyards were "a throat through which the current flows, and the transactions which occur therein are only incidents to this current...."[79]

The court also used the stream of commerce doctrine to uphold the Grain Futures Act of 1922. The shipment of grain to market, its temporary storage, sale and reshipment in large part to other states were all parts of the flow of interstate commerce, Taft wrote in *Board of Trade of Chicago v. Olsen* (1923). This opinion was somewhat ironic since it effectively overturned an earlier decision, also written by Taft, that held unconstitutional a congressional attempt to regulate boards of trade dealing in commodities futures.[80] *(Details, p. 114)*

The court's adoption of the stream of commerce doctrine placed a consequent restriction on the state power to regulate commerce. This was illustrated in the case of *Lemke v. Farmers Grain Co.* (1922) in which the court held that wheat delivered and sold by farmers to North Dakota grain elevators and then resold mostly to buyers in Minnesota was in a stream of interstate commerce. Therefore, the court said, a state statute regulating the price and profit of wheat sales was an interference with the free flow of interstate commerce.[81]

The 'Rule of Reason'

In 1911 the court abandoned its literal interpretation of the language of the Sherman Antitrust Act set out by Justice Harlan in the *Northern Securities* case. A slim majority of the court in the case of *Standard Oil Co. v. United States* adopted the controversial "rule of reason," under which only unreasonable combinations and undue restraints of trade are considered illegal.

The court first discussed the rule in the 1897 case, *United States v. Trans-Missouri Freight Association.* There the majority held that a combination of railroads to set freight rates that all would abide by was illegal even though the rates were reasonable. The majority flatly rejected the argument that the Sherman Antitrust Act applied only to unreasonable combinations. Justice Peckham wrote for the court:

> ...When, therefore, the body of an act pronounces as illegal every contract or combination in restraint of trade or commerce among the several States ... the plain and ordinary meaning of such language is not limited to that kind of contract alone which is unreasonable restraint of trade, but all contracts are included in such language....[82]

Disagreeing with this interpretation, Justice Edward D. White wrote a dissenting opinion:

> The theory upon which the contract is held to be illegal is that even though it be reasonable, and hence valid under the general principles of law, it is yet void, because it conflicts with the act of Congress already referred to. Now, at the outset, it is necessary to understand the full import of this conclusion. As it is conceded that the contract does not unreasonably restrain trade, and that if it does not so unreasonably restrain, it is valid under the general law, the decision, substantially, is that the act of Congress is a departure from the general principles of law, and by its terms destroys the right of individuals or corporations to enter into very many reasonable contracts. But this proposition, I submit, is tantamount to an assertion that the act of Congress is itself unreasonable.[83]

Over the next few years, the majority continued to hold that the antitrust act applied to all combinations, not only those that might be considered unreasonable.

But in 1911, in the case that broke up the Standard Oil complex, the advocates of the rule of reason became the majority.

In an elaborate and lengthy opinion, White, now Chief Justice, traced the development of the "rule of reason" in English common law and its use in the United States at the time the antitrust act was enacted. He then declared that because the act did not enumerate the kinds of contracts and combines it embraced, the act "necessarily called for the exercise of judgment which required that some standard should be resorted to" for determining whether the act had been violated.[84] Clearly, he said, Congress meant that standard to be the rule of reason.

Although he concurred with the majority's conclusion that the Standard Oil combination violated the antitrust act, Justice Harlan criticized the majority for "usurpation ... of the functions" of Congress. By endorsing the rule of reason, Harlan said,

> ...the court has now read into the act of Congress words which are not to be found there, and has thereby done that which it adjudged ... could not be done without violating the Constitution, namely, by interpretation of a statute, changed a public policy declared by the legislative department.[85]

Two weeks later the majority again gave its approval to the rule of reason when it ruled that the tobacco trust must be dissolved. White wrote that the rule "was in accord with all the previous decisions of this court, despite the fact that the contrary view was sometimes erroneously attributed to some of the expressions" in prior decisions.[86]

Harlan's fear, expressed in his Standard Oil dissent, that unreasonableness would prove a difficult standard to apply, was not unwarranted. In 1913 the court found reasonable a combination of manufacturers of shoemaking equipment which controlled between 70 and 80 percent of the market. Because the three manufacturers involved individually controlled about the same percentage of the market before they joined forces, the court found that their combination sought only greater efficiency.[87]

Under this rule, the court held in 1920 that the U.S. Steel Corp. was not in violation of the antitrust act, despite the fact that the corporation had attempted to create a monopoly and failed. "It is against monopoly that the statute is directed, not against an expectation of it," the court wrote.[88]

Declaring in 1918 that "[e]very agreement concerning trade, every regulation of trade, restrains," the court enunciated the procedure it still uses to determine whether or not a combination or trust is reasonable. Justice Louis D. Brandeis, for the court in *Chicago Board of Trade v. United States*, wrote:

>...The true test of legality is whether the restraint imposed is such as merely regulates and perhaps thereby promotes competition or whether it is such as may suppress or even destroy competition. To determine that question the court must ordinarily consider the facts peculiar to the business to which the restraint is applied; its condition before and after the restraint was imposed; the nature of the restraint and its effect, actual or probable. The history of the restraint, the evil believed to exist, the reasons for adopting the particular remedy, the purpose or end sought to be attained, are all relevant facts.[89]

Antitrust and Labor

Efforts to include a specific exemption for labor unions in the 1890 Sherman Act were unsuccessful. As a result, the act was used almost from its passage as an anti-labor measure justifying the issuance of orders halting strikes by labor unions. In 1894, a federal circuit court relied partially on the Sherman Act to uphold an injunction against Eugene V. Debs and other leaders of the Pullman strike on the grounds that the railroad workers had conspired to restrain trade. *(Details, p. 217)*

The Supreme Court upheld the injunction against the strike and the resulting convictions for contempt of the order, resting its opinion on the broad ground that the federal government's responsibility for interstate commerce and the mails gave it the authority to interfere with the strike in order to prevent obstruction of those functions. Of its failure to look to the antitrust act for authority to issue the injunction, the court said: "It must not be understood from this that we dissent from the conclusion of that [circuit] court in reference to the scope of the act...."[90]

That the court agreed the antitrust act could be applied to labor unions was made abundantly clear in its 1908 decision in the Danbury Hatters' case (*Loewe v. Lawlor*). A union attempting to organize workers at a hat factory in Danbury, Conn., was supported by the American Federation of Labor which set up boycotts of stores where the hats were sold in several states.

Speaking for the court, Chief Justice Melville W. Fuller asserted that since the antitrust act covered "any combination whatever" in restraint of trade it extended to labor unions whose activities — as in this case — were "aimed at compelling third parties and strangers involuntarily not to engage in the course of trade except on conditions that the combination imposes...."[91]

Fuller also employed the stream of commerce doctrine to show that the boycotts, although intrastate, had a direct effect on interstate commerce. "If the purposes of the combinations were, as alleged, to prevent any interstate transportation [of the hats] at all, the fact that the means operated at one end before the physical transportation commenced and at the other end after the physical transportation ended was immaterial," Fuller wrote.[92]

As a result of the decision in the Danbury Hatters' case Congress inserted provisions in the Clayton Antitrust Act of 1914 to exempt labor unions from antitrust actions. Section 6 of that act stipulated that labor was "not a commodity or article of commerce." Section 20 provided that "no restraining order or injunction shall be granted by any court of the United States ... in any case between an employer and employees ... unless necessary to prevent irreparable injury to property, or to a property right."

The court did not consider the validity of these sections until 1921 when it narrowed the Clayton Act labor exemption in the case of *Duplex Printing Press Co. v. Deering.* An interstate union wanted to organize workers at a press manufacturer in Michigan. It struck the Michigan plant, and also set up a secondary boycott of the press markets, primarily in the New York City vicinity. The question was whether the Clayton Act provisions prohibited the issuance of an injunction against those persons engaged in the secondary boycott. With three dissenting votes, the court ruled against the union, holding that the Clayton Act exemptions pertained only to legal and normal operations of labor unions. There was nothing in the act, the court said "to exempt such an organization or its members from accountability where it or they depart from its normal and legitimate objects and engage in an actual combination or conspiracy in restraint of trade."[93] The secondary boycott was such a restraint, the justices held.

The *Duplex Printing Press* decision was only the first in a series of cases in the 1920s where the court found basis in the antitrust laws for ruling against labor unions. In 1925, the court held that an intrastate strike against a coal company directly affected commerce and violated the antitrust laws. In 1927, the court overruled two lower federal courts to grant an injunction against a stone-cutters union that had instituted a secondary boycott of stone cut by non-union workers.[94]

To overcome the court's narrow interpretation of the labor exemption in the Clayton Act, Congress in 1932 passed the Norris-LaGuardia Act, which prohibited the issuance of injunctions by federal courts in labor disputes except where unlawful acts were threatened or committed.

The court in *Lauf v. E.G. Shinner & Co.* (1938) upheld the act on the ground that it was within congressional power to determine the jurisdiction of the lower federal courts.[95] The court has maintained that ruling in the face of several subsequent challenges to the law.[96]

In 1941, the court gave additional vigor to the Clayton Act when it sustained a provision of Section 20 of that law

The Court, Congress and Commerce: A Chronology

The following sets out in chronological order major Supreme Court decisions on the power of Congress to tax and to regulate commerce in the United States.

1824 — *Gibbons v. Ogden* — First definition of commerce power: Congress may regulate all commerce affecting more than one state.

1851 — *Cooley v. Port Warden of Philadelphia* — "*Cooley* doctrine" gives Congress authority to regulate areas of commerce national in scope while allowing state to regulate areas of commerce local in nature.

1871 — *The Daniel Ball* — Forerunner of "stream of commerce" doctrine: Congress may regulate boat operating solely intrastate but transporting goods in interstate commerce.

1888 — *Kidd v. Pearson* — Manufacture is not commerce.

1895 — *United States v. E. C. Knight Co.* — Processing is manufacture, not commerce, and does not affect commerce directly; therefore, a sugar processing trust is not a restraint of trade under federal antitrust law.

1903 — *Champion v. Ames* — Congress may use commerce power as police power to outlaw interstate sale and shipment of lottery tickets.

1904 — *McCray v. United States* — Congress may use tax power as police power to place burden on sale of yellow oleo.

1905 — *Swift & Co. v. United States* — "Stream of commerce" doctrine: Congress may regulate intrastate commerce which is a part of a stream of interstate commerce.

1908 — *Adair v. United States* — Labor relations do not directly affect interstate commerce; therefore, Congress may not use its commerce power to prohibit "yellow dog" contracts.

— *Loewe v. Lawlor* — Union boycott is restraint of trade and interstate commerce in violation of antitrust act.

1909 — *First Employers' Liability Case* — Congress lacks power to make employers liable for on-job death of railway employees not involved with interstate commerce.

1911 — *Standard Oil of New Jersey v. United States* — Adoption of "rule of reason": only unreasonable trusts are violations of antitrust act.

1914 — *Shreveport Rate Case* — Congress may regulate intrastate rail rates where such regulation is necessary to ensure effective regulation of interstate rates.

1917 — *Wilson v. New* — Congress may set emergency wage and hour standards for railway workers.

1918 — *Hammer v. Dagenhart* — Congress may not use commerce power as police power to set hour standards for child laborers; such use is unconstitutional attempt to regulate manufacturing, which is not commerce.

1921 — *Duplex Printing Co. v. Deering* — Clayton Act does not exempt unions involved in boycotts from prosecution under antitrust act.

1922 — *Stafford v. Wallace* — "Stream of commerce" doctrine expanded: Congress may regulate unfair business practices in intrastate industries that are part of flow of interstate commerce.

— *Bailey v. Drexel Furniture Co.* — Congress may not use tax power as police power to place high tax on profits of companies employing child laborers; such a use of the tax power is unconstitutional imposition of a penalty, not an effort to raise revenue.

1935 — *Schechter Poultry Corp. v. United States* — "Stream of commerce" doctrine does not allow Congress to regulate company receiving goods from out of state but selling them locally.

— *Railroad Retirement Board v. Alton Railroad Co.* — Congress exceeds scope of commerce clause by enacting pension system for railroad workers.

1936 — *Carter v. Carter Coal Co.* — Mining is not commerce and does not affect it directly; therefore, Congress may not regulate labor relations in coal mining industry. Tax on coal, refundable if producer complies with regulations, is an unconstitutional penalty.

— *United States v. Butler* — Congress may not regulate agricultural production by taxing food processors in order to pay benefits to farmers who reduce production of certain crops.

1937 — *National Labor Relations Board v. Jones & Laughlin Steel Corp.* — Congress may regulate labor relations in manufacturing to prevent possible interference with interstate commerce; effectively overturns *Carter, Schechter* rulings.

— *Helvering v. Davis, Steward Machine Co. v. Davis* — Congress has authority to use tax, spending for general welfare powers to enact tax-benefit plans as part of Social Security, unemployment compensation statutes; effectively overturns *Butler, Alton* rulings.

1939 — *Mulford v. Smith* — Congress may set marketing quotas for agricultural production, regulating commerce at beginning of stream of commerce.

1941 — *United States v. Darby Lumber Co.* — Congress may use commerce power to prohibit from interstate commerce goods made under substandard labor conditions; specifically overturns *Dagenhart* decision.

1942 — *Wickard v. Filburn* — Congress may regulate agricultural production affecting interstate commerce even if produce is not meant for sale.

1964 — *Heart of Atlanta Motel v. United States* — Congress may use commerce power to bar private individuals operating public accommodations that cater to interstate clientele or use goods made in interstate commerce from discriminating on basis of race.

1976 — *National League of Cities v. Usery* — Congress exceeds commerce power when it establishes wage and hour standards for state employees; such standards are an unconstitutional infringement on state sovereignty.

which stated that certain acts such as strikes and secondary boycotts would not be considered violations of any federal law.[97]

In 1945, the court ruled that a union which conspired with manufacturers to boycott a non-union competitor was violating the Sherman Act.[98] But a union's refusal to work for a trucking firm or to take as members any of the persons who worked for the firm was not a violation of the antitrust law but a proper exercise of union rights under the Clayton and Norris-LaGuardia Acts.[99]

A Federal Police Power

Congress has no explicit constitutional mandate to protect public health, public welfare and public morals. Such protections are traditionally the responsibility of the states acting through their police powers. Nonetheless, Congress in the late 1800s began to develop a federal police power to deal with a growing list of social and economic problems that were no longer local but national in scope.

The national legislature used its constitutional grant of authority over interstate commerce to justify much of this regulation, claiming power to regulate any matter that at some point was a part of interstate commerce. As scholar Robert K. Carr described it:

Where the commerce power had previously been used primarily to regulate, foster or promote commerce for its own sake, ... it now seemed that Congress might seek to regulate social and economic practices within the states, provided only that at some point they involved a crossing of state lines.[100]

Initial attempts by Congress to exercise a police power were largely unsuccessful; the court ruled that such regulations could apply only in areas of the United States outside of state boundaries, such as the District of Columbia. In 1870, for example, the court vitiated most of a federal statute barring the sale of certain illuminating oils "except so far as the [prohibition] operates within the United States, but without the limits of any State." [101] The court explained:

...[the] grant of power to regulate commerce among the States has always been understood as limited by its terms; and as a virtual denial of any power to interfere with the internal trade and business of the separate states; except, indeed, as a necessary and proper means for carrying into execution some other power expressly granted or vested.[102]

Lottery Tickets

In 1902, however, the court upheld a federal statute prohibiting the transportation of diseased cattle in interstate commerce.[103] But it was the court's sanction of the new federal police power in a controversial 1903 case that was of greater significance. The court heard arguments three times in the case of *Champion v. Ames (The Lottery Case),* which concerned an 1895 act of Congress making it illegal to transport lottery tickets from a state or foreign country into another state.[104] The statute had been challenged on the grounds that lottery tickets were not commerce and that regulation of them was reserved to the states. It was also argued that Congress could only regulate commerce, and not prohibit it altogether.

The five-man majority, speaking through Justice John Marshall Harlan, declared that lottery tickets were commerce and that their shipment across state lines made them subject to regulation by Congress. The federal regula-tion, Harlan said, did not interfere with the commerce of lottery tickets within the states and so did not infringe on their right to regulate that traffic. In effect, he said, the federal regulation supplemented state regulation:

...As a State may, for the purpose of guarding the morals of its own people, forbid all sales of lottery tickets within its limits, so Congress, for the purpose of guarding the people of the United States against the "wide-spread pestilence of lotteries" and to protect the commerce which concerns all the States, may prohibit the carrying of lottery tickets from one State to another.[105]

Immoral Women

Congressional efforts to curb prostitution were thwarted at first by the Supreme Court. An act of 1907 made it illegal for anyone to harbor an alien woman for purposes of prostitution within three years after her arrival in the country. By a vote of six to three the court held in 1909 that regulation of houses of prostitution was an internal state matter that Congress could not reach.[1]

Continuing concern over reports that women were being held as virtual slaves and forced to engage in prostitution led to adoption in 1910 of the Mann Act, which punished any person found guilty of transporting women for immoral purposes in interstate or foreign commerce. The court in *Hoke v. United States* (1913) unanimously upheld the act, without referring to its decision in the earlier prostitution case. "Of course, it will be said that women are not articles of merchandise but this does not affect the analogy of the cases," wrote Justice Joseph McKenna. He added:

...if the facility of interstate transportation can be taken away from the demoralization of lotteries, the debasement of obscene literature, the contagion of diseased cattle or persons, the impurity of food and drugs, the like facility can be taken away from the systematic enticement to and the enslavement in prostitution and debauchery of women, and, more insistently, of girls.[2]

In subsequent cases, the court upheld enforcement of the Mann Act against persons transporting women across state lines for immoral purposes although there was no commercial gain involved and against Mormons who transported their plural wives across state lines.[3]

---

[1] *Keller v. United States,* 213 U.S. 138 (1909).
[2] *Hoke v. United States,* 227 U.S. 308 at 322 (1913).
[3] *Caminetti v. United States,* 242 U.S. 470 (1917); *Cleveland v. United States,* 329 U.S. 14 (1946).

Doubtful Victory

Five years after the Supreme Court struck down the 1916 child labor law in *Hammer v. Dagenhart,* a journalist interviewed Reuben Dagenhart, one of two brothers whose father had brought the suit to prevent Congress from interfering with his sons' jobs in a North Carolina cotton mill. Reuben was 20 at the time of the 1923 interview. Excerpts follow:

"What benefit ... did you get out of the suit which you won in the United States Supreme Court?"...

"I don't see that I got any benefit. I guess I'd have been a lot better off if they hadn't won it.

"Look at me! A hundred and five pounds, a grown man and no education. I may be mistaken, but I think the years I've put in the cotton mills have stunted my growth. They kept me from getting any schooling. I had to stop school after the third grade and now I need the education I didn't get."...

"Just what did you and John get out of that suit, then?" he was asked.

"Why, we got some automobile rides when them big lawyers from the North was down here. Oh, yes, and they bought both of us a Coca-Cola! That's all we got out of it."

"What did you tell the judge when you were in court?"

"Oh, John and me never was in court. Just Paw was there. John and me was just little kids in short pants. I guess we wouldn't have looked like much in court.... We were working in the mill while the case was going on...."

Reuben hasn't been to school, but his mind has not been idle.

"It would have been a good thing for all the kids in this state if that law they passed had been kept. Of course, they do better now than they used to. You don't see so many babies working in the factories, but you see a lot of them that ought to be going to school."

Source: Labor, Nov. 17, 1923, p. 3, quoted in Leonard F. James, *The Supreme Court in American Life,* 2nd ed. (Glenview, Ill.: Scott, Foresman & Co., 1971), p. 74.

Recalling John Marshall's declaration that the commerce power is plenary, complete and unlimited except by the Constitution, Harlan said that the power to regulate encompassed prohibition.

If Congress finds a subject of interstate commerce noxious, "can it be possible that it must tolerate the traffic, and simply regulate the manner in which it may be carried on?" Harlan asked.[106] On the contrary, he said, "we know of no authority in the Courts to hold that the means thus devised [prohibition of shipment] are not appropriate and necessary to protect the country ... against a species of interstate commerce which ... has become offensive to the entire people of the nation."[107] Harlan also noted that the court had sustained the Sherman Antitrust Act which prohibited contracts that restrained interstate commerce. *(Antitrust act upheld, p. 90)*

Justice Harlan anticipated the arguments of the minority who predicted that the use of the commerce power as a police tool would "defeat the operation" of the 10th Amendment which reserved to the states powers not granted to the federal government. While plenary and complete, the power of Congress over interstate commerce is not arbitrary, Harlan said but is limited by the Constitution and may not infringe rights protected by that document.

This decision, as historian Charles Warren wrote, "disclosed the existence of a hitherto unsuspected field of national power." Warren continued:

...The practical result of the case was the creation of a federal police power — the right to regulate the manner of production, manufacture, sale and transportation of articles and the transportation of persons, through the medium of legislation professing to regulate commerce between the states. Congress took very swift advantage of the new field thus opened to it.[108]

The court sustained many of the statutes Warren referred to, including the Pure Food and Drug Act of 1906, the Mann Act, which penalized persons convicted of transporting women across state lines for immoral purposes, and two statutes regulating safety for railway workers.[109] *(Mann Act, box, p. 95)*

For a dozen years the federal police power appeared well entrenched. But in 1918 the court was to render a decision that left further expansion of that power in momentary doubt. The federal police power collided with states' rights and came out the loser.

Child Labor

In its 1918 decision in the case of *Hammer v. Dagenhart* the court struck down a 1916 act of Congress that sought to discourage employment of children by prohibiting the shipment in interstate commerce of any products made in factories or mines that employed children under 14 or allowed children aged 14 to 16 to work more than a limited number of hours per week.[110] The statute was contested by Roland Dagenhart, whose two teen-aged sons worked in a North Carolina cotton mill. Dagenhart sought an injunction against U.S. District Attorney W. C. Hammer to prevent him from enforcing the act and costing his sons their jobs. *(Box, this page)*

Majority Opinion. By a 5-4 vote, the court declared the 1916 law unconstitutional. Congress, said Justice William R. Day, had exceeded its authority when it prohibited goods made by children from interstate commerce. The power to regulate commerce is the authority "to control the means by which commerce is carried on," and not the "right to forbid commerce from moving," said Day.[111]

This statement required Day to distinguish his holding in the child labor act from the cases in which the court had sanctioned a congressional prohibition against the movement of items such as lottery tickets and adulterated food in interstate commerce. Day did so by declaring these latter articles harmful in themselves, and asserting that their regulation "could only be accomplished by prohibiting the use of the facilities of interstate commerce to effect the evil intended." That "element is wanting in the present case," he said; the goods manufactured by children "are of themselves harmless."[112]

Day did not stop at this point but went on to examine the reasons why Congress enacted the law. "The act in its effect does not regulate transportation among the states," Day said, "but aims to standardize the ages at which children may be employed in mining and manufacturing within the states." [113]

Retreating to the earlier distinction between commerce and manufacture, Day said mining and manufacture were subject only to state regulation. The fact that goods "were intended for interstate commerce transportation does not make their production subject to federal control under the commerce power," he maintained. [114]

In conclusion, the justice stated that the act "not only transcends the authority delegated to Congress over commerce but also exerts a power as to a purely local matter to which the federal authority does not extend." [115]

Holmes Dissent. Justice Oliver Wendell Holmes' dissenting opinion left little doubt that the four minority justices believed the majority's ruling had been motivated in large part by the justices' personal views opposing the child labor act. On its surface, Holmes said, the act was indisputably within the federal commerce power. That being the case, he said, "it seems to me that it is not made any less constitutional because of the indirect effects that it may have (that is, the discouragement of child labor), however obvious it may be that it will have those effects." [116] In support of this proposition, Holmes cited a number of cases in which the court had upheld a regulatory measure without considering the probable effect of the measure.

Nor was it important that the evil was not itself in interstate transportation. "It does not matter whether the supposed evil precedes or follows the transportation," Holmes declared. "It is enough that in the opinion of Congress the transportation encourages the evil." [117]

Holmes also maintained that it was Congress and not the court that should determine when prohibition was necessary to effective regulation, adding that "if there is any matter upon which civilized countries have agreed .... it is the evil of premature and excessive child labor." [118]

The federal law did not interfere with the state police power, asserted Holmes, and in any event the court had made clear that the exercise of the federal commerce power could not be limited by its potential for interfering with intrastate regulation of commerce. States, he said,

...may regulate their internal affairs and their domestic commerce as they like. But when they seek to send their products across the State line they are no longer within their rights. ... Under the Constitution such commerce belongs not to the States but to Congress to regulate. It may carry out its views of public policy whatever indirect effect they may have upon the activities of the States. [119]

Congressional efforts to circumvent the *Hammer v. Dagenhart* ruling proved unsuccessful. Congress in 1919 sought to use its tax power to discourage the use of child labor by placing a high tax on goods that had been manufactured in factories employing youngsters, but the court declared the tax unconstitutional. [120] Congress then passed a constitutional amendment forbidding the employment of children, but the states had not ratified it by the time the court itself in *United States v. Darby Lumber Co.* (1941) overturned its own ruling. [121] *(Child labor tax case, p. 114; United States v. Darby, p. 101)*

Effect of Dagenhart

The court did not rely on the *Dagenhart* ruling much as a precedent, the major exception being the invalidation of the child labor tax law. The justices continued to sanction use of the commerce power as a police tool when it was applied to universally recognized social evils. A few weeks after the child labor case decision, the court unanimously upheld the constitutionality of the 1906 Meat Inspection Act, which called for local inspection of meat products and banned those rejected or not inspected from interstate commerce. [122] Subsequent decisions approved federal statutes prohibiting the interstate transportation of stolen cars, making transportation of kidnapped persons in interstate commerce a federal crime, and preventing the interstate shipment of convict-made goods to those states that prohibited them. [123] Like child labor, the goods involved in these three cases — cars, kidnapped persons and horse collars — were not in and of themselves harmful. Yet the court upheld the federal regulation in all three cases. As it held in the case dealing with the validity of the statute pertaining to stolen cars:

Congress can certainly regulate interstate commerce to the extent of forbidding and punishing the use of such commerce as an agency to promote immorality, dishonesty or the spread of any evil or harm to the people of other states from the state of origin. In doing this, it is merely exercising the police power, for the benefit of the public, within the field of interstate commerce. [124]

The court sanctioned use of the police power more recently when in 1971 it sustained provisions of the 1968 Consumer Credit Protection Act to prohibit loan-sharking. Although individual loan-sharking activities might be wholly intrastate, the court said that it was in a "class of activity" that affected interstate commerce and thus could be regulated under the commerce power. [125]

New Deal and the Commerce Power

Between the court's 1918 ruling in the *Dagenhart* child labor case and the economic crisis of the Great Depression, Congress made little use of the commerce power as a tool for regulating business.

When, under President Roosevelt's guidance, Congress attempted to use federal regulation to stimulate economic recovery, the Supreme Court, still dominated by a small majority strongly disposed toward protection of private property rights — and states' rights — again resisted. The

resulting collision — and the threat by President Roosevelt to increase the size of the court in order to win approval of his New Deal legislation — marked the birth of the modern commerce power. In 1937 the court accepted Justice Benjamin Cardozo's view that the power was equal to the nation's problems. In subsequent years, the court has upheld the use of the commerce power to deal with problems ranging from civil rights violations to environmental pollution.

Black Monday

The centerpiece of Roosevelt's recovery program was the National Industrial Recovery Act (NIRA) of 1933. It declared a "national emergency productive of widespread unemployment and disorganization of industry, which burdens interstate and foreign commerce, affects the public welfare and undermines the standards of living of the American people...." To speed industrial recovery, the NIRA authorized the president to approve codes of fair competition. Each of these codes, among other conditions, had to contain hour and wage standards for workers in the particular industry.

The first inkling of how the Supreme Court would treat the NIRA came in January 1935 when it declared the "hot oil" section of the law an unconstitutional delegation of legislative authority. The provisions permitted the president to prohibit the interstate transportation of oil produced in excess of amounts allowed by the states. The "Hot Oil" case did not deal, however, with the codes of fair competition.[126] *(Details of case, p. 78)*

Five months later, on what came to be known as "black Monday," the court declared the entire NIRA invalid. *Schechter Poultry Corp. v. United States* was a test case brought by the government in hope that a favorable response from the court would encourage industry compliance, which had been flagging.[127] The circumstances involved, however, made it less than an ideal test.

The Schechter brothers bought live poultry shipped into New York City largely from points out of the state, slaughtered it, then sold it locally. They were accused of violating several provisions of the New York City live poultry industry code, including the wage and hour standards and the prohibition against "straight killing" or allowing a customer to select individual poultry for slaughter. They were also charged with selling an "unfit chicken" to a local butcher. As a result, the suit was quickly dubbed the "Sick Chicken Case."

A unanimous Supreme Court held that the Schechters' operation was a local concern that did not directly affect interstate commerce. Federal regulation through the fair competition codes was, therefore, an unconstitutional abridgement of states' rights.

The court noted that the provisions of the code which the Schechters were charged with violating applied to the slaughtering operation and subsequent sale in local markets, activities which the court said were not in interstate commerce. The court also denied that these activities were part of the stream of commerce. Chief Justice Charles Evans Hughes wrote:

> ...The mere fact that there may be a constant flow of commodities into a state does not mean that the flow continues after the property has arrived and has become commingled with the mass of property within the state and is there held solely for local disposition and use.[128]

The court acknowledged that Congress had power not only to regulate interstate commerce but also to protect interstate commerce from burden or injury imposed by those engaged in intrastate activities. The effect of the burden must be direct, however, said the court, recalling the court's distinction between direct and indirect effects first discussed in the 1895 sugar trust case. Said Hughes:

> In determining how far the federal government may go in controlling intrastate transactions upon the ground that they "affect" interstate commerce, there is a necessary and well-established distinction between direct and indirect effects. The precise line can be drawn only as individual cases arise, but the distinction is clear in principle.[129]

That distinction, the court said, was essential to maintenance of the federal system. Without it the federal government would have complete power over domestic affairs of the states and there would be a centralized government.

"It is not the province of the Court," Hughes wrote, "to consider the economic advantages or disadvantages of such a centralized system. It is sufficient to say that the Federal Constitution does not provide for it." [130]

The court found no way that the alleged violations by the Schechters directly affected interstate commerce. It also held that the delegation to the president by Congress of the authority to establish the codes of competition was excessive and therefore unconstitutional. On both these grounds, it declared the NIRA invalid. *(Details of opinion on legislative delegation, p. 78)*

Some scholars have argued that the court, if it had desired, could have upheld the NIRA so far as it was based on the federal power over interstate commerce. Robert K. Carr, for instance, has suggested that the justices could have extended the stream of commerce doctrine to cover the Schechters' business even though it was at the end of the stream.[131]

It should not be overlooked, however, that the court was unanimous and that the justices considered most likely to approve the New Deal legislation found the NIRA, as presented in the "Sick Chicken Case," unconstitutional. Justice Benjamin N. Cardozo, in a concurring opinion for himself and Justice Harlan Fiske Stone, claimed that the distinction between direct and indirect effects on commerce was a matter of degree. But, he added, "[t]o find immediacy or directness [in this case] is to find it almost everywhere." [132]

Coal Codes

No such unanimity marked the next New Deal decision. In *Carter v. Carter Coal Co.* (1936), the court struck down the 1935 Bituminous Coal Conservation Act. The act stated that the production and distribution of coal so closely affected interstate commerce that federal regulation was necessary to stabilize the industry.[133] Passed despite the adverse ruling in *Schechter,* the act authorized fixed prices for coal, provided for collective bargaining rights for coal miners, allowed a two-thirds majority of the industry to establish wage and hour standards for the entire industry and established a tax scheme to ensure compliance with the regulations.

Divided 6-3, the court in May 1936 declared the act unconstitutional. Justice George Sutherland, speaking for the majority, focused first on the labor relations provisions. He declared that mining was production, not commerce, and that the relation between a mine operator and mine workers was purely local in character.

Since mining itself was not in interstate commerce, Sutherland continued, it became necessary to determine if its effect on that commerce was direct. Here, Sutherland set forth a definition of a direct effect that turned not on the degree to which a thing affected interstate commerce but on the manner in which the affect occurred. Sutherland wrote:

...The word "direct" implies that the activity or condition invoked or blamed shall operate proximately — not mediately, remotely, or collaterally — to produce the effect.... And the extent of the effect bears no logical relation to its character. The distinction between a direct and an indirect effect turns, not upon the magnitude of either the cause or the effect, but entirely upon the manner in which the effect has been brought about.[134]

It made no difference, said Sutherland, whether one man mined coal for sale in interstate commerce or several men mined it. Labor problems were local controversies affecting local production. "Such effect as they have upon commerce, however extensive it may be, is secondary and indirect," Sutherland proclaimed.[135]

Nor was mining a part of the stream of commerce. Looking to the ruling in the *Schechter* case, Sutherland said:

...The only perceptible difference between that case and this is that in the *Schechter* case, the federal power was asserted with respect to commodities which had come to rest after their interstate transportation; while here, the case deals with commodities at rest before interstate commerce has begun. That difference is without significance.[136]

Having declared the labor provisions an invalid exercise of federal power under the commerce clause, Sutherland proceeded to hold the price-fixing provisions invalid on the grounds that they were so dependent on the labor provisions, they could not stand on their own. This he determined despite a severability clause in the legislation that said the price-fixing provisions could stand if other provisions were found unconstitutional. *(Principles of severability, box, p. 113)*

The majority also held that the statute was an unconstitutional delegation of legislative powers to the executive branch and to the coal industry. It further held that the tax provisions were not for the purpose of raising revenue but to coerce compliance with the regulations. The taxes were therefore not valid on their own but only if they aided the exercise of the commerce power. Since the commerce power had been exercised unconstitutionally, the tax provisions were also invalid, the majority said.

In a concurring opinion, Chief Justice Hughes disagreed with the majority ruling that the price-fixing provisions were inseparable from the labor provisions. But he agreed that the distinction between direct and indirect effects on interstate commerce was a matter of kind and not degree.

"The power to regulate interstate commerce embraces the power to protect that commerce from injury," Hughes said, and added:

But Congress may not use this protective authority as a pretext ... to regulate activities and relations within the states which affect interstate commerce only indirectly.... If the people desire to give Congress the power to regulate industries within the State, and the relations of employers and employees in those industries, they are at liberty to declare their will in the appropriate manner, but it is not for the court to amend the Constitution by judicial decision.[137]

The Dissent. As historians Alfred H. Kelly and Winfred A. Harbison noted:

The most extraordinary thing about Sutherland's opinion was the absurdity of his contention that while the labor provisions of the act were only indirectly related to interstate commerce, they were nonetheless so intimately related to those portions of the law dealing with interstate commerce as to be inseparable from them.[138]

In fact, Sutherland never discussed the question of whether the price-fixing provisions were in interstate commerce or directly affected it. If he had, he would have had to reconcile his opinion with the *Shreveport Rate Case* precedent permitting federal regulation of intrastate matters that are inextricably mingled with interstate commerce. *(Shreveport Rate Case, p. 88)*

It was this precedent that Cardozo in dissent used to argue the validity of the price-fixing precedents.

The price-fixing provisions, said Cardozo, were valid as they applied to transactions in interstate commerce and to transactions in intrastate commerce if such local transactions "directly or intimately affected" interstate commerce.

Joined by Justices Stone and Louis D. Brandeis, Cardozo then reiterated his *Schechter* opinion that the distinction between direct and indirect effects was one of degree, not kind. "At all events," wrote Cardozo, " 'direct' and 'indirect' ... must not be read too narrowly. The power is as broad as the need that evokes it." [139]

In this instance, that need was great, said Cardozo, writing:

Congress was not condemned to inaction in the face of price wars and wage wars.... Commerce had been choked and burdened; its normal flow had been diverted from one state to another; there had been bankruptcy and waste and ruin alike for capital and for labor.... After making every allowance for difference of opinion as to the most efficient cure, the student of the subject is confronted with the indisputable truth that there were ills to be corrected, and ills that had a direct relation to the maintenance of commerce among the states without friction or diversion. An evil existing, and also the power to correct it, the lawmakers were at liberty to use their own discretion in the selection of the means.[140]

Cardozo's opinion recognized what the majority failed to acknowledge — that the local but widespread economic problems of the depression were national in scope. In protecting state sovereignty and private property rights, the majority almost totally rejected the concept of national supremacy. It did reject the theory that Congress might act to protect what it perceived to be the general welfare. It was this attitude that led to Roosevelt's attempt to moderate the conservative voice of the court through his court-packing plan. *(Details, p. 240)*

Roosevelt, to use an apt cliche, lost the battle but won the war. Congress rejected his court-packing scheme, but not before one of the justices who generally voted with the conservative majority, Owen J. Roberts, did an about-face to convert the more liberal minority into a majority. In April 1937, Cardozo's reasoning in the *Carter* dissent became the majority opinion in a case upholding the 1935 National Labor Relations Act (NLRA).[141]

A National Labor Law

Passed in 1935, the NLRA declared that the denial of the rights of workers to organize and bargain collectively

Regulation of Foreign Commerce

From the beginning, the federal power to regulate foreign commerce has been complete. The constitutional grant "comprehend[s] every species of commercial intercourse between the United States and foreign nations. No sort of trade can be carried on between this country and any other, to which this power does not extend," wrote Chief Justice John Marshall in *Gibbons v. Ogden* (1824), the classic interpretation of the commerce clause.[1]

Using this power, Congress may set tariffs, regulate international shipping, aviation and communications and establish embargoes against unfriendly countries. In conjunction with its powers to coin money, regulate its value and borrow it, Congress may authorize U.S. participation in international financing, banking and monetary affairs.

Exercise of the power to regulate foreign commerce has seldom been challenged in the courts; it was not until 1928 that protective tariffs, long a matter of controversy, came before the Supreme Court and then as a test of the taxing power.[2] Congressional grants of authority to the president to adjust tariff schedules at his discretion have been upheld against challenges that they were improper delegations of power.[3] *(p. 216)*

Federal power over foreign commerce extends to prohibiting that commerce. "The Congress may determine what articles may be imported into this country and the terms upon which importation is permitted. No one can be said to have a vested right to carry on foreign commerce with the United States," wrote the court in 1933.[4]

Under this principle, the court upheld federal statutes prohibiting the importation of inferior and impure tea, prize fight films, and natural sponges from the Gulf of Mexico and the Straits of Florida.[5]

The federal authority over foreign commerce is also exclusive. The Constitution expressly forbade the states to enter into treaties with foreign nations or to lay imposts and duties on foreign imports and exports. The "original package" doctrine first put forward by Chief Justice Marshall in 1827 undergirds the prohibition against state duties on imports.[6] *(Details, p. 329)*

However, in the absence of federal regulation, the Supreme Court has allowed state inspection and quarantine laws to stand, even though they might affect foreign commerce.[7]

---

[1] *Gibbons v. Ogden,* 9 Wheat. 1 at 193-94 (1824).

[2] *J. W. Hampton Jr. & Co. v. United States,* 276 U.S. 394 (1928).

[3] *Field v. Clark,* 143 U.S. 649 (1892); *Buttfield v. Stranahan,* 192 U.S. 470 (1904); *J. W. Hampton Jr. & Co. v. United States,* 276 U.S. 394 (1928).

[4] *Board of Trustees v. United States,* 289 U.S. 48 at 57 (1933).

[5] *Buttfield v. Stranahan,* 192 U.S. 470 (1904); *Weber v. Freed,* 239 U.S. 325 (1915); *The Abby Dodge,* 223 U.S. 166 (1912).

[6] *Brown v. Maryland,* 12 Wheat. 419 (1827).

[7] *Gibbons v. Ogden,* 9 Wheat. 1 (1824); *Compagnie Francaise De Navigation a Vapeur v. Louisiana State Board of Health,* 186 U.S. 380 at 385 (1902).

caused strikes and other labor problems that directly burdened and obstructed interstate commerce. To eliminate the obstruction and guarantee workers' rights, Congress prohibited both employees and employers from engaging in specified unfair labor practices. The act also established a National Labor Relations Board (NLRB) to administer the law and hear charges of violations.

In view of the precedent established in the *Schechter* and *Carter* cases, it seemed likely that the Supreme Court would also invalidate the NLRA's application to employers and employees engaged in manufacturing and production. The question was put to the court in 1937 in the midst of public and congressional debate over Roosevelt's court-packing plan.

The case of *NLRB v. Jones & Laughlin Steel Corp.* arose after the steel company fired 10 union employees from one of its Pennsylvania factories. The employees claimed they had been let go solely because they were union members. The NLRB agreed and ordered the steel company to stop discriminating against its union workers. When the company failed to comply, the NLRB asked a court of appeals to enforce its order. Relying on the *Carter* decision, that court refused the petition, saying Congress did not have the power to regulate local labor relations.

Arguing the case before the Supreme Court, attorneys for the NLRB contended that the Pennsylvania factory was in a stream of commerce, receiving raw materials from and transporting its products to other states through interstate commerce. The corporation argued that the NLRA was regulating labor relations, a local concern not subject to federal regulation.

By a 5-4 vote, the Supreme Court reversed the lower court, sustaining the National Labor Relations Act. Joining Justices Cardozo, Brandeis and Stone to make a majority were Chief Justice Hughes and Justice Roberts. Hughes wrote the majority opinion, relying to a great extent on the reasoning of Cardozo's dissent in the *Carter Coal* case.

Reiterating that Congress has the authority to regulate intrastate matters that directly burdened or obstructed interstate commerce, Hughes said the fact that the employees were engaged in the local activity of manufacturing was not "determinative." The question was what effect a strike of the factory would have on interstate commerce. Hughes continued:

> . . .In view of respondent's far-flung activities, it is idle to say that the effect would be indirect or remote. It is obvious that it would be immediate and might be catastrophic. We are asked to shut our eyes to the plainest facts of our national life and to deal with the question of direct and indirect effects in an intellectual vacuum. . . . When industries organize themselves on a national scale, making their relation to interstate commerce the dominant factor in their activities, how can it be maintained that their industrial labor relations constitute a forbidden field into which Congress may not enter when it is necessary to protect interstate commerce from the paralyzing consequences of industrial war? We have often said that interstate commerce itself is a practical conception. It is equally true that interferences with that commerce must be appraised by a judgment that does not ignore actual experience.[142]

Hughes' majority opinion did not specifically overturn the court's holdings in *Schechter* and *Carter Coal.* But it did do away with Justice Sutherland's artificial and unrealistic definition of what intrastate matters directly affected interstate commerce. Once again a majority held that the distinction was a matter of degree to be determined on a case-by-case basis, and not one of kind which did not take into account the realities of the economic system and the nation's needs.

For the four dissenters, Justice James C. McReynolds said he found no material difference between the *Jones & Laughlin* case and those of *Schechter* and *Carter Coal.* "Every consideration brought forward to uphold the Act before us was applicable to support the Acts held unconstitutional in causes decided within two years," he wrote.[143]

The steel company was not in the middle of the stream of commerce but at the end of one stream when it received the raw materials and at the beginning of a second when it shipped its finished product, the minority justices wrote. As a result, the company was not in interstate commerce and its labor relations were not regulable by the federal government but by the states, McReynolds said. To uphold the NLRA was to give its board "power of control over purely local industry beyond anything heretofore deemed permissible."[144]

Other NLRB Cases

The court upheld the NLRB in four other cases decided the same day as the *Jones & Laughlin* suit. Two of the cases involved a large trailer manufacturing company and a men's clothing manufacturer, both of which sold a large portion of their products interstate.[145] Nevertheless, a labor strike in either of these businesses would not have the catastrophic effect on the national economy that a steel strike would have, and the effect of these decisions was to broaden the court's holding in the steel case.

The third case involved the Associated Press (AP).[146] Holding that interstate communication of any sort was interstate commerce regulable by Congress, the court rejected the AP's argument that the labor law violated the news association's First Amendment right to freedom of press. The NLRA, the court said, has "no relation whatever to the impartial distribution of news." In the fourth case, the court held that a small company running buses between Virginia and the District of Columbia was an instrumentality of interstate commerce subject to the labor relations act.[147]

Three later NLRB cases are also noteworthy. In the first, *Santa Cruz Fruit Packing Co. v. National Labor Relations Board* (1938), the court upheld enforcement of the NLRA against a California fruit and vegetable packing company that sold less than 50 percent of its goods in interstate and foreign commerce. A company lockout of union employees resulted in a strike and refusal by warehousemen, truckers and stevedores to handle the packed food.

"It would be difficult to find a case in which unfair labor practices had a more direct effect upon interstate . . . commerce," the court wrote.[148] The *Santa Cruz* case is significant because the labor problem stopped the goods at the beginning of the stream of interstate commerce — unlike the *Jones & Laughlin* case where a strike would have stopped the goods in midstream.

In the second case, *Consolidated Edison v. National Labor Relations Board* (1938), a utility that was not in interstate commerce was nevertheless subject to the NLRA because of "the dependence of interstate and foreign commerce upon the continuity of the service. . . ."[149] The utility provided electricity, gas and steam to three railroads, the Port of New York, several steamship piers, two telegraph companies and a telephone company.

In the third case, *National Labor Relations Board v. Fainblatt* (1939), the court ruled that the NLRA covered unfair labor practices by a clothing manufacturer that resulted in a strike that reduced significantly the amount of goods normally available for shipment in interstate commerce. The manufacturer's contention that he only indirectly affected interstate commerce because only a small portion of his product was shipped interstate was to no avail. The court said:

> . . .The power of Congress to regulate interstate commerce is plenary and extends to all such commerce be it great or small. . . . The amount of the commerce regulated is of special significance only to the extent that Congress may be taken to have excluded commerce of small volume from the operation of its regulatory measure by express provision or fair implication.[150]

With these decisions, the court drew the powers of the NLRB so broadly that few cases have since challenged the authority of the board. The court had declared that labor problems in almost any industry that depended in any way on interstate commerce for a portion of its business might sufficiently injure or burden interstate commerce so as to demand their compliance with the national labor relations law.

Wages and Hours

Given the new-found willingness of the Supreme Court — evidenced by the NLRB rulings — to construe the commerce power broadly, Congress decided to try again to set federal minimum wage and maximum hours standards.

Since the court in 1918 had held hours limitations for child workers an unwarranted federal intrusion into intrastate matters, wage and hour reform attempts had been restricted to the individual states. For almost two decades, the court had approved state maximum hour statutes, but not until 1937 did it abandon its opposition to state minimum wage laws, which it viewed as violating the freedom of contract. Finally, in 1937, the court upheld a Washington state minimum wage law.[151] *(Details, p. 327)*

The next year Congress passed the Fair Labor Standards Act of 1938, which set a 40-hour work week and an eventual minimum wage of 40 cents an hour with time and a half for overtime. The act covered most workers "engaged in commerce or in the production of goods for commerce." It barred production of goods by workers paid less or working more than the standards prescribed, and, in a provision almost identical to that struck down by the court in the child labor case, *Hammer v. Dagenhart*, it barred the shipment in interstate commerce of any products made in violation of the standards.

A test of the 1938 statute came to the court in 1941 after the government charged Fred W. Darby with violations of the standards.[152] Darby ran a lumber company in Georgia, converting raw wood into finished lumber and selling a large part of it in other states.

The court unanimously upheld the federal minimum wage statute. Justice Harlan Fiske Stone, writing the opinion in *United States v. Darby Lumber Co.*, first considered the power of Congress to prohibit shipment of goods manufactured in violation of the standards:

While manufacture is not of itself interstate commerce the shipment of manufactured goods interstate is such commerce and the prohibition of such shipment by Congress is indubitably a regulation of the commerce. . . .

The motive and purpose of the present regulation is plainly to make effective the Congressional conception of public policy that interstate commerce should not be made the instrument of competition in the distribution of goods produced under substandard labor conditions, which competition is injurious to the commerce and to the states from and to which the commerce flows. The motive and purpose of a regulation of interstate commerce are matters for the legislative judgment upon the exercise of which the Constitution places no restriction and over which the courts are given no control.[153]

Although based on different precedents, Stone realized that this conclusion was directly contrary to the finding in *Hammer v. Dagenhart.* Of that case, Stone wrote:

. . .The distinction on which the decision was rested that Congressional power to prohibit interstate commerce is limited to articles which in themselves have some harmful or deleterious property — a distinction which was novel when made and unsupported by any provision of the Constitution — has long since been abandoned. . . . The thesis of the opinion that the motive of the prohibition or its effect to control in some measure the use or production within the states of the article thus excluded from commerce can operate to deprive the regulation of its constitutional authority has long since ceased to have force. . . .

The conclusion is inescapable that *Hammer v. Dagenhart* was a departure from the principles which have prevailed in the interpretation of the commerce clause both before and since the decision and that such vitality, as a precedent, as it then had has long since been exhausted. It should be and now is overruled.[154]

The court also held that the prohibition of the actual production of goods in violation of the standards was a proper means of protecting interstate commerce. This conclusion, said Stone, did not violate the 10th Amendment reserving to the states those powers not delegated to the federal government. He added:

There is nothing in the history of its [the amendment's] adoption to suggest that it was more than declaratory of the relationship between the national and state governments as it had been established by the Constitution before the amendment, or that its purpose was other than to allay fears that the new national government might seek to exercise powers not granted, and that the states might not be able to exercise fully their reserved powers. . . .

From the beginning and for many years the amendment has been construed as not depriving the national government of authority to resort to all means for the exercise of a granted power which are appropriate and plainly adapted to the permitted end.[155]

The court in this decision re-established a strong federal police power and further extended federal opportunities for regulation of production. The idea that the 10th Amendment restricted the full exercise of federal power was dead. As several scholars have noted, Stone's opinion

brought back to prominence the nationalistic interpretation of the commerce clause first outlined by John Marshall, and the court has not since swerved significantly from this interpretation.

A year later, the court went beyond *Darby* to uphold the wage and hour standards as they applied to employees who maintained a building where the tenants produced goods for sale in interstate commerce.[156] In subsequent cases, the court held that the standards applied to operators of oil well drilling rigs, night watchmen and elevator operators.[157] A few employees were not covered however. In 1943, the court said the minimum wage did not apply to workers for a wholesaler who brought goods outside the state but sold them locally.[158] Nor did the standards apply to maintenance workers in an office building in which some of the tenants were executives and sales personnel for manufacturing goods sold in interstate commerce but where no actual manufacturing occurred.[159]

Writing in 1942, Robert K. Carr said that after the *Darby* decision, "about the only further step the Court might take in its general reasoning concerning the commerce power would be to cease denying that manufacture is not of itself commerce and conclude that where goods are produced for, or affect, interstate trade, the act of production is a phase of the total process of commerce."[160] The court took that step the same year.

Agriculture and Commerce

To replace the Agricultural Adjustment Act declared an unconstitutional infringement on state power in the 1936 decision in *United States v. Butler*, Congress passed a similar act in 1938. Rather than paying farmers to produce less of certain commodities as the first act had, the second act established marketing quotas for the various commodities and penalized producers who exceeded them. *(Butler ruling, p. 117)*

The following year the court upheld the Act against the challenge that it too infringed on the reserved powers of the states by attempting to regulate production. Ironically, the opinion was written by Justice Owen J. Roberts who had written the court's opinion in the *Butler* case. The court found that the 1938 act did not regulate production, but marketing, which was at the "throat" of interstate commerce.[161]

The same broad interpretation was given to the 1937 Agricultural Marketing Act which established milk marketing agreements to control milk prices. The court upheld the act twice in 1939 and again in 1942, rejecting in all three cases the argument that Congress lacked authority to regulate milk produced and sold within a single state.[162] In the 1942 case, *United States v. Wrightwood Dairy Co.,* Chief Justice Harlan Fiske Stone wrote for the court:

. . .Congress plainly has power to regulate the price of milk distributed through the medium of interstate commerce . . . and it possesses every power needed to make that regulation effective. The commerce power is not confined in its exercise to the regulation of commerce among the States. It extends to those activities intrastate which so affect interstate commerce, or the exertion of the power of Congress over it, as to make regulation of them appropriate means to the attainment of a legitimate end, the effective execution of the granted power to regulate interstate commerce. The power of Congress over interstate commerce is plenary and complete in itself, may be exercised to its utmost extent, and acknowledges no limitations other than are prescribed in the Constitution. . . . It follows that no form of State activity can constitutionally thwart the regulatory power granted by the commerce clause to Congress. Hence the reach of that power extends to those intrastate activities which in a substantial way interfere with or obstruct the exercise of the granted power.[163]

Just how "substantial" that intrastate activity had to be was tested later in the year in the case of *Wickard v. Filburn.*[164] Under the 1938 agricultural adjustment act, Wickard had been allotted 11 acres of wheat. He planted 23 acres and harvested 269 bushels more than his quota permitted. He intended to sell what he was allowed, and use the excess for feed and for seed for future crops. Although he did not sell the excess in either intrastate or interstate commerce, he still was penalized for raising more than his quota. Wickard challenged the penalty.

The court's opinion was written by Justice Robert H. Jackson who, after the case was first argued, professed bewilderment as to how Congress could regulate "activities that are neither interstate nor commerce."[165]

Reargument apparently erased his doubts. Upholding Congress' authority to regulate Wickard's production, Jackson wrote:

Whether the subject of the regulation in question was "production," "consumption," or "marketing" is . . . not material for purposes of deciding the question of federal power before us. . . . But even if appellee's activity be local and though it may not be regarded as commerce, it may still, whatever its nature, be reached by Congress if it exerts a substantial economic effect on interstate commerce, and this irrespective of whether such effect is what might at some earlier time have been defined as "direct" or "indirect."[166]

Jackson then pointed out that by growing his own wheat, Wickard would not buy wheat and thus would reduce the market demand:

. . .That appellee's own contribution to the demand for wheat may be trivial by itself is not enough to remove him from the scope of federal regulation where, as here, his contribution, taken together with that of many others similarly situated, is far from trivial. . . . Home-grown wheat in this sense competes with wheat in commerce. The stimulation of commerce is a use of the regulatory function quite as definitely as prohibitions or restrictions thereon. This record leaves us in no doubt that Congress may properly have considered that wheat consumed on the farm where grown, if wholly outside the scheme of regulation, would have a substantial effect in defeating and obstructing its purpose to stimulate trade therein at increased prices.[167]

Thus the court had found a rationale to uphold regulation by Congress of production that was not in commerce. Constitutional historian C. Herman Pritchett has called this case the "high-water mark of commerce clause expansionism."[168]

The Modern Commerce Power

The broad construction of the commerce clause by the court of the late 1930s and early 1940s has continued through the 1970s. Not only was the commerce clause the foundation for ever more detailed supervision of the commercial life of the nation by Congress and executive agencies; it has been used to prohibit racial discrimination in public accommodations, remove restrictions on interstate travel and justify federal regulation of environmental pollutants. In one instance, the court used the commerce clause to give Congress control of a field of commerce it did not want and quickly returned to the states. In only one case in the 40 years after 1937 did the court find that Congress had exceeded the scope of this power.

Racial Discrimination

Early in the nation's history slaveholders realized that Congress might use its power over interstate commerce to prohibit racial discrimination. Slaveowners from time to time expressed this fear, but the commerce power never was wielded against the traffic in human slaves. *(Details p. 376)*

After the Civil War, however, Congress attacked racial discrimination in public accommodations through several different means, all with little success. An 1875 statute, based on the 14th Amendment's guarantees of due process and equal protection of the laws, barred segregation in public accommodations. The Supreme Court in the 1883 *Civil Rights Cases* struck the law down, holding that the 14th Amendment applied only to discriminatory actions by states, not by individuals.[169] Therefore, the amendment could not be used to reach discriminatory action on railroads and other privately owned public carriers and accommodations.

Opponents of racial segregation also tried to use the commerce power to reach discriminatory practices. The Interstate Commerce Commission (ICC), however, dismissed a challenge to segregated railroad facilities based on a section of the Interstate Commerce Act that prohibited "undue or unreasonable prejudice or disadvantage" in such facilities. "The disposition of a delicate and important question of this character, weighted with embarrassments arising from antecedent legal and social conditions, should aim at a result most likely to conduce to peace and order. . .," said the commission, in effect ruling that it would not enforce the prohibition.[170]

An attempt to reach racial segregation on public carriers on the ground that it burdened interstate commerce was successful in *Hall v. DeCuir* (1878) but produced the opposite result — the Louisiana law that was voided would have prohibited segregation.[171] Using the *Cooley* rule, the court said prohibition of segregation was a matter on which there should be national uniformity and thus only Congress could act. Congress acted in passing the Civil Rights Act of 1875, but as already noted, the court struck down that act.

A state statute that required segregation on public carriers was challenged with the hope that the court would apply the reasoning it had in *Hall v. DeCuir,* but instead the court in 1890 ruled that the law affected only intrastate traffic and imposed no burden on interstate commerce.[172] This case was then cited in the famous case of *Plessy v. Ferguson* (1896) as precedent for denying the claim that separate but equal facilities for blacks and whites in railway cars unduly burdened interstate commerce.[173] *(Details, p. 608)*

Although there were subsequent sporadic attempts at ending segregation through the commerce clause, congressional and public interest in resolving the problem waned in the first decades of the 20th century.

Right to Travel: Firmly Established on Shifting Base

The right of a citizen to travel freely in the United States has been supported by the Supreme Court throughout its history. As early as 1849, Chief Justice Roger B. Taney wrote in the *Passenger Cases:*

> ...For all great purposes for which the Federal government was formed we are one people, with one common country. We are all citizens of the United States; and, as members of the same community, must have the right to pass and repass through every part of it without interruption, as freely as in our own States.[1]

But the court has not been consistent in locating the source of this right. The court has struck down some restrictions on an individual's right to travel as impermissible burdens on interstate commerce and others as a violation of the 14th Amendment's "privileges and immunities" clause.

Both arguments were offered in the 1941 case of *Edwards v. California,* which involved the state's "anti-Okie" law penalizing people who brought indigents into the state. Edwards was charged with bringing his jobless and penniless brother-in-law into California from Texas. The court was unanimous in its decision to strike down the California law, but was divided on its reasoning. A majority of five claimed that the state statute was a burden on interstate commerce. The purpose and effect of the law, the majority wrote:

> ...is to prohibit the transportation of indigent persons across the California border. The burden upon interstate commerce is intended and immediate; it is the plain and sole function of the statute. Moreover, the indigent non-residents who are the real victims of the statute are deprived of the opportunity to exert political pressure upon the California

legislature in order to obtain a change in policy.... We think this statute must fall under any known test of the validity of State interference with interstate commerce.[2]

But the other four justices believed the state law invalid because it conflicted with the clause of the 14th Amendment that states: "No State shall make or enforce any law which shall abridge the privileges or immunities of citizens of the United States...." "This Court," wrote Justice Robert H. Jackson, "should ... hold squarely that it is a privilege of citizenship of the United States, protected from state abridgement, to enter any state of the Union, either for temporary sojourn or for the establishment of permanent residence therein and for gaining resultant citizenship thereof. If national citizenship means less than this, it means nothing." [3]

The court has never made a choice between these two bases for the right to travel. In cases upholding the Civil Rights Act of 1964, it said that refusal of public accommodations to blacks traveling interstate was an unconstitutional burden on interstate commerce.[4] *(Commerce and civil rights, this page)*

In another case, the court struck down state laws requiring persons to live in a state for a certain time period before becoming eligible for welfare payments. Such laws violated the right to travel, the majority said, adding that it felt no need to "ascribe the source of this right ... to a particular constitutional provision." [5] In an interesting dissent, Chief Justice Earl Warren and Justice Hugo L. Black found the residence requirements restrictions were not unwarranted when weighed against the purpose — wider state participation in welfare programs — Congress sought to achieve in sanctioning the residence requirements.

---

[1] *The Passenger Cases,* 7 How. 283 at 492 (1849).
[2] *Edwards v. California,* 314 U.S. 160 at 174 (1941).
[3] Id. at 183.

[4] *Heart of Atlanta Motel v. United States,* 379 U.S. 241 (1964); *Katzenbach v. McClung,* 379 U.S. 294 (1964).
[5] *Shapiro v. Thompson,* 394 U.S. 618 at 630 (1969).

Civil Rights and Commerce. Then in 1946 the Supreme Court ruled that segregation on a public carrier burdened interstate commerce. The case of *Morgan v. Virginia* involved a black woman traveling on a bus from Virginia to Maryland.[174] She refused to move to the back of the bus to make her seat available to a white. The court upheld her refusal.

In 1950 the court ruled that separate dining facilities on interstate trains were a violation of the Interstate Commerce Act provision that had gone so long unenforced.[175] In 1955 the ICC announced that it was prohibiting racial discrimination in all trains and buses that crossed state lines.

But it was not until the 1964 Civil Rights Act that Congress attempted again to prohibit racial discrimination in all public accommodations.

Title II of the 1964 act barred discrimination on grounds of race, color, religion or national origin in public accommodations if the discrimination was supported by state law or official action, if lodgings were provided to transient guests or if interstate travelers were served or if a

substantial portion of the goods sold or entertainment provided moved in interstate commerce.

This portion of the act was immediately challenged as unconstitutional. Six months after the statute was enacted, the Supreme Court unanimously upheld Title II. The case of *Heart of Atlanta Motel v. United States* (1964) involved a motel in downtown Atlanta that served out-of-state travelers.[176] The motel challenged the validity of the act on the grounds that Congress had exceeded its power to regulate interstate commerce and had violated Fifth Amendment guarantees by depriving businesses of the right to choose their own customers.

Despite the motel's contention that its business was purely local in character, the court upheld the application to it of Title II. Justice Tom C. Clark explained that Congress' power to regulate interstate commerce gave the authority to regulate local enterprise that "might have a substantial and harmful effect" on that commerce.[177]

That Congress' intent in passing the law was to correct what it considered a moral and social evil in no way undercut the law's constitutionality, Clark continued. The moral implications of the discrimination did "not detract from the overwhelming evidence of the disruptive effect" that discrimination had on interstate commerce, he said.[178]

In a companion case, *Katzenbach v. McClung,* decided the same day, the court upheld Title II as applied to a restaurant in Birmingham, Ala.[179] Ollie's Barbeque did not cater to an interstate clientele but 46 percent of the food it served was meat supplied through interstate commerce.

Five years later, the court in *Daniel v. Paul* (1969) upheld the application of Title II to a small rural recreation area that attracted few interstate travelers and that offered few food products sold in interstate commerce.[180] Justice Hugo Black dissented, saying he would have supported the majority if it had used the 14th Amendment to reach the discriminatory practices at the recreational facility but that he objected to the lengths the majority went to show the connection of that discrimination to interstate commerce.

Insurance

In one instance, the court used the commerce clause to give Congress control of a field of trade it did not want and quickly returned to the states.

Since its 1869 decision in *Paul v. Virginia,* the Supreme Court had held consistently that purely financial or contractual transactions such as insurance were not in commerce, even if the transactions involved parties in different states.[181] This left the states full authority to regulate the insurance business.

In 1944, the Justice Department sought to use the Sherman Antitrust Act to break up a conspiracy of insurance companies that sought to monopolize fire insurance sales in six southern states. Using the precedent established by *Paul v. Virginia,* the companies, all members of the South-Eastern Underwriters Association, contended that they could not be reached by the antitrust act since their business was not in commerce.

Overturning *Paul v. Virginia,* the court in a 4-3 decision ruled against the companies. "No commercial enterprise of any kind which conducts its activities across state lines has been held to be wholly beyond the regulatory power of Congress under the Commerce Clause," wrote Justice Hugo L. Black. "We cannot make an exception for the business of insurance."[182] Congress, not the court, must make the exceptions to the antitrust act, Black concluded.

Because this decision called into question the validity of all state insurance regulations, Congress in 1945 passed the McCarran Act which stated that "no Act of Congress shall be construed to invalidate, impair or supersede" a state law regulating or taxing insurance unless the federal act specifically related to insurance. In 1946 the court upheld the McCarran Act.[183]

Environmental Law

Congress' police power to legislate for the public health and welfare, derived primarily from its commerce power, has become the constitutional basis for federal legislation regulating air and water pollution.

The Water Quality Improvement Act of 1970, the primary vehicle for water pollution prevention and control, states in its declaration of policy that it is enacted in "connection with the exercise of jurisdiction over the waterways of the Nation and in consequence of the benefits resulting to the public health and welfare by the prevention and control of water pollution." Likewise, the primary

purpose given for passage of the Air Quality Act of 1967 is "to promote health and welfare and the productive capacity of [the nation's] population."

While various regulations promulgated under these statutes have been challenged in the courts, the Supreme Court has heard no case challenging the authority of Congress to act in these areas.

State Governments

In 1976 a divided Supreme Court placed the first restrictions in 40 years on congressional exercise of the commerce power. The court struck down the portion of a 1974 act of Congress extending minimum wage and overtime requirements to state and local government employees.[184] Congress, the five-man majority said, was interfering too far into the essential functions of state and local government by imposing the standards. The court also overruled its 1968 decision in *Maryland v. Wirtz,* which upheld extension of minimum wage standards to employees of state schools and hospitals.[185]

Writing for the majority in *National League of Cities v. Usery,* Justice William H. Rehnquist said:

> We have repeatedly recognized that there are attributes of sovereignty attaching to every state government which may not be impaired by Congress not because Congress may lack an affirmative grant of legislative authority to reach the matter, but because the Constitution prohibits it from exercising the authority in that manner....
>
> One undoubted attribute of state sovereignty is the state's power to determine the wages which shall be paid to those whom they employ in order to carry out their governmental functions, what hours those persons will work, and what compensation will be provided where these employees may be called upon to work overtime.[186]

"Congress," Rehnquist concluded, "may not exercise that [commerce] power so as to force directly upon the states its choices as to how essential decisions regarding the conduct of integral governmental functions are to be made."[187]

For the minority, Justice William J. Brennan Jr. described the majority opinion as a "catastrophic judicial body blow at Congress' power under the Commerce Clause."[188] Observing that the court in earlier precedents had ruled that Congress may regulate those economic activities of a state that are validly regulated by Congress if engaged in by private persons, Brennan said the majority was simply "invalidating a congressional judgment with which they disagree."[189]

Also in dissent, Justice John Paul Stevens wrote that he found it difficult to perceive the principle on which the court based its ruling that "the Federal Government may not interfere with a sovereign state's inherent right to pay a substandard wage to the janitor at the state capitol," since the federal government already regulated so many other aspects of the janitor's job, from the withholding of taxes from his paycheck to the environmental regulations he must observe in maintaining the capitol's furnace.[190]

Although Brennan in his minority opinion charged that the majority's reasoning was not far different from the pre-1937 court's "overly restrictive construction of the commerce power," it seemed unlikely that the majority opinion in the 1976 case signified such a retreat.[191] Rehnquist, in a footnote, specifically noted that the court expressed no view about possible congressional attempts "to affect integral operations of state government" through other constitutional powers, such as the spending power and the enforcement clause of the 14th Amendment.[192]

And in a concurring opinion, Justice Harry A. Blackmun said that while he was "not untroubled by certain possible implications" of the decision, he thought the court's "balancing approach" in the case "does not outlaw federal power in areas such as environmental protection where the federal interest is demonstrably greater

and where state facility compliance with imposed federal standards would be essential."[193]

"*National League of Cities v. Usery* may portend a modest resurrection of judicial limitation upon congressional exercise of the commerce power...," wrote the authors of the Library of Congress' annotated Constitution. "But, despite the broad phrasing of the opinion, its accommodation of cases in which Congress has been permitted to regulate and Justice Blackmun's limited concurrence suggested that ... [its] potential ... may be quite restrained."[194]

Footnotes

[1] *Gibbons v. Ogden,* 9 Wheat. 1 at 196 (1824).

[2] *Missouri, Kansas & Texas Railway Co. of Texas v. May,* 194 U.S. 267 at 270 (1904).

[3] Robert L. Stern, "The Commerce Clause and the National Economy," *Harvard Law Review,* LIX (May, July 1946), p. 946.

[4] Charles Warren, *The Making of the Constitution* (Boston: Little, Brown & Co., 1928), p. 16.

[5] *Gibbons v. Ogden,* 9 Wheat. 1 (1824).

[6] Id. at 184.

[7] Charles Warren, *The Supreme Court in United States History,* rev. ed., 2 vols. (Boston: Little, Brown & Co., 1926), I:597.

[8] *Gibbons v. Ogden,* 9 Wheat. 1 at 9 (1824).

[9] Id. at 76.

[10] Id. at 189-90.

[11] Id. at 194.

[12] Id. at 194-95.

[13] Id. at 196-97.

[14] Id. at 227.

[15] Warren, *Supreme Court in History,* I:620-21.

[16] Felix Frankfurter, *The Commerce Clause under Marshall, Taney and Waite* (Chapel Hill, N.C.: University of North Carolina Press, 1937), p. 25.

[17] *Brown v. Maryland,* 12 Wheat. 419 (1827).

[18] *Willson v. Blackbird Creek Marsh Co.,* 2 Pet. 245 (1829).

[19] See, e.g., *New York v. Miln,* 11 Pet. 102 (1837); *The License Cases,* 5 How. 504 (1847); *The Passenger Cases,* 7 How. 283 (1849).

[20] *Cooley v. Port Wardens of Philadelphia,* 12 How. 299 (1852).

[21] *Willson v. Blackbird Marsh Creek Co.,* 2 Pet. 245 (1829).

[22] *Pennsylvania v. Wheeling and Belmont Bridge Co.,* 13 How. 518 (1852).

[23] *Pennsylvania v. Wheeling and Belmont Bridge Co.,* 18 How. 421 at 430 (1856).

[24] *Veazie v. Moor,* 14 How. 568 (1852).

[25] *Gilman v. City of Philadelphia,* 3 Wall. 713 (1866).

[26] *The Daniel Ball,* 10 Wall. 557 at 565 (1871).

[27] *United States v. Chandler-Dunbar Water Co.,* 229 U.S. 53 at 73 (1913).

[28] *Arizona v. California,* 283 U.S. 423 at 455-56 (1931).

[29] *Ashwander v. Tennessee Valley Authority,* 297 U.S. 288 (1936).

[30] *Tennessee Electric Power Co. v. Tennessee Valley Authority,* 306 U.S. 118 (1939).

[31] *United States v. Appalachian Electric Power Co.,* 311 U.S. 377 at 407 (1940).

[32] *United States v. Trans-Missouri Freight Assn.,* 166 U.S. 290 (1897).

[33] *Munn v. Illinois,* 94 U.S. 113 (1877).

[34] *Wabash, St. Louis & Pacific Railway Co. v. Illinois,* 118 U.S. 557 at 577 (1886).

[35] *Interstate Commerce Commission v. Brimson,* 154 U.S. 447 (1894).

[36] *Interstate Commerce Commission v. Cincinnati, New Orleans & Texas Pacific Railway Co.,* 167 U.S. 479 at 494-95, passim, (1897).

[37] Id. at 501.

[38] *Interstate Commerce Commission v. Alabama-Midland Railway Co.,* 168 U.S. 144 (1897).

[39] *Illinois Central Railroad Co. v. Interstate Commerce Commission,* 206 U.S. 41 (1907).

[40] *Interstate Commerce Commission v. Chicago, Rock Island and Pacific Railway Co.,* 218 U.S. 88 at 108 (1910).

[41] *United States v. Atchison, Topeka and Santa Fe Railroad Co.,* 234 U.S. 476 at 486 (1914).

[42] Loren P. Beth, *The Development of the American Constitution 1877-1917* (New York: Harper & Row, Harper Torchbooks, 1971), p. 151.

[43] *Minnesota Rate Cases,* 230 U.S. 252 at 399 (1913).

[44] *Shreveport Rate Case,* 234 U.S. 342 at 351-52 (1914).

[45] *Railroad Commissioner of Wisconsin v. Chicago, Burlington & Quincy Railroad Co.,* 257 U.S. 563 at 589-90 (1922).

[46] *Dayton-Goose Creek Railway Co. v. United States,* 263 U.S. 456 (1924).

[47] *Adair v. United States,* 208 U.S. 161 at 172, 179, passim, (1908).

[48] Id. at 191.

[49] *First Employers' Liability Cases,* 207 U.S. 463 (1908).

[50] *Second Employers' Liability Cases,* 223 U.S. 1 (1912).

[51] *Pennsylvania Railroad Company v. U.S. Railroad Labor Board,* 261 U.S. 72 (1923); *Pennsylvania Railroad System and Allied Lines Federation No. 90 v. Pennsylvania Railroad Company,* 267 U.S. 203 (1925).

[52] *Texas & New Orleans Railroad Co. v. Brotherhood of Railway & Steamship Clerks,* 281 U.S. 548 at 571 (1930).

[53] *Southern Railway Co. v. United States,* 222 U.S. 20 (1911).

[54] *Baltimore & Ohio Railroad Co. v. Interstate Commerce Commission,* 221 U.S. 612 at 619 (1911).

[55] *Wilson v. New,* 243 U.S. 332 (1917).

[56] Id. at 350.

[57] *Railroad Retirement Board v. Alton Railroad Co.,* 295 U.S. 330 at 368 (1935).

[58] Id. at 384.

[59] *Pipe Line Cases,* 234 U.S. 548 at 559, 561, passim (1914).

[60] *Public Utilities Commission of Rhode Island v. Attleboro Steam & Electric Co.,* 273 U.S. 83 (1927); *Federal Power Commission v. Natural Gas Pipeline Co.,* 315 U.S. 575 (1942).

[61] *Pensacola Telegraph Co. v. Western Union Telegraph Co.,* 96 U.S. 1 (1878).

[62] *Federal Radio Commission v. Nelson Bros.,* 289 U.S. 266 at 279 (1933).

[63] *Veazie v. Moor,* 14 How. 568 at 574 (1852).

[64] *Kidd v. Pearson,* 128 U.S. 1 at 20 (1888).

[65] *United States v. E. C. Knight Co.,* 156 U.S. 1 (1895).

[66] Id. at 12.

[67] Id. at 13.

[68] Id. at 16.

[69] Id. at 43.

[70] *Mandeville Island Farms v. American Crystal Sugar Co.,* 334 U.S. 219 at 230 (1948).

[71] *United States v. Trans-Missouri Freight Assn.,* 166 U.S. 290 (1897); *United States v. Joint Traffic Assn.,* 171 U.S. 505 (1898).

[72] *Addystone Pipe & Steel Co. v. United States,* 175 U.S. 211 at 241 (1899).

[73] *Northern Securities Company v. United States,* 193 U.S. 197 at 327 (1904).

[74] Id. at 331.

[75] Id. at 333.

[76] *Swift & Co. v. United States,* 196 U.S. 375 (1905).

[77] Id. at 396-99, passim.

[78] *Board of Trade of Chicago v. Olsen*, 262 U.S. 1 at 35 (1923).

[79] *Stafford v. Wallace*, 258 U.S. 495 at 518 (1922).

[80] *Board of Trade of Chicago v. Olsen*, 262 U.S. 1 (1923), overturning *Hill v. Wallace*, 259 U.S. 44 (1922).

[81] *Lemke v. Farmers Grain Co.*, 258 U.S. 50 (1922); see also: *Eureka Pipeline Co. v. Hallanan*, 257 U.S. 265 (1921); *United Fuel Gas Co. v. Hallanan*, 257 U.S. 277 (1921); *Western Union Telegraph Co. v. Foster*, 247 U.S. 105 (1918).

[82] *United States v. Trans-Missouri Freight Assn.*, 166 U.S. 290 at 328 (1897).

[83] Id. at 344.

[84] *Standard Oil Co. v. United States*, 221 U.S. 1 at 60 (1911).

[85] Id. at 103, 104-05, passim.

[86] *United States v. American Tobacco Co.*, 221 U.S. 106 at 179 (1911).

[87] *United States v. Winslow*, 227 U.S. 202 (1913).

[88] *United States v. United States Steel Corp.*, 251 U.S. 417 (1920).

[89] *Chicago Board of Trade v. United States*, 246 U.S. 231 at 238 (1918).

[90] *In re Debs*, 158 U.S. 564 at 600 (1895).

[91] *Loewe v. Lawlor*, 208 U.S. 274 at 293-94 (1908).

[92] Id. at 301.

[93] *Duplex Printing Press Co. v. Deering*, 254 U.S. 443 at 469 (1921).

[94] *Coronado Coal Co. v. United Mine Workers*, 268 U.S. 295 (1925); *Bedford Cut Stone Co. v. Journeymen Stone Cutters' Assn.*, 274 U.S. 37 (1927).

[95] *Lauf v. E. G. Shinner & Co.*, 303 U.S. 315 (1938).

[96] *New Negro Alliance v. Sanitary Grocery Co.*, 303 U.S. 552 (1938); *Brotherhood of Railroad Trainmen v. Chicago River and Indiana Railroad Co.*, 353 U.S. 30 (1957); *Boys Market v. Retail Clerks Union*, 398 U.S. 235 (1970).

[97] *United States v. Hutcheson*, 312 U.S. 219 (1941).

[98] *Allen Bradley Co. v. Local Union No. 3*, 325 U.S. 797 (1945).

[99] *Hunt v. Crumboch*, 325 U.S. 821 (1945).

[100] Robert K. Carr, *The Supreme Court and Judicial Review* (New York: Farrar & Rinehart Inc., 1942), p. 108.

[101] *United States v. DeWitt*, 9 Wall. 41 at 45 (1870).

[102] Id. at 44.

[103] *Reid v. Colorado*, 187 U.S. 137 (1902).

[104] *Champion v. Ames*, 188 U.S. 321 (1903).

[105] Id. at 357.

[106] Id. at 355.

[107] Id. at 358.

[108] Warren, *Supreme Court in History*, II:735-36.

[109] *Hipolite Egg Co. v. United States*, 220 U.S. 45 (1911); *Hoke v. United States*, 227 U.S. 308 (1913); *Southern Railway Co. v. United States*, 222 U.S. 20 (1911); *Baltimore & Ohio Railroad Co. v. Interstate Commerce Commission*, 221 U.S. 612 (1911).

[110] *Hammer v. Dagenhart*, 247 U.S. 251 (1918).

[111] Id. at 268-69.

[112] Id. at 271.

[113] Id. at 271-72.

[114] Id. at 272.

[115] Id. at 276.

[116] Id. at 277.

[117] Id. at 279-80.

[118] Id. at 280.

[119] Id. at 281.

[120] *Bailey v. Drexel Furniture Co.*, 259 U.S. 20 (1922).

[121] *United States v. Darby Lumber Co.*, 312 U.S. 100 (1941).

[122] *Pittsburgh Melting Co. v. Totten*, 248 U.S. 1 (1918).

[123] *Brooks v. United States*, 267 U.S. 432 (1925); *Gooch v. United States*, 297 U.S. 124 (1936); *Kentucky Whip & Collar Co. v. Illinois Central Railroad Co.*, 299 U.S. 334 (1937).

[124] *Brooks v. United States*, 267 U.S. 432 at 436-37 (1925).

[125] *Perez v. United States*, 402 U.S. 146 (1971).

[126] *Panama Refining Co. v. Ryan*, 293 U.S. 388 (1935)

[127] *Schechter Poultry Corp. v. United States*, 295 U.S. 495 (1935).

[128] Id. at 543.

[129] Id. at 546.

[130] Id. at 549.

[131] Carr, *Supreme Court and Judicial Review*, pp. 118-22.

[132] *Schechter Poultry Corp. v. United States*, 295 U.S. 495 at 554 (1935).

[133] *Carter v. Carter Coal Co.*, 298 U.S. 238 (1936).

[134] Id. at 307-08.

[135] Id. at 309.

[136] Ibid.

[137] Id. at 317-18.

[138] Alfred H. Kelly and Winfred A. Harbison, *The American Constitution; Its Origins and Development*, 5th ed. (New York: W. W. Norton & Co., Inc., 1976), p. 707.

[139] *Carter v. Carter Coal Co.*, 298 U.S. 238 at 328 (1936).

[140] Id. at 331-32.

[141] *National Labor Relations Board v. Jones & Laughlin Steel Corp.*, 301 U.S. 1 (1937).

[142] Id. at 41-42.

[143] Id. at 77.

[144] Id. at 78.

[145] *National Labor Relations Board v. Fruehauf Trailer Co.*, 301 U.S. 49 (1937); *National Labor Relations Board v. Friedman-Harry Marks Clothing Co.*, 301 U.S. 58 (1937).

[146] *Associated Press v. National Labor Relations Board*, 301 U.S. 103 (1937).

[147] *Washington, Virginia & Maryland Coach Co. v. National Labor Relations Board*, 301 U.S. 142 (1937).

[148] *Santa Cruz Fruit Packing Co. v. National Labor Relations Board*, 303 U.S. 453 at 469 (1938).

[149] *Consolidated Edison v. National Labor Relations Board*, 305 U.S. 197 at 220 (1938).

[150] *National Labor Relations Board v. Fainblatt*, 306 U.S. 601 at 606 (1939).

[151] *West Coast Hotel v. Parrish*, 300 U.S. 379 (1937); *Morehead v. Tipaldo*, 298 U.S. 587 (1936); *Adkins v. Children's Hospital*, 261 U.S. 525 (1923); *Bunting v. Oregon*, 243 U.S. 426 (1917).

[152] *United States v. Darby Lumber Co.*, 312 U.S. 100 (1941).

[153] Id. at 113, 115, passim.

[154] Id. at 116-17.

[155] Id. at 124.

[156] *A. B. Kirschbaum v. Walling*, 316 U.S. 517 (1942).

[157] *Warren-Bradshaw Co. v. Hall*, 317 U.S. 88 (1942); *Walton v. Southern Package Corporation*, 320 U.S. 540 (1944); *Borden v. Borella*, 325 U.S. 679 (1945).

[158] *Walling v. Jacksonville Paper Co.*, 317 U.S. 564 (1943).

[159] *10 East 40th St. Bldg. v. Callus*, 325 U.S. 578 (1945).

[160] Carr, *Supreme Court and Judicial Review*, p. 135.

[161] *Mulford v. Smith*, 307 U.S. 38 at 47 (1939).

[162] *United States v. Rock Royal Cooperative*, 307 U.S. 533 (1939); *H. P. Hood & Sons v. United States*, 307 U.S. 588 (1939), *United States v. Wrightwood Dairy Co.*, 315 U.S. 110 (1942).

[163] *United States v. Wrightwood Dairy Co.*, 315 U.S. 110 at 118-19 (1942).

[164] *Wickard v. Filburn*, 317 U.S. 111 (1942).

[165] Quoted in Alpheus T. Mason and William M. Beaney, *The Supreme Court in a Free Society* (Englewood Cliffs, N.J.: Prentice-Hall Inc., 1959), p. 98.

[166] *Wickard v. Filburn*, 317 U.S. 111 at 124-25 (1942).

[167] Id. at 128-29.

[168] C. Herman Pritchett, *The American Constitution* 3rd ed. (New York: McGraw Hill Book Company Inc., 1977), p. 198.

[169] *Civil Rights Cases*, 109 U.S. 3 (1883).

[170] Quoted in C. Herman Pritchett, *The American Constitution*, 1st ed. (New York: McGraw Hill Book Company Inc.,1959) p. 604.

[171] *Hall v. DeCuir*, 95 U.S. 485 (1878).

[172] *Louisville, New Orleans & Texas Railway Co. v. Mississippi*, 133 U.S. 587 (1890).

[173] *Plessy v. Ferguson*, 163 U.S. 537 (1896).

[174] *Morgan v. Virginia*, 328 U.S. 373 (1946).

[175] *Henderson v. United States*, 339 U.S. 816 (1950).

[176] *Heart of Atlanta Motel v. United States*, 379 U.S. 241 (1964).

[177] Id. at 258.

[178] Id. at 257.

[179] *Katzenbach v. McClung,* 379 U.S. 294 (1964).

[180] *Daniel v. Paul,* 395 U.S. 298 (1969).

[181] *Paul v. Virginia,* 8 Wall. 168 (1869).

[182] *United States v. South-Eastern Underwriters Association,* 322 U.S. 533 at 553 (1944).

[183] *Prudential Insurance Co. v. Benjamin,* 328 U.S. 408 (1946).

[184] *National League of Cities v. Usery,* 426 U.S. 833 (1976).

[185] *Maryland v. Wirtz,* 392 U.S. 183 (1968).

[186] *National League of Cities v. Usery,* 426 U.S. 833 at 845 (1976).

[187] Id. at 855.

[188] Id. at 880.

[189] Id. at 867.

[190] Id. at 880.

[191] Id. at 868.

[192] Id. at 852, Note 17.

[193] Id. at 856.

[194] United States Congress, Library of Congress, Congressional Research Service, *The Constitution of the United States; Analysis and Interpretation,* 1976 supplement (Washington, D.C.: Government Printing Office, 1977), p. S. 10.

Fiscal and Monetary Powers

Recognizing that the federal government must have unquestioned power to raise and spend money, the framers set out clear congressional authority to lay and collect taxes, pay the national debt and spend for the common defense and general welfare of the people as the first power enumerated in Article I, Section 8. To make congressional control over fiscal and monetary matters complete, the framers also gave Congress the power to coin money and regulate its value.

The Constitution places only one prohibition on the federal tax power — Congress may not tax exports. Only two of the three constitutional limits on the taxing power have had any lasting significance. The first requires that all duties, imposts and excises be levied uniformly throughout the country. The second requires that all direct taxes be apportioned among the states on the basis of their relative populations. The third limited a federal tax on the importation of slaves to $10 per person.

One major implied limitation has restricted federal power to tax state governments and their instrumentalities.

Because of these few restrictions, both Congress and the Supreme Court have been able to interpret the taxing and spending power liberally. C. Herman Pritchett, in his book *The American Constitution,* noted that adequate revenue and broad power to spend it were absolutely necessary to the conduct of an effective central government. "Consequently," he continued, "the first rule for judicial review of tax statutes is that the heavy burden of proof lies on anyone who would challenge any congressional exercise of fiscal power. In almost every decision touching the constitutionality of federal taxation, the Supreme Court has stressed the breadth of congressional power and the limits of its own reviewing powers." [1]

The three major decisions in which the court has sought to restrain the exercise of congressional power in the taxation and monetary area have had relatively little effect and caused the court great embarrassment. In all three instances, the court's decisions were eventually negated.

The court's 1870 ruling that paper money could not be substituted for gold as legal tender in the payment of certain debts was reversed by the court itself within 15 months. Its 1895 decision overturning the imposition of a federal income tax was nullified when the 16th Amendment was adopted. Some 40 years later the court attempted to limit the power of Congress to spend for the general welfare, striking down the Agricultural Adjustment Act of 1933. But that decision too was soon disavowed by a court faced with President Roosevelt's court-packing plan.

Direct Taxes

While the court has had little difficulty with the meaning of indirect taxes, the definition of direct taxes has been more troublesome. The Constitution is of little assistance, referring only to "capitation, or other direct taxes." Nor is the history of the Constitutional Convention helpful. The apportionment limitation was inserted at the urging of southern states, which wanted to prevent heavy taxation of their lands and slaves, but the convention did not discuss what sorts of levies were direct.

As early as 1796, the government sought court interpretation of this vague phrase in a test case concerning a federal tax on carriages.[2] That the validity of the tax was secondary to securing a definition of direct taxes was evidenced by the fact that the government paid the attorneys on both sides of the issue.[3]

Only head taxes and taxes on land were direct taxes and thus required to be apportioned by population, the court held, finding the carriage tax an indirect use tax. This definition stood as valid for a century until the court in 1895 struck down an income tax as unconstitutional on the grounds that it was a direct tax but was not levied proportionately among the states.[4]

The Income Tax Cases

In the first half of the 19th century, the federal government's revenue needs were modest, easily met by excise taxes and duties on imports. A federal tax on personal income was first imposed during the Civil War to meet the need for additional revenue. The statute, enacted in 1862, levied a tax on individual incomes in excess of $600; the exemption rose to $2,000 in 1870. The law expired in 1872.

That tax, as applied to attorneys' income, was upheld unanimously by the court in 1881 as an indirect tax. The justices once more agreed: the only direct taxes were head taxes and taxes on land.[5]

During the 1870s and 1880s, little interest was shown in enactment of a second income tax law. But as wealth based on land shifted to wealth based on earnings, the 1890s saw increasing pressure for an income tax. After the depression of 1893 reduced federal revenues, Congress yielded, and in 1894 levied a tax of 2 percent on personal incomes in excess of $4,000. Only about 2 percent of the population earned more than this amount.[6] The tax was immediately challenged.

The First Case. Charles Pollock, a stockholder in the Farmers' Loan and Trust Company, sought to enjoin the New York bank from paying what he considered an unconstitutional tax. He claimed the tax was direct and therefore invalid because it was not apportioned on the basis of state populations. It was clear that both Pollock and the bank wanted the law struck down, and that the case had been deliberately arranged to evade the federal ban on suits seeking to stop the collection of taxes.

Although it generally refuses to hear cases in which the opposing parties have agreed to bring the suit, the court set aside its rule in this instance. Because so much was at stake, Pollock and the bank hired the best available attorneys, and the court allowed the U.S. attorney general to appear in behalf of the law even though the government was not a party to the suit.

Attorneys for Pollock argued two basic points. First they said that a tax on the income from land was indistinguishable from a tax on the land itself, and therefore was an unconstitutional direct tax since it had not been apportioned according to the constitutional prescription. Second, they claimed that even if the tax was indirect it was still unconstitutional because as a tax applied only to incomes over a certain amount it did not meet the uniformity test.

Most historians agree that these arguments were weak at best. But the plaintiff's attorneys also portrayed the income tax as a weapon that could be used by a populist government to destroy private property rights, a political argument calculated to appeal to the more economically conservative justices on the bench. "I believe there are private rights of property here to be protected," the prominent attorney Joseph H. Choate declaimed. The income tax law "is communistic in its purposes and tendencies, and is defended here upon principles as communistic, socialistic — what should I call them — populistic as ever have been addressed to any political assembly in the world."[7]

Only eight justices heard the arguments. Justice Howell E. Jackson was absent, ill with the tuberculosis that would shortly kill him. The court handed down its decision April 8, 1895. Six of the eight agreed with Choate that the tax on the income from land was identical to a tax on the land and was thus unconstitutional. But the eight divided evenly on the issue of whether income from personal property was also a direct tax and whether any part of the law was invalid because it did not meet the uniformity test.[8]

Second Income Tax Case. Pollock's attorneys asked for reargument so that the court might settle these crucial points. The court agreed; the arguments were heard, and a full court rendered its second decision only six weeks after the first on May 20, 1895. By a 5-4 vote, the court struck down the entire income tax law as unconstitutional.[9] (Justice Jackson voted with the minority, which meant that one justice who believed the law constitutional during the first case reversed his opinion in the second. Because there is no opinion written and no breakdown given in split decisions, just who the justice was has been the subject of great speculation.)

Chief Justice Melville W. Fuller, speaking for the majority, first reaffirmed the one point settled in the first case: "Taxes on real estate being indisputable direct taxes, taxes on the rents or income of real estate are equally direct taxes."[10]

Fuller next declared that the majority was "of the opinion that taxes on personal property, or on the income from personal property, are likewise direct taxes."[11] Fuller finally held that the remainder of the law was invalid on the principle that the parts of the legislation were so inseparable that if any of them were voided, all of them must fall. Since "it is obvious that by far the largest part of the anticipated revenue" was to come from the tax on income from real estate and personal property, Fuller said, it was equally obvious that the court's decision to strike down those taxes "would leave the burden of the tax to be borne by professions, trades, employments, or vocations; and in that way what was intended as a tax on capital would remain in substance a tax on occupations and labor."[12]

In this decision, the majority avoided addressing the question of what constituted uniformity for the levying of indirect taxes.

To reach its conclusions in both the first and second cases, the court found it necessary to gloss over the precedents. Fuller said that the court's statement in the carriage tax case — that the only direct taxes were those on land itself and head taxes — was only a comment that did not have the force of law. The decision upholding the Civil War income tax involved a tax on earned income, Fuller rationalized in the first *Pollock* case, not on income from land. In the second opinion, Fuller did not even mention the earlier income tax case.

That the extralegal argument in defense of private property rights had its intended effect was reflected in Justice Stephen J. Field's concurring opinion in the first Pollock case. "The present assault upon capital is but the beginning ... the stepping stone to others ... till our political contests will become a war of the poor against the rich," he wrote.[13]

The four dissenters submitted separate opinions, sharply reproving the majority for disregarding a century of precedent and even more sharply criticizing it for the political implications of its ruling. Justice John Marshall Harlan said it perhaps most forcefully:

> The practical effect of the decision today is to give certain kinds of property a position of favoritism and advantage inconsistent with the fundamental principles of our social organization, and to invest them with power and influence that may be perilous to that portion of the American people upon whom rests the larger part of the burden of the government, and who ought not to be subjected to the dominion of aggregated wealth any more than the property of the country should be at the mercy of the lawless.[14]

The criticism of the court's decision was widespread and blunt. The editor of the generally conservative *American Law Review* wrote:

> ...[I]t appears, at least from one of the opinions which was rendered, that the Justice [Field] who rendered it proceeded with an imagination inflamed by the socialistic tendencies of the law, as involving an attack upon private property; a consideration which lay totally outside the scope of his office as a judge interpreting the Constitution. It is speaking truthfully, and therefore not disrespectfully, to say that some of the judges of the Court seem to have no adequate idea

The 'Income Tax' Amendment

Despite the Supreme Court's 1895 holding that a tax on personal income was unconstitutional because it was an unapportioned direct tax, agitation for an income tax continued. Overburdened by payment of a disproportionately high amount of regressive taxes, such as tariffs, levied by the federal government and incensed at the accumulation of greater and greater wealth by fewer and fewer people, laborers and farmers kept the issue alive, adding each election to the number of Democrats and progressive Republicans in Congress who favored an income tax.

Proposals for an income tax took three forms. One proposition was that Congress simply re-enact an income tax statute and hope that the Supreme Court — with several new justices on it — would overturn its 1895 decision. The second called for adoption of a constitutional amendment to eliminate the constitutional requirement that direct taxes be apportioned among the states on the basis of their populations. The third alternative was to fashion an income tax in such a way that it could be called an indirect excise tax and in that way avoid the apportionment problem.

Little action was taken on any of these proposals until 1909, the first year of William Howard Taft's presidency. When he took office, a two-year long depression had depleted government revenues. At the same time, the Republicans had promised during the 1908 campaign to do something about the high tariffs. When the tariff bill was introduced in the Senate, the Democrats offered an income tax rider almost identical to the one declared unconstitutional. "Instead of trying to conform the amendment to the decision of the Court, the amendment distinctly challenges that decision. I do not believe that that opinion is a correct interpretation of the Constitution and I feel confident that an overwhelming majority of the best legal minds in the Republic believe it was erroneous," said Joseph W. Bailey, D-Texas (H 1891-1901; S 1901-1913), chief sponsor of the amendment.[1]

Fearful that the Democrats and insurgent Republicans had enough strength to pass the Bailey proposal, the conservative Senate Republican leadership coun-tered with a proposed constitutional amendment that would permit an income tax without apportionment. Even if the amendment were approved by Congress, the conservatives did not believe enough state legislatures could be persuaded to ratify it.

The amendment was supported by Taft, who believed that passage of a simple income tax statute would injure the Supreme Court by forcing it to choose between loss of prestige (if it overturned its earlier decision) or loss of popularity (if it found a new income tax law unconstitutional).

Despite their fears that the conservative Republican strategy was correct and that the states would not ratify an income tax amendment, the Democrats and progressive Republicans nonetheless favored the amendment in principle and felt bound to vote for it. It passed the Senate on a 77-0 vote in July 1909. The House approved the amendment a week later on a 318-14 vote.

Contrary to expectation, state legislatures did approve the amendment; it became the 16th Amendment to the Constitution on Feb. 25, 1913.

In November 1912, the Democrats won majorities in both houses of Congress. They quickly passed a law reducing tariffs on a number of imports and made up the consequent deficit in revenue by enacting an income tax law. The statute levied a 1 percent tax on all net income above $3,000 for individuals and above $4,000 for married couples living together. An additional graduated tax was levied on incomes above $20,000. According to the Internal Revenue Service, 437,036 income tax returns were filed for 1916, the first tax year.[2] The court had upheld the income tax law in a series of three 1916 cases.

The 16th Amendment was the third constitutional amendment ratified especially to overturn a decision of the Supreme Court. The 11th Amendment was passed to nullify the decision in *Chisholm v. Georgia* (1793) that allowed a citizen of another state or a foreign citizen to sue a state in federal court. The 14th Amendment was passed in part to overturn the decision in *Scott v. Sandford* (1857), which held that blacks could not be citizens of the United States. *(Chisholm v. Georgia, p. 303; Scott v. Sandford, p. 135)*

---

[1] Alpheus T. Mason and William M. Beaney, *The Supreme Court in a Free Society* (Englewood Cliffs, N.J.: Prentice-Hall Inc., 1959), p. 133. Other sources of information for this material include Alfred H. Kelly and Winfred A. Harbison, *The American Constitution; Its Origins and Development,* 5th ed. (New York: W.W. Norton & Com-pany Inc., 1976); Sidney Ratner, *American Taxation: Its History as a Social Force in Democracy* (New York: W.W. Norton & Company Inc., 1942).

[2] Conversation with the Statistics of Income Branch, Statistics Division, Internal Revenue Service, Sept. 19, 1978.

---

of the dividing line between judicial and legislative power, and seem to be incapable of restraining themselves to the mere office of judge.[15]

Dissatisfaction with the decision resulted 18 years later in enactment of the 16th Amendment. The decision also cost the court prestige. Coming in the same year that the court refused to apply the Sherman Antitrust Act to sugar manufacturers and upheld Eugene V. Debs' conviction for his involvement in the Pullman strike, the decision, wrote historian Pritchett, " earned the Court a popular reputa-tion as a tool of special privilege which was not dispelled for forty years." [16]

Retreat. Not deaf to the outcry, the Fuller court did not apply the *Pollock* precedent to succeeding tax cases. Instead the court found the taxes on certain kinds of incomes "incidents of ownership" and thus excise or indirect taxes rather than direct taxes. This reasoning was applied to uphold taxes on commodity exchange sales, inheritances, tobacco and stock sales.[17] The Fuller court also considered indirect a tax on the business of refining sugar that was determined by gross receipts from the sale of sugar.[18] These modifications allowed the court in 1911 to call a tax on corporate income an excise tax "measured by income" on the privilege of doing business.[19]

Ratification of the 16th Amendment in 1913 gave Congress power to impose taxes on income "from whatever source derived, without apportionment among the several States, and without regard to any census or enumerations." *(Passage of amendment, box, p. 111)*

Congress later in that year enacted an income tax law that was upheld by the court in 1916.[20] Implicitly criticizing its 1895 position, the court said that the 16th Amendment gave Congress no new powers of taxation but simply guaranteed that the income tax would never again be "taken out of the category of indirect taxation to which it inherently" belongs.[21]

After 1916 the court's concern shifted from whether a tax was direct or indirect to a determination of what was properly considered income. A major case in this category was *Eisner v. Macomber* (1920) in which the court invalidated a section of the income tax law providing that "a stock dividend shall be considered income, to the amount of its cash value." The court held that stock dividends (as opposed to cash dividends) could not be treated as income. Instead they were capital, and taxes on them were direct and had to be apportioned. Only when the dividends were converted or sold, did they become taxable as income. This holding has been modified, but its basic premise was still operative in the late 1970s.[22]

Uniformity

In 1884 the court held that a tax met the Constitution's requirement of uniformity if it operated the same upon all subjects being taxed. A tax, the court held in the *Head Money Cases,* was not non-uniform simply because the subject being taxed was not distributed uniformly throughout the United States.[23]

The question whether the tax rate had to be uniform — left unanswered in the income tax cases — was finally settled in 1900. Congress had imposed an inheritance tax during the Spanish-American War on legacies of more than $10,000; the tax rate varied with the amount of the bequest and the relationship of the heir to the deceased. The law was challenged on grounds that if it was a direct tax, it was not apportioned, and if it was an indirect tax, it was not uniform.

The court ruled that the tax was indirect, but was uniform within the meaning of the Constitution so long as it applied in the same manner to the same class throughout the United States.[24]

In 1927, the court held that geographic uniformity was not violated by the fact that Florida residents were not able to take advantage of a federal tax deduction for state inheritance taxes because that state did not impose such a tax.[25]

Taxing as Police Power

Since the inception of the nation Congress has used the taxing power as a tool of regulation as well as a source of revenue. The protective tariff was an early example of a regulatory tax.

The second statute passed by the First Congress provided that "it is necessary for the support of government, for the discharge of the debts of the United States and the

Fruit or Vegetable?

The tomato is a vegetable, not a fruit, declared the Supreme Court in a 19th century tariff case. The question arose because fruits could be imported duty-free under an 1883 tariff act, but vegetables were required to pay a duty equal to 10 percent of their value.

Maintaining that tomatoes were fruits, an importer sued the New York port collector to recover back duties. But in the 1893 case of *Nix v. Hedden* (149 U.S. 305), the court held that tomatoes were vegetables. Delivering the opinion of the court, Justice Horace Gray wrote:

Botanically speaking, tomatoes are the fruit of a vine, just as are cucumbers, squashes, beans and peas. But in the common language of the people, whether sellers or consumers of provisions, all these are vegetables, which are grown in kitchen gardens, and which, whether eaten cooked or raw, are, like potatoes, carrots, parsnips, turnips, beets, cauliflower, cabbage, celery and lettuce, usually served at dinner in, with, or after the soup, fish or meats which constitute the principal part of the repast, and not, like fruits generally, as dessert.

encouragement and protection of manufacturers, that duties be laid on goods, wares and merchandise imported."

The validity of such tariffs was much debated and not conclusively settled until 1928. Writing for the court then, Chief Justice William Howard Taft said:

Whatever we may think of the wisdom of a protection policy, we cannot hold it unconstitutional. So long as the motive of Congress and the effect of its legislative action are to secure revenue for the benefit of the general government, the existence of other motives in the selection of the subject of taxes cannot invalidate Congressional action.[26]

When the tax power has been used as a regulatory tool to support or enforce another constitutional power the court has generally sustained it, even if the tax was designed to eliminate the matter taxed. A landmark decision illustrating this view is *Veazie Bank v. Fenno,* decided in 1869.[27]

Congress had placed a 10 percent tax on the circulation of state bank notes in order to give the untaxed national bank notes the competitive edge and drive the state notes out of the market. The court upheld the statute on the ground that it was a legitimate means through which Congress could exercise its constitutional authority to regulate the currency.

The taxing power has also been upheld as an auxiliary to the commerce power. In 1884, the court held that a 50-cent tax on each immigrant levied on shipowners and used to support indigent immigrants was not a use of the tax power as such but rather the exercise of the foreign commerce power.[28] *(Foreign commerce power, box, p. 100)*

In 1940 the court upheld the Bituminous Coal Act of 1937, which imposed a stiff tax on sales of coal in interstate commerce but exempted those producers who agreed to abide by industry price and competition regulations. The court acknowledged that the exemption was intended to force compliance with the code, but said that Congress "may impose penalties in aid of the exercise of any of its enumerated powers," in this case, the commerce clause.[29]

The 1940 ruling effectively overturned the court's decision in *Carter v. Carter Coal Co.* (1936), which held a similar tax in the 1935 Bituminous Coal Conservation Act to be an unconstitutional penalty for non-compliance with the industry regulations rather than a tax designed to raise revenues. [30] *(Details of Carter case, p. 98)*

Colored Oleo

Where the Congress used the taxing power on its own to achieve a desired social or economic goal, the court developed two distinct lines of precedents, just as it had in its early review of the use of the commerce power as a policing mechanism.

The first line essentially held that so long as the tax produced some revenue, the court would not examine the motives behind its imposition.

Thus, just one year after the court sustained use of the commerce power as a police tool in the Lottery Case, it upheld use of the taxing power to attain similar objectives. *McCray v. United States* (1904) involved a federal statute that placed a 10-cents-a-pound tax on oleo colored yellow to resemble butter, but only a 1/4-cent-a-pound tax on un-

---

Separability: Divided It Stands

Separability is the capability of the remaining portions of a statute to stand on their own if one part has been found invalid. If the capability is lacking, a court may declare the entire statute void because of a single flawed provision. As one authority wrote:

> ...Whether or not the judicial determination of partial validity will so disembowel the legislation that it must fall as a whole, or whether the valid portion will be enforced separately is a question of importance second only to the initial determination of validity. That parts of a statute may be enforced separately provided certain conditions are met has become a fundamental legal concept.[1]

Separability, or severability as it is also called, has grown out of the concept that the judiciary should uphold the constitutionality of legislative acts where possible, bolstered by the presumption that the legislature would not intentionally enact invalid laws.

For a court to find a statute separable, the legislature must have intended that it be separable and the statute itself must be capable of separation. To determine whether legislation meant the law to be severable, the court may examine the act's history, its object, context, title and preamble, as well as the legislatively declared existence of an emergency. Legislative intent was one of the reasons the court gave for striking down the general income tax in 1895. Having declared that the tax on income from property was unconstitutional, the court said that would leave only taxes on occupations and labor, adding: "We cannot believe that such was the intention of Congress." [2] *(Details of Income Tax Case, p. 109)*

Despite a severability clause in the Bituminous Coal Conservation Act of 1935, the Supreme Court in 1936 ruled that the price-fixing provisions of the act were inseparable from the labor regulations provisions which it had declared unconstitutional. "The statutory mandate for a [coal industry] code upheld by two legs at once suggests the improbability that Congress would have assented to a code supported by only one," wrote the court.[3] *(Details, p. 98)*

To be capable of being severed, the valid portion of the law must be independent and complete in itself. If voiding part of the law would defeat or change its purpose, the entire act should be declared void.

The court applied this principle in 1935 when it declared the Railroad Retirement Act of 1934 unconstitutional. Finding certain portions of the act invalid, the court said that those portions "so affect the dominant aim of the whole statute as to carry it down with them."[4] *(Details, p. 89)*

Congress commonly includes a severability or saving clause in its legislation that declares if one part of the statute is found unconstitutional, it will not serve to make the rest of the act invalid. The clause is of relatively modern usage and is not critical to a court determination as to separability. Justice Louis D. Brandeis wrote that the saving clause was sometimes an aid in determining legislative intent, "but it is an aid merely, not an inexorable command." [5]

The general rule followed by the court on separability clauses was enunciated in 1929. When a separability clause is included, wrote Justice George Sutherland, the court begins

> ...with the presumption that the legislature intended the act to be divisible; and this presumption must be overcome by considerations which make evident the inseparability of its provisions or the clear probability that the invalid part being eliminated the legislature would not have been satisfied with what remains.[6]

Riders to appropriations or revenue bills are the most typical examples of severability. For instance, the sections of the 1919 Revenue Act imposing a tax on articles made by child labor were ruled unconstitutional in 1922, but the rest of the statute was unaffected.[7] Robert E. Cushman observes that the court has never invalidated an appropriations or revenue bill because one of the riders was found invalid.[8]

---

[1] C. Dallas Sands, *Statutes and Statutory Construction*, 4th ed. (Chicago: Callaghan & Co., 1973), II: 335.

[2] *Pollock v. Farmers' Loan and Trust Co.*, 158 U.S. 601 at 637 (1895).

[3] *Carter v. Carter Coal Co.*, 298 U.S. 238 at 314 (1936).

[4] *Railroad Retirement Board v. Alton Railway Co.*, 295 U.S. 330 at 362 (1935).

[5] *Dorchy v. Kansas*, 264 U.S. 286 at 290 (1924).

[6] *Williams v. Standard Oil Co. of Louisiana*, 278 U.S. 235 at 242 (1929).

[7] *Bailey v. Drexel Furniture Co.*, 259 U.S. 20. (1922).

[8] Robert E. Cushman and Robert F. Cushman, *Cases in Constitutional Law*, 3rd ed. (New York: Appleton-Century-Crofts, 1968), p. 70.

Crime Pays . . . Taxes

The old saw that crime doesn't pay is not true so far as the Internal Revenue Service is concerned.

The Supreme Court has consistently held that income from illegal activities is taxable. "We see no reason . . . why the fact that a business is unlawful should exempt it from paying the taxes that if lawful it would have to pay," wrote Oliver Wendell Holmes Jr. in 1927.[1] As a result, the court has held taxable the income from illegal sales of liquor, extortion and embezzlement.[2]

If taxes are due on illegal incomes, are illegal expenses, such as bribery, deductible? "This by no means follows," said Holmes, "but it will be time enough to consider the question when a taxpayer has the temerity to raise it."[3]

A taxpayer finally did. In 1958 the court was asked to determine if a bookmaking operation could deduct as ordinary and necessary business expenses the salaries of its bookies and the rent it paid. Both paying employees and renting space to conduct illegal activities were against the law in Illinois where the case arose.

Writing for the court, Justice William O. Douglas held that the expenses fit the meaning of the Treasury regulations regarding taxable income and were therefore deductible.[4]

---

[1] *United States v. Sullivan*, 274 U.S. 259 (1927).

[2] *United States v. Sullivan*, 274 U.S. 259 (1927); *Rutkin v. United States*, 343 U.S. 130 (1952); *James v. United States*, 366 U.S. 213 (1961).

[3] *United States v. Sullivan*, 274 U.S. 259 at 264 (1927).

[4] *Commissioner of Internal Revenue v. Sullivan*, 356 U.S. 27 (1958).

colored oleo. The tax was intended clearly to remove the competition to butter by making it too expensive to manufacture colored oleo. It was challenged as an invasion of state police powers and as a violation of due process.[31]

But the court disagreed, holding that the tax was on its face an excise tax and therefore was permissible. "The decisions of this Court," wrote Chief Justice Edward D. White, "lend no support whatever to the assumption that the judiciary may restrain the exercise of a lawful power on the assumption that a wrongful purpose or motive has caused the power to be exerted."[32]

Similar reasoning was used by the court to uphold the Harrison Anti-Narcotics Act of 1914. This statute required people dealing in narcotics to pay a small annual registration fee and to keep certain records. It also made manufacture, sale and shipment of narcotics illegal.

A five-man majority in *United States v. Doremus* upheld the narcotics registration tax in 1919. "The Act may not be declared unconstitutional because its effect may be to accomplish another purpose as well as the raising of revenue," wrote Justice William R. Day.[33] The four dissenters contended that the tax was an exercise of the police power which they believed was reserved to the states.

Child Labor

This dissenting view in *Doremus* was to become the majority position, beginning the second line of precedents,

in the next major tax regulation case. This reasoning held a tax unconstitutional if its primary purpose was the punishment of a certain action, not the raising of revenue.

Bailey v. Drexel Furniture Co. (1922) concerned Congress' second attempt to end child labor.[34] After the court ruled in 1918 that the commerce power could not be used to reach what many considered a despicable practice, Congress turned to the taxing power, imposing a 10 percent tax on the net profits of any company that employed children under a certain age. Although similar to statutory tax schemes the court had approved before, the court nevertheless declared the tax unconstitutional. *(Commerce and child labor, p. 96)*

Chief Justice William Howard Taft, for the eight-justice majority, said the child labor tax was a penalty intended to coerce employers to end their use of child labor:

> Taxes are occasionally imposed . . . on proper subjects with the primary motive of obtaining revenue from them and with the incidental motive of discouraging them by making their continuation onerous. They do not lose their character as taxes because of the incidental motive. But there comes a time in the extension of the penalizing features of the so-called tax when it loses its character as such and becomes a mere penalty with the characteristics of regulation and punishment. Such is the case in the law before us.[35]

Linking the ruling with the holding in the 1918 case, *Hammer v. Dagenhart*, Taft said that just as use of the commerce power to regulate wholly internal matters of the state was invalid, so was use of the taxing power to achieve the same purpose. The consequences of validating such a law were grave, Taft continued. "To give such magic to the word 'tax,' " he said, "would be to break down all constitutional limitation of the powers of Congress and completely wipe out the sovereignty of the States."[36]

Taft distinguished the ruling in the child labor tax case from the holdings in *McCray* and *Doremus* by asserting that the primary purpose of the taxes in the latter case was to raise revenue. He further distinguished the *Doremus* case by claiming that the regulations outlined in the narcotics control statute were necessary to the collection of the tax "and not solely to achievement of some other purpose plainly within state power."[37]

Commentators have questioned the logic of Taft's reasoning. If it was clear that Congress wanted to stop child labor, it was just as clear that Congress intended to terminate the colored oleo industry and closely regulate the manufacture and sale of narcotics. But the significant factor was Taft's implicit claim that the court would determine when a tax became a penalty; the court would be the final authority in determining the primary motive of Congress in imposing a tax.

Taft reinforced the reasoning laid out in the child labor decision by applying it to a second case decided the same day. In an attempt to stop some unethical practices by some of the commodity exchanges, the Futures Trading Act of 1921 imposed a 20-cents-a-bushel tax on all contracts for sales of grain for future delivery, but exempted those sales arranged through boards of trade that met certain requirements set out in the act.

The court struck down the statute. When the stated purpose of the statute is to regulate the boards of trade, wrote Taft, and when the purpose "is so clear from the effect of the provisions of the bill itself, it leaves no ground upon which the provisions . . . can be sustained as a valid exercise of the taxing power."[38] The court in 1923 approved a second attempt to regulate commodity exchanges when it upheld the Grain Futures Act of 1922 as a valid exercise of the commerce power.[39] (Board of Trade of Chicago v. Olsen, details, p. 92)

The Bailey precedent was applied again in 1935 to invalidate a provision of the 1926 Revenue Act which imposed a $1,000 excise tax on liquor dealers doing business in violation of state or local prohibition laws. The court held that the tax was actually a penalty valid only so long as Congress had the authority granted under the 18th Amendment to enforce nationwide prohibition. When the Amendment was repealed (by adoption of the 21st Amendment in 1933), the court said that the $1,000 penalty also fell.[40]

This line of precedent culminated in two 1936 New Deal cases involving the taxing power. In Carter v. Carter Coal Co., the court struck down the Bituminous Coal Conservation Act of 1935 partly because of its provision reducing a coal tax for coal producers who complied with labor regulations set out in the statute. The court found this provision a penalty on producers who refused to comply.[41] In United States v. Butler, the court invalidated a tax on certain food processors, the revenue from which was used to pay farmers to cut their production of certain foods. The court said the tax was part of an unconstitutional regulatory scheme.[42] (Carter case, p. 98; Butler case, p. 117)

Regulatory Tax Upheld

A few months later, following the proposal of Roosevelt's "court-packing" plan, the court in 1937 abandoned this line of precedent and retreated to that first set out in the oleo case. The court upheld the National Firearms Act of 1934, which imposed an annual license tax on manufacturers of and dealers in certain classes of firearms likely to be used by criminals, such as sawed-off shotguns and machine guns. The act, which also required identification of purchasers, clearly was intended to discourage sales of such weapons.

Upholding the validity of the tax, the court struck directly at Taft's opinion in the Bailey child labor tax case. Noting that the license tax produced some revenue, the court added:

> Every tax is in some measure regulatory.... But a tax is not any the less a tax because it has a regulatory effect, ... and it has long been established that an Act of Congress which on its face purports to be an exercise of the taxing power is not any the less so because the tax is burdensome or tends to restrict or suppress the thing taxed.
>
> Inquiry into the hidden motive which may move Congress to exercise a power constitutionally conferred upon it is beyond the competency of the courts.... They will not undertake ... to ascribe to Congress an attempt, under the guise of taxation, to exercise another power denied by the Federal Constitution.[43]

Taxes on marijuana and on gamblers were subsequently upheld with similar reasoning.[44] However, the statute authorizing a tax on persons in the business of accepting wagers also required them to register with the Internal Revenue Service. The court refused to find the registration requirement a violation of the Fifth Amendment's self-incrimination clause, even where the gambler was doing business in a state that prohibited gambling.

Judges and Taxes

The question whether salaries of federal judges — including those of the Supreme Court justices — are immune from the federal income tax was raised by Justice Howell E. Jackson in 1895 during the court's consideration of the 1890 income tax law.

In a letter to Chief Justice Melville W. Fuller, Jackson asked if the income tax conflicted with the constitutional prohibition against reducing a judge's salary during his term of office. "Does that [1890] Act include our salary as members of the Supreme Court?" Jackson queried. "It seems to me that it cannot. That Congress cannot do indirectly what it is prohibited from doing directly."[1]

The question was put aside after the court declared the income tax unconstitutional, but it came up again shortly after the federal income tax law implementing the 16th Amendment was enacted. In 1920, the court agreed with Jackson's assessment and ruled that the salaries of sitting federal judges were immune from the federal income tax.[2] (Income tax cases, 16th Amendment, pp. 109, 111)

Joined by Justice Louis D. Brandeis, Justice Oliver Wendell Holmes Jr. dissented: "[T]he exemption of salaries from diminution is intended to secure the independence of judges on the ground, as it was put by Hamilton in the Federalist, (No. 79), that 'a power over a man's subsistence amounts to a power over his will. ...' That ... seems to me no reason for exonerating [a judge] from the ordinary duties of a citizen, which he shares with all others."[3]

In 1925 the court expanded this immunity to cover judges who were appointed after the income tax law was enacted.[4] Congress subsequently passed a law providing that salaries of judges appointed after its passage would be subject to the income tax. The court upheld this statute in 1939, specifically overruling the earlier cases.[5]

To impose a non-discriminatory income tax on judges' salaries "is merely to recognize that judges are also citizens, and that their particular function in government does not generate an immunity from sharing with their fellow citizens the material burden of the government whose Constitution and laws they are charged with administering," the court wrote.[6]

Holmes until his retirement in 1925 and Brandeis until his retirement in 1939 voluntarily paid federal income tax.

---

[1] Quoted in Leo Pfeffer, This Honorable Court (Boston: Beacon Press, 1965), p. 223; see also Carl Swisher, American Constitutional Development, 2nd ed. (Cambridge: Houghton Mifflin Co., 1954), p. 437.
[2] Evans v. Gore, 253 U.S. 245 (1920).
[3] Id. at 265.
[4] Miles v. Graham, 268 U.S. 501 (1925).
[5] O'Malley v. Woodrough, 307 U.S. 277 (1939).
[6] Id. at 282.

In 1968 and 1969 the court reversed this part of the decision, holding that registration requirements of regulatory tax laws did in fact compel self-incrimination where the activity taxed was unlawful. These decisions in no way diminished the ability of Congress to use the tax power as a regulatory or penalty mechanism, however.[45] *(Self-incrimination, p. 555)*

Federal-State Tax Immunities

"The power to tax involves the power to destroy," declared Chief Justice John Marshall in 1819 setting out the basis for the major implied limitation on the federal government's taxing power.[46]

Marshall announced this maxim as the court ruled that a state could not tax the national bank, intending by this holding to prevent the states from taxing the new and still fragile central government out of existence. In 1842, federal immunity from state taxation was expanded further when the court ruled that states could not tax the incomes of federal officers.[47]

But the immunity conferred by these holdings cut two ways. In 1871, the court held that the federal government could not tax the income of state officials. If the states could not threaten the sovereignty of the federal government by taxing its officers, instrumentalities and property, then neither could the national government use the taxing power to threaten the sovereignty of the states, declared the court.[48]

For a century the court applied this doctrine extensively. Thus, the court held in 1829 that a state could not tax federal stocks and bonds and in 1886 that a state could not tax federally owned real estate.[49] In 1895 the court ruled, as part of the income tax cases, that the national government could not impose a tax on state or municipal bonds.[50] At various times the most tangential of relationships with one or the other level of government conferred immunity upon the taxpayer. For example, in 1931 a federal tax on the sales of motorcycles to a city police department was held invalid.[51]

But gradually, the court began to limit immunities granted to both the federal and state governments. State immunity from federal taxation was restricted to activities of a "strictly governmental nature." States generally were no longer immune from federal taxation on activities which if performed by a private corporation would be taxable. Federal contractors were much less often granted immunity from state taxation and income tax immunity for state and federal officials was overturned in 1938 and 1939.[52]

As the doctrine of immunity stood in the late 1970s, the federal government was prohibited from taxing state government property and instrumentalities. The most significant of these prohibitions continued to bar federal taxation of state and municipal bonds.

Federally owned property was generally immune from state taxation.[53] States were forbidden to tax congressionally chartered fiscal institutions without the consent of Congress, but state property taxes could be levied on other federally chartered corporations.[54] Income from federal securities and tax-exempt bonds was not taxable by the states although the court has ruled that a state may tax the interest accrued on government bonds and estates that included U.S. bonds.[55]

Government contractors generally were subject to state taxes, even if the taxes increased the cost of the contract to the federal government. States generally, however, could not levy a property tax on government property used by a private person in the fulfillment of a government contract, although a privilege tax measured by the value of the government property held, was permissible.[56] *(Details on intergovernmental tax immunities, see p. 357)*

The Power to Spend

The authority of Congress to appropriate and spend money under the necessary and proper clause to carry out any of its enumerated powers has been broadly interpreted by the court. From the initial days of the union, the power to spend money for internal improvements has been justified by the authority given Congress over war, interstate commerce, territories and the mails.

Standing

Use of the spending power has been rarely challenged, partly because the court has made it extremely difficult for either a taxpayer or a state to bring a challenge into court. In a pair of cases considered together in 1923, a taxpayer, Frothingham, and a state, Massachusetts, questioned the validity of a federal grant-in-aid program, a mechanism whereby the federal government gives the states a certain amount of money, generally for a certain purpose and usually with the requirement that the states must meet certain conditions, such as matching the grant.[57] Such programs were just coming into use and were considered by many an infringement of states' rights.

Because Frothingham's "interest in the moneys of the Treasury . . . is comparatively minute and indeterminate" and because "the effect upon future taxation, of any payment out of the funds . . . [is] remote, fluctuating and uncertain," the court held that the taxpayer did not have sufficient injury to sue.[58] This holding was modified subsequently to permit some taxpayers' challenge. *(p. 291)*

The court also ruled that the state, which had sought to sue in behalf of its citizens, had no standing. "It cannot be conceded that a state . . . may institute judicial proceedings to protect citizens of the United States from the operation of the statutes thereof," the court said.[59]

Challenges to spending for internal improvements or public works projects were also rebuffed by the court. In 1938 the court upheld federal loans to municipalities for power projects, ruling that the state-chartered power companies which had questioned the loans had no right to be free from competition and had not suffered sufficient damages to have standing to bring the case as federal taxpayers.[60] This opinion was reinforced in a 1939 decision.[61]

Grants-in-Aid Programs

The court has also refused to limit congressional use of grants-in-aid programs. The first challenge came in the two 1923 cases and concerned the Sheppard-Towner Act which subsidized state maternity and infant welfare programs. The plaintiffs claimed the grant in aid was a subtle form of federal invasion of state sovereignty and that if a state refused the grant, it was a burden on the state's citizens whose federal taxes supported the grants in participating states.

As already noted, the court ruled that neither the taxpayer nor the state had standing to challenge the statute but, in his majority opinion, Justice George Sutherland added some *dicta* that implied the court would uphold grants in aid as constitutional. "Probably," Sutherland said, "it would be sufficient to point out that the powers of the state are not invaded, since the statute imposes no obligation, but simply extends an option which the state is free to accept or reject." [62]

With the passage of time, Sutherland's *dicta* has gained the force of law. In 1947 Oklahoma challenged a provision of the Hatch Act under which its federal highway funds would be reduced if it did not remove a state highway commission officer who had actively participated in partisan politics in violation of the act. The state challenged this requirement as improper federal control over its internal political matters. The court rejected that claim:

> While the United States is not concerned with, and has no power to regulate local political activities as such of State officials, it does have power to fix the terms upon which its money allotments to States shall be disbursed.[63]

Spending for the General Welfare

Article I, Section 8, Clause 1 also gives Congress the power "to provide for the common defense and general welfare." From the beginning there were differences over what spending for the general welfare meant. One view limited it to spending for purposes connected with the powers specifically enumerated in the Constitution. This was the strict interpretation associated with James Madison. "Nothing is more natural nor common," Madison wrote in No. 41 of *The Federalist Papers*, "than first to use a general phrase, and then to explain and qualify it by recital of particulars."[64]

The other view, associated with Alexander Hamilton, was that the general welfare clause conferred upon the government a power independent from those enumerated. This broad construction came to be the accepted view, but it was almost 150 years before the court found it necessary to interpret the clause.

United States v. Butler

When the court finally did render an interpretation of the general welfare clause in 1936, it gave lip service to Hamilton's stance, but then limited that interpretation by claiming that the power to spend had been combined in this instance with the power to tax to regulate a matter outside the scope of the federal government's powers — agricultural production. In other words, the court said Congress had combined the two powers in an improper exercise of the federal police power.

The question before the court in this case was the constitutionality of the Agricultural Adjustment Act of 1933 (AAA), the New Deal measure passed during the first "hundred days" of Roosevelt's presidency to boost farm prices and farmers' purchasing power. The statute provided that an excise tax would be levied on the processors of seven basic food commodities and the proceeds of the tax would be used to pay benefits to farmers who reduced their production of those commodities. The case of *United States v. Butler* arose when Butler, a receiver for a bankrupt cotton mill company, refused to pay the processing tax.[65]

In addition to determining whether the benefit payment scheme was a valid exercise of the power to spend for the general welfare, the court was also required to choose between two lines of precedent to determine the validity of the tax portion of the statute. Under one set of cases, the court could hold that the tax was a valid excise; under the other, the court could declare the tax invalid because in reality it was a penalty designed to regulate a wholly intrastate matter.

As in earlier New Deal cases, the court chose the more restrictive interpretation. Writing for the six-man majority, Justice Owen J. Roberts said the tax was not a tax in the

The Borrowing Power

As political scientists Ogg and Ray point out in their book, *Introduction to American Government,* the power of the federal government to borrow money is not only "expressly conferred in the Constitution, but is one of the very few federal powers entirely unencumbered by restrictions — with the result that Congress may borrow from any lenders, for any purposes, in any amounts, or on any terms, and with or without provision for the repayment of loans, with or without interest."[1]

The power to borrow is so broad that there have been few challenges to it brought to the Supreme Court. Those that have been heard have resulted in decisions which give the widest possible latitude to the government in exercising the power. For example, the court has struck down state taxes on federal bonds and securities on the ground the taxes would impair the central government's ability to borrow money.[2] *(Details, p. 357)*

The only restriction the court has placed on the power to borrow came in one of the 1935 "gold clause" cases, which held that Congress may not change the terms of a loan.[3] *(Details, currency section, p. 118)*

---

[1] Frederick A. Ogg and P. Orman Ray, *Introduction to American Government* (New York: Appleton-Century-Crofts Inc., 1951) p. 527.
[2] *Weston v. City Council of Charleston,* 2 Pet. 449 (1829).
[3] *Perry v. United States* 294 U.S. 330 (1935).

normal sense of the word but "an expropriation of money from one group for the benefit of another" as part of a regulatory device.[66]

This made the tax unconstitutional under the taxing power, although, Roberts said, it might not be invalid if it were enacted as "an expedient regulation" of another enumerated power.[67] This was not the case here either, Roberts continued. Clearly, the enumerated power could not be the power over interstate commerce since agricultural production was an intrastate matter, he said, noting that the government had not argued the validity of the act on the basis of the commerce power.

Roberts then turned to the benefit payments and the general welfare clause. Reviewing the interpretations placed on the clause by Madison and Hamilton, Roberts concluded that Hamilton's was the correct one. "[T]he power of Congres to authorize expenditure of public monies for public purposes is not limited by the first grants of legislative power found in the Constitution," Roberts declared.[68]

Notwithstanding this point, Roberts next declared the crop benefit payments an unconstitutional invasion of the rights reserved to the states. The AAA, he said:

> . . .is a statutory plan to regulate and control agricultural production, a matter beyond the powers delegated to the federal government. The tax, the appropriation of funds raised, and the direction of their disbursement, are but parts of the plan. They are but means to an unconstitutional end.[69]

In contradistinction to Justice Sutherland's *dicta* in the 1923 grant-in-aid cases, Roberts rejected the argument that compliance with the federal statute was voluntary. "The power to confer or withhold unlimited benefits is the power to coerce or destroy," Roberts said.[70]

He also rejected the contention that the national economic emergency empowered Congress to regulate agricultural production:

> It does not help to declare that local conditions throughout the nation have created a situation of national concern; for this is but to say that whenever there is a widespread similarity of local conditions, Congress may ignore constitutional limitations upon its own powers and usurp those reserved to the states. . . . If the act before us is a proper exercise of the federal taxing power, evidently the regulation of all industry throughout the United States may be accomplished by similar exercises of the same power.[71]

Dissent. For the minority, Justice Harlan Fiske Stone argued that regulation contemplated under the AAA was not accomplished by the tax but by the way the proceeds were used. The same regulation could be achieved by spending any Treasury funds, no matter what their source, he said, adding that the processing tax simply defrayed the public expense of the benefit payments.

Stone also castigated the majority's weakening of the spending power and invalidation of the benefit payments. "It is a contradiction in terms to say that there is a power to spend for the national welfare, while rejecting any power to impose conditions reasonably adopted to the attainment of the end which alone would justify the expenditure," he said.[72]

Butler Abandoned

Stone's dissent presaged the stand a court chastened by President Roosevelt's court-packing plan would take a year and a half later. In 1937 the court upheld in two separate cases portions of the 1935 Social Security Act. Although the court in these two decisions did not formally overturn its decision in *Butler*, it effectively left that decision a dead letter.

The first case, *Steward Machine Co. v. Davis* (1937), was a test of the unemployment compensation provisions of a statute that taxed employers; employers could earn a tax credit if they contributed to a federally approved state unemployment compensation insurance system.[73] The law was challenged on the grounds that the tax was not intended to raise revenue but to regulate employment which was an internal matter for the states and that the states had been coerced into yielding a portion of their sovereignty to the federal government.

The challenges were rejected by a 5-4 vote. Justice Roberts who had written the opinion in *Butler* now joined the majority in minimizing its impact.

Justice Benjamin N. Cardozo for the majority first explained its view that Congress had the power to tax employment. "Employment is a business relation . . . without which business could seldom be carried on effectively," he said, adding that the power to tax business extended to the power to tax any of its parts.[74]

The court found the statute no invasion of states' rights or sovereignty but rather an example of cooperation between the national government and the state to overcome the common evil of unemployment. The statute represented a national means to solve what had become a national problem insoluble by the states acting independently of each other. "It is too late today for the argument to be heard with tolerance that in a crisis so extreme the use of the moneys of the nation to relieve the unemployed and their dependents is a use for any purpose narrower than the promotion of the general welfare," Cardozo wrote.[75]

The justice acknowledged that the tax credit granted on the basis of fulfillment of certain conditions was "in some measure a temptation. But to hold that motive or temptation is equivalent to coercion is to plunge the law into endless difficulties." In any event, Cardozo added, the point of coercion had not been reached in the case at hand.[76]

Nor were the conditions themselves coercive, he continued. The states were given a wide range of choice in enacting laws to fulfill the requirements, and they could withdraw at any time from the state-federal cooperative arrangement.

Cardozo distinguished the unemployment compensation case from *Butler* on two other points. Unlike the agricultural production case, the proceeds from the employment tax were not earmarked for a specific group of people but instead went into the general revenues of the country. In the second place, the states specifically had to approve the tax credit by passing a law allowing it, unlike the AAA which attempted to regulate without permission from the states.

Social Security. In the second case, *Helvering v. Davis,* decided the same day by a 7-2 vote, the court upheld the constitutionality of federal old age benefits.[77] In this opinion, Cardozo acknowledged that in spending for the general welfare, a

> . . .line must still be drawn between one welfare and another, between particular and general. Where this shall be placed cannot be known through a formula in advance of the event. There is a middle ground . . . in which discretion is at large. The discretion, however, is not confided to the courts. The discretion belongs to Congress, unless the choice is clearly wrong, a display of arbitrary power, not an exercise of judgment.[78]

Cardozo then went on to show that Congress had not used its discretion arbitrarily in this case but that the statute was warranted by a need to solve a national problem that the states could not cure individually.

Nor could the states oppose what Congress determined to be the national welfare, Cardozo said. "[T]he concept of welfare or the opposite is shaped by Congress, not the states. So the concept be not arbitrary, the locality must yield."[79]

The Currency Powers

The express power "[to] coin Money, regulate the Value thereof, and of foreign Coin, and fix the Standard of Weights and Measures," has been construed, with one brief but significant exception, to give Congress complete control over the nation's currency.

It was in a decision upholding creation of the national bank, established largely to give some stability to the various state and foreign currencies in use during the union's early history, that John Marshall gave his classic definition of the necessary and proper clause.[80] *(Details, p. 73)*

A national currency as such did not exist until the Civil War when Congress in 1862 and 1863 authorized the printing of paper money or "greenbacks" and made these notes legal tender for the payment of debts. In 1869 the court upheld a federal tax that was intended to drive state bank notes out of circulation and leave a single uniform national currency. [81] *(Details, p. 112)*

Also in 1869, the court ruled that greenbacks could not be substituted as payment in cases where the contract specifically stipulated payment in gold, which was then the preferred medium of exchange.[82] Left unanswered was whether a creditor could refuse payment in greenbacks if the contract did not specify gold payment.

This question was raised as early as 1863 in *Roosevelt v. Meyer,* but the court refused to take the case, claiming it did not have jurisdiction.[83] Constitutional scholar Robert G. McCloskey, in his book *The American Supreme Court,* found this claim contrived. "We must assume," McCloskey wrote, "either that the judges were unfamiliar with the law that furnishes their very basis for being, or that they deliberately chose a Pickwickian interpretation in order to avoid deciding, in wartime, a question so central to the conduct of war." [84] The government had issued the paper money to finance its war debts, including the salaries of its fighting men. It could not have afforded to pay them in gold.

First Legal Tender Case

But when the war ended, the court no longer avoided deciding the issue, at least so far as it pertained to contracts entered into prior to 1862, when the paper currency was first issued. The case of *Hepburn v. Griswold* came to the court in 1865.[85] It was argued in 1867 and reargued in 1868. In the words of court historian Charles Warren:

> The probable action of the Court had been the subject of long and excited debate in the community. On the one side, were the National and the State banks, the mortgagees and creditors who demanded payment in gold; lined up with these interests were those men who, on principle, denied the right of the Federal Government to make paper currency legal tender, and opposed legalized cheating through the enforced payment of debts in depreciated currency. On the other side, were the railroads, the municipal corporations, the mortgagors of land and other debtors who now sought to pay, with a depreciated legal tender currency, debts contracted on a gold basis before the war; and with these interests, there were associated all those men who felt strongly that the Government ought not to be deprived of a power which they considered so necessary to its existence in time of war.[86]

Not until Feb. 7, 1870, was the court ready to deliver its opinion. At the time the court had only seven justices. (Congress in 1866 had reduced the size of the court to deprive President Andrew Johnson of an appointment. When Ulysses S. Grant succeeded to the presidency, Congress returned the number of justices to nine, but then refused to confirm Grant's first nominee, Attorney General Ebenezer R. Hoar. And a week before the court announced its *Hepburn* decision, Justice Robert C. Grier retired.)

Thus it was by a 4-3 split that the court invalidated the law. It was the third major act of Congress the court had found unconstitutional. *(Box, next page)*

Rejecting the government's claim that the legal tender laws were a valid means of exercising the war power, the court ruled against the constitutionality of using paper money to pay debts contracted prior to 1862. The opinion was delivered by Chief Justice Salmon P. Chase, who, ironically, as President Lincoln's secretary of the Treasury, had advocated enactment of the legal tender statutes. Lincoln in fact had nominated Chase to the court because, he said, "we wish for a Chief Justice who will sustain what has been done in regard to emancipation and the legal tenders." [87]

For the court, Chase acknowledged that Congress in the exercise of its express powers had the unrestricted right to choose "among means appropriate, plainly adapted, really calculated." [88] But, he said, it was up to the court, not Congress, to decide whether the means chosen was appropriate.

Chase denied that the express power to issue currency implied a power to make that currency legal tender in the payment of debts. Furthermore, Chase said, whatever benefit might come from allowing paper money to be used as legal tender was "far more than outweighed by the losses of property, the derangement of business, the fluctuations of currency and values, and the increase of prices to the people and the government and the long train of evils which flow from the use of irredeemable paper money." [89]

Given that, Chase continued, "[W]e are unable to persuade ourselves that an expedient of this sort is an appropriate and plainly adapted means for the execution of the power to declare and carry on war." [90] Thus Chase concluded that the statutes were not an appropriate use of Congress' implied powers under the necessary and proper clause.

Chase then noted that the statute could be viewed as impairing the obligations of contracts. He acknowledged that Congress under its express power to establish national bankruptcy laws incidentally had the right to impair contract obligations. But, Chase said, "we cannot doubt that a law not made in pursuance of an express power, which necessarily and in its direct operation impairs the obligation of contracts, is inconsistent with the spirit of the Constitution." [91] The legal tender acts were also a similar spiritual violation of the Fifth Amendment's prohibition against taking private property for public use without due process of law, Chase added.

Impact. While the decision applied only to contracts made before the paper currency was issued, Chase's reasoning brought into serious question the validity of using paper money to pay debts incurred after 1862. The consequences, if this were found to be true, were grave. The court itself in the very near future would describe them:

> It is also clear that if we hold the acts invalid as applicable to debts incurred ... which have taken place since their enactment, our decision must cause, throughout the country, great business derangement, widespread distress, and the rankest injustice. The debts which have been contracted since ... 1862 ... constitute, doubtless, by far the greatest portion of the existing indebtedness of the country.... Men have bought and sold, borrowed and lent, and assumed every variety of obligations contemplating that payment might be made with such notes.... If now ... it be established that these debts and obligations can be discharged only by gold coin; ... the government has become an instrument of the grossest injustice; all debtors are loaded with an obligation it was never contemplated they should assume; a large percentage

Significant Acts of Congress . . .

Since the Supreme Court first declared a part of an act of Congress unconstitutional in *Marbury v. Madison* (1803), it has found only 105 federal laws to be in violation of the Constitution. Of those, only a handful have been laws of major significance for Congress, the court and the country. Following is a brief explanation of those statutes and the court decisions. *(Full list of all acts of Congress declared unconstitutional, p. 926)*

Missouri Compromise

In *Dred Scott v. Sandford* (1857), the Supreme Court declared unconstitutional the recently repealed Missouri Compromise of 1820, which prohibited slavery in the Louisiana territories lying north of 36° 30'. Chief Justice Roger B. Taney wrote that slaves were essentially property and that Congress had no authority to regulate local property rights. Taney also held that even free blacks were not and could not become citizens of the United States.

The opinion seriously damaged the court's prestige, and rather than settling the slavery question, as at least some of the justices had hoped, the decision probably hastened the onset of the Civil War. The *Dred Scott* decision was undone by the 13th Amendment, ratified in 1865, prohibiting slavery and by the 14th Amendment, ratified in 1868, making citizens of all persons born in the United States and under its jurisdiction. *(Details, p. 139)*

Test Oath Law

The court in 1867 declared invalid an 1865 Act that required attorneys, as a condition for practicing in federal courts, to swear that they had never engaged in or supported the southern rebellion against the Union. In *Ex parte Garland*, the court said that the statute was an unconstitutional bill of attainder because it punished persons by prohibiting them from practicing their professions. The court also held the statute to be an *ex post facto* law because it was enacted after the commission of the offense.

The court's opinion in this case and other cases coming from the states indicated that it would not review other federal Reconstruction legislation favorably. To avoid this possibility, Congress removed the court's jurisdiction to review cases arising under certain of those laws; it is the only time in the court's history that Congress specified a group of laws the court could not review. *(Details, pp. 263, 667)*

Legal Tender Acts

These acts, passed in 1862 and 1863, made paper money a substitute for gold as legal tender in the payment of public and private debts. In the *First Legal Tender Case (Hepburn v. Griswold,* 1870), the Supreme Court ruled that Congress had exceeded its authority by making paper money legal for the payment of debts incurred before passage of the legal tender laws. The outcry from debtors and the potential economic repercussions from this decision were so great that within 15 months the court — with two new members — reconsidered and overturned its earlier decision, thus establishing paper money as a legal currency (*Knox v. Lee,* 1871). *(Details, p. 119)*

Civil Rights Act of 1875

One of several federal statutes enacted in the first decade after the Civil War to end discrimination against blacks, the Civil Rights Act of 1875 barred discrimination in privately owned public accommodations such as hotels, theaters and railway cars. The court held that neither the 13th nor 14th Amendments gave Congress the power to act to bar private discrimination of this type. The decision was one in a series that vitiated Congress' power to enforce effectively the guarantees given to blacks by the two amendments. It would be almost a century before Congress and the court effectively overturned this series of rulings. *(Civil Rights Cases, details, p. 608)*

Federal Income Tax

The court in 1895 struck down the first general peacetime income tax enacted by Congress (*Pollock v. Farmers' Loan and Trust Co.*). The court held that the section of the statute taxing income from real estate was a direct tax and consequently violated the Constitution's requirement that direct taxes be apportioned among the states. This defect, the court held, was inseparable from the rest of the tax provisions and as a result they all fell. The ruling was overturned in 1913 with the ratification of the 16th Amendment specifically exempting income taxes from an apportionment requirement. *(Details, p. 109)*

'Yellow-Dog' Contracts

Exhibiting its early antipathy to organized labor, the Supreme Court in 1908 declared unconstitutional a section of the 1898 Erdman Act making it unlawful for any

---

is added to every debt, and such must become the demand for gold to satisfy contracts, that ruinous sacrifices, general distress and bankruptcy may be expected. [92]

The narrow margin of the vote, and public perception of such horrors as the court eventually described intensified criticism of the court, which was still suffering the loss of prestige resulting from its ill-fated decision in the *Dred Scott Case* 13 years earlier. *(Details, p. 139)*

Even as Chase was delivering the court's opinion striking down the Legal Tender Act, President Grant sent

the names of his nominees to fill the court's two vacancies to the Senate for confirmation. The nominees were William Strong and Joseph P. Bradley. In light of subsequent events President Grant was charged with 'packing' the court with these appointments.

Second Legal Tender Decision

Strong was confirmed Feb. 18; Bradley, March 21. On April 1, 1870, the court announced that it would hear two more pending legal tender cases (*Knox v. Lee, Parker v. Davis*), and in so doing, would review its decision in the

. . . Struck Down as Unconstitutional

railway employer to require as a condition of employment that his employees not join a labor union *(Adair v. United States)*. The act was an infringement on property rights guaranteed by the Fifth Amendment, the court said. Congress also had exceeded its authority under the commerce clause, the court added, because labor relations were not in interstate commerce and did not directly affect it.

It was not until 1930 that the court sanctioned a federal law guaranteeing railway employees collective bargaining rights and not until 1937 that the court acknowledged that labor relations affected interstate commerce. *(Details, p. 88)*

Child Labor Laws

The court in 1918 struck down a 1916 law that sought to end child labor by prohibiting the shipment in interstate commerce of any goods made by children under a certain age who had worked more than a specified number of hours *(Hammer v. Dagenhart)*. The majority said that Congress was not regulating commerce but manufacture, an authority it did not possess. *(Details, p. 96)*

Congress responded by passing a second statute placing a heavy tax on any goods made by child laborers. The court struck down this statute too, declaring that the tax was not intended to raise revenue but to penalize employers of children *(Bailey v. Drexel Furniture Co., 1922)*. *Hammer v. Dagenhart* was specifically reversed in 1941 when the court upheld a federal minimum wage and maximum hour law that applied to both children and adults *(United States v. Darby)*. *(Details, Bailey case, p. 114, Darby case, p. 101)*

Agricultural Adjustment Act of 1933 (AAA)

Designed to restore farm prices and farmers' purchasing power, the AAA levied an excise tax on seven basic food commodities and used the revenue to pay benefits to farmers who reduced their production of the commodities. Striking down the act in 1936, the majority held that Congress had no constitutional authority to regulate agricultural production. The following year, after President Roosevelt's court-packing threat, the majority approved similar tax/benefit schemes when it upheld federal Social Security and unemployment compensation legislation *(Helvering v. Davis, Steward Machine Co. v. Davis, 1937)*. In 1938 Congress passed a second agricultural adjustment act which substituted marketing quotas for the processing tax and production quotas of the first act. This second act was upheld in *Mulford v. Smith* (1939). *(Details, Butler case, p. 117; Helvering, Steward cases, p. 118)*

National Industrial Recovery Act of 1933 (NIRA)

The centerpiece of President Roosevelt's economic recovery program, the NIRA authorized the president to approve industry-wide fair competition codes containing wage and hour regulations. In the Hot Oil case *(Panama Refining Co. v. Ryan,* 1935), the court struck down as an unconstitutional delegation of legislative power a section of the act that authorized the president to prohibit from interstate commerce so-called "hot" oil produced in violation of state regulations controlling the amount of production. The court held that Congress had not drawn specific enough standards to guide the president in exercising his discretionary authority.

The Hot Oil case was followed quickly by the Sick Chicken case *(Schechter Poultry Corp. v. United States,* 1935) in which a unanimous court struck down the entire NIRA, both because it gave the president too much discretion in establishing and approving the fair competition codes and because it exceeded congressional power by applying to intrastate as well as interstate commerce. *(Details, pp. 78, 98)*

Bituminous Coal Conservation Act of 1935

Passed despite the adverse ruling in the Sick Chicken case, the 1935 coal conservation act authorized fixed prices for coal, provided collective bargaining rights for miners, allowed two-thirds of the industry to establish mandatory wage and hour regulations for the whole industry and set up a tax system to ensure compliance with the regulations. Divided 6-3, the court declared the act an invalid delegation of powers to private industry and an unconstitutional extension of the interstate commerce power. While not directly overruled, this case and the ruling in the Sick Chicken case were effectively nullified in *National Labor Relations Board v. Jones & Laughlin Co.* (1937) when the court accepted congressional assertion of its power to regulate intrastate production. A second coal conservation act, enacted in 1937 and omitting the labor provisions, was upheld in the case of *Sunshine Anthracite Coal Co. v. Adkins* (1940). *(Details of Carter case, p. 98; Jones & Laughlin case, p. 99)*

Hepburn case.[93] And on May 1, 1871, by another slim majority, 5-4, the court overruled its earlier decision. The *Hepburn* decision enjoyed the shortest life — 15 months — of any major decision of the court in the 19th century.

Strong wrote the court's opinion in the *Second Legal Tender Cases,* rebutting point by point the arguments Chief Justice Chase had made in the first decision. With regard to the weakest point of Chase's opinion, his claim that it was the court's duty to determine if Congress had used an appropriate means to implement an express power, Strong responded:

Is it our province to decide that the means selected were beyond the constitutional power of Congress, because we may think other means to the same ends would have been more appropriate and equally efficient?... The degree of the necessity for any congressional enactment, or the relative degree of its appropriateness, ... is for consideration in Congress, not here.[94]

No matter where one stood on the merits of the legal tender issue, the court's quick reversal of itself was almost universally deplored. A later Chief Justice, Charles Evans Hughes, was to call the reversal one of the court's "self-inflicted wounds," and a serious mistake with respect to its effect on public opinion.[95] That effect was summarized in the well-respected *Nation:*

The present action of the Court is to be deplored, first, because this sudden reversal of a former judgment which had been maturely considered after full argument, will weaken popular respect for all decisions of the Court including this one; second, because the value of a judgment does not depend on the number of Judges who concur in it — Judges being weighed, not counted, and because of the rehearing of a cause, in consequence of the number of Judges having been increased, is peculiarly, and for obvious reasons, objectionable, where the number is dependent on the will of the very body whose acts the Court has to review, and which in this very case it is reviewing; and third, because the Judges who have been added to the Bench since the former decision are men who were at the Bar when that decision was rendered, and were interested professionally and personally in having a different decision. We do not mean to insinuate that this has affected their judgment, but we do say that it is not enough for a Judge to be pure; he must be likewise above suspicion; that is, he must not only be honest, but must give no man any reason for thinking him otherwise than honest.[96]

The decision in the *Second Legal Tender Cases* was reaffirmed in 1884 when the court upheld the use of legal tender notes in peacetime.[97] The court in 1872 also reaffirmed its 1869 decision that creditors holding contracts specifically calling for payment in gold did not have to accept paper money in payment.[98] As a consequence, more and more creditors insisted on gold clauses and they were eventually contained in almost every private and public bond.

Gold Clause Cases

But in 1933, to counter gold hoarding and exporting and speculation in foreign exchanges, Congress required all holders to surrender their gold and gold certificates to the Treasury in return for an equivalent amount of paper currency. In an effort to raise prices, Congress next devalued the dollar by lowering its gold content.

As a result of these two acts, Congress in a third act then nullified all gold clauses in contracts. The clauses could not be enforced since gold was no longer in circulation, and the statute also prevented creditors from enforcing collection in enough of the devalued currency to make up the value of the gold stipulated in the contract.

The nullification statute was challenged on several grounds — taking private property without compensation, violating the Fifth Amendment's due process clause, and invading the powers of the states. But in a series of four cases, the court handed Congress and the president one of their few victories of the early New Deal period.

In the first two cases, the court upheld the power of Congress to regulate the value of currency. Chief Justice Charles Evans Hughes, who wrote the 5-4 majority opinions in all four cases, said:

We are not concerned with consequences, in the sense that consequences, however serious, may excuse an invasion of constitutional right. We are concerned with the constitutional power of the Congress over the monetary system of the country and its attempted frustration. Exercising that power, the Congress has undertaken to establish a uniform currency, and parity between kinds of currency, and to make that currency, dollar for dollar, legal tender for the payment of debts. In the light of abundant experience, the Congress was entitled to choose such a uniform monetary system, and to reject a dual system, with respect to all obligations within the range of the exercise of its constitutional authority. The contention that these gold clauses are valid contracts and cannot be struck down proceeds upon the assumption that private parties, and States and municipalities, may make and enforce contracts which may limit that authority. Dismissing that untenable assumption, the facts must be faced. We think that it is clearly shown that these clauses interfere with the exertion of the power granted to the Congress and certainly it is not established that the Congress arbitrarily or capriciously decided that such interferences existed.[99]

In the third case, the plaintiff sought to recover the difference between the gold content of $10,000 in gold certificates and the gold content of the currency he had been issued in replacement for the certificates. Chief Justice Hughes explained that the certificates were a form of currency, rather than a receipt for gold, the implication being that Congress could replace the certificates with another form of currency. But the court held that the plaintiff had not sustained sufficient damage to sue in the Court of Claims where the case had originated, and thus avoided deciding whether the gold certificates were actually contracts with the federal government, and whether their required surrender was a violation of due process.[100]

In the last case, the holder of a government bond sued for the difference between its gold value and the amount he had received for it in devalued dollars. In this instance, the court ruled against the government, declaring that although Congress had the right to abrogate the gold clauses in private contracts, it had no power to do so with regard to contracts to which the government itself was a party. Wrote Hughes:

By virtue of the power to borrow money *"on the credit of the United States,"* the Congress is authorized to pledge that credit as an assurance of payment as stipulated, — as the highest assurance the Government can give, its plighted faith. To say that the Congress may withdraw or ignore that pledge, is to assume that the Constitution contemplates a vain promise, a pledge having no other sanction than the pleasure and convenience of the pledgor. This Court has given no sanction to such a conception of the obligations of our Government.[101]

Hughes, however, softened the blow to the government by holding that the plaintiff, as in the previous case, had not sustained sufficient damages to be entitled to standing in the Court of Claims.

Speaking for the four dissenters in all four cases, Justice James C. McReynolds wrote what has been called "one of the bitterest minority opinions ever recorded." [102] "Just men regard repudiation and spoliation of citizens by their sovereign with abhorrence; but we are asked to affirm that the Constitution has granted power to accomplish both," McReynolds lamented.[103]

Footnotes

[1] C. Herman Pritchett, *The American Constitution*, 3rd ed. (New York: McGraw-Hill Book Co. Inc., 1977), p. 167.

[2] *Hylton v. United States*, 3 Dall. 171 (1796).

[3] Alpheus T. Mason and William M. Beaney, *The Supreme Court in a Free Society*, (Englewood Cliffs, N.J.: Prentice-Hall Inc., 1959), p. 129.

[4] See, for example, *Veazie Bank v. Fenno*, 8 Wall 533 (1869); *Schley v. Rew*, 23 Wall. 331 (1875).

[5] *Springer v. United States*, 102 U.S. 586 (1881).

[6] Carl B. Swisher, *American Constitutional Development*, 2nd ed. (Cambridge, Mass.: The Riverside Press, 1954), p. 448.

[7] Quoted in Mason and Beaney, *Supreme Court in a Free Society*, p. 131.

[8] *Pollock v. Farmers' Loan and Trust Co.*, 157 U.S. 429 (1895).

[9] *Pollock v. Farmers' Loan and Trust Co.*, 158 U.S. 601 (1895).

[10] Id. at 637.

[11] Ibid.

[12] Ibid.

[13] *Pollock v. Farmers' Loan and Trust Co.*, 157 U.S. 429 at 607 (1895).

[14] *Pollock v. Farmers' Loan and Trust Co.*, 158 U.S. 601 at 685 (1895).

[15] Editor's Notes, American Law Review, May-June 1895, p. 472; cited in Leo Pfeffer, *This Honorable Court, A History of the United States Supreme Court*, (Boston: Beacon Press, 1965), p. 222.

[16] Pritchett, *American Constitution*, p. 169.

[17] *Nicol v. Ames*, 173 U.S. 509 (1899); *Knowlton v. Moore*, 178 U.S. 41 (1900); *Patton v. Brady*, 184 U.S. 608 (1902); *Thomas v. United State*, 192 U.S. 363 (1904).

[18] *Spreckles Sugar Refining Co. v. McClain*, 192 U.S. 397 (1904).

[19] *Flint v. Stone Tracy Co.*, 220 U.S. 107 (1911).

[20] *Brushaber v. Union Pacific Railroad Co.*, 240 U.S. 1 (1916); *Stanton v. Baltic Mining Co.*, 240 U.S. 103 (1916); *Tyee Realty Co. v. Anderson*, 240 U.S. 115 (1916).

[21] *Stanton v. Baltic Mining Co.*, 240 U.S. 103 at 112 (1916).

[22] *Eisner v. Macomber*, 252 U.S. 189 (1920).

[23] *Head Money Cases*, 112 U.S. 580 (1884).

[24] *Knowlton v. Moore*, 178 U.S. 41 (1900).

[25] *Florida v. Mellon*, 273 U.S. 12 (1927).

[26] *J. W. Hampton Jr. & Co. v. United States*, 276 U.S. 394 at 412 (1928).

[27] *Veazie Bank v. Fenno*, 8 Wall. 533 (1869).

[28] *Head Money Cases*, 112 U.S. 580 (1884).

[29] *Sunshine Anthracite Coal Co. v. Adkins*, 310 U.S. 381 at 393 (1940).

[30] *Carter v. Carter Coal Co.*, 298 U.S. 238 (1936).

[31] *McCray v. United States*, 195 U.S. 27 (1904).

[32] Id. at 56.

[33] *United States v. Doremus*, 249 U.S. 86 at 94 (1919).

[34] *Bailey v. Drexel Furniture Co.*, 259 U.S. 20 (1922).

[35] Id. at 38.

[36] Ibid.

[37] Id. at 43.

[38] *Hill v. Wallace*, 259 U.S. 44 at 66-67 (1922).

[39] *Board of Trade of Chicago v. Olsen*, 262 U.S. 1 (1923).

[40] *United States v. Constantine*, 296 U.S. 287 (1935).

[41] *Carter v. Carter Coal Co.*, 298 U.S. 238 (1936).

[42] *United States v. Butler*, 297 U.S. 1 (1936).

[43] *Sonzinsky v. United States*, 300 U.S. 506 at 513-14 (1937).

[44] *United States v. Sanchez*, 340 U.S. 42 (1950); *United States v. Kahriger*, 345 U.S. 22 (1953).

[45] *Marchetti v. United States*, 390 U.S. 39 (1968); *Grosso v. United States*, 390 U.S. 62 (1968); *Haynes v. United States*, 390 U.S. 85 (1968); *Leary v. United States*, 395 U.S. 6 (1969).

[46] *McCulloch v. Maryland*, 4 Wheat. 316 at 431 (1819).

[47] *Dobbins v. Erie County*, 16 Pet. 435 (1842).

[48] *Collector v. Day*, 11 Wall. 113 (1871).

[49] *Weston v. City Council of Charleston*, 2 Pet. 449 (1829); *Van Brocklin v. Tennessee*, 117 U.S. 151 (1886).

[50] *Pollock v. Farmers' Loan & Trust Co.*, 157 U.S. 429 (1895).

[51] *Indian Motorcycle Co. v. United States*. 283 U.S. 570 (1931).

[52] *South Carolina v. United States*, 199 U.S. 437 (1905); *Helvering v. Gerhardt*, 304 U.S. 405 (1938); *Graves v. O'Keefe*, 306 U.S. 466 (1939).

[53] *Clallam County v. United States*, 263 U.S. 341 (1923).

[54] *Maricopa County v. Valley Bank*, 318 U.S. 357 (1943); *Pittman v. Home Owners' Corporation*, 308 U.S. 21 (1939); *McCulloch v. Maryland*, 4 Wheat. 316 (1819); *Thomson v. Union Pacific Railroad Co.*, 9 Wall. 579 (1870); *Union Pacific Railroad Co. v. Peniston*, 18 Wall. 5 (1873).

[55] *Northwestern Mutual Life Insurance Co. v. Wisconsin*, 275 U.S. 136 (1927); *Miller v. Milwaukee*, 272 U.S. 173 (1927); *Hibernia Savings Society v. San Francisco*, 200 U.S. 310 (1906); *Plummer v. Coler*, 178 U.S. 115 (1900); *Blodgett v. Silberman*, 277 U.S. 1 (1928).

[56] *Alabama v. King and Boozer*, 314 U.S. 1 (1941); *James v. Dravo Contracting Co.*, 302 U.S. 134 (1937); *United States v. Allegheny County*, 322 U.S. 174 (1944); *United States and Borg-Warner Corp. v. City of Detroit*, 355 U.S. 466 (1958); *United States v. Township of Muskegan*, 355 U.S. 484 (1958).

[57] *Frothingham v. Mellon, Massachusetts v. Mellon*, 262 U.S. 447 (1923).

[58] Id. at 487.

[59] Id. at 485-486.

[60] *Alabama Power Co. v. Ickes*, 302 U.S. 464 (1938).

[61] *Tennessee Electric Power Co. v. Tennessee Valley Authority*, 306 U.S. 118 (1939).

[62] *Frothingham v. Mellon, Massachusetts v. Mellon*, 262 U.S. 447 (1923).

[63] *Oklahoma v. Civil Service Commission*, 330 U.S. 127 at 143 (1947).

[64] *The Federalist Papers*, with an Introduction by Clinton Rossiter (New York: Mentor, 1961), No. 41, p. 263.

[65] *United States v. Butler*, 297 U.S. 1 (1936).

[66] Id. at 61.

[67] Ibid.

[68] Id. at 66.

[69] Id. at 68.

[70] Id. at 71.

[71] Id. at 74-75.

[72] Id. at 85.

[73] *Steward Machine Co. v. Davis*, 301 U.S. 548 (1937).

[74] Id. at 581.

[75] Id. at 586-87.

[76] Id. at 589-90.

[77] *Helvering v. Davis*, 301 U.S. 619 (1937).

[78] Id. at 640.

[79] Id. at 645.

[80] *McCulloch v. Maryland*, 4 Wheat. 316 (1819).

[81] *Veazie Bank v. Fenno*, 8 Wall. 533 (1869).

[82] *Bronson v. Rodes*, 7 Wall. 229 (1869).

[83] *Roosevelt v. Meyer*, 1 Wall. 512 (1863).

[84] Robert G. McCloskey, *The American Supreme Court* (Chicago: University of Chicago Press, 1960), p. 112-113.

[85] *Hepburn v. Griswold*, 8 Wall. 603 (1870).

[86] Charles Warren, *The Supreme Court in United States History*, rev. ed., 2 vol. (Boston: Little, Brown & Co., 1926), II:499.

[87] Id., p. 401.

[88] *Hepburn v. Griswold*, 8 Wall. 603 at 622 (1870).

[89] Id. at 621.

[90] Ibid.

[91] Id. at 623.

[92] *Knox v. Lee, Parker v. Davis*, 12 Wall. 457 at 529-30 (1871).

[93] *Knox v. Lee, Parker v. Davis*, 12 Wall. 457 (1871).

[94] Id. at 542.

[95] Charles Evans Hughes, *The Supreme Court of the United States* (New York: Columbia University Press, 1928), pp. 52-53.

[96] *Nation*. April 27, 1871, quoted in Warren, *Supreme Court in U.S. History*, II:525-26.

[97] *Julliard v. Greenman*, 110 U.S. 421 (1884).

[98] *Trebilcock v. Wilson,* 12 Wall. 687 (1872).

[99] *Norman v. Baltimore & Ohio Railroad Co., United States v. Bankers Trust Co.* (The Gold Clause Cases), 294 U.S. 240 at 316 (1935).

[100] *Nortz v. United States* (The Gold Clause Cases), 294 U.S. 317 (1935).

[101] *Perry v. United States* (The Gold Clause Cases), 294 U.S. 330 at 351 (1935).

[102] Alfred H. Kelly and Winfred A. Harbison, *The American Constitution; Its Origins and Development,* 5th ed. (New York: W. W. Norton & Co. Inc., 1976), p. 696.

[103] *The Gold Clause Cases,* 294 U.S. 240 at 362 (1935).

The Power Over Foreign Affairs

The framers of the Constitution viewed foreign policy as the making of treaties and the waging of war. Wary of entrusting all authority for the conduct of foreign relations to the executive, the authors of the Constitution divided these responsibilities between the president and Congress. The president would conduct war and negotiate treaties while Congress would declare war, raise and maintain armies and ratify treaties.

But congressional influence over foreign policy has not been restricted to the exercise of these shared and somewhat limited powers. Congress also has exclusive authority to regulate foreign commerce and has used its other express powers in conjunction with the necessary and proper clause to shape numerous facets of the nation's foreign policy. Despite the widely recognized prerogatives of the president in foreign relations, Congress too has enormous powers to undergird or undercut presidential foreign policy decisions.

While not insignificant, the Supreme Court's role in this area has been a minor one. Challenges to the foreign policy decisions of Congress and the president come to the court infrequently; and the court has rarely curbed the actions Congress has taken in the exercise of its foreign affairs powers.

The War Power

The Constitution divides responsibility for waging war between the president and Congress. The president is commander in chief of the Army and Navy when they are called into actual service, while Congress is expressly granted power to declare war, raise and support armies, provide and maintain a navy and make rules and regulations to govern the armed forces. Congress may also organize, arm and discipline the state militias, but the states have express authority to train them. *(Presidential war powers, p. 185)*

The power of the federal government to conduct war has never been seriously questioned although the source of that power has been disputed. Chief Justice John Marshall implied in *McCulloch v. Maryland* (1819) that the power to declare war carried with it automatically the power to conduct war.[1] Others have contended, as did Justice George Sutherland in the famous *United States v. Curtiss-Wright Corp.* decision of 1936, that the power to wage war is inherent in the fact of the nation's sovereignty and is not dependent on the enumerated powers of the Constitution.[2]

Still others, among them Alexander Hamilton, contended that the power to wage war comes from the enumerated powers amplified by the necessary and proper clause.[3]

Whatever the source of the power, the Supreme Court has been extremely reluctant to place any limits on it as exercised by either Congress or the president. The court with but few exceptions has heard cases challenging the exercise of the war power only after the war has ended and when there was little chance an adverse decision could harm the successful prosecution of the war — or be disobeyed by the other two branches. The court has sanctioned large congressional delegations of power to the executive branch — a wartime delegation of power has never been held unconstitutional — and has supported large-scale intrusions into state sovereignty and the rights of private citizens and corporations. In those cases where it has declared a statute drawn in wartime unconstitutional, it has almost always done so on the ground that the law abused some other power besides the war power. *(pp. 128-130)*

"In short," constitutional scholar Robert E. Cushman wrote, "what is necessary to win the war Congress may do, and the Supreme Court has shown no inclination to hold void new and drastic war measures."[4]

But at least some of the justices have acknowledged the dangers inherent in such an unchecked power. "No one will question that this power is the most dangerous one to free government in the whole catalogue of powers," wrote Justice Robert H. Jackson in 1948. "It usually is invoked in haste and excitement when calm legislative consideration of constitutional limitation is difficult. It is executed in a time of patriotic fervor that makes moderation unpopular. And, worst of all, it is interpreted by the Judges under the influence of the same passions and pressures."[5]

Declaration of War

While the president as commander in chief has the primary responsibility to conduct war, Congress has the express power to declare it. However, it has formally done so in only five of the nation's conflicts: the War of 1812, the Mexican War, the Spanish-American War, World War I and World War II. No formal declaration was made in the Naval War with France (1798-1800), the First Barbary War (1801-05), the Second Barbary War (1815), the Civil War, the various Mexican-American clashes of 1914-17, the Korean War and the Indochinese War.

From time to time the absence of a formal declaration of war has been challenged before the Supreme Court. In 1800, the court held that Congress need not declare full-scale war but could provide for a limited conflict. "Congress is empowered to declare a general war, or Congress may wage a limited war; limited in place, in objects and in time," wrote Justice Samuel Chase in reference to the Naval War with France. [6]

With Congress in recess at the beginning of the Civil War, President Lincoln declared a blockade of Confederate ports in April 1861. In May 1861 he issued a proclamation increasing the size of the Army and the Navy and calling for 80,000 volunteers. He also ordered 19 new vessels for the Navy and requested $2 million from the Treasury to cover military requisitions.

In July 1861, Congress passed a measure acknowledging that a state of war existed and authorizing the closing of southern ports. On Aug. 6, 1861, Congress adopted a resolution providing that "All the acts, proclamations, and orders of the President respecting the Army and Navy . . . and calling out or relating to the militias or volunteers . . . are hereby approved and in all respects made valid . . . as if they had been issued and done under the previous express authority and direction of the Congress of the United States."

The Supreme Court upheld this retroactive ratification in a group of rulings known as the *Prize Cases* (1863). [7] The cases were brought by owners of vessels that had attempted to run the blockade of the southern ports before Congress

---

"No one will question that this power is the most dangerous one to free government in the whole catalogue of powers. It usually is invoked in haste and excitement when calm legislative consideration of constitutional limitation is difficult. It is executed in a time of patriotic fervor that makes moderation unpopular. And, worst of all, it is interpreted by the Judges under the influence of the same passions and pressures."

—Justice Robert H. Jackson
Woods v. Miller Co., 1948

---

acted to ratify the blockade but had been seized and condemned as "prizes." The owners sued for redress on the ground that no war had been declared between the North and the South.

Observing that "civil war is never solemnly declared," the court said that while a president does not initiate war, he is "bound to accept the challenge without waiting for any special legislative authority." [8] Justice Robert C. Grier for the 5-4 majority continued:

If it were necessary to the technical existence of a war, that it should have a legislative sanction, we will find it in almost every Act passed at the extraordinary session of the Legislature of 1861, which was wholly employed in enacting laws to enable the Government

to prosecute the war with vigor and efficiency. . . . Without admitting that such [a ratification] Act was necessary under the circumstances, it is plain that if the President had in any manner assumed powers which it was necessary should have the authority or sanction of Congress, . . .this ratification has operated to perfectly cure the defect. [9]

Although none of them involved declarations of war, the court has ruled in several cases that subsequent ratification of an executive action or appropriation of money to carry out that action is equivalent to a prior authorization of that action. [10] One of these cases involved a challenge to the president's authority to create war agencies under the First War Powers Act of 1941. The court in 1947 said that "the appropriation by Congress of funds for the use of such agencies stands as confirmation and ratification of the action of the Chief Executive." [11]

Modern Undeclared Wars

During debate on the controversial Indochina War of the 1960s and 1970s, it was contended that declarations of war were outmoded, given the existence of modern nuclear weapons and the need to commit troops overseas in emergencies on a limited war basis. Testifying before the Senate Foreign Relations Committee in 1971, Professor Alpheus T. Mason of Princeton University commented:

The Framers, with deliberate care, made war-making a joint enterprise. Congress is authorized to 'declare war'; the President is designated 'commander in chief.' Technology has expanded the President's role and correspondingly curtailed the power of Congress. Unchanged are the joint responsibilities of the President and Congress. The fact that a congressional declaration of war is no longer practical does not deprive Congress of constitutionally imposed authority in war-making. On the contrary, it is under obligation to readjust its power position. [12]

The Supreme Court, however, refused to inject itself in the argument over whether the war in Vietnam should have been formally declared. Lower federal courts in several instances ruled that challenges to the war as undeclared by Congress raised political questions not resolvable in the courts. The Supreme Court refused all appeals that it review the lower court rulings. [13] *(Box, next page)*

The court, however, was not unanimous in its denials. In *Mora v. McNamara* (1967), brought by three enlisted men seeking to stop their transfer to Vietnam, Justices Potter Stewart and William O. Douglas dissented from the court's refusal to hear the case. Whether a president can commit troops to combat in an undeclared war and whether Congress had in effect declared war through resolution and appropriations, Stewart wrote, were

. . .large and deeply troubling questions. Whether the Court would ultimately reach them depends, of course, upon the resolution of serious preliminary issues of justiciability. We cannot make these problems go away simply by refusing to hear the cases of three obscure Army privates. [14]

Douglas in agreement with Stewart quoted from the majority opinion in another "political question" case, *Nixon v. Herndon* (1927):

"That objection that the subject matter of the suit is political is little more than a play upon words. Of course the petition concerns political action but it

Court, Congress and Cambodian Bombing

The Supreme Court's hesitancy to inject itself into controversies between the executive and legislative branches over exercise of the war power was dramatically illustrated by the events of August 1973. In April of that year, Rep. Elizabeth Holtzman, D-N.Y., and several Air Force officers challenged as unconstitutional the continued bombing of Cambodia after the United States had signed cease-fire agreements in Vietnam and Laos. On June 29, 1973, Congress passed legislation cutting off funding as of Aug. 15 for further bombing operations.

District Court Order

One month later, on July 25, Federal District Judge Orrin G. Judd, ruling in the Holtzman suit, issued a permanent injunction halting all military operations in Cambodia after July 27. Judd did not rule on the constitutionality of the military operations, but stated that he found no congressional authority to fight in Cambodia.[1]

Judge Judd rejected the government's argument that earlier congressional actions had, in effect, approved the bombing. The government contended that the failure of the House June 27 to override a veto of a measure immediately cutting off bombing funds and congressional acceptance of the compromise Aug. 15 bombing cutoff date amounted to legislative approval of Cambodian military activities until that date.

"It cannot be the rule," Judd said, "that the President needs a vote of only one-third plus one of either House in order to conduct a war, but this would be the consequence of holding that Congress must override a Presidential veto in order to terminate hostilities which it has not authorized."[2]

On July 27, the effective date of Judd's order, the 2nd Circuit Court of Appeals, acquiescing in a request by the government, delayed the effect of the injunction and agreed to hear arguments Aug. 8 in the government's appeal of Judd's ruling.

To the Justices

Holtzman appealed this delaying order to Supreme Court Justice Thurgood Marshall, asking reversal.

Marshall Aug. 1 refused to reinstate the injunction. Acknowledging that considering the case on its merits alone, he might well find continued combat in Cambodia unconstitutional, Marshall said he could not make such a momentous decision solely on his own authority:

> . . .It must be recognized that we are writing on an almost entirely clean slate in this area. The stark fact is that although there have been numerous lower court decisions concerning the legality of the war in Southeast Asia, this Court has never considered the problem, and it cannot be doubted that the issues posed are immensely important and complex. . . .

Lurking in this suit are questions of standing, judicial competence, and substantive constitutional law which go to the roots of the division of power in a constitutional democracy. These are the sort of issues which should not be decided precipitously or without the benefit of proper consultation.[3]

Holtzman's attorney then appealed Marshall's refusal to Justice William O. Douglas at his home in Goose Prairie, Wash. The attorney flew to Seattle, drove five hours toward Goose Prairie, and walked the last mile through the woods to deliver the appeal to Douglas' cabin. The justice agreed to hear arguments in the matter on Aug. 3. He ruled from his Goose Prairie home later in the day; his opinion was issued early in the morning of Aug. 4.

This was a "capital case" involving life and death, said Douglas, reinstating the order halting the bombing.

Those about to die might be Cambodian farmers or American pilots and navigators. Douglas continued:

> When a [request for a] stay in a capital case is before us, we do not rule on guilt or innocence. A decision on the merits . . . does not precede the stay. If there is doubt whether due process has been followed, the stay is granted because death is irrevocable. . . . I do not sit today to determine whether the bombing of Cambodia is unconstitutional. . . . [D]enial of the application before me would catapult our airmen as well as Cambodian peasants into the death zone. I do what I think any judge would do in a capital case — vacate the stay entered by the court of appeals.[4]

Within 30 minutes of the receipt of Douglas' decision in Washington, the government asked Chief Justice Warren E. Burger to call the full court into session to review the issue and reverse Douglas' ruling. Under the court's procedural rules, this request went back to Marshall.

After talking to each of the other seven members of the court, Marshall later on Aug. 4 reversed Douglas' ruling, again delaying the effective date of the cutoff order.[5]

Holtzman Aug. 6 asked Marshall to send her suit to the entire court. Marshall refused Aug. 8.

Court of Appeals Decision

Also Aug. 8, the 2nd Circuit Court of Appeals, by a 2-1 vote granted the government's appeal and reversed the district court's original ruling halting military operations in Cambodia. The Supreme Court Aug. 9 refused to review the circuit court of appeals' decision.

Although all bombing of Cambodia ceased as of Aug. 15, the congressionally mandated cutoff date, it is interesting to note that the Department of Defense did not comply with Douglas' reinstatement of the injunction halting the bombing even for the few hours it was in effect. During this period, a department spokesman said that "pending appropriate legal action on this matter, we will abide by the congressional mandate to end the bombing on Aug. 15."

[1] *Holtzman v. Schlesinger,* 361 F. Supp 553 (1973).
[2] Id. at 565.
[3] *Holtzman v. Schlesinger,* 414 U.S. 1304 at 1313-14 (1973).
[4] *Holtzman v. Schlesinger,* 414 U.S. 1316 at 1319-20 passim (1973).
[5] *Holtzman v. Schlesinger,* 414 U.S. 1321 (1973).

alleges and seeks to recover for private damage. That private damage may be caused by such political action and may be recovered for in a suit at law hardly has been doubted for over two hundred years . . . and has been recognized by this Court." [15]

Termination of War

The Constitution makes no provision for the termination of a state of war. While the Supreme Court has indicated there must be some sort of formal termination, it has left a determination of the appropriate means to the two political branches. In l948 the court wrote:

> . . .'The state of war' may be terminated by treaty or legislation or Presidential proclamation. Whatever the mode, its termination is a political act. . . . Whether and when it would be open to this Court to find that a war though merely formally kept alive had in fact ended, is a question too fraught with gravity even to be adequately formulated when not compelled. [16]

Raising Armies

Although the federal government conscripted men into the Army during the Civil War, its authority to raise armies through a compulsory draft was not tested in the federal courts until after Congress adopted the Selective Service Act of 1917.

The law was challenged on several grounds, including the allegation that it violated the 13th Amendment's prohibition against involuntary servitude.

In 1918 the Supreme Court unanimously upheld the law in a series of cases known collectively as the *Selective Draft Law Cases.* [17] The authority to institute the compulsory draft, said Chief Justice Edward D. White, was derived from the express war powers and the necessary and proper clause, strengthened by historical practice. It also derived from the nature of a "just government" whose "duty to the citizen includes the reciprocal obligation of the citizen to render military service in case of need and the right to compel it." [18]

Conscription was not involuntary servitude, said White, reaffirming a 1916 decision in which the court held that the 13th Amendment was intended to cover the kinds of compulsory labor similar to slavery and not those "duties which individuals owe to the States, such as service in the army, militia, on the jury, etc. . . ." [19]

The court has never passed on the question of the constitutionality of a "peacetime" draft. Lower federal courts, however, have upheld the draft in the absence of declared war. [20]

Military Justice

In the exercise of its power to govern and regulate the armed services, Congress has established a military justice system complete with its own laws, courts and appeals.

The Supreme Court has held that it has no jurisdiction to review courts-martial through writs of certiorari but may do so through writs of *habeas corpus.* [21] Traditionally, the court has only reviewed those cases challenging the jurisdiction of military courts over the person tried and the crime committed.

The Fifth Amendment guarantee of indictment by a grand jury in any capital case specifically exempts cases involving "land or naval forces, or . . . the Militia, when in actual service in time of War or public danger. . . ." The court also has indicated that such cases might be exempted from the Sixth Amendment guarantee of trial by jury.[22] This has left in question whether a serviceman is entitled to a civilian trial for a capital offense when he is not in actual service and it is not wartime. In deciding this question the court has generally restricted the instances in which courts-martial are appropriate.

In 1955, for example, the court ruled that once discharged, a soldier may not be court-martialed for an offense committed when he was in the service. [23]

In 1969 a serviceman challenged the jurisdiction of a court-martial to try him for a non-military offense (attempted rape) committed off post while he was on leave. In *O'Callahan v. Parker* the court said courts-martial could try only service-connected crimes. The justices did not explain what they meant by service-connected crimes, but in holding that the serviceman had been improperly court-martialed, the majority pointed out that his offense was committed during peacetime in a territory held by the United States, that it did not relate to his military duties and that the victim was not engaged in any military duties, that the crime was traditionally cognizable by civilian courts which were available to try the offense, and that the commission of the crime did not directly flout military authority or violate military property. [24]

In 1971, another serviceman was court-martialed for the rape and kidnapping on a military post of two women, one of whom worked on the base, the other of whom was visiting her serviceman brother. Although several of the conditions present in the *O'Callahan* case were present in this case, the court held that a crime by a serviceman on a military post violating the security of persons or property on the post was service-connected and that he could be court-martialed rather than stand trial in a civilian court. [25]

While the Uniform Code of Military Justice provides many due process rights to servicemen comparable to those enjoyed under the Constitution by civilians, the court in 1976 held that persons undergoing summary courts-martial did not have a constitutional right to legal counsel. [26]

Wartime Legislation

During wartime Congress, often at the president's behest, has adopted legislation placing extraordinary controls and regulations on all phases of the economy, including matters over which the federal government might not have authority in peacetime. Relatively few of these statutes have been challenged before the Supreme Court and in all but a few cases the court has upheld the extraordinary exercise of power.

Civil War

Desperately in need of money to pay the armed forces and to finance the war effort, Congress in 1862 and 1863 passed laws making Treasury notes legal tender. This meant that creditors had to accept paper money, rather than gold or silver, in the payment of debts.

Challenged in court, the statutes were defended by the government as necessary and proper means of exercising the federal powers over war, commerce and the borrowing of money.

Five years after the war had ended, the Supreme Court in 1870 disagreed. It struck down the Legal Tender Acts claiming that they carried "the doctrine of implied powers very far beyond any extent hitherto given to it." [27]

Little more than a year later, the court in 1871 reversed itself and upheld the Legal Tender Acts. That the acts were appropriate to an exercise of the war powers, that they achieved the desired effect was "not to be doubted," the court now said. "[W]hen a statute has proved effective in the execution of powers confessedly existing, it is not too much to say that it must have some appropriateness to the execution of those powers," the majority wrote. [28] *(Details of Legal Tender Cases, p. 119)*

World War I

War measures enacted during World War I authorized the federal government to force compliance with war contracts, to operate factories producing war goods and to regulate the foreign language press. In conjunction with other express powers, the federal government also ran the nation's railroads, censored mail and controlled radio and cable communication.

Among the more important war measures — and the one that most significantly impinged on traditional state authorities — was the Lever Act of 1917, which authorized

---

". . .Congress, in time of war, unquestionably has the fundamental power . . . to conscript men and to requisition the properties necessary and proper to enable it to raise and support its Armies. Congress furthermore has a primary obligation to bring about whatever production of war equipment and supplies shall be necessary to win a war."

—Justice Harold H. Burton
Lichter v. United States, 1948

---

the federal government to regulate all phases of food and fuel production, including importation, manufacturing and distribution.

In 1921, the court held unconstitutional a section of the Lever Act that provided penalties for anyone who sold necessary food items at an unreasonable price. The section was so vague as to violate the accused's right to due process under the Fifth Amendment and the right to be informed of the nature and cause of the accusation guaranteed by the Sixth Amendment, the court said, adding that "the mere existence of a state of war could not suspend or change the operation upon the power of Congress of the guarantees and limitations" of the two amendments. [29] *(See p. 190)*

The decision was of relatively little significance to the war effort since it came three years after the war had ended, and involved language that would have been easily correctable by Congress. In a 1924 case involving a price-fixing provision of the Lever Act, the court, by deciding the case on other grounds, carefully avoided discussing the constitutional issue of whether the government could set coal prices that resulted in uncompensated losses to the sellers. [30] As one commentator wrote, "it is to be noted that the Court avoided an adverse action on the war measure, in a decision handed down more than five years after the cessation of hostilities." [31]

In a third World War I case, the court firmly upheld the federal takeover of the railroads against a challenge

that it violated states' rights. The specific challenge was to the authority of the Interstate Commerce Commission to set intrastate rail rates. In *Northern Pacific Railway Co. v. North Dakota ex rel Langer* (1919), the court wrote that if a conflict occurs in a sphere which both the federal government and the states have authority to regulate, federal power is paramount. [32]

World War II

Mobilization of private industry and delegation of authority to the president to conduct the war were even more extensive during World War II than they had been in World War I.

Among the more important measures passed by Congress were the Selective Service Act of 1940; the Lend-Lease Act of 1941 which allowed the president to ship supplies to U.S. allies; the First War Powers Act of 1941 which gave the president power to reorganize executive and independent agencies when, in his discretion, reorganization seemed necessary for more effective prosecution of the war; the Second War Powers Act of 1942 which gave the president authority to requisition plants, and to control overseas communications, alien property, and defense contracts; the Emergency Price Control Act of 1942 which established the Office of Price Administration to control the prices of rent and commodities; the War Labor Disputes Act of 1943, authorizing seizure of plants threatened by strike or other labor dispute; and the Renegotiation Act which gave the executive branch authority to require compulsory renegotiation to recapture excessive profits made on war contracts.

During the war itself, the Supreme Court agreed to hear only one major case involving these enormous grants of power. *Yakus v. United States* (1944) challenged the Emergency Price Control Act as an unconstitutional delegation of legislative power to the executive branch. [33] But the court upheld Congress' power to delegate to the Office of Price Administration the authority to set maximum prices and to decide when they should be imposed. The Constitution, the court said,

> . . .does not require that Congress find for itself every fact upon which it desires to base legislative action or that it make for itself detailed determinations which it has declared to be prerequisite to the application of the legislative policy to particular facts and circumstances impossible for Congress itself properly to investigate. The essentials of the legislative function are the determination of the legislative policy and its formulation and promulgation as a defined and binding rule of conduct — here the rule, with penal sanctions, that prices shall not be greater than those fixed by maximum price regulations which conform to standards and will tend to further the policy which Congress has established. These essentials are preserved when Congress has specified the basic conditions of fact upon whose existence or occurrence, ascertained from relevant data by a designated administrative agency, it directs that its statutory command shall be effective. [34]

Only if there were an absence of standards for judging whether the OPA administrator had obeyed the will of Congress in administering the law would this price-fixing statute be unconstitutional, said the court. In this case, the court continued, the standards, "with the aid of the 'statement of the considerations' required to be made by the Administrator, are sufficiently definite . . . to enable Congress, the courts and the public to ascertain whether the Administrator . . . has conformed to those standards." [35]

As in World War I, the court avoided answering the question of whether Congress had the authority under its war powers to empower the executive branch to fix prices. But in the postwar case of *Lichter v. United States* (1948), the court gave some indication of how extensive it believed congressional powers during wartime to be:

> . . .Congress, in time of war, unquestionably has the fundamental power . . . to conscript men and to requisition the properties necessary and proper to enable it to raise and support its Armies. Congress furthermore has a primary obligation to bring about whatever production of war equipment and supplies shall be necessary to win a war." [36]

In the *Lichter* case, the court upheld the Renegotiation Act, which authorized the executive branch to recover excessive profits from war industries, against a challenge of unconstitutional delegation of powers. "A constitutional power implies a power of delegation of authority under it sufficient to effect its purposes," the majority wrote. In no less sweeping terms, the majority continued:

> This power is especially significant in connection with constitutional war powers under which the exercise of broad discretion as to methods to be employed may be essential to an effective use of its war powers by Congress. The degree to which Congress must specify its policies and standards in order that the administrative authority granted may not be an unconstitutional delegation of its own legislative power is not capable of precise definition. In peace or in war it is essential that the Constitution be scrupulously obeyed, and particularly that the respective branches of the Government keep within the powers assigned to each by the Constitution. On the other hand, it is of the highest importance that the fundamental purposes of the Constitution be kept in mind and given effect in order that, through the Constitution, the people of the United States may in time of war as in peace bring to the support of those purposes the full force of their united action. In time of crisis nothing could be more tragic and less expressive of the intent of the people than so to construe their Constitution that by its own terms it would substantially hinder rather than help them in defending their national safety. [37]

Postwar Legislation

After the Civil War, the Supreme Court stated that ". . .the [war] power is not limited to victories in the field. . . . It carries with it inherently the power to guard against the immediate renewal of the conflict and to remedy the evils which have arisen from its use and progress." [38] It is this reasoning that has allowed the court to sanction enforcement of measures based on the war powers long after the actual hostilities have ended.

For example, the court in 1921 upheld a federal statute continuing rent control in the District of Columbia first imposed during World War I when a housing shortage occurred in the nation's capital. [39] The court said the statute's extension was made necessary by the continuing housing shortage resulting from the war emergency. However, in 1924 the court denied another extension of the rent control law. [40] "A law depending upon the existence of an emergency or other certain state of facts to uphold it may

cease to operate if the emergency eases or the facts change even though valid when passed," the court said. [41] In this case, the facts had changed — the government was hiring fewer people and there was more new housing available in the district. If an increased cost of living was all that remained from the war, the court said, that was no justification for a continuation of the rent control measure.

The court has also sanctioned a measure based on the war powers but not enacted until after the hostilities had ended. Ten days after the World War I armistice was signed, Congress under color of the war powers passed a law prohibiting the production, sale and transportation of liquor for the duration of the war emergency. Finding that it was within congressional power to require prohibition in order to conserve manpower and increase efficiency during the demobilization period, the court upheld the law in 1919 and 1920. [42]

A similar issue was addressed in the 1948 case of *Woods v. Miller Co.* questioning the validity of a 1947 statute continuing the rent control program established under the Emergency Price Control Act. [43] The court upheld the statute on the basis of the World War I precedents. But Justice William O. Douglas, writing for the majority, added a note of caution:

> We recognize the force of the argument that the effects of war under modern conditions may be felt in the economy for years and years, and that if the war power can be used in days of peace to treat all the wounds which war inflicts on our society, it may not only swallow up all other powers of Congress but largely obliterate the Ninth and Tenth Amendments [reserving rights and powers to the people of the states] as well. [44]

In a separate concurring opinion, Justice Robert H. Jackson also voiced his misgivings: "I cannot accept the argument that war powers last as long as the effects and consequences of war for if so they are permanent — as permanent as the war debts." [45]

Treaty Powers

The original proposal before the 1787 Constitutional Convention gave the Senate sole authority to make treaties with foreign countries. In the final version that power was shared with the president, who had the "Power, by and with the Advice and Consent of the Senate, to make Treaties. . . ." How equal a partner this phrasing made the Senate in the actual negotiation of treaties was debated for several decades. Some senators advocated that the Senate actually direct treaty-making by proposing negotiations. Such initiative, they said, was the right and duty of the Senate under the Constitution, and was helpful in showing that the United States was united in its demands.

This debate was largely laid to rest in 1936 when the Supreme Court declared: "The President alone negotiates. Into the field of negotiation the Senate cannot intrude, and Congres itself is powerless to invade it." [46] *(p. 201)*

But if the president has the primary treaty powers, Congress nonetheless plays a crucial role through Senate ratification, congressional implementation and repeal.

Ratification

Although the Constitution is silent on the subject, the Senate since 1795 has claimed the right to amend and modify treaties once they have been submitted for ratification. Twice this power has been reviewed and sanctioned by the Supreme Court. Speaking in 1869, the court said:

> In this country, a treaty is something more than a contract, for the Federal Constitution declares it to be the law of the land. If so, before it can become a law, the Senate, in whom rests the authority to ratify it, must agree to it. But the Senate are *[sic]* not required to adopt or reject it as a whole, but may modify or amend it. . . . [47]

In 1901, the court reiterated that the Senate might make ratification conditional upon adoption of amendments to the treaty. [48]

Congressional Implementation

Some treaties are self-executing, and when ratified become the law of the land equivalent to legislative acts. Others once ratified still require Congress to pass enabling legislation to carry out the terms and conditions of the treaty. Chief Justice John Marshall in 1829 described the kinds of treaties needing additional implementation as those where "the terms of the stipulation import a contract — when either of the parties engages to perform a particular act — the treaty addresses itself to the political . . . department; and the legislature must execute the contract, before it can become a rule for the Court." [49]

If the treaty deals with a subject outside the coverage of its enumerated powers, Congress may use its authority under the necessary and proper clause to justify enactment of implementing legislation. It is under this authority that Congress, for example, has conferred judicial power upon American consuls abroad to be exercised over American citizens and has provided for foreign extradition of fugitives from justice. Without a treaty on these subjects, Congress would have no power to act.

An extreme example of this use of the necessary and proper clause in conjunction with treaty-making came in *Missouri v. Holland* (1920). [50] Congress wished to protect certain migratory birds from hunters. When lower federal courts ruled an act of Congress to this effect unconstitutional as an invasion of state sovereignty, the federal government negotiated a treaty with Canada for the protection of the birds. The Senate ratified it and Congress again passed legislation barring hunting of the birds and providing other protections. Because this legislation was to implement the treaty, the Supreme Court upheld it:

> . . .We do not mean to imply that there are no qualifications to the treaty-making power; but they must be ascertained in a different way. It is obvious that there may be matters of the sharpest exigency for the national well-being that an act of Congress could not deal with but that a treaty followed by such an act could, and it is not lightly to be assumed, that in matters requiring national action, "a power which must belong to and somewhere reside in every civilized government" is not to be found. . . . [51]

Several commentators have noted that this opinion "is one of the most far-reaching assertions of national power in our constitutional history." [52]

Historians Alfred Kelly and Winfred Harbison found the implications of the case "astounding. If a treaty could accomplish anything of a national character so long as its subject matter were plausibly related to the general welfare, what limits were there to federal authority, if exercised in pursuance of the treaty-making power?" [53]

No House Treaty Role

An attempt by members of the House of Representatives to gain for that chamber a role in the ratification of the controversial treaty ceding to Panama the Panama Canal and the Canal Zone came to naught in April 1978.

Sixty House members opposed to the treaty argued that because the United States owned the property in question, both the House and Senate needed to give their consent to the disposal of that land, as required by Article IV, Section 3, clause 2 of the Constitution.

A divided Court of Appeals for the District of Columbia held that the Article IV grant was not an "exclusive power" and that the constitutional grant authorizing the Senate to ratify treaties also carried the power to dispose of U.S. property (*Edwards v. Carter*, 1978). The majority wrote:

> [I]t seems that, on its face, the Property Clause is intended not to restrict the scope of the Treaty Clause, but, rather, is intended to permit Congress to accomplish through legislation what may concurrently be accomplished through other means provided by the Constitution.

In dissent, Judge George MacKinnon claimed that the treaty would violate the Constitution and disenfranchise the 435 members of the House of Representatives from voting as members of Congress upon the proposal to dispose of $8 billion dollars worth of canal property belonging to the United States.

Repeal

The court has ruled that a treaty may supersede a prior act of Congress and that an act of Congress may in effect repeal prior treaties or parts of them. [54] In the *Head Money Cases* (1884), the court wrote that there was nothing in a treaty that made it

> . . .irrepealable or unchangeable. The Constitution gives it no superiority over an act of Congress in this respect, which may be repealed or modified by an act of Congress of a later date. Nor is there anything in its essential character, or in the branches of the government by which the treaty is made, which gives it this superior sanctity. . . . In short, we are of opinion that, so far as a treaty made by the United States with any foreign nation can become the subject of judicial cognizance in the courts of this country, it is subject to such acts as Congress may pass for its enforcement, modification or repeal. [55]

Other Foreign Policy Powers

In addition to its war and treaty powers, Congress, as Louis Henkin points out, has general powers that

> . . .enable it to reach virtually where it will in foreign as in domestic affairs, subject only to constitutional prohibitions protecting human rights. The power to tax (Article I, Section 8, Clause 1) has long been a power to regulate through taxation. . . . Major programs depend wholly on the 'spending power' . . . — to 'provide for the common Defence and general Welfare of the

United States' — and it has been used in our day for billions of dollars in foreign aid.

Other, specialized powers also have their international uses: Congress has authorized a network of international agreements under its postal power (Article I, Section 8, Clause 7), and there are international elements in the regulation of patents and copyrights. The express power to govern territory (Article IV, Section 3) may imply authority to acquire territory, and Congress determines whether territory acquired shall be incorporated into the United States. Congress can exercise 'exclusive legislation' in the nation's capital, its diplomatic headquarters (Article I, Section 8, Clause 17). The power to acquire and dispose of property has supported lend-lease and other arms programs and sales or gifts of nuclear reactors or fissionable materials. . . . By implication in the Constitution's grant of maritime jurisdiction to the federal judiciary (Article III, Section 2), Congress can legislate maritime law. . . .[56] *(Box on maritime law, p. 86)*

In addition, the fact that the appointment of ambassadors, public ministers and other diplomatic officers requires the advice and consent of the Senate gives that body a degree of control over foreign relations. The power to appropriate funds for defense, war and general execution of foreign policy rests solely with Congress.

In those cases where it has reviewed these powers the Supreme Court has supported their exercise. For instance, regulation of foreign imports through tariffs was upheld in 1928.[57] As early as 1828 the court endorsed the power to acquire territory through conquest or treaty and in 1883 it supported the power to acquire territory through discovery.[58] In a series of cases in the early 1900s, the court left it up to Congress to determine whether to incorporate a territory into the United States.[59] The power of Congress to dispose of federal property was deemed absolute in 1840.[60] *(Tariffs, p. 112; incorporation of territory, p. 138; property disposal, p. 140)*

The court has never invalidated a spending program or appropriation passed for the common defense.

Footnotes

[1] *McCulloch v. Maryland*, 4 Wheat. 316 (1819).

[2] *United States v. Curtiss-Wright Export Corp.*, 299 U.S. 304 (1936).

[3] *The Federalist Papers*, with an Introduction by Clinton Rossiter (New York, Mentor, 1961), No. 23, p. 152.

[4] Robert E. Cushman, *Leading Constitutional Decisions*, 12th ed. (New York: Appleton-Century-Crofts, 1963), p. 373.

[5] *Woods v. Miller Co.*, 333 U.S. 138 at 147 (1948).

[6] *Bas v. Tingy*, 4 Dall. 37 at 43 (1800).

[7] *Prize Cases*, 2 Black 635 (1863).

[8] Id. at 666.

[9] Id. at 670-71.

[10] See, for example, *Wilson v. Shaw*, 204 U.S. 24 (1907); *Brooks v. Dewar*, 313 U.S. 354 (1941); *Isbrandtsen-Moller Co. v. United States*, 300 U.S. 139 (1937).

[11] *Fleming v. Mohawk Wrecking Co.*, 331 U.S. 111 at 116 (1947).

[12] Senate Foreign Relations Committee, Hearings on War Power Legislation, 91st Congress, 1st Session, 1971 (Washington, Government Printing Office, 1972), p. 254.

[13] See, for example, *Luftig v. McNamara*, 373 F. 2d 664 (D.C. Cir.), cert. denied, 387 U.S. 945 (1967); *Mora v. McNamara*, 387 F. 2d 862 (D.C. Cir.), cert. denied, 389 U.S. 934 (1967).

[14] *Mora v. McNamara*, 389 U.S. 934 at 935 (1967).

[15] Id. at 939, quoting from *Nixon v. Herndon*, 273 U.S. 536 at 540 (1927).

[16] *Ludecke v. Watkins*, 335 U.S. 160 at 168-69 (1948).

[17] *Selective Draft Law Cases*, 245 U.S. 366 (1918).

[18] Id. at 378.

[19] *Butler v. Perry*, 240 U.S. 328 at 333 (1916).

[20] See, for example, *Hart v. United States*, 382 F 2d 1020 (C.A. 3, 1967), cert. denied 391 U.S. 956 (1968); *United States v. Holmes*, 387 F 2d 781 (C.A. 7, 1967), cert. denied, 391 U.S. 936 (1968).

[21] *Ex parte Vallandigham*, 1 Wall. 243 (1864); *Ex parte Milligan*, 4 Wall. 2 (1866); *Ex parte Yerger*, 8 Wall. 85 (1869); *Ex parte Reed*, 100 U.S. 13 (1879).

[22] *Ex parte Milligan*, 4 Wall. 2 (1866); *Ex parte Quirin*, 317 U.S. 1 (1942).

[23] *United States ex rel Toth v. Quarles*, 350 U.S. 11 (1955).

[24] *O'Callahan v. Parker*, 395 U.S. 258 (1969).

[25] *Relford v. Commandant*, 401 U.S. 355 (1971).

[26] *Middendorf v. Henry*, 425 U.S. 25 (1976).

[27] *Hepburn v. Griswold*, 8 Wall. 603 at 617 (1870).

[28] *Knox v. Lee, Parker v. Davis*, 12 Wall. 457 at 543 (1871).

[29] *United States v. Cohen Grocery Co.*, 255 U.S. 81 at 88 (1921).

[30] *Matthew Addy Co. v. United States*, 264 U.S. 239 (1924).

[31] Carl B. Swisher, *American Constitutional Development*, 2nd ed. (Cambridge: Houghton Mifflin Co., The Riverside Press, 1954), p. 638, n. 51.

[32] *Northern Pacific Railway Co. v. North Dakota ex rel Langer*, 250 U.S. 135 (1919).

[33] *Yakus v. United States*, 321 U.S. 414 (1944).

[34] Id. at 424.

[35] Id. at 426.

[36] *Lichter v. United States*, 334 U.S. 742 at 765-66 (1948).

[37] Id. at 778-80.

[38] *Stewart v. Kahn*, 11 Wall. 493 at 507 (1871).

[39] *Block v. Hirsh*, 256 U.S. 135 (1921).

[40] *Chastleton Corp. v. Sinclair*, 264 U.S. 543 (1924).

[41] Id. at 547-48.

[42] *Hamilton v. Kentucky Distilleries and Warehouse Co.*, 251 U.S. 146 (1919); *Ruppert v. Caffey*, 251 U.S. 264 (1920).

[43] *Woods v. Miller Co.*, 333 U.S. 138 (1948).

[44] Id. at 143-44.

[45] Id. at 147.

[46] *United States v. Curtiss-Wright Export Corp.*, 299 U.S. 304 at 319 (1936).

[47] *Haver v. Yaker*, 9 Wall. 32 at 35 (1869).

[48] *Fourteen Diamond Rings v. United States*, 183 U.S. 176 (1901).

[49] *Foster v. Neilson*, 2 Pet. 253 at 314 (1829).

[50] *Missouri v. Holland*, 252 U.S. 416 (1920).

[51] Id. at 433.

[52] Henry Steele Commager, *Documents of American History*, 9th ed. 2 vols. (Englewood Cliffs, N.J.: Prentice-Hall Inc., 1973), II:163.

[53] Alfred H. Kelly and Winfred A. Harbison, *The American Constitution; Its Origins and Development*, 5th ed. (New York: W. W. Norton & Co. Inc., 1976), p. 644.

[54] *The Cherokee Tobacco*, 11 Wall. 616 (1871); *Foster v. Neilson*, 2 Pet. 253 (1829).

[55] *Head Money Cases*, 112 U.S. 580 at 599 (1884).

[56] Louis Henkin, *Foreign Affairs and the Constitution* (New York: W. W. Norton & Co. Inc., Norton Library, 1975), p. 76-77.

[57] *J. W. Hampton Jr. & Co. v. United States*, 276 U.S. 394 (1928).

[58] *American Insurance Co. v. Canter*, 1 Pet. 511 (1828); *United States v. Jones*, 109 U.S. 513 (1883).

[59] *Downes v. Bidwell*, 182 U.S. 244 (1901); *Dorr v. United States*, 195 U.S. 138 (1904).

[60] *United States v. Gratiot*, 14 Pet. 526 (1840).

The Power to Admit States, Govern Territories and Grant Citizenship

The Constitution gives Congress the authority to admit new states, govern territories and establish uniform rules for naturalization of foreign-born persons as citizens.

These three seemingly straightforward grants of power have raised some of the most difficult questions the court has ever been asked to answer. One of these was whether Congress had the power to prohibit slavery in the territories. A second was whether the residents of territories automatically enjoyed the rights and privileges guaranteed by the Constitution. A third question was who qualified for citizenship in the United States. And a fourth, still not finally resolved, is whether Congress may revoke a person's citizenship against his or her will.

New States

Article IV, Section 3 of the Constitution gives Congress the power to admit new states to the Union so long as it does not form a new state by dividing an existing state or by joining parts or all of two or more states without their consent.

Five states have been formed from land that was originally part of the first 13 states. In the first four cases — Vermont, Maine, Kentucky and Tennessee — the ceding states agreed to the division. The fifth state, West Virginia, was formed when the western counties of Virginia that wanted to remain in the Union split away from the rest of the state, which had joined the Confederacy. A special legislature comprised of persons from the western counties was convened to give its approval to the split, but Virginia did not formally agree until after the Civil War concluded. Texas was an independent nation before its admission to the Union in 1845 and California was carved from a region ceded by Mexico in 1848. The remaining 30 states all spent some time as territories before being granted statehood. [1]

Equal Footing

When it adopted the Northwest Ordinance of 1787 providing for the eventual transition of the Northwest Territory into states, the Confederation Congress stipulated that these new states would enter the union on equal footing in all respects with the original states. The Constitutional Convention formally rejected insertion of a similar phrase into Article IV, Section 3, but the "equal footing" principle, at least as it concerns political standing and sovereignty has nevertheless remained a valid guide for Congress and the courts.

Thus, in *Pollard v. Hagan* (1845), the court declared that the "right of . . . every . . . new state to exercise all the powers of government, which belong to and may be exercised by the original states of the Union, must be admitted, and remain unquestioned." [2] "Equality of constitutional right and power is the condition of all the States of the Union, old and new," the court declared again in 1883. [3]

Relying on the equal footing doctrine, Oklahoma challenged a provision in the congressional resolution granting

---

The "right of . . . every . . . new state to exercise all the powers of government, which belong to and may be exercised by the original states of the Union, must be admitted and remain unquestioned."

—Justice John McKinley
Pollard v. Hagan, 1845

---

it statehood which specified that the state's capital must remain at Guthrie for at least seven years. The state legislature moved it to Oklahoma City after only four years. In *Coyle v. Smith* (1911), the court held that Congress could not place in statehood resolutions restrictions on matters wholly under the state's control. The court, through Justice Horace H. Lurton, wrote:

The power is to admit "new States into *this* Union." "This Union" was and is a union of States, equal in power, dignity and authority, each competent to exert that residuum of sovereignty not delegated to the United States by the Constitution itself. To maintain otherwise would be to say that the Union, through the power of Congress to admit new States, might come to be a union of States unequal in power, as including States whose powers were restricted only by the Constitution, with others whose powers had been

The Tidelands Oil Controversy

When oil was discovered off the coasts of California, Texas and Louisiana, the question of who owned the submerged land immediately off the coastal states developed into a raging controversy. Presuming that it owned the land, California leased drilling rights to oil companies as early as 1921. The federal government, however, also claimed ownership of the land and in 1945 brought an original suit against California in the Supreme Court asking the court to prevent the state from exploiting the oil further.

The suit was decided by the Supreme Court in 1947. California argued that the original coastal states held title to the three-mile strip of sea adjacent to their shores and since California entered the Union on an equal footing with the original states, it too held title to the three-mile belt.[1] The federal government contended that it had the right to control the offshore lands because of its responsibility to protect and defend the nation. Moreover, in its exercise of its foreign relations, the federal government asserted it had a right to make whatever agreements were necessary concerning the offshore lands without interference by commitments made by the states.

The Supreme Court found in favor of the federal government. Writing for the majority, Justice Hugo L. Black denied that the original 13 states had title to the three-mile ocean zone. On the contrary, he said:

...the idea of a definite three-mile belt in which an adjacent nation can, if it chooses, exercise broad, if not complete dominion, has apparently at last been generally accepted throughout the world.... That the political agencies of this nation both claim and exercise broad dominion and control over our three-mile marginal belt is now a settled fact.... And this assertion of national dominion over the three-mile belt is binding upon this Court....[2]

Even without this acquisition by assertion, Black said, the federal government would control the offshore lands as "a function of national external sovereignty." He continued:

...The three-mile rule is but a recognition of the necessity that a government next to the sea must be able to protect itself from dangers incident to its location. It must have powers of dominion and regulation in the interest of its revenues, its health, and the security of its people from wars waged on or too near its coasts. And insofar as the nation asserts its rights under international law, whatever of value may be discovered in the seas next to its shores and within its protective belt, will most naturally be appropriated for its use.[3]

The court in 1950 applied its ruling in the California case to assert federal control over Louisiana's coastal lands.[4] In another 1950 case, the court denied Texas' claim that because it was an independent and sovereign nation prior to its admission as a state, it had in fact owned the three-mile strip along its shores.[5] The court acknowledged that this was so, but said that when Texas came into the Union it did so on an equal footing with the other states and thus relinquished its claim to the coastal lands.

These controversial rulings became a campaign issue in the 1952 presidential contest, with the Republicans promising to turn over the three-mile zone to the states if elected. In 1953, the Republican-controlled Congress passed the Submerged Lands Act ceding to the states the mineral rights to lands lying offshore between the low tide mark and the states' historic boundaries, which stretched to between three and 10-1/2 miles from shores. Congress' authority to overturn the effect of the Supreme Court's 1947 ruling and relinquish the lands was upheld in 1954.[6]

---

[1] *United States v. California*, 332 U.S. 19 (1947).
[2] Id. at 33-34.   [3] Id. at 35.
[4] *United States v. Louisiana*, 339 U.S. 699 (1950).

[5] *United States v. Texas*, 339 U.S. 707 (1950).
[6] *Alabama v. Texas*, 347 U.S. 272 (1954); see also *United States v. Louisiana*, 363 U.S. 1 (1960).

---

further restricted by an act of Congress accepted as a condition of admission.[4]

In most instances, the equal footing theory has worked to give new states constitutional rights and powers they did not possess as territories. But in one instance, it required a new state to give up some of its sovereignty. In 1947 the court held that the ocean bed beneath the three-mile coastal limit along the Atlantic Ocean did not belong to the original states, but to the federal government, so states subsequently admitted to the Union did not own the ocean soil along their coasts either. *(Details, box, this page)*

But in 1950 Texas challenged that decision on the ground that as an independent nation before its admission to the Union it had owned its coastal strip. The court acknowledged Texas' original sovereignty but ruled that entry into the Union "entailed a relinquishment of some of her sovereignty," including the coastal strip, in order that the new state be on an equal footing.[5]

Justice William O. Douglas for the court explained:

The "equal footing" clause [in the statehood resolution] prevents extension of the sovereignty of a State into a domain of political and sovereign power of the United States from which the other States have been excluded, just as it prevents a contraction of sovereignty ... which would produce inequality among the states.[6]

But the doctrine has been held not to apply to nonpolitical conditions imposed prior to admission. Before it became a state, Minnesota had agreed not to tax certain lands held by the federal government at the time of Minnesota's admission. Afterwards, some of these lands were granted to a railroad that Minnesota sought to tax. The court sustained the tax restriction agreement, saying it was unaffected by the equal footing doctrine. "...[A] mere agreement in reference to property involves no question of equality of status, but only of the power of a state to deal with the nation ... in reference to such property," the court ruled in 1900.[7]

The Power to Govern the Territories

There is no express constitutional authority for the federal government to acquire territory, but the power is implied in some of the enumerated powers and is considered inherent in the fact of the nation's sovereignty.

"The Constitution confers absolutely upon the government of the Union, the powers of making war and of making treaties; consequently, that government possesses the power of acquiring territory, either by conquest or treaty," declared Chief Justice John Marshall in a frequently cited 1828 case. [8] The court also has held that the nation has an inherent power to acquire territory by discovery. [9]

The only specific grant of power over territories conferred on Congress by the Constitution is contained in Article IV, Section 3, Clause 2. It authorizes the federal legislature "to dispose of and make all needful Rules and Regulations respecting the Territory or other Property belonging to the United States. . . ." With one important exception, the court has consistently interpreted this power broadly and upheld its exercise. Congress, the court said in 1880, "has full and complete legislative authority over the people of the Territories and all the departments of the territorial governments. It may do for the Territories what the people, under the Constitution of the United States, may do for the States." [10] In 1899, the court again ruled that Congress had the same full legislative powers over activities within the territories as state legislatures had in the states. [11] The court also has approved congressional delegation of its legislative powers over local territorial affairs to a territorial legislature elected by its citizens. [12]

Slavery in the Territories

The one exception was the court's 1857 ruling that Congress did not have the authority to prohibit slavery in the territories. [13] The decision in *Scott v. Sandford*, which also denied blacks citizenship in the United States, was possibly the court's greatest strategic error. For instead of resolving the conflict that had divided the nation for decades, as many of the justices participating in the decision apparently had hoped, the ruling contributed to further division of North and South. Three years after the decision the country plunged into civil war.

The Dred Scott decision was equally damaging to the court itself — a "gross abuse of trust" as one eminent historian would describe it [14] — for, rightly or wrongly, much of the public believed that the decision had been motivated by narrow, political concerns and that the court had not acted with the judicious dispassion the public expected of the men who were the final interpreters of the nation's laws.

Background

Slavery in the territories did not become an issue until 1819. With support from both northern and southern delegates, the Confederation Congress prohibited slavery in the Northwest Territory when it passed the Northwest Ordinance in 1787. [15]

But when the Missouri territory applied for statehood in 1819, slavery in the territories became a serious political and constitutional question. In that year there were 11 free states and 11 slave states. Northerners in the House of Representatives pushed through an amendment to the statehood resolution that would have prohibited slavery in the new state despite the fact that many Missourians were slaveholders. Dominated by southerners, the Senate objected to the amendment, claiming that Congress had no constitutional right to impose such a condition on a new state. Ironically, few southerners questioned Congress' right to prohibit slavery in the territories.

The stalemate between the two chambers was not resolved until the following year after Maine also applied for statehood. The Missouri Compromise of 1820 provided for the entry of Maine as a free state and Missouri as a slave state, which maintained the numerical balance between free and slave states. The compromise also prohibited slavery in the remainder of the Louisiana Purchase area that lay north of 36° 30' north latitude, a line that was an extension of Missouri's southern boundary.

A second compromise became necessary when Missouri's constitution was presented to Congress for approval later in 1820. A section of that document barred the entry of free blacks into the new state. Representatives from several northern states that had given free blacks rights of citizenship objected to the provision, claiming it violated the comity clause (Article IV, Section 2, Clause 1) of the Constitution which gave citizens of one state "all Privileges and Immunities of Citizens in the several States." Southerners, on the other hand, contended that free blacks did not have the same rights as whites — they could not vote in federal elections, for example — and thus were not citizens under the Constitution.

The Constitution did not define either federal or state citizenship nor did it clearly stipulate whether those persons defined as citizens by one state retained that status when they moved to another state. In the immediate controversy, Congress reached a compromise that essentially barred Missouri from passing any law that would ban the entry of citizens of another state. Although the two Missouri compromises relieved sectional tensions at the time, they did not answer the greater questions of whether Congress actually had the authority to prohibit slavery in the territories and whether blacks, free or slave, were citizens with all the rights and privileges guaranteed by the Constitution.

With the formal acquisition of Texas in 1846 and the prospect of obtaining more land from Mexico, extension of slavery into the territories again became an issue. This in reality was a thin shield for the real issue which was whether slavery could continue to exist at all.

Once again, northern representatives proposed to bar slavery in the newly acquired territories. They contended that Congress, under the "rules and regulation" clause of Article IV and under the treaty and war powers, had the power to prohibit slavery in the territories. They also noted that Congress had exercised this authority throughout its existence.

Southern opponents argued that slaves were property and that all the sovereign states owned the territories in common. The federal government, they continued, had no right to act against the interests of the sovereign states by barring their property in slaves from any of the territories. A corollary argument was that abolition of slavery was a violation of the Fifth Amendment's due process clause because it took property without just compensation.

The controversy over the western lands was settled in 1850 when Congress produced a three-part compromise. California would enter the Union as a free state. Enforcement of the controversial Fugitive Slave Act would be turned over to the federal government. And the citizens of the newly organized Utah and New Mexico territories would determine whether they would allow slavery at the time those territories became states.

Dred Scott's Case

It was at the beginning of this crisis in 1846 that the slave Dred Scott sought his freedom in the courts.

Scott was originally owned by a family named Blow who in 1833 sold him to an army surgeon, Dr. John Emerson of St. Louis. In 1834, Emerson was transferred to Rock Island, Ill., and later to Fort Snelling in the Wisconsin Territory, returning to St. Louis near the end of 1838. Scott accompanied Emerson throughout this period.

Some time later Emerson died, leaving Scott to his widow, who in the mid 1840s moved to New York depositing Scott into the care of his original owners, the Blows. Opposed to the extension of slavery into the western territories, Henry Blow lent financial support to Scott to test in court whether his residence on free soil in Illinois and the Wisconsin Territory made him a free man. A lower state court found in favor of Scott, but in 1852 the Missouri Supreme Court reversed the decision, holding that under Missouri law, Scott remained a slave.

Strader v. Graham: Precedent

The Missouri Supreme Court may have relied on an 1851 decision of the U.S. Supreme Court that dealt with the precise question whether a slave's sojourn in free territory made him a free man if he returned to a slave state. [16] That case was brought by a man named Graham of Kentucky who owned three slaves. These three were traveling minstrels whom Graham had taken into Ohio to perform. In 1841 the slaves escaped by boat across the Ohio River to Cincinnati and Graham sued Strader, the boat's captain. Strader argued that he had done no wrong because the minstrels were free by virtue of their earlier travels.

The court unanimously dismissed the case for lack of jurisdiction. Wrote Chief Justice Roger B. Taney for the court:

Every state has an undoubted right to determine the *status,* or domestic or social condition, of the persons domiciled within its territory.... There is nothing in the Constitution of the United States that can control the law of Kentucky upon this subject. And the condition of the negroes, therefore, as to freedom or slavery, after their return depended altogether upon the laws of the State, and could not be influenced by the laws of Ohio. It was exclusively in the power of Kentucky to determine for itself whether their employment in another state should or should not make them free on their return. The Court of Appeals have determined, that by the laws of the state they continued to be slaves. And this judgment upon this point is ... conclusive upon this court, and we have no jurisdiction over it. [17]

1820 Compromise Repealed

In 1854 the issue of the extension of slavery into the territories flared up once more. Sen. Stephen A. Douglas (D

1847-1853, PSD 1853-1861) of Illinois and his supporters wanted to organize the area known as Nebraska into a territory and encourage its settlement to improve the feasibility of building a railroad from Illinois to the Pacific Coast. The Nebraska area under the Missouri Compromise was one in which Congress had barred the introduction of slavery. But to secure southern support in Congress for his project, Douglas wrote a bill that repealed the 1820 compromise on slavery and substituted for it popular or squatters' sovereignty which allowed newly organized territories to decide for themselves whether they would allow slavery.

Anti-slavery members of Congress were outraged by the proposal, but with strong pressure from the executive branch, the bill was passed. It led to growing extremism on both sides and to a civil war in Kansas in 1856 between the pro-slavery government at Shawnee, which was regarded by the federal government as legitimate, and the anti-slavery government at Topeka.

A Matter for the Court

It was during these years that more and more people began to look to the Supreme Court for a solution to the slavery question. Historian Carl B. Swisher wrote of the period that while there was skepticism about entrusting a final decision to the courts,

...the belief was growing [that] there might be some point in turning to the judiciary in the hope that it could resolve a conflict which Congress was unable to settle. Many Southerners hoped and expected that the judiciary would decide their way and perhaps give a security which politics could not provide. Many Northerners hoped the courts could in some way find a pattern of rightness not too different from the pattern of their own beliefs. [18]

A court settlement of the issue was clearly what those around Dred Scott were seeking. In 1854, Mrs. Emerson arranged for the sale of Scott to her brother, John F. A. Sanford (misspelled in the court records as Sandford) and in 1853 Scott's attorney brought suit for his freedom in the federal circuit court for Missouri. Suits may be brought in federal court by a citizen of one state against the citizen of another state, so Scott's first task was to show that he was a citizen of Missouri. The circuit court held that Scott, as a black slave, was not a citizen of Missouri and therefore did not have the right to bring suit in federal court. Scott appealed to the Supreme Court.

Faced with a civil war in Kansas over the precise issue of slavery in the territories, a Congress increasingly less able to find a political solution and mounting demands for some final judicial solution, the court agreed to hear the case.

The court first heard arguments in February 1856. But because the justices disagreed on a number of the issues presented and because they feared their disagreement would be used for political ends in the upcoming presidential campaign, adding to the controversy rather than quieting it, the court decided to have the case reargued later in the year.

Narrow Ruling Rejected. Although the circumstances of the two cases were not identical, most historians agree that the court could have dismissed Dred Scott's suit on the same reasoning that it employed in *Strader v. Graham,* that is, that it was up to Missouri to determine whether Scott was slave or free and the court had no authority to interfere with that decision.

After the case was reargued, seven of the nine justices were prepared to restrict themselves to this narrow judgment. One justice, Samuel Nelson, was assigned to write the opinion. But the two dissenters — John McLean, a Republican from Ohio, and Benjamin R. Curtis, a Whig from Massachusetts — announced that their dissents would cover all the issues: whether Dred Scott was a citizen, whether his stay on free soil made him a free man and whether Congress had the authority to prohibit slavery in the territories.

Unwilling to let the dissents go unanswered, each of the seven majority justices decided to write an opinion answering those issues he thought to be in question. Several of the seven were anxious to address the territorial question, partly out of personal belief, partly because they thought a decision might help resolve the dilemma and partly because they thought the public expected the court to address the issue. Several northern papers already had

---

Slaves and the descendants of slaves "are not included, and are not intended to be included, under the word 'citizens' in the Constitution, and can, therefore, claim none of the rights and privileges which that instrument provides for and secures to citizens of the United States."

—Chief Justice Roger B. Taney
Scott v. Sandford, 1857

---

chided the court for an opinion the papers assumed would favor the South. This was not an unreasonable assumption in those days of intense regional feeling since five of the nine justices were from the South.

Newly elected President James Buchanan also put some pressure on the court to decide the territorial slavery issue. In letters to Justices John Catron and Robert C. Grier, Buchanan urged the court to take up this issue so that at his inauguration he might say, as he finally did, that the issue was "a judicial question, which legitimately belongs to the Supreme Court . . . before whom it is now pending and will, it is understood, be speedily and finally settled. To their decision, in common with all good citizens, I shall cheerfully submit, whatever that may be." [19]

Taney's Opinion

The court announced its decision March 6, 1857, two days after Buchanan's inauguration. By a 7-2 vote, the court ruled against Scott. Of the seven opinions written by members of the majority, it is Chief Justice Taney's that is considered to present the formal view of the court.

Taney first dealt with the issue of whether Dred Scott, or any slave or descendant of slaves, could be a citizen under the Constitution. It was Taney's opinion that:

. . .they are not, and that they are not included, and were not intended to be included, under the word "citizens" in the Constitution, and can, therefore, claim none of the rights and privileges which that instrument provides for and secures to citizens of the United States. [20]

Taney drew this conclusion from an examination of historical practices and the intent of the framers of the Constitution. Slaves, he said,

. . .had for more than a century before [the Constitution was ratified] been regarded as being of an inferior order, and altogether unfit to associate with the white race, either in social or political relations; and so far inferior, that they had no rights which the white man was bound to respect; and that the negro might justly and lawfully be reduced to slavery for his benefit. . . . This opinion was at that time fixed and universal in the civilized portion of the white race. [21]

Even the words "all men are created equal" in the Declaration of Independence did not encompass the black race. The authors of that declaration, Taney said,

. . .perfectly understood the meaning of the language they used, and how it would be understood by others; and they knew that it would not in any part of the civilized world, be supposed to embrace the negro race, which, by common consent, had been excluded from civilized Governments and the family of nations, and doomed to slavery. [22]

Taney also touched on the question of whether a person declared a citizen by one state was automatically a citizen of the United States, concluding that this was not so since the Constitution gave the federal government exclusive control over naturalization.

With regard to whether other states were bound to recognize as citizens those granted citizenship by a single state, Taney said:

. . .Each state may still confer [citizenship rights] upon an alien, or anyone it thinks proper. . .; yet he would not be a citizen in the sense in which the word is used in the Constitution . . . nor entitled to sue as such in one of its courts, nor to the privileges and immunities of a citizen in the other States. [23]

Taney also used an examination of pre-Revolutionary War laws in the states to show that slaves, far from being citizens, were actually considered property:

The unhappy black race were separated from the whites by indelible marks, and laws long before established, and were never thought of or spoken of except as property, and when the claims of the owner or the profit of the trader was supposed to need protection. [24]

That slaves were considered property was reflected in the only two provisions of the Constitution that specifically mentioned them, he continued. These provisions, Taney said, "treat them as property, and make it the duty of the government to protect it; no other power, in relation to this race, is to be found in the Constitution." [25]

As was said earlier, Taney might have ended the matter right there, declaring that since Scott was not a citizen under the meaning of the Constitution, he could not bring suit in federal court. But the Chief Justice felt it necessary to discuss whether Scott's residence in the Wisconsin Territory made him a free man. In this way he was able to reach the question of whether Congress had the constitutional authority to bar slavery in the states.

Taney first declared that Congress did not have that power under Article IV, Section 2 of the Constitution. This language, he said allowed Congress to make rules and regulations only for the territories held at the time the Constitution was ratified. "It applied only to the property which the States held in common at that time," Taney said, "and has no reference whatever to any territory or other property which the new sovereignty might afterwards itself acquire." [26]

Taney acknowledged that the federal government had the power to acquire new territory for preparation for statehood, and that Congress could in its discretion determine the form of government the territory would have. But Congress must exercise that power over territories within the confines prescribed by the Constitution. Congress, Taney said,

> . . .has no power of any kind beyond [the Constitution]; and it cannot, when it enters a territory of the United States, put off its character, and assume discretionary or despotic powers which the Constitution has denied to it. It cannot create for itself a new character separated from the citizens of the United States, and the duties it owes them under the provisions of the Constitution. [27]

Among those duties was the duty to protect property, Taney said. Noting that the Fifth Amendment provided that no persons should be deprived of life, liberty or property without due process of law, Taney concluded that

> . . .an Act of Congress, which deprives a citizen . . . of his liberty or property, merely because he came himself or brought his property into a particular Territory of the United States, and who had committed no offense against the laws, could hardly be dignified with the name of due process of law. [28]

Therefore, Taney said, the portion of the Missouri Compromise that prohibited slavery in the northern portion of the Louisiana Purchase was void and Dred Scott had not been freed by his residence there.

Nor was Scott a freeman because of his residence in Illinois. Using the reasoning in *Graham v. Strader,* Taney said that since

> . . .Scott was a slave when taken into the State of Illinois by his owner, and was there held as such, and brought back in that character, his *status,* as free or slave depended on the laws of Missouri, and not of Illinois. [29]

Justices James M. Wayne and Grier for the most part concurred with Taney's opinion, Justice Nelson submitted the original opinion he had written for the court, dismissing the case on the basis of the ruling in *Graham v. Strader.* Justices Peter V. Daniel, John A. Campbell and Catron, using different reasoning, all agreed that Congress had no authority to prohibit slavery in the territories. The dissenters, McLean and Curtis, also filed lengthy opinions, setting out their opposition to the majority.

But it was Taney's opinion that, in historian Bruce Catton's words "reverberated across the land like a thunderclap." [30] Northern papers were quick to criticize the decision and the court. For example, the Washington correspondent for the *New York Tribune* wrote March 7, 1857: "If the action of the Court in this case has been atrocious, the manner of it has been no better. The Court has rushed into politics, voluntarily and without other purpose than to subserve the cause of slavery." [31]

Northern abolitionists particularly scored Taney's statement that blacks were so inferior to whites "that they had no rights which the white man was bound to respect." Taney did say this, but in the context that this was the general belief at the time the Constitution was written and with the *caveat* that the accuracy or inaccuracy of the belief was not a question before the court.

As Taney's biographer, Carl B. Swisher has noted, the "phrase was torn from its context by critics of the decision and published as a statement by Taney that the Negro had no rights which the white man was bound to respect. The error found its way into the history of the period, was repeated in the classrooms of the country and persists to the present day. . . ." [32]

Legal scholars and constitutional historians generally agree that Taney's opinion was questionable in several respects. He made no mention of the fact that Congress had been prohibiting slavery in territories for 70 years or of the fact that Missouri courts had accorded citizenship rights to several blacks considered citizens by other states.

By the modern canons of judicial restraint, Taney erred grievously. He decided on the constitutionality of a federal law when it was not strictly necessary to do so. His opinion applied the law more broadly than was required by the facts of the case. And the court could have observed the rule that no matter how grave the constitutional questions, the court will try to put a construction on a federal law that **will make it valid.** *(Judicial restraint, p. 287)*

It also seems apparent that the justices allowed their own political persuasions to influence their decisions. As constitutional historian Edward S. Corwin wrote: "When . . . the student finds six judges arriving at precisely the same result by three distinct processes of reasoning, he is naturally disposed to surmise that the result may possibly have induced the processes rather than that the processes compelled the result. . . ." [33]

What was the significance of the Dred Scott decision? Rather than dampening the controversy over slavery, the ruling fueled it, perhaps hastening the onset of the war. The finding that blacks, both slave and free, were not and could not be citizens under the Constitution led to the adoption of the 14th Amendment, which itself would play a very complicated role in the development of constitutional law. *(Box, next page)*

But perhaps its greatest impact was on the court itself. A contemporary editorial in the *North American Review* of October 1857 assessed this impact:

> The country will feel the consequences of the decision more deeply and more permanently in the loss of confidence in the sound judicial integrity and strictly legal character of their tribunals, than in anything beside; and this, perhaps, may well be accounted the greatest political calamity which this country, under our forms of government, could sustain. [34]

The Insular Cases

Because the territory acquired in the early decades of the nation's history was intended for eventual statehood, questions of imperialism and colonization over foreign peoples did not arise.

But with the acquisition of Hawaii, Puerto Rico, Guam and the Philippines in 1898, the likelihood of statehood was not assumed and the ensuing debate over American imperialism raised a difficult question.

Did the constitutional rights and guarantees afforded residents of the United States extend to residents of these

Dred Scott Reversed: The 14th Amendment

It took a constitutional amendment to overturn the Supreme Court ruling in the *Dred Scott* case that blacks were not and could not be citizens under the Constitution.

Congress in early 1865 passed the 13th Amendment abolishing slavery. It was ratified toward the end of the year, but hopes that its adoption would encourage the southern states to protect the civil rights of their former black slaves went unrealized. In fact the southern states passed so-called "black codes," which contained harsh vagrancy laws and sterner criminal penalties for blacks than for whites and set up racially segregated schools and other public facilities.

Fearing this indicated the southern states were unchastened by the war and that the 13th Amendment abolishing slavery would prove a hollow promise, Republicans, both radical and moderate, began to push for stronger guarantees of black rights. In order to secure political dominance in the South, the Radical Republicans also wanted to ensure that blacks had the right to vote and to keep former prominent Confederates out of state and federal office.

To these ends, the Republican-controlled Congress passed the Freedmen's Bureau Act and the Civil Rights Act of 1866. Both sought to protect basic rights, and the latter attempted to void by legislation the Supreme Court's denial of citizenship to blacks. But the Civil Rights Act was passed over President Johnson's veto and its constitutionality was doubtful. So Republicans looked to enactment of a constitutional amendment. In April of 1866 the Joint Committee on Reconstruction reported the 14th Amendment. With few changes, the five-part amendment was submitted to the states for ratification in June 1866.

The third and fourth sections of the amendment were of only temporary significance. They prohibited anyone from holding state or federal office (unless authorized by Congress) who had participated in rebellion after taking an oath to support the U.S. Constitution, and denied the responsibility of federal or state governments for debts incurred in aid of rebellion.

The second section of the amendment in effect eliminated the clause of Article I, Section 2, of the Constitution, which directed that only three-fifths of the slave population of a state be counted in apportioning the House of Representatives. This section also provided that if any state abridged the right of its citizens to vote for federal or state officers, the number of its representatives in the House would be reduced in proportion to the numbers denied the vote. In addition to ensuring blacks

the right to vote, this language was intended to dilute the strength of the southern states and Democrats in Congress. But it did not specifically give blacks the right to vote because moderate Republicans feared that such an outright grant might jeopardize ratification of the amendment in those northern states that still restricted black voting rights. As a result, the southern states ignored this section of the amendment, and its inadequacy led quickly to adoption of the 15th Amendment in 1870. *(15th Amendment, p. 477)*

The first section of the 14th Amendment directly overruled the *Dred Scott* decision. It declared that all persons born or naturalized in the United States and subject to its jurisdiction are citizens of the United States and the state in which they live. It also prohibited the states from making any law that abridged the privileges and immunities of citizens of the United States, deprived any person of life, liberty or property without due process of law, or denied anyone equal protection of the laws.

In addition to protecting civil rights of blacks, the original sponsor of this section, Rep. John A. Bingham (R Ohio 1855-63, 1865-73), intended it to override the 1833 Supreme Court ruling in *Barron v. Baltimore,* which held that the first eight amendments of the Bill of Rights protected individual rights only from infringement by the federal government, not by state governments. Bingham intended that the 14th Amendment also would protect these rights from infringment by the states. But the final wording of the section was a prohibition on the states and not a positive grant to Congress to protect civil rights against state encroachment, and the court initially limited Congress' authority to enforce these protections against state infringement. Not until 1925, in the case of *Gitlow v. New York,* would the court begin to apply the 14th Amendment to secure the guarantees of the Bill of Rights against state action. *(Details, p. 388)*

The court was to frustrate the authors of the 14th Amendment even further by applying the rights guarantees intended for persons to businesses instead. This interpretation of the 14th Amendment's due process clause was not abandoned until the New Deal era. *(Details, pp. 583-586)*

After the Second World War, the Supreme Court ruled that the equal protection clause prohibited racial segregation in the schools; and almost 100 years after its ratification, the court upheld federal civil rights legislation based in part on the 14th Amendment. *(Details, pp. 587-623)*

---

new territories? In other words, did the Constitution follow the flag? The court discussed the issue in the *Insular Cases* in the early 1900s before reaching a final conclusion.

No Foreign Country

In the first case, the collector for New York's port continued to collect duties on sugar imported from Puerto Rico after it was annexed, as if it were still a foreign nation. Contending that the island was no longer a foreign country, the sugar owners sued for return of the paid duties.

The court by a 5-4 vote held in *DeLima v. Bidwell* (1901) that Puerto Rico had ceased to be a foreign country so far as the tariff laws were concerned and that the duties had been illegally collected. [35] The controlling precedent, wrote Justice Henry B. Brown, was the decision in *Cross v. Harrison* (1853) in which the court recognized that California had lost its status as a foreign country as soon as ratification of the annexation treaty was officially announced in the new territory. [36] While that opinion did not directly involve the issue at hand in the *DeLima* case,

Power over Federal Property

In addition to granting Congress power over territories, Article IV, Section 3, Clause 2, also gives Congress the power "to dispose of and make all needful Rules and Regulations respecting . . . other Property belonging to the United States."

The power to dispose of public property is considered absolute by the Supreme Court. In an 1840 case, the court denied a contention that Congress could only sell federal land and not lease it. "The disposal must be left to the discretion of Congress," the court asserted. [1]

The authority over disposal of federal property was expanded in 1913 when the court held that the federal government could sell or lease any excess hydroelectric power it might generate in the process of improving the navigability of a stream. [2] And in 1936 the court held that since the construction of a federal dam created the energy from which electric power could be generated, the government had the authority to generate and sell the power. [3]

Congressional authority to make rules and regulations for federally owned property is also absolute and may be delegated to the executive branch. [4] States may not tax federal lands within their boundaries nor may they take actions that would interfere with the federal power to regulate federal lands. [5]

---

[1] *United States v. Gratiot,* 14 Pet. 526 at 538 (1840).

[2] *United States v. Chandler-Dunbar Water Co.,* 229 U.S. 53 (1913).

[3] *Ashwander v. Tennessee Valley Authority,* 297 U.S. 288 (1936).

[4] See, e.g., *United States v. Fitzgerald,* 15 Pet. 407 at 421 (1841); *Sioux Tribe v. United States,* 316 U.S. 317 (1942).

[5] *Van Brocklin v. Tennessee,* 117 U.S. 151 (1886); *Gibson v. Chouteau,* 13 Wall. 92 (1872); *Irvine v. Marshall,* 20 How. 558 (1858); *Emblem v. Lincoln Land Co.,* 184 U.S. 660 (1902).

Brown said, "it is impossible to escape the logical inference from that case that goods carried from San Francisco to New York after the ratification of the treaty would not be considered as imported from a foreign country." [37]

Not the United States

But if Puerto Rico was not a foreign country so far as tariffs were concerned, neither was it part of the United States, said a majority of the court in a second case decided the same day. *Downes v. Bidwell* (1901) upheld a provision of the Foraker Act of 1900 which established special import duties for Puerto Rican goods. [38] The New York port collector imposed the duty on a shipment of oranges and the owners sued, citing the constitutional stricture that all duties must be uniform throughout the United States.

With another 5-4 division, the court ruled against the orange owners. However, the majority could not agree on its reasons. In the official opinion of the court, Justice Brown held that the Constitution applied only to the states and that it was up to Congress to decide if it wished to extend it to the territories. In passing the Foraker Act, Congress had clearly stated its decision not to extend the Constitution to Puerto Rico, Brown said. Thus the duties were not required to be uniform and were therefore legal.

In a concurring opinion, Justice Edward D. White, joined by Justices George Shiras Jr. and Joseph McKenna, put forth for the first time the theory that the Constitution fully applied only to residents in territories that had been formally "incorporated" into the United States either through a ratified treaty or an act of Congress.

In his opinion White envisioned a series of awful consequences that could ensue if the Constitution was automatically extended to acquired territory. He imagined discovery of an unknown island "peopled with an uncivilized race," yet desirable for commercial and strategic purposes. Automatic application of the Constitution could "inflict grave detriment on the United States . . . from . . . the immediate bestowal of citizenship on those absolutely unfit to receive it," White wrote. [39]

He also imagined a war in which the United States would occupy enemy territory. "Would not the war . . . be fraught with danger if the effect of occupation was to necessarily incorporate an alien and hostile people into the United States?" he asked. [40]

Once a treaty containing incorporation provisions is ratified by Congress, the full range of constitutional rights would be effective in the territory, White said. But, he added,

> . . .where a treaty contains no conditions for incorporation, and, above all, where it . . . expressly provides to the contrary, incorporation does not arise until in the wisdom of Congress it is deemed that the acquired territory has reached that state where it is proper that it should enter into and form a part of the American family. [41]

Dissenting, Justice John Marshall Harlan argued that the Constitution must follow the flag:

> In my opinion, Congress has no existence and can exercise no authority outside of the Constitution. Still less is it true that Congress can deal with new territories just as other nations have done or may do with their new territories. This nation is under the control of a written constitution, the supreme law of the land and the only source of the powers which our Government, or any branch or officer of it, may exert at any time or at any place. . . . The idea that this country may acquire territories anywhere upon the earth, by conquest or treaty, and hold them as mere colonies or provinces — the people inhabiting them to enjoy only such rights as Congress chooses to accord to them — is wholly inconsistent with the spirit and genius as well as the words of the Constitution. [42]

Juries. Two years later, White again offered his incorporation theory in a concurring opinion. A Hawaiian named Mankichi had been convicted of manslaughter by a non-unanimous jury during the period after the annexation of Hawaii in 1898 but before its incorporation into the United States in 1900. The annexation act had specified that Hawaiian laws not contrary to the Constitution would apply until such time as the islands were incorporated. Conviction by less than a unanimous jury, legal under Hawaiian law, was challenged as a violation of the Fifth and Sixth Amendments of the Constitution.

The majority opinion, written by Brown, contended that although the annexation act said so, Congress had not really intended to provide the guarantees of the Fifth and Sixth Amendments to Hawaiians. To do so would have required the release of all those persons convicted of crimes

Eminent Domain: An Inherent Power

"The right of eminent domain, that is, the right to take private property for public uses, appertains to every independent government," said the Supreme Court in 1879. "It requires no constitutional recognition; it is an attribute of sovereignty."[1] That the framers of the Constitution believed the federal government to possess this power is evidenced by the clauses in the Fifth Amendment which prohibit the taking of private property without due process of law and payment of just compensation.

An attempt to extend these Fifth Amendment guarantees to the taking of private land by the states failed when the Supreme Court in 1833 held that the first eight amendments to the Constitution protected rights only against infringement by the federal government and not by state governments.[2]

The 14th Amendment, ratified in 1868, prohibited the states from depriving a person of property without due process of the law but made no mention of just compensation. At first the court interpreted this omission to mean that the states did not have to make compensation.[3] But in 1897 the court reversed itself, holding that a state had not provided due process of law if it had not made just compensation: "The mere form of the proceeding instituted against the owner . . . cannot convert the process used into due process of law, if the necessary result be to deprive him of his property without compensation."[4]

Public Use

By virtue of their authority to review eminent domain cases, the courts are the final arbiters of what uses of private land may be considered public. The Supreme Court has traditionally given great weight to the federal legislature's designation of what constitutes a public use, even suggesting in 1946 that the court might not have the authority to review a congressional determination of public use. "We think that it is the function of Congress to decide what type of taking is for a public use and that the agency authorized to do the taking may do so to the full extent of its statutory authority," the court observed.[5]

Public uses include lands used for public buildings, highways and parks and for preserving sites of historical interest, such as battlefields. In 1954, the court upheld the right of Congress to use its power of eminent domain to facilitate slum clearance, urban renewal and the construction of public housing, even though only a small portion of the public would be eligible to live in the housing.[6]

In addition to exercising the eminent domain power itself, Congress may delegate it "to private corporations to be exercised by them in the execution of works in which the public is interested," such as railroad and utility companies.[7]

Just Compensation

The general standard set by the court for determining whether the compensation paid is adequate is the amount a willing buyer would pay to a willing seller in the open market.[8] That amount may be adjusted to account for various contingencies. For instance, the compensation may be reduced if the owner receives a benefit from the taking of the property greater than the benefit to the public at large.[9]

In those instances where the government has infringed on a person's property without actually taking it — for instance, where noise from a nearby airport makes land unfit for the uses its owners intended — the court has established another general rule: "Property is taken in the constitutional sense when inroads are made upon an owner's use of it to an extent that, as between private parties, a servitude [subjecting the property owned by one person to the use of another] has been acquired either by agreement or in the course of time."[10]

In some instances, the court has held that federal or state regulations prohibiting the use of property for certain purposes in order to protect the public welfare are exercises of the police power and not the taking of property under the eminent domain power, which would require compensation. In 1962 the court wrote:

A prohibition simply upon the use of property for purposes that are declared, by valid legislation, to be injurious to the health, morals or safety of the community, cannot, in any just sense, be deemed a taking or appropriation of property for the public benefit. Such legislation does not disturb the owner in the control or use of his property for lawful purposes, nor restrict his right to dispose of it, but is only a declaration by the State that its use by one, for certain forbidden purposes, is prejudicial to the public interests.[11]

In times of war or emergency, the court has held that government actions destroying property or preventing its use for the purposes intended did not constitute a taking entitling the owners to compensation.[12]

---

[1] *Boom Co. v. Patterson*, 98 U.S. 403 at 405 (1879).

[2] *Barron v. Baltimore*, 7 Pet. 243 (1833).

[3] *Davidson v. City of New Orleans*, 96 U.S. 97 (1878).

[4] *Chicago, Burlington & Quincy Railroad Co. v. City of Chicago*, 166 U.S. 226 at 236-37 (1897).

[5] *United States ex rel. Tennessee Valley Authority v. Welch*, 327 U.S. 546 at 551-52 (1946).

[6] *Berman v. Parker*, 348 U.S. 26 (1954).

[7] *Boom Co. v. Patterson*, 98 U.S. 403 at 405 (1879); see also *Noble v. Oklahoma City*, 297 U.S. 481 (1936); *Luxton v. North River Bridge Co.*, 153 U.S. 525 (1894).

[8] *United States v. Miller*, 317 U.S. 369 at 374 (1943); *United States ex rel. Tennessee Valley Authority v. Powelson*, 319 U.S. 266 at 275 (1943).

[9] *Bauman v. Ross*, 167 U.S. 548 (1897).

[10] *United States v. Dickinson*, 331 U.S. 745 at 748 (1947).

[11] *Goldblatt v. Town of Hempstead*, 369 U.S. 590 at 593 (1962).

[12] *United States v. Caltex*, 344 U.S. 149 (1952); *United States v. Central Eureka Mining Co.*, 357 U.S. 155 (1958); *National Board of YMCA v. United States*, 395 U.S. 85 (1969).

by non-unanimous juries after the annexation. "Surely such a result could not have been within the contemplation of Congress," Brown said. [43]

White agreed with Brown's result but reasoned that since the islands were not incorporated at the time of Mankichi's trial, the guarantees of the Fifth and Sixth Amendments did not extend to him.

For the four dissenters, Chief Justice Melville Fuller wrote: "The language [of the annexation act] is plain and unambiguous and to resort to construction or interpretation is absolutely uncalled for. To tamper with words is to eliminate them." [44]

Incorporation Theory Prevails

A few months later, a majority of the court subscribed for the first time to White's incorporation doctrine. *Dorr v. United States* (1904) involved circumstances similar to the Mankichi case. The question was whether a criminal trial in the Philippines held without indictment and heard by a jury of fewer than 12 persons was a violation of the defendant's rights under the Constitution.

It was not, held the court. Justice William R. Day's majority opinion offered a succinct statement approving the incorporation doctrine:

That the United States may have territory, which is not incorporated into the United States as a body politic, we think was recognized by the framers of the Constitution in enacting the Article [Article IV] already considered, giving power over the territories, and is sanctioned by the opinions of the Justices concurring in the judgment in *Downes v. Bidwell....*

Until Congress shall see fit to incorporate territory ceded by treaty in the United States, we regard it as settled by that decision that the territory is to be governed under the power existing in Congress to make laws for such territories and subject to such constitutional restrictions upon the powers of the body as are applicable to the situation. [45]

The incorporation doctrine was quickly reinforced when the court in 1905 voided trial by six-person juries in Alaska on the grounds that Alaska had been largely incorporated into the United States. [46] In 1911, eight justices — Harlan continued to dissent — agreed that since Congress had not incorporated the Philippines, criminal trials did not require 12-member juries. [47] The incorporation theory remained into the 1970s the rule for determining when constitutional rights and guarantees are extended to territorial residents.

Power Over Citizenship and Naturalization

"Citizenship," declared Chief Justice Earl Warren, "*is* man's basic right for it is nothing less than the right to have rights. Remove this priceless possession and there remains a stateless person, disgraced and degraded in the eyes of his countrymen." [48]

Although it refers to "citizens" in several instances, nowhere does the main body of the Constitution define who is a citizen and how one acquires citizenship. The prevailing assumption was that a citizen was a person who was born in the country and who remained under its jurisdiction and protection. This definition, followed in England and known as *jus soli,* was in contrast to the common practice in the rest of Europe of *jus sanguines,* where citizenship was determined by the nationality of the parents.

In its 1857 *Dred Scott* decision, the Supreme Court adopted an extremely narrow definition of citizenship that stood for less than a dozen years. Not only did the court exclude blacks, even native-born free blacks, from citizenship, it held that national citizenship was dependent on and resulted from state citizenship. Wrote Chief Justice Roger B. Taney:

...[E]very person, and every class and description of persons who were at the time of the adoption of the Constitution recognized as citizens in the several States, became also citizens of this new political body; but none other; it was formed by them, and for them and their posterity but for no one else. [49]

This ruling led ultimately to the 14th Amendment, ratified in 1868 at the conclusion of the Civil War. Its first sentence stated: "All persons born or naturalized in the United States and subject to the jurisdiction thereof, are citizens of the United States and of the State wherein they reside." *(Details of Dred Scott case, p. 135, 14th Amendment, p. 139)*

Designed primarily to confer citizenship on blacks, the 14th Amendment made the concept of *jus soli* the law of the land. This was confirmed and further defined in the case of *United States v. Wong Kim Ark* (1898) where the Supreme Court declared that — under the 14th Amendment — children born in the United States to resident alien parents were citizens even if their parents were barred from becoming citizens themselves. The court wrote:

The Fourteenth Amendment affirms the ancient and fundamental rule of citizenship by birth within the territory, in the allegiance and under the protection of the country, including all children here born of resident aliens, with the exceptions or qualifications ... of children of foreign sovereigns or their ministers, or born on public ships, or of enemies within and during hostile occupation of part of our territory, and with the single additional exception of children of members of the Indian tribes owing direct allegiance to their several tribes. [50]

This last exception was eliminated in 1925 when Congress granted citizenship to Indians living in tribes.

Naturalization

Wong Kim Ark's parents could not become citizens because Congress, under its power "to establish a uniform rule of naturalization," in 1882 specifically prohibited citizenship by naturalization to Chinese persons. The court has allowed Congress to establish whatever conditions it deems necessary for citizenship through naturalization.

"Naturalization is a privilege, to be given, qualified or withheld as Congress may determine and which the alien may claim as of right only upon compliance with the terms which Congress imposes," the court said in 1931. In this case, the court was upholding denial of naturalization to a pacifist who wanted to qualify his oath of allegiance by refusing to support war unless he believed it morally justified. [51]

The court has held that Congress may exclude an entire class or race of people from eligibility for citizenship and may expel aliens from the country. Upholding a statute expelling Chinese laborers from the country if they did not obtain a required residence certificate within a specified time the court wrote:

> ...The right of a nation to expel or deport foreigners, who have not been naturalized or taken any steps towards becoming citizens ... is as absolute and unqualified as the right to prohibit and prevent their entrance into the country....
> ...The power to exclude or expel aliens, being a power affecting international relations, is vested in the political departments of the government, and it is to be regulated by treaty or by act of Congress, and to be executed by the executive authority according to the regulations so established.... [52]

Exclusions

After ratification of the 14th Amendment, Congress enacted laws limiting naturalized citizenship to whites and to blacks of African descent. Citizenship was extended to the residents of some, but not all, of the U.S. territories. The residents of Hawaii became citizens in 1900, those of Puerto Rico in 1917 and those of the Virgin Islands in 1927. But the residents of the Philippines were denied citizenship throughout the period the United States held the islands as a trust territory. Other Asians did not fare any better in winning citizenship through naturalization. The final barriers to their naturalization were not removed until passage of the 1952 Immigration and Nationality Act, which barred the use of race as a reason for denying citizenship.

Other conditions set by Congress have excluded from naturalization anarchists, members of the Communist Party and others who advocate the violent overthrow of the country. To qualify for naturalization, an alien must have been a resident of the country for five years and be of good moral character. This latter phrase has been interpreted to exclude drunks, adulterers, polygamists, gamblers, convicted felons and homosexuals.

Conscientious Objectors. The court has generally sustained these exclusions. [53] The primary exception has been its disapproval of the exclusion of conscientious objectors who have refused to swear an oath of allegiance requiring them to bear arms.

Initially, the court agreed that this was a valid exclusion. In one extreme case, the court denied citizenship to a 50-year-old female pacifist, who would not have been required to bear arms in any event. [54] This ruling and two others like it were specifically overturned in the 1946 case of *Girouard v. United States.*

Girouard was a Seventh Day Adventist who refused to swear he would bear arms but said he would serve in a noncombatant position. In a ruling based entirely on its interpretation of the law, not the Constitution, the majority said it could not believe that Congress meant to deny citizenship in a country traditionally protective of religious freedom to those who objected to war on religious grounds. [55]

Four years later, the court ruled that citizenship could be granted to a pacifist who refused to serve in the Army even as a non-combatant. [56] In 1952, Congress formally took notice of the 1946 and 1950 rulings by allowing naturalization of conscientious objectors so long as they agreed to perform approved alternative service.

Denaturalization

As early as 1824, the Supreme Court, speaking through Chief Justice John Marshall, declared there was no difference between a naturalized citizen and one who was native-born. A naturalized citizen, wrote Marshall:

> ...becomes a member of the society, possessing all rights of the native citizen, and standing, in the view of the constitution, on the footing of a native. The constitution does not authorize Congress to enlarge or abridge those rights. The simple power of the national Legislature is to prescribe a uniform rule of naturalization, and the exercise of its power exhausts it, so far as respects the individual. [57]

With one major exception this statement remains true. Naturalized citizens do enjoy the same rights, privileges and responsibilities as do native-born citizens. The exception is that naturalized citizens may be denaturalized.

Fraud. The court has repeatedly held that a naturalized citizen may lose his citizenship if he obtained it fraudulently. "An alien has no moral or constitutional rights to retain the privileges of citizenship" won through fraud, the court said in 1912. [58] The court has also ruled that the lapse of time between naturalization and the time when the fraud is discovered is of no significance. In one case, the court sustained deprivation of naturalization for a man who claimed to be in real estate when in fact he was a bootlegger. The fact that more than 25 years had lapsed between his naturalization and discovery of his fraud made no difference, although the court subsequently barred his deportation. [59]

Bad Faith. Naturalization may also be lost if it was obtained in bad faith. A prime example is the case of *Luria v. United States* where the court upheld denaturalization of a man who apparently never intended to become a permanent resident of the United States at the time he was naturalized. The decision upheld an act of Congress that made residence in a foreign country within five years of naturalization *prima facie* evidence of bad faith. [60]

In 1943, however, the court established a rule that a naturalized citizen could not be denaturalized unless the government could demonstrate by "clear, unequivocal and convincing" evidence that the citizenship had been fraudulently obtained. In *Schneiderman v. United States,* the government sought Schneiderman's denaturalization on the grounds that he had been a member of a Communist organization five years prior to and at the time of his naturalization in 1927. The court acknowledged the existence of a statute that foreclosed naturalization to those who advocated the violent overthrow of the government but said that the government had not proved sufficiently whether the organizations Schneiderman belonged to advocated such violence in a manner that was a clear and present public danger or merely in a doctrinal manner that put forward overthrow of the government simply for consideration and discussion. [61]

It was not until 1946 that the court assented to the denaturalization of a person under the *Schneiderman* rule. Finding clear evidence that Paul Knauer, a naturalized citizen, was a Nazi before, at the time of and after his

The Constitution on Citizenship

The Constitution contains few specific references to citizens and citizenship. The body of the Constitution states only that the president, senators and representatives must be citizens, that citizens of each state shall enjoy the privileges and immunities of all other states and that citizens may bring certain suits in federal court. This last was modified by the 11th Amendment.

Not until ratification of the 14th Amendment in 1868 was language added to the Constitution defining eligibility for citizenship. The Constitution does not even specifically restrict the right to vote to citizens, but citizens are the only people whose right to vote is constitutionally protected.

Following are the passages in the Constitution that refer to citizens:

Article I, Section 2. No Person shall be a Representative who shall not have . . . been seven Years a Citizen of the United States. . . .

Article I, Section 3. No Person shall be a Senator who shall not have . . . been nine Years a Citizen of the United States. . . .

Article II, Section 1. No Person except a natural born Citizen, or a Citizen of the United States, at the time of the Adoption of this Constitution, shall be eligible to the Office of President. . . .

Article III, Section 2. The judicial Power shall extend to all Cases . . . between a State and Citizens of another State;* — between Citizens of different States; — between Citizens of the same State claiming Lands under Grants of different States, and between a State, or the Citizens thereof, and foreign States, Citizens or Subjects.*

Article IV, Section 2. The Citizens of each State shall be entitled to all Privileges and Immunities of Citizens in the several States.

Amendment XI. The Judicial power of the United States shall not be construed to extend to any suit in law or equity, commenced or prosecuted against one of the United States by Citizens of another State, or by Citizens or Subjects of any Foreign State.

Amendment XIV, Section 1. All persons born or naturalized in the United States and subject to the jurisdiction thereof, are citizens of the United States and of the State wherein they reside. No State shall make or enforce any law which shall abridge the privileges and immunities of citizens of the United States. . . .

Section 2. Representatives shall be apportioned among the several States according to their respective numbers, counting the whole number of persons in each State, excluding Indians not taxed. But when the right to vote at any election for the choice of electors for President and Vice President of the United States, Representatives in Congress, the Executive and Judicial officers of a State, or the members of the Legislature thereof, is denied to any of the male inhabitants of such State, being twenty-one years of age, and citizens of the United States, or in any way abridged, except for participation in rebellion, or other crime, the basis of representation therein shall be reduced in the proportion which the number of such male citizens shall bear to the whole number of male citizens twenty-one years of age in such State. . . .

Amendment XV, Section 1. The right of citizens of the United States to vote shall not be denied or abridged by the United States or by any State on account of race, color, or previous condition of servitude.

Amendment XIX. The right of citizens of the United States to vote shall not be denied or abridged by the United States or by any State on account of sex.

Amendment XXIV, Section 1. The right of citizens of the United States to vote in any primary or other election for President or Vice President, for electors for President or Vice President, or for Senator or Representative in Congress, shall not be denied or abridged by the United States or any State by reason of failure to pay any poll tax or other tax.

Amendment XXVI, Section 1. The right of citizens of the United States, who are eighteen years of age or older, to vote shall not be denied or abridged by the United States or by any State on account of age.

* These phrases were modified by the 11th Amendment.

naturalization, the court said that ". . .when an alien takes the oath with reservation or does not in good faith forswear loyalty and allegiance to the old country, the decree of naturalization is obtained by deceit." [62]

In a dissenting opinion that was eventually to gain support of a slim majority of the court, Justice Wiley B. Rutledge, joined by Justice Frank Murphy, said he did not believe a naturalized citizen could be stripped of his citizenship in such a case. "My concern is not for Paul Knauer," Rutledge said. "But if one man's citizenship can thus be taken away, so can that of any other. . . . [A]ny process which takes away their [naturalized] citizenship for causes or by procedures not applicable to native born citizens places them in a separate and an inferior class." [63] Rutledge said he did not believe such a difference was contemplated by the authors of the Constitution when they gave Congress the power to establish uniform naturalization rules.

Eighteen years later, Rutledge's dissent became the majority position in the 1964 case of *Schneider v. Rusk.* [64] The case tested the validity of a provision of the 1952 immigration law which revoked the citizenship of any naturalized citizen who subsequently resided in his or her native land for three continuous years.

Born in Germany, Mrs. Schneider came to the United States as a child and acquired derivative citizenship when her parents were naturalized. As an adult she returned to Germany, married a German national and visited the United States only twice in eight years. Her case came to the court after she was denied a U.S. passport on the ground that she had lived in Germany for three continuous years.

By a 5-3 vote, the court struck down the 1952 provision allowing revocation of Mrs. Schneider's citizenship. Echoing Rutledge and Murphy, and John Marshall before them, Justice William O. Douglas said: "We start from the premise that the rights of citizenship of the native born and of the naturalized person are of the same dignity and are coextensive." [65]

The 1952 provision, Douglas continued, "proceeds on the impermissible assumption that naturalized citizens as a class are less reliable and bear less allegiance to this country than do the native born. This is an assumption that is impossible for us to make. . . . The discrimination aimed at naturalized citizens drastically limits their rights to live and work abroad in a way that other citizens may." [66]

Expatriation

The *Knauer* and the *Schneider* decisions set out the arguments in a continuing debate over whether Congress has the power to revoke the citizenship of any citizen, whether naturalized or native-born.

That a citizen may voluntarily expatriate himself has never been questioned. The court has also held that Congress may stipulate certain acts, the voluntary performance of which would be the equivalent of voluntary expatriation. Thus, in 1915 the court upheld a provision of the Citizenship Act of 1907 by which any female citizen who married an alien surrendered her citizenship in the United States. [67]

That provision was repealed in 1922, but in 1950 the court ruled that a woman who had voluntarily sworn allegiance to Italy in order to marry an Italian citizen had, in essence, forsworn her allegiance to the United State and effectively renounced her citizenship in the United States. [68]

The Immigration and Nationality Act of 1952 contained a long list of circumstances under which a citizen would lose his citizenship. These included voting in a foreign election, being convicted and discharged from the armed services for desertion during time of war and leaving or remaining outside the country to avoid military service. The question was whether the performance of any of these actions amounted to voluntary renunciation of citizenship. If it did not, then their validity turned on whether Congress had the power to revoke citizenship.

Foreign Elections

In the first case to deal fully with this question — *Perez v. Brownell* — a divided court in 1958 upheld the provision revoking citizenship of a person who voted in a foreign election. [69] The majority held that Congress could revoke citizenship as a necessary and proper means of exercising its other powers. In this case, the court viewed this provision as enacted pursuant to Congress' implied power over foreign affairs. Justice Felix Frankfurter said the court could not deny Congress the authority to regulate conduct of Americans — such as voting in foreign elections — that might prove embarrassing or even jeopardize the conduct of foreign relations.

Frankfurter also rejected the argument that the 14th Amendment denied Congress the power to revoke citizenship. "[T]here is nothing in the terms, the context, the history or the manifest purpose of the Fourteenth Amendment to warrant drawing from it a restriction upon the power otherwise possessed by Congress to withdraw citizenship." [70]

Chief Justice Earl Warren dissented:

The Government is without the power to take citizenship away from a native-born or lawfully naturalized American. The Fourteenth Amendment recog-

nizes that this priceless right is immune from the exercise of governmental powers. If the Government determines that certain conduct by United States citizens should be prohibited because of anticipated injurious consequences to the conduct of foreign affairs or to some other legitimate governmental interest, it may within the limits of the Constitution proscribe such activity and assess appropriate punishment. But every exercise of governmental power must find its source in the Constitution. The power to denationalize is not within the letter or the spirit of the powers with which our Government was endowed. The citizen may elect to renounce his citizenship, and under some circumstances he may be found to have abandoned his status by voluntarily performing acts that compromise his undivided allegiance to his country. The mere act of voting in a foreign election, however, without regard to the circumstances attending the participation, is not sufficient to show a voluntary abandonment of citizenship. The record in this case does not disclose any of the circumstances under which this petitioner voted. We know only the bare fact that he cast a ballot. The basic right of American citizenship has been too dearly won to be so lightly lost. [71]

Desertion

The same day it handed down its decision in *Perez,* the court invalidated the provision of the immigration law that revoked citizenship for persons convicted and discharged from the armed services for desertion. In *Trop v. Dulles,* five justices agreed that the provision was unconstitutional but only four agreed on one line of reasoning. For them, Warren again said he did not believe Congress had the power to revoke citizenship. Additionally, he said, revocation of citizenship in this instance was a violation of the Eighth Amendment's proscription against cruel and unusual punishment. This punishment was more cruel than torture, Warren said, for it was "the total destruction of the individual's status in organized society." [72]

Justice William J. Brennan Jr. agreed with the outcome but not with Warren's reasoning. He admitted that his support of the majority in the *Perez* case was paradoxical judged against his position in the present case. But, he said, revocation of citizenship for voting in a foreign election was within the authority of Congress under its powers to regulate foreign affairs. In the *Trop* case, revocation for desertion went beyond any legitimate means of regulation in exercise of the power to raise and maintain armies, he said.

The four dissenters maintained the position they had espoused in the majority opinion in the *Perez* case.

Draft Evasion

Five years later in *Kennedy v. Mendoza-Martinez* (1963), the court struck down the provisions of the immigration act that revoked the citizenship of anyone who left or remained outside the country in order to evade military service.

The sections were invalid, the court said, "because in them Congress has plainly employed the sanction of deprivation of nationality as a punishment . . . without affording the procedural safeguards guaranteed by the Fifth and Sixth Amendments." [73] Deciding the case on these grounds made it unnecessary for the court to choose between the powers of Congress and the rights of citizenship.

Control of Aliens

The congressional power over aliens is absolute and derives from the fact of the nation's sovereignty. This was recognized by the Supreme Court in 1889 as it upheld an act of Congress barring entry of Chinese aliens into the country:

> That the government of the United States, through the action of the legislative department, can exclude aliens from its territory is a proposition which we do not think open to controversy. Jurisdiction over its own territory to that extent is an incident of every independent nation. It is a part of its independence. If it could not exclude aliens, it would be to that extent subject to the control of another power.... The United States, in their relation to foreign countries and their subjects or citizens, are one nation, invested with powers which belong to independent nations, the exercise of which can be invoked for the maintenance of its absolute independence and security throughout its entire territory. [1]

Under this authority, Congress has barred from entry convicts and prostitutes, epileptics, anarchists and professional beggars. It has excluded people because of their race and it has established national origin quotas.

This absolute authority also empowers Congress to regulate to a large extent the conduct of aliens in the country, and to provide that aliens convicted of certain crimes be deported.

The Supreme Court has held that aliens involved in deportation proceedings are entitled to certain constitutional rights, including protections against self-incrimination, unreasonable searches and seizures, cruel and unusual punishment, *ex post facto* laws and bills of attainder and the rights to bail and procedural due process. [2]

Nevertheless, the court did uphold a provision of the Internal Security Act of 1950 that authorized the attorney general to jail without bail aliens who were members of the Communist Party pending a decision on whether they would be deported. [3]

---

[1] *Chae Chang Ping v. United States (Chinese Exclusion Case),* 130 U.S. 581 at 603-4 (1889). See also *Fong Yue Ting v. United States,* 149 U.S. 698 (1893); *Lem Moon Sing v. United States,* 158 U.S. 538 (1895); *Harisiades v. Shaughnessy,* 342 U.S. 580 (1952); *Shaughnessy v. United States ex rel Mezei,* 345 U.S. 206 (1953).

[2] *Kimm v. Rosenberg,* 363 U.S. 405 (1960), *Abel v. United States,* 362 U.S. 217 (1960); *Marcello v. Bonds,* 349 U.S. 302 (1955); *Carlson v. Landon,* 342 U.S. 524 (1952); *Wong Yang Sung v. McGrath,* 339 U.S. 33 (1950).

[3] *Carlson v. Landon,* 342 U.S. 524 (1952).

Foreign Elections Again

In 1967 the court, again divided 5-4, made that choice, declaring the government powerless to revoke citizenship.

The case of *Afroyim v. Rusk* turned on the same issue involved in the *Perez* case. [74] Polish-born Beys Afroyim was a naturalized U.S. citizen who in 1951 voluntarily voted in an Israeli election. He was denied renewal of his passport for that reason.

Urging the court to review its decisions in the *Perez* case, Afroyim maintained that he could lose his U.S. citizenship only through voluntary renunciation. Following the *Perez* precedent, the lower courts ruled that Congress through its implied power over foreign affairs could revoke the citizenship of Americans voting in foreign elections.

Overturning *Perez,* the majority rejected the idea

> ...that, aside from the Fourteenth Amendment, Congress has any general power, express or implied, to take away an American citizen's citizenship without his assent.... In our country the people are sovereign and the government cannot sever its relationship to the people by taking away their citizenship. [75]

Nor could Congress find power to revoke citizenship in the citizenship clause of the 14th Amendment. That clause, the majority said,

> ...provides its own constitutional rule in language calculated completely to control the status of citizenship: 'All persons born or naturalized in the United States ... are citizens of the United States....' There is no indication in these words of a fleeting citizenship, good at the moment it is acquired but subject to destruction by the government at any time. [76]

The majority in a footnote made an exception for persons who obtained their naturalization through fraud.

The four dissenters held to the reasoning of the majority in the *Perez* case. "The Citizenship Clause . . . neither denies nor provides to Congress any power of expatriation...," wrote Justice John Marshall Harlan. He continued:

> ...Once obtained, citizenship is of course protected from arbitrary withdrawal by the constraints placed around the Congress' powers by the Constitution; it is not proper to create from the Citizenship Clause an additional, and entirely unwarranted, restriction upon legislative authority. The construction now placed on the Citizenship Clause rests, in the last analysis, simply on the Court's *ipse dixit,* evincing little more, it is quite apparent, than the present majority's own distaste for the expatriation power. [77]

Non-Residence

Decided by such a narrow vote, the *Afroyim* decision was not considered a definitive answer to the question of congressional power to expatriate citizens. And while it did not overturn the *Afroyim* decision, the case of *Rogers v. Bellei,* decided in 1971, clouded the issue even further. [78]

Bellei was born overseas in 1939 of one American parent and one alien parent. The 1952 immigration law stated that a person of such parentage would be considered a citizen of the United States so long as he or she lived in the United States for five continuous years between the ages of 14 and 28. Bellei only visited the United States briefly on five occasions. Because he did not meet the residence requirement, his citizenship was revoked. He challenged the requirement, but by a 5-4 vote the court upheld the provision.

Writing for the majority, Justice Harry A. Blackmun maintained that Bellei did not qualify for U.S. citizenship under the 14th Amendment. Bellei "was not born in the United States. And he has not been subject to the jurisdiction of the United States," said Blackmun. "All this being so, it seems indisputable that the first sentence of the 14th

Amendment has no application to plaintiff Bellei. He simply is not a Fourteenth-Amendment-first-sentence citizen." [79]

The decision in *Afroyim*, Blackmun continued, was based on the fact that Afroyim was a citizen by virtue of the 14th Amendment. But Bellei was a citizen by an act of Congress, and if Congress may impose conditions that such a person must meet before he can become a citizen, Blackmun said, the majority could see no constitutional reason why it could not impose conditions that must be met after he became a citizen. Blackmun wrote:

...Our National Legislature indulged the foreign-born child with presumptive citizenship subject to subsequent satisfaction of the reasonable residence requirement, rather than to deny him citizenship outright, as concededly it had the power to do, and relegate the child, if he desired American citizenship, to the more arduous requirements of the usual naturalization process. The plaintiff here would force the Congress to choose between unconditional conferment of United States citizenship at birth and deferment of citizenship until a condition precedent is fulfilled. We are not convinced that the Constitution requires so rigid a choice. [80]

The minority held that the *Afroyim* decision controlled this case and that Congress could not revoke Bellei's citizenship. In an unusually bitter dissent, Justice Hugo L. Black wrote:

...Congress could not, until today, consistent with the Fourteenth Amendment enact a law stripping an American of his citizenship which he has never voluntarily renounced or given up. Now the Court, by a vote of five to four through a simple change in its composition, overturns the decision.... This precious Fourteenth Amendment American citizenship should not be blown around by every passing political wind that changes the composition of this Court. I dissent. [81]

Congress repealed this residence requirement in 1978.

Footnotes

[1] C. Herman Pritchett, *The American Constitution* 3rd ed. (New York: McGraw-Hill Book Company, Inc., 1977), p. 55.

[2] *Pollard v. Hagan*, 3 How. 212 at 224 (1845).

[3] *Escanaba Co. v. Chicago*, 107 U.S. 678 at 689 (1883).

[4] *Coyle v. Smith*, 221 U.S. 559 at 567 (1911).

[5] *United States v. Texas*, 339 U.S. 707 at 718 (1950).

[6] Id., at 719-20.

[7] *Stearns v. Minnesota*, 179 U.S. 223 at 245 (1900).

[8] *American Insurance Co. v. Canter*, 1 Pet. 511 at 542 (1828).

[9] *United States v. Jones*, 109 U.S. 513 (1883).

[10] *First National Bank v. Yankton County*, 101 U.S. 129 at 133 (1880).

[11] *Simms v. Simms*, 175 U.S. 162 (1899).

[12] *Binns v. United States*, 194 U.S. 486 (1904).

[13] *Scott v. Sandford*, 19 How. 393 (1857).

[14] Edward S. Corwin, *The Doctrine of Judicial Review, Its Legal and Historical Basis and Other Essays* (Princeton: Princeton University Press, 1914; reprint ed., Gloucester, Mass.: Peter Smith, 1963), p. 157.

[15] General sources for historical background of the *Dred Scott* case include: Alfred H. Kelly and Winfred A. Harbison, *The American Constitution; Its Origins and Development*, 5th ed. (New York: W. W. Norton & Co. Inc., 1976), pp. 234-56, 333-67; Carl B. Swisher, *History of the Supreme Court of the United States:* Vol. V., *The Taney Period, 1836-64* (New York: Macmillan Publishing Co. Inc., 1974), pp. 528-652; Bruce Catton, "The Dred Scott Case," in John A. Garraty, ed., *Quarrels That Have Shaped The Constitution* (New York: Harper & Row, 1964), p. 85.

[16] *Strader v. Graham*, 10 How. 82 (1850).

[17] Id. at 93.

[18] Carl B. Swisher, *American Constitutional Development*, 2nd ed. (Cambridge: Houghton-Mifflin Co., The Riverside Press, 1954), p. 588-89.

[19] James D. Richardson, ed., *A Compilation of the Messages and Papers of the Presidents* (New York: Bureau of National Literature, Inc., 1927), vol. 7, p. 2962.

[20] *Scott v. Sandford*, 19 How. 393 at 404 (1857).

[21] Id. at 407.

[22] Id. at 410.

[23] Id. at 405.

[24] Id. at 410.

[25] Id. at 425.

[26] Id. at 436.

[27] Id. at 449.

[28] Id. at 450.

[29] Id. at 452.

[30] Catton, "Dred Scott", p. 85.

[31] Quoted in Charles Warren, *The Supreme Court in United States History*, rev. ed., 2 vols. (Boston: Little Brown & Co., 1922, 1926), II:304.

[32] Swisher, *American Constitutional Development*, p. 248.

[33] Corwin, *Doctrine of Judicial Review*, p. 156.

[34] Quoted in Warren, *Supreme Court in History*, II:316.

[35] *DeLima v. Bidwell*, 182 U.S. 1 (1901).

[36] *Cross v. Harrison*, 16 How. 164 (1853).

[37] *DeLima v. Bidwell*, 182 U.S. 1 at 187 (1901).

[38] *Downes v. Bidwell*, 182 U.S. 244 (1901).

[39] Id. at 306.

[40] Id. at 307-308.

[41] Id. at 339.

[42] Id. at 380.

[43] *Hawaii v. Mankichi*, 190 U.S. 197 at 216 (1903).

[44] Id. at 223.

[45] *Dorr v. United States*, 195 U.S. 138 at 143 (1904).

[46] *Rasmussen v. United States*, 197 U.S. 516 (1905).

[47] *Dowdell v. United States*, 221 U.S. 325 (1911).

[48] *Perez v. Brownell*, 356 U.S. 44 at 64-65 (1958), Chief Justice Earl Warren dissenting.

[49] *Scott v. Sandford*, 19 How. 393 at 406 (1857).

[50] *United States v. Wong Kim Ark*, 169 U.S. 649 at 693 (1898); see also *Perkins v. Elg*, 307 U.S. 325 (1939).

[51] *United States v. Macintosh*, 283 U.S. 605 at 615 (1931).

[52] *Fong Yue Ting v. United States*, 149 U.S. 698 at 707, 713 passim, (1893).

[53] *Galvan v. Press*, 347 U.S. 522 (1954); *Berenyi v. District Director*, 385 U.S. 630 (1967), Communist Party membership; *Boutilier v. Immigration and Naturalization Service*, 387 U.S. 118 (1967), homosexuals.

[54] *United States v. Schwimmer*, 279 U.S. 644 (1929).

[55] *Girouard v. United States*, 328 U.S. 61 (1946), overturning *United States v. Schwimmer*, 279 U.S. 644 (1929); *United States v. Macintosh*, 283 U.S. 605 (1931); and *United States v. Bland*, 283 U.S. 636 (1931).

[56] *Cohnstaedt v. Immigration and Naturalization Service*, 339 U.S. 901 (1950).

[57] *Osborn v. Bank of United States*, 9 Wheat. 737 at 827 (1824).

[58] *Johannessen v. United States*, 225 U.S. 227 at 241 (1912).

[59] *Costello v. United States*, 365 U.S. 265 (1961).

[60] *Luria v. United States*, 231 U.S. 9 (1913).

[61] *Schneiderman v. United States*, 320 U.S. 118 (1943).

[62] *Knauer v. United States*, 328 U.S. 654 (1946).

[63] Id. at 675-77.
[64] *Schneider v. Rusk,* 377 U.S. 163 (1964).
[65] Id. at 165.
[66] Id. at 168-69.
[67] *Mackenzie v. Hare,* 239 U.S. 299 (1915).
[68] *Savorgnan v. United States,* 338 U.S. 491 (1950).
[69] *Perez v. Brownell,* 356 U.S. 44 (1958).
[70] Id. at 58, note.
[71] Id. at 77-78.
[72] *Trop v. Dulles,* 356 U.S. 86 at 101 (1958).

[73] *Kennedy v. Mendoza-Martinez,* 372 U.S. 144 at 165-66 (1963).
[74] *Afroyim v. Rusk,* 387 U.S. 253 (1967).
[75] Id. at 257.
[76] Id. at 262.
[77] Id. at 292-93.
[78] *Rogers v. Bellei,* 401 U.S. 815 (1971).
[79] Id. at 827.
[80] Id. at 835.
[81] Id. at 836-37.

The Power to Amend the Constitution

Few questions concerning the power of Congress to propose amendments to the Constitution have come to the Supreme Court. More cases of importance have arisen concerning the power of Congress to enforce new amendments.

Several of the 26 amendments that have been added to the Constitution, primarily those conferring a political right, such as voting, empower Congress to enforce them through legislation. The first of these enforcement provisions were part of the three Civil War amendments conferring citizenship and political rights on blacks.

The court of the 1870s and 1880s severely weakened Congress' power to enforce these guarantees, ruling that Congress could reach state discrimination only after it had occurred and individual discrimination not at all. It was almost 100 years before the court, playing a leading part in the civil rights revolution of the 1950s and 1960s, reversed this posture, sustaining a broad enforcement role for Congress.

The Amending Power

Article V of the Constitution states: "The Congress, whenever two thirds of both Houses shall deem it necessary, shall propose Amendments to this Constitution, or, on the Application of the Legislatures of two thirds of the several States, shall call a Convention for proposing Amendments, which, in either Case, shall be valid to all Intents and Purposes, as Part of this Constitution, when ratified by the Legislatures of three fourths of the several States, or by Conventions in three fourths thereof, as the one or the other Mode of Ratification may be proposed by the Congress. . . ."

More than 9,100 proposed amendments to the Constitution had been introduced in Congress by June 1979.[1] Most of them were duplicates of earlier proposals or very similar; some were introduced repeatedly in successive Congresses. Only 33 of these amendments have been submitted to the states for ratification, and only five of those (excluding the pending Equal Rights Amendment and the proposed amendment giving the District of Columbia voting representation in Congress) have not been ratified. All of the submitted amendments were proposed by a two-thirds vote of Congress. A constitutional convention to propose an amendment had not occurred. By mid-1979 more than half the states had petitioned Congress for an

amendment mandating a balanced federal budget. And between 1965 and 1969, 33 states — one short of the necessary two-thirds — petitioned Congress for an amendment to allow one chamber of a state legislature to be apportioned on the basis of geography or political subdivisions, rather than strictly by population. The petition campaign was in response to the Supreme Court decision in *Reynolds v. Sims* (1964), which required both houses of a state legislature to be apportioned on a basis of substantial equality of population. That decision struck not only at gerrymandered state legislatures, but also at those apportioned — on the basis of one state senator for each city, town or country, for example.[2] *(Reynolds v. Sims, p. 492)*

Viewing constitutional amendments as political decisions, the Supreme Court has been reluctant to interfere in the process. Nonetheless, the court has heard several cases challenging the constitutionality of ratified amendments and has handed down a number of decisions affecting procedures for enacting and ratifying amendments.

Constitutional Challenges

State Suits. The first challenge to a constitutional amendment came in 1798, after ratification of the 11th Amendment, which prohibited the citizens of one state from suing another state in federal court without its consent. The question was: What effect did ratification of the amendment have on such suits pending at the time of ratification? To apply the amendment to pending suits, said petitioners, would give it the unconstitutional character of an *ex post facto* law.

In *Hollingsworth v. Virginia*, the court ruled that once the amendment took effect upon ratification, the court had no jurisdiction to hear any case of the type described by the amendment — including pending ones. Therefore, the court dismissed the case.[3]

Prohibition. The constitutional amendment prohibiting the manufacture, sale and transportation of alcoholic beverages enjoyed only a brief life but engendered more Supreme Court cases testing its validity than any other amendment. Most of these cases involved challenges to the way the amendment was ratified *(see below)* but in one case the court was asked to decide whether liquor was a proper subject for a constitutional amendment. The court in 1920 ruled it was.[4]

Women's Vote. The 19th Amendment, granting the vote to women, was challenged on the ground that it made

---

Extension and Rescission

Once it has set a time period for ratification of a proposed constitutional amendment, may Congress then extend that deadline? That is the question posed by opponents of the Equal Rights Amendment (ERA) in challenging the 39-month extension of that amendment's ratification deadline. The extension was approved by Congress in October 1978.

The proposed amendment, which would give men and women equal rights under the law, originally provided seven years for ratification; that time period was set to expire March 22, 1979. The 1978 extension moved the deadline to June 30, 1982. At the time Congress passed the extension, 35 states had ratified the amendment. Three more states were needed to ratify the ERA for it to become the 27th Amendment.

Debate on the extension in both the House and Senate centered on its constitutionality. The question of such an extension had never been considered by the Supreme Court. However, in *Dillon v. Gloss* (1921), the court ruled that Congress had the authority to fix a reasonable time period in which the states must ratify a proposed constitutional amendment.[1] And in the 1939 case of *Coleman v. Miller*, the court held that the question of what constitutes a reasonable time period was a non-justiciable political matter for Congress to determine.[2]

A corollary question concerning the ERA ratification was whether states that had ratified the amendment could subsequently rescind that ratification. As of July 1979, four states — Idaho, Nebraska, South Dakota and Tennessee — had done just that. The Supreme Court may have already answered the question. In its opinion in the *Coleman* case, the court wrote:

> . . .We think that in accordance with . . . historic precedent the question of the efficacy of ratifications by state legislatures, in the light of previous rejection or attempted withdrawal, should be regarded as a political question pertaining to the political departments, with the ultimate authority in the Congress in the exercise of its control over the promulgation of the adoption of the amendment.[3]

[1] *Dillon v. Gloss*, 256 U.S. 368 (1921).
[2] *Coleman v. Miller*, 307 U.S. 433 (1939).
[3] Id. at 450.

tion: He has nothing to do with the proposition, or adoption of amendments to the Constitution," wrote Justice Samuel Chase in 1798.[6]

Two-Thirds Requirements. The court has also ruled that the two-thirds requirement for adoption of a proposed constitutional amendment applies to two-thirds of those members present and voting and not to two-thirds of the entire membership.[7]

Time Limits. Whether a constitutional amendment has to be ratified within a certain time period is unclear. Congress first added a time limit in 1917 when it required that the prohibition amendment be ratified within seven years of its submission to the states. That requirement was challenged in *Dillon v. Gloss* (1921).[8]

The court rejected the challenge, saying that "the fair inference or implication from Article V is that the ratification must be within some reasonable time after the proposal," and that Congress' power to set a time limit was "an incident of its power to designate the mode of ratification."[9]

Not until 1939 did the court hear a case asking what constituted a reasonable time period for ratification. Such a determination, the court said in *Coleman v. Miller*, was a political question for Congress, not the court, to decide.[10]

Moreover, four justices in a concurring opinion called into question the court's finding in *Dillon v. Gloss* that ratification should occur within a reasonable time. Since Congress has exclusive power over the amending process, they wrote, it "cannot be bound by and is under no duty to accept the pronouncements upon that exclusive power by this Court. . . . Therefore any judicial expression . . . is a mere admonition to the Congress in the nature of an advisory opinion, given wholly without constitutional authority."[11] It is significant that the court did not hear a case dealing with Article V for 40 years after its 1939 decision. Five amendments were added to the Constitution during this period. *(Box this page)*

State Ratification Procedures

Who May Ratify. The court has repeatedly held that ratification of constitutional amendments by a state must be accomplished either through the state legislature or by a state convention and that Congress has the sole authority to determine which method will be used for each amendment submitted to the states.[12]

Thus, in 1920 the court ruled that a provision of the Ohio constitution requiring a popular referendum to approve its legislature's ratification of the 18th Amendment was in violation of the federal Constitution.[13] In a second case, the court held that state-required procedures that barred two state legislatures from ratifying the 19th Amendment were in conflict with the federal Constitution.[14] In both cases, the court held that "the function of a state legislature in ratifying a proposed Amendment to the Federal Constitution, like the function of Congress in proposing the Amendment, is a federal function, derived from the Federal Constitution; and it transcends any limitations sought to be imposed by the people of a state."[15]

Ratification and Rejection. Whether a state may rescind its ratification of a constitutional amendment is a political question that Congress must decide, the court has indicated. Tennessee challenged the women's suffrage amendment on the grounds that it was counted as ratifying the 19th Amendment despite the fact that its legislature had subsequently rescinded the ratification. Basing its

such a large addition to the electorate of the few states that had refused to ratify it that it undercut their political autonomy. The court held that the 19th Amendment affected the electorate no more than the 15th Amendment, which forbade voting discrimination on the basis of race, color or previous condition of servitude.[5] The court observed that the latter amendment had been considered valid and enforced by the judiciary for the last half century.

Federal Ratification Procedures

Presidential Veto. The president is not required to sign and cannot block a congressional resolution proposing a constitutional amendment to the states. "The negative of the President applies only to the ordinary cases of legisla-

decision on narrow procedural grounds, the court in 1922 held that official notice of the ratification to the secretary of state was conclusive upon him, and that his certification of ratification was binding on the courts. [16]

In *Coleman v. Miller* (1939), the question was raised whether a state legislature that had first rejected an amendment could reverse itself and ratify it. The court strongly intimated that this was a question only Congress could answer.[17] *(Box, p. 150)*

Congressional decisions, however, have not been consistent. At the direction of Congress, the secretary of state counted the ratifications of the 14th Amendment by Ohio, New Jersey and Oregon despite votes by the three state legislatures to withdraw the ratification. But the secretary of state apparently accepted North Dakota's rescission of its ratification of the 25th Amendment. [18]

Enforcement Power

Seven constitutional amendments contain language conferring on Congress the power to enforce them by "appropriate legislation." These amendments are the three Civil War amendments (the 13th, 14th and 15th); the 19th giving women the vote; the 23rd permitting residents of the District of Columbia to vote for president; the 24th abolishing the poll tax in federal elections, and the 26th setting the minimum voting age at 18 years. The 18th Amendment prohibiting the sale of liquor divided enforcement power between Congress and the states. It was repealed 14 years after its ratification, partly because enforcement proved so ineffective.

The Civil War amendments have required the most significant exercise of the enforcement power. The 13th Amendment, ratified in 1865, abolished slavery. The 14th Amendment, ratified in 1868, made blacks citizens and prohibited states from denying citizens due process and equal protection of the laws. The 15th Amendment, ratified in 1870, prohibited federal and state governments from denying the right to vote to citizens on the basis of race, color or previous condition of servitude. By 1875, Congress had passed seven statutes to implement and enforce these three amendments.

But in its first considerations of the enforcement power the Supreme Court ruled that Congress had exceeded its enforcement authority when it passed many of these statutes. The court narrowed the congressional enforcement power in two ways: Congress could only enforce the guarantees of these amendments against official state acts of discrimination, not against the discriminatory actions of private persons; furthermore, the enforcement power was corrective, to be exercised only after the discriminatory state action occurred.

The Civil Rights Cases

Striking down the Civil Rights Act of 1875 which sought to prohibit discrimination against blacks in public accommodations, the court in 1883 wrote that the power to enforce the due process and equal protection guarantees of the 14th Amendment

...does not invest Congress with power to legislate upon subjects which are within the domain of State legislation; but to provide modes of relief against State legislation, or State action, of the kind referred to. It does not authorize Congress to create a code of municipal law for the regulation of private rights; but to provide modes of redress against the operation of State laws and the action of State officers, executive or judicial, when these are subversive of the fundamental rights specified in the amendment. [19]

In the same case, the court also curbed congressional power to enforce the 13th Amendment's abolition of slavery. The court acknowledged that Congress had the authority "to pass all laws necessary and proper for abolishing all badges and incidents of slavery in the United States." Such laws could guarantee blacks "fundamental rights which are the essence of civil freedom, namely the same right to make and enforce contracts, to sue parties, give evidence and to inherit, purchase, lease, sell and convey property, as is enjoyed by white citizens." [20] But having said this, the court then held that these fundamental rights did not extend to the right of access to public accommodations. "It would be running the slavery argument into the ground to make it apply to every act of discrimination which a person may see fit to make," the court wrote. [21]

Voting Rights

The court generally recognized that Congress had an inherent power to protect a person's right to vote in federal elections. And once it was established that a person had the right to vote in state elections, the court generally upheld Congress' power under the 15th Amendment to enforce that right.

But in other rulings, the court eased the way for the states to continue to discriminate against blacks. In *United States v. Reese* (1876), the court ruled that the 15th Amendment did not confer the right to vote on anyone but simply prohibited racial discrimination in voting. [22] As a result, southern states wrote statutes that prevented blacks from voting even though on their face the laws were not discriminatory. Such statutes required voters to pass literacy tests or pay poll taxes. Occasionally, a state or locality would gerrymander voting districts to dilute the strength of the black vote. Some of the more obviously discriminatory of these state statutes were declared unconstitutional only to be replaced by other forms of discrimination. *(Details of voting rights decisions, p. 477)*

As a result of this body of rulings, Congress was limited to enforcing the Civil War amendments against state infringements through remedial legislation alone. One common form of such corrective legislation was to authorize persons denied their rights in state courts to bring their cases into federal court. Another method was to provide federal civil and criminal penalties for state officials who deprived persons of their rights. *(Removal privilege, p. 258)*

Modern Enforcement

This situation prevailed until the civil rights movement of the 1950s and 1960s prompted passage of new legislation to enforce the guarantees of the Civil War amendments. In reviewing this legislation, the Supreme Court now interpreted the amendments' enforcement clauses expansively, sanctioning congressional authority to prohibit state action before it occurred and, in certain cases, prohibiting racial discrimination by private individuals.

Voting Rights

Two of the cases concerned the constitutionality of the Voting Rights Act of 1965. This statute abolished literacy tests for five years (the abolition was later made permanent) and required states and local political units covered by the law to clear any changes in their election laws with the Justice Department before they took effect. Areas covered by the law — primarily in the South — were those where a literacy test had been in use and where a substantial percentage of the voting-age population was not registered to vote. The bill also authorized sending federal examiners into the covered areas to supervise voter registration.

In *South Carolina v. Katzenbach* (1966) the court upheld the law as a proper exercise of Congress' enforcement powers granted by the 15th Amendment. South Carolina challenged the act as infringing on powers traditionally reserved to the states.

"As against the reserved powers of the States, Congress may use any rational means to effectuate the constitutional prohibition of racial discrimination in voting," the court wrote. While the means used by Congress were "inventive," the court found them appropriate to prohibit voting discrimination. [23]

The second case challenged a provision of the Voting Rights Act that forbade states to bar from voting persons who had completed a certain number of years in an accredited foreign language school even if they could not speak or write English. The question was the effect of this provision on a New York statute requiring that voters be able to speak and write English — a law which disenfranchised most of the state's large Puerto Rican population.

The court upheld the federal provision as a proper means of enforcing both the equal protection clause of the **14th Amendment and the guarantee of the 15th Amendment.** In both instances, the court said, the question was not whether the court agreed with the provision barring such literacy requirements but whether "we perceive a basis upon which Congress might predicate a judgment that the application of New York's English literacy requirement . . . constituted an invidious discrimination in violation of the Equal Protection Clause." [24] That the requirement did violate the equal protection clause was plain, the court said. "Any contrary conclusion would require us to be blind to the realities familiar to the legislators." [25]

Private Discrimination

The court in 1968 broadened its interpretation of the enforcement power conferred by the 13th Amendment. The case of *Jones v. Alfred H. Mayer Co.* concerned an 1866 civil rights law enacted to ensure blacks the same right as whites to make and enforce contracts, sue, inherit, and buy, lease, sell and occupy real estate. Persons who denied others these rights on the grounds of race or previous condition of servitude were guilty of a misdemeanor. The question was whether this law was violated by the refusal of a private individual to sell a house to a black. Although the court had never directly ruled on that issue, it had been assumed that the 13th Amendment, like the 14th and 15th, reached only discrimination by state officials.

The court by a 7-2 vote ruled that the statute did apply to private acts of discrimination. When Congress first enacted the statute granting blacks the right to buy and sell property, "it plainly meant to secure that right against interference from any source whatever, whether governmental or private," the majority wrote. [26]

The issue then was whether the 1866 statute was a proper exercise of the 13th Amendment's enforcement power. The court held that it was:

> . . .Surely, Congress has the power under the Thirteenth Amendment rationally to determine what are the badges and the incidents of slavery, and the authority to translate that determination into effective legislation. Nor can we say that the determination Congress has made is an irrational one. [27]

The court extended the effect of this enforcement power even further when it held in 1971 that a section of the 1866 act prohibited private individuals, such as members of the Ku Klux Klan, from conspiring to prevent blacks from exercising their constitutional rights such as freedom of speech and assembly. [28] In a 1976 decision, the court held that racially segregated private schools which refused to admit black students solely on account of their race violated the provision of the 1866 statute which gave blacks "the same right . . . to make and enforce contracts . . . as is enjoyed by white citizens." [29]

State Sovereignty

Furthermore, in 1976, the court held that the enforcement power granted by the 14th Amendment acts as a limit on the protection which the 11th Amendment provides to the states from undue federal interference in their affairs. By shielding states from federal suits brought by citizens without their consent, that amendment serves as a guarantee of state sovereignty. *(Details, p. 354)*

In the case of *Fitzpatrick v. Bitzer,* the court held that under the enforcement power of the 14th Amendment, Congress acted properly when it amended the 1964 Civil Rights Act to authorize federal judges to hear civil rights complaints brought by citizens against a state — and, upon a finding of discrimination, to order the state to make retroactive payments of benefits to the victims of discrimination.

The affected state — Connecticut — challenged the power of Congress to authorize such federal court orders, arguing that the 11th Amendment protected it from such federal interference in the spending of state funds. The court rejected the state's argument, declaring:

> . . .[W]e think that the Eleventh Amendment, and the principles of state sovereignty which it embodies . . . are necessarily limited by the enforcement provisions . . . of the Fourteenth Amendment. . . . We think that Congress may, in determining what is 'appropriate legislation' for the purpose of enforcing the provisions of the Fourteenth Amendment, provide for private suits against States or state officials which are constitutionally impermissible in other contexts. [30]

Footnotes

[1] Congressional Quarterly. *Guide to Congress,* 2d ed. (Washington, D.C.: Congressional Quarterly, 1976), p. 225; Commerce Clearing House, Congressional Index 1975-76, 1977-78; 1979 (Chicago: Commerce Clearing House, 1975, 1976, 1977, 1978, 1979).

[2] *Reynolds v. Sims,* 377 U.S. 533 (1964).

[3] *Hollingsworth v. Virginia,* 3 Dall. 378 (1798).

[4] *National Prohibition Cases,* 253 U.S. 350 (1920).

[5] *Leser v. Garnett,* 258 U.S. 130 (1920).

[6] *Hollingsworth v. Virginia,* 3 Dall. 378 at 381, note (1798).

[7] *National Prohibition Cases,* 253 U.S. 350 (1920).

[8] *Dillon v. Gloss,* 256 U.S. 368 (1921).

[9] Id. at 375, 376.

[10] *Coleman v. Miller,* 307 U.S. 433 (1939).

[11] Id. at 459.

[12] *United States v. Sprague,* 282 U.S. 716 (1931).

[13] *Hawke v. Smith,* 253 U.S. 221 (1920).

[14] *Leser v. Garnett,* 258 U.S. 130 (1922).

[15] Id. at 137; see also *Hawke v. Smith,* 253 U.S. 221 at 230 (1920).

[16] *Leser v. Garnett,* 258 U.S. 130 (1922).

[17] *Coleman v. Miller,* 307 U.S. 433 at 450 (1939).

[18] Robert E. Cushman and Robert F. Cushman, *Cases in Constitutional Law* (New York: Appleton-Century-Crofts, 1968), p. 8.

[19] *Civil Rights Cases,* 109 U.S. 3 at 11 (1883).

[20] Id. at 22.

[21] Id. at 24.

[22] *United States v. Reese,* 92 U.S. 214 (1876).

[23] *South Carolina v. Katzenbach,* 383 U.S. 301 at 324 (1966).

[24] *Katzenbach v. Morgan,* 384 U.S. 641 at 656 (1966).

[25] Id. at 653.

[26] *Jones v. Alfred H. Mayer Co.,* 392 U.S. 409 at 424 (1968).

[27] Id. at 440-41.

[28] *Griffin v. Breckenridge,* 403 U.S. 88 (1971).

[29] *Runyon v. McCrary,* 427 U.S. 160 (1976).

[30] *Fitzpatrick v. Bitzer,* 427 U.S. 445 at 456 (1976).

Miscellaneous Powers

The Constitution authorizes Congress to make bankruptcy, patent and copyright laws, set standard weights and measures, administer the nation's capital, establish a postal system and punish counterfeiting.

There have been few cases involving the power of weights and measures, and the power to establish penalties for counterfeiting has proved superfluous since Congress may also punish counterfeiting under its power to regulate currency.

The Supreme Court has placed few restrictions on the exercise of the other powers.

Bankruptcy

The power to make "uniform Laws on the subject of Bankruptcies throughout the United States" was exercised only infrequently in the 1800s. Federal laws were enacted in 1800, 1841 and 1867 to meet specific economic crises, but each survived public criticism and political pressure only a few years and then was repealed. In the intervals between federal laws, state bankruptcy laws were controlling. When Congress chose to act in the field, however, it interpreted its powers broadly and this interpretation was usually sanctioned by the Supreme Court.

Rather than restrict the coverage of bankruptcy laws to tradesmen as was the English practice, Congress in its first bankruptcy law extended coverage to bankers, brokers, commodities agents and insurance underwriters. The belief that the grant of power was broad enough to cover such categories of bankrupts was sanctioned by the court in 1902, and the court has since given its implicit approval to laws extending bankruptcy coverage to almost every class of person and corporation. [1] The court has also approved federal laws to rehabilitate the debtor as well as to provide appropriate relief to creditors. [2]

Despite its liberal interpretation of this clause, the Supreme Court has recognized some limitations on the power. Congress must be mindful of a creditor's due process rights guaranteed by the Fifth Amendment. [3] Because the states have incorporation power, a corporation dissolved by a state court decree may not file a petition for reorganization under the federal bankruptcy laws. [4] Nor may Congress place the fiscal affairs of a city, county or other state political unit under the control of a federal bankruptcy court. [5]

Patents and Copyrights

Congressional authority over patents and copyrights comes from Article I, Section 8, Clause 8, which empowers Congress "To promote the Progress of Science and useful Arts, by securing for limited Times to Authors and Inventors the exclusive Right to their respective Writings and Discoveries."

In fashioning copyright and patent laws, Congress must balance two interests. As described by the Library of Congress, these are "the interest of the public in being protected against monopolies and in having ready access and use of new items versus the interest of the country, as a whole, in encouraging invention by rewarding creative persons for their innovations." [6]

There have been no serious challenges to the right of Congress to set standards and conditions for the granting of patents and copyrights within the constitutional limits. But numerous court cases have turned on the question of whether a particular invention meets the standards. [7] This has made the court and not Congress in large measure the final judge of what those standards are.

In a recent case, the court established three tests that an item must pass to be patentable: "Innovation, advancement and things which add to the sum of useful knowledge are inherent requisites in a patent system which by constitutional command must 'promote the Progress of . . . useful Arts.' This is the *standard* expressed in the Constitution and it may not be ignored." [8]

In the famous Trademark Cases of 1879, the court held that trademarks could not be defined either as writing or discoveries and thus were not capable of being copyrighted or patented. [9] Congress could only regulate trademarks through the exercise of its power over interstate commerce.

Postal Power

Clause 7 of Article I, Section 8 gives Congress the power "To establish Post Offices and post Roads." Whether this meant that Congress had the power actually to construct post offices and post roads or simply to designate those that would be used as postal facilities was settled in 1876 when the Supreme Court upheld federal appropriation of land on which to build a post office. [10]

The postal power has been interpreted to include the authority to ensure the speedy delivery and protection of the mail. [11] It was on this principle that the federal government was granted an injunction against leaders of the 1894 Pullman strike that halted mail delivery along with the trains. At the same time, federal troops were sent to Illinois to quell the violence that had erupted. Eugene V. Debs and other labor leaders were convicted of contempt for violating the injunction.

The Supreme Court upheld the convictions and the use of federal troops in 1895, declaring that "[t]he strong arm of the national Government may be put forth to brush away all obstructions to the freedom of interstate commerce or the transportation of the mails." [12]

The postal power also has been interpreted to allow Congress to bar items from the mails that it believes might defraud the public or injure its morals. The first such case was *Ex parte Jackson* (1878), in which the Supreme Court sustained congressional action barring from the mails certain circulars relating to lotteries. [13]

In more recent cases, the court has said that the federal power to exclude matter from the mails is limited by other constitutional guarantees. Thus, in 1965, the court struck down a federal law authorizing the post office not to forward mail it regarded as communist propaganda unless the addressee specifically said he wanted to receive it. [14] Declaring the statute a violation of the First Amendment, the court said the law impinged on the right of a person to receive whatever information he or she wanted to receive. The Congressional Research Service of the Library of Congress notes that this was the first time the court had invalidated a federal statute because it conflicted with the First Amendment. [15] *(Freedom of speech and the mails, p. 431)*

Congress frequently has invoked its postal power to aid it in the exercise of other express powers. Thus, in 1910, the court held that correspondence schools were in interstate commerce, and therefore susceptible to federal regulation, because of their reliance on the mails. [16] In 1938, the court upheld provisions of the Public Utility Holding Company Act requiring gas and electric utilities to register with the Securities and Exchange Commission partially on the ground that such holding companies conducted a large and continuous portion of their business through the mails. [17]

District of Columbia

The power "to exercise exclusive Legislation in all Cases whatsoever, over . . . the Seat of Government of the United States" has been interpreted to mean that Congress may make the laws and appoint the administrators of the District of Columbia or delegate the lawmaking powers to a locally elected government. The local government was partially elected from 1802 when the district was established until 1874 when Congress, in the wake of financial scandals involving city officials, substituted a presidentially appointed commission to administer the district under laws passed by Congress. In 1967, this form of government was changed to a presidentially appointed mayor and city council. In 1973, Congress once again turned over administration of the capital city to a locally elected government although it retained a tight rein on the city's financial affairs and its judicial system and may enact laws for the district at any time.

Residents of the district, although citizens of the United States entitled to all constitutional guarantees, were unable to vote for president until the 23rd Amendment was ratified in 1961.

Congress in 1970 authorized the district to elect one non-voting delegate to the House of Representatives. Because the district is not a state, a constitutional amendment is considered to be necessary to give the district a voting member in the House and representation in the Senate. Congress approved such an amendment late in 1978 and sent it to the states for ratification.

The Supreme Court has had almost no occasion to review the federal administration of the District of Columbia.

Footnotes

[1] *Hanover National Bank v. Moyses*, 186 U.S. 181 (1902); *Continental Bank v. Chicago, Rock Island & Pacific Railway Co.*, 294 U.S. 648 (1935); *United States v. Bekins*, 304 U.S. 27 (1938).

[2] *Continental Bank v. Chicago, Rock Island & Pacific Railway Co.*, 294 U.S. 648 (1935); *Wright v. Vinton Branch*, 300 U.S. 440 (1937); *Adair v. Bank of America Association*, 303 U.S. 350 (1938).

[3] *Louisville Bank v. Radford*, 295 U.S. 555 (1935).

[4] *Chicago Title & Trust Co. v. Wilcox Building Corp.*, 302 U.S. 120 (1937).

[5] *Ashton v. Cameron County District*, 298 U.S. 513 (1936).

[6] U.S. Congress. Library of Congress, Congressional Reference Service. *The Constitution of the United States; Analysis and Interpretation* (Washington, D.C., Government Printing Office, 1973), p. 316.

[7] *Funk Bros. Seed Co. v. Kalo Co.*, 333 U.S. 127 (1948); *Sinclair & Co. v. Interchemical Corp.*, 325 U.S. 327 (1945); *Marconi Wireless Co. v. United States*, 320 U.S. 1 (1943); *Keystone Manufacturing Co. v. Adams*, 151 U.S. 139 (1894); *Diamond Rubber Co. v. Consolidated Tire Co.*, 220 U.S. 428 (1911); *A & P Tea Co. v. Supermarket Equipment Corp.*, 340 U.S. 147 (1950).

[8] *Graham v. John Deere Co.*, 383 U.S. 1 (1966).

[9] *Trade-Mark Cases (United States v. Steffens)*, 100 U.S. 82 (1879).

[10] *Kohl v. United States*, 91 U.S. 367 (1876).

[11] *Ex parte Jackson*, 96 U.S. 727 (1878).

[12] *In re Debs*, 158 U.S. 564 at 582 (1895).

[13] *Ex parte Jackson*, 96 U.S. 727 (1878).

[14] *Lamont v. Postmaster General*, 381 U.S. 301 (1965).

[15] Congressional Reference Service, *Constitution; Analysis and Interpretation*, p. 310, note 10.

[16] *International Textbook Co. v. Pigg*, 217 U.S. 91 (1910).

[17] *Electric Bond & Share Co. v. Securities and Exchange Commission*, 303, U.S. 419 (1938).

The Power to Investigate

In 1792 the House of Representatives decided that rather than ask the president to investigate, it would establish its own special committee to inquire into the circumstances surrounding an Army disaster in 1791. About 1,500 soldiers commanded by Maj. Gen. Arthur St. Clair were on a road- and fort-building expedition in the Northwest Territory when they were attacked by Indians. Some 600 men were killed and another 300 were wounded.

The special committee subpoenaed witnesses, including St. Clair, Secretary of War Henry Knox and Secretary of the Treasury Alexander Hamilton, and the War Department papers concerning the expedition. The committee's final report absolved St. Clair. Blame for the unfortunate episode was placed on the War Department, particularly the quartermaster and supply contractors, who were accused of mismanagement, neglect and delay in supplying necessary equipment, clothing and munitions to the troops. The House took no action on the report and the Federalists prevented its publication because of its reflections on Knox and Hamilton. So began congressional exercise of the right to investigate, one of the most controversial powers Congress possesses. [1]

"...The power of Congress to conduct investigations is inherent in the legislative process. That power is broad.... But broad as is this power of inquiry, it is not unlimited."
—Chief Justice Earl Warren
Watkins v. United States, 1957

The power to investigate is an implied power based on the constitutional assignment in Article I, Section 1, of "all legislative powers herein granted." The authority for legislative bodies to conduct inquiries was established as early as the 16th century by the British House of Commons. The Commons first used this power in determining its membership. It then made increasing use of investigations to assist it in performing lawmaking functions and in overseeing officials responsible for executing the laws and spending funds made available by Parliament.

Investigating committees of the House of Commons had authority to summon witnesses and examine documents, and the Commons could support its committees by punishing uncooperative witnesses for contempt. American colonial legislatures, the Continental Congress and state legislatures relied on these parliamentary precedents in carrying out their own investigations. Thus the power to investigate, to compel the attendance of witnesses and to demand the production of documents was regarded by most members of the early Congresses as an intrinsic part of the power to legislate.

Writing as a graduate student in 1884, Woodrow Wilson asserted that "the informing function of Congress should be preferred even to its legislative function." [2] Serving as the eyes and ears of the two chambers of Congress, investigations have gathered information on the need for legislation, tested the effectiveness of already-enacted legislation, inquired into the qualifications and performance of members and executive branch officials and laid the groundwork for impeachment proceedings.

The practices of some investigatory committees, however — particularly those looking into so-called un-American activities — have been challenged in the courts. While generally giving Congress wide latitude in the exercise of its investigatory power, the Supreme Court has drawn some limits, primarily to protect the rights of witnesses and to maintain the separation of the legislative and judicial powers.

The investigating power and its limits were described in 1957 by Chief Justice Earl Warren:

...The power of Congress to conduct investigations is inherent in the legislative process. That power is broad. It encompasses inquiries concerning the administration of existing laws as well as proposed or possibly needed statutes. It includes surveys of defects in our social, economic or political system for the purpose of enabling the Congress to remedy them. It comprehends probes into departments of the Federal Government to expose corruption, inefficiency or waste. But broad as is this power of inquiry, it is not unlimited. There is no general authority to expose the private affairs of individuals without justification in terms of the functions of Congress.... Nor is the Congress a law enforcement or trial agency. These are functions of the executive and judicial departments of government. No inquiry is an end in itself; it must be related to and in further-ance of a legitimate task of the Congress. [3]

The Contempt Power

Like the investigative power it reinforces, the congressional power to punish for contempt has its source in parliamentary precedents dating from Elizabethan times. No express power to punish for contempt of Congress, except in the case of a member, was granted Congress in the Constitution. But Congress assumed that it had inherent power to jail non-members for contempt without a court order because such power was necessary to enforce its investigatory powers and to protect the integrity of its proceedings.

The House issued its first contempt citation in 1795 against two men who had tried to bribe several members of Congress to support a grant of land to them. It was not until 1821, however, that the Supreme Court was asked whether Congress has the power to punish non-members for actions it considers contempt. In *Anderson v. Dunn*, the court upheld the constitutionality of the summary use of the contempt power by Congress. A denial of power to punish for contempt, the court said, "leads to the total annihilation of the power of the House of Representatives to guard itself from contempts, and leaves it exposed to every indignity and interruption that rudeness, caprice, or even conspiracy, may meditate against it." [4]

The court limited the contempt power, however, "to the least power adequate to the end proposed," and said that imprisonment for contempt of Congress could not extend beyond the adjournment of Congress. [5]

Considering imprisonment only to the end of a legislative session inadequate, Congress in 1857 passed a law, still in effect in amended form (2 U.S.C. 192), making it a

---

Contempt of Congress

Congress in 1857 enacted a statute that allowed it to turn over congressional contempt cases to the federal courts for indictment and trial.

Under this statute, as it has been amended and interpreted, the courts are obligated to provide the defendant all the protections guaranteed defendants in other criminal actions.

The language of the statute, now known as Section 192, says:

Every person who having been summoned as a witness by the authority of either House of Congress to give testimony or to produce papers upon any matter under inquiry before either House, or any joint committee established by a joint or concurrent resolution of the two Houses of Congress, or any committee of either House of Congress, willfully makes default, or who having appeared, refuses to answer any question pertinent to the question under inquiry, shall be deemed guilty of a misdemeanor, punishable by a fine of not more than $1,000 nor less than $100 and imprisonment in a common jail for not less than one month nor more than twelve months. (2 United States Code, Section 192)

---

criminal offense to refuse information demanded by either chamber of Congress.

Even after passage of the 1857 law, Congress preferred to punish persons in contempt itself, reasoning that a few days of confinement might induce a witness to cooperate, while turning him over to a court might put him out of the reach of the investigating committee. However, as the press of legislative business mounted and as court review of summary congressional punishment grew more frequent, Congress increasingly relied on criminal prosecution for contempt under the 1857 statute. The last time either house of Congress itself punished someone for contempt was in 1932. Since then, all contempt citations have been prosecuted under the criminal statute. [6] *(Box, this page)*

Contempt and Judicial Review

The Supreme Court first asserted the right of federal courts to review congressional contempt citations in the 1881 case of *Kilbourn v. Thompson*. [7] The case originated with the refusal of a witness, Hallet Kilbourn, to produce papers demanded by a House committee investigating the failure of the banking firm of Jay Cooke. The House ordered Kilbourn jailed for contempt. Released on a writ of *habeas corpus*, Kilbourn sued the Speaker, members of the investigating committee and the sergeant-at-arms, John Thompson, for false arrest. In defense they contended that congressional exercise of the contempt power must be presumed legitimate and that the courts had no authority to review the exercise.

Sustaining Kilbourn's claim, the court held that the chambers of Congress do not have a general power to punish for contempt:

If they are proceeding in a matter beyond their legitimate cognizance, we are of the opinion that this can be shown, and we cannot give our assent to the principle that, by the mere act of asserting a person to be guilty of contempt, they thereby establish their right to fine and imprison him, beyond the power of any court or any other tribunal whatever to inquire into the grounds on which the order was made. [8]

Contempt Statute Upheld

In 1897, the court upheld the validity of the 1857 statute making contempt of Congress a criminal offense. The act was challenged as an illegal delegation of power from Congress to the courts. The court wrote:

...We grant the Congress could not divest itself, or either of its Houses, of the essential and inherent power to punish for contempt, in cases to which the power of either House properly extended; but because Congress, by the Act of 1857, sought to aid each of the Houses in the discharge of its constitutional functions, it does not follow that any delegation of the power in each to punish for contempt was involved. [9]

The court reiterated this position in 1935 when it ruled that the 1857 statute did not replace but supplemented Congress' authority to bring its own contempt citations. The case concerned a witness who had destroyed papers after a congressional investigating committee had issued a subpoena for them. [10]

Abusive Letter

The court in 1917 held that Congress may not use its contempt power as punishment for punishment's sake.

Marshall v. Gordon arose out of a New York state grand jury investigation and indictment of a member of the House for violations of the Sherman Act.[11]

Upon his indictment, the member asked a House Judiciary subcommittee to investigate Marshall, the district attorney responsible for the member's prosecution. The subcommittee went to New York to make inquiries, whereupon Marshall wrote a letter accusing the subcommittee of interfering with the grand jury proceedings. In the letter, which was made public, Marshall used highly abusive and ill-tempered language, and the House cited him for contempt.

Ruling that the contempt power could be used only where there was actual interference with or resistance to the legislative process, the court wrote:

...[W]e think from the very nature of that power it is clear that it does not embrace punishment for contempt as punishment, since it rests only upon the right of self-preservation, that is, the right to prevent acts which in and of themselves inherently obstruct or prevent the discharge of legislative duty or the refusal to do that which there is an inherent legislative power to compel in order that legislative functions may be performed. [12]

Judicial Review

With its assertion in *Kilbourn* of authority to review the validity of congressional contempt citations, the court also assumed the power to review the legitimacy of congressional investigations. The court held that the House could not punish Kilbourn for contempt because the investigation in which Kilbourn was required as a witness was beyond the authority of the House to conduct.

The House investigation of a bankruptcy case that was still pending in the courts was a judicial exercise that infringed on the separation of powers, said the court in *Kilbourn*. Not only could Congress not validly legislate in this area, but in its resolution establishing the investigating committee Congress had shown no interest in developing legislation as a result of the investigation.

The court said that it was sure

...no person can be punished for contumacy as a witness before either House, unless his testimony is required in a matter into which the House has jurisdiction to inquire, and we feel equally sure that neither of these bodies possesses the general power of making inquiry into the private affairs of the citizen. [13]

Having asserted the right to review congressional inquiries, the court then ruled that congressional power to investigate had at least three limits. Investigations had to be confined to subject areas over which Congress had jurisdiction, their purpose had to be enactment of legislation and they could not merely inquire into the private affairs of citizens.

Limits Qualified

In the next Supreme Court test of the investigation power, the court relaxed two of the limits it had established in the *Kilbourn* case. *In re Chapman* (1897) involved New York stockbroker Elverton R. Chapman, convicted of contempt after he refused to answer an investigating committee's questions about senators' trading in sugar stocks during action on a sugar tariff measure. [14]

The court held that in this instance the Senate had a legitimate interest in knowing whether any of its members had been involved in sugar speculations. As a result it could compel testimony from Chapman on matters he considered private:

...The [committee's] questions were not intrusions into the affairs of the citizen; they did not seek to ascertain any facts as to the conduct, methods, extent or details of the business of the firm in question, but only whether that firm, confessedly engaged in buying and selling stocks, and the particular stock named, was employed by any Senator to buy or sell for him any of that stock, whose market price might be affected by the Senate's action. [15]

Because the investigation was legitimate, the court said that "it was certainly not necessary that the resolution should declare in advance what the Senate meditated doing when the investigation was concluded." [16]

By this decision, the court removed its requirement that Congress must state the legislative purposes of its investigative committees and it narrowed the category of situations in which witnesses might refuse to answer questions put to them by such committees.

McGrain v. Daugherty. In 1927, the court issued a landmark decision, *McGrain v. Daugherty*, in which it affirmed the *Chapman* decision while it firmly established the power of Congress to conduct legislative and oversight investigations. [17]

The case arose during a Senate investigation of Harry M. Daugherty's activities as attorney general under President Harding from 1921 to 1924, and particularly his failure to prosecute the primary instigators of the Teapot Dome oil lease scandal. The Senate subpoenaed the former attorney general's brother, Mally S. Daugherty, but he refused to appear. The Senate then had its sergeant-at-arms, John McGrain, take Daugherty into custody, but Daugherty won release on a writ of *habeas corpus* and challenged the Senate's power to compel him to testify.

Upholding the Senate inquiry, the court ruled that the Senate and the House had the power to compel private persons to appear before investigating committees and answer pertinent questions in aid of the legislative function. The "power of inquiry — with process to enforce it — is an essential and appropriate auxiliary to the legislative function," the court said. [18] It continued:

A legislative body cannot legislate wisely or effectively in the absence of information respecting the conditions which the legislation is intended to affect or change, and where the legislative body does not itself possess the requisite information . . . recourse must be had to others who possess it. Experience has taught that mere requests for such information are often unavailing, and also that information which is volunteered is not always accurate or complete, so some means of compulsion are essential to obtain what is needed. [19]

The court denied Daugherty's contention that the inquiry was actually a trial of his actions, holding instead that it was an inquiry into the "administration of the Department of Justice — whether its functions were being properly discharged or were being neglected and misdirected...." an area in which Congress was competent to legislate. "The only legitimate object the Senate could have in ordering the investigation was to aid it in legislating," the court concluded, "and we think the subject-matter was such that this was the real object. An express avowal of the object would have been better; but . . . was not indispensable." [20]

Witness Rights

But in the same breath with which it gave Congress a broad field in which to conduct investigations, the court limited the investigatory power by reaffirming that witnesses in such investigations did have rights. Neither House nor Senate has authority to compel disclosures about private affairs, said the court in the *Daugherty* case. "[A] witness rightfully may refuse to answer where the bounds of inquiry are exceeded or the questions are not pertinent to the matter under scrutiny." [21]

Pertinency

In the next case involving a congressional investigation, the court confirmed both the broad power and the witness' rights set out in the *Daugherty* case. It upheld a Senate inquiry even though the matter under investigation was also pending in the courts.

Sinclair v. United States (1929) also grew out of the Teapot Dome scandal. Observing that Congress had authority over the naval petroleum reserves, the court said it was legitimate for the Senate to conduct an inquiry into whether legislation to recover the leased oil lands was necessary or desirable, despite the fact that a suit for recovery of the lands had already begun. While Congress may not compel testimony to aid the prosecution of court suits, the court said, its authority "to require pertinent disclosures in aid of its own constitutional power is not abridged because the information sought to be elicited may also be of use in such suits." [22]

The court also used the *Sinclair* case to spell out further what the rights of witnesses appearing before investigating committees were. It reaffirmed the right of a witness to refuse to testify where the question was not pertinent to the matter at hand.

If a witness who refused to answer a question was brought to trial under the 1857 contempt statute, the court said, it was "incumbent upon the United States to plead and show that the question pertained to some matter under investigation." [23] Finally, the court ruled that the pertinency of an inquiry is a question for determination by the courts as a matter of law.

But, the court added, a witness who refused to answer questions could be punished for contempt, as in this case, if he were mistaken as to the law on which he based his refusal. It was no defense that the witness acted in good faith on the advice of counsel, the court held.

Pertinency vs. Balance

The post-World War II quest to uncover subversion in the United States produced a new style of congressional investigation and a host of lawsuits challenging it. Ostensibly seeking to discover the extent of communist infiltration into the government, the labor movement and various other areas of American life, these investigations were used primarily to expose publicly persons suspected of belonging to or being affiliated with the Communist Party.

This purpose was openly acknowledged by Rep. Martin Dies Jr., D-Texas (1931-45, 1953-59), chairman of the House Special Committee to Investigate Un-American Ac-

tivities: "I am not in a position to say whether we can legislate effectively in reference to this matter, but I do know that exposure in a democracy of subversive activities is the most effective weapon that we have in our possession." [24]

As Chief Justice Earl Warren put it in 1957:

This new phase of investigative inquiry involved a broad-scale intrusion into the lives and affairs of private citizens. It brought before the courts novel questions of the appropriate limits of congressional inquiry. . . . In the more recent cases, the emphasis shifted to problems of accommodating the interest of the Government with the rights and privileges of individuals. [25]

The first case the Supreme Court heard in the postwar era testing the right of a congressional committee to investigate against the right of a witness did not involve a member of the Communist Party but rather a publisher of politically conservative books. Edward A. Rumely refused to tell the House Select Committee on Lobbying Activities the names of individuals making bulk purchases of the books he published which were distributed by the Committee for Constitutional Government, an arch-conservative organization. Rumely was convicted of contempt of Congress but a court of appeals reversed the conviction. The Supreme Court upheld the appeals court ruling in *United States v. Rumely* (1953). [26]

A majority of the court avoided the constitutional issue of whether the committee's questions violated Rumely's First Amendment rights by narrowly construing the authority granted by the resolution establishing the committee. The majority held that the mandate to investigate "lobbying activities" was limited to "representations made directly to the Congress, its members or its committees," and excluded attempts to influence Congress directly through public disseminations of literature. [27] Thus its interrogation of Rumely had been outside the committee's power. To interpret the resolution to cover indirect lobbying "raises doubts of constitutionality in view of the prohibition of the First Amendment," wrote Justice Felix Frankfurter for the majority. [28] It was this same narrow interpretation of the meaning of lobbying activities that allowed the court in 1954 to uphold the federal lobby registration act. *(p. 174)*

Justices William O. Douglas and Hugo L. Black did not shy away from the First Amendment issues of the case. Claiming that the authorizing resolution in fact did intend the investigating committee to look into indirect lobbying activities, Douglas and Black said the demand for Rumely's book distribution list was a violation of the First Amendment guarantees of free speech and press. "If the present inquiry were sanctioned, the press would be subjected to harassment that in practical effect might be as serious as censorship," wrote Douglas. [29]

The Watkins Case

The most severe limitations placed by the Supreme Court on the power of congressional investigating committees to inquire into the affairs of private citizens came in the 1957 decision in *Watkins v. United States*. [30]

Watkins was a regional officer of the Farm Equipment Workers Union. Appearing before the House Un-American Activities Committee in 1954, Watson answered fully the questions pertaining to his association with the Communist Party. He also answered questions about persons he knew to be present members of the party.

But Watkins refused to answer questions about persons, who, to the best of his knowledge, had disassociated themselves from the party. "I do not believe that such questions are relevant to the work of this committee nor do I believe that this committee has the right to undertake the public exposure of persons because of their past activities. I may be wrong and the committee may have this power, but until and unless a court of law so holds and directs me to answer, I most firmly refuse to discuss the political activities of my past associates," Watkins said. [31] Convicted of contempt of Congress under the amended 1857 statute, Watkins appealed.

Speaking for the court majority, Chief Justice Warren held Watkins not guilty of contempt of Congress. The situation, Warren said, demanded that the court balance the congressional need for particular information with the individual's interest in privacy. The critical element in this courtly juggling act, he said, "is the existence of, and the weight to be ascribed to, the interest of the Congress in demanding disclosures from an unwilling witness." [32]

The majority, Warren said, had "no doubt that there is no congressional power to expose for the sake of exposure." [33] The only legitimate interest Congress could have in such an investigation as Watkins was subjected to was the furtherance of a legislative purpose. And that required that the instructions authorizing the investigation fully spell out the investigating committee's purpose and jurisdiction, he said. Claiming that it "would be difficult to imagine a less explicit authorizing resolution" than the one establishing the Un-American Activities Committee, Warren said that such an "excessively broad" authorizing resolution

> ...places the courts in an untenable position if they are to strike a balance between the public need for a particular interrogation and the right of citizens to carry on their affairs free from unnecessary governmental interference. It is impossible in such a situation to ascertain whether any legislative purpose justified the disclosures sought and, if so, the importance of that information to the Congress in furtherance of its legislative function. The reason no court can make this critical judgment is that the House of Representatives itself has never made it. [34]

The majority also reaffirmed the holding in the *Sinclair* case that the questions asked must be pertinent to the matter under inquiry. A witness deciding whether to answer a question, Warren wrote, "is entitled to have knowledge of the subject to which the interrogation is deemed pertinent." [35] Such subject matter was not revealed by the authorizing resolution or by the resolution establishing the subcommittee. Although the matter under inquiry was communist infiltration of labor unions, that was not apparent to a majority of the court, and if it was not apparent after trial and appeal, Warren said, it was doubtful the subject matter was apparent at the time of the interrogation.

Warren then stated a rule for ascertaining pertinency of questions to the matter under inquiry:

> ...Unless the subject matter has been made to appear with indisputable clarity, it is the duty of the investigative body, upon objection of the witness on grounds of pertinency, to state for the record the subject under inquiry at that time and the manner in which the propounded questions are pertinent thereto. To be

meaningful, the explanation must describe what the topic under inquiry is and connective reasoning whereby the precise questions relate to it. [36]

This the committee had not done, Warren said, and thus Watkins could not be held in contempt.

Once again the court had said that the congressional power to investigate was broad but not unlimited. One of the limits was that the investigation had to serve a legislative purpose; its purpose could not be solely to expose publicly persons who held unpopular political beliefs or associations. The legislative purpose had to be spelled out in sufficient detail that a witness might know what the purpose was, and the investigating body was required to explain to the witness, if he asked, the relevance of its questions to that purpose.

Most of these limitations had already been set out in previous decisions. The importance of the *Watkins* case was that the court reaffirmed these individual rights in an era fraught with fear that the exercise of those rights could doom the existence of the nation itself.

The Barenblatt Case

The court cited this need for self-preservation two years later when it retreated somewhat from its defense of the rights of witnesses. By 5-4 vote, the court ruled that First Amendment rights may be limited where the public interest outweighs the private interest. [37] Justices John Marshall Harlan and Felix Frankfurter deserted the majority in the *Watkins* case to join the only dissenter in that case, Justice Tom Clark. The other two justices making up the majority in *Barenblatt v. United States* (1959) were Charles E. Whittaker, who did not participate in the *Watkins* case, and Potter Stewart, who had replaced Harold H. Burton on the court. Burton had not participated in the *Watkins* case.

Barenblatt refused to answer questions propounded by a House Un-American Activities subcommittee investigating communist infiltration into higher education. Barenblatt's challenge to his subsequent contempt conviction rested largely on the *Watkins* precedent. He claimed that the committee's authorizing resolution was too vague to determine whether the particular inquiry aimed at Barenblatt was directed toward a legitimate legislative purpose. He also claimed that he was not adequately apprised of the relevance of the questions asked to the subject matter of the inquiry. He also claimed that the questions he refused to answer were an encroachment on his First Amendment rights.

Upholding Barenblatt's contempt conviction, the majority denied all three claims. First, wrote Harlan, Watkins' conviction had been reversed only because he had not been informed fully of the pertinency of the questions he was asked to the subject under investigation. The vagueness of the mandate establishing the committee was only one facet the court examined in its search for the subject matter of the investigation and was not determinative.

In the case at hand, the majority did not agree with Barenblatt's contention that the vagueness of the mandate deprived the subcommittee of its authority to compel his testimony:

> Granting the vagueness of the committee's charter, we may not read it in isolation from its long history in the House of Representatives. Just as legislation is often given meaning by the gloss of legislative reports, administrative interpretations, and long us-

age, so the proper meaning of an authorization to a congressional committee is not to be derived alone from its abstract terms unrelated to the definite content furnished them by the course of congressional actions." [38]

As to the pertinence of the questions asked to the subject of the investigation, the court said the record showed that Barenblatt was well aware of their relevance.

Thus, Harlan continued, the only constitutional issue at stake was "whether the Subcommittee's inquiry into petitioner's past or present membership in the Communist Party transgressed the provisions of the First Amendment, which of course reach and limit congressional investigations." [39]

As the court recognized in the *Watkins* case, an answer to that question, Harlan said, "involves a balancing by the courts of the competing private and public interests at stake in the particular circumstances shown." [40]

On the public side, Harlan observed that Congress had the power to legislate in the field of communist activity in the United States:

> In the last analysis, this power rests on the right of self-preservation.... To suggest that because the Communist Party may also sponsor peaceable political reforms the constitutional issues before us should now be judged as if that Party were just an ordinary political party from the standpoint of national security is to ask this Court to blind itself to policy since the close of World War II. [41]

In other words, Barenblatt's right to conduct theoretical classroom discussions on the nature of communism did not outweigh the committee's right to investigate those who might have advocated the overthrow of the government.

"We conclude," said Harlan, "that the balance between the individual and the governmental interests here at stake must be struck in favor of the latter, and that therefore the provisions of the First Amendment have not been offended." [42]

The Dissent. Speaking for himself, Chief Justice Warren and Justice William O. Douglas, Justice Hugo L. Black charged that the majority had rewritten the First Amendment to read:

> "Congress shall pass no law abridging freedom of speech, press, assembly and petition, unless Congress and the Supreme Court reach the joint conclusion that on balance the interests of the Government in stifling these freedoms is greater than the interest of the people in having them exercised." [43]

The majority's balancing test, Black continued,

> ...leaves out the real interest in Barenblatt's silence, the interest of the people in being able to join organizations, advocate causes, and make political 'mistakes' without later being subject to governmental penalties for having dared to think for themselves.... It is these interests of society, rather than Barenblatt's own right to silence, which I think the court should put on the balance against the demands of the Government.... [44]

In a separate dissent, Justice William J. Brennan Jr. said that:

> ...no purpose for the investigation of Barenblatt is revealed by the record except exposure purely for the sake of exposure. This is not a purpose to which

Barenblatt's rights under the First Amendment can validly be subordinated. An investigation in which the processes of law-making and law-evaluating are submerged entirely in exposure of individual behavior — in adjudication, of a sort, through the exposure process — is outside the constitutional pale of congressional inquiry. [45]

Succeeding Cases

In subsequent cases, the court has continued to employ this balancing approach with mixed results, coming down some times for the witness and other times for Congress.

In *Wilkinson v. United States* and *Braden v. United States*, decided the same day in 1961, the court again found national interests to outweigh individual rights. These cases involved two men who had followed an Un-American Activities subcommittee to Atlanta where the panel conducted an inquiry into the extent of communist propaganda in the South. [46] Both men actively and publicly protested the subcommittee proceedings and were subsequently subpoenaed to appear before it. Wilkinson and Braden refused to answer questions about their Communist Party affiliations and consequently were convicted of contempt. The two men complained that the subcommittee had intended to harass them rather than to elicit any information pertinent to its investigation.

But the court upheld their convictions, saying the investigation was properly authorized and that the questions were pertinent to the subject matter on which legislation could be based.

Four months later, the balance tipped the other way. In *Deutsch v. United States* (1961), the court overturned the contempt conviction of a man who, like Watkins, refused to answer questions on the possible un-American activities of some of his acquaintances. [47] The court held that the government had not proved the pertinency of these questions to the inquiry at hand. Not only must the witness be aware of the relevance of the question at the time he refuses to answer, but the relevance must be proved at the contempt trial, the majority said.

In 1962 the court reversed another contempt conviction, because the indictment for contempt failed to state the subject under investigation at the time of the interrogation. To omit this statement from the indictment violated the Fifth Amendment guarantee of due process and the Sixth Amendment right to be informed of the cause and nature of the accusation, the court said in *Russell v. United States*. [48]

In 1963 the court overturned a contempt conviction on the grounds that the committee involved had violated its own rules when it refused a witness' request for a closed hearing. [49]

In 1966 a unanimous court held that a person could not be convicted of contempt in a criminal proceeding if the investigation at which he refused to answer questions was not authorized by the full committee as required by its own rules and if the full committee had not made a "lawful delegation" to the subcommittee authorizing the inquiry. Justice Abe Fortas wrote that the "jurisdiction of the courts cannot be invoked to impose criminal sanctions in aid of a roving commission." [50]

Of this series of reversals, constitutional scholar C. Herman Pritchett has written:

> ...These reversals were accomplished for the most part without challenging the scope of investigatory power or

querying the motives of the investigators. They were achieved primarily by strict judicial enforcement of the rules on pertinency, authorization, and procedure, plus strict observance of the constitutional standards governing criminal prosecutions. [51]

The Fifth Amendment

Some witnesses in the early Cold War years invoked the Fifth Amendment guarantee against self-incrimination when they refused to answer investigating committee questions. This portion of the Fifth Amendment states that no person "shall be compelled in any criminal case to be a witness against himself." The court previously had interpreted this guarantee to mean that a person could not be required to divulge information that might make him liable to a criminal proceeding. *(Self-incrimination, p. 555)*

Not until 1955 did the Supreme Court consider any contempt of Congress cases against witnesses who invoked the self-incrimination clause. Prior to that it had handed down two important rulings dealing with grand jury investigations. In the first case, *Blau v. United States* (1950), the court acknowledged that admission of communist activity might be incriminating. [52]

In the second case, *Rogers v. United States* (1951), the court ruled that a witness could not invoke the Fifth Amendment privilege after already having answered questions about materially incriminating facts. That case arose after Jane Rogers told a grand jury that she had been treasurer of the Communist Party in Denver. Having made this admission she sought to end her testimony and refused to give the name of the person to whom she had turned over the party's books. A divided Supreme Court ruled that she had waived the right to silence by her initial testimony and that the further questions she had refused to answer did not involve a "reasonable danger of further incrimination." [53]

The validity of the Fifth Amendment as a defense against a contempt of Congress citation was considered by the court in two cases decided the same day in 1955. The circumstances in *Quinn v. United States* and *Emspak v. United States* were similar. Both men had refused to answer certain questions from congressional committees pertaining to their affiliation with the Communist Party. Quinn did not expressly invoke the self-incrimination clause and Emspak's primary defense was that the questions infringed on his First Amendment rights. The court held that the intent of each man to plead the Fifth Amendment was clear.

There is not a "ritualistic formula" involved in invoking the protection, Chief Justice Warren said in the *Quinn* case. "If an objection to a question is made in any language that a committee may reasonably be expected to understand as an attempt to invoke the privilege, it must be respected...," he added. [54]

In the *Emspak* case, Warren said:

...[I]f it is true in these times a stigma may somehow result from a witness' reliance on the Self-Incrimination Clause, a committee should be all the more ready to recognize a veiled claim of the privilege. Otherwise, the great right which the Clause was intended to secure might be effectively frustrated by private pressures. [55]

Immunity

To counter the frequent use of the Fifth Amendment by witnesses before congressional committees, Congress in

Power of Subpoena

The Supreme Court has never questioned the power of the House and Senate and their authorized committees to issue subpoenas to ensure the attendance of witnesses or the production of papers and other documents for examination at congressional investigations.

"Issuance of subpoenas ... has long been held to be a legitimate use by Congress of its power to investigate," the court wrote in *McGrain v. Daugherty* (1927). "Experience has taught that mere requests for ... information often are unavailing...." [1]

In 1975, use of the congressional subpoena power was challenged on First Amendment grounds. The 1975 case arose when the Senate Judiciary Subcommittee on Internal Security issued a subpoena for the bank records of the United States Servicemen's Fund (USSF), a group that protested American involvement in the Indochina War. [2] The records included lists of contributors to the organization. The USSF claimed the subpoena was intended to impede the exercise of First Amendment rights because contributors, fearing that their association with the organization might be made public, would withdraw their support.

The Supreme Court rejected the claim, holding that on its face the subpoena was issued to further a legitimate legislative inquiry. Because members of Congress are constitutionally protected from being questioned for legislative actions, the court said it could not inquire into the motivations for issuing the subpoena. Concurring, Justices Thurgood Marshall, William J. Brennan Jr. and Potter Stewart said they did not read the majority opinion to mean "that the constitutionality of a congressional subpoena is always shielded from more searching judicial inquiry." [3]

---

[1] *McGrain v. Daugherty*, 273 U.S. 135 at 175 (1927).
[2] *Eastland v. United States Servicemen's Fund*, 421 U.S. 491 (1975).
[3] Id. at 515.

1954 amended an immunity statute that had been on the books since 1857. The Immunity Act of 1954 (PL 83-600) permitted either chamber of Congress by majority vote, or a congressional committee by a two-thirds vote, to grant immunity to witnesses in national security investigations, provided an order was first obtained from a U.S. district court judge and also provided the attorney general was notified in advance and given an opportunity to offer objections. The bill also permitted the U.S. district courts to grant immunity to witnesses before the court or grand juries. Witnesses thus immunized were faced with the choice of testifying or going to jail. The Fifth Amendment claim could not be raised.

The Supreme Court upheld the immunity act in *Ullmann v. United States* (1956). Affirming the conviction of William L. Ullmann, who had refused to testify before a grand jury despite a grant of immunity, the court held that the Fifth Amendment self-incrimination clause protected witnesses only against testimony that might lead to conviction on criminal charges. This possibility was ruled out by the grant of immunity. "Once the reason for the privilege ceases, the privilege ceases," Justice Felix Frankfurter wrote for the majority. [56]

Observing that there was no indication that this immunity would protect a person forced to admit he was a communist from the loss of his job or other consequences, Justice William O. Douglas entered a sharp dissent for himself and Justice Hugo L. Black. "My view is that the framers put it beyond the power of Congress to *compel* anyone to confess his crimes," Douglas wrote. [57]

Investigating Elections

Congress has investigative powers inherent in the constitutional right of each chamber to judge the elections, returns and qualifications of its members. That point was settled in two cases involving the 1926 senatorial election in Pennsylvania in which Republican William S. Vare was declared the winner over Democrat William B. Wilson.

The first case, *Reed v. County Commissioners of Delaware County, Pa.* (1928), arose when the Senate established an investigating committee to look into reports of corruption in the election. Chairman James A. Reed, D-Mo., and his committee filed suit to compel local officials to produce the ballot boxes for inspection. Their right to do so was challenged. The court upheld the right of each chamber "to secure information upon which to decide concerning elections," but held that the committee did not have the right to subpoena the ballot boxes because the resolution establishing the committee did not contain the proper authorization. [58]

The second case, *Barry v. United States ex rel. Cunningham* (1929), arose because Thomas W. Cunningham refused to answer certain questions concerning the Vare campaign's contributions. The Senate ordered Cunningham taken into custody. He petitioned for a writ of *habeas corpus*, charging that the Senate had exceeded its power when it arrested him. The court, writing through Justice George Sutherland, disagreed:

> . . .Exercise of the power [to judge elections, returns and qualifications] necessarily involves the ascertainment of facts, the attendance of witnesses, the examination of such witnesses, with the power to compel them to answer pertinent questions, to determine the facts and apply the appropriate rules of law, and, finally, to render a judgment which is beyond the authority of any other tribunal to review. [59]

Footnotes

[1] For general information on St. Clair inquiry, see Marshall E. Dimock, *Congressional Investigating Committees* (Baltimore: The Johns Hopkins Press, 1929; reprint ed., New York: AMS Press Inc., 1971), p. 87-89; Congressional Quarterly, *Guide to Congress*, 2nd ed. (Washington; Congressional Quarterly Inc., 1976), p. 161-62.

[2] Woodrow Wilson, *Congressional Government* (Cleveland: World Publishing Co., Meridian Books, 1965), p. 198.

[3] *Watkins v. United States*, 354 U.S. 178 at 187 (1957).

[4] *Anderson v. Dunn*, 6 Wheat. 204 at 228 (1821).

[5] Id. at 231.

[6] Conversations with the offices of the Parliamentarians of the Senate and the House, September 18, 19, 1978.

[7] *Kilbourn v. Thompson*, 103 U.S. 168 (1881).

[8] Id. at 197.

[9] *In re Chapman*, 166 U.S. 661 at 671-72 (1897).

[10] *Jurney v. MacCracken*, 294 U.S. 125 (1935).

[11] *Marshall v. Gordon*, 243 U.S. 521 (1917).

[12] Id. at 542.

[13] *Kilbourn v. Thompson*, 103 U.S. 168 at 190 (1881).

[14] *In re Chapman*, 166 U.S. 661 (1897).

[15] Id. at 669.

[16] Id. at 670.

[17] *McGrain v. Daugherty*, 273 U.S. 135 (1927).

[18] Id. at 174.

[19] Id. at 175.

[20] Id. at 177-78.

[21] Id. at 176.

[22] *Sinclair v. United States*, 279 U.S. 263 at 295 (1929).

[23] Id. at 296-97.

[24] Quoted in August Raymond Ogden, *The Dies Committee* (Washington, The Catholic University of America Press, 1945), p. 44.

[25] *Watkins v. United States*, 354 U.S. 178 at 195 (1957).

[26] *United States v. Rumely*, 345 U.S. 41 (1953).

[27] Id. at 47.

[28] Id. at 46.

[29] Id. at 57.

[30] *Watkins v. United States*, 354 U.S. 178 (1957).

[31] Quoted in Robert E. Cushman and Robert F. Cushman, *Cases in Constitutional Law*, 3rd ed. (New York: Appleton-Century-Crofts, 1968), p. 112.

[32] *Watkins v. United States*, 354 U.S. 178 at 198 (1957).

[33] Id. at 200.

[34] Id. at 205-206.

[35] Id. at 208-209.

[36] Id. at 214-15.

[37] *Barenblatt v. United States*, 360 U.S. 109 (1959).

[38] Id. at 117.

[39] Id. at 126.

[40] Ibid.

[41] Id. at 127-29.

[42] Id. at 134.

[43] Id. at 143.

[44] Id. at 144.

[45] Id. at 166.

[46] *Wilkinson v. United States*, 365 U.S. 399 (1961); *Braden v. United States*, 365 U.S. 431 (1961).

[47] *Deutsch v. United States*, 367 U.S. 456 (1961).

[48] *Russell v. United States*, 369 U.S. 749 (1962).

[49] *Yellin v. United States*, 374 U.S. 109 (1963).

[50] *Gojack v. United States*, 384 U.S. 702 at 715 (1966).

[51] C. Herman Pritchett, *The American Constitution*, 3rd ed. (New York: McGraw-Hill Book Co., 1977), p. 161.

[52] *Blau v. United States*, 340 U.S. 159 (1950).

[53] *Rogers v. United States*, 340 U.S. 367 at 374 (1951).

[54] *Quinn v. United States*, 349 U.S. 155 at 162-63 (1955).

[55] *Emspak v. United States*, 349 U.S. 190 at 195 (1955).

[56] *Ullmann v. United States*, 350 U.S. 422 at 439 (1956).

[57] Id. at 445.

[58] *Reed v. County Commissioners of Delaware County, Pa.*, 277 U.S. 376 at 380 (1928).

[59] *Barry v. United States ex rel. Cunningham*, 279 U.S. 597 at 613 (1929).

The Power Over Internal Affairs

The first seven sections of Article I of the Constitution set out the duties of the House and the Senate and the powers each chamber has over its internal affairs. Among these are the authority of each house to judge the qualifications and elections of its members, to punish its members, to set the time, place and manner of holding congressional elections, to establish its own rules for conducting official business, and to impeach, try and convict or acquit federal civilian and judicial officers. Observing the doctrine of separation of powers, the Supreme Court has found little necessity to intervene in these internal prerogatives of Congress.

Congress and the court also have recognized a power that is not expressly mentioned in the Constitution — the power of self-preservation. This authority is implicit in the clause that grants senators and representatives immunity from being questioned by the executive or judicial branches for any legislative action. The necessity for Congress to be protected from intimidation and harassment by the other branches has led the court to give a broad interpretation to this so-called speech or debate clause to the extent that immunity has been granted to members of Congress charged with criminal activity.

The power of self-protection has also been used as the authority for enacting laws regulating campaign financing and requiring lobby registration. The court sustained both laws against challenges that they conflicted with First Amendment rights. The court, however, has held that some specific campaign financing regulations impermissibly conflicted with First Amendment guarantees and it has insisted that the lobby registration law applied only to certain narrow categories of lobbyists and lobbying activity.

Qualifications

Clause 1 of Article I, Section 5 of the Constitution states in part: "Each House shall be the judge of the . . . qualifications of its own members. . . ." The Constitution also requires that members meet certain age, citizenship and residency requirements. *(Constitutional qualifications, box p. 166)*

Whether Congress, or either house of Congress, had power to add qualifications for membership beyond those listed by the Constitution, or power to overlook the absence of one of the constitutional requirements, were questions answered sometimes in the affirmative and sometimes in the negative. Until the Supreme Court's negative answer in the 1969 *Powell* case, Congress acted from time to time as if it were entitled to add qualifications as well as to wink at failure to fulfill a constitutional requirement.

Alexander Hamilton initiated discussion of the question in No. 60 of *The Federalist Papers.* "The qualifications of the persons who may . . . be chosen are defined and fixed in the Constitution, and are unalterable by the legislature," Hamilton wrote. [1]

However, later authorities contended that the Constitutional Convention intended to empower Congress to add to the listed qualifications.

Of the three senators-elect the Senate has excluded, only one was refused his seat because he did not meet a qualification added by the Senate — loyalty to the Union during the Civil War. (Loyalty was later made a constitutional requirement by the 14th Amendment.) The other two failed to meet the citizenship requirement. Of the 10 excluded representatives-elect, four were excluded for disloyalty during the Civil War. One was excluded because he did not live in the district he represented. Another House member-elect was excluded because he was a polygamist, a second was excluded for malfeasance, a third for misconduct and two more for seditious activities.

Powell Case

In 1967 the House voted to exclude Rep. Adam Clayton Powell Jr. The exclusion ended one of the stormiest episodes in congressional history and precipitated a Supreme Court ruling that Congress could not add to the constitutional qualifications for membership in Congress.

Pastor of the Abyssinian Baptist Church in Harlem, one of the largest congregations in the country, Powell, a New York Democrat, was elected to the 79th Congress in 1944. Powell was re-elected regularly, served as chairman of the House Committee on Education and Labor from 1961 to 1967, and was considered by many observers to be the most powerful black legislator in the United States.

Powell's downfall was brought about in part by his flamboyant personality and his apparent disregard for the law. In 1958, he was indicted for income tax evasion, but the case was dismissed when the jury was unable to reach a verdict. In 1960 he was convicted of libel. Powell eventually paid the libel judgment but not before he had been held in contempt of court four times and had been found guilty of fraudulently transferring property to avoid paying.

Constitutional Qualifications for Membership in Congress

● A senator must be at least 30 years old and have been a citizen of the United States not less than nine years (Article I, Section 3, Clause 3).

● A representative must be at least 25 years old and have been a citizen not less than seven years (Article I, Section 2, Clause 2).

● Every member of Congress must be, when elected, an inhabitant of the state that he is to represent (Article I, Section 2, Clause 2, and Section 3, Clause 3).

● No one may be a member of Congress who holds any other "Office under the United States" (Article I, Section 6, Clause 2).

● No person may be a senator or a representative who, having previously taken an oath as a member of Congress to support the Constitution, has engaged in rebellion against the United States or given aid or comfort to its enemies, unless Congress has removed such disability by a two-thirds vote of both houses (Fourteenth Amendment, Section 3).

But Powell's real troubles began when some of his congressional activities came to light. In the 1950s and early 1960s, Powell enjoyed several costly pleasure trips at government expense. He was also criticized for taking a female staff member on many trips to Bimini Island in the Bahamas. He paid his wife out of government funds almost $21,000 a year as a clerk while she lived in Puerto Rico. Additionally, in the late 1960s Powell indulged in long absences from Congress. These apparent misuses of public funds and continuing legal problems in New York stirred a great furor among the public and members of the House, who felt he was discrediting the institution.

Re-elected in 1966, Powell arrived in Washington only to have the House Democratic Caucus strip him of his committee chairmanship. The following day, Jan. 10, 1967, the House voted to deny Powell his seat pending an investigation.

The investigating committee recommended that Powell be censured for his misconduct and fined to offset the public funds he had misspent. But the full House rejected these recommendations, voting 307 to 116 March 1, 1967, to exclude Powell from Congress.

Powell ran successfully in the special election to fill his vacancy but did not try to claim his seat. He ran again in 1968, was elected and was seated in Congress, subject to loss of seniority and a $25,000 fine. Meanwhile Powell and several of his constituents had challenged his 1967 exclusion in the courts. Powell sought a declaratory judgment that his exclusion was unconstitutional, a permanent order forbidding House Speaker John W. McCormack, D-Mass. (1928-71), to refuse to administer the oath of office to Powell, the House clerk to refuse to perform duties due a representative, the House sergeant-at-arms to refuse to pay Powell his salary, and the House doorkeeper to threaten not to admit him to the House chamber.

There were two main issues involved in this suit. Could the House add to the Constitution's qualifications for membership? Could the courts properly examine the actions of the House in such cases, order the House not to add to those qualifications, and enforce the order?

The federal district court for the District of Columbia dismissed the suit because it said it did not have jurisdiction over the subject matter. The Court of Appeals, District of Columbia Circuit, affirmed in February 1969 the action of the lower court in dismissing the suit. The court of appeals held that the lower court did have jurisdiction over the subject matter but that the case involved a political question which, if decided, would constitute a violation of the separation of powers and produce an embarrassing confrontation between Congress and the courts. Judge Warren E. Burger wrote the court of appeals decision.

The Supreme Court however, went on to consider and decide the case. The court handed down its ruling in *Powell v. McCormack* in June 1969. [2] The vote was 7-1. For the court, Chief Justice Earl Warren stated that the House had improperly excluded Powell. The case was not moot, Warren said, because of Powell's claim for back salary.

Nor did the speech or debate clause (Article I, Section 6) of the Constitution conferring congressional immunity protect all those named by Powell in his suit from judicial review of their actions pertaining to his exclusion. Warren dismissed the action against McCormack and the other members involved but allowed Powell to maintain his suit against the House employees.

Warren then dismissed the argument that this was a political question the court should not decide. Determination of Powell's right to his seat in the 90th Congress, the court held, required only interpretation of the Constitution, the traditional function of the court.

Turning to that interpretation, Warren said: "Our examination of the relevant historical matters leads us to the conclusion that . . . the Constitution leaves the House without authority to *exclude* any person, duly elected by his constituents, who meets all the requirements for membership expressly prescribed in the Constitution." [3] Since Powell met these requirements, he could not be excluded.

The court did not deny the unquestionable interest of Congress in maintaining its own integrity. In most cases, however, the court felt that that interest could be properly safeguarded by use of each chamber's power to punish or expel its members.

The Supreme Court sent the case back to the court of appeals with instructions to enter a declaratory judgment stating that the House action was unconstitutional and to conduct further proceedings on the unresolved issues of seniority, back pay and the $25,000 fine.

Justice Potter Stewart dissented, holding that the end of the 90th Congress and the seating of Powell in the 91st Congress rendered the case moot.

Power to Punish Members

Article I, Section 5, Clause 2 of the Constitution empowers each chamber of Congress to "punish its Members for disorderly Behavior, and with the Concurrence of two thirds, expel a Member."

Expulsion has been a power little exercised by Congress. Fifteen senators have been expelled, one in 1797 for engaging in a conspiracy against a foreign country and 14 during the Civil War for supporting a rebellion. In the House only three members have been expelled, all of them in 1861 for Civil War activities.

The Senate has used the milder punishment of censure to discipline seven of its members; the House has censured only 19 of its members. From time to time, each chamber has employed other less severe forms of discipline to punish various kinds of misconduct. [4]

The Supreme Court has not been called upon to mediate directly in any of these punishment cases. It is likely the court would consider such a case a non-justiciable political question. The court has indicated that it considers the power to expel a broad one. "The right to expel extends to all cases where the offense is such as in the judgment of the Senate is inconsistent with the trust and duty of a member." [5]

In a 1906 case touching on expulsion, the court upheld a law providing that a member of Congress found guilty of accepting payment for services rendered in connection with a government proceeding "shall . . . be rendered forever thereafter incapable of holding any office . . . under the government of the United States." Convicted under that statute, Sen. Joseph R. Burton, R-Kan. (1901-06), challenged the act's constitutionality on the grounds that it deprived the Senate of its right to decide on expulsion of its members. The court disagreed, writing that the "final judgment of conviction did not operate *ipso facto,* to vacate the seat of the convicted Senator nor compel the Senate to expel him or to regard him as expelled by force alone of the judgment." [6]

Imprisonment

Although neither the House nor the Senate has ever found it necessary, the Supreme Court in 1881 indicated that both chambers of Congress had the power to imprison members for misconduct. In the case of *Kilbourn v. Thompson,* the court said:

> . . .[T]he Constitution expressly empowers each House to punish its own members for disorderly behavior. We see no reason to doubt that this punishment may in a proper case be imprisonment, and that it may be for refusal to obey some rule on that subject made by the House for the preservation of order.
>
> So, also, the *penalty* which each House is authorized to inflict in order to compel the attendance of absent members may be imprisonment, and this may be for a violation of some order or standing rule on the subject. [7]

Powell Case

The most recent court test of the congressional power to punish members came in 1969. Two years earlier, the House of Representatives refused to seat Adam Clayton Powell Jr., D-N.Y., a member of Congress since 1944, because he allegedly misspent government funds and committed other misdeeds. In *Powell v. McCormack* (1969) the court held that Congress could not exclude any member-elect for any reason other than failure to meet one of the constitutionally specified requirements for membership in Congress. [8] Powell met these requirements of age, residence and citizenship. In essence, the court said that the House could not punish Powell for his indiscretions until after it had seated him. *(Details of Powell case, pp. 165-66)*

Congressional Immunity

The concept of legislators having some immunity from legal actions was well established in England and in the Colonies by the time it was made part of the American Constitution. Article I, Section 6 provides that "Senators and Representatives shall . . . in all Cases, except Treason, Felony and Breach of the Peace, be privileged from Arrest during their Attendance at the Session of their respective Houses, and in going to and returning from the same; and for any Speech or Debate in either House, they shall not be questioned in any other Place."

Arrest

The privilege from arrest clause has become practically obsolete, as various court decisions have narrowed its protection. As presently interpreted, the clause applies only to arrests in civil suits, such as non-payment of debts or breach of contract. Even this protection is of little significance since most states do not arrest persons in such actions. Civil arrests were more common at the time the Constitution was written.

The Supreme Court has declared that the privilege from arrest clause does not apply to service of process in either civil or criminal cases. [9] Nor does it apply to arrest in criminal cases. In 1908, the court interpreted the phrase "treason, felony or breach of the peace" to exclude all criminal offenses from the privilege's coverage. [10]

Speech or Debate Clause

Adopted by the Constitutional Convention without discussion or opposition, the speech or debate clause was intended to protect the independence and integrity of Congress and reinforce the separation of powers by preventing the executive and judicial branches from looking into congressional activities for evidence of criminality. Repeatedly, the Supreme Court has stated that the "immunities of the Speech or Debate Clause were not written into the Constitution simply for the personal or private benefit of Members of Congress, but to protect the integrity of the legislative process by insuring the independence of individual legislators." [11]

To ensure that integrity, the court has seen fit to apply the clause to a broader range of legislative activities than just speech and debate and even to protect legislative aides in certain instances. But the court has not construed the clause so broadly as to grant complete immunity from all prosecution or to preclude all judicial review of the activities of individual legislation.

More than Speech. In its first interpretation of the speech or debate clause in *Kilbourn v. Thompson* (1881), the Supreme Court refused "to limit it to words spoken in debate." [12]

The case involved a contempt of Congress citation against Hallet Kilbourn, manager of a District of Columbia real estate pool, for refusing to answer questions before a House committee investigating the bankrupt Jay Cooke and Co. and its interest in the real estate pool. The House ordered Kilbourn jailed for contempt. He sued the Speaker of the House, members of the investigating committee and Sergeant at Arms John G. Thompson for false arrest. The Supreme Court sustained Kilbourn's claim of false arrest on the ground that the investigation was not a legitimate one. *(Details, pp. 158-59)*

The court concluded, however, that the Speaker and the members of the investigating committee could not be prosecuted for the false arrest because the report recommending contempt and the vote to direct Kilbourn's arrest were covered by the speech or debate clause. The court wrote:

> . . .The reason of the rule is as forcible in its application to written reports presented in that body [the

House] by its committees, to resolutions offered which, though in writing, must be reproduced in speech, and to the act of voting, whether it is done vocally or by passing between the tellers. In short, to things generally done in a session of the House by one of its members in relation to the business before it. [13]

Extension to Aides. In its *Kilbourn* decision, the court did not extend the protection of the speech or debate clause to the sergeant at arms who as a result was liable to prosecution for false arrest. A similar holding was made in 1967 in the case of *Dombrowski v. Eastland*. [14] Petitioners charged that Sen. James O. Eastland, D-Miss. (1941, 1943-79), chairman of the Judiciary Committee's Internal Security Subcommittee, and the subcommittee counsel conspired with Louisiana officials to seize the property and records of the petitioners in violation of the Fourth Amendment.

The court, in a *per curiam* decision, held that Eastland was not liable to prosecution but that the subcommittee counsel was. Noting that the record contained no evidence of Eastland's involvement in any activity that he might be liable for, the court said that "legislators engaged in the sphere of legislative activity . . . should be protected not only from the consequences of litigation's results but also from the burden of defending themselves." [15]

As to the subcommittee counsel, the court said there was enough dispute over the facts involved in his alleged collaboration with the state officials to warrant prosecution. The speech and debate clause, though applicable to congressional employees, was not absolute, the court said.

In 1972 the court elaborated on this opinion. *Gravel v. United States* involved Sen. Mike Gravel, D-Alaska, and his actions in releasing portions of the then-classified Pentagon Papers history of U.S. involvement in the Vietnam War. [16]

During the controversy over publication of the Pentagon Papers in 1971 by several newspapers, Gravel on June 29, 1971, convened a special meeting of the Public Works Subcommittee on Public Buildings, of which he was chairman. With the press and public in attendance, Gravel read classified documents from the Pentagon Papers into the subcommittee record. Subsequently, the senator arranged for the verbatim publication of the subcommittee record by Beacon Press.

In August 1971, a federal grand jury in Boston, investigating release of the Pentagon Papers, ordered Gravel aide Leonard S. Rodberg to appear before it. Rodberg had been hired the night Gravel called the session of his subcommittee to read excerpts from the secret documents. He subsequently helped Gravel edit and make arrangements for publication of the papers. Rodberg moved to quash the subpoena on the grounds that he was protected from questioning by the speech or debate clause.

In a 5-4 decision on June 29, 1972, the Supreme Court held that the constitutional immunity of members of Congress from grand jury questioning extended to their aides if the conduct in question would be a protected legislative act if performed by the member himself.

"The day-to-day work of such aides is so critical to the Member's performance that they must be treated as [the Member's] alter egos," wrote Justice Byron R. White for the majority. [17]

However the majority agreed that this protection did not extend to arrangements that were made for the publication of the subcommittee report nor information about the

source of the classified documents. Gravel, as well as Rodberg, could be required to testify to the grand jury about these non-legislative matters, the majority said:

> While the Speech or Debate Clause recognizes speech, voting and other legislative acts as exempt from liability that might attach, it does not privilege either senator or aide to violate an otherwise valid criminal law in preparing for or implementing legislative acts. [18]

Justice Potter Stewart dissented from the ruling insofar as it held that a member of Congress could be forced to tell a grand jury about the sources of information used to prepare for legislative activity. Justices William O. Douglas, William J. Brennan Jr. and Thurgood Marshall argued in dissent that the constitutional immunity protected Gravel, Rodberg and the Beacon Press even from questions concerning the publication of the papers read into the subcommittee record.

Immunity vs. Individual Rights

The speech or debate clause would appear to protect legislators and their aides from prosecution even in cases where their legislative activities have infringed on the constitutional rights of private individuals.

A major case, *Tenney v. Brandhove* (1951), involved the California state legislature but the court's ruling seems applicable to Congress. [19] In the case, Brandhove sued members of a legislative committee investigating un-American activities. Brandhove said their questioning of him was not for a legislative purpose but to harass and intimidate him and to prohibit him from exercising his right of free speech.

The court dismissed Brandhove's suit. "The claim of an unworthy purpose does not destroy the privilege" of congressional immunity, wrote Justice Felix Frankfurter. He continued:

> . . .Legislators are immune from deterrents to the uninhibited discharge of their legislative duty, not for their private indulgence but for the public good. One must not expect uncommon courage even in legislators. In times of political passion, dishonest and vindictive motives are readily attributed to legislative conduct and as readily believed. Courts are not the place for such controversies. Self-discipline and the voters must be the ultimate reliance for discouraging or correcting such abuses. The courts should not go beyond the narrow confines of determining that the committee's inquiry may fairly be deemed within its province. [20]

Justice Douglas dissented: "It is one thing to give great leeway to the legislative right of speech, debate, and investigation. But when a committee perverts its power, brings down on an individual the whole weight of government for an illegal or corrupt purpose, the reason for the immunity ends." [21]

In *Doe v. McMillen* (1973), the court held that members of Congress and their employees — chiefly John McMillen, D-S.C. (1939-73), chairman of the House District of Columbia Committee, the committee's members and employees — were immune from charges that they violated the right of certain children to privacy by naming them as disciplinary and absentee problems in a committee report on the District of Columbia school system. Wrote Justice White:

...The business of Congress is to legislate; Congressmen and aides are absolutely immune when they are legislating. But when they act outside the "sphere of legitimate legislative activity" ... they enjoy no special immunity from local laws protecting the good name or the reputation of the ordinary citizen. [22]

Since the committee members and employees included the names of the children in a report that was a legitimate legislative activity they were immune from prosecution. But the court held that this immunity might not extend to the public printer and the superintendent of documents, also named in the suit. This protection did not cover persons, the court said, "who publish and distribute otherwise actionable materials beyond the reasonable requirements of the legislative function." [23] It was left to the trial court to determine if these defendants had gone beyond those requirements.

In 1975 the court held that a valid subpoena from a congressional committee fell within the protected sphere of legislative activity even if it was claimed that the subpoena was intended to impede the exercise of First Amendment rights. [24] The case involved Sen. Eastland, the Judiciary Subcommittee on Internal Security and the subcommittee counsel. Eastland had issued a subpoena for the bank records of the United States Servicemen's Fund (USSF), as part of the subcommittee's inquiry into the enforcement of the Internal Security Act of 1950. The USSF set up coffeehouses and aided underground military base newspapers, both vehicles for protest against American involvement in Indochina. The courts could not investigate the propriety of the inquiry into the fund's activities beyond determining that such an inquiry was within the jurisdiction of the subcommittee, said the court. If that is determined, "the speech or debate clause is an absolute bar to interference," the court concluded. [25]

In dissent, Justice Douglas claimed that "no official ... may invoke immunity for his actions for which wrongdoers normally suffer." [26]

In the 1979 case of *Hutchinson v. Proxmire,* the court held that the speech or debate clause did not immunize a member of Congress from libel suits for allegedly defamatory statements he made about a person in press releases and newsletters, even though the statements had originally been made on the Senate floor. "Valuable and desirable as it may be" to inform the public of a member's activities, the court said, transmittal of such information in press releases "is not part of the legislative function or the deliberations that make up the legislative process." [27]

Criminal Prosecutions

The Supreme Court in 1966 held, 7-0, that in prosecuting a former member of Congress the executive branch could not inquire into the member's motive for making a speech on the floor, even though the speech was allegedly made for a bribe and was part of an unlawful conspiracy.

United States v. Johnson arose out of the conviction of former Rep. Thomas F. Johnson, D-Md. (1959-63), in June 1963 by a federal jury in Baltimore. [28] The government charged that Johnson, former Rep. Frank W. Boykin, D-Ala. (1935-63), and two officers of a Maryland savings and loan company then under indictment entered into a conspiracy whereby Johnson and Boykin would approach the Justice Department to urge a "review" of the indictment and Johnson would make a speech on the floor of the House defending savings and loan institutions in general. Johnson

---

'To Support the Right of the People'

The basic interpretation of the speech or debate clause comes not from the Supreme Court of the United States but from the Supreme Court of Massachusetts, which included an immunity clause in its 1780 constitution. Charged with slander during a private conversation on the floor, three members of the state's lower chamber invoked the immunity clause. Speaking to the plea, Massachusetts Chief Justice Parsons in 1808 wrote:

These privileges [of immunity] are thus secured, not with the intention of protecting the members against prosecutions for their own benefit, but to support the right of the People, by enabling their representatives to execute the functions of their office without fear of prosecutions, civil or criminal. I therefore think that the article ought not to be construed strictly, but liberally, that the full design of it may be answered. I will not confine it to delivering an opinion, but will extend it to the giving of a vote, to the making of a written report, and to every other act resulting from the nature and the execution of the office. And I would define the article as securing to every member exemption from prosecution for everything said or done by him as a representative, in the exercise of the functions of that office, without inquiring whether the exercise was regular, according to the rules of the House, or irregular and against those rules. I do not confine the member to his place in the House; and I am satisfied that there are cases in which he is entitled to this privilege when not within the walls of the Representatives' Chamber. (*Coffin v. Coffin,* 4 Mass. 1, at 27 (1808)

---

made the speech in June 1960 and it was reprinted by the indicted company and distributed to the public. Johnson and Boykin allegedly received money in the form of "campaign contributions." Johnson's share was put at more than $20,000.

The four men were convicted on seven counts of violating the federal conflict of interest law and one count of conspiring to defraud the United States (President Johnson Dec. 17, 1965, granted Boykin a full pardon.)

The 4th Circuit Court of Appeals in September 1964 set aside Johnson's conspiracy conviction and ordered a retrial on the other counts.

The Supreme Court essentially affirmed the court of appeals ruling. The opinion was written by Justice John Marshall Harlan who said that the precedents did not deal

...with a criminal prosecution based upon an allegation that a member of Congress abused his position by conspiring to give a particular speech in return for remuneration from private interests. However reprehensible such conduct may be, we believe the Speech or Debate Clause extends at least so far as to prevent it from being made the basis of a criminal charge against a member of Congress of conspiring to defraud the United States by impeding the due discharge of government functions. The essence of such a charge in this context is that the Congressman's conduct was improperly motivated, and . . . that is precisely what the Speech or Debate Clause generally forecloses from executive and judicial inquiry. [29]

Emphasizing the narrowness of its holding, the court said the decision did not address whether congressional immunity would extend to a prosecution based on a specifically drawn statute passed by Congress to regulate the conduct of its own members. Nor did it speak to a prosecution for a general criminal statute that did not rely for its proof on the member's motivation for performing his legislative activities. The court said it would allow a new trial of Johnson on the conspiracy charge only if the executive branch could purge all parts of its prosecution offensive to the speech or debate clause. The government chose to drop the conspiracy charge. (On a retrial of the seven conflict-of-interest charges, Johnson was convicted a second time and sentenced to six months in prison.)

Brewster Case. The question whether the government could — without violating congressional immunity under the speech and debate clause — successfully prosecute a member of Congress for taking a bribe in return for casting a vote came before the court in 1972.

Former Sen. Daniel B. Brewster, D-Md. (1963-69), was indicted in 1969 on charges of accepting $24,000 in bribes between 1966 and 1968 from the mail order firm of Spiegel Inc. During that time, Brewster was a member of the Senate Post Office and Civil Service Committee, which was considering proposed changes in postal rates. The indictment alleged that the bribes influenced Brewster's legislative action on these proposals.

In November 1970, a federal district judge in the District of Columbia dismissed the charges against Brewster, stating that the speech or debate clause shielded him from prosecution for bribery related to the performance of legislative acts. The Justice Department immediately asked the Supreme Court to review this decision.

By a 6-3 vote, the court reversed the lower court ruling and held that Brewster could indeed be prosecuted on the bribery charge. Observing that a broad interpretation of the speech or debate clause would immunize almost all legislators' activities, Chief Justice Warren E. Burger stated:

> In its narrowest scope, the Clause is a very large, albeit essential, grant of privilege. It has enabled reckless men to slander and even destroy others with impunity, but that was the conscious choice of the framers. . . . [B]ut the shield does not extend beyond what is necessary to preserve the integrity of the legislative process. [30]

The court has never interpreted the clause "as protecting all conduct *relating* to the legislative process," said Burger. "In every case thus far before this Court, the Speech or Debate Clause has been limited to an act which was clearly part of the legislative process — the *due* functioning of the process." [31]

Turning specifically to the Brewster case, Burger separated the act of taking a bribe from the act of casting a ballot:

> The illegal conduct is taking or agreeing to take money for a promise to act in a certain way. There is no

need for the government to show that [Brewster] fulfilled the alleged illegal bargain; acceptance of the bribe is the violation of the statute, not performance of the illegal promise.

> Taking a bribe is, obviously, no part of the legislative process or function; it is not a legislative act. [32]

By this construction, the court found that, unlike the *Johnson* case, it would not be necessary for the government in prosecuting Brewster to inquire into the legislative acts or their motivations in order to provide a violation of the bribery statute.

In dissent, Justice William J. Brennan Jr. said the majority had taken an artificial view of the charges. The indictment, Brennan said, was not for receipt of money but for receipt of money in exchange for a promise to vote a certain way. To prove this crime, he continued, the government would have to inquire into Brewster's motives and this it was prevented from doing by the immunity clause.

The three dissenters also said that Congress, not the courts, was the proper forum for disciplining the misconduct of its members. "The speech or debate clause does not immunize corrupt congressmen," wrote Justice Byron R. White. "It reserves the power to discipline [them] in the houses of Congress." [33]

Brewster stood trial and was convicted but the conviction was reversed. Before a second trial could begin, Brew-

---

> *". . .the Clause is a very large . . . grant of privilege. It has enabled reckless men to slander and even destroy others with impunity, . . . but the shield does not extend beyond what is necessary to preserve the integrity of the legislative process."*
>
> —Chief Justice Warren E. Burger
> *United States v. Brewster*, 1972

---

ster pleaded no contest to a felony charge of accepting an illegal gratuity while he was a senator.

Dowdy Case. Little more than a year later, the court in 1973 refused to review an appellate court ruling which had reversed the conviction of former Rep. John Dowdy, D-Texas (1952-73), on five of eight conspiracy, bribery and perjury charges. The 4th Circuit Court of Appeals held that the evidence used in Dowdy's trial directly related to the legislative process. It "was an examination of defendant's actions as a Congressman, who was chairman of a subcommittee investigating a complaint, in gathering information in preparation for a possible subcommittee investigatory hearing," the appeals court said. [34]

Although the alleged criminal act — bribery — was the same in the *Dowdy, Johnson* and *Brewster* cases, the major difference was the source of the evidence. In Brewster's case the court found sufficient evidence available outside of Brewster's legislative activities to let the case go forward. In the *Dowdy* and *Johnson* cases, so much of the evidence was based on their legislative activities that introduction of that evidence violated their immunity and was therefore unconstitutional.

Elections Regulation

The Constitution gives the states the authority to set the time, place and manner of holding elections for Congress with the proviso that "Congress may at any time by law make or alter such Regulations, except as to the Places of chusing Senators." (Article I, Section 4, Clause 1)

The first law that Congress passed regulating the time, place or manner of a federal election was an 1842 act requiring that representatives be elected by districts. Congress' first comprehensive regulation of elections was the Enforcement Act of 1870, adopted to enforce the right of blacks to vote granted under the 15th Amendment. Together with two 1871 statutes, the Enforcement Act made it a federal offense to register falsely, bribe voters, interfere with election officials and make false counts of ballots cast. Any election officer who failed to perform a duty required of him in a federal election under either federal or state law was also guilty of a federal offense.

In 1880, the act was challenged as an unconstitutional infringement on the states' right to conduct elections. The suit also questioned whether Congress had the authority to punish state election officers for violations of state election law affecting federal elections.

In *Ex parte Siebold* the court upheld the Enforcement Act:

> ...There is no declaration [in Article I, Section 4] that the regulations shall be made wholly by the State legislature or wholly by Congress. If Congress does not interfere, of course they may be made wholly by the State, but if it chooses to interfere, there is nothing in the words to prevent its doing so, either wholly or partially. On the contrary, their necessary implication is that it may do either. It may either make the regulations, or it may alter them. If it only alters, leaving ... the general organization of the polls to the State, there results a necessary cooperation of the two governments in regulating the subject. But no repugnance in the system of regulations can arise thence; for the power of Congress over the subject is paramount. It may be exercised as and when Congress sees fit to exercise it. When exercised, the action of Congress, so far as it extends and conflicts with the regulations of the State, necessarily supersedes them. [35]

It stood to reason that if Congress could regulate elections, it had the power to enforce its regulations, the court continued. A state election official officiating at a federal election has a responsibility to the federal government as well as to the state and the fact that the official is a state official does not shield him from federal punishment for failure to perform his duty to the United States.

To the argument that Congress cannot punish violations of state election law pertaining to federal elections, the court said: "The State laws which Congress sees no occasion to alter, but which it allows to stand, are in effect adopted by Congress. It simply demands their fulfilment." [36]

In subsequent cases, the court has upheld Congress' authority under Article I, Section 4, to protect against personal violence and intimidation at the polls, and against failure to count all the votes cast. [37]

Primary Elections

Though the court had ruled that congressional authority to regulate the time, manner and place of holding

Justices Who Served in Congress

Of the 101 Supreme Court justices, 27 served in the Senate, the House or both before being seated on the court. Only one justice, David Davis, left the court to serve in Congress. In 1877, the Illinois legislature elected Davis to the U.S. Senate; Davis had served on the court since 1862. Davis was in the Senate for only one term, serving as president *pro tempore* from 1881 to 1883, when he retired.

A list of the men who served both in Congress and on the Supreme Court follows.

Justice	Congressional Service	Court Service
Senate		
William Paterson	1789-Nov. 13, 1790	1793-1806
Oliver Ellsworth	1789-March 8, 1796	1796-1799
Levi Woodbury	1825-31; 1841-1845	1845-1851
David Davis	1877-1883	1862-1877
Salmon P. Chase*	1849-1855; March 4-6, 1861	1864-1873
Stanley Matthews	March 21, 1877-1879	1881-1889
Howell E. Jackson	1881-April 4, 1886	1894-1895
Edward D. White*	1891-March 12, 1894	1894-1921
Hugo L. Black	1927-Aug. 19, 1937	1937-1971
Harold H. Burton	1941-Sept. 30, 1945	1945-1958
Sherman Minton	1935-1941	1949-1956
House		
John Marshall*	1799-June 7, 1800	1801-1835
Joseph Story	May 23, 1808-1809	1811-1845
Gabriel Duvall	Nov. 11, 1794-March 28, 1796	1812-1835
John McLean	1813-1816	1829-1861
Henry Baldwin	1817-May 8, 1822	1830-1844
James M. Wayne	1829-Jan. 13, 1835	1835-1867
Philip B. Barbour	Sept. 19, 1814-1825	1836-1841
Nathan Clifford	1839-1843	1858-1881
William Strong	1847-1851	1870-1880
Joseph McKenna	1885-1892	1898-1925
William H. Moody	Nov. 5, 1895-May 1, 1902	1906-1910
Mahlon Pitney	1895-Jan. 10, 1899	1912-1922
Fred M. Vinson*	Jan. 12, 1924-1929; 1931-May 12, 1938	1946-1953
Both Chambers		
John McKinley	S: Nov. 27, 1826-1831; March 4-April 22, 1837 H: 1833-1835	1837-1852
Lucius Q. C. Lamar	H: 1857-1860; 1873-1877 S: 1877-March 6, 1885	1888-1893
George Sutherland	H: 1901-1903 S: 1905-1917	1922-1938
James F. Byrnes	H: 1911-1925 S: 1931-July 8, 1941	1941-1942

Denotes a Chief Justice.

elections was paramount to state authority, in 1921 it ruled that party primaries were not elections, and that Congress consequently had no right to regulate them.

Newberry v. United States arose when Truman H. Newberry, R-Mich. (1919-22), was convicted for having spent more money than he was allowed under the 1911 campaign expenditure law in his primary race against Henry Ford for the 1918 Republican Senate nomination in Michigan.

Newberry's case was argued before the Supreme Court by Charles Evans Hughes, who had served six years on the court in 1910-16 and would return to it in 1930 as Chief Justice.

The court set the conviction aside by a 5-4 vote. However, on the constitutional question of whether Congress had the power to regulate primaries the court divided 4-4. (Justice Joseph McKenna, who voted to reverse the conviction, was unsure how ratification of the 17th Amendment in 1913 affected Congress' power to act under the 1911 statute.)

The four justices who claimed that Congress did not have authority to regulate primaries wrote that the word election "now has the same general significance as it did when the Constitution came into existence — final choice of an officer by duly qualified electors." [38]

Primaries, the four continued, "are in no sense elections for an office but merely methods by which party adherents agree upon candidates whom they intend to offer and support for ultimate choice by all qualified electors." [39] The manner in which candidates are nominated for federal office "does not directly affect the manner of holding the election," they concluded. [40]

This politically naive view of the role of the primary was assailed by Justice Mahlon Pitney, who observed that the primary had no reason to exist except as preparation for an election. Congressional authority to regulate the manner of holding an election "can mean nothing less," Pitney said,

---

"To say that Congress is without the power to pass appropriate legislation to safeguard . . . [a presidential] election from the improper use of money to influence the result is to deny the nation in a vital particular the power of self-protection."

—Justice George Sutherland
Burroughs and Cannon v. United States, 1934

---

than the ability to regulate "the entire mode of procedure — the essence, not merely the form of conducting the elections." [41]

Pitney's dissent became the majority position twenty years later when the court, in the 1941 case of *United States v. Classic,* reversed its *Newberry* decision. The 1941 case involved a government prosecution, under the 1870 Enforcement Act, of Louisiana election commissioners for altering and falsely counting votes in a primary election. In most cases winning the Democratic nomination to Congress in Louisiana was tantamount to winning the general election. [42]

Writing for the 5-3 majority, Justice Harlan Fiske Stone stated: ". . .[W]e think that the authority of Congress, given by [Article I, Section 4], includes the authority to regulate primary elections when as in this case, they are

a step in the exercise by the people of their choice of representatives in Congress." [43]

The three opposing justices dissented, not on the grounds that Congress did not have the authority to regulate primary elections but on the grounds that the statute making alteration and miscounting of ballots criminal offenses was not specific enough to encompass primaries.

Campaign Financing

Sensitive to charges that corporations exerted undue influence on Congress through unrestrained spending on favored candidates, Congress in 1907 passed the first law regulating campaign financing.

The Tillman Act prohibited corporations and national banks from making any money contributions to any candidate for federal office. A 1910 law required every political committee seeking to influence the election of House members in two or more states to file contribution and spending reports with the clerk of the House. A 1911 law provided similar regulation for Senate races.

In 1925 Congress passed the Federal Corrupt Practices Act setting limits on the amounts candidates for the Senate and House could spend in general elections. Primary elections were omitted because of the court's ruling in the *Newberry* case. The 1925 act also required political committees seeking to influence the election of presidential electors in two or more states to file contribution and spending reports that would be available to the public.

This last provision was challenged in the 1934 case of *Burroughs and Cannon v. United States* as an infringement on the right of the states to appoint their presidential electors in the manner they deemed appropriate (Article II, Section 1, Clause 2). [44] In upholding the federal disclosure provisions as they pertained to presidential electors, the Supreme Court implicitly sanctioned federal regulation of campaign financing in congressional elections.

The provisions, observed Justice George Sutherland for the majority, applied to committees operating in two or more states. Such committees, "if not beyond the power of the state to deal with at all, are beyond its power to deal with adequately," Sutherland said. [45]

Turning to the authority of Congress to supply adequate regulation, Sutherland said that the importance of the election of the president

> . . .and the vital character of its relationship to and effect upon the welfare and safety of the whole people cannot be too strongly stated. To say that Congress is without the power to pass appropriate legislation to safeguard such an election from the improper use of money to influence the result is to deny to the nation in a vital particular the power of self-protection. [46]

First Amendment Conflict. But congressional authority to regulate campaign spending is not unchecked.

In the 1976 decision in the case of *Buckley v. Valeo* the court held that certain provisions of a 1974 campaign financing law violated First Amendment rights. [47]

Among the plaintiffs challenging the 1974 statute were Sen. James L. Buckley, Cons-R N.Y. (1971-77), former Sen. Eugene J. McCarthy, D-Minn. (1959-71), the New York Civil Liberties Union and *Human Events,* a conservative publication.

The plaintiffs did not question Congress' power to regulate campaign financing but claimed that the law's new limits on campaign contributions and expenditures curbed the freedom of contributors and candidates to express themselves in the political marketplace.

The Supreme Court handed down its ruling on Jan. 30, 1976, in an unsigned 137-page opinion. In five separate, signed opinions, several justices concurred with and dissented from separate issues in the case.

In its decision, the court upheld provisions that:
- Set limits on how much individuals and political committees may contribute to candidates.
- Provided for the public financing of presidential primary and general election campaigns.
- Required the disclosure of campaign contributions of more than $100 and campaign expenditures of more than $10.

But the court overturned other features of the law, ruling that the campaign spending limits were unconstitutional violations of the First Amendment guarantee of free expression. For presidential candidates who accepted federal matching funds, however, the ceiling on expenditures remained intact.

"A restriction on the amount of money a person or group can spend on political communication during a campaign necessarily reduces the quantity of expression," the court stated, "by restricting the number of issues discussed, the depth of their exploration and the size of the audience reached. This is because virtually every means of communicating ideas in today's mass society requires the expenditure of money."[48] Only Justice Byron R. White dissented on this point; he would have upheld the limitations.

Although the court acknowledged that both contribution limits and spending limits had First Amendment implications, it distinguished between the two by saying that the act's "expenditure ceilings impose significantly more severe restrictions on protected freedom of political expression and association than do its limitations on financial contributions."[49]

The $1,000 ceiling on the amount an individual could spend on behalf of a candidate was a clear violation of the First Amendment, the opinion said:

> While the . . . ceiling thus fails to serve any substantial government interest in stemming the reality or appearance of corruption in the electoral process, it heavily burdens core First Amendment expression. . . .Advocacy of the election or defeat of candidates for federal office is no less entitled to protection under the First Amendment than the discussion of political policy generally or advocacy of the passage or defeat of legislation.[50]

The court struck down the limits on how much of their own money candidates could spend on their campaigns. "The candidate, no less than any other person, has a First Amendment right to engage in the discussion of public issues and vigorously and tirelessly to advocate his own election and the election of other candidates," the opinion said.[51]

White dissented on expenditure limits. Rejecting the argument that money is speech, he wrote that there are "many expensive campaign activities that are not themselves communicative or remotely related to speech."[52]

Justice Thurgood Marshall rejected the court's reasoning in striking down the limit on how much candidates may spend on their own campaigns. "It would appear to follow," he said, "that the candidate with a substantial personal fortune at his disposal is off to a significant 'head start.'"[53]

Separation of Powers. The court held unanimously that the Federal Election Commission, the agency established to oversee and enforce the campaign financing laws, was unconstitutional. The court said the method of appointment of commissioners violated the Constitution's separation-of-powers and appointments clauses because some members were named by congressional officials but exercised executive powers.

According to the decision, the commission may exercise only those powers Congress is allowed to delegate to congressional committees — investigating and information-gathering. Only if the commission's members were ap-

---

"A restriction on the amount of money a person or group can spend on political communication during a campaign necessarily reduces the quantity of expression. . . ."
—Buckley v. Valeo, 1976

---

pointed by the president, as required under the Constitution's appointments clause, could the commission carry out the administrative and enforcement responsibilities the law originally gave it, the court ruled.

The justices stayed their ruling for 30 days to give the House and Senate time to "reconstitute the commission by law or adopt other valid enforcement mechanisms."[54] As events developed, Congress took more than three months to act and instead of merely reconstituting the commission it passed a considerably expanded campaign financing law.

Election Returns

Because the Constitution makes each house the judge of the election returns of its members, disputed elections have been considered political questions that the court will not review. Only once has the court felt obliged to answer whether a state law interfered with this congressional right.

Roudebush v. Hartke (1972) arose when Rep. Richard L. Roudebush, R-Ind. (1961-72), lost the 1970 Senate election to incumbent Sen. Vance Hartke, D-Ind. (1959-77), by a slim margin.[55] Roudebush asked for a recount by the state and Hartke challenged it on the grounds that the state's recount procedure would interfere with the Senate's right to judge the disputed election returns.

Denying Hartke's challenge, the court said that the state "recount does not prevent the Senate from independently evaluating the election any more than the initial count does. The Senate is free to accept or reject the apparent winner in either count, and, if it chooses, to conduct its own recount."[56] The recount did not change the outcome of the election.

Equal Representation

Hartke was seated by the Senate pending the outcome of the recount, but in an earlier case, the Senate refused to seat the apparent victor of a disputed election until the investigation into alleged misdoings in his campaign were completed. *Barry v. United States ex rel. Cunningham* involved the contested 1926 election of William S. Vare to the Senate from Pennsylvania. One of the issues involved in the case was whether the Senate's refusal to seat Vare pending the outcome of the investigation deprived Pennsylvania of its equal representation. The court concluded it did not:

> ...The equal representation clause is found in Article V, which authorizes and regulates amendments to the Constitution, "provided, ... that no state, without its consent, shall be deprived of its equal suffrage in the Senate." This constitutes a limitation upon the power of amendment and has nothing to do with a situation such as the one here presented. The temporary deprivation of equal representation which results from the refusal of the Senate to seat a member pending inquiry as to his election or qualifications is the necessary consequence of the exercise of a constitutional power, and no more deprives the state of its "equal suffrage" in the constitutional sense than would a vote of the Senate vacating the seat of a sitting member or a vote of expulsion. [57]

Lobby Regulation

The right to lobby Congress — to assert rights, or to win a special privilege or financial benefit for the group applying the pressure or to achieve an ideological goal — is guaranteed by the First Amendment to the Constitution. It provides that "Congress shall make no law ... abridging the freedom of speech or of the press; or the right of the people peaceably to assemble and to petition the Government for redress of grievances."

Pressure groups, whether operating through general campaigns designed to sway public opinion or through direct contact with members of Congress, help to inform both Congress and the public about public issues and make known to Congress the practical aspects of proposed legislation — whom it would help or hurt, who is for or against it. Against these benefits, there are serious liabilities. The most serious is that in pursuing their own objectives, the pressure groups are apt to lead Congress into decisions which benefit the pressure groups but which do not necessarily serve other parts of the public. Occasionally, lobbyists resort to bribery or other unethical tactics in their efforts to influence legislation.

To guard against such lobbying methods, the House in 1876 passed a resolution requiring lobbyists to register with the clerk of the House. Congress subsequently passed a handful of specialized measures regulating certain kinds of lobbying activities, but it was not until 1946 that it enacted a general lobbying regulation law.

Because of the difficulty of imposing meaningful regulation on lobbying without infringing on the constitutional rights of free speech, press, assembly and petition, the 1946 act did not actually regulate. Instead it simply required any person who was hired by someone else for the principal purpose of lobbying Congress to register with the secretary of the Senate and the clerk of the House and to file certain quarterly financial reports so that the lobbyist's activities would be known to Congress and the public. Organizations which solicited or received money for the principal purpose of lobbying Congress did not necessarily have to register, but they did have to file quarterly spending reports with the clerk detailing how much they spent to influence legislation.

Test Case

The National Association of Manufacturers (NAM) brought a test suit in 1948 challenging the validity of the 1946 law. A federal court in the District of Columbia in 1952 held the act unconstitutional because the definitions used in the law were "too indefinite and vague to constitute an ascertainable standard of guilt." [58] Later in the same year, the Supreme Court reversed the lower court on a technicality, leaving the 1946 law in full force but open to future challenge. [59]

Harriss Case. That challenge came in *United States v. Harriss*, actually begun at the same time the NAM case was being pursued. [60] In June 1948, the federal government obtained indictments against several individuals and an organization for alleged violations of the registration and reporting sections of the 1946 lobbying law.

It was charged that, without registering or reporting, New York cotton broker Robert M. Harriss had made payments to Ralph W. Moore, a Washington commodity trader and secretary of the National Farm Committee, for the purpose of pressuring Congress on legislation, and that Moore had made similar payments to James E. McDonald, the agricultural commissioner of Texas, and Tom Linder, the agricultural commissioner of Georgia. A lower court in 1953 held the lobbying law unconstitutional on grounds that it was too vague and indefinite to meet the requirements of due process, and that the registration and reporting requirements violated the rights of free speech, free press, assembly and petition.

In June 1954 the Supreme Court, by a 5-3 vote, reversed the lower court and upheld the constitutionality of the 1946 statute. To do so, it had to interpret the act very narrowly. The statute, the majority said, applied only to lobbyists or organizations who solicited, collected or received contributions in order to conduct their lobbying, and then only to those lobbyists and organizations whose main purpose was to influence legislation.

Furthermore, the court interpreted the act "to refer only to 'lobbying in its commonly accepted sense' — to direct communications with members of Congress on pending or proposed federal legislation." [61]

This limited interpretation omitted from coverage several categories of lobbying organizations, including those that spent money from their own funds to conduct lobbying activities rather than collecting funds specifically for the purpose of lobbying, those who could claim that their primary purpose was something other than attempting to influence legislation, and those whose lobbying activities were confined to influencing the public on legislation or issues — so-called grass-roots lobbying.

But it was only under this limited construction that a majority of the court would find the act constitutional.

Sympathetic to the congressional dilemma, the majority observed that Congress was not trying to prohibit lobbying activities but merely wanted to find out

> ...who is being hired, who is putting up the money and how much. It acted in the same spirit and for a similar purpose in passing the Federal Corrupt Practices Act — to maintain the integrity of a basic governmental process.... Under these circumstances, we believe that Congress, at least within the bounds of the Act as we have construed it, is not constitutionally forbidden to require the disclosure of lobbying activities. To do so would be to deny Congress in large measure the power of self-protection. [62]

In dissent, Justices William O. Douglas, Hugo L. Black and Robert H. Jackson complained that in order to uphold the lobbying act, the court had in essence rewritten it.

The dissenters also contended that the majority's construction made the statute no less vague than it had been:

> The language of the Act is so broad that one who writes a letter or makes a speech or publishes an article or distributes literature or does many of the other things with which appellees are charged has no fair notice when he is close to the prohibited line. No construction we give it today will make clear retroactively the vague standards that confronted appellees when they did the acts now charged against them as criminal. [63]

Rules

The power of the House and Senate each to make its own rules for the conduct of its business was described by Justice David J. Brewer in 1892:

> ...The Constitution empowers each house to determine its rules of proceedings. It may not by its rules ignore constitutional restraints or violate fundamental rights, and there should be a reasonable relation between the mode or method of proceeding established by the rule and the result which is sought to be attained. But within these limitations all matters of method are open to the determination of the house, and it is no impeachment of the rule to say that some other way would be better, more accurate or even more just. It is no objection to the validity of the rule that a different one has been prescribed and in force for a length of time. The power to make rules is not one which once exercised is exhausted. It is a continuous power, always subject to be exercised by the house, and within the limitations suggested, absolute and beyond the challenge of any other body or tribunal. [64]

Twice the court has ruled that where a rule of the House or Senate conflicts with the rights of a private person, the rule must give way. In one of the cases, *United States v. Smith* (1932), the court held that the Senate rules on confirming nominees to executive agencies could not be construed to allow the Senate to reconsider its confirmation of a person already sworn into the office. [65] The court was careful to say that the question before it was how the rule should be interpreted and not its constitutionality.

In the second case, *Christoffel v. United States* (1949), a divided court overturned the perjury conviction of a witness who claimed before a House committee he was not affiliated with the Communist Party. [66] The majority held that while there was a quorum of the committee present at the time the hearing began, there was no proof that the quorum still existed at the time the alleged perjury occurred. Thus, it was not proved that the committee was a "competent tribunal" before which an erroneous statement would amount to perjury.

The four dissenters contended that, once established, a quorum was presumed to continue until a point of no quorum was raised.

The Journal

Article I, Section 5 of the Constitution states that a majority of each house constitutes a quorum to do business. In *United States v. Ballin* (1892), the court held that in disputes over whether a majority was present, the *Congressional Record*, the official journal of the proceedings in each chamber, would be the unchallengeable proof of how many

---

To Protect the General Welfare

In its decision in *United States v. Harriss,* the Supreme Court held that Congress was not constitutionally forbidden to require disclosure of lobbying activities because to do so "would be to deny Congress in large measure the power of self-protection." [1]

This was clearly the intent of Congress when it enacted the 1946 lobby registration law. But one of the statute's authors apparently found some constitutional authority for enactment of the law in the clause that allows Congress to act for the general welfare. Introducing the bill in the Senate, Sen. Robert N. LaFollette Jr., R-Prog. (1925-35), Prog. (1935-47), said:

> In the last analysis, Congress is the center of political gravity under our form of government because it reflects and expresses the popular will in the making of national policy. Too often, however, the true attitude of public opinion is distorted and obscured by the pressures of special-interest groups. Beset by swarms of lobbyists seeking to protect this or that small segment of the economy or to advance this or that narrow interest, legislators find it difficult to discover the real majority will and to legislate in the public interest.
>
> As government control of economic life and its use as an instrument of popular welfare have increased, the activities of these powerful groups have multiplied.... These agents seek to transform the aims and programs of their groups into public policy by having them embodied in general legislation....
>
> A pressure-group economy gives rise to government by whirlpools of special-interest groups in which the national welfare is often neglected. The pulling and hauling of powerful pressure groups create delays and distortions which imperil national safety in wartime and threaten paralysis and bankruptcy in time of peace. The public welfare suffers in the warfare of private groups, and Congress becomes an arena for the rationalization of group and class interests. [2]

---

[1] *United States v. Harriss,* 347 U.S. 612 at 625 (1954).

[2] U.S., Congress, Senate, Legislative Reorganization Act of 1946, S Rept 1400 to accompany S 2177, 79th Congress, 2nd Sess., 1946, pp. 4-5, quoted in Karl Schriftgiesser, *The Lobbyists* (Boston: Little, Brown & Co., 1951), pp. 82-83.

---

members were present. [67] This ruling upheld the most controversial of a new set of rules and procedures adopted by the House in 1890 — the counting of present but non-voting members to make a quorum.

In a second case decided that year, the court upheld a federal statute that had been authenticated by both houses and signed into law by the president despite a showing in the *Congressional Record* that the enacted statute omitted a section that had been passed by both chambers. [68]

Continuing Senate Session

In the 1927 case of *McGrain v. Daugherty*, the court sustained the Senate's claim that it was a continuing body which did not need to reauthorize its committees with each new Congress. It may be true that the House must dissolve since its members "are all elected for the period of a single Congress," the court said, "but it cannot well be the same with the Senate, which is a continuing body whose mem-

bers are elected for a term of six years and so divided into classes that the seats of one-third only become vacant at the end of each Congress, two-thirds always continuing into the next Congress. . . ." [69]

Footnotes

[1] *The Federalist Papers* with an Introduction by Clinton Rossiter (New York: Mentor Books, 1961), p. 371.

[2] *Powell v. McCormack*, 395 U.S. 486 (1969).

[3] Id. at 522.

[4] Congressional Quarterly, *Guide to Congress*, 2nd ed. (Washington, D.C.: Congressional Quarterly Inc., 1976), p. 685-700.

[5] *In re Chapman*, 166 U.S. 661 at 669-70 (1897).

[6] *Burton v. United States*, 202 U.S. 344 at 369 (1906).

[7] *Kilbourn v. Thompson*, 103 U.S. 168 (1881).

[8] *Powell v. McCormack*, 395 U.S. 486 (1969).

[9] *Long v. Ansell*, 293 U.S. 76 (1934); *United States v. Cooper*, 4 Dall. 341 (C.C. Pa. 1800).

[10] *Williamson v. United States*, 207 U.S. 425 (1908).

[11] *United States v. Brewster*, 408 U.S. 501 at 507 (1972).

[12] *Kilbourn v. Thompson*, 103 U.S. 168 at 204 (1881).

[13] Ibid.

[14] *Dombrowski v. Eastland*, 387 U.S. 82 (1967).

[15] Id. at 85; also see *Powell v. McCormack*, 395 U.S. 486 at 505 (1969).

[16] *Gravel v. United States*, 408 U.S. 606 (1972).

[17] Id. at 616-17.

[18] Id. at 626.

[19] *Tenney v. Brandhove*, 341 U.S. 367 (1951).

[20] Id. at 377.

[21] Id. at 383.

[22] *Doe v. McMillan*, 412 U.S. 306 at 324 (1973).

[23] Id. at 315-16.

[24] *Eastland v. United States Servicemen's Fund*, 421 U.S. 491 (1975).

[25] Id. at 503.

[26] Id. at 518.

[27] *Hutchinson v. Proxmire* (1979).

[28] *United States v. Johnson*, 383 U.S. 169 (1966).

[29] Id. at 180.

[30] *United States v. Brewster*, 408 U.S. 501 at 516-17 (1972); see also *United States v. Helstoski* (1979).

[31] Id. at 515-16.

[32] Id. at 526.

[33] Id. at 563.

[34] *United States v. Dowdy*, 479 F.2d 213 at 224 (1973); cert. denied, 414 U.S. 823 (1973).

[35] *Ex parte Siebold*, 100 U.S. 371 at 383-84 (1880).

[36] Id. at 388-89.

[37] *Ex parte Yarbrough*, 110 U.S. 651 (1884); *United States v. Mosely*, 238 U.S. 383 (1915).

[38] *Newberry v. United States*, 256 U.S. 232 at 250 (1921).

[39] Ibid.

[40] Id. at 257.

[41] Id. at 280.

[42] See Louisiana House election results 1920-1942 in Congressional Quarterly, *Guide to U.S. Elections* (Washington, D.C.; Congressional Quarterly Inc., 1975), pp. 742-797.

[43] *United States v. Classic*, 313 U.S. 299 at 317 (1941).

[44] *Burroughs and Cannon v. United States*, 290 U.S. 534 (1934).

[45] Id. at 544-45.

[46] Id. at 545.

[47] *Buckley v. Valeo*, 424 U.S. 1 (1976).

[48] Id. at 19.

[49] Id. at 23.

[50] Id. at 47-48.

[51] Id. at 52.

[52] Id. at 263.

[53] Id. at 288.

[54] Id. at 143.

[55] *Roudebush v. Hartke*, 405 U.S. 15 (1972).

[56] Id. at 25-26.

[57] *Barry v. United States ex rel. Cunningham*, 279 U.S. 597 at 615-16 (1929).

[58] *National Association of Manufacturers v. McGrath*, 103 F. Supp. 510 (D.C. 1952).

[59] *McGrath v. National Association of Manufacturers*, 344 U.S. 804 (1952).

[60] *United States v. Harriss*, 347 U.S. 612 (1954).

[61] Id. at 620.

[62] Id. at 625.

[63] Id. at 632-33.

[64] *United States v. Ballin*, 144 U.S. 1 (1892).

[65] *United States v. Smith*, 286 U.S. 6 (1932).

[66] *Christoffel v. United States*, 338 U.S. 84 (1949).

[67] *United States v. Ballin*, 144 U.S. 1 (1892).

[68] *Field v. Clark*, 143 U.S. 649 (1892).

[69] *McGrain v. Daugherty*, 273 U.S. 135 at 181 (1927).

Selected Bibliography

Baxter, Maurice G. *The Steamboat Monopoly: Gibbons v. Ogden, 1824.* Borzoi Series in United States Constitutional History. New York: Alfred A. Knopf Inc., Borzoi Books, 1972.

Beth, Loren P. *The Development of the American Constitution, 1877-1917.* New York: Harper and Row Publishers Inc. 1971.

Black, Charles L., Jr. *Perspectives in Constitutional Law.* Englewood Cliffs, N.J.: Prentice-Hall Inc., 1963.

Carr, Robert K. *The Supreme Court and Judicial Review.* American Government in Action series. New York: Farrar and Rinehart Inc., 1942.

Claude, Richard. *The Supreme Court and the Electoral Process.* Baltimore: The Johns Hopkins Press, 1970.

Commager, Henry Steele. *Documents of American History.* 2 vols. 9th ed. Englewood Cliffs, N.J.: Prentice-Hall Inc., 1973.

Congressional Quarterly. *Guide to Congress.* 2nd ed. Washington, D.C.: Congressional Quarterly Inc., 1976.

Cortner, Richard C. *The Jones & Laughlin Case.* Borzoi Series in United States Constitutional History. New York: Alfred A. Knopf Inc., Borzoi Books, 1970.

Corwin, Edward S. *The Constitution and What It Means Today.* 12th ed. Princeton: Princeton University Press, 1958.

———. *The Doctrine of Judicial Review: Its Legal and Historical Basis and other Essays.* Princeton: Princeton University Press, 1914; reprint ed., Gloucester, Mass.: Peter Smith, 1963.

Cushman, Robert E. *Leading Constitutional Decisions.* 12th ed. New York: Appleton-Century-Crofts, 1963.

Cushman, Robert E. and Cushman, Robert F. *Cases in Constitutional Law*. 3rd ed. New York: Appleton-Century-Crofts, 1968.

Dimock, Marshall E. *Congressional Investigating Committees*. Baltimore: The Johns Hopkins University Press, 1929; reprint ed., New York: AMS Press Inc., 1971.

Frankfurter, Felix. *The Commerce Clause Under Marshall, Taney and Waite*. Chapel Hill, N.C.: The University of North Carolina Press, 1937.

Freund, Paul A., gen. ed. *History of the Supreme Court of the United States*. New York: Macmillan Publishing Co. Inc., 1974. Vol. 1: *Antecedents and Beginnings to 1801*, by Julius Goebel Jr. Vol. V: *The Taney Period, 1836-64*, by Carl B. Swisher.

Garraty, John A., ed. *Quarrels That Have Shaped the Constitution*. New York: Harper and Row, 1964.

Henkin, Louis. *Foreign Affairs and the Constitution*. New York: W. W. Norton & Co. Inc., The Norton Library, 1975.

Hughes, Charles Evans. *The Supreme Court of the United States: Its Foundations, Methods and Achievements, an Interpretation*. New York: Columbia University Press, 1928.

Jackson, Robert H. *The Struggle for Judicial Supremacy: A Study of a Crisis in American Power Politics*. New York: Random House, Vintage Books, 1941.

James, Leonard F. *The Supreme Court in American Life*. 2nd ed. Glenview, Ill.: Scott, Foresman and Co., 1971.

Kauper, Paul G. *Constitutional Law: Cases and Materials*. Boston: Little, Brown & Co., 1966.

Kelly, Alfred H. and Harbison, Winfred A. *The American Constitution; Its Origins and Development*, 5th ed. New York: W. W. Norton & Company Inc., 1976.

Kurland, Philip B. *Politics, the Constitution and the Warren Court*. Chicago: University of Chicago Press, 1970.

Kutler, Stanley I., ed. *The Supreme Court and the Constitution: Readings in American Constitutional History*. Boston: Houghton Mifflin Co., 1960.

Madison, James; Hamilton, Alexander; and Jay, John. *The Federalist Papers*. Introduction by Clinton Rossiter. New York: The New American Library, Mentor Books, 1961.

Mason, Alpheus T. *The Supreme Court from Taft to Warren*. rev. ed. Baton Rouge: Louisiana State University Press, 1968.

Mason, Alpheus T. and Beaney, William M. *The Supreme Court in a Free Society*. Englewood Cliffs, N.J.: Prentice-Hall Inc., 1959.

McCloskey, Robert G. *The American Supreme Court*. Chicago History of American Civilization series. Chicago: University of Chicago Press, 1960.

Miller, Arthur Selwyn. *The Supreme Court and American Capitalism*. The Supreme Court in American Life series. New York: The Free Press, 1968.

Morgan, Donald G. *Congress and the Constitution: A Study of Responsibility*. Cambridge: The Belknap Press of Harvard University Press, 1966.

Murphy, Walter F. *Congress and the Court: A Case Study in the American Political Process*. Chicago: The University of Chicago Press, 1962.

Pfeffer, Leo. *This Honorable Court: A History of the United States Supreme Court*. Boston: Beacon Press, 1965.

Pollak, Louis H., ed. *The Constitution and the Supreme Court: A Documentary History*. 2 Vols. Cleveland: The World Publishing Co., 1966.

Pritchett, C. Herman. *The American Constitution*. 3rd ed. New York: McGraw-Hill Book Co. Inc., 1977.

_____. *Congress Versus the Supreme Court, 1957-1960*. Minneapolis: University of Minnesota Press, 1961.

Ratner, Sidney. *American Taxation: Its History as a Social Force in Democracy*. New York: W. W. Norton & Co. Inc. 1942.

Schmidhauser, John R. and Berg, Larry L. *The Supreme Court and Congress: Conflict and Interaction, 1945-1968*. Supreme Court in American Life series. New York: The Free Press, 1972.

Swindler, William F. *Court and Constitution in the Twentieth Century: The Old Legality, 1889-1932*. Indianapolis: The Bobbs-Merrill Co. Inc., 1969.

_____. *Court and Constitution in the Twentieth Century: The New Legality, 1932-1968*. Indianapolis: The Bobbs-Merrill Co. Inc., 1970.

Swisher, Carl Brent. *American Constitutional Development*. 2nd ed. Cambridge: Houghton Mifflin Co., The Riverside Press, 1954.

Twiss, Benjamin R. *Lawyers and the Constitution: How Laissez-Faire Came to the Supreme Court*. Princeton: Princeton University Press, 1942.

United States Congress. Library of Congress, Congressional Reference Service. *The Constitution of the United States of America: Analysis and Interpretation*. Washington, D.C.: Government Printing Office, 1973; together with the 1976 Supplement. Washington, D.C.: Government Printing Office, 1977.

Warren, Charles. *The Supreme Court in United States History*. 2 vols. rev. ed. Boston: Little, Brown & Co., 1926.

THE COURT AND THE POWERS OF THE PRESIDENT

Introduction 181

The Commander in Chief...................... 185

The Architect of Foreign Policy.................. 199

The President as Executive 209

The Power to Veto and to Pardon 221

Privilege and Immunity........................ 229

Confrontation: The President v. The Court 235

The Court and the
Powers of the President

Presidential power developed virtually unchecked by the Supreme Court from the nation's founding until the New Deal.

The gradual alteration in the balance of federalism — the shifting of power from the states to federal jurisdiction — broadened the scope and the range of executive authority. Thirty years of continuous crisis, from the New Deal to the Cold War, further accelerated expansion of presidential power.

The Constitution, Justice Robert H. Jackson once reminded the court, was an 18th century sketch for a government — not a finished blueprint.[1] This growth of executive authority could not have been foreseen in 1787, and the accrual of presidential power became far more than the original sum of the executive roles set out by the Constitution.

The 20th century has seen a few major court rulings curbing presidential power.

Most dramatic of these were the short-lived series of anti-New Deal rulings, the 1952 *Steel Seizure* decision and the 1974 Watergate tapes decision which resulted in President Richard M. Nixon's early departure from the White House.[2]

Such cases — and such decisions — have been infrequent in the nation's history.

General Responsibilities

Two factors contribute to the infrequency of Supreme Court rulings on the authority of the chief executive. The constitutional language describing the powers of the president is phrased in very general terms of roles and responsibilities: he is vested with the executive power, he is commander in chief, he is directed to take care that the laws are faithfully executed. This provides an uncertain basis for constitutional challenges to presidential action.

Concurring in the court's action in the *Steel Seizure Case*, Justice Jackson commented on the imprecision of the language employed in the debate over the scope of the president's powers:

> Loose and irresponsible use of adjectives colors all non-legal and much legal discussion of presidential powers. "Inherent" powers, "plenary" powers, "war" powers and "emergency" powers are used, often interchangeably and without fixed or ascertainable meanings.

The vagueness and generality of the clauses that set forth presidential powers afford a plausible basis for pressures within and without the administration for presidential action beyond that supported by those whose responsibility it is to defend his actions in court. The claim of inherent and unrestricted presidential powers has long been a persuasive dialectical weapon in political controversy.[3]

A Special Position

The aura that surrounds the office of the president and its occupant insulates it somewhat from court challenges. George Reedy, a former aide to President Lyndon B. Johnson, noted the monarchic dimension of the modern presidency. Reedy observed that, "the life of the White House is the life of a court," and the men that make up the court "serve the material needs and the desires of a single man."[4]

Political scientist Louis Koenig has remarked in this respect that even if the president "lags in donning monarchic trappings, others will put them on him.... The news media make the confident assumption that the president's countrymen are eager to assign him the role of father figure."[5]

The advantages the presidency thus possesses over other branches of government in capturing the public eye and political support, Justice Jackson has pointed out, makes the task of curbing presidential power even more difficult:

> Executive power has the advantage of concentration in a single head in whose choice the whole Nation has a part, making him the focus of public hopes and expectations.... No other personality in public life can begin to compete with him in access to the public mind through modern methods of communications. By his prestige as head of state and his influence upon public opinion he exerts a leverage upon those who are supposed to check and balance his power which often cancels their effectiveness.[6]

In light of these characteristics, the court has been cautious in locking constitutional horns with the chief executive on matters that juxtaposed their authority and prestige against the president's will.

Divergent Views of Power

Even presidents have held strikingly divergent views on the limits of presidential power. William Howard Taft viewed executive power as limited to the specific powers granted in the Constitution:

> The true view of executive functions . . . is, as I conceive it, that the President can exercise no power which cannot be fairly and reasonably traced to some specific grant of power or justly implied and included within such grant as proper and necessary.[7]

Taft's constitutional view of executive authority prevailed throughout much of the 19th century.

Theodore Roosevelt viewed the presidential office differently. His "stewardship" theory of presidential leadership envisioned an active president acting responsibly on behalf of the public welfare. Roosevelt believed:

> . . .every executive officer . . . was a steward of the people. . . . My belief was that it was not only his right but his duty to do anything that the needs of the nation demanded unless such action was forbidden by the Constitution or by the laws. . . .In other words, I acted for the public welfare . . . whenever and in whatever manner was necessary, unless prevented by direct constitutional or legislative provision.[8]

The broadest assertion of executive authority, however, was Franklin D. Roosevelt's — based on the concept of executive prerogative described by the 17th century English political philosopher John Locke as "power to act according to discretion for the public good, without the prescription of the law, and sometimes even against it. . . ."[9]

Acting on this prerogative theory Roosevelt took steps to cope with Depression and world war, arguing that, as the court itself finally noted, extraordinary times demanded extraordinary measures. The prerogative concept of presidential power carried over into the Cold War but the court slowed its development when it rejected Truman's claim of the extra-statutory authority to seize and operate the nation's steel mills.

The Shield of Joint Action

It is always possible in confrontations with the court that the president will ignore or defy the court. Both Jackson and Lincoln, for example, did so. But early in the nation's history, presidents realized that they held the strongest possible position against judicial challenge when they acted in conjunction with Congress. Joint action by the two political branches of government has consistently provided a high degree of insulation from court challenge.

Again Jackson wrote:

> Presidential powers are not fixed but fluctuate, depending upon their disjunction or conjunction with those of Congress. . . .
>
> When the President acts pursuant to an express or implied authorization of Congress, his authority is at its maximum, for it includes all that he possesses in his own right plus all that Congress can delegate. In these circumstances, and in these only, may he be said . . . to personify the federal sovereignty. If his act is held unconstitutional under these circumstances, it usually means that the Federal Government as an undivided whole lacks power.[10]

When presidents act without the backing of Congress, supported only by their claim of inherent power, they run the high risk of rejection by the court, as Truman and Nixon discovered.

The Foreign Role

In foreign and military matters, the court has upheld the presidential exercise of sweeping power. In the midst of its rulings denying the president authority to cope with the economic crisis at home, the court, in 1936, upheld the president's inherent and virtually unlimited authority to conduct the nation's foreign affairs.[11]

Justice George Sutherland's opinion in this case claimed that the foreign affairs powers emanated from sources different from other presidential powers. This provided the basis for Sutherland's view that the president could act entirely alone in foreign relations matters. Though Sutherland's historical analysis has been criticized, the court has not modified the broad grant of executive power sanctioned by this ruling.

Domestic Power and Privilege

The court, on the other hand, has denied the president such broad inherent power in domestic affairs. When President Truman seized the steel mills during the Korean War to prevent interruption of steel production and supplies, the court rejected the president's claim of the power to take such action, in part because Congress had, some years earlier, decided not to grant the president the power he sought to exercise here.

The court's ruling denying President Nixon an absolute executive privilege to withhold White House tapes sought for use as evidence in a trial specifically recognized the need for a limited privilege to protect documents and information related to foreign affairs. This decision, it is worth noting, came at a time when Congress — far from supporting the president's claim — was considering articles of impeachment against Nixon.

Presidents and Justices

Presidents cannot be certain the men they appoint to the court will support their views on the exercise of presidential power. Thomas Jefferson made several appointments to the bench that he hoped would counteract Chief Justice John Marshall's control over the court's decisions. But Jefferson's effort to reduce Marshall's effectiveness with the court's personnel failed utterly.

When President Lincoln appointed Salmon P. Chase to the bench, Chase was a presidential hopeful and future rival for the nomination. Lincoln made Chase Chief Justice to deflect his presidential ambitions and to harness his legal talents for the administration. Chase, who had advocated passage of the administration's Legal Tender Acts during his term as Treasury secretary, later opposed the Lincoln administration's view in the first *Legal Tender Case,* holding those acts unconstitutional.

Of the four Truman appointments to the bench, Justices Tom Clark and Sherman Minton, appointed in October 1949, were close friends of the president. In the *Steel Seizure* decision, Clark joined with the majority, and Minton dissented.

President Nixon appointed Warren E. Burger Chief Justice because — apart from his judicial qualifications — Burger had been outspoken in his criticism of the Warren court's rulings limiting prosecutors' efforts to convict criminals. Ironically, Burger wrote the court opinion that forced Nixon to resign or face impeachment and trial.

Presidential influence with the men they appoint to the court apparently often ends with the candidate's confirmation.

Several presidents, on the other hand, have maintained close ties with sitting justices. President James Buchanan sought and obtained information from fellow Pennsylvanian Justice Robert C. Grier about how the court would vote on the pending decision in the Dred Scott case. Theodore Roosevelt continued his close ties with Justice William H. Moody after he appointed him to the bench in 1906.

Perhaps the most famous friendship between a president and a justice was that of Franklin D. Roosevelt and Felix Frankfurter. Friends since undergraduate days at Harvard, Roosevelt and Frankfurter maintained a lively correspondence throughout most of their respective careers. After Roosevelt appointed Frankfurter to the Supreme Court in 1939, the two men communicated freely, offering advice and criticism on politics and legal matters. Their correspondence ranged over every conceivable subject from Washington society gossip to matters of administration patronage and political strategy.

President Lyndon B. Johnson appointed his longtime adviser Abe Fortas to the Supreme Court. The congressional investigation of Johnson's nomination of Fortas for the post of Chief Justice revealed that Johnson and Fortas also had continued an active political association after Fortas had been appointed to the bench. Concern over this relationship compounded by political concerns eventually forced Johnson to withdraw the nomination.

The interplay between law and politics — between the court and the president — reaches back to the court's beginnings.

The court is aware of the political consequences of the decisions it makes or chooses not to make. As Finley Peter Dunne's 19th century political cartoon character Mr. Dooley observed, the justices read election returns too. They keep apprised of the nation's political pulse and the tempo of the times.

As Charles Warren observed:

> The Court is not an organism dissociated from the conditions and history of the times in which it exists. It does not formulate and deliver its opinions in a legal vacuum. Its Judges are not abstract and impersonal oracles, but are men whose views are ... affected by inheritance, education and environment and by the impact of history past and present....[12]

Footnotes

[1] *Youngstown Sheet and Tube Co. v. Sawyer,* 343 U.S. 579 at 653 (1952).

[2] *Youngstown Sheet and Tube Co. v. Sawyer,* 343 U.S. 579 (1952); *United States v. Nixon,* 417 U.S. 683 (1974).

[3] *Youngstown Sheet and Tube Co. v. Sawyer,* 343 U.S. 579 at 646-647 (1952).

[4] George E. Reedy, *The Twilight of the Presidency* (New York: New American Library, 1970), p. 4.

[5] Louis Koenig, *The Chief Executive,* 3d ed. (New York: Harcourt Brace Jovanovich, 1975), pp. 3-4.

[6] *Youngstown Sheet and Tube Co. v. Sawyer,* 343 U.S. 579 at 653-654 (1952).

[7] William Howard Taft, *Our Chief Magistrate and His Powers* (New York: Columbia University Press, 1916), p. 144.

[8] Theodore Roosevelt, *An Autobiography* (New York: MacMillan Co., 1920), p. 406.

[9] John Locke, *Second Treatise of Government,* with an Introduction by Charles L. Sherman (New York: Appleton-Century-Crofts, 1937), p. 109.

[10] *Youngstown Sheet and Tube Co. v. Sawyer,* 343 U.S. 579 at 635-636 (1952).

[11] *United States v. Curtiss-Wright Export Corporation,* 299 U.S. 304 (1936).

[12] Charles Warren, *The Supreme Court in United States History,* rev. ed., 2 vols. (Boston: Little, Brown & Co., 1922, 1926), I:2.

The Commander In Chief

The president is the commander of the nation's military forces. The Constitution vests the executive with the role and title of "Commander in Chief of the Army and Navy of the United States, and of the Militia of the several States, when called into the actual service of the United States. . . ."

"These cryptic words have given rise to some of the most persistent controversies in our constitutional history," wrote Justice Robert H. Jackson more than 250 years after the Framers placed those phrases into the Constitution. Jackson, speaking from his experience as attorney general under President Franklin Roosevelt as well as Supreme Court justice, continued: ". . . just what authority goes with the name has plagued Presidential advisors who . . . cannot say where it begins or ends." [1]

One of the first to note the potentially vast scope of this executive role was Alexander Hamilton. Although he wrote initially that it "would amount to nothing more than the supreme command and direction of the military and naval forces, as first general and admiral of the Confederacy," [2] he soon amended that to acknowledge that "the direction of war most peculiarly demands those qualities which distinguish the exercise of power by a single hand." [3]

The men who wrote the Constitution divided the war power between the executive and the legislative departments of government. They gave Congress the power to declare war and the president the power to conduct it. Mistrust of executive power vested in a single individual led to the creation of a unique divided institutional structure for making war. [4] *(War powers of Congress, p. 125)*

Subsequent experience, however, has led to the blurring of the lines between the constitutionally distinct functions, a blurring which has effectively insulated most exercises of the war power from judicial review.

Between 1789 and 1861, presidents regarded their role as commander in chief as purely military in nature. [5] Faced with a civil war, however, President Abraham Lincoln began to expand the presidential war power beyond that original concept. He found constitutional justification for the exercise of broad discretionary powers by fusing the powers of the commander in chief with the executive's general constitutional responsibility to take care that the laws are faithfully executed. [6] The national emergency of secession and war, Lincoln said, required the swift and firm exercise of extraordinary powers by the chief executive. [7]

In two world wars in the 20th century, Presidents Woodrow Wilson and Franklin D. Roosevelt took a similar view of presidential war powers as they further expanded the sphere of those powers in wartime.

Faced with war emergencies, Presidents Wilson and Roosevelt controlled the economy, fixed prices, set priority production targets, ran the transportation system, the mines and industrial plants, detained individuals and groups on the basis of their ethnic origin — many of whom were American citizens not guilty of any crime — and threatened to ignore certain laws that did not comply with their objectives. [8]

The Supreme Court and the War Power

Moreover, this assertion of broad emergency power blurred the constitutional distinction between Congress' authority to declare war and the president's power to direct it. Congress delegated power and provided funds; the president directed policy. Fiscal and legislative support for the president was regarded as congressional sanction of the president's decisions. Thus, the two departments fused their war-making powers, and the court declined to challenge policies adopted and supported by both political branches of government. [9]

Political scientist Glendon Schubert described the trend:

> One very interesting aspect which emerged from the World War II cases . . . was the consistency with which the courts came to conceptualize the fusion or merging of the power of the political branches of the national government so that either the President or the Congress might individually or cojointly exercise any power attributable to the United States as a sovereign state at war. Under this theory, agreement between the President and Congress places any action in time of war beyond the pale of judicial review. [10]

While the exercise of the war power in such a manner insulated the president's acts from judicial scrutiny, it has not prevented the Supreme Court from denying the president the right to use those war powers in time of peace. In the 1952 *Steel Seizure Case* the court rejected President Truman's claim of authority to seize the nation's steel mills during the Korean War. The court ruled that without congressional authorization the president lacked the power to seize the mills.

Undeclared Wars

The Constitution provides Congress with power to declare war but only five of eleven major conflicts fought by the United States abroad have been formally declared wars.

The others were undeclared engagements commenced under presidential claims of authority as commander in chief, custodian of executive power and, after the second world war, under Article XLIII of the United Nations Charter. The effect of these undeclared wars was to dim further the Constitution's separation of congressional and presidential war powers. The modern distinction might be: the president directs the war, Congress funds it.

Congress acted in response to the president's acts or recommendations to declare the War of 1812, the Mexican War (1846-48), the Spanish-American War (1898), and the two world wars (1917-18, 1941-45).

Presidents engaged in hostilities without prior congressional sanction in the Quasi-War with France (1798-1800), two Barbary wars (1801-1805, 1815), Mexican-American border clashes (1914-1917), the Korean War (1950-53) and the Vietnam War (1964-73). Two conflicts — the War of 1812 and the Spanish-American War (1898) — were clearly products of congressional policy.[1]

There have been approximately 137 instances, according to United States Department of State estimates, where the president has authorized the use of armed forces abroad without congressional assent.[2]

---

[1] Louis Koenig, *The Chief Executive*, 3rd ed. (New York: Harcourt Brace Jovanovich, Inc. 1975), p. 217.

[2] U.S. Dept. of State, Research Project 806A (August 1967), "Armed Actions Taken by the United States Without a Declaration of War, 1798-1967."

All in all, the court has examined only a small portion of presidential actions taken under the war powers clause. As Clinton Rossiter has observed, the court has examined only "a tiny fraction of [the president's] significant deeds and decisions as commander in chief, for most of these were by nature challengeable in no court but that of impeachment. . . ."[11]

Early Delegation

Early Supreme Court rulings preserved the distinction between the power of Congress to declare war and the power of the president to conduct it.[12]

In 1795 Congress granted part of its declaratory power to the president when it authorized him to call out the militia of any state to quell resistance to the law. The court sanctioned the president's exercise of discretion to determine when an emergency existed and then to order out the state militia to meet the exigency.[13]

During the War of 1812, several New England states challenged that statute, claiming that neither Congress nor the president had the authority to determine when the state militia should be called out. The New Englanders opposed that war and had refused to place their state troops under federal control.

In the case of *Martin v. Mott* decided in 1827, the court upheld the delegation of that authority as a limited power,

"confined to cases of actual invasion, or of imminent danger of invasion."[14] Justice Joseph Story, who wrote the court's opinion, stated that:

...[A]uthority to decide whether the exigency has arisen, belongs exclusively to the President, and . . . his decision is conclusive upon all other persons. We think that this construction necessarily results from the nature of the power itself, and from the manifest object contemplated by the act of Congress. . . .

Whenever a statute gives a discretionary power to any person, to be exercised by him, upon his own opinion of certain facts, it is a sound rule of construction that the statute constitutes him the sole and exclusive judge of the existence of those facts.[15]

While conceding that the president possessed a limited discretionary power to declare that a crisis existed, the court continued, nevertheless, to regard the president's war power as primarily military in nature. As late as 1850, Chief Justice Roger Brooke Taney observed that under the war power clauses the president's:

... duty and his power are purely military. As Commander in Chief, he is authorized to direct the movements of the naval and military forces placed by law at his command, and to employ them in the manner he may deem most effectual to harass and conquer and subdue the enemy. He may invade the hostile country, and subject it to the sovereignty and authority of the United States. But his conquests do not enlarge the boundaries of this Union, nor extend the operation of our institutions and laws beyond the limits before assigned them by legislative power.[16]

Foreign Wars, 1815-1912

The Supreme Court has never opposed the president's deployment of forces abroad as commander in chief. In the 19th century Presidents assigned naval squadrons to cruise in the Mediterranean (1815), in the Pacific (1821), in the Caribbean (1822), in the South Atlantic (1826), in Far Eastern waters (1835) and along the African coast (1842). These deployments showed the flag, encouraged trade and protected shipping. However, no troops garrisoned American bases on foreign soil as a result of these actions.[17]

In wartime, presidents controlled policy; in peacetime presidents generally deferred to Congress during the 19th century. Thus, between 1836 and 1898, with the exception of the wartime administrations of James K. Polk, Grover Cleveland and Abraham Lincoln, Congress provided the initiative in foreign policy. When the chief executive in peacetime advocated expansionist policies that threatened war — for example Franklin Pierce in Cuba, Secretary of State William H. Seward over Alaska and Ulysses S. Grant in Santo Domingo — Congress blocked such projects.[18]

Polk's Mexican policy forced a declaration of war with that country in 1846. The president directed General Zachary Taylor to occupy disputed territory claimed by Mexico. As a result of an alleged provocation by Mexican troops, Polk asked Congress to declare war.[19] Congressional opposition led a young Whig congressman named Abraham Lincoln to introduce resolutions demanding to know the exact spot where the armed forces clashed. The House censured the president for a war "unnecessarily and unconstitutionally begun," but Congress funded the war, anyway.[20]

President William McKinley's decision to send the battleship *Maine* into Havana harbor led to war with Spain over Cuban independence in 1898. Congress passed a joint resolution authorizing the use of armed force to obtain Cuba's separation from Spain, then followed with a declaration of war when Spain recalled her ambassador and refused to leave Cuba.[21]

But McKinley made the decision to insist on Spain's surrender of the Philippines without congressional consultation. Later he deployed over 100,000 troops to put down the insurrection, led by Emilio Aguinaldo, as part of the movement for Philippine independence. This deployment led to charges in Congress of unilateral war-making by the president.[22]

McKinley also sent several thousand U.S. troops to join an international brigade which rescued Americans trapped in Peking by a Chinese nationalist uprising. Democrats criticized this action but Congress was out of session

and calls for a special session in an election year were to no avail.[23]

President Theodore Roosevelt engineered the revolution in Panama against Colombia to make the "dirt fly" on construction of the isthmian canal. But Roosevelt's less-than-subtle sanction of the Panamanian revolution in November 1903 raised few objections from Congress or the public.[24]

Early in the 20th century, the Supreme Court considered and resolved questions of citizenship and constitutional rights for the inhabitants of newly-acquired non-contiguous U.S. territories. The court, however, never challenged the president's prerogative to conduct war or acquire the territories. *(Insular Cases, p. 138)*

Most of the instances of presidential use of troops without congressional authorization between 1815 and 1912 involved small contingents of forces for limited purposes which had strong public support.

President Lincoln and the Civil War

The first major Supreme Court pronouncement on the war powers of the president came as a result of the broad exercise of those powers by President Abraham Lincoln during the Civil War.

From the outbreak of hostilities at Fort Sumter on April 12, 1861, until Congress convened in special session July 4, 1861, President Lincoln prepared the nation for war without authority from Congress. He acted under his power as commander in chief and his presidential oath to maintain the Constitution and preserve the Union.

On his own authority Lincoln declared the existence of a rebellion, called out the state militia to suppress it and proclaimed a blockade of southern ports — the legal equivalent to a declaration of war. In May, Lincoln called for 40 regiments of United States volunteers to serve for three years. He ordered increases made in the size of the Army and Navy, paid out two million dollars from the federal treasury without specific authorization and indebted the government to the tune of a quarter of a billion dollars in pledged credit. Lincoln also ordered suspension of *habeas corpus* in certain parts of the United States. He directed military commanders to arrest persons engaged in or likely to engage in "treasonable practices."[25]

When Congress convened, Lincoln's July 4, 1861 message to the special session explained the measures taken and recommended steps for the exercise of additional power. Bolstered by a corroborative opinion from Attorney General Edward Bates, Lincoln informed the Congress that public necessity and the preservation of the union required swift and bold action, "whether strictly legal or not." The president said he felt certain Congress would "readily ratify" his actions. He noted that public safety required the "qualified suspension of the privilege of the writ [of *habeas corpus*] which was authorized to be made."[26]

During the special session Congress intermittently debated a joint resolution that sanctioned Lincoln's acts. Nagging doubts about the legality of *habeas corpus* suspension and the port blockades prevented a vote on the approbatory resolution. But a rider attached to a pay bill for Army privates, rushed through Congress at the close of the session, gave approval to the president's acts pertaining

to the militia, the Army, the Navy and the volunteers, stating that they were "in all respects legalized and made valid, to the same intent and with the same effect as if they had been issued and done under the previous express authority and direction of Congress."[27]

Congress made no challenge to Lincoln's management of the war until the December 1861 session. The Joint Committee on the Conduct of the War, established at first to investigate the Union disaster at the first battle of Bull Run, soon expanded the scope of its investigations. Headed by Radical Republican Senator Benjamin F. Wade of Ohio, the committee tried unsuccessfully to wrest control of war policy from the president.[28]

The Prize Cases

When it faced the questions raised by Lincoln's assumption of broad wartime powers, the Supreme Court divided sharply. But by a 5-4 vote in 1863, the court in the *Prize Cases* upheld the president's exercise of the war power to impose the blockade on southern ports.[29]

The *Prize Cases* arose as a challenge to Lincoln's unilateral proclamation of a blockade of those ports, a proclamation made in April 1861 and not in any way ratified by Congress until July. Several neutral vessels were captured and brought to Union ports as prizes early in the blockade. They had been captured as they tried to pass the blockade.

Under international law, ships could legally be taken as prizes only when a conflict had been recognized as a war between two belligerent powers.

Lincoln had consistently refused to recognize the Confederate government as a sovereign — and belligerent — power. He insisted that the conflict was an insurrection, not a war. This view effectively denied the South sovereign status or the possibility of recognition by neutral governments.

Thus, if the court adopted Lincoln's view that the South was not a belligerent, it appeared that it would have to rule that under international law the blockade was illegal — and the vessels improperly seized.

The Opinion

The cases were argued for twelve days in February 1863. Two weeks later, the court announced its decision in favor of Lincoln's position, upholding his power to impose the blockade.

"This greatest of civil wars. . . sprung forth suddenly from the parent brain, a Minerva in the full panoply of war. The President was bound to meet it in the shape it presented itself, without waiting for Congress to baptize it with a name. . . ."

—Justice Robert C. Grier
The *Prize Cases,* 1863

Lincoln's three appointees to the court — Justices Noah H. Swayne, Samuel F. Miller and David Davis — joined with Robert C. Grier and James M. Wayne to form the majority. Grier wrote the opinion which accepted both the president's definition of the conflict and his power to impose the blockade. The majority acknowledged that Congress had the power to declare war, but ruled that the president had to meet the challenge in the emergency until Congress could act:

By the Constitution, Congress alone has the power to declare a national or foreign war. It cannot declare war against a State or any number of States, by virtue of any clause in the Constitution. The Constitution confers on the President the whole executive power. He is bound to take care that the laws be faithfully executed. He is Commander-in-Chief of the Army and Navy of the United States, and of the militia of the several States when called into the actual service of the United States. He has no power to initiate or declare a war either against a foreign nation or a domestic State. But by the Acts of Congress of Feb. 28th, 1795 . . . and 3rd of March, 1807 . . . he is authorized to call out the militia and use the military and naval forces of the United States in case of invasion by foreign nations, and to suppress insurrection against the government of a State or of the United States.

If a war be made by invasion of a foreign nation, the President is not only authorized but bound to resist force, by force. He does not initiate the war, but is bound to accept the challenge without waiting for any special legislative authority. And whether the hostile party be a foreign invader, or States organized in rebellion, it is none the less a war, although the declaration of it be *"unilateral".* . . .

This greatest of civil wars was not gradually developed by popular commotion, tumultous assemblies, or local unorganized insurrections. However long may have been its previous conception, it nevertheless sprung forth suddenly from the parent brain, a Minerva in the full panoply of war. The President was bound to meet it in the shape it presented itself, without waiting for Congress to baptize it with a name; and no name given to it by him or them could change the fact.

It is not the less a civil war, with belligerent parties in hostile array, because it may be called an 'insurrection' by one side, and the insurgents be considered as rebels or traitors. It is not necessary that the independence of the revolted province or State be acknowledged in order to constitute it a party belligerent in a war according to the law of nations. Foreign nations acknowledge it as war by a declaration of neutrality. The condition of neutrality cannot exist unless there be two belligerent parties.[30]

". . .[C]ivil war . . . under our system of government, can exist only by an Act of Congress which requires the assent of two of the great departments of the government, the Executive and the Legislative. . . ."

—Justice Samuel Nelson
The *Prize Cases,* 1863

The Dissent

Justice Samuel Nelson and Justices John Catron, Nathan Clifford and Chief Justice Roger B. Taney found Grier's analysis inadequate. The dissenting justices argued that the war power belonged to Congress and that the blockade was illegal from the time of Lincoln's April proclamation until Congress approved it in July. As to the matter of whether a war existed, Nelson wrote:

. . .[B]efore this insurrection against the established government can be dealt with on the footing of a civil war, within the meaning of the law of nations and the Constitution of the United States, and which will draw after it belligerent rights, it must be recognized or declared by the war making power of the government. No power short of this can change the legal *status* of the government or the relations of its citizens from that of peace to a state of war, or bring into existence all those duties and obligations of neutral third parties growing out of a state of war. The war power of the government must be exercised before this changed condition . . . can be admitted. . . .

. . . we find there that to constitute a civil war in the sense in which we are speaking, before it can exist, in contemplation of law, it must be recognized or declared by the sovereign power of the State, and which sovereign power by our Constitution is lodged in the Congress of the United States — civil war, therefore, under our system of government, can exist only by an Act of Congress which requires the assent of two of the great departments of the government, the Executive and Legislative. . . .

The Acts of 1795 and 1807 did not, and could not, under the Constitution, confer on the President the power of declaring war against a state of this Union, or of deciding that war existed, and upon that ground authorize the capture and confiscation of the property of every citizen of the State whenever it was found on the waters. The laws of war . . . convert every citizen of the hostile State into a public enemy, and treat him accordingly, whatever may have been his previous conduct. This great power over the business and property of the citizen is reserved to the Legislative Department by the express words of the Constitution. It cannot be delegated or surrendered to the Executive. Congress alone can determine whether war exists or should be declared. . . .

I am compelled to the conclusion that no civil war existed between this Government and the States in insurrection until recognized by the Act of Congress 13th July, 1861; that the President does not possess the power under the Constitution to declare war or recognize its existence within the meaning of the law of nations, which carries with it belligerent rights, and thus change the country and all its citizens from a state of peace to a state of war; that this power belongs exclusively to the Congress of the United States and consequently, that the President had no power to set on foot a blockade under the law of nations. . . .[31]

The opinions of Grier and Nelson represented opposing constitutional theories about who might initiate war under the Constitution. But notwithstanding any constitutional shortcomings of his position, Lincoln continued to direct the war. He issued the Emancipation Proclamation of Jan. 1, 1863 under his authority as commander in chief, and this authority to do so was never challenged before the court.

Merryman and Milligan

Article I, Section 9 of the Constitution states: "The Privilege of the Writ of Habeas Corpus shall not be suspended, unless when in Cases of Rebellion or Invasion the public Safety may require it." Under this clause Lincoln suspended the privilege of the writ in sections of the country where military forces attempted to prevent pro-southern sympathizers from disrupting transportation and communications systems. The wartime suspension of *habeas corpus* was challenged as early as 1861 by none other than the Chief Justice of the United States. Lincoln, however, continued to suspend *habeas corpus* during the war. In March 1863, Congress authorized the suspension of the privilege by the president at his discretion.

Early Challenge

In 1861, Chief Justice Roger B. Taney, holding circuit court in Baltimore, ordered federal military officers to justify their detention of John Merryman, a civilian southern sympathizer detained in a military prison for his part in burning railroad bridges near Baltimore, and to show cause why Merryman should not be released for proceedings in a civilian court.[32] Citing Lincoln's suspension order, the military commander refused to respond.

Chief Justice Taney regarded the officer's refusal as a violation of proper judicial procedure. The Chief Justice wrote an opinion that lectured the president on his duty to faithfully execute the laws. Failure to support the proceedings of the court, Taney remarked, amounted to usurpation of civilian authority and the substitution of military government.[33] Taney warned:

> . . .[T]he people of the United States are no longer living under a government of laws, but every citizen holds life, liberty and property at the will and pleasure of the army officer in whose military district he may happen to be found.[34]

To southern sympathizers the *Merryman* case became a symbol of oppression. Merryman eventually was handed over to civilian authorities and indicted for treason.

The question remained unresolved: did the President have the power to order civilians tried by military tribunals in regions outside the war zone where the civil courts remained open? The administration argued that military trials were necessary because the civilian court and peacetime procedures were inadequate to deal with the problem of organized rebellion.

In 1864, the court refused to address the question in the case of Clement L. Vallandigham, a "Copperhead" — a Northern sympathizer with the Confederate cause — a former Democratic Representative from Ohio who denounced Lincoln's war policy in speeches. Vallandigham was arrested and tried by a military commission.

The Supreme Court refused to hear Vallandigham's appeal of that conviction. Justice James Wayne wrote that the court "cannot without disregarding its frequent decisions and interpretation of the Constitution in respect to its judicial power . . . review or pronounce any opinion upon the proceedings of a military commission."[35]

"Martial law cannot arise for a threatened invasion. The necessity must be actual and present; the invasion real, such as effectively closes the courts. . . . Martial rule can never exist where the courts are open and in the proper and unobstructed exercise of their jurisdiction. It is also confined to the locality of actual war."

—Justice David Davis
Ex parte Milligan, 1866

But after the war, the court took on that issue and resolved it — against the president.

The Milligan Case

In 1864, L. P. Milligan was tried by a military commission in Indiana and convicted of conspiracy. He was sentenced to die for his part in a plot to release and arm rebel prisoners and march them into Missouri and Kentucky to cooperate in an invasion of Indiana.

President Andrew Johnson commuted Milligan's sentence to life in prison. Milligan, nevertheless, came to the Supreme Court to challenge his trial and conviction. In 1866, the court unanimously ordered his release, holding that the President had no power to require civilians to be tried by military courts in an area where regular courts continued to function.

Justice David Davis, Lincoln's own nominee to the court, wrote the opinion for the court, condemning Lincoln's use of military tribunals in areas where the civil courts remained open. The court divided 5-4 on the question of whether Congress had the power to authorize military trials under such circumstances.

The decision established that martial law must be confined to "the theater of active military operations."[36]

Davis' opinion, issued in December 1866, after the war emergency had passed, and eight months after the decision itself was announced, held that:

> . . .The Constitution of the United States is a law for rulers and people, equally in war and in peace, and covers with the shield of its protection all classes of men, at all times and under all circumstances. No doctrine, involving more pernicious consequences, was ever invented by the wit of man than that any of its provisions can be suspended during any of the great exigencies of government. . . .Martial law cannot arise from a *threatened* invasion. The necessity must be actual and present; the invasion real, such as effectually closes the courts. . . . Martial rule can never exist where the courts are open, and in the proper and unobstructed exercise of their jurisdiction. It is also confined to the locality of actual war.[37]

The assumption of broad presidential powers in a wartime emergency ended — temporarily — with Lincoln's death and the end of the war.

President Wilson and World War

As a professor at Princeton University, Woodrow Wilson minimized the presidential role in the constitutional system.[38] Moreover, as Wilson's biographer has observed, Wilson did not concern himself with foreign affairs in the years prior to his election as president because "he did not think they were important enough to warrant any diversion from the mainstream of his thought."[39]

President-elect Wilson changed his mind. A month before taking office, Wilson asserted that the chief executive "must be prime minister, and he is the spokesman of the nation in everything."[40]

Wilson's terms as president brought the broadest assertion of presidential powers up to that time. During the world war, Congress cooperated with Wilson and delegated vast authority to the president for the conduct of the war. Legislative sanction of extraordinary presidential actions insulated Wilson's war policy — at home and abroad — from judicial review.

Even before World War I, Wilson ordered U.S. troops to pursue Mexican bandits across the border into Mexico where American troops engaged Mexican regulars in a sporadic border war, during Mexico's revolution and subsequent search for stable and democratic government.[41]

As the war in Europe engulfed the United States, and American troops entered the conflict in 1917, Wilson sought and obtained from Congress broad delegations of power to prepare for war and to mobilize the home front.[42] During the war, Wilson managed the nation's economy by delegating power to a series of war management and war production boards created to coordinate domestic production and supply.

"It is not an army that we must shape and train for war," Wilson explained; "it is a nation."[43]

Wilson commandeered plants and mines; he requisitioned supplies, fixed prices, seized and operated the nation's transportation and communications networks, and managed the production and distribution of foodstuffs. The Council of National Defense, an umbrella agency created by Wilson, administered the economy during the war. Wall Street broker Bernard Baruch, appointed by Wilson to head the War Industries Board, became the nation's virtual economic dictator. The board had no statutory authority whatsoever; Wilson simply created it under his authority as commander in chief.[44]

Wilson's exercise of the war power went unchallenged by the Supreme Court. In part, this was the result of Wilson's obtaining prior congressional approval for all his actions. Issues that raised constitutional questions, moreover, reached the court only after the armistice, when they no longer possessed urgent significance. All three branches of the government seemed to assume that the broad powers exercised by Lincoln during the Civil War carried over for use in foreign wars.

The delegation of legislative power by Congress to the president reached unprecedented heights during World War I. Many statutes simply stated their general objectives and left it to the president to interpret those goals and administer the measures he felt necessary to achieve them.

When the Senate attempted to form a watchdog committee to oversee management of the war, Wilson opposed the measure as a check on his leadership. The House then killed the proposal.[45]

The closest the court came to questioning executive war power during World War I came with its 1921 decision declaring part of the Lever Food Control Act unconstitutional. The Lever Act provided for federal control of the distribution and production of foodstuffs and the marketing of fuel. The bill subjected the nation's economy to whatever regulations the president mandated to guarantee Allied victory. It authorized the president to license the manufacture and distribution of foodstuffs and to seize factories and mines to ensure continued production of defense-related commodities. Section 4 of the act made it a criminal offense to charge excessive prices for commodities.[46] The court invalidated that section of the law because it set no ascertainable standard of guilt, failed to define unjust or unreasonable prices, and was therefore in conflict with the constitutional guarantees of due process of law and of adequate notice to persons accused of crime of the nature and cause of the charge against them.[47]

President Roosevelt and Total War

The concept of expanded presidential powers in wartime, tested in the crisis of civil war and sanctioned by Congress in World War I, underwent further expansion during the 12 years of Franklin D. Roosevelt's tenure in the White House.

In his March 4, 1933, inaugural speech Roosevelt said he would ask Congress, "for the one remaining instrument to meet the crisis — broad Executive power to wage a war against the emergency as great as the power that would be given me if we were in fact invaded by a foreign foe. . . ."[48]

The emergency was the Great Depression. Roosevelt's New Deal legislative program sought to meet economic disaster with emergency measures similar to those employed by Lincoln and Wilson in wartime. The Supreme Court, however, was far more reluctant to sanction these measures than those taken in military crises. *(Details, pp. 240-244.)*

The rise of fascist dictators in Germany and Italy and the expansion of the Japanese empire into China and Southeast Asia changed the focus of the nation from economic recovery to foreign aggression abroad. Although the Neutrality Acts of 1935, 1936 and 1937 required the president to avoid negotiations that might involve the nation in another war, Roosevelt in the prewar years claimed broad executive powers as commander in chief to deal with belligerent nations. The president's personal diplomacy committed the United States to a "neutrality" weighted in favor of Anglo-American interests in Europe against the plans of conquest pursued by Germany, Italy and by Japan in the Far East. [49]

The Supreme Court supported Roosevelt's use of broad powers in the area of foreign policy — and, after war came, of the war power. It recognized the "plenary and exclusive" power the president possessed in foreign affairs and sanctioned the president's use of the executive agreement, as well as treaties, to make binding foreign policy commitments on behalf of the United States. [50] *(See pp. 201-202)*

The president declared a limited national emergency in May 1939 and an unlimited emergency in May 1941. These declarations, though questioned by the Senate at the time, made available to Roosevelt statutory authority to wield extraordinary presidential powers. Roosevelt set out his own theory to justify the exercise of unusual power in the war crisis in a Sept. 7, 1942 message to Congress. The message demanded repeal of certain provisions contained in the Emergency Price Control Act of 1942. (Congress subsequently amended the law to meet the president's objections):

> I ask the Congress to take this action by the first of October. Inaction on your part by that date will leave me with an inescapable responsibility to the people of this country to see to it that the war effort is no longer imperilled by threat of economic chaos.
>
> In the event that the Congress should fail to act, and act adequately, I shall accept the responsibility and I will act....
>
> The President has the powers, under the Constitution and under Congressional acts, to take measures necessary to avert a disaster which would interfere with the winning of the war.
>
> ...the American people can be sure that I will use my powers with a full sense of my responsibility to the Constitution and to my country. The American people can also be sure that I shall not hesitate to use every power vested in me to accomplish the defeat of our enemies in any part of the world where our own safety demands such defeat.
>
> When the war is won, the powers under which I act automatically revert to the people — to whom they belong. [51]

Delegated Power

Woodrow Wilson's management of the economy during World War I had eroded reservations about the constitu-

tionality of a broad federal war power. During the second world war, Congress again delegated vast federal powers to the president to prosecute the war. Roosevelt's war management program caused hardly a stir of protest on constitutional grounds. Congress and the president developed a working partnership to win the war. The assumption that war powers exercised by Lincoln and Wilson carried over to the new emergency prevented confrontation between Roosevelt and the legislative and judicial branches.

The OPA Cases

Roosevelt created a vast number of new administrative agencies responsible to him to conduct the war. By 1945 there were 29 separate agencies grouped under the Office of Emergency Management alone.

The most significant court challenge to the delegation of power during World War II was to the Emergency Price Control Act of Jan. 30, 1942. That act directed the Office of Price Administration (OPA) to set price ceilings on rents and consumer goods and to ration some products in short supply.

Albert Yakus, Benjamin Rottenberg and B. Rottenberg, Inc., were convicted of selling beef at wholesale prices above the maximum prescribed by the OPA. These wholesalers challenged their conviction, arguing that the Emergency Price Control Act was an unconstitutional delegation of legislative power by Congress to the executive.

The Supreme Court upheld the price control act in 1944. [52] In contrast to its rejection of earlier New Deal measures, the court declared this grant of power valid because it contained precise standards to confine the administrator's regulations and orders within fixed limits. Moreover, the court stated, judicial review offered sufficient remedy for transgression of those limits.

In a dissenting opinion, Justice Owen J. Roberts registered his concern over Congress' delegation of power to the executive branch. Roberts posed the question — could Congress suspend any part of the Constitution in wartime? Then, he continued:

> ... My view is that it may not suspend any of the provisions of the instrument. What any of the branches of government do in war must find warrant in the charter and not in its nullification, either directly or stealthily by evasion and equivocation. But if the court puts its decision on the war power I think it should say so. The citizens of this country will then know that in war the function of legislation may be surrendered to an autocrat whose "judgment" will constitute the law; and that his judgment will be enforced by federal officials pursuant to civil judgments, and criminal punishments will be imposed by courts as matters of routine. [53]

In an opinion delivered the same day as the Yakus decision, the court upheld rent control powers of the OPA. [54] Justice William O. Douglas' opinion justified this delegation of power to the OPA Administrator as a necessary wartime measure:

> We need not determine what constitutional limits there are to price fixing legislation. Congress was dealing here with conditions created by activities resulting from a great war effort.... A nation which can demand the lives of its men and women in the waging of that war is under no constitutional necessity of providing a system of price control on the domestic

front which will assure each landlord a "fair return" on his property.[55]

In 1947, the court upheld a similar rent control law as justified by the reduction in residential housing available to veterans demobilized at the end of the war. Again writing for the court, Douglas observed, however, that the court would not approve indefinite extension of wartime controls into peacetime, "to treat all the wounds which war inflicts on our society."[56]

The Supreme Court never upheld challenges to the authority of other wartime agencies or to the authority of the 101 government corporations created by the president and engaged in production, insurance, transportation, banking, housing and other lines of business related to successful prosecution of the war effort.

Furthermore, the court upheld the power of the president to apply sanctions to individuals, labor unions and industries that refused to comply with wartime guidelines. These sanctions had no statutory basis. A retail fuel distributor who admitted violating fuel rationing orders challenged these sanctions. In his case the court ruled that where rationing supported the war effort, presidential sanctions forcing compliance with rationing guidelines were constitutional.[57]

Military Trials

In 1942, the court backed the president's power to set up military commissions to try persons who have committed military crimes but who are not members of the armed forces of the United States. This decision came in the case of *Ex parte Quirin.*[58]

President Roosevelt set up a military commission in 1942 to try eight Nazi saboteurs captured after they entered the United States clandestinely by putting ashore from a German submarine. The military commission tried the saboteurs for offenses against the laws of war. Although the president's proclamation that created the commission specifically denied the eight saboteurs access to American courts, their lawyers obtained a writ of *habeas corpus* that contended the president lacked statutory and constitutional authority to order trial by military commission, that they had been denied constitutional guarantees extended to persons charged with criminal offenses and that they should have been tried in civilian courts.

The court convened a special term to hear the case argued July 29-30, 1942. On July 31, the court ruled that such constitutional requirements did not apply to trials held by military commission for those who entered United States territory as belligerents. It was not necessary for the court to determine the extent of the president's authority as commander in chief to set up military commissions because Congress had authorized military commissions to try offenders against the laws of war. Thus the president's action was more broadly based than Lincoln's use of military commissions struck down in 1866. *(Details, p. 187)*

Ex Parte Quirin also established the authority of civil courts to review a military commission's jurisdiction to try certain persons.[59]

Relocation Program

By Executive Order No. 1066, issued Feb. 19, 1942, President Franklin D. Roosevelt placed Japanese-Americans living on the West Coast under rigid curfew laws and restricted their movements day and night. A congressional resolution of March 21, 1942, supported the president's action. Roosevelt subsequently ordered the removal of all Japanese from the coastal region for the duration of the war as a measure of protection against sabotage by persons of Japanese ancestry.

Instituted under the powers of the commander in chief, the removal program made no distinction between citizens and aliens. Japanese-Americans suffered great economic and psychological distress as the plan was hastily implemented. By the spring of 1942, more than 100,000 Japanese-Americans had been relocated in internment camps by the War Relocation Authority. Seventy thousand American citizens of Japanese ancestry were detained in camps for periods up to four years, subjected to forcible confinement and then resettled in areas away from the Pacific coast.[60]

The constitutionality of the curfew, exclusion and relocation programs came before the Supreme Court in three cases decided in 1943 and 1944. The effect of all three decisions was to uphold this extraordinary exercise of the war power by Congress and the president.

Curfew Case

In June 1943, the court, in *Hirabayashi v. United States,* unanimously upheld the curfew order as applied to U.S. citizens as "within the boundaries of the war power." The court's opinion, written by Chief Justice Harlan Fiske Stone, made clear, however, that the court was not considering "whether the President, acting alone, could lawfully have made the curfew order."[61]

Because Congress had ratified Roosevelt's executive order by statute, the question became that of "the constitutional power of the national government through the joint action of Congress and the executive to impose this restriction as an emergency war measure." The court held that the curfew order was within that jointly exercised power.[62]

Exclusion, Detention

Eighteen months later, in December 1944, the court upheld the exclusion of Japanese-Americans from their West Coast homes. The vote was 6-3 in the case of *Korematsu v. United States.*

The majority relied heavily upon the reasoning of *Hirabayashi* in concluding that it was not outside the power of Congress and the executive, acting together, to impose this exclusion.[63]

The same day, however, the court granted a writ of *habeas corpus* to Mitsuye Endo, a Japanese-American girl, freeing her from one of the detention centers. These centers were intended as "interim places of residence" for persons whose loyalty was being ascertained. After one was determined to be loyal, the intent was that loyal persons be resettled outside the centers.

Endo's loyalty had been determined, but she had not been released from the center for resettlement. The court ordered her release. Without ruling on the constitutionality of the relocation program, the court held that "whatever power the War Relocation Authority may have to detain other classes of citizens, it has no authority to subject citizens who are concededly loyal to its leave procedures."[64]

"The authority to detain a citizen or grant him a conditional release as protection against espionage or sabotage is exhausted at least when his loyalty is conceded," wrote Justice Douglas for the court.[65]

The challenge of total war pointed up the tension between the idea of constitutional government and the demands of military policy and national security. Effective conduct of the war raised cries of executive dictatorship as it had in 1861 and 1917. But so long as the presidential war powers rested on the twin foundations of statutory authority and the prerogatives of the commander in chief, they seemed safe from constitutional challenge.

Postwar Powers

Between 1945 and 1947 postwar differences between the United States and the Soviet Union brought on the Cold War, a state of permanent international crisis and half-war that shaped presidential policy-making for three decades. Superpower rivalries, and this permanent state of ideological war, permitted President Harry S Truman and the next three American presidents to retain control of policy-making in the postwar era. Congress placed few obstacles in the way of presidential formulation of Cold War strategy.

Truman had virtually a free hand in the development of that policy. The Truman Doctrine, the Marshall Plan and "containment" of communism met only token resistance in Congress.

When, six months after communists took control of the mainland of China, communist North Korea invaded South Korea, Truman acted decisively — and unilaterally. On June 27, 1950, he announced that American air and naval forces would aid South Korea to repel the invasion from the north. Truman claimed authority for his actions from the United Nations Security Council vote that condemned North Korea's action and the June 27 resolution that urged U.N. members to assist South Korea.[66] The United States, however, had never signed a specific agreement to assign American forces to the Security Council for "police actions" such as this one.

The initial decision to commit U.S. forces brought some criticism in the Senate of this abuse of the war power. The House, however, broke into applause when it received official news of the president's action.

The Steel Seizure Case

The first modern rebuff to presidential war powers was administered by the court to President Harry S Truman in the *Steel Seizure Case* of 1952. The idea of broad emergency powers in time of cold war as well as hot war met court opposition when Truman took over the nation's steel mills to prevent a strike and ensure continued steel production for the war in Korea. Six members of the court held Truman's seizure an unconstitutional usurpation of powers and ordered the mills returned to private hands.[67]

Truman's seizure order cited no statutory authority for the action. The president's directive stated simply that the action was taken under his powers as commander in chief and in accordance with the Constitution and the laws of the United States. Though a majority of the court agreed that the president had by this action overstepped constitutional boundaries that separated legislative and executive powers, they did not rule out the possibility that such seizures might be legal if done under statutory authority.[68]

Three members of the court, including Chief Justice Fred M. Vinson, dissented, arguing that the president possessed broad executive powers to take such action in the state of emergency created by the Korean War.[69]

Wartime Seizure Power

Presidents since Woodrow Wilson have seized industrial plants to prevent interruption of production during wartime.

The term "government seizure" simply means that the government assumes temporary custody of the property. People responsible for management of the plant or industry continue to operate the industry. Seizure proceedings have been regarded as an effective way to break a stalemate in stalled labor-management contract negotiations to prevent production interruptions in vital industries during a national emergency.

President Franklin D. Roosevelt used regular army troops in a labor strike that occurred on June 5, 1941. The president ordered some 2,000 troops to prevent disruption of aircraft production at the North American Aviation Plant in Los Angeles, Calif. The president's Executive Order explained that it was necessary to send troops to ensure continued production of aircraft while labor and management negotiated an end to the walk out over wages. The government retained control of the plant until July 2, 1941.

The strike was called less than ten days after Roosevelt had proclaimed an unlimited national emergency calling upon employers and employees to cooperate as war approached.[1]

No specific statute authorized the president to seize plants in a labor dispute. The Selective Service Act provided for seizure of plants when they refused to obey government orders to manufacture necessary arms and supplies.

Attorney General Robert H. Jackson's legal opinion justifying the seizure order derived the president's power from the "aggregate" of executive powers set out in the Constitution and federal statutes. Jackson said that the president had the inherent constitutional duty "to exert his civil and military as well as his moral authority to keep the defense effort of the United States a going concern."[2] Congress later authorized presidential seizures of plants involved in a labor dispute with the 1943 War Labor Disputes Act.

The single wartime court test of the seizure power proved inconclusive. After a three-year struggle between Montgomery Ward and Co. and the War Labor Board, the president in 1944 ordered the company's property seized to prevent a work stoppage.

A federal district court ruled that the company engaged in "distribution" and not "production". The president had no general war power to seize the property, the court said.

An appeals court interpreted "production" in broader terms and reversed the lower court. The Supreme Court accepted the case, then dismissed it as moot when the Army returned the property to company control.[3]

---

[1] Bennett M. Rich, *The Presidents and Civil Disorder* (Washington, D.C.: The Brookings Institution, 1941), pp. 177-183.

[2] Ibid. p. 184.

[3] *Montgomery Ward & Co. v. U.S.*, 326 U.S. 690 (1944).

Majority Views. Justice Hugo Black's brief opinion for the court rejected the proposition that either the president's commander-in-chief powers or some inherent executive prerogative powers authorized the seizure:

> Even though "theater of war" be an expanding concept, we cannot with faithfulness to our constitutional system hold that the Commander in Chief of the Armed Forces has the ultimate power as such to take possession of private property in order to keep labor disputes from stopping production. This is a job for the Nation's lawmakers, not for its military authorities. [70]

In a concurring opinion, Justice Robert H. Jackson wrote that the commander in chief clause:

> . . .is sometimes advanced as support for any presidential action, internal or external, involving use of force, the idea being that it vests power to do anything, anywhere, that can be done with an army or navy. . . . But no doctrine that the court could promulgate would seem to me more sinister and alarming than that a President . . . can vastly enlarge his mastery over the internal affairs of the country by his own commitment of the nation's armed forces to some foreign venture. . . . There are indications that the Constitution did not contemplate that the title Commander-in-Chief of the Army and Navy will constitute him also Commander-in-Chief of the country, its industries and its inhabitants. He has no monopoly of "war powers," whatever they are. While Congress cannot deprive the President of the command of the army and navy, only Congress can provide him an army and navy to command. . . .
>
> That military powers of the Commander-in-Chief were not to supercede representative government of internal affairs seems obvious from the Constitution and from elementary American history. . . . Congress, not the Executive, should control utilization of the war power as an instrument of domestic policy. . . . [71]

In Dissent. Chief Justice Vinson's dissenting opinion, joined by Justices Stanley F. Reed and Sherman Minton, was a pragmatic argument in support of the president's action, drawing upon historical precedents and emphasizing the gravity of the threat presented by a steel strike during the Korean conflict.

The dissenters relied primarily on the general executive power, not the commander-in-chief clause:

> Those who suggest that this is a case involving extraordinary powers should be mindful that these are extraordinary times. . . .
>
> The broad executive power granted by Article II to an officer on duty 365 days a year cannot, it is said, be invoked to avert disaster. Instead, the President must confine himself to sending a message to Congress recommending action. Under this messenger-boy concept of the Office, the President cannot even act to preserve legislative programs from destruction so that Congress will have something left to act upon. There is no judicial finding that the executive action was unwarranted because there was in fact no basis for the President's finding of the existence of an emergency, for, under this view, the gravity of the emergency and the immediacy of the threatened disaster are considered irrelevant as a matter of law. . . . Presidents have been in the past, and any man worthy of the Office

should be in the future, free to take at least interim action necessary to execute legislative programs essential to survival of the Nation. . . . [72]

> *". . .the Constitution did not contemplate that the title Commander-in-Chief of the Army and Navy will constitute him also Commander-in-Chief of the country, its industries and its inhabitants. He has no monopoly of 'war powers,' whatever they are. . . ."*
>
> —Justice Robert H. Jackson
> The *Steel Seizure Case,* 1952

China, Cuba and Vietnam

Presidents after Truman received similar congressional *carte blanche* for their foreign policy decisions as the state of permanent crisis continued into the 1950s and 1960s.

Congress in January 1955 authorized President Eisenhower to use force if necessary to defend Chiang Kai Chek's government on Taiwan against the threat of attack from mainland China. In March 1957, Eisenhower sought and received congressional authorization to act to block communist aggression in the Middle East. Sixteen months later, he sent Marines to Lebanon to prevent an outbreak of fighting between warring factions in that country. [73]

President John F. Kennedy obtained a joint congressional resolution on Oct. 3, 1962, authorizing him to use force if necessary to prevent the spread of communism in the Western Hemisphere. The resolution followed discovery of a Soviet supported missile capability in Cuba, 90 miles from the Florida coast. President Kennedy's decision to "quarantine" Cuba to prevent the landing of Soviet ships laden with Russian-built missiles and equipment brought the world to the brink of nuclear war. [74]

As the long war in Southeast Asia began to involve the United States more and more, President Lyndon B. Johnson in 1964 sought and received congressional passage of the Gulf of Tonkin Resolution that read, in part:

> . . .the United States is . . . prepared, as the President determines, to take all necessary steps, including the use of armed force, to assist any member or protocol state of the Southeast Asia Collective Defense Treaty requesting defense of its freedom. [75]

Johnson asked Congress to pass the resolution after **North Vietnamese patrol boats reportedly attacked U.S.** destroyers on patrol in the Gulf of Tonkin. The vote in support of the Southeast Asia Resolution (Tonkin Gulf) was 88-2 in the Senate and 416-0 in the House. Johnson relied on that expression of congressional support, and the broad language of the document, to wage the war in Vietnam. [76]

Military appropriations for defense, approved by Congress, continued to be regarded by some as signalling approval of the president's policies. As in the cases of Lincoln and Wilson, it seemed likely that Presidents Eisenhower, Kennedy and Johnson would have taken the same actions even without the authorizing resolutions.

Commander in the Field, Governor at Home

Within the broad sweep of the power of the commander in chief to conduct war fall a myriad of related duties and powers.

Field Decisions

First among these is the authority to make command decisions for field operations. Presidents have generally delegated that power to the generals — although Lincoln, for example, ordered General McClellan to make a general advance in 1862 to bolster morale and to carry the war into the enemy's territory.

President Wilson settled a command controversy that erupted on the Western Front in 1918. Franklin D.Roosevelt personally participated in the decisions that directed the strategy of World War II, the outcome of the war and postwar territorial divisions.

Truman ordered the atomic bombs dropped at Hiroshima and Nagasaki. Presidents Johnson and Nixon selected or approved targets to be hit by air strikes during the Vietnam conflict.

Thus, exercise of constitutional authority as commander in chief extends to all decision-making powers accorded any supreme military commander under international law.

Military Justice

The commander in chief governs the creation of military commissions and tribunals in territories occupied by United States forces and fixes the limits of their jurisdiction absent congressional limits on this power. The president's authority also endures after hostilities have ceased.[1]

The commander in chief is the ultimate arbiter of all matters involving the enforcement of rules and regulations related to courts martial,[2] including the amendment of the rules during war.[3] However, the president may only dismiss an officer in peacetime as part of a post-court-martial sentence.

The court has never limited the president's wartime dismissal power. The president may displace an officer in the military service by appointing someone else in his place with the advice and consent of the Senate.[4] He may not make additions to the list of military grades and ranks established by Congress.

Conduct of War

In the conduct of war the president may use secret agents to secure information,[5] he may authorize trade with the enemy if Congress approves,[6] and he may compel the aid of citizens and friendly aliens in theatres of military operations.

He may negotiate an armistice to end the fighting and set conditions for the armistice which affect the terms of the subsequent peace agreement.[7]

The president may authorize the occupation of a region or a nation and provide government administration for it,[8] but he cannot annex a region without the approval of Congress.[9]

Control of Property

In time of war, the commander in chief may requisition property for military use — an act which incurs the obligation of the United States to give "just compensation." [10] The court has upheld broad presidential power to use or "take" private property for federal use in wartime. But the government is obligated by the Fifth Amendment to pay "just compensation" to the owners of private property converted or condemned for public use in wartime.[11] Moreover, property taken, but not used, obligates the government to pay compensation.[12]

The president has the power to declare someone an enemy and to order his property seized,[13] and that authority extends to the property of the friendly aliens as well as to enemy aliens. [14]

While the concept of "just compensation" applies to citizens and friendly aliens, no such guarantee extends to alien enemies, nor is there an obligation on the part of the government to respond to suits by enemy aliens for return of seized properties. [15]

The president may under his war power, in addition, fix prices, nullify private contracts[16] and forbid, regulate and control the use of foods and malt liquors.[17]

---

[1] *Madsen v. Kinsella*, 343 U.S. 341 at 348 (1952); *Johnson v. Eisentrager*, 399 U.S. 763 at 789 (1950).

[2] *Swaim v. United States*, 165 U.S. 553 (1897).

[3] *Ex parte Quirin*, 317 U.S. 1 at 28-29 (1942).

[4] *Mullan v. United States*, 140 U.S. 240 (1891); *Wallace v. United States*, 257 U.S. 541 (1922).

[5] *Totten v. United States*, 92 U.S. 105 (1876).

[6] *Hamilton v. Dillon*, 21 Wall. 73 (1875); *Haver v. Yaker*, 9 Wall. 32 (1869).

[7] Protocol of Aug. 12, 1898 (stated in McKinley's Second Annual Message) in Fred L. Israel, ed., *The State of the Union Messages of the Presidents 1790-1966*, 3 vols. (New York: Chelsea House, Robert Hector Publishers, 1966), II:1848-1896; Wilson's Address to Congress (14 Points), in Henry S. Commager, ed. *Documents of American History*, 7th ed. (New York: Appleton-Century-Crofts, 1962), pp. 137-144.

[8] *Santiago v. Nogueras*, 214 U.S. 260 (1909); *Dooley v. United States*, 182 U.S. 222 at 230-231 (1901).

[9] *Fleming v. Page*, 9 How. 603 at 615 (1850).

[10] *Mitchell v. Harmony*, 13 How. 115 (1852); *United States v. Russell*, 13 Wall. 623 (1869).

[11] *Davis v. Newton Coal Co.*, 267 U.S. 292 (1925).

[12] *International Paper Co. v. U.S.*, 282 U.S. 399 at 406 (1931); *U.S. v. CalTec Philippines Inc.*, 344 U.S. 149 (1952).

[13] *Central Union Trust v. Garvan*, 254 U.S. 554 (1921).

[14] *Silesian American Corp. v. Clark*, 332 U.S. 469 (1947).

[15] *Clark v. Uebersee-Finanz-Korp.*, 332 U.S. 480 at 484-486 (1947).

[16] *Addy v. U.S.; Ford v. U.S.*, 264 U.S. 239 at 244-246 (1924).

[17] *Starr v. Campbell*, 208 U.S. 527 (1908); *U.S. v. Standard Brewery Co.*, 251 U.S. 210 (1920).

Vietnam and the War Powers Debate

The longest undeclared war in U.S. history, costing well over $100 billion and 360,000 American dead and wounded, drew to a close Jan. 23, 1973, with the signing of a ceasefire agreement in Paris.

The fullest expression of legal justification for the Vietnam War came from the Legal Adviser of the State Department, Leonard Meeker, in a memorandum submitted March 11, 1966, to the Senate Committee on Foreign Relations. [77] Meeker argued that the framers of the Constitution intended the president to be free to repel sudden attacks without prior congressional sanction, even though in the modern era that attack might occur halfway around the globe. Meeker's memorandum identified 125 historical precedents of congressionally unauthorized executive use of military force. [78] The precedents, however, were mostly minor skirmishes that involved a minimum amount of force or actual fighting: landings to protect citizens, enforcement of laws against piracy, Indian skirmishes, the occupation of Caribbean states, (usually to prevent political instability, economic collapse, or European intervention).

Meeker argued that the Tonkin Gulf Resolution and the SEATO Treaty authorized Johnson to act to defend Southeast Asia against communism. Making perhaps his most telling political point, Meeker noted the large majorities by which Congress had approved the Tonkin Gulf Resolution and its continuing support of the war through appropriation of funds. [79]

Nixon and the War Powers

Even after President Richard M. Nixon signed the Tonkin Gulf repealer measure Jan. 12, 1971, he continued the war in Vietnam under the aegis of the powers of the commander in chief.

The Nixon administration emphasized that Congress was ratifying its policy by approving appropriations for it and declared that the war presented political questions beyond the purview of judicial scrutiny. [80] Nixon officials emphasized the "merger" theory of war powers, pointing out the progressive blurring of the constitutional distinction between Congress' war power and the president's commander in chief role. Distinctions between the power to declare and the power to conduct wars were invidious ones proponents of the theory argued; the nation was in the strongest position when the president and Congress acted in unison. Therefore, Congress should support the president's policies through appropriations with a minimum of dissent so long as the president, in turn, informed the Congress of his political and military decisions on a regular basis. [81] The clear result of this theory was a virtual monopoly of the war power by the president.

Acting on this theory, Nixon, beginning in 1969, authorized secret American air raids in neutral Cambodia without informing Congress. The following year he ordered American forces into Cambodia to destroy supply centers and staging areas used by North Vietnam for its operations in the South.

In 1972, the president, acting on his own initiative, directed the mining of North Vietnamese ports to forestall the flow of arms to guerrilla and regular forces in South Vietnam, a decision that risked collisions with Russian and Chinese supply vessels. In 1973, attempting to force North Vietnam to make a truce, Nixon ordered carpet bombing of Hanoi and Haiphong. Nixon neither sought nor obtained explicit congressional approval for any of his policies with respect to Vietnam and, when the truce was signed, the 1973 Paris Accords had been negotiated by the president's men without congressional participation. [82]

War Powers Act of 1973

In response to recent disregard of its prerogatives by Nixon and his predecessors, Congress on Nov. 7, 1973, passed the War Powers Act over Nixon's veto. [83]

The act authorized the president to undertake limited military action in the absence of a declaration of war. Within 48 hours of such action, the law directed the President to make a report in writing to the Congress. Military action and troop deployment were limited to 60 days renewable for an additional 30 days to effect the safe removal of troops. At any time during the 60-day period, the law stipulated, Congress could order the immediate removal of forces by concurrent resolution, not subject to presidential veto. [84]

While the act appeared to limit presidential discretion, critics pointed out that it could be interpreted as expanding the president's war making capacity. A blank check to commit troops anywhere, at any time, subject only to a 60-90-day limit, indefinitely renewable, appeared to critics as an invitation to havoc or holocaust. Moreover, precisely **how Congress could reverse presidential commitment of troops once deployed, was never spelled out.** [85]

The Courts and the Vietnam War

Federal courts were asked repeatedly in the late 1960s and early 1970s to hold that American involvement in the undeclared war in Southeast Asia was unconstitutional because Congress had never declared it.

The Supreme Court, however, steadily declined to hear cases that raised this issue. [86] This refusal was based on the view that war was a political question. *(Box, p. 127)*

The Court's Role

While the Supreme Court's rulings have served to enlarge the scope of the executive's war power rather than to narrow it, the possibility remains that some court, convinced of the unconstitutionality of a president's course of action, could and would order him to desist.

But the court has generally adhered to the view which Justice Robert H. Jackson set out in the *Steel Seizure Case:*

> We should not use this occasion to circumscribe, much less to contract, the lawful role of the President as Commander-in-Chief. I should indulge the widest latitude of interpretation to sustain his exclusive function to command the instruments of national force, at least when turned against the outside world for the security of our society. But when it is turned inward, not because of rebellion but because of a lawful economic struggle . . . it should have no such indulgence. His command power is not such an absolute . . . but is subject to limitations consistent with a constitutional Republic whose law and policy-making branch is a representative Congress. The purpose of lodging dual titles in one man was to insure that the civilian would control the military, not to enable the military to subordinate the presidential office. No penance would ever expiate the sin against free government of holding that a President can escape control of executive powers by law through assuming his military role. [87]

Footnotes

[1] *Youngstown Sheet and Tube Co. v. Sawyer,* 343 U.S. 579 at 641 (1952).

[2] *The Federalist Papers,* with an Introduction by Clinton Rossiter (New York: New American Library, Mentor Books, 1961), No. 61, pp. 417-418.

[3] Ibid., No. 74, p. 447.

[4] Louis Koenig, *The Chief Executive,* 3d. ed. (New York: Harcourt Brace Jovanovich, 1975), pp. 27-29.

[5] C. Herman Pritchett, *The American Constitution* (New York: McGraw-Hill Book Co., 1959), p. 344.

[6] Arthur M. Schlesinger, Jr., *The Imperial Presidency* (New York: Popular Library, 1973), pp. 68-69.

[7] James D. Richardson, ed. *Messages and Papers of the Presidents,* 20 vols. (New York: Bureau of National Literature, Inc., 1897) VII:3225-3226.

[8] Edward S. Corwin, *The President, Offices and Powers 1787-1957,* 4th rev. ed. (New York: New York University Press, 1957), pp. 229, 235, 255.

[9] Glendon A. Schubert, *The Presidency in the Courts* (Minneapolis: University of Minnesota Press, 1957), pp. 286-290.

[10] Ibid. p. 287.

[11] Clinton Rossiter, *The Supreme Court and the Commander in Chief* (Ithaca, N.Y.: Cornell University Press, 1951), p. 126.

[12] *Talbot v. Seeman,* 1 Cr. 1 (1801); *Bas v. Tingy,* 4 Dall. 37 (1800).

[13] *Martin v. Mott,* 12 Wheat. 19 (1827).

[14] Id. at 29.

[15] Id. at 31-32.

[16] *Fleming v. Page,* 9 How. 603 at 615 (1850).

[17] Richard W. Leopold, *The Growth of American Foreign Policy* (New York: Alfred A. Knopf, 1962), pp.96-98.

[18] W. Taylor Reveley III, "Presidential War-Making: Constitutional Prerogative or Usurpation?", *Virginia Law Review,* 55:1258n-1259n.

[19] Samuel Eliot Morison, Henry Steele Commager and William E. Leuchtenburg, *The Growth of the American Republic,* 2 vols. (New York: Oxford University Press, 1969) I:550-551.

[20] *Congressional Globe,* 30th Cong., 1st sess. 95 (1848).

[21] Richard W. Leopold, *The Growth of American Foreign Policy,* pp. 150-152, 180-188, 212.

[22] Ibid.

[23] Ibid., pp. 215-218.

[24] Ibid., pp. 316-321.

[25] Edward S. Corwin, *The President, Offices and Powers,* pp. 228-230.

[26] Richardson, ed. *Messages and Papers of the Presidents,* VII:3225-3226.

[27] Carl B. Swisher, *American Constitutional Development,* 2d ed. (Cambridge, Mass.: Houghton Mifflin Co., 1954), p. 29.

[28] Elisabeth Joan Doyle, "The Conduct of the War, 1861," in Arthur M. Schlesinger Jr. and Roger Bruns, eds. *Congress Investigates 1792-1974* (New York: Chelsea House, 1975), p. 72.

[29] *The Prize Cases,* 2 Bl. 635 (1863).

[30] Id. at 668-669.

[31] Id. at 688-689, 690, 693, 698.

[32] Carl B. Swisher, *History of the Supreme Court of the United States:* Vol. V, *The Taney Period, 1836-64* (New York: MacMillan Publishing Co., 1974), pp. 844-846.

[33] Ibid. at 847-850.

[34] *Ex parte Merryman* 17 Fed. Cas. (No. 9487) (C.C.D. Md. 1861) quoted in Henry Steele Commager, ed., *Documents of American History,* 7th ed. (New York: Appleton-Century-Crofts, 1963), p. 402.

[35] *Ex parte Vallandigham,* 1 Wall. 243 (1864).

[36] *Ex parte Milligan,* 4 Wall. 2 at 127 (1866).

[37] Id. at 120-121,126-127.

[38] Woodrow Wilson, *Congressional Government* (Boston: Houghton Mifflin Co., 1885).

[39] Arthur Link, *Wilson, the Diplomatist: A Look at His Major Foreign Policies* (New York: Watts, Franklin Inc., 1965) pp. 5-11.

[40] Samuel E. Morison, Henry S. Commager, William E. Leuchtenburg, *The Growth of the American Republic,* II:337.

[41] Ibid. at 349, 353-356.

[42] Alfred H. Kelly and Winfred A. Harbison, *The American Constitution: Its Origin and Development,* 5th ed. (New York: W. W. Norton & Co., 1976), p. 626.

[43] Samuel E. Morison, Henry S. Commager, William E. Leuchtenburg, *The Growth of the American Republic,* II:377.

[44] Edward S. Corwin, *The President, Offices and Powers,* p. 236.

[45] Ibid., p. 235.

[46] *United States Statutes at Large,* Vol. XL, p. 276ff.

[47] *United States v. L. Cohen Grocery Co.,* 255 U.S. 81 at 81-83 (1921).

[48] *The Public Papers and Addresses of Franklin D. Roosevelt,* 5 vols. (New York: Random House, 1938), II:15.

[49] Samuel E. Morison, Henry S. Commager, William E. Leuchtenburg, *The Growth of the American Republic,* II:538-539.

[50] *United States v. Curtiss-Wright Export Corp.,* 299 U.S. 304 (1936); *United States v. Belmont,* 301 U.S. 324 (1937); *United States v. Pink,* 315 U.S. 203 (1942).

[51] *88 Congressional Record* (1942), p. 7044.

[52] *Yakus v. United States,* 321 U.S. 414 (1944).

[53] Id. at 459-460.

[54] *Bowles v. Willingham,* 321 U.S. 504 (1944).

[55] Id. at 519.

[56] *Woods v. Cloyd W. Miller Co.,* 333 U.S. 138 (1948).

[57] *Steuart & Bros. Inc. v. Bowles,* 322 U.S. 398 at 405-406 (1944).

[58] *Ex parte Quirin,* 317 U.S. 1 (1942).

[59] Id. at 46,48.

[60] James M. Burns, *Roosevelt: The Soldier of Freedom* (New York: Harcourt Brace Jovanovich, 1970), pp. 214-217, 266-268.

[61] *Hirabayashi v. United States,* 320 U.S. 81 at 102 (1943).

[62] Id. at 92.

[63] *Korematsu v. United States,* 323 U.S. 214 (1944).

[64] *Ex parte Endo,* 323 U.S. 283 at 297 (1944).

[65] Id. at 302.

[66] "Authority of the President to Repel the Attack in Korea," 23 *Department of State Bulletin,* 173 (1950).

[67] *Youngstown Sheet and Tube Co. v. Sawyer,* 343 U.S. 579 at 641 (1952).

[68] Id. at 585-587.

[69] Id. at 667-668.

[70] Id. at 587.

[71] Id. at 641-644.

[72] Id. at 668,708-709.

[73] Dwight D. Eisenhower, *Waging Peace, 1956-61* (Garden City, N.Y.: Doubleday & Co., 1965), pp. 272-273.

[74] *Public Papers of the Presidents, John F. Kennedy, 1962* (Washington, D.C.: U.S. Government Printing Office, 1963) pp. 806-815.

[75] PL-88-408, 78 *Statutes* 384; *Public Papers of the Presidents, Lyndon B. Johnson, 1963-1964,* 2 vols. (Washington, D.C.: U.S. Government Printing Office, 1965) I:926-932, 946-947.

[76] Lyndon B. Johnson, *The Vantage Point, Perspectives on the Presidency, 1963-1969* (New York: Holt, Rinehart & Winston, 1971), pp. 112-119.

[77] Leonard Meeker, *The Legality of United States' Participation in the Defense of Vietnam,* 54 *State Department Bulletin,* 474 (1966).

[78] Ibid. at 484-489.

[79] Ibid. at 485-486.

[80] Francis D. Wormuth, "The Nixon Theory of the War Power: A Critique," *California Law Review,* 60:624.

[81] *Hearings on U.S. Commitments to Foreign Powers Before the Senate Committee on Foreign Relations,* 90th Cong., 1st sess. (1967) at 108, 140-154.

[82] Kelly and Harbison, *The American Constitution,* p. 1016.

[83] *Guide to Congress,* 2d. ed. (Washington, D.C.: Congressional Quarterly, 1976), pp. 279-280.

[84] Ibid.

[85] Louis W. Koenig, *The Chief Executive,* 3d. ed. (New York: Harcourt Brace Jovanovich, 1975), p. 220.

[86] *Mora v. McNamara,* 387 F. 2d 862 (D.C. Cir.), cert. denied, 389 U.S. 934 (1967); *Luftig v. McNamara,* 373 F. 2d 664 (D.C. Cir.) cert. denied, 387 U.S. 945 (1967); *United States v. Mitchell,* 369 F. 2d 323 (2d Cir. 1966) cert. denied, 386 U.S. 972 (1967); *Velvel v.*

Johnson, 287 F. Supp. 846 (D. Kan. 1968).
[87] *Youngstown Sheet and Tube Co. v. Sawyer,* 343 U.S. 579 at 645-646 (1952).

The Architect of Foreign Policy

The Constitution grants the president the power to make treaties and to receive and appoint ambassadors. In addition to the foreign policy powers asserted by the president as commander in chief, these specific grants of power are the source of the president's authority to conduct the nation's foreign relations and shape its foreign policy.

The treaty-making power has been the more significant grant, and it has been interpreted by the Supreme Court as a broad base for the president's power over foreign policy. The court's traditional view on this matter was foreshadowed by then-Rep. John Marshall's speech on the floor of the House of Representatives in 1800, defending President John Adams' unilateral decision to return a British fugitive to British authorities.

Marshall declared:

> The President is the sole organ of the nation in its external relations, and its sole representative with foreign nations. Of consequence, the demand of a foreign nation can only be made on him. He possesses the whole executive power. . . .[1]

The Constitution, as in the grant of war powers, divided the power over foreign affairs. The Founding Fathers desired a strong executive but not another English monarch. They brought Congress into the treaty-making process. The president was to initiate policy and make treaties with other nations but he had to obtain the consent of two-thirds of the Senate for ratification of a treaty.

The internal tension established in the Constitution with respect to foreign relations powers provided a check on the president. Congress was granted other powers related to foreign relations: notably, the appropriations power, the authority to raise, maintain and regulate the armed forces, and the power "to declare War, grant Letters of Marque and Reprisal, and make rules concerning Captures on Land and Water." Alexander Hamilton noted the reciprocal nature of the treaty-making power when he observed that "The power of making treaties . . . . seems therefore to form a distinct department and to belong, properly neither to the legislative nor to the executive."[2]

The Early Debate

The debate over control of foreign policy began at the Constitutional Convention, when the Founding Fathers pondered the merits of lodging the foreign relations power almost exclusively in the hands of the chief executive.[3]

In 1793, Madison and Hamilton engaged in an exchange of views over the executive prerogative in foreign affairs prompted by the debate over America's neutrality in the wars of the French Revolution.

Hamilton, as "Pacificus," defended President Washington's Neutrality Proclamation and his unilateral promulgation of it. Foreign policy was an executive function, Hamilton declared. Congress had the power to declare war but the president had the power to make treaties and preserve peace until Congress declared war. Thus, Hamilton noted "it belongs to the 'executive power' to do whatever else the law of nations, co-operating with the treaties of the country, enjoin in the intercourse of the United States with foreign powers."[4] Hamilton conceded that executive policy might influence the decision of Congress, but he insisted that each branch of government was free to perform its assigned duties, according to its view of the matter.

At Thomas Jefferson's instigation, James Madison responded to Hamilton's defense of executive prerogative. **Under the pseudonym "Helvidius," Madison defended the** congressional initiative in foreign affairs. He compared Hamilton's assertions of presidential independence to the royal prerogative of British monarchs and asserted that Congress, too, could decide when matters of national policy led to war. Deliberations over grave matters of war and peace could not be foreclosed by the president's decisions, Madison said. What would be the result if Congress declared war and the president proclaimed neutrality? Madison asked.[5]

The question never received a formal reply from Hamilton, but in 1794 Congress passed the first neutrality act superceding the president's proclamation. The neutrality act established a congressional role in declarations of neutrality. Even Jefferson had already conceded, however, that the role of Congress in the negotiation of treaties and in the conduct of diplomacy was a limited one. In 1790, he observed that: "[t]he transaction of business with foreign nations is Executive altogether."[6]

Court Decisions

The Supreme Court has sustained the "sole organ" principle upholding the president's pre-eminence in the conduct of foreign relations, and it has checked challenges to the president's treaty-making power by the states and by the Senate while affirming the president's exclusive role.

But the court has refused to hear other cases that challenged the president's conduct of foreign affairs on the ground that the issue was political in nature, and thus beyond the realm of judicial determination.

The court has extended to the president broad discretionary powers in foreign affairs while it limited or denied the president the same latitude in the exercise of power related to domestic affairs. E. S. Corwin has observed that in the field of foreign affairs "[t]he power to determine the substantive content of American policy is a divided power, with the lion's share falling, usually, though by no means always, to the President."[7]

The States' Role

One of the first foreign policy matters settled by the Supreme Court was the question of the states' role in foreign affairs.

The source of the foreign affairs power was debated in 1795 by Justices William Paterson and James Iredell. Iredell wrote that sovereignty belonged to the states in foreign affairs prior to ratification of the Constitution; with ratification, that sovereignty passed to the national government from the states.

Paterson disagreed. Sovereignty never belonged to the separate states, he argued; the power to conduct foreign relations passed to the national government as an inheritance of power from the Continental Congress.[8] Paterson's view of an inherent foreign affairs power was expanded by the 1936 *Curtiss-Wright* decision.[9]

The outcome of the court's argument in 1795, however, was a flat denial to the states of any control over or role in foreign policy matters. The treaty-making power was not affected by the doctrine of "dual federalism" reserving undelegated powers to the states.

In the case of *Ware v. Hylton* a war law passed by Virginia during the Revolution provided that British-owned property be sequestered and individual debts owed to British citizens be paid to a designated state official. But the 1783 peace treaty permitted British subjects to sue in state courts to collect debts owed them prior to the Revolution.

The year after the Iredell-Paterson debate, the Supreme Court ruled that the treaty provision nullified the state law. Powers reserved to the states by the Tenth Amendment did not include any powers in the field of foreign relations. Justice Samuel Chase observed:

A treaty cannot be the Supreme law of the land, that is of all the United States, if any act of a State Legislature can stand in its way. . . . It is the declared will of the people of the United States that every treaty made, by the authority of the United States shall be superior to the Constitution and laws of any individual state. . . .[10]

Exclusive federal control over foreign relations and the treaty-making power was again asserted by the court in an 1840 case. The state of Vermont had decided to comply with Canada's request to return a fugitive Canadian murderer. Writing for the court, Chief Justice Roger B. Taney denied the state authorities' power to return the prisoner because the United States government had no extradition treaty with Great Britain. Taney wrote that:

It was one of the main objects of our Constitution to make us, so far as regarded our foreign relations, one

people and one nation; and to cut off all communications between foreign governments and the several State authorities.[11]

Justice William O. Douglas reiterated this view in a 1942 court opinion which held that:

Power over external affairs is not shared by the States; it is vested in the national government exclusively. . . . And the policies of the States become wholly irrelevant to judicial inquiry when the United States, acting within its constitutional sphere, seeks enforcement of its foreign policy in the courts.[12]

The Court's Role

In the field of foreign policy, the Supreme Court has often invoked the "political question" doctrine to avoid head-on collisions with the president.

That doctrine rests on the separation of powers theory — that the Supreme Court exercises the judicial power and leaves political, or policy, questions to Congress and the president.

Chief Justice John Marshall in 1829 explained the rule in one of the first cases in which it was applied. The court refused to rule on a boundary dispute between Spain and the United States:

In a controversy between two nations concerning national boundary, it is scarcely possible that the courts of either should refuse to abide by the measures adopted by its own government. There being no common tribunal to decide between them, each determines for itself on its own rights, and if they cannot adjust their differences peaceably, the right remains with the strongest. The judiciary is not that department of the government to which the assertion of its interests against foreign powers is confided. . . . A question like this respecting the boundaries of nations, is . . . more a political than a legal question. . . .[13]

Subsequent court rulings increased the list of political questions. The court either supported the decision of the "political" departments or refused to judge them. These "political questions" include: presidential decisions about the status of belligerents under international law;[14] the determination of when negotiated treaties had been ratified by another signatory nation;[15] decision as to the recognition and treatment of *de jure* and *de facto* governments;[16] judgments about accredited diplomatic representatives to the United States;[17] the length of military occupations under treaty terms;[18] the effective date of treaties;[19] and when tacit consent renewal of lapsed treaties was permissible.[20]

In the landmark "political question" decision of *Baker v. Carr*, Justice William J. Brennan Jr.'s opinion for the court made it clear that the court did not regard all matters touching foreign relations as beyond the court's review. His remarks provided a concise statement of the court's criteria for considering matters that concern foreign relations:

There are sweeping statements to the effect that all questions touching foreign relations are political questions. . . . Yet it is error to suppose that every case or controversy which touches foreign relations lies beyond judicial cognizance. Our cases in this field show a discriminating analysis of the particular question posed, in terms of the history of its management by the political branches, of its susceptibility to judicial handling in the light of its nature and posture in the specific case, and of the possible consequences of judicial action.[21]

The Senate's Role

The Senate role in the foreign policy process is limited to ratification of treaties. The Supreme Court in a 1901 decision defined a valid treaty and the Senate's role in making it:

> Obviously the treaty must contain the whole contract between the parties, and the power of the Senate is limited to a ratification of such terms as have already been agreed upon between the President, acting for the United States, and the commissioners of the other contracting power. The Senate has no right to ratify the treaty and introduce new terms into it, which shall be obligatory upon the other power, although it may refuse its ratification, or make such ratification conditional upon the adoption of amendments to the treaty.[22] *(Details on congressional foreign policy powers, p. 125)*

The 'Sole Negotiator'

The logical result of the court's restrictive view of the roles left for the states, for the court itself, and even for the Senate in foreign affairs was its 1936 decision that the president was the "sole negotiator" of foreign policy.

Improbable as it may seem, a war between Paraguay and Bolivia in 1932 was the catalyst which evoked that broad ruling from the court undergirding the president's primary role in foreign affairs.[23]

Both sides in that war depended upon outside military suppliers. American arms manufacturers, facing a depressed economy at home, exported weapons to the belligerents. Revulsion against the war, isolationist sentiment at home, and pressure from Great Britain and the League of Nations caused the United States to act to end the arms trade.

Congress on May 24, 1934, approved a joint resolution that authorized President Roosevelt to embargo these arms shipments if, in his judgment, an embargo would contribute to ending the war.[24] The resolution provided for fines and imprisonment, or both, for those who violated the embargo. Roosevelt signed the resolution into law May 28, 1934.[25] The resolution in no way restricted or directed his discretion in instituting the embargo.

Roosevelt soon declared an embargo in effect. Curtiss-Wright Export Corporation and two other companies were subsequently convicted of selling aircraft machine guns to Bolivia in violation of the embargo. They challenged the constitutionality of the resolution, arguing that it was an improper delegation of congressional power to the president.

The Supreme Court already had evinced sympathy for such challenges, striking down several major New Deal initiatives in 1935 on that basis.[26] *(Details, pp. 240-243)*

The Curtiss-Wright Decision

The court upheld the embargo resolution. The vote was 7-1. Justice Harlan Fiske Stone took no part in the case. Justice James McReynolds dissented.

Justice George Sutherland's opinion, written for the majority, upheld sweeping executive powers in foreign affairs. The majority distinguished between "external" and "internal" powers of the federal government — foreign policy and domestic policy. Based on his reading of the historical evidence and on his own previous studies of the foreign affairs power, Justice Sutherland concluded that the source of national authority in foreign relations was the British crown, not the separate states. This placed the foreign affairs power on an extra-constitutional footing different from that of the internal powers which passed from the states to the federal government.[27]

Sutherland's opinion elaborated on the theory of external sovereignty argued in 1795 by Justice William Paterson. Sutherland wrote:

> The broad statement that the federal government can exercise no powers except those specifically enumerated in the Constitution, and such implied powers as are necessary and proper to carry into effect the enumerated powers, is categorically true only in respect of our internal affairs. In that field, the primary purpose of the Constitution was to carve from the general mass of legislative powers then possessed by the states such positions as it was thought desirable to vest in the federal government, leaving those not included in the enumeration still in the states. . . . That this doctrine applies only to powers which the state had is self-evident. And since the states severally never possessed international powers, such powers could not have been carved from the mass of state powers but obviously were transmitted to the United States from some other source. . . .
>
> As a result of separation from Great Britain by the colonies, acting as a unit, the powers of external sovereignty passed from the Crown not to the colonies severally, but to the colonies in their collective and corporate capacity as the United States of America. . . . Rulers come and go; governments and forms of government change; but sovereignty survives. A political society cannot endure without a supreme will somewhere. Sovereignty is never held in suspense. When, therefore, the external sovereignty of Great Britain in respect of the colonies ceased, it passed to the Union. . . . It results that the investment of the federal government with the powers of external sovereignty did not depend upon the affirmative grants of the Constitution. The powers to declare and wage war, to conclude peace, to make treaties, to maintain diplomatic relations with other sovereignties, if they had never been mentioned in the Constitution, would have vested in the federal government as necessary concomitants of nationality.[28]

Sutherland then, echoing John Marshall's phrases, asserted the key role in foreign affairs for the president:

> . . . The President alone has the power to speak as a representative of the nation. He makes treaties with the advice and consent of the Senate; but he alone negotiates. Into the field of negotiation the Senate cannot intrude; and Congress is powerless to invade it. . . .
>
> It is important to bear in mind that we are here dealing not alone with an authority vested in the President by an exertion of legislative power, but with such an authority plus the very delicate, plenary and

exclusive power of the President as the sole organ of the federal government in the field of international relations — a power which does not require as a basis for its exercise an act of Congress, but which . . . must be

---

". . .[T]he President alone has the power to speak as a representative of the nation. He makes treaties with the advice and consent of the Senate; but he alone negotiates. . . ."

—Justice George Sutherland
United States v. Curtiss-Wright Export Corporation, 1936

---

exercised in subordination to the applicable provisions of the Constitution.[29]

Delegation of power to the president in the foreign affairs field thus, was not to be judged by the same standards as delegation of power over domestic matters:

> When the President is to be authorized by legislation to act in respect of a matter intended to affect a situation in foreign territory, the legislator properly bears in mind the important consideration that the form of the President's action — or, indeed whether he shall act at all — may well depend, among other things, upon the nature of . . . confidential information which he has or may thereafter receive. . . .This consideration . . . discloses the unwisdom of requiring Congress in this field of governmental power to lay down narrowly definite standards by which the President is to be governed.[30]

The Treaty Power: Its Effect and Its Limits

Treaties — their effect, their relationship to conflicting laws, to the Constitution, and to the allocation of power between the states and the federal government — have been the subject of numerous Supreme Court rulings.

In 1829 Chief Justice John Marshall discussed the nature and the force of a treaty:

> A treaty is in its nature a contract between two nations, not a Legislative Act. It does not generally effect, of itself, the object to be accomplished, especially so far as its operation is infraterritorial; but is carried into execution by the sovereign power of the respective parties to the instrument.
>
> In the United States a different principle is established. Our Constitution declares a treaty to be the law of the land. It is, consequently, to be regarded in courts of justice as equivalent to an Act of the Legislature, whenever it operates of itself without the aid of any legislative provision. But when the terms of the stipulation import a contract — when either of the parties engages to perform a particular act — the treaty addresses itself to the political, not the judicial department; and the Legislature must execute the contract before it can become a rule for the court.[31]

The distinction which Marshall set out — between a self-executing treaty and a non-self-executing treaty, which requires legislative action — survives to the present. A self-executing treaty requires no legislation to put it into effect.

For example, treaties that defined the rights of aliens in the United States would be self-implementing once ratified by the Senate and would bind the courts to enforce their terms.

A non-self-executing treaty, on the other hand, does not take effect until implemented through legislation approved by the "political" departments of the government and would not be enforced by the courts until then.

Treaty Versus Statute

Neither a treaty nor a statute has intrinsic superiority and the later will prevail. In the case of a non-self-

executing treaty, however, congressional acts take precedence. Justice Samuel F. Miller stated the rule in the *Head Money Cases* (1884): "a treaty made by the United States with any foreign nation . . . is subject to such acts as Congress may pass for its enforcement, modification, or repeal." [32]

Despite earlier treaties with several nations that guaranteed free admission of immigrants to the United States, the court upheld a law that placed a tax on immigrants. The majority opinion defined a valid treaty and its relationship to acts of Congress:

> A treaty is primarily a compact between independent nations. It depends for the enforcement of its provisions on the interest and the honor of the governments which are parties to it. If these fail, its infraction becomes the subject of international negotiations and reclamations, so far as the injured party chooses to seek redress, which may in the end be enforced by actual wars. It is obvious that with all this the judicial courts have nothing to do and can give no redress. But a treaty may also contain provisions which confer certain rights upon the citizens or subjects of one of the nations residing in the territorial limits of the other, which partake of the nature of municipal law, and which are capable of enforcement as between private parties in the courts of the country. . . .
>
> A treaty, then, is a law of the land as an act of Congress is, whenever its provisions prescribe a rule by which the rights of the private citizen or subject may be determined. And when such rights are of a nature to be enforced in a court of justice, that court resorts to the treaty for a rule of decision for the case before as it would to a statute. . . .[33]

Missouri v. Holland

A treaty, the court has held, may shift regulation of a matter from state to federal control, thus giving Congress new powers it would not possess without the treaty.

In 1916, the United States, Britain and Canada signed a treaty to protect migratory birds by limiting hunting seasons and by other measures. The treaty stipulated that both the United States and Canada would seek domestic legislation to put the law into effect.

"Acts of Congress are the supreme law of the land only when made in pursuance of the Constitution, while treaties are declared to be so when made under the authority of the United States. . . ."
—Justice Oliver Wendell Holmes Jr.
Missouri v. Holland, 1920

Two previous acts of Congress regulating migratory bird hunting had been struck down in lower federal courts which found them an unconstitutional extension of federal power into an area reserved to the states by the Tenth Amendment. The 1916 treaty was implemented by a 1918 law which regulated the hunting of migratory birds and authorized the Secretary of Agriculture to administer those rules.[34]

Missouri challenged the law. But the court upheld it as necessary to carry treaty provisions into effect.

The plenary nature of the federal treaty-making power, held the court, was sufficient to grant Congress control over matters otherwise ascribed to the states.

The effect of the ruling in *Missouri v. Holland* was to hold that ratification of a treaty could give Congress powers it would not otherwise have. Justice Oliver Wendell Holmes' opinion viewed the treaty power broadly:

> To answer this question it is not enough to refer to the Tenth Amendment, reserving the powers not delegated to the United States, because by Article II, [Section] 2, the power to make treaties is delegated expressly, and by Article VI treaties made under the authority of the United States, along with the Constitution and the laws of the United States made in pursuance thereof, are declared the supreme law of the land. If the treaty is valid there can be no dispute about the validity of the statute under Article I, [Section] 8, as a necessary and proper means to execute the powers of the Government. . . .
>
> It is said that a treaty cannot be valid if it infringes the Constitution, that there are limits, therefore, to the treaty making power, and that one such limit is that what an act of Congress could not do unaided, in derogation of the powers reserved to the States, a treaty cannot do. An earlier act of Congress that attempted by itself and not in pursuance of a treaty to regulate the killing of migratory birds within the States had been held bad in the District Court. . . . Those decisions were supported by arguments that migratory birds were owned by the States in their sovereign capacity for the benefit of their people, and that . . . this control was one that Congress had no power to displace. The same argument is supposed to apply now with equal force.
>
> Whether the two cases were decided rightly or not they cannot be accepted as a test of the treaty power.

Acts of Congress are the supreme law of the land only when made in pursuance of the Constitution, while treaties are declared to be so when made under the authority of the United States. . . . We do not mean to imply that there are no qualifications to the treaty making power; but they must be ascertained in a different way. It is obvious that there may be matters of the sharpest exigency for the national well-being that an act of Congress could not deal with but that a treaty followed by such an act could and it is not lightly to be assumed that, in matters requiring national action, "a power which must belong to and somewhere reside in every civilized government" is not to be found. . . . The treaty in question does not contravene any prohibitory words to be found in the Constitution. The only question is whether it is forbidden by some invisible radiation from the general terms of the Tenth Amendment. . . .

Here a national interest of very nearly the first magnitude is involved. It can be protected only by national action in concert with that of another power. The subject-matter is only transitorily within the state and has no permanent habitat therein. But for the treaty and the statute there soon might be no birds for any power to deal with. We see nothing in the Constitution that compels the government to sit by while a food supply is cut off and the protectors of our forests and our crops are destroyed. It is not sufficient to rely upon the States.[35]

Termination of Treaties

The court has held that the termination of treaties, even those terminable on notice, requires an act of Congress. Legislative repeal of a treaty, however, may violate international obligations undertaken in the treaty provisions. In that case, the court has said the matter:

> . . .becomes the subject of international negotiations and reclamations, so far as the injured party choses to seek redress, which may in the end be enforced by actual war. It is obvious that with all this, the judicial courts have nothing to do and can give no redress.[36]

The court affirmed its support of congressional power to repeal treaties in 1899 when it held that:

> Congress by legislation and so far as the people and authorities of the United States are concerned, could abrogate a treaty made between this country and another country which had been negotiated by the President and approved by the Senate.[37]

An act of Congress has been held to have superceded a conflicting provision of a prior treaty. And although the court has never declared a treaty unconstitutional, it has voided an executive agreement with Canada that conflicted with extant legislation.[38]

Legislative practice and executive opinion support the view that terminating international pacts belongs as a prerogative of sovereignty, to Congress. But the president, in his function of interpreting treaties prior to their enforcement, may find that a treaty has been breached and may decide that a treaty is no longer binding on the United States.[39] The court has stipulated that treaties may be abrogated by agreement between the contracting parties, by the treaty provisions, by congressional repeal, by the president and by the president and the Senate acting jointly.[40]

Constitutional Limits

In 1889, the court discussed the unlimited nature of the treaty power — but made clear that a treaty could be found unconstitutional. The court wrote:

That the treaty power of the United States extends to all proper subjects of negotiation between our government and the governments of other nations, is clear. . . . The treaty power, as expressed in the Constitution, is in terms unlimited except by those restraints which are found in that instrument against the action of the government or of its departments, and those arising from the nature of the government itself and of that of the States. It would not be contended that it extends so far as to authorize what the Constitution forbids, or a change in the character of the government or in that of one of the States, or a cession of any portion of the territory of the latter, without its consent. . . .[41]

The court has never held a treaty unconstitutional but in 1957 it made clear the continuing validity of the view that the treaty power is subject to the limits set by the Constitution. Writing for the court in the case of *Reid v. Covert*, Justice Hugo L. Black stated:

. . .no agreement with a foreign nation can confer power on the Congress, or on any other branch of government, which is free from the restraints of the Constitution. . . . It would be manifestly contrary to

the objectives of those who created the Constitution . . . let alone alien to our entire constitutional history and tradition — to construe Article VI [the Supremacy Clause] as permitting the United States to exercise power under an international agreement without observing constitutional prohibitions. . . .

The prohibitions of the Constitution were designed to apply to all branches of the National Government and they cannot be nullified by the Executive and the Senate combined.

There is nothing new or unique about what we say here. This Court has regularly and uniformly recognized the supremacy of the Constitution over a treaty. . . . This Court has also repeatedly taken the position that an Act of Congress, which must comply with the Constitution, is on a full parity with a treaty, and that when a statute which is subsequent in time is inconsistent with a treaty, the statute to the extent of conflict renders the treaty null. It would be completely anomalous to say that a treaty need not comply with the Constitution when such an agreement can be overridden by a statute that must conform to that instrument.

There is nothing in *State of Missouri v. Holland* . . . which is contrary to the position taken here. There the Court carefully noted that the treaty involved was not inconsistent with any specific provision of the Constitution. The Court was concerned with the Tenth Amendment which reserves to the States or the people all power not delegated to the National Government. To the extent that the United States can validly make treaties, the people and the States have delegated their power to the National Government and the Tenth Amendment is no barrier. [42]

The Use of Executive Agreements

"Every time we open a new privy, we have to have an executive agreement," Secretary of State John Foster Dulles facetiously told a Senate subcommittee in 1953.[43] Dulles exaggerated the problem but underscored the growing preference by presidents to negotiate executive agreements rather than submit treaties for Senate ratification.

Presidents can negotiate executive agreements personally and have the advantage of greater control over the outcome by avoiding Senate debate and delays as in the case of treaty ratification procedures.

In that 1953 hearing Dulles estimated that the U.S. entered into roughly 10,000 executive agreements in connection with the NATO treaty alone.[44]

Of the large number of such agreements, however, only a small percent rested only upon the president's powers in foreign relations or as commander in chief. Many of the agreements, authorized in advance by Congress, rested in addition upon congressional statutes or Senate-ratified treaty provisions.[45] Thus, executive agreements divided into two types: those authorized by Congress and those made on presidential initiative.

Authorized Agreements

Authorized agreements have been made on a wide variety of matters early and often in the nation's history.

Congress authorized officers of the executive branch to enter negotiations when the United States needed to borrow money from foreign countries, and when it appropriated money to pay tribute to the Algerine pirates to prevent attacks on shipping.[46] Moreover, Texas, Hawaii and Samoa became United States possessions by executive agreements approved by congressional resolution.[47] Similar broad grants of authority through congressional approval of executive agreements underlay the president's power to lower tariff barriers and ease restrictions on international trade.

The Lend-Lease Act of March 11, 1941, granted Roosevelt the power to enter into executive agreements to manufacture in government arsenals or "otherwise procure" defense articles and "to sell, transfer, exchange, lease, and lend those war materials to the governments of any country deemed vital to the defense of the United States."[48]

Another form of congressional authorization of presidential agreements was the United Nations Participation Act of Dec. 20, 1945, which permitted the president to negotiate a series of agreements with the United Nations Security Council providing for the number and types of armed forces to be made available to the Council for the purpose of maintaining peace and international security.[49]

Presidents have also negotiated agreements with other nations about the status of forces stationed on foreign soil.

Recognition and Non-Recognition

The twin powers of recognition of foreign governments or the reverse side of the coin — non-recognition — have been powerful tools in the president's conduct of foreign relations. This power has been derived from the Constitution's statement that the executive, "shall receive ambassadors and other public ministers."

Though the president has occasionally sought the cooperation of Congress in recognizing nations, the act of recognition is a presidential function. Presidential power to determine which nation held sovereign jurisdiction over a region has been sustained by the court. In *Williams v. Suffolk Ins. Co.* (1839), the court refused to consider a challenge to President Martin Van Buren's decision not to recognize Argentina's claim of sovereignty over the Falkland Islands.

The opinion defined the narrow purview of the court's scrutiny where executive and/or "political" questions were involved:

> . . .when the executive branch of the government, which is charged with our foreign relations, shall, . . .assume a fact in regard to the sovereignty of any island or country, it is conclusive on the judicial department. . . . And in this view, it is not material to inquire, nor is it the province of the court to determine, whether the executive be right or wrong. It is enough to know, that in the exercise of his constitutional functions, he had decided the

question. Having done this . . . it is obligatory on the people and government of the Union.[1]

An 1897 Senate Foreign Relations Committee report on the subject of recognition concluded that "the executive branch is the sole mouthpiece of the nation in communication with foreign sovereignties." [2]

Non-Recognition

The practice of refusing to recognize governments has largely been a political decision vested in the executive branch and unchallenged by the courts.

President Woodrow Wilson decided not to recognize the *de facto* government of Mexico's Provisional President Huerta in 1913 — an act which hastened Huerta's downfall a year later.[3] Wilson employed the non-recognition policy with considerable discretion and American presidents in the 20th century followed suit.

Every president between the administrations of Wilson and Franklin D. Roosevelt's 1933 policy reversal had refused to recognize the Union of Soviet Socialist Republics.[4] President Herbert Hoover followed the non-recognition principle with respect to the Japanese puppet government (Manchukuo) in Manchuria in 1932.[5]

And every president from Truman to Lyndon B. Johnson refused to recognize the Communist government of mainland China until President Nixon's *de facto* recognition in 1972.[6]

---

[1] *Williams v. Suffolk Ins. Co.*, 13 Pet. 414 at 419-420 (1839).
[2] Senate Doc. No. 56, 54th Cong., 2d Sess. (1897), pp. 20-22.
[3] Samuel Eliot Morison, Henry Steele Commager and William E. Leuchtenburg, *The Growth of the American Republic,* 2 vols. (New York: Oxford University Press, 1969), II:354.

[4] *The Constitution of the United States of America, Analysis and Interpretation* (Washington, D.C.: U.S. Government Printing Office, 1973), p. 544.
[5] Ibid.
[6] Louis Koenig, *The Chief Executive,* 3rd ed. (New York: Harcourt Brace Jovanovich, 1975), p. 217.

These agreements usually afforded American military personnel and their dependents a qualified privilege of trial by United States courts martial while within the jurisdiction of another country.

Presidential Initiatives

In 1817, President James Monroe agreed with Great Britain to limit arms on the Great Lakes. Executive treaty-making, accomplished by an exchange of notes approved by the Senate, took place without an exchange of ratifications. [50] Indian raids along the border between Mexico and the United States led to a series of agreements (1882-1896) that permitted troops of both nations to cross the international border in pursuit of marauding Indians. Presidents took these actions under their commander in chief powers and the court in 1902 found "probable" justification for the agreements:

> While no act of Congress authorizes the department to permit the introduction of foreign troops, the power to give such permission without legislative assent was probably assumed to exist from the authority of the President as commander in chief. . . . [51]

Four justices in dissent, however, said that such acts by the president required treaty or statutory sanction.

President McKinley ended the Spanish-American War by such an agreement, sent troops to China in the face of the Boxer Rebellion and signed a Boxer Indemnity Protocol,[52] along with other European powers — without Senate approval. Secretary of State John Hay agreed to the substance of the "open door" notes that guaranteed Chinese sovereignty and called a halt to the establishment of "spheres of influence" by major powers in China. [53]

President Theodore Roosevelt initialed what amounted to a secret treaty between Japan and the United States that recognized Japan's military protectorate in Korea, as well as agreements that dealt with Japanese immigration (1907) and the balance of power in the Pacific (1908). [54]

Woodrow Wilson's Secretary of State, Robert Lansing (1917), exchanged letters with Japan that recognized that nation's "special interests" in China in return for Japanese recognition of the "open door" policy. [55]

Franklin Roosevelt's use of executive agreements made that procedure a primary instrument for attaining his foreign policy objectives and nearly replaced the treaty-making power in its effect.

He recognized the Soviet Union by an exchange of notes in 1933 and, in the fall of 1940, an executive agreement that provided for hemisphere defense in the event of an attack, changed United States' policy from neutrality to a state of quasi-belligerency with the Axis powers.

The Hull-Lothian agreement of September 2, 1940, authorized the exchange of destroyers for bases. [56] A 1941 agreement with the Danish foreign minister, entered into after Nazi Germany occupied Denmark, permitted the United States to occupy Greenland for defense purposes. [57]

The agreements at Cairo, Teheran, Yalta and Potsdam outlined the territorial and ideological contours of the postwar peace. [58]

Cold War Agreements

Treaty-making reemerged for a time in the Cold War era in the form of multinational defense pacts such as the North Atlantic Treaty Organization (NATO), Southeast Asia Treaty Organization (SEATO), Central Treaty Organization (CENTO) and the United Nations Charter itself.

But executive agreements remained a primary instrument of foreign policy. In 1956, congressional concern about the proliferation of commitments by executive agreement emerged in a Senate bill that would have required the president to submit all such agreement for Senate perusal within 60 days. The House took no action on the measure. [59]

A 1969-1970 study of executive agreements by the Senate Foreign Relations Subcommittee on Security Agreements and Commitments Abroad uncovered many secret agreements made during the 1960s with a variety of counties including Ethiopia, Spain, Laos, Thailand and South Korea.

A 1971 agreement made by the Nixon administration with Portugal for the use of an air base in the Azores and an agreement with Bahrain for naval base facilities on the Persian Gulf stirred the Senate to pass a "sense of the Senate" resolution to the effect that both agreements should have been submitted to the Senate for approval as treaties. [60] In 1972 the Senate voted to cut off funds but the House failed to act on the matter.

In 1972, 1973 and 1974, Congress considered but did not complete action on bills which would have given it the power to veto executive agreements made by the president with other nations. In 1972, Congress did enact a measure which required that the texts of all international agreements be submitted to Congress, but the law did not give Congress the authrity to veto such executive agreements. [61]

The Court and Executive Agreements

During the Roosevelt administration, the Supreme Court upheld the executive agreement as a valid exercise of presidential power.

In the case of *United States v. Belmont,* the court held that the presidential decision to recognize the Soviet Union in 1933, and the executive agreement that gave effect to that policy, constituted a valid international compact. Moreover, the court noted, such agreement, without Senate approval, had the effect of a treaty and overruled conflicting state laws. Justice Sutherland, author of the *Curtiss-Wright* opinion earlier in the term, delivered the court's opinion:

> The recognition, establishment of diplomatic relations, the assignment, and agreements with respect thereto, were all parts of one transaction, resulting in an international compact between the two govern-

ments. That the negotiations, acceptance of the assignment and agreements and understandings in respect thereof were within the competence of the President may not be doubted. Governmental power over internal affairs is distributed between the national government and several states. Governmental power over external affairs is not distributed, but is vested exclusively in the national government. And in respect of what was done here, the Executive had authority to speak as the sole organ of that government.... [62]

> ...[A]n international compact as this was, is not always a treaty which requires the participation of the Senate. There are many such compacts, of which a protocol, a *modus vivendi,* a postal convention, and agreements like that now under consideration are illustrations.... [63]

United States v. Pink

In 1942 — in a decision reminiscent of its 1796 decision in *Ware v. Hylton* first affirming the supremacy of a federal treaty over state law — the court reaffirmed the force and validity of executive agreements.

The 1933 executive agreement that extended diplomatic recognition to the Soviet Union provided that after settlement of U.S. claims against Russian-owned companies, the assets of the company which remained would be returned to the Soviet Union. New York State, however, went to court to prevent the return of the remaining assets of an insurance company with New York offices.

The court upheld the terms of the executive agreement against the state's claims. The majority held that the terms of the agreement bound the state just as if they were treaty provisions, because the president possessed the power to remove obstacles to diplomatic recognition. It was, Justice William O. Douglas said:

> a modest implied power of the President who is the 'sole organ of the Federal Government in the field of international relations' .... It was the judgment of the political department that full recognition of the Soviet Government required the settlement of outstanding problems including the claims of our nationals. ... We would usurp the executive function if we held that the decision was not final and conclusive in the courts. [64]

With respect to state power in the field of foreign affairs or the conflict of state laws with international agreements, Douglas affirmed the long-standing rule that:

> ...state law must yield when it is inconsistent with, or impairs the policy or provisions of, a treaty or of an international compact or agreement. ...The power of a State to refuse enforcement of rights based on foreign law which runs counter to the public policy of the forum ... must give way before the superior Federal policy evidenced by a treaty or international compact or agreement.... [65]

No state had the power to modify an international agreement or to reject part of a policy that underpinned the broader diplomatic policy of recognition of a foreign government, in this case the Soviet Union, wrote Douglas. Such an exercise of state power would be a "dangerous invasion of Federal authority," which "would tend to disturb that equilibrium in our foreign relations which the political departments of our national government had diligently endeavoured to establish...." [66]

Footnotes

[1] *United States Congress, Debates and Proceedings, First Congress, First Session. March 3, 1789 to Eighteenth Congress, First Session, May 27, 1824. [Annals of Congress].* 42 vols., (Washington, D.C.: Gales & Seaton, 1834-1856), X:596, 613-614 (1800).

[2] *The Federalist Papers,* with an Introduction by Clinton Rossiter (New York: New American Library, Mentor Books, 1961), No.75, pp. 450-451.

[3] Max Farrand, ed., rev. ed., *The Records of the Federal Convention of 1787* (New Haven: Yale University Press, 1937), II:183.

[4] "Pacificus," Nos. 1, 3, in John C. Hamilton, ed., *Works of Alexander Hamilton,* 7 vols. (New York: John F. Trow, 1851), VII:76,82-83.

[5] Gailliard Hunt, ed., *The Writings of James Madison,* 9 vols. (New York: G.P. Putnam's Sons, 1900-1910), VI:138-188.

[6] Paul L. Ford, ed., *The Writings of Thomas Jefferson,* 10 vols. (New York: G.P. Putnam's Sons, 1892-1899), V:161-162.

[7] Edward S. Corwin, *The Constitution and What It Means Today,* (Princeton, N.J.: Princeton University Press, 1958), p. 171.

[8] *Penhallow v. Doane,* 3 Dall. 54 at 80-83 (1795).

[9] *United States v. Curtiss-Wright Export Corp.,* 299 U.S. 304 (1936).

[10] *Ware v. Hylton,* 3 Dall. 199 at 236-237 (1796).

[11] *Holmes v. Jennison,* 14 Pet. 540 at 575 (1840).

[12] *United States v. Pink,* 315 U.S. 203 at 233-234 (1942).

[13] *Foster v. Neilson,* 2 Pet. 253 at 307, 309 (1829).

[14] *United States v. Palmer,* 3 Wheat. 610 (1818).

[15] *Doe v. Braden,* 16 How. 635 at 657 (1853).

[16] *Jones v. United States,* 137 U.S. 202 (1890); *Oetjen v. Central Leather Co.,* 246 U.S. 297 (1918).

[17] *In re Baiz,* 135 U.S. 403 (1890).

[18] *Neely v. Henkel,* 180 U.S. 109 (1901).

[19] *Terlinden v. Ames,* 184 U.S. 270 (1902).

[20] *Charlton v. Kelly,* 299 U.S. 447 (1913).

[21] *Baker v. Carr,* 369 U.S. 186 at 212 (1962).

[22] *Fourteen Diamond Rings v. United States,* 183 U.S. 176 at 183 (1901).

[23] *United States v. Curtiss-Wright Corp.,* 299 U.S. 315 (1936).

[24] Charles A. Lofgren, "United States v. Curtiss-Wright: An Historical Assessment," *The Yale Law Journal,* 83 (November 1973):1-13.

[25] 48 Stat. 1744 (1934).

[26] *Schechter Poultry Corp. v. United States,* 295 U.S. 495 (1935); *Carter v. Carter Coal Co.,* 298 U.S. 238 (1936); *Panama Refining Co. v. Ryan,* 293 U.S. 288 (1935).

[27] George Sutherland, *Constitutional Power and World Affairs,* (New York: Columbia University Press, 1919), pp. 25-47, 116-126.

[28] *United States v. Curtiss-Wright Export Corp.,* 299 U.S. 315 at 315-318 (1936).

[29] Id. at 319-320.

[30] Id. at 321-322.

[31] *Foster v. Neilson,* 2 Pet. 253 at 314 (1829).

[32] *Head Money Cases,* 112 U.S. 580 at 598 (1884).

[33] Id. at 598-599.

[34] Migratory Bird Treaty Act, July 3, 1918, c. 128, 40 *Stat.* 755.

[35] *Missouri v. Holland,* 252 U.S. 416 at 432-435 (1920).

[36] *Head Money Cases,* 112 U.S. 580 at 598-599 (1884).

[37] *La Abra Silver Mining Co. v. United States,* 175 U.S. 423 at 460 (1899).

[38] *Whitney v. Robertson,* 124 U.S. 190 (1888); *United States v. Guy W.Capps Inc.,* 348 U.S. 296 (1955).

[39] *Charlton v. Kelly,* 229 U.S. 447 (1913).

[40] *Bas v. Tingy,* 4 Dall. 37 (1800); *Head Money Cases,* 112 U.S. 580 (1884).

[41] *Geofroy v. Riggs,* 133 U.S. 258 at 266-267 (1889).

[42] *Reid v. Covert,* 354 U.S. 1 at 16-18 (1957).

[43] Hearings on S. J. Res. 1 and S. J. Res. 43 Before a Subcommittee of the Senate Judiciary Committee, 83d Cong., 1st sess (1953), p. 877.

[44] Ibid.

[45] *The Constitution of the United States of America, Analysis and Interpretation* (Washington, D.C.: U.S. Government Printing Office, 1973), p. 506.

[46] Wallace McClure, *International Executive Agreements: Democratic Procedure Under the Constitution of the United States* (New York: AMS Press, 1941), p. 41.

[47] Ibid. at 62-70.

[48] Henry S. Commager, ed., *Documents of American History,* 7th ed. (New York: Appleton-Century-Crofts, 1962), pp. 449-450.

[49] "A Decade of American Foreign Policy," Senate Doc., No. 123, 81st Cong., 1st sess. (1950), p. 126.

[50] *The Constitution of the United States, Analysis and Interpretation,* p. 512.

[51] *Tucker v. Alexandroff,* 183 U.S. 424 at 435,467 (1902).

[52] Samuel B. Crandall, *Treaties: Their Making and Enforcement,* 2d ed. (New York: Columbia University Press, 1916), pp. 103-104.

[53] Samuel E. Morison, Henry S. Commager and William E. Leuchtenburg, 2 vols. *The Growth of the American Republic,* II:261-264.

[54] Wallace McClure, *International Executive Agreements,* pp. 96-97.

[55] Henry S. Commager, ed., *Documents of American History,* pp. 45, 52-53, 133-134.

[56] Wallace McClure, *International Executive Agreements,* pp. 391-393.

[57] 4 *State Department Bulletin* (1941), p. 443.

[58] "A Decade of American Foreign Policy, Basic Documents, 1941-1949," Senate Document No. 123, Part 1, 81st Cong., 1st sess. (1950).

[59] Arthur M. Schlesinger Jr., *The Imperial Presidency* (New York: Popular Library, 1973, 1974), pp. 299-300.

[60] Congressional Quarterly, *1972 Almanac* (Washington, D.C.: Congressional Quarterly, 1972), pp. 279-280, 435.

[61] *Congress and the Nation,* Vol.IV, *1973-1976* (Washington, D.C.: Congressional Quarterly, 1977), p. 864.

[62] *United States v. Belmont,* 301 U.S. 324 at 330 (1936).

[63] Id. at 330-331.

[64] *United States v. Pink,* 315 U.S. 203 at 229-230 (1942).

[65] Id. at 230-231.

[66] Id. at 233.

The President As Executive

"The executive Power shall be vested in a President of the United States of America," begins Article II. But the Constitution quickly follows this sweeping statement of power with a correspondingly broad responsibility: the president is obligated to "take Care that the Laws be faithfully executed."

Presidents, justices and scholars have disagreed over the import of the "executive power" provision. Is it a broad grant of inherent executive authority, adding to the enumerated powers which follow? Or is it just a simple designation of office, adding nothing in substantive power?

In practice, the provision has been interpreted as granting presidents virtually all power necessary for management of the executive branch in the public interest. Even William Howard Taft, who adopted the conservative view — that the president's powers were limited to those spelled out in the Constitution or clearly included within those express powers — acted as president on the broader interpretation of executive power.[1]

Not only did pragmatic necessity bolster the broad view of executive power, but those who adopted it also found support for it in the "decision of 1789" — the discussion by the First Congress of the specific powers of the executive. *(Box, p. 213)*

The "take care" clause blended the Founding Fathers' distrust of concentrated power with the practical necessity of vesting administrative and enforcement authority in the president. This provision clearly rendered the president subordinate to the laws he administered.

Through precedent and practice the "faithful execution" clause has come to incorporate a broad series of powers that range from the administrative interpretation of acts of Congress to the declaration of martial law in times of civil disorder or national emergency. The court generally has granted the president broad discretion to act under this clause.

The President's Subordinates

The court also has viewed this clause as early acknowledgement of the Executive's need to carry out many duties through subordinates. The clause does not direct the Executive to faithfully execute the laws — but only to take care that the laws are faithfully executed, a clearly supervisory function.

As early as 1839, the court set out the general rule that the duties and obligations placed on the president by law could be carried out by his subordinates. The case arose under an 1823 law which stated that public money could not be disbursed by officers of the United States except at the president's discretion. The court in the case of *Wilcox v. McConnel* ruled that the chief executive, "speaks and acts through the heads of the several departments in relation to subjects which appertain to their respective duties."[2]

Four years later the court wrote:

The President's duty in general requires his superintendence of the administration; yet this duty cannot require of him to become the administrative officer of every department and bureau, or to perform in person the numerous details incident to services which, nevertheless, he is, in a correct sense, by the Constitution and laws required and expected to perform. This cannot be, 1st. Because, if it were practicable, it would be to absorb the duties and responsibilities of the various departments of the government in the personal action of the one chief executive officer. It cannot be, for the stronger reason, that it is impracticable — nay, impossible.[3]

The Power of Appointment

The president's power to appoint and remove those subordinate officials was a necessary complement to his power to manage the executive branch. Members of the president's administration are responsible for carrying out the duties of the office they have been selected to fill and to serve the president who appointed them.

Article II, section 2, provides that the president:

...shall nominate, and by, and with the advice and consent of the Senate, shall appoint ambassadors, other public ministers and consuls, judges of the Supreme Court, and all other officers of the United States, whose appointments are not herein otherwise provided for, and which shall be established by law; but the Congress may by law vest the appointment of such inferior officers, as they think proper, in the Presidents alone, in the courts of law, or in the heads of departments.

The clause provided four methods of appointment: presidential appointment with Senate confirmation, presidential appointments without Senate confirmation, ap-

Diplomatic Appointments

With establishment of the Foreign Service, Congress reduced the discretionary appointment power with respect to diplomatic posts.

The president completely controlled the appointment and removal of diplomatic ministers during the first 65 years of the nation's history. All matters of grade, rank and compensation were left to his discretion during this period.

One example of the breadth of this power came in 1814. President Madison, with the Senate in recess, appointed three commissioners to negotiate with the British to end the War of 1812.

Opponents in Congress argued that the offices had not been created by statute, hence no vacancies existed to allow the president to appoint peace commissioners.

Madison responded that there were two classes of offices under the Constitution. One included the range of posts created by law to manage the government; the second related to foreign affairs and were diplomatic posts, completely under presidential control and not subject to congressional scrutiny or prior approval. Congress protested, but took no action. The peace made by these commissioners ended the war.[1]

In 1855 Congress created an official list of envoys and ministers in the public service with salary and rank specified for each post.

Today, foreign service appointments are nominally made by the president, but they are governed by the Foreign Service Act of 1946.

The president retains the right and power to appoint ambassadors-at-large as personal emissaries for specific foreign missions without Senate consultation or approval. Such appointments are not regarded as regular ambassadorial or ministerial appointments by Congress or the court.[2]

---

[1] *U.S. Constitution, Analysis and Interpretation* (Washington, D.C.: U.S. Government Printing Office, 1973), p. 520.
[2] Ibid.

---

pointments by courts of law, and appointments by heads of departments. Congress exercises no power to appoint executive officers though it may set qualifications for offices established by statute. Congressional requirements usually have pertained to citizenship, grade, residence, age, political affiliation and professional competence.

The appointment power of the president has been exercised in conformance with a blend of historical precedents, custom, constitutional requirements and statutory provisions established by Congress.

Congress has narrowed the range of officers over whom the president has the discretionary appointment power. The creation of the Civil Service Commission and the steady addition of positions to the professional civil service list has reduced the scope of the president's exercise of the appointment power. Moreover, the establishment of a professional foreign service and the enumeration of the list of diplomatic posts available for presidential appointments also narrowed the president's range of appointments.

The court has decided only a few cases with respect to the appointment process but the decisions made, beginning

with *Marbury v. Madison,* control the president's power to nominate and appoint and limit his discretionary exercise of the removal power.

Marbury v. Madison

The most famous decision made by Chief Justice Marshall, and perhaps the most famous in the court's history, began as a relatively unimportant controversy over a presidential appointment.

William Marbury sought delivery of his commission of appointment as a justice of the peace. In addition to the political significance of the case in constitutional history as the means by which the Marshall court established the principle of judicial review, *Marbury v. Madison* had something to say about the appointment process.[4]

The court held that Marbury should have received his commission, which had been duly signed and sealed, but not delivered. But, Marshall held, the court lacked the power to issue the order commanding Secretary of State James Madison to deliver it. The effect of *Marbury* was that, in making appointments, the president was under no enforceable obligation to deliver a commission, even after the nominee was confirmed by the Senate.

Confirmation and Courtesy

Senate consent to executive appointments was a unique innovation incorporated into the Constitution. The original idea of Senate participation in the selection, as well as confirmation, of nominees never materialized, however. President Washington collided with the Senate over approval of an Indian treaty and subsequently refused to consult the Senate on appointment matters, except to send up nominations for approval. Senate consent to an executive appointment came to mean simply that a majority of the Senate approved the president's nomination.

Presidents have customarily consulted individual senators of their own political party on matters of appointments related to their home states. But policy considerations, as well as political ones, often take precedence over this practice of senatorial courtesy, and failure of the president to extend this courtesy to the appropriate senators usually has not alone resulted in a nominee's rejection.

Once the Senate has approved a nominee, it cannot reverse its decision. In 1930, Senate rules permitted a move for reconsideration and recall of a confirmation resolution within two days after its passage.

In December 1930, President Hoover nominated George O. Smith as chairman of the Federal Power Commission. The Senate, in executive session on Dec. 20, confirmed Smith and ordered the resolution of confirmation sent to the president. Later that same day, the Senate adjourned until Jan. 5, 1931.

The president, notified of Smith's confirmation, delivered the commission of appointment, and Smith took office.

On Jan. 5, the next day the Senate was in session, it voted to reconsider Smith's nomination; a month later, it voted again and refused to confirm it.

President Hoover refused to return the confirmation resolution as requested by the Senate, describing this maneuver as a congressional effort to exercise the power of removal. The Senate then took the matter to court to test Smith's right to continue in office.

When the matter came to the Supreme Court, it upheld Smith's right to the post on the grounds that Senate precedent did not support the Senate's reconsideration of a confirmation action, after the nominee assumed the duties of the office.[5]

Recess Appointments

The Constitution authorizes the president to fill vacant offices during a Senate recess. "Recess" is here held to mean periods longer than a holiday observance or a brief and temporary adjournment. It states:

> The President shall have Power to fill up all Vacancies that may happen during the Recess of the Senate, by granting Commissions which shall expire at the End of their next Session.

If the vacancy occurs with the Senate in session, the president may fill the office with an *ad interim* appointment, if such an appointment is provided for by the statute creating the position.

A recess appointee, however, may not receive the salary of the office until confirmed by the Senate. This practice has prevented the president from using recess appointments to keep men in office whom the Senate would refuse to confirm.[6]

The Removal Power

The Constitution says nothing about the president's power to remove from office the officials he has appointed with the advice and consent of the Senate, although Article II provides for congressional impeachment and removal of some of these officers. The president's power to remove derives from the power to appoint and from the debate concerning the executive power in the First Congress in 1789.

In the first major modern court ruling on the removal power, Chief Justice William Howard Taft, the only former president to head the court, traced the origins of the power back to that debate — on the bill creating the Department of Foreign Affairs. *(Box, p. 213)*

Taft concluded that the removal power was understood in that "decision of 1789" to exist as a complement of the president's power to appoint:

> It is very clear from this history that the exact question which the House voted upon was whether it should recognize and declare the power of the President under the Constitution to remove the Secretary of Foreign Affairs without the advice and consent of the Senate. That was what the vote was taken for . . . there is not the slightest doubt, after an examination of the record, that the vote was, and was intended to be, a legislative declaration that the power to remove officers appointed by the President and the Senate vested in the President alone. . . .[7]

But despite that early decision, there has been much debate over this aspect of executive power. "Controversy pertaining to the scope and limits of the President's power of removal fills a thick chapter of our political and judicial history," wrote Justice Felix Frankfurter in 1958.[8]

President Andrew Jackson asserted the executive's right to remove officials as an essential element of his power to control the personnel within his department. When he **removed his secretary of the Treasury for failure to comply** with a directive to remove government deposits from the

Bank of the United States, the Senate condemned Jackson's removal of the secretary as an assumption of power, "not conferred by the Constitution and laws, but in derogation of both."

Jackson responded with a protest message to the Senate in which he asserted that the executive's removal power was a direct corollary of his responsibility to oversee faithful execution of the laws:

> The whole executive power being invested in the President, who is responsible for its exercise, it is a necessary consequence that he should have a right to employ agents of his own choice to aid him in the performance of his duties, and to discharge them when he is no longer willing to be responsible for their acts. . . .[9]

By 1839, the court acknowledged that, as a practical matter, the president alone exercised the removal power.

Although it was clear the president and the Senate together had the power to remove officers appointed and confirmed by them, "it was very early adopted as the practical construction of the Constitution that this power was vested in the President alone," wrote the court.[10]

The first major challenge by Congress to this executive power came with the Tenure of Office Act of March 2, 1867, enacted amid the conflict between Congress and President Andrew Johnson over Reconstruction. The measure provided that any civil officer appointed by the president with the advice and consent of the Senate could be removed only with Senate approval. The law stripped President Johnson and future presidents of the discretionary removal of power.

Johnson protested the law and removed his secretary of war without complying with its provisions. That action became one of the factors in the impeachment attempt against him.

Modified in the administration of Ulysses S. Grant, the law was repealed in 1887 without any judicial ruling on its constitutionality.

Few presidents were as conscious of the prerogatives of the executive as Woodrow Wilson. A 1919 act of Congress created an executive budget bureau under the president's direction. The legislation established the office of comptroller general and an assistant comptroller of the United States who were to head an independent accounting department. The two officers were to be appointed by the president and confirmed by the Senate to serve during "good behavior." They were to be removed from office only by concurrent resolution of Congress on the grounds of inefficiency, neglect of duty or malfeasance in office.

Wilson favored the idea of a budget bureau but vetoed the measure, objecting that the removal procedure violated the Constitution because it denied the president the power to remove officials he had appointd to office.

Wilson explained that he regarded "the power of removal from office as an essential incident to the appointing power," and so could not "escape the conclusion that the vesting of this power of removal in the Congress is unconstitutional." [11]

President Warren G. Harding subsequently signed a similar bill, the Budget and Accounting Act, on June 10, 1921. [12]

The Case of the Recalcitrant Postmaster

President Wilson fired a postmaster and brought about the first major Supreme Court decision on the removal power. The ruling, in the case of *Myers v. United States,* was handed down in 1926, after Wilson and Myers, the postmaster, had both died. It seemed to grant the president an unlimited power to remove all officers he appointed except judges.

In 1876 Congress passed a law making removal of postmasters subject to Senate consent. President Wilson removed Myers without Senate consent. Myers and his heirs sued, challenging the validity of the removal in light of the 1876 law.

The court upheld the dismissal of Myers, ruling that Congress could not properly limit the executive's removal power in this way.

The opinion of Chief Justice Howard Taft rested heavily on the "decision of 1789" — the decisions made by the First Congress as it passed measures creating the machinery of the executive department. Those early decisions, Taft noted, "have always been regarded . . . as of the greatest weight in the interpretation of the fundamental instrument." [13]

Taft discussed the removal power as it was considered in these sessions:

Mr. Madison and his associates in the discussion in the House dwelt at length upon the necessity there was for construing article 2 to give the President the sole power of removal in his responsibility for the conduct of the executive branch, and enforced this by emphasizing his duty expressly declared in the third section of the article to "take care that the laws be faithfully executed."...

The vesting of the executive power in the President was essentially a grant of the power to execute the laws. But the President alone and unaided could not execute the laws. He must execute them by the assistance of subordinates. This view has since been repeatedly affirmed by this court.... As he is charged specifically to take care that they be faithfully executed, the reasonable implication, even in the absence of express words, was that as part of his executive power he should select those who were to act for him

under his direction in the execution of the laws. The further implication must be, in the absence of any express limitation respecting removals, that as his selection of administrative officers is essential to the execution of the laws by him, so must be his power of removing those for whom he cannot continue to be responsible....

...A veto by the Senate — a part of the legislative branch of the government — upon removals is a much greater limitation upon the executive branch, and a much more serious blending of the legislative with the executive, than a rejection of a proposed appointment. It is not to be implied. The rejection of a nominee of the President for a particular office does not greatly embarrass him in the conscientious discharge of his high duties in the selection of those who are to aid him, because the President usually has an ample field from which to select for office, according to his preference, competent and capable men. The Senate has full power to reject newly proposed appointees whenever the President shall remove the incumbents. Such a check enables the Senate to prevent the filling of offices with bad or incompetent men, or with those against whom there is tenable objection.

The power to prevent the removal of an officer who has served under the President is different from the authority to consent to or reject his appointment. When a nomination is made, it may be presumed that the Senate is, or may become, as well advised as to the fitness of the nominee as the President, but in the nature of things the defects in ability or intelligence or loyalty in the administration of the laws of one who has served as an officer under the President are facts as to which the President, or his trusted subordinates, must be better informed than the Senate, and the power to remove him may therefore be regarded as confined for very sound and practical reasons, to the governmental authority which has administrative control....

...Mr. Madison and his associates pointed out with great force the unreasonable character of the view that the convention intended, without express provision, to give to Congress or the Senate, in case of political or other differences, the means of thwarting the executive in the exercise of his great powers and, in the bearing of his great responsibility by fastening upon him, as subordinate executive officers, men who by their inefficient service under him, by their lack of loyalty to the service, or by their different views of policy might make his taking care that the laws be faithfully executed most difficult or impossible.

Made responsible under the Constitution for the effective enforcement of the law, the President needs as an indispensable aid to meet it the disciplinary influence upon those who act under him of a reserve power of removal. . . . Each head of a department is and must be the President's alter ego in the matters of that department where the President is required by law to exercise authority.

In all such cases, the discretion to be exercised is that of the President in determining the national public interest and in directing the action to be taken by his executive subordinates to protect it. In this field his cabinet officers must do his will. He must place in each member of his official family, and his chief executive subordinates, implicit faith. The moment that he loses confidence in the intelligence, ability, judgment, or loyalty of any one of them, he must have the power to remove him without delay. To require him to file charges and submit them to the consideration of the Senate might make impossible that unity and co-ordination in executive administration essential to effective action.[14]

". . .responsible under the Constitution for the effective enforcement of the law, the President needs as an indispensable aid to meet it the disciplinary influence upon those who act under him of a reserve power of removal. . . ."
—Chief Justice William Howard Taft
Myers v. United States, 1926

The court saw no reason why Congress should be allowed to limit the president's removal of postmasters. Taft wrote:

> There is nothing in the Constitution which permits a distinction between the removal of a head of a department or a bureau, when he discharges a political duty of the President or exercises his discretion, and the removal of executive officers engaged in the discharge of their other normal duties. The imperative reasons requiring an unrestricted power to remove the most important of his subordinates in their most important duties must therefore control the interpretation of the Constitution as to all appointed by him.[15]

Taft's opinion seemed to extend the president's removal power even to officers appointed to independent regulatory commissions:

> . . .there may be duties of a quasi-judicial character imposed on executive officers and members of executive tribunals whose decisions after hearing affect interests of individuals, the discharge of which the President cannot in a particular case properly influence or control. But even in such a case he may consider the decision after its rendition as a reason for removing the officer, on the ground that the discretion regularly entrusted to that officer by statute has not been on the whole intelligently or wisely exercised. Otherwise he does not discharge his own constitutional duty of seeing that the laws be faithfully executed.[16]

In Dissent. Justices James C. McReynolds, Louis D. Brandeis and Oliver Wendell Holmes dissented from the *Myers* ruling. They viewed the 1876 law as a legitimate exercise of congressional authority to impose statutory limits on grants of power. In a separate opinion, Justice McReynolds emphasized that the office in question was that of a postmaster — an inferior and civil position created by Congress:

> . . .The Constitution empowers the President to appoint ambassadors, other public ministers, consuls, judges of the Supreme Court and superior officers, and no statute can interfere therein. But Congress may authorize both appointment and removal of all inferior officers without regard to the President's wishes —

even in direct opposition to them. This important distinction must not be overlooked. And consideration of the complete control which Congress may exercise over inferior officers is enough to show the hollowness of the suggestion that a right to remove them may be inferred from the President's duty to "take care that the laws be faithfully executed." He cannot appoint any inferior officer, however humble, without legislative authorization; but such officers are essential to execution of the laws. Congress may provide as many

---

The 'Decision of 1789'

One of the major tasks facing the first Congress in 1789 was to set up the machinery needed to run the government. The Constitution provided the framework but the legislative measures adopted by the First Congress supplied the structure and organization for each of the branches.

Chief Justice William Howard Taft explained in the court's 1926 opinion in *Myers v. United States* why the court gave such weight to the "decision of 1789" concerning the president's removal power:

> We have devoted much space to this discussion and decision of the question of the presidential power of removal in the First Congress, not because a congressional conclusion on a constitutional issue is conclusive, but first because of our agreement with the reasons upon which it was avowedly based, second because this was the decision of the First Congress on a question of primary importance in the organization of the government made within two years after the Constitutional Convention and within a much shorter time after its ratification, and third because that Congress numbered among its leaders those who had been members of the convention. It must necessarily constitute a precedent upon which many future laws supplying the machinery of the new government would be based and, if erroneous, would be likely to evoke dissent and departure in future Congresses. It would come at once before the executive branch of the government for compliance and might well be brought before the judicial branch for a test of its validity. As we shall see, it was soon accepted as a final decision of the question by all branches of the government.

The "decision of 1789" related to a bill proposed by James Madison to establish an executive department of foreign affairs. It provided that the principal officer was "to be removed from office by the President of the United States." Debate over the removal clause led to a change in wording so that the bill finally read, "whenever the principal officer shall be removed by the President of the United States."

Taft's exhaustive analysis of the "decision of 1789" in *Myers* led to the majority's conclusion that this change reflected the understanding of the First Congress that the president had the sole power to remove executive branch officers.

Source: *Myers v. United States,* 272 U.S. 52 at 136-137 (1926).

or as few of them as it likes. It may place all of them beyond the President's control; but this would not suspend his duty concerning faithful execution of the laws. Removals, however important, are not so necessary as appointments.[17]

Brandeis wrote: "Power to remove . . . a high political officer might conceivably be deemed indispensable to democratic government and, hence, inherent in the President. But power to remove an inferior administrative officer . . . cannot conceivably be deemed an essential of government." [18]

Justice Holmes called the majority's arguments "a spider's web inadequate to control the dominant facts." Holmes noted that the postmaster's position was:

> . . .an office that owes its existence to Congress and that Congress may abolish tomorrow. Its duration and the pay attached to it while it lasts depend on Congress alone. Congress alone confers on the President the power to appoint to it and at any time may transfer the power to other hands. . . . The duty of the President to see that the laws be executed is a duty that does not go beyond the law or require him to achieve more than Congress sees fit to leave within his power.[19]

A few years later, the court adopted the *Myers'* dissenters' focus on the "nature of the office" to limit the broad reach of the removal power asserted in *Myers*.

The Case of the Federal Trade Commissioner

Nine years after the *Myers* ruling the court narrowed the scope of the president's removal power to include only "all purely executive offices." The court explicitly rejected the president's claim to inherent power to remove members of regulatory agencies.

William E. Humphrey was appointed to the Federal Trade Commission (FTC) by President Coolidge and reappointed by President Hoover. When Franklin D. Roosevelt became president, he wanted the conservative Humphrey off the commission in order to appoint a moderate Republican in his place. Roosevelt sought Humphrey's resignation, denied him a personal interview to discuss the matter and then decided to view a later communication from Humphrey as a resignation letter which Roosevelt made effective Oct. 7, 1933.

Humphrey challenged the president's action. He denied any intention to resign and claimed the president had violated the Constitution and the terms of the act that created the FTC. The FTC was an independent quasi-judicial body protected from political removal by the terms of its enabling statute. Members of the FTC were given 7-year terms by the act, with removal from office by the president limited to cause such as inefficiency, neglect of duty or malfeasance in office.

Roosevelt never claimed any wrongdoing on Humphrey's part. Humphrey sued for his salary, but died during the court proceedings; his executor pursued the litigation, now entitled *Humphrey's Executor v. United States.*[20]

The Decision. On May 27, 1935, the "Black Monday" of the court's battle with President Roosevelt over New Deal legislation, the court ruled for Humphrey's executor — and against Roosevelt.

Justice George Sutherland stated, for the unanimous court, that because the Federal Trade Commission was both a quasi-judicial and quasi-legislative body, it was not subject to the unlimited and absolute executive power of removal. The court not only denied the president power to remove members of independent regulatory agencies but also implied that other officers who performed functions not wholly executive in character might not be subject to executive removal.

Sutherland's opinion distinguished between the duties of a postmaster, such as Myers, and the responsibilities of a member of the Federal Trade Commission:

> . . .The office of a postmaster is so essentially unlike the office now involved that the decision in the *Myers* case cannot be accepted as controlling our decision here. A postmaster is an executive officer restricted to the performance of executive functions. He is charged with no duty at all related to either the legislative or judicial power. The actual decision in the *Myers* case finds support in the theory that such an officer is merely one of the units in the executive department, and, hence, inherently subject to the exclusive and illimitable power of removal by the Chief Executive, whose subordinate and aid he is. . . .[21]

The court discarded Taft's dicta in *Myers*, stating that:

> . . .the necessary reach of the decision goes far enough to include all purely executive officers. It goes no farther. . . . Much less does it include an officer who occupies no place in the executive department and who exercises no part of the executive power vested by the Constitution in the President.[22]

Sutherland then explained that the absolute executive removal power extended only to those officers whose functions are purely executive and that "illimitable power of removal is not possessed by the President" over FTC commissioners:

> . . .The authority of Congress, in creating quasi-legislative or quasi-judicial agencies, to require them to act independently of executive control cannot well be doubted; and that authority includes . . . power to fix the period during which they shall continue in office, and to forbid their removal except for cause in the meantime. For it is quite evident that one who holds his office only during the pleasure of another cannot be depended upon to maintain an attitude of independence against the latter's will.[23]

The court thus claimed for Congress the power to set the terms of office and conditions of removal for those offices whose functions were an amalgam of executive-legislative and judicial functions. The court thereby limited the executive removal power, declaring that the extent of that power depended upon the "nature of the office" involved.

> The fundamental necessity of maintaining each of the three general departments of government entirely free from the control or coercive influence, direct or indirect, of either of the others, has often been stressed and is hardly open to serious question. . . . The sound application of a principle that makes one master in his own house precludes him from imposing his control in the house of another. . . .
>
> The power of removal here claimed for the President falls within this principle, since its coercive influence threatens the independence of a commission,

which is not only wholly disconnected from the executive department, but which, as already fully appears, was created by Congress as a means of carrying into operation legislative and judicial powers, and as an agency of the legislative and judicial departments. . . . Whether the power of the president to remove an officer shall prevail over the authority of Congress to condition the power by fixing a definite term and precluding a removal except for cause, will depend upon the character of the office; the *Myers* decision, affirming the power of the President alone to make the removal, is confined to purely executive officers; and as to officers of the kind here under consideration, we hold that no removal can be made during the prescribed term for which the officer is appointed, except for one or more of the causes named in the applicable statute. . . .[24]

In Humphrey's case, Justice Felix Frankfurter wrote more than 20 years later, the court:

. . .drew a sharp line of cleavage between officials who were part of the Executive establishment and were thus removable by virtue of the President's constitutional powers, and those who are members of a body "to exercise its judgment without the leave or hindrance of any other official or any department of the government," . . .as to whom a power of removal exists only if Congress may fairly be said to have conferred it. This sharp differentiation derives from the difference in functions between those who are part of the Executive establishment and those whose tasks require absolute freedom from executive interference.[25]

The Morgan Case. The *Humphrey* decision, however, did not prevent President Roosevelt from removing someone from an office for which Congress had not set terms of removal.

In 1938, Dr. E. A. Morgan, chairman of the Tennessee Valley Authority (TVA), relied on the *Humphrey* ruling in challenging his removal by the president. A federal appeals court ruled that the TVA act did not limit the president's exercise of the removal power. Because the action by the president promoted the smooth functioning of the TVA, the court viewed the removal as within the president's duty to see that the laws were faithfully executed. The Supreme Court declined to review that decision.[26]

The Case of the War Claims Commissioner

In the *Humphrey's Executor* decision, the court seemed to rule that Congress must specify the terms and conditions of removal before courts would limit the executive power of removal. However, a case decided 23 years later extended the *Humphrey* doctrine to limit the president's power to remove quasi-judicial officers even where no specific statutory language set out the terms of their removal. The court thus reinforced the "nature of the office" approach to this question.

President Truman appointed three Democrats to the War Claims Commission, established to settle certain types of claims that grew out of World War II. The commission was to go out of business after it settled all claims. The law made no provision for removal of commissioners.

When President Eisenhower took office in 1953, he wanted to name three Republicans to the commission and so requested the resignations of the three Democratic members. They refused, and Eisenhower removed them.

One of the commissioners named Wiener sued for his salary in the U.S. Court of Claims, arguing that his removal was illegal. The court agreed that his duties had been quasi-judicial, but denied Wiener's claim, relying on the fact that the statute creating the commission had not limited the executive's power to remove its members.[27]

The *Humphrey* ruling did not apply, the court decided, because here there was no explicit statutory explication of the removal procedure for a claims commissioner.[28]

The Supreme Court, with Justice Frankfurter writing the opinion, ruled unanimously for Wiener. The court noted the similarity of facts in this case with the facts in Humphrey:

We start with one certainty. The problem of the President's power to remove members of agencies entrusted with duties of the kind with which the War Claims Commission was charged was within the lively knowledge of Congress. Few contests between Congress and the President have so recurringly had the attention of Congress as that pertaining to the power of removal. . . .

. . .The ground of President Eisenhower's removal of petitioner was precisely the same as President Roosevelt's removal of Humphrey. Both Presidents desired to have Commissioners, one on the Federal Trade Commission, the other on the War Claims Commission, "of my own selection." They wanted these Commissioners to be their men. The terms of removal in the two cases are identic [sic] and express the assumption that the agencies of which the two Commissioners were members were subject in the discharge of their duties to the control of the Executive. An analysis of the Federal Trade Commission Act left this Court in no doubt that such was not the conception of Congress in creating the Federal Trade Commission. The terms of the War Claims Act of 1948 leave no doubt that such was not the conception of Congress regarding the War Claims Commission. . . .[29]

"Few contests between Congress and the President have so recurringly had the attention of Congress as that pertaining to the power of removal. . . ."

—Justice Felix Frankfurter
Wiener v. United States, 1958

Frankfurter, after analyzing the law, concluded that Congress did not intend that the commissioners be subject to the threat of presidential removal:

If, as one must take for granted, the War Claims Act precluded the President from influencing the Commission in passing on a particular claim, *a fortiori* must it be inferred that Congress did not wish to have hang over the Commission the Damocles' sword of removal by the President for no reason other than that he preferred to have on that Commission men of his own choosing.

For such is this case. . . . Judging the matter in all the nakedness in which it is presented, namely, the claim that the President could remove a member of an adjudicatory body like the War Claims Commission merely because he wanted his own appointees on such a Commission, we are compelled to conclude that no such power is given to the President directly by the Constitution, and none is impliedly conferred upon him by statute simply because Congress said nothing about it. The philosophy of *Humphrey's Executor,* in its explicit language as well as its implication, precludes such a claim.[30]

Executive Discretion

Is the president's power to see that the laws are faithfully executed limited simply to carrying out the letter of the laws enacted by Congress? Or does he have power to act, beyond or in conflict with those laws, if he thinks the public interest demands it?

In general, executive practice and court decisions in the 20th century have tended to adopt the more expansive view of executive discretionary power, a view enhanced by the increasing practice of Congress of delegating power to the Executive Branch.

To Protect a Justice

One of the court's first rulings on this overall question of executive power occurred in 1890 in one of the more bizarre cases ever to come before the Supreme Court. Despite the absence of any authorizing statute, the court upheld the power of the president to provide federal protection for a Supreme Court justice whose life was threatened in the course of his judicial duties.

Sarah Althea Terry and her husband David, angry over a decision against their claim to an estate, threatened to kill Justice Stephen J. Field, who had led the panel of judges ruling against them. In response to these threats, the attorney general ordered federal marshals to protect Field. While he was in California on judicial business, Field was attacked by Terry. The deputy marshal protecting Field shot Terry and killed him. California tried to hold the marshal, a man by the name of Neagle, and charge him with murder under state law.

The Supreme Court ruled that California could not try Neagle, because the killing had occurred in the course of his duties under federal law — even though there was no particular federal law authorizing him to protect the justice. Thus the court ordered Neagle released from state custody.

Writing for the court, Justice Samuel F. Miller asked:

Is this duty [to take care that the laws be faithfully executed] limited to the enforcement of Acts of Congress or of treaties of the United States according to their *express terms,* or does it include the rights, duties and obligations growing out of the Constitution itself, our international relations, and all the protection implied by the nature of the government under the Constitution?[31]

The court's answer came as it implicitly adopted the latter view:

In the view we take of the Constitution of the United States, any obligation fairly and properly inferable from that instrument, or any duty of the marshal to be derived from the general scope of his duties under the laws of the United States, is "a law".... It would be a great reproach to the system of government of the

United States, declared to be within its sphere sovereign and supreme, if there is found within the domain of its powers no means of protecting the judges, in the conscientious and faithful discharge of their duties, from the malice and hatred of those upon whom their judgments may operate unfavorably."[32]

To Protect the Public Interest

This broad view of presidential power was reaffirmed by the court in 1915, with its decision in the case of the *United States v. Midwest Oil Co.*

By law, all public lands containing minerals were declared open to occupation, exploration and purchase by citizens. In 1909, however, President William Howard Taft withdrew from further public uses some three million acres in public lands containing oil deposits in order to preserve oil supplies for the use of the Navy.

This withdrawal was challenged by citizens who had subsequently explored and discovered oil on these lands; they cited the law declaring all such lands open to citizen exploration. But the court upheld the president's prerogative to withdraw the lands from private acquisition.

Justice Joseph R. Lamar cited historical precedent as the basis for upholding the president's action:

[The president] ... has, during the past eighty years, without express statutory — but under the claim of power to do so — made a multitude of Executive orders which operated to withdraw public land that would otherwise have been open to private acquisition. They affected every kind of land — mineral and non-mineral. . . .

The President was in a position to know when the public interest required particular portions of the people's lands to be withdrawn from entry or relocation; his action inflicted no wrong upon any private citizen, and being subject to disaffirmance by Congress, could occasion no harm to the interest of the public at large. Congress did not repudiate the power claimed or the withdrawal orders made. On the contrary, it uniformly and repeatedly acquiesced in the practice....

...Government is a practical affair, intended for practical men. Both officers, lawmakers and citizens naturally adjust themselves to any long-continued action of the Executive Department, on the presumption that unauthorized acts would not have been allowed to be so often repeated as to crystallize into a regular practice. . . .[33]

Delegation of Power

Congress vastly expanded the president's discretionary power in the late 19th and early 20th centuries by delegating authority to him, a process continued to the present.

In 1890, Congress provided for the duty-free admission of certain imported items, but gave the president the authority to impose duties on these items if the country of origin began to impose unreasonable duties on American-made goods. In 1892, the court, ruling in the case of *Field v. Clark,* upheld this congressional delegation of power: Congress furnished a remedy and authorized the president to decide when it should be applied. The court held that this delegation did not violate the separation of powers or result in executive lawmaking.[34]

In 1891, Congress authorized the president to set aside public lands in any state or territory as forest reservations.

A subsequent statute authorized the secretary of agriculture to administer these lands, and to make rules governing their use and occupancy. Violations of the rules were punishable by fines or imprisonment or both. This delegated power was challenged as unconstitutional.

The court upheld the president's authority, stating that:

> ...the authority to make administrative rules is not a delegation of legislative power, nor are such rules raised from an administrative level to a legislative character because the violation thereof is punishable as a public offense.[35]

Not until 1935 did the court invalidate a statute on the grounds that it constituted an improper delegation of power from Congress to the president. That ruling was followed with several in that term and the next which found New Deal legislation unconstitutional for this reason. *(Details, pp. 240-244)*

But after its turnabout on the New Deal in 1937, the court also returned to its generally approving view of congressional delegation, a view which has prevailed for more than 40 years.

Limits to Inherent Powers

If the court's rulings in *Neagle* and *Midwest Oil,* and its general inclination to back congressional delegation of power to the executive seemed to imply that there were no limits on the scope of the inherent powers a president could claim, that impression was dramatically corrected in 1952.

A divided court flatly rejected President Harry S Truman's claim of inherent power to seize the nation's steel mills in order to avoid disruption of steel production — and possible disruption of supplies to military forces in Korea. The executive order directing seizure of the mills explained that a work stoppage would jeopardize national defense.

Congress had decided against giving the president such seizure power in the Taft-Hartley Act, passed in 1947; and Truman chose to ignore other provisions of that law which might have been useful in the circumstances, relying instead on a broad view of inherent presidential power.

For the majority, Justice Hugo L. Black wrote that the president was improperly "making" the law he wished to execute:

> In the framework of our Constitution, the President's power to see that the laws are faithfully executed refutes the idea that he is to be a lawmaker. The Constitution limits his function in the lawmaking process to the recommending of laws he thinks wise and the vetoing of laws he thinks bad. . . .[36]

In a concurring opinion, Justice Robert H. Jackson commented:

> Loose and irresponsible use of adjectives colors all non-legal and much legal discussion of presidential powers. "Inherent" powers, "implied" powers, "incidental" powers, "plenary" powers, "war" powers and "emergency" powers are used, often interchangeably and without fixed or ascertainable meanings.
>
> The vagueness and generality of the clauses that set forth presidential powers afford a plausible basis for pressures within and without an adminstration for action beyond that supported by those whose responsibility it is to defend his actions in court. . . .[37]

Executives and Emergencies

The preservation of peace and order in the community is a requirement for successful execution of the laws. Disregard or disobedience of the laws may require the president to act to preserve the peace and restore order in the community.

Since 1792, presidents have possessed statutory authority to use troops to quell disorder when, in their judgment, the disorder hinders the execution of the laws.

Ever since the case of *Martin v. Mott,* decided in 1827, the Supreme Court has steadily backed the president's authority to decide when and if an emergency exists that requires the use of federal troops.

Justice Joseph Story's opinion in that case limited the exercise of the power to times of actual invasion or imminent danger thereof, but affirmed the president's authority "to decide whether the exigency has arisen." Moreover, Story wrote, the decision "belongs exclusively to the president, and . . . his decision is conclusive upon all other persons." [38]

Chief Justice Roger B. Taney reaffirmed the president's authority in such matters in the case of *Luther v. Borden.* Explaining that the president's decision to use troops to keep order was beyond the authority of judges to question, he wrote:

> . . .Judicial power presupposes an established government capable of enacting laws and enforcing their execution. . . . The acceptance of the judicial office is a recognition of the authority of the government from which it is derived. . . .[39]

In emergencies, the president may employ several means short of calling out federal troops. President Jefferson used the *posse comitatus* (a body of persons summoned to assist in the preservation of public peace) to enforce the embargo. President Franklin Pierce's attorney general ruled that federal marshals could command citizens' aid to enforce the Fugitive Slave Act of 1850. During the "bleeding Kansas" episode in the pre-Civil War strife over slavery in the territories, Pierce placed military forces in Kansas under the control of federal marshals to be used as a *posse* to prevent further bloodshed. The most extraordinary *posse* was the group of 75,000 volunteers summoned by Lincoln to suppress the "civil disorder" in 1861. President Eisenhower invoked the same provisions when he dispatched troops to Little Rock, Arkansas, to enforce court-ordered desegregation at Little Rock high school. The court never challenged Eisenhower's action, but in *Cooper v. Aaron* it rejected arguments by opponents of the president's decision who contended that the "faithful execution" clause was not a grant of authority to use federal troops to enforce federal court decrees because they were not statutes and, therefore, not laws of the United States. [40]

President Cleveland and the Pullman Strike

Presidents have used troops to quell labor strikes and attendant civil disorders that threatened the public safety, or disrupted services and functions under federal jurisdiction.

One of the most hotly contested of those assertions of presidential power arose after a strike against the Pullman railroad car company in 1894 paralyzed rail traffic west of Chicago, Illinois. Workers at the Pullman car works went on strike because of a wage reduction order. Members of the

When Executives Disagree...

Chief executives do not always agree on the proper course of action to take in times of civil disorder and emergency, particularly when politics may intervene. President Grover Cleveland's unilateral decision to send troops to Chicago during the 1894 Pullman strike prompted an angry and indignant reply from Illinois Governor John Peter Altgeld. The governor had not requested federal troops, and he claimed Cleveland's action was "unnecessary" and "unjustifiable."

Executive Office, State of Illinois
July 5, 1894.
Hon. Grover Cleveland, President of the United States, Washington, D.C.

Sir: — I am advised that you have ordered Federal troops to go into service in the State of Illinois. Surely the facts have not been correctly presented to you in this case, or you would not have taken this step, for it is entirely unnecessary, and, as it seems to me, unjustifiable. Waiving all questions of courtesy, I will say that the State of Illinois is not only able to take care of itself, but it stands ready to furnish the Federal government any assistance it may need elsewhere. Our military force is ample, and consists of as good soldiers as can be found in the country. . . . [B]ut they have not been ordered out because nobody in Cook county, whether official or private citizen, asked to have their assistance, or even intimated in any way that their assistance was desired or necessary. . . .

I repeat that you have been imposed upon in this matter; but even if by a forced construction it were held that the conditions here came within the letter of the statute, then I submit that local self-government is a fundamental principle of our Constitution. . . .

To absolutely ignore a local government in matters of this kind, when the local government is ready to furnish assistance needed, and is amply able to enforce the law, not only insults the people of this State by imputing to them an inability to govern themselves, or an unwillingness to enforce the law, but is in violation of a basic principle of our institutions. The question of Federal supremacy is in no way involved. No one disputes it for a moment; but, under our Constitution, Federal supremacy and local self-government must go hand in hand, and to ignore the latter is to do violence to the Constitution. . . .

I have the honor to be, yours respectfully,
JOHN P. ALTGELD, Governor of Illinois.

Executive Mansion, Washington, D.C.,
July 5, 1894.
Hon. John P. Altgeld, Governor of Illinois, Springfield, Ill.

Sir: — Federal troops were sent to Chicago in strict accordance with the Constitution and laws of the United States, upon the demand of the post office department that obstruction of the mails should be removed, and upon the representations of the judicial officers of the United States that the process of the Federal courts could not be executed through the ordinary means, and upon competent proof that conspiracies existed against commerce between the States. To meet these conditions, which are clearly within the province of Federal authority, the presence of Federal troops in the city of Chicago was deemed not only proper, but necessary, and there has been no intention of thereby interfering with the plain duty of the local authorities to preserve the peace of the city.

Grover Cleveland.

Executive Office, State of Illinois,
July 6, 1894.
Hon. Grover Cleveland, President of the United States,

Sir: — Your answer to my protest involves some startling conclusions and ignores and evades the question at issue — that is, that the principle of local self-government is just as fundamental in our institutions as is that of Federal supremacy.

First — You calmly assume that the executive has the legal right to order Federal troops into any community of the United States, in the first instance, whenever there is the slightest disturbance, and that he can do this without any regard to the question as to whether that community is able and ready to enforce the law itself. Inasmuch as the executive is the sole judge of the question as to whether any disturbance exists in any part of the country, this assumption means that the executive can send Federal troops into any community in the United States at his pleasure, and keep them there as long as he chooses. If this is the law, then the principle of self-government either never did exist in this country or else has been destroyed. . . .

Second — It is also a fundamental principle in our government that except in times of war the military shall be subordinate to the civil authority. . . . [T]he State troops are ordered out to act under and with the civil authorities. The troops you have ordered to Chicago are not under the civil authorities, and are in no way responsible to them for their conduct. . . .

Inasmuch as the Federal troops can do nothing but what the State troops can do there, and believing that the State is amply able to . . . enforce the law, and believing that the ordering out of the Federal troops was unwarranted, I again ask their withdrawal.

John P. Altgeld

Executive Mansion, Washington, D.C.
July 6, 1894.
While I am still persuaded that I have neither transcended my authority nor duty in the emergency that confronts us, it seems to me that in this hour of danger and public distress, discussion may well give way to active efforts on the part of all in authority to restore obedience to law and to protect life and property.

Grover Cleveland.
Hon. John P. Altgeld,
Governor of Illinois.

Source: Henry S. Commager, ed. *Documents of American History* 7th ed. (Appleton-Century-Crofts, New York, 1963), pp. 609-612.

American Railway Union, with the support of its president, Eugene V. Debs, carried out a secondary boycott against the Pullman company by refusing to service Pullman sleeping cars attached to trains. The mood of the strikers and collisions between strikers and men hired by Pullman to protect company property threatened violence.

President Grover Cleveland dispatched federal troops to Chicago to preserve peace and ordered the U.S. attorney in the city to seek an order halting the Debs boycott on the basis that the strike crippled interstate commerce and interfered with delivery of the mail.

Debs and his associates ignored the court order. They were arrested, convicted of contempt, and sentenced to prison. Debs then petitioned the Supreme Court for a writ of *habeas corpus*. He challenged his detention as illegal because the court order he was charged with ignoring rested on no statutory basis.

Affirming broad executive power to deal with such emergencies the court refused to issue the writ, thereby upholding Debs' conviction. For the court, Justice David J. Brewer wrote:

> . . .The entire strength of the nation may be used to enforce in any part of the land the full and free exercise of all national powers and the security of all rights entrusted by the Constitution to its care. The strong arm of the national government may be put forth to brush away all obstructions to the freedom of interstate commerce or the transportation of the mails. If the emergency arises, the army of the nation, and all its militia, are at the service of the nation to compel obedience to its laws. . . .

> We do not care to place our decision upon this ground alone. Every government, entrusted by the very terms of its being with powers and duties to be exercised and discharged for the general welfare, has a right to apply to its own courts for any proper assistance in the exercise of the one and the discharge of the other. . . .

> . . .it is obvious from these decisions that while it is not the province of the government to interfere in any matter of private controversy between individuals, or to use its great powers to enforce the rights of one against another, yet, whenever the wrongs complained of are such as affect the public at large, and are in respect of matters which by the Constitution are entrusted to the care of the nation, and concerning which the nation owes the duty to all the citizens of securing to them their common rights, then the mere fact that the government has no pecuniary interest in the controversy is not sufficient to exclude it from the courts, or prevent it from taking measures therein to fully discharge those constitutional duties.[41]

Even after Congress restricted the use of injunctions against labor unions these restrictions were not held to forbid government-sought orders to seize and operate mines in the face of a strike, nor did it forbid mine operators from getting court orders preventing government seizures.[42]

Perhaps the best summary of the court's view of executive power in an emergency was set out by the court in a case involving the actions of a state governor in the emergency:

> When it comes to a decision by the head of the State upon a matter involving its life, the ordinary rights of individuals must yield to what he deems the necessities of the moment. Public danger warrants the substitution of executive process for judicial process.[43]

Footnotes

[1] *Myers v. United States,* 272 U.S. 52 (1926).

[2] *Wilcox v. McConnel,* 13 Pet. 498 at 513 (1839).

[3] *Williams v. United States,* 1 How. 290 at 297 (1843).

[4] *Marbury v. Madison,* 1 Cr. 137 (1803).

[5] *United States v. Smith,* 286 U.S. 6 (1932).

[6] C. Herman Pritchett, *The American Constitution* (New York: McGraw-Hill Book Co., 1959), p. 319.

[7] *Myers v. United States,* 272 U.S. 52 at 114 (1926).

[8] *Wiener v. United States,* 357 U.S. 349 at 351 (1958).

[9] James D. Richardson, ed., *Messages and Papers of the Presidents,* 20 vols. (New York: Bureau of National Literature Inc., 1897), III:1304.

[10] *Ex parte Hennen,* 13 Pet. 230 at 257-259 (1839).

[11] Carl B. Swisher, *American Constitutional Development,* 2d ed. (Cambridge, Mass.: Houghton Mifflin Co., 1954), p. 742.

[12] Ibid. at 743.

[13] *Myers v. United States,* 272 U.S. 52 at 174-175 (1926).

[14] Id. at 117, 121-122, 130-134.

[15] Id. at 134.

[16] Id. at 135.

[17] Id. at 192-93.

[18] Id. at 247.

[19] Id. at 177.

[20] *Humphrey's Executor v. United States,* 295 U.S. 602 at 618-619 (1935).

[21] Id. at 627.

[22] Id. at 627-28.

[23] Id. at 629.

[24] Id. at 629-32.

[25] *Wiener v. United States,* 357 U.S. 349 at 353 (1958).

[26] *Morgan v. TVA,* 312 U.S. 701 (1941) cert. denied; C. Herman Pritchett, *The Tennessee Valley Authority: A Study in Public Administration* (Chapel Hill, N.C.: University of North Carolina Press, 1943), pp. 203-16.

[27] *Wiener v. United States,* 357 U.S. 349 (1958).

[28] Id. at 352.

[29] Id. at 353, 354.

[30] Id. at 356.

[31] *In re Neagle,* 135 U.S. 1 at 64 (1890).

[32] Id. at 59.

[33] *United States v. Midwest Oil Co.,* 236 U.S. 459 at 469, 472-473 (1915).

[34] *Field v. Clark,* 143 U.S. 649 (1892).

[35] *United States v. Grimaud,* 220 U.S. 506 at 521 (1911).

[36] *Youngstown Sheet and Tube Co. v. Sawyer,* 343 U.S. 579 at 587 (1952).

[37] Id. at 646-647.

[38] *Martin v. Mott,* 12 Wheat. 19 at 28 (1827).

[39] *Luther v. Borden,* 7 How. 1 at 40 (1849).

[40] *Cooper v. Aaron,* 358 U.S. 1 at 4, 18-19 (1958).

[41] *In re Debs,* 158 U.S. 564 at 582, 584, 586 (1895).

[42] *Youngstown Sheet and Tube Co. v. Sawyer,* 343 U.S. 579 (1952); *United States v. United Mine Workers,* 330 U.S. 258 (1947).

[43] *Moyer v. Peabody,* 212 U.S. 78 at 84-85 (1909).

The Power To Veto And To Pardon

The Constitution equips the president with two means of nullifying particular actions of the other branches of the government: the veto and the pardon.

By use of the veto, a president may kill a measure which Congress has already approved. A veto spells death for a bill, unless each chamber can muster a two-thirds vote in its favor to override the veto.

This quasi-legislative device has developed from an infrequently used tool wielded only against unconstitutional or defective laws into a policy weapon often used in the political struggles between the White House and Congress over the proper shape of legislation.

The pardon power, on the other hand, permits the president to reduce sentences, remit penalties or entirely exempt individuals and classes of persons from sentences imposed by the courts. The only express limitation on the pardon power is that persons impeached may not be pardoned.

This power has been sparingly exercised, and generally, occasions of its use draw little public notice.

The Veto Power

President Franklin D. Roosevelt, who vetoed more bills in all than any other president, is said to have told his aides on more than one occasion, "Give me a bill that I can veto," as a reminder to Congress that every bill which it approves faces possible rejection by the president.[1] While measures occasionally are challenged before the Supreme Court, every bill has to pass political muster in the Oval Office.

Article I of the Constitution provides that the president may veto a bill by returning it to the house of its origin unsigned and accompanied by a statement of objections to the measure. The veto kills the bill unless it is overridden by a two-thirds majority vote of the members of each house.

Perhaps because the Congress and the White House generally accept the politically determined outcome of veto battles, the Supreme Court has never been called upon to judge the validity of a direct veto.

But Article I also provides that:

If any bill shall not be returned by the President within ten days (Sundays excepted) after it shall have been presented to him, the same shall be a law, in like manner as if he had signed it, unless the Congress by their adjournment prevent its return, in which case it shall not be a law.

The section permits a bill to become a law without the president's signature, presumably a measure the president disapproves of but finds it impolitic to veto.

With Congress adjourned, however, the president's failure to sign a bill constitutes an absolute "pocket" veto over the measure because Congress has no opportunity to override the veto. The Supreme Court's only significant decisions on the veto power have attempted to clarify the conditions under which a pocket veto can be used.

Alexander Hamilton considered the "qualified negative" of the veto a shield against encroachment on executive power by the legislative branch and a barrier to hasty enactment of "improper laws."[2] Hamilton viewed the veto power as a means of improving the spirit of cooperation between the president and the Congress, producing further reflection on measures. He argued that the qualified veto was less harsh than an absolute veto. Hamilton declared that the framers:

> . . .have pursued a mean in this business [the veto power], which will both facilitate the exercise of the power vested in this respect in the executive magistrate, and make its efficacy to depend on the sense of a considerable part of the legislative body. . . . A direct and categorical negative has something in the appearance of it more harsh, and more apt to irritate, than the mere suggestion of argumentative objections to be approved or disapproved by those to whom they are addressed.[3]

Presidents and the Veto Power

Use of the veto power has varied, greatly, from president to president. The first six presidents vetoed only ten measures in their entire administrations, usually on constitutional grounds or because of technical flaws in the legislation. Andrew Jackson, however, began to use the veto as a political device to defeat measures he opposed as a matter of political principle, although he vetoed only twelve measures in eight years.

In the entire period up to the Civil War, only 52 bills were vetoed and no presidential veto was overridden until 1866.

President Andrew Johnson used the veto in his battle with Radical Republicans in Congress over control of Reconstruction. Johnson's vetoes were overridden 15 times.

Eight presidents never cast any vetoes, although the most recent of those was President James A. Garfield.

During the late 19th century, many presidential vetoes were cast to block private bills and "pork barrel" legislation.

Presidents Grover Cleveland and Franklin D. Roosevelt cast the most vetoes. Roosevelt cast 631 negatives and Cleveland 584.

Many of Cleveland's vetoes pertained to private bills that awarded individuals pensions or other government benefits.

The New Deal and World War II broadened the scope of legislative activity and brought greater complexity to government legislation, which resulted in a greater number of vetoes cast on substantive legislative measures. Until Roosevelt vetoed a revenue bill it had been assumed that tax measures were exempt from presidential veto.

In all, presidents vetoed 2,342 measures between 1789 and June 30, 1976, with all but 58 of the vetoes cast after 1860. The direct veto had been used 1,355 times, the pocket veto 987. Only 86 times in that period did Congress override a veto.[4]

The Pocket Veto

The Supreme Court's major ruling on the veto power came in 1929 as it attempted to clarify the Constitution's intent with respect to the president's use of the pocket veto.

In the *Pocket Veto Case* of 1929, the court ruled that a bill must be returned to a sitting chamber of Congress. Thus the pocket veto could be used any time that the chamber of a bill's origin was not in session on the tenth day following submission of the bill to the chief executive. Subsequent rulings, however, have undercut both points.

The Pocket Veto Case

A bill giving certain Indian tribes the right to file claims in the U.S. Court of Claims cleared Congress and was sent to President Calvin Coolidge for his signature June 24, 1926.

When the first session of the 69th Congress adjourned nine days later, on July 3, Coolidge had neither signed nor returned the bill. He subsequently took no action on the measure and assumed he had pocket-vetoed it. Congress did not reconvene until December, when the second session began.

Certain Indian tribes in Washington state sought to file claims under the measure, arguing that it had become law without the president's signature because Coolidge had not vetoed it. They argued that a pocket veto could only be used between Congresses, when there was no Congress in existence. The word "adjournment" they read to mean only the final adjournment of a Congress, not simply an adjournment between sessions.

Furthermore, they argued, the "ten days" allowed the president to consider and sign or return legislation meant ten legislative, not calendar, days. Under this interpretation, the ten-day period for this particular bill would have run from June 24 until December 1926.[5]

The Supreme Court rejected those arguments, holding that a pocket veto could properly be used between sessions of Congress. The court concluded that "adjournment" included interim adjournments. Justice Edward T. Sanford wrote the court's opinion in which he described the president's exercise of the pocket veto power:

The Constitution in giving the President a qualified negative over legislation — commonly called a veto — entrusts him with an authority and imposes

upon him an obligation that are of the highest importance, in the execution of which it is made his duty not only to sign bills that he approves in order that they may become law, but to return bills that he disapproves, with his objections, in order that they may be reconsidered by Congress. The faithful and effective exercise of this momentous duty necessarily requires time in which the President may carefully examine and consider a bill and determine, after due deliberation, whether he should approve or disapprove it, and if he disapproves it, formulate his objections for the consideration of Congress. To that end a specified time is given, after the bill has been presented to him, in which he may examine its provisions and either approve it or return it, not approved, for reconsideration . . . . The power thus conferred upon the President cannot be narrowed or cut down by Congress, nor the time within which it is to be exercised lessened, directly or indirectly. And it is just as essential a part of the constitutional provisions, guarding against ill-considered and unwise legislation, that the President, on his part, should have the full time allowed him for determining whether he should approve or disapprove a bill, and if disapproved, for adequately formulating the objections that should be considered by Congress, as it is that Congress, on its part, should have an opportunity to repass the bill over his objections.[6]

Justice Sanford noted that the failure of the bill in question to become law could not "properly be ascribed to the disapproval of the President — who presumably would have returned it before the adjournment if there had been sufficient time in which to complete his consideration and take such action but is attributable solely to the action of Congress in adjourning before the time allowed the President for returning the bill had expired."[7] Moreover, the term "days" meant calendar and not legislative days:

The word "days," when not qualified, means in ordinary and common usage calendar days. This is obviously the meaning in which it is used in the constitutional provision, and is emphasized by the fact that "Sundays" are excepted.[8]

On the question of "adjournment", Sanford wrote:

We think under the constitutional provision the determinative question in reference to an "adjournment" is not whether it is a final adjournment of Congress or an interim adjournment, such as the adjournment of the first session, but whether it is one that "prevents" the President from returning the bill to the House in which it originated within the time allowed. It is clear, we understand, it is not questioned, that since the President may return a bill at any time within the alloted period, he is prevented from returning it, within the meaning of the constitutional provision if by reason of the adjournment it is impossible for him to return it to the House in which it originated on the last day of that period. . . .

We find no substantial basis for the suggestion that although the House in which the bill originated is not in session the bill may nevertheless be returned, consistently with the constitutional mandate, by delivering it, with the President's objections, to an officer or agent of the House, for subsequent delivery to the House when it resumes its sittings at the next session, with the same force and effect as if the bill had been returned to the House on the day it was delivered to such officer or agent. Aside from the fact that Congress has never enacted any statute authorizing any officer or agent of either House to receive for it bills returned by the President during its adjournment, and that there is no rule to that. effect in either House, the delivery of the bill to such officer or agent, even if authorized by Congress itself, would not comply with the constitutional mandate. . . . In short it was plainly the object of the constitutional provision that there should be a timely return of the bill, which should not only be a matter of official record . . . but should enable Congress to proceed immediately with its reconsideration; and that the return of the bill should be an actual and public return to the House itself, and not a fictitious return by a delivery of the bill to some individual which could be given a retroactive effect at a later date when the time for the return of the bill to the House had expired.[9]

The *Wright* Case

Within a decade, the broad sweep of the court's ruling in the *Pocket Veto* cases was limited by a later court decision. In 1938, in the case of *Wright v. United States*, the court held that during a short recess of one chamber — the one to which a vetoed bill must be returned — an official of that chamber could receive a veto message to deliver to the chamber after the recess. Thus, a pocket veto could not be used in those circumstances.[10]

In that case, the court said that the statement in the *Pocket Veto* ruling that a bill must be returned to a sitting chamber "should not be construed so narrowly as to demand that the President must select a precise moment when the House is within the walls of its chambers and that a return is absolutely impossible during a recess however temporary." [11]

In recent years, it has become a routine practice for the House and Senate to appoint their Clerk or Secretary to receive messages from the president during a recess.

The Nixon Pocket Vetoes

President Nixon in December 1970 pocket-vetoed the Family Practice of Medicine Act which would have provided $225 million in support for hospital and medical school programs. The measure was sent to the White House eight days before a six-day Christmas recess. Nixon later announced that he had pocket-vetoed the measure.

In 1973, a federal district judge in the District of Columbia ruled that the veto was invalid because the six-day recess was too brief to justify its use. The court held that the brief adjournment did not prevent Nixon from returning the bill.

In 1976, a second Nixon pocket veto was struck down by a federal court. His veto of the amended Federal Highway Act of 1973 was held invalid. The reason again cited by the court was that both chambers approved agents to receive such messages during the interim period. The government did not appeal.

The effect of these two lower court rulings was to limit the use of the pocket veto to final adjournments, thus nullifying to a great extent the Supreme Court's pronouncement in the *Pocket Veto Case.* [12]

The Power To Sign Bills

For 150 years presidents went to Capitol Hill on the last day of the legislative session in order that they might sign all approved bills by the end of the congressional session.

The custom was based in part upon the belief that all legislative power, including the president's power to sign legislation, expired with the end of a session. It meant, however, that certain bills received only hasty consideration by the president.[1]

Near the conclusion of the June 1920 congressional session President Woodrow Wilson asked the attorney general to determine if bills might be constitutionally approved within the ten days following adjournment. The attorney general reported affirmatively, and Wilson accordingly signed bills into law during this period after an interim adjournment.[2]

At the end of the final 1931 congressional session, President Herbert Hoover, on the advice of his attorney general, began the practice of signing measures after final adjournment.[3] On March 5, 1931, the day after Congress adjourned, Hoover signed a bill.[4] The question of its validity resulted in a Supreme Court decision upholding the president's action.

The court cited:

> . . .the fundamental purpose of the constitutional provision to provide appropriate opportunity for the President to consider the bills presented to him. The importance of maintaining that opportunity unimpaired increases as bills multiply.[5]

The court noted that in the week prior to adjournment 269 bills were sent to the president, of which 184 reached his desk on the last day of the session.[6] The court found no reason why the time for the president's consideration of bills should be cut short because Congress had adjourned:

> No public interest would be conserved by the requirement of hurried and inconsiderate examination of bills in the closing hours of a session, with the result that bills may be approved which **on further consideration would be disapproved.**[7]

The court has not decided, however, whether bills passed less than ten days before the end of a president's term may be approved or vetoed by an incoming president. *Dicta* in the 1932 case suggested that the incoming president would not approve such a bill because it was not submitted to him, but to the previous president. President Truman, however, signed bills sent to the White House before President Roosevelt's death. His authority to do so was not challenged.

[1] Carl B. Swisher, *American Constitutional Development,* 2nd ed. (Cambridge, Mass.: Houghton Mifflin Co., 1954), p. 785.
[2] Ibid., p. 786.
[3] Ibid.
[4] *Edwards v. United States*, 286 U.S. 482 at 493 (1932).
[5] Ibid.
[6] Id.
[7] Id.

The Power to Grant Pardons and Reprieves

With the single exception of persons impeached, the Constitution gives the president the unlimited power "to grant Reprieves and Pardons for Offences against the United States. . . ." A pardon is an exemption from sentence and guilt; a reprieve is the suspension of a sentence or other legally imposed penalties for a temporary period.

The Supreme Court has supported the president's discretion to exercise the pardon power against all challenges. A pardon may be full or partial, absolute or conditional, or general. The president may attach conditions to a pardon, the court has held, so long as they are not contrary to the Constitution or federal laws. [13]

Although acceptance of a pardon is generally considered a necessary act, conditional pardons — and commutations — have been upheld against challenge by the person pardoned. The effect of a full pardon, the court has held, is to end the punishment and blot out the guilt "so that in the eyes of the law the offender is as innocent as if he had never committed the offence." [14]

The early view of the pardon power was set out by Chief Justice John Marshall, who defined a pardon as an act of grace. [15] But a century later, the individual act of mercy had become, as well, in the words of Justice Oliver Wendell Holmes Jr., "part of the Constitutional scheme." [16]

Presidents have issued pardons and granted amnesty — a general pardon to groups or communities — since President Washington issued a general amnesty to the western Pennsylvania "whiskey rebels" in 1795.

The most famous pardon in American history to date was that granted by President Gerald R. Ford on Sept. 8, 1974, to his predecessor, former President Richard M. Nixon, who had resigned the presidency amid allegations of his involvement in crimes related to the Watergate cover-up.

That pardon was "full, free and absolute . . . for all offenses against the United States which he . . . has committed or may have committed" as president. [17] Former President Nixon accepted the pardon with a statement describing it as a "compassionate act." *(Text of pardon, box p. 225)*

The framers of the Constitution granted the president of the United States a pardon power similar to that exercised by the kings of England. [18]

Alexander Hamilton, writing in *The Federalist Papers,* advocated that the use of this power be unfettered:

> Humanity and good policy conspire to dictate that the benign prerogative of pardoning should be as little as possible fettered or embarrassed. The criminal code of every country partakes so much of necessary severity, that without an easy access to exceptions in favor of unfortunate guilt, justice would wear a countenance too sanguinary and cruel. [19]

Acceptance

In one of the court's first rulings on the pardon power, Chief Justice John Marshall stated that acceptance of a pardon by the recipient was a necessary condition of its taking effect. In the case of *United States v. Wilson,* decided in 1833, Marshall wrote:

> A pardon is an act of grace, proceeding from the power entrusted with the execution of the laws, which exempts the individual, on whom it is bestowed, from the punishment the law inflicts for a crime he has committed. It is the private, though official act of the executive magistrate, delivered to the individual for whose benefit it is intended, and not communicated officially to the court. . . . A pardon is a deed, to the validity of which delivery is essential, and delivery is not complete without acceptance. It may then be rejected by the person to whom it is tendered; and if it be rejected, we have discovered no power in a court to force it on him. A pardon may be conditional, and the condition may be more objectionable than the punishment inflicted by the judgment. [20]

This opinion reflected the common-law tradition which viewed the sovereign's pardon as an act of grace — and the common English practice that a pardon or commutation was often granted on the condition that the convicted felon move to another place.

In 1915, the court reaffirmed Marshall's view of the need for acceptance of a pardon. The decision came in the case of *Burdick v. United States.* [21]

George Burdick, city editor of the *New York Tribune,* refused to testify before a federal grand jury investigating customs fraud, saying that his testimony would tend to incriminate him. President Woodrow Wilson then offered Burdick a full and unconditional pardon in connection with any matters he might be questioned about.

Burdick refused the pardon, refused again to testify, and was imprisoned for contempt. But a unanimous Supreme Court upheld his right to reject the pardon, citing Marshall's 1833 opinion.

Justice Joseph McKenna, writing for the court, explained the risk of implied guilt in the granting of pardons to individuals who, although not convicted of a crime, nevertheless accepted a pardon:

> . . . the grace of a pardon . . . may be only in pretense or seeming . . . involving consequences of even greater disgrace than those from which it purports to relieve. Circumstances may be made to bring innocence under the penalties of the law. If so brought, escape by confession of guilt implied in the acceptance of a pardon may be rejected. . . . [22]

The Effect of a Pardon

The leading case defining the effect of a presidential pardon came just after the Civil War. The case involved one of the nation's leading attorneys, southerner Augustus H. Garland, and an 1865 act of Congress which required all attorneys who wished to practice in the Supreme Court and other federal courts to take an oath that declared that they had not aided the Confederate cause by word or deed. [23]

Garland had practiced before the Supreme Court prior to the war. When Arkansas, his home state, joined the Confederacy, he followed the state and served in the Confederate congress. Under the "test oath" requirement imposed by the 1865 law, Garland was forever disqualified from resuming his legal practice before the federal courts.

In July 1865, however, Garland received a full pardon from President Andrew Johnson for all offenses committed, direct or implied, in the Civil War. Garland cited the pardon and asked for permission to practice in federal court although he was still unable, due to his service to the Confederacy, to take the test oath.

Garland argued that the disqualifying Act of Congress, so far as it affected him, was unconstitutional and void as a bill of attainder prohibited by the Constitution. Beyond that, he argued that even if the act was constitutional, the pardon released him from compliance with its provisions.[24]

'The Benign Prerogative of Mercy'

The Supreme Court ruled for Garland on both points. For the first time in the case of *Ex parte Garland*, it struck down an act of Congress by the narrow margin of a 5-4 vote. The majority found the test oath law unconstitutional as a bill of attainder and an *ex post facto* law. *(See box on constitutional limits on Congress, pp. 76-77)*

But even if the law were valid wrote Justice Stephen J. Field for the majority, the pardon placed Garland "beyond the reach of punishment of any kind" for his Civil War role. "It is not within the constitutional power of Congress thus to inflict punishment beyond the reach of executive clemency," Field wrote.[25]

Field then went on to look at the presidential pardon power and its effect on the recipient and on Congress:

> The power thus conferred is unlimited, with the exception stated [impeachment]. It extends to every offence known to the law, and may be exercised at any time after its commission, either before legal proceedings are taken, or during their pendency, or after conviction and judgement. This power of the President is not subject to legislative control. Congress can neither limit the effect of his pardon, nor exclude from its exercise any class of offenders. The benign prerogative of mercy reposed in him cannot be fettered by any legislative restrictions.[26]

Having established the unlimited nature of the president's pardoning power, Field discussed the effect of a presidential pardon on the recipient:

> A pardon reaches both the punishment prescribed for the offense and the guilt of the offender; and when the pardon is full, it releases the punishment and blots out of existence the guilt, so that in the eye of the law the offender is as innocent as if he had never committed the offence. If granted before conviction, it prevents any of the penalties and disabilities consequent upon conviction from attaching; if granted after conviction, it removes the penalties and disabilities, and restores him to all his civil rights; it makes him, as it were, a new man, and gives him a new credit and capacity.[27]

In Dissent

The dissenters, in an opinion written by Justice Samuel F. Miller, focused on the initial question of the constitutionality of the disqualifying law: whether it was an *ex post facto* law and whether Congress could pass laws to ensure the character and loyalty of the nation's lawyers. They found the law a proper exercise of congressional power, and disagreed that the pardon put Garland beyond its reach:

> The right to practice law in the courts . . . is a privilege granted by the law . . . not an absolute right . . . the presidential pardon relieves the party from all

---

Nixon Pardon Proclamation

Following is the text of the proclamation by which President Gerald R. Ford Sept. 8, 1974, pardoned former President Richard M. Nixon:

Richard Nixon became the thirty-seventh President of the United States on January 20, 1969, and was re-elected in 1972 for a second term by the electors of forty-nine of the fifty states. His term in office continued until his resignation on August 9, 1974.

Pursuant to resolutions of the House of Representatives, its Committee on the Judiciary conducted an inquiry and investigation on the impeachment of the President extending over more than eight months. The hearings of the committee and its deliberations, which received wide national publicity over television, radio, and in printed media, resulted in votes adverse to Richard Nixon on recommended articles of impeachment.

As a result of certain acts or omissions occurring before his resignation from the office of President, Richard Nixon has become liable to possible indictment and trial for offenses against the United States. Whether or not he shall be so prosecuted depends on findings of the appropriate grand jury and on the discretion of the authorized prosecutor. Should an indictment ensue, the accused shall then be entitled to a fair trial by an impartial jury, as guaranteed to every individual by the Constitution.

It is believed that a trial of Richard Nixon, if it became necessary, could not fairly begin until a year or more has elapsed. In the meantime, the tranquility to which this nation has been restored by the events of recent weeks could be irreparably lost by the prospects of bringing to trial a former President of the United States. The prospects of such trial will cause prolonged and divisive debate over the propriety of exposing to further punishment and degradation a man who has already paid the unprecedented penalty of relinquishing the highest elective office in the United States.

Now, therefore, I, Gerald R. Ford, President of the United States, pursuant to the pardon power conferred upon me by Article II, Section 2, of the Constitution, have granted and by these presents do grant a full, free, and absolute pardon unto Richard Nixon for all offenses against the United States which he, Richard Nixon, has committed or may have committed or taken part in during the period from January 20, 1969, through August 9, 1974.

In witness whereof, I have hereunto set my hand this 8th day of September in the year of Our Lord Nineteen Hundred Seventy-Four, and of the independence of the United States of America the 199th.

---

the penalties, or in other words, from all the punishment, which the law inflicted for his offence. But it relieves him from nothing more. If the oath required as a condition to practising law is not a punishment, as I think I have shown it is not, then the pardon of the President has no effect in releasing him from the requirement to take it. If it is a qualification which Congress had a right to prescribe as necessary to an attorney, then the President, cannot, by pardon or otherwise, dispense with the law requiring such qualification.

This is not only the plain rule as between the legislative and executive departments of the government, but it is the declaration of common sense. The man who, by counterfeiting, by theft, by murder, or by treason, is rendered unfit to exercise the functions of an attorney or counselor-at-law, may be saved by the executive pardon from the penitentiary or the gallows, but is not thereby restored to the qualifications which are essential to admission to the bar. No doubt it will be found that very many persons among those who cannot take this oath, deserved to be relieved from the prohibition of the law; but this in no wise depends upon the act of the President in giving or refusing a pardon. It remains to the legislative power alone to prescribe under what circumstances this relief shall be extended.[28]

The court thus allowed former Confederates to resume the practice of law in the nation's federal courts. The decision produced a furor in the north and led to legislative efforts to reform the court. Reacting to the ruling, Congress considered barring all ex-Confederates from the practice of law, but the bill was not approved. Garland later became Attorney General of the United States, during the administration of President Grover Cleveland.

Broad, But Not Perpetual

Despite the broad effect of a pardon on a person convicted of or under investigation for a crime, the court has held that a pardon cannot protect an individual who is convicted of a second post-pardon crime.

A New York court tried and convicted a person whose first federal offense had been pardoned. The court nevertheless took the fact of a prior conviction into consideration in determining the penalty for the second offense. The convicted individual challenged consideration of that factor, but the Supreme Court warned that it was a misimpression to think

> that a pardon would operate to limit the power of the United States in punishing crimes against its authority to provide for taking into consideration past offenses committed by the accused as a circumstance of aggravation even although for such past offenses there had been a pardon granted.[29]

The court has held that a pardon restores a convict's competency as a witness in a court of law. The justices found that the disability resulted from the conviction and that the pardon obliterated the effect of the conviction and thus restored the person's competency to testify.[30]

Undoing the Past

However, a pardon cannot make amends for the past, the court has held. It cannot afford compensation for time spent in prison, nor does it restore property rights that have been legally vested in others. The leading case on this aspect of the effects of a presidential pardon arose, like *Ex parte Garland,* out of the Civil War.

The property of a man who served with the Confederacy was condemned and sold for his "treason." After the general pardon issued to ex-Confederates in 1868 by President Andrew Johnson, the former owner of the property sued for the proceeds of the sale. The court denied his claim and declared that a pardon cannot

> ...make amends for the past. It affords no relief for what has been suffered by the offender in his person by imprisonment, forced labor, or otherwise; it does not give compensation for what has been done or suffered, nor does it impose upon the government any obligation to give it. The offense being established by judicial proceedings, that which has been done or suffered when they were in force is presumed to have

been rightly done and justly suffered, and no satisfaction for it can be required... Neither does the pardon affect any rights which have vested in others directly by the execution of the judgment for the offense, or which have been acquired by others whilst that judgment was in force. If, for example, by the judgment a sale of the offender's property has been had, the purchaser will hold the property notwithstanding the subsequent pardon.... The rights of the parties have become vested, and are as complete as if they were acquired in any other legal way. So, also, if the proceeds have been paid into the treasury, the right to them has so far become vested in the United States that they can only be secured to the former owner of the property through an act of Congress. Moneys once in the treasury can only be withdrawn by an appropriation by law. However large, therefore, may be the power of pardon possessed by the President, and however extended may be its application, there is this limit to it, as there is to all his powers, it cannot touch moneys in the Treasury of the United States, except expressly authorized by Act of Congress....[31]

Conditions and Commutations

The questions posed by conditional pardons came before the court after President Lincoln, on Dec. 8, 1863, offered pardons to all Confederates who swore allegiance to the Constitution and the Union. Lincoln's pardon offer, if accepted, would have granted former Confederates the right to restoration of their property taken during the war.

In the case of *United States v. Klein,* decided in 1872, the court upheld the president's right to offer pardon and property restoration in exchange for allegiance:

> It was competent for the President to annex to his offer of pardon any conditions or qualifications he should see fit; but after those conditions and qualifications had been satisfied, the pardon and its connected promises took full effect.[32]

Congress had tried, through legislation, to block the property restoration effect of this pardon. The court rejected that effort:

> To the Executive alone is intrusted the power of pardon; and it is granted without limit. Pardon includes amnesty. It blots out the offense pardoned and removes all its penal consequences. It may be granted on conditions. In these particular pardons that no doubt might exist as to their character, restoration of property was expressly pledged; and the pardon was granted on condition that the person who availed himself of it should take and keep a prescribed oath.
>
> Now, it is clear that the Legislature cannot change the effect of such a pardon any more than the Executive can change a law....[33]

Commutation Challenges

In a series of cases involving the president's exercise of his pardon power to commute — reduce — sentences, the court has held that this aspect of the power may be exercised without the recipient's consent.

William Wells, convicted of murder, was to be hanged on April 23, 1852. On execution day, President Millard Fillmore granted him a conditional pardon, commuting his sentence to life in prison.

Wells accepted the pardon, but challenged the condition as illegal, seeking his release from prison through a writ of *habeas corpus.* His attorneys argued to the Supreme Court that:

> . . . a President granting such a pardon assumes a power not conferred by the Constitution — that he legislates a new punishment into existence, and sentences the convict to suffer it; in this way violating the legislative and judicial power of the government, it being the power of the first to enact laws for the punishment of offences . . . and that of the judiciary, to sentence . . . according to them. [34]

The court in 1856 rejected this argument, upheld the president's power to commute a sentence without the recipient's consent, and concluded:

> . . . it may be said, [that] . . . the condition, when accepted, becomes a substitute for the sentence of the court . . . [and] is substantially the exercise of a new power. But this is not so, for the power to offer a condition, without ability to enforce its acceptance, when accepted by the convict, is the substitution, by himself, of a lesser punishment than the law has imposed upon him, and he cannot complain if the law executes the choice he has made. [35]

In subsequent cases, the court has declared that the president's prerogative includes the power to remit fines, penalties and forfeitures and to pardon contempt of court. [36]

Biddle v. Perovich. Seventy years later, the court reaffirmed its holding in the *Wells* case, ruling that a president could commute a death sentence entirely without the recipient's consent.

Vuco Perovich, convicted of murder in Alaska in 1905 and sentenced to be hanged, received a commuted sentence of life imprisonment from President William Howard Taft in 1909. Authorities moved Perovich to a state penitentiary and then, some years later, to the federal prison at Leavenworth, Kan. Perovich twice applied unsuccessfully for a pardon.

He then applied for release through a writ of *habeas corpus,* arguing that his removal from an Alaskan jail to a federal penitentiary and the president's commutation of his death sentence were effected without his consent and without legal authority.

Perovich's attorney urged the Supreme Court to hold that a sentence could not be commuted without consent. The court rejected that argument, and ruled that consent was not required for commutation of sentence. "When we come to the commutation of death to imprisonment for life," wrote Justice Oliver Wendell Holmes Jr., "it is hard to see how consent has much to do with the effect of the president's action. Supposing that Perovich did not accept the change, he could not have got himself hanged against the Executive order. . . ." [37]

Justice Holmes then set out the modern court's view of the presidential pardon power:

> A pardon in our days is not a private act of grace from an individual happening to possess power. It is part of the Constitutional scheme. When granted it is the determination of the ultimate authority that the public welfare will be better served by inflicting less than what the judgment fixed. . . . Just as the original punishment would be imposed without regard to the prisoner's consent and in the teeth of his will, whether

he liked it or not, the public welfare, not his consent, determines what shall be done. So far as a pardon legitimately cuts down a penalty, it affects the judgment imposing it. [38]

Schick v. Reed. In 1974 the court for a third time rejected a challenge to the power of commutation. President Eisenhower commuted the death sentence of a child murderer to life in prison without possibility of parole, a sentence not at that time authorized by law for the crime of murder.

After serving 20 years, the prisoner sued to require the parole board to consider him eligible for parole on the basis that he had served the equivalent to a "life" sentence, and,

---

"When we come to the commutation of death to imprisonment for life, it is hard to see how [the prisoner's] consent has much to do with the effect of the president's action. Supposing that Perovich did not accept the change, he could not have got himself hanged against the Executive order. . . ."

—Justice Oliver Wendell Holmes Jr.
Biddle v. Perovich, 1927

---

furthermore, that the death penalty had in the interim been outlawed by a Supreme Court decision of 1972. [39]

Schick, the prisoner, argued that he had made a "bad bargain" in exchanging a death sentence for life in prison without opportunity for parole.

The Supreme Court held that the conditional commutation of his sentence was lawful and that intervening events had not undermined its validity. [40] Writing for the court, Chief Justice Warren Burger explained:

> A fair reading of the history of the English pardoning power, from which our Art. II, [section] 2, derives, of the language of that section itself, and of the unbroken practice since 1790 compels the conclusion that the power flows from the Constitution alone, and not from any legislative enactments, and that it cannot be modified, abridged, or diminished by the Congress. Additionally, considerations of public policy and humanitarian impulses support an interpretation of that power so as to permit the attachment of any condition which does not otherwise offend the Constitution. The plain purpose of the broad power conferred . . . was to allow plenary authority in the President to "forgive" the convicted person in part or entirely, to reduce a penalty in terms of a specified number of years, or to alter it with conditions which are in themselves constitutionally unobjectionable. . . . We therefore hold that the pardoning power is an enumerated power of the Constitution and its limitations, if any, must be found in the Constitution itself. [41]

Three justices, however, questioned the, "extra-legal nature of the Executive action." Justice Thurgood Marshall, writing for Justices William O. Douglas and William

J. Brennan, argued that "[I]n commuting a sentence the Chief Executive is not imbued with the constitutional power to create unauthorized punishments."[42]

Footnotes

[1] Louis Koenig, *The Chief Executive*, 3d. ed. (New York: Harcourt Brace Jovanovich, 1975), p. 165

[2] *The Federalist Papers*, with an Introduction by Clinton Rossiter (New York: New American Library, Mentor Books, 1961), No. 73, p. 442.

[3] Ibid. at 445.

[4] *Guide to Congress*, 2d. ed. (Washington, D.C.: Congressional Quarterly, 1976), pp. 628-631.

[5] *Okanogan Indians et al. v. United States (The Pocket Veto Case)*, 279 U.S. 655 (1929).

[6] Id. at 677-679.

[7] Id. at 678-679.

[8] Id. at 679-680.

[9] Id. at 680-681, 683-685.

[10] *Wright v. United States*, 302 U.S. 583 (1938)

[11] Id. at 594.

[12] Congressional Quarterly, *Almanac, 1970* (Washington, D.C.: Congressional Quarterly , 1971), pp. 592-593.

[13] *United States v. Klein*, 13 Wall. 128 (1872).

[14] *Ex parte Garland*, 4 Wall. 333 at 380-381 (1867).

[15] *United States v. Wilson*, 7 Pet. 150 (1833).

[16] *Biddle v. Perovich*, 274 U.S. 480 at 486 (1927).

[17] *Historic Documents of 1974* (Washington, D.C.: Congressional Quarterly, 1975), pp. 816-817.

[18] Edward S. Corwin, *The President: Offices and Powers*, 4th ed. (New York: New York University Press, 1957), pp. 158-159.

[19] *The Federalist Papers*, No. 74, p. 447.

[20] *United States v. Wilson*, 7 Pet. 150 at 160-161 (1833).

[21] *Burdick v. United States*, 236 U.S. 79 (1915).

[22] Id. at 90-91.

[23] Charles Warren, *The Supreme Court in United States History*, rev. ed., 2 vols. (Boston: Little, Brown & Co., 1922, 1926), II:450-451.

[24] *Ex parte Garland*, 4 Wall. 333 at 374-376 (1866).

[25] Id. at 381.

[26] Id. at 380.

[27] Id. at 380-381.

[28] Id. at 396-397

[29] *Carlesi v. New York*, 233 U.S. 51 at 59 (1914).

[30] *Boyd v. United States*, 142 U.S. 450 (1892).

[31] *Knote v. United States*, 95 U.S. 149 at 153-154 (1877).

[32] *United States v. Klein*, 13 Wall. 128 at 142 (1872).

[33] Id. at 147-148.

[34] *Ex parte Wells*, 18 How. 307 at 307-309 (1856).

[35] Id. at 314-315.

[36] *The Laura*, 114 U.S. 411 (1885);*Illinois Central R.R. v. Bosworth*, 133 U.S. 92 (1890); *Ex parte Grossman*, 267 U.S. 87 (1925).

[37] *Biddle v. Perovich*, 274 U.S. 480 at 487 (1927).

[38] Id. at 485-486.

[39] *Furman v. Georgia, Jackson v. Georgia, Branch v. Texas*, 408 U.S. 238 (1972).

[40] *Schick v. Reed*, 419 U.S. 256 (1974).

[41] Id. at 266-267.

[42] Id. at 274.

Privilege and Immunity

Neither executive immunity nor executive privilege are mentioned in the Constitution. The two concepts evolved from the system of separated powers, the basic constitutional design of the three coordinate branches, each insulated from coercion by the others.

Executive immunity has been asserted by presidents and upheld by the Supreme Court as a shield against judicial interference with presidential policy-making. Once a policy is effected, the court may review its results, but a court may not order the president — either as chief executive or as private individual — to take some particular policy action or to refrain from it.

And yet the president is not immune from all challenge to his actions. Article II, Section 4, provides that the other political branch — Congress — may impeach and remove a president from office if it finds him guilty of "Treason, Bribery or other high Crimes and Misdemeanors." The question is unresolved whether a sitting president might be charged and prosecuted for crimes in any court other than a court of impeachment. Once impeached, however, the Constitution is explicit in making the point that an official is then "liable and subject to Indictment, Trial, Judgment and Punishment, according to Law."

Executive privilege, on the other hand, has generally been asserted as the president's prerogative to withhold information, documents, and the testimony of his aides from public or congressional scrutiny. Congress has never fully accepted the principle, although it has been asserted and practiced by presidents since George Washington.

Presidents find the basis for this claim in the separation of powers principle, vaguely stated at the beginning of Article II — "The executive power shall be vested in a President of the United States of America" — and the subsequent clause which directs the president to "take care that the laws be faithfully executed."

The court's rulings on executive privilege have acknowledged the existence of a limited privilege as necessary to protect the national security and the conduct of diplomatic negotiations. The court, however, has denied emphatically any absolute privilege to withhold information under all circumstances.

Executive Immunity

The turmoil of Reconstruction and the troubled presidency of Andrew Johnson provided the backdrop for the leading Supreme Court decision on the immunity of the president, as an official and an individual, from judicial interference with the conduct of his office.

In 1866, the court — in the case of *Ex parte Milligan* — had declared that Lincoln had exceeded his authority in setting up Civil War military commissions outside the war zone. This ruling gave the South reason to hope that the court would also strike down the congressional program of Reconstruction outlined in the Reconstruction Act of 1867. *(Ex parte Milligan, p. 189)*

Mississippi thus came to the Supreme Court asking the justices to order the president to stop carrying out the Reconstruction program. The state challenged both the constitutionality of the laws upon which it was based and the president's authority to carry them out.[1]

In *Marbury v. Madison,* the court had held that a court with jurisdiction could issue a writ to order the president to perform a ministerial duty, a duty as to which he had little discretion.[2] But Mississippi was asking the court to exercise its authority to restrain the president's enforcement of an act of Congress.

The court rejected that request. Chief Justice Salmon P. Chase wrote the court's opinion which distinguished between the ministerial duties of a president and his general responsibility for seeing that the laws were faithfully executed. Ministerial acts, wrote Chase, could be subject to court orders, but acts involving political discretion were beyond judicial reach.

When a court issued an injunction against a political act, it interfered with the operation of the political branches and risked a collision between the judicial and political departments. There were practical reasons to avoid such collisions, explained Chief Justice Chase:

> If the President refuse obedience, it is needless to observe that the Court is without power to enforce its process. If, on the other hand, the President complies . . . and refuses to execute the acts of Congress, is it not clear that a collision may occur between the executive and legislative departments. . . .? May not the House of Representatives impeach the President for such refusal? And in that case could this Court interfere in behalf of the President, thus endangered by compliance with its mandate. . . .?

> A ministerial duty . . . is one in respect to which nothing is left to discretion. It is a simple, definite

duty, arising under conditions admitted or proved to exist, and imposed by law. . . .

Very different is the duty of the President in the exercise of the power to see that the laws are faithfully executed. . . . The duty thus imposed on the President is in no just sense ministerial. It is purely executive and political.

An attempt on the part of the Judicial Department of the Government to enforce the performance of such duties by the President might be justly characterized, in the language of Chief Justice Marshall, as 'an absurd and excessive extravagance.'

It is true that in the instance before us the interposition of the court is not sought to enforce action by the Executive under constitutional legislation, but to restrain such action under legislation alleged to be unconstitutional. But we are unable to perceive that this circumstance takes the case out of the general principles which forbid judicial interference with the exercise of executive discretion. . . .

The Congress is the Legislative Department of the Government; the President is the Executive Department. Neither can be restrained in its action by the Judicial Department; though the acts of both, when performed, are, in proper cases, subject to its cognizance.[3]

Mississippi suggested that the injunctive relief sought might be issued against Johnson as a private citizen if the office of the president was beyond the reach of such an order. But Chase declared that no such distinction could be entertained in the case:

. . . it is plain that relief as against the execution of an Act of Congress by Andrew Johnson, is relief against its execution by the President. A bill praying an injunction against the execution of an act of Congress by the incumbent of the presidential office cannot be received, whether it describes him as President or as citizen of a State.[4]

The court dismissed Georgia's subsequent effort to prevent enforcement of the Reconstruction acts by Secretary of War Stanton and General Ulysses S. Grant.[5] The court refused to issue to these presidential subordinates the order they would not issue to the president. The suit involved political questions and political rights, the court said, and the issue lay beyond the court's jurisdiction.[6] The rights involved were not personal or property rights, the court observed but "the rights of sovereignty, of political jurisdiction, of government, of corporate existence as a State, with all its constitutional powers and privileges."[7]

The President's Men

Thus, held the court, once the president moves into the realm of policy and politics, the court cannot compel him to act or prevent him from acting. Once completed, however, the court may consider a challenge to the results of the president's policies and at that point may review and disallow those policies.

The president's subordinates, however, may be ordered by a court not to carry out a threatened illegal act which would lead to irreparable damage. Those subordinates may also be commanded by a court to carry out some ministerial duty required by law.

In *Kendall v. United States,* the court in 1838 held that the postmaster general could be ordered by a court to

pay an account due without breaching the powers and prerogatives of the president. Justice Smith Thompson's majority opinion discussed the president's discretionary powers, their derivation and exercise:

The theory of the constitution undoubtedly is, that the great powers of the government are divided into separate departments; and so far as these powers derived from the constitution, the departments may be regarded as independent of each other. But beyond that, all are subject to regulations by law, touching the discharge of the duties required to be performed. The executive power is vested in a president; and so far as his powers are derived from the constitution, he is beyond the reach of any other department. . . . But it by no means follows, that every officer in every branch of that department is under the exclusive direction of the president. Such a principle, we apprehend, is not, and certainly cannot be claimed by the president. There are certain political duties imposed upon many officers in the executive department, the discharge of which is under direction of the president. But it would be an alarming doctrine, that congress cannot impose upon any executive officer any duty they may think proper, which is not repugnant to any rights secured and protected by the constitution; and in such cases, the duty and responsibility grow out of and are subject to the control of the law, and not to the direction of the president.[8]

The court rejected the argument that the postmaster general, a presidential Cabinet officer, was under the sole direction of the president. That principle wrote the court:

. . . if carried out in its results to all cases falling within it, would [result in] . . . clothing the President with a power entirely to control legislation of Congress, and paralyze the administration of justice.

To contend that the obligation imposed on the President to see the laws faithfully executied implies a power to forbid their execution, is a novel construction of the Constitution, and entirely inadmissible.[9]

Subsequent rulings by the court have held that subordinate executive officers may be held personally liable for damages wrought by acts in excess of their authority.[10] But some executive immunity protects them from liability for reasonable actions taken in good faith in the performance of their duties.[11] *(Sovereign immunity, p. 261)*

Executive Privilege

Presidents, acknowledging that Congress has the right to inquire into executive branch matters, have from time to time, claimed executive privilege to withhold information from Congress.

These claims, however, have been exceptions to the general rule of compliance with congressional requests for such information. As one investigator has written, in "virtually every incident . . . prior to the Civil War, presidents complied substantially with congressional requests, withholding information only if specifically authorized to do so by Congress."[12]

Since 1954, the incidence of claims of privilege has risen sharply, resulting in a number of Supreme Court pronouncements on the subject.

Until 1974, the legal basis for the privilege was much debated. Attorneys general and others seeking to justify a claim of privilege relied heavily on historical precedents of presidential refusals to provide requested information.[13] The precedents, however, often provided ambiguous support for the privilege.

One writer, after investigating the precedents cited, concluded that, contrary to presidential claims, "Congress prevailed, and got precisely what it sought to get" in most cases.[14] Raoul Berger, author of a book on the question, called executive privilege a "constitutional myth."[15]

In 1974, however, in the case of *United States v. Nixon*, the Supreme Court for the first time placed a constitutional foundation under the privilege.[16] Upholding a limited privilege, the assertion of which must be justified in each case by the executive, the court rejected President Richard Nixon's particular claim of absolute privilege to withhold information. Yet in so doing, the court provided a fortified basis for future presidential claims of privilege.

Presidents and Privilege

Not until 1958 did the phrase "executive privilege" come into use. In that year Justice Stanley F. Reed used it in an opinion.[17]

But the practice described by the phrase began much earlier. President Washington only once denied Congress access to papers, refusing to allow the House to see papers related to negotiation of the controversial Jay Treaty. Washington based his refusal on the fact that the House lacked power under the Constitution to demand treaty-related documents. Washington acknowledged the right of the Senate to have access to those papers.[18]

Chief Justice John Marshall, writing for the court in *Marbury v. Madison*, implicitly acknowledged a basis for some executive privilege:

> By the Constitution of the United States, the President is invested with certain important political powers, in the exercise of which he is to use his own discretion, and is accountable only to his country in his political character and to his own conscience.[19]

Marshall, however, saw limits to the president's prerogative of secrecy:

> ...Questions in their nature political, or which are, by the Constitution and the laws, submitted to the executive, can never be made in this court.
>
> But, if this be not such a question; if, so far from being an intrusion into the secrets of the cabinet ... if it be no intermeddling with a subject over which the executive can be considered as having exercised any control; what is there in the exalted station of the officer, which shall bar a citizen from asserting, in a court of justice, his legal rights, or shall forbid a court to listen to the claim, or to issue a mandamus directing the performance of a duty, not depending on executive discretion, but on particular acts of congress, and the general principles of law?[20]

President Thomas Jefferson, contrary to popular misconception, complied partially when the House requested information from him about the Aaron Burr conspiracy. Jefferson provided the information, withholding the names of individuals mentioned in parts of a letter requested, saying that the names were not pertinent to the House inquiry.

During Burr's 1807 treason trial, Jefferson was subpoenaed to appear, and declined to do so, but he eventually produced the letter sought by Burr's counsel. Presiding

Judge John Marshall again recognized a limited privilege protecting state secrets, but said that the court would weigh the need for secrecy against the need of the accused for the document sought in order that he might have a fair trial.[21]

President Andrew Jackson in 1835 rejected a Senate request for a list of charges against Surveyor-General Gideon Fitz in connection with fraudulent land sales.[22] Presidents Tyler, Polk and Pierce all withheld information demanded by Congress.

The Court and the Privilege

Early in the 20th century the court acknowledged that heads of executive departments could raise claims of executive privilege with respect to court-ordered demands for records of the department or the testimony of department employees.[23]

In 1927, the court held that executive privilege did not protect the executive branch from legitimate legislative investigation. In the case of *McGrain v. Daugherty*, the court upheld the right of the Senate to inquire into the failure of President Warren G. Harding's attorney general to prosecute key figures in the Teapot Dome scandal.[24] *(Details, p. 159)*

National Security. In 1948, the court acknowledged that there were areas of executive power — military and national security matters in particular — where the president might properly refuse to disclose all facts relative to a decision. The case involved a challenge to the president's decision to award certain foreign air travel routes to one company while denying them to a competitor.[25] In the opinion, Justice Robert H. Jackson wrote:

> The President, both as Commander-in-Chief and as the Nation's organ for foreign affairs, has available intelligence services whose reports neither are nor ought to be published to the world. It would be intolerable that courts, without the relevant information, should review and perhaps nullify actions of the Executive taken on information properly held secret.... But even if courts could require full disclosure, the very nature of executive decisions as to foreign policy is political, not judicial. Such decisions are wholly confided by our Constitution to the political departments of the government, Executive and Legislative. They are delicate, complex, and involve large elements of prophecy. They are and should be undertaken only by those directly responsible to the people, whose welfare they advance or imperil. They are decisions of a kind for which the Judiciary has neither aptitude, facilities nor responsibility and have long been held to belong to the domain of political power not subject to judicial intrusion or inquiry.[26]

A Judicial Role. Five years later, the court asserted a judicial role in assessing claims of executive privilege asserted to protect military or national security secrets. The decision in *United States v. Reynolds* set out guidelines for judging such claims.[27]

The widow of a civilian pilot killed in a plane crash during a test of secret military equipment sought copies of investigative reports of the accident. The secretary of the Air Force refused, claiming that the reports were privileged documents.

The Supreme Court accepted that claim, but in doing so declared that in each case of this sort "the court itself must determine whether the circumstances are appropriate for the claim of privilege."[28]

Chief Justice Fred M. Vinson continued:

> In each case, the showing of necessity which is made will determine how far the court should probe in satisfying itself that the occasion for invoking the privilege is appropriate. Where there is a strong showing of necessity, the claim of privilege should not be lightly accepted, but even the most compelling necessity cannot overcome the claim of privilege if the court is ultimately satisfied that military secrets are at stake.[29]

The Modern Privilege

Executive claims of an absolute privilege to withhold information accelerated after 1954, reported a Library of Congress study in 1973.

In 1954, President Dwight D. Eisenhower wrote Defense Secretary Charles Wilson advising him to direct his subordinates not to testify about certain matters during the much-publicized Army-McCarthy hearings.[30]

In the course of that investigation by the Senate Permanent Subcommittee on Investigations, Chairman Joseph R. McCarthy, R. Wis. 1947-1957, insisted that John Adams, counsel for the Army, tell the subcommittee about a meeting held in the attorney general's office with high-level White House staff members.[31]

In response, Adams submitted to the subcommittee copies of a letter from Eisenhower to Wilson invoking executive privilege with respect to testimony by executive department officials. The letter included copies of a memorandum that listed historical precedents of prior successful claims of executive privilege. Eisenhower's letter "became the major authority cited for exercise of 'executive privilege' to refuse information to the Congress for the next seven years...," reported the Library of Congress.[32]

President John F. Kennedy refused a special Senate subcommittee's request for the identity of individuals assigned to edit speeches of military leaders. Kennedy directed Secretary of Defense Robert S. McNamara and all personnel under his jurisdiction not to comply with the committee's request.

Such refusals of information, Kennedy said, would not be automatic. "Each case must be judged on its own merits," the president maintained.[33] Kennedy reaffirmed that position in an exchange of correspondence with Rep. John E. Moss, D-Calif. 1933-1979: "Executive privilege can be invoked only by the President and will not be used without specific Presidential approval."[34]

President Lyndon B. Johnson assured Moss that "the claim of 'executive privilege' will continue to be made only by the President."[35] Moss later received a similar declaration from President Nixon who issued a memorandum to the heads of all executive departments and agencies stating the policy that, "executive privilege will not be used without specific Presidential approval."[36]

The memorandum required that requests to invoke executive privilege in answer to an inquiry from Congress go to the attorney general. If he and the department head agreed the privilege should not be invoked Congress would receive the information. If either or both wished, the issue would be submitted to the president.

Despite these specific declarations, some executive branch officials during the Nixon administration did claim "executive privilege" without presidential approval.[37]

The court denied the president's claim of executive privilege in the 1971 *Pentagon Papers* decision. The Supreme Court held that President Nixon had not satisfied the heavy burden of proof required to enjoin publication of classified material allegedly injurious to national security.[38]

In 1973, the Supreme Court ruled that federal courts lacked power to review executive branch classification decisions which exempted materials from disclosure under the 1966 Freedom of Information Act. Congress subsequently amended the law to allow courts to review classification decisions.[39]

"The privilege is fundamental to the operation of the government and inextricably rooted in the separation of powers under the Constitution. . . . Nowhere in the Constitution . . . is there any explicit reference to a privilege of confidentiality, yet to the extent this interest relates to the effective discharge of a President's powers, it is constitutionally based. . . ."

—Chief Justice Warren Burger
United States v. Nixon, 1974

United States v. Nixon

The most significant Supreme Court decision concerning claims of executive privilege came in 1974 and resulted in the resignation of President Nixon.

The court rebuffed Nixon's claim of an absolute privilege to reject judicial demands for information. The court held that Nixon must surrender to the Watergate Special Prosecutor subpoenaed tapes of White House conversations that occurred between the president and his aides.

The tapes were required for use as evidence in the criminal trial of former White House aides charged with attempting to obstruct justice by covering up White House involvement in the 1972 break-in at the Democratic National Committee headquarters in the Watergate office building.

Background. Special Prosecutor Leon Jaworski in April 1974 obtained a subpoena ordering delivery of certain tapes, memoranda and papers related to specific meetings of the president with particular White House aides.

The president's counsel moved to quash the subpoena, formally claiming executive privilege as a defense against compliance. The district court denied all motions on behalf of Nixon and ordered the president to deliver all the materials requested in the subpoena.

Nixon appealed to the Supreme Court which heard oral arguments July 8 in the cases of *United States v. Nixon, Nixon v. United States.*

On July 24, with Chief Justice Warren E. Burger speaking for a unanimous court, the justices rejected Nixon's claim of privilege. Burger discussed the derivation of executive privilege:

Whatever the nature of the privilege of confidentiality of presidential communications in the exercise of Art. II powers the privilege can be said to derive from the supremacy of each branch within its own assigned area of constitutional duties. Certain powers and privileges flow from the nature of the enumerated powers; the protection of the confidentiality of presidential communications has similar constitutional underpinnings.[40]

The court then observed that:

...neither the doctrine of separation of powers, nor the need for confidentiality of high level communications, without more, can sustain an absolute, unqualified presidential privilege of immunity from judicial process under all circumstances. The President's need for complete candor and objectivity from advisers calls for great deference from the courts. However, when the privilege depends solely on the broad undifferentiated claim of public interest in the confidentiality of such conversations, a confrontation with other values arises. Absent a claim of need to protect military, diplomatic or sensitive national security secrets, we find it difficult to accept the argument that even the very important interest in confidentiality of presidential communications is significantly diminished by protection of such material for *in camera* inspection with all the protection that a district court will be obliged to provide.

The impediment that an absolute, unqualified privilege would place in the way of the primary constitutional duty of the Judicial Branch to do justice in criminal prosecutions would plainly conflict with the function of the courts under Art. III. In designing the structure of our Government and dividing and allocating the sovereign power among three coequal branches, the Framers of the Constitution sought to provide a comprehensive system, but the separate powers were not intended to operate with absolute independence....

To read the Art. II powers of the President as providing an absolute privilege as against a subpoena essential to enforcement of criminal statutes on no more than a generalized claim of the public interest in confidentiality of nonmilitary and nondiplomatic discussions would upset the constitutional balance of "a workable government" and gravely impair the role of the courts under Art. III....[41]

In rejecting this particular claim of privilege, however, the Court for the first time acknowledged a constitutional basis for executive privilege:

A President and those who assist him must be free to explore alternatives in the process of shaping policies and making decisions and to do so in a way many would be unwilling to express except privately. These are the considerations justifying a presumptive privilege for presidential communications. The privilege is fundamental to the operation of government and inextricably rooted in the separation of powers under the Constitution....

Nowhere in the Constitution ... is there any explicit reference to a privilege of confidentiality, yet to the extent this interest relates to the effective discharge of a President's powers, it is constitutionally based....[42]

> "...when the ground for asserting privilege as to subpoenaed materials sought for use in a criminal trial is based only on the generalized interest in confidentiality, it cannot prevail over the fundamental demands of due process of law in the fair administration of criminal justice."
>
> —Chief Justice Warren Burger
> *United States v. Nixon,* 1974

In this case the claim of an absolute privilege failed when weighed against the requirements of evidence in a criminal proceeding. Burger observed:

No case of the Court ... has extended this high degree of deference to a President's generalized interest in confidentiality....

In this case we must weigh the importance of the general privilege of confidentiality of presidential communications in performance of his responsibilities against the inroads of such a privilege on the fair administration of criminal justice. The interest in preserving confidentiality is weighty indeed and entitled to great respect. However we cannot conclude that advisers will be moved to temper the candor of their remarks by the infrequent occasions of disclosure because of the possibility that such conversations will be called for in the context of a criminal prosecution....

A President's acknowledged need for confidentiality in the communications of his office is general in nature, whereas the constitutional need for production of relevant evidence in a criminal proceeding is specific and central to the fair adjudication of a particular criminal case in the administration of justice. Without access to specific facts a criminal prosecution may be totally frustrated. The President's broad interest in confidentiality of communications will not be vitiated by disclosure of a limited number of conversations preliminarily shown to have some bearing on the pending criminal cases.

We conclude that when the ground for asserting privilege as to subpoenaed materials sought for use in a criminal trial is based only on the generalized interest in confidentiality, it cannot prevail over the fundamental demands of due process of law in the fair administration of criminal justice. The generalized assertion of privilege must yield to the demonstrated, specific need for evidence in a pending criminal trial....[43]

The Nixon Papers

In 1977, the Supreme Court rejected a second Nixon claim of executive privilege to restrict access to the records of his administration. Against such a claim, the court upheld a 1974 act of Congress that placed the records, tapes and papers of the Nixon administration in federal custody.[44]

Presidents historically have retained control of their papers and governed both their use and public access to them. But the unusual circumstances surrounding Nixon's departure from office moved Congress to depart from that custom.[45]

Nixon's attorneys argued that by removing control of the papers from the former president, Congress had infringed upon the prerogatives of the president and had opened the way for wide disclosure of privileged matters.

The Supreme Court majority rejected that argument. Justice William J. Brennan Jr. wrote for the court that the president's challenge to the act on these grounds rested on "an archaic view of the separation of powers as requiring three airtight departments of government."[46]

Executive privilege would not be violated by government archivists' screening the papers any more than had Federal Judge John Sirica's private review of the White House tapes used as evidence in the Watergate cover-up trials, Brennan said. The archivists':

> . . .screening constitutes a very limited intrusion by personnel in the Executive Branch sensitive to executive concerns. These very personnel have performed the identical task in each of the presidential libraries without any suggestion that such activity has in any way interfered with executive confidential-

ity. . . . Nor should the American people's ability to reconstruct and come to terms with their history be truncated by an analysis of Presidential privilege that focuses only on the needs of the present.[47]

Chief Justice Warren E. Burger and Justice William H. Rehnquist dissented. Burger argued that the law would severely affect the conduct of executive branch business. The law, Burger stated, would be:

> . . .a 'ghost' at future White House conferences with conferees choosing their words more cautiously because of the enlarged prospect of compelled disclosure to others.[48]

Justice Rehnquist warned that the court's decision "will daily stand as a veritable sword of Damocles over every succeeding President and his advisers."[49]

The Supreme Court weighed Nixon's claim of privilege against the need to preserve intact the records of his administration. The majority as well as the dissenters recognized the existence of a limited privilege but in this instance found the countervailing necessity of the public's right to know to outweigh Nixon's claim.

Footnotes

[1] *Mississippi v. Johnson,* 4 Wall. 475 (1867).

[2] *Marbury v. Madison,* 1 Cr. 137 (1803).

[3] *Mississippi v. Johnson,* 4 Wall. 475 at 500-501, 498-499 (1867).

[4] Id. at 501.

[5] *Georgia v. Stanton,* 6 Wall. 50 (1868).

[6] Id. at 77.

[7] Ibid.

[8] *Kendall v. United States ex. rel. Stokes,* 12 Pet. 524 at 609-610, 613 (1838).

[9] Id. at 613.

[10] *Little v. Bareme,* 2 Cr. 170 (1804); *United States v. Lee,* 106 U.S. 196 (1882); *Bivens v. Six Unknown Named Agents of the Federal Bureau of Narcotics,* 403 U.S. 388 (1971).

[11] *Barr v. Mateo,* 360 U.S. 564 (1959); *Butz v. Economou,* 438 U.S. 478 (1978).

[12] Norman Dorson and Richard Shattuck, "Executive Privilege, the Congress and the Court," *Ohio State Law Journal,* 35:13.

[13] Herman Wollkinson, "Demand of Congressional Committees for Executive Papers," *Federal Bar Journal,* X:103-150; Robert Kramer and Herman Marcuse, "Executive Privilege — A Study of the Period 1953-1960," *George Washington Law Review,* XXIX:623-718, 827-916; Irving Younger, "Congressional Investigations and Executive Secrecy: A Study in Separation of Powers," *University of Pittsburgh Law Review,* 20:757, 773.

[14] J. Russell Wiggins, "Government Operations and the Public's Right to Know," *Federal Bar Journal,* XIX:76.

[15] Raoul Berger, *Executive Privilege: A Constitutional Myth,* (Cambridge, Mass.: Harvard University Press, 1974), p. 1.

[16] *United States v. Nixon,* 418 U.S. 683 (1974).

[17] *Kaiser Aluminum & Chem. Co. v. United States,* 157 F. Supp. 937, 943 (Ct. Cl. 1958).

[18] Raoul Berger, *Executive Privilege: A Constitutional Myth,* pp.178-179, 232-233.

[19] *Marbury v. Madison,* 1 Cr. 138 at 165-166 (1803).

[20] Id. at 170.

[21] Raoul Berger, *Executive Privilege: A Constitutional Myth,* pp.179-181, 187-194.

[22] Id. at 181.

[23] *Boske v. Comingore,* 177 U.S. 459 (1900); *United States ex rel. Touhy v. Ragan, Warden, et. al.* 340 U.S.462 (1951).

[24] *McGrain v. Daugherty,* 273 U.S. 135 (1927).

[25] *Chicago & Southern Airlines v. Waterman S.S. Co.,* 333 U.S. 103, 105 (1948).

[26] Id. at 111.

[27] *United States v. Reynolds,* 345 U.S. 1 at 11 (1953).

[28] Id.

[29] Id.

[30] "The Present Limits of Executive Privilege," Study Prepared by the Government and General Research Division of the Library of Congress, *Congressional Record,* H. 2243-2246 (March 28, 1973). Cited as LC Study.

[31] LC Study, *Congressional Record,* H. 2243-2246 (March 28, 1973).

[32] Eisenhower to Secretary of Defense, May 17, 1954, *Public Papers of the Presidents, Dwight D. Eisenhower, 1954,* (Washington, D.C.: U.S. Government Printing Office, 1960), pp. 483-485.

[33] U.S. Congress, Senate, Committee on Armed Services, Special Preparedness Subcommittee, *Military Cold War and Speech Review Policies, Hearings,* 87th Cong., 2nd sess. (Washington, D.C.: U.S. Government Printing Office, 1962), pp. 508-509.

[34] Ibid.

[35] Johnson to the Hon. John E. Moss, April 2, 1965. *Public Papers of the Presidents, Lyndon B. Johnson, 1965,* 2 vols. (Washington, D.C.: U.S. Government Printing Office, 1966), II:376.

[36] U.S. Congress, Senate, Committee on the Judiciary, Subcommittee on the Separation of Powers, *Executive Privilege: The Withholding of Information by the Executive, Hearings,* 92 Cong., 1st sess. (Washington, D.C.: U.S. Government Printing Office, 1971), p.2.

[37] LC Study, *Congressional Record,* H. 2243-2246 (March 28, 1973).

[38] *New York Times Co. v. United States, United States v. Washington Post,* 403 U.S. 713 (1971).

[39] *Environmental Protection Agency v. Mink,* 410 U.S. 73 (1973); *Congress and the Nation,* Vol. IV (Washington, D.C.: Congressional Quarterly Inc., 1977), pp. 805-806.

[40] *U.S. v. Nixon, Nixon v. U.S.,* 418 U.S. 683 at 705-706 (1974).

[41] Id. at 706-707.

[42] Id. at 708,711.

[43] Id. at 711-713.

[44] *Nixon v. Administrator, General Services Administration,* 433 U.S. 425 (1977).

[45] Id. at 433-435.

[46] Id. at 443.

[47] Id. at 451-452.

[48] Id. at 520.

[49] Id. at 545.

Confrontation: The President v. The Court

Among the most dramatic chapters in American history are those which relate the collision between a president and the Supreme Court. Infrequent though they are, these confrontations span our history — from the Jefferson-Marshall clash of 1803 to the face-off between President Nixon and the Supreme Court in 1974.

Some of these clashes have been personal as well as political, as in the case of fellow Virginians Thomas Jefferson and John Marshall. Others have resulted from the efforts of presidents — Lincoln, Roosevelt and Truman — to use extraordinary powers in extraordinary times.

In some of these chapters the president seems to emerge the victor. In others, the court seems to prevail in the constitutional battle. But in all of them, the shape of the system is altered — as are the powers of the court and the executive to deal with future crises.

Jefferson v. Marshall

The long conflict between the administration of President Thomas Jefferson and the Federalist-dominated Supreme Court led by John Marshall had its roots both in the politics of Virginia and the national debate between Republicans and Federalists over the proper stance for the United States during the European wars following the French Revolution.

President Washington's 1793 proclamation of neutrality effectively terminated the French-American alliance of 1778.[1] Opponents of the policy saw it as evidence of the partiality of the Washington administration to Great Britain. The Jeffersonians feared that this Federalist stance would enmesh the United States in Britain's imperial enterprises.[2]

The political conflict was further heightened by the moves taken by the Federalists, during the "quasi-war" with France (1798-1800), to put the nation on a war footing. During that undeclared maritime conflict, Congress passed the controversial Sedition Acts, intended to silence editors and pamphleteers who attacked President Adams' administration and the defense measures he supported.

During the Quasi-War crisis some 25 persons were arrested for seditious libel under the terms of the Sedition Act.[3] Most of them were Republican editors. Ten were convicted for violations of the act.

One response to the Alien and Sedition Acts came in the form of resolutions adopted by the legislatures of Kentucky and Virginia. The resolutions, drafted by Jefferson and Madison, protested what they perceived to be the dangerous usurpation of power by the central government.[4]

The 'Revolution' of 1800

Jefferson saw his defeat of Adams for the presidency in 1800, and the transfer of power from one political group to another, as a revolution. But the revolution was incomplete. Federalist judges were firmly in control of the fledgling federal courts. And perhaps the most enduring legacy the Federalists left President Jefferson was the new Chief Justice of the United States — John Marshall.[5]

On Jan. 20, 1801, six weeks before the end of his term, John Adams nominated Marshall — then Secretary of State — to head the Supreme Court. The post had been vacant since September 1800 when Oliver Ellsworth resigned.

Adams had first nominated, and the Senate approved, John Jay, who had been the nation's first Chief Justice, but he declined the post, grumbling about ill health and the rigors of riding circuit.

Adams had considered Justice William Cushing for the position, but Cushing was 68 years old and he had declined appointment as Chief Justice in 1796. Justice William Paterson, another promising and younger candidate, was considered but dropped because the president's rival within Federalist ranks, Alexander Hamilton, supported Paterson's candidacy. Moreover, as Cushing was Paterson's senior on the supreme bench, it would appear that Adams slighted Cushing in making the appointment.[6]

Marshall's appointment was opposed in the Senate by members unhappy that Paterson was not nominated, but he was confirmed Jan. 27 in the waning days of the Adams presidency. Marshall received his commission as Chief Justice on Feb. 4, 1801, and took his seat on the bench over which he would preside for 34 years.[7]

Marshall's legal and judicial experience was meager. He had been a successful lawyer in Richmond after only a few months' education at William and Mary College.[8] His mission to France as one of the three American ministers in the abortive WXYZ mission won him a reputation in international law. He had served as a Federalist Representative in the House from Virginia's Richmond district, staunchly supporting President Adams' policies, and then had become Adams' Secretary of State.[9]

Marshall's appointment rankled Jefferson. The two **Virginians had been on opposite sides of the political fence** since the Revolution. Though third cousins, the two men had a mutual antagonism that probably dated to Jefferson's unfortunate term as Governor of Virginia in 1780 when he had been forced to flee the capitol by the approach of the British army. Marshall had served in the revolutionary army and his war experiences undoubtedly bred contempt for Jefferson's failure to face the enemy.[10]

In one of his first official acts as Chief Justice, Marshall administered the oath of office to President Jefferson. While Jefferson's inaugural speech was conciliatory, he moved within the year to repeal the newly enacted Judiciary Act of 1801 passed by the "lame-duck" Federalist congress as a judicial reform measure.

The Judiciary Act of 1801

The 1801 act was an admirable piece of legislation, but its passage was ill-timed. The House passed the law Jan. 20, 1801 — the day of Marshall's nomination — without a single Republican vote. The Senate approved it Feb. 7, and Adams signed the bill on Feb. 13. The law added new circuit judgeships, removed the requirement that Supreme Court justices ride circuit, and reduced the number of justices from six to five by stating that the next vacancy would not be filled.

Adams appointed sixteen new circuit court justices to fill the new posts, as well as a number of marshals and justices of the peace, whose posts were also created by the 1801 Act. In his last full month in office, Adams appointed 217 individuals to public office — of whom 93 were legal or judicial officers.[11]

The Judiciary Act of 1801 was repealed March 31, 1802. An act passed in April restored the number of seats on the Supreme Court to six, fixed one annual term for the court instead of two, and set up six circuits, each presided **over by a Supreme Court justice who would continue to ride circuit.** [12]

Marbury v. Madison

In the rush of business at the end of the Adams administration, Secretary of State Marshall failed to see to the delivery of several commissions of appointment. William Marbury, one of Adams' "midnight appointments" as justice of the peace for the District of Columbia, was among those who did not receive his commission, which Adams had signed and Marshall had sealed. Secretary of State Madison, acting under President Jefferson's orders, refused to deliver the commission at Marbury's request.[13]

Marbury then asked the Supreme Court to order Secretary of State Madison to deliver the commission. At the February 1803 session of the court, it ruled on Marbury's application for the order. In an historic opinion by Marshall, the court held itself powerless to issue such an order, declared part of the Judiciary Act of 1789 unconstitutional and lectured Jefferson on the proper performance of his duties.[14] Marshall's opinion was a bold and politically astute attack on Jefferson and his administration.

The Chief Justice expounded upon Marbury's vested right to the commission and reminded the president he was not above the law:

The commission being signed, the subsequent duty of the secretary of state is prescribed by law, and to be guided by the will of the president. He is to affix the seal of the United States to the commission, and is to record it.

This is not a proceeding which may be varied, if the judgment of the executive shall suggest one more eligible; but is a precise course accurately marked out by law, and is to be strictly pursued. It is the duty of the secretary of state to conform to the law, and in this he is an officer of the United States, bound to obey the laws. He acts, in this respect, . . . under the authority of law and not by the instructions of the president. It is a ministerial act which the law enjoins on a particular officer for a particular purpose.[15]

Marshall protected the court against the charge that it sought to aggrandize power by finding that the court lacked jurisdiction to issue the writ. By so doing, the court for the first time exercised the power to strike down an act of Congress as unconstitutional.

That aspect of the *Marbury* decision did not receive as much attention at the time as the court's lecture to Jefferson.[16] Judicial review had been regarded by many as a necessary adjunct of the constitutional system. The court had earlier assumed that it had this power.[17] *(Details p. 69)*

This was as close as the court and the Jefferson administration came to an institutional collision. But neither Jefferson nor Marshall ceased their efforts to undercut the prestige and power of the other, and of the branches they headed.

Impeachment: A Political Weapon

Jefferson, convinced by *Marbury* that stronger measures were needed to blunt the court's influence under Marshall, turned to the impeachment process.

The Constitution provided only one way to remove judges from office: impeachment for high crimes and misdemeanors. Conviction after impeachment and trial in the Senate required removal from office.

The Jeffersonians interpreted "high crimes and misdemeanors" broadly to allow impeachment for political acts. Their strategy was to use the impeachment process to remove federal judges from the bench for "crimes" such as ethical lapses and irresponsible political statements.

New Hampshire District Court Judge John Pickering was impeached, convicted and removed from office in proceedings begun in February 1803. Jefferson sent a message to the House accompanied by evidence that Pickering was a hopelessly insane drunkard. For the previous three years his behavior on the bench had been irrational and irresponsible. The House impeached Pickering, and the Senate trial came in March 1804.

The Senate convicted Pickering by a 19-7 vote along strict party lines and removed him from office. The impeachment of Pickering settled nothing with respect to the nature of impeachments brought against rational judges whose major crime was political opposition to Jeffersonian principles.

The main issue was Republican use of the impeachment process to remove politically obnoxious Federalist judges. Flawed precedent aside, with Pickering impeached and removed, Republicans went after bigger game.[18]

The Impeachment of Justice Samuel Chase

Republican leaders agreed that Justice Samuel Chase was an excellent impeachment target.[19] He had campaigned for Adams while on the Supreme Court bench, tried and convicted a group of rebels of treason in Pennsylvania for their part in opposing a new tax law (1799-1800), made political harangues from the bench to grand juries, and personally conducted the trial of Republican editor James Thomson Callendar under the Sedition Act.[20] Chase left no doubts about his staunch Federalism; in Republican minds he forfeited any claim to judicial impartiality on the bench.

Moreover, the time was ripe for a counterattack against the judiciary. Republicans still seethed over the lecture Marshall gave Jefferson in *Marbury v. Madison*. With John Randolph of Virginia guiding Republican forces, the House appointed a committee to inquire into Chase's conduct in January 1804. The House voted March 12 to impeach Chase on a strict party-line vote (73-32).[21]

The first seven articles of impeachment recounted Chase's "oppressive" conduct in the trials under the Sedition Act. The last article referred to an address by Chase characterized as an inflammtory diatribe designed to excite unrest against the government of the United States. The charges referred to Chase's outspoken criticism of Republican policies at the state and national levels.[22]

Vice President Aaron Burr, fresh from his duel with Alexander Hamilton, presided over the Senate trial that began in February 1805. Chase's attorneys maintained that an impeachable offense must be one indictable under law. It was clear to observers and participants alike that the independence of the federal judiciary was on trial. Removal of Chase would spur further Republican assaults on the bench.[23]

The vote in the Senate fell short of the necessary two-thirds majority on any of the impeachment articles, and Chase remained on the bench.

Chase's impeachment and trial set a precedent of strict construction of the impeachment clause and bolstered the judiciary's claim of independence from political tampering. The failure of the Chase impeachment was a source of political embarrassment to Jefferson.

The Jeffersonians abandoned the idea of removing federalist judges by impeachment. Federal judges, as a result of the trial, for a time exhibited greater restraint in their conduct and refrained from political lectures while on the bench.

Burr Trial

Vice President Aaron Burr had presided over the trial of Justice Chase. In August 1807, Burr was the defendant, tried for treason in a dramatic trial that saw the Chief Justice of the United States collide again with President Thomas Jefferson.

Marshall heard the case as judge of the United States circuit court for Virginia, but the antagonism between Jefferson and Marshall, and the tenacity with which Jefferson attempted to orchestrate Burr's conviction produced a trial with unmistakable political and personal overtones.[24]

Aaron Burr lost his political power base in New York when he refused to step aside and let Jefferson assume the presidency in the disputed election of 1800. Jefferson won the office after a compromise among the electors assured Jefferson enough electoral votes to win. Burr's failure to acknowledge Jefferson as the legitimate winner in 1800 earned Burr Jefferson's everlasting animosity.

Burr's attempts to recoup his political fortunes led him into a protracted political struggle with Hamilton that

ended with the duel which cost Hamilton his life and Burr all chances of regaining legitimate political power.[25]

Burr went west to revive his political fortunes and assembled a small force of men at Blennerhassett Island in the upper Ohio River. The men and equipment moved down the Mississippi River to New Orleans.[26]

Burr's plans for the band of adventurers have remained obscure, but rumors circulated that Burr intended to separate the Southwest from the Union. At first unconcerned, Jefferson in 1806 issued an order for Burr's arrest. Burr fled but was captured and returned to Richmond for trial.[27]

Marshall's rulings as presiding judge thwarted Jefferson's hopes that Burr would be convicted. The Chief Justice had no affection for Burr, but he refused to permit the court to be stampeded into a conviction simply because Burr was an unpopular and unscrupulous individual.[28]

Marshall ruled first on Burr's request to obtain from President Jefferson, by subpoena, certain letters Burr claimed he needed to provide an adequate defense.[29] Burr's evidentiary claim turned the trial into a polite but intense confrontation between the Chief Justice and the president. Marshall ruled that the evidence sought was germane to the case and issued a subpoena seeking delivery of certain letters to the court in Richmond. The president refused to comply with the subpoena. Jefferson declined to make an appearance at court or to furnish the documents without certain portions deleted,[30] but he did say that transcripts of portions of the letters would be turned over to the court if the material was required. The case turned on other issues, and the subpoena and confrontation faded away.

The exchanges between Jefferson and Marshall were outwardly polite and solicitous of cooperation, but they masked the inner tension of the combatants.

The main issue in the case was Marshall's definition of treason. Burr's attorneys maintained that treason consisted of an actual "levying of war" against the United States. They drew a distinction between the act of war and the advising of it.[31]

The prosecution relied on a broader definition of treason found in English common law that viewed all who contemplated treason as engaging in the act itself. Thus, they argued, Burr was guilty because he advised assembling an armed force and moving it down river to New Orleans.[32]

Marshall ruled that because the prosecution failed to produce two witnesses to the act of treason, or to the procurement of men and arms for the expedition, it had not met the burden of proving the charge of treason.[33] *(Box on treason, p. 398)*

Following Marshall's ruling, the jury found "that Aaron Burr is not proved to be guilty under this indictment by any evidence submitted to us. We therefore find him not guilty."[34]

Antagonism between Marshall and the executive branch subsided when Jefferson retired in 1809. The election of Madison, the appointment of several Republicans to the court, the changing nature of national issues and the demise of Federalism, reduced the grounds of antagonism between the court and the president.

Neither Jefferson nor Marshall "won" the series of confrontations between them. Both men maintained the integrity of their departments. Jefferson had managed to chastise the judiciary through the threat of impeachment, and Marshall raised the prestige of the court and maintained the independence of the judiciary.

Jackson, the Court and the Indians

Andrew Jackson — whose determination to play a strong executive role laid the foundations for the modern concept of presidential power — clashed indirectly with the Supreme Court and claimed for the executive an independent role in constitutional interpretation.

In vetoing the bill to recharter the Second Bank of the United States, Jackson denied that the Supreme Court alone was the ultimate arbiter of constitutional questions. Jackson asserted that the president too might exercise an independent judgment separate from the court and Congress in matters of policy:

> The Congress, the Executive, and the Court must each for itself be guided by its own opinion of the Constitution. Each public officer who takes an oath to support the Constitution swears that he will support it as he understands it, and not as it is understood by others. . . . The opinion of the judges has no more authority over Congress than the opinion of Congress has over the judges, and on that point the President is independent of both. The authority of the Supreme Court must not, therefore, be permitted to control the Congress or the Executive when acting in their legislative capacities, but to have only such influence as the force of their reasoning may deserve.[1]

The theory had its impractical side. If there was no final decision about the constitutionality of a statute, how would serious controversies be resolved? Jackson was vague in his response to that question, and frequently settled matters by sheer force of will, bolstered by his general popularity.[2]

Constitutional conflict between the president and the court threatened to break into open warfare in the early 1830s when the Supreme Court steadfastly rejected the efforts of the state of Georgia to assert its jurisdiction over Cherokee Indians living on Indian land within its boundaries.

The Cherokees had become settled farmers on this land, adopted a constitution, developed an alphabet and proclaimed themselves an independent state. But Georgia, anxious to expel the Indians and open their land for settlement, extended state authority over the region in 1829, declared Indian law nullified by state law and passed measures designed to permit seizure of the Indian lands.[3]

Asserting its newly claimed sovereignty over the region, the Georgia courts convicted a Cherokee named Corn Tassel of murder.[4]

". . .John Marshall has made his decision, now let him enforce it."

—Attributed to President
Andrew Jackson, 1832

The Supreme Court granted Corn Tassel permission to contest his conviction by the state court before the high court. He challenged his conviction on the basis that Georgia had no jurisdiction over Indians and their territory. The state ignored the court's action and executed Corn Tassel on Dec. 24, 1830, before the court could hear his case.[5]

The Supreme Court, faced with such defiance, could do nothing to enforce its authority. President Jackson, sympathetic to the state, did nothing.

Subsequently, the Cherokees asked the Supreme Court to restrain Georgia from enforcing its laws over the Indians. Acting as an independent nation, the Cherokees filed their **request as an original case before the court.** *(Details p. 307)*

The court dismissed the suit, ruling that Indian tribes were not foreign nations, but "domestic dependent nations" under the sovereignty and dominion of the United States.[6]

In still another case, decided in 1832, however, the court ruled against Georgia's claim to jurisdiction over the Cherokees.[7] A missionary among the Indians refused to pay a state license fee required of white persons living in Indian territory. Challenging the fee as **unconstitutional state interference in Indian matters, the missionary took his case** to the court. The court agreed and denied the state power to enforce the fee requirement, ordering him released from prison. The state declared it would resist enforcement of the court's ruling.[8]

President Jackson refused to act. The Supreme Court was powerless to enforce its own ruling. Jackson is alleged to have said: "Well, John Marshall has made his decision, **now let him enforce it."** *(Box p. 239)*

For a few months, the stalemate held. The precedent of defiance of national authority set by Georgia, however, was quickly followed by South Carolina, which declared that it had the power to nullify — through non-enforcement — the controversial tariff act of 1832.[9] That nullification threat prompted Jackson to issue a vigorous rebuttal, asserting federal authority against such a state challenge to enforcement of federal law.[10]

In the light of Jackson's strong stand against nullification, the conflict between Georgia and the court faded. The state realized that President Jackson could not continue to support Georgia's defiance while condemning South Carolina for similar action. *(Details p. 307)*

Lincoln v. Taney

Chief Justice Roger B. Taney helped elect Abraham Lincoln President in 1860. The Supreme Court's 1857 decision in the controversial *Dred Scott* case — in which Taney wrote the major opinion — split the Democratic Party into northern and southern wings over the issue of slavery. That schism gave Lincoln, a Republican, the victory over the northern Democrat Stephen A. Douglas and two southern candidates, John C. Breckinridge and John Bell.

In the *Dred Scott* case, the court held that Congress lacked the power to ban the expansion of slavery into the territories. Lincoln's opposition to this ruling brought him to national prominence in 1858. Running for a Senate seat from Illinois, against Douglas, Lincoln aired his opposition to the decision in a series of seven head-to-head debates on slavery around the state of Illinois. *(Details on ruling p. 135)*

Lincoln promised to do all he could to have the ruling overturned and, as president, he asserted the chief executive's right to seek solutions to such problems as equal to that of the court.

In his first inaugural address, Lincoln declared:

> [I]f the policy of the Government upon vital questions affecting the whole people, is to be irrevocably fixed by decisions of the Supreme Court, the instant they are made in ordinary litigation between parties in personal actions, the people will have ceased to be their own rulers, having to that extent practically resigned their government into the hands of that imminent tribunal."[1]

Against this backdrop of confrontation, the old Jacksonian Democrat Taney and the new Republican president locked horns over Lincoln's suspension of the privilege of the writ of *habeas corpus* during the Civil War.

The antagonism of court and executive, of Taney and Lincoln, intensified with war. Six weeks after the opening guns of the Civil War were heard at Fort Sumter, Taney challenged Lincoln's decision to suspend the privilege of the writ.

John Merryman was arrested by Union soldiers in Maryland and charged with aiding Baltimore secessionists. Imprisoned by the military at Fort McHenry, Merryman obtained a writ of *habeas corpus* challenging his detention. Prison officials refused to comply with the writ, which ordered Merryman's release, citing Lincoln's proclamation suspending the writ when public safety was threatened.[2]

Chief Justice Taney, acting as a circuit judge, issued a contempt citation against the fort commander and demanded the appearance of Merryman at circuit court proceedings in Baltimore. The military commander prevented the writ from being served and refused to deliver up Merryman.

Taney then proceeded to write an opinion holding suspension of the writ unconstitutional.[3] Taney lectured President Lincoln on his duty to enforce the law:

> . . .I can see no ground whatever for supposing that the President in any emergency or in any state of things can authorize the suspension of the privilege of the writ of *habeas corpus,* or arrest a citizen except in aid of the judicial power. He certainly does not faithfully execute the laws if he takes upon himself legislative power by suspending the writ of *habeas corpus* — and the judicial power, also, by arresting and imprisoning a person without the process of law.[4]

Lincoln responded to the Taney opinion in his July 4, 1861, Message to Congress,[5] in which he maintained his theory that wartime emergency measures superceded constitutional niceties.

During the next two years, Lincoln, through Secretary of War Edwin M. Stanton, instituted censorship, military arrest and trial, and continued to suspend or ignore *habeas corpus* requirements in the cases of individuals suspected of aiding the Confederate cause.[6]

The State Department directed arrests through an elaborate network of secret servicemen, federal marshals and military authorities. Hundreds of persons were arrested without being told why. The suspension of *habeas corpus* enabled authorities to hold them without sufficient evidence or legal action until the emergency that led to the arrest passed. Military officers disregarded judicial orders for the release of prisoners. Legal clashes between civil and military authorities were frequent during the war, but the military — backed by the president — held the upper hand.[7]

Did Jackson Really Say That?

Historical research indicates that Andrew Jackson probably never made the famous "John Marshall" remark attributed to him for decades after the crisis between Georgia and the Supreme Court over the Cherokee Indians in 1832.[1]

When the court, led by Chief Justice John Marshall, ruled that Georgia had no jurisdiction over the Cherokee Indians and their lands that lay within the state's boundaries, Jackson allegedly commented: "Well, John Marshall has made his decision, now let him enforce it."

The words reflected Jackson's views, but, like the story of George Washington and the cherry tree episode, Jackson's remarks were probably invented by folklorists to enhance the reputation of a famous man.

The remark was attributed by American journalist and newspaperman Horace Greeley in 1864 to Jackson's reported conversation with George M. Briggs of Massachusetts, a member of Congress at the time of the court's decision.[2]

However, no writer prior to Greeley reported the remark. It reappeared in William G. Sumner's *Life of Andrew Jackson* (1899) and was reprinted by others. John Spencer Bassett, Jackson's biographer, wrote in 1910 that the remark was "a popular tradition. . . . It is not sure that the words were actually uttered, but it is certain, from Jackson's view and temperament, that they might have been spoken." [3]

---

[1] Joseph C. Burke, "The Cherokee Cases: A Study in Law, Politics and Morality," *Stanford Law Review* 21: 500-531.

[2] Horace Greeley, *American Conflict: A History of the Great Rebellion in the United States of America,* 1860-1865, 2 vols. (Westport, Conn.: Greenwood Press, 1969 repr. of 1864 ed.), I:106.

[3] John S. Bassett, *Life of Andrew Jackson,* 2 vols. in 1 (Hamden, Conn.: Shoe String Press, 1967 repr. of 1931 ed.), II:688-692.

In 1862, the administration turned control of arrests over to the War Department. Lincoln declared that all persons resisting the draft or discouraging military enlistments were subject to court martial. Thousands of citizens suspected of disloyalty were arrested, imprisoned and then released without trial after the particular emergency passed.[8] Lincoln elaborated his theory of presidential leadership in an 1863 letter to Erastus Corning, an iron manufacturer and former mayor of Albany, New York:

> Thoroughly imbued with a reverence for the guaranteed rights of individuals, I was slow to adopt the strong measures which by degrees I have been forced to regard as being within the exceptions of the Constitution and as indispensable to the public safety. . . . I concede that the class of arrests complained of can be constitutional only when in cases of rebellion or invasion the public safety may require them; and I insist that in such cases they are constitutional wherever the public safety does require them, as well as in places in which they may prevent the rebellion extending as in those where it may already be prevailing.[9]

Beneath the legal arguments, the clash between Taney and Lincoln rested on differences of opinion about the importance of preserving the Union. Lincoln believed the preservation of the Union was paramount. The federal government in such an emergency could exercise powers that required the temporary sacrifice of civil liberties and civil procedures. Taney, on the other hand, considered the bloodshed and violence and the extra-constitutional actions necessary to preserve the Union a greater disaster than dissolution. [10]

Taney died Oct. 12, 1864. Two years later in the case of *Ex parte Milligan,* the court vindicated his stance in *Merryman* and ruled the president's use of military tribunals outside the war zone unconstitutional. [11] *(Details p. 189)*

Lincoln appointed his secretary of the Treasury, Salmon P. Chase, Chief Justice in Taney's place. In 1870, it was Chief Justice Chase, however, who wrote the court's opinion in the first *Legal Tender Case,* declaring the Lincoln administration's Legal Tender Acts, which authorized the use of paper money during the war, unconstitutional. *(Details p. 119)*

The Court and the Roosevelt Revolution

The stock market crash of 1929 and the ensuing Great Depression were economic crises of proportions unprecedented in American history.

But President Herbert C. Hoover was philosophically unable to view the Depression as more than an economic "adjustment period" and thus continued optimistically to predict that the economy would correct itself. Many business leaders believed Hoover, preaching confidently that prosperity was just around the corner. But the dream of recovery became an American nightmare.

Unemployment reached the 12-million mark, industrial production toppled to less than half of 1929 levels, and by 1933 the entire banking network of the nation was on the verge of collapse. [1] Economic crisis precipitated social crisis. And social discontent found its expression in a major political upheaval.

Hoover: 1929-1932

Hoover did not believe in broad governmental relief or social reform programs. His abiding faith in "rugged individualism" and limited government prevented his espousal of any full-scale economic recovery measures. His constitutional conservatism rejected any suggestion that federal power might be expanded to deal with the crisis.

Thus, it was not surprising when Hoover was repudiated at the polls in 1932. Democratic candidate Franklin Delano Roosevelt, former governor of New York, was elected president by an impressive margin.

The 'Hundred Days'

Roosevelt took office in March 1933; large Democratic majorities controlled both houses of Congress.

In his inaugural address, the Hyde Park, N.Y., aristocrat made clear his view of the economic crisis as a national emergency in which he would exercise "broad executive power to wage a war against the emergency as great as the power that would be given me if we were in fact invaded by a foreign foe." [2]

A special session of Congress was called by the new president, convening on March 9, 1933. In the next "hundred days," the Congress, led by Roosevelt and his "Brain Trust," attacked the Depression on all fronts.

Banking

The Emergency Banking Act of March 9, 1933, retroactively sanctioned a "bank holiday." Roosevelt had earlier closed all the nation's banks and suspended all gold exports and foreign exchange operations. The bill also called for surrender of all gold and gold certificates to the Treasury to be exchanged for an equal amount of other currency.

The purpose of the act was to halt the hoarding of currency and to set the stage for a mild inflationary devaluation of the money supply. The banking measures, the Gold Reserve Act of 1934 and the congressional joint resolution of June 5, 1933, took gold out of circulation, reduced the gold content of the dollar and cancelled the "gold clause" in private contracts which stipulated that a fixed amount of a debt be paid in gold. [3]

Agriculture

The most important agricultural relief measure of the New Deal was the Agricultural Adjustment Act (AAA) of May 12, 1933. The purpose of the AAA was to restore agricultural prices to pre-war (1914) levels — reducing farm production by retiring acreage from use.

The AAA provided for an agreement between farmers and the federal government that the farmer would plant fewer acres and in return would receive better prices for his goods — prices bolstered by a government subsidy. [4] The whole program was financed through a tax on processors of each affected commodity.

Labor and Industry

New Deal efforts to restore industrial production and reduce unemployment operated on a theory of limited industrial self-government. The program attempted to bring about cooperation between large and small manufacturing concerns and their employees.

Thus the National Industrial Recovery Act (NIRA) of June 16, 1933, established "codes of fair competition" for wages, prices and trade practices. The codes, drafted by representatives of business and trade groups, were submitted for approval to the president, who was empowered to prescribe the codes. Once approved, the codes became the standard of commercial practice in a particular industry, with violations punishable as violations of the Federal Trade Commission Act.

In addition, the NIRA stipulated that labor had the right to organize workers for collective bargaining. [5]

TVA

An act of May 18, 1933, created the Tennessee Valley Authority (TVA), a government corporation authorized to construct dams and reservoirs as part of a development project for the Tennessee Valley region. The entire project included flood control, reforestation and agricultural and industrial projects. TVA also produced fertilizer, explosives and, eventually, electric power.

The Constitutional Base

This emergency relief and recovery program had its constitutional basis in emergency executive powers, and the power of Congress to provide for the general welfare and to regulate interstate commerce.

It was the most far-reaching assertion to date of national leadership.

The need for immediate action eliminated the usual procedures of lengthy debate and deliberation. Roosevelt's "Brain Trust" hammered out the legislation in conference with the president and representatives of affected interest groups. Once drafted, the bills were presented to Congress as "must" legislation, and Congress generally responded with alacrity.

New Deal and Old Court

The extraordinary exercise of legislative and executive power reflected and authorized by the New Deal legislation was certain to be tested in the Supreme Court. Several of the key cases which came to the court in the next three years were, in fact, test cases, brought by the administration itself.

The Supreme Court of 1933, however, was hardly a body that could be expected to be receptive to revolutionary uses of federal power.

Six of the justices had sat on the bench since the pre-Depression Twenties — or earlier. Four of them were staunch conservatives: Taft nominee Willis Van Devanter, Wilson choice James C. McReynolds, and two Harding nominees, George Sutherland and Pierce Butler.

Two other justices — Louis D. Brandeis and Harlan Fiske Stone — had been appointed by Wilson and Coolidge, respectively, and tended to take more liberal views on questions of federal power.

The three newest members of the court were all Hoover nominees — Chief Justice Charles Evans Hughes, and Associate Justices Benjamin Cardozo and Owen J. Roberts.

Hughes, a former associate justice, governor of New York, presidential nominee and secretary of state, had been considered a liberal earlier in his career, but had acquired a more conservative reputation as his fame and fortune increased. He was named Chief Justice in 1930, to succeed Chief Justice William Howard Taft.

Roberts, a successful Republican attorney from Pennsylvania, had been named to the court in the same year. Hoover, noting Roberts' progressive reputation, considered him a liberal appointment.[6] Cardozo, a liberal and well-regarded legal scholar and judge, had been appointed by Hoover in 1932.

Hopeful Signs

In 1934, the court seemed to hint that it would take a favorable attitude toward the "emergency" exercise of extraordinary power in the New Deal statutes. In January of that year, the court upheld, against constitutional challenge, a state moratorium law.[7]

Chief Justice Hughes explained that although emergencies did not create power they did empower government to act in ways that might be considered unconstitutional in normal circumstances. The vote in the case, however, was

5-4. Dissenting were Sutherland, Van Devanter, McReynolds and Butler.

Two months later, by an identical vote, the court upheld a state law creating a board empowered to fix minimum and maximum prices for milk.[8] In the majority opinion, Roberts wrote that the state possessed the power to decide and adopt whatever reasonable economic policy toward business promoted the public welfare.

But the hopes raised by these rulings were shattered by key decisions announced in the next two court terms.

The 'Hot Oil' Case

Between January 1935 and June 1936, the Supreme Court ruled against the New Deal in eight out of ten major cases involving New Deal statutes. The court upheld only the emergency monetary legislation of 1933 and the creation of the Tennessee Valley Authority.[9]

The first blow came on Jan. 7, 1935. In the case of *Panama Refining Co. v. Ryan,* the "hot oil" case, the court held unconstitutional the portion of the National Industrial Recovery Act which provided for a code to govern the production of oil and petroleum products. With only Cardozo dissenting, the court held that the contested portion unlawfully delegated legislative power to the president.[10]

Three months later, on May 6, the Railroad Retirement Act was struck down. The court ruled that Congress had exceeded the scope of its power to regulate interstate commerce when it approved the creation of an industry-wide pension system. The vote was 5-4; Roberts sided with the conservatives. Chief Justice Hughes, dissenting with Brandeis, Cardozo and Stone, scolded the majority for placing such "an unwarranted limitation upon the commerce clause of the Constitution."[11]

Black Monday

The most devastating single day of this period, however, came on "Black Monday," May 27, 1935. In unanimous decisions announced that day, the court struck to the heart of President Roosevelt's concept of presidential power.

The court struck down a federal farm mortgage relief act, finding it unfair to creditors.[12]

Then the court, in the case of *Schechter Poultry Corp. v. United States,* held the key portion of the National Industrial Recovery Act unconstitutional.[13]

In a third blow to the power of the executive, the court held that the president lacked any inherent power to remove members of the Federal Trade Commission from their posts.[14] *(Details p. 214)*

The most devastating was the NIRA ruling. Rejection of that recovery plan threatened nullification of the entire New Deal economy program. The NIRA had encouraged the creation of industry-wide, presidentially-approved codes of competition, eventually adopted to govern almost every service trade and industry.

But critics of the NIRA saw it as government interference in matters which should be left to private enterprise. Even before the court heard the *Schechter* case, difficulties with implementing the NIRA had convinced the administration that a major overhaul of the program was needed.[15]

Despite its shortcomings, however, the NIRA had provided needed action in time of crisis. Psychologically, it had worked to restore confidence among the people — in themselves and in the economy, although by 1935 there was also clear evidence that the codes were sometimes used by business to promote their interests at the expense of the public.

Schechter was picked as a test case by the administration, which acknowledged it was not the best vehicle for ascertaining the validity of the NIRA program.[16] It focused on the fair trade provisions affecting the poultry industry. The Schechter brothers of Brooklyn had been convicted of violating both fair trade and the labor provisions of the poultry industry's code.[17]

When the Supreme Court ruled on the matter, it found unanimously that the NIRA was an unconstitutional delegation of legislative power to the president, allowing him to approve the codes for each industry which then had the force of law. Furthermore, wrote Chief Justice Hughes for the majority, allowing trade and industry groups to make the codes in the first place, amounted to delegation of the legislative authority to private citizens. [18]

Roosevelt assessed the implications of the "Black Monday" decisions in a press conference on May 31:

> Is the United States going to decide . . . that their Federal Government shall in the future have no right **under any implied or any court-approved power to** enter into a solution of a national economic problem, but that that national economic problems must be decided only by the States? . . . We thought we were solving it, and now it has been thrown right straight in our faces. We have been relegated to the horse-and-buggy definition of interstate commerce.[19]

States' Rights Rulings

The year 1936 began with still another blow to the New Deal. On Jan. 6, the court struck down the Agricultural Adjustment Act as an unconstitutional invasion of states' rights. The court divided 6-3 on the question and the divisions were bitter ones.[20] Roberts and Chief Justice Hughes voted with the conservatives; Stone, Brandeis and Cardozo dissented.

Writing for the majority in *United States v. Butler,* Justice Roberts set out the view that agriculture was a matter reserved to state, not federal, regulation. The AAA program was an improper use of congressional authority to regulate agriculture, the majority held. The processing tax it imposed was a penalty to force compliance with the AAA acreage reduction program — an impermissible objective and thus an impermissible use of the taxing power.

In May, 1936, the court struck again. The Bituminous Coal Conservation Act was held an unconstitutional invasion of states' rights. The Act, also called the Guffey Act, was the New Deal's effort to control and regulate coal production. It set up a commission to adopt codes to regulate production in various regions and it levied a tax on coal which was partially refunded to operators abiding by the code. The law also guaranteed collective bargaining rights in the industry.[21]

Mining, like agriculture, was a matter for states to regulate, wrote Justice Sutherland for the majority in *Carter v. Carter Coal Co.* The tax in this case, as in *Butler,* was a means to an impermissible end and thus must fall. Congress had overreached its proper power.[22]

A week later, the court struck down the Municipal Bankruptcy Act — again as an invasion of the rights of states. The vote in *Ashton v. Cameron County District* was 5-4. Hughes, Cardozo, Brandeis and Stone dissented.

Writing for the majority, Justice McReynolds held that the law permitting subdivisions of the states to file for bankruptcy to readjust their debt obligations was unconstitutional, an impermissible extension of federal power.[23] The dissenters responded that the voluntary municipal bankruptcy petitions to which the state consented were not an invasion of state sovereignty.[24]

The Roosevelt recovery and reform programs launched in the first Hundred Days did extend federal authority over matters left previously to state authority. The shift in the balance between state and federal power seemed to many to threaten to erode the structure of the Union. Such critics supported the court's strict construction and dual federalism doctrines to counterbalance the New Deal's challenge to the traditional arrangements of power.

Counterattack

If the justices of the Supreme Court read the election results in November 1936, they got a clear message that Roosevelt had overwhelming popular support in his attempt to combat the Depression and its effects. In the 1936 presidential election a moderate economic recovery blended with a sense of pragmatic purpose, Roosevelt's personal charm and his expressed concern for the "little man" to overwhelm the mildly reform-minded Alfred E. Landon, the Republican standard-bearer. Landon's only issue was Roosevelt, and the Republicans had to admit the necessity of many New Deal reforms.[25] Landon carried Maine and Vermont. Roosevelt carried all other states.

The court's opposition to a program and a president with such an overwhelming mandate began to produce a public view of the court as an obstacle to reform. Members of Congress recommended that Congress curtail the court's jurisdiction. Sen. Joseph O'Mahoney, D-Wyo. (1934-53, 1954-56), proposed that the court be required to have a two-thirds majority vote when it declared acts of Congress unconstitutional. Sen. Burton K. Wheeler, D-Mont. (1923-47), **proposed a constitutional amendment that permitted** Congress to override a court decision by a two-thirds vote of both houses.[26]

But the thrust of the counterattack came from Roosevelt. In his second inaugural speech he urged all agencies of the government to cooperate in advancing the common good.[27]

The Plan

On February 5, 1937, Roosevelt sent Congress a message that proposed a judicial "reorganization." The measure would have increased the number of Supreme Court justices to as many as 15, creating one new seat for each justice who, upon reaching the age of 70, declined to retire.[28] Thus, for every justice age 70 or over the president could appoint another one up to a maximum of six. The measure also called for other changes: the addition of a total of fifty new judges for all federal courts; a rule that appeals on constitutional matters move directly to the Supreme Court; a requirement that government attorneys be heard before any court granted an injunction against enforcement of an act of Congress in cases where the act's constitutional status was questioned; and assignment of district judges to congested areas to relieve the backlog and expedite business.[29]

Roosevelt presented the plan as a bill to relieve the justices' workload. In his message he explained that the court's work was "handicapped by insufficient personnel" and by the presence of old judges unable to perform their duties. As Roosevelt put it, "little by little, new facts became blurred through old glasses fitted, as it were, for the needs of another generation." [30]

It was not a characteristic Roosevelt message. It lacked simplicity and clarity. The proposals were too technical and too confusing for easy public comprehension. And the president's purpose was only slightly concealed. It was a "court-packing" scheme to get liberal Roosevelt-appointed justices on the bench to reverse its anti-New Deal stance.

Public Reaction

Roosevelt, however, had miscalculated public reaction to such a proposal. He had not prepared the public or obtained the advice of Senate leaders before introducing the measure.[31] The message, and the remedy suggested, reflected the president's sense of desperate frustration with the court's performance. With a number of important measures pending before the court, the president felt impelled to make certain the New Deal would not be further obstructed by the court. As Robert Jackson would later write, "The Court seemed to have declared the mortality table unconstitutional and a nation was waiting for the President to move." [32]

The plan touched off a widespread and bitter debate in Congress and in the nation. Harold Ickes, Roosevelt's Secretary of the Interior, noted that no other single measure "has caused the spilling of so much printer's ink or led to so many fervent discussions. The President has a first class fight on his hands. Practically all of the newspapers are against him. . . . But the worst of it is that some of the progressives in Congress and outside are lining up with the reactionaries." [33]

At a Democratic victory dinner March 4, 1937, Roosevelt assailed the court for rendering the nation powerless to deal with the problems of economic recovery.[34] In a radio "fireside chat" broadcast a few days later Roosevelt told the American people that the court had:

> . . . cast doubts on the ability of the elected Congress to protect us against catastrophe by meeting squarely our modern social and economic conditions. . . . This plan will save our National Constitution from hardening of the judicial arteries.[35]

But the idea of tampering with the Supreme Court met vigorous public opposition. The public still regarded the nine-member court as the guardian of the Constitution, aloof from politics. The proposal to increase the court's membership was criticized as perverting the Constitution and destroying judicial integrity and independence.[36]

The court-plan fight split the Democrats in Congress. By early March Sen. Burton K. Wheeler, a New Dealer, was leading the fight against the bill, whose supporters in the Senate were led by Carter Glass, D-Va. (1920-46), Joseph Robinson, D-Ark. (1913-37), and Edward Burk, D-Neb. (1935-41).[37] The Republican minority, content to let Democrats fight among themselves over the merits of the plan, remained in the background.

During hearings on the bill by the Senate Judiciary Committee, Sen. Wheeler made public a letter from Chief Justice Charles Evans Hughes that denied every assertion the president had made with respect to the court's work-load and performance. An increase in the number of justices, wrote Hughes, would actually delay the court's work by prolonging deliberation on each case.

Justice Brandeis, convinced that Roosevelt's plan threatened the separation of powers doctrine under the Constitution, added his signature to the letter. Hughes had told Wheeler that in the interest of saving time he had not obtained the signatures of the other justices to the letter. Hughes' remark left Wheeler with the impression that the letter reflected the unanimous opinion of the court. Later research revealed, however, that Justice Stone would not have supported Hughes or signed the letter.[38] However, publication of the Hughes-Brandeis letter damaged chances for passage of the reorganization plan.

A Court Reversal

The court itself dealt the death blow to the court-packing plan with a series of decisions announced between late March and late May 1937 upholding New Deal measures.

On March 29, by a 5-4 vote, the court upheld a state minimum wage law for women — nearly identical to a state law struck down ten months earlier, also by a 5-4 vote.[39] The same day, the court unanimously upheld a revised farm mortgage moratorium act — repassed by Congress after its predecessor was unanimously voided by the court in 1935.[40]

On April 12, again by a 5-4 vote, the court upheld the National Labor Relations Act.[41] And on May 24, by votes of 5-4 and 7-2, the court upheld both the unemployment compensation and the old-age benefits of the Social Security Act.[42]

In each case where the vote was 5-4, Justice Roberts — now in favor of New Deal statutes — cast the deciding vote, abandoning the four conservatives with whom he had voted in previous terms to join Chief Justice Hughes and the three more liberal justices.

Justice Roberts' "switch in time" was long assumed to be a direct response to the court-packing threat. The key case indicating his shift was the minimum wage ruling.

When the court in June 1936 struck down New York state's minimum wage law — citing a 1923 precedent — Roberts had voted with the conservatives to form the five-man majority against the law. They found it an unconstitutional infringement on the freedom of contract.[43]

In December 1936, a similar case from Washington state — *West Coast Hotel v. Parrish* — was argued before the court.[44] On Dec. 19, the justices voted in conference on that case. Justice Harlan Fiske Stone was absent. The court divided 4-4 — with Roberts voting to uphold the law.

The justices decided to await Stone's return and his vote. On Feb. 6 — the day after Roosevelt sent his "judicial reorganization" message to Congress — Stone voted. As he had done in the New York case, he voted to uphold the minimum wage law. With Roberts' already-cast vote, the court was now on its own private record 5-4 to uphold the law. The decision was announced on March 29 after the court-packing battle was under way — but Roberts' switch had occurred long before.

The story of Roberts' switch did not emerge until later. At the time it was widely assumed to show the impact of the president's threat. Felix Frankfurter later obtained from Roberts a memorandum outlining the events related above which made clear that Roberts' change-of-mind preceded the court-packing threat.[45]

Other developments also spelled defeat for the plan. The Supreme Court Retirement Act approved by Roosevelt in March 1937 permitted justices to retire without resigning, retaining pension and other benefits, at age 70. Justice Willis Van Devanter, a New Deal foe, announced May 18 that he would retire at the end of the term, giving Roosevelt his first opportunity to appoint a man to the court.

Sen. "Joe" Robinson, the majority leader in the Senate floor fight on behalf of the Roosevelt plan, died of a heart attack July 14. The Senate recommitted the court-packing bill to the Judiciary Committee July 22.[46]

The administration later accepted a watered down reorganization measure that reformed lower court procedure but included no provision for additional justices on the Supreme Court. Roosevelt signed that bill August 26.[47]

Roosevelt's victory was not without its costs. His proposal and the battle which ensued opened a break in Democratic party ranks that took years to heal. After 1938, a conservative congressional coalition composed of southern Democrats and Republicans blocked New Deal measures with repeated regularity.[48]

Roosevelt made four appointments to the court between 1937 and 1940. Sen. Hugo L. Black replaced Van Devanter in 1937. Stanley F. Reed replaced George Sutherland in 1938. Roosevelt's longtime friend Felix Frankfurter took Cardozo's place in 1939 and Justice William O. Douglas was appointed after Brandeis retired in 1939.

After 1937, the Supreme Court launched a revolution of its own. It repudiated the dual federalism concept that federal power was limited by states' rights. In cases involving labor relations, manufacturing, agriculture and the spending power, the court espoused a broad concept of federal power.

The court gradually repudiated the earlier limits it had imposed on the commerce power. In the 1941 decision in *United States v. Darby,* the court approved federal wage and hour standards prescribed in the Fair Labor Standards Act. In 1939, with its decision in *Mulford v. Smith,* the court upheld the second Agricultural Adjustment Act. And soon the limitation on federal spending imposed in *Butler* was also swept away.[49] *(Details, pp. 101, 118)*

Truman v. The Court

Late in his second term, President Harry S Truman collided with the Supreme Court. The issue was his decision to seize and operate the nation's steel mills in order to avoid a strike which would disrupt production and, Truman felt, jeopardize the U.S. war effort in Korea.

The result was a ruling in which the court declared a halt to the steady expansion of "emergency" executive power which began in the days of Depression and accelerated during World War II.

The decision was announced June 2, 1953. The vote was 6-3. Of the four justices named to the court by Truman, two voted to uphold the president's action and two opposed it.

The Seizure Order

The United Steel Workers of America announced an industry-wide strike, to begin April 9, 1952.[1] Bargaining sessions to avert the strike through a negotiated settlement, encouraged by the efforts of the Wage Stabilization Board (WSB), ended in failure when the plant operators rejected a WSB wage settlement formula.[2]

On April 8, Truman issued an Executive Order to Secretary of Commerce Charles Sawyer directing him to seize and operate the nation's steel mills. The order cited the state of national emergency proclaimed Dec. 16, 1950 — after the Chinese invasion of Korea — and the necessity to maintain uninterrupted steel production during the war. Truman explained his action as a proper exercise of general executive authority granted by Article II, as well as his more specific power as commander in chief.[3]

Truman's advisers calculated that a halt in steel production would endanger the lives of men on the battlefield by reducing supplies of guns and ammunition. They forecast that shortages in steel would limit aircraft production, power plant construction, shipbuilding and atomic weapons research.

The steel companies attacked the order as unconstitutional and went to court,[4] obtaining an injunction in the District of Columbia restraining Secretary of Commerce Sawyer from carrying out the seizure order.

The court of appeals then stayed the district court injunction and the case moved to the Supreme Court for consideration of the constitutional challenge to the president's seizure power.

The Decision

The case of *Youngstown Sheet and Tube Co. v. Sawyer* was argued May 12-13, 1952.

Three weeks later on June 2, the court ruled 6-3 against Truman. In an opinion written by Justice Hugo L. Black, the majority held that the president's seizure of the steel mills was an unconstitutional exercise of power.

The court rejected the theory of executive prerogative implicit in Truman's order. The president lacked statutory authority for the seizure, Black wrote, and neither the commander in chief power, nor any inherent executive prerogative provided authority for it.

The Executive Order was invalid, the court held, because it attempted to make law while the Constitution limited the president "to the recommending of laws he thinks wise and the vetoing of laws he thinks bad." Black relied on the legislative history of the 1947 Labor-Management Relations (Taft-Hartley) Act, in which Congress had decided against authorizing the president to seize strike-bound industrial plants. *(Details pp. 193-194)*

All five other members of the majority wrote concurring opinions. Justices Harold H.Burton and Felix Frankfurter thought the president should have invoked the Taft-Hartley Act provisions for a cooling-off period. They declared that in light of Congress' rejection of such a seizure authority in that act, Truman's order contradicted"the clear will of Congress."[5]

Justice Tom Clark agreed that the president had, in this instance, violated procedures set out by Congress for the settlement of strikes.[6] Justice William O. Douglas wrote that court sanction of Truman's seizure would have expanded Article II of the Constitution to "suit the political conveniences of the present emergency."[7]

Chief Justice Fred M. Vinson, joined by Justices Stanley F. Reed and Sherman Minton dissented, emphasizing the nature of the national emergency and the discretionary power of the president in times of crisis. Vinson found the president's action supportive of congressional intention in that the seizure was for the purpose of insuring steel for weapons to conduct a congressionally supported war in Korea. The Chief Justice's dissent was a pragmatic argument that accepted the view of an expanded executive prerogative as a fact of constitutional life in the 20th century.[8]

Truman later wrote:

> . . .[T]he Supreme Court's decision . . . was a deep disappointment to me. I think Chief Justice Vinson's dissenting opinion hit the nail right on the head, and I am sure that someday his view will come to be recognized as the correct one.[9]

The administration decided not to attempt a settlement. The following week Truman sought legislative authorization for the seizure of the strikebound plants. Congress refused.

The strike lasted fifty-three days — and ended July 24. Six hundred thousand steel workers and 25,000 iron-ore workers who had been on a sympathy strike part of that time had been idled seven weeks. Losses in wages and production were estimated at $2 billion.

Truman claimed that military shortages in certain types of ammunition were experienced in the summer and fall of 1952 as a result of the loss in steel production occasioned by the strike and the court's refusal to sanction his handling of it.[10]

Truman's *Memoirs* gave his personal view of the court's action and the president's powers:

> It is not very realistic for the justices to say that comprehensive powers shall be available to the President only when a war has been declared or when the country has been invaded. We live in an age when hostilities begin without polite exchanges of diplomatic notes. There are no longer sharp distinctions between combatants and noncombatants. . . . Nor can we separate the economic facts from the problems of defense and security. . . . The President, who is Commander-in-Chief and who represents the interest of all the people, must [be] able to act at all times to meet any sudden threat to the nation's security. A wise President will always work with Congress, but when Congress fails to act or is unable to act in a crisis, the President, under the Constitution, must use his powers to safeguard the nation.[11]

Nixon, Watergate and the Court

Richard M. Nixon campaigned for the presidency in 1968 as an anti-court candidate, promising that, if elected, he would by his appointments change the court from one which "coddled" criminals to one which was more responsive to the problems and the needs of law enforcement officers.

Nixon was elected and, in his first term, he placed four new members on the court: Chief Justice Warren Burger, Justices Harry A. Blackmun, Lewis F. Powell Jr. and William H. Rehnquist, all chosen for their conservative views on questions of law and order.

But in the most ironic of circumstances, Nixon in 1974 found himself before the court arguing that he had the right to withhold evidence sought by a prosecutor for use in a criminal trial. The court's response was negative.

After an initial silence, Nixon accepted the court's decision. Two weeks later — realizing the import of that evidence for his own reputation and fate in an ongoing impeachment inquiry — Nixon resigned the presidency.

Nixon's resignation mooted the impeachment proceedings, which had begun as a result of Nixon's response to the investigation of the so-called Watergate scandal.

The burglary of the Democratic National Headquarters offices in the Washington, D.C., Watergate complex in mid-1972, and the attempted cover-up of White House involvement in the affair, was the immediate source of Nixon's troubles.

But it was by no means the only matter which brought him into collision with the Supreme Court.

During his years in office, Nixon's claims of broad executive prerogative to act in the interests of national security, to refuse to spend congressionally provided funds, or to withhold information brought him before the court. In five of the six cases involving Nixon's claims, the court ruled against him.

Pentagon Papers

In June 1971 *The New York Times* and *The Washington Post* began publication of articles based on a top-secret Defense Department analysis of the United States' role in the war in Southeast Asia. Both newspapers had obtained copies of the classified document.

The Nixon administration, criticized for its conduct of the war, attempted to block publication of the articles. Administration attorneys argued that publication would result in a diplomatic imbroglio and would damage the nation's security.[1]

Attorney General John N. Mitchell first asked the newspapers to halt publication. Both refused.

Mitchell then obtained an injunction from a federal court in New York ordering the *Times* to halt publication of the articles. But a federal court in the District of Columbia refused to grant a similar order against the *Post*. Both cases were appealed to the Supreme Court.

The Nixon administration argued that national security interests justified such "prior restraint" of publication; the *Times* and the *Post* responded that such a curb on the freedom of the press violated the First Amendment.

On June 30, 1971, the court ruled 6-3 against the Nixon administration. The majority held that the government had failed to meet the heavy burden of justifying prior restraint based on the claim that publication would damage national security. The court allowed publication of the articles to continue.[2]

The court did not deny that there might be circumstances in which such a restraint might be justified; they simply held that it had not been justified here.[3] *(Details p. 232)*

Wiretapping

A year later, the Nixon administration again lost a national security argument before the court.

Only since 1968 had Congress provided statutory authority for the use of wiretaps or electronic surveillance by law enforcement officers. To minimize the invasion of individual rights which could result, Congress required that every tap or electronic surveillance be approved by a federal judge, who would issue a warrant approving the surveillance. This was part of the Omnibus Crime Control and Safe Streets Act of 1968.[4]

The Nixon administration claimed, however, that this court approval and warrant requirement did not apply to its use of wiretaps to keep track of the activities of domestic groups suspected of subversive activities. These wiretaps were legal, administration lawyers argued, as "a reasonable exercise of the President's power . . . to protect the national security."[5]

Justices From the Cabinet

Thirty-two justices of the Supreme Court — including nine Chief Justices — served as executive branch officials before their appointment to the court. Eighteen held Cabinet-level posts — nine of them were Attorneys General — and another eight served in other posts in the Department of Justice.

Four men — Roger B. Taney, Levi Woodbury, William H. Moody and William Howard Taft — held more than one Cabinet post. Taft held more high executive branch posts than any other justice. He is the only man to serve both as president and Chief Justice of the United States.

The following table lists the justices, the major executive branch positions they held and their years of service.

Justice	Position	Court Service
John Jay*	Secretary for Foreign Affairs under the Articles of Confederation, 1784-1789; U.S. Diplomat, 1794-1795	1789-1795
John Marshall*	Envoy to France, 1797-1798; Secretary of State, 1800-1801	1801-1835
Smith Thompson	Secretary of the Navy, 1818-1823	1823-1843
Gabriel Duvall	Comptroller of the Treasury, 1802-1811	1812-1835
John McLean	Postmaster General, 1823-1829	1829-1861
Roger B. Taney*	Attorney General, 1831-1833; Secretary of the Treasury, 1833-1834	1836-1864
Levi Woodbury	Secretary of the Navy, 1831-1834; Secretary of the Treasury, 1834-1841	1845-1851
Nathan Clifford	Attorney General, 1846-1848	1858-1881
Salmon P. Chase*	Secretary of the Treasury, 1861-1864	1864-1873
Lucius Q. C. Lamar	Secretary of the Interior, 1885-1888	1888-1893
Joseph McKenna	Attorney General, 1897-1898	1898-1925
William H. Moody	Secretary of the Navy, 1902-1904; Attorney General, 1904-1906	1906-1910
Charles E. Hughes*	Secretary of State, 1921-1925	1910-1916; 1930-1941
Willis Van Devanter	Counsel, Interior Department, 1897-1903	1910-1937
James McReynolds	Attorney General, 1913-1914	1914-1941
William H. Taft*	U.S. Solicitor General, 1890-1892; Secretary of War, 1904-1908; President, 1908-1912	1921-1930
Edward T. Sanford	Assistant Attorney General, 1907-1908	1923-1930
Harlan F. Stone*	Attorney General, 1924-1925	1925-1946
Owen J. Roberts	Prosecuting Attorney, Teapot Dome Scandal, 1924	1930-1945
Stanley Reed	Solicitor General, 1935-1938	1938-1957
William O. Douglas	Chairman, Securities and Exchange Commission, 1937-1939	1939-1975
Frank Murphy	Attorney General, 1938-1940	1940-1949
James F. Byrnes	Secretary of State, 1945-1947	1941-1942
Robert H. Jackson	Solicitor General, 1938-1939; Attorney General, 1940-1941	1941-1954
Fred M. Vinson*	Secretary of Treasury, 1945-1946	1946-1953
Tom C. Clark	Attorney General, 1945-1949	1949-1967
Byron R. White	Deputy Attorney General, 1961-1962	1962–
Arthur J. Goldberg	Secretary of Labor, 1961-1962	1962-1965
Abe Fortas	Under Secretary of Interior, 1942-1946	1965-1969
Thurgood Marshall	Solicitor General, 1964-1967	1967–
Warren E. Burger*	Assistant Attorney General, 1953-1955	1969–
William H. Rehnquist	Assistant Attorney General, 1969-1971	1971–

* Denotes Chief Justice

Sources:

Leon Friedman, Fred L. Israel, eds., *The Justices of the United States Supreme Court 1789-1969, Their Lives and Major Opinions,* 5 vols. (New York and London: Chelsea House, 1969, 1978); *Members of Congress Since 1789* (Washington D.C.: Congressional Quarterly, 1977); William F. Swindler, *Court and Constitution in the Twentieth Century,* 2 vols. (Indianapolis and New York: The Bobbs-Merrill Co., 1969, 1970).

By a 6-2 vote, the Supreme Court in 1972 rejected that claim of inherent power. In domestic security matters, wrote Justice Powell, the "convergence of First and Fourth Amendment values" requires strict observance of constitutional safeguards. "[U]nreviewed executive discretion," he warned, "may yield too readily to pressure to obtain incriminating evidence and overlook potential invasions of privacy and protected speech."[6]

Impoundment

When Congress earmarked funds for programs the president wished to curtail, Nixon simply refused to spend the money. This assertion of the power to impound funds gave Nixon the equivalent of an item veto over congressional appropriations bills, a seemingly unchallengeable mechanism to block any program involving federal expenditures.

Nixon was not the first chief executive to try this tool. Presidents Jefferson, Grant and Franklin Roosevelt had impounded funds, and the procedure had been used as an instrument of fiscal policy by Presidents Truman, Eisenhower and Kennedy.[7]

But legislative authority for impoundment could be derived from the language of the authorizing statute in most previous impoundment incidents. Furthermore, if the money impounded was for defense projects, the president could also argue that, as commander in chief, he had authority to withhold spending for such programs.

Nixon, however, used impoundment more frequently than his predecessors. Between 1969 and 1973, he impounded more than $15 billion in funds intended for more than 100 programs. The affected programs included pollution control, housing, public education and other social programs.

On Jan. 31, 1973, Nixon asserted the president's

...constitutional right ... to impound funds and that is, not to spend money, when the spending of money would mean either increasing prices or increasing taxes for all the people, that right is absolutely clear.[8]

But when one particular impoundment of billions in funds authorized for distribution to states under the Water Pollution Control Act of 1972 came before the Supreme Court, the court rejected Nixon's claim of a constitutional power to impound these funds.

The ruling came six months after Nixon had left office. On Feb. 19, 1975, the court held unanimously that Nixon exceeded his authority when he refused to allocate those water pollution funds to the states. The wording of the 1972 act, wrote Justice Byron R. White, left the president no power to withhold the funds. The decision did not set limits for the president's impoundment power generally, but its implication was that Nixon's claim of such a power was a shaky one.[9]

Watergate and the White House Tapes

The most dramatic of confrontations between court and chief executive came between Nixon and the Supreme Court in July 1974. The decision cost Nixon his office.

In July 1973, a witness before the Senate Select Committee on Presidential Campaign Activities revealed that through secret recording devices, many of President Nixon's conversations with his staff had been recorded on tape.

At the time of the revelation, the Watergate affair and alleged White House involvement in it were under investigation by the select committee, a federal grand jury and a Watergate special prosecution force led by Special Prosecutor Archibald Cox.

The disclosure of the taping system set off a year-long battle for certain White House tapes. The tug-of-war eventually brought Nixon's lawyers to the Supreme Court, defending his right to withhold this evidence.

Cox quickly obtained a subpoena for certain tapes which he wished to use as evidence to the grand jury. Nixon refused to comply, setting off a legal battle which culminated in the "Saturday Night Massacre" of late October 1973. The "massacre," resulting from Cox's refusal to stop his efforts to obtain the tapes, included Cox's firing and the resignations of Attorney General Elliot Richardson and his deputy, William Ruckelshaus, both of whom chose to resign rather than follow Nixon's order to fire Cox. Cox was eventually fired by Solicitor General Robert Bork.

The public outcry over Nixon's actions in this episode forced him to turn over some of the subpoenaed tapes — and led to the initiation of a House impeachment inquiry into the president's conduct.[10]

In March 1974, as the House Judiciary Committee's impeachment investigation was getting under way, former Attorney General John N. Mitchell, former presidential assistants John D. Ehrlichman and H. R. (Bob) Haldeman and four other former Nixon aides were indicted for conspiracy to defraud the United States and to obstruct justice. The charges related to their efforts to cover up White House involvement in the Watergate affair.

In mid-April the new Special Prosecutor, Leon Jaworski, obtained a subpoena ordering Nixon to hand over additional taped conversations for use as evidence in the trial of Mitchell and the others.

Nixon's lawyers moved to quash the subpoena. Federal District Judge John J. Sirica refused and denied the motion. Late in the Supreme Court term, the case moved onto its docket. Quickly, the court decided it would review the matter.[11]

In an extraordinary summer argument session, the cases of *U.S. v. Nixon, Nixon v. U.S.* were argued on July 8, 1974. *(Details p. 232-233)*

On July 24, the court ruled. By an 8-0 vote, it rejected Nixon's claim of an absolute executive privilege to withhold the evidence sought by the special prosecutor. Chief Justice Warren Burger, Nixon's own choice to head the court, wrote the opinion. Only Justice Rehnquist, who had served in the Justice Department under Mitchell before moving to the high bench, did not participate in the case.

Nixon, the court said, must surrender the tapes.

Nixon was at the western White House in California when the decision came. For a few hours there was no word of his reaction. Then came a statement that the president accepted the decision.

That evening the House Judiciary Committee began nationally televised debates on the charges against Nixon. Within the week, it had approved three articles of impeachment.[12]

Two weeks later on Aug. 9 Nixon resigned the post of the presidency.[13]

Still More Tapes

Resignation did not end Nixon's battles before the Supreme Court. Soon thereafter, Nixon and the General Services Administrator reached an agreement concerning control of and access to the tapes and papers of the Nixon administration. As had been the case with other former presidents, Nixon was to have control of those materials.

But Congress, sensitive to the unusual circumstances surrounding Nixon's departure from office, passed a law — the Presidential Recordings and Materials Preservation Act — placing those materials in federal custody.[14] Nixon immediately went to court, challenging the law as violating a long list of rights and privileges — including the separation of powers, executive privilege, the right of privacy, First Amendment freedom of expression, the Fourth Amendment's protection against unreasonable search and seizure, the right to equal protection under the law and the constitutional ban on bills of attainder — laws passed to punish individuals.[15]

On June 28, 1977, the court upheld the law by a 7-2 vote.

The majority opinion, written by Justice William J. Brennan Jr., acknowledged that the law might infringe on some of Nixon's rights. But the court then weighed the damage done to the former president as an individual against the public interest in preserving the Nixon materials intact and concluded that the latter outweighed Nixon's claim.

Still another Nixon tapes case was yet to be decided by the Supreme Court. In 1978, Nixon finally won the last of these cases.

On April 18, 1978, by a 5-4 vote, the court granted Nixon's request that lower courts not be allowed to permit broadcasters to copy the White House tapes used as evidence in the trial of Mitchell, Haldeman and Ehrlichman.

The broadcasters were seeking to market the tapes commercially. The court ruled that such access need not be granted immediately — especially since the 1974 act concerning the tapes and other Nixon materials did set up procedures for public access to those items at some future date. [16]

Footnotes: Jefferson

[1] Samuel F. Bemis, *A Diplomatic History of the United States* (New York: Henry Holt & Co., 1936), pp. 95-100.

[2] Samuel E. Morison, Henry S. Commager, William E. Leuchtenburg, *The Growth of the American Republic*, 2 vols. (New York: Oxford University Press, 1969), I:218-319.

[3] James M. Smith, *Freedom's Fetters: The Alien and Sedition Laws and American Civil Liberties* (Ithaca, N.Y.: Cornell University Press, 1956).

[4] Frank M. Anderson, "Contemporary Opinion of the Virginia and Kentucky Resolutions," *American Historical Review*, V:45-63, 225-252; Adrienne Koch, *Jefferson and Madison, The Great Collaboration* (New York: Alfred A. Knopf, 1950).

[5] Eugene P. Link, *Democratic-Republican Societies* (New York: Octagon Books, 1965); Noble E. Cunningham Jr., *The Jeffersonian Republicans: The Formation of Party Organization, 1789-1801* (Chapel Hill, N.C.: University of North Carolina Press, 1957); Alexander DeConde, *The Quasi-War: The Politics and Diplomacy of the Undeclared War with France, 1797-1801* (New York: Charles Scribner's Sons, 1966).

[6] Donald O. Dewey, *Marshall versus Jefferson: The Political Background of Marbury v. Madison* (New York: Alfred A. Knopf, 1970), pp. 3-4.

[7] Ibid. at 5-8.

[8] Leonard Baker, *John Marshall: A Life in Law* (New York: MacMillan Publishing Co., 1974), p. 61.

[9] William Stinchcombe, "The Diplomacy of the WXYZ Affair," *The William and Mary Quarterly*, 3rd Series, XXXIV: 590-617.

[10] Donald O. Dewey, *Marshall versus Jefferson*, p. 31.

[11] Erwin C. Surrency, "The Judiciary Act of 1801," *American Journal of Legal History* 2:53-65; Kathryn Turner, "Federalist Policy and the Judiciary Act of 1801," *William and Mary Quarterly*, 22:3-32; Donald O. Dewey, *Marshall versus Jefferson*, pp. 55, 58-59.

[12] Ibid. at 68-69; Richard E. Ellis, *The Jeffersonian Crisis: Courts and Politics in the Young Republic* (New York: Oxford University Press, 1971), pp. 45, 50-51.

[13] *Marbury v. Madison*, 1 Cr. 137 at 138-139 (1803).

[14] Id. at 173.

[15] Id. at 158.

[16] Donald O. Dewey, *Marshall versus Jefferson*, pp. 135-141.

[17] See: *Holmes v. Walton* (New Jersey, 1780); *Trevett v. Weeden* (Rhode Island, 1786); *Bayard v. Singleton* (North Carolina, 1787); *Ware v. Hylton*, 3 Dall. 199 (1796).

[18] Donald O. Dewey, *Marshall versus Jefferson*, p. 141; Richard E. Ellis, *The Jeffersonian Crisis*, pp. 72-73, 76.

[19] Leonard Baker, *John Marshall*, p. 148; Richard B. Lillich, "The Chase Impeachment," *American Journal of Legal History*, (1960), 4:49-72.

[20] Leonard Baker, *John Marshall*, p. 418-419; Donald O. Dewey, *Marshall versus Jefferson*, pp. 148-149.

[21] Richard E. Ellis, *The Jeffersonian Crisis*, p. 81.

[22] Charles Warren, *The Supreme Court in United States History*, rev ed., 2 vols. (Boston: Little, Brown & Co., 1922, 1926), I:236-237.

[23] Ibid. at 236-237.

[24] Leonard Levy, *Jefferson and Civil Liberties, The Darker Side* (New York: Quadrangle Books, Inc., 1973).

[25] Leonard Baker, *John Marshall*, pp. 452-453.

[26] Thomas P. Abernathy, *The Burr Conspiracy* (New York: Oxford University Press, 1954).

[27] "The Deposition of William Eaton, Esq.," in *Ex parte Bollman, Ex parte Swartout*, 4 Cr. 75 Appendix A at 463-466 (1807).

[28] Leonard Baker, *John Marshall*, pp. 452-453.

[29] Donald O. Dewey, *Marshall versus Jefferson*, pp. 162-163.

[30] *United States v. Burr*, 25 Fed. Cas. 55, 69 (No. 14693) (C.C.Va. 1807).

[31] Raoul Berger, *Executive Privilege: A Constitutional Myth* (Cambridge, Mass.: Harvard University Press, 1974), p. 193.

[32] Bradley Chapin, *The American Law of Treason: Revolutionary and Early National Origins* (Seattle: University of Washington Press, 1964).

[33] Leonard Baker, *John Marshall*, pp. 464-465, 513.

[34] Ibid. at 514-515.

Footnotes: Jackson

[1] James D. Richardson, ed., *Messages and Papers of the Presidents*, 20 vols. (New York: Bureau of National Literature, 1897), III:1145.

[2] Samuel E. Morison, Henry S. Commager, William E. Leuchtenburg, *The Growth of the American Republic*, I:419-423; John W. Ward, *Andrew Jackson: Symbol for an Age* (New York: Oxford University Press, 1962.

[3] Charles Warren, *The Supreme Court in United States History*, I:730-731.

[4] *Johnson v. McIntosh* 8 Wheat. 543 (1823); Charles Warren, *The Supreme Court in United States History*, I:732-733.

[5] Ibid. at 733-734.

[6] *Cherokee Nation v. Georgia*, 5 Pet. 1 (1831).

[7] *Worcester v. Georgia*, 6 Pet. 515 (1832).

[8] Charles Warren, *The Supreme Court in United States History*, I:754.

[9] Samuel E. Morison, Henry S. Commager, William E. Leuchtenburg, *The Growth of the American Republic*, I:438-442.

[10] James D. Richardson, ed., *Messages and Papers of the Presidents*, III:1203-1204.

Footnotes: Lincoln

[1] James D. Richardson, ed., *Messages and Papers of the Presidents*, VII:3210.

[2] *Ex parte Merryman*, Fed. Cas. (No. 9847); Carl B. Swisher, *American Constitutional Development*, 2d ed. (Cambridge, Mass.: Houghton Mifflin Co., 1954), p. 279.

[3] Ibid. at 280-281.

[4] *Ex parte Merryman* in Henry S. Commager, ed., *Documents of American History*, 7th ed. (New York: Appleton-Century-Crofts, 1963), pp. 398-401.

[5] James D. Richardson, ed., *Messages and Papers of the Presidents*, VII:3225-3226.

[6] Carl B. Swisher, *History of the Supreme Court of the United States: Vol.V, The Taney Period, 1836-64* (New York: MacMillan Publishing Co., 1971), pp. 852-853.

[7] Charles Warren, *The Supreme Court in United States History*, II:372-373.

[8] James D. Richardson, ed., *Messages and Papers of the Presidents*, VII:3303-3305.

[9] Lincoln to Erastus Corning, June 12, 1863, in John C. Nicolay and John Hay, eds., *The Complete Works of Abraham Lincoln*, 12 vols. (New York: Francis D. Tandy Co., 1905-1934), VIII:298-314.

[10] Alfred H. Kelly and Winfred A. Harbison, *The American Constitution*, 5th ed. (New York: W. W. Norton & Co., 1976), p. 413.

[11] *Ex parte Milligan*, 4 Wall. 2 (1866).

Footnotes: Roosevelt

[1] Samuel E. Morison, Henry S. Commager, William E. Leuchtenburg, *The Growth of the American Republic*, II:485-487, 502-503.

[2] Samuel I. Rosenman, comp., *The Public Papers and Addresses of Franklin D. Roosevelt*, 5 vols. (New York: Random House, 1938), II, *The Year of Crisis, 1933*, p.15.

[3] William F. Swindler, *Court and Constitution in the 20th Century*, 2 vols. (Indianapolis and New York: Bobbs-Merrill Co., 1970), II:20-21; Samuel E. Morison, Henry S. Commager, William E. Leuchtenburg, *The Growth of the American Republic*, II:484-489.

[4] Carl B. Swisher, *American Constitutional Development*, 2d ed. (Cambridge, Mass.: Houghton Mifflin Co., 1954), pp. 848-859; Henry S. Commager, ed., *Documents of American History*, (New York: Appleton-Century-Crofts, 1963), pp. 242-246.

[5] William F. Swindler, *Court and Constitution in the 20th Century*, II:23-24; *U.S. Statutes at Large*, Vol. XLVIII, p. 195.

[6] Robert H. Jackson, *The Struggle for Judicial Supremacy: A Study of a Crisis in American Power Politics* (New York: Random House, 1941), pp. 83-84; Carl B. Swisher, *American Constitutional Development*, pp. 920-921.

[7] *Home Building and Loan Association v. Blaisdell*, 290 U.S. 398 (1934).

[8] *Nebbia v. New York*, 291 U.S. 502 (1934).

[9] *Norman v. The Baltimore and Ohio Railroad Co.*, 294 U.S. 240 (1935); *John N. Perry v. United States*, 294 U.S. 330 (1935); *Ashwander et. al. v. Tennessee Valley Authority*, 297 U.S. 288 (1936).

[10] *Panama Refining Co. v. Ryan, Amazon Petroleum Corp. v. Ryan*, 293 U.S. 388 (1935).

[11] *Retirement Board v. Alton R. Co.*, 295 U.S. 330 (1935).

[12] *Louisville Bank v. Radford*, 295 U.S. 555 (1935).

[13] *Schechter Poultry Corp. v. United States*, 295 U.S. 495 (1935).

[14] *Humphrey's Executor v. United States*, 295 U.S. 602 (1935).

[15] Robert H. Jackson, *The Struggle for Judicial Supremacy: A Study of a Crisis in American Power Politics*, p. 12.

[16] Ibid. at 113.

[17] Ibid.

[18] *Schechter Poultry Corp. v. United States*, 295 U.S. 495 at 536-539, 541-542 (1935).

[19] Samuel I. Rosenman, comp., *The Public Papers and Addresses of Franklin D. Roosevelt*, IV:215, 221.

[20] *United States v. Butler*, 297 U.S. 1 (1936).

[21] *Carter v. Carter Coal Co.*, 298 U.S. 238 (1936).

[22] Id. at 288-289, 303.

[23] *Ashton v. Cameron County District*, 298 U.S. 513 (1936).

[24] Id. at 542-543.

[25] William F. Swindler, *Court and Constitution in the 20th Century*, II:56.

[26] Alfred H. Kelly and Winfred A. Harbison, *The American Constitution*, p. 714.

[27] Samuel I. Rosenman, comp., *Public Papers and Addresses of Franklin D. Roosevelt*, V:635-636, 638-639, 641-642.

[28] "Reform of the Federal Judiciary," 75th Cong., 1st sess., Sen. Report No. 711.

[29] Henry S. Commager, ed., *Documents of American History*, pp. 382-383.

[30] "Recommendation to Reorganize Judicial Branch," 75th Cong., 1st sess., HR Doc. No. 142.

[31] Harold L. Ickes, *The Secret Diary of Harold L. Ickes*, 3 vols. (New York: Simon and Schuster, 1954), II:7.

[32] Robert H. Jackson, *The Struggle for Judicial Supremacy*, p. 187.

[33] Harold L. Ickes, *The Secret Diary of Harold L. Ickes*, II:74-75.

[34] Ibid. at pp. 88-89.

[35] "Address by the President of the United States," March 9, 1937, in Henry S. Commager, *Documents of American History*, pp. 383-387.

[36] Harold L. Ickes, *The Secret Diary of Harold L. Ickes*, II:74-75, 93, 104, 109, 115, 251; William F. Swindler, *Court and Constitution in the 20th Century*, II:68-71.

[37] Harold L. Ickes, *The Secret Diary of Harold L. Ickes*, II:70, 98, 100, 103, 251, 424, 105-106.

[38] William F. Swindler, *Court and Constitution in the 20th Century*, II: 71-73.

[39] *West Coast Hotel Co. v. Parrish*, 300 U.S. 379 at 390 (1937).

[40] *Wright v. Vinton Branch*, 300 U.S. 440 (1937).

[41] *N.L.R.B. v. Jones & Laughlin Steel Corp.*, 301 U.S. 1 (1937).

[42] *Steward Machine Co. v. Davis*, 301 U.S. 548 (1937); *Helvering v. Davis*, 307 U.S. 619 (1937).

[43] *Morehead v. New York ex rel. Tipaldo*, 298 U.S. 587 (1936).

[44] *West Coast Hotel Co. v. Parrish*, 300 U.S. 379 (1937).

[45] Max Freedman, ann., *Roosevelt and Frankfurter: Their Correspondence, 1928-1945* (Boston: Little, Brown & Co., 1967), pp. 392-395.

[46] "Judiciary Reform Act of 1937, August 24, 1937, in Henry S. Commager, *Documents of American History*, pp. 391-393; Robert H. Jackson, *The Struggle for Judicial Supremacy*, pp.192-193; Harold L. Ickes, *The Secret Diary of Harold L. Ickes*, II:144, 152-153, 170-172.

[47] Alfred H. Kelly and Winfred A. Harbison, *The American Constitution*, p. 718.

[48] James T. Patterson, *Congressional Conservatism and the New Deal,The Growth of the Conservative Coalition in Congress,1933-1939* (Lexington, Ky.: University of Kentucky Press, 1967).

[49] *United States v. Darby*, 312 U.S. 100 (1941); *Mulford v. Smith*, 307 U.S. 38 (1939).

Footnotes: Truman

[1] Harry S Truman, *Memoirs*, 2 vols. (Garden City, N.Y.: Doubleday & Co., 1956), II:465-467.

[2] Ibid. at 468.

[3] Ibid. at 471-472.

[4] Ibid. at 469-470.

[5] *Youngstown Sheet and Tube Co. v. Sawyer*, 343 U.S. 579 at 609 (1952).

[6] Id. at 662.

[7] Id. at 632.

[8] Id. at 668-669.

[9] Harry S Truman, *Memoirs*, II:428.

[10] Ibid. at 477.

[11] Ibid. at 478.

Footnotes: Nixon

[1] *New York Times Co. v. United States; United States v. The Washington Post*, 403 U.S. 713 (1971).

[2] Id. at 714-715.

[3] Id. at 724-725.

[4] 82 *United States Statutes at Large*, 198 ff., PL 90-351.

[5] *United States v. United States District Court*, 407 U.S. 297 at 301 (1972).

[6] Id. at 317.

[7] Alfred H. Kelly and Winfred A. Harbison, *The American Constitution*, pp. 1020-1021.

[8] *Nixon, The Fifth Year of His Presidency* (Washington, D.C.: Congressional Quarterly, 1974), p. 153-A.

[9] *Train v. City of New York*, 420 U.S. 35 (1975); *Train v. Campaign Clean Water*, 420 U.S. 136 (1975).

[10] *Watergate: Chronology of a Crisis* (Washington, D.C.: Congressional Quarterly, 1975), pp. 191-194, 220, 224-225, 293-294, 297, 341-345, 353-362.

[11] Ibid. at 535-537, 600-648.

[12] Ibid. at 689-692, 711-723, 734-742.

[13] Ibid. at 754-756.

[14] PL 93-526 (1974); *Congress and the Nation*, Vol. IV (Washington, D.C.: Congressional Quarterly, 1977), p. 952.

[15] *Richard M. Nixon v. Administrator, General Services Administration*, 433 U.S. 425 (1977).

[16] *Nixon v. Warner Communications Inc. et al.*, 453 U.S. 589 (1978).

Selected Bibliography

Abernathy, Thomas P. *The Burr Conspiracy.* New York: Oxford University Press, 1954.

Alsop, Joseph, and Catledge, Turner. *The 168 Days.* Garden City, N.Y.: Doubleday, Doran & Co., 1938.

Anderson, Frank M. "Contemporary Opinion of the Virginia and Kentucky Resolutions." *American Historical Review.* 5: 45-63, 225-252.

Baker, Leonard. *Back to Back: The Duel Between F.D.R. and the Supreme Court.* New York: Macmillan Publishing Co., 1967.

_____. *John Marshall, A Life in Law.* New York: Macmillan Publishing Co., 1974.

Bassett, John S. *Life of Andrew Jackson.* 2 Vols. Garden City, N.Y.: Doubleday, Doran & Co., 1911.

Bemis, Samuel F. *A Diplomatic History of the United States.* New York: Henry Holt & Co., 1936.

Berger, Raoul. *Executive Privilege: A Constitutional Myth.* Cambridge, Mass.: Harvard University Press, 1974.

Beveridge, Albert. *The Life of John Marshall.* 4 Vols. Boston and New York: Houghton Mifflin Co., 1916-1919.

Binkley, Wilfred E. *Powers of the President.* New York: Doubleday & Co., 1937.

Burns, James M. *Roosevelt: The Lion and the Fox.* New York: Harcourt Brace Jovanovich, 1960.

_____. *Roosevelt: The Soldier of Freedom.* New York: Harcourt Brace Jovanovich, 1970.

Burke, Joseph C. "The Cherokee Cases: A Study in Law, Politics and Morality," *Stanford Law Review,* 21: 500-531.

Chapin, Bradley. *The American Law of Treason: Revolutionary and Early National Origins.* Seattle: University of Washington Press, 1964.

Commager, Henry S.,ed. *Documents of American History.* 7th ed. New York: Appleton-Century-Crofts, 1962.

Congress and the Nation, 1973-1976. Vol. IV. Washington, D.C.: Congressional Quarterly, 1977.

Congressional Quarterly Almanac, 1970. Washington, D.C.: Congressional Quarterly, 1971.

Corwin, Edward S. *The President: Offices and Powers, 1787-1957.* 4th rev. ed. New York: New York University Press, 1957.

_____. *The Constitution and What It Means Today.* Princeton, N.J.: Princeton University Press, 1958.

Cox, Archibald. *The Role of the Supreme Court in American Government.* New York: Oxford University Press, 1976.

Cunningham, Noble E. Jr. *The Jeffersonian Republicans: The Formation of Party Organization, 1789-1801.* Chapel Hill, N.C.: University of North Carolina Press, 1957.

Cushman, Robert F. *Cases in Civil Liberties.* New York: Prentice-Hall, 1968.

DeConde, Alexander. *The Quasi-War: The Politics and Diplomacy of the Undeclared War with France, 1797-1801.* New York: Charles Scribner's Sons, 1966.

Dewey, Donald O. *Marshall versus Jefferson: The Political Background of Marbury v. Madison.* New York: Alfred A. Knopf, 1970.

Dorson, Norman and Shattuck, John H. F. "Executive Privilege, the Congress and the Court." *Ohio State Law Journal:* 34: 1-40.

Doyle, Elisabeth Joan. "The Conduct of the War, 1861." In *Congress Investigates 1792-1974.* Edited by Arthur

M. Schlesinger, Jr. and Roger Bruns. New York: Chelsea House, 1975.

Eisenhower, Dwight D. *Public Papers of the Presidents.* Washington, D.C.: U.S. Government Printing Office, 1950.

Ellis, Richard E. *The Jeffersonian Crisis: Courts and Politics in the Young Republic.* New York: Oxford University Press, 1971.

Farrand, Max, ed. *The Records of the Federal Convention of 1787.* 4 Vols. Rev. ed. New Haven: Yale University Press, 1966.

Faulkner, Robert K. *The Jurisprudence of John Marshall.* Princeton, N.J.: Princeton University Press, 1968.

Ford, Paul L. ed., *The Writings of Thomas Jefferson.* 10 Vols., New York: G. P. Putnam's Sons, 1892-1899.

Freedman, Max, ann. *Roosevelt and Frankfurter, Their Correspondence, 1928-45.* Boston: Little, Brown & Co., 1967.

Friedman, Leon and Israel, Fred L., eds. *The Justices of the United States Supreme Court, 1789-1969, Their Lives and Major Opinions.* 5 Vols. New York and London: Chelsea House Publishers, 1969-78.

Freund, Paul A., gen. ed. *History of the Supreme Court of the United States.* New York: Macmillan Publishing Co., 1971, 1974. Vol. I: *Antecedents and Beginnings to 1801,* by Julius Goebel, Jr.; Vol. V: *The Taney Period, 1836-64,* by Carl B. Swisher; Vol. VI: *Reconstruction and Reunion, 1864-1888, Part One,* by Charles Fairman.

Garraty, John A., ed. *Quarrels That Have Shaped the Constitution.* New York: Harper & Row, 1963.

Guide to Congress. 2nd ed. Washington, D.C.: Congressional Quarterly , 1976.

Hamilton, John C., ed. *The Works of Alexander Hamilton.* 7 Vols. New York: John F. Tow, 1850-1851.

Henkin, Louis. *Foreign Affairs and the Constitution.* New York: W. W. Norton & Co., 1972.

Ickes, Harold L. *The Secret Diary of Harold L. Ickes.* 3 Vols. New York: Simon & Schuster, 1954.

Israel, Fred L., ed. *The State of the Union Messages of the Presidents, 1790-1966.* 13 Vols. New York: Chelsea House, Robert Hector Publishers, 1966.

Jackson, Percival E. *Dissent in the Supreme Court.* Norman, Okla.: University of Oklahoma Press, 1967.

Jackson, Robert H. *The Struggle for Judicial Supremacy.* New York: Random House, 1941.

Johnson, Lyndon B. *Public Papers of the Presidents, 1963-1964.* 2 Vols. Washington, D.C.: U.S. Government Printing Office, 1965.

Kelly, Alfred H. and Harbison, Winfred A. *The American Constitution: Its Origin and Development.* 5th ed. New York: W. W. Norton & Co., 1976.

Kennedy, John F. *Public Papers of the Presidents, 1962.* Washington, D.C.: U.S. Government Printing Office, 1963.

Key, V. O. Jr. *Politics, Parties and Pressure Groups.* 5th ed. New York: Thomas Y. Crowell Co., 1964.

Koch, Adrienne. *Jefferson and Madison, The Great Collaboration.* New York: Alfred A. Knopf, 1950.

Koenig, Louis. *The Chief Executive.* 3rd. ed. New York: Harcourt Brace Jovanovich, 1975.

Kramer, Robert and Marcuse, Herman. "Executive Privilege — A Study of the Period 1953-1960." *George Washington Law Review.* 29: 623-827.

Krislov, Samuel. *The Supreme Court in the Political Process.* New York: Macmillan Publishing Co. Inc., 1965.

Kurland, Philip B. *Politics, the Constitution and the Warren Court.* Chicago: University of Chicago Press, 1970.

Kutler, Stanley I. "Ex Parte McCardle: Judicial Impotency? The Supreme Court and Reconstruction Reconsidered," *American Historical Review,* 72: 835-851.

Laski, Harold J. *The American Presidency: An Interpretation.* New York: Harper & Bros., 1940.

Leopold, Richard W. *The Growth of American Foreign Policy.* New York: Alfred A. Knopf, 1962.

Levy, Leonard. *Legacy of Suppression: Jefferson and Civil Liberties, The Darker Side.* Cambridge, Mass.: Harvard University Press, 1963.

Leuchtenburg, William E. *Franklin D. Roosevelt and the New Deal: 1932-1940.* New York: Harper & Row, 1963.

Lillich, Richard B. "The Chase Impeachment," *American Journal of Legal History.* IV: 49-72.

Link, Arthur. *Wilson, The Diplomatist.* Baltimore: Johns Hopkins Press, 1957.

Link, Eugene P. *Democratic Republican Societies.* New York: Columbia University Press, 1942.

Lofgren, Charles A. "United States v. Curtiss-Wright: An Historical Assessment." *The Yale Law Journal,* 83: 1-32.

Longaker, Richard P. "Andrew Jackson and the Judiciary." *Political Science Quarterly.* 71: 341-364.

Madison, James; Hamilton, Alexander; and Jay, John. *The Federalist Papers.* Introduction by Clinton Rossiter. New York: New American Library, Mentor Books, 1961.

Mason, Alpheus T. and Beaney, William M. *The Supreme Court in a Free Society.* Englewood Cliffs, N.J.: Prentice-Hall, 1959.

McClure, Wallace. *International Executive Agreements: Democratic Procedure Under the Constitution of the United States.* New York: AMS Press, 1941.

Meeker, Leonard. "The Legality of United States' Participation in the Defense of Vietnam." United States Department of State, *Bulletin,* 474 (1966).

Members of Congress Since 1789. Washington, D.C.: Congressional Quarterly, 1977.

Morison, Samuel E., Commager, Henry S. and Leuchtenberg, William E. *The Growth of the American Republic.* 2 Vols. New York: Oxford University Press, 1969.

Morgan, Donald G. *Congress and the Constitution.* Cambridge, Mass.: Harvard University Press, 1966.

Murphy, Paul L. *The Constitution in Crisis Times, 1918-1969.* New York: Harper & Row, 1972.

Neustadt, Richard E. *Presidential Power.* New York: John Wiley & Sons Inc., 1960.

Nicolay, John G. and Hay, John, eds. *The Complete Works of Abraham Lincoln.* 12 Vols. New York: Francis D. Tandy Co., 1905.

Nixon, The Fifth Year of His Presidency. Washington, D.C.: Congressional Quarterly, 1974.

Patterson, James T. *Congressional Conservatism and the New Deal, 1933-1939.* Lexington, Ky.: University of Kentucky Press, 1967.

Peltason, Jack W. *Understanding the Constitution.* 4th ed. New York: Holt, Rinehart & Winston, 1959.

Post, Gordon C. *The Supreme Court and Political Questions.* Baltimore: Johns Hopkins Press, 1936.

Pritchett, C. Herman. *The American Constitution.* New York: McGraw-Hill Co., 1959.

_____. *The Tennessee Valley Authority: A Study in Public Administration.* Chapel Hill, N.C.: University of North Carolina Press, 1943.

Pritchett, C. Herman and Westin, Alan F. *The Third Branch of Government.* New York: Harcourt, Brace & World, 1963.

Randall, James G. *Constitutional Problems Under Lincoln.* Urbana: University of Illinois Press, 1951.

Reveley, W. Taylor III. "Presidential War-Making: Constitutional Prerogative or Usurpation?" *Virginia Law Review,* 55: 1243-1305.

Richardson, James D. ed. *Messages and Papers of the Presidents.* 20 Vols. New York: Bureau of National Literature, Inc., 1897.

Rodell, Fred. *Nine Men: A Political History of the Supreme Court of the United States from 1790-1955.* New York: Random House, 1955.

Rosenman, Samuel I., comp. *The Public Papers and Addresses of Franklin D. Roosevelt.* 5 Vols. New York: Random House, 1955.

Rossiter, Clinton. *The Supreme Court and the Commander in Chief.* Ithaca: Cornell University Press, 1951.

Rostow, Eugene V. "The Japanese American Cases — A Disaster." *Yale Law Journal.* LIV (June 1945), pp. 489-533.

Schlesinger Jr., Arthur M. *The Imperial Presidency.* New York: Popular Library, 1973.

Schubert, Glendon M. *The Presidency in the Courts.* Minneapolis: University of Minnesota Press, 1957.

Smith, James M. *Freedom's Fetters: The Alien and Sedition Laws and American Civil Liberties.* Ithaca: Cornell University Press, 1956.

Stinchcombe, William. "The Diplomacy of the WXYZ Affair." *The William and Mary Quarterly.* 3rd Series, 34: 590-617.

Surrency, Erwin C. "The Judiciary Act of 1801." *American Journal of Legal History.* II: 53-65.

Sutherland, George. *Constitutional Power and World Affairs.* New York: Columbia University Press, 1919.

Swindler, William F. *Court and Constitution in the Twentieth Century, The Old Legality, 1889-1932.* Indianapolis and New York: Bobbs-Merrill Co., 1970.

_____. *Court and Constitution in the Twentieth Century, The New Legality, 1932-1968.* New York and Indianapolis: Bobbs-Merrill Co., 1954.

Taylor, Telford. *The Grand Inquest: the Story of Congressional Investigations.* New York: Simon & Schuster, 1955.

Truman, Harry S. *Memoirs.* 2 Vols. Garden City, New York: Doubleday & Co., 1956.

Turner, Kathryn. "Federalist Policy and the Judiciary Act of 1801." *The William and Mary Quarterly.* 22: 32.

United States Congress. Debates and Proceedings, First Congress, First Session. March 3, 1789, to Eighteenth Congress, First Session, May 27, 1824. [Annals of Congress] 42 Vols. Washington, D.C.: Gales & Seaton, 1834-1856.

U.S. Congress. Library of Congress. Congressional Reference Service. *The Constitution of the United States of America: Analysis and Interpretation.* 1963, 1972 eds. Washington, D.C.: U.S. Government Printing Office, 1964, 1973, 1976 Supplement, 1977.

United States Congress. Senate. "A Decade of American

Foreign Policy, Basic Documents, 1941-1949," Senate Document No. 123, 81st Cong., 1st sess. (1950) pt. 1.

United States Congress. Senate. Committee on Armed Services. Special Preparedness Subcommittee. Military Cold War and Speech Review Policies. Hearings. 87th Cong. 2nd sess. Washington, D.C.: U.S. Government Printing Office, 1971.

United States Congress. Senate. Committee on the Judiciary. Subcommittee on the Separation of Powers. Executive Privilege: The Withholding of Information by the Executive. Hearings. 92nd Cong. 1st sess. Washington, D.C.: U.S. Government Printing Office, 1971.

United States Congress. Senate. Hearings on S. J. Res. 1 and S. J. Res 43 Before a Subcommittee of the Senate Judiciary Committee. 83rd Cong. 1st sess. (1953).

United States Congress. Senate. Hearings on U.S. Commitments to Foreign Powers Before the Senate Committee on Foreign Relations. 90th Cong. 1st sess. (1967).

United States. Department of State. Bulletin No. 23. "Authority of the President to Repel the Attack in Korea." (1950).

United States. Library of Congress. "The Present Limits of Executive Privilege." A Study Prepared by The Government and General Research Division of the Library of Congress. *Congressional Record.* H. 2243-2264 (March 28, 1973).

Warren, Charles. *The Supreme Court in United States History.* 2 Vols. Boston: Little, Brown & Co., 1922, 1926.

Watergate: Chronology of a Crisis. Washington, D.C.: Congressional Quarterly, 1975.

Wiggins, J. Russell, "Government Operations and the Public's Right to Know." *Federal Bar Journal.* 19: 62.

Wilson, Woodrow. *Congressional Government, A Study in American Politics.* Boston: Houghton Mifflin Co., 1885.

—————. *The State.* Boston: D. C. Heath & Co., 1889.

—————. *Constitutional Government in the United States.* New York: Columbia University Press, 1908.

Wolkinson, Herman. "Demand of Congressional Committees for Executive Papers." *Federal Bar Journal.* (April, July, October 1949) X: 103-150.

Wormuth, Francis D. "The Nixon Theory of the War Power: A Critique." *California Law Review.* 60: 623-703.

Younger, Irving. "Congressional Investigations and Executive Secrecy: A Study in Separation of Powers." *University of Pittsburgh Law Review.* 20: 755.

THE COURT AND JUDICIAL POWER

Introduction 255

Federal Jurisdiction 256

Federal Judicial Power. 267

Judicial Restraint. 287

The Court and Judicial Power

During its first twelve years as a nation, the United States had neither a Supreme Court nor any federal system of courts.

This lack seemed to many a major factor contributing to the "national humiliation" which the young nation suffered during the period of its government under the Articles of Confederation.[1]

Article III of the Constitution of 1789 remedied that deficiency with two concise provisions. The first provided that "[t]he judicial power of the United States, shall be vested in one supreme Court," and whatever inferior federal courts Congress "from time to time" saw fit to establish. The second set out the types of cases and controversies that should be considered by a federal — rather than a state — tribunal.

Among the most articulate of the advocates of a federal judiciary was Alexander Hamilton. In *The Federalist Papers,* he argued that an independent system of national courts was "peculiarly essential" in a limited government like that set up by the Constitution. The limits which the Constitution devised to curtail the power of Congress, he wrote, "can be preserved in practice no other way than through the medium of courts of justice, whose duty it must be to declare all acts contrary to the manifest tenor of the Constitution void. Without this, all the reservations of particular rights or privileges would amount to nothing."[2]

National power required national courts, Hamilton wrote:

> . . .if it be possible at any rate to construct a federal government capable of regulating the common concerns and preserving the general tranquility . . . [i]t must stand in need of no intermediate legislations, but must itself be empowered to employ the arm of the ordinary magistrate to execute its own resolutions. The majesty of the national authority must be manifested through the medium of the courts of justice. . . .[3]

A Limited Power

Despite his high hopes for the contribution a national judiciary would make to national power and stability, Hamilton recognized that "the judiciary is beyond comparison the weakest of the three departments . . . it is in continual jeopardy of being over-powered, awed, or influenced by its coordinate branches. . . ."[4]

Congress filled in the skeletal structure of national judicial power with the Judiciary Act of 1789 and subsequent statutes. But it was left chiefly to the Supreme Court to define the jurisdiction of the federal courts — itself included — with precision, and to guide the use of the powers of the federal judiciary. With every decision it has issued since its initial term, the Supreme Court has shaped the power of the federal courts.

The federal judicial power is limited. It extends only to certain types of cases and controversies. And its arsenal is small. Thus it has been necessary that its authority be exercised with care and restraint. Federal judicial power grew slowly, through the interaction of the courts, the president — who peoples its benches — and Congress — which exerts statutory control over much of the jurisdiction and most of the powers of the federal courts.

Judicial Self-Restraint

Questions of jurisdiction, proper remedies, abstention and comity seem technical matters to many — often overlooked by those who find more interest in the substantive issues resolved by the court. But it is the resolution of these seemingly esoteric matters which governs the breadth of access — and the scope of the remedy — available to those who seek redress in the federal courts.

Overall, the Supreme Court has carefully circumscribed its powers, its jurisdiction, and those of the lower federal courts. Felix Frankfurter, writing in the 1920s, described this self-limitation as possibly "the most significant aspect of judicial action in the American constitutional scheme." Such self-denial, he wrote, was "the expression of an energizing philosophy of the distribution of governmental powers. For a court to hold that decision does not belong to it, is merely to recognize that a problem calls for the exercise of initiative and experimentation possessed only by political processes. . . ."[5]

The overriding factor in this self-restraint has been the court's clearly demonstrated awareness of the prerogatives of the other elements of the federal system — its coordinate branches, Congress and the executive — and the states.

Justice Lewis F. Powell Jr. expressed this realization in 1974:

> Repeated and essentially head-on confrontations between the life-tenured branch and the representative branches of the government will not, in the long run, be beneficial to either. The public confidence essential to the former and the vitality critical to the latter may well erode if we do not exercise self-restraint in the

utilization of our power to negative the actions of the other branches.[6]

This concern has infused the court's dealing with questions of jurisdiction and judicial review, requests for orders halting state proceedings or mandating federal action, access to writs of *habeas corpus*, and political matters. After the two most notable periods in which the court abandoned caution in such matters — just before the Civil War and during the New Deal — and deliberately collided with Congress and the executive, it found itself severely criticized for its assertiveness.

An Extraordinary Role

For all its limits — constitutional, statutory and self-imposed — the federal judiciary possesses extraordinary power.

Early in the 20th century — even before the modern expansion of this power — Charles Grove Haines wrote that "the distinguishing characteristic of the American system of government is the extraordinary power and position of the judiciary."

Haines continued:

> The practice of all departments of government to defer to the courts and abide by their decisions, when in a suit between private parties, the majority of justices hold that in their opinion a statute or executive order is unconstitutional and therefore null and void, is the most significant feature of constitutional law in the United States.[7]

Haines wrote before the New Deal confrontation of Congress, the court and the president, before the revolution in civil rights accelerated by court decisions, before the Steel Seizure Case, before the Watergate ruling that drove a president from office.

But his general assessment of modern judicial power was reinforced by those events.

In 1962, another constitutional scholar, Alexander Bickel, wrote, in reference to Hamilton's long-ago description of the federal judiciary and the Supreme Court: "The least dangerous branch of the American government is the most extraordinarily powerful court of law the world has ever known."[8]

Federal Jurisdiction

Judicial power is useless without jurisdiction. Unless a court has jurisdiction over the persons or issues involved in a dispute, its power does not extend to resolve that matter.

In 1869, Chief Justice Salmon P. Chase explained:

> Without jurisdiction the court cannot proceed at all in any cause. Jurisdiction is the power to declare the law, and when it ceases to exist, the only function remaining to the court is that of announcing the fact and dismissing the cause.[9]

Jurisdiction, a lower court once wrote, is the vessel into which judicial power may be poured.[10] Jurisdiction is the prerequisite to the exercise of judicial power.

The primary characteristic of the federal judicial system is that all its courts are courts of limited jurisdiction, in contrast to state courts, which are presumed to have jurisdiction over a case, unless that presumption is disproved.

Most questions of federal court jurisdiction involve the distribution of power between states and the federal government.

"Expansion of the jurisdiction of the federal courts," one scholar reminds us, "diminishes the power of the states."[11]

The Constitutional Possibility

Article III, section 2 of the Constitution, outlines a broad area for the exercise of federal judicial power:

> The Judicial Power shall extend to all Cases, in Law and Equity, arising under this Constitution, the Laws of the United States, and Treaties made, or which shall be made, under their Authority; — to all cases affecting Ambassadors, other public Ministers and Consuls; — to all Cases of admiralty and maritime Jurisdiction; — to Controversies to which the United States shall be a party; — to Controversies between two or more States; — between Citizens of different States; — between Citizens of the same State claiming Lands under Grants of different States, and between a State, or the Citizens thereof, and foreign States, Citizens, or Subjects.

This general grant of jurisdiction divides into two categories: cases which merit federal consideration because of their subject matter — a claim or question arising under the Constitution, federal statutes or treaties, or admiralty or maritime law — and cases which merit federal attention because of the parties involved — the United States, a state, citizens of different states, or representatives of foreign countries.

Article III gave the Supreme Court original jurisdiction over two of the latter category of cases. The court has the right to hear cases initially, before any other court, if they involve ambassadors or other foreign diplomats or if they involve states.

With those exceptions, the Constitution granted Congress the power of determining how much of the broad area outlined in Article III actually came within the jurisdiction of the federal courts.

The Political Reality

The Supreme Court clearly has kept in mind the language of Article III giving Congress complete control over the existence and jurisdiction of all federal courts below the Supreme Court itself.

"[T]he judicial power of the United States," stated the court in 1845 is "dependent for its distribution and organization, and for the modes of its exercise, entirely upon the action of Congress . . ." with some exceptions related to the High Court itself.[12]

Twenty years later, the court reiterated that point: "[T]wo things are necessary to create jurisdiction. . . . The Constitution must have given to the court the capacity to take it, and an Act of Congress must have supplied it."[13]

The Act of 1789

Congress moved quickly to exercise this power. The first Congress enacted the Judiciary Act of 1789. It set up a system of lower federal courts — district courts and circuit courts with limited jurisdiction, spelled out the appellate jurisdiction of the Supreme Court, and gave that court the power to review state court rulings rejecting federal claims.[14] *(Text, p. 949)*

The 1789 act made clear that most cases would be resolved in state courts. Federal district courts were to hear admiralty and maritime matters; circuit courts would hear cases involving disputes between residents of different states, the United States and aliens — and where more than $500 was at stake. Circuit courts also had some limited "federal question" jurisdiction concurrent with state courts, as well as some jurisdiction to hear appeals from district court rulings.

The Supreme Court acquiesced in this congressional limitation of federal jurisdiction. Writing a 1799 decision holding federal courts without jurisdiction over a particular case, Chief Justice Oliver Ellsworth — himself one of the authors of the Judiciary Act — declared that "[a] circuit court . . . is of limited jurisdiction and has cognizance, not of cases generally, but only of a few specially circumstanced. . . ."[15]

Underscoring that point, Justice Samuel Chase added a footnote:

> The notion has frequently been entertained that the federal courts derive their judicial power immediately from the constitution; but the political truth is, that the disposal of the judicial power (except in a few specified instances) belongs to Congress. If Congress has given the power to this court, we possess it, not otherwise; and if Congress has not given the power to us or to any other court, it still remains at the legislative disposal. Besides, Congress is not bound . . . to enlarge the jurisdiction of the federal courts, to every subject, in every form, which the constitution might warrant.[16]

Federal Questions

Although Article III clearly envisioned that federal courts would have the final word on cases raising claims under the Constitution, federal laws and treaties, it was 80 years before Congress granted such jurisdiction to those courts. Until then, most "federal questions" were resolved in state courts, subject to review — if the federal claim were denied — by the Supreme Court.

The 1789 act did grant the Supreme Court the power to consider the constitutionality of state laws — when state courts rejected federally based challenges to them. But the act said nothing about any power of the court to review acts of Congress for their constitutional validity. The court simply assumed that power early in its history. *(pp. 270-271)*

The 1875 Act. In 1875, Congress granted lower federal courts virtually the entire "federal question" jurisdiction outlined in Article III. For the first time, all cases arising under the Constitution, federal laws or treaties could be initiated in federal district courts.

Professors Felix Frankfurter and James M. Landis, half a century later, described the 1875 act as revolutionary:

> From 1789 down to the Civil War the lower federal courts were, in the main, designed as protection to

---

The Jurisdictional Amount

To keep trivial matters out of the federal courts, Congress throughout the nation's history, has set a "jurisdictional amount" — a dollar figure for the amount which must be in controversy before most cases can enter the federal judicial system.

In 1789, the amount was set at $500. In 1887, the figure was quadrupled to $2,000. The next increase was in 1911, to $3,000 — where it remained until 1958, when Congress raised it to $10,000, the current level.

From 1789 until 1925, there was also a jurisdictional amount — of varying levels — required for appeal to the Supreme Court in certain cases. Since 1925 there has been no such requirement.

In the 1970s, the main categories of cases affected by the jurisdictional amount requirement have been diversity cases and some federal question cases. In many modern statutes, Congress has granted federal courts jurisdiction over cases without regard to the amount of money involved. Among the areas in which this requirement for federal jurisdiction is waived by statute are admiralty and maritime cases; bankruptcy matters; cases arising under Acts of Congress regulating commerce; those involving orders of the Interstate Commerce Commission; patent, trademark and copyright cases; internal revenue and customs duty cases; postal matters; most civil rights cases; elections disputes; and cases to which the United States is a party.

Source: Charles Alan Wright, *Handbook of the Law of Federal Courts,* 2d ed. (St. Paul: West Publishing Co., 1970), p. 108.

---

citizens litigating outside of their own states and thereby exposed to the threatened prejudice of unfriendly tribunals. Barring admiralty jurisdiction, the federal courts were subsidiary courts. The Act of 1875 marks a revolution in their function. . . . These courts ceased to be restricted tribunals of fair dealing between citizens of different states and became the primary and powerful reliances for vindicating every right given by the Constitution, the laws and treaties of the United States. Thereafter, any suit asserting such a right could be begun in federal courts; any such action begun in state court could be removed to the federal courts for disposition.[17]

No subsequent jurisdictional statute has so greatly enlarged the jurisdiction of the federal courts. But as Congress has enacted laws reaching into areas left heretofore to state control, "federal question" jurisdiction has become a larger and larger category.

Two areas in which new statutes have brought particular expansion of this category of federal cases are labor law and civil rights law.

Admiralty and Maritime Law

"Like the Constitution itself" wrote Frankfurter and Landis, the Judiciary Act of 1789 "was a response to the practical problems and controversies of our early history."[18] And so, to contemporary eyes, the admiralty and

The Right to Remove Cases...

With the expansion of federal jurisdiction, Congress has also enlarged the right of persons charged initially in state courts to "remove" or transfer those cases into federal courts for trial and final resolution.

The Judiciary Act of 1789, which left most matters to state courts, provided a limited right of removal from state to federal courts in civil suits involving aliens, diversity of residence or of land grant sources, *and* involving more than $500.

In 1815, Congress provided a similar right of removal in all cases involving federal customs officials — and, in 1833, involving federal revenue officials.

The Civil War brought further expansion of this right — to include all persons sued in state courts for actions under federal authority during the war.

The Supreme Court upheld the validity of these removal statutes in 1868:

> It is the right and the duty of the National Government to have its constitution and laws interpreted and applied by its own judicial tribunals. In cases arising under them, properly brought before it, this court is the final arbiter.

Without such a provision for removal, state courts could punish federal officials for carrying out federal law or policy. A government without the power to protect such an official, wrote the court, "would be one of pitiable weakness, and would wholly fail to meet the ends which the framers of the Constitution had in view.[1]

Twelve years later, the court upheld the right of a federal revenue officer, charged with murder for killing a man who was defending an illegal still, to have his trial take place in federal, not state courts.

"If, whenever and wherever a case arises under the Constitution and laws or treaties of the United States, the National Government cannot take control of it," wrote Justice William Strong for the court, "whether it

be civil or criminal, in any stage of its progress, its judicial power is, at least, temporarily silenced, instead of being at all times supreme." [2]

The court viewed the power of Congress to enact removal statutes as part of its power to enact all laws necessary and proper to carry into effect the enumerated powers granted it and the federal courts by the Constitution.

The Modern Right

As Congress enlarged the "federal question" jurisdiction of the federal courts after the Civil War, it also expanded the right of removal.

That right remains firmly established. The defendant in any civil case which could have been initiated in federal court may transfer the case to a federal court. A federal official sued or prosecuted in state court for official acts may remove his case into federal court. And a defendant in any case, civil or criminal, who can show that he is denied, or is unable to enforce, his constitutional civil rights in a state court may have his case transferred into federal court.

Concerned about the impact of this last removal statute on federal-state relationships, the Supreme Court has allowed the removal of such cases only when a defendant has presented convincing evidence that he will be denied his federally assured rights simply by being brought to trial in a state court.

Two pairs of cases illustrate this caution on the part of the court.

The first such "civil rights" removal provision was part of the Civil Rights Act of 1866. On March 1, 1880, the Supreme Court ruled in a pair of cases concerning this right of removal and demonstrated the strict scrutiny they gave such requests.

---

maritime jurisdiction of federal district courts did not appear the limited area it does to modern interpretation. Instead, it reflected a fact of life:

> Trade requires dependable laws and courts. Maritime commerce was then the jugular vein of the Thirteen States. The need for a body of law applicable throughout the nation was recognized by every shade of opinion in the Constitutional Convention.[19]

And so, to ensure that a uniform body of admiralty and maritime law would develop, Congress vested jurisdiction over all such cases in the federal district courts. Although the Supreme Court initially adopted a narrow definition of the waters covered by this grant, it eventually expanded that view to include virtually all navigable and potentially navigable waterways within the country.[20] *(p. 86)*

A Question of Party

To preserve national sovereignty, to provide a neutral forum, and to ensure federal control of foreign relations, the Constitution gave federal courts jurisdiction over cases in

which the United States itself was a party, in cases between states and between citizens of different states, and in cases involving representatives of foreign governments.

United States v.....

Because of the protection of sovereign immunity, most cases involving the United States are initiated by the federal government. *(Box, p. 261)*

When the United States comes into the federal courts as a plaintiff, however, it must satisfy the same requirements as any other party seeking to file a federal suit. It must demonstrate a real interest that is seriously threatened in a manner susceptible of judicial resolution.

The court, however, has made clear that such an interest need not be simply one of property or monetary concern: "The obligations which it [the United States] is under to promote the interest of all, and to prevent the wrongdoing of one resulting in injury to the general welfare, is often of itself sufficient to give it a standing in court." [21] *(General discussion of standing, p. 291)*

Cases brought by the United States against a state are adjudicated in federal court. The first such case before the

...from State into Federal Court

1880 Rulings

Taylor Strauder, a black man charged with murder in West Virginia, was allowed to remove his case for trial from state to federal courts — because he could point to a state law which excluded blacks from jury duty. The court found this law persuasive evidence that he would be denied his equal rights during a state trial.[3]

But Burwell and Lee Reynolds, two black brothers charged with murder in Virginia, were not so lucky. Their claim was similar to Strauder's, but they could cite no state law excluding blacks from the juries of the state. They could only point to the fact that there was no black on the juries which indicted and would try them, arguing that this was evidence of strong community prejudice which would operate to deny them equal rights. Taking a narrow view of state action, the court refused to allow removal of the Reynolds' trial to federal courts.[4]

For the next 80 years, the Supreme Court had no occasion to rule on the scope of this right because there was no law providing for appeal of a federal judge's refusal to allow removal of a case from state court.

1966 Rulings

In one of its first modern statements on this right of removal, the Supreme Court — again in a pair of cases — renewed its insistence upon a careful application of the removal law.

Civil rights demonstrators, charged with trespass under Georgia law for attempting to exercise their right of equal access to public accommodations, secured by the Civil Rights Act of 1964, sought to remove their trials

to federal court. The Supreme Court granted that request.[5]

But on the same day in 1966, the Supreme Court refused to allow removal of a case in which civil rights demonstrators were charged with breach of the peace in violation of Mississippi law.[6]

The difference between the two situations, in the court's view, was the fact that the Georgia demonstrators clearly were exercising a right granted by federal law. But no federal law gave the Mississippi demonstrators the right "to obstruct a public street, to contribute to the delinquency of a minor, to drive an automobile without a license, or to bite a policeman."[7]

Justice Potter Stewart stated the court's view of the authority granted under this law:

The civil rights removal statute does not require and does not permit the judges of the federal courts to put their brethren of the state judiciary on trial. Under ... [that law] the vindication of the defendant's federal rights is left to the state courts except in the rare situations where it can be clearly predicted by reason of the operation of a pervasive and explicit state or federal law that those rights will inevitably be denied by the very act of bringing the defendant to trial in the state court.[8]

Congress could enlarge the conditions under which civil rights cases could be transferred from state to federal courts, Stewart wrote, but "if changes are to be made in the long-settled interpretation of the provisions of this century-old removal statute, it is for Congress and not for this Court to make them."[9]

---

[1] *Nashville v. Cooper,* 6 Wall. 247 at 253 (1868).
[2] *Tennessee v. Davis,* 100 U.S. 257 at 266 (1880).
[3] *Strauder v. West Virginia,* 100 U.S. 303 (1880).
[4] *Virginia v. Rives,* 100 U.S. 313 (1880).

[5] *Georgia v. Rachel,* 384 U.S. 780 (1966).
[6] *City of Greenwood, Miss. v. Peacock,* 384 U.S. 808 (1966).
[7] Id. at 826-827.
[8] Id. at 828.
[9] Id. at 833-834.

Supreme Court arrived in 1890 — with no challenge from the state to Supreme Court jurisdiction. Two years later, however, when the United States sued Texas in the Supreme Court, Texas argued that such federal jurisdiction was an infringement of its sovereignty.

The Supreme Court quickly disposed of that argument: when Texas entered the Union, it had acquiesced in the provisions of Article III extending federal judicial power to *all* cases arising under the Constitution, federal laws or treaties, without regard to the parties involved; *and* to all controversies in which the United States was a party, without regard to the subject of the dispute, *and* granting the Supreme Court original jurisdiction over cases in which states were parties.[22]

The court does not automatically take jurisdiction of all such cases. It has refused those that appeared to present only a difference of opinion and not an actual collision of interests between governments.[23]

State v. State

The Supreme Court has original and exclusive jurisdiction over cases between states. *(Decisions, p. 365)*

As in the case of suits brought by the United States, the court does not necessarily agree to accept jurisdiction over all interstate cases. Refusing to consider a tax-based dispute between Massachusetts and Missouri in 1939, the court explained:

To constitute ... a [justiciable] controversy, it must appear that the complaining State has suffered a wrong through the action of the other State, furnishing ground for judicial redress, or is asserting a right against the other State which is susceptible of judicial enforcement according to the accepted principles of the common law or equity systems of jurisprudence.... In the exercise of our original jurisdiction so as truly to fulfill the constitutional purpose we not only must look to the nature of the interest of the complaining state — the essential quality of the right asserted — but we must also inquire whether recourse to that jurisdiction ... is necessary for the State's protection....[24]

Citizen v. State

Taking the language of Article III literally, the Supreme Court — in its first major decision, issued in 1793 —

overrode claims of state immunity from suits brought without the state's consent, and held that citizens of one state could sue another state in federal court, even over the state's objection.[25]

Within five years, this decision in the case of *Chisholm v. Georgia* was overruled by ratification of the Eleventh Amendment, which narrowed federal jurisdiction to cases *initiated* by a state against citizens of another state or initiated by those citizens against the state *with* its consent. *(Details, pp. 303-304)*

The Supreme Court has original, but not exclusive, jurisdiction over such cases. Only civil cases between states and non-residents may come into federal court under this provision; states may not use federal courts to enforce state criminal laws against non-residents.[26] And the court has held that a state's suit against its own citizens is outside the scope of federal judicial power and can only be initiated in state courts.[27]

Furthermore, when the state is allowed to come into federal court to sue a non-resident — often a corporation — the Supreme Court has required that the state be defending its own interest or the general welfare of its population — not simply the private interest of some individual state resident.[28]

Citizen v. Citizen

"A . . . powerful influence behind the demand for federal courts was due to the friction between individual states which came to the surface after the danger of the common enemy had disappeared," wrote Professors Frankfurter and Landis. "In one respect it gave rise to lively suspicions and hostilities by the citizens of one state towards those of another as well as toward aliens. This fear of parochial prejudice, dealing unjustly with litigants from other states and foreign countries, undermined the sense of security necessary for commercial intercourse." [29]

To ensure a neutral forum for the resolution of disputes between citizens of different states, Congress concurred with the grant of jurisdiction in Article III, giving the new circuit courts authority to hear such "diversity" cases.

The Supreme Court generally has required "complete diversity" of residence, ruling in 1806 that if diversity was the basis for federal jurisdiction over a case, no party on one side of a case could be a citizen of the same state as any party on the other side.[30] In certain types of cases, the court has held that Congress can waive this strict interpretation of the diversity requirement.[31]

A few years after the court announced the strict application of the diversity requirement, it applied a corollary to slow efforts of persons challenging corporate actions to move their cases into federal courts by using diversity of residence as the basis for federal jurisdiction over the dispute.

In 1809, the court held that such a case could come into federal court only if *all* a corporation's stockholders were citizens of a state other than that of the plaintiff.[32] As a result, there was very little corporate litigation in federal courts until 1844, when the Supreme Court overruled itself and decided that, for purposes of determining diversity jurisdiction, a corporation would be assumed to be a citizen of the state in which it was chartered.

This assumption was subsequently replaced by one which viewed all of a corporation's stockholders as citizens of the state of its incorporation.[33] This "developing doctrine of corporate citizenship," noted Frankfurter and Landis,

"enormously extended" the reach of federal diversity jurisdiction.[34]

One primary limitation on diversity cases is the "jurisdictional amount" imposed by law for federal jurisdiction. Initially $500, this amount is now $10,000. Cases between residents of different states involving less than $10,000 are heard by state courts. (Certain types of cases — such as divorce and custody cases — generally are left to state courts regardless of the amount involved.)[35] *(Box, p. 257)*

Since 1890, efforts have been made to abolish federal diversity jurisdiction as an anachronism.

The jurisdiction of federal courts over cases in which citizens of the same states claimed land under grants from different states quickly became obsolete.

Foreign Relations

To ensure that control of foreign relations remained unmistakably in the hands of national — not local and state — authorities, the Constitution granted the federal courts power to hear all cases between a state or American citizens and a foreign state or its citizens or subjects, and all cases involving ambassadors, public ministers or consuls.

After the Supreme Court made clear that a foreign nation, like a state, could be sued in federal court only if it gave its consent to the suit, few such suits arose.[36]

A century later, the court further narrowed this category of cases, ruling that a state could not be sued by a foreign nation without the state's consent.[37]

For more than a century, it has been firmly established that a foreign nation may come into federal court with a civil claim, just as a citizen or domestic corporation may. In 1871, the Supreme Court had "not the slightest difficulty" in upholding the right of Emperor Napoleon III to sue in federal court for damages caused to a French ship which had collided with an American vessel: "A foreign sovereign, as well as any other foreign person, who has a demand of a civil nature against any person here, may prosecute it in our courts. To deny him this privilege would manifest a want of comity and friendly feeling." [38]

That privilege survives for all nations recognized by and at peace with the United States.[39]

Federal jurisdiction over cases involving ambassadors, public ministers and consuls extends only to foreign officials in the United States, not to U.S. officials accredited to foreign governments.[40] Because diplomatic immunity protects most high-ranking figures from lawsuits, most cases involve consuls, or suits brought by diplomatic personnel against U.S. citizens. The Supreme Court has granted state courts jurisdiction over some cases involving consular officials, particularly if the subject of the case is one normally left to the states, like domestic relations. But in so doing, the court indicated that Congress could require that all such cases be heard in federal courts.[41]

Supreme Court Jurisdiction

The Constitution grants the Supreme Court original jurisdiction in "all cases affecting Ambassadors, other public Ministers and Consuls, and those in which a State shall be a Party. . . ."

These cases may be heard initially by the Supreme Court. This original jurisdiction may be exclusive or concurrent, shared with other federal courts or with state courts.

The Sovereign's Immunity

The United States cannot be sued in federal court unless Congress expressly authorizes such lawsuits.

This legal doctrine is a corollary of the theory that the king could do no wrong. It has been applied, wrote a recent Supreme Court justice, "by our courts as vigorously as it had been on behalf of the crown."[1]

This immunity was recognized by the court as early as 1834. Chief Justice John Marshall stated in that year that "the party who institutes such suit [against the United States] must bring his case within the authority of some act of Congress, or the court cannot exercise jurisdiction over it." Subsequently, the court held the federal government immune even from suits seeking recompense for damages or injuries inflicted by its agents or employees.[2]

In 1940, the Supreme Court explained that "the reasons for this immunity partake somewhat of dignity and decorum, somewhat of practical administration, somewhat of the political desirability of an impregnable legal citadel where government as distinct from its functionaries may operate undisturbed by the demands of litigants." However, the court continued, "[a] sense of justice has brought a progressive relaxation by legislative enactments of the rigor of the immunity rule."[3]

This relaxation, through acts of Congress waiving immunity, actually began with a Supreme Court decision in the 1882 case of *United States v. Lee.*[4] George Lee, a son of Robert E. Lee, sued to recover his family home, Arlington, which had been seized by federal officials acting under presidential order and was being used as a cemetery and a fort. The government claimed that such a suit could not be brought because of sovereign immunity.

The Supreme Court, in a 5-4 decision, disagreed and rejected the defense of sovereign immunity. When it was claimed that a federal officer was holding property illegally, a federal court could take jurisdiction to hear out the claim, held the court. The doctrine of sovereign immunity, wrote Justice Samuel F. Miller for the majority, was "not permitted to interfere with the judicial enforcement of the established rights of plaintiffs, when the United States is not a defendant or necessary party to the suit...."[5]

The use of the sovereign immunity defense in such a case, continued Miller, "seems to be opposed to all the principles upon which the rights of the citizen, when brought in collision with the acts of the Government, must be determined. In such cases there is no safety for the citizen, except in the protection of the judicial tribunals, for rights which have been invaded by the officers of the Government, professing to act in its name."[6]

Miller continued:

No man in this country is so high that he is above the law. No officer of the law may set that law at defiance, with impunity. All the officers of the Government, from the highest to the lowest, are creatures of the law and are bound to obey it.

It is the only supreme power in our system of government, and every man who, by accepting office, participates in its functions, is only the more strongly bound to submit to that supremacy, and to observe the limitations which it imposes upon the exercise of the authority which it gives....[7]

Five years later, in 1887, Congress passed the Tucker Act, specifically granting to the Court of Claims and federal district courts jurisdiction over cases such as *United States v. Lee.*

In 1946, Congress approved the Federal Tort Claims Act, waiving the government's immunity to certain personal injury claims against government employees or contractors.

Cases against federal officials generally fall into four categories, Justice Felix Frankfurter once explained. There are cases in which a person seeks a share of government property — or seeks to compel the exercise of official authority. These are not usually allowed to survive in the face of a defense of sovereign immunity.

There are cases in which a person sues a government official because he is threatened or injured by that official's action taken under an allegedly unconstitutional law or in excess of his legal authority. These cases are usually allowed to proceed.[8]

And in cases in which an official is charged with inflicting some common-law injury on another and seeks to invoke sovereign immunity by citing the law or the command of his superior as authority for his action, the court has allowed some such cases to proceed and has found that sovereign immunity blocks others.[9]

---

[1] *Feres v. United States*, 340 U.S. 135 at 139 (1950).

[2] *United States v. Clarke*, 8 Pet. 436 at 444 (1834); *Gibbons v. United States*, 8 Wall. 269 (1869).

[3] *United States v. Shaw*, 309 U.S. 495 at 500-501 (1940).

[4] *United States v. Lee*, 106 U.S. 196 (1882).

[5] Id. at 207-208.

[6] Id. at 218-219.

[7] Id. at 220.

[8] Most recently, see *Butz v. Economou*, 438 U.S. 478 (1978).

[9] *Larson v. Domestic & Foreign Corp.*, 337 U.S. 682 at 705 (1949).

Cases brought under its original jurisdiction comprise a very small portion of the modern court's caseload — and most of those cases involve interstate controversies. Only a very few original cases have been brought involving foreign diplomats.

Congress may not expand or curtail the court's original jurisdiction. That was established by the court in its 1803 decision in *Marbury v. Madison.*

The act of Congress which the court held in that case to be unconstitutional was a provision of the Judiciary Act of 1789. The 13th section of that act authorized the court to issue writs of *mandamus* to federal officials; the court viewed this as an expansion of the original jurisdiction granted to it by the Constitution, and thus unconstitutional. Congress lacked the power to amend that grant, reasoned Marshall:

...It has been insisted ... that as the original grant of jurisdiction to the Supreme and inferior courts, is general and the clause, assigning original jurisdiction to the Supreme Court, contains no negative or restrictive words, the power remains to the legislature, to assign original jurisdiction to that court in other cases than those specified in the article ... provided those cases belong to the judicial power of the United States.

If it had been intended to leave it in the discretion of the legislature to apportion the judicial power between the supreme and inferior courts ... it would certainly have been useless to have proceeded further than to have defined the judicial power, and the tribunals in which it should be vested. The subsequent part of the section [of Article III assigning original jurisdiction to the Supreme Court] is mere surplusage, is entirely without meaning, if such is to be the construction.... It cannot be presumed that any clause in the constitution is intended to be without effect; and, therefore, such a construction is inadmissible ....[42]

Congress, however, has successfully asserted the power to decide whether or not the court's original jurisdiction over certain matters is exclusive or concurrent. In 1789 the Judiciary Act gave the court exclusive jurisdiction over all civil suits between a state and the United States or between two states; while suits between a state and an individual might be heard first in other courts — and only later before the Supreme Court. In addition, the 1789 Act gave the court exclusive jurisdiction over all suits *against* ambassadors, public ministers or their domestics, but not over all cases brought *by* ambassadors or public ministers, nor over all cases involving consuls.

The reasoning behind this division of original jurisdiction was set out by the Supreme Court a century later. The purpose of the grant of original jurisdiction, explained Chief Justice Morrison Waite, was:

> ...to open and keep open the highest court of the Nation, for the determination, in the first instance, of suits involving a State or a diplomatic or commercial representative of a foreign government. So much was due to the rank and dignity of those for whom the provision was made; but to compel a State to resort to this one tribunal for the redress of all its grievances or to deprive an ambassador, public minister or consul of the privilege of suing in any court he chose having jurisdiction ... would be, in many cases, to convert what was intended as a favor into a burden.[43]

Therefore, continued the Chief Justice, "Congress took care to provide that no suit should be brought *against* an ambassador or other public minister except in the Supreme Court, but that he might sue in any court he chose that was open to him...." And, he continued, the same approach gave a state the right — any time it was sued by the United States or another state — to have its case heard originally by the Supreme Court. It could choose to bring its own cases against individuals, however, in any court it chose.[44]

Exercise of the court's original jurisdiction is not mandatory. Just before the Civil War, the state of Kentucky came to the court asking for an order directing the governor of Ohio to return a free black man indicted in Kentucky for helping a fugitive slave to escape. The court

A Federal Common Law?

When federal judges, dealing with diversity cases, resolve matters normally dealt with by state courts and state law, what law do they apply?

This question resulted in one of the most remarkable turnabouts in Supreme Court history — in which the Supreme Court not only overturned a century-old precedent, but declared that precedent-setting ruling unconstitutional.

The Judiciary Act of 1789 provided that "the laws of the several states" should in general "be regarded as the rules of decision in trials at common law" in applicable cases in federal courts. "No issue in the whole field of federal jurisprudence has been more difficult than determining the meaning of this statute," wrote one scholar. "The central question has been whether the decisions of state courts are 'laws of the several states' within the meaning of the statute, and thus of controlling effect in some situations at least in the federal courts." [1]

In 1842 the Supreme Court, in deciding the case of *Swift v. Tyson*, stated that the "laws of the several states" applied in diversity cases by federal courts included only the written statutes of the states — not the common law or interpretation of the statutes set out by the decisions of state courts.[2]

The apparent basis for the ruling, Carl Swisher later wrote, was the belief of the justices that state courts would follow the federal courts' interpretation of the common law, resulting in uniformity of application among the states. But, Swisher noted, "the strategy failed.... State courts continued to follow in their own interpretations, with the result that state courts and federal courts, sitting virtually side by side, were handing down different interpretations ..." of the same law.[3]

In 1938 the Supreme Court took the opportunity presented by a diversity case concerning personal injury and questions of negligence and overruled *Swift v. Tyson*. Furthermore, the court declared its earlier ruling unconstitutional. The Constitution, said the court in *Erie Railroad Co. v. Tompkins*, required that the law in diversity cases be the law of the applicable state — both its written laws and the decisions of its courts. The most essential uniformity was consistency of interpretation and application of a state's laws within its limits — by federal as well as state courts.[4] "There is no federal general common law," stated the court.[5]

---

[1] Charles Alan Wright, *Handbook of the Law of Federal Courts*, 2d ed. (St. Paul: West Publishing Co., 1970), p. 219.
[2] *Swift v. Tyson*, 16 Pet. 1 (1842).
[3] Carl B. Swisher, *American Constitutional Development*, 2d ed. (Cambridge: Houghton Mifflin Co., 1954), p. 980.
[4] *Erie Railroad Co. v. Tompkins*, 304 U.S. 64 (1938).
[5] Id. at 78.

reaffirmed its jurisdiction over such a case — and then declined to issue the requested order.[45]

Several decades later, the court declared that it would not exercise its original jurisdiction over criminal cases between states and citizens of other states. Wisconsin came to the Supreme Court in 1887 seeking assistance in enforcing penalties which state courts had assessed against an out-of-state corporation. The Supreme Court declined to take original jurisdiction over the case. Justice Horace Gray explained:

...the mere fact that a State is the plaintiff is not a conclusive test that the controversy is one in which this court is authorized to grant relief against another State or her citizens.... [T]his court has declined to take jurisdiction of suits between States to compel the performance of obligations which, if the States had been independent nations, could not have been enforced judicially, but only through the political departments of their governments.

The penal laws of a country do not reach beyond its own territory, except when extended by express treaty or statute to offenses committed abroad by its own citizens; and they must be administered in its own courts only, and cannot be enforced by the courts of another country....

[T]he jurisdiction conferred by the Constitution upon this court, in cases to which a State is a party, is limited to controversies of a civil nature....[46]

Appellate Jurisdiction

In all other cases falling within the scope of federal judicial power — aside from those placed in the court's original jurisdiction by the Constitution — Article III grants the court appellate jurisdiction "both as to Law and Fact, with such Exceptions, and under such Regulations as the Congress shall make."

Congress quickly accepted the invitation to make exceptions and regulations concerning the high court's jurisdiction over appeals from lower courts.

The Judiciary Act of 1789 granted the court jurisdiction over appeals from the decisions of the circuit courts in civil cases — so long as more than $2,000 was at stake. Not until 1889 did the Supreme Court have the jurisdiction to hear appeals in criminal cases.

In addition, the famous Section 25 of the Judiciary Act granted the Supreme Court authority to take appeals from rulings of high state courts upholding state laws or state actions against challenge that they are in conflict with the U.S. Constitution, federal laws or treaties.

The Supreme Court has from the first concurred in this assertion of congressional power over its appellate jurisdiction.[47]

In 1866 the court declared:

The original jurisdiction of this court, and its power to receive appellate jurisdiction, are created and defined by the Constitution; and the Legislative Department of the Government can enlarge neither one nor the other. But it is for Congress to determine how far, within the limits of the capacity of this court to take, appellate jurisdiction shall be given, and when conferred, it can be exercised only to the extent and in the manner prescribed by law. In these respects, it is wholly the creature of legislation.[48]

The Case of William McCardle

The full truth of this statement was brought home to the court and the nation three years later.

In 1867 Congress expanded the availability of the writ of *habeas corpus* to persons who felt they were illegally detained by state or federal authority. The 1867 act allowed federal judges to issue such a writ in "all cases where any person may be restrained of his or her liberty, in violation of the Constitution or of any treaty or law of the United States."

The purpose of the postwar law was to provide protection from state prosecution and detention for federal officials enforcing Reconstruction laws in the former confederacy.

Ironically, the first major test of that law came as a result of its use by a southern editor, William McCardle, who had been charged by a military tribunal with impeding Reconstruction through his newspaper articles. McCardle came to the Supreme Court, seeking a writ of *habeas corpus* ordering the military authorities to release him. He contended that the military commission had no jurisdiction to try him, a civilian. It was widely believed, according to histories of the time, that the court would avail itself of this opportunity to declare the Reconstruction Acts themselves unconstitutional.[49]

The first question under consideration in the McCardle case, argued and decided in February 1868, was whether the Supreme Court had jurisdiction to hear an appeal of a lower court's refusal to issue the writ.

The unanimous Supreme Court held that it did. Describing the 1867 Act, it said:

This legislation is of the most comprehensive character. It brings within the *habeas corpus* jurisdiction of every court and of every judge every possible case of privation of liberty contrary to the National Constitution, treaties, or laws. It is impossible to widen this jurisdiction.

And it is to this jurisdiction that the system of appeals is applied. From decisions of a judge or of a district court appeals lie to the Circuit Court, and from the judgment of the Circuit Court to this court.... Every question of substance which the Circuit Court could decide upon the return of the *habeas corpus* ... may be revised here on appeal from its final judgment.[50]

March 1868 was an eventful month. From March 2 until March 9 the Supreme Court heard arguments on the merits of McCardle's appeal for a writ of *habeas corpus*. Three days into the arguments, Chief Justice Salmon P. Chase left the High Court bench for the chair of the presiding official in the Senate impeachment trial of President Andrew Johnson.

On March 12, Congress acted to prevent the court's possible use of the McCardle case to strike down the Reconstruction Acts. As a rider to a revenue bill, Congress added a provision repealing the portion of the 1867 Habeas Corpus Act extending the Supreme Court's appellate jurisdiction over cases arising under it. Despite his own difficult position, President Johnson vetoed the bill March 25. It was repassed over his veto two days later.[51]

A week later, on April 2, the Supreme Court agreed to hear further arguments in the McCardle case, now focusing on the impact of the repeal on the case already argued. The court then delayed matters further by postponing these arguments until its next term, a move much protested by at least two of the justices.

In May President Johnson was acquitted by one vote in the Senate.

In March 1869 the court heard the postponed arguments; on April 12, 1869, it held that Congress had eliminated the court's jurisdiction over the case. Chief Justice Chase spoke for the court; there was no dissenting opinion:

> The provision of the Act of 1867, affirming the appellate jurisdiction of this court in cases of *habeas corpus,* is expressly repealed. It is hardly possible to imagine a plainer instance of positive exception.
>
> We are not at liberty to inquire into the motives of the Legislature. We can only examine into its power under the Constitution; and the power to make exceptions to the appellate jurisdiction of this court is given by express words.
>
> What, then, is the effect of the repealing Act upon the case before us? We cannot doubt as to this. Without jurisdiction the court cannot proceed at all in any cause. . . .
>
> It is quite clear, therefore, that this court cannot proceed to pronounce judgment in this case, for it has no longer jurisdiction of the appeal; and judicial duty is not less fitly performed by declining ungranted jurisdiction than in exercising firmly that which the Constitution and the laws confer.[52]

Later in the year, Chase would comment — in another opinion — that such a repeal of jurisdiction was "unusual and hardly to be justified except upon some imperious public exigency."[53]

Carl Swisher points out that this was, to date, "the only instance in American history in which Congress has rushed to withdraw the appellate jurisdiction of the Supreme Court for the purpose of preventing a decision on the constitutionality of a particular law."[54] (This aspect of the Supreme Court's appellate jurisdiction was restored in 1885.)

But as Charles L. Black Jr. states, the McCardle case "marks the extent of the vulnerability of the Judiciary to congressional control, and hence underlines the significance of Congress' never (except for this case and perhaps one or two other ambiguous and minor instances) having tried to employ this power to hamper judicial review even of its own acts."[55] *(Court-curbing proposals, pp. 665-672)*

The Modern System of Appeals

For the first century of the nation's existence, the Supreme Court was virtually the only federal appeals court. The circuit and district courts functioned as trial courts. The Supreme Court was obliged to rule on all appeals brought from the rulings of those lower courts — as well as those brought under the Judiciary Act of 1789 from state courts.

And, wrote Professors Frankfurter and Landis

> . . .for a hundred years the range of Supreme Court litigation remained practically unchanged. The same types of cases which in 1789 the framers of the Judiciary Act had designated for review by the Supreme Court continued to come before it till 1891. Despite the vast transformation of thirteen seaboard colonies into a great nation, with all that this implied in the growth of judicial business and the emergence of new controversies of vast proportions, a heavy stream of petty litigation reached the Supreme Court.[56]

Especially after the Civil War, the number of cases flowing to the Supreme Court began to swell. First in 1891,

---

A Guide for Discretion

Since Congress in 1925 gave the Supreme Court broad discretion over the decision to review or deny review in most of the cases brought to its attention, the court has adopted certain rules to guide the exercise of this discretion.

One such rule is the "Rule of Four" — a case is accepted for review only if four members of the court feel that it merits full consideration by the court. That rule has since 1925 governed the court's decisions to grant or deny review through use of the writ of certiorari.

More formal and official is the portion of the Rules of the Supreme Court of the United States which states:

> A review on writ of certiorari is not a matter of right, but of sound judicial discretion, and will be granted only where there are special and important reasons therefor. The following, while neither controlling nor fully measuring the court's discretion, indicate the character of reasons which will be considered:
>
> (a) Where a state court has decided a federal question of substance not theretofore determined by this court, or has decided it in a way probably not in accord with applicable decisions of this court.
>
> (b) Where a court of appeals has rendered a decision in conflict with the decision of another court of appeals on the same matter; or has decided an important state or territorial question in a way in conflict with applicable state or territorial law; or has decided an important question of federal law which has not been, but should be, settled by this court; or has decided a federal question in a way in conflict with applicable decisions of this court; or has so far departed from the accepted and usual course of judicial proceedings, or so far sanctioned such a departure by a lower court, as to call for an exercise of this court's power of supervision.
>
> The same general considerations . . . will control in respect of petitions for writs of certiorari to review judgments of the Court of Claims, of the Court of Customs and Patent Appeals, or of any other court whose determinations are by law reviewable on writ of certiorari.

(Rule 19 of the Rules of the Supreme Court of the United States, adopted June 15, 1970.)

---

and then, most notably in 1925, Congress gave the Supreme Court the power to select the most important of these cases for review — and to refuse to review others.

There are two primary routes to Supreme Court review of the decision of an inferior court. The first is through the "writs of right" — first the writ of error issued to state courts under the 1789 Act and then the appeal still in use today. If the court finds that it has jurisdiction over an appeal, it is obligated to decide the issues it raises. The second is through the writ of certiorari — a discretionary writ issued by the court to a lower court ordering that court to send to the High Court the record of the case. In the last

The Duty To Decide

In 1821, Chief Justice John Marshall set out, in clear and certain terms, his view of the Supreme Court's duty to decide all cases which properly fall within its jurisdiction. As history would show, such an approach was deceptively simple; the court would many times disagree on whether a matter was properly before it and was appropriate for decision.

Marshall wrote:

> It is most true that this Court will not take jurisdiction if it should not: but it is equally true, that it must take jurisdiction if it should. The judiciary cannot, as the legislature may, avoid a measure because it approaches the confines of the constitution. We cannot pass it by because it is doubtful. With whatever doubts, with whatever difficulties, a case may be attended, we must decide it, if it be brought before us. We have no more right to decline the exercise of jurisdiction which is given, than to usurp that which is not given. The one or the other would be treason to the constitution. *(Cohens v. Virginia, 6 Wheat. 264 at 404, 1821)*

80 years, most of the cases coming to the court have been transferred from the appeals route to the discretionary certiorari route, giving the court more control over its docket.

The Circuit Court of Appeals

This process began in 1891 with creation by Congress of a new level of federal courts, between the circuit and district courts on the one hand and the Supreme Court on the other. These new courts — circuit courts of appeals — were to hear all appeals from decisions of the district and circuit courts. Their word was to be final in almost all diversity, admiralty, patent, revenue and non-capital criminal cases. (In 1911 Congress abolished the old circuit courts.)

The Circuit Court of Appeals Act of 1891 provided for Supreme Court review of such cases, after their decision by the appeals courts, only if the appeals court judges certified a case to the High Court — or if the Supreme Court decided to grant review through issuing a writ of certiorari. Still granted a right to appeal to the Supreme Court were parties to cases involving constitutional questions, matters of treaty law, jurisdictional questions, capital crimes and conflicting laws.

A Broader Jurisdiction

Early in the 20th century, Congress twice found it necessary to enlarge the court's appellate jurisdiction.

In 1907, the Criminal Appeals Act granted the government the right to appeal directly to the Supreme Court a federal judge's ruling dismissing an indictment, so long as the defendant had not been placed in jeopardy before dismissal of the charges. This statute remedied an omission in the 1891 act, which, the court had ruled in 1892, left the government without this right.[57] Thus, if a federal judge dismissed an indictment, finding the law on which it was based unconstitutional, no appeal of that ruling was possi-

ble. The prosecution was terminated. After a federal district judge thus blocked the Roosevelt administration's prosecution of the Beef Trust, Congress acted to remedy the deficiency in the law.[58]

In 1914 Congress enlarged the power of the Supreme Court to review state court decisions. In 1911 the New York Court of Appeals held that state's workmen's compensation law — the nation's first — unconstitutional under the state and federal constitutions. Because the Supreme Court could only review state court rulings in which the state court *denied* a federal challenge to a state law, or held a federal law invalid, this ruling was outside the scope of judicial review.

And so in 1914, Congress authorized the court to review — through issuing a writ of certiorari — rulings of a high state court upholding, as well as denying, a federal right or challenge.[59] Later, Congress made review of all state court rulings on federal questions subject to Supreme Court discretion — except those where a state court held a federal treaty, law or action invalid or upheld a state law or action against federal challenge.[60] Review in those categories of cases remained obligatory.

The cases coming to the Supreme Court continued to increase in numbers. As early as 1909, President William Howard Taft urged Congress to curtail the appellate jurisdiction of the court to confine it to statutory and constitutional questions.

The 'Judges Bill'

After Taft became Chief Justice in 1921, his campaign for reform shifted into high gear. The result was passage in 1925 of a new judiciary act, often known as the "judges bill" — a reference to the fact that the original legislation was drafted by members of the Supreme Court.[61]

Under the Judiciary Act of 1925, the Supreme Court retains a broad right of review over federal cases — generally to be exercised at the court's discretion. *(Text, p. 960)*

The 1925 Act made the circuit courts of appeals, well-established after three decades, the last word on most cases they decided.

The only cases in which there was an appeal of right from an appeals court ruling were those in which the appeals court held a state law invalid under the Constitution, federal laws or federal treaties. In such cases, review by the Supreme Court was limited to the federal question involved. In all other cases, Supreme Court review of appeals court decisions was available only through the issuance of a writ of certiorari — over which the court had complete discretion.[62]

Under the 1925 act — and for half a century after that — the right of direct appeal to the Supreme Court from district court decisions remained available in cases decided under antitrust or interstate commerce laws; appeals by the United States under the Criminal Appeals Act; suits to halt enforcement of state laws or other official state actions; and suits designed to halt enforcement of Interstate Commerce Commission orders.

(In the 1970s, these direct appeal routes were all redirected by Congress through the courts of appeals. After 1976, direct appeal remained only in cases in which district courts held an act of Congress invalid in a case to which the United States or its employees were a party, and from decisions of three-judge district courts involving reapportionment, some civil rights matters, some voting rights matters and some federal campaign spending cases, as well as decisions of a special railroad reorganization court.)

From state courts, only two types of cases retained a right of direct appeal under the 1925 act — those in which a state law was upheld against a federally based challenge and those in which a federal law or treaty was held invalid.

The court's power to review state court rulings, however, remained — as always — quite limited in contrast to its broad power to review federal court decisions. The court could review only such cases in which substantial federal questions were raised and in which state courts had rendered final judgment.

The Judiciary Act of 1925 stands with the acts of 1789 and 1891 as one of the great organizational statutes in the history of the federal judiciary. For the most part, Chief Justice Taft's hopes for the accomplishments of the new law seem to have been achieved. In late 1925, he wrote in the *Yale Law Journal*:

> The sound theory of the new Act is that litigants have their rights sufficiently protected by the courts of first instance, and by one review in an intermediate appellate federal court. The function of the Supreme Court is conceived to be, not the remedying of a particular litigant's wrong, but the consideration of those cases whose decision involves principles, the application of which are of wide public and governmental interest.[63]

Footnotes

[1] *The Federalist Papers*, with an Introduction by Clinton Rossiter, (New York: New American Library, Mentor Books, 1961), No. 15, pp. 106-107.

[2] Ibid., No. 78, p. 466.

[3] Ibid., No. 16, p. 116.

[4] Ibid., No. 78, pp. 465-466.

[5] Felix Frankfurter, *The Commerce Clause Under Marshall, Taney and Waite* (Chapel Hill, N.C.: The University of North Carolina Press, 1927), pp. 95-96.

[6] *United States v. Richardson*, 418 U.S. 166 at 188 (1974).

[7] Charles G. Haines, *The American Doctrine of Judicial Supremacy* (Berkeley, Calif.: The University of California Press, 1932), pp. 23-24.

[8] Alexander Bickel, *The Least Dangerous Branch* (Indianapolis: Bobbs-Merrill Co., 1962), p. 1.

[9] *Ex parte McCardle*, 7 Wall. 506 at 514 (1869).

[10] 291 F.940 (7th Cir. 1923), revised by *Michaelson v. United States*, 266 U.S. 42 (1924).

[11] Charles Alan Wright, *Handbook of the Law of Federal Courts*, 2d ed. (St. Paul: West Publishing Co., 1970), p. 2.

[12] *Cary v. Curtis*, 3 How. 236 at 245 (1845).

[13] *Nashville v. Cooper*, 6 Wall. 247 at 252 (1868).

[14] See Felix Frankfurter and James M. Landis, *The Business of the Supreme Court: A Study in the Federal Judicial System* (New York: Macmillan Publishing Co., 1928), pp. 1-14; also Julius Goebel Jr., *History of the Supreme Court of the United States: Vol. I, Antecedents and Beginnings to 1801* (New York: Macmillan Publishing Co., 1971), pp. 457-508.

[15] *Turner v. Bank of North America*, 4 Dall. 8 at 11 (1799).

[16] Id. at 10.

[17] Frankfurter and Landis, *The Business of the Supreme Court*, pp. 64-65.

[18] Ibid. pp. 6-7.

[19] Ibid.

[20] *The Thomas Jefferson*, 10 Wheat. 428 (1825); *The Genesee Chief*, 12 How. 443 (1851); *United States v. Appalachian Power Co.* 311 U.S. 377 (1940).

[21] *In re Debs*, 158 U.S. 564 at 584 (1895).

[22] *United States v. Texas*, 143 U.S. 621 (1892).

[23] *United States v. West Virginia*, 295 U.S. 463 at 473-474 (1935).

[24] *Massachusetts v. Missouri*, 308 U.S. 1 at 15, 18 (1939).

[25] *Chisholm v. Georgia*, 2 Dall. 419 (1793).

[26] *Wisconsin v. Pelican Insurance Co.* 127 U.S. 265 (1888).

[27] *California v. Southern Pacific Railway Co.*, 157 U.S. 229 (1895).

[28] *Georgia v. Tennessee Copper Co.*, 206 U.S. 230 (1907); *Georgia v. Pennsylvania R. Co.*, 324 U.S. 439 (1945).

[29] Frankfurter and Landis, *The Business of the Supreme Court*, pp. 8-9.

[30] *Strawbridge v. Curtiss*, 3 Cr. 267 (1806).

[31] *State Farm, Fire & Casualty Co. v. Tashire*, 386 U.S. 523 (1967).

[32] *Bank of the United States v. Deveaux*, 5 Cr. 61 (1809).

[33] *Louisville RR v. Letson*, 2 How. 497 (1844); *Marshall v. Baltimore and Ohio R. Co.*, 16 How. 314 (1854); *Muller v. Dows*, 94 U.S. 444 (1877).

[34] Frankfurter and Landis, *The Business of the Supreme Court*, p. 65, 89; see also Charles Alan Wright, *Handbook*, p. 89.

[35] Charles Alan Wright, *Handbook*, pp. 84-85; *Ex parte Burrus*, 136 U.S. 586 (1890); *Barber v. Barber*, 21 How. 582 (1858).

[36] *The Schooner Exchange v. McFaddon*, 7 Cr. 116 at 146 (1812).

[37] *Monaco v. Mississippi*, 292 U.S. 313 (1934).

[38] *The Ship Sapphire v. Napoleon III*, 11 Wall. 164 at 167 (1871).

[39] *Pfizer Inc. v. Government of India*, 434 U.S. 308 (1978).

[40] *Ex parte Gruber*, 269 U.S. 302 (1925).

[41] *Popovici v. Agler*, 280 U.S. 389 (1930).

[42] *Marbury v. Madison*, 1 Cr. 137 at 174 (1803).

[43] *Ames v. Kansas*, 111 U.S. 449 at 464 (1884).

[44] Id. at 464-465.

[45] *Kentucky v. Dennison*, 24 How. 66 (1861).

[46] *Wisconsin v. Pelican Insurance Company of New Orleans*, 127 U.S. 265 at 287, 288, 289-290, 297 (1888).

[47] *Wiscart v. Dauchy*, 3 Dall. 321 at 327 (1796); *Durousseau v. United States*, 6 Cr. 307 at 314 (1810).

[48] *Daniels v. Chicago & Rock Island Railroad Co.*, 3 Wall. 250 at 254 (1866).

[49] Carl B. Swisher, *American Constitutional Development*, 2d ed. (Cambridge: Houghton Mifflin Co., 1954), p. 324.

[50] *Ex parte McCardle*, 6 Wall. 318 at 325-326, 327 (1868).

[51] Charles Warren, *The Supreme Court in United States History*, 2 vols. (Boston: Little, Brown & Co., 1922, 1926), II:474-485.

[52] *Ex parte McCardle*, 7 Wall. 506 at 514, 515 (1869).

[53] *Ex parte Yerger*, 8 Wall. 85 at 104 (1869).

[54] Swisher, *American Constitutional Development*, p. 325.

[55] Charles L. Black Jr., *Perspectives in Constitutional Law* (Englewood Cliffs, N.J.: Prentice-Hall, 1963) p. 13.

[56] Frankfurter and Landis, *The Business of the Supreme Court*, p. 299.

[57] *United States v. Sanges*, 144 U.S. 310 (1892).

[58] Frankfurter and Landis, *The Business of the Supreme Court*, pp. 113-119.

[59] Ibid., pp. 193-198.

[60] Ibid., p. 211.

[61] Ibid., pp. 255-286.

[62] Charles Alan Wright, *Handbook*, p. 477.

[63] William Howard Taft, "The Jurisdiction of the Supreme Court Under the Act of February 13, 1925," *Yale Law Journal*, November 1925, p. 2, cited in *The Supreme Court from Taft to Warren* by Alpheus T. Mason (Baton Rouge: Louisiana State University Press, 1958) p. 222, note 83.

Federal Judicial Power

Once it is clear that a court has jurisdiction over a case, the scope of judicial power determines what the court may do about the dispute before it. Judicial power was defined by Supreme Court Justice Samuel Miller late in the 19th century as "the power of a court to decide and pronounce a judgment and carry it into effect...."[1]

Federal judicial power includes the power of judicial review — the power to measure the acts of Congress, the actions of the executive, and the laws and practices of the states against the Constitution — and to invalidate those which conflict with the requirements of that basic national charter.

In addition, the courts have the power to enforce their judgments through the use of writs, to punish persons for contempt, to make rules governing the judicial process and admission to the bar.

Judicial Review

"If men were angels, no government would be necessary," wrote James Madison in *The Federalist Papers*. He continued:

> ...If angels were to govern men, neither external nor internal controls on government would be necessary. In framing a government which is to be administered by men over men, the great difficulty lies in this: you must first enable the government to control the governed; and in the next place, oblige it to control itself.[2]

The power of judicial review is one of the major self-control mechanisms of the American system of government. Judicial review — especially as exercised over acts of Congress — is a uniquely American concept. The Constitution makes no mention of this power, but many of those who drafted its language made clear their belief that the Supreme Court must have this power. The court soon assumed its existence and — within 15 years of the framing of the Constitution — exercised it to establish its validity in practice.

And not only does this power operate as a constant admonition to Congress — and the states, who first felt the full force of its workings — but also to the executive. One hundred and seventy-one years after the Supreme Court struck down the first act of Congress, it cited that ruling as it informed a president that he too must comply with the law, even at the cost of disgrace and resignation from office.[3]

The origins of judicial review are obscure. During the colonial period, the Privy Council in London had the power to review and nullify acts of the colonial assemblies. During the revolutionary period, state courts exercised the power to strike down laws found to violate state constitutions, although such rulings usually provoked considerable controversy.[4]

The Constitutional Convention apparently did not discuss judicial review. It did, however, consider and reject a proposal set forth by James Madison which would have lodged the veto power in a council composed of members of the executive and judicial branches. In the debate on this proposal, some members of the convention expressed their belief that "the Judges in their proper official character ...

have a negative on the laws" — and so should not be given the chance to impose "a double negative."[5]

A long and scholarly debate developed over the legitimacy of the power of judicial review as assumed and exercised by the Supreme Court. Some scholars argued that the framers assumed the courts would exercise this power; others found its assumption clear usurpation. As one legal scholar noted several decades ago, the debate has by the 20th century become irrelevant in light of the long tradition of national acquiescence in the exercise of this power within our system.[6]

Review of State Acts

Clearly granted to the Supreme Court, however, was the power to review and reverse certain state court decisions. From 1789 until the Civil War, this was the aspect of judicial review most vigorously exercised, debated, protested and resisted. *(Details, pp. 303-308)*

The Judiciary Act of 1789, of which Oliver Ellsworth was the chief sponsor, expressly granted the Supreme Court this power to review, and reverse or affirm, the final rulings of state courts upholding a state law against a challenge that it was in conflict with the Constitution, federal laws or a federal treaty.

This provision, the 25th section of the act, was viewed as implementing the supremacy clause — the portion of the Constitution which states that the Constitution, federal laws and federal treaties are the supreme law of the land. (Congress in 1914 expanded this aspect of judicial review further, allowing the Supreme Court to review state court decisions finding state laws invalid because they conflicted with the Constitution, federal laws or federal treaties. *(See p. 265)*

Section 25 was highly controversial — especially after the court, in 1810, began exercising this power to hold certain state laws unconstitutional. Twice, in 1816 and 1821, the court firmly rejected state challenges to Section 25 as unconstitutional. First, Justice Joseph Story in *Martin v. Hunter's Lessee* — and then Chief Justice John Marshall in *Cohens v. Virginia* — defended the court's power over such state rulings as essential to preserve national sovereignty.[7] *(Details, pp. 305-306)*

Despite innumerable proposals that Congress abolish or curtail this aspect of judicial review, Congress has not given its final approval to any such measure. Part of the reason that this particular power has survived may lie in the restraint with which it has been exercised by the court. *(See pp. 287-295)*

After Section 25 was amended in 1867, it appeared that Congress, by omitting a restrictive sentence, had granted the court — when reviewing state court decisions — the power to review all the issues in such cases, not simply the federal issue which justified its review in the first place. But the court in 1875 refused to interpret the 1867 amendment as expanding its power in this direction.[8]

In 1945, Justice Robert H. Jackson described the traditional approach of the court in reviewing state court rulings:

> This Court from the time of its foundation has adhered to the principle that it will not review judgments of state courts that rest on adequate and inde-

Judicial Review: Supreme Court . . .

After the Supreme Court, in the second century of its history, began to wield its power of judicial review more often to overturn acts of Congress and decisions of state legislatures, critics of this exercise of power, both on and off the bench, began to charge that the court was acting as a super-legislature.

By striking down as invalid laws with which it did not agree, they argued, the court was engaging in "judicial legislation," substituting its judgment for those of duly elected representatives of the people.

Among the justices most critical of this development in its early stages was John Marshall Harlan, who wrote in dissent from the 1895 ruling overturning the peacetime income tax law:

> . . .Is the judiciary to supervise the action of the legislative branch of the government upon questions of public policy? Are they to override the will of the people, as expressed by their chosen servants, because, in their judgment, the particular means employed by Congress in execution of the powers conferred by the Constitution are not the best that could have been devised, or are not absolutely necessary to accomplish the objects for which the government was established?. . . .
>
> The vast powers committed to the present government may be abused, and taxes may be imposed by Congress which the public necessities do not in fact require, or which may be forbidden by a wise policy. But the remedy for such abuses is to be found at the ballot-box, and in a wholesome public opinion which the representatives of the people will not long, if at all, disregard. . . .[1]

Ten years later, Justice Harlan was joined by Justice Oliver Wendell Holmes Jr. in expressing similar criticism in dissent, as the court struck down New York's law setting maximum hours for bakers. Harlan wrote: "Whether or not this be wise legislation, it is not the province of the court to inquire. Under our system of government, the courts are not concerned with the wisdom or policy of legislation."[2]

Justice Holmes elaborated on this point:

> This case is decided upon an economic theory which a large part of the country does not entertain. If it were a question whether I agreed with that theory, I should desire to study it further and long before making up my mind. But I do not conceive that to be my duty, because I strongly believe that my agreement or disagreement has nothing to do with the right of a majority to embody their opinions in law. It is settled by various decisions of this court that state constitutions and state laws may regulate life in many ways which we as legislators might think as injudicious, or, if you like, as tyrannical as this. . . . But a constitution is not intended to embody a particular economic theory, whether of paternalism . . . or of *laissez faire*. It is made for people of fundamentally different views, and the accident of our finding certain opinions natural and familiar or novel and even shocking ought not to conclude our judgment upon the question whether statutes em-

bodying them conflict with the Constitution of the United States.[3]

Invalidating Legislation

Chief Justice William Howard Taft led the court during the decade of the 1920s, a period during which the court invalidated more legislation than in the half century preceding it. Taft easily accepted the idea that the court did in fact "make" law, dismissing the idea that judges should try to ascertain and apply "the exact intention of those who established the Constitution" as held only by persons who did not understand "the proper administration of justice."[4]

In 1913 he wrote:

> Frequently, new conditions arise which those who were responsible for the written law could not have had in view, and to which existing common law principles have never before been applied, and it becomes necessary for the Court to make applications of both. . . . [Such an application] is not the exercise of legislative power . . . [but] the exercise of a sound judicial discretion in supplementing the provisions of constitutions and laws and custom, which are necessarily incomplete or lacking in detail essential to their proper application, especially to new facts and situations constantly arising. . . . Indeed it is one of the highest and most useful functions that courts have to perform in making a government of law practical and uniformly just.[5]

As might be expected, there were justices serving with Taft who took issue with his view. Among them was Louis D. Brandeis. When the court held invalid a state law setting standard sizes for loaves of bread, Brandeis wrote:

> . . .It is not our function to weigh evidence. Put at its highest, our function is to determine . . . whether the measure enacted in the exercise of an unquestioned police power and of a character inherently unobjectionable, transcends the bounds of reason. That is, whether the provision as applied is so clearly arbitrary or capricious that legislators acting reasonably could not have believed it to be necessary or appropriate for the public welfare.
>
> To decide, as a fact, that the prohibition of excess weights 'is not necessary for the protection of the purchasers. . .'; . . .and that it 'subjects bakers and sellers of bread' to heavy burdens, is in my opinion, an exercise of the powers of a super-legislature — not the performance of the constitutional function of judicial review.[6]

The court majority that so consistently struck down New Deal legislation in the 1930s was not insensitive to similar charges that it was imposing its own will — on Congress, the president and the American people.

In *United States v. Butler* (1936), Justice Owen J. Roberts, whose vote so often during this period meant the difference between the court's declaring a statute valid or invalid, sought to answer these charges by minimizing the court's role:

... Or Super-Legislature?

It is sometimes said that the court assumes a power to overrule or control the action of the people's representatives. This is a misconception.... When an act of Congress is appropriately challenged in the courts as not conforming to the constitutional mandate, the judicial branch of Government has only one duty — to lay the article of the Constitution which is invoked beside the statute which is challenged and to decide whether the latter squares with the former.... The only power [the judiciary] has, if such it may be called, is the power of judgment. This court neither approves nor condemns any legislative policy.[7]

Roberts' claim did not go unanswered. In a strong dissent, Justice Harlan Fiske Stone said that the majority in *Butler* had assumed the very power Roberts said the court did not have. Stone cited two judicial principles:

One is that courts are concerned only with the power to enact statutes, not with their wisdom. The other is that while unconstitutional exercise of power by the executive and legislative branches ... is subject to judicial restraint, the only check upon our own exercise of power is our own sense of self-restraint. For the removal of unwise laws from the statute books appeal lies not to the courts but to the ballot and to the processes of democratic government.... The present levy is held invalid, not for any want of power in Congress to lay such a tax..., but because the use to which its proceeds are put is disapproved.[8]

Justice Benjamin N. Cardozo, another of Roberts' colleagues, had earlier written critically of judges who took the approach Roberts outlined:

Their notion of their duty is to match the colors of the case at hand against the colors of many sample cases spread out upon their desk. The sample nearest in shade supplies the applicable rule. But, of course, no system of living law can be evolved by such a process, and no judge of a high court, worthy of his office, views the function of his place so narrowly. If that were all there was to our calling, there would be little of intellectual interest about it. The man who had the best card index would also be the wisest judge. It is when the colors do not match ... that the serious business of the judge begins.[9]

In the years following resolution of the New Deal crisis — political, economic and judicial — the debate over "judicial legislation" did not die out. If anything, it intensified as the court extended its scrutiny into the area of state laws and practices affecting individual rights.

Reapportionment

When the court in the early 1960s moved into the field of legislative malapportionment, ordering all states to redraw the lines of their legislative districts to make them more equal in population, Chief Justice Earl Warren defended the court's involvement in a matter traditionally left entirely to legislative power:

We are told that the matter of apportioning representation in a state legislature is a complex and many-faceted one. We are advised that States can rationally consider factors other than population in apportioning legislative representation. We are admonished not to restrict the power of the States to impose differing views as to political philosophy on their citizens. We are cautioned about the dangers of entering into political thickets and mathematical quagmires. Our answer is this: a denial of constitutionally protected rights demands judicial protection; our oath and our office require no less of us.[10]

This assertion was vigorously rebutted by the second Justice John Marshall Harlan:

...What is done today deepens my conviction that judicial entry into this realm is profoundly ill-advised and constitutionally impermissible.

...I believe that the vitality of our political system, on which in the last analysis all else depends, is weakened by reliance on the judiciary for political reform; in time a complacent body politic may result.

These decisions also cut deeply into the fabric of our federalism....

Finally, these decisions give support to a current mistaken view of the Constitution and the constitutional function of this Court. This view, in a nutshell, is that every major social ill in this country can find its cure in some constitutional 'principle,' and that this Court should 'take the lead' in promoting reform when other branches of government fail to act. The Constitution is not a panacea for every blot upon the public welfare, nor should this Court, ordained as a judicial body, be thought of as a general haven for reform movements. The Constitution is an instrument of government, fundamental to which is the premise that in a diffusion of governmental authority lies the greatest promise that this Nation will realize liberty for all its citizens. This Court, limited in function in accordance with that premise, does not serve its high purpose when it exceeds its authority, even to satisfy justified impatience with the slow workings of the political process.[11]

---

[1] *Pollock v. Farmers' Loan & Trust Co.*, 158 U.S. 601 at 679-680 (1895).

[2] *Lochner v. New York*, 198 U.S. 45 at 69 (1905).

[3] *Id.*, at 75-76.

[4] Alpheus T. Mason, *The Supreme Court from Taft to Warren* (Baton Rouge: Louisiana State University Press, 1958), p. 46, citing William Howard Taft, *Popular Government*, pp. 222-223.

[5] *Ibid.*

[6] *Burns Baking Company v. Bryan*, 264 U.S. 504 at 533-534 (1923).

[7] *United States v. Butler*, 297 U.S. 1 at 62-63 (1936).

[8] *Id.* at 78-79.

[9] Benjamin N. Cardozo, "The Nature of the Judicial Process" in *Selected Writings*, ed. Margaret E. Hall (New York: Fallon, 1947), p. 113.

[10] *Reynolds v. Sims*, 377 U.S. 533 at 566 (1964).

[11] *Id.* at 624-625.

pendent state grounds. . . . The reason is so obvious that it has rarely been thought to warrant statement. It is found in the partitioning of power between the state and federal judicial systems and in the limitations of our own jurisdiction. Our only power over state judgments is to correct them to the extent that they incorrectly adjudge federal rights. . . .[9]

Review of Acts of Congress

The first case challenging the validity of an act of Congress came to the Supreme Court in 1796. Both sides in the matter — a question of taxation — simply assumed that the Supreme Court could uphold or strike down the act. The court upheld it.[10]

Five years later, just before the end of President John Adams' term in office, Adams named William Marbury a justice of the peace for the District of Columbia. But although Marbury was confirmed and his commission duly signed by Adams, Secretary of State John Marshall failed to deliver the commission before Adams left office. President Thomas Jefferson, Adams' successor, declined to deliver the commission.

Marbury, with former attorney general Charles Lee as his attorney, came to the Supreme Court late in the year, asking the justices to issue a writ of *mandamus* ordering James Madison, Jefferson's Secretary of State, to deliver the commission. In response, the court directed Madison to show cause why they should not issue such an order. Arguments in the case were set for the next term, then scheduled to begin in June 1802.

Congress, however, repealed the law providing for a June court term and replaced it with one providing that the next term would begin in February. As a result, the court did not meet for 14 months, during which Marbury's request hung pending.[11]

Finally the case was argued, and on Feb. 24, 1803, the decision was announced. The court refused to issue the order which Marbury requested.

The refusal came despite their finding, announced by Chief Justice John Marshall, that Marbury had a legal right to his commission, that failure to deliver the commission violated that right, and that a writ of *mandamus* was the proper remedy for such a situation.

The basis for the court's refusal was its finding that it lacked the power to issue the writ in this case because the law which purported to authorize it to issue such orders was unconstitutional.

Section 13 of the Judiciary Act of 1789 specifically authorized the Supreme Court "to issue writs of *mandamus* in cases warranted by the principles and usages of law, to any courts appointed or persons holding office, under the authority of the United States." Citing this provision, Marbury had come directly to the Supreme Court with his request.

With reasoning more notable for its conclusion than its clarity, Marshall found that this provision expanded the court's original jurisdiction:

> It is the essential criterion of appellate jurisdiction, that it revises and corrects the proceedings in a cause already instituted, and does not create that cause. Although, therefore, a mandamus may be directed to courts, yet to issue such a writ to an officer for the delivery of a paper, is in effect the same as to sustain an original action for that paper, and, there-

fore, seems not to belong to appellate, but to original jurisdiction.[12]

Congress, continued the court, had no power to modify its original jurisdiction, and so this grant of authority was unconstitutional and void. The court boldly asserted the power to make this declaration:

> It is emphatically the province and duty of the judicial department to say what the law is. . . .
>
> . . .if a law be in opposition to the constitution; if both the law and the constitution apply to a particular case, so that the court must either decide that case conformably to the law, disregarding the constitution; or conformably to the constitution, disregarding the law; the court must determine which of these conflicting rules governs the case. This is of the very essence of judicial duty.
>
> If, then, the courts are to regard the constitution, and the constitution is superior to any ordinary act of the legislature, the constitution, and not such ordinary act, must govern the case to which they both apply.[13]

To rule to the contrary, Chief Justice Marshall continued:

> . . .would subvert the very foundation of all written constitutions. It would declare that an act which, according to the principles and theory of our government, is entirely void, is yet, in practice, completely obligatory. It would declare that if the legislature shall do what is expressly forbidden, such act, notwithstanding . . . is in reality effectual. It would be giving to the legislature a practical and real omnipotence, with the same breath which professes to restrict their powers within narrow limits. It is prescribing limits, and declaring that those limits may be passed at pleasure.
>
> . . .it thus reduces to nothing what we have deemed the greatest improvement on political institutions, a written constitution. . . .[14]

Defining the Constitution. With that decision, and the firm establishment of the power of the court to nullify unconstitutional acts of Congress, the Supreme Court changed the meaning of the word "constitution." Prior to the founding of the United States, the word was used not to refer to a written basic law but simply to the principles observed in the operation of the government. Every government thus had some constitution; but not every government was bound by its constitution as a supreme law.[15]

With *Marbury v. Madison*, the Supreme Court became the effective instrument for enforcing the supremacy of the U.S. Constitution.[16]

Criticism of judicial review, led after *Marbury* by none other than President Thomas Jefferson himself, continues to the present time. However, as Charles Evans Hughes noted in 1928: "The reasoning of Chief Justice Marshall's opinion has never been answered. . . . The doctrine of judicial review . . . practically is as much a part of our system of government as the judicial office itself." [17]

The Power Exercised

For the first century of the nation's history, the Supreme Court exercised the power of judicial review primarily to enhance national power by striking down state laws and upholding acts of Congress challenged as infringing upon states' rights.

As one scholar wrote, the Marshall Court wielded the power of judicial review "to place its stamp of approval upon the idea of the Constitution as an instrument of expanding national power." [18]

Not until 1857 — 54 years after *Marbury* — did a second act of Congress fall, declared unconstitutional by the Supreme Court. In the infamous *Dred Scott* case, the court held that the Missouri Compromise was unconstitutional because Congress lacked the power to exclude slavery from the territories. That decision, which contributed to intensification of the debate over slavery and its eventual explosion in civil war, also inflicted severe damage upon the court. Hughes later would describe it as the first of three of the court's "self-inflicted wounds . . . a public calamity." [19] *(Details, p. 135)*

Fifteen years after *Dred Scott*, the court dealt itself the second such injury. It first struck down — and 15 months later reversed itself to uphold — the acts of Congress making paper money legal tender in payment of debts incurred before the passage of the acts.[20] *(Details, p. 118)*

In the following century — from 1870 through 1970 — the pace of judicial invalidation of congressional acts quickened. By late in the 1970s, more than 100 acts of Congress had fallen, wholly or in part, before the court's examination. *(List, p. 926)*

As the court exercised this power more frequently, it found itself more and more the center of controversy. Proposals to curb the power of judicial review proliferated. But as one legal scholar wrote at mid-century, such proposals "have been directed mainly, if not always, not against the existence of the power but against the manner or the finality of its exercise." [21]

And the judicial consensus in 1979 seemed to be the same as that set out half a century earlier by Hughes, a man who had served on the court, had left to run for President, and later returned to the court as Chief Justice:

> The dual system of government implies the maintenance of the constitutional restrictions of the powers of Congress as well as of those of the States. The existence of the function of the Supreme Court is a constant monition to Congress. A judicial, as distinguished from a mere political, solution of the questions arising from time to time has its advantages. . . .[22]

The Power to Issue Writs

The Judiciary Act of 1789 authorized all federal courts to issue all writs "which may be necessary for the exercise of their respective jurisdictions, and agreeable to the principles and usages of law."

That provision, slightly reworded, remains the general statutory authority for federal courts to issue orders to carry out their decisions.[23]

Most significant and most controversial of the writs generally employed by the federal courts is the "Great Writ" — the writ of *habeas corpus*. Used to require government officials to justify their decision to hold a person in custody over his objection, this writ has been described with many superlatives as "the best and only sufficient defense of personal freedom." [24]

Other writs used by the courts have included the writ of error, used until early in the 20th century to notify a state court that the Supreme Court was to review one of its rulings; the writ of certiorari, now the most common notice to a lower or state court that the Supreme Court has

granted review of its decision; and the writ of *mandamus,* the writ involved in *Marbury v. Madison.*

A federal court, the Supreme Court has said, may use all these "auxiliary writs as aids in the performance of its duties, when the use of such historic aids is calculated in its sound judgment to achieve the ends of justice entrusted to it." [25]

Habeas Corpus

First in importance of the writs available to the federal courts is the writ of *habeas corpus*. An integral part of the nation's English heritage, this writ is used by a court to inquire into the reasons for a person's detention by government authority.

Habeas corpus, the court noted in 1963, "has time and again played a central role in national crises, wherein the claims of order and of liberty clash most acutely." The court continued:

> Although in form the Great Writ is simply a mode of procedure, its history is inextricably intertwined with the growth of fundamental rights of personal liberty. For its function has been to provide a prompt and efficacious remedy for whatever society deems to be intolerable restraints. Its root principle is that in a civilized society, government must always be accountable to the judiciary for a man's imprisonment: if the imprisonment cannot be shown to conform with the fundamental requirements of law, the individual is entitled to his immediate release.[26]

During the two centuries since the nation's founding, the use of this writ by the federal courts has gradually expanded it into a major instrument for the reform of federal and state criminal procedures.[27]

Federal courts have broad discretion in determining when the issuance of this writ is appropriate to order release of a prisoner. But the Supreme Court has emphasized that "[d]ischarge from conviction through *habeas corpus* is not an act of judicial clemency, but a protection against illegal custody." [28]

There is no time limit within which a prisoner must seek a writ of *habeas corpus* as a remedy for errors at his trial.[29] And the writ may be issued to military as well as civilian authorities.[30]

Release through the writ should not be sought as a substitute for appeal of a conviction. "Mere convenience cannot justify use of the writ as a substitute for an appeal," wrote Justice Felix Frankfurter in 1942. "But dry formalism should not sterilize procedural resources which Congress has made available to the federal courts." [31]

The Supreme Court has declared that the power of federal courts to issue this writ must be given by written law — as it always has been. Despite its antiquity, this assertion is open to debate in light of the express statement in the Constitution forbidding suspension of the privilege of the writ except when the public safety demands it.[32]

The court also has maintained that proceedings begun by a petition for this writ are entirely separate from the question of a defendant's guilt or innocence, and thus are no substitute for a direct appeal of a conviction.[33] The writ has been used in modern times to challenge a lack of jurisdiction of the sentencing court or to charge constitutional error which, if proved, makes the entire detention illegal, regardless of the guilt or innocence of the person detailed.

Restricted Use. For most of the 19th century, the use of the writ of *habeas corpus* by federal courts was strictly limited by two factors:

• The Supreme Court viewed the writ as properly used only to challenge the jurisdiction of the sentencing court. In 1830 the court declared that the inquiry sparked by a request for this writ began and ended with the question of jurisdiction. If a person was detained under the judgment of a court with jurisdiction over him and his case, his detention was lawful.[34]

• And the court faithfully observed the statutory restriction of the federal use of the writ to question the detention of federal prisoners only. In 1845 the court refused to issue such a writ to state officials, even though the state prisoner seeking the writ argued that his state jailers were blocking all his efforts to appeal to the Supreme Court.[35]

Small exceptions to this limitation were approved by Congress in 1833 and 1842 when it extended the use of this writ to order state officials to release federal officers imprisoned for enforcing federal laws, and to order state officials to release foreign nationals detained by a state in violation of a treaty.

Despite these restrictions, in the pre-Civil War period some persons did use a request for a writ of *habeas corpus*, coupled with a writ of certiorari, as a clumsy method of invoking the appellate jurisdiction of the Supreme Court. But few prisoners using this device were successful in obtaining their release.[36]

The Beginning of Expansion. In 1867, there began a century of expansion of the federal right to release through the writ of *habeas corpus*. In that year Congress ended the restriction of this right to federal prisoners.

Intending to prevent state imprisonment of federal officials engaged in Reconstruction programs, Congress authorized federal courts "to grant writs of *habeas corpus* in all cases where any person may be restrained of his or her liberty in violation of the Constitution, or of any treaty or law of the United States." The 1867 Act also provided for review by the Supreme Court of lower court rulings denying *habeas corpus* relief to persons seeking it under this law.

Almost before the ink was dry on the statute, the case of *Ex parte McCardle* was argued before the Supreme Court, and Congress — fearful of a ruling that would invalidate the Reconstruction Acts — repealed this expansion of the Supreme Court's appellate jurisdiction.[37] *(Details, p. 263)*

But despite this backward step, the basic expansion of the federal use of the writ remained intact. Lower federal courts could now use the writ to release state prisoners detained in violation of their federal rights.

And the Supreme Court soon made clear that the 1868 repeal affected only the 1867 enlargement of its appellate jurisdiction. The court's pre-existing jurisdiction over questions of *habeas corpus* relief — although procedurally cumbersome — was still valid. This point was made late in 1869 in the case *Ex parte Yerger.*

Edward Yerger, a civilian, was held by military authorities in Mississippi after his conviction by a military commission for killing an army major. A lower federal court granted his petition for a writ of *habeas corpus*, reviewed the reasons for his detention and found it proper. The Supreme Court agreed to review that decision by the lower court, affirming its continuing authority to exercise appellate jurisdiction to revise such decisions, using the writs of *habeas corpus* and certiorari.[38]

In 1885 Congress restored the jurisdiction of the Supreme Court to consider direct appeals from circuit court rulings denying *habeas corpus* relief. But in the intervening decades, the court continued to use the earlier, clumsier method to review decisions by lower courts on requests for *habeas corpus* relief.

In a set of cases decided in 1880, the court employed this means to consider situations in which persons accused of violating civil rights laws sought release through *habeas corpus*, arguing that the laws under which they were convicted were not constitutional. In each case, the court denied the writ and upheld the challenged law.[39]

Returning to the jurisdictional view of the writ, the Supreme Court based its power to act upon the reasoning that if the law was in fact unconstitutional, then the court which convicted the prisoner lacked jurisdiction to detain him — and so the writ should issue to order his release. The court explained that questions concerning the constitutionality of the law under which an indictment is brought or a conviction obtained affect the foundation of the entire proceeding:

> . . .An unconstitutional law is void, and is as no law. An offense created by it is not a crime. A conviction under it is not merely erroneous, but is illegal and void, and cannot be a legal cause of imprisonment.[40]

Nine years later, after Congress had restored its jurisdiction over lower court denials of *habeas corpus* relief to persons alleging that they were detained in violation of their federal rights, the court found a logical link between the jurisdictional basis for such relief and the new rights-based grounds for the writ:

> . . .It is difficult to see why a conviction and punishment under an unconstitutional law is more violative of a person's constitutional rights, than an unconstitutional conviction and punishment under a valid law. In the first case, it is that the court has no authority to take cognizance of the case; but in the other it has no authority to render judgment against the defendant.[41]

The Modern Writ. Although Congress in its 1867 expansion of the right to *habeas corpus* clearly contemplated federal intervention in state matters, for half a century after the act there were few collisions of state and federal power in this area. This was in part the result of the narrow definition of federal rights, the court's continuing limited view of the issues properly raised by a petition for *habeas corpus* relief, and the fact that most of the Bill of Rights was not applied to protect persons against state action.

As the court expanded the category of federally protected rights, and applied the guarantees of the first eight amendments to the states, the use of the writ to challenge and overturn state convictions became more frequent and more controversial.

The beginning of the development of the modern federal use of the writ of *habeas corpus* to question detention of state prisoners can be traced to the court's 1915 decision in the case of *Frank v. Mangum.* This ruling signaled an end to the court's traditional view that so long as a sentencing court had jurisdiction to impose the challenged sentence, the Supreme Court would not inquire further into the legality of a person's confinement.

In *Frank v. Mangum*, the court refused to order the release of a man convicted of murder by a state court, even though he alleged that he had been denied a fair trial because the court was dominated by a mob. But in its opinion, written by Justice Mahlon Pitney, the court enlarged its traditional view of the responsibility of a federal court to examine state convictions.

First, the court indicated its belief that a court with jurisdiction over a case could lose jurisdiction if it allowed events to deny a defendant his federal rights.

Second, the court held that the 1867 Habeas Corpus Act gave state prisoners the right to "a judicial inquiry in a court of the United States into the very truth and substance of causes of his detention," even if that required the federal court "to look behind and beyond the record of his conviction."[42]

But the court denied *habeas corpus* relief in this case because the defendant's claim of mob domination had been reviewed fully — and rejected — by a state appeals court.

But eight years later, the court granted a similar plea. In the case of *Moore v. Dempsey*, the court, speaking through Justice Oliver Wendell Holmes Jr., declared that:

> . . .if the case is that the whole proceeding is a mask — that counsel, jury and judge were swept to the fatal end by an irresistable wave of public passion, and that the State Courts failed to correct the wrong, neither perfection in the machinery for correction nor the possibility that the trial court and counsel saw no other way of avoiding an immediate outbreak of the mob can prevent this Court from securing to the petitioners their constitutional rights.[43]

And in 1942, the court finally acknowledged that *habeas corpus* relief involved far more than jurisdictional issues:

> . . .the use of the writ in the federal courts to test the constitutional validity of a conviction for crime is not restricted to those cases where the judgment of conviction is void for want of jurisdiction of the trial court to render it. It extends also to those exceptional cases where the conviction has been in disregard of the constitutional rights of the accused and where the writ is the only effective means of preserving his rights.[44]

Subsequently, the court has broadened the power of federal courts, when considering state prisoners' petitions for *habeas corpus*, to redetermine matters already considered and resolved by state courts. In 1953 the court held that federal courts could rehear such a prisoner's claims "on the merits, facts or law" to be certain that his federal rights had been protected.[45]

Ten year later, the court in the case of *Townsend v. Sain*, ruled that although a federal judge might defer to a state court's reliable findings of fact, where the facts remained in dispute, the federal judge should rehear the relevant evidence if there was not a "full and fair evidentiary hearing" on the prisoner's claim in a state court, either at the time of his trial or in subsequent proceedings. Furthermore, the court made clear in that decision that a federal judge should not defer to a state judge's findings of law: "It is the district judge's duty," stated the court, "to apply the applicable federal law . . . independently."[46]

Exhausting State Remedies. To prevent unnecessary collisions between state and federal authority through the exercise of this expanded power of *habeas corpus*, the Supreme Court adopted the general rule that federal courts

State Courts and Habeas Corpus

State courts have the power to issue writs of *habeas corpus*, but federal supremacy places one major restraint on their use of the Great Writ. State judges may not use it to require release of persons held in federal custody.

In the years preceding the Civil War, considerable resistance arose in abolitionist states to federal enforcement of the Fugitive Slave Act. In Wisconsin, after newspaper editor Sherman Booth was convicted for helping fugitive slaves escape, state courts ordered his federal jailers to release him, issuing a writ of *habeas corpus* to them for this purpose.

In 1859 the Supreme Court made clear that such an order exceeded the bounds of state power in the federal system. Federal supremacy, the court held in the case *Ableman v. Booth*, meant that state courts could not use the writ to order release of federal prisoners.[1] *(Details, p. 360)*

More than half a century later, the court modified this ban slightly, ruling that with the consent of the United States, state courts might use the writ to direct federal officials to present a federal prisoner to state court for trial there on state charges.[2]

---

[1] *Ableman v. Booth*, 21 How. 506 (1859).
[2] *Ponzi v. Fessenden*, 258 U.S. 254 (1922); *Smith v. Hooey*, 393 U.S. 374 (1969).

should await completion of state proceedings before ordering release of a state prisoner on *habeas corpus*.

In 1885 the court refused to order the release, before trial, of a state prisoner who sought a writ of *habeas corpus* from federal court. In its decision in *Ex parte Royall*, the court affirmed the power of the federal courts to issue such a pre-trial writ, but urged discretion in the use of that power in the interest of comity and preservation of the balance between state and federal power.[47]

This rule, slowly enlarged on a case-by-case basis, became the "exhaustion requirement" — set out in a 1944 ruling:

> Ordinarily an application for *habeas corpus* by one detained under a state court judgment of conviction for crime will be entertained by a federal court only after all state remedies available, including all appellate remedies in the state courts and in this court by appeal or writ of certiorari, have been exhausted.[48]

Four years later, when the Judicial Code was revised, this requirement was included.

In 1950 the court reaffirmed that this rule meant that a direct challenge to a state conviction should be taken all the way to the Supreme Court before a prisoner could then begin a collateral attack on his conviction by seeking a writ of *habeas corpus* from federal district court. In its opinion the court set out the reasoning upon which such a requirement was based:

> Since the states have the major responsibility for the maintenance of law and order within their borders, the dignity and importance of their role as guardians of the administration of criminal justice merits review of

their acts by this Court before a prisoner, as a matter of routine, may seek release ... in the district courts of the United States. It is this Court's conviction that orderly federal procedure under our dual system of government demands that the state's highest court should ordinarily be subject to reversal only by this Court and that a state's system for the administration of justice should be condemned as constitutionally inadequate only by this Court.[49]

Three years later, the court was more succinct: "A failure to use a state's available remedy, in the absence of some interference or incapacity ... bars federal *habeas corpus*." [50]

Exceptions to the Rule. Although the court had always left open the possibility that it would not enforce the exhaustion requirement in exceptional circumstances, federal courts until 1963 were quite consistent in requiring adherence to the rule.[51]

But in that year, the Supreme Court ruled that a state prisoner's failure to appeal his conviction did not necessarily bar him forever from obtaining *habeas corpus* relief from a federal court. This was the ruling in the case of *Fay v. Noia.*[52]

Noia and two other men were convicted in 1942 of killing a Brooklyn storekeeper. All three were sentenced to life in Sing Sing. The other two men unsuccessfully appealed their convictions; Noia did not. Eventually, the other two won release on federal *habeas corpus*, after a federal judge agreed that their detention was unconstitutional because they had been convicted on the basis of confessions coerced from them.

But despite identical circumstances concerning his confession and conviction, Noia was denied release on *habeas corpus* because he had not exhausted state remedies by appealing his conviction. Noia could not rectify the situation, for his right to appeal had terminated because he did not file for an appeal within 30 days after his conviction.

By a 6-3 vote, the Supreme Court ordered Noia's release, despite his failure to appeal. Writing for the majority, Justice William J. Brennan Jr. declared that it was just this sort of situation, which "affront[ed] ... the conscience of a civilized society," for which *habeas corpus* relief was intended. "If the States withhold effective remedy, the federal courts have the power and the duty to provide it." [53]

The exhaustion requirement meant, wrote Justice Brennan, only that a state prisoner could not obtain federal *habeas corpus* relief unless he had first tried all state remedies still available. Because Noia's right to appeal had expired, his failure to avail himself of it did not foreclose *habeas corpus* relief.

When a federal court was applying this rule to deny relief to a state prisoner, wrote Brennan, it must be certain that a person who had failed to exhaust his state remedies had done so deliberately, that he "understandingly and knowingly forewent the privilege of seeking to vindicate his federal claims in the state courts, whether for strategic, tactical, or any other reasons that can fairly be described as the deliberate by-passing of state procedures...." [54]

Noia's choice not to appeal in 1942, when appeal could have resulted in a new trial and death sentence, could not realistically be viewed as his "considered choice," wrote Brennan, and so should not be held to bar him from *habeas corpus* relief in federal courts.[55]

The court in *Fay v. Noia*, also overruled its 1950 decision which required a person to appeal his conviction all the way to the Supreme Court before seeking federal *habeas corpus* relief. That requirement, held the court in 1963, placed an unnecessary burden on the prisoner and the court.[56]

Recent Rulings. In the 1970s, the Supreme Court narrowed the impact of *Fay v. Noia.* On the one hand, the court held that a prisoner's claim that illegally obtained evidence had been improperly used to convict him could not serve as a basis for federal *habeas corpus* relief — so long as the state had provided him an opportunity for "full and fair litigation" of that claim at an earlier time.[57]

On the other hand, the court narrowed availability of federal *habeas corpus* relief through a stricter application of the exhaustion requirement. The court abandoned the "deliberate bypass" standard of *Fay v. Noia*, under which state prisoners who had not deliberately bypassed their right to assert their federal claim earlier could obtain federal *habeas corpus* review. In its place it adopted, first for federal and then for state prisoners seeking this relief, the rule that an earlier failure to assert a federal claim would bar *habeas corpus* relief unless the prisoner could show *both* good reason for the earlier omission *and* actual prejudice to his case as a result of the claimed violation of his federal right.[58]

Writs of Mandamus

"The remedy of *mandamus* is a drastic one," wrote the Supreme Court in 1976, "to be invoked only in extraordinary situations...." [59]

This extraordinary writ is a court order to a government official requiring him to take some action related to his post. The writ may be peremptory — an absolute and unqualified command. Or it may be an alternative command, giving the individual to whom it is addressed the opportunity to show cause to the court why he should not comply with its order. Companion to the *mandamus* is the writ of prohibition — which bars a government official or lower court from taking certain action.

In modern times, the Supreme Court actually issues very few writs of *mandamus*, even when it finds the person seeking them entitled to such an order. It customarily rules simply that the party is entitled to that remedy, but withholds the issuance of the writ assuming that the official or the lower court will now act in conformity with that ruling.[60]

Early in its history, with its decision in *Marbury v. Madison*, the Supreme Court made clear that this writ was to be used only in cases over which the issuing court already had jurisdiction. In *Marbury v. Madison*, the court held that Marbury was entitled to his commission and that a writ of *mandamus* was the proper remedy for the situation, but it refused to issue that order to Secretary Madison.

The reason for the court's refusal was its finding that it lacked original jurisdiction over the case, which involved neither a state nor a foreign minister.[61] *(Details, pp. 69, 270)*

Subsequent rulings reinforced this requirement, but as the jurisdiction of the federal courts has been expanded, so have the types of cases in which this writ may be used.

The separation of powers has limited the issuance of these writs from federal courts to federal executive officials. Not until 1838 did the Supreme Court rule that any lower federal court could issue such a writ to a federal official in the executive branch.[62]

In *Marbury* the court distinguished between the types of action which a court might order an executive branch official to take and those in which the separation of powers forbids judicial interference. Only ministerial acts, wrote Chief Justice John Marshall, could be the subject of writs of *mandamus*:

> ...Where the head of a department acts in a case, in which executive discretion is to be exercised; in which he is the mere organ of executive will ... any application to a court to control, in any respect, his conduct would be rejected....
>
> But where he is directed by law to do a certain act affecting the absolute rights of individuals, in the performance of which he is not placed under the particular direction of the President, and the performance of which the President cannot lawfully forbid ... in such cases, it is not perceived on what ground the courts ... are further excused from the duty of giving judgment that right be done to an injured individual....[63]

When the court, in 1838, upheld the issuance of a writ of *mandamus* to the Postmaster General, it made clear that it so ruled because the action ordered was "a precise, definite act, purely ministerial, and about which the Postmaster-General had no discretion whatever."[64]

The extraordinary nature of these writs in the federal system has been further underscored by the court's insistence that such writs be issued only to persons who lack any other legal remedy. As early as 1803 and as recently as 1976, the court has reiterated this point:

> As a means of implementing the rule that the writ will issue only in extraordinary circumstances, we have set forth various conditions for its issuance ... [including that] the party seeking issuance of the writ have no other adequate means to attain the relief he desires ... and that he satisfy "the burden of showing that [his] right to issuance of the writ is 'clear and indisputable.'"[65]

It is a general rule within the federal judicial system that only final judgments are reviewable by a higher court — that intermediate rulings should not be reviewed until the trial or proceeding has concluded in a final judgment.

In keeping with this policy, the Supreme Court has resisted most efforts by parties to obtain a writ of *mandamus* to review or undo an interim, or interlocutory, ruling of a lower court. On the other hand, the court has also steadfastly insisted, since early in its history, that the writ of *mandamus* is not to be used as a substitute for a direct appeal from a ruling.[66] In 1947, the court affirmed this last point with particular emphasis:

> Mandamus, prohibition and injunction against judges are drastic and extraordinary remedies.... These remedies should be resorted to only where appeal is a clearly inadequate remedy. We are unwilling to utilize them as a substitute for appeals. As extraordinary remedies, they are reserved for really extraordinary cases.[67]

Mandamus in the Present Court. The most frequent modern use of writs of *mandamus* is by an appellate court to confine a lower court "to a lawful exercise of its prescribed jurisdiction," or to compel it "to exercise its authority when it is its duty to do so...."[68] These writs, the court has made clear, are "meant to be used only in the exceptional case where there is clear abuse of discretion or 'usurpation of judicial power'...."[69]

Most such orders are issued by the court immediately superior to the receiving court, but the Supreme Court possesses the power to issue a writ directly to a district court "where a question of public importance is involved or where the question is of such a nature that it is peculiarly appropriate that such action by this court should be taken."[70] The court also has the power to issue the writ to a state court, so long as the case involved is within the appellate jurisdiction of the Supreme Court.[71]

Although the decision to issue or deny the request for such a writ is left to the discretion of the court to whom the request is addressed, the Supreme Court has not hesitated to overturn what it considers unnecessary use of this writ. In recent cases, the court has held that the writ of *mandamus* should not be used to order a trial judge to reinstate certain pleas, because his decision to dismiss them could be reviewed on appeal.[72]

On the other hand, the court recently has upheld the use of the writ to override trial judges' decisions to appoint a special master to hear a case, to deny a jury trial and to reverse a federal judge's decision that in order to avoid delay in hearing a case, it should be tried in state, not federal court.[73]

Injunctions

Complementing the affirmative function of the writ of *mandamus* is the negative function of the injunction — an order directing someone to halt a course of action that will cause irreparable injury to another, for which no adequate recompense can be made by a subsequent lawsuit.

Injunctions are issued under the equity power of the federal courts — their general responsibility to ensure fairness and justice — rather than their more specific jurisdiction over matters arising under the Constitution and the laws.

Injunctions may be temporary — simply preserving the status quo pending final resolution of the issues in a dispute — or they may be permanent bans on certain courses of action. A federal judge may issue a preliminary or temporary injunction even before deciding whether or not he has jurisdiction over a case. The order must be obeyed until it is reversed or lifted.[74]

Some consider the power to issue injunctions, as well as the other writs, to be inherent in the nature of the federal courts, but the Supreme Court has traditionally held that Congress must authorize the federal courts to issue such orders.

Since 1789 Congress has provided such statutory authority — and has steadily exercised its power to limit the circumstances in which federal courts may issue injunctions. The Judiciary Act of 1789 made clear that equity suits were to be brought only when no legal remedy existed to resolve a dispute.

More specific limitations followed quickly. In 1793 Congress forbade the courts to use injunctions to stay state court proceedings. This Anti-Injunction Act, which set out the fundamental policy of federal non-interference with state judicial proceedings, remains in effect to this day.

In 1867 Congress forbade federal courts to use injunctions to interfere with the assessment or collection of federal taxes. This ban forced the landmark case of *Pollock v. Farmers' Loan & Trust Co.*, which challenged the constitutionality of the peacetime income tax, into the form

'Government By Injunction'

In the early days of organized labor in the United States, federal courts were so receptive to the requests of employers to issue injunctions against boycotts, picketing and other now-legitimate union activity, that this unity of judiciary and management came to be termed "government by injunction."[1] *(Details, pp. 93-95)*

Congress in 1914 attempted to restrict this use of federal injunctive power. Included in the Clayton Act, enacted that year, were provisions forbidding the issuance of federal injunctions in labor disputes unless necessary to prevent irreparable injury to property, and providing a limited right to a jury trial for persons charged with contempt for disobeying such court orders.

But the Supreme Court, with two 1921 decisions, interpreted the Clayton Act restriction into ineffectiveness. With these rulings, the court upheld, as still appropriate, injunctions against a union — rather than against particular employees — and against a variety of "unlawful" labor activities.[2]

A more successful effort to limit "government by injunction" came in 1932 with passage of the Norris-LaGuardia Act. That act prohibited issuance of injunctions by federal courts in labor disputes except after a hearing and findings that the order was necessary to prevent substantial and irreparable injury, the result of unlawful acts; and that the injury inflicted by granting the injunction was outweighed by the injury which would result if it were not granted.

Some questions were raised about the power of Congress to impose such a limit on the equity jurisdiction of the federal courts, but in 1938 the Supreme Court upheld this restriction. Writing for the court, Justice Owen J. Roberts stated that "[t]here can be no question of the power of Congress thus to define and limit the jurisdiction of the inferior courts of the United States."[3]

The Supreme Court has held that this restriction does not foreclose federal injunctions to halt a strike by a union against mines being operated by the government.[4]

And the court upheld the provision of the Taft-Hartley Act, which granted federal courts jurisdiction to issue such an injunction against a strike when it found that the strike affected an entire industry or substantial part of it and, if allowed to continue, would threaten the nation's health or safety.[5]

---

[1] Carl B. Swisher, *American Constitutional Development*, 2d ed. (Cambridge: Houghton Mifflin Co., 1954), pp. 806-812; *In re Debs*, 158 U.S. 564 (1895); *Gompers v. Bucks Stove & Range Co.*, 221 U.S. 417 (1911).

[2] *Duplex Printing Press v. Deering*, 254 U.S. 443 (1921); *American Steel Foundries v. Tri-City Central Trades Council*, 257 U.S. 184 (1921).

[3] *Lauf v. E. G. Shinner & Co.*, 303 U.S. 323 at 330 (1938).

[4] *United States v. United Mine Workers*, 330 U.S. 258 (1947).

[5] *United Steelworkers of America v. United States*, 361 U.S. 39 (1959).

---

of a suit for an injunction from a federal court directing a bank not to pay its federal income taxes.[75]

The extensive use of the injunction by federal courts sympathetic to the efforts of property owners and employers to curtail the activities of organized labor brought the enactment of laws in 1914 and 1932 limiting such "government by injunction." *(Box, this page)*

In similar fashion, Congress in 1910 and 1937 required that injunctions halting enforcement of state laws or acts of Congress challenged as unconstitutional be granted only by panels of three federal judges, not by a single federal judge. Appeals from the decisions of these panels could be taken directly to the Supreme Court. These provisions were repealed in 1976.

In the 1930s, Congress further restricted the use of federal injunctions to interfere with state affairs, forbidding their use to halt the collection or enforcement of public utility rates fixed by state order or the collection of state or local taxes. These bans were not effective in situations where no adequate state remedy was available to persons protesting the rates or the taxes.

During World War II, Congress again demonstrated its power to limit the use of this remedy by the courts. It provided that only one court in the country could enjoin rules or orders issued by the Office of Price Administration. The Supreme Court upheld even this limitation on injunctive relief.[76]

The Other Branches. The question of the Supreme Court's power — or that of any other federal court — to use the injunction to halt the proceedings of either Congress or the Executive Branch arose soon after the Civil War, and was quickly and decisively settled.

When Mississippi came to the court seeking an injunction ordering President Andrew Johnson, as an official or as an individual, to cease enforcing the allegedly unconstitutional Reconstruction Acts, the court held that it lacked the power to issue such an order.

The court reasoned that this request fell under the same general principles set out in the *mandamus* cases of *Marbury v. Madison* and *Kendall v. Stokes,* which "forbid judicial interference with the exercise of executive discretion." Only purely ministerial duties of executive officials were subject to such orders.[77]

In the opinion in this case, *Mississippi v. Johnson,* Chief Justice Salmon P. Chase provided a succinct statement of the court's view of the impropriety of its enjoining the operations of either of the other coordinate branches:

> The Congress is the Legislative Department of the Government; the President is the Executive Department. Neither can be restrained in its action by the Judicial Department; though the acts of both, when performed, are, in proper cases, subject to its cognizance.[78]

This ruling, however, did not prevent federal courts from exercising the power to enjoin federal officials from enforcing an unconstitutional act of Congress, an action which fell into the ministerial category. The courts assumed this power long before any statutory authorization could be found for it, but such an authorization was provided in the 1937 statute requiring that such injunctions be issued by three-judge panels.

Federal Courts and State Power. Few problems regarding the exercise of federal judicial power have been more persistent than those resulting from the power of federal judges to enjoin state officials and halt state proceedings.

It was to that clearly evident point of friction that Congress spoke in 1793 when it passed the Anti-Injunction Act, a nearly complete ban on such federal interference in state affairs.

In recent decades, the court has supplemented that statute with the judicial doctrine of abstention, the rule that federal courts should normally deny requests to halt state enforcement of state laws.

The Anti-Injunction Act. Although its rationale is lost in history, the language of the 1793 act is clear: federal courts should not use injunctions to stay proceedings in state courts unless Congress approves such use of these writs.

The modern version of that law, revised in 1948, states:

A court of the United States may not grant an injunction to stay proceedings in a state court except as expressly authorized by Act of Congress, or where necessary in aid of its jurisdiction or to protect or effectuate its judgments.

Through the years, however, the court has found express exception to this ban in a number of federal laws including removal statutes, those giving federal courts jurisdiction over farm mortgages, federal *habeas corpus* statutes and federal price control laws.[79]

Furthermore, the court found implicit exceptions to this ban that allow it to permit federal courts to halt state court proceedings when necessary to protect jurisdiction of the federal court over a case or to prevent relitigation in state courts of issues already resolved in federal court.[80] (In 1941, the court appeared to abandon this last exception, but seven years later, when the anti-injunction statute was rewritten, this exception was reinstated as proper.[81])

Subsequently, the court has found additional exceptions to the ban in cases brought by the United States, and in cases brought under the civil rights law which authorizes individuals to sue for damages in federal court when they have been deprived of a constitutional right by someone acting under color of state law.[82]

The Anti-Injunction Act applies only when a federal court is asked to halt an ongoing state court proceeding. It does not affect the power of federal courts to order state officers to stop enforcing unconstitutional state laws.

This latter aspect of federal judicial power was recognized by the Supreme Court as early as 1824.[83] And since its 1908 decision in the case *Ex parte Young*, federal judges may issue such injunctions against state officials even before the challenged law is actually ruled invalid.[84]

But to curtail instances of such clear federal intervention in state business, the court has required that persons exhaust their state legislative and administrative remedies before seeking a federal injunction of this sort.[85] And in 1910, Congress limited the power to issue such injunctions to three-judge panels, denying it to a single federal judge acting alone.

The exercise of this power has been tempered by concern for preserving the balance of the federal system. Justice William J. Brennan Jr. expressed this concern in 1965:

...the Court has recognized that federal interference with a State's good-faith administration of its criminal laws is peculiarly inconsistent with our federal framework. It is generally to be assumed that state courts and prosecutors will observe constitutional limitations ... and that the mere possibility of erroneous initial application of constitutional standards will usually not amount to the irreparable injury necessary to justify a disruption of orderly state proceedings.[86]

To win such an injunction a defendant must show a threat of irreparable injury "both great and immediate," substantially more than simply that attendant upon any criminal prosecution or enforcement of the laws.[87]

In a series of rulings in the 1940s, the court reinforced this requirement with a new doctrine of abstention. Under this approach to federal injunctive power, federal judges were generally to refrain from enjoining state officials until state courts had full opportunity to consider the challenged law or practice and revise or interpret it to remove the constitutional problem.[88] The court applied the doctrine both to requests that federal judges halt ongoing state court proceedings and that they halt enforcement of challenged state laws by forbidding any future prosecutions under them.

But the civil rights revolution of the following decades strained this doctrine, and resulted in several exceptions to the court's rule.

In 1963, the court ruled that when a civil rights case involved no question of state law sufficient to resolve the dispute, there was no need to require the persons bringing the case to exhaust state remedies before seeking a federal injunction.[89] Two years later, the court held that there was no reason for federal courts to defer to state proceedings in a case where no possible reinterpretation of state law could bring the challenged provisions within constitutional bounds.[90]

Still another — and even more significant — exception to the abstention doctrine was the apparent result of the Supreme Court's 1965 decision in the case of *Dombrowski v. Pfister*. In that case, the court ruled that abstention was inappropriate in cases in which state laws were "justifiably attacked on their face as abridging free expression or as applied for the purpose of discouraging protected activities."[91]

James A. Dombrowski, executive director of a civil rights group, the Southern Conference Educational Fund, and several of his associates were arrested in 1963 by Louisiana officials and charged with violating that state's laws against subversive activities and communist propaganda. The charges were dropped, but state officials continued to threaten Dombrowski with prosecution. Charging that such threats were part of the state's campaign to discourage civil rights activity, and that the state laws under which the charges had been brought against him violated his First Amendment rights, Dombrowski sought a federal injunction against such alleged harassment.

The Anti-Injunction Act did not apply because there were no pending state court proceedings. But the three-judge panel hearing Dombrowski's request found this an appropriate case for abstention — to give state courts an opportunity to interpret the challenged laws to bring them into line with the First Amendment.

The Supreme Court, by a vote of 5-2, overturned that ruling. Abstention served no legitimate purpose in such a case, held the majority, especially in the face of the clear "chilling effect" which prosecution under the challenged laws would have on the First Amendment freedoms involved.

Many, including a number of federal judges, saw this ruling as greatly broadening the permissible use of federal injunctions to halt or forestall state criminal prosecutions. The decision seemed to allow such orders in cases in which a state law on its face was so vague or so broad as to collide with the First Amendment — even if the particular case involved no showing of bad faith or harassment on the part of state officials, or any other clear threat of irreparable injury.

This interpretation of *Dombrowski* was short-lived. In a set of five cases decided in 1971, the Supreme Court reaffirmed the basic requirement that before an injunction is issued, there must be a showing of threatened irreparable injury. Furthermore, the court made clear that in cases involving ongoing prosecutions "the normal thing to do when federal courts are asked to enjoin pending proceedings in state courts is not to issue such injunctions." [92] This ruling is generally referred to as *Younger v. Harris,* from the name of one of the five decisions handed down together.[93]

Justice Hugo L. Black, who had not participated in the *Dombrowski* decision although a member of the court at the time, wrote the court's opinions. Only Justice William O. Douglas dissented in *Younger,* although several other justices took issue with the application of the abstention doctrine in one of the other cases decided that day.

In each case the court reversed a lower court's decision to enjoin state prosecution based on a law challenged as violating the First Amendment. "[T]he existence of a 'chilling effect,' even in the area of First Amendment rights," wrote Justice Black, "has never been considered a sufficient basis, in and of itself, for prohibiting state action." [94] In his view, *Dombrowski* permitted an injunction because of a clear threat of irreparable injury from a possible prosecution, not because the law at issue was alleged to violate the First Amendment. In these cases the court found no such threat, no showing of bad faith or harassment sufficient to justify an immediate injunction.

The court in *Younger v. Harris* did not base its ruling on the Anti-Injunction Act, but on the broader notion of the "comity" necessary to preserve the federal system. Comity, Black explained, was simply "a proper respect for state functions." [95]

In a series of rulings following *Younger,* the court, by narrowing margins, has extended this doctrine of non-intervention to limit federal injunctions halting state criminal proceedings begun *after* the injunction was requested, and to curtail their use to intervene in some state civil proceedings.[96] In each case, the court has based these extensions of the *Younger* rule on the general principle of comity, rather than on any statutory prohibition.

Declaratory Judgments

A milder and less intrusive judicial remedy than the injunction is the declaratory judgment. In such a ruling, a federal court simply declares conclusively the rights and obligations of the parties in dispute. No coercive or consequential order is necessarily attached to that declaration, although the judgment may be accompanied by, or may serve as the basis for, an injunction.

Because neither the Supreme Court nor other federal courts may issue advisory opinions, the court initially wavered in its view of the propriety of declaratory judgments. The court faced the issue after a number of states adopted laws early in the 20th century authorizing their courts to issue such judgments. When some cases decided in this way found their way to the Supreme Court, the question of the court's jurisdiction over them arose: were they actual "cases and controversies" as required by the Constitution? *(Advisory opinions, p. 287)*

In 1928, the answer seemed to be "no." But five years later, in an apparent change of mind, the court took jurisdiction over such a case.[97]

Congress effectively resolved any remaining doubts with passage of the Federal Declaratory Judgment Act of 1934, specifically authorizing the issuance of such judgments by federal courts in "cases of actual controversy." The Supreme Court upheld the constitutionality of the law three years later.

By confining the use of declaratory judgments to actual controversies, wrote Chief Justice Charles Evans Hughes, the act simply provided a new procedural remedy for the courts to use in cases already within their jurisdiction.[98]

Nevertheless, the line between declaratory judgments and advisory opinions is a thin one. In 1941 the court wrote:

> The difference between an abstract question and a "controversy" contemplated by the Declaratory Judgment Act is necessarily one of degree, and it would be difficult, if it would be possible, to fashion a precise test for determining in every case whether there is such a controversy. Basically, the question in each case is whether the facts alleged, under all the circumstances, show that there is a substantial controversy, between parties having adverse legal interests, of sufficient immediacy and reality to warrant the issuance of a declaratory judgment.[99]

Although it has insisted that "case or controversy" requirements are applied just as strictly to cases seeking declaratory judgments as to other cases, the Supreme Court nevertheless has hesitated to approve resolution of major constitutional questions through such judgments. In 1961 it refused a doctor's request for a declaratory judgment that Connecticut's law against all birth control devices was unconstitutional. Four years later, the court reversed the doctor's conviction for violating that law, and held the statute unconstitutional.[100]

"The Declaratory Judgment Act was an authorization, not a command," the court has stated. "It gave the federal courts competence to make a declaration of rights; it did not impose a duty to do so." [101] Federal courts thus have broad discretion in deciding whether to grant requests for such judgments.

The judgment is available as a remedy in all civil cases except those involving federal taxes, an area Congress excluded in 1935.

Unlike the injunction, a declaratory judgment may be issued even though another adequate remedy for the dispute exists, and even though there are other pending state or federal suits concerning the same matter — although the latter circumstance may bring stricter standards into play on the decision whether to grant the judgment.

Yet the Supreme Court has limited the use of declaratory judgments, particularly when its use would leave a state law unenforceable.

The law barring injunctions against state taxes makes no mention of declaratory judgments, but in 1943 the court applied the abstention doctrine to preclude use of this remedy in such cases as well.[102]

Is a showing of threatened irreparable injury necessary to justify a declaratory judgment against a law under which the person seeking the judgment is being prosecuted or threatened with prosecution? The court has waffled on this point, but the answer appears to be that such a threat must be demonstrated only if the judgment would disrupt ongoing state proceedings. Otherwise, there is no need to prove such possible injury.

Following its seeming relaxation of the abstention doctrine in cases where injunctions were sought against state laws challenged as violating the First Amendment, the court in 1967 seemed to adopt a broader view of the power of federal judges to issue declaratory judgments against such laws as well. (Details, p. 278)

In a New York case, *Zwickler v. Koota,* the court ruled that federal judges had a duty to hear constitutional challenges to state laws and that "escape from that duty is not permissible merely because state courts also have the solemn responsibility" of protecting constitutional rights.

The court held that the abstention doctrine allowed escape from this duty only in special circumstances. Injunctions and declaratory judgments were not twin remedies, ruled the court: when a plaintiff in a single case requested both, the factors in favor and against each remedy should be weighed separately by the Judge.[103]

Injury Standard

But four years later, as part of the complex of decisions known as *Younger v. Harris,* the court made clear that when a declaratory judgment was sought to halt an ongoing state criminal prosecution, only a clear threat of immediate and irreparable injury justified its issuance — the same standard required for an injunction.

The same standards applied, explained Justice Hugo L. Black, because "ordinarily a declaratory judgment will result in precisely the same interference with and disruption of state proceedings that the long-standing policy limiting injunctions was designed to avoid."[104]

But the court subsequently held that there need be no demonstration of irreparable injury to justify a declaratory judgment against a state law, if no prosecution under that law is pending against the person seeking the judgment.[105] When there is no ongoing state proceeding which a judgment would disrupt, "considerations of equity, comity, and federalism have little vitality," the court stated in 1974, thus the individual's right to have his federal claim considered in a federal court is paramount.[106]

"Requiring the federal courts totally to step aside when no state criminal prosecution is pending against the federal plaintiff would turn federalism on its head," wrote Justice William J. Brennan Jr. for a unanimous court.[107]

The court also recently rejected the argument that if there is no pending state prosecution under a challenged law against the person bringing the challenge, there is no real "case or controversy." The court ruled that so long as a genuine threat of enforcement of such a law exists, there is a case or controversy falling within federal jurisdiction.[108]

The Contempt Power

To maintain decorum within the courtroom and to enforce obedience to its orders, courts possess the inherent power to punish persons for contempt.

Contempt may be civil or criminal, depending upon the action involved and the purpose of the penalty imposed.

A judge may punish persons summarily for contempts committed in his presence, but in recent years the Supreme Court has used the due process guarantee to impose some procedural restraints on the exercise of this judicial power.

'Milder Medicine'

Declaratory judgments, wrote Justice William J. Brennan in 1974, were plainly intended by Congress "as an alternative to the strong medicine of the injunction," particularly when that medicine is to be administered to state officials.[1]

Earlier, in a 1971 dissenting opinion, Brennan, joined by Justices Byron R. White and Thurgood Marshall, had outlined the differences between these two forms of judicial relief:

The effects of injunctive and declaratory relief in their impact on the administration of a State's criminal laws are very different.... An injunction barring enforcement of a criminal statute against particular conduct immunizes that conduct from prosecution under the statute. A broad injunction against all enforcement of a statute paralyzes the State's enforcement machinery: the statute is rendered a nullity. A declaratory judgment, on the other hand, is merely a declaration of legal status and rights; it neither mandates nor prohibits state action....

What is clear ... is that even though a declaratory judgment has 'the force and effect of a final judgment,' ...it is a much milder form of relief than an injunction. Though it may be persuasive, it is not ultimately coercive; non-compliance with it may be inappropriate, but is not contempt.[2]

---

[1] *Steffel v. Thompson,* 415 U.S. 452 at 466 (1974).
[2] *Perez v. Ledesma,* 401 U.S. 82 at 124, 125-126 (1971).

The inherent contempt power of the new federal courts was reinforced by the Judiciary Act of 1789, which authorized the courts "to punish by fine or imprisonment, at the[ir] discretion ... all contempts of authority in any cause or hearing before the same."

As early as 1821, the Supreme Court urged restraint in the use of this power, cautioning courts to use "the least possible power adequate to the end proposed."[109]

At least one judge, James H. Peck, disregarded such advice. In 1830, he was impeached for using the contempt power to disbar and imprison a man who had published an article criticizing one of his opinions.

Peck was acquitted, but the event resulted in an 1831 statute, which limited the use of the contempt power to punishing, by fine or imprisonment, three types of offenses: "the misbehavior of any person in their presence, or so near thereto as to obstruct the administration of justice, the misbehavior of any of the officers of said courts in their official transactions, and the disobedience or resistance by any such officer, or by any party, juror, witness, or other person, to any lawful writ, process, order, rule, decree, or command of the said courts."

In 1874, with its decision in *Ex parte Robinson,* the court upheld the limitations imposed upon the use of the contempt power by the 1831 law, reversing the disbarment of an attorney found to be guilty of a contempt of court for actions outside the presence of the judge. The court held

Enforcement Powers

Beyond the power of contempt, federal courts have little equipment with which to enforce their rulings. This is particularly true of the Supreme Court.

In 1890, Justice Samuel F. Miller wrote:

> . . .as has been more than once said in this court, in the division of the powers of government between the three great departments, executive, legislative and judicial, the judicial is the weakest for the purposes of self-protection and for the enforcement of the powers which it exercises. The ministerial officers through whom its commands must be executed are marshals of the United States, and belong emphatically to the Executive Department of the government. They are appointed by the President, with the advice and consent of the Senate. They are removable from office at his pleasure. They are subjected by Act of Congress to the supervision and control of the Department of Justice, in the hands of one of the cabinet officers of the President, and their compensation is provided by Acts of Congress. The same may be said of the district attorneys of the United States, who prosecute and defend the claims of the government in the courts.[1]

"The court's only effective power is the power to persuade," wrote Henry J. Abraham in 1968, and at times that power has failed. Although the writ of *mandamus* is available to compel federal officials to carry out some duties, the court has been reluctant to use it against lower federal court judges, who have been among the most notable resisters in recent years to decisions of the higher court.[2]

Early in the 20th century, one rather remarkable case arose in which the Supreme Court itself exercised the contempt power to punish a person who had deliberately disregarded its order — with tragic consequences. A man named Johnson, sentenced to death by a state court in Tennessee, convinced the Supreme Court to hear his challenge to his conviction. In granting his request for review, the Supreme Court issued an order staying his execution.

Despite that order, Johnson was taken from jail and lynched. After his death, the sheriff with custody over him, one Shipp, was charged by the Attorney General with conspiring in the death of Johnson — and was found guilty of contempt of the Supreme Court, a verdict which resulted in a brief imprisonment.[3]

The Supreme Court acted in this case through a commissioner appointed to take testimony.[4]

---

[1] *In re Neagle*, 135 U.S. 1 at 63 (1890).

[2] Henry J. Abraham, *The Judicial Process*, 2d ed. (New York: Oxford University Press, 1968), p. 231; see also pp. 225-231, 338-340, and Stephen T. Early, *Constitutional Courts of the United States* (Towota, N.J.: Littlefield, Adams & Co., 1977), pp. 64-69, 156-160.

[3] *United States v. Shipp*, 203 U.S. 563 (1906).

[4] Henry M. Hart Jr. and Herbert Wechsler, *The Federal Courts and the Federal System* (Brooklyn: The Foundation Press, 1953) p. 421.

---

that the 1831 law not only limited the types of misconduct punishable as contempt, but also limited the penalties which might be imposed. Disbarment was not among them.[110]

Contumacious Conduct

The essential characteristic of contempt, the court has held, is obstructiveness, blocking the proper judicial functions of the court.

Little question has been raised about the court's power to maintain peace within the courtroom through the use of the contempt power.

As the court declared in 1888:

> . . .it is a settled doctrine . . . that for direct contempts committed in the face of the court . . . the offender may, in its discretion, be instantly apprehended and immediately imprisoned, without trial or issue, and without other proof than its actual knowledge of what occurred;. . . such power, although arbitrary in its nature and liable to abuse, is absolutely essential to the protection of the courts in the discharge of their functions. Without it, judicial tribunals would be at the mercy of the disorderly and the violent, who respect neither the laws . . . nor the officers charged with the duty of administering them.[111]

As recently as 1970, the Supreme Court has affirmed the power of a judge to keep peace in his courtroom, even at the cost of having a defendant bound and gagged or physically removed from the room.[112]

Direct disobedience to a court order is perhaps the most frequent conduct outside the courtroom penalized as contempt. Affirming the contempt conviction of labor leader Eugene Debs for such disobedience in 1895, the court wrote:

> . . .the power of a court to make an order carries with it the equal power to punish for a disobedience of that order, and the inquiry as to the question of disobedience has been, from time immemorial, the special function of the court. . . .[113]

Willful disregard of a court order may be both civil and criminal contempt, the court has ruled.[114]

'The Vicinity of the Court'

Generally, the Supreme Court has viewed the 1831 Act — the limitations of which continue in operation — as allowing use of the contempt power only to punish conduct actually impeding a trial or other judicial proceeding.

In 1918, the court strayed from this view. In the case of *Toledo Newspaper Co. v. United States*, the court — by a 5-2 vote — upheld a contempt citation against a newspaper for publishing articles and cartoons about a railway rate dispute pending in court. The judge viewed the articles as intended to provoke public resistance to his eventual order and to intimidate him.

For the first time, the court approved the use of the power to punish conduct which simply tended to obstruct the courts in carrying out their duty.[115]

Two decades later, the court reversed this ruling and returned to the strict construction of the contempt power as defined by the 1831 law. In the case of *Nye v. United States*, the court reversed the contempt convictions of persons who had successfully used liquor and other methods of persuasion — miles from the courtroom — to convince a plaintiff to drop his case. These actions were reprehensible, stated the court, but were punishable under other laws.

The phrase used in the 1831 law — allowing courts to punish misconduct "in their presence or so near thereto as to obstruct the administration of justice" — meant that the conduct should be geographically near the courtroom or it should not be punished as contempt, held the court. The conduct in this case, although it did obstruct justice, "was not misbehavior in the vicinity of the court disrupting to quiet and order or actually interrupting the court in the conduct of its business."[116]

The Obstinate Witness. The Fifth Amendment guarantees witnesses before courts or grand juries the right to refuse to incriminate themselves. But no other privilege allows persons simply to refuse to answer proper questions addressed to them in those forums. Furthermore, once a witness is granted immunity from prosecution for crimes revealed by his testimony, his privilege of silence ends altogether. False testimony, however, is prosecutable as perjury — whether given by an immunized witness or not.

In 1919, in the case *Ex parte Hudgings,* the Supreme Court held that a witness committing perjury should not be held in contempt as a penalty for his false testimony unless the perjury was clearly an obstructive tactic. "[I]n order to punish perjury . . . as a contempt," wrote Chief Justice Edward D. White for the court, "there must be added to the essential elements of perjury under the general law the further element of obstruction to the court in the performance of its duty."[117]

But the court has backed the use of the contempt power to punish obstinate witnesses who simply refused, for reasons other than self-incrimination, to respond to certain questions. In 1958 Justice Felix Frankfurter commented:

> Whatever differences the potentially drastic power of courts to punish for contempt may have evoked, a doubt has never been uttered that stubborn disobedience of the duty to answer relevant inquiries in a judicial proceeding brings into force the power of the federal courts to punish for contempt.[118]

In 1975 the court in *United States v. Wilson* upheld the use of the summary contempt power to punish an immunized trial witness who persisted in his refusal to respond to questions. Such "intentional obstructions of court proceedings," held the court, could destroy a prosecution. "In an ongoing trial with the judge, jurors, counsel, and witnesses all waiting," wrote Chief Justice Warren Burger, the summary contempt power is "an appropriate remedial tool to discourage witnesses from contumacious refusals to comply with lawful orders essential to prevent a breakdown of the proceedings."[119]

Although grand jury witnesses who refuse to answer questions despite a grant of immunity may be cited for contempt, the court in 1965 held that such punishment may not be summary; it may be imposed only after a hearing at which the accused witness is allowed to defend himself against the charge. This 1965 holding in *Harris v. United States* overruled a 1959 decision allowing summary punishment of grand jury witnesses in this situation.[120]

Attorneys. Lawyers — as officers of the court — have received their share of contempt citations.

In 1952 the court upheld the contempt citations and convictions of the defense attorneys for eleven Communist Party leaders convicted of violating the Smith Act. Lower

court judges reviewing the attorneys' actions during the trial described their conduct as "wilfully obstructive," "abominable," and "outrageous . . . conduct of a kind which no lawyer owes his client, which cannot ever be justified."[121]

But the court continues to insist that the element of obstruction be clear before such a penalty can be properly imposed. In 1962 the court reversed the contempt conviction of an attorney so penalized simply for asserting his right to ask questions until he was stopped by a court official.[122]

Defendants. The court also has upheld the use of the contempt power of federal judges to punish — by additional prison terms — persons convicted of a crime who absconded and were fugitives from justice for a period of years before surrendering to serve the sentences for those crimes.[123]

Civil and Criminal Contempt

Contempt may be civil or criminal in nature. As the justices have had many occasions to acknowledge, it is sometimes difficult to distinguish between the two.

The test developed by the court — and used consistently since 1911 — focuses upon the character and purpose of the penalty imposed. In the case of *Gompers v. Buck's Stove and Range Co.,* the court declared that:

> . . .If it [the penalty] is for civil contempt the punishment is remedial, and for the benefit of the complainant [generally the other party to a case]. But if it is for criminal contempt the sentence is punitive, to vindicate the authority of the court.[124]

Justice Joseph R. Lamar continued:

> . . .imprisonment for civil contempt is ordered where the defendant has refused to do an affirmative act required by the provisions of an order. . . . Imprisonment in such cases . . . is intended to be remedial by coercing the defendant to do what he had refused to do. . . .
>
> For example: if a defendant should refuse to pay alimony . . . he could be committed until he complied with the order. Unless there were special elements of contumacy, the refusal to pay . . . is treated as being rather in resistance to the opposite party than in contempt of the court. . . .[125]

Citing the often-quoted statement that a person imprisoned for civil contempt carries "the keys of the prison in his pocket," Justice Lamar pointed out that such a person "can end the sentence and discharge himself at any moment by doing what he had previously refused to do."[126]

Criminal contempt, on the other hand, results when:

> . . .the defendant does that which he has been commanded not to do, the disobedience is a thing accomplished. Imprisonment cannot undo or remedy what has been done, nor afford any compensation for the pecuniary injury caused by the disobedience. If the sentence is limited to imprisonment for a definite period, the defendant . . . cannot shorten the term by promising not to repeat the offense. Such imprisonment operates . . . solely as punishment. . . .[127]

Summarizing the test, civil contempt consists of the refusal to act as the court commands, a disobedience punished by imprisonment until the person obeys; while criminal contempt consists of doing the forbidden — and being punished for a definite term.

The Court: Supervisor of Federal Courts. . .

By virtue of its position at the apex of the nation's judiciary, the Supreme Court exerts broad supervisory power over the administration of justice in the federal courts.

This responsibility is multi-faceted. Among its elements are the court's power to review the functioning of the lower courts, to propose rules of procedure governing processes in the federal courts and to oversee the admission, conduct and expulsion of members of the federal bar.

All federal courts have an inherent power to supervise their officers, the conduct of litigants, witnesses, attorneys and jurors, and to protect property within their custody.[1]

Furthermore, the Supreme Court has held that it and other federal courts are empowered to appoint persons of special skills to help resolve certain issues. Most prominent of such temporary aides at the Supreme Court level are special masters, whom the court appoints to hear evidence and recommend judgment in original cases involving complex factual matters such as boundary locations. The rationale for the use of such special personnel was set out by Justice Louis D. Brandeis in 1920:

> Courts have (at least in the absence of legislation to the contrary) inherent power to provide themselves with appropriate instruments required for the performance of their duties . . . [including] authority to appoint persons unconnected with the court to aid judges in the performance of specific judicial duties, as they may arise. . . .[2]

General Supervision. The court's general supervisory power over lower federal courts is exercised randomly and sporadically through its decisions reviewing their actions — approving some and rebuking others.

The court at times has taken the opportunity presented by such a case to go beyond the decision required to resolve a particular dispute and to prescribe or clarify rules of procedure.

An example of this mode of exercising the supervisory power is the 1966 Supreme Court decision in the case of *Cheff v. Schnackenberg.*[3] While upholding the lower court's refusal of a jury trial to the plaintiff in that case, the court went on to rule — in its supervisory role — that

anyone sentenced by a federal judge to more than six months in prison for contempt should be given a jury trial.

Several years earlier, the court exercised its supervisory power to reduce a contempt sentence, after the sentencing court had ignored Supreme Court suggestions that a reduction was necessary.[4]

"The Supreme Court's review power," wrote one student of the judicial system, "is probably its most extensively used method for instructing the lower courts in the constitutional or statutory law and procedural niceties they are to apply. Processes of appeal and reversal are parts — most important parts — of the internal control mechanism of the constitutional court system."[5]

"Judicial supervision of the administration of criminal justice in the federal courts," wrote Justice Felix Frankfurter in 1943, "implies the duty of establishing and maintaining civilized standards of procedure and evidence."[6] Frankfurter went on to indicate his belief that such standards might be considerably stiffer than those required by the Constitution itself.

Rule-Making Power. The Judiciary Act of 1789 authorized all federal courts to make rules for the orderly conduct of their business. In addition, Congress has enacted "process acts" to specify certain forms and procedures for use in the federal courts.[7]

In 1825 the Supreme Court sustained the power of Congress to make procedural rules for the federal courts — and also to delegate considerable responsibility for drafting such rules to the courts themselves.[8]

The Supreme Court in the ensuing century set out various rules applying to different types of lawsuits, but not until the 1930s was there a uniform set of rules governing procedures in all federal courts.[9]

In 1933, Congress authorized the Supreme Court to propose rules governing post-verdict proceedings in all federal criminal cases. The following year, it granted similar authority to the court to propose rules of civil procedure, subject to veto by Congress. And in 1940, Congress gave the court authority to propose rules governing criminal case procedures prior to a verdict.

Using advisory committees of distinguished attorneys and legal scholars and judges, the Supreme Court proposed — and Congress approved — the Federal Rules of Civil Procedure, which took effect in 1938, and the Fed-

---

Fourteen years later, in 1925, the Supreme Court reinforced this distinction between civil and criminal contempt, ruling that the president's power of pardon extended to allow pardons of persons convicted of criminal — but not of civil — contempt.[128]

In 1947, the Supreme Court somewhat muddied this distinction between civil and criminal contempt by ruling that the same action could be both — and by upholding the conviction of the United Mine Workers of America and its president, John L. Lewis, on both types of contempt as a result of his and the union's disobedience of a court order forbidding a strike.

"Common sense," wrote Chief Justice Fred M. Vinson, "would recognize that conduct can amount to both civil and criminal contempt. The same acts may justify a court in resorting to coercive and to punitive measures."[129]

The distinction was illuminated again, however, in one small portion of the decision. Lewis and the union argued that the order they had disobeyed was invalid, a violation of statutory restrictions on the use of injunctions in labor disputes. *(Box, p. 276)*

The Supreme Court found the injunction valid, but declared that even if it had been illegally issued, it was to be obeyed — on pain of contempt — until it was reversed "by orderly and proper proceedings." If the injunction had been found invalid, Vinson explained, the civil contempt citation would be set aside — because any duty to obey the order had vanished. But the criminal contempt conviction — punishment for disobedience to an outstanding and unreversed court order — would remain in effect.[130]

In 1966 the court looked to the character of the disobedience and the purpose of the penalty in ruling that

...the Federal Bar, and Federal Procedure

eral Rules of Criminal Procedure, which took effect in 1946. Both have been subsequently amended through this same process of committee drafting, Supreme Court recommendation and congressional examination and approval.[10]

Overseeing the Bar. It is well settled, declared Chief Justice Roger B. Taney in 1857, " ...that it rests exclusively with the court to determine who is qualified to become one of its officers, as an attorney and a counselor, and for what cause he ought to be removed. That power, however, is not an arbitrary and despotic one, to be exercised at the pleasure of the court, or from passion, prejudice, or personal hostility; but it is the duty of the court to exercise and regulate it by a sound and just judicial discretion, whereby the rights and independence of the bar may be as scrupulously guarded and maintained by the court, as the rights and dignity of the court itself." [11]

Ten years later, as the court invalidated the act of Congress imposing a test oath requirement upon all attorneys wishing to practice before federal courts, Justice Stephen Field elaborated upon this aspect of the power of the federal courts:

> ...The order of admission is the judgment of the court that the parties possess the requisite qualifications as attorneys and counselors, and are entitled to appear as such and conduct causes therein. From its entry the parties become officers of the court, and are

responsible to it for professional misconduct. They hold their office only during good behavior and can only be deprived of it for misconduct ascertained and declared by the judgment of the court after opportunity to be heard has been afforded.... Their admission or their exclusion is not the exercise of a mere ministerial power. It is the exercise of judicial power....

> The attorney and counselor being, by the solemn judicial act of the court, clothed with his office, does not hold it as a matter of grace and favor. The right which it confers upon him to appear for suitors, and to argue causes, is something more than a mere indulgence, revocable at the pleasure of the court, or at the command of the Legislature. It is a right of which he can only be deprived by the judgment of the court, for moral or professional delinquency....[12]

Congress may set statutory qualifications for admission to the bar, the court held in that ruling in *Ex parte Garland*, but those qualifications are subject to judicial review and disallowance.

Similarly, the court has ruled in modern times on questions of state bar qualifications and disqualifications, holding that alienage alone is insufficient reason to deny someone admission to a state bar, while backing the decisions of state bar officials to exclude conscientious objectors — and individuals refusing to answer questions concerning possible membership in the Communist Party.[13]

---

[1] U.S. Congress, Library of Congress, Congressional Reference Service, *The Constitution of the United States of America: Analysis and Interpretation* (Washington, D.C.: U.S. Government Printing Office, 1973) pp. 583-584.

[2] *Ex parte Peterson*, 253 U.S. 300 at 312 (1920).

[3] *Cheff v. Schnackenberg*, 384 U.S. 373 at 380 (1966).

[4] *Yates v. United States*, 356 U.S. 363 at 366 (1958).

[5] Stephen T. Early Jr., *Constitutional Courts of the United States* (Totowa, N.J.: Littlefield, Adams & Co., 1977), p. 149; see also pp. 149-156.

[6] *McNabb v. United States*, 318 U.S. 322 at 340 (1943).

[7] Julius Goebel, Jr. *History of the Supreme Court of the United States*: Vol. I, *Antecedents and Beginnings to 1801* (New York: MacMillan Publishing Co., 1971), pp. 509-551.

[8] *Wayman v. Southard*, 10 Wheat. 1 (1825).

[9] Henry M. Hart Jr., Herbert Wechsler, *The Federal Courts and the Federal System* (Brooklyn, N.Y.: The Foundation Press, 1953), p. 577-611.

[10] Charles Alan Wright, *Handbook on the Law of Federal Courts* (St. Paul: West Publishing Co., 1970), pp. 257-263.

[11] *Ex parte Secombe*, 19 How. 9 at 13 (1857).

[12] *Ex parte Garland*, 4 Wall. 333 at 378-379 (1867); see also *Ex parte Robinson*, 19 Wall. 505 (1874).

[13] *In re Griffiths*, 413 U.S. 717 (1973); *Konigsberg v. California*, 366 U.S. 36 (1961) and 353 U.S. 252 (1957); *In re Summers*, 325 U.S. 651 (1945).

---

persons imprisoned for contempt, after refusing to answer grand jury questions despite a grant of immunity, were being penalized for civil contempt. Their disobedience, wrote Justice Tom Clark, was in refusing to do what the court ordered, and their punishment was "for the obvious purpose of compelling the witnesses to obey the orders to testify," and whenever they did so, they would be released.[131]

A Summary Power

"A contempt proceeding," stated the court in 1904, "is *sui generis*" — a unique type of judicial process.[132]

One aspect of this uniqueness is the fact that contempt has traditionally been a summary power — that is, a judge could — on the spot — hold someone in contempt and impose punishment, without any need for a trial before a jury — or many of the other procedural safeguards guaranteed by the Bill of Rights.

The summary nature of this power is directly related to its original purpose — to enable a judge to maintain order in his courtroom. As the Supreme Court, quoting a lower court, wrote in an 1888 ruling:

> The judicial eye witnessed the act and the judicial mind comprehended all the circumstances of aggravation, provocation or mitigation; and the fact being thus judicially established, it only remained for the judicial arm to inflict proper punishment.[133]

A few years later, in upholding the use of the contempt power to punish disobedience of a court order, the court rejected the suggestion that a person charged with contempt of the orders of one court or one judge should be sentenced by another judge. "To submit the question of disobedience to another tribunal, be it a jury or another court, would operate to deprive the proceeding of half its efficiency," stated the court.[134]

An Unbiased Judge

But by 1925, the Supreme Court began to apply some of the elements of the due process guarantee to contempt proceedings.

In that year, the court recommended that when a judge became so personally involved with an allegedly contemptuous course of behavior that he lacked the necessary neutrality to be fair in imposing a sentence, he should turn the matter over to a colleague. In the case of *Cooke v. United States,* Chief Justice William Howard Taft wrote for the majority:

> . . .where conditions do not make it impracticable, or where the delay may not injure public or private right, a judge called upon to act in a case of contempt by personal attack upon him, may, without flinching from his duty properly ask that one of his fellow judges take his place.[135]

Nevertheless, the court continued to defer to the discretion of the trial judge in most such situations.

The most notable example of this judicial deference came in 1952 when the court upheld as proper the criminal contempt citations imposed by Federal Judge Harold Medina upon the attorneys who had, during a long and controversial trial before him, defended 11 men accused of violating the Smith Act in their roles as leaders of the U.S. Communist Party.

Noting that Medina waited until after the trial to cite and sentence them for contempt, the attorneys challenged the summary nature of the contempt proceedings and argued that Medina should have referred the contempt charges to another judge for hearing and sentencing.

Justice Robert H. Jackson set out the reasoning behind the decision to uphold Medina's actions:

> . . .It is almost inevitable that any contempt of a court committed in the presence of the judge during a trial will be an offense against his dignity and authority. At a trial the court is so much the judge and the judge so much the court that the two terms are used interchangeably.... It cannot be that summary punishment is only for such minor contempts as leave the judge indifferent and may be evaded by adding hectoring, abusive and defiant conduct toward the judge as an individual. Such an interpretation would nullify, in practice, the power it purports to grant.[136]

But just two years later, in a less sensational case, *Offutt v. United States,* the court held that a judge who had become involved in a wrangle with a defense attorney presenting a case before him should have sent contempt charges against that attorney to another judge for resolution.

Justice Felix Frankfurter, who had dissented from the ruling upholding Medina's actions, wrote for the court:

> The pith of this rather extraordinary power to punish without the formalities required by the Bill of Rights for the prosecution of federal crimes generally, is that the necessities of the administration of justice require such summary dealing with obstructions to it.

It is a mode of vindicating the majesty of law, in its active manifestation, against obstruction and outrage. The power thus entrusted to a judge is wholly unrelated to his personal sensibilities, be they tender or rugged. But judges also are human, and may . . . quite unwittingly identify offense to self with obstruction to law. Accordingly, this Court has deemed it important that district judges guard against this easy confusion by not sitting themselves in judgment upon misconduct of counsel where the contempt charged is entangled with the judge's personal feeling against the lawyer.[137]

A unanimous court reaffirmed this holding in 1971.[138]

The Right to Trial

As early as the 19th century, the Supreme Court began to place some limits on the summary nature of the contempt power, requiring the use of normal adversary procedures to deal with contempts occurring out of the presence of the court. In 1946 the new rules of federal criminal procedure allowed summary punishment only of conduct seen or heard by the judge and "committed in the actual presence of the court."

All other criminal contempt was to be prosecuted separately, after notice, with a hearing at which a defense to the charge could be presented, and opportunity for release on bail. Furthermore, the rule stated that if the contempt involved "disrespect to or criticism of a judge, that judge is disqualified from presiding at the trial or hearing except with the defendant's consent."

This was not a sudden change. The court had taken the opportunity in earlier cases to state that the presumption of innocence applied in criminal contempt cases, that guilt must be proven beyond a reasonable doubt, that a person charged with contempt could not be compelled to be a witness against himself and that persons accused of contempt other than that occurring in open court should be advised of the charges and should have an opportunity to present a defense against them with the aid of counsel and to call witnesses.[139]

But in a long and unbroken line of cases, the court insisted that persons charged with contempt did not have the right to a trial by jury — except in such unusual cases as those in which Congress by law provided that right.[140] The Sixth Amendment states that "in all criminal prosecutions the accused shall enjoy the right to a speedy and public trial, by an impartial jury...." The court's position was simply that criminal contempt was not a crime in the sense of this amendment and thus its guarantee did not apply.

Citing long lines of precedents, the court in 1958, 1960 and 1964 reaffirmed its position: there was no constitutional right to a jury trial for persons charged with contempt.[141]

Then, almost in passing, the court in 1966 announced that federal courts could not sentence persons to more than six months in prison for criminal contempt unless they had been tried by a jury — or had waived their right to such a trial.[142]

The court's turnabout came in the case of Paul Cheff, who did not benefit because his contempt sentence was for six months — no longer. The court did not base its statement imposing the jury trial requirement upon a constitutional basis but upon its power to supervise the conduct of lower federal courts. *(See box, pp. 282-283)*

Two years later, however, the court placed the requirement of a jury trial for serious criminal contempt charges upon a constitutional basis. On the same day that the court extended the Sixth Amendment right to a jury trial to state proceedings, it ruled that state courts, like federal ones, must accord the right to a jury trial to persons charged with serious criminal contempts.[143]

Writing for the majority, Justice Byron R. White explained:

Our deliberations have convinced us . . . that serious criminal contempts are so nearly like other serious crimes that they are subject to the jury trial provisions of the Constitution, now binding on the states. . . .

Criminal contempt is a crime in the ordinary sense; it is a violation of the law, a public wrong which is punishable by fine or imprisonment or both. . . .

Indeed, in contempt cases an even more compelling argument can be made for providing a right to jury trial as a protection against the arbitrary exercise of official power. Contemptuous conduct, though a public wrong, often strikes at the most vulnerable and human qualities of a judge's temperament. Even when the contempt is not a direct insult to the court or the judge, it frequently represents a rejection of judicial authority, or an interference with the judicial process or with the duties of officers of the court.[144]

White cited the court's 1895 statement in *In re Debs* that contempt proceedings would be less efficient if they were conducted before a court other than that which was the object of the contempt. *(See p. 284)* At this point, he wrote, the modern court disagreed:

. . .in our judgment, when serious punishment for contempt is contemplated, rejecting a demand for jury trial cannot be squared with the Constitution or justified by considerations of efficiency or the desirability of vindicating the authority of the court. . . . Perhaps to some extent we sacrifice efficiency, expedition, and economy, but the choice in favor of jury trial has been made, and retained, in the Constitution.[145]

Six years later, a more closely divided court affirmed this extension of the right to a jury trial in contempt cases. Due process, the court held in 1974, required that persons whose aggregate criminal contempt sentences were more than six months should have a jury trial on the contempt charges against them.[146]

Footnotes

[1] Samuel F. Miller, *Lectures On the Constitution*, (Albany, N.Y.: Banks and Brothers, 1891), p. 314.

[2] *The Federalist Papers*, with an Introduction by Clinton Rossiter (New York: New American Library, Mentor Books, 1961), No. 51, p. 322.

[3] *United States v. Nixon*, 418 U.S. 683 at 705 (1974).

[4] Robert K. Carr, *The Supreme Court and Judicial Review* (New York: Farrar & Rinehart, 1942), p. 43.

[5] Ibid., p. 45, citing Max Farrand, *The Records of the Federal Convention of 1787* (New Haven: Yale University Press, 1911), II:73.

[6] Thomas Reed Powell, *Vagaries and Varieties in Constitutional Interpretation* (New York: Columbia University Press, 1956; reprint ed. New York: AMS Press, 1967), p. 20.

[7] *Martin v. Hunter's Lessee*, 1 Wheat. 304 (1816); *Cohens v. Virginia*, 6 Wheat. 264 (1821).

[8] *Murdock v. Memphis*, 20 Wall. 590 (1875).

[9] *Herb v. Pitcairn*, 324 U.S. 117 at 125-126 (1945).

[10] *United States v. Hylton*, 3 Dall. 171 (1796).

[11] Charles Warren, *The Supreme Court in United States History*, 2 vols. (Boston: Little, Brown & Co., 1922, 1926), II:222-223.

[12] *Marbury v. Madison*, 1 Cr. 137 at 175-176 (1803).

[13] Id. at 177-178.

[14] Id. at 178.

[15] Carl B. Swisher, *American Constitutional Development*, 2d ed. (Cambridge; Houghton Mifflin Co., 1954), p. 10.

[16] Charles G. Haines, *The American Doctrine of Judicial Supremacy* (Berkeley, Calif.: The University of California Press, 1932), pp. 202-203.

[17] Charles Evans Hughes, *The Supreme Court of the United States* (New York: Columbia University Press, 1928), pp. 87-89.

[18] Carr, *The Supreme Court and Judicial Review*, p. 71.

[19] Hughes, *The Supreme Court*, pp. 50-51.

[20] *Hepburn v. Griswold*, 8 Wall. 603 (1870); *Knox v. Lee*, 12 Wall. 457 (1871).

[21] Powell, *Vagaries and Varieties*, p. 18.

[22] Hughes, *The Supreme Court*, pp. 95-96.

[23] The current version of that provision — referred to as the All Writs Act — grants federal courts power to issue "all writs necessary or appropriate in aid of their respective jurisdictions and agreeable to the usages and principles of law." 28 U.S.C. 1651(a)

[24] *Ex parte Yerger*, 8 Wall. 85 at 95 (1869).

[25] *Adams v. United States ex rel. McCann*, 317 U.S. 269 at 273 (1942).

[26] *Fay v. Noia*, 372 U.S. 391 at 401-402 (1963).

[27] U.S. Congress, Library of Congress, Congressional Reference Service, *The Constitution of the United States of America: Analysis and Interpretation* (Washington, D.C.: U.S. Government Printing Office, 1973), pp. 617-618.

[28] *Brown v. Allen*, 344 U.S. 443 at 465 (1953).

[29] *United States v. Smith*, 331 U.S. 469 at 475 (1947).

[30] *Gusik v. Schilder*, 339 U.S. 977 (1950).

[31] *Adams v. United States ex rel. McCann*, 317 U.S. 269 at 274 (1942).

[32] Library of Congress, *The Constitution*, p. 616-617.

[33] *Ex parte Bollman*, 4 Cr. 75 at 101 (1807).

[34] *Ex parte Watkins*, 3 Pet. 193 at 202 (1830).

[35] *Ex parte Dorr*, 3 How. 104 at 105 (1845).

[36] Charles Fairman, *History of the Supreme Court of the United States:* Vol. VI, *Reconstruction and Reunion, 1864-1888, Part One* (New York: MacMillan Publishing Co., 1971), pp. 443-447.

[37] Ibid. p. 451; *Ex parte McCardle*, 7 Wall. 506 (1869).

[38] *Ex parte Yerger*, 8 Wall. 85 (1869).

[39] *Ex parte Virginia*, 100 U.S. 339 (1880); *Ex parte Clarke*, 100 U.S. 399 (1880); *Ex parte Siebold*, 100 U.S. 371 (1880).

[40] *Ex parte Siebold*, 100 U.S. 371 at 376-377 (1880).

[41] *Ex parte Nielsen*, 131 U.S. 176 at 183-184 (1889).

[42] *Frank v. Mangum*, 237 U.S. 309 at 327, 331 (1915).

[43] *Moore v. Dempsey*, 261 U.S. 86 at 91 (1923); see also *Hawk v. Olson*, 326 U.S. 271 at 276 (1945).

[44] *Waley v. Johnston*, 316 U.S. 101 at 104-105 (1942).

[45] *Brown v. Allen*, 344 U.S. 443 at 464-465 (1953).

[46] *Townsend v. Sain*, 372 U.S. 293 at 312, 318 (1963).

[47] *Ex parte Royall*, 117 U.S. 241 (1886).

[48] *Ex parte Hawk*, 321 U.S. 114 at 116-117 (1944); see also *Darr v. Burford*, 339 U.S. 200 at 217 (1950).

[49] *Darr v. Burford*, 339 U.S. 200 at 217 (1950).

[50] *Brown v. Allen*, 344 U.S. 443 at 487 (1953).

[51] *Darr v. Burford*, 339 U.S. 200 at 210, 216 (1950).

[52] *Fay v. Noia*, 372 U.S. 391 (1963).

[53] Id. at 441.

[54] Id. at 438-439.

[55] Id. at 440.

[56] Id. at 435-437.

[57] *Stone v. Powell,* 428 U.S. 465 (1976).

[58] *Davis v. United States,* 411 U.S. 233 (1973); *Francis v. Henderson,* 425 U.S. 536 (1976); *Wainwright v. Sykes,* 433 U.S. 72 (1977).

[59] *Kerr v. United States District Court,* 426 U.S. 394 at 402 (1976).

[60] *United States v. Haley,* 371 U.S. 18 (1962); *Deen v. Hickman,* 358 U.S. 57 (1958).

[61] *Marbury v. Madison,* 1 Cr. 137 (1803).

[62] *McIntire v. Wood,* 7 Cr. 504 (1813); *McCluny v. Silliman,* 6 Wheat. 598 (1821); *Kendall v. Stokes,* 12 Pet. 524 at 624 (1838).

[63] *Marbury v. Madison,* 1 Cr. 137 at 170-171 (1803).

[64] *Kendall v. Stokes,* 12 Pet. 524 at 613 (1838).

[65] *Kerr v. United States District Court,* 426 U.S. 394 at 403 (1976); see also *Marbury v. Madison,* 1 Cr. 137 at 169 (1803); *United States v. Duell,* 172 U.S. 576 at 582 (1899); *Ex parte Republic of Peru,* 318 U.S. 578 at 584 (1943).

[66] *The Bank of Columbia v. Sweeny,* 1 Pet. 567 at 569 (1828).

[67] *Ex parte Fahey,* 332 U.S. 258 at 259-260 (1947); see also *Parr v. United States,* 351 U.S. 513 at 520 (1956); *Roche v. Evaporated Milk Association,* 319 U.S. 21 at 26, 29 (1943).

[68] *Ex parte Republic of Peru,* 318 U.S. 578 at 583 (1943).

[69] *Bankers Life & Casualty v. Holland,* 346 U.S. 379 at 383 (1953).

[70] *Ex parte United States,* 287 U.S. 241 at 248-249 (1932).

[71] *Deen v. Hickman,* 358 U.S. 57 (1957).

[72] *Roche v. Evaporated Milk Association,* 319 U.S. 21 (1943).

[73] *La Buy v. Howes Leather,* 352 U.S. 249 (1957); *Beacon Theatres Inc. v. Westover,* 359 U.S. 500 (1959); *Thermtron Products v. Hermansdorfer,* 423 U.S. 336 (1976).

[74] *United States v. United Mine Workers,* 330 U.S. 258 (1947).

[75] *Pollock v. Farmers' Loan & Trust Co.,* 158 U.S. 601 (1895).

[76] *Lockerty v. Phillips,* 319 U.S. 182 (1943).

[77] *Mississippi v. Johnson,* 4 Wall. 475 at 498-499 (1867).

[78] Id. at 500.

[79] See *Mitchum v. Foster,* 407 U.S. 225 at 234-235 (1972).

[80] Id. at 235-236.

[81] *Toucey v. New York Life Insurance Co.,* 314 U.S. 118 at 139 (1941).

[82] *Leiter Minerals v. United States,* 352 U.S. 220 (1957); *Mitchum v. Foster,* 407 U.S. 225 (1972).

[83] *Osborn v. Bank of the United States,* 9 Wheat. 738 (1824).

[84] *Ex parte Young,* 209 U.S. 123 (1908).

[85] *Prentis v. Atlantic Coast Line Co.,* 211 U.S. 210 (1908).

[86] *Dombrowski v. Pfister,* 380 U.S. 479 at 484-485 (1965).

[87] *Fenner v. Boykin,* 271 U.S. 240 at 244 (1926).

[88] *Beal v. Missouri Pacific R.R. Co.,* 312 U.S. 45 (1941); *Railroad Commission of Texas v. Pullman Co.,* 312 U.S. 496 (1941); *Douglas v. City of Jeannette,* 319 U.S. 157 (1943).

[89] *McNeese v. Board of Education for Community Unit School District,* 373 U.S. 668 (1963).

[90] *Harman v. Forssenius,* 380 U.S. 528 at 534-535 (1965).

[91] *Dombrowski v. Pfister,* 380 U.S. 479 at 489-490 (1965).

[92] *Younger v. Harris,* 401 U.S. 37 at 45 (1971).

[93] *Younger v. Harris,* 401 U.S. 37 (1971); *Samuels v. Mackell, Fernandez v. Mackell,* 401 U.S. 66 (1971); *Byrne v. Karalexis,* 401 U.S. 216 (1971); *Perez v. Ledesma,* 401 U.S. 82 (1971); *Dyson v. Stein,* 401 U.S. 200 (1971).

[94] *Younger v. Harris,* 401 U.S. 37 at 51 (1971).

[95] Id. at 44.

[96] *Hicks v. Miranda,* 422 U.S. 332 (1975); *Huffman v. Pursue Ltd.,* 420 U.S. 592 (1975); *Trainor v. Hernandez,* 431 U.S. 434 (1976); *Juidice v. Vail,* 430 U.S. 327 (1976).

[97] *Willing v. Chicago Auditorium Association,* 277 U.S. 274 at 289 (1928); *Nashville, Chicago & St. Louis Railway Company v. Wallace,* 288 U.S. 249 at 264 (1933).

[98] *Aetna Life Insurance Company v. Haworth,* 300 U.S. 227 (1937).

[99] *Maryland Casualty Co. v. Pacific Coal & Oil Co.,* 312 U.S. 270 at 273 (1941); *Alabama State Federation of Labor v. McAdory,* 325 U.S. 450 at 461 (1945).

[100] *Poe v. Ullman,* 367 U.S. 497 (1961); *Griswold v. Connecticut,* 381 U.S. 479 (1965).

[101] *Public Affairs Associates v. Rickover,* 369 U.S. 111 at 112 (1962); *Brillhart v. Excess Insurance Co.,* 316 U.S. 491 at 494 (1942).

[102] *Great Lakes Dredge and Dock Co. v. Huffman,* 319 U.S. 293 (1943).

[103] *Zwickler v. Koota,* 389 U.S. 241 at 254, 248 (1967).

[104] *Samuels v. Mackell,* 401 U.S. 66 at 72 (1971).

[105] *Steffel v. Thompson,* 415 U.S. 452 (1974); *Ellis v. Dyson,* 421 U.S. 426 (1975).

[106] *Steffel v. Thompson,* 415 U.S. 452 at 462 (1974).

[107] Id. at 472.

[108] *Lake Carriers Association v. MacMullan,* 406 U.S. 498 (1972); *Steffel v. Thompson,* 415 U.S. 452 (1974); *Ellis v. Dyson,* 421 U.S. 426 (1975).

[109] *Anderson v. Dunn,* 6 Wheat. 204 at 231 (1821).

[110] *Ex parte Robinson,* 19 Wall. 505 (1874).

[111] *Ex parte Terry,* 128 U.S. 289 at 313 (1888).

[112] *Illinois v. Allen,* 397 U.S. 337 (1970).

[113] *In re Debs,* 158 U.S. 564 at 594-595 (1895).

[114] *United States v. United Mine Workers,* 330 U.S. 258 (1947).

[115] *Toledo Newspaper Co. v. United States,* 247 U.S. 402 (1918).

[116] *Nye v. United States,* 313 U.S. 33 at 52 (1941).

[117] *Ex parte Hudgings,* 249 U.S. 378 at 383 (1919); see also *In re Michael,* 326 U.S. 224 (1945).

[118] *Brown v. United States,* 356 U.S. 148 at 153 (1958).

[119] *United States v. Wilson,* 421 U.S. 309 at 315-316, 319 (1975).

[120] *Harris v. United States,* 382 U.S. 162 (1965), overruling *Brown v. United States,* 359 U.S. 41 (1959).

[121] *Sacher v. United States,* 343 U.S. 1 at 3 (1952).

[122] *In re McConnell,* 370 U.S. 230 (1962).

[123] *Green v. United States,* 356 U.S. 165 (1958).

[124] *Gompers v. Buck's Stove and Range Co.,* 221 U.S. 418 at 441 (1911).

[125] Id. at 442.

[126] Ibid.

[127] Id. at 442-443.

[128] *Ex parte Grossman,* 267 U.S. 87 (1925).

[129] *United States v. United Mine Workers,* 330 U.S. 258 at 300 (1947).

[130] Id. at 295.

[131] *Shillitani v. United States, Pappadio v. United States,* 384 U.S. 364 at 368 (1966).

[132] *Bessette v. W. B. Conkey,* 194 U.S. 324 at 326 (1904).

[133] *Ex parte Terry,* 128 U.S. 289 at 312 (1888).

[134] *In re Debs,* 158 U.S. 564 at 595 (1895).

[135] *Cooke v. United States,* 267 U.S. 517 at 539 (1925).

[136] *Sacher v. United States,* 343 U.S. 1 at 12 (1952).

[137] *Offutt v. United States,* 348 U.S. 11 at 14 (1954).

[138] *Mayberry v. Pennsylvania,* 400 U.S. 455 (1971).

[139] *Michaelson v. United States,* 266 U.S. 42 at 66 (1924); *Cooke v. United States,* 267 U.S. 517 at 537 (1925).

[140] The Clayton Act of 1914 provides a jury trial for persons charged with contempt for some types of disobedience to court orders; some limited right to jury trial for contempt was provided by portions of the Civil Rights Acts of 1957 and 1964.

[141] *Green v. United States,* 356 U.S. 165 (1958); *Levine v. United States,* 362 U.S. 610 (1960); *United States v. Barnett,* 376 U.S. 681 (1964).

[142] *Cheff v. Schnackenberg,* 384 U.S. 373 (1966).

[143] *Duncan v. Louisiana,* 391 U.S. 145 (1968); *Bloom v. Illinois,* 391 U.S. 194 (1968).

[144] *Bloom v. Illinois,* 391 U.S. 194 at 198, 201, 202 (1968).

[145] Id. at 208, 209.

[146] *Codispoti v. Pennsylvania,* 418 U.S. 506 (1974).

Judicial Restraint

Political and constitutional necessity require the federal courts — limited both in power and in jurisdiction — to exercise their authority with restraint. Most particularly is this true with the Supreme Court. The court has recognized this fact from its earliest years. As one scholar notes, "nearly all of the specific limitations which are said to govern the exercise of judicial review have been announced by the Supreme Court itself." [1]

The rules, principles and doctrines which compose this posture of restraint have evolved as the court has said "yes" to some cases and "no" to others. They usually develop from the "threshold questions" — the seemingly technical issues which the court must resolve before moving on to the "merits," or the substance, of the controversy. The elements of restraint are given sometimes overlapping labels — "case or controversy" requirement, advisory opinion, "mootness," "friendly" suits, test cases, "standing to sue," precedent and *stare decisis,* "political questions," and comity.

For those whose memory of recent debates over judicial activism and judicial restraint is fresh, it may come as a surprise to learn that even during "activist" periods of Supreme Court history the rules have rarely changed. Only their application has varied.

Justices often differ on whether a case is moot, whether a litigant has standing, or whether a question is "political" — but few have advocated discarding any of those standards. In 1938 Justice Louis D. Brandeis set out some of these rules in a form cited so often that it has become a classic exposition of judicial restraint.

The justice — to summarize the Brandeis rules, included in a concurring opinion in the case *Ashwander v. Tennessee Valley Authority* — said that the court avoided deciding many constitutional questions by adhering to the rules that:

● It would not consider the constitutionality of legislation in friendly, non-adversary cases.

● It would not decide any constitutional question before a decision on such matter was necessary.

● It would not set out any constitutional rule broader than warranted by the facts in the particular case before it.

● It would resolve a dispute on a non-constitutional basis rather than a constitutional basis, if possible.

● It would not consider a challenge to a law's validity brought by someone who fails to demonstrate that he has been injured by the law or by someone who had benefited from the law.

● When an act of Congress was challenged as invalid, the court would be certain there was no possible interpretation under which the law could be found constitutional before striking it down as unconstitutional. [2] *(Text of* Ashwander *rules, p. 288)*

These rules, as Chief Justice Earl Warren and others have taken pains to point out, are neither absolute nor purely constitutional. In them, the court has blended political reality, policy considerations and constitutional elements into a posture of judicial restraint — which the court applies as it wishes from case to case. Thus it is quite possible to find major decisions of the court which count as exceptions to every one of Brandeis' rules — as well as to others he did not mention.

Cases and Controversies

The single most basic restriction on the work of the federal courts is the requirement that they decide only "cases or controversies." Article III states that federal judicial power extends to certain types of "cases" and certain "controversies." The Supreme Court has interpreted those words to limit the power of federal courts to resolving disputes between adversary parties whose legal rights and interests are truly in collision.

To qualify, Chief Justice Charles Evans Hughes once explained:

> . . . The controversy must be definite and concrete, touching the legal relations of parties having adverse legal interests. . . . It must be a real and substantial controversy admitting of specific relief through a decree of a conclusive character, as distinguished from an opinion advising what the law would be upon a hypothetical state of facts. [3]

The practical value of this requirement — aside from the limiting function it has on possible federal caseloads — is, in the words of Justice Felix Frankfurter, that real cases and controversies have "that clear concreteness provided when a question emerges precisely framed and necessary for decision from a clash of adversary argument exploring every aspect of a multi-faced situation embracing conflicting and demanding interests." [4]

A more modern term to describe a case or controversy properly before the court is "justiciable." Chief Justice Earl Warren in 1968 described this concept — and its link to the "case or controversy" doctrine. *(Box, p. 289)*

Advisory Opinions

One of the earliest corollaries developed by the court from the Constitution's use of "case" and "controversy" was its firm decision that neither it nor lower federal courts would give advisory opinions. The federal courts do not speak simply to give advice on abstract issues or hypothetical situations.

In 1793, the justices of the Supreme Court politely refused to answer a set of questions submitted to them by Secretary of State Thomas Jefferson, on behalf of President George Washington, concerning neutrality and the court's interpretation of several major treaties with Britain and France. [5] The court indicated in correspondence that it found the issuance of such advisory opinions contrary to the basic separation of powers and functions in the federal government.

More than a century later, the court reaffirmed this stance with its decision in the case, *Muskrat v. United States.* [6]

Congress, desiring to determine the constitutionality of certain laws it had passed concerning Indian lands, authorized certain Indians to sue the United States to obtain a Supreme Court ruling on that question. When the case reached the court in 1911, the court dismissed it as outside its power because no actual dispute existed: all parties to the case were in reality working together to ascertain the constitutionality of the law, not to resolve any actual conflict between legal rights or concrete interests.

Justice Brandeis and Rules of Restraint

In 1938 Justice Louis D. Brandeis delineated, in a concurring opinion in *Ashwander* v. *Tennessee Valley Authority,* a set of court-formulated rules useful in avoiding constitutional decisions. The portion of his opinion setting forth those rules is as follows:

The Court developed, for its own governance in the cases confessedly within its jurisdiction, a series of rules under which it has avoided passing upon a large part of all the constitutional questions pressed upon it for decision. They are:

1. The Court will not pass upon the constitutionality of legislation in a friendly, non-adversary, proceeding, declining because to decide such questions "is legitimate only in the last resort, and as a necessity in the determination of real, earnest and vital controversy between individuals. It never was the thought that, by means of a friendly suit, a party beaten in the legislature could transfer to the courts an inquiry as to the constitutionality of the legislative act." *Chicago & Grand Trunk Ry.* v. *Wellman,* 143 U.S. 339, 345. Compare *Lord* v. *Veazie,* 8 How. 251; *Atherton Mills* v. *Johnston,* 259 U.S. 13, 15.

2 The Court will not "anticipate a question of constitutional law in advance of the necessity of deciding it." *Liverpool, N.Y. & P.S.S. Co.* v. *Emigration Commissioners,* 113 U.S. 33, 39; [1] *Abrams* v. *Van Schaick,* 293 U.S. 188; *Wilshire Oil Co.* v. *United States,* 295 U.S. 100. "It is not the habit of the Court to decide questions of a constitutional nature unless absolutely necessary to a decision of the case." *Burton* v. *United States,* 196 U.S. 283, 295.

3. The Court will not "formulate a rule of constitutional law broader than is required by the precise facts to which it is to be applied." *Liverpool, N.Y. & P.S.S. Co.* v. *Emigration Commissioners, supra.* Compare *Hammond* v. *Schappi Bus Line,* 275 U.S. 164, 169-172.

4. The Court will not pass upon a constitutional question although properly presented by the record, if there is also present some other ground upon which the case may be disposed of. This rule has found most varied application. Thus, if a case can be decided on either of two grounds, one involving a constitutional question, the other a question of statutory construction or general law, the Court will decide only the latter. *Siler* v. *Louisville & Nashville R. Co.,* 213 U.S. 175, 191; *Light* v. *United States,* 220 U.S. 523, 538. Appeals from the highest court of a state challenging its decision of a question under the Federal Constitution are frequently dismissed because the judgment can be sustained on an independent state ground. *Berea College* v. *Kentucky,* 211 U.S. 45, 53.

5. The Court will not pass upon the validity of a statute upon complaint of one who fails to show that he is injured by its operation. [2] *Tyler* v. *The Judges,* 179 U.S. 405; *Hendrick* v. *Maryland,* 235 U.S. 610, 621. Among the many applications of this rule, none is more striking than the denial of the right of challenge to one who lacks a personal or property right. Thus, the challenge by a public official interested only in the performance of his official duty will not be entertained. *Columbus & Greenville Ry.* v. *Miller,* 283 U.S. 96, 99-100. In *Fairchild* v. *Hughes,* 258 U.S. 126, the Court affirmed the dismissal of a suit brought by a citizen who sought to have the Nineteenth Amendment declared unconstitutional. In *Massachusetts* v. *Mellon,* 262 U.S. 447, the challenge of the federal Maternity Act was not entertained although made by the Commonwealth on behalf of all its citizens.

6. The Court will not pass upon the constitutionality of a statute at the instance of one who has availed himself of its benefits. [3] *Great Falls Mfg. Co.* v. *Attorney General,* 124 U.S. 581; *Wall* v. *Parrot Silver & Copper Co.,* 244 U.S. 407, 411-412; *St. Louis Malleable Casting Co.* v. *Prendergast Construction Co.,* 260 U.S. 469.

7. "When the validity of an act of the Congress is drawn in question, and even if a serious doubt of constitutionality is raised, it is a cardinal principle that this Court will first ascertain whether a construction of the statute is fairly possible by which the question may be avoided." *Crowell* v. *Benson,* 285 U.S. 22, 62. [4]

---

[1] E.g., *Ex parte Randolph,* 20 Fed. Cas. No. 11,558, pp. 242, 254; *Charles River Bridge* v. *Warren Bridge,* 11 Pet. 420, 553; *Trade-Mark Cases,* 100 U.S. 82, 96; *Arizona* v. *California,* 283 U.S. 423, 462-464.

[2] E.g., *Hatch* v. *Reardon,* 204 U.S. 152, 160-161; *Corporation Commission* v. *Lowe,* 281 U.S. 431, 438; *Heald* v. *District of Columbia,* 259 U.S. 114, 123; *Sprout* v. *South Bend,* 277 U.S. 163, 167; *Concordia Fire Insurance Co.* v. *Illinois,* 292 U.S. 535, 547.

[3] Compare *Electric Co.* v. *Dow,* 166 U.S. 489; *Pierce* v. *Somerset Ry.,* 171 U.S. 641, 648; *Leonard* v. *Vicksburg, S. & P. R. Co.,* 198 U.S. 416, 422.

[4] E.g., *United States* v. *Delaware & Hudson Co.,* 213 U.S. 366, 407-408; *United States* v. *Jin Fuey Moy,* 241 U.S. 394, 401; *Baender* v. *Barnett,* 255 U.S. 224; *Texas* v. *Eastern Texas R. Co.,* 258 U.S. 204, 217; *Panama R. Co.* v. *Johnson,* 264 U.S. 375, 390; *Linder* v. *United States,* 268 U.S. 5, 17-18; *Missouri Pacific R. Co.* v. *Boone,* 270 U.S. 466, 471-472; *Richmond Screw Anchor Co.* v. *United States,* 275 U.S. 331, 346; *Blodgett* v. *Holden,* 275 U.S. 142, 148; *Lucas* v. *Alexander,* 279 U.S. 573, 577; *Interstate Commerce Commission* v. *Oregon-Washington R. & N. Co.,* 288 U.S. 14, 40.

In the court's opinion, Justice William R. Day wrote that a judgment in such a case would be "no more than an expression of opinion upon the validity of the acts in question."[7] That was not the court's function.

When the use of declaratory judgments by lower courts was begun a few years later, one of the main questions raised by this new remedy was whether or not it was appropriate for use by federal courts, given the case or controversy requirement of federal jurisdiction. The court eventually approved its use. (*Details, p. 278*)

Mootness

A second corollary of this requirement is the rule that the court will not decide a case when circumstances are sufficiently altered by time or events to remove the dispute or conflict of interests. Such cases are then dead, or "moot": for purposes of federal jurisdiction, they no longer exist. There is nothing left for the court to resolve; a judgment would have no effect beyond a mere expression of opinion.

The court has long defined its function as "to decide actual controversies by a judgment which can be carried into effect, and not to give opinions upon moot questions or abstract propositions, or to declare principles or rules of law which cannot affect the matter in issue in the case before it." [8]

One of the more recent instances of the court's refusing to resolve a matter because the case presenting it was moot came in 1974. Marco DeFunis came to the court charging that he had been denied admission to a state university law school in order that his place in the class might be given, under an affirmative action program, to a less qualified minority applicant. DeFunis, in the course of his lawsuit, had obtained a court order directing the school to admit him. By the time his case was argued before the Supreme Court, he was in his final year of law school. The court — in the spring that he would graduate — held the case moot: whatever their decision, it would not have affected DeFunis, who was to graduate regardless. [9]

Exceptions to the Rule

But the court has developed a number of exceptions to the rigid application of this rule. In criminal cases where the defendant has served out his sentence, the court still finds his case viable if there is the possibility he will continue to suffer adverse legal consequences as a result of the conviction he is challenging. [10]

A similar rule applies in civil cases if the challenged judgment or situation may continue to have an adverse effect on the plaintiff.

Such an exception also exists for conduct and situations which are necessarily of short duration, "capable of repetition, yet evading review" if the mootness rule is strictly applied.

A recent example of the application of this "capable of repetition" exception is the 1973 abortion decision in *Doe v. Bolton, Roe v. Wade.* The plaintiffs in the cases challenging state laws against abortions included pregnant women. Given the predictable nine-month term of a pregnancy, and the less predictable but usually slower term of a constitutional case making its way to the Supreme Court, it was no surprise that the women were no longer pregnant when the case arrived at the Supreme Court.

But the court rejected the argument that the end of these pregnancies made the case moot. This, wrote Justice Harry A. Blackmun for the court, was a clear situation in which a condition "capable of repetition" might never win Supreme Court review if the standard of mootness were applied rigidly. [11]

Election cases — challenging the application of certain election law requirements — provide another example of cases where the actual dispute may end — after an election is held — yet the problem remains. [12]

The Tip of An Iceberg

The concept of justiciability — the characteristic which makes a case appropriate for review — was described by Chief Justice Earl Warren in 1968. He linked the concept to the court's self-imposed rules implementing the "case and controversy" doctrine:

The jurisdiction of federal courts is defined and limited by Article III of the Constitution. In terms relevant to the question for decision in this case, the judicial power of federal courts is constitutionally restricted to 'cases' and 'controversies.' As is so often the situation in constitutional adjudication, those two words have an iceberg quality, containing beneath their surface simplicity submerged complexities which go to the very heart of our constitutional form of government. Embodied in the words 'cases' and 'controversies' are two complementary but somewhat different limitations. In part those words limit the business of the federal courts to questions presented in an adversary context and in a form historically viewed as capable of resolution through the judicial process. And in part those words define the role assigned to the judiciary in a tripartite allocation of power to assure that federal courts will not intrude into areas committed to the other branches of government. Justiciability is the term of art employed to give expression to this dual limitation placed upon federal courts by the case-and-controversy doctrine.

Justiciability is itself a concept of uncertain meaning and scope. Its reach is illustrated by the various grounds upon which questions sought to be adjudicated in federal courts have been held not to be justiciable. Thus no justiciable controversy is presented when the parties seek adjudication of only a political question, when the parties are asking for an advisory opinion, when the question sought to be adjudicated has been mooted by subsequent developments, and when there is no standing to maintain the action. . . .

Source: *Flast v. Cohen*, 392 U.S. 83 at 94-95 (1968).

'Friendly' Suits and Test Cases

Taken at face value, the court's insistence on actual cases and disputes involving clearly colliding legal interests precludes its ruling in any "friendly" suits — those in which there is no real or substantial controversy but which each side agrees to pursue in order to attain a mutually desired judicial resolution.

In 1850, Chief Justice Roger B. Taney minced no words when he spoke for the court to dismiss such a case. He found such collusion "contempt of the court, and highly reprehensible." [13]

The classic statement on "friendly suits" came in 1892, when the court backed up a state court's refusal to declare unconstitutional a state law regulating railroad fares. Writing the court's opinion, Justice David J. Brewer explained:

. . . The theory upon which, apparently, this suit was brought is that parties have an appeal from the

Judicial Immunity

One restraint to which judges are not vulnerable in their exercise of judicial power is the threat of civil damage suits. Judges may not be sued for their official actions, no matter how erroneous or injurious these acts may be. That has been a rule of the federal judicial system throughout its history, proclaimed most firmly by the Supreme Court in an 1872 ruling involving the judge who presided over the trial of one of the men accused of the murder of Abraham Lincoln.

In that case of *Bradley v. Fisher,* Justice Stephen Field wrote:

> . . . it is a general principle of the highest importance to the proper administration of justice that a judicial officer, in exercising the authority vested in him, shall be free to act upon his own convictions, without apprehension of personal consequence to himself. Liability to answer to everyone who might feel himself aggrieved by the action of the judge, would be inconsistent with the possession of this freedom, and would destroy that independence without which no judiciary can be either respectable or useful. [1]

Furthermore, stated the court, this immunity was not breached even if the judicial actions protested were taken in bad faith:

> . . . The purity of their motives cannot in this way be the subject of judicial inquiry . . . . If civil actions could be maintained . . . against the judge, because the losing party should see fit to allege in his complaint that the acts of the judge were done with partiality, or maliciously, or corruptly, the protection essential to judicial independence would be entirely swept away. Few persons sufficiently irritated to institute an action against a judge for his judicial acts would hesitate to ascribe any character to the acts which would be essential to the maintenance of the action. [2]

The only situation in which such cases might be allowed was when the challenged acts were taken to affect a matter over which the judge had no jurisdiction.

"[F]or malice or corruption in their action whilst exercising their judicial functions within the general scope of their jurisdiction," the court concluded, "judges . . . can only be reached by public prosecution in the form of impeachment, or in such other form as may be specially prescribed." [3]

The complete protection of this immunity was affirmed by the court in a 1967 ruling. The justices held this immunity unaffected by the federal civil rights law which allows damage suits to be brought against anyone who deprives another person of his civil rights while acting under "color of law."

And in a 1978 decision the court held that this immunity protected a state judge from a damage suit resulting from his allowing a teenager to be sterilized without her knowledge or consent.[4]

Judges, however, enjoy no such immunity from prosecution under the criminal laws if they commit a crime, or engage in other illegal action ouside their judicial office.

Tax Immunity? The Constitution stipulates that the compensation paid to judges shall not be reduced during their time in office. Using this provision as the basis for their holding, the Supreme Court in 1920 ruled that a federal judge appointed to his post before passage of the federal income tax law could not be forced to pay income taxes because to do so would unconstitutionally reduce his salary.

Five years later, the Supreme Court extended this immunity to judges appointed after the income tax law took effect.[5]

But this exemption was short-lived. Congress in 1932 expressly applied the income tax to the salaries of judges taking office after mid-1932. And in 1939, the court upheld the 1932 law and overruled its 1920 decision, stating that to require judges to pay a nondiscriminatory federal income tax was "merely to recognize that judges are also citizens, and that their particular function in government does not generate an immunity from sharing with their fellow citizens the material burden of the government whose Constitution and laws they are charged with administering." [6]

[1] *Bradley v. Fisher,* 13 Wall. 335 at 347 (1872).
[2] Id. at 347, 348.
[3] Id. at 354.
[4] *Pierson v. Ray,* 386 U.S. 547 (1967); *Stump v. Sparkman,*

435 U.S. 349 (1978).
[5] *Evans v. Gore,* 253 U.S. 245 (1920); *Miles v. Graham,* 268 U.S. 501 (1925).
[6] *O'Malley v. Woodrough,* 307 U.S. 277 at 282 (1939).

Legislature to the courts; and that the latter are given an immediate and general supervision of the constitutionality of the acts of the former. Such is not true. Whenever, in pursuance of an honest and actual antagonistic assertion of rights by one individual against another, there is presented a question involving the validity of any Act of any Legislature, state or federal, and the decision necessarily rests on the competency of the Legislature to so enact, the court must, in the exercise of its solemn duties, determine whether the Act be constitutional or not; but such an exercise of power is the ultimate and supreme function of courts.

It is legitimate only in the last resort, and as a necessity in the determination of real, earnest, and vital controversy between individuals. It never was the thought that, by means of a friendly suit, a party beaten in the Legislature could transfer to the courts an inquiry as to the constitutionality of the legislative Act. [14]

Yet some of the landmark decisions in the court's history have come in "friendly" cases, arranged because both sides were interested in obtaining a final judicial determination of a question. Perhaps the first such case was the tax case of *Hylton v. United States*, decided in 1796. In that case the government paid the attorneys for both sides in order to get the case taken all the way to the High Court. [15]

Among other major cases which could have been rejected as friendly suits are *Fletcher v. Peck* (1810), *Dred Scott v. Sandford* (1857) and — only a few years after Justice Brewer's ringing statement — *Pollock v. Farmers' Loan and Trust Co.* (1895). [16] In the last case, brought by a stockholder in a bank seeking an order directing the bank not to pay certain federal income taxes — a result which the bank was happy to encourage — the court held the peacetime federal income tax unconstitutional. Justice Brewer made no comment on the "friendly" nature of the suit. (*Details*, pp. 310, 135, 109)

A more modern example came in 1936, when the court struck down a major New Deal statute in the case of *Carter v. Carter Coal Company*, brought by the president of the company against the company and the other officers, among whom was his own father. [17] (*Details*, p. 98)

In the same vein, although the court has refused to rule on some obviously concocted "test cases" like *Muskrat*, it does not dismiss cases simply because they have been selected by the administration or some pressure group as the proper vehicle to "test" a law. The court's decision to hear or dismiss such a test case usually turns on whether or not it presents an actual conflict of legal rights susceptible of judicial resolution.

'Standing to Sue'

Not only must there be an actual legal dispute to justify a federal case, but such cases may only be brought by persons directly involved in or affected by that dispute. The question of whether a person has a sufficient interest at stake in such a dispute is described as a question of legal "standing." Chief Justice Earl Warren once commented that such questions serve " 'on occasion, as a short-hand expression for all the various elements of justiciability.' "[18]

Basically, the Supreme Court has required that to bring a federal suit, a person must have "such a personal stake in the outcome of the controversy as to assure that concrete adverseness which sharpens the presentation of issues upon which the court so largely depends for illumination of difficult constitutional questions." [19]

In most cases involving private disputes, the injury or interest asserted is clear beyond question. Issues of legal standing, therefore, tend to generate more discussion and debate when they arise in cases in which laws or other government action are challenged as unconstitutional; in these cases, the relationship between the plaintiff and the challenged action is more remote.

Frothingham v. Mellon. Perhaps the best illustration of the way in which the court has addressed the issue of standing to sue is provided by several of the "taxpayer" suits decided over the last half-century.

The first was actually a pair of cases. The state of Massachusetts and Mrs. Frothingham, a federal taxpayer, came to the Supreme Court challenging as unconstitutional the use of federal grants-in-aid to states for maternal and child health programs. Massachusetts argued that such federal aid invaded the powers reserved to the states by the Tenth Amendment; Mrs. Frothingham asserted in addition that such an improper use of her tax money effectively deprived her of her property without due process of law as guaranteed by the Fifth Amendment.

The Supreme Court refused to address those constitutional arguments, finding that neither the state nor the taxpayer had standing to bring the cases in the first place.

Writing for the court in 1923, Justice George Sutherland found the question posed by Massachusetts to be "political, and not judicial in character" and thus outside the court's jurisdiction. [20] In addition, Mrs. Frothingham's interest in the use of federal revenues was "comparatively minute and indeterminable" and the effect of federal payments from those funds upon her future tax burden "so remote, fluctuating, and uncertain," that she lacked an adequate personal interest in the situation to bring the federal challenge. [21] (The court did note, however, that local taxpayers often had sufficient interest at stake to bring justiciable cases challenging local expenditures.)[22]

Sutherland explained the court's reasoning concerning federal taxpayer suits:

> The administration of any statute, likely to produce additional taxation to be imposed upon a vast number of taxpayers, the extent of whose several liability is indefinite and constantly changing, is essentially a matter of public and not of individual concern. If one taxpayer may champion and litigate such a cause, then every other taxpayer may do the same . . . in respect of every other appropriation act and statute whose administration requires the outlay of public money, and whose validity may be questioned. The bare suggestion of such a result, with its attendant inconveniences, goes far to sustain the conclusion which we have reached, that a suit of this character cannot be maintained. [23]

In conclusion, Sutherland reiterated the court's view that its power to review the validity of Acts of Congress was not a general one, but was properly invoked "only when the justification for some direct injury suffered or threatened, presenting a justiciable issue, is made to rest upon such an act." The person invoking the exercise of this aspect of federal judicial power, declared the court, "must be able to show not only that the statute is invalid, but that he has sustained or is immediately in danger of sustaining some direct injury as the result of its enforcement, and not merely that he suffers in some indefinite way in common with people generally." [24]

Until 1968, the court's ruling in *Frothingham v. Mellon* was interpreted to bar virtually all taxpayer efforts to challenge the constitutionality of a federal law, unless the taxpayer could show some additional personal stake in its enforcement.

Flast v. Cohen. In 1968, however, the court modified this rule with its decision in *Flast v. Cohen*. Mrs. Flast, a federal taxpayer, sued Secretary of Health, Education and Welfare Wilbur J. Cohen to halt the use of federal funds under the Elementary and Secondary Education Act of 1965 to aid pupils in parochial, as well as public, schools. This use of her tax monies, argued Mrs. Flast, violated the First Amendment ban on establishment of religion and on government efforts to impede the free exercise of religion.

A three-judge federal panel dismissed her case, citing *Frothingham v. Mellon.*

But the Supreme Court reversed that decision, ruling that a federal taxpayer does have standing to bring constitutional challenges to federal spending and taxing programs when he alleges that they conflict with constitutional provisions restricting the taxing and spending power of Congress. A federal taxpayer, wrote Chief Justice Earl

A Wrong, But No Right

Unless a person can assert a federally protected right or interest which has been injured or threatened with injury, he lacks the essential element of a federal case.

The Latin maxim — *damnum absque injuria* — describes the situation: there is loss, but no injury sufficient to provide a basis for judicial remedy.

In 1938, such a situation was before the court in the case of *Alabama Power Company v. Ickes* (302 U.S. 464). The privately owned company came into federal court seeking to halt federal grants to cities within its service area. The grants were to enable the cities to set up their own utility systems, as competitors to the private system. The company argued that such grants were unlawful and asserted, as the necessary injury, the loss of business it would suffer from such competition.

The Supreme Court dismissed the case. The company had no protected legal or equitable right to operate free of competition, and so it had no standing to challenge the validity of the grants. The court wrote that if the company's business was destroyed or curtailed, "it will be by lawful competition from which no legal wrong results." What the company sought to claim, continued the court, was "damage to something it does not possess — namely, a right to be immune from lawful municipal competition." (at 480)

Warren, "may or may not have the requisite personal stake in the outcome, depending upon the circumstances of the particular case. Therefore, we find no absolute bar in Article III to suits of federal taxpayers challenging allegedly unconstitutional federal taxing and spending programs." [25]

To prove the "requisite personal stake," wrote Warren, a taxpayer must establish a logical connection, or nexus, between his taxpayer status and the claim he brought to the court. In this case, Mrs. Flast had done so, and so the lower federal court should go on to consider the substance of her challenge. The establishment of this connection assured that a taxpayer was not simply seeking "to employ a federal court as a forum in which to air his generalized grievances about the conduct of government or the allocation of power in the Federal System," Warren continued. That was still an impermissible use of the federal courts. [26]

That particular portion of the *Flast* opinion was cited frequently by the court in the 1970s, as it made clear that despite *Flast*, there was still a standing requirement for federal cases.

In 1974, with the decision in *United States v. Richardson*, the court held that a taxpayer did not have standing to challenge the secrecy of the Central Intelligence Agency's budget, a secrecy he alleged to be in direct conflict with the Constitution. Writing for the court, Chief Justice Warren E. Burger explained that this was not a challenge to the power to tax or to spend — the only sort of taxpayer challenge which Flast had addressed — but rather to the laws concerning the CIA. Furthermore, he wrote, Richardson did not allege that as a taxpayer he was suffering any particular concrete injury as a result of this secrecy. [27]

A concurring opinion by Justice Lewis F. Powell Jr. noted the lowering of standing requirements over the three preceding decades, through statutes granting standing to bring certain cases, and through court rulings such as *Baker*

v. Carr, [28] allowing voters to challenge state malapportionment, and *Flast v. Cohen*. However, wrote Powell, despite these developments, "the Court has not broken with the traditional requirement that, in the absence of a specific statutory grant of the right of review, a plaintiff must allege some particularized injury that sets him apart from the man on the street." [29] This point was emphasized by a series of rulings in which the court held that persons lacked standing to challenge military surveillance programs, the membership of some members of Congress in the armed forces reserves, municipal zoning ordinances and the tax-exempt status of certain hospitals. [30]

The Asserted Interest. One area in which the modern court has clearly enlarged access to the federal judiciary is in the categories of interests which may be asserted by citizens and taxpayers in federal cases. The asserted interest may be economic, constitutional, aesthetic, conservationist or recreational — but it still must be personal, rather than general, although in certain voting rights and environmental cases, that requirement too has been applied flexibly. [31]

Although the court generally has insisted that a plaintiff be arguing his own interest as the primary one — not that of a third party — there have been notable exceptions to that rule. [32] As early as 1915, the court allowed alien *employees* to challenge a state law requiring *employers* to hire four times as many residents as aliens. [33] A decade later, the court allowed a religious organization which operated a *parochial school* to challenge a state law penalizing *parents* who did not send their children to public schools. [34]

In situations where it appears unlikely that the persons most directly affected by the challenged law will be able to bring their own legal protest into court, the justices have generally allowed less affected persons to make the challenge. Such was apparently the reasoning behind several cases in which white plaintiffs challenged laws restricting the rights of blacks to live or buy property in certain neighborhoods. [35] And in some recent cases, the court has allowed doctors to challenge laws restricting the advice or treatment they may give their patients. [36]

Organizations whose members are injured by government action may assert the interest of their members in seeking judicial review, but the court has made clear that there must be injury — as well as an interest — in such cases. [37]

States, acting as *parens patriae*, are allowed to bring some federal suits in behalf of their citizens, challenging acts which are injurious to the health or welfare of the entire population. *Massachusetts v. Mellon*, however, made clear that such *parens patriae* suits may not be brought against the federal government. [38]

Political Questions

In his classic discussion of judicial power in the court's opinion in *Marbury v. Madison*, Chief Justice John Marshall declared:

The province of the court, is, solely, to decide on the rights of individuals, not to inquire how the executive, or executive officers, perform duties in which they have a discretion. Questions in their nature political, or which are, by the constitution and laws, submitted to the executive, can never be made in this court. [39]

Since that time, the court has employed this "political question" doctrine as a convenient device for avoiding head-on collisions with Congress, the President or the states on matters ranging from foreign relations to malapportioned congressional districts.

The attributes of this doctrine are quite variable. One modern justice has observed that they "in various settings, diverge, combine, appear and disappear in seeming disorderliness."[40] Several decades earlier, a scholar suggested that expediency was indeed the chief determinant of "political questions."[41]

State Governments

The Constitution provides that the United States shall guarantee to every state a republican form of government. When the question of enforcing that guarantee came to the Supreme Court in 1849, the court made clear that this was indeed a "political question."

The case of *Luther v. Borden* involved two competing groups, each asserting that they were the lawful government of Rhode Island. In the court's opinion, Chief Justice Roger B. Taney stated firmly that "it rests with Congress to decide what government is the established one in a state."[42] Taney continued:

> ... when the senators and representatives of a State are admitted into the councils of the Union, the authority of the government under which they are appointed, as well as its republican character, is recognized by the proper constitutional authority. And its decision is binding on every other department of the government, and could not be questioned in a judicial tribunal.[43]

In the same case, the court displayed a similar deference to the decision of the president, as authorized by law, to call out the militia of a state to suppress an insurrection there.[44]

The court has remained quite consistent in applying the political question doctrine to refuse cases in which persons attempt to use this "guaranty" provision of the Constitution as a basis for challenging state government or state action.[45] Tennessee was unsuccessful, however, when it attempted to use this line of precedents to shield its state legislative apportionment statute from judicial review in *Baker v. Carr.*[46]

Foreign Affairs

The court has generally left questions of foreign policy and foreign affairs to the political branches. In 1829, the court refused to settle an international border question, stating that it was not the role of the judiciary to assert national interests against foreign powers.[47] That point has been steadily reaffirmed throughout the history of the court, based firmly on the court's view that in foreign affairs the nation should speak with a single voice.[48] *(Details, p. 200)*

Legislative Process

In similar fashion, the court has generally used the political question doctrine to refuse to intervene in questions of legislative process or procedure, including issues concerning constitutional amendments, leaving their resolution to Congress or the states.[49]

The exception to that general practice has come in cases raising questions of basic constitutional standards — such as the power of Congress over certain subjects or the propriety of a chamber's excluding a member who meets the constitutional qualifications and has been duly elected — or in matters such as the pocket veto case where the political branches deadlock on an issue.[50] *(Details, pp. 165, 222)*

Legislative Apportionment

For most of the nation's history, the court also viewed challenges to state decisions allocating population among electoral districts as a political question outside the realm of judicial consideration.

In 1946, Justice Felix Frankfurter made clear that this view was based on practical political considerations:

> ... Nothing is clearer than that this controversy [over malapportionment of Illinois congressional districts] concerns matters that bring courts into immediate and active relations with party contests. From the determination of such issues this Court has traditionally held aloof. It is hostile to a democratic system to involve the judiciary in the politics of the people.[51]

Sixteen years later, the court overturned that ruling — and held that its earlier refusal to intervene in apportionment matters was based on an overbroad view of the "political question" doctrine. The decision was *Baker v. Carr,* in which the court held that challenges to malapportionment of state legislatures were justiciable.

After reviewing the line of "political question" cases, Justice William J. Brennan Jr. stated for the majority that:

> ... it is the relationship between the judiciary and the coordinate branches of the Federal Government, and not the federal judiciary's relationship to the States, which gives rise to the 'political question.' ...
> ... The nonjusticiability of a political question is primarily a function of the separation of powers. ....[52]

The basic question of fairness at the heart of the lawsuit which had begun *Baker v. Carr,* Brennan concluded for the court, was a constitutional, not a political, one, and was well within the jurisdiction of the court. Simply "the presence of a matter affecting state government does not [in and of itself] render the case nonjusticiable."[53]

Political Questions and Practical Politics

Writing in 1936, C. Gordon Post described the political question doctrine as a judicial concession founded "in the inadequacy of the judiciary itself." He continued:

> If the court found it better to limit its jurisdiction, to restrict its power of review, it was not because of the doctrine of the separation of powers or because of a lack of rules, but because of expediency. If the court left certain questions pertaining to foreign relations in the hands of the political departments, it was because in our foreign relations a unified front is sensible, practical and expedient. If the court placed the question of whether a state ... possessed or did not possess a republican form of government within the jurisdiction of the political departments, it was because of very practical considerations. If the court was fully conscious that its mandate could not, or would not, be enforced in the particular case, obviously it was more expedient to leave the matter to the political departments exclusively. In general, judicial review or not, the court has found it more expedient to leave the decision of certain questions to governmental bodies more appropriately adapted to decide them.[54]

The Role of Precedent

Supreme Court decisions are final — subject only to infrequent situations in which Congress can and does overrule them by statute, where Congress and the states amend the Constitution to reverse the court, and where the court itself decides to overturn precedent.

The doctrine of *stare decisis* — "let the decision stand" — binds the court to adhere to the decisions of an earlier day. This rule of precedent, wrote one scholar, is linked to "the idea that our law and judicial decisions have a historical continuity — as opposed to a system by which courts might endeavor to render justice in each case anew, as though each case constituted a problem unto itself, in no way related to any previous problems which courts have disposed of." [55]

The doctrine has a very practical basis: the need for stability in law. As Justice Louis D. Brandeis once wrote: "in most matters it is more important that the applicable rule of law be settled than that it be settled right." [56]

And Justice William O. Douglas, no advocate of slavish adherence to precedent, wrote:

> *Stare decisis* provides some moorings so that men may trade and arrange their affairs with confidence. *Stare decisis* serves to take the capricious element out of law and to give stability to a society. It is a strong tie which the future has to the past. [57]

But the application of precedent is not as simple as it might appear. Robert K. Carr explained:

> . . . In actual practice, two cases are rarely, if ever, exactly alike. . . . Thus a judge may have wide discretion in deciding in a given case to follow either precedent A or precedent B, both of which seem to have considerable bearing on the case but which, unfortunately, are completely contradictory to one another. [58]

In more than 100 situations, from 1810 to the present, the court has made exception to the doctrine of *stare decisis* and overruled an earlier decision. Century-old precedents have fallen, as have those barely a year old. [59]

In 1810, the court in the case of *Hudson and Smith v. Guestier* overruled an 1808 decision concerning the jurisdiction of a foreign power over vessels offshore. Chief Justice John Marshall disagreed with the court's decision to overrule the earlier holding. Only two other decisions were overruled by the court during Marshall's tenure as Chief Justice, and only four were reversed by the court during the Chief Justiceship of his successor, Roger B. Taney. [60]

After the Civil War, changing conditions and changing court personnel placed increasing strain on the reverence for precedent. In 1870 the court held the Legal Tender Acts unconstitutional; a year later, with two new members, it reversed itself and upheld the same laws. [61] *(Details, p. 118)*

Twenty-five years later, the court held the statute authorizing a peacetime income tax to be unconstitutional, revising a century-old definition of "direct taxes" — and ignoring previous rulings which would seem to dictate that the court uphold the tax laws. [62] This ruling was itself eventually reversed by adoption of the 16th Amendment in 1913. *(Details, p. 111)*

The Supreme Court of the 20th century has clearly felt itself free to overrule its previous decisions; more than three out of four of the court's self-reversals have come since 1900. The court's reversals on child labor, minimum wage and maximum hour laws, New Deal legislation and state

flag salute laws are among the major chapters in modern Supreme Court history. *(Details, pp. 96-103)*

As its actions have made clear, the modern court views *stare decisis* as "a principle of policy and not a mechanical formula of adherence to the latest decision, however recent and questionable, when such adherence involves collision with a prior doctrine more embracing in its scope, intrinsically sounder, and verified by experience." [63]

The modern court also tends to apply the doctrine more faithfully to questions of statutory law than to constitutional issues. As Justice Stanley Reed explained for the court in 1944:

> . . . we are not unmindful of the desirability of continuity of decision in constitutional questions. However, when convinced of former error, this Court has never felt constrained to follow precedent. In constitutional questions, where correction depends upon amendment, and not upon legislative action this Court throughout its history has freely exercised its power to re-examine the basis of its constitutional decisions. This has long been accepted practice, and this practice has continued to this day. [64]

The rule of precedent is also made more flexible by the court's practice of "distinguishing" a new case from a precedent which would seem to be controlling, pointing out factors which make the two situations different, and justifying a different result. A precedent can eventually be "distinguished" into complete uniqueness — and utter uselessness. This sort of erosion took place during the late 1930s and 1940s with regard to the court's 1896 decision in *Plessy v. Ferguson,* allowing "separate, but equal" facilities for blacks and whites. By the time the court in 1954 officially overruled *Plessy,* the decision's value as a precedent had been destroyed. [65] *(Details, p. 587)*

The rule of precedent creates a certain predictability in the law as proclaimed by the Supreme Court, preserving stability and continuity. But the exceptions to that rule, the departures from the doctrine of *stare decisis,* are one method by which the court adapts the Constitution to new circumstances and new conditions. [66]

The Demands of Comity

The existence of dual judicial systems in the United States — state courts and federal courts — imposes certain peculiar restraints upon the conduct of the federal judiciary. Law enforcement remains primarily the responsibility of state officials; yet the final word on questions of federal law and federal rights is left to the federal courts. The operations of such a dual system require continuing adjustment.

Federal judges have several powerful instruments to wield against improper state action: the writ of *habeas corpus* to order release of a state prisoner detained in violation of his constitutional rights; the injunction to halt improper state proceedings; the declaratory judgment to hold a state law unconstitutional, invalid and unenforceable.

When state action is challenged by persons who ask a federal judge to intervene in state matters, the Supreme Court often counsels restraint, citing the demands of "comity."

Comity, wrote E. S. Corwin, is "a self-imposed rule of judicial morality, whereby independent tribunals of concurrent or coordinate jurisdiction exercise a mutual restraint in order to prevent interference with each other and to avoid collisions of authority." [67]

More simply, Justice Hugo L. Black wrote in 1971, comity is "a proper respect for state functions, a recognition of the fact that the entire country is made up of a Union of separate state governments, and a continuance of the belief that the National Government will fare best if the States and their institutions are left free to perform their separate functions in their separate ways." [68]

Black, years earlier a local police judge, continued:

> . . . This, perhaps for lack of a better and clearer way to describe it, is referred to by many as 'Our Federalism,'. . . . The concept does not mean blind deference to 'States' Rights' any more than it means centralization of control over every important issue in our National Government and its courts. . . . What the concept does represent is a system in which there is sensitivity to the legitimate interest of both State and National Governments, and in which the National Government, anxious though it may be to vindicate

and protect federal rights and federal interests, always endeavors to do so in ways that will not unduly interfere with the legitimate activities of the States. [69]

The demands of comity have produced at least two corollary rules — the requirement that persons who challenge state actions in federal courts first "exhaust" all possible state remedies for their complaint, and the "abstention" doctrine, which requires federal judges to refrain from acting or asserting federal jurisdiction over a matter within state hands until the state courts have had a full opportunity to correct the situation at issue. *(pp. 273, 277)*

The application of these rules by the Supreme Court has led to much debate on and off the bench, particularly in recent decades since the court has applied most of the procedural guarantees of the Bill of Rights to state court proceedings. In the 1960s the Supreme Court tended to find or create new exceptions to these rules of restraint. In the 1970s the court, under different leadership, tended to narrow such exceptions. The process of adjustment continues.

Footnotes

[1] Robert K. Carr, *The Supreme Court and Judicial Review* (New York: Farrar & Rinehart, 1942) p. 185.

[2] *Ashwander v. Tennessee Valley Authority*, 297 U.S. 288 at 346-348 (1938).

[3] *Aetna Life Insurance Company v. Haworth*, 300 U.S. 227 at 240-241 (1937).

[4] *United States v. Fruehauf*, 365 U.S. 146 at 157 (1961).

[5] Alexander M. Bickel, *The Least Dangerous Branch* (Indianapolis: Bobbs-Merrill Co., 1962) pp. 113-114; Charles Warren, *The Supreme Court in United States History*, 2 vols. (Boston: Little, Brown & Co., 1922, 1926), I:110-111.

[6] *Muskrat v. United States*, 219 U.S. 346 (1911).

[7] Id. at 362.

[8] *Mills v. Green*, 159 U.S. 651 at 653 (1895); see also *California v. San Pablo & Tulare Railroad Company*, 149 U.S. 308 at 314 (1893).

[9] *DeFunis v. Odegaard*, 416 U.S. 312 (1974).

[10] *Sibron v. New York*, 392 U.S. 40 (1968); *Benton v. Maryland* 395 U.S. 784 (1969).

[11] *Roe v. Wade*, *Doe v. Bolton*, 410 U.S. 113, 179 (1973); *Southern Pacific Terminal Co. v. Interstate Commerce Commission*, 219 U.S. 498 at 515 (1911).

[12] *Moore v. Ogilvie*, 394 U.S. 814 (1969).

[13] *Lord v. Veazie*, 8 How. 251 at 255 (1850).

[14] *Chicago & Grand Trunk Railway Co. v. Wellman*, 143 U.S. 339 at 344-345 (1892).

[15] *Hylton v. United States*, 3 Dall. 171 (1796).

[16] *Fletcher v. Peck*, 6 Cr. 87 (1810); *Dred Scott v. Sandford*, 19 How. 393 (1857); *Pollock v. Farmers' Loan and Trust Co.*, 157 U.S. 429, 158 U.S. 601 (1895).

[17] *Carter v. Carter Coal Company*, 298 U.S. 238 (1936).

[18] *Flast v. Cohen*, 392 U.S. 83 at 99 (1968).

[19] *Baker v. Carr*, 369 U.S. 186 at 204 (1962).

[20] *Massachusetts v. Mellon*, *Frothingham v. Mellon*, 262 U.S. 447 at 483 (1923).

[21] Id. at 487.

[22] See *Everson v. Board of Education*, 330 U.S. 1 (1947); *Doremus v. Board of Education*, 342 U.S. 429 (1952); *Engel v. Vitale*, 370 U.S. 421 (1962).

[23] *Frothingham v. Mellon*, 262 U.S. 447 at 487 (1923).

[24] Id. at 488.

[25] *Flast v. Cohen*, 392 U.S. 83 at 101 (1968).

[26] Id. at 106.

[27] *United States v. Richardson*, 418 U.S. 166 at 175, 177 (1974).

[28] *Baker v. Carr*, 369 U.S. 186 (1962).

[29] *United States v. Richardson*, 418 U.S. 166 at 193 (1974).

[30] *Laird v. Tatum*, 408 U.S. 1 (1972); *Schlesinger v. Reservists Committee to Stop the War*, 418 U.S. 208 (1974); *Warth v. Seldin*, 422 U.S. 490 (1975); *Simon v. Eastern Kentucky Welfare Rights Organization*, 426 U.S. 26 (1976).

[31] *Association of Data Processing Organizations v. Camp*, 397 U.S. 150 at 154 (1970); *Sierra Club v. Morton*, 405 U.S. 727 at 738-739 (1972); *United States v. Richardson*, 418 U.S. 166 at 193-194 (1974); *Baker v. Carr*, 369 U.S. 186 (1962); *United States v. SCRAP*, 412 U.S. 669 (1973).

[32] *Tileston v. Ullman*, 318 U.S. 44 (1943); *United States v. Raines*, 362 U.S. 17 at 20-24 (1960).

[33] *Truax v. Raich*, 239 U.S. 33 (1915).

[34] *Pierce v. Society of Sisters*, 268 U.S. 510 (1925).

[35] *Buchanan v. Warley*, 245 U.S. 60 (1917); *Barrows v. Jackson* 346 U.S. 249 (1953).

[36] *Griswold v. Connecticut*, 381 U.S. 479 (1965); *Doe v. Bolton*, 410 U.S. 179 (1973); *Singleton v. Wulff*, 428 U.S. 106 (1976).

[37] *Joint Anti-Fascist Refugee Committee v. McGrath*, 341 U.S. 123 (1951); *NAACP v. Alabama ex rel. Patterson*, 357 U.S. 449 (1958); *NAACP v. Button*, 371 U.S. 415 (1963); *Sierra Club v. Morton*, 405 U.S. 727 at 739 (1972).

[38] *Missouri v. Illinois*, 180 U.S. 208 (1901); *Georgia v. Tennessee Copper Company*, 206 U.S. 230 (1907); *Pennsylvania v. West Virginia*, 262 U.S. 553 (1923); *Georgia v. Pennsylvania R. Co.*, 324 U.S. 439 (1945); *Massachusetts v. Mellon*, 262 U.S. 447 (1923).

[39] *Marbury v. Madison*, 1 Cr. 137 at 170 (1803).

[40] *Baker v. Carr*, 369 U.S. 186 at 210 (1962).

[41] C. Gordon Post, *Supreme Court and Political Questions* (Baltimore: Johns Hopkins University Press, 1936; reprint ed. New York: Da Capo Press, 1969) p. 130.

[42] *Luther v. Borden*, 7 How. 1 at 42 (1849).

[43] Id.

[44] Id. at 43; see also *Martin v. Mott*, 12 Wheat. 19 (1827).

[45] *Pacific States Telephone and Telegraph Co. v. Oregon*, 223 U.S. 118 (1912).

[46] *Baker v. Carr*, 369 U.S. 186 at 209-210 (1962).

[47] *Foster v. Neilson*, 2 Pet. 253 at 307 (1829).

[48] *Oetjen v. Central Leather Co.*, 246 U.S. 297 at 302 (1918); *United States v. Curtiss-Wright Export Corporation*, 299 U.S. 304 (1936).

[49] *Hawke v. Smith*, 253 U.S. 221 (1920); *Coleman v. Miller*, 307 U.S. 433 (1939); *Powell v. McCormack*, 395 U.S. 486 (1969).

[50] *Pocket Veto Case*, 279 U.S. 655 (1929).

[51] *Colegrove v. Green*, 328 U.S. 549 at 553-554 (1946).

[52] *Baker v. Carr*, 369 U.S. 186 at 210 (1962).

[53] Id. at 232.

[54] Post, *Supreme Court and Political Questions*, pp. 129-130.

[55] Carr, *Supreme Court and Judicial Review*, pp. 18-19.

[56] *Burnet v. Coronado Oil & Gas Company*, 285 U.S. 393 at 406 (1932).

[57] William O. Douglas, "Stare Decisis," *The Record* of the Association of the Bar of the City of New York, IV (1949), pp. 152-179, reprinted in *The Supreme Court: Views from Inside*, ed. Alan F. Westin (New York: W.W. Norton & Co., 1961), p. 123.

[58] Carr, *Supreme Court and Judicial Review*, pp. 18-19.

[59] Albert P. Blaustein and Andrew H. Field, " 'Overruling' Opinions in the Supreme Court," *Michigan Law Review* 47 (December 1958), pp. 151-194, reprinted in Robert Scigliano, ed. *The Courts: A Reader in the Judicial Process* (Boston: Little, Brown & Co., 1962), pp. 393-408.

[60] *Hudson and Smith v. Guestier*, 6 Cr. 281 (1810), overruling *Rose v. Himely*, 4 Cr. 241 (1808); Blaustein and Field, *op. cit.* p. 397.

[61] *Knox v. Lee*, 12 Wall. 457 (1871) overruling *Hepburn v. Griswold*, 8 Wall. 603 (1870).

[62] *Pollock v. Farmers' Loan and Trust Co.*, 157 U.S. 601 (1895).

[63] *Helvering v. Hallock*, 309 U.S. 106 at 119 (1940).

[64] *Smith v. Allwright*, 321 U.S. 649 at 665-666 (1944) overruling *Grovey v. Townsend*, 295 U.S. 45 (1935).

[65] Blaustein and Field, " 'Overruling' Opinions in the Supreme Court," in *The Courts*, ed. Scigliano, p. 395.

[66] Loren P. Beth, *The Constitution, Politics and the Supreme Court* (New York: Harper & Row, 1962), p. 49.

[67] Edward S. Corwin, ed., *The Constitution of the United States of America: Analysis and Interpretation* (Washington, D.C.: U.S. Government Printing Office, 1953), p. 626.

[68] *Younger v. Harris*, 401 U.S. 37 at 441 (1971).

[69] Id.

Selected Bibliography

Abraham, Henry J. *The Judicial Process,* 2d. ed. rev. New York: Oxford University Press, 1968.

Beth, Loren P. *The Constitution, Politics and the Supreme Court.* New York: Harper & Row, 1962.

Bickel, Alexander M. *The Least Dangerous Branch.* Indianapolis: Bobbs-Merrill Co., 1962.

Black, Charles L. Jr. *Perspectives in Constitutional Law.* Englewood Cliffs, N.J.: Prentice-Hall, 1963.

Carr, Robert K. *The Supreme Court and Judicial Review.* New York: Farrar & Rinehart, 1942.

Corwin, Edward S. *The Constitution of the United States of America.* Washington, D.C.: U.S. Government Printing Office, 1953.

Early, Stephen T. *Constitutional Courts of the United States.* Totowa, N.J.: Littlefield, Adams & Co., 1977.

Frankfurter, Felix, and Landis, James M. *The Business of the Supreme Court: A Study in the Federal Judicial System.* New York: Macmillan Publishing Company, 1928.

Frankfurter, Felix. *The Commerce Clause Under Marshall, Taney and Waite.* Chapel Hill: University of North Carolina Press, 1937.

Freund, Paul A., gen. ed. *History of the Supreme Court of the United States.* New York: Macmillan Publishing Co., 1971, 1974, 1971. Vol. I: *Antecedents and Beginnings to 1801,* by Julius Goebel, Jr.; Vol. V: *The Taney Period, 1836-1964,* by Carl B. Swisher; Vol. VI: *Reconstruction and Reunion, 1864-1888, Part One,* by Charles Fairman.

Haines, Charles G. *The American Doctrine of Judicial Supremacy.* 2d ed. Berkeley, Calif.: University of California Press, 1932.

Hart, Henry M. Jr., and Wechsler, Herbert. *The Federal Courts and the Federal System.* Brooklyn: The Foundation Press, Inc. 1953.

Hughes, Charles Evans. *The Supreme Court of the United States: Its Foundation, Methods and Achievements, An Interpretation.* New York: Columbia University Press, 1928.

Madison, James; Hamilton, Alexander; and Jay, John. *The Federalist Papers.* Introduction by Clinton Rossiter. New York: New American Library, Mentor Books, 1961.

Mason, Alpheus T. *The Supreme Court From Taft To Warren.* Baton Rouge: Louisiana State University Press, 1958.

Post, C. Gordon. *Supreme Court and Political Questions.* Baltimore: Johns Hopkins Press, 1936; reprint ed. New York: Da Capo Press, 1969.

Powell, Thomas Reed. *Vagaries and Varieties in Constitutional Interpretation.* New York: Columbia University Press, 1956; reprint ed. New York: AMS Press, 1967.

Scigliano, Robert, ed. *The Courts: A Reader in the Judicial Process.* Boston: Little, Brown & Co., 1962.

Stern, Robert L., and Gressman, Eugene. *Supreme Court Practice.* 5th ed. Washington, D.C.: Bureau of National Affairs, Inc., 1978.

Swisher, Carl B. *American Constitutional Development.* 2d ed. Cambridge: Houghton Mifflin Co., 1954.

U.S. Congress. Library of Congress. Congressional Reference Service. *The Constitution of the United States of America: Analysis and Interpretation.* Washington, D.C.: U.S. Government Printing Office, 1964, 1973.

Warren, Charles. *The Supreme Court in United States History.* 2 vols. Boston: Little, Brown & Co., 1922, 1926.

Westin, Alan F., ed. *The Supreme Court: Views from Inside.* New York: W.W. Norton & Co., 1961.

Wright, Charles Alan. *Handbook of the Law of Federal Courts,* 2d. ed. St. Paul: West Publishing Co., 1970.

THE COURT AND THE STATES

Introduction 299

Judicial Review and the States 303

The States and the Economy 309

The State and the Individual 337

The State as Sovereign 353

Interstate Relations 365

The Court and the States

"The Constitution looks to an indestructible Union, composed of indestructible States," said the Chief Justice of the United States. The year was 1869, and the Supreme Court had ruled that states lacked the power to secede: The Confederate States, in the court's view, had never left the Union.[1]

Notwithstanding this brave assertion of federal unity, the survival of the Union had seemed far from certain for most of the preceding 80 years. States' rights, interposition, nullification and finally Civil War had all placed the fragile fabric of national authority under intense strain.

In the Reconstruction year of 1869, and many times since, the indestructibility of the states has been called into question. As the national government has gained in strength and authority, the existence of the states as viable governmental units at times has seemed precarious.

The Constitution, written to create the national government, imposes substantial and severe limitations upon the powers and activities of the states. Yet, it assumes their continued operation as effective units of local government.

Gradually, as called upon to interpret the meaning of the Constitution, the Supreme Court has defined those limits upon state powers. Time and again it has struck down state action as in conflict with the Constitution or federal law. This function of the court was particularly significant during the period from the founding of the nation to the Civil War.

But, as Professor Charles Black has pointed out, the court has affirmed the powers of the states even as it has set their limits:

> The states have had to be fenced in, saving their dignity; this is obvious in the nature of the case, and was explicitly provided for in the Constitution and amendments. But the line that marks the limit of their power is necessarily the line that marks the area within which their actions are legitimate.[2]

The National Period

"The general government, though limited as to its objects, is supreme with respect to those objects," wrote Chief Justice John Marshall in 1821:

> With the ample powers confided to this supreme government are connected many express and important limitations on the sovereignty of the states. The powers of the Union, on the great subjects of war,

peace, and commerce . . . are in themselves limitations of the sovereignty of the states. . . .[3]

The success of the Union was by no means a certainty. The confederation that preceded it was a failure: The central government was too weak; the states, too strong.

Overriding all other questions during the nation's first century was the simple one: Would the nation survive? The threat was not from without, but from within. Would centrifugal force — the states' insistence on retaining power that should belong to the national government — force the splintering of the Union?

On the eve of the Civil War, Chief Justice Roger B. Taney would write: "The Constitution was not formed merely to guard the States against danger from foreign nations, but mainly to secure union and harmony at home; for if this object could be attained, there would be but little danger from abroad. . . ."[4]

Until the conflict between states' rights and national power moved onto the battlefields of the Civil War, much of it was focused in the small courtrooms that served as early homes to the U.S. Supreme Court. As Charles Warren, historian of the court's first century, explains:

> The success of the new government depended on the existence of a supreme tribunal, free from local political bias or prejudice, vested with power to give an interpretation to federal laws and treaties which should be uniform throughout the land, to confine the federal authority to its legitimate field of operation, and to control state aggression on the federal domain.[5]

Two of the nation's greatest statesmen, both Virginians, led the national debate of the early decades over the respective rights and powers of the states and the national government. Speaking for the states was Thomas Jefferson, the third president of the United States. Speaking for national supremacy was John Marshall, its fourth Chief Justice.

Three years before Jefferson and Marshall moved into the White House and the Supreme Court chambers, respectively, Jefferson set out his view of the relationship of state to federal power in the Kentucky Resolutions, written to protest congressional enactment of the Alien and Sedition Acts. His view of this relationship contrasted sharply with the "supreme government" view set out by Marshall in 1821.

The Nature of the Union

Four years after the Civil War ended, the Supreme Court — in deciding the case of *Texas v. White* — considered and discussed the meaning of "state" and the nature of the Union.

During the Civil War, the Confederate government of Texas had sold off some of the U.S. bonds in its possession to one George W. White and other purchasers, in return for medical and other needed supplies. After the war, the new government of Texas sued White and the other purchasers to recover title to the bonds. The case was argued before the Supreme Court in February 1869 and was decided on April 12, 1869. The court ruled that Texas could recover title to the bonds, because the actions of the Confederate government were not binding.[1]

Because this case was brought to the court by Texas under the Constitution's grant of original jurisdiction over a case brought by a state, the court first considered the status of the state of Texas. Had it, by its secession and participation in the rebellion against national authority, rendered itself ineligible to bring such suits?

Definition of 'State'

The answer was "no." And in the process of reaching that answer, Chief Justice Salmon P. Chase discussed "the correct idea of a State" and its relationship to the Union:

The word "state" . . . describes sometimes a people or community of individuals united more or less closely in political relations, inhabiting temporarily or permanently the same country; often it denotes only the country or territorial region, inhabited by such a community; not unfrequently it is applied to the government under which the people live; at other times it represents the combined idea of people, territory, and government.

It is not difficult to see that in all these senses the primary conception is that of a people or community. The people, in whatever territory dwelling, either temporarily or permanently, and whether organized under a regular government, or united by looser or less definite relations, constitute the State.

This is undoubtedly the fundamental idea upon which the republican institutions of our own country are established. . . .

In the Constitution the term "state" most frequently expresses the combined idea just noticed of people, territory and government. A State, in the ordinary sense of the Constitution, is a political community of free citizens, occupying a territory of defined boundaries, and organized under a government sanctioned and limited by a written constitution, and established by the consent of the governed. It is the union of such States, under a common constitution, which forms the distinct and

greater political unit, which that Constitution designates as the United States, and makes of the people and States which compose it one people and one country.[2]

Chase then recited the steps Texas took upon seceding:

In all respects, so far as the object could be accomplished by ordinances of the Convention, by Acts of the Legislature, and by votes of the citizens, the relations of Texas to the Union were broken up. . . . Did Texas, in consequence of these Acts, cease to be a State? Or, if not, did the State cease to be a member of the Union? . . .

The Union of the States never was a purely artificial and arbitrary relation. It began among the Colonies, and grew out of common origin, mutual sympathies, kindred principles, similar interests and geographical relations. It was confirmed and strengthened by the necessities of war, and received definite form, and character, and sanction from the Articles of Confederation. By these the Union was solemnly declared to "be perpetual." And when these articles were found to be inadequate . . . the Constitution was ordained "to form a more perfect Union." It is difficult to convey the idea of indissoluble unity more clearly. . . . What can be indissoluble if a perpetual Union, made more perfect, is not?

But the perpetuity and indissolubility of the Union by no means implies the loss of distinct and individual existence, or of the right of self-government by the States. . . . [W]e have already had occasion to remark . . . that "without the States in union, there could be no such political body as the United States." . . . [I]t may be not unreasonably said that the preservation of the States, and the maintenance of their governments are as much within the design and care of the Constitution as the preservation of the Union and the maintenance of the National Government. The Constitution, in all its provisions, looks to an indestructible Union, composed of indestructible States.

When, therefore, Texas became one of the United States, she entered into a [*sic*] indissoluble relation. All the obligations of perpetual union, and all the guaranties of republican government in the Union, attached at once to the State. The Act which consummated her admission into the Union was something more than a compact; it was the incorporation of a new member into the political body. And it was final. . . .[3]

---

[1] *Texas v. White,* 7 Wall. 700 (1869).
[2] Id. at 720-721.
[3] Id. at 724, 725, 726.

The states, wrote Jefferson, "constituted a general government for special purposes, delegated to that government certain definite powers, reserving, each state to itself,

the residuary mass of right to their own self-government . . . Whensoever the general government assumed undelegated powers, its acts are . . . of no force."[6]

By Jefferson's death in 1826, it was clear that Marshall's views, not his, had prevailed. The states were operating under clear and definite constitutional restraints applied firmly by the Supreme Court. The laws of 10 states had fallen as in conflict with federal treaties, as impairing the obligation of contracts, or as interfering too far with the broadly construed powers of Congress.

Six months before his death, Jefferson conceded defeat, as he wrote to a friend:

> I see, as you do ... the rapid strides with which the Federal branch of our Government is advancing towards the usurpation of all the rights reserved to the States, and the consolidation in itself of all powers, foreign and domestic; and that too by constructions which, if legitimate, leave no limits to their power. . . .

> Under the power to regulate commerce, they assume indefinitely that also over agriculture and manufactures. . . . Under the authority to establish postroads, they claim that of cutting down mountains for the construction of roads, of digging canals, and, aided by a little sophistry on the words "general welfare," a right to do, not only the acts to effect that which are sufficiently enumerated and permitted, but whatsoever they shall think or pretend will be for the general welfare.[7]

The process Jefferson so lamented slowed in the decades following his death and that of Marshall in 1835. Chief Justice Taney, Marshall's successor, held views much more congenial to Jefferson's.

During his tenure, the court left undisturbed the basic principles of national supremacy set out by the seminal rulings of the Marshall court. Within that framework, however, the Taney court found room for broad state powers — the power to govern its land, its people and its resources, to ensure the public health and to preserve the public welfare. The rulings recognizing this "police power" survived as good law and strong precedent long after the unfortunate but most famous of the Taney court's rulings in the *Dred Scott* case was overturned, first by war and then by the 14th Amendment.

Preserving the States

During the period of Reconstruction, the Supreme Court protected the southern states from the drastic changes the Radicals in Congress had intended to bring about, specifically in the status and privileges of black citizens. In so doing, the court delayed for almost a century the black man's move toward equality.

Beginning with its decision in the *Slaughterhouse Cases* of 1873, the court limited the list of rights that the 14th Amendment protected against state action. Subsequently it narrowly construed — or struck down as unconstitutional — much of the postwar civil rights legislation.

Half a century later, one scholar would write that had this set of cases been decided otherwise, "the States would have largely lost their autonomy and become, as political entities, only of historical interest. If every civil right possessed by a citizen of a State was to receive the protection of the National Judiciary, and if every case involving such a right was to be subject to its review, the States would be placed in a hopelessly subordinate position. . . . The boundary lines between the States and the National Government would be practically abolished. . . ."[8]

Yet even as this was written, the Supreme Court itself was opening the door to the gradual extension of national protection to the rights of persons threatened by state action.

Protecting Property

In contrast to its feeling, in the post-Civil War period, that the time was not ripe for extension of federal control over the state's treatment of the individual, the Supreme Court did not hesitate to extend federal protection over property threatened by too-vigorous assertion of the state's police powers.

After a brief fling with state regulation in the 1870s and 1880s, the court settled into a laissez-faire posture from which it found the 14th Amendment's due process guarantee just the implement with which to control state regulatory efforts. As the contract clause faded out of use in this fashion, the due process guarantee was wielded more and more.

And using the 10th Amendment's concept of powers reserved to the states — and therefore, the court reasoned, denied to the national government — the court likewise struck down federal regulatory laws as intruding upon the rights of the states. Thus was created a twilight zone, a no-man's land, where regulation could not be effectively imposed by either state or national authority.

The Depression and the New Deal — and the new social and economic realities they created — brought a dramatic end to this period. The court widened the field for state regulation, even as it upheld the extension of federal power deeper than ever into the domain of the states.

Since 1937, explains one scholar, "the Court's function is more like that of a traffic cop — to see that our multiple legislatures, in their many activities, do not collide, to make sure that the road is kept free for national power, which, under the rules laid down in 1789, has the right of way."[9]

Protecting Persons

Even as the court relinquished as no longer necessary its role as guardian of property and commerce against state interference, it began to assert the role of protector of persons against state action.

As written, the Bill of Rights protects persons only against action by the federal government. Early in the nation's history, the court refused to extend those protections to persons threatened by state action.

But in the mid-1920s, the court began using the 14th Amendment's guarantee of due process to protect certain of those individual rights against infringement by the state. First Amendment freedoms of expression were the first to win such protection, followed by due process rights of fair trial and fair treatment for persons suspected or accused of crimes. Then, at mid-century, that amendment's equal protection guarantee came into use as the effective guarantee of individual rights its authors had intended it to be.

Using the equal protection clause as its measure, the court struck down state laws requiring racial segregation in public schools, public transportation and public accommodations, and moved the nation into a new revolution that continues today. Not only black citizens were the beneficiaries of equal protection rulings; in the 1960s and 1970s, the court found the same rationale useful for discarding laws that discriminated against women and aliens as well.

Just as the court's landmark rulings of the Marshall era establishing national supremacy over state rights were met with resistance from the states, so were the rulings of the court under Chief Justice Earl Warren. The court's decision decreeing an end to public school segregation set off a reaction in the southern states comparable in intensity only to the hostility of the previous century's debate over slavery. That antagonism was further inflamed by the Supreme Court's interference with matters previously left entirely to the states — the drawing of electoral district lines and the treatment of criminal suspects. "Impeach Earl Warren" was a frequently seen slogan.

Yet just as Marshall's nationalism was moderated by Taney's recognition of state power, so Warren's tenure was followed by that of Chief Justice Warren E. Burger, who led a court that again gave more weight to the state's right and need to operate with flexibility within the federal system.

In 1971 Justice Hugo L. Black — who came to the court of 1937 as a liberal southern senator and Franklin D. Roosevelt's first appointment to the bench — sounded this theme for the court of the 1970s as he described what he called "Our Federalism":

> . . .a proper respect for state functions, a recognition of the fact that the entire country is made up of a Union of separate state governments, and a continuance of the belief that the National Government will fare best if the States and their institutions are left free to perform their separate functions in their separate ways.[10]

Footnotes

[1] *Texas v. White,* 7 Wall. 700 at 725 (1869).

[2] Charles Lund Black, *The People and the Court* (New York: Macmillan Publishing Co., 1960) p. 143.

[3] *Cohens v. Virginia,* 6 Wheat. 264 at 382 (1821).

[4] *Ableman v. Booth,* 21 How. 506 at 517 (1859).

[5] Charles Warren, *The Supreme Court in United States History,* 2 vols. (Boston: Little, Brown & Co., 1922, 1926) I:5-6.

[6] C. Herman Pritchett, *The American Constitution,* 2d ed (New York: McGraw-Hill Book Co., 1968) p. 65.

[7] Letter to William B. Giles, Dec. 26, 1825, cited in Warren, *The Supreme Court in United States History,* I: 620-621.

[8] Warren, *The Supreme Court in United States History,* II: 547-548.

[9] Alpheus T. Mason, *The Supreme Court from Taft to Warren* (Baton Rouge: Louisiana University Press, 1958) p. 167.

[10] *Younger v. Harris.* 401 U.S. 37 at 44 (1971).

Judicial Review and the States

"I do not think that the United States would come to an end if we lost our power to declare an Act of Congress void," said Justice Oliver Wendell Holmes Jr. "I do think the Union would be imperilled [*sic*] if we could not make that declaration as to the laws of the several states." [1]

While the landmark assertion of judicial review over Acts of Congress in *Marbury v. Madison* was left unused, uncontested and undisturbed for more than half a century after its announcement, the history of the court from its first term to the Civil War is a narrative of continuing controversy over the assertion of its statutory power to review state laws and the decisions of state courts.

During that time, "the chief conflicts arose over the court's decisions restricting the limits of state authority and not over those restricting the limits of congressional power. Discontent with its actions on the latter subject arose, *not* because the Court held an Act of Congress unconstitutional, but rather because it refused to do so." [2]

Sources of Power

Article III of the Constitution grants the federal courts jurisdiction over all controversies between states, those in which the United States is a party, controversies between a state and the citizens of another state, and between a state and foreign states, their citizens or subjects.

The Judiciary Act of 1789 expressly gave the court the power to review state court rulings involving federal issues or claims. *(Text of Section 25, box, this page)*

Resistance: *Chisholm v. Georgia*

No sooner had the court handed down its first major decision than the states' resistance to the assertion of federal judicial power was made clear. Within five years, a new amendment had become part of the Constitution, overruling the court's decision.

The case of *Chisholm v. Georgia* arose when two South Carolinians sued Georgia in the Supreme Court, invoking the jurisdiction granted to the court by Article III. As executors of the estate of a man to whom money was owed by persons whose property the state of Georgia confiscated during the war, the South Carolinians asked Georgia to pay the debt.

The state of Georgia refused to appear before the Supreme Court, denying its authority to hear cases in which a state was the defendant.

Finding clear authority for such suits in Article III, the court on Feb. 18, 1793, upheld the right of citizens of one state to bring a suit against another state in the Supreme Court. Chief Justice John Jay delivered the major opinion. Only Justice James Iredell disagreed. [3]

The Chief Justice took note of the fact that Georgia was at that very time "prosecuting an action in this court against two citizens of South Carolina," while disclaiming the correlative right. Jay commented:

That rule is said to be a bad one, which does not work both ways; the citizens of Georgia are content with a right of suing citizens of other states; but are not

Judicial Review and State Courts

Unlike the power of the Supreme Court to review Acts of Congress to measure their constitutionality, the authority of the court to review acts of state courts is explicitly granted by law — by Section 25 of the Judiciary Act of 1789.

That Act provided:

That a final judgment or decree in any suit, in the highest court of law or equity of a State in which a decision in the suit could be had, where is drawn in question the validity of a treaty or statute of, or an authority exercised under the United States, and the decision is against their validity;

or where is drawn in question the validity of a statute of, or an authority exercised under any State, on the ground of their being repugnant to the constitution, treaties or laws of the United States, and the decision is in favour of such their validity,

or where is drawn in question the construction of any clause of the constitution, or of a treaty, or statute of, or commission held under the United States, and the decision is against the title, right, privilege or exemption specifically set up or claimed by either party under such clause of the said Constitution, treaty, statute or commission, may be re-examined and reversed or affirmed in the Supreme Court of the United States....

content that citizens of other states should have a right to sue them.[4]

To buttress his ruling in support of the court's jurisdiction, Jay said he had no precedents to refer to, but, he explained:

> The extension of the judiciary power of the United States to such controversies appears to me to be wise, because it is honest, and because it is useful ... because it leaves not even the most obscure an [*sic*] friendless citizen without means of obtaining justice from a neighboring state; because it obviates occasions of quarrels between states on account of the claims of their respective citizens; because it recognizes and strongly rests on this great moral truth, that justice is the same whether due from one man or a million, or from a million to one man . . . .[5]

This decision, reports historian Charles Warren, "fell upon the country with a profound shock. . . . The vesting of any such jurisdiction over sovereign states had been expressly disclaimed . . . by the great defenders of the Constitution, during the days of the contest over its adoption."[6]

The day after the ruling, a proposed constitutional amendment to override the decision was introduced in the House of Representatives.

State pride was injured, but more than that was at issue. Already in delicate financial condition after the Revolution, the states feared fiscal disaster if suits such as that upheld in *Chisholm* were brought to recover property confiscated during the war.

Georgia reacted dramatically. The Georgia House approved a measure declaring that anyone who carried out the Supreme Court's decision would be "guilty of felony and shall suffer death, without benefit of clergy, by being hanged." The bill did not become law.[7]

The following year, the U.S. House and Senate approved the proposed amendment.[8] On Jan. 8, 1798, the 11th Amendment was formally added to the Constitution. It states:

> The Judicial power of the United States shall not be construed to extend to any suit in law or equity, commenced or prosecuted against one of the United States by Citizens of another State, or by Citizens or Subjects of any Foreign State.

Chisholm v. Georgia was overruled. The states had won the first battle.

The Supreme Court acquiesced. Within a month of ratification, the court dismissed a suit against the state of Virginia by citizens of another state, citing the amendment in support of its statement that it had no jurisdiction over the matter.[9] *(Further discussion of the amendment, p. 354)*

Supremacy: *Ware v. Hylton*

Similar facts — but a much longer effective life — characterized the court's next major decision, which again involved a clear question of state rights.

Article VI of the Constitution asserts national supremacy, stating that the Constitution, federal laws and treaties are the supreme law of the land and all conflicting state laws or constitutions are invalid.

The treaty of peace with Britain, which ended the Revolutionary War, provided that neither nation would raise any legal obstacle to the recovery of debts due from its citizens to those of the other nation. Large sums of money were affected by this provision. One scholar estimates that in Virginia alone as much as $2 million was owed to British subjects.[10]

Like many other states, Virginia had confiscated the property of British loyalists during the Revolution. And state law had provided that persons owing money to British subjects could satisfy their obligation by making payments to the state.

After the treaty was signed, British creditors came into federal court to sue Virginia debtors for payment of their obligations. Defending the debtors and the state was John Marshall. He argued only this one case before the Supreme Court — and he lost.[11]

Early in 1796 the court ruled — against the debtors, against the state and for the British creditors. The debts must be paid, it held. The state had a moral obligation to return the payments made during the war, but whether it did so or not, the debtors were still liable. This case was entitled *Ware v. Hylton.*[12]

National supremacy was affirmed. "Here is a treaty," wrote Justice William Cushing, "the supreme law, which overrules all state laws upon the subject to all intents and purposes; and that makes the difference."[13]

Resistance: *United States v. Judge Peters*

For almost 15 years after *Ware v. Hylton*, the court — by a cautious approach to the use of its authority to review state court actions — avoided a head-on collision with state power. But in 1809 it found itself head to head with the state of Pennsylvania.

The controversy that culminated in 1809 had begun during the Revolutionary War when Gideon Olmstead and his companions seized a British ship as a prize of war. The ship was sold as a prize vessel, and the proceeds became the object of a tug-of-war between Olmstead and the state of Pennsylvania.

In 1803 a federal judge — Richard Peters — ordered that the money be paid to Olmstead. Instead of complying, the state legislature ordered that it be placed into the state treasury. Until that time, it had been in the personal custody of the state treasurer, a man named David Rittenhouse.

Apparently deterred by the legislature's action, Judge Peters did not actually issue the order directing payment to Olmstead. Finally, in 1808, the 82-year-old Olmstead asked the Supreme Court to direct Peters to issue the order. The state of Pennsylvania responded that such a suit could not be brought in federal court because of the 11th Amendment denial of federal jurisdiction over suits brought by citizens against a state.

The Supreme Court, on Feb. 20, 1809, issued Olmstead's requested order. The court found it necessary to grant his request, explained Chief Justice Marshall, to preserve national supremacy:

> If the legislatures of the several states may, at will, annul the judgments of the courts of the United States, and destroy the rights acquired under those judgments, the constitution itself becomes a solemn mockery, and the nation is deprived of the means of enforcing its laws by the instrumentality of its own tribunals.[14]

On the 11th Amendment defense raised by the state, the court found that it did not apply to this situation simply because the state was not the defendant.

The Supreme Court decision did not settle the matter. The governor of Pennsylvania declared he would use the militia to prevent enforcement of its order, which Judge Peters finally issued on March 24. When the federal marshal attempted to deliver the order to the two women who were executors of the now-deceased Rittenhouse's estate, he was met by the state militia. The marshal called out a posse of 2,000 men. A federal grand jury indicted the militia commander and ordered his arrest for resisting federal law.

The governor asked President James Madison to intervene. Madison declined. The legislature then capitulated, removing the militia, appropriating the money due Olmstead and making the payment; thus the long quarrel ended.[15]

Challenge to Power

The Judiciary Act of 1789 left to the state courts all cases arising within the states, even if they involved some federal question. But to ensure that constitutional principles and federal law were uniformly applied, the act granted, in such cases, the right of appeal to the Supreme Court. The provision granting this right was the much-debated Section 25. *(Text, box, p. 303)*

Section 25 authorized the Supreme Court to re-examine and reverse or affirm the final judgment of the highest court in a state when the state court decided a case involving the Constitution, federal laws or federal treaties and resolved the matter against the federal claim.

In 1914, Congress expanded the scope of this power of review by allowing the Supreme Court to review state court decisions upholding — as well as those denying — a federal claim. *(See p. 265)*

"In view of the extreme jealousy shown by the States from the outset towards the Federal Government, it is a singular fact in our history that this Section was in force 24 years before any State resented its existence or attempted to controvert the right of Congress to enact it," writes Warren.[16]

And when the challenge came, in 1816, it came from Virginia, Marshall's home state. The state court that posed the challenge and denied the power of the Supreme Court to review its decisions was led by Judge Spencer Roane, close friend of Thomas Jefferson and — it is said — the man who would have been Chief Justice instead of John Marshall, had Oliver Ellsworth resigned that post a few months later, and Jefferson, not Adams, been president.[17]

Like *Chisholm* and *Ware*, the facts of this challenge case involved land belonging to British subjects, which Virginia had confiscated and then granted to new owners.

Lord Fairfax owned much land in Virginia, which he willed at his death in 1781 to his nephew, Denny Martin, a British subject. Virginia law not only denied the right of aliens to inherit land within its boundaries but it also claimed that it had confiscated the estate during the Revolution, and subsequently granted portions to other owners, including one David Hunter. Eventually, some of this contested land was purchased by John Marshall's brother — and perhaps even the Chief Justice himself. At any rate, Marshall did not take part in the court's considerations of this case.

First titled *Hunter v. Fairfax's Devisee*, the case came to the court in 1796 — but was postponed due to the death of Hunter's attorney.[18] Almost 15 years passed before a Virginia court upheld Hunter's claim, and the Fairfax heirs moved the matter back to the Supreme Court, where it was argued in 1812 under the name, *Fairfax's Devisee v. Hunter's Lessee.*

In 1813 the court ruled for the British heirs. The vote was 3-1, with Justice William Johnson dissenting and two justices — Marshall being one — not taking part in the case. Justice Joseph Story wrote a forceful opinion, holding that aliens could inherit land in Virginia, state law to the contrary. Thus Denny Martin held title to the disputed lands and the state could not grant title to them to anyone else. The court ordered the Virginia court to issue an order to this effect, settling the case in Martin's favor.[19]

Defiance. Resentful of the ruling and of the damage inflicted by Story's opinion upon the state's confiscation and inheritance laws, the state court refused to follow the Supreme Court's directive. Instead, it decided to consider the question of the constitutionality of the Supreme Court's claimed power to consider the case at all: Was Section 25 of the Judiciary Act constitutional?

Late in 1815 the state court held the section invalid, declaring that the Supreme Court could not constitutionally review state court rulings, and thus it would not obey the court's order:

> The appellate power of the Supreme Court of the United States does not extend to this Court, under a sound construction of the Constitution. . . . So much of the Twenty-fifth Section of the Act . . . to establish the Judicial Courts of the United States as extends the appellate jurisdiction of the Supreme Court to this court, is not in pursuance of the Constitution. . . .

And back went the matter to the Supreme Court.

Again Marshall did not consider the case, now known as *Martin v. Hunter's Lessee.*

The Court's Ruling. Within three months of the state court challenge, the Supreme Court responded with a sweeping affirmance of the validity of Section 25. In its opinion issued on March 20, 1816, the court stated:

> [T]he appellate power of the United States does extend to cases pending in the state courts; and . . . the 25th section of the judiciary act, which authorizes the exercise of this jurisdiction in the specified cases, by a writ of error, is supported by the letter and spirit of the constitution. We find no clause in that instrument which limits this power; and we dare not interpose a limitation where the people have not been disposed to create one.[20]

Justice Story, author of the court's opinion, took the opportunity to deliver a ringing defense of national supremacy:

> The constitution of the United States was ordained and established, not by the states in their sovereign capacities, but emphatically, as the preamble of the constitution declares, by "the people of the United States." There can be no doubt that it was competent to the people to invest the general government with all the powers which they might deem proper and necessary; to extend or restrain these powers according to their own good pleasure, and to give them a paramount and supreme authority. As little doubt can there be that the people had a right to prohibit to the states the exercise of any powers which were, in their judgment, incompatible with the objects of the general compact; to make the powers of the state governments, in given cases, subordinate to those of the nation. . . .[21]

Examining Article III "creating and defining the judicial power of the United States," Story pointed out that:

[i]t is the case, then, and not the court, that gives the jurisdiction [to federal courts]. If the judicial power extends to the case, it will be in vain to search in the letter of the Constitution for any qualification as to the tribunal where it depends.[22]

The Constitution, he continued:

is crowded with provisions which restrain or annul the sovereignty of the states.... When, therefore, the states are stripped of some of the highest attributes of sovereignty, and the same are given to the United States; when the legislatures of the states are, in some respects, under the control of Congress, and in every case are, under the constitution, bound by the paramount authority of the United States; it is certainly difficult to support the argument that the appellate power over the decisions of state courts is contrary to the genius of our institutions. The courts of the United States can, without question, revise the proceedings of the executive and legislative authorities of the states, and if they are found to be contrary to the constitution, may declare them to be of no legal validity. Surely the exercise of the same right over judicial tribunals is not a higher or more dangerous act of sovereign power.[23]

And further, wrote Justice Story:

...[a] motive of another kind, perfectly compatible with the most sincere respect for state tribunals, might induce the grant of appellate power over their decisions. That motive is the importance, and even the necessity of uniformity of decisions throughout the whole United States, upon all subjects within the purview of the constitution. Judges of equal learning and integrity, in different states, might differently interpret a statute, or a treaty of the United States, or even the constitution itself. If there were no revising authority to control these jarring and discordant judgments, and harmonize them into uniformity, the laws, the treaties, and the constitution of the United States would be different in different states, and might, perhaps, never have precisely the same construction, obligation, or efficacy, in any two states. The public mischiefs that would attend such a state of things would be truly deplorable ... the [Supreme Court's] appellate jurisdiction must continue to be the only adequate remedy for such evils.[24]

A Second Challenge

Despite the firmness of the court's decision in *Martin v. Hunter's Lessee,* the Virginia court of appeals, led by Roane, continued to resist the Supreme Court.

A second collision between the two came just five years after the first. This time, Chief Justice Marshall participated; the court again affirmed its power of reviewing state court actions; and the matter was settled.

Although state law forbade the sale of out-of-state lottery tickets in Virginia, two persons named Cohen sold tickets in Virginia to a congressionally authorized lottery in the District of Columbia. They were convicted of violating the Virginia law. But they appealed their conviction to the Supreme Court, arguing that the Virginia law must fall before the conflicting — and overriding — federal law authorizing the lottery and the sale of tickets.

Virginia's response was to argue that the case should be dismissed because the Supreme Court lacked jurisdiction over it.

On March 3, 1821, the court again rejected this argument, holding that it was founded upon a mistaken view of the relationship of the state and federal judicial systems. Writing for the court, Chief Justice Marshall rejected the idea that these systems were totally separate and independent, like those of different sovereign nations:

That the United States form, for many, and for most important purposes, a single nation, has not yet been denied. In war, we are one people. In making peace, we are one people. In all commercial regulations, we are one and the same people. In many other respects, the American people are one; and the government which is alone capable of controlling and managing their interests in all these respects, is the government of the Union. It is their government, and in that character they have no other. America has chosen to be, in many respects, and to many purposes, a nation; and for all these purposes, her government is complete; to all these objects, it is competent. The people have declared, that in the exercise of all powers given for these objects it is supreme. It can, then, in effecting these objects, legitimately control all individuals or governments within the American territory. The constitution and laws of a state, so far as they are repugnant to the constitution and laws of the United States, are absolutely void. These states are constituent parts of the United States. They are members of one great empire — for some purposes sovereign, for some purposes subordinate.

In a government so constituted, is it unreasonable that the judicial power should be competent to give efficacy to the constitutional laws of the legislature? That department can decide on the validity of the constitution or law of a state, if it be repugnant to the constitution or to a law of the United States. Is it unreasonable that it should also be empowered to decide on the judgment of a state tribunal enforcing such unconstitutional law? ... We think it is not.[25]

To hold that the Supreme Court lacked jurisdiction over this and similar cases, Marshall wrote, would have "mischievous consequences":

It would prostrate, it has been said, the government and its laws at the feet of every state in the Union. And would not this be its effect? What power of the government could be executed by its own means, in any state disposed to resist its execution? ... Each member will possess a veto on the will of the whole. ... [26]

No government ought to be so defective in its organization as not to contain within itself the means of securing the execution of its own laws against other dangers than those which occur every day. Courts of justice are the means most usually employed; and it is reasonable to expect that a government should repose on its own courts, rather than on others. There is certainly nothing in the circumstances under which our constitution was formed; nothing in the history of the times, which would justify the opinion that the confidence reposed in the states was so implicit as to leave in them ... the power of resisting, or defeating, in the form of law, the legitimate measures of the Union.[27]

The 11th Amendment had no application here, the court held, because this case was initiated by the state, not the Cohens.

After this resounding decision on the question of jurisdiction, the court's ruling on the merits of the case — against the Cohens and in favor of the state — was merely a postscript. In approving the District of Columbia lottery, the court held, Congress had not intended to authorize the sale of tickets in a state forbidding such a transaction.[28]

Repeal and Resistance

The decade following the Supreme Court's decision in *Cohens v. Virginia* saw the states' battle against judicial review shift to forums other than the Supreme Court.

In Congress there was a series of efforts to repeal Section 25 or otherwise terminate the court's jurisdiction over state court rulings. It was proposed that the Senate become the court of appeals for all cases involving the states — or that a certain number of the justices, above a simple majority, be required to agree in any decision on the validity of a state law. None succeeded.

Georgia and the Cherokees

Perhaps the most celebrated clash of the court and state power followed the decisions affirming judicial review.

During Andrew Jackson's first term in the White House, the court collided with the state of Georgia — and unlike Madison in the Olmstead case, Jackson was on the side of the state.

The Cherokee Indians occupied land within the boundaries of Georgia. The state attempted to assert control over the Indians and these lands with a series of increasingly stringent laws passed during the 1820s. Finally, the Cherokees — acting as an independent nation — filed a request with the Supreme Court, under its original jurisdiction, for an order directing the state to stop enforcing these laws.

Not only did the state of Georgia fail to appear to defend against this request, but even before it was ruled upon, the governor and legislature executed an Indian, convicted of murder under the contested laws, in direct defiance of a Supreme Court notice to the state that it was going to review the murder conviction in light of the challenge to the laws.[29]

In March 1831 the court denied the Cherokees' request, holding that its original jurisdiction did not extend to such a suit because the Cherokees were not a foreign state. "If it be true that wrongs have been inflicted, and that still greater are to be apprehended," wrote Chief Justice Marshall, "this is not the tribunal which can redress the past or prevent the future." [30]

A second challenge to these laws quickly arrived before the court. Georgia law required white persons living in Indian territory to obtain a state license. Two missionaries — Samuel Worcester and Elizur Butler — refused, were convicted and sentenced to four years at hard labor.

They appealed to the Supreme Court, which issued a writ of error to the state court, notifying it to send the record of the case to Washington for review. The order was ignored. The case was argued Feb. 20, 1832, without the appearance of counsel for the state.

On March 3 the court ruled. Federal jurisdiction over the Cherokees was exclusive, therefore the state had no power to pass any laws affecting them. The missionaries' convictions were reversed because the laws under which they were charged were void. Worcester and Butler should be released, said the court.[31]

But it did not actually issue the order directing release before it adjourned its term two weeks later, leaving the matter suspended until its new term in 1833.

There was reason for the court to delay. President Jackson was known to side with the state. Often-repeated but unsubstantiated reports quoted him as saying: "Well, John Marshall has made his decision, now let him enforce it." Whether or not he made such a statement, his failure to act bore out the sentiment.

Justice Story wrote a friend the week of the ruling:

Georgia is full of anger and violence. What she will do it is difficult to say. Probably she will resist the execution of our judgment, and if she does, I do not believe the President will interfere.... The rumor is, that he has told the Georgians he will do nothing.... The court has done its duty. Let the Nation now do theirs. If we have a Government, let its command be obeyed; if we have not, it is as well to know it at once, and to look to consequences.[32]

As the year wore on, Chief Justice Marshall became increasingly pessimistic about the standoff. He wrote to Story:

I yield slowly and reluctantly to the conviction that our Constitution cannot last. I had supposed that North of the Potomack a firm and solid government competent to the security of rational liberty might be preserved. Even that now seems doubtful. The case of the South seems to me to be desperate. Our opinions are incompatible with a united government even among ourselves. The Union has been prolonged thus far by miracles. I fear they cannot continue.[33]

But they did continue, for a while. Events made it politically impossible for Jackson to continue to give even tacit support to Georgia's defiance of the court. Late in 1832, South Carolina, protesting a new tariff law and other intrusions upon state's rights, approved the Nullification Ordinance. It asserted the right of a state to disregard and thereby nullify federal laws it viewed as unconstitutional. The ordinance forbade any appeal to the Supreme Court from state courts in cases involving the ordinance or any federal law.

President Jackson responded by describing the nullification theory as treason. Thus firmly planted on the side of federal power, he could hardly continue to sanction Georgia's disobedience to the court's ruling in the missionary case. Realizing that political fact of life, the governor of Georgia pardoned Worcester and Butler in 1833; they subsequently dropped their case.

Taxes, Slaves and War

State resistance to federal judicial power did not end with the Cherokee controversy. Ohio courts refused for a period of years in the 1850s to carry out a Supreme Court ruling on a tax matter. Also in the 1850s, the supreme court of California held Section 25 of the Judiciary Act invalid — but its legislature ordered the judges to comply with the federal law. And in the years just before the Civil War, a great struggle between state and federal judicial power took place in Wisconsin over the trial of an abolitionist for violating the federal fugitive slave law.[34] *(See p. 360)*

In 1941 Justice Robert H. Jackson would write that such state resistance to the Supreme Court's power to review state laws and state court actions "practically ended with the Civil War":

It is now an accepted part of our constitutional doctrine that conflicts between state legislation and the federal Constitution are to be resolved by the

Supreme Court and, had it not been, it is difficult to see how the Union could have survived.[35]

Events of the 1950s would prove Jackson's statements a bit premature. Yet even the fierce opposition of some areas to the Supreme Court's school desegregation rulings did not manifest itself in a successful drive against the institution of judicial review.

Footnotes

[1] Oliver Wendell Holmes Jr., *Collected Legal Papers.* (New York: Harcourt Brace, 1920), pp. 295-296; Address, Feb. 15, 1913, to Harvard Law School Association of New York.

[2] Charles Warren. *The Supreme Court in United States History,* 2 vols. (Boston: Little, Brown & Co., 1922, 1926), I:5.

[3] *Chisholm v. Georgia,* 2 Dall. 419 (1793).

[4] Id. at 473.

[5] Id. at 478-479.

[6] Warren, *The Supreme Court in United States History,* I:96.

[7] Ibid., pp. 99-101.

[8] The vote in the Senate was 23-2, in the House, 81-9. Ibid., p. 101.

[9] Ibid., p. 102.

[10] Ibid., p. 144.

[11] Ibid., p. 145-146.

[12] *Ware v. Hylton,* 3 Dall. 199 (1796).

[13] Id. at 283.

[14] *United States v. Judge Peters,* 5 Cr. 115 at 136 (1809).

[15] Warren, *The Supreme Court in United States History,* I:374-387; Charles G. Haines, *American Doctrine of Judicial Supremacy,* 2d ed. (Berkeley: University of California Press, 1932) pp. 290-292.

[16] Warren, *The Supreme Court in United States History,* I:443.

[17] Carl B. Swisher. *American Constitutional Development,* 2d ed. (Cambridge: Houghton Mifflin Co., 1954) p. 108.

[18] *Hunter v. Fairfax's Devisee,* 3 Dall. 305 (1796).

[19] *Fairfax's Devisee v. Hunter's Lessee,* 7 Cr. 602 (1813).

[20] *Martin v. Hunter's Lessee,* 1 Wheat. 304 at 351 (1816).

[21] Id. at 324-325.

[22] Id. at 338.

[23] Id. at 343-344.

[24] Id. at 347-348; further details, see Warren, *The Supreme Court in United States History,* I:442-453.

[25] *Cohens v. Virginia,* 6 Wheat. 264 at 413-415 (1821).

[26] Id. at 385.

[27] Id. at 387-388.

[28] Warren, *The Supreme Court in United States History,* I:547-564.

[29] Ibid., pp. 729-779.

[30] *Cherokee Nation v. State of Georgia,* 5 Pet. 1 at 20 (1831).

[31] *Worcester v. Georgia,* 6 Pet. 515 (1832).

[32] Warren, *The Supreme Court in United States History,* I:757, citing *Life and Letters of Joseph Story* (1851), II:83, 86.

[33] Ibid., I:769, citing Massachusetts Historical Society Proceedings, 2d series, XIV.

[34] Warren, *Supreme Court in U.S. History,* II:256-260.

[35] Robert H. Jackson, *The Struggle for Judicial Supremacy,* (New York: Alfred A. Knopf, 1941), p. 17.

The States and the Economy

For the first 150 years of its history, the Supreme Court exerted its greatest influence on the states of the Union through its decisions on matters of economic interest. In case after case — as the justices construed the contract clause, the commerce clause and defined the state's power of taxation — the court determined the relationship of state to federal power.

"Certainly," wrote Thomas Reed Powell in the mid-20th century, "the commerce powers of the nation and the state raise the most perennial and persistent problems of constitutional federalism." [1] The commerce clause, wrote Felix Frankfurter in 1937, "has throughout the Court's history been the chief source of its adjudications regarding federalism." [2]

Anticipating the creation of a national economy, the Constitution granted the federal government the power to regulate interstate and foreign commerce. Supplementing that grant, the Constitution forbade states without congressional consent to tax imports or exports or to impose tonnage duties on incoming ships.

To guarantee the stability of commercial transactions and to protect property against legislative encroachment, the framers of the Constitution included in that document a prohibition on passage of state laws impairing the obligation of contracts. Further, they added language forbidding states to coin money, issue bills of credit or make changes in the legal tender.

Each of these constitutional restrictions on state powers over commerce received its initial interpretation during the tenure of Chief Justice John Marshall. The net impact of these rulings, particularly those interpreting the commerce clause itself, was to establish the court's power to limit state authority. As Frankfurter wrote: "Marshall's use of the commerce clause . . . gave momentum to the doctrine that state authority must be subject to such limitations as the Court finds it necessary to apply for the protection of the national community." [3]

New York saw its steamboat monopoly fall before the court's broad interpretation of the federal power over commerce. Georgia became the first state to have a law declared unconstitutional, when its effort to repeal a corruptly obtained land grant collided with the contract clause.

Maryland was rebuked by the court for taxing vendors of foreign goods. And Missouri was told firmly that it could not issue state loan certificates without violating the Constitution's ban on state issuance of bills of credit.

Once these limits were well established, the court seemed willing to acknowledge that, within the structure of federal supremacy, states retained certain basic powers with which to regulate commerce within their borders.

This broad reserved power, most often called the police power, received the stamp of judicial approval in the 1830s and serves to modern times as a firm basis for a wide variety of state actions to protect its citizens, its public health and morals, and its natural resources.

"Because the 'police power' is a response to the dynamic aspects of society," wrote Frankfurter, "it has eluded attempts at definition. But precisely because it is such a response, it is one of the most fertile doctrinal sources for striking an accommodation between local interests and the demands of the commerce clause." [4]

During the laissez-faire period of the late 19th and early 20th centuries, the justices viewed many of the state laws enacted in exercise of this police power as too vigorous, particularly in their impact on the use of private property. In the due process clause of the 14th Amendment, the conservative court found a useful instrument to counter such laws, many of which fell before the court's finding that they deprived businessmen of their property without due process of law.

The New Deal — and the depression that precipitated it — wrote a conclusion to that period in the court's history. Since 1937, the court has been more tolerant of state regulation of business even as it has upheld the extension of federal power into areas of the economy formerly left entirely to state control. As Powell wrote, the modern court tends "to sanction state action when from the standpoint of practical considerations it interferes with the national economy no more than is deemed to be justified by the importance of the resulting protection of community interests."[5]

The Obligation of Contracts

From the nation's founding to the Civil War, the contract clause served as one of the most effective instruments for establishing federal control over state actions. As one scholar writes:

> The cases of *Fletcher v. Peck* and *Dartmouth College v. Woodward* formed the beginning of an extensive series of restrictions upon state legislation, made possible through the fact that many laws may be

attacked on the ground of infringement of property rights. . . . The [court's early] decisions aligned on the side of nationalism the economic interests of corporate organizations. [6]

Land Grants

In 1810 the court for the first time struck down a state law as unconstitutional. In the case of *Fletcher v. Peck,* the court ruled that grants made by a state legislature cannot be repealed without violating the constitutional prohibition on impairment of contract obligations.

In 1795 the Georgia legislature granted some 35 million acres of land along the Yazoo River to four land speculator companies. The price — for what is now most of the states of Alabama and Mississippi — was $500,000. And approval of the grant was facilitated by the promise of the speculators to many legislators that they would share in the land thus granted.

Chagrined by the obvious bribery, the new legislature elected after the grant revoked it in 1796, and declared all claims resulting from it void. But the land companies already had resold much of the land to innocent purchasers, who now held questionable titles.

A long debate began. Pointing to the corruption that attended the 1795 land grant, Georgia argued that the titles held under it were worthless. The purchasers argued that the state legislature did not have the power to nullify their rights.

Because many of the purchasers lived in New England, the case quickly became a federal problem. After several years of discussion in Congress, the matter moved into the federal courts. One of the attorneys arguing the case before the Supreme Court was Joseph Story, a 30-year-old Massachusetts attorney. Within two years he would sit on the Supreme Court bench, the youngest nominee in its history.

On March 16, 1810, the court ruled. The original land grant was a valid contract; Georgia could not annul the titles granted under it — such an attempt ran headlong into the ban on state action impairing the obligation of contracts.

The court would not inquire into the motives behind approval of the 1795 land grant, wrote Marshall:

> That corruption should find its way into the governments of our infant republics, and contaminate the very source of legislation, or that impure motives should contribute to the passage of law, or the formation of a legislative contract, are circumstances most deeply to be deplored. [7]

> [But] [i]f the title be plainly deduced from a legislative act, which the legislature might constitutionally pass, if the act be clothed with all the requisite forms of a law, a court . . . cannot sustain a suit . . . founded on the allegation that the act is a nullity, in consequence of the impure motives which influenced certain members of the legislature which passed the law. [8]

Marshall explored the implications of upholding Georgia's right to repeal the grant:

> [S]uch powerful objections to a legislative grant . . . may not again exist, yet the principle, on which alone this rescinding act is to be supported, may be applied to every case in which it shall be the will of any legislature to apply it. The principle is this: that a

legislature may, by its own act, devest [sic] the vested estate of any man whatever, for reasons which shall, by itself, be deemed sufficient. [9]

The court rejected that principle.

The court agreed that one legislature could repeal any general legislation passed by a former legislature. Yet the new legislature could not undo any action taken under the repealed law: "The past cannot be recalled by the most absolute power." [10]

"When, then, a law is in its nature a contract, when absolute rights have vested under that contract, a repeal of the law cannot devest those rights. . . ." [11]

Tax Exemptions

Two years later the court extended its interpretation of the contract clause as a restraint on the tendency of state legislators to change their minds. In the case of *New Jersey v. Wilson* in 1812, the court refused to allow a state to modify or revoke a clear contractual grant of exemption from taxes. [12]

The colonial legislature of New Jersey had granted certain lands to the Delaware Indians. Included in the grant was an exemption from taxation for the lands held by the Indians. After the Indians sold this land to other owners, the state tried to tax it. The new owners challenged the tax as a violation of the contract in the original grant — and they won.

The Supreme Court noted that the state could have limited the tax exemption to the period when the land belonged to the Indians — but that it placed no such a

---

The Constitution "was not intended to furnish the corrective for every abuse of power which may be committed by the State governments. The interest, wisdom, and justice of the representative body, and its relations with its constituents, furnish the only security where there is no express contract against unjust and excessive taxation, as well as against unwise legislation generally. . . ."

—Chief Justice John Marshall
Providence Bank v. Billings, 1830

---

condition upon the exemption. Thus the exemption passed with title to the land, and efforts to repeal or ignore it impaired the original obligation.

Eighteen years later, the court made clear that no tax exemption could ever be assumed to be a part of a contract, grant or charter. In the case of *Providence Bank v. Billings,* the court held that "[a]ny privileges which may exempt it [a corporation] from the burthens common to individuals do not flow necessarily from the charter, but must be expressed in it, or they do not exist." [13]

The power to tax could indeed be used as a means of destroying a business — and thereby impairing a contract, Chief Justice Marshall conceded, "but the Constitution of the United States was not intended to furnish the corrective for every abuse of power which may be committed by the State governments. The interest, wisdom and justice of the representative body, and its relations with its constituents, furnish the only security where there is no express contract against unjust and excessive taxation, as well as against unwise legislation generally.... [A]n incorporated bank, unless its charter shall express the exemption, is no more exempted from taxation than an unincorporated company would be, carrying on the same business." [14]

In 1854 the state of Ohio brought this question back before the justices, leading to the first Supreme Court ruling finding a portion of a state's constitution unconstitutional. The state bank of Ohio was chartered under a law which provided that the bank would pay a certain percentage of its profits to the state in lieu of taxes. Subsequently, the state legislature passed a law providing for a tax on banks, and assessed one branch of the state bank $1,266.63 as its share of the new tax.

The bank refused to pay, arguing that the state's effort to impose this new tax on it impaired the contract of the original charter. [15]

The court upheld the bank's exemption from taxes. Justice John McLean wrote the majority opinion. The charter was perfectly clear, he wrote:

> Nothing is left to inference.... The payment was to be in lieu of all taxes to which the Company or stockholders would otherwise be subject. This is the full measure of taxation on the Bank. It is in the place of any other tax which, had it not been for this stipulation, might have been imposed on the Company or stockholders. [16]

> Every valuable privilege given by the charter ... is a contract which cannot be changed by the Legislature, where the power to do so is not reserved in the charter.... A municipal corporation ... may be changed at the will of the Legislature. Such is a public corporation, used for public purposes. But a bank, where the stock is owned by individuals, is a private corporation. [17]

> A state, in granting privileges to a bank ... exercises its sovereignty, and for a public purpose, of which it is the exclusive judge. Under such circumstances, a contract made for a specific tax, as in the case before us, is binding.... Having the power to make the contract, and rights becoming vested under it, it can no more be disregarded nor set aside by a subsequent Legislature, than a grant for land. [18]

Still determined to tax the bank, Ohio amended its state constitution to provide for such a tax. Back came the issue to the Supreme Court. Once again, in 1856, the court reiterated its holding that the effort to tax the bank impermissibly impaired the obligation of the original agreement with the bank. Justice James M. Wayne wrote for the court:

> A change of constitution cannot release a state from contracts made under a constitution which permits them to be made.... The moral obligations never die. If broken by states and nations, though the terms of reproach are not the same with which we are accustomed to designate the faithlessness of individuals, the violation of justice is not the less. [19]

Private Corporate Charters

Fletcher v. Peck extended to agreements involving the state the protection of a clause many had thought protected only agreements between two private parties. Nine years later, the court further extended that protection to shield private corporate charters against alteration or repeal.

This extension came in the landmark case of *Dartmouth College v. Woodward,* decided in 1819.

Dartmouth College in New Hampshire originally was set up by a royal charter. After the formation of the Union, the agreement with the king became an agreement with the state. In 1816 the state legislature passed several laws amending the college's charter to convert it into a university, to enlarge the number of its trustees and otherwise to revise the means and purpose of its operations.

The trustees of the college resisted, charging that these amendments impaired the obligation of the contract implicit in the original charter. In 1818 the case came to the

---

"A change of constitution cannot release a state from contracts made under a constitution which permits them to be made.... The moral obligations never die. If broken by states and nations, though the terms of reproach are not the same with which we are accustomed to designate the faithlessness of individuals, the violation of justice is not the less."

—Justice James M. Wayne
Dodge v. Woolsey, 1856

Supreme Court, with the famous advocate Daniel Webster arguing the college's case. The state defended the changes in the charter by contending that the school was a public corporation subject to such legislative action.

Webster was convincing. In 1819 the court ruled for the college, finding the amendments an unconstitutional impairment of the contract obligation. Chief Justice Marshall wrote the court's opinion.

Simply assuming a much-debated point, Marshall stated that the charter incorporating the private college was a contract within the protection of the Constitution:

> It is a contract made on a valuable consideration. It is a contract for the security and disposition of property. It is a contract, on faith of which real and personal estate has been conveyed to the corporation. It is then a contract within the letter of the constitution, and within its spirit also.... [20]

Marshall conceded that this application of the contract clause probably never occurred to the men who wrote it into the Constitution: "It is more than possible that the preservation of rights of this description was not particularly in the view of the framers of the constitution when the clause under consideration was introduced into that instrument." [21]

But the Chief Justice found no good reason to except these contracts from constitutional protection:

> It is probable that no man ever was, and that no man ever will be, the founder of a college, believing at the time that an act of incorporation constitutes no security for the institution; believing that it is immediately to be deemed a public institution, whose funds are to be governed and applied, not by the will of the donor, but by the will of the legislature. All such gifts are made in the . . . hope, that the charity will flow forever in the channel which the givers have marked out for it. If every man finds in his own bosom strong evidence of the universality of this sentiment, there can be but little reason to imagine that the framers of our constitution were strangers to it, and that, feeling the necessity and policy of giving permanence and security to contracts, of withdrawing them from the influence of legislative bodies, whose fluctuating policy, and repeated interferences, produced the most perplexing and injurious embarrassments, they still deemed it necessary to leave these contracts subject to those interferences. [22]

In his concurring opinion, Justice Joseph Story made clear the avenue by which states could retain the power to make modifications in such charters without violating the Constitution. "If the legislature mean to claim such an authority, it must be reserved in the grant," Story wrote. [23] And most charters granted by the states since that time have contained language reserving to the state the power to repeal or modify them.

For the half century following the *Dartmouth College* decision, the contract clause would produce more litigation than any other part of the Constitution. Charles Warren, historian of the court during this period, wrote that this ruling came at a "peculiarly opportune" time:

> [B]usiness corporations were for the first time becoming a factor in the commerce of the country, and railroad and insurance corporations were, within the next fifteen years, about to become a prominent field for capital. The assurance to investors that rights granted by state legislatures were henceforth to be secure against popular or partisan vacillation, and capricious, political or fraudulent change of legislative policy, greatly encouraged the development of corporate business. [24]

Bankruptcy Laws

Using the contract clause to strike down state insolvency laws, the Supreme Court contributed to the nation's economic chaos during the 1820s.

Two weeks after the *Dartmouth College* decision, the court held New York's insolvency law invalid as impairing the obligation of contracts. The law freed a debtor and discharged him from liability for all previous debts, once he surrendered his remaining property to the state.

Although it was unclear at the time — and thus contributed to the misimpression that all such state laws would be held unconstitutional — the court based its decision on the fact that the New York law freed a debtor from liability for debts contracted *before* the law passed, and thus impaired the obligation of those existing contracts.

In the opinion, Chief Justice Marshall stated that the constitutional power of Congress to pass a uniform bankruptcy law did not, by its mere existence, deny states the power to pass such laws. Until Congress exercised that power, he wrote, states could pass bankruptcy and insolvency laws so long as they did not violate the contract clause. [25]

Eight years later, in 1827, the court cleared up the confusion on this matter, ruling that state laws discharging debts contracted *after* the laws' passage did not violate the contract clause. Argued in 1824 and reargued in 1827, this case, entitled *Ogden v. Saunders,* divided the justices, 4-3, and for the only time in his entire long career as Chief Justice, John Marshall was on the losing side in a constitutional case. [26]

The court upheld a new version of the New York insolvency law, with Justice Bushrod Washington setting out his often-quoted opinion on how the Supreme Court should approach cases challenging a state law:

> It is but a decent respect due to the wisdom, the integrity, and the patriotism of the legislative body, by which any law is passed, to presume in favor of its validity, until its violation of the constitution is proved beyond all reasonable doubt. [27]

Marshall, joined in dissent by Justices Story and Gabriel Duvall, argued that the contract clause forbade any legislative impairment of future as well as existing contracts. The majority's view, he warned, could be used to construe that clause, "into an inanimate, inoperative, unmeaning" provision. [28]

With its rejection of this viewpoint, the court for the first time placed a limit on the protection of the contract clause. This decision concluded the court's expansion of the contract clause as a curb on state legislatures.

During this same term, the court upheld the decision of the Rhode Island legislature to abolish imprisonment as a punishment for debtors. This modification of the remedy for defaulting on contracts did not impair the obligation imposed by the contract, held the court, even though it applied to debtors already in default at the time of its passage. [29] In the first state bankruptcy case, Chief Justice Marshall had written that "without imparing [sic] the obligation of the contract, the remedy may certainly be modified. . . . Imprisonment is no part of the contract, and simply to release the prisoner does not impair its obligation." [30]

But the court made clear that a state could go too far in modifying the remedy provided for enforcing debt obligations. In 1843 it held invalid — under the contract clause — an Illinois law that so altered the remedies for default on mortgages that it effectively impaired the obligation involved. [31]

The Public Interest

Having made clear its insistence upon state respect of contract obligations, the court in the 1830s began to open loopholes in the protection that the contract clause provided to property rights.

Certain state powers were inalienable, the court held; they could not be simply contracted away, even if the state wished to do so. Primary among these paramount powers of the state were its power of eminent domain and its police power. The relationship of these powers to contract obligations was set out by the court in three 19th century cases.

The case that began this narrowing of the contract clause protection was argued in Marshall's last years, set for reargument, and was decided by the court in 1837, during the first term of Chief Justice Roger B. Taney. For some, the decision in *Charles River Bridge v. Warren Bridge* marks the shift from the Marshall court to the Taney court.

In 1785 the Massachusetts legislature chartered a company to build a bridge across the Charles River to Boston, to operate it and to collect tolls from passengers. Quickly, the bridge became profitable; tolls were collected long after its costs were paid. This bridge was called the Charles River Bridge.

Decades later, in 1828, the legislature chartered a second company to build a second bridge across the Charles. Located near the first bridge, the new bridge would be a tollway only until its costs were paid — or for six years, whichever was shorter — and then it would be a free bridge. This new bridge was the Warren Bridge.

Realizing that its business would disappear once it was in competition with a free bridge, the Charles River Bridge Co. challenged the law authorizing the second bridge as impairing the contract in its charter and as destroying the value of its franchise by preventing it from earning the tolls it was authorized to collect.

By the time the case was decided in 1837, the new Warren Bridge was not only built, but was paid for and operating on a toll-free basis.

And the Charles River Bridge Co. lost its case before the court. The vote was 4-3.

"[I]n grants by the public nothing passes by implication," wrote Chief Justice Taney for the court. Without an explicit grant of exclusive privilege in the original bridge company charter, none was assumed to exist to limit the state's power to authorize construction of another bridge. [32]

Taney said the same rule applied in this case that Marshall had applied in the 1830 decision in *Providence Bank v. Billings:* The court would not read into a bank charter an implied grant of privilege against the state. *(p. 310)*

The state power in question in the bridge case was no less vital than the taxing power, wrote Taney. He elaborated:

...the object and end of all government is to promote the happiness and prosperity of the community by which it is established, and it can never be assumed that the government intended to diminish its power of accomplishing the end for which it was created.

And in a country like ours, free, active and enterprising, continually advancing in numbers and wealth; new channels of communication are daily found necessary, both for travel and trade, and are essential to the comfort, convenience and prosperity of the people. A State ought never to be presumed to surrender this power, because, like the taxing power, the whole community have an interest in preserving it undiminished.

And when a corporation alleges that a State has surrendered for seventy years its power of improvement and public accommodation, in a great and important line of travel, along which a vast number of its citizens must daily pass; the community have a right to insist ... "that its abandonment ought not to be presumed, in a case in which the deliberate purpose of the State to abandon it does not appear."

The continued existence of a government would be of no great value, if by implications and presumptions, it was disarmed of the powers necessary to accomplish the ends of its creation, and the functions it was designed to perform, transferred to the hands of privileged corporations....

While the rights of private property are sacredly guarded, we must not forget that the community also have rights, and that the happiness and well being of every citizen depends on their faithful preservation....

The whole community are interested in this inquiry, and they have a right to require that the power of promoting their comfort and convenience, and of advancing the public prosperity, by providing safe, convenient, and cheap ways for the transportation of produce, and the purposes of travel, shall not be construed to have been surrendered or diminished by the State, unless it shall appear by plain words that it was intended to be done. [33]

Considering the implications of the Charles River Bridge claim, Taney noted that turnpikes — like the toll bridge — had in many areas been rendered useless by the coming of the railroad. If the court approved the Charles River Bridge claim, he warned:

[Y]ou will soon find the old turnpike corporations awakening from their sleep, and calling upon this court to put down the improvements which have taken their place.... We shall be thrown back to the improvements of the last century, and obliged to stand still until the claims of the old turnpike corporations shall be satisfied, and they shall consent to permit these States to avail themselves of the lights of modern science.... [34]

The broad power of eminent domain gained further recognition a few years after the *Charles River Bridge* decision, as a result of the court's resolution of a quarrel between the owners of a toll bridge and the town of Brattleboro, Vt.

The owners of the toll bridge had been granted a century-long franchise to build and operate the bridge. But after the state authorized the building of highways, the town of Brattleboro ran a free highway right across the toll bridge, converting it into a free bridge. Although they were compensated by the state, the bridge owners protested that this impaired their charter and the contract obligation it contained.

In 1848 the Supreme Court rejected this claim, upholding a broad state power of eminent domain paramount to contract rights. Justice Peter V. Daniel wrote the court's opinion:

[I]n every political sovereign community there inheres necessarily the right and the duty of guarding its own existence, and of protecting and promoting the interests and welfare of the community at large.... This power, denominated "eminent domain" of the State, is, as its name imports, paramount to all private rights vested under the government, and these last are, by necessary implication, held in subordination to this power, and must yield in every instance to its proper exercise.

The Constitution of the United States ... can, by no rational interpretation, be brought to conflict with this attribute in the States; there is no express delegation of it by the Constitution; and it would imply an incredible fatuity in the States, to ascribe to them the intention to relinquish the power of self-government and self-preservation. [35]

The validity of this ruling was re-emphasized 80 years later, when the court ruled that a state retained this power of eminent domain even in the face of its express agreement to surrender it — and could thus exercise it properly in a way in which it had contracted to forego. [36]

The Police Power

In 1880, with the court's decision in *Stone v. Mississippi*, the police power joined this power of eminent domain on the list of inalienable powers that a state could not surrender permanently.

The "carpetbagger" legislature of Mississippi had chartered a state lottery corporation, the Mississippi Agricultural, Educational and Manufacturing Aid Society. As soon as a new legislature was in power, Mississippi amended its constitution to ban lotteries from the state. The state then sued the society for existing in violation of this prohibition. The society responded with the argument that the state ban was invalid because it impaired the contract obligation of the society's charter.

The court ruled against the lottery. In a brief but weighty opinion, Chief Justice Morrison R. Waite announced the decision of the unanimous court:

All agree that the Legislature cannot bargain away the police power of a State.... Many attempts have been made in this court and elsewhere to define the police power, but never with entire success.... No one denies, however, that it extends to all matters affecting the public health or the public morals.... No Legislature can bargain away the public health or the public morals.... The supervision of both these subjects of governmental power is continuing in its nature, and they are to be dealt with as the special exigencies of the moment may require. Government is organized with a view to their preservation, and cannot devest [sic] itself of the power to provide for them....

Anyone, therefore, who accepts a lottery charter, does so with the implied understanding that the People, in their sovereign capacity ... may resume it at any time when the public good shall require.... [37]

Remedies and Obligations

The climax in the use of the contract clause as a curb on state legislation came just after the Civil War. In the eight years from 1865 to 1873 there were 20 cases in which state laws or actions were held invalid as in conflict with the contract clause. After this point, the combined effect of the eminent domain and police power exceptions to the clause's protection for property began to reduce its restraining force. [38]

The due process clause, for a time, took the place of the contract clause as a shield for property rights. The court linked the two with its statement — in the 1897 case of *Allgeyer v. Louisiana* — that the right to make contracts was an element of the liberty guaranteed by the due process clause. [39] This "freedom of contract" would be used for several decades by the court to curtail state efforts to regulate wages, hours and working conditions. *(p. 326)*

The last major contract clause ruling came during the Depression. Since that time, the contract clause has become no more than "a tail to the due process of law kite ... a fifth wheel to the Constitutional law coach." [40]

In 1933 the Minnesota legislature responded to the plight of the many persons unable to meet mortgage payments during the Depression, and passed a mortgage moratorium act. The law allowed postponement of foreclosure sales and extension of the period during which the property might be retained and redeemed by the defaulting mortgagor. The law was clearly temporary; it was to expire May 1, 1935.

One mortgage holder, Home Building & Loan Association, challenged the law as impairing the obligation of contract contained in the mortgage.

By a vote of 5-4, the Supreme Court upheld the law, emphasizing the emergency conditions which justified its passage. Chief Justice Charles Evans Hughes wrote the opinion in *Home Building & Loan Association v. Blaisdell:*

"Emergency does not create power. Emergency does not increase granted power or remove or diminish the restrictions imposed upon power.... But while emergency does not create power, emergency may furnish the occasion for the exercise of power."

The prohibition in the contract clause "is not an absolute one," Hughes continued, "and is not to be read with literal exactness like a mathematical formula." [41]

The majority, in Hughes' words, declared:

[T]he state ... continues to possess authority to safeguard the vital interests of its people. It does not matter that legislation appropriate to that end 'has the result of modifying or abrogating contracts already in effect.' ...Not only are existing laws read into contracts in order to fix obligations as between the parties, but the reservation of essential attributes of sovereign power is also read into contracts as a postulate of the legal order. The policy of protecting contracts against impairment presupposes the maintenance of a government by virtue of which contractual relations are worth while, — a government which retains adequate authority to secure the peace and good order of society. This principle of harmonizing the constitutional prohibition with the necessary residuum of state power has had progressive recognition in the decisions of this court. [42]

In light of the rulings in *Charles River Bridge v. Warren Bridge, West River Bridge v. Dix, Stone v. Mississippi* and its progeny, Hughes found it untenable to argue that the contract clause prevented "limited and temporary interpositions with respect to the enforcement of contracts if made necessary by a great public calamity such as fire, flood, or earthquake...."

Hughes continued:

The reservation of state power appropriate to such extraordinary conditions may be deemed to be as much a part of all contracts as is the reservation of state power to protect the public interest in the other situations to which we have referred. And if state power exists to give temporary relief from the enforcement of contracts in the presence of disasters due to physical causes such as fire, flood, or earthquake, that power cannot be said to be nonexistent when the urgent public need demanding such relief is produced by other and economic causes....

Where, in earlier days, it was thought that only the concerns of individuals ... were involved, and that those of the state itself were touched only remotely, it has later been found that the fundamental interests of the state are directly affected; and that the question is no longer merely that of one party to a contract as against another, but of the use of reasonable means to safeguard the economic structure upon which the good of all depends. [43]

Making clear the significance of the emergency and temporary nature of the legislation upheld in *Blaisdell*, the court struck down similar but more sweeping laws from other states. [44]

This seemed to end the long line of contract clause cases decided by the court. Edward S. Corwin wrote in 1958: "Till after the Civil War the principal source from which cases stemmed challenging the validity of state legislation, the 'obligation of contracts' clause is today of negligible importance. . . ." [45]

Taking issue with that view, Justice Potter Stewart in 1978 wrote that "the Contract Clause remains part of the Constitution. It is not a dead letter." Stewart wrote the court's opinion striking down part of a state pension law as it was applied to increase the liability and obligations of employers who had pension agreements with their employees in force when the law was passed. [46] The previous term, the court had applied the contract clause to hold that the legislatures of New Jersey and New York had acted unconstitutionally when they changed the terms under which bonds were issued by the Port Authority of New York and New Jersey. [47]

The Control of Commerce

"The spirit of enterprise, which characterizes the commercial part of America, has left no occasion of displaying itself unimproved," wrote Alexander Hamilton in *The Federalist*. "It is not at all probable that this unbridled spirit would pay much respect to those regulations of trade by which particular states might endeavor to secure exclusive benefits to their own citizens. The infractions of these regulations on one side, the efforts to prevent and repeal them, on the other, would naturally lead to outrages, and these to reprisals and war."

Later Hamilton would carry his warning further, predicting that without a strong federal power to regulate interstate and foreign commerce, the United States might soon become like the German Empire "in continual trammels from the multiplicity of the duties which the several princes and states exact upon the merchandises passing through their territories." [48]

Hamilton thus would not have been surprised to hear Justice Felix Frankfurter say, some 175 years later, that "with us, the commerce clause is perhaps the most fruitful and important means for asserting authority against the particularism of state policy." [49]

Unlike the contract clause, which is clearly a restriction on state action, the commerce clause makes no mention of state powers. It simply gives Congress the power "to regulate commerce with foreign nations, and among the several states, and with the Indian tribes."

The Steamboat Monopoly

The restrictive force of this clause was brought home to the states with the court's first ruling on this grant of power to Congress. The decision came in 1824 with *Gibbons v. Ogden*, the case of the New York steamboat monopoly.

Since 1798 Robert R. Livingston and Robert Fulton had held a grant from the New York legislature of the exclusive right to run steamboats in the state's waters. In 1811 Livingston and Fulton secured a similar monopoly for steamship transportation near New Orleans.

The monopoly was a source of aggravation to other states, which passed laws excluding the Livingston-Fulton boats from their waters while granting a monopoly for their

state to another company. Instead of unifying the states, it appeared that the development of steamboat transportation was dividing them further. Arguing this case before the court, Attorney General William Wirt described the situation as one in which New York was almost at war with Ohio, Connecticut and New Jersey. [50]

Aaron Ogden, former New Jersey governor, operated steamboats in New York under license from the monopoly. But Thomas Gibbons, his former partner, was competing with Ogden — and the monopoly — by running steamboats between New York and New Jersey. Although Gibbons was not licensed by the monopoly, his ships were licensed under the federal law governing the coasting trade.

Ogden obtained an order from the New York courts directing Gibbons to stop his competing business. Gibbons took the case to the Supreme Court.

For five days in February 1824 the case was argued before the justices. Daniel Webster argued along with Wirt for the anti-monopoly side.

On March 2 the court announced its decision. It struck down the monopoly as in conflict with the broad federal power to regulate interstate commerce. The court rejected a narrow definition of commerce. Speaking for the court, Chief Justice Marshall defined commerce as intercourse — not simply traffic, or buying and selling alone. And commerce included navigation, as well, the particular subject at issue here. Marshall explained: "The power over commerce, including navigation, was one of the primary objects for which the people of America adopted their government, and must have been contemplated in forming it." [51]

And this federal power did not cease to exist at state borders, continued Marshall:

> Commerce among the states cannot stop at the external boundary line of each state, but may be introduced into the interior. . . . The power of Congress, then, comprehends navigation within the limits of every state in the Union; so far as that navigation may be, in any manner, connected with "commerce with foreign nations, or among the several states, or with the Indian tribes." [52]

New York's effort to confine the use of its waters to the monopoly's ships, thus denying that use to vessels such as Gibbons' — licensed under the federal coasting law — collided with federal regulation of commerce and so must fall, held the court:

> The nullity of any act, inconsistent with the constitution, is produced by the declaration that the constitution is the supreme law. The appropriate application of that part of the clause . . . is to such acts of the state legislature as do not transcend their powers, but though enacted in the execution of acknowledged state powers, interfere with, or are contrary to the laws of Congress, made in pursuance of the constitution. . . . In every such case, the act of Congress . . . is supreme; and the law of the state, though enacted in the exercise of powers not controverted, must yield to it. [53]

Much has been written about the significance of this decision. Felix Frankfurter, later to sit on the Supreme Court, wrote that the theme Marshall first sounded in *Gibbons v. Ogden* became the focal point of the constitutional system — "the doctrine that the commerce clause, by its own force, and without national legislation, puts it into the power of the Court to place limits upon state authority."

"Marshall's use of the commerce clause," he continued, "gave momentum to the doctrine that state authority must be subject to such limitations as the court finds it necessary to apply for the protection of the national community." [54]

In addition to its impact on the nation's constitutional development, the ruling had considerable effect on the Union's economic development, as other observers have noted:

> Steamboat navigation, freed from the restraint of state-created monopolies . . . increased at an astonishing rate. Within a few years steam railroads, encouraged by the freedom of interstate commerce from state restraints, were to begin a practical revolution of internal transportation. The importance of national control of commerce in the rapid economic development is almost incalculable. For many years after 1824 Congress enacted but few important regulatory measures, and commerce was thus free to develop without serious monopolistic or governmental restraint. [55]

Still another scholar emphasizes the latter point, noting:

> Like most of the important cases decided by Chief Justice Marshall, [Gibbons v. Ogden] involved, not the assertion of the power of the federal government over interstate commerce, but acted rather as a prohibition against state activity. Apart from granting coasting licenses, the federal government was not interested in the commerce involved. The decision was an act in defense of laissez-faire, rather than of positive federal control. [56]

An Exclusive Power?

For 30 years after the *Gibbons* ruling, the nation would be preoccupied with the debate over whether the power of Congress to regulate commerce was exclusive — or whether the states retained some concurrent authority in that area.

Underlying this debate was the simmering issue of slavery. Charles Warren wrote:

> [T]hroughout the long years when the question of the extent of the Federal power over commerce was being tested in numerous cases in the Court, that question was, in the minds of Southerners, simply coincident with the question of the extent of the Federal power over slavery. So the long-continued controversy as to whether Congress had exclusive or concurrent jurisdiction over commerce was not a conflict between theories of government, or between Nationalism and State-Rights, or between differing legal construction [sic] of the Constitution, but was simply the naked issue of State or Federal control of slavery. It was little wonder, therefore, that the Judges of the Court prior to the Civil War displayed great hesitation in deciding this momentous controversy. [57]

The particular question left hanging by *Gibbons* was whether the existence of federal power to regulate navigation left the states entirely powerless in that area. In the 1829 case of *Willson v. Blackbird Creek Marsh Co.,* the court held that the states did retain some power over navigation within their borders — at least so long as Congress had not acted to regulate it.

As allowed under state law, the Blackbird Creek Marsh Co. built a dam on the creek of that name in Delaware. The operators of a federally licensed sloop, irritated by the obstruction, rammed and broke the dam. The dam company won a damage judgment in state court against the ship owners, who then appealed to the Supreme Court, arguing that the dam and the authorizing state law were impermissible infringements upon the federal power over navigation.

The mere existence of federal power to regulate navigation on such creeks — if not exercised — did not foreclose state action to regulate such matters, held the court. This was particularly true when the objectives of state action were, as in this case, to preserve the value of property and to enhance the public health. "Measures calculated to produce these objects, provided they do not come into collision with the powers of the general government, are undoubtedly within those which are reserved to the States," wrote Chief Justice Marshall. [58]

The *Willson* decision paved the way for formulation of the concept of the state police power during the era of Chief Justice Taney. That concept served as a useful implement for carving out an area within which state regulation of commerce was permissible. *(Discussion, p. 322)*

For two decades after *Willson*, however, neither the court nor the country found it easy to ascertain the line between permissible and impermissible state regulation affecting commerce. The court's decisions grew more and more unpredictable.

In the 1837 case of *Mayor of New York v. Miln*, the court upheld a New York law that required reports to be filed on all passengers arriving on ships in the city's port. Although the law was challenged as an invasion of the federal power over foreign commerce, the court found no

---

"Marshall's use of the commerce clause gave momentum to the doctrine that state authority must be subject to such limitations as the Court finds it necessary to apply for the protection of the national community."

—Felix Frankfurter, *The Commerce Clause Under Marshall, Taney and Waite,* 1937

---

such intrusion. Instead, the justices viewed the law — intended to minimize the possibility of the immigrant passengers becoming public charges — as a proper exercise of the state police power not in conflict with federal authority. [59]

Four years later, when the question of a state's power to forbid the importation of slaves came to the court, the justices sidestepped a decision on that issue. But all the justices — forced into comment by one justice who decided to air his views on that question — expressed their personal opinions, revealing "almost complete chaos of interpretation." [60]

In 1847 the court decided the *License Cases*, in which it upheld the right of states to require that all sales of alcohol within the state be licensed, even the sales of imported alcohol. Again the court held such a requirement a valid exercise of the police power.

But the six justices wrote nine opinions, none of which could be characterized as a majority's view. Thus the decision provided little guide for future state action. [61]

And two years later, with a similar multiplicity of opinions, the court struck down New York and Massachusetts laws taxing all alien passengers arriving in their ports. The court divided 5-4. Once again there was no opinion that could be identified as having the support of a majority of the justices. [62]

These *Passenger Cases* were argued three times before the court finally decided them in 1849. When they were decided, each justice read his own opinion, a process consuming seven hours. [63]

The numerical majority, led by Justice John McLean, found the taxes a direct infringement of the exclusive federal power over interstate and foreign commerce. The dissenters, led by Chief Justice Taney, viewed the states as having a concurrent power with Congress and saw the tax laws as a proper use of state police power.

Yes and No

At last in 1852 — almost three decades after *Gibbons v. Ogden* — the court managed to formulate its divergent opinions into some sort of rule by which it might be determined whether states could exercise any regulatory authority over matters of interstate and foreign commerce.

The case, *Cooley v. Board of Wardens of the Port of Philadelphia,* turned on the question of whether the state of Pennsylvania could require vessels entering the port of Philadelphia to take on a pilot to enter, or, if they refused, to pay a certain fee. One Cooley refused to take on a pilot or pay the fee, challenging the requirement as an infringement by the state on exclusive federal power over matters of commerce such as pilotage.

Congress in 1789 had enacted a law that said pilots should continue to be regulated by state law until such time as Congress acted to impose a uniform system of regulation on them.

The court upheld Pennsylvania's pilot requirement. Writing the opinion was the most junior justice, Benjamin R. Curtis, a 41-year-old Boston attorney in his first term on the court. Curtis explained that the court found the state law permissible because Congress clearly had intended state regulation of this matter to continue, because Congress had not passed any superseding legislation concerning pilotage, and because the subject was in fact one better dealt with by local regulation.

In explaining this last point, Curtis set out what came to be known as the "*Cooley* rule," used to distinguish matters of exclusive federal control under the commerce power from those where a concurrent federal and state power existed:

> The grant of commercial power to Congress does not contain any terms which expressly exclude the States from exercising an authority over its subject matter. If they are excluded, it must be because the nature of the power, thus granted to Congress, requires that a similar authority should not exist in the States. . . .

> Now, the power to regulate commerce embraces a vast field, containing not only many, but exceedingly various subjects, quite unlike in their nature; some imperatively demanding a single uniform rule, operating equally on the commerce of the United States in every port; and some, like the subject now in question,

as imperatively demanding that diversity, which alone can meet the local necessities of navigation.

> Either absolutely to affirm, or deny, that the nature of this power requires exclusive legislation by Congress, is to lose sight of the nature of the subjects of this power, and to assert concerning all of them, what is really applicable but to a part. Whatever subjects of this power are in their nature national, or admit only of

---

Speed Limits and Mud Flaps

Although railroad rates were removed from state control before the end of the 19th century, the Supreme Court — and Congress — have continued to leave the states considerable authority to regulate interstate traffic in ways protecting the public safety. This, the court has held in a variety of cases, is a permissible exercise of the police power — so long as it does not impose an undue burden on interstate commerce.

In judging the validity of such laws, the court usually weighs the benefits produced by the regulation against the burden it imposes on the regulated vehicles. Thus, as early as 1910, the court upheld Georgia's speed limit for interstate trains; but later it struck down Georgia's requirement that trains slow at all grade crossings. The effect of this latter requirement was to double the travel time of some trains whose routes took them past as many crossings as one each minute. [1]

In the Motor Carrier Act of 1935, Congress left to the state the regulation of the size and weight of interstate motor vehicles traveling through its territory. Subsequently, the court upheld South Carolina's limits on the size of trucks and trailers, even though they were substantially stricter than those of adjoining states. [2]

In 1945 the court struck down Arizona's law restricting the length of railroad trains operating within the state. Although Congress had not regulated that subject, the court held that the limits placed by the law were so in conflict with the railroad industry's usual train length that they burdened commerce, and did not so benefit the public safety that they could be justified. [3] In general, the court held, states have more control over the highways than over the railroads within their boundaries.

In 1959 the court held that Illinois burdened commerce by requiring that trucks passing through the state have a certain kind of rear-fender mudguard different from the usual mudflap — which Illinois declared illegal. [4] And in 1978 the court struck down Wisconsin's ban on double-trailer trucks. The court held that the state did not provide any proof that this ban enhanced the safety of highway traffic, and so it must fall as an undue burden on interstate commerce. [5]

---

[1] *Southern Railway Co. v. King,* 217 U.S. 524 (1910); *Seaboard Air Line R. Co. v. Blackwell,* 244 U.S. 310 (1917).
[2] *South Carolina Highway Department v. Barnwell Brothers,* 303 U.S. 177 (1938).
[3] *Southern Pacific Co. v. Arizona,* 325 U.S. 761 (1945).
[4] *Bibb v. Navajo Freight Lines,* 359 U.S. 520 (1959).
[5] *Raymond Motor Transportation Inc. v. Rice,* 434 U.S. 429 (1978).

one uniform system, or plan of regulation, may justly be said to be of such a nature as to require exclusive legislation by Congress. That this cannot be affirmed of laws for the regulation of pilots and pilotage is plain. . . . [A]lthough Congress has legislated on this subject, its legislation manifests an intention . . . not to regulate this subject, but to leave its regulation to the several States. [64]

A century later, one constitutional scholar would describe the *Cooley* decision this way:

> To the question whether the power of Congress is exclusive, Mr. Justice Curtis took a great step forward by answering, "Yes, and no." This is the wisest initial answer to give to many questions that embrace such a variety and diversity of issues that no single answer can possibly be suitable for all. [65]

The line-drawing process that the *Cooley* rule demanded was a difficult one. During the same term when the rule was announced, the court held that Virginia had impermissibly built a bridge across the Ohio River, and infringed on the federal power to regulate interstate commerce. The bridge was too low for some boats to pass under. Although the facts of the case seemed similar, except in scale, to those of the Blackbird Creek decision, the court decided against the state.

By licensing ships under the coasting law to navigate the Ohio River, held the court, Congress clearly had asserted its authority over traffic there. In the earlier case, it was doubtful whether federal power had been extended over small creeks. "No state law can hinder or obstruct the free use of a license granted under an Act of Congress," wrote Justice McLean for the court. [66]

Congress overrode this decision. By passing a law authorizing the already-built bridge, it removed any objection to its existence as in conflict with congressional power. This was the first time that Congress directly blocked the effect of a court decision. In 1856 the court reviewed and upheld this act as within the power of Congress to regulate navigation. [67]

National Concerns

Railroad rates and immigration were two subjects to which the court applied the *Cooley* rule and found them to fall within the category of issues requiring exclusive federal regulation.

Immigration. Immigration had been an issue in the *Miln* case of 1837 and again in the *Passenger Cases* of 1849. In the former, the court had upheld a state requirement of reports on all incoming alien passengers; in the latter, it had struck down state taxes on all incoming aliens.

By the 1870s immigration clearly had become a matter of national concern. In 1876 the court voided New York, Louisiana and California laws that attempted to regulate immigration — and reduce the burden it might place on its finances — by requiring the owners of every ship bringing immigrants into the state to give bond for each alien. In the New York case the bond was $300 a passenger; payment could be waived by payment of a $1.50-per-person tax within 24 hours of landing. The states defended these laws as "a suitable regulation . . . to protect its cities and towns from the expense of supporting persons who are paupers or diseased, or helpless women and children, coming from foreign countries."

But the Supreme Court saw these laws as merely imposing a tax on the privilege of landing passengers in the state. That was impermissible interference with federal power over foreign commerce. Writing for the court, Justice Samuel Miller explained that the transportation of persons from foreign lands to this country had become foreign commerce, the regulation of which was exclusively reserved to Congress. Over such a subject, the state could not exercise its police power:

> [T]he matter of these statutes may be and ought to be the subject of a uniform system or plan. The laws which govern the right to land passengers in the United States from other countries ought to be the same in New York, Boston, New Orleans and San Francisco. . . . [T]his whole subject has been confided to Congress by the Constitution. [68]

Emphasizing this point again in the companion California case, Justice Miller wrote:

> The passage of laws which concern the admission of citizens and subjects of foreign nations to our shore belongs to Congress, and not to the states. . . . If it be otherwise, a single state can, at her pleasure, embroil us in disastrous quarrels with other nations. [69]

One result of these decisions was the passage by Congress, in 1882, of the nations' first general immigration law.

Railroad Rates. By the Civil War, commerce was moving across country by rail as well as water. Reflecting this shift, many of the court's post-war commerce clause rulings focused on the efforts of states to regulate the railroads.

For a time the court flirted with state regulation of railroad rates. But as the rail networks expanded across the United States, it became clear that the intrastate operations of an interstate railroad was hardly the subject for local regulation. In 1886 the court issued a decision to that effect — a major factor in the creation by Congress of the Interstate Commerce Commission in 1887.

In many states it was pressure from farmers that resulted in the passage of state laws regulating railroad rates. Particularly successful in this effort was the secret order called the National Grange, which won passage of a number of laws regulating how much railroads could charge farmers to carry their produce to market. In like fashion, some states passed laws to regulate rates that grain elevator companies could charge to store the farmers' grain.

In 1877 the Supreme Court appeared to sanction such state regulation of these businesses with its decision in a set of cases involving both railroad and grain elevator rate regulation. These decisions are referred to as the *Granger Cases,* or by the title of the grain elevator case, *Munn v. Illinois.* [70]

Acknowledging that these matters fell within the purview of federal power, the court nevertheless upheld the state laws. Writing in the Wisconsin railroad rate case, Chief Justice Morrison R. Waite stated:

> Until Congress acts in reference to the relations of this Company to interstate commerce, it is certainly within the power of Wisconsin to regulate its fares, etc., so far as they are of domestic concern. With the people of Wisconsin, this Company has domestic relations. Incidentally, these may reach beyond the State. But certainly, until Congress undertakes to legislate for

those who are without the State, Wisconsin may provide for those within, even though it may indirectly affect those without. [71]

To limit the implications of the grant of this power to the states, the court devised the criteria of "public interest" with which to distinguish those businesses that might be subject to state regulation from those that could not be. Chief Justice Waite outlined the rationale:

> Property does become clothed with a public interest when used in a manner to make it of public consequence and affect the community at large. When, therefore, one devotes his property to a use in which the public has an interest, he, in effect, grants to the public an interest in that use, and must submit to be controlled by the public for the common good, to the extent of the interest he has thus created. [72]

State regulation of grain elevators survived for several decades, upheld by the court again in 1892. [73]

But state power to regulate railroad rates was soon sharply curtailed. In 1886 — less than a decade after the

---

"The passage of laws which concern the admission of citizens and subjects of foreign nations to our shore belongs to Congress, and not to the states.... If it be otherwise, a single state can, at her pleasure, embroil us in disastrous quarrels with other nations."

—Justice Samuel Miller
Chy Lung v. Freeman, 1876

Granger Cases — the Supreme Court held that if a railroad was part of an interstate network, states could not regulate its rates, even for the intrastate portion of a trip. [74] Speaking for the court, Justice Miller wrote:

> It cannot be too strongly insisted upon, that the right of continuous transportation from one end of the country to the other is essential in modern times to that freedom of commerce from the restraints which the States might choose to impose upon it, that the commerce clause was intended to secure. This clause ... was among the most important of the subjects which prompted the formation of the Constitution.... And it would be a very feeble and almost useless provision, but poorly adapted to secure the entire freedom of commerce among the States which was deemed essential to a more perfect union by the framers ... if, at every stage of the transportation of goods and chattels through the country, the State within whose limits a part of this transportation must be done could impose regulations concerning the price, compensation, or taxation, or any other restrictive regulation interfering with and seriously embarrassing this commerce.... [75]
>
> [I]t is not, and never has been, the deliberate opinion of a majority of this court that a statute of a State which attempts to regulate the fares and charges

by railroad companies within its limits, for a transportation which constitutes a part of commerce among the States, is a valid law.... [76]

> As restricted to a transportation which begins and ends within the limits of the State, it may be very just and equitable, and it certainly is the province of the State Legislature to determine that question. But when it is attempted to apply to transportation through an entire series of States a principle of this kind, and each one ... shall attempt to establish its own rates of transportation ... the deleterious influence upon the freedom of commerce among the States and upon the transit of goods through those States cannot be overestimated. That this species of regulation is one which must be, if established at all, of a general and national character, and cannot be safely and wisely remitted to local rules and local regulations, we think it is clear.... [77]

The next year, Congress enacted the long-pending legislation to create the Interstate Commerce Commission, whose primary mission was the regulation of interstate railroad systems. States were still able to regulate purely intrastate railroad rates, and to exercise their police power to regulate other aspects of railroad operations, under judicial supervision to ensure that the states did not burden interstate commerce or deny the railroad due process of law.

With passage of the Interstate Commerce Act, Congress began to extend affirmative federal control over commerce. The period thus ended when most of the Supreme Court's commerce clause rulings viewed the clause chiefly as a limit on state power. The exercise of federal power in this area brought a whole new set of commerce clause issues to the court, phrased in terms of national, not state, authority. *(Chapter on Congress, p. 87)*

Local Concerns

But if the court saw it necessary to remove the issues of immigration and railroad regulation from state control, it by no means left the states bereft of power over economic matters. Between the Civil War and the New Deal, the court held that insurance, liquor, manufacturing, segregation, agriculture and child labor were all matters of strictly local concern. After the first years of the New Deal, the line between local and national matters — preserved chiefly through the doctrine of dual federalism — became indistinct and of relatively little importance. *(p. 97)*

Insurance. In 1869 the court held that the business of insurance regulation should be left to the states. The justices upheld a state law requiring out-of-state insurance companies to obtain a state license and post bond with the state of Virginia before doing business there. This was a proper local law governing local transactions, held the court in the case of *Paul v. Virginia.* [78]

And this remained the law for 75 years. During World War II, several fire insurance companies were indicted under federal antitrust law, and they raised as their defense the fact that insurance was outside the category of "commerce," which was the subject of the Sherman Antitrust Act under which the charges were brought. The government contested this claim — and the Supreme Court rejected it.

The court upheld the indictment in 1944 and thus brought insurance within the definition of commerce subject to federal regulation. Writing for the court, Justice Hugo L. Black said:

No commercial enterprise of any kind which conducts its activities across state lines has been held to be wholly beyond the regulatory power of Congress under the Commerce Clause. We cannot make an exception of the business of insurance. [79]

In all cases in which the Court has relied upon the proposition that "the business of insurance is not commerce," its attention was focused on the validity of state statutes — the extent to which the Commerce Clause automatically deprived states of the power to regulate the insurance business. Since Congress had at no time attempted to control the insurance business, invalidation of the state statutes would practically have been equivalent to granting insurance companies engaged in interstate activities a blanket license to operate without legal restraint. [80]

Congress, however, quickly handed this subject back to the state legislatures, passing a law exempting the insurance business from the reach of all but a few major federal antitrust and labor laws. In 1946 the Supreme Court upheld this action.[81]

Manufacturing

By defining commerce to exclude manufacturing or production, the Supreme Court effectively placed a number of issues beyond federal reach and within state control.

In 1888 the court upheld an Iowa law that forbade the manufacture of liquor in Iowa for sale outside the state as well as in the state. In so doing, Justice Lucius Quintus Cincinnatus Lamar proclaimed:

No distinction is more popular to the common mind, or more clearly expressed in economic and political literature, than that between manufactures and commerce. Manufacture is transformation — the fashioning of raw materials into a change of form for use. The functions of commerce are different. The buying and selling and the transportation incidental thereto constitute commerce; and the regulation of commerce in the constitutional sense embraces the regulation at least of such transportation. . . .

If it be held that the term includes the regulation of all such manufactures as are intended to be the subject of commercial transactions in the future, it is impossible to deny that it would also include all productive industries that contemplate the same thing. The result would be that Congress would be invested, to the exclusion of the States, with the power to regulate, not only manufacture, but also agriculture, horticulture, stock raising, domestic fisheries, mining — in short, every branch of human industry. . . .

The power being vested in Congress and denied to the States, it would follow as an inevitable result that the duty would devolve on Congress to regulate all of these delicate, multiform, and vital interests — interests which in their nature are, and must be, local in all the details of their successful management. [82]

It does not follow that, because the products of a domestic manufacture may ultimately become the subjects of interstate commerce . . . the legislation of the State respecting such manufacture is an attempted exercise of the power of commerce exclusively conferred upon Congress. [83]

Seven years later, this distinction used in the liquor case to uphold state regulation was exercised again — this

time to preclude federal regulation. In the *Sugar Trust* case of 1895, the court held that the Sherman Antitrust Act, enacted under the federal commerce power, could not be used as a basis for prosecuting sugar manufacturers.

Wrote Chief Justice Melville W. Fuller:

Commerce succeeds to manufacture, and is not a part of it. The power to regulate commerce is the power to prescribe the rule by which commerce shall be governed, and is a power independent of the power to suppress monopoly. [84]

The relief of the citizens of each state from the burden of monopoly was left with the states to deal with, and this court has recognized their possession of that power even to the extent of holding that an employment or business carried on by private individuals, when it becomes a matter of such public interest and importance as to create a common charge or burden upon the citizen; in other words, when it becomes a practical monopoly, to which the citizen is compelled to resort . . . is subject to regulation by state legislative power. . . .

It is vital that the independence of the commercial power and of the police power, and the delimitation between them, however sometimes perplexing, should

---

Garbage and Commerce

"All objects of interstate trade merit Commerce Clause protection; none is excluded by definition at the outset," stated the Supreme Court in 1978, including garbage within that constitution protection.[1]

By a 7-2 vote, the court struck down — as an infringement of federal power to regulate commerce — a New Jersey law forbidding the importation of solid or liquid waste originated or collected out of state. Justice Potter Stewart wrote the court's opinion; Justice William H. Rehnquist and Chief Justice Warren E. Burger dissented.

New Jersey, whose landfills had for years been used by the cities of Philadelphia and New York as depositories for their garbage, sought to preserve the remaining landfill space within its boundaries for dumping its own garbage. But the court found that the state had chosen a constitutionally impermissible means of achieving that end. Wrote Stewart:

[W]hatever New Jersey's ultimate purpose, it may not be accomplished by discriminating against articles of commerce coming from outside the State unless there is some reason, apart from their origin, to treat them differently.

[This law] falls squarely within the area that the Commerce Clause puts off-limits to state regulation. On its face, it imposes on out-of-state commercial interests the full burden of conserving the State's remaining landfill space. . . . What is crucial is the attempt by one State to isolate itself from a problem common to many by erecting a barrier against the movement of interstate trade.[2]

---

[1] *Philadelphia v. New Jersey*, 437 U.S. 617 at 622 (1978).
[2] Id. at 626-27, 628.

always be recognized and observed, for while the one furnishes the strongest bond of union, the other is essential to the preservation of the autonomy of the states as required by our dual form of government.....[85]

In subsequent similar decisions, the court held mining, lumbering, fishing, farming, the production of oil and the generation of electric power all outside the scope of the federal commerce power and hence, within the scope of state regulation. [86]

Although the court did not directly overrule these particular decisions separating manufacture and commerce, in the late 1930s it simply abandoned the distinction, upholding federal laws that did regulate manufacturing, such as the National Labor Relations Act. [87] Similarly, it upheld the Agricultural Adjustment Act of 1938, setting marketing quotas for farm products. This, the court reasoned, regulated farm production at the point where it entered interstate commerce, the marketing warehouse. The justices dismissed the argument that not all products regulated were sold in interstate commerce. [88]

And three years later the court upheld the application of these quotas to a farmer who grew wheat — in excess of his quota — only for use on his own farm. Despite the lack of any clear connection between the excess wheat on this farm and interstate commerce, the court sustained the reach of federal power. Justice Robert H. Jackson explained the court's rationale: If the price of wheat rose high enough, the farmer would be induced to put his wheat into interstate commerce — and if he didn't, he would use it for his own purposes and thus not buy wheat in interstate commerce that he otherwise would need to buy. "Home-grown wheat in this sense competes with wheat in commerce," Jackson said. [89]

At the same time, the court continued to sanction state regulation of production. A few months after the farmer's wheat decision, the court upheld California's detailed system for regulating raisin production and marketing, even to the point of controlling the flow of raisins into interstate commerce to maintain a certain price level. [90]

Segregation. Within one 15-year period in the late 19th century, the court used the *Cooley* rule to deny one state the power to prohibit racial discrimination on steamboats while granting another state the authority to decree racial segregation on trains.

When Josephine DeCuir, "a person of color," boarded *The Governor Allen*, a Mississippi River steamboat, to travel from New Orleans to another point in Louisiana, she sought a seat in the cabin set aside for white persons. She was denied entrance, and subsequently sued the steamboat owners for violating an 1869 state law forbidding racial discrimination on common carriers.

The state courts found that this law affected interstate commerce and thus was invalid. On appeal, the Supreme Court in 1878 declared itself bound by this finding of the state courts and thus ruled against DeCuir and against the law. Under the *Cooley* rule, the justices held that equal access to steamboat accommodations was a matter for national regulation. State regulation of such matters, if it affected interstate commerce, burdened interstate commerce.

Chief Justice Waite explained:

If each State was at liberty to regulate the conduct of carriers while within its jurisdiction, the confusion likely to follow could not but be productive of great inconvenience and unnecessary hardship. Each State could provide for its own passengers and regulate the transportation of its own freight, regardless of the interests of others. Nay more, it could prescribe the rules by which the carrier must be governed within the State in respect to passengers and property brought from without. On one side of the river . . . he might be required to observe one set of rules, and on the other another. Commerce cannot flourish in the midst of such embarrassments. [91]

If the public good requires such legislation [decreeing equal access], it must come from Congress and not from the States. [92]

Just 12 years later, however, the court upheld a Mississippi law requiring railroads doing business in the state to provide separate accommodations for black and white passengers. In this case, unlike the *DeCuir* case, the state court held that this law applied solely to intrastate railroad operations and, in accord with that finding, the Supreme Court in 1890 held it no burden on interstate commerce. [93]

In dissent, Justice John Marshall Harlan found Chief Justice Waite's comments in the earlier case "entirely pertinent to the case before us. . . . It is difficult to understand how a state enactment, requiring the separation of the white and black races on interstate carriers of passengers, is a regulation of commerce among the States, while a similar enactment forbidding such separation is not. . . ." [94]

In 1896, in the famous case of *Plessy v. Ferguson*, the court upheld "separate but equal" accommodations on common carriers again — this time against challenge as a violation of the 14th Amendment. Harlan dissented again. [95]

It was 56 years before the court reversed its 1890 ruling allowing Mississippi to require railroads to segregate passengers. In 1946 the court declared that "seating arrangements for the different races in interstate motor travel require a single uniform rule to promote and protect national travel." Hence the justices struck down a Virginia law requiring black passengers to ride in the rear of interstate buses, and reversed the conviction of one Irene Morgan who refused to move to comply with that law. [96]

The end to tolerance of local segregation of any segment of interstate transportation came in the mid-1950s with an Interstate Commerce Commission rule terminating racial segregation on all interstate trains and buses and in all public waiting rooms in railway and bus stations. In 1956 the Supreme Court affirmed a lower court's ruling striking down such segregation in intrastate transportation as a violation of the 14th Amendment. [97]

Child Labor. Perhaps the most extreme of the court's cases reserving areas of the economy for strictly state or local supervision were its child labor rulings of 1918 and 1922, striking down the efforts of Congress to prohibit child labor.

These rulings depended upon the dichotomy between manufacturing and commerce — and upon the 10th Amendment reservation of powers to the states and the accompanying doctrine of dual federalism, the idea that the state governments and the national government operated within neatly defined and separated domains, within which each was supreme.

The first child labor case was that of *Hammer v. Dagenhart*. Congress had attempted to forbid the use of the channels of interstate commerce to products of factories, quarries or mines employing children under 14 years of age.

This, held the court, intruded too far upon state concerns. Justice William R. Day wrote for the majority:

> Over interstate transportation . . . the regulatory power of Congress is ample, but the production of articles, intended for interstate commerce, is a matter of local regulation. . . .
>
> There is no power vested in Congress to require the states to exercise their police power to prevent possible unfair competition. . . .
>
> The grant of power to Congress . . . was to enable it to regulate such commerce, and not to give it authority to control the states in their exercise of the police power over local trade and manufacture.
>
> The grant of authority over a purely federal matter was not intended to destroy the local power always existing and carefully reserved to the states in the Tenth Amendment to the Constitution. [98]
>
> . . .[I]f Congress can thus regulate matters entrusted to local authority by prohibition of the movement of commodities in interstate commerce, all freedom of commerce will be at an end, and the power of the states over local matters may be eliminated, and thus our system of government practically destroyed. [99]

In candid dissent, Justice Oliver Wendell Holmes Jr. declared:

> The Act does not meddle with anything belonging to the states. They may regulate their internal affairs and their domestic commerce as they like. But when they seek to send their products across the State line they are no longer within their rights. If there were no Constitution and no Congress their power to cross the line would depend upon their neighbors. Under the Constitution such commerce belongs not to the States but to Congress to regulate. It may carry out its views of public policy whatever indirect effect they may have on the activities of the States. . . . [100]

Four years later, the court struck down a second congressional effort to discourage child labor — this time through the use of the taxing power. Chief Justice William Howard Taft, speaking for the majority, set out the same objections that Day had voiced:

> Grant the validity of this law, and all that Congress would need to do hereafter, in seeking to take over to its control any one of the great number of subjects of public interest, jurisdiction of which the states have never parted with, and which are reserved to them by the 10th Amendment, would be to enact a detailed measure of complete regulation of the subject and enforce it by a so-called tax. . . . To give such magic to the word "tax" would be to break down all constitutional limitation of Congress and completely wipe out the sovereignty of the states. [101]

These two rulings stood until 1941, when the court overruled *Hammer v. Dagenhart*, and discarded the doctrine of dual federalism, as it upheld the Fair Labor Standards Act, which — among other provisions — prohibited child labor. The case bringing this landmark opinion was *United States v. Darby*.

Writing for the court, Justice Harlan Fiske Stone declared that:

> Such regulation is not a forbidden invasion of state power merely because either its motive or its conse-

quence is to restrict the use of articles of commerce within the states of destination. . . . Whatever their motive and purpose, regulations of commerce which do not infringe some constitutional prohibition are within the plenary power conferred on Congress by the Commerce Clause. . . .

> The power of Congress over interstate commerce . . . extends to the activities intrastate which so affect interstate commerce or the exercise of the power of Congress over it as to make regulation of them appropriate means to the attainment of a legitimate end, the exercise of the granted power of Congress to regulate interstate commerce. . . . [102]

A Changing Answer

A century after Justice Curtis formulated the *Cooley* rule to bring some clarity into the confusion of the exclusive and concurrent commerce power debate, the answer to the questions that debate posed still seemed to be "Yes, and No." As Thomas Reed Powell wrote in the mid-1950s:

> Once it was thought that the test of what states may do is what the nation may not do, or that the test of what the states may not do is what the nation may do, but the criteria are no longer so clear cut as that. The involutions of state power must be considered with a greater particularity than can be compressed into a formula. [103]

The Police Power

The 10th Amendment reserves to the states and the people "the powers not delegated to the United States by the Constitution nor prohibited by it to the states." Early in the nation's history, the Supreme Court began to recognize that one of the most important of these reserved powers is that called the police power, the power to govern its people, and to regulate the use of its land and its resources to ensure the public welfare.

The police power, in effect, grants the states some power to affect interstate commerce. As Thomas Reed Powell has written:

> By this judicial invention there is no constitutional division between concurrent and exclusive power over commerce. The power of Congress is concurrent with that of the states; the power of the states is concurrent with that of Congress. The exercise of state power, however, is subject to several restrictions. It must not impose regulation in conflict with regulations of Congress. It must not, even in the absence of conflict, impose regulations if Congress, by what it has done, is deemed to have "occupied the entire field." [104]

Oddly enough, the first recognition by the court of this power came even as Chief Justice Marshall was asserting the sweeping federal power over commerce. In the opinion resolving the case of *Gibbons v. Ogden*, Marshall acknowledged the power of a state "to regulate its police, its domestic trade, and to govern its own citizens." This power, he continued, might even enable the state to legislate — concurrently with Congress — on the subject of navigation.

And earlier in the opinion, he had mentioned the state's power to require inspection of items departing the state before they entered into the stream of interstate or foreign commerce. Inspection laws, Marshall wrote, "form a portion of that immense mass of legislation which embraces everything within the territory of a state not surrendered to the general government. . . . Inspection laws, quarantine laws, health laws of every description, as well as laws for regulating the internal commerce of a state, and those which respect turnpike-roads, ferries, etc. are component parts of this mass." [105]

Five years later in *Willson v. Blackbird Creek Marsh Co.*, Marshall appeared to base the court's approval of a state-built dam across a small creek upon the power of the state to act to preserve property values and enhance the public health. [106]

But it was during the tenure of Chief Justice Roger B. Taney that the concept of this power was first fully enunciated by the court. In the opinion of the court in the case of *Charles River Bridge v. Warren Bridge*, Taney spoke of the importance of protecting the states' "power over their own internal police and improvement, which is so necessary to their well being and prosperity." [107]

Within the same month as the *Charles River Bridge* decision, the court gave its first extended exposition of the police power as it ruled in the case of *The Mayor of New York v. Miln.*

In an effort to lighten the burden immigration placed upon its port city, New York law required the master of any ship arriving in New York Harbor from outside the state to report to the mayor the birthplace, previous residence, age and occupation of every passenger. George Miln, owner of the ship *Emily*, did not comply and was sued by the state for the penalties he thus incurred. In his defense, Miln argued that the state law was invalid, that it regulated foreign commerce and navigation in conflict with federal power over those areas.

The Supreme Court rejected that defense. Writing for the majority, Justice Philip Barbour stated that:

the [challenged] act is not a regulation of commerce, but of police, and . . . being thus considered, it was passed in the exercise of a power which rightfully belonged to the States. . . . It is apparent . . . that the object of the Legislature was to prevent New York from being burdened by an influx of persons brought thither in ships . . . and for that purpose a report was required . . . that the necessary steps might be taken by the city authorities to prevent them from becoming chargeable as paupers. [108]

Gibbons v. Ogden did not control the decision because this case concerned regulation of state territory, not of navigation, wrote Justice Barbour. And here there was no colliding federal law, he continued; so even under the reasoning of *Gibbons v. Ogden* the New York law could stand. Barbour wrote for the majority:

But we do not place our opinion on this ground. We choose rather to plant ourselves on what we consider impregnable positions. They are these: That a State has the same undeniable and unlimited jurisdiction over all persons and things within its territorial limits, as any foreign nation, where that jurisdiction is not surrendered or restrained by the Constitution of the United States. That, by virtue of this, it is not only the right, but the bounden and solemn duty of a State, to advance the safety, happiness and prosperity of its people, and to provide for its general welfare, by any and every act of legislation which it may deem to be

The Perils of Colored Oleo

To the modern view, one of the oddest sets of police power laws and accompanying Supreme Court decisions involved the efforts of states to protect their citizens from the "perils" of colored oleo.

Pennsylvania, ostensibly to protect the public health and to prevent fraud — the selling of oleo as butter — banned the sale of colored oleomargarine within the state. In 1888 the Supreme Court held this a reasonable exercise of the state police power. [1]

Six years later, the original package doctrine notwithstanding, the court upheld a Massachusetts law that forbade the sale of imported margarine in the original package — if the margarine was colored to resemble butter. [2] Due to the risk of fraud, the court found this a different question from that resolved — against a state ban on the sale of imported liquor in the original package — in the case of *Leisy v. Hardin. (See discussion, p. 325)*

Subsequent rulings modified the scope of state power over colored margarine, but in 1902 Congress passed a law providing that oleomargarine was subject to state regulation upon arrival within the limits of the state.

---

[1] *Powell v. Pennsylvania*, 127 U.S. 678 (1888).
[2] *Plumley v. Massachusetts*, 155 U.S. 461 (1894).

conducive to these ends; where the power over the particular subject, or the manner of its exercise is not surrendered or restrained, in the manner just stated. That all those powers which relate to merely municipal legislation, or what may, perhaps, more properly be called internal police, are not thus surrendered or restrained; and that, consequently, in relation to these, the authority of a State is complete, unqualified and exclusive.

In regard to the particular subject of this case, the court held that the power exercised was encompassed in the recognized power of a state to pass and enforce inspection and quarantine laws, which operated directly upon items in interstate and foreign commerce, delaying and sometimes even destroying them:

We think it as competent and as necessary for a State to provide precautionary measures against the moral pestilence of paupers, vagabonds, and possibly convicts, as it is to guard against the physical pestilence which may arise from unsound and infectious articles imported, or from a ship, the crew of which may be laboring under an infectious disease. [109]

The significance of the development of this concept by the Supreme Court under Chief Justice Taney — and of the underlying doctrine of dual federalism as a limit on federal power — has been described by Alpheus T. Mason and William M. Beaney:

[I]n the context of his times, state police power was the only available weapon with which government could face the pressing problems of the day. In a period in which the national government was not yet prepared to deal realistically with economic and social problems, national supremacy had the effect of posing the unexercised commerce power of Congress, or the contract clause, as barriers to any governmental action. Taney's dual federalism ... enabled the state to deal experimentally with problems that the national government would not face until another half-century had elapsed. Thus Marshall and Taney left as legacies two official conceptions of federalism [national supremacy and dual federalism] that succeeding justices were free to apply as their inclinations or the needs of the time dictated. [110]

The police power has been employed for a variety of ends: to control entry to the state, to protect the public health and public morals, to ensure public safety, to regulate business and to regulate working conditions. The court has by no means approved all of the uses to which the states have put the police power. A number fell as interfering with the federal power to regulate commerce; others fell as interfering with the freedom of contract or the liberty of property. But, nevertheless, the police power has served as a broad basis for state efforts to control economic and business matters for the public good.

Control of Entry

After *Miln* recognized some state power to control the entry of persons, the court in 1839 indicated that states possessed a correlative power to exclude out-of-state corporations from doing business within their boundaries. In that ruling, however, in the case of the *Bank of Augusta v. Earle,* the court held that it would be assumed — absent clear evidence to the contrary — that a state gave its consent to the conduct of business by an out-of-state corporation. [111]

Although the right to exclude a foreign corporation obviously included the right to place conditions on such an entity's conduct of business within the state, the court some four decades later made clear that a state could not exercise this power to place an undue burden on an out-of-state corporation wishing to engage in interstate commerce within the state. This 1877 decision in the case of *Pensacola Telegraph Co. v. Western Union* made clear, notes one commentator, that the state's power to exclude foreign corporations was subject to "the overriding force of a congressional license to carry on interstate commerce," in this case, communication by telegraphic messages. [112]

In the 1841 case of *Groves v. Slaughter* the court managed to sidestep a decision on the question of the state's power to ban the entry of out-of-state slaves — although the justices took the opportunity to air personal views on the matter that were quite diverse. [113]

And in the *Passenger Cases* of 1849 the court held — by a narrow margin — that the federal commerce power clearly limited the state's power to control the entry of persons. Striking down state laws taxing entering aliens, the court, in the words of Justice John McLean, held:

the police power of the State cannot draw within its jurisdiction objects which lie beyond it. It meets the commercial power of the Union in dealing with subjects under the protection of that power, yet it can only be exercised under peculiar emergencies and to a limited extent. In guarding the safety, the health, and morals of its citizens, a State is restricted to appropriate and constitutional means.

In dissent, Chief Justice Taney and his colleagues argued that "the several States have a right to remove from among their people, and to prevent from entering the State, any person, or class or description of persons, whom it may deem dangerous or injurious to the interests and welfare of its citizens." [114]

But the majority's view in the *Passenger Cases* has prevailed to modern times. In 1876 the court held that control of immigration from abroad was a matter exempt from state regulation and entrusted exclusively to Congress. And in 1941 it struck down — as an obstruction of interstate commerce — a California law that penalized persons bringing poor people into the state to live. [115]

Public Health and Morals

Perhaps the most widely acknowledged objective for the exercise of the police power is the protection of the public health, the focus of the quarantine and inspection laws about which Chief Justice Marshall commented in *Gibbons v. Ogden.*

When the court in 1847 upheld state laws licensing the sale of alcohol, one of the few points upon which the justices could agree was the paramount responsibility of the state to use the police power to protect its public health and to preserve public morals. Justice McLean set forth his views:

The acknowledged police power of a State extends often to the destruction of property. A nuisance may be abated.... Merchandise from a port where a contagious disease prevails, being liable to communicate the disease, may be excluded; and in extreme cases, it may be thrown into the sea. This comes in direct conflict with the regulation of commerce; and yet no one doubts the local power. It is a power essential to self-preservation.... It is, indeed, the law of nature, and is possessed by man in his individual capacity. He may resist that which does him harm, whether he be assailed by an assassin, or approached by poison. And it is the settled construction of every regulation of commerce, that, under the sanction of its general laws, no person can introduce into a community malignant diseases, or anything which contaminates its morals, or endangers its safety.... From the explosive nature of gunpowder, a city may exclude it. Now this is an article of commerce, and is not known to carry infectious disease; yet to guard against a contingent injury, a city may prohibit its introduction.

When in the appropriate exercise of these federal and State powers, contingently and incidentally the lines of action run into each other; if the State power be necessary to the preservation of the morals, the health, or safety of the community, it must be maintained. [116]

No better illustration of the complexities of applying this police power for the purpose of safeguarding public health and morals can be provided than by the long series of rulings handed down by the court from these *License Cases* of 1847 well into the 20th century concerning state power to regulate all aspects of the subject of intoxicating liquors.

In 1874 the court upheld Iowa's prohibition of the sale of liquor, even that owned at the time of the law's passage. [117] In 1887 the court upheld a Kansas law that forbade both the manufacture and sale of intoxicating liquor. Writing for the court, Justice John Marshall Harlan made clear that the police power was not without limits:

If ... a statute purporting to have been enacted to protect the public health, the public morals, or the public safety, has no real or substantial relation to those objects, or is a palpable invasion of rights secured by the fundamental law, it is the duty of the courts to so adjudge. . . .

[But in this case, we] cannot shut out of view the fact, within the knowledge of all, that the public health, the public morals, and the public safety, may be endangered by the general use of intoxicating drinks; nor the fact, established by statistics accessible to everyone, that the idleness, disorder, pauperism, and crime existing in the country are, in some degree at least, traceable to this evil. If, therefore, a State deems the absolute prohibition of the manufacture and sale, within her limits, of intoxicating liquors for other than medical, scientific and manufacturing purposes, to be necessary to the peace and security of society, the courts cannot, without usurping legislative functions, override the will of the people as thus expressed by their chosen representatives. [118]

The following year the court upheld a state's ban on the manufacture of liquor in the state for export, but struck down a ban on the importation of liquor into that state. The ban on importation, the court held, interfered with interstate commerce. [119]

And two years later, the court further weakened state power over the importation of liquor by holding that a state could not forbid the first sale of such liquor in its original package. This ruling in the case of *Leisy v. Hardin* was based on the doctrine — first announced in the 1827 case of *Brown v. Maryland* —that as long as an imported product remained in the package in which it had entered the state — it was beyond state regulation or taxation. [120]

Iowa had banned the sale of imported liquor in any package. Leisy, a Peoria, Ill., brewer, shipped liquor to Keokuk, Iowa, where it was seized by Hardin, a law enforcement officer. Leisy challenged Iowa's ban on the first sale of imported liquor as infringing upon the federally protected flow of interstate commerce. The court agreed with Leisy and struck down that portion of the law. Writing for the court, Chief Justice Melville W. Fuller stated:

Up to that point of time [after the first sale in the original package], we hold that, in the absence of congressional permission to do so, the State had no power to interfere by seizure, or any other action, in prohibition of importation and sale by the foreign nonresident importer. Whatever our individual views may be, as to the deleterious or dangerous qualities of particular articles, we cannot hold that any articles which Congress recognizes as subjects of interstate commerce are not such, or . . . can be controlled by state laws amounting to regulations, while they retain that character. [121]

Fuller's opinion invited Congress to act. In 1890 — the year of the decision — Congress approved the Wilson Act, stripping imported liquor of the protection of interstate commerce — or the original package. The law stated that upon arrival in a state, intoxicating liquors were subject to whatever police power laws the state wished to pass, just as if the liquor had been produced in the state and not imported. In 1891 the Supreme Court approved the act. [122]

Congress subsequently acted to place the subject of alcohol control even more completely under state authority. The Webb-Kenyon Act of 1913 forbade the shipment of liquor into any state where its use or sale would violate state law. In 1917 the court upheld state power under this law to forbid the entry of intoxicating liquor. [123]

And the addition of the 21st Amendment (repeal of Prohibition) to the Constitution in 1933 placed the matter entirely under state control, stating that "the transportation or importation into any State, Territory, or possession of the United States for delivery or use therein of intoxicating liquors, in violation of the laws thereof, is hereby prohibited." The court has construed the power granted by this amendment broadly, holding only that states may not forbid the sale of liquor on federal property, that Congress may continue to regulate the importation of liquor from abroad, and that a state may only place reasonable restrictions on the passage of liquor through its territory. [124]

'Public Interest' Regulation

From its 1877 decision in *Munn v. Illinois* until 1934, the Supreme Court used the doctrine of the "public interest" as its standard for determining the types of businesses that states might properly regulate. Businesses that appeared to the justices to be "clothed with a public interest" might be regulated; others that lacked this characteristic were to remain free of state control.

Explaining the logic of this standard, Chief Justice Morrison R. Waite wrote in *Munn v. Illinois* that under the police power "the government regulates the conduct of its citizens one towards another, and the manner in which each shall use his own property, when such regulation becomes necessary for the public good. . . . Property does become clothed with a public interest when used in a manner to make it of public consequence, and affect the community at large." [125] (Details, p. 318)

The "public interest" doctrine survived for half a century but, as a standard for decisions by courts or state legislatures, it never acquired any clear meaning. The court held that bakeries, meatpackers, ticketscalpers, employment agencies, gas stations and ice vendors were not businesses "clothed with a public interest" — but that railroads, public utilities, grain elevators, stockyards, fire insurance companies and tobacco warehouses were. [126]

In 1934 the court abandoned this rationale for state regulation with its decision in the case of *Nebbia v. New York*. The court held that New York could set the acceptable range of prices to be charged for milk within the state. States could regulate virtually any business for the public good, held the court, so long as the regulation was reasonable and effected through appropriate means. Discarding the *Munn* approach, Justice Owen J. Roberts wrote for the majority:

It is clear there is no closed class or category of businesses affected with a public interest. . . . The function of courts . . . is to determine in each case whether circumstances vindicate the challenged regulation as a reasonable exertion of governmental authority or condemn it as arbitrary or discriminatory. . . . The phrase "affected with a public interest" can, in the nature of things, mean no more than that an industry, for adequate reason, is subject to control for the public good. . . . [T]here can be no doubt that upon proper occasion and by appropriate measures the state may regulate a business in any of its aspects. . . .

The Constitution does not secure to any one liberty to conduct his business in such fashion as to inflict injury upon the public at large, or upon any substantial group of the people. Price control, like any other form of regulation, is unconstitutional only if arbitrary, discriminatory, or demonstrably irrelevant to the policy the legislature is free to adopt, and hence an unnecessary and unwarranted interference with individual liberty. [127]

Wages and Hours

With the waning of the contract clause as a useful instrument to counter the increasingly vigorous assertions of the police power to regulate the use of property or the conduct of business, the 14th Amendment's due process clause took its place. The Supreme Court moved into a period of laissez-faire rulings, finding that there were some areas of business that neither federal nor state power could reach.

As a companion to this philosophy, the court began espousing the doctrine of "freedom of contract" — a part of the liberty protected by the 14th Amendment. Thus armed, the court for decades dealt unkindly with the efforts of states to control the hours — and later the wages — of workers within their jurisdiction.

The first of these laws considered fully by the Supreme Court — in 1898 — was upheld. Utah limited to eight hours a day the period that miners could work in underground mines except in an emergency. This law was challenged as denying both the worker and the employer their freedom of contract.

In the case of *Holden v. Hardy,* the court rejected that challenge and found the law a proper exercise of the police power by the state to protect its citizens' health by limiting the amount of time they spent in admittedly hazardous and unhealthy conditions. [128]

Bakery Workers: *Lochner.* Seven years later, however, health considerations did not weigh so heavily when the court considered — and struck down — New York's law limiting the hours that bakery employees might work. The court found this an infringement of the liberty of contract without due process of law.

Justice Rufus Peckham wrote for the majority in *Lochner v. New York:*

Clean and wholesome bread does not depend upon whether the baker works but ten hours per day or only sixty hours a week. The limitation of the hours of labor does not come within the police power on that ground.

It is a question of which of two powers or rights shall prevail — the power of the state to legislate or the right of the individual to liberty of person and freedom of contract.... We think the limit of the police power has been reached and passed in this case. There is ... no reasonable foundation for holding this to be necessary or appropriate as a health law to safeguard the public health.... We think that there can be no fair doubt that the trade of a baker, in and of itself, is not an unhealthy one to that degree which would authorize the legislature to interfere with the right to labor, and with the right of free contract on the part of the individual, either as employer or employee.

[If the court upheld this law] no trade, no occupation, no mode of earning one's living, could escape this all-pervading power, and the acts of the legislature in limiting the hours of labor in all employments would be valid, although such limitation might seriously cripple the ability of the laborer to support himself and his family....

Statutes of the nature of that under review, limiting the hours in which grown and intelligent men may labor to earn their living, are mere meddlesome interferences with the rights of the individual, and they are not saved from condemnation by the claim that they are passed in the exercise of the police power and upon the subject of the health of the individual whose rights are interfered with, unless there be some fair ground ... to say that there is material danger to the public health, or to the health of the employees, if the hours of labor are not curtailed. [129]

Laundry Women: *Muller.* The vote in *Lochner* was 5-4. And the narrowness of that balance came into focus three years later, when the court — in the case of *Muller v. Oregon* (1908), upheld Oregon's law setting a maximum 10-hour day for women working in laundries.

Arguing this case for Oregon was Louis D. Brandeis, later to become one of the court's most famous justices. In this case, he used what came to be called a "Brandeis brief" — briefs heavily buttressd with sociological and statistical information intended to support the legal argument. The court, in its opinion, paid a rare compliment to Brandeis by mentioning his brief and him, by name. The information was apparently convincing. The court upheld the law unanimously. [130]

Where the hazards of the occupation had distinguished *Hardy* from *Lochner,* sex apparently made the difference between *Lochner* and *Muller.* State regulation of working hours for women was seen as valid in light of the fact that women were thought to be physically less strong than men and that longer working hours were considered likely to impair their childbearing function.

And 10 years later, in 1917, the court upheld still another maximum hours law from Oregon — this one setting the 10-hour day as the maximum for all industrial

---

"Clean and wholesome bread does not depend upon whether the baker works but ten hours per day or only sixty hours a week. The limitation of the hours of labor does not come within the police power on that ground."

—Justice Rufus Peckham
Lochner v. New York, 1905

---

workers. The vote was 5-3; Justice Brandeis — counsel when these cases began — did not take part in the ruling.

Justice Joseph McKenna wrote the majority opinion in the case of *Bunting v. Oregon.* The opinion indicated that the court had given the benefit of the doubt to the law:

It is enough for our decision if the legislation under review was passed in the exercise of an admitted power of government.... There is a contention made that the law ... is not either necessary or useful "for the preservation of the health of employees...." The record contains no facts to support the contention....[131]

This ruling established the right of states to limit the hours of work for men and women in almost all occupations, free of challenge under the due process clause, so long as the standard imposed had some clear relationship to the society's health and safety.

Wages of Women, Children. But *Lochner* was not altogether dead, and soon reappeared as the court began striking down state and federal efforts to regulate wages. In 1923 the court invalidated a law enacted by Congress for the District of Columbia that set a minimum wage for women and children workers.

In this case of *Adkins v. Children's Hospital,* the vote was 5-3; Brandeis again did not participate. The opinion was written by Justice George Sutherland, who had been named to the court in 1922. Felix Frankfurter filed a long Brandeis brief demonstrating the unhappy effects of substandard wages on women. Although Frankfurter would later become a member of the court, the majority here found his statistics of little relevance to the validity of the law.

This was "simply and exclusively a price-fixing law," wrote Sutherland, "confined to adult women . . . who are legally as capable of contracting for themselves as men." A law could not prescribe the proper wage to preserve the health and moral character of a woman, he said. And it was lopsided, requiring an employer to pay a worker a certain amount regardless of whether he found the worker that valuable.

"A statute which prescribes payment . . . solely with relation to circumstances apart from the contract of employment, the business affected by it and the work done under it," Sutherland concluded, "is so clearly the product of a naked, arbitrary exercise of power that it cannot be allowed to stand under the Constitution." [132]

In dissent, Chief Justice William Howard Taft expressed his surprise at the revival of the doctrine of freedom of contract, saying that he thought *Lochner* had been overruled after *Muller* and *Bunting.*

Also in dissent, Justice Oliver Wendell Holmes Jr. wrote:

> This statute does not compel anybody to pay anything. It simply forbids employment at rates below those fixed as the minimum requirement of health and right living. It is safe to assume that women will not be employed at even the lowest wages allowed unless they earn them, or unless the employer's business can sustain the burden. In short, the law in its character and operation is like hundreds of so-called police laws that have been upheld. [133]

Holmes said he did not understand "the principle on which the power to fix a minimum for the wages of women can be denied by those who admit the power to fix a maximum for their hours of work. . . . I perceive no difference in the kind or degree of interference with liberty . . . between one case and the other." [134]

The court remained adamant. Fourteen years after *Adkins,* the court struck down a New York minimum wage law for women and children. The vote was 5-4, resolving the case of *Morehead v. Tipaldo* against the state. The four justices still serving who had formed the *Adkins* majority were joined by Justice Owen J. Roberts, who had been appointed to the court after the earlier ruling. This decision was announced in the spring of 1936.

Writing for the majority, Justice Pierce Butler declared any minimum wage law a violation of due process: "[T]he

state is without power by any form of legislation to prohibit, change or nullify contracts between employers and adult women workers as to the amount of wage to be paid." [135]

The dissenters — Chief Justice Charles Evans Hughes, Justices Brandeis, Benjamin Cardozo and Harlan Fiske Stone — viewed the matter as of broader concern to the community. Justice Stone wrote:

> We have had opportunity to perceive more clearly that a wage insufficient to support the worker does not visit its consequences upon him alone; that it may affect profoundly the entire economic structure of society and, in any case, that it casts on every taxpayer, and on government itself, the burden of solving the problems of poverty, subsistence, health and morals of large numbers in the community. Because of their nature and extent, these are public problems. A generation ago they were for the individual to solve; today they are the burden of the nation. [136]

Within a year, the court had reversed itself and overruled *Adkins.* In 1937, in the midst of the court-packing fight, the court — by a 5-4 vote — upheld Washington State's law setting minimum wages for women and children workers. Elsie Parrish, a chambermaid, had sued the hotel

---

"The exploitation of a class of workers who are in an unequal position with respect to bargaining power and are thus relatively defenseless against the denial of a living wage is not only detrimental to their health and well being but casts a direct burden for their support upon the community. . . ."

—Chief Justice Charles Evans Hughes
West Coast Hotel Co. v. Parrish, 1937

---

for which she worked to recover the difference between her pay and the minimum wage, under the state law, of $14.50 a week. The West Coast Hotel Co. used *Adkins* as its defense.

Justice Roberts, who had voted against the New York law, joined the dissenters from that case to form a majority upholding the Washington law in the decision known as *West Coast Hotel Co. v. Parrish.*

Chief Justice Hughes wrote the opinion:

> What can be closer to the public interest than the health of women and their protection from unscrupulous and overreaching employers? And if the protection of women is a legitimate end of the exercise of state power, how can it be said that the requirement of the payment of a minimum wage fairly fixed in order to meet the very necessities of existence is not an admissible means to that end? . . . The Legislature had the right to consider that its minimum wage requirements would be an important aid in carrying out its policy of protection. The adoption of similar requirements by

many states evidences a deep-seated conviction both as to the presence of the evil and as to the means adapted to check it. Legislative response to that conviction cannot be regarded as arbitrary or capricious and that is all we have to decide. Even if the wisdom of the policy be regarded as debatable and its effects uncertain, still the Legislature is entitled to its judgment. [137]

Recent economic experience, wrote Hughes, required the court to take a broader view of the purposes for which states might exercise their police power. The theory of the freedom of contract, upon which *Lochner* had been based, was defective when applied to situations where the contracting parties were clearly not of equal bargaining power:

> The exploitation of a class of workers who are in an unequal position with respect to bargaining power and are thus relatively defenseless against the denial of a living wage is not only detrimental to their health and well being but casts a direct burden for their support upon the community. What these workers lose in wages the taxpayers are called upon to pay. The bare cost of living must be met. . . . The community is not bound to provide what is in effect a subsidy for unconscionable employers. The community may direct its law-making power to correct the abuse which springs from their selfish disregard of the public interest. [138]

Fair Labor Standards Act. Within a year, federal power had been extended into this area so recently opened to state regulation. Congress approved the Fair Labor Standards Act, setting minimum wage and maximum hour standards for businesses using the facilities of interstate commerce.

The act provided criminal penalties for violating these standards, and a lumber company president named Darby was indicted for such offenses. His case became a test of the constitutionality of the act. In the 1941 decision in *United States v. Darby*, the court upheld the federal authority under the commerce power to impose such standards. [139]

Congress later extended the protection of these standards through amendments to the act. In 1966 it included the employees of state hospitals, schools and institutions. Two years later, in the case of *Maryland v. Wirtz*, the court upheld this extension, against challenge from the states that it encroached too far on their own internal affairs. [140]

In 1974 Congress went even further to eliminate the traditional exemption for state government employees from the minimum wage and overtime standards of the Act. In 1976 the Supreme Court overruled *Maryland v. Wirtz* and held the 1974 changes in the act unconstitutional. Congress had intruded too far into the internal affairs of the states, held the court, 5-4: "[B]oth the minimum wage and the maximum hour provisions will impermissibly interfere with the integral governmental functions" of the states. [141] *(Page 363)*

The Taxing of Commerce

The Constitution imposes two limitations upon the state's power to raise revenue through taxes. The first is implicit in the commerce clause; the second is an explicit ban upon state duties on imports or exports, or state-imposed tonnage duties, unless Congress should consent to such state taxes.

Most of the court's interpretation of the taxing powers of the states has been inextricably entwined with the

---

A Tax on Exports

The Supreme Court has had relatively few opportunities to elaborate on the application of the Export-Import Clause of the Constitution to exports. By far most of the rulings on this ban on state taxes have dealt with the subject of state efforts to tax imported goods.

But in 1860 the court considered — and struck down — California's effort to impose a stamp tax on bills of lading of gold to be taken out of the state. Writing for the court, Chief Justice Roger B. Taney found little difference between this tax and the license law voided by the court in *Brown v. Maryland*, its first ruling on the clause.

"A bill of lading . . . is invariably associated with every cargo of merchandise exported to a foreign country, and consequently a duty upon that is, in substance and effect, a duty on the article exported," wrote Taney. "And if the law of California is constitutional, then every cargo of every description exported from the United States may be made to pay an export duty to the State, provided the tax is imposed in the form of a tax on the bill of lading, and this in direct opposition to the plain and express prohibition in the Constitution." *(Almy v. California,* 24 How. 169 at 174, 1860)

In subsequent cases interpreting this clause with respect to exports, however, the court has generally attempted to preserve the state's right to tax an item so long as it appears possible that the item will not actually leave the state.

---

court's developing view of the commerce clause. Justice Felix Frankfurter wrote in 1946:

> The power of the state to tax and the limitations upon that power imposed by the commerce clause have necessitated a long continuous process of judicial adjustment. The need for such adjustment is inherent in a federal government like ours, where the same transaction has aspects that may concern the interests and involve the authority of both the central government and the constituent states. . . . To attempt to harmonize all that has been said in the past would neither clarify what has gone before nor guide the future. Suffice it to say that especially in this field opinions must be read in the setting of the particular case and as the product of preoccupation with their special facts. [142]

This approach is less than satisfactory for many judges and legislators who attempt to gauge the proper reach of state taxes. "This case-by-case approach," noted Justice Byron R. White 20 years after Frankfurter wrote, "has left 'much room for controversy and confusion and little in the way of precise guides to the States in the exercise of their indispensable power of taxation.' " [143]

A Concurrent Power

The major difference between the commerce and the taxing powers, in a constitutional sense, is that the taxing power may be exercised concurrently by the state and federal governments over the same item or area, while the commerce power may not be.

In *Gibbons v. Ogden*, Chief Justice Marshall discussed the distinction:

Although many of the powers formerly exercised by the states, are transferred to the government of the Union, yet the state governments remain, and constitute a most important part of our system. The power of taxation is indispensable to their existence, and is a power which, in its own nature, is capable of residing in, and being exercised by, different authorities at the same time....

Congress is authorized to lay and collect taxes, etc., to pay the debts, and provide for the common defense and general welfare of the United States. This does not interfere with the power of the states to tax for the support of their own governments; nor is the exercise of that power by the states an exercise of any portion of the power that is granted to the United States. In imposing taxes for state purposes, they are not doing what Congress is empowered to do. Congress is not empowered to tax for those purposes which are within the exclusive province of the states. When, then, each government exercises the power of taxation, neither is exercising the power of the other....[144]

A Limited Power

But even before Marshall wrote these words, the court — in its first major ruling affecting the state's power to tax, *McCulloch v. Maryland* — had made clear the limit that federal power placed upon that exercise of state sovereignty.

The tax question involved the power of the state of Maryland to tax a branch of the Bank of the United States, located in Baltimore. The tax was instituted by the state as an anti-bank move, intended to curtail the issuance of bank notes by the bank. Such a use of the state taxing power was improper, held the court, a violation of the Constitution's provision that federal law is supreme over the states.

Marshall explained:

[T]he Constitution and the laws made in pursuance thereof are supreme; ...they control the constitution and laws of the respective states, and cannot be controlled by them....

[T]he power to tax involves the power to destroy; ...the power to destroy may defeat and render useless the power to create; ...there is a plain repugnance, in conferring on one government a power to control the constitutional measures of another, which other, with respect to those very measures, is declared to be supreme....[145]

The consequences of allowing such a tax were then described by the Chief Justice:

If the states may tax one instrument, employed by the government in the execution of its powers, they may tax any and every other instrument. They may tax the mail; they may tax the mint; they may tax patent rights; they may tax the papers of the custom-house; they may tax judicial process; they may tax all the means employed by the government, to an excess which would defeat all the ends of government. This was not intended by the American people. They did not design to make their government dependent on the states.[146]

Limiting the sweep of the ruling, Marshall concluded:

This opinion does not deprive the states of any resources which they originally possessed. It does not

extend to a tax paid by the real property of the bank, in common with other real property within the state, nor to a tax imposed on the interest which the citizens of Maryland may hold in this institution, in common with other property of the same description throughout the State. But this is a tax on the operations of the Bank, and is, consequently, a tax on the operation of an instrument employed by the government of the Union to carry its powers into execution. Such a tax must be unconstitutional.[147]

Taxing Imports

Within eight years, Maryland — and its use of the tax power — was back before the Supreme Court. Its lawyer was Roger B. Taney. The case was *Brown v. Maryland.*

The purpose of the constitutional ban on state taxes on imports and exports was to prevent discrimination against imports and against states within the interior of the coun-

---

The "power to tax involves the power to destroy; ... the power to destroy may defeat and render useless the power to create...."

—Chief Justice John Marshall
McCulloch v. Maryland, 1819

---

try. State taxes could be used to make imported goods more expensive than similar domestic goods. And if coastal states were allowed to tax incoming goods passing on to other states, they could impose a considerable burden on the citizens of those interior states.

Maryland law required persons who sold imported goods to purchase licenses. The law was challenged as violating the ban on import taxes and as interfering with the federal regulation of interstate and foreign commerce.

The court agreed with the challenge on both points. The license requirement was basically an indirect tax on imports. Chief Justice Marshall wrote:

The constitutional prohibition on the states to lay a duty on imports ... may certainly come in conflict with their acknowledged power to tax persons and property within their territory. The power, and the restriction on it, though quite distinguishable when they do not approach each other, may yet, like the intervening colors between white and black, approach so nearly as to perplex the understanding....

It is sufficient for the present to say, generally, that when the importer has so acted upon the thing imported that it has become incorporated and mixed up with the mass of property in the country, it has, perhaps, lost its distinctive character as an import, and has become subject to the taxing power of the state; but while remaining the property of the importer, in his warehouse, in the original form or package in which it was imported, a tax upon it is too plainly a duty on imports to escape the prohibition in the constitution....

This indictment is against the importer, for selling a package of dry goods in the form in which it was imported, without a license. This state of things is changed if he sells them, or otherwise mixes them with the general property of the state, by breaking up his packages, and traveling with them as an itinerant peddler. In the first case, the tax intercepts the import, as an import, on its way to become incorporated with the general mass of property, and denies it the privilege of becoming so incorporated until it shall have contributed to the revenue of the state. [148]

Thus, with this ruling in *Brown v. Maryland,* wrote Felix Frankfurter more than a century later, Chief Justice Marshall "gave powerful practical application to the possibilities intimated in *Gibbons v. Ogden.* Imminent in the commerce clause were severe limitations upon the power of the states to tax as well as to regulate commerce." [149]

And the "original package" doctrine that Marshall first set out in this case would stand for decades as a valid limit on the exercise of state tax and police powers.

In concluding the opinion in *Brown v. Maryland,* Marshall commented: "[W]e suppose the principles laid down in this case . . . apply equally to importations from a sister state," as well as to importation of goods from foreign countries. [150]

Forty-two years later, auctioneer L. P. Woodruff cited this comment in his challenge to the sales tax Mobile, Ala., placed on goods he brought into the state and sold, in their original package, at auction. Under *Brown v. Maryland* Woodruff claimed that the tax was in violation of the export-import clause. [151]

Not so, held the Supreme Court in 1869, dismissing Marshall's comment and limiting the prohibition on state import taxes to imports from foreign countries. Justice Samuel Miller, writing for the court, explained the effect such a broad exemption from state taxes would have:

[T]he merchant of Chicago who buys his goods in New York and sells at wholesale in the original packages, may have his millions employed in trade for half a lifetime and escape all state, county, and city taxes: for all that he is worth is invested in goods which he claims to be protected as imports from New York. Neither the State nor the city which protects his life and property can make him contribute a dollar to support its government, improve its thoroughfares or educate its children. [152]

Two points were thus settled by this decision in *Woodruff v. Parham:* The state power to tax goods imported from other states is not hindered by the export-import clause — and once interstate transportation of those goods has ended, a state may tax them, even in their original package.

So the protection of the original package — against state taxes — terminated earlier for goods from other states than for goods from other countries.

This point was reaffirmed in the court's 1885 decision in the case of *Brown v. Houston.* There the court held that Louisiana could tax coal from Pennsylvania even while it was still on the barges in which it had entered the state. [153]

Foreign Goods

But for almost 200 years the Supreme Court steadfastly rejected all state efforts to tax imported foreign goods so long as those goods retained their character as imports.

In 1872 the court refused to allow a state to tax such goods — even just as property like any other within the state. Adolph Low of San Francisco, an importer, was assessed a state property tax upon some $10,000 worth of French champagne he had imported and had stored in its original package, awaiting sale. The tax on the champagne also fell upon all other personal and real property in the state, based upon its value.

Low came to the Supreme Court, arguing that this tax violated the ban of the export-import clause. He won his case. The court struck down the tax with its decision in the case of *Low v. Austin.*

Brown v. Maryland and the original package doctrine governed this case, wrote Justice Stephen Field:

In that case it was also held that the authority given to import, necessarily carried with it a right to sell the goods in the form and condition, that is, in the bale or package, in which they were imported; and that the exaction of a license tax for permission to sell in such case was not only invalid as being in conflict with the constitutional prohibition . . . but also as an interference with the power of Congress to regulate commerce with foreign nations. [154]

It made no difference that the tax did not fall directly upon imports as a class, but simply upon the whole category of citizen-owned property. The original package doctrine still prevented their taxation:

The question is not as to the extent of the tax, or its equality with respect to taxes on other property, but as to the power of the State to levy any tax. . . . Imports, therefore, whilst retaining their distinctive character as such, must be treated as being without the jurisdiction of the taxing power of the State. [155]

The court subsequently extended this principle even further, holding that a state could not tax imports brought into a state for the importer's own use. [156]

And then, in 1976, *Low v. Austin* was overruled. The court held that a state could assess a value-based property tax upon imported tires stored in a warehouse awaiting sale. *Low v. Austin* had been based upon a misinterpretation of *Brown v. Maryland,* explained Justice William J. Brennan Jr. for the court in the case of *Michelin Tire Corp. v. Wages.* Such a non-discriminatory tax was not prohibited:

[S]uch an exaction, unlike discriminatory state taxation against imported goods as imports, was not regarded as an impediment that severely hampered commerce or constituted a form of tribute by seaboard States to the disadvantage of the other States. It is obvious that such nondiscriminatory property taxation can have no impact whatsoever on the Federal Government's exclusive regulation of foreign commerce. . . .

Unlike imposts and duties, which are essentially taxes on the commercial privilege of bringing goods into a country, such property taxes are taxes by which a State apportions the cost of such services as police and fire protection among the beneficiaries according to their respective wealth; there is no reason why an importer should not bear his share of these costs along with his competitors handling only domestic goods. The Import-Export Clause clearly prohibits state taxation based on the foreign origin of the imported goods, but it cannot be read to accord imported goods preferential treatment that permits escape from uniform taxes imposed without regard to foreign origin for services which the State supplies. [157]

Commerce and Taxes

Justice Tom C. Clark wrote in 1959:

Commerce between the States having grown up like Topsy, the Congress meanwhile not having undertaken to regulate taxation of it, and the States having understandably persisted in their efforts to get some return for the substantial benefits they have afforded it, there is little wonder that there has been no end of cases testing out state tax levies.

The resulting judicial application of constitutional principles to specific state statutes leaves much room for controversy and confusion and little in the way of precise guides to the States in the exercise of their indispensable power of taxation. This Court alone has handed down some three hundred full-dress opinions. . . . [T]he decisions have been "not always clear . . . consistent or reconcilable. . . ." From the quagmire there emerge, however, some firm peaks of decision which remain unquestioned.

[The commerce clause] requires that interstate commerce shall be free from any direct restrictions or impositions by the States [including any burdens imposed by state taxes]. Nor may a State impose a tax which discriminates against interstate commerce either by providing a direct commercial advantage to local business . . . or by subjecting interstate commerce to the burden of "multiple taxation." [158]

Railroad Cases. The application of these principles to the questions involved is best illustrated by several sets of cases.

The first involves railroads, and the effort of the State of Pennsylvania to tax the Philadelphia & Reading Railroad. The state imposed a tonnage tax on freight that the railroad moved through the state. And it imposed a tax on the gross receipts of the company.

On March 3, 1873, the Supreme Court ruled in two cases, each challenging one of these taxes as in conflict with the commerce clause.

The court struck down the tonnage tax, as in conflict with the requirement that interstate commerce be unimpeded by the states. Writing for the court, Justice William Strong declared:

It is of national importance that over that subject [transportation of people or products through a state or from one state to another] there should be but one regulating power, for if one State can directly tax persons or property passing through it, or tax them indirectly by levying a tax upon their transportation, every other may, and thus commercial intercourse between States remote from each other may be destroyed. The produce of Western States may thus be effectually excluded from Eastern markets, for though it might bear the imposition of a single tax, it would be crushed under the load of many. It was to guard against the possibility of such commercial embarrassments, no doubt, that the power of regulating commerce among other States was conferred upon the Federal Government. [159]

But on the same day, the court upheld Pennsylvania's tax upon the gross receipts of the railroad even though some of those receipts resulted from interstate commerce.

Again Justice Strong wrote the opinion, starting from the proposition that

every tax upon personal property or upon occupations, business or franchises, affects more or less the subjects and the operations of commerce. Yet it is not everything that affects commerce that amounts to a regulation of it, within the meaning of the Constitution. We think it may safely be asserted that the States have authority to tax the estate, real and personal, of all their corporations, including carrying companies, precisely as they may tax similar property when belonging to natural persons, and to the same extent. . . . A power to tax to this extent may be essential to the healthy existence of the state governments and the Federal Constitution ought not to be so construed as to impair, much less destroy, anything that is necessary to their efficient existence.

Strong then proceeded to apply a version of the "original package" doctrine to the issue:

While it must be conceded that a tax upon interstate transportation is invalid, there seems to be no stronger reason for denying the power of a State to tax the fruits of such transportation after they have become intermingled with the general property of the carrier, than there is for denying her power to tax goods which have been imported, after their original packages have been broken, and after they have been mixed with the mass of personal property in the country. [160]

Given the ruling of the court that a state could not tax goods still moving in interstate commerce, but could tax them — even in their original package — once the interstate movement ended, the question obviously occurs as to the definition of an interstate journey's beginning and end.

The general principles developed by the court hold that interstate commerce begins once an item is surrendered to a common carrier for transportation or otherwise begins its journey out of the state. The journey — and the protection of interstate commerce — ends when the items arrive at their destination, usually defined as in the possession of the person to whom they are sent. Temporary and unexpected interruptions in the journey do not terminate the protection of the commerce clause against state taxation, but a true break in the journey may allow a state to tax items in commerce. [161]

Following the decision upholding Pennsylvania's gross receipts tax as applied to railroads, the court has dealt with a variety of state efforts to tax interstate corporations doing business within the state. The court has upheld both net income and gross receipts taxes so long as they are fairly apportioned to reflect the share of the company's overall business done in the state and to accord with the services and protection provided by the state to the company. [162]

'Privilege' Cases. The second set of cases illustrating the court's effort to apply the commerce clause requirement carefully but not too strictly to state taxation involves the question of state taxes on "the privilege of doing interstate business."

In the 1869 case of *Paul v. Virginia,* the court held that Virginia could impose conditions upon its grant to an out-of-state insurance company of the right to do business in the state. Virginia's law required the company to obtain a license and to deposit security bonds of $30,000 to $50,000 with the state treasurer. [163]

But when Kentucky sought to enforce its law requiring out-of-state express companies to obtain a state license before carrying on business in the state, the United States

Express Co. protested that this requirement was an infringement of the federal power to regulate commerce. The case came to the Supreme Court in 1890 and was decided — against the state — in 1891.

"To carry on interstate commerce is not a franchise or a privilege granted by the State," wrote Justice Joseph P. Bradley, "it is a right which every citizen of the United States is entitled to exercise under the Constitution and laws of the United States. . . ." A state could not use a license tax to exclude or burden corporations engaged in interstate commerce. Distinguishing the *Paul* decision, Bradley wrote: "The case is entirely different from that of foreign corporations seeking to do a business which does not belong to the regulating power of Congress." Insurance, the court had held in *Paul v. Virginia,* was not subject to that congressional power. *(p. 319)*

And the court rejected any defense of the Kentucky law as an exercise of the police power: "[I]t does not follow that everything which the Legislature of a State may deem essential for the good order of society and the well being of its citizens can be set up against the exclusive power of Congress to regulate the operations of foreign and interstate commerce."[164]

For almost a century, with increasing confusion and diminishing effect, the court adhered to this rule. As one scholar writes:

> The question whether state taxes bore so heavily upon interstate commerce as to be an unconstitutional burden arose perennially. If a generalization is to be made at all, it is perhaps to the effect that the principles involved became less clear with the passing years, and the decisions rested more obviously upon the beliefs of the Court as to what in each case would best serve the public welfare. The lines of the original-package doctrine . . . became increasingly blurred as decisions dealt with such matters as natural gas and electricity which only in a highly figurative sense could be thought of as in packages at all. The principle that state control began when the article shipped in interstate commerce came to rest in the state was likewise blurred because of the fact that so many of the items of interstate commerce could not be thought of as coming to rest. The absence of a clear line marking the taxing jurisdiction of the state resulted, not from any particular line of decisions of the Supreme Court, but from the nature of commerce itself and the nature of the federal system. . . .[165]

By 1977 the Supreme Court realized that the prohibition of taxes on "the privilege of doing interstate business" had become little more than a formalism, "a trap for the unwary draftsman" of a state tax law.

In that year, the court discarded its opposition to all taxes described in this way and adopted the practical approach already in evidence in most of its modern state tax rulings. Rejecting the challenge of an interstate motor carrier to a Mississippi tax, Justice Harry A. Blackmun explained the court's decision. Citing several of the other recent state tax cases, he noted that they "considered not the formal language of the tax statute, but rather the practical effect, and have sustained a tax against Commerce Clause challenge when the tax is applied to an activity with a substantial nexus with the taxing state, is fairly apportioned, does not discriminate against interstate commerce and is fairly related to the services provided by the State. . . .

"[The modern court] consistently has indicated that 'interstate commerce may be made to pay its way,' and has moved toward a standard of permissibility of state taxation based upon its actual effect rather than its legal terminology."[166]

In this case, finding that the challenged tax resulted in no effect forbidden by the Commerce Clause, the court upheld it. The full measure of this about-face by the court was illustrated the following year, in 1978, when the court approved a Washington State tax on stevedoring virtually identical to one it had twice held an unconstitutional burden on interstate commerce.[167]

Peddlers and Drummers

The third set of cases begin with the "peddlers and drummers" decisions of the late 19th century. They illustrate the intricate nature of the task of deciding when a state tax discriminates against interstate commerce and when one does not.

Peddlers traveled through the country in the 19th century, carrying with them the goods they sold. Drummers, on the other hand, carried only samples, taking orders from their customers for future delivery. The distinction became significant when states tried to tax the peddlers and the drummers, and were challenged in this effort as interfering with interstate commerce. The court's decisions came in the cases of *Welton v. Missouri* and *Robbins v. Shelby County Taxing District.*

M. M. Welton was a peddler in Missouri; he sold sewing machines produced in another state. In 1876 the Supreme Court held that Missouri could not require Welton to obtain a license for his peddling, because the law imposing that requirement affected only persons selling

---

The modern court "consistently has indicated that 'interstate commerce may be made to pay its way,' and has moved toward a standard of permissibility of state taxation based upon its actual effect rather than legal terminology."

—Justice Harry A. Blackmun
Complete Auto Transit Inc. v. Brady, 1977

---

out-of-state goods and so discriminated against interstate commerce in violation of the commerce clause. The commerce clause protects a commodity "even after it has entered the State," wrote Justice Stephen Field, "from any burdens imposed by reason of its foreign origin."[168]

Four years later, however, the court upheld Tennessee's requirement that all peddlers of sewing machines obtain licenses, even as that requirement applied to an agent of a Connecticut-based manufacturer. Justice Noah Swayne wrote for the court:

> In all cases of this class, it is a test question whether there is any discrimination in favor of the State or of the citizens of the State which enacted the law. Wherever there is, such discrimination is fatal. . . . In the case before us, the statute . . . makes no such

discrimination. It applies alike to sewing machines manufactured in the State and out of it. The exaction is not an unusual or unreasonable one. The State, putting all such machines upon the same footing . . . had an unquestionable right to impose the burden. [169]

Seven years later, however, the court held that the commerce clause forbade states to place any sort of license requirement or tax on drummers, who take orders in one state for future deliveries of goods from another state. These deliveries are interstate commerce, held the court, and thus are not subject to state taxes.

Sabine Robbins sold stationery, by displaying samples and taking orders, in Memphis, Tenn. The stationery came from Ohio. Tennessee law required all such "drummers" to obtain a license, whether they were employed by in-state or out-of-state firms. Robbins failed to comply and was fined. He challenged his fine by arguing that the drummers' license improperly interfered with interstate commerce.

The Supreme Court, in 1887, agreed. Writing for the majority, Justice Joseph Bradley held that "to tax the sale of such [out-of-state] goods, or the offer to sell them, before they are brought into the State . . . seems to us clearly a tax on interstate commerce itself." The fact that the license requirement applied also to the persons who sold in-state goods was irrelevant.

> Interstate commerce cannot be taxed at all, even though the same amount of tax should be laid on domestic commerce. . . . The negotiation of sales of goods which are in another State, for the purpose of introducing them into the State in which the negotiation is made, is interstate commerce.

This particular license tax discriminated against out-of-state businesses who had little alternative to this mode of selling, while in-state businesses could simply open stores in the state where they had their offices anyway. "This kind of taxation is usually imposed at the instance and solicitation of domestic dealers, as a means of protecting them from foreign competition," wrote Bradley.

If this sort of tax were upheld, he concluded, "[T]he confusion into which the commerce of the country would be thrown . . . would be but a repetition of the disorder which prevailed under the Articles of Confederation." [170]

This principle from the *Robbins* case was later extended to protect mail-order businesses from state taxes, particularly the sales taxes increasingly adopted by states. Those taxes affected only local sales, not those from out-of-state merchants.

In an effort to impose an equal tax burden on sales from out-of-state sources, states developed the concept of a "use tax" — a tax on the in-state use of an item acquired from an out-of-state seller. This tax was equivalent to the "sales tax" imposed on the in-state purchase of a similar item.

This "use tax" was quickly challenged as in conflict with the commerce clause. But the Supreme Court in 1937 found it non-discriminatory and thus permissible. Its decision came in the case of *Henneford v. Silas Mason Co.*

Writing for the court, Justice Benjamin Cardozo explained that the tax was incurred after any interstate commerce had ceased, that the tax did not hamper commerce or discriminate against interstate commerce: "When the account is made up, the stranger from afar is subject to no greater burdens as a consequence of ownership than the dweller within the gates. The one pays upon one activity or incident, and the other upon another, but the sum is the same when the reckoning is closed." [171]

Subsequently, the court held that a state imposing a use tax may require the out-of-state seller to collect it, so long as there is a sufficient connection between the state and the out-of-state seller to support imposition of this duty. The connection can be the fact that the seller has local agents in the taxing state, that a mail-order company has retail outlets in the taxing state, or even that a company which runs a mail-order business has offices within the taxing state which solicit advertising for a magazine also published by the mail-order company. [172]

But the basic principle of *Welton* and *Robbins* survives as the effective guide for state taxation in this area. In 1977 the court cited *Welton* as it struck down a New York tax that burdened stock transactions taking place on out-of-state stock exchanges, not the New York Stock Exchange or the New York-based American Stock Exchange. Writing for the court, Justice Byron R. White noted that the consequence of the New York tax was that "the flow of securities sales is diverted from the most economically efficient channels and directed to New York. This diversion of interstate commerce and diminution of free competition in securities sales are wholly inconsistent with the free trade purpose of the Commerce Clause." [173]

Coins, Currency and Credit

The Constitution flatly forbids states to coin money, issue bills of credit or make any changes in the legal tender. As Justice John McLean commented once: "Here is an act inhibited in terms so precise that they cannot be mistaken. They are susceptible of but one construction." [1]

In light of such clarity, it is not surprising that the Supreme Court has ruled on these prohibitions only a few times in its history. And most of the rulings have dealt with the prohibition on state issuance of bills of credit.

In 1830 the court ruled that this ban foreclosed a state from issuing loan certificates. [2] Seven years later, however, it found that the ban did not extend to preclude a state-chartered bank from issuing notes, even if the state owned all the bank's stock. [3]

But the leeway that this appeared to afford the states in this area was sharply curtailed just after the Civil War, when the court held that the national power over the currency was broad enough to sanction the use of the taxing power of Congress to drive state bank notes out of circulation altogether. [4]

---

[1] *Briscoe v. Bank of Kentucky,* 11 Pet. 257 at 318 (1837).
[2] *Craig v. Missouri,* 4 Pet. 410 (1830).
[3] *Briscoe v. Bank of Kentucky,* 11 Pet. 257 (1837).
[4] *Veazie Bank v. Fenno,* 8 Wall. 533 (1869).

Footnotes

[1] Thomas Reed Powell, *Vagaries and Varieties in Constitutional Interpretation* (New York: AMS Press, 1967), p. 85.

[2] Felix Frankfurter. *The Commerce Clause Under Marshall, Taney and Waite* (Chapel Hill: University of North Carolina Press, 1937), pp. 66-67.

[3] Ibid., pp. 18-19.

[4] Ibid., p. 27.

[5] Thomas Reed Powell, *Vagaries and Varieties*, p. 176.

[6] Charles G. Haines, *American Doctrine of Judicial Supremacy*, 2d ed. (Berkeley: University of California Press, 1932), pp. 313-314.

[7] *Fletcher v. Peck*, 6 Cr. 87 at 130 (1810).

[8] Id. at 131.

[9] Id. at 134.

[10] Id. at 135.

[11] Ibid.

[12] *New Jersey v. Wilson*, 7 Cr. 164 (1812).

[13] *The Providence Bank v. Billings*, 4 Pet. 514 at 562 (1830).

[14] Id. at 563.

[15] *Piqua Branch of the State Bank of Ohio v. Knoop*, 16 How. 369 (1854).

[16] Id. at 378.

[17] Id. at 380.

[18] Id. at 389.

[19] *Dodge v. Woolsey*, 18 How. 331 at 360 (1856); see Charles Warren, *The Supreme Court in United States History*, 2 vols. (Boston: Little, Brown & Co., 1922, 1926), II:250-255.

[20] *Dartmouth College v. Woodward*, 4 Wheat. 519 at 644 (1819).

[21] Id.

[22] Id. at 647-648.

[23] Id. at 712.

[24] Warren, *The Supreme Court in United States History*, I: 491.

[25] *Sturges v. Crowninshield*, 4 Wheat. 122 (1819).

[26] *Ogden v. Saunders*, 12 Wheat. 213 (1827).

[27] Id. at 270.

[28] Id. at 339.

[29] *Mason v. Haile*, 12 Wheat. 370 (1827).

[30] *Sturges v. Crowninshield*, 4 Wheat. 122 at 201 (1819).

[31] *Bronson v. Kinzie*, 1 How. 311 (1843).

[32] *Charles River Bridge v. Warren Bridge*, 11 Pet. 420 at 546 (1837).

[33] Id. at 547-550.

[34] Id. at 552-553.

[35] *West River Bridge Co. v. Dix.*, 6 How. 530 at 531-532 (1848).

[36] *Pennsylvania Hospital v. Philadelphia*, 245 U.S. 20 (1917).

[37] *Stone v. Mississippi*, 101 U.S. 814 at 817-819, 821 (1880).

[38] Library of Congress, *The Constitution of the United States of America: Analysis and Interpretation* (Washington: U.S. Government Printing Office: 1964), p. 409-410.

[39] *Allgeyer v. Louisiana*, 165 U.S. 578 (1897).

[40] Library of Congress, *The Constitution*, p. 410.

[41] *Home Building & Loan Association v. Blaisdell*, 290 U.S. 398 at 425-426, 428 (1934)

[42] Id. at 434-435.

[43] Id. at 439-440.

[44] *W. B. Worthen Co. v. Thomas*, 292 U.S. 426 (1934); *Worthen Co. v. Kavanaugh*, 295 U.S. 56 (1935).

[45] Edward S. Corwin, *The Constitution and What It Means Today*, 12th ed. (Princeton: Princeton University Press, 1958), p. 85.

[46] *Allied Structural Steel Co. v. Spannaus*, 438 U.S. 234 at 241 (1978).

[47] *United States Trust Co. v. New Jersey*, 431 U.S. 1 (1977).

[48] *The Federalist Papers*, with an Introduction by Clinton Rossiter (New York: New American Library, Mentor Books, 1961), No. 7, p. 63; No. 22, p. 145.

[49] Felix Frankfurter, "Some Observations on the Nature of the Judicial Process of Supreme Court Litigation." Proceedings of the American Philosophical Society, 98:233, 1954, reprinted in Alan F. Westin, ed., *The Supreme Court: Views from Inside* (New York: W. W. Norton & Co., 1961), p. 39.

[50] Warren, *The Supreme Court in United States History*, I:598.

[51] *Gibbons v. Ogden*, 9 Wheat. 1 at 189-190 (1824).

[52] Id. at 194, 196.

[53] Id. at 210-211.

[54] Felix Frankfurter, *The Commerce Clause*, pp. 18-19.

[55] Alfred H. Kelly, Winfred A. Harbison, *The American Constitution*, 4th ed. (New York: W. W. Norton & Co., 1970), p. 296.

[56] Carl B. Swisher, *American Constitutional Development*, 2d ed. (Cambridge: Houghton Mifflin Co., 1954), p. 193.

[57] Warren, *The Supreme Court in United States History*, II:627-628.

[58] *Willson v. Blackbird Creek Marsh Co.*, 2 Pet. 245 at 251 (1829).

[59] *Mayor of New York v. Miln*, 11 Pet. 102 (1837).

[60] *Groves v. Slaughter*, 15 Pet. 449 (1841); see Swisher, *American Constitutional Development*, p. 198.

[61] *Thurlow v. Massachusetts, Fletcher v. Rhode Island, Peirce v. New Hampshire*, 5 How. 504 (1847).

[62] *Smith v. Turner, Norris v. Boston*, 7 How. 283 (1849).

[63] Warren, *The Supreme Court in United States History*, II:178.

[64] *Cooley v. Board of Wardens of the Port of Philadelphia*, 12 How. 299 at 318-320 (1852).

[65] Powell, *Vagaries and Varieties*, p. 152.

[66] *Pennsylvania v. Wheeling & Belmont Bridge Co.*, 13 How. 518 at 566 (1852).

[67] Warren, *The Supreme Court in United States History*, II:236.

[68] *Henderson v. Wickham, Commissioners of Immigration v. The North German Lloyd, Chy Lung v. Freeman*, 92 U.S. 259, 275 at 273 (1876).

[69] Id. at 280.

[70] *Chicago, Burlington & Quincy Railroad Co. v. Iowa*, 94 U.S. 155; *The Chicago, Milwaukee & St. Paul Railroad Co. v. Ackley*, 94 U.S. 179; *Peik v. Chicago & Northwestern Railway Co.*, 94 U.S. 164; *The Winona & St. Peter Railroad Co. v. Blake*, 94 U.S. 180; *Stone v. Wisconsin*, 94 U.S. 181; *Munn v. Illinois*, 94 U.S. 113 (1877).

[71] *Peik v. Chicago & Northwestern Railway Co.*, 94 U.S. 164 at 178 (1877).

[72] *Munn v. Illinois*, 94 U.S. 113 at 126.

[73] *Budd v. New York*, 143 U.S. 517 (1892).

[74] *Wabash, St. Louis & Pacific Railway Co. v. Illinois*, 118 U.S. 557 (1886).

[75] Id. at 573.

[76] Id. at 575.

[77] Id. at 577.

[78] *Paul v. Virginia*, 8 Wall. 168 (1869).

[79] *United States v. Southeastern Underwriters Association*, 322 U.S. 533 at 553 (1944).

[80] Id. at 544.

[81] *Prudential Insurance Co. v. Benjamin, Robertson v. California*, 328 U.S. 408 (1946).

[82] *Kidd v. Pearson*, 128 U.S. 1 at 20, 21 (1888).

[83] Id. at 22-23.

[84] *United States v. E. C. Knight Co.*, 156 U.S. 1 at 12 (1895).

[85] Id. at 11, 13.

[86] *Oliver Iron Mining Co. v. Lord*, 262 U.S. 172 (1923); *Coe v. Errol*, 116 U.S. 517 (1886); *Champlin Refining Co. v. Corporation Commission*, 286 U.S. 210 (1932); *Utah Power & Light v. Pfost*, 286 U.S. 165 (1932).

[87] *National Labor Relations Board v. Jones & Laughlin Steel Corp.*, 301 U.S. 1 (1937).

[88] *Mulford v. Smith*, 307 U.S. 38 (1939).

[89] *Wickard v. Filburn*, 317 U.S. 111 at 128 (1942).

[90] *Parker v. Brown*, 317 U.S. 341 (1942).

[91] *Hall v. DeCuir*, 95 U.S. 485 at 489 (1878).

[92] Id. at 490.

[93] *Louisville, New Orleans & Texas Railway Company v. Mississippi*, 133 U.S. 587 (1890).

[94] Id. at 594.

[95] *Plessy v. Ferguson*, 163 U.S. 537 (1896).

[96] *Morgan v. Virginia*, 328 U.S. 373 (1946).

[97] *Gayle v. Browder*, 352 U.S. 903 (1956).

[98] *Hammer v. Dagenhart*, 247 U.S. 251 at 272-274 (1918).

[99] Id. at 276-277.

[100] Id. at 281.

[101] *Bailey v. Drexel Furniture Co.*, 259 U.S. 20 at 38 (1922).

[102] *United States v. Darby*, 312 U.S. 100 at 114, 115, 118 (1941).

[103] Powell, *Vagaries and Varieties*, p. 85.

[104] Ibid. at 162-163.

[105] *Gibbons v. Ogden*, 9 Wheat. 1 at 208, 203 (1824).

[106] *Willson v. Blackbird Creek Marsh Co.*, 2 Pet. 245 (1829).

[107] *Charles River Bridge v. Warren Bridge*, 11. Pet. 420 at 552 (1837).

[108] *Mayor of New York v. Miln*, 11 Pet. 102 at 132-133 (1837).

[109] Id. at 139, 142.

[110] Alpheus T. Mason, William M. Beaney, *The Supreme Court in a Free Society* (Englewood Cliffs: Prentice-Hall, 1959), p. 82.

[111] *Bank of Augusta v. Earle*, 13 Pet. 519 (1839).

[112] Frankfurter, *The Commerce Clause*, p. 106; *Pensacola Telegraph Co. v. Western Union*, 96 U.S. 1 (1877).

[113] *Groves v. Slaughter*, 15 Pet. 449 (1841).

[114] *Smith v. Turner, Norris v. Boston*, 7 How. 283 at 408, 467 (1847).

[115] *Henderson v. Wickham*, 92 U.S. 259 (1876); *Edwards v. California*, 314 U.S. 160 (1941).

[116] *Thurlow v. Massachusetts, Fletcher v. Rhode Island, Peirce v. New Hampshire*, 5 How. 504 at 589-590, 592 (1847).

[117] *Bartemeyer v. Iowa*, 18 Wall. 129 (1874).

[118] *Mugler v. Kansas*, 123 U.S. 623 at 691-692 (1887).

[119] *Kidd v. Pearson*, 128 U.S. 1 (1888); *Bowman v. Chicago & Northwestern Railroad Co.*, 125 U.S. 465 (1888).

[120] *Leisy v. Hardin*, 135 U.S. 100 (1890); *Brown v. Maryland*, 12 Wheat. 419 (1827).

[121] *Leisy v. Hardin*, 135 U.S. 100 at 124-125.

[122] *In re Rahrer*, 140 U.S. 545 (1891).

[123] *Clark Distilling Co. v. Western Maryland Railway*, 242 U S. 311 (1917).

[124] *Collins v. Yosemite Park and Curry Co.*, 304 U.S. 518 (1938); *Jameson & Co. v. Morgenthau*, 307 U.S. 171 (1939); *Duckworth v. Arkansas*, 314 U.S. 390 (1941); *Carter v. Virginia*, 321 U.S. 131 (1944).

[125] *Munn v. Illinois*, 94 U.S. 113 at 125-126 (1877).

[126] *Burns Baking Co. v. Bryan*, 264 U.S. 504 (1924); *Wolff Packing Co. v. Industrial Court*, 262 U.S. 522 (1923); *Tyson and Brother v. Banton*, 273 U.S. 418 (1927); *Ribnik v. McBride*, 277 U.S. 350 (1928); *Williams v. Standard Oil Co.*, 278 U.S. 235 (1929); *New State Ice Co. v. Liebmann*, 285 U.S. 262 (1932); *Cotting v. Kansas City Stock Yards Co.*, 183 U.S. 79 (1901); *Townsend v. Yeomans*, 301 U.S. 441 (1937); *German Alliance Ins. Co. v. Kansas*, 233 U.S. 389 (1914).

[127] *Nebbia v. New York*, 291 U.S. 502 at 536-537, 539 (1934).

[128] *Holden v. Hardy*, 169 U.S. 366 (1898).

[129] *Lochner v. New York*, 198 U.S. 45 at 57-58, 59, 61 (1905).

[130] *Muller v. Oregon*, 208 U.S. 412 (1908).

[131] *Bunting v. Oregon*, 243 U.S. 426 at 438, 439 (1917).

[132] *Adkins v. Children's Hospital*, 261 U.S. 525 at 554, 559 (1923).

[133] Id. at 570.

[134] Id. at 569.

[135] *Morehead v. Tipaldo*, 298 U.S. 587 at 611 (1936).

[136] Id. at 635.

[137] *West Coast Hotel v. Parrish*, 300 U.S. 379 at 398, 399 (1937).

[138] Id. at 399, 400.

[139] *United States v. Darby*, 312 U.S. 100 (1941).

[140] *Maryland v. Wirtz*, 392 U.S. 183 (1968).

[141] *National League of Cities v. Usery*, 426 U.S. 833 at 851 (1976).

[142] *Freeman v. Hewit*, 329 U.S. 249 at 251 (1946).

[143] *Boston Stock Exchange v. State Tax Commission*, 429 U.S. 318 at 329 (1977).

[144] *Gibbons v. Ogden*, 9 Wheat. 1 at 199 (1824).

[145] *McCulloch v. Maryland*, 4 Wheat. 316 at 426, 431 (1819).

[146] Id. at 432.

[147] Id. at 436-437.

[148] *Brown v. Maryland*, 12 Wheat. 419 at 441-442, 443 (1827).

[149] Frankfurter, *The Commerce Clause*, p. 149.

[150] *Brown v. Maryland*, 12 Wheat. 419 at 449 (1819).

[151] *Woodruff v. Parham*, 8 Wall. 123 (1869).

[152] Id. at 137.

[153] *Brown v. Houston*, 114 U.S. 622 (1885).

[154] *Low v. Austin*, 13 Wall. 29 at 33 (1872).

[155] Id. at 34-35.

[156] *Hooven & Allison Co. v. Evatt*, 324 U.S. 652 (1945).

[157] *Michelin Tire Corp. v. Wages*, 423 U.S. 276 at 286, 287 (1976).

[158] *Northwestern States Portland Cement Co. v. Minnesota*, 358 U.S. 450 at 457-458 (1959).

[159] *State Freight Tax Case, Philadelphia & Reading RR v. Pennsylvania*, 15 Wall. 232 at 280 (1873).

[160] *State Tax on Railroad Gross Receipts, Philadelphia & Reading RR Co. v. Pennsylvania*, 15 Wall. 284 at 293, 295 (1873).

[161] *Coe v. Errol*, 116 U.S. 517 (1886), *General Oil v. Crain*, 209 U.S. 211 (1908).

[162] *Western Union Telegraph Co. v. Massachusetts*, 125 U.S. 530 (1888); *Hans Rees' Sons v. North Carolina*, 283 U.S. 123 (1931); *United States Glue Co. v. Oak Creek*, 247 U.S. 321 (1918); *Maine v. Grand Trunk Railway Co.*, 142 U.S. 217 (1891); *Wisconsin v. J. C. Penney Co.*, 311 U.S. 432 (1940); *General Motors Corp. v. Washington*, 377 U.S. 436 (1964); *Northwestern States Portland Cement Co. v. Minnesota*, 358 U.S. 450 (1959).

[163] *Paul v. Virginia*, 8 Wall. 168 (1869).

[164] *Crutcher v. Kentucky*, 141 U.S. 47 at 57, 59, 60 (1891).

[165] Swisher, *American Constitutional Development*, p. 844.

[166] *Complete Auto Transit Inc. v. Brady*, 430 U.S. 274 at 279, 281 (1977).

[167] *Department of Revenue of the State of Washington v. Association of Washington Stevedoring Companies*, 435 U.S. 734 (1978).

[168] *Welton v. Missouri*, 91 U.S. 275 at 282 (1876).

[169] *Howe Machine Co. v. Gage*, 100 U.S. 676 at 679 (1880).

[170] *Robbins v. Shelby County Taxing District*, 120 U.S. 489 at 497-499 (1887).

[171] *Henneford v. Silas Mason Co.*, 300 U.S. 577 at 584 (1937).

[172] *Felt & Tarrant Co. v. Gallagher*, 306 U.S. 62 (1939); *Nelson v. Sears, Roebuck & Co.*, 312 U.S. 359 (1941); *Nelson v. Montgomery Ward & Co.*, 312 U.S. 373 (1941); *Scripto v. Carson*, 362 U.S. 207 (1960); *National Geographic Society v. California Board of Equalization*, 430 U.S. 551 (1977).

[173] *Boston Stock Exchange v. State Tax Commission*, 429 U.S. 318 at 336 (1977).

The State and the Individual

On its face, the Constitution imposes few restraints on how a state deals with an individual.

Early in its history, the court ruled that the guarantees of individual rights in the first 10 Amendments, the Bill of Rights, did not apply directly to the states — a ruling the court has yet to overturn.

Although the court addressed the issue of slavery in a variety of ways, it was never from the perspective of a human rights question. Slaves were property.

Even after the addition of the 13th, 14th and 15th Amendments to the Constitution, the Supreme Court refused for decades to interpret these amendments to expand the list of civil rights protected against state action. Citing the doctrine of reserved state powers, the court held that most civil rights questions still remained within the purview of the states.

Not until the 20th century did the court begin to employ the 14th Amendment's guarantees of due process and equal protection to apply to state actions the most fundamental of the guarantees of the Bill of Rights. The revolution thus begun is still continuing.

The Constitution

The Constitution forbade states or the federal government to pass any bill of attainder or *ex post facto* law. Until the 20th century, these were the only explicit constitutional provisions interpreted by the Supreme Court to restrain state actions affecting the individual.

An *ex post facto* law is one that operates retrospectively, to make an earlier action invalid, illegal or criminal. A bill of attainder, in English law, was an act of Parliament declaring a person guilty of treason, sentencing him to die and confiscating his property. In American law, a bill of attainder has simply come to mean any measure that punishes an individual without a trial.

There is some evidence that those who wrote the ban on *ex post facto* laws into the Constitution intended it to protect property as well as persons, to apply to civil as well as criminal laws.

But the Supreme Court — in its first ruling on this portion of the Constitution — nullified such intent. Rejecting the contention of a person named Calder that a state law nullifying his title to certain property was in conflict with this provision, the court held that the ban on *ex post facto* laws applied only to criminal legislation.

Writing for the court, Justice Samuel Chase set out its views:

> I do not think it [the prohibition] was inserted to secure the citizen in his private rights, of either property or contracts . . . the restriction not to pass any *ex post facto* law, was to secure the person of the subject from injury, or punishment, in consequence of such law.

> I do not consider any law *ex post facto,* within the prohibition, that mollifies the rigor of the criminal law; but only those that create, or aggravate the crime; or increase the punishment; or change the rules of evidence, for the purpose of conviction.[1]

It is the view of some scholars that the later rulings of the Marshall court interpreting broadly the protection of the contract clause for property rights — against legislative amendment or nullification — were an effort to regain the protection for property lost through this narrow interpretation of the *ex post facto* clause.[2]

In later rulings on this language, the court has held that it does not forbid a state to make any retroactive changes in its trial procedure and rules of evidence. The court has simply limited those changes that may be applied to the trials of persons who committed crimes before the change to those that work to the advantage of the defendant. In a pair of cases decided in 1898, the court, for example, held that a state could alter the rules of evidence to allow the admission of additional evidence, in cases already set for trial before the change because that was simply a change in procedures, but that it could not reduce the size of a jury for the trial of crimes already committed, because it was easier to convince fewer jurors to convict a defendant.[3]

In a more recent ruling, the Supreme Court in 1977 refused to use this clause to invalidate a death sentence imposed upon a man convicted of murder. He had argued that it should operate to nullify his sentence because the capital punishment law in operation at the time of the murders was subsequently declared unconstitutional and invalid — and he was sentenced under a new law passed after that court decision.

By a 6-3 vote the court rejected his claim, holding that the change from the old law to the new one was simply procedural and that in fact the new law worked more to the benefit of the defendant.[4] Also in 1977, the court held that

Congress had not violated this ban when it took the papers and tapes of the Nixon administration out of the custody of former President Nixon and placed them under government control.[5]

The first broad application of the bills of attainder ban, along with the *ex post facto* prohibition, came soon after the Civil War. A number of states and Congress enacted laws requiring persons who wished to engage in a variety of activities to take "test oaths" to ensure their loyalty to the Union.

In Missouri the test oath requirement was particularly severe. Before any person could vote, hold or run for office, practice law, teach, hold property in trust for a religious organization or serve as a clergyman, he was required to take a sweeping oath that he had always been loyal to the United States and that he had never, by act or word, given any aid or support to any enemy. The effect of the law was to exclude from those activities anyone who had even voiced sympathy with the Confederacy.

John A. Cummings, a Catholic priest, refused to be sworn and was convicted and sentenced for acting as a priest without taking the oath. He challenged the requirement as a violation of the constitutional prohibitions on bills of attainder and *ex post facto* laws.

The court agreed with his challenge on both points. In an opinion written by Justice Stephen Field, it declared:

> We admit . . . that among the rights reserved to the States is the right of each State to determine the qualifications for office, and the conditions upon which its citizens may exercise their various callings and pursuits within its jurisdiction. . . . But it by no means follows that, under the form of creating a qualification or attaching a condition, the States can, in effect, inflict a punishment for a past act which was not punishable at the time it was committed.

The disabilities imposed by Missouri upon persons who did not take the oath certainly could be considered punishments, Field wrote:

The state could not constitutionally pass a law that declared Cummings personally, or all clergymen, guilty of

---

"The Constitution deals with substance, not shadows. Its inhibition [against ex post facto *laws] was leveled at the thing, not the name. It intended that the rights of the citizen would be secure against deprivation for past conduct by legislative enactment, under any form, however disguised. . . ."*

—Justice Stephen Field
Cummings v. Missouri, 1867

---

any crime, and, likewise, it could not pass a law *assuming* such guilt, Field wrote.

The Constitution deals with substance, not shadows. Its inhibition was leveled at the thing, not the name. It intended that the rights of the citizen would

be secure against deprivation for past conduct by legislative enactment, under any form, however disguised . . . .[6]

The court also held the federal test oath invalid.[7]

In subsequent rulings, the court has relaxed somewhat its opposition to after-the-fact disqualifications of persons for certain actions. It has held that the state's police power — as applied to protect the public health — justified its forbidding a person convicted of a felony to resume the practice of medicine. And it has upheld the right of a state to exclude convicted felons from holding certain labor union offices. The court also has permitted states to require its public employees to take loyalty oaths, so long as they are narrowly drawn and carefully applied.[8]

The Bill of Rights

In paving its streets, the city of Baltimore disrupted the course of certain streams, which then dumped debris and gravel into Baltimore Harbor around the wharf owned by a man named Barron. As a result the value of Barron's wharf was destroyed; the water around it had been made too shallow for vessels to approach to off-load at the wharf.

Barron sued the city of Baltimore and took his case to the Supreme Court, arguing that the Fifth Amendment guarantee against the government's taking private property for public use without just compensation required the city to compensate him for his loss.

Barron lost again at the Supreme Court. Chief Justice John Marshall, speaking for the court, refused to apply any of the provisions of the Bill of Rights to state action: "These amendments contain no expression indicating an intention to apply them to the State governments. This court cannot so apply them."[9]

The Civil War Amendments

Few stranger chapters can be found in the history of the court than the story of the way in which the justices, after the Civil War, read the 13th, 14th and 15th Amendments to the Constitution so narrowly that they frustrated almost entirely the intentions of the men who drafted them and worked for their incorporation into the Constitution.

The amendments' sponsors intended to extend federal protection to citizens against state action infringing the rights already protected by the Bill of Rights against federal action. The court rejected this interpretation for decades.

Servitude and Discrimination

"Neither slavery nor involuntary servitude, except as a punishment for crime whereof the party shall have been duly convicted, shall exist within the United States, or any place subject to their jurisdiction," reads the 13th Amendment, abolishing slavery and authorizing Congress to pass legislation enforcing that ban.

Although it conceded that this amendment empowered Congress to pass laws to abolish "all badges and incidents of slavery," the court in the *Civil Rights Cases* of 1883 refused to view racial discrimination as a "badge of slavery."

Writing for the court, Justice Joseph Bradley stated:

> Congress did not assume, under the authority given by the 13th Amendment, to adjust what may be

called the social rights of men and races in the community; but only to declare and vindicate those fundamental rights which appertain to the essence of citizenship, and the enjoyment or deprivation of which constitutes the essential distinction between freedom and slavery .... It would be running the slavery argument into the ground, to make it apply to every act of discrimination which a person may see fit to make as to the guests he will entertain, or as to the people he will take into his coach or cab or car, or admit to his concert or theater, or deal with in other matters of intercourse or business ....[10]

Early in the 20th century, the court did cite this amendment to strike down state peonage laws, which required a person who defaulted on a contract either to go to jail or to go to work for his creditor to "work off" his default.[11]

The court has, however, recognized a number of established exceptions to the "involuntary servitude" banned by

" . . . It would be running the slavery argument into the ground, to make it apply to every act of discrimination which a person may see fit to make as to the guests he will entertain, or as to the people he takes into his coach or cab or car, or admit to his concert or theater, or deal with in other matters of intercourse or business . . . ."

—Justice Joseph Bradley
Civil Rights Cases, 1883

the 13th Amendment — among them work for the state on state roads, jury duty and compulsory military service.[12]

Privileges and Immunities

"All persons born or naturalized in the United States, and subject to the jurisdiction thereof, are citizens of the United States and of the State wherein they reside," states the first section of the 14th Amendment, overruling the court's holding in *Dred Scott v. Sandford* that blacks were not citizens.

The same section of the amendment, clearly directed against state action, further declares that "No State shall make or enforce any law which shall abridge the privileges or immunities of citizens of the United States; nor shall any State deprive any person of life, liberty, or property, without due process of law; nor deny to any person within its jurisdiction the equal protection of the laws."

Adopted in 1868, this amendment contained four other sections, only one of which — giving Congress the authority to pass appropriate enforcing laws — is pertinent here.

During congressional consideration of the 14th Amendment, advocates of the measure in both chambers made clear their belief that it would extend federal protection for a broad range of basic rights, including those guaranteed by the Bill of Rights, to persons denied them by state action.[13]

Slaughterhouse Cases. Five years after the amendment was ratified, the Supreme Court ruled that it did not give citizens the full protection of the Bill of Rights against actions by the states.

Oddly enough, it was butchers, not black men, bringing these landmark cases. New Orleans butchers charged that the state of Louisiana had violated the 14th Amendment by granting to one company the exclusive right to operate a slaughterhouse in New Orleans.

This monopoly, the butchers charged, deprived them of their right to carry on their business, a right included among the privileges and immunities guaranteed by the first section of the amendment. These cases were known collectively as the *Slaughterhouse Cases.*[14]

The monopoly was granted in 1869; the next year the case reached the Supreme Court. It was argued in 1872 and then re-argued in 1873. Representing the butchers was former Justice John A. Campbell of Alabama, who had left the court when his state seceded from the Union. He placed the burden of his argument on the privileges and immunities section of the amendment, although reference was made to the due process and equal protection guarantees as well.

On April 14, 1873 — eight years after the end of the Civil War — the court issued its opinion. The vote was 5-4; the majority opinion was written by Justice Samuel F. Miller. Dissenting were Chief Justice Salmon P. Chase, Stephen Field, Noah Swayne and Joseph Bradley.

The monopoly was granted by the state in the exercise of its police power, wrote Miller. It did not forbid the protesting butchers to practice their trade — it merely required them to do so at a particular slaughterhouse. By law, all other slaughterhouses in the area were to be closed.

Considering the citizenship section of the amendment, Miller made an important distinction: "It is quite clear, then, that there is a citizenship of the United States and a citizenship of a State, which are distinct from each other and which depend upon different characteristics or circumstances in the individual."

Moving on to the next portion of the amendment, Miller continued:

Of the privileges and immunities of the citizens of the United States, and of the privileges and immunities of the citizens of the State, and what they respectively are, we will presently consider; but we wish to state here that it is only the former which are placed by this clause under the protection of the Federal Constitution, and that the latter, whatever they may be, are not intended to have any additional protection by this paragraph of the Amendment.[15]

With the exception of the Constitution's language forbidding states to pass *ex post facto* laws, bills of attainder and laws impairing the obligation of contract, Miller wrote:

...the entire domain of the privileges and immunities of citizens of the States lay within the constitutional and legislative power of the States, and without that of the Federal Government. Was it the purpose of the 14th Amendment ... to transfer the security and protection of all the civil rights which we have mentioned, from the States to the Federal Government? And where it is declared that Congress shall have the power to enforce that article, was it intended to bring within the power of Congress the entire domain of civil rights heretofore belonging exclusively to the States?

All this and more must follow, if the proposition of the plaintiffs . . . [the butchers] be sound. . . . [S]uch a construction . . . would constitute this court a perpetual censor upon all legislation of the States, on the civil rights of their own citizens, with authority to nullify such as it did not approve as consistent with those rights, as they existed at the time of the adoption of this amendment. . . .

We are convinced that no such results were intended by the Congress which proposed these Amendments, nor by the Legislatures of the States, which ratified them. . . .

Thus, the butchers' challenge to the monopoly failed, for "the privileges and immunities relied on in the argument are those which belong to citizens of the States as such, and . . . are left to the state governments for security and protection, and not by this article placed under the special care of the Federal Government." "The argument has not been much pressed in these cases that the defendants' charter deprives the plaintiffs of their property without due process of law, or that it denies to them the equal protection of the law," added Miller. However, he did go on to say that "under no construction of that provision that we have ever seen, or any that we deem admissible, can the restraint imposed by the State of Louisiana upon the exercise of their trade by the butchers of New Orleans be held to be a deprivation of property within the meaning of that provision." [16]

Dissenting Opinions. In dissent, Justice Field argued that the 14th Amendment did extend protection to citizens against the deprivation of their common rights by state legislation:

The fundamental rights, privileges and immunities which belong to him as a free man and a free citizen, now belong to him as a citizen of the United States, and are not dependent upon his citizenship of any State. . . . They do not derive their existence from its legislation, and cannot be destroyed by its power.

To hold the majority's view, confining this protection to the privileges and immunities specifically or implicitly set out as belonging to U.S. citizens, rendered this portion of the amendment "a vain and idle enactment, which accomplished nothing, and most unnecessarily excited Congress and the people on its passage. With privileges and immunities thus designated no State could ever have interfered by its laws, and no new constitutional provision was required to inhibit such interference . . . . But if the Amendment refers to the natural and inalienable rights which belong to all citizens, the inhibition has a profound significance and consequence." [17]

Not surprisingly, the 14th Amendment so interpreted provided little protection for any of the disadvantaged groups who sought its shelter in the next half-century — blacks, women, aliens and criminal defendants.

Civil Rights Cases. In the opinion in the *Slaughterhouse Cases* Justice Miller stated his doubts that "any action of a State not directed by way of discrimination against the negroes as a class, or on account of their race, will ever be held to come within the purview of this [equal protection] provision. It is so clearly a provision for that race and that emergency. . . ." [18]

Yet, 10 years later, in its decision in the *Civil Rights Cases* of 1883, the court so narrowly interpreted the amend-

ment's protection for black citizens that even Miller's limited view of the equal protection clause seemed too broad. And during those years the court struck down a number of the laws Congress had passed — under the power granted by the Civil War amendments — to enforce those amendments. This narrowing process consisted of two elements: a limited category of federally protected rights and an insistence that the 14th Amendment reached only state, not private action. [19]

In the *Civil Rights Cases,* the court struck down the Civil Rights Act of 1875 as beyond the power granted to Congress by the enforcing section of the 14th Amendment. That act made it a crime to deny equal access and enjoyment of public accommodations to black persons. There were five such cases grouped under the rubric of the *Civil Rights Cases* and decided together by the court: *United States v. Stanley* from Kansas, *United States v. Ryan* from California, *United States v. Nichols* from Missouri, *United States v. Singleton* from New York, and *Robinson v. Memphis and Charleston Railroad Co.* from Tennessee.

In the *Stanley* and *Nichols* cases, the defendants were charged with refusing to allow blacks equal access to inns and hotels; in the *Ryan* and *Singleton* cases, they were persons who had refused to allow black people to sit in a certain part of theaters in San Francisco and in New York; the *Robinson* case resulted from a railroad conductor's refusal to allow a black woman to ride in the "ladies' car" on the train.

The court voted 8-1 to strike down the Civil Rights Act. Writing for the majority Justice Bradley found the reason simple: The 14th Amendment forbade state action, not "individual invasion of individual rights . . . ." Bradley continued:

. . . It does not invest Congress with power to legislate upon subjects which are within the domain of state legislation; but to provide modes of relief against state legislation or state action. . . . It does not authorize Congress to create a code of municipal law for the regulation of private rights; but to provide modes of redress against the operation of state laws, and the action of state officers executive or judicial, when these are subversive of the fundamental rights specified in the Amendment.

Such legislation [as Congress is authorized to pass] cannot properly cover the whole domain of rights. . . . That would be to establish a code of municipal law regulative of all private rights between man and man in society. It would be to make Congress take the place of the State Legislatures, and to supersede them. . . . [T]he legislation which Congress is authorized to adopt in this behalf is not general legislation upon the rights of the citizen, but corrective legislation, that is, such as may be necessary and proper for counteracting such laws as the States may adopt or enforce. . . .

In this connection it is proper to state that civil rights, such as are guarantied [*sic*] by the Constitution against state aggression, cannot be impaired by the wrongful acts of individuals, unsupported by state authority. . . . The wrongful act of an individual, unsupported by any such authority, is simply a private wrong, or a crime of that individual, an invasion of the rights of the injured party, it is true, whether they affect his person, his property or his reputation; but if not sanctioned in some way by the State, or not done under state authority, his rights remain in full force and may presumably be vindicated by resort to the laws of the State for redress.[20]

Harlan's Dissent. In dissent, Justice John Marshall Harlan lamented:

> Constitutional provisions, adopted in the interest of liberty, and for the purpose of securing, through national legislation, if need be, rights inhering in a state of freedom and belonging to American citizenship, have been so construed as to defeat the ends the people desired to accomplish, which they attempted to accomplish, and which they supposed they had accomplished by changes in their fundamental law.

Harlan viewed Congress as authorized under both the 13th and 14th Amendments to pass legislation barring private racial discrimination:

> If, then, exemption from discrimination, in respect of civil rights, is a new constitutional right . . . and I do not see how this can now be questioned . . . why may not the nation, by means of its own legislation of a primary direct character, guard, protect and enforce that right? It is a right and privilege which the nation conferred.[21]

Harlan's dissent had no effect on his colleagues. Thirteen years later, he would again dissent alone, as the court in the famous and now-overruled case of *Plessy v. Ferguson* held state-imposed racial segregation no violation of the rights guaranteed to citizens by the 14th Amendment. The majority found such segregation on railway cars a proper

---

"If, then, exemption from discrimination, in respect of civil rights, is a new constitutional right . . . and I do not see how this can now be questioned . . . why may not the nation, by means of its own legislation of a primary direct character, guard, protect and enforce that right? It is a right and privilege which the nation conferred."

—Justice John Marshall Harlan, dissenting
Civil Rights Cases, 1883

---

and reasonable exercise of the state police power. Writing for the court, Justice Henry B. Brown stated, "The object of the amendment was undoubtedly to enforce the absolute equality of the two races before the law, but in the nature of things, it could not have been intended to abolish distinctions based upon color, or to enforce social, as distinguished from political, equality . . . ."

Brown rejected the "assumption that the enforced separation of the two races stamps the colored race with a badge of inferiority." He continued:

> If this be so, it is not by reason of anything found in the act, but solely because the colored race chooses to put

that construction upon it . . . . The [plaintiff's] argument also assumes that social prejudices may be overcome by legislation, and that equal rights cannot be secured to the negro except by an enforced commingling of the two races. We cannot accept this proposition. If the two races are to meet on terms of social equality, it must be the result of natural affinities, a mutual appreciation of each other's merits and a voluntary consent of individuals.[22]

For 60 years, *Plessy* would stand to allow states to enforce "separate but equal" rules, despite the 14th Amendment's command of equal protection.

Not only did black citizens find little aid in the court's view of the 14th Amendment; but the same plight afflicted women. In 1873 the court refused to apply the 14th Amendment's privileges and immunities clause to require a state to license a woman to practice law in its courts.[23] And two years later it ruled that a state did not deny a woman privileges and immunities guaranteed by the 14th Amendment by refusing to allow her to vote.[24]

Charles Warren comments that by 1875, the year of this ruling, "it now became evident that the privileges and immunities clause of the Amendment, as construed by the Court, afforded slight protection to an individual and no protection to a corporation, affected by oppressive state legislation."[25]

Nor were state laws discriminating against aliens doomed by the 14th Amendment. In only one ruling during the late 19th century did the court strike down any municipal ordinance or state law as denying aliens equal protection of the law.[26]

And the 14th Amendment was of no aid to criminal defendants in state courts. In 1884 the court refused to use the 14th Amendment's due process guarantee to require that a state, in prosecuting someone for a capital crime, first obtain a grand jury indictment.[27]

The Right to Vote

"The right of citizens of the United States to vote shall not be denied or abridged by the United States or by any State on account of race, color, or previous condition of servitude," states the first section of the 15th Amendment. The second section gives Congress the power to enforce that ban.

This constitutional protection too shrank in the postwar years. The Supreme Court, in 1876, handed down a pair of decisions that effectively nullified the 1870 law Congress had passed to enforce this guarantee of the right to vote.

'Exemption from Discrimination.' Adhering closely to the wording of the amendment, the court in the case of *United States v. Reese* struck down the parts of the law that provided punishment for state election officials who refused to accept or count black votes or who otherwise obstructed citizens from voting. The court held that the penalties covered a broader range of behavior than that proscribed by the amendment, and hence must fall.

"The Fifteenth Amendment does not confer the right of suffrage upon anyone," wrote Chief Justice Morrison Waite for the court. But, Waite continued, the "Amendment has invested the citizens of the United States with a new constitutional right which is within the protecting power of Congress. That right is exemption from discrimination in the exercise of the elective franchise on account of race, color or previous condition of servitude." But the law at issue was too broad, covering actions outside the jurisdiction of Congress as well as those within. Thus it must be struck down: "Within its legitimate sphere, Congress is supreme and beyond the control of the courts; but if it steps outside of its constitutional limitation . . . the courts . . . must, annul its encroachments upon the reserved power of the States and the people."[28]

The same day — March 27, 1876 — the court issued its opinion in the case of *United States v. Cruikshank* in which the 1870 act had been used to bring charges against several persons for using violence and fraud to keep blacks from exercising a number of constitutional rights — among them the right of assembly, the right to petition for redress of grievances, the right to bear arms and the right to vote. Again, the court held that these actions were outside federal jurisdiction, that the rights allegedly interfered with were not federally protected rights and thus Congress could not prescribe punishment for persons who violated them.

Wrote Chief Justice Waite:

> The Government of the United States is one of delegated powers alone. Its authority is defined and limited by the Constitution. All powers not granted to it by that instrument are reserved to the States or the people. No rights can be acquired under the Constitution or laws of the United States, except such as the Government of the United States has the authority to grant or secure. All that cannot be so granted or secured are left under the protection of the States.

The 14th Amendment, the Chief Justice continued, "adds nothing to the rights of one citizen as against another. It simply furnishes an additional guarantee against any encroachment by the States upon the fundamental rights which belong to every citizen as a member of society."

Again, Waite made the point announced in *Reese:*

> The right to vote in the States comes from the States; but the right of exemption from the prohibited discrimination comes from the United States. The first has not been granted or secured by the Constitution of the United States; but the last has been.

In this case there was no explicit charge that the fraud and violence that occurred had been intended to prevent blacks from voting on account of their race, and so, Waite could say that "it does not appear that it was their intent to interfere with any right granted or secured by the Constitution or laws of the United States." Although, he commented, "[w]e may suspect that 'race' was the cause of the hostility; . . . it is not so averred."[29]

But the court did not entirely undercut the force of the 15th Amendment. In 1884 it upheld the convictions of several members of the Ku Klux Klan who had beaten up a black man to keep him from voting in federal elections. These convictions were obtained under the portions of the 1870 enforcement law that remained in effect after the court's rulings in *Reese* and *Cruikshank.*

"If this government is anything more than a mere aggregation of delegated agents of other States and governments, each of which is superior to the General Government, it must have the power to protect the elections on which its existence depends from violence and corruption," wrote Justice Samuel Miller for the court in the 1884 decision in the case entitled *Ex parte Yarbrough.*

In some circumstances, Miller continued, the 15th Amendment did grant blacks the right to vote, "and Con-

gress had the power to protect and enforce that right."[30]

Circumvention. *Ex parte Yarbrough* and federal enforcement power notwithstanding, the southern states adopted and used a number of devices that successfully kept most blacks from voting for most of a century after the Civil War. Judicial action to outlaw these devices were belated.

The first such device to fall was the "grandfather" clause, setting some literacy or other standard that prospective voters must meet — unless they or their father or grandfather were a registered voter in the years before adoption of the 15th Amendment. In 1915 the Supreme Court struck down such a clause implemented by the state

---

The court rejects the assumption "that the enforced separation of the two races stamps the colored race with a badge of inferiority. If this be so, it is not by reason of anything found in this act, but solely because the colored race chooses to put that construction upon it . . . ."

—Justice Henry B. Brown
Plessy v. Ferguson, 1896

---

of Oklahoma, finding it a clear violation of the amendment. Oklahoma then required all persons who had not voted in the 1914 election to register within two weeks in order to become voters. In 1939 the court held this requirement also in violation of the 15th Amendment.[31]

The "white primary" was used effectively to disenfranchise blacks until the court in 1944 held the "white primary" impermissible as a violation of the equal protection guarantee and the 15th Amendment.[32]

In 1898 the court held that neither poll taxes nor a literacy test violated the amendment and, as recently as 1960, the Supreme Court upheld a North Carolina literacy requirement for voters.[33] However, in 1964 the adoption of the 24th Amendment forbade the use of poll taxes in federal elections, and in 1966 the Supreme Court held a state's poll tax for state elections a denial of equal protection.[34] Four years later the court upheld a 1970 act of Congress suspending all use of literacy tests. Such a ban was a proper implementation of the 15th Amendment, held the court.[35]

And even before it moved into the general "political thicket" of reapportionment, the court in 1960 struck down the racial gerrymandering of electoral districts as in violation of the 15th Amendment guarantee.[36] *(Details, p. 483-484)*

The Guarantee of Due Process

It was doubly ironic that the first extended use of the due process clause by the Supreme Court was to protect business against regulation by the state. This portion of the 14th Amendment, which was enacted to protect persons, was thereby turned into a shield for property. And the provision first tested before the court in an unsuccessful effort to claim its protection for the right to carry on business would, by the end of the 19th century, take the place of the contract clause as business' most effective weapon against state regulation.

The first decision signalling this development appeared to be a defeat for propertied interests. In the 1897 case of *Allgeyer v. Louisiana,* the court held that due process protected a citizen's right to do business with out-of-state as well as in-state insurance firms.

But in writing the court's opinion Justice Rufus Peckham set out for the first time from the bench the theory that the liberty protected by the due process guarantee of the 14th Amendment included the right to make contracts, free of state interference.

Liberty, wrote Peckham, includes "not only the right of the citizen to be free from the merely physical restraint of his person . . . but the term is deemed to embrace the right of the citizen to be free in the enjoyment of all his faculties; to be free to use them in all lawful ways; to live and work where he will; to earn his livelihood by any lawful calling; to pursue any livelihood or avocation, and for that purpose to enter into all contracts which may be proper, necessary and essential to his carrying out to a successful conclusion the purposes above mentioned." [37]

Within that year the court held that due process required a state, in taking private property for public use — by requiring a railroad to pay for crossing facilities and flagmen — must provide just compensation to the owner.[38] And in 1898 the court held that courts should review the railroad rates set by state commissions to ensure that they did not deprive the railroad company of due process by failing to provide a fair return on its investment.[39]

From these precedents, the court had little philosophical distance to travel to its ruling in *Lochner v. New York,* invalidating New York's maximum hours law for bakers as violating the freedom of contract and, hence, due process. *Lochner* was the first in a long series of rulings in which the court used this theory to strike down state efforts to set maximum hours or minimum wages for workers. *(pp. 326-327)*

'Substantive Due Process'

This use of due process — to examine and test the constitutional validity of the substance of a law, not simply the procedures it provides — is called "substantive due process." The effect of its use during the early portion of the 20th century is described by one scholar:

> From the standpoint of the development of the federal system, the rise of substantive due process meant two things: one, that a national agency — the Supreme Court — was to decide (in many instances) what the states could and could not do; it thus meant a diminution of state autonomy. Second, to the extent that the Court used substantive due process to frustrate state attempts to regulate business, there would be more pressure exerted by nonbusiness interests for the national government to act, thus accelerating the march to Washington and the accretion of power in the hands of federal officials.

The conservative justices who espoused this use of substantive due process were thus "unwitting nationalists in the battle over the nature of the federal system." [40]

The court would employ this approach — and the theory of freedom of contract — until the New Deal was well under way.

The State and Privacy

A right of personal privacy — which protects the individual from the interference of the state — began to emerge in Supreme Court decisions of the 1960s and 1970s.

Without any consensus as to the constitutional foundation for such a right, the court agreed that it required an end to state laws prohibiting the use of contraceptives, criminalizing all abortions, and making it illegal to possess obscene material in one's own home for one's personal use.

"We deal with a right of privacy older than the Bill of Rights," wrote Justice William O. Douglas when the Supreme Court struck down a Connecticut law forbidding the use — or counseling of the use — of contraceptives by anyone in the state.[1] Also suggested as the basis for this holding and this right were the due process guarantee of the 14th Amendment, the 'penumbra' of the privacy interests protected by the First, Third, Fourth and Fifth Amendments, and the Ninth Amendment's statement that the enumeration of rights in the Constitution is not complete and exclusive and that other rights are "retained by the people."

Four years later, the court held that a state could not forbid the mere possession of obscene material. This holding was based in part upon the fundamental First Amendment right "to receive information and ideas, regardless of their social worth," but also in part upon the "right to be free, except in very limited circumstances, from unwanted governmental intrusions into one's privacy." The state had no right to control the content of a person's thoughts, held the court.[2]

And in the most controversial of the privacy-related rulings of recent terms, the court in 1973 used the right of privacy as the basis for its holding that states could not stand in the way of women who decided, early in a pregnancy, to terminate it through an abortion.

Noting the conflicting views as to the constitutional basis for the right of privacy, Justice Harry A. Blackmun stated firmly that "[t]his right of privacy, whether it be founded in the Fourteenth Amendment's concept of personal liberty and restrictions upon state action, as we feel it is, or . . . in the Ninth Amendment's reservation of rights to the people, is broad enough to encompass a woman's decision whether or not to terminate her pregnancy."[3] The court did recognize the right and interest of the state to regulate the factors or conditions governing that decision as pregnancy progressed toward the time at which a live child could be born and live outside the mother.

---

[1] *Griswold v. Connecticut,* 381 U.S. 479 at 486 (1965).
[2] *Stanley v. Georgia,* 394 U.S. 557 (1969).
[3] *Roe v. Wade, Doe v. Bolton,* 410 U.S. 113 at 153 (1973).

The Quiet Revolution

The first crack in the court's refusal to apply the Bill of Rights to protect individuals against state action came quietly and with little argument.

In 1925 the court was considering Benjamin Gitlow's argument that his right to due process of law — and his First Amendment freedom of expression — were violated by the state of New York. Gitlow, a member of the Socialist Party, was indicted for publishing and distributing allegedly subversive documents. The charges were based on New York's criminal anarchy law, which forbade the use of language or the distribution of publications advocating the forcible overthrow of organized government.

Gitlow argued that this law also violated the due process guarantee because under it the state could punish someone for speaking his thoughts, without any evidence that concrete or substantive evil was likely to result.

His argument simply assumed that the "liberty" protected by the 14th Amendment's due process clause included the First Amendment guarantees of freedom of speech and of the press.

The court upheld Gitlow's prosecution, finding the state law not in conflict with the due process guarantee.

But in its opinion, written by the conservative Justice Edward Terry Sanford, the court merely assumed that Gitlow was correct: The 14th Amendment due process clause *did* apply the First Amendment's protections to persons threatened by state action.

"For present purposes," wrote Sanford, "we may and do assume that freedom of speech and of the press — which are protected by the 1st Amendment from abridgment by Congress —are among the fundamental personal rights and 'liberties' protected by the due process clause of the 14th Amendment from impairment by the states ...." [41] However, the court held, the New York law did not violate those rights.

The door thus was open to the gradual, case-by-case process of the following decades, as the court would use the due process guarantee of the 14th Amendment to apply to the states those protections of the Bill of Rights it found to be fundamental.

Six years later, in the case of *Stromberg v. California*, the court for the first time struck down a state law as violating freedom of speech. [42]

Beneficiary of the ruling was Yetta Stromberg, a young woman who conducted a daily flag salute ceremony in a Young Communist League children's camp; the flags involved were those of Soviet Russia and the Communist Party. She was convicted of violating California's "red-flag" law, which forbade the display of a red flag for propaganda or protest purposes. The law denied Stromberg the freedom for political expression and discussion, wrote Chief Justice Charles Evans Hughes, finding it too broad to withstand challenge under the now-applicable First Amendment standards.

Freedom of the press was also now protected against state action. In 1931 the court invalidated, for the first time, a state law as infringing on freedom of the press. Struck down by the court was a Minnesota law that allowed a newspaper or magazine publishing scandalous, malicious, defamatory or obscene material to be "padlocked" as a nuisance by an injunction. If the newspaper were published despite the injunction the publisher could be convicted of contempt of court. The "padlocking" would be terminated only if the judge approving it was convinced that the publication would be unobjectionable in the future. [43]

In 1934 the court held that freedom of religion was protected against state action by the due process guarantee. In the particular case decided, the court held that although the guarantee did apply, a state university did not abridge

a student's freedom of religion by requiring him to take military drill. [44]

Three years later, freedom of assembly was granted the same protection, as the court overturned the conviction of a Communist Party member for conducting a party meeting. [45]

And in 1947 the court made clear that not only the First Amendment freedoms but also the First Amendment guarantee against establishment of religion was protected by due process. [46] Again, in the particular case decided, the court held that this guarantee was not infringed upon by a school board policy of reimbursing parents for the costs of transporting their children to school, parochial as well as public. This was the first in a long and complicated series of rulings as the court has worked to determine what forms of state aid might be constitutionally provided to church-related schools. *(Details, p. 466)*

The court then expanded the reach of the First Amendment protection against state action to encompass the expression of ideas in handbills, meetings and demonstrations and participation in patriotic programs. *(Details, p. 406)*

In 1938 the court held that a city could not require everyone who wished to distribute any publication — by hand or otherwise — in the city to obtain written permission to do so. Overturning the conviction of a Jehovah's Witness for failing to obtain such permission, the court held the ordinance a violation of the freedom of the press, a freedom that included "every sort of publication which affords a vehicle of information and opinion." [47]

In 1939 the justices held that a city could regulate but not absolutely deny the use of public parks, roads and buildings to organizations wishing to use them for meetings and other forms of communication. [48]

Jehovah's Witnesses are taught that saluting a flag is contrary to the teachings of the Bible. The conflict between this teaching and the requirement of many public schools that children daily salute the U.S. flag came to the court in the case of the *Minersville School District v. Gobitis*.

With its decision in this case, announced in 1940, the court appeared to halt its expansion of First Amendment protection against state action. By an 8-1 vote, the court rejected the argument that the flag salute requirement abridged the freedom of religion guaranteed to the Jehovah's Witnesses' children. [49]

But only three years later — in the middle of World War II — the court reversed itself. In the case of the *West Virginia Board of Education v. Barnette*, the court ruled that the state could not compel children to participate in a patriotic ceremony when to do so violated their religious beliefs.

Wrote Justice Robert H. Jackson for the court:

> If there is any fixed star in our constitutional constellation, it is that no official ... can prescribe what shall be orthodox in politics, nationalism, religion or other matters.... We think the action of the local authorities in compelling the flag salute and pledge transcends constitutional limitations on their power and invades the sphere of intellect and spirit which it is the purpose of the First Amendment ... to reserve from all official control. [50]

Fair Criminal Procedures

After the court began to extend First Amendment protections against state action, pressure began to build for a similar extension of other guarantees in the Bill of Rights, in particular those intended to protect persons charged with crimes.

Right to Counsel. In 1932 the court began this process. The right first extended was the right to counsel, guaranteed in federal cases by the Sixth Amendment. The case was that of the black "Scottsboro boys" charged with raping two white women on a freight train passing through Alabama.

Taken off the train and jailed in Scottsboro, the black men were never asked whether they wished to have the aid of lawyers, and the first case came to trial with no defense

---

"[I]n a capital case, where the defendant is unable to employ counsel, and is incapable adequately of making his own defense because of ignorance, feeblemindedness, illiteracy, or the like, it is the duty of the court . . . to assign counsel for him as a necessary requisite of due process of law. . . ."

—Justice George Sutherland
Powell v. Alabama, 1932

---

attorney present. Lawyers eventually did act as defense counsel; the defendants were convicted.

The Supreme Court reversed their convictions, holding in *Powell v. Alabama* that the denial of the right to the effective aid of legal counsel was, in the circumstances of this case, a denial of due process under the 14th Amendment.

Writing for the court, Justice George Sutherland declared:

[I]n a capital case, where the defendant is unable to employ counsel, and is incapable adequately of making his own defense because of ignorance, feeblemindedness, illiteracy, or the like, it is the duty of the court, whether requested or not, to assign counsel for him as a necessary requisite of due process of law; and that duty is not discharged by an assignment at such a time or under such circumstances as to preclude the giving of effective aid in the preparation and trial of the case. To hold otherwise would be to ignore the fundamental postulate . . . "that there are certain immutable principles of justice which inhere in the very idea of free government which no member of the Union may disregard." [51]

Ten years later, the court limited the effect of this holding by ruling in *Betts v. Brady* that "[t]he due process clause of the Fourteenth Amendment does not incorporate, as such, the specific guarantees found in the Sixth Amendment although a denial by a state of rights or privileges specifically embodied in that . . . may . . . operate, in a given case, to deprive a litigant of due process of law. . . ." Thus the justices refused to require that the state must always furnish counsel to a defendant charged with a crime and unable to employ his own lawyer. [52]

But 31 years after *Powell*, in 1963, the Supreme Court overruled *Betts v. Brady* and held that the Sixth Amendment right to counsel was incorporated in the due process clause and that every defendant in a state criminal trial, just as in a federal trial, was guaranteed representation by counsel whom he employed or who was appointed for him by the court. This ruling came in the case of *Gideon v. Wainright*. [53] *(Details, p. 567)*

Judge and Jury. Early in the century, the court extended to state courts the requirement that a person tried for a crime be tried by an impartial judge. In 1927 the court struck down an Ohio law that allowed a city's mayor to try bootleggers, and to put half the fines assessed and collected into the city coffers.

"It certainly violates the Fourteenth Amendment," wrote Chief Justice William Howard Taft, "and deprives a defendant in a criminal case of due process of law, to subject his liberty or property to the judgment of a court the judge of which has a direct, personal, substantial pecuniary interest in reaching a conclusion against him in his case." [54]

Although it was not until 1968 that the right to a jury trial was extended to state criminal defendants, the court held decades earlier that if a jury was provided, it must be fairly chosen. In 1923 the court ruled that five black men convicted in Arkansas of murdering a white man were denied due process because of the atmosphere in which their jury was selected and their trial conducted.

And in another case arising out of the prosecution of the "Scottsboro boys," the court reversed their convictions after a second trial, ruling that due process had been denied them because blacks had been excluded from the juries that indicted and tried them. Subsequently the court ruled that indictments of blacks by grand juries from which blacks were excluded were invalid. [55]

In two decisions in 1876 and 1900 the court held that the 14th Amendment did not require states to provide jury trials to persons accused of crimes, although the Sixth Amendment provided such a guarantee for persons charged with federal crimes. In 1968, in the case of *Duncan v. Louisiana*, the court reversed those earlier rulings and extended the jury trial guarantee to state criminal defendants. [56] *(Details, p. 530)*

Earlier in 1965, the court had applied still another element of the fair trial guarantee to state courts — the right to confront witnesses against oneself. [57]

Fifth Amendment Protections. Few constitutional guarantees have generated as much controversy as the Fifth Amendment right not to be forced to incriminate oneself.

One aspect of this right is the right to remain silent when accused, and to refuse to testify in one's own defense.

In 1908 the court held that this privilege was not protected in state proceedings by the due process guarantee, declining to forbid a state judge to comment on a defendant's silence. [58]

More than 50 years later, in 1964, the court overruled that holding. In the case of *Malloy v. Hogan*, the justices extended this Fifth Amendment protection to persons charged with state crimes. The following year, the court held it unfair for a judge or prosecutor to comment adversely during a trial upon a defendant's failure to testify in his own behalf. [59]

As early as 1936, the court began to use the Fifth Amendment to forbid the use in state trials of forced confessions. That year the court reversed the murder convictions of three blacks because they were in part based upon confessions extracted from them through torture. This was a clear denial of due process, held the court.[60]

Malloy v. Hogan and *Gideon v. Wainwright* were combined by the court into a foundation for two of its most criticized rulings of the 1960s. In the case of *Escobedo v. Illinois*, the court ruled that a confession of murder could not be used against Escobedo because it was obtained after intensive police interrogation during which Escobedo was denied his request to see a lawyer. The confession was thus obtained in clear violation of his constitutional right to counsel and could not properly be used against him, held the court.[61]

Two years later, with its decision in the case of *Miranda v. Arizona,* the court kindled further controversy. Applying this "exclusionary rule" against illegally or unconstitutionally obtained evidence, the court held that confessions could not be used as evidence if they were obtained from suspects interrogated by police without being advised of their rights to remain silent and to obtain legal counsel.

In *Miranda,* the court required that police inform persons who were held in custody of their right to remain silent, of the fact that anything they said could be used against them in court, and of their right to have assistance of counsel before and during interrogation, even if they could not afford to hire an attorney themselves.[62]

Law enforcement officials charged that such decisions made their tasks impossible. Congress considered acting to reverse the rulings, and these decisions were criticized again and again during the 1968 presidential campaign.

A less controversial portion of the Fifth Amendment protects persons against being tried twice for the same action by the same sovereign. Because the federal system includes two systems of justice — one state and one national, every person is subject to both criminal jurisdictions and may — without violating this guarantee — be tried by both for crimes arising from the same actions.[63]

Not until 1969 did the court extend the guarantee against double jeopardy to protect persons from being tried twice by a state for the same actions. Thirty-two years earlier, the court had held that this guarantee did not protect state defendants.

In that 1937 decision, in *Palko v. Connecticut,* Justice Benjamin Cardozo explained why the court viewed some of the guarantees of the Bill of Rights as applied to the states while others were not. Certain rights like the right to a jury trial were valuable, he wrote, yet "they are not of the very essence of a scheme of ordered liberty. To abolish them is not to violate a 'principle of justice so rooted in the traditions and conscience of our people as to be ranked as fundamental.'"

Other rights, which are applied to the states through the 14th Amendment, are of such importance, wrote Cardozo, "that neither liberty nor justice would exist if they were sacrificed .... This is true, for illustration, of freedom of thought and speech."

In 1969 the court overruled this holding to the extent it restricted the double jeopardy guarantee to federal defendants. In *Benton v. Maryland,* the court held that this guarantee was indeed fundamental to the American system of justice.[64] *(Details, pp. 571-573)*

Unreasonable Search and Seizure. The Fourth Amendment protects citizens from searches and seizures that are unreasonable. In 1949 a Colorado abortionist challenged his conviction because it was based on records seized from his office by officers acting without a warrant.

The Supreme Court stated that the Fourth Amendment freedom from unreasonable searches was a necessary part of the concept of "ordered liberty" — to which Cardozo had referred in *Palko* — and thus was protected by the 14th Amendment against state action.[65]

As early as 1914, the court had held that evidence obtained in searches violating the Fourth Amendment could not be used in federal courts.[66] But in this 1949 state case, the court did not forbid the use of evidence even if it was unconstitutionally obtained.

In 1961 the court reversed this stance and excluded such evidence from use at state trials as well as federal ones. In the court's opinion in *Mapp v. Ohio,* Justice Tom C. Clark explained:

> The ignoble shortcut to conviction left open to the State [by the court's failure to apply the exclusionary rule earlier] tends to destroy the entire system of constitutional restraints on which the liberties of the people rest. Having once recognized that the right to privacy embodied in the Fourth Amendment is enforceable against the States, and that the right to be secure against rude invasions of privacy by state officers is, therefore, constitutional in origin, we can no longer permit that right to remain an empty promise.[67]

The Fourth Amendment forbids only *unreasonable* searches and seizures. A long line of cases raises the question of what is "reasonable" in various circumstances. In 1963 the court held that the same standards were to be used to judge the reasonableness of searches and seizures by state as by federal officers.[68] Subsequently the court has upheld as reasonable "stop-and-frisk" searches by police, searches of the area within reach of a recently arrested suspect, and certain car searches — all without warrants.[69] *(Details, pp. 544-547)*

Cruel Punishment. The Eighth Amendment forbids cruel and unusual punishment.

In a bizarre Louisiana case, Willie Francis, a convicted murderer, prepared for his death by electrocution, sat in the portable electric chair, heard the switch pulled — and nothing happened. The chair failed to function. Francis was then returned to his cell to await repair of the chair and a second "execution." In the meantime, he challenged this "sentence" as cruel and unusual punishment.

The Supreme Court assumed, but did not actually rule, that the Eighth Amendment applied to the states. But even if the standard applied, the justices found that it had not been violated in Francis' case.[70]

In 1962 the court directly applied this prohibition to the states. It struck down a California law that made drug addiction a crime.[71]

In the 1970s the court considered two sets of cases challenging the death penalty as cruel and unusual — and unconstitutional — punishment. In the first set, decided in 1972, the court effectively invalidated all existing capital punishment laws by holding that the procedures they provided for imposition of the death sentence violated due process. The procedures left so much discretion to the judge or jury imposing the sentence, held the court, that the result was a system under which receiving a death sentence was as arbitrary and irrational as being struck by lightning.[72]

Four years later, the court held that death, in and of itself, was not an unconstitutionally cruel and unusual punishment for persons convicted of first-degree murder. But it did strike down laws that made death the mandatory sentence for persons convicted of first-degree murder. The due process guarantee, the court held, required individualized consideration of a crime and the criminal, before such a final sentence was imposed.[73]

Juvenile Rights. The court also has extended certain of the guarantees of the Bill of Rights to juvenile court proceedings. They include the right of a juvenile to be notified of charges against him, to have the aid of counsel, to confront witnesses against him, to be informed of his right to remain silent, and to be found guilty — or delinquent — beyond a reasonable doubt.

The court has refused, however, to extend the right to a jury trial to juvenile court proceedings, which by their nature are less formal than regular criminal court proceedings. To require a jury trial, the court reasoned, would unnecessarily rigidify and formalize the operations of the juvenile courts.[74]

The Guarantee of Equal Protection

For the first 70 years after it became a part of the Constitution, the 14th Amendment's guarantee of equal protection of the laws seemed useless. Despite it, the court steadfastly upheld the "separate but equal" segregation codes of the southern states. And in only one of the first 10 cases brought under this provision, did a challenge to a state law succeed.[75]

Not until 1938 did the court begin re-examining segregation laws with an eye to the equality they were supposed to preserve. Not until the civil rights revolution of the 1950s and 1960s did the equal protection clause take on the meaning its authors had intended.

Voting Rights

The right to vote — for which the court had provided only narrow federal protection under the 15th Amendment — was brought within the protection of the 14th Amendment by a series of rulings culminating in the court's famous "one person, one vote" edict of 1964.

'White Primaries.' But before the issue of malapportionment was addressed directly by the court, it confronted one of the most effective anti-black electoral devices — the white primary.

In a campaign spending case decided in 1921, the court appeared to limit federal regulation of elections to the final general election of an officer, excluding any regulation of primary contests.[76]

Within this understanding, many states in the South felt free to forbid blacks to vote in Democratic primaries which were, in most of the South, the actual election because little or no Republican opposition to a Democratic nominee ever surfaced.

The first time that such a "white primary" law came to the court, in 1927, the court struck it down as a clear violation of the equal protection guarantee.[77]

Texas, the state involved in that case, next passed a law empowering the state's political parties to set the qualifications for primary voters; the Democratic Party then exercised that power to exclude blacks from eligibility as primary voters. In 1932 the court held that law unconstitutional. The party had acted as the agent of the state, it held, and thus its action fell under the equal protection clause with which it clearly conflicted.[78]

Persisting in its effort to keep black voters from participating in its electoral processes, the Texas Democratic

Party then voted to confine party membership to whites. Because there was no connection to the state in this case, the Supreme Court upheld that exclusion in its decision in the case of *Grovey v. Townsend* in 1935.[79]

But this form of discrimination did not survive much longer. In 1941 the court held that primary elections were, in many states, an integral part of the process of electing members of Congress. Thus, Congress had the authority to regulate such primaries.[80] Three years later, with the case of *Smith v. Allwright,* the court reversed *Grovey.* It redefined state action to include political parties that followed state regulation of primary elections and thereby became state agencies, in that respect. Thus, racial discrimination by political parties in primary voting came under the ban of the 15th Amendment.[81] *(Details, p. 481)*

Poll Taxes and Literacy Tests. In the late 19th century the court had upheld the use of a poll tax and an "understanding" or literacy test to screen out illiterate persons who wished to vote. In 1964, after such devices had been abandoned by most states, the 24th Amendment was added to the Constitution to prohibit the use of poll taxes to abridge the right to vote in federal elections. And in 1966 the court struck down poll tax requirements for state elections, finding them a violation of the equal protection guarantee.[82]

Voting Rights Act. The continuing success of many southern states in keeping black citizens from voting moved Congress to enact progressively stronger civil rights laws during the 1950s and 1960s authorizing federal action to counter such obstruction. By 1965, however, the lack of success of these new laws — coupled with the dramatic and brutal resistance of certain areas in the South to black demonstrations expressing the frustration of black voters — made clear that Congress must act forcefully.

The result was the Voting Rights Act of 1965, which prohibited the use of any test or device as a qualification for voting in any state where less than half the voting age population was registered — or voted — at the time of the 1964 presidential election. That test applied the act to six southern states and a number of counties in other states. South Carolina, one of the affected states, immediately challenged the act as a violation of the constitutional reservation to the states of the power to set voter qualifications. A three-judge federal court agreed with the state, but the Supreme Court did not. The justices upheld the law as an appropriate exercise of congressional power to enforce the 15th Amendment.[83]

Reapportionment Revolution

The most far-reaching extension of Supreme Court power into state affairs mandated by the court under Chief Justice Earl Warren came with its reapportionment rulings. In 1962 the court ended years of abstention from the sensitive political issue of redistricting and reapportionment, and agreed to assess the fairness of congressional and state legislative district lines.

Only 16 years earlier, in the case of *Colegrove v. Green,* the court had refused to intervene in such matters, despite enormous disparity in population between state electoral districts. Justice Felix Frankfurter had explained:

From the determination of such issues this Court has traditionally held aloof. It is hostile to a democratic system to involve the judiciary in the politics of the people .... Courts ought not to enter this political thicket. The remedy for unfairness in districting is to secure State legislatures that will apportion properly, or to invoke the ample powers of Congress.[84]

But less than 20 years later the court reversed that holding to rule that challenges to the fairness of the apportionment of state legislatures were, in fact, proper matters for the federal courts to resolve.

In the landmark case of *Baker v. Carr* the court directed a lower federal court to hear the challenge of certain Tennessee voters that the malapportionment of the state legislature denied them equal protection of laws under the 14th Amendment. At that time the Tennessee legislature had not been reapportioned for more than 60 years, during which there had been substantial shifts in population, chiefly from rural to urban areas.

Writing for the court, Justice William J. Brennan Jr. reviewed the history of the "political question" doctrine of judicial restraint, and concluded that the equal protection claim here did not require decision of any truly political question and that the case was not removed from the purview of federal courts by the fact that it affected state government. "The right asserted is within the reach of judicial protection under the Fourteenth Amendment," he stated.[85]

'One Person, One Vote' Rule. The following year, the court struck down Georgia's county unit system of electing

---

"The conception of political equality from the Declaration of Independence, to Lincoln's Gettysburg Address, to the Fifteenth, Seventeenth and Nineteenth Amendments can mean only one thing — one person, one vote."

—Justice William O. Douglas
Gray v. Sanders, 1963

---

state officials and set out the guidelines for the fair apportionment of legislative representation:

Once the geographical unit for which a representative is to be chosen is designated, all who participate in the election are to have an equal vote — whatever their race, whatever their sex, whatever their occupation, whatever their income and wherever their home may be in that geographical unit. This is required by the Equal Protection Clause of the Fourteenth Amendment.

Writing for the court in this case, Justice William O. Douglas concluded with the statement:

The conception of political equality from the Declaration of Independence, to Lincoln's Gettysburg Address, to the Fifteenth, Seventeenth, and Nineteenth Amendments can mean only one thing — one person, one vote.[86]

The following year this standard was applied by the court to require congressional redistricting and state legislative reapportionment.[87]

Although in subsequent cases the court set the strict rule of mathematical equality for newly drawn districts, it

relaxed that standard in 1973 for state legislative districts, approving the creation of districts that were "as nearly of equal population as practicable" and allowing some legitimately based divergence from strict equality.[88] *(Details, p. 495)*

Housing, Schools and Marriage

Even before the court began to wield the equal protection clause in behalf of voters, however, it began to use it to strike down the racial segregation that had come to characterize so many parts of American life after the Civil War.

As early as 1917, the court made its first move against housing segregation. In that year, it struck down a Louisville, Kentucky, residential segregation ordinance — as an unconstitutional interference with the right of a property owner to sell his real estate to whomever he pleased.

But what could not be accomplished legally by city action could be achieved by private agreement, and so "restrictive covenants" flourished. A purchaser accepting a contract or title with such a covenant agreed not to sell the real estate to a black person. This was clearly private action, unreachable under the 14th Amendment, according to the *Civil Rights Cases* decision. Yet in 1948 the court effectively circumvented the "private action" limitation, by holding that any state action to enforce such a covenant would violate the 14th Amendment.[89]

In subsequent rulings, the court held that state voters could not amend their constitution to restrict the efforts of state or local government to end racial discrimination, nor could they require that all fair housing laws be approved by referendum. Where discrimination is not clearly based on race, however, the court has hesitated to strike down such voter-approval requirements or to overturn local decisions concerning housing.[90]

Early in the 20th century, the court extended its tolerance of segregation, signaled by *Plessy v. Ferguson*'s "separate but equal" holding, to the setting of schools, upholding a Kentucky law that forbade colleges to teach whites and blacks at the same time and in the same place.[91]

School segregation began to come under scrutiny by the Supreme Court in the 1930s, beginning at the graduate school level. In 1938 the court held that a state providing graduate education in law to white students must, under the equal protection guarantee, offer substantially similar education to black state residents. The court rejected the state's offer to pay a black student's tuition in an out-of-state law school. The state was obligated, held the court in the case of *Missouri ex rel. Gaines v. Canada,* to provide equal protection within its own borders.

Chief Justice Charles Evans Hughes wrote:

That obligation is imposed by the Constitution upon the States severally as governmental entities, — each responsible for its own laws establishing the rights and duties of persons within its borders. It is an obligation the burden of which cannot be cast by one State upon another .... That separate responsibility of each State within its own sphere is of the essence of statehood....[92]

This holding was reaffirmed in 1948. And in 1950 the court struck down one state university's practice of making a black graduate student sit at special seats and tables in classrooms, cafeteria and library.[93]

On the same day as the latter ruling, the court ordered the University of Texas Law School to admit a qualified black student. The newly created "black" law school in the state did not provide equal opportunity for a legal education, held the court. A qualified black student had a constitutional right to a state-provided legal education equal to that offered to qualified white students, declared the justices in the case of *Sweatt v. Painter.*[94]

Then, in 1954, the court extended this principle to elementary and secondary education with the famous decisions known by the title, *Brown v. Board of Education of Topeka.*[95] The "separate but equal" doctrine was ruled unconstitutional, as applied to public schools, a clear denial of equal protection of the laws. *Plessy v. Ferguson* was overruled. *(p. 592)*

The reaction of the southern states was belligerent. The following year in the second *Brown* decision, the court required states to move with "all deliberate speed" in carrying out the mandate to end public school segregation.[96]

Implementation was slow and painful, continuing for decades after the ruling. In a long line of follow-up rulings, the court steadfastly rejected state and local efforts to obstruct or circumvent its requirements and made clear that it would sanction substantial changes in and costs to a school system as the price for carrying out the edict of *Brown.* Although *Brown,* decided upon an equal protection basis, dealt with states where segregated schools had been required by law, the court did not hesitate to require an end to public school segregation in states that had not had such laws.[97]

And in still another use of the equal protection clause to end state discrimination, the court in 1967 held that the 14th Amendment guarantee was violated by a state law that prohibited the intermarriage of persons of different races.[98]

Rich and Poor

The court has been more reluctant to strike down discrimination based on economic status than that based on race.

In 1973, for example, it refused to invalidate the property tax-based systems through which most states finance their public schools. Texas' financing system had been challenged as denying equal protection to students who lived in poorer districts where the property tax produced less revenue. "The consideration and initiation of fundamental reforms with respect to state taxation and education are matters reserved for the legislative process of the different states," wrote Justice Lewis F. Powell Jr. for the court, refusing to intervene.[99]

But the court has held that the equal protection guarantee forbids states to deny divorces to people too poor to pay the usual court fees, or to require poor people to stay in prison to "work off" a fine they cannot pay while people who can pay the fine are released earlier, even when convicted of the same offense.

A state must provide a poor defendant a free transcript of his trial when such is necessary for him to appeal his conviction, and it must provide legal counsel to all persons charged with any offense for which they are imprisoned and who cannot afford to pay their own attorney.[100]

The Rights of Aliens

The only successful equal protection challenge among the first cases brought to the Supreme Court in the decade after the 14th Amendment was added to the Constitution involved the rights to aliens. Yick Wo, a Chinese resident of

San Francisco, was denied the license necessary to run a laundry in the city, as were all other Chinese laundry operators. Although the license requirement was superficially non-discriminatory, it obviously was enforced in such a way as to deny equal protection. The Supreme Court struck it down in 1886.[101]

Although the court, out of respect for the state's right to control property and resources within its territory, upheld state laws requiring that all persons working on its public works projects be citizens, and denying to aliens (who were ineligible to become citizens) the right to acquire certain state land, it has never given a state *carte blanche* to discriminate against lawfully admitted aliens.[102]

In 1915 the court used the equal protection guarantee to void an Arizona law requiring that an employer hire four citizens for every alien he employed.[103]

And in 1948 the court struck down a California law that denied aliens ineligible for citizenship the right to obtain the licenses necessary to earn a living as commercial fishermen. The guarantee of equal protection, stated the court, meant that "all persons lawfully in this country shall abide 'in any state' on an equality of legal privileges with all citizens under nondiscriminatory law." A state could not deny aliens the right to earn a living in the same way citizens did.[104]

That same year another California law fell before an equal protection challenge from aliens. That law — intended to prevent alien parents from buying land through their native-born citizen children — forbade ineligible aliens to pay for land being sold to a citizen.[105]

In the 1970s the court further expanded the rights of aliens, even, in some cases, to receive benefits provided by a state. The court held that states could not deny resident aliens welfare benefits, the right to practice law in the state or the right to be considered for state civil service jobs. In 1977 the court held that a state could not exclude resident aliens from eligibility for state scholarships, but in 1978 and 1979, the court upheld New York laws requiring state policemen and public school teachers to be citizens.[106] *(Details, p. 625)*

The Rights of Women

Least successful of the plaintiffs under the equal protection clause are women. As noted earlier, their efforts to use other portions of the 14th Amendment to challenge state refusals to admit women to the practice of law or to register women to vote were quickly rejected by the court in the 19th century. *(p. 631)*

In 1904 the court not only rejected an equal protection challenge to a state law forbidding women to work in saloons, but went on to hold that a state could by law bar women from even entering such places. As recently as 1948, the court again upheld a state law forbidding women to work as barmaids, unless they were married to or the child of the bar owner.[107]

Sex was simply considered a valid reason for state discrimination. In 1961 the court upheld a Florida law that "exempted" women from jury duty on the basis of their function as "the center of home and family life."[108]

Ten years later, however, the court began to apply the equal protection test more strictly against state laws that discriminated simply on the basis of sex. In a case involving the appointment of an executor for a deceased child, the court struck down an Idaho law that gave preference to male relatives over female relatives in selecting among equally qualified executors. "To give a mandatory preference to members of either sex over members of the other, merely to accomplish the elimination of hearings on the merits, is to make the very kind of arbitrary legislative choice forbidden by the Equal Protection Clause," wrote Chief Justice Warren E. Burger for the court. [109]

And four years later the court overruled its 1961 decision concerning women and jury duty, holding that state laws exempting women from jury duty violated the requirement that a jury be drawn from a fair cross-section of the community. Such a general exclusion of women from the group eligible for jury duty was not rational, held the court. [110]

Also in 1975, the court overturned a Utah law that set different ages at which men and women were considered adults. In 1977 it followed this with a ruling striking down an Oklahoma law setting different drinking ages for men and women, and an Alabama law which, by setting minimum height and weight requirements for prison guards, effectively denied such jobs to most women in the state. [111]

But the court had not, by the late 1970s, adopted the stiff standard for testing sex discrimination by states that it used to judge race discrimination. States merely had to

prove that laws discriminating on the basis of sex were reasonable and related to the achievement of important governmental goals. On the other hand, a law discriminating on the basis of race would be held constitutional only if it was found necessary to serve a compelling state interest.

And the court still maintained some vestiges of the view that women should be protected. In 1974, with liberal Justice William O. Douglas writing the opinion, the court upheld a Florida law giving widows — but not widowers — a special property tax exemption. [112] And in 1977, after striking down the height and weight requirements for prison guards, the court nevertheless upheld a state regulation excluding women from certain prison guard jobs, holding that their sex made them vulnerable to attack in all-male prisons and thus disqualified them for the job of preserving security there. [113]

The court was also reluctant to make states revise their disability insurance programs to include coverage for pregnant women unable to work for a time during or after pregnancy and childbirth. The decision to exclude women in this category from coverage of an otherwise comprehensive plan was upheld by the court as rational in light of the state's fiscal objectives. [114]

Footnotes

[1] *Calder v. Bull*, 3 Dall. 386 at 390, 391 (1798).
[2] Alpheus T. Mason and William M. Beaney, *The Supreme Court in a Free Society* (Englewood Cliffs: Prentice-Hall, 1959), p. 197.
[3] *Thompson v. Missouri*, 171 U.S. 380 (1898); *Thompson v. Utah*, 170 U.S. 343 (1898).
[4] *Dobbert v. Florida*, 432 U.S. 282 (1977).
[5] *Nixon v. Administrator of General Services*, 433 U.S. 425 (1977).
[6] *Cummings v. Missouri*, 4 Wall. 277 at 319, 325 (1867).
[7] *Ex parte Garland*, 4 Wall. 333 (1867).
[8] *Hawker v. New York*, 170 U.S. 189 (1898); *DeVeau v. Braisted*, 363 U.S. 144 (1960); *Garner v. Board of Public Works*, 341 U.S. 716 (1951); *Cole v. Richardson*, 405 U.S. 676 (1972); *Elfbrandt v. Russell*, 384 U.S. 11 (1966).
[9] *Barron v. Baltimore*, 7 Pet. 243 at 250 (1833).
[10] *The Civil Rights Cases*, 109 U.S. 3 at 22, 24-25 (1883).
[11] *Bailey v. Alabama*, 219 U.S. 219 (1911).
[12] *Butler v. Perry*, 240 U.S. 328 (1916); *Arver v. United States (Selective Draft Law Cases)*, 245 U.S. 366 (1918).
[13] Carl B. Swisher, *American Constitutional Development*, 2d ed. (Cambridge: Houghton Mifflin Co., 1954), pp. 330-333, citing 36 Congressional Globe, 1089-1090, 2542, 2765-2766, and 44 Congressional Globe, Appendix 84.
[14] *The Butchers' Benevolent Association of New Orleans v. The Crescent City Livestock Landing and Slaughterhouse Company, Esteben v. Louisiana (The Slaughterhouse Cases)*, 16 Wall. 36 (1873).
[15] Id. at 74.
[16] Id. at 77-78, 80-81.
[17] Id. at 95-96.
[18] Id. at 81.
[19] *United States v. Reese*, 92 U.S. 214 (1876); *United States v. Cruikshank*, 92 U.S. 542 (1876); *United States v. Harris*, 106 U.S. 629 (1883).
[20] *The Civil Rights Cases*, 109 U.S. 3 at 11, 13-14, 17 (1883).
[21] Id. at 26, 50.
[22] *Plessy v. Ferguson*, 163 U.S. 537 at 544, 551 (1896).
[23] *Bradwell v. The State*, 16 Wall. 130 (1873).
[24] *Minor v. Happersett*, 21 Wall. 162 (1875).
[25] Charles Warren, *The Supreme Court in United States History*, 2 vols. (Boston: Little, Brown & Co., 1922, 1926), II:567.
[26] *Yick Wo v. Hopkins*, 118 U.S. 356 (1886).
[27] *Hurtado v. California*, 110 U.S. 516 (1884).
[28] *United States v. Reese*, 92 U.S. 214 at 217-218, 221 (1876).
[29] *United States v. Cruikshank*, 92 U.S. 542 at 551, 554, 546 (1876).
[30] *Ex parte Yarbrough*, 110 U.S. 651 at 657-658, 665 (1884).
[31] *Guinn v. United States*, 238 U.S. 347 (1915); *Lane v. Wilson*, 307 U.S. 368 (1939).
[32] *United States v. Classic*, 313 U.S. 299 (1941); *Smith v. Allwright*, 321 U.S. 649 (1944).
[33] *Williams v. Mississippi*, 170 U.S. 213 (1898); *Lassiter v. Northampton County Board of Elections*, 360 U.S. 45 (1960).
[34] *Harper v. Virginia Board of Education*, 383 U.S. 663 (1966).
[35] *Oregon v. Mitchell, Texas v. Mitchell, United States v. Idaho, United States v. Arizona*, 400 U.S. 112 (1970).
[36] *Gomillion v. Lightfoot*, 364 U.S. 339 (1960).
[37] *Allgeyer v. Louisiana*, 165 U.S. 578 at 589 (1897).
[38] *Chicago, Burlington & Quincy Railroad Co. v. Chicago*, 166 U.S. 226 (1897).
[39] *Smyth v. Ames*, 169 U.S. 466 (1898).
[40] Loren P. Beth, *The Development of the American Constitution: 1877-1917* (New York: Harper & Row, 1971), pp. 67-68.
[41] *Gitlow v. New York*, 268 U.S. 652 at 666 (1925).
[42] *Stromberg v. California*, 283 U.S. 259 (1931).
[43] *Near v. Minnesota*, 283 U.S. 697 (1931).
[44] *Hamilton v. Board of Regents*, 293 U.S. 245 (1934).
[45] *De Jonge v. Oregon*, 299 U.S. 353 (1937).
[46] *Everson v. Board of Education*, 330 U.S. 1 (1947).
[47] *Lovell v. Griffin*, 303 U.S. 444 (1938); *Cantwell v. Connecticut*, 310 U.S. 296 (1940).
[48] *Hague v. CIO*, 307 U.S. 496 (1939).
[49] *Minersville School District v. Gobitis*, 310 U.S. 586 (1940).
[50] *West Virginia State Board of Education v. Barnette*, 319 U.S. 624 at 642 (1943).
[51] *Powell v. Alabama*, 287 U.S. 45 at 71-72 (1932).
[52] *Betts v. Brady*, 316 U.S. 455 at 461-462 (1942).
[53] *Gideon v. Wainwright*, 372 U.S. 335 (1963).
[54] *Tumey v. Ohio*, 273 U.S. 510 at 523 (1927).
[55] *Moore v. Dempsey*, 261 U.S. 86 (1923); *Norris v. Alabama*, 294 U.S. 587 (1935); *Smith v. Texas*, 311 U.S. 128 (1940).
[56] *Walker v. Sauvinet*, 92 U.S. 90 (1876); *Maxwell v. Dow*, 176 U.S. 581 (1900); *Duncan v. Louisiana*, 391 U.S. 145 (1968).
[57] *Pointer v. Texas*, 380 U.S. 400 (1965).
[58] *Twining v. New Jersey*, 211 U.S. 78 (1908).
[59] *Malloy v. Hogan*, 378 U.S. 1 (1964); *Griffin v. California*, 381 U.S. 957 (1965).

[60] *Brown v. Mississippi*, 297 U.S. 278 (1936).

[61] *Escobedo v. Illinois*, 378 U.S. 478 (1964).

[62] *Miranda v. Arizona*, 384 U.S. 436 (1966).

[63] *United States v. Lanza*, 260 U.S. 377 (1922).

[64] *Palko v. Connecticut*, 302 U.S. 319 at 325-326 (1937); *Benton v. Maryland*, 395 U.S. 784 (1969).

[65] *Wolf v. Colorado*, 338 U.S. 25 (1949).

[66] *Weeks v. United States*, 232 U.S. 383 (1914).

[67] *Mapp v. Ohio*, 367 U.S. 643 at 660 (1961).

[68] *Ker v. California*, 374 U.S. 23 (1963).

[69] *Terry v. Ohio*, 392 U.S. 1 (1968); *Chimel v. California*, 395 U.S. 752 (1969); *Schneckloth v. Bustamonte*, 412 U.S. 218 (1973); *Cady v. Dombrowski*, 413 U.S. 433 (1973); *Gustafson v. Florida, United States v. Robinson*, 414 U.S. 260, 218 (1973); *Cardwell v. Lewis*, 417 U.S. 583 (1974); *South Dakota v. Opperman*, 428 U.S. 364 (1976).

[70] *Louisiana ex. rel. Francis v. Resweber*, 329 U.S. 459 (1947).

[71] *Robinson v. California*, 370 U.S. 660 (1962).

[72] *Furman v. Georgia*, 408 U.S. 238 (1972).

[73] *Gregg v. Georgia*, 428 U.S. 153 (1976); *Woodson v. North Carolina, Roberts v. Louisiana*, 428 U.S. 380, 325 (1976).

[74] *In re Gault*, 387 U.S. 1 (1967); *In re Winship*, 397 U.S. 358 (1970); *McKeiver v. Pennsylvania*, 403 U.S. 528 (1971).

[75] *Yick Wo v. Hopkins*, 118 U.S. 356 (1886); Warren, *The Supreme Court in United States History*, II:596.

[76] *Newberry v. United States*, 256 U.S. 232 (1921).

[77] *Nixon v. Herndon*, 273 U.S. 536 (1927).

[78] *Nixon v. Condon*, 286 U.S. 73 (1932).

[79] *Grovey v. Townsend*, 295 U.S. 45 (1935).

[80] *United States v. Classic*, 313 U.S. 45 (1941).

[81] *Smith v. Allwright*, 321 U.S. 649 (1944).

[82] *Harper v. Virginia Board of Elections*, 383 U.S. 663 (1966).

[83] *South Carolina v. Katzenbach*, 393 U.S. 301 (1966).

[84] *Colegrove v. Green*, 328 U.S. 549 at 553-554, 556 (1946).

[85] *Baker v. Carr*, 369 U.S. 186 at 237 (1962).

[86] *Gray v. Sanders*, 372 U.S. 368 at 379, 381 (1963).

[87] *Reynolds v. Sims*, 377 U.S. 533 (1964); *Wesberry v. Sanders*, 376 U.S. 1 (1964).

[88] *Kirkpatrick v. Preisler*, 394 U.S. 526 (1969); *Mahan v. Howell*, 410 U.S. 315 (1973).

[89] *Buchanan v. Warley*, 245 U.S. 601 (1917); *Shelley v. Kraemer*, 334 U.S. 1 (1948).

[90] *Reitman v. Mulkey*, 387 U.S. 369 (1967); *Hunter v. Erickson*, 393 U.S. 385 (1969); *James v. Valtierra*, 402 U.S. 137 (1971); *Village of Arlington Heights v. Metropolitan Housing Development Corp.*, 429 U.S. 252 (1977).

[91] *Berea College v. Kentucky*, 211 U.S. 45 (1908).

[92] *Missouri ex rel. Gaines v. Canada*, 305 U.S. 337 at 350 (1938).

[93] *Sipuel v. University of Oklahoma*, 332 U.S. 631 (1948); *McLaurin v. Oklahoma State Regents*, 339 U.S. 637 (1950).

[94] *Sweatt v. Painter*, 339 U.S. 629 (1950).

[95] *Brown v. Board of Education of Topeka*, 347 U.S. 483 (1954).

[96] *Brown v. Board of Education of Topeka (II)*, 349 U.S. 294 (1955).

[97] *Cooper v. Aaron*, 358 U.S. 1 (1958); *Griffin v. School Board*, 377 U.S. 218 (1964); *Green v. County School Board*, 391 U.S. 430 (1968); *Swann v. Charlotte-Mecklenburg Board of Education*, 402 U.S. 1 (1971); *Keyes v. Denver School District #1*, 413 U.S. 921 (1973).

[98] *Loving v. Virginia*, 399 U.S. 1 (1967).

[99] *San Antonio Independent School District v. Rodriguez*, 411 U.S. 1 (1973).

[100] *Boddie v. Connecticut*, 401 U.S. 371 (1971); *Williams v. Illinois*, 399 U.S. 235 (1970); *Griffin v. Illinois*, 351 U.S. 12 (1955); *Argersinger v. Hamlin*, 407 U.S. 25 (1972).

[101] *Yick Wo v. Hopkins*, 118 U.S. 356 (1886).

[102] *Heim v. McCall*, 239 U.S. 175 (1915); *Terrace v. Thompson*, 263 U.S. 197 (1923).

[103] *Truax v. Raich*, 239 U.S. 33 (1915).

[104] *Takahashi v. Fish & Game Commission*, 334 U.S. 410 (1948).

[105] *Oyama v. California*, 332 U.S. 633 (1948).

[106] *Graham v. Richardson*, 403 U.S. 365 (1971); *In re Griffiths*, 413 U.S. 717 (1973); *Sugarman v. Dougall*, 403 U.S. 634 (1973); *Nyquist v. Mauclet*, 422 U.S. 1 (1977); *Foley v. Connelie*, 435 U.S. 291 (1978); *Ambach v. Norwick* (1979).

[107] *Cronin v. Adams*, 192 U.S. 108 (1904); *Goesaert v. Cleary*, 335 U.S. 465 (1948).

[108] *Hoyt v. Florida*, 368 U.S. 57 (1961).

[109] *Reed v. Reed*, 404 U.S. 71 at 76 (1971).

[110] *Taylor v. Louisiana*, 419 U.S. 522 (1975).

[111] *Stanton v. Stanton*, 421 U.S. 7 (1975); *Craig v. Boren*, 429 U.S. 190 (1976); *Dothard v. Rawlinson*, 433 U.S. 321 (1977).

[112] *Kahn v. Shevin*, 416 U.S. 351 (1974).

[113] *Dothard v. Rawlinson*, 433 U.S. 321 (1977).

[114] *Geduldig v. Aiello*, 417 U.S. 484 (1974).

The State as Sovereign

With the firm establishment of the court's power of judicial review of state action, of Congress' broad power over interstate and foreign commerce, and of the application of many of the provisions of the Bill of Rights to state action, what rights or powers do the states have left?

The Constitution itself provides a partial answer. The 10th Amendment declares that the powers not given to the federal government by the Constitution nor removed from the arsenal of the states by the Constitution are reserved for the states and the people. And the 11th Amendment grants states freedom from being unwillingly hauled into federal court by citizens having non-constitutional complaints.

And the court itself, while ever maintaining the framework of federal supremacy, has affirmed a variety of powers for the states — the power over elections, the powers of its courts, the broad police power over its land and its people, the power to tax, and the power to form compacts with other states for the resolution of matters of mutual concern.

The well-founded fear of the original 13 states that a strong national government would limit their own power and sovereignty was a major obstacle to ratification of the Constitution.

James Madison wrote in *The Federalist Papers* to calm such fears:

> The powers delegated by the proposed Constitution to the federal government are few and defined. Those which are to remain in the State governments are numerous and indefinite. The former will be exercised principally on external objects, as war, peace, negotiation, and foreign commerce; with which last the power of taxation will, for the most part, be connected. The powers reserved to the several States will extend to all the objects which, in the ordinary course of affairs, concern the lives, liberties, and properties of the people, and the internal order, improvement and prosperity of the State. [1]

Reserved State Powers

To write this view into the Constitution, the first Congress approved the 10th Amendment, which states: "The powers not delegated to the United States by the Constitution, nor prohibited by it to the States, are reserved to the States respectively, or to the people."

In an action that would gain significance with the years, Congress — before approving this provision — rejected an amendment that would have inserted the word "expressly" before the word "delegated." Such an insertion, if approved, would have severely limited — or altogether prevented — any expansion of national power through the doctrine of implied powers.

Until well into the 20th century, the 10th Amendment was wielded, with varying degrees of success, to curtail federal power, particularly federal power over the economy in areas claimed to be reserved for state regulation. The subjects thus "reserved" ranged from child labor to farm production.

The first effort to use the 10th Amendment to curtail federal power was a distinct failure. Maryland based its challenge to the Second Bank of the United States upon the argument that the Constitution did not grant Congress the power to create corporations and that the 10th Amendment thereby reserved such power to the states. Furthermore, the state argued that the power of taxation — except for taxes on imports and exports — was reserved to the state, giving Maryland the right to tax the bank if Congress had the right to create it.

Speaking for the court, Chief Justice John Marshall in 1819 firmly rejected both prongs of the state's argument — and the concept that the 10th Amendment provided the states with an instrument to limit national power. "[T]he states have no power, by taxation or otherwise, to retard, impede, burden, or in any manner control the operations of the constitutional laws enacted by Congress to carry into execution the powers vested in the general government," Marshall wrote. And the absence of the word "expressly" from the amendment left it up to the court to decide if a particular power had been granted the national government — a decision to be made in light of its interpretation of the constitutional system as a whole. [2]

Five years later, in 1824, Marshall felt it necessary, in concluding his opinion in the New York steamboat case, to issue a further warning against a broad interpretation of the 10th Amendment:

> Powerful and ingenious minds, taking as postulates, that the powers expressly granted to the government of the Union are to be contracted ... into the narrowest possible compass, and that the original powers of the States are retained, if any possible

construction will retain them, may . . . explain away the constitution . . . and leave it a magnificent structure indeed, to look at, but totally unfit for use. [3]

'Dual Federalism'

During the tenure of Marshall's successor, Chief Justice Roger B. Taney, 10th Amendment arguments received a friendlier hearing, and the court began to develop the concept of "dual federalism." In this view, the respective domains of state and federal government are neatly defined: Each government is sovereign and supreme within its own sphere, and the enumerated powers of the central government are limited by the reserved powers of the state.

During its laissez-faire period — which extended into the mid-1930s — the court used the 10th Amendment to limit federal power, even while it, at the same time, used the concept of due process to limit state power to regulate property, thus creating a "twilight zone" within the economy where no effective regulation existed. During this period the court wielded the 10th Amendment to restrict the reach of the federal antitrust laws, to nullify federal efforts to limit or prohibit child labor, and to strike down key New Deal programs such as those intended to regulate agriculture, to aid bankrupt cities and to restore order in the coal industry. [4]

In the child labor and agriculture cases, in particular, the court did what the first Congress had refused to do and in effect inserted the word "expressly" into the 10th Amendment to qualify the enumerated powers of the federal government.

Wrote Justice Owen J. Roberts in 1936:

> From the accepted doctrine that the United States is a government of delegated powers, it follows that those not expressly granted or reasonably to be implied from such as are conferred, are reserved to the states or to the people. To forestall any suggestion to the contrary, the Tenth Amendment was adopted. The same proposition, otherwise stated, is that powers not granted are prohibited. [5]

The court was not consistent in its application of the reserved powers doctrine. During the early part of the century, it rejected 10th Amendment challenges to the exercise of the federal police power over lotteries, prostitution, colored oleo and the repeal of prohibition. [6]

But its 1930s insistence on 10th Amendment restrictions on national power provoked Roosevelt's "court-packing" plan — and soon both "dual federalism" and the reserved powers doctrine were discarded by the court's majority. In 1937 the court rebuffed a 10th Amendment challenge to the Social Security Act as intruding upon the powers of the states. In its opinion, Justice Benjamin Cardozo acknowledged that changing economic and political facts made it necessary now for the national government to assume functions once considered the proper responsibility of state and local authority. The court subsequently approved new versions of the agriculture, coal and bankruptcy legislation it had struck down just a few years earlier as intruding upon the reserved powers of the states. [7]

'Cooperative Federalism'

In 1941 the court formally interred the 10th Amendment, with its decision in the case of the *United States v. Darby* upholding the Fair Labor Standards Act which, among other provisions, prohibited child labor. Finding the

act constitutional as it extended federal regulation over working conditions in virtually all major sectors of the economy, Justice Harlan Fiske Stone wrote:

> Our conclusion is unaffected by the Tenth Amendment. . . . The amendment states but a truism that all is retained which has not been surrendered. There is nothing in the history of its adoption to suggest that it was more than declaratory of the relationship between national and state governments as it had been established by the Constitution before the amendment or that its purpose was other than to allay fears that the new national government might seek to exercise powers not granted, and that the states might not be able to exercise fully their reserved powers. . . . From the beginning and for many years the amendment has been construed as not depriving the national government of authority to resort to all means for the exercise of a granted power which are appropriate and plainly adapted to the permitted end. [8]

Dual federalism was replaced by cooperative federalism. The court abandoned the effort of neatly defining the boundaries of state and federal power over matters of mutual interest. Instead it has in recent years sanctioned an overlapping system of complementary state and federal regulation.

Liability to Lawsuits

The states were stunned by the Supreme Court's first major ruling. In 1793 the court held that a state could be hauled into federal court, without its consent, if it was sued by the citizens of another state. Quickly, Congress approved and the states ratified the 11th Amendment to overrule that decision in the case of *Chisholm v. Georgia*; the new amendment was in place by 1798. [9] *(p. 303)*

As added to the Constitution, the 11th Amendment denied federal jurisdiction over any "suit in law or equity" brought against a state by citizens of another state or of a foreign state."

The amendment did not expressly forbid federal courts from taking jurisdiction over suits brought against a state by its own citizens, but the Supreme Court in 1890 held that the amendment did bar such suits. Later, the court also read the amendment to forbid suits brought by a foreign nation against a state without its consent.[10]

Nor did the amendment forbid suits against a state brought under the Constitution, an omission which became significant only in the 20th century. [11]

States' Protection Narrowed

The Supreme Court has narrowed the protection that this amendment provides to the states. The first shrinkage occurred in 1824, when the court held that this immunity did not protect a state official who was acting under an unconstitutional state law or who was exceeding his properly granted authority. This ruling was announced in the case of *Osborn v. Bank of the United States.* [12]

Half a century later, the bar imposed by the 11th Amendment appeared to deny any federal remedy to citizens holding bonds repudiated by the financially strained southern states. In frustration, some groups began to demand repeal of the 11th Amendment. [13]

The Supreme Court, however, resolved the impasse. In an 1885 case involving the bond situation in Virginia, the

Acts Voided as Infringing on State Powers

Of the more than 100 Acts of Congress struck down by the Supreme Court over the last 190 years, more than a dozen have been found invalid because Congress had reached too far into matters that were left to the states to regulate. Among the laws so invalidated were:

● The Fair Labor Standards Act as amended to extend minimum wage and overtime provisions to employees of state and local governments. (*National League of Cities v. Usery,* 426 U.S. 833, 1976)

● The Voting Rights Act Amendments of 1970 insofar as they reduced to 18 the voting age for state and local, as well as federal, elections. This change subsequently was made through the 26th Amendment. (*Oregon v. Mitchell,* 400 U.S. 223, 1970)

● The first Municipal Bankruptcy Act of the New Deal, which provided for the readjustment of municipal indebtedness. The court later approved a revised version of this law. (*Ashton v. Cameron County District,* 298 U.S. 513, 1936)

● The Home Owners' Loan Act of the New Deal insofar as it provided for the conversion of state building and loan associations into federal associations. (*Hopkins Savings Assn. v. Cleary,* 296 U.S. 315, 1935)

● The first Bituminous Coal Conservation Act to regulate the mining industry, a matter left to that time entirely to the states. The court later approved a revised coal industry regulation law. (*Carter v. Carter Coal Company,* 298 U.S. 238, 1936)

● The New Deal's first Agricultural Adjustment Act regulating agricultural production, a matter left heretofore entirely to the states. The court later approved a new Agricultural Adjustment Act. (*United States v. Butler,* 297 U.S. 1, 1936)

● The Futures Trading Act, which taxed sales of grain for future delivery, a matter not in interstate commerce, according to the court. (*Hill v. Wallace,* 259 U.S. 44, 1922)

● The Child Labor Tax Act of 1919 and the Child Labor Law of 1916, both of which sought to prohibit the employment of children under a certain age in factories or mills. (*Bailey v. Drexel Furniture Co.,* 259 U.S. 20, 1922; *Hammer v. Dagenhart,* 247 U.S. 251, 1918)

● The Federal Corrupt Practices Act insofar as it limited the spending of a senatorial candidate in his primary campaign. This ruling, limiting federal power over elections to the general elections alone, was later overruled. (*Newberry v. United States,* 256 U.S. 232, 1921)

● The Oklahoma Enabling Act, which conditioned the admission of Oklahoma to the Union in part on the requirement that its state capital should not be moved before 1913. Such a decision was left to the discretion of other states, held the court, and to impose that condition upon a state's admission to the Union placed it on an unequal footing with the other states. (*Coyle v. Smith,* 221 U.S. 559, 1911)

● The Federal Employers' Liability Act, which regulated the liability of common carriers operating intrastate as well as interstate. The court later upheld a similar law applying only to interstate carriers. (*The Employers' Liability Cases,* 207 U.S. 463, 1908)

● The Immigration Act of 1907 insofar as it penalized the harboring of a prostitute who was an alien. The court held that once aliens are admitted to the country, control over such matters passed to the states. (*Keller v. United States,* 213 U.S. 138, 1909)

● The Civil Rights Act of 1875 insofar as it penalized individuals who denied equal access to blacks seeking entry to public accommodations. (*The Civil Rights Cases,* 109 U.S. 3, 1883)

● The original trademark law applying to trademarks for exclusive use within the United States, which, the court found, applied to intrastate as well as interstate commerce. (*The Trademark Cases,* 100 U.S. 82, 1879)

● The Internal Revenue Act of 1867 insofar as it banned the sale of illuminating oil within a state if it was flammable at too low a temperature. This was simply a police regulation, held the court, and should be left to state officials. (*United States v. DeWitt,* 9 Wall. 41, 1870)

The court also held, in the late 19th century, that the federal income tax law was void insofar as it applied to the salaries of state officials, and that a city — as an agent of the state — was exempt from federal taxes on the interest paid on municipal bonds. This first ruling was later overturned by the court. (*Collector v. Day,* 11 Wall. 113, 1871; *United States v. Railroad Co.,* 17 Wall. 322, 1873)

And the court has held that there are certain areas in which Congress may not delegate power to the states. In the case of *Knickerbocker Ice Co. v. Stewart* in 1920, the court held that Congress could not delegate to states the power of setting maritime workers' rights and remedies, in terms of workmen's compensation, for on-the-job injuries. This delegation, held the court, defeated the need — and the constitutional intention — of a uniform maritime law. A second effort of Congress to achieve the same end was struck down in 1924. (*Knickerbocker Ice Co. v. Stewart,* 253 U.S. 149, 1920; *Washington v. Dawson & Co.,* 264 U.S. 219, 1924)

court allowed suits against state officials who were carrying out an unconstitutional law or otherwise exceeding their proper authority. In such circumstances, held the court, the official acts as an individual and can be sued as such. The 11th Amendment did not bar such suits.

In that and later rulings, the court has reasoned that the amendment was intended to forbid the use of the courts by citizens seeking to compel a state to take some affirmative action or to exercise its authority in some non-ministerial and discretionary matter. [14]

In subsequent cases, the court has also held that the 11th Amendment provides no protection for state officials who damage property or injure persons in deliberate and negligent disregard of state law or individual rights. [15] Reaffirming that point in a 1974 case brought against state officials by the parents of children killed during an anti-war demonstration, the court stated: "The Eleventh Amendment provides no shield for a state official confronted by a claim that he had deprived another of a federal right under color of state law." [16]

Halting State Action

Questions of the immunity of a sovereign state from the compulsion of court orders again arise when a federal court is asked to halt enforcement of a state law that allegedly violates the constitutional rights of citizens.

Since 1908 the Supreme Court has allowed federal judges to grant such requests, temporarily enjoining the enforcement of a state law until its constitutional validity is ruled upon. Subsequent to that ruling — in the case of *Ex parte Young* — Congress required that such orders be issued, not by a single federal judge, but by a panel of three judges. [17]

Such orders may operate only prospectively, that is, they may halt only future actions under a challenged law; in general, they may not require a state to remedy injuries already inflicted by actions under such a law.[18]

However, the court held in 1976 that Congress could by law — as an exercise of its power to enforce the guarantees of the 14th Amendment — set aside immunity from retroactive relief and require states to make remedial payments to victims of state discrimination, in this particular case, state employees. [19]

And in 1978 the court upheld as a proper exercise of federal judicial power an award of attorneys' fees from the state to the prison inmates who had brought a successful suit challenging state prison conditions as unconstitutional.

When a state refuses to comply with a federal court order, Justice John Paul Stevens wrote for the court in that case, such a financial penalty might well be the most effective way to ensure compliance: "The principles of federalism that inform Eleventh Amendment doctrine surely do not require federal courts to enforce their decrees only by sending high state officials to jail."[20]

Furthermore, Stevens noted, court costs had been awarded against states since at least the middle of the 19th century. The 11th Amendment had never, he said, been viewed as forbidding those awards.

Political Powers

In no area of state affairs has the Supreme Court been more reluctant to intervene than in questions of state political power. This reluctance to involve itself in political questions was evident as early as the court's decision in the 1849 case of *Luther v. Borden.* [21]

The case arose under Article IV of the Constitution, which provides that "[T]he United States shall guarantee to every State in this Union a republican form of government." The dispute involved two competing groups claiming to be the legitimate government of the state of Rhode Island. The court refused to resolve this "political question," holding that enforcement of the constitutional guarantee was a matter for Congress, not the courts.

On the basis of this same "political question" doctrine, the court in 1912 declined to decide whether or not Oregon — by adopting the direct legislative devices of the initiative and the referendum — had destroyed its republican form of government and thus its own lawful authority. The court held that Congress, by seating the U.S. senators and House members from Oregon, had sanctioned these changes in the character of the state government. [22]

Electoral Districts

The Constitution, besides providing that "the times, places and manner of holding elections for Senators and Representatives, shall be prescribed in each state by the legislature thereof," also grants Congress some power to regulate the subject.

Congress first exercised this authority in 1842, requiring states to divide themselves into districts for the election of House members. Subsequent laws also required that these districts be compact — that is, not gerrymandered. But after a 1929 act omitted that requirement, the court ruled in 1932 that without such statutory authority, it could not act to correct a state's gerrymandered districts. [23]

Until 1962 the court held steadfastly to the position that malapportionment of legislative districts was a "political question," not for the courts to resolve. But to leave this matter to the legislators elected from those very districts was clearly to prevent any improvement in the situation. In 1962 the court discarded this "political question" response to the problem with its decision in the case of *Baker v. Carr.* Using the 14th Amendment's equal protection guarantee as the basis for its intervention, the court entered the "political thicket" and ordered states to draw new congressional and state legislative district lines to ensure the equality of votes cast within the state. [24]

These rulings resulted in a long line of Supreme Court cases concerning implementation of the "one person, one vote" rule. And in 1973, while maintaining the standard of strict mathematical equality for congressional districts, the court did relax that standard slightly for state legislative districts. Some deviation might be justified, wrote Justice William H. Rehnquist for the court, citing a statement from an earlier reapportionment ruling: "So long as the divergences from a strict population standard are based on legitimate consideration incident to the effectuation of a rational state policy, some deviations from the equal population principle are constitutionally permissible with respect to the apportionment of seats. . ." in the state legislature. [25]

Primaries, Qualifications

Until 1941 the control of primary elections was left entirely to the states. This tradition was reinforced by a Supreme Court ruling in 1921 that appeared to read the Constitution's references to "elections" to mean only the general election, not preliminary contests. [26]

But in 1941 that interpretation was overturned by the court, which held that in states where primary elections were an integral part of the process of electing members of Congress, congressional power to regulate elections extended over them. [27]

States have long been conceded the power to set qualifications for voters, but the national government — chiefly through the amending process — possesses the power to declare certain qualifications unreasonable. That power was exercised in the 15th, 19th and 26th Amendments, forbidding states to deny the right to vote because of race, sex or age — so long as the prospective voter is at least 18 years of age. State challenges to this means of expanding the electorate were disposed of by the court in 1922 with the dismissal of Tennessee's argument that its political autonomy had been destroyed by the 19th Amendment, which added many new voters to its electorate without its consent. [28]

And in 1970 the Supreme Court ruled that Congress by statute can lower the voting age only for federal elections — not for state and local ones. That ruling led to the approval and ratification of the 26th Amendment, which lowered the voting age to 18 for all elections. In that same decision, the court upheld an act of Congress that restricted residence requirements to 30 days for presidential elections and forbade the use of literacy tests in all elections. [29]

The most comprehensive federal scheme of regulation for the conduct of elections by states was approved by Congress in the Voting Rights Act of 1965, legislation enacted in response to the continuing efforts of some parts of the South to deny qualified black residents the right to vote. The act authorized federal supervision of elections in those areas, forbade the affected states to use any literacy test or similar device to qualify voters, and required federal approval of any change in their voting laws, practices or procedures.

The states of South Carolina and New York (affected because of a provision concerning tests for non-English-speaking voters) quickly challenged the law as an invasion of the reserved rights of the states to set voter qualifications. The Supreme Court rejected this argument and upheld the law: "As against the reserved powers of the States, Congress may use any rational means to effectuate the constitutional prohibition of racial discrimination in voting." [30]

In less dramatic decisions, the Supreme Court in modern times also has struck down state election laws which made it unreasonably difficult for third parties to win a place on a ballot, required excessively high filing fees for candidates, or set unreasonable primary registration requirements and long residency requirements for voters. [31]

The Taxing Power

Apart from the commerce clause, the court has imposed three other limiting principles upon the state's power to raise money through taxes: 1) The tax must be imposed on persons or property or activities within its own jurisdiction, 2) the tax must be for public purposes, and 3) it cannot fall directly upon the federal government.

A series of post-Civil War rulings established the first principle. [32] The second was settled by the court's 1875 decision in the case of *Loan Association v. Topeka.* The court struck down Kansas' law authorizing a tax to pay for city bonds issued to assist a private bridge-building corporation. Writing for the court, Justice Samuel Miller was candid in condemning such an action:

> To lay, with one hand, the power of the government on the property of the citizen, and with the other to bestow it upon favored individuals to aid private enterprises and build up private fortunes, is none the less a robbery because it is done under the forms of law and is called taxation. [33]

And the third principle, set out emphatically by Chief Justice John Marshall in the 1819 ruling in *McCulloch v. Maryland,* denies states the right to use taxes to hinder the operations of the federal government. [34]

After settling the question of the state's power to tax the Bank of the United States, the court in 1829 issued the first in a series of rulings protecting government securities from state taxation. State taxes on federal stock, bonds, and even national bank shares, without congressional consent, impermissibly interfere with the federal power to borrow, a power expressly granted by the Constitution, held the court. [35]

In 1886 the court for the first time ruled that a state may not tax federally owned real estate, a holding that has been expanded to include most federally owned property. [36]

Intergovernmental Immunity

In announcing the court's decision in *McCulloch v. Maryland* — which in essence survives to the present — Chief Justice Marshall asserted that "the power to tax involves the power to destroy." [37] This statement became the basis for a long and involved series of rulings in which the court — for a time — granted to federal and state governments and their officials immunity, each from taxation by the other.

The first of these rulings came in 1842 with the case of *Dobbins v. Erie County.* [38] The court held that a state could not tax the income of federal revenue officers without impermissibly interfering with federal functions. Thirty years later, the court granted a corresponding immunity to state officials, with its ruling in the case of *Collector v. Day,* striking down a federal tax on the salary of a state judge. [39]

In 1895 the court granted state and municipal bonds — and the interest they generated — immunity from federal taxation similar to that already enjoyed by national securities from state taxes. This was part of the court's income tax ruling in the case of *Pollock v. Farmers' Loan & Trust Co.* [40]

Some limit on this immunity — for state governments — was recognized in 1905, when the court held that only governmental functions of state governments were immune from federal taxes. Thus it upheld the imposition of federal taxes on the state-run liquor business in South Carolina. [41]

Notwithstanding this decision, the court continued to elaborate on the intergovernmental tax immunity question for three more decades. It struck down a federal tax on motorcycles that were to be sold to a city police department. [42] Also falling as impermissible were state taxes on income from federally granted copyrights and patents, on gasoline sold to the federal government, and on income from leases of public lands. [43] But the end of this body of rulings was in sight even as some of these last decisions were announced late in the 1920s. In dissent from the gasoline tax case, Justice Oliver Wendell Holmes Jr. met Marshall's assertion head-on and declared: "The power to tax is not the power to destroy while this court sits." [44]

Diluted Immunity

Beginning with reversal of the copyright royalties income case in 1932, the court dropped its effort to preserve this immunity in such extended form. In the 1938 decision in *Helvering v. Gerhardt* and the 1939 ruling in *Graves v. New York ex rel. O'Keefe,* the court overruled *Dobbins* and *Collector.* [45]

The immunity granted to state officials in *Collector,* explained Justice Harlan Fiske Stone in the *Helvering* opinion, "was sustained only because it was one deemed necessary to protect the states from destruction by federal taxation of those governmental functions which they were exercising when the Constitution was adopted and which were essential to their continued existence." Such immunity is not justified "where the tax laid upon individuals affects the state only as the burden is passed on to it by the taxpayer. . . ." [46]

No longer does state immunity from federal taxes impose any substantial limitation on federal power. The most significant remaining example of such immunity is that granted to the income from state and municipal bonds.

Federal immunity from state taxes protects the property, institutions and activities of the federal government, but it no longer extends to persons merely doing business with the state — even if state taxes mean higher costs to the federal government. [47]

Early in its exposition of the Constitution's prohibition on state action impairing the obligation of contracts, the court applied this contract clause to the state's power to grant and revoke exemptions from state taxes. Unless a reservation of state right to modify or nullify such a grant of exemption is included in the granting agreement, the contract clause forbids a state to rescind or modify such an exemption. The major impact of these holdings is simply to guarantee that states include such reservation clauses in such grants. [48] *(See p. 310)*

The Police Power

Broadest of the powers reserved to the states is the police power — the authority of the state to govern its citizens, its land and its resources, and to restrict individual freedom to protect or promote the public good.

Most of the Supreme Court's rulings on this power concern its impact on foreign or interstate commerce. Yet states exercise this power in a multitude of ways that affect only matters within their borders.

One use of the police power is illustrated by the state's grant of a slaughterhouse monopoly upheld in the 1873 ruling in the *Slaughterhouse Cases.* The court upheld the monopoly against a constitutional challenge, finding it a proper exercise of the police power. Justice Samuel Miller acknowledged, for the court, that this power "is, and must be from its very nature, incapable of any very exact definition or limitation. Upon it depends the security of social order, the life and health of the citizen, the comfort of an existence in a thickly populated community, the enjoyment of private and social life, and the beneficial use of property." [49]

And in an earlier judicial description of the power, Justice Philip Barbour explained that under it the states had "the same undeniable and unlimited jurisdiction over all persons and things within its territorial limits, as any foreign nation, where that jurisdiction is not surrendered or restrained by the Constitution...." [50]

The Supreme Court considers this internal use of the police power only when it is challenged as violating some constitutional right. When a state comes to the court to defend its use of this power against such a challenge, the court usually adopts a balancing approach, weighing the benefits that the contested law provides the general public against the alleged constitutional cost.

The court has, in these decisions, recognized that the states have wide latitude to act to protect their natural resources from damage or diversion, to protect property values and the general quality of life in an area by the use of zoning requirements, and to protect the public health and morals through quarantine and health and even some censorship laws.

Environmental Protection

"It is a fair and reasonable demand on the part of a sovereign," wrote Justice Oliver Wendell Holmes Jr. in one of the first state environmental cases before the court, "that the air over its territory should not be polluted on a great scale...." And so in 1907 the court upheld Georgia's successful effort to win a court order directing a Tennessee copper company to stop its outpouring of sulphurous fumes that were destroying all vegetation in the vicinity in both states. [51]

The following year the court upheld New Jersey's right to prohibit diversion of water from its streams to New York. And in 1922 the justices, at the request of Wyoming, ordered Colorado to stop its diversion of the Laramie River. [52]

This principle has its limits. In 1923 the court refused to allow West Virginia to retain within the state and for its own use all the natural gas produced there. But the court has approved state laws prohibiting the waste of its natural resources by companies exploiting them. [53]

And when Congress began enacting national environmental protection measures, the court continued to uphold non-conflicting state legislation. In 1973 the court upheld Florida's water pollution law as complementary to federal legislation concerning oil spills in navigable waters. The court reasoned that Congress had not pre-empted all state regulation of such matters and that the state could exercise its police power over maritime activities currently with the federal government. Five years later, however, the court struck down Washington State's laws setting standards for the size and type of oil tankers permitted in Puget Sound, finding that they conflicted with federal law and the intent of Congress to set uniform national standards for such ships. [54]

Zoning

The validity of the state's power — through zoning ordinances — to govern land use was recognized by the court early in the 20th century. In 1915 it upheld a city's prohibition of brickmaking in a certain area, although the effect of the ban was virtually to put one brickmaker out of business. This ban was challenged by the brickmaker as a due process violation; the court did not agree. [55]

But two years later it did strike down the housing segregation ordinance of Louisville, Ky., which forbade blacks and whites to live in areas inhabited predominantly by members of the other race. This restriction, held the

---

Fish, But Not All Fowl

Under the police power, states have broad authority over fish and game, and can prohibit, allow or license hunting and fishing within their borders. In one of the more peculiar chapters in federal-state relations, the national government used the treaty power to take the subject of migratory birds out of state control.

Spurred by conservationist concern, Congress in 1913 enacted a law strictly regulating the killing of birds that migrated from state to state. Several federal courts held this law invalid, dealing with a subject Congress had no power to control.

But before any Supreme Court ruling was obtained on the matter, the United States in 1916 signed a treaty with Canada providing for the protection of migratory birds. Using the treaty as the basis for its action, Congress in 1918 enacted a new migratory bird protection law.

The state of Missouri challenged this as an invasion of the rights reserved to the states. But the court upheld the law on the basis that the treaty had removed the subject of migratory birds from state to federal jurisdiction. *(Missouri v. Holland,* 252 U.S. 416, 1920)

court, interfered too far with the right of property, effectively denying persons the right to sell to black purchasers. [56]

In 1926 came the landmark zoning ruling as the court upheld a city ordinance that excluded apartment houses from certain residential neighborhoods. This limitation was challenged in *Euclid v. Ambler Realty Co.* as a due process violation of the individual's freedom to put his property to whatever use he desired. The court heard the case argued twice.

In the court's opinion upholding the restriction, Justice George Sutherland said changing conditions justified regulations that, half a century earlier, "probably would have been rejected as arbitrary." The ordinance, he said, was a justifiable use of the police power to prevent a form of local nuisance:

> A nuisance may be merely a right thing in the wrong place — like a pig in the parlor instead of the barnyard. If the validity of the legislative classification for zoning purposes be fairly debatable, the legislative judgment must be allowed to control.

In this case, the city had decided that apartment houses created disadvantages for homeowners in an area, "interfering by their height and bulk with the free circulation of air and monopolizing the rays of the sun which otherwise would fall upon the smaller homes, and bringing . . . the disturbing noises incident to increased traffic and business . . . depriving children of the privilege of quiet and open spaces for play. . . ."

And that value judgment would be allowed to stand. [57]

With this approach the court consistently rebuffed challenges to zoning ordinances. In 1954 the court upheld the use of the federal police power in a slum-clearance project intended to result in a more attractive community. Justice William O. Douglas wrote that "[i]t is within the power of the legislature to determine that the community should be beautiful as well as healthy, spacious as well as clean, well-balanced as well as carefully patrolled."

And 20 years later, Douglas spoke for the court as it upheld a zoning ordinance adopted by the village of Belle Terre, N.Y., which restricted occupancy of its homes to single families, excluding groups of more than two unrelated persons:

> The regimes of boarding houses, fraternity houses, and the like present urban problems. More people occupy a given space; more cars rather continuously pass by; more cars are parked; noise travels with crowds.
>
> A quiet place where yards are wide, people few, and motor vehicles restricted are legitimate guidelines in a land use project addressed to family needs. . . . The police power is not confined to elimination of filth, stench, and unhealthy places. It is ample to lay out zones where family values, youth values, and the blessings of quiet seclusion, and clean air make the area a sanctuary for people. [58]

The court subsequently upheld Detroit's use of zoning power to require that adult movie theaters and adult bookstores be dispersed within the city. And it sustained — against an equal protection challenge — a suburb's refusal to modify its zoning requirements for one area to allow the construction there of a racially integrated low-income housing complex. [59] Finding New York's historic preservation law an exercise of power analogous to zoning laws, the court

upheld it in 1978 against a property owner's challenge that it constituted a governmental "taking" of property without just compensation. [60]

The court has set some limits on the exercise of this police power. Just two years after the *Euclid* decision, the court rejected a Seattle ordinance that required the written consent of property owners in a neighborhood before a home for the aged could be built there. The justices found it unlikely that the old folks' home could result in any injury, inconvenience or annoyance to the community. [61]

And in 1977 the court struck down a village ordinance that denied a grandmother the right to live in the same household with her sons and grandsons. The vote was 5-4. Writing for the majority, Justice Lewis F. Powell Jr. declared that the challenged ordinance "slice[d] deeply into the family itself . . . select[ing] certain categories of relatives who may live together and declar[ing] that others may not. . . . When a city undertakes such intrusive regulation of the family, neither *Belle Terre* nor *Euclid* governs; the usual judicial deference to the legislature is inappropriate." [62]

Pornography

The recurring problem of obscenity has called into play a wide variety of state and city police power laws and regulations intended to prohibit or curtail the distribution of offensive sexually oriented films, books and magazines within communities. This exercise of the police power has come before the court in a long series of cases in which the persons whose activities are banned or restricted argue that the state is impermissibly infringing upon their First Amendment freedoms.

Although it approved state censorship of movies as early as 1915, the court reversed this holding in 1952 and brought movies within the protection of the First Amendment. [63]

Subsequently the court held that obscene material is not protected against state action by the First Amendment. But while working to formulate a useful definition of obscenity, the court has dealt with challenges to obscenity laws of states and companion city regulations on a case-by-case basis. The primary concern of the court has been to ensure that state and local anti-obscenity efforts do not sweep so broadly that they curtail forms of expression protected by the First Amendment. [64]

The court has moved carefully. It has refused to deny states all power of censorship, but it has set out some guidelines for censorship laws to follow. [65] It has allowed state courts to halt the sale of indecent materials so long as there is a speedy hearing to determine if in fact the objectionable materials are obscene. It has struck down state grants of broad authority to police to seize any items they consider obscene, as well as state laws making it a crime to possess obscene books for sale, or official efforts to curtail distribution of particular named magazines and books. [66]

In 1973 the court reaffirmed state power to regulate obscene material. In that decision the court set out new guidelines for the definition of obscenity, giving added weight to local community standards. But in 1974 it made clear that jury decisions on obscenity are subject to judicial review. The following year the court reaffirmed its insistence on carefully drawn anti-obscenity ordinances, striking down a Florida city's ordinance forbidding drive-in theater operators to show films containing nudity on screens visible from public places. [67]

A Clash of Courts

During the turbulent decade before the outbreak of the Civil War, the controversial Federal Fugitive Slave Act set off an extended tug-of-war between federal and state judicial power, centering around one Sherman Booth, an abolitionist newspaper editor.

In 1854 Booth, a resident of Milwaukee, Wis., was arrested there and charged with violating the law by helping a fugitive slave escape from a federal marshal.

From jail he sought the aid of a state supreme court judge, who — like most people in Wisconsin — was not in sympathy with slavery or the federal law requiring the return of runaway slaves. The state judge issued a writ of *habeas corpus* to the federal marshal, Stephen Ableman, holding Booth, and ordered Booth's release. Ableman complied, but asked the U.S. Supreme Court to review the case. Before the court heard arguments in the case, federal and state authorities clashed again. In 1855 Booth was indicted by a federal grand jury for violating the Federal Fugitive Slave Act. He was tried, convicted and sentenced to one month in prison and a $1,000 fine.

Three days after being sentenced, Booth again appealed to the Wisconsin courts for relief. The following day the court issued a writ of *habeas corpus* and ordered his release. The attorney general of the United States took this case to the Supreme Court.

Not until 1859 was the matter resolved by the court, but when the decision came it was a vigorous assertion of national judicial supremacy. In writing the opinion, Chief Justice Roger B. Taney noted that it was the first time the state courts had tried to assert their supremacy over federal courts in cases arising under the Constitution and U.S. laws.

That assertion was soundly rejected by a unanimous court.

It would seem to be hardly necessary to do more than to state the result to which these decisions of the state courts must inevitably lead. . . . [N]o one will suppose that a government which has now lasted nearly seventy years, enforcing its laws by its own tribunals, and preserving the union of the States, could have lasted a single year, or fulfilled the high trusts committed to it, if the offenses against its laws could not have been punished without the consent of the State in which the culprit was found. . . .

[A]lthough the State of Wisconsin is sovereign within its territorial limits to certain extent, yet that sovereignty is limited and restricted by the Constitution of the United States. And the powers of the General Government, and of the State, although both exist and are exercised within the same territorial limits, are yet separate and distinct sovereignties, acting separately and independently of each other, within their respective spheres. And the sphere of action appropriated to the United States is as far beyond the reach of the judicial process issued by a state judge or a state court, as if the line of division was traced by landmarks and monuments visible to the eye. (*Ableman v. Booth*, 21 How. 506 at 514-516, 1859)

Public Health

The most drastic exercises of the police power upheld by the court have come under the use of this power to protect the public health. In 1905 the court rejected a man's challenge to the compulsory vaccination ordinance adopted by the city of Cambridge, Mass., to protect its populace against smallpox. Justice John Marshall Harlan wrote the court's opinion rejecting the challenge to this requirement as depriving a citizen of his personal liberty without due process of law:

Upon the principle of self-defense, of paramount necessity, a community has the right to protect itself against an epidemic of disease which threatens the safety of its members. . . . [I]n every well-ordered society charged with the duty of conserving the safety of its members the rights of the individual in respect of his liberty may at times, under the pressure of great dangers be subject to such restraint . . . as the safety of the general public may demand. . . . [68]

Twenty-two years later, the court applied this rationale to justify Virginia's decision, under state law, to sterilize Carrie Buck, a mentally defective woman with a "feeble-minded" mother and a "feeble-minded" child. This was not a deprivation of rights without due process, held the court. Justice Holmes wrote:

. . . the principle that sustains compulsory vaccination is broad enough to cover cutting the Fallopian tubes.

We have seen more than once that the public welfare may call upon the best citizens for their lives. It would be strange if it could not call upon those who already sap the strength of the State for these lesser sacrifices . . . in order to prevent our being swamped with incompetence. . . . Three generations of imbeciles are enough. [69]

Although this case has not been directly overruled, it was effectively nullified by the court when in 1942 the justices struck down a similar Oklahoma law as a violation of equal protection. [70]

The Judicial Power

Federal judicial power clearly curtails the power of state courts. Most significant of these restraints is the Supreme Court's power to review the rulings of state courts on federal claims and questions.

Initially granted by Congress in 1789, contested in the Olmstead controversy of 1809 and challenged by Virginia in 1816 and 1821, the power was ringingly upheld by the courts in *Martin v. Hunter's Lessee* and *Cohens v. Virginia.* (See pp. 305-307)

Once the power of the Supreme Court to have the last word on any federal question was made certain, however, the court seemed quite willing, for decades, to leave large categories of litigation to the state courts. Until the mid-19th century, almost all corporate and criminal litigation — as well as much admiralty litigation — was left to state courts.

In 1809 the court ruled that federal jurisdiction did not include cases brought by or against a corporation unless all the corporate stockholders lived in a state other than that of the opposing party.

Charles Warren states:

THE COURT AND THE STATES

As a result of this decision the reports of Supreme Court and of the Circuit Courts during the first forty years thereafter reveal an almost complete absence of cases in which corporations (other than banking and insurance) were litigants; and the development of a body of corporation law by the Federal Courts was postponed to a late date in their history.

Thirty-six years later, the court effectively reversed itself on this point, holding that a corporation was assumed to be a citizen of the state in which it was chartered. Thus, any suit brought by or against a citizen of another state was properly within federal jurisdiction because of the diversity of citizenship. [71]

In the same term that it decided *Martin v. Hunter's Lessee*, the court ruled that federal courts lacked any criminal jurisdiction except that which would be created by passage of federal laws declaring certain crimes to be federal ones. [72]

Until the mid-19th century much of admiralty law was left to state courts, despite the Judiciary Act's explicit grant of admiralty jurisdiction to federal district courts. In 1825 the court adopted a narrow definition of federal admiralty jurisdiction, limited to waters affected by the ebb and flow of the tides. This left most of the nation's inland waterways under state control. [73]

However, as steamboat traffic and barge traffic increased, the court reconsidered that definition, and reversed it in 1851. Chief Justice Roger B. Taney was frank about the impact of economic reality upon the court's opinion: "[T]he conviction that this definition of admiralty powers was narrower than the Constitution contemplated, has been growing stronger every day with the growing commerce on the lakes and navigable rivers of the western States." The court ruled that federal admiralty courts had jurisdiction over all public navigable waters upon which interstate or foreign commerce was carried.

Fifteen years later, the court completed the removal of such matters from state courts, asserting exclusive federal jurisdiction over admiralty cases. States could still pass laws providing remedies in maritime accidents, but they could be enforced only in federal courts. This removed an "immense class of cases" from the state courts, reported Warren. [74]

Concurrency and Cooperation

During the early years of the nation's existence, the federal government frankly depended on state courts to enforce some federal laws, such as the Fugitive Slave Act of 1793, and the Embargo Acts of Jefferson's administration. Local hostility to the intent of some of these laws caused a cessation of this practice, but the court in this century has twice affirmed federal power to require states to enforce federal laws. [75]

And in 1880 the court ruled that state election judges charged with supervising elections of state and congressional officers were properly charged with violating federal civil rights laws by stuffing the ballot box, also a violation of state law. [76]

Interference

Even after the establishment of the power of judicial review, questions steadily recurred of interference by state courts in federal matters and federal courts in state court matters. The court ruled that state courts could not enjoin the judgment of a federal court or order a federal official to

Antitrust Immunity

Recognizing that "the states are sovereign, save only as Congress may constitutionally subtract from their authority," the Supreme Court in 1943 held that the Sherman Antitrust Act was not intended to prevent states from adopting policies or programs that restrained competition in some portion of the state's economy.

This was the ruling in the case of *Parker v. Brown* (317 U.S. 341), in which California's raisin marketing program — which clearly operated to limit competition among raisin growers — was challenged as in conflict with federal antitrust and agricultural laws. The court upheld the state's program.

Chief Justice Harlan Fiske Stone explained the reasoning behind its finding that states were immune from the federal antitrust law:

> We find nothing in the language of the Sherman Act or in its history which suggests that its purpose was to restrain a state or its officers or agents from activities directed by its legislature. In a dual system of government in which, under the Constitution, the states are sovereign, save only as Congress may constitutionally subtract from their authority, an unexpressed purpose to nullify a state's control over its officers and agents is not lightly to be attributed to Congress.
>
> The Sherman Act makes no mention of the state as such, and gives no hint that it was intended to restrain state action or official action directed by a state.... There is no suggestion of a purpose to restrain state action in the Act's legislative history. The sponsor of the bill which was ultimately enacted as the Sherman Act declared that it prevented only "business combinations"....
>
> True, a state does not give immunity to those who violated the Sherman Act by authorizing them to violate it, or by declaring that their action is lawful ... and we have no question of the state ... becoming a participant in a private agreement or combination by others for restraint of trade.... Here the state command ... is not rendered unlawful by the Sherman Act since ... it must be taken to be a prohibition of individual and not state action....
>
> The state in adopting and enforcing the prorate program made no contract or agreement and entered into no conspiracy in restraint of trade or to establish monopoly but, as sovereign, imposed the restraint as an act of government which the Sherman Act did not undertake to prohibit. (317 U.S. 341 at 350-352.)

Twenty-five years later, in 1978, the court held that this immunity did not extend to cities, unless their anticompetitive conduct was undertaken in carrying out state policy to replace competition with regulation or monopoly. This decision came in *City of Lafayette, La. v. Louisiana Power & Light Co.* (435 U.S. 389).

perform some duty by issuing a writ of *mandamus;* that states could not regulate the processes of federal courts; that a state court's interpretation of state laws was not binding on federal courts. [77]

This last holding was substantially modified in 1938, after almost a century. The Supreme Court then held that in the absence of an applicable and controlling federal law or constitutional provision, federal courts should apply the appropriate state law to a situation before it. [78]

The court also has ruled that a federal court may not take property out of state court custody, and that a state may not seize property attached by a federal court. [79]

Since its landmark 1859 ruling in the case of *Ableman v. Booth,* the court has steadfastly denied to state courts the power to order federal officials to release a person they hold in custody. *(See box, p. 360)*

But federal courts retain the power to issue a writ of *habeas corpus* to state officials ordering the release of a person held in custody in violation of his constitutional rights.

The Judiciary Act of 1789 authorized federal courts to issue writs of *habeas corpus* as necessary "in the exercise of their respective jurisdictions," but until after the Civil War that writ could be used only to order the release of federal, not state, prisoners. In 1867 Congress expanded this *habeas corpus* power to allow use of the writ to order the release of any person held "in violation of the Constitution or of any treaty or law of the United States."

This expansion of *habeas corpus* gave a new instrument to state prisoners who felt that their conviction had been obtained in a way which violated their constitutional rights. The Supreme Court generally has required, however, that before a state prisoner uses this means of challenging his conviction in federal court he exhaust all possible avenues to challenge the conviction within the state court system. In the 1960s and 1970s, the Supreme Court was divided over how strictly to apply this "exhaustion of remedies" requirement. In 1963 the court held that a prisoner who missed the opportunity to raise federally based challenges to his conviction in state courts was not foreclosed by that failure from requesting a federal court to issue a writ of *habeas corpus.* [80]

In the mid-1970s, the court seemed to modify this holding and to return to its insistence on compliance with all state requirements before moving into the federal courts. In a 1977 ruling denying *habeas corpus* relief to a Florida prisoner who had failed to raise his constitutional claim at the proper time in state courts, Justice William H. Rehnquist spoke of the need for ensuring that the state trial of a person charged with a state crime was the " 'main event,' so to speak, rather than a 'tryout on the road' for what will later be the determinative federal habeas hearing." [81]

Injunctions

Another exercise of federal power over state court proceedings is the use of the injunction, issued by a federal judge, ordering state officials to stop enforcing a state law, or ordering state judicial proceedings to halt. In 1793 Congress unconditionally forbade such federal interference with state court proceedings. But since that time several exceptions have been made to the ban. Federal courts may interfere in this way 1) when authorized by Congress, 2) when necessary to protect their own jurisdiction, and 3) to carry out their judgments.

And in 1908 the Supreme Court added an exception with its ruling in the case of *Ex parte Young.* There it held that a person about to be tried in state court could obtain a federal order halting the trial if he could show that he would suffer irreparable damage if tried. [82]

No Foreign Affairs!

The Constitution strictly forbade states to involve themselves in foreign affairs. It prohibited the formation of treaties, alliances, confederations; it required the consent of Congress for states to tax imports, exports or freight brought into their ports; it forbade states to maintain troops or ships of war in peacetime, or to conclude any agreement or compact with a foreign power; and it prohibited states from engaging in war unless they were invaded or otherwise in imminent danger.

These provisions left relatively little need for interpretation by the Supreme Court. One of the court's first rulings made quite clear the supremacy of federal treaties over conflicting state laws [1] — and in 1920 the court affirmed the power of a treaty to remove from state jurisdiction a subject, in this case migratory birds, normally left to its control. [2] *(See box, p. 358)*

In 1841 the court held that the Constitution's ban on states making treaties denied a state the power even to return a fugitive to a foreign state. [3]

One small crack in the court's opposition to state laws involving matters of foreign import appeared just after World War I, when the court upheld state espionage laws as a proper exercise of state police power. [4]

But several decades later, in 1956, the court overturned that holding, ruling that the Smith Act of 1940, a national sedition act, had pre-empted all state power over espionage and sedition directed against the federal government. [5] *(Details, p. 513)*

---

[1] *Ware v. Hylton,* 3 Dall. 199 (1796).
[2] *Missouri v. Holland,* 252 U.S. 416 (1920).
[3] *Holmes v. Jennison,* 14 Pet. 540 (1840).
[4] *Gilbert v. Minnesota,* 254 U.S. 325 (1920).
[5] *Pennsylvania v. Nelson,* 350 U.S. 497 (1956).

Amid the tense civil rights conflicts of the 1960s, the court appeared to broaden this exception to allow federal judges to halt state court proceedings when defendants claimed that the state laws under which they were charged violated their First Amendment freedom of expression. In a particular case decided by the court in 1965, *Dombrowski v. Pfister,* the court held that such a threat existed and that it was a proper use of federal power to halt the enforcement of the challenged law until it was determined valid or invalid. [83]

Defendants prosecuted under state laws subject to this sort of First Amendment challenge took full advantage of this ruling, producing a wave of petitions to federal courts and a resulting flood of federal injunctions to halt enforcement of such state laws.

In 1971 the court curtailed this trend. "[T]he normal thing to do when federal courts are asked to enjoin pending proceedings in state courts is not to issue such injunctions," wrote Justice Hugo L. Black. Black explained that federal courts should abstain from such interference in state business unless there was an immediate threat of irreparable injury resulting from continuation of the trial or enforcement of the law, unless the challenged law was flagrantly unconstitutional, or unless there had been official disregard of the law. [84]

This policy of federal abstention was based upon "the notion of 'comity,' " wrote Black. He defined that notion:

... a proper respect for state functions, a recognition of the fact that the entire country is made up of a Union of separate state governments, and a continuance of the belief that the National Government will fare best if the States and their institutions are left free to perform their separate functions in their separate ways. This, perhaps for lack of a better and clearer way to describe it, is referred to by many as 'Our Federalism,' ... The concept does not mean blind deference to 'States' Rights' any more than it means centralization of control over every important issue in our National Government and its courts. The Framers rejected both these courses. What the concept does represent is a system in which there is sensitivity to the legitimate interests of both State and National Governments, and in which the National Government, anxious though it may be to vindicate and protect federal rights and federal interests, always endeavors to do so in ways that will not unduly interfere with the legitimate activities of the States. [85]

The Power to Govern

Although the Supreme Court ruled firmly — after the end of the Civil War — that states have no power to secede from the Union, the court has left to the states a wide area of freedom concerning the conduct of their internal government. [86]

In the 19th century, the court upheld the state's power to move a county seat — or to reduce the pay of its officers. Both actions were challenged as violating the contract clause. [87]

In the 1960s Congress extended the reach of the federal minimum wage and overtime requirements to the employees of state schools and hospitals, and the court at first upheld this action as a proper use of the congressional power over interstate commerce. [88] But in 1976, ruling in a case testing a later congressional extension of these standards to all state and local government employees, the court reversed its earlier ruling and struck down such federal interference in state business.

Justice William H. Rehnquist wrote for the court:

One undoubted attribute of state sovereignty is the States' power to determine the wages which shall be paid to those whom they employ in order to carry out their governmental functions, what hours those persons will work, and what compensation will be provided where those employees may be called upon to work overtime. ...

[B]oth the minimum wage and the maximum hour provisions will impermissibly interfere with the integral governmental functions of these bodies. ... If Congress may withdraw from the States the authority to make those fundamental employment decisions upon which their systems for performance of these functions must rest, we think there would be little left of the States' " 'separate and independent existence.' "[89]

In dissent, describing the current degree of federal control over matters within a state, Justice John Paul Stevens questioned the principle upon which the court based its holding that "the Federal Government may not interfere with a sovereign state's inherent right to pay a substandard wage to the janitor at the state capitol" in light of the fact that "the Federal Government may ... require the State to act impartially when it hires or fires the janitor, to withhold taxes from his pay check, to observe safety regulations when he is performing his job, to forbid him from dumping too much soft coal in the capitol furnace, from dumping untreated refuse in an adjacent waterway, from overloading a state-owned garbage truck or from driving either the truck or the governor's limousine over 55 miles an hour." [90]

Within a week of that ruling, the court asserted federal supervision over another aspect of state and local government hiring and firing, with a decision that the First Amendment demanded an end to the practice by newly elected local officials in Cook County (Ill.) of firing all employees who were not of the same political party as themselves. Such patronage firings, held the court, violated the freedoms of political belief and association.[91]

Footnotes

[1] *The Federalist Papers*, with an Introduction by Clinton Rossiter (New York: New American Library, Mentor Books, 1961), No. 45, pp. 292-293.

[2] *McCulloch v. Maryland*, 4 Wheat. 316 at 436 (1819).

[3] *Gibbons v. Ogden*, 9 Wheat. 1 at 222 (1824).

[4] *United States v. E. C. Knight*, 156 U.S. 1 (1895); *Hammer v. Dagenhart*, 247 U.S. 251 (1918); *Bailey v. Drexel Furniture Co.*, 259 U.S. 20 (1922); *United States v. Butler*, 297 U.S. 1 (1936); *Ashton v. Cameron County*, 298 U.S. 513 (1936); *Carter v. Carter Coal Co.*, 298 U.S. 238 (1936).

[5] *United States v. Butler*, 297 U.S. 1 at 68 (1936).

[6] *Champion v. Ames*, 188 U.S. 321 (1903); *McCray v. United States*, 195 U.S. 27 (1904); *Rhode Island v. Palmer*, 253 U.S. 350 (1920); *Hoke v. United States*, 227 U.S. 308 (1913).

[7] *Steward Machine Co. v. Davis*, 301 U.S. 548 (1937); *Mulford v. Smith*, 307 U.S. 38 (1939); *Sunshine Anthracite Coal Co. v. Adkins*, 310 U.S. 381 (1940); *Chicot County Drainage District v. Baxter State Bank*, 308 U.S. 371 (1940).

[8] *United States v. Darby Lumber Co.*, 312 U.S. 100 at 123-125 (1941).

[9] *Chisholm v. Georgia*, 2 Dall. 419 (1793).

[10] *Hans v. Louisiana*, 134 U.S. 1 (1890); *Monaco v. Mississippi*, 292 U.S. 313 (1934).

[11] Thomas Reed Powell, *Vagaries and Varieties in Constitutional Interpretation* (New York: AMS Press, 1967), p. 19.

[12] *Osborn v. Bank of the United States*, 9 Wheat. 738 (1824).

[13] Charles Warren, *The Supreme Court in United States History*, 2 vols. (Boston: Little, Brown & Co., 1922, 1926), II:665.

[14] *Poindexter v. Greenhow*, 114 U.S. 270 (1885).

[15] *Johnson v. Lankford*, 245 U.S. 541 (1918).

[16] *Scheuer v. Rhodes*, 416 U.S. 233 at 237 (1974).

[17] *Ex parte Young*, 209 U.S. 123 (1908). In 1976 Congress eliminated this requirement, returning to the situation in which a single federal judge may halt enforcement of an allegedly unconstitutional state law. *Congress and the Nation*, Vol. IV, p. 616.

[18] *Edelman v. Jordan*, 415 U.S. 651 (1974).

[19] *Fitzpatrick v. Bitzer*, 427 U.S. 445 (1976).

[20] *Hutto v. Finney*, 437 U.S. 678 at 691 (1978).

[21] *Luther v. Borden*, 7 How. 1 (1849).

[22] *Pacific States Telephone & Telegraph Co. v. Oregon*, 223 U.S. 118 (1912).

[23] *Wood v. Broom*, 287 U.S. 1 (1932).

[24] *Colegrove v. Green*, 328 U.S. 549 (1946); *Baker v. Carr*, 369 U.S. 186 (1962); *Wesberry v. Sanders*, 376 U.S. 1 (1964); *Reynolds v. Sims*, 377 U.S. 533 (1964).

[25] *Mahan v. Howell*, 410 U.S. 315 (1973).

[26] *Newberry v. United States*, 256 U.S. 232 (1921).

[27] *United States v. Classic,* 313 U.S. 299 (1941).

[28] *Leser v. Garnett,* 258 U.S. 130 (1922).

[29] *Oregon v. Mitchell, Texas v. Mitchell, United States v. Idaho, United States v. Arizona,* 400 U.S. 112 (1970).

[30] *South Carolina v. Katzenbach,* 383 U.S. 301 at 324 (1966); *Katzenbach v. Morgan,* 384 U.S. 641 (1966).

[31] *Williams v. Rhodes,* 393 U.S. 23 (1968); *Bullock v. Carter,* 405 U.S. 134 (1972); *Lubin v. Panish,* 415 U.S. 709 (1974); *Kusper v. Pontikes,* 414 U.S. 51 (1973); *Dunn v. Blumstein,* 405 U.S. 330 (1972).

[32] Warren, *Supreme Court in U.S. History,* II:569.

[33] *Loan Association v. Topeka,* 20 Wall. 655 at 664 (1875).

[34] *McCulloch v. Maryland,* 4 Wheat. 316 (1819).

[35] *Weston v. City Council of Charleston,* 2 Pet. 449 (1829); *Bank of Commerce v. New York,* 2 Bl. 620, 635 (1863); *Bank Tax Cases,* 2 Wall. 200 (1865).

[36] *Van Brocklin v. Tennessee,* 117 U.S. 151 (1886).

[37] *McCulloch v. Maryland,* 4 Wheat. 316 at 431 (1819).

[38] *Dobbins v. Erie County,* 16 Pet. 435 (1842).

[39] *Collector v. Day,* 11 Wall. 113 (1871).

[40] *Pollock v. Farmer's Loan & Trust Co.,* 158 U.S. 601 (1895).

[41] *South Carolina v. United States,* 199 U.S. 437 (1905).

[42] *Indian Motorcycle Co. v. United States,* 283 U.S. 570 (1931).

[43] *Long v. Rockwood,* 277 U.S. 142 (1928); *Panhandle Oil Co. v. Mississippi,* 277 U.S. 218 (1928); *Gillespie v. Oklahoma,* 257 U.S. 501 (1922).

[44] *Panhandle Oil Co. v. Mississippi,* 277 U.S. 218 at 223 (1928).

[45] *Fox Film Corp. v. Doyal,* 286 U.S. 123 (1932); *Helvering v. Gerhardt,* 304 U.S. 405 (1938); *Graves v. New York ex. rel. O'Keefe,* 306 U.S. 466 (1939).

[46] *Helvering v. Gerhardt,* 304 U.S. at 414, 419-420 (1938).

[47] *United States v. Allegheny County,* 322 U.S. 174 (1944); *Alabama v. King & Boozer,* 314 U.S. 1 (1941).

[48] *New Jersey v. Wilson,* 7 Cr. 164 (1810); *The Providence Bank v. Billings,* 4 Pet. 514 (1830).

[49] *The Slaughterhouse Cases,* 16 Wall. 36 at 62 (1873).

[50] *Mayor of New York v. Miln,* 11 Pet. 102 at 139 (1837).

[51] *Georgia v. Tennessee Copper Co.,* 206 U.S. 230 at 238 (1907).

[52] *Hudson Water Co. v. McCarter,* 209 U.S. 349 (1908); *Wyoming v. Colorado* 259 U.S. 419 (1922).

[53] *Pennsylvania v. West Virginia,* 262 U.S. 553 (1923); *Bandini Petroleum Co. v. Superior Court,* 284 U.S. 1 (1931); *Champlin Refining Co. v. Commission,* 286 U.S. 210 (1932).

[54] *Askew v. American Waterways Operators Inc.,* 411 U.S. 325 (1973); *Ray v. Atlantic Richfield Co.,* 435 U.S. 151 (1978).

[55] *Hadacheck v. Los Angeles,* 239 U.S. 394 (1915).

[56] *Buchanan v. Warley,* 245 U.S. 60 (1917).

[57] *Euclid v. Ambler Realty Co.,* 272 U.S. 365 at 387, 388, 394 (1926).

[58] *Berman v. Parker,* 348 U.S. 26 at 33 (1954); *Village of Belle Terre v. Boraas,* 416 U.S. 1 at 9 (1974).

[59] *Young v. American Mini Theatres Inc.,* 427 U.S. 50 (1976); *Village of Arlington Heights v. Metropolitan Housing Development Corp.* 429 U.S. 252 (1977).

[60] *Penn Central Transportation Co. v. New York City,* 438 U.S. 104 (1978).

[61] *Washington ex rel. Seattle Trust Co. v. Roberge,* 278 U.S. 116 (1928).

[62] *Moore v. City of East Cleveland,* 431 U.S. 494 at 498-99 (1977).

[63] *Mutual Film Corp. v. Industrial Commission,* 236 U.S. 230 (1915); *Burstyn v. Wilson,* 343 U.S. 495 (1952).

[64] *Roth v. United States,* 354 U.S. 476 (1957).

[65] *Times Film Corp. v. Chicago,* 365 U.S. 43 (1961); *Freedman v. Maryland,* 380 U.S. 51 (1965).

[66] *Kingsley Books v. Brown,* 354 U.S. 436 (1957); *Smith v. California,* 361 U.S. 147 (1959); *Marcus v. Search Warrant,* 376 U.S. 717 (1961); *Bantam Books Inc. v. Sullivan,* 372 U.S. 58 (1963).

[67] *Miller v. California,* 413 U.S. 15 (1973); *Jenkins v. Georgia,* 418 U.S. 152 (1974); *Erznoznik v. City of Jacksonville,* 422 U.S. 205 (1975).

[68] *Jacobson v. Massachusetts,* 197 U.S. 11 at 27, 29 (1905).

[69] *Buck v. Bell,* 274 U.S. 200 at 207 (1927).

[70] *Skinner v. Oklahoma,* 316 U.S. 535 (1942).

[71] *Bank of the United States v. Deveaux,* 5 Cr. 61 (1809); Warren, *The Supreme Court in United States History,* I:391; *Louisville Railroad v. Letson,* 2 How. 497 (1845).

[72] *United States v. Hudson and Goodwin,* 7 Cr. 32 (1812); *United States v. Coolidge,* 1 Wheat. 415 (1816).

[73] *The Thomas Jefferson,* 10 Wheat. 428 (1825).

[74] *The Propeller Genessee Chief v. Fitzhugh,* 12 How. 443 at 451 (1851); *The Moses Taylor, The Hine v. Trevor,* 4 Wall. 411, 555 (1866); Warren, *The Supreme Court in United States History,* II:415.

[75] *Second Employers' Liability Cases,* 223 U.S. 1 (1912); *Testa v. Katz,* 330 U.S. 386 (1947).

[76] *Ex parte Siebold,* 100 U.S. 371 (1880).

[77] *McKim v. Voorhees,* 7 Cr. 279 (1812); *McCluny v. Silliman,* 6 Wheat. 598 (1821); *Wayman v. Southard,* 10 Wheat. 1 (1825); *Swift v. Tyson,* 16 Pet. 1 (1842); *Martin v. Waddell's Lessee,* 16 Pet. 367 (1842).

[78] *Erie Railroad Co. v. Tompkins,* 304 U.S. 64 (1938).

[79] *Peck v. Jenness,* 7 How. 612 (1848); *Taylor v. Carryl,* 20 How. 583 (1858); *Freeman v. Howe,* 24 How. 450 (1861).

[80] *Fay v. Noia,* 372 U.S. 391 (1963).

[81] *Wainwright v. Sykes,* 433 U.S. 72 at 90 (1977).

[82] *Ex parte Young,* 209 U.S. 123 (1908).

[83] *Dombrowski v. Pfister,* 380 U.S. 479 (1965).

[84] *Younger v. Harris,* 401 U.S. 37 at 45 (1971).

[85] Id. at 44.

[86] *Texas v. White,* 7 Wall. 700 (1869).

[87] *Newton v. Commissioners,* 100 U.S. 548 (1880); *Butler v. Pennsylvania,* 10 How. 402 (1851).

[88] *Maryland v. Wirtz,* 392 U.S. 183 (1968).

[89] *National League of Cities v. Usery,* 426 U.S. 833 at 845, 851 (1976).

[90] Id. at 880.

[91] *Elrod v. Burns,* 427 U.S. 347 (1976).

Interstate Relations

Interstate relations, which in the 20th century are a matter to which the average citizen gives little thought, were a cause of great concern to the men who wrote the Constitution. The Confederation — the first effort to unite the former colonies into one nation — had failed. As the framers labored at the constitutional convention, they were well aware of the situation that Charles Warren would later describe:

> [T]he differences between the States — economic, social, religious, commercial — were in some instances as great as the differences between many of the nations of Europe today; and out of these differences arose materially hostile and discriminating state legislation. . . . Pierce Butler of South Carolina said, in the Federal Convention, that he considered the interests of the Southern States and of the Eastern States "to be as different as the interests of Russia and Turkey." [1]

To facilitate smooth relationships between the newly linked states, the Constitution adopted some of the principles of international relations and converted them into provisions governing the relationships of the states.

And so Article IV requires each state to give "full faith and credit" to the public acts of the other states, to grant all citizens of all states certain privileges and immunities, and to surrender a fugitive to the state where he is sought.

And although the Constitution denies states the sovereign right to make treaties or alliances, it did give some recognition to the potential usefulness of interstate agreements by providing, in Article I, that states could — with congressional consent — enter into compacts with each other.

Full Faith and Credit

"Full faith and credit shall be given in each state to the public acts, records, and judicial proceedings of every other state." Congress is authorized by the Constitution to provide for the implementation of this provision, and it did so in laws passed in 1790 and 1804.

The meaning of the "full faith and credit" clause is simple: One state must treat the final judgment of the courts of another state as conclusive, settling the issues raised by the case. In 1813 the court rejected the argument that the clause meant only that one state's judgment should be considered as important evidence when a second

state's courts considered the same facts and the same question. [2]

However, the judgment of one state can be enforced or implemented in a second state only through that state's courts — where the second state, if opposed to the judgment, can usually block enforcement.

Furthermore, the first state's judgment can be challenged in the second state with the claim that the first state court did not have jurisdiction over the matter decided, or otherwise disregarded necessary technical points. Most modern cases arising under the "full faith and credit" clause involve questions of jurisdiction — especially called into play in cases when a divorce is granted to a temporary resident of a state. Most states now, however, recognize divorces granted in other states. [3]

This requirement affects only civil matters, not criminal cases. One state does not enforce the criminal laws of another, chiefly because a person has the right to be tried for a crime in the place where the crime was committed — and the courts of other jurisdictions have no right to try him. [4]

E. S. Corwin wrote of this clause:

> There are few clauses of the Constitution, the literal possibilities of which have been so little developed. Congress has the power under the clause to decree the effect that the statutes of one State shall have in other States . . . power to enact standards whereby uniformity of State legislation may be secured as to almost any matter with which interstate recognition of private rights would be useful and valuable. [5]

But Congress has exercised this power very little.

Privileges and Immunities

"The citizens of each state shall be entitled to all privileges and immunities of citizens in the several states," declares the Constitution, leaving open the definition of those "privileges and immunities."

The primary purpose of this requirement, wrote Justice Samuel Miller a century after its adoption, was to require states to treat the citizens of other states in the same way as their own, "to declare to the several States, that whatever those rights, as you grant or establish them to your own citizens, or as you limit or qualify, or impose restrictions on their exercise, the same, neither more nor less, shall be the measure of the rights of citizens of other states [when they are] within your jurisdiction." [6]

As to the definition of these privileges and immunities, Miller referred to the case of *Corfield v. Coryell*, decided in 1823 by Justice Bushrod Washington, sitting as a circuit judge. Washington held that despite this clause, New Jersey could forbid out-of-state persons from gathering oysters in New Jersey. The privileges and immunities that New Jersey — and other states — were bound to grant all states' citizens were more general ones, such as the right to be protected by the government, the right to property, the right to travel through or live in a state other than the state of one's usual residence, the right to bring lawsuits.

In 1869 the court held that this privileges and immunities clause did not protect corporations from discriminatory treatment by states other than those where they were chartered. And the court has allowed states to distinguish in some areas between residents and non-residents, upholding reasonable residency requirements and reasonably different non-resident license fees for persons who wish to obtain fish and game licenses, business licenses, the right to practice a profession, to vote in state elections or to run for state office. [7]

A state may not tax non-residents (with a commuter's tax for example) if no comparable tax is imposed on its residents. [8] And a state may not make medical services that are legal for its residents, such as abortions, illegal for non-residents to obtain within its borders. [9]

Rendition

To offset the fact that states are not required to enforce each other's criminal laws, the Constitution states that "[a] person charged in any state with treason, felony, or other crime, who shall flee from justice, and be found in another state, shall, on demand of the executive authority of the state from which he fled, be delivered up, to be removed to the state having jurisdiction of the crime."

In its major ruling on this point, however, the Supreme Court effectively nullified this requirement. The court in 1861 held that this clause imposed a moral obligation on the governor of Ohio to surrender a fugitive to Kentucky, where he had been indicted for helping a slave to escape. But the court then ruled that the national government, whether through the courts or other means, could not compel the surrender of this fugitive. Such federal coercion of state officials would be unconstitutional, it held in the case of *Kentucky v. Dennison*. [10]

The resulting ineffectiveness of this clause has been somewhat offset by the enactment of a federal law making it a crime to flee from state to state to avoid prosecution and the adoption, by most states, of a uniform extradition act.

Compacts Between the States

Although Article I declares that "no state shall, without the consent of Congress . . . enter into any Agreement or Compact with another state," the Supreme Court has never invalidated any compact on the basis that it lacked congressional approval.

The court adopted a relaxed approach to this requirement of congressional consent when it ruled in 1893 that Congress, by its silence, had given its approval to a compact settling a boundary dispute between Virginia and Tennessee. [11] Writing in that case, Justice Stephen Field interpreted the requirement of formal congressional consent

to apply only to "the formation of any combination tending to the increase of political power in the States, which may encroach upon or impair the supremacy of the United States or interfere with their rightful management of particular subjects placed under their entire control." [12]

And so compacts that do not tend to increase the power of the states vis-à-vis that of the national government or otherwise infringe on national prerogatives are assumed — in the absence of congressional action to the contrary — to have the requisite consent.

Since New York and New Jersey resolved their longstanding dispute over New York Harbor in the 1830s with a compact, ending their pending case before the Supreme Court, many states have found them useful means of joining together to resolve mutual problems — from boundaries to resource conservation to pollution control. In one of the court's most recent rulings on the compact clause, it upheld — as valid without express congressional consent — the MultiState Tax Compact in which more than a dozen states joined to improve their methods of taxing interstate corporations. [13]

The court further strengthened the usefulness of compacts when it ruled, in 1951, that once a state has adopted a compact — and the approval of Congress is granted or assumed — the state cannot unilaterally withdraw from it. [14]

Interstate Lawsuits

When — despite these facilitating provisions of the Constitution — two states find themselves suing each other, it is the exclusive function of the Supreme Court to hear the case. This power of the court to settle disputes between states of the Union, at odds as states, is one of the most unique characteristics of the American judicial system.

Addressing the centennial celebration of the Supreme Court in 1889 Justice Stephen Field explained:

> Controversies between different States of the world respecting their boundaries, rights of soil, and jurisdiction have been the fruitful source of irritation between their people, and not infrequently of blood conflicts. . . .
>
> Between the States in this country, under the Articles of Confederation, there were also numerous conflicts as to boundaries and consequent rights. . . . [But] by the judicial article of the Constitution, all such controversies are withdrawn from the arbitrament of war to the arbitrament of law. [15]

Article III specifically extends federal judicial power to controversies between two or more states. But it was decades before the court settled such a controversy on its merits. The first case between states — between New York and Connecticut — arrived at the court in 1799, but was dismissed before it was decided. [16]

Thirty years later, the state of New Jersey brought to the court its quarrel with New York over control of the port of New York. New York refused to acknowledge the Supreme Court's jurisdiction over the dispute. Chief Justice Marshall firmly rejected the state's claim of immunity from the court's reach in such a matter, but the states then resolved their problems by compact, ending their case before the court. The compact adopted was the ancestor of that establishing the Port of New York Authority. [17]

In 1846 — after the case had been before it for eight years — the court settled its first boundary dispute between states. At issue was 150 square miles claimed by both Rhode Island and Massachusetts. Once again, before the court could get to the merits of the dispute, it was obliged to assert its authority to decide such interstate matters, an authority disputed by Massachusetts. The court reaffirmed that authority — and then decided the case in favor of Massachusetts. [18]

Missouri and Iowa almost went to war with each other over some 2,000 square miles of contested territory, each state calling out its militia, before the Supreme Court decided the case — in favor of Iowa — in 1850. By this decision, the court placed that territory in a free state rather than a slave one, no small issue at the time. [19]

The settlement of that dispute drew notice in Congress, where one senator commented:

> In Europe armies run [boundary] lines and they run them with bayonets and cannon. They are marked with ruin and devastation. In our country, they are run by an order of the Court. They are run by an unarmed surveyor with his chain and his compass, and the monuments which he puts down are not monuments of devastation but peaceable ones. [20]

Only months before the onset of the Civil War, the general acknowledgment of the Supreme Court's power over such matters was exemplified by the submission to the court of a boundary dispute between the states of Alabama and Georgia. [21]

After the war, boundary disputes multiplied, many involving changes in the courses of the rivers or channels that had marked an original boundary. But by that period in history, the court's authority to resolve such matters was so generally accepted that they came naturally to the justices for settlement.

And the variety of interstate issues coming to the court increased greatly. The classic post-war interstate case — between Virginia and West Virginia — involved West Virginia's agreement, upon becoming a separate state, to assume a certain portion of Virginia's state debt. Soon after the end of the war, Virginia opened negotiations with West Virginia for payment of that share; West Virginia resisted. In 1906 Virginia brought the matter to the Supreme Court, which declared that it did have jurisdiction over this sort of interstate dispute, and that West Virginia — by 1915 — owed Virginia some $12 million.

West Virginia still refused to pay. Virginia asked the Supreme Court to order the West Virginia legislature to impose a tax to raise the money to pay the debt. Realizing that if it granted this unprecedented request, it might well be met with resistance from West Virginia, the court delayed. The justices scheduled arguments on the question of how they might enforce such an order.

West Virginia finally agreed to pay the debt, without the necessity of an order from the Supreme Court, and enacted a bond issue that did pay it off. [22]

Earlier, the court had held that South Dakota, which owned North Carolina bonds, could not only sue North Carolina to recover money due, but could also foreclose, if need be, on the security pledged to back the bonds. [23]

In the long series of water-related disputes that began with that between New York and New Jersey in 1829, the court has been quite willing to hear states argue their points — but hesitant to order one state to act — or cease acting — without strong proof by the complaining state of the need for such a judicial decree.

Early in the century, the court heard Missouri argue — in defense of its citizens' health — that Illinois should be ordered to halt its diversion of sewage into the Mississippi River, because it was thereby exposing the citizens of Missouri to the risk of typhoid. The court did not issue such an order, holding that Missouri had not proved its case. [24]

Similarly, the court heard Kansas argue for an order halting Colorado's diversion of the Arkansas River, but held in 1907 that Kansas had not presented sufficient evidence to support issuance of the order. Fifteen years later, however, in 1922, the court did grant Wyoming an injunction halting Colorado's diversion of the Laramie River. [25]

Footnotes

[1] Charles Warren, *The Supreme Court and Sovereign States*, (Princeton: Princeton University Press, 1924), p. 9.

[2] *Mills v. Duryee*, 7 Cr. 481 (1813).

[3] *Atherton v. Atherton*, 181 U.S. 155 (1901); *Haddock v. Haddock*, 201 U.S. 562 (1906); *Williams v. North Carolina*, 317 U.S. 387 (1942) and 325 U.S. 226 (1945); *Sherrer v. Sherrer*, 334 U.S. 343 (1948).

[4] *Huntington v. Attrile*, 146 U.S. 657 (1892).

[5] Edward S. Corwin, *The Constitution and What It Means Today*, 12th ed. (Princeton: Princeton University Press, 1958), p. 166.

[6] *The Slaughterhouse Cases*, 16 Wall. 36 at 77 (1873).

[7] *Paul v. Virginia*, 8 Wall. 168 (1869); *McCready v. Virginia*, 94 U.S. 391 (1877); *Toomer v. Witsell*, 334 U.S. 385 (1948); *LaTourette v. McMaster*, 248 U.S. 465 (1919); *Blake v. McClung*, 172 U.S. 239 (1898).

[8] *Ward v. Maryland*, 12 Wall. 418 (1871); *Austin v. New Hampshire*, 420 U.S. 656 (1975).

[9] *Doe v. Bolton*, 410 U.S. 179 (1973).

[10] *Kentucky v. Dennison*, 24 How. 66 (1861).

[11] *Virginia v. Tennessee*, 148 U.S. 503 (1893).

[12] Id. at 517-518.

[13] *United States Steel Corp. v. MultiState Tax Commission*, 434 U.S. 452 (1978).

[14] *West Virginia ex rel. Dyer v. Sims*, 341 U.S. 22 (1951).

[15] Hampton L. Carson, *The Supreme Court of the United States: Its History* (Philadelphia: A.R. Keller Co., 1892), p. 708.

[16] Warren, *The Supreme Court and Sovereign States*, pp. 38-39.

[17] *New Jersey v. New York*, 3 Pet. 461 (1830); also 5 Pet. 284 (1831); also 6 Pet. 323 (1832).

[18] *Rhode Island v. Massachusetts*, 4 How. 591 (1846).

[19] *Missouri v. Iowa*, 7 How. 660 (1849) and 10 How. 1 (1850).

[20] Charles Warren, *The Supreme Court in United States History*, 2 vols. (Boston: Little, Brown & Co., 1922, 1926) II:298.

[21] *Alabama v. Georgia*, 23 How. 509 (1860).

[22] *Virginia v. West Virginia*, 238 U.S. 202 (1915), 241 U.S. 531 (1916), and 246 U.S. 565 (1918).

[23] *South Dakota v. North Carolina*, 192 U.S. 286 (1904).

[24] *Missouri v. Illinois*, 180 U.S. 208 (1901).

[25] *Kansas v. Colorado*, 206 U.S. 46 (1907); *Wyoming v. Colorado*, 259 U.S. 419 (1922).

Selected Bibliography

Beth, Loren P. *The Development of the American Constitution: 1877-1917.* New York: Harper & Row. 1971.

Black, Charles L. Jr. *The People and the Court.* New York: MacMillan Publishing Co., 1960.

Carson, Hampton L. *The Supreme Court of the United States: Its History.* Philadelphia: A. R. Keller Co. 1892.

Carr, Robert K. *The Supreme Court and Judicial Review.* New York: Farrar & Rinehart, 1942.

The Constitution of the United States of America: Analysis and Interpretation. Washington: U.S. Government Printing Office, 1973, 1964.

Corwin, Edward S. *The Constitution and What it Means Today,* 12th ed. Princeton: Princeton University Press, 1958.

The Federalist Papers, with an Introduction by Clinton Rossiter. New York: New American Library, Mentor Books, 1961.

Frankfurter, Felix. *The Commerce Clause Under Marshall, Taney and Waite.* Chapel Hill: University of North Carolina Press, 1937.

Freund, Paul A. *The Supreme Court of the United States: Its Business, Purposes, and Performances.* Cleveland: Meridian Books, World Publishing Co., 1961.

Haines, Charles G. *The American Doctrine of Judicial Supremacy,* 2nd ed. Berkeley, Calif.: University of California Press, 1932.

Jackson, Robert H. *The Struggle for Judicial Supremacy.* New York: Alfred A. Knopf, 1941.

Kelly, Alfred H., and Harbison, Winfred A. *The American Constitution,* 4th ed. New York: W.W. Norton & Co., 1970.

Mason, Alpheus T. *The Supreme Court from Taft to Warren.* Baton Rouge: Louisiana State University Press, 1958.

Mason, Alpheus T., and Beaney, William M. *The Supreme Court in a Free Society.* Englewood Cliffs: Prentice-Hall, 1959.

Powell, Thomas Reed. *Vagaries and Varieties in Constitutional Interpretation.* New York: Columbia University Press, 1956; reprint ed. AMS Press, 1967.

Pritchett, C. Herman. *The American Constitution,* 2d ed. New York: McGraw-Hill Book Co., 1968.

Swindler, William F. *Court and Constitution in the Twentieth Century,* 2 vols. Indianapolis: Bobbs-Merrill Co., 1969, 1970.

Swisher, Carl B. *American Constitutional Development,* 2d ed. Cambridge: Houghton Mifflin Co., 1954.

Warren, Charles. *The Supreme Court in United States History,* 2 vols. Boston: Little, Brown & Co., 1922, 1926.

———— *The Supreme Court and Sovereign States.* Princeton: Princeton University Press, 1924.

Westin, Alan F., ed. *The Supreme Court: Views from Inside.* New York: W.W. Norton & Co., 1961.

PART III

THE COURT AND THE INDIVIDUAL

Introduction 373

Freedom for Ideas 387

The Rights of Political Participation 475

Due Process and Individual Rights 523

Equal Rights.................................. 583

Supreme Court Building Facade.
Photo by Dan De Vay.

The Court and the Individual

The Supreme Court's role as guardian of the rights and liberties of the individual is a new one, a responsibility assumed only in the 20th century.

For most of its history, the court had little to say about such questions. Preoccupied with defining the relationship of nation to state, state to state, and government to business, the court found little occasion and less reason to deal with individual rights.

One major reason for the absence of such matters from the court's docket until the 20th century was the lack of any broad constitutional basis for the assertion of individual rights against government action.

The Constitution itself contains few provisions touching individual rights; and those few have been infrequently invoked. The Bill of Rights operated solely against federal action — at least until adoption of the 14th Amendment in 1868.

That amendment's guarantees of the privileges and immunities of U.S. citizens, due process of law and equal protection were designed to extend the protection of the Bill of Rights to individuals threatened by state action.

But not until half a century after its ratification was the purpose of this amendment in any way fulfilled. In the 1920s the court finally began to read its guarantees as its authors had intended.

By the 1970s the promises of due process and equal protection had been construed to apply most of the guarantees of the Bill of Rights to the states. Questions of individual rights versus government authority consumed more and more of the court's time, becoming its most controversial and pressing business.

A Narrow Base: 1789-1865

The Supreme Court deals with cases which arise under the Constitution and the laws of the United States.

Only half a dozen sentences in the original Constitution dealt directly with matters of individual rights. The Constitution does forbid suspension of the privilege of the writ of *habeas corpus* except in time of public emergency.[1] And it prohibits the passage of bills of attainder or *ex post facto* laws.[2] For almost all crimes, the Constitution requires jury trials in the state where the crime was committed;[3] it defines the crime of treason, sets the standard of evidence and limits the penalty for that crime.[4] And it provides for extradition of fugitives[5] and forbids religious tests for federal office-holders.[6]

The Demand for a Bill of Rights

Not surprisingly, many persons active in the formulation of the new government — with all-too-fresh memories of governmental oppression — found the lack of more comprehensive guarantees of individual rights a serious deficiency. Historian Charles Warren described the situation:

> Men on all sides contended that, while the first object of a Constitution was to establish a government, its second object, equally important, must be to protect the people against the government. That was something which all history and all human experience had taught.
>
> The first thing that most of the colonies had done, on separating from Great Britain, had been to assure to the people a Bill of Rights, safeguarding against state legislative despotism those human rights which they regarded as fundamental. Having protected themselves by specific restrictions on the power of their state legislatures, the people of this country were in no mood to set up and accept a new national government, without similar checks and restraints. As soon as the proposed Constitution was published, the demand for a national Bill of Rights was heard on all sides. . . .[7]

Practical concerns motivated this demand, Warren wrote:

> . . .They were thinking of facts, not theories. They had lived through bitter years, when they had seen governments, both royal and state, trample on the human rights which they and their ancestors in the colonies and in England had fought so hard to secure. In the seven years prior to the signing of the federal Constitution, they had seen the legislatures of four states . . . deprive their citizens of the right to jury trial in civil cases. They had seen the state legislatures . . . pass bills of attainder sentencing men to death or banishment without a criminal trial by jury. They had seen the legislatures of nearly all the states deprive persons of their property without due process, by the passage of laws allowing tender of worthless paper and other property in payment of debts and of judgments. They had seen a Massachusetts legislature impair the freedom of the press by confiscatory taxation. They had seen the royal government quarter troops on the inhabitants in time of peace and deny to the people the

right of assembly and of petition. They had seen the King's officials search their houses without lawful warrants. They knew that what government had done in the past, government might attempt in the future, whether its ruling power should be royal, state, or national — king, governor, legislature, or Congress. And they determined that, in America, such ruling power should be definitely curbed at the outset. There should be no uncontrolled power in the government of American citizens. Rightly had Jefferson said, "an elective despotism was not the government we fought for." [8]

Thus, a number of the states which ratified the Constitution did so only with the assurance that a top priority of the First Congress would be the approval of a Bill of Rights to be added to the Constitution.

The Bill of Rights

In June 1789 James Madison of Virginia introduced a dozen proposed constitutional amendments in the First Congress, a Bill of Rights generally modeled after existing state bills of rights. Congress approved 10 of the amendments in September 1791, and they took effect in December after ratification by the requisite number of states. [9]

The first eight of these amendments are the Bill of Rights. As Chief Justice Earl Warren noted, its provisions do not guarantee novel rights, but do "summarize in a striking and effective manner the personal and public liberties which Americans [of that time] . . . regarded as their due and as being properly beyond the reach of any government. . . ." [10]

The Bill of Rights was conceived to protect the individual against the government. Chief Justice Warren continued:

The men of our First Congress . . . knew . . . that whatever form it may assume, government is potentially as dangerous a thing as it is a necessary one. They knew that power must be lodged somewhere to prevent anarchy within and conquest from without, but that this power could be abused to the detriment of their liberties. [11]

The guarantees perform an affirmative as well as a negative function, Zechariah Chafee Jr. points out:

They fix a certain point to halt the government abruptly with a "thus far and no farther"; but long before that point is reached they urge upon every official of the three branches of the state a constant regard for certain declared fundamental policies of American life. [12]

The first of these amendments protects freedom of thought and belief. It forbids Congress to restrict freedom of religion, speech, the press, peaceable assembly and petition.

The Second Amendment ensures the right of the states to maintain militia and, in connection with that state right, the right of the people to keep and bear arms. The Third Amendment restricts government power to quarter soldiers in people's homes. Neither has been the subject of many cases before the federal courts. [13]

The Fourth Amendment forbids any violation of a person's right to be secure in his person, house, papers and effects against unreasonable searches or seizures. This security is to be ensured by allowing issuance of search or arrest warrants only if there is probable cause for the intrusion and if the person to be arrested or the place to be searched and the objects sought are described precisely.

The Fifth Amendment requires indictment of all persons charged in civilian proceedings with capital or otherwise serious crimes. It forbids trying a person twice for the same offense or compelling a person to incriminate himself. It states that no one should be deprived of life, liberty or property without due process of law, and protects private property against being taken for public use without just compensation.

The Sixth Amendment sets out certain requirements for criminal trials, guaranteeing a speedy and public jury trial for all persons accused of crime, with an impartial jury selected from the area of the crime. The defendant is further guaranteed the right to be notified of the charge against him, to confront witnesses testifying against him, to compel witnesses to come to testify in his favor, and to have the aid of an attorney in his defense.

The Seventh Amendment, long since outmoded by inflation, provides for a jury trial in all common law suits involving more than $20.

The Eighth Amendment forbids excessive bail, excessive fines, and cruel and unusual punishment.

(The Ninth and Tenth Amendments do not guarantee specific rights.)

The Judicial Role

Madison, father of these amendments, expected the federal courts to play a major role in implementing their guarantees. "Independent tribunals of justice will consider themselves in a peculiar manner the guardians of those rights; they [the courts] will be an impenetrable bulwark against every assumption of power in the Legislative or Executive; they will naturally be led to resist every encroachment upon rights expressly stipulated for in the Constitution by the declaration of rights," he told his fellow members of Congress. [14]

But the Supreme Court itself had little occasion to apply these promises in its first 130 years.

The stringent Alien and Sedition Acts of 1798 — severe infringements of the rights and liberties of the individual, particularly those freedoms protected by the First Amendment — were never challenged before the High Court. The acts expired early in 1801. It is worth noting, however, that most of the early members of the court, in their roles as circuit judges, presided over trials of persons charged with sedition, and displayed no disinclination to enforce that law. [15]

Slavery, despite the prolonged national debate it engendered, was never dealt with by the court as a matter of individual rights. The few pronouncements by the court on the issue demonstrate clearly that the justices saw it as a matter of property rights, not human rights. *(Box, p. 376)*

Barron v. Baltimore

Furthermore, the court in 1833 made clear that the Bill of Rights provided no protection against state action, but only against that of federal authority.

The case of *Barron v. Baltimore* arose when the owner of a wharf challenged city action which seriously impaired the value of his wharf by creating shoals and shallows around it. Barron described this as a "taking" of his property without just compensation, in violation of the Fifth Amendment. [16]

But when Barron's case came before the Supreme Court, Chief Justice Marshall found the question it posed to be "of great importance, but not of much difficulty." Marshall described Barron's argument: the Fifth Amendment "being in favor of the liberty of the citizen ought to be so construed as to restrain the legislative power of a State, as well as that of the United States."[17]

That argument could not prevail, however, continued the Chief Justice; the Bill of Rights was adopted to secure individual rights against the "apprehended encroachments of the general government — not against those of the local governments."[18] The court could find no indication that Congress intended the Bill of Rights to safeguard the individual against state action, and it would not undertake such an extension of those provisions on its own. Marshall concluded:

> ...Had Congress engaged in the extraordinary occupation of improving the constitutions of the several States by affording the people additional protection from the exercise of power by their own governments in matters which concerned themselves alone, they would have declared this purpose in plain and intelligible language.[19]

Barron v. Baltimore stands to this day, unreversed in its precise finding — that Congress, in approving the Bill of Rights, did not intend them to protect the individual against state action but only against action by federal officials.

The Civil War Amendments

After the Civil War, Congress attempted to overturn the restrictions which *Barron v. Baltimore* placed on the guarantees of the Bill of Rights.

Three constitutional amendments, often called the Civil War Amendments, were approved by Congress and ratified by the states after the end of that conflict.

The 13th Amendment, adopted in 1865, abolished slavery and involuntary servitude, except for persons sentenced to such service as punishment for crime. Congress is authorized by the amendment to pass laws to enforce this guarantee.

The 15th Amendment, adopted in 1870, forbids state or federal authorities to deny or abridge the right of U.S. citizens to vote because of race, color, or previous condition of servitude. It, too, authorized Congress to pass legislation enforcing its prohibition.

The 14th Amendment, the most complex and most litigated of the three, was adopted in 1868. It declares that all persons born or naturalized in the United States are citizens. This is the Constitution's only definition of citizenship.

In addition, the amendment forbids states to abridge by law any privilege or immunity of U.S. citizens, to deprive any person of life, liberty or property without due process of law, or to deny to any person the equal protection of the law.

These guarantees are the heart of the amendment, and they, too, are undergirded by a grant of power to Congress to enforce them through legislation. They have been the foundation of the modern revolution in civil rights and criminal procedure, although for decades after their addition to the Constitution they seemed almost useless as protection for individual rights.

The Intent of Congress

The privileges and immunities, due process and equal protection clauses were intended by their author, Rep. John A. Bingham, R-Ohio (1855-1863, 1865-1873), to extend the guarantees of the Bill of Rights against state action. Bingham thought that the privileges and immunities section of the 14th Amendment would be the chief vehicle for this extension.

In 1871 Bingham explained his view of this portion of the amendment, in response to a query from a fellow member of the House. He stated that "the privileges and immunities of citizens of the United States ... are chiefly defined in the first eight amendments to the Constitution.... These eight articles ... were never limitations upon the power of the States, until made so by the Fourteenth Amendment."[20]

During Senate consideration of the amendment, the chief Senate spokesman in behalf of the proposal had stated that "the great object of the first section of this amendment is ... to restrain the power of the States and compel them at all times to respect these great fundamental guarantees."[21]

During the process of ratification, however, the other sections of the amendment — concerning apportionment of representatives among the states, the holding of federal posts by persons who had forsaken such offices to support the rebellious states, and the validity of the public debt — were given far more attention than section 1.

Frustration of the Promise

Almost a century would pass before the hopes explicit in the adoption of the 13th, 14th and 15th Amendments were fulfilled. In large part, the frustration of their promises was the work of the Supreme Court.

Partly in response to waning public enthusiasm for Reconstruction, partly out of concern for healing the wounds of war, partly just because the nation had not yet developed its sensitivity to issues of individual rights, the court in the post-war decades severely curtailed the operation of these Civil War Amendments to protect individual citizens.

The restrictive interpretation of these amendments came in two lines of rulings. In one, the court defined narrowly the privileges and immunities, due process and equal protection clauses of the 14th Amendment, and the similar substantive phrases of the 13th and 15th Amendments. In the second, the court confined rigidly the enforcement power which these three amendments granted Congress.

Early in the 1870s the court first indicated its limited view of the effect of these amendments. The privileges and immunities of U.S. citizenship were a brief list, the court held, and did not include, for example, the right to vote.[22] The 13th Amendment did no more than abolish the institution of slavery, the court ruled; and the 15th Amendment did not grant to anyone a federal right to vote, only the right to exercise the state-granted franchise free of racial discrimination.[23]

In the mid-1880s the court held that the due process guarantee did not extend the specific protections of the Bill of Rights against state action.[24] And a decade later, it found no denial of equal protection in the requirement of segregated public facilities for blacks and whites.[25]

Furthermore, the court refused to acknowledge that the enforcement clauses of these amendments significantly

The Court and the Issue of Slavery . . .

Slavery played a behind-the-scenes role in the early constitutional development of the United States, but not until after the Civil War did the status of the nation's blacks become a question of individual rights rather than property rights. Carl B. Swisher described the impact of slavery upon pre-Civil War constitutional history:

Concern for the preservation of slavery furnished the driving power back of theories of state rights and of limitation upon the power of the federal government which for many decades hampered the expansion of federal power. Concern for the protection of slavery entered into the interpretation of the commerce clause . . . of clauses having to do with the rights of citizenship, and of other important constitutional provisions. The clash of interest between slavery and non-slavery groups brought on the crisis of a civil war which threatened the complete destruction of the American constitutional system.[1]

Historian Charles Warren viewed the slavery issue as underlying the early debate over the scope of the commerce power:

[T]hroughout the long years when the question of the extent of the federal power over commerce was being tested in numerous cases in the court, that question was, in the minds of Southerners, simply coincident with the question of the extent of the Federal power over slavery.[2]

The question of slavery came to the court in its first decades only as a question of international or commercial law, of states' rights and federal power — not as a human rights issue.

The court gave firm support to federal power over the subject of fugitive slaves. At the same time, it left as much as possible to the states the question of the status of slaves who had spent time in both slave and free areas. The court's divergence from this position — in the *Dred Scott* case of 1857 — added fuel to the conflagration that burst out in civil war.

International Law

In the first case involving slavery decided by the court, the justices held that the slave trade, though by 1825 illegal in the United States, was not illegal under international law. The case involved slaves who arrived in the United States after being removed from a vessel captured by an American warship.

Chief Justice Marshall made clear in his opinion that the legality of the situation alone, not its morality, was before the court. He wrote:

In examining claims of this momentous importance; claims in which the sacred rights of liberty and of property come in conflict with each other . . . this Court must not yield to feelings which might seduce it from the path of duty, but must obey the mandates of the law. . . . Whatever might be the answer of a moralist to this question, a jurist must search for its legal solution in those principles of action which are sanctioned by the usages, the national acts, and the general assent of that portion of the world of which he considers himself as a part. . . .[3]

Commercial Law

Four years later, the court ruled that a slave who died in an abortive rescue attempt after a steamboat fire was a passenger, not freight, for purposes of his owners' damage suit against the vessels involved.

"A slave has volition, and has feelings which cannot be entirely disregarded," wrote Chief Justice Marshall. "He cannot be stowed away as a common package. . . . The carrier has not, and cannot have, the same absolute control over him that he has over inanimate matter. In the nature of things, and in his character, he resembles a passenger, and not a package of goods."[4]

In 1841 the court was faced with a case challenging Mississippi's ban on the importation of slaves. But the justices found a way to decide the case without ruling directly on the importation ban.[5]

enlarged federal power to protect individual rights. The enforcement power granted to Congress to implement these provisions was rigidly confined by state prerogatives, it held. *(Details, p. 151)*

Congress enacted a number of major statutes to enforce the 13th, 14th and 15th Amendments. By the end of the century, most of their provisions had either been declared invalid by the court, repealed directly or rendered obsolete by subsequent legislation.[26] Charles Warren, writing early in the 20th century, described the effect of the Civil War Amendments upon the nation's black citizens, as a result of these Supreme Court decisions:

The first section of the 14th Amendment is a prohibitory measure, and the prohibitions operate against the states only, and not against acts of private persons; the fifth section only gives Congress power, by general legislation, to enforce these prohibitions, and Congress may, within bounds, provide the modes of

redress against individuals when a State has violated the prohibitions; and though Congress cannot act directly against the states, Congress may regulate the method of appeal to United States courts by any persons whose right under the Amendment has been affected by action of the states. As to the 15th Amendment, though theoretically it is capable of being enforced to a certain extent by direct congressional action, Congress has, in fact, taken few steps toward such enforcement; and only a few acts of a state or of a state officer have been found by the courts to violate it. Meanwhile, the southern states, by constitutional and statutory provisions, which have been in general upheld by the court, have found methods of limiting the negro right to vote. . . .[27]

Early in the 20th century, one student of these court rulings declared that the enforcement acts were struck down because "they were in fact out of joint with the times.

... A Question of Legality, Not Morality

Fugitive Slave Laws

As the tension between slave and free states built, and the operations of the underground railway accelerated, an increasing number of cases challenged the federal fugitive slave law, enacted in 1793 to govern the return of fugitive slaves from one state to another.

In 1842 the court affirmed the exclusive power of Congress over fugitive slave matters. The justices struck down a Pennsylvania law providing that before a fugitive was delivered up to his alleged owner or representative, a hearing should be held before a magistrate to determine the validity of the claim to the supposed fugitive slave.[6]

Six years later the court reaffirmed the validity of the federal fugitive slave law and specifically disclaimed any power to resolve the moral dilemma it posed: "[S]ome notice should be taken of the argument, urging on us a disregard of the Constitution and the act of Congress in respect to this subject, on account of the supposed inexpediency and invalidity of all laws recognizing slavery or any right of property in man. But that is a political question, settled by each state for itself; and the federal power over it is limited and regulated by the people of the states in the Constitution itself, as one of its sacred compromises, and which we possess no authority as a judicial body to modify or overrule."[7]

On the eve of the Civil War, the court resolved the most famous of the fugitive slave cases, *Ableman v. Booth.*

Sherman Booth, an abolitionist editor, was prosecuted under the federal fugitive slave law for helping a fugitive slave to escape. The state courts of Wisconsin, Booth's residence, repeatedly issued writs of *habeas cor-*

pus, ordering federal authorities to release Booth from custody, basing their order on the view that the federal fugitive slave law was unconstitutional. The court in March 1859 resoundingly defended the freedom of federal courts from such state interference — and upheld Booth's conviction.[8]

Slave or Free?

The first case in which the court was asked to decide what effect residence in a free state or territory had on the status of a slave came to the court in 1850 — and was resolved with restraint and without incident. The persons involved were held as slaves in Kentucky, worked for a time in the free state of Ohio, but returned to Kentucky to live. The court held that their status depended on the state where they were residing. No constitutional provision controlled state action on this matter, it held.[9]

The court reached a similar conclusion seven years later in the landmark case of *Dred Scott v. Sandford,* but unfortunately it did not stop there.

In this case, the alleged slave, Dred Scott, brought the case on his own behalf. By holding that Scott's status was determined by the law of the state in which he now lived — the slave state of Missouri — the court also held that he could not bring the suit, as a slave, and thus it had no jurisdiction over the matter at all.

But the court went on to hold that slaves were not citizens and that Congress lacked the power to exclude slavery from the territories.[10]

The issue of slavery then became a matter that was to be resolved only on the battlefield; the Supreme Court did not speak again on the subject.

---

[1] Carl B. Swisher, *American Constitutional Development,* 2d ed. (Cambridge: Houghton Mifflin Co., 1954), p. 230.

[2] Charles Warren, *The Supreme Court in United States History,* 2 vols. (Boston: Litle, Brown & Co., 1922, 1926), I:627.

[3] *The Antelope,* 10 Wheat. 66 at 114, 121 (1825).

[4] *Boyce v. Anderson,* 2 Pet. 150 at 154-5 (1829).

[5] *Groves v. Slaughter,* 15 Pet. 449 (1841).

[6] *Prigg v. Pennsylvania,* 16 Pet. 539 (1842).

[7] *Jones v. Van Zandt,* 5 How. 215 at 231 (1848).

[8] *Ableman v. Booth,* 21 How. 506 (1859).

[9] *Strader v. Graham,* 10 How. 52 (1851).

[10] *Dred Scott v. Sandford,* 19 How. 393 (1857).

They did not square with public consciousness, either North or South. They belonged . . . to a more arbitrary period. They fitted a condition of war, not of peace, and suggested autocracy, rather than a democracy!"[28]

But eventually the court's narrow view of these amendments gave way to a more expansive one — and these amendments provided the groundwork for the modern revolution in civil and criminal rights.

Congress facilitated this shift in federal judicial concern with more technical, but equally important, legislation. In 1867 Congress expanded the class of persons who could ask a federal court to issue a writ of *habeas corpus* ordering their release from custody. The new law allowed persons detained by state officials to use this mode of obtaining release if they could show that their detention was in violation of their constitutional rights. In 1875 Congress gave federal courts the right to hear all cases arising under the Constitution or federal laws. And several

years later, it authorized the Supreme Court to hear appeals in criminal cases. *(Details, pp. 257, 272)*

Property, Not People

But in one of the most ironic chapters in Supreme Court history, these new powers and guarantees were for half a century wielded with much more effect to protect property than to protect persons.

Developing the doctrine of substantive due process, the court found the 14th Amendment a useful tool for striking down a wide range of "progressive" state laws — ranging from those setting minimum wages and maximum hours for working men and women to consumer-oriented measures concerning weights and measures of items produced for sale. *(See box, pp. 526, 527)*

Only a few isolated cases provided some hope that the court would eventually exercise its authority to protect the individual against the government.

In 1886 the court held that the equal protection clause assured aliens the right to run laundries in San Francisco free of discriminatory application of licensing requirements by city officials.[29]

The same year, the court held that the Fourth and Fifth Amendments provided absolute protection from federal seizure for an individual's private papers.[30] Twenty-eight years later — in 1914 — the court provided for enforcement of this protection through an "exclusionary rule" — declaring that persons from whom federal agents took evidence illegally had the right to demand that the evidence be excluded from use in federal court.[31]

In 1915 the court invoked the 14th Amendment to strike down state laws restricting the right of aliens to work.[32] During that term, the court also held that the 15th Amendment was violated by Oklahoma's use of a grandfather clause which effectively required all blacks — and only blacks — to take a literacy test before being qualified to vote.[33]

World War I brought the most restrictive set of federal laws concerning speech and the press since 1798. Challenged as violating the First Amendment, these laws were upheld by the Supreme Court — but the cases posing these questions to the court set off the still-continuing process of formulating standards by which to judge the validity of such governmental restrictions on individual freedom.

Broadening Protection: 1925-1938

However, the court still viewed the Bill of Rights as operating only against federal, not state, action. Because state authorities exert far more impact upon the everyday lives of individual citizens than their federal counterparts, this continuing adherence to the effective result of *Barron v. Baltimore* — notwithstanding the intervening adoption of the 14th Amendment — left most citizens inadequately protected against arbitrary, coercive and unfair state government action.

Protection Assumed

The waning of this view — and the beginning of the expansion of federal protection for individual rights — is marked by the court's 1925 ruling in the case of *Gitlow v. New York.*

Benjamin Gitlow, a left-wing socialist, was indicted for violating New York's criminal anarchy law by publishing and distributing subversive documents describing his political beliefs. He came to the Supreme Court arguing that the state law was unconstitutional — a violation of the First Amendment.[34]

The court upheld the law, but in so doing, the majority stated that it now assumed "that freedom of speech and of the press — which are protected by the First Amendment from abridgment by Congress — are among the fundamental personal rights and 'liberties' protected by the due process clause of the Fourteenth Amendment from impairment by the states."[35]

Thus the court began reading into the guarantee of due process the rights and liberties set out in the Bill of Rights. This process, variously described as the incorporation or absorption of the Bill of Rights into the 14th Amendment, continued for a full 45 years. By the mid-1970s, the court had extended the Bill of Rights at last to the point that Rep. Bingham had initially intended a century earlier, when Congress approved Section 1 of the 14th Amendment.

Protection Asserted

The first rights subsumed under the due process clause and thus protected against state action were those set out in the First Amendment. In 1931 the court for the first time struck down state laws as infringing on the freedom to speak and the freedom of the press.[36] In 1934 it assumed that freedom of religion was likewise protected against state infringement.[37] And in 1937 the court held the right of peaceable assembly to be so protected.[38]

The court also began in the 1930s to enforce the equal protection guarantee against racial discrimination by state officials — and to use the due process clause to require fundamental fairness in state dealings with criminal suspects.

The groundwork for revolution was laid.

A Double Standard

As the federal courts, led by the Supreme Court, began to assume the role intended for them by Madison and the drafters of the 14th Amendment, the court hinted that it would apply a stricter standard to laws challenged as infringing on individual rights than it used for those attacked as abridging economic rights.

In the case of *United States v. Carolene Products Co.,* decided in 1938, the court upheld a federal law barring interstate shipment of certain types of skimmed milk.[39] This ruling reflected the court's shift away from disapproval of all such laws as interfering too much with states' rights and the free flow of commerce.

Writing for the majority, Justice Harlan Fiske Stone said that the court would now uphold economic regulation that was challenged as unconstitutional, so long as the regulation had a rational basis.[40]

But in a footnote to that statement, the famous Footnote 4, Stone suggested that "[t]here may be narrower scope for operation of the presumption of constitutionality when legislation appears on its face to be within a specific prohibition of the Constitution, such as those of the first ten Amendments. . . ."[41] *(Text of footnote, p. 379)*

This meant, said Robert H. Jackson several years later, that the "presumption of validity which attaches in general to legislative acts is frankly reversed in the case of interferences with free speech and free assembly."[42] He explained the reasoning behind this double standard:

> Ordinarily, legislation whose basis in economic wisdom is uncertain can be redressed by the processes of the ballot box or the pressures of opinion. But when the channels of opinion or of peaceful persuasion are corrupted or clogged, these political correctives can no longer be relied on, and the democratic system is threatened at its most vital point. In that event the Court, by intervening, restores the processes of democratic government; it does not disrupt them.[43]

Freedom for Ideas

The First Amendment protects the unrestricted exchange of ideas against government suppression. The guarantees of freedom for speech, press and religion have been "first" in several ways — the first listed in the Bill of Rights and the first of those amendments to be fully applied against state action.

Furthermore, many argue, this amendment is in fact first in importance among the Constitution's guarantees of individual rights. Such a "preferred position" is usually linked to the function of these freedoms in maintaining an environment that fosters responsive democratic government.

In 1937 Chief Justice Charles Evans Hughes explained this viewpoint:

> The greater the importance of safeguarding the community from incitement to the overthrow of our institutions by force and violence, the more imperative is the need to preserve inviolate the constitutional rights of free speech, free press and free assembly in order to maintain the opportunity for free political discussion, to the end that government may be responsive to the will of the people and that changes, if desired, may be obtained by peaceful means. Therein lies the security of the Republic, the very foundation of constitutional government.[44]

A Charter for Government

Eight years later, Justice Wiley B. Rutledge assimilated the court's acknowledgment of its new role in respect to the rights of the individual, the view of the First Amendment freedoms as "preferred," and the stricter test for laws challenged as violating that freedom:

> The case confronts us again with the duty our system places on this Court to say where the individual's freedom ends and the State's power begins. Choice on that border, now as always delicate, is perhaps more so where the usual presumption supporting legislation is balanced by the preferred place given in our scheme to the great, the indispensable democratic freedoms secured by the First Amendment.... That priority gives these liberties a sanctity and a sanction not permitting dubious intrusions. And it is the character of the right, not of the limitation, which determines what standard governs the choice....
>
> For these reasons any attempt to restrict those liberties must be justified by clear public interest, threatened not doubtfully or remotely, but by clear and present danger. The rational connection between the remedy provided and the evil to be curbed, which in other contexts might support legislation against attack on due process grounds, will not suffice. These rights rest on firmer foundation.[45]

"The First Amendment," added Justice Rutledge later in his opinion, "is a charter for government, not for an institution of learning." [46]

Concurring, Justice Robert H. Jackson wrote:

> ...it cannot be the duty, because it is not the right, of the state to protect the public against false doctrine. The very purpose of the First Amendment is to foreclose public authority from assuming a guardianship of the public mind through regulating the press, speech and religion. In this field every person must be his own watchman for truth, because the forefathers did not trust any government to separate the true from the false for us....
>
> This liberty was not protected because the forefathers expected its use would always be agreeable to those in authority or that its exercise would always be wise, temperate, or useful to society.
>
> As I read their intentions, this liberty was protected because they knew of no other way by which free men could conduct representative democracy.[47]

'Footnote Four'

In a footnote to its decision in *United States v. Carolene Products Co.*, the court in 1938 foreshadowed its shift in concern from economic to individual rights:

[4] There may be narrower scope for operation of the presumption of constitutionality when legislation appears on its face to be within a specific prohibition of the Constitution, such as those of the first ten Amendments, which are deemed equally specific when held to be embraced within the Fourteenth. See Stromberg v. California, 283 U.S. 359, 369, 370, 51 S.Ct. 532, 535, 536, 75 L. Ed. 1117, 73 A.L.R. 1484; Lovell v. Griffin, 303 U.S. 444, 58 S.Ct. 666, 82 L. Ed. 949, decided March 28, 1938.

It is unnecessary to consider now whether legislation which restricts those political processes which can ordinarily be expected to bring about repeal of undesirable legislation, is to be subjected to more exacting judicial scrutiny under general prohibition of the Fourteenth Amendment than are most other types of legislation. On restriction upon the right to vote, see Nixon v. Herndon, 273 U.S. 536, 47 S.Ct. 446, 71 L.Ed. 759; Nixon v. Condon, 286 U.S. 73, 52 S.Ct. 484, 76 L.Ed. 984, 88 A.L.R. 458; on restraints upon the dissemination of information, see Near v. Minnesota, 283 U.S. 697, 713-714, 718-720, 722, 51 S.Ct. 625; 630, 632, 633, 75 L.Ed. 1357; Grosjean v. American Press Co., 297 U.S. 233, 56 S.Ct. 444, 80 L.Ed. 660; Lovell v. Griffin, supra; on interferences with political organizations, see Stromberg v. California, supra, 283 U.S. 359, 369, 51 S.Ct. 532, 535, 75 L.Ed. 1117, 73 A.L.R. 1484; Fiske v. Kansas, 274 U.S. 380 47 S.Ct. 655, 71 L.Ed. 1108; Whitney v. California, 274 U.S. 357, 373-378, 47 S.Ct. 641, 647, 649, 71 L.Ed. 1095; Herndon v. Lowry, 301 U.S. 242, 57 S.Ct. 732, 81 L.Ed. 1066; and see Holmes, J., in Gitlow v. New York, 268 U.S. 652, 673, 45 S.Ct. 625, 69 L.Ed. 1138; as to prohibition of peaceable assembly, see De Jonge v. Oregon, 299 U.S. 353, 365, 57 S.Ct. 255, 260, 81 L.Ed. 278.

Nor need we enquire whether similar considerations enter into the review of statutes directed at particular religions, Pierce v. Society of Sisters, 268 U.S. 510, 45 S.Ct. 571, 69 L.Ed. 1070, 39 A.L.R. 468, or national, Meyer v. Nebraska, 262 U.S. 390, 43 S.Ct. 625, 67 L.Ed. 1042, 29 A.L.R. 1446; Bartels v. Iowa, 262 U.S. 404, 43 S.Ct. 628, 67 L.Ed. 1047; Farrington v. Tokushige, 273 U.S. 284, 47 S.Ct. 406, 71 L.Ed. 646, or racial minorities. Nixon v. Herndon, supra; Nixon v. Condon, supra; whether prejudice against discrete, and insular minorities may be a special condition which tends seriously to curtail the operation of those political processes ordinarily to be relied upon to protect minorities, and which may call for a correspondingly more searching judicial inquiry. Compare McCulloch v. Maryland, 4 Wheat. 316, 428, 4 L.Ed. 579; South Carolina State Highway Department v. Barnwell Bros., 303 U.S. 177, 58 S.Ct. 510, 82 L.Ed. 734, decided February 14, 1938, note 2, and cases cited.

More recently, Justice William J. Brennan Jr. in 1979 discussed the way in which the First Amendment operates to "foster the values of democratic self-government":

> The First Amendment bars the State from imposing upon its citizens an authoritative vision of truth. It forbids the State from interfering with the communicative processes through which its citizens exercise and prepare to exercise their rights of self-government. And the Amendment shields those who would censure the State or expose its abuses.[48]

No Absolute Right

But neither the intrinsic importance of free expression nor its "societal function" result in the First Amendment's operating as an absolute ban on all official restrictions on speech, the press, assembly or religion.

The collective good — the nation's security or the public's safety — warrants some restriction on the individual's freedom to speak, to publish, to gather in groups and to exercise his religious beliefs. The task of the court has been to balance the community's interest against the individual's rights, to determine when order and safety demand that limits be set to individual freedom.

Wartime, the Cold War and the civil rights movement created the atmosphere within which the Supreme Court has worked to reconcile these competing concerns. The court's course has been an uneven one: It has discarded "tests" for determining permissible government constraints almost as soon as it has developed them.

The much-mentioned "clear and present danger" test, although little-used by the court in recent decades, nevertheless stands as a symbol of the basic position held by the court on free speech questions: Only for very good reason may the government suppress speech — and the court will evaluate the reasons.

The issue of freedom of the press has come more and more frequently before the court in recent years. The court has steadfastly rejected all prior restraints upon publication — most dramatically in the Pentagon Papers case of 1971. And while it has rejected efforts by the news media to expand the protection of the First Amendment into special privileges for the press, it has extended new protection to the news media from libel suits brought by public officials or public figures.

Freedom of religion, a guarantee reflecting the original purpose of many of the nation's earliest settlers, has been at issue in some of the court's most controversial modern rulings. While it has generally upheld laws enacted to enhance the public welfare against challenges that they incidentally curtail the freedom to exercise one's religious beliefs, the court has turned strict scrutiny on laws challenged as violating the amendment's ban on the establishment of religion. Such scrutiny has resulted in such decisions as those rejecting state efforts to require or allow devotional exercises in public schools or to use public funds to aid parochial schools.

Political Rights

For the first 130 years of American history, the privilege of political participation was strictly limited. Until well into the 20th century, the right to vote was the prerogative of the adult white man, and often only of those adult white men who could pay a poll tax, pass a literacy test or meet other qualifications.

The Constitution barely mentions the right to vote; and there is no mention at all of the right to have that vote counted equally with others nor of the protected freedom of political association.

Yet within the last half-century, these rights have won judicial recognition and protection. By 1979, the right to vote belonged to virtually all citizens 18 years of age and older, regardless of sex or race.

In the 17 years since the court abandoned its traditional aloofness from the issue of electoral districting, the right to have one's vote count as equal to those of other city or state residents has become firmly established. As it has implemented that right, the court has redistributed the balance of political power in every state of the Union.

Unrestricted political association — the freedom to associate with others who share one's political views — has been recognized as an individual right and an institutional one.

Although the court during the peak of Cold War upheld state and federal programs and statutes curtailing the exercise of this freedom, the court of the 1970s has made clear that it considers this freedom to be the core of those which the First Amendment was intended to protect.

The Suffrage

Congress, not the court, has led in expansion of the suffrage. Three constitutional amendments were required to lower the barriers of race, sex and age.

Indeed, it was the court's narrow view of the privileges, immunities and rights protected by the Civil War Amendments which necessitated adoption of the 19th Amendment to enfranchise women[49] and which rendered the 15th Amendment a hollow promise for most of a century.[50]

After the Civil War, despite the clear language of the 14th and 15th Amendments, the court continued to defer to state power to set voter qualifications, steadily upholding a variety of devices used to exclude blacks from the suffrage. In the 20th century the court slowly asserted itself and began to strike down the most blatant of these mechanisms — the grandfather clause in 1915, the white primary in 1927 and again in 1944.[51]

But it was left for Congress to take the lead, as it did in the 1960s, abolishing poll tax requirements through a constitutional amendment, suspending literacy tests, and imposing federal control over the electoral machinery of states with high minority population and low voter registration or participation.

At that time the court's role — although secondary — was crucial. A century earlier, the court had undercut similar efforts by Congress to guarantee the right to vote against racial discrimination, adopting a constricted view of the power of Congress to enforce the constitutional amendments adopted in the wake of the Civil War.

But in the 1960s the court gave full backing to the exercise of unprecedented federal power to guarantee civil rights to the nation's blacks.

The most aggressive and effective of the major civil rights statutes of that era was the Voting Rights Act of 1965, which superimposed federal power and federal machinery upon the electoral processes of states which had long denied blacks the right to vote.

In 1966 the court upheld the law against every point of a multi-faceted constitutional challenge by the affected states.[52]

Within five years of the law's enactment, more than one million blacks had been newly registered to vote.

Redistricting Revolution

In stark contrast with the court's reluctance to enforce the clear ban of the 15th Amendment was its unexpected plunge into the subject of legislative redistricting and malapportionment of legislative power.

After decades of declaring such issues "political" and unsuitable for judicial resolution, the court in 1962 changed its mind.

In the case of *Baker v. Carr,* the court announced its reversal, holding that constitutionally based challenges to the malapportionment of state legislative bodies were "federal questions" which federal courts might properly consider.[53]

Although the court in 1962 went no further than that declaration, *Baker v. Carr* set off a still-reverberating judicial revolution.

The following year, the justices declared that the 14th Amendment's guarantee of equal protection — when applied to voting rights — meant "one person, one vote."[54] Each vote cast in an electoral district in a state or in a city should be of equal weight with every other. The application of this rule to federal and state electoral divisions revolutionized the political base of every legislative body of any significance in the nation.

Beliefs and Association

Out of the unlikely context of the anti-subversive and anti-civil rights measures of the 1950s and 1960s, the protected freedom of political association won judicial affirmation.

In addition to its constitutional basis in the First Amendment, the right of association has a clear practical basis: no point-of-view can win recognition in the increasingly complex American society without organized backing.

War slowed the progress of this right toward acknowledged constitutional status. During World War II and the subsequent Cold War, Congress and state legislatures sought to protect the nation against subversion with laws and programs which declared communism and similar political beliefs and affiliations criminal, tantamount to treason.

As it had during the Civil War and World War I, the Supreme Court reflected its sensitivity to the national mood with initial decisions upholding the validity of these anti-subversive devices. The court backed the power of Congress to enact laws which effectively made participation in Communist Party activities illegal by anyone aware of the party's aims. The court seemed to sanction the use of guilt by association as a basis for depriving or denying persons jobs.

Yet within a few years of these rulings, the court began to circumscribe narrowly the methods by which such laws could be enforced. Enforcement became so difficult that, in many instances, it was altogether abandoned.

In one line of rulings beginning in 1957, the court set out strict standards of proof for government efforts to prosecute persons who were members of the U.S. Communist Party. Simple association could not properly serve as the basis for denying a person a job, firing him, depriving him of his U.S. passport, or refusing him admission to the bar, held the court.[55]

Almost simultaneously, in another series of decisions, the court began to give full recognition to the right of association. These rulings, most of which dealt with civil rights activists, soon had their impact on the court's view of

legislation penalizing simple membership in "subversive" organizations.[56]

By 1967 the right had gained clear constitutional status. As Justice Byron R. White wrote:

> The right of association is not mentioned in the Constitution. It is a judicial construct appended to the First Amendment rights to speak freely, to assemble, and to petition for redress of grievances. While the right of association has deep roots in history and is supported by the inescapable necessity for group action in a republic as large and complex as ours, it has only recently blossomed as the controlling factor in constitutional litigation; its contours as yet lack delineation. . . .[57]

In the 1970s the court began to define those contours as it applied the right of association to curtail the exercise of state power over radical student groups, national political party delegations, independent candidates and party-switching voters. The court also held that the practice of patronage firing infringed on this freedom.

Equality Before The Law

The 14th Amendment's promise of equal protection of the laws was intended, said one of its key advocates, Sen. Jacob M. Howard (R Mich. 1862-1871), to give "to the humblest, the poorest, the most despised of the race, the same rights and the same protection before the law as it gives to the most powerful, the most wealthy, or the most haughty."[58]

Not until well past the middle of the next century, however, was the protection of this guarantee actually extended to the nation's black citizens, to aliens, to women, the poor and the illegitimate. And even then, the extension was less than complete.

Early Rulings

At first, the Supreme Court seemed in accord with the design of this portion of the 14th Amendment. The equal protection clause, wrote Justice Samuel F. Miller in 1873, was clearly meant to guarantee equal treatment of blacks. He expressed doubt "whether any action of a State not directed by way of discrimination against the negroes as a class . . . will ever be held to come within the purview of this provision."[59]

Six years later, the court used the equal protection clause to strike down a state law excluding blacks from jury duty. The equal protection guarantee, declared the court, meant that "the law in the States shall be the same for the black as for the white; that all persons, whether colored or white, shall stand equal before the laws of the States. . . ."[60]

The Erosion of Protection

But this declaration soon eroded into superficiality. In 1883 — with its rulings in the *Civil Rights Cases* — the court held that the 14th Amendment applied only to state, not individual, action; that individual discrimination did not violate the 13th Amendment; and that Congress could act only to remedy discrimination by a state, not to prevent it before it occurred.[61]

A decade later, in 1896, the court in the case of *Plessy v. Ferguson* held reasonable Louisiana's requirement of "equal but separate" accommodations for black and white passengers on railway trains.[62] This ruling, wrote one commentator, left the 14th Amendment's guarantees "virtually nonexistent except as a bulwark of the rights of corporations."[63]

Plessy was the logical outcome of a conservative view of the power of the law. In the majority opinion, written by Justice Henry B. Brown, the court declared:

> If the two races are to meet upon terms of social equality, it must be the result of natural affinities, a mutual appreciation of each other's merits and a voluntary consent of individuals.... Legislation is powerless to eradicate racial instincts or to abolish distinctions based upon physical differences, and the attempt to do so can only result in accentuating the difficulties of the present situation. If the civil and political rights of both races be equal one cannot be inferior to the other civilly or politically. If one race be inferior to the other socially, the Constitution of the United States cannot put them upon the same plane.[64]

Business interests, generally more able than individuals to present their views to the court in the late 19th and early 20th century, did not hesitate to use the equal protection clause as a basis from which to challenge state taxes, police regulations and labor laws.

They too met with no more than a modicum of success. The court adopted rationality as the test for such challenges and would uphold all such laws so long as they had a reasonable basis. Nevertheless, businessmen persisted, and economic cases accounted for the vast majority of equal protection questions before the court until 1960.[65]

The Modern View

On the 70th anniversary of its adoption — in 1938 — the 14th Amendment began to take on new strength in its intended role as protector of individual rights.

In the first of a line of rulings which would erode the declaration of *Plessy v. Ferguson* into uselessness, the Supreme Court in 1938 held that a state which maintained no "black" law school violated the equal protection promise when it refused to admit a black resident to its "white" state law school, just because of his race.[66]

Six years later, even as the court upheld the war power of the federal government to remove Japanese-Americans from their West Coast homes, the justices signaled their waning tolerance for laws using racial classifications.

In the court's opinion in the case of *Korematsu v. United States*, the majority stated that "all legal restrictions which curtail the civil rights of a single racial group are immediately suspect" as violations of the 14th Amendment's guarantee of equal protection. Such laws were subject to "the most rigid scrutiny," declared the court. "Pressing public necessity may sometimes justify the existence of such restrictions; racial antagonism never can."[67]

Led by the National Association for the Advancement of Colored People and its legal defense fund, civil rights groups quickly accepted this clear judicial invitation to challenge the segregation which pervaded American life. In several subsequent cases decided in the late 1940s, the justices indicated their increasing skepticism as to whether separate facilities could ever be truly equal.

Finally, in its ruling in the cases entitled *Brown v. Board of Education*, the court in 1954 abandoned the "separate but equal" doctrine, and held state segregation of public schools clearly unconstitutional.[68] Eighty-six years after adoption of the 14th Amendment, the court had at last set the nation on the road to fulfilling the promise of equal protection.

But although the court now mandated a change in the nation's direction, progress was slow. In the 1960s the frustration of the nation's blacks erupted in protests, boycotts, sit-ins, demonstrations. The reaction was often violent.

The compound of protest and reaction sparked congressional action. In 1964 Congress passed the most comprehensive civil rights measure since Reconstruction. The Civil Rights Act of 1964 translated the guarantee of equal protection into a statutory requirement of equal opportunity in employment and equal access to public facilities for blacks and whites. Irving Brant wrote that the 1964 Act brought to fruition "all that a once-aroused nation had attempted" in adopting the 14th Amendment.[69]

The Act was immediately challenged as unconstitutional and just as quickly upheld by a unanimous Supreme Court.[70]

In 1968 Congress approved a federal Fair Housing Act. The court reinforced its provisions with a broadened interpretation of the Civil Rights Act of 1866, which guaranteed similar rights of equal treatment to blacks and whites seeking to sell, buy or rent housing.[71]

The Expanding Guarantee

In the 1970s the Supreme Court faced a range of "second-generation" questions raised by the national effort to ensure equal treatment for blacks and whites. The justices wrestled with the problem of defining proper remedies for past discrimination. White plaintiffs charged that employers engaged in "reverse discrimination" — penalizing innocent members of the majority group in order to compensate minority group members for past unfairness.

The protection of the 14th Amendment's guarantee of equality before the law was broadened during the 1970s as the court brought aliens and women within its scope. In 1971 the court formally declared alienage, like race, to be in all circumstances a suspect classification upon which to base laws. Absent a compelling state justification, such laws would be held invalid.[72]

Women fared less well. By the end of the decade, the court had not gone so far as to declare sex a suspect classification in all circumstances.

But in 1971 the court for the first time nullified a state law because it violated the equal protection guarantee by treating men and women differently without a sufficient justification.[73] In subsequent rulings, the court struck down a variety of federal regulations and state laws for this same reason.

Fundamental Fairness

The Constitution twice promises the individual that government will not deprive him of life, liberty or property without due process of law.

Neither of these guarantees — in the Fifth and 14th Amendments — protects absolutely against loss of life, liberty or property. They simply assure the individual that this deprivation will occur only after the government has adhered to certain standard approved procedures.

But what is due process for the person faced with a sentence of death, or life in prison, or loss of his property?

The Supreme Court has spent more than a century answering that question.

The first time it considered the matter, it noted that the phrase "due process" probably meant no more to those who wrote it into the Bill of Rights than simply "by the law of the land" — that is, by accepted legal procedures.[74]

From that matter-of-fact origin, however, the guarantee of due process has expanded into the basic constitutional assurance to the individual that the government will deal fairly with him, even when it suspects or charges him with serious crimes.

The close relationship between procedure and substance, particularly in the nation's judicial system, was pointed out by Justice Wiley B. Rutledge in 1947. "At times," he wrote, "the way in which courts perform their function becomes as important as what they do in the result. In some respects matters of procedure constitute the very essence of ordered liberty under the Constitution."[75]

Incomplete Definition

Despite the many landmark due process decisions which dot the history of the Supreme Court in the 20th century, the definition of due process remains incomplete. Justice Felix Frankfurter explained why:

> Due process of law . . . conveys neither formal nor fixed nor narrow requirements. It is the compendious expression for all those rights which the courts must enforce because they are basic to our free society. But basic rights do not become petrified as of any one time, even though, as a matter of human experience, some may not too rhetorically be called eternal verities. It is of the very nature of a free society to advance in its standards of what is deemed reasonable and right. Representing as it does a living principle, due process is not confined within a permanent catalogue of what may at a given time be deemed the limits or the essentials of fundamental rights.[76]

Frankfurter wrote that in 1949. In the next two decades the court would expand the meaning of due process to encompass virtually all the specific guarantees of the Bill of Rights.

The Long Debate

The Fifth Amendment contains the original due process guarantee. But *Barron v. Baltimore* made plain that its reach was limited to federal action.

The 14th Amendment, added in 1868, included a similar guarantee, specifically directed against state action. But in one of history's odd turn-abouts, this provision was used initially by the court as a means of dismantling state economic regulation. At the same time, the justices were refusing to read into the due process clause any requirement that states use the indictment process for persons charged with capital crimes, or that they provide 12-man juries to try persons charged with serious crimes, or that they observe the privilege against compelled self-incrimination.[77]

For a century after 1868, the court and legal scholars argued over whether or not the 14th Amendment's due process guarantee "incorporated" or "absorbed" the Bill of Rights — making each particular guarantee applicable against state action.

As the debate continued from decision to decision, it tended to obscure the growing consensus among the justices that due process meant more than "by the law of the land" — that it indeed represented a promise of fundamental fairness. Frankfurter described it as "representing a pro-

found attitude of fairness between man and man, and more particularly between the individual and the government. . . ."[78] Eventually, this consensus rendered the "incorporation" debate moot.

The Beginning of Expansion

The enlargement of the meaning of due process was begun in the 1920s by a fundamentally conservative court. Inherent in the concept of due process, it declared, were the guarantees that one's trial would be free from mob domination, that the judge would be impartial, that the jury would be representative of the community, and that one should have the effective aid of an attorney.[79] These the court first recognized as essential in particular cases — where the crimes were serious and the defendant young, ignorant or a member of a minority group.

In the 1930s the court began to apply constitutional standards to the evidence used by state prosecutors. Confessions extracted by torture could not fairly be used against the persons so forced to incriminate themselves, held the court — decades before it formally extended the Fifth Amendment privilege against compelled self-incrimination to state defendants.[80]

In the 1940s the court simply assumed that the ban on cruel and unusual punishment applied to the states as well as the federal government.[81] It held that the Fourth Amendment guarantee of personal security against unreasonable search and seizure applied against state action, but declined to require state judges to exclude evidence seized in violation of that guarantee.[82]

The Due Process Revolution

The decade of the 1960s saw the most rapid expansion of the meaning of due process. Led by Chief Justice Earl Warren, the Supreme Court firmly applied the guarantees of the Fourth, Fifth, Sixth and Eighth Amendments against state action.

In 1960 the court forbade federal agents to use evidence seized illegally by state agents. In 1961 it required the exclusion of illegally obtained evidence from state trials.[83]

Since 1938 all federal defendants had been guaranteed the aid of an attorney. In 1963 the Supreme Court finally closed the gap between the right of state and federal defendants in that regard. The court declared that all persons charged with serious crimes in state court were assured the aid of an attorney, appointed by the court and paid by the state, if necessary.[84]

Rejecting "the notion that the Fourteenth Amendment applies to the states only a 'watered-down subjective version of the Bill of Rights,' " the court in 1964 held that state suspects, like federal ones, are protected against being forced to incriminate themselves.[85] In 1965 the court held that this privilege also barred adverse comment, by judge or prosecutor, on a defendant's failure to testify in his own defense.[86] Also that year, the court held that due process required states to provide a defendant with the right to confront and cross-examine persons who testified against him.[87]

In 1967 the court held that states were obliged to provide a speedy trial to criminal defendants.[88] In 1968 it added the requirements of a jury trial for all persons charged by the state with serious crimes.[89] Then, on the last day of Chief Justice Warren's tenure, the court in 1969 applied the ban on double jeopardy to state criminal proceedings.[90]

The Bill of Rights had effectively — and controversially — at last been nationalized.

But the process is a continuing one, as the decisions of the last decade have shown. In the words of Justice Frankfurter, " 'due process', unlike some legal rules, is not a technical conception with a fixed content. . . . Due process is not a mechanical instrument. It is not a yardstick. It is a process. It is a delicate process of adjustment. . . ."[91]

Footnotes

[1] Article I, Section 9, Clause 2.

[2] Article I, Section 9, Clause 3.

[3] Article III, Section 2, Clause 3.

[4] Article III, Section 2.

[5] Article IV, Section 2, Clause 2.

[6] Article VI, Section 3.

[7] Charles Warren, *Congress, the Constitution and the Supreme Court* (Boston: Little, Brown & Co., 1925), pp. 79-80.

[8] Ibid., pp. 81-82.

[9] Irving Brant, *The Bill of Rights* (Indianapolis: Bobbs-Merrill Co., 1965), pp. 42-67; Julius Goebel Jr., *History of the Supreme Court of the United States*, Vol. I: *Antecedents and Beginnings to 1801* (New York: Macmillan Publishing Co., 1971), Chapter X, pp. 413-456.

[10] Henry M. Christman, ed. *The Public Papers of Chief Justice Earl Warren* (New York: Simon & Schuster, 1959), p. 70.

[11] Ibid.

[12] Zechariah Chafee Jr., *Free Speech in the United States* (Cambridge: Harvard University Press, 1941; reprint ed., New York: Atheneum, 1969), pp. 6-7.

[13] Brant, *Bill of Rights*, p. 486; see also Goebel, *Antecedents and Beginnings*, pp. 633-651.

[14] Brant, *Bill of Rights*, pp. 49-50.

[15] Ibid., p. 314; see also Goebel, *Antecedents and Beginnings*, pp. 633-651.

[16] *Barron v. Baltimore*, 7 Pet. 243 (1833).

[17] Id. at 247.

[18] Id. at 250.

[19] Ibid.

[20] Brant, *Bill of Rights*, p. 333; see also Carl B. Swisher, *American Constitutional Development*, 2d ed. (Cambridge: Houghton Mifflin Co., 1954), p. 331.

[21] Brant, *Bill of Rights*, p. 336.

[22] *The Slaughterhouse Cases*, 16 Wall. 36 (1873); *Minor v. Happersett*, 21 Wall. 162 (1875).

[23] *United States v. Reese*, 92 U.S. 214 (1876); *United States v. Cruikshank*, 92 U.S. 542 (1876).

[24] *Hurtado v. California*, 110 U.S. 516 (1884).

[25] *Plessy v. Ferguson*, 163 U.S. 537 (1896).

[26] Charles Warren. *The Supreme Court in United States History*, 2 vols. (Boston: Little, Brown & Co., 1922, 1926), II:618.

[27] Ibid., p. 617.

[28] William W. Davis, *The Federal Enforcement Acts*, Studies on Southern History and Politics (1914), cited in Warren, *The Supreme Court in United States History*, II:618.

[29] *Yick Wo v. Hopkins*, 118 U.S. 356 (1886).

[30] *Boyd v. United States*, 116 U.S. 616 (1886).

[31] *Weeks v. United States*, 232 U.S. 383 (1914).

[32] *Truax v. Raich*, 239 U.S. 33 (1915).

[33] *Guinn v. United States*, 238 U.S. 347 (1915).

[34] *Gitlow v. New York*, 268 U.S. 652 (1925).

[35] Id. at 666.

[36] *Stromberg v. California*, 283 U.S. 259 (1931); *Near v. Minnesota*, 283 U.S. 697 (1931).

[37] *Hamilton v. Board of Regents*, 293 U.S. 245 (1934).

[38] *DeJonge v. Oregon*, 299 U.S. 353 (1937).

[39] *United States v. Carolene Products Co.*, 304 U.S. 144 (1938).

[40] Id. at 152.

[41] Ibid.

[42] Robert H. Jackson, *The Struggle for Judicial Supremacy* (New York: Random House, Vintage Books, 1941), pp. 284-285.

[43] Ibid.

[44] *DeJonge v. Oregon*, 299 U.S. 353 at 365 (1937).

[45] *Thomas v. Collins*, 323 U.S. 516 at 529-530 (1945).

[46] Id. at 537.

[47] Id. at 545-546.

[48] *Herbert v. Lando* (1979).

[49] *Minor v. Happersett*, 21 Wall. 162 (1875).

[50] *United States v. Reese* (1876) 92 U.S. 214 (1876); *United States v. Cruikshank*, 92 U.S. 542 (1876).

[51] *Guinn v. United States*, 238 U.S. 347 (1915); *Nixon v. Herndon*, 273 U.S. 536 (1927); *Smith v. Allwright*, 321 U.S. 649 (1944).

[52] *South Carolina v. Katzenbach*, 383 U.S. 301 (1966).

[53] *Baker v. Carr*, 369 U.S. 186 (1962).

[54] *Gray v. Sanders*, 372 U.S. 368 (1963).

[55] *Yates v. United States*, 354 U.S. 298; *Scales v. United States*, 367 U.S. 203 (1961); *Noto v. United States*, 367 U.S. 290 (1961); *Elfbrandt v. Russell*, 384 U.S. 11 (1966); *Aptheker v. Secretary of State*, 378 U.S. 500 (1964); *Schware v. Board of Bar Examiners*, 353 U.S. 232 (1957); *Keyishian v. Board of Regents*, 385 U.S. 589 (1967); *United States v. Robel*, 389 U.S. 258 (1967).

[56] *National Association for the Advancement of Colored People (NAACP) v. Alabama*, 357 U.S. 449 (1958); *NAACP v. Button*, 371 U.S. 415 (1963).

[57] *United States v. Robel*, 389 U.S. 258 at 282-283 (1967).

[58] Brant, *Bill of Rights*, p. 337.

[59] *The Slaughterhouse Cases*, 16 Wall. 36 at 81 (1873).

[60] *Strauder v. West Virginia*, 100 U.S. 303 at 307 (1880).

[61] *The Civil Rights Cases*, 100 U.S. 3 (1883).

[62] *Plessy v. Ferguson*, 163 U.S. 537 (1896).

[63] Brant, *Bill of Rights*, p. 367.

[64] *Plessy v. Ferguson*, 163 U.S. 537 at 551-552 (1896).

[65] Robert J. Harris, *The Quest for Equality* (Baton Rouge: Louisiana State University Press, 1960), p. 59; cited by C. Herman Pritchett, *The American Constitution*, 2d ed. (New York: McGraw-Hill Book Co., 1968), p. 682.

[66] *Missouri ex rel. Gaines v. Canada*, 305 U.S. 337 (1938).

[67] *Korematsu v. United States*, 323 U.S. 214 at 216 (1944).

[68] *Brown v. Board of Education*, 347 U.S. 483 (1954).

[69] Brant, *Bill of Rights*, p. 377.

[70] *Heart of Atlanta Motel v. United States*, 379 U.S. 241 (1964).

[71] *Jones v. Alfred H. Mayer Co.*, 392 U.S. 409 (1968).

[72] *Graham v. Richardson*, 403 U.S. 365 (1971).

[73] *Reed v. Reed*, 404 U.S. 71 (1971).

[74] *Murray's Lessee v. Hoboken Land & Improvement Co.*, 18 How. 272 (1856).

[75] *United States v. United Mine Workers*, 330 U.S. 258 at 342 (1947).

[76] *Wolf v. Colorado*, 338 U.S. 25 at 27 (1949).

[77] *Hurtado v. California*, 110 U.S. 516 (1884); *Maxwell v. Dow*, 176 U.S. 581 (1900); *Twining v. New Jersey*, 211 U.S. 78 (1908).

[78] *Joint Anti-Fascist Refugee Committee v. McGrath*, 341 U.S. 123 at 162 (1951).

[79] *Moore v. Dempsey*, 261 U.S. 86 (1923); *Tumey v. Ohio*, 273 U.S. 510 (1927); *Norris v. Alabama*, 294 U.S. 587 (1935); *Powell v. Alabama*, 287 U.S. 45 (1932).

[80] *Brown v. Mississippi*, 297 U.S. 278 (1936).

[81] *Louisiana ex rel. Francis v. Resweber*, 329 U.S. 459 (1947).

[82] *Wolf v. Colorado*, 338 U.S. 25 (1949).

[83] *Elkins v. United States*, 364 U.S. 206 (1960); *Mapp v. Ohio*, 367 U.S. 643.

[84] *Gideon v. Wainwright*, 372 U.S. 335 (1963).

[85] *Malloy v. Hogan*, 378 U.S. 1 at 10-11 (1964).

[86] *Griffin v. California*, 380 U.S. 609 (1965).

[87] *Pointer v. Texas*, 380 U.S. 400 (1965).

[88] *Klopfer v. North Carolina*, 386 U.S. 213 (1967).

[89] *Duncan v. Louisiana*, 391 U.S. 145 (1968).

[90] *Benton v. Maryland*, 395 U.S. 784 (1969).

[91] *Joint Anti-Fascist Refugee Committee v. McGrath*, 341 U.S. 123 at 163 (1951).

FREEDOM FOR IDEAS

Freedom of Expression 387

Freedom of Speech 395

Freedom of the Press. 423

Freedom of Religion 451

"Freedom of expression is the well-spring of our civilization...."

Justice Felix Frankfurter
Dennis v. United States, 1951

Freedom for Ideas

Of all the liberties guaranteed the individual by the Bill of Rights, the freedoms of the First Amendment are perhaps the most widely cherished. Won at the cost of revolution and separation from the mother country, the freedoms of speech, press, religion, peaceable assembly and petition are values fundamental to the American concepts of individual freedom and representative self-government.

Freedom for individual expression of ideas and opinions reflects belief in the worth of each individual member of society. So too does the decision to entrust the government of that society to the will of its members.

As a result, the "First Amendment protects two kinds of interests on free speech," wrote Professor Zechariah Chafee Jr. "There is an individual interest, the need of many men to express their opinions on matters vital to them if life is to be worth living, and a social interest in the attainment of truth, so that the country may not only adopt the wisest course of action but carry it out in the wisest way." [1]

The freedom of the one is necessary for the viability of the other. As Professor Thomas I. Emerson observed, freedom of individual expression is essential to the preservation of a stable community in the face of ever-changing political, economic and social circumstances, to the maintenance of "the precarious balance between healthy cleavage and necessary consensus." [2]

An End and A Means

Suppression of free expression, on the other hand, would endanger both the personal development and liberty of the individual and the stability of representative government. In the words of constitutional historian Thomas M. Cooley,

> Repression of full and free discussion is dangerous in any government resting upon the will of the people. The people cannot fail to believe that they are deprived of rights, and will be certain to become discontented, when their discussion of public measures is sought to be circumscribed by the judgment of others upon their temperance or fairness. They must be left at liberty to speak with the freedom which the magnitude of the supposed wrongs appears in their minds to demand; and if they exceed all the proper bounds of moderation, the consolation must be, that the evil likely to spring from the violent discussion will probably be less, and

its correction by public sentiment more speedy, than if the terrors of the law were brought to bear to prevent the discussion. [3]

Justice Louis D. Brandeis, writing in 1927, eloquently explained this relationship of the First Amendment freedoms to the individual and his government:

> Those who won our independence believed that the final end of the State was to make men free to develop their faculties; and that in its government the deliberative forces should prevail over the arbitrary. They valued liberty both as an end and as a means. They believed liberty to be the secret of happiness and courage to be the secret of liberty. They believed that freedom to think as you will and to speak as you think are means indispensable to the discovery and spread of political truth; that without free speech and assembly discussion would be futile; that with them, discussion affords ordinarily adequate protection against the dissemination of noxious doctrine; that the greatest menace to freedom is an inert people; that public discussion is a political duty; and that this should be a fundamental principle of the American government. They recognized the risks to which all human institutions are subject. But they knew that order cannot be secured merely through fear of punishment for its infraction; that it is hazardous to discourage thought, hope and imagination; that fear breeds repression; that repression breeds hate; that hate menaces stable government; that the path of safety lies in the opportunity to discuss freely supposed grievances and proposed remedies; and that the fitting remedy for evil counsels is good ones. Believing in the power of reason as applied through public discussion, they eschewed silence coerced by law — the argument of force in its worst form. Recognizing the occasional tyrannies of governing majorities, they amended the Constitution so that free speech and assembly should be guaranteed. [4]

The First Amendment

The First Amendment states: "Congress shall make no law respecting an establishment of religion, or prohibiting the free exercise thereof; or abridging the freedom of speech, or of the press; or the right of the people peaceably to assemble, and to petition the Government for a redress of grievances."

Given the fundamental character of these rights, it seems somewhat ironic that they were not enumerated in the main body of the Constitution. In that document, the framers sought to prevent federal infringement of certain crucial personal rights by prohibiting Congress specifically from enacting *ex post facto* laws and bills of attainder, requiring religious oaths from government officers, and by limiting suspension of the writ of *habeas corpus*.

The Constitution's authors were apparently convinced, however, that the limited powers given the central government and their division among three separate and co-equal branches of government were sufficient guarantees against

---

". . .[F]reedom to think as you will and to speak as you think are means indispensable to the discovery and spread of political truth. . . ."

Justice Louis D. Brandeis
Whitney v. California, 1927

---

abuse of the freedoms of belief and expression. Many of the framers also thought any enumeration of individual rights was bound to be incomplete and would imply that those freedoms not listed were not protected against government impingement.

Participants in the state ratifying conventions were unsatisfied with these explanations. Some of the colonies agreed to ratify the Constitution only on the condition that these and other critical rights — such as indictment and trial by jury — be added to the Constitution. The First Congress approved 12 amendments protecting individual rights and submitted them to the states in the fall of 1789. Two of these amendments — dealing with apportionment of U.S. Representatives and compensation of members of Congress — failed to win ratification. The other 10 amendments were made part of the Constitution late in 1791.

No Absolute Rights

For nearly 130 years, the Supreme Court had very little occasion to review the First Amendment and interpret its constitutional limitations.

Seven years after ratification of the amendment, Congress, fearing war with France, curtailed the exercise of free speech and press by passing the Sedition Act of 1798. The law proved so unpopular that it precipitated the fall of the Federalist Party that sponsored it and was allowed to expire before constitutional challenges to it reached the Supreme Court. In the late 1800s the court reviewed a pair of federal territorial laws that outlawed polygamy. The laws were challenged as abridging the free exercise of religion. The court held that polygamy was a crime in the eyes of the law and society and could not be justified as a religious practice. The laws barring it therefore did not violate the First Amendment.

Not until World War I, when Congress enacted new sedition and espionage acts, was the Supreme Court forced

to consider whether the First Amendment's prohibition against federal interference with speech, press, religion and assembly was absolute or whether certain emergencies might limit its protection.

In a series of nine cases testing the constitutionality of these two wartime laws, the Supreme Court made clear that the guarantees of free speech and press were less than absolute. The justices, however, disagreed on the point at which government might properly move to curb exercises of these freedoms.

The States and Speech

At this same time, the court began to consider whether the First Amendment extended to prohibit state as well as federal abridgment of its guarantees.

The First Amendment explicitly prohibits only Congress from abridging its guaranteed freedoms.

In *Barron v. Baltimore* (1833), the court ruled that the eight amendments comprising the Bill of Rights were restrictions solely on the federal government and not on the states. [5] In 1868, the 14th Amendment was added to the Constitution. It forbade the states to deprive anyone of "liberty" without due process of the law. By 1890 the court had defined "liberty" to include economic and property rights, thereby protecting them from infringement by the states. Personal liberties remained outside the court's interpretation of the 14th Amendment. But as constitutional historians Alpheus T. Mason and William M. Beaney observed, "This illogical position could not long endure." [6]

Application of the First Amendment strictures to state action began with the case of *Gilbert v. Minnesota* in 1920. Justice Brandeis, dissenting, said he could not believe "that the liberty guaranteed by the Fourteenth Amendment includes only liberty to acquire and enjoy property." [7]

Nonetheless, as late as 1922 a majority of the court still declared: "[T]he Constitution of the United States imposes upon the States no obligation to confer upon those within their jurisdiction . . . the right of free speech." [8]

One year later, in 1923, the court began to include personal freedoms in the definition of liberty protected by the 14th Amendment. Liberty, the majority wrote in *Meyer v. Nebraska*,

> . . .denotes not merely freedom from bodily restraint but also the right of the individual to contract, to engage in any of the common occupations of life, to acquire useful knowledge, to marry, establish a home and bring up children, to worship God according to the dictates of his own conscience, and generally to enjoy those privileges long recognized at common law as essential to the orderly pursuit of happiness by free men. . . . The established doctrine is that this liberty may not be interfered with, under the guise of protected public interest, by legislative action which is arbitrary or without reasonable relation to some purpose within the competency of the State to effect. [9]

Two years later the court with little explanation stated that the First Amendment guarantees of free speech and free press were applicable to the states. In *Gitlow v. New York* (1925), it wrote:

> For present purposes we may and do assume that freedom of speech and of the press — which are protected by the First Amendment from abridgment by Congress — are among the fundamental personal rights and "liberties" protected by the due process

clause of the Fourteenth Amendment from impairment by the States. [10]

State Laws and Religious Freedom

That same year, the court also moved toward including religious liberty within this protection, as it struck down an Oregon law requiring all children to attend public schools. In *Pierce v. Society of Sisters* (1925) the court said that the right of parents to rear their children as they saw fit included the right to send those children to private and parochial schools. [11]

But a majority of the court did not explicitly apply the First Amendment ban on governmental interference with free exercise of religion to the states until 1940. Then, in *Cantwell v. Connecticut,* the court declared that the 14th Amendment "has rendered the legislatures of the states as incompetent as Congress to enact" such restrictions. The states were specifically barred from passing any laws respecting establishment of religion by the 1947 ruling in *Everson v. Board of Education.* [12]

The States, the Press and Assembly

In 1931 the Supreme Court, for the first time, struck down a state law as an unconstitutional prior restraint on the press. This action came in *Near v. Minnesota.* Six years

---

The right of assembly "cannot be denied without violating those fundamental principles of liberty and justice which lie at the base of all civil and political institutions...."

Chief Justice Charles Evans Hughes
De Jonge v. Oregon, 1937

---

later, the court held that the freedom of assembly was guaranteed against state infringement by the First and 14th Amendments. In the case of *DeJonge v. Oregon,* the court held the right of peaceful assembly to be equally as fundamental as the rights of free speech and press and therefore equally entitled to protection from restriction by the states. The right of assembly, the court wrote, "is one that cannot be denied without violating those fundamental principles of liberty and justice which lie at the base of all civil and political institutions, principles which the Fourteenth Amendment embodies in the general terms of its due process clause." [13]

Government Restraints

The restraints which government places on exercise of First Amendment rights are of two basic kinds — suppression of the utterance before it is spoken or published and punishment of the person who made the offending utterance.

Prohibition of prior restraints — censorship, severe taxation and licensing systems, for example — is particularly vital to ensure freedom of the press. The English legal commentator, Sir William Blackstone, thought that liberty

of the press lay entirely in allowing "no previous restraints upon publications and not in freedom from censure for criminal matter when published." [14]

But the First Amendment has been interpreted by the Supreme Court to limit subsequent punishment as well as prior restraint. As Thomas M. Cooley wrote,

> ...[t]he mere exemption from previous restraints cannot be all that is secured by the constitutional provisions, inasmuch as of words to be uttered orally there can be no previous censorship, and the liberty of the press might be rendered a mockery and a delusion, and the phrase itself a byword, if, while every man was at liberty to publish what he pleased, the public authorities might nevertheless punish him for harmless publications.... Their [the First Amendment guarantees] purpose has evidently been to protect parties in the free publication of matters of public concern, to secure their right to a free discussion of public events and public measures, and to enable every citizen at any time to bring the government and any person in authority to the bar of public opinion by any just criticism upon their conduct in the exercise of the authority which the people have conferred upon them.... The evils to be prevented were not the censorship of the press merely, but any action of the government by means of which it might prevent such free and general discussion of public matters as seems absolutely essential to prepare the people for an intelligent exercise of their rights as citizens. [15]

No Absolute Bar

Although the First Amendment is stated absolutely — "Congress [and by incorporation through the 14th Amendment, the states] shall make no law ..." — few contend that the amendment is an absolute ban on governmental restrictions of the amendment's guarantees.

Most justices and other constitutional scholars distinguish between pure expression and expression that is in itself conduct or that incites conduct. The first, with a few exceptions, is absolutely protected against governmental infringement; the second is not. Although the court was speaking specifically of the freedom of religion, its explanation of this distinction in *Cantwell v. Connecticut* (1940) may be applied to all First Amendment freedoms: "[T]he Amendment embraces two concepts, — freedom to believe and freedom to act. The first is absolute but, in the nature of things the second cannot be. Conduct remains subject to regulation for the protection of society." [16]

Unprotected Speech

Some forms of expression that fall outside protection of the First Amendment are fairly obvious. Few would apply First Amendment protection to a person who counsels murder or, as Justice Oliver Wendell Holmes Jr. said, to a "man falsely shouting fire in a theater and causing a panic." Few would argue that publishers are free to print deliberately false and defamatory material about public or private individuals. Few would hold that a state may not require vaccination against deadly communicable diseases even if such immunization is contrary to individual religious belief and practice.

The outer bounds of First Amendment protection are not fixed. The Supreme Court initially held commercial speech — that which proposed a financial transaction — to be outside the amendment's reach. In a series of recent cases, the court has reversed that position.

The court once ruled that libelous statements were unprotected; it has since held false and defamatory statements about public officials and figures to be protected unless actual malice is proved.

Obscenity is still considered beyond the scope of the First Amendment, but even there the standards for determining what is obscene and what is not have undergone significant change in recent decades, bringing some material under protection that might not have been covered several years ago.

Speech and Conduct

Commercial speech, libel and obscene material are examples of pure expression. What has proved even more difficult for the court to determine with clarity and consistency is the precise point at which expression becomes conduct that breaches the bounds of First Amendment protection and is then subject to government restraint and regulation.

Assume, for example, that a man is making an intemperate speech on a controversial issue on a public street corner to whoever cares to listen. Does the First Amendment protect him totally against punishment for any consequences that speech might have? If not, must the government wait to stop the speech until his listeners take action either against the speaker or the object of his speech? Or may it stop him at the point that it thinks his words will lead to a breach of the peace? Or is it permissible for the government, knowing from past experience that the speaker is a rabble-rouser, to prevent him from speaking at all?

Finding an answer to these questions is made more difficult by the emotional overlay carried by many forms of expression. The voicing of a popular opinion held by a

---

The "freedom to differ is not limited to things that do not matter much."

Justice Robert H. Jackson
West Virginia State Board of Education v. Barnette, 1943

---

majority is unlikely to raise any First Amendment challenge. But as Justice Robert H. Jackson once observed, "freedom to differ is not limited to things that do not matter much." [17]

It is the unpopular opinion and minority position on matters of crucial concern that are most likely to draw hostility and hatred from the majority upon whose good will the rights of the minority depend for their continued meaning. And if the unpopular opinion is perceived as a threat to a way of life or a form of government, it may prompt the majority to petition the government to repress the expression. Such suppression is just what the First Amendment was designed to curb, explained Justice Holmes in a 1919 dissenting opinion:

> Persecution for the expression of opinions seems to me perfectly logical. . . . But when men have realized that time has upset many fighting faiths, they may come to believe even more than they believe the very

foundations of their own conduct that the ultimate good desired is better reached by free trade in ideas — that the best test of truth is the power of the thought to get itself accepted in the competition of the market, and that truth is the only ground upon which their wishes safely can be carried out. That at any rate is the theory of our Constitution. [18]

The Task of Balancing

The Supreme Court's job has been to balance the scales so that personal rights are restricted only so much as needed to preserve an organized and orderly society. This has not been an easy task, for some justices give more weight to certain factors in the equation than others. If, for instance, a judge believes the preservation of First Amendment rights to be worth more than the tranquillity of the established society, the judge may require the society to

---

". . .[T]he best test of truth is the power of the thought to get itself accepted in the competition of the market. . . ."

Justice Oliver Wendell Holmes Jr., dissenting
Abrams v. United States, 1919

---

show that the expression places it in some grave and immediate jeopardy. If, on the other hand, the judge gives the need for an orderly society the same or greater weight than the need for free expression, even a small degree of disruption may be enough for him to justify governmental restraint of the threatening idea.

The Absolute Position

Very few justices have believed that the First Amendment is absolute, that the government may under no circumstances restrict the exercise of free speech, press, religion or assembly.

Justice Hugo L. Black held this view. "[T]he Amendment provides in simple words that Congress shall make no law . . . abridging freedom of speech or of the press," he wrote in one case. "I read 'no law abridging' to mean no law abridging. . . ." [19]

Black elaborated on this theme in a 1961 dissenting opinion:

> . . .I believe that the First Amendment's unequivocal command that there shall be no abridgment of the rights of free speech and assembly shows that the men who drafted our Bill of Rights did all the "balancing" that was to be done in this field. . . . [T]he very object of adopting the First Amendment, as well as the other provisions of the Bill of Rights, was to put the freedoms protected there completely out of the area of any congressional control that may be attempted through the exercise of precisely those powers that are now being used to "balance" the Bill of Rights out of existence. [20]

Black's view of the First Amendment meant that he would extend its protection to obscene materials and to libelous statements. But even Black placed certain kinds of expression outside the reach of the First Amendment. In 1949 he wrote an opinion holding that a particular instance of picketing was so intertwined with illegal labor practices as to lose any First Amendment protection it might otherwise have. And in two cases in the mid-1960s, Black contended that civil rights demonstrations were not protected if they occurred in inappropriate places. *(Details, p. 415)*

Preferred Position

If they have not considered First Amendment rights to be absolute, the great majority of justices still have accorded them a preferred position when weighed against competing rights and interests. This preferred position arises from the judicial belief that preservation of these rights is so essential to the maintenance of democratic values as to warrant special judicial consideration.

This view was first broached by Justice Benjamin N. Cardozo. In a 1937 case he suggested that because the freedom of "thought and speech . . . is the matrix, the indispensable condition, of nearly every other form of freedom," First Amendment rights were on a "different plane of social and moral values" than the other rights and freedoms guaranteed by the Bill of Rights. [21]

Freedom of "thought and speech . . . is the matrix, the indispensable condition, of nearly every other form of freedom. . . ."

Justice Benjamin N. Cardozo
Palko v. Connecticut, 1937

Cardozo's statement was followed in 1938 by a broad hint that the court might apply stricter standards to test the validity of laws restricting First Amendment rights than it did in cases involving property and economic rights. Traditionally the court deferred to legislative judgment in enacting statutes levying taxes and regulating business. So long as there was a reasonable basis for the regulation, the court would presume it constitutional.

But in the famous *Carolene Products* footnote, Justice Harlan Fiske Stone wrote that "[T]here may be a narrower scope for operation of the presumption of constitutionality when legislation appears on its face to be within a specific prohibition of the Constitution, such as those of the first ten amendments. . . ."[22] *(Text of footnote, p. 379)*

The following year, all but one member of the court endorsed the premise implicit in that footnote. "Mere legislative preferences or beliefs respecting matters of public convenience may . . . be insufficient to justify such [regulation] as diminishes the exercise of rights [of freedom of speech and press] so vital to the maintenance of democratic institutions," the majority wrote. Furthermore, it was the duty of the courts "to weigh the circumstances and to appraise the substantiality of the reasons advanced" to support regulation of First Amendment rights rather than to defer to legislative judgment.[23]

This special treatment of the First Amendment came to be known as the "preferred position," a phrase first used by Stone, then Chief Justice, in a dissent in *Jones v.*

Opelika (1942). Perhaps fittingly, the phrase was first used in a majority opinion in the decision that overturned *Jones.* In the case of *Murdock v. Pennsylvania* (1943) the majority flatly stated that "[f]reedom of press, freedom of speech, freedom of religion are in a preferred position."[24]

The fullest elaboration of this attitude came in the 1945 case of *Thomas v. Collins.* In a plurality opinion, Justice Wiley B. Rutledge wrote that it was the court's duty

> . . .to say where the individual's freedom ends and the State's power begins. Choice on that border, now as always delicate, is perhaps more so where the usual presumption supporting legislation is balanced by the preferred place given in our scheme to the great, the indispensable democratic freedoms secured by the First Amendment. . . . That priority gives these liberties a sanctity and a sanction not permitting dubious intrusions. . . .
>
> . . .[A]ny attempt to restrict those liberties must be justified by clear public interest, threatened not doubtfully or remotely, but by clear and present danger. The rational connection between the remedy provided and the evil to be curbed, which in other contexts might support legislation against attack on due process grounds, will not suffice. These rights rest on firmer foundation. Accordingly, whatever occasion would restrain orderly discussion and persuasion, at appropriate time and place, must have clear support in public danger, actual or impending. Only the gravest abuses, endangering paramount interests, give occasion for permissible limitation. [25]

Use of the phrase "preferred position" faded away, but the court has not abandoned the concept. A majority of the court considers statutes that limit First Amendment rights highly suspect, requiring close judicial attention and compelling justification for their existence.

Chief Justice Warren E. Burger stated the court majority's consensus on this matter in a 1978 case:

> Deference to a legislative finding cannot limit judicial inquiry when First Amendment rights are at stake. . . . A legislature appropriately inquires into and may declare the reasons impelling legislative action but the judicial function commands analysis of whether the specific conduct charged falls within the reach of the statute and if so whether the legislation is consonant with the Constitution. Were it otherwise, the scope of freedom of speech and of the press would be subject to legislative definition and the function of the First Amendment as a check on legislative power would be nullified. [26]

Deference to the Legislature

A few justices opposed the use of the preferred position concept. Chief among these was Felix Frankfurter, a vigorous advocate of judicial restraint. In a 1949 case, he characterized the preferred position approach to the First Amendment as "a mischievous phrase, if it carries the thought, which it may subtly imply, that any law touching communication is infected with presumptive invalidity."[27]

When he balanced First Amendment rights against competing interests, Frankfurter placed great weight on legislative judgment. In a 1951 case, he wrote:

> . . .Free speech cases are not an exception to the principle that we are not legislators, that direct policy-

Restraints on Expression . . .

The Supreme Court has never held the freedoms of speech, press, religion and assembly to be absolute or unabridgeable. Although it has written specific rules for determining whether speech is obscene or libelous, the court has been unable to settle on a general standard for determining at what point a form of expression becomes sufficiently threatening to society to justify its being regulated or otherwise restrained by government.

Clear and Present Danger

The first time the Supreme Court ruled directly on the extent to which government might limit speech, Justice Oliver Wendell Holmes Jr. proposed the "clear and present danger" test as the standard for such regulation. The case, *Schenck v. United States* (1919), was the first of several challenging convictions under the World War I espionage and sedition acts which made it a federal crime to obstruct the U.S. war effort.

Writing for a unanimous court, Holmes said:

> The question in every case is whether the words are used in such circumstances and are of such a nature as to create a clear and present danger that they will bring about the substantive evils that Congress has a right to prevent. It is a question of proximity and degree. [1]

In the eyes of the justices, the fact that the country was engaged in a war made Schenck's efforts to obstruct recruitment a clear and present danger punishable under federal law. *(Details, p. 397)*

'Bad Tendency'

Eight months later, a majority of the court moved away from the clear and present danger standard toward what became known as the "bad tendency" test. Simply stated, this test held that government may punish any speech that tends to interfere with the successful prosecution of a war effort, no matter how remote in time or unlikely the effect of the interference might be.

The majority applied the bad tendency test in several cases.[2] But in 1937 it renewed reliance on the clear and present danger doctrine.

The case concerned a black Communist who went to Georgia to solicit members for the Communist Party and to encourage black Georgians to demand equal rights with whites. He was convicted under a state law because a trial court found that his speeches and documents had a dangerous tendency to incite insurrection.

A majority of the court overturned the conviction on the ground that the speech and documents did not threaten "a clear and present danger of forcible obstruction of a particular state function."[3] *(Details, p. 405)*

Non-Seditious Speech

Until 1937 the court had considered free-speech questions primarily in the context of seditious speech — utterances that threatened the viability of the established governing and economic system.

After 1937 the court began to review more cases weighing the constitutional guarantee of free speech against state limitations designed to preserve public peace. In these cases it frequently employed the clear and present danger test. Thus in 1940 the court held that a state could not constitutionally punish a person for peacefully picketing an employer with whom he had a labor dispute.[4]

In another 1940 case the court overturned the conviction for breach of the peace of a Jehovah's Witness whose attack on other religions highly incensed two passersby who had consented to listen to it. In the absence of a definitive statute making such conduct a clear and present danger to a substantial interest of the state, the court said the situation had threatened no "clear and present menace to public peace and order." [5] *(Details, p. 408)*

It soon became apparent that the justices could seldom reach a consensus on whether a danger was "clear and present." In 1949 a majority of the court held that the clear and present danger to public order was not threatened by a speaker whose speech in a private hall sparked a near-riot by several hundred protestors gathered outside the hall. But in 1951 the court upheld the conviction of a speaker whose utterances caused one listener to threaten to stop the speaker from continuing his remarks. Here the court majority held that a clear and present danger of greater disorder warranted restraint of the speaker. [6] *(Details, pp. 408-409)*

Subversive Speech

The widely held fear that the American system of government was in danger of subversion by communists led to enactment of a federal law outlawing membership in the Communist Party and the advocacy of the violent overthrow of the established government. *(Discussion of political associations, p. 499)*

The question whether this act was an unconstitutional infringement on free speech came to the Supreme Court in the 1951 case of *Dennis v. United States*. A majority of the court upheld the federal law using a substantially revised version of the clear and present danger test.

The justices read the traditional rule as being applicable only when the probability of success of the intended dangerous effect was imminent. Finding this an inadequate protection from subversive activity that included advocacy of the future overthrow of the government by force, Chief Justice Fred M. Vinson wrote that the clear and present danger test must be reinterpreted as follows: "In each case [courts] must ask whether the gravity of the 'evil' discounted by its improbability, justified such invasion of free speech as is necessary to avoid the danger."[7]

Balancing Doctrine

With this restatement, the original meaning of the clear and present danger test appeared to be lost. The doctrine was little used after the 1957 case of *Yates v. United States.*[8]

It was replaced for a time by the so-called balancing doctrine, in which the court weighed the value of preserving free speech against the value of preserving whatever

. . . The Search for a Standard

governmental interest that speech might adversely affect. This standard made its first appearance in a 1950 decision in which the court sustained a federal law which denied the protection of the National Labor Relations Act to any union whose officers failed to swear that they were not communists and did not believe in the violent overthrow of the government.

The court majority found that the law's primary purpose was to prevent the possibility that a union official would use his power to force a strike in order to advance the communist cause. In the court's view this law limited speech only incidentally. The court found application of the clear and present danger test inappropriate and turned instead to the balancing test:

> When particular conduct is regulated in the interest of public order, and the regulation results in an indirect, conditional, partial abridgment of speech, the duty of the courts is to determine which of these two conflicting interests demands the greater protection under the particular circumstances presented.[9]

Since the government's interest in preventing disruption of the economy was greater than the interest of a relatively few people in preserving their right to free speech, the court came down in favor of the government.

Throughout the Cold War period, the court employed the balancing test to determine the validity of numerous state and federal laws restricting the speech and actions of individuals associated with the Communist Party and other allegedly subversive organizations.[10]

But when the court was asked to weigh the interest of a state in obtaining the membership lists of a state branch of the NAACP against the members' right to privacy in association, it balanced the scales in favor of the right of association. However, the court did not apply the balancing test to other 1960s civil rights cases involving picketing and demonstrations. And in 1967 the court specifically rejected the use of that test in a national security case.[11]

Incitement Test

The court disposed of some of the Cold War cases by using what has been called the incitement test. This test distinguished between the advocacy of unlawful conduct (such as the violent overthrow of the government) as abstract doctrine, and advocacy that actually incited

action. The first was protected by the First Amendment, the second was not.[12]

Vagueness Test

Recognizing the inadequacy of these substantive tests, the court has come to rely on several tests that focus on the challenged statute rather than on the conduct or speech it regulates. The three standards most frequently employed are statutory vagueness, facial overbreadth and the least restrictive means test. They are based on the premise that over-inclusive restrictions might cause some persons to refrain from exercising their constitutionally protected freedoms.

The first use of the vagueness test in a First Amendment case came in 1931 when the Supreme Court reversed a conviction under California's "red flag" law on the ground that it was so vague that it permitted punishment of innocent speech.[13]

Least Restrictive Means

A statute which is overly broad restricts forms of expression that are protected as well as those that are not. Under the least restrictive means test, government may only restrain expression as much as necessary to achieve its purpose: "[E]ven though the governmental purpose be legitimate and substantial, that purpose cannot be pursued by means that broadly stifle fundamental personal liberties when the end can more narrowly be achieved."[14]

Statutes deficient in any of these respects may be challenged by persons whose speech may in fact be properly punished by the state under the law. In a 1964 case the court explained:

> Although a statute may be neither vague, overbroad, nor otherwise invalid as applied to the conduct charged against a particular defendant, he is permitted to raise its vagueness or unconstitutional overbreadth as applied to others. And if the law is found deficient in one of these respects, it may not be applied to him either, until and unless a satisfactory limiting construction is placed on the statute. The statute, in effect, is stricken down on its face. This result is deemed justified since the otherwise continued existence of the statute in unnarrowed form would tend to suppress constitutionally protected rights.[15]

---

[1] *Schenck v. United States*, 249 U.S. 47 at 52 (1919).

[2] See, for example, *Abrams v. United States*, 250 U.S. 616 (1919); *Pierce v. United States*, 252 U.S. 239 (1920); *Gitlow v. New York*, 268 U.S. 652 (1925).

[3] *Herndon v. Lowry*, 301 U.S. 242 at 261 (1937).

[4] *Thornhill v. Alabama*, 310 U.S. 88 (1940).

[5] *Cantwell v. Connecticut*, 310 U.S. 296 at 311 (1940).

[6] *Terminiello v. Chicago*, 337 U.S. 1 (1949); *Feiner v. New York*, 340 U.S. 315 (1951).

[7] *Dennis v. United States*, 341 U.S. 494 at 510 (1951).

[8] *Yates v. United States*, 354 U.S. 298 (1957).

[9] *American Communications Association v. Douds*, 339 U.S. 382 at 399 (1950).

[10] See, for example, *Konigsberg v. State Bar of California*, 366 U.S. 36 (1961).

[11] *NAACP v. Alabama ex rel. Patterson*, 357 U.S. 449 (1958); *Edwards v. South Carolina*, 372 U.S. 229 (1963); *Cox v. Louisiana*, 379 U.S. 536 (1965); *Brown v. Louisiana*, 383 U.S. 131 (1966); *Adderly v. Florida*, 385 U.S. 39 (1967); *United States v. Robel*, 389 U.S. 258 (1967).

[12] *Brandenburg v. Ohio*, 395 U.S. 444 (1969).

[13] *Stromberg v. California*, 283 U.S. 359 (1931).

[14] *Shelton v. Tucker*, 364 U.S. 479 at 488 (1960).

[15] *Coates v. Cincinnati*, 402 U.S. 611 at 619-20 (1971).

making is not our province. How best to reconcile competing interests is the business of legislatures, and the balance they strike is a judgment not to be displaced by ours, but to be respected unless outside the pale of fair judgment. [28]

The Standards

The Supreme Court has developed a number of guidelines to help it find the proper balance between the values of free expression and the need for curtailing that freedom in the public interest. Many of them have fallen into disuse. None of them has been applied continuously or consistently.

Perhaps the best known of these guidelines is the "clear and present danger" rule, which postulates that government may repress expression only when the danger generated by that expression is so great and immediate that its impact will be felt before there is time for open discussion to cure the danger. Seldom used now, the clear and present danger rule has been subjected to numerous modifications.

A second rule, also seldom used, is the "bad tendency" test. Under this guideline restraint is permitted if it can be shown that the expression has a "bad tendency," that is, a tendency to bring about an evil that government may properly try to prevent.

Still another is the *ad hoc* balancing test, where all the factors in a particular situation are weighed against each other, and the most compelling argument prevails.

Furthermore, the court will hold a restrictive statute unconstitutionally vague if a person cannot easily know what expression is or is not restricted by it. A statute may be impermissibly broad if it draws under its coverage protected as well as unprotected expression. In some in-stances, the court has held statutes invalid because the legislature could have employed means of achieving the same goal with less restriction of free expression.

Using these guidelines, the modern court has ruled that freedom of speech, assembly and religion may be regulated as to their time, place and manner, so long as the regulation is applied to all equally and unarbitrarily. Governments may restrict the free exercise of religion in pursuit of a compelling secular purpose, so long as the means used to achieve that purpose affect religious practices only indirectly and are the only means by which the purpose can be achieved. A state may aid religious institutions if the aid is indirect, is designed to achieve a secular purpose and avoids excessive entanglement between church and state.

It is clear, as Thomas I. Emerson and others have pointed out, that the court has been unable to find a single comprehensive approach to First Amendment questions.

During periods of external threat the court has sustained government repression of expression while paying lip service to the theories of why repression should not be permitted. But as soon as the danger seems to have passed, the court has begun to strike down such repressive legislation.

Perhaps this imperfect process is no more than its authors expected from the guarantees of the First Amendment. In 1802 Thomas Jefferson, in a letter to a friend, referred to the adoption four years earlier of the Alien and Sedition Acts despite the clear constitutional prohibitions against such a suppression of free speech and press. Jefferson observed:

> It is still certain that tho' written constitutions may be violated in moments of passion or delusion, yet they furnish a text to which those who are watchful may again rally and recall the people; they fix too for the people principles for their political creed. [29]

Footnotes

[1] Zechariah Chafee Jr., *Free Speech in the United States* (Cambridge: Harvard University Press, 1941; reprint ed. New York: Atheneum, 1969), p. 33.

[2] Thomas I. Emerson, *The System of Freedom of Expression* (New York: Random House, Vintage Books, 1970), p. 7.

[3] Thomas M. Cooley, *A Treatise on Constitutional Limitations,* 8th ed., 2 vols. (Boston: Little, Brown & Co., 1927), II:901.

[4] *Whitney v. California,* 274 U.S. 357 at 375-376 (1927).

[5] *Barron v. Baltimore,* 7 Pet. 243 (1833).

[6] Alpheus T. Mason and William M. Beaney, *The Supreme Court in a Free Society* (New York: W. W. Norton & Co., 1968), p. 289.

[7] *Gilbert v. Minnesota,* 254 U.S. 325 at 343 (1920).

[8] *Prudential Insurance Co. v. Cheek,* 259 U.S. 530 at 538 (1922).

[9] *Meyer v. Nebraska,* 262 U.S. 390 at 399-400 (1923).

[10] *Gitlow v. New York,* 268 U.S. 652 at 666 (1925).

[11] *Pierce v. Society of Sisters,* 268 U.S. 510 (1925).

[12] *Cantwell v. Connecticut,* 310 U.S. 296 at 303 (1940); *Everson v. Board of Education,* 330 U.S. 1 (1947).

[13] *Near v. Minnesota,* 283 U.S. 697 (1931); *DeJonge v. Oregon,* 299 US. 353 at 364 (1937).

[14] William Blackstone, *Commentaries on the Laws of England,* quoted in Chafee, *Free Speech,* p. 9.

[15] Cooley, *Constitutional Limitations,* II:885-86.

[16] *Cantwell v. Connecticut,* 310 U.S. 296 at 303-04 (1940).

[17] *West Virginia State Board of Education v. Barnette,* 319 U.S. 624 at 642 (1943).

[18] *Abrams v. United States,* 250 U.S. 616 at 630 (1919).

[19] *Smith v. California,* 361 U.S. 147 at 157 (1959).

[20] *Konigsberg v. State Board of California,* 366 U.S. 36 at 61 (1961).

[21] *Palko v. Connecticut,* 302 U.S. 319 at 327, 326 (1937).

[22] *United States v. Carolene Products,* 304 U.S. 144 at 152, fn. 4 (1938).

[23] *Schneider v. Irvington,* 308 U.S. 147 at 161 (1939).

[24] *Murdock v. Pennsylvania,* 319 U.S. 105 at 115 (1943). overturning *Jones v. Opelika,* 316 U.S. 584 (1942).

[25] *Thomas v. Collins,* 323 U.S. 516 at 529-30 (1945).

[26] *Landmark Communications Inc. v. Virginia,* 435 U.S. 829 at 843-44 (1978).

[27] *Kovacs v. Cooper,* 336 U.S. 77 at 90 (1949).

[28] *Dennis v. United States,* 341 U.S. 494 at 539-40 (1951).

[29] Thomas Jefferson to Dr. Priestly, June 19, 1802, quoted in John P. Frank, *Marble Palace: The Supreme Court in American Life* (New York: Alfred A. Knopf, 1958), p. 196.

Freedom of Speech

Speech is the basic vehicle for communicating ideas, thoughts and beliefs. The right to speak freely is therefore necessary to the free flow of ideas considered so crucial to the successful maintenance of representative government in the United States. It was this concept that the authors of the First Amendment acknowledged when they prohibited government from abridging the freedom of speech.

But though the First Amendment states its protection absolutely, few contend that the right is without limit. And there are forms of speech that few believe deserve any First Amendment protection whatsoever. The task for the Supreme Court, then, has been to answer two fundamental questions raised by the constitutional guarantee of free speech: What constitutes protected speech and under what circumstances may such speech be curbed?

The court has divided speech into two general categories, pure speech and what some of its members call "speech plus."

Pure Speech

Verbal expression of thought and opinion, whether spoken calmly in the privacy of one's home or delivered passionately in a soapbox harangue, is the purest form of speech and the most common. Constitutional historian C. Herman Pritchett has observed that the "distinctive qualities of pure speech are that it relies for effect only on the power of the ideas or emotions that are communicated by speech and that usually the audience is a voluntary one which chooses to listen to the speaker's message." [1]

Because it does not interfere with or inconvenience others to any great extent, pure speech is subject to the least amount of government control. The Supreme Court, however, recognizes the right of government to curb and punish pure speech that threatens or incites others to threaten the national security or public safety. It also acknowledges that government has a right to regulate pure speech that does interfere with others, such as speech amplified by a loudspeaker.

The greatest official restrictions on pure speech have come during times of war or other external threats to the nation's security. The court has upheld both federal and state controls on seditious and subversive speech during these periods. It has also sustained punishment of non-seditious speech that stimulates a violent and hostile reaction from its listeners. But because the court considers the varying circumstances attending each free speech case, it has been unable to develop and apply consistently a standard for determining the point at which the threat to national security or public safety warrants a restriction on or punishment of the speech.

Unprotected Speech. Certain forms of pure speech and expression fall outside the protection of the First Amendment because they are not essential to communication of ideas and are of little social value. "Fighting words" — those public insults calculated to elicit a violent response from the listener — fall into this category, as does obscenity. Here again, however, the court has had great difficulty settling on a standard defining obscenity.

Initially the court also held speech that advertised products and services to be outside the protection of the First Amendment. In recent decisions, however, the court has recognized that the ideas and information conveyed by advertisements are of substantial value to the consuming public and so has drawn commercial speech under First Amendment coverage.

Symbolic Speech

Expression that is not verbal but that makes a statement symbolically has also been considered pure speech by the court. For example, it has upheld as the equivalent of pure speech the right of students to wear armbands and to fly the flag upside down in symbolic protest of the Vietnam War. Although such symbolism may make itself felt on an involuntary audience, it relies for effect, like pure speech, primarily on evocation of an idea or emotion. The court has also held, however, that symbolic speech, like pure speech, may be so intertwined with conduct that state regulation of the conduct also permits regulation of the speech.

'Speech Plus'

"Speech plus" combines the rights of speech and assembly with a course of conduct — usually parading, demonstrating or picketing. According to Pritchett, "speech plus" involves:

> . . . physical movement of the participants, who rely less upon the persuasive influence of speech to achieve their purposes and more upon the public impact of assembling, marching and patrolling. Their purpose is to bring a point of view — by signs, slogans, singing or their mere presence — to the attention of the

widest possible public, including those uninterested or even hostile. [2]

The court has upheld the right of persons to engage in speech plus conduct but at the same time it has accorded government the right to regulate the conduct aspect to ensure public safety and order. Such regulation must be precisely drawn and applied in a nondiscriminatory fashion. The government also must have a legitimate and substantial interest to justify the regulation, and the regulation must restrict the speech aspect as little as possible.

Labor Picketing. One area of speech plus conduct has been held by the court to have almost no First Amendment protection. Although the court at first ruled that the information conveyed to the public by labor picketing merited some degree of First Amendment protection, later decisions have virtually reversed this holding. Peaceful labor picketing is protected under federal labor law, however.

Private and Public Property

The Supreme Court has firmly established that government may not prevent most public property from being used for public speech and assembly. It has made an exception, however, of public property, such as a jailyard, that is dedicated to specific uses making it an inappropriate public forum.

Because it bars abridgment of speech only by government, the First Amendment is generally not pertinent to speech that occurs on private property. Here, too, there are exceptions. The court has held that the First Amendment does apply to privately owned company towns that provide all the services to its residents that a municipally-owned town would.

But the owners of private property dedicated to specific public purposes — a shopping mall, for example — may restrict speech on their property that is not directly related to the public use of the property.

Seditious Speech and the Safety of the State

Just seven years after ratification of the First Amendment prohibiting government abridgment of speech, the Federalist-dominated Congress passed the Sedition Act of 1798. Among other provisions this act set stiff penalties for false, scandalous or malicious writings about the president, either chamber of Congress, or the government, if published with intent to defame any of them, excite hatred against them, stir up sedition or aid foreign countries hostile to the United States.

Republicans, against whom the act was primarily directed, charged that it abridged the freedoms of speech and press but no challenge found its way to the Supreme Court. The act expired after two years. Although only 25 people were arrested and 10 convicted under the act, it was extremely unpopular and is credited with bringing about the demise of the Federalist Party. Upon taking office in 1801, Republican Thomas Jefferson pardoned all those convicted under it, and several years later Congress refunded their fines, with interest.

Although the martial law imposed in some areas during the Civil War substantially curtailed freedoms of speech and press, the constitutionality of these actions was never presented directly to the Supreme Court, and it was not until the United States entered World War I that Congress again passed legislation restricting free speech and free press.

Espionage and Sedition

The Espionage Act of 1917 made it a crime to publish or make false statements with the intent to interfere with the operation of the armed forces or to cause insubordination, disloyalty or mutiny in the armed forces or to obstruct recruiting and enlistment efforts.

The Sedition Act of 1918 made it a crime to say or do anything to obstruct the sale of government war bonds; or to utter, print, write or publish anything intended to cause contempt and scorn for the government of the United States, the Constitution, the flag or the uniform of the armed forces; or to say or write anything urging interference with defense production. The act also made it a crime to advocate, teach, defend or suggest engaging in any of that conduct proscribed by the law.

Challenges to these two laws reached the Supreme Court in 1919 and 1920 — after World War I ended — and presented the court with its first opportunity to define the extent of the protection afforded by the First Amendment. Was the right of free speech absolute, or could its exercise be restrained? If the latter, under what circumstances and to what extent might free speech be limited?

The court's answer to the first question was that free speech was not absolute. Under certain circumstances Congress could forbid and punish speech it considered seditious. In those early cases, the court never seriously examined the federal acts themselves, as it later would scrutinize state laws curbing free speech. Instead, the court deferred to the congressional judgment that the speech and conduct prohibited by the laws would be detrimental to the success of the war effort.

The court did not answer the question of acceptable limits to free speech as easily or as firmly. Although the first decisions were unanimous, the court quickly divided on this point, with the substantial majority ruling that speech and publications that had the tendency to bring about evils that Congress wished to prevent could be punished. The proofs required to show that speakers or publishers intended their remarks to have evil effects were not particularly strict. In balancing preservation of First Amendment rights against preservation of existing government form and policies, this majority found the latter interest to have greater weight.

Justice Oliver Wendell Holmes Jr. and Louis D. Brandeis were an eloquent minority. They held that, to be restricted, speech or publication must raise an immediate danger that its intended effect would damage the war effort. They would require that intent to achieve this effect be proved more by evidence than inference.

The *Schenck* Case

The first of six major seditious speech cases, *Schenck v. United States* (1919), involved the secretary of the Socialist Party and others convicted of conspiring to cause insubordination in the armed forces and to obstruct recruiting and enlistment efforts. Schenck printed and distributed some 15,000 leaflets opposing the recently passed Selective Service law; many of these leaflets were mailed to draftees.

Justice Holmes, who wrote the unanimous opinion affirming the convictions, described the message: "In impassioned language it intimated that conscription was despotism in its worst form and a monstrous wrong against humanity in the interest of Wall Street's chosen few." The leaflet urged its readers to assert their right to oppose the draft. Again in Holmes' words, the pamphlet

> ...described the arguments on the other side [in favor of the draft] as coming from cunning politicians and a mercenary capitalist press, and even silent consent to the conscription law as helping to support an infamous conspiracy. It denied the power to send our citizens away to foreign shores to shoot up the people of other lands, and added that words could not express the condemnation such cold-blooded ruthlessness deserves, &c, &c, winding up "You must do your share to maintain, support and uphold the rights of the people of this country." [3]

At his trial Schenck did not deny that the intended effect of this circular was to persuade people to resist conscription. But he argued that such expression was protected by the First Amendment. The court, however, rejected this contention. "We admit that in many places and in ordinary times the defendants in saying all that was said in the circular would have been within their constitutional rights," Holmes wrote. "But the character of every act depends upon the circumstances in which it is done." [4] Holmes then framed what became known as the "clear and present danger" doctrine. If the spoken or printed words raised a clear and present danger of bringing about the evils that Congress had the constitutional authority to prevent, the First Amendment protections of free speech and press must give way and the words may be punished. *(Development of doctrine, p. 392)*

In Holmes' view, Schenck's words, printed during wartime and with the admitted intent to persuade men to refuse induction, presented such a clear and present danger. "When a nation is at war," he wrote, "many things that might be said in time of peace are such a hindrance to its effort that their utterance will not be endured so long as men fight and that no Court could regard them as protected by any constitutional right." [5]

"When a nation is at war, many things that might be said in time of peace are such a hindrance to its effort that their utterance will not be endured...."

Justice Oliver Wendell Holmes Jr.
Schenck v. United States, 1919.

It made no difference that Schenck and his compatriots had not succeeded in obstructing recruitment. "The statute ... punishes conspiracies to obstruct as well as actual obstruction," Holmes concluded. "If the act, (speaking or circulating a paper), its tendency and the intent with which it is done are the same, we perceive no ground for saying that success alone warrants making the act a crime." [6]

The *Frohwerk* Case

The next two cases, decided on the same day a week after the *Schenck* decision, also unanimously affirmed convictions under the espionage and sedition laws. But in both cases, the evidence showing intent to create a clear and present danger was less convincing than in the *Schenck* case.

In *Frohwerk v. United States* (1919), Justice Holmes indicated that had more evidence been presented, the defendant might well have been acquitted. Frohwerk had placed in a German-language newspaper 12 articles that the government considered attempts to cause disloyalty and insubordination among the armed forces.

Writing the opinion, Holmes said there was little in the language of the articles to distinguish them from the language Schenck used in his leaflets. But from the trial record, the court was unable to determine whether the circumstances surrounding the publishing and distribution of the articles were such that no clear and present danger was raised:

> ...It may be that all this might be said or written even in time of war in circumstances that would not make it a crime. We do not lose our right to condemn either measures or men because the Country is at war. It does not appear that there was any special effort to reach men who were subject to the draft.... But we must take the case on the record as it is, and on that record it is impossible to say that it might not have been found that the circulation of the paper was in quarters where a little breath would be enough to kindle a flame and that the fact was known and relied upon by those who sent the paper out. [7]

The *Debs* Case

In the second case decided that day in 1919 the court upheld the conviction of well-known Socialist Eugene V. Debs for violating the espionage act by a speech he gave in Canton, Ohio. The government alleged the speech was intended to interfere with recruiting and to incite insubordination in the armed forces.

Debs' speech was primarily about socialism. He discussed its growing popularity and predicted its eventual success. However, he also spoke in support of several people serving sentences for violations of the espionage and sedition acts, saying of one that if she was guilty, then so was he. And he made the statements that "you need to know that you are fit for something better than slavery and cannon fodder" and "You have your lives to lose; you certainly ought to have the right to declare war if you consider a war necessary." On this evidence, a trial jury convicted Debs.

The Supreme Court affirmed the conviction. Based on these statements, wrote Holmes, a jury could reasonably conclude that Debs was opposed "not only [to] war in general but this war, and that the opposition was so expressed that its natural and intended effect would be to obstruct recruiting." [8]

Treason

Article III, Sec. 3 of the Constitution specifically defines treason against the United States as consisting "only in levying War against them, or in adhering to their Enemies, giving them Aid and Comfort. No Person shall be convicted of Treason unless on the Testimony of two Witnesses to the same overt Act, or on Confession in open Court."

The Supreme Court has reviewed only three charges of treason, all arising from World War II incidents. Two of these decisions left interpretation of part of the law in some doubt; the third added little to the discussion.

In *Cramer v. United States* (1945), Cramer befriended two of the German saboteurs who were landed in the United States in 1942 to sabotage the American war effort. He met twice with them in public places and held some money in safekeeping for one of them. Cramer was charged with giving aid and comfort to the enemy but the Supreme Court held by a 5-4 decision that Cramer's traitorous intent had not been proved and that eating and drinking with the enemy did not establish guilt. [1]

The 1947 case of *Haupt v. United States* grew out of the same incident. Haupt was the father of one of the saboteurs and was convicted of giving aid and comfort to the enemy after he sheltered his son, helped him try to find employment in a bomb sight factory and bought him an automobile. Sustaining the conviction by a 8-1 vote, the court held that sheltering the enemy was an overt act that gave aid and comfort and there was no further need to prove that Haupt had traitorous intent when he took in his son. [2]

In the third case, *Kawakita v. United States* (1952), the court held that charges of treason against the United States could be brought against an American citizen who had committed a treasonous act against the United States in a foreign country. [3]

------

[1] *Cramer v. United States,* 325 U.S. 1 (1945).
[2] *Haupt v. United States,* 330 U.S. 631 (1947).
[3] *Kawakita v. United States,* 343 U.S. 717 (1952).

The court then considered whether Debs actually intended his speech to have this effect. Here Holmes looked at evidence showing that just before speaking Debs endorsed the view that U.S. involvement in World War I was unjustifiable and should be opposed by all means. Such evidence "that the defendant accepted this view . . . at the time that he made his speech is evidence that if in that speech he used words tending to obstruct the recruiting service he meant that they should have that effect," Holmes said. [9]

The *Abrams* Case

Eight months later, in November 1919, the court issued its first divided decision in a seditious speech case.

Abrams v. United States concerned the convictions of five Russian-born immigrants for writing, publishing and distributing in New York City two allegedly seditious pamphlets criticizing the U.S. government for sending troops into Russia in 1918. One of the pamphlets described President Wilson as a coward and a hypocrite, implying that the real reason for sending troops to Russia was not to protect supplies for use in the war against Germany but to aid those fighting takeover of Russia by communist revolutionaries. The pamphlet also described capitalism as the "one enemy of the workers."

The second pamphlet, printed in Yiddish, warned workers in munitions factories that their products would be used to kill Russians as well as Germans. It called for a general strike. The five distributed some of these pamphlets by tossing them from a window; others were circulated secretly around the city. The five were each sentenced to 20 years imprisonment.

A seven-justice majority upheld the convictions. Justice John H. Clarke, writing for the majority, quickly dismissed the direct free speech issue by citing the *Schenck* and *Frohwerk* cases as precedents. The only question the court need answer, Clarke said, was whether there was sufficient evidence presented to the jury to sustain its guilty verdict.

Clarke quoted sections of the two pamphlets — the evidence in the case — and from these excerpts concluded:

. . .the plain purpose of their propaganda was to excite, at the supreme crisis of war, disaffection, sedition, riots, and, as they hoped, revolution, in this country for the purpose of embarrassing and if possible defeating the military plans of the [U.S.] Government in Europe. . . . Thus it is clear not only that some evidence but that much persuasive evidence was before the jury tending to prove that the defendants were guilty as charged. . . . [10]

In Dissent. This reasoning strayed too far from the clear and present danger test to win the concurrence of Holmes and Brandeis. Holmes agreed with the majority that the five defendants had advocated a general strike and

------

"It is only the present danger of immediate evil or an intent to bring it about that warrants Congress in setting a limit to the expression of opinion. . . ."

Justice Oliver Wendell Holmes, Jr., dissenting
Abrams v. United States, 1919

------

curtailment of war materials production, but he questioned whether their intent to actually hinder the war effort had been proved. Holmes contended that the espionage and sedition acts must be construed to require conviction of a speaker only if it is proved that he intended his speech to have the criminal effect proscribed by the law and that the speech must produce or be intended to produce a "clear and imminent danger that it will bring about forthwith certain substantive evils that the United States constitutionally may seek to prevent."

Continuing, Holmes wrote:

But as against dangers peculiar to war, as against others, the principle of the right to free speech is always the same. It is only the present danger of immediate evil or an intent to bring it about that warrants Congress in setting a limit to the expression of opinion where private rights are not concerned. Congress certainly cannot forbid all effort to change the mind of the country. Now nobody can suppose that the surreptitious publishing of a silly leaflet by an unknown man, without more, would present any immediate danger that its opinions would hinder the success of the government arms or have any appreciable tendency to do so. [11]

Only the Yiddish pamphlet criticizing the U.S. intervention in Russia could afford "even a foundation" for the government's charge, Holmes said.

The *Schaefer* Case

In the next case the court majority moved even further away from Holmes' clear and present danger test. *Schaefer v. United States* (1920) arose after five officers of a Philadelphia German-language newspaper were convicted of publishing false news items with the intent to promote Germany's success in the war and hamper recruiting efforts. The articles, generally unfavorable to the U.S. war effort, were reprinted from other publications, but the paper's officers had either added to or omitted parts of the text. One article was found objectionable solely because one word had been mistranslated so that "bread lines" read "bread riots."

Six of the justices voted to reverse the convictions of two of the men but sustained the convictions of the other three. Speaking through Justice Joseph McKenna, the majority said it had no doubt that the statements were deliberately falsified, "the purpose being to represent that the war was not demanded by the people but was the result of the machinations of executive power...." [12]

Nor, said the majority, was it unreasonable for a jury to conclude that the additions and omissions were made with the intent that the reprinted articles would have the effect alleged. To readers, McKenna wrote, the articles' "derisive contempt may have been truly descriptive of American feebleness and inability to combat Germany's prowess, and thereby [may have served] to chill and check the ardency of patriotism...." [13]

Furthermore, the majority held that there was no need to show that the articles presented an immediate danger but only that they tended to have a bad effect. Were the articles, McKenna asked,

> ...the mere expression of peevish discontent, aimless, vapid and innocuous? We cannot so conclude. We must take them at their word, as the jury did, and ascribe to them a more active and sinister purpose. They were the publications of a newspaper, deliberately prepared, systematic, always of the same trend, more specific in some instances, it may be, than in others. Their effect or the persons affected could not be shown, nor was it necessary. The tendency of the articles and their efficacy were enough for offense ... and to have required more would have made the law useless. It was passed in precaution. The incidence of its violation might not be immediately seen, evil appearing only in disaster, the result of disloyalty engendered and the spirit of mutiny. [14]

Brandeis Dissent. Holmes and Brandeis would have acquitted all five defendants on the ground that the articles did not raise a clear and present danger to the government's war efforts. Of one of the reprints, Brandeis wrote:

> It is not apparent on a reading of this article ... how it could rationally be held to tend even remotely or indirectly to obstruct recruiting. But ... the test to be

applied ... is not the remote or possible effect. There must be the clear and present danger. Certainly men judging in calmness and with this test presented to them could not reasonably have said that this coarse and heavy humor immediately threatened the success of recruiting. [15]

Brandeis not only chided the majority for failing to apply the test in its review of the case but criticized the lower courts for failing to offer the test to the jury as the standard to be used. Instead, the jury had been instructed to convict if they found that any of the articles would diminish "our will to win" the war.

Brandeis concluded with a strong warning against restricting free speech too readily:

> ...To hold that such harmless additions to or omissions from news items and such impotent expressions of editorial opinion, as were shown here, can afford the basis even of a prosecution will doubtless discourage criticism of the policies of the Government. To hold that such publications can be suppressed as false reports, subjects to new perils the constitutional liberty of the press.... Nor will this grave danger end with the passing of the war. The constitutional right of free speech has been declared to be the same in peace and in war. In peace, too, men may differ widely as to what loyalty to our country demands; and an intolerant majority, swayed by passion or by fear, may be prone in the future, as it has often been in the past, to stamp as disloyal opinions with which it disagrees. Convictions such as these, besides abridging freedom of speech, threaten freedom of thought and of belief. [16]

Justice Clarke also dissented, but not on free speech grounds.

The *Pierce* Case

The final major case in this series centered on a pamphlet entitled "The Price We Pay," written by an eminent Episcopal clergyman and published by the Socialist Party.

A federal district judge in Baltimore acquitted several persons accused of violating the espionage act by distributing the pamphlet in that city. The judge found that the booklet was an attempt to recruit persons to the Socialist Party and its philosophy and not an attempt to persuade them to interfere with the war effort.

However, an Albany, N.Y., judge and jury found the latter to be true. Consequently, several persons who distributed the pamphlet in Albany were convicted of conspiring to attempt to cause insubordination in the armed forces. They appealed to the Supreme Court on the ground that the government failed to show intent to cause insubordination or to prove that distribution of the pamphlet created a clear and present danger that insubordination would result.

Seven justices upheld the convictions in *Pierce v. United States* (1920). Much of their reasoning hinged on the fact that a jury could conclude that several of the statements were false, and that the distributors knew them to be false or distributed them without any regard for whether the statements were false or not. Among those statements the court majority thought a jury might consider false were the following:

● "Into your homes the recruiting officers are coming. They will take your sons of military age and impress them into the army.... And still the recruiting officers will come; seizing age after age, mounting up to the elder ones and taking the younger ones as they grow to soldier size."

● "The Attorney General of the United States is so busy sending to prison men who do not stand up when the Star Spangled Banner is played, that he has no time to protect the food supply from gamblers."

● "Our entry into [the war] was determined by the certainty that if the allies do not win, J. P. Morgan's loans to the allies will be repudiated, and those American investors who bit on his promises would be hooked."

A jury would also be warranted in concluding that such statements, when circulated, would have a tendency to cause insubordination and that that was the intent of the distributors. Even if a jury was not agreed on the probable effect of the pamphlet, said Justice Mahlon Pitney,

> ...at least the jury fairly might believe that, under the circumstances existing, it would have a tendency to cause insubordination, disloyalty and refusal of duty in the military and naval forces.... Evidently it was intended, as the jury found, to interfere with the conscription and recruitment services; to cause men eligible for the service to evade the draft; to bring home to them, and especially to their parents, sisters, wives, and sweethearts, a sense of impending personal loss, calculated to discourage the young men from entering the service....[17]

In Dissent. Holmes and Brandeis dissented in an opinion written by Brandeis. They disagreed that the statements cited by the majority were false. The first, regarding recruiting, was eventually proved true. The second, concerning the attorney general, was false if taken literally but was clearly meant to suggest that the attorney general might better spend his time than prosecuting people for allegedly seditious statements. The third, regarding the reason for U.S. entry into the war, was an expression of opinion rather than fact. To buttress this last statement, Brandeis noted that some members of Congress found the loans instrumental in the government's decision to enter the war. Brandeis then said:

> ...To hold that a jury may make punishable statements of conclusions or of opinion, like those here involved, by declaring them to be statements of facts and to be false would practically deny members of small political parties freedom of criticism and of discussion in times when feelings run high and the questions involved are deemed fundamental.[18]

Furthermore, Brandeis continued, even if the statements were false, the government offered no proof showing that the men who distributed the pamphlet knew they were false. Nor was there any proof that the pamphlet was distributed with the intent to dampen military morale. The defendants did not even distribute the pamphlet to military men, Brandeis observed. And finally, he said, there was no indication that distribution of "The Price We Pay" raised a clear and present danger of causing insubordination.

Brandeis again concluded with a warning that the court majority had placed the guarantee of free speech in a precarious position:

> The fundamental right of free men to strive for better conditions through new legislation and new institutions will not be preserved, if efforts to secure it by argument to fellow citizens may be construed as criminal incitement to disobey the existing law —

merely, because the argument presented seems to those exercising judicial power to be unfair in its portrayal of existing evils, mistaken in its assumptions, unsound in reasoning or intemperate in language.[19]

The *Hartzel* Case

Distance in time from actual war combat brought calmer voices to the debate on seditious speech. The 1918 sedition law was repealed in 1921, and many of those convicted of violating it, including Debs, were ultimately pardoned or had their sentences reduced.

The Espionage Act was still in force when the United States entered World War II. The Supreme Court reviewed only one conviction made under it during this period. The case concerned a man who printed and sent out several articles urging in hostile and intemperate language that the white race stop fighting each other and band together to war against the yellow races.

The question in *Hartzel v. United States* (1944) was not whether what Hartzel said fell within the reach of the federal law, but whether there was enough evidence to sustain his conviction, the same question prominent in the last three World War I cases. A five-justice majority concluded that the government had not proved beyond a reasonable doubt that Hartzel had intended his statements to incite insubordination in the armed forces.[20]

State Sedition Laws

From time to time, states perceived their internal security to be threatened by radical political forces and, like the federal government, they sought to minimize those threats by restricting the exercise of free speech, free press and free assembly.

The first round of such state laws was enacted after President McKinley was assassinated in 1901 by a professed anarchist. The model for these criminal anarchy laws — and for the federal Smith Act of 1940 — was New York's 1902 law which defined criminal anarchy as "the doctrine that organized government should be overthrown by force or violence, or by assassination of the executive head or any of the executive officials of government, or by any unlawful means." The law made it a felony for anyone to advocate criminal anarchy by speech or by printing and distributing any material advocating or teaching the doctrine.

Following World War I and the communist revolution of 1917, 33 states enacted peacetime sedition or criminal syndicalism statutes. Similar to but broader than the criminal anarchy laws, these statutes made it unlawful to advocate, teach or aid the commission of a crime, sabotage or other unlawful act of violence in order to bring about political change or a change in industrial ownership. These laws also made it unlawful to organize or knowingly become a member of an organization that advocated criminal syndicalism.

The Supreme Court initially sustained the constitutionality and application of these laws, but by the late 1930s the court began to reverse convictions in lower courts, holding either that the law was too vague or broad or that it had been applied to persons whose advocacy of overthrow of the government presented no immediate threat.

During the Cold War years, states focused exclusively on preventing communist infiltration of government. Many required public employees to swear that they did not advocate forceful overthrow of the government. Persons refusing to take such oaths were liable to dismissal; those who lied were subject to prosecution for perjury.

At first the court sustained convictions under these laws, but as the threat of infiltration receded, the court began to find several of the loyalty oath statutes unconstitutionally vague. In some instances, the court found their application violative of due process requirements. *(Loyalty oath cases, pp. 508-516).*

By the late 1960s, the fear that communists would destroy the established order was replaced by concern that the public peace was in jeopardy from civil rights activitists, anti-war protestors and members of the so-called New Left. Once again, several states turned to their criminal anarchy and syndicalism laws to restrain the disturbing speech that came from dissident elements of the society. In its first review of this latest application of a criminal syndicalism law, however, the court drew into doubt the validity of all such laws. The First Amendment protected the advocacy of forceful overthrow of the government, the court said, unless that advocacy actually incited someone to undertake such action.

The *Gitlow* Case

The first of these state sedition laws to be tested in the Supreme Court was New York's criminal anarchy law.

Benjamin Gitlow, a member of the left wing of the Socialist Party, was convicted under the law for printing and distributing some 16,000 copies of the "Left Wing Manifesto." This tract repudiated the moderate stance of the main body of the Socialist Party and called for the overthrow of the democratic state by *"class action* of the proletariat *in any form* having as its objective the conquest of the power of the state." It also urged the proletariat to "organize its own state *for the coercion and suppression of the bourgeoisie."*

Gitlow appealed his conviction to the Supreme Court on the ground that the statute unconstitutionally restricted his rights of free speech and free press by condemning certain classes of speech without considering whether they presented a clear and present danger of bringing about the evil that the state had the right to prevent.

Gitlow won one of his arguments. The First Amendment explicitly prohibited only Congress, and not the states, from restricting free speech. Gitlow argued, however, that the First Amendment rights of free speech and free press were implicit in the concept of liberty guaranteed by the 14th Amendment. The Supreme Court agreed, almost casually, with this contention. *(Details, p. 388)*

But a majority of the court nonetheless sustained the conviction in *Gitlow v. New York* (1925). The majority, writing through Justice Edward T. Sanford, first held that Gitlow's manifesto fell within the speech proscribed by the law. It was neither abstract doctrine nor the "mere prediction that industrial disturbances and revolutionary mass strikes will result spontaneously in an inevitable process of evolution in the economic system." [21] Instead, the manifesto urged mass strikes for the purpose of fomenting industrial disturbance and revolutionary action to overthrow the organized government.

The court next held that the state was within its police power when it punished "those who abuse this freedom [of expression] by utterances inimical to the public welfare, tending to corrupt public morals, incite to crime, or disturb the public peace...." [22]

The state need not show that such utterances created a clear and present danger of inciting overthrow of the government but only that they tended to have that effect. Sanford explained:

> ... That utterances inciting to the overthrow of organized government by unlawful means present a sufficient danger of substantive evil to bring their punishment within the range of legislative discretion is clear. Such utterances, by their very nature, involve danger to the public peace and to the security of the State. They threaten breaches of the peace and ultimate revolution. And the immediate danger is none the less real and substantial, because the effect of a given utterance cannot be accurately foreseen. The State cannot reasonably be required to measure the danger from every such utterance in the nice balance of a jeweler's scale. A single revolutionary spark may kindle a fire that, smouldering for a time, may burst into a sweeping and destructive conflagration. It cannot be said that the state is acting arbitrarily or unreasonably when in the exercise of its judgment as to the measures necessary to protect the public peace and safety, it seeks to extinguish the spark without waiting until it has enkindled the flame or blazed into the conflagration. It cannot reasonably be required to defer the adoption of measures for its own peace and safety until the revolutionary utterances lead to actual disturbances of the public peace or imminent and immediate danger of its own destruction; but it may, in the exercise of its judgment, suppress the threatened danger in its incipiency. [23]

Having upheld the authority of the state to determine that a certain class of speech presented a danger, the majority then refused to consider whether the First Amendment protected specific utterances falling within that class.

The First Amendment does not protect "those who abuse this freedom [of expression] by utterances inimical to the public welfare, tending to corrupt public morals, incite to crime, or disturb the public peace...."

Justice Edward T. Sanford
Gitlow v. New York, 1925

The majority's reasoning was different from the court's traditional approach to convictions under federal sedition laws, which condemned certain kinds of actions. Under those laws, speech was unprotected only if the government could prove that the circumstances in which it was uttered made it the equivalent of the proscribed action.

Holmes Dissenting. Justices Holmes and Brandeis dissented, arguing that the clear and present danger test should be applied to state, as well as to federal, statutes restricting the right of free speech. If that test is applied to Gitlow's case, wrote Holmes,

> ... it is manifest that there was no present danger of an attempt to overthrow the government by force on the part of the admittedly small minority who shared [Gitlow's] views. It is said that this manifesto was more than a theory, that it was an incitement. Every

The Right and Freedom of Association . . .

The right of an individual to associate freely with others who share similar beliefs and aspirations is not explicitly granted by the original Constitution or the Bill of Rights. But the Supreme Court has recognized this right as implicit in the First Amendment guarantees of free speech and assembly and in the 14th Amendment's concept of liberty.

Early Rulings

The court's development of the right of association is of recent vintage. In 1927 a majority of the justices upheld the conviction of a woman for violating California's criminal syndicalism law by associating with people in an organization that advocated overthrow of the government by unlawful means. [1]

And in 1928, the court upheld conviction of a Ku Klux Klan officer who disobeyed a New York statute which required certain organizations to file membership lists with the state. In an opinion from which only one justice dissented, the court held the statute a proper exercise of the state's police power.[2]

Although it was not specifically discussed, the right to be free of guilt by association underlay the court's decision in *DeJonge v. Oregon* (1937). In this case the court distinguished between the illegal intent of the Communist Party to overthrow the U.S. government and the protected right of one of its members to speak and assemble for lawful purposes, albeit under the party's auspices.[3] *(Details, p. 405)*

At no time in America's history has the right of association been more sorely tested than during the Cold War years, when millions of Americans believed the national security threatened by communist subversion. Numerous challenges to anti-subversive laws raised the issue whether political associations were constitutionally protected. Although this contention won a few adherents on the court, none of the decisions in the late 1940s and early 1950s involving subversive activities were ever grounded on a right of association. *(Further discussion, p. 499)*

The NAACP Cases

The court began to recognize a constitutionally protected right of association late in the 1950s. The series of cases in which this development occurred dealt not with membership in the Communist Party, which advocated action that, if taken, would have been illegal, but with membership in the National Association for the Advancement of Colored People (NAACP), an organization that pursued legal goals. The cases arose when several southern states, incensed by the civil rights association's pivotal role in Supreme Court rulings abolishing state-imposed segregation, moved to prevent the NAACP from continuing its activities within their borders.

The NAACP challenged these measures before the Supreme Court, which not only held that the right of association was implicit in the First and 14th Amendments but also that it stood on an equal plane with the explicitly guaranteed freedoms of speech, press, assembly and religion.

Disclosure of Membership

The first of the NAACP cases arose in Alabama. Like many other states, Alabama had a statute requiring all out-of-state corporations to register with the state before doing business there. Although local branches of the NAACP had operated in Alabama since 1918, the NAACP had never registered under the statute, nor had the state indicated it should do so.

Then, in 1956, the state attorney general, charging the NAACP with failure to comply with the registration statute, asked for and was granted a temporary restraining order prohibiting the NAACP from conducting futher business in the state. The attorney general also requested, and the state court ordered, that the NAACP supply him with certain records, including lists of all its Alabama members.

The NAACP eventually produced all the records requested except the membership lists. The state court held the organization in contempt, fining it $100,000.

The Supreme Court unanimously reversed the contempt conviction with its decision in the case of *NAACP v. Alabama ex rel. Patterson* (1958). Justice John Marshall Harlan wrote the court opinion:

> Effective advocacy of both public and private points of view, particularly controversial ones, is undeniably enhanced by group association, as this Court has more than once recognized by remarking upon the close nexus between the freedoms of speech and assembly. . . . It is beyond debate that freedom to engage in association for the advancement of beliefs and ideas is an inseparable aspect of the "liberty" assured by the Due Process Clause of the Fourteenth Amendment. . . . [S]tate action which may have the effect of curtailing the freedom to associate is subject to the closest scrutiny.[4]

Furthermore, said Harlan, the right of association also entails the right to privacy in that association. "It is hardly a novel perception that compelled disclosure of affiliation with groups engaged in advocacy may constitute [an] effective . . . restraint on freedom of association," Harlan said.[5]

Turning to the NAACP case, he then observed that the association had offered unrebutted evidence that previous public disclosures of its membership had resulted in economic reprisal, loss of employment, and physical violence to members. The court held that Alabama had not presented any sufficient reason to justify such an infringement of this protected right.

The reversal of the contempt citation was not the end of this particular story, however. The court sent the case back to the state trial court for a decision on whether the NAACP had violated Alabama law by failing to register to do business. Eventually, the state court issued a permanent injuction forbidding the NAACP to operate in the state.[6] Upon appeal, the Supreme Court again reversed the state court in a unanimous decision in 1967.[7]

Teachers' Associations

In 1960 the court struck down an even more subtle attempt to discourage membership in the NAACP.

. . . An Implicit First Amendment Guarantee

Arkansas law required teachers in state-supported schools to file affidavits listing all the organizations they had belonged to or contributed to within the last five years. It was widely understood that this requirement was aimed at exposing teachers who belonged to the NAACP. The case of *Shelton v. Tucker* (1960) came to the Supreme Court after teachers whose contracts were not renewed because they refused to comply with the statute charged that the law violated their rights to personal, academic and associational liberties.

Writing for the five-justice majority, Justice Potter Stewart said there was no question that a state might, in an appropriate investigation of the fitness and competence of its teachers, consider their associational ties.

In this case, the majority held that the state had gone too far. The law's "comprehensive interference with associational freedom goes far beyond what might be justified in the exercise of the State's legitimate inquiry into the fitness and competency of its teachers," Stewart wrote.[8]

Litigation and Solicitation

Using a different method in its attempt to curb NAACP activities, Virginia in 1956 amended its regulations governing ethical conduct of attorneys to forbid solicitation of clients by an agent of an organization that litigates a case in which it is not a party and has no pecuniary interest.

Litigation aid, including apprising persons that they might have a claim, is one of the primary methods the NAACP uses in its work for racial equality. The organization brought suit to stop enforcement of Virginia's new rule, arguing that it infringed its right to associate to help persons seek legal redress of violations of their constitutional rights.

By a 6-3 vote, the Supreme Court held in *NAACP v. Button* (1963) that Virginia's statute impermissibly infringed on the right of association.

As one commentator has noted, the opinion, written by Justice William J. Brennan Jr., was "notable as extending the concept of expression to a point" that no previous decision of the court had reached.[9] Brennan wrote:

> . . . [A]bstract discussion is not the only species of communication which the Constitution protects: the First Amendment also protects vigorous advocacy, certainly of lawful ends, against government intrusion. . . . In the context of NAACP objectives, litigation is not a technique of resolving private differences; it is a means for achieving the lawful

objective of equality of treatment by all government . . . for the members of the Negro community in this country. It is thus a form of political expression. . . . And under the conditions of modern government, litigation may well be the sole practicable avenue open to a minority to petition for redress of grievances.

> We need not, in order to find constitutional protection for the kind of cooperative, organizational activity disclosed by this record, whereby Negroes seek through lawful means to achieve legitimate political ends, subsume such activity under a narrow, literal conception of freedom of speech, petition or assembly. For there is no longer any doubt that the First and Fourteenth Amendments protect certain forms of orderly group activity.[10]

The majority held that Virginia's statute was impermissibly vague, risking the "gravest danger of smothering all discussion looking to the eventual institution of litigation" on behalf of minority group members, and that the state had not shown a sufficiently compelling reason for restricting this right to associate.[11]

Fifteen years later the court by a 7-1 vote reaffirmed *Button*, declaring that "collective activity undertaken to obtain meaningful access to the courts is a fundamental right within the protection of the First Amendment." That holding came in the case of *In re Primus* (1978), in which the court overturned a state bar's public reprimand of an attorney affiliated with the American Civil Liberties Union for soliciting clients.[12]

Legislative Investigation

The final NAACP case in this series involved state action challenging the right of members of an association to retain the privacy of that association. A committee established by the Florida legislature to investigate communist activity in the state obtained information that some 14 former or present Communist Party members might be members of the Florida NAACP. The committee called as a witness the president of the Miami branch of the NAACP and asked him to verify this information. He refused and was convicted of contempt. The Supreme Court overturned the conviction by a 5-4 vote in *Gibson v. Florida Legislative Investigating Committee* (1963).[13]

Writing for the majority, Justice Arthur J. Goldberg said that the investigating committee had not presented enough evidence showing a substantial connection between the NAACP and Communists to warrant the intrusion into the right of association.

---

[1] *Whitney v. California*, 274 U.S. 357 (1927).
[2] *Bryant v. Zimmerman*, 278 U.S. 63 (1928).
[3] *DeJonge v. Oregon*, 299 U.S. 353 (1937).
[4] *NAACP v. Alabama ex rel. Patterson*, 357 U.S. 44 at 460-61 (1958).
[5] Id. at 461.
[6] *NAACP v. Alabama ex rel. Patterson*, 360 U.S. 240 (1959); *NAACP v. Gallion*, 368 U.S. 16 (1961).
[7] *NAACP v. Alabama ex rel. Flowers*, 377 U.S. 288 (1964); see also *Louisiana ex rel. Gremillion v. NAACP*, 366 U.S. 293 (1961); *Bates v. City of Little Rock*, 361 U.S. 516 (1960).
[8] *Shelton v. Tucker*, 364 U.S. 379 at 490 (1960).
[9] Thomas I. Emerson, *The System of Freedom of Expression* (New York: Random House, Vintage Books, 1970), p. 429.
[10] *NAACP v. Button*, 371 U.S. 415 at 429-30 (1963).
[11] Id. at 434.
[12] *In re Primus*, 436 U.S. 412 at 426 (1978), quoting *United Transportation Union v. Michigan Bar*, 401 U.S. 576 at 585 (1971).
[13] *Gibson v. Florida Legislative Investigating Committee*, 372 U.S. 539 (1963).

idea is an incitement. It offers itself for belief and if believed it is acted on unless some other belief outweighs it or some failure of energy stifles the movement at its birth. The only difference between the expression of an opinion and an incitement in the narrower sense is the speaker's enthusiasm for the result. Eloquence may set fire to reason. But whatever may be thought of the redundant discourse before us it had no chance of starting a present conflagration. If in the long run the beliefs expressed in proletarian dictatorship are destined to be accepted by the dominant forces of the community, the only meaning of free speech is that they should be given their chance and have their way. [24]

The *Whitney* Case

The next state sedition law tested in the Supreme Court was California's criminal syndicalism statute.

Anita Whitney, a niece of former Supreme Court Justice Stephen J. Field, participated in a convention establishing the California branch of the new Communist Labor Party.

At the convention, Whitney advocated adoption of a resolution dedicating the party to seek political change through the ballot, but this proposition was rejected in favor of a resolution urging revolutionary class struggle as the means to overthrow capitalism. Despite her defeat, Whitney continued to participate in the convention. She also continued her membership in the party for a time and attended one or two more meetings.

Although she testified that she had no intention of helping to create an unlawful organization, Whitney was convicted of violating the portion of the California law prohibiting organization of and participation in groups advocating criminal syndicalism.

A unanimous Supreme Court sustained her conviction. After holding that the state statute was not unconstitutionally vague, Justice Sanford said the majority saw little to distinguish Whitney's actions from Gitlow's manifesto. In fact, Whitney's actions in assembling with others to form a group advocating forceful overthrow of the government posed an even greater danger to the state. Sanford wrote:

> The essence of the offense denounced by the Act is the combining with others in an association for the accomplishment of the desired ends through the advocacy and use of criminal and unlawful methods. It partakes of the nature of a criminal conspiracy.... That such united and joint action involves even greater danger to the public peace and security than the isolated utterances and acts of individuals is clear. We cannot hold that, as here applied, the Act is an unreasonable or arbitrary exercise of the police power of the State, unwarrantedly infringing any right of free speech, assembly or association, or that those persons are protected from punishment by the due process clause who abuse such rights by joining and furthering an organization thus menacing the peace and welfare of the state. [25]

Speaking Separately. Justices Holmes and Brandeis concurred with the majority in a separate opinion written by Brandeis that sounded more like a dissent. Under the California statute, Brandeis wrote,

> ... [t]he mere act of assisting in forming a society for teaching syndicalism, of becoming a member of it, or of assembly with others for that purpose is given the

dynamic quality of crime. There is guilt although the society may not contemplate immediate promulgation of the doctrine. Thus the accused is to be punished, not for contempt, incitement or conspiracy, but for a step in preparation, which, if it threatens the public order at all, does so only remotely. The novelty in the prohibition introduced is that the statute aims, not at the practice of criminal syndicalism, nor even directly at the preaching of it, but at association with those who propose to preach it. [26]

Brandeis did not deny that the freedom of assembly, like the freedoms of speech and press, could be restricted by the state, but he again insisted that the restriction be permitted only if the assembly presented a clear and present danger of resulting in the intended evil. The danger must be imminent and serious, he wrote; fear of danger is not enough to restrict the First Amendment freedoms:

> ... To justify suppression of free speech there must be reasonable ground to fear that serious evil will result if free speech is practiced. There must be reasonable ground to believe that the danger apprehended is imminent. There must be reasonable ground to believe that the evil to be prevented is a serious one. Every denunciation of existing law tends in some measure to increase the probability that there will be violation of it. Condonation of a breach enhances the probability. Expressions of approval add to the probability. Propagation of the criminal state of mind by teaching syndicalism increases it. Advocacy of law-breaking heightens it still further. But even advocacy of violation, however reprehensible morally, is not a justification for denying free speech where the advocacy falls short of incitement and there is nothing to indicate that the advocacy would be immediately acted on. The wide difference between advocacy and incitement, between preparation and attempt, between assembling and conspiracy, must be borne in mind. In order to support a finding of clear and present danger it must be shown either that immediate serious violence was to be expected or was advocated, or that the past conduct furnished reason to believe that such advocacy was then contemplated....
>
> ... The fact that speech is likely to result in some violence or in destruction of property is not enough to justify its suppression. There must be the probability of serious injury to the State. Among free men, the deterrents ordinarily to be applied to prevent crime are education and punishment for violations of the law, not abridgment of the rights of free speech and assembly. [27]

Although they believed that under these standards the California law improperly restricted Whitney's rights of free speech and assembly, Brandeis and Holmes felt compelled to concur in Whitney's conviction for technical reasons. A few months later, the California governor pardoned Whitney, basing much of his reasoning on Brandeis' opinion.

The *Fiske* Case

The same day that it decided *Whitney*, the Supreme Court reversed for the first time a conviction under a state criminal syndicalism act. The decision in *Fiske v. Kansas* (1927) was the court's first ruling since the amendment was adopted that a government had unconstitutionally restrained free speech.

Fiske, an organizer for International Workers of the World (IWW), was convicted for violating Kansas' syndicalism law, which was similar to California's. The only evidence introduced at his trial to show the unlawful nature of the organization was the IWW preamble, which read in part: "Between these two classes a struggle must go on until the workers of the world organize as a class, take possession of the earth, and the machinery of production and abolish the wage system."

The trial jury apparently assumed that this class struggle would involve the violent overthrow of the government, which would make the IWW and participation in it unlawful under the Kansas statute. But the Supreme Court reversed the decision, holding that there was no evidence

---

"The fact that speech is likely to result in some violence or in destruction of property is not enough to justify its suppression."

Justice Louis D. Brandeis
Whitney v. California, 1927

---

specifically showing that the IWW actually advocated violence or other criminal acts as methods of bringing about political and industrial change. [28]

The Fiske decision proved a turning point in the court's rulings on state criminal syndicalism laws. It heard three more major cases testing the constitutionality of these laws as applied in particular circumstances and, in all three cases, reversed convictions under such laws.

The *DeJonge* Case

Two of these three cases came to the court in 1937, 10 years after *Fiske. DeJonge v. Oregon* arose after the defendant was convicted for conducting a public meeting under Communist Party auspices. DeJonge maintained he was innocent because he had not advocated or taught any criminal doctrine at the meeting, but merely discussed issues of public concern. The state courts, however, interpreted the statute to make criminal any participation in any meeting sponsored by an organization that advocated at any time the forceful overthrow of the established government.

A unanimous court reversed DeJonge's conviction, holding that the state's interpretation of the statute was unnecessarily restrictive of the rights of free speech and assembly. In one of the court's first expositions on the right of assembly, Chief Justice Charles Evans Hughes wrote:

> ...peaceable assembly for lawful discussion cannot be made a crime. The holding of meetings for peaceable political action cannot be proscribed. Those who assist in the conduct of such meetings cannot be branded as criminals on that score. The question, if the rights of free speech and peaceable assembly are to be preserved, is not as to the auspices under which the meeting is held but as to its purpose; not as to the relations of the speakers, but whether their utterances transcend the bounds of the freedom of speech which the Constitution protects. If the persons assembling have committed crimes elsewhere, if they have formed or are engaged in a conspiracy against the public peace

and order, they may be prosecuted for their conspiracy or other violation of valid laws. But it is a different matter when the State, instead of prosecuting them for such offense, seizes upon mere participation in a peaceable assembly and a lawful public discussion as the basis for a criminal charge. [29]

The *Herndon* Case

In a second case decided in 1937, a majority of the court abandoned the "bad tendency" test adopted in *Gitlow* in favor of something more like the clear and present danger standard.

Herndon v. Lowry (1937) concerned a black organizer sent to Atlanta to recruit members for the Communist Party. He held three meetings and signed up a few members. He had with him membership blanks, literature on the Communist Party and a booklet entitled "The Communist Position on the Negro Question." This booklet called for self-determination for blacks living in the southern "black belt." The booklet envisioned a black-dominated government separate from the rest of the United States. To achieve this goal, the tract advocated strikes, boycotts and a revolutionary power struggle against the white ruling class.

Herndon was arrested and convicted of violating a Georgia law which made it unlawful for anyone to attempt to persuade anyone else to participate in an insurrection against the organized government. Herndon appealed his conviction on the grounds that he had said or done nothing to create any immediate danger of an insurrection.

A five-justice majority of the Supreme Court agreed, holding the state statute to be too vague and too broad. The state needed to show more than that Herndon's words and actions might tend to incite others to insurrection at some future time. Justice Owen J. Roberts wrote:

> The power of a state to abridge freedom of speech and of assembly is the exception rather than the rule and penalizing even of utterances of a defined character must find its justification in a reasonable apprehension of danger to organized government. The judgment of the legislature is not unfettered. The limitation upon individual liberty must have appropriate relation to the safety of the state. [30]

The majority could not concur with the state court's view that Herndon was guilty if he intended an insurrection to occur "at any time within which he might reasonably expect his influence to continue to be directly operative in causing such action by those whom he sought to induce."

"The power of a state to abridge freedom of speech and of assembly is the exception rather than the rule...."

Justice Owen J. Roberts
Herndon v. Lowry, 1937

This view left a jury without any precise standard for measuring guilt, Roberts said, and could conceivably allow a jury to convict a person simply because it disagreed with his opinion:

The statute, as construed and applied, amounts merely to a dragnet which may enmesh anyone who agitates for a change of government if a jury can be persuaded that he ought to have foreseen his words would have some effect in the future conduct of others. No reasonably ascertainable standard of guilt is prescribed. So vague and indeterminate are the boundaries thus set to the freedom of speech and assembly that the law necessarily violates the guarantee of liberty embodied in the Fourteenth Amendment. [31]

In Dissent. The four dissenters would have used the bad tendency test to uphold the conviction. They said Herndon's possession of the booklets on black self-determination showed that he intended to distribute them, and noted that he had not denied that intention. They also said it was apparent that by endorsing the self-determination plan, Herndon was advocating insurrection. "Proposing these measures was nothing short of advising a resort to force and violence, for all know that such measures could not be effected otherwise," they wrote. [32]

The *Brandenburg* Case

State criminal syndicalism laws enjoyed a re-emergence in the late 1960s as states sought ways to restrain both civil rights and anti-war activists. The court, however, in a 1969 *per curiam* opinion called into question the continuing validity of most criminal syndicalism laws.

In the case of *Brandenburg v. Ohio,* the court extended the *Herndon* decision by setting out what has been called the "incitement" test. This standard distinguishes between advocacy of the use of force as an abstract doctrine, which is protected by the First Amendment, and actual incitement to use force, which is not protected.

The case concerned the leader of a Ku Klux Klan group who invited a newsman and photographer to film a Klan rally. Parts of the film were subsequently broadcast both locally and nationally. These showed several armed men burning a wooden cross. They also showed Brandenburg giving a speech in which he said that "if our President, our Congress, our Supreme Court, continues to suppress the white Caucasian race, it's possible that there might have to be some revengance [sic] taken." As a result of the film, Brandenburg was convicted of violating Ohio's criminal syndicalism act.

The Supreme Court reversed the conviction in an unsigned opinion. It observed that the *Brandenburg* case was similar to *Whitney.* Both had assembled with others in a group that advocated unlawful means to change the political order. Although the court sustained Whitney's conviction in 1927,

> . . . later decisions have fashioned the principle that the constitutional guarantees of free speech and free press do not permit a State to forbid or proscribe advocacy of the use of force or of law violation except where such advocacy is directed to inciting or producing imminent lawless action and is likely to incite or produce such action. . . . Measured by this test, Ohio's Criminal Syndicalism Act cannot be sustained. [33]

The court thus also specifically overturned its *Whitney* ruling.

Public Speech and Public Safety

More prevalent than speech that threatens national security is public speech that is perceived to jeopardize community order. The Supreme Court's role here has been much the same as its role in the national security cases — to find the balance among the right of an individual to make a public speech, the right of his listeners to assemble to hear that speech, and the obligation of the state to maintain public order, safety and tranquillity.

If the incident involves only verbal or symbolic expression, the balance tips in favor of the right to speak. Government may place no restraint on or punish such speech unless it threatens or actually harms public safety, the court has held.

However, because the court examines the individual circumstances of each case, the point at which speech becomes an incitement or a threat to the welfare of the community has varied considerably from case to case. In both its national security and public safety decisions involving the right of free speech, the court has been unable to devise an acceptable general standard for measuring the point at which First Amendment protection must give way to government restriction on speech.

While government may not place any prior restraints on speech, the court has ruled that it may regulate the time, place and manner of speech that is likely to interfere with other rightful uses of public property. This is especially true of speech that is combined with potentially disruptive conduct such as parading or demonstrating.

But the court has insisted that such regulations be precisely drawn to restrict speech only as much as is necessary and that they be applied and enforced in a non-discriminatory manner.

Permits, Peace and Prior Restraint

Until the Supreme Court construed the First Amendment to apply to the states, it conceded to municipalities absolute authority to regulate and even prohibit speech on public property. In 1897 the court sustained the validity of a Boston ordinance prohibiting public speeches on Boston Common without a permit from the mayor. The Supreme Court endorsed the holding of the Massachusetts Supreme Court, which, in an opinion written by Oliver Wendell Holmes Jr., declared that a legislature:

> . . .as representative of the public . . . may and does exercise control over the use which the public may make of such places. . . . For the legislature absolutely or constitutionally to forbid public speaking in a highway or public park is no more an infringement of the rights of a member of the public than for the owner of a private house to forbid it in his house.[34]

Fighting Words: Insult to Injury

"Fighting words," words that are so insulting as to provoke violence from the person they are addressed to, are generally unprotected by the First Amendment guarantee of free speech.

The Supreme Court first made this point in the 1942 case of *Chaplinsky v. New Hampshire.* Chaplinsky, a Jehovah's Witness, provoked a public disturbance when he publicly assailed another religion as "a racket," and called a police officer "a God damned racketeer" and "a damned Fascist." He was convicted of violating a state statute making it a crime to call another person "offensive and derisive names" in public.

The Supreme Court sustained the conviction, upholding the statute against a challenge that it violated the guarantee of free speech. "[R]esort to epithets or to personal abuse is not in any proper sense communication of information or opinion safeguarded by the Constitution . . .," the unanimous court wrote. It then said:

> Allowing the broadest scope to the language and purpose of the . . . Amendment, it is well understood that the right of free speech is not absolute at all times and under all circumstances. There are certain well-defined and narrowly limited classes of speech, the prevention and punishment of which has never been thought to raise any Constitutional problem. These include the lewd and obscene, the profane, the libelous, and the insulting or "fighting" words — those which by their very utterance inflict injury or tend to incite an immediate breach of the peace. It has been well observed that such utterances are no essential part of any exposition of ideas, and are of such slight social value as a step to truth that any benefit that may be derived from them is clearly outweighed by the social interest in order and morality. [1]

But the court in *Chaplinsky* was willing to uphold the statute only because the state court had narrowly construed its language to apply to fighting words and no other speech.

The Supreme Court has continued to insist that statutes setting penalties for fighting words be narrowly drawn and strictly interpreted. Thus, in 1972, the court affirmed the reversal of a conviction under a Georgia law of a man who had called a police officer a "son of a bitch" and threatened the officer with physical abuse. The Supreme Court concluded that the state court's interpretation of the statute was too broad, making it applicable to protected speech as well as to fighting words. [2]

Profanity

In 1971, the court ruled that a state may not punish as a criminal offense the public display of an offensive word, when the word is used as an expression of legitimate protest and the display does not result in a breach of the peace.

In protest of the Vietnam War, Paul Cohen wore into a Los Angeles courthouse a jacket inscribed with the slogan "Fuck the Draft." He was arrested and convicted under a state breach of the peace law making "offensive conduct" a crime.

Writing for the majority in *Cohen v. California* (1971), Justice John Marshall Harlan described the offending slogan not as conduct but as speech expressing a political viewpoint. Such expression is entitled to First Amendment protection, Harlan said, unless it provoked or intended to provoke a breach of the peace, of which there was no evidence in this case.

The state could not properly prohibit public display of the offending expletive, Harlan continued. For if a state had the power to outlaw public use of one word, he wrote, it could outlaw the use of other words and such action would run "a substantial risk of suppressing ideas in the process. Indeed, governments might soon seize upon the censorship of particular words as a convenient guise for banning the expression of unpopular views."[3]

The court later held that the Federal Communications Commission could regulate the times at which radio and television may broadcast offensive words.[4] *(Details, p. 446)*

---

[1] *Chaplinsky v. New Hampshire,* 315 U.S. 568 at 571, 572 (1942).

[2] *Gooding v. Wilson,* 405 U.S. 518 (1972); see also *Lewis v. City of New Orleans,* 415 U.S. 130 (1974).

[3] *Cohen v. California,* 403 U.S. 15 at 26 (1971).

[4] *Federal Communications Commission v. Pacifica Foundation,* 438 U.S. 726 (1978).

Some 40 years passed before the court was obliged to rule again on this question. By that time, it had decided that the First Amendment acted as a bar against state infringement of free speech. In line with that view, the court was beginning to give special scrutiny to cases claiming that government was abridging free speech.

The case of *Hague v. C.I.O.* (1939) arose out of Jersey City, N.J., Mayor Frank Hague's opposition to attempts to organize workers in the city into closed-shop unions.

To discourage these organizing efforts, Hague harassed members of the Committee for Industrial Organization (C.I.O.), searching them when they entered the city, arresting them for distributing union literature and forcibly throwing some of them out of the city. He also refused to grant any member of the union the permit required by city ordinance before a public speech could be made on public property. The C.I.O. brought suit to stop Hague from enforcing this statute.

The Supreme Court granted the injunction against continued enforcement of the ordinance. Writing for two members of the majority, Justice Owen J. Roberts said that the right to speak and assemble in public was a privilege and immunity of national citizenship that states and cities could not abridge:

> Wherever the title of streets and parks may rest, they have immemorially been held in trust for the use of the public and, time out of mind, have been used for purposes of assembly, communicating thoughts between citizens, and discussing public questions. Such

use of the streets and public places has, from ancient times, been a part of the privileges, immunities, rights and liberties of citizens. The privilege of a citizen of the United States to use the streets and parks for communication of views on national questions may be regulated in the interest of all; it is not absolute, but relative, and must be exercised in subordination to the general comfort and convenience, and in consonance with peace and good order; but it must not, in the guise of regulation, be abridged or denied. [35]

In a concurring opinion, Justices Harlan Fiske Stone and Stanley F. Reed viewed the rights of free speech and assembly as included not in the privileges and immunities clause of the 14th Amendment but in that amendment's prohibition against state deprivation of personal liberty without due process of law. Under the due process guarantee these rights were secured to all persons in the United States and not just to citizens. This broader view was eventually accepted by a majority of the court's members.

In the *Hague* case, Roberts indicated that states and cities might regulate certain aspects of public speaking. In a 1941 decision, the court elaborated on this, holding that the time, manner and place of public speeches or other forms of expression could be regulated so long as the regulation was precisely and narrowly drawn and applied neutrally to all speakers and demonstrators. [36] *(Details, Cox v. New Hampshire, p. 413)*

Disturbing the Peace

Having established in the *Hague* case the right of individuals to communicate ideas in public places, the court was quickly faced with the question whether the First Amendment protected speech that sparked a breach of the peace.

Speech to Passersby. The first case raising this issue concerned a Jehovah's Witness named Jesse Cantwell. Seeking converts to his faith in New Haven, Conn., in 1938, Cantwell stopped two men on a sidewalk and asked if he could play a phonograph record for them. They agreed, and he played "Enemies," which attacked organized religion in general and Catholicism in particular. The two men, both Catholics, were offended and told Cantwell to go away. There was no violence or other disturbance. Nonetheless, Cantwell was convicted of inciting others to a breach of the peace.

The Supreme Court reversed the conviction in *Cantwell v. Connecticut* (1940), finding the ordinance making breach of the peace a crime too vague as applied to Cantwell:

The offense known as breach of the peace embraces a great variety of conduct destroying or menacing public order and tranquility. It includes not only violent acts but acts and words likely to produce violence in others. No one would have the hardihood to suggest that the principle of freedom of speech sanctions incitement to riot or that religious liberty connotes the privilege to exhort others to physical attack upon those belonging to another sect. When clear and present danger of riot, disorder, interference with traffic upon the public streets, or other immediate threat to public safety, peace or order, appears, the power of the State to prevent or punish is obvious. Equally obvious is it that a State may not unduly suppress free communication of views, religious or other, under the guise of conserving desirable conditions. Here we have

a situation analogous to a conviction under a statute sweeping in a great variety of conduct under a general and indefinite characterization, and leaving to the executive and judicial branches too wide a discretion in its application. [37]

Looking at the facts of the situation, the court said it found "no assault or threatening of bodily harm, no truculent bearing, no intentional discourtesy, no personal abuse." Absent a statute narrowly drawn to define and punish the conduct Cantwell engaged in, his conduct, the court said, "raised no such clear and present menace to public peace and order as to render him liable" under the general breach of the peace statute. [38]

Near Riot. The next breach-of-the-peace case raised the question to what extent the First Amendment protected speech which provoked a near-riot.

Terminiello was a defrocked Catholic priest who in 1946 spoke at a private meeting in Chicago sponsored by the Christian Veterans of America. In his speech Terminiello virulently attacked Jews, blacks and the Roosevelt administration but did not urge his 800 listeners to take any specific action.

While he spoke, some 1,000 protestors gathered outside the hall, shouting, throwing rocks through windows and trying to break into the meeting. The police restrained the mob with difficulty. As a result of the disturbance Terminiello was arrested for and convicted of disorderly conduct under an ordinance which made it illegal for anyone to aid in a "breach of the peace or a diversion tending to a breach of the peace."

By a 5-4 vote, the Supreme Court reversed Terminiello's conviction without reaching the constitutional issues involved. Instead, the majority held that the trial judge had improperly instructed the jury when he defined a breach of the peace as speech that "stirs the public to anger, invites dispute, brings about a condition of unrest, or creates a disturbance." Some parts of this instruction, the majority felt, would punish speech protected by the First Amendment, and since it was not apparent under which part the jury had convicted Terminiello, the conviction must fall.

Justice William O. Douglas explained the majority position in *Terminiello v. Chicago* (1949):

. . . [A] function of free speech under our system of government is to invite dispute. It may indeed best serve its high purpose when it induces a condition of unrest, creates dissatisfaction with conditions as they are, or even stirs people to anger. Speech is often provocative and challenging. It may strike at prejudices and preconceptions and have profound unsettling effects as it presses for acceptance of an idea. That is why freedom of speech, though not absolute, . . . is nevertheless protected against censorship or punishment, unless shown likely to produce a clear and present danger of a serious substantive evil that rises far above public inconvenience, annoyance or unrest. . . . There is no room under our Constitution for a more restrictive view. For the alternative would lead to standardization of ideas either by legislatures, courts, or dominant political or community groups. [39]

Chief Justice Fred M. Vinson dissented, contending that Terminiello's speech consisted of "fighting words" that are outside the protection of the First Amendment. *(Fighting words, box, p. 407)*

Loud Sounds and Free Speech

Does a city impermissibly interfere with freedom of speech by regulating the use of loudspeakers and other amplification devices? This question has come to the Supreme Court twice, and its decisions have left the answer in some confusion.

The case of *Saia v. New York* (1948) brought before the court a Lockport, N.Y., ordinance that prohibited the use of sound equipment without permission from the chief of police. Samuel Saia, a Jehovah's Witness, obtained a permit to amplify religious lectures he gave in a public park. Because some people complained — apparently about the noise rather than the content of the lecture — Saia's permit was not renewed. He spoke with the loudspeaker anyway and was arrested and convicted of violating the ordinance. He countered that the ordinance violated his right to free speech.

Noise and Sound

By a 5-4 decision, the Supreme Court struck down the ordinance because it set no standards to guide the police chief in granting or denying permits. Writing for the majority, Justice William O. Douglas explained:

> The present ordinance would be a dangerous weapon if it were allowed to get a hold on our public life. Noise can be regulated by regulating decibels [rather than by barring loudspeakers]. The hours and place of public discussion can be controlled. . . . Any abuses which loud-speakers create can be controlled by narrowly drawn statutes. When a city allows an official to ban them in his uncontrolled discretion, it sanctions a device for suppression of free communication of ideas. [1]

In dissent, Justice Felix Frankfurter insisted that a city has a right to regulate the use of sound amplification to protect the privacy of other users of the park. "Surely there is not a constitutional right to force unwilling people to listen," he said. [2] In a separate dissent, Justice Robert H. Jackson drew a distinction between speech and amplification of speech. Regulating amplification, even prohibiting it altogether, in no way interfered with the freedom of speech itself, he said.

The following year, the four dissenters in *Saia* and Chief Justice Fred M. Vinson made up a new majority that sustained a Trenton, N.J., ordinance prohibiting the use on all public streets of any sound equipment that emitted "loud and raucous noise."

This language might have been interpreted as barring all use of sound equipment in city streets, but, a three-justice plurality in *Kovacs v. Cooper* (1949), for whom Justice Stanley F. Reed spoke, distinguished between "loud and raucous noise" and other sounds which might come from amplifying systems.

Reed agreed that "[a]bsolute prohibition within municipal limits of all sound amplification, even though reasonably regulated in place, time and volume is undesirable and probably unconstitutional as an unreasonable interference with normal activities." But regulation of noise was permissible. The ordinance, Reed said, in no way restricts "communication of ideas or discussion of issues by the human voice, by newspapers, by pamphlets. . . ." [3]

Frankfurter and Jackson wrote separate concurring opinions. Justice Hugo L. Black in dissent disagreed with Reed's interpretation of the ordinance, contending that it in fact prohibited all sound amplification. This repudiation of *Saia*, he wrote, was "a dangerous and unjustifiable breach in the constitutional barriers designed to insure freedom of expression." [4]

Sound and Streetcars

In a third sound amplification case, the court majority held that individuals do not have an absolute right to privacy in public places. A private transit company in the District of Columbia piped music, occasionally interspersed with commercials into its streetcars. Despite a challenge from passengers that the practice violated their right to privacy, the programming was approved by the local public utilities commission.

The Supreme Court held that courts had no authority to interfere with such a decision by the commission so long as it was arrived at through proper procedures. Since the commission had done this, the court sustained its approval of the programming.

Justice Douglas dissented, calling the programming "a form of coercion to make people listen." [5]

---

[1] *Saia v. New York*, 334 U.S. 558 at 562 (1948).
[2] Id. at 563.
[3] *Kovacs v. Cooper*, 336 U.S. 77 at 81-82, 89 (1949).
[4] Id. at 101-102.
[5] *Public Utilities Commission of the District of Columbia v. Pollak*, 343 U.S. 451 at 468 (1952).

In a separate dissent joined by Justices Felix Frankfurter and Harold H. Burton, Justice Robert H. Jackson maintained that Terminiello's speech created a "clear and present danger" that a riot would ensue and that the authorities were entitled to act to preserve the public peace "at least so long as danger to public order is not invoked in bad faith, as a cover for censorship or suppression." In conclusion, Jackson wrote:

> . . . The choice [for the courts] is not between order and liberty. It is between liberty with order and anarchy without either. There is danger that, if the court does not temper its doctrinaire logic with a little practical wisdom, it will convert the constitutional Bill of Rights into a suicide pact. [40]

Street Meeting. Two years later the Supreme Court drew closer to Jackson's position when it affirmed the breach of the peace conviction of a student whose streetcorner speech seemed much less threatening to public order than Terminiello's.

The different conclusions in these two cases illustrate the difficulty the court has had in settling on a general standard by which to determine when speech oversteps the bounds of First Amendment protection and becomes subject to punishment. *(Box on general standards, pp. 392-93)*

Irving Feiner spoke at an open-air meeting in Syracuse, N.Y., inviting listeners to attend a meeting that evening of the Progressive Party. In the course of his speech, Feiner made insulting remarks about President Truman, the American Legion and the mayor of Syracuse. He also urged blacks to fight for equal rights. Someone complained to the police, who sent two officers to investigate. The crowd was restless and some passersby were jostled and forced into the street. Finally one listener told the officers that if they did not stop Feiner, he would. The police then asked Feiner to stop speaking. When he refused they arrested him for breach of the peace.

The six justices voting to sustain the conviction in *Feiner v. New York* (1951) found that the police had acted not to suppress speech but to preserve public order. Chief Justice Vinson wrote:

> We are well aware that the ordinary murmurings and objections of a hostile audience cannot be allowed to silence a speaker, and are also mindful of the possible danger of giving overzealous police officials complete discretion to break up otherwise lawful public meetings. . . . But we are not faced here with such a situation. It is one thing to say that the police cannot be used as an instrument for the oppression of unpopular views, and another to say that, when as here the speaker passes the bounds of argument or persuasion and undertakes incitement to riot, they are powerless to prevent a breach of the peace. [41]

In dissent, Justice Hugo L. Black said that the majority's decision in effect made the police censors of public speech. Instead, the duty of the police should be to protect the speaker in the exercise of his First Amendment rights, even if that necessitates the arrest of those who would interfere, he said. Justices Douglas and Sherman Minton also dissented.

Prior Restraint

In contrast with its difficulty in defining the point at which speech incites breaches of the peace and therefore loses its First Amendment protection, the court has steadfastly rejected state efforts to place prior restraints on speech.

In 1931 the court held that an injunction against continued publication of a newspaper was an unconstitutional prior restraint of the press. [42] In 1940 it held that a statute which permitted city officials to determine what was a religious cause and what was not amounted to an unconstitutional restraint on the free exercise of religion. [43] But not until 1945 did the court overturn a state statute as an improper prior restraint on speech.

Union Organizer. The case of *Thomas v. Collins* arose after Thomas, a union organizer, refused to apply for the organizer's permit required by Texas law. The state issued an injunction to stop Thomas from soliciting for union members. He made a speech advocating union membership anyway and was convicted of contempt. He appealed to the Supreme Court, which overturned his contempt conviction by a 5-4 vote.

Elaborating on the reasoning behind the court's earlier permit decisions, Justice Wiley B. Rutledge said it was clear that the injunction against soliciting restrained Thomas' right to speak and the rights of the workers to

assemble to hear him. The statute prohibiting solicitation without a permit was so imprecise that it in essence forbid "any language which conveys, or reasonably could be found to convey, the meaning of invitation," Rutledge said. "How one might 'laud unionism,' as the State and the State Supreme Court concede Thomas was free to do, yet in these circumstances not imply an invitation, is hard to conceive," he said. [44]

Consequently the law operated in this case to require Thomas to register in order to make a public speech. This was incompatible with the guarantees of the First Amendment, Rutledge said:

> If the exercise of the rights of free speech and assembly cannot be made a crime, we do not think this can be accomplished by the device of requiring previous registration as a condition for exercising them and making such a condition the foundation for restraining in advance their exercise. [45]

The dissenters would have affirmed Thomas' conviction. Justice Roberts contended that the contempt conviction was based not on Thomas' speech but on his explicit solicitation of workers to join the union in violation of the order not to solicit without a permit. The dissenters thought the registration requirement was well within the powers of the state to regulate business transactions.

Street Speaker. A solid majority of the court struck down as an unconstitutional prior restraint a permit system as applied to a specific speaker in the case of *Kunz v. New York*, decided the same day in 1951 as the *Feiner* case.

New York City had an ordinance that barred worship services on public streets without a permit. Kunz, an ordained Baptist minister, had been granted a permit for one year but his application for renewal was rejected because his vituperative denunciations of Catholics and Jews had created public disturbances. When Kunz spoke without the permit, he was convicted and fined $10. He appealed his conviction to the Supreme Court, which overturned it by an 8-1 vote.

Writing for the majority, Chief Justice Vinson rejected as too arbitrary the New York court's rationale that the permit had been revoked "for good reasons." He said:

> . . . We have here . . . an ordinance which gives an administrative official discretionary power to control in advance the right of citizens to speak on religious matters on the streets of New York. As such, the ordinance is clearly invalid as a prior restraint on the exercise of First Amendment rights. [46]

In lone dissent, Justice Jackson contended that Kunz' speeches were filled with "fighting words," the kind of verbal abuses and insults which were likely to incite violent response and which city officials were entitled to restrain.

"The question . . . is not whether New York could, if it tried, silence Kunz, but whether it must place its streets at his service to hurl insults at the passer-by," Jackson said. [47]

Symbolic Speech

Symbolic speech, the expression of ideas and beliefs through symbols rather than words, has generally been held to be protected under the First Amendment. Recent examples of symbolic speech are the burning of draft cards to protest the Vietnam War and the burning of bras to proclaim women's liberation.

Red Flags

The Supreme Court first dealt with the issue of symbolic speech in 1931 when it found California's "red flag" law unconstitutional. The statute made it a crime to raise a red flag as a symbol of opposition to organized government, or as "an invitation . . . to anarchistic action, or as an aid to propaganda that is of a seditious character." A state jury convicted Yetta Stromberg of raising a reproduction of the Soviet flag every morning at a children's summer camp, but it did not say under which part of the law it convicted her.

The Supreme Court held that the first clause of the statute was an unconstitutional restriction of free speech because conceivably the flying of any banner symbolizing advocacy of a change in government through peaceful means could be penalized. Such punishment would violate the right of free speech. Because it was possible that the jury had believed Stromberg guilty of violating only this clause of the law, its unconstitutionality rendered her conviction a denial of due process. Chief Justice Charles Evans Hughes wrote:

> The maintenance of the opportunity for free political discussion to the end that government may be responsive to the will of the people and that changes may be obtained by lawful means, an opportunity essential to the security of the Republic, is a fundamental principle of our constitutional system. A statute which upon its face, and as authoritatively construed, is so vague and indefinite as to permit the punishment of the fair use of this opportunity is repugnant to the guaranty of liberty contained in the Fourteenth Amendment. [48]

Saluting the Flag

The fullest exposition of symbolism as a form of communication protected by the First Amendment came in the court's decision in the second wartime "flag salute" case. There the court ruled that states could not compel school children to pledge allegiance to the American flag. *(Details, p. 457)*

Writing for the majority in *West Virginia State Board of Education v. Barnette* (1943), Justice Robert H. Jackson said:

> There is no doubt that, in connection with the pledges, the flag salute is a form of utterance. Symbolism is a primitive but effective way of communicating ideas. The use of an emblem or flag to symbolize some system, idea, institution, or personality, is a short cut from mind to mind. Causes and nations, political parties, lodges and ecclesiastical groups seek to knit the loyalty of their followings to a flag or banner, a color or design. The State announces rank, function, and authority through crowns and maces, uniforms and black robes, the church speaks through the Cross, the Crucifix, the altar and shrine, and clerical raiment. Symbols of State often convey political ideas just as religious symbols come to convey theological ones. Associated with many of these symbols are appropriate gestures of acceptance or respect: a salute, a bowed or bared head, a bended knee. A person gets from a symbol the meaning he puts into it, and what is one man's comfort and inspiration is another's jest and scorn. [49]

Right to Remain Silent

The First Amendment guarantees individuals the right to speak freely. The Supreme Court has also held that this guarantee includes a right to remain silent. In other words, the state may not coerce or compel a person to state a position or belief that he does not voluntarily endorse.

Among the most dramatic examples of this right are the two 1940 cases arising from the refusal of children of Jehovah's Witnesses to salute the American flag in school. In their view, pledging allegiance to the flag violated their religious belief that they should not worship graven images.

The first time the court considered this matter it held that the flag salute requirement did not violate religious freedom, but three years later the court reversed itself to rule that compulsory flag salutes did abridge the freedom guaranteed by the First Amendment for speech and religious belief. [1] *(Details of cases, p. 457)*

More recently, the court held that the individual's First Amendment freedom included the right to refuse to carry a state-required ideological message on his car license plates.

George Maynard was convicted of a misdemeanor for obscuring the motto on his New Hampshire license plate, which read "Live Free or Die." Affirming a lower court's reversal of Maynard's conviction, the Supreme Court said, "[T]he right of freedom of thought protected by the First Amendment against state action includes both the right to speak freely and the right to refrain from speaking at all." [2]

---

[1] *Minersville School District v. Gobitis*, 310 U.S. 586 (1940), overruled by *West Virginia State Board of Education v. Barnette*, 319 U.S. 624 (1943).
[2] *Wooley v. Maynard*, 430 U.S. 705 at 714 (1977).

The First Amendment, Jackson said, no more permitted a state to compel allegiance to a symbol of the organized government than it permitted the state to punish someone who used a symbol to express peaceful opposition to organized government.

Sit-In Demonstrations

Another form of symbolic speech reviewed by the Supreme Court was the student sit-in of the early 1960s. To protest racial discrimination in public accommodations, blacks requested service at "whites only" lunch counters, and remained there quietly until ejected or arrested.

At least one justice believed that these sit-ins were a form of expression guaranteed constitutional protection under some circumstances. In a concurring opinion in *Garner v. Louisiana* (1961), Justice John Marshall Harlan wrote that a sit-in was:

> . . . as much a part of the "free trade in ideas" . . . as is verbal expression, more commonly thought of as "speech." It, like speech, appeals to good sense and to "the power of reason as applied through public discussion" . . . just as much, if not more than, a public oration delivered from a soapbox at a street corner. This Court has never limited the right to speak . . . to mere verbal expression. [50]

But the court in this and other sit-in cases avoided answering the question whether the First and Fourteenth Amendments protected the protestors from conviction for trespassing on private property. [51]

Anti-War Protests

The unpopularity of the Vietnam War generated several symbolic speech cases. In *United States v. O'Brien* (1968), the Supreme Court refused to view draft card burning, an expression of protest to the war and the draft, as symbolic speech protected by the First Amendment. "We cannot accept the view that an apparently limitless variety of conduct can be labeled 'speech' whenever the person engaging in the conduct intends thereby to express an idea," the majority said. Even if that view were adopted, the majority continued, the First Amendment would not protect draft card burning:

> This Court has held that when "speech" and "nonspeech" elements are combined in the same course of conduct, a sufficiently important governmental interest in regulating the nonspeech element can justify incidental limitations on First Amendment freedoms. [52]

Here, the majority said, Congress had a substantial interest in maintaining the draft registration system as part of its duty to raise and maintain armies.

In 1969, however, the Supreme Court ruled that school officials improperly suspended students for wearing black armbands in symbolic protest of the Indochina War. The officials said they based the suspensions on their fear that the armbands might create a disturbance among the students. However, the majority wrote in *Tinker v. Des Moines School District,*

> ... undifferentiated fear or apprehension of disturbance is not enough to overcome the right to freedom of expression.... In order for the State in the person of school officials to justify prohibition of a particular expression of opinion, it must be able to show that its action was caused by something more than a mere desire to avoid the discomfort and unpleasantness that always accompany an unpopular viewpoint. [53]

Street Theater. In yet another form of protest against the Vietnam War, an actor wore an army uniform while he and others performed a protest play on a sidewalk outside an army induction center in Houston. The play depicted U.S. soldiers killing Vietnamese women and children. The actor was arrested and convicted of violating a federal law which made it a crime to wear an official military uniform in a theatrical production that was unfavorable to the armed forces.

The Supreme Court unanimously overturned the conviction in *Schacht v. United States* (1970), concluding that the wearing of the uniform was part of the actor's speech. "An actor, like everyone else in our country enjoys a constitutional right to freedom of speech, including the right openly to criticize the Government during a dramatic performance," the court said. [54]

Protest and the Flag

The Supreme Court in three modern cases reversed convictions of persons who used the American flag to symbolize opposition to government policy and the course of public events. In two of these, the court avoided the question whether such symbolism constituted expression protected by the First Amendment.

Street v. New York (1968) concerned a man who protested the shooting of civil rights activist James Meredith by publicly burning a flag while declaring: "If they did that to Meredith, we don't need an American flag."

He was convicted under a New York law which made it illegal to mutilate a flag or to cast contempt upon it either by words or conduct. Overturning the conviction, the Supreme Court said the statute as applied to Street was too broad because it permitted the punishment of his words, which were protected by the First and Fourteenth Amendments. [55]

In the second case, the court overturned the conviction of a man who wore a small flag on the seat of his pants. In *Smith v. Goguen* (1974), the court said the Massachusetts statute, which made contemptuous treatment of the flag a crime, was unconstitutionally vague because it "fails to draw reasonably clear lines between the kinds of non-ceremonial treatment [of the flag] that are criminal and those that are not." [56]

In the third case, the Supreme Court reached the constitutional issue. *Spence v. Washington* (1974) arose when a student flew a flag, on which he had superimposed a peace symbol, upside down from his apartment window. The student was protesting the recent U.S. invasion of Cambodia and the shooting of four Kent State University student protestors. He was arrested and convicted for violating a Washington statute prohibiting defacement of the flag.

In a *per curiam* opinion, the court majority overturned the conviction, holding that the student's conduct was a form of symbolic speech protected under the First Amendment. The majority wrote:

> ... [T]here can be little doubt that appellant communicated through the use of symbols.... [This communication] was a pointed expression of anguish by appellant about the then-current domestic and foreign affairs of his government. An intent to convey a particularized message was present, and in the surrounding circumstances the likelihood was great that the message would be understood by those who viewed it. [57]

Since the communication was protected by the First Amendment, the majority continued, the state could punish the communication only if it clashed with some substantial state interest. But there was no evidence that the flag caused a breach of the peace, and the possibility that some passersby might be offended by the message was not sufficient to warrant restraint of speech.

For a three-justice minority, Justice William H. Rehnquist contended that the state had a valid interest in "preserving the character of the flag." He said the statute did not infringe on the right of free expression but "simply withdraws a unique national symbol from the roster of materials that may be used as a background for communications." [58]

The Freedom of Assembly

The right to assemble peaceably was first recognized by the Supreme Court as one of the privileges and immunities of national citizenship. Writing in the 1876 case of *United States v. Cruikshank,* the court said:

The right of the people peaceably to assemble for the purpose of petitioning Congress for a redress of grievances, or for any thing else connected with the powers or the duties of the national government, is an attribute of national citizenship, and, as such, under the protection of, and guaranteed by, the United States. The very idea of a government, republican in form, implies a right on the part of its citizens to meet peaceably for consultation in respect to public affairs and to petition for a redress of grievances. [59]

The court did not again address the issue of the right of assembly until the 1937 case of *DeJonge v. Oregon*. Then a majority of the court recognized, first, that the right of assembly was on an equal status with the rights of free speech and free press, and, second, that it was applicable to the states through the due process clause of the 14th Amendment.

As a result of this First Amendment protection, the court said that "peaceable assembly for lawful discussion cannot be made a crime."[60] *(Details, DeJonge case, p. 405)*

Two years later in the case of *Hague v. C.I.O.* a plurality of three justices again held that the right of peaceable assembly was protected by the privileges and immunities clause of the 14th Amendment. But two other justices found this right included in the "liberty" guaran-

---

. . .[P]eaceable assembly for lawful discussion cannot be made a crime."

Chief Justice Charles Evans Hughes
DeJonge v. Oregon, 1937

---

teed by the 14th Amendment due process clause. It is this broader view that has prevailed.[61] *(Details, Hague case, p. 407)*

Parades and Demonstrations

The right peacefully to parade or demonstrate to make known a group's views or to support or oppose an issue of public policy is based on the twin guarantees of the rights of free speech and free assembly.

But because parading and demonstrating involves conduct that might interfere with the ability of other members of the public to use the same public places, they have always been considered subject to greater regulation than exercises of pure speech and assembly.

To preserve the freedoms of speech and assembly, the Supreme Court has insisted that parade and demonstration regulations be precisely worded and applied in non-discriminatory fashion. To preserve the public welfare, the court has held that not all public places are appropriate sites for public protests.

Time, Place and Manner

The basic precedent for the court's rulings on parades and demonstrations was the 1941 case of *Cox v. New Hampshire*. Cox was one of 68 Jehovah's Witnesses convicted of violating a statute prohibiting parading without a permit. He challenged the statute as an improper infringe-

---

The Right of Petition

The First Amendment right "to petition the Government for a redress of grievances" had its origins in the Magna Carta and the development of the English parliamentary system. One of the earliest exercises of the right in the United States occurred in the 1830s when Congress received scores of petitions seeking abolition of slavery in the District of Columbia. The right of petition was later invoked by the unemployed petitioners of Coxey's army of 1894, the bonus marchers in 1932 and participants in the Poor People's Campaign of 1968.

Petitioners are not restricted to seeking redress of grievances only from Congress. They may petition administrative agencies and, of course, the courts. Application of the First Amendment to the states through the due process clause of the 14th Amendment has also ensured citizens the right to make their views known to state governments.

Nor is petition of government limited solely to seeking a redress of grievances. Individuals, citizen groups and corporations all lobby government in efforts to persuade it to adopt policies that will benefit their particular interests. The only significant Supreme Court decisions on the right of petition have come in the lobbying area, and they are of limited scope. In its major decision, the court upheld the authority of Congress to require certain lobbyists to register. *(United States v. Harriss, 1954; details, lobby regulation, p. 174)*

---

ment on his rights of free speech and assembly, but the Supreme Court rejected his argument in a unanimous decision. As construed and applied, the court said, the ordinance did not allow denial of permits because the views of the paraders might be unpopular; the ordinance was intended only to ensure that paraders would not unduly interfere with others using the streets. Chief Justice Charles Evans Hughes explained:

> If a municipality has authority to control the use of its public streets for parades and processions, as it undoubtedly has, it cannot be denied authority to give consideration, without unfair discrimination, to time, place and manner in relation to the other proper uses of the streets. [62]

Civil Rights Protests

Cases arising out of the civil rights movement of the late 1950s and 1960s gave the court the opportunity to explore more fully the extent of First Amendment protection for peaceable demonstrations and protests.

In a series of cases arising out of non-violent demonstrations in southern states, the Supreme Court ruled that peaceful protests conducted according to valid regulations on public property designated for general use were protected by the First Amendment. But peaceful protests on public property reserved for specific purposes might not be protected.

Breach of Peace. The first case in this series arose in Columbia, S.C., where in early 1961 some 180 black high school and college students marched to the state capitol grounds to protest discrimination. Between 200 and 300 people gathered to watch the peaceful demonstration.

The Court and Civil Disobedience

Is a person ever justified in ignoring a law restricting First Amendment freedoms and proceeding to speak or meet in defiance of the law? As with most free speech questions the Supreme Court has answered both yes and no — depending on the circumstances.

Disobedience Permitted

A person may disobey the law if it is obviously unconstitutional as it is written. In a long line of cases that includes *Cantwell v. Connecticut* (1940), *Kunz v. New York* (1951) and *Niemotko v. Maryland* (1951), the court has reversed convictions of persons who spoke or met without a permit, finding that the statute requiring the permit was unconstitutional. *(Details, Cantwell, p. 419, Kunz, p. 410, Niemotko, p. 454)*

The Supreme Court fully stated this rule in *Shuttlesworth v. City of Birmingham* (1969).

The Rev. Fred L. Shuttlesworth was convicted for violating a Birmingham, Ala., ordinance that made it an offense to participate in a public demonstration without a permit. Because the ordinance gave city officials complete discretion to determine to whom they would grant permits, the court held that the ordinance was unconstitutional. For the unanimous court, Justice Potter Stewart wrote that the ordinance

> . . . fell squarely within the ambit of the many decisions of this Court over the last 30 years, holding that a law subjecting the exercise of First Amendment freedoms to the prior restraint of a license, without narrow, objective, and definite standards to guide the licensing authority, is unconstitutional. . . . And our decisions have made clear that a person faced with such an unconstitutional licensing law may ignore it, and engage with impunity in the exercise of the right of free expression for which the law purports to require a license. [1]

Defiance Disapproved

But the court has held that a person may not violate with impunity a law restricting First Amendment rights if that law is valid but was simply applied to him improperly. In *Poulos v. New Hampshire* (1953), the defendant was arbitrarily denied a permit to conduct a religious meeting. He went ahead with the meeting, and when arrested for defying the ordinance, claimed it would have taken too long to appeal the improper denial through legal channels.

The court sustained the conviction, stating:

> It must be admitted that judicial correction of arbitrary refusal by administrators to perform official duties under valid laws is exulcerating and costly. But to allow applicants to proceed without the required permits to run businesses, erect structures, purchase firearms, . . . hold public meetings

without prior safety arrangements or take other unauthorized action is apt to cause breaches of the peace or cause public dangers. The valid requirements of license are for the good of the applicants and the public. It would be unreal to say that such official failures to act in accordance with state law, redressable by state judicial procedures, are state acts violative of the Federal Constitution. Delay is unfortunate, but the expense and annoyance of litigation is a price citizens must pay for life in an orderly society where the rights of the First Amendment have a real and abiding meaning. [2]

Injunction Defied

Nor may a person defy with impunity an injunction issued to restrain a meeting or demonstration, even if the injunction may be invalid. This situation arose in the controversial case of *Walker v. City of Birmingham* (1967).

In 1963 the Southern Christian Leadership Conference under the guidance of Dr. Martin Luther King Jr. sponsored a number of demonstrations in Birmingham protesting racial discrimination.

City officials, clearly unsympathetic to the cause of the demonstrators, refused to issue them the required parade permits. Many of the demonstrators paraded anyhow, and after several days a state court on April 10 issued an injunction ordering King and his supporters to stop parading without a permit. With no hope of being granted a permit and no time to fight the injunction in court, the black civil rights activists went ahead with planned demonstrations on Good Friday, April 12, and Easter, April 14. King and seven others were later arrested and convicted of contempt of court.

The Supreme Court upheld the convictions by a 5-4 vote. The majority acknowledged that the parade permit ordinance might be unconstitutional on its face. But it held that the demonstrators should have obeyed the injunction while they could challenge its validity in *(See contempt discussion, p. 279)*

Justice Stewart wrote for the majority, quoting the court's opinion in a similar case decided early in the 20th century:

> An injunction duly issuing out of a court of general jurisdiction with equity powers, upon pleadings properly invoking its action, and served upon persons made parties therein and within the jurisdiction, must be obeyed by them, however erroneous the action of the court may be. . . . [3]

The four dissenters in three separate opinions argued that the ordinance and the *ex parte* injunction enforcing it were clearly invalid and that the protestors had the right to continue unpenalized in the exercise of their First Amendment freedoms.

[1] *Shuttlesworth v. City of Birmingham*, 394 U.S. 147 at 150-51 (1969).
[2] *Poulos v. New Hampshire*, 345 U.S. 395 at 409 (1953).
[3] *Walker v. City of Birmingham*, 388 U.S. 307 at 314 (1967) quoting *Howat v. State of Kansas*, 258 U.S. 181 at 189-190 (1922); see also *Carroll v. President and Commissioners of Princess Anne*, 393 U.S. 175 (1968).

Although there was no threat of violence or other disturbance, the police grew concerned that trouble might flare up and so ordered the demonstrators to disperse within 15 minutes. The students refused, continuing to listen to speeches by their leader and to sing. The police arrested the students, who were subsequently convicted of breach of the peace.

The Supreme Court overturned the convictions in *Edwards v. South Carolina* (1963). [63] The court accepted the state courts' finding that the students' conduct constituted a breach of the peace under state law. But the justices held that the state law was unconstitutionally broad because it penalized the exercise of free speech, assembly and petition for redress of grievances "in their most pristine and classic form." Justice Potter Stewart wrote for the court:

> . . . These petitioners were convicted of an offense so generalized as to be, in the words of the South Carolina Supreme Court, "not susceptible of exact definition." And they were convicted upon evidence which showed no more than that the opinions which they were peaceably expressing were sufficiently opposed to the views of the majority of the community to attract a crowd and necessitate police protection. [64]

Recalling that the majority in *Terminiello v. Chicago* (1949) had held provocative and unsettling speech to be constitutionally protected, Stewart declared that "the Fourteenth Amendment does not permit a State to make criminal the peaceful expression of unpopular views." [65]

In lone dissent, Justice Tom C. Clark would have upheld the convictions on the grounds that the police had made a good faith effort to preserve the peace and did not intend to suppress speech.

Similar circumstances attended the arrest and conviction of the Rev. B. Elton Cox for breach of the peace in Baton Rouge, La. In 1961 Cox led some 2,000 black college students in a two-and-one-half block march from the state capitol to a courthouse where 23 other students were in jail for their attempts to integrate white lunch counters.

Prior to the march, police officials asked Cox to abandon the demonstration, but he refused. The march was orderly. Once at the courthouse, Cox and the students complied with police instructions to stay on the sidewalk on one side of the street. Between 100 and 300 white onlookers watched the students wave picket signs and sing patriotic and religious songs. Cox then made a speech explaining the reasons for the demonstration. At its conclusion, he observed that it was lunchtime and urged the marchers to seek service at white lunch counters.

At this point the sheriff ordered the demonstrators to disperse immediately. Soon after that the police fired a tear gas cannister into the crowd and the demonstrators left the courthouse area without further incident.

The following day Cox was arrested and subsequently convicted of disturbing the peace. By a 7-2 vote, the Supreme Court set aside the conviction in *Cox v. Louisiana* (1965). As in *Edwards,* the majority found Louisiana's breach of the peace statute unconstitutionally broad in scope because it penalized persons who were lawfully exercising their rights of free speech, assembly and petition.[66]

Courthouse Picketing. In a second case arising from the same set of circumstances, the court by a 5-4 vote overturned Cox' conviction for violating a Louisiana statute prohibiting picketing or parading "in or near" a courthouse. [67]

The court sustained the validity of the statute. The state had a substantial interest in adopting safeguards to preserve the administration of justice from outside influence and control, the majority said, and the statute was precisely drawn so that it did not restrict the rights of free speech and assembly but instead regulated conduct which, though entwined with speech and assembly, was not constitutionally protected.

But the court also held that the term "near" was so vague that it was not unreasonable for Cox to rely on the interpretation of the police as to how close they might come to the courthouse. By specifically confining the demonstration to a particular segment of the sidewalk, the police had in effect given permission for the demonstration to take place at that particular place. Thus the statute had been applied improperly to convict Cox.

Library Protest. The following year a majority of the court overturned convictions for breach of the peace brought against five black men who staged a peaceful and orderly protest against racial segregation by refusing to leave a library reserved for white use.

A five-justice majority held this demonstration to be constitutionally protected in the case of *Brown v. Louisiana* (1966). The First Amendment freedoms "embrace appropriate types of action which certainly include the right in a peaceable and orderly manner to protest by silent and reproachful presence, in a place where the protestant has every right to be, the unconstitutional segregation of public facilities," the majority wrote. [68]

In dissent, Justice Black maintained that the First Amendment did not "guarantee to any person the right to use someone else's property, even that owned by the government and dedicated to other purposes, as a stage to express dissident ideas." [69]

Jailhouse Demonstration. Black's views won the adherence of a majority in a case decided later in 1966. *Adderly v. Florida* arose after blacks demonstrated at a county jail to protest the arrests of several students who had tried to integrate a public but segregated theater. The demonstrators were convicted of criminal trespass.

Writing the opinion for the five-justice majority, Black acknowledged that the jail, like the capitol grounds in *Edwards,* was public property but there the similarities ended. "Traditionally, state capitol grounds are open to the public. Jails, built for security purposes, are not," he said. Black continued:

> . . . The State, no less than a private owner of property, has power to preserve the property under its control for the use to which it is lawfully dedicated. For this reason there is no merit to the [demonstrators'] argument that they had a constitutional right to stay on the property over the jail custodian's objections, because this "area chosen for the peaceful civil rights demonstration was not only 'reasonable' but also particularly appropriate. . . ." Such an argument has as its major unarticulated premise the assumption that people who want to propagandize protests or views have a constitutional right to do so whenever and however and wherever they please. That concept of constitutional law was vigorously and forthrightly rejected in [previous cases]. . . . We reject it again. [70]

For the four dissenters, Justice William O. Douglas said the majority was effectively negating the *Edwards* and *Cox* precedents. Douglas wrote:

Public Speech on Private Property . . .

The First Amendment prohibits only government action abridging the freedom of speech. Most First Amendment cases thus involve situations in which speech occurs or is abridged in a public forum or on public property.

Some private property is dedicated to public use, however, and there the question arises whether the property owner becomes subject to the First Amendment prohibition. If that is so, then a private owner may place no more restrictions on exercises of the First Amendment on his property than a government may place on free speech spoken on municipally held property.

The Company Town

The court first confronted this issue in the 1946 case of *Marsh v. Alabama.* Chickasaw, Ala., a suburb of Mobile, was wholly owned by a private corporation. A Jehovah's Witness, Grace Marsh, passed out handbills on a Chickasaw street in violation of a regulation forbidding such distribution. She challenged her subsequent arrest and conviction, claiming that her First Amendment rights had been infringed.

A majority of the Supreme Court agreed. Save for its private ownership, wrote Justice Hugo L. Black, Chickasaw had all the characteristics of any other American town. And its residents had the same interest as residents of municipally owned towns in keeping channels of communication open. "There is no more reason for depriving these people of the liberties guaranteed by the First and Fourteenth Amendments than there is for curtailing these freedoms with respect to any other citizens," Black said. [1]

Picketing and Private Malls - I

In 1968 the court relied on *Marsh v. Alabama* when it forbade the owner of a private shopping mall to prohibit union picketing of a store in the mall. A non-union supermarket in a privately owned mall near Altoona, Pa., was picketed by members of a food employees union who wished to point out that the supermarket did not employ union workers or abide by union pay and working condi-

tion requirements. The owners of the store and the shopping center won an injunction forbidding picketing in the mall and its private parking lots.

By a 6-3 vote, the Supreme Court declared the injunction invalid in *Amalgamated Food Employees Union Local 590 v. Logan Valley Plaza* (1968). Noting the similarities between the shopping center and the business district in the company town involved in *Marsh,* Justice Thurgood Marshall observed that the general public had unrestricted access to the mall and that it served as the functional equivalent of a town business district. These circumstances, the majority said, rendered the mall public for purposes of the First Amendment, and consequently its owners could not invoke state trespass laws to prohibit picketing that advanced the communication of ideas. Marshall noted the narrowness of the ruling:

> . . .All we decide here is that because the shopping center serves as the community business block "and is freely accessible and open to the people in the area and those passing through" . . . the State may not delegate the power, through the use of its trespass laws, wholly to exclude those members of the public wishing to exercise their First Amendment rights on the premises in a manner and for a purpose generally consonant with the use to which the property is actually put. [2]

Justice Black dissented, contending that the majority erred in its reliance on *Marsh* as a precedent. *Marsh* held that the First Amendment applied when the private property had taken on *all* of the aspects of a town, he said, adding that:

> . . .I can find nothing in *Marsh* which indicates that if one of these features is present, e.g., a business district, this is sufficient for the Court to confiscate a part of an owner's private property and give its use to people who want to picket on it. [3]

Handbill Protests in Shopping Centers

Within four years a majority of the court qualified the

The jailhouse, like an executive mansion, a legislative chamber, a courthouse, or the statehouse itself . . . is one of the seats of government, whether it be the Tower of London, the Bastille, or a small county jail. And when it houses political prisoners or those who many think are unjustly held, it is an obvious center for protest. . . . Conventional methods of petitioning may be, and often have been, shut off to large groups of our citizens. . . . Those who do not control television and radio, those who cannot afford to advertise in newspapers or circulate elaborate pamphlets may have only a more limited type of access to public officials. Their methods should not be condemned as tactics of obstruction and harassment as long as the assembly and petition are peaceable, as these were. [71]

Residential Area. In 1969 the court upheld the right of peaceful demonstrators to parade in a residential neighborhood, on the public sidewalks near Chicago Mayor Richard

Daley's home to urge desegregation of Chicago public schools. White residents grew threatening and, to ward off potential violence, police asked the marchers to disperse. They refused and were arrested. Five were convicted of disorderly conduct.

In a unanimous decision in *Gregory v. City of Chicago* the Supreme Court overturned the convictions. Because there was no evidence that the marchers' conduct had been disorderly the court said the convictions violated due process. The court also said that the "march, if peaceful and orderly, falls well within the sphere of conduct protected by the First Amendment." [72]

Labor Picketing

The question of how much protection the First Amendment affords labor picketing has deeply troubled the Supreme Court. Picketing clearly conveys a message to the

. . . The First Amendment Restricted

ruling in *Logan Valley Plaza,* holding that owners of a private shopping mall could prohibit the distribution of leaflets unrelated to business conducted in the mall.

The circumstances in *Lloyd Corporation, Ltd. v. Tanner* (1972) were similar to those in *Marsh* with one major difference. The Lloyd Center was not a company town but a privately owned and operated shopping mall that prohibited the circulation of handbills. Inside the mall, several people attempted to distribute handbills inviting the general public to attend a meeting to protest the Vietnam War. When asked to desist, they did, but then brought suit charging they had been denied their right to free speech.

By a 5-4 vote the Supreme Court rejected the charge. Writing for the majority, Justice Lewis F. Powell Jr. held that although the shopping mall served the public it still maintained its private character:

> . . .The invitation is to come to the Center to do business with the tenants. . . . There is no open-ended invitation to the public to use the Center for any and all purposes, however incompatible with the interests of both the stores and the shoppers whom they serve. . . . This Court has never held that a trespasser or an uninvited guest may exercise general rights of free speech on property privately owned and used nondiscriminatorily for private purposes only. [4]

Writing for the dissenters, Justice Marshall saw nothing to distinguish this case from the court's holdings in *Marsh* and *Logan Valley Plaza.*

Picketing and Private Malls - II

Four years later, the court moved a step closer to divesting speech on private property used for specific public purposes of any First Amendment protection. But

a majority of the court still refused to overturn the *Logan Valley Plaza* decision, leaving the issue in some confusion.

Hudgens v. National Labor Relations Board (1976) arose after striking employees of a shoe company warehouse decided also to picket the company's retail stores. One of these was situated in a shopping mall whose owners threatened to have the pickets arrested for trespassing if they did not desist. The pickets withdrew but challenged the owners' threat as an unfair labor practice under the National Labor Relations Act.

Before answering that question, the Supreme Court majority felt it necessary to determine whether the picketing was entitled to any First Amendment protection. A majority concluded it was not. Three of the members of the majority held that the *Lloyd* decision had in effect overruled the *Logan Valley Plaza* decision and that, consequently, uninvited speech on private property was not protected. The three other justices comprising the majority did not believe that the *Logan Valley Plaza* decision had been overruled. But they distinguished between the pickets in that case who conveyed information about the operation of a store actually located in the mall and the pickets in *Hudgens* who tried to convey information about a warehouse located away from the mall.

Justices Marshall and William J. Brennan Jr. dissented. Marshall insisted that when an owner of a private shopping mall invited the public onto his property to conduct business he gave up a degree of privacy to the interests of the public. One of those public interests was "communicating with one another on subjects relating to businesses that occupy" the shopping center. "As far as these groups are concerned," said Marshall, "the shopping center owner has assumed the traditional role of the state in its control of historical First Amendment forums." [5]

---

[1] *Marsh v. Alabama,* 326 U.S. 501 at 508-9 (1946); see also *Tucker v. Texas,* 326 U.S. 517 (1946).

[2] *Amalgamated Food Employees Union Local 590 v. Logan Valley Plaza,* 391 U.S. 308 at 319-20 (1968).

[3] Id. at 332.

[4] *Lloyd Corporation, Ltd. v. Tanner,* 407 U.S. 551 at 564-65, 568 (1972).

[5] *Hudgens v. National Labor Relations Board,* 424 U.S. 507 at 543 (1967).

---

public about the issues in labor disputes and is therefore a form of expression. But unlike most other sorts of parades and demonstrations, picketing also uses economic pressure and coercion to bring about better working conditions and, as conduct, is regulable by government.

Permissible Pickets

Initially courts considered all labor picketing illegal.

As labor unions grew in power and acceptability, that view began to change. In a 1921 decision the Supreme Court permitted a union to post one picket at each entrance and exit of a factory for the purpose of explaining a union grievance against the employer. Although the First Amendment issue of free speech was not directly raised in this case, the court acknowledged that "[w]e are a social people and the accosting by one of another in an inoffensive way and an offer by one to communicate and discuss information with a view to influence the other's action are not

regarded as aggression or a violation of the other's rights." [73]

In a 1937 decision, the court moved closer to the First Amendment question. In *Senn v. Tile Layers Union,* it upheld a Wisconsin statute permitting peaceful picketing against a challenge that such picketing constituted a "taking" of the employer's property without due process of law guaranteed by the Fourteenth Amendment. "Clearly, the means which the state authorizes — picketing and publicity — are not prohibited by the Fourteenth Amendment. Members of a union might . . . make known the facts of a labor dispute, for freedom of speech is guaranteed by the Federal Constitution," Justice Louis D. Brandeis wrote for a slim majority. [74]

Full Protection

Three years later, in 1940 a substantial majority of the court drew industrial picketing under the protective wing of the First Amendment. In *Thornhill v. Alabama* (1940) Byron Thornhill appealed his conviction under an Alabama law which forbade picketing. He argued that the statute violated his rights of free speech, assembly and petition for redress of grievances.

Speaking through Justice Frank Murphy, eight justices held the anti-picketing statute to be invalid. "In the circumstances of our times the dissemination of information concerning the facts of a labor dispute must be regarded as within that area of free discussion that is guaranteed by the Constitution," Murphy wrote. [75]

That the picketing might result in some degree of economic coercion did not divest it of its First Amendment protection. Murphy explained:

> . . .It may be that effective exercise of the means of advancing public knowledge may persuade some of those reached to refrain from entering into advantageous relations with the business establishment which is the scene of the dispute. Every expression of opinion on matters that are important has the potentiality of inducing action in the interests of one rather than another group in society. But the group in power at any moment may not impose penal sanctions on peaceful and truthful discussion of matters of public interest merely on a showing that others may thereby be persuaded to take action inconsistent with its interests.[76]

The following year the court in *AFL v. Swing* (1941) relied on *Thornhill* to hold that the First Amendment guarantee of free speech was infringed by a state policy limiting picketing to cases where union members had a dispute with their employer, forbidding organizational picketing by unions hoping to persuade non-union workers to join. [77]

Prior Restraint of Violence

But in another case decided the same day as *AFL v. Swing,* a majority of the court indicated that the First Amendment did not foreclose prior restraint of picketing in the interest of public safety. By a 6-3 vote, the majority upheld an injunction forbidding a union of milk wagon drivers to engage in picketing because their past picketing had resulted in violence. Justice Felix Frankfurter wrote the opinion for the majority in *Milk Wagon Drivers Union v. Meadowmoor Dairies Inc.* (1941).

"Peaceful picketing is the workingman's means of communication," said Frankfurter, but the First Amendment does not protect "utterance in a context of violence" that becomes "part of an instrument of force." Under the circumstances of the case, he continued, "it could justifiably be concluded that the momentum of fear generated by past violence would survive even though future picketing might be wholly peaceful." [78]

Three dissenters contended that the injunction as it applied to future peaceful picketing by the union was too broad.

Third-Party Picketing

In 1942 the court delivered somewhat conflicting decisions on the permissibility of picketing of persons not directly involved in a labor dispute. The conclusion of the two holdings seemed to be that a third party to a labor dispute could be picketed only if the union had no other means to make its views on the dispute effectively known.

In the case of *Bakery and Pastry Drivers v. Wohl* the court lifted an injunction against a union of bakery truck drivers who had picketed bakeries and groceries using non-union drivers in order to induce the non-union drivers to give some of their work to union drivers. The court majority observed that the mobility and "middle-man" status of the non-union drivers separated them from the public. Therefore picketing those who did business with them was "the only way to make views, admittedly accurate and peaceful, known." [79]

But in a second case decided the same day, the court sustained an injunction against a carpenters union, forbidding it to picket a cafe owned by a man whose nearby house was being built by a non-union contractor. The five-justice majority noted that the union's real complaint was with the contractor and that the injunction permitted picketing against his other business enterprises. "As a means of communication of the facts of a labor dispute, peaceful picketing may be a phase of the constitutional right of free utterance," the majority wrote. "But recognition of peaceful picketing as an exercise of free speech does not imply that the state must be without power to confine the sphere of communication to that directly related to the dispute," it concluded in *Carpenters and Joiners Union v. Ritter's Cafe* (1942).[80]

In both these cases the majority recognized that industrial picketing, in Justice William O. Douglas' words,

> . . .is more than free speech, since it involves patrol of a particular locality and since the very presence of a picket line may induce action of one kind or another, quite irrespective of the nature of the ideas which are being disseminated. Hence those aspects of picketing make it the subject of restrictive regulation. [81]

Illegal Conduct

The court moved another step away from *Thornhill* in 1949. Picketing as "conduct" may in some circumstances be so intertwined with illegal labor practices that states may prohibit it, held a unanimous court in *Giboney v. Empire Storage and Ice Co.*

A Missouri court issued an injunction against a union of ice drivers who had picketed an ice company in order to persuade the company to refuse to sell ice to non-union drivers. Other unions had observed the picket line, and the company's sales fell by 85 percent. If the company had entered into the proposed union agreement, however, it would have thus violated Missouri's restraint of trade law.

The union contended that because its picketing publicized the facts about the labor dispute it was therefore entitled to First Amendment protection. The Supreme Court rejected this thesis. In an opinion written by Justice Hugo L. Black, the court found that the picketing was an integral part of conduct which violated a valid state law and was therefore not protected by the First Amendment. Black wrote: "It has never been deemed an abridgement of freedom of speech or press to make a course of conduct illegal merely because the conduct was in part initiated, evidenced or carried out by means of language." [82]

State Regulation

In a series of cases beginning with *Giboney* and continuing with three decisions in 1950, the court effectively reversed *Thornhill,* making clear that the expressive aspects of picketing did not protect it from state regulation and prohibition. If the purpose of the picketing could be construed as contrary to state statute or policy, the court would hold a state-imposed injunction valid.

The first of the 1950 cases blended the aspects of industrial picketing and civil rights demonstrations. In *Hughes v. Superior Court of California,* the court upheld an injunction forbidding picketing by blacks trying to force a grocer to hire a certain percentage of black employees. Although no state law prohibited racial hiring quotas, the California judge who issued the injunction held the picketing inimical to the state's policy of supporting nondiscrimination. Upholding this judgment, the court through Justice Frankfurter stated:

> . . .It has been amply recognized that picketing, not being the equivalent of speech as a matter of fact, is not its inevitable legal equivalent. Picketing is not beyond the control of a State if the manner in which picketing is conducted or the purpose which it seeks to effectuate gives ground for its disallowance. [83]

In two other cases decided the same day, the court upheld injunctions against picketing aimed at forcing an employer to pressure his employees to choose the picketing union as their bargaining representative, and against picketing to compel a family business with no employees to operate by union standards. [84]

In the 1953 case of *Local Plumbers Union #10 v. Graham* the court again held that the speech aspects of picketing did not protect it from regulation. The union claimed that the picketing simply announced to the public that the picketed employer hired non-union workers, but the Supreme Court found that the major purpose of the picketing was to force the employer to replace his non-union employees with union workers, action which would violate the state's "right-to-work" law. [85]

In 1957 the court upheld an injunction against unions engaged in organizational picketing of a non-union gravel pit. Such picketing violated a state law making it an unfair labor practice for anyone to force an employer "to interfere with any of his employees in the enjoyment of their legal rights."

Writing for the majority in *International Brotherhood of Teamsters, Local 695 v. Vogt,* Justice Frankfurter reviewed the line of cases decided by the court since the *Thornhill* finding that picketing was protected by the First Amendment.

Thornhill was still valid, Frankfurter said, because "[s]tate courts, no more than state legislatures, can enact blanket prohibitions against picketing." But, he added, the cases decided since then had

> . . .established a broad field in which a state, in enforcing some public policy, whether of its criminal or its civil law, and whether announced by its legislature or its courts, could constitutionally enjoin peaceful picketing aimed at preventing effectuation of that policy. [86]

For the three dissenters, Justice Douglas said that the majority had completely abandoned *Thornhill.* Douglas urged the court to return to the proposition that the First Amendment protects from state restriction all picketing that is not violent or a part of illegal conduct:

> . . .[W]here, as here, there is no rioting, no mass picketing, no violence, no disorder, no fisticuffs, no

coercion — indeed nothing but speech, the principles announced in *Thornhill* . . . should give the advocacy of one side of a dispute First Amendment protection. [87]

In 1968 the court held that the First Amendment forbade a state to delegate to the owner of a shopping mall the power to restrict labor picketing of a store in the mall. But the continuing validity of this decision has since been called into question, and the decision in the *Vogt* case stands as the court's position on labor picketing's relation to the First Amendment.[88] *(See box, pp. 416-417)*

Soliciting and Canvassing

Door-to-door non-commercial solicitation of a neighborhood by persons seeking financial and moral support for their particular religious, political or civic cause squarely sets the freedoms of speech, press and religion against the right of privacy in one's home. Must the right to disseminate ideas give way to privacy or does privacy yield to the uninvited dissemination of ideas?

Professor Zechariah Chafee argued that privacy may be the value more worthy of preservation:

> . . .Of all the methods of spreading unpopular ideas . . . [solicitation] seems the least entitled to extensive [First Amendment] protection. The possibilities of persuasion are slight compared with the certainties of annoyance. Great as is the value of exposing citizens to novel views, home is one place where a man ought to be able to shut himself up in his own ideas if he desires. [89]

But the Supreme Court has generally held in solicitation cases that freedom of ideas takes precedence over privacy. To protect their citizens from annoyance, governments may regulate the time and manner of solicitation, and to protect the public from fraud or crime, governments may require solicitors to identify themselves. But such regulations must be narrowly drawn and precisely defined to avoid infringing First Amendment rights.

One of the first solicitation ordinances to fall under Supreme Court scrutiny was a Connecticut statute that prohibited solicitation of money or services without the approval of the secretary of the local public welfare office. The secretary had the discretion to determine if the solicitation was in behalf of a *bona fide* religion or charitable cause.

The Supreme Court struck down the statute, in *Cantwell v. Connecticut* (1940):

> . . .Without doubt a State may protect its citizens from fraudulent solicitation by requiring a stranger in the community, before permitting him publicly to solicit funds for any purpose, to establish his identity and his authority to act for the cause which he purports to represent. The State is likewise free to regulate the time and manner of solicitation generally, in the interest of public safety, peace, comfort or convenience. But to condition the solicitation of aid for the perpetuation of religious views or systems upon a license, the grant of which rests in the exercise of a determination by state authority as to what is a religious cause, is to lay a forbidden burden upon the exercise of liberty protected by the Constitution. [90]

Although continuing to uphold the authority of a town to require solicitors to meet identification requirements, the

Financing Political Speech

When Congress or state legislatures place limits on the amounts individuals, corporations and unions may contribute to candidates or political campaigns and on the amounts candidates may spend, they are restricting the right of free speech.

In three early cases the Supreme Court avoided the question whether the Federal Corrupt Practices Act unconstitutionally restricted free speech by prohibiting any corporation or labor union from making a contribution to or expenditures on behalf of any candidate for federal office. [1]

Then, in the 1976 case of *Buckley v. Valeo* challenging the constitutionality of the Federal Election Campaign Act of 1974, the court upheld the law's limits on campaign contributions but struck down, as violating free speech, limits on campaign spending. [2] *(Details, p. 172)*

In 1978 the court also called into question the validity of the Corrupt Practices Act prohibition on corporate contributions when it struck down, 5-4, a Massachusetts law which forbade corporations to spend money to influence voters' decisions on referendum issues.

The state law offended the First Amendment guarantee of freedom of speech, wrote Justice Lewis F. Powell Jr. for the majority in *First National Bank of Boston v. Bellotti:*

> ...If the speakers here were not corporations, no one would suggest that the State could silence their proposed speech. It is the type of speech indispensable to decisionmaking in a democracy, and this is no less true because the speech comes from a corporation rather than an individual. The inherent worth of the speech in terms of its capacity for informing the public does not depend upon the identity of the source, whether corporation, association, union or individual. [3]

Powell was careful to distinguish the holding in this case from other portions of the state law which forbid corporate contributions to political candidates. "The risk of corruption perceived in cases involving candidate elections ... simply is not present in a vote on a public issue," Powell said. [4]

For three of the dissenters, Justice Byron R. White warned against the threat of corporate domination of political discussion and electoral processes. Corporate expression and individual expression are not interchangeable values, White contended. "Ideas which are not a product of individual choice are entitled to less First Amendment protection," he said. [5]

Justice William H. Rehnquist dissented for a different reason, citing his view of the "limited application of the First Amendment to the States." [6]

---

[1] *United States v. CIO,* 335 U.S. 106 (1948); *United States v. United Auto Workers,* 352 U.S. 567 (1957); *Pipefitters v. United States,* 407 U.S. 385 (1972).
[2] *Buckley v. Valeo,* 424 U.S. 1 (1976).
[3] *First National Bank of Boston v. Bellotti,* 435 U.S. 765 at 777 (1978).
[4] Id. at 790.   [5] Id. at 807.   [6] Id. at 823.

court in 1976 ruled a New Jersey town ordinance too vague to meet First Amendment standards. The ordinance did not adequately specify what solicitors it covered nor what those covered must do to be in compliance, the court said in *Hynes v. Oradell.* [91]

Membership Solicitation

The 1945 case of *Thomas v. Collins* brought to the court a First Amendment challenge to a Texas law that required all labor union organizers to register with the state before soliciting union members there.

To test the statute, union organizer R. J. Thomas announced that he would solicit members without registering. A Texas court issued an order restraining Thomas from addressing an organizing rally without the proper credentials, but he defied the order and was subsequently convicted of contempt. Thomas challenged the registration requirement as violating his right of free speech.

The Supreme Court agreed, holding that the First Amendment clearly protected a speech made to solicit persons for membership in a lawful organization:

> That there was restriction upon Thomas' right to speak and the right of the workers to hear what he had to say, there can be no doubt. The threat of the restraining order, backed by the power of contempt, and of arrest for crime, hung over every word.... We think a requirement that one must register before he undertakes to make a public speech to enlist support for a lawful movement is quite incompatible with the requirements of the First Amendment. [92]

Doorbells

In 1943 the court in the case of *Martin v. Struthers* struck down a Struthers, Ohio, ordinance which prohibited all distributors of handbills or other advertisements from knocking on doors or ringing bells to ensure that residents would receive the flyer.

Ignoring this ordinance, a Jehovah's Witness distributed a flyer, which advertised a religious meeting, in a neighborhood where many of the residents were night workers and consequently slept in the daytime. He was arrested and defended himself with the claim that the ordinance was unconstitutional.

The court agreed, by a 5-4 vote. "While door to door distributors of literature may be either a nuisance or a blind for criminal activities, they may also be useful members of society engaged in dissemination of ideas...," wrote Justice Hugo L. Black for the majority. He enumerated a number of causes that depended on door-to-door solicitation for their success, observing that this form of dissemination of ideas "is essential to the poorly financed causes of little people." [93] The First Amendment prohibited the community from substituting its judgment for that of an individual in determining whether the individual may receive information, Black said.

In dissent, Stanley F. Reed maintained that the ordinance did not violate any First Amendment right but simply respected a homeowner's privacy:

> ...No ideas are being suppressed. No censorship is involved. The freedom to teach or preach by word or book is unabridged, save only the right to call a householder to the door of his house to receive the summoner's message. [94]

Commercial Speech

Initially, the Supreme Court held that commercial speech — advertising — was unprotected by the First Amendment and therefore subject to regulation and even prohibition by the states. But in a series of decisions in the 1970s, the court has changed its mind. Finding that commercial speech provides information to which the consuming public has a right, the court has struck down state and local prohibitions of certain advertisements. The court continued to emphasize, however, that commercial advertising is subject to regulation to prevent false, deceptive and misleading information and to specify the time, place and manner of publication and distribution.

Unprotected Speech

Commercial speech was first discussed by the court in *Schneider v. Irvington* (1939), in which it ruled that the First Amendment prohibited a city from requiring a person soliciting for religious causes to first obtain permission from city officials. However, the court cautioned, "[w]e are not to be taken as holding that commercial solicitation and canvassing may not be subjected to such regulation as the ordinance [concerned in this case] requires." [95]

Schneider was followed by the court's unanimous opinion in *Valentine v. Chrestensen* (1942), the case which became the early precedent on commercial speech. Here the court held that the First Amendment did not protect commercial hand bills even if one side of a handbill contained a statement protesting an ordinance prohibiting the circulation of commercial handbills:

> This court has unequivocally held that the streets are proper places for the exercise of the freedom of communicating information and disseminating opinion and that, though the states and municipalities may appropriately regulate the privilege in the public interest, they may not unduly burden or proscribe its employment in these public thoroughfares. We are equally clear that the Constitution imposes no such restraint on government as respects purely commercial advertising. Whether, and to what extent, one may promote or pursue a gainful occupation in the streets, to what extent such activity shall be adjudged a derogation of the public right of the user, are matters for legislative judgment. [96]

In a 1951 case, salesmen of nationally-known magazines claimed that freedom of the press was infringed by ordinances prohibiting door-to-door solicitation for subscriptions without prior consent of the homeowners. The court rejected the claim. "We agree that the fact that periodicals are sold does not put them beyond the protection of the First Amendment. The selling, however, brings into the transaction a commercial feature," the court wrote. [97]

Communication of Information

This commercial feature was enough to allow states to bar door-to-door solicitation, but it was not enough to deprive a paid political advertisement of all First Amendment protection. In the landmark libel case of *New York Times v. Sullivan* (1964), the court held that an advertisement seeking support for the civil rights movement

> . . .was not a commercial advertisement in the sense in which the word was used in *Chrestensen*. It communi-

cated information, expressed opinion, recited grievances, protested claimed abuses, and sought financial support on behalf of a movement whose existence and objectives are matters of the highest public interest. . . . That the Times was paid for publishing this advertisement is as immaterial in this connection as is the fact that newspapers and books are sold. . . . Any other conclusion would discourage newspapers from carrying 'editorial advertisements' of this type. . . . [98]

This reasoning in the *Times* case was implemented in 1975 when the court held that Virginia violated the First Amendment when it punished a local newspaper editor for printing an advertisement concerning the availability of legal abortions in New York. The advertisement did more than propose a commercial transaction, the court said in *Bigelow v. Virginia*. It also conveyed information not only to women who might be interested in seeking an abortion but to people interested in the general issue of whether abortions should be legalized. [99]

The Consumer's Right

The following year, in *Virginia State Board of Pharmacy v. Virginia Citizens Consumer Council, Inc.*, the court majority abandoned its distinction between advertising which publicly conveyed important information and thereby merited some First Amendment protection and that which did not.

Agreeing with a lower court that Virginia could not constitutionally forbid pharmacists to advertise the prices of prescription drugs, the court wrote:

> Advertising, however tasteless and excessive it sometimes may seem, is nonetheless dissemination of information as to who is producing and selling what product, for what reason, and at what price. So long as we preserve a predominantly free enterprise economy, the allocation of our resources in large measure will be made through numerous private economic decisions. It is a matter of public interest that those decisions, in the aggregate, be intelligent and well informed. To this end, the free flow of commercial information is indispensable. . . . And if it is indispensable to the proper allocation of resources in a free enterprise system, it is also indispensable to the formation of intelligent opinions as to how that system ought to be regulated or altered. Therefore, even if the First Amendment were thought to be primarily an instrument to enlighten public decisionmaking in a democracy, we could not say that the free flow of information does not serve that goal. [100]

In subsequent cases the court used this reasoning to rule that a state could not prohibit advertisement of contraceptives, advertisement of prices for routine legal services or the posting of "For Sale" and "Sold" signs in private yards. [101] Using traditional First Amendment tests, the court found that the right of the public to the commercial information outweighed any interest the government had in suppressing that information.

In a fourth case, however, the court held that the First Amendment was not violated by a state bar's disciplinary action against an attorney who solicited clients in person, for pecuniary gain, under circumstances which posed dangers of fraud, undue influence and intimidation — all of which was conduct the court thought the state had a right to prevent. [102]

Footnotes

[1] C. Herman Pritchett, *The American Constitution*, 3d ed. (New York: McGraw-Hill Book Co., 1977), p. 314.

[2] Ibid., p. 317.

[3] *Schenck v. United States*, 249 U.S. 47 at 51 (1919).

[4] Id. at 52.

[5] Ibid.

[6] Ibid.

[7] *Frohwerk v. United States*, 249 U.S. 204 at 208-9 (1919).

[8] *Debs v. United States*, 249 U.S. 211 at 215 (1919).

[9] Id. at 216.

[10] *Abrams v. United States*, 250 U.S. 616 at 623 (1919).

[11] Id. at 627, 628.

[12] *Schaefer v. United States*, 251 U.S. 466 at 481 (1920).

[13] Id. at 478.

[14] Id. at 479.

[15] Id. at 486.

[16] Id. at 493-95.

[17] *Pierce v. United States*, 252 U.S. 239 at 249 (1929).

[18] Id. at 269.

[19] Id. at 273; the three minor decisions in this series were: *Sugarman v. United States*, 249 U.S. 182 (1919); *Stilson v. United States*, 250 U.S. 583 (1919); *O'Connell v. United States*, 253 U.S. 142 (1920).

[20] *Hartzel v. United States*, 322 U.S. 680 (1944).

[21] *Gitlow v. New York*, 268 U.S. 652 at 665 (1925).

[22] Id. at 667.

[23] Id. at 669.

[24] Id. at 673.

[25] *Whitney v. California*, 274 U.S. 357 at 371-72 (1927).

[26] Id. at 373.

[27] Id. at 376, 378.

[28] *Fiske v. Kansas*, 274 U.S. 380 (1927).

[29] *DeJonge v. Oregon*, 299 U.S. 353 at 365 (1937).

[30] *Herndon v. Lowry*, 301 U.S. 242 at 258 (1937).

[31] Id. at 263-64.

[32] Id. at 276.

[33] *Brandenburg v. Ohio*, 395 U.S. 444 at 447-48 (1969).

[34] *Davis v. Massachusetts*, 167 U.S. 43 at 47 (1897).

[35] *Hague v. C.I.O.*, 307 U.S. 496 at 515-16 (1939).

[36] *Cox v. New Hampshire*, 312 U.S. 569 (1941).

[37] *Cantwell v. Connecticut*, 310 U.S. 296 at 308 (1940).

[38] Id. at 310, 311.

[39] *Terminiello v. Chicago*, 337 U.S. 1 at 4-5 (1949).

[40] Id. at 37.

[41] *Feiner v. New York*, 340 U.S. 315 at 320-21 (1951).

[42] *Near v. Minnesota*, 283 U.S. 697 (1931).

[43] *Cantwell v. Connecticut*, 310 U.S. 296 (1940).

[44] *Thomas v. Collins*, 323 U.S. 516 at 534-35 (1945).

[45] Id. at 540.

[46] *Kunz v. New York*, 340 U.S. 290 at 293 (1951).

[47] Id. at 298.

[48] *Stromberg v. California*, 283 U.S. 359 at 369 (1931).

[49] *West Virginia State Board of Education v. Barnette*, 319 U.S. 624 at 632-33 (1943).

[50] *Garner v. Louisiana*, 368 U.S. 157 (1961).

[51] See, for example, *Peterson v. City of Greenville*, 373 U.S. 244 (1963); *Shuttlesworth v. City of Birmingham*, 373 U.S. 262 (1963); *Lombard v. Louisiana*, 373 U.S. 267 (1963); *Gober v. City of Birmingham*, 373 U.S. 374 (1963); *Avent v. North Carolina*, 373 U.S. 375 (1963).

[52] *United States v. O'Brien*, 391 U.S. 367 at 376 (1968).

[53] *Tinker v. Des Moines School District*, 393 U.S. 503 at 508-9 (1969).

[54] *Schacht v. United States*, 398 U.S. 58 at 63 (1970).

[55] *Street v. New York*, 394 U.S. 576 (1969).

[56] *Smith v. Goguen*, 415 U.S. 566 at 574 (1974).

[57] *Spence v. Washington*, 418 U.S. 405 at 410-11 (1974).

[58] Id. at 423.

[59] *United States v. Cruikshank*, 92 U.S. 542 at 552 (1876).

[60] *DeJonge v. Oregon*, 299 U.S. 353 at 365 (1937).

[61] *Hague v. C.I.O.*, 307 U.S. 496 (1939).

[62] *Cox v. New Hampshire*, 312 U.S. 569 at 576 (1941).

[63] *Edwards v. South Carolina*, 372 U.S. 229 (1963); see also *Fields v. South Carolina*, 375 U.S. 44 (1963); *Cameron v. Johnson*, 390 U.S. 611 (1968).

[64] *Edwards v. South Carolina*, 372 U.S. 229 at 235, 237 (1963).

[65] Id. at 237; *Terminiello v. Chicago*, 337 U.S. 1 (1949).

[66] *Cox v. Louisiana*, 379 U.S. 536 (1965).

[67] *Cox v. Louisiana*, 379 U.S. 559 (1965).

[68] *Brown v. Louisiana*, 383 U.S. 131 at 142 (1966).

[69] Id. at 166.

[70] *Adderly v. Florida*, 385 U.S. 39 at 41, 47-48 (1966).

[71] Id. at 49-51.

[72] *Gregory v. City of Chicago*, 394 U.S. 111 at 112 (1969).

[73] *American Steel Foundries v. Tri-City Central Trades Council*, 257 U.S. 184 at 204 (1921).

[74] *Senn v. Tile Layers Union*, 301 U.S. 468 at 478 (1937).

[75] *Thornhill v. Alabama*, 310 U.S. 88 at 102 (1940).

[76] Id. at 104; see also *Carlson v. California*, 310 U.S. 106 (1940).

[77] *AFL v. Swing*, 312 U.S. 321 (1941).

[78] *Milk Wagon Drivers Union v. Meadowmoor Dairies, Inc.*, 312 U.S. 287 at 293, 294 (1941).

[79] *Bakery and Pastry Drivers v. Wohl*, 315 U.S. 769 at 775 (1942).

[80] *Carpenters and Joiners Union v. Ritter's Cafe*, 315 U.S. 722 at 727 (1942).

[81] *Bakery and Pastry Drivers v. Wohl*, 315 U.S. 769 at 776-77 (1942).

[82] *Giboney v. Empire Storage & Ice Co.*, 336 U.S. 490 at 502 (1949).

[83] *Hughes v. Superior Court of California*, 339 U.S. 460 at 465-66 (1950).

[84] *Building Service Employees Union v. Gazzam*, 339 U.S. 532 (1950); *International Brotherhood of Teamsters v. Hanke*, 339 U.S. 470 (1950).

[85] *Local Plumbers Union #10 v. Graham*, 345 U.S. 192 (1953).

[86] *International Brotherhood of Teamsters, Local 695 v. Vogt*, 354 U.S. 284 at 294-95, 293 (1957).

[87] Id. at 296.

[88] *Amalgamated Food Employees Union v. Logan Valley Plaza*, 391 U.S. 308 (1968), qualified by *Lloyd Corp. Ltd. v. Tanner*, 407 U.S. 551 (1972) and *Hudgens v. National Labor Relations Board*, 424 U.S. 507 (1976).

[89] Zechariah Chafee Jr., *Free Speech in the United States* (Cambridge: Harvard University Press, 1941; reprint ed., New York: Atheneum, 1969), p. 405-6.

[90] *Cantwell v. Connecticut*, 310 U.S. 296 at 306-7 (1940); see also *Schneider v. Irvington*, 308 U.S. 147 (1939); *Largent v. Texas*, 318 U.S. 418 (1943).

[91] *Hynes v. Oradell*, 425 U.S. 610 (1976).

[92] *Thomas v. Collins*, 323 U.S. 516 at 534, 540 (1945); see also *Staub v. City of Baxley*, 355 U.S. 313 (1958).

[93] *Martin v. City of Struthers*, 319 U.S. 141 at 145, 146 (1943).

[94] Id. at 154-55.

[95] *Schneider v. Irvington*, 308 U.S. 147 at 165 (1939).

[96] *Valentine v. Chrestensen*, 316 U.S. 52 at 54 (1942).

[97] *Breard v. City of Alexandria*, 341 U.S. 622 at 642 (1951).

[98] *New York Times Co. v. Sullivan*, 376 U.S. 254 at 266 (1964).

[99] *Bigelow v. Virginia*, 421 U.S. 809 (1975).

[100] *Virginia State Board of Pharmacy v. Virginia Citizens Consumer Council, Inc.*, 425 U.S. 748 at 765 (1976).

[101] *Carey v. Population Services International*, 431 U.S. 678 (1977); *Bates v. Arizona State Bar*, 433 U.S. 350 (1977); *Linmark Associates Inc. v. Township of Willingboro*, 431 U.S. 85 (1977).

[102] *Ohralik v. Ohio State Bar Association*, 436 U.S. 447 (1978); see also *Friedman v. Rogers* (1979).

Freedom of the Press

Much of the significance of free speech would be lost if speech could not be freely printed and circulated. Not only is it virtually impossible for a single individual to disseminate his views on public matters without help from the press — including, in modern times, the broadcast media — but it is also impossible for individuals otherwise to procure for themselves the information they need to make informed judgments on the conduct of government and other matters of public concern.

Thomas Jefferson spelled out the importance of this informing function in 1787, criticizing omission of a free press guarantee from the Constitution. Writing from France, where he had been during the Constitutional Convention, Jefferson said:

> The people are the only censors of their governors; and even their errors will tend to keep these to the true principles of their institution. To punish these errors too severely would be to suppress the only safeguard of the public liberty. The way to prevent these irregular interpositions of the people is to give them full information of their affairs thru the channel of the public papers, & to contrive that those papers should penetrate the whole mass of the people. The basis of our government being the opinion of the people, the very first object should be to keep that right; and were it left to me to decide whether we should have a government without newspapers or newspapers without a government, I should not hesitate for a moment to prefer the latter. [1]

Nearly 200 years later, Justice Lewis F. Powell Jr. stated the same case for a free press in the context of modern communications:

> . . .An informed public depends on accurate and effective reporting by the news media. No individual can obtain for himself the information needed for the intelligent discharge of his political responsibilities. For most citizens the prospect of personal familiarity with newsworthy events is hopelessly unrealistic. In seeking out the news the press therefore acts as an agent of the public at large. It is the means by which the people receive that free flow of information and ideas essential to intelligent self-government. By enabling the public to assert meaningful control over the political process, the press performs a crucial function in effecting the societal purpose of the First Amendment. [2]

The First Amendment is premised on the view that its societal purpose can only be achieved if publishers are free to determine for themselves what they will print. Though the First Amendment is usually thought of in terms of individual freedom, it is the societal value that the Supreme Court has stressed in its decisions upholding the guarantee of a free press.

Meaning of the Guarantee

At the least, the guarantee of freedom of the press means freedom from prior restraint or censorship. At the most, the guarantee also means that governments may not punish the press for what it publishes. As is true of the other guarantees of the First Amendment, this absolute position has been subscribed to by only a handful of Supreme Court justices. The vast majority of the court has viewed freedom of the press, like free speech, free assembly and the free exercise of religion, as subject to certain restrictions.

Prior Restraint

The Supreme Court has struck down a number of laws that have acted as prior restraints on the press. This list includes statutes that forbade continued publication of malicious criticisms of government officials, prohibited circulation of non-commercial handbills or placed a discriminatory tax on some newspapers.

In 1971 the Supreme Court rejected a request by the Nixon administration to order several newspapers to stop printing excerpts from classified documents that detailed the history of U.S. involvement in the Indochina War. The court said the government had failed to show sufficient justification for restraining continued publication of the documents.

But in that case and others the court has strongly implied that prior restraints might be permissible under certain extreme circumstances, to prevent, for example, disclosure of the movement of troops during war or inciting others to violence.

The court also has upheld the right of government to regulate certain aspects of publishing, including labor and business practices and the manner and place of distribution of circulars and handbills. These regulations may from time to time work as prior restraints on the press.

Subsequent Punishment

The court has not guarded the press quite so rigorously against subsequent punishment as against prior restraint.

During World War I it upheld the convictions of several persons for publication of articles the court found in violation of the espionage and sedition acts. *(Seditious speech, p. 396)*

Libel, the printed defamation of an individual, was long thought by the court to be outside the protection of the First Amendment. But in the 1960s the court began to reverse this posture, extending publishers considerable protection against libel suits brought by public officials and public figures. The court has held that the First Amendment affords less protection from libel suits brought by private individuals, although the line distinguishing private individuals from public figures is often blurred.

A corollary question faced by the court is whether the First Amendment protects the press against claims that published articles or broadcast reports have impermissibly interfered with individual privacy. In the few cases it has decided involving this issue, the court has ruled against the privacy claims unless the claimants could prove that the publisher acted with actual malice or displayed reckless disregard for the truth of the report.

The court still considers obscene publications to be outside the protection of the First Amendment and subject both to prior restraint and subsequent punishment. The justices, however, have had great difficulty in defining what material is obscene, and it is likely that the standard for that determination will continue to evolve as societal mores change. *(Box, pp. 428-29)*

The Press and Justice

In the mid-20th century freedom of the press has upon occasion collided with the right to impartial and fair administration of justice. Comprehensive reporting of the workings of the justice system is crucial to its fair administration. But news reports — especially of sensational crimes

— may injure a defendant's rights by prejudicing the community against him.

In a series of cases decided in the early 1960s the court set out some guidelines that courts should follow to protect the rights of the accused with minimal restriction on freedom of the press.

One response of trial judges to this conflict has been the so-called "gag rule" under which the trial court restricts the information the press may report about certain trials. In 1976 the court reviewed such a gag order and found it an unconstitutional prior restraint. But by declining subsequently to review lower court decisions, the court also has upheld several contempt citations against reporters who defied gag rules.

Access and Confidentiality

In recent years the Supreme Court has ruled against the arguments of the press that the First Amendment guarantees them special privileges in two important and complicated areas. The first is the matter of access to news. Does the special role of the press in the workings of an effective representative government entitle reporters to special access to potential news sources? Gag rules are just one aspect of this access question. Another aspect — whether reporters should have special access to prisons to view conditions and interview inmates — has been answered negatively by a majority of the court.

The second and perhaps more troubling area is that of confidentiality. Can reporters be required to divulge the identity of their news sources to court officials and other law enforcement officers investigating alleged criminal activities? Reporters contend that their relationship with news sources should be privileged just as are the relationships between doctor and patient, lawyer and client, and husband and wife. But the court has so far rejected this argument, holding that a reporter has no more constitutional right to withhold information that might help in the prosecution of a crime than does an ordinary citizen.

In another ruling disappointing to the press, the court held that the First Amendment does not require police to use subpoenas instead of search warrants when it seeks evidence of a crime from newspaper offices and files.

Prior Restraint: Censorship

Writing of the effect of censorship on the press, Prof. Thomas I. Emerson has said:

> . . .A system of prior restraint is in many ways more inhibiting than a system of subsequent punishment: It is likely to bring under government scrutiny a far wider range of expression; it shuts off communication before it takes place; suppression by a stroke of the pen is more likely to be applied than suppression through a criminal process; the procedures do not require attention to the safeguards of the criminal process; the system allows less opportunity for public appraisal and criticism; the dynamics of the system drive toward excesses, as the history of all censorship shows. [3]

It was a history of excesses that impelled the addition of the free press guarantee to the First Amendment. Prior restraint of the press had been widely practiced — and sharply attacked — in England where both church and state authorities had imposed a licensing system on the press from the development of the printing press in the 15th century until 1695, when the licensing laws were finally repealed. Indirect censorship through heavy taxation also was common.

Several of the colonies also attempted to censor the press from time to time, but these efforts proved so unpopular that they were generally quite shortlived.

Consequently, when the guarantee of freedom of the press was written it was widely assumed to mean freedom from prior restraint. And, in fact, few prior restraints have been imposed on the press throughout U.S. history.

Public Nuisance

Not until 1931 did the Supreme Court review a case questioning the propriety of prior restraint of the press. The case — *Near v. Minnesota* — concerned an unusual Minnesota statute which prohibited as a public nuisance publication of malicious, scandalous and defamatory newspapers, magazines and other publications. The truth of the defamatory allegations was a defense only if the allegations were made with good motive and for justifiable ends.

In 1927 the county attorney for Hennepin County sought an injunction under this statute to halt continued publication of a weekly periodical which had charged that county officials were derelict in their duties regarding a Jewish gangster who operated gambling, bootlegging and racketeering operations in Minneapolis. The articles charged that the police chief was in collusion with the gangster, that a member of the grand jury investigating the rackets was sympathetic to the gangsters, and that the county attorney seeking the injunction had failed to take adequate measures to stop the vice operations.

The publication was clearly something of a scandal sheet, and its managers seemed clearly prejudiced against Jews.

A state court issued a temporary injunction forbidding continued publication of the newspaper. At the ensuing trial it was concluded the paper had violated the state statute, and a permanent injunction forbidding further publication of the paper was issued. At every opportunity, Near, the manager of the paper, raised the argument that the law as applied to his paper violated his rights under the 14th Amendment. When the state supreme court affirmed the order for the permanent injunction, Near appealed to the Supreme Court.

By a 5-4 vote, the Supreme Court lifted the injunction, holding that the Minnesota statute was an unconstitutional prior restraint on the press in violation of the First and 14th Amendments.

'Essence of Censorship.' Admittedly, the statute did not operate exactly like the old English licensing laws which required editors to submit all articles to government censors for approval prior to publication, wrote Chief Justice Charles Evans Hughes for the majority. Nonetheless, he continued:

> [i]f we cut through mere details of procedure, the operation and effect of the statute in substance is that public authorities may bring the owner or publisher of a newspaper or periodical before a judge upon a charge of conducting a business of publishing scandalous and defamatory matter — in particular that the matter consists of charges against public officers of official dereliction — and unless the owner or publisher is able and disposed to bring competent evidence to satisfy the judge that the charges are true and are published with good motives and for justifiable ends, his newspaper or periodical is suppressed and further publication is made punishable as a contempt. This is of the essence of censorship. [4]

Acknowledging that freedom of the press from prior restraint was not absolute, Hughes suggested four exceptional situations in which government censorship might be permissible: publication of crucial war information such as the number and location of troops; obscene publications; publications inciting "acts of violence" against the community or violent overthrow of the government; and publications that invade "private rights."

The nature of these exceptions, none of which applied in the pending case, placed "in a strong light the general conception that liberty of the press, historically considered and taken up by the Federal Constitution, has meant, principally although not exclusively, immunity from prior restraints or censorship," Hughes wrote. [5]

Nor had the passage of time lessened the necessity for that immunity, he continued:

> . . .While reckless assaults upon public men, and efforts to bring obloquy upon those who are endeavoring faithfully to discharge official duties, exert a baleful influence and deserve the severest condemnation in public opinion, it cannot be said that this abuse is greater, and it is believed to be less, than that which characterized the period in which our institutions took shape. Meanwhile, the administration of government has become more complex, the opportunities for malfeasance and corruption have multiplied, crime has grown to most serious proportions, and the danger of its protection by unfaithful officials and of the impairment of the fundamental security of life and property by criminal alliances and neglect, emphasizes the primary need of a vigilant and courageous press, especially in great cities. The fact that the liberty of the press may be abused by miscreant purveyors of scandal does not make any the less necessary the immunity of the press from previous restraint in dealing with official misconduct. Subsequent punishment for such abuses as may exist is the appropriate remedy, consistent with constitutional privilege. [6]

Hughes said the Minnesota statute could not be justified on the grounds that a publisher might avoid its penalties by showing that the defamatory material was true and printed with good motives and for justifiable ends. This would place the legislature in the position of deciding what were good motives and justifiable ends and thus "be but a step to a complete system of censorship." [7]

Nor was the statute justified because it was intended to prevent scandals which might disturb the public peace and even provoke assaults and the commission of other crimes. "Charges of reprehensible conduct, and in particular of official malfeasance, unquestionably create a public scandal," Hughes wrote, "but the theory of the constitutional guaranty is that even a more serious public evil would be caused by authority to prevent publication." [8]

The four dissenters, in an opinion written by Justice Pierce Butler, contended that the Minnesota law did not "operate as a *previous* restraint . . . within the proper meaning of that phrase." The restraint occurred only after publication of articles adjudged to constitute a public nuisance and served only to prohibit further illegal publications of the same kind. "There is nothing in the statute purporting to prohibit publications that have not been adjudged to constitute a nuisance," Butler said. [9]

Furthermore, the dissenters thought the threat of subsequent punishment inadequate to protect against this sort of evil. Libel laws are ineffective against false and malicious assaults printed by "insolvent publishers who may have purpose and sufficient capacity to contrive to put into effect a scheme . . . for oppression, blackmail or extortion," they wrote. [10]

The Press, Laws and Taxes

When the court in 1936 struck down certain state taxes on the press as an unconstitutional prior restraint, Justice George Sutherland made clear for the majority that the First Amendment did not immunize newspapers from payment of ordinary business taxes. [1] The court has also made it clear that the First Amendment does not exempt the press from compliance with general laws regulating business and labor relations.

"The publisher of a newspaper has no special immunity from the application of general laws," the court said in 1937, ruling that the National Labor Relations Act was applicable to the press. [2] Likewise it held that the press must abide by federal minimum wage and maximum hour standards. [3]

The court also has held that the press is subject to antitrust laws. In *Associated Press v. United States* (1945), Justice Hugo L. Black said that antitrust laws were vital to preservation of a free press:

...The First Amendment, far from providing an argument against application of the Sherman [Antitrust] Act, here provides powerful reasons to the contrary. That Amendment rests on the assumption that the widest possible dissemination of information from diverse and antagonistic sources is essential to the welfare of the public, that a free press is a condition of a free society. Surely a command that the government itself shall not impede the free flow of ideas does not afford nongovernment combinations a refuge if they impose restraints upon that constitutionally guaranteed freedom. Freedom to publish means freedom for all and not for some. Freedom to publish is guaranteed by the Constitution, but freedom to combine to keep others from publishing is not. [4]

[1] *Grosjean v. American Press Company*, 297 U.S. 233 (1936).

[2] *Associated Press v. National Labor Relations Board*, 301 U.S. 103 at 132 (1937).

[3] *Oklahoma Press Publishing Co. v. Walling*, 327 U.S. 186 (1946).

[4] *Associated Press v. United States*, 326 U.S. 1 at 20 (1945); see also: *Lorain Journal Co. v. United States*, 342 U.S. 143 (1951); *United States v. Radio Corporation of America*, 358 U.S. 334 (1959); *Citizen Publishing Company v. United States*, 394 U.S. 131 (1969); *United States v. Greater Buffalo Press, Inc.*, 402 U.S. 549 (1971).

Restrictive Taxation

The Supreme Court prohibited the use of a more traditional kind of prior restraint in the 1936 case of *Grosjean v. American Press Co.*

The Louisiana legislature under the direction of Gov. Huey Long placed a state tax of 2 percent on the gross receipts of newspapers that sold advertisements and had circulations in excess of 20,000 per week. The tax was billed as a tax on the privilege of doing business, but it had been calculated to affect only nine big city newspapers opposed to the Long regime. The papers immediately sought an injunction in federal district court to stop enforcement of

the law on the grounds that the tax violated freedom of the press and, because smaller newspapers were exempt, denied equal protection of the laws.

The federal district court issued the injunction and a unanimous Supreme Court affirmed that decision solely on First Amendment grounds. The tax "operates as a restraint in a double sense," wrote Justice George Sutherland. "First, its effect is to curtail the amount of revenue realized from advertising, and, second, its direct tendency is to restrict circulation." [11]

Sutherland then reviewed the history of restrictive taxation of the press. The British Parliament had frequently imposed so-called "taxes on knowledge" to suppress criticism of the government. Despite strong opposition, these stamp taxes persisted until 1855. Massachusetts in 1785 and 1786 imposed both a stamp tax and an advertising tax on newspapers and magazines, but hostility to the taxes was so strong that they were quickly repealed.

Given this background, Sutherland said, the framers of the First Amendment must have meant to prohibit the imposition of such taxes. He continued:

The predominant purpose of the grant of immunity here invoked was to preserve an untrammeled press as a vital source of public information. The newspapers, magazines and other journals of the country, it is safe to say, have shed and continue to shed, more light on the public and business affairs of the nation than any other instrumentality of publicity; and since informed public opinion is the most potent of all restraints upon misgovernment, the suppression or abridgement of the publicity afforded by a free press cannot be regarded otherwise than with grave concern. The tax here involved is bad not because it takes money from the pockets of the ... [newspapers]. If that were all, a wholly different question would be presented. It is bad because, in the light of its history and of its present setting, it is seen to be a deliberate and calculated device in the guise of a tax to limit the circulation of information to which the public is entitled in virtue of the constitutional guaranties. A free press stands as one of the great interpreters between the government and the people. To allow it to be fettered is to fetter ourselves. [12]

Handbills

The Supreme Court has always considered handbills, leaflets, circulars and other types of flyers containing an individual or group opinion on public issues to be a part of the press entitled to First Amendment protection.

Chief Justice Charles Evans Hughes voiced this principle in 1938:

The liberty of the press is not confined to newspapers and periodicals. It necessarily embraces pamphlets and leaflets. These indeed have been historic weapons in the defense of liberty, as the pamphlets of Thomas Paine and others in our own history abundantly attest. The press in its historic connotation comprehends every sort of publication which affords a vehicle of information and opinion. [13]

Consequently, the court has been unsympathetic to efforts of municipalities to restrict distribution of such handbills on public property. The arguments that some restriction is necessary to protect the public from fraud or

The Command to Publish

If freedom of the press means that government may not stop the press from printing, neither may government command the press to print. The Supreme Court has only found one exception to the rule that government may not dictate the form and content of what the press prints.

The 'Help-Wanted' Case

In 1973 the court upheld a government order to a newspaper forbidding it to place help-wanted advertisements under columns labeled "Jobs — Male Interest" and "Jobs — Female Interest" in violation of an ordinance that prohibited discrimination by sex in employment. The court reached that decision by a 5-4 vote. The majority explained that the help-wanted ads were commercial speech unprotected by the First Amendment and that the column heads added by the newspaper were indistinguishable from that speech. (*Commercial speech, p. 421*)

Furthermore, the majority said in *Pittsburgh Press Co. v. Pittsburgh Commission on Human Relations* (1973), even if commercial speech merited First Amendment protection, illegal commercial speech did not:

...The advertisements, as embroidered by their placement, signaled that the advertisers were likely to show an illegal sex preference in their hiring decisions. Any First Amendment interest which might be served by advertising an ordinary commercial proposal and which might arguably outweigh the governmental interest supporting the regulation is altogether absent when the commercial activity itself is illegal and the restriction on advertising is incidental to a valid limitation on economic activity. [1]

The Right of Reply

In a decision handed down the following year, the court emphasized the narrowness of the *Pittsburgh Press* holding when it struck down a Florida statute that required newspapers to grant political candidates equal space to reply to the paper's criticism and attacks on their public records.

Writing for a unanimous court in *Miami Herald Publishing Co. v. Tornillo* (1974), Chief Justice Warren E. Burger carefully reviewed the arguments in favor of the law, acknowledging that the diminishing number of newspapers and the concentration of media ownership meant that frequently only one view of an issue was published. "Chains of newspapers, national newspapers, national wire and news services, and one-newspaper towns, are the dominant features of a press that has become noncompetitive and enormously powerful and influential in its capacity to manipulate popular opinion and change the course of events," he wrote. [2]

But a governmental command to print specific information collides with the freedom of the press guaranteed by the First Amendment, he said, and under the decisions of the court

...any such compulsion to publish that which " 'reason' tells them should not be published" is unconstitutional. A responsible press is an undoubtedly desirable goal, but press responsibility is not mandated by the Constitution and like many other virtues it cannot be legislated. [3]

In conclusion, Burger wrote:

...A newspaper is more than a passive receptacle or conduit for news, comment and advertising. The choice of material to go into a newspaper, and the decisions made as to limitations on the size and content of the paper, and treatment of public issues and public officials — whether fair or unfair — constitute the exercise of editorial control and judgment. It has yet to be demonstrated how governmental regulation of this crucial process can be exercised consistent with First Amendment guarantees of a free press as they have evolved to this time. [4]

[1] *Pittsburgh Press Co. v. Pittsburgh Commission on Human Relations*, 413 U.S. 376 at 389 (1973).
[2] *Miami Herald Publishing Co. v. Tornillo*, 418 U.S. 241 at 249 (1974).
[3] Id. at 256.
[4] Id. at 258.

to keep the streets clean have not been considered sufficient to justify the resulting infringement on the freedoms of speech and press. The court has only limited distribution of non-commercial handbills when distribution has occurred on private property dedicated to specific public purposes. (*Box, p. 416*)

The Lovell Case. The first test of a city ordinance controlling distribution of handbills came in the 1938 case of *Lovell v. Griffin*. Alma Lovell, a Jehovah's Witness, distributed religious tracts in Griffin, Ga., in violation of an ordinance which prohibited circulation of literature of any kind without written permission from the city manager. The Supreme Court struck down the ordinance as an unconstitutional prior restraint on the press. Chief Justice Hughes wrote for a unanimous court:

...The ordinance prohibits the distribution of literature of any kind at any time, at any place, and in any manner without a permit from the City Manager.... Whatever the motive which induced its adoption, its character is such that it strikes at the very foundation of the freedom of the press by subjecting it to license and censorship. [14]

The Handbill Cases. In a series of cases considered together in 1939, the Supreme Court struck down four ordinances seeking to regulate handbill circulation.

The first of these cases, *Schneider v. Irvington*, again involved a Jehovah's Witness who was convicted of canvassing and distributing religious tracts without the required permit. The court held that this ordinance, like the one in *Lovell*, left too much to official discretion. [15]

Obscenity: An Elusive Definition. . .

The Supreme Court has never considered obscenity to be protected by the First Amendment. Obscenity is one of the categories of expression that is unprotected because it is "no essential part of any exposition of ideas, and [is] of . . . slight social value as a step to truth. . . ." [1]

But placing obscenity outside the protection of the First Amendment has not ended the matter, only shifted the focus of judicial effort to the problem of defining what is obscene and what is not. The problem has proved a frustrating one; the only criterion that the court has consistently agreed upon is that to be obscene, material must deal with sex.

Neither Profanity Nor Violence

Blasphemous or sacrilegious expression is not considered obscene by the court, nor, generally, are scatological profanities. Violence has been found obscene only when linked with sex.

As Justice John Marshall Harlan explained in a case in which the court ruled that the phrase "Fuck the Draft" worn on a jacket in a public courthouse was not obscene: "Whatever else may be necessary to give rise to the States' broader power to prohibit obscene expression, such expression must be, in some significant way, erotic." [2]

Early Standards

It was not until the Victorian era that laws restricting the dissemination of obscene materials began to develop. The earliest court standard defining obscenity was stated by a British court in the case of *Regina v. Hicklin* (1868): "whether the tendency of the matter charged as obscenity is to deprave and corrupt those whose minds are open to such immoral influences, and into whose hands a publication of this sort may fall." [3]

That test, used extensively by American courts, covered a wide range of material.

As Prof. Thomas I. Emerson observes, the *Hicklin* test "brought within the ban of the obscenity statutes any publication containing isolated passages that the courts felt would tend to exert an immoral influence on susceptible persons." [4]

As the moral standards of the Victorian era began to be rejected as too rigid, so did the Hicklin test. In 1933 Appeals Court Judge Augustus Hand proposed a new standard:

> While any construction of the statute that will fit all cases is difficult, we believe that the proper test of whether a given book is obscene is in its dominant effect. In applying this test, relevancy of the objectionable parts to the theme, the established reputation of the work in the estimation of approved critics, if the book is modern, and the verdict of the past, if it is ancient, are persuasive pieces of evidence; for works of art are not likely to sustain a high position with no better warrant for their existence than their obscene content. [5]

This meant that a publication of literary merit should not be judged obscene on the basis of particular passages taken out of context.

The *Roth* Standard

The Supreme Court did not express any opinion on a definition of obscenity until 1957 when it considered both a federal and a state obscenity law.

Roth v. United States concerned a federal statute making it a crime to mail materials that were "obscene, lewd, lascivious or filthy," while *Alberts v. California* concerned a state law making it illegal to publish, sell, distribute or advertise any "obscene or indecent" material. The majority relied heavily on Hand's test in drawing up what became known as the "*Roth* standard."

The five-justice majority first declared that obscene matter is not entitled to any protection from the First Amendment. Justice William J. Brennan Jr. wrote:

> . . .All ideas having even the slightest redeeming social importance — unorthodox ideas, controversial ideas, even ideas hateful to the prevailing climate of opinion — have the full protection of the guaranties, unless excludable because they encroach upon the limited area of more important interests. But implicit in the history of the First Amendment is the rejection of obscenity as utterly without redeeming social importance. [6]

Brennan then proposed a definition of obscenity and a standard for determining what was obscene:

> . . .[S]ex and obscenity are not synonymous. Obscene material is material which deals with sex in a manner appealing to prurient interest. The portrayal of sex, e.g., in art, literature, and scientific works, is not itself sufficient reason to deny material the constitutional protection of freedom of speech and press. . . . It is therefore vital that the standards for judging obscenity safeguard the protection of freedom of speech and press for material which does not treat sex in a manner appealing to prurient interest. [7]

The standard for making this determination, Brennan said, was "whether to the average person, applying contemporary standards, the dominant theme of the material taken as a whole appeals to the prurient interest." [8]

Having found that the trial courts in both the *Roth* and *Albert* cases had applied this standard and had found the material in question obscene, the majority upheld convictions under both the federal and state laws.

Roth Redefined

The court grew increasingly fragmented on obscenity questions after the *Roth* decision. Seldom did a majority agree on application of a single standard to the materials in question. Nonetheless, several important refinements of the *Roth* standard gained a measure of acceptance.

...And A Changing Standard

In the 1962 case of *Manual Enterprises v. Day*, Justice Harlan wrote a prevailing opinion in which he held that, to be obscene, material must not only appeal to prurient interest but also be patently offensive. That is, he wrote, obscene materials are those "so offensive on their face as to affront current community standards of decency."[9]

Because the case involved a federal obscenity statute, Harlan thought the community and the standards of decency should be national in scope.

Two years later in *Jacobellis v. Ohio* (1964), Justice Brennan's prevailing opinion added the requirement that the materials in question must be found "utterly without redeeming social importance."[10]

Confusion

The height of confusion over a definition of obscenity was reached on one day in 1967 when the court, in deciding three obscenity cases, issued 14 separate opinions.

In one of these cases the court ruled that the book *Fanny Hill* was not obscene. The test to be applied, the prevailing opinion held, was that the dominant theme of the book must appeal to prurient interest, that the book must be found patently offensive when judged by contemporary community standards and that it must be found utterly without redeeming social value.

Since the trial court had found that the book might have "some minimal literary value," it was not obscene under the test.[11]

In a second case decided the same day, the court came up with a fourth and separate test. This "pandering" test held that material which might not be obscene on its own merits could become so if it was placed "against a background of commercial exploitation of erotica solely for the sake of their prurient appeal."[12]

Retreat

After this point the court retreated, indicating in a 1967 *per curiam* opinion in *Redrup v. New York* that it would sustain obscenity convictions only to protect juveniles or unwilling adults from exposure to obscene materials or in cases of pandering.[13]

Over the next few years the court reversed a number of obscenity convictions because they did not fall into these categories.

The *Miller* Standard

Then in 1973 a majority of the court, albeit a slim one, endorsed for the first time since the 1957 *Roth* decision a standard for determining what was obscene. This new standard gave governments at all levels much more latitude to ban obscene materials than did the *Roth* test.

Writing for the five-justice majority in *Miller v. California* (1973), Chief Justice Warren E. Burger held that states could regulate:

...works which depict or describe sexual conduct. That conduct must be specifically defined by the applicable state law, as written or authoritatively construed. A state offense must also be limited to works which, taken as a whole, appeal to the prurient interest in sex, which portray sexual conduct in a patently offensive way, and which, taken as a whole, do not have serious literary, artistic, political or scientific value.[14]

Under this standard, Burger said, the majority intended to exclude only hard-core materials from First Amendment protection. As a guideline, he suggested that such materials were those which included "patently offensive representations or descriptions of ultimate sexual acts, normal or perverted, actual or simulated" and "patently offensive representations or descriptions of masturbation, excretory functions, and lewd exhibition of the genitals."[15]

The majority specifically rejected the *Jacobellis* test that to be obscene, materials must be "utterly without redeeming social value." It also rejected the idea that the community standard must be national in scope. "It is neither realistic nor constitutionally sound to read the First Amendment as requiring that the people of Maine or Mississippi accept public depiction of conduct found tolerable in Las Vegas or New York City," Burger wrote.[16]

The majority stressed that First Amendment values would be adequately protected by this standard. Burger noted that appellate courts had the authority to "conduct an independent review of constitutional claims when necessary."[17]

The following year, the court did just that when it overturned a Georgia jury's finding that the movie "Carnal Knowledge" was obscene. Holding that local juries did not "have unbridled discretion" to determine what is patently offensive, the court in *Jenkins v. Georgia* (1974) found nothing in the movie that fit its *Miller* standards for what might constitute hard-core obscenity.[18]

---

[1] *Chaplinsky v. New Hampshire*, 315 U.S. 568 at 572 (1942).

[2] *Cohen v. California*, 403 U.S. 15 at 20 (1971).

[3] *Regina v. Hicklin*, L.R. 3 Q.B. 360 at 371 (1868), quoted in Thomas I. Emerson, *The System of Freedom of Expression* (New York: Random House, Vintage Books, 1970), p. 469.

[4] Emerson, *System*, p. 469.

[5] *United States v. One Book Entitled "Ulysses"*, 72 F. 2d 705 at 708 (2d Cir. 1934).

[6] *Roth v. United States, Alberts v. California*, 354 U.S. 476 at 484 (1957).

[7] Id. at 487-88.

[8] Id. at 489.

[9] *Manual Enterprises v. Day*, 370 U.S. 478 at 482 (1962).

[10] *Jacobellis v. Ohio*, 378 U.S. 184 at 191 (1964).

[11] *A Book Named "John Cleland's Memoirs of a Woman of Pleasure" v. Attorney General of Massachusetts*, 383 U.S. 413 at 419 (1966).

[12] *Ginzburg v. United States*, 383 U.S. 463 at 466 (1966).

[13] *Redrup v. New York*, 386 U.S. 767 (1967).

[14] *Miller v. California*, 413 U.S. 15 at 24 (1973).

[15] Id at 25.

[16] Id. at 32.

[17] Id. at 25.

[18] *Jenkins v. Georgia*, 418 U.S. 153 (1974).

Prior Restraint and Obscenity

In its landmark ruling in *Near v. Minnesota*, the Supreme Court majority indicated that obscenity was one form of expression that might be subject to prior restraint.

Twenty-six years later, in its first case dealing directly with that question, a five-justice majority upheld, against a challenge of unconstitutional prior restraint, a New York statute that allowed public officials to seek injunctions against the sale of obscene publications.

Contrary to the discussion in *Near*, the majority indicated that the First Amendment might protect even obscene publications from licensing or censorship before publication. But this challenged statute was not such a prior restraint. Instead, the majority said, it "studiously withholds restraint upon matters not already published and not yet found to be offensive." As such it was a valid means "for the seizure and destruction of the instruments of ascertained wrongdoing. . . ." [1]

In another 5-4 decision, the court upheld in 1961 a Chicago ordinance which prohibited public showings of movies found to be obscene at a prior screening. In this case, *Times Film Corp. v. City of Chicago*, the majority held that the doctrine of prior restraint was not absolute and that the censorship procedure was a valid means for controlling the dissemination of obscene movies. For the dissenters, Chief Justice Earl Warren said the majority decision "gives formal sanction to censorship in its purest and most far-reaching form. . . ." [2]

In 1965 the court sought to limit the impact of this decision by prescribing strict procedural rules authorities must follow when censoring films. The burden of proving the film obscene falls on the censor who must license it quickly or seek a restraining order in court. Furthermore, the entire censorship process must "assure a prompt final judicial decision." The court has been consistent in enforcing these procedural safeguards. [3]

---

[1] *Kingsley Books v. Brown*, 354 U.S. 436 at 445, 444 (1957).
[2] *Times Film Corp. v. City of Chicago*, 365 U.S. 43 at 55 (1961).
[3] *Freedman v. Maryland*, 380 U.S. 51 at 59 (1965); see also *Southeastern Promotions, Ltd. v. Conrad*, 420 U.S. 546 (1975), *Roaden v. Kentucky*, 413 U.S. 496 (1973).

The other three cases involved ordinances that prohibited all distribution of handbills on public streets. Here, the court held such flat prohibition impermissible under the First Amendment rights of speech and press. [16]

Justice Owen J. Roberts attempted to explain how a city might properly regulate circulation of handbills:

Municipal authorities, as trustees for the public, have the duty to keep their communities' streets open and available for movement of people and property, the primary purpose to which the streets are dedicated. So long as legislation to this end does not abridge the constitutional liberty of one rightfully upon the street

to impart information through speech or the distribution of literature, it may lawfully regulate the conduct of those using the streets. For example, a person could not exercise this liberty by taking his stand in the middle of a crowded street, contrary to traffic regulations, and maintain his position to the stoppage of all traffic; a group of distributors could not insist upon a constitutional right to form a cordon across the street and to allow no pedestrian to pass who did not accept a tendered leaflet; nor does the guarantee of freedom of speech or of the press deprive a municipality of power to enact regulations against throwing literature broadcast in the streets. Prohibition of such conduct would not abridge the constitutional liberty since such activity bears no necessary relationship to the freedom to speak, write, print or distribute information or opinion. [17]

The majority also said that the desire to prevent litter was not a sufficient reason to limit circulation of handbills. Litter, wrote Roberts, was the indirect consequence of the constitutional protection. Cities could prevent litter by other methods.

To the argument that cities should be permitted to prohibit the dissemination of handbills in public streets so long as other public places were available for such distribution, Roberts wrote that "one is not to have the exercise of his liberty of expression in appropriate places abridged on the plea that it may be exercised in some other place." [18]

Anonymous Handbills. In a 1960 case the Supreme Court struck down a Los Angeles ordinance that required all handbills to include the name and address of the person preparing, sponsoring or distributing them.

"There can be no doubt that such an identification requirement would tend to restrict freedom to distribute information and thereby freedom of expression," wrote Justice Hugo L. Black in *Talley v. California.* [19] Throughout history, he observed, persecuted groups and sects have had to resort to anonymous criticism of oppressive practices to avoid further persecutions.

Three justices dissented, maintaining that the court should weigh the state's interest in preventing fraud against the individual's claimed rights. In the present case, they said there was no evidence that the person preparing the handbills would have been subjected to harassment or other injury by publication of his name and address on the circulars.

Injunctions. In a 1971 case, the Supreme Court ruled that a temporary injunction against the continued publication of certain handbills was an unconstitutional abridgment of the freedoms of speech and press.

The case of *Organization for a Better Austin v. Keefe* arose when an organization which sought to maintain the racial stability of its neighborhood grew upset with the tactics Keefe used to induce whites to sell their homes to blacks. After Keefe denied the allegations and refused to cooperate with the association, it began to circulate handbills in Keefe's neighborhood describing what it considered to be his unsavory real estate activities. Keefe then sought and was granted the injunction.

The Supreme Court held that "the injunction, so far as it imposes prior restraint on speech and publication, constitutes an impermissible restraint on First Amendment rights." The fact that the association's aim in circulating the handbills was to coerce Keefe into cooperation with it was "not fundamentally different from the function of a newspaper," the majority said. Nor could the injunction be justified as protecting Keefe's privacy. Keefe was "not attempting to stop the flow of information into his own household, but to the public." [20]

Election-Day Editorials

The basic need to protect free discussion of governmental affairs lay at the heart of the court's 1966 decision to strike down an Alabama statute which made it a crime to solicit votes on election day.

A newspaper editor who printed an editorial on election day urging his readers to vote a certain way on a ballot proposition was convicted under this law. A statute setting criminal penalties "for publishing editorials such as the one here silences the press at a time when it can be most effective," wrote Justice Hugo L. Black for the majority in *Mills v. Alabama.* "It is difficult to conceive of a more obvious and flagrant abridgment of the constitutionally guaranteed freedom of the press." [21]

The Pentagon Papers

Publication in June 1971 of articles based upon a classified history of U.S. involvement in Vietnam precipitated an unprecedented confrontation between the federal government and the press.

The 47-volume, 7,000-page history, which soon became known as the "Pentagon Papers," covered the Truman, Eisenhower, Kennedy and Johnson administrations. It indicated that the U.S. government was more involved in the Vietnamese civil war at almost every stage than U.S. officials had ever publicly admitted.

Copies of the Pentagon Papers were made available to the press by Daniel Ellsberg, an analyst who had helped prepare the report and then become an anti-war activist.

The *New York Times* was the first newspaper to publish articles based on the papers; the first installment appeared in its June 13, 1971, edition. The following day, after the second installment appeared, the Justice Department asked the *Times* to return the documents and to halt publication of the series. The articles, they said, would cause "irreparable injury to the defense interests of the U.S." The *Times* refused to comply.

On June 15, U.S. District Court Judge Murray I. Gurfein granted the temporary restraining order requested by the Justice Department against the *Times,* to be in effect until he could hold hearings on the government's request for a permanent injunction.

After the hearings, Gurfein ruled June 19 that the government was not entitled to a permanent injunction against the *Times'* publication of further articles. But Judge Irving R. Kaufman of the U.S. Court of Appeals immediately granted a restraining order against the *Times,* at the Justice Department's request, to permit the government to appeal Judge Gurfein's decision. The appeals court June 23 returned the case to the lower court for further secret hearings and extended until June 25 a restraining order against the *Times.* The *Times* on June 24 petitioned the Supreme Court to review the Court of Appeals order.

The government also sought to restrain the *Washington Post,* which had published its first Pentagon Papers article June 18, from further publications. The *Post* case arrived at the Supreme Court through an involved succession of hearings and temporary restraining orders similar to those in the *Times* case. However, both the district court

Freedom to Circulate

"Liberty of circulating is as essential to that freedom [of the press] as liberty of publishing; indeed, without the circulation, the publication would be of little value," the Supreme Court said as early as 1878. [1]

But in that case and others, the court nonetheless upheld the right of Congress to prohibit the use of the mails to circulate materials considered injurious to public morals.

Circulation through the mails of publications espousing unpopular political opinions and doctrines has also been restricted. During World Wars I and II the government permitted the postmaster general to withdraw second-class mailing privileges from publications that violated the espionage laws. In 1921 the court upheld this delegation of authority when it sustained the postmaster general's withdrawal of second-class mail rates from the socialist newspaper, *Milwaukee Leader,* without directly addressing the First Amendment questions implied in the case. [2]

The court appeared more willing to protect publications that clearly posed no threat to national security. In 1946 it ruled that the postmaster general had exceeded his authority when he withdrew second class mail privileges from *Esquire* magazine because he determined the magazine's contents fell outside the matter eligible for the special mailing rates. The court said that Congress had authorized the postmaster general to decide only whether publications contained "information of a public character, literature or art" and not "whether the contents meet some standard of the public good or welfare." [3]

The court also extended some protection to dissident publications in 1965 when it struck down a 1962 federal statute permitting the postmaster general to deliver "communist political propaganda" only at the would-be recipient's specific request. [4]

Circulation of Obscenity

Because obscenity has no First Amendment protection, the court has consistently sustained federal statutes restricting its dissemination. In 1957 the court upheld a law prohibiting the mailing of obscene materials and in 1970 it sustained a federal statute allowing individuals to request the post office not to deliver them obscene materials. [5] In other cases the court has upheld the right of Congress to bar importation of obscene matter and to prohibit transport of such matter by common carrier through interstate commerce. [6]

---

[1] *Ex parte Jackson,* 96 U.S. 727 at 733 (1878); see also *In re Rapier,* 143 U.S. 110 (1892).

[2] *United States ex rel. Milwaukee Social Democratic Publishing Co. v. Burleson,* 255 U.S. 407 (1921).

[3] *Hannegan v. Esquire,* 327 U.S. 146 at 158-159 (1946).

[4] *Lamont v. Postmaster General,* 381 U.S. 301 (1965).

[5] *Roth v. United States,* 354 U.S. 476 (1957); *Rowan v. Post Office Department,* 397 U.S. 728 (1970).

[6] *United States v. Thirty-seven Photographs,* 402 U.S. 363 (1971); *United States v. 12 200-Ft. Reels of Super 8mm. Film,* 413 U.S. 123 (1973); *United States v. Orito,* 413 U.S. 139 (1973).

and the court of appeals in Washington refused the Justice Department's request for a permanent injunction against the *Post.* The government appealed to the Supreme Court on June 24.

The court heard arguments on June 26 and announced its decision four days later. By a 6-3 vote, the court June 30 ruled that the government had failed to meet "the heavy burden of showing justification" for restraining further publications of the Pentagon Papers. [22]

Each of the nine justices wrote a separate opinion. Taken together, these opinions covered the wide range of sentiment that exists when a First Amendment right must be weighed against national security claims.

The Majority

In separate concurring opinions, Justices Hugo L. Black and William O. Douglas maintained that freedom of the press was absolute and could not be abridged by the government under any circumstances.

"[E]very moment's continuance of the injunctions against these newspapers amounts to a flagrant, indefensible, and continuing violation of the First Amendment," Black asserted in the last opinion he would write. "Both the history and language of the First Amendment support the view that the press must be left free to publish news, whatever the source, without censorship, injunctions or prior restraints." [23]

Douglas wrote: "The First Amendment provides that 'Congress shall make no law . . . abridging the freedom of speech or of the press.' That leaves, in my view, no room for governmental restraint on the press." [24]

Justice William J. Brennan Jr. thought the government might properly restrain the press in certain clear emergencies. But the circumstances of this case did not present such an emergency, Brennan said, and there should have been no injunctive restraint. The government sought the injunction on the grounds that the publication "could," "might," or "may" damage national security, Brennan said. "But the First Amendment tolerates absolutely no prior judicial restraints of the press predicated upon surmise or conjecture that untoward consequences may result." [25]

Justices Potter Stewart and Byron R. White both thought that prior restraints might be permissible under certain conditions and that disclosure of some of the information in the Pentagon Papers might be harmful to national interests. "But I cannot say that disclosure of any of them [the papers] will surely result in direct, immediate, and irreparable damage to our Nation or its people," concluded Stewart. "That being so, there can under the First Amendment be but one judicial resolution of the issues before us." [26]

White said he concurred with the majority "only because of the concededly extraordinary protection against prior restraints enjoyed by the press under our constitutional system." The government's position, White said, is that the necessity to preserve national security is so great that the president is entitled

> . . .to an injunction against publication of a newspaper story whenever he can convince a court that the information to be revealed threatens "grave and irreparable" injury to the public interest; and the injunction should issue whether or not . . . publication would be lawful . . . and regardless of the circumstances by which the newspaper came into possession of the information.

At least in the absence of legislation by Congress. . ., I am quite unable to agree that the inherent powers of the Executive and the courts reach so far as to authorize remedies having such a sweeping potential for inhibiting publications by the press. [27]

The critical factor for Justice Thurgood Marshall was that Congress had twice refused to give the president authority to prohibit publications disclosing matters of national security or to make such disclosures criminal. It would be a violation of the doctrine of separation of powers, Marshall said,

> . . .for this Court to use its power of contempt to prevent behavior that Congress has specifically declined to prohibit. . . .The Constitution provides that Congress shall make laws, the President execute laws, and courts interpret law. . . . It did not provide for government by injunction in which the courts and the Executive can "make law" without regard to the action of Congress. [28]

The Dissenters

Chief Justice Warren E. Burger and Justices John Marshall Harlan and Harry A. Blackmun dissented. All three lamented the haste with which the cases had been decided. Holding that the press did not enjoy absolute protection from prior restraint, Burger said that the exception which might permit restraint "may be lurking in these cases and would have been flushed had they been properly considered in the trial courts, free from unwarranted deadlines and frenetic pressures." [29]

Burger also thought the papers had been derelict in their duty to report the discovery of stolen property or secret government documents. That duty "rests on taxi drivers, Justices and the *New York Times,*" he said. [30]

Justice Harlan listed a number of questions which he said should and would have been considered if the cases had been deliberated more fully. On the merits of the cases, Harlan said the judiciary should not "redetermine for itself the probable impact of disclosure on the national security." [31]

Therefore, Harlan would have sent the cases back to the lower courts for further proceedings, during which time he would have permitted the temporary restraining orders to remain in effect. Harlan said he could "not believe that the doctrine prohibiting prior restraints reaches to the point of preventing courts from maintaining the *status quo* long enough to act responsibly in matters of such national importance. . . ." [32]

In his dissent, Justice Blackmun wrote:

> The First Amendment, after all, is only one part of the entire Constitution. Article II . . . vests in the Executive Branch primary power over the conduct of foreign affairs. . . . Each provision of the Constitution is important and I cannot subscribe to a doctrine of unlimited absolutism for the First Amendment at the cost of downgrading other provisions. . . . What is needed here is a weighing, upon properly developed standards, of the broad right of the press to print and of the very narrow right of the government to prevent. [33]

Subsequent Punishment. The three dissenters and Stewart and White from the majority indicated that they believed the newspapers might be subject to criminal penalties for publishing classified government documents. But the question never arose. The government's prosecution of Daniel Ellsberg for espionage, theft and conspiracy for leaking the papers was dismissed because of government misconduct. The government brought no further prosecutions.

Subsequent Punishment: Libel

Libel is the defamation of character or reputation in print or by other visual means such as television or cartoon. The general belief that publishers should be punished for printing defamatory statements can be traced back to the efforts of state and church authorities in England to suppress seditious criticism of their policies.

There is disagreement in the academic community over whether the First Amendment guarantee of freedom of the press was intended to prohibit Congress from enacting seditious libel laws — laws providing punishment for those who print defamatory statements about government officials and policies. Whatever the case, the Federalist-dominated Congress enacted such a libel law in 1798, but it proved extremely unpopular and was allowed to expire two years later. Although the validity of the 1798 law was never challenged before the Supreme Court, later justices assumed it was unconstitutional. [34]

In any event, Congress has never again enacted a law making general criticism of government officials and their conduct unlawful. It is now well accepted that general criticism of government policies and officials is protected by the First Amendment, although specific types of criticism may be punishable. The Sedition Act of 1918, for example, set penalties for interfering with the war effort and the Smith Act of 1940 punished those who conspired to advocate otherthrow of the government. Both types of conduct are considered by the court to be outside the protection of the First Amendment.

Civil Libel

In the area of libel of private individuals, the dilemma is to balance the need for open discussion of public issues and personalities against protection for individuals against false, irresponsible and malicious publications. Absolute immunity from libel suits is granted to judges, legislators and executive officials. Qualified federal immunity is granted to certain professionals such as doctors and lawyers. But publishers historically have been liable to damage suits. Libelous publications include those which charge that an individual is guilty of a criminal offense, carries a dread disease such as leprosy, is incompetent in his profession or employment or, if a public official, is guilty of misconduct.

In the United States, truth is a defense to a libel charge. But truth is often expensive to prove. And when the truth involves a matter of judgment, as in a political opinion, it may be impossible to prove. Clearly, placing this burden of proof on publishers can lead to self-censorship, a hesitancy to print information about public officials and others influential in public life. Such self-censorship in turn impairs the societal function of the press in a democratic system.

Cognizant of the restriction that libel laws placed on a free press, several states early in the 20th century began to enact laws protecting publishers from libel suits in all cases except those where the publisher printed his charges in actual malice. The seminal decision came from the Kansas Supreme Court in the 1908 case of *Coleman v. MacLennan,* in which a political candidate sued a newspaper publisher for libel:

> ...[W]here an article is published and circulated among voters for the ... purpose of giving what the defendant believes to be truthful information concerning a candidate for public office, and for the purpose of enabling such voters to cast their ballots more intelligently, and the whole thing is done in good faith, and without malice, the article is privileged, although the principal matters contained in the article may be untrue in fact and derogatory to the character of the plaintiff, and in such a case the burden is on the plaintiff to show actual malice in the publication of the article. [35]

Nearly 50 years later the U.S. Supreme Court adopted this "actual malice" rule for libel suits brought against publishers by public officials and other personalities in the public eye.

In the interim the court repeatedly stated its view — in *dicta* — that libel was outside the protection of the First Amendment. "There are certain well-defined and narrowly limited classes of speech, the prevention and punishment of which have never been thought to raise any Constitutional problem," the court wrote in *Chaplinsky v. New Hampshire* (1942). "These include the lewd and obscene, the profane, the libelous, and the insulting or 'fighting' words...." [36] Similar statements were made in other decisions; only once before 1964 did the court review a libel case, but one that concerned group libel and not individual civil libel. *(Box, p. 435)*

New York Times v. Sullivan

The case in which the Supreme Court reconsidered its opinions — and revised the rules for libel — was *New York Times Co. v. Sullivan* (1964).

L. B. Sullivan was an elected commissioner of the city of Montgomery, Ala., responsible for the police department. He sued *The New York Times* and four black clergymen for libel as a result of an advertisement the clergymen had placed in the newspaper on March 29, 1960.

The ad, entitled "Heed Their Rising Voices," called attention to the fledgling struggle for civil rights in the South, and appealed for funds to support the black student movement, the "struggle for the right-to-vote" and the legal defense of civil rights leader Dr. Martin Luther King Jr., who had been indicted for perjury in Montgomery.

The Suit

The heart of the advertisement was a recitation of the violence with which the civil rights movement had been met. The basis for Sullivan's libel suit was contained in two of these paragraphs. They read:

> In Montgomery, Alabama, after students sang "My Country, 'Tis of Thee" on the State Capitol steps,

433

their leaders were expelled from school, and truckloads of police armed with shotguns and tear-gas ringed the Alabama State College Campus. When the entire student body protested to state authorities by refusing to re-register, their dining hall was padlocked in an attempt to starve them into submission. . . .

Again and again the Southern violators have answered Dr. King's peaceful protests with intimidation and violence. They have bombed his home almost killing his wife and child. They have assaulted his person. They have arrested him seven times — for "speeding," "loitering" and similar "offenses." And now they have charged him with "perjury" — a *felony* under which they could imprison him for *ten years*. . . . [37]

Although the advertisement did not refer to him personally, Sullivan contended that the references to police included him. He also contended that because arrests are usually made by police, the "they" in "They have arrested" Dr. King referred to him, and that the "they" who made the arrests were equated with the "they" who bombed King's home and assaulted him.

The two paragraphs contained conceded errors. The students sang the National Anthem, not "My Country, 'Tis of Thee." Several students were expelled from the school for demanding service at an all-white lunch counter, but not for leading the demonstration at the capital. Police were deployed near the campus but they did not "ring" it. Students protested the expulsions by boycotting classes for a day, not by refusing to re-register. The campus dining room was never padlocked; the only students denied access to it were those who did not have meal tickets. King had been arrested four times, not seven times.

The suit was tried under Alabama libel law, and Sullivan was awarded damages of $500,000. Other plaintiffs in Alabama brought suits against the *Times* seeking damages totaling $5.6 million.

The Supreme Court Decision

The *Times* appealed the decision to the Supreme Court, which unanimously reversed it.

Writing for six of the justices, Justice William J. Brennan Jr. dismissed the court's earlier *dicta* viewing all libel as outside the protection of the First Amendment. "None of . . . [those] cases sustained the use of libel laws to impose sanctions upon expression critical of the official conduct of public officials," he said. "[L]ibel can claim no talismanic immunity from constitutional limitations. It must be measured by standards that satisfy the First Amendment." [38]

At the outset Brennan distinguished the civil rights advertisement from the kind of commercial speech that the court had held unprotected by the First Amendment. The ad primarily communicated information about a public issue of great concern, he said. *(Commercial speech, p. 421)*

Reviewing the role of a free press in a democratic society, Brennan said:

. . .we consider this case against the background of a profound national commitment to the principle that debate on public issues should be uninhibited, robust, and wide-open, and that it may well include vehement, caustic, and sometimes unpleasantly sharp attacks on government and public officials. . . . The present advertisement, as an expression of grievance and protest on one of the major public issues of our time, would

seem clearly to qualify for the constitutional protection. The question is whether it forfeits that protection by the falsity of some of its factual statements and by its alleged defamation of . . . [Sullivan]. [39]

The courts, said Brennan, have recognized that "erroneous statement is inevitable in free debate, and that it must be protected if the freedoms of expression are to have the 'breathing space' that they 'need . . . to survive.' "[40]

This was true of speech about public officials as well as public issues, Brennan said:

. . .A rule compelling the critic of official conduct to guarantee the truth of all his factual assertions — and to do so on pain of libel judgments virtually unlimited in amount — leads to a comparable "self-censorship". . . . Under such a rule, would-be critics of official conduct may be deterred from voicing their criticism, even though it is believed to be true and even though it is in fact true, because of doubt whether it can be proved in court or fear of the expense of having to do so. . . . The rule thus dampens the vigor and limits the variety of public debate. It is inconsistent with the First and Fourteenth Amendments. [41]

Drawing heavily on the 1908 Kansas decision in *Coleman v. MacLennan*, Brennan then set out the standard for determining whether defamatory statements about public officials fell within the protection of the First Amendment:

The constitutional guarantees require, we think, a federal rule that prohibits a public official from recovering damages for a defamatory falsehood relating to his official conduct unless he proves that the statement was made with 'actual malice' — that is, with knowledge that it was false or with reckless disregard of whether it was false or not. [42]

Applying that rule to the circumstances of the *Sullivan* case, the court found that there was no evidence that the individual clergymen knew their statements to be false or were reckless in that regard. Although the *Times* had information in its news files that would have corrected some of the errors contained in the advertisement, the court did not find that the *Times* personnel had acted with any actual malice. The evidence against the *Times,* said Brennan, "supports at most a finding of negligence in failing to discover the misstatements, and is constitutionally insufficient to show the recklessness that is required for a finding of actual malice." [43]

In a concurring opinion, Justice Hugo L. Black, joined by Justice William O. Douglas, contended that the First and 14th Amendments prevented a state from ever awarding libel damages to a public official for false statements made about his public conduct. The newspaper and the individual clergymen "had an absolute, unconditional constitutional right to publish in the *Times* advertisement their criticisms of the Montgomery agencies and officials," he wrote. [44]

In another concurring opinion, Justice Arthur J. Goldberg, again joined by Douglas, also held that the First Amendment provided an absolute right to criticize the public conduct of public officials. He also questioned how much protection the "actual malice" rule would afford publishers. Can "freedom of speech which all agree is constitutionally protected . . . be effectively safeguarded by a rule allowing the imposition of liability upon a jury's evaluation of the speaker's state of mind"? he asked. [45]

Follow-Up Rulings

In a series of subsequent decisions, the court elaborated on its *New York Times* rule. In *Garrison v. Louisiana* (1964), the court ruled that the actual malice rule limited state power to impose criminal as well as civil sanctions against persons criticizing the official conduct of public officials. In 1968 the court ruled that to prove reckless disregard for the truth or falsity of the allegedly libelous statement there must be "sufficient evidence to permit the conclusion that the defendant in fact entertained serious doubts as to the truth of his publications." [46]

Proof of Malice. In the 1979 case of *Herbert v. Lando,* the court by a 6-3 vote held that the *New York Times* actual malice standard required inquiry into the editorial process — the pre-publication thoughts, conclusions and conversations of editors and reporters — by persons who charge they have been libeled by the product of that process. The decision was viewed as a defeat for the press which had contended the First Amendment protected the editorial process from such scrutiny.

Writing for the six-justice majority, Justice White said nothing in the First Amendment restricted a person alleging libel from obtaining the evidence necessary to prove actual malice under the *New York Times* rule. To the contrary, White said,

> ...*New York Times* and its progeny made it essential to proving liability that plaintiffs [alleging libel] focus on the conduct and state of mind of the defendant [publishers]. To be liable, the alleged defamer of public officials or of public figures must know or have reason to suspect that his publication is false. In other cases [brought by private individuals] proof of some kind of fault, negligence perhaps, is essential to recovery. Inevitably, unless liability is to be completely foreclosed, the thoughts and editorial processes of the alleged defamer would be open to examination. [47]

Who May Sue. The problem which has most seriously divided the court is determining against what category of person the *New York Times* rule operates. All the justices agreed that public officials must show actual malice to win damages, and in 1966 the court further defined "public officials."

In a pair of cases the following year, the court applied the rule in cases involving a "public figure."

In 1971 a narrow majority of the court held that to win damages in libel suits involving matters of public concern and interest private individuals must also show actual malice. But in two subsequent rulings, the court appears to have shifted its position to allow states to set less stringent standards of proof than actual malice for private citizens alleging libel.

Public Officials

Two years after the decision in *New York Times Co. v. Sullivan,* the court further defined what it meant by public officials in the 1966 case of *Rosenblatt v. Baer.* The former supervisor of a county ski resort sued a newspaper columnist for an allegedly libelous statement about his management of the recreation area. Without being instructed to use the *New York Times* rule, the jury found in favor of the supervisor. By an 8-1 vote the Supreme Court reversed. But the justices disagreed on their reasons for reversal.

Group Libel

From time to time states have sought to quell racial and religious intolerance and unrest by enacting group libel laws — laws that make it illegal for anyone to defame groups of people.

Such laws clearly act as a restraint on the freedom of the press to discuss public issues concerning particular groups. But in the only case it has heard on the validity of group libel laws, the Supreme Court sustained such a law, holding that the First Amendment offered no protection for such defamatory statements.

The case of *Beauharnais v. Illinois* (1952) concerned Joseph Beauharnais, who presided over an organization called the White Circle League. He distributed on Chicago streets leaflets making clearly racist statements about blacks and calling on the mayor and city council to protect white residents and neighborhoods against harassment by blacks.

Beauharnais was arrested and convicted of violating an Illinois group libel statute that made it illegal to publish anything defamatory or derogatory about "a class of citizens of any race, color, creed or religion." He appealed his conviction, but the Supreme Court sustained it by a 5-4 vote.

Writing for the majority, Justice Felix Frankfurter observed that it would be libelous to accuse an individual falsely of being a rapist or robber. And, said Frankfurter, "if an utterance directed at an individual may be the object of criminal sanctions, we cannot deny to a State power to punish the same utterance directed at a defined group" unless the state had acted arbitrarily when it passed its group libel law. [1]

Frankfurter did not mention the First Amendment until the end of his opinion. He then held it irrelevant to this case on the basis of the court's earlier *dicta* that it afforded no protection for libel.

In a separate dissenting opinion, Justice William O. Douglas wrote:

> Today a white man stands convicted for protesting in unseemly language against our decisions invalidating restrictive covenants. Tomorrow a negro will be hailed before a court for denouncing lynch law in heated terms. . . . Intemperate speech is a distinctive characteristic of man. Hot-heads blow off and release destructive energy in the process. . . . So it has been from the beginning; and so it will be throughout time. The Framers of the Constitution knew human nature as well as we do. [2]

The viability of the *Beauharnais* decision as a precedent has been called into serious question by the court's later decisions that both civil and criminal libels are within the scope of the First Amendment protections, but the court has not reconsidered the 1952 decision. [3]

---

[1] *Beauharnais v. Illinois,* 343 U.S. 250 at 258 (1952).
[2] Id. at 286-287.
[3] See *The New York Times Co. v. Sullivan,* 376 U.S. 254 (1964); *Garrison v. Louisiana,* 379 U.S. 64 (1964); *Ashton v. Kentucky,* 384 U.S. 195 (1966).

The Right to Publicity

In August 1972 an Ohio television station filmed, without the performer's consent, the entire 15-second act of Hugo Zacchini, a "human cannonball" whose "act" consisted of being shot from a cannon into a net some 200 feet away.

After the station showed the film clip on its nightly news program as an item of interest, Zacchini sued, charging that the television station had appropriated his right to control publicity concerning his performance.

The Ohio supreme court ruled in favor of the television station. Unless Zacchini showed that the station intentionally meant to harm him or to use the film for some private purpose, then its airing of Zacchini's act was protected by the First and 14th Amendments, held the state court.

By a 5-4 vote, the Supreme Court overturned that decision in *Zacchini v. Scripps-Howard Broadcasting Co.* (1977)

"Wherever the line in particular situations is to be drawn between media reports that are protected and those that are not, we are quite sure that the First and Fourteenth Amendments do not immunize the media when they broadcast a performer's entire act without his consent," wrote Justice Byron R. White for the majority. "The Constitution no more prevents a State from requiring . . . [the television station] to compensate petitioner for broadcasting his act on television than it would privilege . . . [the station] to film and broadcast a copyrighted dramatic work without liability to the copyright owner."

Three of the dissenters held that the broadcast was privileged under the First and 14th Amendments. The film was a simple report on a newsworthy event and shown as part of an ordinary daily news report. The broadcast was therefore no more than "a routine example of the press fulfilling the informing function so vital to our system." (433 U.S. 562 at 574-75, 580, 1977)

Justice Brennan, who wrote the formal court opinion in which only two other justices concurred, defined "public official":

There is, first, a strong interest in debate on public issues, and second, a strong interest in debate about those persons who are in a position significantly to influence the resolution of those issues. Criticism of government is at the very center of the constitutionally protected area of free discussion. Criticism of those responsible for government operations must be free, lest criticism of government itself be penalized. It is clear, therefore, that the "public official" designation applies at the very least to those among the hierarchy of government employees who have, or appear to the public to have, substantial responsibility for or control over the conduct of governmental affairs. . . . Where a position in government has such apparent importance that the public has an independent interest in the qualifications and performance of the person who holds it, beyond the general public interest in the qualifications and performance of all government employees, both elements we identified in *New York Times* are

present and the *New York Times* malice standards apply. [48]

Although this has come to be the accepted definition of "public official," a majority of the court did not initially endorse it. Justice Tom C. Clark concurred in the judgment without an opinion. Justice Douglas concurred, but thought the question should turn on whether the alleged libel involved a public issue rather than a public official. Justice Potter Stewart also agreed with the judgment but cautioned that the actual malice rule should be applied only "where a State's law of defamation has been unconstitutionally converted into a law of seditious libel." [49]

Justice John Marshall Harlan concurred with the judgment but disagreed with part of Brennan's opinion. Justice Black concurred, maintaining that the First and 14th Amendments forbade all libel judgments against newspaper comment on public issues. Justice Abe Fortas dissented for technical reasons.

Candidates. The court was considerably more unified in 1971 when it ruled that candidates for public office were public officials and that the *New York Times* rule protected publishers from libel charges resulting from their decision to print information on the criminal records of these persons. [50]

Public Figures

The wide diversity of views on the applicability of the actual malice rule was again evident in two 1967 decisions in which a majority of the court held that the *New York Times* rule applied to persons who were not public officials but were nonetheless in the public eye.

The first of these cases, *Curtis Publishing Co. v. Butts*, concerned a libel action brought by former University of Georgia athletic director Wallace Butts against *The Saturday Evening Post*, which was owned by the Curtis Publishing Co.

The *Post* had printed a story in which it alleged that Butts had "fixed" a football game by revealing his team's offensive and defensive plays to the opposing coach, Paul Bryant of the University of Alabama.

At his trial, completed before the Supreme Court issued its malice rule, Butts admitted talking to Bryant but said he had revealed nothing of value to him. Butts was supported by expert witnesses, and there was substantial evidence that the *Post* investigation of the allegation had been gravely inadequate. The jury found in Butts' favor and the final award was $480,000. After the *New York Times* rule was issued, the publishing company asked for another trial which the state courts denied.

The second case, *Associated Press v. Walker*, concerned an allegedly libelous eyewitness news report that former general Edwin A. Walker had led rioters against federal marshals who were trying to maintain order at the University of Mississippi during turmoil over the enrollment of a black student, James Meredith. Walker, who had commanded federal troops guarding black students who tried to enter a Little Rock, Ark., high school in 1958, was awarded $500,000 in compensatory damages. *(Little Rock incident, resulting cases, p. 597)*

The Supreme Court unanimously reversed the award in Walker's case but by a 5-4 vote upheld the award of damages to Butts. [51]

All of the justices agreed that both Butts and Walker were public figures, but four of the justices would not have

The Press and Personal Privacy

Freedom of the press might be justifiably curtailed, wrote Chief Justice Charles Evans Hughes in *Near v. Minnesota* (1931), to prevent the invasion of "private rights." *(Near ruling, p. 425; privacy, p. 644)*

Although the specific question whether government may prevent publication of articles that threaten to invade a person's privacy has not come before the court, the court has dealt with the question of whether publications may be punished for infringing individual privacy.

The 'Desperate Hours' Case

The first of these cases, *Time Inc. v. Hill* (1967), concerned a claim of privacy by a family who had been held hostage in their Pennsylvania home in 1952 by three escaped convicts. The convicts treated the family politely and released them unharmed.

In 1953 a book entitled *The Desperate Hours* was published; it recounted a story similar to the Hill family's experience but, unlike the actual event, the convicts in the story treated their captives violently. The novel was made into a play and later a film. In an article on the play, *Life* magazine sent actors to the former Hill house where they were photographed acting scenes from the play. The article characterized the play as a re-enactment of the Hill incident.

Hill sued the magazine under a New York right of privacy statute which made it a misdemeanor for anyone to use without consent another's name for commercial purposes. The jury found in favor of Hill and the state appeals courts affirmed that judgment.

The Supreme Court reversed on a 6-3 vote.[1] The Hill family was newsworthy, albeit involuntarily, observed Justice William J. Brennan Jr. for the majority. The New York statute as interpreted by the state's courts permitted newsworthy persons to recover upon showing only that the report or article was fictionalized. But, said Brennan, the actual malice standard set out in *New York Times Co. v. Sullivan* (1964) must be applied to this case even though private individuals are involved.[2] Brennan wrote:

> The guarantees for speech and press are not the preserve of political expression or comment upon public affairs, essential as those are to healthy government. One need only pick up any newspaper or magazine to comprehend the vast range of published matter which exposes persons to public view, both private citizens and public officials. Exposure of the self to others in varying degrees is a concomitant of life in a civilized community. The risk of this exposure is an essential incident of a society which places a primary value on freedom of speech and of press.... We have no doubt that the subject of the *Life* article ... is a matter of public interest.... Erroneous statement is no less inevitable in such a case than in the case of comment upon public affairs, and in both, if innocent or merely negligent, "...it must be protected if the freedoms of expres-

sion are to have the 'breathing space' that they 'need ... to survive'...."

> ...We create a grave risk of serious impairment of the indispensable service of a free press in a free society if we saddle the press with the impossible burden of verifying to a certainty the facts associated in news articles with a person's name, picture or portrait, particularly as related to nondefamatory matter.[3]

Because the jury had not been instructed that it could award damages to the Hills only if it found the article had been published with actual malice, the majority sent the case back to the lower courts for further proceedings.

Calculated Falsehood

In the next case, however, the court found that a jury had been justified in finding that false statements had been printed with reckless disregard for the truth.

Cantrell v. Forest City Publishing Co. (1974) concerned a published report on the family of a man who had been killed in a bridge collapse. Among the admitted misrepresentations in the article were "quotes" from the man's widow, who had not been interviewed by the reporter. This was a "calculated falsehood," the majority said, portraying the Cantrell family "in a false light through knowing or reckless untruth."[4]

Court Records

In the 1975 case of *Cox Broadcasting Corporation v. Cohn*, the Supreme Court struck down a Georgia law making it illegal to broadcast the names of rape victims.

The father of a girl who had died as a result of an assault and rape brought suit against a television station owned by the Cox Broadcasting Corporation for reporting his daughter's name in two of their news reports. The reporter testified that he had obtained the name of the rape victim at an open court hearing at which five of the six men indicted for the crime pleaded guilty.

The Supreme Court struck down the Georgia law by an 8-1 vote. The First and 14th Amendments do not allow states to "impose sanctions for the publication of truthful information contained in official court records open to public inspection," the majority said. On the issue of privacy, the majority wrote:

> ...If there are privacy interests to be protected in judicial proceedings, the States must respond by means which avoid public documentation or other exposure of private information. Their political institutions must weigh the interests in privacy with the interests of the public to know and of the press to publish.[5]

In 1979, a unanimous court struck down a state law that forbade newspapers, but not other forms of the press, from reporting the names of juveniles involved in criminal proceedings.[6]

---

[1] *Time Inc., v. Hill*, 385 U.S. 374 (1967).
[2] *The New York Times Co. v. Sullivan*, 376 U.S. 254 (1964).
[3] *Time Inc. v. Hill*, 385 U.S. 374 at 388, 389 passim (1967).
[4] *Cantrell v. Forest City Publishing Co.*, 419 U.S. 245 at 253 (1974).
[5] *Cox Broadcasting Corp. v. Cohn*, 420 U.S. 469 at 495, 496 (1975).
[6] *Smith v. Daily Mail* (1979).

applied the actual malice rule to their cases. Three of the remaining five justices would have applied the actual malice rule and two of the justices believed that freedom of the press absolutely protected publishers from being sued for libel.

The Opinion. Writing the formal opinion for the court, Justice Harlan, joined by Clark, Stewart and Fortas, concluded that Butts and Walker were "public figures." (Chief Justice Earl Warren, the fifth member of the majority, agreed with Harlan's result but not with his reasoning.)

"Butts may have attained that status by position alone and Walker by his purposeful activity amounting to a thrusting of his personality into the 'vortex' of an important public controversy...," Harlan said. Both men "commanded sufficient public interest and had sufficient access to the means of counter-argument to be able to 'expose through discussion the falsehood and fallacies' of the defamatory statements." [52]

But those four justices would apply a less strict rule than the actual malice test in libel cases brought by such public figures. Harlan wrote:

> ...a "public figure" who is not a public official may also recover damages for a defamatory falsehood whose substance makes substantial danger to reputation apparent, on a showing of highly unreasonable conduct constituting an extreme departure from the standards of investigation and reporting ordinarily adhered to by reasonable publishers. [53]

Using this standard, Harlan found that the *Post* had failed to exercise elementary journalistic precautions to determine if the allegation against Butts was true. Therefore the libel award to Butts must be sustained, he said.

But the award to Walker must be overturned, Harlan said, because nothing in the evidence suggests a "departure from accepted publishing standards." [54]

The remaining five justices agreed with Chief Justice Earl Warren that public figures must prove actual malice under the *New York Times* rule to win libel damages. Warren wrote:

> ...[I]t is plain that although they are not subject to the restraints of the political process, "public figures," like "public officials," often play an influential role in ordering society. And surely as a class these "public figures" have as ready access as "public officials" to mass media of communication, both to influence policy and to counter criticism of their views and activities. Our citizenry has a legitimate and substantial interest in the conduct of such persons, and freedom of the press to engage in uninhibited debate about their involvement in public issues and events is as crucial as it is in the case of "public officials." The fact that they are not amenable to the restraints of the political process only underscores the legitimate and substantial nature of the interest, since it means that public opinion may be the only instrument by which society can attempt to influence their conduct. [55]

Applying the *New York Times* rule, it was evident that Walker had not proved actual malice and thus his judgment must be reversed, Warren said. But in the Butts case, the magazine's conduct showed the "degree of reckless disregard for the truth" that constituted actual malice under the rule.

Justices Brennan and Byron R. White concurred with Warren in requiring public figures to prove malice and in

reversing the award in the Walker case, but they would have also reversed the award in the Butts case on the grounds that the jury instructions did not conform with the actual malice standard. Justices Black and Douglas also would have reversed the Butts award on the grounds that the First and 14th Amendments did not permit any libel judgments against the press for publication of articles on matters of public interest.

Private Individuals

The court splintered into four positions the first time it considered whether private individuals must prove actual malice to win damages for libel.

George Rosenbloom, a distributor of nudist magazines, was arrested in a police crackdown on pornography. A local radio station reported that Rosenbloom had been arrested for possession of obscene literature. After he was acquitted of criminal obscenity charges, Rosenbloom sued the radio station for libel. A jury awarded him $750,000, but an appeals court reversed on the grounds that the jury should have been required to apply the *New York Times* actual malice standard to the case.

The Supreme Court affirmed the appeals court decision by a 5-3 ruling in the case of *Rosenbloom v. Metromedia Inc.* (1971).

Chief Justice Warren E. Burger and Justices Brennan and Harry A. Blackmun agreed that the actual malice rule should be applied to all discussion of public issues even if the discussion includes defamatory statements about private individuals.

The First Amendment was intended to protect discussion of public issues, Brennan said, and an issue does not become less public

> ...merely because a private individual is involved.... The public's primary interest is in the event; the public focus is on the conduct of the participant and the content, effect, and significance of the conduct, not the participant's prior anonymity or notoriety. [56]

Justice Black concurred, maintaining that the guarantee of a free press protected publishers against all libel suits. Justice White also concurred, holding that the *New York Times* rule protected newspapers who praised public officials, in this case the police who undertook the pornography investigation, and criticized their adversaries.

In dissent, Justices Marshall, Stewart and Harlan said they would not apply the actual malice rule to libel cases involving private individuals. Justice Douglas did not participate.

The *Gertz* Decision

Three years later the court shifted, adopting the *Rosenbloom* dissenters' position that the actual malice rule did not apply in libel cases brought by private individuals. Five justices endorsed this view in the case of *Gertz v. Robert Welch, Inc.* (1974).

Elmer Gertz was an attorney who sued a Chicago policeman in behalf of the family of a youth killed by the officer. *American Opinion*, the journal of the John Birch Society, printed an article in 1969 characterizing Gertz as a "Leninist" with a criminal record who was part of a communist conspiracy to discredit local police forces. Charging that the allegations were false, Gertz sued the journal for damages.

The jury found his claims valid and awarded him $50,000 in damages, but the trial court overruled the jury. Using *Rosenbloom* as a precedent, the court said that the First Amendment protected publishers from libel suits in connection with discussions of public interest even if they defamed private individuals unless the individual could prove actual malice on the part of the publisher. A court of appeals agreed with this ruling, but the Supreme Court reversed on a 5-4 vote.

The five-man majority included the two new members of the court, Lewis F. Powell Jr. and William H. Rehnquist, who had succeeded Justices Black and Harlan late in 1971. Voting with them were *Rosenbloom* dissenters Marshall and Stewart and, with reservations, Justice Blackmun.

The *New York Times* rule is not appropriate in libel cases involving private individuals, wrote Justice Powell for the majority. Private citizens lack the access of public officials and public figures to "channels of effective communication" to combat allegations about their conduct, he observed. Furthermore, private individuals, unlike public officials and figures, have not voluntarily subjected themselves to public scrutiny. A private person, Powell wrote,

> . . .has relinquished no part of his interest in the protection of his own good name, and consequently he has a more compelling call on the courts for redress of injury inflicted by defamatory falsehood. Thus, private individuals are not only more vulnerable to injury than public officials and public figures; they are also more deserving of recovery. [57]

Therefore, Powell continued, "so long as they do not impose liability without fault, the States may define for themselves the appropriate standard of liability for a publisher or broadcaster of defamatory falsehood injurious to a private individual." [58]

To avoid undesirable self-censorship by the press, Powell cautioned, the liability of publications to private-person libel suits must be limited. Therefore, private individuals who proved, for example, only that a publisher had been negligent when he printed false defamatory statements could recover damages only for the actual injury to his reputation.

Punitive or presumed damages could be awarded only on a showing that actual malice, as defined by the *New York Times* rule, was intended, Powell held.

Turning to the case at hand, Powell held that Gertz was a private individual despite his active participation in community and professional affairs:

> . . .Absent clear evidence of general fame or notoriety in the community, and pervasive involvement in the affairs of society, an individual should not be deemed a public personality for all aspects of his life. It is preferable to reduce the public-figure question to a more meaningful context by looking to the nature and extent of an individual's participation in the particular controversy giving rise to the defamation. [59]

The majority sent the case back for a new trial, holding, on the one hand, that the jury should not have been allowed to award damages without a finding of fault on the part of *American Opinion,* and, on the other hand, that the trial court had erred in holding that the actual malice standard should be applied.

Justice Blackmun said that although he would prefer to extend the actual malice standard to such a case, he would join the opinion by Powell in order to make a firm

majority and allow "the court to come to rest in the defamation area." [60]

In separate dissents, Chief Justice Burger and Justice Brennan, joined by Justice Douglas, maintained that discussions of public interest, including those touching private persons, should be protected by the actual malice rule. Justice White also dissented, claiming that the majority opinion made it almost impossible for a private individual to defend his reputation successfully since he must prove not only that the offending statement was false but also that it was made negligently.

Gertz Reaffirmed

The court reaffirmed the principles of the *Gertz* decision in the 1976 case of *Time v. Firestone.* In its December 22, 1967, issue, *Time* magazine carried an item in its "Milestones" section announcing the divorce of Russell A. Firestone Jr., heir to the tire fortune, from his third wife, Mary Alice Sullivan. In that item the magazine wrote: "The 17-month intermittent trial produced enough testimony of extramarital adventures on both sides, said the judge, 'to make Dr. Freud's hair curl.' "

This report, as *Time* was soon to discover, was less than accurate. Although Firestone's suit for divorce had charged his wife with adultery and extreme cruelty, the judge in granting him the divorce did not specify that those charges were the grounds upon which the divorce was granted.

When *Time* refused her request for a retraction of the item, the former Mrs. Firestone filed a libel suit against the magazine. She won a $100,000 damage judgment.

Time appealed, claiming that Mrs. Firestone was a public figure and therefore must prove actual malice to win the suit. The magazine also argued that reports of court proceedings are of sufficient public interest that they cannot be the basis for libel judgments — even if erroneous or false and defamatory — unless it is proved that they were published maliciously.

The Supreme Court rejected both of *Time*'s arguments by a 5-3 vote, sending the case back to Florida courts to determine whether or not *Time* had been negligent in failing to check the accuracy of the report or was otherwise at fault.

Writing for the majority, Justice Rehnquist stated that Mrs. Firestone was not a public figure despite her involvement in the sensational divorce case. She "did not assume any role of especial prominence in the affairs of society . . . and she did not thrust herself to the forefront of any particular public controversy in order to influence the resolution of the issues involved in it." [61]

Rehnquist noted that the justices had already rejected, in the *Gertz* case, use of the actual malice rule for all reports of court proceedings. The public interest in such reports, he added, was sufficiently protected under a 1975 decision forbidding the states to allow the media to be sued for reporting true information available to the public in official court records. *(1975 case, p. 437)*

Justice White dissented, saying that the libel award should be upheld. Justice Brennan also dissented, arguing that the first Amendment protected reporting of public judicial proceedings unless actual malice was proved. The third dissenter, Justice Marshall, thought Mrs. Firestone was a public figure and that the *New York Times* actual malice rule should therefore apply.

In two 1979 cases, the court again upheld the *Gertz* decision, ruling that private individuals who were placed in the public eye involuntarily were not "public figures" and therefore did not have to prove actual malice under the *New York Times* rule in order to bring a successful libel suit. [62]

Free Press v. Fair Trial

The First Amendment guarantee of freedom of the press seems on occasion to conflict with the Sixth Amendment's guarantee of trial by an impartial jury.

As Justice Tom C. Clark wrote in 1966:

A responsible press has always been regarded as the handmaiden of effective judicial administration, especially in the criminal field.... The press does not simply publish information about trials, but guards against the miscarriage of justice by subjecting the police, prosecutors, and judicial processes to extensive public scrutiny and criticism. [63]

In this way the public may assure itself that justice is attained, to the benefit both of society and of the individual defendant.

The conflict of this freedom with this right arises from the Constitution's promise that a defendant shall be judged by an impartial jury solely on evidence produced in court, and that both judge and jury shall be free from outside influence. But in cases concerning prominent people or sensational crimes, pretrial publicity can so saturate a community that the pool of unbiased potential jurors is significantly diminished. News accounts and editorials may influence jurors and judges while a case is pending. The question then is what, if any, restrictions on the free press are constitutionally permissible in order to ensure a fair trial.

Contempt of Court

The Supreme Court has exhibited little tolerance for efforts by judges to restrict criticism of them and their official conduct. From time to time judges have held in contempt publishers, editors and writers who have criticized them — while a case was still pending — for the way they have handled it.

The argument in support of such punishment is that public criticism of a judge might influence or coerce him to rule in a way that will maintáin the good will of the publisher and the community at large at the expense of fairness to the parties in the case.

Federal Courts. The potential for judicial abuse of the contempt power prompted Congress in 1831 to enact a law forbidding the use of contempt citations to punish misbehavior other than that which occurred in court "or so near thereto as to obstruct the administration of justice." In a 1918 case the Supreme Court allowed the use of the contempt power to curtail a newspaper's criticisms of a judge's conduct concerning a pending case. [64]

In 1941, however, the court overruled its earlier decision, holding that the phrase "so near thereto" meant only physical proximity. Thus, federal law as presently construed gives published criticisms of federal judicial conduct absolute protection from summary contempt proceedings.[65] *(Discussion of contempt power, p. 279)*

State Courts. In 1907, the several years before the Supreme Court held that the First Amendment freedoms were protected against state action by the 14th Amendment, the court sustained a contempt citation against a newspaper publisher for publishing articles and a cartoon critical of a court's actions on pending cases.

If the court determines that a critical publication tends to interfere with the fair administration of justice, wrote Justice Oliver Wendell Holmes Jr., then the publisher may be punished. "When a case is finished, the courts are subject to the same criticism as other people, but the propriety and necessity of preventing interference with the court of justice by premature statement, argument or intimidation hardly can be denied," he said. [66]

Since 1925, when the Supreme Court made the First Amendment applicable to the states, it has not sustained any contempt citation issued by a judge against a newspaper critical of his actions on a case that is still pending. *(First Amendment and the states, p. 388)*

The leading decision in this area is *Bridges v. California* (1941), in which the court overturned by a 5-4 vote contempt rulings against both a labor leader and an anti-union Los Angeles newspaper.

While a motion for a new trial was pending in a dispute between two competing longshoremen's unions, Bridges, the president of one of the unions, sent a telegram to the U.S. secretary of labor describing as outrageous the judge's initial decision favoring the competing union. Bridges threatened to strike the entire Pacific coast if the original decision were allowed to stand. The telegram was reprinted in several California newspapers.

A companion case to *Bridges, Times-Mirror Co. v. Superior Court of California,* involved a *Los Angeles Times* editorial which urged a trial judge to give severe sentences to two union members found guilty of beating up non-union truck drivers.

Writing for the five-justice majority overturning the contempt citation against the newspaper, Justice Hugo L. Black said that punishment for contempt improperly restricted freedom of the press. If the contempt citations were allowed to stand, Black said,

...anyone who might wish to give public expression to his views on a pending case involving no matter what problem of public interest, just at the time his audience would be most receptive, would be as effectively discouraged as if a deliberate statutory scheme of censorship had been adopted. [67]

Such a restriction on freedom of the press would be permissible only if the criticism raised a clear and present danger that a substantive evil would result, Black continued. But the only dangers cited by the court in this case were that the articles might result in disrespect for the court and unfair administration of justice. Black quickly dismissed the first of these rationales:

...The assumption that respect for the judiciary can be won by shielding judges from published criticism wrongly appraises the character of American public opinion. For it is a prized American privilege to speak one's mind, although not always with perfect good taste, on all public institutions. And an enforced

Commissions and Confidentiality

A state may not fine a newspaper for printing a true report of confidential proceedings of a state commission considering disciplinary action against a sitting state judge. This was the Supreme Court's unanimous holding in the case of *Landmark Communications Inc. v. Virginia* (435 U.S. 829, 1978).

After the Norfolk (Va.) *Virginian-Pilot* printed an accurate report of an inquiry by the state judicial review commission into the conduct of a sitting judge named in the article, the newspaper was indicted, tried, convicted and fined $500 for violating state law by breaching the confidentiality of the commission's proceedings.

The state justified the law as it applied in this case as necessary to protect public confidence in the judicial process, to protect the reputation of judges and to protect persons who might bring complaints to the commission. The court held that those interests justified the law protecting the confidentiality of proceedings before the commission, but they did not justify imposing criminal penalties on news media, uninvolved in the commission's proceedings, who breached that confidentiality.

silence, however limited, solely in the name of preserving the dignity of the bench, would probably engender resentment, suspicion, and contempt much more than it would enhance respect. [68]

Nor did the court find any evidence that the articles in question created a clear and present danger of interfering with the fair administration of justice. The judge in the *Los Angeles Times* case was likely to know that a lenient sentence for the two union members would result in adverse criticisms from the paper. "To regard it [the editorial], therefore, as in itself of substantial influence upon the course of justice would be to impute to judges a lack of firmness, wisdom, or honor, which we cannot accept as a major premise," Black wrote. [69]

Likewise, the judge in the *Bridges* case was likely to realize that his decision might result in a labor strike. "If he was not intimidated by the facts themselves," Black said, "we do not believe that the most explicit statement of them could have sidetracked the course of justice." [70]

Speaking for the dissenters, Justice Felix Frankfurter said the judges were within their rights to punish comments that had a "reasonable tendency" to interfere with the impartial dispensation of justice. Frankfurter wrote:

> . . .Freedom of expression can hardly carry implications that nullify the guarantees of impartial trials. And since courts are the ultimate resorts for vindicating the Bill of Rights, a state may surely authorize appropriate historic means [the contempt power] to assure that the process for such vindication be not wrenched from its rational tracks into the more primitive melee of passion and pressure. The need is great that courts be criticized, but just as great that they be allowed to do their duty. [71]

In *Pennekamp v. Florida* (1946), the court by an 8-0 vote reaffirmed its opinion that editorial comment on the court's handling of a pending case did not present a clear

and present danger of interfering with the fair administration of justice and was therefore not punishable. "In the borderline instances where it is difficult to say upon which side the alleged offense falls, we think the specific freedom of public comment should weigh heavily against a possible tendency to influence pending cases," the court said. [72]

The following year, the court in *Craig v. Harney* (1947) overturned a contempt citation for articles which gave an unfair and inaccurate account of a trial. The majority found that neither the articles nor a critical editorial constituted "an imminent and serious threat to the ability of the court to give fair consideration" to the pending case. [73]

Although the court almost totally abandoned use of the clear and present danger test in other contexts during the 1950s, it reaffirmed the use of that test in contempt cases in 1962. *(Discussion of standard, p. 392)*

In *Wood v. Georgia*, the court reversed the contempt citation of a county sheriff who denounced a county judge's order to a grand jury to investigate rumors of purchased votes and other corrupting practices as a "political attempt to intimidate" black voters. The lower court held that the sheriff's criticism, publicized in several news accounts, created a clear and present danger of influencing the grand jury. The Supreme Court disagreed, observing that the lower courts had made no attempt to show how the criticism created "a substantive evil actually designed to impede the course of justice. . . ." [74]

Pre-trial Publicity

The press contempt cases concerned criticism of judges and their conduct. A more frequent threat to the fair administration of justice is posed by publications that cast defendants in a case in such a bad light that their rights to fair treatment are jeopardized. In those instances the court has held that trial courts should take regulatory actions to protect the right to a fair trial with the least possible restriction on a free press.

Defense attorneys frequently have claimed that news reports were so inflammatory and pervasive as to deny their clients due process. The Supreme Court rejected such a claim in the 1951 case of *Stroble v. California,* noting that the publicity had receded six weeks before the trial, that the defendant had not requested a change of venue and that his publicized confession was voluntary and placed in evidence in open trial. [75]

In 1959 the court overturned a federal conviction because jurors had been exposed through news accounts to information that was not admitted in evidence at the trial. [76]

Two years later the Supreme Court for the first time reversed a state conviction on grounds that pre-trial publicity had denied the defendant due process.

In *Irvin v. Dowd* (1961), defendant Irvin had been arrested and indicted for one of six murders committed in and around Evansville, Ind. Shortly after Irvin's arrest, the police sent out press releases saying that he had confessed to all six crimes. The news media covered the crimes and the confession extensively; it also reported on previous crimes in which Irvin had been implicated. Irvin's attorney won a change of venue to a neighboring rural county which was just as saturated by the same news reports. A request for a second change of venue was denied.

The pervasiveness of the news reports was evident during jury selection. Of the 420 potential jurors asked, 370 said that they had some opinion about Irvin's guilt. Eight of the 12 jurors selected said they thought he was guilty.

Given these circumstances, a unanimous Supreme Court found that the jury did not meet the constitutional standard of impartiality. Justice Clark, who wrote the opinion, cautioned, however, that it was not necessary for jurors to

> ...be totally ignorant of the facts and issues involved. In these days of swift, widespread and diverse methods of communication, an important case can be expected to arouse the interest of the public in the vicinity, and scarcely any of those best qualified to serve as jurors will not have formed some impression or opinion as to the merits of the case. This is particularly true in criminal cases. To hold that the mere existence of any preconceived notion as to the guilt or innocence of an accused, without more, is sufficient to rebut the presumption of a prospective juror's impartiality would be to establish impossible standards. [77]

The following year, a narrow majority of the court held that pre-trial publicity had not worked to deny Teamsters Union president David D. Beck a fair trial on charges of grand larceny. The adverse publicity, stemming largely from a U.S. Senate investigation, had been diluted by time and by the presence of other labor leaders also under investigation, and both the grand jury and petit jury had been carefully questioned to avoid selection of those unduly influenced by media reports, the majority said. [78]

But in *Rideau v. Louisiana* (1963), a majority of the court held that a murder defendant whose filmed confession was broadcast and seen by three jurors had been denied due process when his effort to win a change of venue was rejected. Clark dissented, arguing that there was no evidence showing that the telecast confession had indelibly marked the minds of the jurors. [79]

Conduct of Trial

The very presence of working news reporters in and near a courtroom during the course of a trial may also jeopardize its fairness.

In 1965 the court had little trouble holding that the presence of television cameras, radio microphones and newspaper photographers at the pre-trial hearing and trial of financier Billy Sol Estes denied Estes his right to a fair trial. "[V]ideotapes of these hearings clearly illustrate that the picture presented was not one of that judicial serenity and calm to which petitioner was entitled," the court said. [80]

Three years later, in 1966, the Supreme Court in the case of *Sheppard v. Maxwell* laid out some ground rules to ensure fair trials with minimal restriction on the operation of a free press.

The Sheppard Case

The 1954 bludgeon murder of a pregnant woman in her suburban Cleveland home and the subsequent arrest, trial and conviction of her husband, Dr. Sam Sheppard, for that murder excited some of the most intense and sensational press coverage the country has witnessed.

Pre-trial publicity as much as proclaimed Sheppard's guilt. Reporters had access to witnesses during the trial itself and frequently published information damaging to Sheppard that could have come only from the prosecuting

attorneys. Some of this information was never introduced as evidence.

Reporters in the courtroom were seated inside the bar only a few feet from the jury and from Sheppard and his counsel. Sheppard, jurors, witnesses and counsel were constantly beseiged by reporters and photographers as they entered and left the courtroom.

"The fact is that bedlam reigned at the courthouse during the trial and newsmen took over practically the entire courtroom," said the Supreme Court, overturning Sheppard's conviction by an 8-1 vote. "The carnival atmosphere at trial could easily have been avoided since the courtroom and courthouse premises are subject to control of the court," the majority wrote. "[T]he presence of the press at judicial proceedings must be limited when it is apparent that the accused might otherwise be prejudiced or disadvantaged." [81]

Change of venue and postponement of the trial until publicity dies down would be proper if pre-trial publicity threatens the fair administration of justice, the court said. Once the trial has begun, the judge may limit the number of reporters permitted in the courtroom and place strict controls on their conduct while there. Witnesses and jurors should be isolated from the press, and the jury may be sequestered to prevent it from being influenced by trial coverage.

The majority also indicated that the judge should have acted to prevent officials from releasing certain information to the press:

> ...[T]he trial court might well have proscribed extrajudicial statements by any lawyer, party, witness or court official which divulged prejudicial matters, such as the refusal of Sheppard to submit to an interrogation or take any lie detector tests; any statement made by Sheppard to officials; the identity of prospective witnesses or their probable testimony; any belief in guilt or innocence; or like statements concerning the merits of the case....
>
> Being advised of the great public interest in the case, the mass coverage of the press, and the potential prejudicial impact of publicity, the court could also have requested the appropriate city and county officials to promulgate a regulation with respect to dissemination of information about the case by their employees. In addition, reporters who wrote or broadcast prejudicial stories could have been warned as to the impropriety of publishing material not introduced in the proceedings.... In this manner, Sheppard's right to a trial free from outside interference would have been given added protection without corresponding curtailment of the news media. [82]

Gag Rules

One of the results of the *Sheppard* case was the increased use of so-called "gag rules," under which the press is barred by judicial order from publishing articles containing certain types of information about pending court cases. Refusal to comply with the order may result in being held in contempt of court.

Such orders are clearly a prior restraint on publication, and their constitutionality has been challenged repeatedly by the press.

In the court's only full-scale review of a gag rule, all nine justices held the challenged order an unconstitutional prior restraint on the press. Only three justices, however, said that all gag rules were unconstitutional. Four felt they might be permissible under some circumstances. The remaining two justices indicated their inclination to agree that all gag rules were unconstitutional but were unwilling to make that finding based on the pending case.

The murder of six members of a family in the small town of Sutherland, Neb., in October 1975 was followed by the arrest of Erwin Charles Simants, who was charged with the crimes. Because of the nature of the crimes and the location — a rural area with a relatively small number of potential jurors — the judge issued a gag order on the day of the preliminary hearing. Although that hearing took place in open court, the press was forbidden to report any of the testimony given or the evidence presented.

The order subsequently was upheld but modified by state courts. As finally effective it forbade the reporting before trial of any confessions or admissions by Simants (except those made directly to the media) and of any other facts strongly implicating him in the crime.

The order remained in effect until the jury was chosen early in January 1976; it then expired. In December 1975 the Supreme Court agreed to hear arguments in the Nebraska Press Association's appeal from the Nebraska supreme court decision upholding the order. Before the case was argued in April, Simants had been convicted and sentenced to death.

Writing the court's opinion in *Nebraska Press Association v. Stuart* (1976), Chief Justice Warren E. Burger said there was no need for the First Amendment freedom of the press to collide with the Sixth Amendment guarantee of right to a fair trial. The judge could have used less dramatic means than the gag order to ensure that excessive publicity did not make it impossible to assemble an unbiased jury and conduct a fair trial, such as many of the methods recommended in the *Sheppard* opinion.

"[P]rior restraints on speech and publication are the most serious and the least tolerable infringement on First Amendment rights," Burger wrote. "A prior restraint . . . has an immediate and irreversible sanction. If it can be said that a threat of criminal or civil sanctions after publication

'chills' speech, prior restraint 'freezes' it at least for the time."[83] *(Prior restraint, p. 424)*

Furthermore, said Burger, the right to report evidence given in an open courtroom is a settled principle. "[O]nce a public hearing had been held, what transpired there could not be subject to prior restraint."[84]

Moreover, it was not clear, said Burger, that the publicity which the judge feared would have biased all potential jurors to the point of making a fair trial impossible or that other measures besides a gag order would not have worked as well to protect Simants' right to a fair trial. Neither was it established that the gag order actually provided that protection.

But the Chief Justice refused to rule out the possibility that the circumstances of some particular case might justify imposition of a gag rule. "This Court has frequently denied that First Amendment rights are absolute and has consistently rejected the proposition that a prior restraint can never be employed," he said.[85]

"The right to a fair trial by a jury of one's peers is unquestionably one of the most precious and sacred safeguards enshrined in the Bill of Rights," wrote Justice William J. Brennan Jr. in a concurring opinion joined by Justices Thurgood Marshall and Potter Stewart. But, Brennan added, "I would hold . . . that resort to prior restraints on the freedom of the press is a constitutionally impermissible method for enforcing that right." Judges have less drastic means of ensuring fair trials than by prohibiting press "discussion of public affairs," he said.[86]

Closed Hearings

In 1979, the court in the case of *Gannett Co. v. DePasquale* rejected the claim of a newspaper chain that it had a constitutional right, under the First and the Sixth Amendments, to attend a pre-trial hearing on suppression of evidence in a murder case.[87]

By a vote of 5-4, the court held that the judge in the case had properly granted the request of the defendants to keep press and public out of the hearing.[88]

Access and Confidentiality

In a very practical sense, the public has delegated to the press the job of gathering, sifting through and reporting the news that will help it shape its political, economic and social views of the world and the individual's place in it. As the public's surrogate the press attends and reports on events that the vast majority of the public does not or cannot attend.

In recent years the news gathering process has been the subject of several Supreme Court cases as the justices have considered whether the First Amendment guarantees the press special access to or special protection for its news sources. The court generally has refused to adopt such an expansive view of the First Amendment freedom.

Privilege of Access

Does the First Amendment require government to grant members of the press special access to institutions and persons not available to the general public?

The Supreme Court has confronted this question on only two occasions; both dealt with government bars on access to prisons and prison inmates. On both occasions, the court held that the press had no greater access to such institutions than that enjoyed by the general public.

Inmate Interviews

In a pair of cases decided together in June 1974, the court weighed the right of the public to know about prison conditions and the right of reporters to gather news within the prison system against society's interest in secure prisons. The court sustained, by 5-4 votes, federal and California prison regulations which bar interviews by reporters with inmates they request by name to see.[89]

By a 6-3 vote the court also ruled that the First Amendment rights of inmates may legitimately be constrained by certain considerations of the penal system, such as security, rehabilitation and discipline.[90] *(Inmates and free speech, box, next page)*

Inmates and Free Speech

Even prison rules limiting inmate communications with persons outside the prison walls must be measured against the First Amendment, held a unanimous Supreme Court in *Procunier v. Martinez* (1974). The justices thus invalidated California regulations allowing prison mailroom officials wide discretion to censor letters to or from inmates.

The traditional "hands-off" policy of the federal courts toward prison regulations is rooted in a realistic appreciation of the fact that "the problems of prisons ... are complex and intractable, and ... not readily susceptible of resolution by decree," Justice Lewis F. Powell Jr. explained. [1]

However, he continued, "[w]hen a prison regulation or practice offends a fundamental constitutional guaranteee, federal courts will discharge their duty to protect constitutional rights. . . . This is such a case." [2]

The court recognized that censorship of inmate mail jeopardized the First Amendment rights of those free persons who wished to communicate with prisoners. But it also acknowledged that the government had a legitimate interest in maintaining order in penal institutions, an interest that might justify the imposition of certain restraints on inmate correspondence.

To determine whether a censorship regulation constituted an impermissible restraint on First Amendment liberties, the court set out a two-part test: the regulation must further a substantial government interest — not simply the suppression of criticism or other expression — and the restraint on speech imposed by the regulation "must be no greater than is necessary or essential to the protection of the particular governmental interest involved." [3]

The court also held that the inmate and author must be informed of the censorship of a particular letter.

In a second case decided later in the year, the court held that states were under no First Amendment obligation to permit prisoners to have face-to-face interviews with news reporters. An inmate's First Amendment rights might legitimately be constrained by security, rehabilitative and discipline considerations, the court said in *Procunier v. Hillery* (1974). Referring to its decision in *Procunier v. Martinez*, the court pointed to the mail as one alternative means inmates had of communicating with persons outside the prison. [4]

---

[1] *Procunier v. Martinez,* 416 U.S. 396 at 404-5 (1974).
[2] Id. at 405-6.
[3] Id. at 413.
[4] *Procunier v. Hillery,* 417 U.S. 817 (1974).

The ban did not mean that reporters had no access to the prisons, the majority stressed in *Pell v. Procunier, Saxbe v. Washington Post* (1974). Reporters could communicate with specific inmates through the mail. Furthermore, both the California and federal prison systems permitted reporters to visit prisons and to talk with inmates they met in the course of their supervised tour, or with inmates selected by prison officials.

But nothing in the First or 14th Amendments required "government to afford the press special access to information not shared by members of the public generally." [91]

In a dissenting opinion joined by two other justices, Justice Lewis F. Powell Jr. saw the ban on interviews as "impermissibly restrain[ing] the ability of the press to perform its constitutionally established function of informing the people on the conduct of their government." [92] Elaborating on this point, Powell said the government had no legitimate interest in withholding the information reporters might gather in personal interviews:

> . . .Quite to the contrary, federal prisons are public institutions. The administration of these institutions, the effectiveness of their rehabilitative programs, the conditions of confinement they maintain, and the experiences of the individuals incarcerated therein are all matters of legitimate societal interest and concern. Respondents [the reporters] do not assert a right to force disclosure of confidential information or to invade in any way the decisionmaking process of governmental officials. Neither do they seek to question any inmate who does not wish to be interviewed. They only seek to be free of an exceptionless prohibition against a method of newsgathering that is essential to effective reporting in the prison context. [93]

County Jails

In 1978 the court by a 4-3 vote reaffirmed its holding that reporters have no right to greater access than the general public to state institutions like prisons.

In 1972 a federal judge found conditions in an Alameda County, Calif., jail to be so shocking as to constitute cruel and unusual punishment. As a result, television station KQED sought access to the prison to interview inmates and film conditions there.

The county sheriff agreed to begin monthly scheduled tours of the prison open to the press and general public but prohibited the use of cameras or sound equipment as well as interviews with inmates. KQED then won an order from a federal judge directing the sheriff to grant the press wider access, to allow the interviews and the use of sound and camera equipment. The sheriff appealed in the case of *Houchins v. KQED, Inc.*

Neither the First nor 14th Amendment mandates "a right of access to government information or sources of information within the government's control," wrote Chief Justice Burger, announcing the decision in an opinion only two other justices joined. The First Amendment does not guarantee access to information, but only the freedom to communicate information once acquired. "[U]ntil the political branches decree otherwise, as they are free to do, the media has no special right of access to the Alameda County Jail different from or greater than that accorded the public generally," Burger wrote. [94]

The fourth member of the majority, Justice Stewart, agreed only that the order was too broad. The three dissenters — Justices William J. Brennan Jr., John Paul

Both the state and federal regulations prohibiting face-to-face interviews were apparently written to curtail the so-called "big wheel" phenomenon, the situation in which the influence of certain inmates is so enhanced by publicity that disruption and disciplinary problems result.

The majority, with Justice Potter Stewart writing the opinions, held that prison officials were justified in adopting the ban on interviews to minimize disruptive behavior.

Stevens and Powell — argued that "information-gathering is entitled to some measure of constitutional protection . . . not for the private benefit of those who might qualify as representatives of the 'press' but to insure that the citizens are fully informed regarding matters of public interest. . . ." [95] Two justices — Thurgood Marshall and Harry A. Blackmun — did not participate.

Protecting Confidentiality

Does the First Amendment allow reporters to withhold information from the government in order to protect a news source? Members of the press contend that the threat of potential exposure will dry up news sources who, for a variety of reasons, will provide information to reporters only if they are assured confidentiality. Not only will the individual reporter's effectiveness be damaged by forced disclosure, they contend, but the public will also suffer, losing information that it is entitled to have. For these reasons they argue that the First Amendment protects the confidentiality of news sources, even if the sources reveal to the reporter information about crimes.

Several states have enacted laws shielding reporters from demands of grand juries, courts and other investigating bodies for confidential or unpublished information they have collected in their work.

But a bare majority of the Supreme Court has held that reporters do not have a constitutional privilege to refuse to answer legitimate inquiries from law enforcement officers and court officials.

Grand Jury Investigations

In 1972 the court considered together three cases in which reporters challenged grand jury subpoenas for confidential information thought to be in their possession. These cases concerned:

• Paul M. Branzburg, an investigative reporter for the Louisville *Courier-Journal* who wrote several articles based on personal observations of drug users whom he had promised not to identify. He was then subpoenaed by a grand jury to testify on what he had observed.

• Paul Pappas, a television newsman who was allowed to visit a Black Panthers headquarters during a period of civil unrest on the condition that he not report what he saw. He later was subpoenaed to testify about that visit.

• Earl Caldwell, a black reporter for *The New York Times* who gained the confidence of Black Panthers in the San Francisco area and wrote several articles about them. He was then called to testify before a grand jury on alleged criminal activity among the Panthers.

State courts in the *Branzburg* and *Pappas* cases ruled that the reporters must provide the information sought to the grand juries. The two reporters appealed.

In the *Caldwell* case, a federal court of appeals reversed a lower court, holding that freedom of the press protected Caldwell not only from testifying but even from appearing before the grand jury. The Justice Department appealed this ruling to the Supreme Court.

The Decision

By a 5-4 vote the Supreme Court sustained the state courts in *Branzburg v. Hayes* and *In re Pappas,* and reversed the appeals court in *United States v. Caldwell.* "Until now the only testimonial privilege for unofficial witnesses that is rooted in the Federal Constitution is the

Fifth Amendment privilege against self-incrimination," wrote Justice Byron R. White for the majority. "We are asked to create another by interpreting the First Amendment to grant newsmen a testimonial privilege that other citizens do not enjoy. This we decline to do." [96]

The majority denied that any infringement of First Amendment rights was involved in these cases:

> We do not question the significance of free speech, press or assembly to the country's welfare. Nor is it suggested that news gathering does not qualify for First Amendment protection; without some protection for seeking out the news, freedom of the press could be eviscerated. But this case involves no intrusions upon speech or assembly, no prior restraint or restriction on what the press may publish and no express or implied command that the press publish what it prefers to withhold. No exaction or tax for the privilege of publishing, and no penalty, civil or criminal, related to the content of published material is at issue here. The use of confidential sources by the press is not forbidden or restricted; reporters remain free to seek news from any source by means within the law. No attempt is made to require the press to publish its sources of information or indiscriminately to disclose them on request. [97]

White observed that the First Amendment did not protect the press from obeying other valid laws such as labor and antitrust regulations. The authority of grand juries to subpoena witnesses was vital to their task:

> . . .Fair and effective law enforcement aimed at providing security for the person and property of the individual is a fundamental function of government, and the grand jury plays an important constitutionally mandated role in this process. On the records now before us, we perceive no basis for holding that the public interest in law enforcement and in ensuring effective grand jury proceedings is insufficient to override the consequential, but uncertain, burden on newsgathering which is said to result from insisting that reporters, like other citizens, respond to relevant questions put to them in the course of a valid grand jury investigation or criminal trial. [98]

The majority thought that potential exposure would affect few of a reporter's confidential news sources. "Only where news sources themselves are implicated in crime or possess information relevant to the grand jury's task need they or the reporter be concerned about grand jury subpoenas," White wrote. Nor can we "seriously entertain the notion that the First Amendment protects a newsman's agreement to conceal the criminal conduct of his source . . . on the theory that it is better to write about crime than to do something about it," he said. [99]

The majority's "crabbed view of the First Amendment reflects a disturbing insensitivity to the critical role of an independent press in our society," wrote Justice Potter Stewart in a dissent which Justices Thurgood Marshall and William J. Brennan Jr. joined. The majority decision "invites state and federal authorities to undermine the historic independence of the press by attempting to annex the journalistic profession as an investigative arm of government." [100]

Stewart contended that a reporter had a constitutional right to maintain a confidential relationship with news sources. The right to publish must include the right to gather news, he said, and that right in turn must include a

Radio and Television Broadcasting. . .

The modern expansion of the "press" to include radio and television broadcasters has generated some new First Amendment issues.

Because there are only a limited number of broadcast frequencies, the government has found it necessary to allocate access to them through a licensing system. Such a system would normally be considered prior restraint violative of the freedoms of speech and of the press. But as the Supreme Court noted in 1969, "[w]ithout government control the . . . [media] would be of little use because of the cacophony of competing voices, none of which could be clearly and predictably heard." [1]

The court has sustained the right of the Federal Communications Commission (FCC) to determine who shall receive broadcast licenses, but emphasized that such determinations must be made on neutral principles that do not favor one broadcaster over another because of the particular views espoused. "Congress did not authorize the Commission to choose among applicants upon the basis of their political, economic or social views or upon any other capricious basis," the court wrote in 1943. [2]

Right of Reply

The unique nature of the broadcast media does not place it altogether outside the protection of the First Amendment. But the freedom guaranteed to those who wish to broadcast is a different variety, subject to requirements such as the "fairness doctrine."

The FCC has determined that the public interest in diverse viewpoints requires broadcasters to give individuals whose viewpoints or records are attacked on the air an opportunity to respond to the charges. The commission also requires broadcasters who editorialize to give a right of reply to opposing viewpoints. The repliers need not pay for the air time they use.

This so-called "fairness doctrine" was challenged as a violation of the broadcasters' First Amendment rights to determine the content of broadcasts free from governmental interference.

The Supreme Court rejected this argument in a unanimous decision in 1969. "Where there are substantially more individuals who want to broadcast than there are frequencies to allocate, it is idle to posit an unabridgeable First Amendment right to broadcast comparable to the right of every individual to speak, write, or publish," wrote Justice Byron R. White in *Red Lion Broadcasting Co. v. Federal Communications Commission* (1969). [3]

The First Amendment right of viewers and listeners to diverse viewpoints on matters of political, economic and social concern are paramount to the rights of broadcasters, White said:

. . .A license permits broadcasting, but the licensee has no constitutional right to be the one who holds the license or to monopolize a radio frequency to the exclusion of his fellow citizens. There is nothing in the First Amendment which prevents the Government from requiring a licensee to share his frequency with others and to conduct himself as a proxy or fiduciary with obligations to present those views and voices which are representative of his community and which would otherwise, by necessity, be barred from the airwaves. [4]

Right to Broadcast

Conversely, the Supreme Court has ruled that radio and television stations are not required by the First Amendment's guarantee to sell time to all individuals and groups who wish to expound their views on public issues across the airwaves. The court announced this decision in *Columbia Broadcasting System v. Democratic National Committee* (1973) by a vote of 7-2.

Six of the justices, led by Chief Justice Warren E. Burger, held that while the fairness doctrine did require broadcasters to provide a right of reply to opposing views, Congress had firmly rejected the idea that all persons wishing to air their views should have access to broadcast facilities. The "fairness doctrine" makes the broadcaster responsible for adequate coverage of public issues in a manner which fairly reflects different viewpoints, the six agreed, but since every viewpoint cannot be aired, Congress and the FCC have appropriately left it to the broadcaster to exercise journalistic discretion in selecting those which present a fair picture of the issue.

Five of the six justices saw the basic question as "not whether there is to be discussion of controversial issues of public importance in the broadcast media, but rather who shall determine what issues are to be discussed by whom, and when." [5] Providing a right of access to the airwaves would work chiefly to benefit persons who could afford to buy the time, and these persons could not be held accountable for fairness, they said.

Justice William O. Douglas agreed with the outcome of the majority's reasoning but went beyond its opinion to contend that the First Amendment actually prohibited the government from requiring broadcasters to accept such paid editorial advertisements. Broadcasters, Douglas wrote, are entitled to the same protection under the guarantee of a free press that newspapers receive.

Justices William J. Brennan Jr. and Thurgood Marshall dissented. By approving the broadcasters' policy of refusing to sell such air time the government was abridging the right of its citizens to free speech, they wrote.

The public nature of the airwaves, the preferred status given to broadcasters to whom the government granted the right to use a certain frequency, the extensive government regulation of broadcast programming, and FCC approval of the challenged policy all combined to make that refusal government action clearly violating the

---

right to confidentiality. Surveys have shown that "an unbridled subpoena power will substantially impair the flow of news to the public" from persons in sensitive areas involving governmental and political figures, financial affairs, political dissidents and minority groups. A reporter's immunity to grand jury probes is not a personal right but the right of the public to maintain an access to information of public concern, Stewart said. [101]

...Permissible Prior Restraint

First Amendment ban, Brennan said. The public's First Amendment interest "in the reception of a full spectrum of views presented in a vigorous and uninhibited manner on controversial issues of public importance" was thwarted by a policy of refusing paid editorials. Such a policy gave broadcasters nearly exclusive control over the "selection of issues and viewpoints to be covered, the manner of presentation, and, perhaps most important, who shall speak." The "fairness doctrine" was insufficient to ensure this necessary wide-open exchange of views, said Brennan. [6]

Content and Context

The Supreme Court in 1978 upheld against a First Amendment challenge the power of the FCC to limit the hours during which radio stations may broadcast certain material which, although offensive to many listeners, is not obscene.

About two o'clock one afternoon, a New York radio station owned by the Pacifica Foundation aired a recorded monologue by humorist George Carlin. Entitled "Filthy Words," the monologue satirized society's attitude toward certain words, in particular seven which are generally barred from use on radio and television. In the monologue, Carlin lists the seven "dirty words" (shit, piss, fuck, cunt, cocksucker, motherfucker and tits) and then uses them in various forms throughout the recording.

After receiving a parent's complaint that his young son had heard the monologue, the FCC issued an order to the station restricting the hours at which such an "offensive" program could be broadcast. Pacifica Foundation challenged the order, arguing that the FCC was regulating the content of a program in violation of the guarantee of free speech.

"No such absolute rule [forbidding government regulation of content] is mandated by the Constitution," said Justice John Paul Stevens for the five-justice majority in *Federal Communications Commission v. Pacifica Foundation* (1978). "[B]oth the content and the context of speech are critical elements of First Amendment analysis...." [7]

While "some uses of even the most offensive words are unquestionably protected" by the First Amendment, "the constitutional protection accorded to ... such pa-

tently offensive ... language [as used in the monologue] need not be the same in every context.... Words that are commonplace in one setting are shocking in another," he said. [8]

The context of the broadcast justified the FCC's regulation, the majority concluded. Because the broadcast media has established a "uniquely pervasive presence," offensive material which is broadcast reaches people in the privacy of their homes "where the individual's right to be let alone plainly outweighs the First Amendment rights of an intruder." Furthermore, the broadcast was "uniquely accessible to children, even those too young to read," and the court has held in the past that speech otherwise protected by the First Amendment might be regulated to protect the welfare of children. [9]

The four dissenters held that the majority could and should have avoided dealing with the constitutional issue by simply holding that the Communications Act of 1934 allowed the FCC to ban or restrict the broadcast only of obscene materials.

Media Cross-Ownership

The Supreme Court upheld in 1978 the authority of the FCC to decree an end to common ownership of a community's single newspaper and its only radio or television station against a challenge that the ban on cross-media ownership violated freedom of the press.

The commission has broad power "to regulate broadcasting in the 'public interest,'" wrote Justice Marshall for the unanimous court. The FCC issued its order to encourage diversity of ownership that could possibly result in diversity of viewpoints aired within a community. This was a valid public interest and a rational means of reaching that goal, Marshall said in *Federal Communications Commission v. National Citizens Committee for Broadcasting*. [10]

Under the FCC regulations, existing combinations were allowed to continue in operation, with the exception of those that owned the only newspaper and the only broadcast outlet in a community or the only newspaper and the only television station in the community. In these monopoly situations, divestiture of either the newspaper or the broadcast outlet was required within five years, unless some reason to waive the requirement was shown.

---

[1] *Red Lion Broadcasting Co. v. Federal Communications Commission*, 395 U.S. 367 at 376 (1969).

[2] *National Broadcasting Company v. United States*, 319 U.S. 190 at 226 (1943).

[3] *Red Lion Broadcasting Co. v. Federal Communications Commission*, 395 U.S. 367 at 388 (1969).

[4] Id. at 389.

[5] *Columbia Broadcasting System, Inc. v. Democratic National Committee*, 412 U.S. 94 at 130 (1973).

[6] Id. at 184, 187.

[7] *Federal Communications Commission v. Pacifica Foundation*, 438 U.S. 726 at 744 (1978).

[8] Id. at 746-47.

[9] Id. at 748, 749.

[10] *Federal Communications Commission v. National Citizens Committee for Broadcasting*, 436 U.S. 775 (1978).

But Stewart did not believe the immunity was absolute. When weighed against other constitutional rights such as the fair administration of justice, First Amendment rights must be given a preferred position, he said, and

government must show a compelling reason for restricting them.

Stewart then offered a rule for determining when a reporter may be required to appear before a grand jury:

...I would hold that the government must (1) show that there is probable cause to believe that the newsman has information which is clearly relevant to a specific probable violation of law; (2) demonstrate that the information sought cannot be obtained by alternative means less destructive of First Amendment rights; and (3) demonstrate a compelling and overriding interest in the information. [102]

Justice William O. Douglas also dissented, holding the First Amendment immunized reporters from grand jury investigations unless they were implicated in a crime.

Since it issued this decision, the court has declined to review several lower court orders finding reporters in contempt for refusing to reveal confidential sources to law enforcement and court officials. [103]

Newsroom Searches

The Supreme Court sanctioned a different threat to confidentiality when it ruled in *Zurcher v. The Stanford Daily* (1978) that the First Amendment does not protect newspaper offices from warranted police searches for information or evidence.

The lineup of the justices was almost identical to that in the 1972 cases. Justice Brennan did not participate; Justice Stevens dissented as had Justice Douglas (whom Stevens succeeded) in the earlier case. By a 5-3 vote, the court rejected the argument of the nation's press that police should use subpoenas, not search warrants, to obtain information or evidence from news files, at least so long as the reporter or newspaper was not suspected of any involvement in criminal activity.

A subpoena is a less intrusive means for obtaining evidence than is a search by police armed with a warrant. The subpoena requires a person to search his own home, office or files for certain specified items. The search warrant authorizes police, unannounced, to enter a home or office by force if necessary to search for the particular material the warrant describes.

Furthermore, a person faced with a search warrant has no opportunity to contest the search before it takes place. But a person subpoenaed to produce information may move to quash the subpoena.

The case arose from a 1971 police search of the offices of *The Stanford Daily,* the campus newspaper of Stanford University. The search occurred after conflict between police and demonstrators at Stanford University Hospital resulted in injury to nine policemen. Police obtained a warrant to search the files, wastebaskets, desks and photo laboratories at the *Daily's* offices; the object of the fruitless search was evidence of the identity of the demonstrators responsible for the police injuries.

The Decision

The Supreme Court majority argued that the men who wrote the Fourth Amendment were well aware of the conflict between the government and the press, and if they had felt that special procedures were needed when the government wanted information in the possession of the press, they would have said so.

The First Amendment guarantee of a free press that can gather, analyze and publish news without governmental interference is sufficiently protected by the Fourth Amendment requirement that searches be reasonable and that warrants be issued by neutral magistrates, wrote Justice White for the majority. He continued:

Properly administered, the preconditions for a warrant — probable cause, specificity with respect to the place to be searched and the things to be seized, and overall reasonableness — should afford sufficient protection against the harms that are assertedly threatened by warrants for searching newspaper offices. [104]

Magistrates could ensure that the search not interfere with actual timely publication of a newspaper — and that the warrant be specific enough to prevent officers from rummaging "at large in newspaper files" or intruding into editorial decisions. White also said the majority was no more persuaded than it had been in 1972 "that confidential sources will disappear and that the press will suppress news because of fears of warranted searches." [105]

Justice Stewart, joined by Justice Marshall, found it

...self-evident that police searches of newspaper offices burden the freedom of the press.... [I]t cannot be denied that confidential information may be exposed to the eyes of police officers who execute a search warrant by rummaging through the files, cabinets, desks and wastebaskets of a newsroom. Since the indisputable effect of such searches will thus be to prevent a newsman from being able to promise confidentiality to his potential sources, it seems obvious to me that a journalist's access to information, and thus the public's will thereby be impaired.... The end result, wholly inimical to the First Amendment, will be a diminishing flow of potentially important information to the public. [106]

Justice John Paul Stevens based his disagreement with the majority not on the free press argument but entirely on his belief that mere documentary evidence in the possession of an innocent third party should be sought by subpoena rather than search warrant.

Footnotes

[1] Quoted in Willard Grosvenor Bleyer, *Main Currents in the History of American Journalism* (Boston: Houghton Mifflin Co., 1927), p. 103.

[2] Dissenting opinion in *Saxbe v. Washington Post,* 417 U.S. 843 at 863 (1974).

[3] Thomas I. Emerson, *The System of Freedom of Expression* (New York: Random House, Vintage Books, 1970), p. 506.

[4] *Near v. Minnesota,* 283 U.S. 697 at 713 (1931).

[5] Id. at 716.

[6] Id. at 720.

[7] Id. at 721.

[8] Id. at 722.

[9] Id. at 735, 736.

[10] Id. at 738.

[11] *Grosjean v. American Press Co.,* 297 U.S. 233 at 244-45 (1936).

[12] Id. at 250.

[13] *Lovell v. Griffin,* 303 U.S. 444 at 452 (1938).

[14] Id. at 451.

[15] *Schneider v. Irvington,* 308 U.S. 147 (1939); see also *Jamison v. Texas,* 318 U.S. 413 (1943).

[16] Specific names of these three cases are: *Kim Young v. California, Snyder v. Milwaukee, Nichols v. Massachusetts,* 308 U.S. 147 (1939).

[17] *Schneider v. Irvington*, 308 U.S. 147 at 160-61 (1939).

[18] Id. at 163.

[19] *Talley v. California*, 362 U.S. 60 at 64 (1960).

[20] *Organization for a Better Austin v. Keefe*, 402 U.S. 415 at 418, 419, 420 (1971).

[21] *Mills v. Alabama*, 384 U.S. 214 at 219 (1966).

[22] *New York Times Co. v. United States*, 403 U.S. 713 at 714 (1971).

[23] Id. at 715, 717.

[24] Id. at 720.

[25] Id. at 725-26.

[26] Id. at 730.

[27] Id. at 730-31, 732.

[28] Id. at 742.

[29] Id. at 749.

[30] Id. at 751.

[31] Id. at 757.

[32] Id. at 759.

[33] Id. at 761.

[34] See Holmes' dissent in *Abrams v. United States*, 250 U.S. 616 at 630 (1919); Black and Douglas opinion in *Beauharnais v. Illinois*, 343 U.S. 250 at 272 (1952); majority opinion in *The New York Times Co. v. Sullivan*, 376 U.S. 254 (1964).

[35] *Coleman v. MacLennan*, 98 P 281 at 281-82 (1908).

[36] *Chaplinsky v. New Hampshire*, 315 U.S. 568 at 571-72 (1942); see also *Beauharnais v. Illinois*, 343 U.S. 250 (1952); *Near v. Minnesota*, 283 U.S. 697 (1931); *Roth v. United States*, 354 U.S. 476 (1957).

[37] *The New York Times Co. v. Sullivan*, 376 U.S. 254 at 257-58 (1964).

[38] Id. at 268, 269.

[39] Id. at 270-71.

[40] Id. at 271-72.

[41] Id. at 279.

[42] Id. at 279-80.

[43] Id. at 288.

[44] Id. at 293.

[45] Id. at 300.

[46] *Garrison v. Louisiana*, 379 U.S. 64 (1964); *Ashton v. Kentucky*, 384 U.S. 195 (1966); *St. Amant v. Thompson*, 390 U.S. 727 at 731 (1968); *Greenbelt Cooperative Publishing Assn. v. Bresler*, 398 U.S. 6 (1970); *Time Inc. v. Pape*, 401 U.S. 279 (1971).

[47] *Herbert v. Lando* (1979).

[48] *Rosenblatt v. Baer*, 383 U.S. 75 at 85-86 (1966).

[49] Id. at 93.

[50] *Monitor Patriot Co. v. Roy*, 401 U.S. 265 (1971); see also *Ocala Star-Banner Co. v. Damron*, 401 U.S. 295 (1971).

[51] *Curtis Publishing Co. v. Butts, Associated Press v. Walker*, 388 U.S. 130 (1967).

[52] Id. at 155.

[53] Ibid.

[54] Id. at 159.

[55] Id. at 164.

[56] *Rosenbloom v. Metromedia Inc.*, 403 U.S. 29 at 43 (1971).

[57] *Gertz v. Robert Welch, Inc.*, 418 U.S. 323 at 345 (1974).

[58] Id. at 347.

[59] Id. at 352.

[60] Id. at 354.

[61] *Time Inc. v. Firestone*, 424 U.S. 448 at 453 (1976).

[62] *Wolston v. Readers' Digest Assn., Inc.* (1979); *Hutchinson v. Proxmire* (1979).

[63] *Sheppard v. Maxwell*, 384 U.S. 333 at 350 (1966).

[64] *Toledo Newspaper Co. v. United States*, 247 U.S. 402 (1918).

[65] *Nye v. United States*, 313 U.S. 33 (1941).

[66] *Patterson v. Colorado*, 205 U.S. 454 at 463 (1907).

[67] *Bridges v. California, Times-Mirror Co. v. Superior Court of California*, 314 U.S. 252 at 269 (1941).

[68] Id. at 270-71.

[69] Id. at 273.

[70] Id. at 278.

[71] Id. at 284.

[72] *Pennekamp v. Florida*, 328 U.S. 331 at 347 (1946).

[73] *Craig v. Harney*, 331 U.S. 367 at 378 (1947).

[74] *Wood v. Georgia*, 370 U.S. 375 at 389 (1962).

[75] *Stroble v. California*, 343 U.S. 181 (1951).

[76] *Marshall v. United States*, 360 U.S. 310 (1959).

[77] *Irvin v. Dowd*, 366 U.S. 717 at 722-23 (1961).

[78] *Beck v. Washington*, 369 U.S. 541 (1962).

[79] *Rideau v. Louisiana*, 373 U.S. 723 (1963).

[80] *Estes v. Texas*, 381 U.S. 532 at 536 (1965).

[81] *Sheppard v. Maxwell*, 384 U.S. 333 at 355, 358 (1966).

[82] Id. at 361-62.

[83] *Nebraska Press Association v. Stuart*, 427 U.S. 539 at 559 (1976).

[84] Id. at 568; see also *Cox Broadcasting Corp. v. Cohn*, 420 U.S. 469 (1975).

[85] *Nebraska Press Association v. Stuart*, 427 U.S. 539 at 570 (1976).

[86] Id. at 572.

[87] *Gannett Co. Inc. v. DePasquale* (1979).

[88] Ibid.

[89] *Saxbe v. Washington Post Co.*, 417 U.S. 843 (1974); *Pell v. Procunier*, 417 U.S. 817 (1974).

[90] *Procunier v. Hillery*, 417 U.S. 817 (1974).

[91] *Pell v. Procunier*, 417 U.S. 817 at 834 (1974).

[92] Id. at 835.

[93] *Saxbe v. Washington Post Co.*, 417 U.S. 843 at 861 (1974).

[94] *Houchins v. KQED, Inc.*, 438 U.S. 1 at 15-16 (1978).

[95] Id. at 32.

[96] *Branzburg v. Hayes, In re Pappas, United States v. Caldwell*, 408 U.S. 665 at 689-90 (1972).

[97] Id. at 681-82.

[98] Id. at 690-91.

[99] Id. at 691, 692.

[100] Id. at 725.

[101] Id. at 732-33.

[102] Id. at 743.

[103] See, for example, *Hubbard Broadcasting Co. v. Ammerman*, 436 U.S. 906 (1978); *Tribune Publishing Co. v. Caldero*, 434 U.S. 930 (1977); *The New York Times Co. v. New Jersey* (1978).

[104] *Zurcher v. The Stanford Daily*, 436 U.S. 547 at 565 (1978).

[105] Id. at 566.

[106] Id. at 571-73.

Freedom of Religion

It is unthinkable to most Americans that the government could or would dictate what religious beliefs individuals must hold and what church they must attend. The freedom to believe as one chooses, or not to believe at all, is as basic to the concept of American democracy as the rights of free speech and press.

The First Amendment's guarantees of free exercise of religion and separation of church and state were the direct products of colonial experience. Many of the colonies were established by settlers fleeing from religious persecution, primarily in Anglican-dominated England.

Some of the colonialists were themselves intolerant, persecuting those whose religious beliefs and practices were different from their own. Several colonies forbade Catholics and/or non-Christians to hold certain offices and jobs. For a time, six of the colonies established a state religion.

Other colonies, however, notably Rhode Island, Pennsylvania and Delaware, tolerated a high degree of religious diversity. Still others, including some of those who originally tolerated only a single religion, eventually lent public support to several different faiths. [1]

First Freedom

Thus, by the time of the Revolution, belief in religious toleration was well-established, and when the First Amendment was written in 1789, it was religious freedom that led the list of rights Congress was forbidden to abridge. As Justice Joseph Story wrote in his commentaries on the Constitution:

It was under a solemn consciousness of the dangers from ecclesiastical ambition, the bigotry of spiritual pride, and the intolerance of sects, thus exemplified in our domestic as well as in foreign annals, that it was deemed advisable to exclude from the national government all power to act upon the subject. [2]

The Supreme Court has never viewed either of the religion clauses — "Congress shall make no law respecting an establishment of religion, or prohibiting the free exercise thereof" — as absolute. Freedom to believe *is* absolute, but freedom to *practice* that belief may be circumscribed by government under certain conditions. Government may not directly aid religion, but secular programs that indirectly benefit religious institutions may be permissible.

To Ensure Neutrality

The court's task has been to ensure that government remains neutral toward religion. As Chief Justice Warren E. Burger explained in 1970:

The course of constitutional neutrality in this area cannot be an absolutely straight line; rigidity could well defeat the basic purpose of these provisions, which is to insure that no religion be sponsored or favored, none commanded and none inhibited. The general principle deducible from the First Amendment and all that has been said by the Court is this: that we will not tolerate either governmentally established religion or governmental interference with religion. Short of those expressly proscribed governmental acts there is room for play in the joints productive of a benevolent neutrality which will permit religious exercise to exist without sponsorship and without interference.

Each value judgment under the Religion Clauses must therefore turn on whether particular acts in question are intended to establish or interfere with religious beliefs and practices or have the effect of doing so. Adherence to the policy of neutrality that derives from an accommodation of the Establishment and Free Exercise Clauses has prevented the kind of involvement that would tip the balance toward government control of churches or governmental restraint on religious practice. [3]

Judicial Tests

To maintain this neutrality, the court has developed tests that it applies to the circumstances of each case challenging a supposed violation of the religion clauses.

If a law allegedly interferes with the free exercise of religion, the court will first examine the statute to see if it carefully describes the conduct that may be restricted. The statute may not be vague or too broad, nor may it leave too much to the discretion of the officials administering it. It may not discriminate on the basis of religion.

If the statute is carefully drawn and its purpose and effect are to achieve a secular goal, such as setting the time and place of open-air religious meetings to minimize disruption to other members of the public, the restriction likely will be permitted, even if it occasionally restricts a religious exercise.

In recent decisions, the court has been more protective of religious freedom, requiring the government to show that it has a compelling reason for taking any action which indirectly restricts religious liberty, and that no means less restrictive of religious freedom could have accomplished the same secular goal.

If a government action is alleged to constitute an establishment of religion, the government can successfully defend it only by showing that both the purpose and effect of the action are secular and not intended to aid religion and that the government involvement with religion required by the challenge action is not excessive and does not require continued governmental surveillance of the religious institutions affected.

These, however, are only the general rules. A reading of the cases shows they were not always applied uniformly.

The Free Exercise of Religion

Freedom of religion is inextricably bound up with the other freedoms guaranteed by the First and 14th Amendments. Without the freedoms of speech and press, the expression and circulation of religious beliefs and doctrines would be impossible. Without the freedoms of assembly and association, the right to participate with others in public and private religious worship would be curtailed.

So interwoven are these freedoms that both before and after the court held in 1940 that the 14th Amendment protected the free exercise of religion from restriction by the states, it resolved many cases challenging state infringements on religious liberty by relying on the freedoms of speech and press.

The court held in *Lovell v. Griffin* (1938) that a municipal prohibition against distribution of handbills without a permit as enforced against a Jehovah's Witness passing out religious circulars was an unconstitutional prior restraint on freedom of the press. And in *Kunz v. New York* (1951), the court held that arbitrary denial of a public speech permit to a Baptist minister was a violation of the rights of free speech and assembly as well as of religious liberty.[4] *(Details, Lovell case, p. 426, Kunz case, pp. 410, 454)*

As a result of this close relationship, the Supreme Court uses many of the same tests that it uses to test restrictions on free speech and press to determine if government has impermissibly restricted free exercise of religion.

In general the Supreme Court has ruled that states and the federal government may restrict the free exercise of religion if the exercise involves fraud or other criminal

---

"Crime is not the less odious because sanctioned by what any particular sect may designate as religion."

—Justice Stephen J. Field
Davis v. Beason, 1890

---

activity and there is no other means of protecting the public. Government also may restrict religious practices that threaten public peace and order, but only if the restriction is nondiscriminatory, narrowly drawn and precisely applied.

The court also has upheld the right of government, in some circumstances, to compel an individual to take an action contrary to his or her religious belief. As the rule was stated late in the 1970s, such a compulsory law will stand against a First Amendment challenge if its primary purpose and effect is to advance a valid secular goal and if the means chosen are calculated to have the least possible restrictive effect on free exercise of religion.

Religion and Criminal Law

In its first direct pronouncement on the First Amendment's protection for the free exercise of religion, the Supreme Court held in 1879 that polygamy was a crime and could not be excused as a religious practice.

Reynolds v. United States (1879) brought to the court a Mormon's challenge to the constitutionality of a federal law barring plural marriages in Utah territory. Observing that bigamy and polygamy were considered punishable offenses in every state, the court found "it . . . impossible to believe that the constitutional guaranty of religious freedom was intended to prohibit legislation in respect to this most important feature of social life."[5]

Eleven years later the court elaborated on this reasoning when it upheld an Idaho territorial statute denying the vote to bigamists, polygamists and those who advocated plural marriages. In *Davis v. Beason* (1890), the court for the first time distinguished between protected belief and unprotected conduct:

. . .It was never intended or supposed that the [First] Amendment could be evoked as a protection against legislation for the punishment of acts inimical to the peace, good order and morals of society. With man's relations to his Maker and the obligations he may think they impose, and the manner in which an expression shall be made by him of his belief on those subjects, no interference can be permitted provided always the laws of society designed to secure its peace and prosperity, and the morals of its people, are not interfered with. However free the exercise of religion may be, it must be subordinate to the criminal laws of the country, passed with reference to actions regarded by general consent as properly the subjects of punitive legislation. [6]

Justice Stephen J. Field, who wrote the court's opinion, concluded succinctly: "Crime is not the less odious because sanctioned by what any particular sect may designate as religion." [7]

Fraud

The exercise of religious freedom through solicitation of funds to maintain the religion has occasionally been re-

Religion: An Evolving Definition

As the nation's tolerance for religious diversity has broadened, so has the Supreme Court's definition of beliefs it considers religious and therefore entitled to First Amendment protection.

Originally the court considered religion in the traditional Judeo-Christian sense, which demanded belief in a divine being. "The term 'religion' has reference to one's views of his relations to his Creator, and the obligations they impose of reverence for his being and character, and of obedience to his will," the court said in the 1890 case of *Davis v. Beason.* [1]

This view of religion still prevailed in 1931, when Chief Justice Charles Evans Hughes wrote in a dissent that "[t]he essence of religion is belief in a relation to God involving duties superior to those arising from any human relation." [2] This definition became the foundation for the definition adopted by Congress in 1948 of the belief one must hold to qualify for exemption from military service as a conscientious objector. *(Box, p. 457)*

In the 1940s the court began to move toward a more expansive interpretation of "religion," accepting beliefs that were neither orthodox nor theistically based. In 1943 Justice Felix Frankfurter quoted with approval the words of Federal Judge Augustus Hand:

> It is unnecessary to attempt a definition of religion; the content of the term is found in the history of the human race and is incapable of compression into a few words. Religious belief arises from a sense of the inadequacy of reason as a means of relating the individual to his fellowmen and to his universe.... [I]t may justly be regarded as a response of the individual to an inward mentor, call it conscience or God, that is for many persons at the present time the equivalent of what has always been thought a religious impulse. [3]

The following year Justice William O. Douglas, speaking for the court majority, said that the free exercise of religion "embraces the right to maintain theories of life and of death and of the hereafter which are rank heresy to followers of the orthodox faiths."[4] In 1953 Douglas again spoke for the court when he wrote that "it is no business of courts to say that which is religious practice or activity for one group is not religion under the protection of the First Amendment." [5]

As one commentator noted, these decisions made clear that "the classification of a belief as religion does not depend upon the tenets of its creed." [6]

The breadth of the court's modern definition of religion was perhaps most clearly stated in its 1961 decision in *Torcaso v. Watkins:*

> ...neither a State nor the federal government can constitutionally force a person 'to profess a belief or disbelief in any religion.' Neither can constitutionally pass laws nor impose requirements which aid all religions as against non-believers, and neither can aid those religions based on a belief in the existence of God as against those religions founded on different beliefs. [7]

In 1965 the court reaffirmed its *Torcaso* judgment, viewing as religious any sincere and meaningful belief which occupies a place in the possessor's life parallel to the place God holds in the faith of an orthodox believer. The court expanded this definition in 1970 to include moral and ethical beliefs held with the strength of traditional religious convictions. [8]

---

[1] *Davis v. Beason,* 133 U.S. 333 at 342 (1890).

[2] *United States v. Macintosh,* 283 U.S. 605 at 633-34 (1931).

[3] *United States v. Kauten,* 133 F. 2d 703 at 708 (1943), quoted by Justice Felix Frankfurter, dissenting, in *West Virginia State Board of Education v. Barnette,* 319 U.S. 624 at 658-59 (1943).

[4] *United States v. Ballard,* 322 U.S. 78 at 86 (1944).

[5] *Fowler v. Rhode Island,* 345 U.S. 67 at 70 (1953).

[6] "Toward a Constitutional Definition of Religion," *Harvard Law Review* 91 (March 1978) 5:1056.

[7] *Torcaso v. Watkins,* 367 U.S. 488 at 495 (1961).

[8] *United States v. Seeger,* 380 U.S. 163 at 166 (1965); *Welsh v. United States,* 398 U.S. 333 (1970).

---

stricted by states and municipalities wishing to protect their citizens from fraud.

In *Cantwell v. Connecticut* (1940), the court laid out the type of restriction that might be permitted:

> Nothing we have said is intended even remotely to imply that, under the cloak of religion, persons may, with impunity, commit fraud upon the public.... Even the exercise of religion may be at some slight inconvenience in order that a State may protect its citizens from injury. Without doubt a State may protect its citizens from fraudulent solicitation by requiring a stranger in the community ... to establish his identity and his authority to act for the cause which he purports to represent. The State is likewise free to regulate the time and manner of solicitation generally, in the interest of public safety, peace, comfort or convenience....[8]

In *Martin v. City of Struthers* (1943), the court majority held that the possibility that some persons might use house-to-house solicitations as opportunities to commit crimes did not warrant an ordinance prohibiting all solicitors from ringing doorbells to summon the occupants of the house. The court said that the municipality must find a way of preventing crime that was less restrictive of those persons soliciting for sincere causes.[9] *(Details, p. 420)*

The 'I Am' Movement

Only once has the Supreme Court dealt with the question whether a movement designated as religious by its founders was actually fraudulent.

Guy Ballard, the leader of the "I Am" movement, at one point had some three million followers. He and two relatives claimed that their teachings had been dictated by God, that Jesus had personally appeared to them and that they could cure both curable and incurable disesases. They were indicted by the federal government for mail fraud.

The sole question before the Supreme Court in *United States v. Ballard* (1944) was whether the trial jury had been properly instructed that it need not determine whether the Ballards' beliefs were true but only whether the Ballards believed them to be true.

A majority of the Supreme Court found the instruction proper. Religious freedom, wrote Justice William O. Douglas,

> ... embraces the right to maintain theories of life and of death and of the hereafter which are rank heresy to followers of the orthodox faiths. Heresy trials are foreign to our Constitution. Men may believe what they cannot prove. They may not be put to the proof of their religious doctrines or beliefs.... The religious views espoused by respondents might seem incredible, if not preposterous, to most people. But if those doctrines are subject to trial before a jury charged with finding their truth or falsity, then the same can be done with the religious beliefs of any sect. [10]

Chief Justice Harlan Fiske Stone dissented, saying that a jury could properly be instructed to determine whether the representations were true or false. Stone said he saw no reason why the government could not submit evidence, for instance, showing that Ballard had never cured anyone of a disease. Justice Robert H. Jackson also dissented, on the ground that the case should have been dismissed altogether. *(Court definitions of religion, box, p. 453)*

Child Labor Laws

Laws that make employment of children under a certain age a crime have been upheld against claims that they impinge on religious liberty.

In 1944 the court sustained a Massachusetts statute that prohibited girls younger than 18 from selling newspapers on the streets.

The law had been applied to forbid a nine-year-old Jehovah's Witness from distributing religious literature. The state's interest in protecting children from the harmful effects of child labor "is not nullified merely because the parent grounds his claim to control the child's course of conduct on religion or conscience," the court wrote in *Prince v. Massachusetts.* [11]

Religion and Social Order

On balance, society's need for order and tranquility may at times be strong enough to warrant restriction of religious liberty. But the Supreme Court has made it clear that such restrictions must be narrowly drawn and uniformly applied.

The conflict between public order and religious liberty was first raised in *Cantwell v. Connecticut* (1940). Jesse Cantwell, a Jehovah's Witness, played a recording that attacked the Catholic Church for two passersby who were Catholic. When they indicated their displeasure with the message, he stopped the record and moved on. The next day he was arrested for breach of the peace.

The Supreme Court overturned the conviction, finding the statute defining breach of the peace too broad, "sweeping in a great variety of conduct under a general and indefinite characterization." [12] This vagueness left too much discretion to officials charged with applying it.

Cantwell, the majority said, had not started a riot or caused anyone else to take action that amounted to a breach of the peace. He therefore raised no "clear and present menace to public peace and order as to render him liable to conviction of the common law offense in question," the court concluded. [13] *(Details, p. 408)*

Permits

The court also ruled that permit systems requiring speakers, demonstrators and paraders to seek a license before undertaking their activity were valid only if narrowly drawn and precisely applied. In *Cantwell*, the court struck down a statute that forbade solicitation for religious causes without a permit because the law allowed a state official discretion to withhold permits if he did not think the cause was a religious one. "[T]o condition the solicitation of aid for the perpetuation of religious views or systems upon a license, the grant of which rests in the exercise of a determination by state authority as to what is a religious cause, is to lay a forbidden burden upon the exercise of [religious] liberty...," the court wrote. [14]

In *Cox v. New Hampshire* (1941), the court upheld conviction of a group of Jehovah's Witnesses who paraded on public streets without obtaining the required permit. The court said that statute was not enacted or applied with intent to restrict religious freedom. Rather, it was intended simply to determine the time, manner and place of parades so as to minimize public disruption and disorder. Such a precisely drawn and applied statute did not unconstitutionally impinge on religious liberty. [15] *(Details, p. 413)*

In *Kunz v. New York* (1951), the court reversed the conviction of a Baptist minister who continued to give highly inflammatory public street sermons even though his permit to speak on the streets had not been renewed because earlier speeches had caused disorder. The court said that "an ordinance which gives an administrative official discretionary power to control in advance the right of citizens to speak on religious matters on the streets ... is clearly invalid as a prior restraint on the exercise of First Amendment rights." [16] *(Details, p. 410)*

In another 1951 case the Supreme Court ruled that a city could not deny a permit for a public meeting to a group whose religious views it disapproved.

Jehovah's Witnesses applied for a permit to hold a religious meeting in Havre de Grace, Md. The permit was denied after officials questioned the Witnesses about their religious beliefs. The Witnesses held their meeting despite the permit denial and were consequently arrested for disorderly conduct.

The Supreme Court reversed their convictions in *Niemotko v. Maryland* (1951). Denial of a permit to one religious group when permits had been granted to other religious meetings amounted to a denial of equal protection, the court said. [17]

Two years later, the court reversed the conviction of a Jehovah's Witness who spoke at an open-air meeting in violation of a Pawtucket, R.I., ordinance prohibiting religious addresses in public parks.

During the trial, the state admitted that it had allowed ministers of other churches to deliver sermons at church services held in public parks. The court ruled that such

Jehovah's Witnesses: Definers of Freedom

It is a measure of the success of the First Amendment guarantee of the free exercise of religion that its broad interpretation has evolved almost solely in connection with one of the most reviled religious sects in American history. "Probably no sect since the early days of the Mormon Church has been as much a thorn in the communal side and as much a victim of communal hate and persecution as Jehovah's Witnesses," writes one commentator.[1]

Jehovah's Witnesses were originally followers of Charles T. Russell, a Presbyterian who grew disillusioned with all existing religious organizations and began to fashion a new religion in the late 1860s and early 1870s. His followers were first known as Russellites, adopting the name Jehovah's Witnesses after Joseph F. Rutherford succeeded Russell in 1931. In 1884 the sect established the Watchtower Bible and Tract Society to print and disseminate religious literature distributed by the Witnesses.

In 1931 the Witnesses described their mission as follows:

As Jehovah's Witnesses our sole and only purpose is to be entirely obedient to his commandments; to make known that he is the only true and almighty God; that his Word is true and that his name is entitled to all honor and glory; that Christ is God's King, whom he has placed upon his throne of authority; that his kingdom is now come, and in obedience to the Lord's commandments we must now declare this good news as a testimony or witness to the nations and to inform the rulers and the people of and concerning Satan's cruel and oppressive organization, and particularly with reference to Christendom, which is the most wicked part of that visible organization, which great act will be quickly followed by Christ the King's bringing to the obedient peoples of earth peace and prosperity, liberty and health, happiness and everlasting life; that God's kingdom is the hope of the world and there is no other, and that this message must be delivered by those who are identified as Jehovah's Witnesses.[2]

To carry this message across the country, the Witnesses organized Watchtower Campaigns in the 1930s and 1940s. Each house in a town would be visited by a Witness. If the occupants were willing, the Witness would give them literature, usually for a monetary contribution, and play a phonograph record. The gist of the message is that organized religions, and the Roman Catholic Church in particular, are rackets. A typical publication, entitled *Enemies*, claimed that:

...the greatest racket ever invented and practiced is that of religion. The most cruel and seductive public enemy is that which employs religion to carry on the racket, and by which means the people are deceived and the name of Almighty God is reproached. There are numerous systems of religion, but the most subtle, fraudulent and injurious to humankind is that which is generally labeled the 'Christian religion,' because it has the appearance of a worshipful devotion to the Supreme Being, and thereby easily misleads many honest and sincere persons.[3]

Under a chapter entitled "Song of the Harlot," the booklet says: "Referring now to the foregoing scriptural definition of harlot: what religious system exactly fits the prophecies recorded in God's Word? There is but one answer, and that is, the Roman Catholic Church...."[4]

Understandably, the Witnesses were not popular in many communities. On more than one occasion members of the sect met with violence from those affronted by the Witnesses' views. Several communities enacted laws to curb the activities of the Witnesses, and it was these laws that the Witnesses challenged in court. According to constitutional historian Robert F. Cushman, members of the sect brought some 30 major cases testing the principles of religious freedom to the Supreme Court since 1938. In most of those cases, the court ruled in their favor.[5]

The first case brought by the Witnesses was *Lovell v. Griffin* (1938), in which the court held that religious handbills were entitled to protection of freedom of the press. In another important case, *Cantwell v. Connecticut* (1940), the court held, first, that the 14th Amendment prohibited abridgment by the states of the free exercise of religion; second, that public officials did not have the authority to determine that some causes were religious and others were not; and third, that a breach of the peace law as applied to a Jehovah's Witness whose message angered two passersby was overbroad and vague and therefore unconstitutional.[6]

Other significant decisions upheld the right of Witnesses to solicit from door to door and to ring homeowners' doorbells, to refuse to salute the flag and to be exempt from peddler's fees on sales of their literature.[7]

---

[1] Leo Pfeffer, *Church, State and Freedom*, rev. ed. (Boston: Beacon Press, 1967), p. 650; Pfeffer and Justice Robert H. Jackson's dissenting opinion in *Douglas v. City of Jeannette*, 319 U.S. 157 (1943) served as the main sources for this information.

[2] Quoted by Pfeffer, *Church, State and Freedom*, p. 651.

[3] Quoted by Justice Jackson, *Douglas v. City of Jeannette*, 319 U.S. 157 at 171 (1943).

[4] Ibid.

[5] Robert F. Cushman, *Cases in Civil Liberties*, 2d ed. (Englewood Cliffs, N.J.: Prentice-Hall, 1976), p. 305.

[6] *Lovell v. Griffin*, 303 U.S. 444 (1938); *Cantwell v. Connecticut*, 310 U.S. 296 (1940).

[7] *Martin v. City of Struthers*, 319 U.S. 141 (1943); *West Virginia State Board of Education v. Barnette*, 319 U.S. 624 (1943), overruling *Minersville School District v. Gobitis*, 310 U.S. 586 (1940); *Murdock v. Pennsylvania*, 319 U.S. 105 (1943), overruling *Jones v. Opelika*, 316 U.S. 584 (1942).

unequal treatment constituted an improper establishment of religion. "To call the words which one minister speaks to his congregation a sermon, immune from regulation, and the words of another minister an address, subject to regulation, is merely an indirect way of preferring one religion over another," the court said in *Fowler v. Rhode Island* (1953).[18]

License Fees

The validity of license fees imposed on peddlers was challenged by Jehovah's Witnesses who contested the application of the fees to Witnesses who sold religious literature from door to door.

At first review, the court sustained the license fees. In *Jones v. Opelika* (1942), a five-justice majority ruled that the solicitations were more commercial than religious:

> When proponents of religious or social theories use the ordinary commercial methods of sales of articles to raise propaganda funds, it is a natural and proper exercise of the power of the state to charge reasonable fees for the privilege of canvassing. Careful as we may and should be to protect the freedoms safeguarded by the Bill of Rights, it is difficult to see in such enactments a shadow of prohibition of the exercise of religion or of abridgement of the freedom of speech or the press. It is prohibition and unjustifiable abridgement which is interdicted, not taxation.[19] *(Commercial speech, p. 421)*

The following year, Justice James F. Byrnes, who had voted with the majority, resigned and was replaced by Wiley B. Rutledge, a liberal. The court decided to consider the license fee issue a second time and this time struck it down, again by a 5-4 vote.

The case generating the reversal concerned a Jeannette, Pa., ordinance which placed a tax of $1.50 a day on the privilege of door-to-door solicitation. It also required all persons taking orders for or delivering goods door-to-door to obtain a license from the city.

Without obtaining such a license, Jehovah's Witnesses went from house to house in the town soliciting new members. They requested "contributions" of specific amounts from persons showing an interest in their books

---

"Freedom of speech, freedom of the press, freedom of religion are available to all, not merely to those who can pay their own way."

Justice William O. Douglas
Murdock v. Pennsylvania, 1943

---

and pamphlets but on occasion gave the literature free of charge to residents who were unable to pay. Arrested and convicted of violating the ordinance, the Witnesses claimed it unconstitutionally restricted their religious liberty.

"A state may not impose a charge for the enjoyment of a right granted by the federal constitution," the majority said in *Murdock v. Pennsylvania* (1943), overruling its decision in *Jones v. Opelika*.[20]

The majority held that because Jehovah's Witnesses believe that each Witness is a minister ordained by God to preach the gospel, the license fee constituted a tax on the free exercise of religion. Soliciting new adherents by personal visitation and the sale of religious tracts was an evangelical activity that "occupies the same high estate under the First Amendment as do worship in the churches and preaching from the pulpits," the five justices wrote.[21]

Unlike the majority in *Opelika*, this majority did not hold that the commercial aspects of religious solicitation deprived it of its First Amendment protection:

> ...[T]he mere fact that the religious literature is "sold" by itinerant preachers rather than "donated" does not transform evangelism into a commercial enterprise. If it did, then the passing of the collection plate in church would make the church service a commercial project. The constitutional rights of those spreading their religious beliefs through the spoken and printed word are not to be gauged by standards governing retailers or wholesalers of books.... It is plain that a religious organization needs funds to remain a going concern. But an itinerant evangelist, however misguided or intolerant he may be, does not become a mere book agent by selling the Bible or religious tracts to help defray his expenses or to sustain him. Freedom of speech, freedom of the press, freedom of religion are available to all, not merely to those who can pay their own way.[22]

Religion and Political Duty

Under what circumstances may government compel a person to set aside or subordinate his or her religious beliefs in order to fulfill some officially imposed duty? The Supreme Court generally has upheld statutes aimed clearly at maintaining or improving the public health and welfare even if those laws indirectly infringe on religious liberty.

In 1905 a state law requiring compulsory vaccination against smallpox was sustained against such a challenge, brought by Seventh Day Adventists opposed to it on religious grounds. The court ruled in *Jacobson v. Massachusetts* that the legislature had acted reasonably to require vaccination in order to suppress a disease that threatened the entire population.[23]

The Supreme Court, however, has remained silent on the question whether the state can force a person to accept medical treatment, including blood transfusions, if such treatment would violate his religious beliefs. Although a number of well-publicized cases have arisen in lower courts, the Supreme Court so far has chosen not to adjudicate the issue.

Private Schools

In several instances the court has determined that the government's interest in imposing a duty upon individual citizens is not great enough to warrant the intrusion on free exercise of religion. The shifting weights accorded government interests and religious liberty in different situations are illustrated by two early decisions.

In the 1925 case of *Pierce v. Society of Sisters*, the court ruled that Oregon could not constitutionally compel all school children to attend public schools. Such compulsion violated the liberty of parents to direct the upbringing of their children, a liberty which includes the right to send children to parochial schools.[24]

But in 1934 the court held that a college student's conscientious objection to war did not excuse him from attending mandatory classes in military science and tactics at the University of California. [25]

The Flag Salute Cases - I

By far the most dramatic cases to pose to the Supreme Court the question of government compulsion versus religious liberty involved school children and the American flag. Could government demand that children be forced to salute the American flag against their religious beliefs?

If, in retrospect, it is difficult to understand how such an issue drew so much judicial and public attention, it should be remembered that these particular cases arose as first Europe and then the United States entered World War II. Displays of patriotism and loyalty assumed a new importance.

Lillian and William Gobitis, aged 12 and 10 respectively, were expelled from a Minersville, Pa., school in 1936 for refusing to participate in daily flag salute ceremonies. The children were Jehovah's Witnesses who had been taught not to worship any graven image.

The children's parents appealed to the local school board to make an exception for their children to the flag salute requirement. When the school board refused, Gobitis placed the children in a private school and then sued to recover the additional school costs and to stop the school board from requiring the flag salute as a condition for attendance in the public schools.

A federal district court in Philadelphia and then the court of appeals upheld Gobitis' position. The school board appealed to the Supreme Court.

On three earlier occasions the Supreme Court in brief, unsigned opinions had dismissed challenges to flag salute requirements, saying that they posed no substantial federal question. But in each of those cases the result of the dismissal was to sustain the requirement. [26] A dismissal of the Gobitis case would have left the lower court decisions in place, striking down the requirement.

The court granted review, and the case of *Minersville School District v. Gobitis* was argued in the spring of 1940. The Gobitis children were represented by attorneys for the American Civil Liberties Union; a "friend of the court" brief was filed by the American Bar Association in their behalf.

The Supreme Court voted 8-1, however, to reverse the lower courts and sustain the flag salute requirement.

Religious liberty must give way to political authority, wrote Justice Felix Frankfurter for the majority, at least so long as that authority was not used directly to promote or restrict religion. "Certainly the affirmative pursuit of one's convictions about the ultimate mystery of the universe and man's relation to it is placed beyond the reach of the law," he wrote. On the other hand, he said, the "mere possession of religious convictions which contradict the relevant concerns of a political society does not relieve the citizen from the discharge of political responsibilities." [27]

Was the flag salute a relevant political concern? Frankfurter sidestepped the question, writing that national unity was the basis for national security and that the court should defer to the local determination that a compulsory flag salute was an effective means of creating that unity:

...The influences which help toward a common feeling for the common country are manifold. Some may seem harsh and others no doubt are foolish. Surely, however, the end is legitimate. And the effective means for its attainment are still so uncertain and

Religion and War

Since it instituted compulsory conscription in 1917, Congress has exempted from military service those persons who object to war for religious reasons.

In 1917 the exemption was relatively narrow, extending only to adherents of a "well-recognized religious sect or organization . . . whose existing creed or principles [forbid] its members to participate in war in any form. . . ."

Congress expanded the exemption in 1940 to include any persons who "by reason of their religious training and belief are conscientiously opposed to participation in war in any form." In 1948 Congress defined "religious training and belief" to mean "an individual's belief in a relation to a Supreme Being involving duties superior to those arising from any human relation but [not including] essentially political, sociological, or philosophical views or a merely personal moral code."

In 1965 this definition was challenged as discriminating against those persons holding strong "religious" convictions but not believing in a Supreme Being in the orthodox sense. The Supreme Court sidestepped the issue by interpreting Congress' definition very broadly. The "test of belief 'in a relation to a Supreme Being' is whether a given belief that is sincere and meaningful occupies a place in the life of its possessor parallel to that filled by the orthodox belief in God of one who clearly qualifies for exemption," the court said in *United States v. Seeger*. [1]

In 1970 the court went even further and construed the exemption to include those persons who objected to all war on moral and ethical grounds. To come within the meaning of the law, wrote Justice Hugo L. Black for the court in *Welsh v. United States*, opposition to the war must "stem from the registrant's moral, ethical, or religious beliefs about what is right and wrong and . . . these beliefs [must] be held with the strength of traditional religious convictions." [2]

But the Supreme Court subsequently rejected a contention that conscription unconstitutionally infringed on the religious liberty of those opposed to a particular war as unjust. The court acknowledged that this ruling impinged on those religions that counseled their members to refuse participation in unjust wars but to fight in those that were just. But the court said that Congress had acted reasonably and neutrally when it decided that the danger of infringing religious liberty did not outweigh the government interest in maintaining a fairly administered draft service; fairness would be threatened by the difficulty of separating sincere conscientious objectors to a particular war from fraudulent claimants. [3]

The court in another case held that a federal law giving veterans' benefits only to persons who had performed active duty did not unconstitutionally discriminate against conscientious objectors who had performed alternative service. [4]

---

[1] *United States v. Seeger*, 380 U.S. 163 at 165-66 (1965).
[2] *Welsh v. United States*, 398 U.S. 333 at 340 (1970).
[3] *Gillette v. United States*, 401 U.S. 437 (1971).
[4] *Johnson v. Robison*, 415 U.S. 361 (1974).

so unauthenticated by science as to preclude us from putting the widely prevalent belief in flag-saluting beyond the pale of legislative power. It mocks reason and denies our whole history to find in the allowance of a requirement to salute our flag on fitting occasions the seeds of sanction for obeisance to a leader.

The wisdom of training children in patriotic impulses by those compulsions which necessarily pervade so much of the educational process is not for our independent judgment. [28]

Though the members of the court might find "that the deepest patriotism is best engendered by giving unfettered scope to the most crochety beliefs," it was not for the court but for the school board to determine that granting the

---

The "mere possession of religious convictions which contradict the relevant concerns of a political society does not relieve the citizen from the discharge of political responsibilities."

Justice Felix Frankfurter
Minersville School District v. Gobitis, 1940

Gobitis children an exemption from the salute "might cast doubts in the minds of other children which would themselves weaken the effect of the exercise," Frankfurter wrote. [29]

Only Justice Harlan Fiske Stone dissented, choosing religious liberty over political authority. The compulsory salute, Stone said,

> . . .does more than suppress freedom of speech and more than prohibit the free exercise of religion, which concededly are forbidden by the First Amendment. . . . For by this law the state seeks to coerce these children to express a sentiment which, as they interpret it, they do not entertain, and which violates their deepest religious convictions. [30]

Moreover, Stone said the school board could have found ways to instill patriotism in its students without compelling an affirmation some students were unwilling to give:

> . . .The very essence of the liberty which they [the First and 14th Amendments] guaranty [sic] is the freedom of the individual from compulsion as to what he shall think and what he shall say, at least where the compulsion is to bear false witness to his religion. If these guaranties are to have any meaning they must, I think, be deemed to withhold from the state any authority to compel belief or the expression of it where that expression violates religious convictions, whatever may be the legislative view of the desirability of such compulsion. [31]

The majority's reluctance to review legislative judgment was in this case "no more than the surrender of the constitutional protection of the liberty of small minorities to the popular will," Stone said. [32]

Reaction. The press and the legal profession responded unfavorably to the majority decision. One commentator noted that more than 170 leading newspapers condemned the decision while only a few supported it. [33] Law review articles almost universally opposed the decision.

Two years after the *Gobitis* decision, Justices Hugo L. Black, William O. Douglas and Frank Murphy announced in a dissent from the majority's holding in an unrelated case that they had changed their minds about compulsory flag salutes.

In *Jones v. Opelika* (1942), the majority upheld a statute imposing peddler's fees on Jehovah's Witnesses selling religious publications door to door. Dissenting from this decision as an unconstitutional suppression of the free exercise of religion, Black, Douglas and Murphy described the majority position as a logical extension of the principles in the *Gobitis* ruling. They wrote:

> . . .Since we joined in the opinion in the *Gobitis* case, we think this is an appropriate occasion to state that we now believe that it was . . . wrongly decided. Certainly our democratic form of government functioning under the historic Bill of Rights has a high responsibility to accommodate itself to the religious views of minorities however unpopular and unorthodox those views may be. The First Amendment does not put the right freely to exercise religion in a subordinate position. We fear, however, that the opinion in these and in the *Gobitis* case do exactly that. [34]

The Flag Salute Cases - II

The reversal of position by Black, Douglas and Murphy and the appointment in 1943 of Justice Wiley B. Rutledge, a libertarian with well-established views favoring freedom of religion, indicated that at least four justices might join now-Chief Justice Stone in overruling *Gobitis* if the flag salute issue were reconsidered. That opportunity arose in 1943.

The case in which the court overturned *Gobitis* was *West Virginia State Board of Education v. Barnette.* After the *Gobitis* decision, the West Virginia board of education required all schools to make flag salutes part of their daily routine in which all teachers and pupils must participate. Not only would children be expelled if they refused to salute the flag, they would be declared "unlawfully absent" from school and subject to delinquent proceedings. Parents of such children were subject to fine and imprisonment. Several families of Jehovah's Witnesses affected by this decree sued for an injunction to stop its enforcement. The federal district court agreed to issue the injunction and the state school board appealed that decision directly to the Supreme Court.

By a 6-3 vote the Supreme Court upheld the lower federal court and reversed *Gobitis.* Writing the opinion, which was announced on Flag Day, 1943, Justice Robert H. Jackson rejected the *Gobitis* view that the courts should defer to the legislative judgment in this matter. "The very purpose of a Bill of Rights was to withdraw certain subjects from the vicissitudes of political controversy, to place them beyond the reach of majorities and officials and to establish them as legal principles to be applied by the courts," he said. [35]

Jackson then turned to the heart of the issue. "National unity as an end which officials may foster by persuasion and example is not in question," he wrote. "The problem is whether under our Constitution compulsion as here employed is a permissible means for its achievement." Jackson's answer was negative. "Compulsory unification of opinion achieves only the unanimity of the graveyard," he said. [36]

For Jackson, the issues raised by the compulsory flag salute reached beyond questions of religious liberty to broader concerns for the individual's personal liberty. In what many readers consider one of the most elegant passages in Supreme Court prose, he wrote:

> The case is made difficult not because the principles of its decision are obscure but because the flag involved is our own. Nevertheless, we apply the limitations of the Constitution with no fear that freedom to be intellectually and spiritually diverse or even contrary will disintegrate the social organization. To believe that patriotism will not flourish if patriotic ceremonies are voluntary and spontaneous instead of a compulsory routine is to make an unflattering estimate of the appeal of our institutions to free minds. We can have intellectual individualism and the rich cultural diversities that we owe to exceptional minds only at the price of occasional eccentricity and abnormal attitudes. When they are so harmless to others or to the State as those we deal with here, the price is not too great. But freedom to differ is not limited to things that do not matter much. That would be a mere shadow of freedom. The test of its substance is the right to differ as to things that touch the heart of the existing order.
>
> If there is any fixed star in our constitutional constellation, it is that no official, high or petty, can prescribe what shall be orthodox in politics, nationalism, religion or other matters of opinion or force citizens to confess by word or act their faith therein. If there are any circumstances which permit an exception, they do not now occur to us. [37]

Justices Black, Douglas and Murphy wrote concurring opinions explaining their change of mind. In dissent, Justices Owen J. Roberts and Stanley F. Reed simply stated that they agreed with the majority opinion in *Gobitis*.

But Justice Frankfurter's dissent rivaled Jackson's majority opinion in eloquence. Insisting that the majority had failed to exercise proper judicial restraint, Frankfurter maintained that it was within the constitutional authority

---

"If there is any fixed star in our constitutional constellation, it is that no official . . . can prescribe what shall be orthodox in politics, nationalism, religion or other matters of opinion. . . ."

Justice Robert H. Jackson
West Virginia State Board of Education v. Barnette, 1943

---

of the state school board to demand that public school children salute the American flag. Reading the majority a lecture on their duties as interpreters of the Constitution, Frankfurter began with an unusual personal reference to his own Jewish heritage:

> One who belongs to the most vilified and persecuted minority in history is not likely to be insensible to the freedoms guaranteed by our Constitution. Were my purely personal attitude relevant I should wholeheartedly associate myself with the general libertarian views in the Court's opinion, representing as they do the thought and action of a lifetime. But as judges we are neither Jew nor Gentile, neither Catholic nor agnostic. . . . As a member of this Court I am not justified in writing my private notions of policy into the Constitution, no matter how deeply I may cherish them or how mischievous I may deem their disregard. The duty of a judge who must decide which of two claims before the Court shall prevail, that of a State to enact and enforce laws within its general competence or that of an individual to refuse obedience because of the demands of his conscience, is not that of an ordinary person. It can never be emphasized too much that one's own opinion about the wisdom or evil of a law should be excluded altogether when one is doing one's duty on the bench. The only opinion of our own even looking in that direction that is material is our opinion whether legislators could in reason have enacted such a law. In the light of all the circumstances, including the history of this question in this Court, it would require more daring than I possess to deny that reasonable legislators could have taken the action which is before us for review. . . . I cannot bring my mind to believe that the "liberty" secured by the Due Process Clause gives this Court the authority to deny to the State of West Virginia the attainment of that which we all recognize as a legitimate legislative end, namely, the promotion of good citizenship, by employment of the means here chosen. [38]

Sunday Closing Laws

In 1961 the court set out the modern rule for determining when a state may properly compel obedience to a secular law that conflicts with religious beliefs.

The rule was stated as the court upheld the validity of Sunday closing laws, challenged as restricting the free exercise of religion. That claim was raised by an Orthodox Jew who observed the Jewish Sabbath, closing his clothing and furniture store on Saturday. To make up the lost revenue, he opened the store on Sunday. When Pennsylvania enacted a Sunday closing law in 1959, he challenged its constitutionality.

The Supreme Court found that the law did not violate the First Amendment. Sunday closing of commercial enterprises was an effective means for achieving the valid state purpose of providing citizens with a uniform day of rest. Although it operated indirectly to make observance of certain religious practices more expensive, the Sunday closing law did not make any religious practice illegal, the majority observed in *Braunfeld v. Brown* (1961).

The court then announced the rule for judging whether a state law unconstitutionally restricts the exercise of religious liberty:

> . . .If the purpose or effect of a law is to impede the observance of one or all religions or is to discriminate invidiously between religions, that law is constitutionally invalid even though the burden may be characterized as being only indirect. But if the State regulates conduct by enacting a general law within its power, the purpose and effect of which is to advance the State's

secular goals, the statute is valid despite its indirect burden on religious observance unless the State may accomplish its purpose by means which do not impose such a burden. [39]

Unemployment Compensation

Two years later the court significantly modified its *Braunfeld* ruling by declaring that only a compelling state interest could justify limitations on religious liberty.

Sherbert v. Verner (1963) arose after Adell Sherbert was fired from her South Carolina textile mill job because, as a Seventh Day Adventist, she refused to work on Saturdays. Because she refused available work, the state denied her unemployment compensation benefits.

Overturning the state ruling by a 7-2 vote, the court, speaking through Justice William J. Brennan Jr., explained that the state's action forced Sherbert either to abandon her religious principles in order to work, or to maintain her religious precepts and forfeit unemployment compensation benefits. "Governmental imposition of such a choice puts the same kind of burden upon the free exercise of religion as would a fine imposed against appellant for her Saturday worship," Brennan wrote.[40]

Brennan contended that the state could limit the exercise of an individual's religion only for a compelling state interest. "Only the gravest abuses, endangering paramount interests, give occasion for permissible limitation," he said. Prevention of fraudulent claims was the only reason the state advanced for denying benefits to Sherbert, Brennan noted. To justify that denial, he wrote, the state must show that it cannot prevent such fraud by means that are less restrictive of religious liberty. [41]

In dissent, Justices John Marshall Harlan and Byron R. White held that the court should have abided by its *Braunfeld* rule. Unemployment compensation was intended to help people when there was no work available, not to aid those who, for whatever reason, refused available work. Maintenance of such a distinction was a valid goal of the state, which affected religion only indirectly, they said.

Compulsory School Attendance

The *Sherbert* ruling was reinforced by the court's 1972 decision in *Wisconsin v. Yoder*. Old Order Amish parents refused to send their children to school beyond grade eight; this violated Wisconsin's law compelling all children to attend school until they reached age 16. The parents asserted that high school education engendered values contrary to Amish beliefs which hold that salvation may be obtained only by living in religious, agrarian communities separate from the world and worldly influences.

Expert witnesses testified that compulsory high school education might result not only in psychological harm to Amish children confused by trying to fit into two different worlds, but also in destruction of the Amish community.

Despite this testimony, the Wisconsin trial and appeals courts upheld compulsory attendance as a reasonable and constitutional means of promoting a valid state interest.

The state supreme court reversed, ruling that the state had not shown that its interest in compelling attendance was sufficient to justify the infringement on the free exercise of religion. The Supreme Court affirmed that holding.

Chief Justice Warren E. Burger wrote the court's opinion. He acknowledged that the provision of public schools was one of the primary functions of the state. But, he added:

. . .a state's interest in universal education, however highly we rank it, is not totally free from a balancing process when it impinges on fundamental rights and interests, such as those specifically protected by the Free Exercise Clause of the First Amendment, and the traditional interest of parents with respect to the religious upbringing of their children so long as they . . . "prepare [them] for additional obligations."[42]

The court accepted the evidence showing that the traditional Amish community life was based on convictions that would be weakened by forcing teenage children to attend public schools. The court also noted that the Amish provided their children with alternative modes of informal vocational education that accommodated all the interests the state advanced in support of its compulsory attendance law. In light of this, the state must show "with more particularity [than it had] how its admittedly strong interest in compulsory education would be adversely affected by granting an exception to the Amish," Burger concluded. [43]

Religion and Oath-Taking

Article VI of the Constitution states that "no religious Test shall ever be required as a Qualification to any Office or public Trust under the United States."

The Supreme Court in 1961 ruled that under the First Amendment, states also are prohibited from requiring religious test oaths.

Ray Torcaso, appointed a notary public in Maryland, was denied his commission when he refused to declare his belief in God, a part of the oath notaries public were required by Maryland law to take. Torcaso sued, challenging the oath as abridging his religious liberty.

A unanimous Supreme Court struck down the oath requirement in *Torcaso v. Watkins* (1961). Justice Hugo L. Black wrote:

We repeat and again affirm that neither a State nor the Federal Government can constitutionally force a person "to profess a belief or disbelief in any religion." Neither can constitutionally pass laws or impose requirements which aid all religions as against nonbelievers, and neither can aid those religions based on a belief in the existence of God as against those religions founded on different beliefs. [44]

Naturalization Cases

The Supreme Court thus stated unequivocally that a state may not require a person to swear to a belief he or she does not hold. But may government require a person to swear a non-religious oath contrary to his religious beliefs? In a series of cases concerning pacifist applicants for U.S. citizenship, the Supreme Court first said "yes" and then said "no."

The naturalization oath requires applicants for citizenship to swear "to support and defend the Constitution and the law of the United States of America against all enemies, foreign and domestic." The naturalization service interpreted this to require that would-be citizens be willing to bear arms in defense of the country. It therefore denied citizenship to two women pacifists and to a 54-year old Yale Divinity School professor who said he would fight only in wars he believed to be morally justified.

Although the three were qualified in every other way to be citizens and were extremely unlikely ever to be called into active service, the court upheld the naturalization service's position as reasonable in 1929 in *United States v. Schwimmer* and again in 1931.[45]

Following World War II, the court reconsidered and reversed these holdings. Again the majority did not reach the constitutional issue but dealt only with the statutory interpretation of the oath.

Girouard v. United States (1946) concerned a Canadian Seventh-Day Adventist who agreed to serve as a non-combatant in the armed forces but refused to bear arms because killing conflicted with his religious beliefs. The majority noted that the oath did not expressly require naturalized citizens to swear to bear arms and ruled that this interpretation need not be read into the oath. Congress, the majority said, could not have intended to deny citizenship in a country noted for its protection of religious beliefs to persons whose religious beliefs prevented them from bearing arms.[46]

The year before it overruled its early decisions in the pacifist naturalization cases, the Supreme Court upheld the Illinois bar's decision to deny admission to an attorney because its required oath conflicted with his beliefs.[47]

That decision has never been overruled, but its effect has been weakened by subsequent decisions. Among the more recent of these was the court's 1978 ruling in *McDaniel v. Paty* in which the court struck down as unconstitutional a Tennessee law that forbade clergymen to hold state offices.[48]

Writing the court's opinion, Chief Justice Burger relied on *Sherbert v. Verner* as precedent, saying that the state law unconstitutionally restricted the right of free exercise of religion by making it conditional on a willingness to give up the right to seek public office.[49]

Justices Potter Stewart, William J. Brennan Jr. and Thurgood Marshall used *Torcaso* as precedent, and Marshall and Brennan held that the law also violated the establishment clause.[50] Justice Byron R. White held that the law denied clergymen equal protection of the laws.

Establishment of Religion

The establishment clause of the First Amendment prohibits Congress from making any law "respecting an establishment of religion." This means that Congress is not only forbidden to designate a national church but also to support directly one or all religions in any way.

The two men most responsible for its inclusion in the Bill of Rights construed the clause absolutely. Thomas Jefferson and James Madison thought that the prohibition of establishment meant that a presidential proclamation of Thanksgiving Day was just as improper as a tax exemption for churches.[51]

The Supreme Court, which specifically declared the establishment clause applicable to the states in 1947, has never adopted this absolutist position. In its first decision on the clause, the court sustained a federal construction grant to a Roman Catholic hospital. The court held that the hospital's purpose was secular and that it did not discriminate among its patients on the basis of religion. The aid therefore only indirectly benefited the church.[52]

Since that decision in 1899, only two areas of national life have raised significant establishment questions — public schools and taxes. The court has sustained the practice of exempting churches from taxes on the grounds that to tax them would be to entangle government excessively with religion. For much the same reason, the court has also declined to review legal questions involving intra-church controversies. *(Box, next page)*

The court has barred religious exercises in tax-supported public schools as unconstitutional government advancement of religion. Prayer recitations, Bible readings and religious instruction, when denominational, favor one religion over others; when non-denominational, they favor all religion over non-religious beliefs, the court has said.

The court, however, has adopted what it describes as a "benevolent neutrality" toward government financial aid to parochial schools. If the aid is secular in its purpose and effect and does not entangle the government excessively in its administration, it is permissible, even if it indirectly benefits the church schools.

Not all justices agree, however, on what aid is secular and what is not. For example, a majority of the court continues to hold that state textbook loan programs to parochial schools are proper. But a minority insists that because textbooks are essential to the business of teaching, their loan to church-affiliated schools is an unconstitutional establishment of religion.

Tax Exemptions

Historically, the federal government, every state and the District of Columbia have exempted churches from paying property and income taxes.

In 1970 the Supreme Court sustained these exemptions by an 8-1 vote. The case, *Walz v. Tax Commission*, arose when a property owner in New York challenged the state's property tax exemption for religious institutions as an establishment of religion. He contended that the exemption meant that non-exempt property owners made an involuntary contribution to churches.

Writing for the majority, Chief Justice Warren E. Burger observed that churches were only one of several institutions — including hospitals, libraries, historical and patriotic organizations — exempted from paying property taxes. Such exemptions reflected the state's decision that these groups provided beneficial and stabilizing influences in the community and that their activities might be hampered or destroyed by the need to pay property taxes. "We cannot read New York's statute as attempting to establish religion," wrote Burger; "it is simply sparing the exercise of religion from the burden of property taxation levied on private profit institutions."[53]

Thus the exemption met the existing test for determining whether government policy constituted improper establishment of religion: Both the purpose and effect of the exemption were primarily secular, having only an indirect benefit to religion.

But to this test, the court in *Walz* added a new one: whether the exemption resulted in excessive government

Internal Church Disputes

The Supreme Court has been reluctant to involve itself in the internal disputes that occasionally arise within churches. Where judicial intervention is unavoidable, the court has insisted that the judiciary decline to decide questions of religious doctrine.

This rule was first developed in the case of *Watson v. Jones* (1872), which involved a dispute over church property between a national church organization and local churches that had withdrawn from the national hierarchy. Although the case was decided on common law grounds, it had clear First Amendment overtones:

> All who unite themselves to [the central church] do so with an implied consent to [its] government, and are bound to submit to it. But it would be a vain consent, and would lead to the total subversion of such religious bodies, if anyone aggrieved by one of their decisions could appeal to the secular courts and have [it] reversed.[1]

In 1952, the Supreme Court said that the First Amendment guarantee of freedom of religion gave religious organizations an "independence from secular control or manipulations — in short, power to decide for themselves, free from state interference, matters of church government as well as those of faith and doctrine."[2]

In 1969, the court again held that both religion clauses forbid court interference with religious doctrine:

> First Amendment values are plainly jeopardized when church property litigation is made to turn on the resolution by civil courts of controversies over religious doctrine and practice. If civil courts undertake to resolve such controversies in order to adjudicate the property dispute, the hazards are ever present of inhibiting the free development of religious doctrine and of implicating secular interests in matters of purely ecclesiastical concern.... The Amendment therefore commands civil courts to decide church property disputes without resolving underlying controversies over religious doctrines.[3]

The judicial role is therefore limited to examining the church rules and determining that they have been applied appropriately. As Justice Louis D. Brandeis put it in a 1929 decision, "In the absence of fraud, collusion, or arbitrariness, the decisions of the proper church tribunals on matters purely ecclesiastical, although affecting civil rights, are accepted in litigation before the secular courts as conclusive...."[4]

---

[1] *Watson v. Jones*, 13 Wall. 679 at 728-29 (1872).
[2] *Kedroff v. St. Nicholas Cathedral*, 344 U.S. 94 at 116 (1952); see also *Kreshik v. St. Nicholas Cathedral*, 363 U.S. 190 (1960).
[3] *Presbyterian Church in the United States v. Mary Elizabeth Blue Hull Memorial Presbyterian Church*, 393 U.S. 440 at 449 (1969).
[4] *Gonzalez v. Archbishop*, 280 U.S. 1 at 16 (1929); see also *Serbian Eastern Orthodox Diocese v. Milivojevich*, 426 U.S. 696 (1976).

involvement with religion. To answer this question, Burger said the court must consider whether the alternative of taxing the property would result in more or less entanglement than continuing the exemption.

Observing that taxation would require government valuation of church property, and possibly tax liens and foreclosures, Burger concluded that the "hazards of churches supporting government are hardly less in their potential than the hazards of government supporting churches." Tax exemption, on the other hand, created "only a minimal and remote involvement between church and state.... It restricts the fiscal relationship between church and state, and tends to complement and reinforce the desired separation insulating each from the other."[54]

Religion and Public Schools

"We are a religious people whose institutions presuppose a Supreme Being," wrote Justice William O. Douglas in 1952.[55]

The nation's governmental institutions reflect this belief daily. Each session of the House and Senate opens with a prayer. The Supreme Court begins its sessions with an invocation asking that "God save the United States and this honorable court." Our currency proclaims, "In God We Trust," while we acknowledge that we are "one nation, under God," each time we recite the Pledge of Allegiance.

These official and public affirmations of religious belief have not escaped legal challenge, but the Supreme Court has dismissed most of them summarily.

In 1964, for example, the court refused without comment to review a lower court decision which held that despite inclusion of the phrase "under God" in the Pledge of Allegiance, the First Amendment did not bar the New York Education Commission from recommending that the pledge be recited in schools. In 1971 the court declined to review a lower court decision refusing to stop astronauts from praying on television for God's blessing for a successful trip to the moon. In the same ruling, the lower court had also rejected a challenge to the phrase "So help me God" contained in the oath witnesses are required to take in many court trials. And in 1979 the court refused to review a challenge to the words "In God We Trust" on currency.[56]

Although the court has been reluctant to proscribe this sort of government-sponsored public expression of religious belief on the part of adults, it has flatly prohibited states from requiring or permitting religious exercises by children in public elementary and secondary schools.

Released Time

The first two Supreme Court rulings concerning religious exercises in public schools involved "released time" programs. Employed by school districts across the country, these programs released students from regular classwork, usually once a week, to receive religious instruction. In some cases the students received the instruction in their regular classrooms; sometimes they met in another schoolroom; at other times they met in churches or synagogues. Students participated in the programs voluntarily. Students who did not participate had a study period during the time religious instruction was given.

The first of the released time cases was *Illinois ex rel. McCollum v. Board of Education* (1948). The Champaign, Ill., school board operated a released time program in which religion teachers came into the public schools once a week to give one half-hour of religious instruction to voluntary participants. The program was challenged as a violation of the First Amendment's establishment clause by the atheist mother of a fifth grader, the only pupil in his class who did not participate in the program.

By an 8-1 vote, the Supreme Court declared the program unconstitutional.

"Pupils compelled by law to go to school for secular education are released in part from their legal duty upon the condition that they attend religious classes," wrote Justice Hugo L. Black for the majority. "This is beyond all question a utilization of the tax-established and tax-supported public school system to aid religious groups to spread their faith." [57]

Four justices concurred in the judgment in a separate opinion. Not only did the program violate the establishment clause because its actual operation tended to advance certain religions over others, they said, it also threatened to impede the free exercise of religion. Justice Felix Frankfurter explained:

> Religious education so conducted on school time and property is patently woven into the working scheme of the school. The Champaign arrangement thus presents powerful elements of inherent pressure by the school system in the interest of religious sects.... That a child is offered an alternative may reduce the constraint; it does not eliminate the operation of influence by the school in matters sacred to conscience and outside the school's domain. The law of imitation operates, and nonconformity is not an outstanding characteristic of children. The result is an obvious pressure upon children to attend. Again, while the Champaign school population represents only a fraction of the more than two hundred and fifty sects of the nation, not even all the practicing sects in Champaign are willing or able to provide religious instruction.... As a result, the public school system of Champaign actively furthers inculcation in the religious tenets of some faiths, and in the process sharpens the consciousness of religious differences at least among some of the children committed to its care....[58]

Four years later the court upheld New York City's released time program, in which religious instruction was given during the school day but not in the public schools. In *Zorach v. Clausen* (1952), the court held, by a 6-3 vote, that this program did not violate the establishment clause. "The First Amendment ... does not say that in every and all respects there shall be a separation of Church and State," wrote Justice Douglas, noting that governments provided churches with general services such as police and fire protection and that public officials frequently said prayers before undertaking their official chores. [59]

The New York program did not significantly aid religion; it simply required that "the public schools do no more than accommodate their schedules to a program of outside religious instruction." To hold that they may not "would be to find in the Constitution a requirement that the government show a callous indifference to religious groups." [60]

Government, continued Douglas,

> ...may not coerce anyone to attend church, to observe a religious holiday, or to take religious instruction. But it can close its doors or suspend its operations as to those who want to repair to their religious

Monkey Laws

One of the most celebrated trials in all American history was the 1925 Scopes case, in which teacher John Scopes was convicted and fined $100 for teaching the Darwinian theory of evolution in violation of a Tennessee law that made it illegal to teach anything other than a literal Biblical theory of man's creation.

Scopes' conviction was subsequently reversed by the state supreme court for technical reasons, although the statute was permitted to stand, and was never challenged before the U.S. Supreme Court. [1]

But 43 years later the Supreme Court was given an opportunity to rule on the same issue in the case of *Epperson v. Arkansas.*

In this case a public school biology teacher challenged the state law which forbade teachers in state-supported schools from teaching or using textbooks which teach "the theory or doctrine that mankind ascended or descended from a lower order of animals."

By a 9-0 vote the court struck down this law as a violation of the First Amendment prohibition on establishment of religion and its guarantee of the free exercise of religion. "The overriding fact is that Arkansas' law selects from the body of knowledge a particular segment which it proscribes for the sole reason that it is deemed to conflict with a particular religious doctrine; that is, with a particular interpretation of the Book of Genesis by a particular religious group." [2]

---

[1] *Scopes v. State,* 154 Tenn. 105, 289 S.W. 363 (1927).
[2] *Epperson v. Arkansas,* 393 U.S. 97 at 103 (1968).

sanctuary for worship or instruction. No more than that is undertaken here. [61]

Justices Black, Frankfurter and Robert H. Jackson wrote separate dissenting opinions. All three held that the program was coercive and a direct aid to religion. Black wrote:

> ...Here the sole question is whether New York can use its compulsory education laws to help religious sects get attendants presumably too unenthusiastic to go unless moved to do so by the pressure of this state machinery.... Any use of such coercive power by the state to help or hinder some religious sects or to prefer all religious sects over nonbelievers or vice versa is just what I think the First Amendment forbids. [62]

School Prayer

A decade after the *Zorach* decision, the Supreme Court set off an intense new round of controversy over church-and-state matters with its decisions banning school prayer and Bible reading as regular devotional exercises in public schools. Such exercises, often coupled with recitation of the Pledge of Allegiance, were common occurrences in classrooms across the country.

As early as 1930 the Supreme Court dismissed for lack of a federal question a state court's refusal to direct the Washington state school superintendent to require Bible reading in public schools.

The question of Bible readings in public schools came to the court again in 1952, but the court again dismissed the suit, this time because the parents of the child involved no longer had standing to sue because the child had already graduated from school. [63]

Another 10 years passed before the court directly confronted the issue of the constitutionality of devotional practices in public schools. The case of *Engle v. Vitale* arose after New York's State Board of Regents recommended to school districts that they adopt a specified non-denominational prayer to be repeated voluntarily by students at the beginning of each school day. The brief prayer read: "Almighty God, we acknowledge our dependence upon Thee, and we beg Thy blessings upon us, our parents, our teachers and our country."

The prayer was not universally adopted throughout the state. New York City, for example, chose instead to have its students recite the verse of the hymn "America" that asks God's protection for the country.

The school board of New Hyde Park, N.Y., adopted the recommended prayer, however. Parents of 10 pupils in the school district, with the support of the New York Civil Liberties Union, brought suit, claiming that the prayer was contrary to their religious beliefs and practices and that its adoption and use violated the establishment clause. The state courts upheld the prayer on the condition that no student be compelled to participate.

By a 6-1 vote the Supreme Court reversed the state courts, holding that this use of the prayer was "wholly inconsistent with the Establishment Clause." In an opinion written by Justice Black, the majority explained its view:

> ...[T]he constitutional prohibition against laws respecting an establishment of religion must at least mean that in this country it is no part of the business of government to compose official prayers for any group of the American people to recite as a part of a religious program carried on by government. [64]

The fact that the prayer was non-denominational and that students who did not wish to participate could remain

---

"(T)he constitutional prohibition against laws respecting an establishment of religion must at least mean that . . . it is no part of the business of government to compose official prayers for any group of the American people to recite as part of a religious program carried on by government."

Justice Hugo L. Black
Engel v. Vitale, 1962

---

silent or leave the room did not free the prayer "from the limitations of the Establishment Clause." Black wrote:

> ...The Establishment Clause, unlike the Free Exercise Clause, does not depend upon any showing of direct governmental compulsion and is violated by the enactment of laws which establish an official religion whether those laws operate directly to coerce nonobserving individuals or not. This is not to say, of

course, that laws officially prescribing a particular form of religious worship do not involve coercion of such individuals. When the power, prestige and financial support of government is placed behind a particular religious belief, the indirect coercive pressure upon religious minorities to conform to the prevailing officially approved religion is plain. [65]

In response to the argument that the prayer, if an establishment of religion at all, was a relatively insignifi-

---

"I cannot see how an 'official religion' is established by letting those who want to say a prayer say it."

Justice Potter Stewart, dissenting,
Engel v. Vitale, 1962

---

cant and harmless encroachment, Black quoted James Madison, the chief author of the First Amendment:

> ...[I]t is proper to take alarm at the first experiment on our liberties.... Who does not see that the same authority which can establish Christianity, in exclusion of all other Religions, may establish with the same ease any particular sect of Christians, in exclusion of all other Sects? [66]

Asserting that "the Court has misapplied a great constitutional principle," Justice Potter Stewart dissented. "I cannot see how an 'official religion' is established by letting those who want to say a prayer say it," he said. [67] Stewart compared the regents' prayer to other state-sanctioned religious exercises, such as the reference to God in the pledge to the flag, in the president's oath of office and in the formal opening of each day's session of the court itself:

> I do not believe that this Court, or the Congress, or the President has by the actions and practices I have mentioned established an "official religion" in violation of the Constitution. And I do not believe the State of New York has done so in this case. What each has done has been to recognize and to follow the deeply entrenched and highly cherished spiritual traditions of our Nation — traditions which come down to us from those who almost two hundred years ago avowed their "firm Reliance on the Protection of divine Providence" when they proclaimed the freedom and independence of this brave new world. [68]

Bible Readings

A year later, the court affirmed its "school prayer" decision, declaring unconstitutional the practice of daily Bible readings in public school classrooms.

Two cases, *School District of Abington Township v. Schempp* and *Murray v. Curlett,* were considered together. The *Schempp* case concerned a Pennsylvania statute that required the reading of at least 10 verses from the Bible each day, followed by recitation of the Lord's Prayer and the pledge to the flag. Pupils were excused from participating at the request of their parents. The Schempps asserted that certain literal Bible readings were contrary to their

School Prayer and Congressional Backlash

"The Supreme Court has made God unconstitutional." That statement, made by Sen. Sam Ervin, D-N.C. (1954-74), typified general reaction to the Supreme Court's 1962 school prayer decision.[1]

Members of Congress, governors, even a former president all spoke out in opposition to the decision. And although the ruling was greeted favorably by the Jewish community and many Christian leaders, several Protestant and Catholic clergymen expressed shock. "I am shocked and frightened that the Supreme Court has declared unconstitutional a simple and voluntary declaration of belief in God by public school children," said Francis Cardinal Spellman. "The decision strikes at the very heart of the Godly tradition in which America's children have for so long been raised."[2]

Reaction to the Supreme Court's Bible-reading decision was just as adverse and outspoken. "Why should the majority be so severely penalized by the protests of a handful?" asked evangelist Billy Graham.[3]

And despite the opposition of most major religious organizations to any constitutional amendment to overturn the rulings, mail advocating such an amendment flooded into congressional offices.

Becker Amendment

Rep. Frank J. Becker, R-N.Y. (1953-65), introduced a proposed constitutional amendment after the court announced its school prayer decision. That amendment provided that nothing in the Constitution should be interpreted to bar "the offering, reading from, or listening to prayer or biblical scriptures, if participation therein is on a voluntary basis, in any government or public school institution or place."

The House Judiciary Committee took no action on the proposal, and after the 1963 Bible-reading ruling, Becker filed a petition discharging that committee from consideration of the amendment. (If such a petition is signed by a majority of House members, the amendment may be brought directly to the House floor for debate.)

Although Judiciary Committee Chairman Emanuel Celler, D-N.Y., 1923-73, had made plain his opposition to the amendment, he attempted to diffuse the discharge petition drive by agreeing in 1964 to hold hearings on the issue. Once hearings were held, the committee took no further action; Celler said it had found no way to approve a constitutional amendment without infringing upon existing constitutional guarantees of freedom of religion.

Dirksen Amendment

Despite the lack of congressional action, the school prayer issue did not disappear. In mid-1965, a court of appeals upheld the action of a New York principal who had refused a request by a group of children that time be set aside for them during school hours to recite two prayers. The Supreme Court refused to review this decision, as in 1968 it refused to review a court order barring the compulsory recitation by public school kindergarten children of a thank-you verse. And in 1971 the court declined to review a New Jersey court decision barring the school-board approved practice in one school district of providing a pre-school period during which prayers were read from the *Congressional Record* to anyone who wished to attend.[4]

Responding to the first of these decisions, Senate Minority Leader Everett McKinley Dirksen, R-Ill., 1951-69, proposed in 1966 an amendment stating that the Constitution should not be interpreted to bar any public school authority from providing for or permitting the voluntary participation of students in prayer. His amendment specifically stated that it did not authorize any government official to prescribe the form or content of a prayer.

In September 1966 the Senate agreed to substitute the text of this proposed constitutional amendment for that of a pending bill. But the Senate then failed, by nine votes, to give the Dirksen amendment the two-thirds vote needed for passage of a constitutional amendment.

Wylie Amendment

For a few years, congressional interest in a school prayer amendment waned. Then, at the urging of a grassroots organization called the Prayer Campaign Committee, Rep. Chalmers P. Wylie, R-Ohio, began to circulate another petition among House members to discharge from a still-opposed House Judiciary Committee a proposed amendment similar to the Dirksen amendment. By September 1971 a majority of the House had signed Wylie's petition and the amendment came to the House floor for debate. On Nov. 8, 1971, the amendment failed by 28 votes to win the approval of the necessary two-thirds majority. The vote was 240-162.

Since that vote no serious effort has been made in either the House or Senate to pass a constitutional amendment permitting voluntary prayer in public schools.

---

[1] Quoted in Leo Pfeffer, *Church, State and Freedom*, rev. ed. (Boston: Beacon Press, 1967), p. 466.

[2] Ibid., p. 467.

[3] Quoted in Congressional Quarterly, "Restore Prayers in Schools: The Move that Failed," *Education for a Nation*

(Washington, D.C.: Congressional Quarterly, 1972), p. 38.

[4] *Stein v. Oshinsky*, 382 U.S. 957 (1965); *DeKalb County Community School District 428 v. DeSpain*, 390 U.S. 906 (1968); *Board of Education of Netcong, N.J. v. State Board of Education*, 401 U.S. 1013 (1971).

Unitarian religious beliefs and brought suit to stop the readings. In the *Murray* case, the challenged reading was required not by state law but by a 1905 city rule. Madalyn Murray and her student son, William, were atheists. They contended that the daily religious exercises placed "a premium on belief as against non-belief and subject[ed] their freedom of conscience to the rule of the majority." They asked that the readings be stopped.

By an 8-1 vote the court held that the Bible readings in both cases were unconstitutional. The readings were clearly religious exercises prescribed as part of the school curriculum for students compelled by law to attend school. They were held in state buildings and supervised by teachers paid by the state. By these actions the state abandoned the neutrality toward religion demanded by the establishment clause. Justice Tom C. Clark wrote for the majority:

> The place of religion in our society is an exalted one, achieved through a long tradition of reliance on the home, the church and the inviolable citadel of the individual heart and mind. We have come to recognize through bitter experience that it is not within the power of government to invade that citadel, whether its purpose or effect be to aid or oppose, to advance or retard. In the relationship between man and religion, the State is firmly committed to a position of neutrality. [69]

It was no defense that the Bible reading exercises might be "relatively minor" encroachments on the First Amendment. "The breach of neutrality that is today a trickling stream may all too soon become a raging torrent," Clark wrote. [70] Nor did the ruling set up a "religion of secularism" in the schools. Schools could permit the study of the Bible for its literary and historical merits; they were only prohibited from using the Bible as part of a devotional exercise.

Finally, Clark said that the ruling did not deny the majority its right to the free exercise of religion. "While the Free Exercise Clause clearly prohibits the use of state action to deny the rights of free exercise to *anyone*, it has never meant that a majority could use the machinery of the State to practice its beliefs." [71]

Opposition from the public to the two school prayer decisions ran high, encouraging both chambers of Congress to consider constitutional amendments that would overrule the decisions. Neither the House nor the Senate was able to produce the two-thirds votes needed to send a proposed amendment to the states for ratification. *(Reaction, box, p. 465)*

State Aid to Parochial Schools

The first suit challenging state aid to church-related schools reached the Supreme Court in the 1930 case of *Cochran v. Louisiana Board of Education.* [72]

Louisiana furnished all school children in the state, including those attending parochial schools, secular textbooks paid for with public funds. Cochran, a taxpayer, challenged the statute. Because the court in 1930 had not yet specifically stated that the 14th Amendment incorporated the religious guarantees of the First Amendment, Cochran's contention was that this use of public funds violated the 14th Amendment's prohibition against state action depriving persons of their property without due process of law.

Rejecting this assertion, the Supreme Court adopted the "child benefit" theory, holding that the provision of free textbooks was designed to further the education of all children in the state and not to benefit church-related schools.

The 1947 case of *Everson v. Board of Education,* in which the court specifically applied the establishment clause to the states, was also the first case in which the court was required to consider whether the clause barred

public aid to church-operated schools. Elaborating on its reasoning in *Cochran,* the court by a 5-4 vote ruled that while the establishment clause forbade states from aiding religion, it did not prohibit the states from granting aid to all children in the state without regard to their religious beliefs.

Everson concerned a New Jersey statute that permitted local boards of education to reimburse parents for the costs of sending their children to school on public transportation. Arch Everson, a local taxpayer, challenged as an impermissible establishment of religion the reimbursement of parents of parochial school students.

Writing for the majority, Justice Hugo L. Black offered what would become an often quoted description of the meaning of the establishment clause:

> The "establishment of religion" clause of the First Amendment means at least this: Neither a state nor the Federal Government can set up a church. Neither can pass laws which aid one religion, aid all religions or prefer one religion over another. Neither can force nor

---

"Neither a state nor the Federal Government can set up a church. Neither can pass laws which aid one religion, aid all religions or prefer one religion over another. Neither can force nor influence a person to go to or to remain away from church against his will or force him to profess a belief or disbelief in any religion."

Justice Hugo L. Black
Everson v. Board of Education, 1947

---

influence a person to go to or to remain away from church against his will or force him to profess a belief or disbelief in any religion. No person can be punished for entertaining or professing any religious beliefs or disbeliefs, for church attendance or non-attendance. No tax in any amount, large or small, can be levied to support any religious activities or institutions, whatever they may be called, or whatever form they may adopt to teach or practice religion. Neither a state nor the Federal Government can, openly or secretly, participate in the affairs of any religious organizations or groups and *vice versa.* In the words of Jefferson, the clause against establishment of religion by law was intended to erect "a wall of separation between Church and State." [73]

Having said that, however, the majority proceeded to uphold the New Jersey statute on the ground that it did not aid religion but was instead public welfare legislation benefiting children rather than schools:

> ...It is undoubtedly true that children are helped to get to church schools. There is even a possibility that some of the children might not be sent to the church schools if the parents were compelled to pay their children's bus fares out of their own pockets when transportation to a public school would have been paid

for by the State. . . . Similarly, parents might be reluctant to permit their children to attend [church] schools which the state had cut off from such general government services as ordinary police and fire protection, connections for sewage disposal, public highways and sidewalks. Of course, cutting off church schools from these services, so separate and so indisputably marked off from the religious function, would make it far more difficult for the schools to operate. But such is obviously not the purpose of the First Amendment. That Amendment requires the state to be a neutral in its relations with groups of religious believers and nonbelievers; it does not require the state to be their adversary. State power is no more to be used so as to handicap religions, than it is to favor them. [74]

The legislation, concluded Black, "does no more than provide a general program to help parents get their children, regardless of their religion, safely and expeditiously to and from accredited schools." [75]

Dissent. For the four dissenters, Justice Wiley B. Rutledge agreed with the majority that the establishment clause "forbids state support, financial or other, of religion in any guise, form or degree. It outlaws all use of public funds for religious purposes." But to cast this particular case in terms of public welfare, as the majority does, is to ignore "the religious factor and its essential connection with the transportation, thereby leaving out the only vital element in the case," said Rutledge. [76]

Publicly supported transportation of parochial school children benefits not only their secular education but also their religious education, Rutledge asserted. In conclusion he wrote:

> Two great drives are constantly in motion to abridge, in the name of education, the complete division of religion and civil authority which our forefathers made. One is to introduce religious education and observances into the public schools. The other, to obtain public funds for the aid and support of various private religious schools. . . . In my opinion, both avenues were closed by the Constitution. Neither should be opened by this Court. [77]

Textbooks

It was evident from the *Everson* decision that despite Justice Black's extremely broad interpretation of the establishment clause, the line of separation between church and state was, as a later justice would put it, "a blurred, indistinct and variable barrier depending on all the circumstances of a particular relationship." [78]

The court now needed to devise some criterion for assessing whether state aid to church schools breached that barrier.

In the 20 years between *Everson* and the next state aid case, the Supreme Court decided the school prayer cases, ruling that the establishment clause did not permit public schools to use prayers and Bible reading as part of their daily exercises and that such exercises violated the clause because they were sectarian in purpose and their primary effect was to advance religion.

The court first applied these guidelines to a question of state aid to church-related schools in the 1968 case of *Board of Education of Central School District No. 1 v. Allen.*

The circumstances were similar to those of the *Cochran* case. New York required local school boards to lend textbooks purchased with public funds to seventh through twelfth grade students, including those attending parochial schools. The New York requirement was challenged as a violation of the establishment clause. The New York Court of Appeals upheld the requirement and, by a 6-3 vote, the Supreme Court affirmed that decision.

Writing for the majority, Justice Byron R. White explained that the purpose of the requirement was secular, to further the educational opportunities of students regardless of whether they attended public or private schools. Because the subject matter of the books was secular, the loan program neither advanced nor inhibited religion, White said.

To the claim that books were critical to the teaching process and that the primary goal of parochial schools was to teach religion, White observed that the court "has long recognized that religious schools pursue two goals, religious instruction and secular education." Without more evidence, White said the majority could not state that "all teaching in a sectarian school is religious or that the processes of secular and religious training are so intertwined that secular textbooks furnished to students by the public are in fact instrumental in the teaching of religion." [79]

The majority also held that the loan program conformed to the *Everson* "child-benefit" precedent. "[N]o funds or books are furnished to parochial schools, and the financial benefit is to parents and children, not to schools," White wrote. [80]

In separate dissents, Justices William O. Douglas and Abe Fortas contended that although local public school boards would approve the books for use, in actual practice sectarian authorities would choose the books to be used in the church schools.

Justice Black also dissented, distinguishing between non-ideological aid such as transportation or school lunch — which was permissible — and books, which were related to substantive religious views and beliefs, and thus, in his view, were impermissible forms of state aid.

'Parochiaid'

The *Allen* case was decided at a time when rising educational costs compelled more and more parochial school officials to seek direct financial aid from the states. Faced with their own fiscal problems, many states with large numbers of parochial school students were willing to comply on the premise that it would be less expensive to give the church schools aid than to absorb their students into the public system if they were forced to close.

Several states — notably New York, Pennsylvania and Ohio — passed statutes authorizing such direct aid as teacher salary subsidies, tuition reimbursements and tuition tax credits. The favorable decision in the *Allen* case and support for such programs from President Nixon and many members of Congress encouraged church and state officials to hope that these so-called "parochiaid" programs might pass constitutional scrutiny. They were to be disappointed.

Teacher Payments

The first challenges to these direct aid laws reached the court in 1971. *Lemon v. Kurtzman* and its companion cases concerned a Rhode Island statute that authorized a salary supplement to certain non-public school teachers and a Pennsylvania law that established a program to reimburse non-public schools for teachers' salaries, textbooks and instructional materials. In practice, the Rhode Island law benefited only Roman Catholic schools while the Pennsylvania law affected more than 20 percent of the students in the state. Both laws stipulated that recipient teachers must teach only secular subjects. The Pennsylvania law stipulated that the textbooks and instructional materials also be secular in nature.

The court struck down both state laws by unanimous votes. In doing so it added a new requirement to the test for permissible state aid.

Writing the court's opinion, Chief Justice Warren E. Burger said such aid not only must have a secular legislative purpose and a primary effect that neither advanced nor inhibited religion, but it also must not foster "an excessive government entanglement with religion."[81] The latter requirement was drawn from a 1970 ruling upholding property tax exemptions for church property. (*Walz v. Tax Commission, p. 461*)

To determine whether state entanglement with religion is excessive, Burger said, the court "must examine the character and purposes of the institutions that are benefited, the nature of the aid that the State provides, and the resulting relationship between the government and the religious authority."[82]

Applying this new test to the Rhode Island statute, the majority found that teacher salary supplements did result in excessive state entanglement with religion. Without continual monitoring, the state could not know with certainty whether a parochial school teacher was presenting subject matter to pupils in the required neutral manner, Burger said. Simple assurances were not sufficient, he said:

> ...We need not and do not assume that teachers in parochial schools will be guilty of bad faith or any conscious design to evade the limitations imposed by the statute and the First Amendment. We simply recognize that a dedicated religious person, teaching in a school affiliated with his or her faith and operated to inculcate its tenets, will inevitably experience great difficulty in remaining religiously neutral.[83]

The only way to ensure that teachers will remain neutral, Burger said, is through "comprehensive, discriminating and continuing state surveillance." Such constant contact between state and church amounted to excessive entanglement.[84]

By the same reasoning, the salary reimbursement portion of the Pennsylvania statute was also invalid, Burger said. Furthermore, the portion of the Pennsylvania law reimbursing church schools for textbooks and instructional materials constituted direct aid to the school rather than to the pupils and their parents.

School Maintenance

Using the same three-part test, the court in 1973 struck down New York statutes that authorized maintenance and repair grants to certain private and parochial schools, reimbursed low-income parents of non-public school students for a portion of the school tuition and allowed tax credits to parents of non-public school students who did not qualify for the tuition reimbursements.

Writing for the majority in *Committee for Public Education and Religious Liberty v. Nyquist,* Justice Lewis F. Powell Jr. said that nothing in the statute stipulated that maintenance grants should be used only for secular purposes. Because the state grant could easily be used to "maintain the school chapel, or [cover] the cost of renovating classrooms in which religion is taught, or the cost of heating and lighting those same facilities," the majority could not deny that the primary effect of the grant was to subsidize directly "the religious activities of sectarian elementary and secondary schools" in violation of the establishment clause.[85]

Tuition Grants

The tuition reimbursement law also unconstitutionally advanced religion, the majority held. Even though it appeared to aid parents, its obvious and primary effect was to aid church schools. Powell wrote:

> ...[I]t is precisely the function of New York's law to provide assistance to private schools, the great majority of which are sectarian. By reimbursing parents for a portion of their tuition bill, the State seeks to relieve their financial burdens sufficiently to assure that they continue to have the option to send their children to religion-oriented schools. And while the other purposes for that aid — to perpetuate a pluralistic educational environment and to protect the fiscal integrity of overburdened public schools — are certainly unexceptionable, the effect of the aid is unmistakably to provide desired financial support for nonpublic, sectarian institutions.[86]

It made no difference to the majority that parents might spend the reimbursement money on something other than tuition:

> ...[I]f the grants are offered as an incentive to parents to send their children to sectarian schools by making unrestricted cash payments to them, the Establishment Clause is violated whether or not the actual dollars given eventually find their way into the sectarian institutions. Whether the grant is labeled a reimbursement, a reward or a subsidy, its substantive impact is still the same.[87]

Tax Credits

The majority concluded that the tax credit provisions served to advance religion for the same reasons tuition grants did. Under either the tuition reimbursement or the tax credit, the parent "receives the same form of encouragement and reward for sending his children to nonpublic schools," Powell wrote.[88]

Dissenting from the majority on the questions of tuition reimbursement and tax credits, Chief Justice Burger and Justice William H. Rehnquist contended that the programs aided parents and not schools. Justice Byron R. White would have upheld all three programs. He said that the primary effect of the statutes was not to advance religion but to "preserve the secular functions" of parochial schools.

Testing Services

On the same day as the *Nyquist* decision, June 25, 1973, the court struck down a similar tuition reimbursement plan enacted by Pennsylvania officials.[89] And in a third case, the court held invalid another New York law which appropriated $28 million in per-pupil payments to non-public schools to cover the costs of testing and maintaining state-mandated pupil records. Most of the funds were spent on testing — both state-mandated standardized tests and those prepared by teachers to measure the progress of students in regular course work.

The court found that the statute was invalid as it related to this latter sort of testing because "despite the obviously integral role of testing in the total teaching process," it made no attempt to ensure that teacher-prepared tests were "free of religious instruction." Thus the grants used for testing had the primary effect of advancing religion. And because the court could not determine which part of the grants was spent on potentially religious activities and which on permissible secular activities, it invalidated the entire statute. [90]

Other State Services

In two subsequent cases, *Meek v. Pittinger* (1975) and *Wolman v. Walter* (1977), the court again used its three-level test to measure the constitutionality of a variety of state services. Under these rulings, the court allowed states to provide church-affiliated schools with loaned textbooks, standardized testing and scoring services, and speech and hearing diagnostic services. Therapeutic, guidance and remedial education services could be provided by public school board employees to parochial school students at sites away from the schools, although similar services provided at the schools were impermissible.

The court in *Wolman* ruled unconstitutional an Ohio law that permitted the state to pay the costs of transportation for parochial school field trips. The majority held that because the schools determined the timing and destination of field trips, they and not parents were the true beneficiaries of the statute, and thus could not be reimbursed.

"The field trips are an integral part of the educational experience," the majority said, "and where the teacher works within and for a sectarian institution, an unacceptable risk of fostering of religion is an inevitable byproduct." [91]

The court also held impermissible as a violation of the establishment clause the loan of instructional materials and equipment either to sectarian schools themselves or to their pupils.

Ruling out direct loans to schools in *Meek,* the court held that even though the materials were secular in nature the loan "has the unconstitutional primary effect of advancing religion because of the predominantly religious character of the schools benefiting from the Act." [92] In the later *Wolman* case, the majority said it saw no significant difference between lending materials to schools and lending them to pupils; "the state aid inevitably flows in part in support of the religious role of the schools," it said. [93]

Federal Aid to Parochial Schools

Federal taxpayers, the court ruled in 1923, did not have a substantial interest in or suffer direct injury from federal decisions on spending, and therefore could not challenge such decisions in court. [94]

Then, in the 1968 case of *Flast v. Cohen,* the court modified this rule to permit such taxpayer suits under certain circumstances. Challenges to federal spending would be permitted if they attacked a spending or tax program, rather than a regulatory policy, and if the taxpayer could show that the alleged misspending violated a constitutional restriction on congressional spending and taxing powers. *(Standing to sue, p. 291)*

Mrs. Flast challenged as an unconstitutional establishment of religion a program of federal aid to both public and parochial school children. Congress in 1965 had based this education aid program on the "child benefit" theory. Title I of the Elementary and Secondary Education Act of 1965, the major federal aid program, gave grants to educationally disadvantaged children regardless of whether they attended public or private schools.

The Supreme Court in 1968 ruled that Mrs. Flast could bring her suit challenging this program because the establishment clause "operates as a specific constitutional limitation upon the exercise by Congress of the taxing and spending power...." [95]

Flast's challenge never returned to the Supreme Court for a decision on the merits of her argument. Another case did, but the justices sidestepped the constitutional issue.

The case of *Wheeler v. Barrera* (1974) was brought by parents of non-public school students in Missouri who complained that their children were not receiving the same Title I benefits as eligible children attending public schools.

The court held that in order to continue receiving Title I funds, the state must comply with the federal requirement to provide parochial school students with remedial services comparable to those given public school students. But, the court said, these services did not have to be identical. And because such a program had not yet been instituted, the court declined to rule whether the provision of publicly employed teachers to teach parochial school students in their own schools would violate the establishment clause. [96]

Aid to Church Colleges

Unlike its lengthy deliberations over government aid to elementary and secondary schools, the Supreme Court had little difficulty in upholding direct government aid to church-affiliated colleges and universities.

In three cases decided in the 1970s, the court approved state and federal programs aiding sectarian institutions of higher education.

In *Tilton v. Richardson* (1971), the first of these cases, the court upheld federal construction grants to church-affiliated colleges under the Higher Education Facilities Act of 1963. This federal statute permitted church-related schools to receive grants with the understanding that no federally financed building would be used for sectarian purposes.

Writing the opinion for the five-justice majority, Chief Justice Warren E. Burger said that because the grants were available to both secular and sectarian schools the law met the test that government aid be secular in purpose. The majority did not find the involvement between the federal government and church-related schools likely to be excessive. The buildings themselves were religiously neutral in character, and since religious indoctrination was not the primary purpose of the colleges, the necessity for government surveillance to maintain the separation between religious and secular education was minimal.

Nor did the federal law advance religion. There was no evidence, said Burger, that "religion seeps into the use of any of these facilities." [97]

The majority, however, did declare unconstitutional a section of the law that permitted the schools to use the buildings for sectarian purposes after 20 years.

Underlying the majority's decision was its presumption that there is a significant difference between the religious aspects of church-related colleges and church-related primary and secondary schools, and between impressionable youngsters and more skeptical young adults. As Burger explained it:

...[C]ollege students are less impressionable and less susceptible to religious indoctrination.... The skepticism of the college student is not an inconsiderable barrier to any attempt or tendency to subvert the congressional objectives and limitations. Furthermore, by their very nature, college and postgraduate courses tend to limit the opportunities for sectarian influence by virtue of their own internal disciplines. Many church-related colleges and universities are characterized by a high degree of academic freedom and seek to evoke free and critical responses from their students.[98]

Justice William O. Douglas, speaking for three of the dissenters, objected to the federal law on the grounds that no federal tax revenues should be used to support religious activities of any sort. Justice Brennan also dissented.

Using the *Tilton* decision as a precedent, the court in 1973 and 1976 upheld respectively a South Carolina statute that allowed the state to issue revenue bonds to finance construction of secular facilities at secular and sectarian colleges and universities, and a Maryland program of general annual grants to private colleges, including church-related schools. [99]

Footnotes

[1] Sources on history of religious freedom in the United States included Loren P. Beth, *The American Theory of Church and State* (Gainesville: University of Florida Press, 1958) and Leo Pfeffer, *Church, State and Freedom*, rev. ed. (Boston: Beacon Press, 1967).

[2] Joseph Story, *Commentaries on the Constitution of the United States*, Sec. 1879; cited in Charles Evans Hughes, *The Supreme Court of the United States: Its Foundations, Methods and Achievements, An Interpretation* (New York: Columbia University Press, 1928), p. 161.

[3] *Walz v. Tax Commission*, 397 U.S. 664 at 669-70 (1970).

[4] *Lovell v. Griffin*, 303 U.S. 444 (1938); *Kunz v. New York*, 340 U.S. 290 (1951).

[5] *Reynolds v. United States*, 98 U.S. 145 at 165 (1879).

[6] *Davis v. Beason*, 133 U.S. 333 at 342-43 (1890).

[7] Id. at 345; see also *Cleveland v. United States*, 329 U.S. 14 (1946).

[8] *Cantwell v. Connecticut*, 310 U.S. 296 at 306-7 (1940).

[9] *Martin v. City of Struthers*, 319 U.S. 141 (1943).

[10] *United States v. Ballard*, 322 U.S. 78 at 86, 87 (1944).

[11] *Prince v. Massachusetts*, 321 U.S. 158 at 166 (1944).

[12] *Cantwell v. Connecticut*, 310 U.S. 296 at 308 (1940).

[13] Id. at 311.

[14] Id. at 307; see also *Schneider v. Irvington*, 308 U.S. 147 (1939); *Martin v. City of Struthers*, 319 U.S. 141 (1943).

[15] *Cox v. New Hampshire*, 312 U.S. 569 (1941).

[16] *Kunz v. New York*, 340 U.S. 290 at 293 (1951).

[17] *Niemotko v. Maryland*, 340 U.S. 268 (1951).

[18] *Fowler v. Rhode Island*, 345 U.S. 67 at 70 (1953).

[19] *Jones v. Opelika*, 316 U.S. 584 at 597 (1942).

[20] *Murdock v. Pennsylvania*, 319 U.S. 105 at 113 (1943).

[21] Id. at 109.

[22] Id. at 111; see also *Follett v. City of McCormick*, 321 U.S. 573 (1944).

[23] *Jacobson v. Masschusetts*, 197 U.S. 11 (1905).

[24] *Pierce v. Society of Sisters*, 268 U.S. 510 (1925).

[25] *Hamilton v. California Board of Regents*, 293 U.S. 245 (1934).

[26] *Leoles v. Landers*, 302 U.S. 656 (1937); *Hering v. State Board of Education*, 303 U.S. 624 (1938); *Gabrielli v. Knickerbocker, Johnson v. Town of Deerfield*, 306 U.S. 621 (1939).

[27] *Minersville School District v. Gobitis*, 310 U.S. 586 at 593, 594-95 (1940).

[28] Id. at 598.

[29] Id. at 598, 600.

[30] Id. at 601.

[31] Id. at 604.

[32] Id. at 606.

[33] Irving Dilliard, "The Flag-Salute Cases," in John A. Garraty, ed., *Quarrels That Have Shaped the Constitution* (New York: Harper & Row, 1964), p. 234.

[34] *Jones v. Opelika*, 316 U.S. 584 at 623-24 (1942).

[35] *West Virginia State Board of Education v. Barnette*, 319 U.S. 624 at 638 (1943).

[36] Id. at 640, 641.

[37] Id. at 641-42.

[38] Id. at 646-47.

[39] *Braunfeld v. Brown*, 366 U.S. 599 at 607 (1961); see also *Gallagher v. Crown Kosher Super Market*, 366 U.S. 617 (1961).

[40] *Sherbert v. Verner*, 374 U.S. 398 at 404 (1963).

[41] Id. at 406, quoting *Thomas v. Collins*, 323 U.S. 516 at 530 (1945).

[42] *Wisconsin v. Yoder*, 406 U.S. 205 at 214 (1972).

[43] Id. at 236.

[44] *Torcaso v. Watkins*, 367 U.S. 488 at 495 (1961).

[45] *United States v. Schwimmer*, 279 U.S. 644 (1929); *United States v. Macintosh*, 283 U.S. 605 (1931); *United States v. Bland*, 283 U.S. 636 (1931).

[46] *Girouard v. United States*, 328 U.S. 61 (1946), overturning *United States v. Schwimmer*, 279 U.S. 644 (1929); *United States v. Macintosh*, 283 U.S. 605 (1931); *United States v. Bland*, 283 U.S. 636 (1931).

[47] *In re Summers*, 325 U.S. 561 (1945).

[48] *McDaniel v. Paty*, 435 U.S. 618 (1978).

[49] *Sherbert v. Verner*, 374 U.S. 398 (1963).

[50] *Torcaso v. Watkins*, 367 U.S. 488 (1961).

[51] C. Herman Pritchett, *The American Constitution*, 3d ed. (New York: McGraw-Hill Book Co., 1977), p. 402.

[52] *Bradfield v. Roberts*, 175 U.S. 291 (1899); see also *Quick Bear v. Leupp*, 210 U.S. 50 (1908).

[53] *Walz v. Tax Commission*, 397 U.S. 664 at 673 (1970).

[54] Id. at 675, 676.

[55] *Zorach v. Clausen*, 343 U.S. 306 at 313 (1952).

[56] *Lewis v. Allen*, 379 U.S. 923 (1964); *O'Hair v. Paine*, 432 F 2d 66 (CA 5, 1971); *O'Hair v. Blumenthal* (1979).

[57] *Illinois ex rel. McCollum v. Board of Education*, 333 U.S. 203 at 210 (1948).

[58] Id. at 227-28.

[59] *Zorach v. Clausen*, 343 U.S. 306 at 312 (1952).

[60] Id. at 315, 314.

[61] Id. at 314.

[62] Id. at 318.

[63] *Clithero v. Schowalter*, 284 U.S. 573 (1930); *Doremus v. Board of Education*, 342 U.S. 429 (1952).

[64] *Engel v. Vitale*, 370 U.S. 421 at 425 (1962).

[65] Id. at 430-31.

[66] Id. at 436, quoting James Madison, "Memorial and Remonstrance Against Religious Assessments."

[67] Id. at 445.

[68] Id. at 450.

[69] *School District of Abington Township v. Schempp, Murray v. Curlett*, 374 U.S. 203 at 226 (1963).

[70] Id. at 225.

[71] Id. at 226.

[72] *Cochran v. Louisiana Board of Education*, 281 U.S. 370 (1930).

[73] *Everson v. Board of Education*, 330 U.S. 1 at 15-16 (1947).

[74] Id. at 17-18.

[75] Id. at 18.

[76] Id. at 33, 50.

[77] Id. at 63.

[78] *Lemon v. Kurtzman,* 403 U.S. 602 at 614 (1971).

[79] *Board of Education of Central School District No. 1 v. Allen,* 392 U.S. 236 at 245, 248 (1968).

[80] Id. at 243-44.

[81] *Lemon v. Kurtzman,* 403 U.S. 602 at 613 (1971), quoting *Walz v. Tax Commission,* 397 U.S. 664 at 674 (1970).

[82] Id. at 615.

[83] Id. at 618.

[84] Id. at 619.

[85] *Committee for Public Education and Religious Liberty v. Nyquist,* 413 U.S. 756 at 774 (1973).

[86] Id. at 783.

[87] Id. at 786.

[88] Id. at 791.

[89] *Sloan v. Lemon,* 413 U.S. 825 (1973).

[90] *Levitt v. Committee for Public Education and Religious Liberty,* 413 U.S. 472 at 480 (1973).

[91] *Wolman v. Walter,* 433 U.S. 229 at 254 (1977).

[92] *Meek v. Pittinger,* 421 U.S. 349 at 363 (1975).

[93] *Wolman v. Walter,* 433 U.S. 229 at 250 (1977).

[94] *Frothingham v. Mellon,* 262 U.S. 447 (1923).

[95] *Flast v. Cohen,* 392 U.S. 83 at 104 (1968).

[96] *Wheeler v. Barrera,* 417 U.S. 402 (1974).

[97] *Tilton v. Richardson,* 403 U.S. 672 at 681 (1971).

[98] Id. at 686.

[99] *Hunt v. McNair,* 413 U.S. 734 (1973); *Roemer v. Maryland Board of Public Works,* 426 U.S. 736 (1976).

Selected Bibliography

Barker, Lucius J. and Barker, Twiley W. Jr. *Civil Liberties and the Constitution: Cases and Commentaries,* 3d ed. Englewood Cliffs, N.J.: Prentice-Hall, 1978.

Beth, Loren P. *The American Theory of Church and State.* Gainesville: University of Florida Press, 1958.

Brant, Irving. *The Bill of Rights: Its Origin and Meaning.* Indianapolis: Bobbs-Merrill Co., 1965.

Chafee, Zechariah Jr. *Free Speech in the United States.* Cambridge: Harvard University Press, 1941. Reprinted by New York: Atheneum, 1969.

Congressional Quarterly. *Guide to Congress.* 2d ed. Washington, D.C.: Congressional Quarterly Inc., 1976.

Cooley, Thomas M. *A Treatise on the Constitutional Limitations Which Rest Upon the Legislative Power of the States of the American Union* (with large additions, consideration of amendments, and giving the results of recent cases, by Walter Carrington). 8th ed. 2 vols. Boston: Little, Brown & Co., 1927.

Cushman, Robert F. *Cases in Civil Liberties.* 2d ed. Englewood Cliffs, N.J.: Prentice-Hall, 1976.

Dowling, Noel T. *Cases on Constitutional Law.* 6th ed. Brooklyn: The Foundation Press, Inc., 1959.

Emerson, Thomas I. *The System of Freedom of Expression.* New York: Random House, Vintage Books, 1970.

Emerson, Thomas I. and Hutchins, Robert M. *Political and Civil Rights in the United States: A Collection of Legal and Related Materials.* 2d ed. 2 vols. Buffalo: Dennis & Co., 1958.

Frank, John P. *Marble Palace: The Supreme Court in American Life.* New York: Alfred A. Knopf, 1958.

Freund, Paul A., Sutherland, Arthur E., Howe, Mark DeWolfe, and Brown, Ernest J. *Constitutional Law:* *Cases and Other Problems.* 2 vols. Boston: Little, Brown & Co., 1954.

Gellhorn, Walter. *American Rights: The Constitution in Action.* New York: Macmillan Publishing Co., 1960.

Kalven, Harry Jr. *The Negro and the First Amendment.* Chicago: University of Chicago Press, Phoenix Books, 1966.

Kelly, Alfred H. and Harbison, Winfred A. *The American Constitution: Its Origins and Development.* 5th ed. New York: W. W. Norton & Co., 1976.

Konvitz, Milton R. *Fundamental Liberties of a Free People: Religion, Speech, Press, Assembly.* Ithaca, N.Y.: Cornell University Press, 1957.

Levy, Leonard W. *Freedom of Speech and Press in Early American History: Legacy of Suppression.* New York: Harper & Row, Harper Torchbooks, 1963.

Madison, James, Hamilton, Alexander, and Jay, John. *The Federalist Papers,* Introduction by Clinton Rossiter. New York: Mentor Books, 1961.

Mason, Alpheus T. and Beaney, William M. *The Supreme Court in a Free Society.* Englewood Cliffs, N.J.: Prentice-Hall, 1959.

Murphy, Paul L. *The Constitution in Crisis Times, 1918-1969.* New York: Harper & Row, Harper Torchbooks, 1972.

Pfeffer, Leo. *Church, State and Freedom.* rev. ed., Boston: Beacon Press, 1967.

Pritchett, C. Herman. *The American Constitution.* 3d ed. New York: McGraw-Hill Book Co., 1977.

Shapiro, Martin M., ed. *The Supreme Court and Constitutional Rights: Readings in Constitutional Law.* Atlanta: Scott, Foresman & Co., 1967.

THE RIGHTS OF POLITICAL PARTICIPATION

Introduction 475

The Right to Vote 477

The Right to an Equal Vote 489

Freedom of Political Association 499

The Rights of Political Participation

Democracy, it has been noted, is a form of government which will never be completely achieved.

The political history of the United States has been the continuing effort to translate the ideals of equality and freedom into political reality. But the elusiveness of these goals is reflected in a long line of Supreme Court decisions which deal with questions concerning the right to vote, the right to have the vote counted equally with all others, and the freedom to associate with persons of similar political views.

The Right to Vote

The right to cast a vote is the cornerstone of the democratic political system. Yet the Constitution makes little mention of that right — and, for well over a century, the Supreme Court maintained that its source was state, not federal, citizenship.

To remedy this paucity of reference to the suffrage, the Constitution has five times been amended to extend and protect this basic political right.

In the nation's earliest years, the right to vote was the exclusive prerogative of free white adult property-owning males. Property qualifications were the first restriction abandoned, although vestiges of that requirement remained for more than a century in the form of poll taxes.

The Civil War — and the amendments which marked its close — seemed to promise a new age of broadened political participation. The privileges and immunities clause of the 14th Amendment appeared to many to guarantee all citizens — female as well as male, black as well as white — the right to vote.

But within a decade of its adoption, the Supreme Court made clear that the amendment had no such practical effect. The Constitution of the United States, declared the court, still granted no one the right to vote. That was still a state prerogative. The ruling, in a case brought on behalf of a woman seeking to vote, sparked a 45-year-long drive for another constitutional amendment, which did grant women the right to vote.

The 15th Amendment spoke plainly: The suffrage was not to be restricted because of the race, color or previous slavery of the potential voter. Yet, insulated from federal action by court decisions which perpetuated the view that voter qualifications and election regulations were exclusively state responsibilities, state officials successfully em- ployed a variety of devices — literacy tests, grandfather clauses, poll taxes, white primaries — to circumvent the amendment's intent for most of another century.

Although the Supreme Court began as early as 1915 to edge toward a new view of the amendments and the protection they provided for the right to vote, it was Congress, spurred by the modern civil rights movement, which led in the eventual fulfillment of the promise of the 15th Amendment. The Voting Rights Act of 1965 at last secured to the nation's black citizens the right to vote. The act asserted federal authority over electoral matters left since 1789 in the hands of state officials.

Once Congress acted, the Supreme Court steadily backed its power to ensure the right to vote. The court heard out the challenges of the states to the new law — and then rejected them resoundingly. In a series of rulings which were a mirror image of those postwar decisions of the 1870s and 1880s, the court gave the broadest possible reading to the 15th Amendment, the power of Congress to enforce it, and to the 1965 act, making it the most effective civil rights law ever enacted.

The Right To An Equal Vote

Even as the court's modern voting rights decisions underwrote the expansion of the right to vote at all, its plunge into the political morass of redistricting cases revolutionized the balance of political power both within Congress and in every state legislature in the nation.

Electoral districts within state boundaries had been a fact of life since early in the 19th century when Congress first directed all states with more than one member in the House of Representatives to elect those House members from separate, compact and contiguous districts. Later in the century, the national legislature required that its electoral districts within each state also be as nearly equal in population as was practicable.

But in 1929, Congress omitted those requirements from its revision of the law. A few years later, the Supreme Court found the omission purposeful. Lifting these requirements for congressional districts came just as the nation's population was shifting from primarily rural areas to become an urban majority. For 40 years this shift was not reflected in the nation's legislatures.

Farm and rural interests continued to dominate in Congress and in state legislatures. Efforts by urban residents to have district lines redrawn to reflect their new strength — and to win equal weight for their votes — failed.

In large part these attempts were blocked by the insistence of federal courts, led by the Supreme Court, that such challenges were political matters outside judicial power, best dealt with by the malapportioned legislatures which were the heart of the problem. As late as 1946, the court explicitly reaffirmed this view, describing redistricting challenges as a "political thicket" it would not enter.

But within 16 years the court reversed itself. In 1962 it took the first step into this thicket, ruling that redistricting cases might, after all, present questions susceptible to judicial resolution. This ruling opened the doors of the federal courts to a multitude of suits challenging state and congressional districting and apportionment structures.

As it dealt with these subsequent cases, the court translated the 14th Amendment's guarantee of equal protection into the rule of "one person, one vote" as the proper measure for redistricting plans. Within a decade it appeared that the standard was in some ways a dual one, applied to require that a state's congressional districts be almost precisely equal in population, while allowing its own legislative electoral districts to vary further from the ideal of precise equality.

In subsequent rulings, the court also extended the application of this "one person, one vote" rule to a variety of local electoral districts.

Political Association

The right to vote receives little mention in the Constitution, but the freedom of political association receives none at all. The constitutional source for this recognized element of American political life is found in the modern rulings of the Supreme Court.

The court has made clear in decisions concerning communists and civil rights activists, radicals and Republicans, that it considers the freedom to associate with persons of like political views — without penalty from the government — to be an essential corollary of the First Amendment freedoms of speech, peaceable assembly and the right to petition the government for redress of grievances.

Like other First Amendment rights — but unlike the right to vote — the freedom of political association may legitimately be restricted by government in order to further other major interests. Thus political association cases present the court with the task of reconciling individual freedom and the government's need to preserve public peace and national security.

Such reconciliation takes place through a process of weighing and balancing, which inevitably reflects the social and political context in which the justices live and work. Thus it should be no surprise that during periods of severe external threat — wartime and Cold War — the court has upheld substantial restrictions upon the exercise of this right.

Nowhere is this more obvious than in the line of decisions of the 1950s and 1960s concerning the efforts of Congress, the Executive Branch and state legislatures to curtail the spread of domestic communism and to protect government against infiltration by disloyal persons.

In its early 1950s rulings on these laws and programs, the court found their restrictive impact on individual freedom justified. As the threat eased, however, the court found challenges to these laws more and more persuasive. In response, it tightened the standards of proof to ensure that persons were not penalized simply for "guilt by association" or abstract advocacy of revolution, but only for actions which clearly threatened the nation's security. Eventually, this line of rulings vitiated the internal security laws into complete ineffectiveness.

The right of political association — finally recognized even in internal security cases — found its clearest definition, however, in cases involving homegrown forms of activism and more traditional political activities. In the 1960s, the court forbade states to interfere with the right of civil rights activists to associate and work for the advancement of blacks and other minorities. Such associations could not be penalized by the state, held the court. Later rulings recognized the right of national political parties to this freedom — interpreted to shield those parties from the interference of state courts — and the right of persons holding different views from those of an elected officeholder to keep their jobs nonetheless.

The Right to Vote

Among the most significant characteristics of the continuing American experiment in popular government is the gradual broadening of the suffrage. In 1792 only propertied white males were granted the privilege of voting. By 1972 that right was possessed by all Americans 18 or older — blacks and whites, women and men.

The Constitution barely mentions the right to vote. It provides for the direct election of members of the House of Representatives, permits states to set voter qualifications, and gives the states the authority to set the times, places and manner of elections for senators and representatives. Article I, section 4, does, however, reserve to Congress the power to override, by law, such state-made election rules.

Early in the history of the republic, popular pressure forced states to drop the restrictive property qualification for voting. The Constitution subsequently has been amended five times to extend the vote to formerly disenfranchised groups.

The 15th Amendment, added in 1870, prohibited denial of the right to vote for reasons of race, color or previous condition of servitude.

Women, who had sought to win the right to vote through judicial interpretation of the "privileges and immunities" clause of the 14th Amendment, were rebuffed in that effort by the Supreme Court. Uniting into an organized women's suffrage movement, they worked and fought for half a century for the right to vote. Finally, in 1920, the addition of the 19th Amendment forbade restriction of the suffrage on account of sex.

In 1961 the 23rd Amendment granted residents of the nation's capital, the District of Columbia, the right to vote in presidential elections. In 1964 the 24th Amendment ended all efforts to restrict the right to vote because of lack of wealth or property, outlawing use of a poll tax as a means of abridging the right to vote in federal elections.

Then the age for political participation was formally lowered by the 26th Amendment, ratified in 1971, granting all citizens 18 and older the right to vote in federal elections. With this amendment — and new civil rights legislation finally implementing the 15th Amendment — virtually every adult citizen possessed the right to vote in the nation's elections by 1972.

The Right and the Power: A Narrow View

No other constitutional promise has gone so long unfulfilled as that of the 15th Amendment. Despite the clear language forbidding abridgment of the right to vote because of race or color, state officials succeeded for almost a full century in denying black citizens the right to vote or to play any significant role in state or national politics.

The Supreme Court, by its acquiescence, played a critical role in creating this anomalous situation.

The right to vote was viewed by many as doubly guaranteed by the Civil War amendments — protected by the provision of the 14th Amendment safeguarding the privileges and immunities of citizens against state infringement and by the clear language of the 15th Amendment forbidding abridgment of the right to vote because of race, color, or previous condition of servitude.

In addition, voting rights for blacks had been made a condition for readmission to the union for the rebellious states of the Confederacy.

And yet, after the presidential election of 1876, the issue of Negro voting rights was again left to state control. As the southern states returned to white rule under "restored" governments, they passed laws which effectively defeated the purposes of the 14th and 15th Amendments.

The Supreme Court created the environment for such systematic state obstruction with a set of rulings in which it adopted the narrowest possible view of the impact of the 14th and 15th Amendments upon the individual's right to vote. The court held that the right to vote was chiefly governed by state laws; that its source was the state, not the U.S. Constitution; and that Congress had only limited power to interfere in state regulation of electoral matters.

No Privilege Or Immunity

The first of these restrictive rulings came in 1875 with the court's decision in the case of *Minor v. Happersett*. The court took the opportunity presented by that case to declare that the U.S. Constitution did not confer the right to vote upon anyone.

And so, the court denied the effort of Mrs. Francis Minor to win the right to vote as one of the privileges and immunities of U.S. citizenship guaranteed against state abridgment by the 14th Amendment.

The case of *Minor v. Happersett* was brought by Francis Minor, a St. Louis attorney, on behalf of his wife, president of the Missouri Woman Suffrage Association. The Minors argued that the right to vote was a privilege of U.S. citizenship, protected by the first section of the 14th Amendment. Therefore, the Minors concluded, states could not deny women the right to vote.

Missouri law, however, limited suffrage to males. Happersett, an election registrar, refused to register Mrs. Minor, and the couple filed suit.

In keeping with the narrow view of the privileges and immunities clause set out two years earlier in *The Slaughterhouse Cases,* the Supreme Court rejected the Minors' argument. Chief Justice Morrison R. Waite wrote for the court that the right to vote was not a privilege or immunity of federal citizenship. The suffrage, Waite stated, had never been coextensive with citizenship:

> The United States has no voters in the States of its creation....
> ...[T]he Constitution of the United States does not confer the right of suffrage upon anyone....

It was still up to the states, Waite said, to define voter qualifications — even for federal elections:

> The [Fourteenth] Amendment did not add to the privileges and immunities of a citizen. It simply furnished an additional guaranty for the protection of such as he already had....
> It is clear, therefore, we think, that the Constitution has not added the right of suffrage to the privileges and immunities of citizenship as they existed at the time it was adopted.[1]

No Federal Voting Right

The following year, the court adopted a similar narrow view of the 15th Amendment.

In two cases — *United States v. Reese* and *United States v. Cruikshank* — the court overturned federal convictions of persons charged with violating the 1870 act enforcing the 15th Amendment's guarantee against denial of voting rights because of race.

In the *Reese* case, state election officials were convicted for violating the law by refusing to receive or count a black man's vote. The court overturned the convictions, finding the section of the law under which they were charged technically defective.

The court, again through Chief Justice Waite, stated that "[t]he Fifteenth Amendment does not confer the right of suffrage upon anyone ... [but] has invested the citizens of the United States with a new constitutional right ... exemption from discrimination in the exercise of the elective franchise on account of race, color or previous condition of servitude."[2]

United States v. Cruikshank, decided that same day in 1876, dealt with one of the ninety-six indictments resulting from a massacre of sixty blacks in Colfax, La., in 1873. Disputes over local elections allegedly led William J. Cruikshank and others to shoot down a posse of blacks who had seized the Colfax courthouse.

Cruikshank and his confederates were indicted under the enforcement act for conspiring to intimidate blacks to prevent their exercise of constitutional rights, including the right to vote. The Supreme Court declared the indictment defective because "it is nowhere alleged in these counts that the wrong contemplated against the rights of these citizens was on account of their race or color."[3]

Chief Justice Waite delivered the opinion of the court. He declared again that the amendment added nothing to the rights a citizen possessed:

> It simply furnishes an additional guaranty as against any encroachment by the States upon the

fundamental rights which belong to every citizen as a member of society.... The power of the National Government is limited to the enforcement of this guaranty....

> The right to vote in the States comes from the States; but the right of exemption from the prohibited discrimination comes from the United States. The first has not been granted or secured by the Constitution of the United States; but the last has been.
> Inasmuch, therefore, as it does not appear in these counts that the intent of the defendants was to prevent these parties from exercising their right to vote on account of their race..., it does not appear that it was their intent to interfere with any right granted or secured by the Constitution or laws of the United States. We may suspect that race was the cause of the hostility; but it is not so averred.[4]

Exceptions to the View

Despite this limiting interpretation of the new constitutional language concerning the right to vote, the court upheld federal power to regulate elections generally under the provisions of Article I.

In 1880, in the case of *Ex parte Siebold* — which did not involve charges of racial discrimination — the court upheld federal power to ensure that elections of federal officials be fairly conducted. Siebold, a state election official, was convicted of violating federal law by stuffing a ballot box in an election of state and federal officers.

The court upheld his conviction, citing Article I, section 4, to justify federal regulation of the actions of state election officials. Article I, section 4, gave Congress broad concurrent powers to regulate elections along with and independent of state power in that area.[5]

Over the next three decades the court reaffirmed this position in similar cases.[6]

The Yarbrough Case

The court's narrow view of the 15th Amendment also underwent some modification in its 1884 ruling in the case of *Ex parte Yarbrough,* the only early case in which the court backed the use of federal power to punish the action of private individuals for obstructing the right to vote in a federal election.

In *Yarbrough,* the court held that once an individual acquired the right to vote for federal officers — by meeting state-set voter qualifications — that right was accorded federal protection.

Jasper Yarbrough, a member of the Ku Klux Klan, and some fellow Klansmen attacked a Negro named Berry Saunders and beat him up to prevent his voting in a congressional election. Yarbrough was convicted and sentenced to prison for violating the 1870 Enforcement Act by conspiring to prevent a citizen from voting.

He challenged his conviction, arguing that the 1870 law was unconstitutional, because Congress lacked the authority to act to protect the right to vote in federal elections. The court, however, upheld his conviction, the federal law, and congressional power to protect the right to vote.

Justice Samuel Miller, writing for the majority, made clear that the right to vote for members of Congress was derived from the federal Constitution — not state laws — and was subject to federal protection:

> That a government whose essential character is republican ... has no power to secure this election

from the influence of violence, of corruption, and of fraud, is a proposition so startling as to arrest attention. . . .

If this government is anything more than a mere aggregation of delegated agents of other States and governments, each of which is superior to the General Government, it must have the power to protect the elections on which its existence depends from violence and corruption.

If it has not this power, it is left helpless before the two great natural and historical enemies of all republics, open violence and insidious corruption. . . .

. . .The States in prescribing the qualifications for the most numerous branch of their own Legislatures, do not do this with reference to the election for members of Congress. . . . They define who are to vote for the popular branch of their own legislature, and the Constitution of the United States says the same persons shall vote for members of Congress in that State. It adopts the qualification thus furnished as the qualification of its own electors for members of Congress.

It is not true, therefore, that electors for members of Congress owe their right to vote to the state law in any sense which makes the exercise of the right to depend exclusively on the law of the State.

Counsel for petitioners, seizing upon the expression found in the opinion of the court in the case of *Minor v. Happersett* (1875) . . . that "the Constitution of the United States does not confer the right of suffrage upon any one," . . . insists that the voters in this case do not owe their right to vote in any sense to that instrument.

But the court was combating the argument that this right was conferred on all citizens, and therefore upon women as well as men.

In opposition to that idea, it was said the Constitution adopts as the qualification for voters of members of Congress that which prevails in the State where the voting is to be done; therefore, said the opinion, the right is not definitely conferred on any person or class of persons by the Constitution alone, because you have to look to the law of the State for the description of the class. But the court did not intend to say that when the class or the person is thus ascertained, his right to vote for a member of Congress was not fundamentally based upon the Constitution, which created the office of member of Congress, and declared it should be elective, and pointed to the means of ascertaining who should be electors. . . .[7]

The 15th Amendment, said the court, did operate in some circumstances as the source of a right to vote. And Congress did have the authority "to protect the citizen in the exercise of rights conferred by the Constitution of the United States essential to the healthy organization of the government itself. . . ."[8]

And so, the opinion concluded:

If the Government of the United States has within its constitutional domain no authority to provide against these evils [violence and corruption of elections], if the very sources of power may be poisoned by corruption or controlled by violence and outrage, without legal restraint, then, indeed, is the country in danger and its best powers, its highest purposes, the hopes which it inspires . . . are at the mercy of the combinations of those who respect no right but brute force, on the one hand, and unprincipled corruptionists on the other.[9]

But despite this opinion, the court in general maintained for decades that in the absence of state action, the acts of private individuals to deny the rights of others to vote were outside the reach of federal power. In 1903, the court stated that the provisions of the 1870 Enforcement Act which might be interpreted "to punish purely individual action [to interfere with voting rights] cannot be sustained as an appropriate exercise of the power conferred by the 15th Amendment upon Congress."[10]

The Pattern of Exclusion

Encouraged by the court's limiting view of the federal right to vote and of federal power to enforce that right, many southern states during the period from 1890 to 1910 rewrote their constitutions or added new requirements for voters to exclude blacks from participation in the political process.[11] The court by and large left major elements of the program of disenfranchisement untouched for decades.

The strategy of exclusion employed many methods, among them literacy tests, grandfather clauses, all-white primaries, poll taxes and the racial gerrymander.

Grandfather clauses were held unconstitutional in 1915, and white primaries were finally ruled invalid in 1944. But not until Congress acted did the court strike down the use of poll taxes and literacy tests.

Ancestry and Literacy

For seventy years, from 1898 until 1969, the Supreme Court steadily upheld the validity of literacy tests for voters.

Williams v. Mississippi: 1898

In 1898 the court first upheld the validity of literacy tests as voter qualification devices. In the case of *Williams v. Mississippi*, a Negro man was indicted for murder by an all-white grand jury. The jurors were selected from the list of registered voters who had, among other qualifications, passed such a literacy test. Williams challenged the use of the test as unconstitutional.

Williams' attorneys argued that his conviction was invalid because the laws under which the grand jury was selected allowed discrimination in voter registration, thereby violating the equal protection guarantee of the 14th Amendment.

Justice Joseph McKenna, writing for the court's majority, refused to find the Mississippi statutes in violation of the equal protection clause. The "evil" was not the laws themselves, he wrote, for they did not on their face discriminate against blacks; the only evil resulted from the effect of their discriminatory administration.[12]

Grandfather Clauses

Seventeen years later, however, the Supreme Court held impermissible Oklahoma's combined use of a literacy test and a "grandfather" clause.

The state required all voters to pass a literacy test *or to* show that their ancestors were entitled to vote in 1866. This requirement was challenged as a violation of the 15th Amendment, because in operation it exempted most white males from the literacy test requirement and permitted voter registrars to test primarily blacks, whose ancestors in most cases had not been eligible to vote in 1866.

The state defended its system by arguing that the clause did not deny blacks the right to vote outright; it simply required them all to take the literacy tests. The 15th Amendment, the state continued, did not confer the right to vote on all Negroes; it merely prevented states from denying them the right to vote on purely racial grounds.

With its 1915 decision in the case of *Guinn v. United States,* the court began moving toward its modern view of the amendment. Unanimously, the court struck down Oklahoma's system as an unconstitutional evasion of the 15th Amendment. Chief Justice Edward D. White wrote the court's opinion.

In that opinion, however, the court continued to affirm state power to require voters to demonstrate some measure of literacy, stating that the establishment of a literacy test requirement was "but the exercise by the state of a lawful power . . . not subject to our supervision. . . ."[13]

Guinn had limited impact on black voting rights in the South because it dealt only with the grandfather clause. The case, however, was the first in which the court in a voting rights case looked beyond nondiscriminatory form to discover discriminatory substance.

(In a second Oklahoma case decided that same day, the court upheld the federal indictments — under the Reconstruction Civil Rights Acts — of county election officials who refused to count certain persons' votes. The court, in the case of *United States v. Mosely,* declared that: "[T]he right to have one's vote counted is as open to protection by Congress as the right to put a ballot in a box.")[14]

Oklahoma subsequently adopted a requirement that all voters register within a twelve-day period, exempting from the requirement those who had voted in the 1914 elections, prior to the *Guinn* decision. In 1939 the court held this too was an unconstitutional attempt to disenfranchise blacks in violation of the 15th Amendment.

Justice Felix Frankfurter, writing for the majority, said that the 15th Amendment "nullifies sophisticated as well as simple-minded modes of discrimination. It hits onerous procedural requirements which effectively handicap exercise of the francise by the colored race although the abstract right to vote may remain unrestricted as to race."[15]

Tests of Understanding

In addition to strict literacy tests, some states also required voters to "understand and explain" an article of the Constitution. The vagueness of one such provision was nullified by a federal court as an arbitrary grant of power to election officials who could and did administer the literacy test in a racially discriminatory fashion and thus violated the 15th Amendment. The fact that the provision itself made no mention of race did not save it from being unconstitutional. The Supreme Court affirmed this ruling in 1949.[16]

But the court continued to uphold state power to require that its voters demonstrate some measure of literacy. In 1959 the Supreme Court upheld North Carolina's requirement that all voters be able to read and write a section of the state constitution in English. Such a test was not, on its face, a violation of the 14th, 15th or 17th Amendments, the court held in the case of *Lassiter v. Northampton County Board of Elections.*

Justice William O. Douglas' opinion for the majority stressed that the state had an interest in securing an independent and intelligent electorate. How the state achieved that objective, Douglas said, was a policy question outside the court's purview:

> Literacy and intelligence are obviously not synonymous. Illiterate people may be intelligent voters. Yet in our society . . . a state might conclude that only those who are literate should exercise the franchise. . . . We do not sit in judgment on the wisdom of that policy. We cannot say, however, that it is not an allowable one measured by constitutional standards.
>
> Of course a literacy test, fair on its face, may be employed to perpetuate that discrimination which the 15th Amendment was designed to uproot. No such influence is charged here. . . . The present requirement, applicable to members of all races . . . seems to us one fair way of determining whether a person is literate. . . . Certainly we cannot condemn it on its face as a device unrelated to the desire of North Carolina to raise the standards for people of all races who cast the ballot." [17]

But six years later, the court held Louisiana's test requiring voters to display a reasonable knowledge and understanding of any section of the state or federal constitution to be a violation of the 15th Amendment.

The court's unanimous opinion, written by Justice Hugo L. Black, viewed the requirement in light of the history of voter discrimination in the state:

> The applicant facing a registrar in Louisiana thus has been compelled to leave his voting fate to that official's uncontrolled power to determine whether the applicant's understanding of the Federal or State Constitution is satisfactory. As the evidence showed, colored people, even some with the most advanced education and scholarship, were declared by voting registrars with less education to have an unsatisfactory understanding of the Constitution of Louisiana or of the United States. This is not a test but a trap, sufficient to stop even the most brilliant man on his way to the voting booth. The cherished right of people in a country like ours to vote cannot be obliterated by the use of laws like this, which leave the voting fate of a citizen to the passing whim or impulse of an individual registrar.[18]

Suspension of Literacy Tests

In 1965, Congress, as part of the Voting Rights Act, suspended all literacy tests and similar devices in all areas where less than half the population of voting age had been registered or had voted in the 1964 presidential election.

The act was immediately challenged as infringing upon state power to oversee elections. In *South Carolina v. Katzenbach,* decided in 1966, the Supreme Court upheld Congress' power to pass the law and backed all its major provisions, including that suspending literacy tests.[19]

Chief Justice Earl Warren, who delivered the opinion of the court, wrote that the provision of the act suspending literacy tests:

> ...was clearly a legitimate response to the problem, for which there is ample precedent [in Fifteenth Amendment cases].... Underlying the response was the feeling that States and political subdivisions which had been allowing white illiterates to vote for years could not sincerely complain about "dilution" of their electorates through the registration of Negro illiterates. Congress knew that continuance of the tests and devices in use at the present time, no matter how fairly administered in the future, would freeze the effect of past discrimination in favor of unqualified white registrants. Congress permissably rejected the alternative of requiring a complete re-registration of all voters, believing that this would be too harsh on many whites who had enjoyed the franchise for their entire adult lives.[20]

The opinion in *South Carolina v. Katzenbach*, announced on March 7, 1966, was followed three months later by two decisions that prevented states from disqualifying potential voters simply because they were unable to read or write English.[21]

Reinstatement Denied

Three years later, in 1969, the court rejected the effort of a North Carolina county to have the literacy test reinstated — under provisions of the 1965 law. The court declared that counties and states which had denied blacks their equal educational opportunity, by operating separate and unequal schools for blacks and whites, had denied blacks the opportunity to acquire the skills necessary to pass a literacy test. And so, the court held in the case of *Gaston County v. United States*, reinstatement of a literacy test would simply perpetuate the effects of the dual, unequal educational system which had so long operated to disenfranchise blacks.[22]

Justice John Marshall Harlan wrote for the court that although Gaston County recently had shown considerable progress in voter registration and in equalizing educational opportunity:

> Affording today's Negro youth equal educational opportunity will doubtless prepare them to meet, on equal terms, whatever standards of literacy are required when they reach voting age. It does nothing for their parents, however. From this record, we cannot escape the sad truth that throughout the years, Gaston County systematically deprived its black citizens of the educational opportunities it granted to its white citizens. "Impartial" administration of the literacy test today would serve only to perpetuate those inequities in a different form.[23]

The 1965 act, extended for five years in 1970, was amended at that time to suspend literacy tests nationwide and to bring more areas under coverage of its provisions. The Supreme Court upheld the nationwide ban on literacy tests in the 1970 case of *Oregon v. Mitchell.*[24] In that case, Justice Hugo L. Black explained that such a ban, in light of the long history of discriminatory literacy tests, was well within the power of Congress to enforce the 15th Amendment. In 1975 the law was amended to abolish all literacy tests permanently.

White Primaries

Southern politics was so completely dominated by the Democratic Party during the first half of the 20th century that the Democratic primary was in most areas the only significant part of the election process. Winning the primary was tantamount to election. Being excluded from voting in the primary was equivalent to being excluded from voting altogether.

But not until 1941 did the Supreme Court make clear that Congress had the power to regulate primary, as well as general, elections.

In fact, in a 1921 decision involving campaign spending — *Newberry v. United States* — the court seemed to say that Congress lacked this power to regulate primary elections.[25] *(Details, pp. 171-172)*

This court-created doubt about the reach of federal power encouraged the eleven states that had comprised the Confederacy to begin systematic exclusion of blacks from participation in the primary. The Democratic Party was often organized on a statewide or county basis as a private club or association which could freely exclude blacks.

The effort of Texas to use the white primary to shut blacks out of participation in the political process came before the Supreme Court in five cases, decided in 1927, 1932, 1935, 1944 and 1953.

Nixon v. Herndon: 1927

In 1923, the Texas legislature passed a law forbidding blacks to vote in the state Democratic primary. Dr. L. A. Nixon, a black resident of El Paso, challenged the law, arguing that it clearly violated the 14th and 15th Amendments.

In the case of *Nixon v. Herndon*, decided in 1927, the Supreme Court agreed with Nixon's 14th Amendment claim.

Justice Oliver Wendell Holmes Jr. wrote for a unanimous court that "a more direct and obvious infringement" of the equal protection guarantee was hard to imagine. The court found it unnecessary to consider Nixon's 15th Amendment claim.[26]

Nixon v. Condon: 1932

After the 1927 *Herndon* decision, the legislature authorized state political parties' executive committees to establish their own qualifications for voting in the primary. Dr. Nixon again sued, challenging the law as racially discriminatory.

Attorneys for the state argued that the 14th Amendment's equal protection clause did not apply because the party, not state officials, set up the allegedly discriminatory standards.

With Justice Benjamin N. Cardozo writing for the five-man majority, the court held, in 1932, that the executive committee of the Democratic Party acted as a delegate of the state in setting voter qualifications, that its action was equivalent to state action and thus within the scope of the equal protection guarantee which it violated.[27]

Grovey v. Townsend: 1935

The Texas Democratic party forthwith, without state direction or authorization, voted to limit party membership to whites.

In 1935, with its decision in the case of *Grovey v. Townsend*, the Supreme Court unanimously held that the political party in this instance was not acting as a creature of the state and that its action was thus unreachable under either the 14th or 15th Amendments. The court in this case viewed the political party as a private club, a voluntary association of private individuals, whose actions — even in controlling access to the vote — were not restricted by the Constitution.[28]

United States v. Classic: 1941

Only six years later, however, the court began to cut away the foundation on which *Grovey v. Townsend* was based.

In 1941 — in the case of *United States v. Classic* — the court discarded the *Newberry* restriction on federal power to regulate primary elections.

Classic was not a racial discrimination case at all. Classic, an overzealous opponent of Louisiana governor Huey Long, was convicted of falsifying election returns. His conviction was based on the federal law that made it a crime "to injure, oppress, threaten or intimidate any citizen in the free exercise or enjoyment of any right or privilege secured to him by the Constitution." He challenged his conviction, arguing that the right to vote in a primary election was not a right secured by the Constitution.

The prosecution in the *Classic* case was initiated by the then-new civil rights section of the Justice Department set up by Attorney General Frank Murphy and later directed by Attorney General Robert Jackson, both of whom became members of the Supreme Court. The case was argued before the court by Herbert Wechsler, a former law clerk to Justice Harlan Fiske Stone and by Attorney General Jackson.

The court upheld Classic's conviction, ruling that the white primary was an integral part of the election process. The authority of Congress under Article I, section 4, to regulate elections included the authority to regulate primary elections, wrote Justice Stone, "when, as in this case, they are a step in the exercise by the people of their choice of representatives in Congress."[29]

Smith v. Allwright: 1944

Three years later, in 1944, the court overturned *Grovey* and held the all-white primary unconstitutional.

The case of *Smith v. Allwright* arose out of the refusal of S. S. Allwright, a county election official, to permit Lonnie E. Smith, a black man, to vote in the 1940 Texas Democratic primary.

Smith sued Allwright for damages for this deprivation of his civil rights. Lower federal courts denied Smith the right to bring suit, citing *Grovey v. Townsend* as placing this sort of discrimination beyond federal control.

Smith was represented before the Supreme Court by two attorneys for the National Association for the Advancement of Colored People, William H. Hastie and Thurgood Marshall, both later distinguished judges, with Marshall becoming the first black member of the Supreme Court. The court heard oral arguments twice in the case. On April 3, 1944, the court held the white primary as a violation of the 15th Amendment.

The seven justices appointed by Roosevelt since the *Grovey* decision, along with Harlan Fiske Stone, who had voted with the majority in *Grovey*, found state action evident in the number of state laws regulating primary elections.

Only Justice Owen J. Roberts sounded a dissenting voice as the court overturned *Grovey v. Townsend*, a decision not yet a decade old.

Writing for the majority, Justice Stanley Reed linked *Classic* and *Smith v. Allwright*:

> The fusing by the *Classic* case of the primary and general elections into a single instrumentality for choice of officers has a definite bearing on the permissibility under the Constitution of excluding Negroes from primaries.... *Classic* bears upon *Grovey v. Townsend* not because exclusion of Negroes from primaries is any more or less state action by reason of the unitary character of the electoral process but because the recognition of the place of the primary in the electoral scheme makes clear that state delegation to a party of the power to fix the qualifications of primary elections is delegation of a state function that may make the party's action the action of the state.[30]

Thus, held the court, Allwright's action was state action abridging Smith's right to vote just because of his race, a clear violation of the 15th Amendment.

Justice Roberts, author of the court's opinion in *Grovey*, warned that by overruling such a recent decision, the court "tends to bring adjudications of this tribunal into the same class as a restricted railroad ticket, good for this day and train only."[31]

Terry v. Adams: 1953

In 1953, with still another Supreme Court decision, the relentless effort of Texas Democrats — and politicians in other southern states — to maintain the white primary at last came to an end.

Since 1889, the Jaybird Party, an all-white Democratic organization in one Texas county, had declared itself a private club and had submitted political candidates' names in an unofficial county white primary. The successful candidate in the Jaybird primary inevitably entered and won the following Democratic primary and general election.

The court struck down this strategem as a violation of the 15th Amendment, finding the use of racially exclusive private clubs as a political caucus for electing candidates a violation of the 15th Amendment.

Justice Hugo L. Black wrote in the majority opinion in the case of *Terry v. Adams*:

> [T]he Jaybird primary has become an integral part, indeed the only effective part, of the elective process that determines who shall rule and govern in the county. The effect of the whole procedure, Jaybird primary plus Democratic primary plus general election, is to do precisely that which the Fifteenth Amendment forbids — strip Negroes of every vestige of influence in selecting the officials who control the local county matters that intimately touch the daily lives of citizens.[32]

Poll Taxes

In the early days of the republic, poll taxes replaced land-holding, property and other more burdensome requirements for voters, but most poll taxes were eliminated by the time of the Civil War.

This sort of tax was revived in the early 1890s, however, as one of the devices used to restrict the suffrage to white voters in the South. The ostensible reason for re-introduction of the poll tax was to "cleanse" the state of such election abuses as repeat voting.

A Legitimate Tax

In 1937 the Supreme Court upheld the constitutionality of the poll tax against the challenge that it violated the equal protection guarantee of the 14th Amendment. In the case of *Breedlove v. Suttles,* the court held that the tax assessed upon voters by Georgia was a legitimate means of raising revenue. It was not a denial of equal protection, held the court, because, on its face, it applied to Negro and white voters alike.

The court, for whom Justice Pierce Butler wrote the opinion, rejected the notion that the Georgia tax was an impermissible levy on a federally guaranteed right.[33]

After the Populist era many states had voluntarily dropped use of the poll tax. Proposals to abolish it were introduced in every Congress from 1939 to 1962. By 1960 only four states still required its payment by voters. In August 1962, the House approved a constitutional amendment —already accepted by the Senate — which outlawed poll taxes in federal elections.

Constitutional Amendment

The poll tax ban was ratified as the 24th Amendment Jan. 23, 1964. The first Supreme Court decision interpreting the amendment came in 1965. The court in the case of *Harman v. Forssenius* struck down Virginia's effort to anticipate the poll tax ban by giving voters in federal elections the option of paying the levy or filing a certificate of residence before each election.

The court held that the re-registration/residence requirement for persons who chose to exercise their right to vote without paying a poll tax subverted the effect of the 24th Amendment.[34]

In 1966 the court held the poll tax an unconstitutional requirement for voting in state and local elections as well. "Wealth, like race, creed, or color is not germane to one's ability to participate intelligently in the electoral process," wrote Justice William O. Douglas for the court in the case of *Harper v. State Board of Elections.* Thus the court struck down Virginia's $1.50 poll tax as a violation of the equal protection clause, overruling *Breedlove v. Suttles.*[35]

Douglas explained the court's reasoning:

> We conclude that a State violates the Equal Protection Clause of the Fourteenth Amendment whenever it makes the affluence of the voter or payment of any fee an electoral standard. Voter qualifications have no relation to wealth nor to paying or not paying this or any other tax. . . .
>
> To introduce wealth or payment of a fee as a measure of a voter's qualifications is to introduce a capricious or irrelevant factor. . . . In this context — that is, as a condition of obtaining a ballot — the requirement of fee paying causes an 'invidious' discrimination . . . that runs afoul of the Equal Protection Clause.[36]

Justices Hugo L. Black and John Marshall Harlan wrote dissenting opinions. Black argued that the majority was merely incorporating its notion of good government policy into the Constitution. Justice Harlan, with whom Justice Potter Stewart concurred in dissent, described the majority opinion as "wholly inadequate" to explain why a poll tax was "irrational or invidious."[37]

The Racial Gerrymander

Even as the white primary, literacy tests and poll taxes were disappearing from the electoral framework of the South, the Supreme Court struck down the use of still another device used to disenfranchise black voters.

Northern and southern states both made some use of the racial gerrymander — the practice of drawing election district boundary lines in order to dilute or eliminate any concentration of black voting strength in a single district.

In 1960 the case of *Gomillion v. Lightfoot* brought this practice before the Supreme Court, which found it a clear violation of the 15th Amendment. The court's ruling in this case was notable for two other reasons: it pre-dated by two years the court's abandonment of its traditional hands-off policy toward redistricting and reapportionment questions in general, and the majority opinion was written by Justice Felix Frankfurter, who had been the court's most articulate spokesman for this hands-off policy. *(Details, p. 490)*

Alabama law, challenged in the *Gomillion* case, redefined the boundaries of the city of Tuskegee, Ala., to exclude virtually all black voters. The excluded blacks sought a court order halting enforcement of the law, which had changed the shape of the city limits from a square to a 28-sided figure, removing all but four or five qualified black voters from within the city while not removing a single white voter.

Professor C. G. Gomillion of Tuskegee Institute, and the other affected black citizens argued both that the gerrymander denied them due process and equal protection under the 14th Amendment and that it infringed their right to vote in violation of the 15th Amendment.

The Supreme Court unanimously declared the gerrymander unconstitutional. The right of the states to control the boundaries of their political subdivisions is subject to constitutional limitation, it held.

Justice Frankfurter wrote the court's opinion. Frankfurter had been the author of the court's opinion in the 1946 case of *Colegrove v. Green,* which declared that the court ought not to enter the "political thicket" of redistricting questions because they were political questions beyond the competence of the courts to resolve.[38]

Frankfurter distinguished between the *Gomillion* and *Colegrove* cases, pointing out that *Colegrove* involved involuntary non-racial disparities in districts created by population shifts, not state action, while *Gomillion,* on the other hand, involved intentional racial discrimination by the state:

> When a legislature thus singles out a readily isolated segment of a racial minority for special discriminatory treatment, it violates the Fifteenth Amendment. In no case involving unequal weight in voting distribution that has come before the court did the decision sanction a differentiation on racial lines whereby approval was given to unequivocal withdrawal of the vote solely from colored citizens. Apart from all else, these considerations lift this controversy out of the so-called "political" arena and into the conventional sphere of constitutional litigation. . . .
>
> While in form this is merely an act redefining metes and bounds, if the allegations are established, the inescapable human effect of this essay in geometry and geography is to despoil colored citizens, and only colored citizens, of their theretofore enjoyed voting rights.[39]

Justice Charles E. Whittaker's concurring opinion pointed out that this application of the 15th Amendment extended the meaning of that amendment, guaranteeing not only the right to vote but also the right to vote in a particular district. The equal protection clause of the 14th Amendment would have been a preferable basis for the ruling, Whittaker wrote:

> [I]nasmuch as no one has the right to vote in a political division, or in a local election concerning only an area in which he does not reside, it would seem to follow that one's right to vote in Division A is not abridged by a redistricting that places his residence in Division B *if* he there enjoys the same voting privileges as all others in that Division.

But it does seem clear to me that accomplishment of a State's purpose . . . of "fencing Negro citizens out of" Division A and into Division B is an unlawful segregation of races of citizens in violation of the Equal Protection Clause of the Fourteenth Amendment. . . .[40]

The Manhattan Mosaic

In 1962, Manhattan voters brought suit charging that a New York congressional districting law was irrational, discriminatory, unequal and segregated voters by race and national origin, concentrating white voters in the 17th — "Silk Stocking" — district, and non-white and Puerto Rican voters in the 18th, 19th and 20th congressional districts.

The Supreme Court found no constitutional violation. Its opinion noted that since Manhattan was a mosaic of ethnic and racial groups, almost any combination of arbitrarily drawn congressional district lines would result in some pattern of racial imbalance subject to challenge as unconstitutional.[41] *(Later ruling, p. 494)*

The Right and the Power: A Broad View

Although the court had struck down the use of grandfather clauses and white primaries before 1950, it was Congress which at last asserted federal power to ensure the right of black citizens to vote.

A constitutional amendment ratified in 1964 outlawed the use of poll taxes in federal elections; the Voting Rights Act of 1965 suspended use of literacy tests and set up federal machinery to protect the opportunity of blacks to register and vote.

Congress began reasserting its authority to enforce the 15th Amendment in 1957. The amendment authorizes Congress to pass appropriate legislation to enforce it. But in the years immediately after adoption of the amendment, efforts to pass enforcing legislation were proscribed by the court's restrictive view of this power. *(Details, p. 151)*

The Civil Rights Act of 1957 set up the Civil Rights Commission, which was charged, among other tasks, with studying the problem of voter discrimination. The act also authorized the attorney general to bring lawsuits to halt public and private interference with the right of blacks to vote, and expanded federal jurisdiction over such suits.

The investigatory procedures of the commission and the authorization of federal voting rights suits were upheld by the Supreme Court in 1960.[42]

Responding to reports that progress in securing voting rights for blacks was still slow even under the provisions of the 1957 Act, Congress in 1960 passed a measure which permitted the U.S. attorney general to sue a state for deprivation of voting rights if the individuals named initially as defendants — usually voting registrars — should leave office.

This provision remedied a situation which had arisen in a suit brought by the United States against Alabama voting officials.[43]

In addition, Title VI of the 1960 law authorized the appointment of special federal "voting referees" to oversee voter registration in selected counties where a federal court found a pattern of voter discrimination to exist.

The Civil Rights Act of 1964, in its first title, mandated state adoption of standard procedures and requirements for all persons seeking to register to vote. The law also required local officials to justify rejecting an applicant who had completed the sixth grade or had equivalent evidence of intellectual competence. Other provisions of the 1964 law expedited the movement of voting rights cases to the Supreme Court.[44]

In two cases brought under the 1964 Act, the Supreme Court sanctioned the government's efforts to break the pattern of case-by-case litigation of voting rights violations. The court upheld federal power to challenge a state's entire constitutional legal framework for voter registration and conduct of elections.[45]

The Voting Rights Act

But progress was still slow. In Dallas County, Ala., three new federal laws and four years of litigation produced the registration of only 383 black voters out of a potential pool of 15,000 blacks of voting age.

On March 8, 1965, the Rev. Martin Luther King Jr. led a "Walk for Freedom" to dramatize the need for additional efforts in behalf of registering black voters in Selma — the county seat of Dallas County — and elsewhere in the South. The violence of the reaction of local white law enforcement officers and white bystanders to King's peaceful demonstration drew nationwide attention to the dimensions of the problem.

A week later, President Lyndon B. Johnson addressed a joint session of Congress to ask passage of a new voting rights measure to close the legal loopholes that had so long allowed local officials to stall black voter registration. Johnson explained that "no law that we now have on the books . . . can ensure the right to vote when local officials are determined to deny it."[46]

Later that month, testifying before a Senate committee on the need for such legislation, NAACP official Roy Wilkins — appearing on behalf of the Leadership Conference on Civil Rights — urged Congress to "transform this retail litigation method of registration into a wholesale administration procedure registering all who seek to exercise their democratic birthright."[47]

State Requirements: Age, Residence, Property

States historically have imposed qualifications upon voters other than racially motivated ones. Recent Supreme Court rulings, however, have limited state power to impose such voter requirements when they are related to age, residence for any extended period, or property ownership.

Nevertheless, as recently as 1974 the court affirmed the power of states to exclude convicted felons from the exercise of the franchise. In 1968, in the case of *Green v. New York City Board of Elections,* the court upheld a New York law which barred convicted, unpardoned felons from voting.[1]

In 1974 the court reaffirmed that position, ruling that denial of the right to vote to convicted felons did not violate the 14th Amendment.[2]

Age and Residence

In 1970 the court upheld the power of Congress to lower age and residence requirements for participation in federal elections, although not for state or local elections.[3]

Only eleven years earlier, the court had declared that states had broad powers to set age and residence rules for voters:

> The states have long been held to have broad powers to determine the conditions under which the right of suffrage may be exercised.... Residence requirements, and age ... are obvious examples indicating factors which a State may take into consideration in determining the qualification of voters.[4]

Following that ruling, the court in 1972 seemed to limit all state-imposed residency requirements for voters to 30 days. In a case involving Tennessee's residency requirement of one year prior to registration as a voter, the court held that requirement invalid, saying that the state had shown no compelling state interest to justify such a lengthy residency requirement.[5] This decision in

Dunn v. Blumstein sidestepped, but did not overrule, a 1904 decision upholding a similar Maryland requirement that a voter file a declaration of intent to register one year before his enrollment on the voter lists.[6]

But the court later left standing Arizona's rule cutting off voter registration 50 days before a primary. The court indicated that the state had shown the 50-day period necessary to permit preparation of accurate voter lists.[7]

In an earlier ruling, the court had held that a state could not prevent military personnel stationed within its borders from establishing residence for purposes of voting in the state.[8] And, the court held in 1970, a state could not deny the right to vote to persons living in a federal enclave within the state, if those persons were otherwise treated as state residents.[9]

Property Ownership

By the mid-1970s, property requirements for voting in general elections had disappeared from the American electoral process.

In a set of modern rulings, the court made clear that the equal protection guarantee of the 14th Amendment was offended by state efforts to so restrict the right to vote.

In 1969 the court struck down Louisiana's law which limited to property tax-payers the right to vote in elections to approve issuance of utility revenue bonds.[10] The same day, the court held that the equal protection guarantee assured all residents — not merely those who owned or leased property or who had children in the public schools — the right to vote in school district elections.[11]

In 1970 the court applied the same principle to strike down state efforts to exclude non-property owners from voting in elections held to approve the issue of general obligation bonds.[12] The court later struck down laws which limited the right to vote in city bond elections to persons who owned taxable property.[13]

---

[1] *Green v. New York City Board of Elections,* 389 U.S. 1048 (1968).

[2] *Richardson v. Ramirez,* 418 U.S. 24 (1974).

[3] *Oregon v. Mitchell, Texas v. Mitchell, United States v. Idaho, United States v. Arizona,* 400 U.S. 112 (1970).

[4] *Lassiter v. Northampton County Board of Elections,* 360 U.S. 45 at 51 (1959).

[5] *Dunn v. Blumstein,* 405 U.S. 330 (1972).

[6] *Pope v. Williams,* 193 U.S. 621 (1903).

[7] *Marston v. Lewis,* 410 U.S. 679 (1973); *Burns v. Fortson,* 410 U.S. 686 (1973).

[8] *Carrington v. Rash,* 380 U.S. 89 (1965).

[9] *Evans v. Cornman,* 398 U.S. 419 (1970).

[10] *Cipriano v. City of Houma,* 395 U.S. 701 (1969).

[11] *Kramer v. Union Free School District No. 15,* 395 U.S. 818 (1969).

[12] *Phoenix v. Kolodzieski,* 399 U.S. 204 (1970).

[13] *Hill v. Stone,* 421 U.S. 289 (1975).

Within five months, Congress had approved the sweeping Voting Rights Act of 1965 — signed by President Johnson Aug. 6, 1965.

The law suspended literacy tests and provided for the appointment of federal supervisors of voter registration in all states and counties where literacy tests (or similar qualifying devices) were in effect as of Nov. 1, 1964, and where less than 50 percent of the voting age residents were

registered to vote or did vote in the 1964 presidential election.

The law established criminal penalties for persons found guilty of interfering with the voting rights of others. State or county governments brought under the coverage of the law due to low voter registration or participation were required to obtain federal approval of any new voting laws, standards, practices or procedures before implementing them. A covered state or county could "escape" from the law's provisions if it could convince a three-judge federal court in the District of Columbia that no racial discrimination in registration or voting had occurred in the previous five years.

The act placed federal registration machinery in six southern states (Alabama, Georgia, Mississippi, South Carolina, Louisiana and Virginia), Alaska, 28 counties in North Carolina, three counties in Arizona and one in Idaho.

It was the most effective civil rights legislation ever enacted. Within four years, almost one million blacks had registered to vote under its provisions.[48]

Judicial Support

Not surprisingly, this unprecedented assertion of federal power over electoral and voting matters was immediately challenged as exceeding the constitutional authority of Congress and encroaching on states' rights.

But in 1966, in direct contrast to its post-Civil War rulings, the Supreme Court firmly backed the power of Congress to pass such a law.

The case challenging the act was *South Carolina v. Katzenbach.* The state asked the court to halt implementation of the law, charging that Congress had overstepped itself in suspending state voting standards, authorizing the use of federal election examiners, and adopting a "triggering" formula which resulted in its affecting some states, but not others.

At the court's invitation, Alabama, Georgia, Louisiana, Mississippi and Virginia filed briefs in support of South Carolina's challenge. Twenty other states filed briefs in support of the law.

South Carolina charged that by suspending voter qualification "tests and devices" in some states, Congress violated the principle that all states were equal. It also alleged that the law denied the affected states due process of law by simply presuming that high minority population coupled with low voter participation demonstrated the existence of racially discriminatory voting practices. Due process was also denied, argued South Carolina, by the law's failure to allow judicial review of the findings putting the law into effect in a state. Furthermore, the state maintained, the act was an unconstitutional bill of attainder, punishing certain states — and it violated the separation of powers by using legislative means to find certain states guilty of discrimination.

Taking a far broader view both of the right to vote and congressional power to enforce and protect that right than had the court of the 1870s and 1880s, the Supreme Court in 1966 rejected all constitutional challenges to the act.

"Congress," wrote Chief Justice Earl Warren for eight members of the court, "has full remedial powers to effectuate the constitutional prohibition against racial discrimination in voting." [49]

Warren continued:

The Voting Rights Act was designed by Congress to banish the blight of racial discrimination in voting, which has infected the electoral process in parts of our country for nearly a century.... Congress assumed the power to prescribe these remedies from §2 of the Fifteenth Amendment, which authorizes the National Legislature to effectuate by "appropriate" measures the constitutional prohibition against racial discrimination in voting. We hold that the sections of the Act

which are properly before us are an appropriate means for carrying out Congress' constitutional responsibilities and are consonant with all other provisions of the Constitution. We therefore deny South Carolina's request that enforcement of these sections of the act be enjoined.[50]

Warren then responded to the challenges to each of the particular provisions of the Act.

With respect to the coverage formula, Warren said that it was "rational in both practice and theory." The suspension of tests and devices "was a legitimate response to the problem for which there is ample precedent in Fifteenth Amendment cases...." The federal approval requirement for new voting rules in the states covered by the act, Warren observed, "may have been an uncommon exercise of congressional power, as South Carolina contends, but the Court has recognized that exceptional conditions can justify legislative measures not otherwise appropriate." The appointment of federal election examiners was "clearly an appropriate response to the problem, closely related to remedies authorized in prior cases." [51]

Justice Hugo L. Black concurred in part and dissented in part. He agreed that Congress had the power under the 15th Amendment to suspend literacy tests, and to authorize federal examiners to register qualified voters. But Black objected to the provisions that suspended any changes in state voting laws until the state obtained approval of the change from the attorney general or the federal district court in the District of Columbia. This provision, Black argued, "so distorts our constitutional structure of government as to render any distinction drawn in the Constitution between state and federal power almost meaningless." [52]

Also in 1966, in the case of *Katzenbach v. Morgan,* the court upheld the portion of the Voting Rights Act which permitted persons educated in accredited "American-flag" schools to vote even if they were unable to read and write English. The provision was aimed at enfranchising Puerto Ricans educated in such schools, living in the United States, but unable to demonstrate literacy in English.[53]

Subsequent Rulings

Although the basic constitutionality of the Voting Rights Act was now settled, a steady stream of voting rights cases came to the court in the late 1960s and the 1970s, testing the scope and application of the law. The court steadfastly backed the act and the broadest possible interpretation and application of its provisions.

In the 1969 case of *Gaston County v. United States,* the court refused to allow a North Carolina county to reinstate a literacy test. Writing the court's opinion, Justice John Marshall Harlan linked the county's earlier maintenance of segregated schools and the literacy level of its blacks, and declared that to reinstitute the literacy qualification for voters would simply perpetuate the inequality of the denial of equal educational opportunity.[54] *(Details, p. 480)*

In a number of other cases the court upheld the preclearance requirement for a wide variety of laws and practices affecting the right to vote.[55]

In 1978 the court even extended the requirement to apply to a county school board's rule that any employee running for state office must take leave from his post without pay during the period of active candidacy. The court held both that the rule was a voting standard, practice or procedure subject to the requirement and that the county school board was a political subdivision subject

The Right to Run for Public Office

In the late 1960s and 1970s, the Supreme Court struck down a number of state-imposed restrictions on the right to run for public office, in most cases ruling that the restrictions violated the 14th Amendment's guarantee of equal protection.

Nominating Petitions

In 1969 the court held that a state law requiring valid nominating petitions for independent presidential electors to include the signatures of at least 200 persons from each of 50 counties — among the total of 25,000 signatures required — violated the "one person, one vote" rule. By setting this arbitrary quota for each of that many counties, held the court, the law discriminated against voters residing in the more heavily populated counties of the state.[1] With this ruling in the case of *Moore v. Ogilvie,* the court reversed a 1948 decision upholding the same requirement.[2]

Filing Fees

Three years later, in 1972, the court struck down a state's practice of basing the size of filing fees for candidates on the estimated total cost of an election. This practice, held the court, discriminated against candidates who could not afford to pay large fees.[3]

In 1974 the court held it unconstitutional for a state to set mandatory high filing fees in order to prevent poor people from running for office.[4]

Campaign Spending

In a broad-ranging decision relying heavily on First Amendment principles, the Supreme Court in the 1976 case of *Buckley v. Valeo* struck down congressionally-set limits on the amount candidates for president might spend. In that same ruling, however, the justices upheld the limits placed on individual contributions to campaigns and on the contributions of corporate political action committees.[5] *(Details, pp. 172-173)*

New Parties

Two other recent rulings reduced the burden which states may impose upon new political parties seeking to win a place on the state ballot.

In a 1968 ruling in a case initiated by the American Independent Party, the court struck down Ohio's substantially more burdensome requirements for small or newly organized parties wishing to obtain a place on the ballot. The court declared that laws which placed heavier burdens on parties other than the Republican and Democratic parties violated the guarantee of equal protection.[6]

Qualifying for a Ballot

Six years later, however, the court held that a state might properly require new and minority parties seeking a ballot spot to secure a certain number of voter signatures endorsing its effort — and to require that those signatures belong to persons who had not voted in a party primary or otherwise participated in another party's nominating process during that year. This restriction, held the court, was simply a reasonable means for the state to use in protecting the integrity of its nominating process.[7]

---

[1] *Moore v. Ogilvie,* 394 U.S. 814 (1969).
[2] *MacDougall v. Green,* 335 U.S. 281 (1948).
[3] *Bullock v. Carter,* 405 U.S. 134 (1972).
[4] *Lubin v. Panish,* 415 U.S. 709 (1974).

[5] *Buckley v. Valeo,* 424 U.S. 1 (1976).
[6] *Williams v. Rhodes,* 393 U.S. 23 (1968).
[7] *American Party of Texas v. White, Hainsworth v. White,* 415 U.S. 767 (1974).

---

to the provisions of the Voting Rights Act. Four justices dissented on the first point; three on the second.[56]

Earlier, the court held that annexation of contiguous areas by communities covered by the act was prohibited without prior federal approval.[57]

In 1975, however, the court held in the case of *Richmond v. United States* that a federally approved annexation plan did not violate the Voting Rights Act — even if it reduced the percentage of black voters in the city's population — so long as there were legitimate objective reasons for the annexation.[58]

In two cases decided in 1977 — *Briscoe v. Bell* and *Morris v. Gressette* — the court also sustained the act's limits on judicial review of the formula which put the law into effect in certain areas, and on judicial review of the attorney general's decision to approve changes in voting laws or practices.[59]

Despite its willingness to affirm the sweeping provisions of the 1965 law as originally enacted and as amended, the court has refused to interpret it as forbidding all use of

racial criteria in redistricting or as requiring that blacks be given proportional representation on elected bodies.

In its 1976 decision in the case of *Beer v. United States,* the court upheld a city's reapportionment of the districts from which city council members were chosen. The change resulted in an increase in the number of black council members, but not in a proportional representation of black voters among the council members. The court held that the Voting Rights Act was satisfied so long as such changes did not reduce the voting strength of racial minorities.[60]

And — although the court in its 1960 ruling in *Gomillion v. Lightfoot* had held as unconstitutional any redistricting that was clearly intended to deny or dilute the right of blacks to vote — it held in 1977 that states could still use some racial criteria in drawing electoral districts for members of the state legislature.

In the case of *United Jewish Organizations of Williamsburgh v. Carey,* the court upheld New York's 1974 redistricting law which purposely redrew certain districts with non-white majorities of at least 65 percent. The county affected in the case was one of three in the state which had been brought under the coverage of the Voting Rights Act by the 1970 amendments to that law.

The Hasidic Jewish community of the Williamsburgh section of Brooklyn objected to the redrawn lines because the new boundaries divided their voting strength between two districts. The Jewish community argued that such use of racial criteria in the redistricting plan deprived them of equal protection guaranteed by the 14th Amendment and diluted their voting strength in violation of the 15th Amendment.

The Constitution does not prevent all use of racial criteria in districting and apportionment, wrote Justice

Byron R. White for seven members of the majority. Nor, he continued, does it "prevent a State subject to the Voting Rights Act from deliberately creating or preserving black majorities in particular districts in order to ensure that its reapportionment plan complies with [the act]. . . ."

"There is no doubt," White continued, that the state in drawing new district lines, "deliberately used race in a purposeful manner. But its plan represented no racial slur or stigma with respect to whites or any other race, and we discern no discrimination violative of the Fourteenth Amendment nor any abridgment of the right to vote on account of race within the meaning of the Fifteenth Amendment."[61]

Footnotes

[1] *Minor v. Happersett,* 88 U.S. 627 at 629 (1874).

[2] *United States v. Reese,* 92 U.S. 563 at 564 (1876).

[3] *United States v. Cruikshank,* 92 U.S. 542 at 555 (1876).

[4] Id. at 554-556.

[5] *Ex parte Siebold,* 100 U.S. 371 (1880).

[6] *Ex parte Clarke,* 100 U.S. 399 (1880); *United States v. Gale,* 109 U.S. 65 (1883); *In re Coy,* 127 U.S. 731 (1888); *United States v. Mosley,* 238 U.S. 383 (1915).

[7] *Ex parte Yarbrough,* 110 U.S. 651 at 657-658, 663-664 (1884).

[8] Id. at 666.

[9] Id. at 667.

[10] *James v. Bowman,* 190 U.S. 127 at 139 (1903).

[11] C. Vann Woodward, *The Strange Career of Jim Crow,* 2nd rev. ed. (New York: Oxford University Press, 1966), pp. 82-93.

[12] *Williams v. Mississippi,* 170 U.S. 213 at 225 (1898).

[13] *Guinn v. United States,* 238 U.S. 347 at 366 (1915).

[14] *United States v. Mosley,* 238 U.S. 383 at 386 (1915).

[15] *Lane v. Wilson,* 307 U.S. 268 at 275 (1939).

[16] *Davis v. Schnell,* 336 U.S. 933 (1949).

[17] *Lassiter v. Northampton County Board of Elections,* 360 U.S. 45 at 51-54 (1959).

[18] *Louisiana v. United States,* 380 U.S. 145 at 152-153 (1965).

[19] *South Carolina v. Katzenbach,* 383 U.S. 301 (1966).

[20] Id. at 328, 334.

[21] *Katzenbach v. Morgan,* 384 U.S. 641 (1966); *Cardona v. Power,* 384 U.S. 672 (1966).

[22] *Gaston County v. United States,* 395 U.S. 285 (1969).

[23] Id. at 296-297.

[24] *Oregon v. Mitchell,* 400 U.S. 112 (1970).

[25] *Newberry v. United States,* 256 U.S. 232 (1921).

[26] *Nixon v. Herndon,* 273 U.S. 536 at 541 (1927).

[27] *Nixon v. Condon,* 286 U.S. 73 (1932).

[28] *Grovey v. Townsend,* 295 U.S. 45 (1935).

[29] *United States v. Classic,* 313 U.S. 299 at 317 (1941).

[30] *Smith v. Allwright,* 321 U.S. 649 at 660 (1944).

[31] Id. at 669.

[32] *Terry v. Adams,* 345 U.S. 461 at 469-470 (1953).

[33] *Breedlove v. Suttles,* 302 U.S. 277 (1937).

[34] *Harman v. Forssenius,* 380 U.S. 528 (1965).

[35] *Harper v. Virginia State Board of Elections,* 383 U.S. 663 at 668 (1966).

[36] Id. at 666, 668.

[37] Id. at 683, 686.

[38] *Colegrove v. Green,* 328 U.S. 549 (1946).

[39] *Gomillion v. Lightfoot,* 364 U.S. 339 at 346-347 (1960).

[40] Id. at 349.

[41] *Wright v. Rockefeller,* 376 U.S. 52 (1964).

[42] *United States v. Raines,* 362 U.S. 17 (1960); *Hannah v. Larch,* 363 U.S. 420 (1960).

[43] Congressional Quarterly, *Congress and the Nation,* Vol. I (Washington: Congressional Quarterly, 1965) p. 1628; *United States v. Alabama,* 362 U.S. 602 (1960).

[44] Congressional Quarterly. *Congress and the Nation,* I: 1638.

[45] *United States v. Louisiana,* 380 U.S. 145 (1965); *United States v. Mississippi,* 380 U.S. 128 (1965).

[46] Lyndon B. Johnson, *Public Papers of the Presidents of the United States, Lyndon B. Johnson, 1965,* Book I (Washington: U.S. Government Printing Office, 1966) March 15, 1965, p. 282.

[47] U.S. Congress. Senate. Judiciary Committee. Voting Rights (Part II), Statement of Roy Wilkins, 89th Cong. 1st Sess. 1965, p. 1005.

[48] Congressional Quarterly. *Congress and the Nation,* Vol. II (Washington: Congressional Quarterly, 1969) p. 354, 356-365.

[49] *South Carolina v. Katzenbach,* 383 U.S. 301 at 326 (1966).

[50] Id. at 308.

[51] Id. at 330, 334, 336.

[52] Id. at 358.

[53] *Katzenbach v. Morgan,* 384 U.S. 641 (1966).

[54] *Gaston County v. United States,* 395 U.S. 285 (1969).

[55] *Allen v. Virginia Board of Elections,* 393 U.S. 544 (1969); *Hadnott v. Amos,* 394 U.S. 358 (1969).

[56] *Dougherty County Board of Education v. White,* 435 U.S. 921 (1978).

[57] *Perkins v. Mathews,* 400 U.S. 379 (1971).

[58] *Richmond v. United States,* 422 U.S. 358 (1975).

[59] *Briscoe v. Bell,* 432 U.S. 404 (1977); *Morris v. Gressette,* 432 U.S. 491 (1977).

[60] *Beer v. United States,* 425 U.S. 130 (1976).

[61] *United Jewish Organizations of Williamsburgh v. Carey,* 430 U.S. 144 at 161, 165 (1977).

The Right to an Equal Vote

In the early 1960s, as Congress was moving with judicial backing to fulfill at last the promise of the 15th Amendment, the Supreme Court sparked a second revolution in the nation's electoral system — this one based on the demands of the equal protection guarantee of the 14th Amendment.

In 1962, the court abandoned its long-standing policy of non-interference in the malapportionment of population among a state's electoral districts. By the end of the decade, the court's rulings had required that almost all the nation's legislative and congressional district lines be redrawn.

The equal protection guarantee, ruled the court, meant that one person's vote should be counted equally with another's. Thus the standard by which these redistricting efforts were measured was that of "one person, one vote."

Congress, Districts and People

Article I, section 4 of the Constitution gives Congress the power to override state-set rules governing the election of senators and representatives. The section reads:

> The Times, Places and Manner of holding Elections for Senators and Representatives shall be prescribed in each State by the Legislature thereof; but the Congress may at any time by Law make or alter such Regulations, except as to the Places of chusing Senators.

Congress exercised this power in 1842 to require that members of the House be elected from separate districts within each state. In 1872 Congress added the requirement that these districts be of approximately equal population. Subsequent reapportionment statutes, including those enacted in 1901 and 1911, contained the specification that congressional districts be "contiguous and compact territory and containing as nearly as practicable an equal number of inhabitants." [1]

But the next such law, passed in 1929, omitted these requirements; the Supreme Court in 1932 held the omission intentional and the standards thus no longer in effect. In the case of *Wood v. Broom*, the court upheld a Mississippi redistricting law which failed to provide compact, contiguous and population-equal districts. [2]

This omission — and its interpretation by the Supreme Court — came at a critical time in the nation's demographic history.

The 1920 census showed that, for the first time, more Americans lived in cities than in rural settings. The implication was clear: eventually the voice of the farmer in the legislature and in Congress would grow fainter, while that of the city dweller would increase in strength.

But for 40 years, with the help of a hands-off policy on the part of the Supreme Court, rural interests successfully delayed the full political impact of this shift in population.

The court steadfastly held that challenges to malapportionment were political questions, placed outside its purview by the separation of powers. In 1946, refusing to intervene in Illinois — where there was as much as an 800,000-person difference between the largest and smallest congressional districts, the court reaffirmed its intention to stay out of the "political thicket" of redistricting and reapportionment.

But within two decades the court reversed that stance of restraint. With the decision announced in the 1962 case of *Baker v. Carr*, the court abandoned its view that malapportionment was a strictly political question. In subsequent rulings the court moved into the thicket, requiring the redrawing of state legislative and congressional district lines to ensure each voter's ballot an equal weight in the state electoral process.

'The Political Thicket'

The case of *Colegrove v. Green* was brought to the Supreme Court in 1946 by a Northwestern University professor of political science, Kenneth W. Colegrove. He challenged Illinois' congressional districts as so unequal in population that they in fact denied voters in the more populous districts the equal protection of the law guaranteed them by the 14th Amendment. The numerical disparity between these districts, he pointed out, was as large as 800,000 persons.

The Supreme Court, divided 4-3, threw out his case without addressing the equal protection issue. Justice Robert H. Jackson did not take part in the decision; the seat of the Chief Justice was vacant — Chief Justice Harlan Fiske Stone died two months before the decision was announced in June 1946. [3]

Justice Felix Frankfurter wrote the opinion announcing the decision, joined in that opinion by Justices Stanley F. Reed and Harold H. Burton. Frankfurter noted that the case could be resolved simply on the same basis as *Wood v. Broom*: Since Congress had omitted the equal population standard from the reapportionment law now in effect, there was no such requirement for states to follow in drawing district lines.

But practical considerations as well dictated the court's decision not to intervene here, Frankfurter continued:

...due regard for the effective working of our Government revealed this issue to be of a peculiarly political nature and therefore not meet for judicial determination. . . .

Nothing is clearer than that this controversy concerns matters that bring courts into immediate and active relations with party contests. From the determination of such issues this Court has traditionally held aloof. It is hostile to a democratic system to involve the judiciary in the politics of the people. . . .

...due regard for the Constitution as a viable system precludes judicial correction [of the evils protested here]. Authority for dealing with such problems resides elsewhere. . . . The short of it is that the Constitution [Article I, section 4] has conferred upon Congress exclusive authority to secure fair representation by the States in the popular House and left to that House determination whether States have fulfilled their responsibility. If Congress failed in exercising its powers, whereby standards of fairness are offended, the remedy ultimately lies with the people. Whether Congress faithfully discharges its duty or not, the subject has been committed to the exclusive control of Congress. . . .

To sustain this action would cut very deep into the very being of Congress. Courts ought not to enter this political thicket. The remedy for unfairness in districting is to secure State legislatures that will apportion properly, or to invoke the ample powers of Congress. . . .[4]

The critical fourth vote was cast by Justice Wiley B. Rutledge, who wrote a separate opinion explaining that he did not endorse the position set out by Frankfurter that issues of districting were not proper matters for judicial determination, but that in this case he thought the court properly dismissed the matter in order to avoid collision with the political departments of the government.[5]

Justice Hugo L. Black, William O. Douglas and Frank Murphy dissented, finding the matter well within the power of the federal courts to redress constitutional grievances caused by state action.

Black wrote: "What is involved here is the right to vote guaranteed by the Federal Constitution. It has always been the rule that where a federally protected right has been invaded the federal courts will provide the remedy to rectify the wrong done."[6]

Population disparities such as those in this case clearly violated the 14th Amendment, the dissenters concluded, and the court should grant relief for such a violation.

Colegrove stood for 16 years as a firmly planted obstacle to judicial inquiry into the apportionment of state legislatures, as well as into the distribution of population among congressional districts.

Race and Redistricting

But in 1960 — with Justice Frankfurter delivering the court's opinion — the Supreme Court made an exception to its refusal to intervene in such matters.

Civil rights and redistricting converged in the case of *Gomillion v. Lightfoot*, and the Supreme Court was persuaded by a claim of racial discrimination to strike down the Alabama law which redrew the city of Tuskegee's voting boundary lines to eliminate nearly every black voter from the city's limits.[7] *(Details, p. 483)*

Justice Frankfurter drew a clear line between redistricting challenges based on the 14th Amendment, like *Colegrove,* and 15th Amendment challenges to racial redistricting, like *Gomillion:*

The decisive facts in this case ... are wholly different from the considerations found controlling in *Colegrove.*

That case involved a complaint of discriminatory apportionment of congressional districts. The appellants in *Colegrove* complained only of a dilution of the strength of their votes as a result of legislative inaction over a course of many years. The petitioners here complain that affirmative legislative action deprives them of their vote and the consequent advantages that the ballot affords. . . .

When a state exercises power wholly within the domain of state interest, it is insulated from federal judicial review. But such insulation is not carried over when state power is used as an instrument of circumventing a federally protected right.[8]

Baker v. Carr

By 1962, only three members of the *Colegrove* court remained on the bench: Frankfurter, Black and Douglas — the latter two, dissenters from the 1946 ruling.

By that year, as well, studies made clear that the once mild over-representation of rural voters in state legislatures had become an extreme one.

Rural districts held nearly twice as many seats as they would have been entitled to by apportionment on a population basis alone. A similar substantial degree of population imbalance, though by no means as acute, also existed with respect to congressional districts in most states.

In the 1962 Tennessee redistricting case of *Baker v. Carr,* the Supreme Court took its first step into the political thicket of legislative reapportionment.

In *Baker v. Carr,* the court by a 6-2 vote ruled that constitutional challenges to legislative malapportionment could properly be considered by federal courts. Such claims were "justiciable," held the court in the decision announced on March 26, 1962, abandoning the view that they were political questions outside the competence of the courts.[9]

The court stopped there. It did not go on to address the merits of the challenge to malapportionment.

Background

The Tennessee legislature had failed to reapportion itself for sixty years, despite the fact that the state constitution required decennial reapportionment after each census.

By 1960, population shifts from rural to urban regions of the state had created dramatic disparities in the pattern of representation for state house and senate seats. Justice Tom C. Clark noted the extent of the problem in his concurring opinion in *Baker v. Carr,* pointing out that two-thirds of the members of the state senate were elected by slightly more than one-third of the state's population, while two-thirds of the members of the house were elected by 40 percent of the state's voters.[10]

Appeals to the legislature to reapportion itself were futile. A suit brought in state court was rejected on the grounds that state courts — like federal courts — should stay out of such legislative matters. The city dwellers who brought the state suit then appealed to the federal courts, charging that the "unconstitutional and obsolete" apportionment system denied them the equal protection of the laws promised by the 14th Amendment.

The Opinion

Justice William J. Brennan Jr. wrote the court's opinion in *Baker v. Carr.*

With surprising ease, the majority resolved the question of federal jurisdiction over the case. The complaint clearly arose under one of the provisions of the U.S. Constitution, Brennan wrote, so it fell within the federal judicial power as defined in Article III: "An unbroken line of our precedents sustains the federal courts' jurisdiction of the subject matter of federal constitutional claims of this nature."[11]

Then, turning to the question of the voters' standing to bring the case, Brennan explained that they did have such standing because they had been deprived of an interest which they sought to defend:

> These appellants seek relief in order to protect or vindicate an interest of their own.... Their constitutional claim is, in substance, that the 1901 statute [setting up the existing districting and apportionment structure] constitutes arbitrary and capricious state action, offensive to the Fourteenth Amendment in its irrational disregard of the standard of apportionment prescribed by the State's Constitution or of any standard, effecting a gross disproportion of representation to voting population.[12]

This holding did not require the court to go on to decide the merits of the voters' allegations, Brennan wrote. But he did go on to consider the critical question of the justiciability of the issue — its suitability to judicial solution. *(Discussion of justiciability and standing, pp. 289, 291)*

Did this suit present a "political question" outside the proper scope of the Supreme Court's consideration?

The answer was "no," Brennan explained:

> ...the mere fact that the suit seeks protection of a political right does not mean it presents a political question.... It is argued that apportionment cases, whatever the actual wording of the complaint, can involve no federal constitutional right except one resting on the guaranty of a republican form of government, and that complaints based on that clause have been held to present political questions which are nonjusticiable.
> We hold that the claim pleaded here neither rests upon nor implicates the Guaranty Clause and that its justiciability is therefore not foreclosed by our decisions of cases involving that clause. The District Court misinterpreted *Colegrove v. Green* and other decisions of this Court on which it relied.[13]

(The guaranty clause to which Brennan referred is the provision in Article IV of the Constitution which states that the United States shall guarantee to every state a republican form of government. One of the first major expositions of the "political question" doctrine in the 1849 case of *Luther v. Borden* involved this guarantee. The court held its enforcement to be a political question, left to the political branches — Congress and the president — and outside judicial competence.)[14] *(Details, p. 293)*

Justice Charles E. Whittaker, who retired a week later, did not participate in the decision.

Concurring Opinions

Justices Douglas, Clark and Potter Stewart wrote concurring opinions.

Douglas emphasized the court's frequent role as protector of voting rights.

Clark would have gone on to consider the merits of the particular complaint and grant relief: "[No] one, not even the State nor the dissenters, has come up with any rational basis for Tennessee's apportionment statute."[15] Nevertheless, Clark recommended that federal courts intrude in **reapportionment matters only as a last resort.**

Stewart reiterated that the court had decided only that such 14th Amendment challenges to malapportionment were justiciable matters and that the persons bringing this case had standing to sue.

Dissenting Opinions

Justices Frankfurter and John Marshall Harlan dissented. In what was his last major opinion, Frankfurter criticized the majority for "[s]uch a massive repudiation of the experience of our whole past in asserting destructively novel judicial power...." The court had, he argued, allowed a "hypothetical claim resting on abstract assumptions" to become "the basis for affording illusory relief for a particular evil even though it foreshadows deeper and more pervasive difficulties in consequence." [16]

Frankfurter went on to say that to give judges the task of "accommodating the incommensurable factors of policy" involved in reapportionment plans was "to attribute ... omnicompetence to judges." By this decision, he wrote, the Supreme Court gave the nation's courts the power "to devise what should constitute the proper composition of the legislatures of the fifty States." The court had overlooked the fact, he added, "that there is not under our Constitution a judicial remedy for every political mischief, for every undesirable exercise of legislative power." [17]

Justice Harlan found the Tennessee plan rational, and wrote that he found "nothing in the Equal Protection Clause or elsewhere in the Federal Constitution which expressly or impliedly supports the view that state legislatures must be so structured as to reflect with approximate equality the voice of every voter.... In short, there is nothing in the Federal Constitution to prevent a State, acting not irrationally, from choosing any electoral legislative structure it thinks best suited to the interests, temper, and customs of its people." [18]

Harlan concluded with a strong criticism of the majority's action, saying that "what the Court is doing reflects more an adventure in judicial experimentation than a solid piece of constitutional adjudication." [19]

'One Person, One Vote'

The decision in *Baker v. Carr* opened the doors of federal courtrooms across the country to litigants challenging state and congressional apportionment systems. But that ruling provided no standards to guide federal judges in measuring the validity of challenged systems.

With its subsequent rulings in 1963 and 1964, the Supreme Court formulated a standard, known far and wide as the "one man, one vote" or "one person, one vote" rule.

Participating in the decisions announcing this rule were two new members of the court. After the ruling in *Baker v. Carr,* Justices Whittaker and Frankfurter both retired. President John F. Kennedy appointed Byron R. White to replace Whittaker and Arthur J. Goldberg to succeed Frankfurter.

The Rule Announced

The "one person, one vote" rule was first set out by the court almost exactly one year after its decision in *Baker v. Carr.* But the case in which the announcement came did not involve legislative districts.

In the ruling in the case of *Gray v. Sanders,* the court found that Georgia's county-unit primary system for electing state officials — a system which weighted votes to give advantage to rural districts in statewide primary elections — denied voters the equal protection of the laws.

Justice Douglas' opinion for eight members of the court rejected the state's effort to defend this weighted vote system by analogy to the electoral college system. The electoral college system was included in the Constitution because of specific historical concerns, Douglas wrote, but that inclusion "implied nothing about the use of an analogous system by a State in a statewide election." [20]

All votes in a statewide election must have equal weight, held the court:

How then can one person be given twice or 10 times the voting power of another person in a statewide election merely because he lives in a rural area or because he lives in the smallest rural county? Once the geographical unit for which a representative is to be chosen is designated, all who participate in the election are to have an equal vote — whatever their race, whatever their sex, whatever their occupation, whatever their income, and wherever their home may be in that geographical unit. This is required by the Equal Protection Clause of the Fourteenth Amendment. The concept of "we the people" under the Constitution visualizes no preferred class of voters but equality among those who meet the basic qualification. The idea that every voter is equal to every other voter in his State, when he casts his ballot in favor of one of several competing candidates, underlies many of our decisions.... The conception of political equality from the Declaration of Independence to Lincoln's Gettysburg Address, to the Fifteenth, Seventeenth, and Nineteenth Amendments can mean only one thing — one person, one vote. [21]

Justice Harlan again dissented:

The Court's holding surely ... flies in the face of history ... "one person, one vote" has never been the universally accepted political philosophy in England, the American Colonies, or in the United States.... I do not understand how, on the basis of these mere numbers, unilluminated as they are by any of the complex and subtle political factors involved, a court of law can say, except by judicial fiat, that these disparities are in themselves constitutionally invidious. [22]

The Rule Applied

The court's rulings in *Baker* and *Gray* concerned the equal weighting and counting of votes cast in state elections. In 1964, deciding the case of *Wesberry v. Sanders,* the court applied the "one person, one vote" principle to congressional districts and set equality, not rationality, as the standard for congressional redistricting.

Voters in Georgia's fifth congressional district — which included Atlanta — complained that the population of their congressional district was more than twice the ideal state average of 394,312 persons-per-district. By its failure to re-district, the state denied them equal protection of the laws, they charged. They also challenged Georgia's apportionment scheme as a violation of Article I, Section 2 of the Constitution that declares that members of the House of Representatives are to be elected "by the people."

A federal district court dismissed the case in 1962, but the Supreme Court by a 6-3 vote reversed the lower court decision in February 1964.

Justice Black, speaking for six members of the court, explained:

We hold that, construed in its historical context, the command of Art. I, Sec. 2, that Representatives be chosen 'by the People of the several States' means that as nearly as is practicable, one man's vote in a congressional election is to be worth as much as another's....

To say that a vote is worth more in one district than in another would not only run counter to our fundamental ideas of democratic government, it would cast aside the principle of a House of Representatives elected "by the People."

While it may not be possible to draw congressional districts with mathematical precision, that is no excuse for ignoring our Constitution's plain objective of making equal representation for equal numbers the fundamental goal of the House of Representatives. [23]

Black's view was sharply attacked by Justice Harlan, who dissented:

The upshot of all this is that the language of Art. I, [Sections] 2 and 4, the surrounding text, and the relevant history are all in strong and consistent direct contradiction of the Court's holding. The constitutional scheme vests in the States plenary power to regulate the conduct of elections for Representatives, and, in order to protect the Federal Government, provides for congressional supervision of the States' exercise of their power. Within this scheme, the appellants do not have the right which they assert, in the absence of provision for equal districts by the Georgia Legislature or the Congress. The constitutional right which the Court creates is manufactured out of whole cloth. [24]

Justice Black did not invoke the equal protection clause in the case. Speculation as to why Black based this ruling on historical grounds rather than on the 14th Amendment suggests that his choice was a compromise among members of the court. [25]

Four months later, however, eight members agreed on the requirements of the 14th Amendment for state reapportionment.

State Legislative Districts

By a vote of 8-1, the Supreme Court on June 15, 1964, ruled that the 14th Amendment required equally populated electoral districts for both houses of bicameral state legislatures.

This decision is known by the title of a case from Alabama, *Reynolds v. Sims.* But since the case was accompanied to the Supreme Court by a number of others concerning other state legislatures, the court's decision immediately affected reapportionment in New York, Maryland, Virginia, Delaware and Colorado as well. Ultimately, every state legislature felt the impact of *Reynolds v. Sims.*

Writing for the court what he would often describe as the most significant opinion of his judicial career, Chief Justice Earl Warren stated that the "controlling criterion" for any reapportionment plan must be equal population.[26]

The court rejected the suggestion that a state might, by analogy to the federal system, constitute one house of its legislature on the basis of population and the other on an area basis.[27]

The Equal Protection Clause required substantially equal representation of all citizens. The court did not provide any precise formula for defining "substantially equal" and left it to lower courts to work out a useful standard.

Justice Harlan — the lone dissenter — said the court's rule had no constitutional basis, and that the drafters of the 14th Amendment had not meant to give the federal government authority to intervene in the internal organization of state legislatures.

Majority Opinion. Chief Justice Warren, in the majority opinion in *Reynolds v. Sims,* set forth the reasoning behind "one person, one vote" rule with clarity and firmness:

The right to vote freely for the candidate of one's choice is of the essence of a democratic society, and any restrictions on that right strike at the heart of representative government. And the right of suffrage can be denied by a debasement of suffrage or dilution of the weight of a citizen's vote just as effectively as by wholly prohibiting the free exercise of the franchise....

Legislators represent people, not trees or acres. Legislators are elected by voters, not farms or cities or economic interests. As long as ours is a representative

---

"Legislators represent people, not trees or acres. Legislators are elected by voters, not farms or cities or economic interests."

Chief Justice Earl Warren
Reynolds v. Sims, 1964

---

form of government, and our legislatures are those instruments of government elected directly by and directly representative of the people, the right to elect legislators in a free and unimpaired fashion is a bedrock of our political system....

...The fact that an individual lives here or there is not a legitimate reason for overweighting or diluting the efficacy of his vote. The complexions of societies and civilizations change, often with amazing rapidity. A nation once primarily rural in character becomes predominantly urban. Representation schemes once fair and equitable become archaic and outdated. But

the basic principle of representative government remains, and must remain, unchanged — the weight of a citizen's vote cannot be made to depend on where he lives. Population is, of necessity, the starting point for consideration and the controlling criterion for judgment in legislative apportionment controversies. A citizen, a qualified voter, is no more nor no less so because he lives in the city or on the farm. This is the clear and strong command of our Constitution's Equal Protection Clause. This is an essential part of the concept of a government of laws and not men....

The Equal Protection Clause demands no less than substantially equal state legislative representation for all citizens, of all places as well as of all races.

We hold that as a basic constitutional standard, the Equal Protection Clause requires that the seats in both houses of a bicameral state legislature must be apportioned on a population basis. Simply stated, an individual's right to vote for state legislators is unconstitutionally impaired when its weight is in substantial fashion diluted when compared with votes of citizens living in other parts of the State.[28]

The court's opinion recognized the impossibility of **attaining mathematical precision in election district populations:**

...the Equal Protection Clause requires that a State make an honest and good faith effort to construct districts, in both houses of its legislature, as nearly of equal population as is practicable. We realize that it is a practical impossibility to arrange legislative districts so that each one has an identical number of residents, or citizens, or voters. Mathematical exactness or precision is hardly a workable constitutional requirement.[29]

Warren wrote that in applying the equal population principle:

...somewhat more flexibility may therefore be constitutionally permissible with respect to state legislative apportionment than in congressional districting.... For the present, we deem it expedient not to attempt to spell out any precise constitutional tests. What is marginally permissible in one State may be unsatisfactory in another, depending on the particular circumstances of the case. Developing a body of doctrine on a case-by-case basis appears to us to provide the most satisfactory means of arriving at detailed constitutional requirements in the area of state legislative apportionment."[30]

Dissenting Opinion. Justice Harlan again dissented, arguing that judicial intervention in reapportionment questions was "profoundly ill advised and constitutionally impermissible." This series of decisions, Harlan said, would weaken the vitality of the political system and "cut deeply into the fabric of our federalism." The court's ruling gave "support to a current mistaken view of the Constitution and the constitutional function of this Court. This view, in a nutshell, is that every major social ill in this country can find its cure in some constitutional 'principle,' and that this Court should 'take the lead' in promoting reform when other branches of government fail to act. The Constitution is not a panacea for every blot upon the public welfare, nor should this court, ordained as a judicial body, be thought of **as a haven for reform movements....**"[31]

Congressional Districts: Strict Equality

Five years elapsed between the court's admonition in *Wesberry v. Sanders,* urging states to make a good-faith effort to construct congressional districts as nearly of equal population as is practicable, and the court's next application of constitutional standards to congressional redistricting.

In 1967 the court hinted at the strict stance it would adopt two years later. With two unsigned opinions, the court sent back to Indiana and Missouri for revision those two states' redistricting plans for congressional districts — because they allowed variations of as much as 20 percent from the average district population.[32]

Two years later, Missouri's revised plan returned to the court for full review. With its decision in the case of *Kirkpatrick v. Preisler,* the court by a 6-3 vote rejected the plan. It was unacceptable, held the majority, because it allowed a variation of as much as 3.1 percent from perfectly equal population districts.[33]

The court thus made clear its strict application of "one person, one vote" to congressional redistricting. Minor deviations from the strict equal-population principle were permissible only when the state provided substantial evidence that the variation was unavoidable.

Writing for the majority, Justice Brennan declared that there was no "fixed numerical or percentage population variance small enough to be considered *de minimis* and to satisfy without question the 'as nearly as practicable' standard."[34]

Brennan continued:

> The whole thrust of the 'as nearly as practicable' approach is inconsistent with adoption of fixed numerical standards which excuse population variances without regard to the circumstances of each particular case....
>
> The extent to which equality may practicably be achieved may differ from State to State and from district to district.... Unless population variances among congressional districts are shown to have resulted despite such effort, the State must justify each variance, no matter how small....
>
> ...to consider a certain range of variances *de minimis* would encourage legislators to strive for that range rather than for equality 'as nearly as practicable.' ...to accept population variances, large or small, in order to create districts with specific interest orientations is antithetical to the basic premise of the constitutional command to provide equal representation for equal numbers of people.[35]

Justice Abe Fortas concurred with the majority but felt that the court had set a standard of "near-perfection" difficult to achieve:

> Whatever might be the merits of insistence on absolute equality if it could be obtained, the majority's pursuit of precision is a search for a will-o'-the wisp. The fact is that any solution to the apportionment and districting problem is at best an approximation because it is based upon figures which are always to some degree obsolete. No purpose is served by an insistence on precision which is unattainable because of the inherent imprecisions in the population data on which districting must be based.[36]

Justices Harlan, Stewart, and Byron R. White dissented. White called the majority's ruling "an unduly rigid and unwarranted application of the Equal Protection Clause which will unnecessarily involve the courts in the abrasive task of drawing district lines."[37] Harlan wrote that the decision transformed "a political slogan into a constitutional absolute. Strait indeed is the path of the righteous legislator. Slide rule in hand, he must avoid all thought of county lines, local traditions, politics, history, and economics, so as to achieve the magic formula: one man, one vote."[38]

In another congressional redistricting case decided the same day, the court in *Wells v. Rockefeller* rejected New York's redistricting plan as out of line with equal protection standards.

The New York plan resulted in districts of nearly equal size within regions of the state, but not of equal population throughout the state. That was unacceptable, held the court, in light of the fact that the state could not and did not claim that its legislators had made a good-faith effort to achieve precise mathematical equality among its congressional districts.

Brennan wrote again for the court:

> To accept a scheme such as New York's would permit groups of districts with defined interest orientations to be over-represented at the expense of districts with different interest orientations. Equality of population among districts in a substate is not a justification for inequality among all the districts in the State.[39]

Practical Results

The effect of this line of rulings from *Baker* through *Kirkpatrick* was felt in every state. By the end of the 1960s, 39 of the 45 states which elect more than one member of the House had redrawn their district lines. But since the new districts were based on 1960 census figures, population shifts during the decade left the new districts far from equal in population.

The redistricting following the 1970 census, however, resulted in substantial progress toward population equality among each state's congressional districts. Three hundred eighty-five of the 435 members of the House of Representatives elected in 1972 were chosen from districts which varied less than one percent from their state's average congressional district population.[40]

Equality Reaffirmed

In 1973 the court unanimously reaffirmed the strict standard for congressional districts set out in *Kirkpatrick.* The court invalidated Texas' 1971 redistricting plan which allowed a difference of almost five percent between the most populous and the least populous congressional district.[41]

Justice White, writing the opinion in the case of *White v. Weiser,* said that these differences were avoidable.

Chief Justice Warren E. Burger, Justices William H. Rehnquist and Lewis F. Powell Jr. concurred, but added that had they been members of the court in 1969, they would have dissented from the rule of strict equality set out in *Kirkpatrick v. Preisler.*

State Legislative Districts: More Leeway

Baker v. Carr began the revolution in the state legislatures of the nation, allowing federal courts to become involved in the question of malapportionment. *Reynolds v. Sims* marked the second phase in the process, establishing the "one person, one vote" standards for new legislative districting plans.

The third and longest phase of the modernization of state legislative representation was characterized by the Supreme Court's effort to resolve the tension between the goal of equal population, demanded by the 14th Amendment, and state definitions of democratic representation which often took other factors than population into account.

In this effort, which extended over a decade and a half after *Reynolds v. Sims,* the court indicated a preference for single-member, not multi-member, electoral districts; a continuing insistence that reapportionment is primarily a legislative, not a judicial, responsibility; and, since 1973, a greater tolerance of deviation from equal population for state than for congressional districts.

Multi-Member Districts

In 1965, in the case of *Fortson v. Dorsey,* the Supreme Court refused to hold unconstitutional Georgia's use of single- and multi-member districts for electing members of the state senate — a system which was challenged as intended to minimize the voting strength of certain minority groups.

Although the court held that those allegations had not been proved, Justice Brennan in the court's opinion made clear that the court was not giving blanket approval to multi-member districts:

It might well be that, designedly or otherwise, a multi-member constituency apportionment scheme, under the circumstances of a particular scheme, would operate to minimize or cancel out the voting strength of racial or political elements of the voting population. When this is demonstrated it will be time enough to consider whether the system still passes constitutional muster.[42]

The following year, the court refused to disturb a similar electoral system for Hawaii's senate, emphasizing that the task of setting up such systems was basically that of legislators, not judges.[43]

And again in 1971, in a case from Indiana, the court refused to hold that multi-member districts were *per se* unconstitutional, requiring proof that the particular districts challenged in fact operated to dilute the votes of certain groups or certain persons.[44]

Two years later, however, the court did require the disestablishment of two multi-member districts for electing members of the Texas house, holding them impermissible in light of the history of political discrimination against blacks and Mexican-Americans residing in those areas.[45]

Population Equality

Beginning in 1967, with its decision in the Florida case of *Swann v. Adams,* the court defined the outer limits of population variance for state legislative districts. In that case, the court held unconstitutional Florida's plan, which had deviations of as much as 30 and 40 percent from population equality.

Minor variations from equality would be tolerated if there were special justifications for it, held the court, but it would be left to the state to prove the justification sufficient.

Justice White wrote the opinion for the seven-man majority:

Reynolds v. Sims . . . recognized that mathematical exactness is not required in state apportionment plans. *De minimis* variations are unavoidable, but variations of 30 percent among senate districts and 40 percent among house districts can hardly be deemed *de minimis* and none of our cases suggests that differences of this magnitude will be approved without a satisfactory explanation grounded on acceptable state policy.[46]

White said that the court in *Reynolds* had limited the permissible deviations to "minor variations" brought about by "legitimate considerations incident to the effectuation of a rational state policy . . . such . . .as the integrity of political subdivisions, the maintenance of compactness and contiguity in legislative districts or the recognition of natural or historical boundary lines." [47]

Justice Harlan, joined by Justice Stewart, dissented, saying that Florida's plan made sense as a rational state policy. Harlan noted that in striking down the plan "because neither the State nor the District Court justified the relatively minor variations in population among some of the districts," the court "seems to me to stand on its head the usual rule governing this Court's approach to legislative enactments, state as well as federal, which is . . . that they come to us with a strong presumption of regularity and constitutionality." [48]

After the court's insistence in the 1969 decision in *Kirkpatrick v. Preisler* that congressional districts be precisely equal in population, doubts arose about the flexibility left to states in drawing state legislative electoral districts not absolutely equal in the number of inhabitants.

More Flexible Standards

But in 1973, the court in the case of *Mahan v. Howell* reiterated the more relaxed application of the "one person, one vote" standard to state legislative districts. The court declared that "in the implementation of the basic constitutional principle — equality of population among the districts — more flexibility was constitutionally permissible with respect to state legislative reapportionment than in congressional redistricting." [49]

Virginia's legislative reapportionment statute, enacted after the 1970 census, allowed as much as a 16.4 percent deviation from equal population in the districts from which members of the state house were elected. When this was challenged in federal court as too wide a disparity, the lower court agreed, citing *Kirkpatrick v. Preisler* and *Wells v. Rockefeller,* although both concerned congressional districts.

By a 5-3 vote, the Supreme Court reversed the lower court, with Justice William H. Rehnquist speaking for the majority. Justice Lewis F. Powell Jr. did not participate in

'One Man, One Vote' At City Hall

In several recent rulings, the Supreme Court has **extended the application of the** "one person, one vote" rule to some local, as well as state and national, electoral districts.

In 1967 the court ruled that county school board members, each representing a local school board, from districts of disparate population, were not subject to this rule because the county board performed administrative, not legislative, functions.[1]

But in the case of *Avery v. Midland County,* decided in 1968, the court ruled that when a state delegates lawmaking power to local government and provides for election by district of the officials exercising that power, those districts must be of substantially equal population.[2]

Two years later the court in 1970 ruled that the "one person, one vote" rule must be applied to any election — state or local — of persons performing governmental functions:

If one person's vote is given less weight through unequal apportionment, his right to equal voting participation is impaired just as much when he votes for a school board member as when he votes for a state legislator.... [T]he crucial consideration is the right of each qualified voter to participate on an equal footing in the election process.[3]

Three years later, however, the court held that the constitutional guarantee of equal protection did not demand that the "one person, one vote" rule be applied to special-purpose electoral districts such as those devised to regulate water supplies in the West. In such districts, the court held, states may restrict the franchise to landowners and weigh the votes of each person according to the property he owns.[4]

---

[1] *Sailors v. Board of Education,* 387 U.S. 105 (1967); see also *Dusch v. Davis,* 387 U.S. 112 (1967).

[2] *Avery v. Midland County,* 390 U.S. 474 (1968).

[3] *Hadley v. Junior College District of Metropolitan Kansas City, Mo.,* 397 U.S. 50 at 55 (1970).

[4] *Salyer Land Co. v. Tulare Water District; Associated Enterprises Inc. v. Toltec Watershed Improvement District,* 410 U.S. 743 (1973).

---

the decision. Justices Brennan, William O. Douglas and Thurgood Marshall dissented.

The court upheld the state districting plan, finding the population variance not excessive.

Justice Rehnquist cited *Reynolds v. Sims* in support of the majority's view that some deviation from equal population was permissible for state legislative districts so long as it was justified by rational state policy. He explained the reason behind the court's application of different standards to state and congressional redistricting plans:

...almost invariably, there is a significantly larger number of seats in state legislative bodies to be distributed within a State than congressional seats and ... therefore it may be feasible for a State to use political subdivision lines to a greater extent in establishing

state legislative districts while still affording adequate statewide representation....

By contrast, the court in *Wesberry v. Sanders* ... recognized no excuse for the failure to meet the objection of equal representation for equal numbers of people in congressional districting other than the practical impossibility of drawing equal districts with mathematical precision. Thus, whereas population alone has been the sole criterion of constitutionality in congressional redistricting under Art. I ... broader latitude has been afforded the State under the Equal Protection Clause in state legislative redistricting because of the considerations enumerated in *Reynolds v. Sims*.... The dichotomy between the two lines of cases has consistently been maintained....

Application of the "absolute equality" test of *Kirkpatrick* and *Wells* to state legislative redistricting may impair the normal functioning of state and local governments....

We hold that the legislature's plan for apportionment of the House of Delegates may reasonably be said to advance the rational state policy of respecting the boundaries of political subdivisions. The remaining inquiry is whether the population disparities among the districts which have resulted from the pursuit of this plan exceed constitutional limits. We conclude that they do not.[50]

Rehnquist noted, however, that the 16 percent deviation from equality "may well approach tolerable limits."

In dissent, Justice William J. Brennan Jr., joined by Justices William O. Douglas and Thurgood Marshall, argued for a stricter application of the "one person, one vote" principle, saying:

The principal question presented for our decision is whether on the facts of this case an asserted state interest in preserving the integrity of county lines can justify the resulting substantial deviations from population equality....

...The Constitution does not permit a State to relegate considerations of equality to secondary status and reserve as the primary goal of apportionment the service of some other state interest.[51]

Several months later in 1973, the court, in the case of *Gaffney v. Cummings,* upheld Connecticut's reapportionment of its legislature, despite a maximum deviation of 7.8 percent from mathematical equality in the population of the districts.[52]

Justice White wrote for the majority that state legislative reapportionment plans need not place an "unrealistic emphasis on raw population figures" when to do so might "submerge ... other considerations and itself furnish a ready tool for ignoring factors that in day-to-day operation are important to an acceptable representation and apportionment arrangement."[53]

White also warned that strict adherence to arithmetic could frustrate achievement of the goal of fair and effective representation "by making the standards of reapportionment so difficult to satisfy that the reapportionment task is recurringly removed from legislative hands and performed by federal courts...."[54]

He continued:

We doubt that the Fourteenth Amendment requires repeated displacement of otherwise appropriate state decision making in the name of essentially minor deviations from perfect census population equality that no one, with confidence, can say will deprive any person of fair and effective representation in his state legislature.

That the Court was not deterred by the hazards of the political thicket when it undertook to adjudicate the reapportionment cases does not mean that it should become bogged down in a vast, intractable apportionment slough, particularly when there is little if anything to be accomplished by doing so.[55]

The same day it announced its decision upholding Connecticut's reapportionment in *Gaffney*, the court in the case of *White v. Regester* upheld a similar plan for the Texas legislature, despite a 9.9 percent variation in the populations of the largest and smallest districts. In the same case, however, the court required revision of the plan to eliminate two multi-member districts in areas with histories of discrimination against racial and ethnic minority-group voters.[56]

Court Plans: A Closer Look

Two years later, in 1975, the court distinguished between the standards it applied to state redistricting plans drawn by legislators and to those drawn by judges. Stricter standards applied to the latter.

In the North Dakota case of *Chapman v. Meier*, the court disapproved a court-ordered plan for the state legisla-

ture which allowed up to 20 percent population variance among districts.[57]

Court-ordered redistricting plans should not include multi-member districts or allow more than a minimal variation from the goal of equal population, held the court, unless unique state features or significant state policy justified those characteristics.

Justice Harry A. Blackmun spoke for the unanimous court, stating that "absent particularly pressing features calling for multi-member districts, a United States district court should refrain from imposing them upon a State."[58]

A 20-percent population variance, he continued, was not permissible "simply because there is no particular racial or political group whose voting power is minimized or cancelled." Moreover, Blackmun stated, neither sparse population nor the geographic division of the state by the Missouri River, "warrant[ed] departure from population equality." [59]

Reaffirming this position in the 1977 case of *Connor v. Finch*, the court, by a 7-1 vote, overturned a court-ordered reapportionment plan for the Mississippi state legislature because it allowed population variations of up to 16.5 percent in senate districts and of up to 19.3 percent among house districts. The population variance was defended as necessary to preserve the integrity of county lines within legislative districts.[60]

But the court found this insufficient in light of the stricter standards set out in *Chapman v. Meier* for court-ordered plans.

Footnotes

[1] For general background, see Congressional Quarterly, *Guide to U.S. Elections* (Washington: Congressional Quarterly 1975), pp. 523-539.

[2] *Wood v. Broom*, 287 U.S. 1 (1932).

[3] *Colegrove v. Green*, 328 U.S. 549 (1946).

[4] Id. at 552, 553-554, 556.

[5] Id. at 564.

[6] Id. at 574.

[7] *Gomillion v. Lightfoot*, 364 U.S. 339 (1960).

[8] Id. at 346, 347.

[9] *Baker v. Carr*, 369 U.S. 186 (1962).

[10] Id. at 253.

[11] Id. at 201.

[12] Id. at 207.

[13] Id. at 209.

[14] *Luther v. Borden*, 7 How. 1 (1849).

[15] *Baker v. Carr*, 369 U.S. 186 at 258 (1962).

[16] Id. at 267.

[17] Id. at 268-270.

[18] Id. at 332, 334.

[19] Id. at 339.

[20] *Gray v. Sanders*, 372 U.S. 368 at 378 (1963).

[21] Id. at 379-381.

[22] Id. at 384, 388.

[23] *Wesberry v. Sanders*, 376 U.S. 1 at 7-8 (1964).

[24] Id. at 42.

[25] Richard O. Claude, *The Supreme Court and the Electoral Process* (Baltimore: The John Hopkins Press, 1970), pp. 213n.-214n.

[26] *Reynolds v. Sims*, 377 U.S. 533 at 567 (1964).

[27] Id. at 573-574.

[28] Id. at 555, 562, 567-568.

[29] Id. at 577.

[30] Id. at 578.

[31] Id. at 624-625.

[32] *Duddleston v. Grills*, 385 U.S. 455 (1967); *Kirkpatrick v. Preisler*, 385 U.S. 450 (1967).

[33] *Kirkpatrick v. Preisler*, 394 U.S. 526 (1969).

[34] Id. at 530.

[35] Id. at 530-531, 533.

[36] Id. at 538-539.

[37] Id. at 553.

[38] Id. at 549-550.

[39] *Wells v. Rockefeller*, 394 U.S. 542 at 546 (1969).

[40] Congressional Quarterly, *Guide to U.S. Elections* (Washington: Congressional Quarterly, 1975), p. 538.

[41] *White v. Weiser*, 412 U.S. 783 (1973).

[42] *Fortson v. Dorsey*, 379 U.S. 433 at 439 (1965).

[43] *Burns v. Richardson*, 384 U.S. 73 (1966).

[44] *Whitcomb v. Chavis*, 403 U.S. 124 (1971).

[45] *White v. Regester*, 412 U.S. 755 (1973).

[46] *Swann v Adams*, 385 U.S. 440 at 444 (1967).

[47] Ibid.

[48] Id. at 447.

[49] *Mahan v. Howell*, 410 U.S. 315 at 321 (1973).

[50] Id. at 321-323, 328.

[51] Id. at 339-340.

[52] *Gaffney v. Cummings*, 412 U.S. 736 (1973).

[53] Id. at 749.

[54] Ibid.

[55] Id. at 749-750.

[56] *White v. Regester*, 412 U.S. 755 (1973).

[57] *Chapman v. Meier*, 420 U.S. 1 (1975).

[58] Id. at 19.

[59] Id. at 24-25.

[60] *Connor v. Finch*, 431 U.S. 407 (1977).

Freedom of Political Association

The freedom to espouse any political belief and to associate with others sharing that belief is, in the words of the modern Supreme Court, "the core of those activities protected by the First Amendment."[1]

Judicial recognition of this freedom is exclusively a development of the mid-20th century. A corollary of the First Amendment freedoms of speech and belief, the judicially-enunciated right of political association traces its origin to many of the post-World War I rulings in which the court first attempted to reconcile the government's need to protect itself against internal subversion with the First Amendment protection for free speech.

This freedom is not absolute, the court has made clear, condoning its curtailment, especially during times of national peril when the line between freedom of political association and treasonable conspiracy becomes blurred.

In its longest series of rulings on this freedom — those involving the anti-subversive programs of the Cold War era — the court labored to strike the proper balance between individual freedom and national security. If traced decision by decision, the constitutional freedom seems ill-defined.

But the court by the end of that effort — which consumed almost two decades — seemed firm on one point: individuals have a constitutional right not to be penalized simply through guilt by association, simply because they are members of a particular group. Any government-imposed penalty may properly be imposed only after it is shown that their association involves active, knowing participation in efforts to bring about violent revolution.

Internal Security Laws

The nation's first internal security laws were enacted within the same decade as the Bill of Rights. The Alien and Sedition Acts of 1798, among their other controversial provisions, set severe penalties for persons found guilty of criticizing the government or government officials. Convictions under these laws — some obtained before Supreme Court justices sitting as circuit judges — aroused public indignation, but the laws expired before they were ever challenged before the Supreme Court itself.

During the Civil War, military officials imposed many restrictions upon individual rights and expression. But, again, the constitutionality of those actions which seemed to infringe First Amendment rights was never questioned before the court.

The Supreme Court first found itself face to face with the question of permissible government restrictions upon political belief and expression in 1919. During World War I, Congress passed the Espionage Act of 1917 and the Sedition

Act of 1918 to penalize persons who spoke or published statements with the intent of interfering with the nation's military success, or with the effect of bringing the flag, the Constitution, the government or the military uniform into disrepute, or of promoting the cause of the enemy. Hundreds of persons were convicted of violating these laws.

In a series of cases decided after the end of the war, the court upheld these laws but began to formulate tests to gauge when such restriction by the government of speech and expression was permissible.[2]

Increasing concern about the threat of communism, which intensified after the end of World War II, sparked the passage of federal laws intended to protect the nation against communist subversion. These laws restricted the exercise — by persons holding certain views — of the freedom of political belief, expression and association. In the long line of cases which arose under these laws the modern court attempted to reconcile the demands of political freedom with the requirements of internal security.

The First Decisions

The famous if often-disregarded "clear and present danger" test for determining when official restriction or punishment may be imposed upon the exercise of the right to speak was set out by the court in 1919 in the case of *Schenck v. United States.*

Schenck was convicted under the Espionage Act for mailing out circulars to men eligible for the military draft urging them to resist the draft; which he described as unconstitutional despotism.

Although the court upheld his conviction, finding that his actions constituted a clear and present threat that illegal action would result, it did set out a famous standard for determining when such restriction by the government was permissible. Writing for the unanimous court, Justice Oliver Wendell Holmes Jr. declared:

> The most stringent protection of free speech would not protect a man in falsely shouting fire in a theatre and causing a panic. It does not even protect a man from an injunction against uttering words that may have all the effect of force. . . . The question in every case is whether the words used are used in such circumstances and are of such a nature as to create a clear and present danger that they will bring about the substantive evils that Congress has a right to prevent.[3]

Finding similar danger in the actions of two other men convicted under that law, the court in the same month — March 1919 — upheld their convictions.

Later in 1919 — and again in 1920 — Holmes dissented with Justice Louis D. Brandeis when the court upheld three more convictions under the World War I Espionage and Sedition Acts.

In these cases, to the dismay of Justices Holmes and Brandeis, the court adopted a more relaxed standard for government curtailment of free expression of political ideas. The majority espoused the view that the "bad tendency" of an individual's speech or action, rather than the actual threat of danger, was sufficient to justify punishment. The new test, stated the majority, did not require that an utterance's "effect or the persons affected . . . be shown. . . . The tendency of the articles and their efficacy were enough for offense . . ." [4]

In dissent, Justice Brandeis opposed this "bad tendency" test both because it eliminated consideration of the speaker's intent and because it ignored the relevance of the likelihood that danger would result. He restated the "clear and present danger" test in the case of *Schaefer v. United States,* saying:

> This is a rule of reason. Correctly applied, it will preserve the right of free speech both from suppression by tyrannous majorities and from abuse by irresponsible, fanatical minorities. [5]

Gitlow and *Whitney*: State Restrictions

The 1920s were a period of intolerance in the United States. Many states, following the example of Congress, passed laws penalizing persons for expressing or acting upon views of political truth which were perceived as subversive. In 1925 and again in 1927, the court upheld convictions of persons holding such views. In both instances, Holmes and Brandeis disagreed with the majority's view that the clear and present danger test had no application at all to laws that punished advocacy of the forcible overthrow of government.

In the case of *Gitlow* v. *United States* the court in 1925 upheld the conviction of Benjamin Gitlow, a leader of the left wing of the Socialist Party, for violating provisions of the New York criminal anarchy statute by publishing thousands of copies of a manifesto setting out his beliefs.

The decision is particularly important in it the court for the first time assumed that the First Amendment freedoms of speech and the press protected from abridgment by Congress were among the fundamental personal liberties protected by the 14th Amendment against impairment by the states.

But the court made clear that the First Amendment "does not confer an absolute right to speak or publish, without responsibility, whatever one may chose." [6]

And, it emphasized, challenges to state laws alleged to restrict the freedom of speech or the press must overcome a strong presumption in favor of the constitutionality of state legislation. If the state thought the statute necessary, and the court agreed, then the only other question was whether the language used or the action punished was prohibited by the state law.

In 1927 the court upheld the conviction of Anita Whitney — who happened to be the niece of former Supreme Court Justice Stephen J. Field — for violating the California Syndicalism Act of 1919 by her part in organizing the California Communist Labor Party. Whitney had participated in the convention setting up the state party and was an alternate member of its state executive committee. With the decision in *Whitney v. California,* the majority of the court appeared to allow persons to be punished simply for associating with groups which espoused potentially illegal acts.

Justices Holmes and Brandeis agreed in upholding the conviction, because the clear and present danger test had not been used as part of Whitney's defense at trial. But in a concurring opinion that often read like a dissent, Brandeis challenged laws which exalted order over liberty:

> Those who won our independence by revolution were not cowards. They did not fear political change. They did not exalt order at the cost of liberty. To courageous, self-reliant men, with confidence in the power of free and fearless reasoning applied through the processes of popular government, no danger flowing from speech can be deemed clear and present, unless the incidence of the evil apprehended is so imminent that it may befall before there is opportunity for full discussion. If there be time to expose through discussion the falsehood and fallacies, to avert the evil by the processes of education, the remedy to be applied is more speech, not enforced silence. Only an emergency can justify repression. Such must be the rule if authority is to be reconciled with freedom. [7]

Enlarging Freedom: 1937

During the decade of the 1930s, the Supreme Court, now under the leadership of Chief Justice Charles Evans Hughes, extended *Gitlow's* protection of First Amendment freedoms against state action, while it repudiated the guilt-by-association rule which it seemed to adopt in *Whitney.*

In 1931 the court reversed the conviction of Yetta Stromberg, a supervisor in a youth camp operated by the Young Communist League in California, for violating the state law prohibiting display of a red flag as an "emblem of opposition to organized government." Such a flag was raised by Stromberg each morning at the camp for a flag-salute ceremony. In holding the state law invalid under the due process guarantee of the 14th Amendment, the court ignored Stromberg's Communist Party affiliation. [8]

Six years later, in 1937, the court overturned the conviction of a man named De Jonge for violating Oregon's criminal syndicalism law when he presided over a public meeting called by the Communist Party to protest police brutality in a longshoreman's strike. That same year, the court reversed the conviction of a Communist organizer in Georgia for attempting to recruit members and distributing literature about the party. [9]

In each case the court focused upon the actions of the individual, emphasizing personal guilt rather than guilt by association. In the court's opinion in De Jonge's case, Chief Justice Hughes wrote that the state could not punish a person making a lawful speech simply because the speech was sponsored by an allegedly "subversive" organization.

Hughes' opinion made no reference to the "clear and present danger" test. He assumed that incitement to violence would not be protected by the First Amendment. The essence of his opinion for the unanimous court was an affirmation of the political value of the rights of free speech and association:

> The greater the importance of safeguarding the community from incitements to the overthrow of our institutions by force and violence, the more imperative is the need to preserve inviolate the constitutional rights of free speech, free press and free assembly in order to maintain the opportunity for free political

discussion, to the end that government may be responsive to the will of the people and that changes, if desired, may be obtained by peaceful means. Therein lies the security of the Republic, the very foundation of constitutional government.... The question, if the

rights of free speech and peaceable assembly are to be preserved, is not as to the auspices under which the meeting is held but as to its purpose; not as to the relations of the speakers, but whether their utterances transcend the bounds of the freedom of speech....[10]

Communism and Cold War

World communism posed a double-edged threat to the survival of the American system.

Militarily, the spread of communist-dominated regimes across the globe posed the most serious external challenge the West had ever faced.

And ideologically, the appeal of communist theory to some in the United States resulted in enactment of laws intended to curtail the advocacy of those ideas and penalize those who espoused them. Some observers of this reaction wondered if legislators at home would in fact strangle the very freedoms which military and diplomatic personnel abroad were working to preserve.

Justice William O. Douglas wrote in 1951, reflecting this concern:

> In days of great tension when feelings run high, it is a temptation to take shortcuts by borrowing from the totalitarian techniques of our opponents. But when we do, we set in motion a subversive influence of our own design that destroys us from within.[11]

The three major federal laws enacted to discourage the growth of communist-affiliated organizations in the United States were the Smith Act of 1940, the McCarran Act of 1950 and the Communist Control Act of 1954.

The Smith Act made it a crime to advocate the violent overthrow of the government or to organize or to belong to any group advocating such revolutionary action. The McCarran Act required all communist-action or communist-front groups to register with the Justice Department and disclose their membership lists; that law further penalized members of such groups by prohibiting their holding of government or defense-related jobs or using U.S. passports. The Communist Control Act of 1954 declared that the Communist Party was an instrument of treasonable conspiracy against the U.S. government and thus deprived of all the rights and privileges of political parties and legal entities in the United States.

Debate over the constitutionality of these laws — and the loyalty-security programs and oath requirements which accompanied them — resounded frequently in the nation's courtrooms, including that of the Supreme Court. One's conclusion turned upon one's view of communism — was it a valid political movement, espousal of which and association with which was protected by the First Amendment? Or was it a treasonable conspiracy, which the Constitution itself viewed as punishable?[12]

In the first decade of the Cold War, the Supreme Court — reflecting the mood of the nation — generally upheld the provisions and application of these laws. In so doing, the majority avoided ruling directly on the challenge that they impermissibly abridged the First Amendment guarantee of freedom of political association.

Then, beginning in 1957, as the Cold War thawed, the court began to restrict their application, finding them often used in too sweeping a fashion. The Constitution specifies

that no one shall be found guilty of treason without evidence of overt treasonous acts. The Supreme Court began to insist that these internal security laws be used only to penalize persons who knowingly and actively sought to promote communist revolution in the United States, not simply to punish persons who had at some time found other social and economic or philosophical tenets of the movement attractive.

In the decade from 1957 through 1967, the coalescence of a libertarian majority on the court under Chief Justice Earl Warren resulted in decisions which forced the government to cease prosecuting persons under the Smith Act, to abandon its effort to force registration of the Communist Party and other Communist-affiliated groups, and to cease denying passports and defense-industry jobs to members of such groups.

In addition, the court — which had earlier condoned the use of loyalty oaths by state and local governments attempting to ensure the loyalty of their employees — struck down many such oaths as improper restrictions upon the freedom to believe and to speak freely and to associate with others of like belief.

The loyalty-oath controversies stemmed from the requirement in Article VI of the Constitution requiring state and federal officeholders to swear to uphold the Constitution of the United States. Congress and state legislatures, however, had imposed other oaths deemed appropriate as a condition of public office.

The Smith Act

The Alien Registration Act of 1940 required all aliens living in the United States to register with the government; any found to have past ties to "subversive organizations" could be deported. *(Box, p. 503)*

But Title I of that act — the Smith Act — affected citizens as well as aliens. Intended to thwart communist activity in the United States, the measure was the nation's first peacetime sedition law since the infamous Sedition Act of 1798. Yet it attracted little attention at the time of its passage in 1940. Thomas I. Emerson observes that: "Enactment of the bill reflected not so much a deliberate national determination that the measure was necessary to protect internal security as an unwillingness of members of Congress to vote against legislation directed at the Communist Party." [13]

The Smith Act made it a crime "to knowingly or willfully advocate, abet, advise, or teach the duty, necessity, desirability, or propriety of overthrowing or destroying any government in the United States by force or violence...." It forbade the publication or display of printed matter teaching or advocating forcible overthrow of the government.

And in language directly curtailing the freedom of association, the law made it a crime to organize any group teaching, advocating or encouraging the overthrow or destruction of government by force or to become a "knowing" member of any organization or group dedicated to the violent overthrow of any government in the United States.

In 1948 the government indicted eleven leaders of the Communist Party in the United States, charging them with violating the Smith Act by conspiring to form groups teaching the overthrow of the government by force or violence. The eleven were convicted after a long and sensational trial.

In upholding the convictions, Judge Learned Hand spoke for the federal court of appeals and used a "sliding scale" rule for applying the clear-and-present-danger test in sedition cases: "In each case [courts] must ask whether the gravity of the 'evil,' discounted by its improbability, justifies such invasion of free speech as is necessary to avoid the danger," Hand said.[14]

The Act Upheld: Dennis

In 1951 the Supreme Court by a vote of 6-2 upheld the convictions — and the constitutionality of the Smith Act. Justice Tom C. Clark did not take part in the court's decision in *Dennis v. United States.* The eight voting members of the court disagreed widely over the proper way to measure the validity of sedition laws against the restraints they placed on First Amendment freedoms of expression and association.

Chief Justice Fred M. Vinson, speaking for Justices Stanley F. Reed, Harold H. Burton and Sherman Minton, gave lip service to the "clear and present danger" test but seemed in fact to apply the "sliding scale" rule. The Smith Act, wrote Vinson, did not allow persons to be punished simply for peaceful study and discussion of revolutionary concepts: "Congress did not intend to eradicate the free discussion of political theories, to destroy the traditional rights of Americans to discuss and evaluate ideas without fear of governmental sanction." [15]

Yet, on the other hand, the Chief Justice wrote:

Overthrow of the Government by force and violence is certainly a substantial enough interest for the Government to limit speech. Indeed, this is the ultimate value of any society, for if a society cannot protect its very structure from armed internal attack, it must follow that no subordinate value can be protected. If, then, this interest may be protected, the literal problem which is presented is what has been meant by the use of the phrase "clear and present danger" of the utterances bringing about the evil within the power of Congress to punish.

Obviously, the words cannot mean that before the Government may act, it must wait until the *putsch* is about to be executed, the plans have been laid and the signal is awaited. If Government is aware that a group aiming at its overthrow is attempting to indoctrinate its members and to commit them to a course whereby they will strike when the leaders feel the circumstances permit, action by the Government is required.... Certainly an attempt to overthrow the Government by force, even though doomed from the outset because of inadequate numbers or power of the revolutionists is a sufficient evil for Congress to prevent....

The damage which such attempts create both physically and politically to a nation makes it impossible to measure the validity in terms of the probability of success....

The formation ... of such a highly organized conspiracy, with rigidly disciplined members subject to call when the leaders ... felt that the time had come for action, coupled with the inflammable nature of world conditions ... convince us that their convictions were justified.... And this analysis disposes of the contention that a conspiracy to advocate, as distinguished from the advocacy itself, cannot be constitutionally restrained, because it comprises only the preparation. It is the existence of the conspiracy which creates the danger.... If the ingredients of the reaction are present we cannot bind the Government to wait until the catalyst is added....

...Petitioners intended to overthrow the Government of the United States as speedily as the circumstances would permit. Their conspiracy to organize the Communist Party and to teach and advocate the overthrow of the Government of the United States by force and violence created a "clear and present danger" of an attempt to overthrow the Government by force and violence. They were properly and constitutionally convicted for violation of the Smith Act.[16]

In a lengthy concurring opinion, Justice Felix Frankfurter observed:

Suppressing advocates of overthrow inevitably will also silence critics who do not advocate overthrow but fear that their criticism may be so construed. No matter how clear we may be that the defendants now before us are preparing to overthrow our Government at the propitious moment, it is self-delusion to think that we can punish them for their advocacy without adding to the risks run by loyal citizens who honestly believe in some of the reforms these defendants advance. It is a sobering fact that in sustaining the convictions before us we can hardly escape restriction on the interchange of ideas.[17]

First Amendment guarantees must be balanced against the nation's need to protect itself, Frankfurter stated:

The appellants maintain that they have a right to advocate a political theory, so long, at least, as their advocacy does not create an immediate danger of obvious magnitude to the very existence of our present scheme of society. On the other hand, the Government asserts the right to safeguard the security of the Nation by such a measure as the Smith Act. Our judgment is thus solicited on a conflict of interests of the utmost concern to the well-being of the country.[18]

The responsibility for reconciling this conflict of values lay primarily with Congress, not the court, wrote Frankfurter. The court should only set aside the laws reflecting the judgment of Congress in such matters if it found no reasonable basis for the judgment, or if it found the law too indefinite to meet the demands of due process or breaching the separation of powers. The court was responsible for ensuring fair procedures in the enforcement of the law and for requiring substantial proof to justify conviction, but "[b]eyond these powers we must not go; we must scrupulously observe the narrow limits of judicial authority even though self-restraint is alone set over us." [19]

Justice Robert H. Jackson, in his concurring opinion, declared that the "clear and present danger" test was inadequate when applied to laws intended to curtail the spread of the communist conspiracy:

The authors of the clear and present danger test never applied it to a case like this, nor would I. If applied as it is proposed here, it means that the Communist plotting is protected during its period of incubation; its preliminary stages of organization and preparation are immune from the law; the Government can move only after imminent action is manifest, when it would, of course, be too late.[20]

The law of conspiracy was "an awkward and inept remedy" when applied to the threat of subversion presented by the Communist Party, which Jackson described as "a state within a state, an authoritarian dictatorship within a republic." But despite the awkwardness of the instrument, Jackson wrote, he found no constitutional reason for denying the government its use: "There is no constitutional right to gang up on the Government."[21]

Justices Hugo L. Black and William O. Douglas dissented. Black argued that the conspiracy section of the Smith Act should be held void as a prior restraint on the exercise of First Amendment freedoms of speech and the press. Black noted that the eleven Communist leaders had not been charged with an actual attempt to overthrow the government but only with agreeing "to assemble and to talk and publish certain ideas at a later date. The indictment is that they conspired to organize the Communist Party and to use speech or newspapers ... to teach and advocate the forcible overthrow of the Government. No matter how it is worded, this is a virulent form of prior censorship of speech and press, which I believe the First Amendment forbids."[22]

Douglas also reminded his colleagues that the defendants were not on trial for conspiring to overthrow the government, but only for organizing groups advocating its overthrow. He warned of the "vice of treating speech as the equivalent of overt acts of a treasonable or seditious character," noting that the Constitution allowed punishment for treason only upon evidence of overt treasonable acts:

[N]ever until today has anyone seriously thought that the ancient law of conspiracy could constitutionally be used to turn speech into seditious conduct. Yet that is precisely what is suggested. ... We deal here with speech alone, not with speech *plus* acts of sabotage or unlawful conduct. Not a single seditious act is charged in the indictment. ...

Free speech has occupied an exalted position because of the high service it has given our society. Its protection is essential to the very existence of a democracy. ... We have founded our political system on it. It has been the safeguard of every religious, political, philosophical, economic, and racial group amongst us. We have counted on it to keep us from embracing what is cheap and false; we have trusted the common sense of our people to choose the doctrine true to our genius and to reject the rest. ... We have above all else feared the political censor. ...

There comes a time when even speech loses its constitutional immunity. Speech innocuous one year may at another time fan such destructive flames that it must be halted in the interests of the safety of the Republic. That is the meaning of the clear and present danger test. When conditions are so critical that there will be no time to avoid the evil that the speech threatens, it is time to call a halt. Otherwise, free speech which is the strength of the Nation will be the cause of its destruction.

Aliens and Communism

Congress, by virtue of its control over immigration and naturalization, has virtually unlimited power to regulate the activities of aliens in the United States and to deport those it finds undesirable. But in several decisions, the modern Supreme Court has curtailed this power when it is used to penalize aliens for membership in the Communist Party.

Party membership alone — without evidence of the member's advocacy of forcible or violent overthrow of the government — was insufficient reason to revoke an individual's naturalization, the court ruled in 1943. By a 6-3 vote in the case of *Schneiderman v. United States,* the court reversed the government's decision to revoke naturalization papers granted to William Schneiderman in 1927 when he was a member of the Communist Party.[1]

The Alien Registration Act of 1940 provided for deportation of aliens who were members of the Communist Party. In 1952 the court upheld the application of this provision even to aliens whose membership had terminated before the 1940 law took effect.[2]

Congress included similar provisions in the Internal Security Act of 1950 and the Immigration and Nationality Act of 1952.

In 1954 the court upheld deportation of a resident alien because of his Communist Party membership, even though it was not clear that he was aware of the party's advocacy of the violent overthrow of the government. Congress, said the court, had virtually unrestricted power to deport aliens.[3]

But in 1957 and 1963, the court applied stricter standards to similar deportation decisions. In the cases of *Rowoldt v. Perfetto* and *Gastelum-Quinones v. Kennedy,* the court required the government to prove not only that the alien was a member of the party but also that he understood the political implications of that membership — before it might permissibly order him to leave the country.[4]

Writing for the court in the *Gastelum-Quinones* case, Justice Arthur J. Goldberg explained:

... there is a great practical and legal difference between those who firmly attach themselves to the Communist Party being aware of all of the aims and purposes attributed to it, and those who temporarily join the Party, knowing nothing of its international relationships and believing it to be a group solely trying to remedy unsatisfactory social or economic conditions, carry out trade-union objectives, eliminate racial discrimination, combat unemployment, or alleviate distress and poverty. ...[5]

[1] *Schneiderman v. United States,* 320 U.S. 118 (1943).
[2] *Harisiades v. Shaughnessy,* 342 U.S. 580 (1952).
[3] *Galvan v. Press,* 347 U.S. 522 (1954).
[4] *Rowoldt v. Perfetto,* 355 U.S. 115 (1957); *Gastelum-Quinones v. Kennedy,* 374 U.S. 469 (1963).
[5] *Gastelum-Quinones v. Kennedy,* 374 U.S. 469 at 473 (1963).

Yet free speech is the rule, not the exception. The restraint to be constitutional must be based on more than fear, on more than passionate opposition... on more than a revolted dislike for its contents....

Free speech — the glory of our system of government — should not be sacrificed on anything less than plain and objective proof of danger that the evil advocated is imminent. On this record no one can say that petitioners and their converts are in such a strategic position as to have even the slightest chance of achieving their aims.[23]

In the wake of the *Dennis* decision, new Smith Act conspiracy prosecutions were brought involving 121 defendants — all second-rank U.S. Communist Party officials. Other prosecutions were also brought against individuals for their party membership. Convictions were secured in every case brought to trial between 1951 and 1956. The courts of appeal affirmed the convictions and the Supreme Court denied petitions for review.

Strict Standards of Proof: *Yates*

Late in 1955, however, the court agreed to review the convictions of 14 persons charged with Smith Act violations.

The decision of the court in these cases, generally known by the name of one, *Yates v. United States,* was announced in June 1957. By imposing strict standards of proof upon the government in such prosecutions, the court effectively curtailed further use of the Smith Act to prosecute members of the American Communist Party. The decision marked a major shift in the court's attitude toward the Smith Act, although it left untouched its earlier declaration in *Dennis* that the act was constitutinal.

The defendants who brought before the court the cases of *Yates v. United States, Schneiderman v. United States* and *Richmond v. United States,* were charged with organizing and participating in a conspiracy, namely the Communist Party of the United States, to advocate the overthrow of the government by force.

By a 6-1 vote, the Supreme Court in the *Yates* decision found that the government had waited too long to indict these persons for their involvement in the organization of the party in the United States, that the trial judge had erred in his instructions to the jury concerning what they must find to convict the defendants on the advocacy charges, and that the evidence in several cases was insufficient to prove the charges. The court reversed all the convictions, acquitting those of the defendants against whom the evidence was insufficient and ordering new trials for the others. Not participating in the ruling were Justice William J. Brennan Jr. and Justice Charles E. Whittaker.[24]

The majority took a narrow view of the scope of the Smith Act provision making it unlawful to organize a group advocating violent overthrow of the government. The majority, explained Justice John Marshall Harlan in the court's opinion, defined "organize" in respect to the formation of the U.S. Communist Party as an activity that took place in 1945 with the party's founding in this country, rejecting the government's definition of "organize" as an ongoing process. Because the defendants were not indicted on this charge until 1951, the three-year statute of limitations on such charges rendered that part of the indictment invalid, held the court.

Harlan wrote:

Stated most simply, the problem is to choose between two possible answers to the question: when was the Communist Party "organized"? Petitioners contend that the only natural answer to the question is the formation date — in this case, 1945. The Government would have us answer the question by saying that the Party today is still not completely "organized"; that "organizing" is a continuing process that does not end until the entity is dissolved....

We conclude ... that since the Communist Party came into being in 1945, and the indictment was not returned until 1951, the three-year statute of limitations had run on the "organizing" charge, and required the withdrawal of that part of the indictment from the jury's consideration.[25]

Furthermore, held the court, the trial judge had misinterpreted the court's meaning in the *Dennis* decision when he instructed the jury. He failed to distinguish properly between advocacy of an abstract doctrine, a protected activity, and advocacy intended to promote unlawful action, a punishable activity under the Smith Act. In restating Vinson's ruling in *Dennis,* Justice Harlan discarded the clear and present danger test altogether. In *Dennis,* he wrote, the punishable advocacy did not create any danger of immediate revolution but "was aimed at building up a seditious group and maintaining it in readiness for action at a propitious time." [26]

Harlan continued:

In failing to distinguish between advocacy of forcible overthrow as an abstract doctrine and advocacy of action to that end, the District Court appears to have been led astray by the holding in *Dennis* that advocacy of violent action to be taken at some future time was enough.... The District Court apparently thought that *Dennis* obliterated the traditional dividing line between advocacy of abstract doctrine and advocacy of action....

The essence of the *Dennis* holding was that indoctrination of a group in preparation for future violent action, as well as exhortation to immediate action, by advocacy found to be directed to "action for the accomplishment" of forcible overthrow, to violence as "a rule or principle of action," and employing "language of incitement," ... is not constitutionally protected when the group is of sufficient size and cohesiveness, is sufficiently oriented towards action, and other circumstances are such as reasonable to justify apprehension that action will occur.

This is quite a different thing from the view of the District Court here that mere doctrinal justification of forcible overthrow, if engaged in with the intent to accomplish overthrow, is punishable *per se* under the Smith Act. That sort of advocacy, even though uttered with the hope that it may ultimately lead to violent revolution, is too remote from concrete action to be regarded as the kind of indoctrination preparatory to action which was condemned in *Dennis....*

The essential distinction is that those to whom the advocacy is addressed must be urged to *do* something, now or in the future, rather than merely to *believe* in something....

We recognize that distinctions between advocacy and teaching of abstract doctrines, with evil intent, and that which is directed to stirring people to action, are often subtle and difficult to grasp, for in a broad sense, as Mr. Justice Holmes said. . . "Every idea is an incitement." But the very subtlety of these distinctions required the most clear and explicit instructions with reference to them. . . .[27]

The court, wrote Harlan, also found the evidence of advocacy geared to action deficient in a number of the cases: "however much one may abhor even the abstract preaching of forcible overthrow or believe that forcible overthrow is the ultimate purpose to which the Communist Party is dedicated, it is upon the evidence in the record that the petitioners must be judged in this case."[28]

Justices Black and Douglas concurred in part and dissented in part. Both felt that all the prosecutions of these defendants should be dropped because the Smith Act provisions upon which the charges were based "abridge freedom of speech, press and assembly in violation of the First Amendment."[29]

"I believe that the First Amendment forbids Congress to punish people for talking about public affairs, whether or not such discussion incites to action, legal or illegal," Black wrote.[30]

In a separate dissenting opinion Justice Clark said that all of the convictions should be upheld, in line with *Dennis*. Clark noted that although the Communists in *Yates* were lower in the hierarchy than those defendants in *Dennis*, they served "in the same army and were engaged in the same mission."[31]

The *Yates* requirement that the government show a connection between advocacy and action, between participation in the Communist Party and forcible overthrow of the government, ended most Smith Act prosecutions. The government decided to drop charges against those of the *Yates* defendants who, in light of the court's ruling, could have been retried.

Membership Prosecutions

Despite the court's narrow view of the Smith Act's "organizing" and "advocating" provisions, prosecutions remained possible under the clause which forbade "knowing" membership in any group advocating forcible overthrow of the government. When coupled with the registration provisions of the 1950 McCarran Act, this provision seemed to constitute compulsory self-incrimination in violation of the Fifth Amendment guarantee against such coercion. *(McCarran Act, pp. 505-506)*

In 1961, the Supreme Court for the first time reviewed convictions of persons under the membership clause. In those rulings, the court upheld the constitutionality of the provision, but measured the government's proof in such cases against the strict *Yates* standard of evidence.

In the case of *Scales v. United States,* the court affirmed the conviction of Junius Scales, director of a Communist training school, and upheld the constitutionality of the membership clause. The vote was 5-4. Justices Black, Douglas, Brennan and Chief Justice Earl Warren dissented.

Justice Harlan, again the spokesman for the majority, distinguished between active, "knowing" membership and passive, merely nominal membership in a subversive organization. The membership clause, properly applied, did not violate the First Amendment guarantees of free political expression and association, he explained. In *Dennis*, the court had established two points in that regard:

. . .the advocacy with which we are here concerned is not constitutionally protected speech, and. . .that a combination to promote such advocacy, albeit under the aegis of what purports to be a political party, is not such association as is protected by the First Amendment.

We can discern no reason why membership, when it constitutes a purposeful form of complicity in a group engaging in this same forbidden advocacy, should receive any greater degree of protection from the guarantees of that amendment.[32]

Harlan continued:

. . .The clause does not make criminal all association with an organization which has been shown to engage in illegal advocacy. There must be clear proof that a defendant "specifically intend[s] to accomplish [the aims of the organization] by resort to violence.". . . Thus the member for whom the organization is a vehicle for the advancement of legitimate aims and policies does not fall within the ban of the statute: he lacks the requisite specific intent "to bring about the overthrow of the government as speedily as circumstances would permit." Such a person may be foolish, deluded, or perhaps merely optimistic, but he is not by this statute made a criminal.[33]

Justices Douglas, Brennan and Chief Justice Warren based their dissent primarily on the view that the 1950 Internal Security Act specifically immunized persons from prosecution under the Smith Act membership clause.

In a separate opinion, Justice Douglas charged that the court in this decision was legalizing guilt by association, an action with which he strongly disagreed. In his separate opinion, Justice Black reiterated his view that the First Amendment "absolutely forbids Congress to outlaw membership in a political party or similar association merely because one of the philosophical tenets of that group is that the existing government should be overthrown by force at some distant time in the future when circumstances may permit."[34]

In a companion case, *Noto v. United States,* the court reversed the membership clause conviction of John Francis Noto, holding the evidence insufficient under the *Yates* rule to justify the conviction. There was no dissent from the decision to reverse the conviction. Justice Harlan wrote for the court:

. . .the mere abstract teaching of Communist theory, including the teaching of the moral propriety or even moral necessity for a resort to force and violence, is not the same as preparing a group for violent action and steeling it to such action. There must be some substantial direct or circumstantial evidence of a call to violence now or in the future which is both sufficiently strong and sufficiently pervasive to lend color to the otherwise ambiguous theoretical material regarding Communist Party teaching, and to justify the inference that such a call to violence may fairly be imputed to the Party as a whole, and not merely to some narrow segment of it.[35]

The McCarran Act

Deeming the Smith Act insufficient protection against the domestic communist movement, Congress in 1950 approved the Internal Security — or McCarran — Act, over a veto by President Harry S Truman. The purpose of the act was to expose party leaders and members of communist-front groups by requiring that all communist-front and communist-action organizations register with the attorney general. Public exposure, it was thought, would curtail the activities of such groups.

Title I of the McCarran Act established a five-member, presidentially appointed Subversive Activities Control Board (SACB) to determine, subject to judicial review, whether a particular organization was a communist-action or communist-front group and whether certain individuals were among the members.

Once the SACB decided that an organization was such a communist group, the organization was required to register with the Justice Department, providing to the government lists of its officers and members. Members of registered groups were barred from federal jobs, jobs in defense-related industries and from applying for or using U.S. passports.[36]

The penalties for failure to register were heavy fines and long prison terms. Compliance with the law, however, made the subject a likely candidate for investigation by a legislative committee or prosecution under the Smith Act. The act did, however, state that holding offices in, or being a member of a communist organization should not in itself be a crime and that registration should not be used as evidence against a person being prosecuted for violating any criminal law.

In November 1950 the attorney general filed a petition with the SACB to compel the Communist Party of the United States to register as a communist-action organization. That action commenced an unsuccessful fifteen-year battle to force registration of the party. The judicial record involved three decisions by the court of appeals and two reviews by the Supreme Court. The case record included 15,000 pages of testimony and 507 documentary exhibits. The SACB twice ordered the party to register. Both orders were appealed to the courts by the party.[37]

Registration Order Upheld

In 1961, the Supreme Court upheld the second registration order, in an apparent victory for the government. The case of *Communist Party v. Subversive Activities Control Board* was decided by a 5-4 vote. The majority rejected the party's arguments that the registration provisions were unconstitutional as a bill of attainder and as violations of the First Amendment's guarantees of freedom.[38] *(Bill of attainder rulings, p. 76)*

Justice Frankfurter, writing for Justices Clark, Harlan, Charles E. Whittaker and Potter Stewart, found — in one of the longest opinions in the court's history — that the evidence confirmed the SACB ruling that the party was a communist-action group within the scope of the McCarran Act registration provisions. The provisions of that law did not constitute a bill of attainder, Frankfurter declared:

> It attaches not to specified organizations but to described activities in which an organization may or may not engage. The singling out of an individual for legislatively prescribed punishment constitutes an attainder whether the individual is called by name or described in terms of conduct which, because it is past conduct, operates only as a designation of particular persons.... The Subversive Activities Control Act is not of that kind. It requires the registration only of

organizations which, after the date of the Act, are found to be under the direction, domination, or control of certain foreign powers and to operate primarily to advance certain objectives.[39]

Nor, held the majority, did the law violate First Amendment guarantees. Other federal statutes demanded registration and disclosure, Frankfurter noted. In requiring registration Congress balanced private rights of free speech and association against the public interest in disclosure:

> Where the mask of anonymity which an organization's members wear serves the double purpose of protecting them from popular prejudice and of enabling them to cover over a foreign-directed conspiracy, infiltrate into other groups, and enlist the support of persons who would not, if the truth were revealed, lend their support ... it would be a distortion of the First Amendment to hold that it prohibits Congress from removing the mask.[40]

Frankfurter emphasized the foreign-dominated character of the Communist Party in the United States:

> ... There is no attempt here to impose stifling obligations upon the proponents of a particular political creed as such, or even to check the importation of particular political ideas from abroad for propagation here. The Act compels the registration of organized groups which have been made the instruments of a long-continued, systematic, disciplined activity directed by a foreign power and purposing to overthrow existing government in this country.[41]

The majority found it premature to consider the challenge that the registration provisions violated the Fifth Amendment privilege against compelled self-incrimination, pointing out that this privilege must be claimed by an individual and that it was not now evident that the party officers would make such a claim. In similar fashion, the majority refused to rule on the constitutionality of any other sanctions which might be imposed upon members of the party, once it was registered.

Chief Justice Warren and Justices Brennan, Black and Douglas dissented in separate opinions, citing a wide variety of reasons for their disagreement with the majority.

Chief Justice Warren would have remanded the case to the SACB for reconsideration of credibility of the testimony of two key government witnesses.

Justice Black protested that the Subversive Activities Control Act of 1950 effectively outlawed the Communist Party, a direct violation of the First Amendment:

> The first banning of an association because it advocates hated ideas — whether that association be called a political party or not — marks a fateful moment in the history of a free country. That moment seems to have arrived for this country.... This whole Act, with its pains and penalties, embarks this country, for the first time, on the dangerous adventure of outlawing groups that preach doctrines nearly all Americans detest. When the practice of outlawing parties and various public groups begins, no one can say where it will end. In most countries such a practice once begun ends with a one-party government.[42]

Justices Douglas and Brennan found the registration provisions in violation of the Fifth Amendment. Justice Douglas wrote:

Politics, Passports and the Right to Travel

One of the sanctions placed upon members of the Communist Party by Cold War legislation designed to protect the national security was the denial of the privilege of a U.S. passport.

The Passport Act of 1926, the basis for modern passport administration, placed control over passports in the Department of State, authorizing it to deny issuance of travel documents to applicants with criminal records and those who were not U.S. citizens.

From 1917 until 1931, passports generally were refused to members of the American Communist Party. During the Cold War, the State Department resumed the practice of denying passports to Communist Party members and others associated with the party. The 1950 McCarran Act forbade members of any registered communist political action or front organization to apply for or use a passport.

Although the registration provisions were successfully resisted by the party and other groups, the State Department nevertheless denied passports to a number of individuals thought or known to be communists, acting under its own rules and the discretion granted it by the Immigration and Nationality Act of 1952.

In the case of *Kent v. Dulles,* decided in 1958, the Supreme Court held that Congress had not authorized the Secretary of State to deny passports to persons because of the applicant's belief or associations. Furthermore, held the court, the right to travel is an aspect of liberty of which the citizen cannot be deprived without due process of law. The court, by a 5-4 vote, reversed the State Department's denial of a passport to artist Rockwell Kent, who desired to use it to travel to a meeting of the World Council of Peace in Helsinki, Finland. The Secretary of State denied the passport to Kent after he refused to submit an affidavit disclaiming any affiliation with Communist groups.

For the majority, Justice William O. Douglas wrote:

> . . .we are dealing here with citizens who have neither been accused of crimes or found guilty. They are being denied their freedom of movement solely because of their refusal to be subjected to inquiry into their beliefs and associations. They do not seek to escape the law nor to violate it. They may or may not be Communists. But assuming they are, the

only law which Congress has passed expressly curtailing the movement of Communists across our borders has not yet become effective. It would therefore be strange to infer that pending the effectiveness of that law, the Secretary has been silently granted by Congress the larger, the more pervasive power to curtail in his discretion the free movement of citizens in order to satisfy himself about their beliefs or associations.[1]

The dissenting justices — Harold H. Burton, John Marshall Harlan, Charles E. Whittaker and Tom C. Clark — found the Secretary's decision proper under the discretion granted him by existing law.

In the wake of the *Kent* decision, the Eisenhower administration requested Congress to pass a statute expressly authorizing the State Department to deny passports to persons with communist affiliations. Congress did not enact such a measure.[2]

The court's decision in the 1961 case of *Communist Party v. Subversive Activities Control Board* upheld the order to the party to register under the McCarran Act and made operative the provisions of the act that denied passports to Communist Party members. *(Details of decision, p. 506)*

The State Department revoked the passports of several leading Communist Party officials including Herbert Aptheker, one of the party's leading intellectuals. In its 1964 decision in the case of *Aptheker v. Secretary of State* the court declared the passport denial provisions of the McCarran Act unconstitutional as infringements of the freedom to travel. The vote was 6-3.

Writing for the majority, Justice Arthur J. Goldberg explained that the law violated the guarantee of due process by failing to distinguish between knowing and unknowing party membership and by arbitrarily excluding any consideration of the purpose of the proposed travel.[3]

Justices Harlan, Clark and Byron R. White dissented.

The following year, the court in the case of *Zemel v. Rusk* upheld the power of the State Department to impose geographic area limitations on the use of U.S. passports.[4] But several subsequent decisions made clear that such limitations, although valid, are practically unenforceable.[5]

---

[1] *Kent v. Dulles,* 357 U.S. 117 at 130 (1950).
[2] *Congress and the Nation,* Vol. I (Washington: Congressional Quarterly, 1965): p. 1650.

[3] *Aptheker v. Secretary of State,* 378 U.S. 500 (1964).
[4] *Zemel v. Rusk,* 381 U.S. 1 (1965).
[5] *United States v. Laub,* 385 U.S. 475 (1967); *Travis v. United States,* 385 U.S. 491 (1967).

Signing as an officer or director of the Communist Party — an ingredient of an offense that results in punishment — must be done under the mandate of law. That is compulsory incrimination of those individuals and, in my view, a plain violation of the Fifth Amendment.[43]

Enforcing Provisions Nullified

But as subsequent rulings made clear, the court had upheld only the power of Congress to require registration of

communist-front and communist-action groups; it would not give similar sanction to the implementing provisions of the McCarran Act.

In 1964 the court held invalid the passport restrictions imposed by the act on members of registered organizations. *(Box, above)* In 1965, in the case of *Albertson v. Subversive Activities Control Board,* the court held that the registration requirements, when applied to individuals, violated the Fifth Amendment privilege against compelled self-incrimination.

And in 1967, the court declared unconstitutional that provision which barred members of registered organizations from jobs in defense-related facilities.

Congress responded, first by rewriting the registration provisions, and eventually by allowing the SACB to die.[44]

Registration and Incrimination

Most severe of these court-inflicted blows to the McCarran Act was its 1965 ruling in *Albertson v. Subversive Activities Control Board,* a sequel to the 1961 decision upholding the SACB registration order to the Communist Party.

Party officers refused to comply with a final notice from the Justice Department which set Nov. 19, 1961, as the deadline for registration of the party. The government subsequently obtained criminal indictments against the party for its failure to register, and an SACB order directed party officers to register personally.

The officers refused and appealed to the federal courts, citing their Fifth Amendment privilege against self-incrimination as justification for their refusal.

With the court's decision in the case of *Albertson v. Subversive Activities Control Board,* the officers of the Communist Party won a clear-cut victory. The court held unanimously that the information sought in the registration forms included material that was self-incriminatory. Thus, compulsion to register did violate the officers' Fifth Amendment privilege. Brennan wrote the court's opinion.

The court rejected the government's argument that the information sought through the registration forms was no more incriminating than that on a tax return. While questions on tax returns were "neutral on their face and directed at the public at large," wrote Brennan, the registration questions were aimed at "a highly selective group inherently suspect of criminal activities." Continuing, he explained that in this case the Fifth Amendment privilege was asserted "not . . . in an essentially non-criminal and regulatory area of inquiry, but against an inquiry in an area permeated with criminal statutes where response to any of the form's questions in context might involve the petitioners in the admission of a crucial element of a crime." [45]

This ruling effectively ended the long effort by the government to force registration of the party.[46]

Association and Jobs

Two years later, in the case of *United States v. Robel,* the court declared that the McCarran Act also abridged the right of political association insofar as it denied all members of communist-action or communist-front organizations the right to hold jobs in defense-related industries. The ban, held the court by a vote of 6-2, was too broad, taking in all types of members, not simply active and knowing advocates of violent revolution.

Robel, a member of the Communist Party, worked as a machinist in a Seattle shipyard determined by the Secretary of Defense to be a defense facility. He stayed on the job after the final registration deadline for the party and so was charged with violation of the act.

Chief Justice Warren's opinion for the six-man majority viewed this portion of the law as establishing guilt purely by association:

> When Congress' exercise of one of its enumerated powers clashes with those individual liberties protected by the Bill of Rights, it is our "delicate and difficult" task to determine whether the resulting re-

striction on freedom can be tolerated. . . . The Government emphasizes that the purpose of . . . [the contested ban] is to reduce the threat of sabotage and espionage in the nation's defense plants. The Government's interest in such a prophylactic measure is not insubstantial. But it cannot be doubted that the means chosen to implement that governmental purpose in this instance cut deeply into the right of association. [It] . . . put appellee to the choice of surrendering his organizational affiliation, regardless of whether his membership threatened the security of a defense facility or giving up his job. . . . The statute quite literally establishes guilt by association alone, without any need to establish that an individual's association poses the threat feared by the Government in proscribing it. The inhibiting effect on the exercise of First Amendment rights is clear. . . .

Warren added, however, that "nothing we hold today should be read to deny Congress the power under narrowly drawn legislation to keep from sensitive positions in defense facilities those who would use their positions to disrupt the Nation's production facilities." [47]

Justices Byron R. White and Harlan dissented. White wrote that in Robel's case:

> . . . the interest in anticipating and preventing espionage or sabotage would outweigh the deterrent impact of job disqualification. . . . In the case before us the Court simply disagrees with the Congress and the Defense Department, ruling that Robel does not present a sufficient danger to the national security to require him to choose between membership in the Communist Party and his employment in a defense facility. . . . I much prefer the judgment of Congress and the Executive Branch that the interest of respondent in remaining a member of the Communist Party . . . is less substantial than the public interest in excluding him from employment in critical defense industries.[48]

In the fall of 1967 Congress revised the definition of communist-front organization in the McCarran Act. Another amendment to the act eliminated the registration requirement and authorized the SACB to place on a public register the names of individuals and organizations it found to be communist.

In 1968 Attorney General Ramsey Clark asked the board to conduct hearings on seven individuals thought to be members of the Communist Party. The SACB issued orders against three of the individuals, declaring them to be members of a communist-action organization. The Board's order was set aside by the District of Columbia Court of Appeals in 1969, holding that mere membership in the Communist Party was protected by the First Amendment.[49]

Federal Loyalty Programs

To ensure that only "loyal" persons held federal jobs, Presidents Harry S Truman and Dwight Eisenhower instituted federal loyalty programs which provoked considerable constitutional controversy.

Critics of the programs argued that through it the government penalized persons for a state of mind rather than for overt acts of disloyalty, and dismissed persons from jobs purely on the grounds of "guilt by association."

Defenders of the program pointed out that there was no constitutional right to hold a government job — and that the government had a right to protect itself from internal subversion. Moreover, dismissal from a government job did not imply guilt but only that some question existed as to one's fitness for government employment.

The Truman Program

In 1947 President Truman by executive order established a loyalty program for all civilian employees of the Executive Branch. Executive Order 9835 established a Loyalty Review Board within the Civil Service Commission to coordinate agency loyalty policies and to serve as the final board of appeal in loyalty dismissal cases. Loyalty investigations were required for all present government employees and for all applicants for government jobs. Dismissal of individuals from government posts or denial of a job was permitted when "on all the evidence, reasonable grounds exist for belief that the person involved is disloyal to the Government of the United States." (In 1951, this standard was modified to allow dismissal when "there is a reasonable doubt as to the loyalty of the person involved.")

In the 1940s, Congress authorized summary dismissal of employees of the Departments of State, Defense, Army, Navy, Air Force and the Atomic Energy Commission when dismissal was considered necessary or advisable in the interest of national security. In 1950 Congress extended this authority to additional departments, including Treasury, Commerce and Justice.

The Eisenhower Program

In 1953 President Eisenhower extended this summary dismissal power to all executive branch agencies and replaced the Truman loyalty program with a more stringent loyalty-security program established by Executive Order 10450.

Under the Eisenhower program a suspected employee bore the burden of proving his employment "clearly consistent" with national security. The order also sanctioned dismissal for reasons other than disloyalty: for example, personal behavior, sexual misconduct, excessive use of drugs or alcohol, and physical or mental disorders.[50]

Loyalty Programs Sustained

The Supreme Court never squarely addressed the substantial constitutional questions raised by the federal loyalty and security programs, although it did rule in a number of cases during the 1950s concerning individuals who contested their dismissal on a variety of grounds.

Three primary constitutional provisions were implicated in the government's effort to ensure the loyalty of its employees: the First Amendment guarantees of freedom of expression and political association; the Fifth Amendment guarantee that government would not deprive one of liberty or property without due process of law; and the Article I ban on the passage of bills of attainder.

Only the due process question received any extended consideration by the court in these cases.

The first rulings on the federal loyalty program came in 1951.

In its decision in the case of *Joint Anti-Fascist Refugee Committee v. McGrath,* the court upheld the authority of the attorney general, under the Truman loyalty program, to maintain and furnish to the Loyalty Review Board a list of allegedly subversive organizations.

The court held, however, that the attorney general had exceeded that authority and acted arbitrarily in placing the names of three particular organizations — including the Anti-Fascist Refugee Committee — on that list.

The vote was 5-3. Justice Tom C. Clark, attorney general when the case was filed, did not participate in the court's decision.

Justice Harold H. Burton — joined only by Justice Douglas — wrote the opinion announcing the judgment of the court. That opinion carefully avoided the First Amendment issues of political association raised by use of this list.

In concurring opinions, Justices Black, Douglas, Frankfurter and Robert H. Jackson questioned the constitutionality of the list in light of the guarantee of due process and the prohibition on a bill of attainder.

Justice Frankfurter wrote that although the designation as "communist" actually imposed no legal sanction on the listed organizations,

> . . . in the conditions of our time such designation drastically restricts the organizations, if it does not proscribe them. . . . Yet, designation has been made without notice, without disclosure of any reasons justifying it, without opportunity to meet the undisclosed evidence or suspicion on which designation may have been based, and without opportunity to establish affirmatively that the aims and acts of the organization are innocent. . . .

Frankfurter concluded that such action

> . . . to maim or decapitate, on the mere say-so of the Attorney General, an organization to all outward-seeming engaged in lawful objectives is so devoid of fundamental fairness as to offend the Due Process Clause of the Fifth Amendment.[51]

Justices Stanley Reed, Sherman Minton and Chief Justice Fred M. Vinson dissented, finding the due process guarantee inapplicable and rejecting any First Amendment challenge to use of the list:

> So long as petitioners are permitted to voice their political ideas . . . it is hard to understand how any advocate of freedom of expression can assert that their right has been unconstitutionally abridged. As nothing in the orders or regulations concerning this list limits the teachings or support of these organizations, we do not believe that any right of theirs under the First Amendment is abridged by publication of the list.[52]

On the same day, the court, evenly divided 4-4, upheld, without opinion, the decision of the loyalty board to dismiss Dorothy Bailey, a training officer in the United States Employment Service. Justice Clark again did not participate in the decision.

The even division within the court left standing an appeals court ruling finding Bailey's removal valid. Because there was no constitutional right to federal employment, her dismissal did not violate due process; and the majority of the lower court continued, the First Amendment did not bar removal of persons from office for political reasons. There was no opinion from the Supreme Court, as is the practice in cases which evenly divide the justices.[53]

In several subsequent cases, the court ruled dismissals on loyalty or security grounds improper on procedural grounds.

In 1955 the court ruled that the Loyalty Review Board had exceeded its authority in discharging a public health officer as a security risk, after the officer had twice been cleared of any suspicion of disloyalty by agency loyalty boards.[54]

In 1956 the court held unjustified the summary dismissal of an inspector with the Food and Drug Administration on loyalty grounds. The court ruled that dismissal from a non-sensitive position could not be justified as necessary in the interest of national security.[55]

Loyalty Procedures Improper

In 1959, however, the court weakened the federal government's effort to carry out its loyalty program by casting doubt on the propriety of the procedures used in revoking security clearances and dismissing employees on the basis of information from anonymous sources. With its ruling in the case of *Greene v. McElroy,* the court forced the president to revise those procedures.[56]

William L. Greene lost his job as vice president of an engineering firm engaged in defense contract work after his security clearance was revoked. The review board revoking the clearance relied on confidential reports, never available to Greene, even though he appeared at the hearings of the board to respond to the charges against him.

As a result of loss of his clearance, Greene was unable to find another job in the field of aeronautical engineering. He challenged the revocation of his clearance as depriving him of his livelihood and thus of liberty and property without the due process of law guaranteed by the Fifth Amendment.

The court by an 8-1 vote agreed that the denial of access to the evidence against him had been improper, depriving Greene of the opportunity to respond to and rebut the charges. Neither Congress nor the President had authorized the Defense Department thus to classify the employees of a contractor as security risks without giving them the opportunity to confront and examine the evidence against them, held the court.

Chief Justice Warren, writing for five members of the majority, carefully narrowed the reach of the ruling:

> ...[P]etitioner's work opportunities have been severely limited on the basis of a fact determination rendered after a hearing which failed to comport with our traditional ideas of fair procedure. The type of hearing was the product of administrative decision not explicitly authorized by either Congress or the President. Whether those procedures under the circumstances comport with the Constitution we do not decide. Nor do we decide whether the President has inherent authority to create such a program, whether congressional action is necessary, or what the limits on executive or legislative authority may be. We decide only that in the absence of explicit authorization from the President or Congress the respondents were not empowered to deprive petitioner of his job in a proceeding in which he was not afforded the safeguards of confrontation and cross-examination.[57]

Justices Frankfurter, Harlan and Whittaker concurred with the court's judgment.

Justice Clark dissented, arguing that no one has "a constitutional right to have access to the Government military secrets.... What for anyone else would be considered a privilege at best has for Greene been enshrouded in constitutional protection. This sleight of hand is too much for me."

Clark warned that the majority opinion was casting a cloud over the entire federal loyalty-security program which could result in "a rout of our internal security."[58]

Early in 1960 President Eisenhower issued an executive order restricting the use of informants whose identities must be protected and granting additional rights to persons accused as security risks to confront and cross-examine their accusers.[59]

In 1961, however, the court, divided 5-4, upheld the national security dismissal of a short-order cook in a cafeteria on the premises of the Naval Gun Factory in Washington, D.C. The court held this action well within the authority granted by Congress to the executive to control military bases.[60]

Loyalty Oaths and Labor

Concomitant with the institution of the federal loyalty-security program was the proliferation of requirements that persons holding certain posts take loyalty oaths or sign affidavits to demonstrate their loyalty to the United States government. In a long line of rulings, the Supreme Court first upheld and then circumscribed both the use and the usefulness of such requirements.

Labor Affidavit Upheld

Concern over Communist infiltration of the labor movement and "political strikes" spurred Congress to include in the Taft-Hartley Act, the Labor Management Relations Act of 1947, a provision requiring officers of all labor organizations wishing to benefit from the protections and guarantees of federal labor law to sign affidavits that they were not members of, or affiliated, with the Communist Party, that they did not believe in or hold membership in any organization teaching or believing in the forcible, illegal or unconstitutional overthrow of the federal government.

Unions whose officers did not sign such affidavits were denied all protection of and services from the National Labor Relations Board.

In 1950, the Supreme Court upheld that requirement as within the power of Congress. In the case of *American Communications Association v. Douds,* Chief Justice Vinson explained:

> There can be no doubt that Congress may, under its constitutional power to regulate commerce among the several States, attempt to prevent political strikes and other kinds of direct action designed to burden and interrupt the free flow of commerce.[61]

The affidavit requirement, held the court, was a reasonable means of attaining that end:

> Congress could rationally find that the Communist Party is not like other political parties in its utilization of positions of union leadership as means by which to bring about strikes and other obstructions of commerce for purposes of political advantage....[62]

The court recognized, continued the Chief Justice, that:

> By exerting pressures on unions to deny office to Communists and others identified therein,... [the affidavit requirement] undoubtedly lessens the threat to interstate commerce, but it has the further necessary effect of discouraging the exercise of political

rights protected by the First Amendment. Men who hold union offices often have little choice but to renounce Communism or give up their offices. . . .[63]

But in response to the challenge that the affidavit requirement was an unconstitutional curtailment of individual freedom, Vinson wrote that the requirement:

> . . . does not interfere with speech because Congress fears the consequences of speech; it regulates harmful conduct which Congress has determined is carried on by persons who may be identified by their political affiliations and beliefs. The [National Labor Relations] Board does not contend that political strikes, the substantive evil at which. . . [the requirement] is aimed, are the present or impending products of advocacy of the doctrines of Communism or the expression of belief in overthrow of the Government by force. . . .Speech may be fought with speech. Falsehoods and fallacies must be exposed, not suppressed, unless there is not sufficient time to avert the evil consequences of noxious doctrine by argument and education. That is the command of the First Amendment. But force may and must be met with force. . . . [The affidavit requirement] is designed to protect the public not against what Communists and others identified therein advocate or believe, but against what Congress has concluded they have done and are likely to do again.[64]

Justices Clark, Sherman Minton and Douglas did not take part in this decision.

Justice Frankfurter concurred in upholding the membership portion of the affidavit but dissented from the majority opinion upholding the portion involving belief alone.

Justice Robert H. Jackson also concurred in part and dissented in part, making a similar distinction between the membership and the belief portions of the affidavit:

> . . . all parts of this oath which require disclosure of overt acts of affiliation or membership in the Communist Party are within the competence of Congress to enact. . . any parts of it that call for a disclosure of belief unconnected with any overt act are beyond its power.[65]

Earlier in his opinion, Jackson had phrased his view in less abstract terms:

> . . . I think that under our system, it is time enough for the law to lay hold of the citizen when he acts illegally, or in some rare circumstances when his thoughts are given illegal utterance. I think we must let his mind alone.[66]

In a vigorous dissenting opinion, Justice Hugo L. Black criticized his colleagues for allowing the government to restrict the right to think:

> Freedom to think is inevitably abridged when beliefs are penalized by imposition of civil disabilities. . . . Like anyone else, individual Communists who commit overt acts in violation of valid laws can and should be punished. But the postulate of the First Amendment is that our free institutions can be maintained without proscribing or penalizing political belief, speech, press, assembly, or party affiliation. This is a far bolder philosophy than despotic rulers can afford to follow. It is the heart of the system on which our freedom depends.[67]

Labor Office Ban Voided

In 1959, Congress replaced the affidavit requirement — which proved ineffective since some Communists were willing to take the oath and risk prosecution for perjury — with a flat prohibition against members of the Communist Party holding any union office. The new section of the federal labor law, part of the Management Reporting and Disclosure Act of 1959, also disqualified anyone who had been a member of the party during the last five years.[68]

In 1965, the Supreme Court held this ban unconstitutional as a violation of the provision forbidding Congress to pass bills of attainder.

In the case of *United States v. Brown,* Archie Brown, a member of the Communist Party, challenged the operation of the law which forbade him to serve on the executive board of a local of the International Longshoremen's and Warehousemen's Union. He also based his challenge on First and Fifth Amendment grounds, but the court found it unnecessary to consider those.

By a 5-4 vote the Supreme Court ruled in his favor. Chief Justice Earl Warren wrote the majority opinion:

> Congress undoubtedly possesses power under the Commerce Clause to enact legislation designed to keep from positions affecting interstate commerce persons who may use such positions to bring about political strikes. In . . . [this prohibition] however, Congress has exceeded the authority granted it by the Constitution. The statute does not set forth a generally applicable rule decreeing that any person who commits certain acts or possesses certain characteristics (acts and characteristics which, in Congress' view, make them likely to initiate political strikes) shall not hold union office, and leave to courts and juries the job of deciding what persons have committed the specified acts or possess the specified characteristics. Instead, it designates in no uncertain terms the persons who possess the feared characteristics and therefore cannot hold union office without incurring criminal liability — members of the Communist Party. . . .
>
> We do not hold today that Congress cannot weed dangerous persons out of the labor movement. . . . Rather, we make again the point . . . that Congress must accomplish such results by rules of general applicability. It cannot specify the people upon whom the sanction it prescribes is to be levied. Under our Constitution, Congress possesses full legislative authority, but the task of adjudication must be left to other tribunals.[69]

In dissent, Justice Byron R. White, joined by Justices Tom C. Clark, John Marshall Harlan and Potter Stewart, criticized the majority's distinction between the legislative function of making rules and the judicial function in applying those rules to particular individuals or groups. White wrote that the court took "too narrow [a] view of the legislative process."[70]

In two other cases related to the non-Communist affidavit requirement, the court in the 1960s reversed convictions of union members who had sworn falsely that they were not Communists. The court decided both cases without dealing with the First Amendment claim of freedom of political association or the Fifth Amendment privilege protecting individuals against compelled self-incrimination.[71]

Teachers and Oaths

The most prevalent state legislative reaction to the fear of communist subversion was enactment of a law requiring public employees — in particular, teachers — to take a loyalty oath affirming that they had not been and were not members of the Communist Party.

During the 1950s, the court generally upheld the constitutionality of such oaths, but by 1967 it had reversed most of those early rulings, finding that most oaths relied too heavily upon guilt by association and demanded too little in the way of evidence of actual involvement in subversive activity.

In the 1970s, the court upheld several laws requiring state employees to take affirmative oaths promising to uphold the Constitution and to oppose the violent overthrow of the government.

Gerende and Garner

The court's first loyalty oath rulings came in 1951. In April of that year, with its decision in the case of *Gerende v. Board of Supervisors of Elections,* the court upheld Maryland's law requiring every candidate for public office to file an affidavit disavowing involvement in any attempt to overthrow the government by force or violence.[72]

Two months later, on the same day that it upheld the constitutionality of the Smith Act, the court in the case of *Garner v. Board of Public Works of the City of Los Angeles* upheld as constitutional a Los Angeles ordinance requiring city employees to affirm their loyalty both through oath and affidavit.

The contested ordinance required public employees both to sign an affidavit stating whether or not they were or ever had been members of the Communist Party and to swear that they had not advocated the overthrow of state or federal government in the previous five years, that they were not and had not during that period been affiliated with any group advocating such overthrow and that they would not advocate such overthrow or become a member of such a group during the period they held a city job.

Seventeen employees refused to comply with the ordinance and were dismissed. They sued for reinstatement, challenging the oath and affidavit requirement as unconstitutional as a bill of attainder, an *ex post facto* law, and a violation of their freedom of speech, assembly and right to petition the government for redress of grievances.[73]

The court upheld the affidavit requirement by a vote of 7-2, but the oath only by a 5-4 division.

Justice Tom Clark, writing for the majority, explained that they did not view the ordinance as a bill of attainder because it did not punish anyone, but simply set standards of qualification and eligibility for city jobs. It was not a *ex post facto* law, he continued, because it involved activity which for the seven previous years had been proscribed for city employees. The majority did not address the First Amendment issues directly.

Justices Felix Frankfurter and Harold H. Burton concurred in the decision to uphold the affidavit requirement, but dissented from the majority's ruling upholding the oath. Frankfurter wrote:

> The Constitution does not guarantee public employment. City, State and Nation are not confined to making provisions appropriate for securing competent professional discharge of the functions pertaining to diverse governmental jobs. They may also assure themselves of fidelity to the very presuppositions of our scheme of government on the part of those who seek to serve it.[74]

Frankfurter explained that he would have overturned the oath requirement because it was "not limited to affiliation with organizations known at the time to have advocated overthrow of government.... How can anyone be sure that an organization with which he affiliates will not at some time in the future be found...to advocate overthrow of government by 'unlawful means'?"[75]

Burton found the retroactive nature of the oath invalid under the court's decisions concerning bills of attainder and *ex post facto* laws.

Justices Black and William O. Douglas found all aspects of the requirement objectionable, holding both the oath and the affidavit requirements invalid as bills of attainder.

Loyalty Dismissals

Loyalty-oath requirements for state or city employees usually were linked with programs for the removal of public employees whose loyalty was suspect.

In 1952 the Supreme Court upheld a New York law setting up a state list of subversive organizations — those advocating the violent overthrow of the government — and providing that membership in any listed organization would constitute *prima facie* evidence justifying dismissal from a public post.

The law was intended primarily to ensure the doctrinal orthodoxy of teachers and other officials in the New York public school system. Before dismissal, an individual who was a member of such an organization was entitled to a full hearing and judicial review of the decision to dismiss him.

With its decision in the case of *Adler v. Board of Education of City of New York,* the court by a 6-3 vote sustained the law.[76]

For the majority, Justice Sherman Minton wrote:

> That the school authorities have the right and the duty to screen the officials, teachers and employees as to their fitness to maintain the integrity of the schools as a part of ordered society, cannot be doubted. One's associates, past and present, as well as one's conduct, may properly be considered in determining fitness and loyalty. From time immemorial, one's reputation has been determined in part by the company he keeps.[77]

Disqualification from a job under the law, wrote Minton, did not deny one the right of free speech and assembly. "His freedom of choice between membership in the organization and employment in the school system might be limited, but not his freedom of speech or assembly...."[78]

Justices Frankfurter, Black and Douglas dissented. Justice Frankfurter argued that the court should have dismissed the case without ruling on the law. Justices Douglas and Black found the law a violation of the First Amendment. It "proceeds on a principle repugnant to our society — guilt by association," wrote Douglas.[79]

Douglas elaborated:

> Youthful indiscretions, mistaken causes, misguided enthusiasms — all long forgotten — become the ghosts of a harrowing present. Any organization committed to a liberal cause, any group organized to revolt against a hysterical trend, any committee launched to sponsor an unpopular program becomes suspect. These are the organizations into which Com-

munists often infiltrate. Their presence infects the whole, even though the project was not conceived in sin. A teacher caught in that mesh is almost certain to stand condemned. Fearing condemnation, she [*sic*] will tend to shrink from any association that stirs controversy. In that manner freedom of expression will be stifled. . . .

What happens under this law is typical of what happens in a police state. Teachers are under constant surveillance; their pasts are combed for signs of disloyalty; their utterances are watched for cues to dangerous thoughts. A pall is cast over the classrooms. There can be no real academic freedom in that environment. Where suspicion fills the air and holds scholars in line for fear of their jobs, there can be no exercise of the free intellect. . . .

Of course the school systems . . . need not become cells for Communist activities; and the classrooms need not become forums for propagandizing the Marxist creed. But the guilt of the teacher should turn on overt acts. So long as she is a law-abiding citizen, so long as her performance within the public school system meets professional standards, her private life, her political philosophy, her social creed should not be the cause of reprisals against her.[80]

Initial Limitation

But late in the same year as the *Adler* ruling, the Supreme Court unanimously struck down an Oklahoma loyalty program which penalized knowing *and* unknowing members of certain proscribed organizations.

The law challenged in the case of *Wieman v. Updegraff* required all state officers and employees to take a loyalty oath and excluded from public jobs those persons who had been members of certain organizations, regardless of their knowledge of the organization's purposes.

With this ruling the court began to impose limits upon state loyalty oaths by requiring, at the least, that membership be a conscious endorsement of an organization's aims and doctrines before it was used as a basis for a state-imposed penalty.

Justice Clark, in the court's opinion, made clear that in *Garner* and *Adler* only "knowing" membership resulted in disqualification for or dismissal from a public job. But under Oklahoma law, "membership alone disqualifies," wrote Clark.[81]

This was a critical difference:

. . . the fact of association alone [under the challenged law] determines disloyalty and disqualification; it matters not whether association existed innocently or knowingly. To thus inhibit individual freedom of movement is to stifle the flow of democratic expression and controversy at one of its chief sources. . . . Indiscriminate classification of innocent with knowing activity must fall as an assertion of arbitrary power. The oath offends due process.[82]

Justice Jackson, who had not heard the case argued, did not participate in the decision.

Penalizing the Privilege

Four years later, the court held it unconstitutional for a state or city automatically to dismiss an employee if he invoked his constitutional privilege against self-incrimination to avoid answering questions about his political associations.

States and Sedition

In addition to enacting loyalty oath requirements and loyalty dismissal programs, many states during the 1940s and 1950s passed their own sedition laws to punish persons for plotting to overthrow the U.S. government.

In 1956, however, the Supreme Court held that Congress had pre-empted such state laws, occupying the field of federal sedition prosecutions with passage of the Smith Act, the McCarran Act and the Communist Control Act.

This decision in the case of *Pennsylvania v. Nelson* limited state sedition statutes to punishing sedition against state or local — not federal — government.

Steve Nelson, an avowed communist, had been convicted for violating Pennsylvania's sedition law by his words and actions concerning the federal government. He was sentenced to serve 20 years in prison, and to pay a $10,000 fine and prosecution costs of $13,000. The state supreme court held that the state law had been superseded by the Smith Act — a ruling the Supreme Court upheld and extended.

Writing the majority opinion, Chief Justice Earl Warren surveyed the relevant provisions of the Smith, McCarran and Communist Control Acts and declared:

. . . the conclusion is inescapable that Congress has intended to occupy the field of sedition. Taken as a whole they evince a congressional plan which makes it reasonable to determine that no room has been left for the States to supplement it. Therefore, a state sedition statute is superseded regardless of whether it purports to supplement the federal law.[1]

"Since 1939," he noted, "in order to avoid a hampering of uniform enforcement of its program by sporadic local prosecutions, the Federal Government has urged local authorities not to intervene in such matters, but to turn over to the federal authorities immediately and unevaluated all information concerning subversive activities." [2]

Justices Stanley F. Reed, Harold H. Burton and Sherman Minton dissented.

Following the decision, all pending proceedings under state sedition laws were dismissed or abandoned. Congress considered a measure reversing the court's decision but did not complete action on such a bill.

In 1965 the court further curtailed state subversion laws, holding Louisiana's Subversive Activities Criminal Control Act unconstitutionally vague.[3] And in 1969 the court in the case of *Brandenburg v. Ohio* struck down Ohio's Criminal Syndicalism Act, declaring illegal the use of advocacy of violence, crime, sabotage and terrorism to accomplish industrial or political reform. This ruling overturned the court's 1927 decision in *Whitney v. California*, upholding an almost identical California law.[4] *(Details, p. 500)*

---

[1] *Pennsylvania v. Nelson*, 350 U.S. 497 at 504 (1956).
[2] *Id.* at 505-506.
[3] *Dombrowski v. Pfister*, 380 U.S. 479 (1965).
[4] *Brandenburg v. Ohio*, 395 U.S. 444 (1969), overturning *Whitney v. California*, 274 U.S. 357 (1927).

At issue in the case of *Slochower v. Board of Higher Education of New York City* was the city's summary dismissal of a Brooklyn College professor because, in testimony before the Senate internal security subcommittee, he had refused to answer questions about his political associations before 1941, invoking the Fifth Amendment. Slochower was suspended without notice, hearing, or an opportunity to explain or discuss the reasons for the termination of his tenure. This action came under a provision of the city charter which automatically terminated the tenure of any public official who invoked the Fifth Amendment to avoid answering questions related to official conduct.

Slochower sued, challenging his dismissal as improper and the city charter provision as unconstitutional because it penalized the exercise of a federally guaranteed constitutional right.

The court ruled in his favor — but upon different grounds.

Summary dismissal, the court held by a 5-4 vote, violated Slochower's right to due process of law. The city board of education, wrote Justice Clark for the majority, had erred in treating his assertion of his Fifth Amendment privilege as a "conclusive presumption of guilt."

Such interpretation of the assertion of a constitutional right was impermissible, Clark continued: "The privilege against self-incrimination would be reduced to a hollow mockery if its exercise could be taken as equivalent to a confession of guilt. . . ."[83] Since no valid inference of guilt could be made, the court sustained Slochower's claim of privilege before the Senate subcommittee and ruled that there was no basis for his dismissal.

Justice Reed, speaking also for Justices Burton and Minton, dissented, arguing that "the city does have reasonable ground to require its employees either to give evidence regarding facts of official conduct within their knowledge or to give up the positions they hold."[84] Justice John Marshall Harlan, in a separate dissenting opinion, wrote that the majority had "misconceived" the nature of the city charter provision in question and had "unduly circumscribed the power of the State to ensure the qualifications of its teachers."[85]

The State's Right To Inquire

In two 1958 decisions however, the court again upheld the right of states to question employees about their associations, in examining their overall qualifications for state employment.

In *Lerner v. Casey,* a subway conductor refused to tell his superiors whether or not he was a member of the Communist Party. He was dismissed as a person of doubtful loyalty and reliability.[86] In the case of *Beilan v. Board of Public Education, School District of Philadelphia,* a school teacher who refused to tell his superintendent whether he had earlier held a position in the Communist Party was dismissed as incompetent.[87]

The five-man majority in both cases — Harlan, Burton, Frankfurter, Clark and Charles E. Whittaker — stressed that the subway conductor and the school teacher were dismissed because they refused to answer questions put by their employers — action that constituted evidence of incompetency and unreliability.

In a concurring opinion, Justice Frankfurter said the two employees were "terminated because of their refusals to answer questions relevant. . .to an inquiry by their supervisors into their dependability. When these two employees were discharged, they were not labelled "disloyal." They were discharged because governmental authorities, like other employers, sought to satisfy themselves of the dependability of employees in relation to their duties."[88]

In dissent, Chief Justice Earl Warren, and Justices William J. Brennan, Black and Douglas argued that the two employees had been branded disloyal by the inquiry into their political associations and activities. In his dissenting opinion, Brennan wrote, "more is at stake here than the loss of positions of public employment for unreliability or incompetence. Rather, it is the simultaneous public labeling of the employees as disloyal that gives rise to our concern."[89]

The Shift of the Sixties

With a series of decisions begining in 1958 — initially involving civil rights, not communist, groups — the Supreme Court gave formal recognition to a First Amendment freedom of political association. *(Details, pp. 402-403)*

In line with this development came a clear shift in the court's willingness to back government inquiry into the affiliations of its employees and government-imposed penalties upon persons whose affiliations seemed suspect. The *Aptheker* and *Robel* rulings of 1964 and 1967 reflected the change. *(Details, pp. 507-508)*

And the court, in a set of rulings in the mid-1960s, effectively reversed most of its key decisions upholding state government loyalty oath and loyalty program requirements, finding that they were too broad to comport with the freedom guaranteed by the First Amendment.

The first of these freedom-of-association rulings was the 1958 decision in the case of the *National Advancement of Colored People v. Alabama.*[90]

Two years later the court struck down a state law which required public school teachers to file affidavits listing all their organizational memberships. In its opinion in the case of *Shelton v Tucker,* the court found this requirement to go "far beyond what might be justified in the exercise of the State's legitimate inquiry into the fitness and competency of its teachers."[91]

The following year, the court first applied this new view to loyalty oaths, striking down a Florida law which required state employees to swear that they had never lent "aid, support, advice, counsel or influence to the Communist Party." Employees who did not sign such an oath were fired.

In its opinion in this case of *Cramp v. Board of Public Instruction,* the court held this oath far too vague, "completely lacking in. . .terms susceptible of objective measurement."[92] A law describing prohibited acts " 'in terms so vague that men of common intelligence must necessarily guess at its meaning and differ as to its application violates the first essential of due process of law,' " wrote Justice Potter Stewart for the unanimous court.[93]

In 1964 Washington State's loyalty oath for teachers was struck down on the basis of similar reasoning.[94] And in 1966 and 1967, this shift culminated in decisions effectively nullifying *Gerende v. Board of Supervisors of Elections, Garner v. Board of Public Works,* and *Adler v. Board of Education of New York City.*

Elfbrandt and Garner

The first of these rulings came in the case of *Elfbrandt v. Russell.* Barbara Elfbrandt, a Quaker teacher in Arizona, challenged the constitutionality of the state laws which

Politics, Loyalty and Admission to the Bar

Concerned about Communist infiltration of the legal profession, several states began in the 1950s inquiring into the political affiliation and associations of persons seeking admission to the practice of law in the state.

This line of inquiry — and state decisions to deny admission to certain persons whose responses were deemed unsatisfactory — produced a line of Supreme Court decisions stretching almost two decades.

The first case was that of George Anastaplo. When Illinois bar examiners questioned him about his political beliefs, Anastaplo refused, on principle, to respond at all to such questions, asserting that they invaded areas protected by the First and 14th Amendments from state infringement. He was denied admission to the bar. In 1955 the Supreme Court upheld that denial by refusing to review his appeal of that action.[1]

Affiliation Alone

But two years later, in 1957, the court ruled in two cases that questionable political affiliations alone, or the simple refusal to answer questions about one's political associations, did not give a state a basis for concluding that an applicant lacked the proper moral character for admission to the practice of law.

In the case of *Schware v. New Mexico Board of Bar Examiners,* the board concluded that Rudolph Schware lacked the requisite "good moral character" for admission because he had used aliases for several years during the 1930s to obtain jobs in businesses that discriminated against Jews, because he had been arrested several times and because he had been a member of the Communist Party from 1932-1940.

The Supreme Court unanimously reversed the board's decision. Justice Hugo L. Black wrote the opinion, refuting the board's inference that because Schware had belonged to the Communist Party he was of bad moral character.[2]

Raphael Konigsberg was denied admission to the California bar because he, like Anastaplo, refused to answer questions about his political affiliations. The court overturned the state's action the same day that it reversed the lower court decision in Schware's case. Konigsberg's record of public and military service testified sufficiently to his loyalty, held the court, reversing the state board's ruling as contrary to the evidence.[3]

Refusal to Answer

But, as both Anastaplo and Konigsberg discovered, Supreme Court reversal of the state's initial refusal to admit them to the practice of law did not guarantee them admission.

On the basis of *Schware* and *Konigsberg,* Anastaplo asked Illinois to reconsider his application for admission to the bar. After lengthy proceedings, the state again rejected it.

In 1961, the Supreme Court by a 5-4 vote upheld the state's action. The majority based its decision on the view that the state had a legitimate interest in examining the qualifications of persons seeking to practice law in the state — and that questions about his political background were a proper element in that examination. By continuing to refuse to answer those questions, Anastaplo, the court held, obstructed the state's inquiry, and denial of admission was a legitimate response.[4]

A second ruling in Konigsberg's case was announced the same day. Also by a 5-4 vote, the court upheld California bar officials' refusal to admit Konigsberg — not because of concern about his character but simply because he too persisted in his refusal to answer questions germane to its inquiry, thereby obstructing the state's examining process.[5]

Evidence of Character

Ten years later, in two decisions announced the same day in 1971, the Supreme Court appeared to mark the boundary line for such questioning of candidates for admission to the bar. By a vote of 5-4, the court held that the First Amendment forbade a state to exclude an applicant from admission to the bar solely on the basis of his refusal to state whether or not he had ever belonged to an organization advocating the violent overthrow of the government — without any other evidence of disloyalty or unfitness. Justice Black wrote the opinion; dissenting were Justices Harlan, Byron R. White, Harry A. Blackmun and Chief Justice Warren Burger.[6]

But the same day, with Justice Potter Stewart joining those dissenters from the earlier case, the court, by a 5-4 vote, held that states could require applicants for admission to the bar to be of good moral character and loyal to the Constitution — even when the "loyalty" requirement included taking an oath in support of the state and federal constitutions and responding to two questions concerning membership in any organization advocating overthrow of the government by force or violence, with the specific intent of furthering that goal.[7]

In this case, the majority was careful to point out that there was no indication that any applicant had been denied admission to the bar because of his answers to these questions or his refusal to answer them. "It is well settled," wrote Justice Stewart, "that Bar Examiners may ask about Communist affiliation as a preliminary to further inquiry into the nature of the association and may exclude an applicant for refusal to answer."[8]

---

[1] *In re Anastaplo,* 348 U.S. 946 (1955).

[2] *Schware v. New Mexico Board of Bar Examiners,* 353 U.S. 232 (1957).

[3] *Konigsberg v. State Bar of California,* 353 U.S. 252 (1957).

[4] *In re Anastaplo,* 366 U.S. 82 (1961).

[5] *Konigsberg v. State Bar of California,* 366 U.S. 36 (1961).

[6] *In re Stolar, Baird v. State Bar of Arizona,* 401 U.S. 23 (1971).

[7] *Law Students Civil Rights Research Council v. Wadmond,* 401 U.S. 154 (1971).

[8] Id. at 165-166.

required state employees to take a loyalty oath. The oath itself simply affirmed support for the constitution and laws of the state and the United States, but the state legislature had by law provided that the oath would be considered violated by knowing membership in the Communist Party. The law made clear that any employee who took the oath and at the time or later became a willing, knowing member of the Communist Party could be prosecuted for perjury.

By a 5-4 vote, the Supreme Court held this combination of oath and interpretative statute too broad to meet constitutional standards. Justice William O. Douglas wrote the majority opinion, explaining that the major flaw was the failure of the state to acknowledge that many people might join organizations such as the Communist Party without actually sharing the organization's unlawful purposes. The challenged law, he continued, was predicated on the doctrine of guilt by association:

> Those who join an organization but do not share its unlawful purposes and who do not participate in its unlawful activities surely pose no threat, either as citizens or as public employees. . . .This Act threatens the cherished freedom of association protected by the First Amendment, made applicable to the States through the Fourteenth Amendment. . . .A law which applies to membership without the "specific intent" to further the illegal aims of the organization infringes unnecessarily on protected freedoms. It rests on the doctrine of "guilt by association" which has no place here.[95]

With this ruling, the court effectively, if implicitly, overturned its *Garner* decision upholding the same sort of oath.

The four dissenting justices, Byron R. White, Clark, Harlan and Stewart said that the oath should be upheld in light of the court's earlier decisions acknowledging the right of states to condition public employment upon the requirement that employees abstain from knowing membership in subversive organizations.

Keyishian and *Adler*

The following year, the court struck down the New York law which it had upheld in its 1952 *Adler* ruling. The vote in the case of *Keyishian v. Board of Regents of the University of the State of New York* was again 5-4. Justice William J. Brennan Jr. spoke for the majority.

The law authorized the board of regents to prepare a list of subversive organizations and to deny jobs to teachers belonging to those organizations. The law made membership in the Communist Party *prima facie* evidence for disqualification from employment. Four university faculty members subject to dismissal under the law challenged its constitutionality.

The court found the law too vague — and too sweeping, penalizing "[m]ere knowing membership without a specific intent to further the unlawful aims" of the Communist Party.[96] The question of vagueness, noted Brennan, had not been placed before the court in *Adler*. The majority described New York's complex of criminal anarchy and loyalty laws as "a highly efficient *in terrorem* mechanism" which operated to curtail First Amendment freedom:

> It would be a bold teacher who would not stay as far as possible from utterances or acts which might jeopardize his living by enmeshing him in this intricate machinery. . . .
> Our Nation is deeply committed to safeguarding academic freedom, which is of transcendent value to all of us and not merely to the teachers concerned. That freedom is therefore a special concern of the First Amendment, which does not tolerate laws that cast a pall of orthodoxy over the classroom.[97]

Four justices — Clark, Harlan, Stewart and White — dissented. Justice Clark, writing for the dissenters, declared: "[T]he majority has by its broadside swept away one of our most precious rights, namely, the right of self preservation . . . ."[98]

A few months later, the court by a vote of 6-3 struck down the Maryland loyalty oath law which it had upheld in the 1951 *Gerende* ruling.

Writing for the court, Justice Douglas explained that the oath was so vague that it violated the due process guarantee of the 14th Amendment. Its capricious application could "deter the flowering of academic freedom as much as successive suits for perjury," he wrote.[99]

Justices Harlan, Stewart and White dissented.

Political Association in the 1970s

As the threat of domestic subversion seemed to ebb, and questions of domestic politics came again into the foreground of national attention, the Supreme Court during the 1970s issued a number of decisions defining various aspects of the freedom of political association.

Loyalty Oaths

The court generally backed state power to require employees to take affirmatively-worded loyalty oaths, declaring their support for the existing system of constitutional government rather than disavowing any affiliation with groups intending to overthrow that system.

In 1971 the court upheld a state requirement that teachers take such an oath, making clear in its opinion that persons could be properly dismissed for refusing to take such an oath only if they were first given a hearing on the reasons for their refusal.[100] The following year, the court by a vote of 4-3 upheld a state requirement that all its employees swear to "oppose the overthrow of the government by force, violence or by any illegal or unconstitutional method."[101]

Also in 1971 and 1972, the court upheld state requirements that applicants for admission to the state bar take affirmative oaths of loyalty to the state and federal constitutions. But the court at the same time limited strictly the power of state officials to penalize those who would not take such oaths.[102] *(See box, p. 515)*

In 1974, the court held unanimously that a state infringed the First Amendment freedom of political association by requiring political parties seeking a place on its ballot to swear that they did not advocate the violent overthrow of local, state or federal government.

In the court's opinion in the case of *Communist Party of Indiana v. Whitcomb,* Justice Brennan reaffirmed the court's view that " 'the constitutional guarantees of free

Politics and Public Employees

The First Amendment's guarantee of freedom for political association does not deny Congress and state legislatures the power to limit the political activity of public employees.

The Supreme Court first made this point in 1947, and reaffirmed it as recently as 1973. The limited infringement of such laws upon the right of political association, ruled the court, is quite justified by the government's interest in having its employees chosen on the basis of merit, not political loyalty.

The end of the spoils system for filling federal posts brought with it laws limiting the political activities of government workers. In 1876 Congress prohibited government employees from requesting, giving, or receiving money for political purposes from any federal official. The Civil Service Act of 1883 forbade federal officials to use their position or authority to coerce or influence the political action of their subordinates.

The Hatch Act of 1939 prohibited federal employees from taking active part in political campaigns or the management of political party activities. Civil Service Commission regulations subsequently have denied government workers the right to participate in the following political activities: running for office, distributing campaign literature, taking an active role in political campaigns, circulating nominating petitions, attending political conventions as other than a spectator and publishing or signing a letter soliciting votes for a candidate.

In 1947, the Supreme Court in the case of *United Public Workers v. Mitchell,* upheld such restrictions on the political activities of government employees. The vote was 4-3. Justices Frank Murphy and Robert H. Jackson did not take part in the decision. Justices Wiley Rutledge, Hugo L. Black and William O. Douglas dissented.

Justice Stanley F. Reed, speaking for four members of the court, declared that the court saw no constitutional objection to the finding of Congress that an efficient public service was best obtained by prohibiting active participation by public employees in political campaigns. The conclusion was a reasonable one, well

within the power of Congress over federal employees. Reed continued:

> For regulation of employees it is not necessary that the act regulated be anything more than an act reasonably deemed by Congress to interfere with the efficiency of the public service. . . .

We have said that Congress may regulate the political conduct of Government employees "within reasonable limits," even though the regulation trenches to some extent upon unfettered political action. The determination of the extent to which political activities of governmental employees shall be regulated lies primarily in Congress. Courts will interfere only when such regulation passes beyond the generally existing conception of governmental power.[1]

Reed added, however, that the concept of government power might change, indicating that some future court might find these restrictions impermissible.

But sixteen years later, in 1973, the court again rebuffed First Amendment challenges to federal and state prohibitions on partisan political activity by public employees. By a 6-3 vote, the court again upheld the validity of the Hatch Act.

Justice Byron R. White wrote for the majority in the case of *Civil Service Commission v. Letter Carriers:*

> [I]t is in the best interest of the country, indeed essential, that federal service should depend upon meritorious performance rather than political service, and that the political influence of federal employees on others and on the electoral process should be limited.[2]

Justices Douglas, William J. Brennan Jr. and Thurgood Marshall dissented.

In a companion case — *Broadrick v. Oklahoma State Personnel Board* — the court by a vote of 5-4 sustained a state law prohibiting employees from partisan political activity.[3] Justice Potter Stewart, who voted with the majority in the Hatch Act case, joined the dissenters in the state case.

---

[1] *United Public Workers v. Mitchell,* 330 U.S. 75 at 101, 102 (1947).

[2] *Civil Service Commission v. Letter Carriers,* 413

U.S. 548 at 557 (1973).

[3] *Broadrick v. Oklahoma State Personnel Board,* 413 U.S. 601 (1973).

---

speech and free press do not permit a State to forbid or proscribe advocacy of the use of force or of law violation except where such advocacy is directed to inciting or producing imminent lawless action and is likely to incite or produce such action.' "[103]

Political Parties

Political parties — and in one case a radical student organization — won court rulings making clear their right of association, and the point at which state officials could limit its exercise.

In the 1972 case of *Healy v. James,* the court held that without evidence that the group would have adverse effects on campus life, university officials could not constitutionally refuse to recognize a local chapter of the radical organization, Students for a Democratic Society.[104]

Several decisions in the next two years set out the court's view on the permissible restrictions a state might place on persons wishing to change political parties, as voters or candidates. In 1973 the court upheld a state requirement that voters who wished to vote in a party's primary have enrolled in that party at least 30 days before the last general election.[105]

Later in the year, the court held that the First Amendment limited the scope of such a state requirement. The court struck down as abridging the right of political association a state rule forbidding a person to vote in the primary of one party if he had voted in that of another party within the preceding 23 months.[106] Early in 1974, however, the court upheld a state requirement that independent candidates disaffiliate themselves from a party one year before the primary election of the year in which they wish to run as independents.[107]

In 1975 the court held that national political parties, as well as individuals, have a constitutional right of political association. In the case of *Cousins v. Wigoda*, the court held that this right was infringed by state court efforts to penalize one set of state delegates who were seated at the Democratic National Convention, by convention decision, instead of another set of delegates from the state. The case arose out of the 1972 convention — to which two opposing sets of Democratic delegates went from Illinois, one committed to the presidential candidacy of Sen. George S. McGovern (D S.D.) and the other set chosen and led by then-Mayor Richard J. Daley of Chicago.[108]

Patronage Firing

Twice — in 1947 and 1973 — the court has upheld federal and state laws restricting the partisan political activity of federal and state workers, finding the curtailment of First Amendment rights justified by the interest in having government jobs filled on the basis of merit, not political loyalty. *(Box p. 517)*

In a 1976 decision, the court dealt with the other side of the patronage hiring issue — patronage firing. And in that decision, the court held that the freedom of political association was violated by that practice.

The case of *Elrod v. Burns*, like *Cousins*, arose in Illinois. It had been the practice that all employees of the Cook County sheriff's office, who were not covered by civil service regulations and who were not of the same party as the newly-elected sheriff, were fired by the incoming sheriff — who would then replace them with persons of political affiliation similar to his.

This, held the court by a 5-3 vote, violated the First Amendment.

Writing for the court, Justice Brennan explained:

> . . . though freedom of belief is central, "[t]he First Amendment protects political association as well as political expression". . . . There can no longer be doubt that freedom to associate with others for the common advancement of political beliefs and ideas is a form of

"orderly activity" protected by the First and Fourteenth Amendments. . . .[109]

Brennan cited as precedent the decision in the *Keyishian* case nine years earlier, noting that in that case the court "squarely held that political association alone could not, consistently with the First Amendment, constitute adequate ground for denying public employment." [110] *(Details, p. 516)*

Then, moving to weigh the state's justification for patronage firing against its curtailment of individual freedom, Brennan cited the cases in which the court had upheld the Hatch Act limitations on partisan political activity by government employees — *United Public Workers v. Mitchell*, and *Civil Service Commission v. Letter Carriers*.[111] Those limitations were upheld, he explained, as a justifiable way of eliminating patronage — the very practice which Illinois now argued to preserve.

By forbidding the firing of persons simply because of their political affiliation, Brennan continued, the court was not outlawing political parties:

> Parties are free to exist and their concomitant activities are free to continue. We require only that the rights of every citizen to believe as he will and to act and associate according to his beliefs be free to continue as well.

> In summary, patronage dismissals severely restrict political belief and association. Though there is a vital need for government efficiency and effectiveness, such dismissals are on balance not the least restrictive means for fostering that end. . . .patronage dismissals cannot be justified by their contribution to the proper functioning of our democratic process through their assistance to partisan politics since political parties are nurtured by other, less intrusive and equally effective methods. More fundamentally, however, any contribution of patronage dismissals to the democratic process does not suffice to override their severe encroachment on First Amendment freedoms. . . .[112]

Justices Lewis F. Powell, William H. Rehnquist and Chief Justice Warren E. Burger dissented, holding that the patronage system contributed to the democratization of politics and to sustaining grass-roots interest in government — considerations that outweighed the limited intrusion of patronage firing on First Amendment freedoms.

Footnotes

[1] *Elrod v. Burns*, 427 U.S. 347 at 356 (1976).
[2] *Schenck v. United States*, 249 U.S. 47 (1919); *Frohwerk v. United States*, 249 U.S. 204 (1919); *Debs. v. United States*, 249 U.S. 211 (1919).
[3] *Schenck v. United States*, 249 U.S. 47 at 52 (1919).
[4] *Schaefer v. United States*, 251 U.S. 466 at 482 (1920).
[5] Id. at 479.
[6] *Gitlow v. New York*, 268 U.S. 652 at 666 (1925).
[7] *Whitney v. California*, 274 U.S. 357 at 377 (1927).
[8] *Stromberg v. California*, 283 U.S. 359 (1931).
[9] *DeJonge v. Oregon*, 299 U.S. 353 (1937); *Herndon v. Lowry*, 301 U.S. 242 (1937).
[10] *DeJonge v. Oregon*, 299 U.S. 353 at 365 (1937).
[11] *Joint Anti-Fascist Refugee Committee v. McGrath*, 341 U.S. 123 at 174 (1951).
[12] *Congress and the Nation*, Vol. I (Washington: Congressional Quarterly, 1965), pp. 1645-1670.

[13] Thomas I. Emerson, *The System of Freedom of Expression.* (New York: Random House, 1970), p. 110.
[14] *Dennis v. United States*, 341 U.S. 494 at 510 (1951).
[15] Id. at 502.
[16] Id at 509, 510-511, 516-517.
[17] Id. at 549.
[18] Id. at 518-520.
[19] Id. at 525-526.
[20] Id. at 570.
[21] Id. at 577.
[22] Id. at 579.
[23] Id. at 584-585, 590.
[24] *Yates v. United States*, 354 U.S. 298 (1957); see also the court's review of Yates' convictions for contempt: *Yates v. United States*, 355 U.S. 66 (1957); 356 U.S. 363 (1958).
[25] *Yates v. United States*, 354 U.S. 298 at 306-307, 312 (1957).
[26] Id. at 321.

27 Id. at 320-322, 324-325, 326-327.
28 Id. at 329-330.
29 Id. at 339.
30 Id at 340.
31 Id. at 345.
32 Scales v. United States, 367 U.S. 203 at 228-229 (1961).
33 Id. at 229-230.
34 Id. at 260.
35 Noto v. United States, 367 U.S. 290 at 297-298 (1961).
36 Congress and the Nation, Vol. I, pp. 1650-1651.
37 Ibid. p. 1653.
38 Communist Party v. Subversive Activities Control Board, 367 U.S. 1 (1961).
39 Id. at 86.
40 Id. at 102-103.
41 Id. at 105.
42 Id. at 137, 145.
43 Id. at 181.
44 Congress and the Nation, Vol. II, pp. 413-415; Vol. III, p. 489; Vol. IV, p. 570.
45 Albertson v. Subversive Activities Control Board, 382 U.S. 70 at 79 (1965).
46 Congress and the Nation, Vol. II, p. 418.
47 United States v. Robel, 389 U.S. 258 at 265, 266-267 (1967).
48 Id. at 285.
49 Boorda v. Subversive Activities Control Board, 421 F. 2d 1142 (D.C. Cir. 1969).
50 General background on loyalty programs, Congress and the Nation, Vol. I, pp. 1663-1668.
51 Joint Anti-Fascist Refugee Committee v. McGrath, 341 U.S. 123 at 161 (1951).
52 Id. at 200.
53 Bailey v. Richardson, 341 U.S. 918 (1951).
54 Peters v. Hobby, 349 U.S. 331 (1955).
55 Cole v. Young, 351 U.S. 536 (1956); see also Service v. Dulles, 354 U.S. 363 (1957).
56 Greene v. McElroy, 360 U.S. 474 (1959).
57 Id. at 508.
58 Id. at 511, 524.
59 Congress and the Nation, Vol. I, pp. 1667-1668.
60 Cafeteria and Restaurant Workers Union v. McElroy, 367 U.S. 886 (1961).
61 American Communications Association v. Douds, 339 U.S. 382 at 390 (1950).
62 Id. at 391.
63 Id. at 393.
64 Id. at 396.
65 Id. at 445.
66 Id. at 444.
67 Id. at 446, 452-453.
68 Congress and the Nation, Vol. I, pp. 568, 611.
69 United States v. Brown, 381 U.S. 437 at 449-450, 461 (1965).
70 Id. at 474.
71 Killian v. United States, 368 U.S. 231 (1961); Raymond

Dennis et al. v. United States, 384 U.S. 855 (1966).
72 Gerende v. Board of Supervisors of Elections, 341 U.S. 56 (1951).
73 Garner v. Board of Public Works of the City of Los Angeles, 341 U.S. 716 (1951).
74 Id. at 724-725.
75 Id. at 726, 728.
76 Adler v. Board of Education of New York City, 342 U.S. 485 (1952).
77 Id. at 493.
78 Ibid.
79 Id. at 508.
80 Id. at 509, 510, 511.
81 Wieman v. Updegraff, 344 U.S. 183 at 190 (1952).
82 Id. at 191.
83 Slochower v. Board of Higher Education of New York City, 350 U.S. 551 at 557 (1956).
84 Id. at 561.
85 Id. at 565.
86 Lerner v. Casey, 357 U.S. 468 (1958).
87 Beilan v. Board of Public Education, School District of Philadelphia, 357 U.S. 399 (1958).
88 Id at 410.
89 Id. at 418; see also Speiser v. Randall, 357 U.S. 513 (1958).
90 National Association for the Advancement of Colored People v. Alabama, 357 U.S. 449 (1958).
91 Shelton v. Tucker, 364 U.S. 479 at 490 (1960).
92 Cramp v. Board of Public Instruction, Orange County, Fla., 368 U.S. 278 at 286 (1961).
93 Id. at 287.
94 Baggett v. Bullitt, 377 U.S. 360 at 367 (1964).
95 Elfbrandt v. Russell, 384 U.S. at 17-19 (1966).
96 Keyishian v. Board of Regents of the University of the State of New York, 385 U.S. 589 at 606 (1967).
97 Id. at 601, 603.
98 Id. at 628.
99 Whitehill v. Elkins, 389 U.S. 54 at 62 (1967).
100 Connell v. Higginbotham, 403 U.S. 207 (1971).
101 Cole v. Richardson, 405 U.S. 676 (1972).
102 In re Stolar, Baird v. State Bar of Arizona, 401 U.S. 23, 1 (1971); Law Students Civil Rights Research Council v. Wadmond, 401 U.S. 154 (1971).
103 Communist Party of Indiana v. Whitcomb, 414 U.S. 441 at 448 (1974).
104 Healy v. James, 408 U.S. 169 (1972).
105 Rosario v. Rockefeller, 410 U.S. 752 (1973).
106 Kusper v. Pontikes, 414 U.S. 51 (1973).
107 Storer v. Brown, Frommhagen v. Brown, 415 U.S. 724 (1974).
108 Cousins v. Wigoda, 419 U.S. 477 (1975).
109 Elrod v. Burns, 427 U.S. 347 at 357 (1975).
110 Id. at 358.
111 United Public Workers v. Mitchell, 330 U.S. 75 (1947); Civil Service Commission v. Letter Carriers, 413 U.S. 548 (1973).
112 Elrod v. Burns, 427 U.S. 347 at 372-373.

Selected Bibliography

Atleson, James B. "The Aftermath of *Baker* v. *Carr:* An Adventure in Judicial Experimentation." *California Law Review* 51 (1963): 535-572.

Auerbach, Carl E. "The Reapportionment Cases: One Person, One Vote — One Vote, One Value," *Supreme Court Review 1964:* 1-87.

Baker, Gordon E. *The Reapportionment Revolution.* New York: Random House, 1966.

Banzhaf, John F., III "Multi-Member Electoral Districts — Do They Violate the 'One Man, One Vote' Principle?" *Yale Law Journal* 75 (1966): 1309-1338.

Barth, Alan, *The Loyalty of Free Men.* New York: Viking Press, 1951.

Berry, Mary F., *Black Resistance/White Law: A History of Constitutional Racism in America.* New York: Appleton-Century-Crofts, 1971.

Bickel, Alexander M. "The Voting Rights Cases." *Supreme Court Review 1966:* 79-102.

Bontecou, Eleanor. *The Federal Loyalty-Security Program.* Ithaca, N.Y.: Cornell University Press, 1953.

Brown, Ralph S. Jr. *Loyalty and Security: Employment Tests in the United States.* New Haven: Yale University Press, 1958.

Carr, Robert K. *Federal Protection of Civil Rights.* Ithaca: Cornell University Press, 1947.

Chafee, Zechariah Jr., *Free Speech in the United States.* Cambridge, Mass.: Harvard University Press, 1941.

—————. *The Blessings of Liberty.* Philadelphia: Lippincott, 1956.

Chase, Harold W. *Security and Liberty: The Problem of Native Communists, 1947-1955,* Garden City, N.Y.: Doubleday & Co., 1954.

Claude, Richard O. *The Supreme Court and the Electoral Process.* Baltimore: Johns Hopkins Press, 1970.

Cook, Thomas I. *Democratic Rights versus Communist Activity.* New York: Doubleday & Co., 1954.

Cortner, Richard C. *The Apportionment Cases.* Knoxville, Tenn.: University of Tennessee Press, 1970.

Cushman, Robert E. *Civil Liberties in the United States.* Ithaca, N.Y.: Cornell University Press, 1956.

DeGrazia, Alfred. *Essay on Apportionment and Representative Government.* Washington, D.C.: American Enterprise Institute, 1963.

—————. *Public and Republic: Political Representation in America.* New York: Alfred Knopf, 1961.

Dixon, Robert G. Jr. *Democratic Representation: Reapportionment in Law and Politics.* New York: Oxford University Press, 1968.

Elliott, Ward E. Y. *The Rise of Guardian Democracy: The Supreme Court's Role in Voting Rights Disputes, 1845-1969.* Cambridge, Mass.: Harvard University Press, 1974.

Emerson, Thomas I. and Haber, David. *Political and Civil Rights in the United States.* 2 Vols. Buffalo, New York: Dennis and Co., 1958.

Emerson, Thomas I. *The System of Freedom of Expression.* New York: Random House, 1970.

Fraenkel, Osmond K. *The Supreme Court and Civil Liberties.* Dobbs Ferry, N.Y.: Oceana, 1960.

Gellhorn, Walter, *American Rights: The Constitution in Action,* New York: MacMillan Publishing Co., 1960.

—————. *Security, Loyalty and Science.* Ithaca, N.Y.: Cornell University Press, 1950.

—————. *The States and Subversion.* Ithaca, N.Y.: Cornell University Press, 1952.

Hanson, Royce. *The Political Thicket: Reapportionment and Constitutional Democracy.* Englewood Cliffs, N.J.: Prentice-Hall, 1966.

Irwin, William P. "Representation and Election: The Reapportionment Cases in Retrospect." *Michigan Law Review* 67 (1969): 73-82.

Konvitz, Milton R. *Fundamental Liberties of a Free People.* Ithaca, N.Y.: Cornell University Press, 1957.

Latham, Earl. *The Communist Controversy in Washington.* Cambridge, Mass.: Harvard University Press, 1966.

McKay, Robert. *Reapportionment: The Law and Politics of Equal Representation.* New York: Twentieth Century Fund, 1965.

Meiklejohn, Alexander, *Political Freedom: The Constitutional Powers of the People.* New York: Harper & Row, 1960.

Mendelson, Wallace E. "Clear and Present Danger — From *Schenck* to *Dennis.*" *Columbia Law Review* 52 (1952): 313-333.

Murray, Robert K. *Red Scare: A Study in National Hysteria, 1919-1920.* Minneapolis: University of Minnesota Press, 1955.

Myrdal, Gunnar. *An American Dilemma.* New York: Harper & Row, 1944.

Nathanson, Nathaniel L. "The Communist Trial and the Clear and Present Danger Test." *Harvard Law Review* LXIII (1950): 1167-75.

Polsby, Nelson W. ed. *Reapportionment in the 1970s.* Berkeley, Los Angeles, Calif.: University of California Press, 1971.

Pritchett, C. Herman. *Congress versus the Supreme Court, 1957-1960.* Minneapolis: University of Minnesota Press, 1961.

—————. *The Political Offender and the Warren Court.* Boston: Boston University Press, 1958.

Schaar, John H. *Loyalty in America.* Berkeley and Los Angeles: University of California Press, 1957.

Schubert, Glendon. *Reapportionment.* New York: Charles Scribner's, 1965.

Woodward, C. Vann. *Origins of the New South, 1877-1913.* Baton Rouge, La.: Louisiana State University Press, 1951.

—————. *The Strange Career of Jim Crow.* 2nd rev. ed. New York: Oxford University Press, 1966.

DUE PROCESS AND INDIVIDUAL RIGHTS

Introduction 523

Search and Seizure. 539

Self-Incrimination. 555

The Aid of Legal Counsel. 565

Double Jeopardy 571

Cruel and Unusual Punishment. 575

Due Process and Individual Rights

Due process of law is such a broad and flexible concept that it eludes precise definition. Most essentially, it embodies a promise to the individual that his government will treat him fairly.

In the mid-twentieth century the Supreme Court expanded that implicit guarantee to embrace a wide range of rights, including those specifically delineated in the Fourth, Fifth, Sixth and Eighth Amendments — guarantees until then applicable only against federal action, not against state infringement.

Due process is primarily a guarantee of fair procedures, of *how* the government must or must not do something, not of *what* they must or must not do. Justice William O. Douglas noted the importance of procedure, pointing out that most of the provisions of the Bill of Rights were procedural. "It is procedure," he wrote, "that spells much of the difference between rule by law and rule by whim or caprice. Steadfast adherence to strict procedural safeguards is our main assurance that there will be equal justice under law." [1]

Procedural rights are perhaps of most significance for persons charged with crimes. These rights provide an individual accused of a crime assurance that he will receive fair treatment by the authorities. Every criminal case is a legal contest between the individual and government. A crime is an offense against society. And government is society's agency to prosecute the offender. But it is an uneven match. The power of the individual defendant is no match for the power of government unless the individual has guarantees he will be treated fairly.

Procedural rights are not based on sentimental concern for the criminal. The guarantees were not devised to coddle criminals or provide technical loopholes through which dangerous persons escape the consequences of their acts.

"Due process of law is not, primarily, the right of the accused," David Fellman has written. "It is basically the community's assurance that prosecutors, judges and juries will behave properly, within rules distilled from long centuries of concrete experience." [2]

Although the procedural safeguards of the Bill of Rights are known primarily for their importance to persons suspected or accused of crime, they operate as well to shield all individuals against any arbitrary, despotic or unduly intrusive government action.

These provisions assure an individual charged with a crime:

- notice of the nature and cause of the charge against him;
- a speedy and public trial by an impartial jury of the area where the crime was committed;
- opportunity to confront witnesses accusing him and to compel witnesses in his favor to appear;
- the aid of an attorney in preparing and presenting his defense.

Furthermore, these guarantees promise the individual that he will not be:

- subjected to unreasonable searches or baseless arrests by government officials;
- compelled to incriminate himself;
- deprived of his life, his liberty or his property without due process of law;
- tried for a serious offense without being formally charged in an indictment;
- tried twice for the same action by the same sovereign;
- subject to excessive bail or excessive fines;
- sentenced to suffer cruel and unusual punishment.

Originally, these particular guarantees applied directly only to persons tried in federal courts, even though most persons charged with crimes in the United States are tried in state and local courts.

But since 1868 the 14th Amendment has guaranteed the individual due process and equal protection from state, as well as federal, authorities. Beginning in the 1930s, the Supreme Court has read those guarantees as extending many of the specific procedural protections of the Bill of Rights to state defendants.

The process reached its climax in the 1960s, but the revolutionary decisions of that time were rooted in decisions of the 1920s and 1930s. Under the leadership of Chief Justices William Howard Taft and Charles Evans Hughes, the court first began to apply the fundamental requirements of fair procedure to state trials, even while individual justices wrangled over whether or not the 14th Amendment guarantee of due process so "incorporated" the Bill of Rights as to extend all its specific guarantees to defendants in state cases.

Initially, the court rejected any "wholesale" incorporation theory, preferring a more "selective" approach. The majority began developing a list of "fundamental" rights which they said the states must observe under the due process clause: the right to legal counsel in certain cases, the ban on cruel and unusual punishment and the guarantee against unreasonable search and seizure.

The "selective incorporation" debate came to a dramatic end in the 1960s. In a series of rulings, the court resoundingly rejected any idea that only a "watered-down" Bill of Rights applied to the states. The court extended to state defendants the protection of the controversial exclusionary rule, the right to appointed counsel, the privilege against compelled self-incrimination, the right to confront prosecution witnesses, the right to a speedy trial, the right to a jury trial and the protection against double jeopardy.

Due Process: Early Views

Early in its history, during the tenure of Chief Justice John Marshall, the Supreme Court held that the Bill of Rights limited only federal, not state, action.

In 1833 the Supreme Court set out this conclusion in its ruling in the case of *Barron v. Baltimore.*[3]

With Chief Justice Marshall writing the opinion, the court rejected the argument of a Baltimore wharf-owner that the Fifth Amendment provision declaring that persons whose private property was taken for public use should be justly compensated should apply against all government action, not just federal government action. Marshall wrote that this was not the intent of those who approved and ratified the Bill of Rights:

> The Constitution was ordained and established by the people of the United States for themselves, for their own government, and not for the government of the individual States.... The powers they conferred on this government were to be exercised by itself; and the limitations on power, if expressed in general terms, are naturally, and, we think, necessarily applicable to the government created by the instrument.
>
> ...the provision in the fifth amendment to the Constitution, declaring that private property shall not be taken for public use without just compensation, is intended solely as a limitation on the exercise of power by the government of the United States, and is not applicable to the legislation of the States.[4]

Congress and Due Process

But although the justices refused to extend the Fifth Amendment's guarantee of due process against *state* action, the court in 1856 applied that guarantee to legislative action by Congress, making clear that all branches of the *federal* government were bound by its promise of fair procedures.

In the case of *Murray's Lessee v. Hoboken Land and Improvement Company,* the court upheld an act of Congress authorizing the Treasury Department to issue warrants against the property of federal revenue collectors who were indebted to the federal government.[5] The law had been challenged as allowing the taking of property without due process.

In the majority opinion written by Justice Benjamin R. Curtis, the court began its effort to define due process. Curtis described due process as any process which did not conflict with specific constitutional provisions or established judicial practices. Curtis wrote:

> That the warrant now in question is legal process, is not denied. It was issued in conformity with an act of Congress. But is it "due process of law?" The Constitution contains no description of those processes which it was intended to allow or forbid. It does not even declare what principles are to be applied to ascertain whether it be due process. It is manifest that it was not left to the legislative power to enact any process which might be devised. The article is a restraint on the legislative as well as on the executive and judicial powers of the government, and cannot be so construed as to leave Congress free to make any process "due process of law," by its mere will. To what principles, then, are we to resort to ascertain whether this process enacted by Congress, is due process? To this the answer must be twofold. We must examine the Constitution itself, to see whether this process be in conflict with any of its provisions. If not found to be so, we must look to those settled usages and modes of proceeding existing in the common and statute law of England, before the emigration of our ancestors and which are shown not to have been unsuited to their civil and political condition by having been acted on by them after the settlement of this country.[6]

Substantive Due Process

Twelve years after that ruling, the 14th Amendment became part of the Constitution, forbidding the states to deprive any person of life, liberty or property without due process of law.

Oddly, this due process guarantee was initially used with a great deal more effect to protect property than life or liberty. This was the result of the development of the doctrine of substantive due process — the view that the substance, as well as the procedures, of a law must comply with due process. *(Box p. 526-527)*

In the mid-20th century, Justice Robert H. Jackson compared the two types of due process:

> Procedural due process is more elemental and less flexible than substantive due process. It yields less to the times, varies less with conditions, and defers much less to legislative judgment. Insofar as it is technical law, it must be a specialized responsibility within the competence of the judiciary on which they do not bend before political branches of the Government, as they should on matters of policy which comprise substantive law.[7]

Due Process and the States

For 65 years after the 14th Amendment was ratified, its due process clause provided little, if any, protection to persons tried in state and local courts.

In 1884 the court held that due process did not require states to use indictments to charge persons with capital crimes, despite the Fifth Amendment provisions requiring indictments in similar federal cases. In 1900 the court held that the due process guarantee did not require states to use twelve-man juries. In 1908 the court held that the Fifth

Amendment privilege against compelled self-incrimination did not protect state defendants.

Hurtado v. California

In the indictment case, *Hurtado v. California,* the court upheld the murder conviction and death sentence of Joseph Hurtado, who had been charged without an indictment.[8] He challenged his conviction, arguing that under Justice Curtis' definition of due process in *Hoboken* — as that process which did not conflict with specific constitutional provisions — he had been denied due process.

The court's ruling, relaxing the earlier standard for the demands of due process upon state criminal procedures, blurred the *Hoboken* definition.

Writing for the court, Justice Stanley Matthews redefined due process as "any legal proceeding enforced by public authority, whether sanctioned by age and custom, or newly devised in the discretion of the legislative power, in furtherance of the general public good, which regards, and preserves these principles of liberty and justice. . . ."[9]

However, Matthews continued:

It is not every Act, legislative in form, that is law. Law is something more than mere will exerted as an act of power. It must be not a special rule for a particular person or a particular case, . . .thus excluding, as not due process of law, Acts of attainder, Bills of pains and penalties, Acts of confiscation, Acts reversing judgments, and Acts directly transferring one man's estate to another, legislative judgments and decrees, and other similar, special, partial and arbitrary exertions of power under the forms of legislation. Arbitrary power, enforcing its edicts to the injury of the persons and property of its subjects, is not law, whether manifested as the decree of a personal monarch or of an impersonal multitude.[10]

Adopting reasoning diametrically opposed to that of Curtis in *Hoboken,* the majority ruled that because the Fifth Amendment expressly included *both* the indictment requirement *and* the due process guarantee, the indictment requirement was obviously not included as an element of due process.

In dissent, Justice John Marshall Harlan set out what would come to be called the "incorporation" approach. In his view, the 14th Amendment guarantee of due process "incorporated" many of the specific guarantees of the Bill of Rights, effectively nullifying *Barron v. Baltimore* by applying them against state action.

Harlan argued that the court's reasoning in *Hurtado* could open the door for states to deny defendants many other rights:

. . .If the presence in the Fifth Amendment of a specific provision for grand juries in capital cases, alongside the provision for due process of law in proceedings involving life, liberty or property, is held to prove that "due process of law" did not, in the judgment of the framers of the Constitution, necessarily require a grand jury in capital cases, inexorable logic would require it to be, likewise, held that the right not to be put twice in jeopardy of life and limb for the same offense, nor compelled in a criminal case to testify against one's self—rights and immunities also specifically recognized in the Fifth Amendment—were not protected by that due process of law required by the settled usages and proceedings existing under the common and statute law of England at the settlement of this country. More than that, other Amendments of the Constitution proposed at the same time, expressly recognize the right of persons to just compensation for private property taken for public use; their right, when accused of crime, to be informed of the nature and cause of the accusation against them, and to a speedy and public trial, by an impartial jury of the State and district wherein the crime was committed; to be confronted by the witnesses against them; and to have compulsory process for obtaining witnesses in their favor. Will it be claimed that these rights were not secured by the "law of the land" or by "due process of law," as declared and established at the foundation of our government?[11]

Eventually the court would adopt an approach of "selective incorporation" of the guarantees of the Bill of Rights into the due process clause of the 14th Amendment.

Selective Incorporation

Justice Samuel F. Miller described this approach in an 1877 decision, discussing the court's role in defining what due process required of state action. Miller wrote:

If . . . it were possible to define what it is for a State to deprive a person of life, liberty or property without due process of law, in terms which would cover every exercise of power thus forbidden to the State, and exclude those which are not, no more useful construction could be furnished by this or any other court to any part of the fundamental law.

But, apart from the imminent risk of failure to give any definition which would be at once perspicuous, comprehensive and satisfactory, there is wisdom, we think, in the ascertaining of the intent and application of such an important phrase in the Federal Constitution, by the gradual process of judicial inclusion and exclusion, as the cases presented for decision shall require, with the reasoning on which such decisions may be founded. This court is, after an experience of nearly a century, still engaged in defining the obligation of contracts, the regulation of commerce, and other powers conferred on the Federal Government, or limitations imposed upon the States.[12]

Maxwell v. Dow

In 1900 the court ruled in the case of *Maxwell v. Dow* that the 14th Amendment did not require state juries to be composed of twelve persons.

Justice Harlan again dissented, protesting the contrast between the court's vigorous use of substantive due process and its reluctance to enforce procedural due process. He wrote:

If then the 'due process of law' required by the Fourteenth Amendment does not allow a State to take private property without just compensation, but does allow the life or liberty of the citizen to be taken in a mode that is repugnant to the settled usages and the modes of proceeding authorized at the time the Constitution was adopted and which was expressly forbidden in the National Bill of Rights, it would seem that the protection of private property is of more consequence than the protection of the life and liberty of the citizen.[13]

The Protection of Substantive Due Process ...

With the development of the doctrine of substantive due process, the Supreme Court appointed itself the guardian of property rights against restrictive state legislation. The court scrutinized state regulatory laws focusing on what states chose to regulate rather than on how they regulated it.

This development transformed a guarantee of procedural fairness for persons into a legal foundation for the court to monitor state economic regulations.

A Developing Concept

Substantive due process was first hinted at in a dissenting opinion in the *Slaughterhouse Cases* in 1873.

In this ruling the court rejected a 14th Amendment challenge to a state grant of a slaughterhouse monopoly. Butchers in New Orleans, deprived of the opportunity to practice their trade by this state action, attacked it as an abridgement of their privileges and immunities, a denial of equal protection and a violation of due process.

The majority of the court ruled against them, but Justice Joseph P. Bradley agreed in dissent with their contention that "a law which prohibits a large class of citizens from adopting ... or from following a lawful employment ... does deprive them of liberty as well as property, without due process of law." [1]

Four years later, in the case of *Munn v. Illinois*, the court edged closer to adopting Bradley's view. Although the justices voted to uphold a state law that regulated grain elevator rates, they did so only after considering the substance of the business regulated.

The court found that grain storage was one of a class of businesses "affected with a public interest" and thus subject to such state regulation. [2]

This decision was the first in a line of rulings stretching over half a century, in which the court looked to the character of the activity regulated to determine whether it was properly subject to state regulation.

In the 1877 case of *Mugler v. Kansas,* concerning a state prohibition law, Justice John Marshall Harlan explained the court's view of its responsibility for scrutinizing the substance of challenged laws:

> The courts are not bound by mere forms, nor are they to be misled by mere pretenses. They are at liberty — indeed, are under a solemn duty — to look at the substance of things, whenever they enter upon the inquiry whether the legislature has transcended the limits of its authority. If, therefore, a statute purporting to have been enacted to protect the public health, the public morals, or the public safety, has no real or substantial relation to those objects, or is a palpable invasion of rights secured by the fundamental law, it is the duty of the courts to so adjudge, and thereby give effect to the Constitution. [3]

Three years later, in 1890, the court in the case of *Chicago, Milwaukee and St. Paul R.R. Co. v. Minnesota,* first used substantive due process to strike down a state law regulating economic matters, ruling that the courts should have the final word on the reasonableness of railroad rates. [4] And in 1898 the court declared that courts should review public utility rates for reasonableness and to see that they allowed a fair return to the utility. [5]

Freedom of Contract

Although many laws in which states exercised their police power were challenged as a denial of due process, the Supreme Court generally found those laws valid, [6] but in the areas of rate-setting, price regulation, and wage and hour laws, the court was far less disposed to defer to the judgment of state legislators.

Wage and hour legislation was often found by the court to infringe upon "freedom of contract" — an aspect of liberty first acknowledged by the court in the case of *Allgeyer v. Louisiana,* decided in 1897. In that ruling the court declared that the personal liberty which the due process guarantee protected included the individual's right "to live and work where he will; to earn his livelihood by any lawful calling; to pursue any livelihood or avocation, and for that purpose to enter into all contracts which may be proper, necessary and essential to his carrying out to a successful conclusion the purposes above mentioned." [7]

With these doctrines — that business affected with a public interest was properly subject to state regulation, and that government should not interfere with the individual's freedom of contract — the Supreme Court plunged into its new role as judge of the substance of state economic regulation.

Under the "public interest" rubric, the court upheld state regulation of such varied matters as insurance and stockyards. [8] But beginning in the 1920s, the court found fewer and fewer areas of economic life to be properly included in this category. [9]

In its effort to protect the "freedom of contract," the court struck down a number of the first wage and hour laws passed by the states. In 1898, in the case of *Holden v. Hardy,* [10] the court upheld a law setting the ten-hour day as the maximum which miners might work. But seven years later, in the case of *Lochner v. New York,* [11] the court struck down a state law setting the ten-hour day and the sixty-hour week as the maximum for bakers.

The court saw a critical difference between the working conditions of mines and bakeries. Miners worked in palpably unhealthy conditions, to which their exposure should be limited; bakers were subject to less risk of injury or illness in their working environment. Subsequently, however, the court dropped its opposition to maximum-hour laws. [12] But it was not so tolerant when it considered the first minimum-wage statutes.

In its 1923 decision in the case of *Adkins v. Children's Hospital,* the court struck down the District of Columbia's minimum wage law for women. Justice George Sutherland, for the five-man majority, described the law as "simply and exclusively a price-fixing law" in violation of the freedom of contract. [13]

The Demise of Substantive Due Process

The Depression and the New Deal created pressures which inexorably forced the court to drop its use of substantive due process to monitor economic regulation.

... From Property Rights to Privacy Concerns

Beginning in 1934 with its ruling in the case of *Nebbia v. New York,* the court abdicated its role as "super-legislature," leaving decisions on the wisdom and appropriateness of economic legislation to legislators. In *Nebbia,* the court upheld a state law regulating milk prices, even though the milk industry was not one "affected with a public interest." [14] The court thus ceased to distinguish between some lines of business and others for the purpose of finding some subject to state regulation and others exempt.

Nevertheless, the court continued to use the "freedom of contract" doctrine to nullify a state minimum wage law for women. In the case of *Morehead v. Tipaldo,* a five-man majority in 1936 declared:

> The right to make contracts about one's affairs is a part of the liberty protected by the due process clause. Within this liberty are provisions of contracts between employer and employee fixing the wages to be paid.... [15]

But the tide of public opinion had already turned against this sort of judicial second-guessing. In 1936 both major parties repudiated the *Morehead* decision.

The following year, after President Franklin D. Roosevelt had brandished his plan to "pack" the court, the justices reversed themselves. In the case of *West Coast Hotel v. Parrish,* the court upheld a Washington state minimum wage law for women, overruling *Adkins* and *Morehead.* [16]

Four years later, with its decision in *United States v. Darby Lumber Co.,* the court upheld federal power to set minimum-wage and maximum-hour standards for workers involved in interstate commerce. [17] Also in 1941, the court upheld a state law regulating the fees which employment agencies might charge. [18] And in 1944 the court terminated the judicial role in rate-making. [19]

In the 1941 employment-agency fee ruling, *Olsen v. Nebraska,* Justice William O. Douglas wrote for the unanimous court: "We are not concerned ... with the wisdom, need, or appropriateness of the legislation. Differences of opinion on that score suggest a choice which 'should be left where ... it was left by the Constitution — to the states and to Congress.' " [20]

In 1952, the justices again stated that they no longer "sit as a superlegislature to weigh the wisdom of legislation nor to decide whether the policy it expresses offends the public welfare." [21]

From Property to Privacy

Yet even as the court sounded the epitaph for the use of substantive due process to justify its supervision of economic regulation, it was developing a line of rulings under the equal protection guarantee which would lead it back to the consideration of the substance of state legislation.

In 1942 the court in the case of *Skinner v. Oklahoma* struck down a state law which allowed habitual criminals to be sterilized. This law was a denial of equal protection, held the court, because of its substance — because it allowed the state to deprive an individual of "one of the basic civil rights of man." [22]

Matters of personal choice in family life have been the primary beneficiary of the "new substantive due process" approach foreshadowed in *Skinner.*

The landmark ruling in this area was the court's 1965 declaration in *Griswold v. Connecticut* that privacy was a value protected by the Constitution. [23] In that case, the court struck down a state law forbidding all use of birth control devices. Although Justice Douglas, writing the majority opinion, was careful not to rest the conclusion upon the due process clause, Justice Hugo L. Black — in dissent — found the ruling a direct descendant of *Lochner v. New York.* This too was substantive due process, he warned, and it was "no less dangerous when used to enforce this Court's views about personal rights than those about economic rights." [24]

Footnotes

[1] *The Slaughterhouse Cases,* 16 Wall. 36 at 122 (1873).

[2] *Munn v. Illinois,* 94 U.S. 113 (1877).

[3] *Mugler v. Kansas,* 123 U.S. 623 at 661 (1887).

[4] *Chicago, Milwaukee and St. Paul R.R. Co. v. Minnesota,* 134 U.S. 418 (1890).

[5] *Smyth v. Ames,* 169 U.S. 466 (1898).

[6] *Powell v. Pennsylvania,* 127 U.S. 678 (1888); *Jacobson v. Massachusetts,* 197 U.S. 11 (1905); *Austin v. Tennessee,* 179 U.S. 343 (1900); *Packer Corp. v. Utah,* 285 U.S. 105 (1932); *Euclid v. Ambler Realty Co.,* 272 U.S. 365 (1926).

[7] *Allgeyer v. Louisiana,* 165 U.S. 578 at 589 (1897).

[8] *German Alliance Insurance Co. v. Lewis,* 233 U.S. 389 (1914); *Cotting v. Godard,* 183 U.S. 79 (1901).

[9] *Tyson & Brother v. Banton,* 273 U.S. 418 (1927); *Ribnik v. McBride,* 277 U.S. 350 (1928); *Wolff Packing Co. v. Court of Industrial Relations,* 262 U.S. 522 (1923); *Burns Baking Co. v. Bryan,* 264 U.S. 504 (1924).

[10] *Holden v. Hardy,* 169 U.S. 366 (1898).

[11] *Lochner v. New York,* 198 U.S. 45 (1905).

[12] *Muller v. Oregon,* 208 U.S. 412 (1908); *Bunting v. Oregon,* 243 U.S. 426 (1917). For examples of substantive due process and labor matters, see *Adair v. United States,* 208 U.S. 161 (1908); *Coppage v. Kansas,* 236 U.S. 1 (1915); *Lincoln Federal Labor Union v. Northwestern Iron & Metal Co.,* 335 U.S. 525 (1949).

[13] *Adkins v. Children's Hospital,* 261 U.S. 525 at 554 (1923).

[14] *Nebbia v. New York,* 291 U.S. 502 (1934); see also *Petersen Baking Co. v. Burns,* 290 U.S. 570 (1934).

[15] *Morehead v. Tipaldo,* 298 U.S. 587 at 610 (1936).

[16] *West Coast Hotel v. Parrish,* 300 U.S. 379 (1937).

[17] *United States v. Darby Lumber Co.,* 312 U.S. 100 (1941).

[18] *Olsen v. Nebraska,* 313 U.S. 236 (1941).

[19] *Federal Power Commission v. Hope Natural Gas,* 320 U.S. 591 (1944).

[20] *Olsen v. Nebraska,* 313 U.S. 236 at 246 (1941).

[21] *Day-Brite Lighting, Inc. v. Missouri,* 342 U.S. 421 at 423 (1952); see also *Williamson v. Lee Optical of Oklahoma,* 348 U.S. 483 (1955).

[22] *Skinner v. Oklahoma,* 316 U.S. 535 (1942).

[23] *Griswold v. Connecticut,* 381 U.S. 479 (1965); see also *Eisenstadt v. Baird,* 405 U.S. 438 (1972); *Roe v. Wade,* 410 U.S. 113 (1973); *Doe v. Bolton,* 410 U.S. 179 (1973).

[24] *Griswold v. Connecticut,* 381 U.S. 479 at 522 (1965).

Twining v. New Jersey

Eight years later the court in the case of *Twining v. New Jersey* refused to hold that due process was denied state defendants by a judge's calling the jury's attention to the defendant's failure to testify in his own defense, implying that such silence was an admission of guilt. The defendants had claimed that the judge's comments violated their Fifth Amendment right to remain silent rather than incriminate themselves. They argued that this right was a fundamental "privilege or immunity" of federal citizenship protected against state action by the 14th Amendment.

The court rejected the claim and upheld the decision of the state court sustaining conviction. Justice William H. Moody's opinion for the majority also denied that the 14th Amendment guarantee of due process extended the protection of the first eight amendments against state action:

> . . .The essential elements of due process of law, already established . . . are singularly few, though of wide application and deep significance. . . . Due process requires that the court which assumes to determine the rights of parties shall have jurisdiction . . . and that there shall be notice and opportunity for hearing given the parties. . . .[14]

But Justice Moody left open the possibility that additional due process requirements could be imposed upon the states:

> It is possible that some of the personal rights safeguarded by the first eight Amendments against national action may also be safeguarded against state action, because a denial of them would be a denial of due process of law. . . . If this is so, it is not because those rights are enumerated in the first eight Amendments, but because they are of such a nature that they are included in the conception of due process of law.[15]

'Fundamental' Rights

This emphasis on rights became increasingly prevalent in the 1920s and 1930s as the court began to rule that some rights were so fundamental to fair treatment that the due process guarantee required states to observe them.

In the case of *Palko v. Connecticut*, decided in 1937, the court explained its view that some rights were "implicit in the concept of ordered liberty" and thus protected by due process against state infringement. In *Palko*, however, the court again rejected the "incorporation" theory.

Palko had been tried twice by Connecticut for the same murder. He challenged his conviction, arguing that the second trial violated the Fifth Amendment guarantee against double jeopardy. The court refused to reverse his conviction, declaring that the protection against double jeopardy was not one of those rights which due process required the states to observe.

For the court, Justice Benjamin N. Cardozo gave a "status report" on due process and state action:

> The right to trial by jury and the immunity from prosecution except as the result of an indictment may have value and importance. Even so, they are not of the very essence of a scheme of ordered liberty. To abolish them is not to violate a "principle of justice so rooted in the traditions and conscience of our people as to be ranked as fundamental." . . .What is true of jury trials and indictments is true also, as the cases show, of the immunity from compulsory self-incrimination. . . . This too might be lost, and justice still be done. . . . The exclusion of these immunities and privileges from the privileges and immunities protected against the action of the states has not been arbitrary or casual. It has been dictated by a study and appreciation of the meaning, the essential implications, of liberty itself.
>
> We reach a different plane of social and moral values when we pass to the privileges and immunities that have been taken over from the earlier articles of the federal bill of rights and brought within the Fourteenth Amendment by a process of absorption. . . . [T]he process of absorption has had its source in the belief that neither liberty nor justice would exist if they were sacrificed. . . . This is true . . . of freedom of thought and speech. . . . Fundamental too in the concept of due process, and so in that of liberty, is the thought that condemnation shall be rendered only after trial. . . . The hearing, moreover, must be a real one, not a sham or a pretense, *Moore v. Dempsey.* . . . For that reason, ignorant defendants in a capital case were held to have been condemned unlawfully when in truth, though not in form, they were refused the aid of counsel, *Powell v. Alabama.*[16]

A decade later, with its decision in the case of *Adamson v. California*, the court reaffirmed its *Twining* holding that the self-incrimination guarantee did not operate against state action — and its general view that the 14th Amendment did not incorporate the Bill of Rights.[17]

Arguing for the "incorporation" theory and dissenting from *Adamson* were four members of the court — Justices Hugo L. Black, Frank Murphy, William O. Douglas and Wiley B. Rutledge. They argued that the 14th Amendment was originally intended "to extend to all the people of the nation the complete protection of the Bill of Rights."[18] Black and Douglas would continue to serve on the court through the 1960s — and find their views at last espoused by a majority of the court as it extended virtually all those protections to all persons.

Footnotes

[1] *Joint Anti-Fascist Refugee Committee v. McGrath*, 341 U.S. 123 at 179 (1951).

[2] David Fellman, *The Defendant's Rights* (New York: Rinehart & Co., Inc., 1958), pp. 3-4.

[3] *Barron v. Baltimore*, 7 Pet. 243 (1833).

[4] Id. at 247, 250-251.

[5] *Murray's Lessee v. Hoboken Land and Improvement Co.*, 18 How. 272 (1856).

[6] Id. at 276-277.

[7] *Shaughnessy v. United States ex rel. Mezei*, 345 U.S. 206 at 224 (1953).

[8] *Hurtado v. California*, 110 U.S. 516 (1884); see also *Pennoyer v. Neff*, 95 U.S. 714 (1878).

[9] *Hurtado v. California*, 110 U.S. 516 at 537 (1884).

[10] Id. at 535-536.

[11] Id. at 547-548.

[12] *Davidson v. New Orleans*, 95 U.S. 97 at 104 (1877).

[13] *Maxwell v. Dow*, 1976 U.S. 581 at 614 (1900).

[14] *Twining v. New Jersey*, 211 U.S. 78 at 110-111 (1908).

[15] Id. at 99.

[16] *Palko v. Connecticut*, 302 U.S. 319 at 325 (1937).

[17] *Adamson v. California*, 332 U.S. 46 at 53 (1947).

[18] Id. at 89.

A Fair Trial

Anyone accused of a crime is constitutionally guaranteed certain essential rights: a hearing on the charges against him, an opportunity to force the government to prove the charges, and a chance to present a rebuttal to that evidence.

In the 1920s the Supreme Court began to use the due process clause to require that states ensure that trials be held free of mob domination, and be conducted before an impartial judge and a fairly chosen jury.

Trial Atmosphere

As early as 1915, the court acknowledged that a trial could be so dominated by outside pressures that its outcome would deny the defendant due process. The court refused, however, to intervene in the case of *Frank v. Mangum,* finding that the state in that instance provided the defendant sufficient opportunity through appellate review to win correction of this denial of his rights.[1]

Eight years later, however, the court approved federal intervention to order release of five black men convicted of murder in Arkansas and sentenced to die, following a trial so dominated by racial tensions that it became a travesty of justice. Justice Oliver Wendell Holmes Jr. wrote in the case of *Moore v. Dempsey:*

> ...if the case is that the whole proceeding is a mask — that counsel, jury, and judge were swept to the fatal end by an irresistible wave of public passion, and that the state courts failed to correct that wrong — neither perfection in the machinery for correction nor the possibility that the trial court and counsel saw no other way of avoiding an immediate outbreak of the mob can prevent this court from securing to the petitioners their constitutional rights.[2]

An Unbiased Judge

Four years after *Moore v. Dempsey,* the court in 1927 applied the due process clause to require that state and local trials be held before impartial judges without any personal stake in their outcome.

In the case of *Tumey v. Ohio,* the court held unconstitutional a system which permitted the presiding judge to take a portion of every fine he assessed against persons found guilty of violating the state's prohibition law.[3]

Writing for the court, Chief Justice William Howard Taft declared:

> All matters of judicial qualification may not involve constitutional validity. Thus matters of kinship, personal bias, state policy, remoteness of interest would seem to generally be matters merely of legislative discretion.... But it certainly violates the 14th Amendment and deprives a defendant in a criminal case of due process of law to subject his liberty or property to the judgment of a court, the judge of which has a direct, personal, substantial pecuniary interest in reaching a conclusion against him in his case.[4]

The court emphasized that the judge's interest must be both personal and substantial. In 1928 it limited the effect of *Tumey* when it held that, in a town where the mayor-

judge received a fixed salary for his duties, payment of half the fines to the town treasury did not violate due process of law.[5]

In 1972, however, the court ruled that due process was denied persons charged with traffic offenses and tried by the mayor of another Ohio township. The court based its decision on the fact that the fines collected from traffic violators provided a substantial portion of village revenues.

Justice William J. Brennan Jr. reasoned, in the majority opinion, that although the mayor received no personal benefit or income from convictions, the "possible temptation" to convict "may . . . exist when the mayor's executive responsibilities for village finances may make him partisan to maintain the high level of contributions from the mayor's court."[6]

Non-Lawyer Judges

But in 1976 the court held that although due process requires that a judge be impartial, it does not require that he be an attorney.

In the case of *North v. Russell,* the court considered a due process challenge to Kentucky's two-tiered state court system under which small towns were permitted to employ non-lawyer judges for police courts.

Lonnie North challenged his conviction by such a court and a non-lawyer judge for drunken driving, claiming that it violated his right to due process. The Supreme Court rejected this argument and upheld the use of non-lawyer judges in cases involving minor offenses.

Chief Justice Warren E. Burger, speaking for five of the six members of the majority, wrote:

> Our concern in prior cases with judicial functions being performed by nonjudicial officers has also been directed at the need for independent, neutral and detached judgment, not at legal training....
>
> We conclude that the Kentucky two-tier trial court system with lay judicial officers in the first tier in smaller cities and an appeal of right with a *de novo* trial before a traditionally law-trained judge in the second does not violate either the due process or equal protection guarantees of the Constitution of the United States....[7]

Justices Potter Stewart and Thurgood Marshall dissented. They found the use of non-lawyer judges a violation of the guarantees of due process and of the assistance of legal counsel.

Trial By Jury

The system of trial by jury is a distinctive feature of the Anglo-American system of justice, dating back as far as the 14th century.

The men who wrote the Constitution included in Article III the flat requirement that "The Trial of all Crimes, except in Cases of Impeachment, shall be by Jury."

Not content with this single provision, those who drafted the Bill of Rights included additional guarantees of that right in the grand jury requirement of the Fifth Amendment, in the "speedy and public trial by an impartial jury" requirement of the Sixth Amendment, and in the soon-outdated requirement of the Seventh Amendment for jury trials in common-law suits involving more than $20.

This right has been the subject of many recent Supreme Court rulings concerning the size of juries, the requirement that verdicts be unanimous, methods of selecting juries, and the waiver of the right to a jury trial by a guilty plea, usually the outcome of plea bargaining.

In federal cases — where Article III applies — the court has been unwavering in its view that a jury in a criminal case must consist of 12 persons and must reach a unanimous verdict. (In federal civil cases, however, the court has held that juries may be as small as six members.[8])

In the case of *Patton v. United States,* the court spelled out its view of the meaning of a jury trial:

> That it means a trial by jury as understood and applied at common law, and includes all the essential elements as they were recognized in this country and England when the Constitution was adopted, is not open to question. Those elements were: (1) That the jury should consist of twelve men, neither more nor less; (2) that the trial should be in the presence and under the superintendence of a judge having power to instruct them as to the law and advise them in respect of the facts; and (3) that the verdict should be unanimous.[9]

State Trials

Not for a full century after adoption of the due process clause, however, did the court hold that the requirement of trial by jury spelled out in the Sixth Amendment applied to the states.

In the case of *Walker v. Sauvinet,* decided in 1876, the court held that the Seventh Amendment right to trial by jury in civil cases was not a privilege or immunity of federal citizenship protected against state action.[10]

Then, in *Maxwell v. Dow* (1900), the court ruled that neither the privileges and immunities clause of the 14th Amendment nor that amendment's due process clause required that state juries consist of twelve persons. Elaborating on that point, the court declared further that "[t]rial by jury has never been affirmed to be a necessary requisite of due process of law." [11]

With a line of decisions beginning in the 1930s, however, the court made clear that *if* a state provided a trial by jury to a defendant, it was required to use fair procedures in selecting a jury which would represent a cross-section of the community and would be relatively unbiased. *(Details, p. 532)*

Not until 1968, however, on the centennial of the adoption of the 14th Amendment, did the court hold that the right to trial by jury for persons charged with serious crimes was sufficiently fundamental to require its application to the states.

In the case of *Duncan v. Louisiana,* the court applied the Sixth Amendment right to a jury trial to the states, finding it a necessary ingredient of due process.[12]

Gary Duncan, charged with battery in Louisiana courts, was denied a jury trial, convicted and sentenced to a fine and two years in prison. Duncan appealed to the Supreme Court, arguing that this denial of a jury trial violated his right to due process. The Supreme Court agreed. For the court Justice Byron R. White wrote:

> Because we believe that trial by jury is fundamental to the American scheme of justice, we hold that the Fourteenth Amendment guarantees a right of jury trial in all criminal cases which — were they to be tried in a federal court — would come within the Sixth Amendment's guarantee.[13]

The application of the right to jury trial to the states resulted in two new questions for the court. Were states now required to comply with federal practice by providing that all juries be composed of twelve persons? Must all state jury verdicts be unanimous?

Small Juries

The answer to the first question came quickly — and it was in the negative. In the case of *Williams v. Florida,* decided in 1970, the court held it proper for states to use juries composed of as few as six persons, at least in trying non-capital cases.[14]

Williams was tried for robbery by a six-man jury which Florida law allowed in all non-capital cases.

Writing for the court, Justice White acknowledged:

> We do not pretend to be able to divine precisely what the word "jury" imported to the Framers, the First Congress, or the States in 1789. It may well be that the usual expectation was that the jury would consist of 12, and that hence, the most likely conclusion to be drawn is simply that little thought was actually given to the specific question we face today. But there is absolutely no indication in "the intent of the Framers" of an explicit decision to equate the constitutional and common law characteristics of the jury. Nothing in this history suggests, then, that we do violence to the letter of the Constitution by turning to other than purely historical considerations to determine which features of the jury system, as it existed at common law, were preserved in the Constitution. The relevant inquiry, as we see it, must be the function which the particular feature performs and its relation to the purposes of the jury trial. Measured by this standard, the 12-man requirement cannot be regarded as an indispensable component of the Sixth Amendment. . . .
>
> . . .[T]he essential feature of a jury obviously lies in the interposition between the accused and his accuser of the common-sense judgment of a group of laymen, and in the community participation and shared responsibility which results from the group's determination of guilt or innocence. The performance of this role is not a function of the particular number of the body which makes up the jury. To be sure the number should probably be large enough to promote group deliberation, free from outside attempts at intimidation, and to provide a fair possibility for obtaining a representative cross section of the community. But we find little reason to think that these goals are in any meaningful sense less likely to be achieved when the jury numbers six, than when it numbers 12 — particularly if the requirement of unanimity is retained. And, certainly the reliability of the jury as a factfinder hardly seems likely to be a function of its size.[15]

In 1978 the court made plain that juries must consist of at least six persons, rejecting Georgia's use of a five-person jury.[16]

Serious Crimes

On the same day that the court resolved the question of jury size for states with the *Williams* ruling, it answered another question raised by the application of the Sixth Amendment right to the states: what crimes were serious enough to require states to provide a jury trial? In the case of *Baldwin v. New York,* the court held that states must provide trial by jury for all persons charged with offenses which could be punished by more than six months in prison.[17]

Unanimous Juries

In 1972 the court held that state juries need not reach their verdicts unanimously. This ruling came in a pair of cases — *Johnson v. Louisiana* and *Apodaca v. Oregon.*[18]

In the Louisiana case, the court upheld a state jury's 9-3 verdict convicting a man of robbery. Writing for the majority, Justice White declared that "want of jury unanimity is not to be equated with the existence of a reasonable doubt" concerning a defendant's guilt.

The court majority rejected the defendant's argument "that in order to give substance to the reasonable doubt standard which the State, by virtue of the Due Process Clause of the Fourteenth Amendment, must satisfy in criminal cases . . . that clause must be construed to require a unanimous jury verdict in all criminal cases." [19]

White wrote:

> . . .this Court has never held jury unanimity to be a requisite of due process of law. . . . Appellant offers no evidence that majority jurors simply ignore the reasonable doubts of their colleagues or otherwise act irresponsibly in casting their votes in favor of conviction, and before we alter our own longstanding perceptions about jury behavior and overturn a considered legislative judgment that unanimity is not essential to reasoned jury verdicts, we must have some basis for doing so other than unsupported assumptions. . . .
>
> Of course, the State's proof could perhaps be regarded as more certain if it had convinced all 12 jurors instead of only nine. . . . But the fact remains that nine jurors — a substantial majority of the jury — were convinced by the evidence. In our view disagreement of three jurors does not alone establish reasonable doubt. . . . That rational men disagree is not in itself equivalent to a failure of proof by the State, nor does it indicate infidelity to the reasonable-doubt standard.[20]

In the Oregon case, Robert Apodaca and two other men had been convicted of burglary, larceny and assault with a deadly weapon. The men had been convicted by twelve-member juries voting 11-1 and 10-2 for a verdict of guilty; Oregon law required that juries reach their verdicts by no less a majority than 10-2.

Despite the lack of jury unanimity the Supreme Court affirmed these convictions, using reasoning similar to that in the Louisiana case.

In 1979 the court in the case of *Burch v. Louisiana* faced a question posed by the "intersection" of its decisions allowing states to use juries of fewer than twelve persons and those allowing state juries to reach their verdicts by less than unanimous votes.

In that case, the court held that a jury as small as six persons must reach its verdict unanimously. The court held that a defendant charged with a non-petty crime was denied his Sixth Amendment right to trial by jury if the

---

Due Process for Delinquents

Juveniles, the court has ruled, possess some, but not all, of the due process rights assured to adults through the due process clause and the Sixth Amendment.

Juvenile court proceedings generally are considered civil, not criminal, hearings. They are designed to shelter a young offender from the exposure of a public trial, giving him the opportunity to begin anew without the handicap of publicity or a criminal record.

Until 1967 only general elements of due process and fair treatment were applied to these proceedings. But in 1967 the court in the case *In re Gault* held that juveniles charged with violating the law did have the right to confront and cross-examine persons presenting the evidence against them. Furthermore, the court declared that juveniles had the same rights as adults to notice, aid of counsel, and protection against self-incrimination.[1]

In 1970 the court held that due process required that juveniles be found delinquent by proof "beyond a reasonable doubt" — rather than by any lesser standard.

In the case of *In re Winship,* the justices found that Samuel Winship, a 12-year-old found guilty "by a preponderance of the evidence" of stealing money from a woman's pocketbook, had been denied his due process rights. The standard of proof of guilt "beyond a reasonable doubt" was an essential element of due process and fair treatment applicable to juvenile as well as adult proceedings, held the court.[2]

The following year, however, in the cases of *McKeiver v. Pennsylvania* and *In re Burrus,* the court refused to extend the right to trial by jury to juvenile court proceedings.[3]

Justice Harry A. Blackmun explained the reasoning of the court:

> If the jury trial were to be injected into the juvenile court system as a matter of right, it would bring with it into that system the traditional delay, the formality and the clamor of the adversary system and, possibly, the public trial. . . .
>
> If the formalities of the criminal adjudicative process are to be superimposed upon the juvenile court system, there is little need for its separate existence. Perhaps that ultimate disillusionment will come one day, but for the moment we are disinclined to give impetus to it.[4]

Four years later, the court extended the Fifth Amendment protection against double jeopardy to minors, ruling that a juvenile found in juvenile court to have violated the law could not subsequently be tried for the same action as an adult.[5]

---

[1] *In re Gault,* 387 U.S. 1 (1967).
[2] *In re Winship,* 397 U.S. 358 (1970).
[3] *McKeiver v. Pennsylvania, In re Burrus,* 403 U.S. 528 (1971).
[4] Id. at 550-551.
[5] *Breed v. Jones,* 421 U.S. 519 at 529 (1975).

state allowed him to be convicted by a less than unanimous vote of a six-man jury.[21]

A Fair Cross-Section

Ostensibly, the fairness of an individual's trial is further safeguarded by the selection of an impartial jury. The defendant is protected against bias due to his or her race, sex, employment or class by the "cross-section" principle that forbids systematic exclusion of identifiable segments of the community from empanelment on juries. Long before *Duncan v. Louisiana* required states to provide jury trials in most cases, the court was demanding that state juries, if provided, be fairly selected.

"It is part of the established tradition in the use of juries as instruments of public justice," declared the court in a 1940 decision, "that the jury be a body truly representative of the community. For racial discrimination to result in the exclusion from jury service of otherwise qualified groups not only violates our Constitution and the laws enacted under it but is at war with our basic concepts of a democratic society and a representative government." [22]

Three decades later, the court reiterated this point in two rulings — in 1975 and 1979 — holding that state laws were unconstitutional if they resulted in the virtual exclusion of women from juries. In these rulings, the court reaffirmed the fair cross-section requirement as fundamental to the Sixth Amendment right to a jury trial.[23]

Congress incorporated this principle into the Federal Jury Selection and Service Act of 1968, which — a century after adoption of the 14th Amendment — forbade discrimination in the selection of jury panels based on race, color, religion, sex, national origin or economic status.[24]

Racial Bias

Racial discrimination in jury selection has been the subject of Supreme Court rulings since 1880. Both the due process and the equal protection guarantees of the 14th Amendment furnish a basis for judicial review of state jury selection practices alleged to be discriminatory. Most often the equal protection clause has served as the more effective of the two provisions in nullifying state discrimination in this area.

Such was the case in 1880 when the court struck down Virginia and West Virginia laws which clearly excluded blacks from jury service and thus violated the promise of equal protection.[25] But the court made clear in another decision the same year that it would not require state officials to ensure that blacks actually did serve on juries.[26] In other words, the mere absence of black jurors from any particular panel would not serve as a constitutional basis for challenging the jury's decision.

For the next half-century, this superficial approach to ensuring blacks equal protection in jury selection procedures prevailed. Without proof of statutory discrimination, blacks continued to be excluded from local juries in case after case.

Then, in 1935, in the "Second Scottsboro Case" — *Norris v. Alabama* — the court looked behind the language of the state law to its effect — and found its effect unconstitutional.[27]

One of the "Scottsboro boys," Clarence Norris, a Negro convicted of raping a white woman, challenged his conviction as a violation of equal protection, pointing out that blacks were systematically eliminated from the pools from which state jurors — including those who indicted and tried him — were chosen. When his case came to the Supreme Court, the court reversed his conviction.

Writing for the court, Chief Justice Charles Evans Hughes described the court's responsibility as "to inquire not merely whether it [the equal protection guarantee] was denied in express terms but also whether it was denied in substance and effect." [28] Pointing out that no black had served on a jury in that county within the memory of any person living, Chief Justice Hughes found that and related evidence sufficient basis for reversing Norris' conviction as unconstitutional.

Twelve years later, in the case of *Patton v. Mississippi*, the court found similar justification for reversing the murder conviction of a black man indicted and convicted by all-white juries.

The Supreme Court held the long exclusion of blacks from juries a denial of equal protection. Justice Hugo L. Black delivered the opinion of a unanimous court:

> When a jury selection plan, whatever it is, operates in such way as always to result in the complete and long-continued exclusion of any representative at all from a large group of negroes, or any other racial group, indictments and verdicts returned against them by juries thus selected cannot stand . . . our holding does not mean that a guilty defendant must go free. For indictments can be returned and convictions can be obtained by juries selected as the Constitution commands.[29]

In subsequent cases, the court upheld good-faith efforts by state officials to secure competent juries representative of the community. In 1953 the court approved the use of taxpayers' rolls as the basis from which names were selected for jury service.[30]

The court then began to rule against token selection of blacks for jury duty, or systems of jury selection which made it easy for selecting officials to exclude blacks. Examples of the latter came in the case of *Avery v. Georgia* — in which the court struck down a system using different colored pieces of paper for black persons eligible for jury duty than for white persons eligible — and in *Whitus v. Georgia*, in which the justices invalidated the selection of jurors from tax records maintained on racially separate bases.[31]

In 1954, with its decision in *Hernandez v. Texas*, the court held that the 14th Amendment forbade the systematic or arbitrary exclusion of any substantial racial group in the population from jury service. A unanimous court ruled that in a county where 14 percent of the population was of Mexican or Latin-American descent, it violated equal protection to exclude all such persons from juries.[32]

Blue Ribbon Juries

The Supreme Court has upheld the use of specially qualified panels of jurors for difficult cases. The court has held that such panels do not deny equal protection or due process. The key case was *Fay v. New York*, decided in 1947.[33]

New York law forbade selection of jury panels on the basis of race, creed, color or occupation but provided for the use of "blue ribbon" juries. Two union officials convicted by a "blue ribbon" jury of conspiracy and extortion claimed that these panels excluded laborers, craftsmen and service employees, discriminating against certain economic classes

Due Process: The Right To Notice

Formal notice of charges — or of legal proceedings affecting one's rights — is one of the essential elements of due process. All parties who are to become involved in legal proceedings must be informed in advance of trial of the specific charges against them to give them time to prepare their defense or, in the case of modern class action cases, to withdraw from the affected class.

The Supreme Court has held that in civil and criminal proceedings alike, notice must be given promptly and with sufficient specificity to permit preparation of an adequate defense. In addition, the court has recently extended the due process requirement of notice to protect consumers from a unilateral seizure of property by creditors and to shield individuals from some administrative actions.

The concept of notice is included in both the Fifth and Sixth Amendments. The Fifth Amendment provides that no one "shall be held to answer for a capital, or otherwise infamous crime, unless on a presentment or indictment of a Grand Jury, except in cases arising in the land or naval forces, or in the militia. . . ." The Supreme Court in its 1884 ruling in *Hurtado v. California* held that this requirement of an indictment applied only to persons charged with federal crimes. That decision has never been reversed.[1]

The Sixth Amendment states that in *all* criminal prosecutions the defendant has the right "to be informed of the nature and cause of the accusation" against him. This more general rule has been accepted by virtually all jurisdictions as basic to a fair trial.

Both the Sixth Amendment and due process require that laws describing certain actions as criminal be sufficiently specific to place persons on notice as to what acts are proscribed. As the court wrote in 1926, "a statute which either forbids or requires the doing of an act in terms so vague that men of common intelligence must necessarily guess at its meaning and differ as to its application, violates the first essential of due process of law."[2]

In line with this reasoning, the court has held "void for vagueness" laws which do not define with reasonable specificity the nature of forbidden conduct, and has set aside indictments which are insufficiently precise in stating the charges against an individual.

In testing laws challenged as unconstitutionally vague, the court must balance the right to notice against the imprecision of language and the political considerations inherent in the process of writing laws. Justice Tom C. Clark in 1952 set out the court's view of these factors:

A criminal statute must be sufficiently definite to give notice of the required conduct to one who would avoid its penalties, and to guide the judge in its application and the lawyer in defending one charged with its violation. But few words possess the precision of mathematical symbols, most statutes must deal with untold and unforeseen variations in factual situations, and the practical necessities of discharging the business of government inevitably limit the specificity with which legislators can spell out prohibitions. Consequently, no more than a reasonable degree of certainty can be demanded. Nor is it unfair to require that one who deliberately goes perilously close to an area of proscribed conduct shall take the risk that he may cross the line.[3]

In recent rulings, the Supreme Court has extended the concept of notice, holding that it is required in a variety of situations outside of those occurring in the enforcement of the criminal law.

In two cases, decided in 1969 and 1972, the court held that due process required that consumers be notified before their wages were garnished or property repossessed for non-payment of debts.[4]

The court in 1970 applied the notice requirement to termination of welfare benefits.[5] Two years later, it held that a teacher fired after ten years of service was entitled to notice and a hearing.[6] And in 1975, the court held that students were entitled to notice of charges before they were suspended from public schools for misbehavior.[7]

---

[1] *Hurtado v. California*, 110 U.S. 516 (1884).
[2] *Connally v. General Construction Co.*, 269 U.S. 385 at 391 (1926).
[3] *Boyce Motor Lines, Inc. v. United States*, 342 U.S. 337 at 340 (1952).

[4] *Sniadach v. Family Finance Corp. et al.*, 395 U.S. 337 (1969); *Fuentes v. Shevin*, 407 U.S. 67 (1972).
[5] *Goldberg v. Kelly*, 397 U.S. 254 (1970).
[6] *Perry v. Sinderman*, 408 U.S. 593 (1972).
[7] *Goss v. Lopez*, 419 U.S. 565 (1975).

---

and thus violating the due process and equal protection guarantees of the 14th Amendment.

The court upheld the system and the convictions. Justice Robert H. Jackson delivered the majority opinion:

We fail to perceive on its face any constitutional offense in the statutory standards prescribed for the special panel. The Act does not exclude, or authorize the clerk to exclude, any person or class because of race, creed, color or occupation. It imposes no qualification of an economic nature beyond that imposed by the concededly valid general panel statute. Each of the grounds of elimination is reasonably and closely related to the juror's suitability for the kind of service the special panel requires or to his fitness to judge the kind of cases for which it is most frequently utilized. Not all of the grounds of elimination would appear relevant to the issues of the present case. But we know of no right of defendants to have a specially constituted panel which would include all persons who might be fitted to hear their particular and unique case. . . .[34]

In dissent, Justices Frank Murphy, Hugo L. Black, Wiley B. Rutledge and William O. Douglas protested that use of blue ribbon juries conflicted with the fair cross-section requirement. Murphy wrote:

. . .There is no constitutional right to a jury drawn from a group of uneducated and unintelligent persons.

Compulsory Process

The defendant's right to present a defense includes the right to use subpoenas and similar legal processes to compel witnesses to appear in his behalf at trial.

In 1967 the Supreme Court extended this right to persons charged with crimes by the states. In the case of *Washington v. Texas* the court declared that:

> The right to offer the testimony of witnesses, and to compel their attendance if necessary, is in plain terms the right to present a defense, the right to present the defendant's version of the facts as well as the prosecution's to the jury so it may decide where the truth lies. Just as an accused has a right to confront the prosecution's witnesses for the purpose of challenging their testimony, he has the right to present his own witnesses to establish a defense. This right is a fundamental element of due process of law. (*Washington v. Texas,* 388 U.S. 14 at 19, 1967).

Nor is there any right to a jury chosen solely from those at the lower end of the economic and social scale. But there is a constitutional right to a jury drawn from a group which represents a cross-section of the community. And a cross-section of the community includes persons with varying degrees of training and intelligence and with varying economic and social positions. Under our Constitution, the jury is not to be made the representative of the most intelligent, the most wealthy or the most successful, nor of the least intelligent, the least wealthy or the least successful. It is a democratic institution, representative of all qualified classes of people.[35]

Women On Juries

Although the court as early as 1946 disapproved of the exclusion of women from federal jury panels, it took 30 more years before it applied that principle to state juries.[36] As recently as 1961, in the case of *Hoyt v. Florida,* the court upheld a Florida statute which made jury service by women voluntary. Women interested in being included on jury lists had to record with the county their willingness to serve.[37]

Gwendolyn Hoyt — accused of murdering her husband with a baseball bat — challenged the constitutionality of the statute. Failure to include women on the jury, she claimed, denied women defendants the equal protection of the law.

The court rejected this argument, saying that Florida law did not exclude all women from jury service, but simply permitted them to avail themselves of a broad exemption from that duty. The court noted that 17 states granted women such a privilege.

For the court, Justice John Marshall Harlan wrote that "woman is still regarded as the center of home and family life." In light of that, he continued, "[w]e cannot say that it is constitutionally impermissible for a State . . . to conclude that a woman should be relieved from the civic duty of jury service unless she herself determines that such service is consistent with her own special responsibilities."[38]

But fourteen years later the court overturned *Hoyt.* In the case of *Taylor v. Louisiana,* announced in 1975, the court found state laws which generally exempted women from jury duty were unconstitutional because they were in conflict with the Sixth Amendment right of a defendant to be tried by an impartial jury drawn from a fair cross-section of the community.[39] *(See also p. 532)*

In 1978 the court reaffirmed this position, striking down a Missouri law which exempted women from jury duty upon their request. Leaving room for states to exempt persons responsible for the care of children and other dependents from jury duty, the court held that this broader, sex-based exemption denied defendants their right to a jury which fairly represented their community.[40]

Speedy Trial

As early as 1905, the Supreme Court made clear that the right to a speedy trial was a relative matter, "consistent with delays and depend[ent] upon circumstances."[41]

The court has adopted a balancing approach in cases where a defendant has allegedly been denied this right. In each case, the justices weigh the particular facts to determine the reasons for the delay and the effect of the delay on the defendant.

In *United States v. Provoo,* decided in 1955, the court upheld dismissal of an indictment of a defendant who — although ready for trial since 1951 and protesting governmental requests for delay — had not been tried. The court explained that the lapse of time, the death or disappearance of witnesses, and the protracted confinement of the defendant had seriously jeopardized his opportunity to defend himself.[42]

Dismissal of the charges, the unanimous court held firmly in 1973, is the only appropriate remedy for denial of this right. In the case of *Strunk v. United States* the court found reduction of sentence insufficient remedy for delay of trial to the point that the right was denied.[43]

The court has held that this right does not apply to delays before a person is accused of a crime, but, rather, only to the interval between arrest and trial.

In a 1971 ruling, Justice Byron R. White explained this view:

> . . .[T]he Sixth Amendment speedy trial provision has no application until the putative defendant becomes an "accused". . . .
>
> . . .On its face, the protection of the amendment is activated only when a criminal prosecution has begun and extends only to those persons who have been "accused" in the course of that prosecution. These provisions would seem to afford no protection to those not yet accused, nor would they seem to require the Government to discover, investigate, and accuse any person within any particular period of time. . . .[44]

In 1977 the court reaffirmed this point. In the case of *United States v. Lovasco,* the justices rejected the argument of a defendant that he had been denied due process by a good-faith investigative delay between the commission of an offense and the time of his indictment.[45]

Justice Thurgood Marshall wrote for the court:

> . . .prosecutors do not deviate from "fundamental conceptions of justice" when they defer seeking indictments until they have probable cause to believe an accused is guilty; indeed it is unprofessional conduct for a prosecutor to recommend an indictment on less than probable cause. . . . From the perspective of po-

tential defendants, requiring prosecutions to commence when probable cause is established is undesirable because it would increase the likelihood of unwarranted charges being filed, and would add to the time during which defendants stand accused but untried....

Penalizing prosecutors who defer action ... would subordinate the goal of "orderly expedition" to that of "mere speed." This the Due Process Clause does not require. We therefore hold that to prosecute a defendant following investigative delay does not deprive him of due process, even if his defense might have been somewhat prejudiced by the lapse of time.[46]

Speedy Trial and the States

In the 1967 case of *Klopfer v. North Carolina*, the court held that the due process clause required protection of the right to speedy trial against abridgment by the states.[47]

The court unanimously struck down a North Carolina law which allowed indefinite postponement of a criminal prosecution without dismissal of the indictment. The defendant would remain at liberty, but the prosecutor could restore the case to the docket at any time that a judge agreed such action to be appropriate.

Speaking for the court, Chief Justice Earl Warren explained that this procedure "clearly denies the petitioner the right to a speedy trial which we hold is guaranteed to him by the Sixth Amendment.... We hold here that the right to a speedy trial is as fundamental as any of the rights secured by the Sixth Amendment." [48]

Speed, Balance and Congress

Federal and state officials operated until the 1970s on the assumption that an accused's failure to demand a speedy trial meant that he acquiesced in delay of proceedings.

In a 1972 ruling in *Barker v. Wingo*, the court rejected the view "that a defendant who fails to demand a speedy trial forever waives his right." [49]

Justice Lewis F. Powell Jr. wrote for the court to reaffirm its "balancing approach" to speedy trial claims:

The approach we accept is a balancing test, in which the conduct of both the prosecution and the defendant are weighed.

A balancing test necessarily compels courts to approach speedy-trial cases on an *ad-hoc* basis. We can do little more than identify some of the factors which courts should assess in determining whether a particular defendant has been deprived of his right. Though some might express them in different ways, we identify four such factors: Length of delay, the reason for the delay, the defendant's assertion of his right, and prejudice to the defendant....

We regard none of the four factors identified above as either a necessary or sufficient condition to the finding of a deprivation of the right of speedy trial. Rather they are related factors and must be considered together with such other circumstances as may be relevant. In sum, these factors have no talismanic qualities; courts must still engage in a difficult and sensitive balancing process. But, because we are dealing with a fundamental right of the accused, this process must be carried out with full recognition that the accused's interest in a speedy trial is specifically affirmed in the Constitution.[50]

The Disruptive Defendant

Inherent in the defendant's right to confront and cross-examine those persons who testify against him is the right to be present at his trial.[1]

In 1970, however, the Supreme Court held that this right was not absolute and that a defendant who persistently disrupted trial proceedings by noisy and disorderly conduct was not denied his constitutional rights when the judge had him removed from the courtroom.

In that case, *Illinois v. Allen*, the defendant had constantly interrupted the trial proceedings with noisy outbursts and insulting language. The judge finally ordered him removed from the courtroom until he agreed to behave.

At the conclusion of the trial — which resulted in his conviction — the defendant, Allen, filed a petition for *habeas corpus* relief, claiming that he had been denied his right to a fair trial because of his enforced absence from the courtroom during the presentation of most of the state's case against him.

A unanimous Supreme Court rejected that argument. Justice Hugo L. Black wrote:

It is essential to the proper administration of criminal justice that dignity, order, and decorum be the hallmarks of all court proceedings in our country. The flagrant disregard in the courtroom of elementary standards of proper conduct should not and cannot be tolerated. We believe trial judges confronted with disruptive, contumacious, stubbornly defiant defendants must be given sufficient discretion to meet the circumstances of each case. No one formula for maintaining the appropriate courtroom atmosphere will be best in all situations. We think there are at least three constitutionally permissible ways for a trial judge to handle an obstreperous defendant like Allen: (1) bind and gag him, thereby keeping him present; (2) cite him for contempt; (3) take him out of the courtroom until he promises to conduct himself properly.[2]

[1] *Lewis v. United States*, 146 U.S. 370 (1892).
[2] *Illinois v. Allen*, 397 U.S. 337 at 333-334 (1970); see also *Mayberry v. Pennsylvania*, 400 U.S. 455 (1971).

The ruling in *Barker v. Wingo* prompted Congress — against the advice of the Justice Department and federal judges — to pass the Speedy Trial Act of 1974 in an effort demand a reduction in delays in federal trials. The act established a 100-day deadline between arrest or indictment and trial. The deadline was to take effect after a phase-in period during which progressively tighter deadlines were imposed on trial schedules. Failure to meet the deadline would result in dismissal of the charges in most cases.[51]

Confrontation of Witnesses

The Sixth Amendment guarantees federal defendants the right to confront and cross-examine their accusers. In the case of *Mattox v. United States*, decided in 1895, the

Supreme Court defined the purpose of this confrontation rule:

> The primary object . . . was to prevent depositions or ex parte affidavits . . . being used against the prisoner in lieu of a personal examination and cross-examination of the witness in which the accused has an opportunity, not only of testing the recollection and sifting the conscience of the witness, but of compelling him to stand face to face with the jury in order that they may look at him, and judge by his demeanor upon the stand and manner in which he gives his testimony whether he is worthy of belief.[52]

Subsequently, the court struck down an act of Congress as violating this right by allowing the record of a case in which persons were convicted of stealing government property to be used as evidence — at the trial of the person charged with *receiving* that property — that the property *was* stolen. In the opinion, the court further explained the purpose of this confrontation clause:

> . . .a fact which can be primarily established only by witnesses cannot be proved against an accused . . . except by witnesses who confront him at the trial, upon whom he can look while being tried, whom he is entitled to cross-examine, and whose testimony he may impeach. . . . The presumption of the innocence of an accused attends him throughout the trial, and has relation to every fact that must be established to prove his guilt beyond a reasonable doubt.[53]

This presumption was denied the defendant in this case, held the court, because "he was put upon the defensive almost from the outset of the trial by reason alone of what appeared to have been *said* in another criminal prosecution with which he was not connected and at which he was not entitled to be represented."[54]

Many of the court's pronouncements on the confrontation clause have focused on efforts by prosecutors to use hearsay evidence — prior, out-of-court statements of persons unavailable to testify and be cross-examined — at trial.

In general, the court allows use of such evidence only when there is sufficient reason to consider it credible.[55]

In the case of *Pointer v. Texas,* decided in 1965, the court held this right of confrontation to be "a fundamental right essential to a fair trial in a criminal prosecution" and therefore applicable to defendants in state trials through the due process clause.[56]

Pointer involved a trial where a state prosecutor attempted to use the transcript of a witness's testimony taken at a preliminary hearing, where he was not subject to cross-examination. The prosecutor had made no effort to secure the personal appearance of the witness at the trial. The court threw out such evidence.

The Right to A Public Trial

The Sixth Amendment guarantees persons charged with crimes a public, as well as a speedy, trial.

In a 1979 decision, the Supreme Court held that this guarantee of a public trial is solely for the benefit of the defendant. The court rejected the argument that the public in general and the press in particular share in this guarantee.

In the case of *Gannett Co. v. DePasquale,* the court upheld the right of a trial judge to close to the press and the public a pretrial hearing on evidence in a murder case.

Writing for the majority, Justice Potter Stewart pointed out that "[t]o safeguard the due process rights of the accused, a trial judge has an affirmative constitutional duty to minimize the effects of prejudicial pretrial publicity." And, Stewart noted, one of the most effective means of minimizing such publicity is to shut the public and the press out of pretrial proceedings.

"The Sixth Amendment," Stewart continued, "surrounds a criminal trial with guarantees . . . that have as their overriding purpose the protection of the accused from prosecutorial and judicial abuses. Among the guarantees that the Amendment provides to a person charged with the commission of a criminal offense, and to him alone, is the 'right to a speedy and public trial, by an impartial jury.' The Constitution nowhere mentions any right of access to a criminal trial on the part of the public; its guarantee, like the others enumerated, is personal to the accused. . . ."

Although in recent years the court seems to have relaxed some of its earlier restrictions on the use of hearsay evidence or out-of-court statements, it reaffirmed in other rulings announced in the 1970s the high priority it placed upon this right in assuring a fair trial.[57]

In 1973 the court by an 8-1 vote held that a defendant on trial for murder had been denied a fair trial and due process by the state judge's strict application of the hearsay rule to prevent the introduction of testimony by three men to whom a fourth man had confessed the crime with which the defendant was charged.[58]

And in 1974, with Chief Justice Warren E. Burger writing the opinion, the court held that a defendant was denied his right of confrontation when the trial judge forbade cross-examination of a key witness, a juvenile, about his delinquency record and probationary status, matters which could have impeached the credibility of his testimony.[59]

Footnotes

[1] *Frank v. Mangum,* 237 U.S. 309 (1915).
[2] *Moore v. Dempsey,* 261 U.S. 86 at 91 (1923).
[3] *Tumey v. Ohio,* 273 U.S. 510 (1927).
[4] Id. at 523.
[5] *Dugan v. Ohio,* 277 U.S. 261 (1928).
[6] *Ward v. Village of Monroeville,* 409 U.S. 57 at 60 (1972).
[7] *North v. Russell,* 427 U.S. 328 at 337, 339 (1976). See

also: *Fisher v. Pace,* 336 U.S. 155 (1949); *Sacher v. United States,* 343 U.S. 1 (1952).
[8] *Colgrove v. Battin,* 413 U.S. 149 (1973).
[9] *Patton v. United States,* 281 U.S. 276 at 288 (1930); see also *Singer v. United States,* 380 U.S. 24 (1965).
[10] *Walker v. Sauvinet,* 92 U.S. 90 (1876).
[11] *Maxwell v. Dow,* 176 U.S. 581 at 603 (1900).
[12] *Duncan v. Louisiana,* 391 U.S. 145 (1968).
[13] Id. at 149.
[14] *Williams v. Florida,* 399 U.S. 78 (1970).

[15] Id. at 98-101.

[16] *Ballew v. Georgia,* 435 U.S. 223 (1978).

[17] *Baldwin v. New York,* 399 U.S. 66 (1970).

[18] *Johnson v. Louisiana,* 406 U.S. 356 (1972); *Apodaca v. Oregon,* 406 U.S. 404 (1972).

[19] *Johnson v. Louisiana,* 406 U.S. 356 at 359 (1972).

[20] Id. at 359, 362.

[21] *Burch v. Louisiana* (1979).

[22] *Smith v. Texas,* 311 U.S. 128 at 130 (1940).

[23] *Taylor v. Louisiana,* 419 U.S. 522 (1975); *Duren v. Missouri* (1979).

[24] Congressional Quarterly, *Congress and the Nation,* Vol. II (Washington, D.C.: Congressional Quarterly, 1969), p. 385.

[25] *Ex parte Virginia,* 100 U.S. 339 (1880); *Strauder v. West Virginia,* 100 U.S. 303 (1880); see also *Rose v. Mitchell* (1979).

[26] *Virginia v. Rives,* 100 U.S. 313 (1880).

[27] *Norris v. Alabama,* 294 U.S. 587 (1935).

[28] Id. at 590.

[29] *Patton v. Mississippi,* 332 U.S. 463 at 468-469 (1947).

[30] *Brown v. Allen,* 344 U.S. 443 (1953).

[31] *Cassell v. Texas,* 339 U.S. 282 (1950); *Whitus v. Georgia,* 385 U.S. 545 (1967); *Avery v. Georgia,* 345 U.S. 559 (1952).

[32] *Hernandez v. Texas,* 347 U.S. 475 (1954).

[33] *Fay v. New York,* 332 U.S. 261 (1947); see also *Moore v. New York,* 333 U.S. 565 (1948).

[34] *Fay v. New York,* 332 U.S. 261 at 270-271 (1947).

[35] Id. at 299-300.

[36] *Ballard v. U.S.,* 329 U.S. 187 (1946).

[37] *Hoyt v. Florida,* 368 U.S. 57 (1961).

[38] Id. at 62.

[39] *Taylor v. Louisiana,* 419 U.S. 522 (1975).

[40] *Duren v. Missouri* (1979).

[41] *Beavers v. Haubert,* 198 U.S. 77 at 87 (1905).

[42] *United States v. Provoo,* 350 U.S. 857 (1955); see also *Pollard v. United States,* 352 U.S. 354 (1957); *United States v. Ewell,* 383 U.S. 116 (1966).

[43] *Strunk v. United States,* 412 U.S. 434 (1973).

[44] *United States v. Marion,* 404 U.S. 307 at 313 (1971).

[45] *United States v. Lovasco,* 431 U.S. 783 (1977).

[46] Id. at 790-791, 795-796.

[47] *Klopfer v. North Carolina,* 386 U.S. 213 (1967).

[48] Id. at 222-223.

[49] *Barker v. Wingo,* 407 U.S. 514 (1972).

[50] Id. at 530, 533.

[51] Congressional Quarterly, *Congress and the Nation,* Vol. IV (Washington, D.C.: Congressional Quarterly, 1977), p. 576.

[52] *Mattox v. United States,* 156 U.S. 237 at 242-243 (1895).

[53] *Kirby v. United States,* 174 U.S. 47 at 55 (1899).

[54] Id. at 56.

[55] *Motes v. United States,* 178 U.S. 458 (1900); *Reynolds v. United States,* 98 U.S. 145 (1879); *Robertson v. Baldwin,* 165 U.S. 275 (1897); *Mattox v. United States,* 156 U.S. 237 (1895); *Bruton v. United States,* 391 U.S. 123 (1968); *Della Paoli v. United States,* 352 U.S. 232 (1957).

[56] *Pointer v. Texas,* 380 U.S. 400 (1965); see also *Douglas v. Alabama,* 380 U.S. 415 (1965).

[57] *California v. Green,* 399 U.S. 149 (1970); *Dutton v. Evans,* 400 U.S. 74 (1970); see also *Nelson v. O'Neil,* 402 U.S. 622 (1971); *Harrington v. California,* 395 U.S. 250 (1969); *Schneble v. Florida,* 405 U.S. 427 (1972).

[58] *Chambers v. Mississippi,* 410 U.S. 284 (1973).

[59] *Davis v. Alaska,* 415 U.S. 308 (1974).

Search and Seizure

"The security of one's privacy against arbitrary intrusion by the police," wrote Justice Felix Frankfurter in 1946, "is basic to a free society."

"The knock at the door, whether by day or by night," continued Frankfurter, "as a prelude to a search, without authority of law but solely on the authority of the police, did not need the commentary of recent history to be condemned as inconsistent with the conception of human rights enshrined in the history and the basic constitutional documents of English-speaking peoples." [1]

The Fourth Amendment's guarantee of the "right of the people to be secure in their persons, houses, papers and effects, against unreasonable searches and seizures" was intended to protect the individual against this sort of arbitrary invasion of his privacy by police or other authorities. Fresh in the minds of the men who drafted that language was the British use of general warrants and "writs of assistance" to justify the searches of homes by government agents seeking smugglers and others who violated trade and navigation laws.

The guarantee of personal security against unreasonable search and seizure is buttressed by the second portion of the amendment, the warrant clause. It underscores the "reasonableness" requirement for searches and seizures by stating that "no Warrants shall issue, but upon probable cause, supported by Oath or affirmation, and particularly describing the place to be searched and the person or things to be seized."

The Supreme Court has held that a valid warrant — one issued by a neutral and detached magistrate upon his finding of probable cause — is an essential element of compliance with the Fourth Amendment prohibition against unreasonable search and seizure.

This is perhaps the single most stable element in Fourth Amendment doctrine. As the court itself acknowledged in 1967, "translation of the abstract prohibition against 'unreasonable searches and seizures' into workable guidelines for the decision of particular cases is a difficult task which has for many years divided the members of this court.

"Nevertheless, one governing principle, justified by history and by current experience, has consistently been followed: except in certain carefully defined classes of cases, a search of private property without proper consent is 'unreasonable' unless it has been authorized by a valid search warrant." [2]

The warrant must be sufficiently specific to remove the element of discretion from those persons who are to execute it. The court has recognized two primary exceptions to the warrant requirement for searches: a search related to a lawful arrest and a search of a moving vehicle may be conducted without warrants. In recent years the court has resisted arguments that it create new exceptions to the requirement. [3]

The court has adopted a controversial method of enforcing the Fourth Amendment guarantee. That method is the "exclusionary rule" — the court's insistence that evidence obtained in violation of the Fourth Amendment rights of a defendant may not be used as evidence against him. This rule has been in effect in federal courts since 1914. *(Box, pp. 548-549)*

But not until 1949 did the Supreme Court consider the argument that the Fourth Amendment guarantee and the exclusionary rule should apply to state defendants. The court in the case of *Wolf v. Colorado* seemed to say that the rights protected by the Fourth Amendment were so basic to "the concept of ordered liberty" that they were protected against state action through the due process clause of the 14th Amendment. Nevertheless, the court in *Wolf* expressly declined to apply the exclusionary rule against state officials, refusing to require state judges to enforce the Fourth Amendment guarantee by excluding evidence obtained illegally. [4]

In 1961, however, the court reversed *Wolf* insofar as the application of the exclusionary rule was concerned. In the case of *Mapp v. Ohio*, the court extended the full protection of the guarantee to state defendants. [5] Two years later in the case of *Ker v. California* the court stated that the Fourth Amendment guarantee as applied to state action was in all respects the same as that applied to federal action. [6]

The Neutral Magistrate

Search and arrest warrants must be issued by a neutral and detached magistrate if they are to conform to constitutional standards.

Justice Robert H. Jackson, writing the court's opinion in a 1948 case, explained the importance of this requirement:

> The point of the Fourth Amendment, which often is not grasped by zealous officers, is not that it denies

Private Searches: No Protection

The Fourth Amendment protects individuals only against searches and seizures by government agents, not against such actions if they are undertaken by private individuals.

The Supreme Court set out this rule in its 1921 decision in the case of *Burdeau v. McDowell.* McDowell, officer of a company, was dismissed. His former employers blew open the lock on his private office safe, broke the lock on his desk drawer, and delivered the contents of desk and safe to the Justice Department, which was investigating McDowell's role in a mail fraud scheme.

McDowell challenged the seizure of the evidence as a violation of his right to be secure in his "papers and effects" against unreasonable search and seizure. The Supreme Court rebuffed his challenge, holding that the Fourth Amendment reached only government action; actions by private individuals, as in McDowell's case, were outside the amendment's protection. McDowell could, the court noted, institute a private suit against those individuals who took his papers and turned them over to the government. *(Burdeau v. McDowell,* 256 U.S. 465, 1921)

law enforcement the support of the usual inferences which reasonable men draw from evidence. Its protection consists in requiring that those inferences be drawn by a neutral and detached magistrate instead of being judged by the officer engaged in the often competitive enterprise of ferreting out crime. Any assumption that evidence sufficient to support a magistrate's disinterested determination to issue a search warrant will justify the officers in making a search without a warrant would reduce the Amendment to a nullity and leave the people's homes secure only in the discretion of police officers.... When the right of privacy must reasonably yield to the right of search is, as a rule, to be decided by a judicial officer, not by a policeman or Government enforcement agent.[7]

The court emphasized the importance of this requirement in the 1971 case of *Coolidge v. New Hampshire.* In that case, the court forbade the use of evidence obtained in a police search based on a warrant issued by the state official who was the chief investigator and prosecutor in the case. "Since he was not the neutral and detached magistrate required by the Constitution," stated the court, "the search stands on no firmer ground than if there had been no warrant at all."[8]

The following year, however, the court ruled that municipal court clerks may issue search warrants in cases involving the breach of municipal laws.

The court stated that there was no Fourth Amendment "commandment ... that all warrant authority must reside exclusively in a lawyer or judge." Justice Lewis F. Powell Jr. wrote the court's opinion, declaring:

The substance of the Constitution's warrant requirements does not turn on the labelling of the issuing party. The warrant traditionally has represented an independent assurance that a search and arrest will not proceed without probable cause to believe that a crime

has been committed and that the person or place named in the warrant is involved in the crime. Thus an issuing magistrate must meet two tests. He must be neutral and detached, and he must be capable of determining whether probable cause exists for the requested arrest or search.... If ... detachment and capacity do conjoin, the magistrate has satisfied the Fourth Amendment's purpose....[9]

Probable Cause

A magistrate must find "probable cause" before he issues a search or arrest warrant. "Probable cause" has been variously defined, but the court has made clear, on one hand, that while the term "means less than evidence which would justify condemnation,"[10] on the other hand it does require "belief that the law was being violated on the premises to be searched; and ... the facts ... are such that a reasonably discreet and prudent man would be led to believe that there was a commission of the offense charged...."[11]

A warrant is not valid, the court has held, if it is based only upon a sworn allegation without adequate support in fact. In the 1933 case of *Nathanson v. United States,* the court set out this rule:

Under the Fourth Amendment, an officer may not properly issue a warrant to search a private dwelling unless he can find probable cause therefore from facts or circumstances presented to him under oath or affirmation. Mere affirmance of belief or suspicion is not enough.[12]

The court has held valid, however, warrants based on hearsay, and has not required direct personal observation of the facts or circumstances justifying the warrant by the individual who seeks it.[13] But the magistrate must be satisfied that the informant, whose identity need not be disclosed, is credible or his information reliable.[14]

In 1978 the court for the first time held that a defendant who claims that police obtained evidence against him only after the police or their informants lied in order to convince a magistrate that there was probable cause for a search should be granted a hearing on his claim.

Justice Harry A. Blackmun, writing for the court in the case of *Franks v. Delaware,* made clear the majority's view that "a warrant ... would be reduced to a nullity if a police officer was able to use deliberately falsified allegations to demonstrate probable cause...."[15]

Search With Consent

Only if an individual cannot or does not consent to a search of his "person, house, papers and effects" are police required to obtain a warrant to justify the search. Voluntary consent of the individual who owns or occupies the place to be searched validates the search.

But, the court held in 1973, the individual who is asked to consent to a search need not be informed that he may refuse to give consent.

In the case of *Schneckloth v. Bustamonte* the court discussed the elements of voluntary consent. The majority, for whom Justice Potter Stewart wrote, concluded:

We hold only that when the subject of a search is not in custody and the State attempts to justify the search on the basis of his consent, the Fourth and

Fourteenth Amendments require that it demonstrate that the consent was in fact voluntarily given, and not the result of duress or coercion, express or implied. Voluntariness is a question of fact to be determined from all the circumstances, and while the subject's knowledge of a right to refuse is a factor to be taken into account, the prosecution is not required to demonstrate such knowledge as a prerequisite to establishing a voluntary consent.[16]

Justices William J. Brennan Jr., William O. Douglas and Thurgood Marshall dissented, saying that they failed to see "how our citizens can meaningfully be said to have waived something as precious as a constitutional guarantee without ever being aware of its existence."[17]

The following year, in the case of *United States v. Matlock,* the court held that when one occupant of a house consents to search of the premises, the search is proper and evidence uncovered in it may be used against another occupant.[18]

Property, Papers and Effects

The Supreme Court's first major ruling on the scope of the Fourth Amendment's protection for individual privacy and security came in 1886. The case was *Boyd v. United States.*[19]

The key points of the decision were its holdings that the Fourth Amendment protected individuals against subpoenas — as well as physical searches — for private business papers, and that the Fourth Amendment forbade the use of such subpoenas as unreasonable if they forced the person to whom they were directed to produce self-incriminating evidence.

The Boyds had contracted with the federal government to furnish plate glass for a post office and courthouse building in Philadelphia. They agreed to discount the price of the glass in return for permission to import it duty-free. Subsequently, the government charged that the Boyds had taken advantage of the agreement by importing more glass than the contract permitted.

The government sought forfeiture of the contract. At trial the judge ordered the Boyds to produce the invoice showing the amount of imported glass they had received. Under protest, the Boyds complied with the order. They were convicted.

The Supreme Court, however, reversed their conviction and ordered a new trial, declaring that the subpoena had violated both their Fourth and Fifth Amendment rights. Writing for the majority, Justice Joseph P. Bradley explained:

It is our opinion, therefore, that a compulsory production of a man's private papers to establish a criminal charge against him or to forfeit his property is within the scope of the Fourth Amendment to the Constitution, in all cases in which a search and seizure would be. . . .

Bradley concluded that compulsory production of a man's private papers was an unreasonable search and seizure under the Fourth Amendment, saying:

The principles laid down in this opinion affect the very essence of constitutional liberty and security . . . they apply to all invasions, on the part of the Government and its employees, of the sanctity of a man's home and the privacies of life. It is not the breaking of

his doors and the rummaging of his drawers that constitutes the essence of the offence; but it is the invasion of his indefeasible right of personal security, personal liberty and private property, where that right has never been forfeited by his conviction of some public offense. . . . Breaking into a house and opening boxes and drawers are circumstances of aggravation; but any forcible and compulsory extortion of a man's own testimony or of his private papers to be used as evidence to convict him of crime or to forfeit his goods is within the condemnation of that judgment. In this regard the Fourth and Fifth Amendments run almost into each other. . . .

We have already noticed the intimate relation between the two Amendments. They throw great light on each other. For the "unreasonable searches and seizures" condemned in the Fourth Amendment are almost always made for the purpose of compelling a man to give evidence against himself, which in criminal cases is condemned in the Fifth Amendment; and compelling a man "in a criminal case to be a witness against himself," which is condemned in the Fifth Amendment, throws light on the question as to what is an "unreasonable search and seizure" within the meaning of the Fourth Amendment. And we have been unable to perceive that the seizure of a man's private books and papers to be used in evidence against him is substantially different from compelling him to be a witness against himself.[20]

The Exclusionary Rule

In order to avoid the cumbersome and expensive remedy of retrial for persons convicted on the basis of evidence seized in violation of their Fourth Amendment rights, the court in 1914 adopted the "exclusionary rule."

Set out first by the court in the case of *Weeks v. United States,* the rule allows a defendant who feels that evidence obtained in violation of his rights will be used against him to require the trial court to exclude it from use.[21]

Weeks was arrested without a warrant. Federal agents searched his home, also without a warrant, and took from it documents and letters used as evidence against him at trial. After his conviction, he challenged the conviction as obtained in violation of his rights.

The Supreme Court agreed. In the court's opinion Justice William R. Day explained that exclusion of such evidence was necessary in order to discourage unlawful practices by law enforcement agents:

. . .The tendency of those who execute the criminal laws of the country to obtain conviction by means of unlawful seizures and enforced confessions . . . should find no sanction in the judgments of the courts, which are charged . . . with the support of the Constitution. . . .

. . .If letters and private documents can thus be seized and held and used in evidence against a citizen accused of an offense, the protection of the 4th Amendment, declaring his right to be secure against such searches and seizures, is of no value, and, so far as those thus placed are concerned, might as well be stricken from the Constitution. . . .[22]

The court concluded both that the seizure of the letters by a federal agent and the refusal of the judge to honor Week's request for their return before they were used as evidence were violations of his constitutional rights.

'Mere Evidence'

The court's next major Fourth Amendment decision — *Gouled v. United States* — set out the rule that "mere evidence" could not properly be seized by government officials, even with a search warrant. In *Gouled,* the court also held that a search of a place to which access had been gained by stealth rather than force still fell within the searches prohibited by the Fourth Amendment.[23]

In the *Gouled* case, an acquaintance of Felix Gouled called upon him at his office on the pretext of paying a friendly visit. The "visit," as it turned out, was at the direction of federal agents; Gouled was suspected of attempting to defraud the government in regard to some defense contracts. During the "visit," the acquaintance removed some documents from the premises while Gouled was out of the room. Those documents were later introduced as evidence against Gouled, who was convicted of conspiracy to defraud the government. He challenged the use of the documents as evidence, arguing that it violated his Fourth and Fifth Amendment rights.

The Supreme Court upheld his challenge, applying *Weeks* to exclude both the letters taken by the visitor and additional evidence obtained as a result of the first seizure. The court's ruling was based on the surreptitious and warrantless nature of the search, and on the nature of the letters seized. The letters were "mere evidence," and thus were outside the zone of reasonable seizures.

The court of the late nineteenth and early twentieth centuries was very sensitive to property interests. Both in *Boyd* and *Gouled* the court indicated that the government had a right to seize from an individual only that property to which the individual himself had no right — or an inferior one to the government. With this reasoning, the only proper targets of search warrants were the fruits and instruments of crime and contraband.

Writing for the court, Justice John H. Clarke set out this "mere evidence" rule:

> Although search warrants have ... been used in many cases ever since the adoption of the Constitution, and although their use has been extended from time to time to meet new cases within the old rules, nevertheless it is clear that, at common law and as the result of the *Boyd* and *Weeks Cases* ... they may not be used as a means of gaining access to a man's house or office and papers solely for the purpose of making search to secure evidence to be used against him in a criminal or penal proceeding, but that they may be resorted to only when a primary right to such search and seizure may be found in the interest which the public or the complainant may have in the property to be seized, or in the right to the possession of it, or when a valid exercise of the police power renders possession of the property by the accused unlawful, and provides that it may be taken.[24]

Although this rule severely limits the use of search warrants, in practice its impact was less dramatic. Congress never authorized the use of search warrants for mere evidence, and the Federal Rules of Criminal Procedure limited the objects of federal warrants to instrumentalities and fruits of crime.

Lower courts, however, construed those categories broadly, including many things only remotely connected with a crime as instruments of the crime. By the time the court discarded the rule in 1967, Justice William J. Brennan Jr. would remark that so many exceptions to the rule had been created — and such confusion over what was evidence and what was an instrument of crime — that it was questionable what effect the rule still had.

Searches for Evidence

The court abandoned the "mere evidence" rule in 1967, announcing this shift in its decision in the case of *Warden v. Hayden.*[25]

Hayden, a robbery suspect, was arrested in his home. In a warrantless search of the house by police at the time of his arrest, clothing was found which matched that described by witnesses as worn by the robber, and weapons allegedly used in the hold-up were seized.

Hayden was convicted of armed robbery on the basis of this evidence. He appealed his conviction, claiming that the clothing was seized in violation of the *Gouled* ruling against seizure of mere evidence.

By an 8-1 vote, the court rejected his challenge and discarded the "mere evidence" rule. Justice Brennan wrote the majority opinion, declaring:

> Nothing in the language of the Fourth Amendment supports the distinction between "mere evidence" and instrumentalities, fruits of crime, or contraband. On its face, the provision assures the "right of the people to be secure in their persons, houses, papers and effects...," without regard to the use to which any of these things are applied. This "right of the people" is certainly unrelated to the "mere evidence" limitation. Privacy is disturbed no more by a search directed to a purely evidentiary object than it is by a search directed to an instrumentality, fruit, or contraband. A magistrate can intervene in both situations, and the requirements of probable cause and specificity can be preserved intact. Moreover, nothing in the nature of property seized as evidence renders it more private than property seized, for example, as an instrumentality; quite the opposite may be true. Indeed, the distinction is wholly irrational, since, depending on the circumstances, the same "papers and effects" may be "mere evidence" in one case and "instrumentality" in another....[26]

Brennan declared discredited the twin premises upon which the court in *Gouled* based the "mere evidence" rule — "that property interests control the right of the government to search and seize" and "that government may not seize evidence simply for the purpose of proving crime."[27]

Privacy, not property, was the primary interest protected by the Fourth Amendment, reasoned the majority, and "[t]he requirements of the Fourth Amendment can secure the same protection of privacy whether the search is for 'mere evidence' or for fruits, instrumentalities or contraband."[28]

In conclusion, Brennan wrote:

> The "mere evidence" limitation has spawned exceptions so numerous and confusion so great, in fact, that it is questionable whether it affords meaningful protection. But if its rejection does enlarge the area of permissible searches, the intrusions are nevertheless made after fulfilling the probable cause and particularity requirements of the Fourth Amendment and after the intervention of "a neutral and detached magis-

trate...." ...The Fourth Amendment allows intrusions upon privacy under these circumstances, and there is no viable reason to distinguish intrusions to secure "mere evidence" from intrusions to secure fruits, instrumentalities, or contraband.[29]

Justice Abe Fortas, joined by Chief Justice Earl Warren, agreed that Hayden's clothing was properly used as evidence against him, but criticized the majority's repudiation of the "mere evidence" rule as needless and dangerous.

In dissent, Justice William O. Douglas argued that there were two zones of privacy — one which was completely protected from official intrusion and one which could be invaded by a reasonable, usually warranted, search by government agents. Douglas would place "personal effects" like Hayden's clothes in the first category. He explained:

> The right of privacy protected by the Fourth Amendment relates in part of course to the precincts of the home or the office. But it does not make them sanctuaries where the law can never reach.... A policeman in "hot pursuit" or an officer with a search warrant can enter any house, any room, any building, any office. The privacy of those *places* is of course protected against invasion except in limited situations. The full privacy protected by the Fourth Amendment is, however, reached when we come to books, phamphlets [*sic*], papers, letters, documents, and other personal effects. Unless they are contraband or instruments of the crime, they may not be reached by any warrant nor may they be lawfully seized by the police who are in "hot pursuit." By reason of the Fourth Amendment the police may not rummage around among these personal effects, no matter how formally perfect their authority may appear to be. They may not seize them. If they do, those articles may not be used as evidence. Any invasion whatsoever of those personal effects is "unreasonable" within the meaning of the Fourth Amendment....[30]

To Douglas, "the constitutional philosophy" was clear:

> The personal effects and possessions of the individual (all contraband and the like excepted) are sacrosanct from prying eyes, from the long arm of the law, from any rummaging by police. Privacy involves the choice of the individual to disclose or to reveal what he believes, what he thinks, what he possesses. The article may be a nondescript work of art, a manuscript of a book, a personal account book, a diary, invoices, personal clothing, jewelry, or what not....[31]

Douglas concluded:

> That there is a zone that no police can enter — whether in "hot pursuit" or armed with a meticulously proper warrant — has been emphasized by *Boyd* and by *Gouled.* They have been consistently and continuously approved. I would adhere to them and leave with the individual the choice of opening his private effects (apart from contraband and the like) to the police or keeping their contents and their integrity inviolate. The existence of that choice is the very essence of the right of privacy. Without it the Fourth Amendment and the Fifth are ready instruments for the police state that the Framers sought to avoid.[32]

Recent Rulings

The abolition of the "mere evidence" rule curtailed notably the protection of the Fourth Amendment for private papers.

In two 1976 decisions, the court implicitly made this point. In the case of *United States v. Miller* the court ruled that bank records of a depositor's transactions were not private papers protected by the amendment.[33] And in the case of *Andresen v. Maryland,* the court undercut the *Boyd* ruling to allow the use of an attorney's business records as evidence against him.[34] Because police had a warrant for the search in which they seized those papers, there was no valid Fourth Amendment challenge to their use, the court held. And the justices rejected the attorney's argument that, as in *Boyd,* the use of these papers against him violated his Fifth Amendment privilege against compelled self-incrimination.

Two years later, the court rejected the argument of a campus newspaper that a search of its offices by police with a warrant violated the First and the Fourth Amendments. The *Stanford Daily* offices were searched by police looking for photographs or notes revealing the identity of individual demonstrators responsible for injuries to police during a protest. Such documents were clearly "mere evidence," and there was no allegation that the newspaper or any of its employees had engaged in any wrongdoing. The newspaper contended that police should have subpoenaed the information, rather than searching its offices.

The court, however, rejected that argument, ruling that the Fourth Amendment did not restrict permissible searches to those places occupied by persons suspected of crimes. "Under existing law," wrote Justice Byron R. White for the majority in the case of *Zurcher v. The Stanford Daily,* "valid warrants may be issued to search *any* property, whether or not occupied by a third party, at which there is probable cause to believe that the fruits, instrumentalities, or evidence of a crime will be found." [35]

Justice John Paul Stevens, one of the dissenters from the *Zurcher* decision, took this opportunity to express his concern about the implications of *Warden v. Hayden:*

> ...Countless law abiding citizens ... may have documents in their possession that relate to an ongoing criminal investigation. The consequences of subjecting this large category of persons to unannounced police searches are extremely serious....[36]

Signalling his disagreement with the abandonment of the rule forbidding seizure of mere evidence, Stevens continued:

> Possession of contraband or the proceeds or tools of crime gives rise to two inferences: that the custodian is involved in the criminal activity, and that, if given notice of an intended search, he will conceal or destroy what is being sought. The probability of criminal culpability justifies the invasion of his privacy; the need to accomplish the law enforcement purpose of the search justifies acting without advance notice and by force, if necessary....
>
> Mere possession of documentary evidence, however, is much less likely to demonstrate that the custodian is guilty of any wrongdoing....
>
> The only conceivable justification for an unannounced search of an innocent citizen is the fear that, if notice were given, he would conceal or destroy the

object of the search. Probable cause to believe that the custodian is a criminal, or that he holds a criminal's weapons, spoils, or the like, justifies that fear.... But if nothing said under oath in the warrant application demonstrates the need for an unannounced search by force, the probable cause requirement is not satisfied. In the absence of some other showing of reasonableness, the ensuing search violates the Fourth Amendment.[37]

Arrests and Searches

The Supreme Court has never applied the warrant requirement of the Fourth Amendment as strictly to arrests — "seizures" of one's person — as it has to "searches." The court has applied the common law rule to arrests, approving warrantless arrests by law enforcement officers for crimes committed in their presence and for other crimes where there are reasonable grounds for their action.[38]

In 1925 the court stated that "[t]he usual rule is that a police officer may arrest without warrant one believed by the officer upon reasonable cause to have been guilty of a felony."[39]

Half a century later, the court noted that it had never invalidated an arrest supported by probable cause just because the arresting officer did not have an arrest warrant. To impose a warrant requirement on all arrests, the court said, would "constitute an intolerable handicap for legitimate law enforcement."[40]

Probable cause, however, is essential to justify a warrantless arrest.[41] The court has declared unconstitutional the warrantless detention of suspects apprehended in a police dragnet, declaring that such "investigatory arrests" must be authorized by warrants if the evidence they uncover is to be used in court.[42]

In the 1976 case of *United States v. Watson*, the court upheld the warrantless arrest of a suspect in a public place, based upon probable cause.[43] Justice Byron R. White, in the majority opinion, elaborated on the court's view of the warrant requirement for arrests:

Law enforcement officers may find it wise to seek arrest warrants where practicable to do so, and their judgments about probable cause may be more readily accepted where backed by a warrant issued by a magistrate.... But we decline to transform this judicial preference into a constitutional rule when the judgment of the Nation and Congress has for so long been to authorize warrantless public arrests on probable cause rather than to encumber criminal prosecutions with endless litigation with respect to the existence of exigent circumstances, whether it was practicable to get a warrant, whether the suspect was about to flee, and the like.[44]

Justice Thurgood Marshall dissented, joined by Justice William J. Brennan Jr., saying:

A warrant requirement for arrests would ... minimize the possibility that such an intrusion into the individual's sacred sphere of personal privacy would occur on less than probable cause. Primarily for this reason, a warrant is required for searches. Surely there is no reason to place greater trust in the partisan assessment of a police officer that there is probable cause for an arrest than in his determination that probable cause exists for a search.[45]

Later in the same term, the court upheld the warrantless arrest by police of a suspect in her own home, into which police officers followed her after they saw her standing on her front porch. This ruling came in the case of *United States v. Santana*.[46]

Justice William H. Rehnquist wrote the majority opinion, explaining that under the court's interpretations of the Fourth Amendment, the suspect's front porch was a "public" place:

She was not in an area where she had any expectation of privacy.... She was not merely visible to the public but as exposed to public view, speech, hearing and touch as if she had been standing completely outside her house....

We thus conclude that a suspect may not defeat an arrest which has been set in motion in a public place, and is therefore proper under *Watson*, by the expedient of escaping to a private place.[47]

Justices Marshall and Brennan again dissented, arguing that "in the absence of exigent circumstances, the police may not arrest a subject without a warrant...."[48]

Searches Incident to Arrest

When police arrest a suspect, the court has held that it is reasonable — even without a search warrant — for them to search both the person arrested and, to some limited extent, his immediate surroundings. The justices have viewed such searches as necessary to protect the lives of the arresting officers, to prevent the fugitive's escape, and to prohibit the destruction of evidence.

In a 1925 decision, the court in the case of *Agnello v. United States* acknowledged this exception to the warrant requirement:

The right without a search warrant contemporaneously to search persons lawfully arrested while committing crime, and to search the place where the arrest is made in order to find and seize things connected with the crime as its fruits, or as the means by which it was committed, as well as weapons and other things to effect an escape from custody is not to be doubted.[49]

Twenty-two years later, in the case of *Harris v. United States*, the court gave a broad reading to this exception for warrantless searches.[50]

Harris was arrested in his apartment by FBI agents and charged with mail fraud and forgery. Without a search warrant, the agents searched his entire apartment for five hours. They found no evidence of mail fraud or forgery, but they did discover several stolen Selective Service draft cards. Harris was subsequently convicted for illegal possession of those cards.

He challenged the validity of the search and the seizure of the cards, but the court upheld the search as valid, incident to his arrest. Harris was in control of the entire four-room apartment, it reasoned, and thus the search could extend beyond the room in which he was arrested.

Chief Justice Fred M. Vinson declared for the majority that "[s]earch and seizure incident to lawful arrest is a practice of ancient origin and has long been an integral part of the law-enforcement procedures of the United States...."[51]

Justices Felix Frankfurter, Frank Murphy, Robert H. Jackson and Wiley B. Rutledge dissented. Justice Murphy wrote:

The Court today has resurrected and approved, in effect, the use of the odious general warrant or writ of assistance, presumably outlawed forever from our society by the Fourth Amendment. A warrant of arrest, without more, is now sufficient to justify an unlimited search of a man's home from cellar to garret for evidence of any crime, provided only that he is arrested in his home. Probable cause for the search need not be shown; an oath or affirmation is unnecessary; no description of the place to be searched or the things to be seized need be given; and the magistrate's judgment that these requirements have been satisfied is now dispensed with. In short, all the restrictions put upon the issuance and execution of search warrants by the Fourth Amendment are now dead letters as to those who are arrested in their homes.[52]

The following year, however, the court seemed to narrow the definition of a search which was permissible, without a warrant, pursuant to a valid arrest. The case of *Trupiano v. United States* involved the arrest of several persons on a farm in New Jersey for operating an illegal still — and the seizure, without a warrant, of the still, which the arresting agents had observed in operation during the arrest.[53]

The Supreme Court held the warrantless arrest valid, but not the seizure of the still. For the majority, Justice Murphy wrote that no reason was offered why the federal agents could not have obtained a search warrant before moving in to make the arrest "except [their] indifference to the legal process for search and seizure which the Constitution contemplated."[54]

Murphy continued:

A search or seizure without a warrant as an incident to a lawful arrest has always been considered to be a strictly limited right. It grows out of the inherent necessities of the situation at the time of the arrest. But there must be something more in the way of necessity than merely a lawful arrest.... Otherwise the exception swallows the general principle, making a search warrant completely unnecessary wherever there is a lawful arrest, and so there must be some other factor in the situation that would make it unreasonable or impracticable to require the arresting officer to equip himself with a search warrant.[55]

Later in 1948, the court reiterated this last point in its ruling in *McDonald v. United States:*

Where ... officers are not responding to an emergency, there must be compelling reasons to justify the absence of a search warrant. A search without a warrant demands exceptional circumstances.... We cannot ... excuse the absence of a search warrant without a showing by those who seek exemption from the constitutional mandate that the exigencies of the situation made that course imperative.[56]

Although the "exigent circumstances" requirement of *McDonald* for warrantless searches generally has survived, *Trupiano*'s insistence that a warrant be required whenever obtaining one was practicable was short-lived.

In 1950 the court in the case of *United States v. Rabinowitz* declared that "[t]o the extent that *Trupiano* ... requires a search warrant solely upon the basis of the practicability of procuring it rather than upon the reasonableness of the search after a lawful arrest, that case is overruled."[57]

'Stop and Frisk' Searches

The Supreme Court has held that the police practice of stopping suspicious persons and "frisking" them for weapons is a reasonable "search" within the boundaries of the Fourth Amendment. The court has found such searches permissible even without a search warrant or enough information to constitute probable cause for arrest.

In its 1968 decision in the case of *Terry v. Ohio,* Chief Justice Earl Warren announced that the majority agreed "that there must be a narrowly drawn authority to permit a reasonable search for weapons for the protection of the police officer, where he has reason to believe that he is dealing with an armed and dangerous individual, regardless of whether he has probable cause to arrest the individual for a crime. The officer need not be absolutely certain that the individual is armed; the issue is whether a reasonably prudent man in the circumstances would be warranted in the belief that his safety or that of others was in danger." [1]

The limited nature of this authority was emphasized by the court in a companion case to *Terry: Sibron v. New York.* In *Sibron,* the court held impermissible a police officer's search of a suspect, finding it in violation of the *Terry* standard. Chief Justice Warren explained the difference in the two cases:

The search for weapons approved in *Terry* consisted solely of a limited patting of the outer clothing of the suspect for concealed objects which might be used as instruments of assault. Only when he discovered such objects did the officer in *Terry* place his hands in the pockets of the man he searched. In this case, with no attempt at an initial limited exploration for arms, [the] patrolman ... thrust his hand into Sibron's pocket and took from him envelopes of heroin.... The search was not reasonably limited in scope to the accomplishment of the only goal which might conceivably have justified its inception — the protection of the officer by disarming a potentially dangerous man. Such a search violates the guarantee of the Fourth Amendment, which protects the sanctity of the person against unreasonable intrusions on the part of all government agents.[2]

Four years later, the court in the case of *Adams v. Williams* upheld as proper an officer's stopping a motorist, based upon an informant's tip, reaching into the car and taking a handgun from the person's waistband. The gun was not visible from outside the car; the policeman would not have known of its existence without the informant's tip.[3] The court stated that "[s]o long as the officer is entitled to make a forcible stop and has reason to believe that the suspect is armed and dangerous, he may conduct a weapons search limited in scope to this protective purpose...." [4]

---

[1] *Terry v. Ohio,* 392 U.S. 1 at 27 (1968).
[2] *Sibron v. New York,* 392 U.S. 40 at 65-66 (1968).
[3] *Adams v. Williams,* 407 U.S. 143 (1972).
[4] Id. at 146.

Border Searches

Since the earliest days of the nation's history Congress has authorized warrantless searches of persons entering the country at its borders. Until quite recently it was assumed that such searches were outside the scope of the Fourth Amendment guarantee.

But in a series of rulings in the mid-1970s, the Supreme Court held that the Fourth Amendment did apply to at least some such searches — those which were part of the U.S. Border Patrol's effort to control illegal immigration across the United States-Mexico border. The two types of stops and searches involved were those by roving patrols and those conducted at fixed checkpoints.

In 1973 the court in the case of *Almeida-Sanchez v. United States,* held that roving patrols violated the Fourth Amendment guarantee when they searched vehicles as far as 100 miles from the border without a search warrant or probable cause to suspect that the car contained illegal aliens.[1]

Two years later the unanimous court extended *Almeida-Sanchez* to hold that roving patrols could not even stop a car for questioning of its occupants unless there was more cause for stopping it than simply the fact that the occupants appeared to be Mexican.[2] The same day, the court held that border patrol officers at fixed checkpoints away from the border itself must have probable cause or a warrant before they searched cars at the checkpoint without the driver's consent.[3]

But the following year, the court held that border patrol officers need not have probable cause or a warrant before they stopped cars for brief questioning at fixed checkpoints. Justice Lewis F. Powell Jr. made clear the court's distinction between searches and stops for questioning:

> While the need to make routine checkpoint stops is great, the consequent intrusion on Fourth Amendment interests is quite limited. . . .
>
> Neither the vehicle nor its occupants is searched, and visual inspection of the vehicle is limited to what can be seen without a search. This objective intrusion — the stop itself, the questioning, and the visual inspection — also existed in roving-patrol stops. But we view checkpoint stops in a different light because the subjective intrusion — the generating of concern or even fright on the part of lawful travelers — is appreciably less in the case of a checkpoint stop. . . .
>
> . . .the reasonableness of the procedures followed in making these checkpoint stops makes the resulting intrusion on the interests of the motorists minimal. On the other hand, the purpose of the stops is legitimate and in the public interest. . . . Accordingly, we hold that the stops and questioning at issue may be made in the absence of any individualized suspicion at reasonably located checkpoints.[4]

[1] *Almeida-Sanchez v. United States,* 413 U.S. 266 (1973).
[2] *United States v. Brignoni-Ponce,* 422 U.S. 873 (1975).
[3] *United States v. Ortiz,* 422 U.S. 891 (1975).
[4] *United States v. Martinez-Fuerte, Sifuentes v. United States,* 428 U.S. 543 at 557-558, 561-562 (1976).

In *Rabinowitz* the court separated the question of the reasonableness of a search doctrine from the warrant requirement.

Justice Sherman Minton explained:

> What is a reasonable search is not to be determined by any fixed formula. The Constitution does not define what are 'unreasonable' searches and, regrettably, in our discipline we have no ready litmus-paper test. The recurring questions of the reasonableness of searches must find resolution in the facts and circumstances of each case. . . .
>
> The relevant test is not whether it is reasonable to procure a search warrant, but whether the search was reasonable. That criterion in turn depends on the facts and circumstances — the total atmosphere of the case.[58]

The attempted separation of the reasonableness standard from the warrant requirement and the use of the "total atmosphere" test resulted in considerable confusion over what sort of warrantless searches were permissible incident to a valid arrest.[59]

In 1969 the court overruled *Rabinowitz* and *Harris* and returned to the view that the warrant and reasonableness requirements were indeed linked. This shift was announced in the case of *Chimel v. California.*[60] The court overturned a burglary conviction because it was based on evidence seized without a warrant incident to arrest, but from too extensive a search to be justified by the arrest alone.

Searches incident to arrest were only reasonable insofar as they involved the person arrested and the area immediately under his control — from which he could obtain a weapon or within which he could destroy evidence, declared the court.

Justice Potter Stewart wrote for the majority:

> No consideration relevant to the Fourth Amendment suggests any point of rational limitation, once the search is allowed to go beyond the area from which the person arrested might obtain weapons or evidentiary items. The only reasoned distinction is one between a search of the person arrested and the area within his reach on the one hand, and more extensive searches on the other. . . .
>
> The search here went far beyond the petitioner's person and the area from within which he might have obtained either a weapon or something that could have been used as evidence against him. There was no constitutional justification, in the absence of a search warrant, for extending the search beyond that area. The scope of the search was, therefore, "unreasonable" under the Fourth and Fourteenth Amendments, and the petitioner's conviction cannot stand.[61]

Justice Byron R. White, joined by Justice Hugo L. Black, dissented:

> . . .where as here the existence of probable cause is independently established and would justify a warrant for a broader search for evidence, I would follow past cases and permit such a search to be carried out without a warrant, since the fact of arrest supplies an exigent circumstance justifying police action before the evidence can be removed, and also alerts the suspect to the fact of the search so that he can immediately seek judicial determination of probable cause in an adversary proceeding and appropriate redress.[62]

The following year in the case of *Vale v. Louisiana* the court held that a street arrest of a narcotics suspect did not constitute an "exigent circumstance" to justify a warrantless search of his house.[63]

Then, in *Coolidge v. New Hampshire,* decided in 1971, the court ruled that the arrest of a suspect inside his house did not justify a search of his automobile parked in the driveway.[64]

But the court has never retreated from its view that a suspect under lawful arrest may properly be subjected to full search of his person without a warrant, that such a search is reasonable under the Fourth Amendment, and that evidence found in such a search is admissible.

The court reaffirmed these points in its 1973 ruling in the cases of *United States v. Robinson* and *Gustafson v. Florida,* both involving motorists stopped for violations of auto or traffic laws and found to possess illegal drugs. The subsequent narcotics convictions of both were upheld by the court.[65]

Automobile Searches

In addition to the exception recognized to the warrant requirement for searches incident to arrest, the court since 1925 has allowed some warrantless searches of moving vehicles, especially automobiles.

The landmark case in the law involving automobile searches is *Carroll v. United States,* decided in 1925.[66] George Carroll was convicted of transporting liquor for sale in violation of the federal prohibition law and the 18th Amendment. The contraband liquor used as evidence against him had been taken from his car by federal agents acting without a search warrant.

But the Supreme Court sustained Carroll's conviction against his contention that this seizure violated his Fourth Amendment rights. Writing for the court, Chief Justice William Howard Taft explained:

> . . .the guaranty of freedom from unreasonable searches and seizures by the Fourth Amendment has been construed, practically since the beginning of the government, as recognizing a necessary difference between a search of a store, dwelling house, or other structure in respect of which a proper official warrant readily may be obtained and a search of a ship, motor boat, wagon, or automobile for contraband goods, where it is not practicable to secure a warrant, because the vehicle can be quickly moved out of the locality or jurisdiction in which the warrant must be sought.[67]

Subsequent rulings involving police searches of automobiles, without warrants, for contraband, have made clear the breadth of this exception to the warrant requirements. In a 1931 case the court upheld the search of a parked car as reasonable, since police could not know when the suspect might move it.[68]

The court in a 1948 decision appeared to limit this exception to situations in which Congress had authorized warrantless searches of moving vehicles suspected as involved in the violation of federal laws.[69] But the following year the justices in the case of *Brinegar v. United States* upheld, as reasonable, warrantless searches of automobiles whenever police had probable cause to believe the cars were involved in illegal activity.[70]

This remains the rule, as the court has repeatedly emphasized in cases in which it has refused to declare

evidence to be admissible when it was discovered in a search for which probable cause was lacking.[71]

State Police and Auto Searches

After the court in *Mapp v. Ohio* applied the exclusionary rule to state proceedings — and in *Ker v. California* declared the same standards for state and federal action under the Fourth Amendment — the court's rulings concerning warrantless auto searches by state police continued to apply the same limits imposed on federal authorities.

The court generally has given state police broad leeway in such searches. It has upheld the search of a car without a warrant as long as a week after the arrest of its owner, when the government had a proprietary interest in the car since it was subject to forfeiture under state law.[72] It has allowed police to make such searches of autos after they have been towed to the police garage from the site of an arrest.[73]

The justices have refused to exclude evidence obtained in the routine warrantless search of an impounded vehicle as inadmissible,[74] or to require that a warrant be obtained before police take paint samples from the exterior of a car parked in a public parking lot.[75]

In 1978 the court in the case of *Rakas v. Illinois* held that passengers did not have the right to challenge the warrantless search of the vehicle in which they were riding or the use of evidence seized in that search against them. That decision tied the Fourth Amendment rights of persons riding in automobiles more closely to property concepts than it had in earlier cases.

For the five-man majority, Justice William H. Rehnquist emphasized that Fourth Amendment rights could only be asserted by the person whose privacy was invaded: "A person who is aggrieved by an illegal search and seizure only through the introduction of damaging evidence secured by a search of a third person's premises or property has not had any of his Fourth Amendment rights infringed." [76]

The warrantless search in this case was proper because it was based on probable cause: the car fit the description of a getaway car used in a nearby robbery. And because the passengers did not claim that they owned either the car or the items seized, they could not challenge the search, the seizure or the use of discovered evidence against them as a violation of the Fourth Amendment guarantee.

The four dissenting justices, for whom Justice Byron R. White wrote, criticized the majority for implying that the Fourth Amendment protected property interests rather than privacy interest. The court in this ruling, wrote White, was declaring "open season" for auto searches.[77]

Four months later, however, the court appeared to allay White's fears with its 8-1 decision in the case of *Delaware v. Prouse.* With White writing the majority opinion and Rehnquist as the lone dissenter, the court held impermissible the state police practice of randomly stopping motorists — without any probable cause to suspect a crime or illegal activity — to check their driver's license and auto registration. The court decided that such "seizures" of the person and any subsequent searches violated the Fourth Amendment and that evidence of a drug law violation discovered in a car after such a random stop could not be admitted as evidence in state court.[78]

Electronic Eavesdropping

Not until 1967 did the Supreme Court bring electronic eavesdropping and surveillance techniques within the scope

The Exclusionary Rule: Effective Remedy

In 1914 the Supreme Court announced the controversial "exclusionary rule" which prohibited the use in federal courts of evidence seized by federal agents in violation of the Fourth Amendment prohibition against unreasonable search and seizure. The rule was set out by the court in the case of *Weeks v. United States.*[1] It has subsequently been applied to forbid the use of evidence taken in violation of other constitutional rights as well, in particular the Fifth Amendment privilege against self-incrimination and the Sixth Amendment right to counsel.

For 47 years, however, the rule did not operate in state trials, where evidence seized in unreasonable searches could — as far as the Supreme Court was concerned — be used without violating the Constitution's guarantees. Not until 1961, with its ruling in the case of *Mapp v. Ohio,* did the court extend this rule to state trials.[2]

The application of the rule has been the subject of much legal controversy. By denying prosecutors the use of certain evidence, the rule can sometimes cause the collapse of the government's case and the freeing of a person against whom there is strong evidence of guilt. As Justice Benjamin Cardozo wrote before he came to the Supreme Court bench, "The criminal is to go free because the constable has blundered."[3]

Some, including Chief Justice Warren E. Burger, feel that this is too high a price for society to pay for what may have been inadvertent violations of constitutional guarantees. Burger has suggested that the rule should be abandoned and replaced with some less costly remedy — such as a law authorizing persons whose rights are so violated by law enforcement officers to sue the particular offending individuals for monetary damages.

In a 1920 ruling in the case of *Silverthorne Lumber Co. v. United States,* the court made clear that the exclusionary rule announced in *Weeks* forbade *all* use of illegally obtained evidence in federal courts. The court in that case ordered the government to return to the owner physical evidence illegally seized by federal officials, and ordered the exclusion of evidence photocopied from those originals.[4]

Justice Oliver Wendell Holmes, Jr., speaking for the majority, ruled the photocopied evidence inadmissible, saying that "[t]he essence of a provision forbidding the acquisition of evidence in a certain way is that not merely evidence so acquired shall not be used before the court, but that it shall not be used at all."[5]

In 1954, however, the court held that narcotics illegally seized by federal officials, while not admissible as evidence at trial, could be used to impeach the defendant's credibility after he had testified that he had never used them.[6]

In other decisions, the court made clear that only the person whose rights were violated by the search and seizure could invoke the exclusionary rule.[7]

Wolf v. Colorado

In 1949 the court held in the case of *Wolf v. Colorado* that the Fourth Amendment guarantee protected individuals against state as well as federal action. The court declined, however, to apply the exclusionary rule to enforce this guarantee against state officials.[8]

In *Wolf* a deputy sheriff had seized a doctor's appointment book without a warrant, interrogated patients whose names he found in the book and thereby obtained evidence to charge Wolf with performing illegal abortions.

Wolf challenged the use of such evidence, arguing that it had been illegally seized and should be excluded. The court, however, sustained his conviction.

Justice Felix Frankfurter wrote for the majority that:

> . . .the immediate question is whether the basic right to protect against arbitrary intrusion by the police demands the exclusion of logically relevant evidence obtained by an unreasonable search and seizure because, in a federal prosecution for a federal crime, it would be excluded. . . . When we find that in fact most of the English-speaking world does not regard as vital to such protection the exclusion of evidence thus obtained, we must hesitate to treat this remedy as an essential ingredient of the right. . . .
>
> Granting that in practice the exclusion of evidence may be an effective way of deterring unreasonable searches, it is not for this Court to condemn as falling below the minimal standards assured by the Due Process Clause a State's reliance upon other methods which, if consistently enforced, would be equally effective. . . .
>
> We hold, therefore, that in a prosecution in a State court for a State crime the Fourteenth Amendment does not forbid the admission of evidence obtained by an unreasonable search and seizure.[9]

But even though the court in *Wolf* refused to apply the rule to exclude *all* illegally seized evidence from use in state courts, there were some instances of police conduct so shocking to the court that it reversed convictions thereby obtained.

One such case was *Rochin v. California,* decided in 1952.

In *Rochin,* state police officers had "seized" evidence from a suspect by pumping his stomach to recover two capsules of drugs which he had swallowed at the time of his arrest. The court held the resulting conviction invalid. Frankfurter wrote the opinion for the unanimous court, decrying such methods as "conduct that shocks the conscience, . . . methods too close to the rack and the screw to permit of constitutional differentiation."[10]

But the court's earlier refusal to exclude all illegally obtained evidence was subsequently reaffirmed in cases involving eavesdropping, illegal entry, and the taking of a blood sample from an unconscious injured suspect.[11]

The "Silver Platter" Doctrine

The Supreme Court in *Weeks v. United States* announced two rules of evidence for federal courts.

One, of course, was the exclusionary rule: federal prosecutors could not use evidence obtained by federal agents in violation of the Fourth Amendment protection against unreasonable search and seizure.

. . . or Expensive Constitutional Right?

The second rule became known as the "silver platter" doctrine: federal prosecutors *could* use evidence obtained by *state* agents through unreasonable search and seizure, if that evidence was obtained without federal participation and was turned over to the federal officials.

The apparent incongruity of these two rules was explained by the court's view in 1914 that the Fourth Amendment did not apply to state action.

But after the court reversed that view in *Wolf v. Colorado* in 1949, the "silver platter" doctrine survived for eleven more years. Finally, in *Elkins v. United States,* the court in 1960 repudiated that practice. Writing for the court, Justice Potter Stewart declared:

> . . .surely no distinction can logically be drawn between evidence obtained in violation of the Fourth Amendment and that obtained in violation of the Fourteenth [through which the ban against unreasonable search and seizure was applicable to the states]. The Constitution is flouted equally in either case. To the victim it matters not whether his constitutional right has been invaded by a federal agent or by a state officer.[12]

Mapp v. Ohio

The Supreme Court extended the exclusionary rule to the states in the case of *Mapp v. Ohio,* decided in 1961. In *Mapp,* the court finally declared that "the exclusionary rule is an essential part of both the Fourth and Fourteenth Amendments. . . ."[13]

Cleveland police, suspecting that a law violator was hiding in a certain house, broke in the door, manhandled the woman resident, a Miss Mapp, and searched the entire premises without a warrant. A trunk containing obscene materials was found in the house. Mapp was tried and convicted for possession of obscene materials.

The Supreme Court overturned Mapp's conviction because the evidence used against her had been unconstitutionally seized. Justice Tom C. Clark wrote the majority opinion, in which the court reversed *Wolf* insofar as it dealt with the exclusionary rule:

> Nothing can destroy a government more quickly than its failure to observe its own laws, or worse, its disregard of the charter of its own existence. . . .

> The ignoble shortcut to conviction left open to the State [by allowing use of illegally obtained evi-

dence] tends to destroy the entire system of constitutional restraints on which the liberties of the people rest. Having once recognized that the right to privacy embodied in the Fourth Amendment is enforceable against the States, and that the right to be secure against rude invasions of privacy by state officers is, therefore, constitutional in origin, we can no longer permit that right to remain an empty promise.[14]

Justices Frankfurter, John Marshall Harlan and Charles E. Whittaker dissented.

In 1965 the court held that the *Mapp* decision would not be retroactively applied to overturn state criminal convictions which occurred prior to the new standard's promulgation in 1961. In the case of *Linkletter v. Walker,* the court stated that *Mapp* applied only to cases on direct review at the time of the 1961 ruling and to later cases.[15]

The court in the 1970s has limited the use of the exclusionary rule to overturn convictions. Chief Justice Warren E. Burger said in the case of *Bivens v. Six Unknown Named Agents,* decided in 1971, that he preferred an alternative remedy for the problem of illegal action by the government to obtain evidence. Burger has suggested that a person whose Fourth Amendment rights had been so violated might be authorized by Congress to sue the offending officials.[16]

In line with Burger's reservations about the usefulness of the exclusionary rule, the court in 1974 refused to apply the rule to forbid the use of illegally obtained evidence by persons questioning witnesses before grand juries.[17]

In 1976 the court in the cases of *Stone v. Powell* and *Wolff v. Rice* ruled that federal courts were under no constitutional obligation to use the writ of *habeas corpus* to order release of persons who argued that their convictions in state courts had been obtained with illegally seized evidence.

So long as the state has provided an opportunity for a full, fair hearing of the defendant's challenge to that evidence, held the court, there was no constitutional obligation for federal courts to use the writ of *habeas corpus* to enforce the exclusionary rule.[18]

The same year, the court held that the exclusionary rule did not forbid the use, in federal civil proceedings, of evidence improperly seized by state officials acting in good faith.[19]

---

[1] *Weeks v. United States,* 232 U.S. 383 (1914).

[2] *Mapp v. Ohio,* 367 U.S. 643 (1961).

[3] *People v. Defore,* 242 N.Y. 13 at 21, 150 N.E. 585 (1926).

[4] *Silverthorne Lumber Co. v. United States,* 251 U.S. 385 (1921).

[5] Id. at 392.

[6] *Walder v. United States,* 347 U.S. 62 (1954); see also *Stefanelli v. Minard,* 342 U.S. 117 (1951).

[7] *Goldstein v. United States,* 316 U.S. 114 (1942).

[8] *Wolf v. Colorado,* 338 U.S. 25 (1949).

[9] Id. at 28-29, 31, 33.

[10] *Rochin v. California,* 342 U.S. 165 (1952).

[11] *Irvine v. California,* 347 U.S. 128 (1954); *Breithaupt v. Abrams,* 352 U.S. 432 (1957).

[12] *Elkins v. United States,* 364 U.S. 206 at 215 (1960).

[13] *Mapp v. Ohio,* 367 U.S. 643 at 657 (1961).

[14] Id. at 659, 660.

[15] *Linkletter v. Walker,* 381 U.S. 618 (1965).

[16] *Bivens v. Six Unknown Named Agents,* 403 U.S. 388 (1971); see also *Monroe v. Pape,* 365 U.S. 176 (1961).

[17] *United States v. Calandra,* 414 U.S. 338 (1974).

[18] *Stone v. Powell, Wolff v. Rice,* 428 U.S. 465 (1976).

[19] *United States. v. Janis,* 428 U.S. 433 (1976).

The Fourth Amendment and Administrative Searches:

The Fourth Amendment requires building, health and fire inspectors to obtain warrants for administrative searches of private premises, the court has ruled in recent years. But the justices have also held that warrants for such searches do not need to meet the same strict "probable cause" standards mandated for warrants in criminal investigations.

On the other hand, the court has held that interviews of clients in their homes by welfare workers are not searches within the meaning of the Fourth Amendment. And it has allowed warrantless inspections of establishments selling guns or liquor — businesses regulated by federal law.

Health Inspections

In the 1959 case of *Frank v. Maryland,* the court upheld the warrantless inspection of a private dwelling by a city health official seeking the source of a rat infestation. In its opinion, the court stated that the protection of the Fourth Amendment did not extend to such situations:

> No evidence for criminal prosecution is sought to be seized. Appellant is simply directed to do what he could have been ordered to do without any inspection, and what he cannot properly resist, namely, act in a manner consistent with the maintenance of minimum community standards of health. . . .[1]

Housing Inspections

But only eight years later the court overturned the *Frank* decision. In the case of *Camara v. Municipal Court,* it declared that administrative searches were indeed "significant intrusions upon the interests protected by the Fourth Amendment."

Camara refused to permit a housing inspector of the San Francisco Health Department to make a routine inspection of his apartment without a search warrant. The court upheld Camara's position, stating:

> We may agree that a routine inspection of the physical condition of private property is a less hostile intrusion than the typical policeman's search for the fruits and instrumentalities of crime. For this reason alone, *Frank* differed from the great bulk of Fourth Amendment cases. . . . But we cannot agree that the Fourth Amendment interests at stake in these inspection cases are merely "peripheral." It is surely anomalous to say that the individual and his private property are fully protected by the Fourth Amendment only when the individual is suspected of criminal behavior.[2]

In a second ruling announced the same day as *Camara,* the court declared that government agents must obtain a warrant for administrative entries into the non-public portions of commercial establishments. In the case of *See v. City of Seattle,* the court established broad guidelines for such searches.[3]

Occupational Safety Inspections

The court in the 1978 case of *Marshall v. Barlow's, Inc.,* denied government inspectors from the Occupational Safety and Health Administration the right to make warrantless random safety inspections of non-public working areas on business premises over the owner's objection. If consent was not given to the search, a warrant must be obtained.

Relying on the *Camara* decision, the court held that the "Warrant Clause of the Fourth Amendment protects commercial buildings as well as private homes. . . . That an employee is free to report, and the Government is free to use, any evidence of non-compliance with OSHA that the employee observes furnishes no justification for fed-

---

of the Fourth Amendment guarantee of security against unreasonable search and seizure.

From 1928 until 1967, the court had held firmly that the Fourth Amendment applied only when there was physical entry or trespass and the seizure of tangible items; it did not apply to overheard conversations.

This rule was first set out in the 1928 case of *Olmstead v. United States,* which involved a bootlegging operation against which evidence was gathered through the use of wiretaps on telephone conversations.

The participants challenged this method of obtaining evidence against them, arguing that it violated their Fourth Amendment rights. The court, with Chief Justice William Howard Taft writing its opinion, rejected that claim:

> The well-known historical purpose of the 4th Amendment, directed against general warrants and writs of assistance, was to prevent the use of governmental force to search a man's house, his person, his papers, and his effects, and to prevent their seizure against his will. . . .
>
> The Amendment itself shows that the search is to be of material things — the person, the house, his

papers or his effects. The description of the warrant necessary to make the proceeding lawful is that it must specify the place to be searched and the person or *things* to be seized. . . .

> The Amendment does not forbid what was done here. There was no searching. There was no seizure. The evidence was secured by the use of the sense of hearing and that only. There was no entry of the houses or offices of the defendants. . . .
>
> The language of the Amendment can not be extended and expanded to include telephone wires reaching to the whole world from the defendant's house or office. . . .
>
> Congress may, of course, protect the secrecy of telephone messages by making them, when intercepted, inadmissible in evidence in Federal criminal trials. . . . But the courts may not adopt such a policy by attributing an enlarged and unusual meaning to the 4th Amendment.[79]

In dissent, Justice Oliver Wendell Holmes Jr. wrote: ". . .apart from the Constitution, the government ought not to use evidence obtained, and only obtainable, by a crimi-

Building, Health, Fire and Welfare Inspections

eral agents to enter a place of business from which the public is restricted and to conduct their own warrantless search." [4]

Guns and Liquor

The court has made exceptions to the warrant requirement for administrative searches of premises occupied by gun dealers and liquor establishments, both of which are regulated by federal law. The court has ruled that the premises of such business establishments may be inspected during regular business hours by government agents without a warrant.

In the case of *Colonnade Catering Corp. v. United States,* decided in 1970, the court held that in certain industries subject to particular government oversight there can be no expectation of privacy for the proprietor or the premises of the enterprise.

A federal agent of the alcohol and tobacco tax division of the Internal Revenue Service made a warrantless inspection of a locked storeroom and forcibly seized illegal liquor. Justice William O. Douglas, writing the opinion for the majority, stated that "Congress has broad power to design such powers of inspection under the liquor laws as it deems necessary to meet the evils at hand." [5]

In the 1972 case of *United States v. Biswell,* the court upheld the warrantless search of a pawnbroker's storeroom by a federal agent who discovered two illegal weapons there. Relying on the *Colonnade Catering* decision, the court majority declared:

...where, as here, regulatory inspections further urgent federal interest, and the possibilities of abuse and the threat to privacy are not of impressive dimensions, the inspection may proceed without a warrant where specifically authorized by statute. [6]

Arson Investigations

In 1978 the court held that fire officials inspecting the premises on which a suspicious fire occurred must generally have a warrant, unless the inspection occurs during or immediately after the fire.

In the case of *Michigan v. Tyler* the court held:

...an entry to fight a fire requires no warrant, and ... once in the building, officials may remain there for a reasonable time to investigate the cause of the fire. Thereafter, additional entries to investigate the ... fire must be made pursuant to the warrant procedures governing administrative searches. [7]

Welfare Visits

In the case of *Wyman v. James,* decided in 1970, the court held that home visits by a welfare worker to a prospective client raised no valid Fourth Amendment issues. The majority, in the words of Justice Harry A. Blackmun, agreed that the visit might be both "rehabilitative and investigative," but found nevertheless that it did not reach the dimensions of "a search in the traditional criminal law context" and therefore "does not fall within the Fourth Amendment's proscription." [8]

---

[1] *Frank v. Maryland,* 359 U.S. 360 at 366 (1959).
[2] *Camara v. Municipal Court,* 387 U.S. 523 at 530 (1967).
[3] *See v. City of Seattle,* 387 U.S. 541 (1967).
[4] *Marshall v. Barlows, Inc.,* 436 U.S. 307 at 311, 315 (1978).

[5] *Colonnade Catering Corp. v. United States,* 397 U.S. 72 at 76 (1970).
[6] *United States v. Biswell,* 406 U.S. 311 at 317 (1972).
[7] *Michigan v. Tyler,* 436 U.S. 499 at 511 (1978).
[8] *Wyman v. James,* 400 U.S. 309 at 317-318 (1971).

---

nal act. . . . I think it a less evil that some criminals should escape than that the government should play an ignoble part. . . ." [80]

Justice Louis D. Brandeis also dissented, arguing that wiretapping was clearly a search within the meaning of the Fourth Amendment, which he described as intended to protect "the sanctities of a man's home and the privacies of life." He added that the Fourth Amendment guarantee must, to retain its validity, be read with an awareness of new threats to the security it was intended to protect:

Subtler and more far-reaching means of invading privacy have become available to the government. Discovery and invention have made it possible for the government, by means far more effective than stretching upon the rack, to obtain disclosure in court of what is whispered in the closet. . . . [81]

Furthermore, Brandeis argued, wiretapping was itself a crime under federal law, and government agents should not be allowed to commit crimes to catch criminals:

Decency, security, and liberty alike demand that government officials shall be subjected to the same

rules of conduct that are commands to the citizen. In a government of laws, existence of the government will be imperiled if it fails to observe the law scrupulously. Our government is the potent, the omnipresent, teacher. For good or ill, it teaches the whole people by its example. Crime is contagious. If the government becomes a law-breaker, it breeds contempt for law; it invites every man to become a law unto himself; it invites anarchy. To declare that in the administration of the criminal law the end justifies the means — to declare that the government may commit crimes in order to secure the conviction of a private criminal — would bring terrible retribution. Against that pernicious doctrine this court should resolutely set its face. [82]

In 1934 Congress included in the Federal Communications Act the statement that "no person not being authorized by the sender shall intercept any communication and divulge or publish the existence, contents, substance, purport, effect or meaning of such intercepted communication to any person."

Three years later, in the case of *Nardone v. United States,* the court read this provision as forbidding federal

'Seizure' of Physical Traits

The Supreme Court has consistently held since 1910 that certain physical characteristics which individuals consistently display to the public are not protected by the Fourth Amendment from government "seizure" and use as evidence.

Writing for the court in a 1910 ruling, Justice Oliver Wendell Holmes Jr. held that an individual was not compelled to incriminate himself when he was forced to reveal certain physical characteristics. The Fifth Amendment, wrote Holmes, did not demand "an exclusion of his body as evidence when it may be material." [1]

This principle was subsequently extended to rebut Fourth Amendment challenges to the use of such evidence as voice samples and handwriting examples obtained from suspects. [2]

The court also has held that minor intrusions on a suspect's body do not violate the Fourth Amendment. But it has outlawed more drastic intrusions as offending both the Fourth Amendment and the "sense of justice."

Thus while the court has upheld the extraction of blood samples and the taking of fingernail scrapings from suspects, it has rejected the use of a stomach pump to obtain — from a suspect's digestive system — evidence of narcotics possesion. [3] *(See box, p. 548)*

---

[1] *Holt v. United States,* 218 U.S. 245 at 253 (1910).

[2] *United States v. Dionisio,* 410 U.S. 1 (1973); *United States v. Mara,* 410 U.S. 19 (1973); *United States v. Wade,* 388 U.S. 218 (1967); *Gilbert v. California,* 388 U.S. 263 (1967).

[3] *Rochin v. California,* 342 U.S. 165 (1952); *Breithaupt v. Abram,* 352 U.S. 432 (1957); *Schmerber v. California,* 384 U.S. 757 (1966); *Cupp v. Murphy,* 412 U.S. 291 (1973).

---

agents, as well as all other persons, to intercept and disclose telephone messages by the use of wiretaps. In that and a similar case in 1939, the court excluded from use in federal courts any evidence obtained, directly or indirectly, from wiretaps. [83]

Two wartime rulings announced in 1942, however, allowed some use of evidence obtained by electronic surveillance.

In the case of *Goldstein v. United States,* the court held that wiretap evidence could be used against persons other than those whose conversations had been overheard and whose Fourth Amendment security was therefore violated. [84] And in *Goldman v. United States,* the court held that the use of a "bug" — an electronic listening device, not a wiretap on telephone lines — was not in violation of the Communications Act provision, which applied only to actual interference with communication wires and telephone lines. [85]

In 1961, however, the court began to take a tougher view of electronic surveillance as an impermissible intrusion into personal privacy.

In the case of *Silverman v. United States,* the court held that the Fourth Amendment was violated by the use of a "spike-mike" driven into a building wall to allow police to overhear conversations within the building. The fact that the device, although tiny, actually penetrated the building wall was sufficient, in the court's view, to constitute physical intrusion in violation of the search-and-seizure provision. [86]

Then, six years later, the court finally abandoned the *Olmstead* view and brought electronic surveillance of all types within the proscription of the Fourth Amendment.

The case of *Katz v. United States* involved the use of evidence obtained by government agents who placed a listening device on the outside of a public telephone booth and through it obtained information from telephone conversations which led to the prosecution of individuals involved in illegal bookmaking activities. [87]

Justice Potter Stewart delivered the majority opinion: "The fact that the electronic device employed . . . did not happen to penetrate the wall of the booth can have no constitutional significance," wrote Stewart. [88] He continued:

> . . .the Fourth Amendment protects people, not places. What a person knowingly exposes to the public, even in his own home or office, is not a subject of Fourth Amendment protection. . . . But what he seeks to preserve as private, even in an area accessible to the public, may be constitutionally protected. . . .
>
> . . .[W]hat he [Katz] sought to exclude when he entered the booth was not the intruding eye — it was the uninvited ear. He did not shed his right to do so simply because he made his calls from a place where he might be seen. [89]

Justice Hugo L. Black, in dissent, adhered to the *Olmstead* view that words cannot be "seized."

Two years later, in 1969, the court made clear its intention of penalizing government agents for engaging in improper electronic surveillance. In the cases of *Alderman v. United States, Butenko v. United States,* and *Ivanov v. United States,* the court held that the government must turn over all material obtained by illegal surveillance to the defendant whose Fourth Amendment rights had been violated by its collection and against whom such evidence might be used. The defendant could then examine the information in order to ascertain what parts of it the government might plan to use against him and to challenge its use. [90]

The government, dismayed by this ruling, chose to drop a number of prosecutions rather than disclose the method and the content of some particular instances of surveillance.

Statutory Authorization

Following *Katz,* Congress in the 1968 Crime Control and Safe Streets Act provided for the first time statutory authorization for the federal use of judicially approved wiretaps and other forms of electronic surveillance. The law set out specific procedures to be followed by federal agents in obtaining approval for such surveillance, first from Justice Department officials and then from a federal judge who would issue a warrant for this type of "search-and-seizure."

The law provided that applications for warrants must be approved either by the attorney general himself or by a specially designated assistant attorney general. [91]

In two decisions early in the 1970s, the court signaled its determination to apply the warrant requirement to wiretaps at least as strictly as it applied it to other types of searches.

In 1972 the court unanimously rejected the contention of the Nixon administration that the 1968 law did not require judicial approval of warrants for wiretaps or surveil-lance in national security cases.[92]

Two years later, the court effectively nullified hun-dreds of criminal prosecutions based on evidence obtained by surveillance — with its finding that Attorney General John N. Mitchell had not himself signed the applications for the warrants authorizing the surveillance and had

allowed an aide other than the designated assistant attor-ney general to approve the applications.[93]

In 1979, however, the court held that because Congress must have recognized that most electronic "bugs" can only be installed by agents who secretly enter the premises, warrants authorizing such surveillance need not explicitly authorize covert entry.[94]

Footnotes

[1] *Wolf v. Colorado*, 338 U.S. 25 at 27-28 (1949).

[2] *Camara v. Municipal Court*, 387 U.S. 523 at 528-529 (1967).

[3] *GM Leasing Corporation v. United States*, 429 U.S. 338 (1977); *Michigan v. Tyler*, 436 U.S. 499 (1978); *Mincey v. Arizona*, 437 U.S. 385 (1978).

[4] *Wolf v. Colorado*, 338 U.S. 25 (1949).

[5] *Mapp v. Ohio*, 367 U.S. 643 (1961).

[6] *Ker v. California*, 374 U.S. 23 (1963).

[7] *Johnson v. United States*, 333 U.S. 10 at 13-14 (1948).

[8] *Coolidge v. New Hampshire*, 403 U.S. 443 at 453 (1971); see also *Lo-Ji Sales v. New York* (1979).

[9] *Shadwick v. City of Tampa Fla.*, 407 U.S. 345 at 350 (1972).

[10] *Locke v. United States*, 7 Cr. 339 at 348 (1813).

[11] *Dumbra v. United States*, 268 U.S. 435 at 441 (1925); see also *Byars v. United States*, 273 U.S. 28 (1927); *Draper v. United States*, 358 U.S. 307 (1959).

[12] *Nathanson v. United States*, 290 U.S. 41 at 47 (1933); see also *Giordanello v. United States*, 357 U.S. 480 (1958); *Aguilar v. Texas*, 378 U.S. 108 (1964); *Spinelli v. United States*, 393 U.S. 410 (1969); *United States v. Ventresca*, 380 U.S. 102 at 108-109 (1965).

[13] *Jones v. United States*, 362 U.S. 257 (1960).

[14] *Rugendorf v. United States*, 367 U.S. 528 (1964); *McCray v. Illinois*, 386 U.S. 300 (1967); see also *Whitely v. Warden*, 401 U.S. 560 (1971); *United States v. Harris*, 403 U.S. 573 (1971); *Adams v. Williams*, 407 U.S. 143 (1972).

[15] *Franks v. Delaware*, 438 U.S. 154 at 168 (1978).

[16] *Schneckloth v. Bustamonte*, 412 U.S. 218 at 248-249 (1973).

[17] Id. at 277.

[18] *United States v. Matlock*, 415 U.S. 164 (1974).

[19] *Boyd v. United States*, 116 U.S. 616 (1886).

[20] Id. at 630, 633.

[21] *Weeks v. United States*, 232 U.S. 383 (1914).

[22] Id. at 392-393.

[23] *Gouled v. United States*, 255 U.S. 298 (1921).

[24] Id. at 309.

[25] *Warden v. Hayden*, 387 U.S. 294 (1967).

[26] Id. at 301-302.

[27] Id. at 304, 306.

[28] Id. at 306-307.

[29] Id. at 309-310.

[30] Id. at 320.

[31] Id. at 323.

[32] Id. at 325.

[33] *United States v. Miller*, 425 U.S. 435 (1976).

[34] *Andresen v. Maryland*, 427 U.S. 463 (1976).

[35] *Zurcher v. The Stanford Daily*, 436 U.S. 547 at 554 (1978).

[36] Id. at 579.

[37] Id. at 581-583.

[38] *Ex parte Burford*, 3 Cr. 448 (1805); *Kurtz v. Moffitt*, 115 U.S. 487 (1885).

[39] *Carroll v. United States*, 267 U.S. 132 at 156 (1925).

[40] *Gerstein v. Pugh*, 420 U.S. 103 at 113 (1975).

[41] *Ker v. California*, 374 U.S. 23 (1963).

[42] *Davis v. Mississippi*, 394 U.S. 721 at 727 (1969); *Dunaway v. New York* (1979).

[43] *United States v. Watson*, 423 U.S. 411 (1976).

[44] Id. at 423-424.

[45] Id. at 447.

[46] *United States v. Santana*, 427 U.S. 38 (1976); see *Johnson v. United States*, 333 U.S. 10 at 16, note 7 (1948) for use of the term "hot pursuit."

[47] *United States v. Santana*, 427 U.S. 38 at 42-43 (1976).

[48] Id. at 45.

[49] *Agnello v. United States*, 269 U.S. 20 at 30 (1925); see also *Marron v. United States* 275 U.S. 192 (1927).

[50] *Harris v. United States*, 331 U.S. 145 (1947).

[51] Id. at 150-151.

[52] Id. at 183.

[53] *Trupiano v. United States*, 334 U.S. 699 at 706 (1948).

[54] Id. at 708.

[55] Ibid.

[56] *McDonald v. United States*, 335 U.S. 451 at 454, 456 (1948).

[57] *United States v. Rabinowitz*, 339 U.S. 56 at 66 (1950).

[58] Id. at 63, 66.

[59] *Kremen v. United States*, 353 U.S. 346 (1957); *Abel v. United States*, 362 U.S. 217 at 238; *Chapman v. United States*, 365 U.S. 610 (1961); *Ker v. California*, 374 U.S. 23 (1963).

[60] *Chimel v. California*, 395 U.S. 752 (1969).

[61] Id. at 766, 768.

[62] Id. at 780.

[63] *Vale v. Louisiana*, 399 U.S. 30 (1970).

[64] *Coolidge v. New Hampshire*, 403 U.S. 443 (1971); see also *United States v. Edwards*, 415 U.S. 800 (1974).

[65] *United States v. Robinson*, 414 U.S. 218 (1973); *Gustafson v. Florida*, 414 U.S. 260 (1973).

[66] *Carroll v. United States*, 267 U.S. 132 (1925).

[67] Id. at 153.

[68] *Husty v. United States*, 282 U.S. 694 (1931); see also *Scher v. United States*, 305 U.S. 251 (1938).

[69] *United States v. Di Re*, 332 U.S. 581 (1948).

[70] *Brinegar v. United States*, 338 U.S. 160 (1949).

[71] *Henry v. United States*, 361 U.S. 98 (1959); *Rios v. United States*, 364 U.S. 253 (1960).

[72] *Cooper v. California*, 386 U.S. 58 (1967).

[73] *Chambers v. Maroney*, 399 U.S. 42 (1970); *Preston v. United States*, 376 U.S. 364 (1964).

[74] *Cady v. Dombrowski*, 413 U.S. 433 (1973); *South Dakota v. Opperman*, 428 U.S. 364 (1976).

[75] *Cardwell v. Lewis*, 417 U.S. 583 (1974).

[76] *Rakas v. Illinois*, 439 U.S. 128 (1978).

[77] Id. at 409.

[78] *Delaware v. Prouse* (1979).

[79] *Olmstead v. United States*, 277 U.S. 438 at 463-466 (1928).

[80] Id. at 469-470.

[81] Id. at 473.

[82] Id. at 485.

[83] *Nardone v. United States*, 302 U.S. 379 (1937); *Weiss v. United States*, 308 U.S. 321 (1939); *Nardone v. United States*, 308 U.S. 338 (1939); see also *Rathbun v. United States*, 355 U.S. 107 (1957); *Benanti v. United States*, 355 U.S. 96 (1957).

[84] *Goldstein v. United States*, 316 U.S. 114 (1942).

[85] *Goldman v. United States*, 316 U.S. 129 (1942); see also *On Lee v. United States*, 343 U.S. 747 (1952).

[86] *Silverman v. United States*, 365 U.S. 505 (1961); see also *Wong Sun v. United States*, 371 U.S. 471 (1963); *Berger v. New York*, 388 U.S. 41 (1967); *Osborn v. United States*, 385 U.S. 323 (1966).

[87] *Katz v. United States*, 389 U.S. 247 (1967).

[88] Id. at 353.

[89] Id. at 351.

[90] *Alderman v. United States, Butenko v. United States, Ivanov v. United States*, 394 U.S. 165 (1969).

[91] Congressional Quarterly, *Congress and the Nation*, Vol. II (Washington, D.C.: Congressional Quarterly, 1969), pp. 326-327.

[92] *United States v. U.S. District Court*, 407 U.S. 297 (1972).

[93] *United States v. Giordano*, 416 U.S. 505 (1974).

[94] *Dalia v. United States* (1979).

Self-Incrimination

The fundamental meaning of the Fifth Amendment privilege against self-incrimination is clear: no one "shall be compelled in any criminal case to be a witness against himself. . . ."

A person may not be forced to confess, required to testify, or otherwise to provide evidence which could convict himself. When charged with a crime, an individual defendant is free to plead not guilty. And no inference of guilt may be drawn either from his decision not to testify at his own trial or to remain silent when interrogated by police.[1]

The privilege is not an absolute right to silence. It must be claimed; it is considered waived unless invoked. And when it is claimed, it is for the judge to decide whether or not the assertion of the privilege is justified.[2] The accused waives that right when he agrees to testify in his own defense, and thus becomes subject to cross-examination.

A witness called to testify before a grand jury, a congressional committee or an administrative hearing risks a contempt citation if he refuses to appear. Once on the stand, however, he may refuse to answer particular questions on the grounds that the answers will tend to incriminate him.[3] But he may not assert the privilege just because he fears other adverse consequences of his testimony — such as public ridicule or general disrepute.[4]

And once incriminating facts have been revealed voluntarily, a witness cannot then assert his Fifth Amendment privilege to avoid disclosure of future details.[5]

The privilege is a personal one and may not be invoked to protect anyone else. It is to be asserted only by "natural" persons, not by corporations, labor unions or other organizations.[6]

Individuals in possession of public records or those of an organization cannot claim the Fifth Amendment privilege to protect those records, even if they contain information incriminating to the witness himself. Only purely personal and private documents and papers in the possession of the owner are protected by the privilege.[7]

The court has affirmed repeatedly that innocent persons as well as guilty ones may invoke this privilege. In doing so, the court both rejects the assumption that anyone who "takes the Fifth" must be guilty, and invalidates efforts by state officials to penalize public employees who assert this privilege. The court has declared it unconstitutional for a state to punish employees who refuse to testify about employment-related activities, after being ordered to

waive their privilege against self-incrimination. It has reversed convictions of public employees based on testimony obtained through such coercion, and held that states may not fire persons just because they invoke this privilege.[8] *(Details, pp. 512-516)*

Congress, in the course of regulating certain forms of business and political activity which it found highly susceptible of illegal diversion or influence, has passed a number of federal laws requiring detailed records, reports, registration and/or tax payments related to membership in some groups, to drug and firearms transactions, or to gambling.

Until the 1960s the court generally upheld such registration and tax provisions,[9] but beginning with its decision in the Communist Party registration case of *Albertson v. Subversive Activities Control Board* in 1965, the court held that compliance with such requirements violated the Fifth Amendment.[10] *(Details, p. 508)*

In the late 1960s and early 1970s, the court struck down many of these registration provisions on Fifth Amendment grounds. Congress subsequently re-wrote some of the offending laws to omit the self-incriminatory provisions.[11]

Privilege and Immunity

Immunity statutes, in use throughout American history, represent the government's effort to reconcile its need for information with the Fifth Amendment privilege against compelled self-incrimination.

These laws protect individuals who furnish information to the government from prosecutions based on their own coerced testimony. Most immunity laws contain an exception for perjury: if the immunized witness provides false information, he is subject to prosecution for perjury using his words.

Justice Lewis F. Powell Jr. noted in a recent ruling that immunity laws "seek a rational accommodation between the imperatives of the privilege and the legitimate demands of government to compel citizens to testify."[12]

The modern court has condoned as constitutional a narrower form of immunity than that approved by the court in the 19th century.

Early statutes allowed immunization of witnesses from prosecution for any crime revealed in their testimony, a so-called "immunity bath." Later statutes, however, allowed some indirect use of immunized testimony to obtain other evidence of the witness' wrongdoing.

In 1892, in one of its earliest rulings concerning the Fifth Amendment privilege, the Supreme Court held this more limited immunity to be insufficient protection for the witness.

In the case of *Counselman v. Hitchcock,* the court unanimously ordered the release from custody of Charles Counselman, a railroad official, held in contempt of court after he declined to answer certain questions from a grand jury, asserting his constitutional privilege against compelled self-incrimination. Counselman challenged his detention as a violation of his Fifth Amendment rights and sought release through a writ of *habeas corpus.* The Supreme Court agreed with his challenge.

In its opinion, written by Justice Samuel Blatchford, the court held that grand jury witnesses, as well as persons already charged with crimes, could assert this privilege.

In addition, the court found this limited immunity, which left the witness still subject to indirect use of his testimony against him, insufficient because it "does not supply a complete protection from all the perils against which the constitutional prohibition was designed to guard, and is not a full substitute for that prohibition."[13]

"In view of the constitutional provision," concluded Justice Blatchford, "a statutory enactment, to be valid, must afford absolute immunity against future prosecution for the offense to which the question relates." [14]

This decision was interpreted as a requirement that immunity must protect a witness from all prosecution for the criminal "transactions" revealed in immunized testimony, not just against the "use" of the testimony itself as evidence.

Concerned that the Fifth Amendment privilege could be used to block inquiry into alleged violations of the Interstate Commerce Act, Congress in 1892 provided that witnesses appearing in ICC investigations could be granted this type of "transactional" immunity.

Brown v. Walker

In 1896, by a 5-4 vote, the court upheld the new law in the case of *Brown v. Walker.* In so doing, the court made clear that the privilege was to be claimed only to protect the witness himself, not any third party, and only to protect him from prosecution, not simply from "personal odium and disgrace."

The court upheld the punishment of Brown, a railway company auditor, for contempt, after he refused to answer certain questions from a grand jury, claiming his Fifth Amendment privilege. The court held that this assertion was not appropriate, since the privilege was being claimed to shield others from prosecution.

Justice Henry B. Brown, speaking for the majority, viewed the privilege against self-incrimination as meaning only that the witness was secure from criminal prosecution. The opinion said that such an interpretation established an appropriate equilibrium between the private right and the public welfare. Brown wrote that:

The clause of the Constitution in question is obviously susceptible of two interpretations. If it be construed literally, as authorizing the witness to refuse to disclose any fact which might tend to incriminate, disgrace, or expose him to unfavorable comments, then, as he must necessarily to a large extent determine upon his own conscience and responsibility whether his answer to the proposed question will have that tendency ... the practical result would be, that no

one could be compelled to testify to a material fact in a criminal case. . . . If, upon the other hand, the object of the provision be to secure the witness against a criminal prosecution, which might be aided directly or indirectly by his disclosure, then, if no such prosecution be possible, — in other words, if his testimony operate as a complete pardon for the offense to which it relates, — a statute absolutely securing to him such immunity from prosecution would satisfy the demands of the clause in question. . . .

It can only be said in general that the clause should be construed, as it was doubtless designed, to effect a practical and beneficent purpose — not necessarily to protect witnesses against every possible detriment which might happen to them from their testimony, nor to unduly impede, hinder, or obstruct the administration of criminal justice. . . .

The design of the constitutional privilege is not to aid the witness in vindicating his character but to protect him against being compelled to furnish evidence to convict him of a criminal charge. . . . While the constitutional provision in question is justly regarded as one of the most valuable prerogatives of the citizen, its object is fully accomplished by the statutory immunity, and we are therefore of opinion that the witness was compellable to answer. . . . [15]

The issue of what constituted true immunity was again raised during the 1950s when the Eisenhower administration proposed, and Congress approved, the Immunity Act of 1954. Its purpose was to prevent witnesses, called to testify in government subversion inquiries, from refusing to answer questions on grounds of self-incrimination. The act granted immunity from prosecution for criminal activity revealed during compelled testimony.

But the law was challenged in congressional testimony by Communist Party members who alleged that the 1954 act did not provide true immunity in light of the many disabilities — including loss of employment and public criticism — imposed on party members.

In 1956 the court upheld the 1954 act in the case of *Ullmann v. United States.* Justice Felix Frankfurter, speaking for seven members of the majority, cited *Brown v. Walker,* describing the 1893 immunity statute upheld in *Brown* as having become "part of our constitutional fabric." [16]

Frankfurter continued:

We are not dealing here with one of the vague, undefinable, admonitory provisions of the Constitution whose scope is inevitably addressed to changing circumstances . . . the history of the privilege establishes not only that it is not to be interpreted literally, but also that its sole concern is . . . with the danger to a witness forced to give testimony leading to the infliction of 'penalties affixed to the criminal acts . . .' . . . .Immunity displaces the danger. Once the reason for the privilege ceases, the privilege ceases. [17]

Justices William O. Douglas and Hugo L. Black dissented, urging the court to overrule *Brown v. Walker* and adopt the literal view "that the right of silence created by the Fifth Amendment is beyond the reach of Congress."[18]

Douglas wrote:

. . . the Fifth Amendment was written in part to prevent any Congress, any court, and any prosecutor from prying open the lips of an accused to make incriminating statements against his will. The Fifth Amendment protects the conscience and the dignity of the individual, as well as his safety and security, against the compulsion of the government. . . .

The critical point is that the Constitution places the right of silence *beyond the reach of government.* The Fifth Amendment stands between the citizen and his government. When public opinion casts a person into the outer darkness, as happens today when a person is exposed as a Communist, the government brings infamy on the head of the witness when it compels disclosure. That is precisely what the Fifth Amendment prohibits. [19]

'Use' Immunity

In the Organized Crime Control Act of 1970, Congress approved a more limited grant of "use" immunity to witnesses in organized crime cases. Rather than providing immunity from prosecution for any offense in which the witness was implicated through his testimony, the law simply forbade the use of any of his compelled testimony or derivative evidence against him. Under the 1970 Act, however, a witness could be prosecuted for crimes mentioned in his testimony if the evidence used in the prosecution was developed independently of his testimony. [20]

In the case of *Kastigar v. United States,* the court found this narrower "use" immunity constitutional:

The privilege has never been construed to mean that one who invokes it cannot subsequently be prosecuted. Its sole concern is to afford protection against being forced to give testimony leading to the infliction of 'penalties affixed to . . . criminal acts.' Immunity from the use of compelled testimony, as well as evidence derived directly and indirectly therefrom affords this protection. [21]

The court found this "use" immunity sufficient, because the law allowing it required the state — in prosecuting an immunized witness — to show that its evidence had not been derived from his immunized testimony.

Justice Lewis F. Powell Jr. wrote:

A person accorded this immunity . . . and subsequently prosecuted, is not dependent for the preservation of his rights upon the integrity and good faith of the prosecuting authorities. . . . This burden of proof which we reaffirm as appropriate . . . imposes on the prosecution the affirmative duty to prove that the evidence it proposes to use is derived from a legitimate source wholly independent of the compelled testimony. [22]

Justices Douglas and Thurgood Marshall dissented. Douglas wrote:

When we allow the prosecution to offer only "use" immunity we allow it to grant far less than it has taken away. For while the precise testimony that is compelled may not be used, leads from that testimony may be pursued and used to convict the witness. My view is that the Framers put it beyond the power of Congress to *compel* anyone to confess his crimes. . . . Government acts in an ignoble way when it stoops to the end which we authorize today. [23]

The States and Self-Incrimination

Twice — in 1908 and 1947 — the Supreme Court rejected arguments that the due process guarantee of the 14th Amendment extended the privilege against self-incrimination to state defendants. In both cases, the court permitted state officials to draw unfavorable inferences from a defendant's failure to testify in his own behalf.

In *Twining v. New Jersey,* decided in 1908, the court stated that the privilege was not inherent in due process, but "separate from and independent of" it. [24] In 1947 the court reaffirmed this stance with its decision in the case of *Adamson v. California,* refusing to find the privilege essential to a system of "ordered liberty." [25]

Furthermore, the court in several cases held that the Fifth Amendment did not protect an individual from a state's use of testimony compelled by federal authority or from federal use of testimony compelled by state authority. [26]

Malloy v. Hogan

But in 1964, in the case of *Malloy v. Hogan,* the court reconsidered *Twining* and *Adamson,* and declared that the Fifth Amendment guarantee against self-incrimination did extend to state proceedings.

Malloy, convicted of illegal gambling activities, refused to testify before a state investigation of gambling operations in Hartford County, Conn. Malloy claimed that to testify would compel him to incriminate himself. He was held in contempt and sentenced to prison.

Malloy appealed, but the Connecticut supreme court held that the Fifth Amendment's privilege against self-incrimination was not available to a witness in a state proceeding.

The Supreme Court by a 5-4 vote reversed the state court and upheld Malloy's claim, holding that the 14th Amendment guaranteed him the protection of the Fifth Amendment's privilege against self-incrimination.

Justice William J. Brennan Jr. wrote the majority opinion, declaring:

The Fourteenth Amendment secures against state invasion the same privilege that the Fifth Amendment guarantees against federal infringement — the right of a person to remain silent unless he chooses to speak in the unfettered exercise of his own will, and to suffer no penalty . . . for such silence. . . .

It would be incongruous to have different standards determine the validity of a claim of privilege based on the same feared prosecution, depending on whether the claim was asserted in a state or federal court. Therefore, the same standards must determine whether an accused's silence in either a federal or state proceeding is justified. . . . It must be considered irrelevant that the petitioner was a witness in a statutory inquiry and not a defendant in a criminal prosecution, for it has long been settled that the privilege protects witnesses in similar federal inquiries. . . . [27]

Justices Byron R. White, Potter Stewart, John Marshall Harlan and Tom C. Clark dissented from what they viewed as the step-by-step incorporation of the first eight amendments under the due process clause of the 14th Amendment. Justice Harlan wrote:

The consequence of such an approach . . . is inevitable disregard of all relevant differences which may exist between state and federal criminal law and its enforcement....

The Court's approach in the present case is in fact nothing more or less than "incorporation" in snatches. If, however, the Due Process Clause *is* something more than a reference to the Bill of Rights and protects only those rights which derive from fundamental principles ... it is just as contrary to precedent and just as illogical to incorporate the provisions of the Bill of Rights one at a time as it is to incorporate them all at once. [28]

On the same day the court announced its decision in *Malloy v. Hogan* — June 15, 1964 — it decided the case of *Murphy v. The Waterfront Commission of New York Harbor.* In that case the court declared that the Fifth Amendment protects a state witness against incrimination under federal as well as state law and a federal witness against incrimination under state as well as federal law. Immunity granted under federal law protected against state prosecution and vice versa.

Murphy, subpoenaed to testify about a work stoppage at New Jersey piers, refused to answer questions on the grounds that his answers would tend to incriminate him. Granted immunity under New York and New Jersey laws, Murphy still refused to testify because the immunity failed to protect him from federal prosecution. The court held Murphy in contempt.

The Supreme Court vacated the contempt judgment. Justice Arthur J. Goldberg's opinion for a unanimous court set out the constitutional rule:

> ... a state witness may not be compelled to give testimony which may be incriminating under federal law unless the compelled testimony and its fruits cannot be used in any manner by federal officials in connection with a criminal prosecution against him. We conclude, moreover, that in order to implement this constitutional rule and accommodate the interests of the State and Federal Governments in investigating and prosecuting crime, the Federal Government must be prohibited from making any such use of compelled testimony and its fruits. [29]

The following year, the court reinforced the *Malloy* ruling with its decision in *Griffin v. California.* Effectively reversing *Twining* and *Adamson* in their specific holdings concerning judicial or prosecutorial comment on the silence of defendants, the court held that the Fifth Amendment "forbids either comment by the prosecution on the accused's silence or instructions by the court that such silence is evidence of guilt." [30]

Writing for the court in *Griffin,* Justice William O. Douglas explained:

> ... comment on the refusal to testify is a remnant of the 'inquisitorial system of criminal justice,' ... which the Fifth Amendment outlaws. It is a penalty imposed by courts for exercising a constitutional privilege. It cuts down on the privilege by making its assertion costly. [31]

Coerced Confessions

Confessions, the court stated long ago, are "among the most effectual proofs in the law" but they are admissible as evidence only when given voluntarily. [32] This has long been the rule in federal courts, where the Fifth Amendment

clearly applies. [33] Since 1936 the same rule has governed the use of confessions in state courts. The inevitable question with which the court has thus been faced time and again is how to determine when a confession is voluntary.

In its first ruling on the use of confessions, the court in 1884 defined as involuntary a confession which "appears to have been made, either in consequence of inducements of a temporal nature ... or because of a threat or promise ... which, operating upon the fears or hopes of the accused ... deprive him of that freedom of will or self-control essential to make his confession voluntary within the meaning of the law." [34]

In 1896 the court restated the standard for determining when a confession was admissible: "In short, the true test of admissibility is that the confession is made freely, voluntarily, and without compulsion or inducement of any sort." [35]

This test, as the court acknowledged in a decision the following year, had to be applied in each and every case in which the use of a confession was challenged. Judgment should be made through "consideration of the circumstances surrounding, and the facts established to exist, in reference to the confession, in order to determine whether it was shown to have been voluntarily made." In all federal trials, the resolution of this issue was controlled by the Fifth Amendment command that no person be compelled to incriminate himself. [36]

Delay in charging a suspect with a crime was one of the first factors pointed out by the court as of significant value in making this determination. Several federal laws made clear that when a person was arrested, he should be taken promptly before a magistrate and charged.

In 1943 the Supreme Court gave compelling force to this requirement by holding that confessions obtained after "unnecessary delay" in a suspect's arraignment could not be used as evidence in federal court.

In the case of *McNabb v. United States,* the court overturned the convictions of several men for murdering a federal revenue agent. The most important elements in the prosecution's case were incriminating statements made by the defendants after three days of questioning by federal officers in the absence of any defense counsel and before they were formally charged with any crime.

The court based its decision on the statutory requirements of prompt arraignment, and on the court's general power to supervise the functioning of the federal judicial system, rather than on the Fifth Amendment.

Writing for the majority, Justice Felix Frankfurter explained that the court's supervisory role obligated it to establish and maintain "civilized standards of procedure and evidence" for federal courts. [37] The purpose of the ban on unnecessary delay between arrest and arraignment, he continued, was plain:

> A democratic society, in which respect for the dignity of all men is central, naturally guards against the misuse of the law enforcement process. Zeal in tracking down crime is not in itself an assurance of soberness of judgment. Disinterestedness in law enforcement does not alone prevent disregard of cherished liberties. Experience has therefore counseled that safeguards must be provided against the dangers of the overzealous as well as the despotic. The awful instruments of the criminal law cannot be entrusted to a single functionary. The complicated process of criminal justice is therefore divided into different parts,

responsibility for which is separately vested in the various participants upon whom the criminal law relies for its vindication. Legislation . . . requiring that the police must with reasonable promptness show legal cause for detaining arrested persons, constitutes an important safeguard — not only in assuring protection for the innocent but also in securing conviction of the guilty by methods that commend themselves to a progressive and self-confident society. For this procedural requirement checks resort to those reprehensible practices known as the "third degree" which, though universally rejected as indefensible, still find their way into use. It aims to avoid all the evil implications of secret interrogation of persons accused of crime. It reflects not a sentimental but a sturdy view of law enforcement. It outlaws easy but self-defeating ways in which brutality is substituted for brains as an instrument of crime detection. [38]

The Federal Rules of Criminal Procedure subsequently incorporated this rule, and in 1957 the court in the case of *Mallory v. United States* reaffirmed its importance. With that ruling, the court nullified a death sentence imposed upon a rapist who "confessed" to the crime during a delay of more than eighteen hours between his arrest and his arraignment. The court warned that such "unwarranted detention" could lead "to tempting utilization of intensive interrogation, easily gliding into the evils of 'the third degree' " — precisely what the rule was intended to avoid.[39]

Mallory generated fierce criticism of the court and prompted Congress to revise the statutory rule to allow some use of evidence obtained during such delays. In 1968 Congress included in the Crime Control and Safe Streets Act a provision stating that delay in arraignment was not an absolute bar to federal use of a confession obtained during the period of delay. *(Details, p. 677)*

State Courts and Coerced Confessions

Decades before it specifically applied the Fifth Amendment privilege against state action, the Supreme Court unanimously forbade states to use coerced confessions to convict persons of crimes.

The concept of basic fairness implicit in the 14th Amendment guarantee of due process served as the basis for the court's declaration of this prohibition in its 1936 ruling in *Brown v. Mississippi*. With that decision the court for the first time overturned a state conviction because it was obtained by using a confession extracted by torture.

Mississippi defended its use of this confession by citing the 1908 decision in *Twining v. New Jersey* — that state defendants did not enjoy the protection of the Fifth Amendment privilege against compelled self-incrimination.

The court rejected that defense, stating flatly that "the question of the right of the state to withdraw the privilege against self-incrimination is not here involved." [40] Chief Justice Charles Evans Hughes saw a distinction between "compulsion" forbidden by the Fifth Amendment and "compulsion" forbidden by the 14th Amendment's due process clause:

> . . . The compulsion to which the . . . [Fifth Amendment] refer[s] is that of the processes of justice by which the accused may be called as a witness and required to testify. Compulsion by torture to extort a confession is a different matter. . . .
>
> Because a state may dispense with a jury trial, it does not follow that it may substitute trial by ordeal.

The rack and torture chamber may not be substituted for the witness stand. . . . It would be difficult to conceive of methods more revolting to the sense of justice than those taken to procure the confessions of these petitioners, and the use of the confessions thus obtained as the basis for conviction and sentence was a clear denial of due process. [41]

Over the next three decades, the court judged each case in which state use of a confession was challenged by looking at the "totality of the circumstances" surrounding the arrest and interrogation procedures followed, seeking to determine whether a confession was voluntary and admissible as evidence, or coerced and thus inadmissible. In these cases Chief Justice Hughes' neat distinction between physical coercion and other forms of compulsion soon became blurred.

In 1940 the court affirmed its *Brown* ruling in the case of *Chambers v. Florida*. In the *Chambers* case, four black men had been convicted of murder on the basis of confessions obtained after days of being held incommunicado and interrogated by law enforcement officials. The unanimous court overturned their convictions, acknowledging that psychological coercion, as well as physical torture, could produce involuntary confessions whose use violated due process.

Justice Hugo L. Black wrote the court's opinion, declaring:

> The determination to preserve an accused's right to procedural due process sprang in large part from knowledge of the historical truth that the rights and liberties of people accused of crime could not be safely entrusted to secret inquisitorial processes. . . .
>
> For five days petitioners were subjected to interrogations culminating in . . . [an] all night examination. Over a period of five days they steadily refused to confess and disclaimed any guilt. The very circumstances surrounding their confinement and their questioning without any formal charges having been brought, were such as to fill petitioners with terror and frightful misgivings. Some were practically strangers in the community. . . . The haunting fear of mob violence was around them in an atmosphere charged with excitement and public indignation. . . . To permit human lives to be forfeited upon confessions thus obtained would make of the constitutional requirement of due process of law a meaningless symbol. . . .
>
> Due process of law, preserved for all by our Constitution, commands that no such practice as that disclosed by this record shall send any accused to his death. [42]

The court in subsequent decisions acknowledged that some situations were so inherently coercive that evidence produced from them was inadmissible, but not until the mid-1960s did it develop any hard-and-fast rules concerning the admissibility of prolonged interrogation of suspects in police custody. [43]

Voluntariness, not veracity, was the key to the decision on whether or not a confession was admissible. As Justice Felix Frankfurter explained in the court's 1961 decision in *Rogers v. Richmond:*

> Our decisions . . . have made clear that convictions following the admission into evidence of confessions which are involuntary . . . cannot stand. This is so not because such confessions are unlikely to be true but

because the methods used to extract them offend an underlying principle in the enforcement of our criminal law: that ours is an accusatorial and not an inquisitorial system — a system in which the State must establish guilt by evidence independently and freely secured and may not by coercion prove its own charge against an accused out of his own mouth. [44]

Confessions and Counsel

The Fifth Amendment privilege against compelled self-incrimination was effectively linked with the Sixth Amendment right to counsel by the court's mid-1960s rulings in the cases of *Escobedo v. Illinois* and *Miranda v. Arizona.*

The court as recently as 1958 had held that confessions could be voluntary and admissible even when obtained from a suspect who was denied the opportunity to consult with legal counsel during his interrogation by police. [45]

But in 1964 the court reversed its position on such matters. In the case of *Massiah v. United States* the court declared that an indicted person could not properly be questioned or otherwise persuaded to make incriminating remarks in the absence of his lawyer. [46] Coupled with the court's ruling later that term in *Malloy v. Hogan,* extending the Fifth Amendment privilege to state defendants, *Massiah* laid the ground work for *Escobedo.*

A week after the *Malloy* ruling, the court announced its decision in the case of Danny Escobedo, convicted of murder in Illinois on the basis of his own words. In *Escobedo v. Illinois* the court discarded the voluntarism standard for determining the admissibility of confessions, moving away from the "totality of the circumstances" approach to concentrate on the procedures followed by police in obtaining a confession. [47]

Escobedo repeatedly asked for and was denied the opportunity to see his attorney during his interrogation by police. Incriminating statements he made during this time were used as evidence against him. He challenged his conviction as a denial of his right to counsel. The court agreed with that argument, but linked denial of that right to the fact that Escobedo had not been adequately informed of his constitutional right to remain silent rather than to be forced to incriminate himself.

Justice Arthur J. Goldberg wrote the majority opinion. The vote in the case was 5-4. Dissenting were Justices John Marshall Harlan, Byron R. White, Tom C. Clark and Potter Stewart.

The year before, the court had declared in the case of *Gideon v. Wainwright* that the Sixth Amendment required that every person accused of a serious crime be provided the aid of an attorney. [48] Justice Goldberg reasoned in *Escobedo* that the right guaranteed in *Gideon* would be a hollow one if it did not apply until after police obtained a confession. Goldberg wrote:

> We have . . . learned . . . that no system of criminal justice can, or should, survive if it comes to depend for its continued effectiveness on the citizens' abdication through unawareness of their constitutional rights. No system worth preserving should have to *fear* that if an accused is permitted to consult with a lawyer, he will become aware of, and exercise, these rights. If the exercise of constitutional rights will thwart the effectiveness of a system of law enforcement, then there is something very wrong with that system.

We hold, therefore, that where, as here, the investigation is no longer a general inquiry into an unsolved crime but has begun to focus on a particular suspect, the suspect has been taken into police custody, the police carry out a process of interrogations that lends itself to eliciting incriminating statements, the suspect has requested and been denied an opportunity to consult with his lawyer, and the police have not effectively warned him of his absolute constitutional right to remain silent, the accused has been denied "the Assistance of Counsel" in violation of the Sixth Amendment . . . and that no statement elicited by police during the interrogation may be used against him at a criminal trial. [49]

Justice White's dissenting opinion, joined by Justices Clark and Stewart, criticized the majority's holding that any admission made by an arrested suspect who asked for and was denied the opportunity to see his lawyer was inadmissible as evidence:

> By abandoning the voluntary-involuntary test for admissibility of confessions, the Court seems driven by the notion that it is uncivilized law enforcement to use an accused's own admissions against him at his trial. It attempts to find a home for this new and nebulous rule of due process by attaching it to the right of counsel guaranteed in the federal system by the Sixth Amendment and binding upon the States by virtue of the due process guarantee of the Fourteenth Amendment. . . . The right to counsel now not only entitles the accused to counsel's advice and aid in preparing for trial but stands as an impenetrable barrier to any interrogation once the accused has become a suspect. [50]

Miranda v. Arizona

Two years after *Escobedo,* the Supreme Court in the case of *Miranda v. Arizona*[51] set out "concrete constitutional guidelines" for the custodial interrogation practices of state and local police.[52]

Ernesto Miranda was convicted of kidnapping and rape in Arizona. The prosecution used as evidence against Miranda statements he had made to police during his interrogation. He was not advised of his rights to remain silent and to consult an attorney. Miranda challenged his conviction as obtained in violation of the Fifth Amendment privilege.

By the same 5-4 vote as in *Escobedo,* the court upheld his challenge. It ruled that prosecutors were constitutionally forbidden to use incriminating statements obtained from suspects during interrogation unless strict procedural safeguards had been followed to guarantee that the individual was aware of his constitutional rights to remain silent and to have the aid of an attorney.

" The presence of counsel," stated Chief Justice Earl Warren for the majority, was "the adequate protective device" to "insure that statements made in the government-established atmosphere are not the product of compulsion."[53]

Warren, summarizing the court's holding, said:

> . . . the prosecution may not use statements, whether exculpatory or inculpatory, stemming from custodial interrogation of the defendant unless it demonstrates the use of procedural safeguards effective to secure the privilege against self-incrimination. By custodial interrogation, we mean questioning initiated by

law enforcement officers after a person has been taken into custody or otherwise deprived of his freedom of action in any significant way. As for the procedural safeguards to be employed, unless other fully effective means are devised to inform accused persons of their right of silence and to assure a continuous opportunity to exercise it, the following measures are required. Prior to any questioning, the person must be warned that he has a right to remain silent, that any statement he does make may be used as evidence against him, and that he has a right to the presence of an attorney, either retained or appointed. The defendant may waive effectuation of these rights, provided the waiver is made voluntarily, knowingly and intelligently. If, however, he indicates in any manner and at any stage of the process, that he wishes to consult with an attorney before speaking there can be no questioning. Likewise, if the individual is alone and indicates in any manner that he does not wish to be interrogated, the police may not question him. The mere fact that he may have answered some questions or have volunteered some statements on his own does not deprive him of the right to refrain from answering any further inquiries until he has consulted with an attorney and thereafter consents to be questioned. [54]

The Fifth Amendment, continued Warren, required that whenever a suspect indicated, before or during interrogation, that he wished to remain silent, all interrogation must cease. "At this point he has shown that he intends to exercise his Fifth Amendment privilege," wrote the Chief Justice. Therefore "any statement taken after the person invokes his privilege cannot be other than the product of compulsion, subtle or otherwise." [55]

As in *Escobedo*, Justices Clark, Harlan, White and Stewart dissented, arguing that they felt the court should continue to use the "totality of the circumstances" approach to determining the admissibility of confessions. Jutice Harlan criticized the ruling as "poor constitutional law." He continued:

> I think it must be frankly recognized at the outset that police questioning allowable under due process precedents may inherently entail some pressure on the suspect and may seek advantage in his ignorance or weaknesses.... Until today, the role of the Constitution has been only to sift out *undue* pressure, not to assure spontaneous confessions. The Court's new rules aim to offset these minor pressures and disadvantages intrinsic to any kind of police interrogation. The rules do not serve due process interests in preventing blatant coercion since ... they do nothing to contain the policeman who is prepared to lie from the start.... [56]

Justice White said that the majority misread the Fifth Amendment prohibition against compelled self-incrimination:

> Confessions and incriminating admissions, as such, are not forbidden evidence; only those which are compelled are banned. I doubt that the Court observes these distinctions today....
>
> The obvious underpinning of the Court's decision is a deep-seated distrust of all confessions....
>
> The rule announced today .... is a deliberate calculus to prevent interrogations, to reduce the incidence of confessions and pleas of guilty and to increase the number of trials. Criminal trials, no matter how

efficient the police are, are not sure bets for the prosecution, nor should they be if the evidence is not forthcoming.... There is, in my view, every reason to believe that a good many criminal defendants, who otherwise would have been convicted on what this Court has previously thought to be the most satisfactory kind of evidence, will now, under this new version of the Fifth Amendment, either not be tried at all or will be acquitted if the State's evidence, minus the confession, is put to the test of litigation. [57]

A week after *Miranda* was announced, the court held that it would not apply the decision retroactively to invalidate convictions obtained in trials begun before its announcement on June 13, 1966. A similar rule applied in cases to which *Escobedo* might apply, held the court. [58]

Mallory v. United States, Escobedo v. Illinois, and *Miranda v. Arizona,* together with rulings extending the specific protections of the Bill of Rights to state defendants, brought criticism of the Warren Court to a crescendo in the late 1960s.

One of the major themes of the 1968 presidential campaign was "law and order" — a phrase which Richard Nixon, the successful candidate, used as a basis for his criticism of the court's rulings.

Also in 1968, Congress — responding to similar complaints that the court was in fact encouraging crime by impeding law enforcement officers in their duties — included in the 1968 Crime Control and Safe Streets Act provisions intended to blunt or overrule the effect of *Mallory* and *Miranda*. By stating that confessions could be used in federal courts whenever the judge found them voluntary, Congress attempted to abandon the procedural guidelines set out in *Miranda* and return to the old voluntary-involuntary test for prosecutorial use of incriminating statements. The 1968 law, however, affected only federal trials, not state trials. The states remained bound by the *Miranda* requirements. *(Details, p. 679)*

Despite opposition to its ruling in *Miranda*, the Supreme Court stood by that decision. Early in 1969 the court held that *Miranda* required that police, before questioning an individual in his own home, warn him of his constitutional rights once he was effectively in their custody. [59]

Miranda and the Burger Court

President-elect Nixon had promised during his 1968 presidential campaign to appoint men to the Supreme Court who would be less receptive to the arguments of criminal defendants and more responsive to the reasoning of law enforcement officers. Even before the election, Chief Justice Warren had announced his plans to retire.

In the spring of 1969, Nixon named — and the Senate confirmed — Warren E. Burger, a conservative appeals court judge, as Warren's successor. In 1970 Burger was joined on the bench by another Nixon appointee, Harry A. Blackmun. And in 1971 Nixon filled two more seats on the court with Justices Lewis F. Powell Jr. and William H. Rehnquist.

But despite numerous opportunities, the court with its new Chief Justice and new members did not overturn *Miranda*. The court in the 1970s did, however, decline to extend the *Miranda* requirements to persons other than suspects in police custody — and it did allow some indirect use of statements from persons not warned of their rights.

Justice and the Plea Bargain . . .

The plea bargain — in which a defendant exchanges his plea of guilty for a prosecutor's promise of less severe punishment than could be expected after trial — has become a fixture of the American system of criminal justice. Two political scientists writing in 1978 noted that the guilty plea had become "a mainstay of the criminal justice system in state and federal courts where 80 percent or more of the serious cases and 90 percent or more of the less serious offenses are resolved through pleas of guilty."[1]

There is neither a constitutional nor a statutory basis for plea bargaining. Its origin and survival are based on practical considerations: it serves the interests of the prosecutor, the judge and accused parties who wish to trade the right to trial for more lenient sentences.

As the Supreme Court explained in a 1977 ruling:

> Whatever might be the situation in an ideal world, the fact is that the guilty plea and the often concomitant plea bargain are important components of this country's criminal justice system. Properly administered, they can benefit all concerned. The defendant avoids extended pretrial incarceration and the anxieties and uncertainties of a trial; he gains a speedy disposition of his case, the chance to acknowledge his guilt, and a prompt start in realizing whatever potential there may be for rehabilitation. Judges and prosecutors conserve vital and scarce resources. The public is protected from the risks posed by those charged with criminal offenses who are at large on bail while awaiting completion of criminal proceedings.[2]

Recent Recognition

In 1970 the court for the first time formally recognized the previously unacknowledged practice of plea bargaining. In the case of *Brady v. United States,* the court upheld its use, finding that it provided a "mutuality of advantage" for the state and for the defendant.[3]

Brady was charged with kidnapping under provisions of a federal law which provided for imposition of the death sentence for that crime upon the recommendation of a jury after trial. Brady pleaded guilty, foregoing trial and thereby ensuring that he would not receive the death penalty.

Nine years later the court in the 1968 case of *United States v. Jackson* struck down that portion of the federal kidnapping law under which Brady had been charged, arguing that by allowing a death sentence *only* after trial, the law had the "inevitable effect" of penalizing both the

exercise of the Fifth Amendment right *not* to plead guilty and the Sixth Amendment right to trial by jury.[4]

Brady cited this ruling in challenging his conviction, claiming that his guilty plea was invalid because it was "coerced" by unconstitutional provisions and by his desire to avoid the death penalty.

With an opinion written by Justice Byron R. White, the court unanimously sustained the plea bargaining process and Brady's conviction. White wrote:

> For a defendant who sees slight possibility of acquittal, the advantages of pleading guilty and limiting the probable penalty are obvious — his exposure is reduced, the correctional processes can begin immediately, and the practical burdens of a trial are eliminated. For the State there are also advantages — the more promptly imposed punishment after an admission of guilt may more effectively attain the objective of punishment; and with the avoidance of trial scarce judicial and prosecutorial resources are conserved. . . . It is this mutuality of advantage which perhaps explains the fact that at present well over three-fourths of the criminal convictions in this country rest on pleas of guilty. . . .
>
> Of course, that the prevalence of guilty pleas is explainable does not necessarily validate those pleas nor the system which produces them. But we cannot hold that it is unconstitutional for the State to extend a benefit to a defendant who in turn extends a substantial benefit to the State and who demonstrates by his plea that he is ready and willing to admit his crime. . . .
>
> A contrary holding would require the States and Federal Government to forbid guilty pleas altogether, to provide a single invariable penalty for each crime defined by the statutes. . . . In any event, it would be necessary to forbid prosecutors and judges to accept guilty pleas to selected counts, to lesser included offenses, or to reduced charges. The Fifth Amendment does not reach so far.[5]

The same day that the court announced its ruling in *Brady,* it refused in another guilty plea case to hold invalid a guilty plea entered with the advice of an attorney but challenged as induced by the prosecution's use of a coerced confession and the bad advice of "incompetent counsel."[6]

Keeping the Bargain

In later rulings the court has emphasized that guilty pleas are admissible only if knowingly and voluntarily

---

The first of these rulings came in 1971 in the case of *Harris v. New York.* By a 5-4 vote, the court held that although statements made by a defendant before trial and before he was advised of his rights could not be used as evidence against him, those statements could be used to impeach his credibility as a witness if he took the stand in his own defense and made statements conflicting with those made before trial.

For the majority, Chief Justice Burger observed:

Some comments in the *Miranda* opinion can indeed be read as indicating a bar to use of an uncounseled statement for any purpose, but discussion of that issue was not at all necessary to the Court's holding, and cannot be regarded as controlling. *Miranda* barred the prosecution from making its case with statements of an accused while in custody prior to having or effectively waiving counsel. It does not follow from *Miranda* that evidence inadmissible against an

. . . A Guilty Plea, A Lesser Penalty

made — although it has condoned some forms of pressure in the plea negotiations — and it has held that prosecutors must keep their part of the bargain.

The court made this last point in its December 1971 ruling in the case of *Santobello v. New York*. The court held that the state's failure to keep its commitment to recommend a reduced sentence in exchange for a guilty plea required that the defendant be given the opportunity for a trial.

Chief Justice Warren E. Burger delivered the opinion of the court, saying:

> This phase of the process of criminal justice and the adjudicative element in accepting a plea of guilty, must be attended by safeguards to insure the defendant what is reasonably due in the circumstances. Those circumstances will vary, but a constant factor is that when a plea rests in any significant degree on a promise or agreement of the prosecutor, so that it can be said to be part of the inducement or consideration, such promise must be fulfilled. [7]

In 1973 the court in case of *Tollett v. Henderson* refused to allow a defendant who had pleaded guilty to murder to challenge his conviction by arguing that the grand jury which indicted him was unfairly selected.

Writing for the majority, Justice William H. Rehnquist explained that a guilty plea represented a break in the chain of events which have preceded it in the law enforcement process. "When a criminal defendant has solemnly admitted in open court that he is in fact guilty of the offense with which he is charged, he may not thereafter raise independent claims relating to the deprivation of constitutional rights that occurred prior to the entry of the plea," wrote Rehnquist. [8]

A Voluntary Plea

To be valid, a guilty plea must be voluntarily made and entered with full knowledge of its implications. The court emphasized that point in 1976, setting aside a second-degree murder conviction of a man who pleaded guilty without realizing that he was admitting that he *intended* to kill his victim.

The court held that a defendant's failure to receive adequate notice of the offense to which he pleaded guilty resulted in an involuntary plea. [9]

Prosecutorial Pressure

The Supreme Court held in 1978, however, that due process does not deprive the prosecutor of valid bargaining tools. By a 5-4 vote, the justices backed a prosecutor's threat of an additional justified indictment if the defendant did not accept the offer of a plea bargain.

The court announced this decision in the case of *Bordenkircher v. Hayes*. Hayes had two prior felony convictions and had been charged with a third felony. In plea negotiations the prosecutor offered to recommend a reduced sentence in return for a guilty plea — and threatened that if the bargain was not accepted he would reindict Hayes under a "habitual criminal" law which would have made him subject to a mandatory life sentence if convicted.

Hayes rejected the bargain, was reindicted and convicted, and received a life sentence. He challenged the prosecutor's actions as "vindictive;" the court rejected that challenge.

Justice Potter Stewart delivered the majority opinion saying:

> . . . in the "give-and-take" of plea bargaining, there is no . . . element of punishment or retaliation so long as the accused is free to accept or reject the prosecutor's offer. . . .
>
> There is no doubt that the breadth of discretion that our country's legal system vests in prosecuting attorneys carries with it the potential for both individual and institutional abuse. And broad though that discretion may be, there are undoubtedly constitutional limits upon its exercise. We hold only that the course of conduct engaged in by the prosecutor in this case, which no more than openly presented the defendant with the unpleasant alternatives of foregoing trial or facing charges on which he was plainly subject to prosecution, did not violate the Due Process Clause of the Fourteenth Amendment. [10]

---

[1] Alpheus T. Mason and William M. Beaney, *American Constitutional Law*, 6th ed. (Englewood Cliffs, N.J.: Prentice-Hall, 1978) p. 669.

[2] *Blackledge v. Allison*, 431 U.S. 63 at 71 (1977).

[3] *Brady v. United States*, 397 U.S. 742 at 752 (1970); see also *Boykin v. Alabama*, 395 U.S. 238 (1969).

[4] *United States v. Jackson*, 390 U.S. 570 (1968).

[5] *Brady v. United States*, 397 U.S. 742 at 752-753 (1970); see also *North Carolina v. Alford*, 400 U.S. 25 (1970).

[6] *McMann v. Richardson*, 397 U.S. 759 (1970).

[7] *Santobello v. New York*, 404 U.S. 257 at 262 (1971).

[8] *Tollett v. Henderson*, 411 U.S. 258 at 267 (1973).

[9] *Henderson v. Morgan*, 426 U.S. 637 (1976).

[10] *Bordenkircher v. Hayes*, 434 U.S. 357 at 363, 365 (1978); see also *Corbitt v. New Jersey*, 439 U.S. 212 (1978).

---

accused in the prosecution's case in chief is barred for all purposes, provided of course that the trustworthiness of the evidence satisfies legal standards. . . .

The shield provided by *Miranda* cannot be perverted into a license to use perjury by way of a defense, free from the risk of confrontation with prior inconsistent utterances. [60]

Justices Hugo L. Black, William J. Brennan Jr., William O. Douglas and Thurgood Marshall dissented, warning that this ruling "goes far toward undoing much of the progress made in conforming police methods to the Constitution." [61]

Three years later, the court in *Michigan v. Tucker* upheld the prosecution's use of a statement made by a suspect not fully warned of his rights as a "lead" for locating a prosecution witness. Writing the majority opinion, Justice Rehnquist emphasized that the procedures which *Miranda* required were safeguards for constitutional rights, but were not in themselves constitutionally guaranteed. [62]

In 1975 the court in *Oregon v. Hass* reaffirmed its *Harris* decision. [63] Later that year, the court ruled that although a suspect's assertion of his right to silence must terminate police interrogation of him about one crime, it does not foreclose subsequent police efforts, after an interval and a second warning of his rights, to question him about another crime. This was the holding in the case of *Michigan v. Mosley.* [64]

And in 1976 the court in the case of *United States v. Mandujano* refused to require that *Miranda* warnings be given to grand jury witnesses before they testify — even though they may be potential defendants. [65]

Three years later the court held that a juvenile suspect's request to see his probation officer did not constitute an assertion of his Fifth Amendment privilege and did not require police to cease questioning him. [66]

Footnotes

[1] *Bruno v. United States,* 308 U.S. 287 (1939); *Griffin v. California,* 380 U.S. 609 (1965); *United States v. Hale,* 422 U.S. 171 (1975); *Doyle v. Ohio, Wood v. Ohio,* 427 U.S. 610 (1976).
[2] *Hoffman v. United States,* 341 U.S. 479 (1951); *Mason v. United States,* 244 U.S. 362 (1917); *Rogers v. United States,* 340 U.S. 367 (1951); *United States v. Monia,* 317 U.S. 424 (1943).
[3] *Emspak v. United States,* 349 U.S. 190 (1955).
[4] *Heike v. United States,* 227 U.S. 131 (1913); *Brown v. Walker,* 161 U.S. 591 (1896).
[5] *Rogers v. United States,* 340 U.S. 367 at 372-374 (1951); see also *Blau v. United States,* 340 U.S. 159 (1950).
[6] *Hale v. Henkel,* 201 U.S. 43 (1906); *United States v. White,* 322 U.S. 694 (1944); *Bellis v. United States,* 417 U.S. 85 (1974).
[7] *Wilson v. United States,* 221 U.S. 361 (1911); *Shapiro v. United States,* 335 U.S. 1 (1948); see also *Mancusi v. DeForte,* 392 U.S. 364 (1968); *Couch v. United States,* 409 U.S. 322 (1973); *United States v. Kasmir, Fisher v. United States,* 425 U.S. 391 (1976).
[8] *Garrity v. New Jersey,* 385 U.S. 493 (1967); *Spevack v. Klein,* 385 U.S. 511 (1967); *Slochower v. Board of Higher Education of New York City,* 350 U.S. 551 (1956); *Garner v. Broderick,* 392 U.S. 273 (1968); *Lefkowitz v. Cunningham,* 431 U.S. 801 (1977).
[9] *United States v. Doremus,* 249 U.S. 86 (1919); *United States v. Sanchez,* 340 U.S. 42 (1950); *Sonzinsky v. United States,* 300 U.S. 506 (1937); *United States v. Kahriger,* 345 U.S. 22 (1953).
[10] *Albertson v. Subversive Activities Control Board,* 382 U.S. 70 (1965).
[11] *Grosso v. United States,* 390 U.S. 62 (1968); *Marchetti v. United States,* 390 U.S. 39 (1968); *Haynes v. United States,* 390 U.S. 85 (1968); *Leary v. United States,* 395 U.S. 6 (1969); see also *Minor v. United States, Buie v. United States,* 396 U.S. 87 (1969), *United States v. Freed,* 41 U.S. 601 (1971).
[12] *Kastigar v. United States,* 406 U.S. 441 at 446 (1972).
[13] *Counselman v. Hitchcock,* 142 U.S. 547 at 585-586 (1892).
[14] Id.
[15] *Brown v. Walker,* 161 U.S. 591 at 595, 596, 605-606, 610 (1896).
[16] *Ullmann v. United States,* 350 U.S. 422 at 438 (1956).
[17] Id. at 438-439.
[18] Id. at 440.
[19] Id. at 449, 454.
[20] Congressional Quarterly, *Congress and the Nation,* Vol. III (Washington, D.C.: Congressional Quarterly, 1973), p. 273.
[21] *Kastigar v. United States,* 406 U.S. 441 at 453 (1972).
[22] Id. at 460.
[23] Id. at 466-467.
[24] *Twining v. New Jersey,* 211 U.S. 78 at 106 (1908).
[25] *Adamson v. California,* 332 U.S. 46 at 54 (1947).
[26] *United States v. Murdock,* 284 U.S. 141 (1931); *Feldman v. United States,* 322 U.S. 487 (1944); *Knapp v. Schweitzer,* 357 U.S. 371 (1958).

[27] *Malloy v. Hogan,* 378 U.S. 1 at 8, 11 (1964).
[28] Id. at 16, 27.
[29] *Murphy v. The Waterfront Commission of New York Harbor,* 378 U.S. 52 at 79 (1964).
[30] *Griffin v. California,* 380 U.S. 609 at 615 (1965).
[31] Id. at 614; see also *Lakeside v. Oregon,* 435 U.S. 333 (1978).
[32] *Hopt v. Utah,* 110 U.S. 574 at 585 (1884).
[33] *Bram v. United States,* 168 U.S. 532 (1897).
[34] *Hopt v. Utah,* 110 U.S. 574 at 584-585 (1884).
[35] *Wilson v. United States,* 162 U.S. 613 at 623 (1896).
[36] *Bram v. United States,* 168 U.S. 532, at 561, 542 (1897).
[37] *McNabb v. United States,* 318 U.S. 332 at 340 (1943).
[38] Id. at 343-344.
[39] *Mallory v. United States,* 354 U.S. 449 at 453 (1957).
[40] *Brown v. Mississippi,* 297 U.S. 278 at 285 (1935).
[41] Id. at 285-286.
[42] *Chambers v. Florida,* 309 U.S. 227 at 237, 239-240, 241 (1940).
[43] *Lisenba v. California,* 314 U.S. 219 (1941); *Ashcraft v. Tennessee,* 322 U.S. 143 (1944); *Fikes v. Alabama,* 352 U.S. 191 (1957); *Spano v. New York,* 360 U.S. 315 (1959); *Lynumn v. Illinois,* 372 U.S. 528 (1963); *Townsend v. Sain,* 372 U.S. 293 (1963); *Haynes v. Washington,* 373 U.S. 503 (1963).
[44] *Rogers v. Richmond,* 365 U.S. 534 at 540-541 (1961); see also *Stein v. New York,* 346 U.S. 156 (1953); *Jackson v. Denno,* 378 U.S. 368 (1964).
[45] *Crooker v. California,* 357 U.S. 433 (1958); *Cicencia v. LaGay,* 357 U.S. 504 (1958), overruled by *Miranda v. Arizona,* 384 U.S. 436 (1966).
[46] *Massiah v. United States,* 377 U.S. 201 (1964).
[47] *Escobedo v. Illinois,* 378 U.S. 478 (1964).
[48] *Gideon v. Wainwright,* 372 U.S. 335 (1963).
[49] *Escobedo v. Illinois,* 378 U.S. 478 at 490-491 (1964).
[50] Id. at 496.
[51] *Miranda v. Arizona,* 384 U.S. 436 (1966), was one of four cases reviewed by the court and resolved together. The other cases were: *Vignera v. New York, Westover v. United States, California v. Stewart.*
[52] *Miranda v. Arizona,* 384 U.S. 436 at 441-442 (1966).
[53] Id. at 466.
[54] Id. at 444-445.
[55] Id. at 474.
[56] Id. at 515-516.
[57] Id. at 536, 537, 541-542.
[58] *Johnson v. New Jersey,* 384 U.S. 719 (1966).
[59] *Orozco v. Texas,* 394 U.S. 324 (1969).
[60] *Harris v. New York,* 401 U.S. 222 at 224, 226 (1971).
[61] Id. at 232.
[62] *Michigan v. Tucker,* 417 U.S. 433 (1974).
[63] *Oregon v. Hass,* 420 U.S. 714 (1975).
[64] *Michigan v. Mosley,* 423 U.S. 96 (1975).
[65] *United States v. Mandujano,* 425 U.S. 564 (1976.).
[66] *Fare v. Michael C.* (1979).

The Aid of Legal Counsel

The Sixth Amendment stipulates that "in all criminal prosecutions, the accused shall enjoy the right . . . to have the assistance of counsel for his defense."

Despite this unambiguous language, however, only persons charged with federal crimes punishable by death have been guaranteed this right throughout American history. [1] The right of all other defendants, federal and state, to the aid of an attorney has traditionally depended upon their ability to hire and pay their own lawyer.

But beginning in the 1930s, the Supreme Court vastly enlarged the class of persons who have the right to legal counsel — appointed and paid by the state if necessary — in preparing and presenting a defense. In 1932 the court declared this right so fundamental that the 14th Amendment's due process clause required states to provide the effective aid of counsel to all defendants charged with capital crimes. [2] Six years later, the court held that the Sixth Amendment required that all federal defendants be provided an attorney. [3]

This expansion of the Sixth Amendment right to counsel continued in the 1960s and 1970s, when the court ruled that the Sixth Amendment guaranteed the aid of an attorney to all state defendants charged with crimes that could be considered serious. [4]

A Fundamental Right

The court's first modern ruling on the right to counsel came in the "First Scottsboro Case" — *Powell v. Alabama* — decided in 1932.

Nine illiterate young black men, aged 13 to 21, were charged with the rape of two white girls on a freight train passing through Tennessee and Alabama. Their trial was held in Scottsboro, Ala., where community hostility to the defendants was intense.

The trial judge appointed all members of the local bar to serve as defense counsel. When the trial began, no attorney from the local bar appeared to represent the defendants. The judge, on the morning of the trial, appointed a local lawyer who undertook the task with reluctance. The defendants were convicted.

They challenged their convictions, arguing that they were effectively denied aid of counsel because they did not have the opportunity to consult with their lawyer and prepare a defense. The Supreme Court, divided 7-2, agreed.

Writing for the court, Justice George Sutherland explained:

It is hardly necessary to say that the right to counsel being conceded, a defendant should be afforded a fair opportunity to secure counsel of his own choice. Not only was that not done here, but such designation of counsel as was attempted was either so indefinite or so close upon the trial as to amount to a denial of effective and substantial aid. . . . [5]

The action of the judge in appointing all members of the local bar as defense counsel was "little more than an expansive gesture" that resulted in no aid to the defendants in the critical pre-trial period, the court said. [6]

Citing the court's acknowledgement in *Twining v. New Jersey* two dozen years earlier that some of the rights guaranteed in the Bill of Rights might be so fundamental that a denial of them by a state would be a denial of due process, the court declared that "the right to the aid of counsel is of this fundamental character." [7] *(Details, p. 528)*

In the Scottsboro case, the court's decision leaned heavily upon the circumstances of the case and the characteristics of the defendants in finding the denial of effective aid of counsel a denial of due process. Sutherland wrote:

In the light of the facts . . . . the ignorance and illiteracy of the defendants, their youth, the circumstances of public hostility, the imprisonment and the close surveillance of the defendants by the military forces, the fact that their friends and families were all in other states and communication with them necessarily difficult, and above all that they stood in deadly peril of their lives — we think the failure of the trial court to give them reasonable time and opportunity to secure counsel was a clear denial of due process.

But . . . assuming their inability, even if opportunity had been given, to employ counsel, as the trial court evidently did assume, we are of opinion that, under the circumstances just stated, the necessity of counsel was so vital and imperative that the failure of the trial court to make an effective appointment of counsel was likewise a denial of due process within the meaning of the Fourteenth Amendment. Whether this would be so in other criminal prosecutions, or under other circumstances, we need not determine. All that it

'The Guiding Hand of Counsel'

One of the classic descriptions of the importance of the aid of an attorney at trial came in the landmark 1932 decision in *Powell v. Alabama*, the "First Scottsboro case."

Writing for the court, Justice George Sutherland discussed the basic requirements of due process:

> It has never been doubted by this court, or any other so far as we know, that notice and hearing are preliminary steps essential to the passing of an enforceable judgment, and that they, together with a legally competent tribunal having jurisdiction of the case, constitute basic elements of the constitutional requirement of due process....
>
> What, then, does a hearing include? Historically and in practice, in our own country at least, it has always included the right to the aid of counsel when desired and provided by the party asserting the right. The right to be heard would be, in many cases, of little avail if it did not comprehend the right to be heard by counsel. Even the intelligent and educated layman has small and sometimes no skill in the science of law. If charged with crime, he is incapable, generally, of determining for himself whether the indictment is good or bad. He is unfamiliar with the rules of evidence. Left without the aid of counsel he may be put on trial without a proper charge, and convicted upon incompetent evidence, or evidence irrelevant to the issue or otherwise inadmissible. He lacks both the skill and knowledge adequately to prepare his defense, even though he have a perfect one. He requires the guiding hand of counsel at every step in the proceedings against him. Without it, though he be not guilty, he faces the danger of conviction because he does not know how to establish his innocence. If that be true of men of intelligence, how much more true is it of the ignorant and illiterate, or those of feeble intellect. If in any case, civil or criminal, a state or federal court were arbitrarily to refuse to hear a party by counsel, employed by and appearing for him, it reasonably may not be doubted that such a refusal would be a denial of a hearing, and, therefore, of due process in the constitutional sense. (*Powell v. Alabama*, 287 U.S. 45 at 68-69, 1932)

is necessary now to decide, as we do decide, is that in a capital case, where the defendant is unable to employ counsel, and is incapable adequately of making his own defense because of ignorance, feeblemindedness, illiteracy or the like, it is the duty of the court, whether requested or not, to assign counsel for him as a necessary requisite of due process of law; and that duty is not discharged by an assignment at such a time or under such circumstances as to preclude the giving of effective aid in the preparation and trial of the case. [8]

The Federal Rule

Since 1790, federal law implementing the Sixth Amendment guarantee has required that persons charged with capital crimes in federal courts be provided an attorney. [9] In 1938 the court held that the Sixth Amendment required this assurance for *all* federal defendants. This was the ruling in the case of *Johnson v. Zerbst.* [10]

John Johnson, a Marine, was charged with passing counterfeit money. He was tried and convicted in civil court without the aid of an attorney to act in his defense. He challenged his conviction as obtained in violation of his constitutional rights.

The Supreme Court found his argument persuasive, and upheld his claim. Justice Hugo L. Black spoke for a majority of the court:

> ... The Sixth Amendment ... embodies a realistic recognition of the obvious truth that the average defendant does not have the professional legal skill to protect himself when brought before a tribunal with power to take his life or liberty, wherein the prosecution is presented by experienced and learned counsel. That which is simple, orderly and necessary to the lawyer — to the untrained laymen ... may appear intricate, complex, and mysterious....
>
> ... The Sixth Amendment withholds from federal courts, in all criminal proceedings, the power and authority to deprive an accused of his life or liberty unless he has or waives the assistance of counsel....
>
> ... While an accused may waive the right to counsel, whether there is a proper waiver should be clearly determined by the trial court, and it would be fitting and appropriate for that determination to appear upon the record....
>
> Since the Sixth Amendment constitutionally entitles one charged with crime to the assistance of counsel, compliance with this constitutional mandate is an essential jurisdictional prerequisite to a federal court's authority to deprive an accused of his life or liberty [unless the right has been properly waived].... If the accused, however, is not represented by counsel and has not competently and intelligently waived his constitutional right, the Sixth Amendment stands as a jurisdictional bar to a valid conviction and sentence depriving him of his life or his liberty. [11]

The Appointment of Counsel

Johnson v. Zerbst, with its emphatic declaration of the right of federal defendants to have an attorney, provided no aid to state defendants. And for 30 years after *Powell v. Alabama*, the court refused to rule that the Sixth Amendment, in addition to the general due process guarantee of the 14th Amendment, extended the right to legal counsel to state defendants.

The primary effect of this judicial posture was to withhold the aid of counsel from indigent state defendants charged with non-capital crimes.

The court first declared, in the 1942 case of *Betts v. Brady*, that "appointment of counsel is not a fundamental right" for such state defendants. [12] The due process guarantee of the 14th Amendment, held the court, did not require states to appoint counsel in every criminal case where it was requested by the defendant. A state legislature might choose to write such a requirement into state law, the court added.

The vote of the court in this case was 6-3. Justice Owen J. Roberts delivered the majority opinion, stating:

The Sixth Amendment of the national Constitution applies only to trials in federal courts. The due process clause of the Fourteenth Amendment does not incorporate, as such, the specific guarantees found in the Sixth Amendment although a denial by a state of rights or privileges specifically embodied in that and others of the first eight amendments may, in certain circumstances, or in connection with other elements, operate, in a given case, to deprive a litigant of due process of law in violation of the Fourteenth. Due process of law is secured against invasion by the federal Government by the Fifth Amendment and is safeguarded against state action in identical words by the Fourteenth. The phrase formulates a concept less rigid and more fluid than those envisaged in other specific and particular provisions of the Bill of Rights. Its application is less a matter of rule. Asserted denial is to be tested by an appraisal of the totality of facts in a given case. That which may, in one setting, constitute a denial of fundamental fairness, shocking to the universal sense of justice, may, in other circumstances, and in the light of other considerations, fall short of such denial.[13]

Justice Roberts acknowledged that the indirect impact of *Johnson v. Zerbst* was to raise the question "whether the constraint laid by the [Sixth] amendment upon the national courts expresses a rule so fundamental and essential to a fair trial, and so, to due process of law, that it is made obligatory upon the States by the Fourteenth Amendment."[14]

The court majority's answer was "no." Justice Roberts wrote that Betts — unlike Powell of the Scottsboro case — was a man 43 years old, "of ordinary intelligence and ability." He was not so handicapped by lack of counsel that he was denied the fundamental fairness promised by the due process clause. And so, concluded the court, while "the Fourteenth Amendment prohibits the conviction and incarceration of one whose trial is offensive to the common and fundamental ideas of fairness and right, and while want of counsel in a particular case may result in a conviction lacking in such fundamental fairness, we cannot say that the amendment embodies an inexorable command that no trial for any offense, or in any court, can be fairly conducted and justice accorded a defendant who is not represented by counsel."[15]

Justice Hugo L. Black, joind by Justices Frank Murphy and William O. Douglas in dissent, urged that the same rule apply in state as in federal courts:

A practice cannot be reconciled with "common and fundamental ideas of fairness and right," which subjects innocent men to increased dangers of conviction merely because of their poverty. . . .

Denial to the poor of the request for counsel in proceedings based on charges of serious crime has long been regarded as shocking to the "universal sense of justice" throughout this country. . . .[16]

Under the *Betts* rule, then, the court considered the special circumstances of each case to determine if denial of counsel denied the defendant fair treatment. The court upheld some of the state convictions challenged due to lack of counsel, but in most cases it found circumstances which warranted reversal. Among those were the conduct of the trial judge, the youth or ignorance or lack of legal sophistication of the defendants.[17]

Gideon v. Wainwright

In 1963 the Supreme Court unanimously discarded this case-by-case approach, overruling *Betts v. Brady* to hold that the right to the assistance of counsel was so fundamental that the 14th Amendment due process clause extended the Sixth Amendment guarantee to state defendants.

States were henceforth required to provide counsel for all defendants charged with felonies and unable to pay a lawyer. This was the decision in the case of *Gideon v. Wainwright.*[18] Clarence Earl Gideon, an indigent, was tried and convicted in a Florida state court of a felony — breaking and entering a poolroom to commit a misdemeanor. He requested and was denied a court-appointed attorney; the judge based his refusal of this request on the fact that Gideon's crime — unlike that in the *Powell* case — was not a capital one. Gideon thus conducted his own defense.

Convicted and sentenced to spend five years in prison, Gideon prepared his own petitions asking a federal court to declare his conviction invalid because it was obtained in violation of his constitutional right to counsel, and to order his release. The Supreme Court finally agreed to hear Gideon's case, and appointed a well-known Washington attorney, Abe Fortas, to argue on his behalf. The court specifically requested that both sides in the case argue the additional question: should *Betts v. Brady* be reconsidered?

The court's opinion in *Gideon*, reconsidering and reversing *Betts v. Brady*, was written by Justice Black, who had dissented from *Betts*. Looking back to *Powell v. Alabama*, in which the court had described the right to counsel as fundamental to a fair trial, Black wrote:

The fact is that the Court in *Betts v. Brady* made an abrupt break with its own well-considered precedents. In returning to these old precedents, sounder we believe than the new, we but restore constitutional principles established to achieve a fair system of justice. Not only these precedents but also reason and reflection require us to recognize that in our adversary system of criminal justice, any person haled into court, who is too poor to hire a lawyer, cannot be assured a fair trial unless counsel is provided for him. This seems to us to be an obvious truth. . . . Lawyers to prosecute are everywhere deemed essential to protect the public's interest in an orderly society. . . . That government hires lawyers to prosecute and defendants who have the money hire lawyers to defend are the strongest indications of the widespread belief that lawyers in criminal courts are necessities, not luxuries. . . .[19]

The 'Adequate Protective Device'

In 1964 the Supreme Court further tightened its requirement that states observe the right to counsel. With its controversial ruling in *Escobedo v. Illinois*, the court linked that right to the Fifth Amendment privilege against self-incrimination. In *Escobedo*, a divided court held that a suspect in custody had an absolute right to the aid of an attorney during police interrogation.[20] *(Details, p. 560)*

Two years later, with its decision in the case of *Miranda v. Arizona*, the court declared the presence of counsel "the adequate protective device necessary to make the process of police interrogation conform to the dictates of the [Fifth Amendment] privilege."[21]

The Right Not To Have A Lawyer

In a case which seemed to turn inside-out the court's series of rulings expanding the right of defendants in state courts to have the assistance of an attorney (at public expense if necessary), the Supreme Court in 1975 held that defendants also have the right to *refuse* legal assistance.

In the case of *Faretta v. California*, decided by a vote of 6-3, the court ruled that individuals have the right to conduct their own defense and to reject counsel who have been appointed to represent them.

Writing for the majority, Justice Potter Stewart acknowledged that recognition of this right seemed "to cut against the grain of this court's decisions holding that the Constitution requires that no accused can be convicted and imprisoned unless he has been accorded the right to the assistance of counsel." However, Stewart continued, "it is one thing to hold that every defendant, rich or poor, has the right to the assistance of counsel, and quite another to say that a state may compel a defendant to accept a lawyer he does not want."(*Faretta v. California*, 422 U.S. 806 at 832-833, 1975).

"Accordingly, we hold," wrote Chief Justice Earl Warren, "that an individual held for interrogation must be clearly informed that he has the right to consult with a lawyer and to have the lawyer with him during interrogation."[22]

In 1972 the court held that the right to counsel applied not only to state defendants charged with felonies, but in all trials of persons for offenses serious enough to warrant a jail sentence. Speaking for the unanimous court in the case of *Argersinger v. Hamlin*, Justice William O. Douglas looked back both to *Powell* and *Gideon:*

Both *Powell* and *Gideon* involved felonies. But their rationale has relevance to any criminal trial, where an accused is deprived of liberty. *Powell* and *Gideon* suggest that there are certain fundamental rights applicable to all such criminal prosecutions....

The requirement of counsel may well be necessary for a fair trial even in a petty offense prosecution. We are by no means convinced that legal and constitutional questions involved in a case that actually leads to imprisonment even for a brief period are any less complex than when a person can be sent off for six months or more....

Under the rule we announce today, every judge will know when the trial of a misdemeanor starts that no imprisonment may be imposed, even though local law permits it, unless the accused is represented by counsel.[23]

In 1979 the court limited the application of the *Argersinger* ruling, holding that the right to counsel did not apply in trials of lesser offenses where no sentence of imprisonment was imposed, even though such a sentence could have been imposed.[24]

The 'Critical Stage'

In *Powell v. Alabama*, the court in 1932 indicated the importance of timing in the provision of legal assistance to a defendant.[25] The court described the period between arrest and trial as a critical one in the preparation of a defense. Many of the court's subsequent rulings on the right to counsel have focused on the definition of a "critical stage" at which the right to counsel applies, at which time counsel must be made available if requested by the suspect or defendant.

In *Hamilton v. Alabama*, decided in 1961, the court held that arraignment, at least in some states, was such a critical stage.[26] Later, *Escobedo* and *Miranda* emphatically held that the right applied once a suspect was in custody and subject to interrogation.[27]

In 1967 the court in the case of *United States v. Wade* — and its state counterpart, *Gilbert v. California* — held that police line-ups also were such a critical stage.[28] The court declared in-court identification of defendants based on pre-trial lineups from which defendant's counsel was absent, to be inadmissible.

Writing for a unanimous court in *Wade*, Justice William J. Brennan Jr. observed:

... the principle of *Powell v. Alabama* and succeeding cases requires that we scrutinize *any* pretrial confrontation of the accused to determine whether the presence of his counsel is necessary to preserve the defendant's basic right to a fair trial as affected by his right meaningfully to cross-examine the witnesses against him and to have effective assistance of counsel at the trial itself.[29]

In *Gilbert*, the court applied the same rule to state proceedings.

Wade was quickly undercut by Congress. In the Crime Control and Safe Streets Act of 1968, Congress included a provision allowing use of such line-up identification evidence at trial in federal courts, even if obtained in the absence of counsel. (*Details, p. 679*)

And in 1972 the court further limited the effect of *Wade* and *Gilbert*. The defendants in those cases had already been indicted when they were placed in the lineup. In the case of *Kirby v. Illinois*, the court ruled in 1972 that the right to counsel did not apply to persons in such line-ups who had not yet been indicted. The right did not take effect, the court held, until "formal prosecutorial proceedings" were underway.[30]

For the majority Justice Potter Stewart explained:

The initiation of judicial criminal proceedings is far from a mere formalism. It is the starting point of our whole system of adversary criminal justice. For it is only then that the Government has committed itself to prosecute and only then that the adverse positions of Government and defendant have solidified. It is then that a defendant finds himself faced with the prosecutorial forces of organized society, and immersed in the intricacies of substantive and procedural criminal law. It is this point, therefore, that marks the commencement of the "criminal prosecutions" to which alone the explicit guarantees of the Sixth Amendment are applicable.[31]

The principle of *Wade* and *Gilbert* was further eroded in 1973 when the court held that it was not necessary for a defendant's attorney to be present at a post-indictment photographic identification session with potential witnesses.[32]

Counsel for Appeals

At the other end of the criminal justice process — appeal of conviction — the court in 1974 called a halt to the gradual extension of the right to appointed counsel.

In the case of *Ross v. Moffit* the court held that the state's constitutional obligation to provide appointed counsel for indigents appealing their convictions did not extend past the point where their right to appeal had been effectively exhausted.[33]

'Effective' Aid

As the court made clear in *Powell v. Alabama*, the effective aid of counsel means more than the mere physical presence of an attorney at trial.

In Powell the court held that the judge's gesture of appointing the entire local bar as defense counsel — and the failure of any particular individuals to assume that role before trial — deprived the defendants of the *effective* aid of counsel.

Other factors can deprive a defendant of the sort of legal representation to which the Sixth Amendment — or due process generally — entitles him.

Conflict of interest is one such element. In the 1942 case of *Glasser v. United States,* the Supreme Court found that a judge had denied defendants the effective aid of counsel by requiring a single attorney to represent them both.[34] In that opinion, the majority declared:

> Upon the trial judge rests the duty of seeing that the trial is conducted with solicitude for the essential rights of the accused. . . . Of equal importance with the duty of the court to see that an accused has the assistance of counsel is its duty to refrain from

embarassing counsel in the defense of an accused by insisting, or indeed, even suggesting, that counsel undertake to concurrently represent interests which might diverge from those of his first client, when the possibility of that divergence is brought home to the court.[35]

In 1978 the court elaborated on that point, stating in the case of *Holloway v. Arkansas:*

> Joint representation of conflicting interests is suspect because of what it tends to prevent the attorney from doing. . . . Generally speaking, a conflict may . . . prevent an attorney from challenging the admission of evidence prejudicial to one client but perhaps favorable to another, or from arguing at the sentencing hearing the relative involvement and culpability of his clients in order to minimize the culpability of one by emphasizing that of another. . . . The mere physical presence of an attorney does not fulfill the Sixth Amendment guarantee when the advocate's conflicting obligations has [sic] effectively sealed his lips on crucial matters.[36]

Competent Counsel

Competence of counsel, however, is more difficult to challenge. The court in the 1970s rejected the effort of several persons to challenge their convictions, based on guilty pleas, with the argument that they were the result of advice from incompetent counsel. The court declared that defendants must assume a certain degree of risk that their attorneys would make some "ordinary error" in assessing the facts of their case and the law which applied, and that such error was not a basis for reversing a conviction.[37]

Footnotes

[1] 1 *Stat.* 73, 92 (1789); 1 *Stat.* 112, 118 (1790), now 18 *United States Code* 563.

[2] *Powell v. Alabama,* 287 U.S. 45 (1932).

[3] *Johnson v. Zerbst,* 304 U.S. 458 (1938).

[4] *Gideon v. Wainwright,* 372 U.S. 335 (1963); *Argersinger v. Hamlin,* 407 U.S. 25 (1972).

[5] *Powell v. Alabama,* 287 U.S. 45 at 53 (1932).

[6] Id. at 56-57.

[7] Id. at 68.

[8] Id. at 71.

[9] 1 *Stat.* 73, 92 (1789); 1 *Stat.* 112, 118 (1790); now 18 *United States Code* 563.

[10] *Johnson v. Zerbst,* 304 U.S. 458 (1938).

[11] Id. at 462-463, 465, 467-468.

[12] *Betts v. Brady,* 316 U.S. 455 (1942).

[13] Id. at 461-462.

[14] Id. at 465.

[15] Id. at 473.

[16] Id. at 476.

[17] *Canizio v. New York,* 327 U.S. 82 (1946); *Bute v. Illinois,* 333 U.S. 640 (1948); *Tomkins v. Missouri,* 323 U.S. 485 (1945); *Townsend v. Burk,* 334 U.S. 736 (1948); *White v. Ragen,* 324 U.S. 760 (1945); *DeMeerleer v. Michigan,* 329 U.S. 663 (1947); *Marino v. Ragen,* 332 U.S. 561 (1947); *Rice v. Olsen,* 324 U.S. 786 (1945).

[18] *Gideon v. Wainwright,* 372 U.S. 335 (1963).

[19] Id. at 343-344.

[20] *Escobedo v. Illinois,* 378 U.S. 478 (1964).

[21] *Miranda v. Arizona,* 384 U.S. 436 at 466 (1966).

[22] Id. at 471.

[23] *Argersinger v. Hamlin,* 407 U.S. 25 at 32-33, 40 (1972).

[24] *Scott v. Illinois* (1979).

[25] *Powell v. Alabama,* 287 U.S. 45 (1932).

[26] *Hamilton v. Alabama,* 368 U.S. 52 (1961).

[27] *Escobedo v. Illinois,* 378 U.S. 478 (1964); *Miranda v. Arizona,* 384 U.S. 436 (1966).

[28] *United States v. Wade,* 388 U.S. 218 (1967); *Gilbert v. California,* 388 U.S. 263 (1967).

[29] *United States v. Wade,* 388 U.S. 218 at 227 (1967).

[30] *Kirby v. Illinois,* 406 U.S. 682 (1972); but see also *Coleman v. Alabama,* 399 U.S. 1 (1970).

[31] *Kirby v. Illinois,* 406 U.S. 682 at 689-690 (1972).

[32] *United States v. Ash,* 413 U.S. 300 (1973).

[33] *Ross v. Moffit,* 417 U.S. 600 (1974).

[34] *Glasser v. United States,* 315 U.S. 60 (1942).

[35] Id. at 71, 76.

[36] *Holloway v. Arkansas,* 435 U.S. 475 at 489-490 (1978).

[37] *Mann v. Richardson,* 397 U.S. 759 (1970); *Tollett v. Henderson,* 411 U.S. 258 (1973).

Double Jeopardy

To restrain the government from repeatedly prosecuting an individual for one particular offense, the prohibition against double jeopardy — two trials for one offense — was included in the Fifth Amendment.

The Supreme Court has held that this guarantee protects an individual both against multiple prosecutions for the same offense and against multiple punishments for the same crime.

Until 1969 the double jeopardy clause applied only to federal prosecutions. In that year the Supreme Court in the case of *Benton v. Maryland* held that the due process guarantee of the 14th Amendment extended this protection to persons tried by states as well.[1]

A defendant is placed in jeopardy at the time his jury is sworn in,[2] although if a mistrial is declared under certain circumstances[3] or if the jury fails to agree on a verdict,[4] the double jeopardy clause does not forbid his re-trial.

If he is convicted, he may waive his immunity against double jeopardy and seek a new trial, or he may appeal the verdict to a higher court. If the conviction is set aside for a reason other than insufficient evidence, he may be tried again for the same offense.[5]

If he is acquitted, the double jeopardy clause absolutely bars any further prosecution of him for that crime, even if the acquittal was the result of error.[6]

Dual Sovereigns

The Fifth Amendment double jeopardy guarantee, however, protects only against repeated prosecutions by a single sovereign government. Thus, it is not violated when a person is tried on both state and federal charges arising from a single offense. Many acts are offenses under both federal and state laws.

The court established this rule in the 1922 case of *United States v. Lanza.* Lanza was convicted for violating Washington state's prohibition law. Then he was indicted on the same grounds for violating the federal prohibition law. The federal district judge dismissed his indictment as a violation of the double jeopardy guarantee. The government appealed the dismissal and the Supreme Court reversed it, by a vote of 6-3.

Chief Justice William Howard Taft wrote for the court:

> We have here two sovereignties, deriving power from different sources, capable of dealing with the same subject-matter within the same territory. Each may, without interference by the other, enact laws to secure prohibition. . . . Each government, in determining what shall be an offense against its peace and dignity, is exercising its own sovereignty, not that of the other.
>
> It follows that an act denounced as a crime by both national and state sovereignties is an offense against the peace and dignity of both, and may be punished by each. The 5th Amendment, like all the other guaranties in the first eight amendments, applies only to proceedings by the Federal government . . . and the double jeopardy therein forbidden is a second prosecution under authority of the Federal government after a first trial for the same offense under the same authority. Here the same act was an offense against the state of Washington, because a violation of its law, and also an offense against the United States under the National Prohibition Act. The defendants thus committed two different offenses by the same act, and a conviction by a court of Washington of the offense against that state is not a conviction of the different offense against the United States, and so is not double jeopardy. . . .[7]

The *Lanza* rule survives. In 1959 the court reaffirmed its opinion that multiple prosecutions by different sovereigns for the same offense did not violate the double jeopardy clause.[8] However, because a state and a city are not separate sovereigns, the double jeopardy guarantee does protect an individual against prosecution by both for one offense.[9]

The separate sovereignties doctrine was applied by the court in the 1978 case of *United States v. Wheeler.* There the court ruled that the double jeopardy clause did not protect an American Indian defendant convicted in tribal court from being tried by federal authorities for the same offense.[10]

Appeal and Retrial

The double jeopardy clause also protects an individual who successfully appeals his conviction on a lesser charge from being retried on the original, greater charge.

In the 1957 case of *Green v. United States,* the court ruled that Green, tried for first-degree murder but convicted of murder in the second degree — a verdict which he successfully appealed — could not be tried again for first degree murder after he won a new trial on appeal. The court said that Green had been once in jeopardy for first-degree murder and that appeal of his conviction for a different crime did not constitute a waiver of his protection against double jeopardy. The court explained:

> The underlying idea, one that is deeply ingrained in at least the Anglo-American system of jurisprudence, is that the State with all its resources and power should not be allowed to make repeated attempts to convict an individual for an alleged offense, thereby subjecting him to embarrassment, expense and ordeal and compelling him to live in a continuing state of anxiety and insecurity, as well as enhancing the possibility that even though innocent he may be found guilty.[11]

States and Double Jeopardy

In 1937 — in the often-cited decision in *Palko v. Connecticut* — the court rejected the argument that the 14th Amendment due process clause applied the double jeopardy guarantee to state action.

Palko was convicted of second-degree murder and sentenced to life imprisonment. The state sought and won a new trial claiming that legal errors had occurred at trial. At a second trial Palko was found guilty of first-degree murder and sentenced to die. He challenged his second conviction as a violation of the double jeopardy guarantee and of due process.

The court rejected this argument, excluding the double jeopardy guarantee from the list of guarantees which had been "absorbed" into due process. That protection, Justice Benjamin N. Cardozo wrote for the majority, was not "of the very essence of a scheme of ordered liberty."[12] He then elaborated:

> Is that kind of double jeopardy to which the statute has subjected him a hardship so acute and shocking that our polity will not endure it? Does it violate those "fundamental principles of liberty and justice which lie at the base of all our civil and political institutions?".... The answer surely must be "no." ... The state is not attempting to wear the accused out by a multitude of cases with accumulated trials. It asks no more than this, that the case against him shall go on until there shall be a trial free from the corrosion of substantial legal error.... This is not cruelty at all, nor even vexation in any immoderate degree. If the trial had been infected with error adverse to the accused, there might be here review at his instance, and as often as necessary to purge the vicious taint. A reciprocal privilege, subject at all times to the discretion of the presiding judge ... has now been granted to the state. There is here no seismic innovation. The edifice of justice stands, its symmetry, to many, greater than before.[13]

Thirty-two years later, in 1969, the court overruled *Palko*. In the last announced decision of the Warren Court, the court in the case of *Benton v. Maryland* declared that the double jeopardy clause did apply to the states through the due process guarantee of the 14th Amendment.

Justice Thurgood Marshall delivered the majority opinion:

Our recent cases have thoroughly rejected the *Palko* notion that basic constitutional rights can be denied by the States so long as the totality of the circumstances does not disclose a denial of "fundamental fairness." Once it is decided that a particular Bill of Rights guarantee is "fundamental to the American scheme of justice," ... the same constitutional standards apply against both the State and Federal Governments. *Palko's* roots had thus been cut away years ago. We today only recognize the inevitable.[14]

Justices John Marshall Harlan and Potter Stewart dissented from this "march toward 'incorporating' much, if not all, of the Federal Bill of Rights into the Due Process Clause."[15]

Appeal and Resentencing

The same day the court announced its decision in *Benton* — June 23, 1969 — it held in the case of *North Carolina v. Pearce* that the double jeopardy guarantee limited the authority of a judge to impose a harsher sentence than the original upon a defendant whose first conviction had been set aside and who had been granted a new trial.[16] In 1973, however, the court refused to apply these limitations to re-sentencing by a *jury* after re-trial.[17]

The court held that unless there were objective reasons related to the conduct of the defendant after the imposition of the first sentence, and unless those reasons were set out in the record of the case, the judge could not impose a harsher sentence after retrial. Furthermore, the court held that time already served on the first sentence must be credited against the new sentence.

Pearce was convicted of assault with intent to rape and sentenced to 12 to 15 years in prison. After serving several years, he won reversal of his conviction and a new trial. Convicted in the second trial, Pearce was sentenced to eight years in prison. When this new sentence was added to the time he had already served, it amounted to a longer sentence than the original one.

Justice Potter Stewart wrote the court's opinion holding the new sentence a violation of the double jeopardy guarantee unless the time already served was credited against it:

> The Court has held today, in *Benton v. Maryland* ... that the Fifth Amendment guarantee against double jeopardy is enforceable against the States through the Fourteenth Amendment. That guarantee has been said to consist of three separate constitutional protections. It protects against a second prosecution for the same offense after acquittal. It protects against a second prosecution for the same offense after conviction. And it protects against multiple punishments for the same offense. This last protection is what is necessarily implicated in any consideration of the question whether, in the imposition of sentence for the same offense after retrial, the Constitution requires that credit must be given for punishment already endured....
>
> We hold that the constitutional guarantee against multiple punishments for the same offense absolutely requires that punishment already exacted must be fully "credited" in imposing sentence upon a new conviction for the same offense. If upon a new trial, the defendant is acquitted, there is no way the years he spent in prison can be returned to him. But if he is

reconvicted, those years can and must be returned — by subtracting them from whatever new sentence is imposed.[18]

Acquittals and Appeals

In the mid-1970s, the Supreme Court in several rulings began to expand the government's right to appeal a judge's decision to dismiss charges against a defendant after the trial was underway. Such appeals had been thought impermissible under the general rule that the prosecution may not appeal a verdict of acquittal.

In 1975 the court in the case of *United States v. Wilson* held that the double jeopardy guarantee did not foreclose a government appeal of a trial judge's decision to dismiss charges against a defendant who had already been found guilty as charged.[19]

The court reasoned that the double jeopardy clause did not foreclose an appeal of such a post-verdict dismissal of charges inasmuch as the success of the appeal would only result in reinstatement of the verdict, not in a new trial for the same offense.

In another case decided that same day, the court seemed to make the possibility of further proceedings against the defendant a crucial element in determining the permissibility of such appeals. In the case of *United States v. Jenkins,* the court held that the double jeopardy clause did forbid the government to appeal a ruling dismissing an indictment when a successful appeal might result in further proceedings in the case.[20]

Three years later, however, the court overruled *Jenkins* with its decision in the case of *United States v. Scott.*[21] By a 5-4 vote, the court held that the government could appeal a trial judge's decision to grant a motion from the defendant to dismiss the charges in mid-trial. The court held that the double jeopardy guarantee did not forbid an appeal of that ruling — or retrial of the defendant — because a defendant, in seeking dismissal of the charges based on grounds unrelated to his guilt or innocence, had made a voluntary choice to risk retrial for the same offense. The double jeopardy clause, held the majority, protected an individual against government oppression through multiple prosecutions, but not against the consequences of his own voluntary choice.

Footnotes

[1] *Benton v. Maryland,* 395 U.S. 784 (1969).
[2] *Downum v. United States,* 372 U.S. 734 (1963); *Crist v. Bretz,* 437 U.S. 28 (1978).
[3] *Wade v. Hunter,* 336 U.S. 684 (1949); *United States v. Dinitz,* 424 U.S. 600 (1976); *Lee v. United States,* 432 U.S. 23 (1977).
[4] *United States v. Perez,* 9 Wheat. 579 (1824).
[5] *United States v. Ball,* 163 U.S. 662 (1896).
[6] *United States v. Sanges,* 144 U.S. 310 (1892); *United States v. Ball,* 163 U.S. 662 (1896); *Fong Foo v. United States,* 369 U.S. 141 (1962); *Sanabria v. United States,* 437 U.S. 54 (1978).
[7] *United States v. Lanza,* 260 U.S. 377 at 382 (1922).
[8] *Abbate v. United States,* 359 U.S. 187 (1959); *Bartkus v. Illinois,* 359 U.S. 121 (1959); see also *Petite v. United States,* 361 U.S. 529 (1960).

[9] *Waller v. Florida,* 397 U.S. 387 (1970).
[10] *United States v. Wheeler,* 435 U.S. 313 (1978).
[11] *Green v. United States,* 355 U.S. 184 at 187-188 (1957); see also *Price v. Georgia,* 398 U.S. 323 (1970).
[12] *Palko v. Connecticut,* 302 U.S. 319 at 325 (1937).
[13] Id. at 328.
[14] *Benton v. Maryland,* 395 U.S. 784 at 795 (1969).
[15] Id. at 808.
[16] *North Carolina v. Pearce,* 395 U.S. 711 (1969).
[17] *Chaffin v. Stynchcombe,* 412 U.S. 17 (1973).
[18] *North Carolina v. Pearce,* 395 U.S. 711 at 717 (1969).
[19] *United States v. Wilson,* 420 U.S. 332 (1975).
[20] *United States v. Jenkins,* 420 U.S. 358 (1975).
[21] *United States v. Scott,* 437 U.S. 82 (1978).

Cruel and Unusual Punishment

The Eighth Amendment prohibits cruel and unusual punishment, but leaves open the definition of what is "cruel and unusual."

The Supreme Court has interpreted this prohibition flexibly, measuring punishments challenged as in violation of it against "evolving standards of decency." While it has refused, for example, to outlaw the death penalty as invariably cruel and unusual, it has applied that constitutional standard to prohibit states from imposing prison sentences upon those found "guilty" of drug addiction. The court has generally indicated that it would apply the amendment to prohibit punishments it found barbaric or disproportionate to the crime punished.

Too Severe A Penalty

Since early in the 20th century, the Supreme Court has weighed the severity of a challenged sentence against the seriousness of the crime punished. In 1910 the court in the case of *Weems v. United States* decided the Eighth Amendment ban had been violated by a law which allowed a person convicted of falsifying a public record to be assessed a heavy fine, sentenced to fifteen years at hard labor and subjected to several other sanctions.[1]

Nearly half a century later, the court in the 1958 case, *Trop v. Dulles,* reversed a military court's decision to strip of U.S. citizenship a man who had been convicted of desertion during wartime.

Four members of the court, for whom Chief Justice Earl Warren spoke, found such "denationalization" a cruel and unusual punishment "forbidden by the principle of civilized treatment guaranteed by the Eighth Amendment."[2]

Warren then set out an oft-quoted description of this constitutional provision:

> The exact scope of the constitutional phrase "cruel and unusual" has not been detailed by this Court.... The basic concept underlying the Eighth Amendment is nothing less than the dignity of man. While the State has the power to punish, the Amendment stands to assure that this power be exercised within the limits of civilized standards. Fines, imprisonment and even execution may be imposed depending upon the enormity of the crime, but any technique outside the bounds of these traditional penalties is constitutionally

suspect.... The Court [has] recognized ... that the words of the Amendment are not precise, and that their scope is not static. The Amendment must draw its meaning from the evolving standards of decency that mark the progress of a maturing society.[3]

Death, Drugs and the States

Capital punishment has been discussed by the Supreme Court in virtually every "cruel and unusual punishment" case it has decided, whether or not the death penalty was the punishment challenged in the particular case at hand.

In a decision in 1892, the court refused to apply the Eighth Amendment ban to state action.[4] In the mid-20th century that position was quietly abandoned, but not until 1962 did the court hold that a state violated that prohibition by authorizing an unusually cruel punishment.

Willie Francis and Death

One of the most bizarre of the court's death penalty cases was that of *Louisiana ex rel. Francis v. Resweber,* decided in 1947.

Willie Francis had been sentenced to death by electrocution. On the appointed day Francis was put in the electric chair, the switch was thrown — and nothing happened. A mechanical failure in the operating mechanism prevented the electricity from reaching Francis.

Francis then appealed to the Supreme Court, asking them to forbid the state a second execution attempt because it would constitute cruel and unusual punishment. The court denied Francis' appeal, by a vote of 5-4.[5]

Speaking for the majority, Justice Stanley F. Reed assumed that the Eighth Amendment ban applied to state action, but did not find that action in Francis' case to be cruel and unusual:

> ...the fact that petitioner has already been subjected to a current of electricity does not make his subsequent execution any more cruel in the constitutional sense than any other execution. The cruelty against which the Constitution protects a convicted man is cruelty inherent in the method of punishment, not the necessary suffering involved in any method employed to extinguish life humanely. The fact that an unforeseeable accident prevented the prompt consum-

mation of the sentence cannot, it seems to us, add an element of cruelty to a subsequent execution. There is no purpose to inflict unnecessary pain nor any unnecessary pain involved in the proposed execution.... We cannot agree that the hardship imposed upon the petitioner rises to that level of hardship denounced as denial of due process because of cruelty.[6]

Justice Harold H. Burton, joined by Justices William O. Douglas, Frank Murphy and Wiley B. Rutledge, dissented.

Lawrence Robinson and Drugs

Fifteen years after refusing to halt Willie Francis' execution, the court in 1962 for the first time used the Eighth Amendment to invalidate a state law.

In the case of *Robinson v. California* the court held it impermissibly cruel and unusual punishment for a state to impose prison sentences upon persons found to be drug addicts.

Justice Potter Stewart wrote the majority opinion for six members of the court:

> This statute ... is not one which punishes a person for the use of narcotics, for their purchase, sale or possession, or for antisocial or disorderly behavior resulting from their administration. It is not a law which even purports to provide or require medical treatment. Rather, we deal with a statute which makes the "status" of narcotic addiction a criminal offense....
>
> It is unlikely that any State ... would attempt to make it a criminal offense for a person to be mentally ill, or a leper, or to be afflicted with a venereal disease ... in the light of contemporary human knowledge, a law which made a criminal offense of such a disease would doubtless be universally thought to be an infliction of cruel and unusual punishment in violation of the Eighth and Fourteenth Amendments....
>
> ...We hold that a state law which imprisons a person thus afflicted as a criminal ... inflicts a cruel and unusual punishment in violation of the Fourteenth Amendment."[7]

Justices Byron R. White and Tom C. Clark dissented.

Leroy Powell and Liquor

In 1968 the court refused to apply its *Robinson* ruling to forbid states to punish public drunkenness.

In the case of *Powell v. Texas,* the court upheld a Texas law under which Leroy Powell had been convicted of being intoxicated in a public place. He attacked the law as cruel and unusual punishment, because it punished him for being a chronic alcoholic.

By a 5-4 vote, the court rejected that challenge. Justice Thurgood Marshall delivered the majority opinion, distinguishing the law in *Powell* from that in *Robinson:*

> ...appellant was convicted, not for being a chronic alcoholic, but for being in public while drunk on a particular occasion. The State of Texas thus has not sought to punish a mere status, as California did in *Robinson*; nor has it attempted to regulate appellant's behavior in the privacy of his own home. Rather, it has imposed upon appellant a criminal sanction for public behavior which may create substantial health and safety hazards, both for appellant and for members of the general public, and which offends the moral and

esthetic sensibilities of a large segment of the community....[8]

Justice Abe Fortas, William O. Douglas, William J. Brennan Jr. and Potter Stewart dissented.

Capital Punishment

In the decade from 1968 through 1978 the Supreme Court zig-zagged its way through a series of rulings on the question of capital punishment.

Jury Selection

The first in this line of rulings came in the case of *Witherspoon v. Illinois,* decided in 1968.

In that case the court held that states could not exclude from juries in capital cases all persons opposed to the death penalty. Such exclusion of a sizable group, held the court, resulted in a jury which was not fairly representative of the community. *(Jury selection, pp. 529-534)*

Justice Potter Stewart spoke for the majority:

> ...in a nation less than half of whose people believe in the death penalty, a jury composed exclusively of such people [those favoring capital punishment] cannot speak for the community. Culled of all who harbor doubts about the wisdom of capital punishment — of all who would be reluctant to pronounce the extreme penalty — such a jury can speak only for a distinct and dwindling minority.... In its quest for a jury capable of imposing the death penalty, the State produced a jury uncommonly willing to condemn a man to die.[9]

Jury Discretion

Three years later the court upheld, against a due process challenge, state laws which left completely to the discretion of the jury the decision whether to impose a sentence of death upon a particular defendant. This was the court's ruling in the 1971 case of *McGautha v. California,* reached by a 6-3 vote.

Justice John Marshall Harlan, speaking for six members of the court, declared that:

> In light of history, experience, and the present limitations of human knowledge, we find it quite impossible to say that committing to the untrammeled discretion of the jury the power to pronounce life or death in capital cases is offensive to anything in the Constitution.[10]

In dissent, Justices William J. Brennan Jr., Thurgood Marshall and William O. Douglas argued that states should be required to set guidelines for this irrevocable jury decision.

The Furman Decision

Only a year later, however, the court effectively reversed *McGautha.*

By a 5-4 vote, the court in the cases of *Furman v. Georgia, Jackson v. Georgia* and *Branch v. Texas* invalidated all existing death penalty statutes.

State laws like those of Georgia and Texas, held the majority, left too much discretion to juries in imposing this ultimate penalty. The result was a "wanton and freakish" pattern of its use which violated the Eighth Amendment ban on cruel and unusual punishments.[11]

The Right To Bail: Neither Absolute Nor Excessive

The Eighth Amendment states that "[e]xcessive bail shall not be required. . . ." Throughout U.S. history, federal law has provided that persons arrested for noncapital offenses shall be granted the right to post bail and win release to participate in preparing their defense.

Bail is money or property pledged by an accused person to guarantee his appearance at trial. The accused is thus permitted to go free on bond. Failure to appear at trial — "jumping bail" — carries criminal penalties, plus forfeiture of the pledged bond.

The Supreme Court has held that a presumption in favor of granting bail exists in the Bill of Rights. Justice Horace Gray wrote in 1895:

> The statutes of the United States have been framed upon the theory that a person accused of crime shall not, until he has been finally adjudged guilty in the court of last resort, be absolutely compelled to undergo imprisonment or punishment, but may be admitted to bail, not only after arrest and before trial, but after conviction and pending a writ of error.[1]

The Eighth Amendment's bail provisions limit federal courts, not state courts. The court ruled in the case of *McKane v. Durston*, decided in 1894, that the Eighth Amendment provision on bail did not apply to the states.[2]

The Federal Rules of Criminal Procedure provide that the amount of bail shall be determined by the nature and circumstances of the offense, the weight of the evidence, the defendant's ability to pay and his general character.[3]

Under the 1966 Bail Reform Act, almost all persons charged with noncapital federal offenses are able to obtain release on personal recognizance or unsecured bond.[4]

The leading Supreme Court decision on the question of excessive bail is *Stack v. Boyle*, decided in 1951. Twelve Communist leaders in California were indicted for conspiracy under the Smith Act. Bail was fixed at $50,000 for each defendant. The defendants moved to reduce the amount of bail on the grounds that it was excessive in violation of the Eighth Amendment.

The Supreme Court agreed. Chief Justice Fred M. Vinson delivered the opinion of the court saying:

> This traditional right to freedom before conviction permits the unhampered preparation of a defense, and serves to prevent the infliction of punishment prior to conviction. . . . Unless this right to bail before trial is preserved, the presumption of innocence, secured only after centuries of struggle, would lose its meaning.
>
> The right to release before trial is conditioned upon the accused's giving adequate assurance that he will stand trial and submit to sentence if found guilty. . . . Bail set at a figure higher than an amount reasonably calculated to fulfill this purpose is "excessive" under the Eighth Amendment. . . .
>
> If bail in an amount greater than that usually fixed for serious charges of crimes is required in the case of any of the petitioners, that is a matter to which evidence should be directed in a hearing. . . . In the absence of such a showing, we are of the opinion that the fixing of bail before trial in these cases cannot be squared with the statutory and constitutional standards for admission to bail. . . .
>
> . . .bail has not been fixed by proper methods in this case and . . . petitioners' remedy is by motion to reduce bail. . . .[5]

The following spring, however, the court held that the Eighth Amendment did not guarantee an absolute right to bail. Certain alien Communists had been detained prior to a final determination on their deportation. Their application for bail was denied by the attorney general acting under provisions of the 1950 Internal Security Act.

The court divided 5-4 in rejecting their argument that bail should be granted.

Justice Stanley F. Reed, writing for the majority in the case of *Carlson v. Landon*, stated that the Eighth Amendment did not guarantee all persons detained by federal authority the right to be released on bail:

> The bail clause was lifted with slight changes from the English Bill of Rights Act. In England that clause has never been thought to accord a right to bail in all cases, but merely to provide that bail shall not be excessive in those cases where it is proper to grant bail. When this clause was carried over into our Bill of Rights, nothing was said that indicated any different concept. The Eighth Amendment has not prevented Congress from defining the classes of cases in which bail shall be allowed in this country. Thus, in criminal cases, bail is not compulsory where the punishment may be death. Indeed, the very language of the Amendment fails to say all arrests must be bailable. We think, clearly, here that the Eighth Amendment does not require that bail be allowed under the circumstances of these cases.[6]

Justices Hugo L. Black, Felix Frankfurter, William O. Douglas and Harold H. Burton dissented. Black wrote:

> The plain purpose of our bail Amendment was to make it impossible for any agency of Government, even the Congress, to authorize keeping people imprisoned a moment longer than was necessary to assure their attendance to answer whatever legal burden or obligation might thereafter be validly imposed upon them. . . .[7]

---

[1] *Hudson v. Parker*, 156 U.S. 277 at 285 (1895).
[2] *McKane v. Durston*, 153 U.S. 684 (1894).
[3] Federal Rules of Criminal Procedure, Rule 46(c).
[4] Congressional Quarterly, *Congress and the Nation*, Vol. II

(Washington, D.C.: Congressional Quarterly, 1969), p. 315-316.
[5] *Stack v. Boyle*, 342 U.S. 1 at 4-5, 6, 7 (1951).
[6] *Carlson v. Landon*, 342 U.S. 524 at 545-546 (1952).
[7] Id. at 557-558.

Where the court had rejected a 14th Amendment due process challenge to such laws in *McGautha*, it upheld an Eighth Amendment challenge in *Furman*.

The majority was composed of the five justices who had served under Chief Justice Warren: Justices Douglas, Brennan, Stewart, White and Marshall. Each wrote a separate opinion. Dissenting were the four members named to the court by President Richard M. Nixon — Chief Justice Warren E. Burger, Justices Harry A. Blackmun, Lewis F. Powell Jr. and William H. Rehnquist.

Justice Douglas wrote:

> Under these laws no standards govern the selection of the penalty. People live or die, dependent on the whim of one man or of 12....
>
> ...these discretionary statutes are unconstitutional in their operation. They are pregnant with discrimination and discrimination is an ingredient not compatible with the idea of equal protection of the laws that is implicit in the ban on "cruel and unusual" punishments.[12]

Justice Brennan found the death penalty "uniquely degrading to human dignity"[13] no matter how it was imposed:

> Death is an unusually severe and degrading punishment; there is a strong probability that it is inflicted arbitrarily; its rejection by contemporary society is virtually total; and there is no reason to believe that it serves any penal purpose more effectively than the less severe punishment of imprisonment. The function of these principles is to enable a court to determine whether a punishment comports with human dignity. Death, quite simply, does not.[14]

Justice Stewart found the method of the use of this penalty under existing law to be the critical point in his decision:

> These death sentences are cruel and unusual in the same way that being struck by lightning is cruel and unusual. For, of all the people convicted of rapes and murders in 1967 and 1968, many just as reprehensible as these, the petitioners are among a capriciously selected random handful upon whom the sentence of death has in fact been imposed ... the Eighth and Fourteenth Amendments cannot tolerate the infliction of a sentence of death under legal systems that permit this unique penalty to be so wantonly and so freakishly imposed.[15]

Justice White took a similar view:

> The imposition and execution of the death penalty are obviously cruel in the dictionary sense. But the penalty has not been considered cruel and unusual punishment in the constitutional sense because it was thought justified by the social ends it was deemed to serve. At the moment that it ceases realistically to further these purposes, however, the emerging question is whether its imposition ... would violate the Eighth Amendment. It is my view that it would, for its imposition would then be the pointless and needless extinction of life with only marginal contributions to any discernible social or public purposes....
>
> It is ... my judgment that this point has been reached with respect to capital punishment as it is presently administered under the statutes involved in these cases....[16]

Justice Marshall found the death penalty both "excessive" and "morally unacceptable":

> Assuming knowledge of all the facts presently available regarding capital punishment, the average citizen would, in my opinion, find it shocking to his conscience and sense of justice. For this reason alone capital punishment cannot stand.[17]

Chief Justice Burger, writing for the dissenting justices, based their position in large part on their view of the respective roles of judges and legislators:

> If legislatures come to doubt the efficacy of capital punishment, they can abolish it, either completely or on a selective basis. If new evidence persuades them that they have acted unwisely, they can reverse their field and reinstate the penalty to the extent it is thought warranted. An Eighth Amendment ruling by judges cannot be made with such flexibility or discriminating precision....[18]

State Reaction

The *Furman* decision effectively struck down all existing state death penalty laws. The court, however, seemed to leave open two avenues which states could follow in enacting new laws, limiting jury discretion sufficiently to ensure that the death penalty would be imposed in a less capricious manner.

States could, on one hand, remove almost all discretion from the decision by making death the mandatory punishment for certain crimes. Or the states could provide a two-stage procedure in capital cases — a trial at which the issue of guilt or innocence was determined and then, for those persons found guilty, a second proceeding at which evidence might be presented before the decision was reached on whether or not to impose a sentence of death.

Thirty-five states passed new death penalty statutes. Ten chose the mandatory route; the other 25, the two-stage procedure.

In 1976 both types of new laws were back before the Supreme Court. And the court again was asked to declare whether death in and of itself was a cruel and unusual — hence unconstitutional — punishment for any crime in the United States.

Death Penalty Upheld

In the case of *Gregg v. Georgia* and two companion cases, *Proffitt v. Florida* and *Jurek v. Texas*, the court refused to declare the death penalty unconstitutional in all circumstances. Only Justices Brennan and Marshall dissented from that holding.

Justice Potter Stewart set out the majority position on this central point:

> ...we are concerned here only with the imposition of capital punishment for the crime of murder, and when a life has been taken deliberately by the offender, we cannot say that the punishment is invariably disproportionate to the crime. It is an extreme sanction, suitable to the most extreme of crimes.[19]

So the court would not overrule the judgment of state legislatures and declare capital punishment *per se* unconstitutional. Justice Stewart continued:

> Considerations of federalism, as well as respect for the ability of a legislature to evaluate, in terms of its

particular State, the moral consensus concerning the death penalty and its social utility as a sanction, require us to conclude, in the absence of more convincing evidence, that the infliction of death as a punishment for murder is not without justification and thus is not unconstitutionally severe....

...We hold that the death penalty is not a form of punishment that may never be imposed, regardless of the circumstances of the offense, regardless of the character of the offender, and regardless of the procedure followed in reaching the decision to impose it.[20]

Justices Brennan and Marshall dissented. Brennan argued that death was now an uncivilized and unconstitutional punishment, writing that the court "inescapably has the duty, as the ultimate arbiter of the meaning of our Constitution, to say whether, when individuals condemned to death stand before our Bar, "moral concepts" require us to hold that the law has progressed to the point where we should declare that the punishment of death, like punishments on the rack, the screw and the wheel, is no longer morally tolerable in our civilized society...."[21]

Justice Marshall found death an excessive, shocking, and unjust punishment in all cases, and would declare it invariably cruel and unusual punishment, forbidden by the Eighth Amendment.

Two-Stage Procedure Valid. The court in *Gregg,* *Jurek* and *Proffitt* also upheld as constitutional the new two-stage procedure adopted by Georgia, Florida, Texas and 22 other states for imposing the death sentence.

This procedure, wrote Justice Stewart, met the objections which had caused the court in *Furman* to invalidate the then-existing state laws:

The basic concern of *Furman* centered on those defendants who were being condemned to death capriciously and arbitrarily. Under the procedures before the Court in that case, sentencing authorities were not directed to give attention to the nature or circumstances of the crime committed or to the character or record of the defendant. Left unguided, juries imposed the death sentence in a way that could only be called freakish. The new ... sentencing procedures, by contrast, focus the jury's attention on the particularized nature of the crime and the particularized characteristics of the individual defendant. While the jury is permitted to consider any aggravating or mitigating circumstances, it must find and identify at least one statutory aggravating factor before it may impose a penalty of death. In this way the jury's discretion is channeled. No longer can a jury wantonly and freakishly impose the death sentence; it is always circumscribed by the legislative guidelines....[22]

Mandatory Death Penalty Invalid. In two other cases decided the same day — July 2, 1976 — the court struck down state laws which made death the mandatory penalty for first-degree murder. This ruling came in the cases of *Woodson v. North Carolina* and *Roberts v. Louisiana.*[23]

The court divided 5-4 in these cases; Justices Brennan and Marshall became part of the majority with Justices Stewart, Powell and John Paul Stevens. Dissenting were Chief Justice Burger, Justices Blackmun, White and Rehnquist.

The court majority held that mandatory death penalty statutes "simply papered over the problem of unguided and unchecked jury discretion" and were constitutionally unsatisfactory because they failed to allow room for consideration of the individual defendant and the particular crime.[24]

The majority refused to approve "[a] process that accords no significance to relevant facets of the character and record of the individual offender or the circumstances of the particular offense," finding that such a process "excludes from consideration in fixing the ultimate punishment of death the possibility of compassionate or mitigating factors stemming from the diverse frailties of humankind."[25]

The majority opinion concluded:

...we believe that in capital cases the fundamental respect for humanity underlying the Eighth Amendment ... requires consideration of the character and record of the individual offender and the circumstances of the particular offense as a constitutionally indispensable part of the process of inflicting the penalty of death.[26]

The following year, the court used similar reasoning in striking down a state law which made death the mandatory sentence for anyone convicted of the first-degree murder of a police officer.[27]

A Continuing Review

Even after its 1976 rulings, the court continued to face a number of questions concerning cruel and unusual punishment and the death penalty.

In 1977, in the case of *Coker v. Georgia,* the court held that death was an excessive penalty for the crime of rape, striking down state laws which made rape a capital crime.[28]

And in 1978 the court invalidated Ohio's death penalty law for murder because it limited too strictly the sort of mitigating factors which could be considered in the decision whether or not to impose the death penalty. Chief Justice Burger wrote the opinion for the court in the cases of *Lockett v. Ohio, Bell v. Ohio.* Only Justice Rehnquist dissented.[29]

Footnotes

[1] *Weems v. United States,* 217 U.S. 349 (1910).
[2] *Trop v. Dulles,* 356 U.S. 86 at 99 (1958).
[3] Id. at 99-101.
[4] *O'Neil v. Vermont,* 144 U.S. 323 (1892).
[5] *Louisiana ex. rel. Francis v. Resweber,* 329 U.S. 459 (1947).
[6] Id. at 464.
[7] *Robinson v. California,* 370 U.S. 660 at 666, 667 (1962).
[8] *Powell v. Texas,* 392 U.S. 514 at 532 (1968).
[9] *Witherspoon v. Illinois,* 391 U.S. 510 at 520-521 (1968).
[10] *McGautha v. California,* 402 U.S. 183 at 207 (1971).

[11] *Furman v. Georgia, Jackson v. Georgia, Branch v. Texas,* 408 U.S. 238 (1972).
[12] Id. at 253, 256-257.
[13] Id. at 291.
[14] Id. at 305.
[15] Id. at 309-310.
[16] Id. at 312-313.
[17] Id. at 369.
[18] Id. at 404.
[19] *Gregg v. Georgia,* 428 U.S. 153 at 187 (1976); *Proffitt v. Florida,* 428 U.S. 325 (1976); *Jurek v. Texas,* 428 U.S. 262 (1976).

[20] *Gregg v. Georgia*, 428 U.S. 153 at 186-187 (1976).
[21] Id. at 229.
[22] Id. at 206-207.
[23] *Woodson v. North Carolina*, 428 U.S. 280 (1976); *Roberts v. Louisiana*, 428 U.S. 325 (1976).
[24] *Woodson v. North Carolina*, 428 U.S. 280 at 302 (1976).

[25] Id. at 304.
[26] Id.
[27] *Roberts v. Louisiana*, 431 U.S. 633 (1977).
[28] *Coker v. Georgia*, 433 U.S. 583 (1977).
[29] *Lockett v. Ohio*, 438 U.S. 586 (1978); *Bell v. Ohio*, 438 U.S. 637 (1978).

Selected Bibliography

Allen, Francis A. "Federalism and the Fourth Amendment: A Requiem for *Wolf*," *Supreme Court Review, 1961*. Chicago: University of Chicago Press, 1961.

Amsterdam, Anthony. "Perspectives on the Fourth Amendment," 58 *Minnesota Law Review* (1974):349.

Barnett, Edward L. Jr. "Personal Rights, Property Rights and the Fourth Amendment," *Supreme Court Review, 1960*. Chicago: University of Chicago Press, 1960.

Beaney, William M. "The Constitutional Right to Privacy in the Supreme Court," *Supreme Court Review, 1962*. Chicago: University of Chicago Press, 1962.

————. *The Right to Counsel in American Courts*. Ann Arbor: University of Michigan Press, 1955.

Black, Charles L. *Capital Punishment: The Inevitability of Caprice and Mistake*. New York: W. W. Norton & Co., 1974.

Emerson, Thomas I., and Haber, David. *Political and Civil Rights in the United States*. 2d ed., 2 vols. Buffalo: Dennis, 1958.

Fellman, David. *The Defendant's Rights*. New York: Holt, Rinehart & Winston, 1958.

Fingarette, Herbert. "Addiction and Criminal Responsibility," 84 *Yale Law Journal* (1975):413.

Graham, Fred P. *The Self-Inflicted Wound*. New York: Macmillan Publishing Co., 1970.

Green, John Raeburn. "The Bill of Rights, the Fourteenth Amendment and the Supreme Court," 46 *Michigan Law Review* (1948):869.

————. "The Supreme Court, the Bill of Rights and the States," 97 *University of Pennsylvania Law Review* (1949):608.

Griswold, Erwin N. *Search and Seizure: A Dilemma of the Supreme Court*. Lincoln: University of Nebraska Press, 1975.

————. *The Fifth Amendment Today*. Cambridge, Mass.: Harvard University Press, 1955.

Hall, Livingston; Kamisar, Yale; LaFave, Wayne R.; and Israel, Jerrold H. *Modern Criminal Procedure*. St. Paul: West Publishing Co., 1969.

Israel, Jerrold H. "*Gideon v. Wainwright*: The Art of Overruling," *Supreme Court Review, 1963*. Chicago. University of Chicago Press, 1963.

Kalven, Harry A. Jr., and Zeisel, Hans. *The American Jury*. Boston: Little, Brown & Co., 1966.

Kaplan, John. "The Limits of the Exclusionary Rule," 26 *Stanford Law Review* (1974):1027.

LaFave, Wayne R. " 'Case-by-Case Adjudication' versus 'Standardized Procedures': The *Robinson* Dilemma," *Supreme Court Review, 1974*. Chicago: University of Chicago Press, 1974.

Landynski, Jacob W. *Searches and Seizures and the Supreme Court*. Baltimore: Johns Hopkins University Press, 1966.

Levy, Leonard W. *Against the Law: The Nixon Court and Criminal Justice*. New York: Harper & Row, 1974.

————. *Origins of the Fifth Amendment*. New York: Oxford University Press, 1968.

Lewis, Anthony. *Gideon's Trumpet*. New York: Random House, 1964.

Mason, Alpheus T., and Beaney, William M. *American Constitutional Law*. 6th ed. Englewood Cliffs, N.J.: Prentice-Hall, 1978.

Meltsnev, Michael. *Cruel and Unusual Punishment*. New York: Random House, 1973.

Murphy, Patrick T. *Our Kindly Parent The State: The Juvenile Justice System and How It Works*. New York: Viking Press, 1973.

Oaks, Dallin. "Studying the Exclusionary Rule in Searches and Seizures," 37 *University of Chicago Law Review* (1970):665.

Pritchett, C. Herman. *The American Constitution*. 3d ed. New York: McGraw-Hill Book Co., 1977.

Rossum, Ralph A. "New Rights and Old Wrongs: The Supreme Court and the Problem of Retroactivity," 23 *Emory Law Journal* (1974):381.

White, James B. "The Fourth Amendment as a Way of Talking About People: A Study of *Robinson* and *Matlock*," *Supreme Court Review, 1974*. Chicago: University of Chicago Press, 1974.

EQUAL RIGHTS

Introduction 583

Racial Equality 587

Aliens and Equal Protection 625

Sex Discrimination and Legal Equality 631

Poverty and Equal Protection 641

Equal Rights

The 14th Amendment to the Constitution forbids any state to "deny any person within its jurisdiction the equal protection of the laws." Upholding that right of equal protection, the Supreme Court in 1954 struck down state laws segregating blacks from whites in public schools, touching off a civil rights revolution which has widened to include other forms of discrimination and which has not yet reached its conclusion.

The guarantee of equal protection now prohibits arbitrary discrimination against women and illegitimate children, aliens and the poor. Equal protection may be violated by laws that restrict a person's right to vote, to travel from state to state or to marry whomever he or she pleases. The equal protection clause has become both the weapon securing and the armor safeguarding the civil rights of classes of people who have suffered or might otherwise become victims of invidious and arbitrary discrimination.

In the later decades of the 20th century, the equal protection clause has become so well established as a shield against discrimination that it may be forgotten that this interpretation of the clause is a modern, and continuing, development. The 14th Amendment, ratified in 1868, was intended primarily to prevent discrimination against the blacks whose citizenship it confirmed. But the Supreme Court soon interpreted it into a useless tool for this purpose. Segregation of the races became an apparently unassailable fact of life in the late 19th and 20th centuries, while the equal protection clause was invoked primarily — although not often successfully — against allegedly unfair and unequal taxation and regulation of economic and commercial affairs. Not until the late 1930s did the clause begin to protect those persons originally intended as its primary beneficiaries.

The Measure of Discrimination

Whether applied to civil rights or property rights, the equal protection clause has never been interpreted by the court to mean that a law must treat all classes it affects with absolute equality.

Laws by their very nature distinguish between categories of people, classes of property and kinds of actions. For the most part, such distinctions are desirable, even necessary in an organized society. But some may be capricious or malicious and thereby deny equal protection to the classi-

fied group. Thus the question a court must answer whenever a law is challenged as a violation of equal protection is not whether a classification may be made but whether the classification that is made is permissible.

Traditional Standard

The first standard developed by the Supreme Court for measuring a particular classification against the equal protection guarantee grew largely out of its review of state tax and economic regulation. In this area the court during the first third of the 20th century deferred more often than not to the judgment of the states.

Not surprisingly, its standard for review of such alleged violations was minimal. The court was satisfied that a classification was valid if a state could show that it had a reasonable basis. This traditional standard for testing the validity of classifications — still pertinent to appropriate cases today — was summarized by the court in a 1911 decision:

> The equal protection clause of the Fourteenth Amendment does not take from the State the power to classify in the adoption of police laws, but admits of the exercise of a wide scope of discretion in that regard, and avoids what is done only when it is without any reasonable basis and is therefore purely arbitrary....
>
> A classification having some reasonable basis does not offend against the clause merely because it is not made with mathematical nicety or because in practice it results in some inequality....
>
> When the classification in such a law is called in question, if any state of facts reasonably can be conceived that would sustain it, the existence of that state of facts at the time the law was enacted must be assumed....
>
> One who assails the classification in such a law must carry the burden of showing that it does not rest upon any reasonable basis, but is essentially arbitrary. [1]

Invoking only this permissive standard, the court upheld few challenges to laws on equal protection grounds. As the court itself noted in 1927, the clause had become no more than "the usual last resort of constitutional arguments." [2]

Modern Standard

The court's shift in focus from property rights to individual rights in the late 1930s led it to develop a more probing standard for examining charges of denial of equal protection. Under this so-called active standard, classifications that are "inherently suspect" or that affect what the court considers to be fundamental rights or interests require a greater degree of justification for their existence than simple rationality. A state must prove not only that it has a compelling governmental interest for making the challenged classification, but also that it can achieve that interest in no other way.

The development of this modern standard came in separate stages. In 1944 the court declared race to be a suspect category requiring this heightened judicial scrutiny. But the court then did not expressly apply this standard in its most important decision on racial discrimination, the 1954 ruling striking down state-imposed school segregation as a violation of equal protection. Classifications by alienage came in for heightened review as early as 1948, but not until 1971 did the court explicitly describe alienage as a suspect category.

As early as 1942, the court indicated that the equal protection clause protected all individuals from state deprivation of certain fundamental rights. But 20 years passed before the court began to elaborate on this premise.

Much of the development of this modern equal protection standard has occurred since 1964. In that year Congress passed the 1964 Civil Rights Act, which prohibited discrimination on the grounds of race, color, national origin or religion in most privately-owned public accommodations. It also prohibited job discrimination on these grounds and on the basis of sex.

In 1965 passage of the Voting Rights Act authorized federal action to enforce the rights of blacks to vote. In 1968 Congress barred discrimination in the sale and rental of most housing.

As a result of these federal laws, minorities and other groups traditionally victimized by discrimination brought more and more suits charging a denial of equal protection. In reviewing these cases, the court has moved further and further from the traditional "reasonable basis" standard.

Suspect Categories

Race and alienage are the only two categories to which the Supreme Court has accorded "suspect" status.

Racial Equality

The court first declared race a suspect category in 1944. The case was *Korematsu v. United States* and involved a U.S. citizen of Japanese descent who defied a World War II military order requiring all persons of Japanese descent living on the West Coast to report to relocation centers. The court ruled against Korematsu and held that the wartime emergency necessitated the unusual detention. But in so deciding, it announced that it would give classifications by race increased attention:

It should be noted . . . that all legal restrictions which curtail the civil rights of a single racial group are immediately suspect. That is not to say that all such restrictions are unconstitutional. It is to say that courts must subject them to the most rigid scrutiny. Pressing

public necessity may sometimes justify the existence of such restrictions; racial antagonism never can. [3]

Ten years later, its 1954 school desegregation decisions made abundantly clear the meaning of "rigid scrutiny."

But it was not until 1967 that the court expressly acknowledged that all racial classifications were "inherently suspect." This rather anticlimactic declaration came in a case in which the court struck down a Virginia statute which made it a crime for residents to enter into interracial marriages. *(Racial equality, p. 587)*

Alienage

As early as 1886, the court held that the 14th Amendment protected aliens as well as citizens. But during the next 60 years, the court, applying the traditional standard of review, found most statutes challenged as discriminating against aliens were in fact based on some reasonable — and therefore permissible — objective.

In 1948 the court began to require more than simple rationality to justify such laws. But not until 1971 did the court explicitly acknowledge that such classifications were inherently suspect, requiring a compelling interest as justification.

"Aliens as a class are a prime example of a 'discrete and insular' minority . . . for whom . . . heightened judicial solicitude is appropriate," said the court.[4]

However, because the Constitution gives Congress exclusive authority over naturalization and, by extension, immigration, the Court has been reluctant to judge federal alienage classification laws as strictly as similar state laws. *(Alienage, p. 625)*

Sex Discrimination

All the modern cases challenging discrimination on the basis of sex have occurred since 1969. The court has applied the traditional standard of review to the majority of them, and more often than not found that the state had a rational basis to justify treating women differently from men.

In one line of decisions, however, the court has held that classifications by sex were impermissible. On the grounds of administrative efficiency, the statutes struck down in these cases presumed that all men behaved in one way and all women in another, failing to allow for any variation from the unproved assumption. The court found such presumptions arbitrary, too broad and unjustified by mere administrative convenience.

In one of its more recent cases, a slim majority of the court adopted a test that fell between the "reasonable basis" standard and the "compelling governmental interest" test. This standard requires the state to show that its sex-based classification was necessary to achieve some *"important* governmental objective." [5]

Job Discrimination

The court has upheld both the 1964 Civil Rights Act ban on job discrimination on the grounds of sex and the 1963 Equal Pay Act requiring that men and women be paid the same for the same work.

But the court has steadily refused to describe differential treatment of pregnant women as sex discrimination. Such a classification is based not on gender but on physical condition, a majority of the court has held, ruling that classification by physical condition did not violate either the equal protection clause or the 1964 Civil Rights Act. *(Sex discrimination, p. 631)*

Poverty and Illegitimacy

The court has refused to apply the compelling interest standard to test laws that discriminate against illegitimate children and the poor. Nonetheless, it has treated most cases involving classification by legitimacy with more than minimal scrutiny, striking down several laws distinguishing illegitimate children from their legitimate siblings on the grounds that such classifications were arbitrary and archaic. The court has found discrimination against the poor unconstitutional when it deprives the indigent of a fundamental right or interest. But the court has not applied the equal protection clause to protect the poverty-stricken from deprivation of rights not considered "fundamental."

Fundamental Interests

The court first articulated its "fundamental interest" standard in the 1942 case of *Skinner v. Oklahoma*. The justices were unanimous as they struck down an Oklahoma statute that authorized sterilization of criminals who had committed two felonies "involving moral turpitude:"

> ...We are dealing here with legislation which involves one of the basic civil rights of man. Marriage and procreation are fundamental to the very existence and survival of the race. The power to sterilize, if exercised, may have subtle, far-reaching and devastating effects. In evil or reckless hands it can cause races or types which are inimical to the dominant group to wither and disappear. There is no redemption for the individual whom the law touches.... He is forever deprived of a basic liberty. We mention these matters ... merely in emphasis of our view that strict scrutiny of the classification which a State makes in a sterilization law is essential, lest unwittingly or otherwise invidious discriminations are made against groups or types of individuals in violation of the constitutional guaranty of just and equal laws. [6]

Voting Rights

The fundamental interest doctrine next emerged in 1964, when the court held that the equal protection guarantee required states to create electoral districts each of which had substantially the same number of voters. In the case of *Reynolds v. Sims*, the court wrote:

> Undoubtedly, the right of suffrage is a fundamental matter in a free and democratic society. Especially since the right to exercise the franchise in a free and unimpaired manner is preservative of other basic civil and political rights, any alleged infringement of the right of citizens to vote must be carefully and meticulously scrutinized. [7]

In 1969, the court elaborated:

> ...[I]f a challenged state statute grants the right to vote to some *bona fide* residents of requisite age and citizenship and denies the franchise to others, the Court must determine whether the exclusions are necessary to promote a compelling state interest.
>
> ...[T]he deference usually given to the judgment of legislators does not extend to decisions concerning which resident citizens may participate in the election of legislators and other public officials.... [W]hen we are reviewing statutes which deny some residents the right to vote, the general presumption of constitution-

Federal Equal Protection

Nowhere does the Constitution explicitly require the federal government to ensure equal protection of its laws against arbitrary discrimination. The Supreme Court, however, has found this requirement implicit in the Fifth Amendment's guarantee of due process of law. The court explained this finding in the 1954 case of *Bolling v. Sharpe* in which it struck down the federal government's requirement that black and white pupils in the District of Columbia attend separate schools:

> ...The Fifth Amendment ... does not contain an equal protection clause as does the Fourteenth Amendment which applies only to the states. But the concepts of equal protection and due process, both stemming from our American ideal of fairness, are not mutually exclusive. The "equal protection of the law" is a more explicit safeguard of prohibited unfairness than "due process of law," and, therefore, we do not imply that the two are always interchangeable phrases. But, as this Court has recognized, discrimination may be so unjustifiable as to be violative of due process. (347 U.S. 483 at 499, 1954.)

The court has reaffirmed this finding in several later cases: *Weinberger v. Wiesenfeld*, 420 U.S. 636 at 638, note 2 (1975); *Buckley v. Valeo*, 424 U.S. 1 at 93 (1976); *Hampton v. Mow Sun Wong*, 426 U.S. 88 at 100 (1976); *Passman v. Davis*, (1979).

ality afforded state statutes and the traditional approval given state classifications if the Court can conceive of a "rational basis" for the distinctions made are not applicable. [8]

Applying this stricter standard, the court has struck down a number of statutes because they restricted the right to vote. States have no compelling reason to deny the right to vote to persons simply because they have not resided in the state for a certain period of time, or because they are too poor to pay a poll tax. Filing fees that prevent poor candidates from seeking office also are unconstitutional, as are statutes that keep off the ballot all candidates except those belonging to the two major political parties. *(Voting participation cases, p. 643)*

Right to Travel

Durational residency requirements also violate another fundamental interest guarded by the equal protection clause — the right to travel unrestricted from state to state. The court has debated for several decades the source of this right, sometimes finding it in the interstate commerce clause of Article I of the Constitution, at other times in the privileges and immunities clause of the 14th Amendment. In a 1966 decision the court abandoned the debate:

> ...The constitutional right to travel from one State to another ... occupies a position fundamental to the concept of our Federal Union. It is a right that has been firmly established and repeatedly recognized.... Although there have been recurring differences in emphasis within the Court as to the source of the constitutional right of interstate travel, there is no

need here to canvass those differences further. All have agreed that the right exists. [9]

Using this reasoning, the court in 1969 declared requirements that persons live in a state for a certain period of time before becoming eligible for welfare benefits to be a violation of equal protection and thus unconstitutional. The court said such requirements unconstitutionally restricted the poor in the exercise of their right to travel interstate.

Access to Justice

The Supreme Court has designated one other such matter a fundamental right. That right — access to justice — has been foreclosed at times to poor people who could not afford the fees required either to file suit or hire an attorney, or pay for a transcript to prepare an appeal. In many of these instances, the court has held that the fee requirement impermissibly violated the indigent's guarantee of due process as well as equal protection of the laws. *(Access to justice, p. 641)*

Doctrine Criticized

The fundamental interest doctrine has been criticized from the bench, first by Justice John Marshall Harlan and then by Justice William H. Rehnquist, who replaced Har-

lan on the bench. Both men contended that the court exceeds its power when it selects certain rights and interests for special protection. Harlan wrote in 1969:

> . . .[W]hen a statute affects only matters not mentioned in the Federal Constitution and is not arbitrary or irrational, I must reiterate that I know of nothing which entitles this Court to pick out particular human activities, characterize them as "fundamental," and give them added protection under an unusually stringent equal protection test. [10]

Rehnquist added in 1972 that "[t]his body of doctrine created by the Court can only be described as a judicial superstructure, awkwardly engrafted upon the Constitution itself. " [11]

Since 1969 the court has refused to classify any other right or interest as fundamental. Although it hinted in 1969 that it might place "food, shelter and other necessities of life" in the fundamental-right category, the court in 1972 held that the assurance of adequate housing was not a fundamental interest. [12] And in 1973 a majority of the court held that the right to an education was neither explicitly nor implicitly guaranteed by the Constitution. The majority added that it was "not the province of this Court to create substantive constitutional rights in the name of guaranteeing equal protection of the laws." [13]

Footnotes

[1] *Lindsley v. Natural Carbonic Gas Co.* 220 U.S. 61 at 78-79 (1911); see also *McGowan v. Maryland*, 366 U.S. 420 (1961); *Williamson v. Lee Optical Co.*, 348 U.S. 483 (1955); *Kotch v. Board of River Pilot Commissioners*, 330 U.S. 552 (1947); *Royster Guano Co. v. Virginia*, 253 U.S. 412 (1920).
[2] *Buck v. Bell*, 274 U.S. 200 at 208 (1927).
[3] *Korematsu v. United States*, 323 U.S. 214 at 216 (1944).
[4] *Graham v. Richardson*, 403 U.S. 365 at 372 (1971).
[5] *Craig v. Boren*, 429 U.S. 190 at 197 (1976).
[6] *Skinner v. Oklahoma*, 316 U.S. 535 at 541 (1942).

[7] *Reynolds v. Sims*, 377 U.S. 533 at 561-62 (1964).
[8] *Kramer v. Union Free School District*, 395 U.S. 621 at 627-28 (1969).
[9] *United States v. Guest*, 383 U.S. 745 at 757, 759 (1966).
[10] *Shapiro v. Thompson*, 394 U.S. 618 at 662 (1969).
[11] *Weber v. Aetna Casualty & Surety Co.*, 406 U.S. 164 at 179 (1972).
[12] *Shapiro v. Thompson*, 394 U.S. 618 at 627 (1969); *Lindsey v. Normet*, 405 U.S. 56 (1972).
[13] *San Antonio Independent School District v. Rodriguez*, 411 U.S. 1 at 33 (1973).

Racial Equality

The 14th Amendment, said the Supreme Court in 1880,

> ...was designed to assure to the colored race the enjoyment of all the civil rights that under the law are enjoyed by white persons, and to give to that race the protection of the general government, in that enjoyment, whenever it should be denied by the States. It not only gave citizenship and the privileges of citizenship to persons of color, but it denied to any State the power to withhold from them the equal protection of the laws, and authorized Congress to enforce its provisions. . . .[1]

But another 75 years would pass before black people would receive any substantial benefit from the 14th Amendment's protections. Even as the court spoke, southern states had begun to separate white from black in what would result in almost complete social, legal and political segregation of the two races.

The court itself played a role in creating the climate that allowed segregation to flourish. In its first actions regarding blacks after the Civil War, the court admitted a black attorney to the Supreme Court bar and ruled that a black woman could sue for damages a railroad company that had forcibly removed her from a train after she refused to sit in the "colored" car.[2]

A Narrowed Protection

But in the 1873 *Slaughterhouse Cases*, the court divided 5-4 in ruling that citizens held two distinct types of citizenship, one federal and one state. The 14th Amendment, the majority held, protected a person only from state infringement on such privileges and immunities of national citizenship as the right to petition the federal government and the right to vote in federal elections. The privileges and immunities conferred by citizenship in a state were outside federal protection. This decision, intact today, divested the privileges and immunities clause of any substantive protection it might have afforded citizens of either race.[3] *(Details of case, p. 339)*

In the *Slaughterhouse* opinion, the majority characterized the amendment's equal protection clause as primarily of use to protect blacks from unjust discrimination. In deciding the 1880 case of *Strauder v. West Virginia*, the court utilized the clause to strike down a state law that barred blacks from jury service.

The Civil Rights Cases

Three years later, however, the court significantly narrowed the protection of the clause for blacks. In the 1883 *Civil Rights Cases*, the court nullified an 1875 federal law that gave all persons regardless of color "the full and equal enjoyment" of public transportation, inns, theaters and "other places of public amusement."[4] The court held that the 14th Amendment prohibited only state-imposed discrimination, and not that imposed by individuals acting privately. Congress therefore had overstepped its authority when it sought to stop private businessmen from discriminating against blacks. Furthermore, the court said, the amendment only empowered Congress to remedy acts of state discrimination; Congress could not enact a general law in anticipation of state discriminatory actions.

By 1883, the fervor of Reconstruction had worn thin. As one historian wrote, "Other than Negroes and their faithful friends, the people were tired of giving special protection to the former slaves. It was felt to be time for the return to power of the dominant factions in the several communities."[5]

Against this background, the decision in the *Civil Rights Cases* had particular significance. Political scientist Alan F. Westin attributed to it two primary effects:

> . . .[F]irst, it destroyed the delicate balance of federal guarantee, Negro protest and private enlightenment which was producing a steadily widening area of peacefully integrated public facilities in the North and South during the 1870s and early 1880s. Second, it had an immediate and profound effect on national and state politics as they related to the Negro. By denying Congress power to protect the Negro's rights to equal treatment, the Supreme Court wiped the issue of civil rights from the Republican party's agenda of national responsibility. At the same time, those Southern political leaders who saw anti-Negro politics as the most promising avenue to power could now rally the "poor whites" to the banner of segregation.[6]

'Separate But Equal'

Thirteen years later the Supreme Court in 1896 sanctioned the "separate but equal" doctrine developed to justify state-imposed racial segregation. In its decision in the case of *Plessy v. Ferguson*, a majority of the court held that so long as the facilities provided blacks were equal to those provided whites, state laws requiring segregation did not violate the equal protection or due process clauses of the 14th Amendment. Nor did the court view separation of the races as pinning on blacks a badge of slavery in violation of the 13th Amendment. [7]

In the wake of this decision, state-ordered segregation invaded almost every aspect of daily life in the former Confederate states. Blacks throughout the South were required to use separate streetcars, waiting rooms, toilets and water fountains. They attended different schools and were segregated in parks and theaters, mental hospitals and prisons. At the same time, blacks were almost completely disenfranchised in those states by such devices as the poll tax, property and literacy tests and the white primary. *(Details of voting rights cases, p. 477)*

Although there was comparatively little official segregation in northern and western states, whites there generally regarded blacks as inferiors and there was little intermingling of the two races.

When the United States entered its brief but intense period of imperialism at the end of the 19th century, bringing some eight million non-whites under its domination, northern attitudes grew steadily more sympathetic to the racist views of southern whites.

As the U.S. Civil Rights Commission wrote in understatement: at the end of the 19th century, the "very concept of civil rights seemed to have passed out of existence, and the prospects for the future were not encouraging." [8]

World War I

During the first third of the 20th century, segregation by law appeared firmly entrenched, but the events that would lead to its demise were taking shape. The National Association for the Advancement of Colored People (NAACP), which would lead the court fight to end racial discrimination, was founded in 1909; the National Urban League in 1911. World War I contributed markedly to rising black aspirations.

Many of the 360,000 blacks who fought to make the world safe for democracy began to wonder when they might begin to enjoy democracy's benefits. The Great War also spurred a black migration to the north where blacks found defense industry work.

Racial tension escalated. In the first year after the war concluded, more than 70 blacks were lynched. The Ku Klux Klan enjoyed revived popularity in the North and South. In 1919 bloody race riots broke out in 25 cities across the nation. Historian John Hope Franklin described this time as "the greatest period of interracial strife the nation had ever witnessed." [9]

In three cases concerning segregation in schools the Supreme Court refused to review the "separate but equal" doctrine, although in 1914 it did strike down a state law because it did not provide blacks with exactly the same train accommodations it provided whites.

In 1917 the court struck down a municipal ordinance that prohibited blacks from living on the same streets as whites. This decision did not end residential segregation, however, because private restrictive covenants quickly replaced the illegal ordinances. These covenants, attached to the deed or title to property, forbade the white owner to sell to blacks. The Supreme Court upheld the covenants in 1926, reiterating its view that the 14th Amendment did not reach private discriminatory actions.

The Depression and World War II

Blacks as a group were among the most severely burdened by the Great Depression of the 1930s. Although many blacks had left the Republican Party to vote for Woodrow Wilson in 1912, only to be disillusioned when he did little to advance their civil rights, many thousands more swung their support to Franklin Delano Roosevelt in the 1936 and 1940 elections. The Democratic administration did try to improve the economic condition of both races, but segregation continued unabated. Blacks nonetheless had won recognition as a political power, and by the 1940s militant individuals and organized groups demanding an end to segregation were beginning to make themselves heard.

These demands steadily gained adherents as the ironies of World War II became increasingly apparent. The inconsistency of sending black and white soldiers to fight against Germany's vile racial policies while continuing to practice racial segregation at home became too obvious to ignore.

The Cold War further intensified this paradox. Communist countries pointed to American racial policies in an effort to undermine the appeal of the democratic system that the United States was attempting to persuade the rest of the world to adopt. No reasonable person could deny the irony, as C. Vann Woodward observed, of the United States' competing with the Soviet Union for the friendship of the yellow races of the Orient and the black races of Africa while continuing to treat members of both those races in the United States as second-class citizens.

Against this setting the Supreme Court began to take a closer look at the laws that discriminated on the basis of race.

Shift in Focus

From the end of the Civil War until 1937, the Supreme Court's primary concern was the protection of business from what it considered excessive regulation by the federal government. When these *laissez-faire* views jeopardized Roosevelt's New Deal programs, the president threatened in 1937 to "pack" the court with additional justices who would construe the Constitution to support his economic policies.

The court responded by relaxing its vigilant attitude toward economic regulation and shifting its focus to individual rights and liberties.

A harbinger of this shift came in a 1938 footnote to an otherwise routine decision. In that note, Justice Harlan Fiske Stone implied that the court might soon be required to decide whether

> ... statutes directed at particular religions, ... or national ... or racial minorities, ... [or] whether prejudice against discrete and insular minorities may be a special condition, which tends seriously to curtail the operation of those political processes ordinarily to be relied upon to protect minorities and which may call for a correspondingly more searching judicial inquiry. [10] *(Text of footnote, box, p. 379)*

In the same year, the court ruled that the "separate but equal" rule required a state to provide law schools for blacks if it provided them for whites, even though there might be only a single black law student. The court also upheld the right of blacks to picket an employer to persuade him to hire more black workers.

Closer Scrutiny

In 1944, six years after Stone's footnote comment, the court announced that it would give closer scrutiny to laws that treated one race differently from another, upholding such distinctions only if they were justified by a pressing governmental need. In that same year, the court held it unconstitutional for states to exclude black voters from primary elections and, in the first modern decision on job discrimination, the court ruled in favor of black railroad workers.

In 1948 the court took another look at restrictive covenants, ruling that although the 14th Amendment did not prohibit them, it did prohibit states from enforcing them. With this decision, the court began its expansion of the definition of state action covered by the 14th Amendment to include private discriminatory action promoted in any way by official state action, even if the state action itself was not discriminatory.

But the decisions that portended the most for the future of black civil rights dealt with the question of whether separate facilities could be equal.

On June 5, 1950, the court held first that Texas violated the equal protection clause because its black state law school was not the equivalent of the white school either in tangible aspects — such as the number of books in the library — or in intangible aspects such as the prestige of its faculty and alumni. In a second case decided the same day, the court ruled that Oklahoma violated the equal protection guarantee when it separated a black from his white colleagues in classes, the library and the cafeteria.

Separate, Not Equal

Four years later in the public school desegregation cases, familiarly known as *Brown v. Board of Education*, the unanimous court declared that separation of the races in public schools was "inherently unequal." [11] After sixty years, the *Plessy* doctrine — and a way of life for an entire section of the nation — had been officially renounced.

The *Brown* decisions, wrote Professor G. Theodore Mitau,

> . . .acknowledged judicially what many people had known or felt for a long time: Segregation was morally indefensible, socially irrational and politically undemocratic. It perpetuated a racial myth which imprisoned American values at home and weakened America's leadership abroad. Equally important to many, it defiled this country's claim to stand as a world model of freedom and human dignity in defense of which whites and Negroes fought side by side in all of this nation's major wars. [12]

In 1955 the court issued guidelines directing school officials to desegregate schools with "all deliberate speed." Although many states complied with the court order, many others embarked on programs of "massive resistance" in defiance of the Supreme Court order.

Arkansas' governor in 1958 called out the state's national guard to prevent black students from entering a formerly all-white high school in Little Rock. In extraordinary session, the Supreme Court demanded unanimously that the state cease its resistance and that the students be admitted to the school.

For 10 years after the *Brown* decision, however, the court left it to lower courts to implement school desegrega-

tion. The pace was slow: by 1964 less than 2 percent of black pupils in the former Confederate states were attending desegregated schools. [13]

During this same decade, however, the court frequently cited the *Brown* decision as precedent for rulings striking down other forms of segregation throughout the South, in parks and beaches, traffic courts and theaters, railroad cars and bus terminals.

Civil Rights Revolution

These decisions spurred a revolution in civil rights. Blacks were no longer willing to let whites deny them their rights. Beginning in 1957 with a Montgomery, Ala., bus boycott led by Dr. Martin Luther King Jr., blacks organized to protest racial segregation and discrimination in jobs, housing and public accommodations. The student sit-ins and "Freedom Rides" of the early 1960s sensitized the rest of the nation to the black dilemma; the violence with which whites frequently countered black demonstrations drew the nation's sympathy.

The year that marked the 100th anniversary of the Emancipation Proclamation was particularly turbulent. In May 1963, police loosed dogs and turned high-pressure fire hoses on demonstrators in Birmingham, Ala., provoking sympathy protests in several other cities. In August, 200,000 blacks and whites marched peacefully in Washington, D.C., to present black demands for equal treatment before Congress, the president and a closely-watching country. One month later, a bomb thrown into a black church in Birmingham killed four little girls. On Nov. 22, an assassin shot and killed President John F. Kennedy, an unequivocal advocate of civil rights.

Hope, frustration and outrage impelled Congress in 1964 to approve the most comprehensive civil rights act since Reconstruction. It barred discrimination in most public accommodations, prohibited job discrimination on the basis of race and established a procedure for withholding federal funds from any program, including schools, that continued to discriminate against blacks.

'Not Enough Speed'

That year also marked the end of the court's silence on continuing questions of school desegregation. There has been "too much deliberation and not enough speed" in desegregating public schools, the court declared, holding that a county could not close its schools to avoid desegregating them. Later in the year, the court upheld that section of the 1964 Civil Rights Acts barring racial discrimination in most private accommodations. In 1966 the court upheld Congress' 1965 Voting Rights Act.

In 1968 the court reinterpreted an 1866 civil rights law as barring private individuals from refusing to sell their homes to persons of a different race.

The court in 1968 also declared that state and school officials must do more than simply end segregation, and that they had a duty to take affirmative action to ensure effective school desegregation. The court also gave lower courts new guidelines for determining if desegregation efforts were sincere.

The Question of Remedy

Chief Justice Earl Warren's replacement in 1969 by Chief Justice Warren E. Burger coincided with a new phase in the civil rights movement and the court's role in it. It was clear that racial discrimination was illegal; the court's task was now to define the scope of remedies available to victims of racial discrimination.

The Burger court approved a wide variety of measures to remedy school segregation, including busing, gerrymandered attendance zones, limited use of mathematical ratios and compensatory education programs. The court also extended the obligation to desegregate to non-southern school districts where existing segregation had not been imposed by law but rather through school-board policy or action.

At the same time, however, the court insisted that these remedies be tailored to fit the extent of the proven discrimination. Thus a multi-district busing plan was found too sweeping a remedy when deliberate discrimination had been found in only one of the affected districts. In another instance, a district-wide plan was held to be too broad because the proven discrimination had not been shown to infect the entire school district. The court also held that once a school district was desegregated, school officials were not required to remedy the re-segregation if it resulted from residential patterns rather than from official state action.

After the court reinterpreted the 1866 Civil Rights Act to bar housing discrimination by private individuals, it also read the act to prohibit private schools from refusing to admit black pupils and to invalidate neighborhood recreational association policies excluding black homeowners and renters from membership. In a major case in which federal and city housing officials admitted they had been guilty of intentionally segregating the races in public housing projects, the court backed a lower court's metropolitan area-wide remedy. But in a second case, where a community was charged with exercising its zoning power to exclude blacks by excluding low-income housing, the court held there was no constitutional violation because there was no evidence that the charges were true and that the zoning decision was motivated by racial considerations.

When charges of racial discrimination in employment have been brought under Title VII of the Civil Rights Act of 1964 prohibiting such discrimination, the court has placed the burden of proving non-discrimination on the employer. Few employers have met this test. But when charges of job discrimination have been brought under the 14th Amendment, the court shifted the burden to the employees, requiring them to prove that the employer intended to discriminate; the discriminatory effect of an employment policy is not sufficient proof of intent. Few employees have met this test. Where job discrimination has been proved, however, the court has sanctioned far-reaching remedies, including awards of back pay and retroactive seniority.

The success of the black civil rights movement encouraged other victims of discrimination, particularly women, to assert their right to equal treatment. It has also prompted some members of the majority to complain that they have suffered from "reverse discrimination" — that is, that affirmative action programs to remedy past minority discrimination have in turn discriminated against whites.

The court has held that the 1964 Civil Rights Act provides remedies to whites as well as blacks who have been discriminated against in employment because of their race and that it bars universities receiving federal funds from setting aside a specific number of seats in each class for minority applicants. But the court remains divided on the broader question of whether the equal protection clause of the 14th Amendment permits employers and school officials to adopt race-conscious policies to remedy society's past discriminations.

Equal Educational Opportunity

When the Supreme Court in 1896 ruled that separate public facilities for blacks and whites did not violate the equal protection clause of the 14th Amendment, it pointed to the nation's schools as "the most common instance" of this segregative practice. "Establishment of separate schools for white and colored children has been held to be a valid exercise of the legislative power," the court said in *Plessy v. Ferguson*, "even by courts of States where the political rights of the colored race have been longest and most earnestly enforced." [14]

Boston, 1849

The court was referring to the fact that in an 1849 ruling, a Massachusetts court first sanctioned separate schools for the two races. The city of Boston had maintained separate schools for blacks and whites since 1820. Sarah Roberts, a five-year-old black child, was forced, as a result of this segregation, to walk past five white primary schools on her way to the black school. When repeated attempts to place her in one of the closer white schools failed, Sarah's father hired Charles Sumner, the future senator and abolitionist, and went to court.

Appearing before Massachusetts Chief Justice Lemuel Shaw in *Roberts v. City of Boston* (1849), Sumner made one of his most eloquent pleas, contending that the segregated schools violated state law which held all persons, "without distinction of age or sex, birth or color, origin or condition," to be equal before the law. Noting the general soundness of Sumner's contention, the state supreme court nonetheless rejected Roberts' challenge. Shaw wrote that

> . . .when this great principle [of equality before the law] comes to be applied to the actual and various conditions of persons in society, it will not warrant the assertion, that men and women are legally clothed with the same civil and political powers, and that children and adults are legally to have the same functions and be subject to the same treatment; but only that the rights of all, as they are settled and regulated by law, are equally entitled to the paternal consideration and protection of the law, for their maintenance and security. What those rights are, to which individuals, in the infinite variety of circumstances by which they are surrounded in society, are entitled, must depend on laws adapted to their respective relations and conditions. [15]

To Sumner's contention that segregation "brand[s] a whole race with the stigma of inferiority and degradation," Shaw responded:

It is urged, that this maintenance of separate schools tends to deepen and perpetuate the odious distinction of caste, founded in a deep-rooted prejudice in public opinion. This prejudice, if it exists, is not created by law, and probably cannot be changed by laws. [16]

Massachusetts prohibited dual school systems six years after the *Roberts* decision. In citing this case to support its decision in *Plessy*, the court overlooked the fact that the state case was decided almost twenty years before ratification of the 14th Amendment made blacks citizens and required the states to give all citizens equal protection of the laws.

Plessy and Schools

While the *Plessy* decision did not deal directly with school segregation, the Supreme Court in that opinion clearly condoned the practice. The court confirmed this position in three subsequent cases challenging the "separate" half of the "separate but equal" doctrine as states applied it to schools. In all three instances, the court bowed to the right of the state to run its own schools, refusing to consider the constitutional question of whether state-required segregation denied black children equal protection of the laws.

Georgia, 1899

The first of these cases was *Cumming v. Richmond (Ga.) County Board of Education*, decided in 1899, three years after *Plessy*. The school board had discontinued operating the black high school in order to use the building as an additional facility for black primary school pupils. The board continued to operate a high school for white girls and one for white boys. Blacks in the county sought an injunction to prevent taxes from being used to operate the white schools until a black high school was re-established.

Refusing to grant the injunction, the court said it would not address the constitutional issue of equal protection because it was not raised in the case. The court then said:

> . . .while all admit that the benefits and burdens of public taxation must be shared by citizens without discrimination against any class on account of their race, the education of the people in schools maintained by state taxation is a matter belonging to the respective States, and any interference on the part of the federal authority with the management of such schools cannot be justified except in the case of a clear and unmistakable disregard of rights secured by the supreme law of the land. [17]

Ironically, this opinion was written by Justice John Marshall Harlan, who had so vigorously dissented from the *Plessy* decision. *(Details, p. 609)*

Kentucky, 1908

In 1908, Berea College, a private Christian school incorporated in Kentucky, challenged in the Supreme Court a state law requiring that any institution which taught both blacks and whites must conduct separate classes for the two races.

The school said the state had illegally impaired the school's charter by denying it the right to teach students of both races together. The court rejected the challenge,

holding that since the college could still teach members of both races, the law had not significantly injured the school's charter. [18]

Mississippi, 1927

Twenty years later, a girl of Chinese descent challenged her assignment to an all-black school in Mississippi as a denial of equal protection of the laws. In *Gong Lum v. Rice* (1927), the court upheld her assignment to the black school, saying that the question raised by her challenge "has been many times decided to be within the constitutional power of the state legislature to settle without intervention of the federal courts under the Federal Constitution." [19]

Separate and Unequal

In none of these early cases did the court consider whether the segregated facilities were in fact equal. Nor was school segregation challenged on that specific basis.

In the 1930s, the National Association for the Advancement of Colored People (NAACP) — determined that the "separate-but-equal" doctrine was most vulnerable on this point. Studies of dual school systems, particularly in the South, showed disproportionate amounts of money spent on white and black school facilities, materials, salaries and transportation.

For a number of reasons, the NAACP decided first to attack the lack of equality in institutions of higher education. Inequality of facilities and instruction was even more apparent at the university level than at the primary and secondary school levels. Frequently, the state provided no school at all to blacks seeking certain advanced degrees. And NAACP officials reasoned that integration of a college or university by a few black students represented less of a threat to the segregated southern lifestyle than did wholesale integration of entire school districts. [20]

Missouri, 1938

In 1938 the Supreme Court decided the first of these cases, *Missouri Ex rel. Gaines v. Canada*. Because there were no black law schools in Missouri, Lloyd Gaines, a qualified black undergraduate, applied to the all-white University of Missouri Law School, which refused him admission solely because of his race. The school said it would pay Gaines' tuition at any law school in an adjacent state that would accept him. At the time, law schools in Kansas, Nebraska, Iowa and Illinois accepted black out-of-state students. This solution was unacceptable to Gaines, who sued to compel the University of Missouri to admit him.

By a 6-2 vote, the Supreme Court ruled that Gaines had been denied equal protection and that he was entitled to be admitted to the state's all-white law school. Dismissing the state's contention that it intended to establish a black law school when it became practical, Chief Justice Charles Evans Hughes wrote:

> . . .The question here is not of a duty of the State to supply legal training, or of the quality of the training which it does supply, but of its duty when it provides such training to furnish it to the residents of the State upon the basis of an equality of right. By the operation of the laws of Missouri, a privilege has been created for white law students which is denied to Negroes by reason of their race. [21]

The majority also rejected as inadequate the state's promise to pay tuition at an out-of-state school:

> ...We find it impossible to conclude that what otherwise would be an unconstitutional discrimination, with respect to the legal right to the enjoyment of opportunities within the State, can be justified by requiring resort to opportunities elsewhere. That resort may mitigate the inconvenience of the discrimination but cannot serve to validate it. [22]

Oklahoma, 1948

Ten years later, the court reaffirmed this ruling in the case of *Sipuel v. Board of Regents of the University of Oklahoma* (1948) in which a black law school applicant had been refused admission to the University of Oklahoma because of her race. In a *per curiam* opinion, the court said the state must provide Sipuel with legal training "in conformity with the equal protection clause...." [23]

Texas, 1950

The next case, *Sweatt v. Painter* (1950), focused directly on the inequality of two state institutions at which legal training was provided. Refused admission to the all-white University of Texas law school, Heman Sweatt sued in state court. The court agreed that Sweatt had been denied equal protection but gave the state time to create a black law school. Sweatt, however, refused to apply to the new school on the ground that its instruction would be inferior to that he would receive at the University of Texas. After state courts held the new school "equal" to the long-established University of Texas law school, Sweatt appealed to the Supreme Court.

Unanimously, the court ordered that Sweatt be admitted to the University of Texas. The court "cannot find substantial equality in the educational opportunities offered white and Negro law students by the state," wrote Chief Justice Fred M. Vinson. He elaborated:

> ...In terms of number of the faculty, variety of courses and opportunity for specialization, size of the student body, scope of the library, availability of law review and similar activities, the University of Texas Law School is superior. What is more important, the University of Texas Law School possesses to a far greater degree those qualities which are incapable of objective measurement but which make for greatness in a law school. Such qualities, to name but a few, include reputation of the faculty, experience of the administration, position and influence of the alumni, standing in the community, traditions and prestige. It is difficult to believe that one who had a free choice between these law schools would consider the question close. [24]

For the first time, the court had ordered a state to admit a black to an all-white school because the education provided by a black school was inferior. But Vinson said the court saw no necessity to go on — as Sweatt's attorney, Thurgood Marshall, had asked it to do — to re-examine the separate but equal doctrine "in the light of contemporary knowledge respecting the purposes of the Fourteenth Amendment and the effects of racial segregation." [25]

Oklahoma, 1950

A second case decided the same day, June 5, 1950, cast even more doubt upon the premise that separate could be equal. A black student admitted to the all-white University of Oklahoma as a candidate for a doctorate in education was assigned to a special seat in the classroom and to special tables in the library and cafeteria. The Supreme Court in *McLaurin v. Oklahoma State Regents for Higher Education* (1950) held that such state-imposed requirements produced inequities that could not be tolerated. The restrictions, the court wrote, "impair and inhibit [McLaurin's] ability to study, to engage in discussion and exchange views with other students, and, in general, to learn his profession." [26]

Implicit in this decision was the fact that it was only McLaurin's segregation from the rest of the students that made his treatment unequal. He heard the same lectures, had access to the same books and ate the same food.

Brown v. Board of Education

Even as the court announced its decisions in *Sweatt* and *McLaurin*, the five cases in which the court would make the implicit explicit were taking shape. In each of the five cases, parents of black school children asked lower courts to order school boards to stop enforcing laws requiring or permitting segregated schools.

The Cases

The challenge that gave the landmark school desegregation decision its name, *Brown v. Board of Education of Topeka*, was brought in 1951 by Oliver Brown in behalf of his daughter Linda. [27]

Under Kansas law permitting cities with populations over 15,000 to operate dual school systems, Topeka had opted to segregate its primary schools. As a result Linda Brown was forced to walk 20 blocks to an all-black grade school rather than attend an all-white school in her neighborhood. Several other black families eventually joined the challenge.

In 1951 a federal district court found Topeka's segregation detrimental to black children but found no constitutional violation because the black and white primary schools were substantially equal with respect to buildings, curricula, transportation and teachers.

The case of *Briggs v. Elliott* was actually the first of the cases to reach the Supreme Court. Federal proceedings began in 1950 when parents of black elementary and secondary school-aged children in Clarendon County, S.C., asked a federal district court to enjoin enforcement of state constitutional and statutory provisions requiring segregation in public schools. The court denied the request, but found the black schools inferior to the white ones and ordered the school board to equalize the schools immediately. The court refused, however, to order the school board to admit black children to the white school while the equalization took place. The children's parents then appealed to the Supreme Court, which in 1952 returned the case to the lower court to consider a report on the progress of the equalization program. The lower court found that the school board had either achieved substantial equality in all areas or soon would, and it again upheld the separate but equal doctrine. The case then returned to the Supreme Court.

Davis v. County School Board of Prince Edward County, Va. was almost identical to the *Briggs* case. Parents of black high school students sued to stop enforcement of the state's constitutional provisions requiring separate schools. While the district court found the black high school to be inferior and ordered its equalization, it upheld the validity of the segregation provisions. It also refused to admit the black students to white high schools while the black schools were being brought up to par with the white schools.

The fourth case, *Gebhart v. Belton,* involved the schools of New Castle County, Del. As in the other cases, parents of black children sued to stop enforcement of the constitutional provisions mandating a dual school system, but unlike the other cases, the state court granted the request. Finding the black schools inferior on a number of points, the court ordered white schools to admit black children. The state supreme court affirmed the decree which the school board then appealed to the U.S. Supreme Court.

The fifth case, although argued with the other four, was decided separately. [28] *Bolling v. Sharpe* concerned District of Columbia public schools. Because the 14th Amendment's guarantee of equal protection of the laws applies only to states, parents of black pupils based their challenge to school segregation in the District on the Fifth Amendment's guarantee of due process of the laws. A district court dismissed the suit, and the Supreme Court granted review of the dismissal.

Together, the five cases brought under judicial consideration both grade school pupils and high school students, mandatory segregation laws and permissive ones, the equal protection clause of the 14th Amendment and the due process clause of the Fifth Amendment. Geographically, the five cases came from two southern states, one border state, a plains state and the nation's capital. As one commentator noted, that "wide geographical range gave the anticipated decision a national flavor and would blunt any claim that the South was being made a whipping boy." [29]

Moreover, in all five cases the lower courts found that education offered black students was substantially equal, or soon would be, to that given in the white schools. Thus the primary question presented to the Supreme Court was whether public school segregation *per se* was unconstitutional.

The Arguments

The school cases were argued in December 1952. In June 1953 the court requested reargument, asking the attorneys to address themselves to three main questions.

● What historical evidence was there that the framers of the 14th Amendment intended it to apply to segregation in public schools?

● If the answer to the first question was inconclusive, was it within the power of the court to abolish segregation?

● If school segregation was found unconstitutional, what approach should the court take to end it?

Reargument was heard in December 1953. Two months earlier former California Governor Earl Warren had become Chief Justice, replacing Vinson, who had died in September of a heart attack. Because Congress had already adjourned when he was named, Warren presided over the court by virtue of a recess appointment until his unanimous confirmation on March 1, 1954.

Although there were several lawyers on both sides, the two leading adversaries were Thurgood Marshall, director of the NAACP Legal Defense and Educational Fund, which had been instrumental in guiding the challenge to school segregation through the courts, and John W. Davis, former U.S. representative (D-W.Va., 1911-13), former solicitor general (1913-18), ambassador to Great Britain (1918-21); the 1924 Democratic presidential nominee and a pre-eminent attorney who had argued more cases before the Supreme Court than any other lawyer of his era.

Marshall, then 45, would become in 1967 the first black to sit on the Supreme Court. Davis, at 80, was making his final appearance before the court, arguing in behalf of South Carolina in the *Briggs* case for the continuation of school segregation.

It is one of the ironies of these cases that in 1915 Davis as solicitor general had successfully persuaded the court to strike down Oklahoma's "grandfather clause" that prohibited blacks from voting. In that case, the fledgling NAACP supported Davis' position in its first friend-of-the-court brief.[30] *(Details, p. 480)*

Davis was first to present an answer to the court's three questions. He contended that the framers of the 14th Amendment never intended it to bar segregation in the nation's public schools. In addition to an intensive examination of the legislative history surrounding enactment of the amendment, Davis also recited the names of the states both north and south that instituted or continued to conduct segregated schools after the amendment was ratified; several of these same states had voted to ratify.

To the question whether the court had the authority on its own to overturn the separate but equal doctrine, Davis reminded the court that the doctrine had been upheld not only by the lower courts but by the Supreme Court, and therefore become part of the law of the land. "[S]omewhere, sometime to every principle comes a moment of repose when it has been so often announced, so confidently relied upon, so long continued, that it passes the limits of judicial discretion and disturbance," he said. [31]

Making clear what he thought of earlier expert testimony concerning the detrimental effects of segregation on black children, Davis rhetorically asked what impact a desegregation order might have on a predominantly black school district such as Clarendon County:

> . . .If it is done on the mathematical basis, with 30 children as a maximum . . . you would have 27 Negro children and three whites in one school room. Would that make the children any happier? Would they learn any more quickly? Would their lives be more serene?
>
> Children of that age are not the most considerate animals in the world, as we all know. Would the terrible psychological disaster being wrought, according to some . . ., to the colored child be removed if he had three white children sitting somewhere in the same school room?
>
> Would white children be prevented from getting a distorted idea of racial relations if they sat with 27 Negro children? I have posed that question because it is the very one that cannot be denied. [32]

Davis also said he did not believe the courts had the power to tell the states how to desegregate their schools. "Your Honors do not sit, and cannot sit as a glorified Board of Education for the State of South Carolina or any other state. Neither can the District Court," he declared. Davis then concluded:

> Let me say this for the State of South Carolina. . . . It believes that its legislation is not offensive to the Constitution of the United States.

Famous Footnote: *Plessy* Refuted

One of the more controversial footnotes in Supreme Court history is footnote 11 in *Brown v. Board of Education* (1954). That footnote cited seven sociological and psychological studies of the effects of racial segregation, support for the court's contention that segregation on the basis of race generated a feeling of inferiority among blacks that might never be erased. The text of the footnote follows:

[11] K.B. Clark, Effect of Prejudice and Discrimination on Personality Development (Midcentury White House Conference on Children and Youth, 1950); Witner and Kotinsky, Personality in the Making (152), c. VI; Deutscher and Chein, The Psychological Effects of Enforced Segregation; A Survey of Social Science Opinion, 26 J. Psychol. 259 (1948); Chien, What are the Psychological Effects of Segregation Under Conditions of Equal Facilities?, 3 Int. J. Opinion and Attitude Res. 229 (1949); Brameld, Educational Costs, in Discrimination and National Welfare (MacIver, ed., 1949), 44-48; Frazier, The Negro in the United States (1949), 674-681. And see generally Myrdal, An American Dilemma (1944). [1]

In his book *Simple Justice*, Richard Kluger quotes Chief Justice Earl Warren as saying of the footnote:

"We included it because I thought the point it made was the antithesis of what was said in *Plessy*. They had said there that if there was any harm intended, it was solely in the mind of the Negro. I thought these things — these cited sources — were sufficient to note as being in contradistinction to that statement in *Plessy*." [2]

Kluger's research indicates that at least two of the justices questioned inclusion of the footnote in the school desegregation opinion, but their objections were minor compared to those that came from critics of the decision. Mississippi Sen. James O. Eastland, (D, 1941, 1943-79) in a May 27, 1954, speech in the Senate said:

The Supreme Court could not find the authority for its decisions in the wording of the 14th Amendment, in the history of the amendment or in the decision of any court. Instead, the Court was forced to resort to the unprecedented authority of a group of recent partisan books on sociology and psychology. If this is the judicial calibre of the Court, what can the Nation expect from it in the future? What is to prevent the Court from citing as an authority in some future decision the works of Karl Marx? [3]

Even some who favored desegregation were displeased with the footnote. "It is one thing to use the current scientific findings, however ephemeral they may be, in order to ascertain whether the legislature has acted reasonably, in adopting some scheme of social or economic regulation. . . . It is quite another thing to have our fundamental rights rise, fall or change along with the latest fashions of psychological literature," wrote Professor Edmond Cahn. [4]

Another respected law professor, Alexander Bickel, concluded:

It was a mistake to do it this way. If you're going to invoke sociology and psychology, do it right. . . . No matter how it had been done, no doubt, the enemies of the opinion were certain to seize upon it and proclaim the ruling unjudicial and illegal. The opinion therefore should have said straightforwardly that *Plessy* was based on a self-invented philosophy, no less psychologically oriented than the Court was being now in citing these sources that justify the holding that segregation inflicted damage. It was clear, though, that Warren wanted to present as small a target as possible, and that was wise. He did not want to go out to the country wearing a Hussar's uniform. [5]

---

[1] *Brown v. Board of Education,* 347 U.S. 483 at 495 (1954).
[2] Richard Kluger, *Simple Justice; The History of Brown v. Board of Education and Black America's Struggle for Equality* (New York: Alfred A. Knopf, 1976), p. 706.

[3] U.S. Congress. Senate. *Congressional Record,* May 27, 1954, 100:7252.
[4] Edmond Cahn, *Jurisprudence,* 30 New York University Law Review 150, 159 (1955).
[5] Kluger, *Simple Justice,* p. 707.

It is confident of its good faith and intention to produce equality for all of its children of whatever race or color. It is convinced that the happiness, the progress and the welfare of these children is best promoted in segregated schools, and it thinks it a thousand pities that by this controversy there should be urged the return to an experiment which gives no more promise of success today than when it was written into their Constitution during what I call the tragic era.

I am reminded — and I hope it won't be treated as a reflection on anybody — of Aesop's fable of the dog and the meat: The dog, with a fine piece of meat in his mouth, crossed a bridge and saw the shadow in the stream and plunged for it and lost both substance and shadow.

Here is equal education, not promised, not prophesied, but present. Shall it be thrown away on some fancied question of racial prestige? [33]

Marshall's response to Davis the following day illustrated the difference in the two men's styles and philosophies:

. . .I got the feeling on hearing the discussion yesterday that when you put a white child in a school with a whole lot of colored children, the child would fall apart or something. Everybody knows that is not true.

Those same kids in Virginia and South Carolina — and I have seen them do it — they play in the streets together, they play on their farms together, they go down the road together, they separate to go to school, they come out of school and play ball together. They have to be separated in school.

There is some magic to it. You can have them voting together, you can have them not restricted because of law in the houses they live in. You can have them going to the same state university and the same college, but if they go to elementary and high school, the world will fall apart. . . . They can't take race out of this case. From the day this case was filed until this moment, nobody has in any form or fashion . . . done anything to distinguish this [segregation] statute from the Black Codes, which they must admit, because nobody can dispute . . . the Fourteenth Amendment was intended to deprive the states of power to enforce Black Codes or anything else like it.

. . .[T]he only way that this Court can decide this case in opposition to our position, is that there must be some reason which gives the state the right to make a classification that they can make in regard to nothing else in regard to Negroes, and we submit the only way to arrive at this decision is to find that for some reason Negroes are inferior to all other human beings. . . .

It can't be because of slavery in the past, because there are very few groups in this country that haven't had slavery some place back in the history of their groups. It can't be color because there are Negroes as white as the drifted snow, with blue eyes, and they are just as segregated as the colored man.

The only thing [it] can be is an inherent determination that the people who were formerly in slavery, regardless of anything else, shall be kept as near that stage as possible, and now is the time, we submit, that this Court should make it clear that that is not what our Constitution stands for. [34]

The Decision

All nine justices — including Robert H. Jackson, who had left a hospital bed — were present May 17, 1954, when Chief Justice Warren read the unanimous decision in *Brown v. Board of Education.* The opinion, described by many as the most socially and ideologically significant decision in the court's history, was just 13 paragraphs long.

Warren quickly disposed of the court's first question — whether the framers of the 14th Amendment intended it to bar school segregation. The evidence was inconclusive.

The Chief Justice then turned to the "separate but equal" doctrine. Unlike the *Sweatt* case, he said, children attending the segregated public schools in these cases were — or soon would be — receiving substantially equal treatment so far as "tangible" factors were concerned. Therefore, said Warren, the court must look at the "effect of segregation itself on public education." [35]

That assessment could not be made by turning the clock back to 1868 when the amendment was adopted or to 1896 when the *Plessy* decision was written.

"We must consider public education in the light of its full development and its present place in American life throughout the Nation," wrote Warren. "Only in this way can it be determined if segregation in public schools deprives these plaintiffs of the equal protection of the laws."[36]

The court found that education was "perhaps the most important function" of state and local government, as evidenced by their compulsory attendance laws and considerable expenditures. Education, wrote Warren, was the foundation of good citizenship and the basis for professional training and adjustment to society.

"In these days, it is doubtful that any child may reasonably be expected to succeed in life if he is denied the opportunity of an education," said Warren, adding that where the state had undertaken to make education available it must be available to all on equal terms. [37]

The question is then, said Warren, "Does segregation of children in public schools solely on the basis of race, even though the physical facilities and other 'tangible' factors may be equal, deprive the children of the minority group of equal educational opportunities?"

The court's answer: "We believe that it does."[38]

Observing that intangible factors were considered in finding the treatment accorded Sweatt and McLaurin unequal, Warren said:

Such considerations apply with added force to children in grade and high schools. To separate them from others of similar age and qualifications solely because of their race generates a feeling of inferiority as to their status in the community that may affect their hearts and minds in a way unlikely ever to be undone. [39]

This belief "was amply supported by modern authority," Warren asserted, citing in a famous footnote, seven sociological studies on the detrimental effects of enforced racial segregation. *(Box, p. 594)*

Warren now stated the court's historic conclusion:

We conclude that in the field of public education the doctrine of "separate but equal" has no place. Separate educational facilities are inherently unequal. Therefore, we hold that the plaintiffs and others similarly situated for whom the actions have been brought are, by reason of the segregation complained of, deprived of the equal protection of the laws guaranteed by the Fourteenth Amendment. [40]

In the District of Columbia case, considered separately from the other four because it involved a question of due process under the Fifth Amendment, Warren wrote:

. . .Liberty under law extends to the full range of conduct which the individual is free to pursue, and it cannot be restricted except for a proper governmental objective. Segregation in public education is not reasonably related to any proper governmental objective, and thus it imposes on Negro children of the District of Columbia a burden that constitutes an arbitrary deprivation of their liberty in violation of the Due Process Clause.

In view of our decision that the Constitution prohibits the states from maintaining racially segregated public schools, it would be unthinkable that the same Constitution would impose a lesser duty on the Federal Government. [41]

In both the state cases and the District of Columbia suit, the court postponed its decision on a remedy for the school segregation until after the opposing sides had presented their views on that question.

All Deliberate Speed

Among the issues the court asked the parties to address in argument on appropriate remedies were:

● Should the Supreme Court formulate a detailed decree in each of the five cases, and if so, what specific issues should be addressed?

● Should the court appoint a special master to take evidence and then make specific recommendations to the court on the contents of the decrees?

● Should the court remand the cases to the lower courts to fashion the decrees, and if so, what directions and procedural guidelines should the Supreme Court give the lower courts?

● Should black pupils be admitted to schools of their choice "forthwith" or might desegregation be brought about gradually?

In addition to hearing from the parties involved in the five cases, the court invited the United States and all of the other states that required or permitted segregated public schools to submit their answers to these questions. The United States, Florida, North Carolina, Arkansas, Oklahoma, Maryland and Texas accepted the invitation and participated in the oral argument in April 1955. Several other states declined the invitation.

On May 31, 1955, Chief Justice Warren announced the court's final decision in an opinion commonly known as *Brown II,* to distinguish it from the 1954 decision known as *Brown I.* Warren first noted that the District of Columbia and the school districts in Kansas and Delaware had made substantial progress toward desegregation in the year since the first *Brown* decision was handed down but that Virginia and South Carolina were awaiting the court's final decision before acting. He then moved to the heart of the matter:

Full implementation of these constitutional principles may require solution of varied local school problems. School authorities have the primary responsibility for elucidating, assessing, and solving these problems; courts will have to consider whether the action of school authorities constitutes good faith implementation of the governing constitutional principles. Because of their proximity to local conditions and the possible need for further hearings, the courts which originally heard these cases can best perform this judicial appraisal. Accordingly, we believe it appropriate to remand the cases to those courts.

In fashioning and effectuating the decrees, the courts will be guided by equitable principles. . . . At stake is the personal interest of the plaintiffs in admission to public schools as soon as practicable on a nondiscriminatory basis. To effectuate this interest may call for elimination of a variety of obstacles in making the transition to school systems operated in accordance with the constitutional principles set forth in our May 17, 1954, decision. Courts of equity may properly take into account the public interest in the elimination of such obstacles in a systematic and effective manner. But it should go without saying that the vitality of these constitutional principles cannot be allowed to yield simply because of disagreement with them.

While giving weight to these public and private considerations, the courts will require that the defendants make a prompt and reasonable start toward full compliance with our May 17, 1954, ruling. Once such a start has been made, the courts may find that additional time is necessary to carry out the ruling in an effective manner. The burden rests upon the defendants to establish that such time is necessary in the public interest and is consistent with good faith compliance at the earliest practicable date. To that end, the courts may consider problems related to adminis-

tration, arising from the physical condition of the school plant, the school transportation system, personnel, revision of school districts and attendance areas into compact units to achieve a system of determining admission to the public schools on a nonracial basis, and revision of local laws and regulations which may be necessary in solving the foregoing problems. They will also consider the adequacy of any plans the defendants may propose to meet these problems and to effectuate a transition to a racially nondiscriminatory school system. During this period of transition, the courts will retain jurisdiction of these cases. [42]

Desegregation of public schools, Warren concluded, was to proceed "with all deliberate speed." [43]

Reaction

Reaction to the two *Brown* decisions was immediate.

At one extreme were those committed to segregation as a way of life. They castigated the court, called the decisions a usurpation of state prerogatives and urged defiance. The height of the rhetoric opposing the *Brown* decisions may have been the March 1956 "Declaration of Constitutional Principles," a tract signed by 101 of 128 members of Congress from 11 southern and border states. The signers called the *Brown* decisions "a clear abuse of judicial power," and commended those states that intended to "resist enforced integration by any means." [44]

At the other end of the spectrum were those who hailed the demise of the "separate but equal" doctrine as long overdue but felt that the court seriously erred in *Brown II* by not ordering immediate desegregation. Many found themselves somewhere in the middle, unhappy with the command to desegregate but unwilling to defy it.

Resistance

Massive resistance — a phrase coined by Virginia Sen. Harry F. Byrd (D, 1933-65) — did not begin in earnest until late 1955 and early 1956.

Relieved that the court had not ordered immediate desegregation, many Southern leaders opposed to desegregation apparently presumed that lower courts would ignore or otherwise delay implementation of the *Brown* decisions. By January 1956, however, nineteen lower courts had used the *Brown* precedents to invalidate school segregation and, as historian C. Vann Woodward characterized it, "[s]omething very much like panic seized many parts of the South . . ., a panic bred of insecurity and fear." [45] White Citizens Councils created to preserve segregation spread throughout the South. The NAACP was barred from operating in some states. And many state and local officials sought ways to delay desegregation in the schools.

Official resistance took three main paths. Several states enacted "interposition" statutes declaring the *Brown* decisions of no effect. Mississippi and Louisiana also passed laws claiming that the decisions did not affect the states' execution of their police powers and then requiring school segregation in order to promote public health and morals and preserve the public peace. *(General background on state police power, p. 358)*

Several states also adopted superficially neutral laws that resulted in separation of pupils by race. Among these types of statutes were laws that assigned pupils to specific schools and classes on the basis of their scholastic aptitude and achievement. Since black children had rarely received adequate educations, they were thus easily isolated.

Another tactic was to allow pupils to attend any public school (of the correct grade level) they chose. Few blacks had the courage to attend hostile white schools, and even fewer whites chose to attend black schools. Some states barred public funds to any school district that integrated; others permitted public schools to close rather than to accept black children. In some instances, compulsory attendance laws were repealed and in still other cases states and localities allocated public funds to private segregated schools. Many states employed more than one of these methods to perpetuate segregation in the public schools.

Brown as Precedent

Adverse reaction to the desegregation decision did not deter the court from applying it to other areas of life. In 1955 the court ordered the University of Alabama to admit two blacks to its undergraduate program. [46] In March 1956, the court in a *per curiam* opinion declared in *Florida ex rel Hawkins v. Board of Control* that it would not permit institutes of higher education to delay desegregation. [47] Beginning with the 1954 case of *Muir v. Louisville Park Theatrical Assn.*, the court, in brief orders that cited *Brown* as authority, struck down the separate but equal doctrine as it applied to state-imposed segregation of public places such as public parks, and vehicles of interstate transportation.[48] *(Public accommodations, p. 607)*

Resistance Rebuked

In 1958 the court first addressed the problem of massive resistance. The occasion was the case of *Cooper v. Aaron,* in which Arkansas officials openly defied the court's order to abandon segregation.

Less than a week after the Supreme Court struck down the separate but equal doctrine, the Little Rock, Ark., school board announced its intention to develop a desegregation plan for the city schools. One year later — a week before the court announced its decision in *Brown II* — the school board approved a plan that called for gradual desegregation beginning with Central High School in the fall of 1957. Meanwhile, the state adopted a constitutional amendment commanding the legislature to oppose the *Brown* decisions. In response, the state legislature enacted a law permitting children in racially mixed schools to ignore compulsory attendance laws.

On Sept. 2, 1957, Gov. Orval Faubus sent units of the Arkansas National Guard to Central High to prevent nine black students scheduled to attend the school from entering. Obeying a federal district court order, the school board proceeded with its integration plan and on Sept. 4 the nine students tried to enter the school, only to find their way blocked by guardsmen standing shoulder to shoulder, along with a mob of hostile onlookers. This situation prevailed until Sept. 20, when Faubus decided to obey a court order and withdraw the troops.

On Sept. 23, the black students entered the high school but were quickly removed by police when a mob outside grew unruly. Two days later, President Eisenhower sent federal troops to protect the blacks as they entered and left the school. Federal troops remained there until Nov. 27, when they were replaced by federalized national guardsmen who remained for the duration of the school year.

In the face of both official and public hostility to its desegregation plan, the school board in February 1958 asked the district court for permission to withdraw the

black students from Central High and to postpone any further desegregation for two and a half years. Finding the situation at Central intolerable, the court agreed to the board's request. An appeals court reversed the decision, and the school board appealed the reversal to the Supreme Court.

A Special Term

The court convened a special summer term Aug. 28, 1958, in order to render its opinion before the school year began. Arguments were heard Sept. 11, 1958. On Sept. 12, the court issued an unsigned *per curiam* opinion affirming the appeals court's denial of the postponement. On Sept. 29, the court issued its formal opinion, which sharply rebuked Gov. Faubus and the Arkansas legislature for their obstructive actions. [49]

The court indicated its sympathy for the Little Rock school board which, it said, had acted in good faith, but added that the "constitutional rights of [black] respondents are not to be sacrificed or yielded to the violence and disorder which have followed upon the actions of the Governor and Legislature." [50] The court then reminded those officials that the 14th Amendment prohibited state officials from denying anyone equal protection of the laws and said that it would not tolerate any state action perpetuating segregation in schools:

> . . .State support of segregated schools through any arrangement, management, funds or property cannot be squared with the [14th] Amendment's command that no State shall deny to any person within its jurisdiction the equal protection of the laws. . . . The basic decision in *Brown* was unanimously reached by this Court only after the case had been briefed and twice argued and the issues had been given the most serious consideration. Since the first *Brown* opinion three new Justices have come to the Court. They are at one with the Justices still on the Court who participated in that basic decision as to its correctness, and that decision is now unanimously reaffirmed. The principles announced in that decision and the obedience of the States to them, according to the command of the Constitution, are indispensable for the protection of the freedoms guaranteed by our fundamental charter for all of us. Our constitutional ideal of equal justice under law is thus made a living truth. [51]

To emphasize the gravity with which they viewed the defiance of the Arkansas officials, each of the nine justices personally signed the opinion.

Governor Faubus and the Arkansas legislature chose to ignore this warning. With approval of the legislature, Faubus closed all four Little Rock high schools, which remained closed for the entire 1958-59 school year. In June 1959 a federal district court declared the statute authorizing the closing a violation of the due process and equal protection clauses, and the Supreme Court affirmed that opinion. [52] Little Rock high schools opened to black and white students in the fall of 1959.

Other Decisions

Despite its protestation in the Arkansas case that it would not tolerate schemes to evade segregation, the court in November 1958 affirmed without opinion an appeals court decision upholding Alabama's pupil placement law as constitutional on its face. (The lower court had made clear,

De Facto Segregation: Gary, Denver and Dayton

The 14th Amendment prohibits state action denying persons the equal protection of the law. It thus clearly applies to *de jure* segregation — that which is imposed by law. It was *de jure* segregation that the court declared unconstitutional in the *Brown* case and it was *de jure* segregation that existed throughout most southern and border states.

School segregation also existed, however, in many northern and western communities, particularly in central cities. But most of the northern and western states either never required segregation or repealed their segregation laws decades before the *Brown* decision. Their so-called *de facto* segregation was a result not of law but of economic status, residential patterns and other non-legal factors that did not seem to fall within the scope of the equal protection clause.

In 1964 the Supreme Court refused to review a lower court decision which declared that because racial imbalance in Gary, Ind., schools resulted from residential patterns, not state or school board action, it was not unconstitutional, and school authorities were not required to take affirmative action to eliminate it.[1]

Denver

In 1973, almost 20 years after *Brown*, the court decided the first school segregation case from a state that had not imposed separation by law. In the case of *Keyes v. School District #1, Denver*, the court, by a 7-1 vote, ruled that under certain circumstances segregation in such school systems was unconstitutional.

The case concerned two sets of schools in the Denver, Colo., school system: some already found segregated by deliberate actions of the school board, and core city schools, which were segregated but not — a lower court had held — as a result of school board action. The Supreme Court directed the lower court to determine whether the school board's deliberate action in regard to the first set of schools so affected the other schools that it made the entire district a dual system. If not, the court was to move on to consider proof, which the school board must produce, that the core city schools were not intentionally segregated. If the proof was not persuasive, the court should order desegregation.

With this decision the court expanded the definition of *de jure* segregation to include that fostered by intentional school board policies, even in the absence of state law. Without a showing of intent to segregate, however, no constitutional wrong existed. "We emphasize that the differentiating factor between *de jure* segregation and so-called *de facto* segregation . . . is *purpose* or *intent* to segregate," Justice William J. Brennan Jr. wrote.[2]

The majority indicated that the deliberate segregation of some of a system's schools made the entire system a segregated one:

. . .[C]ommon sense dictates the conclusion that racially inspired school board actions have an impact beyond the particular schools that are the subjects of those actions. . . . Plainly a finding of intentional segregation as to a portion of a school system is not devoid of probative value in assessing the school authorities' intent with respect to other parts of the same school system.[3]

Although he agreed with the decision, Justice Lewis F. Powell Jr. disagreed with the majority's retention of the *de jure, de facto* distinction. He contended that the court should adopt instead the rule that "where segregated public schools exist within a school district to a substantial degree, there is a *prima facie* case that the duly constituted public authorities . . . are sufficiently responsible [for the segregation] . . . to warrant imposing upon them a nationally applicable burden to demonstrate they nevertheless are operating a genuinely integrated school system."[4] Justice William O. Douglas agreed that there was no constitutional distinction.

Discriminatory Intent

In two subsequent cases, the court clearly indicated it would not adopt Powell's proposed rule.

The first case concerned Austin, Texas. Lower courts held that a school board policy of assigning students to schools closest to their homes, resulting in 45 percent of the Mexican-American students attending schools that were 60 percent black or Mexican-American, constituted *prima facie* evidence of *de jure* segregation in violation of the equal protection clause.[5]

With an unsigned opinion, the court in 1976 returned the case to the lower courts for reconsideration in light of its opinion in the case of *Washington v. Davis* (1976). In that case, which concerned employment discrimination, the court had ruled that a racially discriminatory impact was not sufficient evidence to prove unconstitutional discrimination; some racially discriminatory purpose or intent had to be shown in order for the discrimination to violate the 14th Amendment's guarantee of equal protection.[6] *(Details, box p. 620)*

Dayton

In its 1977 decision in *Dayton (Ohio) Board of Education v. Brinkman*, the court held that a lower court erred when it found the existence of racial imbalance in city schools proof of deliberate segregation.

But two years later, in mid-1979, the court seemed to abandon its *de jure, de facto* distinction, upholding massive court-ordered busing plans for the school systems of Columbus and Dayton, Ohio. In both, the court agreed with a lower court's decision that the systems were unconstitutionally segregated.[7]

---

[1] *Bell v. School, City of Gary*, 324 F 2d 209 (1963), cert. denied. 377 U.S. 924 (1964).

[2] *Keyes v. School District #1, Denver*, 413 U.S. 189 at 208 (1973); see also *Columbus (Ohio) Board of Education v. Penick* (1979).

[3] Id. at 203, 207 passim.

[4] Id. at 224.

[5] *Austin Independent School Board v. United States*, 429 U.S. 190 (1976).

[6] *Washington v. Davis*, 426 U.S. 229 (1976).

[7] *Dayton (Ohio) Board of Education v. Brinkman*, 433 U.S. 406 at 413 (1977); see also *Dayton Board of Education v. Brinkman, Columbus Board of Education v. Penick* (1979).

however, that the law might be found unconstitutional if its application resulted in racial discrimination.) [53]

In two 1959 cases, the Supreme Court refused to review lower court rulings requiring that all state remedies for segregation be exhausted before a case could move into federal court. [54]

Over the next three years, the court affirmed lower court decisions striking down Louisiana laws clearly designed to continue school segregation. [55]

Then in June 1963, the court began to express its impatience with dilatory and evasive tactics. In the first signed school case opinion since *Cooper v. Aaron*, the court struck down a transfer scheme which worked to preserve segregated schools. Reversing the lower courts' approval of transfer plans in two Tennessee cities that allowed students assigned to schools where they were in the minority to transfer to schools where their race was in the majority, the unanimous court in *Goss v. Board of Education of Knoxville* (1963) declared that because it was "readily apparent" that the plan would continue segregation, it was therefore unconstitutional. [56]

In a second case in 1963, the court ruled that where federal rights were at stake, all state remedies did not need to be exhausted before seeking relief in federal court. [57]

Too Much Deliberation

The following year, a full ten years after *Brown I*, the court announced it had had enough delays.

The case of *Griffin v. County School Board of Prince Edward County* (1964) originated in the same Virginia county involved in the *Brown* decision. Despite that decision, the county's schools remained segregated. In 1959 the county closed its schools rather than obey a lower court order to desegregate. The county then replaced the public schools for whites with private schools, partially financed by public funds. The county offered to set up similar segregated "private" schools for blacks. The blacks refused the offer and pursued the legal battle for integrated public schools. Consequently, black children in Prince Edward County could not attend public school there from 1959 until 1963. Finally, federal, state and local officials cooperated to open some desegregated public schools in the county.

In 1961, a federal district court ordered a halt in the flow of public funds to the all-white private schools. In 1962 it ordered the county to reopen the public schools, ruling that it could not constitutionally close the schools to avoid segregating them while all the other public schools in the state remained open. The county appealed the ruling to the Supreme Court.

"Whatever nonracial grounds might support a State's allowing a county to abandon public schools, the object must be a constitutional one, and grounds of race and opposition to desegregation do not qualify as constitutional," the court said in 1964 affirming the lower court order. [58]

Dismissing the county's contention that the state courts should have been given an opportunity to determine whether the schools should be opened before the federal district court acted, the court declared:

> . . . [W]e hold that the issues here imperatively call for decision now. The case has been delayed since 1951 by resistance at the state and county level, by legislation, and by lawsuits. The original plaintiffs have doubtless all passed high school age. There has been

entirely too much deliberation and not enough speed in enforcing the constitutional rights which we held in *Brown* . . . had been denied Prince Edward County Negro children. [59]

The court spoke even more sharply in a November 1965 ruling. "Delays in desegregating public school systems are no longer tolerable," the justices declared in the unsigned *per curiam* opinion in *Bradley v. School Board of City of Richmond*. [60] Three weeks later, in *Rogers v. Paul*, the court in another *per curiam* opinion ordered an Arkansas school district to permit a black student "immediate transfer" to an all-white high school, adding that "those similarly situated" might transfer as well. [61] In December 1967 the court affirmed without opinion lower court rulings requiring Alabama to desegregate its schools. It was the first time that a state was ordered to take such action; previously, desegregation orders had been directed only to local school systems. [62]

Affirmative Duty

Then, in May 1968, the Supreme Court put its foot down.

The unanimous court ordered still-segregated school systems to devise desegregation plans that promised to be effective. In *Green v. County School Board of New Kent County, Va.* the court held that the county's freedom-of-choice plan did not accomplish the goals set out in *Brown I* and *Brown II*.

Freedom-of-choice plans allowed students to choose which school within the district they wanted to attend. Details varied from district to district, but in most instances custom and residential patterns served to keep the schools under such plans racially segregated.

Rural New Kent County, with a population divided almost evenly between whites and blacks, was originally segregated by Virginia law. In 1965 the school board adopted a freedom-of-choice plan but, as the Supreme Court noted, in three years of operation no white pupil chose to attend the black school and only 15 percent of the black children were enrolled in the formerly all-white school.

In an opinion written by Justice William J. Brennan Jr., the court said the school board's adoption of a freedom-of-choice plan did not fulfill its obligation to desegregate the county schools:

> In the context of the state-imposed segregated pattern of long standing, the fact that in 1965 the Board opened the doors of the former "white" school to Negro children and of the "Negro" school to white children merely begins, not ends, our inquiry whether the Board has taken steps adequate to abolish its dual, segregated system. *Brown II* was a call for the dismantling of well-entrenched dual systems tempered by an awareness that complex and multifaceted problems would arise which would require time and flexibility for a successful resolution. School boards such as the respondent then operating state-compelled dual systems were nevertheless clearly charged with the affirmative duty to take whatever steps might be necessary to convert to a unitary system in which racial discrimination would be eliminated root and branch. [63]

Observing that it had taken 11 years after *Brown I* for the district to begin desegregating, Brennan continued:

Two Races, Two Districts?

One of the methods some areas adopted to avoid desegregation was the division of a school district into two parts in such a way that most black children would attend the schools of one district and most white children the schools of the other. The Supreme Court did not view this ploy sympathetically. In two cases decided in 1972, it struck down such efforts.

The case of *Wright v. Emporia City Council* concerned a Virginia city whose schools were part of the surrounding county school system. The county was ordered to desegregate its schools. The city then petitioned to operate its own school system. Although both city and county school systems would have had a majority of black students, the county schools would have been more black if the city school district were created than if the city's students were part of a county-wide desegregation plan.

By a 5-4 vote, the court ruled that because the city's proposal would hinder the desegregation process it was impermissible. "Certainly desegregation is not achieved by splitting a single school system operating 'white schools' and 'Negro schools' into two new systems, each operating unitary schools within its borders, where one of the two new systems is, in fact, 'white' and the other is, in fact, Negro," the majority stated. [1]

The four dissenters denied that creation of the second school system would interfere with the desegregation process. A second system should not be rejected if its only effect was a slightly greater racial imbalance in both school systems, they said.

In the second case, the court was unanimous in its opinion that the creation of a new school district was impermissible. The case of *United States v. Scotland Neck City Board of Education* involved the North Carolina legislature's creation of a school district for the city of Scotland Neck, which had been part of a county school system — at that time in the process of implementing a desegregation plan. The court said there was no question that the statute was motivated by a desire to create a predominantly white school system in the city — and so it must be struck down. [2]

---

[1] *Wright v. Emporia City Council*, 407 U.S. 451 at 463 (1972).

[2] *United States v. Scotland Neck Board of Education*, 407 U.S. 484 (1972).

...This deliberate perpetuation of the unconstitutional dual system can only have compounded the harm of such a system.... Moreover, a plan that at this late date fails to provide meaningful assurance of prompt and effective disestablishment of a dual system is also intolerable.... The burden on a school board today is to come forward with a plan that promises realistically to work, and promises realistically to work *now*. [64]

Effective Remedy

The court refused to say that any one type of desegregation plan promised to be more effective than another, leaving it up to each individual school district to fashion a remedy best suited to its situation and needs. But it did give the district courts some guidance in assessing the effectiveness of desegregation plans. Brennan wrote:

...It is incumbent upon the district court to weigh that claim [of plan effectiveness] in light of the facts at hand and ... any alternatives which may be shown as feasible and more promising in their effectiveness. Where the court finds the board to be acting in good faith and the proposed plan to have real prospects for dismantling the state-imposed dual system "at the earliest practicable date," then the plan may be said to provide effective relief. Of course, the availability to the board of other, more promising courses of action may indicate a lack of good faith; and at the least it places a heavy burden upon the board to explain its preference for an apparently less effective method. [65]

While it did not rule out freedom-of-choice plans entirely, the court said experience indicated they were usually ineffective. Certainly, the court said, New Kent County's plan was ineffective. There "the plan has operated simply to burden children and their parents with a responsibility which *Brown II* places squarely on the School Board." The court ordered the board to formulate a new plan that promised to convert the county schools "to a system, without a 'white' school and a 'Negro' school, but just schools." [66]

In two other cases decided the same day, the court applied the *Green* principles to find a freedom-of-choice plan in an Arkansas school district and a free transfer plan in Jackson, Tenn., unlikely to achieve desegregation. [67]

The *Green* case was the last major school desegregation case in which Chief Justice Earl Warren participated.

In the first case heard by the court after Warren E. Burger replaced Warren, who retired in June 1969, the court reversed an appeals court order that allowed indefinite postponement of desegregation in 33 Mississippi school districts so long as they took "significant steps" in the forthcoming school year to dismantle their dual school systems.

The court's brief decision in the case of *Alexander v. Holmes Board of Education* (1969) took on added significance because the Nixon administration had argued for allowing delay. In an unsigned opinion, the court said that the standard of "all deliberate speed" was "no longer constitutionally permissible," and ordered the school districts to begin immediate operation of unitary school systems. The court defined these as "systems within which no person is to be effectively excluded from any school because of race or color." [68]

The Scope of the Remedy

Chief Justice Burger's appointment to the court roughly coincided with a shift in the focus of school desegregation cases. With the *Green* decision, it became clear that schools could no longer avoid the duty to desegregate; the question now was what methods could be used to accomplish that end? A major issue was whether schools were required to reflect the racial balance that existed in the community. Would neighborhood schools, whatever their racial balance, satisfy the desegregation requirement so long as they were open to students of all races? Or must pupils be bused beyond normal geographic school zones to achieve some sort of racial balance?

The Swann Decision

In 1971 the Supreme Court indicated it expected school officials to choose from among a broad range of desegregation tools those that would most effectively eliminate segregation in their district. In a unanimous decision, the court ruled in the case of *Swann v. Charlotte-Mecklenburg County Board of Education* that busing, racial balance quotas and gerrymandered school districts were all appropriate interim methods of eliminating the vestiges of school segregation.

The case arose from controversy over the desegregation of the Charlotte-Mecklenburg County, N.C., school system. That system in 1969-70 contained 84,000 students, 71 percent white and 29 percent black. In that year almost 29,000 of those students were bused to school in an effort to desegregate the school system.

Of the 24,000 black students, 21,000 lived within the city of Charlotte. Because of the smaller number and dispersed residences of black pupils in the rural part of the county, there were no all-black schools in that part of the system. But in the city, most schools remained racially identifiable, and two of every three of the city's black students attended one of 25 schools which were 98-100 percent black. Three of every four of the area's white students attended obviously white schools.

In February 1970 a federal district judge ordered 13,000 additional students bused. More than 9,000 of the additional pupils to be bused were elementary school-aged children. Under the order, no school remained all black, and the effort was made to reach a 71-29 white-black ratio in each school, reflecting the overall white-black ratio in the system.

The 4th Circuit Court of Appeals first delayed the effect, then reversed the elementary school part of the plan as imposing an unreasonable burden upon the school board. The NAACP Legal Defense Fund representing the black parents concerned, appealed to the Supreme Court, arguing that the entire order should have been left intact. The school board also appealed, arguing that more of the order should have been modified.

Chief Justice Burger wrote the court's opinion. He pointed out that federal courts became involved in the desegregation process only when local school authorities failed to fulfill their obligation to eliminate the dual school system. If school authorities did so default — as the lower federal court found that the Charlotte school board had in the *Swann* case — then the federal judge had wide discretion in selecting the means of desegregating the school system. Burger then discussed the four main problem areas presented in *Swann.*

Racial Balance. The court held that the federal district court had properly used mathematical ratios of whites and blacks as "a starting point in the process of shaping a remedy. . . ."

However, Burger wrote, a court could not require "as a matter of substantive constitutional right" any specific degree of racial mixing: "The constitutional command to desegregate schools does not mean that every school in every community must always reflect the racial composition of the school system as a whole." [69]

One-Race Schools. The court acknowledged that residential patterns often resulted in schools that were attended only by children of one race. The presence of such schools did not necessarily indicate a still-segregated system but, wrote Burger, school authorities or the district court:

. . .should make every effort to achieve the greatest possible degree of actual desegregation and will thus necessarily be concerned with the elimination of one-race schools. No *per se* rule can adequately embrace all the difficulties of reconciling the competing interests involved; but in a system with a history of segregation, the need for remedial criteria of sufficient specificity to assure a school authority's compliance with its constitutional duty warrants a presumption against schools that are substantially disproportionate in their racial composition. . . . [T]he burden upon the school authorities will be to satisfy the court that their racial composition is not the result of present or past discriminatory action on their part. [70]

The court endorsed plans that allowed a child attending a school where his race was a majority to transfer to a school where his race was in a minority. But to be successful, the justices added, such plans must assure the transferring pupil available space in the school and free transportation.

Attendance Zones. To overcome the effects of segregated residential patterns, the court endorsed drastic gerrymandering of school districts and pairing, clustering and grouping of schools that were not necessarily contiguous. "As an interim corrective measure, this cannot be said to be beyond the broad remedial powers of a court," the Chief Justice wrote. [71]

Busing. Bus transportation of students had been an "integral part of the public education system for years," Burger wrote, and was a permissible remedial technique to help achieve desegregation. The court conceded that objections to busing might be valid "when the time or distance of travel is so great as to either risk the health of the children or significantly impinge on the educational process." The limits to busing would vary with many factors, "but probably with none more than the age" of the children, the court said. [72]

The court acknowledged that some of these remedies might be "administratively awkward, inconvenient and even bizarre in some situations and may impose burdens on some; but all awkwardness and inconvenience cannot be avoided in the interim period when the remedial adjustments are being made to eliminate the dual school systems." [73]

The court was careful to say that its decision did not deal with *de facto* segregation, discrimination resulting from factors other than state law. Nor did it reach the question of what action might be taken against schools that were segregated as a result of "other types of state action, without any discriminatory action by the school authorities." [74]

In reference to the potential problem of resegregation, which might occur after achievement of a unitary school system, the court concluded its opinion:

. . .Neither school authorities nor district courts are constitutionally required to make year-by-year adjustments of the racial composition of student bodies once the affirmative duty to desegregate has been accomplished and racial discrimination through official action is eliminated from the system. This does not mean that federal courts are without power to deal with future problems; but in the absence of a showing that either the school authorities or some other agency of the state has deliberately attempted to fix or alter demographic patterns to affect the racial composition

Discrimination and Private Schools . . .

One result of the school desegregation controversy was an increase in the number of children attending private schools, many created specifically as havens for those opposing desegregation.

As early as 1925, the Supreme Court had acknowledged the right of parents to send their children to private schools. In the case of *Pierce v. Society of Sisters,* the court ruled that an Oregon statute requiring all children to attend public schools "unreasonably interferes with the liberty of parents and guardians to direct the upbringing and education of children under their control." [1]

This holding, coupled with the court's view that the 14th Amendment did not prohibit acts of private discrimination, appeared to immunize private schools with racially discriminatory admissions policies from desegregation efforts. However, two Supreme Court rulings in the 1970s curtailed the forms of support which state and local governments could provide to racially discriminatory private schools. And in a third case the court significantly narrowed the freedom of such schools to engage in racial discrimination.

Schoolbooks

In the first case, *Norwood v. Harrison* (1973), a unanimous court held that it was not constitutionally permissible for Mississippi to lend textbooks to private schools that discriminated on the basis of race. Lending textbooks constituted direct state aid in violation of the 14th Amendment, the court said. (In other cases the court has held that the First Amendment's clause prohibiting government establishment of religion bars states from lending textbooks to parochial schools but not from lending them to children who attend those schools.) *(Details, p. 466)*

Noting that it had affirmed lower court rulings barring state tuition grants to students attending racially discriminatory private schools, Chief Justice Warren E. Burger wrote:

> . . .Free textbooks, like tuition grants directed to private school students, are a form of financial assist-

ance inuring to the benefit of the private schools themselves. An inescapable educational cost for students in both public and private schools is the expense of providing all necessary learning materials. When, as here, that necessary expense is borne by the State, the economic consequence is to give aid to the enterprise; if the school engages in discriminatory practices the State by tangible aid in the form of textbooks thereby supports such discrimination. Racial discrimination in state-operated schools is barred by the Constitution and "(i)t is also axiomatic that a State may not induce, encourage or promote private persons to accomplish what it is constitutionally forbidden to accomplish.". . . [2]

The court rejected Mississippi's contention that to deny such private schools state aid would deny them equal protection of the laws.

"It has never been held that if private schools are not given some share of public funds allocated for education that such schools are isolated into a classification violative of the Equal Protection Clause," Burger wrote. "It is one thing to say that a State may not prohibit the maintenance of private schools and quite another to say that such schools must, as a matter of equal protection, receive state aid." [3]

Athletic Facilities

The following year, the court affirmed a lower court order forbidding Montgomery, Ala., to permit exclusive use of its park and recreational facilities by racially discriminatory private schools. Such permission "created, in effect, 'enclaves of segregation,' " which deprived black children and their families of equal access to the parks, the court said in the case of *Gilmore v. City of Montgomery* (1974). [4]

Furthermore, the court said, the city's action contravened a court order to desegregate its public schools. Justice Harry A. Blackmun explained that the city's permission for exclusive use of public recreational facilities enhanced the attractiveness of segregated private

---

of the schools, further intervention by a district court should not be necessary. [75]

Related Rulings

The court handed down three other related school desegregation decisions the same day — April 20, 1971. In the case of *North Carolina State Board of Education v. Swann,* the court struck down a state law that forbade school systems to bus or assign students to schools on the basis of race. The court said the law was invalid because it prevented implementation of desegregation plans:

> . . .[I]f a state-imposed limitation on a school authority's discretion operates to inhibit or obstruct the operation of a unitary school system or impede the disestablishing of a dual school system, it must fall; state policy must give way when it operates to hinder vindication of federal constitutional guarantees. . . .

> [T]he statute exploits an apparently neutral form to control school assignment plans by directing that they be "color-blind"; that requirement, against the background of segregation, would render illusory the promise of *Brown.* . . . Just as the race of students must be considered in determining whether a constitutional violation has occurred, so also must race be considered in formulating a remedy. To forbid, at this stage, all assignments made on the basis of race would deprive school authorities of the one tool absolutely essential to fulfillment of their constitutional obligation to eliminate existing dual school systems. [76]

In the case of *Davis v. Board of School Commissioners of Mobile, County, Ala.,* the court ordered an appeals court to re-examine its desegregation order for Mobile, Ala., in light of the guidelines set down in *Swann.* The court said the appeals court had not considered all the available

. . . State Aid and Admissions

schools — formed in reaction to the school desegregation order — by enabling them to offer athletic programs to their students largely at public expense.

Because the city thereby provided the schools with stadiums and other recreational facilities, the schools were able to spend money they would have spent on athletic programs on other educational projects. At the same time, the schools realized revenue from the concessions operated at the stadiums and other facilities.

"We are persuaded...," concluded Blackmun, "that this assistance significantly tended to undermine the federal court order mandating the establishment and maintenance of a unitary school system in Montgomery."[5]

However, the court was unable to decide whether state permission for the segregated private schools to use the facilities in common with other school children and private non-school organizations involved the city government so directly in the segregated actions of the private schools as to violate the Constitution.

Admissions Policies

Racially discriminatory admissions policies of private schools were directly challenged in the 1976 cases of *Runyon v. McCrary* and *Fairfax-Brewster School v. Gonzales*. Two private schools in northern Virginia, Bobbe's Private School and Fairfax-Brewster School, refused to admit Michael McCrary and Colin Gonzalez solely because they were black. Their parents filed suit on behalf of the boys, charging that discriminatory admissions policies violated the 1866 Civil Rights Act which gives "all persons within the jurisdiction of the United States the same right . . . to make and enforce contracts

... as is enjoyed by white citizens." A federal district court and court of appeals agreed with the parents, and the Supreme Court affirmed the lower courts by a 7-2 vote.[6]

For the majority, Justice Potter Stewart rejected the argument that the 1866 law did not reach private contracts. That claim was inconsistent with the court's earlier rulings, said Stewart, in particular the 1968 decision in the case of *Jones v. Alfred H. Mayer Co.* In that decision, the court held that a companion provision of the 1866 act forbade private racial discrimination in the sale or rental of property.[7] *(Details, p. 616)*

Stewart then rejected the arguments that application of the 1866 law to admissions policies violated the constitutional right of parents to have their children associate only with certain persons and to send their children to schools that promote racial segregation. "[P]arents have a First Amendment right to send their children to educational institutions that promote the belief that racial segregation is desirable, and ... the children have an equal right to attend such institutions," Stewart wrote. "But it does not follow that the *practice* of excluding racial minorities from such institutions is also protected" by the right of association.[8]

Dissenting for himself and Justice William H. Rehnquist, Justice Byron R. White took issue with the extension of the contract provision of the 1866 law to private action. No person, black or white, has a right to enter into a contract with an unwilling party no matter what the person's motive is for refusing to contract, White said.

"[T]he statute means what it says and no more, i.e., that it outlaws any legal rule disabling any person from making or enforcing a contract, but does not prohibit racially motivated refusals to contract," he added.[9]

---

[1] *Pierce v. Society of Sisters*, 268 U.S. 510 at 534-35 (1925).

[2] *Norwood v. Harrison*, 413 U.S. 455 at 463-65 (1973); for state tuition grants cases, see *Brown v. South Carolina Board of Education*, 296 F. Supp. 199 (S.C. 1968), affirmed *per curiam* 393 U.S. 222 (1968); *Poindexter v. Louisiana Finance Commission*, 275 F. Supp. 833 (E D La. 1967), affirmed *per curiam* 389 U.S. 571 (1968).

[3] *Norwood v. Harrison*, 413 U.S. 455 at 462 (1973).

[4] *Gilmore v. City of Montgomery*, 417 U.S. 556 at 566 (1974).

[5] Id., at 569.

[6] *Runyon v. McCrary, Fairfax-Brewster School v. Gonzalez*, 427 U.S. 160 (1976).

[7] *Jones v. Alfred H. Mayer Co.*, 392 U.S. 409 (1969).

[8] *Runyon v. McCrary*, 427 U.S. 160 at 176 (1976).

[9] Id., at 195.

---

techniques for desegregation. The plan included no busing for black children attending predominantly black high schools, and its insistence on geographically unified school zones tended to preserve single-race schools.[77]

In the third case, *McDaniel v. Barresi*, the court upheld a Georgia county desegregation plan which assigned black pupils living in heavily black areas to schools in other attendance zones. The state supreme court had declared the plan invalid on the grounds that busing only black pupils denied equal protection of the laws. But the Supreme Court said the school board had acted properly in considering race as a factor in a desegregation plan.[78]

'Tailoring' the Remedy

By 1971 opposition to court-ordered desegregation focused on the school bus. The near-universal antipathy to

busing did not cause the Supreme Court to retract its opinion that busing was an appropriate remedy for segregation, but in 1974 the court began to insist that the scope of the remedy not exceed the extent of the violation causing the segregation.

Cross-District Busing

The first time the court considered the question of whether federal courts could require consolidation of and busing between separate school districts as part of a desegregation plan, it was unable to reach a conclusion.

The case of *Richmond School Board v. Virginia State Board of Education* (1973) came to the court after a federal district judge ordered school officials to consolidate the predominantly black Richmond school district with the two neighboring majority-white county systems in order to desegregate the city schools.[79] The court of appeals overturned the order as too drastic.

Equal Protection and Affirmative Action . . .

Two of the more controversial equal protection cases before the court in the 1970s questioned whether affirmative action programs — designed to compensate for past discrimination against blacks and other minorities — themselves denied equal protection of the laws by favoring minority over majority group members.

Initially sidestepping the issue in 1974, the court in 1978 and 1979 sought to provide an answer to this question.

● In 1978 the court held that Title VI of the Civil Rights Act of 1964, which barred discrimination in any program receiving federal financial assistance, prohibited state universities from setting racial quotas for their entering classes. But in the same decision, the court said that the equal protection clause of the 14th Amendment did not forbid state universities to consider race as one of the factors determining acceptance or rejection of a student application.

● In 1979 the court held that Title VII of the 1964 Civil Rights Act, which barred employment discrimination, did not prohibit employers from voluntarily establishing affirmative action training programs.

The *DeFunis* Case

In the 1974 case of *DeFunis v. Odegaard*, a five-justice majority avoided a ruling on the reverse discrimination issue by finding the case moot, no longer presenting a live controversy. The white plaintiff, who charged that he was denied admission to a state law school in order that the school might accept a less-qualified minority student, had been admitted under court order. He was scheduled to graduate from law school in the spring of 1974, only months after the court heard arguments in his case. The majority held that the case was moot since their decision on the equal protection issue would have no effect on the plaintiff. The dissenting justices would have preferred to resolve the substantive question. [1] *(Discussion of mootness, p. 289)*

The *Bakke* Case

When the court in 1978 finally dealt with a live case of reverse discrimination, it handed down a split decision. By a 5-4 vote, the court ruled that state universities may not set aside a fixed quota of seats in each class for minority group members, denying white applicants the opportunity to compete for those places. At the same time, a different five-justice majority held that it is constitutionally permissible for admissions officers to consider race as one of the complex of factors that determine which applicant is accepted and which rejected.

Background

Allan Bakke, a 38-year-old white engineer, was twice denied admission to the medical school at the University of California at Davis. To ensure minority representation in the student body, the university had set aside 16 seats in each 100-member medical school class for minority applicants.

Challenging the program as a violation of his constitutional right to equal protection of the laws, Bakke contended that he would have been admitted had it not been for this rigid preference system. In each year his application was rejected, the school did accept some minority applicants with qualifications inferior to Bakke's.

Quotas

Justice Lewis F. Powell Jr. was the only justice who agreed with both halves of the decision in *University of California Regents v. Bakke*. On the first decision setting aside the Davis quota system, Powell voted with Chief Justice Warren E. Burger and Justices William H. Rehnquist, Potter Stewart and John Paul Stevens. These four viewed the Bakke case as a "controversy between two specific litigants" which could be settled by applying the 1964 Civil Rights Act and which did not require consideration of constitutional issues. Title VI of the 1964 act, this majority pointed out, barred any discrimination on the ground of race, color or national origin in any program receiving federal financial assistance. When that ban was placed alongside the facts of the case, it was clear to Burger, Rehnquist, Stewart and Stevens that the university had violated the statute.

As Stevens explained:

> The University, through its special admissions policy, excluded Bakke from participation in its program of medical education because of his race. The University also acknowledges that it was, and still is, receiving federal financial assistance. . . . The meaning of the Title VI ban on exclusion is crystal clear: Race cannot be the basis of excluding anyone from participation in a federally funded program. [2]

Powell's reasoning on this point differed from the four. Where they found no constitutional involvement, he found the scope of the Title VI ban and the equal protection clause of the 14th Amendment identical — what violated one therefore violated the other. And so he based his vote against the university's preference system on both the law and the Constitution.

The Davis special admissions program used an "explicit racial classification," Powell noted. Such classifications were not always unconstitutional, he continued, "[b]ut when a state's distribution of benefits or imposition of burdens hinges on . . . the color of a person's skin or ancestry, that individual is entitled to a demonstration that the challenged classification is necessary to promote a substantial state interest." Powell could find no substantial interest that justified establishment of the university's specific quota system. Not even the desire to remedy past discrimination was a sufficient justification, he said; such a desire was based on "an amorphous concept of injury that may be ageless in its reach into the past." [3]

Affirmative Action

But Powell's belief that not all racial classifications were unconstitutional led him to vote with the other four

. . . The Right and the Double-Edged Remedy

justices to approve the use of some race-conscious affirmative action programs. These four were Justices William J. Brennan Jr., Thurgood Marshall, Harry A. Blackmun and Byron R. White.

Powell's vote endorsing this position was cautious; he would limit the use of these programs to situations in which past discrimination had been proved. The other four contended that the university's wish to remedy past societal discrimination was sufficient justification. For the four, Brennan wrote:

> Government may take race into account when it acts not to demean or insult any racial group, but to remedy disadvantages cast on minorities by past racial prejudice, at least when appropriate findings have been made by judicial, legislative, or administrative bodies with competence to act in this area. [4]

The four endorsed the broad remedial use of race-conscious programs, even in situations where no specific constitutional violation had been found.

The *Weber* Case

The 1979 case did not raise the constitutional issue of equal protection. It posed only the question whether the Title VII prohibition against racial discrimination in employment barred an employer from establishing an affirmative action training program that preferred blacks over whites.

By a 5-2 vote, the court held that Title VII did not bar such a program. Stewart, who had voted against racial quotas in the *Bakke* case, joined the four justices who had endorsed use of race-conscious programs in that case to form the majority in *Weber*. Chief Justice Burger and Rehnquist dissented; Powell and Stevens did not participate in the case.

Background

In 1974 Kaiser Aluminum and the United Steelworkers of America agreed upon an affirmative action plan that reserved 50 percent of all in-plant craft training slots for minorities. The agreement was a voluntary effort to increase the number of minority participants holding skilled jobs in the aluminum industry.

Brian Weber, a white, applied for a training program at the Kaiser plant where he worked in Gramercy, La. He was rejected. Weber, who had more seniority than the most junior black accepted for the program, charged that he had been a victim of "reverse discrimination." He won at both the federal district court and the court of appeals levels. The union, the company and the Justice Department then asked the Supreme Court to review the appeals court decision in three separate cases — *United Steelworkers of America v. Weber, Kaiser Aluminum & Chemical Corp. v. Weber, United*

States v. Weber — which the court consolidated for argument and decision. [5]

Permissible Plan

Reversing the lower courts, the majority said that in passing Title VII Congress could not have intended to prohibit private employers from voluntarily instituting affirmative action plans to open opportunities for blacks in job areas traditionally closed to them:

> . . .It would be ironic indeed if a law triggered by a Nation's concern over centuries of racial injustice and intended to improve the lot of those who had "been excluded from the American dream for so long" . . . constituted the first legislative prohibition of all voluntary, private, race-conscious efforts to abolish traditional patterns of racial segregation and hierarchy. [6]

The majority carefully distinguished between the language of Title VII prohibiting racial discrimination in employment and Title VI, the section of the act reviewed in the *Bakke* case and held by a majority of the court to mean that programs receiving federal aid could not discriminate on the basis of race. In Title VI, Brennan said for the majority, "Congress was legislating to assure federal funds would not be used in an improper manner. Title VII, by contrast was enacted pursuant to the Commerce power to regulate purely private decisionmaking and was not intended to incorporate and particularize the commands of the Fifth and Fourteenth Amendments" which guarantee equal protection of the laws against federal and state infringement. [7]

In separate dissents Chief Justice Burger and Rehnquist objected to the majority's interpretation of Title VII and its legislative history. The court's judgment, Burger wrote:

> . . .is contrary to the explicit language of the statute and arrived at by means wholly incompatible with long-established principles of separation of powers. Under the guise of statutory "construction," the Court effectively rewrites Title VII to achieve what it regards as a desirable result. It "amends" the statute to do precisely what both its sponsors and its opponents agreed the statute was not *intended* to do. [8]

Rehnquist also claimed that the majority had contorted the language of Title VII. The majority opinion, he said, is "reminiscent not of jurists such as Hale, Holmes and Hughes, but of escape artists such as Houdini. . . ." The court, he continued, "eludes clear statutory language, 'uncontradicted' legislative history, and uniform precedent in concluding that employers are, after all, permitted to consider race in making employment decisions." [9]

---

[1] *DeFunis v. Odegaard*, 416 U.S. 312 (1974).

[2] *University of California Regents v. Bakke*, 438 U.S. 265 at 412, 418 (1978).

[3] Id. at 320, 307.

[4] Id. at 325.

[5] *United Steelworkers of America v. Weber, Kaiser Alumi-*

num & Chemical Corp. v. Weber, United States v. Weber (1979).

[6] Id.

[7] Id.

[8] Id.

[9] Id.

The Supreme Court divided 4-4, automatically upholding the court of appeals. Justice Lewis F. Powell Jr. did not participate in the case; he had formerly served on both the Richmond and Virginia school boards. There was no court opinion and, because of the even vote, the case carried no weight as precedent.

First Detroit Case. Little more than a year later, the court by a 5-4 vote struck down a district court plan to desegregate Detroit, Mich., schools by busing students among 54 school districts in three counties. The majority held that a multi-district remedy was not appropriate unless all of the districts involved were found responsible for the segregation to be remedied.

The case of *Milliken v. Bradley* (1974) originated when a federal district judge concluded that both the Detroit school board and state officials had taken actions that fostered school segregation in the city. Because the city school system was predominantly black, the judge declared that a plan limited to its boundaries would fail to provide meaningful desegregation of the schools. He therefore ordered the multi-district remedy. "[S]chool district lines are simply matters of political convenience and may not be used to deny constitutional rights," the judge ruled. [80] A court of appeals affirmed the order.

The Supreme Court majority overturned the order. Chief Justice Burger explained that both lower courts erred when they assumed that desegregation could not be achieved unless the Detroit schools reflected the racial balance of the surrounding metropolitan area. Although "boundary lines may be bridged where there has been a constitutional violation calling for interdistrict relief," wrote Burger, "...the notion that school district lines may be casually ignored or treated as a mere administrative convenience is contrary to the history of public education in our country." [81]

In any school desegregation case, said Burger, the scope of the remedy should not exceed the extent of the violation. He continued:

> ...Before the boundaries of separate and autonomous school districts may be set aside by consolidating the separate units for remedial purposes or by imposing a cross-district remedy, it must first be shown that there has been a constitutional violation within one district that produces a significant segregative effect in another district. Specifically, it must be shown that racially discriminatory acts of the state or local school districts, or of a single school district have been a substantial cause of interdistrict segregation. Thus an interdistrict remedy might be in order where the racially discriminatory acts of one or more school districts caused racial segregation in an adjacent district or where district lines have been deliberately drawn on the basis of race. In such circumstances, an interdistrict remedy would be appropriate to eliminate the interdistrict segregation directly caused by the constitutional violation. Conversely, without an interdistrict violation and interdistrict effect, there is no constitutional wrong calling for an interdistrict remedy.[82]

Since none of the other 53 school districts had been shown to practice segregation or to have been affected by Detroit's segregation, the proposed remedy was "wholly impermissible," the majority concluded.

Nor did the fact that state officials contributed to the segregation empower the federal court to order the multi-district remedy. "Disparate treatment of white and Negro students occurred within the Detroit school system, and not elsewhere, and on this record the remedy must be limited to that system," Burger wrote. [83]

Writing for the four dissenters, Justice Thurgood Marshall asserted that without an inter-district remedy "Negro children in Detroit will receive the same separate and inherently unequal education in the future as they have been unconstitutionally afforded in the past." [84] Marshall insisted that the segregative actions of state officials justified the multi-district remedy:

> ...The essential foundation of interdistrict relief in this case was not to correct conditions within outlying districts.... Instead, interdistrict relief was seen as a necessary part of any meaningful effort by the State of Michigan to remedy the state-caused segregation within the city of Detroit.[85]

Second Detroit Case. The Supreme Court remanded the *Milliken* case to the district court to fashion a new remedy that affected only the Detroit city schools. In an opinion affirmed by the appeals court, the district court ordered the school board as part of the new remedy to institute comprehensive remedial education, testing, training, counseling and guidance programs in the city schools. It also directed the state to pay half the costs of implementing these programs. These two parts of the remedy were appealed to the Supreme Court, which upheld them in 1977 by a 9-0 vote.

The court found the comprehensive remedial programs appropriate to remedy the educational conditions caused by the segregation. "Pupil assignment alone does not automatically remedy the impact of previous unlawful educational isolation; the consequences linger and can be dealt with only by independent measures," the court said. [86]

The justices also held that the order to the state to pay half the costs was not equivalent, as the state claimed, to an award for damages. In a non-school-related case, the court in 1974 had ruled that the 11th Amendment protected states against such payments of damages. [87] But the school payments amounted to prospective relief "designed to wipe out continuing conditions of inequality" caused in part by the state, held the court. [88]

System-Wide Remedies

In the 1974 *Milliken* decision, the court held that where segregation affected only one school district, a multi-district remedy was excessive. In 1977 the court held that where segregation did not affect an entire school district, a system-wide desegregation plan was excessive.

A federal district court found in the case of *Dayton (Ohio) Board of Education v. Brinkman* that the city school board had discriminated against minority students in three specific instances. After a court of appeals rejected more limited remedies, the district court proposed a desegregation plan that involved the entire school district. The appeals court affirmed this plan.

The Supreme Court struck the plan down by an 8-0 vote. In an opinion written by Justice William H. Rehnquist, the court questioned the validity of the district court's finding of discrimination in two of the instances and observed that the discrimination in the third affected only high school students. Under these circumstances, the court said, the appeals court overstepped its proper role when it ordered the district court to develop a system-wide plan

Bilingual Education

A unanimous Supreme Court in the case of *Lau v. Nichols* (414 U.S. 563, 1974) ruled that a public school system must make some effort to ensure that its non-English-speaking students are equipped with language skills necessary to profit from their required attendance at school. Non-English-speaking Chinese students in San Francisco charged that the city school board's failure to provide them with bilingual lessons or remedial English resulted in unequal educational opportunities and violated the 14th Amendment.

The court found it unnecessary to address the equal protection issue, ruling that the school board had violated the 1964 Civil Rights Act, which forbade discrimination based on national origin, race or color in any program receiving federal aid, and a Department of Health, Education and Welfare regulation requiring such school districts "to rectify . . . language deficiency" to ensure that instruction was meaningful to non-English speaking pupils.

---

without disputing the district court's findings of fact or legal opinion. Rehnquist wrote:

> The duty of both the District Court and of the Court of Appeals in a case such as this, where mandatory segregation by law of the races in the schools has long since ceased, is to first determine whether there was any action in the conduct of the business of the school board which was intended to, and did in fact, discriminate against minority pupils, teachers or staff. . . . If such violations are found, the District Court in the first instance, subject to review by the Court of Appeals, must determine how much incremental segregative effect these violations had on the racial distribution of the Dayton school population as presently constituted, when that distribution is compared to what it would have been in the absence of such constitutional violations. The remedy must be designed to redress that difference, and only if there has been a systemwide impact may there be a systemwide remedy. [89]

In 1979 the court held that the board's discrimination had a systemwide impact and thus necessitated a systemwide remedy.

A Continuing Balance

The court in the *Swann* decision said that once a school system was desegregated, school authorities would not be required to make annual adjustments in order to maintain a specific racial balance in each school. In the 1976 case of *Pasadena City Board of Education v. Spangler,* the court elaborated on that *Swann* statement.

The Pasadena, Calif., school board adopted a desegregation plan stipulating that as of the 1970-71 school year, no school in the district could have a majority of students of a minority race. In 1974 the school board asked the court to lift the "no-majority" requirement or to modify it. Observing that the board had complied with that requirement only in the initial year of the plan's implementation, the district court refused the request. It held that the requirement was applicable every year, even though residential patterns and other factors outside the school board's control resulted in the changing racial composition of the schools. A court of appeals affirmed the decision on most points, and the board appealed to the Supreme Court.

By a 6-2 vote, the court reversed the district court, holding that its literal interpretation of the requirement required the board to maintain a specific racial balance, which the Supreme Court in the *Swann* case said it would disapprove. The majority wrote:

> No one disputes that the initial implementation of the plan accomplished [its] objective. That being the case, the District Court was not entitled to require the [school district] to rearrange its attendance zones each year so as to ensure that the racial mix desired by the court was maintained in perpetuity. For having once implemented a racially neutral attendance pattern in order to remedy the perceived constitutional violations on the part of the defendants [the school board], the District Court has fully performed its function of providing the appropriate remedy for previous racially discriminatory attendance patterns. [90]

Joined in dissent by Justice William J. Brennan Jr., Justice Thurgood Marshall noted that the desegregation plan fulfilled the no-majority requirement only for one year and that without its continued maintenance immediate resegregation of the school system was likely. Because a lasting unitary school system had therefore apparently not been achieved, Marshall said the majority's application of the *Swann* statement to this case was improper. The *Swann* statement, wrote Marshall,

> . . .recognizes on the one hand that a fully desegregated school system may not be compelled to adjust its attendance zones to conform to changing demographic patterns. But on the other hand, it also appears to recognize that *until* such a unitary system is established, a district court may act with broad discretion — discretion which includes the adjustment of attendance zones — so that the goal of a wholly unitary system might be sooner achieved. [91]

Travel and Public Accommodations

During the first few years after the Civil War, blacks in many localities were afforded substantially the same treatment in public places as were whites.

During the decade of the 1870s there was little state-imposed segregation of the races in transportation or in public accommodations; in fact, three states — Massachusetts, New York and Kansas — specifically prohibited separation of the races in public places. Whether to accept the patronage of blacks was left largely to individual choice, and the majority of operators of public transport systems, hotels, restaurants, theaters and other amusements admitted blacks — if not always to first class accommodations, then at least to second class ones. [92]

Nonetheless, many proprietors, especially in the rural South, refused to serve blacks. Enactment of the 1866 Civil Rights Act, which specifically granted blacks the same rights as whites to bring lawsuits, encourage blacks to challenge these exclusions. Although many of these suits were successful, some courts upheld the right of individual proprietors to deny service to whomever they chose.

In an attempt to reverse these court decisions, the Republican Congress enacted the Civil Rights Act of 1875, declaring that "all persons within the jurisdiction of the United States shall be entitled to the full and equal enjoyment of the accommodations ... of inns, public conveyances on land or water, theaters, and other places of public amusement; subject only to the conditions and limitations established by law, and applicable alike to citizens of every race or color." Persons violating the act were subject to fine or imprisonment.

The Civil Rights Cases

This 1875 act promptly became the basis for several dozen suits protesting denial of equal treatment to blacks. Federal courts in several states upheld the constitutionality of the act, while others found it invalid. Five of these cases — known collectively as the *Civil Rights Cases* — eventually reached the Supreme Court. They involved theaters in New York and California that would not seat blacks, a hotel in Missouri and a restaurant in Kansas that would not serve blacks, and a train in Tennessee that prohibited a black woman from riding in the "ladies" car. *(United States v. Singleton, United States v. Ryan, United States v. Nichols, United States v. Stanley, Robinson & Wife v. Memphis and Charleston Railroad Company.)*

Deciding these cases by an 8-1 vote, the court in 1883 declared that Congress had exceeded its authority to enforce the 13th and 14th Amendments in passing the 1875 Act, and so it was invalid. The 14th Amendment applied only to discriminatory *state* actions, the court reminded Congress. "Individual invasion of individual rights is not the subject-matter of the amendment," the court asserted.[93]

Nor did private discrimination against blacks violate the 13th Amendment abolishing slavery, said the majority:

> ...such an act of refusal has nothing to do with slavery or involuntary servitude.... It would be running the slavery argument into the ground to make it apply to every act of discrimination which a person may see fit to make as to the guests he will entertain, or as to the people he will take into his coach or cab or car, or admit to his concert or theater....[94]

Although public opinion generally supported the court's decision in these *Civil Rights Cases,* four states in 1884 barred discrimination in public places. By 1897, 11 more states — all in the North and West — had enacted similar laws. Those that were challenged were sustained as a proper exercise of state police power.[95]

Segregation and Commerce

The decision in the *Civil Rights Cases* left open the possibility that Congress, through its commerce power, might bar private discrimination against blacks on public carriers. The Constitution gave Congress authority to regulate interstate commerce. By the close of the Civil War, the court had interpreted that authority to mean that states could regulate only local commerce that had no significant impact on other states.

In 1878 a unanimous Supreme Court had declared unconstitutional a Louisiana law *forbidding* segregation on public carriers. So far as the state law required desegregation on carriers that traveled interstate, it was a burden on interstate commerce, the court said in *Hall v. DeCuir.* Prohibition of segregation in interstate transportation was a matter on which there should be national uniformity and thus only Congress could adopt that policy. "If each state was at liberty to regulate the conduct of carriers while within its jurisdiction, the confusion likely to follow could not but be productive of great inconvenience and unnecessary hardship," the court concluded.[96]

Hoping that the court would apply this same reasoning to strike down state segregation laws, opponents of segregation in 1890 challenged a Mississippi law *requiring* segregation on public transportation. Their hopes went unfulfilled. Distinguishing the 1890 case of *Louisville, New Orleans & Texas Railway v. Mississippi* from the *DeCuir* decision on a technicality, the court ruled that the Mississippi law applied only to intrastate traffic and was therefore within a state's power to regulate local commerce.[97]

Plessy v. Ferguson

Six years later the Supreme Court gave its blessing to segregation in the case of *Plessy v. Ferguson.* The case was a deliberate test of the constitutionality of a Louisiana statute requiring separate but equal railroad accommodations for the races. Louisiana was one of six states that by 1896 had enacted such "Jim Crow" laws segregating blacks from whites on trains.

The suit was brought by Homer Plessy, a citizen of the United States and a Louisiana resident who was one-eighth black and appeared white. Plessy bought a first class ticket to travel from New Orleans to Covington, La., and took a seat in the coach reserved for whites. When he refused to move to the black coach, he was arrested. The state courts upheld the constitutionality of the state law. Plessy then appealed to the Supreme Court, which in 1896 affirmed the holdings of the state courts.

The Majority: A Reasonable Rule

Writing for the majority, Justice Henry B. Brown said the state law did not infringe on congressional authority over commerce. "In the present case," said Brown, "no question of interference with interstate commerce can possibly arise, since the East Louisiana Railway appears to have been purely a local line, with both its termini within the State...."[98]

Nor did the state statute violate the 13th Amendment:

> A statute which implies merely a legal distinction between the white and colored races — a distinction which is founded in the color of the two races, and which must always exist so long as white men are distinguished from the other race by color — has no tendency to destroy the legal equality of the two races, or reestablish a state of involuntary servitude.[99]

Plessy's challenge to the law as a violation of the 14th Amendment also failed, the majority said, because that amendment guaranteed only political equality and did not encompass what the court considered social distinctions:

> The object of the [14th] Amendment was undoubtedly to enforce the absolute equality of the two races before the law, but in the nature of things it could

not have been intended to abolish distinctions based upon color, or to enforce social, as distinguished from political equality, or a commingling of the two races upon terms unsatisfactory to either. Laws permitting, and even requiring, their separation in places where they are liable to be brought into contact do not necessarily imply the inferiority of either race to the other, and have been generally recognized as within the competency of the state legislatures in the exercise of their police powers. [100]

The question then, Brown continued, was whether the law was an unreasonable use of the state's police power. Noting that the court thought it reasonable for a state to consider the traditions and customs of its people and to want to protect their comfort and peace, Brown wrote:

> ...we cannot say that a law which authorizes or even requires the separation of the two races in public conveyances is unreasonable, or more obnoxious to the Fourteenth Amendment than the act of Congress requiring separate schools for colored children in the District of Columbia, the constitutionality of which does not seem to have been questioned, or the corresponding acts of state legislatures.

> We consider the underlying fallacy of [Plessy's] argument to consist in the assumption that the enforced separation of the two races stamps the colored race with a badge of inferiority. If this be so, it is not by reason of anything found in the act, but solely because the colored race chooses to put this construction upon it.... Legislation is powerless to eradicate racial instincts or to abolish distinctions based upon physical differences, and the attempt to do so can only result in accentuating the difficulties of the present situation. If the civil and political rights of both races be equal one cannot be inferior to the other civilly, or politically. If one race be inferior to the other socially, the Constitution of the United States cannot put them upon the same plane. [101]

The Dissent: A Colorblind Constitution

In lone dissent, as in the *Civil Rights Cases*, Justice John Marshall Harlan predicted that the decision would prove "quite as pernicious" as had the 1857 *Dred Scott* decision. The Kentucky-born Harlan, himself a former slaveholder, acknowledged that whites were the dominant race in prestige, education, wealth and power. "But in view of the Constitution," he declared, "in the eye of the law, there is in this country no superior, dominant, ruling class of citizens. There is no caste here. Our Constitution is colorblind and neither knows nor tolerates classes among citizens."[102] *(Dred Scott case, p. 135)*

Charging that the majority had glossed over the fact that the Louisiana law segregated blacks because whites considered them inferior, Harlan wrote:

> The arbitrary separation of citizens, on the basis of race, while they are on a public highway, is a badge of servitude wholly inconsistent with the civil freedom and the equality before the law established by the Constitution. It cannot be justified upon any legal grounds.... We boast of the freedom enjoyed by our people above all other peoples. But it is difficult to reconcile that boast with a state of the law, which, practically, puts the brand of servitude and degradation upon a large number of our fellow-citizens, our equals

before the law. The thin disguise of "equal" accommodations for passengers in railroad coaches will not mislead any one, nor atone for the wrong this day done. [103]

Equal Treatment

During the next six decades, the court's stance in regard to segregation on public carriers was similar to that it maintained on school segregation cases. The court upheld the right of the states to separate the races but required that their treatment be equal.

This insistence on equal treatment in transportation was first apparent in the 1914 case of *McCabe v. Atchison, Topeka & Santa Fe Railroad.* Oklahoma law required companies operating trains within the state to provide separate coaches for whites and blacks. McCabe sued the railroad because it provided sleeping cars for whites but none for blacks.

The railroad argued that there was not sufficient demand by blacks for sleeping car accommodations. The court rejected this defense. In an opinion written by Justice Charles Evans Hughes, the court said the railway's contention:

> ...makes the constitutional right depend upon the number of persons who may be discriminated against, whereas the essence of the constitutional right is that it is a personal one. Whether or not particular facilities shall be provided may doubtless be conditioned upon there being a reasonable demand therefore, but, if facilities are provided, substantial equality of treatment of persons traveling under like conditions cannot be refused. It is the individual who is entitled to the equal protection of the laws, and if he is denied by a common carrier, acting in the matter under the authority of a state law, a facility or convenience in the course of his journey which under substantially the same circumstances is furnished to another traveler, he may properly complain that his constitutional privilege has been invaded. [104]

In 1941 the court extended the principle in the *McCabe* case to that of an interstate traveler. A black member of the U.S. House of Representatives, Arthur W. Mitchell (D Ill., 1935-43), held a first-class ticket for a trip from Chicago to Hot Springs, Ark. When the train reached the Arkansas border, Mitchell was required by state law to move to a car reserved for blacks where there were no first class accommodations.

Mitchell challenged the state law as a violation of the Interstate Commerce Act of 1887, which prohibited public carriers from subjecting "any person ... to any undue or unreasonable prejudice or disadvantage in any respect whatsoever." The Interstate Commerce Commission (ICC) dismissed the complaint, but Mitchell appealed to the Supreme Court, which held he was entitled to first class accommodations just as any white would be. The court, however, did not question Arkansas' right to require the segregated coaches. [105]

Morgan v. Virginia

Five years later, the court took a significant step toward overturning segregation in public interstate transportation. The case of *Morgan v. Virginia* (1946) concerned a black woman traveling on a bus from Virginia to Maryland who defied a Virginia law when she refused to move to the back of the bus to make her seat available to whites.

Noting that 10 states specifically required segregation in interstate bus travel and that 18 specifically prohibited it, the court said that a "burden [on interstate commerce] might arise from a state statute which requires interstate passengers to order their movements on the vehicle in accordance with local rather than national requirements." [106] The court held that "seating arrangements for the different races in interstate motor travel require a single, uniform rule to promote and protect national travel." [107] Thus the state law was in violation of the commerce clause.

In 1948 the court upheld a Michigan law prohibiting segregation in public transportation; the law did not interfere with Congress' power to regulate interstate and foreign commerce, it said. In 1950 the court struck down segregated but unequal dining facilities on trains. In 1953 the court applied two seldom-used laws to prohibit restaurants in the District of Columbia from discriminating against blacks. [108]

Plessy Overturned

Then, in 1954, the Supreme Court renounced in its decision in the *Brown* case the "separate but equal" doctrine as it applied to public schools. [109] Beginning with the case of *Muir v. Louisville Park Theatrical Assn.* (1954), the court summarily declared that state-imposed segregation in public accommodations and transportation was unconstitutional as well. Relying on its decision in *Brown,* the court in quick succession ordered an end to state-imposed segregation on public beaches, municipal golf courses, vehicles of interstate transportation, in public parks, municipal auditoriums and athletic contests, seating in traffic court, and in prisons and jails. [110]

Most of these decisions were issued without opinion. In 1963, however, the court issued a full opinion in one case to emphasize its expectation that the states would proceed expeditiously to eliminate state-imposed segregation in public areas. The question in the case of *Watson v. Memphis* (1963) was whether the Tennessee city should be granted more time to desegregate its public parks and other municipal facilities. Warning that it would not countenance indefinite delays, the court said:

> The rights here asserted are, like all such rights, *present* rights; they are not merely hopes to some *future* enjoyment of some formalistic constitutional promise. The basic guarantees of our Constitution are warrants for the here and now and, unless there is an overwhelmingly compelling reason, they are to be promptly fulfilled. [111]

Swimming Pools

In contrast to its continued insistence on school desegregation, a sharply divided court held in 1971 that a city under a court order to desegregate its public facilities could close its public swimming pools rather than operate them on an integrated basis.

For the five-man majority in *Palmer v. Thompson,* Justice Hugo L. Black maintained that the 14th Amendment did not impose an affirmative obligation on a local government to maintain public swimming pools. And, said Black, so long as the city government denied the same facility to both races, it was not violating the equal protection clause.

Discriminatory Wills

In two sets of cases, the Supreme Court has held that the 14th Amendment forbids a state agency, but not a private one, from acting as trustee for wills that discriminate against blacks.

In 1957 the court considered the case of *Pennsylvania v. Board of Directors of City Trusts of Philadelphia,* concerning a will which left money in trust for the establishment and maintenance of a school for poor white orphan boys. The trust was administered by a state agency. The case arose when the agency refused admittance to two black orphan boys.

In a *per curiam* opinion, the Supreme Court said the agency's refusal to admit the two boys amounted to state discrimination in violation of the 14th Amendment.

Administration of the school was then turned over to private trustees who continued to follow the discriminatory terms of the will. This policy was again challenged, but the court in 1958 refused to review it.[1]

A decade later, in 1966, the court decided a case concerning a park in Macon, Ga., which, under the terms of the will bequeathing the land, could only serve whites. In this case the court held that even though the city, refusing to operate the park on a segregated basis, had turned over its management to private trustees, the park retained a public character that made it subject to the prohibitions of the 14th Amendment. [2]

As a result of this decision, the park reverted to the original heirs and was closed to the public. A group of blacks sued, claiming the closing violated their right to equal protection of the laws. But the court in 1970 found no constitutional violation. Closing the park to the public did not treat one race differently from the other, but deprived both blacks and whites equally of the facility, the majority said. [3]

---

[1] *Pennsylvania v. Board of Directors of City Trusts of Philadelphia,* 353 U.S. 230 (1957); 357 U.S. 570 (1958).
[2] *Evans v. Newton,* 382 U.S. 296 (1966).
[3] *Evans v. Abney,* 396 U.S. 435 (1970); see also *Palmer v. Thompson,* 403 U.S. 217 (1971).

For the dissenters, Justice Byron R. White said that "a state may not have an official stance against desegregating public facilities in response to a desegregation order.... The fact is that closing the pools is an expression of public policy that Negroes are unfit to associate with whites." [112]

Semi-Public Business

In a pair of cases, the court in 1960 and 1961 prohibited racial discrimination by privately owned businesses operated on public property. The case of *Boynton v. Virginia* (1960) concerned a privately owned restaurant in an interstate bus terminal. The restaurant refused to serve a black interstate traveler. The question presented to the court was whether the refusal violated the Interstate Commerce Act. The court decided it did:

> ...[I]f the bus carrier has volunteered to make terminal and restaurant facilities and service available to its interstate passengers as a regular part of their transportation, and the terminal and restaurant have acquiesced and cooperated in this undertaking, the

terminal and restaurant must perform these services without discriminations prohibited by the Act. In performance of these services under such conditions, the terminal and the restaurant stand in the place of the bus company.... [113]

The second case involved an intrastate situation and a constitutional question rather than a question of statutory law. The case of *Burton v. Wilmington Parking Authority* (1961) concerned the Eagle restaurant, which leased space in a city-owned parking building. The parking authority rented out the space in order to procure additional revenue to redeem its bonds. When the restaurant refused to serve a black, the question was whether the restaurant was so closely associated with the municipal parking authority as to make its discriminatory action state action in violation of the equal protection clause.

"Only by sifting facts and weighing circumstances can the nonobvious involvement of the State in private conduct be attributed its true significance," the court said in answering the question. [114] It then pointed out that the land on which the parking garage and restaurant sat was publicly owned and that the restaurant was there for the purpose of maintaining the public garage as a self-sustaining entity. Thus, the court concluded that:

> The State has so far insinuated itself into a position of interdependence with [the] Eagle [restaurant] that it must be recognized as a joint participant in the challenged activity, which, on that account, cannot be considered to have been so "purely private" as to fall without the scope of the Fourteenth Amendment. [115]

The Sit-In Cases

The *Boynton* and *Burton* cases served as precedent for a series of cases decided in 1962 commonly known as the "Sit-In Cases." Four of these concerned young blacks who had been convicted of criminal trespass after they had protested racially discriminatory policies of privately-owned stores and restaurants by seeking service at "whites only" lunch counters and tables. The fifth case involved two ministers convicted of aiding and abetting persons to commit criminal trespass by encouraging them to participate in one of the sit-in demonstrations.

The Supreme Court decided most of this type of case involving civil rights activists on First Amendment grounds. The sit-in cases were the only major ones decided on equal protection grounds. In each of the cases, a majority of the court found sufficient state involvement with the private act of discrimination to warrant coverage by the 14th Amendment's equal protection clause.

In the first case decided, *Peterson v. City of Greenville,* an eight-justice majority overturned the convictions of 10 youthful protestors who attempted to desegregate a department store lunch counter in Greenville, S.C. A city ordinance required racial segregation of public eating places. By having the protestors arrested, the store's managers did what the ordinance required, and therefore, held the court, the subsequent convictions amounted to state enforcement of the city ordinance denying equal protection. It was no defense that the store managers would have brought criminal trespass charges in the absence of the ordinance, the majority said:

> When a state agency passes a law compelling persons to discriminate against other persons because

of race, and the State's criminal processes are employed in a way which enforces the discrimination mandated by that law, such a palpable violation of the Fourteenth Amendment cannot be saved by attempting to separate the mental urges of the discriminators. [116]

The *Peterson* case then became the rule for overturning similar criminal trespass convictions in *Gober v. City of Birmingham* and *Avent v. North Carolina.* [117] In both cases, city ordinances required separation of the races in eating places. Then, having overturned the trespass convictions in *Gober,* the court overturned the aiding and abetting convictions of the two ministers who had urged participation in that sit-in. "It is generally recognized that there can be no conviction for aiding and abetting someone to do an innocent act," the majority wrote in *Shuttlesworth v. Birmingham.* [118]

In the final case, *Lombard v. Louisiana,* there was no law requiring segregated eating places in New Orleans. Nonetheless, the court found that public statements of the city mayor and police chief effectively "required" that public eating facilities be segregated. If it is constitutionally impermissible for a state to enact a law segregating the races, "the State cannot achieve the same result by an official command which has at least as much coercive effect as an ordinance," the justices said. [119]

Individual Discrimination

Still, most private owners of hotels, stores, restaurants, theaters and other public accommodations remained "without the scope of the Fourteenth Amendment" until passage in 1964 of the most comprehensive civil rights act since 1875. The act barred discrimination in employment, provided new guarantees to ensure blacks the right to vote, and authorized the federal government to seek court orders for the desegregation of public schools.

Title II of the act was aimed at discrimination in public accommodations. It prohibited discrimination on grounds of race, color, religion or national origin in public accommodations if the discrimination was supported by state law or other official action, if lodgings or other service were provided to interstate travelers or if a substantial portion of the goods sold or entertainment provided moved in interstate commerce.

There was no question that the 14th Amendment barred state officials from requiring or supporting segregation in public places. But the power of Congress to use the commerce clause as authority for barring private discrimination was uncertain. A case challenging that exercise of the commerce power reached the Supreme Court just six months after the 1964 law was enacted.

Heart of Atlanta Motel

The case of *Heart of Atlanta Motel v. United States* (1964) involved a motel in downtown Atlanta that refused to serve blacks in defiance of the new federal law. The motel owner charged that Congress had exceeded its authority under the commerce clause when it enacted Title II, and that the property owner's Fifth Amendment rights were denied when Congress deprived him of the freedom to choose his customers.

A unanimous Supreme Court upheld Title II. Writing for the court, Justice Tom Clark first outlined the interstate aspect of the motel's business, noting that it was accessible to interstate travelers, that it sought out-of-state patrons by advertising in nationally circulated publications and that 75 percent of its guests were interstate travelers. Clark then cited the testimony at the congressional hearings on the act which showed that blacks were frequently discouraged from traveling because of the difficulty encountered in obtaining accommodations. Congress had reasonably concluded that discrimination was an impediment to interstate travel, the court said.

Clark next turned to the commerce power of Congress, finding that Congress had the authority not only to regulate interstate commerce but also to regulate intrastate matters that affected interstate commerce:

> ...[T]he power of Congress to promote interstate commerce includes the power to regulate the local incidents thereof, including local activities in both the States of origin and destination, which might have a substantial and harmful effect upon that commerce. One need only examine the evidence ... to see that Congress may — as it has — prohibit racial discrimination by motels serving travelers, however "local" their operations may appear. [120]

The court also said that it made no difference that Congress had used its power under the commerce clause to achieve a moral goal. That fact, wrote Clark

> ...does not detract from the overwhelming evidence of the disruptive effect that racial discrimination has had on commercial intercourse. It was this burden which empowered Congress to enact appropriate legislation, and, given this basis for the exercise of its power, Congress was not restricted by the fact that the particular obstruction to interstate commerce with which it was dealing was also deemed a moral and social wrong. [121]

The court also rejected the claim that Title II violated the motel owner's Fifth Amendment rights. Congress acted reasonably to prohibit racial discrimination, the court said, noting that 32 states had similar civil rights laws in effect. Furthermore, the court said, "in a long line of cases this Court has rejected the claim that the prohibition of racial discrimination in public accommodations interferes with personal liberty." [122]

The court's decision upholding the constitutionality of the use of the commerce power to bar private discrimination seemed to conflict with the decision in the 1883 *Civil Rights Cases* that Congress lacked the power to enforce the 13th and 14th Amendments by barring private acts of discrimination in public accommodations. The court said in its 1964 ruling that it found the 1883 decision "without precedential value" since Congress in 1875 had not limited prohibition of discrimination to those businesses that impinged on interstate commerce. Wrote Clark of that case:

> ...Since the commerce power was not relied on by the Government and was without support in the [trial] record it is understandable that the Court narrowed its inquiry and excluded the Commerce Clause as a possible source of power. In any event, it is clear that such a limitation renders the opinion devoid of authority for the proposition that the Commerce Clause gives no power to Congress to regulate discriminatory practices now found substantially to affect interstate commerce. [123]

Private Clubs

The freedom to associate with persons of one's own choosing is held to be protected by the First Amendment. Consequently, private clubs with racially discriminatory admissions policies are generally considered beyond the reach of the 14th Amendment.

In one recent instance, the Supreme Court was asked to decide whether the issuance of a liquor license by the state to a private club that discriminated against blacks amounted to discriminatory state action in violation of the 14th Amendment. By a 6-3 vote, the court held in the case of *Moose Lodge 107 v. Irvis* (1972) it did not. [1] The majority said the court had never forbidden a state to provide services to a private individual or group that practiced discrimination. Such a ruling would mean that the state could not provide vital essentials such as fire and police protection, electricity and water to private individuals who discriminate.

The degree of state involvement necessary to constitute state action varies from case to case, the majority continued. In this situation, the liquor regulations, with one exception, in no way promoted discrimination and therefore did not involve the state in the private discriminatory policy, they concluded. The exception was the liquor board's requirement that all club bylaws be obeyed. The majority found that in cases where the bylaws restricted membership by race, the state regulation amounted to enforcement of a discriminatory practice and the requirement should not be applied to the private club.

In a second case, the court rejected the claim of a community recreation association that it was a private club exempt from the 1964 Civil Rights Act. The association limited membership in its swimming pool to white residents of the community and their white guests. In *Tillman v. Wheaton-Haven Recreation Association* (1973), the court ruled that the association was not entitled to the exemption because it had no selection criteria for membership other than race and residence in the community. [2]

---

[1] *Moose Lodge 107 v. Irvis,* 407 U.S. 163 (1972).
[2] *Tillman v. Wheaton-Haven Recreational Association, Inc.,* 410 U.S. 431 (1973).

Ollie's Barbecue

In the companion case of *Katzenbach v. McClung* (1964), the court upheld the section of Title II barring discrimination by private proprietors who served to their clientele goods that moved in interstate commerce. Ollie's Barbecue, a Birmingham, Ala., restaurant that discriminated against blacks, did not seek to serve customers from out of state, but 46 percent of the food it served was supplied through interstate commerce.

The restaurant claimed that the amount of food it purchased in interstate commerce was insignificant compared to the total amount of food in interstate commerce. The court rejected this argument. The restaurant's purchase might be insignificant, the court said, but added to all other purchases of food through interstate commerce by persons who discriminate against blacks, the impact on interstate commerce was far from insignificant. [124]

Commerce and Recreation

Five years later, in the 1969 decision in *Daniel v. Paul*, the court upheld Title II as applied to a small recreational area not far from Little Rock, Ark. The area admitted only whites, but claimed it did not fall under the prohibitions of Title II because it did not deliberately seek interstate travelers and sold few food items purchased through interstate commerce.

The court disagreed. The few food items the amusement area sold were composed of ingredients produced in other states, the court said. Furthermore, the facility advertised for customers in Little Rock and at a military base, and it was unreasonable for it to think that these ads would not attract some interstate travelers. [125]

Justice Hugo L. Black objected to the lengths the majority went to to show the connection between the recreational area and interstate commerce. He said he would have supported the majority if it had held that the 14th Amendment, rather than the commerce clause, empowered Congress to prohibit discrimination in public places.

The Right to Fair Housing

Even as the Supreme Court in the *Civil Rights Cases* of 1883 held that Congress lacked authority to protect blacks against private persons who refused them public accommodations, it acknowledged the power of Congress to erase "the necessary incidents of slavery" and "to secure to all citizens of every race and color, without regard to previous servitude, those fundamental rights which are the essence of civil freedom." Among these, the court said, was the right "to inherit, purchase, lease, sell and convey property...." [126]

With this statement the court by indirection upheld the Civil Rights Act of 1866, enacted by Congress to enforce the 13th Amendment, which abolished slavery. The act gave blacks the same rights as whites to buy, lease, hold and sell property. *(Text of 1866 Act, box, p. 614)*

State Discrimination

However, as southern and border states and cities adopted more statutes and ordinances segregating whites from blacks, even this fundamental right fell victim to "Jim Crow" laws. Ordinances that segregated neighborhoods by restricting some blocks to whites and others to blacks were enacted by several cities in the early 1900s. In 1917 the Supreme Court struck down this type of housing law.

The case of *Buchanan v. Warley* (1917) arose in Louisville, Ky., where a city ordinance forbade members of one race to buy, reside on or sell property on streets where a majority of the residents were of the other race. Buchanan, a white property owner, entered into a contract for the sale of his property to a black man named Warley. When Warley found the Louisville law prevented him from living on the property, he exercised a contract proviso allowing him to break his agreement to purchase. Buchanan then sued for performance of the contract and charged that the Louisville ordinance violated the 14th Amendment. Defenders of the ordinance claimed that it was a valid exercise of the city's police power to prevent racial conflict, maintain racial purity and prevent deterioration in property values.

The Supreme Court acknowledged that the police power was broad, but it also recalled the court's 1883 opinion that acquisition, use and disposal of property were fundamental rights available to all citizens without regard to race or color. The court then unanimously struck down the city ordinance. Justice William R. Day wrote for the court:

That there exists a serious and difficult problem arising from a feeling of race hostility which the law is powerless to control, and to which it must give a measure of consideration, may be freely admitted. But its solution cannot be promoted by depriving citizens of their constitutional rights and privileges.... The right which the ordinance annulled was the civil right of a white man to dispose of his property if he saw fit to do so to a person of color, and of a colored person to make such disposition to a white person.... We think this attempt to prevent the alienation of the property in question ... was not a legitimate exercise of the police power of the state, and is in direct violation of the fundamental law enacted in the Fourteenth Amendment of the Constitution preventing state interference with property rights except by due process of law. [127]

The court subsequently upheld several lower court decisions invalidating similar state and local laws on the basis of the *Buchanan* decision. [128]

Restrictive Covenants

Officially imposed housing segregation was quickly replaced in many localities by private restrictive covenants. Under such covenants, the white residents of a particular block or neighborhood agreed to refuse to sell or lease their homes to blacks.

A challenge to the constitutional validity of such private covenants came before the Supreme Court in 1926. Adhering to its earlier rulings that Congress had no authority to protect individuals from private discrimination, the court dismissed the case of *Corrigan v. Buckley* (1926). The arguments that the covenant violated the Fifth, 13th and 14th Amendments, the court said, were

...entirely lacking in substance or color of merit. The Fifth Amendment "is a limitation only upon the powers of the General Government," ... and is not directed against the action of individuals. The Thirteenth Amendment denouncing slavery ... does not in other matters protect the individual rights of persons of the Negro race.... And the prohibitions of the Fourteenth Amendment "have reference to state action exclusively, and not to any action of private individuals." [129]

No State Enforcement

The court thus upheld the validity of private covenants.

But 22 years later, it effectively nullified them by forbidding the state to enforce them. The case of *Shelley v.*

Civil Rights Act of 1866

Congress enacted the Civil Rights Act of 1866 to enforce the newly ratified 13th Amendment prohibiting slavery. Following is the text of the portion of the Civil Rights Act which the Supreme Court in 1968 held to bar individuals from discriminating against racial minorities in the sale or rental of housing:

Section 1. Be it enacted by the Senate and House of Representatives of the United States of America in Congress assembled, That all persons in the United States and not subject to any foreign power, ... are hereby declared to be citizens of the United States; and such citizens, of every race and color, without regard to any previous condition of servitude ... shall have the same right, in every State and Territory in the United States, to make and enforce contracts, to sue, be parties, and give evidence, to inherit, purchase, lease, sell, hold, and convey real and personal property, and to full and equal benefit of all laws and proceedings for the security of person and property, as is enjoyed by white citizens, and shall be subject to like punishment, pains, and penalties, and to none other, any law, statute, ordinance, regulation, or custom, to the contrary notwithstanding.

Section 2. That any person who, under color of any law, statute, ordinance, regulation, or custom, shall subject, or cause to be subjected, any inhabitant of any State or Territory to the deprivation of any right secured or protected by this act, or to different punishment, pains, or penalties on account of such person having at any time been held in a condition of slavery or involuntary servitude, ... or by reason of his color or race, than is prescribed for the punishment of white persons, shall be deemed guilty of a misdemeanor, and, on conviction, shall be punished by fine not exceeding one thousand dollars, or imprisonment not exceeding one year, or both, in the discretion of the court.

Kraemer (1948) arose when a black couple bought property to which a restrictive covenant applied. A white couple who owned restricted property in the same neighborhood sued to stop the Shelleys from taking possession of the property. The trial court denied that request, holding that the covenant was not effective because it had not been signed by all the property owners in the affected area. The supreme court of Missouri reversed the decision, ruling the covenant effective and not a violation of the Shelleys' rights under the 14th Amendment. The Shelleys appealed to the Supreme Court, where their case was combined with a similar one, *McGhee v. Sipes.* [130]

Writing for a unanimous court (although three members did not participate), Chief Justice Fred M. Vinson repeated the court's earlier opinion that the 14th Amendment does not reach "private conduct, however discriminatory or wrongful." Therefore, Vinson wrote, private restrictive covenants "effectuated by voluntary adherence to their terms" are not in violation of the amendment. [131]

However, the Chief Justice continued, official actions by state courts and judicial officers have never been considered to be outside the scope of the 14th Amendment. In the two cases before the court, Vinson said,

...the States have made available to [private] individuals the full coercive power of government to deny to petitioners, on the grounds of race or color, the enjoyment of property rights in premises which petitioners are willing and financially able to acquire and which the grantors are willing to sell. The difference between judicial enforcement and nonenforcement of the restrictive covenants is the difference to petitioners between being denied rights of property available to other members of the community and being accorded full enjoyment of these rights on an equal footing....

We hold that in granting judicial enforcement of the restrictive agreements in these cases, the States have denied petitioners the equal protection of the laws and that, therefore, the action of the state courts cannot stand. [132]

Two companion cases (*Hurd v. Hodge, Urciola v. Hodge,* 1948) challenged restrictive covenants in the District of Columbia. Because the 14th Amendment applied only to states, the district covenants were alleged to violate the due process clause of the Fifth Amendment. But the court found it unnecessary to address the constitutional issue, holding instead that the district courts were barred from enforcing the covenants by the Civil Rights Act of 1866. [133]

No Penalty

The court expanded its *Shelley v. Kraemer* ruling five years later in the case of *Barrows v. Jackson* (1953) when it ruled that state courts could not require a person who had violated a restrictive covenant to pay damages to other covenantors who claimed her action had reduced their property's value.

Court enforcement of such a damage claim constitutes state action that violates the 14th Amendment if it denies any class the equal protection of the laws, the court said. "If a state court awards damages for breach of a restrictive covenant," the court reasoned, "a prospective seller of restricted land will either refuse to sell to non-Caucasians or else will require non-Caucasians to pay a higher price to meet the damage which the seller may incur." [134] In either event, the court concluded, non-Caucasians would be denied equal protection.

Housing Referenda

In 1967 the court applied its philosophy in *Shelley v. Kraemer* to nullify a state constitutional amendment.

The case of *Reitman v. Mulkey* arose after California voters in 1964 approved a constitutional amendment prohibiting the state from abridging the right of any person to sell or refuse to sell his property to anyone for any reason. The amendment effectively nullified several state fair housing laws.

When the Mulkeys sued Reitman on the grounds that he had declined to rent them an apartment solely because they were black, Reitman moved for dismissal of their complaint claiming that the newly-enacted constitutional amendment made their complaint null and void. The California supreme court, however, held that by the amendment the state had acted "to make private discriminations legally possible" and thus violated the equal protection clause of the 14th Amendment.

By a 5-4 vote, the Supreme Court affirmed the California high court ruling. For the majority, Justice Byron R. White wrote that adoption of the amendment meant:

...[t]he right to discriminate, including the right to discriminate on racial grounds, was now embodied in the State's basic charter, immune from legislative, executive or judicial regulation at any level of the state government. Those practicing racial discriminations need no longer rely solely on their personal choice. They could now invoke express constitutional authority, free from censure or interference of any kind from official sources. [135]

Justice John Marshall Harlan, writing for the dissenters, said the amendment was neutral on its face and did not violate the equal protection clause. By maintaining that the amendment actually encourages private discrimination, Harlan said, the majority "is forging a slippery and unfortunate criterion by which to measure the constitutionality of a statute simply permissive in purpose and effect, and inoffensive on its face." [136]

Two years later the court struck down a newly-added provision of the Akron, Ohio, city charter that required a majority of voters to approve any ordinance dealing with racial, religious or ancestral discrimination in housing.

Noting that the charter did not require similar referenda for other housing matters, such as rent control, public housing and building codes, the majority in *Hunter v. Erickson* (1969) held that the charter singled out a special class of people for special treatment in violation of the equal protection clause. "[T]he State may no more disadvantage any particular group by making it more difficult to enact legislation in its behalf than it may dilute any person's vote or give any group a smaller representation than another of comparable size," the majority wrote. [137]

Justice Hugo L. Black dissented, protesting "against use of the Equal Protection Clause to bar States from repealing laws that the Court wants the States to retain." [138]

In the 1971 case of *James v. Valtierra*, however, the court upheld a California constitutional amendment providing that no local government agency could construct low-income housing projects without first receiving the approval of a majority of those voting in a local referendum.

Distinguishing this holding from that in *Hunter*, the majority said the city charter at issue in *Hunter* created a classification based solely upon race, while the constitutional amendment involved in the *James* case "requires referendum approval for any low-rent public housing project, not only for projects which will be occupied by a racial minority." [139]

In dissent, Justice Thurgood Marshall contended that the California amendment created a classification based on poverty that violated the equal protection clause as much as did classifications based on race. "It is far too late in the day to contend that the Fourteenth Amendment prohibits only racial discrimination," Marshall wrote, "and, to me, singling out the poor to bear a burden not placed on any other class of citizens tramples the values that the Fourteenth Amendment was designed to protect." [140] *(Poverty and equal protection, p. 641)*

Individual Discrimination

Despite the court's rulings on state enforcement of restrictive covenants and housing referenda, blacks and other minorities still had little protection from housing discrimination by individual home and apartment owners.

The Right to Challenge

Ordinarily, the Supreme Court does not allow a person to come before it to defend the rights of third parties. However, the court has sometimes bent this rule in its review of housing discrimination cases. *(Discussion of standing, p. 291)*

The case of *Barrows v. Jackson* (1953) concerned a woman who violated a restrictive convenant by selling her property to blacks. Other covenantors in the neighborhood sued her for damages, claiming that her action reduced their property values. The restrictive covenant did not affect the constitutional rights of the white seller who had breached its terms, but in defense of her action, she argued that the covenant infringed on the rights of racial minorities by forbidding them to buy homes in the neighborhood. The court allowed her to make this defense in behalf of third parties. The reasons for ordinarily prohibiting such a defense were "outweighed [in this case] by the need to protect the fundamental rights which would be denied by permitting the damages action to be maintained," the court said. [1]

In 1972 the court again took a broad view of the right to bring housing discrimination cases. Two white tenants in an apartment building claimed that their landlord's discriminatory policy against non-whites harmed them by denying them social, business and professional advantages gained from associations with minorities. The tenants filed a complaint with the federal Department of Housing and Urban Development (HUD) under Section 810 of the 1968 Civil Rights Act.

When the complaint reached trial, a federal district court held that the tenants were not within the class of persons entitled to sue under the 1968 act. The Supreme Court reversed the lower court in the case of *Trafficante v. Metropolitan Life Insurance Co.*

"We can give vitality to [section] 810...," wrote Justice William O. Douglas, "only by a generous construction which gives standing to sue to all in the same housing unit who are injured by racial discrimination in the management of those facilities within the coverage of the statute." [2]

But the court has not consistently been so generous in construing standing to challenge alleged housing discrimination. In the 1975 case of *Warth v. Seldin*, a five-justice majority deflected an effort to attack a town's zoning ordinance as effectively excluding low- and moderate-income persons from living in the town. The majority held that none of the groups seeking to bring the suit had the legal standing to do so because none could show that a decision in their favor invalidating the zoning ordinance would have a direct ameliorative effect on the injury that they claimed to suffer as a result of its operation. [3]

[1] *Barrows v. Jackson,* 346 U.S. 249 at 257 (1953).
[2] *Trafficante v. Metropolitan Life Insurance Company,* 409 U.S. 205 at 212 (1972); see also *Gladstone Realtors v. Village of Bellwood* (1979).
[3] *Warth v. Seldin,* 422 U.S. 490 (1975).

An Old Law, New Life

Then, in 1968, just weeks after Congress enacted the first federal fair housing law, the Supreme Court by a 7-2 vote held that the 1866 Civil Rights Act barred individual as well as state-backed discrimination in the sale and rental of housing. The case was brought by Joseph Lee Jones, who contended that the Alfred H. Mayer Co. violated the 1866 act by refusing to sell him a home in the Paddock Woods section of St. Louis County, Mo., because he was black.

A federal district court dismissed the case; the court of appeals affirmed the dismissal on the grounds that the 1866 act (in modern form Section 1982 of Title 42 of the U.S. Code) applied only to state discrimination and not to the segregative actions of private individuals.

The Supreme Court reversed the court of appeals. Writing for the majority in *Jones v. Alfred H. Mayer Co.* (1968), Justice Potter Stewart said that the legislative history of the 1866 act persuaded the court that Congress intended to ban private and state-backed discrimination:

> In light of the concerns that led Congress to adopt it and the contents of the debates that preceded its passage, it is clear that the Act was designed to do just what its terms suggest: to prohibit all racial discrimination, whether or not under color of law, with respect to the rights enumerated therein — including the right to purchase or lease property. [141]

The question was then — did Congress have the power to enact the 1866 act? For the answer, Stewart looked to the 13th Amendment rather than to the equal protection clause of the 14th Amendment. The 13th Amendment was adopted to remove the "badges of slavery" from the nation's blacks, Stewart observed, and gave Congress the power to enforce that removal. Stewart continued:

> If Congress has power under the Thirteenth Amendment to eradicate conditions that prevent Negroes from buying and renting property because of their race or color, then no federal statute calculated to achieve that objective can be thought to exceed the constitutional power of Congress simply because it reaches beyond state action to regulate the conduct of private individuals.... Surely Congress has the power under the Thirteenth Amendment rationally to determine what are the badges and the incidents of slavery, and the authority to translate that determination into effective legislation. Nor can we say that the determination Congress has made is an irrational one.... [W]hen racial discrimination herds men into ghettoes and makes their ability to buy property turn on the color of their skin, then it too is a relic of slavery....
>
> At the very least, the freedom that Congress is empowered to secure under the Thirteenth Amendment includes the freedom to buy whatever a white man can buy, the right to live wherever a white man can live. If Congress cannot say that being a free man means at least this much, then the Thirteenth Amendment made a promise the Nation cannot keep. [142]

Justice Harlan, dissenting for himself and Justice White, said that the 1866 act was meant only to protect people from state-imposed discrimination.

Community Clubs, Pools

In 1969 the court held that the 1866 act also prohibited a community recreational club from refusing membership to a black man who received a club share as part of his lease of a home in the neighborhood. [143]

And in 1973, the court ruled that a community recreation area violated the 1866 Civil Rights Act when it limited membership in its swimming pools to white residents of the community and their white guests. In the case of *Tillman v. Wheaton-Haven Recreation Association,* a unanimous court wrote:

> When an organization links membership benefits to residence in a narrow geographical area, that decision infuses those benefits into the bundle of rights for which an individual pays when buying or leasing within the area. The mandate of [the 1866 Civil Rights Act] then operates to guarantee a nonwhite resident, who purchases, leases or holds this property, the same rights as are enjoyed by a white resident. [144]

Remedies for Housing Discrimination

Although the court has struck down several varieties of housing discrimination, it has had little occasion to consider remedies for that discrimination.

In the one case the court has heard on the remedy issue, however, it unanimously upheld the power of a federal judge to order a metropolitan area-wide remedy for segregated public housing in Chicago.

The question in the case of *Hills v. Gautreaux* (1976) was whether the remedy for racial discrimination in public housing caused by state and federal officials must be confined to the city in which the discrimination occurred or could include the surrounding metropolitan area. [145] In holding that the remedy need not be restricted to the city alone, the court made an important distinction between the facts in this case and those in the case decided by its 1974 ruling in *Milliken v. Bradley,* which overturned a metropolitan area-wide plan of school desegregation. [146] *(Milliken decision, p. 606)*

In the Hills case, the Chicago Housing Authority (CHA) was found guilty of discrimination in placing most of the city's public housing in black ghettoes, and the Department of Housing and Urban Development (HUD) was found guilty of sanctioning and aiding this discriminatory public housing program. A court of appeals ordered a metropolitan area-wide plan to eliminate the segregated public housing system, but HUD asked the Supreme Court to reverse it, citing *Milliken v. Bradley.*

Distinguishing between the two cases, Justice Potter Stewart said the court struck down the school desegregation plan because "there was no finding of unconstitutional action on the part of the suburban school officials and no demonstration that the violations committed in the operation of the Detroit school system had any significant segregative effects in the suburbs." [147]

The situation in the Chicago housing case was different, Stewart's opinion said. HUD did not contest the finding that it had violated the Constitution and the 1964 Civil Rights Act, nor did it dispute the appropriateness of its being ordered to help develop public housing in desegregated neighborhoods:

> The critical distinction between HUD and the suburban school districts in *Milliken* is that HUD has been found to have violated the Constitution.... Nothing in the Milliken decision suggests a *per se* rule that federal courts lack authority to order parties found to have violated the Constitution to undertake reme-

The Zoning Power and Fair Housing

Since 1926, when it first upheld a comprehensive zoning law, the Supreme Court has seldom interfered with state exercise of police power to restrict the uses to which specific parcels of land may be put. This has been true even in the face of challenges that a zoning law violated the equal protection clause of the 14th Amendment. *(Zoning power, p. 358)*

Such a challenge was raised in 1974 against a New York village's zoning ordinance that prohibited more than two unrelated persons from sharing a single-family home. The ordinance placed no limit on the number of family members that could share a house. Rejecting an equal protection challenge to the ordinance, the court wrote that the zoning law was a reasonable means of attaining a permissable objective — the preservation of the family character of the village.[1] *(Details, p. 359)*

Arlington Heights, Ill.

In 1977 the court again turned back a challenge to a local zoning decision as in violation of the equal protection clause. The case of *Village of Arlington Heights v. Metropolitan Housing Development Corporation* arose when a housing developer requested the predominantly white Chicago suburb of Arlington Heights to rezone certain land so that the developer could build housing for low- and moderate-income persons of both races there. When the zoning officials refused the request, the developer took the case to court, charging the denial was motivated by a desire to keep black families from moving into the suburb.

By a 5-3 vote, the Supreme Court upheld the village's refusal to rezone. The court said there was no evidence that the refusal was racially motivated. Instead the evidence showed that the zoning decision was motivated by legitimate desires to protect property values by allowing only single-family homes in the area and to preserve the integrity of the zoning plan.[2]

Without evidence of discriminatory intent, wrote Justice Lewis F. Powell Jr. for the majority, the fact that the refusal to rezone had a racially discriminatory effect was "without independent constitutional significance." The court referred back to its mid-1976 job discrimina-

tion ruling in the case of *Washington v. Davis.*[3] There, said Powell, the court made clear "that official action will not be held unconstitutional solely because it results in a racially disproportionate impact.... Proof of racially discriminatory intent or purpose is required to show a violation of the Equal Protection Clause."[4] *(Washington v. Davis, p. 620)*

Motivation

Powell then discussed factors that might be examined to determine whether a decision had been motivated by racial discrimination. These included the potential impact of the decision, the historical background, the specific sequence of events leading up to the decision, departures from normal procedures and the legislative or administrative history, he said.

For example, Powell said, the Arlington Heights decision to refuse to rezone would appear in a different light if the village had not consistently applied its zoning policy, if unusual procedures had been followed in handling this particular request or if the zoning for the particular parcel had been recently changed from multi-family to single-family use.

Justice Byron R. White, author of the majority opinion in *Washington v. Davis*, dissented, saying that the majority should not have applied the ruling to the *Arlington Heights* case before giving the court of appeals the chance to do so. The *Davis* decision was handed down by the Supreme Court after the appeals court ruled in the *Arlington Heights* case.

The court sent the case back to the court of appeals to consider whether the zoning decision violated the Fair Housing Act of 1968. In July 1977, that court held that the village's refusal to rezone would violate the act if it had a discriminatory effect even though there was no intent to discriminate. "Conduct that has the necessary and forseeable consequences of perpetuating segregation can be as deleterious as purposefully discriminating conduct in frustrating" the national goal of integrated housing, the appeals court wrote.[5] It then sent the case back to federal district court to determine if the effect of the refusal was discriminatory.

---

[1] *Village of Belle Terre v. Boraas*, 416 U.S. 1 (1974).
[2] *Village of Arlington Heights v. Metropolitan Housing Development Corporation*, 429 U.S. 252 (1977).
[3] *Washington v. Davis*, 426 U.S. 229 (1976).

[4] *Village of Arlington Heights v. Metropolitan Housing Development Corporation*, 429 U.S. 252 at 264-65 (1977).
[5] *Metropolitan Housing Development Corporation v. Village of Arlington Heights*, 558 F. 2d 1283 at 1289 (1977).

---

dial efforts beyond the municipal boundaries of the city where the violation occurred.[148]
The court's opinion continued:

...[I]t is entirely appropriate and consistent with *Milliken* to order CHA and HUD to attempt to create housing alternatives for the respondents [the black plaintiffs] in the Chicago suburbs. Here the wrong committed by HUD confined the respondents to segregated public housing. The relevant geographic area for purposes of the respondents' housing option is the Chicago housing market, not the Chicago city limits.... To foreclose such relief solely because HUD's constitutional violation took place within the city

limits of Chicago would transform *Milliken*'s principled limitation on the exercise of federal judicial authority into an arbitrary ... shield for those found to have engaged in unconstitutional conduct.[149]

A metropolitan remedy need not impermissibly interfere with local governments which had not been involved in the unconstitutional segregation, Stewart continued:

The remedial decree would neither force suburban governments to submit public housing proposals to HUD nor displace the rights and powers accorded local government entities under federal or state housing statutes or existing land-use laws. The order would have the same effect on the suburban governments as a discretionary decision by HUD to use its statutory powers to provide the respondents with alternatives to the racially segregated Chicago public housing system created by CHA and HUD. [150]

In 1977 the court seemed to limit the potential impact of the *Gautreaux* decision. In the case of *Village of Arling-*

ton Heights v. Metropolitan Housing Development Corporation, the court said that, without a showing of discriminatory motive, the village's refusal to rezone property to permit building of a housing development for low- and moderate-income persons of both races did not violate the 14th Amendment. [151] The court's decision left open the possibility that the zoning decision might have violated the 1968 Fair Housing Act. *(Details, box, p. 617)*

Equality of Employment Opportunity

Civil war and emancipation did little to free blacks from job discrimination. Most of the southern states quickly enacted Black Codes restricting the kinds of jobs blacks could hold, thereby limiting competition with white workers and forcing Negroes to continue as farm and plantation workers.

One of the harshest of these codes was enacted by South Carolina. It prohibited a black from working as an artisan or mechanic unless he obtained a license that cost $10 and from becoming a shopkeeper unless he had a license costing $100. Licenses were issued by judges who decided whether the black applicants were skilled and morally fit for the work.

The only jobs that blacks could obtain without a license were as farm workers or servants, and in both cases they were required to sign labor contracts with their employers. In South Carolina, as in many other southern states, failure to fulfill the labor contract was a crime, and a black worker could avoid a jail term only by agreeing to work off the original contract, his fine for defaulting and court costs. The Supreme Court struck down such peonage laws as unconstitutional in the early 1900s. [152]

Despite industrialization, blacks remained relegated to low-paying, unskilled jobs that promised little, if any, advancement. Even if a black qualified for a better job, he was often passed over in favor of a white employee. Until the states in the mid-1940s began to enact fair employment laws, few blacks who had been refused jobs strictly because of their race had any legal recourse. The employer-employee relationship was considered private and thus outside the protection of the 14th Amendment. Private employers and labor unions could discriminate against blacks with impunity and many of them did. [153]

Early Rulings

Because there were so few legal protections available, only a handful of employment discrimination cases reached the court before 1964, the year that Congress prohibited such job bias. In almost all of these early cases, however, the Supreme Court interpreted available law to protect blacks.

Picketing

The first of these cases came in 1938. Blacks organized a picket line outside a District of Columbia grocery to force the proprietor to hire blacks. A federal court ordered the picketing stopped; the blacks charged that the order violated the Norris-LaGuardia Act, which prohibited federal courts from issuing injunctions in legal labor disputes. The issue before the Supreme Court was whether picketing to force someone to hire blacks was a legal labor objective

within the meaning of the law. By a 7-2 vote, the court held that it was:

> . . .Race discrimination by an employer may be reasonably deemed more unfair and less excusable than discrimination against workers on the ground of union affiliation. There is no justification . . . for limiting [the act's] definition of labor disputes and cases arising therefrom by excluding those which arise with respect to discrimination in terms and condition of employment based upon differences of race or color. [154]

This ruling was modified in 1950 when the court held that picketing to demand that a store owner increase the number of blacks he employed constituted discrimination against already-hired white clerks. [155]

Railway Unions

The first case involving labor union discrimination came in 1944 when the court was asked to decide whether a union acting under federal law as the exclusive bargaining agent for a class of workers was obligated by that law to represent all those workers without regard to race.

The case of *Steele v. Louisville and Nashville Railroad Co.* involved the Brotherhood of Locomotive Firemen, the exclusive bargaining representative for train firemen of 21 railroad companies. The union, which excluded blacks from membership, agreed with the railroad companies to amend the work contract to end all employment of blacks as firemen. As a result, Steele, a black fireman, was reassigned to more difficult, less remunerative work and his job given to a white man with less seniority and no more qualifications than Steele possessed.

In an opinion that carefully avoided any constitutional issues, the court ruled that the Railway Labor Act of 1930, as amended, compelled the exclusive bargaining agent for an entire class of employees to represent all those employees fairly "without hostile discrimination" against any of them. The court also held that Steele had properly brought the case in federal court. [156]

The court reached a similar conclusion in the 1952 case of *Brotherhood of Railroad Trainmen v. Howard.* In this case, a white brakemen's union threatened to strike unless the railroad company fired all its black "train porters," who performed the same functions as brakemen, and replaced them with white union members. Unlike the blacks in the *Steele* case, however, the black train porters had long been represented by their own union. Nonetheless, a majority of the Supreme Court saw no significant difference in the two cases. The black "train porters are threatened with loss of their jobs because they are not white and for no other reason,. . ." wrote Justice Hugo L. Black. "The Federal [Railway Labor] Act . . . prohibits bargaining agents it authorizes from using their position and power to destroy colored workers' jobs in order to bestow them on white workers." [157]

State Anti-Discrimination Laws

Black workers won another measure of job protection in 1945 when the court upheld the validity of state fair employment laws. The New York Civil Rights Act contained a provision — one of the first of its kind ever enacted — prohibiting a union from denying membership on the basis of race, creed or color. The Railway Mail Association, which represented postal clerks in New York and other states and which limited its membership to whites and Indians, appealed the state's judgment that this law applied to its policy of excluding blacks. The association claimed the state law violated the organization's right to due process and equal protection of the laws and encroached on Congress' power to regulate the mails. The Supreme Court denied all three claims:

> We see no constitutional basis for the contention that a state cannot protect workers from exclusion solely on the basis of race, color or creed by an organization functioning under the protection of the state, which holds itself out to represent the general business needs of employees. [158]

The question whether a state fair employment practices act as applied to a company doing interstate business placed an impermissible burden on interstate commerce came to the court in the case of *Colorado Anti-Discrimination Commission v. Continental Airlines* (1963). [159]

A black man named Marion Green applied for a job as a pilot with the interstate airline, which had its headquarters in Denver. He was rejected solely because of his race. The Colorado Anti-Discrimination Commission found the company had discriminated in violation of state law and ordered it to give Green the first opening in its next training course. A state court overruled the order, however, on the grounds that the state law unduly burdened interstate commerce.

The Supreme Court reversed the trial court and upheld the commission's order. The state anti-discrimination law did not conflict with or frustrate any federal law that might also regulate employment discrimination by airlines, said the court. Nor did it deny the airlines any rights granted by Congress. Unlike several cases in which the court has found that state-required racial separation of passengers in public transportation unduly burdened interstate commerce, the court found hiring within a state, even for an interstate job, a "much more localized matter." Furthermore, the potential for diverse and conflicting hiring regulations among the states, which might hamper interstate commerce, was "virtually nonexistent," the court said. *(Discrimination in interstate transportation, p. 608)*

The 1964 Civil Rights Act

The following year, Congress enacted the first federal law prohibiting job discrimination. Title VII of the Civil Rights Act of 1964 prohibited employers of and unions representing more than 25 workers, union hiring halls and employment agencies from discriminating on the grounds of race, color, religion, sex or national origin in the hiring, classification, training or promotion of anyone. The act also created the Equal Employment Opportunities Commission (EEOC) to hear complaints and seek compliance with the law.

In 1972 Congress strengthened the act by extending coverage to employers and unions with 15 or more employees or members, state and local governments and educational institutions. The only major group left uncovered were federal government employees. The 1972 act also enabled the EEOC to go into federal court to enforce the law. Federal courts were authorized to order employers to remedy proven discrimination by reinstating or hiring the employees concerned, with or without awarding them back pay, and by any other remedial measures the courts found appropriate.

Job Qualifications

The Supreme Court first fully discussed the scope of Title VII in its 1971 decision in *Griggs v. Duke Power Co.* Black employees charged that the North Carolina power company had unfairly discriminated when it required them to have a high school diploma or pass a generalized intelligence test as a condition for employment or promotion. The black workers claimed that neither requirement was related to successful job performance, that the requirements disqualified a substantially higher number of blacks than whites and that the jobs in question had been filled by whites under the company's former longstanding policy of giving whites first preference.

By an 8-0 vote, the court ruled that under those circumstances the job qualification requirements were discriminatory. Chief Justice Warren E. Burger set out the court's interpretation of Title VII:

> . . .[T]he Act does not command that any person be hired simply because he was formerly the subject of discrimination, or because he is a member of a minority group. Discriminatory preference for any group, minority or majority, is precisely and only what Congress has proscribed. What is required by Congress is the removal of artificial, arbitrary, and unnecessary barriers to employment when the barriers operate invidiously to discriminate on the basis of racial or other impermissible classification. [160]

Any test that operates to exclude blacks, even one that is neutral on its face, must be shown to have a significant relation to job performance, Burger continued. Neither the requirement for a high school diploma nor the intelligence test had this relation. The court agreed that there was no evidence that the company had intended to discriminate against its black employees, but, wrote Burger, "Congress directed the thrust of the Act to the consequences of employment practices, not simply the motivation." [161]

The Supreme Court in 1975 reaffirmed that tests which excluded more blacks than whites and were not proven to be job-related were discriminatory. [162]

Illegal Protests

A unanimous court held in 1973 that the 1964 Civil Rights Act did not require a company to rehire a black employee who had engaged in deliberate unlawful protests against it. But neither was the company permitted to use the protests as a pretext for refusing to rehire the employee just because of his race. The former employee should have an opportunity to prove that the employer was using the illegal protest as an excuse to carry out a discriminatory

The Question of Intent

Distinguishing between cases based on the Constitution's guarantee of equal protection and those based on federal civil rights laws, the Supreme Court in the mid-1970s began to emphasize that it was far more difficult to prove certain actions unconstitutional than to prove them illegal.

The seminal case in this development was that of *Washington v. Davis*, decided by the court in 1976. In that case, the court ruled that in order to prove an employer guilty of discrimination violating the 14th Amendment's equal protection guarantee, one must not only prove that his action was discriminatory in effect but also that it was motivated by an intent to discriminate.

The case arose when two blacks challenged as unconstitutionally discriminatory the District of Columbia police department's requirement that recruits pass a verbal ability test. The two men backed their challenge by noting that the number of black police officers was not proportionate to the racial mix of the city, that more blacks than whites failed the test and that the test was not significantly related to job performance.

Their challenge was based not on the Civil Rights Act of 1964, however, but on the due process clause of the Fifth Amendment, which the court has found to include an implicit equal protection guarantee. *(Details, box, p. 585)*

A federal district court rejected the challenge. There was no evidence that the police department intended to discriminate against black applicants, it ruled. The number of new black recruits was roughly the same proportion as the racial mix of people of the same age residing in the recruiting area, and the challenged test was job-related, the court held. The appeals court reversed this ruling on the basis of a 1971 Supreme Court ruling concerning a Civil Rights Act challenge to job qualification tests. *(Details, p. 619)*

The Supreme Court, however, agreed with the district court, ruling by a 7-2 vote that there was no constitutional violation without some proof of discriminatory motivation on the part of the police department in addition to the apparently discriminatory impact of the qualification test. Justice Byron R. White wrote that the court had "not held that a law, neutral on its face and serving ends otherwise within the power of the government to pursue, is invalid under the Equal Protection Clause simply because it may affect a greater proportion of one race than another."[1]

The court subsequently applied this principle — that a law or other official action must reflect some racially discriminatory purpose to be in violation of the equal protection guarantee — in other areas of discrimination, including schools and housing. [2] *(School case, p. 606; housing case, p. 616)*

---

[1] *Washington v. Davis*, 426 U.S. 229 at 242 (1976).

[2] *Austin Independent School District v. United States*, 429 U.S. 990 (1976); *Village of Arlington Heights v. Metropolitan Housing Development Corporation*, 429 U.S. 252 (1977).

hiring policy in violation of Title VII, the court said in *McDonnell Douglas Corp. v. Green* (1973). If he could not show this, the refusal to rehire him should stand. [163]

Proof of Discrimination

In the 1978 case of *Furnco Construction Corp. v. Waters*, the Supreme Court held that an appeals court erred when it ordered a construction company to adopt non-discriminatory hiring practices before the company had been found guilty of job discrimination. The court also said that an employer may point to the fact that he has hired a substantial number of black workers as part of his proof that he is not guilty of discrimination. But, wrote the court, "a racially balanced work force cannot immunize an employer from liability for specific acts of discrimination." [164]

Remedies

The Supreme Court has upheld the broad authority of lower federal courts under Title VII to award back wages and retirement benefits to persons who have suffered illegal job discrimination.

Back Pay. The first such case was *Albemarle Paper Co. v. Moody* (1975). A federal district court found that the North Carolina paper mill had discriminated against blacks prior to enactment of Title VII and that the effects of that discrimination were apparent for several years afterward. But because the company no longer discriminated against its black employees, the lower court decided against a back-pay award. A court of appeals reversed that decision, and the paper mill appealed the reversal to the Supreme Court.

By a 7-1 vote, the court ruled that back pay was a proper remedy for such past job discrimination. For the majority, Justice Potter Stewart wrote:

> ...If employers faced only the prospect of an injunctive order, they would have little incentive to shun practices of dubious legality. It is the reasonably certain prospect of a backpay award that "provide[s] the spur or catalyst which causes employers and unions to self-examine and to self-evaluate their employment practices and to endeavor to eliminate, so far as possible, the last vestiges of an unfortunate and ignominious page in this country's history." ...It is also the purpose of Title VII to make persons whole for the injuries suffered on account of unlawful employment discrimination. [165]

Back pay should be awarded in most cases where job discrimination in violation of Title VII has been proved, the majority held, even in cases such as this one, where the employer had acted in good faith to end previous discrimination. If back pay were awarded only for acts of bad faith, the majority said, "the remedy would become a punishment for moral turpitude, rather than a compensation for workers' injuries.... [A] worker's injury is no less real simply because his employer did not inflict it in 'bad faith.' " [166]

In the case of *Fitzpatrick v. Bitzer* (1976), the court upheld the award of retroactive retirement benefits to male employees of the state of Connecticut who had been required by state law to work longer than women employees before they could retire.[167] *(Details, p. 638)*

Seniority Rights. The court also has upheld the authority of federal courts under Title VII to award retroactive seniority rights to persons denied employment or promotion by discriminatory policies.

In its first ruling on this issue, the court in the case of *Franks v. Bowman Transportation Co., Inc.* (1976) held by a 5-3 vote that lower courts could award seniority dating back to the time the application for employment was improperly rejected. Retroactive seniority was an appropriate remedy for job discrimination and such awards should be made in most cases where a seniority system exists and discrimination is proved, the court said.

Such awards are necessary to fulfill the "make-whole" purposes of Title VII, held the court. Without them, Justice William J. Brennan Jr. wrote, the victim of job discrimination "will never obtain his rightful place in the hierarchy of seniority according to which these various employment benefits are distributed. He will perpetually remain subordinate to persons who, but for the illegal discrimination, would have been in respect to entitlement to these benefits his inferiors." [168]

The majority did not distinguish between benefit seniority, which determines such matters as length of vacation and pension benefits, and competitive seniority, which determines such issues as the order in which employees are laid off and rehired, promoted and transferred.

In dissent, Justice Lewis F. Powell Jr. opposed the award of retroactive competitive seniority since it did not affect the employer but rather "the rights and expectations of perfectly innocent employees. The economic benefits awarded discrimination victims would be derived not at the expense of the employer but at the expense of other workers." [169]

Retroactive Seniority Limited. Little more than a year later, the court qualified its holding in the 1976 case when it barred the award of retroactive seniority benefits further back than July 2, 1965, the effective date of the 1964 Civil Rights Act.

In Title VII of that act Congress specifically included language which immunized existing *bona fide* seniority systems from attack as discriminatory. By a 7-2 vote, the court held that this immunity precluded any award of retroactive seniority benefits that would have been accumulated prior to July 2, 1965, absent racial discrimination.

This case — *Teamsters v. United States, T.I.M.E.-D.C. v. United States* (1977) — concerned a nationwide trucking firm and the truckers' union. [170] Lower federal courts found that the firm systematically denied inter-city line-driver jobs to blacks and Spanish-surnamed employees and applicants. Seniority became an issue in determining the remedy for this discrimination.

Under the company's collective bargaining agreement with the Teamsters, competitive seniority for a line driver was counted from the time he took the post, not from the time he joined the company in another position. Thus a black employee transferring to the line-driver job would be required to give up any competitive seniority he had accumulated in his previous position.

Black *and* White

Title VII of the 1964 Civil Rights Act prohibits racial job discrimination against whites as well as blacks, the court ruled in 1976.

In the case of *McDonald v. Santa Fe Trail Transportation Co.*, a freight company fired two white men who had stolen 60 cans of anti-freeze, but the firm did not dismiss a black man who had also participated in the theft.

The court held this differential treatment a clear violation of Title VII. Both the language of the act and the legislative history make plain that whites are to be protected from job discrimination as well as members of racial minorities, said Justice Thurgood Marshall. "While Santa Fe may decide that participation in a theft of cargo may render an employee unqualified for employment, this criterion must be 'applied, alike to members of all races,' and Title VII is violated if . . . it was not." (427 U.S. 273 at 283, 1976)

By a 7-2 vote, the court held that the two white men were also protected from such treatment by a provision of the 1866 Civil Rights Act, embodied in existing law as Section 1981 of Title 42 of the United States Code. The section declares that "all persons within the jurisdiction of the United States shall have the same right . . . to make and enforce contracts . . . as is enjoyed by white citizens. . . ." *(Box, p. 614)*

Citing the *Franks* case, the court held unanimously that persons discriminated against after the effective date of the 1964 act were entitled to retroactive seniority as far back as that date. But with Justices Brennan and Thurgood Marshall dissenting, the court refused to order seniority awards stretching back further than July 2, 1965, for victims of discrimination.

Were it not for the specific immunity granted by the act to *bona fide* seniority systems, wrote Stewart for the majority, the seniority system challenged in this case would probably have been found invalid. But both the language of the immunization provision and the legislative history demonstrated that an

> . . . otherwise neutral, legitimate seniority system does not become unlawful under Title VII simply because it may perpetuate pre-Act discrimination. Congress did not intend to make it illegal for employees with vested seniority rights to continue to exercise those rights, even at the expense of pre-Act discriminatees. [171]

Marshall and Brennan based their dissent on their view that a seniority system which perpetuated the effect of pre-1965 discrimination was not a *bona fide* system protected by the Title VII immunity provision.

Footnotes

[1] *Strauder v. West Virginia*, 100 U.S. 303 at 306-07 (1880).

[2] John P. Frank, *Marble Palace: The Supreme Court in American Life* (New York: Alfred A. Knopf, 1961), p. 204; other sources include John Hope Franklin, *From Slavery to Freedom: A History of Negro Americans*, 3d ed. (New York: Random House, Vintage Books, 1969); John A. Garraty, ed., *Quarrels That Have Shaped the Constitution* (New York: Harper & Row, 1964); United States Commission on Civil Rights, *Freedom to the Free: Century of Emancipation, 1863-1963* (Washington, D.C.: U.S. Government Printing Office, 1963); C. Vann Woodward, *The Strange Career of Jim Crow*, 2d rev. ed. (New York: Oxford University Press, 1966).

[3] *Slaughterhouse Cases*, 16 Wall. 36 (1873).

[4] *Civil Rights Cases*, 109 U.S. 3 (1883).

[5] Carl B. Swisher, "Dred Scott One Hundred Years After,"

The Journal of Politics, May 1957, pp. 167-174, quoted in Frank, *Marble Palace,* p. 205.

[6] Alan F. Westin, "The Case of the Prejudiced Doorkeeper," *Quarrels That Have Shaped the Constitution,* p. 143.

[7] *Plessy v. Ferguson,* 163 U.S. 537 (1896).

[8] United States Commission on Civil Rights, *Freedom to the Free,* p. 71.

[9] Franklin, *From Slavery to Freedom,* p. 480.

[10] *United States v. Carolene Products Co.,* 304 U.S. 144 at 152-53, footnote 4 (1938).

[11] *Brown v. Board of Education of Topeka,* 347 U.S. 483 (1954).

[12] G. Theodore Mitau, *Decade of Decision; The Supreme Court and the Constitutional Revolution, 1954-1964* (New York: Charles Scribner's Sons, 1967), pp. 62-63.

[13] Franklin, *From Slavery to Freedom,* p. 644.

[14] *Plessy v. Ferguson,* 163 U.S. 537 at 544 (1896).

[15] *Roberts v. City of Boston,* 59 Mass. 198 at 206 (1849).

[16] Id. at 209.

[17] *Cumming v. Richmond County Board of Education,* 175 U.S. 528 at 545 (1899).

[18] *Berea College v. Kentucky,* 211 U.S. 45 (1908).

[19] *Gong Lum v. Rice,* 275 U.S. 78 at 86 (1927).

[20] For general background, see Alfred H. Kelly and Winfred A. Harbison, *The American Constitution; Its Origins and Development,* 5th ed. (New York: W. W. Norton & Co., 1976), p. 860; Richard Kluger, *Simple Justice* (New York: Alfred A. Knopf, 1976), pp. 126-137.

[21] *Missouri ex rel. Gaines v. Canada,* 305 U.S. 337 at 349 (1938).

[22] Id. at 350.

[23] *Sipuel v. Board of Regents of the University of Oklahoma,* 332 U.S. 631 at 633 (1948).

[24] *Sweatt v. Painter,* 339 U.S. 629 at 633-34 (1950).

[25] Id. at 636.

[26] *McLaurin v. Oklahoma State Regents for Higher Education,* 339 U.S. 637 at 641 (1950).

[27] *Brown v. Board of Education of Topeka, Briggs v. Elliott, Davis v. County School Board of Prince Edward County, Va., Gebhart v. Belton,* 347 U.S. 483 (1954).

[28] *Bolling v. Sharpe,* 347 U.S. 497 (1954).

[29] Loren Miller, *The Petitioners: The Story of the Supreme Court of the United States and the Negro* (New York: Random House, Pantheon Books, 1966), p. 345.

[30] *Guinn v. United States,* 238 U.S. 347 (1915); see also Kluger, *Simple Justice,* p. 527.

[31] Quoted in Leon Friedman, ed., *Argument: The Oral Argument Before the Supreme Court in Brown v. Board of Education of Topeka, 1952-55* (New York: Chelsea House Publishers, 1969), p. 215.

[32] Ibid.

[33] Ibid., p. 216.

[34] Ibid, pp. 239-40.

[35] *Brown v. Board of Education of Topeka,* 347 U.S. 483 at 492 (1954).

[36] Id. at 492-93.

[37] Id. at 493.

[38] Ibid.

[39] Id. at 494.

[40] Id. at 495.

[41] *Bolling v. Sharpe,* 347 U.S. 497 at 499-500 (1954).

[42] *Brown v. Board of Education of Topeka,* 349 U.S. 294 at 299-301 (1955).

[43] Id. at 301.

[44] U.S. Congress, Senate, "Declaration of Constitutional Principles," March 12, 1956, *Congressional Record,* 102:4460.

[45] Woodward, *Strange Career of Jim Crow,* p. 154.

[46] *Lucy v. Adams,* 350 U.S. 1 (1955).

[47] *Florida ex rel Hawkins v. Board of Control,* 350 U.S. 413 (1956).

[48] *Muir v. Louisville Park Theatrical Assn.,* 347 U.S. 971 (1954); see also: *Mayor and City Council of Baltimore v. Dawson,* 350 U.S. 877 (1955); *Holmes v. City of Atlanta,* 350 U.S. 879 (1955); *New Orleans City Park Improvement Assn. v. Detiege,* 358 U.S. 54 (1959); *Gayle v. Browder,* 352 U.S. 903 (1956); *Wright v. Georgia,* 373 U.S. 284 (1963).

[49] *Cooper v. Aaron,* 358 U.S. 1 (1958).

[50] Id. at 16.

[51] Id. at 19-20.

[52] *Faubus v. Aaron,* 361 U.S. 197 (1959).

[53] *Shuttlesworth v. Birmingham Board of Education,* 162 F Supp. 372, affirmed 358 U.S. 101 (1958).

[54] *Holt v. Raleigh,* 265 F 2d 95, cert. denied, 361 U.S. 818 (1959); *Covington v. Edwards,* 264 F 2d 780, cert. denied, 361 U.S. 840 (1959).

[55] *Bush v. Orleans Parish School Board,* 364 U.S. 500 (1960); *Orleans Parish School Board v. Bush,* 365 U.S. 569 (1961); *St. Helena Parish School Board v. Hall,* 368 U.S. 515 (1962).

[56] *Goss v. Board of Education of Knoxville,* 373 U.S. 683 (1963).

[57] *McNeese v. Board of Education for Community School District 187, Cahokia, Ill.,* 373 U.S. 668 (1963).

[58] *Griffin v. County School Board of Prince Edward County,* 377 U.S. 218 at 231 (1964).

[59] Id. at 229.

[60] *Bradley v. School Board, City of Richmond,* 382 U.S. 103 (1965).

[61] *Rogers v. Paul,* 382 U.S. 198 (1965).

[62] *Wallace v. United States, Bibb County Board of Education v. United States,* 386 U.S. 976 (1967).

[63] *Green v. County School Board of New Kent County, Va.,* 391 U.S. 430 at 437-38 (1968).

[64] Id. at 438-39.

[65] Id. at 439.

[66] Id. at 441, 442.

[67] *Raney v. Board of Education of Gould School District,* 391 U.S. 443 (1968); *Monroe v. Board of Commissioners, City of Jackson,* 391 U.S. 450 (1968).

[68] *Alexander v. Holmes Board of Education,* 396 U.S. 19 (1969); see also *Carter v. West Feliciana Parish School Board,* 396 U.S. 290 (1970); *Northcross v. Board of Education, City of Memphis,* 397 U.S. 232 (1970).

[69] *Swann v. Charlotte-Mecklenburg County Board of Education,* 402 U.S. 1 at 25, 24 (1971).

[70] Id. at 26.

[71] Id. at 27.

[72] Id. at 30-31.

[73] Id. at 28.

[74] Id. at 23.

[75] Id. at 31-32.

[76] *North Carolina State Board of Education v. Swann,* 402 U.S. 43 at 45-46 (1971).

[77] *Davis v. Board of School Commissioners of Mobile County, Ala.,* 402 U.S. 33 (1971).

[78] *McDaniel v. Barresi,* 402 U.S. 39 (1971).

[79] *Richmond School Board v. Virginia State Board of Education,* 412 U.S. 92 (1973).

[80] Quoted by Chief Justice Warren E. Burger in *Milliken v. Bradley,* 418 U.S. 717 at 733 (1974).

[81] Id. at 741.

[82] Id. at 744-45.

[83] Id. at 746.

[84] Id. at 782.

[85] Id. at 789.

[86] *Milliken v. Bradley,* 433 U.S. 267 at 287-88 (1977).

[87] *Edelman v. Jordan,* 415 U.S. 651 (1974).

[88] *Milliken v. Bradley,* 433 U.S. 267 at 290 (1977).

[89] *Dayton (Ohio) Board of Education v. Brinkman,* 433 U.S. 406 at 420 (1977); *Dayton Board of Education v. Brinkman* (1979).

[90] *Pasadena City Board of Education v. Spangler,* 427 U.S. 424 at 437 (1976).

[91] Id. at 443.

[92] For general historical background in this area, see Commission on Civil Rights, *Freedom to the Free,* pp. 60-71; Woodward, "The Case of the Louisiana Traveler," *Quarrels That Have Shaped the Constitution,* p. 145; Woodward, *Strange Career of Jim Crow.*

[93] *Civil Rights Cases,* 109 U.S. 3 at 11 (1883).

94 Id. at 24.

95 Milton Konvitz and Theodore Leskes, *A Century of Civil Rights, with a Study of State Law Against Discrimination* (New York: Columbia University Press, 1961), p. 157. The states that passed anti-discrimination laws were: Connecticut, Iowa, New Jersey and Ohio in 1884; Colorado, Illinois, Indiana, Michigan, Minnesota, Nebraska and Rhode Island in 1885; Pennsylvania in 1887; Washington in 1890, Wisconsin in 1895, and California in 1897.

96 *Hall v. DeCuir*, 95 U.S. 485 at 489 (1878).

97 *Louisville, New Orleans and Texas Railway v. Mississippi*, 133 U.S. 587 (1890).

98 *Plessy v. Ferguson*, 163 U.S. 537 at 548 (1896).

99 Id. at 543.

100 Id. at 544.

101 Id. at 550-51.

102 Id. at 559.

103 Id. at 560-61.

104 *McCabe v. Atchison, Topeka and Santa Fe Railroad*, 235 U.S. 151 at 161-62 (1914).

105 *Mitchell v. United States*, 313 U.S. 80 (1941).

106 *Morgan v. Virginia*, 328 U.S. 373 at 380-81 (1946).

107 Id. at 386.

108 *Bob-Lo Excursion Co. v. Michigan*, 333 U.S. 28 (1948); *Henderson v. United States*, 339 U.S. 816 (1950); *District of Columbia v. Thompson Co.*, 346 U.S. 100 (1953).

109 *Brown v. Board of Education of Topeka*, 347 U.S. 483 (1954).

110 *Mayor and City Council of Baltimore v. Dawson*, 350 U.S. 877 (1955); *Holmes v. City of Atlanta*, 350 U.S. 879 (1955); *New Orleans City Park Improvement Assn. v. Detiege*, 358 U.S. 54 (1959); *Gayle v. Browder*, 352 U.S. 903 (1956); *Muir v. Louisville Park Theatrical Assn.*, 347 U.S. 971 (1954); *Wright v. Georgia*, 373 U.S. 284 (1963); *Schiro v. Bynum*, 375 U.S. 395 (1964); *State Athletic Commission v. Dorsey*, 359 U.S. 533 (1959); *Johnson v. Virginia*, 373 U.S. 61 (1963); *Lee v. Washington*, 390 U.S. 333 (1968).

111 *Watson v. City of Memphis*, 373 U.S. 526 at 533 (1963).

112 *Palmer v. Thompson*, 403 U.S. 217 (1971).

113 *Boynton v. Virginia*, 364 U.S. 454 at 460-461 (1960).

114 *Burton v. Wilmington Parking Authority*, 365 U.S. 715 at 722 (1961).

115 Id. at 725.

116 *Peterson v. City of Greenville*, 373 U.S. 244 at 248 (1963).

117 *Gober v. City of Birmingham*, 373 U.S. 374 (1963); *Avent v. North Carolina*, 373 U.S. 375 (1963).

118 *Shuttlesworth v. Birmingham*, 373 U.S. 262 at 265 (1963).

119 *Lombard v. Louisiana*, 373 U.S. 267 at 273 (1963).

120 *Heart of Atlanta Motel v. United States*, 379 U.S. 241 at 258 (1964).

121 Id. at 257.

122 Id. at 260.

123 Id. at 252.

124 *Katzenbach v. McClung*, 379 U.S. 294 (1964).

125 *Daniel v. Paul*, 395 U.S. 298 (1969).

126 *The Civil Rights Cases*, 109 U.S. 3 at 22 (1883).

127 *Buchanan v. Warley*, 245 U.S. 60 at 80-82 (1917).

128 See, for example, *Harmon v. Tyler*, 273 U.S. 668 (1927); *City of Richmond v. Deans*, 281 U.S. 704 (1930).

129 *Corrigan v. Buckley*, 271 U.S. 323 at 330 (1926).

130 *Shelley v. Kraemer, McGhee v. Sipes*, 334 U.S. 1 (1948).

131 Id. at 13.

132 Id. at 19-20.

133 *Hurd v. Hodge, Urciola v. Hodge*, 334 U.S. 24 (1948).

134 *Barrows v. Jackson*, 346 U.S. 249 at 254 (1953).

135 *Reitman v. Mulkey*, 387 U.S. 369 at 377 (1967).

136 Id. at 393.

137 *Hunter v. Erickson*, 393 U.S. 385 at 393 (1969).

138 Id. at 396-97.

139 *James v. Valtierra*, 402 U.S. 137 at 141 (1971).

140 Id. at 145.

141 *Jones v. Alfred H. Mayer Co.*, 392 U.S. 409 at 436 (1968).

142 Id. at 438-43, passim.

143 *Sullivan v. Little Hunting Park, Inc.*, 396 U.S. 229 (1969).

144 *Tillman v. Wheaton-Haven Recreational Association*, 410 U.S. 431 at 437 (1973).

145 *Hills v. Gautreaux*, 425 U.S. 284 (1976).

146 *Milliken v. Bradley*, 418 U.S. 717 (1974).

147 *Hills v. Gautreaux*, 425 U.S. 284 at 294 (1976).

148 Id. at 297.

149 Id. at 298-300.

150 Id. at 306.

151 *Village of Arlington Heights v. Metropolitan Housing Development Corporation*, 429 U.S. 252 (1977).

152 *Bailey v. Alabama*, 219 U.S. 219 (1911); *United States v. Reynolds*, 235 U.S. 133 (1914); see also *Taylor v. Georgia*, 315 U.S. 25 (1942); *Pollock v. Williams*, 322 U.S. 4 (1944).

153 For general historical accounts of black job discrimination, see Miller, *The Petitioners*; Woodward, *Strange Career of Jim Crow*.

154 *New Negro Alliance v. Sanitary Grocery Co.*, 303 U.S. 552 at 561 (1938).

155 *Hughes v. Superior Court*, 339 U.S. 460 (1950).

156 *Steele v. Louisville and Nashville Railroad Company*, 323 U.S. 192 (1944); see also *Tunstall v. Brotherhood*, 323 U.S. 210 (1944); *Graham v. Brotherhood*, 338 U.S. 232 (1949); *Conley v. Gibson*, 355 U.S. 41 (1957).

157 *Brotherhood of Railroad Trainmen v. Howard*, 343 U.S. 768 at 774 (1951); see also *Syres v. Oil Workers International Union*, 350 U.S. 892 (1955).

158 *Railway Mail Association v. Corsi*, 326 U.S. 88 (1945).

159 *Colorado Anti-Discrimination Commission v. Continental Airlines*, 372 U.S. 714 (1963).

160 *Griggs v. Duke Power Co.*, 401 U.S. 424 at 430-31 (1971).

161 Id. at 432.

162 *Albemarle Paper Company v. Moody*, 422 U.S. 405 (1975).

163 *McDonnell Douglas Corporation v. Green*, 411 U.S. 807 (1973).

164 *Furnco Construction Corporation v. Waters*, 438 U.S. 567 at 579 (1978).

165 *Albemarle Paper Company v. Moody*, 422 U.S. 405 at 417-18 (1975).

166 Id. at 422.

167 *Fitzpatrick v. Bitzer*, 427 U.S. 445 (1976).

168 *Franks v. Bowman Transportation Co., Inc.*, 424 U.S. 747 at 768 (1976).

169 Id. at 788-89.

170 *Teamsters v. United States, T.I.M.E.-D.C. v. United States*, 431 U.S. 324 (1977).

171 Id. at 354.

Aliens and Equal Protection

Congress has exclusive authority to determine who may enter the country, but once an alien is admitted to the United States, he or she is entitled to the equal protection of its laws. In 1886 the court declared that the 14th Amendment protected persons, not just citizens. The Supreme Court in the case of *Yick Wo v. Hopkins* wrote that the Civil War amendment applied "to all *persons* within the territorial jurisdiction, without regard to any differences of race, of color, or of nationality; and the equal protection of the laws is a pledge of the protection of equal laws."[1]

It was 85 years before the Supreme Court in 1971 declared alienage, like race, a suspect category justifiable only by a compelling government interest. But beginning with the *Yick Wo* case, the court, with one period of exception, required states to show more than a merely rational basis for a legal distinction between aliens and citizens. As a result, aliens initially fared better under the court's application of the 14th Amendment's equal protection clause than did the blacks who were expected by the authors of the clause to be its prime beneficiaries.

Early Victories

Yick Wo involved a San Francisco ordinance which, in order to minimize fire hazards, required operators of wooden laundries to obtain a license from the city. Although his laundry had been declared safe by city fire and health officials, Yick Wo was denied a renewal of his license. When he discovered that most Chinese owners of wooden laundries had been denied permits, while most white laundry owners were granted them, he sued, charging that he had been denied equal protection of the laws.

Sustaining the charge, a unanimous Supreme Court wrote:

> . . .Though the law itself be fair on its face and impartial in appearance, yet, if it is applied and administered by public authority with an evil eye and an unequal hand, so as practically to make unjust and illegal discriminations between persons in similar circumstances, material to their rights, the denial of equal justice is still within the prohibition of the Constitution.[2]

Since the city offered no explanation for its discrimination, "the conclusion cannot be resisted, that no reason for it exists except hostility to the race and nationality to which the petitioners [Chinese launderers] belong, and which in the eye of the law is not justified," the court wrote.[3]

The Right to Work

Yick Wo's case involved his right to earn a living, a right which the court said was "essential to the enjoyment of life." The court amplified this holding in the 1915 case of *Truax v. Raich.* Arizona law required that 80 percent of the workers in establishments with more than five employees be U.S. citizens. When a restaurant owner fired Mike Raich, an Austrian native, in order to comply with the statute, Raich charged that he had been denied equal protection. Agreeing, the Supreme Court declared the state law unconstitutional. Justice Charles Evans Hughes wrote the opinion:

> It requires no argument to show that the right to work for a living in the common occupations of the community is of the very essence of the personal freedom and opportunity that it was the purpose of the [14th] Amendment to secure. . . . If this could be refused solely upon the ground of race or nationality, the prohibition of the denial to any person of the equal protection of the laws would be a barren form of words."[4]

Period of Exceptions

Within 12 years the *Raich* decision itself would prove rather barren. In 1915, the country was already growing suspicious of and antagonistic toward immigrants from certain countries. The prejudice, which would peak in the 1920s, is described by historians Alfred H. Kelly and Winfred A. Harbison:

> . . .The average middle class "old American" of the twenties believed firmly that both the Communist and anarchist menaces and the contemporary alarming increase in urban crime were due to the presence of undesirable aliens in the country. Much contemporary xenophobic sentiment also was laden with religious and racial prejudice. Conservative Protestants feared and resented the recent heavy influx of Catholic immigrants from Italy and Poland, while the swarthy new-

comers from southern and eastern Europe as well as those from Japan and Asia were looked upon as "unassimilable" and a threat to American racial purity."[5]

In response, Congress passed laws requiring deportation of aliens convicted of crimes and subversive activity and established the immigration quota system based on national origin. The quotas heavily favored the immigrants of northwest Europe. In 1924 Congress passed a second law that effectively barred most immigration from Asia.

Nor was the Supreme Court immune to this public sentiment. Beginning in 1914, it condoned state laws excluding aliens from certain activities and jobs cloaked with a special public interest. In 1877 the court ruled in the case of *McCready v. Virginia* that Virginia could prohibit residents of other states from planting oysters in its tidal streams. The right to use such streams was a property right, the court said, and the privilege and immunity clause did not invest "the citizens of one state . . . with any interest in the common property of the citizens of another state."[6]

The court extended this special public interest rule to aliens in a 1914 case in which it upheld a Pennsylvania statute forbidding aliens to shoot wild game and, to that end, to possess shotguns and rifles. Wild game, like a tidal stream, was a natural resource that a state may preserve for its own citizens "if it pleases," the court said in *Patsone v. Pennsylvania*. To that purpose, the state may make classifications, and if the class "discriminated against is or reasonably might be considered to define those from whom the evil mainly is to be feared," the classification is permissible, wrote Justice Oliver Wendell Holmes Jr.[7] No evidence was presented to support a contention that aliens shot more game than any other class, but the majority would not say the state was wrong in identifying aliens "as the peculiar source of the evil that it desired to prevent."[8]

In two 1915 decisions, the court used the special public interest test to uphold the right of a state to confine hiring on state public works projects to U.S. citizens.[9]

Alien Land Laws

In the early 1920s, several western states seeking to discourage Japanese immigration passed laws barring aliens ineligible for citizenship from owning or leasing agricultural lands.

The court in 1922 interpreted the federal laws restricting citizenship as allowing only whites and blacks of African descent to become citizens.[10] As a result, the alien land laws applied primarily to Japanese aliens.

In a series of 1923 decisions, the court upheld these laws. Since the federal government recognized two classes of aliens — those who were eligible for citizenship and those who were not, the states were not required to justify state laws making the same distinction. "The rule established by Congress on this subject, in and of itself, furnishes a reasonable basis for classification in a state law. . .," the court said in the case of *Terrace v. Thompson*.[11]

Job Restrictions

In 1927 the court appeared to abandon its 1915 decision that states may not deny aliens opportunities to hold "the common occupations of the community" solely because they were aliens. At the same time the court adopted a more relaxed standard of review for state classifications based on alienage.

The case of *Clarke v. Deckebach* (1927) concerned a Cincinnati ordinance that barred aliens from operating pool

and billiards halls. The Ohio city justified this classification by arguing that pool halls were evil places frequented by lawbreakers and were the scenes of many crimes. Because aliens were less familiar with the laws and customs of the country, their operation of these pool halls constituted a menace to the public, the city claimed.

Upholding the ordinance, the unanimous court said that while the 14th Amendment prohibits "plainly irrational discrimination against aliens. . ., it does not follow that alien race and allegiance may not bear in some instances such a relation to a legitimate object of legislation as to be made the basis of a permissible classification."[12]

Enunciating its new standard of scrutiny, the court wrote:

> It is enough for present purposes that the ordinance, in the light of facts admitted or generally assumed, does not preclude the possibility of a rational basis for the legislative judgment and that we have no such knowledge of local conditions as would enable us to say that it is clearly wrong.
>
> It was competent for the city to make such a choice, not shown to be irrational, by excluding from the conduct of a dubious business an entire class rather than its objectionable members selected by more empirical means.[13]

The 14th Amendment no longer protected aliens seeking to work at ordinary jobs. The court now allowed a city or state to deny rights to all aliens on the presumption that some aliens would act in an unacceptable manner. It was left to the alien class to prove the presumption irrational. Fortunately for aliens, this standard was relatively shortlived.

A Closer Scrutiny

The court first indicated a changed attitude toward questions of alienage and national origin in two World War II cases which concerned U.S. citizens of Oriental descent Both cases involved Japanese-Americans who had failed to comply with military orders first restricting the movements of Japanese-Americans living on the West Coast and then confining them to detention camps for eventual relocation away from the Pacific coast. In both cases the court held that such extreme discrimination against these citizens was justified by the necessities of war and the need to protect the country from the possibility that some disloyal Japanese-Americans might collaborate with the Japanese enemy. But in both cases the court said distinctions based on race and ancestry merited close scrutiny and could be justified only by such "pressing public necessity" as the war.[14] *(Details, pp. 192, 584)*

Land Laws

In 1948 the court effectively reversed its position on alien land laws. The case of *Oyama v. California* involved a Japanese alien who had purchased some agricultural property as a gift to his minor son, a U.S. citizen by birth. Oyama was then appointed his son's guardian which allowed him to work the land for the benefit of his son. The state charged Oyama with attempting to evade the alien land law, and Oyama in turn charged that both he and his son were denied equal protection of the laws by that law.

The Supreme Court ruled, 6-3, that the state law did deprive the citizen son of equal protection:

There remains the question of whether discrimination between citizens on the basis of their racial descent, as revealed in this case, is justifiable. Here we start with the proposition that only the most exceptional circumstances can excuse discrimination on that basis in the face of the equal protection clause and a federal statute giving all citizens the right to own land.... The only justification urged upon us by the State is that the discrimination is necessary to prevent evasion of the Alien Land Law.... In the light most favorable to the State, this case presents a conflict between the State's right to formulate a policy of landholding within its bounds and the right of American citizens to own land anywhere in the United States. When these two rights clash, the rights of a citizen may not be subordinated merely because of his father's country of origin. [15]

The majority did not reach the question of whether the alien father had been denied equal protection of the laws. But the decision stripped the law of much of its effectiveness.

Fishing Rights

Six months later, the court, by a 7-2 vote, rejected its reasoning in the 1927 *Deckebach* case and returned to its earlier position that the right to earn a living was a liberty that could not be denied an alien solely on the basis of race or national origin.

The case of *Takahashi v. Fish and Game Commission* (1948) involved a 1943 California law that prohibited alien Japanese from fishing in the state's coastal waters. In 1945 the state amended the law to extend the ban to all aliens ineligible for citizenship, but a 1946 federal law making Filipinos and persons of races indigenous to India eligible for citizenship effectively restricted the disability imposed by the state law to Japanese aliens. Takahashi, a fisherman denied a license, charged that he had been denied equal protection of the law.

Sustaining the charge, the Supreme Court reversed its previous position that a state could make the same alienage classifications as the federal government. "It does not follow...," wrote Justice Hugo L. Black for the majority, "that because the United States regulates immigration and naturalization in part on the basis of race and color classifications, a state can adopt one or more of the same classifications...." [16]

The Constitution gave Congress complete authority over admission and naturalization of aliens. "State laws which impose discriminatory burdens upon the entrance or residence of aliens lawfully within the United States conflict with this constitutionally derived federal power to regulate immigration," he wrote. [17]

Furthermore, the majority rejected California's claim that the fish in its offshore waters were a natural resource that the state could reserve for its own citizens under the special public interest rule:

...To whatever extent the fish in the three-mile belt off California may be "capable of ownership" by California, we think that the "ownership" is inadequate to justify California in excluding any or all aliens who are lawful residents of the State from making a living by fishing in the ocean off its shores while permitting all others to do so. [18]

The Modern Standard

Questions of discrimination against aliens did not become an issue before the court again until the 1970s.

In its first important aliens case of this period, *Graham v. Richardson* (1971), a unanimous court asserted that

...classifications based on alienage, like those based on nationality or race, are inherently suspect and subject to close judicial scrutiny. Aliens as a class are a prime example of a "discrete and insular" minority ... for whom such heightened judicial solicitude is appropriate. [19]

Graham concerned an Arizona statute that restricted certain welfare benefits to citizens and aliens who had resided in the United States for at least 15 years. A second case, consolidated with *Graham,* tested a Pennsylvania statute which denied certain welfare benefits to all aliens. By its declaration that classification by alienage was inherently suspect, the court required states to show a compelling governmental interest to justify making that distinction.

The claim that the special public interest rule allowed a state to "preserve limited welfare benefits for its own citizens is inadequate" to justify the classification, the court said. [20] Conserving limited financial resources is a valid state interest, the court continued, but a state may not accomplish that by making an otherwise invidious classification.

Aliens as well as residents pay state and federal taxes. "There can be no 'special public interest' in tax revenues to which aliens have contributed on an equal basis with the residents of the State," the court said. [21]

No Compelling Interest

Over the next few years, the court applied "close judicial scrutiny" and found no compelling interest in several state laws denying aliens certain benefits or the opportunity to work in certain professions. The court struck down a Connecticut law that barred aliens from being licensed as lawyers, a Puerto Rico law that barred them from becoming engineers, and a New York law that excluded aliens from the state's competitive civil service. It also struck down a New York law that excluded resident aliens who did not intend to become citizens from eligibility for state financial aid for higher education. [22]

Potential Exemption. In the case concerning its competitive civil service, New York contended it should be allowed to exclude aliens from governmental policy-making positions because aliens might not be "free of competing obligations to another power." [23] The court observed that not all members of the competitive civil service held policy-formulating positions. At the same time, the state allowed aliens to serve in other branches of the state civil service in both policy-making and non-policy-making jobs. Applying strict scrutiny, the court held that the statute must fall because it "is neither narrowly confined nor precise in its application." [24]

But in *dicta* at the end of that unanimous opinion, the court said states might require a person to be a citizen in order to exercise certain rights, such as voting, or to hold certain positions essential to the maintenance of representative government. Among these positions were "state elective or important nonelective executive, legislative, and judicial positions, for officers who participate directly in the formulation, execution, or review of broad public policy perform functions that go to the heart of representative government." [25] The court added that its scrutiny would "not be so demanding where we deal with matters resting firmly within the State's constitutional prerogatives." [26]

State Police. In 1978 this statement provided the basis for a decision in which the Supreme Court, by a 6-3 vote, upheld a New York statute requiring all its state police to be U.S. citizens. Writing for the majority, Chief Justice Warren E. Burger found police among the category of those who participated in making or carrying out governmental policy and whom, therefore, the state could require to be citizens. Burger explained: "The essence of our holdings to date is that although we extend to aliens the right to education and public welfare, along with the ability to earn a livelihood and engage in licensed professions, the right to govern is reserved to citizens."[27]

And because the right to govern fell within the state's constitutional prerogatives, the state needed only to prove that it had a rational basis for excluding aliens from police positions. Because police generally exercise a wide variety of discretionary powers that have a significant impact on citizens, the majority felt it was rational for the state to restrict such jobs to citizens. "Clearly the exercise of police authority calls for a very high degree of judgment and discretion, the abuse or misuse of which can have serious impact on individuals," Burger said. "In short, it would be as anomalous to conclude that citizens may be subjected to the broad discretionary powers of noncitizen police officers as it would be to say that judicial officers and jurors with power to judge citizens may be aliens." [28]

In 1979 the court, by a 5-4 vote, sustained a New York law prohibiting aliens who refuse to apply for U.S. citizenship the opportunity to work as public school teachers. Because teachers played a critical role in developing the attitudes of their students toward government, society and the political process, they fell into the category of occupations "so bound up with the operation of the State as a governmental entity" as to restrict those jobs to citizens, the majority wrote. [29]

Aliens and the Federal Government

No matter what standard the court finally settles on to determine whether the states have deprived aliens of equal protection of the laws, it appears unlikely that it will change its standard of review for judging federal laws that treat aliens and citizens differently. Because the Constitution gives Congress absolute authority over admission and naturalization, the Supreme Court requires Congress only to present some rational basis for making a distinction between citizen and alien or between some aliens and other aliens. *(Power over immigration, p. 146)*

Medicare Benefits

The most recent exposition of this standard came in the 1976 case of *Mathews v. Diaz*, in which a unanimous court upheld a Medicare regulation denying aliens who were not permanent residents living in the country for at least five years eligibility for supplementary medical benefits. The court wrote:

> . . .[T]he fact that Congress has provided some welfare benefits for citizens does not require it to provide like benefits for *all aliens*. Neither the overnight visitor, the unfriendly agent of a hostile foreign power, the resident diplomat, nor the illegal entrant, can advance even a colorable constitutional claim to a share in the bounty that a conscientious sovereign makes available to its own citizens and *some* of its guests. The decision to share that bounty with our guests may take into account the character of the relationship between the alien and this country: Congress may decide that as the alien's tie grows stronger, so does the strength of his claim to an equal share of the munificence. . . .
>
> . . .In short, it is unquestionably reasonable for Congress to make an alien's eligibility depend on both the character and the duration of his residence. Since neither requirement is wholly irrational, this case essentially involves nothing more than a claim that it

would have been more reasonable for Congress to select somewhat different requirements of the same kind. [30]

And because the benefit issue raised was a question of degree rather than kind, the court said it was "especially reluctant to question the exercise of congressional judgment." [31]

Civil Service Jobs

In a second case decided the same day, the court, by a 5-4 vote, ruled that the Civil Service Commission violated the Fifth Amendment due process guarantee by excluding all aliens from the federal competitive civil service and therefore denying them the opportunity for employment in a major sector of the economy. The denial affected an aspect of liberty protected by the Fifth Amendment, the majority said in *Hampton v. Mow Sun Wong*:

> Since these resident...[aliens] were admitted as a result of decisions made by the Congress and the President . . . due process requires that the decision to impose that deprivation of an important liberty be made either at a comparable level of government or, if it is permitted to be made by the Civil Service Commission, that it be justified by reasons which are properly the concern of that agency. [32]

The only reason offered that properly concerned the agency was administrative efficiency, the majority continued. And while it was reasonable for the agency to make a single rule applicable to all aliens, such an arbitrary rule did not outweigh "the public interest in avoiding the wholesale deprivation of employment opportunities caused" by the rule, which therefore must fall. [33]

Three months later, on Sept. 2, 1976, President Ford issued an executive order authorizing the Civil Service Commission to continue to exclude non-citizens from the federal competitive civil service.

Footnotes

[1] *Yick Wo v. Hopkins,* 118 U.S. 356 at 369 (1886).

[2] Id. at 373-74.

[3] Id. at 374.

[4] *Truax v. Raich,* 239 U.S. 33 at 41 (1915).

[5] Alfred H. Kelly and Winfred A. Harbison, *The American Constitution; Its Origins and Development,* 5th ed. (New York: W. W. Norton & Co., 1976), p. 666.

[6] *McCready v. Virginia,* 94 U.S. 391 at 395 (1877).

[7] *Patsone v. Pennsylvania,* 232 U.S. 138 at 144 (1914).

[8] Ibid.

[9] *Heim v. McCall,* 239 U.S. 175 (1915); *Crane v. New York,* 239 U.S. 195 (1915).

[10] *Ozawa v. United States,* 260 U.S. 178 (1922).

[11] *Terrace v. Thompson,* 263 U.S. 197 at 220 (1923); see also *Porterfield v. Webb,* 263 U.S. 225 (1923); *Webb v. O'Brien,* 263 U.S. 313 (1923); *Frick v. Webb,* 263 U.S. 326 (1923); *Cockrill v. California,* 268 U.S. 258 (1925).

[12] *Clarke v. Deckebach,* 274 U.S. 392 at 396 (1927).

[13] Id. at 397.

[14] *Hirabayshi v. United States,* 320 U.S. 81 (1943); *Korematsu v. United States,* 323 U.S. 214 (1944).

[15] *Oyama v. California,* 332 U.S. 633 at 646 (1948).

[16] *Takahashi v. Fish and Game Commission,* 334 U.S. 410 at 418 (1948).

[17] Id. at 419.

[18] Id. at 421.

[19] *Graham v. Richardson,* 403 U.S. 365 at 372 (1971).

[20] Id. at 374.

[21] Id. at 376.

[22] *In re Griffiths,* 413 U.S. 717 (1973); *Examining Board of Engineers, Architects and Surveyors v. de Otero,* 426 U.S. 572 (1976); *Sugarman v. Dougall,* 413 U.S. 634 (1973); *Nyquist v. Mauclet,* 432 U.S. 1 (1977).

[23] *Sugarman v. Dougall,* 413 U.S. 634 at 641 (1973).

[24] Id. at 643.

[25] Id. at 647.

[26] Id. at 648.

[27] *Foley v. Connelie,* 435 U.S. 291 at 297 (1978).

[28] Id. at 298-99.

[29] *Ambach v. Norwick* (1979).

[30] *Mathews v. Diaz,* 426 U.S. 67 at 80-83, passim (1976).

[31] Id. at 84.

[32] *Hampton v. Mow Sun Wong,* 426 U.S. 88 at 116 (1976).

[33] Id. at 115.

Sex Discrimination and Legal Equality

While it took the Supreme Court almost a century to extend the guarantee of equal protection to victims of racial discrimination, it took even longer for the court to extend the same guarantee to victims of sex discrimination.

Not until the 1970s did the court begin a re-examination of the equal protection guarantee as it applied to discrimination between men and women. As the court neared the end of its first decade of this review, the judicial standard by which gender-based discrimination was measured was still uncertain. While the court had taken some important steps toward placing men and women on an equal footing before the law, at the same time it had upheld some laws based on traditional beliefs about the respective roles of men and women.

Early Paternalism

The Supreme Court's judicial attitude toward women and their role in the political and economic life of the nation has generally reflected the prevailing societal attitude. In its early cases, the court either avoided the issue of discrimination against women or adopted a protectionist philosophy, described by some as "romantic paternalism," to justify such discrimination.

The Right to Practice Law

This view of woman as wife, mother and homemaker was quite apparent in the 1873 case of *Bradwell v. Illinois.* A Chicago woman appealed to the Supreme Court, contesting the state's denial of a license to practice law solely on the grounds that she was female.

In the court opinion, Justice Samuel F. Miller did not discuss the gender issue but simply held that the 14th Amendment did not affect state authority to regulate admission of members to its bar. But in a concurring opinion, Justice Joseph P. Bradley gave judicial cognizance to the then-common belief that women were unfit by nature to hold certain occupations:

> ... [T]he civil law, as well as nature herself, has always recognized a wide difference in the respective spheres and destinies of man and woman. Man is, or should be, woman's protector and defender. The natural and proper timidity and delicacy which belongs to the female sex evidently unfits it for many of the occupations of civil life. The constitution of the family

organization, which is founded in divine ordinance, as well as in the nature of things, indicates the domestic sphere as that which properly belongs to the domain and functions of womanhood. [1]

The Right to Vote

If the 14th Amendment did not compel the states to admit women to the bar, neither did it compel them to allow women to vote or to serve on juries. In the case of *Minor v. Happersett* (1875), the court held that although women were citizens, the right to vote was not a privilege or immunity of national citizenship before adoption of the 14th Amendment, nor did the amendment add suffrage to the privileges and immunities of national citizenship. Therefore, the national government could not require states to permit women to vote. [2] In this respect, women fared worse than blacks, whose right to vote was specifically protected by the 15th Amendment. Not until ratification in 1920 of the 19th Amendment were women assured of the right to vote. *(Details of voting discrimination cases, p. 477)*

The court in 1880 ruled that the 14th Amendment did not prohibit the states from excluding women from jury duty. This position was reaffirmed as recently as 1961 but was overturned by the court's decision in the 1975 case of *Taylor v. Louisiana.* [3] *(Details of cases, box, p. 637)*

Working Conditions

The court also employed "romantic paternalism" to uphold laws intended to protect women's morals. In 1904 it affirmed the validity of a Denver ordinance prohibiting the sale of liquor to women and barring women from working in bars or stores where liquor was sold. [4] Four decades later — in the 1948 case of *Goesaert v. Cleary,* the court sustained a Michigan law that forbade a woman to serve as a bartender unless she was the wife or daughter of the bar's owner. The majority thought it was reasonable for Michigan to believe "that the oversight assured through ownership of a bar by a barmaid's husband or father minimizes hardships that may confront a barmaid without such protecting oversight." [5]

But three justices disagreed, contending that the statute made an unjustifiable and therefore unconstitutional distinction between male and female bar owners. "A male bar owner, although he himself is always absent from his bar, may employ his wife and daughter as barmaids," they wrote, while a "female [bar] owner may neither work as a barmaid herself nor employ her daughter in that position." [6] The three implied that the real purpose of the statute was not to protect women's morals but men's jobs.

The protectionist attitude was also evident in the court's response to other cases involving working women. In the early 1900s, the court upheld state laws setting maximum hours and minimum wages for women while holding similar regulations for men a violation of the right to contract their labor. The typical justification of this distinction was provided by the court's 1908 decision in *Muller v. Oregon*, backing a state law which set maximum hours for women laundry workers. The unanimous court wrote:

> The two sexes differ in structure of body, in the functions to be performed by each, in the amount of physical strength, in the capacity for long-continued labor, particularly when done standing, the influence of vigorous health upon the future well-being of the race, the self-reliance which enables one to assert full rights, and in the capacity to maintain the struggle for subsistence. This difference justifies a difference in legislation and upholds that which is designed to compensate for some of the burdens which rest upon [women]. [7]

Reassessment

The civil rights movement of the 1950s and 1960s aroused a new national sensitivity to other forms of discrimination, including that based on sex. Even a cursory examination showed that the traditional protectionist view of women as wives and mothers had contributed substantially to the discrimination they suffered in a modern era where more and more women worked to support themselves and their families. Because women had been expected to remain at home, they were generally less well-educated than men. As a result, women seeking jobs outside the home generally qualified only for low-paying, low-skill jobs where opportunities for advancement were limited. Frequently women were paid less than men who performed the same job, often on the theory that women's earnings were less vital to the support of their families than men's. Certain legal rights and benefits accrued to women only through their presumed dependency on their husbands and not to them as individuals. As a lower court wrote in 1971: "The pedestal upon which women have been placed has, ... upon closer inspection, been revealed as a cage." [8]

Congress began to act to remedy some of the more obvious inequities in 1963 when it adopted the Equal Pay Act. Title VII of the 1964 Civil Rights Act prohibited employment discrimination on the basis of sex. In 1972 Congress barred gender-based discrimination in all education programs that received federal support. It also sent to the states for ratification the proposed Equal Rights Amendment, which would guarantee women and men equal rights under the law. In 1973 it approved a bill prohibiting lenders from denying credit on the basis of sex or marital status.

Cases challenging sex discrimination in various forms began to reach the court in the 1970s. While the court consistently held that classifications based on sex were subject to judicial examination as possible violations of the equal protection guarantee, it was unable during that decade to reach agreement on the standard it would apply to decide whether such classifications were justified and constitutional.

The Search for A Standard

Rationality was the standard applied in the first case, *Reed v. Reed*, decided in 1971. The case arose after a minor child in Idaho died intestate (without a will). His adoptive parents, Sally and Cecil Reed, were separated; both filed competing petitions to serve as administrator of the child's estate. The court awarded the appointment to the father because the Idaho statute designating those eligible to administer intestate estates gave preference to males. Sally Reed challenged the statute as a violation of the equal protection clause of the 14th Amendment.

For the first time the Supreme Court held a state law invalid because it discriminated against women. In an opinion written by Chief Justice Warren E. Burger, a unanimous Supreme Court struck down the Idaho statute. Quoting from a 1920 decision, Burger said that to be constitutionally permissible, a gender-based classification "must be reasonable, not arbitrary, and must rest upon some ground of difference having a fair and substantial relation to the object of the legislation so that all persons similarly circumstanced shall be treated alike." [9]

Applying that standard to the Idaho statute, the court could find no rational basis for giving men preference over women. The statute's purpose was to reduce the work of probate courts by eliminating one source of controversy in probate cases, the court said. But "[t]o give a mandatory preference to members of either sex over members of the other, merely to accomplish the elimination of hearings on the merits, is to make the very kind of arbitrary legislative choice forbidden by the Equal Protection Clause...," the court concluded. [10]

Using this standard, the court in several subsequent cases upheld gender-based classifications, sustaining:

● A Florida property tax exemption for widows but not widowers. The majority found the exemption "reasonably designed to further the state policy of cushioning the financial impact of spousal loss upon the sex for whom that loss imposes a disproportionately heavy burden." *(Kahn v. Shevin,* 1974) [11]

● A federal law that allows certain female naval officers to serve longer than male officers before mandatory discharge upon failure to win promotion. Observing that female officers could not compete with male officers to win promotion through combat or sea duty, the majority thought it reasonable for Congress to give them a longer period in which to earn advancement. *(Schlesinger v. Ballard,* 1975) [12]

● A Social Security regulation that denies survivors' benefits to widows married less than three months before their husband's death. The majority said such denials were a rational means of preventing sham marriages solely for the purpose of obtaining Social Security benefits. *(Weinberger v. Salfi,* 1975) [13]

● A Social Security regulation providing benefits to married women under age 62 with a minor dependent whose husbands were retired or disabled but not to divorced women in the same circumstances. *(Mathews v. deCastro,* 1976) [14]

In 1975 the court used the rationality standard to strike down a Utah law that required divorced fathers to support their sons to age 21 but their daughters only to age 18. The court in this case of *Stanton v. Stanton* rejected arguments that boys needed the longer period of parental support to obtain education and training, and that girls needed a shorter period of support because they tended to mature and marry earlier than males. Present realities make education for girls as important as for boys, the majority said. "And if any weight remains in this day in the claim of earlier maturity of the female, with a concomitant inference of absence of need for support beyond 18, we fail to perceive its unquestioned truth or its significance," the court added. [15]

Stricter Standard Advocated

As early as 1973, four members of the court argued for adoption of a stricter standard for gender-based laws. The case of *Frontiero v. Richardson* involved a female Air Force officer who sought increased benefits for her husband as a dependent. Her request was denied because the law stipulated that while wives of members of the uniformed services were assumed to be dependents eligible for additional benefits, husbands were not and must prove actual dependence in order to be eligible.

Because the law involved was a federal law, the Air Force officer could not challenge it under the 14th Amendment's guarantee of equal protection of the laws against state action. Instead she challenged the law as a violation of the due process clause of the Fifth Amendment, which applies to federal action. Although the Fifth Amendment does not specifically guarantee equal protection, the court has long held that some discriminations are so unjustifiable as to be violations of the amendment's due process guarantee. *(Box, p. 585)*

The Supreme Court struck the law down by an 8-1 vote. In a plurality opinion announcing the court's decision, Justice William J. Brennan Jr. contended that gender-based classifications, like distinctions based on race and alienage, were inherently suspect. Brennan observed that a person's sex was a non-controllable and immutable characteristic, and added:

> ...what differentiates sex from such nonsuspect statuses as intelligence or physical disability, and aligns it with the recognized suspect criteria, is that the sex characteristic frequently bears no relation to ability to perform or contribute to society. As a result, statutory distinctions between the sexes often have the effect of invidiously relegating the entire class of females to inferior legal status without regard to the actual capabilities of its individual members. [16]

Such inherently suspect classifications may be justified only by a compelling governmental interest, argued Brennan. But, he said, the government's only purpose for the gender-based distinction in this case appeared to be administrative convenience, and even under the less exacting standard of rationality, gender-based classifications made solely to suit administrative convenience were constitutionally impermissible.

Only three other justices agreed with Brennan's reasoning, and so his view that gender-based classifications were inherently suspect remained simply an opinion without the force of law.

Justice Lewis F. Powell Jr., for himself, Chief Justice Burger and Justice Harry A. Blackmun said he agreed that the classification under consideration violated the due process clause. He objected, however, to placing sex-based classifications among those considered inherently suspect and justifiable only by a compelling government interest. He maintained that application of the rationality standard to this case would have resulted in the same outcome.

Justice Potter Stewart concurred in the result without subscribing to either Brennan's or Powell's opinion.

Arbitrary Presumptions

In *Frontiero*, the law fell because the legislators had made the unproven assumption that wives depended on their husbands for support while men did not so depend on their wives. Because this assumption did not take into account those situations where wives were financially independent of their husbands and where husbands were in fact dependent on their wives, the court held that the law was too broad and therefore a violation of the equal protection guarantee.

In two subsequent cases, the court found similar presumptions invalid. In a 1975 decision, the court struck down a Social Security Act provision that provided survivors' benefits to widows with small children but not to widowers with small children. Finding this distinction the same as the invalid classification in the *Frontiero* case, the court ruled that it violated the due process clause by providing working women fewer benefits for their Social Security contributions than working men received.

The distinction challenged here was based on an "archaic and overbroad" generalization, said the court in the case of *Weinberger v. Wiesenfeld*. The idea that men more frequently than women are the primary supporters of their families is "not without empirical support," Justice Brennan wrote. "But such a gender-based generalization cannot suffice to justify the denigration of the efforts of women who do work and whose earnings contribute significantly to their families' support." [17]

Pointing out that the intended purpose of the benefit was to allow a mother to stay home to care for her young children, Brennan said the distinction between surviving mothers and surviving fathers was "entirely irrational.... It is no less important for a child to be cared for by its sole surviving parent when that parent is male rather than female." [18]

In a similar case, a five-justice majority invalidated a Social Security Act provision that provided survivors' benefits to widows regardless of their financial dependence on their husbands, but to widowers only if they proved they had received more than half their income from their wives. In this case of *Califano v. Goldfarb* (1977), four members of the majority found that the provision impermissibly discriminated against female wage earners by diminishing the protection, relative to male wage earners, that they provided for their families. Justice Brennan wrote:

> ...The only conceivable justification for writing the presumption of wives' dependency into the statute is the assumption, not verified by the Government ... but based simply on "archaic and overbroad" generalizations ... that it would save the Government time, money and effort simply to pay benefits to all widows, rather than to require proof of dependency of both sexes. We held in *Frontiero,* and again in *Wiesenfeld,* and therefore hold again here, that such assumptions do not suffice to justify a gender-based discrimination in the distribution of employment-related benefits. [19]

The fifth member of the majority, Justice John Paul Stevens found that the provision impermissibly discriminated against dependent widowers rather than their working wives.

For the minority, Justice William H. Rehnquist argued that the classification was a rational one substantially

Unwed Fathers, Illegitimate Children

Illegitimate children and their fathers are among the groups most recently brought under the scope of the equal protection clause. Many states and several federal laws deny illegitimate children rights and benefits that are granted to legitimate children. Other state laws presume that fathers have no fundamental interest in their illegitimate offspring.

In its recent decisions, the Supreme Court has required more than a rational basis to justify different treatment of legitimate and illegitimate children. But it has not made illegitimacy one of the suspect classifications justifiable only by a compelling government interest. In most instances the court has rejected such a classification as unconstitutional when it irrationally punishes the child for the "wrong" of its parents.

In 1972, as it struck down a state law that denied illegitimate children any share in workers' compensation survivors' benefits paid automatically to legitimate children, the court said:

> The status of illegitimacy has expressed through the ages society's condemnation of irresponsible liaisons beyond the bonds of marriage. But visiting this condemnation on the head of an infant is illogical and unjust. Moreover, imposing disabilities on the illegitimate child is contrary to the basic concept of our system that legal burdens should bear some relationship to individual responsibility or wrongdoing. Obviously, no child is responsible for his birth and penalizing the illegitimate child is an ineffectual — as well as an unjust — way of deterring the parent. [1]

Using similar reasoning, the court struck down state laws forbidding illegitimate children to recover damages in the wrongful death of their mother and, conversely, a mother from recovering damages for the wrongful death of her illegitimate child. [2] It also voided a state law giving legitimate, but not illegitimate, children an enforceable right to support from their natural fathers. [3]

Inheritance and Illegitimacy

The court has been ambivalent about laws restricting the rights of illegitimate children to inherit from their fathers when their fathers die intestate — without a written will.

In 1971, the court, by a 5-4 vote, upheld a state law that prevented an acknowledged illegitimate child from inheriting property from her father, who died intestate. To strike down the law, said the majority, would be an unwarranted interference with an exercise of state power. The father could have written a will designating his illegitimate child as an heir or could have legitimated her, the majority pointed out. [4]

But six years later, the court appeared to repudiate this decision when it struck down an Illinois statute that allowed illegitimate children to inherit intestate only from their mothers while legitimate children could inherit from both parents in the absence of a will. [5]

In 1978, however, the court appeared to waver again on this point, upholding, by a 5-4 vote, a New York law which forbade illegitimate children to inherit from their

intestate fathers unless the father had acknowledged his paternity in a court proceeding during his lifetime. [6]

Federal Laws and Benefits

The court has evidenced similar indecision in its rulings on federal laws which distinguish between legitimate and illegitimate children.

In 1974 the court struck down a Social Security Act provision that denied disability insurance benefits to some illegitimate children while allowing such benefits to other illegitimate children and all legitimate children. [7]

But in 1976 the court upheld a Social Security provision requiring certain illegitimate children to prove actual dependence on their deceased parent in order to be eligible for surviving children's benefits. Such proof was not required for legitimate children. [8]

Unwed Fathers

In the case of *Stanley v. Illinois,* an unwed father of children whose mother had died challenged a state statute that made his children wards of the state without giving him an opportunity to prove his fitness as a parent. The law provided a fitness hearing in such circumstances for legitimate parents and unwed mothers.

The court in 1972 ruled that due process entitled the father to such a hearing and that denial of the hearing constituted a violation of equal protection. The only viable reason for denying unwed fathers such hearings was administrative convenience, an insufficient justification for the classification, the court said. [9]

In 1978, however, the court upheld a state law that allowed an unwed father to veto the adoption of his child only if he legitimated the child. The court noted a distinction between unwed fathers who by legitimating their children showed a willingness to assume the responsibilities of parenthood and those unwed fathers who did not legitimate their children, showing little concern for their well-being. [10]

But in 1979 the court struck down a state law that gave the natural mother, but not the natural father, the right to veto their child's adoption. The distinction made by the law was not sufficiently related to the state's interest in facilitating adoption, the majority held. [11]

---

[1] *Weber v. Aetna Casualty and Surety Co.,* 406 U.S. 164 at 175 (1972).

[2] *Levy v. Louisiana,* 391 U.S. 68 (1968); *Glona v. American Guarantee and Liability Insurance Co.,* 391 U.S. 73 (1968); see also *Parham v. Hughes* (1979).

[3] *Gomez v. Perez,* 409 U.S. 535 (1973).

[4] *Labine v. Vincent,* 401 U.S. 532 (1971).

[5] *Trimble v. Gordon,* 430 U.S. 762 (1977).

[6] *Lalli v. Lalli,* 439 U.S. 259 (1978).

[7] *Jimenez v. Weinberger,* 417 U.S. 628 (1974).

[8] *Mathews v. Lucas,* 427 U.S. 495 (1976).

[9] *Stanley v. Illinois,* 405 U.S. 645 (1972).

[10] *Quilloin v. Walcott,* 434 U.S. 246 (1978).

[11] *Caban v. Mohammed* (1979).

related to the intended goal, which Rehnquist defined as a wish to aid "the characteristically [economically] depressed condition of aged widows." [20]

'Important Objectives'

Although he had been unable to convince a majority of the court that gender-based discrimination was so invidious as to require a compelling government interest to justify it, Justice Brennan in 1976 did win majority support for a standard that appeared midway between the standards of rationality and a compelling governmental interest.

The case of *Craig v. Boren* (1976) involved a challenge to an Oklahoma law that permitted the sale of 3.2 beer to women at age 18 but not to men until age 21. Four justices agreed with Brennan that to "withstand constitutional challenge . . . classifications by gender must serve important governmental objectives and must be substantially related to achievement of those objectives." [21] It was not enough that the classification was rational, Brennan said; the distinction must serve some "important governmental objective."

Applying this standard, the majority found that Oklahoma's desire to promote traffic safety was an important goal, but that the gender-based distinction prohibiting the sale, but not the possession, of a low-alcohol beverage to males under 21 was not substantially related to the attainment of that objective. The classification was therefore invalid.

Job Discrimination

The child-bearing function of women has been the major factor interrupting their pattern of employment outside the home. Employers have used potential pregnancy as a primary argument against hiring, training and promoting women and their restrictive policies on pregnancy have been a major target of women's rights advocates who see this issue as the heart of sex discrimination.

The Supreme Court has found cases dealing with pregnancy-related discrimination difficult. A majority of the court has held in several instances that pregnancy classifications do not discriminate between men and women but rather between pregnant persons and nonpregnant persons. Such hairsplitting led one justice to protest that discrimination against pregnant persons was by definition sex discrimination. "[I]t is the capacity to become pregnant which primarily differentiates the female from the male," wrote Justice John Paul Stevens in a 1976 case. [22]

Maternity Leave

In January 1974 the court by a 7-2 vote held that employers violated the due process guarantee by enforcing mandatory pregnancy leave policies requiring all pregnant women to leave their jobs at the same specified time in pregnancy. The cases of *Cleveland Board of Education v. LeFleur* and *Cohen v. Chesterfield County School Board*, decided together, involved school board policies that forced teachers to stop teaching midway through pregnancy.

"[F]reedom of personal choice in matters of marriage and family life is one of the liberties protected by the due process clause, . . ." the majority wrote; due process requires that maternity leave regulations "not needlessly, arbitrarily, or capriciously impinge upon this vital area of a teacher's constitutional liberty." [23]

The court rejected the school boards' arguments that mandatory leave policies ensured continuity of instruction by giving the school time to find qualified substitute teachers. Such an absolute requirement violated the test of rationality, the court said, because in many instances it would interrupt continuity by requiring a teacher to leave her classroom in the middle of a term.

"As long as the teachers are required to give substantial advance notice of their condition, the choice of firm dates later in pregnancy would serve the boards' objectives just as well, while imposing a far lesser burden on the women's exercise of constitutionally protected freedom," the majority wrote. [24]

The court also held that the regulations were too broad because they presumed that all women reaching the fifth or sixth month of pregnancy were physically incapable of continuing in their jobs. Such a presumption, which denies a pregnant woman the opportunity to prove she is fit to continue working, is contrary to the due process guarantees of the Fifth and 14th Amendments, the majority said.

"If legislative bodies are to be permitted to draw a general line anywhere short of the delivery room, I can find no judicial standard of measurement which says the lines drawn here are invalid," said Justice William E. Rehnquist, dissenting for himself and Chief Justice Warren E. Burger. [25]

State Disability Insurance

Six months later, the court in the case of *Geduldig v. Aiello* upheld a state disability insurance program that excluded coverage of disabilities related to normal pregnancy and childbirth. The exclusion was challenged as a violation of the equal protection guarantee. The six-justice majority said the exclusion was based on physical condition, not sex. For them, Justice Potter Stewart wrote:

The California insurance program does not exclude anyone from benefit eligibility because of gender but merely removes one physical condition — pregnancy — from the list of compensable disabilities. While it is true that only women can become pregnant, it does not follow that every legislative classification concerning pregnancy is a sex-based classification. . . . Normal pregnancy is an objectively identifiable physical condition with unique characteristics. Absent a showing that distinctions involving pregnancy are mere pretexts designed to effect an invidious discrimination against the members of one sex or the other, lawmakers are constitutionally free to include or exclude pregnancy from the coverage of legislation such as this on any reasonable basis, just as with respect to any other physical condition. [26]

The question then became simply whether the exclusion was reasonable. Stewart observed that disability coverage for pregnancy would increase costs that would have to be offset by increased employee contributions, changes in other coverage, or lower benefit levels. He continued:

The state has a legitimate interest in maintaining the self-supporting nature of its insurance program. Similarly, it has an interest in distributing the available resources in such a way as to keep benefit payments at an adequate level for disabilities that are covered, rather than to cover all disabilities inadequately. Finally, California has a legitimate concern in maintaining the contribution rate at a level that will not unduly burden participating employees, particularly low-income employees who may be most in need of the disability insurance.

These policies provide an objective and wholly non-invidious basis for the State's decision not to create a more comprehensive insurance program than it has. There is no evidence in the record that the selection of the risks insured by the program worked to discriminate against any definable group or class in terms of the aggregate risk protection derived by that group or class from the program. There is no risk from which men are protected and women are not. Likewise, there is no risk from which women are protected and men are not.

The appellee [Aiello] simply contends that, although she has received insurance protection equivalent to that provided all other participating employees, she has suffered discrimination because she encountered a risk that was outside the program's protection.... [W]e hold that this contention is not a valid one under the Equal Protection Clause of the Fourteenth Amendment. [27]

For the three dissenters, Justice Brennan said the majority should have applied a stricter standard in reviewing the case. "In the past, when a legislative classification has turned on gender, the Court has justifiably applied a standard of judicial scrutiny more strict than that generally accorded economic or social welfare programs," he wrote. [28] Brennan said the proper standard would regard gender-based classifications as inherently suspect, justifiable only to achieve a compelling government interest that could not otherwise be met.

But Brennan also thought the majority applied the standard it did use erroneously:

...[T]he economic effects caused by pregnancy-related disabilities are functionally indistinguishable from the effects caused by any other disability: wages are lost due to a physical inability to work, and medical expenses are incurred for the delivery of the child and for post-partum care. In my view, by singling out for less favorable treatment a gender-linked disability peculiar to women, the State has created a double standard for disability compensation: a limitation is imposed upon the disabilities for which women workers may recover, while men receive full compensation for all disabilities suffered, including those that affect only or primarily their sex.... Such dissimilar treatment of men and women, on the basis of physical characteristics inextricably linked to one sex, inevitably constitutes sex discrimination. [29]

Private Disability Plans

In subsequent cases, lower courts distinguished between that state plan — challenged as violating the constitutional guarantee of equal protection — and private disability insurance plans — challenged as conflicting with the sex discrimination ban of the 1964 Civil Rights Act. In separate cases, six federal courts of appeals agreed that such an exclusion did violate the 1964 law.

The General Electric Co., loser in one of these cases, appealed successfully to the Supreme Court. The majority saw no distinction between private plans attacked under the 1964 Act and state plans challenged as a violation of equal protection. "[E]xclusion of pregnancy from a disability benefits plan providing general coverage is not a gender-based discrimination at all," wrote Rehnquist for the six-justice majority in *General Electric Co. v. Gilbert* (1976).[30]

The plan covered some risks, but not others; there was no risk from which men were protected, but not women, or vice versa. Rehnquist wrote:

[I]t is impossible to find any gender-based discriminatory effect in this scheme simply because women disabled as a result of pregnancy do not receive benefits; that is to say, gender-based discrimination does not result simply because an employer's disability benefits plan is less than all-inclusive.... To hold otherwise would endanger the commonsense notion that an employer who has no disability benefits program at all does not violate Title VII [of the 1964 Act]. [31]

"Surely it offends common sense to suggest . . . that a classification revolving around pregnancy is not, at the minimum, strongly 'sex related,' " wrote Justice Brennan in dissent. "Pregnancy exclusions . . . both financially burden women workers and act to break down the continuity of the employment relationship, thereby exacerbating women's comparatively transient role in the labor force." [32]

Sick Pay and Seniority

Almost exactly one year after the *General Electric* decision, the court ruled that under the 1964 Civil Rights Act, employers may refuse sick pay to women employees absent from work due to pregnancy and childbirth, but they may not divest those women of their accumulated seniority merely because they take maternity leave. The justices all concurred in the ruling in the case of *Nashville Gas Co. v. Satty* (1977).

For the court, Justice Rehnquist wrote that the gas company's seniority policy was a clear violation of the 1964 act's Title VII, which prohibited employment discrimination on the basis of sex. Although the policy appeared to be a neutral rule — simply divesting of seniority all persons who took leaves of absence from work for any reason other than illness (a category from which childbirth-related absences were excluded) — its effect was clearly discriminatory, depriving far more women than men of job opportunities and adversely affecting their status as employees.

The denial of sick pay was permissible, wrote Rehnquist, under the same reasoning which upheld the denial of disability benefits payments. That issue was sent back to lower courts for reconsideration in light of the intervening *General Electric* decision.

Attempting to distinguish the seniority policy from the sick pay and disability benefits policies, Rehnquist emphasized that the gas company:

...has not merely refused to extend to women a benefit [sick pay, disability insurance] that men cannot and do not receive, but has imposed on women a substantial burden that men need not suffer. The distinction between benefits and burdens is more than one of semantics. We held in Gilbert that . . . [Title VII] did not require that greater economic benefits be paid to one sex or the other "because of their differing roles in the scheme of human existence." . . . But that holding does not allow us to read . . . [Title VII] to permit an employer to burden female employees in such a way as to deprive them of employment opportunities because of their different role.[33]

Finding this distinction somewhat confusing, Justice John Paul Stevens in a concurring opinion described the difference between the two policies as one of short-term versus long-term effect. Denial of sick pay did not affect the woman worker beyond the period of her leave; loss of seniority resulted in permanent disadvantage, Stevens said.

In a concurring opinion, Justices Brennan, Powell and Thurgood Marshall suggested that upon re-examination the lower court might find that the combination of the seniority and sick pay policies did violate Title VII by resulting in less net compensation for women than for men employees.

Legislative Resolution

Frustrated by the court's refusal to modify its ruling in the *Gilbert* case, women's rights activists turned to Congress for relief. Congress responded in October 1978 by amending Title VII to prohibit discrimination against pregnant women in any area of employment, including hiring, promotion, seniority rights and job security. The amendment also required employers who offered health insurance and temporary disability plans to provide coverage to women for pregnancy, childbirth and related medical conditions. A legal challenge to the amendment's validity was anticipated.

Children and Mothers

Despite the court's rulings on these pregnancy cases, the 1964 Civil Rights Act Title VII ban on employment discrimination by sex has not been a hollow prohibition.

The first Title VII sex discrimination case to come to the Supreme Court was *Phillips v. Martin Marietta Corp.* (1971). The case concerned the company's policy of refusing to hire women with preschool-aged children, although it hired men regardless of their children's ages. In an unsigned opinion, the court said that Title VII did not permit such a distinction unless it was "a bona fide occupational qualification reasonably necessary to the normal operation of that particular business or enterprise." [34]

Equal Pay

The court implicitly upheld the Equal Pay Act of 1963 in its 1974 decision in *Corning Glass Works v. Brennan.* [35] The court found discriminatory a company policy that paid higher wages to men working on the night shift than to women working on the day shift, even though both did the same work. To compensate for the less attractive night work, the court said the company could pay a night-shift differential, but base wages for men and women must remain the same for the same job, regardless of which shift each worked.

Jobs in Prisons

In the 1977 case of *Dothard v. Rawlinson,* the court for the first time struck down as discrimination on the basis of sex a state law that set minimum height and weight requirements for certain jobs, in this case that of a prison guard.

Dianne Rawlinson was rejected for a job as a prison guard in Alabama because she did not meet the requirement that guards be 5'2" tall and weigh at least 120 pounds. She challenged the law on the grounds that it would disqualify more than 40 percent of the women in the country but less than one percent of the men.

Women on Jury Duty

For nearly 100 years, the Supreme Court held that because a woman's place was in the home, she did not have to peform jury duty unless she expressed a wish to do so. Exclusion of women from state court jury panels did not violate the 14th Amendment, the court ruled in the 1880 case of *Strauder v. West Virginia.* [1] This opinion was reaffirmed in the 1961 case of *Hoyt v. Florida.*

Hoyt sought to overturn her murder conviction on the ground that Florida's jury selection procedures were unconstitutional. The statute required that only women who had registered for jury duty could be called; the effect of the statute was to exclude most women from service. However, the court majority found the statute valid. "[W]oman is still regarded as the center of home and family life," wrote Justice John Marshall Harlan. "We cannot say that it is constitutionally impermissible for a State . . . to conclude that a woman should be relieved from the civic duty of jury service unless she herself determines that such service is consistent with her own special responsibilities." [2]

A Fair Cross-Section

Fourteen years later the court reversed itself. In the 1975 case of *Taylor v. Louisiana,* it ruled that exemption of women from juries was unconstitutional. The case arose after Billy Taylor, convicted of a crime by an all-male jury, challenged the Louisiana law that exempted women from jury service unless they specifically announced a willingness to serve, charging that it denied him his right to a fair trial. The court agreed, reasoning that a jury comprised of a fair cross-section of the community was fundamental to the right to jury trial guaranteed by the Sixth Amendment. That guarantee was denied "if the jury pool is made up of only special segments of the populace or if large, distinctive groups are excluded from the pool," the majority said. Since 53 percent of the community was female — and thereby a large distinctive group — the question then became whether women served "such a distinctive role" that their exclusion from jury service was justifiable.

The majority answered that it was

> . . .no longer tenable to hold that women as a class may be excluded or given automatic exemptions based solely on sex if the consequence is that criminal jury venires are almost totally male. . . . If it was ever the case that women were unqualified to sit on juries or were so situated that none of them could be required to perform jury service, that time has long since passed. [3]

---

[1] *Strauder v. West Virginia,* 100 U.S. 303 (1880).
[2] *Hoyt v. Florida,* 368 U.S. 57 at 62 (1961).
[3] *Taylor v. Louisiana,* 419 U.S. 522 at 537 (1975).

The court ruled this was valid *prima facie* evidence of sex discrimination because the apparently neutral physical requirements "select applicants for hire in a significantly discriminatory pattern." The state was then required to show that the height and weight requirements had a "manifest relationship" to the job in question. This the state failed to do, the court said. [36]

The court did uphold, however, a provision of the Alabama statute that prohibited women from filling "contact" positions which brought prison guards into close proximity with inmates. In this case, the majority said an employee's "very womanhood" would make her vulnerable to sexual and other attacks by inmates and thus "undermine her capacity to provide the security that is the essence of a correctional counselor's responsibility." [37]

Justices Brennan and Marshall dissented. The majority decision "perpetuates one of the most insidious of the old myths about women — that women, wittingly or not, are seductive sexual objects," wrote Marshall. The majority, he said, makes women "pay the price in lost job opportunities for the threat of depraved conduct by prison inmates. . . . The proper response to inevitable attacks on both female and male guards is . . . to take swift and sure punitive actions against the inmate offenders." [38]

Pension Contributions

In 1978 the court by a 5-3 vote ruled that a municipal employer could not require female employees to make higher contributions to a pension fund than male employees earning the same salary.

In the case of *Los Angeles v. Manhart,* the city contended that the differential contributions were not based on sex, but on longevity, a factor "other than sex" that did not violate either the Equal Pay Act or the 1964 Civil Rights Act. Justice John Paul Stevens for the majority acknowledged that women generally lived longer than men and that without the differential, men would, in effect, subsidize the pension benefits eventually paid to women. Stevens said, however, that such subsidies were the essence of group insurance:

> . . .Treating different classes of risk as though they were the same for purposes of group insurance is a common practice which has never been considered inherently unfair. To insure the flabby and the fit as though they were equivalent risks may be more common than treating men and women alike; but nothing more than habit makes one "subsidy" seem less fair than the other. [39]

Stevens emphasized that the 1964 Civil Rights Act protected the individual from discrimination: "Even a true generalization about the class is an insufficient reason for disqualifying an individual to whom the generalization does not apply." [40] Even though most women lived longer than most men, many women workers who paid the larger contribution would not, in fact, live longer than some of their male colleagues, Stevens pointed out.

In dissent, Chief Justice Burger wrote that if employers

> . . .are to operate economically workable group pension programs, it is only rational to permit them to

rely on statistically sound and proven disparities in longevity between men and women. Indeed, it seems to me irrational to assume Congress intended to outlaw use of the fact that, for whatever reasons or combination of reasons, women as a class outlive men. . . .

An effect upon pension plans so revolutionary and discriminatory — this time favorable to women at the expense of men — should not be read into the statute without either a clear statement of that intent in the statute, or some reliable indication in the legislative history that this was Congress' purpose. [41]

Remedies

The majority may have been influenced by Burger's warning of the decision's revolutionary effect on pension plans. By a 7-1 vote, the court reversed the lower court order awarding retroactive relief to the women contributors. In this instance the majority felt that retroactive relief was inappropriate because it "could be devastating for a pension fund." [42] Payment of the award from the pension fund would diminish the fund's assets; that might then prove inadequate to meet obligations, which in turn might decrease benefits to all employees or increase the contribution rates for current employees, the court said.

In lone dissent on this point, Justice Marshall said the majority had been shown no proof that a retroactive award would have the predicted "devastating" effect on the pension fund. He contended that repayment to women of their earlier excessive contributions was the only way to make the women whole for the discrimination they had suffered.

In an earlier case involving remedies for proven sex discrimination, the court held that the 11th Amendment, which prohibits private suits in federal courts against unwilling states, did not protect a state from an order to pay retroactive benefits to employees who were discriminated against by the state. Congress through its 1972 amendments to the 1964 Civil Rights Act empowered federal judges to order states to make such awards.

In the case of *Fitzpatrick v. Bitzer* (1976), the court upheld a federal court order to Connecticut to pay retroactive benefits to men who had been forced by state law to work longer than women employees before they could retire. [43] The court said Congress had the power to enforce the guarantees of the 14th Amendment by authorizing such orders requiring expenditures of states funds. States, by ratifying that amendment, surrendered some of their sovereign immunity to such federal orders, it said. *(11th Amendment immunity, p. 303)*

The court in other cases has upheld the authority of federal judges to award back pay and seniority benefits to victims of job discrimination. [44] Although these cases dealt with job discrimination on the basis of race, the court has given no indication that the same remedies would not apply to proven instances of job discrimination on the basis of sex. *(Details, p. 620)*

Footnotes

[1] *Bradwell v. Illinois,* 16 Wall. 130 at 141 (1873).
[2] *Minor v. Happersett,* 21 Wall. 162 (1875).
[3] *Strauder v. West Virginia,* 100 U.S. 303 (1880); *Hoyt v. Florida,* 368 U.S. 57 (1961) overruled by *Taylor v. Louisiana,* 419 U.S. 522 (1975).
[4] *Cronin v. Adams,* 192 U.S. 108 (1904).
[5] *Goesaert v. Cleary,* 335 U.S. 464 at 466 (1948).
[6] Id. at 468.

[7] *Muller v. Oregon,* 208 U.S. 412 at 422-23 (1908); see also *Riley v. Massachusetts,* 232 U.S. 671 (1914); *Miller v. Wilson,* 236 U.S. 373 (1915); *Bosley v. McLaughlin,* 236 U.S. 385 (1915); *West Coast Hotel v. Parrish,* 300 U.S. 379 (1937).
[8] *Sail'er Inn, Inc. v. Kirby,* 5 Cal. 3d 1.20, 485 P 2d 529 (1971).
[9] *Reed v. Reed,* 404 U.S. 71 at 76 (1971), quoting *Royster Guano Co. v. Virginia,* 253 U.S. 412 at 415 (1920).
[10] *Reed v. Reed,* 404 U.S. 71 at 76 (1971).

[11] *Kahn v. Shevin,* 416 U.S. 351 (1974).

[12] *Schlesinger v. Ballard,* 419 U.S. 498 (1975).

[13] *Weinberger v. Salfi,* 422 U.S. 749 (1975).

[14] *Mathews v. deCastro,* 429 U.S. 181 (1976).

[15] *Stanton v. Stanton,* 421 U.S. 7 at 15 (1975).

[16] *Frontiero v. Richardson,* 411 U.S. 677 at 686-87 (1973).

[17] *Weinberger v. Wiesenfeld,* 420 U.S. 636 at 645 (1975).

[18] Id. at 651-52.

[19] *Califano v. Goldfarb,* 430 U.S. 199 at 217 (1977).

[20] Id. at 242.

[21] *Craig v. Boren,* 429 U.S. 190 at 197 (1976); see also *Orr v. Orr* (1979).

[22] *General Electric Co. v. Gilbert,* 429 U.S. 125 at 162 (1976).

[23] *Cleveland Board of Education v. LaFleur, Cohen v. Chesterfield County School Board,* 414 U.S. 632 at 639-40 (1974).

[24] Id. at 643.

[25] Id. at 660.

[26] *Geduldig v. Aiello,* 417 U.S. 484 at 496-97, footnote 20 (1974).

[27] Id. at 496-97.

[28] Id. at 502.

[29] Id. at 500-01.

[30] *General Electric Co. v. Gilbert,* 429 U.S. 125 at 136 (1976).

[31] Id. at 138-39.

[32] Id. at 149, 158.

[33] *Nashville Gas Co. v. Satty,* 434 U.S. 136 at 142 (1977).

[34] *Phillips v. Martin-Marietta Corp.,* 400 U.S. 542 (1971).

[35] *Corning Glass Works v. Brennan,* 417 U.S. 188 (1974).

[36] *Dothard v. Rawlinson,* 433 U.S. 321 at 329 (1977).

[37] Id. at 336.

[38] Id. at 345-46.

[39] *Los Angeles v. Manhart,* 435 U.S. 702 at 710 (1978).

[40] Id. at 708.

[41] Id. at 726.

[42] Id. at 722.

[43] *Fitzpatrick v. Bitzer,* 427 U.S. 445 (1976).

[44] See, for example, *Albemarle Paper Co. v. Moody,* 422 U.S. 405 (1975); *Franks v. Bowman Transportation Co.,* 424 U.S. 747 (1976); *Teamsters v. United States, T.I.M.E.-D.C. v. United States,* 431 U.S. 324 (1977).

Poverty and Equal Protection

Discrimination based on relative wealth has never been found inherently unconstitutional by the court, even though individual justices in recent years have endorsed that belief.

The Supreme Court has found classifications based upon wealth in violation of the equal protection guarantee, however, when they work to deprive poor people of certain fundamental rights and interests and there is no compelling state interest to justify the discrimination.

On this basis, the court has invalidated classifications by wealth that impede access to justice, the right to travel freely between states, and the right to vote and run for public office.

Efforts to persuade the court to classify all distinctions based on wealth as inherently suspect and to raise vital interests, such as education, to the status of fundamental rights have been unsuccessful. Where the court has found that a classification by wealth does not involve a fundamental interest, it has applied the traditional equal protection test in which the state must only show a rational basis to justify the distinction between rich and poor.

Access to Justice

The first time the Supreme Court found a classification based on wealth to be a violation of equal protection was in the 1956 case of *Griffin v. Illinois.* Judson Griffin and James Crenshaw were convicted of armed robbery in Illinois. Because they were indigent, the two asked for a free transcript of their trial for use in preparing an appeal. After their request was refused, the two charged that the refusal denied them due process and equal protection as guaranteed by the 14th Amendment. By a 5-4 vote, the Supreme Court agreed. However, only four justices subscribed to the opinion written by Justice Hugo L. Black, who said:

> . . .Both equal protection and due process emphasize the central aim of our entire judicial system — all people charged with crime must, so far as the law is concerned, "stand on an equality before the bar of justice in every American court." . . .Surely no one would contend that either a State or the Federal Government could constitutionally provide that defendants unable to pay court costs in advance should be denied the right to plead not guilty or to defend themselves in court. Such a law would make the

constitutional promise of a fair trial a worthless thing. Notice, the right to be heard, and the right to counsel would under such circumstances be meaningless promises to the poor. In criminal trials a State can no more discriminate on account of poverty than on account of religion, race, or color. Plainly the ability to pay costs in advance bears no rational relationship to a defendant's guilt or innocence and could not be used as an excuse to deprive a defendant of a fair trial. [1]

An Equal Right to Appeal

A state is not required by the Constitution to provide an appeals procedure. But if it chooses to do so it may not limit access to it on the basis of wealth, Black continued. "There can be no equal justice where the kind of a trial a man gets depends on the amount of money he has." [2]

Justice Felix Frankfurter concurred in the judgment with a separate opinion.

The four dissenters held the denial neither a deprivation of due process nor of equal protection. So long as Illinois followed its established procedure for appellate review, the dissenters said, due process had not been violated. And so long as the state opened its appeals procedure to all defendants convicted of the same crime, it did not violate equal protection even though

> . . .some may not be able to avail themselves of the full appeal because of their poverty. . . . The Constitution requires the equal protection of the law, but it does not require the States to provide equal financial means for all defendants to avail themselves of such laws. [3]

By 1971, however, the entire court apparently agreed that poverty alone should not bar an indigent from appealing his conviction. In *Mayer v. Chicago,* a unanimous court expanded the *Griffin* ruling to hold that a state's refusal to provide a free transcript to a man so that he might appeal his misdemeanor conviction was a violation of equal protection. "The size of the defendant's pocketbook bears no more relationship to his guilt or innocence in a nonfelony than in a felony case," the court declared. [4]

But in 1976 the court limited the circumstances under which the federal government must provide transcripts at public expense. In *United States v. MacCollum,* the court declared that indigent inmates did not have an unlimited constitutional right to a free transcript of their trial. Congress did not violate the equal protection guarantee implicit in the Fifth Amendment when it made provision of such a transcript conditional upon a finding that the challenge to the conviction was not frivolous and that the transcript was necessary to resolve the issues presented.

These conditions, the five-justice majority conceded,

> . . .place an indigent in somewhat less advantageous position than a person of means. But neither the Equal Protection Clause of the Fourteenth Amendment nor . . . the Fifth Amendment . . . guarantees "absolute equality or precisely equal advantages". . . . In the context of a criminal proceeding, they require only an "adequate opportunity to present [one's] claims fairly. . . ." [5]

The Right to Legal Counsel

In 1963, on the same day that the Supreme Court held in *Gideon v. Wainwright* that a state violated due process when it refused to provide court-appointed attorneys to indigents charged with felonies, the court also held that a state violated equal protection if it provided attorneys to indigents appealing convictions only when the appellate court decided legal counsel would be advantageous to the success of the appeal. For the majority in the case of *Douglas v. California,* Justice William O. Douglas wrote:

> . . .There is lacking that equality demanded by the Fourteenth Amendment where the rich man, who appeals as of right, enjoys the benefit of counsel's examination into the record, research of the law, and marshalling of arguments on his behalf, while the indigent, already burdened by a preliminary determination that his case is without merit, is forced to shift for himself. [6]

Justice John Marshall Harlan, who dissented in *Griffin* also dissented in *Douglas,* arguing that the court should have relied on the due process clause rather than the equal protection guarantee to invalidate the state law:

> The States, of course, are prohibited by the Equal Protection Clause from discriminating between "rich" and "poor" *as such* in the formulation and application of their laws. But it is a far different thing to suggest that this provision prevents the State from adopting a law of general applicability that may affect the poor more harshly than it does the rich, or, on the other hand, from making some effort to redress economic imbalances while not eliminating them entirely. [7]

In subsequent cases the court held that neither due process nor equal protection required a state to provide a convicted defendant with counsel so that he could seek discretionary review of his case in the state's higher courts or in the Supreme Court — rather than an appeal to which he had a right. Nor did a state deny equal protection when it required a convicted indigent who subsequently became capable of repayment to reimburse the state for the costs of his court-appointed attorney.[8]

Court Costs

Justice Harlan eventually persuaded a majority of the court that due process was the proper constitutional basis for striking down state laws discriminating against the poor. People who could not afford the $60 in court costs associated with divorce proceedings were barred by Con-

necticut from filing for separation. Ruling against the state law in the 1971 case of *Boddie v. Connecticut,* Justice Harlan for the majority pointed out that the only way to obtain a divorce was in court. The state, by denying access to court to persons too poor to pay the fees amounted — in the absence of a "sufficient countervailing" justification from the state — to a denial of due process. Harlan acknowledged that the state had an interest in curbing frivolous suits and in using court fees to offset court costs. But these reasons were not sufficient, he said, "to override the interest of these [indigents] in having access to the only avenue open for dissolving their . . . marriages." [9]

Justices Douglas and William J. Brennan Jr. concurred in the result but argued that the case presented a classic denial of equal protection. "Affluence does not pass muster under the Equal Protection Clause for determining who must remain married and who shall be allowed to separate," wrote Douglas. [10]

Bankruptcy

By a 5-4 vote the court did sustain, however, a federal law that required indigents to pay the usual fee in order to declare bankruptcy. "There is no constitutional right to obtain a discharge of one's debts in bankruptcy," the majority wrote in *United States v. Kras* (1973). [11] Since the right to file for bankruptcy was not a fundamental one, the majority ruled that the federal government need only meet the rationality test. And since it was reasonable that the bankruptcy system be self-sufficient, the government met the test. In dissent, Justice Potter Stewart said he could not agree with a decision that made "some of the poor too poor even to go bankrupt." [12]

Fines and Terms

In two unanimous decisions, the court has held that states may not substitute imprisonment for a fine that an indigent is unable to pay. In the 1970 case of *Williams v. Illinois,* the court said that states could not hold poor people in prison beyond the length of the maximum sentence merely to work off a fine they were unable to pay. Forty-seven of the 50 states allowed such further imprisonment. Writing for the court, Chief Justice Warren E. Burger said:

> On its face the statute extends to all defendants an apparently equal opportunity for limiting confinement to the statutory maximum simply by satisfying a money judgment. In fact, this is an illusory choice for Williams or any indigent who . . . is without funds. . . . By making the maximum confinement contingent upon one's ability to pay, the State has visited different consequences on two categories of people. . . . [13]

In 1971 the court ruled that a "$30 or 30 days" sentence was also an unconstitutional denial of equal protection. That provision of the 14th Amendment held the court, barred any state or municipality from limiting punishment for an offense to a fine for those who could pay, but expanding punishment for the same offense to imprisonment for those who could not.[14]

The Right to Travel

Although the Supreme Court has never finally settled on which clause of the Constitution protects an individual's right to travel from state to state, since 1966 it has been established that this is one of the fundamental constitutionally protected rights.[15] *(Right to travel, p. 104)*

In 1969 the court struck down two state laws and a District of Columbia statute setting residence requirements for welfare recipients as unconstitutionally restricting this right to travel. In the case of *Shapiro v. Thompson*, the court ruled, by a 6-3 vote, that the residency requirements infringed on the right of poor people to move from state to state and thereby denied them due process and equal protection of the laws. "[A]ny classification which serves to penalize the exercise of that right [to travel], unless shown to be necessary to promote a *compelling* governmental interest is unconstitutional," the majority said. [16] The majority recognized the state's valid interest in maintaining the fiscal integrity of its welfare plan, but found this interest not a compelling justification for making "invidious distinctions between classes of its citizens...." [17]

The court reiterated its *Shapiro* holding in 1974 when it ruled that Arizona violated the equal protection clause by requiring indigent persons to live in a county for a year before becoming eligible for free non-emergency medical care.[18]

Political Rights

The court in recent years has ruled consistently that states may not place financial impediments in the way of a person's right to vote or otherwise participate in the political process. Rights associated with political participation have been determined by the court to be of fundamental interest to citizens and classifications that prevent some group of people from participating may be justified only by a compelling governmental interest. *(Details, p. 585)*

The poll tax was the major financial barrier to voting for many people for years. Originally conceived of as an additional source of revenue, the poll tax became in the early 1900s a discriminatory tool to bar blacks from voting.

In the 1937 case of *Breedlove v. Suttles*, the court turned aside a charge that the poll tax denied equal protection of the laws, upholding it as a valid source of revenue. [19] In the 1966 case of *Harper v. Virginia State Board of Elections*, the court overruled its 1937 decision on the ground that the poll tax denied equal protection to the poor by depriving them of the freedom to exercise their right to vote. "Wealth, like race, creed, or color, is not germane to one's ability to participate intelligently in the electoral process," the majority declared.[20] *(Details, p. 483)*

Filing Fees

In two cases, the court has held that states may not use filing fee requirements to keep poor candidates off the ballot. Such restrictions not only violate the guarantee of equal protection to candidates but also to voters by limiting the choice of candidates, the court reasoned.

Bullock v. Carter (1972) concerned a Texas statute that based the size of primary election filing fees on the costs of conducting those elections. The fees ran as high as $8,900 for some races.

The court held that keeping spurious candidates off the ballot was a legitimate state objective, but that the method selected to achieve that objective was arbitrary since some serious candidates were unable to pay the high filing fees while some frivolous candidates could afford them. The test applied to the challenged law was not as demanding as the compelling interest test generally used for classifications

---

Family Matters

The court has held that some matters of family and marital relations are of fundamental interest and that therefore classifications which restrict these relationships can be justified only by a compelling reason. However, in 1970 the court ruled that a state statute that appeared to discriminate against large families was constitutional because it had a rational basis. The case of *Dandridge v. Williams* concerned a Maryland law that limited the maximum amount of welfare a family could receive. This meant that large families received less per child in benefits than families with fewer children. Large poor families consequently charged that the state had impermissibly denied them equal protection.

The court majority disagreed, holding that the statute did not deliberately discriminate against large families but was simply a reasonable means for a state to use to allocate scarce welfare funds. *(Dandridge v. Williams,* 397 U.S. 471, 1970)

---

affecting fundamental interests, but it was more rigorous than the traditional equal protection test which simply required the state to show that the challenged classification had a rational basis. [21]

The ruling in *Bullock* was expanded in 1974 when the court held that California could not deny an indigent candidate a ballot spot simply because he was too poor to pay the filing fee, no matter how reasonable that fee was. In *Lubin v. Panish*, the court said the state must provide alternative means for indigents to qualify for a ballot position. [22]

Education and Wealth

In a single 1973 decision, the court refused to make classifications by wealth inherently suspect or to give education the status of a "fundamental interest." This meant that the court would not closely scrutinize a state's decision to finance public schools from local property taxes — even though that decision resulted in wide disparities in the amount spent per pupil in different districts. Nor did the state have to prove that its financing system served a compelling state interest. As a result, the court, by a 5-4 vote, upheld this system of financing public education, challenged as a denial of equal protection of the laws.

Background

In the early 1970s, school districts in every state but Hawaii operated primarily with money raised from taxing the real property within the district. Variations in districts — the amount of taxable property, the value of the property and the tax rate — resulted in widely differing amounts that school districts in the same state could afford to spend for the education of their children. In Texas, where the case of *San Antonio School District v. Rodriguez* arose, the wealthiest district spent $594 for each schoolchild while the poorest spent only $356.

A bombshell shook the foundations of this traditional structure of public school financing on Aug. 30, 1971, when the California Supreme Court declared this method unconstitutional because it resulted in less being spent to educate a child in one school district than in another. [23]

Personal Liberty and Privacy...

An individual's right to privacy in making decisions concerning marriage, procreation and child-rearing is recognized by the Supreme Court as a basic constitutionally protected right with which government may not casually interfere.

This right is not explicitly mentioned in the Constitution. Its source has thus been a matter of considerable disagreement among members of the court. But a majority of them consistently have agreed that the right to personal privacy does exist.

The court dates its recognition of this category of personal rights to its decision in the 1923 case of *Meyer v. Nebraska.* Nebraska law forbade any school from teaching a modern foreign language other than English to children in the first eight grades. The Supreme Court held that the statute violated the 14th Amendment's due process guarantee by depriving the teacher who had been convicted of violating it and the affected parents and children of a measure of personal liberty:

> ...Without doubt, it [liberty] denotes not merely freedom from bodily restraint but also the right of the individual to contract, to engage in any of the common occupations of life, to acquire useful knowledge, to marry, establish a home and bring up children, to worship God according to the dictates of his own conscience, and generally to enjoy those privileges long recognized at common law as essential to the orderly pursuit of happiness by free men.[1]

Two years later the court struck down as a similar violation of the 14th Amendment an Oregon law that required all children to attend public schools. The court in the case of *Pierce v. Society of Sisters* declared that the statute "unreasonably interferes with the liberty of parents . . . to direct the upbringing and education of [their] children. . . ."[2]

Marriage and Procreation

In a 1942 case, the court's development of protection for the right of personal privacy was reinforced by its evolving fundamental-interest standard for classifications under the equal protection clause.

Oklahoma law provided for sterilization of certain convicted felons. In the case of *Skinner v. Oklahoma,* the Supreme Court held the law invalid as a violation of equal protection because it did not treat all persons convicted of similar crimes in a similar way.

In so ruling, the court stated that marriage and procreation were "fundamental to the very existence and survival of the race."[3] Laws that affected such fundamental rights were subject to close scrutiny by the courts, the court continued, and could be justified only by a pressing governmental objective. *(Details, p. 585)*

The court affirmed this view in the 1967 case of *Loving v. Virginia* in which it struck down a Virginia law that punished persons who entered into interracial marriages. The state law violated the equal protection clause because it used a racial classification without justification by any compelling state interest. The court also held that such a state law violated the 14th Amendment's guarantee of due process:

> . . .The freedom to marry has long been recognized as one of the vital personal rights essential to the orderly pursuit of happiness by free men. . . . To deny this fundamental freedom on so unsupportable a basis as the racial classification embodied in these statutes . . . is surely to deprive all the State's citizens of liberty without due process of law. The Fourteenth Amendment requires that the freedom of choice to marry not be restricted by invidious racial discriminations. Under our Constitution, the freedom to marry or not marry a person of another race resides with the individual and cannot be infringed by the State.[4]

Contraceptives

In 1965 the court held that a state unconstitutionally interfered with personal privacy in the marriage relationship when it prohibited anyone, including married couples, from using contraceptives. The vote was 7-2 in the decision in *Griswold v. Connecticut.* The members of the majority varied on their reasons for that conclusion.

Justice William O. Douglas, who wrote the court's formal opinion, held that the right of personal privacy was an independent right implicit in the First, Third, Fourth, Fifth and Ninth Amendments. "[S]pecific guarantees in the Bill of Rights have penumbras, formed by emanations from those guarantees that help give them life and substance. . . . Various guarantees create zones of privacy," Douglas wrote.[5]

Marriage was within a protected zone of privacy, Douglas continued, and the state impermissibly invaded that zone by prohibiting married couples from using contraceptives. "Would we allow the police to search the sacred precincts of marital bedrooms for telltale signs of the use of contraceptives? The very idea is repulsive to the notions of privacy surrounding the marriage relationship," he concluded.[6]

In a concurring opinion, Justice Arthur J. Goldberg, writing for himself, Chief Justice Earl Warren and Justice William J. Brennan Jr., claimed that the right to personal privacy, including privacy in marriage, was a right " 'retained by the people' within the meaning of the Ninth Amendment," which states that the "enumeration in the Constitution of certain rights shall not be construed to deny or disparage others retained by the people."[7]

Similar rulings followed from several other state and federal courts. In Texas, the parents of Mexican-American pupils in San Antonio brought a similar suit, and in December 1971, a federal court found the Texas system unconstitutional. The state appealed to the Supreme Court.

The Opinion

Critical to the holding of the five-justice majority — for whom Justice Lewis F. Powell wrote — were its findings that:

● The Texas system did not disadvantage an identifiable group of poor persons.

...Constitutionally Protected Rights

Justice John Marshall Harlan contended that marriage was one of the basic values that the court had found "implicit in the concept of ordered liberty" protected by the 14th Amendment. [8] Justice Byron R. White held that because marriage was a fundamental interest, the Connecticut law deprived married couples of " 'liberty' without due process of law, as that concept is used in the Fourteenth Amendment." [9]

Justices Potter Stewart and Hugo L. Black in dissent found no right of personal privacy either expressed or implied in the Constitution. Stewart said he thought the Connecticut law was "silly," but held that the only proper way to attack it was through legislative repeal.

In 1972 the court declined to adopt any of these lines of reasoning in striking down a state law that permitted the distribution of contraceptives to single persons for disease control but not for birth control purposes. The court held the law invalid as a violation of the equal protection guarantee. [10]

Abortion

In 1973 the Supreme Court held that the right of personal privacy extended to the qualified right of a woman to decide to have an abortion. Therefore, it held that state laws forbidding all elective abortions were unconstitutional. In reaching this decision, the seven-justice majority found it unnecessary to pinpoint the constitutional source of this right to personal privacy.

"The Constitution does not explicitly mention any right of privacy," wrote Justice Harry A. Blackmun. "In a line of decisions, however, ... the Court has recognized that a right of personal privacy, or a guarantee of certain areas or zones of privacy does exist under the Constitution." [11] Blackmun then summarized the court's decisions in this area, citing the varied opinions as to the source of this right. He continued:

> ...These decisions make it clear that only personal rights that can be deemed "fundamental" or "implicit in the concept of ordered liberty" ... are included in this guarantee of personal privacy. They also make it clear that the right has some extension to activities relating to marriage ... , procreation ... ,

contraception ... , family relationships ... , and child rearing and education.... [12]

Whatever its source, Blackmun continued, "[t]his right of privacy ... is broad enough to encompass a woman's decision whether or not to terminate her pregnancy. The detriment that the State would impose upon the pregnant woman by denying this choice altogether is apparent." [13]

But, Blackmun cautioned, the woman's right to decide to terminate a pregnancy is a qualified one:

> ...[A] state may properly assert important interests in safeguarding health, in maintaining medical standards, and in protecting potential life. At some point in pregnancy, these respective interests become sufficiently compelling to sustain regulation of the factors that govern the abortion decision. [14]

The court then ruled that in the first trimester of pregnancy the state had no interest sufficiently compelling to warrant interference in a decision to abort. In the second trimester, when an abortion was more likely to affect the health of the mother adversely than continuation of the pregnancy, the court held that the state had a compelling interest in protecting her and could therefore regulate the abortion procedure.

In the third trimester, when the fetus presumably could live on its own, the state's compelling interest lay in protecting that life. To that end the court said a state could forbid abortions in the third trimester except when necessary to protect the life or health of the mother.

The Right Extended

In a subsequent case, the court extended even further the right of privacy for a woman to make a decision to abort.

In the case of *Planned Parenthood of Central Missouri v. Danforth,* the court held that states could not require either the consent of the husband, or — if the woman was an unmarried minor — the consent of her parents, as a condition for terminating pregnancy in the first trimester. [15]

---

[1] *Meyer v. Nebraska,* 262 U.S. 390 at 399 (1923).

[2] *Pierce v. Society of Sisters,* 268 U.S. 510 at 534-35 (1925).

[3] *Skinner v. Oklahoma,* 316 U.S. 535 at 541 (1942).

[4] *Loving v. Virginia,* 388 U.S. 1 at 12 (1967).

[5] *Griswold v. Connecticut,* 381 U.S. 479 at 484 (1965).

[6] Id. at 485-86.

[7] Id. at 499.

[8] Id. at 500, quoting from *Palko v. Connecticut,* 302

U.S. 319 at 325 (1937).

[9] Id. at 502.

[10] *Eisenstadt v. Baird,* 405 U.S. 438 (1972).

[11] *Roe v. Wade,* 410 U.S. 113 at 152 (1973).

[12] Id. at 152-53.

[13] Id. at 153.

[14] Id. at 154.

[15] *Planned Parenthood of Central Missouri v. Danforth,* 428 U.S. 52 (1976); see also *Bellotti v. Baird* (1979).

● The right to an education is not guaranteed explicitly or implicitly by the Constitution.

In previous cases classifications by wealth were found unconstitutionally discriminatory, wrote Powell, because the groups or individuals affected "were completely unable to pay for some desired benefit, and as a consequence, they

sustained an absolute deprivation of a meaningful opportunity to enjoy that benefit." But in the *Rodriguez* case, Powell continued, there was no showing that the financing system disadvantaged any definable indigent group or that the poorest people were concentrated in the poorest school districts. He explained:

...The argument here is not that the children in districts having relatively low assessable property values are receiving no public education; rather, it is that they are receiving a poorer quality education than that available to children in districts having more assessable wealth. Apart from the unsettled and disputed question whether the quality of education may be determined by the amount of money expended for it, a sufficient answer . . . is that at least where wealth is involved, the Equal Protection Clause does not require absolute equality or precisely equal advantages.[24]

Asserting that fundamental rights or interests were "the rights and liberties protected by the Constitution," Powell said the majority found no explicit or implicit constitutional protection for education.

"It is not the province of this Court to create substantive constitutional rights in the name of guaranteeing equal protection of the laws," Powell said. ". . .[T]he undisputed importance of education will not alone cause this Court to depart from the usual standard for reviewing a State's societal and economic legislation."[25]

The question then remaining was whether it was reasonable for the state to use the property tax to finance public schools. The majority concluded that it was rational:

...[T]o the extent that the Texas system of school finance results in unequal expenditures between children who happen to reside in different districts, we cannot say that such disparities are the product of a system that is so irrational as to be invidiously discriminatory.... The Texas plan is not the result of hurried, ill-conceived legislation. It certainly is not the product of purposeful discrimination against any group or class. On the contrary, it is rooted in decades of experience in Texas and elsewhere, and in major part is the product of responsible studies by qualified peo-

ple. . . . One must also remember that the system here challenged is not peculiar to Texas. . . . In its essential characteristics, the Texas plan for financing public education reflects what many educators for a half century have thought was an enlightened approach to a problem for which there is no perfect solution. We are unwilling to assume for ourselves a level of wisdom superior to that of legislators, scholars, and educational authorities in 50 States, especially where the alternatives proposed are only recently conceived and nowhere yet tested. The constitutional standard under the Equal Protection Clause is whether the challenged state action rationally furthers a legitimate state purpose or interest.... We hold that the Texas plan abundantly satisfies this standard.[26]

The Dissent

The four dissenters wanted to overturn the Texas system. Justices Douglas and Thurgood Marshall contended that classification by wealth demanded strict scrutiny and that education was a fundamental interest. Children in property-poor districts were unconstitutionally discriminated against, wrote Marshall, and the court should not judge the instrument of their discrimination against the "lenient standard of rationality which we have traditionally applied . . . in the context of economic and commercial matters."[27]

Marshall rejected "the majority's labored efforts to demonstrate that fundamental interests . . . encompass only established rights which we are somehow bound to recognize from the text of the Constitution itself."[28] The right to an education was fundamental, he said, because it was so intimately related to such rights as the right of expressing and receiving information and ideas as guaranteed by the First Amendment. Justices Douglas, Byron R. White and William J. Brennan Jr. said that the school financing system did not meet the rationality test.

Footnotes

[1] *Griffin v. Illinois,* 351 U.S. 12 at 12-13 (1956).

[2] Id. at 19.

[3] Id. at 28-29.

[4] *Mayer v. Chicago,* 404 U.S. 189 at 196 (1971).

[5] *United States v. MacCollum,* 426 U.S. 317 at 324 (1976).

[6] *Douglas v. California,* 372 U.S. 353 at 357-58 (1963).

[7] Id. at 361.

[8] *Ross v. Moffitt,* 417 U.S. 600 (1974); *Fuller v. Oregon,* 417 U.S. 40 (1974).

[9] *Boddie v. Connecticut,* 401 U.S. 371 at 381 (1971).

[10] Id. at 386.

[11] *United States v. Kras,* 409 U.S. 434 at 446 (1973).

[12] Id. at 457.

[13] *Williams v. Illinois,* 399 U.S. 235 (1970).

[14] *Tate v. Short,* 401 U.S. 395 (1971).

[15] *United States v. Guest,* 383 U.S. 745 (1966).

[16] *Shapiro v. Thompson,* 394 U.S. 618 at 634 (1969).

[17] Id. at 633.

[18] *Memorial Hospital v. Maricopa County,* 415 U.S. 250 (1974).

[19] *Breedlove v. Suttles,* 302 U.S. 277 (1937).

[20] *Harper v. Virginia State Board of Elections,* 383 U.S. 663 at 668 (1966).

[21] *Bullock v. Carter,* 405 U.S. 134 (1972).

[22] *Lubin v. Panish,* 415 U.S. 709 (1974).

[23] *Serrano v. Priest,* 96 Cal. Rptr. 601, 487 P. 2d 1241; 5 Cal. 3d 584 (1971).

[24] *San Antonio Independent School District v. Rodriguez,* 411 U.S. 1 at 23-24 (1973).

[25] Id. at 33, 35.

[26] Id. at 54-55.

[27] Id. at 98.

[28] Id. at 99.

Selected Bibliography

Berger, Morroe. *Equality by Statute: The Revolution in Civil Rights,* rev. ed. Garden City, N.Y.: Doubleday & Co., Anchor Books, 1968.

Bickel, Alexander, M. *Politics and the Warren Court.* New York: Harper & Row, 1965.

Black, Charles Jr. "The Lawfulness of the Segregation Decisions." *The Yale Law Journal* 69 (January 1960):421.

Blaustein, Albert P., and Ferguson, Clarence Clyde Jr. *Desegration and the Law; The Meaning and Effect of the School Segregation Cases.* New Brunswick, N.J.: Rutgers University Press, 1957.

Claude, Richard. *The Supreme Court and the Electoral Process.* Baltimore: The Johns Hopkins Press, 1970.

Cushman, Robert F. *Cases in Civil Liberties.* 2d ed. Englewood Cliffs, N.J.: Prentice-Hall, 1976.

"Developments in the Law: Equal Protection." *Harvard Law Review* 82 (March 1969):1065.

Frank, John P. *Marble Palace: The Supreme Court in American Life.* New York: Alfred A. Knopf, 1961.

Franklin, John Hope. *From Slavery to Freedom: A History of Negro Americans.* 3d ed. New York: Random House, Vintage Books, 1969.

Friedman, Leon, ed. *Argument: The Oral Argument Before The Supreme Court in Brown v. Board of Education of Topeka, 1952-55.* New York: Chelsea House Publishers, 1969.

Garraty, John A., ed. *Quarrels That Have Shaped the Constitution.* New York: Harper & Row, 1964.

Guenther, Gerald. "In Search of Evolving Doctrine on a Changing Court: A Model for Newer Equal Protection." *Harvard Law Review* 86 (November 1971):1.

Karst, Kenneth L. "Equal Citizenship Under the Fourteenth Amendment." *Harvard Law Review* 91 (November 1977):1.

Kelly, Alfred H., and Harbison, Winfred A. *The American Constitution; Its Origins and Development,* 5th ed. New York: W. W. Norton & Co., 1976.

Kluger, Richard. *Simple Justice: The History of Brown v. Board of Education and Black America's Struggle for Equality.* New York: Alfred A. Knopf, 1976.

Konvitz, Milton R., and Leskes, Theodore. *A Century of Civil Rights, with a Study of State Law Against Discrimination.* New York: Columbia University Press, 1961.

Kurland, Philip B. *Politics, The Constitution and The Warren Court.* Chicago: The University of Chicago Press, 1970.

Miller, Loren. *The Petitioners: The Story of the Supreme Court of the United States and the Negro.* New York: Random House, Pantheon Books, 1966.

Mitau, G. Theodore. *Decade of Decision: The Supreme Court and the Constitutional Revolution, 1954-1964.* New York: Charles Scribner's Sons, 1967.

Pollak, Louis H., ed. *The Constitution and the Supreme Court: A Documentary History,* Vol. II. Cleveland: World Publishing Co., 1966.

_____. "Racial Discrimination and Judicial Integrity: A Reply to Professor Wechsler." *University of Pennsylvania Law Review* 108 (November 1959):1.

Pritchett, C. Herman, *The American Constitution.* 3d ed. New York: McGraw-Hill Book Co., 1977.

Tussman, Joseph and tenBroek, Jacobus. "The Equal Protection of the Laws." *California Law Review* 37:341.

United States Commission on Civil Rights. *Freedom to the Free: Century of Emancipation, 1863-1963.* Washington, D.C.: U.S. Government Printing Office, 1963.

_____. *Twenty Years After Brown: The Shadows of the Past.* Washington, D.C.: U.S. Government Printing Office, 1974.

U. S. Congress. Library of Congress. Congressional Reference Service. *The Constitution of the United States of America: Analysis and Interpretation.* 1963, 1972 eds. Washington, D.C.: U.S. Government Printing Office, 1964, 1973; 1976 Supplement, 1977.

Wechsler, Herbert. "Toward Neutral Principles of Constitutional Law." *Harvard Law Review* 73 (November 1959):31.

Woodward, C. Vann. *The Strange Career of Jim Crow.* 2d ed. New York: Oxford University Press, 1966.

PART IV

PRESSURES ON THE COURT

Congressional Pressure 653

Presidential Pressure 683

Public Opinion 695

The Court and the Press 705

"The Contemplation of Justice," one of two
Statues Flanking the West Front Entrance of
the Supreme Court.

Photo by Laura B. Weiss

Congressional Pressure

Congress and the Supreme Court are separate but interdependent branches of the federal government. The Supreme Court defines the limits of congressional authority, while Congress confirms the court's members, sets its jurisdiction and pays its bills. Just as the court has used its judicial review powers to influence the shape of federal legislation, so Congress has tried from time to time to use its powers over the court to influence the outcome of particular rulings.

Congress can influence the Supreme Court in three general ways — through selection, confirmation and impeachment of individual justices; through institutional and jurisdictional changes; and through direct reversal of specific court decisions.

The Justices

Congressional influence over selection and confirmation of Supreme Court justices is relatively insignificant. There is no established procedure for Congress to advise the president on his choice of a nominee, although a majority in both houses has at least twice successfully petitioned the chief executive to nominate a particular person to a court vacancy.

The Constitution requires Senate confirmation of all Supreme Court nominees, and the Senate has taken this responsibility seriously, giving most nominees very careful scrutiny. Of the 139 nominations to the high court, the Senate has rejected 26. All but five of these rejections occurred in the 18th and 19th centuries, most of them largely for partisan political reasons. It should be remembered, too, that even though Senate rejection of a nomination obviously adversely affects the rejected nominee, it is more directly a pressure on the president than on the sitting members of the court.

For a variety of reasons, Congress' power to impeach Supreme Court justices also has been of little significance. Only one justice has been impeached — Samuel Chase in 1804 — and he was acquitted by the Senate. Another justice, Abe Fortas, resigned in 1969 under threat of impeachment, but Justice William O. Douglas, accused a year later of committing similar improprieties, not only did not resign but was cleared of all the charges.

Money. Congress through its appropriations process controls all of the money for operation and maintenance of the federal judicial system including the Supreme Court. It also sets the levels of the justices' salaries. Congress has never tried to pressure the court by deliberately withholding operational funds. In 1964, however, after the court handed down a series of controversial rulings, a majority in Congress voted to deny the justices as large a pay increase as other high-ranking federal employees received.

The Institution

Congress has been least successful in influencing the court by making changes in the institution itself and in its procedures and functions. Only once has it stopped the court from taking action by revoking its power to review a case while the case was pending. Proposals to limit the court's jurisdiction so that it may not review federal legislation on specific subjects are offered whenever the court issues a particularly controversial decision or series of rulings, but none of these proposals has been approved.

Congress has tried to influence the philosophical composition of the court by changing its size. This ploy apparently worked once when, after finding a particular statute unconstitutional by a 4-3 vote, the court was increased by two, reconsideration occurred, and the earlier decision was reversed by a 5-4 vote. Proposals to require unanimity or a two-thirds vote of the justices to declare federal statutes or state laws unconstitutional have also been advocated throughout the court's history, but none ever emerged from Congress.

The Decisions

Congress has been far more adept at reversing specific court decisions than at eliminating whole areas from Supreme Court review. Reversal may come about through simple legislation, if the court's decision is based on statutory construction and interpretation, or through constitutional amendment, if the decision is an interpretation of a constitutional provision. The first constitutional amendment overturning a Supreme Court decision was the 11th, ratified in 1795; the first legislative reversal came in 1852.

Periods of Confrontation

There have been several major periods of confrontation between Congress and the court. The first of these occurred in the early 1800s as the national leadership passed from the Federalists to the Republicans. The last occurred in the mid-1950s and 1960s, when conservative members of Congress constantly challenged the liberal decisions on social issues handed down by the Warren court.

Adams v. Jefferson

In the 1800 elections, the Federalists lost to the Republicans, and Thomas Jefferson was elected to replace President John Adams. In an effort to ensure the presence of some Federalist influence in the national government, the Federalists in the final days of the Adams administration passed legislation creating 16 new circuit court judgeships and several justice of the peace positions. The Federalists also stipulated that when the next vacancy occurred on the court, it would go unfilled and the number of justices would be reduced by one. Adams quickly appointed Federalists to the new judgeships, but his midnight appointments came so late that some of the appointees never received their commissions, and their suit to force the Jefferson administration to honor the Adams appointments resulted in the famous *Marbury v. Madison* decision. *(Details, p. 69)*

Once Republicans were ensconced in office, they abolished the new judgeships and raised the number of justices back to six. They also postponed the next Supreme Court term so that the court would be unable to hear quickly an anticipated suit challenging the validity of the repeal. When the court did meet again in 1803, it sustained the repeal. Still not satisfied, the Republicans decided to attack the Federalists on the Supreme Court through impeachment, selecting as their first target Justice Samuel Chase, a man who had used his position on the bench to advance Federalist doctrine.

The House impeached Chase on a party-line vote, but Republicans did not hold together in the Senate and he was acquitted. The House then passed a bill to authorize the president to remove a justice at the request of a majority of the House and Senate, but that effort also died in the Senate. After those two defeats, Republicans ended their broadside attack on the Federalist judiciary, choosing instead to fill vacancies with individuals of their own persuasion as opportunities arose.

Federal Power v. States Rights

In the 1820s and early 1830s controversial decisions expanding the powers of the national government at the expense of state sovereignty led Congress to try unsuccessfully to remove the court's jurisdiction to hear cases challenging the validity of state laws. Repeal of this power would have prevented the court from reviewing the validity of any state law and would have resulted in conflict and confusion among the states. The proposals were, however, soundly defeated in the House in 1831.

Reconstruction and the Court

Congress had its greatest successes in curbing the court during the post-Civil War Reconstruction era. In addition to reducing the number of justices, as vacancies occurred, to seven from 10 in order to prevent President Andrew Johnson from making any appointments to the court, Congress also repealed the court's jurisdiction to review certain denials of writs of *habeas corpus*. The repeal, which the court ultimately sustained (but which was eventually reversed by Congress), prevented it from rendering an opinion in a pending case concerning the constitutionality of the congressional program of Reconstruction.

Once Johnson left office, the court quickly raised the number of justices to nine. The additional seats proved critical to the court's quick reversal of its decision that Congress could not make paper money a substitute currency for gold in the payment of debts.

Progressive Attacks

Progressives in Congress in the early 1920s tried to pressure the economically and socially conservative court into rendering more liberal decisions, but these attempts were singularly unsuccessful. Few of them won any consideration at all. Among the proposals was legislation to require two-thirds of the justices to concur in decisions declaring federal statutes unconstitutional and a measure to permit Congress to overrule the Supreme Court's decision that a federal law was invalid by repassing the statute with a two-thirds majority.

New Deal Crisis

Although an economically conservative court clashed with Congress when it declared invalid most of the early New Deal legislation in the 1930s, the court's real confrontation was with President Franklin D. Roosevelt, who sought to moderate the court's conservatism by "packing" the court with additional members. The plan was extremely unpopular; a majority in Congress opposed it, enacting instead legislation making retirement for elderly justices more financially attractive. Although Roosevelt's plan was defeated, at the cost of a serious rift in the Democratic party, his goal was achieved.

In decisions reached before the court-packing plan was unveiled but not announced until afterwards, the court indicated that it was adopting a broader view of federal economic regulatory powers. The court reinforced its new stance by sustaining re-enactment of much of the New Deal legislation it had previously found unconstitutional. And within months of enactment of the liberalized retirement bill, one of the conservative stalwarts on the court announced his resignation. Roosevelt was then able to begin to make appointments strengthening the liberal faction on the court.

The Warren Court

During the 16 years Earl Warren was Chief Justice (1953-69), the court consistently sustained individual and minority interests against what many citizens considered to be the best interests of the community. Warren began his career on the court by writing the opinion declaring segregation in public schools unconstitutional. Under his guidance the court — often by narrow margins — sustained procedural rights for alleged wrongdoers and criminals, upheld the civil rights of blacks and other racial minorities, granted First Amendment protections to alleged subversives, narrowly defined what material was obscene and could therefore be banned, prohibited officially prescribed prayer and religious observances in public schools and ordered state legislatures to reapportion on the basis of "one person, one vote."

Each of these decisions outraged some segment of the population. Complaints that the court was too permissive and that its decisions would lead to the moral downfall of the country abounded, and demands for Warren's impeachment were displayed on billboards across the country.

Responding to their constituents and their own more conservative political and social philosophies, several groups in Congress tried to curb the Warren court, but very few of these attempts were successful and even fewer had any real effect on the court. Efforts to cut back the court's jurisdiction to review certain kinds of federal and state legislation failed, as did several attempts to reverse specific decisions by legislation or constitutional amendment. Congress did succeed in reversing one decision relating to subversive activities and in modifying three decisions relating to criminal procedures in federal courts. The court itself, under Warren and his successor Warren E. Burger, modified more of the disputed decisions than did Congress.

The court of the 1970s has a significantly more conservative cast than the Warren court. Nonetheless, a few of its decisions, including acceptance of forced busing as a method to achieve racial desegregation in public schools and its bar on state prohibition of abortions, have elicited loud but ineffective calls from Congress for statutory reversal and jurisdictional curbs on the court.

While Congress has rarely been successful — outside of reversing decisions by legislation — in directly pressuring the court, it is impossible to measure how much, if any, indirect pressure consideration of court-limiting proposals places on the court. Perhaps the overall impact of such

congressional efforts has been not to weaken the court's authority but to strengthen it. Each time Congress attempts to curb the court and fails, the public perception is heightened that the court as an institution is unassailable and that its decisions, except in extreme circumstances, are final.

Writing of congressional unwillingness to limit — with one exception — the court's power to review legislation, Professor Charles L. Black has said:

> . . .Nothing so clearly defines the political status of judicial review in a democracy as the fact that Congress might at any time have worried it to death's door. The point is not what we might think about the constitutional merits of any one of these [limiting] steps; it rather inheres in the unbroken demonstration of congressional unwillingness even to try to hamper a judicial function which sometimes results in overturning Congress' own laws. No explaining away can rob this massive historic fact of its own impressiveness. [1]

---

[1] Charles L. Black Jr., *Perspectives in Constitutional Law* (Englewood Cliffs, N.J.: Prentice-Hall, 1963), p. 13.

Individual Pressures

Selection

Congress as an institution has little influence on the selection of nominees to the Supreme Court. Although the Constitution in Article II, Section 2, stipulates that the president shall appoint Supreme Court justices by and with the advice and consent of the Senate, the advisory role usually occurs after the fact as the Senate considers confirmation of the appointee.

An individual senator or representative, particularly one who is personally close to the president, may wield some unofficial influence in the selection process. And because the Senate adheres to the custom of senatorial courtesy — it is most reluctant to confirm a nominee who is repugnant to a senator of the nominee's home state — presidents do well to assure themselves in advance that their nominees will not be objectionable to the pertinent senators.

In at least two instances, a majority of the Senate and House successfully petitioned the president to nominate a specific individual. In 1862, 129 of 140 House members and all but four senators signed a petition urging President Lincoln to nominate Samuel F. Miller of Iowa to the vacancy caused by the death of Justice Peter V. Daniel. The Senate confirmed Miller's nomination, which also had been endorsed by numerous other politicians and lawyers, within half an hour of receiving it. [1]

After Justice Robert C. Grier announced his resignation in December 1869, members of Congress submitted a petition to President Grant asking him to name former Secretary of War Edwin M. Stanton to the seat. Pending in the Senate was the nomination of Grant's attorney general, Ebenezer R. Hoar, to a second vacancy on the court. Hoar's nomination had run into some difficulty and, although Stanton was not Grant's first choice, the president acceded

to the congressional request, thinking that the nomination might enhance Hoar's confirmation chances. But Grant's strategy never bore fruit. Stanton was confirmed immediately upon nomination but died four days later of heart trouble. The Senate subsequently rejected Hoar in February 1870. [2]

Qualifications

While the Constitution specifies qualifications that the president and members of Congress must meet, it sets no corresponding requirements for Supreme Court justices. Proposals to establish qualifications for the court have been made throughout the nation's history, but few have received more than passing attention in Congress.

The most frequent recommendations are that justices be natural-born citizens, of a minimum age, and have a certain number of years of judicial experience. This last suggestion may grow into an informal requirement. Pressure from the legal community and the increasing complexity of the law have made prior experience on the bench an important consideration in the selection of nominees.

Rejections

While it may not play a significant part in the selection of justices, the Senate has a crucial role in the confirmation of Supreme Court nominees. Article II, Section 2 of the Constitution provides that no nominee shall be seated unless confirmed by the Senate. Of the 139 men nominated to a seat on the Supreme Court, the Senate has rejected 26, nearly one-fifth. By contrast, the Senate has denied confirmation of only eight Cabinet nominees.

Supreme Court Nominees Not Confirmed by the Senate

From 1789 through mid-1979, 26 Supreme Court nominations have failed to receive Senate confirmation. Of these, 11 have been rejected outright and the remainder withdrawn or allowed to lapse when Senate rejection appeared imminent. Following is the complete list of nominees failing to receive confirmation:

Nominee	President	Date of Nomination	Senate Action	Date of Senate Action
John Rutledge (for Chief Justice)	Washington	July 1, 1795	Rejected (10-14)	Dec. 15, 1795
Alexander Wolcott	Madison	Feb. 4, 1811	Rejected (9-24)	Feb. 13, 1811
John J. Crittenden	John Quincy Adams	Dec. 17, 1828	Postponed	Feb. 12, 1829
Roger Brooke Taney	Jackson	Jan. 15, 1835	Postponed (24-21)*	March 3, 1835
John C. Spencer	Tyler	Jan. 9, 1844	Rejected (21-26)	Jan. 31, 1844
Reuben H. Walworth	Tyler	March 13, 1844	Withdrawn	
Edward King	Tyler	June 5, 1844	Postponed	June 15, 1844
Edward King	Tyler	Dec. 4, 1844	Withdrawn	
John M. Read	Tyler	Feb. 7, 1845	Not Acted Upon	
George W. Woodward	Polk	Dec. 23, 1845	Rejected (20-29)	Jan. 22, 1846
Edward A. Bradford	Fillmore	Aug. 16, 1852	Not Acted Upon	
George E. Badger	Fillmore	Jan. 10, 1853	Postponed	Feb. 11, 1853
William C. Micou	Fillmore	Feb. 24, 1853	Not Acted Upon	
Jeremiah S. Black	Buchanan	Feb. 5, 1861	Rejected (25-26)	Feb. 21, 1861
Henry Stanbery	Andrew Johnson	April 16, 1866	Not Acted Upon	
Ebenezer R. Hoar	Grant	Dec. 15, 1869	Rejected (24-33)	Feb. 3, 1870
George H. Williams (for Chief Justice)	Grant	Dec. 1, 1873	Withdrawn	
Caleb Cushing (for Chief Justice)	Grant	Jan. 9, 1874	Withdrawn	
Stanley Matthews	Hayes	Jan. 26, 1881	Not Acted Upon**	
William B. Hornblower	Cleveland	Sept. 19, 1893	Rejected (24-30)	Jan. 15, 1894
Wheeler H. Peckham	Cleveland	Jan. 22, 1894	Rejected (32-41)	Feb. 16, 1894
John J. Parker	Hoover	March 21, 1930	Rejected (39-41)	May 7, 1930
Abe Fortas (for Chief Justice)	Lyndon Johnson	June 26, 1968	Withdrawn	
Homer Thornberry	Lyndon Johnson	June 26, 1968	Not Acted Upon	
Clement F. Haynsworth Jr.	Nixon	Aug. 18, 1969	Rejected (45-55)	Nov. 21, 1969
G. Harrold Carswell	Nixon	Jan. 19, 1970	Rejected (45-51)	April 8, 1970

* Later nominated for Chief Justice and confirmed.

** Later nominated and confirmed.

Source: Library of Congress, Congressional Research Service

Competence

Only two Supreme Court nominees have gone unconfirmed primarily on the grounds that they were professionally unqualified.[3] In 1873 President Grant nominated his attorney general, George H. Williams, to be Chief Justice. Williams had served as chief justice of the Oregon Territory, but his record was undistinguished and there were many more qualified men that Grant could have chosen. When the Senate showed signs of balking at the nomination, Williams asked that his name be withdrawn.

Nearly 100 years later, President Nixon's 1970 appointment of G. Harrold Carswell was rejected largely because of Carswell's mediocre juridical record. A second Nixon nominee, Clement F. Haynsworth Jr., although well-qualified judicially, was rejected in part because he appeared insensitive to ethical improprieties and participated in cases where his financial interest might have involved him in conflicts of interest. Similar allegations of impropriety led

to the resignation of Justice Abe Fortas in 1969. *(Details of Fortas resignation, p. 660)*

Partisan Politics

By far, most Senate rejections of Supreme Court nominees have been grounded on political considerations. The primary factor in the rejection of 12 nominees was the "lame duck" status of the nominating president or the fact that the party in control of the Senate forecast victory for its presidential candidate in upcoming elections.

Both problems afflicted the court nominations of President John Tyler, who has the dubious distinction of having more nominees rejected than any other president. Tyler had an opportunity to fill two vacancies, but only one of his six nominations was confirmed by the Senate. One nominee was rejected because his politics offended the party ruling the Senate. Two appointments were killed because the Senate — anticipating correctly that Tyler would not be his party's candidate for election — wanted to hold the vacancies open. And two, including one whom Tyler re-nominated, were rejected after the election of 1844, before the victor — Democrat James K. Polk — assumed office.

Ironically, Tyler also made his only confirmed nomination during this period. As historian Charles Warren observed, Tyler's choice of Samuel Nelson "was so preeminently a wise one that the Senate at once confirmed it. . . ." [4] But the Senate's refusal to confirm any of Tyler's nominations to the second seat helped create the longest vacancy in Supreme Court history. *(Box, p. 784)*

Other "lame duck" presidents whose nominees were rejected include John Quincy Adams, Millard Fillmore, James Buchanan and Lyndon B. Johnson. *(Details, p. 691)*

Several nominations were rejected because a majority of the Senate objected to specific political views or actions of the nominee. Thus Washington's nomination of John Rutledge for Chief Justice was refused because Rutledge had publicly attacked the Jay Treaty. Although it became apparent during the confirmation process that Rutledge suffered from occasional fits of insanity, historian Warren wrote that ". . .[t]he excited political situation . . . was such that irrespective of Rutledge's mental condition his rejection by the Senate was certain. . . ." [5]

Senate Whigs rejected future Chief Justice Roger B. Taney first as treasury secretary — forcing him to resign his recess appointment — and then as an associate justice because he had carried out President Jackson's orders to remove government deposits from the Bank of the United States.

James Madison's appointment of Alexander Wolcott failed in part because of his strict enforcement of the embargo and nonintercourse laws during his tenure as customs collector. James K. Polk's nomination of George W. Woodward fell in part because Woodward held what were described as "native American sentiments" offensive to Irish-Americans and other ethnic groups.

The distinguished lawyer Jeremiah S. Black was not only a lame duck appointment when President Buchanan nominated him a month before Abraham Lincoln was inaugurated, but also a northerner whose views on slavery were unacceptable to abolitionists. The Senate objected to Ebenezer R. Hoar for several reasons, two of which were that he had opposed the impeachment of President Johnson and had supported civil service reform. Rutherford B. Hayes' nomination of Stanley Matthews was initially rejected partly for political reasons and partly for ethical considerations, but upon renomination he was confirmed.

In 1930 the American Federation of Labor and the NAACP mounted a successful lobbying campaign against confirmation of Herbert Hoover's appointee, John J. Parker. A well-qualified federal judge from North Carolina, Parker was accused of insensitivity to labor and racial problems. Civil rights activists might well have rued their success. Parker continued as a judge on the Fourth Circuit Court of Appeals where he handed down some of the earliest and most influential decisions in favor of black rights. The man elevated to the Supreme Court in his stead, Owen J. Roberts, was not so supportive on civil rights issues.

One nominee was denied the position of Chief Justice because the Senate could not decide what his political views were. In addition to being 74 at the time of his nomination in 1874, Caleb Cushing had been a Whig, a Tyler Whig, a Democrat, a Johnson Constitutional Conservative and a Republican. Those shifting allegiances gained

him so many political enemies that Senate opposition forced President Grant to withdraw the nomination.

Perhaps the most pointed political rejection of a nominee was the treatment of Henry Stanbery, President Andrew Johnson's attorney general. Stanbery was well-liked, but the president was not. To deny Johnson any opportunity to make appointments to the high court, Radical Republicans in Congress engineered the passage of legislation to reduce the number of justices from 10 to seven as vacancies occurred. The seat to which Stanbery had been appointed was thus abolished and his nomination never considered. *(Details, p. 664)*

Senatorial Courtesy

A feud between a president and a senator prompted the only two rejections made solely on the grounds of senatorial courtesy. When Justice Samuel Blatchford died, President Grover Cleveland sought to replace him with another New Yorker. Sen. David B. Hill, D-N.Y. (1892-97), made several suggestions, but because he and Cleveland opposed each other on patronage matters, Cleveland ignored his recommendations and nominated New York attorney William B. Hornblower. Hill prevailed upon his colleagues, and the Senate rejected the nomination.

Undaunted, Cleveland next proposed another New Yorker, Wheeler Peckham. Again Hill objected and again the Senate followed his wishes. To Hill's surprise, Cleveland abandoned his intention to nominate a New Yorker and instead named Edward D. White of Louisiana, then serving as the Senate's Democratic Majority Leader. He was confirmed the same day he was nominated.

In most instances the Senate confirms sitting or former senators with little or no inquiry or opposition. One exception to that tradition was the rejection of George E. Badger, W-N.C. (1846-55). President Fillmore, a Whig, named Badger, also a Whig, to the court just three months before the inauguration of Democrat Franklin Pierce. Although it was highly irregular to reject one of its own members, the Democrat-controlled Senate wanted Pierce to fill the vacancy. As a result, Badger's nomination was permanently postponed by a one-vote margin, 26-25.

Controversial Confirmations

Perhaps because there has been some effort to submerge political considerations in favor of judicial experience when selecting and confirming Supreme Court nominees, fewer rejections have occurred in recent years. The Senate has refused to confirm only four nominees as associate justice and one as Chief Justice in the 20th century, compared to a total of 21 appointees rejected in the 19th century.

Four other 20th century nominations, however, have evoked sharp criticism — those of Louis D. Brandeis in 1916, Harlan Fiske Stone in 1925, Charles Evans Hughes in 1930 and Hugo L. Black in 1937. To this list might be added Thurgood Marshall, the first black named to the court. The Senate Judiciary Committee in 1961 and 1962 held up Marshall's confirmation as a judge of the Second Circuit Court of Appeals for a year before approving it. In 1965 the same committee approved Marshall's appointment as solicitor general in less than a month. But when President Johnson named him to the Supreme Court in 1967, southern members of the Senate committee subjected Marshall to intense questioning about his opinions and judicial philosophy. Marshall was nonetheless confirmed by a comfortable 69-11 vote.

Action on the Brandeis nomination a half century earlier was delayed for months by the Senate Judiciary Committee as it pondered the nominee's "radical views." While opposition to the nomination focused on Brandeis' liberal economic, political and social posture, there is evidence that much of it was motivated by anti-Semitic prejudice.

At the time of his nomination, Stone was attorney general and was in the midst of concluding a prosecution for participation in an oil-land fraud against Burton K. Wheeler, a recently elected and influential Democratic senator from Montana. Wheeler was eventually acquitted of the charges but with the aid of his home state colleague, Sen. Thomas J. Walsh, he fought Stone's nomination so vigorously on the Senate floor that it was recommitted for further investigation by the judiciary committee. Stone then personally appeared before the committee, something no previous Supreme Court nominee had done. Subjected to hostile questioning, Stone's performance was impressive, and the committee again recommended that he be confirmed. The full Senate concurred by a vote of 71-6.

Hughes' nomination as Chief Justice in 1930 was attacked primarily because the country was entering the Great Depression and his views were considered too conservative for the times. Black encountered difficulties after he was confirmed because he had once been a member of the Ku Klux Klan. But he repudiated his Klan involvement in a dramatic radio broadcast and criticism waned.

Removal from Office

The Constitution stipulates that Supreme Court justices, like all other federal judges, are appointed for life "during good behavior." A judge may die in office or retire, but the only method specified by the Constitution for forcible removal of a federal judge is through impeachment in the House and conviction by two-thirds of the Senate.

From time to time the other two branches of the federal government have thought to change the philosophical direction of the Supreme Court by proposing that justices serve a limited number of years. Thomas Jefferson, for example, wanted to limit the tenure of justices to six years with reappointment subject to approval of both the House and Senate. Such a scheme would have allowed the Republican president and Congress to replace the Federalists on the court with justices more in keeping with their political philosophy.

In more recent years, Sen. James O. Eastland, D-Miss. (1941, 1943-79), and Rep. Thomas G. Abernethy, D-Miss. (1943-73), offered a constitutional amendment to limit terms of justices to four years and to require Senate approval of incumbent justices within six months of the ratification of the proposed amendment. This proposal, made in 1957, showed the Mississippians' displeasure with a number of the Warren court's liberal rulings, including its decisions striking down state-imposed racial segregation.

None of the proposals to limit tenure have come close to passage. But proposals suggesting ways other than impeachment to remove judges who are physically or mentally incompetent or who conduct themselves unethically or improperly have received serious consideration. The Senate approved such a proposal in 1978 but the House took no action. *(Box, p. 659)*

Impeachment

Article II, Section 4 of the Constitution states that "... all Civil Officers of the United States shall be removed from office on Impeachment for, and conviction of, Treason, Bribery, or other high Crimes and Misdemeanors."

The crimes of treason and bribery as grounds for impeachment have roused little debate because treason is defined elsewhere in the Constitution and bribery is well-defined in the criminal code. But there has been much debate throughout the nation's history as to what the Constitution's authors meant by the phrase "high crimes and misdemeanors." Did they intend it to be read narrowly to mean that a judge could be removed from office only if he committed some indictable offense? Or did the framers intend that the phrase be construed broadly so that impeachment might be used as a political weapon?

This broad construction was the one held by the men who brought the only successful impeachment action against a Supreme Court justice. In 1804 Republican members of the House of Representatives impeached Federalist Justice Samuel Chase for misconduct. Their intent, if the Senate convicted Chase, was to then impeach other Federalist members of the Supreme Court, including the Republicans' *bête noire*, Chief Justice John Marshall. But the Senate failed to convict Chase, Republicans abandoned their plan and Marshall's Federalist philosophy dominated the court until his death in 1835.

Only two other justices have faced serious impeachment threats. Abe Fortas resigned from the court in 1969 after the House threatened to begin an impeachment inquiry into Fortas' association with an industrialist convicted of securities irregularities. On two separate occasions the House investigated impeachment charges against William O. Douglas, first in 1953 because of his temporary stay of execution of two convicted spies, and again in 1970. This second attempt was spurred by conservative Republicans partly in retaliation for the Senate's rejection of two Nixon appointees, partly to reprimand the court for issuing several decisions conservatives disapproved and partly to punish Douglas for what they considered his inappropriate judicial and extra-judicial behavior. In neither instance did proceedings progress beyond the inquiry stage.

Chase Impeachment

The impeachment and trial of Justice Chase for partisan, harsh and unfair judicial behavior while riding circuit had its roots in the Republican desire to rid the federal judiciary of Federalist influence. When Jefferson was elected president and Republicans gained control of Congress in 1800, the judiciary became the last Federalist stronghold in the national government.

Outgoing Federalist President John Adams sought to ensure continuation of his party's judicial influence by having Congress enact laws creating 16 new circuit court judgeships and several justice of the peace positions. He then filled these new posts with last-minute appointments who quickly became known as "midnight judges."

The Republican Congress repealed the 1801 Judiciary Act creating the circuit court judgeships in 1802 and the Supreme Court upheld the repeal in 1803. [6] In the same year, Chief Justice Marshall, an ardent Federalist, announced the court's unanimous decision in *Marbury v. Madison,* the case in which one of Adams' midnight appointees sued the court to order the Jefferson administration to give him his commission. Marshall ruled that the court did not have the constitutional authority to issue such an order, but in so doing he sharply rebuked President Jefferson and asserted for the court the power to declare acts of Congress unconstitutional.[7] *(Details of case, p. 69)*

This decision convinced Republicans that they should move against the court. Already they had used impeachment as a tool of intimidation, threatening to institute impeachment inquiries if the court refused to approve repeal of the 1801 act or ruled against Jefferson in the *Marbury* case.

Other events were conspiring to make the idea of impeachment attractive. In January 1803 the Pennsylvania legislature had impeached and convicted a state judge of "high crimes and misdemeanors" even though it was evident his only "crime" was being an active Federalist. In early February of the same year, Jefferson sent to the House of Representatives documents complaining of the behavior of U.S. District Judge John Pickering of New Hampshire. As one commentator described it, Pickering "was making a daily spectacle of himself on the bench because of intoxication aggravated by copious and blasphemous profanity."[8] The House responded immediately, passing a resolution impeaching Pickering March 2, 1803. He was subsequently convicted and removed from office.

Then, in May 1803, Justice Chase provided the Republicans with the excuse they needed to move against a member of the Supreme Court.

The Charges. An active patriot during the Revolutionary War, Chase was a signer of the Declaration of Independence and chief justice of Maryland before his appointment to the Supreme Court by President Washington in 1796. Chase's legal ability and integrity were unquestioned. But his personality made him unpopular with contemporaries who found him arrogant, arbitrary and guilty of using his position as a judge to advance his Federalist beliefs. As an associate justice, Chase openly approved passage of the hated Alien and Sedition Acts and actively campaigned for Adams' re-election in 1800. These activities drew the enmity of many, but the greatest opprobrium fell on Chase for some of his judicial decisions.

The justice was severely condemned for his arbitrary and intemperate treatment of the sedition trial of Republican printer James T. Callender, who was indicted for writing during the 1800 presidential campaign: "Take your choice, then, between Adams, war and beggary, and Jefferson, peace and competency." Among other inappropriate conduct, Chase was apparently so rude to Callender's attorneys that they left the courtroom altogether.

The justice also was sharply criticized for his conduct of the trial of John Fries, the Pennsylvania farmer who had organized the Whiskey Rebellion against payment of the 1798 "war taxes." Although Fries and his men were armed, little violence occurred. Chase nonetheless insisted that the grand jury indict Fries for treason; he then found Fries guilty and sentenced him to death. To avoid public outrage, Adams subsequently pardoned the farmer.

On yet another occasion, Chase refused to discharge a Delaware grand jury that had ignored his hints that it should indict a Wilmington publisher Chase thought guilty of publishing seditious statements. Finally, in May 1803, Chase delivered what was described as a political harangue to a Baltimore grand jury in which he denounced the Republican administration and its policies.

Enraged at this extra-judicial behavior, Jefferson wrote May 13, 1803, to Rep. Joseph R. Nicholson of Maryland:

Other Removal Methods?

Is impeachment the only permissible method for removing a Supreme Court justice or other federal judge from office?

Because impeachment is so seldom used — only nine federal judges have been impeached; only four convicted — it is widely viewed as an inadequate deterrent to misconduct on the bench. "[A]n impracticable thing — a mere scarecrow," Thomas Jefferson called it after an impeachment attempt against Supreme Court Justice Samuel Chase failed in 1805.

Furthermore, a judge may be impeached and convicted only for commission of treason, bribery or high crimes and misdemeanors. But there has never been a conclusive answer to the question what constitutes a high crime or misdemeanor. Can a judge be impeached for non-criminal but nevertheless improper judicial conduct? How can a judge who is physically or mentally unable to continue in office be removed?

These questions have prompted Congress to explore alternative methods for removal of judges. After Chase's acquittal in 1805, for example, Rep. John Randolph, the chief House prosecutor, rushed to the House floor and proposed a constitutional amendment that would permit the president to remove a justice at the request of a majority of both houses of Congress. The proposal was not approved. *(Details, p. 660)*

A more modern approach was approved by the Senate in 1978. It passed a bill which would have created a commission of 12 federal judges to hear complaints against federal judges and prosecute the most serious ones before a new Court on Judicial Conduct and Disability. That court would be authorized to order involuntary retirement, removal, censure or dismissal of a judge in complaints involving lower court judges. In any case involving a Supreme Court justice, the new court could prepare reports to the House recommending that the justice be impeached or censured, but would be unable to remove the justice on its own authority.

The House took no action on the measure, but that bill, several variations of it and methods establishing disciplinary rather than removal procedures were introduced in both chambers in 1979.

You must have heard of the extraordinary charge of Chace [sic] to the Grand Jury at Baltimore? Ought this seditious and official attack on the principles of our Constitution, and on the proceedings of a state, to go unpunished? and to whom so pointedly as yourself will the public look for the necessary measures? I ask these questions for your consideration, for myself it is better that I should not interfere.[9]

House Republicans took Jefferson's broad hint. In January 1804, just as the Senate was beginning Judge Pickering's impeachment trial, Rep. John Randolph of Virginia proposed an impeachment resolution against Chase in the House. Randolph made eight specific charges against Chase. Six of them dealt with his conduct of the Callender and Fries trials, the seventh with his conduct before the Delaware grand jury and the eighth with his diatribe to the Baltimore grand jury.

Just an hour after the Senate voted March 12 to remove Pickering from office, the full House voted to impeach Chase. The vote was 73-32, split along strictly partisan lines.

Senate Trial. The Senate chamber was filled with spectators, including Chief Justice Marshall and the associate justices, as Chase's trial began Jan. 2, 1805. Vice President Aaron Burr, who had recently killed Alexander Hamilton in a duel, presided over the trial. John Randolph led the team of House managers who prosecuted Chase; his associates included Nicholson, George W. Campbell of Tennessee, Caesar Rodney of Delaware and Peter Early of Georgia. Defending Chase was a battery of able lawyers, including a celebrated orator, Maryland Attorney General Luther Martin, and former Rep. Robert Goodloe Harper, Philip Barton Key, Joseph Hopkinson and former U.S. Attorney General Charles Lee.

Chase himself appeared before the Senate on the opening day of the trial to read a statement in which he maintained he had not engaged in impeachable conduct:

> To these articles . . . I say that I have committed no crime or misdemeanor whatsoever for which I am subject to impeachment according to the Constitution of the United States. I deny, with a few exceptions, the acts with which I am charged; I shall contend, that all acts admitted to have been done by me were *legal*, and I deny, in every instance, the *improper* intentions with which the acts charged are alleged to have been done, and in which their supposed criminality altogether consists. [10]

Chase asked for a delay in the trial so that he could prepare his defense and was granted a month. When the proceedings resumed in February, 52 witnesses, including Marshall, testified before the Senate. Marshall's principal biographer, Albert J. Beveridge, wrote that the Chief Justice's performance was marked by trepidation and that his responses were not favorable to Chase's cause. Marshall's demeanor may have been caused by his worry that should Chase be convicted, Marshall was sure to be the next target. In a letter to Chase dated Jan. 23, 1804, Marshall even suggested that impeachment might be avoided by giving Congress the authority to reverse decisions of the court declaring federal laws unconstitutional. [11] *(Details, p. 71)*

Once testimony was complete, the major debate focused on whether a justice must have committed an indictable crime to be impeached and convicted. While Chase might have comported himself in a highly questionable manner, he had done nothing in violation of any federal law.

The House managers argued that offensive conduct was sufficient for impeachment. Rep. Campbell contended:

> Impeachment, . . . according to the meaning of the Constitution, may fairly be considered a kind of inquest into the conduct of an officer [of the United States], merely as it regards his office; the manner in which he performs the duties thereof; and the effects that his conduct therein may have on society. It is more in the nature of a civil investigation than of a criminal prosecution. [12]

In Chase's behalf, attorney Hopkinson argued that

> . . .no judge can be impeached and removed from office for any act or offense for which he could not be indicted. . . . I maintain as a most important and indispensable principle, that no man should be criminally accused, no man can be criminally condemned, but for the violation of some known law by which he was bound to govern himself. Nothing is so necessary to justice and to safety as that the criminal code should be certain and known. Let the judge, as well as the citizen, precisely know the path he has to walk in, and what he may or may not do. [13]

On March 1, 1805, the Senate was ready to vote. Of the 34 members present, 25 were Republicans, nine were Federalists. Since 23 votes were needed for conviction, the Republicans could carry the day if they voted together. But at least six Republicans sided with the Federalists on each vote, and Chase was acquitted of all eight charges. On one charge the vote was unanimous in Chase's favor. The closest vote came on the complaint that triggered the impeachment — Chase's political harangue to the grand jury. Eighteen senators found Chase guilty; sixteen, not guilty.

Several factors accounted for Chase's acquittal. Manager Randolph's popularity in the House did not extend to the Senate. He may further have reduced his influence by boastfulness and by his extremely broad interpretation of the power of impeachment. There is also evidence that more moderate Republicans were miffed at his opposition in the House to some of their legislative proposals. By all accounts, the case presented by the House managers was inept compared to that of Chase's defenders. Besides, Jefferson — having goaded the House into initiating the impeachment to begin with — took no further part in the proceedings.

Randolph's response to the acquittal was immediate. He strode to the House floor and offered a constitutional amendment to provide for the removal of Supreme Court justices by the president at the request of a majority of both houses of Congress. The House approved the amendment by a 68-33 vote, but the proposal never emerged from the Senate.

The outcome of the trial meant that the Republicans were forced to give up their plans for further impeachments and that Federalist judges on both the Supreme Court and inferior federal courts were secure for the first time since Jefferson's election. The exercise probably proved that impeachment and conviction could not succeed if motivated primarily by politically partisan reasons. But the episode did not resolve the fundamental constitutional question whether only indictable offenses are impeachable. Some 165 years later when members of Congress sought to impeach Justice Douglas primarily for political reasons, the leader of the movement raised the identical question when he argued that "an impeachable offense is whatever a majority of the House of Representatives considers it to be at a given moment in history." [14]

Fortas Resignation

In 1969 Abe Fortas became the first Supreme Court justice to resign under threat of impeachment. Only eight months earlier the Senate had refused to act on President Johnson's proposal to elevate Fortas from associate justice to Chief Justice to replace retiring Earl Warren.

Fortas' resignation came just 10 days after *Life* magazine published on May 4, 1969, an article in which it reported that Fortas accepted in January 1966 a $20,000 check from a family foundation established by multimillionaire industrialist Louis E. Wolfson. Fortas had agreed to act as an adviser to the foundation, which worked to improve community relations and racial and religious cooperation. In September 1966 Wolfson was indicted (and subsequently convicted) for selling unregistered securities. According to the article, Fortas returned the $20,000 to Wolfson in December 1966 and severed his connection with the foundation.

The same day the *Life* article was published, Fortas issued a statement declaring that he did not feel the fee implied any inducement for him to try to influence Wolfson's case.

His statement did not reassure many members of Congress who thought that the justice had violated Canon 25 of "The Canons of Judicial Ethics," prepared in 1922 for the American Bar Association by a committee headed by Chief Justice William Howard Taft. The canon said that a "judge should avoid giving any ground for any reasonable suspicion that he is utilizing the power or prestige of his office to persuade or coerce others to patronize or contribute, either to the success of private business, or to charitable enterprises."

On May 11, Rep. H. R. Gross, R-Iowa (1949-75), announced that he had prepared articles of impeachment against Fortas to present to the House within a "reasonable" time if the justice did not resign. The articles, Gross said, accused Fortas of malfeasance, misconduct and impropriety. Calls for resignation began to come not only from the conservative Republicans and southern Democrats who had blocked his confirmation as Chief Justice but also from liberal Democrats who had supported him in the earlier fight.

On May 13 Rep. Clark MacGregor, R-Minn. (1961-71), apparently with the blessing of the Nixon administration, proposed a preliminary inquiry into the affair by the House Judiciary Committee. The following day Fortas tendered his resignation to President Nixon, who promptly accepted it.

In a letter of explanation to Chief Justice Warren, Fortas maintained that he had done nothing wrong. But he said he feared that continued controversy over his association with the foundation would "adversely affect the work and position of the Court" and that his resignation "will enable the Court to proceed with its vital work free from extraneous stress."[15] *(Text of letter, p. 983)*

Douglas Impeachment Attempts

Twice during Justice William O. Douglas' unprecedentedly long tenure on the Supreme Court bench, the House initiated unsuccessful impeachment proceedings against him. Appointed to the court in 1939, Douglas quickly became one of the most controversial justices in history. His staunchly liberal views, his outspoken opinions and his several marriages, two to women considerably younger than he, made him the target of continuing criticism.

The first attempt to impeach him began after Douglas, on June 17, 1953, temporarily stayed the executions of convicted spies Julius and Ethel Rosenberg. One day later, Rep. W. M. (Don) Wheeler, D-Ga. (1947-55), introduced a resolution of impeachment, and the House Judiciary Committee immediately appointed a special subcommittee of inquiry. On June 19 the full Supreme Court overruled Douglas, setting aside the stay, and the Rosenbergs were executed. At the single subcommittee hearing, Wheeler was

---

Retirement Plans

In one area, inaction by Congress placed pressure on the justices of the Supreme Court. For the first 80 years of the court's existence, Congress made no pension provisions for justices who wished to retire. As a result, several of them stayed on the court until their deaths even though they were physically and mentally incapable of performing their duties adequately.

That situation was somewhat remedied by passage of the Act of April 10, 1869, in which Congress provided that any federal justice who reached 70 years of age and had 10 years of service could resign and receive a pension equal to his salary at the time of resignation.

New Deal Retirement Law

Some historians have suggested that if Congress had not been so stingy in the first place, the Supreme Court crisis of the New Deal period might have been avoided. At the time that President Roosevelt in 1936 announced his plan to rid the court of aged conservatives who were blocking implementation of most of his economic recovery program, all members of the federal judiciary except Supreme Court justices were allowed to retire from regular service rather than resign outright. Judges who retired were still entitled to the salary of the office and any increases in that salary.

Supreme Court justices, however, had to resign, which meant that their pensions were subject to the same fluctuations as other retired government officials. When Justice Oliver Wendell Holmes Jr. was prevailed upon to resign in 1932, his pension amounted to $10,000 a year — half his annual pay as an associate justice — because the Hoover administration, thinking to economize, set that amount as the maximum pension for former government employees.

Chief Justice Charles Evans Hughes thought later that two of the more conservative members of the court would have joined Holmes and retired if Congress had not been so penurious. As it was, Justices Willis Van Devanter and George Sutherland remained on the court, forming the nucleus of the conservative majority that struck down one New Deal law after another.

In response to Roosevelt's court-packing proposal, which it opposed, Congress quickly approved the Supreme Court Retirement Act of 1937, which permitted justices aged 70 with 10 years of service — or aged 65 with 15 years of service — to retire at full salary rather than resign.

The statute quickly proved effective. Roosevelt signed it into law March 1, 1937. On May 18, Justice Van Devanter announced his retirement.

Sources: William F. Swindler, *Court and Constitution in the Twentieth Century, The New Legality, 1932-1968*, Indianapolis, Bobbs-Merrill Co., 1970; Charles Fairman, *History of the Supreme Court of the United States: Vol. VI, Reconstruction and Reunion, 1864-88, Part One*, New York, Macmillan Publishing Co., 1971; Leonard Baker, *Back to Back: The Duel Between FDR and the Supreme Court*, New York, Macmillan Publishing Co., 1967.

---

the only witness to testify, and the full committee July 7 tabled the impeachment resolution.

Second Attempt. The second serious attempt to impeach Douglas followed on the heels of the resignation

A Familiar Complaint

At least one justice has resigned from the Supreme Court in large part because the salary was too low. Justice Benjamin R. Curtis resigned Sept. 30, 1857, at the age of 48. As an associate justice he earned $4,500 annually. Curtis was also greatly disturbed by the majority holding in the Dred Scott case, decided in March 1857. An abolitionist, Curtis was one of two dissenters in that decision.

Prior to his resignation, Curtis explained his plight in a letter to his good friend, Boston historian and educator George Ticknor:

Before [September] I shall have to come to a decision upon a matter of great moment to myself, — whether to continue to hold my present office. The expenses of living have so largely increased, that I do not find it practicable to live on my salary, even now; and, as my younger children will soon call for much increased expenses of education, I shall soon find it difficult to meet expenses by my entire income. Indeed I do not think I can do so without changing, in important particulars, my mode of life. Added to this, I cannot have a house in Washington, and I must either live apart from my family for four to six months every year while I go there, or subject them to a kind of migrant life in boarding-houses, neither congenial or useful. I had hoped it would prove otherwise, and looked forward to being able to have a house there for six months in a year. But what with the increase of luxury and the greatly enhanced prices there, I have now no hope of being able to do this. . . . Such is the actual state of the case as respects my duty to my family. Then as regards the court and the public, I say to you *in confidence,* that I can not feel that confidence in the court, and that willingness to cooperate with them which are essential to the satisfactory discharge of my duties as a member of that body; and I do not expect its condition to be improved. . . . I believe my retirement would be felt to be a loss which would not presently be fully supplied. But I do not myself think it of great public importance that I should remain where I believe I can exercise little beneficial influence and I think all might abstain from blaming me when they remember that I have devoted six of the best years of my life to the public service, at great pecuniary loss, which the interest of my family will not permit me longer to incur. I have no right to blame the public for not being willing to pay a larger salary; but they have no right to blame me for declining it on account of its inadequacy.

Source: Benjamin R. Curtis, *The Life and Writings of Benjamin Robbins Curtis* (Boston: Little, Brown & Co., 1879), p. 155; quoted by John R. Schmidhauser and Larry L. Berg, *The Supreme Court and Congress: Conflict and Interaction, 1945-1968* (New York: The Free Press, 1972), pp. 64-65.

under threat of impeachment of Abe Fortas in 1969 and the Senate rejections in 1969 and 1970 of two Nixon nominees, Clement F. Haynsworth Jr. and G. Harrold Carswell, to fill the vacancy.

On April 15, 1970, House Minority Leader Gerald R. Ford, R-Mich. (1949-73), made five major charges against Douglas in a floor speech. Douglas, Ford said, had engaged in "gross impropriety" when he did not disqualify himself from sitting on obscenity cases involving publisher Ralph Ginzburg. In March 1969 one of Ginzburg's publications had paid Douglas $350 for an article Douglas had written. Ford also objected that an article by Douglas had appeared in the same *Evergreen Review* issue as photographs of nudes.

The minority leader also charged that a book written by Douglas, entitled *Points of Rebellion,* could be construed to advocate violent overthrow of the existing political order and therefore violated the standard of good behavior.

The most serious charge against Douglas was that — in violation of federal law — he practiced law through his association with Albert Parvin and the Albert Parvin Foundation. Parvin was a multimillionaire industrialist who had an interest in a Las Vegas hotel and gambling casino; his foundation was established to promote international cooperation through education. There were allegations that the foundation received a substantial portion of its funding from gambling interests.

Ford charged that Douglas assisted in the incorporation of the foundation and gave the institution legal advice in dealing with an Internal Revenue Service investigation. Douglas maintained that he acted only as an advisor to the foundation, for which he received $12,000 a year plus travel expenses. The justice voluntarily ended his association with the foundation in May 1969.

Finally, Ford criticized Douglas' role as a consultant to the Center for the Study of Democratic Institutions at the same time that the center was a recipient of Parvin Foundation funds.

Ford urged creation of a special House committee to investigate these charges, but Douglas supporter Andrew Jacobs Jr., D-Ind., successfully offered an impeachment resolution to be referred to the House Judiciary Committee, where Douglas was likely to receive sympathetic treatment.

On April 21, 1970, the Judiciary Committee established a special five-member subcommittee to investigate Ford's charges. After months of hearings and deliberations, the subcommittee Dec. 3 voted 3-1 with one abstention that it had found no grounds for impeachment of Douglas.

In its formal report the subcommittee said that Douglas had not violated either judicial ethics or federal law when he failed to disqualify himself from the Ginzburg obscenity cases or when he received payment from one of the Ginzburg publications for the article he had written. Nor was Douglas guilty of practicing law on behalf of the Parvin Foundation. Another attorney assumed responsibility for incorporating the foundation and it retained outside tax counsel during the IRS investigation. Douglas had done nothing unethical or illegal when he accepted payment from the foundation in return for his consulting services. The subcommittee said it considered other charges made against Douglas on the basis of his relationship to Parvin and the foundation but found them "difficult to analyze because of the extreme tenuousness of the circumstantial evidence." The committee also cleared Douglas of the charges concerning his association with the Center for the Study of Democratic Institutions.

On the other charges, the subcommittee found that Douglas had no control over publication by *Evergreen Review* of his writings; the arrangements had been made by Douglas' publisher without his knowledge. The charges that *Points of Rebellion* encouraged violence were based on a misinterpretation of the book, the subcommittee concluded. [16]

Douglas remained on the court another five years, retiring in November 1975 after a debilitating stroke made it impossible for him to maintain his rigorous work schedule.

Salaries

Article III, Section 1 of the Constitution bars Congress from reducing the salaries of Supreme Court justices, but the legislature has absolute control over increases in wages and over appropriations for the operation of the court itself. Only once — in 1964 — has Congress deliberately exercised this power of the purse to show its displeasure with court rulings.

In 1789 Congress set the initial salary of the associate justices at $3,500 per year. As of mid-1979 associate justices were paid $72,000 per year and entitled to an annual cost-of-living increase. Since that provision was legislated in 1975, Congress has suspended all but one cost-of-living increase. Traditionally, the Chief Justice has been paid more than his colleagues. John Jay earned $4,000 as the first Chief Justice; Warren Burger earned $75,000 per year as of mid-1979. *(Box on salary increases, p. 774)*

Like most working people, the justices have not always been satisfied with the level of their compensation. At least one justice resigned from the court partially because he was unable to support his family in the manner he desired on his court salary. *(Box, p. 662)*

Reduction and Raises. During congressional debate in 1866 over reducing the size of the court, Chief Justice Salmon P. Chase urged a three-seat reduction so that the salaries of the remaining justices might be raised. In a June 15, 1866, letter to Associate Justice Samuel F. Miller, Chase wrote:

It is very important — if it is important that adequate salaries should be paid to the Judges of the Supreme Court [—] that the number of Judges should be reduced proportionately as vacancies may occur, to seven. I think that the salaries of the highest Judicial Officers of the Nation ought not to be less than those of the highest Military Officers: and at least an approximation might be made if the number were not so large, and especially if by the reduction of the number the means of increase would ultimately be supplied. [17]

In 1866 the Chief Justice was paid $6,500 a year; associate justices, $6,000. Chase apparently had in mind an increase to $12,000 for himself and an increase to $10,000 for his associates. Congress did provide for reduction of the court to seven as justices either died or retired, but it did not increase their salaries. The next pay raise occurred in 1871, when the salary of associate justices was increased to $8,000 and that of the Chief Justice to $8,500. *(Size of the court, p. 664)*

1964 Salary Controversy

In 1964 Congress considered legislation authorizing the first increases in pay for top-level federal employees since 1955. The House approved a $7,500 increase for members of Congress and all federal judges, including Supreme Court justices. But when the bill reached the Senate floor, the Senate, by a vote of 46-40, adopted an amendment to reduce the increase for the justices to $2,500. A compromise was struck in House-Senate conference, and the increase for the justices was set at $4,500 — $3,000 less than the increase for other federal executives.

The amendment's chief sponsor, Sen. Gordon Allott, R-Colo. (1955-73), insisted that the reduced increase would establish the "semblance of equity" between justices and members of Congress. With the $7,500 increase, members of Congress would receive $30,000; with the $4,500 increase, associate justices would earn $39,500. But there was little doubt in anyone's mind that the amendment was approved out of congressional pique over several recent decisions handed down by the Warren court on such issues as obscenity, school prayer, desegregation and loyalty-security programs. The *American Bar Association Journal* printed in an editorial:

The reason for this discriminating provision seems inescapably an effort on the part of Congress to punish members of our highest Court for performing their constitutional duty of deciding cases as they see them. If indeed this was the purpose, it was unworthy of the principle of the division of powers of our government. But even worse it is an affront to the principle of the independence of the judiciary. [18]

Congress was not to be intimidated by such criticisms. In 1965 the House after heated debate rejected a measure that would have increased Supreme Court salaries by $3,000 retroactive to Jan. 1, 1965. This would have provided the justices with the same increase awarded to members of Congress and other federal judges. The Supreme Court justices did not receive another raise until 1969, when associate justices' salaries were increased to $60,000, compared to $42,500 for members of Congress, and the Chief Justice's salary was increased to $62,500.

Footnotes

[1] Henry J. Abraham, *Justices and Presidents: A Political History of the Supreme Court* (New York: Oxford University Press, 1974), p. 109.

[2] Ibid., p. 118; see also Charles Warren, *The Supreme Court in United States History*, rev. ed. 2 vols. (Boston: Little, Brown & Co., 1922, 1926), II:501.

[3] Sources for the information contained in this section on rejections came primarily from: Abraham, *Justices and Presidents;* Warren, *Supreme Court in History;* and Congressional Quarterly, *Congress and the Nation*, 4 vols. (Washington, D.C.: Congressional

Quarterly, 1965, 1969, 1973, 1977).

[4] Warren, *Supreme Court in History*, II:119.

[5] Ibid., I:137.

[6] *Stuart v. Laird*, 1 Cr. 299 (1803).

[7] *Marbury v. Madison*, 1 Cr. 137 (1803).

[8] Irving Brant, *Impeachment: Trials and Errors* (New York: Alfred A. Knopf, 1972), p. 48.

[9] Leonard Baker, *John Marshall: A Life in Law* (New York: Macmillan Publishing Co., 1974), p. 418.

[10] Brant, *Impeachment*, p. 64.

[11] Beveridge's account of Chase impeachment in Albert J. Beveridge, *The Life of John Marshall*, 4 vols. (Cambridge:

Houghton Mifflin Co., The Riverside Press, 1919), III:157-222.

[12] Brant, *Impeachment*, p. 65.

[13] Ibid., pp. 67-68.

[14] House Minority Leader Gerald R. Ford statement of April 15, 1970, quoted in Brant, *Impeachment*, pp. 79-80.

[15] Summary of events leading to resignation, Congressional Quarterly, *1969 CQ Almanac* (Washington, D.C.: Congressional Quarterly, 1969), pp. 136-39.

[16] Summary of impeachment proceedings: Congressional

Quarterly, *1970 CQ Almanac* (Washington, D.C.: Congressional Quarterly, 1970), pp. 1025-27.

[17] Charles Fairman, *History of the Supreme Court of the United States:* Vol. VI, *Reconstruction and Reunion, 1864-88, Part One* (New York: Macmillan Publishing Co., 1971), p. 163-64.

[18] *American Bar Association Journal*, p. 1151 (1964), quoted by John R. Schmidhauser and Larry L. Berg, *The Supreme Court and Congress: Conflict and Interaction, 1945-68* (New York: The Free Press, 1972), p. 9.

Institutional and Procedural Pressures

Congress sometimes tries to influence the Supreme Court by enacting legislation that affects the court as an institution or its procedures rather than its individual members. To influence the outcome of certain decisions, Congress has changed the size of the court, repealed its jurisdiction over certain kinds of cases and even abolished a court term.

But Congress has considered many more efforts to pressure the court than it has approved. Proposals to require two-thirds of the court to concur in order to declare an act of Congress or state statute unconstitutional have never been approved and seldom were even seriously considered. The major proposal for a change in the size of the court — President Franklin Roosevelt's plan to add six new members to the court — failed because a majority in Congress opposed it. And only once has Congress successfully removed a threat to its legislative policies by repealing the court's jurisdiction; several other attempts have been defeated, most of them by large margins.

Size of the Court

Congress has increased or reduced the number of justices on the Supreme Court seven times in its nearly 200-year history. Generally laws decreasing the number of justices have been motivated by a desire to punish the president; increases have been aimed at influencing the philosophical balance of the court itself. [1]

The Judiciary Act of 1789 set the number of Supreme Court seats at six. In the last days of John Adams' presidency, however, Congress reduced the number to five. Ailing Justice William Cushing was not expected to live much longer, and the out-going Federalists wanted to deny incoming Republican President Thomas Jefferson an opportunity to name Cushing's replacement. The reduction in size never occurred. In 1802 the Republican-controlled Congress repealed the 1801 law and restored the number of justices to six. (Cushing lived until 1810 and it was Madison who named his successor.)

In 1807 Congress increased the number of justices by one, to seven, primarily because of the population growth in Kentucky, Tennessee and Ohio. Justice Thomas Todd of Kentucky was the first justice to fill this new seat.

In 1837 Congress increased the court by two, to nine, again because of the increasing population and expansion of the country into the West and Southwest. Presidents Madison, Monroe and John Quincy Adams had each urged Congress to enlarge the court so that the additional judges might ease some of the backlog of cases in the circuit courts, but Congress refused because it did not want the sitting president to name the justices. *(Circuit court duty, box, p. 754)*

The Judiciary Act of 1837 was passed on the last day of President Jackson's term. Jackson signed the bill and immediately named John Catron and William Smith to the seats. Both men were confirmed, but Smith then declined the appointment.

The next increase, to 10 justices, came in the midst of the Civil War. On the surface the increase was justified again by the westward expansion. The law created a 10th circuit comprised of California and Oregon and later Nevada. But the additional seat meant President Lincoln could appoint a justice who would help ensure that the court majority would decide issues in favor of the Union. Lincoln had already made three appointments to the court in 1862, but his control of the court was still not firm. The same day that the 1863 Judiciary Act went into effect, the court upheld Lincoln's extraordinary exercise of his war powers by a slim 5-4 vote. To the new seat Lincoln appointed Californian Stephen J. Field, who did support the president on war issues. *(Details, The Prize Cases, p. 187)*

Congress was not so accommodating of Lincoln's successor, Andrew Johnson. When Justice Catron died in 1865, Johnson nominated Attorney General Henry Stanbery, who was exceptionally well-qualified for the position. However, the majority in Congress was so opposed to Johnson's Reconstruction policies, and so fearful that his appointees to the court might rule against its own Reconstruction programs, that it responded by reducing the number of seats on the court from 10 to seven. The vacancy to which Stanbery was nominated therefore no longer existed, and no action was taken on his appointment. The court was reduced to eight members when Justice James M. Wayne died in July 1867.

No further vacancies occurred during Johnson's tenure. Little more than a month after General Grant was inaugurated in March 1869, Congress passed another judiciary act raising the number of justices to nine. Because the court had only fallen to eight in number, this meant that Grant only had one new seat to fill. But the resignation of Justice Robert C. Grier gave Grant two vacancies to fill in his first year in office. The president's first appointee was rejected; his second died just four days after confirmation. *(Details, p. 655)*

Grant then nominated William Strong and Joseph P. Bradley just hours after the court declared in *Hepburn v. Griswold* (1870) that the substitution of paper money for gold as legal tender for the payment of contracts entered into before 1862 was unconstitutional. Shortly after Strong and Bradley were confirmed in February and March respectively, the court voted to reconsider its decision in the legal tender case. Fifteen months after declaring "greenbacks" unconstitutional, the court reversed itself by a 5-4 vote and

---

More is Less

In March 1838, at the end of the first term following the addition of two new seats to the Supreme Court, Justice Joseph Story implied in a letter that the increased number had led to decreased efficiency:

> You may ask how the Judges got along together? We made very slow progress, and did less in the same time than I ever knew. The addition to our number has most sensibly affected our facility as well as rapidity of doing business. "Many men of many minds" require a great deal of discussion to compel them to come to definite results; and we found ourselves often involved in long and very tedious debates. I verily believe, if there were twelve Judges, we should do no business at all, or at least very little.

Source: Charles Warren, *The Supreme Court in United States History*, rev. ed., 2 vols. (Boston: Little, Brown & Co., 1922, 1926), II:42.

---

held that paper money was legal for the payment of all contracts. Because both of Grant's appointees voted in favor of reversal and because of the timing of their appointments, Grant was charged with "packing the court," but these allegations have since been considered unwarranted. *(Details, court-packing charges, p. 689; legal tender cases, p. 118)*

Later Court-Packing Attempts

Congress has not added to nor subtracted from the number of seats on the Supreme Court since 1869, although members of Congress frustrated by court decisions have continued to propose changes in the size of the court.

The most serious of these proposals in the 20th century came not from Congress but from the president. Franklin D. Roosevelt proposed in 1937 that the number of justices be raised to 15. Ostensibly to improve the efficiency of the court, the increase was in reality designed to allow Roosevelt to appoint new justices who could be depended upon to support the constitutionality of his New Deal programs, several of which had been struck down by the existing court.

The plan was unpopular with both the public and Congress and was not enacted, but much of the threat to the court's independence was defused by the court itself. Shortly after the proposal was made public, the court upheld in quick succession a Washington minimum wage law and the federal National Labor Relations Act, indicating that the court was now willing to sanction broad federal regulation of private enterprise. *(Details, court-packing plan, p. 689)*

Extraordinary Majority

Members of Congress occasionally have sought to restrain exercise of the court's review powers by requiring that it find acts of Congress or state laws unconstitutional only if an extraordinary majority of the justices concurs in the decision. Most of these proposals have required that two-thirds of the justices concur; some of the more extreme ones have urged that such decisions be unanimous.

The first proposal requiring an extraordinary majority to be considered seriously by Congress was offered in the 1820s after the court ruled against the states in two controversial land claim suits. [2] Although the court's vote was not announced, it was widely thought that because of absences and dissents the cases had been decided by less than a majority vote.

At the behest of Kentucky, one of the states affected by the decisions, Kentucky Sen. Richard M. Johnson, D (H 1807-19; 1829-37; S 1819-29) asked the Senate Judiciary Committee to consider increasing the number of justices to 10 and requiring seven of them to agree in decisions rendering state laws invalid. The committee recommended against increasing the size of the court, but did report a bill to require five of the seven members to concur before the court could nullify state laws. However, the full Senate voted to recommit this bill.

Similar bills offered in both the House and Senate in the next few years also failed, but their consideration may have had the intended effect on the court. In 1834 Chief Justice John Marshall announced that the court would delay a decision in the case of *New York v. Miln*, saying: "The practice of this Court is not (except in cases of absolute necessity) to deliver any judgment in cases where constitutional questions are involved unless four [of the seven] judges concur in opinion, thus making the decision that of a majority of the whole Court." The case was not decided until 1837; then five of the seven justices concurred in the judgment. [3] *(New York v. Miln, p. 316)*

Other proposals would give Congress the final authority to determine the validity of its own legislation. One such proposal, offered by Sen. Robert M. LaFollette, R-Wis. (H 1885-91; S 1906-25), would have allowed Congress to reverse Supreme Court decisions holding federal legislation invalid by repassing the invalidated law by a two-thirds majority vote. Like similar proposals, it died in committee.

Terms

Congress has absolute power to set the terms of the Supreme Court. It once used this power to delay a particular decision by abolishing a term altogether.

In 1802 the Republican-dominated Congress repealed the 1801 Judiciary Act. That statute, enacted by the Federalist lame duck Congress, created several new federal judgeships which outgoing President John Adams promptly filled with Federalists, who in 1802 challenged the repeal. Concerned that the Supreme Court — which was composed completely of Federalists — would find the 1802 repeal unconstitutional, possibly on grounds that the Constitution forbids Congress to reduce judges' salaries, the Republicans postponed the court's next term.

During debate on the legislation, Delaware Federalist Rep. James A. Bayard (H 1797-1803; S 1804-13) opposed the delay, asking the House:

> Could a more dangerous precedent than this be established? May it not lead to the virtual abolition of a Court, the existence of which is guaranteed by the Constitution? If the functions of the Court can be extended by law for fourteen months, what time will arrest us before we arrive at ten or twenty years? [4]

When the court convened 14 months later in February 1803, it upheld the repeal in *Stuart v. Laird* (1803). Congress has not since utilized this method to restrain the court.

Removal of Jurisdiction

Removal of the Supreme Court's authority to review certain categories of cases has been considered throughout U.S. history as one of the more serious threats to the independence of the court. The Constitution authorizes Congress "to make exceptions" to the court's appellate jurisdiction. Although this language probably was not intended as a political weapon, Congress has viewed it as such during three major confrontations with the court.

The first attempt to remove some of the court's jurisdiction came in the 1820s and 1830s when Congress sought unsuccessfully to repeal Section 25 of the Judiciary Act of 1789. This section gave the court power to review high state court decisions upholding state laws challenged as in conflict with the federal Constitution, federal law or treaties.

Only once has Congress repealed the Supreme Court's jurisdiction in order to stop the court from issuing a decision. This occurred in 1868 when Congress repealed the court's power to review federal court denials of writs of *habeas corpus.* The repeal was specifically intended to prevent the court from hearing a *habeas corpus* appeal that called into question the constitutionality of the Reconstruction Acts of 1867.

In the last 25 years Congress has considered legislation to repeal the court's authority to review specific subjects, such as internal security programs, certain criminal procedures, local education problems such as desegregation and school prayer, and state laws forbidding abortions. Although the court's decisions in all of these areas were controversial and generated an outpouring of opposition from the public and members of Congress, none of the jurisdictional repeal attempts were successful.

There has been much scholarly debate on whether the Constitution's authors intended to give Congress absolute control over the court's authority to take appeals from lower court decisions. Justice Felix Frankfurter was one constitutional expert who believed that Congress could "withdraw appellate jurisdiction once conferred" even if the withdrawal affected a pending case. [5] Justice William O. Douglas, on the other hand, thought it unlikely that the court would uphold the constitutionality of repeal legislation. [6] Still others, such as Justice Owen J. Roberts in 1949 and the American Bar Association in 1950, have sought to resolve the dilemma by recommending adoption of a constitutional amendment to make the court and not Congress the determiner of the court's appellate jurisdiction.

In his book analyzing Congress' failure to curb the court during the mid- and late-1950s, constitutional historian C. Herman Pritchett makes the argument that the constitutional grant of authority to control the court's appellate jurisdiction is now largely an anachronism, having been repealed in effect

> . . .by the passage of time and by the recognition that exercise of such power would be in the truest sense subversive of the American tradition of an independent judiciary. . . . Congress can no longer claim with good conscience the authority granted by Article III, Section 2, and every time proposals to exercise such authority are rejected . . . the Court's control over its appellate jurisdiction is correspondingly strengthened. [7]

Section 25

The first congressional attempts to repeal Supreme Court jurisdiction were occasioned by the court's early decisions overturning state laws. Section 25 of the Judiciary Act of 1789 authorized the Supreme Court to review, and uphold or declare invalid, decisions of the states' highest courts upholding state laws challenged as conflicting with the federal Constitution, federal statutes or treaties. With each successive ruling striking down a state law, opposition to Section 25 grew among states' rights proponents. After the Supreme Court emphatically upheld its review power under Section 25 in the case of *Cohens v. Virginia* (1821), several states appealed to their congressional delegations to remove this review power from the court. [8]

The first proposal along these lines was introduced in the Senate in 1821. Sen. Richard M. Johnson of Kentucky proposed a constitutional amendment to give the Senate appellate jurisdiction in cases raising a federal question where a state was a party. This suggestion received little support, primarily because small states held the balance of power in the Senate and were considered likely to prefer a strong national government.

The following year, legislation to repeal the court's Section 25 review power was introduced, but it received little attention then or in the next few years. However, the court's rulings against state sovereignty in *Craig v. Missouri* (1830) and *Cherokee Nation v. Georgia* (1831), coupled with Georgia's outright defiance of the court, generated a major clash over the proper balance of power between the states and the federal government. [9]

As part of that confrontation the House ordered its Judiciary Committee to report a measure repealing Section 25. The committee made its report Jan. 24, 1831, declaring that it was

> . . .no more necessary to the harmonious action of the Federal and State governments, that the Federal court should have power to control the decisions of State courts by appeal, than that the Federal legislature should have power to control the legislation of the States, or the Federal Executive a State Executive, by negative. [10]

Repeal of Section 25 was viewed as a grave threat by members of the court. Chief Justice John Marshall wrote that the "crisis of our Constitution is now upon us," while Justice Joseph Story lamented that "if the Twenty-Fifth Section is repealed, the Constitution is practically gone." [11]

In a letter written after the repeal crisis had passed, former President James Madison commented on its seriousness:

> The jurisdiction claimed for the Federal Judiciary is truly the only defensive armor of the Federal Government, or rather for the Constitution and laws of the United States. Strip it of that armor, and the door is wide open for nullification, anarchy and convulsion. . . . [12]

The measure was never fully debated in the House. Using parliamentary tactics, court supporters were able to repulse the repeal movement by a wide margin. Moves to repeal the section were made in later years but none came any closer to passage.

Although Marshall's court feared the consequences of a successful repeal drive, a later court resisted efforts to expand its Section 25 appellate jurisdiction. In the Act of Feb. 5, 1867, Congress changed the wording of the section so that it could be interpreted to allow the Supreme Court to review all errors of law in high state court decisions and not just those concerned with federal questions. It appeared that Congress might well have intended such an expansion to counter any obstruction to the federal judicial system from the recently rebellious states. Nonetheless, in the 1874 case of *Murdock v. Memphis*, the court held that the 1867 law had not changed Section 25 in any way. Congress did not explicitly amend the section until 1914. [13] *(Changes in appellate jurisdiction, pp. 263-266*

The McCardle Case

Only once in the nation's history has Congress prevented the Supreme Court from deciding a pending case by repealing its appellate jurisdiction over the subject matter of the case.

The extraordinary action was taken by a Congress dominated by Radical Republicans who wanted to prohibit the Supreme Court from reviewing the constitutionality of the Reconstruction Acts of 1867. Those acts substituted military rule for civilian government in the 10 southern states that initially refused to rejoin the Union and established procedures for those states to follow to gain readmittance and representation in the federal government.

The Supreme Court twice avoided ruling on the constitutionality of the Reconstruction acts. In April 1867, just before the acts were scheduled to take effect, the state of Mississippi asked the court for permission to seek an injunction to stop the president from implementing them. The court unanimously rejected the request in *Mississippi v. Johnson*, holding that the president's duties under the acts were political and that therefore the court was without jurisdiction to order the injunction. [14]

The court in May dismissed a similar request by Georgia and Mississippi officials asking that the secretary of war and the commanders of the five military districts be stopped from enforcing the Reconstruction acts. The court again held that the suit raised political questions over which it had no jurisdiction. [15]

Reconstruction Attacked

It was not until November 1867, several months after military rule was established in the southern states, that the events which would touch off the confrontation between the court and Congress began. William H. McCardle, the editor of the *Vicksburg* (Miss.) *Times*, was not loath to express editorially his distaste for Reconstruction and his views that blacks should be excluded from participation in government and the 14th Amendment left unratified. His editorials continually attacked imposition of military government in the South and the actions of the commanding generals. In one editorial, he called the five district commanders "infamous, cowardly, and abandoned villains . . . who should have their heads shaved, their ears cropped, their foreheads branded, and their precious persons lodged in a penitentiary."

In other columns the editor advised white Mississippians to avoid voting in the election to call for a constitutional convention and promised to publish the names of the "sneaks" and "scoundrels" who ignored this advice. [16]

McCardle reserved his bitterest criticisms for Major General Edward O. C. Ord, the commanding general of the Fourth Military District, which included Mississippi and Arkansas.

Ord finally had McCardle arrested and held for trial by a military tribunal, charging him with disturbing the peace, inciting insurrection, slowing the pace of Reconstruction and printing libelous statements.

The Tables Turned

A protection against illegal imprisonment, a writ of *habeas corpus* orders a person holding a prisoner to explain why the prisoner is being held. Seeking to protect blacks and federal officials in the South from harassment by white southerners, Congress in February 1867 enacted a statute expanding the Supreme Court's jurisdiction to review denials of writs of *habeas corpus*.

Prior to the 1867 law, the court had no appellate jurisdiction over lower court denials *of habeas corpus* relief. The 1867 statute permitted appeals from federal circuit courts to the Supreme Court in "all cases where any person may be restrained of his or her liberty in violation of the Constitution or of any treaty or law of the United States," and sought his release through a writ of *habeas corpus*.

The statute was not intended to protect southern whites, but McCardle sought a writ of *habeas corpus* in a federal circuit court, charging that the Reconstruction acts which allowed his arrest and trial by military tribunal were unconstitutional. When the circuit court denied the writ, he appealed directly to the Supreme Court.

Rumors abounded that the Supreme Court would use McCardle's case to declare the Reconstruction acts unconstitutional. In 1866 the court had held unanimously that it was illegal for a military commission to try a civilian when civilian courts were available, and five of the justices had gone so far as to say they did not think Congress had the power under any circumstances to authorize military trials of civilians where civilian courts were open. Many observers interpreted this decision in *Ex parte Milligan* to indicate that the court would not respond favorably to the military rule imposed in the South. [17]

But the Radical Republicans could not afford to have the Reconstruction acts declared unconstitutional until after they had solidified their political power in the South and had forced the southern states to ratify the 14th Amendment as the price for readmittance to the Union.

Thus when McCardle's attorney, Jeremiah S. Black, appealed to the Supreme Court in December 1867 to act quickly on the case, Republicans in the House moved just as quickly to stave off an adverse ruling. In January 1868 the House Judiciary Committee reported and the House passed a bill to require two-thirds of the justices to concur in decisions finding federal laws unconstitutional.

According to historian Charles Warren, this measure had little public support, and the Senate postponed action on it indefinitely. [18] Moreover, it was widely believed that the measure would have failed to accomplish its purpose; of the eight justices then on the court, at least five were thought to believe the Reconstruction acts invalid.

Meanwhile, the Supreme Court agreed to Black's request and set arguments for the first week in March. The government's attorney, Sen. Lyman Trumbull, R-Ill. (1855-73), sought to end the matter by moving for a dismissal of the case on the grounds that the Supreme Court did not have jurisdiction. But the court denied the motion Feb. 17, 1868.

Arguments on the merits in *Ex parte McCardle* began March 2, the same day the House approved the first of the articles of impeachment against President Johnson. [19] McCardle's attorneys included Black, who had been nominated as an associate justice of the Supreme Court by President Buchanan in the last months of his term but was rejected by the Senate in 1861 largely because Senate Republicans wanted to hold the vacancy open for President Lincoln to fill. Another attorney for McCardle was David

Dudley Field, brother to Justice Stephen J. Field, who was sitting on the case.

Because he considered the Reconstruction acts unconstitutional, Attorney General Henry Stanbery refused to argue the government's position; his place was taken by Trumbull and the eminent attorney Matthew Hale Carpenter. By all accounts, the arguments by both sides were impressive.

Jurisdiction Repealed

Arguments concluded March 9. On March 12 the Radical Republicans in Congress made their move. Pending in the House was an insignificant Senate-passed bill to expand the Supreme Court's appellate jurisdiction to cases concerning customs and revenue officers. James F. Wilson, R-Iowa (H 1861-69; S 1883-95), chairman of the House Judiciary Committee, offered an amendment to repeal the 1867 grant of appellate jurisdiction over *habeas corpus* cases and to prohibit the court from acting on any appeals then pending. Democrats and moderate Republicans who might have opposed Wilson's measure apparently did not understand what was happening, and the amendment was passed without debate or objection. The bill as amended was then returned to the Senate, which approved it later in the same day by a 32-6 vote.

President Johnson waited as long as possible before vetoing the bill to see if the Supreme Court would defy Congress and decide the *McCardle* case before its jurisdiction was removed. But though the court met in conference March 21, it announced no decision on the case, taking note instead of the repeal bill and saying it would postpone a decision on the case until action on the legislation was concluded. Justices Field and Robert C. Grier objected to the postponement, Field writing later that the "Judges had all formed their conclusions, and no excuse was urged that more time was wanted for examination." [20]

Johnson vetoed the bill March 25, declaring that the repeal "establishes a precedent which, if followed, may eventually sweep away every check on arbitrary and unconstitutional legislation." [21]

March 30 was the court's next opinion day. When it became obvious that the justices would say nothing about the *McCardle* case, attorney Black asked that the effect of the repeal legislation on the case be argued formally before the court. The court agreed, but also agreed to a postponement until the December 1868 term to give government attorneys time to prepare their arguments.

Justice Grier also objected to this delay, reading the following statement in open court:

> This case was fully argued in the beginning of this month. It is a case which involves the liberty and rights, not only of the appellant, but of millions of our fellow citizens. The country and the parties had a right to expect that [the case] would receive the immediate and solemn attention of the Court. By the postponement of this case, we shall be subject ourselves, whether justly or unjustly, to the imputation that we have evaded the performance of a duty imposed on us by the Constitution, and waited for the Legislative interposition to supersede our action, and relieve us from responsibility. I am not willing to be a partaker of the eulogy or opprobrium that may follow. I can only say . . . I am ashamed that such opprobrium should be cast upon the Court, and that it cannot be refuted. [22]

Grier was not the only one to decry the court's apparent submission to Congress. Gideon Welles, Lincoln's secretary of the Navy and close ally and a noted diarist, wrote that the "Judges of the Supreme Court have caved in, fallen through, failed in the *McCardle* case." [23] Former Justice Benjamin R. Curtis, who defended President Johnson at his impeachment trial, said that "Congress with the acquiescence of the country, has subdued the Supreme Court, as well as the President." [24] And Black in an April 1868 letter wrote that "the Court stood still to be ravished and did not even hallo while the thing was getting done. . . ." [25]

Final Submission

Final arguments in the *McCardle* case were anticlimactic. On April 12 the court issued a unanimous decision upholding the repeal measure and dismissing the case for lack of jurisdiction. Chief Justice Salmon P. Chase wrote that the Constitution gave Congress authority to make exceptions to the court's appellate jurisdiction and that Congress had expressly exercised that authority when it repealed the court's right to review denials of writs of *habeas corpus:*

> We are not at liberty to inquire into the motive of the legislature. We can only examine into its power under the Constitution, and the power to make exceptions to the appellate jurisdiction of this Court is given by express words. What, then, is the effect of the repealing act upon the case before us? We cannot doubt as to this. Without jurisdiction the Court cannot proceed at all in any cause. Jurisdiction is power to declare the law, and when it ceases to exist, the only function remaining to the Court is that of announcing the fact and dismissing the cause. . . . [26]

Aftermath

Less than a month later, Chase confirmed the belief that the court would have declared at least part of the Reconstruction acts unconstitutional. "I may say to you," he wrote to a district judge, "that had the merits of the McCardle Case been decided the Court would doubtless have held that his imprisonment for trial before a military commission was illegal." [27]

As it turned out, McCardle was never brought to trial. By the time the Supreme Court dismissed his case in 1869, Major General Ord was no longer the commanding officer in McCardle's military district. His replacement dropped the charges.

Historian Charles Fairman points out one major irony of the *McCardle case.* Had the Supreme Court defied Congress and issued a decision declaring the Reconstruction acts invalid, it is possible that the 14th Amendment to the Constitution would not have been ratified. One of the provisions of the Reconstruction acts required the 10 recalcitrant southern states to approve the amendment in order to gain reentry into the Union. Ratification of the amendment could only occur if some of the southern states approved it. As Fairman wrote, "one must believe that if Congress had failed to bring the weight of its authority to bear upon the ten States as then organized, there would have been no Fourteenth Amendment." [28]

Ex parte Yerger

A McCardle-type confrontation between Congress and the court concerning jurisdiction over *habeas corpus* granted the court by the Judiciary Act of 1789 was narrowly avoided late in 1869. *Ex parte Yerger* concerned the imprisonment, conviction for murder and sentencing of another Mississippi newspaper editor by a military tribunal. [29] Edward M. Yerger applied to the Supreme Court for an original writ of *habeas corpus*, charging, as McCardle had, that it was unconstitutional for military tribunals to try civilians for civilian crimes.

The court agreed to hear the case. A bill was immediately introduced in the Senate to remove the court's jurisdiction in all cases involving the constitutionality of the Reconstruction acts and over all writs of *habeas corpus* until Reconstruction was completed. A second proposal would have prohibited Supreme Court review of any federal act.

Before the Senate could act, a compromise was struck between Yerger's lawyers and the attorney general. His case was removed to civilian court and his petition for the writ of *habeas corpus* withdrawn. No further congressional action was taken on the proposed jurisdictional limitations.

Recent Repeal Efforts

The 1954 appointment of former California Gov. Earl Warren as Chief Justice of the United States initiated a period unique in the nation's history when the court led other governmental institutions in protecting individual rights from majority discrimination. The first major ruling of the Warren court struck down segregation in public schools, overturning 60 years of officially-sanctioned racial discrimination.

These Warren court decisions inspired a series of anti-court efforts by members of Congress. Perhaps the most serious of these occurred in 1957-58 when southerners opposed to desegregation allied with other conservative members of Congress who thought the court's decisions protecting individuals alleged to have participated in Communist activities threatened to undermine the nation's security. In addition to trying to reverse the individual decisions, the groups launched two major attacks on the court's power to review certain classes of cases. But despite the conservative alliance and widespread opposition to the court's decisions, Congress ultimately refused to adopt either court-curb proposal.

Jenner-Butler Bill

The broader of the two assaults on the jurisdiction of the court during this uneasy period was initiated in the Senate by William E. Jenner, R-Ind. (1944-45, 1947-59). [30] His bill (S 2646), introduced in July 1957, would have barred the Supreme Court from accepting appeals in five categories:

● Cases involving the powers of congressional investigating committees and contempt of Congress proceedings. This was aimed at *Watkins v. United States* (354 U.S. 178, 1957), in which the court ruled that a witness before the House Un-American Activities Committee had not been guilty of contempt of Congress for refusing to answer certain questions because the scope of the committee's inquiry had not been clearly defined by Congress and the committee had failed to show the pertinency of its questions to its investigation. *(Details, p. 160)*

● Cases involving federal laws and regulations governing hiring and firing of government employees on loyalty grounds. This provision was directed at the court's ruling in *Cole v. Young* (351 U.S. 536, 1956), which held that loyalty-

security procedures under the Summary Suspension Act of 1950 applied only to "sensitive" jobs and not to all federal employment. *(Details, p. 510)*

● Cases involving school regulations dealing with subversive activities by teachers. This was directed at the court's jurisdiction to review cases like *Slochower v. Board of Higher Education of the City of New York* (350 U.S. 551, 1956), in which the court ruled that New York City could not dismiss a city college professor from his job merely for refusing to cooperate with a congressional committee investigating subversive activities but had to grant him all the procedural rights due under state and city laws regulating employment of teachers suspected of engaging in forbidden activities. *(Details, p. 514)*

● Cases involving state laws and regulations punishing subversive activities directed against the federal government. This provision was aimed at the court's ruling in *Pennsylvania v. Nelson* (350 U.S. 497, 1956), in which it held that provisions of the Pennsylvania Sedition Act punishing subversive activities directed against the federal government were invalid because Congress had pre-empted this field of legislation when it passed the 1940 Smith Act. *(Details, box, p. 513)*

● Cases involving state regulations for admission to the bar, aimed at cases like *Konigsberg v. State Bar of California* (366 U.S. 36, 1957), in which the court ruled that an applicant could not be denied admission to a state bar solely because he refused to answer questions about past or present Communist Party membership. *(Details, p. 515)*

The "extreme liberal wing of the court" has "become a majority," Jenner said, Aug. 7, 1957, the opening day of hearings on his bill, "and we witness today the spectacle of a court constantly changing the law, and even changing the meaning of the Constitution, in an apparent determination to make the law of the land what the court thinks it should be." [31]

But solving the problem by removing the court's jurisdiction proved too strong a medicine for many witnesses, who perceived this threat to the independence of the judiciary as a graver danger to national security than that posed by the communists.

At the suggestion of Sen. John Marshall Butler, R-Md. (1951-63), Jenner's bill was substantially amended by the Senate Judiciary Committee. As reported in May 1958, only one section of the original Jenner proposal — the provision barring the Supreme Court from reviewing state bar admission rules — was retained. Instead of repealing the court's jurisdiction to review the other categories of cases, the committee recommended language to overturn the particular offending decisions.

To nullify the *Nelson* decision, the reported bill provided that no past or future federal anti-subversive laws should be construed by the courts as prohibiting enforcement of otherwise valid state laws punishing seditious activities directed at the state or federal government. To nullify the *Watkins* decision, the bill provided that each chamber of Congress would be the final judge of whether questions put to witnesses by investigating committees were pertinent to the authorized purpose of the committee's inquiry. The measure also provided that a person accused of contempt of Congress could not argue that the questions were not pertinent unless he had raised that objection at the time the question was asked.

The Butler amendment left the *Slochower* and *Cole* decisions standing. But it moved to overturn a court ruling that the original Jenner bill had not touched. In *Yates v.*

Internal Security Rulings: Only One Reversed

Distressed by many of the Supreme Court's rulings on internal security cases, Congress tried between 1957 and 1959 not only to remove the court's jurisdiction to review such cases but also to reverse specifically the objectionable rulings. Only one of these attempts — modifying the decision in *Jencks v. United States* (353 U.S. 657, 1957) — was successful; the rest failed, most of them in the Senate, where the two efforts to repeal jurisdiction also foundered.

The Victory

The Supreme Court in June 1957 reversed the conviction of labor leader Clinton E. Jencks, charged with perjury for swearing he was not a Communist. The five-justice majority held that reports filed by FBI-paid informants alleging Jencks' participation in Communist Party activities should have been made available to Jencks' defense attorneys when requested. The majority ruled that the prosecution either must turn over to the defense directly any portion of statements previously made by government witnesses that related to their trial testimony or drop the case.

Justice Tom C. Clark, a former U.S. attorney general, dissented, along with Justices Harold H. Burton and John Marshall Harlan. (Justice Charles E. Whittaker did not participate.) Clark said that unless Congress nullified the decision through new legislation, "those intelligence agencies of our government engaged in law enforcement may as well close up shop." He added that the decision would result in a "Roman holiday" for criminals to "rummage" through secret files.

Clark's dissent was seized upon by those in Congress opposed to the court's decision. They also drew strength from the fact that the majority had not specified any right of the prosecution to withhold from the defense any irrelevant portions of testimony requested by the defense. As a result, lower courts were left to their own interpretations of the ruling, and the government was ordered in a number of subsequent trials to produce entire files in a case, regardless of relevancy. Several important prosecutions were dismissed because the government refused to produce the requested files.

At the behest of the White House, the Justice Department and the FBI, the House and Senate Judiciary Committees both moved quickly to report bills to narrow the impact of the *Jencks* decision. The Senate passed its version by voice vote Aug. 26, 1957; the House passed its measure a day later with only 17 dissenting votes. Both chambers agreed overwhelmingly Aug. 30 to a compromise version, and President Eisenhower signed the bill into law Sept. 2.

PL 85-269 did not reverse the *Jencks* decision but restricted it. Following testimony by a government witness, a defendant in a criminal case could request relevant pre-trial statements made by that witness so long as the statement was written and signed by the witness or was a transcription of oral statements made at the time the statements were given. The statute also authorized the trial judge to screen requested statements for relevance.

The Defeats

Reversal of another court decision came within a hairbreadth of passage. In the 1956 case of *Cole v. Young* (351 U.S. 536) the court held that federal employee security procedures applied only to sensitive jobs and that government employees in non-sensitive jobs could not be summarily dismissed for suspected disloyalty.

The Senate in August 1957 approved a bill (S 1411) to permit government supervisors to transfer suspected security risks from sensitive to non-sensitive jobs instead of suspending them. In July 1958 the House approved an amended version of S 1411 which extended federal employee security procedures to all government employees so that anyone suspected of subversive activities could be summarily dismissed.

The final compromise version was identical to the House amendment but limited to one year. The House passed it by voice vote but the compromise was never taken up in the Senate and died at adjournment. In 1959 House and Senate committees held hearings on the issue but no further action was taken.

Yates Bill. The House in 1958 and 1959 approved measures to reverse the portion of the court ruling in *Yates v. United States* (354 U.S. 298, 1957) that defined the word "organize" to mean only the act of initially bringing together a group of people. The legislation would have redefined the word to make it a crime not only to bring into being a group seeking to overthrow the government by force but also to conduct continuing organizational activities. A similar provision was included in the Jenner-Butler bill killed in the Senate in 1958. The Senate took no action on the 1958 House-passed bill; in 1959 a Senate subcommittee approved the House bill, but the full committee did not act on it.

Passport Control. After the Supreme Court held in *Kent v. Dulles* (357 U.S. 116, 1958) that Congress had not authorized the State Department to deny passports to American citizens affiliated with the Communist Party, the department proposed legislation to Congress to overturn the decision. The House passed an amended version of the proposal by voice vote but a threatened filibuster in the Senate blocked consideration there. The House passed similar legislation again in 1959, but although three Senate subcommittees held hearings on the issue, no bill was reported to the Senate floor.

Sources: Walter F. Murphy, *Congress and the Court: A Case Study in the American Political Process* (University of Chicago Press, 1962); C. Herman Pritchett, *Congress Versus the Supreme Court, 1957-60* (Minneapolis: University of Minnesota Press, 1961; reprint ed., New York; DaCapo Press, 1973); Congressional Quarterly, *Congress and the Nation*, Vol. I (Washington, D.C.: Congressional Quarterly, 1965); Congressional Quarterly, *CQ Almanac*, Vols. 13, 14, 15, 16 (Washington, D.C.: Congressional Quarterly, 1957, 1958, 1959, 1960).

Pressure on Congress

In the midst of the 1957-59 congressional effort to reverse Supreme Court decisions on internal security measures and to limit its jurisdiction over such cases, Congress received outside pressure to act from two influential sources.

The first of these was the Conference of Chief Justices of the states, which charged that recent Supreme Court decisions in a number of areas were significantly eroding the power of the states in the federal system. In a document entitled "Report of the Committee on Federal-State Relationships as Affected by Judicial Decisions," adopted Aug. 23, 1958, the judges contended that "the overall tendency of the Supreme Court over the last 25 years or more has been to press the extension of federal power and to press it rapidly" and that the court "too often has tended to adopt the role of policy-maker without proper judicial restraint." In conclusion, the conference stated its "grave concern as to whether individual views of the members of the court as from time to time constituted, or of a majority thereof, as to what is wise or desirable do not unconsciously override a more dispassionate consideration of what is or is not constitutionally warranted."

A second report, this one a set of resolutions urging Congress to "correct legislative defects in the field of internal security revealed by particular [court] decisions," was adopted by the American Bar Association's House of Delegates Feb. 24, 1959. The ABA specifically opposed legislation to remove any court jurisdiction, but it urged adoption of legislation to reverse the court's rulings in *Pennsylvania v. Nelson* (1956), *Yates v. United States* (1957), *Cole v. Young* (1956) and *Watkins v. United States* (1957).

Because these reports coincided with the views of members of Congress opposed to the court, they were cited frequently throughout the debate on the Jenner-Butler bill as expert testimony to buttress arguments to curb the court.

United States (354 U.S. 298, 1957), the court ruled that the 1940 Smith Act did not prohibit "advocacy of forcible overthrow of the government as an abstract doctrine" but only as an incitement to action. The court also held that the act's prohibition against organizing a group seeking to overthrow the government by force applied only to the original act of bringing the group into being and not to continued organizational activity such as recruitment of members. *(Details, p. 504)*

As reported, the compromise Jenner-Butler bill made all teaching and advocacy of forcible overthrow of the government a crime under the Smith Act. It also redefined the term "organize" to include both initial and continuing organizational activities.

The bill did not come to the Senate floor until Aug. 20, 1958, one of the last days of the session. Senate Majority Leader Lyndon B. Johnson, D-Texas (H 1937-49; S 1949-61), apparently had hoped he could avoid bringing it up for consideration altogether, but under pressure from southern colleagues and knowing that he had the votes to defeat it, he allowed it to be offered as an amendment to a minor House-passed bill (HR 6789) dealing with appeals from

rulings of federal administrative agencies. After long supporting speeches by Jenner and Butler, and rebuttals by judiciary committee opponents, Thomas C. Hennings Jr., D-Mo. (H 1935-48; S 1951-60), and Alexander Wiley, R-Wis. (1939-63), Hennings offered a motion to table the Jenner-Butler bill. The motion was adopted by a 49-41 vote, and the bill was killed. Measures similar to individual parts of it were subsequently considered in the House and Senate, but none were enacted. *(Box, p. 670)*

Implied Pre-emption

The second attempt during this period to repeal Supreme Court jurisdiction was more limited in scope but came closer to passage. Under the pre-emption doctrine — based on Article IV, Section 2, making federal laws the "supreme law of the land" — courts have invalidated state laws because Congress stated an intention to pre-empt a given field of legislation, because there was a conflict between the federal and state law, or because the court inferred an intention by Congress to pre-empt the field.

It was to prohibit this "pre-emption by implication" that HR 3, the most important of several anti-pre-emption proposals, was offered. Its primary provision stated that: "No act of Congress shall be construed as indicating an intent on the part of Congress to occupy the field in which such act operates, to the exclusion of all state laws on the same subject matter, unless such act contains an express provision to that effect or unless there is a direct and positive conflict between such act and a state law so that the two cannot be reconciled or consistently stand together."

HR 3 was introduced in the House in 1955 by Rules Committee Chairman Howard W. Smith, D-Va. (1931-67), after the Pennsylvania Supreme Court held in 1954 that the 1940 Smith Act pre-empted provisions of state anti-sedition laws that punished persons found guilty of subversive activities directed against the federal government. The ruling, when affirmed by the U.S. Supreme Court in *Pennsylvania v. Nelson* (1956), affected anti-subversive laws of 43 states. Smith, who wrote the 1940 act affected by the ruling, said the court decision was "the first intimation I have ever had . . . that Congress ever had the faintest notion of nullifying the concurrent jurisdiction of the respective sovereign states to pursue also their own prosecution for subversive activities."[32]

1956 Action. The House Judiciary Committee reported HR 3 in July 1956 after narrowing it so that it would only overturn the *Nelson* decision. The Senate Judiciary Committee also reported bills similar to the original Smith proposal and the narrower version reported in the House, but neither chamber acted on the legislation.

1958 Action. Smith re-introduced HR 3 in 1957. Spurred by opposition to the Supreme Court's ruling in *Nelson*, the House Judiciary Committee reported both a modified version of HR 3 and a bill which would overturn only the *Nelson* decision. The full House adopted HR 3 July 17, 1958, on a 241-155 vote after merging it with the narrower bill.

Similar bills were reported to the full Senate. When one was called up for consideration Aug. 20, 1958, immediately after the Senate voted to table the Jenner-Butler bill, Sen. John L. McClellan, D-Ark. (1943-78), offered an amendment to substitute the House-passed version of HR 3 for the Senate bill. Opponents tried to kill the amendment by offering a motion to table it, but that failed on a 39-46 vote. Over protests from the measure's supporters, Majority

Leader Johnson won adjournment until the following day. Although it looked as if the McClellan amendment had enough votes for adoption, Johnson and other opponents of HR 3 lobbied hard throughout Aug. 21. The lobbying paid off when a motion to recommit the bill to the Judiciary Committee was agreed to by a one-vote margin, 41-40.

Recommittal ended further consideration of HR 3 in the 85th Congress. In 1959, the House again approved HR 3, although with diminished enthusiasm. Smith continued

to introduce the measure for several more years, but it was never again considered by the full House or Senate.

The change in the congressional attitude on the preemption issue between 1958 and 1959 has been attributed to several factors, including an influx of "pro-court" Northern Democrats into the Senate after the 1958 elections, a series of rulings giving the states wider latitude over business matters, and court affirmation that the states could prosecute subversive activities directed against them.

Footnotes

[1] Sources for the information on changes in the size of the court included: Henry J. Abraham, *Justices and Presidents: A Political History of Appointments to the Supreme Court* (New York: Oxford University Press, 1974); and Charles Warren, *The Supreme Court in United States History*, rev. ed., 2 vols. (Boston: Little, Brown & Co., 1922, 1926).

[2] *Martin v. Hunter's Lessee*, 1 Wheat. 304 (1816); *Green v. Biddle*, 8 Wheat. 1 (1823).

[3] Quoted in Walter F. Murphy, *Congress and the Court: A Case Study in the American Political Process* (Chicago: University of Chicago Press, 1962), p. 23.

[4] Warren, *Supreme Court in History*, I:223.

[5] *National Mutual Insurance Co. v. Tidewater Transfer Co.*, 337 U.S. 582 at 655 (1949).

[6] *Glidden Co. v. Zdanok*, 370 U.S. 530 (1962).

[7] C. Herman Pritchett, *Congress Versus the Supreme Court, 1957-60* (Minneapolis: University of Minnesota Press, 1961; reprint ed., New York: DaCapo Press, 1973), p. 122-23.

[8] *Cohens v. Virginia*, 6 Wheat. 264 (1821); major sources for the information on attempts to repeal Section 25 were Warren, *Supreme Court in History*, and Murphy, *Congress and the Court.*

[9] *Craig v. Missouri*, 4 Pet. 410 (1930); *Cherokee Nation v. Georgia*, 5 Pet. 1 (1831).

[10] Murphy, *Congress and the Court*, p. 24.

[11] Warren, *Supreme Court in History*, I:727, 740.

[12] Ibid., I:740.

[13] *Murdock v. Memphis*, 20 Wall. 590 (1874).

[14] *Mississippi v. Johnson*, 4 Wall. 475 (1867).

[15] *Georgia v. Stanton*, 6 Wall. 50 (1867).

[16] Charles Fairman, *History of the Supreme Court of the United States:* Vol. VI, *Reconstruction and Reunion, 1864-88, Part One* (New York: Macmillan Publishing Co., 1971), p. 416, 420-21.

[17] *Ex parte Milligan*, 4 Wall. 2 (1866).

[18] Warren, *Supreme Court in History*, II:466-67.

[19] *Ex parte McCardle*, 7 Wall. 506 (1869).

[20] Julius J. Marke, *Vignettes of Legal History* (South Hackensack, N.J.: Fred B. Rothman & Co., 1965), p. 157.

[21] President Andrew Johnson's veto message to Congress, March 25, 1868, quoted by Ralph R. Martig, "Congress and the Appellate Jurisdiction of the Supreme Court," *Michigan Law Review* 34 (March 1936):664.

[22] Warren, *Supreme Court in History*, II:482.

[23] Ibid., II:483.

[24] Ibid.

[25] Fairman, *Reconstruction and Reunion*, p. 478.

[26] *Ex parte McCardle*, 7 Wall. 506 at 514-15 (1869).

[27] Fairman, *Reconstruction and Reunion*, p. 494.

[28] Ibid., p. 510.

[29] *Ex parte Yerger*, 8 Wall. 85 (1869).

[30] Major sources for the material included in this section were: Murphy, *Congress and the Court*; Pritchett, *Congress Versus the Supreme Court*; John R. Schmidhauser and Larry L. Berg, *The Supreme Court and Congress: Conflict and Interaction, 1945-1968* (New York: The Free Press, 1972); Congressional Quarterly, *CQ Almanac*, Vols. 12, 13, 14, 15 (Washington, D.C.:Congressional Quarterly, 1956, 1957, 1958, 1959).

[31] Congressional Quarterly, *1958 CQ Almanac*, p. 294.

[32] Congressional Quarterly, *1956 CQ Almanac*, p. 586.

Reversals of Rulings

Of all its methods of influencing the Supreme Court, Congress has had most success in reversing individual rulings either through adoption of a constitutional amendment or passage of legislation.

Four of the 26 amendments to the Constitution were adopted specifically to overrule the Supreme Court's interpretation of that document. The amendments reversed the court's rulings on the ability of citizens of one state to bring suit against another state, the application of the Bill of Rights to the states, the income tax and the 18-year-old vote.

But it is difficult and time-consuming to amend the Constitution. Each chamber of Congress must approve the proposed amendment by a two-thirds vote and it must then be ratified by three-fourths of all the states. Moreover, there is long-standing and deeply held sentiment that amendments to the Constitution should not be adopted every time there is a significant disagreement with a Supreme Court ruling. As a result, most proposals for such constitutional amendments never emerge from Congress.

The more frequent way of reversing the Supreme Court

is for Congress to repass the offending statute after modifying it to meet the court's objections. This kind of reversal though simple legislation is easily accomplished if the court has interpreted a statute contrary to the construction intended by Congress. The House and Senate may then pass new legislation explicitly setting forth their intention. In many cases of this type, the court in its opinion will suggest the course the legislation should take to achieve its original purpose.

Reversal is not so easily accomplished when the court and Congress are at politically philosophical odds. Twice Congress passed legislation to end child labor, for example, and twice the Supreme Court ruled that such legislation was not within Congress' power to enact. That its interpretation was based on philosophical differences rather than purely constitutional considerations was evident when the court reversed these two decisions several years later. In the mid-1930s it appeared that a similar confrontation would develop over New Deal legislation, but the court's reexamination of its position on congressional authority to regulate economic matters eased the crisis.

In several instances in recent years, Congress has passed reversal legislation that has had little real effect because Congress has not had comprehensive jurisdiction over the subject in question. In 1968, for example, Congress passed additions to an anti-crime bill overturning several court rulings on the admissibility into evidence of criminal confessions. However, the legislation affected only federal courts, which hear a very small fraction of all criminal cases; procedures for confessions in state courts were left untouched.

Whether such limited reversals have an indirect effect by warning the court that it may be reaching politically unacceptable limits probably depends on a multitude of factors, including the nature of the issue involved, the strength of the congressional opposition, the position of the president and the public consensus.

Constitutional Amendments

Congress and the states have allied on four occasions to overturn Supreme Court decisions through constitutional amendments. Several other proposed amendments to nullify unpopular high court rulings have been offered but have not been approved either by the requisite two-thirds majority of both the House and Senate or by three-fourths of the states.

States Rights

The 11th Amendment, ratified in 1795, was the first amendment adopted to negate a Supreme Court decision; it is the only constitutional amendment that actually removed part of the jurisdiction of the federal courts. The other three only overturned specific rulings of the court.

Article III, Section 2 of the Constitution gave to the Supreme Court jurisdiction over cases arising between a state and citizens of another state or of a foreign country. During the writing of the Constitution opponents of a strong central government opposed this grant, claiming that it would jeopardize the sovereignty of the individual states. But these fears were successfully allayed when proponents of the grant argued that it would only permit suits where the state was the plaintiff. As historian Charles Warren explained:

> . . .The right of the Federal Judiciary to summon a State as defendant and to adjudicate its rights and liabilities had been the subject of deep apprehension and of active debate at the time of the adoption of the Constitution; but the existence of any such right had been disclaimed by many of the most eminent advocates of the new Federal Government, and it was largely owing to their successful dissipation of the fear of the existence of such Federal power that the Constitution was finally adopted. [1]

But the Federalist assurances proved empty promises. The first case brought to the Supreme Court in the February 1791 term was a suit by Dutch bankers against the state of Maryland. [2] And the case that would lead directly to adoption of the 11th Amendment was brought to the court in the August 1792 term.

A South Carolinian named Chisholm, acting as executor for a British creditor, sued the state of Georgia for property confiscated from an Englishman. Chisholm had as his attorney Edmund Randolph, who despite his position as the first U.S. attorney general continued his private law practice.

The court postponed arguments in the case of *Chisholm v. Georgia* until February 1793. When the time came, Georgia officials refused to appear before the court, claiming that the federal judiciary had no jurisdiction over the case. Randolph made his case in behalf of Chisholm, and when he was finished the justices asked if anyone in the court would like to respond. No one did. The court announced its decision Feb. 18, 1793, upholding the right of citizens of one state to sue in federal court another state for breach of contract. [3] *(Details of decision, pp. 303-304)*

The decision, according to Warren, "fell upon the country with a profound shock." [4] Anti-Federalists argued that the decision compromised the sovereignty of the states and made them nothing more than corporations. But the real fear was that the decision would lead to a proliferation of citizen suits against the states that would further jeopardize their already precarious financial plights. Warren wrote:

> . . .In the crucial condition of the finance of most of the States at that time, only disaster was to be expected if suits could be successfully maintained by holders of State issues of paper and other credits, or by Loyalist refugees to recover property confiscated or sequestered by the States; and that this was no theoretical danger was shown by the immediate institution of such suits against the States in South Carolina, Georgia, Virginia and Massachusetts. [5]

Amendment Proposed. The day after the *Chisholm* decision was announced, a resolution proposing a constitutional amendment to bar citizen suits against states was offered in the House. A similar resolution proposed in the Senate was tabled Feb. 25. That resolution was reintroduced in the Senate Jan. 2, 1794, and passed 12 days later by a 23-2 vote. The House approved it March 4, 1794, by an 81-9 vote.

Three-fourths of the states approved the amendment in less than a year, but almost four years passed before its ratification was officially recognized. Then President John Adams sent a message to Congress Jan. 8, 1798, stating that three-fourths of the states having acted, the amendment "may now be deemed to be a part of the Constitution."

The Supreme Court acquiesced in the amendment in February 1798 when it dismissed the case of *Hollingsworth v. Virginia,* in which shareholders of a company sued for losses resulting from Virginia's nullification of the company's title to land in the state. The court said that ratification of the 11th Amendment had removed its jurisdiction "in any case, past or future, in which a State was sued by citizens of another State, or by citizens or subjects of any foreign States." [6] Later interpretations of this amendment, however, have narrowed the protection it provides the states. *(Details, p. 354)*

Citizenship and Civil Rights

After the surrender of the Confederacy in 1865, one of Congress' first actions was adoption of the 13th Amendment abolishing slavery. The states ratified the amendment late in 1865, but expectations that it would compel the rebel states to protect the civil rights of former black slaves went unfulfilled as the South adopted black codes and continued its oppressive treatment of the former slaves.

Congress responded by enacting federal laws to give blacks some measure of protection, but because the constitutionality of one of the most important of these laws — the

Civil Rights Act of 1866 — was in doubt, the legislature looked to enactment of a constitutional amendment to force the South to give blacks their civil rights.

A specially created Joint Committee on Reconstruction drafted the 14th Amendment in early 1866. Although the political attention of the day was focused on the amendment's second section, which unsuccessfully sought to ensure black voting rights, the first section of the amendment ultimately provided more protection to both blacks and whites.

As proposed by Rep. John A. Bingham, R-Ohio (1855-63, 1865-73), this section gave Congress power to make laws "to secure to the citizens of each state all privileges and immunities of citizens in the several states, and to all persons in the several states equal protection in the rights of life, liberty and property." [7] Bingham's intention was to undo the effect of the Supreme Court's ruling in the 1833 case of *Barron v. Baltimore,* which held that the first eight amendments to the Constitution protected individual rights only against infringement by the federal government and not by the states. [8]

As amended by the joint committee, passed by Congress and ratified by the states, the section did not give Congress a positive grant of power to guard against infringement by the states but simply prohibited the states from making any law that abridged the privileges and immunities of citizens of the United States; deprived any persons of life, liberty or property without due process of the law; or denied anyone equal protection of the laws.

Although the record indicates that Bingham expected this amended version to have the same effect as his initial proposal, several rulings by the Supreme Court in the 1870s and 1880s so narrowly construed the language of the first section that it afforded little of its intended protection to any citizens. It was not until 1925 that the court began to use the 14th Amendment to secure the guarantees of the Bill of Rights against state action, and it was the mid-1900s before the court began to extend equal protection of the laws to blacks. *(Details, pp. 388, 583)*

The first section of the 14th Amendment also overturned another Supreme Court ruling — the Dred Scott decision of 1857 — which held that blacks were not and could never become U.S. citizens. [9] The Senate added a single sentence to the language already approved by the House declaring that all persons born or naturalized in the United States and subject to its jurisdiction are citizens of the United States. Although the Dred Scott case was not mentioned during debate, it was clear that the Senate addition was intended to nullify that unfortunate court ruling. *(Details, Dred Scott case, p. 135)*

The debate shows that there was some opposition to the provision because it applied to Chinese and other then-unpopular ethnic groups. Nonetheless, it was approved by both the House and Senate and, upon ratification of the 14th Amendment in 1868, became the only definition of citizenship to appear in the Constitution.

Income Taxes

When the Supreme Court struck down a general federal income tax law in 1895 because it was not apportioned according to constitutional dictates, Chief Justice Melville W. Fuller invited Congress to overturn the court's ruling. "If it be true that the Constitution should have been so framed that a tax of this kind could be laid, the instrument defines the way for its amendment," Fuller wrote in *Pollock v. Farmers' Loan and Trust Co.* (1895). [10]

Article I, Section 9, clause 4 of the Constitution forbids Congress to levy any direct tax that is not apportioned by population. For the first 100 years of the nation's life, the court held that only per capita taxes and taxes on land were direct taxes. But in the 1895 income tax cases, the court held that taxes on income from real estate were also direct and must be levied proportionately among the states. *(Details, p. 109)*

The decision was highly unpopular with laborers and farmers who felt they were burdened with payment of disproportionately high amounts of indirect taxes, such as tariffs. With each election they returned to Congress more and more Democrats and progressive Republicans who favored enactment of an income tax. But nothing concrete happened until 1909. Then a two-year-long depression which had depleted government revenues and a Republican campaign promise to do something about the high tariffs made consideration of an income tax imperative.

When the Republican tariff bill was introduced, Democrats seized on it, offering an amendment almost identical to the income tax law that had been declared unconstitutional in 1895. Conservative Republicans opposed to the tax countered with a proposal for a constitutional amendment to permit an income tax without apportionment. For support they turned to President William Howard Taft, who favored an amendment over legislation. In a message to Congress he observed that simple re-enactment of the income tax law would undoubtedly encounter "protracted litigation" before it could take effect. He also suggested that congressional defiance of the court's rulings would "not strengthen public confidence in the stability of judicial construction of the Constitution." [11]

Conservative Republicans banked on the hope that even if the amendment were approved by Congress, not enough state legislatures would ratify it. Democrats and progressive Republicans largely agreed with this analysis but felt philosophically compelled to vote for the amendment anyway.

The amendment was submitted to the states in 1909. Contrary to all expectations, the requisite number of state legislatures ratified the amendment in less than four years and it became part of the Constitution Feb. 25, 1913. *(Details, p. 111)*

The Right to Vote

Adoption of the fourth amendment to overturn a Supreme Court decision occurred with the apparent cooperation of the court itself.

As one of the amendments to the Voting Rights Act of 1965 Congress enacted in 1970 a provision lowering the voting age for federal, state and local elections to 18 years. President Nixon objected to the provision even as he signed it into law in June 1970. He said he favored lowering the voting age but believed "along with most of the Nation's leading constitutional scholars — that Congress has no power to enact it by simple statute, but rather it requires a constitutional amendment." [12]

The Nixon administration quickly brought suit to test the validity of the legislative measure, and the Supreme Court cooperated by deciding the case just six months after the measure was signed into law. By a 5-4 vote, the court ruled in December 1970 that Congress had the authority to lower the voting age for federal elections but not for state and local elections. [13]

This decision created immense administrative difficulties for the 47 states that did not allow 18-year-olds to vote.

State election officials and legislators said the task of producing dual registration books, ballots and voting machines could not be completed in time for the 1972 elections. Amendments to state constitutions changing voting age requirements would have been difficult if not impossible for some states to approve before 1972.

To assist the states, an amendment to the Constitution to lower the voting age to 18 years in all elections was introduced in both houses of Congress early in 1971. The Senate approved the amendment unanimously March 10, 1971. The House adopted it by a 401-19 vote March 23. The states also acted in record time, ratifying the amendment July 1, 1971, just three months and seven days after it was submitted to them.

Child Labor Amendment

Although Congress adopted an amendment to overturn a pair of Supreme Court decisions on child labor, the amendment failed to win ratification by a sufficient number of states before the Supreme Court itself overruled its earlier decisions.

In 1916 Congress sought to discourage employment of children by enacting a law forbidding the shipment in interstate commerce of goods made by child laborers. The validity of the statute was challenged, and the Supreme Court declared it unconstitutional in *Hammer v. Dagenhart* (1918). [14] In passing the statute, the court said, Congress was attempting to regulate not interstate commerce but labor, which was a matter reserved to the states for regulation under the 10th Amendment. *(Details, p. 96)*

Congress retaliated to this holding in February 1919, enacting a second child labor law which placed a tax of 10 percent on the net profits of any company employing children. But the court declared this statute unconstitutional too, in *Bailey v. Drexel Furniture Co.* (1922), ruling that the tax was intended not to raise revenue but to penalize employers.[15] *(Details, p. 114)*

Still unwilling to concede the fight to the court, Congress in June 1924 submitted to the states a constitutional amendment which would give Congress authority to outlaw child labor. By 1938, however, only 28 of the 48 states had ratified the amendment. In that year Congress again utilized its constitutional power to regulate interstate commerce and enacted a child labor law as part of the federal minimum wage statute. In 1941 the Supreme Court upheld the 1938 law in *United States v. Darby Lumber Co.*, specifically reversing its 1918 ruling in *Dagenhart*. Since then there have been no further ratifications of the still-pending amendment.[16] *(Details, Darby case, p. 101)*

Other Proposed Amendments

Numerous other proposed constitutional amendments to invalidate Supreme Court decisions have failed to win congressional approval. Three of them, proposed in recent years, were intended to overrule the court's controversial reapportionment, school prayer and busing decisions.

Reapportionment. A revolution in the apportionment of state legislatures was precipitated by the Supreme Court in 1962 when it held in *Baker v. Carr* that the judiciary could entertain suits challenging malapportionment. The decision overturned a line of legal precedent holding that the makeup of state legislatures was not a justiciable matter, but was political in nature, and that citizens had no standing to sue to effect a change.[17]

That decision did not generate much congressional opposition, but in 1964 the court in *Reynolds v. Sims* applied its "one-person, one-vote" rule to state legislatures, holding that both chambers must be apportioned on a basis of substantial equality of population.[18] The decision struck not only at malapportioned state legislatures but also at those apportioned — sometimes by terms of the state constitution — on the basis of one state senator for each city, town and county, regardless of population. *(Details of decisions, p. 492)*

The decision was opposed by many rural organizations and state legislators whose strength in the state legislatures was bound to be undermined by the ruling. They lost no time in making their views known to Congress, which responded quickly but ineffectively to the court ruling. Within two months of the decision, the House passed a bill denying federal courts jurisdiction over state reapportionment; it died at the end of the session when the Senate failed to act. In the Senate a six-week filibuster by liberals stymied an attempt by Senate Minority Leader Everett McKinley Dirksen, R-Ill. (H-1933-49; S-1951-69), to require the court to delay reapportionment orders until January 1966. Dirksen said such a delay would give Congress time to consider a constitutional amendment overturning the court decision.

In 1965 and again in 1966 Dirksen tried to secure Senate passage of a constitutional amendment that would allow states to apportion one chamber of their legislatures on the basis of factors other than population. In both years, although a majority of the Senate approved the proposal, Dirksen's effort fell seven votes short of the two-thirds needed for approval of a constitutional amendment.

Discouraged by failure to win Senate approval, advocates of the constitutional amendment turned to the state legislatures themselves. By 1969, 33 states — one short of the two-thirds necessary — had submitted petitions to Congress calling for a constitutional convention to propose a reapportionment amendment. No further action had occurred as of mid-1979.

School Prayer. At about the same time it was causing havoc with the state legislatures, the Supreme Court created additional public controversy by ruling in 1962 and again in 1963 that the First Amendment's prohibition against establishment of religion barred officially prescribed or supported religious observances in public schools.[19] *(Details of decisions, pp. 463-466)*

Although most major religious organizations were opposed to any constitutional amendments overriding these decisions, mail advocating such an amendment flooded into congressional offices. The House Judiciary Committee reluctantly held hearings on proposed amendments in 1964 but took no further action. In the Senate, Minority Leader Dirksen offered a proposed amendment in 1966, but the Senate failed by nine votes to approve it by the necessary two-thirds majority.

Little more happened on the proposals until 1971, when an intense two-year grass-roots campaign succeeded in dislodging a school prayer amendment from the House Judiciary Committee. But this effort too was unsuccessful when less than two-thirds of the House members voting failed to approve the amendment. *(Details, box, p. 465)*

School Busing. In 1979 supporters of an amendment to ban school busing for desegregation purposes also managed to bypass the House Judiciary Committee but ultimately failed when the House July 24 rejected the amendment, 209-216.

Legislative Reversals

A speedier and frequently more successful method than the constitutional amendment for reversing Supreme Court decisions is congressional reversal or modification by legislative enactment.

The court generally acquiesces in such legislative overrides. Its opinions often actually suggest that Congress reenact the measure in question after tailoring it to remove the court's objections to its validity.

The justices do not always bow to congressional efforts to void court decisions by legislation, however. After the court declared unconstitutional the 1916 child labor law, which barred shipment in interstate commerce of goods made by children, Congress passed a second measure placing a prohibitively high tax on profits of such goods. The court declared this law invalid too. Congress then approved a constitutional amendment forbidding child labor but fewer than the necessary two-thirds of the states ratified it before the Supreme Court itself reversed its earlier holdings. *(Details, pp. 96, 101)*

Early Examples

According to historian Charles Warren, Congress first reversed the Supreme Court by legislation in 1852. In *Pennsylvania v. Wheeling and Belmont Bridge Co.* (1852), the court ruled that because a bridge built across the Ohio River obstructed interstate commerce and violated a congressionally-sanctioned compact between Kentucky and Virginia, it must either be raised so that ships could pass under it or be taken down.

Congress immediately passed a law reversing this decision by declaring that the bridge did not obstruct interstate commerce and requiring instead that ships be refitted so that they could pass under the bridge. In 1856 the court sustained this legislative reversal.[20] *(Details, p. 85)*

Congressional reversal by legislation occurred again after the court held in 1890 that in the absence of congressional authorization, liquor in its original container imported into a state through interstate commerce was not subject to state prohibition laws. Accepting the court's implicit invitation, Congress later in the year permitted the states to prohibit such shipments of liquor, and the court upheld that statute in 1891.[21]

ICC. In another early example, changing court personnel and shifting attitudes of sitting justices apparently combined to uphold congressional modification of the court's rulings on the powers of the Interstate Commerce Commission (ICC). Congress in 1887 had created the ICC, the first federal regulatory agency, to provide uniform regulation of interstate railroad rates and to end unethical rebate and price-fixing practices. The Supreme Court in 1894 sustained the authority of Congress to create the agency. But in a series of cases decided in the next three years the court, which was dominated by men opposed to any governmental regulation impinging on the free development of business and industry, stripped the agency of all of its essential regulatory powers. The most damaging ruling held that the ICC had no rate-making powers and implied that Congress could not constitutionally delegate such powers to it.[22]

The decisions led to a resumption of all the unsavory practices that prompted the need to create such an agency in the first place. In the face of growing demands for reform from the public — and even from some of the railroad companies — Congress decided to confront the court. In 1906 it enacted the Hepburn Act, which specifically authorized the commission to adjust rates it judged to be unreasonable and unfair.

The court upheld that grant of power in 1910. Encouraged, Congress then gave the ICC authority to set original rates. Several railroads challenged this statute as an unconstitutional delegation of power, but the court in 1914 said that contention was "without merit," thus completely reversing its earlier decisions.[23] *(Details, p. 87)*

Civil Rights

In one area, more than 80 years passed between a Supreme Court decision and its reversal by legislation. In 1883 the court held unconstitutional the Civil Rights Act of 1875, which made it a misdemeanor for any individual to discriminate against another individual on account of race in the use of public accommodations, transportation or public entertainment. The court specifically ruled that Congress had exceeded its power under the 13th and 14th Amendments when it enacted the statute. [24]

Not until passage of the 1964 Civil Rights Act did Congress reverse the 1883 ruling. In that statute, Congress used its authority to regulate interstate commerce to bar racial discrimination in public accommodations that serve interstate travelers or that sell goods or provide entertainment, a substantial portion of which moves through interstate commerce.

Six months after this statute was signed into law, the court unanimously sustained its constitutionality.[25] *(Details, p. 611)*

Unions and Antitrust

One particularly prolonged and hostile confrontation between the court and Congress centered on whether labor unions were exempt from federal antitrust law. The 1894 statute making combinations in restraint of trade illegal was silent on the question of labor unions, and in 1908 the court ruled that certain union practices, including the boycott, were illegal restraints of trade punishable under the antitrust law. [26]

That decision impelled Congress to add provisions to the Clayton Act of 1914 that specifically exempted from the reach of the antitrust law labor unions pursuing lawful objectives.

The Clayton Act also stipulated that federal courts could not issue injunctions in any labor disputes unless necessary to prevent irreparable property damage.

Seven years later the Supreme Court subverted the intent of the Clayton Act. In a 1921 decision it interpreted the anti-injunction language so narrowly that injunctions against striking workers became almost commonplace. The court also held that, the Clayton Act notwithstanding, certain union practices illegally interfered with commerce and still fell afoul of the antitrust law. [27]

Congress made the next move, enacting the Norris-LaGuardia Act in 1932 to reverse the court's 1921 decision and restore the vitality of the Clayton Act's provisions. A challenge to the 1932 statute did not reach the court until 1938, a year after the majority conceded that Congress as part of its authority to regulate interstate commerce had broad powers to regulate labor relations. Then, in a pair of cases, the court upheld the constitutionality of the Norris-LaGuardia Act, ruling that Congress had clearly passed it to "obviate the results of the judicial construction" of the Clayton Act. [28]

New Deal Legislation

The New Deal period saw Congress overturn the court on more important measures than in any other period in the country's history. At President Franklin D. Roosevelt's instigation, Congress in the early and mid-1930s enacted several statutes aimed at ending the Great Depression and restoring the nation's economic well-being. Of eight major statutes, the Supreme Court upheld only two — an act establishing the Tennessee Valley Authority and legislation abolishing gold clauses in public and private contracts.

At first frustrated by the economically conservative court majority's unwillingness to sustain most of the New Deal programs and then encouraged by the court's apparent economic liberalization in 1937, Congress revised five of the six laws the court had declared invalid. The court subsequently sustained all of the modified versions that were challenged. In lieu of the National Industrial Recovery Act, Congress enacted the National Labor Relations Act, which the court also sustained.

The six original statutes, the cases striking them down, the revised laws and the cases sustaining their validity were:

● National Industrial Recovery Act of 1933, struck down in *Panama Refining Co. v. Ryan* (1935) and *Schechter Poultry Co. v. United States* (1935), replaced by the National Labor Relations Act of 1935, upheld in *National Labor Relations Board v. Jones & Laughlin Steel Corp.* (1937). [29]

● Railroad Retirement Pension Act of 1934, struck down in *Railroad Retirement Board v. Alton* (1935), replaced by railroad retirement acts adopted in 1935, 1937 and 1938, which were never challenged before the Supreme Court. [30]

● Frazier-Lemke Farm Mortgage Act of 1934, struck down in *Louisville Joint Stock Land Bank v. Radford* (1935), modified by Frazier-Lemke Act of 1935, upheld in *Wright v. Vinson Branch* (1937). [31]

● Agricultural Adjustment Act of 1933, struck down in *United States v. Butler* (1936), modified in Agricultural Adjustment Act of 1937, upheld in *Mulford v. Smith* (1939). [32]

● Bituminous Coal Conservation Act of 1935, struck down by *Carter v. Carter Coal Co.* (1936), modified in Bituminous Coal Act of 1937, upheld in *Sunshine Anthracite Coal Co. v. Adkins* (1940). [33]

● Municipal Bankruptcy Act of 1934, struck down in *Ashton v. Cameron County District* (1936), modified in Municipal Bankruptcy Act of 1937, upheld in *United States v. Bekins* (1938). [34]

Insurance Regulation

Congress has used its power to reverse the court to rid itself of regulatory functions it has not wanted. In 1944, for example, the Supreme Court issued a ruling which gave Congress control over insurance, a matter that traditionally had been regulated by the states even though transactions were often conducted through interstate commerce. [35] Congress wanted no part of this new responsibility and in 1945 passed a law returning the authority to regulate insurance to the states. The court upheld this delegation of control in 1946. [36]

Tidelands Oil

Congress in one instance successfully overruled both the court and a president. In the 1947 case of *United States v. California*, the Supreme Court ruled that the federal

government, not the states, owned the three-mile strip of oil-rich submerged land adjacent to the ocean shores. Legislation to reverse this ruling was introduced in 1948, 1949 and 1950 but was not approved. After the court reaffirmed its 1947 ruling in two 1950 cases affecting Louisiana and Texas, Congress in 1951 passed a law giving ownership of the tidelands to the states. [37] President Truman, whose administration had brought the 1947 suit claiming federal ownership, vetoed it.

No attempt was made to override the veto, but the question of who was to control the submerged lands became a major campaign issue in the 1952 presidential elections, with Republicans promising to restore the lands and their oil deposits to the states. The Republicans won the election, and Congress in 1953 enacted the Submerged Lands Act ceding to the states the mineral rights to lands lying offshore between the low tide mark and the states' historic boundaries. The Supreme Court upheld this cession in 1954. [38]

Recent Reversals

Two of the most recent congressional reversals of Supreme Court decisions concerned pregnant women and small fish. Congress in 1978 required employers to include benefits for pregnancy, childbirth and related medical conditions in their health insurance and temporary disability plans. This measure overturned a 1976 court ruling that pregnancy did not have to be covered by such plans. [39]

In another 1978 statute Congress modified the Endangered Species Act of 1973 to reverse the court's 1978 ruling that a TVA dam could not be put into operation because it would destroy the only habitat of a tiny fish called the snail darter. [40] The modification authorized a special Cabinet-level board to decide whether to allow operation of federally funded public works projects even if they threatened the existence of an endangered species.

Congress was less receptive to proposals to reverse the controversial court decisions upholding abortion and forced school busing to overcome racial segregation. Unable to overturn the court's 1973 decision forbidding states to deny abortions, Congress since 1975 has prohibited federal funds from being used to pay for abortions except under certain circumstances. The legislation, however, primarily affects poor women receiving Medicaid payments; privately funded abortions are not touched by the measure.

Since 1975 Congress also has approved language to prohibit the Department of Health, Education and Welfare from requiring busing of any student beyond the school closest to his home that offers the course of study sought by the student. The legislation had no effect on federal courts which order most of the busing undertaken to alleviate racial segregation in schools.

Criminals and Confessions

Congressional modification of several Supreme Court decisions in the 1950s and 1960s setting procedures for procuring and placing into evidence confessions from suspected criminals also had little direct effect on those decisions. The procedures were designed to protect the rights of alleged criminals and were loudly criticized by citizens and law enforcement officers who said they coddled the criminal at the expense of the innocent public. Responding to this outcry, Congress tried for 10 years to reverse one of the earliest of these rulings but to no avail. Then, in 1968, rising crime rates, urban riots and the

Congress and the Supreme Court's Workload

Almost since the beginning of the court's history, justices have complained that the workload is too heavy and that Congress should act to ease the burden.

The first major complaint centered on the justices' circuit-riding duties. After a century of urging, Congress eventually removed these, but by then the number of appeals that the Supreme Court was required by law to hear had swollen to almost unmanageable proportions. Congress finally gave the court more discretion to choose the cases it reviews on the merits, but several categories of cases still require mandatory review. And in the last two decades, Congress has substantially contributed to the court's workload by enacting several laws that require federal judicial review.

Circuit Court Duties

In addition to establishing the size and jurisdiction of the Supreme Court, the Judiciary Act of 1789 required Supreme Court justices to "ride circuit." Under the terms of the act, two justices sat with one district court judge at circuit courts in each of three circuits. In 1792 the six Supreme Court justices were required to attend a total of 27 circuit courts a year in addition to two sessions of the Supreme Court. (Details, circuit riding, box p. 754; text, 1789 judiciary act, p. 949)

As the country expanded westward, circuit riding duties grew steadily more burdensome — one justice reported that he travelled 10,000 miles in 1838 to fulfill his circuit court responsibilities.[1] But Congress refused to do much more than tinker with the federal court system until 1891, when it finally established a separate system of circuit courts of appeals. Even then the appeals courts were to be composed of one justice and two circuit judges, although the law allowed a district judge to sit in place of the justice.

This exception soon became the rule, and in 1911 Congress finally relieved Supreme Court justices of all circuit court duties.

Mandatory Jurisdiction

The Supreme Court's caseload began to increase dramatically after the Civil War. Factors involved in this increase included a rise in the number of diversity cases (cases involving citizens of different states), suits stemming from Reconstruction legislation and congressional enlargement of the court's jurisdiction.

In 1914 Congress began to ease this caseload by increasing the kinds of cases the Supreme Court could review at its own discretion by writ of certiorari. At about the same time, it began to cut back on the categories of cases that the court was required to review. This shift from largely mandatory to primarily discretionary judicial review culminated in the Judiciary Act of 1925, the last major reform of the court's jurisdiction. The act's revisions increased the court's jurisdiction and expanded considerably the number of cases appealed to the court but reduced considerably the percentage of cases the court was required to review on the merits. In its 1923 term, 39 percent of the cases filed required review by the court. In the 1930 term, that proportion had fallen to 15 percent.[2] (Text, 1925 act, p. 960)

The solution was only temporary. By 1976 less than 10 percent of the cases brought to the Supreme Court fell under its mandatory jurisdiction. However, these cases comprised slightly less than half of all cases argued and decided with full opinions that year.[3] Recommendations to abolish the remaining categories of cases that the court was obliged to review were being considered in Congress in mid-1979.

Legislated Burdens

Congress has created much of the modern explosion in the federal court workload through adoption of legislation that places new burdens on those courts. The Speedy Trial Act of 1974, for example, required that by 1980 all federal criminal defendants be tried within 180 days of their arrest.

To alleviate some of the crush of this new work, Chief Justice Warren E. Burger in 1972 urged Congress to include a "court impact statement" with legislation. If every committee reporting a measure that would affect the federal courts included such an impact statement with the report, Burger says, Congress would then be aware of those consequences and might more readily provide the system more resources with which to deal with the judicial impact of new laws. (Details, other recommendations, box, p. 736)

Federal judges also contend that the workload could be relieved if Congress itself would make more of the difficult policy decisions in the course of enacting legislation, rather than passing these decisions on to administrators to make under judicial supervision. "The prevailing passion of Congress for judicial review is the central fact of life at the moment for federal judges at all levels of the system," wrote Justice Carl McGowan of the Court of Appeals for the District of Columbia Circuit late in 1976.[4]

Congress has yet to pay significant attention to this viewpoint. Among recent laws which have added new categories of cases to the federal court load are the National Environmental Policy Act of 1969, the 1970 Clean Air Amendments, the 1970 Occupational Health and Safety Act, the 1972 Black Lung Benefits Act, the Consumer Product Safety Act of 1972, the Employee Retirement Income Security Act of 1974 and the Tax Reform Act of 1976.

[1] Felix Frankfurter and James M. Landis, The Business of the Supreme Court; A Study in the Federal Judicial System (New York: Macmillan Publishing Co., 1928), p. 49.

[2] Gerhard Casper and Richard A. Posner, The Workload of the Supreme Court (Chicago: American Bar Foundation, 1976), p. 20.

[3] U.S., Congress, Senate, The Supreme Court Jurisdiction Act of 1979, S. Rept 96-35 to Accompany S 450, 96th Cong., 1st Sess., 1979, p. 6.

[4] Quoted in Congressional Quarterly, "Judicial Workload: The Courtroom Explosion," The Supreme Court: Justice and the Law, 2d ed. (Washington, D.C.: Congressional Quarterly, 1977), p. 130.

assassinations of civil rights leader Martin Luther King Jr. and presidential candidate Robert F. Kennedy supplied the impetus needed, and Congress, over the objections of the president, enacted legislation to modify some of these decisions. However, the legislation affected only federal courts, in which only about 7 percent of all criminal cases are heard; the vast majority come to state courts.

The Mallory Decision. In 1943 the court in *McNabb v. United States* ruled that a confession obtained by police during an "unnecessary delay" in a suspect's arraignment could not be used as evidence in federal court, even if the confession had been given voluntarily.[41] Critics immediately claimed that the *McNabb* ruling would retard federal law enforcement, and shortly after the decision was made a bill restricting its effect was approved by the House. It died in the Senate. Similar bills introduced in the next two Congresses also languished.

Then in 1957 the Supreme Court sparked new opposition when it reaffirmed the *McNabb* decision and overturned the rape conviction of Andrew Mallory.[42] District of Columbia police had arrested Mallory and questioned him for several hours before he confessed. No attempt was made to bring official charges against him during this period although arraigning magistrates were available in the same building throughout the time Mallory was being questioned. There was no evidence that police coerced Mallory into making an involuntary confession. The Supreme Court nonetheless held that because police had not complied with the *McNabb* doctrine and the Federal Rules of Criminal Procedure which require prompt arraignment, Mallory had been detained illegally and his confession was therefore inadmissible as evidence. *(Details, p. 559)*

Congressional Reaction. Reaction to the *Mallory* decision was immediate and widespread. To many members of Congress the decision was yet another indication that the Supreme Court under the guidance of Chief Justice Earl Warren was out of step with society and overreaching its judicial bounds. A subcommittee of the House Judiciary Committee created specifically to examine controversial decisions of the Warren Court began hearings on proposals to reverse the *Mallory* decision less than a month after it was handed down, and the House in July 1958 passed "corrective" legislation by an overwhelming vote of 294-79. The House measure barred federal courts from disqualifying confessions otherwise admissible as evidence in criminal cases solely because of delay in arraigning the suspect.

The Senate passed the bill after amending it to permit federal courts to throw out confessions obtained during unreasonable delays in arraignment. The House-Senate conference committee struck a compromise, which stated that a reasonable delay in arraignment would not disqualify a confession "provided that such delay is to be considered as an element in determining the voluntary or involuntary nature of such confessions and statements."

The House approved the compromise language easily, but in the Senate an opponent of the bill raised a point of order that conferees had inserted new matter into a conference report in violation of Senate Rule 27. Vice President Richard M. Nixon, who would be elected president on a law-and-order platform in 1968, was presiding. He sustained the point of order and the legislation was killed.

In 1959 the House again passed its version of the *Mallory* reversal legislation, but the Senate took no action and the issue cooled during the early 1960s.

Miranda and Wade Decisions. Then the court handed down two more decisions that again prompted

Congress to act. In the 1966 case of *Miranda v. Arizona* the court set out a new rule for police to follow in interrogating suspects. Under the so-called "Miranda rights" rule, confessions were inadmissible as evidence in state or federal criminal trials if the accused had not been informed of his right to remain silent, if he had not been warned that any statement he made might be used against him and if he had not been informed of his right to have an attorney present during the police interrogation.[43] *(Details, p. 560)*

A 1967 decision also contributed to charges that the court was "soft" on criminals. In *United States v. Wade* the court held that identification of a defendant based solely on a police lineup staged when the defendant's attorney was not present was inadmissible. The majority said such a procedure violated the defendant's Sixth Amendment right to counsel.[44] *(Details, p. 568)*

These decisions brought an outpouring of public sentiment to the president and Congress to reverse the court. In 1967 President Johnson proposed a crime control act to provide federal financial assistance to local law enforcement agencies. The House passed an amended version of the legislation and sent it to the Senate, where the Judiciary Subcommittee on Criminal Laws and Procedures added several provisions to modify the controversial Supreme Court decisions and to limit the court's jurisdiction to review such cases in the future.

The Johnson administration opposed the subcommittee amendments, and when the bill reached the Senate floor in May 1968, liberals succeeded in deleting the provisions limiting the court's jurisdiction. They were unable, however, to defeat the amendments designed to modify the *Miranda, Mallory* and *Wade* decisions. As passed by the Senate, these sections:

● Modified the *Miranda* decision by making confessions admissible in evidence if voluntarily given. The trial judge would determine any question of voluntariness by taking into consideration the circumstances surrounding the act of confessing. The circumstances were to include the time between arrest and arraignment if the confession were given after arrest but before arraignment; whether the defendant knew the nature of the offense with which he was charged or of which he was suspected; whether he had been advised or knew that he was not required to make any statement and that such statement could be used against him; whether he had been advised prior to questioning of his right to counsel; and whether he was without the assistance of counsel when questioned and when giving the confession. No single factor need be conclusive on the issue of voluntariness.

● Modified the *Mallory* decision to provide that a confession made by a person in custody of law officers was not to be inadmissible as evidence solely because of delay in arraigning the defendant if the confession were found to be voluntary, if the weight to be given the confession were left to jury determination and if the confession were given within six hours immediately following arrest. The measure also provided that confessions given after six hours without arraignment might be admissible if the trial judge found the further delay to be reasonable.

● Modified the *Wade* decision to provide that the testimony of an eyewitness that he saw the accused commit the crime for which he was being tried was to be admissible in evidence in any federal criminal trial.

The amended Senate bill came to the House floor just hours after an assassin shot presidential candidate Robert F. Kennedy in a Los Angeles hotel kitchen. Although opponents of the Senate amendments moved to send the bill to a House-Senate conference where they hoped the provisions could be deleted, the House was anxious to approve crime-control legislation and the motion was

rejected on a 60-318 vote. The House then adopted the Senate version of the bill unchanged.

Although he opposed the criminal procedures modifications provisions, President Johnson signed the bill.

Footnotes

[1] Charles Warren, *The Supreme Court in United States History,* rev. ed., 2 vols. (Boston: Little, Brown & Co., 1922, 1926), I:91.

[2] *Vanstophorst v. Maryland.* No report of this case was made in the February, 1791 term; see Warren, *Supreme Court in U.S. History,* I:91.

[3] *Chisholm v. Georgia,* 2 Dall. 419 (1793).

[4] Warren, *Supreme Court in History,* I:96.

[5] Ibid., p. 99.

[6] *Hollingsworth v. Virginia,* 3 Dall. 378 at 381 (1798).

[7] Carl Brent Swisher, *American Constitutional Development,* 2d ed. (Cambridge: Houghton Mifflin Co., The Riverside Press, 1954), p. 331.

[8] *Barron v. Baltimore,* 7 Pet. 243 (1833).

[9] *Scott v. Sandford,* 19 How. 393 (1857).

[10] *Pollock v. Farmers' Loan and Trust Co.,* 158 U.S. 601 at 635 (1895).

[11] Alfred H. Kelly and Winfred A. Harbison, *The American Constitution; Its Origins and Development,* 5th ed. (New York: W. W. Norton & Co., 1976), p. 586.

[12] Richard M. Nixon, *Public Papers of the Presidents of the United States, 1970* (Washington, D.C.: U.S. Government Printing Office, 1971), p. 521.

[13] *Oregon v. Mitchell,* 400 U.S. 112 (1970).

[14] *Hammer v. Dagenhart,* 247 U.S. 251 (1918).

[15] *Bailey v. Drexel Furniture Co.,* 259 U.S. 20 (1922).

[16] *United States v. Darby Lumber Co.,* 312 U.S. 100 (1941).

[17] *Baker v. Carr,* 369 U.S. 186 (1962).

[18] *Reynolds v. Sims,* 377 U.S. 533 (1964).

[19] *Engel v. Vitale,* 370 U.S. 421 (1962); *School District of Abington Township v. Schempp,* 374 U.S. 203 (1963).

[20] *Pennsylvania v. Wheeling and Belmont Bridge Co.,* 13 How. 518 (1852); 18 How. 421 (1856).

[21] *Leisy v. Hardin,* 135 U.S. 100 (1890); *In re Rahrer,* 140 U.S. 545 (1891).

[22] *Interstate Commerce Commission v. Brimson,* 154 U.S. 447 (1894); *Interstate Commerce Commission v. Cincinnati, New Orleans & Texas Pacific Railway Co.,* 167 U.S. 479 (1897); *Interstate Commerce Commission v. Alabama-Midland Railway Co.,* 168 U.S. 144 (1897).

[23] *Interstate Commerce Commission v. Chicago, Rock Island and Pacific Railway Co.,* 218 U.S. 88 (1910); *United States v. Atchison, Topeka and Santa Fe Railroad Co.,* 234 U.S. 476 at 486 (1914).

[24] *Civil Rights Cases,* 109 U.S. 3 (1883).

[25] *Heart of Atlanta Motel v. United States,* 379 U.S. 241 (1964).

[26] *Loewe v. Lawlor (The Danbury Hatters Case),* 208 U.S. 274 (1908).

[27] *Duplex Printing Press Co. v. Deering,* 254 U.S. 443 (1921).

[28] *Lauf v. E. G. Shinner & Co.,* 303 U.S. 315 (1938); *New Negro Alliance v. Sanitary Grocery Co.,* 303 U.S. 552 (1938).

[29] *Panama Refining Co. v. Ryan,* 293 U.S. 388 (1935); *Schechter Poultry Co. v. United States,* 295 U.S. 495 (1935); *National Labor Relations Board v. Jones & Laughlin Steel Corp.,* 301 U.S. 1 (1937).

[30] *Railroad Retirement Board v. Alton,* 295 U.S. 330 (1935).

[31] *Louisville Joint Stock Land Bank v. Radford,* 295 U.S. 555 (1935); *Wright v. Vinton Branch,* 300 U.S. 440 (1937).

[32] *United States v. Butler,* 297 U.S. 1 (1936); *Mulford v. Smith,* 307 U.S. 38 (1939).

[33] *Carter v. Carter Coal Co.,* 298 U.S. 238 (1936); *Sunshine Anthracite Coal Co. v. Adkins,* 310 U.S. 381 (1940).

[34] *Ashton v. Cameron County District,* 298 U.S. 512 (1936); *United States v. Bekins,* 304 U.S. 27 (1938).

[35] *United States v. South-Eastern Underwriters Assn.,* 322 U.S. 533 (1944).

[36] *Prudential Insurance Co. v. Benjamin,* 328 U.S. 408 (1946).

[37] *United States v. California,* 332 U.S. 19 (1947); *United States v. Louisiana,* 339 U.S. 699 (1950); *United States v. Texas,* 339 U.S. 707 (1950).

[38] *Alabama v. Texas,* 347 U.S. 272 (1954); see also *United States v. Louisiana,* 363 U.S. 1 (1960).

[39] *General Electric Co. v. Gilbert,* 429 U.S. 125 (1976).

[40] *Tennessee Valley Authority v. Hill,* 437 U.S. 153 (1978).

[41] *McNabb v. United States,* 318 U.S. 332 (1943).

[42] *Mallory v. United States,* 354 U.S. 449 (1957); major sources for material included in this section were Congressional Quarterly, *CQ Almanac,* Vols. 14, 15, 24 (Washington, D.C.: Congressional Quarterly, 1958, 1959, 1968).

[43] *Miranda v. Arizona,* 384 U.S. 436 (1966).

[44] *United States v. Wade,* 388 U.S. 218 (1967).

Selected Bibliography

Abraham, Henry J. *Justices and Presidents: A Political History of Appointments to the Supreme Court.* New York: Oxford University Press, 1974.

Baker, Leonard. *Back to Back: The Duel Between FDR and The Supreme Court.* New York: Macmillan Publishing Co., 1967.

————. *John Marshall: A Life in Law.* New York: Macmillan Publishing Co., 1974.

Beveridge, Albert J. *The Life of John Marshall.* 4 vols. Cambridge: Houghton Mifflin Co., The Riverside Press, 1919.

Black, Charles L. Jr. *Perspectives in Constitutional Law.* Englewood Cliffs, N.J.: Prentice-Hall, 1973.

Brant, Irving. "Appellate Jurisdiction: Congressional Abuse of the Exceptions Clause." 53 *Oregon Law Review* 3 (Fall 1973).

————. *Impeachment: Trials and Errors.* New York: Alfred A. Knopf, 1972.

Casper, Gerhard and Posner, Richard A. *The Workload of the Supreme Court.* Chicago: American Bar Foundation, 1976.

Choper, J. H. "Supreme Court and the Political Branches: Democratic Theory and Practice." 122 *University of Pennsylvania Law Review* 810 (April 1974).

"Congress vs. Court: The Legislative Arsenal." 10 *Villanova Law Review* 347 (Winter 1965).

Curtis, Charles P. Jr. *Lions Under the Throne.* Cambridge: Houghton Mifflin Co., The Riverside Press, 1947.

Elliott, Shelden D. "Court Curbing Proposals in Congress." 33 *Notre Dame Lawyer* 597 (August 1958).

Fite, Katherine B. and Rubinstein, Louis Baruch. "Curbing the Supreme Court — State Experiences and Federal Proposals." 35 *Michigan Law Review* 762 (March 1937).

Frankfurter, Felix and Landis, James M. *The Business of The Supreme Court: A Study in the Federal Judicial System.* New York: Macmillan Publishing Co., 1928.

Freund, Paul A., gen. ed. *History of the Supreme Court of the United States.* New York: Macmillan Publishing Co., 1971, 1974, 1971. Vol. 1: *Antecedents and Beginnings to 1801,* by Julius Goebel Jr.; Vol. V: *The Taney Period, 1836-1864,* by Carl B. Swisher; Vol. VI: *Reconstruction and Reunion, 1864-1888, Part One,* by Charles Fairman.

Hart, Henry M. Jr. "The Power of Congress to Limit the Jurisdiction of Federal Courts: An Exercise in Dialectic." 66 *Harvard Law Review* 1362 (June 1953).

Hughes, Charles Evans. *The Supreme Court of the United States: Its Foundations, Methods and Achievements, An Interpretation.* New York: Columbia University Press, 1928.

Jackson, Robert H. *The Struggle for Judicial Supremacy: A Study of a Crisis in American Power Politics.* New York: Random House, Vintage Books, 1941.

Kelly, Alfred H. and Harbison, Winfred A. *The American Constitution; Its Origins and Development,* 5th ed. New York: W. W. Norton & Co., 1976.

Kurland, Philip B. *Politics, the Constitution and the Warren Court.* Chicago: University of Chicago Press, 1970.

Marke, Julius J. *Vignettes of Legal History.* South Hackensack, N.J.: Fred B. Rothman & Co., 1965.

Martig, Ralph R. "Congress and the Appellate Jurisdiction of the Supreme Court." 34 *Michigan Law Review* 650 (March 1936).

Murphy, Walter F. *Congress and the Court: A Case Study in the American Political Process.* Chicago: University of Chicago Press, 1962.

Nagel, Stuart S. "Court-Curbing Periods in American History," 18 *The Vanderbilt Law Review* 925 (June 1965).

Pritchett, C. Herman. *Congress Versus the Supreme Court, 1957-60.* Minneapolis: University of Minnesota Press, 1961; reprint ed. New York: Da Capo Press, 1973.

Ratner, Leonard G. "Congressional Power over the Appellate Jurisdiction of the Supreme Court." 109 *University of Pennsylvania Law Review* 157 (December 1960).

Schmidhauser, John R. and Berg, Larry L. *The Supreme Court and Congress: Conflict and Interaction, 1945-1968.* New York: The Free Press, 1972.

Stumpf, Harry P. "Congressional Response to Supreme Court Rulings: The Interaction of Law and Politics." 14 *Journal of Public Law* 382 (1965).

Swindler, William F. *Court and Constitution in the Twentieth Century: The Old Legality, 1889-1932.* Indianapolis: Bobbs-Merrill Co., 1969.

_____. *Court and Constitution in the Twentieth Century: The New Legality, 1932-1968.* Indianapolis: Bobbs-Merrill Co., 1970.

Swisher, Carl Brent. *American Constitutional Development.* 2d ed. Cambridge: Houghton Mifflin Co., The Riverside Press, 1954.

Vose, Clement E. *Constitutional Change: Amendment Politics and Supreme Court Litigation Since 1900.* Lexington, Mass: D.C. Heath & Co., Lexington Books, 1972.

Warren, Charles. *Congress, the Constitution and the Supreme Court.* Boston: Little, Brown & Co., 1925.

_____. "Legislative and Judicial Attacks on the Supreme Court of the United States." 47 *American Law Review* 4 (January-February 1913).

_____. *The Supreme Court in United States History.* rev. ed. 2 vols. Boston: Little, Brown & Co., 1922, 1926.

Presidential Pressure

The major way in which a president exerts influence over the Supreme Court is through his power to select its members. And presidents throughout history have been well aware that the justices they select will shape public policy.

All presidents attempt to place on the court justices — usually from their own political party — whose views coincide with their own, an effort that has met with varying degrees of success. Presidents Jefferson, Jackson, Lincoln, Franklin D. Roosevelt and Richard M. Nixon have been the most successful in influencing the court's conduct through judicial appointments.

Presidents also have attempted to influence the court by criticizing the judiciary or the court's earlier decisions during presidential election campaigns. In 1800, 1860, 1896, 1924, 1936 and 1968, presidential candidates challenged the court's effect on public policy.

As political scientist Robert M. Scigliano has described the intersecting relationship between the court and the president:

> In their contemporary relationship, the Presidency has gained considerable influence over the Supreme Court.
>
> Yet the President cannot be said to dominate the Court. . . .
>
> Tension continues to exist between the two institutions. . . . A President cannot be sure that he is getting what he thinks he is getting in his appointments, a person may change his views after joining the Court, and the judicial obligation calls upon a justice to heed the Constitution and the laws, and not Presidential positions.[1]

Opportunities for Appointments

A vacancy on the Supreme Court has occurred, on the average, about every two years. A president thus can expect to have at least one appointment per term.[2]

But there have been periods when the court seemed to defy the actuarial tables and its membership remained stable for a much longer period, denying the incumbent president the opportunity to make an appointment to the court. Franklin D. Roosevelt, for example, served a full term as president before a vacancy occurred on the court.

Richard M. Nixon, on the other hand, had an opportunity to appoint a new Chief Justice during his first year in office. Nixon then made three more appointments to the court during his first term.

Qualifications

Presidents have considered a variety of criteria in selecting justices. Among the most consistent factors in these selections are merit, friendship, geographical and religious balance and ideology.

Almost all presidents have agreed that a court nominee should have some legal training; but judicial experience has not been considered particularly important. Many distinguished appointees — including eight Chief Justices — had no prior judicial experience.[3]

Of the modern presidents, Franklin D. Roosevelt appointed six men who had no judicial experience: Chief Justice Harlan Fiske Stone and Associate Justices Stanley F. Reed, Felix Frankfurter, William O. Douglas, James F. Byrnes and Robert H. Jackson. President Eisenhower, after appointing Earl Warren Chief Justice of the United States, insisted that all future nominees have judicial experience. (Warren had none.)

Harry S Truman appointed two men without judicial experience: Harold H. Burton and Tom C. Clark. Neither of President John F. Kennedy's two appointees, Arthur J. Goldberg and Byron R. White, had judicial experience. Nor did a Lyndon Johnson appointee, Abe Fortas; nor Nixon nominees William H. Rehnquist and Lewis F. Powell Jr.

Merit

Almost every one of the more than one hundred individuals who have served on the court had some record of public service prior to their appointment. Many had held offices in the executive branch, or had served as state or federal judges, senators, members of the House, governors or law professors.[4]

High ethical standards, as well as experience in public life, are criteria presidents seek in a nominee. Louis D. Brandeis' nomination successfully weathered a challenge from charges that he had engaged in improper practices as an attorney. But the nominations of Clement F. Haynsworth, and Abe Fortas as Chief Justice failed to win approval by the Senate because of questions raised about possible conflicts of interest.

Friendship

Personal friendship has been the reason for several nominations to the court. William Howard Taft's nomination of Horace H. Lurton, Woodrow Wilson's selection of Brandeis, Harry Truman's choice of Harold H. Burton and John F. Kennedy's preference for Byron R. White all had some basis in personal friendship.

President Johnson selected a reluctant Abe Fortas for the bench in 1965 on the basis of personal friendship. And in 1968 Johnson unsuccessfully proposed an old Texas political associate, Homer Thornberry, to fill Fortas' seat.

Geographical Representation

Justices have come from 31 of the 50 states, and states have not been represented in any substantially equal appointment pattern. New York has been the home of 15 justices. Pennsylvania had 11 citizens nominated to the court, Massachusetts 10, Ohio nine, and Virginia and Kentucky six. No other states have been so frequently represented.[5]

Early in the court's history, geographical balance was a major consideration in selecting nominees. Because of the justices' function as circuit judges, it was usually felt that each geographic area should have a spokesman on the court. Until the Civil War, this resulted in a "New England seat," a "Virginia seat," a "New York seat" and a "Pennsylvania seat." With the nation's post-Civil War expansion and the end of the justices' circuit-riding duties, this tradition faded.

Religious Balance

The notion of sectarian religious representation has developed out of the fact that Americans are a pluralistic society and a politically group-conscious people. Thus the idea of a "Roman Catholic seat" and a "Jewish seat" on the court has developed as a way of acknowledging the role of these religious minority groups in the nation.

The "Catholic Seat." Chief Justice Roger B. Taney was the first to hold the "Catholic seat." Since Grover Cleveland appointed Edward D. White to that seat in 1894, it has been held by Joseph McKenna, Pierce Butler, Frank Murphy and William J. Brennan Jr.

Truman's appointment of Tom C. Clark in 1949 after Murphy's death interrupted the tradition, but Eisenhower's appointment of Brennan in 1956 restored the notion of a "Catholic seat." The selection was regarded, in part, as an appeal to Catholic voters.

The "Jewish Seat." The "Jewish seat," established in 1916 with the appointment of Louis D. Brandeis, was filled by Justices Felix Frankfurter (1938), Arthur J. Goldberg (1963) and Abe Fortas (1965). (Benjamin N. Cardozo, a Jew, served along with Brandeis.) In 1969 President Nixon again broke the tradition by nominating three Protestants in succession to the seat Fortas vacated.

Subtler Influences

The special representational concerns of the Republican and Democratic parties may govern, to some extent, the choice of nominees to the court. Black and Jewish support of the Democratic party enhances the likelihood that Democratic presidents will continue to consider those groups in making their selections.

In 1967 President Lyndon B. Johnson nominated Thurgood Marshall as the first black justice of the Supreme Court. Marshall had been counsel for the National Association for the Advancement of Colored People (NAACP) and one of the attorneys responsible for arguing successfully the 1954 court decision in *Brown v. Board of Education, Topeka, Kan.* — the school desegregation case. Marshall served as Solicitor General of the United States prior to appointment to the court.

Ideology has been a significant factor in several presidents' appointments to the high bench. President Theodore Roosevelt wrote to Sen. Henry Cabot Lodge, R-Mass., during the consideration of Horace H. Lurton for appointment to the court, explaining that Lurton was "right" on all the important issues:

> The nominal politics of the man has nothing to do with his actions on the bench. His real politics are all important.... On every question that would come before the bench, he has so far shown himself to be in much closer touch with the policies in which you and I believe.[6]

Lodge agreed, but wondered why a Republican who held the same opinions could not be found. He suggested William H. Moody, the attorney general. "Teddy" Roosevelt appointed Moody in 1906. Lurton was subsequently nominated to the court in 1909 by William Howard Taft.

Party Loyalty

Presidents generally nominate members of their own party to the court. But presidents have occasionally nominated members of the opposition party.

Republican presidents have appointed nine Democratic justices, and Democratic presidents have named three Republicans to the court. Whig President John Tyler appointed Democrat Samuel Nelson. Republican Presidents Abraham Lincoln, Benjamin Harrison, William Howard Taft, Warren G. Harding, Herbert Hoover, Dwight D. Eisenhower and Richard M. Nixon appointed nominal Democrats.

Taft appointed Democrats Horace H. Lurton, Edward D. White (promoted to Chief Justice) and Joseph R. Lamar. The other GOP presidents who successfully nominated Democrats were Lincoln (Stephen J. Field), Benjamin Harrison (Howell E. Jackson), Harding (Pierce Butler), Hoover (Benjamin Cardozo), Eisenhower (William J. Brennan Jr.) and Nixon (Lewis F. Powell Jr.).

Among Democratic presidents, Woodrow Wilson appointed Louis D. Brandeis, Franklin D. Roosevelt appointed Harlan F. Stone Chief Justice, and Harry Truman put Republican Senator Harold H. Burton on the court.

Outside Influences

The appointment of a justice to the Supreme Court of the United States involves a complex pattern of personal and political transactions between the president and the individuals and groups seeking to influence that nomination.

Among the more important influence groups are the members of the president's administration, the sitting justices of the Supreme Court and the legal community.

The Attorney General

The president normally seeks the advice of his chief legal officer, the attorney general. In 1840 the attorney

Appointments and Disappointments

Despite their best efforts to name persons to the court who share their views, presidents frequently have been disappointed because their appointees failed to follow presidential political philosophy in their court opinions.

Donning the court robe does seem to make a difference in the appointees' views. Justice Felix Frankfurter, when asked if appointment to the court changed a person's views, allegedly retorted — "If he is any good he does."[1]

Chief Justice Earl Warren, reflecting on 16 years' service on the court, said he did not see "how a man could be on the Court and not change his views substantially over a period of years . . . for change you must if you are to do your duty on the Supreme Court."[2]

Charles Warren, historian of the court, wrote that "nothing is more striking in the history of the Court than the manner in which the hopes of those who expected a judge to follow the political views of the President appointing him are disappointed."[3]

Jefferson and Marshall

Presidents Thomas Jefferson and James Madison would have agreed. They repeatedly registered their disappointment at the failure of the judges they appointed to the court to resist the powerful and dominating influence of Chief Justice John Marshall.

Madison failed to take Jefferson's advice against the appointment of Joseph Story to the court. Jefferson warned Madison that Story would side with Marshall on important legal questions — and Jefferson proved correct. Story not only joined Marshall in his interpretation of the Constitution but occasionally showed himself even more nationalistic than the Chief Justice.

Roosevelt and Holmes

Theodore Roosevelt named Oliver Wendell Holmes Jr. to the court; Holmes then voted against the administration's antitrust efforts — most notably in the 1904 case of *Northern Securities v. United States.* Holmes' unexpected dissent left the government with a narrow 5-4 majority upholding the dissolution of the Northern Securities Company railroad conglomerate.

After the decision, Roosevelt, referring to Holmes' defection, said that he "could carve out of a banana a Judge with more backbone than that!" Holmes reportedly smiled when told of the remark. Later, at a White House dinner, Holmes remarked to a labor leader and fellow guest: "What you want is favor, not justice. But when I am on my job, I don't give a damn what you or Mr. Roosevelt want."[4]

Woodrow Wilson had reason to regret the appointment of James C. McReynolds to the bench when that justice proved to hold the opposite of Wilson's viewpoint on almost every question the administration argued before the court.

Calvin Coolidge's sole appointee, Harlan F. Stone, sided within a year of his appointment with the liberal Holmes-Brandeis wing of the court.

President Harry S Truman noted that "packing the Supreme Court simply can't be done . . . I've tried and it won't work. . . . Whenever you put a man on the Supreme Court he ceases to be your friend."[5]

And Truman should have known. In the important *Steel Seizure Case,* decided in 1952, the four Truman appointees divided 2-2 in the case which ruled the president's seizure of the steel mills unconstitutional. *(Details, pp. 193-194)*

Eisenhower and Warren

President Eisenhower later described as a "mistake" his decision to appoint Earl Warren Chief Justice. Warren's leadership commenced a judicial "revolution" that greatly disturbed the Republican president.

But Warren's appointment made good political sense in 1953. Warren had delivered California delegates to "Ike" at the Republican national nominating convention in 1952. Warren's removal from the California political scene, where he had proven an immensely popular three-term governor, placated conservative California Republican leaders, including Vice President Richard M. Nixon and Senate Majority Leader William F. Knowland, both of whom disliked Warren's progressive Republican views.

But when Eisenhower was asked if he had made any mistakes during his presidency he quipped, "Yes, two, and they are both sitting on the Supreme Court." The former president thus registered his disappointment at the liberalism of Earl Warren and of Justice William J. Brennan Jr.[6]

Nixon and Watergate

Though his views are not known, former President Richard M. Nixon had ample cause to disagree with the decisions of the court to which he appointed four men.

Although the justices Nixon selected held views consonant with his on many issues, some of them voted to reject Nixon's positions on abortion, aid to parochial schools, school desegregation, busing, and electronic surveillance.

Nixon's most dramatic confrontation with the court came in 1974, when it ruled against his claim of an absolute executive privilege to withhold White House tapes sought for use as evidence in the trial of his former aides. The vote was 8-0. The ruling led to Nixon's resignation two weeks later. *(Details, pp. 245-248)*

---

[1] Henry J. Abraham, *Justices and Presidents: A Political History of Appointments to the Supreme Court* (New York: Oxford University Press, 1974), p. 63.

[2] Anthony Lewis, "A Talk with Warren on Crime, the Court, the Country," *New York Times Magazine,* Oct. 19, 1969, pp. 128-129.

[3] Charles Warren, *The Supreme Court in United States History,* rev. ed., 2 vols. (Boston: Little, Brown & Co., 1922, 1926), I:22.

[4] Abraham, *Justices and Presidents,* p. 62.

[5] Ibid., p. 63

[6] Ibid., p. 246.

general assumed responsibility for judicial appointments, taking over the function from the secretary of state. Since that time the attorney general has become the president's liaison with the principal interest groups and individuals involved in the screening and selection of qualified candidates for appointment to the court.[7]

The Senate's Role

The Senate's power to confirm or reject presidential nominees to the court has resulted in the rejection of 26 out of 136 nominations in nearly two centuries of the court's history. In the 19th century one out of three nominees was rejected by the Senate. In the 20th century only four nominees have been rejected. [8]

The Senate has rejected the president's choice because of the appointee's position on public issues, opposition to the prevailing views on the court, the political characteristics of the nominee or his perceived lack of judicial qualifications.

In the tradition of senatorial courtesy, the Senate will not confirm a nominee opposed by the senators from the nominee's homestate, at least if they are members of the president's political party.

Application of senatorial courtesy accounted for several rejections of Supreme Court nominees in the 19th century — but that tradition has rarely been mentioned in connection with Supreme Court nominations in modern times.

The Senate rejected President Grover Cleveland's nominees William Hornblower (1893) and Wheeler H. Peckham (1894), both of New York. Sen. David B. Hill, D-N.Y., invoked senatorial courtesy to block the nominations in each instance because Cleveland had failed to consult with him about their selection. Cleveland then refused to name a third New Yorker and chose instead Edward D. White, D-La., the Democratic Majority Leader in the Senate.

Senatorial courtesy was a prominent factor in the rejection of Reuben H. Walworth of New York — the choice of President John Tyler. And it was a factor in the Senate negative given to James K. Polk's nomination of Pennsylvanian George W. Woodward in 1845. [9]

The Justices' Role

Sitting justices have rarely hesitated to voice their suggestions of especially qualified nominees for vacant seats. Some justices have offered negative advice. Joseph P. Bradley prepared a report about those who would be qualified to succeed him and concluded that no candidate from his native New Jersey possessed the necessary qualifications.

In the 19th century justices often lobbied effectively with presidents to urge appointment of certain candidates. Justices John Catron and Benjamin R. Curtis, for example, urged President Franklin Pierce to nominate John A. Campbell to the court. Their representations to Pierce included letters of support for Campbell from all the remaining sitting justices.[10]

Among other justices who successfully urged presidents to appoint certain individuals to the court were: Robert C. Grier for William Strong in 1870, Noah H. Swayne for Joseph P. Bradley in 1870, Morrison R. Waite for William B. Woods in 1880, Samuel F. Miller for David J. Brewer in 1889 and Henry B. Brown for Howell E. Jackson in 1893.[11]

Taft: Champion Influencer

William Howard Taft was the only president to become Chief Justice of the United States, thus enjoying a unique double opportunity to influence the personnel and work of the court. During Warren G. Harding's presidency, Taft either selected or approved three of the four men Harding appointed to the court — George Sutherland, Pierce Butler and Edward T. Sanford.

Taft also had lobbied for his own appointment as Chief Justice. In 1920 the ex-president let it be known to newly elected President Harding that he wanted the job. Taft had named Edward D. White Chief Justice and, Taft told Harding, "many times in the past . . . [White] had said he was holding the office for me and that he would give it back to a Republican administration." [12] On June 30, 1921, Harding appointed Taft Chief Justice.

Taft's most prodigious subsequent lobbying effort on presidential appointments resulted in Pierce Butler's appointment to the court. He orchestrated a letter-writing campaign recommending Butler and played down the talents of other potential nominees. Taft dismissed the candidacy of Judge Benjamin N. Cardozo of the New York Court of Appeals because, Taft wrote, Cardozo was "a Jew and a Democrat . . . [and] . . . a progressive judge." Judge Learned Hand, Taft warned, "would almost certainly herd with Brandeis and be a dissenter." [13]

The Chief Justice sought and obtained endorsements for Butler from the Minnesota congressional delegation, members of the church hierarchy — Butler was a Roman Catholic — and from local bar associations across the nation. Harding succumbed to the pressure and sent Butler's nomination to the Senate where, despite considerable opposition from Senate progressives, he won approval.

When Mahlon Pitney resigned in 1922, Taft heartily approved of Harding's choice, Edward T. Sanford. Taft and Sanford had been acquaintances since Theodore Roosevelt's administration. Some observers felt that Sanford was so close to Taft that the Chief Justice had two votes on the bench.

Their friendship and judicial affinity had a final coincidence: they died on the same day in 1930.[14]

Chief Justice Taft's influence over Harding's appointments to the court gave that body a decidedly conservative majority during the 1920s — ending only with Franklin D. Roosevelt's appointments to the court after 1937.

Hughes and Stone

Other Chief Justices have influenced presidential decisions on Supreme Court appointments.

Charles Evans Hughes counseled three presidents on appointments. Herbert Hoover sought Hughes' advice in naming a replacement for Oliver Wendell Holmes in 1931. The president particularly wanted to know Hughes' opinion of fellow New Yorker Benjamin N. Cardozo.[15]

In 1941 Hughes wanted President Roosevelt to name Harlan Fiske Stone as his successor as Chief Justice. Harry S Truman also consulted Hughes in 1946 on his choice of a Chief Justice after Stone's death.[16]

Hoover also sought and obtained Stone's advice on filling the Holmes seat. Stone was so convinced of Cardozo's qualifications that he sent several memoranda to Hoover recommending Cardozo in preference to alternate candidates. Stone tried to overcome Hoover's reservations about appointing another Jewish justice, even offering his own resignation from the court to make room for Cardozo.[17]

Hoover appointed Cardozo February 15, 1932; he was confirmed nine days later. Of the Cardozo nomination one author wrote:

> The appointment and confirmation of Benjamin Cardozo . . . violated nearly all the "rules of the game." Judge Cardozo was a New Yorker, and there were already two judges from that state on the bench — Stone and Hughes. He was a nominal Democrat, and his 'real' politics, highly tinged with liberalism, differed sharply from those of President Hoover. Moreover, he was a Jew and there was already one Jewish judge in the person of Louis Brandeis. Cardozo's selection is inexplicable except in terms of his pre-eminent position among American jurists and the overwhelming pressures on his behalf from leaders of the bench and bar throughout the land.[18]

The Role of the ABA

Since World War II, the American Bar Association (ABA) — through its standing committee on the federal judiciary — also has played some role in passing on the legal and intellectual qualifications of those selected for consideration as Supreme Court justices.

Established in 1945-46, the committee began with the nomination of William J. Brennan Jr. in 1956 to rate prospective justices as professionally qualified or unqualified. This system of rating nominees continued with every nomination until Harry A. Blackmun's appointment in 1970.

Public criticism in the wake of the Senate's rejection of Clement F. Haynsworth Jr. and G. Harrold Carswell, whom the committee had rated as "highly qualified" and "qualified" respectively, resulted in a change in the ABA rating system to three categories — "highly qualified," "not opposed" and "not qualified."

Attorney General John N. Mitchell wrote the chairman of the committee in July 1970 to say that the Nixon administration would submit names of potential Supreme Court nominees to the ABA for preliminary screening prior to sending the president's choice for the seat to the Senate.

But the agreement dissolved almost immediately when names of prospective Nixon nominees to fill the vacant seats occasioned by the retirements of Justices John Marshall Harlan and Hugo L. Black reached the press while the ABA Committee was studying their qualifications. The administration, suspecting a news leak in the committee, withdrew support of the practice.

Despite this rebuff, the ABA conducted its own investigation of the qualifications of Lewis F. Powell Jr. and William H. Rehnquist — named to succeed Harlan and Black. The ABA submitted the findings to the Senate Judiciary Committee. The ABA approved both men — Powell unanimously as "one of the best lawyers available." Rehnquist received nine votes for a highly qualified rating, but three committee members said merely that they were "not opposed" to his appointment.[19]

Politics and Appointments

The political motivations in a president's selection of Supreme Court nominees are less blatant than they used to be.

In the early days of the republic the court was — in addition to its inchoate judicial function — an open political battlefield between the competing interests of Federalists and Republicans as each party sought to impose its ideology on the government of the new nation.

George Washington, W. D. Coles wrote, "initiated the system of appointing political adherents only, to places on the Supreme Bench. That system has seldom been departed from." [20]

Nevertheless, although political affinities are still a factor — doubtless the prevailing one — in selection of nominees to the court, the political element has become less openly partisan and manipulative as the court has evolved into a more equal and autonomous component of the federal system.

The evolution of the court into such a relatively independent institution can be attributed in part to its growing stature under the weight of experience and tradition, and to the justices' sense of destiny and momentous undertaking as they assume their duties. In any event, service on the court, however politically determined, began to engender a spirit of higher motive and unpredictable judgment that came more and more to confound the political expectations of those who made it possible.

The rigid party-line ideology of the Senate became more amorphous, with liberal and conservative factions of each party uniting on common ideological ground in considering court appointees.

But in the beginning, the president's power to appoint Supreme Court justices was considered an out-and-out political opportunity — and soon proved to be a political hornet's nest.

The Marshall Appointment

President John Adams appointed John Marshall Chief Justice because he wanted a loyal Federalist on the bench who would preserve the party's principles in the wake of Jefferson's election as president in 1800.

But Marshall was not Adams' first choice. The president had re-appointed John Jay Chief Justice, but Jay, who had served as the first Chief Justice, declined, because he felt the fledgling court lacked "energy, weight, and dignity."

Adams considered other candidates for the post. With little consultation and no fanfare he finally settled on Marshall, and sent up the nomination Jan. 20, 1801 — about two months before he left the White House.

The Senate exhibited little enthusiasm for Marshall — less because its members opposed Marshall than because they preferred to see Associate Justice William Paterson elevated to the post of Chief Justice.

Adams remained firm. The Federalist-dominated Senate realized that if they rejected Marshall, Adams might send them a "spite" nominee, or worse, and the post would be left vacant for Jefferson to fill.[21]

The Senate approved Marshall's nomination Jan. 27, 1801. No other single appointment affected the early court or the young nation more profoundly. From the court, Marshall championed the principles of federalism for 34 years. His dominance over the court and its members is indicated by the fact that he personally delivered the court's opinions in 519 of the 1,215 decisions handed down between 1801 and 1835. Marshall wrote 36 of the 62 decisions on major constitutional questions announced during his tenure.[22]

Unlike many of his successors, Adams was proud of his nominee. In 1826 he observed:

> My gift of John Marshall to the people of the United States was the proudest act of my life. There is no act of my life on which I reflect with more pleasure.[23]

McLean and Taney

President Jackson's appointment of John McLean to the Supreme Court illustrates the reasons a president may ignore political loyalty in such choices.

Postmaster General McLean, a constant and persistant aspirant to high office, had been postmaster general under both Presidents Monroe and John Quincy Adams. In the intraparty struggles for the presidency McLean somehow maintained cordial ties with both the Adams and Jackson forces in the tumultuous election of 1828.

Jackson kept McLean on as postmaster general even though he did not really trust him. But he knew McLean was a popular figure in the West, and he did not wish to risk a political fight with McLean early in his administration.

McLean promised to abandon his presidential aspirations, in return for which Jackson nominated him to the vacant seat on the Supreme Court.

McLean, however, failed to live up to his end of the bargain. While on the bench he became a presidential candidate four times, taking on the colors of a political chameleon. In 1832 he was the Anti-Masonic candidate; in 1836 he ran as an Independent, in 1842 as a Whig and a Free-Soiler, and in 1856 as a Republican. Unsuccessful in all four efforts, he served on the court until his death in 1861.[24]

In contrast to the McLean selection was Jackson's appointment of Roger B. Taney as Chief Justice. With the resignation of Justice Gabriel Duvall in January 1835, Jackson appointed Taney, his loyal supporter and Treasury secretary, to the vacant seat. Taney had complied with Jackson's order to remove government deposits from the Bank of the United States during Jackson's war against the bank.

The Senate countered the Taney nomination by postponing consideration on the last day of the 1835 session — effectively killing it. On that same day, moreover, the Senate passed a bill abolishing the vacant seat. The House of Representatives refused to go along with that move, however.

Then, on July 6, 1835, Chief Justice John Marshall died. Now Jackson had two seats to fill. Daniel Webster and Associate Justice Joseph Story were mentioned as candidates for the Chief Justice's chair. Jackson even

received suggestions that he promote John McLean to the highest judicial post.

In December Jackson nominated Philip Barbour of Virginia to fill the Duvall seat and Taney to succeed Marshall as Chief Justice. After three months of debate in the Senate both appointments were confirmed in March 1836.

Taney presided as Chief Justice for 28 years, earning a reputation as a great champion of states' rights. His best known opinion, however, in the case of *Dred Scott* — an aberration in an otherwise notable judicial career — hastened the onset of war and contributed to the court's eclipse during and after the Civil War.

Salmon P. Chase

Chief Justice Taney died Oct. 12, 1864. In the midst of civil war, President Lincoln sought as a replacement for Taney a Chief Justice who would support him on matters of war policy and who could help close the widening breach in the Republican Party over Lincoln's conduct of the war.

Salmon Portland Chase was, from the outset, a serious candidate for the nomination. Chase had been governor, senator from Ohio and Lincoln's secretary of the Treasury. He was a talented public servant and seemed to hold the "right" opinions on the issues Lincoln considered important.

But Chase was a political schemer — and he wanted desperately to be president. He had sought the Republican nomination in 1856 and in 1860, and even after becoming Chief Justice he vied for the 1868 presidential nomination of both parties.

Lincoln considered other political candidates for the post, including Associate Justices James M. Wayne and Noah H. Swayne, Secretary of State William H. Seward, Secretary of War Edwin M. Stanton and Montgomery Blair, Lincoln's former postmaster general. Blair was Lincoln's personal choice for the post, a distinguished public servant with roots in the original Free Soil movement that became the Republican Party and a bitter foe of Chase.

But Lincoln appointed Chase — whom he did not trust — and not Blair — whom he trusted implicitly — because he believed that Chase commanded greater respect among Republicans and Unionists of all varieties and would help to unify the party and the nation. The Senate immediately confirmed the nomination.

Lincoln was assassinated four months later. Chief Justice Chase found himself presiding over challenges both to the slain president's wartime policies and postwar plans for conciliation with the South, and to Congress' punitive reconstruction legislation. By most accounts, Chase — notwithstanding his continuing political ambitions — acted with even-handed judicial restraint aimed at forestalling the court's involvement in politics.

His reluctance to preside at the trial for treason of former Confederate President Jefferson Davis contributed to the eventual dismissal of charges against Davis; and his fair handling of the impeachment trial of Andrew Johnson is considered an important factor in the president's acquittal.

As Chief Justice, Chase joined the court majority in *Ex parte Milligan* (1866), which limited the authority of military tribunals over civilians. *(p. 189)* In the *Slaughterhouse Cases,* he dissented from the opinion allowing the maintenance of civil rights under state jurisdiction. *(p. 339)*

But Chase's main divergence from Lincoln's wartime policies came in the 1870-71 *Legal Tender Cases.* Chase delivered the opinion holding unconstitutional the Civil War legislation making paper money legal tender — even though he had been Treasury secretary when the legislation was enacted. He dissented when the decision was reversed in 1871.

Grant 'Packs' the Court

The most successful, if unintentional, "court-packing" ever accomplished by a president came in 1870. The result of President Ulysses S. Grant's appointment of two men to the court in 1870 led to the rapid reversal of the first decision involving the government's power to make paper money legal tender.

In April 1869 Congress increased the size of the court to nine, giving Grant the opportunity to fill an extra seat. Then, in December 1869, Justice Robert C. Grier resigned, giving Grant another vacancy to fill. Grant chose Edwin M. Stanton and Attorney General Ebenezer Hoar to fill the vacancies. Stanton was quickly confirmed but died suddenly four days after his confirmation. The Senate then rejected Hoar's nomination.

In February 1870 Grant nominated Joseph P. Bradley and William Strong to the vacancies. The former was a Republican railroad lawyer and the latter was a former Pennsylvania supreme court justice.

Grant made the nominations even as the court was announcing its decision in the case of *Hepburn v. Griswold*. By a 4 to 3 vote, the court declared the Legal Tender Act of 1862 unconstitutional. That law made greenbacks — paper money — legal tender for payment of debts. Those supporting the gold standard for currency opposed the court's ruling, arguing that it permitted debtors to pay off their debts in cheap currency.

Chief Justice Salmon P. Chase wrote the majority opinion, holding the law invalid insofar as it allowed the use of paper money to pay off debts contracted before its passage. Three Republican justices — Miller, Swayne and Davis, all Lincoln appointees — dissented, arguing that a federal power with respect to money included the right to make paper money legal tender.

The Senate confirmed the Bradley and Strong nominations, and they took their seats in the spring of 1870, during which the court agreed to hear a second legal tender case argued.

A year later the court, in the case of *Knox v. Lee*, reversed *Hepburn v. Griswold*. The vote was 5-4. Justices Bradley and Strong joined the three dissenters in *Hepburn* to form a majority in *Knox*.

Scholars have subsequently debated whether Grant intentionally "packed" the court to get the legal tender ruling reversed. Charles Warren, historian of the Supreme Court, absolved Grant of the charge, saying that the president did not know in advance of the court's ruling when he appointed Bradley and Strong and that under any circumstances Grant would have appointed men to the court who agreed with his views on the money question.

But evidence not available when Warren wrote his history indicates that Grant did have prior knowledge of the outcome of the *Hepburn* case. Grant's secretary of the Treasury, George S. Boutwell, received word from Chief Justice Chase two weeks before the decision was announced what the outcome would be. That information most likely was passed to Grant. Moreover, several years after the event, Grant said he had desired in his appointments of Strong and Bradley a court decision that would sustain the constitutionality of legal tender. He got his wish.[25]

Roosevelt's Would-Be Court

The selection and confirmation of individual nominees to the court have not been the only factors in the struggle between the president and Congress for a politically acceptable court. Both from time to time have attempted to juggle the size of the court's membership in order to achieve a judicial consensus more to their liking.

The term "court-packing" is usually associated not with Grant's appointments but with President Franklin D. Roosevelt's blatant bid in 1937 to reshape the court into an instrument of his will. The attempt was the most transparent example yet of a president's political pressure on the court — and it landed Roosevelt in his biggest political controversy up to that time.

In 1935 and 1936 the court in a series of 5-4 and 6-3 decisions had struck down every important measure of Roosevelt's New Deal program. The so-called "Four Horsemen" — Justices Willis Van Devanter, James C. McReynolds, George Sutherland and Pierce Butler — were totally antagonistic to New Deal philosophy that called for government spending and work projects to help farmers, labor and business survive the Depression. They were often joined by Chief Justice Charles Evans Hughes and Justice Owen J. Roberts to form an anti-New Deal majority. *(Further details, p. 241)*

Roosevelt won a stunning re-election victory in 1936 and on the strength of that popular mandate redoubled his efforts to prevent the "nine old men" on the Supreme Court from obstructing his legislative programs. But his "court reform" bill — permitting a president to add a justice to the Supreme Court for every justice over 70 who refused to retire, for a total of 15 justices — was really a plan to pack the court, and it offended some of FDR's ardent supporters in the Congress and on the bench.

But the potential confrontation was averted. By the time the bill was unfavorably reported by the Senate Judiciary Committee, Roosevelt had begun to get more cooperation from a court suddenly more amenable to his legislation and had gained the opportunity to appoint one new justice to a recently vacated seat.

The court had signaled a more hospitable attitude toward the New Deal in three decisions in the spring of 1937 upholding major administration acts. And Van Devanter's retirement announcement came while the Judiciary Committee was considering the court-packing bill.

That gave Roosevelt the chance to name his first appointee to the court, and he nominated a full-fledged New Dealer, Alabama Sen. Hugo L. Black — the first of eight appointments he would make before the end of 1943. As a result of Roosevelt's attack on the court and his new appointments, the thrust and focus of its decisions changed drastically in the next few years.

A Chief Justice Retires

The retirement of Chief Justice Charles Evans Hughes in 1941 gave President Roosevelt the opportunity to name a man of his choice to that position. He picked a Republican. He did so in the hope of increasing bipartisan political support for his administration in the face of World War II.

When the 80-year-old Chief Justice on June 2, 1941, announced his retirement effective July 1, 1941, Roosevelt felt no urgency to move quickly to fill the post.

The president had two candidates in mind: Associate Justice Harlan Fiske Stone and Attorney General Robert H. Jackson.

Roosevelt preferred Jackson, his attorney general and a New Deal loyalist. The retiring Hughes, on the other hand, felt Stone's record on the court merited his elevation to Chief Justice.

Roosevelt also discussed the nomination with Justice Felix Frankfurter. When asked which of the two men he preferred, Frankfurter told the president:

> On personal grounds I'd prefer Bob [Jackson]. While I've known Stone longer and our relations are excellent and happy, I feel closer friendship with Bob. But from the national interest I am bound to say that there is no reason for preferring Bob to Stone — quite the contrary. Stone is senior and qualified professionally to be C.J. But for me the decisive consideration, considering the fact that Stone is qualified, is that Bob is of your personal and political family, as it were, while Stone is a Republican. . . . When war does come, the country should feel you are . . . the Nation's President, and not a partisan President. Few things would contribute as much to confidence in you as a national and not as a partisan president than for you to name a Republican, who has the profession's confidence, as Chief Justice.[26]

Roosevelt discussed the nomination with Jackson, who assured the president he agreed with Frankfurter's analysis. And Jackson personally delivered the news to Stone of his appointment as Chief Justice.

Stone was confirmed by a voice vote. The president later appointed Jackson to the seat left vacant by Stone's elevation to the position of Chief Justice.

Seeking Harmony

After Stone's death in 1946, President Harry S Truman appointed Fred M. Vinson Chief Justice of the United States because Vinson was an able administrator with broad experience in public service — and because he was Truman's friend. Vinson had served with Truman in the Senate. When Truman became president Vinson served as his Treasury secretary and *ex officio* advisor.

At the time of Stone's death the court was seriously divided by personality clashes among the justices — especially the feud between Justices Jackson and Hugo L. Black described by one of Black's biographers as "the bitterest internecine controversy in the court's history."[27]

Among many other things, the long-simmering antagonism involved Jackson's charges that Black had been guilty of conflict of interest by participating in two decisions in 1944 and 1945.[28] Black had criticized Jackson's leave of absence from the court in 1945-46 to serve as U.S. prosecutor at the Nazi war crimes trial at Nuremberg, Germany — a trial Black called a "high-grade lynching party."[29]

Truman sought the advice of former Chief Justice Hughes and former Associate Justice Owen J. Roberts about the appointment. Both men urged Truman to appoint someone who could restore peace among the members of the court. That apparently ruled out Jackson — believed by many, evidently including Jackson himself, to be heir apparent to the Chief Justiceship.[30]

Truman nominated Vinson June 7, 1946, and he was quickly confirmed two weeks later, amid a further volley of mutual public criticism between Jackson and Black.

In seven years as Chief Justice Vinson muted the clashes between members of the court but he did not restore harmony. There were proportionally more 5-to-4 decisions during the Vinson period than in any other era in the court's history. Vinson died in 1953 — disappointed and unhappy with the results of his term as Chief Justice.[31]

Creating a Vacancy

In 1965, President Lyndon B. Johnson persuaded Arthur J. Goldberg to leave the court to create a vacancy to which Johnson could appoint his friend and trusted adviser Abe Fortas.

Johnson appealed to Goldberg's sense of duty and public service, urging him to resign from the court to become United States Ambassador to the United Nations. Goldberg allowed himself to be persuaded, genuinely hoping that the U.N. forum would be the arena to negotiate an end to the war in Vietnam.

Goldberg, from a poor immigrant family background, had been general counsel for the nation's largest labor unions before becoming secretary of labor in the Kennedy administration. Both Chief Justice Earl Warren and Justice Felix Frankfurter approved of Goldberg's appointment in 1962 as Frankfurter's successor.

But Goldberg was to serve only three years. President Johnson, fresh from an election victory, wanted to put someone of his choice on the court.

After coaxing Goldberg off the court, Johnson had to persuade a reluctant Abe Fortas to take the seat. Johnson invited Fortas to the White House on July 18, 1965, on the pretext of seeking his advice on another matter. The president then simply informed Fortas that he was going over to the East Wing of the White House to nominate Fortas for the Supreme Court.

The pre-arranged session included Goldberg and his family. The resigning justice did not hide his disappointment at leaving the court, saying: "I shall not, Mr. President, conceal the pain with which I leave the court after three years of service. It has been the richest and most satisfying period of my career."[32]

Delaying a Vacancy

When Chief Justice Earl Warren in 1968 announced his intention to retire, he gave President Johnson an opportunity to appoint his successor in the nation's highest judicial post. But Johnson had become a "lame duck" president, declaring in March 1968 that he would not be a candidate for re-election. Nevertheless, Johnson took advantage of the Warren retirement announcement and nominated Justice Fortas as Chief Justice.

The Senate refused to confirm Fortas. Republicans, hopeful of winning the White House, wanted to "save" the vacancy for the Republican president-to-be to fill. Fortas' continuing role as an unofficial adviser to the president on policy matters while on the court and his acceptance of fees for a series of university seminars created enough doubts among enough senators to forestall confirmation in 1968.

Fortas' nomination cleared the Senate Judiciary Committee but ran into a filibuster on the floor. A motion to end the filibuster failed and Fortas then asked the president to withdraw his name from nomination.

Richard Nixon, the Republican candidate, won election as president soon thereafter, and in May 1969 he named his choice, Warren E. Burger, Chief Justice.

By the time Burger was sworn in, Fortas had left the court. In May 1969 *Life* magazine reported that Fortas in 1966 accepted, and then returned, a large fee from the Louis E. Wolfson family foundation. Millionaire Wolfson was later sent to prison for illegal stock manipulations.[33] Rather than face a full-scale inquiry, and possible impeachment proceedings, Fortas resigned May 15, 1969. *(Text, letter of resignation, p. 983)*

The 'Save the Seat' Syndrome

The refusal of the Senate to confirm Fortas' nomination as Chief Justice was a modern example of the "save the seat" strategem — a familiar phenomenon in the 19th century. In that century, many late-term nominees to the court were denied confirmation simply because the Senate, for partisan reasons, wished to save the seat for an incoming president to fill. Thus incoming presidents had an opportunity to place their stamp on the court at the outset of their term.

The Senate in early 1829, for example, refused to confirm lame-duck President John Quincy Adams' nomination of John J. Crittenden to the court, thus "saving" the vacancy for President Andrew Jackson to fill.

The unluckiest president with respect to court appointments was John Tyler. Five of his nominations failed to win Senate approval because Tyler was without a solid political base of his own after Whig President William Henry Harrison died in office in 1841.

Tyler's first four nominees to the court met Senate rejection after the president's policies had collided with those advocated by Henry Clay's rival Whig Party supporters in the Senate. Tyler's fifth nominee — proposed in February 1845 after Democrat James K. Polk had won the 1844 presidential election — was a well-known Philadelphia lawyer, John M. Read, who had political ties with both the Whigs and Democrats.

The Senate postponed consideration of the nomination made by the "lame duck" Tyler and adjourned. President Polk thus began his term in office with the opportunity of filling Henry Baldwin's still-vacant seat. After rejecting Polk's first nominee the Senate confirmed Robert C. Grier in August 1846.

After Franklin Pierce won the 1852 election, President Millard Fillmore, by then a "lame duck," named Sen. George E. Badger of North Carolina to the court. The Senate postponed the nomination — an unusual breach of the Senate tradition that usually grants immediate confirmation to a senator's appointment to the court.

Fillmore refused to accept defeat. He then named a prominent Louisiana lawyer — William Micou — but the Senate again refused to act, allowing Pierce to fill that vacancy at the outset of his administration.

In 1861, at the end of his presidential term, President James Buchanan, a Democrat, tried to fill the seat vacated by Peter V. Daniel. Buchanan found a worthy candidate in Pennsylvanian Jeremiah S. Black — a strong believer in the Union but not an abolitionist. Moreover, Black had been chief justice of the Pennsylvania supreme court and attorney general of the United States.

But it was too late. In less than a month Lincoln would assume the presidency. Republicans in the Senate were not anxious to deny the first Republican president the opportunity to make the court appointment. Black was denied confirmation, 25-26.

Rutherford B. Hayes, an avowed one-term president, in late January 1881 nominated his friend and former college classmate, Stanley Matthews of Ohio, to the seat made vacant by Noah H. Swayne's retirement.

Matthews had had a successful career as a public servant, but he had been a political maverick. One major drawback to his candidacy, however, was that Matthews served as a prominent counsel to financier Jay Gould. The Senate Judiciary Committee refused to report the nomination for floor action, and it appeared Matthews' nomination was dead until Hayes' successor, James A. Garfield, renominated Matthews for the post in 1881. He was confirmed by the narrowest of margins — 24-23.

20th Century Instances

William Howard Taft laid the groundwork for his own subsequent appointment as Chief Justice in 1921 when, as president in 1910, he chose the veteran justice Edward D. White for the post rather than the younger candidate — Justice Charles Evans Hughes.

Earlier in 1910 Taft had appointed Hughes to the court, filling the vacancy created by David J. Brewer's death.

Taft had considered Hughes a threat to his own presidential nomination in 1908. And Hughes was recognized as presidential "timber" within Republican ranks.

At the time of the appointment Taft dangled before Hughes the prospect of becoming Chief Justice when that vacancy occurred. Taft wrote Hughes that he had no reservations about promoting an associate justice to Chief Justice. Then, in a remarkably equivocal addendum, Taft wrote:

> Don't misunderstand me as to the Chief Justiceship. I mean if that office were now open, I should offer it to you and it is probable that if it were to become vacant during my term, I should promote you to it; but, of course, conditions change, so that it would not be right for me to say by way of promise what I would do in the future. Nor, on the other hand, would I have you think that your declination now would prevent my offering you the higher position, should conditions remain as they are.[34]

Hughes got the message and accepted, but conditions did change. In July 1910 Chief Justice Melville W. Fuller died and in December 1910 Taft appointed Louisianan White, 65, a Catholic and a Democrat, to replace him. The public — not to mention Hughes — had expected Taft to name Hughes to the post. Hughes later resigned from the court in 1916 to run for the presidency.[35]

White already had served on the court 17 years when Taft named him Chief Justice. He was an able administrator whose views coincided with those of Taft. And because White was not a young man, the president counted on White's retirement, resignation or death — preferably during a Republican administration — to create a vacancy on the court's top spot, which Taft hoped to fill.

Taft did not conceal his ambitions. When he signed White's commission as Chief Justice he remarked aloud: "There is nothing I would have loved more than being Chief Justice of the United States. I cannot help seeing the irony in the fact that I, who desired that office so much, should now be signing the commission of another man."[36]

White died May 21, 1921. After considerable lobbying by Taft on his own behalf, President Warren G. Harding appointed him Chief Justice of the United States. He served until 1930, when President Hoover appointed as Taft's successor the man Taft had decided not to make Chief Justice — Charles Evans Hughes.

The Court as a Campaign Issue

The Supreme Court — its personnel as well as its positions — has been a recurring issue in presidential campaigns since 1800. The candidates of both major parties, and those of some third parties, have found the court's rulings on a variety of issues — from slavery to taxes and criminal procedure — handy targets for election-year rhetoric.

Presidents Jefferson, Lincoln, Franklin D. Roosevelt and Richard M. Nixon most successfully implemented their campaign criticism of the court. Each of those presidents influenced the court's decisions through their appointments and policies.

Thomas Jefferson

During the election of 1800 Jeffersonian Republicans charged that the federal judiciary was a solid Federalist phalanx intent upon destroying republican liberties.

Jeffersonians also criticized the fact that both Chief Justice John Jay and his successor in that post, Oliver Ellsworth, accepted diplomatic assignments from Presidents Washington and Adams repectively. And Jay had then negotiated the treaty that bore his name — a treaty reviled by all Jeffersonians as pro-British.

James T. Callender, the notorious Jeffersonian pamphleteer, wrote in his 1800 election campaign pamphlet, *The Prospect Before Us:* "Think of the gross and audacious prostitution of the federal bench by the successive selection of foreign ambassadors from that body." [37]

When Jefferson became president, he launched an attack on the judicial branch, encouraging Congress first to repeal the Judiciary Act of 1801 and then to impeach an associate justice, Samuel Chase, for his "crimes" of making political diatribes from the bench.

The Jeffersonians succeeded in repealing the 1801 act but failed in their efforts to impeach Chase. *(Details, pp. 658-660)*

On the whole Jefferson got what he wanted. The judiciary toned down their grand jury charges, and the appointment of Jeffersonian Republicans to all levels of the judiciary ended charges that the federal bench was a Federalist sanctuary. Nevertheless, all of Jefferson's court appointees subsequently succumbed to the influence of Jefferson's Federalist arch-enemy, Chief Justice John Marshall.

The Election of 1860

The court's decision in the 1857 case of *Dred Scott v. Sandford* permanently disrupted the fragile structure of political compromise and adjustment between North and South on the issue of the expansion of slavery into the territories beyond the Mississippi River.

The decision gave Abraham Lincoln an issue that carried him to the White House. The whole existence of the Republican Party rested on the twin pillars of free land and free men in the territories west of the Mississippi.

Republicans chose Lincoln as their standard-bearer in 1860 — in large part because of his simple and eloquent refutation of the slavery expansion argument made by Sen. Stephen A. Douglas in Illinois' 1858 Senate race.

Lincoln refused to compromise on the expansion question, explaining:

> Now, I confess myself as belonging to the class in the country who *[sic]* contemplates slavery as a moral,

social, and political evil, having due regard for its actual existence among us and the difficulties of getting rid of it in any satisfactory way, and to all constitutional obligations which have been thrown about it; but nevertheless, [I] desire a policy that looks to the prevention of it as a wrong, and looks hopefully to the time when as a wrong it may come to an end.[38]

The *Dred Scott* decision left anti-slavery advocates in a dilemma. If Congress could not act to halt the spread of slavery, then who could? The decision — and the court — were primary campaign issues in 1860. Republicans argued that the court's statements on the power of Congress were simply *dicta* — comments extraneous to resolution of the case itself and hence not binding as constitutional law.

Republicans argued that the *Dred Scott* ruling could be overturned by a future court if Republicans gained control of both Congress and the White House, thus winning the opportunity to appoint loyal Republicans to the court. Several Republicans, including Ben Wade and Roscoe Conkling, demanded that the court be "packed" with Republicans should Lincoln win the election.

The Republican platform of 1860 sharply criticized the *Dred Scott* decision:

> ...the new dogma that the Constitution, of its own force, carries slavery into any or all of the territories of the United States, is a dangerous political heresy, at variance with the explicit provisions of that instrument itself, with contemporaneous exposition, and with legislative and judicial precedent; is revolutionary in its tendency, and subversive of the peace and harmony of the country ... the normal condition of all territory of the United States is that of freedom.... [39]

Lincon won the election, but war, rather than his nominations to the court, ultimately overruled *Dred Scott.*

The Income Tax Issue

In 1895 the court held the federal income tax unconstitutional in the case of *Pollock v. Farmer's Loan and Trust Co. (Details, pp. 109-112)*

The opinion angered progressives in Congress and other reformers who felt that the decision protected private vested rights and frustrated Congress' attempts to make the wealthy pay their fair share of taxes. Farmers and laborers considered the decision another victory of the rich and powerful.

The income tax ruling became an issue in the 1896 presidential campaign. The Democratic Party favored the income tax and decried such judicial "usurpation" of legislative power. Its candidate, William Jennings Bryan, in his famous "Cross of Gold" speech at the Democratic National Convention in Chicago in July 1896, said:

> They criticize us for our criticism of the Supreme Court of the United States.... They say that we passed an unconstitutional law; we deny it. The income tax law was not unconstitutional when it was passed; it was not unconstitutional when it went before the Supreme Court for the first time; it did not become unconstitutional until one of the judges changed his mind, and we cannot be expected to know when a judge will change his mind. The income tax is just. It simply intends to put the burdens of government justly upon the backs of the people. I am in favor of an income tax. When I find a man who is not willing to

share of the burdens of government which protects him, I find a man who is unworthy to enjoy the blessings of a government like ours."[40]

But Bryan lost, and not until ratification of the 16th Amendment in 1913 did Congress overturn the effect of the court's 1895 decision.

LaFollette on the Attack

In the 1924 election, Progressives made the Supreme Court's opposition to reform legislation a campaign issue.

Sen. Robert M. LaFollette, R-Wis., was the Progressive Party candidate for president in 1924. He argued that the day had come "when the Federal judiciary must be made — to some extent, at least — subject to the will of the people, or we must abandon the pretense that the people rule in this country. . . . We cannot live under a system of government where we are forced to amend the Constitution every time we want to pass a progressive law. The remedy must adequately cope with the disease, or there is no use applying it."[41]

LaFollette's remedy was a single constitutional amendment that sharply curtailed the power of judicial review, denying any lower federal court authority to declare an act of Congress unconstitutional and providing that when the Supreme Court declared an act of Congress unconstitutional, Congress could override that decision by re-enacting the law.

The 1924 Progressive Party platform stated:

> . . .We favor submitting to the people, for their considerate judgment, a constitutional amendment providing that Congress may by enacting a statute make it effective over a judicial veto.[42]

But 1924 was not a year for reformers. Prosperity and "normalcy" were on the rise, and the nation voted to keep Calvin Coolidge at the helm. The court, Coolidge said in response to LaFollette's criticism, was the chief defender of the American way of life — the chief obstacle preventing "breakdown [of] the guarantees of our fundamental law." [43]

"Fighting Bob" LaFollette died in 1925. His amendment was never adopted.

The Election of 1968

In the presidential campaign of 1968, Richard M. Nixon made clear that if elected he intended to use his power of appointment to remake the Supreme Court in the image of his own conservative value system.

Nixon severely criticized the Warren Court during a "law and order" campaign alleging that the court's decisions in the area of criminal procedure were "seriously hamstringing the peace forces in our society and strengthening the criminal forces." [44]

Soon after taking office in 1969 Nixon appointed Warren Earl Burger Chief Justice of the United States. Burger had a reputation as a hard-line "law and order" judge on the court of appeals for the District of Columbia.[45] He was quickly confirmed.

But Nixon's effort to name a second conservative to fill the seat left vacant by Abe Fortas' resignation ran into trouble.

During the campaign Nixon had said he would nominate a southerner to the court who had a conservative judicial philosophy. In November 1969 the Senate rejected Nixon's first southern nominee, Judge Clement F.

Arguing the President's Case

When the administration goes into the Supreme Court, the president's lawyer is the solicitor general of the United States. He or one of his staff argues the administration's side of a case. In other cases, to which the government is not a party but nevertheless has an interest in the decision, the solicitor general files an *amicus curiae* — "friend of the court" — brief.

The government has been very successful in arguing cases before the court. A 1971 study of the government's performance before the Supreme Court concluded:

> Throughout its history the United States has won most of its cases in the Supreme Court, and at a level of success which has not varied by very much from one period to another. An examination of the Court's opinions, chosen at ten-year intervals starting at 1800, shows that the government won 62 percent of its litigation there during the nineteenth century, and so far has won 64 percent of it during this century.[1]

The government's record in cases where it filed as *amicus curiae* is even better. The position endorsed by the government prevailed in as many as 87 percent of the cases in some terms after World War II. For the terms between 1958 and 1967 the government's rate of success in such cases averaged 71 percent.[2]

---

[1] Robert G. Scigliano, *The Supreme Court and the Presidency* (New York: The Free Press, 1971), p. 177.
[2] Ibid., p. 180.

Haynsworth of the court of appeals, fourth circuit, because of his participation in deciding cases in which, it was charged, he had a financial interest.

Nixon then submitted the name of G. Harrold Carswell, another conservative southerner who was a judge of the court of appeals, fifth circuit. Carswell's record as a staunch segregationist, and his lack of intellectual qualities and legal skill resulted in the Senate's rejection of his nomination in April 1970.

Nixon subsequently filled the Fortas seat with Minnesotan Harry A. Blackmun — a conservative member of the court of appeals for the eighth circuit and a friend of the Chief Justice.

Then in 1971 the retirements of Hugo L. Black and John Marshall Harlan gave Nixon two more seats on the court to fill. He named Lewis F. Powell Jr. to Black's seat. Powell was a distinguished Virginia lawyer who had served as president of the American Bar Association.

To Harlan's seat Nixon nominated assistant attorney general William H. Rehnquist. Harvard Law Professor Paul Freund described Rehnquist as "very conservative" but with a "brilliant and powerful" mind. Both men were confirmed in 1971.

By the end of 1971 — his third year as president — Nixon had appointed four members of the court. He had fulfilled his campaign pledges. The court's subsequent rulings on criminal law reflected the conservative views of Burger and the new associate justices.

Footnotes

[1] Robert G. Scigliano, *The Supreme Court and the Presidency* (New York: The Free Press, 1971), pp. 207-208.

[2] Ibid., p. 86.

[3] Henry J. Abraham, *Justices and Presidents: A Political History of Appointees to the Supreme Court* (New York: Oxford University Press, 1974), pp. 42-44.

[4] Ibid., Table III, p. 53.

[5] Ibid., pp. 56-58.

[6] Henry Cabot Lodge, *Selections from the Correspondence of Theodore Roosevelt and Henry Cabot Lodge, 1884-1918,* 2 vols. (New York: Charles Scribner's Sons, 1925) II:228, 230-231.

[7] Daniel S. McHargue, "Appointments to the Supreme Court of the United States: The Factors that have Affected Appointments, 1789-1932," (Ph.D. Dissertation, Political Science Department, University of California at Los Angeles, 1949), p. 549.

[8] Abraham, *Justices and Presidents,* p. 31.

[9] Ibid., p. 18.

[10] Ibid., p. 104.

[11] Ibid., p. 20.

[12] Alpheus T. Mason, *William Howard Taft: Chief Justice* (New York: Simon & Schuster, 1965), p. 76ff.

[13] Ibid., pp. 170-171.

[14] Leon Friedman and Fred L. Israel, eds. *The Justices of the United States Supreme Court, 1789-1969,* 4 vols. (New York: Chelsea House Publishers, R. R. Bowker, 1969), III: 2209.

[15] Abraham, *Justices and Presidents,* p. 22.

[16] Ibid., pp. 216, 226.

[17] Alpheus T. Mason, *Harlan Fiske Stone: Pillar of the Law* (New York: Viking Press, 1956), p. 336.

[18] Peter Odegaard, *American Politics,* 2d ed. (New York: Harper & Bros., 1947), p. 172.

[19] Abraham, *Justices and Presidents,* pp. 264-265.

[20] Odegaard, *American Politics,* p. 169.

[21] Charles Warren, *The Supreme Court in United States History,* rev. ed., 2 vols. (Boston: Little, Brown & Co., 1922, 1926), I:176-177.

[22] Robert J. Steamer, *The Supreme Court in Crisis: A History of Conflict* (Amherst, Mass.: The University of Massachusetts Press, 1971), p. 35.

[23] Warren, *Supreme Court in U.S. History,* I:178.

[24] Abraham, *Justices and Presidents,* p. 88.

[25] Warren, *Supreme Court in U.S. History,* II:515-527; Sidney Ratner, "Was the Supreme Court Packed by President Grant?," *Political Science Quarterly,* 50 (September 1935):343-358.

[26] Mason, *Harlan Fiske Stone,* pp. 566-567.

[27] Gerald T. Dunne, *Hugo Black and the Judicial Revolution* (New York: Simon & Schuster, 1977), p. 225.

[28] *Tennessee Coal, Iron and Railroad Co. v. Muscola Local 123* 321 U.S. 590 (1944); *Jewell Ridge Coal Corp. v. Local 6167 U.M.W.* 325 U.S. 161 (1945).

[29] Dunne, *Hugo Black and the Judicial Revolution,* p. 241.

[30] Ibid., pp. 240-248.

[31] Abraham, *Justices and Presidents,* pp. 227-228.

[32] Ibid., pp. 259-260.

[33] Robert Shogan, *A Question of Judgment, The Fortas Case and the Struggle for the Supreme Court* (Indianapolis: Bobbs-Merrill Co., 1972), pp. 233-236.

[34] Merlo J. Pusey, *Charles Evans Hughes,* 2 vols. (New York: MacMillan Publishing Co., 1951), I:271.

[35] Henry F. Pringle, *The Life and Times of William Howard Taft,* 2 vols. (New York: Farrar & Rinehart, 1939), II:535.

[36] Alpheus T. Mason, *William Howard Taft: Chief Justice,* p. 39.

[37] Warren, *Supreme Court in U.S. History,* I:167.

[38] Arthur M. Schlesinger Jr. and Fred L. Israel, eds., *History of American Presidential Elections, 1789-1968,* 4 vols. (New York: Chelsea House Publishers, 1971), II:1110-1111.

[39] Ibid., p. 1126.

[40] Ibid., p. 1847.

[41] William F. Swindler, *Court and Constitution in the 20th Century,* 2 vols. (Indianapolis: Bobbs-Merrill Co., 1969), I, *The Old Legality 1889-1932,* pp. 283-284.

[42] Schlesinger and Israel, *American Presidential Elections,* III: 2520.

[43] Alfred H. Kelly and Winfred A. Harbison, *The American Constitution,* 5th ed. (New York: W. W. Norton Co., 1976), p. 647.

[44] Ibid., p. 981.

[45] Stephen J. Wasby, *The Supreme Court in the Federal Judicial System* (New York: Holt, Rinehart & Winston, 1978), p. 95.

Selected Bibliography

Abraham, Henry J. *Justices and Presidents: A Political History of Appointments to the Supreme Court.* New York: Oxford University Press, 1974.

Danelski, David J. *A Supreme Court Justice is Appointed.* New York: Random House, 1964.

Dunne, Gerald T. *Hugo Black and the Judicial Revolution.* New York: Simon & Schuster, 1977.

Kelly, Alfred H., and Harbison, Winfred A. *The American Constitution.* 5th ed. New York: W. W. Norton & Co., 1976.

Mason, Alpheus T. *Harlan Fiske Stone: Pillar of the Law.* New York: Viking Press, 1956.

———. *William Howard Taft: Chief Justice.* New York: Simon & Schuster, 1965.

McHargue, Daniel S., "Appointments to the Supreme Court of the United States: The Factors that Have Affected Appointments, 1789-1932."(Ph.D. Dissertation, Political Science Department, University of California at Los Angeles, 1949).

Odegaard, Peter, *American Politics.* 2d ed. New York: Harper & Bros., 1947.

Pringle, Henry F. *The Life and Times of William Howard Taft.* 2 vols. New York: Farrar & Rinehart, 1939.

Pusey, Merlo F., *Charles Evans Hughes.* 2 vols. New York: MacMillan Publishing Co., 1951.

Ratner, Sidney F. "Was the Supreme Court Packed by President Grant?" *Political Science Quarterly* 50:343 (September 1935).

Schlesinger, Arthur M. Jr. and Israel, Fred L., eds., *History of American Presidential Elections.* 4 vols. New York: Chelsea House Publishers, 1971.

Scigliano, Robert G. *The Supreme Court and the Presidency.* New York: The Free Press, 1971.

Shogan, Robert. *A Question of Judgment: The Fortas Case and the Struggle for the Supreme Court.* Indianapolis: Bobbs-Merrill Co., 1972.

Steamer, Robert J. *The Supreme Court in Crisis: A History of Conflict.* Amherst, Mass.: University of Massachusetts Press, 1971.

Swindler, William F. *Court and Constitution in the 20th Century.* 2 vols. Indianapolis: Bobbs-Merrill Co., 1969.

Warren, Charles. *The Supreme Court in United States History.* Boston: Little, Brown & Co., 1922, 1926.

Wasby, Stephen J. *The Supreme Court in the Federal Judicial System.* New York: Holt, Rinehart & Winston, 1978.

Public Opinion

The Declaration of Independence appealed to two ultimate sources of legitimacy — natural law and the consent of the governed.

"The laws of nature and of nature's God," the rebellious colonists said, entitled them to establish their own sovereign state. Moreover, they held it self-evident that all men are "created" equal and endowed by their "Creator" with "unalienable" rights.

But the signers of the Declaration of Independence also asserted that the government of this new country derived its just powers "from the consent of the governed." Thus public opinion, as well as natural law, was from the beginning invoked as the foundation of the new state.

While rights may be unalienable, the Creator's plan self-evident, and nature's law unchanging, public opinion is none of these. Thus from its inception a tension was built into the American political system between the popular will and eternal principles. That tension is reflected in the Supreme Court, which is expected to be at once independent of, and responsive to, public opinion.

In its function as interpreter of the Constitution, the Supreme Court is applying a fundamental document which was approved by elected officials and can be amended by elected officials, and therefore reflects public opinion. The difficult process of amending the Constitution was intended to ensure that amendments would reflect the settled opinion of most citizens rather than the whim of a transient majority. But the possibility of amendment distinguishes the document from laws intended to be immutable and wholly immune to the pressures of public opinion.

Yet the American public often invests the Constitution with an aura of sanctity and permanence akin to religious sentiment, and the Supreme Court often shares in the public's reverence for its fundamental law. Because of that, and the court's pomp and obeisance to tradition, the public often regards it with more uncritical respect than it does the politicians it elects and rejects. In the public eye, the court is aloof from the haggling of politicians, above the compromising among selfish interests that is so much of the art of democratic politics. Thus public opinion itself tends to insulate the Supreme Court from the more ephemeral changes in public sentiment.

This image of the Supreme Court, however, is double-edged. Because the justices' opinions are inevitably, if not always consciously, influenced by the interests of major sections of the public, popular expectations that the Su-preme Court will be motivated solely by reason and high ideals are often disappointed. None are so quick to see a betrayal of principle in the court's reasonings as those whose ox has just been gored by one of its decisions. When that happens, reverence for the court may turn into cynicism and scorn. This has happened often enough that a mischievous disrespect for the Supreme Court is also part of American tradition, coexisting with esteem for the court's lofty detachment.

The court's aloofness from the popular will finds ultimate expression in its power of judicial review of legislation. A law passed by an elected Congress and signed by an elected president, or enacted by elected state legislatures, can be overturned by nine — or even five — unelected judges. The justification for their power over elected officials lies in the supremacy of the Constitution and in acceptance of the court as its upholder. The interpretation of the Constitution announced by a majority of the justices, no matter how controversial it may be, is in theory as "final" as the Constitution itself. According to long-accepted tradition, the other institutions of government and the public are obligated to accept the court's decisions, which can be reversed only by the court itself or by a constitutional amendment.

In fact, however, the response of other institutions and the public to Supreme Court interpretations of the Constitution and other federal law is a factor in its deliberations, and the court itself not infrequently revises its earlier rulings. Moreover, the Supreme Court usually has hesitated to oppose the popular will expressed through the elected branches of government, both out of respect for the democratic principles it is supposed to protect and from fear of retaliation or noncompliance.

Nevertheless, because the justices' tenure of office — unlike that of the president and Congress — is not subject to changes in public opinion through election, the changing views of new generations are often under-represented among nine men entitled to remain on the bench as long as they live.

Even if they want to respond to changing opinion, the justices are to some degree restrained by the written Constitution, although this restraint should not be exaggerated. The evocative and laconic vagueness of the Constitution — which intelligent and honest men trained in the law can, and usually do, interpret in different ways — allows the Supreme Court the flexibility both to assert its fundamentally enduring principles and to respond to that other source of government authority in the United States — the tradition of popular sovereignty.

The Bill of Rights by its language requires the court to decide case-by-case such questions as: What searches are "unreasonable?" What process is "due" a suspect in certain circumstances? What punishment is "cruel" and "unusual"? *(pp. 539, 523, 575)*

In answering these recurring questions, the modern court has freely acknowledged its reliance on public opinion. Decisions on such invidious issues as capital punishment no doubt owe as much to the public consensus as they do to legal precedent.

Foundations of Independence

The Supreme Court was intended as a non-elected check on the political branches of the federal government, and to that end the men who wrote the Constitution insulated the court from the more passionate and evanescent extremes of public sentiment. The United States prided itself on avoiding the bloody, retributive excesses of the French Revolution — which it helped inspire — and today looks in horror on the violent aftermaths of revolution in trouble spots around the world.

Even in a time of turbulent revolution and the collapse of established authority, the Founding Fathers feared mob rule. The Constitution — with its checks and balances and guarantee of a fair trial — was designed to prevent the new republic from becoming a tyranny of the majority. The independence of a Supreme Court, its members appointed for life, reflected this suspicion of truly "popular" government.

So the colonists generally avoided the worst excesses of revolutionary justice and soon re-established and even strengthened guarantees of civil liberties. During the first decade of the new republic, as Americans witnessed a bloody mockery of justice in the executions of the French Revolution, the Federalists took their stand against unrestrained popular government, and through the genius of the Federalist Chief Justice John Marshall fashioned the Supreme Court into a powerful check on the elected institutions of the young state.

Government by Law

The independence of the judiciary had deep roots in English history, resting ultimately on the belief that a free society must be governed by laws rather than by men. To ensure that the rights of Englishmen were protected and limited by the known dictates of the laws rather than the unpredictable ethics of the rulers, the English courts had a well-established tradition of independence, one that would enable them even to rule against the king.

In America, the replacement of a hereditary executive by an elected one did not diminish Americans' determination to have an independent judiciary. Indeed, the new regime in America pushed the ideal of judicial independence beyond English tradition. The principle of judicial review of legislation, first explicitly claimed by Chief Justice John Marshall's court in 1803 *(Marbury v. Madison)*, gave the Supreme Court a degree of autonomy unprecedented in any court in England, where the supremacy of Parliament had no limits except its own veneration of an unwritten constitution. Because the colonists had rebelled against acts of Parliament which they felt denied them the traditional rights of Englishmen, it is not surprising that

they wanted constitutional limits on the power of their new legislature, or that they soon accepted the Supreme Court's role as the guardian of those limits. *(pp. 69-79)*

Popular sovereignty was also an ideal of the reigning intellectual persuasion of that day, the Enlightenment, which advocated a belief in "natural" law, to be found in such self-evident truths as the equality of all men and their unalienable rights.

Limited Powers

Explicit guarantees of rights were only part of the Constitution's safeguards against a potential tyranny of the majority. The authority of Congress and of the president was implicitly limited by the enumeration of their powers and explicitly limited by various prohibitions. The Constitution does not make clear who is to determine when those limits have been exceeded, but because the whole constitutional system of checks and balances is based on the belief that institutions are little inclined to limit their own power, the Supreme Court functions within the spirit of the Constitution in claiming the right to set limits for the other branches.

In disputes *between* the executive and legislative branches the court also can appear in the role of an outside arbiter. Moreover, the fact that the court is not subject to the same popular demands as the elected institutions of government reduces the pressure for it to acquiesce in popular usurpations of power by either of the other branches.

In such confrontations, however, the court's lack of a popular political base often places it at a disadvantage vis-à-vis Congress and the White House, which can point to a recent popular mandate. Thus the same independence of public opinion that fosters respect for the court's impartiality may undermine faith in its democratic legitimacy.

Since the division of sovereignty agreed upon when the Constitution was ratified was defined in a legal document, it was natural enough to expect the court to interpret its own provisions, and to do so according to judicial criteria rather than perceptions of change in public opinion. The Supreme Court's independence of public opinion thus enhanced its credibility as manager of the Constitution's boundaries between national and state sovereignty.

However, because a *national* court could not be considered a wholly disinterested party in disputes between national and state interests, the states resisted — sometimes with outright defiance — the Supreme Court's early assertions of supremacy. Under Chief Justice Marshall a series of landmark decisions gradually built up the power of the national court, but it required a civil war to settle finally the question of national sovereignty. *(pp. 303-308)*

Disputes over the boundaries between federal and state power continue in modern times, but the jurisdiction of the national court over such issues is no longer in question.

Judicial Function

The Supreme Court has no occasion to interpret the Constitution except when a lawsuit requires such interpretation, and even in those cases the court has a tradition of avoiding constitutional issues if narrower legal grounds suffice to settle the suit. *(p. 287)*

This reduction of great issues to litigation between two parties enables the court to emphasize its insistence on law, rather than public opinion or politics. But this source of authority has its limits. When the court under the guise of judicial impartiality makes judgments which the public deems to be politically motivated, its pronouncements may be viewed as disingenuous. The justices then are accused of "making" law while pretending only to apply established laws, and public acceptance of the Supreme Court's decisions is undermined by the feeling that the court has usurped legislative power and, moreover, has done so with less than total frankness. *(pp. 268-269)*

The charge of making rather than applying law is a frequent one, especially among those who feel disadvantaged by a Supreme Court decision. But belief that the court can be a wholly impartial spokesman for the Constitution has always been a myth, and in the last half-century there has been wider recognition that the court, too, is a political institution that must choose among competing interpretations of a document that means different things to different and often incompatible sections of the public.

Intangible Influences

It is usually difficult to determine whether, or to what extent, a particular decision has been influenced by public opinion. The justices themselves rarely admit that they are swayed by popular, rather than judicial, considerations. To base an interpretation of the Constitution on public opinion would seem to vitiate the purpose of assigning the function of interpretation to an unelected body, thus undermining the Supreme Court's credibility even with the public whose opinion it sought to follow.

Still, the same historical events and trends that shape public opinion also influence judges, and the judges' opinions may resemble those of the public not because they are following popular views but because they have shared the same historical experience.

The fact that public opinion is usually divided, often ambivalent and generally subject to change gives the justices considerable latitude in responding to it. It is only natural that a justice tends to be more responsive to the sentiments of the sector of society that shaped his pre-court experiences. But elevation to the Supreme Court may broaden an individual's awareness of, and sympathy for, elements of the public which his previous position did not require him to consider.

The traditional image of the Supreme Court also exerts pressure on the justices' behavior. However responsive a justice may be to prevailing opinions, the public generally expects his behavior to be judicious. Thurman Arnold noted "the impelling force of dignified and rational procedure upon the judges who invent it."[1]

However intangible, that appearance of dignity and reason is central to the court's function of reassuring the people of the permanence and stability of their political system. Fear of impulsiveness in popular self-government permeates the American political system, whose checks and balances provide an antidote to hasty decisions that might not survive sober second thought. Thus the requirement that a law be approved by two legislative chambers and signed by the president, as well as the possibility of its review by the Supreme Court, tempers the passions and fashions of popular sentiment. Such caution provides the legislative safety net that has allowed the nation to risk so many political innovations.

The Court and Change

Although the Supreme Court is less responsive to public opinion than are America's elected institutions, it, too, reflects the changing trends and values of the nation that alter, among other things, the public's understanding of the Constitution and the truths Americans hold to be "self-evident."

Because the pressure of public opinion influences the court primarily through processes of change in society and politics, the nature of that influence can best be examined by considering it in the context of historical events and trends.

Early Federal-State Relations

After declaring their independence, the first generation of Americans had to decide what kind of state they would create to replace England's 13 colonies. The Articles of Confederation failed to serve the needs of the new nation, and both the public and its statesmen knew why: Too little power was given to national institutions, too much to the states.

The colonial experience, however, had bred a closer identification with local than with national communities. The former colonists recognized the need for a stronger national government than that provided under the Articles of Confederation, but at the same time they were reluctant to grant powers to national authorities so soon after liberating themselves from the distant power of the British government.

The Constitution turned the resulting dispute over national unity and states' rights into an opportunity. The balance of federal and state power, like the separation of powers and the system of checks and balances within the federal government, served as a limitation on the power of the rulers. Thus the rights of individuals — ever precarious in contests with those of governments — were to be protected by keeping the governments in the United States divided and competing. In this way a foundation was laid for a loyalty above that of either state or nation, a loyalty to a system in which both state and national governments enjoyed legitimate sovereignty.

It was to this public loyalty to a Constitution above both state and national governments that the Supreme Court would have to appeal in its contests with both of them.

Chisholm v. Georgia. The court's first attempt to limit state sovereignty resulted in emphatic public repudiation. In 1793 the court ruled in *Chisholm v. Georgia* that a state could be sued in federal court by a citizen of another state.[2] A constitutional amendment to reverse the decision carried in the Senate by a vote of 23 to 2 and in the House by 81 to 9. This near-unanimity among elected legislators gave some indication, in an age without opinion polls, of the breadth of public opposition to the Supreme Court's decision.

The intensity of this opposition was evident in numerous vehement newspaper editorials, too, but found perhaps its most eloquent expression in a bill passed by the Georgia House of Representatives providing that any official who executed a court order allowed under the decision should be declared "guilty of felony and shall suffer death, without benefit of clergy, by being hanged."[3] The bill never was passed, but the sentiments behind it were well-known to the Supreme Court justices.

In fact, when Attorney General Edmund Randolph argued for the plaintiff against the state of Georgia he acknowledged that his motion was "unpopular," adding that his own state, Virginia, "whose will must always be dear to me," had also opposed the position he was taking.

Randolph said that "on ordinary occasions, these dignified opinions might influence me greatly," but that it would be "official perfidy" for him to yield to these opinions on a question of "constitutional right."[4]

Current events also shaped public reaction to the decision. The states feared, not without reason, that if they could be sued by individuals, then an avalanche of claims by holders of state issues of paper and other credits and by Loyalist refugees seeking recovery of confiscated property would jeopardize their precarious finances.

The fact that the plaintiffs in such cases were often Tories who had opposed the revolution did not engender sympathy for their constitutional claims by a citizenry which considered itself heir to the revolution. The public antagonism toward the Tories was also indirectly related to a sense of grievance against the national authority being upheld by the Supreme Court. Fear and distrust of remote British authority had been transferred, to some extent, to the new centralized national government.

Thus one newspaper writer said that the Supreme Court's ruling against Georgia "involved more danger to the liberties of America than the claims of the British Parliament to tax us without our consent," and others warned that the ruling was only the first step toward a standing army and even a monarchy.[5] Such fears were doubtless exaggerated, but for those whose memories of colonial rule were still vivid, anxieties about losing their hard-won self-rule did not seem unrealistic.

The 11th Amendment. The reversal of the *Chisholm* decision by the 11th Amendment, ratified in January 1798, may have reassured those anxious to preserve states' rights, but it also served to reinforce the authority of a strong national court.

The fact that it required a constitutional amendment to overturn a Supreme Court ruling against a state actually confirmed its power. The idea that the Supreme Court's interpretation of the Constitution is final, and therefore can only be changed by amending the Constitution, was implicit in the campaign for the 11th Amendment. While this finality of court opinions was still to be contested in major constitutional conflicts, the use of the amendment process — rather than action by other branches of the federal government or defiance by state governments — set an important precedent.

The 11th Amendment also strengthened the court by teaching it a lesson. It impressed upon the justices the risks of direct confrontation with a popular viewpoint that is both widely shared and deeply felt. A judicious respect for public opinion was evident in subsequent decisions by the early court, whose self-restraint became a foundation of its growing power. Under the tutelage of Chief Justice Marshall, who was a master at combining restraint and boldness, the Supreme Court nursed public opinion toward respect for the federal government — particularly for the federal judiciary.

Marshall in 1801 had begun his 34-year tenure as Chief Justice severely handicapped by the trend of public opinion. His Federalist Party by then had badly alienated the public, and its opponents had swept into power with solid majorities in Congress, and a powerful leader, Thomas Jefferson, in the White House.

The federal judiciary, composed almost entirely of ardent Federalists, shared in the opprobrium cast upon the defeated party. The partisanship they had shown from the bench, especially in enforcing the Alien and Sedition Acts of 1798 against critics of the national administration,

provoked a potent combination of distrust in the public and anger in the new Republican administration.

When the outgoing Federalists, in the Judiciary Act of 1801, created and filled new federal judgeships and reduced the number of Supreme Court justices from six to five so that Jefferson could not fill the next vacancy, it seemed the last straw. The Federalists appeared determined to flout public opinion, reversing the verdict of the 1800 election by entrenching unelected judges for life in the judicial branch. It is scarcely surprising that the new president was determined to curb the power of the federal (and Federalist) judiciary and felt he had a popular mandate to do so.

The effort in 1805 to impeach Samuel Chase, the most partisan of the Federalist justices, nearly succeeded, and had it done so the Republicans probably would have pursued other judicial opponents of their aims, including Marshall. *(Details, p. 658)*

In that event, according to one historian, "the doctrine of an independent judiciary would have foundered and the whole future history of the court might have been profoundly different."[6]

Marbury v. Madison. With Jefferson hostile both to the judiciary and to assertions of national power against state sovereignty, Marshall and his colleagues had to be cautious in advancing the nationalist cause. Their manner of dealing with Jefferson's administration was typified by the *Marbury v. Madison* decision.[7] In this case Marshall laid down the constitutional precedent for judicial review of a national statute, but in doing so satisfied the immediate political objective of Jefferson's party — the denial of a judicial post to one of President Adams' last-minute Federalist appointees. With their political objective secured, it would have been difficult for the Republicans to arouse public hostility to a legal precedent with no immediate consequences. *(Details, p. 267)*

The long-range consequences of *Marbury*, however, made it a landmark case in American constitutional history, exemplifying the concern with far-reaching consequences that has given the Supreme Court, over the years, an influence that survives the shifting moods of public opinion and elected politicians.

It was not until 1810 that the Supreme Court felt sure enough of its growing authority to confront assertions of state sovereignty directly by overturning a state law. In his opinion in *Fletcher v. Peck*, Marshall expressed the case for restraint in judicial review:

> Whether a law be void for its repugnancy to the Constitution is, at all times, a question of much delicacy, which ought seldom, if ever, to be decided in the affirmative in a doubtful case.... It is not on slight implication and vague conjecture that the Legislature is to be pronounced to have transcended its powers, and its acts to be considered as void. The opposition between the Constitution and the law should be such that the judge feels a clear and strong conviction of their incompatibility with each other.[8]

This spirit of restraint, reflected not only in the justices' rhetoric but in decisions favorable to the states as well as to the national government, inhibited the consolidation of local opinion against the Supreme Court. As long as advocates of states' rights had reason to believe the court might rule in their favor in the future, they could more easily tolerate decisions that restricted state authority. It would have been difficult, in any case, for anti-nationalist views to present a national challenge to the Supreme Court for the simple reason that their own centrifugal sentiments kept them disunited. As Robert G. McCloskey observed:

> . . .if Virginia had a problem today that Maryland did not share, Virginia's outraged protest in the name of states' rights would attract little support from Maryland any more than Maryland's similar protest tomorrow would bring Virginia rushing to her standard. Both states were being true to the fractional principle that lay at the heart of the states' rights doctrine. But, because of their adherence to that principle, the Supreme Court, with its eye steadily on a single target, was spared the calamity of confronting a united opposition.[9]

A Sense of Nationhood

While Marshall's court was gradually laying down the great constitutional precedents for national supremacy, public opinion as a whole was growing more accustomed to a sense of nationhood. The Supreme Court both benefited from this evolution and fostered its development. It contributed to nation-building not only by decisions whose overall trend favored national institutions, but by attracting public respect for its role as a symbol of principles on which the nation agreed — the supremacy of law as expressed in the Constitution, and the interpretation of the law through reasoned argument in open debate.

The Supreme Court also contributed to national unity by refusing to take a doctrinaire and uncompromising position against states' rights. It is doubtful that the Union could have been preserved, let alone that it could have so swiftly incorporated vast new territories, without granting sufficient local autonomy to its diverse peoples and regions.

By respecting regional interests, the Supreme Court helped to ensure that authority over the society was not overconcentrated and local and individual freedom was recognized even as a new nation was being created.

Race Relations

It is difficult for nations to tolerate continual internal division. The American system of government is unusual in its willingness to risk internal conflict by preserving and even perpetuating conflicting ideas, sanctioning dispute and giving refuge to unpopular viewpoints.

But while the American system of internal conflict has proved, over time, to be highly creative, it suffered a traumatic, violent breakdown in the Civil War. When the conflict between state and national sovereignties became inextricably merged with the issue of slavery, the Supreme Court could no longer balance their rival claims.

Dred Scott Decision

The slavery issue aroused such passions that there was little hope nine unelected justices could manage them. When they attempted to do so, in *Dred Scott v. Sandford* (1857), they dealt the Supreme Court the most crippling blow in its history.[10] *(See p. 135)*

In deciding that Scott was still a slave despite having traveled in free territory, the court declared that black people could not be citizens and that Congress could not control slavery in the territories. Public opinion in the North was outraged by this decision and found expression in a storm of abuse beyond anything the court had yet encountered. While the South welcomed the decision, the

support of a region preparing to secede if it did not get its way offered little solace to a national court viewed with loathing and contempt in the region loyal to the national government.

The great esteem in which the public held the court in the early 1850s, an esteem carefully nurtured over decades by the discretion of Chief Justices Marshall and Roger B. Taney, was shaken to its foundations by this one divisive opinion. Looking back at the decision, historians have observed that the court asserted more authority than the case required or the public would tolerate, and have cited it as the leading object lesson in the need for judicial restraint.

The authority of the court would in any case have been severely tried by the war that soon broke out, but the *Dred Scott* decision robbed it of the public support that might have enabled it to challenge wartime suspensions of constitutional rights.

When Taney, acting as a circuit judge,[11] ordered that a Maryland secessionist held in military prison be brought before him on a writ of *habeas corpus* and the commanding general defied the order, Taney called upon President Lincoln to "perform his constitutional duty." The northern press that had railed against the *Dred Scott* decision now reviled Taney for supporting "traitors," and the president paid no heed.

During the war the justices generally avoided confrontations with the president and Congress, and by 1863 Taney wrote that he saw no hope that the court would "ever again be restored to the authority and rank which the Constitution intended to confer upon it. The supremacy of the military power over the civil seems to be established, and the public mind has acquiesced in it and sanctioned it."[12]

Civil Rights

The anomaly of a race deprived of rights in a land dedicated to the proposition that all men are created equal was not ended by the violent upheaval it spawned. Both in the South and elsewhere, Negroes were still regarded and treated as members of an inferior race.

Nearly a hundred years after the *Dred Scott* decision alienated northern opinion, the Supreme Court in a decision almost equally bold outraged the South by requiring an end to segregation of the races in public schools (*Brown v. Board of Education of Topeka*).[13]

Underlying this reversal in the court's position was an incipient transformation of American attitudes toward race relations. The Supreme Court was able to challenge passionately-held southern attitudes because of the state of opinion in the rest of the country. Civil rights advocates, both black and white, ardently supported the court, a larger section of the public was basically sympathetic to the pursuit of racial equality, and most others outside the South — whatever their attitudes toward Negroes — were unwilling seriously to challenge a unanimous Supreme Court pursuing the ideal of equality.

The constitutionality of the *Brown* decision and the reasoning of the court were not unequivocally endorsed in the North, but southern efforts to defy the court found no champions outside the South in the 1950s, and generally the country resolved to see the court's new doctrine enforced. Even a reluctant President Eisenhower felt he had no choice but to back up the court with military force in the integration of public schools in Arkansas, in 1957.

After the Civil War northern members of Congress had been intent on requiring racial equality through constitutional amendment and legislation, but as the ardor of Reconstruction abated, the Supreme Court narrowly construed the new amendments and overturned the civil rights legislation with only scattered northern protests. *(Details, p. 151)* Justice John Marshall Harlan, in a lonely dissent in the *Civil Rights Cases* of 1883,[14] objected that the court was sacrificing both the "substance and the spirit" of the 14th Amendment, but the ruling, as Robert S. Hirschfield observed, "probably reflected the prevailing national sentiment". He continued:

> ...in the post-Reconstruction period of industrial development and increased business activity, there was a widespread desire to forget the antagonisms of the past and concentrate on the opportunities of the present.... The plight of the Negro was largely ignored and the issue of racial equality was relegated to the background of the constitutional arena.[15]

In 1896 the Supreme Court gave constitutional sanction to racial segregation in *Plessy v. Ferguson,* asserting that the state of Louisiana had not violated the 14th Amendment by requiring separate railway accommodations as long as those accommodations were equal.[16]

This "separate but equal" doctrine dominated the court's approach to race relations until it was explicitly overturned in 1954. Starting in 1938 the justices began using the doctrine to improve conditions for blacks by insisting on integration unless separate facilities were *truly* equal,[17] but not until the *Brown* decision did the Supreme Court assert that separate educational facilities were "inherently" unequal.

The unanimous opinion, delivered by Chief Justice Earl Warren, said that "To separate [Negro students] from others of similar age and qualifications solely because of their race generates a feeling of inferiority as to their status in the community that may affect their hearts and minds in a way unlikely ever to be undone." After citing with approval a lower court opinion that segregation, because it is usually interpreted as denoting Negro inferiority, "affects the motivation of a child to learn" and tends to retard "the educational and mental development of Negro children," the court observed:

> Whatever may have been the extent of psychological knowledge at the time of *Plessy v. Ferguson,* this finding is amply supported by modern authority.[18]

This statement, and its supporting footnote listing some of the "modern authorities" backing the court's opinion, became a target of critics who doubted whether it was judicious to decide constitutional questions on the basis of current social science. *(Details, p. 592)*

But whatever the legal merits of citing social scientists' findings, Warren's opinion accurately identified a major source of influence on the Supreme Court. Just as the authors of the Declaration of Independence had drawn upon the ideas of 18th-century political theorists to determine what truths to hold "self-evident," so modern justices, consciously or not, share ideas emanating from the intellectual community of their era. Intellectual leaders influence the justices both directly and through their influence on public opinion. There can be no doubt that modern social and behavioral sciences had altered attitudes toward race relations in large sectors of public opinion before the Supreme Court directly invoked their authority.

Mere ideas, however, were not enough to explain the shift in public opinion between *Plessy* and *Brown.* After all,

the idea that all men are created equal had been an American doctrine from the moment of the nation's birth. Before that idea could be applied to black descendants of slaves, there had to be a change of heart as well as mind.

One factor contributing to changed feelings toward blacks among the white majority was the experience of the Second World War. The ideals for which Americans — black and white — were summoned to sacrifice their lives and fortunes made it more difficult, after the war, to champion racial discrimination openly. The armed forces, not surprisingly, were one of the first institutions to feel the impact of this postwar mood, when their longstanding practices of racial segregation were revoked by President Truman in a 1948 executive order.

During the 1950s and '60s, the civil rights movement was to have a great impact on all three branches of the federal government. Civil rights groups, labor unions and churches joined in the campaign, using demonstrations, marches, sit-ins, lobbying and litigation to bring pressure on every level of government and on private businesses and institutions. At the time of the 1954 *Brown* decision many felt that the Supreme Court had advanced dangerously far ahead of public opinion, but the events of the following years suggest that at the very least the justices had tapped a reservoir of popular sentiment waiting to find expression.

Perhaps the most fundamental changes leading the Supreme Court to reverse its established policies on race relations were changes in the black community in the 20th century. Migration to northern cities gave many blacks greater economic opportunity and social mobility and in many ways increased both their self-confidence and their dissatisfaction with racial inequality. New black lobbies increasingly demanded an end to discriminatory practices and gradually developed the means to make their demands felt.

The National Association for the Advancement of Colored People (NAACP) assumed a leading role in this movement, and litigation became its most effective means of securing minority rights and educating American opinion. The cases the NAACP brought into the courts not only won precedents expanding legal rights of blacks, but called the public's attention to the contradiction between the ideals expressed in the Declaration of Independence and the Constitution and the nation's treatment of its minorities.

The skillful management of judicial challenges and other strategies in a well-planned program to secure racial equality influenced public opinion in a less direct way. Together with the achievements of blacks in other areas, it helped erode the stereotype of Negroes as naturally irresponsible and unintelligent. The spectacle of educational inequalities imposed on black children became increasingly intolerable to conscientious whites as well as to blacks themselves.

Nevertheless, public reaction to *Brown v. Board of Education* and other of its civil rights decisions put the court in a difficult position. "Massive resistance" to the racial integration mandated by the court demonstrated the risk involved in decisions that moved too far ahead of public opinion — at least in a large region of the country. At the same time, liberal critics argued that the court's dictum that integration proceed with "all deliberate speed" was too cautious an approach to an inequity in absolute human rights that demanded immediate resolution.

In any event, the court — though legal challenges on both sides abounded — took a low-keyed approach to the civil rights issue in the years following its landmark decisions. Only after Congress joined the civil rights push with a spate of rights legislation in the 1960s — reflecting an even wider public endorsement of racial integration — did the court issue further significant civil rights rulings. And most of these, rather than breaking more new ground, simply placed a judicial imprimatur on the constitutionality of Congress' legislation. *(Details, pp. 610-621)*

Response to Crisis

The Depression and its remedies challenged the nation profoundly. The crisis — sudden in its impact — signalled permanent changes in the allocation and use of power in the United States.

The economic and social upheaval of the Depression made unmistakably clear to the entire nation that the economics of an agrarian frontier society, in which individual initiative was believed capable of solving most individual economic problems, had been replaced by a complex industrial economy of interdependence whose problems could only be solved by national action.

The public demanded from government a swift and powerful response to its economic catastrophe. But the long-range consequences of emergency measures taken to deal with the crisis were controversial.

In its role as the guardian of the traditional values expressed in the Constitution, the Supreme Court had a responsibility to insist that the American public consider, in the midst of alarm and confusion, what was to become of truths long held to be self-evident. While the urgency of the situation called for swift action, the permanence of the changes called for detached and dispassionate reflection. Thus the Depression — not to mention the era of global war that followed it — tested whether or not an 18th-century invention like the Supreme Court, the creature of an "Age of Reason," could still play a useful role in an era of rapid, profound, and continuing change.

To do so, the modern Supreme Court would have to deal with the same fundamental conflict that had marked its entire history, but would have to do so in an age of more or less perpetual crisis.

Reason Amid Panic

During the Depression the Supreme Court was challenged not merely by public opinion, but by a public despair. The panic that followed the "crash" of 1929 had deepened into a "fathomless pessimism" by the time President Roosevelt came to the White House in March 1933. Unemployment had reached between 10 and 15 million, national income had fallen by more than 50 percent, farm foreclosures and business failures had reached epidemic proportions, industrial production had dwindled to a trickle, and the recovery efforts of the Hoover administration had proved woefully inadequate to lift the nation from its strange and dismal condition. Roosevelt's overwhelming victory over Hoover in the 1932 elections, with a popular vote of 22,800,000 to 15,750,000, clearly gave the government a mandate for change. Between the November election and Roosevelt's inauguration in March, 1933, the inaction of the lame-duck Congress reinforced the national sense of paralysis, but in a stirring inaugural address the new president promised to mobilize the nation as if for war.

William E. Leuchtenburg described the impact of that speech:

In declaring there was nothing to fear but fear, Roosevelt had minted no new platitude; Hoover had said the same thing repeatedly for three years. Yet Roosevelt had nonetheless made his greatest single contribution to the politics of the 1930s: the instillation of hope and courage in the people. He made clear that the time of waiting was over, that he had the people's interests at heart, and that he would mobilize the power of the government to help them.[19]

During the next week the new president received almost half a million letters. He had achieved a public image in sharp contrast to that of Hoover, as Leuchtenburg noted, an image "of a man who knew how to lead and had faith in the future." [20] In his famous first "Hundred Days," Roosevelt rushed through Congress a deluge of legislation amounting to a government incursion into economic affairs hitherto left largely to the states and private enterprise.

The program won lopsided majorities in Congress. But the Supreme Court, which had compiled a generally conservative record on economic regulation, proved to be another matter.

The court's overall tendency in the late 19th and early 20th centuries was to constitutionalize the principles of laissez-faire economic theory. This policy grew even more pronounced in the 1920s. "The temper of the times," Robert G. McCloskey observed, "signalized by conservative Republican electoral triumphs and by the withering of the progressive spirit in public policy, was infectious. . . . Now the judges were confident that they spoke for the nation when they defended laissez-faire." [21]

Still, the Depression confronted at least some of the Supreme Court justices with doubts about the sanctity of familiar economic principles. In two decisions in 1934 the court upheld a Minnesota mortgage moratorium and a New York law fixing minimum and maximum prices for milk despite prevailing contrary precedents of interpretations of the Constitution's contract and due-process clauses *(Home Building and Loan Assn. v. Blaisdell* and *Nebbia v. New York).*[22] *(Details, pp. 314, 325)*

In ruling on the Minnesota law, enacted in the midst of farmer protests and lawlessness, Chief Justice Hughes' majority opinion took note of the emergency situation as justification for a temporary suspension of contracts. "While emergency does not create power," he observed, "emergency may furnish the occasion for the exercise of power." But in recognizing a reserve power of states to abridge contracts to "safeguard the economic structure upon which the good of all depends," Hughes also noted structural economic trends that had been evident long before the emergency and would continue after it:

> The settlement and consequent contraction of the public domain, the pressure of a constantly increasing density of population, the interrelation of the activities of our people and the complexity of our economic interests, have inevitably led to an increased use of the economic organization of society in order to protect the very bases of individual opportunity.[23]

Four justices, Van Devanter, McReynolds, Sutherland and Butler, bitterly disagreed with the majority on the mortgage and milk-price decisions, warning that the court must not "yield to the voice of an impatient majority stirred by distressful exigency." [24]

These four were to continue to oppose a strict-constructionist and laissez-faire approach to government efforts to regulate the stricken economy.

Court v. White House

Early in 1935 these conservatives were joined by four other justices in striking down the petroleum code established under the National Industrial Recovery Act (NIRA) enacted by the New Deal in Roosevelt's first Hundred Days,[25] and a few months later all nine justices joined in a unanimous decision condemning the entire NIRA as unconstitutional.[26]

These 8-1 and 9-0 majorities are worth recalling when the judgment of the consistently anti-New Deal justices is challenged in the light of hindsight. The New Deal's ardent supporters as well as its critics on the court found this legislation, drafted in haste and giving the White House vast and ill-defined power, an affront even to a broadly interpreted Constitution.

By this time much of the public, too, had become disenchanted with the confusion wrought by the NIRA's attempts to establish regulatory codes for hundreds of industries large and small. But President Roosevelt called the NIRA ruling more important than any since the *Dred Scott* case, and complained that the country had been "relegated to the horse-and-buggy definition of interstate commerce." *(Details pp. 98, 242)*

Following the NIRA rulings, the four conservative justices were joined by Justice Roberts and sometimes Chief Justice Hughes in striking down one key piece of New Deal legislation after another. The court's majority was aware that its decisions ran counter to public opinion, which had handed the New Deal a solid endorsement in the 1934 congressional elections. Justice Roberts, speaking for the majority in overturning the Agricultural Adjustment Act of 1933, replied to those who criticized the court for obstructing the popular will:

> It is sometimes said that the court assumes a power to overrule or control the action of the people's representatives. This is a misconception. The Constitution is the supreme law of the land ordained and established by the people. All legislation must conform to the principles it lays down. When an act of Congress is appropriately challenged in the courts as not conforming to the constitutional mandate, the judicial branch of the government has only one duty — to lay the article of the Constitution which is invoked beside the statute which is challenged and to decide whether the latter squares with the former. All the court does, or can do, is to announce its considered judgment upon the question. The only power it has, if such it may be called, is the power of judgment.[27]

Justice Stone, joined in dissent by Brandeis and Cardozo, called Roberts' narrow interpretation of the spending power "a tortured construction of the Constitution" and challenged the majority's attitude toward the elected branches of the government. "Courts are not the only agency of government," he said, "that must be assumed to have the capacity to govern." Stone further warned that it was dangerous to assume "that the responsibility for the preservation of our institutions is the exclusive concern of any one of the three branches of government."[28]

The existence of the Supreme Court as a powerful and independent institution was threatened directly the following year. After the 1936 elections, in which he carried every state except Maine and Vermont and rolled up a popular vote margin of 27,751,597 to 16,679,583, President Roosevelt sent Congress a plan to add as many as six new justices to the Supreme Court. Such a move would both have ensured

a comfortable court majority for New Deal legislation and set a precedent denying the court any real independence.

Paul L. Murphy explained Roosevelt's tactics:

> The president had come to feel that large elements of public opinion were now aware, especially in light of growingly more hostile dissent by liberal minority justices, that the obstacle to New Deal success lay not in the Constitution itself but in the composition of this particular court. Here he clearly underestimated the degree of blind public adherence to both as stable symbols in unstable times.[29]

Although his party now held majorities of 75 to 17 in the Senate and 333 to 89 in the House, Roosevelt's "court packing" plan was rejected by Congress. In part, the legislators' loyalty to traditional checks and balances and their doubts about excessive power in the executive branch made them reluctant to undermine the independence of a coordinate branch of government. But Congress also was responding to the public, which, in a deluge of mail to its representatives, rushed to the defense of the court. The Senate Judiciary Committee in June rejected Roosevelt's plan as an attempt to make the judiciary "subservient to the pressures of public opinion of the hour." *(Judiciary Committee report, p. 971)*

The Court Preserved

Had the Supreme Court continued to flout public opinion and its elected representatives, however, it is probable that Congress soon would have sought some kind of court "reform." But while the court-packing plan was being heatedly debated, the court provided the "switch in time that saved nine." By a 5 to 4 decision on April 12, 1937,[30] the court reversed its interpretation of the Constitution's commerce clause to uphold the Wagner Act, which guaranteed labor's right to organize and bargain collectively. This constitutional reversal was soon followed by others validating New Deal legislation. The court-packing plan was defeated and in August, Roosevelt named Hugo Black to replace Willis Van Devanter, strengthening the new liberal bent of the court majority.

At no time in its history has the Supreme Court so obviously responded to the pressure of public opinion with a major shift in its philosophy. And yet its sudden reversal hardly confirmed the cynics' view that the justices "follow the election returns." Even after the overwhelming expression of popular support for Roosevelt's program in the 1936 elections, four of the five justices who had consistently opposed New Deal legislation continued to do so.

And even in defeat the stubbornness of the four dissenting judges served a good purpose: it clarified the fundamental issues by forcing politicians and the public to consider and reconsider the long-range consequences and the philosophical significance of short-term expedients; and it made it more likely that once a new national consensus was achieved it would be recognized as such. Those opposed to the "welfare state" could more readily accept the nation's new direction because they had had their day in court, and the architects of the new economic order could administer and adapt it with greater confidence because their mandate had been thoroughly tested.

Thus the independence of the unelected court, before it was overwhelmed, served one of its basic purposes in the American political system. It ensured that before a great revolution became the law of the land it had won much more than the support of a small or temporary majority.

Footnotes

[1] Thurman Arnold, *The Symbols of Government* (New York: Harcourt Brace and World, 1935; reprint. ed, 1962), p. 145.

[2] *Chisholm v. Georgia*, 2 Dall. 419 (1793).

[3] Charles Warren, *The Supreme Court in United States History*, 2 vols. (Boston: Little, Brown & Co., 1922, 1926) I:100.

[4] Ibid., I:94.

[5] Ibid., I:97.

[6] Robert G. McCloskey, *The American Supreme Court* (Chicago: University of Chicago Press, 1960), p. 45-46.

[7] *Marbury v. Madison*, 1 Cr. 137 (1803).

[8] *Fletcher v. Peck*, 6 Cr. 87 at 128 (1810).

[9] McCloskey, *American Supreme Court*, p. 59.

[10] *Dred Scott v. Sandford*, 19 How. 393 (1857).

[11] *Ex parte Merryman*, 17 Fed. Cas. 144 (No. 9487) (C.C.D. Md.) (1861).

[12] Warren, *Supreme Court in U. S. History*, II:374.

[13] *Brown v. Board of Education of Topeka*, 347 U.S. 483 (1954).

[14] *Civil Rights Cases*, 109 U.S. 3 (1883).

[15] Robert S. Hirschfield, *The Constitution and the Court* (New York: Random House, 1962), p. 63.

[16] *Plessy v. Ferguson*, 163 U.S. 537 (1896).

[17] *Missouri ex rel. Gaines v. Canada*, 305 U.S. 337 (1938).

[18] *Brown v. Board of Education of Topeka*, 347 U.S. 483 at 494 (1954).

[19] William E. Leuchtenburg, *Franklin D. Roosevelt and the New Deal* (New York: Harper & Row, Harper Torchbooks, 1963), p. 42.

[20] Ibid., p. 42.

[21] McCloskey, *American Supreme Court*, p. 158.

[22] *Home Building and Loan Association Co. v. Blaisdell*, 290 U.S. 398 (1934); *Nebbia v. New York*, 291 U.S. 502 (1934).

[23] *Home Building and Loan Association Co. v. Blaisdell*, 290 U.S. 398 at 426, 442 (1934).

[24] Quoted in McCloskey, *American Supreme Court*, p. 164.

[25] *Panama Refining Co. v. Ryan*, 293 U.S. 388 (1935).

[26] *Schechter Poultry Corp. v. United States*, 295 U.S. 495 (1935).

[27] *United States v. Butler*, 297 U.S. 1 at 62-63 (1936).

[28] Id. at 87-88.

[29] Paul L. Murphy, *The Constitution in Crisis Times: 1918-1969* (New York: Harper & Row, Harper Torchbooks, 1972), p. 152.

[30] *National Labor Relations Board v. Jones & Laughlin Steel Corp.*, 301 U.S. 1 (1937).

Selected Bibliography

Arnold, Thurman. *The Symbols of Government*. New York: Harcourt Brace and World Inc., 1935; reprint ed., 1962.

Hirschfield, Robert S. *The Constitution and the Court*. New York: Random House, 1962.

Leuchtenburg, William E. *Franklin D. Roosevelt and the New Deal*. New York: Harper & Row, Harper Torchbooks, 1963.

McCloskey, Robert G. *The American Supreme Court*. Chicago: University of Chicago Press, 1960.

Murphy, Paul L. *The Constitution in Crisis Times: 1918-1969*. New York: Harper & Row, Harper Torchbooks, 1972.

Warren, Charles. *The Supreme Court in United States History*. 2 vols. Boston: Little, Brown & Co., 1922, 1926.

The Court and the Press

"The reaction of the people to judicially-declared law has been an especially important factor in the development of the country," wrote Charles Warren, the noted Supreme Court historian, "for while the judges' decision makes law, it is often the people's view of the decision that makes history.

"Hence, the effect produced on contemporary public opinion has frequently been of more consequence than the actual decision itself," he continued, "and in estimating this effect, regard must be paid to the fact that, while the law comes to lawyers through the official reports of judicial decisions, it reaches the people of the country filtered through the medium of the news-columns and editorials of partisan newspapers and often exaggerated, distorted and colored by political comment." [1]

This assessment in the 1920s, while not entirely flattering to the reporters and newspapers that today attempt to cover the Supreme Court seriously and accurately, acknowledged that the press has played a role in the process by which word of major decisions reaches the people, in the understanding of what the court has done and, to some extent from time to time, in the justices' understanding of how those decisions affect the world outside.

There have been long stretches in the nation's history when the Supreme Court made little news, when its members deferred with regularity to the actions of the executive and legislative branches, interpreted the Constitution as narrowly and infrequently as possible and kept busy debating legal niceties that were largely of interest to small groups of lawyers and merchants.

As a result, when the court roused itself to assertive action, as it did during the years under Chief Justice Earl Warren, much of the public was astonished and not infrequently angered to discover that this relatively obscure group of nine men held immense power over their lives.

Correspondingly, covering the Supreme Court for a newspaper or one of the broadcast media has been considered an up-and-down sort of assignment. When the court has bold members and when broad social ferment is presenting them with important disputes to resolve, the court can be one of the most demanding and rewarding "beats" for a Washington reporter.

At any time, exciting or routine, it is entirely different from almost any other kind of journalistic beat. A reporter who covers the White House or Congress normally has access to senior and junior staff members and to trained public information aides, if not to the principals themselves, when background is needed. The leak of theoretically private information by someone whose purpose may be thereby served is a way of life.

At the Supreme Court, however, there are virtually no staff sources, no access at all to the principals, and the public information officer distributes little information beyond the official statements of the court. Unauthorized leaks about court activities are regarded as roughly equivalent to breaches of national security. A friendly law professor can sometimes help assess the impact of a ruling in his specialized area, but, otherwise, covering the court involves papers — briefs and opinions — rather than people.

Press coverage has had one of its most demonstrable effects on the Supreme Court in recent years when confirmation of presidential nominees to the court was concerned. Reports on alleged liabilities of such men, sometimes originating from special interest groups and sometimes uncovered by the press itself, have clearly influenced voting in the Senate and thus had direct impact on the makeup of the court.

The extent of influence of the press on the actual deliberations of the court is much more difficult to chart. The justices are almost inescapably aware of widespread public interest in a particular highly publicized case; large numbers of friend-of-the-court briefs signal this situation just as clearly as do numerous news reports.

Members of the court, legally trained and normally well-experienced as judges, are highly unlikely to be influenced by prior press accounts of a case or of its oral argument, as opposed to their own reading of the record. In addition, media reaction to argument of a case, whether in news accounts or editorials, has very little time to make itself felt, if at all. Ordinarily, the justices vote on a case, at least tentatively, within three to five days after they hear it.

The long-range impact of press reaction to a controversial decision poses yet another question, one not so easily answered. Even though judicial purists would deny it, there seems little doubt that public opinion, shaped to some degree by the press, has some effect on the way the courts in general decide cases. This is a much more gradual and invisible process than, for example, the way media coverage and viewpoint may affect an election after an intensive campaign.

The doctrine of *stare decisis*, which simply expresses the institutional conservatism of the judicial process, severely curtails reversals of policy that appear to reflect public opinion, but such reversals do happen. The Supreme Court's 1943 reversal of its 1940 ruling that compulsory flag salute laws for public schools violated constitutional freedom-of-religion guarantees could not have been entirely unrelated to the fact that more than 150 newspapers editorialized against the first ruling.

In the final analysis, however, all but a very small percentage of Americans for nearly 200 years have learned about the Supreme Court exclusively through the medium of newspapers and, later, radio and television. A major share of the history of the institution has been written by the reporters who covered its activities and commented on them (before that role passed to the editorial writers), and the interaction between the press and the public it serves, on one hand, and the men who work at the summit of the federal judiciary, on the other, is a significant part of the story of both.

Early Years: 1790-1850

Coverage

In the early days of the republic, information about cases before the Supreme Court and its decisions reached the public in somewhat irregular fashion, as did most information about government. As a classic example, the first sentence of the official record of the first session of the court in 1790 was wrong. It called the body "the Supreme Judicial Court of the United States," following the nomenclature of Massachusetts but not that of the Constitution.

Not until 1804 was the first volume issued of what were to become the official reports of court decisions, an absolute necessity for anyone attempting to practice law. William Cranch, chief justice of the Circuit Court of the District of Columbia, took it upon himself to assemble and publish the decisions of the 1801-1804 terms, and succeeding ones.

Until that time, it had been very difficult for judges and lawyers, much less the general public, to obtain copies of the court's rulings. A rare exception had been *Marbury v. Madison* in 1803, when a summary of the Marshall opinion was widely printed in the newspapers, arousing considerable comment.

In a preface to his first volume of reports, Cranch emphasized the need for uniformity in the law, with an accurate record of Supreme Court decisions enabling judges everywhere to conform. "Every case decided is a check upon the Judge," the compiler wrote. "He cannot decide a similar case differently without strong reasons, which, for his own justification, he will wish to make public. The avenues of corruption are thus obstructed and the sources of litigation closed." [2]

Until 1874 this service for the new nation's judges and lawyers was continued by a series of private decision compilers, whose names are preserved in the formal citations used to identify a decision or a quotation from it, such as 4 Cranch 95. Then they became United States Reports, prepared by the Government Printing Office, and the volume and page citations became impersonal — 1 U.S. 12 and so on. *(Reporting of decisions, p. 873)*

For a number of years, newspaper coverage of arguments before the court and its subsequent decisions was sporadic, concentrating on a few controversial cases and all but ignoring many of the rest. In 1819, for the first time, the *National Intelligencer* began printing a daily list of all cases argued and decisions handed down.

Inaccurate reporting and misinterpretation of Supreme Court decisions by the press were serious problems almost from the start. In 1803 several papers printed an erroneous account of the opinion in *Marbury v. Madison,* which said the court had made a distinction between its authority within the District of Columbia and in the states elsewhere.

This mistake originally appeared in the *Alexandria Advertiser* and was picked up, as was the custom then, by the *Georgia Republican* and the *Boston Gazette.* The error did little damage, however, because all three papers correctly reported the outcome of the decision.

A more serious example of inaccurate reporting occurred in 1819 when the justices ruled on a challenge to the constitutionality of a New York State bankruptcy law. Because no federal law governed that subject at the time, the issues in the case were thus critically important to businessmen as well as ordinary citizens.

The court invalidated the state law, insofar as it enabled a debtor to free himself from a debt that had been contracted before the statute went into effect. But the first newspaper accounts of an admittedly murky opinion reported that the court had held that states had no authority to pass bankruptcy laws generally.

"This opinion has given much alarm to many persons," the *Niles Register* of Baltimore declared. [3] According to a New York paper, the inaccurate version "caused a very considerable sensation in the city, and we do not wonder at it." [4] A Baltimore paper cautioned that "nothing but the publication of the entire opinion can possibly allay the fermentation that is excited." [5]

Twelve days after the decision, an accurate article was printed in a New York paper, and the furor began to subside. But the full text of the opinion in the case, *Sturges v. Crowninshield,* was not published for some time, and a simultaneous period of economic uncertainty in the nation compounded problems created by the initial mistake. *(Details, p. 312)*

Errors aside, the chief characteristic of press coverage of the court during its formative years was political partisanship. Most of the papers were closely allied with a party — the Federalists or the Republicans during the early days, later the Whigs or the Jacksonian Democrats — and their accounts were highly colored by this alignment.

Objectivity was not the style of the day, either in reporting arguments before the court by noted lawyers or in presenting the facts behind a controversial decision. This unabashed bias was particularly notable in accounts of stormy confirmation battles in the Senate and the highly political attempt to impeach Justice Samuel Chase.

But the newspapers of this period, incomplete and partisan as they were, were the principal means of informing the public and influencing opinion. They printed little of what we call news today and their circulation was initially very limited, largely by the absence of transportation.

But, as the republic grew, so did the influence of the press. Julius Goebel Jr. notes: "Relying as they did for filler upon clippings from whatever out-of-town newspapers that might come to hand, it was possible for a subscriber to a Boston or New York journal to learn belatedly of an event or opinion published weeks earlier in South Carolina or Virginia." [6]

Confirmation Battles

In these early years, the press occasionally played a role in determining the Supreme.Court's membership, by serving as an open forum for criticism of controversial nominees, some of whom were subsequently rejected by the Senate. During this period, most American newspapers were highly partisan, containing as much outspoken opinion as fact and making little attempt to distinguish between editorials and news accounts.

In 1795, when the first Chief Justice, John Jay, resigned to become governor of New York, John Rutledge of South Carolina sought and obtained President Washington's nomination for the vacant seat. Just before the August term of the court was to begin, newspaper accounts reached the North of a speech Rutledge had given in Charleston, denouncing the treaty Jay had negotiated with Britain a month earlier, which had already been ratified by the Senate.

Some of these stories were clearly inaccurate; a Boston paper described Rutledge as having spoken "mounted upon the head of a hogshead, haranguing a mob," when the speech was actually delivered in a Charleston church. But Federalist treaty supporters were outraged and accused Rutledge of insanity and bringing "ruin and disgrace" to the country. [7] The *Columbian Centinel* of Boston, a leading Federalist paper, attacked the nominee's character and charged he could not pay his debts. Other papers, in the South and elsewhere, defended him.

Rutledge sat as a recess appointee on the court, which proceeded to decide only two cases during a short session. But he never returned. The president sent his nomination to the Senate, which rejected it 14 to 10 the following December. The *Columbian Centinel* rejoiced that the senators had considered Rutledge's treaty speech an "impudent and virulent attack" on them "by a very unfit person for a Chief Justice." [8] *(Details, p. 657)*

In 1811 President Madison nominated for a vacancy on the court a Connecticut Republican whose political credentials were considerably stronger than his legal qualifications, Alexander Wolcott, a one-time customs collector.

Once again the Federalist press charged into the breach. The *Columbian Centinel* observed that "even those most acquainted with modern degeneracy were astounded at this abominable nomination." [9] The *Connecticut Courant* said it had hoped for a nominee "less disgusting to the moral sense of the community and whose private virtues or legal knowledge might have afforded some security from his political depravity." [10] Other papers commented adversely on his personal habits and morals.

Even Republican leaders were hard-put to defend Wolcott, and the Senate denied him confirmation by a 24-9 vote. Historian Charles Warren, noting that Wolcott later endorsed the expulsion of any judge who declared a law unconstitutional, concluded that "it was fortunate for the course of American legal history that he did not secure this position on the Supreme Bench." [11]

In 1835 another controversy erupted when President Jackson nominated Roger B. Taney to the court. The Senate had earlier refused to confirm Taney as secretary of

the Treasury because he had removed government deposits from the United States Bank, at Jackson's behest. Taney's acknowledged legal skills — he had also served as attorney general — were virtually ignored during the ensuing political debate.

A Boston Whig paper argued that the Senate could not confirm him for the court without reversing in the process "the sentence they passed on Mr. Taney's outrageous violation of the law and the Constitution while he was in the cabinet." [12] A New York paper said that judgeships "are not in the gift solely of the Executive and that subservancy to his will or truckling to his behests is not enough to secure them. . . ." [13] After two months of maneuvering, the Senate shelved the Taney nomination by a 24-21 vote on the last day of its session in March 1835.

Nine months later, however, Jackson nominated Taney to succeed John Marshall as Chief Justice. A somewhat realigned Senate confirmed him, 29 to 15, and he served with considerable distinction until his death 28 years later. *(Details, p. 688)*

The press' role in these early confirmation battles was very different from its role today. Newspapers then were the principal means of serious public and political communication. They circulated, though somewhat slowly, up and down the coast of the narrow new nation, rather than only locally. A week-old article from one city that struck a responsive chord with an editor elsewhere would be reprinted in full, sometimes in several different papers. Frequently papers also printed ostensibly private letters that proved influential in shaping political reaction.

Cases

Marbury v. Madison (1803) was a squabble over presidential patronage that escalated into a contest for authority between Congress and the Supreme Court. It involved an attempt to force President Jefferson to award minor judgeships to men chosen by President John Adams in the closing hours of his administration. The case thus attracted considerable attention from the pro-Adams Federalist press, including the *New York Evening Post*, the *Connecticut Courant* and the *Columbian Centinel*.

Although the decision is remembered today for establishing the court's power to declare an act of Congress unconstitutional, contemporary press coverage focused instead on the political conflict between Chief Justice Marshall and the Federalist would-be justices of the peace, on one hand, and President Jefferson and his fellow Republicans on the other.

Chief Justice Marshall held that the Adams appointees were entitled to their commissions as judges but that Congress had gone beyond constitutional limits in authorizing the Supreme Court to order Cabinet officers to issue those commissions. *(Related details, pp. 69, 235)*

Federalist newspapers, not surprisingly, regarded the ruling as a rebuke of Jefferson. But a number of the most prominent Republican papers, which could have been expected to defend the president and denounce the court's validation of the commissions, were strangely silent. As a group, they did not feel compelled to criticize Marshall's holding that the court had the right to review the constitutionality of acts of Congress. One Republican paper, the *Virginia Argus*, ran a series of articles questioning Marshall's power to rule against Jefferson on the issue of the judges' commissions in one breath while denying Supreme Court jurisdiction over the case in the next.

Journalistic Extremism: Early Years

In the early 19th century, American newspapers felt very little restraint about printing the most vituperative attacks on the Supreme Court and its decisions. A favorite vehicle for such unbridled criticism was a series of letters signed with a pseudonym. A particularly virulent but characteristic example of this species appeared in 1819 in the *General Advertiser* of Philadelphia, signed "Brutus" and commenting on the decision in *McCulloch v. Maryland:*

"...the opinion of that tribunal now before the world is a perfect model of that prejudiced judgment and *ex parte* consideration of a subject that springs from a predetermined resolution to accomplish a desired object, which shows but one side of the question, views but one relation of the principles in controversy and studiously avoids all allusion to the most essential and the principal leading features in the discussion: the foundation of social obligation, the purpose of government, the rights of the people and the liberty of the states.

"These principles and rights are rigorously excluded from all consideration in this argument; and the power, the authority and the supremacy of the Federal government is made the irrefutable, the original source and the sole origin, and the despotic arbiter of a question which challenges and denies the extent of that supremacy of power, that unresisting vigor of authority....

"Never was a bad cause worse supported by constellated talents, learning and wisdom of a Bench of Supreme Judges. It seems as if nature had revolted from the debasing task assigned them; and that their reason and their judgment had forsaken them, upon an instinctive horror and disgust from the destructive purposes they were pledged to fulfill, in defiance of all human rights, human joys and divine commandments...."

The *Washington Federalist* first printed a series of letters from "an unlearned layman," contending that the justices lacked the power to review acts of Congress. Then the paper printed a reply that argued: "...if a law conflict with the Constitution, the judges are bound to declare which is paramount. The judges here arrogate no power. It is not they who speak — it is the Constitution, or rather, the people."[14] That was virtually the only contemporary exchange published on the issue of judicial review that history has come to regard as the chief legacy of *Marbury.*

In some instances, the highly partisan press of this period devoted more attention to the Supreme Court than newspapers do today. The *Charleston Courier,* a leading Federalist paper, published in little more than a month in 1803 two news reports and four lengthy editorials on *Marbury v. Madison,* plus a summary of the decision taken from the *National Intelligencer* and later the full text of the opinion.

Dartmouth College v. Woodward (1819) attracted very little attention when it was argued and decided, apparently because neither the bar nor the press anticipated how important the issue in the case would become in the economic development of the country. The question before the Supreme Court was whether the New Hampshire legis-lature, having granted Dartmouth College a corporate charter, could later rewrite that charter without impairing a contract, conduct forbidden by the federal Constitution. (For generations of loyal Dartmouth alumni, this case was immortalized by the response of Daniel Webster, one of the winning attorneys, to an inquiring justice: "It is, sir, as I have said, a small college, and yet there are those who love it.")

When the case was argued in 1818, the court was stalemated. The *National Intelligencer* said that a decision would be postponed until the next term because there was no majority since "some of the judges have not come to an opinion on the case. Those of the judges who have formed opinions do not agree."[15] Only the Boston and New Hampshire papers covered the arguments, and their accounts illustrate the highly subjective reporting of the era.

The *Columbian Centinel* of Boston informed its readers that "our friend Webster never made a happier effort. To a most elaborate and lucid argument he united a dignified and pathetic peroration which charmed and melted his hearers."[16] The *Boston Daily Advertiser* said that Webster "enchained the court and the audience with an argument which, for weight of authority, force of reasoning and power of eloquence, has seldom been equalled in this or any court."[17]

Nearly a year later when the 1819 term opened, the justices decided the case, holding 5-1 that the charter of a private corporation was a contract and thus invalidating the legislature's attempt to change the Dartmouth charter. The result was not only significant in confirming the supremacy of the Constitution over state legislation but also in assuring business corporations security against improper interference by lawmakers. *(Details, p. 311)*

But corporations were still in their infancy at the time, and the press paid scant attention. There was no mention of the decision in the *Niles Register,* a Baltimore weekly that normally summarized all legal events of consequence. The New York papers barely touched on the case, merely calling the opinion "a most able and elaborate production" and "a learned and able paper."[18]

The decision overruled the state courts, which had upheld their legislature, and the *New Hampshire Gazette* was bold enough to suggest incompetence by the losing attorneys: "Had the case been fairly laid before the court, no man, without impeaching their integrity or their common sense, can doubt but their decision would have confirmed that of the Superior Court in this state."[19]

McCulloch v. Maryland (1819), by contrast, aroused widespread interest around the country from the beginning, and the court's opinion was reprinted in full by many papers, whether or not they agreed with the outcome.

At issue, as several papers emphasized early, was the power of states to tax the Bank of the United States. The case was obviously momentous in the determination of state and federal rights, and the justices heard arguments for nine days. But it took them only three days to rule unanimously that Congress had exclusive jurisdiction over the bank, which it had chartered as a federal agency, and that the state tax was thus invalid. *(Details, p. 73)*

The press reacted along political and geographical lines, with the Federalist papers of the North and East generally favorable. Typical was the *Boston Daily Advertiser,* whose Washington correspondent called the ruling "one of the most able judgments, I will venture to say, ever delivered in this court, and when it is read will satisfy all minds."[20]

That prediction proved false as most Republican papers in the South and West denounced the decision as an unwarranted invasion of states' rights. The *Natchez Press* observed that "our privileges as a people have of late been so frittered away that we may as well inter at once the form of a Constitution, of which the spirit has been murdered." [21] The *Niles Register* in Maryland also attacked the ruling, charging that "a deadly blow has been struck at the sovereignty of the states and from a quarter so far removed from the people as to be hardly accessible to public opinion," an early example of the accusations of unresponsiveness that the court still confronts today.[22]

The *General Advertiser* in Philadelphia went beyond the issues in the case to attack editorially Chief Justice Marshall's opinion for displaying "a most lamentable sophistry, a most lame and impotent logic, and . . . the most flimsy and false attempt at reasoning that can be found in the annals of any nation." [23]

Gibbons v. Ogden (1824) represented a direct confrontation between states' rights advocates and a strong federal government. It was a legal challenge to a longstanding steamboat monopoly granted two prominent Republican politicians by the New York legislature, brought by a would-be competitor who refused to obtain a license from them for his New York-New Jersey ferry line.

Other states had granted similar monopolies, and some had retaliated with bans on ships licensed by adjacent states. As a result, arguments before the court attracted detailed newspaper coverage. "You can form no idea what interest this decision excites at Washington," the *New York Statesman* reported. [24] The court's opinion was ready in three weeks.

Chief Justice Marshall announced the court's finding that the New York law was an unconstitutional interference with Congress' right to regulate commerce. *(Details, p. 83-84)*

For once, newspaper reaction was largely nonpartisan, with journals all over the country praising the Marshall opinion whatever their political affiliation. New Yorkers particularly resented the state-imposed monopoly, and the *New York Evening Post* called the ruling "one of the most able and solemn opinions that has ever been delivered in any court." [25] For the *New York Commercial Advertiser*, it was "one of the most powerful efforts of the human mind that has ever been displayed from the bench of any court." [26]

Reaction elsewhere in the country was similar. The *National Gazette* called the decision a "masterpiece of judicial reasoning," [27] and the *Georgia Journal* published the entire opinion because it found the case "one of such vast interest and importance to our country." [28] Some concern for state authority was voiced; the *Richmond Enquirer* foresaw the possibility that "the state governments would moulder into ruins." [29]

The Cherokee Cases (1830-32) involved the refusal of a state to honor an order of the court, a precursor of the doctrine of nullification that precipitated the Civil War. A 1791 federal treaty had granted the Cherokees land in Georgia, but the state legislature attempted to take it away in 1829. When the Indians filed an original suit in the Supreme Court, state officials refused to participate. Subsequently, the Georgia governor ignored another Supreme Court writ after state authorities had arrested a Cherokee for murder within Indian property.

The *Boston Courier*, a Whig paper, charged that "the integrity and permanence of the union are at stake." [30]

Representing the Jackson administration, the *United States Telegraph* contended that the confrontation demonstrated "the absurdity of the doctrine which contends that the court is clothed with supreme and absolute control over the states." [31] But the *New York Daily Advertiser* saw a concerted effort "to curtail the constitutional jurisdiction and destroy the influence and independence of the Supreme Court." [32]

The court ruled it had no jurisdiction to decide the first Cherokee case, but a second opportunity arose in 1831 when Georgia arrested two missionaries living in Indian country without a license. In March 1832 the court struck down the state licensing law as unconstitutional, holding that the federal government had exclusive jurisdiction over the Cherokees and their reservation. *(Details, pp. 239, 307)*

President Jackson is supposed to have responded: "Well, John Marshall has made his decision, now let him enforce it," but there is considerable doubt about the authenticity of that quote. Georgia officals continued to ignore the Supreme Court, and Whig papers supported the court while those backing Jackson counseled moderation. *(Details, p. 239)*

Subsequently, the Georgia legislature passed a nullification ordinance, rejecting Supreme Court jurisdiction. Congress, at President Jackson's behest, countered with the Force Bill to give federal authorities adequate power to deal with the situation. At that point, Georgia, realizing that Jackson was adamant, pardoned the two missionaries, and the constitutional crisis was averted.

Impeachment Efforts

Only once, in 1805, was a Supreme Court justice formally charged by the House of Representatives with impeachable offenses and then tried by the Senate. Justice Samuel Chase survived this largely political attack, in part with the assistance of the press of the period, even including some Republican papers presumably dedicated to his removal.

The abortive Chase impeachment effort was important because it freed the justices from the threat of congressional retaliation for one or more decisions that had angered a president and the lawmakers of his party.

Chase had won the enmity of the Republicans both for actively opposing Jefferson in the 1800 presidential campaign and for his conduct of the sedition trials of two prominent party members. Charging that the judge's disposition was arbitrary and his temper ferocious, the *Aurora* observed that "few men, perhaps, hold a humbler estimation among his fellow citizens." [33]

With the full approval of President Jefferson, the Republicans seized on a lengthy charge that Justice Chase had delivered to a Baltimore grand jury in 1803 as evidence that he should be removed from the bench. The *National Intelligencer* printed an account of that charge, in which the judge attacked congressional legislation and called the administration "weak, relaxed and not adequate to a discharge of their functions" and primarily interested in "a continuance in unfairly acquired power." [34]

Although its accuracy was later disputed, this article was widely reprinted around the country, and the Chase charge was attacked or defended according to the partisan position of the reprinting paper. The *Charleston Courier*, for example, accused the president and his allies of "conspiring for the overthrow of that third branch of the Constitution — the judiciary. . . ." [35]

In January 1804 the House named a committee to investigate impeachment of Justice Chase, and the debate continued to rage in the press. "Never, never was the bench so much disgraced as by Judge Chase," declared the *Aurora*[36] while the *Connecticut Courant* accused Congress of attempting "to level with the dust the national judiciary, or at least to render it completely subordinate...."[37]

The House voted articles of impeachment early in 1804, citing misconduct during the sedition trial and the Baltimore grand jury charge. The Senate heard the case, then found Chase not guilty. *(Details, p. 658)*

According to historian Charles Warren, the refusal of the Senate to impeach Chase had a "profound effect ... on the course of American legal history,"[38] sidetracking contemporary Republican plans to move against other justices and discrediting the theory that impeachment could be used to remove justices with whom Congress disagreed, without any proof of crime or misdemeanor.

Middle Years: 1850-1900

Coverage

The Supreme Court was a participant, all too passively in the eyes of some, in the tumultuous events of the last half of the 19th century when the issue of slavery tore the country apart and the Civil War ultimately left a legacy of institutionalized discrimination smoldering beneath the surface of reconstituted national self-satisfaction.

Throughout the crisis, the press held up a mirror to the deep emotional divisions in the nation that finally produced armed camps, literally as well as figuratively. The abolitionist and radical Republican papers subjected the court to an unprecedented level of substantive, professional and political criticism during the course of the *Dred Scott Case* in 1856-57. Opposition organs replied in kind.

If *Scott v. Sandford* showed a Democratic majority on the court lining up politically behind the South and slavery, the *Legal Tender Cases* two dozen years later demonstrated that judicial venality was bipartisan, with a freshly minted Republican majority promptly reversing a 15-month old Supreme Court ruling and sending shock waves through the press and public.

But time slowly brought the country back together, and the bitterness engendered by the slavery issue subsided. By 1883, when the court declared federal anti-discrimination laws unconstitutional in the *Civil Rights Cases,* only one justice dissented, and a good deal of the press reaction was favorable. By 1896, when the court upheld state Jim Crow laws in *Plessy v. Ferguson,* newspapers — apart from the black press of the day — paid little attention.

During these 50 years, the press continued to play an instrumental role in Senate confirmation of new justices. Two lame-duck presidents, Fillmore and Buchanan, tried but failed to place their choices on the bench. The Senate's refusal to confirm these nominees was attributed, at least in part, to newspaper criticism.

Problems of the availability of court opinions continued to plague the press. When in 1842 the *Newark Daily Advertiser* could not get the text of a fugitive slave ruling, it suggested that the official reporter publish it in pamphlet form "as a mere matter of pecuniary speculation."[39] Lack of the same opinion did not deter *The Baltimore Sun* from saying that the decision was "all that Maryland can desire, and will be particularly agreeable to the slaveholders of the South."[40]

Newspapers were not the only ones inconvenienced by the court's primitive information policy. When the federal fugitive slave law was upheld against state interference in *Ableman v. Booth* (1859), Chief Justice Taney ordered the clerk not to give out copies of the opinion until it had been printed in the official reports. Six weeks after the decision had been handed down, Attorney General J. S. Black had to get special permission from the Chief Justice to obtain a copy for his official use.

Reporters continued to include in their Supreme Court stories comments that would be regarded today as highly editorial. Discussing the arguments in a martial law case, *The New York Tribune* called one attorney's presentation "long beyond the patience of most listeners."[41]

The justices themselves sometimes responded to newspaper criticism in unorthodox fashion. After the court had decided to reaffirm the constitutionality of the federal fugitive slave act, but before the opinion was printed, Justice John McLean wrote an anonymous letter to a newspaper, protesting criticism of the decision and defending the court against accusations that it universally favored owners over slaves.

During this era of strong feelings on the slavery issue, the attention of the public became a widely sought commodity, and partisans on both sides sought space in any kind of publication. In one of the fugitive slave cases, arguments by the antislavery lawyers, Salmon P. Chase and William H. Seward, were privately printed and widely circulated for propaganda purposes.

But the official reporter of the period, Benjamin Howard, refused to include the arguments in full in his U.S. Reports, arousing some suspicion that his personal sympathies on the question were involved. Historian Carl Swisher notes that in the past Howard had "often incurred widespread criticism for dumping into the reports materials of all kinds to expand the size of his volumes (but) here reversed his usual custom."[42]

Cases

Dred Scott v. Sandford (1857) launched the court — and the country as well — into one of the stormiest periods in its history. The decision in the slavery case aroused bitter criticism in the press, and the court as an institution sank to the lowest level of public esteem and confidence before or since.

Throughout the controversy, newspapers as the dominant means of communication played a major role in highlighting the issues before the court and later in reflecting the impassioned outrage that the decision inspired in many areas, foreshadowing the agonizing division of the Civil War.

Scott was a Negro slave from Missouri who went to court in 1846, charging that he had become a free man when his former master took him into free territory, irrespective of his return to Missouri later. After losing in state court in 1852, then in U.S. Circuit Court two years later, he carried an appeal to the Supreme Court.

At issue were whether a slave could be a citizen with power to sue in the federal courts and whether Congress had the authority to prohibit slavery in the territories, as it originally had in the Missouri Compromise.

The leading abolitionist paper of the North, *The New York Tribune,* printed a running account of the court's secret deliberations after the case had been argued. At one early juncture, the paper reported, apparently with considerable accuracy, the position of each justice. In retrospect, it seems clear that Justice John McLean was providing regular leaks to one of the *Tribune's* Washington reporters, a highly unusual practice even for a politically-inclined justice in those days.

After three months without a decision, the justices called for reargument and were praised by the *New York Courier* for deliberative wisdom. The case was largely ignored during the 1856 presidential campaign, but when it came before the court again in December, the *Courier* said "it may well be regarded as the most important that has been brought before that tribunal." [43]

The political issue of slavery had become inflammatory, and a correspondent of the *Independent* reported that, in the reargument, "the prejudices of the judges were appealed to, until I came to the realization of the fact that our supreme court is composed of men, mere men after all, with the like passions and prejudices of the masses." [44]

The justices did not take up the case in conference for another two months, but the newspapers were filled with rumors and conjecture. With southern Democrats making up a majority of the court, the abolitionist *New York Tribune* declared: "If the court is to take a political bias, and to give a political decision, then let us by all means have it distinctly, and now. The public mind is in a condition to receive it with the contempt it deserves." [45]

Early in March 1857 Chief Justice Taney handed down the majority opinion in the 7-2 decision, holding that Negroes were not citizens and thus unable to sue in the courts; not content to rest there, the court declared that Congress had no power to exclude slavery from the territories. From contemporary accounts, it appears that the court had no idea what a firestorm of opposition the ruling would set off. *(Details, p. 135)*

One day later, the *New York Independent* said: "If there be not aroused a spirit of resistance and indignation which shall wipe out this decision and all its results, as the lightning wipes out the object it falls upon, then indeed are the days of our republic numbered, and the patriot shall see might only beyond the storms of revolution and blood." [46] The *New York Evening Post* charged that a majority of the justices "have consented to become parties to a combination with the Administration to transfer the political control of the government to the hands of the slave oligarchy." [47]

But Democratic papers in both the North and South defended the court against its fervent attackers and counseled moderation. The *New York Herald* warned that disobedience of the court's ruling would constitute "rebellion, treason and revolution." [48] The *Pennsylanian* attacked the "black Republican press, brimful of elements of sedition, treason and insurrection." [49] The administration's voice in Washington, the *Daily Union,* predicted, somewhat rashly as events proved, that the decision "would exert the most powerful and salutary influence throughout the United States." [50]

Court Reporters

Intense public interest in the *Dred Scott* decision focused attention on the informal monopoly enjoyed by the reporter of the Supreme Court, in this instance Benjamin Howard. His public salary was only $1,300 a year, but a banner case enabled him to sell more copies of the volume in which it appeared and even print it separately in pamphlet form.

The Democratic-controlled Senate, strongly supporting the majority opinion and anxious to publicize it broadly, decided to print 20,000 copies. Howard protested that his income would suffer as a result, so the Senate voted to pay him $1,500 and agreed not to distribute its reprint until after his bound volume and pamphlet version had appeared.

The court itself had ruled in 1834 that its opinions could not be copyrighted, but the Senate concluded that Howard had a fair claim to compensation.

Source: Charles Grove Haines and Foster H. Sherwood, *The Role of the Supreme Court in American Government and Politics: 1835-1864,* (Berkeley: University of California Press, 1957), p. 432.

And the *St. Louis Evening News* observed that the decision "has roused the lately torpid Northern pulpit into a factitious frenzy on the stale Negro question and incited the preachers to a fresh crusade against the judges." [51]

In this critical case, the justices became their own publicists. The McLean dissent was read in church the day after he delivered it, obviously with his cooperation, and printed in the *Cincinnati Gazette,* enabling the justice to circulate copies around the country. Justice John Catron, who had voted with the majority but split with Chief Justice Taney on some key questions, assumed — incorrectly as it developed — that the *Washington Union,* the administration paper, would not carry his opinion, and so he had it separately printed in the *Nashville Daily Union and American.*

Some conservative historians have since argued that press coverage of the *Dred Scott* decision was more responsible for inflaming public opinion and ultimately precipitating the Civil War than was the decision itself. Charles Warren, writing in 1922, quoted with approval a *Harper's Weekly* prediction that "however repugnant the Dred Scott decision may be to the feelings of a portion of the Northern states, it can have no practical effects injurious to our tranquility or to our institutions." [52]

"Had the country been influenced by editorials like these," Warren commented, "rather than by the hysterical, virulent and false outpourings of the *Tribune* and the *Independent,* the court's action would have had less effect on history, but it was otherwise destined." [53]

Six months later, the *North American Review* concluded that "The country will feel the consequences of the decision more deeply and more permanently in the loss of confidence in the sound judicial integrity and strictly legal character of their tribunals than in anything beside." [54] But Warren insisted 65 years later that "the loss of confidence in the court was due not merely to the court's decision but to the false and malignant criticisms and portrayals of the court which were spread widely through the North by influential newspapers...." [55]

Reporting Opinions

The divisive character of the *Dred Scott* decision was dramatically illustrated by the court itself in a dispute over making public the language of the majority opinion and dissents. The day after Chief Justice Taney had read the majority opinion in court, Justice Benjamin Curtis, one of the two dissenters, filed his opinion with the clerk based on what he had heard and said from the bench. He gave a copy to a Boston newspaper, and it was widely reprinted.

Nearly a month later, Curtis heard Taney was revising the majority opinion. He asked the clerk for a copy and was told the Chief Justice had forbidden its release until all opinions were printed in the official reports. For the next two months, the two justices engaged in an angry exchange of letters over the issue.

Taney was obviously reacting bitterly to comparisons being made in the abolitionist press between his oral opinion and Curtis' written dissent. The Chief Justice wrote his colleague that "the opinion of the court on former occasions has been assailed in political journals and by political partisans before the opinion itself could be published, yet this is the first instance in the history of the Supreme Court in which the assault was commenced by the publication of the opinion of a dissenting judge."

Curtis had already given some thought to leaving the court, where his $6,000 salary compared unfavorably with the rewards of private practice. His dispute with the Chief Justice settled the matter, and he resigned on Sept. 1, 1857. President Buchanan refused to issue the customary statement of praise for the justice's service that his attorney general had prepared.

"And so the Dred Scott case further deepened its impact of ill will," historian Carl B. Swisher wrote, "and on the Supreme Court an able jurist withdrew to be replaced for more than two decades by a mediocre Buchanan appointment (Nathan Clifford)."

Chief Justice Taney still tried to have the last word. He drafted for the official report of the case a headnote three pages long that summarized his opinion, including those parts that did not enjoy the support of a majority of his colleagues.

Sources: Charles Grove Haines and Foster H. Sherwood, *The Role of the Supreme Court in American Government and Politics: 1835-1864* (Berkeley: University of California Press, 1957), pp. 425-429; Carl B. Swisher, *History of the Supreme Court of the United States:* Vol. V, *The Taney Period, 1836-64* (New York: Macmillan Publishing Company, Inc., 1971), p. 657.

The Legal Tender Cases of 1870-1871. These decisions brought the court again to a low level of public esteem. Once again, press coverage played a significant part in creating the widespread view that the court was not only undependable but also subject to the most obvious political manipulation.

The issue here, while not as inflammatory as slavery, was an outgrowth of the Civil War: did Congress have the power to make paper treasury notes as good as gold for the payment of debts? The financial stakes were high. If the wartime acts were sustained, debtors could settle with depreciated paper money; if not, they would need much more costly gold. *(Details, p. 118)*

State courts had generally upheld the Legal Tender Acts, according to the *Nation*, "being in closer dependence on popular opinion . . . on such an exceedingly delicate subject as the value and power of the currency." [56] The *Chicago Republican* suggested that the court "should not now work universal ruin" but instead withhold any decision that would invalidate paper money. [57]

The case of *Hepburn v. Griswold* was argued in 1867 and reargued a year later, but a majority did not result because of vacancies on the court. By November 1869 a majority had agreed privately that the law was unconstitutional but delayed announcement while opinions were being reconciled.

Meanwhile, press speculation was conspicuously inaccurate. In January 1870 *The New York Times* said that "no consideration has yet been had in the case by the Court" and predicted another reargument. [58] On Feb. 1 *The New York Tribune* said "there is ground for believing that the decision will not go into the question of the constitutionality of the law." [59]

A week later a 4-3 majority of the court decided the *Hepburn* case, holding that the Legal Tender Acts exceeded Congress' war powers, impaired the obligation of contracts and were thus unconstitutional. Early reaction was mild, apparently because it was assumed that only contracts signed before the laws were passed were affected. When lawyers concluded that the ruling invalidated paper money for all contracts, before and after, panic set in among those who foresaw disastrous financial consequences for the entire nation.

On the same day the court decided the *Legal Tender Case,* President Grant sent two new Supreme Court nominations to the Senate. Within two months they were confirmed and the government had moved for rehearing of two other pending legal tender cases that dealt with contracts made after the acts, thus reopening an issue that had been widely regarded as settled. The revamped court granted the motion by a 5-4 vote.

The press reacted strongly, with the *Nation* observing: "We find very little difference of opinion in the press as to the gross impropriety (to use a very mild term) of the reopening of the Legal Tender decision. It is, in every way one looks at it, a blunder." [60] The *Springfield Republican* expressed a hope that "the country is to be spared this great wrong and scandal of a reversal." [61] The *American Law Review* warned that the court could not reverse the ruling in *Hepburn* "without degrading itself in the eyes of all intelligent men, and this fact we should think the new members of the court would recognize quite as distinctly as the old." [62]

But the court ordered yet another reargument of the constitutional question and on May 1, 1871, reversed *Hepburn,* decided 15 months earlier. The two new Grant justices joined with the former minority in the 5-4 ruling. The *Springfield Republican* predicted the reversal "will greatly aggravate the growing contempt for what has long been the most respected and the most influential department of our government, its judiciary." [63] The *Nation* said the move would "weaken popular respect for all decisions of the court, including this last one." [64] Despite its outspoken Republican position, *The New York Tribune* said "it will not be easy to restore public respect and reverence for the tribunal which this decision has sacrificed." [65]

A collection of papers, influenced more by economic stability than judicial impartiality, defended both the outcome of the case and the character of the new justices.

But Historian Charles Warren concluded that the reversal was "a very grave mistake — and a mistake which for many years impaired the people's confidence, not in the honesty but in the impartiality and good sense of the court." [66]

The Civil Rights Cases. By the time the court decided the *Civil Rights Cases* (1883), the climate of public opinion had begun to shift away from the fevered antagonism of the Civil War. The court, with a single dissent by Justice John Marshall Harlan, struck down as unconstitutional an 1875 statute that had prohibited discrimination of any kind in places of public accommodation.

The majority held that the 14th Amendment had not given Congress authority to invade areas of state authority, concluding that "it would be running the slavery argument into the ground to make it apply to every act of discrimination which a person may see fit to make as to the guest he will entertain." *(Details, p. 608)*

Press reaction was generally favorable. "The fact is," observed *The New York Times*, "that as long as we have state governments, within their field of action we cannot by national authority prevent the consequences of misgovernment." [67] The once-radical *Independent* acknowledged that "several leading colored men have expressed great indignation and disappointment" but concluded that "the court is clearly right." [68] The *Chicago Tribune, The Washington Post* and the *Louisville Courier-Journal* all expressed support for the ruling.

However, the case did provoke considerable public debate, including a number of editorials, rallies and proposals for countervailing legislation. Frederick C. Douglass, the black editor, protested that the court had exposed the Negro to any kind of treatment his oppressors could devise: "They can put him in a smoking car or baggage car . . . take him or leave him at a railroad station, exclude him from inns, drive him from all places of amusement or instruction, without the least fear that the national government will interfere for the protection of his liberty." [69]

This era of public indignation and strong conviction, in which the court became a major target, drew to an ignominious close in 1896 with the decision of *Plessy v. Ferguson,* which upheld the constitutionality of separate-but-equal facilities for blacks. State legislatures enacting Jim Crow laws, the court held, were entitled to take into consideration "the established usages, customs and traditions of the people and . . . the promotion of their comfort and the preservation of the public peace and good order."

Outside the Negro press, newspapers paid scant if any attention to the ruling, and there were almost no editorials. It remained for the *Richmond Times,* four years later, to sum up the case: "God Almighty drew the color line, and it cannot be obliterated. The negro must stay on his side of the line, and the white man must stay on his side, and the sooner both races recognize this fact and accept it, the better it will be for both." [70] *(Details, p. 608)*

Confirmation Battles

During the latter half of the 19th century, presidents did not hesitate to make appointments to the Supreme Court during their last days in office, and the press was instrumental on several occasions in calling public attention to the political factors involved.

Franklin Pierce, a Democrat, was elected president in 1852, but before he was to take office the following March, outgoing President Millard Fillmore nominated a fellow-Whig, Senator George Badger of North Carolina, to a vacancy on the court. An earlier Fillmore nomination for the seat had died when the Senate adjourned without acting on it.

Democrats controlled the Senate, but Fillmore had hoped a fellow senator, even of the minority party, might be confirmed. An Alabama paper saw this as "a corrupt effort to seduce the independence of the Senate by the kindly sentiments that exist in that body for one of its members." [71]

The Democratic papers of the South attacked Badger as less acceptable on the slavery issue than a Northern abolitionist. Even the Whig press was less than enthusiastic. *The New York Tribune* called for his confirmation but conceded that "as a statesman, he is of no account, and as a politican detestable." [72]

A month after the nomination, the Senate voted 26-24 to postpone consideration for another three weeks, a clear indication that Badger would not be confirmed. *The New York Times* protested that it was "one of those purely party operations . . . there was no possible objection . . . except that he is a Whig." [73] After Pierce took office, he immediately nominated a Democrat, John Archibald Campbell of Alabama, who won Senate confirmation in four days. *(Details, p. 657)*

Eight years later, the political tables were turned. President James Buchanan, a Democrat with only one month left in his term, named Jeremiah Black, his secretary of State and former attorney general, to a vacancy on the court. Republicans insisted that the selection should be made by their incoming president, Abraham Lincoln.

The situation was complicated by vacancies in the Senate caused by resignations of members from seceding states and by the bitter opposition to Black of Stephen Douglas and his Democratic followers. Echoing the position of the anti-slavery press, *The New York Tribune* observed: "In all the extensive range of his most unhappy selections for office, Mr. Buchanan has never hit upon a single nomination more eminently unfit to be made." [74]

The Senate rejected Black by a 26-25 vote, and President Lincoln, after delays caused by the outbreak of war, filled the vacancy. *(Details, p. 657)*

Just after the war, Congress reduced the number of Supreme Court seats to seven to deprive President Andrew Johnson of a nomination, but when he was succeeded by President Ulysses Grant in 1869, Congress restored the number to nine. Grant named his attorney general, Ebenezer Rockwood Hoar of Massachusetts, to the vacancy. Initial reaction was favorable.

The *Nation* called the appointment "an admirable one." [75] *The New York Times* said of Hoar: "His distinguished abilities are conceded and his elevation to the Supreme Bench is received with profound satisfaction by all." [76] *Harper's Weekly* called the choice "one of the best that could have been made." [77]

But as attorney general, Hoar had offended a number of senators by persuading President Grant to reject their political selections for judgeships and by his personal attitude toward the lawmakers. Historian Charles Warren said his "brusque manners had given great offense;" [78] the *New York Herald* said he treated the senators with "supercilious contempt." [79]

The president attempted to rescue the Hoar nomination by appeasing the Senate with the selection, five days later, of Edwin Stanton of Pennsylvania for a second court vacancy created by a sudden resignation. The former

Early Leaks

The dream of every Supreme Court reporter — having an informant actually on the bench — was apparently realized at least once. Ten days before the court announced its decision in the *Wheeling Bridge Case* in 1852, the *New York Tribune* reported that the majority would require removal or elevation of a bridge across the Ohio River because it interfered with interstate commerce. The story, which identified Justice John McLean as author of the opinion, proved accurate.

Two years later, after Congress had preserved the bridge by legislation, it was destroyed by a windstorm. Ignoring an injunction, the bridge company began reconstruction, and the case came back before the court. In February 1856 the *Tribune* said a majority would hold the protective statute constitutional, thus effectively reversing its earlier ruling. In April the court did just that. *(Details, p. 85)*

Observing that the *Tribune* "seems to have had a trustworthy pipeline to the Supreme Court," historian Carl B. Swisher wrote that the paper "was well served by its news source — from the nature of the comment apparently one of the dissenting justices." One of them was Justice John McLean.

Later the same year, the same paper was able to provide its readers with a running account of the court's secret discussions of the *Dred Scott* case, again apparently coming from a dissenting justice who sympathized with the *Tribune's* anti-slavery position. The only justice who dissented in both the bridge and slave cases was McLean.

Source: *New York Tribune*, Feb. 19, 1856, quoted in Carl B. Swisher, *History of the Supreme Court of the United States:* Vol. V, *The Taney Period, 1836-64* (New York: Macmillan Publishing Company, Inc., 1971), p. 416.

secretary of war was confirmed immediately, but he died of a heart attack four days later, and Hoar's prospects for Senate approval failed to improve. Six weeks later, the Senate refused to confirm him by a 33-24 vote. *(Details, p. 657)*

President Grant did not fare any better with another attorney general when he nominated George Williams of Oregon as Chief Justice in 1873 to succeed Salmon Chase.

The move startled both the organized bar and the public, which had been little impressed by the nominee as a senator or Cabinet officer.

The *American Law Review* called the selection "a disappointment to all who had hoped that the seat of Marshall might be filled by a fitting successor" and said that Grant "has not improved the opportunity to make such a choice from the eminent lawyers of the country as the people had a right to expect." [80]

The *Nation* called it "rather odd that the chief of a court which has to pass on the most complicated controversies of a great commercial country should be chosen from the bar of a frontier state like Oregon...." [81] The *Independent* observed that "the general feeling of the public is that the President might and should have done better...." [82]

So widespread was public protest that the Senate Judiciary Committee voted to reconsider its approval of confirmation. Five weeks after he had proposed it, Grant withdrew the nomination, at Williams' request. Twenty-five years later, Williams wrote that he had been nominated "without my knowledge or consent" and that "the reasons for the Republican opposition to me in the Senate were not such as were given to the public by the newspapers." [83]

Undaunted, President Grant turned to Caleb Cushing of Massachusetts as his new candidate for Chief Justice. The nominee had also served as attorney general and had experience on the supreme judicial court of his home state. He was, however, 74 years old and, according to Charles Warren, "a man of exceedingly unstable character," having switched political parties four or five times. [84]

Press reaction, especially among Republican papers, was strongly adverse. The *New York Tribune* called the nomination "incongruous" and "objectionable." [85] *Harper's Weekly* attacked Cushing as "a pro-slavery Democrat whose views have been notoriously in opposition to those by virtue of which the war was carried on." [86] The *Nation* said that "the President has at last entered the small circle of eminent lawyers, and then with great care has chosen the worst man in it." [87]

The president and the Senate were spared a decision on Cushing's merits, however, when a 13-year-old letter of recommendation from the nominee to Jefferson Davis, then president of the Confederate States, came to light. Although the letter contained no evidence of disloyalty, several senators said it compelled them to vote against Cushing, and Grant withdrew the nomination four days after he had made it.

20th Century: 1900-1950

Coverage

During the first half of the 20th century, the Supreme Court moved through a phase of relative somnolence that reflected national prosperity and wartime unity into one of its most critical eras as an institution, as the Depression brought radical changes in the role of the federal government and sharp constitutional challenges to those changes.

Generally, during the first three decades of the new century, the court did not play a major part in governing the country and, as a result, received relatively little attention from the newspapers.

But the advent of the Depression brought sweeping change. President Franklin D. Roosevelt persuaded Congress that powerful government intervention was required in the nation's economic and social affairs, and the challenges posed to the resulting legislation focused a strong spotlight on the justices and their work. Press coverage broadened and deepened as the nation realized that the fate of the New Deal hung on the response of the court.

The resulting story was good fodder for the news media of the day. First, the relatively conservative court, which had been all but invisible during the terms of Calvin Coolidge and Herbert Hoover, made news by consistently finding New Deal measures unconstitutional. Then the president launched an unprecedented attack against the justices, proposing that the court be enlarged with the obvious expectation that his appointees would shift its philosophical balance.

The ensuing controversy turned Supreme Court reporters into combat correspondents. The justices, completely unused to such an adversary role, attempted to defend their institution. Editorial pages around the country, generally Republican, erupted with charges that Roosevelt was trying to trample on the Constitution. Then, for whatever reason, the court shifted and began upholding New Deal legislation. It was a journalistic field-day.

Roughly around the turn of the century, newspaper reporting of the court, as of other government activities, had begun to come of age, shifting its emphasis from the highly editorial articles that were common during the 1800s to more or less straight accounts of the facts. The trend was faster and more pronounced in some areas of the country than others, but the old personalized journalism was largely a thing of the past by the time the New Deal revived the court's prominence.

As a result, press commentary on Supreme Court rulings moved from the news columns of the nation's papers to their editorial pages. To the extent that the court responds to public opinion in reaching its decisions or in modifying past decisions to conform to changed conditions — a controversial matter from colonial times until the present day — such movement must be measured against newspapers' editorial comment rather than news stories during the first half of the 20th century and thereafter.

During this period, a new and much more timely source of news reporting — radio broadcasting — first began playing a major part in coverage of the court. Generally, then as now, radio news accounts tended to lose in detail what they gained in immediacy, leaving newspapers and specialized legal journals as the principal source of information about all but the simplest cases decided by the court.

Cases

President Franklin D. Roosevelt's New Deal presented the Supreme Court with the most serious challenges in its history, in both judicial and political terms. Congress, at the president's behest, had enacted an imposing body of innovative legislation; many of the new laws aroused sufficient public opposition to wind up in the courts, where they posed a series of issues of great complexity and controversy.

When, from the viewpoint of the White House, the court proved too inflexible to adjust to new concepts of executive and legislative authority aimed at meeting the economic crisis of the Great Depression, the president launched a frontal attack on the institution itself.

Nominally, that attack failed; Roosevelt's attempt to reshape the philosophy of the court by expanding its membership aroused nearly fanatical opposition and never won congressional endorsement. But the mere proposal apparently had such impact on the court — the question is still sharply debated — that the president achieved his underlying goal of more favorable consideration for his programs. Or so it appears today.

Press coverage of this fascinating era, while very different from that of earlier years, played a role in the unfolding events, if only by informing the public of the daily skirmishes between the White House and the justices and

their defenders. The voice of the press, now emanating from the editorial pages of the nation's newspapers rather than their news columns, was not always a steady guide to the controversy.

The N.R.A. Decision of 1935. In May of 1935, when the court declared the National Recovery Administration unconstitutional, *The Washington Star* exulted: "The Supreme Court, almost in the twinkling of an eye, yesterday re-established the Constitution of the United States." The justices "turned back those who have sought to set Federal power above law" and reversed "a tendency toward government domination ... that bordered on dictatorship."[88] *(Details of ruling, pp. 78, 98)*

Comparable enthusiasm was voiced elsewhere. *The New York Herald-Tribune* said with satisfaction of President Roosevelt: "the damage to his prestige is great. He is shown ... to have been leading the country down a blind alley." [89] The *Los Angeles Times:* "The days of a virtually uncontrolled one-man dictatorship in the United States are at an end." [90] *The Denver Post:* "...the Constitution still stands and cannot be stretched by any group of well-meaning but visionary theorists to set up any kind of a political despotism." [91]

Even papers more favorable to the Roosevelt administration expressed little sorrow at the passing of the N.R.A. "Perhaps the decision will mean the end of slovenly legislative procedure," *The Boston Herald* observed. [92] Refusing to become excited, *The New York Times* said: "The judges simply pronounce to be dead a statute which the great mass of the people had already decided to be dead," and their ruling "seems so far to have met with general approval." [93]

The A.A.A. Decision of 1936. Eight months later, when the court pulled down another pillar of the New Deal, the Agricultural Adjustment Administration, the president's press critics took it in stride. *The Washington Star* predicted that the ruling "presages the ultimate invalidation of many more New Deal laws," observing that the decision "should not come as a surprise to the nation ... indeed, the surprising thing would have been for the court to upheld the A.A.A." [94] *(Details of ruling, p. 117)*

The New York Herald-Tribune praised the opinion, saying "the unceremonious fashion in which it sweeps aside the various subterfuges of the law should be a warning to those optimistic New Dealers who had thought to hoodwink the court and evade the Congress by trick or glibly stated purpose." [95]

Other newspapers reacted by reflecting more localized interests. *The Kansas City Star* said the ruling had "precipitated an immediate crisis" among farmers who had participated in the program. [96] *The Chattanooga Times* called for a constitutional amendment to continue the

---

'Landslide' Johnson

While controversy over President Franklin D. Roosevelt's plan to increase the size of the Supreme Court was at its height, a special election was held in the 10th Congressional District of Texas. Of the eight candidates competing, only one endorsed the president's "packing" proposal, and he won. His victory was "a vote of confidence" in the court plan, the new representative, Lyndon B. Johnson, told *The New York Times.*

Source: *The New York Times,* April 11, 1937, quoted in Leonard Baker, *Back to Back* (New York: Macmillan Publishing Company, Inc., 1967), p. 188.

A.A.A. and the T.V.A., which now appeared threatened. [97] The *Lincoln (Neb.) State Journal* inveighed against farmers who "took those checks, swapped away the right to manage their own properties, voted as A.A.A. agents told them to and pretended to be grateful." [98]

"Packing" the Court. Then came the turning point. On Feb. 5, 1937, Roosevelt proposed enlarging the membership of the court to as many as 15 justices; he argued that the federal courts as a whole needed manpower, but his transparent purpose was to dilute the Supreme Court majority hostile to his legislation into a minority by new appointments. *(Details of court-packing fight, p. 240)*

Press reaction was swift and largely critical, ranging from outrage on the right to mannerly questioning by papers that had generally supported the New Deal.

The Washington Star accused the President of "indirection, savoring strongly of subterfuge," and questioned whether the nine-man court "will have enough to do to keep it busy through March." [99]

The New York Herald-Tribune said the court plan would "end the American state as it has existed throughout the long years of its life" and reduce the Constitution to "a paper shell." [100] The *Hartford Courant* suggested that the president might better have said openly: "Let me appoint six judges to the Supreme Court, and they will see to it that the Constitution does not stand in the way of what I want to do." [101]

Calling the plan "a program of almost devilish ingenuity," the *Los Angeles Times* declared; "It is a hard thing to say of the President of the United States, but the fact remains this program cannot be offered in good faith." [102] The *San Francisco Chronicle* said it was "an open declaration of war on the Supreme Court, which is none the less direct because its first attack is on the flank." [103]

Roosevelt sympathizers were hard put to defend the plan. "The historic truth is," the *Des Moines Register* observed, "that no matter how great and good a man may be, executive aggrandisement is not safe for democracy." [104] *The New York Times* said Roosevelt had laid himself open to charges that he was trying "to do by indirection what he cannot do directly," and raised the question of whether this amounted to "political sharp practice, a thing Americans are not yet ready to condone under the name of judicial reform." [105]

The *St. Paul Pioneer Press* and *The Kansas City Star* argued that such a change in the court should be accomplished, if at all, by constitutional amendment rather than statute. Otherwise, the Minnesota paper said, "the Constitution is to be reduced to a mere generality and the court to become a changeling." [106] The *Star* maintained the people should decide such a drastic shift in power and called the "packing" legislation "a short cut . . . in the specious guise of expediting justice." [107]

Support for the New Deal. Then, with almost dazzling swiftness, the entire situation changed. Little more than two months after the "packing" plan had been unveiled, the court began handing down decisions upholding instead of dismantling the New Deal. In March 1937 the justices upheld a state minimum wage and two weeks later the federal Wagner Act, guaranteeing collective bargaining rights to workers. *The New York Times* proclaimed that "the new majority of the court has made legal history." *(Details pp. 99, 327)*

"What more can the Roosevelt Administration reasonably ask. . .?" the *Times* inquired, suggesting that the Wagner Act ruling provided "an excellent opportunity to

. . . withdraw with good grace from the packing proposal." [108] There was general agreement elsewhere. The *Los Angeles Times* said the court had "disproved the President's contention that it is biased and prejudiced against New Deal legislation." [109] The *San Francisco Chronicle* observed that if the ruling doomed "Mr. Roosevelt's rash anti-constitutional revolutionary coup d'etat, believers in representative democratic government breathe easier." [110] The *Chattanooga Times* said, "After these decisions . . . there seems to be left little ground on which the President can stand." [111]

Six weeks later, when the court upheld the new Social Security system, *The New York Times* news account said the ruling "showed that the majority of the court now tends to favor the liberal aims of the Administration," and the paper editorially called the decision "another historic step in the process of adapting the great charter of American democracy to the changing needs of the times." [112] *(Details, p. 118)*

Somewhat more skeptically, *The Wall Street Journal* pointed out that "the court passes only upon the power of Congress to enact such a statute, not upon its wisdom or the rightness of a complex law as it stands." The *Journal* argued that the decision "again enhances the Federal domain; it impairs state sovereignty to the extent that no state can now assert its right to hold its industries free of social burdens like these." [113]

The Washington Star questioned the need for any further debate on the "discredited" court reorganization plan, "a dangerous redesign of the American form of government." [114] *The Washington Post* agreed, saying the court "has driven another nail in the coffin of the President's plan to enlarge the court's membership . . . removing the last flimsy argument." [115]

Whether public reaction to the packing plan, reflected by the press, had been overwhelmingly hostile or whether President Roosevelt felt he had achieved his aim by threat, the proposal to expand the court was never pressed seriously again.

The Court and the Stars and Stripes. During the World War II years, a pair of Supreme Court decisions indicated that the justices were indeed attentive to adverse, widespread press reaction.

In June 1940 the court held 8 to 1 that public schools can compel pupils to salute the American flag, even if the salute violates their religious beliefs.

Initial press response was supportive. *The New York Times* was not disturbed by the court's upholding the compulsory salute statute, while observing that "reverence for which the flag stands is more important than any gesture." [116] *The Washington Star* cautioned its readers that the decision "does not mean that the safeguards against impairment of freedom of worship have been relaxed in the slightest degree." [117]

But, as time passed, more and more reflective editorial writers concluded that the decision had been a mistake, and more than 150 papers ended up criticizing the decision. For example, the *St. Louis Post Dispatch* concluded: "We think its decision is a violation of American principle. We think it is a surrender to popular hysteria. If patriotism depends on such things as this — upon violation of a fundamental right of religious freedom — then it becomes not a noble emotion of love for country but something to be rammed down our throats by the law." [118]

Three years later, the justices reversed their former decision and invalidated flag salute laws as a violation of religious freedom. *The New York Times* remained cautious, acknowledging that the earlier ruling had aroused "an emotion of dislike" and concluding that "the voluntary principle is the essence of civil rights as of common sense."[119] *(Details, p. 457)*

The Washington Star agreed with the majority that "the tribute to the flag becomes a meaningless gesture when forced" but was otherwise not enthusiastic. "There will be grave doubts," the paper concluded, as to the wisdom of the ruling "that compliance with a reasonable regulation, applied almost universally to promote good citizenship, depends on nothing more than the whim of the individual. By that logic the dissidents become the rule-makers, and no regulation is safe."[120]

The Modern Era: 1950-1979

Coverage

The Supreme Court has probably made news more consistently in the years since 1950 than at any other time in the nation's past. Under Chief Justice Earl Warren (1953-69), the court became a mighty engine of government in a way it rarely had been before. Under Chief Justice Warren E. Burger, that machine has braked somewhat but is far from immobile.

Because of the sweeping and controversial nature of many of the court's more recent decisions, contemporary press coverage has been among the most intensive that the institution has received over the years. As in the past, the news media conveyed the pronouncements of the court to the public, analyzed the impact on the nation and relayed citizen reaction back to the nine justices if they chose to read, watch and listen.

The second half of the 20th century added a new dimension to coverage of the court: television. While its cameras were and are barred from the courtroom — although admitted experimentally to lower courts — television hired reporters with legal training and worked to encapsulate and illustrate major decisions for the broader audience their new medium commanded.

Newspapers, increasingly aware of television competition, tended to compress the kind of exhaustive coverage given landmark cases of the past, but more papers assigned more reporters with better legal knowledge to cover the court's overall activities more thoroughly. The value of a permanent written record for judges, law professors and lawyers was not diminished by the prevalence of broadcast reporting.

It was no more possible during this modern era than it ever had been to prove or disprove Finley Peter Dunne's dictum that "the Supreme Court follows the election returns." The most that could be said was that a highly sophisticated communications system made more information, opinion and reaction available to the court than ever before, for whatever judicial notice its members might take.

The 16 years of the activist Warren court produced news that tested the press' reportorial ability: the abolition of public school segregation, the requirement that members of Congress and both houses of all state legislatures be elected from districts accurately balanced as to population, a long series of rulings protecting the constitutional rights of criminal defendants against abuse by law enforcement officials.

The Burger court continued to make news, moving incrementally away from the Warren court's positions on criminal law and in other areas, winning applause in some legal circles and criticism in others. But its decisions on abortion, obscenity, capital punishment and affirmative action presented as large a challenge to reporters and editorial writers as had many rulings by the preceding court.

The early years of the Burger court also brought an unprecedented pair of controversies over confirmation of proposed new justices. The press not only circulated criticism of President Richard Nixon's appointees, Clement F. Haynsworth Jr. and G. Harrold Carswell, to the public, but, in some instances, helped uncover information about them that contributed to their rejection by the Senate.

Cases

So far during the second half of the 20th century, the Supreme Court has never been far from the spotlight of press attention. With the exception of the New Deal court-packing controversy, the court was probably never the focus of such intense public attention and criticism as it was during the years after Earl Warren became Chief Justice in 1953. After Warren Burger succeeded him in 1969, supporters and critics of the previous era exchanged roles, but the court itself continued as a major center of news and controversy.

Desegregating the Public Schools. The high mark of the court's prominence as a powerful agency of government almost certainly came in May of 1954 when the justices ruled unanimously that racial segregation in the public schools was unconstitutional. Recognizing that revolutionary forces had been set in motion, the great majority of the nation's newspapers reacted with caution, rather than exultation or outrage. Most significantly, few of the bitterest critics raised the prospect of resistance. *(Details of ruling, p. 592)*

The New York Times was so restrained as to make its view seem rather equivocal today. "The court is not talking of that sort of equality which produces interracial marriage," the paper assured the nation. "It is not talking of a social system at all." Acknowledging serious problems ahead, the *Times* concluded that "little by little ... we move toward a more perfect democracy."[121]

The Washington Post said the decision "affords all Americans an occasion for pride and gratification" and will ultimately prove "profoundly healthy and healing."[122] The more conservative *Washington Star* observed that "concern over a dubious assumption of power by the court ... does not alter the fact that this decision finds much support in wisdom and fairness."[123]

Reaction from the South was, understandably, less favorable. *The New Orleans Times-Picayune* predicted that in "the immediate future, the decision will do no service either to education or racial accommodation" and concluded that "the disappointment and frustration of the majority of southerners at the revolutionary overturn of practice and usage cannot immediately result in the improvement of race relations." [124]

The *Louisville Courier-Journal* said that "the end of the world has not come for the South or for the nation. The Supreme Court's ruling is not itself a revolution. It is rather acceptance of a process that has been going on a long time — people everywhere could well match the court's moderation and caution." [125]

The *Atlanta Constitution* observed that the ruling "does not mean that Negro and white children will go to school together this fall." [126]

The *Chicago Tribune* salvaged something from the ruling in a grudging editorial. "The principle established by this decision is not that anybody has to give up any of his prejudices," the paper said. "The principle is the much simpler one that the state governments, North and South, must regard all men as created equal so far as opportunities at the disposal of the state are concerned." [127]

The *Houston Chronicle* warned that "racial friction may be increased rather than diminished and . . . endless litigation may arise to plague the Southern states" as they comply. [128] The *Jackson (Miss.) Clarion-Ledger* said: "May 17, 1954, may be recorded by future historians as a black day of tragedy for the South and for both races, but we can conduct ourselves in such fashion as to cause historians to record that we faced that tragedy and crisis with wisdom, courage, faith and determination." [129]

A year later, when the court ordered compliance with its desegregation edict with "all deliberate speed," southern newspapers were considerably less exercised than they had been at the original decision. The court, said the *Raleigh News and Observer*, "has gone about as far as any Southerner could have expected" in refusing to set an arbitrary timetable . . . . [130] The *Atlanta Constitution* called the ruling "much more mild and less specific in tone than had been anticipated." [131]

The *New York Times* said the implementing decision was "perhaps not wholly satisfactory for anybody" but concluded that "the error of a static and ineffective edict has been avoided." [132] The *Wilmington (Del.) Morning News* called it "a pretty sensible decision" that displayed "no lack of firmness" but "understanding of local feelings and respect for local control." [133]

"One Man, One Vote." The Warren court had more than one revolution in store for the American people. In 1964 the court ruled that both houses of state legislatures must be apportioned according to population, rather than geography or custom. The result was a massive redistribution of power away from rural areas to the cities and suburbs, and press response was sharply divided.

The *New York Times* declared that "as a matter of equity, the court is clearly right" in correcting the "historic injustice" that limited the influence of cities in state legislatures. [134] Echoing this reaction, *The Washington Post* said the ruling "goes a long way toward establishing democracy in America" and "will be magnificently liberating" because "rural domination in the state legislatures has created a paralyzing tyranny." [135] *(Details of case, p. 491)*

But *The Wall Street Journal* was unhappy. "It was clearly wrong for the states for so many years to deny effective voice to their urban minorities," the *Journal* conceded. "But it is hardly less wrong for the nation now to go to the other extreme of muzzling rural minorities." [136]

The Washington Star observed that there was "no longer cause for surprise that the court makes its decisions

. . . on the basis of its personalized idea of what is right — what is good for us. . . . We may wonder whether our system of government benefits when justices do what voters will not do." The paper concluded, however, that "the practical and moral effects of the rulings probably will be for the good." [137]

Criminal Justice. The vigor with which the press praised or belabored the Warren court was nowhere more visible than in the highly controversial area of law enforcement. The court's dedication to ensuring the rights of the accused to fair treatment in criminal prosecutions, at the possible expense of convictions, sharply divided commentary in the news media; a classic example was the *Miranda* case, in which the court mandated a code of protection for suspects who were to be interrogated by the police.

The decision, said *The Washington Star*, "will be received with rejoicing by every thug in the land" and "will grievously handicap the police and make it much easier for a criminal to beat the rap." Chief Justice Warren's opinion was "a murky torrent of words" that "will largely destroy the traditional police function at least as far as interrogation is concerned." [138] *(Details of case, p. 560)*

Across town, *The Washington Post* observed with satisfaction that "the Supreme Court is determined to take all this jazz about civil liberty seriously" and "insists upon reading the Constitution as though it had been intended as a charter of freedom."

But even the court's supporters could not agree entirely. The *Post* called the Warren opinion "admirable" for specifying permissible police procedures "with clarity and accuracy." [139] But *The New York Times*, while supporting the decision as a whole, found the listing of procedures "regrettable" as an "over-hasty trespass into the legislative area." The *Times* also criticized the majority for "downgrading the reliability and worth of all confessions" in some unnecessary language.

While predicting that the *Miranda* ruling "will erase some of the discrimination against the poor" in criminal cases, the *Times* said that "experience may well validate the fear expressed by the dissenting justices that law enforcement will be handicapped. . . ." [140]

The Burger Court. The post-Warren court proved hard to define. While much of its work outside the area of criminal law aroused relatively little interest in the press, there were a number of striking exceptions: major rulings legalizing all but end-of-term abortions, redefining pornography to restrict its circulation, reinstating capital punishment and narrowly sustaining the principle of affirmative action in education for victims of historic discrimination.

Executive Privilege. Almost certainly the most notorious case that Chief Justice Burger and his colleagues dealt with during their early years was the Nixon tapes dispute, producing a unanimous 1974 ruling requiring the president to surrender recordings of 64 White House conversations for use as evidence in the Watergate cover-up trial. It led directly to the conviction of a number of high administration officials and to the resignation of the president to avoid a House vote on articles of impeachment against him. *(Details, p. 247)*

Press coverage of the case was intensive throughout. When the Supreme Court agreed to hear the case on an accelerated basis on May 31, the story was played as the most important of the day. Subsequent exchange of briefs and oral argument on July 8 all produced front-page stories although they contained little new information.

When the decision came down on July 24, the nation's newspapers voiced a thundering chorus of grateful affirmation, tempered in some cases by past Republican loyalties. *The Wall Street Journal,* for example, saw the ruling as "a common sense resolution of the immediate problems involved" rather than the rescue of the Republic.

"Surely it is healthier," the *Journal* observed, "to have the President's arguments based not in defiance of the courts but in compliance with them." The paper expressed editorial gratitude for President Nixon's announcement that he would surrender the tapes, on behalf of "those of us who have been struggling to keep an open mind." [141]

Similarly, *The Washington Star* called the decision "historic, definitive and above all correct" but was able to take some solace from the court's recognition, for the first time, of the existence of executive privilege in the White House. That will make for "a more careful and cleaner presidency;" otherwise the courts "would have required the President and his advisors to conduct the nation's business in a fishbowl, a situation that would be intolerable and unworkable." [142]

The New York Times praised the court for reaffirming "the supremacy of law over Presidential pretensions" and establishing that "the presidency cannot be used as a sanctuary for miscreants." "If this nation was to remain the Republic established by the authors of the Constitution," the *Times* declared, "the court could only have ruled as it did." [143]

The Washington Post paid one of its relatively rare tributes to Chief Justice Burger, for "a particularly sound and skillful opinion . . . nicely reconciling the conflicting interests of confidentiality for the President and the right of due process for criminal defendants." The paper concluded ruefully that "it is a measure of how far we have come when a President of the United States can hope to earn favor by not defying a decision by the Supreme Court." [144]

Confirmation Battles

The Senate confirmation battles over two of President Richard Nixon's nominees for the Supreme Court — first, Clement F. Haynsworth Jr., chief judge of the U.S. Court of Appeals for the fourth circuit, and then G. Harrold Carswell, a junior judge on the U.S. Court of Appeals, fifth circuit — provided dramatic examples of the role of the news media in influencing the actions of public officials, both directly and indirectly.

During the confirmation disputes, newspapers, and to a lesser extent radio and television, served two functions. They circulated growing criticism of the two Nixon nominees to the public, which, in turn, brought constituent pressure on members of the Senate to vote against the president's choices. But some of that critical information was actually the product of investigative reporting into the backgrounds of the two judges, producing far more significant information than the Federal Bureau of Investigation had furnished to the White House.

Unforeseen Opposition. No one really anticipated either of the controversies. The Senate had not denied confirmation to a Supreme Court nominee since 1930. The first two Nixon choices, Chief Justice Warren E. Burger and Associate Justice Harry A. Blackmun, had aroused little opposition in the Democratic-controlled Senate despite their relatively conservative judicial views. When Judge Haynsworth was named in 1969, he appeared headed for the same sort of gentle treatment.

The Fortas Affair

Only one justice has ever resigned from the Supreme Court under public pressure. He was Abe Fortas, who, in less than five years on the high bench, nearly rose to the pinnacle of becoming Chief Justice and eleven months later was forced to step down under circumstances that bordered on disgrace.

While Fortas had been a controversial figure throughout his judicial service, it was an example of journalistic enterprise that effectively ended his career. William Lambert, an investigative reporter for *Life* magazine, uncovered the fact that the justice had agreed to accept $20,000 a year for his lifetime, and then for his wife's, from a foundation in return for "continuing services."

What made the charges of unethical behavior even more damning was the fact that the foundation's head was Louis E. Wolfson, then serving a prison term for selling unregistered securities. The American Bar Association later declared that Fortas' retention of a high-paying client while on the bench had been "clearly contrary" to the canons of ethics.

For Fortas, it had been a mighty fall. When he was named to the court by President Lyndon B. Johnson in 1965, *The New York Times* said the move "gives every promise of proving an exceptional appointment" since the nominee had "many qualities . . . other than political shrewdness and presidential gratitude." *The Washington Post* praised Fortas for "his intellectual capacity, his legal experience and his deep concern over civil liberties and civil rights," and the strongly Republican *Washington Star* called him "a most able, respected and scholarly lawyer."

Three years later, an attempt by President Johnson to make Fortas Chief Justice foundered in a Senate filibuster amid charges that he had accepted high lecture fees while on the bench and had continued to serve as a major White House advisor, raising obvious conflict-of-interest problems.

When he resigned in 1969, *The New York Times* approved, saying the justice had "helped preserve the reputation for the integrity of the nation's highest court, which his own actions had so severely shaken." *The Washington Star* agreed that the move "should free the court of the shadow cast upon it by the Fortas indiscretions, and this is the most important thing." Calling the resignation "imperative," *The Washington Post* said that "the outcome is tragic in the true dramatic sense of the term for it entails the destruction of a man of great stature and great promise."

Sources: *The New York Times,* July 29, 1965; *The Washington Post,* July 30, 1965; *The Washington Star,* July 29, 1965; *The New York Times,* May 16, 1969; *The Washington Star,* May 16, 1969; *The Washington Post,* May 16, 1969.

Newspaper reaction at first was guarded but not hostile. *The Washington Star* called the choice of the South Carolinian "both a logical and an excellent one" if the president's purpose was "to bring the court back to a more balanced, a more central position." The newspaper acknowledged that the nominee was "something of an unknown quantity" and observed prophetically that possible conflict of interest questions were "not without troublesome aspects." [145]

The New York Times said the candidate was "disappointing . . . an obscure judge with little reputation for . . . depth, social sensitivity and philosophic insight" and said his record was "marked by an extremely cautious reluctance to interpret the Constitution in the light of changing conditions." [146] *The Washington Post* agreed that Haynsworth was "not particularly distinguished . . . a symbol rather than a man" and found his record that of "a competent jurist . . . nothing more, nothing less." [147]

Then, gradually, conflict charges against the nominee began to mount, based on his considerable stock holdings. He had ruled for a corporation in a labor case while he owned stock in a company that did business with the corporation. He bought stock in a corporation after he had voted in its favor on a case but before the decision was announced. Organized labor came out against his confirmation, as did a number of civil rights groups.

Backers of the nomination held rallying news conferences and spoke out on the Senate floor. The Senate Judiciary Committee approved the nomination, but the vote was 10 to 7. Finally, in late November after a number of Republican defections, the Senate rejected Judge Haynsworth by a 55-45 vote, the largest negative reaction ever accorded a Supreme Court nominee.

The Washington Star, which had supported Haynsworth throughout the three-month debate, insisted that there had been "insufficient evidence to brand Judge Haynsworth as anti-Negro, anti-labor or unethical in his financial dealings." [148]

The New York Times, however, called the Senate vote "a political setback of stunning proportions" for Nixon. The *Times* had called on the president to withdraw the nomination but had not urged senators to vote against Haynsworth because the president's right to select his own court nominees "outweighs the inadequacies and improprieties alleged against Judge Haynsworth." The paper concluded it was "better for the court and the country" that the nomination had been defeated, rather than approved by a narrow margin. [149]

Judicial Competence. Two months later, President Nixon sent to the Senate the nomination of another southern conservative, G. Harrold Carswell of Florida, to fill the continuing vacancy. Both the candidate and the controversy his confirmation debate aroused proved to be even more astonishing than the Haynsworth affair.

Press reaction to Judge Carswell fell short of enthusiasm by varying degrees. *The Washington Star* saw the nominee's philosophy as "several degrees to the right of our own . . . but no red-necked reactionary." The paper predicted that "this time the nomination (of a southerner) will stick" because "Carswell, from all accounts, has been investigated with uncommon diligence." [150]

The *Star* news stories displayed comparable foresight. "Fast Okay Likely for Carswell" the front-page headline read, and the story predicted that the new justice would be on the bench when the court reconvened a month later.

The Washington Post called it "unfortunate" that the president "did not see fit to reward one of the truly distinguished judges (of the South)," maintaining that Carswell's performance on the bench "does not lift him even to the top layer" of the Republicans named to judgeships in the South during the 1950s by President Dwight D. Eisenhower. [151]

Even more pointedly, *The New York Times* expressed "shock" that the president had proposed a nominee "totally lacking in professional distinction . . . wholly unknown

for cogent opinions or learned writing." But the editorial more or less conceded his confirmation, saying he "may in time grow in wisdom." [152]

Despite the fact that he owned no stock at all, Judge Carswell was in trouble almost immediately. Two days after his designation, a television reporter uncovered a militant white-supremacist speech he had made in 1948 and printed on the front page of a weekly newspaper he owned. Then came the story of how he had participated in converting a public golf course in Tallahassee into an all-white private club rather than desegregate it. Feminist groups joined the labor and civil rights coalition of the Haynsworth resistance.

Witnesses told of Judge Carswell's hostility from the bench to Negro civil rights attorneys. The dean of the Yale Law School said Carswell had "the most slender credentials of any man put forward in this century for the Supreme Court." The Judiciary Committee supported him, 13 to 4, but a floor vote was delayed as reports accumulated of the nominee's participation in discriminatory activities.

The Washington Star remained steadfast, saying that the judge "certainly should be approved. His apparent lack of judicial brilliance is not the point" and "his detractors have not made a convincing case against him." [153] But *The New York Times* called his participation in the golf course transaction "shameful" and urged "a rejection of this unworthy nominee" who had displayed "callous disregard of both the law and civil rights." [154]

Late in March both *The Washington Post* and *The New York Times* reported Senate support for Carswell ebbing but probably not seriously enough to prevent his confirmation. Opponents launched delaying tactics to allow wider circulation of adverse information about the nominee. Some Republican backers shifted to an undecided posture. The White House mustered a statement of support by southern judges. President Nixon charged the Senate with trying to usurp his constitutional powers.

On the eve of the final vote, *The Washington Star* predicted that "chances are, it's all over but the confirmation" while acknowledging that "our enthusiasm for Judge Carswell is, quite frankly, restrained." [155] *The Washington Post*, which had favored Judge Haynsworth's confirmation, said Carswell should be rejected because "he lacks the essential qualities." [156] *The New York Times*, two days before the vote, called confirmation "simply incomprehensible;" [157] on the morning of the vote, the paper called the nomination "an insult to the Congress, a denigration of the court and an affront to the faith of the American people in the quality of their government." [158]

When the Senate rejected the Carswell nomination by a 51-45 vote, the newspapers reacted more or less predictably. The *Star* reaffirmed its belief that Judge Carswell had been properly qualified and said that the Senate had been "wrong" if its vote was based on "his social or judicial philosophy." The paper urged that "Mr. Nixon should stick to his guns" in picking still another conservative Supreme Court candidate. [159]

The Washington Post urged the president to choose someone with "impeccable credentials" like Chief Justice Burger, "a man of quality in his intellectual capacity as well as his personal life." [160] *The New York Times* called the Senate decision "a triumph of constitutional responsibility over political partisanship" and observed that "the dismal experience of past weeks must emphasize to the president the urgency of turning quickly to the nomination of a first-rate jurist." [161]

Covering the High Court

The relationship between the Supreme Court and the news media has been an uneasy one over the years. This is hardly surprising since the court, almost by definition, is a rigid, tradition-bound and intensely secretive institution while the press is, by necessity, adaptive, exploratory and devoted as a matter of principle to the elimination of governmental secrecy.

Historically, the court has made the minimum possible accommodation to the need for public information. For many years, the justices regarded other judges and lawyers as their proper constituency and felt they could and should be reached through legal publications. The lay public was largely ignored.

At one time in the last century, Chief Justice Roger B. Taney ordered that no court opinions be made public until they had been printed in the official bound reports. Chief Justice Warren E. Burger reportedly considered eliminating the working-press' room from the courthouse altogether and letting reporters pick up opinions from the clerk, but he rejected the idea.

Only some 20 years ago, reporters with deadline problems — which meant all of them — had to sit in the courtroom and take notes while opinions were being read in full, because texts were not handed out until the justices had concluded, often well into the afternoon.

Conflict between the two institutions, the judiciary and the press, peaked during the Warren court when cross-complaints of botched reporting and impossible working conditions were freely exchanged. Chief Justice Burger has concerned himself with public information access more than any of his predecessors. Although he adopted very few suggested reforms, he acknowledged the problem and made himself available to discuss solutions — a considerable advance, from the viewpoint of the press.

Judicial Expertise in the Press

One focus of past criticism from the legal profession of Supreme Court coverage was the lack of legal training of the reporters, but that pattern has shifted considerably. During one recent term, a half-dozen of the court regulars, nearly half the reporters concentrating primarily on the court, were law school graduates. Several more with a year of law study in special programs at Harvard and Yale have worked the beat with distinction.

The current roster lists nearly 50 reporters who devote all or part of their time to covering the court. A number of these are also assigned to the Department of Justice, which provides a further need for background in the law. But only the two major wire services — the Associated Press and United Press International — and four newspapers — *The Washington Post, The New York Times, The Wall Street Journal* and the *Los Angeles Times* — assign correspondents whose sole responsibility is covering the court and legal affairs.

Keeping Their Distance

Direct contact between the justices and the reporters who cover their pronouncements is very limited, almost non-existent. Print journalists may sit in the courtroom and observe the justices as they present summaries of their opinions and question attorneys during oral argument. Broadcast journalists have the same right, but no more;

they may not record any of the proceedings for radio or television.

Press seating in the courtroom is adequate for about 20 reporters. When major cases attract larger attendance, many reporters are seated where they can hear but not see the bench, and identifying a speaking justice is often difficult.

The court provides an office for its public information officer, another for his staff, and a room for reporters that is frequently crowded on decision days. Those who cover the court regularly have semi-private alcoves for their own desks and telephones. Others must scramble for a limited number of public desks, typewriters and telephones.

Only one set of briefs on each of the cases before the court is available to assist the press corps. (The major wire services have one set apiece, which are jealously but not always successfully guarded against pilferage.) A reporter can run into long delays in getting access to briefs on a newsworthy case.

A separate room is provided in which radio correspondents can record their news broadcasts, but there is no provision for television at all. Cameras have not been allowed in the building since 1975, when Justice William O. Douglas held a news conference when he returned to duty after suffering a stroke. As a result, the networks "illustrate" their stories on decisions with film from the site of the case and shots of their correspondents standing in front of the courthouse.

A number of lawyers, including notably Attorney General Griffin B. Bell, have proposed that television be permitted to record oral argument and decision ceremonies in the courtroom. Chief Justice Burger is known to oppose this innovation strongly, so any experiment in that direction will almost certainly await his retirement.

Services offered reporters covering the court are limited. Copies of opinions are distributed in the information office as soon as the author begins reading a précis from the bench. Sometimes a justice will adlib a colorful phrase or even a small joke in his summary, but a reporter must be in the courtroom to catch it; there are no transcripts of court proceedings available until days later. Reporters who want a same-day transcript of argument of an important case must make their own private arrangements.

The court's public information officer, aided by two assistants, is primarily a mechanic. He hands out copies of the court's orders and opinions, supervises the small library of briefs and past decisions and answers a wide range of inquiries from the public at large.

But he does not attempt to provide reporters covering the court with any sort of legal assistance or guidance. No experienced correspondent expects such an official to interpret the legal rationale or impact of a Supreme Court decision. No occupant of the job in the past 30 years has been remotely qualified for such a role, and even a skilled attorney would be unlikely to go beyond the specific language of any opinion.

But there are a variety of procedural questions involved in some decisions that are both complicated and important as news, and the information officer does not provide any answers. Reporters have suggested that the court make a staff lawyer available for this kind of question: Did the court's action in remanding for further pro-

Burger and the Right to Privacy

Since 1970, Chief Justice Warren E. Burger has refused to allow television cameras to cover his public appearances.

The matter came to a head in February 1979 when Burger insisted that camera crews be turned away from a meeting of the American Bar Association at which Burger gave a speech. The ABA, in an implicit criticism of Burger's policy, subsequently endorsed an "open-meetings policy."

Burger held his ground, however. In a statement released by the court's public information office on May 18, 1979, Burger announced that he planned to continue the no-media rule.

Among other reasons cited by the information office for upholding the ban, the announcement noted that "Eye sensitivity is such that the Chief Justice cannot see his notes when lights are excessive."

But Burger was clearly motivated by displeasure at the behavior of television reporters, who "at ABA meetings as well as elsewhere accosted the Chief Justice in hotel lobbies, on streets, and in other public places, thrusting microphones at him for impromptu press conferences with questions on subjects wholly inappropriate for comment by any judge," among other indignities.

Burger based his position on the traditions of the judiciary as well as his First Amendment rights:

Any TV claim of a First Amendment right to accost a Justice or Judge with microphones in public places and private gatherings ignores what Mr. Justice Brandeis, Mr. Justice Douglas and others have said: that the First Amendment is a collection of rights, not least of which is the right to be let alone, a principle embedded firmly in American tradition. . . .

There is a long tradition of isolation of judges from day-to-day controversy. That tradition means not only that judges do not take part in political affairs or other public controversies but that it is inappropriate for them to be involved with matters not relating to the administration of justice. Judges are not free as legislators and members of the Executive Branch, who are appropriately concerned with such problems. The tradition is well established that limits judges in giving interviews; comment on legal and judicial subjects are [*sic*] made primarily in judicial opinions. This is not a new limitation on judges. It has been traditionally followed by Chief Justices, Justices and most judges since it became generally agreed that the judiciary should be insulated as much as possible from public controversies. First Amendment rights of judicial officers must be exercised with restraint and within limits; others should respect this tradition.

include the volume of potentially newsworthy material that is issued at one time, the legal and factual complexity of some of the cases and the short time in which reporters for wire services and afternoon newspapers must deal with both volume and complexity.

A Tough Beat

During the history of Supreme Court coverage, there have been times when inaccurate or simply wrong reporting seemed more prevalent; the latter days of the Warren court are an example. Usually, such periods provoke some self-criticism by the press and generate efforts to improve working conditions that can contribute to such inaccuracy.

Volume. To help the press deal with the thousands of cases on its docket, the court provides limited advance warning on which ones it will probably announce that it has decided to accept for review or reject on a given Monday. A week or so before these "orders" are handed down, a list of case numbers is provided reporters on a not-for-publication basis. (Actually, any interested party could find it on the pressroom bulletin board.) The numbers are those of cases the court proposes to take up at its conference that Friday. Not every case on the list will be accepted or rejected the following Monday, but the court is committed not to depart from the list and spring surprises.

No comparable warning is provided, however, when the court decides a case it has accepted and heard argued. The public information officer tells reporters a few days in advance how many decisions will be handed down on a given day, without any hint of which ones they will be. (The night before the court's decision in the 1978 Bakke "reverse discrimination" case, a semi-official source, who may or may not have been acting for the court, tipped off a few reporters as to the timing but not the result of the decision. Such tips are very rare.)

Time. Most of the mistakes in Supreme Court reporting are made by reporters for wire services or afternoon newspapers who must file stories as rapidly as possible after decisions are handed down. Radio correspondents normally have a little more time in which to compose much shorter dispatches.

The court has attempted to help solve this problem by issuing headnotes (summaries of the majority opinion) along with its full text, giving reporters with imminent deadlines a news capsule from which to work. Until a few years ago, these headnotes appeared for the first time when the court opinions were published in bound volumes, months — even years — later.

For some time reporters have urged court officials to institute a "lock-up," distributing opinions or an orders list with a strict release time two hours later, so that the hectic, error-prone rush into print or onto the air could be avoided. Highly sensitive to untimely security leaks, the court has not been willing to test this system, even when reporters agreed to be literally locked up.

While not so critical, time can be a serious problem for morning newspaper reporters as well. On heavy decision days, particularly at the end of a term, a reporter for a morning paper that expects full Supreme Court coverage can often work without a break from 10 a.m. to an early evening deadline to handle the day's material.

Complexity. In the uncherished past, all Supreme Court decisions for a given week were handed down on Monday, along with orders accepting or rejecting cases, and the result was often chaos. Sometimes there was simply too

ceedings a case in which the lower court found a state law unconstitutional uphold the constitutionality of the law? Such guidance could improve reporting accuracy without involving any gratuitous interpretation of a court decision.

Lack of legal guidance is only one of the problems that confront reporters covering the Supreme Court. Others

much material to be read, analyzed and reported adequately. Mistakes resulted and significant cases went unreported.

In 1965 the court began spacing out its decisions, handing down a few on Tuesday and Wednesday mornings when it was in session for oral argument. This practice improved the accuracy and balance of court coverage substantially, but congestion remains a problem at term's end, when a tired court is unwilling to sit a few days longer, merely to time its decisions in the interest of better public understanding.

In recent years, the court has moved cautiously toward handing down decisions in related groups, which reporters naturally regard as constructive. In addition, cases of little or no news interest are also apportioned to make heavy days a little lighter.

During most of the 1970s, Supreme Court reporters had access to a weekly publication called "Preview," in which cases accepted for decision were summarized and their significance assessed by various law professors. This was a cooperative project of the Association of American Law Schools, the American Law Institute and the American Bar Association. Quality of these summaries varied, but most reporters found them useful.

Secret Chambers

One problem in Supreme Court coverage that appears to be nearly insoluble involves secrecy and security. In virtually every agency of the executive and legislative branches, reporters have access to the men and women who make the news, opportunity to question them about public business and learn something, in the process, about their character and personality.

At the Supreme Court, this is not true. A justice obviously cannot discuss a case pending before the court. If he talks about a recent decision, his comments have a tendency to revise its content or to prejudge the next similar case or both. If he talks for the record about any issue that may come before the court, he puts his impartiality in question. As a result, members of the court seldom talk with reporters at all, rarely grant on-the-record interviews and almost never hold news conferences.

Reporters sometimes encounter justices at Washington social events, but resulting conversations are closely circumscribed, tending to be limited to sports, hobbies and the weather. After the resignation of Justice Abe Fortas following revelation of his outside activities, members of the court became even more reclusive, limiting public appearances of any kind.

What amounts to a communications barrier between the justices and the media has been particularly vexing to reporters when a member of the court disqualifies himself from participating in a decision. The motive is almost always praiseworthy and the reason usually routine — a past association with a lawyer or organization involved or stock holdings that might suggest a conflict of interest.

But, by tradition, the court refuses to explain why one of its nine members has abstained, evidently regarding this as a matter of idle press curiosity rather than legitimate public interest. As evidence to the contrary, such an abstention can result in a deadlocked 4-to-4 court that has the effect of denying the appealing party the Supreme Court review that the justices had agreed to provide, a situation that would seem to merit some modest public explanation.

Press Access to the Court Building

Following the 1979 leak to ABC-TV reporter Tim O'Brien of a pending court opinion, the court's public information officer, Barrett McGurn, issued rules governing the press' access to the Supreme Court building.

McGurn emphasized that the guidelines were for the most part restatements of existing policy — some of which were being ignored by reporters — and that exceptions could be made for members of the media who asked permission from the public information office. Following are the 1979 rules:

> Parts of the Building are, of course, closed at all times to all but Court personnel. These include the garage and the basement area in general, the ground floor section beyond the ladies' restroom, the Justices' chambers and access corridors on the first floor, and all of the second and third floors including the Library. Where members of the media need access to these areas, escorts will be provided by the Public Information Office, the Marshal or other Court officers.
>
> Transcripts of Oral Arguments are available for examination in the Public Information Office, room 29.
>
> The Court Building is open to the public from 9 a.m. to 4:30 p.m. weekdays. In addition the Clerk's Office is open from 9 a.m. to noon on Saturdays. Accredited news personnel are free to consult the Clerk's Office during the Saturday open hours.
>
> During non-public hours all visitors to the Building are required to sign in and out at the Building entrance desk. Accredited news personnel may use the press area (rooms 30, 31 and 32) and the adjacent food machine section and restrooms from 8 a.m. to 10 p.m. seven days a week. Where additional time is required arrangements may be made through the Public Information Office. During the non-public hours all other areas of the Building are closed.

Speaking Out-of-Chambers. Occasionally Chief Justice Burger has gone beyond his working-conditions talks with reporters. Once he ventured into the press room to introduce a visiting dignitary, but reporters began asking him questions about a meeting of the Judicial Conference then taking place, and he fled in dismay. (Burger applies the same security blanket to this regulatory agency for the federal court system that he does to his own bench, closing all meetings and releasing carefully edited descriptions of its actions, with little explanation available.)

From time to time justices make outside speeches, often bland from a news point of view for the same reasons that inhibit their social conversation. But there are exceptions. Two justices, for example, used speeches to voice their opposition to creation of a National Court of Appeals, a project nurtured but not formally endorsed by the Chief Justice. Occasionally a justice's speech may involve such controversies within the legal profession or issues in judicial administration.

Since these speeches provide one of the rare opportunities for reporters to observe a justice off the bench, there are recurrent complaints that the public information officer does not provide advance notice of such speeches, or, if he does, fails to make texts available.

Leaking the News

The intense atmosphere of security that envelops the decisions and procedures of the court is bound to present a challenge to some enterprising reporters. In all other agencies of government, news leaks — the private release of information in advance of official schedule — are regarded as regrettable but inescapable. At the Supreme Court, they are regarded as a violation of sacred trust.

Meticulous precautions against premature disclosure of court decisions are based on well-grounded fear that an unscrupulous investor could profit at the expense of the innocent if he had advance knowledge of the outcome of one of the many cases with great economic impact. But that is not where the few recent leaks have occurred.

In 1973 *Time* magazine predicted the gist of the court's historic abortion decision and the 7-2 vote more than a week before it was handed down. (The magazine appears on Sunday, and the Chief Justice reportedly held back the opinion, which was to have been released the following day, for a week.) The news business took this scoop in stride, but the court did not. Among various new security measures, Chief Justice Burger ordered all the court clerks — top-ranking young law school graduates who serve each justice for a year as part of a very exclusive apprenticeship — not to speak to or be seen with reporters in the future.

Nevertheless, four years later the secrecy of the court conference was violated again. National Public Radio made headlines by reporting that the justices had voted, 5 to 3, against reviewing the convictions of three defendants in the Watergate cover-up case, and that Chief Justice Burger had personally delayed for a week the scheduled announcement of that decision in hope of recruiting the necessary fourth vote to obtain review. Three of the four men named to the high court by President Richard Nixon, the account went, supported re-examining the Watergate convictions, but the fourth disqualified himself.

The story, obtained by NPR reporter Nina Totenberg, was confirmed by *The New York Times,* with a cautionary note that it was not unusual for any justice to seek and obtain a week's postponement of any tentative decision of the conference.

The source of the Totenberg leak was not identified, but the episode served notice on a startled court that anything smacking of political maneuver inside the sacrosanct conference might find its way into the news.

In the spring of 1979, an ABC-TV reporter correctly reported in advance the outcome of a Supreme Court opinion regarding the right of courts to question newsmen about their thoughts while writing stories. Soon afterwards, a Government Printing Office linotyper assigned to the court's printing unit, was reassigned — without disciplinary action or loss of civil service status — at the request of Chief Justice Warren E. Burger, despite the linotyper's protestation of innocence in disclosure of the information.

Footnotes

[1] Charles Warren, *The Supreme Court in United States History,* rev. ed. (Boston: Little Brown & Co., 1926), vol. 1, p. 3.

[2] Ibid., p. 288.

[3] *Niles Register,* Feb. 27, 1819, quoted in ibid., p. 494.

[4] *New York Evening Post,* Feb. 20, 1819, quoted in ibid., p. 494.

[5] *Baltimore Federal Republican* cited in *Independent Chronicle,* March 6, 1819, quoted in ibid., p. 494.

[6] Julius Goebel Jr., *History of the Supreme Court of the United States:* vol. 1, *Antecedents and Beginnings to 1801* (New York: Macmillan Publishing Company, Inc., 1971), p. 255.

[7] Letter of Oliver Wolcott, July 28, 1795, quoted in Warren, *The Supreme Court in United States History,* vol. 1, p. 131.

[8] *Columbian Centinel,* Dec. 26, 1795, quoted in ibid., p. 137.

[9] *Columbian Centinel,* Feb. 23, 1811, quoted in ibid., p. 411.

[10] *Connecticut Courant,* Feb. 20, 1811, quoted in ibid., p. 411.

[11] Ibid., p. 413.

[12] *Columbian Centinel,* Jan. 22, 1835, quoted in ibid., p. 799.

[13] *New York Courier,* Jan. 19, 1835, quoted in ibid., p. 799.

[14] *Washington Federalist,* April 29, 1803, quoted in ibid., p. 253.

[15] *National Intelligencer,* March 13, 1818, quoted in ibid., p. 480.

[16] *Columbian Centinel,* March 24, 1818, quoted in ibid., p. 482.

[17] *Boston Daily Advertiser,* March 23, 1818, quoted in ibid., p. 482.

[18] *New York Evening Post,* Feb. 5, 1819; *New York Commercial Advertiser,* Feb. 6, 1819, quoted in ibid., p. 488.

[19] Ibid., p. 489.

[20] *Boston Daily Advertiser,* March 13, 1819, quoted in ibid., p. 512.

[21] *Natchez Press* quoted in *Niles Register,* May 22, 1819, quoted in ibid., p. 519.

[22] *Niles Register,* March 13, 1819, quoted in ibid., p. 522.

[23] *General Advertiser,* March 17, 1819, quoted in ibid., p. 523.

[24] *New York Statesman,* Feb. 9, 1824, quoted in ibid., p. 604.

[25] *New York Evening Post,* March 5, 1824, quoted in ibid., p. 612.

[26] *New York Commercial Advertiser,* March 12, 1824, quoted in ibid., p. 612.

[27] *National Gazette,* March 29, 1824, quoted in ibid., p. 613.

[28] *Georgia Journal,* April 6, 1824, quoted in ibid., p. 614.

[29] *Richmond Enquirer,* March 16, 1824, quoted in ibid., p. 618.

[30] *Boston Courier,* Jan. 21, 1831, quoted in ibid., p. 734.

[31] *United States Telegraph,* Jan. 7, 1831, quoted in ibid., p. 734.

[32] *New York Daily Advertiser,* Jan. 13, 1831, quoted in ibid., p. 736.

[33] *Aurora,* Jan. 15, 1801, quoted in ibid., p. 273.

[34] *National Intelligencer,* May 20, 1803, quoted in ibid., p. 276.

[35] *Charleston Courier,* June 9, 1803, quoted in ibid., p. 277.

[36] *Aurora,* March 22, 1804, quoted in ibid., p. 280.

[37] *Connecticut Courant,* Feb. 27, 1805, quoted in ibid., p. 280.

[38] Ibid., pp. 292-93.

[39] *Newark Daily Advertiser,* March 5, 1842, quoted in Carl B. Swisher, *History of the Supreme Court of the United States:* vol. V, *The Taney Period, 1836-64* (New York: Macmillan Publishing Company, Inc., 1971), p. 543.

[40] *The Baltimore Sun,* March 3, 1842, quoted in ibid., p. 543.

[41] *The New York Tribune,* Jan. 5, 1849, quoted in ibid., p. 526.

[42] Ibid., p. 552.

[43] *New York Courier,* Dec. 18, 1856, quoted in Warren, *The Supreme Court in United States History,* vol. 2, p. 286.

[44] *Independent,* Jan. 1, 1857, quoted in ibid., p. 287.

[45] *The The New York Tribune,* Jan. 9, 1857, quoted in Swisher, *History of the Supreme Court of the United States:* vol. V, *The Taney Period, 1836-64,* p. 615.

[46] *New York Independent,* March 12, 1857, quoted in Warren, *The Supreme Court in United States History,* vol. 2, p. 306.

[47] *New York Evening Post,* March 7, 1857, quoted in ibid., p. 307.

[48] *New York Herald,* March 12, 1857, quoted in ibid., p. 309.

[49] *Pennsylvanian*, quoted in ibid., p. 311.

[50] *Daily Union*, March 7, 1857, quoted in ibid., p. 312.

[51] *St. Louis Evening News*, April 15, 1857, quoted in Charles Grove Haines and Foster H. Sherwood, *The Role of the Supreme Court in American Government and Politics: 1835-64* (Berkeley: University of California Press, 1957), p. 431.

[52] *Harper's Weekly*, March 28, 1857, quoted in Warren, *The Supreme Court in United States History*, vol. 2, p. 315.

[53] Ibid., p. 315.

[54] *North American Review*, LXXXV, 1857, quoted in ibid., p. 316.

[55] Ibid., p. 317.

[56] *Nation*, Feb. 10, 1869, quoted in ibid., p. 500.

[57] *Chicago Republican*, Dec. 21, 1868, quoted in ibid., p. 500.

[58] *The New York Times*, Jan. 4, 1870, quoted in ibid., p. 509.

[59] *The New York Tribune*, Feb. 1, 1870, quoted in ibid., p. 510.

[60] *Nation*, April 17, 1870, quoted in ibid., p. 521.

[61] *Springfield Republican*, April 8, 1870, quoted in ibid., p. 522.

[62] *American Law Review*, V, 1870, quoted in ibid., p. 523.

[63] *Springfield Republican*, May 5, 1871, quoted in ibid., p. 525.

[64] *Nation*, May 27, 1871, quoted in ibid., p. 525.

[65] *The New York Tribune*, May 2, 1871, quoted in ibid., p. 526.

[66] Ibid., p. 522.

[67] *The New York Times*, Jan. 24, 1883, quoted in ibid., p. 522.

[68] *Independent*, Oct. 25, 1883, quoted in ibid., p. 614.

[69] John A. Garraty, ed., *Quarrels That Have Shaped the Constitution* (New York: Harper & Row, 1964), p. 138.

[70] *Richmond Times*, Jan. 1, 1900, quoted in ibid., p. 158.

[71] *Mobile Register*, quoted in *Washington Union*, Feb. 3, 1853, quoted in Warren, *The Supreme Court in United States History*, vol. 2, p. 243.

[72] *The New York Tribune*, Jan. 8, 1853, quoted in ibid., p. 244.

[73] *The New York Times*, Feb. 16, 1853, quoted in ibid., p. 245.

[74] *The New York Tribune*, Jan. 29, 1861, quoted in ibid., p. 364.

[75] *Nation*, Dec. 2, 1869, quoted in ibid., p. 502.

[76] *The New York Times*, Dec. 16, 1869, quoted in ibid., p. 502.

[77] *Harper's Weekly*, Jan. 1, 1870, quoted in ibid., p. 502.

[78] Ibid., p. 503.

[79] *New York Herald*, Dec. 21, 1869, quoted in ibid., p. 503.

[80] *American Law Review*, Jan. 1874, quoted in ibid., pp. 553-55.

[81] *Nation*, Dec. 4, 1873, quoted in ibid., p. 555.

[82] *Independent*, Dec. 12, 1873, quoted in ibid., p. 556.

[83] *Yale Law Journal*, VIII, 1899, quoted in ibid., p. 556.

[84] Ibid., p. 557.

[85] *The New York Tribune*, Jan. 10, 12, 1874, quoted in ibid., p. 557.

[86] *Harper's Weekly*, Feb. 7, 1874, quoted in ibid., p. 557.

[87] *Nation*, Jan. 15, 1874, quoted in ibid., p. 557.

[88] *The Washington Star*, May 28, 1935.

[89] *The New York Herald-Tribune*, May 28, 1935.

[90] *Los Angeles Times*, May 28, 1935.

[91] *The Denver Post*, May 28, 1935.

[92] *The Boston Herald*, May 28, 1935.

[93] *The New York Times*, May 28, 1935.

[94] *The Washington Star*, Jan. 7, 1936.

[95] *The New York Herald-Tribune*, Jan. 7, 1936.

[96] *The Kansas City Star*, Jan. 7, 1936.

[97] *Chattanooga Times*, Jan. 7, 1936.

[98] *Lincoln (Neb.) State Journal*, Jan. 7, 1936.

[99] *The Washington Star*, Feb. 5, 1937.

[100] *The New York Herald-Tribune*, Feb. 6, 1937.

[101] *Hartford Courant*, Feb. 6, 1937.

[102] *Los Angeles Times*, Feb. 6, 1937.

[103] *San Francisco Chronicle*, Feb. 6, 1937.

[104] *Des Moines Register*, Feb. 6, 1937.

[105] *The New York Times*, Feb. 6, 1937.

[106] *St. Paul Pioneer Press*, Feb. 6, 1937.

[107] *The Kansas City Star*, Feb. 6, 1937.

[108] *The New York Times*, April 13, 1937.

[109] *Los Angeles Times*, April 13, 1937.

[110] *San Francisco Chronicle*, April 13, 1937.

[111] *Chattanooga Times*, April 13, 1937.

[112] *The New York Times*, May 25, 1937.

[113] *The Wall Street Journal*, May 25, 1937.

[114] *The Washington Star*, May 25, 1937.

[115] *The Washington Post*, May 25, 1937.

[116] *The New York Times*, June 5, 1940.

[117] *The Washington Star*, June 4, 1940.

[118] *St. Louis Post Dispatch*, as quoted in *Quarrels that have Shaped the Constitution*, ed. John A. Garraty, (New York: Harper & Row, 1964), p. 234.

[119] *The New York Times*, June 19, 1943.

[120] *The Washington Star*, June 16, 1943.

[121] *The New York Times*, May 18, 1954.

[122] *The Washington Post*, May 18, 1954.

[123] *The Washington Star*, May 18, 1954.

[124] *The New Orleans Times-Picayune*, May 18, 1954.

[125] *Louisville Courier-Journal*, May 18, 1954.

[126] *Atlanta Constitution*, May 18, 1954.

[127] *Chicago Tribune*, May 18, 1954.

[128] *Houston Chronicle*, May 18, 1954.

[129] *Jackson (Miss.) Clarion-Ledger*, May 18, 1954.

[130] *Raleigh News and Observer*, June 1, 1955.

[131] *Atlanta Constitution*, June 1, 1955.

[132] *The New York Times*, June 1, 1955.

[133] *Wilmington (Del.) Morning News*, June 1, 1955.

[134] *The New York Times*, June 16, 1964.

[135] *The Washington Post*, June 17, 1964.

[136] *The Wall Street Journal*, June 16, 1964.

[137] *The Washington Star*, June 16, 1964.

[138] *The Washington Star*, June 15, 1966.

[139] *The Washington Post*, June 15, 1966.

[140] *The New York Times*, June 14, 1966.

[141] *The Wall Street Journal*, July 25, 1974.

[142] *The Washington Star*, July 25, 1974.

[143] *The New York Times*, July 25, 1974.

[144] *The Washington Post*, July 25, 1974.

[145] *The Washington Star*, Aug. 19, 1969.

[146] *The New York Times*, Aug. 18, 1969.

[147] *The Washington Post*, Aug. 19, 1969.

[148] *The Washington Star*, Nov. 22, 1969.

[149] *The New York Times*, Nov. 22, 1969.

[150] *The Washington Star*, Jan. 20, 1970.

[151] *The Washington Post*, Jan. 21, 1970.

[152] *The New York Times*, Jan. 21, 1970.

[153] *The Washington Star*, Feb. 18, 1970.

[154] *The New York Times*, Feb. 27, 1970.

[155] *The Washington Star*, April 7, 1970.

[156] *The Washington Post*, April 6, 1970.

[157] *The New York Times*, April 6, 1970.

[158] *The New York Times*, April 8, 1970.

[159] *The Washington Star*, April 9, 1970.

[160] *The Washington Post*, April 9, 1970.

[161] *The New York Times*, April 9, 1970.

Selected Bibliography

Freund, Paul A., gen. ed. *History of the Supreme Court of the United States.* New York: Macmillan Co., 1971, 1974. Vol. I: *Antecedents and Beginnings to 1801*, by Julius Goebel Jr.; Vol. V: *The Taney Period*, by Carl B. Swisher.

Garraty, John A., ed. *Quarrels that Have Shaped the Constitution.* New York: Harper and Row, 1964.

Haines, Charles G. and Sherwood, F.H., *The Role of the Supreme Court in American Government and Politics: 1835-1864.* Berkeley: U. of California Press, 1957.

Warren, Charles. *The Supreme Court in United States History*, 2 vols. Boston: Little, Brown & Co., 1926.

PART V

THE COURT AT WORK

Operations of the Court................................. 732

Traditions of the Court............................... 744

The Chief Justice 748

The Justices 753

Supporting Personnel 759

Supporting Organizations....................... 767

Housing the Court............................... 769

The Cost of the Court........................... 773

Supreme Court Building at Night.
United Press International, 9/23/71

The Court at Work

Constitutionally and politically, the Supreme Court is a branch of the federal government coequal with Congress and the presidency. In some ways it is the most powerful, since it can declare the actions of the president illegal and the legislation of Congress unconstitutional.

Still, the Supreme Court seems dwarfed by the sprawling bureaucracies of the legislative and executive components of government. The court is, after all, only nine men, housed within a single building at One First Street Northeast in the nation's capital. Its budget is but a fraction of those appropriated each year for Congress and the executive branch.

Nevertheless, the court is hardly aloof from the long-range and everyday problems of management, procedure, maintenance and personnel faced by any other institution. Like Congress — or the local department store, for that matter — it must be administered, budgeted, staffed and locked up after work each day. And it is the apex of a substantial federal judicial system that includes 95 district courts, 11 courts of appeal and three special courts, along with their judges and attendant staff.

The administrative aspects of the court's operations are, then, considerable, even if they do not rival those that have spawned the huge bureaucracies that serve the executive branch and Congress. Chief Justices from John Jay to Warren Burger have wrestled with the problems of ensuring smooth functioning of the court's managerial machinery in order to allow the judges to concentrate on dispassionate consideration of matters of law.

The ideal tableau of the court — and certainly the image that it has sought to perpetuate over the years — is one of nine wise, just and serene jurists sitting to render, with irreproachable integrity, decisions crucial to the conduct of national life.

That this image has been maintained so well for nearly two centuries testifies, to a remarkable degree, to its accuracy. The high standards necessary both to effective judicial performance and public trust have indeed been consistently maintained by a succession of mostly able jurists who were also men of exemplary personal demeanor. There have been few scandals involving the justices, and the embarrassments the court has suffered have been resolved openly and expeditiously. With some notable exceptions, the political affinities of the justices have been more implicit than overt.

The Court's Image

But to some extent the court's sacrosanct image is also more apparent than real. The court, of course, has no public relations mechanism as such, but the longstanding internal traditions of the institution effectively serve that function. Its insistence on the secrecy of its deliberations, in particular, protects the justices from disclosure of any of the fractiousness or ineptitude that certainly must occur from time to time. The elaborate courtesy and obeisance to seniority on the court also serve its image as an august deliberative body aloof from contentious bickering and disharmony. Its imposing headquarters, the "marble palace," softens the memory of the many years during which the justices were shunted from one "mean and dingy" makeshift office to another. The image notwithstanding, the court as a bureaucracy and administrative body continues to face many workaday challenges.

These involve matters much more important than the mere operation and upkeep of the court itself, although these are substantial. Most centrally, the court must select which cases to review, and when to review them, from the burgeoning volume of litigation that seeks its attention every year, and to render decisions after adequate consideration and in definitive language.

These problems have mushroomed during the past two, increasingly litigious, decades. Between 1960 and 1976, the number of new cases filed in federal district courts rose from 89,112 to 171,617. It is from this labyrinth of casework that the Supreme Court is expected judiciously to cull the legal issues most worthy of its judgment. In the same period — 1960 to 1976 — the court's own docket more than doubled, from 2,296 to 4,730.

So the august tribunal of justices is also, perforce, a beleaguered bureaucracy. In March 1971, the present Chief Justice, Warren E. Burger, told the National Conference on the Judiciary that he had begun work

> . . .by giving priority to methods and machinery, to procedure and techniques, to management and administration of judicial resources, even over the much-needed re-examination of substantive legal institutions that are out of date. That re-examination is important, but it is inevitably a long-range undertaking and it can wait. . . .[1]

Operations of the Court

The Constitution makes the Supreme Court the final arbiter in "cases" and "controversies" arising under the Constitution or the laws of the United States. As the interpreter of the law, the court is often viewed as the least mutable and most tradition-bound of the three branches of the federal government.

Yet as the Supreme Court nears the end of its second century of existence, it has undergone innumerable changes. A few of these changes have been mandated by law. Almost all of them, however, were made because members of the court felt they would provide a more efficient or a more equitable way of dealing with the court's responsibilities. Some of the charges are embodied in court rules; others are informal adaptations to needs and circumstances.

The Schedule of the Term

The court's annual schedule reflects both continuity and change. During its formal annual sessions, certain times are set aside for oral argument, for conferences, for the writing of opinions and for the announcement of decisions. With the ever-increasing number of cases they face each year, the justices are confronted with a tremendous — some say excessive — amount of work during the regular term, which now lasts between eight and nine months.

Their work does not end when the session is finished, however. During the summer recess, the justices receive new cases to consider. About a fourth of the applications for review filed during the term are read by the justices and their law clerks during the summer interim.

Annual Terms

By law, the Supreme Court begins its regular annual session on the first Monday in October "and may hold such adjourned or special terms as may be necessary." [2]

The regular session, known as the October term, now lasts about nine months. Adjournment, which is not determined by statute or court rules, generally occurs in late June or early July of the following year when the court has taken action on the last case argued before it during the term. The increasing caseload that has faced the court has resulted in longer sessions. Adjournment of the 1954 term, for example, occurred on June 6, 1955, while the October 1975 term did not end until July 6, 1976.

Adjournment takes place when a court order, announced by the Chief Justice in open court and entered in the court's journal, is issued. It states that "All cases submitted and all business before the Court at this term in readiness for disposition having been disposed of, it is ordered by this Court that all cases on the docket be, and they are hereby, continued to the next term." [3]

Over the years, the annual sessions of the court have been changed a number of times. During the first decade of its existence, 1790-1801, the court met twice a year, in February and August. The justices had few cases during these years and the early sessions were devoted largely to organization and discussions of lawyers' qualifications. The first case did not reach the court until 1791; the first formal opinion was not handed down until 1792, in the court's third year.

Despite the dearth of casework during the early semi-annual sessions, the Chief Justice and five associate justices had enough to do. The Judiciary Act of 1789, in addition to mandating the February and August sessions, required the justices to travel through the country to preside over the circuit courts — a time-consuming task that continued, except for a brief period, until circuit riding was finally abolished in 1891 and circuit courts of appeal were established.

The Judiciary Act of 1801 called for court terms beginning in June and December. The Judiciary Act of 1802 restored the February term of the court but not the August term. This resulted in a 14-month adjournment — from December 1801 until February 1803.

At the beginning of the 1827 term, Congress changed the opening day of the new term to the second Monday in January. This was done to give the justices more time to ride their circuits.

The opening day of the term was changed to the second Monday in December by an act of June 17, 1844. By this statute, Charles Warren wrote, the justices "were relieved of holding more than one Term of the Circuit Court within any District of such Circuit, in any one year. The result of this provision was to enable the Court to sit later each spring in Washington; and in alternate years thereafter it made a practice of sitting through March, adjourning through April and sitting again in May." [4]

An act of Jan. 24, 1873, moved the beginning of the term from the first Monday in December to the second Monday in October. Since 1917 terms have begun on the first Monday in October.

Special Sessions

The statute and rule covering the annual session of the court also permit the justices to hold special or adjourned terms after the regular session is over. Special sessions are called to deal with urgent matters that cannot be postponed until the next session.

There have been few special or adjourned sessions in the court's history: only four cases have been decided in special session. It has been far more common for the court to consider important cases that arise toward the end of the term simply by delaying the end of the regular term until action is completed.

The four cases for which special sessions were called are:

● *Ex parte Quirin.* The court convened a special term, July 29, 1942, heard arguments on July 29 and July 30 and, on July 31, upheld a military court's jurisdiction over the trial of Nazi saboteurs smuggled ashore from a German submarine. A formal opinion in the case was released on Oct. 29, 1942.

● *Rosenberg v. United States.* Three days after the end of the October 1952 term, the Supreme Court on June 18, 1953, convened a special term to consider a stay of execution ordered by Justice William O. Douglas for Ethel and Julius Rosenberg, convicted of divulging information about the atomic bomb to the Soviet Union. Arguments were heard on June 18, and the court vacated the stay on June 19. The Rosenbergs were executed that day. The court's opinion in the case was released July 16, 1953.

● *Cooper v. Aaron.* In a special session convened Aug. 28, 1958, the court unanimously upheld a lower court order enforcing a desegregation plan for Little Rock High School. The order was opposed by state officials in Arkansas. The court heard arguments on Aug. 28 and Sept. 11, and issued its decision on Sept. 12. City schools were to open in Little Rock on Sept. 15, but Gov. Orval Faubus closed them after the court's decision. A formal opinion in the case was released Sept. 29, 1958.

● *O'Brien v. Brown.* The court convened a special session July 6, 1972, to consider the seating of delegates from California and Illinois at the Democratic National Convention which was to open July 10. The court decided, by a vote of 6-3 on July 7, 1972, to return the California and Illinois cases to the convention and to let the convention itself, rather than the court, decide the matter.

Among the decisions made by the court after postponing adjournment of the regular term, the most recent and most famous is *United States v. Nixon.* In that case the court on July 24, 1974, unanimously denied President Richard M. Nixon's claim of absolute executive privilege to withhold documents requested by the Watergate Special Prosecutor.

Other important decisions handed down after delaying adjournment include *Wilson v. Girard,* handed down on July 11, 1957, and *New York Times v. U.S., U.S. v. Washington Post,* decided on June 30, 1971. The former involved the right of Japanese courts to try American soldiers; the latter rebuffed the effort by the Nixon administration to bar publication of the Pentagon Papers. [5]

Opening Day

Opening day ceremonies of the new term have changed considerably since the court first met on Feb. 1, 1790. Chief Justice John Jay was forced to postpone the first formal session for a day because some of the justices were unable to reach New York City — at that time the nation's capital and home of the court. It began proceedings the next day in a crowded courtroom and with an empty docket.

From 1917 to 1975, when the annual session began on the first Monday in October, the opening day and week were spent in conference. The justices discussed cases that had not been disposed of during the previous term and some of the petitions that had reached the court during the summer recess. The decisions arrived at during this initial conference on which cases to accept for oral argument were announced on the second Monday of October.

At the beginning of the October 1975 term, this practice was changed. That year the justices reassembled for this initial conference during the last week in September. When the justices convened formally on Monday, Oct. 6, 1975, oral arguments began.

Schedule of Arguments

At least four justices must request that a case be argued before it can be approved for a hearing. Until 1955, the court often heard oral arguments five days a week. Friday arguments were dropped when the court's conference was moved to that day. Arguments are now heard on Monday, Tuesday, Wednesday and, rarely, Thursday, for about seven two-week sessions, beginning in the first week in October and ending in the last week of April or the first week of May.

There usually are two consecutive weeks of oral arguments during this period, with two-week or longer recesses during which the justices consider the cases and deal with other court business.

Since the early 1800s — when justices heard oral arguments from 11 a.m. until 4 or 5 p.m. — the schedule for hearing arguments has been changed several times in continuing efforts toward a more manageable daily calendar.

The present schedule for oral arguments — 10 a.m. to noon and 1-3 p.m. — began during the 1969 term. Since most cases receive one hour apiece for argument, that means the court can hear twelve cases a week.

The time provided for oral argument had been limited to two hours — one hour for each side — under a rule of the court adopted March 12, 1849. Cases which the court felt could be covered in a shorter period were placed on a "summary calendar," under which arguments were limited to a half hour for each side. That practice was revived during the 1940s and one hour's argument became the current limit in 1970. Exceptions to the hour-per-case time limit must be sought and granted before arguments begin.

Schedule of Conferences

In the court's early years, conferences often were held in the evenings or on weekends, sometimes in the common boardinghouse that the justices shared. The number of cases for which review was sought and the cases awaiting a final decision determined when and how often conferences were held. Later, Saturday was set aside as the regular conference day. Under a 1955 court order that ended Friday oral arguments, Friday became conference day.

Until recently, a court held its first conferences during opening week, following its formal call to order on the first Monday in October. But in 1975, to streamline the procedure, the justices began meeting in the last week in September, before the official convening of the annual session.

At its initial conference, the court attempts to resolve leftover matters — appeals, petitions for certiorari, etc. — from the previous session. The September conference allows the court to announce its orders on these matters by opening day rather than a week after the formal convening.

During its term, the court holds conferences each Friday during the weeks when oral arguments are heard, and on the Friday just before the two-week oral argument periods. To reduce the workload of its Friday sessions, the court in recent years also has begun holding Wednesday conferences during the weeks when oral arguments are scheduled.

It is in conference that the justices discuss the cases which have been argued during the preceding weeks, and the appeals and petitions asking the court to grant review and hear arguments in other cases. Prior to each of the Friday conferences, the Chief Justice circulates a "discuss list" — a list of cases in which review is sought which are deemed important enough for discussion in conference.

Appeals are placed on the "discuss list" almost automatically, but as many as three-quarters of the petitions for certiorari are never placed on the list and are denied review without discussion by the court. No case is denied review, however, without at least an initial examination by the justices or their clerks. Any justice can have any case placed on the court's conference agenda for discussion.

Most of the cases scheduled for the "discuss list" are also denied review in the end, but only after discussion by the justices during the conference.

Although the last oral arguments have been heard by late April or early May of each year, the conferences of the justices continue until the end of the term to consider cases remaining on the court's agenda.

All conferences are held in strict secrecy, with no legal assistants or staff present. The attendance of six justices constitutes a quorum. Conferences begin with handshakes all around. The Chief Justice is the first to speak in discussing a case; he is followed by each justice in order of seniority.

Decision Days

In the court's early years, conferences were held whenever the justices decided one was necessary — sometimes in the evening or on weekends. Similarly, decisions were announced whenever they were ready. There was no formal or informal schedule for conferences or for the announcement of decisions.

The tradition of announcing decisions on Monday — "Decision Monday" — began in 1857, apparently without any formal announcement or rule to that effect. This practice continued until the court announced on April 5, 1965, that "commencing the week of April 26, 1965, it will no longer adhere to the practice of reporting its decisions only at Monday sessions and that in the future they will be reported as they become ready for decision at any session of the Court." [6]

Like the announcement of opinions, the day for release of the court's "orders list" — the summary of the court's action granting or denying review — has changed over the years.

During the 19th century, the court's summary orders were often announced on Friday, which was called "Motion Day." The practice of posting orders on Monday evolved gradually.

During the first three months of the 1971 term, orders were announced on Tuesday; on Jan. 10, 1972, Monday was established as the day for posting orders. When urgent or important matters arise, the court's summary orders may be announced on a day other than Monday. And when the last oral arguments of the term have been heard, the court may release decisions and written opinions, as well as the orders list, on Mondays.

At present, the orders list is posted at the beginning of the Monday session. It is not orally announced and can be obtained from the clerk and the public information officer.

Unlike its orders, decisions of the court are usually announced orally in open court. The justice who wrote the opinion announces the court's decision, and justices writing concurring or dissenting opinions may state their views as well. When more than one decision is to be rendered, the justices who wrote the opinion make their announcements in reverse order of seniority.

Sometimes all or a large portion of the opinion is read aloud. More often, the author will summarize the opinion or simply announce the result and state that a written opinion has been filed.

Reviewing Cases

In determining whether to accept a case for review, the court has considerable discretion, subject only to the restraints imposed by the Constitution and Congress.

Article III, Section 2 of the Constitution provides that "In all Cases affecting Ambassadors, other public Ministers and Consuls, and those in which a State shall be Party, the Supreme Court shall have original jurisdiction. In all the other Cases . . . the Supreme Court shall have appellate Jurisdiction, both as to Law and act, with such Exceptions, and under such Regulations as the Congress shall make."

Original jurisdiction refers to the right of the Supreme Court to hear a case before any other court does. Appellate jurisdiction is the right to review the decision of a lower court. The vast majority of cases reaching the Supreme Court are appeals from rulings of the lower courts; generally only a handful of original jurisdiction cases are filed each term.

Since enactment of the Judiciary Act of 1925, the Supreme Court has had almost complete discretion to decide for itself what cases it would hear. [7]

Methods of Appeal

Cases come to the Supreme Court in several ways. They may come through writs of certiorari, appeals, petitions and requests for certification.

In seeking a writ of certiorari, a litigant who has lost a case in a lower court petitions the Supreme Court to review the case, setting out the reasons why review should be granted. If the petitition is granted, the court requests from the lower court a certified record of the case.

Supreme Court rules provide that:

> . . .[W]henever a petition for writ of certiorari to review a decision of any court is granted, the clerk shall enter an order to that effect, and shall forthwith notify the court below and counsel of record of the granting of the petition. If the record has not previously been filed, the clerk of this court shall request the clerk of the court possessed of the record to certify it and transmit it to this court. A formal writ shall not issue unless specially directed. [8]

The main difference between the certiorari and appeal routes is that the court has complete discretion to grant a request for a writ of certiorari but is under more obligation to accept and decide a case which comes on appeal. *(Details, pp. 256-266)*

Most cases reach the Supreme Court by means of the writ of certiorari. In the relatively few cases to reach the court by means of appeal, the appellant must file a jurisdictional statement explaining why his case qualifies for review and why the court should grant it a hearing. With increasing frequency in recent years, the justices have been disposing of these cases by deciding them summarily, without oral argument or formal opinion.

Those whose petitions for certiorari have been granted by the court must pay the court's standard $100 fee for docketing the case and the cost of printing briefs. Persons unable to afford the fee or the often considerable cost of printing briefs may file *in forma pauperis* (in the character or manner of a pauper) petitions. The rules governing *in forma pauperis* proceedings state:

> . . .[A]ny court of the United States may authorize the commencement, prosecution or defense of any suit, action or proceeding, civil or criminal, or appeal therein, without prepayment of fees and costs or security therefor, by a person who makes affidavit that he is unable to pay such costs or give security therefor. Such affidavit shall state the nature of the action,

defense or appeal and affiant's belief that he is entitled to redress. . . . An appeal may not be taken in forma pauperis if the trial court certifies in writing that it is not taken in good faith. [9]

Another, seldom used, method of appeal is certification, the request by a lower court — usually a court of appeals — for a final answer to questions of law in a particular case. The Supreme Court, after examining the certificate, may order the case argued before it.

Process of Review

Each year the court is asked to review some 4,000 to 5,000 cases. All petitions are examined by the clerk of the court and his staff; those found to be in reasonably proper form are placed on the docket and given a number. Prior to 1970, there were two dockets, an appellate docket for petitions for certiorari and appeals in cases where the docketing fee was paid, and a miscellaneous docket for *in forma pauperis* petitions and appeals and other requests not qualifying for the appellate docket. When a case on the miscellaneous docket was accepted for review, it was transferred to the appellate docket and renumbered.

Under the 1970 revision of court rules, all cases except those falling within the court's original jurisdiction are placed on single docket, known simply as "the docket." Only in the numbering of the cases is a distinction made between prepaid and *in forma pauperis* cases on the docket. Beginning with the 1971 term, prepaid cases were labeled with the year and the number. The first case filed in 1978, for example, would be designated 78-1. *In forma pauperis* cases contain the year and begin with the number 5001. The second *in forma pauperis* case filed in 1978 would thus be number 78-5002. [10]

Cases on the original docket were unaffected by the 1970 revision. The original docket remains a separate and distinct docket, but cases on it that are carried over to the next term are no longer renumbered; they retain the docket numbers assigned to them when they were filed.

Each justice, aided by his law clerks, is responsible for reviewing all cases on the dockets. In recent years a number of justices have used a "cert pool" system in this review. Their clerks work together to examine cases, writing a pool memo on several petitions. The memo is then given to the justices, who determine if more research is needed. (Other justices prefer to use a system in which they or their clerks review each petition themselves.)

Former Justice William O. Douglas called the review of cases on the dockets "in many respects the most important and interesting of all our functions." Others, apparently, have found it time-consuming and tedious and support the "cert pool" as a mechanism to reduce the burden on the justices and their staffs.

Justice John Paul Stevens, however, withdrew from the pool, saying that it did not save him or his clerks any time.

Petitions on the docket vary from elegantly printed and bound documents, of which multiple copies are submitted to the court, to single sheets of prison stationery scribbled in pencil and filled with grammatical and spelling errors. All are considered by the justices, however, in the process of deciding which ones merit review.

To Grant or Deny Review

The decision whether to grant or deny review of a case is made in conference. Conferences are held in the confer-ence room adjacent to the Chief Justice's chambers. Justices are summoned to the conference room by a buzzer, usually between 9:30 and 10:00 a.m. They shake hands with each other, take their appointed seats, and the Chief Justice begins the discussion.

The "Discuss List"

A few days before the conference convenes, the chief justice compiles a "discuss list" — a list of cases deemed important enough for discussion and a vote.

Appeals are placed on the "discuss list" almost automatically, but as many as three-quarters of the petitions for certiorari are denied a place on the list and thus rejected without further consideration. Any justice can have a case placed on "discuss list" simply by requesting that it be done.

Conferences are held in strict secrecy; only the justices attend, and no legal assistants or staff are present. The junior associate justice acts as doorman and messenger, sending for reference material and receiving messages and data at the door. The secrecy has worked well; unlike other parts of the federal government, there have been very few leaks about what transpires during the conferences. *(Details, pp. 714, 724)*

At the start of the conference, the Chief Justice makes a brief statement outlining the facts of each case. Then each justice, beginning with the senior associate justice, comments on the case.

The last to speak, the junior associate justice, discusses the case and votes on whether the court should accept the case for review. The other justices, in reverse order of seniority, then vote on whether to grant review. (This is the same procedure followed in deciding cases already argued.) A traditional but unwritten rule specifies that it takes four affirmative votes to have a case scheduled for oral argument.

The 'Orders List'

Petitions for certiorari, appeal, and *in forma pauperis* that are approved for review or denied review during conference are placed on a certified orders list to be released the following Monday in open court, announcing what cases will be set for later argument and which have been denied a hearing.

Arguments

The clerk of the court, once the court announces it will hear a case, arranges the schedule for oral argument. He must see that cases are arranged "in the first instance in the order in which they are ordered set down for argument, . . . subject to modification in the light of availability of appendices, extensions of time to file briefs, and of orders granting motions to advance or postpone or specially setting particular cases for argument." [11] Cases generally are heard not sooner than three months after the court has agreed to review them. Under special circumstances, the date scheduled for oral argument can be advanced or postponed.

About two to three weeks before oral argument takes place, the justices receive the briefs and records from counsel in the case. The measure of attention the brief receives — from a thorough and exhaustive study to a cursory glance — depends both on the nature of the case and the work habits of the particular justice.

Changes in the Workload of the Supreme Court

The Supreme Court's caseload has more than doubled during the past two decades. The increased workload is responsible for advancing the court's first conference from early October to the last week in September; for the inclusion of Wednesdays in the conference schedule and other changes in procedures; and for increasing the number of staff members available to cope with the growing number of cases facing the court each term.

Chief Justice Warren E. Burger has warned repeatedly that unless something is done to curb that workload it may be soon be "impossible" for a Chief Justice "to perform his duties well and survive very long." [1]

A glance at the number of cases on the court's docket over the years illustrates its growing burden. In 1803, 13 years after the court first convened, there were only 51 cases on the docket; seven years later, the number was 98. As the number of cases filed each year increased, Congress in 1837 created two additional circuits and added two justices to the seven then on the Supreme Court.

By 1845 there were 173 cases on the docket, and the number kept increasing. It grew to 253 cases in 1850, 310 in 1860, and 636 in 1870. A temporary increase in the number of justices to 10 in 1863 and the creation of several more circuit judges in 1869 did little to stem the tide. In 1880 there were 1,212 cases on the docket and a decade later there were 1,816.

More and More Cases

The Court of Appeals Act of 1891 had a dramatic impact on the caseload of the Supreme Court. The number of new cases dropped to 379 in 1891 and to 275 in 1892.

In the years that followed, however, Congress passed a spate of new laws creating opportunities for litigation, which consequently increased the court's workload. There were 723 cases on the court's docket in the 1900 term and 1,116 in the 1910 term.

Although the Judiciary Act of 1925 gave the court considerable discretion in granting review and greatly reduced the number of cases meriting oral arguments, the number of cases on the docket continued to increase. There were 1,039 cases on the docket in 1930; 1,109 in 1940; 1,321 in 1950; 2,296 in 1960; 4,212 in 1970; and 4,761 in 1975.

The dramatic rise in the court's caseload, particularly after 1960, was due primarily to the increase in *in forma pauperis* filings and to congressional enactment of environmental, civil rights, consumer, safety, and social welfare legislation. Petitions *in forma pauperis* grew from 517 in 1951 to about 2,000 a year in the early 1970s.

But while the number of cases filed each year and the number on each term's docket have increased enormously, the number scheduled for oral argument has grown hardly at all. As one observer of the court pointed out in 1975, the court "was hearing about 150 cases on the merits in 1925; it was hearing about 150 cases on the merits twenty-five years ago. It hears about 150 cases on the merits today." [2]

Studying the Problem

The growing gap between the number of cases on the docket and the number on which oral arguments are heard has aroused concern that the court is neglecting many important cases.

To investigate the matter, several study groups were formed in the 1970s. One, the Study Group on the Caseload of the Supreme Court, was set up by Chief Justice Warren E. Burger in the fall of 1971 and headed by Professor Paul A. Freund of Harvard Law School. Another, the Commission on Revision of the Appellate Court system, was set up by Congress in 1972 and headed by Sen. Roman L. Hruska (R Neb.).

The court's study group issued its report in December 1972, warning that:

> ...The statistics of the Court's current workload, both in absolute terms and in the mounting trend, are impressive evidence that the conditions essential for the performance of the Court's mission do not exist. For an ordinary appellate court, the burgeoning volume of cases would be a staggering burden; for the Supreme Court, the pressures of the docket are incompatible with the appropriate fulfillment of its historic and essential functions. [3]

To ease the burden on the court, the study group recommended the creation of a National Court of Appeals. The new court would be headquartered in Washington and — except for cases involving original jurisdiction — be given jurisdiction to consider all cases now within the Supreme Court's jurisdiction. The National Court of Appeals would screen all cases coming to the Supreme Court, denying review in some, deciding some itself and certifying the more important cases to the Supreme Court for disposition.

The Hruska commission likewise endorsed the creation of a new National Court of Appeals in its 1975 report. But the function of the proposed new court had changed. Instead of sending cases on to the justices, this new body would decide cases of lesser importance referred to it by the Supreme Court. [4]

The high court, the judicial branch and the legal profession have divided on these and other recommendations to lessen its workload. Until there is some consensus there is little likelihood that any dramatic measures will be forthcoming.

---

[1] "The Role of the Judiciary in America," speech sponsored by the American Enterprise Institute for Public Policy Research, Dec. 14, 1978.

[2] Erwin N. Griswold, "Rationing Justice — The Supreme Court's Caseload and What the Court Does Not Do," 60 *Cornell Law Review* (1975):339.

[3] *Report of the Study Group on the Caseload of the Supreme Court* (Washington, D.C.: U.S. Government Printing Office, 1972).

[4] *Report of the Commission on Revision of the Appellate Court System* (Washington, D.C.: U.S. Government Printing Office, 1975).

Essential, or a Formality?

As one of the two public functions of the court, oral arguments are viewed by some as very important. Others dispute their significance, contending that by the time a case is heard most of the justices have already made up their minds.

A number of justices have indicated that oral arguments serve a useful purpose. Chief Justice Charles Evans Hughes wrote that "the desirability . . . of a full exposition by oral argument in the highest court is not to be gainsaid" because it provides "a great saving of time of the court in the examination of extended records and briefs, to obtain the grasp of the case that is made possible by oral discussion and to be able more quickly to separate the wheat from the chaff." [12]

More recently, Justice William J. Brennan, Jr. was quoted as saying: "Oral argument is the absolute indispensable ingredient of appellate advocacy. . . . Often my whole notion of what a case is about crystallizes at oral argument. This happens even though I read the briefs before oral argument." [13]

Time Limits

Like many other aspects of the court's operations, the time allotted for oral argument, as well as the atmosphere in which arguments were heard, has undergone considerable change over the years. In the early years of the court, arguments in a single case would often continue for days.

For the spectators who crowded the courtroom, oral arguments provided high entertainment. Women in Washington once flocked to hear the popular and dashing Henry Clay argue before the court in the 19th century. Arguments at least once were adjourned so that counsel could sober up. In one case, a case was reargued so that a late-arriving woman could hear the part she had missed. [14]

The increasing number of cases heard by the court made the continuation of such practices impossible. Under a rule of the court adopted March 12, 1849, counsel was allowed no more than two hours to present his argument. The two-hour allowance for oral argument continued until the early 20th century.

In between his terms on the court, Charles Evans Hughes wrote in 1928: "In the early period when cases were few, the Court could permit extended argument. At a more recent time, and until a few years ago, two hours was the regular allowance to each side and in very important cases, that time was extended. This allowance has been reduced to an hour, unless special permission is granted, and even in cases of great importance the Court has refused to hear arguments for more than an hour and a half on each side. This restriction is due to the crowded calendar of the court." [15]

In 1970 the time allowed each side for oral argument was reduced from one hour to 30 minutes. Again, the period for oral argument was reduced to save the court's time.

Since the time allotted must include time for any questions the justices may wish to ask, the actual time for presentation may be considerably shorter than 30 minutes.

Under rules of the court as revised in 1970, unless additional time has been granted, one counsel only will be heard for each side, except by special permission when there are several parties on the same side. Divided arguments are not favored by the court. Before the revision, when cases were allowed one hour per side, the court allowed two counsel to be heard for each side.

Although more than one attorney participating in an argument per side is "not favored by the court," counsel for an *amicus curiae* may participate in oral argument if the party supported by the *amicus* allows him to use part of its argument time or the court itself grants a motion allowing argument by counsel for the "friend of the court." (*Amicus curiae* — literally "a friend of the court" — is a person who volunteers or is invited to take part in matters before the court but is not a party in the case.) That motion must show, the rules state, that the *amicus*' argument "is thought to provide assistance to the court not otherwise available." [16]

Because the court is reluctant to extend the time that each side is given for oral argument and because *amicus curiae* participation in oral argument would often necessitate such an extension, the court is generally unreceptive to such motions. And counsel in a case is usually equally unreceptive to a request that he give an *amicus* counsel any of the precious minutes which he has to argue the case.

Court rules provide advice to counsel presenting oral arguments before the court: "Oral argument should undertake to emphasize and clarify the written argument appearing in the briefs theretofore filed." That same rule warns that the court "looks with disfavor on any oral argument that is read from a prepared text." [17] During the 1974 term, two justices interrupted an attorney who was reading from a prepared text and called his attention to the rule. Most attorneys appearing before the court use an outline or notes to make sure they cover the important points.

Circulating the Argument

The Supreme Court has tape-recorded oral arguments since 1955. In 1968 the court, in addition to its own recording, began contracting with private firms to tape and transcribe all oral arguments. The contract stipulates that the transcript "shall include everything spoken in argument, by Court, counsel, or others, and nothing shall be omitted from the transcript unless the Chief Justice or Presiding Justice so directs." But "the names of Justices asking questions shall not be recorded or transcribed; questions shall indicated by the letter 'Q'." [18]

The marshal of the court keeps the court's tape during the term when oral arguments are presented. During that time use of these tapes usually is limited to the justices and their law clerks. At the end of the term, the tapes are sent to the National Archives. Three years after an argument has been heard, persons wishing to listen to the tape or buy a copy of the transcript can apply to the marshal for permission to do so.

Transcripts made by the private firm can be acquired more quickly. These transcripts usually are available less than a week after oral arguments are heard. Four copies are delivered to the marshal of the court, who transmits them to the Library of Congress. Interested persons can copy them in longhand or by typewriter but cannot photograph or photocopy them.

Those who purchase the transcripts from the firm must agree that they will not themselves, and will not permit any other party, "to make a photographic, electrostatic or other facsimile copy" of any of the transcripts. [19] Transcripts usually run from 40 to 50 pages for one hour of oral argument. During the 1977 term, transcripts were sold at a rate of $3.75 per page.

In recent years there have been many proposals that arguments should be taped for television and radio use. To date, the court has shown little enthusiasm for these proposals.

Use of Briefs

A major problem facing counsel in preparing an oral argument is his uncertainty about the extent to which the justices and their law clerks have examined his briefs. Nearly twenty years ago Justice Brennan wrote that "most of the members of the present Court follow the practice of reading the briefs before argument. Some of us, and I am one, often have a bench memorandum prepared before argument. This memorandum digests the facts and the arguments of both sides, highlighting the matters about which I may want to question counsel at the argument. Often I have an independent research made in advance of argument and incorporate the results in the bench memorandum." [20]

Nevertheless, an attorney cannot be sure that other justices will devote such attention to their briefs. If the brief has been thoroughly digested by the justices, he can use his arguments to highlight certain elements. But if it has merely been scanned — and perhaps largely forgotten — in the interval between the reading and the oral argument, he will want to go into considerable detail about the nature of the case and the facts involved. Most lawyers therefore prepare their argument on the assumption that the justices know relatively little about their particular case but are well-acquainted with the general principles of relevant law.

The brief of the petitioner or appellant must be filed within 45 days of the court's announced decision to hear the case. Except in *in forma pauperis* cases, 40 copies of the brief must be filed with the court. For *in forma pauperis* proceedings, the party must file one typed copy with the clerk and send one typed copy to each of the other parties in the case. The opposing brief from the respondent or appellee is to be filed within 30 days of his receipt of the brief of the petitioner or appellant. Either party may appeal to the clerk for an extension of time in filing the brief.

The form and organization of the brief is covered by rules 39 and 40 of the court.

Court rules set no limit on the number of pages in a brief. But they do warn that briefs "must be compact, logically arranged with proper heading, concise, and free from burdensome, irrelevant, immaterial and scandalous matter." [21] Briefs that do not comply with these requirements may be disregarded by the court.

In a 1974 case, for example, the court declared that one party's brief did not comply with court rules with respect to conciseness, statement of questions without unnecessary detail, and printing of appendices. [22] Accordingly, the court directed counsel to file a brief complying with the rules within 20 days. [23]

Court rules 39 and 40 set forth the elements that a brief should contain. These are: (1) Index and Table of Cases; (2) Opinions Below, "a reference to the official and unofficial reports of the opinions delivered in the courts below"; (3) Jurisdiction, "a concise statement of the grounds on which the jurisdiction of this court is invoked"; (4) Questions Presented; (5) Statutes Involved; (6) Statement, "a concise statement of the case containing all that is material to the consideration of the questions presented"; (7) Summary of Argument; (8) Argument, which exhibits "clearly the points of fact and of law being presented, citing the authorities and statutes relied upon"; and (9) Conclusion,

"a statement specifying with particularity the relief requested and names of counsel."

Questioning

During oral argument the justices may interrupt with questions or remarks as often as they wish. On the average, questions are likely to consume about a third of counsel's allotted half-hour of argument. Unless counsel has been granted special permission extending his 30-minute limit, he can continue talking after his time has expired only to answer questions.

The frequency of questioning, as well as the manner in which questions are asked, depends on the style of the justices and their interest in a particular case. Former Justice William O. Douglas, for example, had a reputation for asking relatively few but very incisive questions. Justice Lewis F. Powell Jr. tends to be extremely courteous. Justice Thurgood Marshall often shows considerable impatience with overblown rhetoric.

Questions from the justices have been known to upset and unnerve counsel by interrupting his rehearsed argument and introducing an unexpected element. Nevertheless, questioning has several advantages. It serves to alert counsel about what aspects of the case need further elaboration or more information. For the court, questions can bring out weak points in an argument — and sometimes strengthen it. The late Chief Justice Charles Evans Hughes wrote:

> The judges of the Supreme Court are quite free in addressing questions to counsel during argument. The Bar is divided as to the wisdom of this practice in courts of last resort. Some think that as a rule the court will get at the case more quickly if counsel are permitted to present it in their own way. Well-prepared and experienced counsel, however, do not object to inquiries from the bench, if the time allowed for argument is not unduly curtailed, as they would much prefer to have the opportunity of knowing the difficulties in the minds of the court and of attempting to meet them rather than to have them concealed and presented in conference when counsel are not present. They prefer an open attack to a masked battery. From the standpoint of the bench, the desirability of questions is quite obvious as the judges are not there to listen to speeches but to decide the case. They have an irrepressible desire for immediate knowledge as to the points to be determined. [24]

It is advisable that attorneys answer the justices' questions immediately and directly. Several justices have made known their annoyance when informed by counsel that their inquiry will be answered later in the oral argument. As Justice Robert H. Jackson advised in 1951, "never . . . postpone answer to a question, for that always gives an impression of evasion. It is better immediately to answer the question, even though you do so in short form and suggest that you expect to amplify and support your answer later." [25]

Court anecdotes probably tell as much about the proceedings of the court during oral argument as does any careful study of the rules and procedures. Perhaps the most famous anecdote concerns the late Chief Justice Charles Evans Hughes. Hughes, a stickler for observance of the time limit for oral argument, is reported to have informed a leader of the New York Bar that his argument was over when the lawyer was uttering the word "if." [26]

In the late 19th century the justices occasionally left to have lunch behind a curtain in back of the bench when argument was particularly lengthy and inconsequential. Argument proceeded without the justices and amidst a clatter of china. [27]

The late Justice Felix Frankfurter was renowned for treating counsel, as well as his fellow justices, much as he had his students when he was a professor. This annoyed many lawyers presenting arguments and was resented by other justices who complained about Frankfurter's professorial questioning and his pedantic, if erudite, lectures.[28] Former Justice Douglas was known to write opinions or articles during the presentation of oral argument. [29]

Conferences

Cases on which oral argument has been heard are usually decided in conference. During the Wednesday afternoon conference, the four cases that were argued the previous Monday are discussed and decided. At the all-day Friday conference, the eight cases argued on the preceding Tuesday and Wednesday are discussed and decided. These conferences also consider new motions, appeals and petitions.

Conferences are conducted in complete secrecy. No secretaries, clerks, stenographers or pages are allowed into the room.

This practice began many years ago when the justices became convinced that there was a leak, a premature report of a decision. Suspicion focused on two page boys who waited upon the justices in the conference room. Despite the fact that the pages were later cleared when a member of the bar confessed that he had merely made an educated guess about the court's decision in a particular case, conferences have henceforth been attended only by the justices themselves.

In 1979 the substance of an opinion — and even the identity of its author — were correctly reported in the press several days before its announcement. A typesetter assigned to the court was then dismissed. *(Box, p. 745)*

In the court's early years conferences were held in the Washington boardinghouses in which the justices resided. The justices now meet in the elegant, oak-paneled, book-lined conference chamber near the Chief Justice's suite. There are nine chairs around the large rectangular table, each bearing the nameplate of the justice who sits there. The Chief Justice sits at the east end of the table and the senior associate justice at the west end. The other justices take their place in order of seniority. The junior justice is charged with sending for and receiving documents or other information the court needs. Justice Tom C. Clark, the junior justice from 1949 until 1954, once remarked: "For five years, I was the highest-paid doorkeeper in the world." [30]

Discussion Procedure

On entering the conference room the justices shake hands with each other, a symbol of harmony that began in the 1880s. The Chief Justice begins the conference by calling the first case to be decided and discussing it. When he is finished, the senior associate justice speaks, followed by the other justices in order of seniority.

The justices theoretically can speak for as long as they wish without any time limitation imposed. Nevertheless, Chief Justice Charles Evans Hughes — impatient with long

and occasionally irrelevant discourses during conference — convinced the other justices to limit the time they spent discussing a case. The record of the number of cases decided during Hughes tenure as chief justice indicates that discussion and debate of the cases were considerably curtailed. As the number of cases considered during conference has grown, subsequent courts have tended to follow Hughes' example.

Similarly, the justice whose turn it is to speak during conference is supposed never to be interrupted. But according to an often-repeated story, Justice Oliver Wendell Holmes Jr. did just that to Justice John Marshall Harlan early in this century. As Harlan was presenting his argument in a particular case, Holmes interrupted with "That won't wash! That won't wash!" Chief Justice Melville W. Fuller allegedly relieved the tension with the remark: "But I just keep scrubbing away, scrubbing away." [31]

Other than these procedural arrangements, little is known about what actually transpires in conference. Athough discussions generally are said to be polite and orderly, they occasionally can be acrimonious. Likewise, consideration of the issues in a particular case is usually full and probing, but decisions sometimes are reached before all the justices are satisfied that the issues have been fully explored.

Voting

Once a case has been discussed, voting begins with the junior justice — the last in order of discussion and the first to vote. Voting proceeds up the order of seniority, a custom thought to have been instituted to protect the young justices from being influenced by their elders. The Chief Justice is the last to vote. It takes a majority vote to decide a case — five votes if all nine justices are participating.

Opinions

After the justices have voted on a case, the writing of the opinion or opinions begins. An opinion is a reasoned argument explaining the legal issues in the case and the precedents on which the opinion is based.

Any justice may decide to write a separate opinion. If he is in agreement with the court's decision but disagrees with some of the reasoning in the majority opinion, he may write a concurring opinion giving his reasoning. If he disagrees with the majority, he may write a dissenting opinion or simply go on record as a dissenter without an opinion. More than one justice can sign a concurring or a dissenting opinion.

Writing opinions is often a long and tedious process but a highly important one. The way in which a majority opinion is written can have a tremendous impact on the lives of Americans.

The impact of a particular opinion depends to some extent on who writes it, how he writes it and the extent of support of or dissent from the opinion by the other justices.

The amount of time consumed between the vote on a case and the announcement of the decision varies from case to case. In simple cases where few points of law are at issue, the opinion sometimes can be written and cleared by the other justices in a week or less. In more complex cases, especially those with several dissenting or concurring opinions, it can take six months or more. Some cases may have to be reargued or the initial decision reversed after the drafts of opinions have been circulated.

Assignment Procedure

Soon after a case is decided in conference, the task of writing the majority opinion is assigned. The Chief Justice assigns the task in cases in which he voted in the majority. In cases in which he was in the minority, the senior associate justice voting with the majority assigns the job of writing those majority opinions.

The assigning justice may consider the points made by majority justices during the conference discussion, the workload of the other justices, the need to avoid the more extreme opinions within the majority and expertise in the particular area of law involved in a case. (For an example of this last factor, most of the court's major rulings on the issue of abortion have been explained through majority opinions written by Justice Harry A. Blackmun, who developed his expertise in medical law during his legal career, which included work with the famous Mayo Clinic in Minnesota, his home state.)

Chief Justice Charles Evans Hughes sometimes assigned "conservative" opinions to "liberal" justices and "liberal" opinions to "conservative" justices to avoid giving any impression that the court was divided along ideological lines.

The assignment of opinions can create morale problems among members of the court. Justices have become annoyed and angered when not assigned to write opinions in cases of particular interest to them or directed to write them in routine, uninteresting cases. In 1898 Justice John Marshall Harlan wrote to Chief Justice Melville W. Fuller and complained: "Two Saturdays in succession you have not assigned to me any case but have assigned cases and important ones to Justice [Horace] Gray. I was in the majority in each case assigned to him." [32]

More recently, rumors circulated about ill-will between Chief Justice Warren E. Burger and former Justice William O. Douglas. In a 1972 abortion case, Douglas was said to believe that Burger had abused his power by voting with the majority in order to assign the writing of the majority opinion although, Douglas alleged, Burger's sympathies lay with the minority. Douglas threatened to file a scathing dissent on Burger's alleged misuse of the assignment powers but was dissuaded from doing so by his colleagues, who argued that the court's reputation would suffer if the dissent were publicized. [33]

Methods of Writing

The style of writing a court opinion, a majority opinion or concurring or dissenting opinions depends primarily on the individual justice. In some cases, the justice may prefer to write a restricted and limited opinion; in others, he may prefer a broader approach to the subject. His decision is likely to be influenced by the need to satisfy the other justices who voted with him in the majority.

It usually takes about three weeks to prepare an opinion. But the time spent varies from justice to justice. Justice Oliver Wendell Holmes Jr. was reportedly able to write an opinion over a weekend. Justices Hugo L. Black and Louis D. Brandeis were noted for reading widely on all aspects of a case before writing their opinions. Justice Frankfurter was a perfectionist who often prepared as many as 30 or more drafts for each opinion.

Justices use their law clerks to obtain and sift through the material needed to write an opinion. There has been speculation that some clerks actually ghostwrite a justice's opinion — or at least that justices sometimes tell a clerk what they want in an opinion and allow the clerk to write the first draft.

On the other hand, Justice Douglas was said to give his clerks little or nothing to do in writing or organizing his written opinions. The traditional secrecy which surrounds each justice's office and work habits makes verification of such reports about the clerks' role in opinion-writing very difficult.

When a justice is satisfied that the opinion he has written is conclusive or "unanswerable," it is sent to the print shop in the court's basement. There the draft of the opinion is printed under rigid security. Each copy of the draft opinion is numbered to prevent the removal of extra copies from the premises.

Circulation of Drafts

Once the drafts are printed and circulated, the justices — particularly those in the majority and those filing joint, concurring or dissenting opinions — discuss the drafts by memo, at lunch or over a private telephone line that does not go through the switchboard.

Often the suggestions and criticisms require the author carefully to juggle opposing views. To retain a majority, the author of the draft opinion frequently feels he must make major emendations to oblige justices who are unhappy with the initial draft. Some opinions have to be rewritten repeatedly before the majority is satisfied.

The Nixon Opinion. One illustration of the difficulty of writing a majority opinion is provided by Chief Justice Burger's problems in the case of the Nixon White House tapes. In mid-1974 the court voted unanimously that the president must turn over the tapes sought as evidence in the Watergate "coverup" case, rejecting the argument that he could invoke executive privilege to withhold them.

After the decision had been reached, Burger assigned the opinion to himself. To save time, Burger circulated the draft opinion piece-by-piece. The other justices were dissatisfied with what they were seeing. Many began writing their own version of the opinion. Burger, while annoyed, was forced to compromise. The final result, handed down on July 24, 1974, in *United States v. Nixon*, [34] was a rather unusual joint product, with a number of justices writing various parts of the final opinion. But, although a joint effort, the final opinion was issued in Burger's name. [35]

Vote Changes

One reason for the secrecy surrounding the circulation of drafts is that some of the justices who voted with the majority may find the majority draft opinion so unpersuasive — or one or more of the dissenting drafts so convincing — that he may change his vote.

If enough justices alter their votes, the majority may shift, so that a former dissent becomes instead the majority opinion. When a new majority emerges from this process, the task of writing, printing and circulating a new majority draft begins all over again.

Tradition of Unanimous Opinions

Over the past few decades there has been considerable concern about the lack of unanimity in court decisions and the frequent use of dissenting and concurring opinions. The chief argument in favor of greater unanimity is that it increases the authority of — and hence the respect for — the court's decisions. More than 20 years ago Judge Learned Hand wrote that "disunity cancels the impact of monolithic solidarity on which the authority of a bench of judges so largely depends." [36]

Such disunity actually has a long tradition, at odds with the relative harmony the court likes to project. It was not until Chief Justice John Marshall, took his seat on the court in 1801 that the aspiration toward unanimity became the norm. Before Marshall, each justice would announce his own opinion and the reason for it. These separate (or "*seriatim*") opinions were the custom during the first decade of the court's existence.

During Marshall's 35 years on the high court, the practice of *seriatim* opinions was largely abandoned. In his first four years as Chief Justice, 26 opinions were handed down. Of these, Marshall delivered 24 and the senior associate justice only two. The court's ostensible unanimity was disturbed only once during these four years, by a one-sentence concurring opinion by Justice Samuel Chase in 1804. [37]

While Marshall's insistence on unanimity did much to dispel the early court's image as a bickering and dissension-filled forum and to increase its respect and esteem by the public, it did not meet with universal approval.

Jefferson and Marshall. One of Marshall's strongest critics was President Thomas Jefferson, a Republican who often — and vociferously — expressed displeasure over the court's decisions under Marshall, a Federalist.

In a letter to Thomas Richie, dated Dec. 25, 1820, Jefferson wrote that he had long favored a return to "the sound practice of the primitive court" of delivering *seriatim* opinions. Of Marshall's changes, he wrote: "An opinion is huddled up in conclave, perhaps by a majority of one, delivered as if unanimous, and with the silent acquiescence of lazy or timid associates, by a crafty chief judge, who sophisticates the law to his own mind, by the turn of his own reasoning." [38]

The Tradition of Dissent

During the first decade of its existence, the court followed the custom of the King's Bench of Great Britain in issuing *seriatim* opinions. Unlike the King's Bench, however, the Supreme Court delivered *seriatim* opinions in reverse order of seniority. The first case in which a full opinion was published was *State of Georgia v. Brailsford* (1792). The first opinion in the published record of that case was given by a justice who disagreed with the majority in the case.

The first real dissent, and most of the few other dissents to surface during Marshall's tenure, came from William Johnson of South Carolina, a Jefferson appointee. Soon after coming to the court, Johnson delivered what amounted to a dissenting opinion in *Huidekoper's Lessee v. Douglass* (1805).

In a letter to Jefferson, dated Dec. 10, 1822, Johnson complained about the adverse reaction to his concurring or dissenting opinions. "Some Case soon occurred in which I differed from my Brethren, and I felt it a thing of Course to deliver my Opinion. But, during the rest of the Session, I heard nothing but lectures on the Indecency of Judges cutting at each other." [39]

Under Marshall's successor, Chief Justice Roger B. Taney, dissent became more frequent. Unlike Marshall, Taney did not insist upon delivering the sole opinion for the court.

Nevertheless, Marshall's tradition of court unity continued for many years after his death. Until the early years of this century, the court generally gave single opinions with only an occasional concurrence or dissent. Concurring or dissenting opinions were issued in only about a tenth of the cases decided in the middle and late 19th century.

While the increasing use of concurring and dissenting opinions after Marshall's death has been criticized, particularly during this century, it was, according to some observers, almost inevitable. Charles P. Curtis Jr., for example, has written that "if you require unanimity, you make compromise inevitable, in the Court as everywhere else. Compromise is as alien to the feelings of the judicial process as what Solomon offered to do with the baby was to the feelings of the mother." [40] Even the high apostle of unanimity, John Marshall, filed nine dissents and one special concurrence during his 35 years as Chief Justice.

Dissenting opinions usually are defended by a recitation of cases in which a carefully reasoned dissent became, in time, the basis of a new majority opinion. But such turnabouts are infrequent. Justice Oliver Wendell Holmes Jr., the "Great Dissenter," issued 173 formal dissents — but fewer than 10 percent of these had any impact on subsequent reversals of court decisions.

A dissenting justice may hope that his dissent will convince a majority of the other justices that his opinion is the correct one or that a later court will vindicate his views. A dissenting justice is able to avoid the process of revising and compromising his opinion which often faces the author of the majority opinion. The dissenter generally has only himself to please, a fact which makes many well-written and well-reasoned dissents more memorable than the majority opinion in the case.

The most frequently quoted defense of dissent on the court was given by Chief Justice Charles Evans Hughes, who wrote that "[a] dissent in a court of last resort is an appeal to the brooding spirit of the law, to the intelligence of a future day, when a later decision may possibly correct the error into which the dissenting judge believes the court to have been betrayed." [41]

Hughes was by no means an unqualified advocate of dissent and is believed on a number of occasions to have yielded his dissent to join the majority without further argument. The words preceding his statement about "an appeal to the brooding spirit of the law" are probably more indicative of Hughes' feelings about dissent:

> There are some who think it desirable that dissents should not be disclosed as they detract from the forces of the judgment. Undoubtedly, they do. When unanimity can be obtained without sacrifice of conviction, it strongly commends the decision to public confidence. But unanimity which is merely formal, which is recorded at the expense of strong conflicting views, is not desirable in a court of last resort, whatever may be the effect upon public opinion at the time. This is so because what must ultimately sustain the court in public confidence is the character and independence of the judges. They are not there simply to decide cases, but to decide them as they think they should be decided, and while it may be regrettable that they cannot always agree, it is better that their independence should be maintained and recognized than that unanimity should be secured through its sacrifice. [42]

A list of the "great dissenters" compiled by Karl M. Zobell includes those few who exercised dissent "in a manner which was — either because of a particular notable dissenting opinion, or because of the sheer weight of dissents filed — of historical or jurisprudential significance." According to Zobell, the great dissenters were:

● Justice William Johnson (1804-1834), who "did not choose to conceal his ideas when they differed from those of the majority." During his time on the court he wrote almost half of the 70 dissenting opinions filed in those years. Johnson differed with the majority most frequently in three areas — judicial versus legislative power, the sanctity of property and the role of the states.

● Justice Benjamin R. Curtis (1851-1857), who "seldom dissented" during his six years on the court. But his last opinion — a dissent in the case of *Dred Scott v. Sandford*, (1857) — "was subsequently vindicated by the will of the people, and constitutional amendment; it is thus recalled as a landmark opinion in the history of American judicature."

● Justice John Marshall Harlan (1877-1911), a prodigious dissenter who delivered 380 dissents. He is most famous for his lone dissent against the "separate but equal" doctrine upheld in *Plessy v. Ferguson.*

"It was Harlan's lot to read the law differently than did the majority of his brethren in numerous cases, only to have his views adopted by the legislature or by the court years after his death," Zobell said.

● Justice Oliver Wendell Holmes Jr. (1902-1932), who "actually dissented less frequently during his tenure than did the average of his brethren — once in every 33 cases." But "Holmes' dissents had a way of later becoming correct expositions of the law, as defined by the court or as effected by the Legislature, not only more frequently, but sooner than did those of Harlan." The effect of Holmes on the use of dissent cannot be overestimated. During the so-called Holmes era, "dissent became an instrument by which justices asserted a personal, or individual, responsibility which they viewed as of a higher order than the institutional responsibility owed by each to the court, or by the court to the public." [43]

Other justices who almost certainly should be added to any list of "great dissenters" are Louis D. Brandeis (1916-1939), Benjamin N. Cardozo (1932-1938), Chief Justice Harlan Fiske Stone (1925-1946) and Felix Frankfurter (1939-1962). All served during a time of increasing court division and dissension, when New Deal legislation was being tested in the courts.

Concurring Opinions

For those convinced that dissents damage the prestige of the court and the impact of its decisions, concurring opinions are similarly distasteful. Concurrence is, in many ways, a variation on the *seriatim* opinions of the 1790s. A concurring opinion indicates that the justice who wrote it agrees in general with the majority opinion but has reservations about the way it was written, the reasoning behind it, or specific points in it.

During John Marshall's tenure as Chief Justice, dissents were often masked as concurring opinions. Justice Johnson was a master at this, too, but he also wrote a number of concurring opinions supporting decisions of the Federalist majority but not the reasoning behind those decisions. In the case of *Martin v. Hunter's Lessee*, for example, Johnson wrote in a concurring opinion: "I flatter myself that the full extent of the constitutional revisory power may be secured to the United States, and the benefits of it to the individual, without ever resorting to compulsory or restrictive process upon the state tribunals; a right which, I repeat again, Congress has not asserted; nor has this court asserted, nor does there appear any necessity for asserting." [44]

The justice most prone recently to issuing concurring opinions was Felix Frankfurter (1939-1962). During the 1955-56 term, the court handed down 94 opinions. Of these, 21 included concurring opinions and 14 of them were written by Frankfurter.

The case of *United States v. United Mine Workers*, decided in 1947, provides one example of the problems and vexations accounting for and arising from the use of concurring opinions. [45] Chief Justice Fred M. Vinson and Justices Stanley F. Reed and Harold H. Burton voted against the United Mine Workers for two reasons. Justices Wiley B. Rutledge and Frank Murphy both dissented on the same grounds. Justices Frankfurter and Robert H. Jackson agreed with Vinson, Reed and Burton on one of the grounds but rejected the other. Justice Hugo L. Black and William O. Douglas concurred with Vinson for the reason that Frankfurter and Jackson had rejected, but rejected the argument that Frankfurter had approved. The result was that five justices supported the result for one reason, five justices supported it for another reason, and four justices were opposed for both reasons.

Issuing the Opinion

When the drafts of an opinion — including dissents and concurring views — have been written, circulated, discussed and revised, if necessary, the final versions are sent to be printed.

Final opinions are typed by the justices' secretaries and given to the printer in the Supreme Court building. Between the time that the print shop receives the opinions and they are announced in court, they are kept under the same rigid security as the original drafts. After they are printed, they are proofread in the office of the reporter of decisions. Shortly before the case is announced in court, the reporter adds a "headnote" or syllabus summarizing the decision, accompanied by a "lineup" showing how each justice voted.

Only about 200 copies of this "bench opinion" — or "slip opinion" — are made. As the "bench opinions" are announced in court, copies are distributed to lawyers and reporters in the courtroom and to journalists and others in the public information office. Another copy, with any necessary corrections on it, is also sent to the U.S. Government Printing Office. It is reprinted there for inclusion in *United States Reports*, the official record of Supreme Court opinions.

Announcement of Opinions

The public announcement of opinions in court is probably the court's most dramatic function. It also may be the most expendable. Depending on who delivers the opinion and how, announcements can take a considerable amount of the court's time. Opinions are simultaneously given to the public information officer and reporter of decisions for distribution.

Nevertheless, those who are in the courtroom to hear the announcement of a ruling are participating in a very old tradition. The actual delivery may be tedious or exciting, depending on the nature of the case and the eloquence of the opinion and the style of its oral delivery.

Differences between the opinion as actually spoken and its written counterpart, while of little legal or practical importance, can add a certain interest. Once, Justice James C. McReynolds allegedly became so agitated in delivering one dissent that he added: "The Constitution is gone." [46]

In this century, the court has reduced the amount of time spent in delivering opinions. Before Charles Evans Hughes became Chief Justice in 1930, the court generally read long opinions word for word. Some opinions took days to announce early in the court's history. As the workload increased, this practice came to be regarded as a waste of the court's time. Hughes encouraged the delivery of summaries of the opinion. The justice who has written the majority opinion now generally delivers only a summary, and dissenting justices often do the same with their opinions.

Reporting of Decisions

The importance — and difficulty — of adequately reporting Supreme Court decisions cannot be underestimated. Few people read the full Supreme Court opinions, and accounts in the news media often are superficial. Consequently, the American public frequently has little idea of the reasons for and meaning of decisions that affect their lives.

Justice Felix Frankfurter was acutely aware of this problem. "The evolution of our constitutional law is the work of the initiate," he wrote in 1932. "But its ultimate sway depends upon its acceptance by the thought of the nation. The meaning of the Supreme Court decisions ought not therefore to be shrouded in esoteric mystery. It ought to be possible to make clear to lay understanding the exact scope of constitutional doctrines that underlie decisions." [47]

In a 1967 magazine article, Gilbert Cranberg of the Des Moines, Iowa, *Register and Tribune* quoted one columnist who described the Supreme Court as:

> ...the worst reported and the worst judged institution in the American system of government....
>
> The wholesale shunning of what the Court says leaves most of the country dependent on second-hand reports. It would be difficult to devise handicaps more devastating to an understanding of the Court than those that hobble news reporting of its rulings.... Where Congressmen, subordinate administrators and Presidents are frequently eager to explain and defend their policies, Justices of the Supreme Court emerge from isolation only to read their opinions.... No Justice is available to discuss or clarify the opinion he has written. [48]

Formal Reporting

Cranberg estimated that in 1967 "the total circulation of Supreme Court opinions is probably no more than 20,000. Most of the texts are located in forbidding legal libraries and inaccessible private law offices. Because there are no more than 300,000 lawyers in the United States, it's apparent that even many of the nation's attorneys do not actually read the court opinions." [49]

While total circulation of formal court opinions is now considerably higher than it was in 1967, the psychological impediments to reading them are still there. As Cranberg noted, "poring over Supreme Court texts seemed about as inviting as an evening of wading through a technical manual. Indeed, the deadly, all-but-indigestible legalese I expected to find was there in abundance, but to my delighted surprise there was also a gold mine of information and often exciting, absorbing reading." [50]

As noted earlier, the reporter of decisions edits the opinions and supervises their publication in the official *United States Reports*. The court's decisions first appear in the preliminary prints of the *United States Reports,* usually a few months after the opinions have been issued. On the cover of each preliminary report, there is a message to users requesting them "to notify the Reporter of Decisions ... of any typographical or other formal errors, in order that corrections may be made before the bound volume goes to press." The bound volume usually appears a few months after the preliminary prints.

Copies of preliminary prints are sold by the U.S. Government Printing Office for $50 a term, payable in advance. Each bound volume, which generally contains two to four of the preliminary prints, seldom exceeds 900 pages. The price of a bound volume depends on its length; in recent years the price has ranged from $10 to $20. Individual slip-sheet opinions are sold by the same source at $120 a term. Single copies of a specific court decision vary in size with the length of the opinion and can range in price from 35 cents to more than $2.

The Office of the Clerk of the Court sends copies of the opinions to counsel in each case. A limited number of opinions are available in the clerk's office within a few days after the opinion is announced. There is no charge for these. The opinions are also included in *The United States Law Week,* published by The Bureau of National Affairs, Inc., and *Supreme Court Bulletin,* published by Commerce Clearing House.

News Media

Relatively few people make the effort and take the time to read the opinions of the court, so most Americans must rely on the news media to learn what the court has decided.

Since the late 18th century, however, many — perhaps most — of the opinions handed down by the court have not even been reported. *(Details, p. 706)*

Nevertheless, efforts have been made in the mid-20th century to improve media coverage of the Supreme Court. Justice Felix Frankfurter played a considerable role in that improvement. His biographer, Liva Baker, wrote:

> Frankfurter's concern for public understanding of the Supreme Court took him into a long running fight with *The New York Times.* The press, Frankfurter believed, had a semipublic function and a semipublic responsibility. The *Times,* as the one documentary paper in the nation, should, he thought, furnish its readers the kind of competence in its reporting of the Supreme Court that it furnished in other fields. It should, Frankfurter was fond of saying, cover the Supreme Court at least as well as the World Series.
>
> Beginning in 1933, Frankfurter barraged Arthur Hays Sulzberger, publisher of the *Times,* with letters in which he was outspokenly critical of its failings — and equally outspokenly congratulatory of its triumphs. Finally, in the mid-1950s, a young reporter and Pulitzer Prize winner named Anthony Lewis was sent to Harvard Law School for a year, then assigned to cover the Supreme Court. The *Times* expanded and deepened its Court coverage; a significant by-product

of this development was the effect on other prominent newspapers which, encouraged by the *Times,* sought to improve their reporting of Court news and bring it up to World Series levels. [51]

Supreme Court justices have long felt that their opinions must speak for themselves and that efforts by the justices or by the public information office to explain or interpret the court's opinions are unnecessary. Nevertheless, the court has taken a number of actions in recent years to make it easier for the news media to digest the written opinions in the limited time available.

These changes include:
* Announcement of opinions on days other than Monday so that the press would have a smaller list of cases to report on each day.
* The use of headnotes since 1970, which makes it easier for reporters to plow through hundreds of pages of written opinions.
* The availability of *Preview of United States Supreme Court Cases,* a background analysis of the cases pending before the court.

The *Preview* is published weekly, from September to April, by the Association of American Law Schools and the American Law Institute-American Bar Association Committee on Continuing Professional Education. Prepared by law school professors, it outlines the background, importance and issues in all cases awaiting a final court decision.

The court's public information officer releases opinions to the news media shortly after they are announced. Some of the country's major newspapers and national news media have their own offices near the public information office, so court opinions can be transmitted quickly to their headquarters. *(Details, p. 722)*

Other Channels

In addition to the formal and press reporting of court opinions, there are a number of other, often impromptu, methods of publicizing its rulings. Various lobbying groups are rarely shy about speaking out on court opinions which meet with their approval or provoke their disapproval. In the 1960s and early 1970s, court decisions on issues like school desegregation, prayer in the schools, capital punishment and abortion resulted in an avalanche of publicity from groups both supportive of and hostile to the opinions.

When Supreme Court justices were still riding circuit, they usually maintained strong contacts with people, particularly lawyers and local judges, in the communities they served. Through these contacts, they were able to inform community leaders about recent court rulings and the legal principles on which those opinions were based.

In those days and at the present time, the legal fraternity also has provided a forum for discussing and clarifying court opinions through meetings of bar associations and publication of scholarly articles.

Traditions of the Court

Tradition plays a major role in the operations of the Supreme Court. The court's insistence on the historic continuity of its procedures, and its strict adherence to conventions of secrecy and formal decorum, have yielded little to the changing moods and social patterns of the contemporary world outside its chambers.

At best, this overlapping network of traditions gives the court an aura of substance, dignity and caution that befits the nation's highest institution of law — and the public's confidence in the integrity, sobriety of purpose and independence from outside pressure of its justices. But to some critics, much of the court's tenacious adherence to its formal traditions of procedure and behavior reflect an anachronistic set of values that undergird and constrict the effective functioning of the modern court.

Despite continuing efforts to streamline its procedures and find more efficient ways to cope with change, the court remains the most traditional of the three major branches of government.

Some traditional aspects of the court seem merely quaint. Modern justices are still reluctant to take part in Washington's cocktail party circuit, a regular stop for congressmen, diplomats and administration officials. Justices still employ a full-time seamstress to mend their robes and use quill pens made from the feathers of purebred white geese. While most lawyers no longer don frock coats and striped trousers to appear before the court, attorneys from the solicitor general's office still dress in the cutaways.

Other traditions are much more substantive and more controversial. Proposed changes in convention such as the mandatory retirement of justices, televising court sessions

and security measures to prevent press leaks are issues which continue to generate debate.

Even the more informal or irreverent of the justices have found the traditions of the court of sufficient importance to observe and preserve them. Justice Felix Frankfurter, for example, was a man who "brought a sense of informality and impish humor to the august tribunal. He would wave from the bench at friends among the spectators. He once escorted the child of a visiting Australian law school dean into the empty courtroom and let her sit on each of the justices' chairs. When Mrs. Charles Fahy came to court to hear her husband, the solicitor general from 1941 to 1945, argue a case, Frankfurter once teased her with this note scribbled from the bench: 'Anyhow — I'm for your hat!' He teased his own law clerks incessantly. He whistled in the marble halls, anything from 'The Stars and Stripes Forever' to the sextet from 'Lucia.' "

But "underneath the gaiety and banter there was a seriousness of purpose equal to anything Frankfurter had undertaken in his life. He approached the court with a kind of religious awe; he was indefatigable in guarding its traditions, and he felt, said Chief Justice Earl Warren, 'the burden of carrying on the traditions of the court more than any man.' " [52]

Secrecy

Among the court's most important traditions is secrecy. Secrecy applies not only to formal deliberations but to disclosure of personal disagreements and animosities among the justices as well. The unwritten code of secrecy has made the court the most leakproof of Washington institutions. Nevertheless, there have been and continue to be occasional glimpses into its inner workings and conflicts.

The practice of allowing no one except the justices themselves in the conference room began years ago with the mistaken impression that a page, secretary, clerk or stenographer had leaked a decision. Subsequent leaks, including instances in 1973, 1977 and 1979, have moved the justices to take measures to prevent further premature disclosures or unwarranted gossip. *(See pp. 714, 724)*

In addition to the rather infrequent revelations by an inquisitive press, justices and their law clerks have occasionally revealed something about the court's inner workings and conflicts in their writings and speeches. Probably the two best known examples were the use of the papers of Chief Justice Harlan Fiske Stone and Justice Louis D. Brandeis.

When Stone died in 1946, his widow turned over all the Chief Justice's files and papers to Alpheus T. Mason. In his biography of Stone,[53] Mason revealed much of the court's day-to-day operations, including feuds between liberal and conservative justices. Alexander Bickel used Brandeis' papers to show the justice's contribution to court solidarity, quoting Chief Justice William Howard Taft as saying of Brandeis, "He thinks much of the court and is anxious to have it consistent and strong, and he pulls his weight in the boat." [54]

Justices have good reason to maintain the veil of secrecy that surrounds their conference deliberations and their personal relations with other members of the court. Widespread disclosure of what goes on in conference could reduce public esteem for the court and its rulings. When leaks do occur, the court refuses to confirm or deny their accuracy, and the justices are loath to reveal instances of infighting and conflict among themselves lest they demean the dignity of the court and encourage further quarreling among the justices.

Courtesy

Both in and out of court, the justices seek to present an image of formality and courtesy. Before they go into the courtroom and at the beginning of their private conferences, the justices shake hands with each other. This practice began in the late 19th century when Chief Justice Melville W. Fuller decided that it was a good idea to remind the justices that differences of opinion did not preclude overall harmony of purpose.[55] In court and in their written opinions, the justices address each other as "my brother" or "my dissenting brothers." But the image of fraternal harmony is occasionally undermined by personal, ideological and legal differences among justices with strong views and even stronger egos.

In his book on Justice Samuel F. Miller (1862-90), Charles Fairman quoted Miller as having told a friend that Chief Justice Morrison R. Waite (1874-88) was "mediocre" and that "I can't make a great Chief Justice out of a small man." Miller was equally critical of fellow Justices Nathan Clifford, Noah Haynes Swayne and David Davis. "I can't make Clifford and Swayne, who are too old, resign, or keep the Chief Justice from giving them cases to write opinions in which their garrulity is often mixed with mischief. I can't hinder Davis from governing every act of his life by his hope of the Presidency." [56]

More than a decade before his appointment as Chief Justice, President William Howard Taft indicated his dis-

---

Inside the Conference Room

An unusual and well-publicized leak from the Supreme Court occurred in 1979 when ABC-TV news reporter Tim O'Brien broadcast the results of two cases which had not yet been formally announced in open court. On April 16 O'Brien revealed that Justice Byron R. White would deliver the majority opinion in an important libel case which would allow public figures offended by a report to inquire into the journalist's "state of mind."

Two days later the court, with Justice White speaking for the majority, ruled that public figures could indeed look into the "state of mind" of a journalist and the editorial process when suing for allegedly libelous reporting. O'Brien also reported that during the conference discussion of the case, the justices became involved in an angry and vociferous shouting match about the decision.

On April 17 O'Brien reported that Chief Justice Warren E. Burger had written the opinion in a still unannounced case in which the court ruled against the effort of prison inmates to expand their "due process" rights in parole hearings. After the two ABC-TV broadcasts, Burger was said by court sources to have ordered an immediate investigation.

The court itself made no public comment about the O'Brien reports, and O'Brien refused to reveal how or from whom he obtained the information. Within a week, however, it was reported that Chief Justice Burger had fired a typesetter from the court's print shop. The typesetter, John Tucci, worked for the U.S. Government Printing Office in the court's basement printing shop. Tucci, who would have had access to the opinion before it was released in court, denied that he had leaked the information to O'Brien.

---

taste for some of the justices. "The condition of the Supreme Court is pitiable, and yet those old fools hold on with a tenacity that is most discouraging," Taft said in 1910. "Really, the Chief Justice Fuller is almost senile; Harlan does no work; Brewer is so deaf that he cannot hear and has got beyond the point of the commonest accuracy in writing his opinions; Brewer and Harlan sleep almost through all the arguments. I don't know what can be done. It is most discouraging to the active men on the bench." [57]

Once he became Chief Justice in 1921, Taft was publicly far less critical of the other justices. Still, Taft's efforts to control the disputes and acrimony among the justices "at times exhausted his supply of good nature, and he sometimes betrayed his own irritations by very sharp remarks in letters." One of these letters, written in 1929, when Justice Harlan Fiske Stone was being considered as Taft's successor, alleged that "Stone is not a leader and would have a good deal of difficulty in massing the Court." John P. Frank recounts how, when Stone was appointed in 1925, "he was welcomed into the little extra-court meetings of the Taft bloc of conservative justices, and then, after a time, was dropped from those conventions when it appeared that he might be dangerously 'progressive.' " [58]

Perhaps the most publicized public airing of judicial antagonisms was the attack by Justice Robert H. Jackson against Justice Hugo L. Black in 1946. Jackson had wanted and expected to become Chief Justice when Harlan Fiske Stone died. Instead, President Truman nominated Fred M.

Vinson, and Jackson blamed Black for blocking his appointment as Chief Justice.

When Vinson was nominated, Jackson was serving as chief of a tribunal trying German war criminals in Nuremberg. Jackson responded to news of the appointment with a vitriolic letter to the Senate and House Judiciary committees. In that letter, Jackson denounced Black for participating in a case in which, Jackson charged, Black should have disqualified himself. That case involved the United Mine Workers, who were being represented by a former law partner of Black's, Crampton Harris. Unmentioned in the letter was the fact that Black and Harris had ceased being partners 19 years earlier and had seen each other hardly at all since that time. Black did not reply to the charge, nor did he mention that he had disqualified himself in all cases involving the Federal Communications Commission because his brother-in-law was a member of the FCC.

An earlier example of lack of judicial courtesy involved Chief Justice Roger B. Taney and Justice Benjamin R. Curtis in the famous *Dred Scott* decision of 1857. [59] In that case nine separate opinions were filed, with Taney speaking for the majority of the court. Taney represented the southern point of view and Curtis the northern, or abolitionist, side on the question of slavery in the territories. The Chief Justice made Curtis' dissent in the case far more difficult to write by refusing to allow Curtis to see the other opinions before completing his dissent. Shortly after the opinions were finally released, Curtis resigned from the court.

Justice James C. McReynolds is often cited as a man whose lack of courtesy made life on the court difficult for his fellow justices. McReynolds, who was appointed by President Woodrow Wilson in 1914 and served until 1941, was described by John P. Frank as "the total antithesis of everything Wilson stood for and . . . the most fanatic and hard-bitten conservative extremist ever to grace the Court." [60] McReynolds showed considerable antagonism to the more liberal members of the court and to the Jewish justices, Louis D. Brandeis and Benjamin N. Cardozo.

Rare Discourtesies

Frank has noted that "far more striking than the Court's disputes over the years is the absence of personal friction among the judges, and the extent to which normal tendencies of irritability are controlled rather than exposed. When one considers how easily a bench of nine could march off in nine different directions, one's principal impression may well be not how often but how seldom this occurs. An instance of a [Justice James C.] McReynolds snarling in bare-toothed anti-Semitic hostility at his Jewish brothers on the Court is overbalanced by the real personal sympathy" among the justices. "This degree of respectful personal interrelations is by no means restricted to Justices who . . . were essentially like-minded." [61]

The desire of most justices to maintain these "respectful personal interrelations" has made outbursts like Justice Jackson's rare. Disagreements among justices are far more likely to be exhibited in subtler ways.

A common method of criticizing another justice is to cite his words or previous opinions to prove the inconsistency of his views on a particular issue or opinion. Jackson, for example, was fond of quoting the statements that Justice Black had made when he was a senator from Alabama. Many of these criticisms are so subtle that they go unnoticed by everyone except those privy to the relationships between the justices.

Seniority

The system of seniority affects such court procedures as conference discussion and voting, announcement of opinions, and seating in the courtroom. It is also a determining factor in assignment of office space. Only the Chief Justice is exempt from such traditional obeisance to seniority.

During conferences, discussion of cases begins with the Chief Justice and proceeds down the line of seniority to the junior associate justice. The junior justice has the task of sending for and receiving documents or other information the court may need. Voting on the cases begins with the junior justice and proceeds up the line of seniority to the Chief Justice.

When opinions are announced in the courtroom, the justices who wrote the opinions announce them in reverse order of seniority. The Chief Justice is seated in the center of the winged mahogany bench. The senior associate justice sits at his immediate right and the second senior associate justice at his immediate left. In alternating order of seniority, the other justices take their places, with the junior associate justice at the far left of the bench and the second newest appointee at the far right.

Like the seating on the bench, the three-room offices of the justices are assigned according to seniority. Since there are only seven suites inside the so-called "golden gates" — the large bronze doors that seal the justices off from the public — the two junior justices usually occupy the offices on the public corridor just outside. One exception to this rule was Justice William O. Douglas, who until 1962 chose to keep the office he had been assigned as the most junior justice when he came to the court in 1939. Over the next 23 years, 12 justices with less seniority than Douglas moved to suites inside the door. In 1962, when Justice Frankfurter retired, Douglas at last decided to move inside the "golden gates."

In 1979, Justices William H. Rehnquist and John Paul Stevens occupy space outside the gates.

Continuity

Continuity is not merely an image that the court seeks to perpetuate but is inherent in the nature of the institution.

The main factor in the continuity of the court, of course, is that its justices are appointed for life — and for most members, that has been literally true. The majority of justices either have died while still on the bench or retired near the end of their careers.

Only 102 justices have been confirmed for court service in the nearly two centuries since its establishment. (One — Edwin M. Stanton — died after confirmation before taking his seat on the bench.) None has been removed from the bench involuntarily — although several have resigned under pressure — and few have given up the prestige and accoutrements of the court for another career. Just as change is central to Congress and the presidency through periodic elections, continuity is built into the court through longevity of service. The average length of service of all justices of the court, including current members, has been about 15 years. More than half of them served for at least that long.

William O. Douglas served longer than any other justice in the court's history. When he retired on Nov. 12, 1975, he had been on the high bench for more than 36 years.

Augustus H. Garland once reportedly told President Grover Cleveland, who wished to appoint him to the court, that he thought himself unqualified because a justice should serve for at least 20 years and he doubted that he would live that long.

Turnover

The justices' long service on the court is the most integral aspect of its continuity. With a new member added only every two years or so, successive courts assume their own collective identity, as the same justices work together over the space of decades. Each new member, however different in ideology and temperament from his associates, can make only an incremental difference. He is influential as an instrument of change by a factor of only one-ninth — less so, really, given the deferential role imposed upon him by the tradition of seniority.

While it is customary to refer to influential courts by the names of their Chief Justices — "The Marshall Court" or "The Warren Court" — such designations are somewhat misleading. Although the leadership and judicial ideology of each Chief Justice is without doubt a strong element in the direction "his" court takes and the innovations it generates, the makeup of each court is to a large degree fortuitous.

The Chief Justice, after all, usually inherits his associates when he takes office and does not himself choose new ones as vacancies occur — although his counsel may be covertly sought by a president. For the most part, a Chief Justice works with the associates he has been given, often nominated by a president and confirmed by a Congress of a different political persuasion from his own.

"The Warren Court," for example, is considered the most liberal and activist of modern times. Yet its chief, Earl Warren, was a Republican appointee who took command of a bench manned entirely by eight veteran justices appointed by the liberal Democratic Roosevelt-Truman administrations. In subsequent years — although the court absorbed four nominees of Warren's sponsor, Dwight Eisenhower — the "Warren Court's" number also came to include four appointees of Democratic Presidents Kennedy and Johnson.

The direction of the "Warren Court's" successor — the clearly more conservative "Burger Court" — can easily be attributed to the judicial attitudes of its Chief Justice, Warren E. Burger, and his three fellow-Nixon appointees. But it also encompasses three Eisenhower-Kennedy-Johnson holdovers and a moderate, John Paul Stevens, appointed by Nixon's successor, Gerald Ford.

Whether tending to be monolithic in its judgments or closely divided along liberal/conservative lines — or simply unpredictable — the membership of the court is, in other words, determined in large part by slowly evolving circumstances: by the political party in power as vacancies occur, by the length of time a court has sat together, and finally by the mere durability of each justice, surviving changes in the court and in the times.

Precedent

Another substantive factor in the court's essential continuity is its reliance on precedent in arriving at decisions. Except in rare cases where there is no judicial opinion to be cited, any decision is based primarily on earlier relevant opinions of the Supreme Court or lower courts as interpreted in light of the case under consideration.

The most dramatic and far-reaching of the court's decisions have been instances where a court has arrived at a clear-cut reversal of an earlier court's landmark opinion, especially one where basic constitutional questions are involved. The 1954 decision in *Brown v. Board of Education* represented a watershed reversal of more than a century of earlier court decisions in civil rights cases — decisions which the "Warren Court," in effect, declared to have been unconstitutional.

But whatever the court's decision — and it is far more common to uphold or modify an earlier court's judgment than to reverse it outright — it is so rooted in precedent that it marks a further stage in a judicial continuum rather than an original judgment that stands on its own.

For some justices, precedent has been the only consideration. Justice Owen J. Roberts, for example, issued this scathing dissent in January 1944 when the court overturned an admiralty case it had decided 16 years earlier. "The evil resulting from overruling earlier considered decisions must be evident," Roberts contended. "[T]he law becomes not a chart to govern conduct but a game of chance.... [T]he administration of justice will fall into disrepute. Respect for tribunals must fall when the bar and the public come to understand that nothing that has been said in prior adjudication has force in a current controversy."[62]

Justice Frankfurter joined in Roberts' dissent in the case. Yet four years earlier, Frankfurter had this to say about reversing previous court decisions: "We recognize that stare decisis [adherence to precedent] embodies an important social policy. It represents an element of continuity in law, and is rooted in the psychologic need to satisfy reasonable expectations. But stare decisis is a principle of policy and not a mechanical formula of adherence to the latest decision, however recent and questionable, when such adherence involves collision with a prior doctrine more embracing in its scope, intrinsically sounder, and verified by experience.... This Court, unlike the House of Lords, has from the beginning rejected a doctrine of disability at self-correction."[63] *(Further details, p. 294)*

The Chief Justice

For the most part, the office of Chief Justice of the Supreme Court has developed as it has through the leadership and initiative of the men who have held the job.

There is scant statutory authority for the office or its duties. The Constitution only mentions the title once: "When the President of the United States is tried, the Chief Justice shall preside." [64] The Judiciary Act of 1789 specifies only "That the supreme court of the United States shall consist of a chief justice and five associate justices." *(Judiciary Act of 1789, pp. 949-956)*

Indeed, in the very early years of the court, there was little indication that the title of Chief Justice would become such an important and prestigious one. As John P. Frank noted:

> The great and yet intangible difference between the Chief and his Associates is the prestige that, rightly or wrongly, tradition attaches to the Chief Justiceship. Popular mythology makes the Chief Justiceship much of what it is, in part because there have been some very great Chief Justices whose personal glory has rubbed off on the office, and partly because of popular esteem for the very idea of 'Chief.'

Yet because of tradition, popular perception of the office, or other intangible factors, the Chief Justice is widely perceived as more than *primus inter pares,* or "first among equals." Although he casts only one vote in accepting and deciding cases, as Frank pointed out:

> ...his formal title is a trifle different: he is Chief Justice of the United States, and his fellows are Justices of the Supreme Court. He administers the oath of office to the President. He presides when the Court is in public session, and at its secret conferences. He also presides over the judicial conference of the judges of the lower courts, and he has the not inconsiderable duty of assigning the writing of most of the opinions of his brothers. He is the chief administrative officer of the Court.[65]

First Among Equals

The first three Chief Justices were not held in especially high esteem. The first, John Jay, came to the court in 1789 and resigned six years later, on June 29, 1795, after having concluded the peace treaty with England and having been elected governor of New York.[66]

His successor, John Rutledge, had first been appointed to the court in 1790 but resigned as a justice the next year to accept the post of chief justice of South Carolina. After Jay's election, Rutledge wrote to President Washington that he would accept the Chief Justiceship "if you think me as fit as any other person and have not made choice of one to succeed him [Jay]." [67]

Washington immediately accepted Rutledge's suggestion, and Rutledge was sworn in as Chief Justice on Aug. 12, 1795. But before the Senate came back into session to confirm him, reports of Rutledge's earlier criticism of the Jay Treaty provoked a storm of controversy. When the Senate returned in December, there were, in addition to the outrage arising from Rutledge's criticism of the Jay Treaty, persistent rumors that the new Chief Justice was mentally

unbalanced. Later that month, the Senate rejected the nomination by a vote of 14 to 10.

Washington next offered the Chief Justiceship to Henry Clay, but Clay declined the offer, as did Justice William Cushing. Washington then nominated Oliver Ellsworth, who served from 1796 until he reigned in 1800. President John Adams named former Chief Justice Jay to succeed Ellsworth, but Jay refused to return to his old post, largely because of the onerous circuit duties imposed upon the justices. Adams then chose John Marshall.

John Marshall

Marshall's great achievement was to increase public respect for the Supreme Court. When he became Chief Justice in 1801 the court was held in low esteem, and its rulings, embodied in often unclear and confusing *seriatim* opinions, did little to enhance the prestige of the third branch of the government.

By his insistence on unanimity and the avoidance of dissenting and concurring opinions, Marshall — and to a far lesser extent, his successor, Roger B. Taney (1836-64) — gave the court the prestige it needed to deal effectively with many of the conflicts and controversies that were confronting the country. President Thomas Jefferson, who sought to break Federalist control of the court, encouraged dissent but was successful only in his appointment of Jeffersonian loyalist William Johnson. Following the deaths of Justices William Cushing and Samuel Chase, Jefferson wrote to his successor, James Madison, in 1811 that "it will be difficult to find a character of firmness enough to preserve his independence on the same bench with Marshall."

According to Frank, a Chief Justice:

> ...must get his real eminence not from the office but from the qualities he brings to it. He must possess the mysterious quality of leadership. In this respect the outstanding Chief was Marshall, who for 35 years presided over a Court largely populated by Justices of an opposing political party. Moreover, his Court, because of the very newness of the Constitution it was expounding, dealt with some of the greatest questions of history. Nonetheless, Marshall dominated his Court as has no other Chief Justice. He wrote most of its important opinions, and his dissents are remarkable for their rarity. . . . More important, Marshall brought a first-class mind and a thoroughly engaging personality into second-class company. The Court when he came to it was lazy and quite willing to let him do the work.[68]

William Howard Taft

The only Chief Justice who had served as president (1909-1913), William Howard Taft, came to the court in 1921 and immediately embarked on efforts to modernize the U.S. judicial system. His greatest contributions to the court came in his role as administrator rather than as judge or legal scholar.

A year after his appointment, Taft succeeded in persuading Congress to establish the Judicial Conference of Senior Circuit Judges — now the Judicial Conference of the United States — the governing body for the administration of the federal judicial system. *(See p. 767)*

More important to the Supreme Court itself was Chief Justice Taft's work in convincing Congress to enact the Judiciary Act of 1925. That law gave the court — then suffering a severe backlog of cases —almost unlimited discretion in deciding which cases to accept for review. As a result, the caseload — at least for a time — became more manageable, and the court was able to devote more time and energy to constitutional issues and important questions of federal law.

James F. Simon noted Taft's contribution as Chief Justice:

> Some experts rate Chief Justice William Howard Taft as one of the Court greats, not because of his opinions, but because of his devoted efforts to reform an antiquated court system.... In his first year as Chief Justice Taft crisscrossed the country in a whistle stop campaign for reform of the courts. He spoke to bar associations, argued his case in legal periodicals and testified at length before the House and Senate judiciary committees. His efforts were handsomely rewarded the next year when Congress passed a judicial reform act that streamlined the federal judicial system by coordinating the activities of the far-flung federal districts and bringing them under surer executive control of the Chief Justice. That accomplished, Taft turned his attention to the problem of court congestion in the Supreme Court docket. "We made our preparations with care," he later said, "and it proved to be easier than we supposed." (Taft's reward was the Judges Bill of 1925....) Before he was through, Chief Justice Taft's arm-twisting (he thought nothing of calling the chairman of the judiciary committee or even talking to the president about his reforms) had succeeded in winning the Court its first permanent home — the present Supreme Court building.[69]

Charles Evans Hughes

Another great Chief Justice, Charles Evans Hughes, called attention to the "personality and character" of the office before he himself assumed it in 1930:

> The Chief Justice as the head of the Court has an outstanding position, but in a small body of able men with equal authority in the making of decisions, it is evident that his actual influence will depend upon the strength of his character and the demonstration of his ability in the intimate relations of the judges. It is safe to say that no member of the Supreme Court is under any illusion as to the mental equipment of his brethren. Constant and close association discloses the strength and exposes the weaknesses of each. Courage of conviction, sound learning, familiarity with precedents, exact knowledge due to painstaking study of the cases under consideration cannot fail to command that profound respect which is always yielded to intellectual power conscientiously applied. That influence can be exerted by any member of the Court, whatever his rank in order of precedence. [70]

Hughes served as an associate justice from 1910-16 under the often indecisive, occasionally rambling Chief Justice Edward D. White. During those years, Hughes became acutely aware of the need for leadership by a Chief Justice in conference discussions and in the assignment of opinions. He also came to appreciate the value of harmony among the nine justices.

Constitutional Duty

In the only presidential impeachment trial in the nation's history, Chief Justice Salmon P. Chase — as presiding officer of the trial — may well have prevented President Andrew Johnson's conviction by the Senate in 1868. Mary Ann Harrell has pointed out that "Johnson's political enemies wanted a quick conviction. The Constitution, however, required the Chief Justice to preside; and Chase insisted on presiding as a judge, while the Senate tried legal issues as a court should. The Radicals had to let him rule on points of law; Chase gave the President's lawyers a chance to be heard. Johnson escaped conviction by one vote."

Source: Mary Ann Harrell, *Equal Justice Under Law: The Supreme Court in American Life* (Washington, D.C.: The Foundation of the Federal Bar Association with the cooperation of the National Geographic Society, 1975), p. 53.

Years after Hughes' death, former Justice Owen J. Roberts described Hughes as "the greatest of a great line of Chief Justices." During conferences, Roberts said, "his presentation of the facts of a case was full and impartial. His summary of the legal questions arising out of the facts was equally complete, dealing with opposing contentions so as to make them stand out clearly.... After the Chief Justice had finished his statement of the case and others took up the discussion, I have never known him to interrupt or to get into an argument with the Justice who was speaking. He would wait until the discussion had closed and then briefly and succinctly call attention to the matters developed in the discussion as to which he agreed or disagreed, giving his reasons." [71]

During oral argument and in assigning opinions, Hughes was said to show similar control and consideration. Counsel who were nervous or long-winded were often saved by a simple question from Hughes which sought to clarify or rephrase arguments they had presented poorly. "I know of no instance," Justice Roberts said, "where a lawyer had reason to feel rebuked or hurt by anything the Chief Justice said or did." [72]

Hughes described the assigning of opinions as "my most delicate task.... I endeavored to do this with due regard to the feelings of the senior Justices and to give to each Justice the same proportion of important cases while at the same time equalizing so far as possible the burden of work. Of course, in making assignments I often had in mind the special fitness of a Justice for writing in the particular case." [73]

In assigning opinions, Hughes also tried to avoid extreme points of view and let the centrist view prevail. As Merlo Pusey pointed out in his study of Hughes, "When a Justice with a reputation as a liberal voted with the majority on the conservative side of a question, he usually got the opinion to write. The same was true in the case of a conservative voting on the liberal side. Hughes' constant effort was to enhance public confidence in the entire court as an independent and impartial tribunal." [74]

Hughes also could be extremely considerate of the other justices. When he had voted with the majority at the Saturday conference, he usually had the opinion-writing assignment delivered to the appropriate justice that same night. Knowing that Justice Cardozo, who had suffered a heart attack before coming to the court in 1932, would

Earl Warren and the *Brown* Decision

Chief Justice Warren's personal qualities and his amiable relationship with the other justices played a major role in the court's unanimous ruling in *Brown v. Board of Education.* That landmark decision, written by Warren and handed down on May 17, 1954, declared racial segregation in public schools inherently discriminatory and therefore in contravention of the equal protection clause of the Fourteenth Amendment.

The *Brown* decision was a catalyst fo the civil rights revolution of the late 1950s and 1960s. The opinion doubtless would have been far less important and far-reaching had it not been unanimous. Had there been dissenting or concurring opinions, the impact of the decision would have been reduced, and opponents of desegregation would have been given the opening to challenge the decision. Warren's achievement in securing unanimity was remarkable in itself. Equally remarkable was the fact that he had been Chief Justice only a few months when the decision was handed down.

In *Simple Justice,* his book on the *Brown* decision, Richard Kluger wrote that:

> . . .some time between late February and late March, the court voted at one of its Saturday conferences on the school-segregation cases. The date is in doubt because the justices had agreed that the case was of such magnitude that no word ought to leak out before the decision was announced. . . . The vote was apparently eight to strike down segregation and one, [Justice Stanley F.] Reed, to uphold it. But it was far from certain whether Jackson was going to file a separate concurrence or whether Frankfurter might or whether the two of them might agree on one. . . . Warren, of course, wished to avoid concurring opinions; the fewer voices with which the Court spoke, the better. And he did not give up his hope that Stanley Reed, in the end, would abandon his dissenting position. The Chief assigned himself the all-important task of writing the majority opinion.

On March 30, Justice Jackson suffered a serious heart attack. It was suspected that Jackson, along with Frankfurter, might issue a concurring opinion in the case.

Warren, who had been working on the majority opinion, did not circulate his draft until May 7. Justices Burton, Black, Douglas, Minton and Clark responded quickly and enthusiastically, making only a few minor suggestions for change.

"It was with the three remaining members of the Court [Frankfurter, Jackson Reed] that Warren could have anticipated problems: any of them might still

choose to write his own opinion," Kluger wrote. But Frankfurter "had from the beginning been working for a unified Court. Nothing could have been worse, for the Court or the nation itself, than a flurry of conflicting opinions that would confuse and anger the American people. So long as the Chief was willing to fashion his opinion in a frank, carefully modulated way, Frankfurter had intended to go along." Warren's draft apparently met with Frankfurter's approval.

"Warren personally delivered his draft opinions to Jackson's hospital room and left them for the ailing Justice to study." After having his clerk, Barrett Prettyman, read the draft, Jackson "was willing to settle for one whose principal virtue seemed to be its temperate tone." Prettyman was quoted by Kluger as saying that the "genius of the Warren opinion was that it was so simple and unobtrusive. [Warren] had come from political life and had a keen sense of what you could say in this opinion without getting everybody's back up. His opinion took the sting off the decision, it wasn't accusatory, and it didn't pretend that the Fourteenth Amendment was more helpful than the history suggested — he didn't equivocate on that point."

Justice Reed then remained the only holdout. According to Kluger, Reed's position on the *Brown* case "stemmed from a deeply held conviction that the nation had been taking big strides in race relations and that the Court's decision to outlaw separate schools threatened to impede that march, if not halt it altogether." Warren met many times with Reed and, according to Reed's clerk, George Mickum, had this to say in one of their last meetings: "Stan, you're all by yourself in this now. You've got to decide whether it's really the best thing for the country."

Warren, according to Mickum, "was not particularly eloquent and certainly not bombastic. Throughout, the Chief Justice was quite low-key and very sensitive to the problems that the decision would present to the South. He empathized with Justice Reed's concern. But he was quite firm on the Court's need for unanimity on a matter of this sensitivity." Mickum added that "I really think he [Reed] was really troubled by the possible consequences of his position. Because he was a Southerner, even a lone dissent by him would give a lot of people a lot of grist for making trouble. For the good of the country, he put aside his own basis for dissent." At a conference on May 15, the justices at last accepted — unanimously — Warren's opinion in the *Brown* case.

Source: Richard Kluger, *Simple Justice: Brown v. Board of Education and Black America's Struggle for Equality* (New York: Altred A. Knopt, 1976), pp. 694-699.

begin work on an assignment immediately after getting it, Hughes delayed the delivery of Cardozo's assignments until Sunday. And — so that Cardozo would not be aware of this practice — he also delayed delivering the assignments to Justice Van Devanter, who lived in the same apartment house as Cardozo. Similar tact was used when the other justices gave Hughes "the highly unpleasant duty" of asking for the resignation of 90-year-old Justice Holmes.

Harlan Fiske Stone

In contrast to Hughes' efficient administration of court business, his successor as Chief Justice, Harlan Fiske Stone, was unable or unwilling to maintain such control of the court. Stone allowed conference discussions to go on as long as the other justices wished and made little effort to minimize disagreements and dissents. According to John P. Frank, "Stone is a notable example of a judge completely competent in his own individual duties of judging who was yet unable to function well as Chief."

During Stone's tenure as Chief Justice, Frank continued, "the high efficiency of the Court began to deteriorate, the Court was much more frequently divided than usual, and the opinions of at least some of its members indulged in a stridency of tone which diminished the prestige of the tribunal. Personal relations within the Court were most unhappy. Why? Stone's occasional testiness and vanity made him very difficult to work with. A partisan battler himself, he could not rise above the fray to bring calm leadership into the controversies of others. . . . He was given to tactless comment about his colleagues." [75]

Earl Warren

Chief Justice Earl Warren was temperamentally the opposite of Stone in many respects. Toward the other justices, he was usually temperate and good-natured. Warren had been named Chief Justice by President Eisenhower in October 1953 and had been confirmed unanimously by the Senate on March 1, 1954. Three days after his confirmation, columnist James Reston of *The New York Times* wrote that the new Chief Justice appeared to display at conferences and in court "an ability to concentrate on the concrete; a capacity to do his homework; a sensitive, friendly manner, wholly devoid of pretense, and a self-command and natural dignity so useful in presiding over the court." [76]

Warren's affability and low-key persuasiveness — as much as the liberal affinities of the associate justices he inherited from Democratic presidents — were responsible for leading the Supreme Court into a revolutionary era of ideological decision-making. *Brown v. Board of Education*[77] and other opinions of the Warren era were catalysts of social reform. They also unleashed a storm of protest from those who feared expanding the rights of blacks, the poor, criminals and the underprivileged.

Despite his low-keyed, amiable relationships with his fellow justices, however, Warren could show a gritty leadership. On two occasions in early 1962, Warren publicly rebuked senior justice Felix Frankfurter for expanding his written opinion as he announced it in open court and for lecturing the other justices when he delivered a dissenting opinion.

Warren E. Burger

Since becoming Chief Justice in 1969, Warren E. Burger, like his conservative predecessor William Howard Taft, has functioned more effectively as an administrator of the U.S. court system and as a representative of the courts before Congress, than as a leader in judicial philosophy. Burger has been tireless in his efforts to streamline the courts and to make the ever-increasing caseload of both the Supreme Court and the lower federal courts more manageable. *(See box p. 736)*

Burger has been subjected to considerable criticism as a Chief Justice. He has been blamed for antagonizing some of the other justices and for failing to control the "increasingly unharmonious" relations on the court.

Nevertheless, a lawyer who clerked on the court during the 1977 term defends the Chief Justice and points out that "Burger has tried more than most to bring the justices together by compromising his own position. Some are strong-willed people who just won't bend — and he can't force them." [78]

Head of the Judicial System

In addition to his duties on the Supreme Court, the Chief Justice is also chairman of the Judicial Conference of the United States, chairman of the Board of the Federal Judicial Center, and supervises the Administrative Office of the United States Courts. Chief Justice Burger has estimated that he spends about a third of his time on administrative tasks that do not directly involve the other justices.

Judicial Conference of the U.S. The Judicial Conference, the body which governs administration of the federal judicial system, was set up in 1922 by Chief Justice William Howard Taft. A former lower court judge as well as a former president, Taft felt the federal judiciary needed a forum for coordination.

The conference consists of the Chief Justice, its chairman, and 24 members — the 11 chief justices of the U.S. courts of appeal, a district court judge elected by his peers in each circuit, and the chief judges of the Court of Claims and the Court of Customs and Patent Appeals. *(See p. 767.)*

Federal Judicial Center. The center was created by Congress in 1967 as a research, training and planning arm of the federal judiciary. Headquartered in Washington, D.C., its seven-member board meets four times a year. It was in his capacity as chairman of the Federal Judicial Center that Chief Justice Burger established the Study Group on the Caseload of the Supreme Court in 1972. *(See p. 767)*

Administrative Office of the U.S. Courts. The Administrative Office serves as the "housekeeper" and statistician for the federal court system. It was established by Congress in 1939 to take over the administrative duties that had been performed by the attorney general's office. Among other things, it fixes the salaries of all lower-court personnel except judges and supervises the administrative functions of these courts. *(See p. 767)*

Extra-Judicial Roles

In addition to his responsibilities as head of the Supreme Court and of the federal judicial system, Congress has also made the Chief Justice a member of the Board of Regents of the Smithsonian Institution and a member of the Board of Trustees of the National Gallery of Art and of the Joseph H. Hirshhorn Museum and Sculpture Garden.

The Constitution gives justices of the Supreme Court no other duty than to serve as justices, and the Chief Justice no other additional duty than to preside over Senate impeachment proceedings. Nevertheless, a number of Chief Justices have taken on additional tasks, and several of them have been severely criticized for involving the court in non-judicial, often controversial issues.

Political Involvement

One reason why Chief Justices have taken on non-judicial tasks may be that so many of them were prominent in politics and retained an activist political temperament upon assuming command of the high court. John Marshall, Roger Taney, Salmon P. Chase, Charles Evans Hughes, Harlan Fiske Stone and Fred M. Vinson had been Cabinet members. William Howard Taft had been president. Edward D. White had been a U.S. Senator. Earl Warren had been Governor of California. In fact, only two Chief Justices have come essentially from the bar: Morrison R. Waite (1874-1888) and Melville W. Fuller (1888-1910).

Advising the President

During his first term, President Washington, without judicial advisers of his own, sent the court 29 questions on international law and treaties at a time when he was trying to keep the new country out of the war between Britain and France. The court refused to give advice, maintaining that the Constitution gave them no authority to share executive power or to issue advisory opinions to a president.

Nevertheless, Chief Justice Warren E. Burger has pointed out that "although the members of the first Supreme Court wisely resisted President Washington's request for advisory opinions and declined to perform other functions which they deemed to be executive in nature, there is little doubt that Chief Justice Jay gave advice to Washington over the dinner table and even in writing." [79]

Diplomatic Missions

Jay did more for President Washington than just that. Before becoming Chief Justice, he had served as interim secretary of state. At the president's request, Jay undertook a successful diplomatic mission to Great Britain in 1794 to try to patch up quarrels over British troops in the American Northwest and private debts to British creditors.

The Jay Treaty, which the Chief Justice negotiated during the visit, may have prevented another war between Britain and the United States, but it involved Jay and the court in partisan controversy. (So did Jay's decision to run twice for governor of New York while still Chief Justice.)

While the Senate confirmed Jay's nomination as envoy to Britain by a vote of 18 to 8 on April 19, 1794, objections to such double duty were raised that would resurface when Jay was renominated to the Chief Justiceship in 1800.

During three days of Senate debate on the nomination, a resolution was offered which maintained that "to permit Judges of the Supreme Court to hold at the same time any other office of employment emanating from and holden at the pleasure of the Executive is contrary to the spirit of the Constitution and as tending to expose them to the influence of the Executive, is mischievous and impolitic."

Similar, although more subdued, criticism befell Jay's successor Oliver Ellsworth for accepting President Adams' appointment as envoy to France in early 1799.

Chief Justice Harlan Fiske Stone referred to the impact on the court of the Jay and Ellsworth missions in a letter to President Franklin D. Roosevelt on July 20, 1942.

"We must not forget that it is the judgment of history that two of my predecessors, Jay and Ellsworth, failed in the obligation of their office and impaired their legitimate influence by participation in executive action in the negotiation of treaties," Stone wrote. "True, they repaired their mistake in part by resigning their commissions before resuming their judicial duties, but it is not by mere chance that every Chief Justice since has confined his activities strictly to the performance of his judicial duties." [80]

Investigatory Commissions

Chief Justice Stone's letter to Roosevelt was written in response to the president's suggestion that Stone conduct an investigation into the uses of rubber during World War II. Stone declined the offer, saying, "I cannot rightly yield to my desire to render for you a service which as a private citizen I should not only feel bound to do but one which I should undertake with zeal and enthusiasm."

Stone's main reason for rejecting the assignment was that "a judge and especially the Chief Justice cannot engage in political debate or make public defense of his acts. When his action is judicial he may always rely upon the support of the defined record upon which his action is based and of the opinion in which he and his associates unite as stating the grounds for decision. But when he participates in the action of the executive or legislative departments of government he is without those supports. He exposes himself to attack and indeed invites it, which because of his peculiar situation, inevitably impairs his value as a judge and the appropriate influence of his office." [81]

Chief Justice Earl Warren proved more willing to accept a non-judicial public duty after the assassination of President John F. Kennedy in 1963. For heading the so-called Warren Commission, which investigated and reported upon the assassination, he was, however, subjected to considerable criticism.

Perquisites

The Chief Justice has a number of special perquisites. In addition to an annual salary of $75,000 a year and to the attention and respect that surrounds the office, he also has four law clerks (including a special assistant), three secretaries and a messenger. The Chief Justice is also provided with a car and chauffeur, paid for by the government.

In 1972 Congress authorized the Chief Justice to "appoint an Administrative Assistant who shall serve at the pleasure of the Chief Justice and shall perform such duties as may be assigned to him by the Chief Justice." The statute authorizing the appointment of an administrative assistant says nothing about the functions and duties of such a position; it is left to the Chief Justice to determine how and in what areas he will work.

Chief Justice Burger has had his administrative assistant operate "exclusively in areas outside the Chief Justice's judicial functions as a member of the Supreme Court."

Under Burger, he has provided "(1) research and analysis supportive of the Chief Justice's public addresses and statements; (2) monitoring of literature and developments in the fields of judicial administration and court improvement; (3) liaison with the many legal and judicial groups and individuals dealing with problems in those fields, including assistance in organizing legal conferences; (4) assistance in the task of explaining to the public the role of the Supreme Court and the federal judicial system; and (5) assistance to the Chief Justice in his overall supervisory responsibilities with respect to the institutional operations of the Supreme Court, such as the supervision and coordination of the various offices of the Court." [82]

The Justices

From 1790 until 1979, only 101 men have served as Supreme Court justices. On average, a new justice joins the court every 22 months. Every president who has served a full term or more has made at least one appointment. That so few justices have served is due, of course, to the fact that justices are appointed for life and most of them are loath to give up a position of such prestige and influence.

How Large a Bench?

Another factor in the low turnover has been the fact that the court has remained the same size since 1869. In the Judiciary Act of 1789, Congress established the number of justices, including the Chief Justice, at six. The Judiciary Act of 1801, enacted one month before President John Adams' term expired, reduced the number to five, to prevent the newly-elected president, Thomas Jefferson, from filling any vacancies. Congress in 1802 repealed the 1801 law, bringing the number of Supreme Court justices back to six.

The Judiciary Act of 1807 increased the number to seven, primarily because of the increasing judicial work. In 1827 Congress added two new seats, bringing the number to nine, the size it has remained ever since, except during the Civil War period. The Judiciary Act of 1863 increased the number of justices to ten, but in 1866 Congress cut the court's size down to seven to prevent President Andrew Johnson from filling vacancies with appointees who would reflect his views about the unconstitutionality of Reconstruction legislation.

The last adjustment in court size came with the Judiciary Act of 1869, which increased it to nine seats. The act mandated "That the Supreme Court of the United States shall hereafter consist of the Chief Justice of the United States and eight associate justices, any six of whom shall constitute a quorum; and for the purposes of this act there shall be appointed an additional associate justice of said court."

The last major effort to change the number of members on the court was President Franklin D. Roosevelt's aborted "court-packing" attempt in 1937 to add justices who ostensibly would be more sympathetic to his New Deal legislative proposals than were the sitting justices. In opposition to the plan, several justices argued "that a Court of nine is as large a court as is manageable. The Court could do its work, except for writing of the opinions, a good deal better if it were five rather than nine. Every man who is added to the Court adds another voice in counsel, and the most difficult work of the Court ... is that that is done around the counsel table; and if you make the Court a convention instead of a small body of experts, you will simply confuse counsel. It will confuse counsel within the Court, and will cloud the work of the Court and deteriorate and degenerate it." [83]

Since the failure of Roosevelt's plan, there have been no further efforts to increase the number of justices, nor are there likely to be any in the foreseeable future. During the 19th century, the main reason for increasing the number of justices was the burden of circuit duty: as new circuits were added, more justices were needed to attend sessions of the courts in these circuits. Circuit-riding duties of the justices ended in 1891. *(See box, next page)*

In the past — and to a lesser extent today — a justice usually was appointed from the circuit in which he was to serve. Factors other than regional ones that a president generally considers in nominating a man to be a justice of the Supreme Court are the likelihood of his winning Senate confirmation, his ability and reputation, his ideological position, his political affiliation and beliefs and his religion.

Confirmation

Since the late 18th century, the Senate has formally rejected only 11 court nominees. (The last two were President Richard Nixon's appointees Clement F. Haynsworth Jr. and G. Harrold Carswell.) In addition to the nominations that the Senate has formally rejected, 13 others have been denied confirmation without a vote.

A Judicial 'Family'

Depending on shifting traditions and circumstances, members of the court have sometimes behaved more like a close-knit, chummy family, at others more like a group of dignitaries on their most scrupulously formal behavior.

In the early years of the court, particularly after John Marshall became Chief Justice in 1801, the justices usually lived together during the term in the same boardinghouse and shared their meals together. During the Marshall years, when the court was in session, the justices were together during oral arguments, usually from 11 a.m. until 4 p.m. each day and during conference after 7 p.m. After the conferences, the justices often dined and socialized with each other.

During the early years of the 19th century, Charles Warren has written, "the Judges of the Court appear to have been assiduous diners-out." [84] John Quincy Adams, then secretary of state, wrote in his diary on March 8, 1821: "We had the Judiciary company to dine with us, this day. Chief Justice Marshall, the Judges Johnson, Story and Todd, the Attorney-General Wirt, and late District Attorney Walter Jones; also Messrs. Harper, Hopkinson, D. B. Ogden, J. Sergeant, Webster, Wheaton and Winder, all counsellors of the Court. ... We had a very pleasant and convivial party." [85]

At this time, the justices "lived for the most part in the same lodgings," Warren continued, and "their intercourse was necessarily of the closest kind, off as well as on the bench." Charles Sumner, later the radical Republican senator from Massachusetts and outspoken abolitionist, wrote in a letter of March 3, 1834: "All the judges board together, having rooms in the same house and taking their meals from the same table, except Judge McLean whose wife is with him, and who consequently has a separate table, though in the same house. I dined with them yesterday. ... No conversation is forbidden, and nothing which goes to cause cheerfulness, if not hilarity. The world and all its things are talked of as much as on any other day." [86]

In a letter of March 8, 1812, Justice Joseph Story described the life of the justices in their common boardinghouse. "It is certainly true, that Judges here live with perfect harmony, and as agreeably as absence from friends and families could make our residence. Our intercourse is perfectly familiar and unrestrained, and our social hours, when undisturbed with the labors of the law, are passed in gay and frank conversation, which at once enlivens and instructs." [87]

Many of the justices continued to share a common boardinghouse until after the Civil War. In the late 19th century, however, as the terms of the court grew longer, the justices abandoned the boardinghouses, moved their families to Washington and set up their own homes.

Some of the familial aspects of the earlier days remain. It is rare for one justice to allow his animosity toward another to come to public attention. Justices rarely criticize the views of their colleagues, except in their written opinions. And there have been repeated instances when the other justices have taken on extra work or exhibited extra kindness toward a justice who was physically or mentally unwell. Still, the secrecy and isolation of the court tend to make the camaraderie of the boardinghouse days all but impossible today.

Individualism

History, tradition and the nature of the court's work limit severely the opportunities of its members to demonstrate their individual views and traits.

In the early years of the court, several factors encouraged the growth of individualism. One was the practice of delivering *seriatim* opinions, resulting in the issuance of no single opinion of the court. Chief Justice Marshall ended *seriatim* opinions, but the increasing use of dissenting and concurring opinions after his tenure had a similar effect.

Of judicial independence and individualism, Wesley McCune wrote:

Were it not for one institution, the dissenting opinion, anyone who accepted appointment to the Court would almost immediately lose his individual identity, except for what he could retain in Washington society or during summer vacations. If justices wrote only majority opinions, blended to fit the views of five or more justices, the name on the opinion would mean little and the Court would become as impersonal as a big bank. But through dissents justices have asserted their personal views. Thus, each justice can build a reputation even after arriving on the Court, in addition, of course, to shaping future law by protesting that of the present. [88]

The justices' early circuit-riding responsibilities also encouraged individualism. While on the circuit, the justices operated not as a group but as individual judges with as much discretionary power as they wished to exert.

Another factor favoring independence was the lack of office space before the new court building was completed in 1935. Until then, most of the justices worked in their own homes, seeing the other justices only when oral arguments were heard or conferences held.

Even after occupying their offices in the new court building, however, the justices seldom approached the "old-boy" closeness of the boardinghouse days. After taking his seat on the court in 1972, Justice Lewis F. Powell Jr. confessed:

I had thought of the Court as a collegial body in which the most characteristic activities would be consultation and cooperative deliberation aided by a strong supportive staff. I was in for more than a little surprise.... The Court is perhaps one of the last

Circuit-Riding

Circuit-riding was a tremendous burden for most justices, and there were numerous complaints from the justices about the intolerable conditions that circuit duties imposed on them.

In a letter to the president on Aug. 19, 1792, for example, all the justices wrote:

We really, sir, find the burdens laid upon us so excessive that we cannot forbear representing them in strong and explicit terms.... That the task of holding twenty-seven Circuit Courts a year, in the different States, from New Hampshire to Georgia, besides two sessions of the Supreme Court at Philadelphia, in the two most severe seasons of the year, is a task which, considering the extent of the United States and the small number of Judges, is too burdensome. That to require of the Judges to pass the greater part of their days on the road, and at inns, and at a distance from their families, is a requisition which, in their opinion, should not be made unless in cases of necessity.

The president transmitted that letter to Congress, but Congress, then and for almost 100 years thereafter, refused to abolish the circuit-riding duties. Thus the justices, many of them old and in ill health, faced days of difficult and often impossible travel, inadequate lodgings, bad food and epidemics and disease.

Until circuit duties were finally abolished in 1891, many unsuccessful bills had been introduced in Congress to free Supreme Court justices from this onerous task.

In a speech on the Senate floor on Jan. 12, 1819, Sen. Abner Lacock, D-Pa., summed up the major reasons for congressional defeat of the bills. If the justices were relieved of circuit duties, Lacock argued, they would become "completely cloistered within the City of Washington, and their decisions, instead of emanating from enlarged and liberalized minds, would assume a severe and local character." They might also become "another appendage of the Executive authority" to be subjected to the "dazzling splendors of the palace and the drawing room" and the "flattery and soothing attention of a designing Executive."

Congress finally acted to end the justices' circuit-riding duties when it approved the Circuit Court of Appeals Act of 1891. *(Text, p. 957)* That act established a new set of appeals courts between the district courts and the Supreme Court.

Each justice still has jurisdiction over one or more of the 11 federal circuits and may issue injunctions, grant bail or stay an execution in these circuits. Requests for an injunction, bail or a stay of execution go first to the presiding justice in that circuit. If denied, the application may then be made to one of the other justices.

citadels of jealously preserved individualism.... Indeed a justice may go through an entire term without being once in the chambers of all the other members of the Court.

Powell describes the justices and their staffs as "nine small independent law firms." [89]

Retirement

Neither the Constitution nor the law has anything to say about when or under what circumstances a justice should retire from service on the Supreme Court. Justices are appointed for life and "shall hold their Offices during good Behavior," according to Article III, Section 1 of the Constitution.

Forty-four justices have resigned from the court; one was impeached, tried and acquitted; a few have been threatened with impeachment.

Of the 44 who resigned, most did so because of old age or mental or physical ill health.

Forty-seven justices died while on the court. Three who had announced their retirements died before their resignations took effect. Other reasons for resigning have included matters of conscience, the desire to do other work and the threat of scandal or impeachment.

Until 1869, to keep drawing a salary, many older justices stayed on the job. Until that year, a retired justice received no compensation for his service after retirement. The Judiciary Statute of 1869 provided that any judge who had served on any federal court for at least 10 years, and was 70 or older, could resign from the bench and continue to receive his regular salary until he died.

The law now provides that a justice, if he wishes, may retire at age 70 after having served 10 years or at age 65 after 15 years of service, with compensation commensurate with his salary.

But despite old age or poor health, a number of justices have resisted leaving their seats until subjected to considerable pressure from their colleagues on the court.

After the election of President Andrew Jackson in 1832, Chief Justice John Marshall and Justice Gabriel Duvall (1811-1835), both in failing health, were reluctant to resign because they feared that the "radical" new president would choose equally "radical" new justices to take their places. Marshall remained on the court until his death in 1835, and Duvall submitted his resignation the same year after learning that Jackson intended to nominate as his successor Roger B. Taney, of whom Duvall approved.

By 1869 it was apparent that Justice Robert C. Grier (1846-1870) was both physically and mentally unable to carry out his duties. Early the next year, all the other justices formed a committee to tell Grier that "it was their unanimous opinion that he ought to resign." Soon after being told that by the committee, Grier submitted his resignation.

In his book on the Supreme Court, Charles Evans Hughes recounts the difficulties that the justices had in convincing Justice Stephen J. Field (1863-1897) to resign.

Some justices have stayed too long on the bench. An unfortunate illustration was that of Justice Grier who had failed perceptibly at the time of the first argument of the legal tender case. As the decision was delayed, he did not participate in it. A committee of the Court waited upon Justice Grier to advise him of the desirability of his retirement and the unfortunate consequences of his being in a position to cast a deciding vote in an important case when he was not able properly to address himself to it.

Justice Field tarried too long on the bench. . . . It occurred to the other members of the Court that Justice Field had served on a committee which waited upon Justice Grier to suggest his retirement, and it was

thought that recalling that to his memory might aid him to decide to retire. Justice Harlan was deputed to make the suggestion. He went over to Justice Field, who was sitting alone on a settee in the robing room apparently oblivious of his surroundings, and after arousing him gradually approached the question, asking if he did not recall how anxious the Court had become with respect to Justice Grier's condition and the feeling of the other Justices that in his own interest and in that of the Court he should give up his work. Justice Harlan asked if Justice Field did not remember what had been said to Justice Grier on that occasion. The old man listened, gradually became alert and finally, with his eyes blazing with the old fire of youth, he burst out:

'Yes! And a dirtier day's work I never did in my life!'

That was the end of that effort of the brethren of the Court to induce Justice Field's retirement; he did resign not long after. [90]

In recounting the Grier and Field resignations, Hughes also described the "agreeable spectacle of Justice Holmes at eighty-five doing his share of work, or even more, with the same energy and brilliance that he showed twenty years ago." [91] But in 1932 after he had become Chief Justice, Hughes was obliged to suggest to Holmes, then 90 years old, that he resign. Holmes, doubtless recalling the Grier and Field cases, resigned immediately.

Motives for Resignation

At least three justices have resigned because of the dictates of conscience. Justice John A. Campbell (1853-1861) resigned soon after the outbreak of the Civil War to return to his native Alabama despite the fact that he had opposed secession and had freed all of his own slaves. Justice Benjamin R. Curtis (1851-1857) resigned after disagreeing with Chief Justice Taney over the Dred Scott decision; Curtis, a strong advocate of freedom for slaves once they were on free territory, felt he could no longer serve on a court which had issued the Dred Scott decision, and retired, for that and other reasons. *(See box, p. 662)* Justice Tom C. Clark (1949-1967) resigned to avoid any possible charges of conflict-of-interest after his son, Ramsey, was appointed attorney general.

A number of justices left the court to run for elective office or to take other work. The first Chief Justice, John Jay, resigned in 1795 to become governor of New York. Five years later, he declined reappointment as Chief Justice because he felt that the court lacked "the energy, weight and dignity which are essential to its affording due support to the national government." [92]

Justice Charles Evans Hughes resigned in 1916 to run unsuccessfully for the presidency. Fourteen years later he returned as Chief Justice. Arthur J. Goldberg resigned in 1965 to become U.S. ambassador to the United Nations.

Abe Fortas, the only justice ever to resign amidst charges of judicial misconduct, submitted his resignation on May 14, 1969, a few days after *Life* magazine had published reports that Fortas, during his first year on the court, had received the first of what were to be annual fees of $20,000 from the family foundation of Louis Wolfson. Wolfson was later convicted of violating federal securities laws. In submitting his resignation, Fortas denied any wrongdoing, saying that the fee in question had been returned and the relationship terminated. He was resigning

Compulsory Retirement?

There have been repeated — if so far unsuccessful — suggestions that a constitutional amendment be enacted to require justices of the Supreme Court to retire at age 70 or 75. Justice Owen J. Roberts expressed his support for such a proposal more than 30 years ago:

"I believe it is a wise provision. First of all, it will forestall the basis of the last attack on the court, the extreme age of the justices, and the fact that superannuated old gentlemen hung on there long after their usefulness had ceased. More than that, it tends to provide for each administration an opportunity to add new personnel to the Court, which, I think, is a good thing." [1]

Charles Fairman has written that "there are two distinct reasons for urging some scheme for compulsory retirement" of Supreme Court justices. "There is, first, the actual impairment of mental and physical powers. . . . A second reason for insuring renewal of the Court involves considerations of a different order. Rigidity of thought and obsolescence of social outlook, though more objective, may be no less real than the waning of bodily powers. When a majority of the Court cling to views of public policy no longer entertained by the community or shared by the political branches of government, a conflict arises which must be resolved." [2]

---

[1] Speech to the Association of the Bar of the City of New York, Dec. 11, 1948.

[2] Charles Fairman, "The Retirement of Federal Judges," *Harvard Law Review,* January 1938, p. 397.

---

nevertheless, he said, to quiet the controversy and enable the court to "proceed with its work without the harassment of debate concerning one of its members." [93] *(Text p. 983)*

Impeachment Attempts

Only a few justices have faced impeachment. The first was Samuel Chase (1796-1811). Of the eight articles of impeachment that the House voted against him in late 1804, six concerned his alleged arbitrary and improper actions at the treason and sedition trials of John Fries and James G. Callender in 1800. In its articles of impeachment, the House charged that his partisan behavior in and out of court amounted to "high Crimes and Misdemeanors" under the Constitution.

The Senate trial began on Feb. 4, 1805. Although 25 of the 34 members of the Senate were Republicans, Chase was acquitted on all counts on March 1. Soon after the acquittal, Chase's and Marshall's adversary, President Jefferson, acknowledged that the impeachment of justices was "a farce which will not be tried again."

Jefferson proved prophetic, except for several inchoate efforts in recent years to impeach Justice William O. Douglas (1939-1975) and Chief Justice Earl Warren (1953-1969).

The first impeachment attempt against Douglas came after he had stayed the execution of convicted spies Julius and Ethel Rosenberg in 1953. That resolution was tabled by the Senate Judiciary Committee after a one-day hearing.

The second effort came on April 15, 1970, a week after the Senate's rejection of President Nixon's nomination of G. Harrold Carswell to the Supreme Court. In a speech on the House floor on that date, Minority Leader Gerald R. Ford, R-Mich., charged that Douglas (1) had not disqualified himself from a 1970 Supreme Court case involving Ralph Ginzburg, publisher of *Eros* magazine, although Douglas had received $350 for a 1969 article in another magazine published by Ginzburg; (2) had allegedly sanctioned revolution in his book, *Points of Rebellion* (Random House, 1970); (3) was the author of an article entitled "Redress in Revolution" in the April 1970 issue of *Evergreen Review,* which contained a number of nude photographs; (4) practiced law in violation of federal statutes by assisting in the establishment of the Albert Parvin Foundation in 1960 and in giving the foundation legal advice; and (5) served as a consultant of the "leftish" Center for the Study of Democratic Institutions at a time when the center was the recipient of Parvin Foundation funds.

On Dec. 3, 1970, a special House subcommittee created to investigate the charges against Douglas concluded that there were no grounds for impeachment.

The efforts to impeach Chief Justice Warren never got as far as those against Douglas. Most of the opposition to Warren came from right-wing groups angered over the Warren Court's expansion of individual, civil and criminal rights. The demand for Warren's impeachment was confined, for the most part, to the fulminations of the John Birch Society and to a grass-roots bumper-sticker campaign throughout the South.

Extra-Judicial Activities

A Supreme Court justice cannot be compelled to take any extra-judicial assignments but is free to engage in such activities if he wishes to. The use of this freedom has sparked considerable controversy both inside the court and among its critics. It was Justice Douglas' extra-judicial activities that prompted the 1970 impeachment effort against him.

A Yen for Politics

The extra-judicial activities that cause most concern are those in which a political motive is suspected. Before 1900, the political activities of the justices involved a generally less-than-subtle quest for elective office or outright endorsement of or opposition to political candidates.

As Justice Owen J. Roberts pointed out in a 1948 speech, "every justice who has ever sat on that Court who was bitten by political ambition and has actively promoted his own candidacy for office has hurt his own career as a judge and has hurt the Court." [94]

The early justices did not hesitate to campaign openly for their party's candidates. Justices Samuel Chase (1796-1811) and Bushrod Washington (1799-1829) campaigned actively for presidential candidates John Adams and Charles Pinckney, respectively, in 1800. Chase's campaigning was denounced by the anti-Federalist press, which complained, somewhat disingenuously, that he was neglecting his court duties.

Other political-minded 19th century justices included Smith Thompson (1823-1843), John McLean (1830-1861), Salmon P. Chase (the Chief Justice — 1864-1873 — who presided over the Senate impeachment trial of President Andrew Johnson), David Davis (1862-1877) and Stephen J.

Field (1863-1897). Like Chief Justice Jay before him, Justice Thompson, a Democrat, ran for governor of New York in 1828 but, unlike Jay, conducted an all-out campaign — which he lost.

Justice McLean, who before coming to the court in 1830 had served in the Cabinets of Presidents James Monroe and John Quincy Adams, sought and failed to receive his party's presidential nomination in 1836, 1848, 1852 and 1856. Referring to McLean specifically and to the tendency of justices during that period to become involved in politics, Alexander Bickel wrote "that the recurrence of justices with manifest political aspirations would in time destroy an institution whose strength derives from consent based on confidence." The conduct of justices acting upon their "manifest political aspirations," Bickel continued, "is awkward, unseemly and may give occasion for dire suspicions." [95]

Before his appointment as Chief Justice in 1864, Salmon P. Chase had been a U.S. senator, a governor, a Cabinet member and a presidential candidate. His political activities did not cease on the court. From the bench in 1868 he unsuccessfully sought the presidential nomination of both parties.

Justice David Davis accepted nomination as a minor party candidate for president in 1872 before resigning from the court in 1877 to serve in the Senate. Stephen J. Field periodically indicated his availability for the Democratic presidential nomination.

Far fewer justices have sought elective office in the 20th century. Charles Evans Hughes resigned his seat on the court to run for president in 1916. Justice Robert H. Jackson was approached to run for governor of New York. Presidents Roosevelt in 1944 and Truman in 1948 both considered Justice William O. Douglas as a running mate. After President Eisenhower suffered a heart attack, Chief Justice Earl Warren was widely considered a possible Republican presidential nominee in 1956.

1876 Electoral Commission

One ostensibly public-spirited activity on the part of five justices ended up involving the court in one of its most serious political controversies when Justices Nathan Clifford (1858-1881), Samuel F. Miller (1862-1890), Stephen J. Field (1863-1897), William Strong (1870-1880) and Joseph P. Bradley (1870-1892) were appointed to serve on the electoral commission which resolved the disputed presidential election between Democratic candidate Samuel J. Tilden and Republican candidate Rutherford B. Hayes in 1876.

Congress set up the commission in January 1877 and specified that it be composed of 15 members: three Republicans and two Democrats from the Senate, two Republicans and three Democrats from the House and two Democrats and two Republicans from the Supreme Court. The court itself was to choose a fifth justice. The court finally selected Bradley, a Republican. Dexter Perkins and Glyndon G. Van Deusen wrote that "Justice Bradley, at first in favor of giving Florida's electoral vote to Tilden, changed his mind between midnight and the morning of the day the decision was announced; there is considerable evidence that he yielded to Republican pressure." [96] The commission's vote, announced Feb. 10, 1877, favored Hayes, and Congress acquiesced on March 2, 1877.

Charles Warren pointed out that the justices' service on this commission did not enhance the court's prestige.

"The partisan excitement caused by this election and by the inauguration of Hayes led some newspapers to assert that public confidence in the judges had been weakened, and that the country would be the less willing to accept the doctrines laid down by the Court." [97]

'Public Service'

Some 20th century justices have ignored the lesson of the Hayes-Tilden Electoral Commission that participation on supposedly non-partisan commissions or investigative bodies can involve the court in political controversy. Among these instances were the participation of Justice Joseph R. Lamar (1911-1916) in international arbitration cases; Justice Owen J. Roberts' role on the German-American Mixed Claims Commission and the Pearl Harbor Review Commission and, most controversially, Justice Robert H. Jackson's prosecution of Nazi war criminals at the Nuremberg Nazi trials, and Chief Justice Earl Warren's role as head of a seven-member commission to investigate the assassination of President John F. Kennedy.

Jackson at Nuremberg. Several justices were troubled by Jackson's one-year absence from the court because of his war-trial duties. Chief Justice Harlan F. Stone had opposed Jackson's acceptance of the assignment, and some of the other justices were angry about the extra work that Jackson's absence imposed on them. The situation became even worse after Stone's death in April 1946.

As John P. Frank wrote: "Taking a justice away from his primary duty can be done only at the expense of that duty. Stone's acute bitterness over the burdens placed upon the court by the absence of Jackson (who, Stone sputtered, was off running a lynching bee at Nuremberg) is understandable. Such extra-judicial work may also involve justices in controversies that lower the prestige so valuable to the court." [98]

But the fact that the court did suffer some loss of prestige because of Jackson's role at Nuremberg had less to do with the workload burdens placed on the other justices than with Jackson's assault on Justice Hugo L. Black, issued from Nuremberg. "The most recent direct outbreak of one justice against another was Jackson's attack on Black at the time of the appointment of Chief Justice Vinson in 1946. Jackson, who was abroad at Nuremberg trying German war criminals at the time and who had deeply desired the place for himself, apparently felt that Black was in some way responsible for the appointment of Vinson. He issued a vitriolic public statement denouncing Black for having participated in a certain case in which Jackson felt that Black should have disqualified himself." Amidst the publicity that the statement received, Justice Black "maintained a complete silence." [99]

Somewhat surprisingly, Justice Felix Frankfurter did not share his colleagues' resentment of Jackson's role in the Nuremberg trials. Years before his appointment to the Supreme Court in 1939 and after his retirement in 1962, Justice Frankfurter opposed the participation of justices in any public activities that were not strictly relevant to their judicial responsibilities.

In 1929, for example, Professor Frankfurter had written that "In suggesting that judges engage in public activities off the bench, we are in danger of forgetting that it is the business of judges to be judges. . . . It is necessary for judges to be less worldly than others in order to be more judicial." [100] After his retirement as a Supreme Court justice in 1962, Frankfurter also criticized Chief Justice Earl Warren's decision to head the investigation of President Kennedy's assassination.

Although Frankfurter resigned immediately from the American Civil Liberties Union, the National Association for the Advancement of Colored People and even the Harvard Club when named to the court, he nevertheless served on several presidential and national commissions while serving as a member of the court.

The Warren Commission. To ascertain all the facts and circumstances relating to the assassination of President Kennedy, President Johnson created a seven-man investigating commission on Nov. 29, 1963. Chief Justice Warren agreed to head the commission, which also included Sens. Richard B. Russell, D-Ga., and John Sherman Cooper, R-Ky.; Reps. Hale Boggs, D-La., and Gerald R. Ford, R-Mich.; Allen W. Dulles, former director of the CIA; and John J. McCloy, former disarmament adviser to President Kennedy.

The Warren Commission released its findings on Sept. 27, 1964, concluding that Lee Harvey Oswald, "acting alone and without advice or assistance," had shot President Kennedy. Before the report was released, critics of Warren's performance on the court denounced the Chief Justice for neglecting his judicial duties and for participating in such a "political" undertaking. After the findings were released, those convinced that there had been a "conspiracy" joined in the criticism.

White House Advisers

Justice Frankfurter's continuing interest in political and other non-judicial matters was particularly evident in his role as adviser to President Franklin D. Roosevelt on a variety of matters, foreign and domestic. During the spring and summer of 1939, for example, Frankfurter sent almost 300 notes to Roosevelt warning of the threat posed by Hitler and advising the president of the actions that should be taken to counter the German threat. These and subsequent actions led observers to label Frankfurter the "outside insider in the Roosevelt administration." [101]

Supreme Court justices have been giving advice to presidents and other elected officials since the time of the first Chief Justice, John Jay. This informal relationship generally has resulted in criticism of the justices and the court. When President Roosevelt indicated at a press conference in September 1939 that he had discussed the situation in Europe with Justices Harlan Fiske Stone and Felix Frankfurter, there was a storm of protest over the involvement of justices in the foreign policy deliberations and decisions of the executive branch. Stone thereafter refused all invitations to confer with the president. Frankfurter, however, continued advising Roosevelt and his successors.

A more recent example is the advice that Justice Abe Fortas continued to give President Lyndon Johnson after Fortas' appointment to the court in 1965. Fortas' role as an adviser to Johnson was a major factor in his failure to win Senate confirmation as Chief Justice in 1968. It likely played some part in events leading to Fortas' resignation from the court in May 1969.

James F. Simon described the circumstances leading to Fortas' resignation. In the summer of 1968: "President Johnson named Associate Justice Abe Fortas to succeed Chief Justice Warren. At first, anti-Fortas forces, led by Republican Senator Robert P. Griffin of Michigan, opposed the nomination primarily because it had been made by a

'lame duck' president. At the Senate's confirmation hearings, Fortas ran into deeper trouble. The chief justice-designate, it was learned, had counseled the president on national policy and had even done some behind-the-scenes lobbying on the president's behalf while sitting on the Supreme Court. Later, when Fortas admitted that he had received $15,000 for conducting a series of seminars at American University, his ethics as well as his politics were brought into question. As a result, his nomination as Chief Justice languished and was finally withdrawn by President Johnson." [102]

Fortas retained his seat as an associate justice. But in May 1969, *Life* magazine revealed that since becoming a justice Fortas had accepted — and then returned several months later — $20,000 from a charitable foundation controlled by the family of indicted stock manipulator Louis E. Wolfson. Shortly thereafter, Fortas resigned. In a letter to Chief Justice Earl Warren on May 14, 1969, Fortas stated:

> There has been no wrongdoing on my part....
> There has been no default in the performance of my judicial duties in accordance with the high standards of the office I hold. So far as I am concerned, the welfare and maximum effectiveness of the Court to perform its critical role in our system of government are factors that are paramount to all others. It is this consideration that prompts my resignation which, I hope, by terminating the public controversy, will permit the Court to proceed with its work without the harassment of debate concerning one of its members. [103] *(Complete text, p. 983)*

Perquisites

The scandal surrounding Justice Fortas' acceptance of a fee from the Wolfson Foundation prompted Chief Justice Warren, shortly before his resignation, to urge adoption of a judicial code of ethics requiring judges to file an annual report on investments, assets, income, gifts and liabilities and prohibiting them from accepting compensation other than their judicial salaries.

In 1973 the Judicial Conference, under Chief Justice Warren Burger, adopted resolutions asking judges to report gifts of more than $100 and any income from outside work. Indebtedness or stock earnings need not be reported. The ethics code for federal judges does not require Supreme Court justices to file income disclosure reports. But most of the justices have periodically submitted such statements to the Supreme Court clerk reporting their outside income and gifts.

Since each justice is paid an annual salary of $72,000 — the Chief Justice makes $75,000 — there is little need for a justice to seek outside sources of income. This was not always the case, however. Some of the early justices were so strapped for money and so penuriously reimbursed for their services on the court that they were obliged to seek additional sources of income. *(Salaries of the Justices, p. 774)*

Justices have a number of perquisites. These include two secretaries, a messenger and three law clerks. Like the Chief Justice, they also have their own offices, the services of a court barber and the use of the court dining room, exercise room and library. Unlike the Chief Justice, however, the associate justices are not provided with a government-paid car and chauffeur and must get to and from work on their own.

Supporting Personnel

Compared to the executive and legislative branches of the federal government, the Supreme Court employs few people and spends relatively little money. Only about 300 people now work for the court, and its recent annual budgets have been in the comparatively modest $10-million range.

Some court employees, like the clerk of the court, the marshal, the reporter of decisions, the press officer, the librarian and their staffs, as well as pages and security officers, are appointed by the court. The law clerks are chosen by the justices themselves. In addition, several other groups work with the court but are not employees of it. These include the Office of Solicitor General, the Supreme Court bar, the Federal Judicial Center, the Administrative Office of the U.S. Courts, the U.S. Judicial Conference and the Supreme Court Historical Association.

Solicitor General

The solicitor general, the third highest-ranked official in the Department of Justice, is appointed by the president to represent the U.S. government before the Supreme Court. He decides which cases the government should ask the court to review and what the government's legal position toward them will be. He and his staff prepare the government's briefs and supporting data and argue the government's case before the court. When he chooses not to argue a case himself he assigns the task to one of his staff. A few cases of particular importance may be argued by the attorney general, the solicitor general's superior.

One observer who spent many years in the Office of the Solicitor General wrote that the solicitor general "may not unfairly be described as the highest government official who acts primarily as a lawyer. He has few administrative responsibilities; he can devote his time to studying the legal problems which come before him. Moreover, he must stand on his own feet when he is presenting the most important government cases to the Supreme Court. . . . The solicitor general regards himself — and the Supreme Court regards him — not only as an officer of the executive branch but also as an officer of the Court." [104]

The principal duties of the solicitor general's office are to decide which cases the government should appeal from the lower courts, to review the briefs in those cases written by branches of the Justice Department or the independent agencies of the government, and to participate in oral arguments before the court. The briefs that are reviewed can be approved without change or totally rewritten. Most are revised and modified to some extent in collaboration with the author of the draft.

The Office of the Solicitor General has a heavy workload. During the October 1975 term, for example, the solicitor general participated in 2,219 cases — about 47 percent of the court's total caseload. And of the 179 cases argued in that term, the solicitor general was a party or *amicus curiae* in 121 of them. Lawyers from the solicitor general's office are the only attorneys who still wear frock coats and striped trousers when presenting oral arguments.

The solicitor general is under considerable pressure to limit the number of cases that he brings before the court. As Robert L. Stern noted, this pressure is "partly self-serving and partly not." On the more objective level, the solicitor general

> . . .is aware of the necessity from the standpoint of the effective administration of the judicial system of restricting the number of cases taken to the Supreme Court to the number that the Court can hear. This alone permits the Court to give adequate consideration to the important matters which the highest tribunal in the land should decide. . . . A heavy additional burden would be imposed on the Court if the government, with its great volume of litigation, disregarded that policy and acted like the normal litigant who wants to take one more shot at reversing a decision which is obviously wrong because he lost.

> The selfish reason for the Solicitor General's self-restraint in petitioning for certiorari is to give the Court confidence in government petitions. It is hoped and believed — although no one who has not been on the Court can be sure — that the Court will realize that the Solicitor General will not assert that an issue is of general importance unless it is — and that confidence in the Solicitor General's attempt to adhere to the Court's own standards will cause the Court to grant more government petitions. [105]

The post of solicitor general was created by Congress in 1870 with the establishment of the Department of Justice. Before that time, the functions of the solicitor general were carried out by the attorney general. Congress explained that its purpose in establishing the new office was to provide "a staff of law officers sufficiently numerous and of sufficient ability to transact this law business of the Government in all parts of the United States." The law also said that the solicitor general should be "a man of sufficient learning, ability and experience that he can be sent . . . into any court wherever the government has any interest in litigation, and there present the case of the United States as it should be presented." [106]

At present, the solicitor general is paid the Executive Level III salary of $52,500 a year.

As far as the general public is concerned, solicitors general are fairly anonymous figures, although several — Taft, Reed, Jackson and Thurgood Marshall — later became justices of the Supreme Court. One recent exception was Robert H. Bork (1973-77). Bork's notoriety, however, had nothing to do with his court-related duties but, rather, with his role in the famous "Saturday Night Massacre" following President Nixon's decision to fire special Watergate prosecutor Archibald Cox — himself a former solicitor general (1961-65) — on Oct. 20, 1973. Attorney General Elliot Richardson and Deputy Attorney General William Ruckelshaus resigned rather than obey Nixon's order to fire Cox. After the resignations of Richardson and Ruckelshaus, Bork, as the highest-ranked official left in the Justice Department, took command and fired Cox.

Clerk of the Court

The clerk of the court is the chief administrative officer of the court, and his office is responsible for conducting almost all its business. The office was established by the

Solicitors General

Name	Term		State of Origin	President
Benjamin H. Bristow	Oct. 11, 1870	Nov. 15, 1872	Kentucky	Grant
Samuel F. Phillips	Nov. 15, 1872	May 3, 1885	North Carolina	Grant
John Goode	May 1, 1885	Aug. 5, 1886	Virginia	Cleveland
George A. Jenks	July 30, 1886	May 29, 1889	Pennsylvania	Cleveland
Orlow W. Chapman	May 29, 1889	Jan. 19, 1890	New York	Harrison
William Howard Taft	Feb. 4, 1890	Mar. 20, 1892	Ohio	Harrison
Charles H. Aldrich	Mar. 21, 1892	May 28, 1893	Illinois	Harrison
Lawrence Maxwell Jr.	Apr. 6, 1893	Jan. 30, 1895	Ohio	Cleveland
Holmes Conrad	Feb. 6, 1895	July 8, 1897	Virginia	Cleveland
John K. Richards	July 1, 1897	Mar. 16, 1903	Ohio	McKinley
Henry M. Hoyt	Feb. 25, 1903	Mar. 31, 1909	Pennsylvania	Roosevelt
Lloyd Wheaton Bowers	Apr. 1, 1909	Sept. 9, 1910	Illinois	Taft
Frederick W. Lehman	Dec. 12, 1910	July 15, 1912	Missouri	Taft
William Marshall Bullitt	July 16, 1912	Mar. 11, 1913	Kentucky	Taft
John William Davis	Aug. 30, 1913	Nov. 26, 1918	West Virginia	Wilson
Alexander C. King	Nov. 27, 1918	May 23, 1920	Georgia	Wilson
William L. Frierson	June 1, 1920	June 30, 1921	Tennessee	Wilson
James M. Beck	June 30, 1921	June 7, 1925	New Jersey	Harding
William D. Mitchell	June 4, 1925	Mar. 5, 1929	Minnesota	Coolidge
Charles Evans Hughes Jr.	May 27, 1929	Apr. 16, 1930	New York	Hoover
Thomas D. Thacher	Mar. 22, 1930	May 4, 1933	New York	Hoover
James Crawford Biggs	May 4, 1933	Mar. 24, 1935	North Carolina	Roosevelt
Stanley Reed	Mar. 23, 1935	Jan. 30, 1938	Kentucky	Roosevelt
Robert H. Jackson	Mar. 5, 1938	Jan. 17, 1940	New York	Roosevelt
Francis Biddle	Jan. 22, 1940	Sept. 4, 1941	Pennsylvania	Roosevelt
Charles Fahy	Nov. 15, 1941	Sept. 27, 1945	New Mexico	Roosevelt
J. Howard McGrath	Oct. 4, 1945	Oct. 7, 1946	Rhode Island	Truman
Philip B. Perlman	July 30, 1947	Aug. 15, 1952	Maryland	Truman
Walter J. Cummings Jr.	Dec. 2, 1952	Mar. 1, 1953	Illinois	Truman
Simon E. Sobeloff	Feb. 10, 1954	July 19, 1956	Maryland	Eisenhower
J. Lee Rankin	Aug. 4, 1956	Jan. 23, 1961	Nebraska	Eisenhower
Archibald Cox	Jan. 24, 1961	July 31, 1965	Massachusetts	Kennedy
Thurgood Marshall	Aug. 11, 1965	Aug. 30, 1967	New York	Johnson
Erwin N. Griswold	Oct. 12, 1967	June 25, 1973	Massachusetts	Johnson
Robert H. Bork	June 26, 1973	Jan. 20, 1977	Connecticut	Nixon
Wade Hampton McCree Jr.	March 4, 1977		Michigan	Carter

first formal rule of the court, adopted in February 1790. Through the years, the clerk's duties have increased enormously. The clerk now has the largest staff at the court — more than thirty people.

The responsibilities of the clerk of the court have recently been outlined as including:

(a) the administration of the court's dockets and argument calendars;

(b) the receipt and recording of all motions, petitions, jurisdictional statements, briefs and other documents filed with the court;

(c) the distribution of those various papers to the justices;

(d) the collection of filing fees and the assessment of costs;

(e) the preparation and maintenance of the court's order list and journal, upon which are entered all the court's formal judgments and mandates;

(f) the preparation of the court's formal judgments and mandates;

(g) the notification to counsel and lower courts of all formal actions taken by the court, including written opinions;

(h) the supervision of the printing of briefs and appendices after review has been granted in *in forma pauperis* cases;

(i) the requesting and securing of the certified record below upon the grant of review or other direction of the court;

(j) the supervision of the admission of attorneys to the Supreme Court bar, as well as occasional disbarments;

(k) the constant giving of procedural advice, by telephone, mail and in person, to those counsel and litigants who need assistance or assurance as to the court's rules and procedures.

To help the clerk and his staff carry out these many functions, a computerized information system was installed in 1976. [107]

To date, there have been only 16 clerks of the court. Four of them served for a quarter of a century or more: Elias B. Caldwell (1800-1825); William T. Carroll (1827-1863); J. H. McKenney (1880-1913) and C. Elmore Cropley (1927-1952). The first clerk, John Tucker, was selected on the third day of the court's first session, Feb. 3, 1790, to oversee the courtroom and library, manage subordinate

Clerks of the Supreme Court

Name	Term	State of Origin
John Tucker	1790-1791	Massachusetts
Samuel Bayard	1791-1800	Pennsylvania
Elias B. Caldwell	1800-1825	New Jersey
William Griffith	1826-1827	New Jersey
William T. Carroll	1827-1863	Maryland
D. W. Middleton	1863-1880	District of Columbia
J. H. McKenney	1880-1913	Maryland
James D. Maher	1913-1921	New York
William R. Stansbury	1921-1927	District of Columbia
C. Elmore Cropley	1927-1952	District of Columbia
Harold B. Willey	1952-1956	Oregon
John T. Fey	1956-1958	Virginia
James R. Browning	1958-1961	Montana
John F. Davis	1961-1970	Maine
E. Robert Seaver	1970-1972	Missouri
Michael Rodak Jr.	1972-	West Virginia

employees, collect the salaries of the justices and find them lodgings when necessary.

The 1790 rule that established the position of clerk prohibited him from practicing law before the court while he was a clerk. In the early years the clerk performed many of the duties later taken over by the reporter and the marshal. So varied were the responsibilities of the early clerks that they were described as a combination business manager-errand boy for the justices and the lawyers who appeared before the court.

The importance of the clerk was summed up nearly a century ago by a man who had had considerable experience with the clerk's office, Augustus H. Garland, former governor of Arkansas, former Democratic senator from that state and former U.S. attorney general.

Garland wrote:

It is well to note that it is quite important for lawyers practicing in that Court to see much of the Clerk's office and to know its workings. If any motion is to be had or proceedings asked in Court not specifically provided for by law or rule, it is wise to seek advice there beforehand. . . . Many useless and sometimes unpleasant collisions between the Court and counsel are avoided by this precaution. Even the oldest and most experienced attorneys are not ashamed to consult the Clerk's office and they do not hesitate to do so.[108]

Although the Office of the Clerk of the Court was established in 1790, provision was not made for his salary until nine years later. In 1799 Congress provided "That the compensation to the Clerk of the Supreme Court of the United States shall be as follows, to wit: for his attendance in Court, ten dollars per day, and for his other services, double the fees of the clerk of the Supreme Court of the state in which the Supreme Court of the United States shall be holden."[109]

For almost 100 years the office of the clerk was self-supporting. It paid salaries and other expenses of its operations out of filing fees. The generous fees and other allowances gave some of the early clerks a handsome annual stipend. In 1881, for example, the clerk's net income was almost $30,000 a year — only slightly less than the president's and considerably more than the justices'.[110] Strict accountability for the court's funds was not imposed until 1883. The filing fees now go to the U.S. Treasury, and Congress appropriates the money for the salaries and expenses of the clerk's office. The clerk now has an annual salary of $47,500.

Marshal of the Court

The post of marshal of the court was not formally established until 1867. Many of the duties assigned to the marshal at that time were performed by the marshal of the district in which the court was located. Between 1794 and 1867, for example, the 12 men who served as marshal of the District of Columbia also served, informally, as marshal of the court. The first of these was David Lennox and the last was David Gooding.

In the Judiciary Act of 1867, Congress first gave the court authority to appoint a marshal and, if necessary, to remove him from his post, and to fix his compensation. Several of his tasks, which included ensuring the security of the court, overseeing its protocol functions and supervising payment of its expenses, formerly had been performed by the clerk of the court.

The marshal's current functions include maintaining order in the building and in the courtroom: he directs the court's police force of about seven men and women. They supervise the security of the building and check the brief-cases and purses of all visitors who enter the building. The marshal and his aides also receive visiting dignitaries and escort the justices to formal functions outside the court. He supervises inaugural ceremonies for new justices and arranges memorial services for those who have died.

During public sessions of the court, the marshal (or his deputy) and the clerk — both dressed in cutaways — station themselves at either end of the bench. At exactly 10 a.m., the marshal pounds the gavel and announces: "The Honorable, the Chief Justice and the Associate Justices of the Supreme Court of the United States." As the justices take their seats, he calls for silence by crying "Oyez" ("Hear ye") three times and announces: "All persons having business before the honorable, the Supreme Court of the United States, are admonished to draw near and give their attention, for the court is now sitting. God save the United States and this honorable Court."

The marshal is responsible for seating arrangements during the public sessions and may refuse admission to

Marshals of the Court

Richard C. Parsons (1867-1872)
John C. Nicolay (1872-1887)
John Montgomery Wright (1888-1915)
Frank Key Green (1915-1938)
Thomas E. Waggaman (1938-1952)
T. Perry Lippitt (1952-1972)
Frank M. Hepler (1972-1976)
Alfred Wong (1976-   )

anyone whose attire or conduct does not meet court standards. During oral argument, the marshal or his assistant flashes the white and red lights to warn counsel that his time for presenting arguments is about to expire.

The marshal also serves as the court's business manager and paymaster. He pays the salaries of the justices and all other court employees and disburses other court funds. In addition, the marshal is directed to "serve and execute all process and orders issued by the Court or a member thereof." Today, the marshal of the court delegates the actual serving of papers — usually disbarment orders — to U.S. marshals. In earlier days, serving of papers was sometimes more dramatic.

Marshal Frank K. Green (1915-38), for example, served a subpoena on business tycoon J. Pierpont Morgan Jr. when government officials were trying to regain possession of Martha Washington's will, which Morgan's father had allegedly stolen. Upon receiving the subpoena, Morgan returned the will.

The marshal also appoints and has jurisdiction over the court's messengers, who replaced the court pages in the early 1970s.

The marshal currently receives an annual salary of $42,000.

Reporter of Decisions

The reporter of decisions is responsible for editing the opinions of the court and supervising their printing and publication in the official *United States Reports*. Publication is a slow process. The reporter and his staff of ten check all citations after the opinions of the justices have been delivered, correct typographical and other errors in the opinions and add the headnotes, the voting lineup of the justices and the names of counsel that now appear in the published version of the opinions.

The court's orders and decisions are first circulated as "Preliminary Prints." Users of these preliminary prints are "requested to notify the reporter of decisions . . . of any typographical or other formal errors, in order that corrections may be made before the bound volume goes to press." The orders and decisions are printed by the U.S. Government Printing Office and sold by the Superintendent of Documents.

The post of reporter of decisions had a rather informal beginning. The first reporter, Alexander J. Dallas (1790-1800), was self-appointed. Before the court moved to Philadelphia, Dallas had published a volume on Pennsylvania court decisions. When the court began meeting in Philadelphia in 1791, Dallas' book contained the cases of both the Pennsylvania court and the Supreme Court. Most accounts of the early Supreme Court indicate that Dallas, a lawyer, undertook the first reports as a public service. Dallas — who was also a journalist, editor, patron of the arts and secretary of the Treasury (1814-1816) — published four volumes of decisions covering the Supreme Court's first decade.

Dallas was succeeded unofficially by William Cranch in 1802.

While reporting on the court's decisions, Cranch continued to sit as a judge and later chief justice of the circuit court in Washington, D.C. During Cranch's service as reporter of decisions, the justices began supplementing their oral opinions with written texts in important cases. This was of immeasurable assistance to Cranch and subsequent reporters. Cranch, whose reports were highly praised

Reporters of Decisions

Name	Term of Office
Alexander J. Dallas	1790-1800
William Cranch	1801-1815
Henry Wheaton	1816-1827
Richard Peters Jr.	1828-1842
Benjamin C. Howard	1843-1860
Jeremiah S. Black	1861-1862
John W. Wallace	1867-1874
William T. Otto	1875-1882
J. C. Bancroft Davis	1883-1902
Charles Henry Butler	1902-1915
Ernest Knaebel	1916-1943
Walter Wyatt	1946-1963
Henry Putzel Jr.	1964-1979
Henry C. Lind	1979-

for their accuracy and clarity, believed that public scrutiny of opinions was needed to keep the justices from making arbitrary decisions.

Cranch's successor, Henry Wheaton, was the first reporter formally appointed by the court. In 1816 Congress provided for publication of court decisions and, a year later, set the reporter's salary at $1,000 a year. The Judiciary Act of 1817 mandated that, for this salary, the reporter had to publish each opinion within six months of a decision and provide 80 copies to the secretary of state for distribution. The reports continued to be sold to the public, at $5 a volume, and the reporter was still able to share in the profits, such as they were.

After he retired in 1827 to become minister to Denmark, Wheaton and his successor, Richard Peters Jr., became involved themselves in a Supreme Court case. [111]

Peters was determined to increase the then-meager sales of the reports and his own profits as well. He therefore decided to revise and streamline the earlier reports and publish them in "Peters' Condensed Reports" at a price of $36. Since the purchase of Peters' reports would make it unnecessary for the interested public to purchase Wheaton's reports, the former reporter of decisions sued Peters, charging a violation of copyright. The court ruled, however, that court opinions were in the public domain.

As Augustus H. Garland noted in his book on the Supreme Court, "The office of the Reporter is not a . . . bed of roses. The work is constant, arduous and exacting. A failure to give full scope in the syllabus . . . to the utterances of a judge brings wrath upon him." [112] Reporters Benjamin C. Howard (1843-1860) and John W. Wallace (1867-1874) felt the wrath of several justices.

In 1855 Justice Peter V. Daniel (1842-1860) wrote to reporter Howard complaining that his name had not been inserted at the beginning of his dissenting opinion and that he was henceforth uncertain that he would allow his dissents to be published in the reports. Unfortunately for Howard, he had omitted Daniel's name. Justices Noah H. Swayne (1862-1881) and Nathan Clifford (1858-1881) complained that reporter Wallace failed to publish their opinions or butchered them with his editing.

Wallace was the last reporter to have his name identified with the court's published reports. The first 90 volumes of the reports were titled 1-4 Dall.; 1-15 Cranch; 1-12

Wheat. 1-16 Pet.; 1-24 How.; 1-2 Black and 1-23 Wall. After 1874 the name of the reporter was no longer used as part of the formal citation.

The reporter of decisions is now paid an annual salary of $45,500. The first two reporters, Dallas and Cranch, were paid no salary at all and relied on the sale of their reports or on outside jobs for their income. Congress provided an annual stipend of $1,000 a year; reporters were still obliged to rely on sales of the reports or to moonlight to supplement their incomes. Henry Wheaton, for example, argued a number of cases before the Supreme Court and then reported them.

Supreme Court Bar

When the Supreme Court first convened in February 1790, one of its first actions was to establish qualifications for lawyers who wished to practice before the court. Rule 2, adopted at that time, provided that "it shall be requisite to the admission of attorneys and counsellors to practice in this court, that they shall have been such for three years past in the Supreme Court of the State to which they respectively belong, and that their private and professional character shall appear to be fair."

Qualifications

The two requirements for admission to the Supreme Court bar — acceptable personal and professional character, and qualification to practice before a state's or territory's highest court — have remained the same since 1790. In nearly 200 years since the court was established, some 150,000 attorneys have been admitted to the Supreme Court bar. Some 6,000 are now admitted each year.

The bar of the Supreme Court has been called "a heterogeneous collection of individual lawyers located in all parts of the nation. There is no permanent or formal leadership." [113] Although some lawyers seek admission to the Supreme Court bar merely for their own personal prestige, membership does have a real function. No attorney can enter an appearance in a case or by himself process any case to completion unless he is a member of the Supreme Court bar.[114] A non-member may work on a case, but at least one member of the bar must sponsor any case filed with the court.

The Royal Exchange, New York City, first home of the U.S. Supreme Court.

New Offices

During the 1970s two new support offices were added at the Supreme Court — the legal office and the curatorial office.

Created in 1973, the legal office is composed of two attorneys, known as legal officers, who assist the court with procedural questions arising from petitions for writs of certiorari and applications for extraordinary relief. They also aid some justices with their circuit duties.

The curatorial office was created in 1974 to maintain records of gifts to the court, to care for its historical collection, to develop exhibits and to answer questions from the public concerning court history and the historical collection.

A lawyer who believes he meets the two requirements for admission to the bar must submit two documents to the clerk of the court: (1) "a certificate from the presiding judge or clerk of the proper court evidencing his admission to practice there and that he is presently in good standing, and (2) his personal statement, on a form approved by the Court and furnished by the Clerk, which shall be endorsed by two members of this Court who are not related to the applicant." [115] Applications are screened by the clerk of the court's office, and lawyers whose applications are in order are notified by the clerk.

Before 1970 lawyers had only one means of entry which still applies — an oral motion in open court. The attorney selects a day when the court is in public session and notifies the clerk. The applicant then finds a standing member of the Supreme Court bar who is willing and able to appear in court with him. Early on the morning of his swearing-in, he appears at the office of the admissions clerk and pays a $25 admission fee. When the court convenes at 10 a.m. on the appointed day, the Chief Justice announces that admissions will be entertained at that time. The clerk then calls the sponsor to the rostrum, he requests that the applicant be admitted to the bar, and the Chief Justice announces that the motion is granted.

After all the motions have been made and granted, the new members are welcomed by the Chief Justice, and the clerk of the court administers the oath to the group.

In 1970, largely as a result of the increasing amount of time being spent on the oral motions in open session, the court began allowing applicants to submit written motions without making a formal appearance. These so-called "mail-order admissions" now constitute 80 percent or more of all admissions to the Supreme Court bar.

Attorneys can be disbarred or can resign from the Supreme Court bar. Disbarment generally follows a showing that an attorney has been disbarred from practice in some jurisdiction or "has been guilty of conduct unbecoming a member of the bar of this Court." [116]

To some observers, including John P. Frank, modern members of the Supreme Court bar seem to lack the dramatic flair and oratorical genius that 19th century legal luminaries like Daniel Webster, Henry Clay, John C. Calhoun and Augustus H. Garland exhibited when presenting arguments before the court.

"The most striking difference between the argument of the 19th century and that of today is the difference in the lawyers themselves. In the 19th century, there was a Supreme Court bar, a group of lawyers in or about Washington for at least portions of the year to whom other lawyers sent their cases in the same fashion that a New York lawyer today might send a piece of San Francisco business to a San Francisco lawyer," writes Frank. [117]

But, he continued, "the ease of modern transportation coupled with the desire of individual lawyers to have the experience of appearing in the Supreme Court have almost totally destroyed the system of a Supreme Court bar, so that today a very small number of appearances makes a man an unusually experienced Supreme Court practitioner. The number of lawyers under the age of sixty engaged solely in private practice who have appeared before the court a substantial number of times could be quickly counted. Today the lawyer from Little Rock takes in his own case, whereas in 1880 he would have retained A. H. Garland, who as attorney general and private counsel argued 130 cases. Jeremiah Sullivan Black presented 16 cases between 1861 and 1865 and won 13, including eight reversals of lower courts. Today a very experienced private practitioner may have argued five cases in a lifetime." [118]

Press Officer

The court's press (or public information) office is responsible for answering questions from the public and the news media and distributing information about the court and the justices. The press officer is the public spokesman for the court in matters other than the interpretation of its opinions and orders. As has been noted, the justices believe that their opinions and orders must speak for themselves.

The public information office releases the opinions and orders of the court to the press soon after they are announced in open court. The court's informal orders, the schedule of court sessions and conferences, the activities of the justices, and changes in court procedures are usually placed on a bulletin board in the public information office. Special announcements about the court or the justices are released by the office.

Some of the major news media have offices next to the public information office. The press and the public also can read the file on current petitions, motions, briefs, responses and jurisdictional statements there.

The current public information officer is only the court's third since the post was established in 1935. His salary is $42,000 a year. The public information office has a staff of three. [119]

Librarian

The Supreme Court library, which contains about 250,000 volumes, is located on the third floor of the court building. Rule 2(1) of the court limits its use "to members of the bar of this Court, to members of Congress and the law offices of the executive or other departments of the Government." Usually, however, the library will grant access to its books to members of the public or press who specify a particular research interest.

Since 1887, when the post of librarian was created, there have been seven court librarians. The librarian's salary is now $45,000 a year.

In the early years of the court, the justices had no library of their own, and it was not until 1812 that Congress allowed the justices to use the Library of Congress. In 1832, after repeated refusals to give the court its own library, Congress gave the justices the 2,011 law books in the Library of Congress but insisted that congressmen retain

Old City Hall, Philadelphia, home of the Supreme Court, 1791-1800.

the right to use them as well. Since the court had no librarian at the time, the clerk of the court was put in charge of the books. By 1863 the number of law books had increased to almost 16,000. In 1884 the marshal of the court was given responsibility for the court's collection of books. The post of librarian, created in 1887, remained in the marshal's department until Congress made it a separate office in 1948.

The library has the most complete available set of the printed briefs, records and appendices of court cases. It also contains all federal, state and regional reports; federal and state statutory codes; legal periodicals; legal treatises; and digests and legislative and administrative source material. There are also special collections in international law, military law, British law, patent and trademark law and Supreme Court history.

When the clerk was in charge of the library in the 19th century, lawyers and others allowed to use the library could borrow no more than three books from the library at one time. The books had to be returned within a "reasonable" time. For books that were not returned within a "reasonable" time, the clerk imposed a fine of $1 a day on the

borrower. If a book was lost, the borrower had to pay twice the value of the lost book. This rule was changed to protect the court's collection. Books and other material cannot now be removed from the building, although members of the Supreme Court bar may request that material be sent to them when they are arguing a case.

Law Clerks

As the number of cases has increased over the years, the justices have relied more and more on their law clerks. In 1979 there are 32 law clerks serving the nine justices — almost twice the number employed 10 years ago. The Chief Justice and five most senior associate justices have four clerks each, while the other three justices manage with two or three clerks. The clerks are hired by the individual justices, usually for one year, and are paid $23,087 a year for their services. Some clerks, however, stay longer than a year.

The justices have complete discretion in hiring the law clerks they want. The clerks are generally selected from candidates at the top of their classes in the country's most prestigious law schools. Some have previously clerked for a lower court judge. The nature and amount of a clerk's work depends on the work habits of the particular justice. Years ago, Justice Brandeis once asked his clerk to check every page of every volume of *United States Reports* for information that Brandeis wanted. Justice Hugo L. Black insisted that some of his clerks play tennis with him. Chief Justice Stone liked his clerks to accompany him on his walks.

As John P. Frank, who clerked for Justice Black in the early 1950s, pointed out, "the tasks of the clerks are very much the product of the whims of their justices. In general, it is the job of the clerk to be eyes and legs for his judge, finding and bringing in useful materials." [120] The two major functions of the clerks are to read, analyze and often prepare memoranda for the justices on the thousands of cases that reach the court each year and to help otherwise in whatever way a justice expects in preparing the opinion that he will deliver.

Over the years, law clerks occasionally have been the subject of controversy. In the late 1950s, for example, conservative critics claimed that the court was a hotbed of radicalism and even communism. Because some of these critics were convinced that the clerks had a strong effect on the court's more liberal opinions, they convinced a few conservative congressmen to propose that appointments of law clerks be subject to Senate confirmation. While these efforts failed, there has been continuing debate and concern about just how much influence the clerks have on the opinions of the justices.

It has even been charged that law clerks have on occasion written the opinion issued in the name of the justices, but there has been no proof that any clerk has actually authored an opinion. How much of the preliminary writing a clerk may do is a well-guarded secret.

Three of the current justices served as law clerks: Justice Byron R. White clerked for Chief Justice Fred M. Vinson in 1946-47, Justice John Paul Stevens clerked for Justice Wiley B. Rutledge in 1947-48, and Justice William H. Rehnquist clerked for Justice Robert H. Jackson in 1952-53. All three tend to minimize the influence the clerks have on the justices and their opinions.

Justice Stevens has written that "an interesting loyalty develops betweeen clerks and their Justices. It is much like a lawyer-client relationship, close and confidential. Like a lawyer, a clerk can't tell his client, the Justice, what to do. He can only suggest what can happen if he does or doesn't do something." [121]

Justice White has said that "we couldn't get our work done without the clerks. But I don't think they influence the results here all that much. I like 'em around to hear their various views. When I served as a clerk, I don't think anything I ever did or said influenced my Justice. I felt I was doing Chief Justice Vinson a service by making sure that relevant considerations were placed before him, such as opinions from other courts, law journals, ideas of my own — things he wouldn't have time to dig up on his own." [122]

More than 20 years ago, William H. Rehnquist described his activities as clerk to Justice Jackson. "On a couple of occasions each term, Justice Jackson would ask each clerk to draft an opinion for him along lines which he suggested. If the clerk were reasonably faithful to his instructions and reasonably diligent in his work, the Justice would be quite charitable with his black pencil and paste pot. The result reached in these opinions was no less the product of Justice Jackson than those he drafted himself; in literary style, these opinions generally suffered by compari-

son with those which he had drafted. . . . The specter of the law clerk as a legal Rasputin, exerting an important influence on the cases actually decided by the Court, may be discarded at once. No published biographical materials dealing with any of the Justices suggest any such influence. I certainly learned of none during the time I spent as Clerk." [123]

Rehnquist — considered perhaps the most conservative member of the current court — criticized the clerks of the 1951-1952 terms not for their influence but their political bias. "After conceding a wide diversity of opinion among the clerks themselves, and further conceding the difficulties and possible inaccuracies inherent in political cataloguing of people, it is nonetheless fair to say that the political cast of the clerks as a group was to the 'left' of either the nation or the Court. Some of the tenets of the 'liberal' point of view which commanded the sympathy of a majority of the clerks I knew were: extreme solicitude for the claims of Communists and other criminal defendants, expansion of federal power at the expense of State power, great sympathy toward any government regulation of business — in short, the political philosophy now espoused by the Court under Chief Justice Earl Warren." [124]

Whatever the impact of the clerks on the justices and their opinions has been, they almost always remain in the shadows, inaccessible to the public and the press. The clerks talk among themselves about the views and personalities of their justices, but rarely has a clerk discussed clashes among the justices or leaked news about an opinion until it is announced in court. Such unwritten rules, as well as a clerk's loyalty to the justice he serves, account for the anonymity that surrounds the clerks during their time as staff members of the court.

The first law clerk was hired by Justice Horace Gray in 1882. As early as 1850 the justices had sought congressional approval for the hiring of an "investigating clerk" to help each justice and to copy opinions. When that request was not granted, some of the justices used employees of the court clerk's office to help them.

Justice Gray's law clerk, who had been the top graduate of Harvard Law School, served primarily as a servant and a barber, paid by the justice himself. It was not until 1886 that Congress provided $1,600 a year for a "stenographic clerk" for each justice. In the years that followed, clerks often served considerably longer than the one year they generally serve now. Chief Justices Charles Evans Hughes and William Howard Taft and Justice Frank Murphy employed law clerks who served for five years or more.

Messengers

The former page system — similar to that still used in the Congress — has been phased out in recent years and replaced by a messenger system. Messengers now are selected by the marshal of the court and perform most of the duties that the pages had performed. Each justice has one personal messenger of his own, and the court employs about six additional full-time messengers. The messengers, some of whom are college students or even college graduates, earn from $9,391 to $16,920 a year.

Before they were replaced by messengers, pages were appointed by the marshal. The early pages were chosen when they were high school freshmen; in later years, some of the young men and women who were chosen were night law school students.

When the court was in session, the pages waited behind the bench to pass notes from one justice to another, to fill water glasses or to obtain reference material from the library. When the court was not in session, they performed whatever errands the justices or other court officials needed. Robert Higbie, a former page who now works in the court's library, recounts how, as a young teen-ager, he and another page raced to open a door for Justice William O. Douglas. Once Higbie slipped and Douglas admonished him: "Next time, young man, wear rubbers."

Supporting Organizations

Four other organizations have an impact directly or indirectly on how the court operates, on its workload or the amount of public interest in the court. These organizations are the U.S. Judicial Conference, the Administrative Office of the U.S. Courts, the Federal Judicial Center and the Supreme Court Historical Association.

U.S. Judicial Conference

The Judicial Conference of the United States is the governing body for the administration of the federal judicial system. It has been called the system's "board of trustees" or "board of directors." By law, the conference is charged with carrying on "a continuous study of . . . the general rules of practice and procedure" and recommending "such changes in and addition to those rules as the Conference may deem desirable to promote simplicity in procedure, fairness in administration, the just determination of litigation and the elimination of unjustifiable expense and delay." [125]

The conference has committees or panels on court administration, budget, judicial conduct, judicial activities, review, the federal magistrates system, the bankruptcy system, the probation system, criminal law, the jury system, intercircuit assignments, rules of practice and procedure, Pacific territories, admission to practice standards and, since 1977, a special "Committee on the Bicentennial of Independence and the Constitution."

Congress, at the urging of Chief Justice William Howard Taft, created the judicial conference, then called the Judicial Conference of Senior Circuit Judges, in 1922. The conference originally consisted of the Chief Justice of the Supreme Court, the chief judges of the nine circuit courts of appeal, and the attorney general, who was at that time responsible for the administrative affairs of the courts.

Until 1940 the reports of the conference were included in the annual reports of the attorney general. When the Administrative Office of the United States Courts was created in 1939, administrative responsibility over the courts was transferred from the attorney general to the new office. The administrative office has operated under the supervision and direction of the judicial conference since that time.

The number of members on the conference has more than doubled since 1922. In the 1950s the chief judge of the U.S. Court of Claims and the U.S. Court of Customs and Patent Appeals as well as a district court judge representing each judicial circuit joined the Chief Justice and the chief judges of the 11 circuits as members of the judicial conference. In late 1978 two bankruptcy judges were added, bringing the number of members to 27. The conference has no separate budget of its own, and whatever staff assistance is needed is provided by the Administrative Office of the U.S. Courts.

Administrative Office

As its name indicates, the administrative office is responsible for supervising the administration, pay and employee benefits of the support personnel of the federal court system, except for the Supreme Court. The administrative office also reports on the procedures and caseloads of the federal courts, again except for the Supreme Court. The director and deputy director are appointed by the Supreme Court and are responsible for preparing and submitting the budgets of all 11 U.S. circuit courts of appeal and the U.S. district courts.

The administrative office is responsible for supervising federal probation officers. It also publishes, in cooperation with the Bureau of Prisons, a quarterly magazine called *Federal Probation,* which describes itself as a journal "of correctional philosophy and practice." The office's bankruptcy division administers the offices of the United States bankruptcy judges and, since 1968, the administrative affairs of United States magistrates. When the federal public defender organizations and community defender organizations were created by the Criminal Justice Act of 1970, the administrative office was given the responsibility for their budgets and payrolls as well.

Created by Congress in 1939, the Administrative Office of the U.S. Courts operates under the direction of the Judicial Conference of the United States. The director submits a report about the activities of the office, the situation of the federal courts and any recommendations for improvement to the annual meeting of the judicial conference, to Congress and to the attorney general. At present, about 450 people work in the administrative office. In fiscal year 1978, the office had a budget of $11,750,000.

Federal Judicial Center

The Federal Judicial Center was created by Congress in 1967 "to further the development and adoption of improved judicial administration in the courts of the United States." The center serves as the research, training and development arm of the federal judiciary. Its seven member board, headed by the Chief Justice, includes two judges from the U.S. circuit courts, three from the U.S. district courts and the director of the Administrative Office of the U.S. Courts. The board meets four times a year and the center's policy decisions are made at these meetings.

The center, located in the Dolley Madison House in Washington, D.C., holds about 100 education and training seminars each year and undertakes research projects. One such project is the development of a computerized management information system for improved administration in the courts.

The results of the center's research projects are often passed on to the U.S. Judicial Conference to assist it in making recommendations for improvement in the federal court system. The center's staff — about 100 people — is employed to carry out the board's policy decisions and the center's educational and research projects. The center's annual budget is now slightly more than $8 million.

The center's most publicized and controversial project was its 1972 report of the Federal Judicial Center Study Group on the Caseload of the Supreme Court. As chairman of the center, Chief Justice Warren E. Burger chose seven respected court-seasoned lawyers to serve on the study group. The group, chaired by Professor Paul A. Freund of Harvard Law School, studied the problem for a year.

In December 1972 its report was issued. One of its major conclusions was that "The statistics of the Court's current workload, both in absolute terms and in the mounting trend, are impressive evidence that the conditions essential for the performance of the Court's mission do not exist. For an ordinary appellate court the burgeoning volume of cases would be a staggering burden; for the Supreme Court the pressures of the docket are incompatible with the appropriate fulfillment of its historic and essential functions." [126]

The study group's first and most controversial recommendation for relieving the court's workload was the creation of a National Court of Appeals. *(See box, p. 736.)*

Historical Society

The Supreme Court Historical Society was founded in November 1974 as a non-profit group to increase public interest in and knowledge about the Supreme Court and the federal court system. The society collects and preserves data and memorabilia about the court's early history. The brainchild of Chief Justice Warren E. Burger, it is modeled after the White House and Capitol historical societies. It publicizes the judiciary's — particularly the Supreme Court's — contribution to the country's history on both scholarly and popular levels.

The money to operate the society comes primarily from its 2,200 members. Membership fees range from $25 a year for a regular member to $50,000 for a "benefactor" or top-ranked life member. Members include students (who pay only $5 a year), individuals, firms and foundations. The society has committees for acquisitions, exhibits, oral history and publications and publishes a quarterly newsletter and an annual yearbook. The staff includes a director, three office employees and four researchers.

The brochure sent to prospective members contends that the society "receives no governmental financial support." In September 1976, however, it did receive a five-year, $25,000-a-year matching grant from a division of the National Archives — the National Historical Publications and Records Commission — to prepare a comprehensive documentary history of the Supreme Court from 1789-1800. The need to raise matching funds from private sources for the project has encouraged the society to solicit new members and to publicize the increasing number of items it offers for sale to members and to the public in a kiosk in the Supreme Court foyer.

Supreme Court Chamber, U.S. Capitol, 1860-1935.

Housing the Court

Between Feb. 1, 1790, when the Supreme Court first met in New York City, and Oct. 7, 1935, when the justices first convened in their present building at One First Street Northeast in Washington, D.C., the court held session in about a dozen different places. Thus, during the court's first 145 years of existence, the justices moved, on average, once every 12 years.

Early Days

Some of these early courtrooms were shared with other courts. After the court moved to Washington in 1801, it held formal sessions in various rooms of the Capitol and, according to some sources, in two taverns as well. [127] Some of the premises provided for the court in the Capitol have been described by commentators of that time as "mean and dingy" and "little better than a dungeon." [128] Their present headquarters, by contrast, has been called a "marble palace." [129]

New York City

The Supreme Court first met on Feb. 1, 1790, in New York City, then the nation's temporary capital. The court held session at the Royal Exchange Building at the intersection of Broad and Water Streets in what is now Manhattan's financial district. The courtroom occupied the second floor of the gambrel-roofed, cupola-topped building. There was an open-air market on the first floor of the building and the courtroom on the second floor was a room 60 feet long with a vaulted ceiling.

The justices stayed in New York for two terms. The first lasted from Feb. 1-Feb. 10, 1790, and the second for only two days, Aug. 2-3, 1790. There were no cases on the court's docket during these two terms and the justices spent their time at such duties as appointing a court crier — now called clerk of the court — and admitting lawyers to the bar.

Philadelphia

Before the end of the second term, Congress had voted on July 16, 1790, to move the capital from New York to Philadelphia. The Supreme Court joined the rest of the federal government there for its next session, which began on Feb. 7, 1791, at Independence Hall, then known as "The State House." With no cases to attend to, the court adjourned the next day.

When the court was moved to Philadelphia, it was understood that the justices would sit in City Hall, but that building was not completed until the summer of 1791, in time for the court's August 1791 term. The justices met in the east wing of the new City Hall, which also housed the state and municipal court.

Those courts usually met at different times from the Supreme Court. In March 1796, however, the "Mayor's Court" was scheduled to hold a session in the same first-floor courtroom that the Supreme Court was using. As a result, the Supreme Court vacated the courtroom and held session in the chambers of the Common Council on the second floor of the building.

The court remained in City Hall until the end of the August 1800 term. City Hall also housed the U.S. Congress, which occupied the west wing, and the Pennsylvania legislature, which met in the central part of the building. The records indicate that while in City Hall, the justices often kept late hours to hear oral arguments and that there they began wearing robes for the first time.

Washington, D.C.

The act of July 16, 1790, which transferred the seat of the federal government from New York to Philadelphia, also provided for a subsequent and permanent move to Washington, D.C. That law specified that the final move would take place on the "first Monday in December, in the year one thousand eight hundred." By that time, enough of the Capitol and the White House had been completed for the government to move. Congress and the president were subjected to considerable criticism because the buildings they were to occupy were labeled too palatial and extravagant for a young democracy.

For the Supreme Court, however, there were no accommodations at all. A House committee in 1796 had pointed out that a "building for the Judiciary" was needed, and in 1798 Alexander White, a commissioner for the Federal City, had suggested appropriating funds for one. But two weeks before the court moved to Washington, it was still seeking a place to conduct its business.

Courtrooms in the Capitol

Faced with the imminent convening of the homeless Supreme Court in Washington, Congress on Jan. 23, 1801, passed a resolution providing that "leave be given to the Commissioners of the City of Washington to use one of the rooms on the first floor of the Capitol for holding the present session of the Supreme Court of the United States."

Since only the north wing of the Capitol was ready for occupancy at that time, Congress assigned the court a small room — 24 feet by 30 feet, 31 feet high and rounded at the south end — in the east basement, or first floor, entrance hall. There, the court held its first session in Washington on Feb. 2, 1801. It was the first of a series of often makeshift, hand-me-down quarters assigned by Congress to the court before the completion of its present building in 1935.

By 1807 the entire north wing of the Capitol was in dire need of renovation. In a letter to Chief Justice John Marshall on Sept. 17, 1807, Benjamin Henry Latrobe, the Architect of the Capitol and Surveyor of Public Buildings, suggested that the court move "for the next session into the Library formerly occupied by the House of Representatives."

There the court remained for the February and summer 1808 terms. But as Latrobe indicated in a letter to President James Monroe on Sept. 6, 1809, "the Library became so inconvenient and cold that the Supreme Court preferred to sit at Long's Tavern" during the February 1809 term. Long's Tavern, where the first inaugural ball was held, was located on First Street Southeast, where the Library of Congress now stands.

On Feb. 5, 1810, the court returned to the Capitol and met in a courtroom especially designed for it. Located in the basement beneath the new Senate chamber, the court-

Supreme Court Building, completed 1935.

room was also used by the U.S. Circuit Court and probably by the Orphan's Court of the District of Columbia. The noted Philadelphia lawyer, Charles J. Ingersoll, provided this description of the new courtroom:

> Under the Senate Chamber, is the Hall of Justice, the ceiling of which is not unfancifully formed by the arches that support the former. The Judges in their robes of solemn black are raised on seats of grave mahogany; and below them is the bar; and behind that an arcade, still higher, so contrived as to afford auditors double rows of terrace seats thrown in segments round the transverse arch under which the Judges sit. . . . When I went into the Court of Justice yesterday, one side of the fine forensic colonnade was occupied by a party of ladies, who, after loitering some time in the gallery of the Representatives, had sauntered into the hall, and, were, with their attendants, sacrificing some impatient moments to the inscrutable mysteries of pleading. On the opposite side was a group of Indians, who are here on a visit to the President in their native costume, their straight black hair hanging in plaits down their tawny shoulders, with mockassins

on their feet, rings in their ears and noses, and large plates of silver on their arms and breasts. [130]

The court remained in the new courtroom until the Capitol was burned by the British on Aug. 24, 1814, during the War of 1812. The British are said to have used Supreme Court documents to start the fire. When the Capitol was burned, Congress moved to the temporary "Brick Capitol" at the site of the present Supreme Court building, then — during the two years that the Capitol was being restored — to a house rented from Daniel Carroll. That house, which the court used from Feb. 6, 1815, until July 1, 1816, subsequently became Bell Tavern.

The court returned to the Capitol for its February 1817 term and occupied an undestroyed section in the north wing until 1819. It was this room that was described as "mean and dingy" and "little better than a dungeon." [131] The court remained there until the February 1819 term, when its regular courtroom beneath the Senate chamber was repaired.

The courtroom, which the justices were to occupy until 1860, was the object of both praise and criticism. It was on the court's first day in the restored courtroom — Feb. 2,

1819 — that the decision in the Dartmouth College Case was announced, a decision that made the court headline news throughout the country. [132] On the same day that the Dartmouth case was decided, the *National Intelligencer* reported: "We are highly pleased to find that the Courtroom in the Capitol is in a state fit for the reception of the Supreme Court.... It is ... considerably more agreeable than that which was produced on entering the same apartment, previous to the re-modification of it made necessary by the conflagration of the interior of the Capitol." [133]

Many observers took a dimmer view of the courtroom. The *New York Statesman,* for example, described it as "not in a style which comports with the dignity of that body, or which wears a comparison with the other halls of the Capitol. In the first place, it is like going down cellar to reach it. The room is on the basement story in an obscure part of the north wing. In arriving at it, you pass a labyrinth, and almost need the clue of Ariadne to guide you to the sanctuary of the blind goddess. A stranger might traverse the dark avenues of the Capitol for a week, without finding the remote corner in which Justice is administered to the American Republic." [134] Other critics noted that the chamber was so small that the justices had to put on their robes in full view of the spectators.

Whatever its shortcomings, the courtroom at least lent a new aura of stability and permanence to the previously peripatetic court. The court remained in the basement courtroom for 41 years, surviving fires in 1851 and 1852. After the court moved to its new chambers in 1860, the courtroom became part of the law library of Congress.

In 1860, with the Civil War imminent, the court moved from the basement to the old Senate chamber on the first floor of the Capitol. The new courtroom was located on the east side of the main corridor between the rotunda and the current Senate chamber. The large room, with a dozen anterooms for office space and storage, was by far the most commodious and imposing quarters the court had occupied. The galleries had been removed when the Senate moved to its new chambers, giving the courtroom an aura of spaciousness.

The justices sat on a raised platform behind a balustrade. In back of the balustrade was an arched doorway topped by a gilded American eagle and flanked by ten marble columns. The justices faced a large semi-circular colonnaded chamber. The area just in front of the bench was used for the presentation of arguments and it was ringed by wooden benches for the spectators. There were red drapes and carpets, and busts of former Chief Justices lined the walls.

Despite the dignity and spaciousness of the courtroom, the adjoining office space was cramped and inadequate. There was no dining hall, for example, and the justices were forced to use the robing room for their meals. The conference room, where the justices met to discuss cases and render their decisions, also served as the court's library. Because of the reluctance of some of the justices to opening the conference room windows, the room was frequently closed and stuffy. The clerk's office was similarly close and cluttered.

None of the justices had individual office space in the Capitol, and each had to provide for his own and his staff's working quarters at a time when spacious housing in Washington was difficult to find. Nevertheless, the justices held sessions in these quarters for 75 years, with two exceptions. An explosion of illuminating gas on Nov. 6, 1898, forced the court to hold the Nov. 7 and Nov. 14 sessions in the Senate District of Columbia Committee room. During reconstruction of the courtroom from October to Dec. 9, 1901, sessions were held in the Senate Judiciary Committee room.

President — later Chief Justice — William Howard Taft began promoting the idea of a separate building for the Supreme Court around 1912. Taft continued to advocate the construction of a Supreme Court building when he became Chief Justice in 1921. At Taft's persistent urging, Congress finally relented in 1929 and authorized funds for the construction of a permanent dwelling for the court. During the construction of the new building, the court continued to sit in the old Senate chamber. Its last major decision announced there, at the end of the 1934 term, was that striking down President Roosevelt's National Industrial Recovery Act.

New Court Building

The Supreme Court held its first session in the new building at One First Street Northeast, across the plaza from the Capitol, on Oct. 7, 1935. A hundred and forty-five years after it first met in New York, 134 years after it moved to Washington and six years after Congress had appropriated $9,740,000 for a permanent residence, the nation's highest tribunal finally had a home of its own.

In laying the cornerstone for the new building on Oct. 13, 1932, Chief Justice Charles Evans Hughes paid tribute to his predecessor, William Howard Taft, who had died two years before. "This building," Hughes said, "is the result of his intelligent persistence." The site chosen for the new court had been the location of the "Brick Capitol" that was used by Congress after the British burned the Capitol in 1814.

Architect Cass Gilbert was commissioned to design the edifice and, in May 1929, submitted a plan for "a building of dignity and importance suitable for its use as a permanent home of the Supreme Court of the United States." Chief Justice Taft died in 1930 and Gilbert in 1934, but the project was continued under Chief Justice Hughes and architects Cass Gilbert Jr. and John R. Rockart, under the supervision of Architect of the Capitol David Lynn.

The architects chose the Corinthian style of Greek architecture which would blend most harmoniously with the congressional buildings on Capitol Hill. The dimensions of the building were 385 feet east and west, from front to back, and 304 feet north and south. At its height, the building rises four stories above the ground level.

Marble was selected as the primary material to be used, and more than $3 million — almost a third of the building's cost — was spent on domestic and foreign marble. Pure Vermont marble was used for the exterior of the building. A thousand freight cars were needed to haul the stone from Vermont. Georgia marble flecked with crystal was quarried for the four inner courts, while a creamy Alabama marble was used for most of the walls and floors of corridors and entrance halls.

For the court's Great Hall — its showcase — and the courtroom at the end of the Great Hall, architect Gilbert insisted on Ivory Vein Marble from Spain for the walls and Light Sienna Old Convent marble from the Montarrenti quarry in Italy for the huge columns. The Italian marble was shipped to finishers in Knoxville, Tenn., and they made the blocks into 30-foot columns and shipped them to Washington. Darker Italian and African marble was used for the floor.

Most of the floors are of oak, and the doors and walls of most offices are of American-quartered white oak. Bronze and mahogany were also used. The roof was made from cream-colored Roman tile set on bronze strips over lead-coated copper on a slab of watertight concrete. As Wesley McCune noted, the "Court might succumb to a political storm, but it will never be driven out by any kind of inclement weather." [135] The building includes two self-supporting marble spiral staircases from the garage to the top floor. The only other spiral staircases like those in the court are in the Vatican and the Paris Opéra.

Since its completion in 1935, the Supreme Court building has been a subject of both outspoken praise and equally outspoken criticism. It has been described as both a "marble palace" and a "marble mausoleum." Its admirers speak in terms of structural simplicity, austerity, beauty, and dignity. For them, it is a fitting monument epitomizing the words on the front entrance of the building, "Equal Justice Under Law."

Despite general public approval of the new building, it has had numerous critics. In the 1930s, the authors of the Federal Writers' Project *Guide to Washington* wrote that "the building has a cold, abstract, almost anonymous beauty but is lacking in that power which comes from a more direct expression of purpose." Chief Justice Harlan Fiske Stone called it "almost bombastically pretentious" and "wholly inappropriate for a quiet group of old boys such as the Supreme Court." Another justice said that the court would be "nine black beetles in the Temple of Karnak." Another asked: "What are we supposed to do, ride in on nine elephants?" [136]

The building was designed so that the justices need not enter public areas except when hearing oral arguments and announcing their opinions. A private elevator connects the underground garage with the corridor, closed to the public, where the justices' offices are located.

The basement of the Supreme Court building contains — in addition to the garage — a printing press and offices for the guards and maintenance help.

The second floor contains the justices' dining room and library and the Office of the Reporter of Decisions and other offices.

On the third floor is the library, paneled in hand-carved oak, and on the fourth floor there is a gymnasium and storage area.

The public is allowed to see only the ground floor, where the public information office is located, and the first floor, which houses the courtroom.

When Congress in 1929 authorized $9,740,000 for the construction of the court building, it was expected then that extra funds for necessary furnishings would have to be appropriated. Nevertheless, the final and complete cost of the building, in addition to all the furnishings, was below the authorization, and $94,000 was returned to the U.S. Treasury. It is estimated that replacing the building today would run to well over $100 million.

Architecture

On the steps to the main entrance of the building are a pair of huge marble candelabra with carved panels representing justice, holding sword and scales, and the "three fates," who are weaving the thread of life. On either side of the steps are two marble figures by sculptor James Earle Fraser. On the left side is a female — the "contemplation of justice" — and on the right is a male — the "guardian or authority of law."

At the entrance of the building is a pediment filled with sculptures representing "liberty enthroned," guarded by "order" and "authority." On either side are groups depicting "council and research." Panels on the main door were sculptured by John Donnelly Jr. and depict scenes in the development of the law. Along both sides of the great hall are busts of former Chief Justices, heraldic devices and medallion profiles of lawgivers.

From the great hall, oak doors open into the courtroom, or court chamber. Measuring 82 feet by 91 feet with a 44-foot ceiling, the room has 24 columns of Italian marble. Overhead, along all four sides of the room, are marble panels sculptured by Adolph A. Weinman. Directly above the bench are two figures, depicting "majesty of the law" and "power of government." Between these figures is a tableau of the Ten Commandments. At the far left is a group representing "safeguard of the rights of the people" and "genii of wisdom and statescraft." At the far right is "the defense of human rights."

On the wall to the right of incoming visitors are figures of historical lawmakers of the pre-Christian era — Menes, Hammurabi, Moses, Solomon, Lycurgus, Solon, Draco, Confucius and Augustus. These are flanked by figures symbolizing "fame" and "history." To the left of visitors are lawmakers of the Christian era — Napoleon, Marshall, Blackstone, Grotius, Saint Louis, King John, Charlemagne, Mohammed and Justinian. They are flanked by figures representing "liberty," "peace" and "philosophy."

New Quarters?

When the building was finished in 1935, it was widely regarded as the permanent home of the United States Supreme Court. But in recent years, court officials have complained that the building "is bursting at the seams" [137] and that the court needs more space. In 1978, Chief Justice Warren E. Burger gave his blessing to a group of federal planners who are attempting to find an alternate location for the court.

The present building, these planners contend, could not be expanded without destroying the architectural integrity of the building. Among the alternatives being considered are to move the court to a new location on Capitol Hill and convert the present building into a legal museum or turn it over to the Library of Congress for a visiting scholars center; to expand below ground level and take over adjacent property; and to select as a site a new "judicial campus" in "monumental Washington" — somewhere between the Lincoln Memorial and the Capitol.

Those favoring a move from Capitol Hill to a new "judicial campus" contend that the court has remained in the shadow of Congress since 1800 and needs a new and separate location to symbolize its role as the third and co-equal branch of the government. Planning is still in the early stages and a final decision, which will require years of study and the approval of several federal agencies, the court and Congress, is not expected for at least several years.

Cost of the Court

Compared to its two coequal branches of the government, the executive branch and Congress, the Supreme Court seems a relatively inexpensive operation. In fiscal year 1979, for example, the high court received $9,690,000 for the salaries of the nine justices and more than 300 employees and other expenses, and $1,450,000 for care of the building and grounds. That same fiscal year, the Executive Office of the President requested $83.2 million, and Congress, with more than 18,000 employees, asked for $1.2 billion. [138]

Supreme Court Budget

The Supreme Court budget for each fiscal year is drawn up in the Office of the Marshal of the Court. It is submitted by Oct. 15 — nearly a year in advance — to the Office of Management and Budget (OMB). (The fiscal year begins the following Oct. 1.)

The OMB is prohibited by statute from making any changes in the proposed budget for the federal judiciary before submitting it — along with proposed executive and legislative budgets — to Congress in January.

Supreme Court requests in the president's budget document have been divided into two categories — salaries and expenses of the Supreme Court, and care of buildings and grounds — since fiscal year 1977. Before that, there were five categories: salaries; printing; miscellaneous expenses; car for the Chief Justice; and books for the Supreme Court.

Federal Judiciary

For the 95 district courts, the 11 circuit courts, the Court of Claims, the Court of Customs and Patent Appeals and the Customs Court, the budget process before submission to Congress involves several steps that are not applicable to the Supreme Court. The budget of each lower court requires consideration by the Administrative Office of the U.S. Courts and the Judicial Conference of the United States, which have no jurisdiction over the Supreme Court.

The various offices of the district courts submit their budget requirements for the next fiscal year to the chief judge of their district, who sends them to the administrative office in Washington by May 1 of the preceding fiscal year. The chief judge of the three special courts follows the same procedure.

The chief judge of the 11 circuit courts has been assisted since 1972 by a "circuit executive" whose duties include preparing the budget requests. Like those of the district and special courts, the proposed budget for the circuits must be submitted to the administrative office by May 1.

Budget requests are evaluated by specialists on the basis of productivity, in May and June. The conclusions are reviewed by the director of the administrative office, then sent to a committee of judges for review before they are delivered to the judicial conference for approval.

Committees of the judicial conference review the requests, make recommendations and send them to the budget committee for evaluation and further recommendations.

The judicial conference meets, usually in September, to consider the committees' recommendations and prepare a final version of the requests, which are then returned to the financial management division of the administrative office and submitted to the Office of Management and Budget (OMB) by Oct. 15.

The fiscal 1979 budget request for the federal judiciary — minus Supreme Court funds — was $521.1 million.

Congressional Consideration

Before the president sends the budget to Congress, the Administrative Office of the U.S. Courts submits justifications for the funds requested to the subcommittees of the congressional appropriations committees that will first consider the requests — the Senate subcommittee on State, Justice, Commerce and the Judiciary and the House subcommittee on the Departments of State, Justice and Commerce, the Judiciary and Related Agencies. Subcommittee hearings on the proposed budget generally begin in late January or early February.

The subcommittees hold public hearings at which a justice of the Supreme Court, the chairman of the Judicial Conference Budget Committee, the chief judges of the special courts and experts on the budget from the Administrative Office of the U.S. Courts are called to justify the budget requests. When the hearings are over, the subcommittees vote on appropriations bills and send them to a vote by the full Senate and House Appropriations Committees, followed by a final vote on the floors of the House and Senate. The Judiciary's budget requests are often reduced by Congress.

The funds Congress appropriates for the Supreme Court now go directly to the court and are spent by the marshal for salaries of the justices and other employees and for court needs. Before 1935, Congress channeled money for the Supreme Court through the Justice Department. The allocation of funds for the other federal courts is handled by the financial management division of the Administrative Office of the U.S. Courts. The division submits recommendations on the allocation to the director of the administrative office, who makes the final decision on how the money is disbursed.

Salaries of the Justices

Supreme Court justices in recent years have expressed no complaint about the salaries that Congress has set for them — $72,000 a year for justices, and $75,000 for the Chief Justice. In 1975, Congress passed a law providing cost-of-living salary increases for the federal judiciary.

Service on the Supreme Court was not always so remunerative. On Sept. 23, 1789, Congress set the salary of an associate justice at $3,500 a year and for the Chief Justice at $4,000 a year.

That salary was not increased until 1819. When Congress was urged to raise the salaries in 1816, Justice Joseph Story (1812-1845) prepared a memorandum complaining that "the necessaries and comforts of life, the manner of living and the habits of ordinary expenses, in the same rank of society, have, between 1789 and 1815, increased in price from one hundred to two hundred percent. The business of the Judges of the Supreme Court, both at the Law Term in February and on the Circuits, has during the same period increased in more than a quadruple ratio and is increasing annually." [139] Congress was unreceptive at that time to Story's and other pleas for a pay raise for the justices.

Retirement System

For almost a century, many Supreme Court justices were caught in a dilemma: low salaries and no retirement plan. Many left the bench to accept more lucrative employment elsewhere. Justice Story, for one, did not. In 1816, when Congress refused to increase his and the other associate justices' salaries from $3,500, Story declined an offer to take over Charles Pinckney's law practice in Baltimore. Had he accepted the offer, he would have been assured of an income of at least $10,000 a year.

Until 1869 justices who were unable to carry out their duties because of age or disability often hesitated to submit resignations because there were no retirement benefits.

It was in large measure the incapacity of Justices Robert C. Grier (1846-1870) and Samuel Nelson (1845-1872) that prompted Congress to provide in the Judiciary Act of April 10, 1869, "that any judge of any court of the United States, who, having held his commission as such at least ten years, shall, after having attained the age of seventy years, resign his office, shall thereafter, during the residue of his natural life, receive the same salary which was by law payable to him at the time of his resignation."

The Judiciary Act of 1869 made no provisions for retirement benefits for a justice who became incapacitated before reaching age 70 or before 10 years of service on the court. That omission was subsequently remedied, and the U.S. Code now contains provisions for resignation or retirement for age and retirement for disability.

Before 1937, justices who left the court for any reason had to resign rather than retire, which meant that their pensions were subject to fluctuating civil service guidelines. That policy was changed with the Supreme Court Retirement Act of 1937. *(Details, p. 755)*

The law now provides that:

> Any justice or judge of the United States appointed to hold office during good behavior who resigns after attaining the age of seventy years and after serving at least ten years continuously or otherwise shall, during the remainder of his lifetime, continue to receive the salary which he was receiving when he resigned. Any justice or judge of the United States . . . may retain his office but retire from regular active service after attaining the age of seventy years and after serving at least ten years continuously or otherwise, or after attaining the age of sixty-five years and after serving at least fifteen years continuously or

Salaries		
Years	**Chief Justice**	**Associate Justices**
1789-1819	$ 4,000	$ 3,500
1819-1855	$ 5,000	$ 4,500
1855-1871	$ 6,500	$ 6,000
1871-1873	$ 8,500	$ 8,000
1873-1903	$10,500	$10,000
1903-1911	$13,000	$12,500
1911-1926	$15,000	$14,500
1926-1946	$20,500	$20,000
1946-1955	$25,500	$25,000
1955-1964	$35,500	$35,000
1964-1969	$40,000	$39,500
1969-1975	$62,500	$60,000
1975-1977*	$65,625	$63,000
1977-	$75,000	$72,000

* A cost of living adjustment equal to 5 percent of regular salary.

otherwise. He shall, during the remainder of his lifetime, continue to receive the salary of the office. [140]

Any justice or judge of the United States appointed to hold office during good behavior who becomes permanently disabled from performing his duties may retire from regular active service. . . . Any justice or judge of the United States desiring to retire under this section shall certify to the President his disability in writing. Whenever an associate justice of the Supreme Court, a chief judge of a circuit or the chief judge of the Court of Claims, Court of Customs and Patent Appeals or Customs Court, desires to retire under this section, he shall furnish to the President a certificate of disability signed by the Chief Justice of the United States. . . . [141]

Each justice or judge retiring under this section after serving ten years continuously or otherwise shall, during the remainder of his lifetime, receive the salary of the office. A justice or judge retiring under this section who has served less than ten years in all shall, during the remainder of his lifetime, receive one-half the salary of the office. [142]

A justice of the Supreme Court who is unable to perform his duties cannot be forced to resign. Congress, however, has provided that other federal judges deemed to be "unable to discharge efficiently all the duties of his office by reason of permanent mental or physical disability" can be replaced by the president with Senate approval. [143]

Footnotes

¹ Court Reform — Priority to Methods and Machinery," Speech by Chief Justice Warren E. Burger, March 12, 1971, to the National Conference on the Judiciary, Williamsburg, Va.

² Supreme Court Rule 3(1).

³ Robert L. Stern and Eugene Gressman, *Supreme Court Practice*, (Washington, D.C.: Bureau of National Affairs, 1978), p. 4.

⁴ Charles Warren, *The Supreme Court in United States History*, rev. ed., 2 vols. (Little, Brown & Co., Boston, 1922, 1926) II:148.

⁵ *United States v. Nixon*, 419 U.S. 683 (1974); *Wilson v. Girard*, 354 U.S. 524 (1957); *New York Times Co. v. United States, Washington Post v. United States*, 403 U.S. 713 (1971).

⁶ *Supreme Court Journal*, April 5, 1965; quoted in Stern and Gressman, *Supreme Court Practice* p. 10.

⁷ John P. Frank, *Marble Palace: The Supreme Court in American Life* (New York: Alfred A. Knopf, 1958), p. 15.

⁸ Supreme Court Rule 25(1).

⁹ 28 U.S.C. 1915(a).

¹⁰ Rules of the Supreme Court of the United States, adopted June 15, 1970.

¹¹ Supreme Court Rule 43.

¹² Charles Evans Hughes, *The Supreme Court of the United States* (New York: Columbia University Press, 1928), pp. 62-63.

¹³ Quoted in Harvard Law School Occasional Pamphlet Number Nine (1967), p. 22.

¹⁴ Frank, *Marble Palace*, pp. 91-92.

¹⁵ Hughes, *The Supreme Court of the United States*, p. 61.

¹⁶ Supreme Court Rule 44(7).

¹⁷ Supreme Court Rule 44(1).

¹⁸ Stern and Gressman, *Supreme Court Practice*, p. 741.

¹⁹ Ibid.

²⁰ William J. Brennan Jr., "State Court Decisions and the Supreme Court," 31 *Pennsylvania Bar Association Quarterly* (1960):403-404.

²¹ Supreme Court Rule 40(1).

²² Supreme Court Rules 39 and 40.

²³ *Huffman v. Pursue, Ltd.*, 419 U.S. 892 (1974).

²⁴ Hughes, *The Supreme Court of the United States*, p. 62.

²⁵ Robert H. Jackson, "Advocacy Before the Supreme Court: Suggestions for Effective Case Presentations," 101 *American Bar Association Journal* (1951):862.

²⁶ Frank, *Marble Palace*, p. 92.

²⁷ Ibid., p. 93.

²⁸ Ibid., p. 105.

²⁹ Ibid.

³⁰ Quoted by Richard L. Williams, "Justices Run 'Nine Little Law Firms' at Supreme Court," *Smithsonian*, February 1977.

³¹ Willard L. King, *Melville Weston Fuller* (New York: Macmillan Publishing Co., 1950), p. 290.

³² Ibid., p. 245.

³³ Glen Elsasser and Jay Fuller, "The Hidden Face of the Supreme Court," *Chicago Tribune Magazine*, April 23, 1978, p. 50.

³⁴ *United States v. Nixon*, 419 U.S. 683 (1974).

³⁵ Elsasser and Fuller, "The Hidden Face," pp. 50-57.

³⁶ Learned Hand, *The Bill of Rights* (Cambridge: Harvard University Press, 1958), p. 72.

³⁷ *Head & Amory v. Providence Ins. Co.*, 2 Cr. 127 (1804).

³⁸ Quoted in Warren, *The Supreme Court in United States History*, I:654.

³⁹ Ibid., p. 655.

⁴⁰ Charles P. Curtis Jr., *Lions Under the Throne* (Fairfield, N.J.: Kelley Press, 1947), p. 76.

⁴¹ Hughes, *The Supreme Court of the United States*, p. 68.

⁴² Ibid., p. 67-68.

⁴³ Karl M. Zobell, "Division of Opinion in the Supreme Court: A History of Judicial Disintegration," 44 *Cornell Law Quarterly*, (1959): 186-214.

⁴⁴ *Martin v. Hunter's Lessee*, 1 Wheat. 304, 381 (1816).

⁴⁵ *United States v. United Mine Workers*, 330 U.S. 258 (1947).

⁴⁶ Frank, *Marble Palace*, p. 121.

⁴⁷ *The New York Times*, Nov. 13, 1932.

⁴⁸ Gilbert Cranberg, "What Did the Supreme Court Say," *Saturday Review*, April 8, 1967.

⁴⁹ Ibid.

⁵⁰ Ibid.

⁵¹ Liva Baker, *Felix Frankfurter* (New York: Coward-McCann, 1969), p. 218.

⁵² Ibid., pp. 216-217.

⁵³ Alpheus T. Mason, *Harlan Fiske Stone* (New York: Viking Press, 1956).

⁵⁴ Alexander Bickel, *The Unpublished Opinions of Justice Brandeis* (Cambridge: Harvard University Press, 1957), p. 203.

⁵⁵ Mary Ann Harrell, *Equal Justice Under Law: The Supreme Court in American Life* (Washington, D.C.: The Foundation of the American Bar Association with the cooperation of the National Geographic Society, 1975), p. 127.

⁵⁶ Charles Fairman, *Mr. Justice Miller* (Cambridge: Harvard University Press, 1939), pp. 373-374.

⁵⁷ Henry F. Pringle, *Life and Times of William Howard Taft*, 2 vols. (New York: Farrar & Rinehart, 1939), I:529-530.

⁵⁸ Frank, *Marble Palace*, pp. 76, 81, 264-265.

⁵⁹ *Dred Scott v. Sandford*, 19 How. 393 (1857).

⁶⁰ Frank, *Marble Palace*, p. 45.

⁶¹ Ibid., p. 259.

⁶² *Mahnich v. Southern Steamship Co.*, 321 U.S. 96 at 112-113 (1944).

⁶³ *Helvering v. Hallock*, 309 U.S. 106 at 119, 121 (1940).

⁶⁴ Art. I, section 3, clause 6.

⁶⁵ Frank, *Marble Palace*, p. 71.

⁶⁶ Warren, *The Supreme Court in United States History*, I:124.

⁶⁷ Quoted in Warren, *The Supreme Court in United States History*, I:127.

⁶⁸ Frank, *Marble Palace*, pp. 78-79.

⁶⁹ James F. Simon, *In His Own Image: The Supreme Court in Richard Nixon's America* (New York: David McKay Company, 1973), pp. 92-93.

⁷⁰ Hughes, *The Supreme Court of the United States*, p. 57.

⁷¹ Address to the Association of the Bar of the City of New York, Dec. 12, 1948.

⁷² Ibid.

⁷³ Merlo Pusey, *Charles Evans Hughes*, 2 vols. (New York: Columbia University Press, 1963), II:678.

⁷⁴ Id., p. 679.

⁷⁵ Frank, *Marble Palace*, pp. 80-81.

⁷⁶ *The New York Times*, March 4, 1954.

⁷⁷ *Brown v. Board of Education*, 347 U.S. 483 (1954).

⁷⁸ Quoted by David F. Pike, "Supreme Court: Trials and Tribulations," *U.S. News & World Report*, March 26, 1979, p. 34.

⁷⁹ Address to the National Archives, Sept. 21, 1978.

⁸⁰ Letter to Franklin D. Roosevelt, July 20, 1942.

⁸¹ Ibid.

⁸² Stern and Gressman, *Supreme Court Practice*, pp. 26-27.

⁸³ Charles Evans Hughes, Letter to Congress, March 21, 1937.

⁸⁴ Charles Warren, *The Supreme Court in United States History*, I:471.

⁸⁵ Ibid., p. 87.

⁸⁶ Ibid., p. 792.

⁸⁷ Ibid., p. 473.

⁸⁸ Wesley McCune, *The Nine Young Men* (New York: Harper & Brothers, 1947), p. 238.

⁸⁹ Quoted by Richard L. William, "Justices Run 'Nine Little Law Firms' at Supreme Court," *Smithsonian*, February 1977, p. 89.

⁹⁰ Hughes, *The Supreme Court of the United States*, pp. 75-76.

⁹¹ Ibid., p. 76.

⁹² Warren, *The Supreme Court in United States History*, I:173.

⁹³ Letter to Chief Justice Earl Warren, May 14, 1969.

⁹⁴ Address to the Association of the Bar of the City of New York, Dec. 11, 1948.

⁹⁵ Alexander Bickel, *Politics and the Warren Court* (New York: Harper & Row, 1965), p. 137.

⁹⁶ Dexter Perkins and Glyndon G. Van Deusen, *The United States of America*, 2 vols. (New York: Macmillan Publishing Co., 1962), II:64.

[97] Warren, *The Supreme Court in United States History,* II:583.

[98] Frank, *Marble Palace,* p. 269.

[99] Ibid., pp. 258-259.

[100] *The Boston Herald,* Nov. 15, 1929.

[101] Baker, *Felix Frankfurter,* p. 237; see also, Joseph P. Lash, *From the Diaries of Felix Frankfurter* (New York: W. W. Norton and Company, 1975).

[102] Simon, *In His Own Image: The Supreme Court in Richard Nixon's America,* p. 102.

[103] Letter to Chief Justice Earl Warren, May 14, 1969.

[104] Robert L. Stern, "The Solicitor General and Administrative Agency Litigation," *American Bar Association Journal,* Feb. 1960, pp. 154-155.

[105] Ibid., p. 156.

[106] 28 U.S.C. 505.

[107] Stern and Gressman, *Supreme Court Practice,* pp. 17-18.

[108] Augustus H. Garland, *Experience in the Supreme Court of the United States, with Some Reflections and Suggestions as to That Tribunal* (Washington, D.C.: John Byrne and Company 1898), p. 12., quoted in Stern and Gressman, *Supreme Court Practice,* p. 18.

[109] 1 Stat. 624, 625.

[110] Charles Fairman, "The Retirement of Federal Judges," *Harvard Law Review,* January 1938, p. 417.

[111] *Wheaton v. Peters,* 8 Pet. 591 (1834).

[112] Garland, *Experience in the Supreme Court of the United States,* quoted in Supreme Court Information Office, "The Docket Sheet," Vol. 13, No. 3 (Summer, 1976), p. 4.

[113] Stern and Gressman, *Supreme Court Practice,* pp. 909-910.

[114] Supreme Court Rule 5.

[115] Supreme Court Rule 5(2).

[116] Supreme Court Rule 8.

[117] Frank, *The Marble Palace,* p. 93.

[118] Ibid., pp. 93-94.

[119] Telephone interview with Barrett McGurn, April 16, 1979.

[120] Frank, *The Marble Palace,* p. 116.

[121] Quoted by Richard L. Williams in "Justices Run 'Nine Little Law Firms' at Supreme Court," *Smithsonian,* February 1977, p. 88.

[122] Id., pp. 90-91.

[123] William H. Rehnquist, "Who Writes Decisions of the Supreme Court," *U.S. News & World Report,* Dec. 13, 1957, p. 74.

[124] Ibid., p. 75.

[125] 28 U.S.C. 331, as amended in 1961.

[126] *Report of the Study Group on the Caseload of the Supreme Court* (Federal Judicial Center, 1972), p. 8.

[127] "The Supreme Court — Its Homes Past and Present," American Bar Association Journal, Vol 27 (1941):283-289.

[128] Warren, *The Supreme Court in United States History,* I:164.

[129] Frank, *Marble Palace.*

[130] Quoted by Warren, *The Supreme Court in United States History,* I:457-458.

[131] Id., p. 459.

[132] *Dartmouth College v. Woodward,* 4 Wheat. 518 (1819).

[133] *National Intelligencer,* Feb. 2, 1819, quoted in Warren, *The Supreme Court in United States History,* I:460.

[134] *New York Statesman,* Feb. 7, 1824, quoted in Ibid.

[135] McCune, *The Nine Young Men,* p. 2.

[136] Quoted in Harrell, "Equal Justice Under Law: The Supreme Court in American Life," p. 116.

[137] Quoted by Lawrence L. Knutson, Associated Press, Jan. 16, 1978.

[138] *Appendix to the Budget for Fiscal Year 1980, The Budget of the U.S. Government* (Washington, D.C.: U.S. Government Printing Office, 1979), pp. 51-52.

[139] William Waldo Story, ed., *Life and Letters of Joseph Story,* 2 vols. (Boston: Little & Brown, 1851), I:302.

[140] 28 U.S.C. 371.

[141] 28 U.S.C. 372.

[142] Ibid.

[143] 28 U.S.C. 372(b).

Selected Bibliography

American Bar Association. "The Supreme Court — Its Homes Past and Present." 27 *ABA Journal* (1941).

Baker, Liva. *Felix Frankfurter.* New York: Coward-McCann, 1969.

Bickel, Alexander M. *The Caseload of the Supreme Court.* Washington, D.C.: American Enterprise Institute for Public Policy Research, 1973.

———. *Politics and the Warren Court.* New York: Harper & Row, 1965.

———. *The Unpublished Opinions of Justice Brandeis.* Cambridge: Harvard University Press, 1957.

Brennan, William J. Jr. "State Court Decisions and the Supreme Court." 31 *Pennsylvania Bar Association Quarterly* (1960).

Cranberg, Gilbert. "What Did the Supreme Court Say." *Saturday Review.* April 8, 1967.

Curtis, Charles P. Jr. *Lions Under the Throne.* Fairfield, N.J.: Kelley Press, 1947.

Elsasser, Glenn, and Fuller, Jack. "The Hidden Face of the Supreme Court." *Chicago Tribune Magazine,* April 23, 1978.

Fairman, Charles. *Mr. Justice Miller.* Cambridge: Harvard University Press, 1939.

Frank, John P. *Marble Palace: The Supreme Court in American Life.* New York: Alfred A. Knopf, 1961.

Freund, Paul A. *The Supreme Court of the United States.* Cleveland and New York: Meridian Books, 1961.

Hand, Learned. *The Bill of Rights.* Cambridge: Harvard University Press, 1958.

Harrell, Mary Ann. *Equal Justice Under Law: The Supreme Court in American Life.* Washington, D.C.: The Foundation of the Federal Bar Association with the cooperation of the National Geographic Society, 1975.

Hughes, Charles Evans. *The Supreme Court of the United States.* New York: Columbia University Press, 1928.

Jackson, Robert H. "Advocacy Before the Supreme Court: Suggestions for Effective Case Presentations." 101 *American Bar Association Journal* (1951).

King, Willard L. *Melville Weston Fuller.* New York: Macmillan Publishing Co., 1950.

Kluger, Richard. *Simple Justice: Brown v. Board of Education and Black America's Struggle for Equality.* New York: Alfred A. Knopf, 1976.

Lash, Joseph P. *From the Diaries of Felix Frankfurter.* W. W. Norton & Co., 1975.

Mason, Alpheus T. *Harlan Fiske Stone.* New York: Viking Press, 1956.

McCune, Wesley. *The Nine Young Men.* New York: Harper & Brothers, 1947.

Pfeffer, Leo. *This Honorable Court: A History of the United States Supreme Court.* Boston: Beacon Press, 1965.

Pringle, Henry F. *Life and Times of William Howard Taft.* New York: Farrar & Rinehart, 1939.

Pusey, Merlo. *Charles Evans Hughes.* New York: Columbia University Press, 1963.

Simon, James F. *In His Own Image: The Supreme Court in Richard Nixon's America.* New York: David McKay Co., 1973.

Stern, Robert L., and Gressman, Eugene. *Supreme Court Practice.* Washington, D.C.: Bureau of National Affairs, 1978.

Warren, Charles. *The Supreme Court in United States History.* rev. ed. 2 vols. Boston: Little, Brown & Co., 1922, 1926.

Williams, Richard L. "Justice Run 'Nine Little Law Firms' at Supreme Court," *Smithsonian,* February 1977.

———. "Supreme Court of the United States: The Staff That Keeps It Operating." *Smithsonian,* January 1977.

Zobell, Karl M. "Division of Opinion in the Supreme Court: A History of Judicial Disintegration." 44 *Cornell Law Quarterly* (1959).

PART VI

MEMBERS OF THE COURT

Overview 783

Biographies 793

View of Justices' Bench, Supreme Court Chamber.
Architect of the Capitol Photo No. 35571

Members of the Court

Even though it is now almost 200 years old, the Supreme Court has had only 101 members, making it one of the most exclusive as well as long-lasting government entities in the world.

All 101 justices have been men, and 100 have been white. All but 11 have been Protestants.

Yet the court has exhibited diversity in other ways — politically, geographically, and in the age, personality and previous service of its individual members. And there have been periodic breakthroughs when appointees with innovative ideas or controversial backgrounds first attained a seat on the court. The first Roman Catholic was appointed in 1835, the first Jew in 1916, the first black in 1967. No woman has yet been nominated to the court, although two women were on a list being considered by President Richard M. Nixon in 1971.

There are in fact no constitutional or statutory qualifications at all for serving on the Supreme Court. The Constitution simply states that "the judicial power of the United States shall be vested in one Supreme Court" as well as any lower federal courts the Congress may establish (Article III, Section 1) and that the president "...by and with the Advice and Consent of the Senate, shall appoint ... Judges of the Supreme Court...." There is no age limitation, no requirement that judges be native-born citizens, nor even a requirement that appointees have a legal background.

Naturally, informal criteria for membership quickly developed. Every nominee to the court has been a lawyer. And over the years a myriad of other factors have entered into the process of presidential selection. Some of them became long-lasting traditions with virtually the force of a formal requirement. Others were as fleeting as the personal friendship between an incumbent president and his nominee.

The First Justices

George Washington, as the first president, had the responsibility of choosing the original six justices of the Supreme Court. The type of men he chose and the reasons he chose them foreshadowed the process of selection carried out by his successors.

In naming the first justices, Washington paid close attention to their politics, which at that time meant primarily loyalty to the new Constitution. Of the six original appointees, three had attended the Philadelphia convention which formulated the Constitution, and the other three had supported its adoption. John Jay, the first Chief Justice, was co-author with Alexander Hamilton and James Madison of *The Federalist Papers*, a series of influential essays published in New York supporting ratification of the Constitution.

During his two terms of office (1789-97), Washington had occasion to make five additional Supreme Court appointments. All were staunch supporters of the Constitution and the new federal government.

Another of Washington's major considerations was geographical. The new states were a disparate group that had barely held together during the fight for independence and the confederation government of the 1780s. To help bind them more closely together, Washington consciously tried to represent each geographical area of the country in the nation's new supreme tribunal.

His first six appointees consisted of three northerners — Chief Justice John Jay from New York and Associate Justices William Cushing of Massachusetts and James Wilson of Pennsylvania — and three southerners — John Blair of Virginia, James Iredell of North Carolina and John Rutledge of South Carolina. The five later appointees were Oliver Ellsworth of Connecticut, Thomas Johnson and Samuel Chase of Maryland, William Paterson of New Jersey and Rutledge, appointed a second time. Thus by the time Washington left office, nine of the original 13 states had already achieved representation on the Supreme Court.

Appointment Opportunities

With a total of 11, Washington still holds the record for the number of Supreme Court appointments made by any president. The second highest total — nine — belongs to President Franklin D. Roosevelt, the only president to serve more than two terms. Roosevelt also came closest since Washington to naming the entire membership of the court — only two justices who served prior to the Roosevelt years were still on the court at the time of his death. And one of them — Harlan Fiske Stone — Roosevelt elevated from associate justice to Chief Justice.

Presidents Andrew Jackson (1829-37) and William Howard Taft (1909-13) had the next highest number of justices appointed with six each. Taft holds the record for a one-term president. Next in order are Abraham Lincoln

Longest Vacancies

The longest vacancy in the court's history lasted for two years, three months and 23 days. During that period the Senate rejected four nominations by two presidents to the seat, and future President James Buchanan declined three invitations to fill the vacancy.

When Justice Henry Baldwin died April 21, 1844, John Tyler was president. Elected vice president on the Whig ticket in 1840, Tyler broke with the party after he had become president upon William Henry Harrison's death in 1841. From then on, he was a president essentially without a party or personal popularity. At the time of Baldwin's death, one Tyler nomination to the court had already been rejected and a second was pending. Tyler first offered the Baldwin vacancy to Buchanan, who, like Baldwin, was a Pennsylvanian. When he declined, the president nominated Philadelphia attorney Edward King to the seat.

Followers of Henry Clay, however, who controlled the Senate, thought Clay would win the presidency in that year's election, and they voted in June 1844 to postpone consideration of both King's nomination and Tyler's pending appointment of Reuben H. Walworth to the second vacancy. Tyler resubmitted King's name in December. Again the Senate refused to act, and Tyler was forced to withdraw the appointment.

By this time, Tyler was a lame duck president and Clay had lost the election to Democrat James K. Polk. Nonetheless, Tyler in February 1845 named John M. Read, a Philadelphia attorney who had support among the Democrats and the Clay Whigs in the Senate. But the Senate failed to act on the nomination before adjournment, and the vacancy was left for Polk to fill.

Polk had only slightly better luck with his appointments. After six months in office he offered the position to Buchanan, who again refused it. Another few months passed before Polk formally nominated George W. Woodward to the Baldwin vacancy in December 1845.

Woodward turned out to be a hapless choice. He was opposed by one of the senators from his home state, Pennsylvania, and his extreme "American nativist" views made him unpopular with many other senators. His nomination was rejected on a 20-29 vote in January 1846. Polk then asked Buchanan once again to take the seat. Buchanan accepted but later changed his mind

and declined a third time. The president then turned to Robert C. Grier, a district court judge from Pennsylvania who proved acceptable to almost everyone. The Senate confirmed him Aug. 4, 1846, the day following his nomination.

Daniel Vacancy

The second-longest vacancy lasted almost as long as the first — two years, one month and 16 days. It occurred when Justice Peter V. Daniel of Virginia died May 31, 1860. At this point four of the remaining justices were northerners; four were from the South. Naturally, the South wanted then-President James Buchanan to replace Daniel with another southerner; the North urged a nomination from one of its states.

Buchanan took a long time making up his mind. In February 1861, nearly eight months after the vacancy occurred, he nominated Secretary of State Jeremiah S. Black, a former chief justice of the Pennsylvania supreme court and U.S. attorney general. Black might have proved acceptable to southern senators, but many of them had already resigned from the Senate to join the Confederacy. Though he supported the Union, Black was not an abolitionist, and his nomination drew criticism from the northern anti-slavery press. Black also was opposed by Democrat Stephen A. Douglas, who had just lost the presidential election to Abraham Lincoln. Finally, Republicans in the Senate were not anxious to help fill a vacancy that they could leave open for the incoming Republican president. Had Buchanan acted earlier, it is likely that Black would have been confirmed. As it was, the Senate rejected his nomination by a one-vote margin, 25-26.

Buchanan made no further attempt to fill the Daniel vacancy. Lincoln, who soon had two more seats on the court to fill, did not name anyone to the Daniel seat until July 1862 — more than a year after his inauguration. His choice was Samuel F. Miller, a well-respected Iowa attorney. Miller's nomination had been urged by a majority of both the House and Senate and by other politicians and members of the legal profession. The Senate confirmed his nomination within half an hour of receiving it July 16, 1862.

Sources: Henry J. Abraham. *Justices and Presidents: A Political History of Appointments to the Supreme Court.* New York: Oxford University Press, 1974; Charles Warren. *The Supreme Court in United States History,* rev. ed. 2 vols. Boston: Little, Brown & Company, 1922, 1926.

(1861-65) and Dwight D. Eisenhower (1953-61) with five each.

Three presidents — excluding Jimmy Carter, who as of mid-1979 had no Supreme Court vacancies to fill — made no appointments to the Supreme Court. William Henry Harrison (1841) and Zachary Taylor (1849-50) both died in office before any vacancies occurred. Andrew Johnson (1865-69), who served just six weeks short of a full term, had no chance to make a court appointment because of his rancorous political battle with Congress over Reconstruction. So bitter did the struggle become that Congress in effect took away Johnson's power of appointment by pass-

ing legislation in 1866 to reduce the court to seven members from 10 as vacancies should occur.

The legislation was occasioned by the death of Justice John Catron in 1865 and Johnson's nomination in 1866 of Henry Stanbery to replace him. The Senate took no action on Stanbery's nomination and instead passed the bill reducing the size of the court. When Justice James Wayne died in 1867, the membership of the court automatically dropped to eight. In 1869, when the Republicans had recaptured the White House, they enacted legislation increasing the court to nine seats, allowing President Ulysses S. Grant to make a nomination.

Non-partisan Appointments

As political parties became an established fact of American political life, each of the major parties sought to appoint members to the Supreme Court who would espouse their view of what the federal government should and should not do.

As Washington had appointed supporters of the new Constitution, so most presidents have selected nominees with whom they were philosophically and politically in accord. Whenever a president goes to the opposite political party to find a nominee, it is the exception rather than the rule.

The first clear-cut instance of a president of one party appointing a member of the other to the Supreme Court was Republican Abraham Lincoln's selection of Democrat Stephen J. Field of California in 1863. President John Tyler, elected vice president as a Whig in 1840, appointed Democrat Samuel Nelson to the court in 1845, but by that time Tyler was no longer identified with either major political party.

After Lincoln's example, Republican presidents occasionally appointed Democrats to the court. President Benjamin Harrison selected Democrat Howell E. Jackson of Tennessee in 1893; Warren G. Harding appointed Democrat Pierce Butler in 1922; Herbert Hoover appointed Democrat Benjamin N. Cardozo in 1932; Dwight D. Eisenhower appointed Democrat William J. Brennan Jr. in 1956; and Richard Nixon appointed Democrat Lewis F. Powell Jr. in 1971. Republican William Howard Taft was the only president to appoint more than one member of the opposite party to the court. Three of his six nominees to the court were Democrats — Edward D. White, whom he elevated from associate justice to Chief Justice, and Horace Lurton and Joseph R. Lamar, southern Democrats appointed respectively in 1909 and 1910.

Only three Democrats appointed Republicans to the court. Woodrow Wilson named Louis D. Brandeis, a nominal Republican, to the bench in 1916. Franklin D. Roosevelt elevated Republican Harlan Fiske Stone from associate justice to Chief Justice in 1941. Harry S Truman appointed Republican Sen. Harold H. Burton of Ohio, an old friend and Senate colleague, in 1945.

Lobbying for a Nomination

Presidential selection of justices is usually the result of a balancing of factors and a sifting of potential candidates before the president finally makes up his mind. But on a few occasions in American history, a president's choice has all but been made for him by overwhelming pressure for a particular nominee.

One of the more dramatic instances of this process occurred in 1853, when President Franklin Pierce nominated John A. Campbell of Alabama for a spot on the court. Campbell was a 41-year-old lawyer who had such a brilliant reputation that the Supreme Court justices decided they wanted him as a colleague. As a result, the entire membership of the court wrote to Pierce requesting Campbell's nomination. To emphasize their point, they sent two justices to the president to deliver the letters in person. Pierce complied, and Campbell was confirmed within four days.

In 1862 President Lincoln was looking for a new justice from the Midwest. The Iowa congressional delegation began pressing for the appointment of Samuel F. Miller, a doctor and lawyer who had helped form the Iowa Republican Party and had a strong reputation for moral and intellec-

tual integrity. The movement grew rapidly until 129 of 140 House members and all but four senators had signed a petition for Miller's nomination. With such massive and unprecedented congressional support, Miller received Lincoln's approval despite his lack of any judicial experience. He became the first justice from west of the Mississippi River.

In 1932 a strong national movement began for the appointment of Benjamin Cardozo, chief judge of the New York court of appeals, to the Supreme Court. Cardozo was a Democrat, while the president who was to make the appointment, Herbert Hoover, was a Republican. Furthermore, Cardozo was Jewish and there was already one Jew on the court, Louis D. Brandeis. Under these circumstances, it was considered unlikely Hoover would make the nomination.

But Cardozo's record was so impressive that a groundswell of support arose for him. Deans and faculty members of the nation's leading law schools, chief judges of other state courts, labor and business leaders, and powerful senators all urged Hoover to choose Cardozo. Despite his desire to appoint a western Republican, Hoover finally yielded and nominated Cardozo, who was confirmed without opposition.

Geographical Factors

George Washington's weighing of geographical factors in appointing the first justices continued as a tradition for over a century. It was re-enforced by the justices' duty under the Judiciary Act of 1789 to attend circuit court sessions. Presidents strove not only for geographical balance in their appointments, but considered it important that each justice be a native of the circuit over which he presided.

But the burdensome attendance requirement was curtailed by legislation during the 19th century until it became optional in 1891 and was abolished altogether in 1911. In the 20th century, geography became less and less a consideration in Supreme Court nominations, although as recently as 1970 President Nixon made an issue of it in the failure of the Senate to confirm two southerners — Clement Haynsworth Jr. and G. Harrold Carswell — to the court. Nixon claimed the Senate would not confirm a conservative southerner and turned to Minnesotan Harry A. Blackmun instead.

In its heyday, the geographical factor was sometimes almost sacrosanct. The most enduring example was the so-called New England seat, which was occupied by a New Englander, usually from Massachusetts, from 1789 to 1932. There was also a seat for a New Yorker from 1806 to 1894 and a Maryland-Virginia seat from 1789 to 1860. *(Details, box, next page)*

Geography had strong political ramifications as well. This was especially so in the case of the South. With the growth of sectional differences, particularly over the slavery issue, before the Civil War, the South felt itself to be on the defensive. One of the ways it sought to defend its interests was to gain a majority on the Supreme Court. And, indeed, five of the nine justices in 1860 were from slaveholding states.

With the coming of the Civil War, the sectional balance of power shifted. Four of the five southern justices died between 1860 and 1867, and another — Justice John A. Campbell of Alabama — resigned to join the Confederate cause.

Regional Seats on the Supreme Court

Geography was a prime consideration in the appointment of Supreme Court justices throughout the 19th century. Presidents found it expedient to have each of the expanding nation's rival sections represented on the court. Whenever a justice died or resigned, his replacement usually came from the same state or a neighboring one. In addition, the justices' circuit duties, which required them to attend court sessions in their circuits periodically, made it desirable for each justice to be a native of the circuit over which he presided.

The 'New England Seat'

The most notable instance of geographical continuity was the seat traditionally held by a New Englander. William Cushing of Massachusetts was appointed an associate justice by President George Washington in 1789. From then until 1932, the seat was held by a New England appointee, usually from Massachusetts.

When Cushing died after 21 years on the court, President James Madison looked to New England for a successor. He offered the post to both former Attorney General Levi Lincoln and John Quincy Adams, both from Massachusetts, but they declined. After Madison's nomination of Alexander Wolcott of Connecticut was turned down by the Senate, the president turned back to Massachusetts and selected Joseph Story, at 32 the youngest justice ever chosen.

Story served 34 years, dying in 1845. James K. Polk, who was then president, chose to continue the New England tradition of holding the seat by appointing Levi Woodbury of New Hampshire, a prominent Jacksonian who had served as governor, U.S. senator, secretary of the Navy, and secretary of the Treasury.

Woodbury's tenure lasted less than six years, and it fell to President Millard Fillmore to find a successor. He chose Benjamin Curtis, another Massachusetts native.

Curtis resigned in 1857 after only five and a half years, largely because of his acrimonious relations with other members of the Taney court. President James Buchanan, mindful of the continued need for a New Englander on the court, chose Nathan Clifford of Maine, a former attorney general.

Clifford served until his death in July 1881, shortly after President James A. Garfield was shot. When Garfield died in September his successor, Chester Arthur, chose the chief justice of the Massachusetts supreme court, Horace Gray, to replace Clifford.

Gray served until 1902, when he was succeeded by another Massachusetts supreme court chief justice, Oliver Wendell Holmes Jr., appointed by President Theodore Roosevelt.

By the time of Holmes' appointment, however, the significance of geography had declined as a qualification for selection to the Supreme Court. President Theodore Roosevelt, in particular, was disdainful of such a prerequisite and it was mostly accidental that Holmes came from Massachusetts. Nevertheless, his selection extended for another 30 years the tradition of the "New England seat."

After Holmes' resignation in 1932, President Herbert Hoover chose as his successor Benjamin N. Cardozo, chief judge of New York State's highest court, thus ending the Supreme Court's longest-lasting geographical tradition. And while Cardozo's successor, Felix Frankfurter, was a resident of Massachusetts, that fact apparently played no role in his selection.

The 'New York Seat'

New York was another longtime holder of a specific seat on the Supreme Court. With the appointment of Justice Henry Brockholst Livingston by President Thomas Jefferson in 1806, a tradition began which continued until New Yorkers themselves ended it in 1894 by their internal quarreling.

Livingston served until his death in 1823. President James Monroe offered the post indirectly to Martin Van Buren, then a U.S. senator, but received a non-committal response. The president then chose Smith Thompson of New York, his secretary of the Navy. Thompson served for 20 years. His death in 1843 came at an inopportune moment politically: President John Tyler was disliked by both Democrats and Whigs and had little political leverage. His attempts to choose a successor to Thompson met with repeated failure, the Senate defeating one nominee and forcing another to withdraw. Finally, at the last moment before leaving office in 1845, Tyler found a New Yorker acceptable to the Senate for the post. He was Samuel Nelson, who continued to serve until his resignation in December 1872.

Two more New Yorkers held the seat after Nelson's retirement, Ward Hunt from 1873 to 1882 and Samuel Blatchford from 1882 to 1893. But then a bitter quarrel between New Yorkers over the seat ended the tradition.

The two main New York antagonists were President Grover Cleveland and Sen. David B. Hill, old political enemies. Cleveland twice nominated a New Yorker for the post, and twice Hill used senatorial courtesy to object to the nominees. In both cases, the Senate followed its own tradition of honoring a senator's objection to a nominee of his own party from his own state and rejected Cleveland's choices. On his third try to fill the vacancy, Cleveland abandoned New York and chose U.S. Senator Edward D. White of Louisiana, who was confirmed immediately by his colleagues.

The 'Virginia-Maryland Seat'

Virginia and Maryland shared a seat on the Supreme Court from the first appointments in 1789 until the Civil War. John Blair of Virginia, appointed by President Washington, served until 1796. Washington chose as his successor Samuel Chase of Maryland. After his death in 1811, another Marylander, Gabriel Duvall, was given the seat. Upon his resignation in 1835, the seat went back to Virginia, with Philip P. Barbour holding it from 1836 to 1841 and Peter V. Daniel from 1841 to 1860. With the coming of the Civil War, there was a realignment of circuits as well as the desire of the new Republican administration to appoint more northerners and westerners to the court. The Maryland-Virginia tradition was ended when Iowan Samuel F. Miller was appointed as Daniel's successor by President Abraham Lincoln.

Not one of these justices was replaced by a southerner. Thus by 1870 every Supreme Court seat was held by a northerner or westerner. But with the gradual decline of bitterness over the war, southern members again began to appear on the court. President Rutherford B. Hayes, who sought to reconcile relations between the North and South, made the first move by appointing William B. Woods of Georgia in 1880. Woods was not a native southerner, having migrated there after the Civil War. But despite this "carpetbagger" background, he was never identified with the corruption and profligacy associated with the Reconstruction era. As a federal judge for the fifth — deep-South — circuit, he gained the respect of his neighbors for his fairness and honesty.

The first native southerner appointed to the court after the Civil War was Woods' successor, Lucius Q. C. Lamar of Mississippi, appointed by President Grover Cleveland in 1888. Lamar had personally drafted Mississippi's ordinance of secession in 1861 and had served the Confederacy both as a military officer and as a diplomatic envoy to Europe. So his accession to the court was an even more significant symbol of reconciliation between the sections than Woods' appointment eight years earlier.

Thirty-one states have contributed justices to the Supreme Court. New York has by far the highest total, with 13, followed by Ohio with ten and Massachusetts with eight. Several major states have had only one justice, including Texas, Indiana and Missouri — as have such small states as Utah, Maine and Wyoming.

Of the 19 states which have never had a native on the court, most are smaller western states. Only six of the 19 are east of the Mississippi River. The largest state never to have had a justice is Florida, the ninth most populous state according to the 1970 census.

The lack of representation on the court from some of the smaller states resulted in a controversy during the 1950s when North Dakota's outspoken maverick Sen. William Langer began opposing all non-North Dakotan Supreme Court nominees as a protest against big-state nominees. Langer was chairman of the Senate Judiciary Committee during the 83rd Congress (1953-55). In 1954 he joined in delaying tactics against the nomination of Earl Warren as Chief Justice, managing to hold off confirmation for two months. He continued his struggle for the next six years, until his death in 1959.

Only Lawyers

All of President Washington's appointees were lawyers, and no president has deviated from this precedent. The legal education of the justices has changed radically over the years, however. Until the mid-19th century, it was traditional for aspiring lawyers to study privately in a law office until they had learned the law sufficiently to pass the bar. There were no law schools as such in the early years, although some universities had courses in law. John Marshall, for example, attended a course of law lectures at William and Mary College in the 1770s. Two of the earliest justices — John Rutledge and John Blair — received their legal education in England, at the Inns of Court. A modern justice, Frank Murphy (1940-49), also studied there.

Of the 54 justices (including Rutledge and Blair) who attended law school, by far the largest number (12) attended Harvard. Yale taught eight justices law and Columbia five. The first justice to receive a law degree from an American university was Benjamin R. Curtis, who got his from Harvard in 1832.

But it was not until 1957 that the Supreme Court was composed, for the first time, entirely of law school graduates. Before that, many had attended law school, but had not received degrees. The last justice never to have attended law school was James F. Byrnes, who served from 1941 to 1942. The son of poor Irish immigrants, Byrnes never even graduated from high school. He left school at the age of 14, worked as a law clerk and eventually became a court stenographer. Reading law in his spare time, Byrnes passed the bar at the age of 24.

The last justice not to have a law degree was Stanley F. Reed, who served from 1938 to 1957. He attended both the University of Virginia and Columbia law schools, but received a degree from neither.

Pre-court Experience

Judges. Most justices have been active either in politics or in judicial office before coming to the Supreme Court. In fact, only one justice — George Shiras Jr. — had never engaged in political or judicial activities before his appointment. A total of 60 justices had some judicial experience — federal or state — before coming to the Supreme Court. Surprisingly, there have been many more who had experience on the state level (42) than on the federal level (25). (There is an overlap in the figures because seven justices had both federal and state judicial offices.)

All except two of President Washington's appointees had state judicial experience, the president believing that such experience was important for justices of the new federal court. But it was not until 1826 that a justice with previous federal judicial experience was appointed. He was Robert Trimble, who had served nine years as a U.S. district judge before being elevated to the Supreme Court.

Even after Trimble's appointment, judges with federal judicial experience continued to be a rarity on the Supreme Court. By 1880 only two other federal judges — Philip P. Barbour in 1836 and Peter V. Daniel in 1841 — had made it to the highest court. After 1880, when federal circuit judge William B. Woods was appointed, the pace picked up, and federal judicial experience became an increasingly important criterion for appointment to the Supreme Court. In 1979 five of the nine sitting justices, a majority, had held previous federal judicial office.

Politicians. Many justices have come from a political background, serving in Congress, as governors or as members of a Cabinet. One president, William Howard Taft, was later appointed to the court, as Chief Justice, in 1921.

More than a fourth of all justices — 27 — held congressional office before their elevation to the court. An additional six justices sat in the Continental Congress in the 1770s or 1780s.

The first justice who had a congressional background was William Paterson, who had served in the Senate from 1789 to 1790. Chief Justice John Marshall was the first justice with Cabinet experience, having held the post of secretary of State from 1800 to 1801.

Only a few incumbent members of Congress have been directly nominated to the Supreme Court. Only one incumbent House member, James M. Wayne in 1835, has ever been named to the court, and six incumbent senators: Oliver Ellsworth in 1796, John McKinley in 1837, Levi Woodbury in 1846, Edward D. White in 1894, Hugo L. Black in 1937 and Harold H. Burton in 1945.

The Senate has traditionally confirmed its own members without much debate. But in January 1853 when lame-

Catholic and Jewish Justices

The overwhelming Protestant complexion of the Supreme Court has been broken only 11 times; 90 of the 101 justices have been of Protestant background.

The first Catholic nominee, Chief Justice Roger B. Taney, was controversial not because of his religion, but because of his close alliance with his sponsor, the highly political Andrew Jackson.

Not until 1894 — 30 years after Taney's death — was the second Catholic, Edward D. White, appointed; he became Chief Justice 16 years later. White's religion, like Taney's, was not an issue. Both men were from traditional Catholic regions, and their faith had not been a factor during their long political careers. In President McKinley's 1897 appointment of Catholic Joseph McKenna, geography was the overriding factor; he replaced another Californian, Stephen J. Field.

Pierce Butler was the next Catholic appointee. President Warren G. Harding named him to the bench in 1922, largely because of Butler's political base. He was a Democrat, and Harding wanted to make a show of bipartisanship.

On Butler's death in late 1939, President Franklin D. Roosevelt picked as his successor Frank Murphy, an Irish Catholic politician who had been mayor of Detroit, governor of Michigan, and was then serving as Roosevelt's attorney general. In 1949, when Murphy died, President Truman broke the continuity of a Catholic seat on the court by naming a Protestant, Tom C. Clark. For the first time since 1894, there was no Catholic on the court.

Of all the Catholic appointments, that of William J. Brennan Jr. by President Eisenhower in 1956 attracted the most notice, although it too was relatively non-controversial. But it was an election year and the Republicans were making a strong appeal to normally Democratic Catholic voters in the big cities. Some saw Brennan's appointment as part of that GOP strategy, although Eisenhower insisted it was an appointment made purely on merit.

Much more controversial than any of the Catholic nominees was Louis D. Brandeis, the first Jewish justice, named by President Wilson in 1916. Brandeis was already a figure of great controversy because of his views on social and economic matters. Conservatives bitterly fought his nomination, and there was an element of anti-Semitism in some of the opposition. When Brandeis took his seat on the court, Justice McReynolds refused to speak to him for three years and once refused to sit next to him for a court picture-taking session.

Herbert Hoover's nomination of Benjamin N. Cardozo in 1932 established a so-called Jewish seat on the Supreme Court. Justice Felix Frankfurter replaced Cardozo in 1939. He in turn was replaced by Justice Arthur J. Goldberg in 1962. And when Goldberg resigned his court position to become U.S. Ambassador to the United Nations, President Lyndon B. Johnson chose Abe Fortas to replace him.

But with Justice Fortas' resignation in 1969, President Richard M. Nixon broke the tradition of a "Jewish seat" by choosing Harry A. Blackmun of Minnesota, a Protestant.

duck President Millard Fillmore nominated Whig Sen. George Badger of North Carolina to the court, the Democratic Senate postponed the nomination until the close of the congressional session in March. Then the new Democratic president, Franklin Pierce, was able to nominate his own man. The postponement of Badger's nomination was a polite way of defeating a colleague's nomination, avoiding an outright rejection.

Sen. White's nomination came about after a bitter quarrel between President Grover Cleveland and Sen. David B. Hill of New York resulted in the Senate's rejection of two Cleveland nominees from New York. Cleveland then turned to the Senate for one of its own members, White, and that body quickly approved him. *(See p. 657)*

Sen. Hugo. L. Black's 1937 nomination was surrounded by controversy. Sen. Joseph T. Robinson of Arkansas, the Senate majority leader who had led the fight for President Franklin D. Roosevelt's so-called "court-packing" plan, was expected to get the nomination but died suddenly. So Roosevelt picked Black, one of the few southern senators other than Robinson who had championed the president in the court battle. Black's support of the controversial bill — plus what some felt was his general lack of qualifications for the Supreme Court — led to a brief but acrimonious fight over his nomination. After he was confirmed, publicity grew over his one-time membership in the Ku Klux Klan, and charges were made that he was still a member. But in a nationwide radio address, Black denied any racial or religious intolerance on his part and defused the criticism.

The last Supreme Court appointee with any previous congressional service was Sherman Minton in 1949. He had served as a U.S. senator from Indiana from 1935 to 1941, then was appointed to a circuit court of appeals judgeship. Since the retirement of Justice Black in 1971, no Supreme Court member has had any congressional experience.

Cabinet Members. Since John Adams' secretary of state, John Marshall, was appointed to the Supreme Court, 22 other Cabinet secretaries became justices, 13 of them appointed while still serving in the Cabinet. Heading the list of Cabinet positions that led to Supreme Court seats is that of attorney general. Nine attorneys general, including seven incumbents, have been appointed to the court. Next came secretaries of the Treasury (four), secretaries of state (three) and secretaries of the Navy (three). One postmaster general, one secretary of the interior, one secretary of war and one secretary of labor were appointed to the court.

The appointment of incumbent attorneys general has been largely a 20th-century phenomenon: Six of the seven appointments occurred after 1900. The other occurred just before that, when President William McKinley appointed his attorney general, Joseph McKenna. The 20th-century incumbents named to the court were William H. Moody, appointed by Theodore Roosevelt in 1906; James C. McReynolds (Wilson, 1914); Harlan Fiske Stone (Coolidge, 1925); Frank Murphy (Franklin D. Roosevelt, 1940); Robert H. Jackson (Roosevelt, 1941); and Tom C. Clark (Truman, 1949).

In the 19th century two men who had served as attorney general eventually were elevated to the Supreme Court, but appointment followed their Cabinet service by some years. They were Roger B. Taney, appointed Chief Justice by President Andrew Jackson in 1835, after serving as Jackson's attorney general from 1831 to 1833, and Nathan Clifford, appointed to the court by President James Buchanan in 1857 after service as James K. Polk's attorney general from 1846 to 1848.

Foreign-Born Justices

Since the Constitution makes no stipulation that Supreme Court justices must be native-born Americans, presidents are free to name foreign-born members to the court.

In all, six Supreme Court justices were born outside the United States, although one was the son of an American missionary who was temporarily living abroad. Of the remaining five, four were born in the British Isles. Only one — Felix Frankfurter — was born in a non-English-speaking country.

President George Washington appointed three of the foreign-born justices. The others were selected by Presidents Benjamin Harrison, Warren G. Harding and Franklin D. Roosevelt.

The six justices born outside the United States, in order of their appointment, are:

● James Wilson, born Sept. 14, 1742, in Caskardy, Scotland. Wilson grew up in Scotland and was educated at St. Andrews University in preparation for a career in the ministry. But in 1765 he sailed for America, where he studied law and went into land speculation. A signer of the Declaration of Independence, Wilson also was a member of the 1787 Constitutional Convention and its committee of detail, which was responsible for writing the first draft of the Constitution. In 1789 President Washington appointed Wilson one of the original members of the Supreme Court. In the late 1790s, Wilson's land speculations failed and he was jailed twice for debt while riding circuit and died in a dingy inn in North Carolina.

● James Iredell, born Oct. 5, 1751, in Lewes, England. Iredell was born into an old English family allegedly descended indirectly from Oliver Cromwell's son-in-law. Through family connections, Iredell received an appointment as colonial comptroller of customs at Edenton, N.C., at the age of 17. After six years he was promoted to collector of the port of Edenton. Iredell identified with the colonial cause and resigned his job as collector in 1776. While serving in his colonial offices, Iredell had studied law and began practice in 1770. In 1788 he was a strong supporter of the new federal Constitution and worked for its ratification by North Carolina. President Washington appointed him a Supreme Court justice in 1790. He served until his death in 1799 at the age of 47, the youngest justice ever to die on the court.

● William Paterson, born Dec. 24, 1745, in County Antrim, Ireland. Paterson emigrated to America with his parents when he was only two years old. He received his education at Princeton University and then read law,

opening his own law practice in 1769. Paterson was active in New Jersey affairs during the Revolutionary and Confederation periods, and served as a delegate to the Constitutional Convention in 1787. He was a member of the First Senate in 1789-90 and as a member of the Judiciary Committee helped write the Judiciary Act of 1789. Later, he codified the laws of the state of New Jersey, and in association with Alexander Hamilton laid out plans for the industrial city of Paterson. He was appointed to the Supreme Court by President Washington in 1793 and served until his death in 1806.

● David J. Brewer, born Jan. 30, 1837, in Smyrna, Turkey. Brewer was a member of an old New England family whose father was serving as a Congregational missionary in Turkey. The family returned to the United States soon after Brewer's birth. Brewer sought his fortune in Kansas and spent most of his career in the Kansas court system and lower federal courts. He was elevated to the Supreme Court by President Benjamin Harrison in 1890. Brewer's mother was the sister of Supreme Court Justice Stephen J. Field (1863-97) and Cyrus W. Field, promoter of the first Atlantic cable.

● George Sutherland, born March 25, 1862, in Buckinghamshire, England. Sutherland's father converted to Mormonism about the time of George's birth and moved his family to the Utah Territory. Although the senior Sutherland soon deserted the Mormons, the family remained in Utah, where George was educated at Brigham Young University. When Utah entered the Union as a state in 1896, Sutherland was elected to the state legislature. In 1900 he won a seat in the U.S. House and went on to serve two terms in the U.S. Senate (1905-17) before being defeated for re-election. While in the Senate, he formed a close friendship to a fellow senator, Warren G. Harding of Ohio. When Harding became president, he appointed Sutherland to the Supreme Court. Later, Sutherland became one of the justices known as implacable foes of President Franklin D. Roosevelt's New Deal.

● Felix Frankfurter, born Nov. 15, 1882, in Vienna, Austria. Frankfurter came to the United States with his parents in 1894 and grew up on the lower East Side of New York City. He achieved a brilliant academic record at City College and Harvard Law School, entering practice in New York City. In 1914 he joined the Harvard Law faculty and remained there, with time out for some governmental service during World War I, until his appointment to the Supreme Court by President Franklin D. Roosevelt in 1939.

The last Supreme Court justice with Cabinet experience was Tom C. Clark (1949-67), once Truman's attorney general.

Governors. Only five governors or former governors have ever been appointed to the Supreme Court. The most recent — and the most famous — was California Gov. Earl Warren, appointed Chief Justice by President Eisenhower in 1953. Warren had a long politicl career behind him, having served as attorney general of California before winning three terms as governor of his state. In 1948 he was

the Republican nominee for vice president and was briefly a candidate for the presidential nomination in 1952.

The only other incumbent governor ever appointed to the court was Charles Evans Hughes of New York, chosen by President Taft in 1910. Hughes was a reform governor who had conducted investigations into fraudulent insurance practices in New York before being elected governor in 1906. He left the court in 1916 to run for president on the Republican ticket, losing narrowly to Woodrow Wilson. Later he served as secretary of state under Presidents

Harding and Coolidge and returned to the court in 1930 as Chief Justice.

The three other former governors appointed to the Supreme Court were Levi Woodbury of New Hampshire in 1846 (governor, 1823-24), Salmon P. Chase of Ohio in 1864 (governor, 1856-60), and Frank Murphy of Michigan in 1940 (governor, 1937-39).

Generation Gaps

The age at which justices joined the court has varied widely. The oldest person ever initially appointed was Horace H. Lurton, who was 65 when he went on the court in 1910. Two Chief Justices were older than that when they achieved their office, but they had already served on the court previously: Harlan Fiske Stone was 68, in 1941; and Charles Evans Hughes 67, in 1930.

Representing the younger generation, Justices William Johnson and Joseph Story were both only 32 when they were appointed in 1804 and 1811 respectively. Story was younger than Johnson by about a month.

Only two other justices were under 40 when appointed: Bushrod Washington, nephew of the president, who was 36 when appointed in 1798, and James Iredell, who was 38 when appointed in 1790. Iredell also was the youngest justice to die on the court — 48 when he died in 1799.

The youngest justice in the 20th century was William O. Douglas, who was 40 when appointed in 1939.

The oldest justice ever on the court was Oliver Wendell Holmes, who retired at 90 in 1932, the court's only nonagenarian. The second-oldest member, Chief Justice Roger B. Taney, was 87 when he died in 1864. All other justices who reached 80 retired from the bench. They were Louis D. Brandeis and Gabriel Duvall, both 82, Joseph McKenna and Stephen J. Field, both 81, and Samuel Nelson, 80.

The youngest member ever to leave the court was Benjamin Curtis, who resigned in 1857 at 47. Others who left the court before the age of 50 were Justices Iredell, dead at 48, Alfred Moore, who retired at 48, and John Jay and John A. Campbell, who retired at 49. Jay also holds the record for number of years survived after leaving the court — 34 years. In modern times, Justice James F. Byrnes lived 29 years after resigning from the court in 1942.

Longevity

Length of service on the court has also varied greatly, from 15 months to 36 years. Justice James F. Byrnes served the shortest time, being confirmed by the Senate June 12, 1941, but resigning on Oct. 3, 1942, to become director of the World War II Office of Economic Stabilization.

Justice Thomas Johnson, who served from 1791 to 1793, was on the court only 16 months. Although he retired because of ill health, he lived another 26 years, dying at the age of 87.

Edwin Stanton, the controversial secretary of war during the Lincoln and Andrew Johnson administrations, was nominated for the Supreme Court by President Grant. The Senate confirmed him on Dec. 20, 1869, but Stanton died suddenly of a heart attack on Dec. 24. Since he did not have a chance to begin his service on the court, he is not considered to have been a justice.

In January 1974 Justice William O. Douglas broke the old longevity record for service on the court, held since December 1897 by Stephen J. Field, who had served 34 years and nine months when he resigned. Douglas went on to serve until November 1975, when he resigned after 36 years and seven months on the court.

Chief Justice John Marshall established the first longevity record by serving for 34 years and five months between 1801 and 1835. That record held until Field broke it in 1897.

Other justices who served 30 years or longer include Hugo L. Black (34 years, 1 month), the first John Marshall Harlan and Joseph Story (33 years each), James Wayne (32 years), John McLean (31 years), and Bushrod Washington and William Johnson (30 years each).

Black's 34 years occurred in an era of such changing membership on the court that he served at one time or another with 28 different justices, more than a quarter of the court's entire membership throughout its history.

Four or five years is usually the longest the court goes without a change in justices. But there was one lengthy period — 12 years — when the court maintained the same membership intact. That was from 1811, when Joseph Story was confirmed, to 1823, when Justice Henry Brockholst Livingston died.

Infirmity

Longevity of service sometimes leads to questions of disability, as justices age and are no longer capable of carrying a full load of casework. By early 1870, Justice Robert C. Grier was nearly 76. His mental and physical powers were obviously impaired and he often seemed confused and feeble. Grier complied when a committee of his fellow justices finally approached him to urge his resignation. He died eight months later.

Among the justices urging Grier's retirement was Stephen J. Field. Ironically, a quarter of a century later, Field found himself in the same position as Grier. His powers had visibly declined and he was taking less and less part in court proceedings. The other justices finally began hinting strongly that Field resign. But Field insisted on staying on the court long enough to break Chief Justice John Marshall's record for length of service on the court.

A Disabled Court. In 1880 the court was manned by an especially infirm set of justices; three of the nine were incapacitated. Justice Ward Hunt had suffered a paralytic stroke in 1879 and took no further part in court proceedings, but he refused to resign because he was not eligible for a full pension under the law then in effect. Finally, after three years, Congress passed a special law exempting Hunt from the terms of the pension law, granting him retirement at full pay if he would resign from the court within 30 days of enactment of the exemption. Hunt resigned the same day.

Justice Nathan Clifford also had suffered a stroke which prevented him from participating in court activities. But Clifford also refused to resign, hoping to live long enough for a Democratic president to name a successor. At the time, Clifford was the only Democrat left on the court who had been named by a Democratic president. But he died while Republicans were still in power.

While Hunt and Clifford were both incapacitated, Justice Noah Swayne's mental acuity was noticeably declining. He was finally persuaded to resign by President Rutherford B. Hayes, with the promise that Swayne's friend and fellow Ohioan Stanley Matthews would be chosen as his successor.

The most recent case of a court disability was that of Justice William O. Douglas, who suffered a stroke in January 1975. At first, Douglas attempted to continue his duties, but in November 1975 he resigned, citing the pain and physical disability resulting from the stroke.

Controversial Justices

The only time a justice clearly has been driven from the court by outside pressure occurred in 1969, when Justice Abe Fortas resigned. The resignation followed by less than eight months a successful Senate filibuster against President Lyndon B. Johnson's nomination of Fortas to be Chief Justice. Fortas' departure from the court climaxed a furor brought on by the disclosure early in May 1969 that he had received and held for 11 months a $20,000 fee from the family foundation of a man later imprisoned for illegal stock manipulation.

A year after Fortas' resignation, an attempt was made to bring impeachment charges against Justice Douglas. General dissatisfaction with Douglas' liberal views and controversial lifestyle — combined with frustration over the Senate's rejection of two of President Nixon's conservative southern nominees — seemed to spark the action. House Republican leader Gerald R. Ford of Michigan, who led the attempt to impeach Douglas, charged among other things that the justice had practiced law in violation of federal law, had failed to disqualify himself in cases in which he had an interest, and violated standards of good behavior by allegedly advocating revolution. A special House Judiciary subcommittee created to investigate the charges found no grounds for impeachment.

The only Supreme Court justice ever to be impeached was Samuel Chase. A staunch Federalist who had rankled Jeffersonians with his partisan political statements and vigorous prosecution of the Alien and Sedition Acts, Chase was impeached by the House in 1804. But his critics failed to achieve the necessary two-thirds majority in the Senate for conviction. *(For details of the Fortas, Douglas and Chase cases, see pp. 658-663)*

Questionable Behavior

Other, less heralded cases, have occurred from time to time that resulted in increased criticism of the justices. One early controversy surfaced in 1857, when the nation was awaiting the court's decision in the *Dred Scott* case. Justices Robert C. Grier and John Catron wrote privately to the incoming president, James Buchanan, detailing the court's discussions and foretelling the final decision. Buchanan was glad of the news and was able to say in his inaugural address that the decision was expected to come soon and that he and all Americans should acquiesce in it. But divulging the court's decision before it is publicly announced is generally considered to be unethical.

Another controversy arose 14 years later in the so-called Legal Tender Cases. The court, with two vacancies, had found the Civil War legal tender acts unconstitutional. But then President Grant named two justices to fill the vacancies, and the court voted to rehear the case. With the two new justices — William Strong and Joseph P. Bradley — voting with the majority, the court now found the legal tender acts constitutional. It was charged that Grant had appointed the two knowing in advance that they would vote to reverse the court's previous decision. But historians have not turned up any evidence that there was any explicit arrangement involved.

Political activity by Supreme Court justices has usually been frowned upon — especially in the 19th century, when several justices manifested a hunger for their party's presidential nomination.

Justice John McLean entertained presidential ambitions throughout his long Supreme Court career (1829-61)

Relatives on the Court

Several sets of relatives have served as Supreme Court justices. In two instances, they were on the court at the same time. There have been no father-son combinations, but one grandfather-grandson, one uncle-nephew and one father-in-law-son-in-law tandem. At least one pair of cousins served on the court.

The two John Marshall Harlans were grandfather and grandson. The elder Harlan, a Kentucky politician, was put on the court by President Rutherford B. Hayes in 1877 and served until 1911 — one of the longest periods of service in court history. His grandson and namesake was born and grew up in Chicago, but made his career as a highly successful Wall Street lawyer. His service extended from his appointment by President Dwight D. Eisenhower in 1954 until his resignation in September 1971.

Stephen J. Field was appointed to the Supreme Court by President Abraham Lincoln in 1863. Twenty-six years later, in 1889, he was still on the court when President Benjamin Harrison named his nephew, David J. Brewer, as an associate justice. Brewer was Field's sister's son. The two served together on the court from 1889 to Field's death in 1897.

Although Justice Stanley Matthews was only four years older than Justice Horace Gray, Matthews became Gray's posthumous father-in-law. Both justices were appointed in 1881, Matthews by President James A. Garfield and Gray later in the year by President Chester Arthur. They served together on the court until Matthews' death in March 1889. In June of the same year, Gray, a 61-year-old bachelor, married Matthews' daughter Jane.

The two Lamars who served on the court — Lucius Quintus Cincinnatus Lamar of Mississippi and Joseph Rucker Lamar of Georgia — were cousins. They were descendants of a Huguenot family that settled in the colonies in the 1600s. Lucius served on the court from 1888 to 1893, the first native-born southerner to be appointed after the Civil War. Joseph, appointed by President William Howard Taft, served from 1910 to 1916. Other prominent members of the same family were Mirabeau Buonaparte Lamar, second president of the Republic of Texas (1838-41), and Gazzaway Bugg Lamar, merchant, banker, and Confederate agent.

and flirted with several political parties at various stages. In 1856 he received 190 votes on an informal first ballot at the first Republican national convention. He also sought the Republican presidential nomination in 1860.

Chief Justice Salmon P. Chase had aspired to the presidency before going on the bench, losing the Republican nomination to Lincoln in 1860. In 1864, while serving as Lincoln's secretary of the Treasury, he allowed himself to become the focus of an anti-Lincoln group within the Republican Party. During his service on the court, in both 1868 and 1872, he made no secret of his still-burning presidential ambitions and allowed friends to maneuver politically for him.

In 1877 the Supreme Court was thrust into the election process when a dispute arose as to the outcome of the 1876 presidential election. To resolve the problem, Congress created a special electoral commission that included five

Supreme Court justices. Each chamber of Congress also chose five members, the Democratic House choosing five Democrats and the Republican Senate choosing five Republicans.

The five justices were supposed to be divided evenly politically — two Democrats, Nathan Clifford and Stephen J. Field, two Republicans, Samuel F. Miller and William Strong, and one independent, David Davis. Davis, however, withdrew from consideration because he had been elected a U.S. senator from Illinois. Justice Joseph P. Bradley, a Republican, was substituted for Justice Davis, making the overall lineup on the commission 8 to 7 in favor of the Republicans.

The three Republican justices loyally supported the claims of Republican presidential aspirant Rutherford B. Hayes on all questions, and the two Democratic justices backed Democratic nominee Samuel J. Tilden.

The result was the election of Hayes. Justice Clifford, the chairman of the commission, was so contemptuous of the outcome that he called Hayes an illegitimate president and refused to enter the White House during his incumbency.

The Justices of the Supreme Court: Biographies in Brief

This directory includes vital statistics and brief accounts of the lives and public careers of each of the 101 justices of the Supreme Court through mid-1979. They are listed in the chronological order of their appointment to the court; the dates beneath each justice's name indicate his period of service.

Sources used in compiling these biographies included: individual biographies of the justices; *The Justices of the United States Supreme Court 1789-1969: Their Lives and Major Opinions*, ed. Leon Friedman and Fred L. Israel, R.

R. Bowker Company, New York, 1969; *Dictionary of American Biography*, Charles Scribner's Sons, New York, 1928-1936; *Encyclopedia of American Biography*, ed. John A. Garraty, Harper & Row, New York 1974; *Encyclopedia Americana*, Americana Corp., New York, 1968; *Encyclopedia Britannica*, Encyclopedia Britannica Corp., Chicago, 1973; *Who Was Who in America*, Marquis-Who's Who, Inc., Chicago, 1968; and several histories, chiefly Charles Warren, *The Supreme Court in United States History*, 2 vols, Little, Brown & Co., Boston, 1922, 1926.

John Jay

(1789-1795)

Born: Dec. 12, 1745, New York, N.Y.

Education: privately tutored; attended boarding school; graduated from King's College (later Columbia University), 1764; clerked in law office of Benjamin Kissam, admitted to the bar in 1768.

Official Positions: secretary, royal boundary commission, 1773; member, New York Committee of 51, 1774; delegate, Continental Congress, 1774, 1775, 1777, president, 1778-79; delegate, New York provincial congress, 1776-77; chief justice, New York State, 1777-78; minister to Spain, 1779; secretary of foreign affairs, 1784-89; envoy to Great Britain, 1794-95; governor, New York, 1795-1801.

Supreme Court Appointment: nominated Chief Justice by President George Washington Sept. 24, 1789; confirmed by the Senate Sept. 26, 1789, by a voice vote; replaced on the court by John Marshall, nominated by President John Adams.

Family: married Sarah Van Brugh Livingston, April 28, 1774, died 1802; five daughters and two sons.

Died: May 17, 1829, Bedford, N.Y.

Personal Background

John Jay, the first Chief Justice of the United States, was descended from two of New York's most prominent families. His mother was Dutch, his father a wealthy merchant descended from French Huguenots.

The youngest of eight children, Jay grew up on the family farm at Rye, N.Y. He was taught Latin by his mother and attended a boarding school in New Rochelle for three years. Following more private tutoring, he entered

King's College and graduated at the age of 19. He was admitted to the bar four years later.

In 1774 Jay married Sarah Van Brugh Livingston, daughter of William Livingston, later governor of New Jersey during the Revolution. The couple had seven children, one of whom became a lawyer and active abolitionist. John Jay, Jay's grandson, served as minister to Austria in the early 1870s.

In his retirement years, Jay pursued his interest in agriculture and devoted time to the Episcopal Church. He was one of the founders of the American Bible Society and was elected its president in 1821. He opposed the War of 1812.

Public Career

During his many years of public service, Jay developed a reputation for fairness and honesty. Prior to the presidential election of 1800, Alexander Hamilton urged Governor Jay to call a special session of the New York legislature and change the state's election laws to ensure New York would deliver Federalist votes. Although a strong Federalist, Jay refused, writing to Hamilton that he would be "proposing a measure for party purposes which I think it would not become me to adopt."

Jay represented his state at both the first and second Continental Congresses. Although he was not present for the signing of the Declaration of Independence, he worked for its ratification in New York. At this time he also helped to draft the new state constitution.

In December 1778 Jay was elected president of the Continental Congress. The following September, he was sent to Spain in an attempt to win diplomatic recognition and large amounts of economic aid. Although the mission was at best only a modest success, it did provide Jay with important diplomatic experience. In 1783 Jay helped negotiate the Treaty of Paris, which formally ended the Revolutionary War.

Although he was not a member of the Constitutional Convention in 1787, Jay recognized the need for a stronger union while serving as secretary of foreign affairs. He contributed five essays to *The Federalist Papers* arguing for support of the new Constitution. In the presidential election of 1789 Jay received nine electoral votes.

While organizing his first administration, George Washington first offered Jay the position of secretary of

State. When Jay declined, the president named him Chief Justice of the new Supreme Court. In this position, Jay helped pave the way for a strong, independent national judiciary.

In 1794 Jay, while still Chief Justice, was sent to England in an effort to ease growing hostilities between that country and the United States. The result was the controversial Jay Treaty, which outraged many at home who felt it surrendered too many American rights.

When he returned from the treaty negotiations Jay discovered he had been elected governor of New York, a position he had run for and lost in 1792. He promptly resigned as Chief Justice and served as governor for two three-year terms.

During his tenure Jay supported the gradual freeing of slaves and instituted a revision of the state criminal code. He became interested in prisoner welfare and recommended the construction of a model penitentiary. He also reduced the number of crimes carrying the death penalty.

Following the resignation of Oliver Ellsworth, President Adams, in December 1800, nominated Jay for a second term as Chief Justice. Although he was immediately confirmed by the Senate, Jay refused the office for health reasons and also, as he wrote Adams, because the court lacked "the energy, weight, and dignity which are essential to its affording due support to the national government."

Jay lived in retirement on his 800-acre estate in Westchester County, N.Y., for 28 years until his death at 83 in 1829.

John Rutledge

(1789-1791)

Born: ca. September 1739, Charleston, S.C.

Education: privately tutored; studied law at the Middle Temple in England; called to the English bar in 1760.

Official Positions: member, South Carolina Commons House of Assembly, 1761-76; South Carolina attorney general pro tem, 1764-65; delegate, Stamp Act Congress, 1765; member, Continental Congress, 1774-76, 1782-83; president, South Carolina General Assembly, 1776-78; governor, South Carolina, 1779-82; judge of the Court of Chancery of South Carolina, 1784-91; chief, South Carolina delegation to the Constitutional Convention, 1787; member, South Carolina convention to ratify U.S. Constitution, 1788; chief justice, South Carolina supreme court, 1791-1795; member, South Carolina Assembly, 1798-99.

Supreme Court Appointment: nominated associate justice by President George Washington September 24, 1789; confirmed by the Senate Sept. 26, 1789, by a voice vote; replaced on the court by Thomas Johnson, nominated by President Washington.

Family: married Elizabeth Grimké May 1, 1763, died 1792; ten children.

Died: June 21, 1800, in Charleston, S.C.

Personal Background

Sarah Hext Rutledge was only 15 years old when she gave birth to her first son, John, in 1739. When her husband, Dr. John Rutledge, died in 1750, she was left a wealthy widow with seven children at the age of 26.

As a youth, John Rutledge studied law in the office of Andrew Rutledge, who was both his uncle and grandfather, and Speaker of the South Carolina Commons House of Assembly. Later he read for two years under Charleston lawyer James Parsons and then sailed for England, where he studied at the Inns of Court in London.

The wealthy Rutledge family, together with the Pinckneys, exerted great influence over South Carolina politics toward the end of the 18th century. John Rutledge's brother Edward, a law partner of Thomas Pinckney, was a signer of the Declaration of Independence and a delegate to the Constitutional Convention in Philadelphia; he was elected governor of South Carolina in 1798. Hugh Rutledge, another brother, also was a member of the South Carolina bar.

In 1763 Rutledge married Elizabeth Grimké, member of an old Charleston family and aunt of Angelina and Sarah Moore Grimké, two of South Carolina's most famous abolitionists and reformers. One of Rutledge's children, John Jr., became a member of the U.S. House of Representatives.

Public Career

Almost immediately upon his return to South Carolina from England in 1761, Rutledge became a leading member of the local bar. He had been home only three months when he was elected to the provincial legislature. In 1764 he was appointed attorney general by the King's governor in an attempt to win his support in a power struggle between the crown and the assembly. Rutledge held the position for 10 months but did not take sides against the assembly.

At the age of 25 Rutledge was the youngest delegate to the Stamp Act Congress in New York in 1765. There he served as chairman of the committee that drafted a petition to the King demanding repeal of the Stamp Act. The demand was met the following year.

In 1774 Rutledge headed the South Carolina delegation to the Continental Congress, which included his brother Edward and Edward's father-in-law, Henry Middleton. At the Congress in Philadelphia, Rutledge allied with other conservatives in supporting colonial rights but opposing separation from the mother country. When the Congress proposed an economic boycott against Britain, he convinced them to allow one product to continue to be traded — South Carolina's principal export, rice.

Rutledge continued to serve in the Continental Congress in 1775 but returned to South Carolina in December of that year to help form a new state government. A new constitution was written, calling for the formation of a new state assembly. Rutledge was elected president of the assembly in March 1776. In 1778 he resigned rather than accept a new, more liberal and democratic state constitution. In the face of a British invasion the following year, however, he was made governor by the assembly and given broad emergency powers.

South Carolina fell to the British in the summer of 1780. After the British army moved to Virginia in 1781, Rutledge returned to South Carolina to help restore civil authority. In 1784 he was appointed chief judge of the new state court of chancery.

At the Constitutional Convention in 1787 Rutledge served on the select committee that produced the first draft of the Constitution. He is responsible for writing the "supremacy clause," which states that the Constitution and laws of the United States "shall be the supreme law of the land."

Most of his attention, however, was directed toward protecting wealthy, anti-democratic interests. He successfully opposed, for example, an immediate ban on the slave trade. In 1789 South Carolina's electors cast their vice-presidential votes for Rutledge, in recognition of his service to the state.

Rutledge accepted President Washington's offer to become an associate justice of the Supreme Court in 1789. But although he participated in circuit court duties, he never sat as a justice due to personal illness and the inaction of the court. In February 1791 Rutledge resigned to accept what he considered to be a more prestigious position — chief justice of the supreme court of South Carolina.

The importance of the U.S. Supreme Court was gradually increasing, however, and in 1795 Rutledge wrote Washington of his desire to succeed John Jay as Chief Justice. Although he presided as a recess appointee over the August term of the court, his nomination as Chief Justice was rejected by the Senate in December 1795 because of his public opposition to the Jay Treaty with England.

Rutledge attempted to drown himself after hearing news of his Senate rejection and suffered lapses of sanity until the end of his life. He died in June 1800 at the age of 60.

William Cushing

(1789-1810)

Born: March 1, 1732, Scituate, Mass.

Education: graduated Harvard, 1751, honorary LL.D., 1785; honorary A.M., Yale, 1753; studied law under Jeremiah Gridley, admitted to the bar in 1755.

Official Positions: judge, probate court for Lincoln County, Mass. (now Maine), 1760-61; judge, Superior Court of Massachusetts Bay province, 1772-77; chief justice, Superior Court of the Commonwealth of Massachusetts, 1777-80, Supreme Judicial Court, 1780-89; member, Massachusetts Constitutional Convention, 1779; vice president, Massachusetts Convention, which ratified federal constitution, 1788; delegate to electoral college, 1788.

Supreme Court Appointment: nominated associate justice by President George Washington Sept. 24, 1789; confirmed by the Senate Sept. 26, 1789, by a voice vote; replaced on court by Joseph Story, nominated by President Madison.

Family: married Hannah Phillips, 1774.

Died: Sept. 13, 1810, Scituate, Mass.

Personal Background

William Cushing was a member of one of colonial Massachusetts' oldest and most prominent families. He

Margins of Confirmation

More often than not, the Senate's actual confirmation of a Supreme Court nominee is a formality. Deference to the president usually prevails over whatever reservations members may have aired during committee and floor debate, so that 73 nominees have been approved by voice vote with no recorded opposition. (Five men confirmed in this fashion subsequently declined to serve.)

Three justices were confirmed by unanimous roll-call votes. In two other cases, the nominee was officially confirmed by voice vote, but an individual senator put his opposition into the record: Sen. Joseph McCarthy, R-Wis., to the confirmation of Justice William J. Brennan Jr. in 1957, and Sen. Strom Thurmond, R-S.C., to that of Arthur J. Goldberg in 1962.

Close Calls

A number of justices, however, were approved for court service by the skin of their teeth. One vote allowed the confirmation of Stanley Matthews, confirmed by a 24-23 vote in 1881; a three-vote margin, 26-23, confirmed Nathan Clifford in 1858; and Lucius Q. C. Lamar squeaked by, 32-28, in 1888.

Other nominees who attracted substantial opposition — more than 10 votes against confirmation — were Chief Justice Roger B. Taney, 29-15 in 1836; Philip P. Barbour, 30-11, 1836; William Smith, 23-18, 1837 (Smith declined the seat); John Catron, 28-15, 1837; Edwin M. Stanton, 46-11, 1869; Roscoe Conkling, 39-12, 1882 (he declined); Chief Justice Melville W. Fuller, 41-20, 1888; David J. Brewer, 53-11, 1889; Mahlon Pitney, 50-26, 1912; Louis D. Brandeis, 47-22, 1916; Chief Justice Charles E. Hughes, 52-26, 1930; Hugo L. Black, 63-16, 1937; Sherman Minton, 48-16, 1949; John M. Harlan, 71-11, 1955; Potter Stewart, 70-17, 1959; Thurgood Marshall, 69-11, 1967; and William H. Rehnquist, 68-26, 1971.

Also-Rans

A few votes also made the difference in Senate decisions to reject court appointees. Among the almost-justices were Jeremiah S. Black, defeated by a single vote, 25-26, in 1861; John J. Parker, 39-41, 1930; John Rutledge's appointment as Chief Justice, 10-14, 1795; John C. Spencer, 21-26, 1844; George W. Woodward, 20-29, 1845; Ebenezer R. Hoar, 24-33, 1870; William B. Hornblower, 24-30, 1894; Wheeler H. Peckham, 32-41, 1894; Clement Haynsworth Jr., 45-55, 1969; and G. Harrold Carswell, 45-51, 1970. (Confirmation votes for each justice appear in these pages, and in the list of appointments, pp. 946-948.)

was descended on his mother's side from John Cotton, the 17th century New England Puritan minister. Both his father and grandfather served in the government of the Massachusetts Bay province.

Cushing graduated from Harvard in 1751. After teaching for a year in Roxbury, Mass., he began studying law under Jeremiah Gridley in Boston. In 1755 he opened private practice in his home town of Scituate.

In 1760 Cushing moved to what is now Dresden, Maine, to become justice of the peace and judge of pro-bates. He was not an accomplished lawyer and seemed unable to make decisions. Before long, he had lost most of his corporate business to other lawyers.

In 1774 Cushing married Hannah Phillips of Middletown, Conn.

Public Career

When Cushing's father, John Cushing, decided to retire from the provincial superior court in 1772, he insisted that his son succeed him as judge. Although William Cushing was not the colonial government's first choice, he nonetheless was appointed to the position that year.

In 1774 Cushing reluctantly allied himself with the colonials by refusing to accept his salary through the British government. Although his decision did not come until the state legislature began preparing impeachment proceedings against him, he now began to be perceived as a supporter of the revolutionary cause. This belief was strengthened when he was denied a seat on the governor's council because of his stand.

In 1775 the new revolutionary government of Massachusetts reorganized the judicial system but retained Cushing as senior associate justice of the superior court. In 1777 he was elevated to chief justice.

Although Cushing played only a small role in the state constitutional convention of 1779, he actively supported ratification of the Constitution. He also served as vice president of the state convention that ratified the document in 1788.

Cushing was one of Washington's original appointees to the Supreme Court in 1789. He was the only justice to wear a full wig but quickly abandoned that practice.

In 1794 Cushing was persuaded to run against Samuel Adams for governor of Massachusetts — while retaining his court seat — but lost by a two-to-one margin. In 1795 he declined an offer from Washington to succeed John Jay as Chief Justice. As senior associate justice, however, he presided over the court when Chief Justice Ellsworth was absent.

Cushing remained on the bench until his death in 1810, delivering 19 opinions during his 21-year tenure.

James Wilson
(1789-1798)

Born: Sept. 14, 1742, Caskardy, Scotland.

Education: attended University of St. Andrews (Scotland); read law in office of John Dickinson, admitted to the bar in 1767; honorary M.A., College of Philadelphia, 1776, honorary LL.D., 1790.

Official Positions: delegate, first Provincial Convention at Philadelphia, 1774; delegate, Continental Congress, 1775-77, 1783, 1785-87; delegate, U.S. Constitutional Convention, 1787; delegate, Pennsylvania convention to ratify U.S. Constitution, 1787.

Supreme Court Appointment: nominated associate justice by President George Washington Sept. 24, 1789; confirmed by the Senate Sept. 26, 1789, by a voice vote; replaced on the court by Bushrod Washington, nominated by President John Adams.

Family: married, first, Rachel Bird, Nov. 5, 1771, died 1786, six children; second, Hannah Gray, Sept. 19, 1793, one son died in infancy.

Died: Aug. 21, 1798, Edenton, N.C.

Personal Background

James Wilson was born in the Scottish Lowlands, the son of a Caskardy farmer. Though the family had little money, his devout Calvinist parents were determined that James be educated for the ministry.

After study in local grammar schools, Wilson at 14 won a scholarship to St. Andrews University and matriculated in the fall of 1757. During his fifth year, he entered the university's divinity school but was forced to leave for financial reasons when his father died.

To help support his family, he took a job as a private tutor but left the position to study accounting and bookkeeping in Edinburgh. In 1765 he decided against becoming a clerk and sailed for America.

After studying law in the new country, Wilson became one of its foremost legal scholars. Described as a man of extreme energy, he was driven by a desire for wealth and fame, constantly involved in various speculation schemes, primarily in land. He was part-owner of the Somerset Mills on the Delaware River and president of the Illinois and Wabash Co., which had vast western land holdings.

From 1777 to 1787, Wilson devoted most of his energy to developing new business interests. As his financial commitments built, he continued to seek new investments. But the credit cycle eventually caught up with Wilson. As an associate justice, he travelled the southern circuit in constant fear of being thrown in jail for bad debts.

Public Career

Wilson arrived in Philadelphia in the fall of 1765 and immediately obtained a tutorship at the College of Philadelphia. Teaching tired him, however, and he saw a better opportunity in law. He soon began reading in the office of John Dickinson, a prominent attorney who had studied at the Inns of Court.

In 1768 Wilson opened private practice in Reading, Pa. Two years later, he moved west to Carlisle, where his practice expanded rapidly. By 1774 he was practicing in seven counties, specializing in land law.

In 1775 Wilson was elected a delegate to the Continental Congress, where he served on several committees. He aligned himself with other members of the Pennsylvania delegation in opposing separation from England. In the end, however, he followed the state assembly's instructions and signed the Declaration of Independence.

Wilson's opposition to the Pennsylvania constitution of 1776 attracted criticism from state populists and earned him a reputation as a conservative aristocrat. That reputation grew when he developed an active practice in Philadelphia defending wealthy Tories and other rich businessmen. In 1779 he was forced to barricade his home against an armed attack by a riotous mob angered over high inflation and food shortages. He eventually had to go into hiding.

At the Constitutional Convention in 1787, Wilson was a member of the committee of detail, responsible for writing the first draft of the Constitution. Although his populist foes refused to believe it, Wilson was a fervent advocate of popular sovereignty and democracy who supported popular election of the president and members of both the Senate and House. One of the first to envision the principle of judicial review, Wilson fought for a strong national judiciary and a powerful presidency. He saw no conflict between the ideal of popular rule and a strong national government since, in his view, the national government existed only by virtue of the popular will. Wilson is credited with incorporating this idea of popular sovereignty into the Constitution.

As the new national government was being formed, Wilson hoped for federal office and offered his name to Washington as Chief Justice of the new Supreme Court. Washington appointed John Jay instead and named Wilson an associate justice.

Of the original Washington appointees to the Supreme Court, Wilson was its most accomplished legal scholar. A pamphlet he had published in 1774 presaged the concept of "dominion status" that serves today as the official guiding principle of the British Commonwealth.

His defense of the Bank of North America in 1785 anticipated constitutional opinions delivered by Chief Justice Marshall at least 25 years later. In 1964 Associate Justice Hugo Black cited Wilson in *Wesberry v. Sanders* as a supporting source for the "one-man-one-vote" principle.

Around 1796 Wilson's investment schemes began to collapse around him. While riding circuit, he was chased by angry creditors who caught up with him in Burlington, N.J., and had him jailed. He then sought refuge in Edenton, N.C. — the hometown of fellow Justice James Iredell — but was soon discovered and imprisoned again. Eventually released, he remained in Edenton in ill health. He died at 55 in a dingy inn next to the Edenton Court House.

John Blair Jr.
(1789-1796)

Born: 1732, Williamsburg, Va.

Education: graduated with honors from College of William and Mary, 1754; studied law at Middle Temple, London, 1755-56.

Official Positions: member, Virginia House of Burgesses, 1766-1770; clerk, Virginia Governor's Council, 1770-75; delegate, Virginia Constitutional Convention, 1776; member, Virginia Governor's Council, 1776; judge, Virginia General Court, 1777-78; chief justice, 1779; judge, first Virginia Court of Appeals, 1780-89; delegate, U.S. Constitutional Convention, 1787; judge, Virginia Supreme Court of Appeals, 1789.

Supreme Court Appointment: nominated associate justice by President George Washington Sept. 24, 1789; confirmed by the Senate Sept. 26, 1789, by a voice vote; replaced on court by Samuel Chase, nominated by President Washington.

Family: married Jean Balfour, died 1792.

Died: Aug. 31, 1800, Williamsburg, Va.

Personal Background

John Blair Jr. was the son of one of Virginia's most prominent colonial officials, a member of the House of Burgesses and a member of the Governor's Council. He was also acting governor of the state in 1758 and 1768.

The family owned rich land holdings, and young John — one of 10 children — was given an excellent education. In 1754 he graduated from the College of William and Mary, which had been founded by his great-uncle James Blair. After studying law at the Middle Temple in London, he returned home to Williamsburg and began practicing law.

A slightly built man, six feet tall with thinning red hair, Blair toward the end of his life suffered from chronic headaches, possibly brought on by the rigors of riding circuit. His wife, Jean Balfour, died in 1796 from a chronic illness which was described at the time as hysteria.

Public Career

Blair entered the Virginia House of Burgesses in 1766 at the age of 34. A conservative, he opposed the defiant resolutions of Patrick Henry condemning the Stamp Act, but joined with leading merchants in agreeing to boycott specific British imports.

In 1770 Blair resigned his seat to become clerk of the governor's council, the first of several state offices and judgeships. In 1782, while serving as a judge on the state's first court of appeals, he sided with the majority decision in *Commonwealth v. Caton* that the court could declare legislative acts unconstitutional.

Although not a leading participant in the Constitutional Convention of 1787, Blair firmly supported ratification and was one of three Virginia delegates who signed the new document.

When the Virginia judicial system was reorganized in 1789, Blair sat on the new supreme court of appeals for three months until his appointment as one of the original justices of the U.S. Supreme Court. Because of his wife's illness and the relative inactivity of the court, he did not attend all its sessions. He finally resigned in January 1796 after his wife's death and his own growing ill-health.

In 1799 Blair wrote to his sister of being "struck with a strange disorder . . . depriving me of nearly all the powers of mind." He died on Aug. 31, 1800, at his home in Williamsburg.

James Iredell
(1790-1799)

Born: Lewes, England, Oct. 5, 1751.

Education: educated in England; read law under Samuel Johnston of North Carolina; licensed to practice, 1770-71.

Recess Appointments

If a vacancy occurs on the Supreme Court when the Senate is not in session, the president may make a recess appointment. The appointee may be sworn in as a justice and participate actively in the deliberations and decisions of the court. When the Senate reconvenes, the president must then formally nominate the appointee, who is then subject to Senate confirmation. If confirmed, the justice will be sworn in a second time.

Of the 15 recess appointments in the court's history, only five have taken their seats on the bench before being confirmed by the Senate. Four of these men were eventually confirmed when the Senate reconvened — Benjamin R. Curtis, appointed and confirmed in December 1851; Earl Warren, appointed as Chief Justice in September 1953 and confirmed in March 1954; William J. Brennan Jr., appointed in October 1956 and confirmed in 1957; and Potter Stewart, appointed in January 1959 and confirmed in May 1959.

The fifth recess appointee who took his seat before his confirmation was ultimately rejected by the Senate. When John Jay resigned as the nation's first Chief Justice in June 1795, John Rutledge asked President Washington to appoint him to the vacancy. A Federalist, Rutledge had served for a year and a half as one of the first associate justices, resigning in 1791.

Washington complied with the request and gave Rutledge a recess appointment. Rutledge presided over the August 1795 term of the court at which two cases were heard and decided. When the Senate convened at the end of the year, it refused to confirm Rutledge's formal nomination, rejecting him Dec. 15, 1795, by a 10-14 vote. Reports that Rutledge suffered a mental disability no doubt played some role in his rejection. But the deciding factor was his outspoken opposition to the Jay Treaty, which made him appear disloyal to his own political party.

The ten men who received recess appointments but who did not take their place on the court until after formal confirmation by the Senate were: Thomas Johnson, confirmed in 1791; Bushrod Washington, confirmed in 1798; Alfred Moore, confirmed in 1799; Brockholst Livingston, confirmed in 1806; Smith Thompson, confirmed in 1823; John McKinley, confirmed in 1837; Levi Woodbury, confirmed in 1846; David Davis, confirmed in 1862; John Marshall Harlan, confirmed in 1877; and Oliver Wendell Holmes Jr., confirmed in 1902.

Sources: Henry J. Abraham. *Justices and Presidents: A Political History of Appointments to the Supreme Court.* New York: Oxford University Press, 1974. U.S. Senate Judiciary Committee. *Nomination of Potter Stewart.* Executive Rept. No. 2, 86th Cong., 1st Sess., Minority Views.

Official Positions: comptroller of customs, Edenton, N.C., 1768-1774; collector of customs, Port of North Carolina, 1774-76; judge, Superior Court of North Carolina, 1778; attorney general, North Carolina, 1779-1781; member, North Carolina Council of State, 1787; delegate, North Carolina convention for ratification of federal Constitution, 1788.

Supreme Court Appointment: nominated associate justice by President George Washington Feb. 8, 1790; confirmed by the Senate Feb. 10, 1790, by a voice vote; replaced on court by Alfred Moore, nominated by President John Adams.

Family: married Hannah Johnston, July 18, 1773; three children.

Died: Oct. 20, 1799, Edenton, N.C.

Personal Background

James Iredell was born into an English family reputedly descended from Oliver Cromwell's son-in-law, Henry Ireton. The family was forced to change its name, so the story goes, following the return of Charles II to the throne.

When James' merchant father, Francis, became ill in the early 1760s, James was able through family connections to acquire a position in America in 1868 as comptroller of the customs in Edenton, N.C. During his six years in that job he read law in the office of Samuel Johnston and began practice in December 1770. In 1773 he married his mentor's sister, Hannah Johnston.

Because of a slight lisp, Iredell was not effective as a public speaker but was a prolific writer of letters and essays. Many of these writings survive today and reveal a clear, candid style.

Public Career

Although a new immigrant and an employee of the British, Iredell nevertheless soon found himself in support of the American revolutionary cause. In 1776 he resigned from his job as collector for the crown at the port of Edenton.

Iredell then served on a commission to redraft North Carolina law in conformance with the state's new independent status. When a new state judicial court system was created the following year, he was chosen one of three superior court judges — a position he reluctantly accepted. But the rigors of travelling circuit were burdensome for him, and he resigned after a few months to return to private law practice.

From 1779 to 1781, Iredell served as state attorney general. In 1787 the legislature appointed him to collect and revise all state laws; the new code appeared in 1791.

After the war Iredell had aligned himself with conservative leaders who favored a strong government and adherence to the peace treaty terms of 1783. In 1786 he stated that the state constitution had the power to limit the state legislature — a novel idea at the time.

Iredell's most influential work, written under the pen name of "Marcus," was his defense of the new federal Constitution. The tract, which appeared at the same time as the first issues of the Jefferson-Hamilton-Jay pro-Constitutional *Federalist Papers*, refuted George Mason's 11 objections to the document.

At the state ratification convention in 1788, Iredell served as floor leader of the Federalists, a position that brought him to the attention of George Washington. When Robert Harrison declined to serve on the Supreme Court in 1790, the president decided to appoint Iredell because, as Washington noted in his diary, "in addition to the reputation he sustains for abilities, legal knowledge and respectability of character, he is of a State of some importance in the Union that has given no character to a federal office."

Iredell served on the court for nine years, riding the southern circuit five times between 1790 and 1794. In dissent from *Chisholm v. Georgia*, he argued that a state could not be sued by a citizen from another state — a position later added to the Constitution by the 11th

Amendment. In 1798 he set a precedent for *Marbury v. Madison* in arguing for the right of courts to declare laws unconstitutional *(Calder v. Bull).*

Iredell died in 1799 at 48 in his home in Edenton.

Thomas Johnson
(1791-1793)

Born: Nov. 4, 1732, Calvert County, Md.

Education: educated at home; studied law under Stephen Bordley; admitted to the bar, 1760.

Official Positions: delegate, Maryland Provincial Assembly, 1762; delegate, Annapolis Convention of 1774; member, Continental Congress, 1774-1777; delegate, first constitutional convention of Maryland, 1776; first governor of Maryland, 1777-1779; member, Maryland House of Delegates, 1780, 1786, 1787; member, Maryland convention for ratification of the federal Constitution, 1788; chief judge, general court of Maryland, 1790-91; member, board of commissioners of the Federal City, 1791-94.

Supreme Court Appointment: nominated associate justice by President George Washington Nov. 1, 1791, to replace John Rutledge, who resigned; confirmed by the Senate Nov. 7, 1791, by a voice vote; replaced on court by William Paterson, nominated by President Washington.

Family: married Ann Jennings, Feb. 16, 1766, died 1794; three boys and five girls, one of whom died in infancy.

Died: Oct. 26, 1819, Frederick, Md.

Personal Background

Born to Thomas and Dorcas Sedgwick Johnson in 1732, Thomas Johnson was one of 12 children. He received no formal education as a youth but trained in the office of Thomas Jennings, clerk of the Maryland provincial court in Annapolis. Following that apprenticeship, Johnson worked and studied in the office of Stephen Bordley, an Annapolis attorney. He was admitted to the bar in 1760.

During the Revolution Johnson served as first brigadier-general of the Maryland militia. In 1777 he was responsible for leading almost 2,000 men from Frederick, Md., to Gen. Washington's headquarters in New Jersey.

After the war Johnson revived a plan he had dreamed of as early as 1770 — to improve navigation along the Potomac River and open a passageway to the west coast. To this end, he helped organize the state-chartered Potomac Company in 1785, with his good friend George Washington as its president. The company eventually proved unprofitable.

In 1766 Johnson married Ann Jennings, the daughter of his old employer in the provincial court. They were married for 28 years, until her death in 1794.

Public Career

Johnson began his career as a Maryland statesman in 1762 when he was chosen a delegate to the Maryland Provincial Assembly from Anne Arundel County. As a member of the first Continental Congress in Philadelphia, he served on the committee that drafted a petition of grievances to King George III. In 1775 it was Thomas Johnson who placed the name of George Washington in nomination before the Congress for the position of commander-in-chief of the Continental Army.

Johnson was absent from Philadelphia the day the Declaration of Independence was signed. However, he thoroughly supported the document and voted for Maryland's independence on July 6, 1776. He also helped to write the new state constitution that year.

During the Revolution Johnson served three consecutive terms as governor of Maryland and played a key role in keeping Washington's army manned and equipped.

Declining to serve a fourth term as governor, Johnson entered the Maryland house of delegates in 1780, where he helped prepare legislation determining the jurisdiction of the state admiralty court. As a member of the state ratification convention in 1788, he worked for approval of the new federal Constitution. Two years later he became chief judge of the Maryland general court.

Johnson was nominated associate justice of the Supreme Court in August 1791. Hesitant because of the rigors of riding circuit, he was assured by Chief Justice Jay that every attempt would be made to bring him relief. When assigned to the southern circuit, however, including all territory south of the Potomac, he was unable to persuade Jay to rotate assignments. Citing ill health, he resigned from the bench after serving little more than a year. He wrote only one opinion during his tenure.

Johnson, however, continued in public life as a member of the commission appointed by Washington to plan the new national capital on the Potomac. That commission selected the design submitted by Pierre L'Enfant and voted to name the new city "Washington." Johnson was present when the cornerstone of the new Capitol building was laid in September 1793.

In 1795 Johnson refused an offer from President Washington to serve as secretary of state. He retired to Frederick, Md., where he died at the age of 86.

William Paterson
(1793-1806)

Born: Dec. 24, 1745, County Antrim, Ireland.

Education: graduated from College of New Jersey (Princeton), 1763, Master of Arts, 1766; studied law under Richard Stockton; admitted to the bar, 1769.

Official Positions: member, New Jersey Provincial Congress, 1775-76; delegate, New Jersey State Constitutional Convention, 1776; New Jersey attorney general, 1776-83; delegate, U.S. Constitutional Convention, 1787; U.S. senator, 1789-1790; governor, New Jersey, 1790-93.

The Men Who Never Served

One Supreme Court nominee was confirmed by the Senate but died before he could take his seat on the court.

Edwin M. Stanton — President Lincoln's fiery secretary of war who became the chief cabinet opponent of Lincoln's successor, Andrew Johnson — resigned his post in 1868 after Congress' effort to impeach Johnson failed.

The next year, Stanton's congressional supporters persuaded President Grant to appoint Stanton, already in failing health, to a court seat. He was quickly confirmed, on Dec. 20, 1869, but died four days later.

Seven other nominees were confirmed but declined the appointment.

Supreme Court Appointment: nominated associate justice by President George Washington March 4, 1793, to replace Thomas Johnson, who resigned; confirmed by the Senate March 4, 1793, by a voice vote; replaced on court by H. Brockholst Livingston, nominated by President Jefferson.

Family: married, first, Cornelia Bell, Feb. 9, 1779, died 1783, three children; second, Euphemia White, 1785.

Died: September 9, 1806, Albany, N.Y.

Personal Background

Born in Ireland, William Paterson emigrated to America with his parents when he was two years old. The family lived in several places before settling in Princeton, N.J., where William's father, Richard, began manufacturing tin plate and selling general merchandise. He also made successful real estate investments which helped to pay for William's education.

At the college of New Jersey (Princeton), Paterson was a fellow student of Oliver Ellsworth, who would later become Chief Justice of the Supreme Court. With Ellsworth and others, Paterson founded the Well-Meaning Society (later the Cliosophic Club) as a forum for lively discussions on the political issues of the day.

In 1766 Paterson received a Master of Arts degree from Princeton and the same year began reading law in the office of Richard Stockton. In 1769 he opened his own practice in New Bromley, about 30 miles from Princeton. There was little demand for his services, however, and in 1772 he returned to the college town.

Paterson married twice. With his first wife, Cornelia Bell, he lived on a farm on the Raritan River west of New Brunswick. She died in 1783 after the birth of their third child. Two years later Paterson married her close friend, Euphemia White.

Public Career

Paterson was elected as a delegate from Somerset County to the provincial congress of New Jersey in 1775, where he served as assistant secretary and later secretary. In 1776 he helped write the state constitution and was chosen attorney general. During this period Paterson also was a member of the state legislative council, a county minuteman officer and a member of the council of safety.

In May 1787 Paterson was chosen a delegate to the Constitutional Convention in Philadelphia, where he was responsible for introducing the New Jersey Plan, proposing a unicameral legislature giving each state an equal vote. Despite failure of that plan, Paterson signed the Constitution and worked for its adoption in New Jersey.

As a member of the judiciary committee of the new U.S. Senate, Paterson was responsible, along with his old classmate Oliver Ellsworth, for writing the Judiciary Act of 1789. He left the Senate in 1790 when he was chosen governor and chancellor of the state of New Jersey.

In this capacity, Paterson codified the laws of the state and updated the procedural rules for the common-law and chancery courts. With the assistance of Alexander Hamilton, he laid plans for an industrial town on the Passaic River, to be named Paterson.

Appointed to the Supreme Court in 1793, Paterson — while riding circuit — tried several cases arising out of the Whiskey Rebellion in western Pennsylvania. He took a Federalist position in a number of sedition trials.

When Oliver Ellsworth resigned as Chief Justice in 1800, President Adams refused to elevate Paterson to the position because of his close alliance with Alexander Hamilton. In 1804 Paterson missed a session of the court because of failing health and in 1806 decided to travel to Ballston Springs, N.Y., for treatment. He made the trip only as far as his daughter's home in Albany, where he died on Sept. 9.

Samuel Chase

(1796-1811)

Born: April 17, 1741, Somerset County, Md.

Education: tutored by father; studied law in Annapolis law office; admitted to bar in 1761.

Official Positions: member, Maryland General Assembly, 1764-84; delegate, Continental Congress, 1774-78, 1784-85; member, Maryland Committee of Correspondence, 1774; member, Maryland Convention and Council of Safety, 1775; judge, Baltimore Criminal Court, 1788-96; chief judge, General Court of Maryland, 1791-96.

Supreme Court Appointment: nominated associate justice by President George Washington Jan. 26, 1796, to replace John Blair, who resigned; confirmed by the Senate Jan. 27, 1796, by a voice vote; replaced on court by Gabriel Duvall, nominated by President Washington.

Family: married, first, Anne Baldwin May 21, 1762, who died; second, Hannah Kilty Giles, March 3, 1784, four children.

Died: June 19, 1811, Baltimore, Md.

Personal Background

Samuel Chase's mother, Martha Walker, died when he was still a child. His father, Thomas Chase, an Episcopal clergyman, tutored him at home and gave him a foundation in the classics. At 18, Chase began studying law in the office of Hammond and Hall in Annapolis. Two years later, in 1761, he was admitted to the bar and began practicing in the mayor's court of Annapolis. Chase lived in the state capital until 1786, when he moved to Baltimore.

During his lifetime Chase invested in several business schemes that later caused him embarrassment. In 1778, when his efforts to corner the flour market through speculation were discovered, he was dismissed as a member of the Maryland delegation to the Continental Congress for two years.

Chase also was involved in two war-supply partnerships and owned many iron and coal properties. These businesses were largely failures, and in 1789 he was forced to declare personal bankruptcy.

About six feet in height, Chase had a large head and brownish-red complexion that earned him the nickname "bacon face" among his law colleagues. He was a signer of the Declaration of Independence and a fervent patriot whose career was marked by turbulence, sensation and controversy.

Public Career

When Chase entered the Maryland general assembly in 1764 he took immediate opposition to the policies of the British-appointed governor of the colony. As a member of the "Sons of Liberty," he participated in riotous demonstrations, incurring the wrath of the Annapolis mayor and aldermen who called him a "busy, restless incendiary, a ringleader of mobs, a foul-mouthed and inflaming son of discord."

In 1778 Chase served on no fewer than 30 committees of the Continental Congress. As a delegate from Maryland, he urged that the colonies unite in an economic boycott of England. He served with Benjamin Franklin and Charles Carroll on a commission sent to Montreal to persuade Canada to join with the colonies against Great Britain. The mission failed.

Instrumental in achieving support in Maryland for the Declaration of Independence, Chase did not favor adoption of the new Constitution, arguing it would institute an elitist government and not a government of the people. He wrote a series of articles against ratification under the pen name of "Caution."

As a judge, his abusive and overbearing manner won him few friends. Displeased over the fact that Chase held two judgeships simultaneously, the Maryland assembly at one point tried to strip him from all public offices, but the vote fell short.

It was his impeachment trial in 1805 that was to bring him the most publicity. By the time Chase reached the Supreme Court he had become a radical Federalist. As an associate justice, he took an active part in Federalist politics and campaigned hard for the Alien and Sedition Acts. Biased and dogmatic, he sought the indictment of Republican newspaper editors who sided against the Federalists.

Chase's greatest political impropriety came on May 2, 1803, when he gave an impassioned speech to a grand jury against democratic "mobocracy." He was impeached by the House on March 12, 1804. Although most senators agreed that Chase had acted poorly on the bench, there were not enough votes to convict him of "high crimes," and he kept his seat on the court. There have been no other impeachments of Supreme Court justices.

Following the trial, Chase sank into oblivion. By then, John Marshall dominated the court, and Chase was often ill from gout and unable to attend meetings. He died in 1811.

Oliver Ellsworth
(1796-1800)

Born: April 29, 1745, Windsor, Conn.

Education: B.A., Princeton, 1766; honorary LL.D., Yale (1790), Princeton (1790) and Dartmouth (1797).

Official Positions: member, Connecticut General Assembly, 1773-1776; state's attorney, Hartford Co., 1777-85; delegate to Continental Congress, 1777-84; member, Connecticut Council of Safety, 1779; member, Governor's Council, 1780-85, 1801-07; judge, Connecticut Superior Court, 1785-89; delegate, Constitutional Convention, 1787; member, U.S. Senate 1789-96; commissioner to France, 1799-1800.

Supreme Court Appointment: nominated Chief Justice by President George Washington March 3, 1796, to replace John Jay, who resigned; confirmed by the Senate March 4, 1796, by a 21-1 vote; succeeded on court by John Marshall, nominated by President John Adams.

Family: married Abigail Wolcott, 1771; four sons and three daughters survived infancy.

Died: Nov. 26, 1807, Windsor, Conn.

Personal Background

Oliver Ellsworth's great-grandfather immigrated in the middle of the 17th century from Yorkshire, England, to Windsor, Conn., where the future second Chief Justice was born to captain David Ellsworth and Jemima Leavitt in 1745.

After studying under a Bethlehem, Conn., minister, Ellsworth entered Yale at 17. For reasons that are now unclear, he left Yale at the end of his sophomore year and enrolled in Princeton, where he engaged in lively discussions about colonial politics and sharpened his debating skills.

After graduating from Princeton, Ellsworth began studying for the ministry at the urging of his father. Theology did not hold his interest long, however, and he soon turned to law. After four years of training he was admitted to the bar in 1777.

Ellsworth had little money in the early years of his practice. After marrying 16-year-old Abigail Wolcott in 1772, he settled on a farm that had belonged to his father and worked the land himself. When the Hartford court was in session, he walked to the town and back, a total of 20 miles.

Ellsworth's financial situation changed dramatically, however, as his practice grew. By 1780 he had become a leading member of the Connecticut bar and was well on his way toward acquiring a large fortune.

According to contemporary accounts, Ellsworth was a good conversationalist and elegant dresser who enjoyed frequent pinches of snuff. A tall, robust man, he was in the habit of talking to himself and was prone to obstinacy. Aaron Burr is said to have remarked: "If Ellsworth had happened to spell the name of the Deity wih two d's, it would have taken the Senate three weeks to expunge the superfluous letter."

Deeply religious, Ellsworth was an active member of the Congregationalist Church and returned to the study of theology after his retirement from the court. He also advocated improved farming techniques for Connecticut and wrote a regular advice column on the subject.

Public Career

Although his name is not among the signers of the Constitution, Ellsworth deserves to be included in any list of the nation's "founding fathers." Principal author of the Judiciary Act of 1789 and co-author of the Connecticut Compromise, Ellsworth originated the name for the new American government when he suggested the appellation "United States" in a resolution being considered by the Constitutional Convention.

Ellsworth's political career began in 1773 when he was elected to the Connecticut general assembly. In 1775 he was appointed one of five members of the committee of the pay table, which controlled the state's Revolutionary War expenditures. He also was a Connecticut delegate to the Continental Congress during the Revolution and served on many of its committees, including one that heard appeals from admiralty courts.

In 1787 Ellsworth was elected a member of the Connecticut delegation to the Constitutional Convention and helped devise the famous "Connecticut Compromise" that ended the dispute between large and small states over representation in the federal legislature.

Ellsworth had to leave the convention before it ended to attend to judicial business in Connecticut, and was not present for the signing of the newly drafted Constitution. He worked hard for its ratification in Connecticut, however.

In 1789 Ellsworth became one of Connecticut's first two U.S. senators. His administrative skills were immediately put to use as he helped draft the first set of Senate rules and organize the army, a U.S. Post Office and a census. Ellsworth engineered the conference report on the Bill of Rights and helped draft the measure that admitted North Carolina to the union. It was Ellsworth's idea to force Rhode Island to join the federation by imposing an economic boycott.

A staunch supporter of Hamilton's monetary policies, Ellsworth had by this time become a strong Federalist. His most important work in the Senate came when he was chosen to head a committee to draft a bill organizing the federal judiciary. The bill, which provided for the initial structure of the Supreme Court, the district courts and the circuit courts, became the Judiciary Act of 1789.

When John Jay resigned as Chief Justice of the Supreme Court in 1795, President Washington appointed John Rutledge as his successor. The Senate refused to confirm Rutledge, however, and Washington chose to elevate Associate Justice William Cushing. When Cushing declined, the nomination fell to Ellsworth.

Ellsworth had been on the court only three years when President Adams sent him to France with two other envoys in an effort to soften hostilities between France and the United States. The mission, plagued by transportation difficulties and only a partial success, took its toll on Ellsworth's health.

Before returning home, Ellsworth notified Adams of his resignation as Chief Justice. He lived on his estate in Windsor until his death in 1807.

Bushrod Washington
(1798-1829)

Born: June 5, 1762, Westmoreland County, Va.

Education: privately tutored; graduated College of William and Mary, 1778; read law under James Wilson; member, Virginia bar; honorary LL.D. degrees from Harvard, Princeton and University of Pennsylvania.

Official Positions: member, Virginia House of Delegates, 1787; member, Virginia convention to ratify U.S. Constitution, 1788.

Supreme Court Appointment: nominated associate justice by President John Adams Dec. 19, 1798, to replace James Wilson, who died; confirmed by the Senate Dec. 20, 1798, by a voice vote; succeeded on court by Henry Baldwin, nominated by President Jackson.

Family: married Julia Ann Blackburn, 1785; no children.

Died: Nov. 26, 1829, in Philadelphia, Pa.

Personal Background

Bushrod Washington received his first name from his mother, Hannah Bushrod, a member of one of Virginia's oldest colonial families. His father, John Augustine Washington, was a brother of George Washington and served as a member of the Virginia legislature and magistrate of Westmoreland County, Va.

As a boy Bushrod was privately tutored. He graduated from the College of William and Mary at 16 and was a founding member of Phi Beta Kappa, then a secret social club. He was a student in George Wythe's law course at the same time as John Marshall.

Toward the end of the Revolution, Washington enlisted as a private in the Continental Army. He was present when Cornwallis surrendered at Yorktown in October 1781. After the war, Washington studied law for two years under the Philadelphia lawyer James Wilson, whom he would later succeed on the Supreme Court.

Biographical sources remember Bushrod Washington as a confirmed user of snuff and an untidy dresser, blind in one eye. According to most accounts, he also was considered to be a diligent and methodical student of the law. In the words of his colleague, Justice Joseph Story: "His mind was solid, rather than brilliant; sagacious and searching, rather than quick or eager; slow, but not torpid. . . ."

In 1785 Washington married Julia Ann Blackburn, the daughter of an aide-de-camp to Gen. Washington during the Revolution. She is said to have been at his side constantly, even when he made his rounds as a circuit judge. She was with him when he died in Philadelphia and died herself during the trip home to attend the funeral.

When George Washington died in 1799 with no children of his own, he left his Mount Vernon estate, including all his public and private papers, to his nephew Bushrod. The former president had provided that his slaves be freed when his wife Martha died. But Bushrod refused to carry out this request and in 1821 sold more than 50 of the slaves to two men from Louisiana, separating families in the process.

For this action he was bitterly attacked in several journals of the day. He dismissed the criticism by arguing the slaves were his property to do with as he saw fit. In 1816 Washington had been elected the first president of the American Colonization Society, established to transport free blacks to Africa — a movement that was criticized by abolitionists.

Public Career

Washington began private law practice in Westmoreland County, Va., and later in Alexandria, Va., where he specialized in chancery cases. In 1787, with encouragement from his uncle, he ran for the Virginia House of Delegates and was elected. The following year he was sent as a delegate to the state ratification convention and successfully argued, along with Marshall and Madison, for state approval of the new federal Constitution.

Around 1790 Washington moved to Richmond, where he developed a successful law practice and trained many law students, including Henry Clay. During this period he also served as reporter for the court of appeals and spent much of his time writing two volumes of reports of cases argued before the court.

During his tenure on the court, Washington was often associated with Chief Justice Marshall and Justice Story. Indeed, Justice William Johnson, another member of the Marshall court, once complained that Marshall and Washington "are commonly estimated as a single judge." Washington and Marshall disagreed in only three cases during their joint tenure.

Alfred Moore
(1799-1804)

Born: May 21, 1755, New Hanover County, N.C.

Education: educated in Boston; studied law under his father; received law license, 1775.

Official Positions: member, North Carolina legislature, 1782, 1792; North Carolina attorney general, 1782-91; trustee, University of North Carolina, 1789-1807; North Carolina Superior Court judge, 1799.

Supreme Court Appointment: nominated associate justice by President John Adams, Dec. 6, 1799, to replace James Iredell, who died; confirmed by the Senate Dec. 10, 1799, by a voice vote; succeeded on court by William Johnson, nominated by President Jefferson.

Family: married Susanna Eagles.

Died: Oct. 15, 1810, Bladen County, N.C.

Personal Background

Alfred Moore was born in 1755, the son of a North Carolina colonial judge. He was descended from Roger

Moore, a leader of the 1641 Irish Rebellion, and James Moore, governor of South Carolina in the early 18th century.

Seeking the best education for their son, Moore's parents sent him to school in Boston. After completing his studies there, Moore returned home and read law under his father. At the age of 20 he was licensed to practice law.

During the Revolution Moore served as a captain in a Continental regiment commanded by his uncle, Colonel James Moore. He saw action in several successful battles, but, after his father died in 1777, left the army and returned to the family plantation to be with his mother. He continued his activities against the British by joining the local militia and participating in raids on troops stationed in Wilmington. The British plundered his property in retaliation.

Public Career

Following brief service in the North Carolina legislature, Moore became state attorney general in 1782, succeeding James Iredell, his predecessor on the Supreme Court, and during that time became a leader of the state bar.

A strong Federalist, Moore lost election as a delegate to the state constitutional ratifying convention, but was instrumental in getting the state finally to approve in 1789.

Moore resigned as attorney general in 1791 when the state legislature created a new office of solicitor general, giving it the same powers and salary as the attorney general. Moore claimed the new office was unconstitutional.

In 1792 Moore was elected to the state legislature again, but three years later lost a race for the U.S. Senate by one vote in the legislature. In 1798 he was appointed by President John Adams as one of three commissioners to negotiate a treaty with the Cherokee Indians, but he withdrew from the discussions before the treaty was signed. In 1799 he served as a judge on the North Carolina Superior Court.

When Justice James Iredell died in 1799, Adams looked to North Carolina for a replacement. William R. Davie was apparently the first choice, but he had just been made a diplomatic agent to France, so the nomination went to Moore.

Moore exerted little influence during his five years on the court and wrote only one opinion. He resigned in 1804, citing ill-health, and returned home to work on the development of the University of North Carolina. He died in North Carolina on Oct. 15, 1810, at the home of his son-in-law.

John Marshall
(1801-1835)

Born: Sept. 24, 1755, Germantown, Va.

Education: tutored at home; self-taught in law; attended one course of law lectures at College of William and Mary, 1780; member, Phi Beta Kappa.

Official Positions: member, Virginia House of Delegates, 1782-85, 1787-90, 1795-96; member, Executive Council of State, 1782-84; recorder, Richmond City Hustings Court, 1785-88; delegate, state convention for ratification of federal Constitution, 1788; minister to France, 1797-98; member, U.S. House of Representatives, 1799-1800; U.S. secretary of state, 1800-1801; member, Virginia Constitutional Convention, 1829.

Supreme Court Appointment: nominated Chief Justice by President John Adams Jan. 20, 1801, to replace Oliver Ellsworth, who resigned; confirmed by the Senate Jan. 27, 1801, by a voice vote; replaced on court by Roger B. Taney, nominated by President Jackson.

Family: Married Mary Willis Ambler, Jan. 3, 1783, died Dec. 25, 1831; ten children.

Died: July 6, 1835, Philadelphia, Pa.

Personal Background

The first of 15 children, John Marshall was born in a log cabin on the Virginia frontier near Germantown. His father, descended from Welsh immigrants, was an assistant surveyor to George Washington and member of the Virginia House of Burgesses. His mother was the daughter of an educated Scottish clergyman.

As a youth, Marshall was tutored by two clergymen but his primary teacher was his father, who introduced him to the study of English literature and Blackstone's Commentaries.

During the Revolutionary War, young Marshall participated in the siege of Norfolk as a member of the Culpeper Minute Men and was present at Brandywine, Monmouth, Stony Point and Valley Forge as a member of the third Virginia Regiment. In 1779 he returned home to await another assignment but was never recalled. He left the Continental Army with the rank of captain in 1781.

Marshall's only formal instruction in the law came in 1780 when he attended George Wythe's course of law lectures at the College of William and Mary. He was admitted to the bar that same year and gradually developed a lucrative practice, specializing in defending Virginians against their pre-Revolutionary War British creditors.

In January 1783 Marshall married Mary Willis Ambler, daughter of the Virginia state treasurer, and established a home in Richmond. The couple had ten children, only six of whom survived to maturity. Marshall spent many years attending to the needs of his wife, who suffered from a chronic illness and nervousness.

From 1796 until about 1806, Marshall's life was dominated by the pressures of meeting debts incurred by a land investment he had made in the northern neck of Virginia. It has been speculated that his need for money motivated him to write *The Life of George Washington*, which appeared in five volumes from 1804 to 1807. The book was written too quickly, and when Jefferson ordered postmasters, who doubled as salesmen for the book's publisher, not to take orders for it, the opportunity for large sales was lost.

The leisurely pace of the Supreme Court in its early days was well suited to the personality of Marshall, who had grown to enjoy relaxation and the outdoors as a boy. The Chief Justice enjoyed socializing in the clubs and saloons of Richmond and kept a fine supply of personal wines. He is said to have excelled at the game of quoits (similar to horseshoes), and was also known to take a turn at whist, backgammon and tenpins.

Marshall was Master of his Masonic lodge in Richmond and served as Masonic Grand Master of Virginia for several years. He was a member of the American Colonization Society, which worked toward the transfer of freed slaves to Africa, and belonged to the Washington Historical Monument Society and several literary societies.

Public Career

Marshall was elected to the Virginia House of Delegates from Fauquier County in 1782 and 1784. He reentered the House in 1787 and was instrumental in Virginia's ratification of the new U.S. Constitution. At the state ratifying convention his primary attention was directed to the need for judicial review. By 1789 Marshall was considered to be a leading Federalist in the state.

Marshall refused many appointments in the Federalist administrations of Washington and Adams, including U.S. attorney general in 1795, associate justice of the Supreme Court in 1798 and secretary of war in 1800. In 1796 he refused an appointment by President Adams as minister to France, but the following year agreed to serve as one of three special envoys sent to smooth relations with that country. This mission, known as the "XYZ affair," failed when French diplomats demanded a bribe as a condition for negotiation. Congress, however, was greatly impressed by the stubborn resistance of the American emissaries, and Marshall received a generous grant as a reward for his participation.

In 1799 Marshall was persuaded by Washington to run for the U.S. House of Representatives as a Federalist from Richmond. His career in the House was brief, however, for in 1800 he became of secretary of state under Adams. When Adams retired to his home in Massachusetts for a few months that year, Marshall served as the effective head of government.

When Oliver Ellsworth resigned as Chief Justice of the Supreme Court on Sept. 30, 1800, Adams offered the position to John Jay, who had been the court's first Chief Justice. When Jay declined, the Federalists urged Adams to elevate associate Justice William Paterson. But Adams nominated Marshall instead.

As the primary founder of the American system of constitutional law, including the doctrine of judicial review, Marshall participated in more than 1,000 Supreme Court decisions, writing more than 500 of them himself. In 1807 he presided over the treason trial of Aaron Burr in the Richmond circuit court, locking horns with Jefferson, who sought conviction. Burr was acquitted.

In 1831, at age 76, Marshall underwent successful surgery in Philadelphia for the removal of kidney stones. Three years later, he developed an enlarged liver and his health declined rapidly. When Marshall died on July 6, 1835, three months short of 80, the Liberty Bell cracked as it tolled in mourning.

William Johnson

(1804-1834)

Born: Dec. 17, 1771, Charleston, S.C.

Education: graduated Princeton, 1790; studied law under Charles Cotesworth Pinckney; admitted to bar in 1793.

Official Positions: member, South Carolina House of Representatives, 1794-98, Speaker, 1798; judge, Court of Common Pleas, 1799-1804.

Supreme Court Appointment: nominated associate justice by President Thomas Jefferson on March 22, 1804, to replace Alfred Moore, who resigned; confirmed by the Senate March 24, 1804, by a voice vote; replaced on court by James M. Wayne, nominated by President Jackson.

Family: married Sarah Bennett, March 20, 1794; eight children, six of whom died in childhood; two adopted.

Died: Aug. 4, 1834, Brooklyn, N.Y.

Personal Background

William Johnson's father, also named William, was a blacksmith, legislator and Revolutionary patriot who moved from New York to South Carolina in the early 1760s. When the British captured Charleston during the war, the Johnson family was exiled from their home and William's father sent to detention in Florida. After several months, the family was eventually reunited in Philadelphia and returned to South Carolina together.

Young William graduated first in his class from Princeton in 1790. Returning to Charleston, he began reading law under Charles Cotesworth Pinckney, a prominent adviser to President Washington who had studied at the Inns of Court. Johnson joined the bar in 1793.

The following year, Johnson married Sarah Bennett, sister of Thomas Bennett, who later would become governor of South Carolina. The couple had eight children but only two survived to maturity. They eventually adopted two refugee children from Santo Domingo.

A member of the American Philosophical Society, Johnson retained an interest in education and literature all his life. He was one of the primary founders of the University of South Carolina and in 1822 published a two-volume biography of Revolutionary War General Nathanael Greene. Johnson also published a *Eulogy of Thomas Jefferson* in 1826.

Public Career

Johnson's political career began in 1794 when he entered the South Carolina house of representatives as a member of Jefferson's new Republican party. Following service as speaker in 1798, Johnson was chosen one of three judges to sit on the state's highest court, the Court of Common Pleas. Here, he gained experience riding circuit and dealing with the burgeoning judicial questions concerning federal and state relations. In 1804 Johnson became Jefferson's first Republican nominee to the Supreme Court, replacing Alfred Moore.

At least until 1830, Johnson was the most independent of the justices on the Marshall Court, and has been called "the first great Court dissenter." Fighting against the wishes of powerful — some would say dictatorial — Chief Justice Marshall, Johnson eventually succeeded in establishing dissenting opinions as accepted court practice.

Johnson once wrote Jefferson that the court was no "bed of roses," and in the first part of his career on the bench tried to obtain another appointment. He remained on the court, however, until his death following surgery in 1834 in Brooklyn.

Henry Brockholst Livingston
(1806-1823)

Born: Nov. 25, 1757, New York City.

Education: graduated from College of New Jersey (Princeton), 1774; honorary LL.D., Harvard (1810), Princeton; studied law under Peter Yates; admitted to bar in 1783.

Official Positions: member, New York Assembly, 12th session, 24th session, 25th session; judge, New York State supreme court, 1802-07.

Supreme Court Appointment: nominated associate justice by President Thomas Jefferson Dec. 13, 1806, to replace William Paterson, who died; confirmed by the Senate Dec. 17, 1806, by a voice vote; replaced on court by Smith Thompson, nominated by President Monroe.

Family: married, first, Catharine Keteltas, five children; second, Ann Ludlow, three children; third, Catharine Kortright, three children.

Died: March 18, 1823, Washington, D.C.

Personal Background

As a member of the powerful Livingston family of New York, Brockholst Livingston was born into the colonial aristocracy. His father, William Livingston, was governor of New Jersey and a leader in the New York opposition to British colonial policies.

Young Livingston was graduated from Princeton in 1774, where he was a classmate of James Madison, and joined the Continental Army at the outbreak of the Revolution. As a commissioned major, he served under Generals Schuyler and St. Clair and participated in the siege of Ticonderoga. He was also an aide to Benedict Arnold during the Saratoga campaign and was present at Gen. John Burgoyne's surrender in 1777. Livingston left the army with the rank of lieutenant colonel.

After the war, Livingston travelled to Spain to serve as private secretary to his brother-in-law, John Jay, then serving as the American minister there. During this time, Livingston began to form a personal dislike for Jay.

Although Livingston was considered an affable and genial man, there appears to have been a violent side to his personality. He killed one man in a duel in 1798 and is believed to have fought several others. An assassination attempt was made on his life in 1785.

Livingston married three times and had a total of 11 children. A devotee of history, he was co-founder of the New York Historical Society and one of its vice presidents. He served as trustee and treasurer of Columbia University from 1784 until the end of his life and was instrumental in organizing the New York public school system.

Public Career

Livingston — who began emphasizing the middle name Brockholst, probably to avoid confusion with two cousins also named Henry — was elected to the New York Assembly in 1786. He also began practicing law at this time, working closely with Alexander Hamilton.

During these years, Livingston began a conversion, along with other members of his family, from Federalism to anti-Federalism. By 1792 he was bitterly attacking the campaign of John Jay for the New York governorship and succeeded in denying Jay a crucial bloc of votes. When Jay returned from negotiating a treaty with England in 1794, Livingston was at the forefront of voices critical of Jay and his agreement.

As the New York anti-Federalist alliance of the Burr, Clinton and Livingston factions reached its height around 1800, several Livingstons received high appointments. In 1802 Brockholst Livingston joined two of his relatives-by-marriage on the New York supreme court. He served for five years, specializing in commercial law.

In 1804 Livingston was considered seriously for an opening on the Supreme Court, but the position went instead to William Johnson. In 1806, however, Livingston was nominated by Jefferson to fill the vacancy created by the death of William Paterson.

Livingston died in 1823, after serving 16 years on the bench.

Thomas Todd

(1807-1826)

Born: Jan. 23, 1765, King and Queen County, Va.

Education: graduated from Liberty Hall (now Washington and Lee University), Lexington, Va., 1783; read law under Harry Innes; admitted to bar in 1788.

Official Positions: clerk, federal district for Kentucky, 1792-1801; clerk, Kentucky house of representatives, 1792-1801; clerk, Kentucky court of appeals (supreme court), 1799-1801; judge, Kentucky court of appeals, 1801-1806; chief justice, 1806-07.

Supreme Court Appointment: nominated associate justice by President Thomas Jefferson on Feb. 28, 1807, to fill a newly created seat; confirmed by the Senate March 3, 1807, by a voice vote; replaced on court by Robert Trimble, nominated by President John Q. Adams.

Family: married, first, Elizabeth Harris, 1788, five children; second, Lucy Payne, 1812, three children.

Died: Feb. 7, 1826, Frankfort, Ky.

Personal Background

Thomas Todd was only 18 months old when his father died. He was 11 when his mother died, and from then on was raised by a guardian. The family owned large tracts of land handed down since the 17th century. But Thomas was excluded from inheriting any of this by primogeniture.

Todd's mother, Elizabeth, managed to leave her son money she had accumulated through managing a successful boarding house, and Thomas used it to acquire a solid education in the classics. Most of the inheritance, however,

was eventually lost because of mismanagement on the part of the guardian.

At age 16, Todd served in the Revolutionary War for six months, returning home to attend Liberty Hall (now Washington and Lee University) in Lexington, Va. After graduation, he accepted an invitation from Harry Innes, a distant relative and respected member of the Virginia legislature, to tutor Innes' daughters in exchange for room, board and law instruction.

In 1784, when Innes was asked to move to Danville, Ky. (then part of Virginia), to set up a district court in the area, Todd made the move with the family. It was at this time that the Kentucky area of Virginia held the first of five conventions seeking admission to the Union as a separate state. Through his friendship with Innes, Todd was able to act as clerk for each convention.

With his first wife, Elizabeth, Todd had five children, one of whom, Charles Stewart, became Minister to Russia in 1841. When Elizabeth died in 1811, Todd married Dolley Madison's sister, Lucy Payne, in the East Room of the White House the following year.

During his lifetime, Todd accumulated over 7,200 acres in Kentucky. He also owned stock in two companies involved in waterway and public highway transportation.

Public Career

Todd joined the Virginia bar in 1788 and soon developed a specialty in land law. When Kentucky became a state in 1792, he served as secretary to the new Kentucky legislature. In 1799, when the state supreme court was created, Todd was chosen to be its chief clerk.

In 1801 Kentucky Governor James Garrard appointed Todd to fill a newly created fourth seat on the state court. At the age of 41, Todd was named its chief justice. Most of the cases handled by the court during his tenure involved land title disputes, and the chief justice developed a reputation for being fair and honest in settling complicated land controversies.

In 1807 the federal Judiciary Act of 1789 was amended to create a new federal court circuit made up of Tennessee, Kentucky and Ohio. On the recommendation of the congressmen from those states, President Jefferson chose Todd to preside over this new circuit as the sixth associate justice on the Supreme Court.

During his years on the bench, Todd missed five entire court terms because of personal and health reasons. He delivered only 14 opinions during his tenure, and of these, only one was a dissent.

Joseph Story

(1811-1845)

Born: Sept. 18, 1779, Marblehead, Mass.

Education: attended Marblehead Academy; graduated from Harvard, 1798, LL.D., 1821; read law under Samuel Sewall and Samuel Putnam; admitted to bar, 1801.

Official Positions: member, Massachusetts legislature, 1805-1808; speaker of the house, 1811; U.S. Representative, 1808-09; delegate, Massachusetts constitutional convention, 1820.

Supreme Court Appointment: nominated by President James Madison Nov. 15, 1811, to replace William Cushing, who died; confirmed by the Senate Nov. 18, 1811, by a voice vote; replaced on court by Levi Woodbury, nominated by President Polk.

Family: married, first, Mary Lynde Oliver, Dec. 9, 1804, died June 1805; second, Sarah Waldo Wetmore, Aug. 27, 1808, seven children.

Died: Sept. 10, 1845, Cambridge, Mass.

Personal Background

Joseph Story was descended from an old New England family. His father participated in the Boston Tea Party in 1773. Following a disagreement with a fellow classmate, Joseph was forced to leave Marblehead Academy before completing his college preparatory studies. By constantly studying on his own through the fall of 1794, however, he was able to enroll in Harvard in time for the 1795 term. Such drive and diligence were to characterize much of Story's life.

After graduating (second in his class) from Harvard in 1798, Story began reading law, sometimes for 14 hours a day, in the Marblehead office of Samuel Sewall, later chief justice of the Massachusetts supreme court. When Sewall was appointed to a judgeship, Story completed his studies under Samuel Putnam in Salem, Mass.

Admitted to the bar in 1801, Story began practice in Salem. The county bar was dominated by the Federalist establishment, however, and Story, a Republican-Democrat, was exposed to a good deal of prejudice. In the beginning he considered moving to Baltimore, but as his practice grew in prestige and influence, he chose to remain in Salem.

Story was an ardent poetry lover throughout his life. He was known by his hometown friends as "the poet of Marblehead." In 1805 he published "The Power of Solitude," a long, effusive poem written in heroic couplets. When his father and his wife of only seven months both died in 1806, Story, in a fit of sorrow, burned all copies of the poem he could find. Story experienced tragedy several times in his life; he lost five of his seven children by his second marriage.

An avid conversationalist, Story enjoyed music, drawing and painting. Besides being a writer, Story was an able public speaker and eulogist. He delivered the annual Fourth of July oration in Salem in 1804 and in 1826 delivered the Phi Beta Kappa oration at Harvard.

Public Career

Story served for three years in the Massachusetts legislature and then entered the U.S. Congress in 1808. During his one term of service in the House, he was blamed by Jefferson for the repeal of Jefferson's foreign trade embargo, and lost further points with his party by calling for a plan to strengthen the U.S. Navy. In January 1811 Story returned to the Massachusetts legislature and was elected speaker of the house. By November of that year he had become one of the two youngest men ever to sit on the Supreme Court. (The other was William Johnson.)

Only 32 years old and with no court experience, Story had not been Madison's first choice for the job, but Levi Lincoln and John Quincy Adams had both declined. Alexander Wolcott had been rejected by the Senate. Although he had a few financial reservations about taking the job, Story accepted the position as a great honor.

A supporter of higher learning for women, Story retained an active interest in education for most of his life. In 1819 he was elected to the Harvard Board of Overseers and became a fellow of the Harvard Corporation six years later. In 1829, Story moved from Salem to Cambridge, Mass., to become professor of law at his alma mater. He played a key role in the foundation of Harvard Law School. He is also credited, along with Chancellor James Kent of New York, with founding the equity system of jurisprudence as practiced in the United States today.

While teaching at Harvard, Story wrote his nine *Commentaries* on the law. Each of these works went through many editions, and one — *Commentaries on the Constitution* (1833) — was published in French, Spanish and German. By this time Story had achieved an international reputation.

In addition to the *Commentaries,* Story wrote legal essays for the North American Review and the American Law Review, and contributed unsigned articles to the *Encyclopedia Americana.* His court opinions, though often accused of being tedious, are seminal works in the history of American national law.

On the court, Story rarely disagreed with the strong nationalism of Chief Justice Marshall. In fact, it was Story's opinion in *Martin v. Hunter's Lessee* (1816) that established the appellate supremacy of the Supreme Court over state courts in civil cases involving federal statutes and treaties.

When Marshall died in 1835, Story undoubtedly coveted the chief justiceship, and his colleagues generally agreed he should be appointed. But Story was anathema to Andrew Jackson (he once called Story the "most dangerous man in America"), and Roger Taney received the nomination instead.

Story's nine years on the Taney Court were spent largely in dissent and by the beginning of the 1845 term he was prepared to resign. He refused to leave until he had attended to all his unfinished business, however, and in the fall of 1845 suddenly became ill and died on September 10, 1845.

Gabriel Duvall
(1812-1835)

Born: Dec. 6, 1752, Prince Georges County, Md.

Eduation: classical preparatory schooling; studied law.

Official Positions: clerk, Maryland Convention, 1775-77; clerk, Maryland House of Delegates, 1777-87; member,

Maryland State Council, 1782-85; member, Maryland House of Delegates, 1787-94; U.S. Representative, 1794-96; chief justice, General Court of Maryland, 1796-1802; presidential elector, 1796, 1800; first Comptroller of the Treasury, 1802-1811.

Supreme Court Appointment: nominated associate justice by President James Madison, Nov. 15, 1811, to replace Samuel Chase, who died; confirmed by the Senate Nov. 18, 1811, by a voice vote; replaced on court by Philip Barbour, nominated by President Jackson.

Family: married, first, Mary Bryce, July 24, 1787, died March 24, 1790, one son; second, Jane Gibbon, May 5, 1795, died April 1834.

Died: March 6, 1844, Prince Georges County, Md.

Personal Background

Descended from a family of French Huguenots, Gabriel Duvall was the sixth of ten children born on the family plantation known as "Marietta." The farm land, located on the South River near Buena Vista, Md., had been assigned to Duvall's great-grandfather by Lord Baltimore.

Duvall was active in the Revolutionary War, serving as mustermaster and commissary of stores for the Maryland troops, and later as a private in the Maryland militia. Toward the end of the war, he helped protect confiscated British property.

In 1787, at the age of 35, Duvall married Mary Bryce, daughter of Captain Robert Bryce of Annapolis. She died three years later, shortly after the birth of their son. In 1795 Duvall married Jane Gibbon, who died in 1834 shortly before Duvall resigned from the Supreme Court.

Public Career

Duvall's first public appointment came in 1775 when he was made clerk of the Maryland Convention. When the Maryland state government was created in 1777, he was named clerk for the house of delegates.

In 1787 Duvall was elected to the Maryland house of delegates, where he served until 1794. He was also chosen to attend the Constitutional Convention in Philadelphia, but decided along with the four others elected from Maryland not to attend.

Duvall entered the third Congress of the United States in 1794 as a Republican-Democrat. Two years later he resigned to become chief justice of the general court of Maryland. As chief justice, Duvall also served as recorder of the mayor's court in Annapolis, and it was in this capacity that he heard Roger Taney deliver his first speech as a member of the bar.

Duvall was chosen by President Thomas Jefferson to be the first comptroller of the Treasury in 1802. Nine years later he was nominated by President James Madison to serve on the Supreme Court.

During his 23 years on the bench, Duvall generally voted with Chief Justice Marshall. His most notable dissent came in the Dartmouth College case, although he wrote no formal opinion.

By the end of his tenure on the court, Duvall was 82 years old. His deafness and frequent absence had become an embarrassment and his resignation in 1835 came as a great relief to court observers.

Duvall spent his last years working on his family history and devoting attention to his son and nieces and nephews. He died in 1844 at the age of 91.

Smith Thompson
(1823-1843)

Born: ca. Jan. 17, 1768, Dutchess County, N.Y.

Education: graduated Princeton, 1788; read law under James Kent; admitted to bar, 1792; honorary law doctorates from Yale, 1824, Princeton, 1824, and Harvard, 1835.

Official Positions: member, New York state legislature, 1800; member, New York Constitutional Convention, 1801; associate justice, New York supreme court, 1802-14; appointed to New York State Board of Regents, 1813; chief justice, New York supreme court, 1814-18; U.S. Secretary of Navy, 1819-23.

Supreme Court Appointment: nominated associate justice by President James Monroe Dec. 8, 1823, to replace Brockholst Livingston, who died; confirmed by the Senate Dec. 19, 1823, by a voice vote; replaced on court by Samuel Nelson, nominated by President Tyler.

Family: married, first, Sarah Livingston, died Sept. 22, 1833, two sons and two daughters; second, Eliza Livingston, two daughters and one son.

Died: Dec. 18, 1843, Poughkeepsie, N.Y.

Personal Background

Smith Thompson's public career was inevitably shaped by his personal ties and social connections. His father, Ezra Thompson, was a successful New York farmer and a well known anti-Federalist in state politics. More important, however, were Thompson's links to the powerful Livingston family, an important force in New York politics at the end of the 18th century.

Thompson was born around 1768 — the exact date is unclear — in Dutchess County, N.Y., between the Hudson River and the Connecticut border. After graduating from Princeton in 1788, he taught school and read law under James Kent, a well-respected jurist, then working in Poughkeepsie. In 1793 Thompson joined the law practice of Kent and Gilbert Livingston, an old friend of his father.

Thompson married Livingston's daughter, Sarah, in 1794, and thus became a member of that fractious family. When Sarah died in 1833, he married her first cousin, Eliza Livingston. By this time, however, the family's influence was on the decline.

Public Career

Thompson's public career got off to a quick start in 1800 when he entered the state legislature as a member of the Livingston wing of the anti-Federalist Republican party. The next year he attended the state constitutional convention and received an appointment as district attorney for the middle district of New York. Before he had a chance to assume those duties, however, he was appointed to the state supreme court and immediately assumed that position.

During his tenure on the state bench, Thompson served with two of his cousins by marriage. One of these men, Brockholst Livingston, preceded Thompson to the U.S. Supreme Court in 1806.

In addition to his family relations, Thompson was joined on the state court by James Kent, his old friend and mentor. When Kent stepped down as its chief justice in 1814 to become chancellor of New York, Thompson succeeded him.

Thompson became secretary of the Navy under President Monroe in 1819, probably through the influence of Martin Van Buren, a rising young New York politician and ally of Thompson. As Navy secretary, Thompson had few administrative duties and spent a good deal of his time dabbling in New York politics, working, at times, with Van Buren. He also made no secret of his presidential ambitions during this period.

When Brockholst Livingston died in 1823, Thompson was immediately thought of as a contender for the vacancy on the Supreme Court, along with chancellor Kent. Thompson delayed expressing formal interest in the seat, however, hoping with Van Buren's help to mount a campaign drive for the 1824 presidential election. Van Buren disappointed him in the end, however, and Thompson accepted the court appointment from Monroe. Thompson continued to harbor political ambitions while on the Supreme Court and in 1828 decided to run for governor of New York. He lost to his old friend, Martin Van Buren, in a bitter and dramatic campaign.

While on the court, Thompson became part of a group that began to pull away from the strong nationalism of Chief Justice John Marshall. In 1827 he joined in overruling Marshall in *Ogden v. Saunders* when he voted in support of state bankruptcy laws. His most notable opinion came in *Kendall v. United States* (1838) when he argued against President Jackson that the executive branch was not exempt from judicial control. The passage was later omitted from the printed opinion at the request of the U.S. attorney general.

Robert Trimble
(1826-1828)

Born: Nov. 17, 1776, Augusta County, Va.

Education: Bourbon Academy; Kentucky Academy; read law under George Nicholas and James Brown; admitted to bar in 1803.

Official Positions: Kentucky State Representative, 1802; Kentucky Court of Appeals Judge, 1807-09; U.S. District Attorney for Kentucky, 1813-17; U.S. District Judge, 1817-26.

Supreme Court Appointment: nominated associate justice by President John Quincy Adams on April 11, 1826, to replace Thomas Todd, who died; confirmed on May 9, 1826, by a 27-5 vote. Replaced on court by John McLean, nominated by President Jackson.

Family: married Nancy Timberlake, Aug. 18, 1803; at least 10 children.

Died: Aug. 25, 1828, Paris, Ky.

Personal Background

Robert Trimble was the son of an early Kentucky pioneer who hunted game and scouted for Indians. It appears young Trimble studied at the Bourbon Academy in Kentucky and after teaching for a short time attended the Kentucky Academy (later Transylvania University) in Woodford County. Following his study at the Kentucky Academy, Trimble read law under George Nicholas and James Brown, who later became Minister to France.

Public Career

Trimble began private practice in Paris, Ky., in about 1800. In 1802 he entered the Kentucky House of Representatives and in 1807 was appointed justice of the Kentucky Court of Appeals. He resigned the judgeship in 1808, claiming the yearly salary of $1,000 was too low to support his large and growing family.

Trimble also refused the chief justiceship of Kentucky in 1810 for financial reasons, and declined to run for the U.S. Senate in 1812. Although he twice refused to accept the law professorship at Transylvania University, he served as a trustee of the school for many years.

Trimble's decision to concentrate on his private law practice instead of public service proved profitable. By 1817 he had earned a sizable amount of money and owned a number of slaves. That year he decided to accept the nomination by President Madison to be the federal district judge for Kentucky. He served for eight years.

Trimble — Adams' only appointment to the U.S. Supreme Court — was chosen for his judicial belief in strong national power over state power, a position that had not won him many friends in Kentucky. During his two years on the Supreme Court bench, he was a strong supporter of Chief Justice Marshall, although they disagreed in *Ogden v. Saunders* over the power of the states to enact insolvency laws.

John McLean
(1829-1861)

Born: March 11, 1785, Morris County, N.J.

Education: attended local school; privately tutored; read law in office of Arthur St. Clair Jr.

Official Positions: examiner, U.S. Land Office, 1811-12; U.S. representative, 1813-16, chairman, Committee on Accounts; judge, Ohio Supreme Court, 1816-22; commissioner, General Land Office, 1822-23; U.S. postmaster general, 1823-29.

Supreme Court Appointment: nominated associate justice by President Andrew Jackson March 6, 1829, to replace Robert Trimble, who died; confirmed by the Senate March 7, 1829, by a voice vote; replaced on court by Noah H. Swayne, nominated by President Lincoln.

Family: married, first, Rebecca Edwards, 1807, died 1840, four daughters and three sons; second, Sarah Bella Ludlow Garrard, 1843, one son, died in childbirth.

Died: April 4, 1861, Cincinnati, Ohio.

Personal Background

John McLean's father, Fergus, was a Scotch-Irish weaver who immigrated to New Jersey in 1775. After his marriage to a New Jersey woman and the birth of several children, Fergus moved his family first to western Virginia, then Kentucky and finally in 1797 settled on a farm near Lebanon, Ohio, about forty miles north of Cincinnati. Young John attended the county school and later earned enough money as a farmhand to hire two Presbyterian ministers to tutor him.

In 1804 he began two years of work as an apprentice to the clerk of the Hamilton County Court of Common Pleas in Cincinnati. At the same time, he was able to study law with Arthur St. Clair, a respected Cincinnati lawyer.

Following his admission to the bar in 1807, McLean married Rebecca Edwards of Newport, Ky., and returned to Lebanon, where he opened a printing office. In a short time, he began publishing the Lebanon *Western Star* newspaper, a weekly journal supportive of Jeffersonian politics. In 1810, however, McLean relinquished the printshop to his brother, Nathaniel, and devoted all of his time to law practice.

McLean experienced a profound religious conversion in 1811 and remained a devout Methodist for the rest of his life. He participated actively in church affairs and was chosen honorary president of the American Sunday School Union in 1849.

Public Career

McLean was elected to Congress in 1812. During his two terms of service, he supported the war measures of the Madison administration, and opposed creation of the second Bank of the United States. In 1816 McLean resigned from the House and was elected to one of four judgeships on the Ohio Supreme Court, serving for three years.

McLean worked hard for the nomination and election of James Monroe to the presidency in 1816, and in 1822 Monroe returned the favor by appointing McLean commissioner of the General Land Office. A year later he was made postmaster general.

McLean was well-liked by the postal employees and proved to be a skilled administrator. The postal service greatly expanded under his leadership, and by 1828 the department was the largest agency in the executive branch.

By this time, McLean had become an astute politician. He managed to keep his job as postmaster general under John Quincy Adams while establishing ties with many of Andrew Jackson's men at the same time. When Jackson became president in 1829, Robert Trimble's seat on the Supreme Court was still vacant because of Senate political maneuverings, and McLean was nominated to fill it. His most famous opinion during his 36 years on the bench was his dissent in the *Dred Scott* case, which was eventually reflected in the 14th Amendment to the Constitution.

McLean entertained presidential ambitions throughout his Supreme Court career and flirted with several political parties at various stages. In 1856 he received 190 votes on an informal presidential ballot taken at the first Republican national convention in Philadelphia. Thaddeus Stevens pushed his candidacy four years later, but the effort was blocked by Ohio Republicans.

McLean died of pneumonia in 1861.

Henry Baldwin
(1830-1844)

Born: Jan. 14, 1780, New Haven, Conn.

Education: Hopkins Grammar School, 1793; Yale College, 1797, LL.D., 1830; studied law under Alexander J. Dallas.

Official Positions: U.S. Representative, F-Pa., 1817-1822; chairman, Committee on Domestic Manufactures.

Supreme Court Appointment: nominated associate justice by President Andrew Jackson, Jan. 4, 1830, to replace Bushrod Washington, who died; confirmed by the Senate Jan. 6, 1830, by a 41-2 vote; replaced on court by Robert C. Grier, nominated by President Polk.

Family: married, first, Marianna Norton, 1802, died 1803, one son, Henry; second, Sally Ellicott, 1805.

Died: April 21, 1844, Philadelphia, Pa.

Personal Background

Born in New Haven, Conn., Baldwin was the product of a New England heritage going all the way back to the seventeenth century. His half-brother, Abraham, was a representative to both the Continental Congress and the Constitutional Convention and a U.S. Senator from Georgia.

As a boy, Henry lived on the family farm near New Haven but moved to the city when he entered Yale College. Upon graduation in 1797, he clerked in the law office of Alexander J. Dallas, a prominent Philadelphia attorney, and was soon admitted to the Philadelphia bar. Following this, Baldwin decided to settle in Pittsburgh, then a young city which afforded opportunities for a beginning lawyer.

Baldwin settled easily and quickly into the Pittsburgh community, joining the county bar and making many friends. With Tarleton Bates and Walter Forward, he formed a successful law firm known as the "Great Triumvirate of Early Pittsburgh." During this period, Baldwin developed a reputation for his well-written law briefs, which he prepared in his large personal law library, considered to be one of the finest in the "West."

In only a short time, Baldwin and his law partners became known for their political leadership as well as their legal skill. Together, they published a newspaper called *The Tree of Liberty*, which supported a faction of the Republican party in western Pennsylvania. Through his work in the party and in Pittsburgh civic affairs, Baldwin became a popular and prominent leader in the community by his mid-twenties. Before long, he was affectionately known as the "Idol of Pennsylvania" and the "Pride of Pittsburgh."

Despite all of his political and legal activity, Baldwin found time to involve himself in business affairs. He was part owner of at least three mills in Pennsylvania in addition to a profitable woolen mill in Steubenville, Ohio.

Public Career

Baldwin, the manufacturer, entered Congress in 1817 as a supporter of higher tariffs and as a spokesman for Pittsburgh's economic growth interests. He resigned from the House in 1822 for health reasons, but after two years of rest returned to his role as unofficial political leader of Allegheny County. In 1823 he urged Andrew Jackson to run for the presidency and throughout John Quincy Adams' administration was a close adviser to Jackson on western Pennsylvania politics.

When Justice Bushrod Washington died in 1829, President Jackson decided to nominate Baldwin to fill the seat, against the wishes of Vice President Calhoun, who supported another candidate.

Baldwin's career on the bench was erratic. In the beginning, he supported the liberal interpretations of Chief Justice Marshall, but later refused to embrace either strict or broad construction of the Constitution.

Baldwin is reported to have suffered temporary mental derangements toward the end of his life. Biographical sources do not elaborate on this except to say he did not get along well with other justices on the bench, and his closest friends were suspicious of his nonconforming and peculiar habits. As early as 1832, Roger B. Taney had advised President Jackson not to take legal action against the Bank of the United States because the case would be tried in Philadelphia and Baldwin would be unreliable as presiding judge. Baldwin, then 52, had already begun to suffer lapses of reason.

Baldwin was said to be occasionally violent and ungovernable on the bench toward the end of his life. In 1844, when he died of paralysis, he was deeply in debt and his friends had to take up a collection to pay his funeral expenses.

James Moore Wayne

(1835-1867)

Born: ca. 1790, Savannah, Ga.

Education: Princeton University, 1808, honorary LL.B., 1849; read law under three lawyers including Judge Charles Chauncey of New Haven.

Official Positions: member, Georgia House of Representatives, 1815-16; mayor, Savannah, 1817-19; judge, Savannah Court of Common Pleas, 1820-22; Georgia superior court, 1822-28; U.S. Representative, D-Ga., 1829-35, chairman, Committee on Foreign Relations.

Supreme Court Appointment: nominated associate justice by President Andrew Jackson, Jan. 7, 1835, to replace William Johnson, who died; confirmed by the Senate Jan. 9, 1835 by a voice vote.

Family: married Mary Johnston Campbell, 1813; three children.

Died: July 5, 1867, Washington, D.C.

Personal Background

James Wayne was born in Georgia, the son of a British army officer. He was the twelfth of thirteen children. As a boy, James lived on the family rice plantation outside of Savannah and was educated by an Irish tutor. He progressed so quickly in his studies that he was ready to enter the College of New Jersey (now Princeton) at the age of 14. Shortly after his graduation in 1808, James' father died and his brother-in-law, Richard Stites, became his guardian.

Wayne had begun to study law under a prominent Savannah lawyer, John Y. Noel, and after his father's death, he studied at Yale under Judge Charles Chauncey for almost two years. Upon returning to Savannah, he read in the office of his brother-in-law and in 1810 went into partnership with Samuel M. Bond.

During the War of 1812, Wayne served as an officer in a volunteer Georgia militia unit called the Chatham Light Dragoons. In 1813 he married Mary Johnston Campbell of Richmond, Va. The couple had three children.

Public Career

In 1815 Wayne was elected to the Georgia legislature, serving two years. At age 27 he became mayor of Savannah, but resigned after two years to resume his law practice. At the end of 1819, he was elected to sit on Savannah's Court of Common Pleas and in 1822 was appointed to a superior court judgeship. The court provided him with much hard work and the opportunity for public recognition.

Wayne entered Congress in 1829 and served for three terms. During this period he became a strong ally of the Jackson administration. By 1835 he was considered a leading Unionist Democrat and was nominated to the Supreme Court by President Jackson.

Unlike his colleague, Justice Campbell of Alabama, Wayne refused to leave the bench when secession came and remained a strong Union supporter throughout the Civil War. It was an agonizing period for the justice, who was disowned by his home state and accused of being an enemy alien by a Confederate court.

At war's end, Wayne opposed the punitive Reconstruction measures taken against the South and refused to hold circuit court in states under military Reconstruction rule. He did not live to see the end of Reconstruction, dying of typhoid in 1867.

Roger Brooke Taney

(1836-1864)

Born: March 17, 1777, Calvert County, Md.

Education: graduated from Dickinson College in Pennsylvania, 1795, honorary LL.D.; read law in office of Judge Jeremiah Chase in Annapolis.

Official Positions: member, Maryland House of Delegates 1799-1800; Maryland State Senator, 1816-21; Maryland Attorney General, 1827-31; chairman, Jackson Central Committee for Maryland, 1827-28; U.S. Attorney General, 1831-33; acting Secretary of War, 1831; U.S. Secretary of the Treasury, 1833-34 (appointment rejected by Senate).

Supreme Court Appointment: nominated Chief Justice by President Andrew Jackson, Dec. 28, 1835, to replace John Marshall, who died; confirmed by Senate on March 15, 1836, by a 29-15 vote; replaced on court by Salmon P. Chase, nominated by President Lincoln.

Family: married Anne P. C. Key, Jan. 7, 1806; six daughters, one son died in infancy.

Died: Oct. 12, 1864, Washington, D.C.

Personal Background

Roger Taney was descended on both sides from prominent Maryland families. His mother's family, named Brooke, first arrived in the state in 1650, complete with fox hounds and other trappings of aristocracy. The first Taney arrived about 1660 as an indentured servant but was able to acquire a large amount of property and became a member of the landed Maryland tidewater gentry.

Taney was born in Calvert County, Md., on his father's tobacco plantation. He was educated in local rural schools and privately tutored by a Princeton student. In 1795, at the age of 18, he graduated first in his class from Dickinson College in Pennsylvania.

As his father's second son, Taney was not in line to inherit the family property and so decided on a career in law and politics. For three years, he was an apprentice lawyer in the office of Judge Jeremiah Chase of the Maryland General Court in Annapolis. He was admitted to the bar in 1799.

In 1806 Taney married Anne Key, daughter of a prominent farmer and the sister of Francis Scott Key. Since Taney was a devout Roman Catholic and his wife an Episcopalian, they agreed to raise their sons as Catholics and their daughters as Episcopalians.

Public Career

Taney began his political career as a member of the Federalist party, serving one term in the Maryland legislature from 1799 to 1800. After being defeated for re-election, he moved from Calvert County to Frederick, where he began to develop a profitable law practice.

In 1803 Taney was beaten again in an attempt to return to the House of Delegates. Despite this setback, he began to achieve prominence in the Frederick community as a lawyer and politician. He was to live there for more than 20 years.

In supporting the War of 1812, Taney split with the majority of Maryland Federalists. But in 1816, as a result of shifting political loyalties, he was elected to the state senate and became a dominant figure in party politics.

Taney's senate term expired in 1821. In 1823 he settled in Baltimore, where he continued his successful law practice and political activities. By this time, the Federalist party had virtually disintegrated and Taney threw his support to the Jackson Democrats. He led Jackson's 1828 presidential campaign in Maryland and served as the state's attorney general from 1827 until 1831. At that time, he was named U.S. attorney general for the Jackson administration and left Baltimore for Washington.

It was at this stage in his career that Taney played a leading role in the controversy over the second Bank of the

United States, helping to write Jackson's message in 1832 vetoing the bank's recharter. The next year, when Secretary of Treasury William Duane refused to withdraw federal deposits from the national bank, Duane was dismissed by Jackson and replaced by Taney, who promptly carried out the action.

Taney held the Treasury job for nine months, presiding over a new system of state bank depositories called "pet banks." Jackson, who had delayed as long as he could, was eventually forced to submit Taney's nomination as Treasury secretary to the Senate. In June 1836, Taney was rejected by the Senate and forced to resign.

In 1835 Jackson appointed Taney to replace aging Supreme Court Justice Gabriel Duvall, but the nomination was indefinitely postponed by a close Senate vote. Ten months later, Jackson proposed Taney's name again, this time to fill the seat left vacant by the death of Chief Justice Marshall. To the horror of the Whigs, who considered him much too radical, Taney was confirmed as Chief Justice on March 15, 1836.

Philip Pendleton Barbour

(1836-1841)

Born: May 25, 1783, Orange County, Va.

Education: read law on his own; attended one session at College of William and Mary, 1801.

Official Positions: member, Virginia House of Delegates from Orange Co., 1812-14; U.S. Representative, 1814-25, 1827-30; Speaker of the House, 1821-23; state judge, General Court for the Eastern District of Virginia, 1825-27; president, Virginia Constitutional Convention, 1829-30; U.S. District Judge, Court of Eastern Virginia, 1830-36.

Supreme Court Appointment: nominated associate justice by President Andrew Jackson, Dec. 28, 1835, to replace Gabriel Duvall, who resigned; confirmed by the Senate, March 15, 1836, by a 30-11 vote; replaced on court by Peter Vivian Daniel, nominated by President Van Buren.

Family: married Frances Todd Johnson, 1804; seven children.

Died: Feb. 25, 1841, in Washington, D.C.

Personal Background

Philip Barbour was a country gentleman from one of Virginia's oldest families. Descended from a Scottish merchant who settled in the state in the seventeenth century, Philip's father, Thomas Barbour, was a member of the Virginia House of Burgesses and a prosperous Orange County planter. James Barbour, Philip's older brother, was a Virginia governor, a U.S. senator and secretary of war under President John Quincy Adams.

As a boy, Philip received his early education in the local schools, excelling in languages and classical literature. At the age of 17, he read law for a short time and then moved to Kentucky to begin practice. He soon returned to his home state, however, and borrowed money to enroll in the College of William and Mary. He attended only one session and left to resume his law practice. After two years, he had earned enough money to marry Frances Johnson, the daughter of an Orange County landowner. James Barbour had married Frances' sister 12 years earlier.

Public Career

Philip Barbour was elected to the Virginia House of Delegates in 1812. Two years later he won a seat in the U.S. Congress and, in a philosophical split with his brother, allied with a group of older Republicans who espoused strict construction and limited federal power.

Barbour served as Speaker of the House from 1821 until he was defeated by Henry Clay in 1823. In 1824 he chose not to run for re-election to his House seat.

After declining an offer from Thomas Jefferson to teach law at the University of Virginia, Barbour became a state judge on the general court for the eastern district of Virginia, serving for almost two years. In 1827 he returned to Congress and ran again for speaker, losing this time to fellow-Virginian Andrew Stevenson.

By this time Barbour was politically aligned with the Democratic forces of Andrew Jackson. After being passed over for a Jackson cabinet position in 1829, he was chosen president of the Virginia Constitutional Convention to replace the ailing James Monroe. In votes taken by the convention, he sided with the landed interests of the conservative eastern slaveholders against the claims of the westerners who later were to form a separate state, West Virginia.

In 1830 Barbour accepted an appointment as federal district court judge for eastern Virginia. During the national election of 1832, he was touted as a vice presidential candidate over Jackson's choice, Martin Van Buren. But party regulars, fearing the election might be thrown into the Senate, persuaded Barbour to withdraw his candidacy and support Van Buren as the nominee.

Barbour became an associate justice at the age of 53. In his short term on the bench — only five years — he generally followed the Taney court's drift toward a narrowing of corporate immunity and greater consideration of social and economic concerns.

Barbour became ill in early February 1841. By the end of the month, however, his health seemed to have improved and on Feb. 24 he attended a conference with other justices until ten o'clock at night. The next morning he was found dead of a heart attack.

Official Positions: judge, Tennessee Supreme Court of Errors and Appeals, 1824-31; first chief justice of Tennessee, 1831-34.

Supreme Court Appointment: nominated associate justice by President Andrew Jackson March 3, 1837, to fill a newly created seat; confirmed by the Senate March 8, 1837, by a 28-15 vote. Seat abolished by Congress; later recreated and filled by Joseph P. Bradley, nominated by President Grant.

Family: married, wife's name not available.

Died: May 30, 1865, Nashville, Tenn.

Personal Background

Little is known about John Catron's early years. Born about 1786, of German ancestry, he is believed to have lived first in Virginia and then Kentucky. His family was poor, and young Catron probably had little formal education, if any. In 1812 Catron moved to the Cumberland Mountain region of Tennessee and served under Andrew Jackson in the War of 1812. He joined the bar in 1815 and practiced in the Cumberland Mountain area until 1818, when he settled in Nashville and became an active member of the Davidson County bar. By this time he had developed a specialty in land law.

Catron was a successful businessman as well as a lawyer. With his brother George and a third partner, he owned and operated the profitable Buffalo Iron Works from 1827 until 1833 when he sold his interest in the business. He later reinvested in the company but kept himself out of its management.

Public Career

In 1824 the Tennessee legislature created a new seat on the Supreme Court of Errors and Appeals — the state's highest court — and Catron was elected to fill the post. In 1831 he became the court's first chief justice but resigned in 1834 when the court was abolished by judicial reorganization.

After leaving the bench, Catron turned his attention to private practice and politics. In 1836 he directed Martin Van Buren's presidential campaign in Tennessee. As a result of his party loyalty and diligence, Catron was picked by outgoing President Jackson in 1837 to fill one of two newly created seats on the Supreme Court. (The other was filled by John McKinley.) The appointment came on Jackson's final day in office.

On the court, Catron supported states' rights and in 1857 sided with the "pro-Southern" majority in the *Dred Scott* case. He refused to support the Confederacy, however, and was forced to leave Nashville after Tennessee seceded from the Union.

John Catron
(1837-1865)

Born: ca. 1786, Pennsylvania.
Education: self-educated.

John McKinley
(1837-1852)

Born: May 1, 1780, Culpeper County, Va.

Education: read law on his own and was admitted to the bar in 1800.

Official Positions: Alabama state representative, sessions of 1820, 1831 and 1836; U.S. Senator, 1826-31 and 1837; U.S. Representative, 1833-35.

Supreme Court Appointment: nominated associate justice by President Martin Van Buren Sept. 18, 1837, for a newly created Supreme Court seat; confirmed by the Senate Sept. 25, 1837, by a voice vote; replaced by John A. Campbell, nominated by President Pierce.

Family: married, first, Juliana Bryan; second, Elizabeth Armistead.

Died: July 19, 1852, Louisville, Ky.

Personal Background

Born in Virginia, McKinley at an early age moved to frontier Kentucky with his family. His father, a physician, gave McKinley an interest in studying for an acceptable profession. Young McKinley read law and was admitted to the bar in 1800.

After practicing in Frankfort, the state capital, and in Louisville, the state's main commercial center, McKinley set out for Alabama, a newly-thriving territory about to be admitted to the union. He settled in Huntsville, and soon became a part of the so-called Georgia machine, a group of locally prominent lawyers, planters and businessmen, mostly from Georgia, who dominated north Alabama socially and politically.

Public Career

Once settled in Huntsville, McKinley entered politics. He was elected to the Alabama legislature for the session of 1820. Then, in 1822, he missed election by the state legislature to the U.S. Senate by only one vote. Four years later, the seat opened up again with the death of the incumbent, and this time McKinley took it, by a margin of three votes.

During his term in the Senate, he stood for strict construction of the Constitution and a liberal reform of federal land policies, defending small landholders against speculators. McKinley was defeated for re-election to the Senate by Alabama Gov. Gabriel Moore in 1831.

During the 1820s McKinley had switched from support of Henry Clay to Andrew Jackson. Thereafter, he remained an ardent Jacksonian. In 1832 he was elected to the U.S. House and supported Jackson's campaign against the Bank of the United States. McKinley further proved his loyalty to Jackson by supporting Martin Van Buren, Jackson's choice for the vice presidency in 1832 and for the presidency in 1836.

Elected once again to the U.S. Senate in 1837, McKinley was picked for the Supreme Court by President Van Buren before the new Congress met, so he never got to serve his second Senate term. Congress had enacted a bill increasing the court from seven members to nine in the waning days of Jackson's term. After William Smith of Alabama had turned down Jackson's nomination to one of the new seats, it fell to the newly inaugurated President Van Buren to pick another man. His choice was McKinley.

McKinley's fifteen years on the bench were quiet. He stood by his states' rights and pro-slavery views to the last.

McKinley's circuit-riding duties — which he estimated at 10,000 miles a year — contributed to his failing health. When he died in 1852, Chief Justice Taney eulogized him as a "sound" lawyer, "faithful and assiduous. . . ."

Peter Vivian Daniel
(1841-1860)

Born: April 24, 1784, Stafford County, Va.

Education: attended Princeton University, 1802-03.

Official Position: member, Virginia House of Delegates, 1809-12; Virginia Privy Council, 1812-35; lieutenant governor of Virginia, 1818-35; U.S. district judge, eastern district of Virginia, 1836-41.

Supreme Court Appointment: nominated associate justice by President Van Buren Feb. 26, 1841, to replace Justice Philip Barbour, who died; confirmed by the Senate March 2, 1841, by a 22-5 vote; replaced on court by Samuel F. Miller, nominated by President Lincoln.

Family: married, first, Lucy Randolph, 1809, died 1847; second, Elizabeth Harris, 1853; two children.

Died: May 31, 1860, Richmond, Va.

Personal Background

Daniel was a member of an old Virginia family which went back to the early days of the colony. It was a landed family, with a sizeable estate, "Crow's Nest," where Daniel was born and brought up. His early education was by private tutors. He spent one year at Princeton, but returned to Virginia and moved to Richmond to study law in the office of Edmund Randolph.

Randolph had been both attorney general and secretary of state in George Washington's administration, and Daniel's association with him gained him access to the inner circle of Virginia political power. Daniel's marriage to Randolph's daughter Lucy further cemented the connection.

Public Career

In 1809 Daniel was elected to the Virginia house of delegates, where he served until elected to the Virginia privy council, an executive advisory and review body, in 1812. In 1818 he was chosen lieutenant governor of Virginia while continuing to serve on the privy council. He remained in both capacities for the next 17 years.

A loyal Jacksonian Democrat, Daniel supported President Andrew Jackson in his attack on the Bank of the United States. At one point, Jackson offered him the post of attorney general, but Daniel turned it down because of its inadequate salary. Because of his support of Jackson, Daniel was denied re-election in 1835 to his positions as privy councilor and lieutenant governor. The next year, Jackson appointed him federal district judge for eastern Virginia.

Daniel's elevation to the Supreme Court came suddenly. Justice Philip Barbour died Feb. 24, 1841, only a week before Democratic President Martin Van Buren was to turn over his office to the new Whig administration of William Henry Harrison. To ensure that the court seat remained in Democratic hands, Van Buren nominated

Daniel only two days after Barbour's death, and the Democratic-controlled Senate confirmed the appointment on March 2, two days before adjournment.

Daniel remained on the court for 19 years, a vestige of the Jeffersonian school's advocacy of states' rights and a weak central government. He died on the eve of the Civil War and was not replaced on the court for two years. The delay occurred because the Republicans took power and restructured the circuit court system to cut the number of southern circuits and increase those in the midwest and west.

Samuel Nelson
(1845-1872)

Born: Nov. 10, 1792, Hebron, N.Y.

Education: graduated, Middlebury College, 1813.

Official Positions: postmaster, Cortland, N.Y., 1820-23; presidential elector, 1820; judge, sixth circuit of New York, 1823-31; associate justice, New York supreme court, 1831-37; chief justice, New York supreme court, 1837-45; member, Alabama Claims Commission, 1871.

Supreme Court Appointment: nominated associate justice by President John Tyler Feb. 4, 1845, to replace Justice Smith Thompson, who died; confirmed by the Senate Feb. 14, 1845, by a voice vote; replaced on court by Ward Hunt, nominated by President Grant.

Family: married, first, Pamela Woods, 1819, died 1822, one son; second, Catherine Ann Russell, ca. 1825, two daughters, one son.

Died: Dec. 13, 1873, Cooperstown, N.Y.

Personal Background

Descended from Scotch-Irish parents who immigrated to America in the 1760s, Nelson spent his boyhood on farms in upstate New York. He attended local district schools, where his interest in his studies at first led him to plan a career in the ministry.

After graduation from Middlebury College in 1813, however, Nelson decided to study law instead. He clerked in a law office in Salem, N.Y., was admitted to the bar in 1817, and settled in Cortland, a small but thriving county seat in central New York. After establishing a successful law practice there, Nelson became involved in politics, identifying with the Democratic-Republicans and later with the Jackson-Van Buren wing of the Democratic party.

Public Career

In 1820 Nelson served as a presidential elector, voting for President James Monroe, and was appointed postmaster of Cortland, a position he held for three years. Also during that period, in 1821, Nelson was a delegate to the state constitutional convention, where he advocated the abolition of property qualifications for voting.

Beginning in 1823, Nelson embarked on a career in the judiciary which was to last for nearly 50 years. His first judicial position was as a judge of the sixth circuit of New York (1823-31). In 1831 he was elevated to the state supreme court and in 1837 became chief justice. From there he went to the U.S. Supreme Court in 1845.

Nelson's nomination for the Supreme Court in the waning days of the Tyler adminstration came as a complete surprise. Two previous Tyler nominees had been turned down by the Senate, and several other prominent persons had declined offers of appointment. But Nelson's reputation as a careful and uncontroversial jurist, combined with his Democratic background, were received favorably, and the Democratic-controlled Senate confirmed him with little contention.

Most of Nelson's 27 years on the court were unspectacular. He achieved some brief notoriety in the secession crisis of 1860-61 when he joined with Justice John A. Campbell to try to conciliate the North and South and avoid the Civil War. Nelson was also considered for the Democratic presidential nomination in 1860, but nothing came of it.

In 1871 President Grant appointed Nelson a member of the commission to settle the Alabama claims dispute against Great Britain. It was his hard work on the commission which finally broke Nelson's health, and he retired from the court the next year.

Levi Woodbury
(1845-1851)

Born: Dec. 22, 1789, Francestown, N.H.

Education: Dartmouth College, graduated with honors, 1809; Tapping Reeve Law School, ca. 1810.

Official Positions: clerk, New Hampshire state senate, 1816; associate justice, New Hampshire superior court, 1817-23; governor, New Hampshire, 1823-24; speaker, New Hampshire state house, 1825; U.S. Senator, 1825-31 and 1841-45; Secretary of the Navy, 1831-34; Secretary of the Treasury, 1834-41.

Supreme Court Appointment: nominated associate justice by President James K. Polk Dec. 23, 1845, to replace Justice Joseph Story, who died; confirmed by the Senate Jan. 3, 1846, by voice vote; replaced on court by Benjamin R. Curtis, nominated by President Fillmore.

Family: married Elizabeth Williams Clapp, June 1819; four daughters, one son.

Died: Sept. 4, 1851, Portsmouth, N.H.

Personal Background

The second of ten children, Woodbury was born into an old New England family which traced its American roots back to 1630. Originally settled in Massachusetts, some of the family's descendants moved to New Hampshire in the late 1700s, where Woodbury was born in 1789.

Woodbury graduated from Dartmouth College with honors in 1809 and then began the study of law. While he studied privately with practicing lawyers — as was then the custom — he also briefly attended a law school in Litchfield, Conn., making him the first Supreme Court justice to have attended a law school.

After being admitted to the bar in 1812, Woodbury practiced in his native Francestown and in nearby Portsmouth, the main commercial center of the state, from 1812 to 1816. But his interests soon turned to politics, and he held some kind of political office almost constantly from 1816 to his appointment to the Supreme Court in 1845.

Public Career

Woodbury started his climb up the political ladder in 1816 when he was appointed clerk of the state senate. After serving a year, he was put on the New Hampshire superior court, where he remained until 1823, when he became a successful insurgent candidate for governor of New Hampshire, beating the entrenched Democratic-Republican machine of Isaac Hill.

Woodbury was defeated for re-election in 1824, but came back the next year to win a seat in the state house and was elected speaker. Shortly thereafter, the legislature elected him to the U.S. Senate, where he served from 1825 to 1831.

Upon his retirement from the Senate, Woodbury was made secretary of the Navy in President Andrew Jackson's cabinet reorganization of 1831. He made little mark in that office, but in 1834 he was suddenly elevated to the crucial post of secretary of the Treasury in the midst of Jackson's war on the Bank of the United States. Jackson had gone through three Treasury secretaries, including later Chief Justice Roger B. Taney, in a little over a year. Woodbury loyally cooperated with Jackson's policies, although with some reservations, and remained as head of the Treasury through the administration of Martin Van Buren (1837-41).

Upon leaving the cabinet, Woodbury was chosen to serve once again in the U.S. Senate, where he was sitting when Polk tapped him for the Supreme Court.

Woodbury served for less than six years on the court, dying in 1851. He was a contender for the Democratic presidential nomination in 1848, but lost to Lewis Cass.

Aug. 4, 1846, by a voice vote; replaced on court by William Strong, nominated by President Grant.

Family: married Isabella Rose, 1829.
Died: Sept. 26, 1870, Philadelphia, Pa.

Personal Background

The eldest of 11 children, Grier was born into a family of Presbyterian ministers. Both his father and his maternal grandfather followed that vocation.

Grier was taught by his father until the age of 17, then entered Dickinson College as a junior and finished in one year. He then became a teacher in the Northumberland Academy, succeeding his father as principal in 1815.

But Grier's interests turned to the law, which he studied privately, passing the bar in 1817. He set up practice first in Bloomsburg, but soon moved to the county seat of Danville, Pa., where he became a prominent local attorney.

Public Career

A solid Jacksonian Democrat, Grier came to the attention of the Democratic politicians in Harrisburg. As a result, he got a patronage appointment as president judge of the district court of Allegheny County in 1833, a job he held for the next 13 years, establishing a reputation as a thorough and knowledgeable judge.

In 1844 Supreme Court Justice Henry Baldwin of Pennsylvania died, and a long effort began to fill his seat. It took more than two years for the spot to be filled finally by Grier. President Tyler had made two nominations; the first was withdrawn and the second got no action from the Democratic Senate. Tyler left office in March 1845, and the task of filling the vacancy fell to President Polk.

Polk also had difficulty finding a justice, first offering the position to future president James Buchanan. When Buchanan turned it down, Polk nominated George Woodward, but the Senate refused to confirm him. Finally, Polk selected Grier, who was confirmed.

Grier served on the court for nearly a quarter-century. Toward the end of his service, his mental and physical powers waned to the point that he was barely functioning. Finally, a committee of his colleagues called on him to urge his retirement. He took their advice and resigned in February 1870. He died seven months later.

Robert Cooper Grier
(1846-1870)

Born: March 5, 1794, Cumberland County, Pa.
Education: Dickinson College, graduated 1812.
Official Positions: president judge, district court of Allegheny Co. Pa., 1833-46.
Supreme Court Appointment: nominated associate justice by President James K. Polk Aug. 3, 1846, to replace Justice Henry Baldwin, who died; confirmed by the Senate

Benjamin Robbins Curtis
(1851-1857)

Born: Nov. 4, 1809, Watertown, Mass.
Education: Harvard University, graduated 1829 with highest honors; Harvard Law School, graduated 1832.
Official Positions: Massachusetts state representative, 1849-51.

Supreme Court Appointment: nominated associate justice by President Millard Fillmore Dec. 11, 1851, to replace Justice Levi Woodbury, who died; confirmed by the Senate Dec. 29, 1851, by a voice vote; replaced on court by Nathan Clifford, nominated by President Buchanan.

Family: married, first, Eliza Maria Woodward, 1833, died 1844, five children; second, Anna Wroe Curtis, 1846, died 1860, three children; third, Maria Malleville Allen, 1861, four children.

Died: Sept. 15, 1874, Newport, R.I.

Personal Background

Curtis was the son of a Massachusetts ship captain whose ancestors settled New England in the 1630s. His father died while on a voyage abroad when Curtis was a child. He was raised by his mother with help from his half-uncle, George Ticknor, a Harvard professor and author.

When Curtis was ready to enter Harvard University in 1825, his mother moved to Cambridge and ran a boarding school for students there to support herself and her family. Curtis graduated from Harvard in 1829 and immediately entered Harvard Law School, from which he graduated in 1832 after taking a year off in 1831 to set up a law practice in Northfield, Mass., a small town in the Connecticut River Valley.

In 1834 Curtis moved to Boston to join the law practice of his distant cousin, Charles Pelham Curtis. After the death of his first wife, Curtis married his law partner's daughter in 1846.

Public Career

Elected to the Massachusetts house in 1849, Curtis chaired a commission which designed a sweeping reform of judicial proceedings in the state. A conservative Whig, Curtis was a strong supporter of Daniel Webster. He rallied behind the senator during the crisis of 1850 when Webster was working for compromise of the territorial and slave issues and was being denounced for his efforts by Massachusetts abolitionists.

In 1851, when President Fillmore was looking for a replacement for the late Justice Levi Woodbury, Webster, then serving as Fillmore's secretary of state, recommended Curtis. Curtis' relations with his colleagues on the court, especially with Chief Justice Taney, became so acrimonious during court arguments over the *Dred Scott* case and other pre-Civil War controversies that he decided to leave the court and resigned on Sept. 30, 1857.

Curtis believed strongly in preserving the Union through compromise. In his court activities, he upheld and enforced the unpopular fugitive slave law. But he drew the line at the *Dred Scott* decision; he was one of two justices who dissented from that highly criticized opinion.

Curtis devoted the remainder of his life to a lucrative law practice in Boston. He appeared before the Supreme Court on numerous occasions to argue for his clients. Politically, he remained a conservative, objecting to some of the emergency measures taken by President Lincoln, including the Emancipation Proclamation and the suspension of *habeas corpus*.

He also opposed the radical Reconstruction policies of congressional Republicans during Andrew Johnson's administration. In 1868 he served as the leading counsel for President Johnson during the impeachment proceedings. Johnson offered Curtis the position of attorney general, but he declined.

John Archibald Campbell
(1853-1861)

Born: June 24, 1811, Washington, Ga.

Education: Franklin College (now the University of Georgia), graduated with first honors, 1825; attended U.S. Military Academy at West Point, 1825-28.

Official Positions: Alabama state representative, sessions of 1837 and 1843; assistant secretary of war, Confederate States of America, 1862-65.

Supreme Court Appointment: nominated associate justice by President Franklin Pierce March 22, 1853, to replace Justice John McKinley, who died; confirmed by the Senate March 25, 1853, by a voice vote; replaced on court by David Davis, nominated by President Lincoln.

Family: married Anna Esther Goldthwaite in the early 1830s; five children.

Died: March 2, 1889, Baltimore, Md.

Personal Background

Born into a family of Scotch and Scotch-Irish descent, Campbell was a child prodigy. He entered college at the age of 11, graduating at 14. He then attended West Point for three years before withdrawing to return home to support the family after the death of his father. A year later, at the age of 18, he was admitted to the bar by special act of the Georgia legislature.

In 1830 Campbell moved to Alabama to begin his legal career, settling first in Montgomery, where he met and married Anna Esther Goldthwaite, member of a prominent Alabama family. They moved to Mobile in 1837 and Campbell was elected to the first of two terms in the state legislature.

Public Career

Campbell quickly became one of the leading lawyers in Alabama, and before long his reputation spread nationally. Twice he declined appointment to the Alabama supreme court. He was a delegate to the Nashville convention of 1850, convened to protect southern rights in the face of what they saw as northern encroachment, especially on the slavery question. Campbell was a moderating influence at the convention, writing many of the resolutions which finally were adopted.

Campbell was selected for the Supreme Court after a Democratic Senate had refused to act on three choices nominated by Whig President Millard Fillmore. When Fillmore was replaced by Democrat Franklin Pierce in March 1853, Democrats were able to appoint one of their own to the court. Campbell's selection was made in an unprecedented fashion. The Supreme Court justices wanted the new president to nominate Campbell and sent a delegation to Pierce to make their wish known. Pierce complied.

Campbell's service on the bench was cut short by the Civil War. He opposed secession and was hopeful that slavery would slowly disappear if the South was left alone. He himself freed all his slaves upon his Supreme Court appointment, and thereafter hired only free blacks as servants. During the secession crisis, he attempted to serve as a mediator between the seceding states and the new Lincoln administration.

But when the die was cast and hostilities broke out, he resigned his court position and returned to the South, settling in New Orleans. In 1862, he was invited to join the Confederate government and accepted the position of assistant secretary of war in charge of administering the conscription law. He remained in that position until the fall of the Confederacy in 1865.

After a few months of detention by the Union, Campbell was freed and returned to New Orleans, where he built up a prosperous and prestigious law practice. He argued before the Supreme Court on numerous occasions in the quarter-century before his death.

Nathan Clifford
(1858-1881)

Born: Aug. 18, 1803, Rumney, N.H.

Education: studied law in office of Josiah Quincy in Rumney, admitted to New Hampshire bar, 1827.

Official Positions: Maine state representative, 1830-34; attorney general of Maine, 1834-38; U.S. Representative, 1839-43; U.S. Attorney General, 1846-48; Minister to Mexico, 1849-49.

Supreme Court Appointment: nominated associate justice by President James Buchanan Dec. 9, 1857, to replace Benjamin R. Curtis, who resigned; confirmed by the Senate Jan. 12, 1858, by a 26-23 vote; replaced on court by Horace Gray, nominated by President Arthur.

Family: married Hannah Ayer, ca. 1828; six children.

Died: July 25, 1881, Cornish, Maine.

Personal Background

Clifford was the son of a New Hampshire farmer whose American roots went back three generations. His grandfather was an officer in the Revolutionary War.

Clifford attended the local academies for his early education, then studied law in the office of Josiah Quincy, a prominent attorney in Rumney, N.H. Clifford was admitted to the bar in 1827 and moved to Newfield, Maine, to begin practice. There he met and married a local woman, Hannah Ayer.

Clifford was a staunch Jacksonian Democrat, maintaining his early political beliefs throughout his long life and political career.

Public Career

Clifford entered public life soon after beginning his law practice in Maine. In 1830, at the age of 27, he was elected to the lower house of the Maine legislature. He was re-elected for three more one-year terms, and served the last two years as speaker. He was then elected attorney general of the state by the legislature, serving four years. After that, he won two terms in the U.S. House, but was defeated for election to a third term.

Clifford's defeat in 1843 marked the end of the first phase of his political career. He then returned to law practice in Maine for three years. He had earned a reputation as a hard worker and received attention for the thoroughness of his preparation.

In 1846 President Polk chose Clifford as attorney general. Polk needed New England representation in his Cabinet, and Clifford supported the administration's ideas.

During his service in the Polk Cabinet, Clifford played a key role in mediating the many disputes between Polk and his secretary of state, James Buchanan. Polk was vigorously pursuing his war with Mexico, while Buchanan advocated a more cautious policy. Buchanan liked and trusted Clifford, and when he became president would appoint Clifford to the Supreme Court.

In 1848 Polk entrusted Clifford with a diplomatic mission. He was sent to Mexico with the purpose of getting Mexico to ratify the peace treaty ending the war. Clifford did so and stayed on to become U.S. minister to the Mexican government from 1848-49. With a new Whig adminstration in Washington in 1849, Clifford returned to Maine to resume law practice, this time in the more populous and prosperous city of Portland.

When a Supreme Court vacancy occurred in late 1857, Buchanan chose Clifford to fill it. There was strong criticism against the nomination; Clifford was looked upon in the North as a "doughface" — a northern man with southern principles. Clifford had supported Buchanan administration policies which many northerners thought favored the South. But Clifford was confirmed in a close vote.

In 1877, Clifford — still on the court — served as chairman of the electoral commission set up to decide the disputed presidential election of 1876. He voted with the Democrats for Tilden, but the Republican, Rutherford B. Hayes, won by one vote. Clifford always considered Hayes an illegitimate president, and refused to enter the White House during his presidency.

In 1880 Clifford suffered a stroke which prevented him from taking any futher active role in court proceedings. He refused to resign, however, hoping to live until a Democratic president could name his successor. But he died while the Republicans were still in power.

Noah Haynes Swayne
(1862-1881)

Born: Dec. 7, 1804, Frederick County, Va.

Education: studied law privately and was admitted to the bar in Warrenton, Va., in 1823.

Official Positions: Coshocton County prosecuting attorney, 1826-29; Ohio state representative, 1830 and 1836; U.S. attorney for Ohio, 1830-41; Columbus City councilman, 1834.

Supreme Court Appointment: nominated associate justice by President Abraham Lincoln Jan. 21, 1862, to replace John McLean, who died; confirmed by the Senate Jan. 24, 1862, by a 38-1 vote; replaced on court by Stanley Matthews, nominated by President Hayes and renominated by President Garfield.

Family: married Sarah Ann Wager, 1832; four sons, one daughter.

Died: June 8, 1884, New York City.

Personal Background

Although born in the slave-holding state of Virginia, Swayne was the son of antislavery Quaker parents of Pennsylvania origin. He studied medicine as a youth, but after the death of his teacher he switched to law.

Following his admission to the bar, Swayne migrated to the free state of Ohio because of his opposition to slavery. During his long legal career in that state, he was involved in cases defending runaway slaves. When he married Sarah Ann Wager, a Virginian who owned slaves, she freed them at his insistence.

Public Career

Shortly after settling in Ohio, Swayne became involved in politics as a Jacksonian Democrat. He was elected prosecuting attorney of Coshocton County in 1826 and to the Ohio legislature in 1829. In 1830 President Andrew Jackson appointed him U.S. attorney for Ohio, and he served throughout the rest of Jackson's administration as well as that of Martin Van Buren. During his service as U.S. attorney, he also developed a successful private law practice and served on the Columbus city council and once again in the state legislature.

Swayne's political activity ebbed in the 1840s, but resurged in the 1850s when the slavery issue began tearing the nation apart. Swayne's antislavery convictions drove him from the Democratic Party, and he supported the presidential candidate of the new Republican Party, John Charles Fremont, in 1856. Swayne also served in the 1850s as a member of a state committee overseeing Ohio's finances, which had fallen into disorder.

Although Swayne had no judicial experience and was not well known outside Ohio, Lincoln nevertheless made him his first appointment to the Supreme Court. The vacancy was caused by the death of Justice John McLean, a close friend of Swayne's, and McLean had let it be known that he wanted Swayne to succeed him on the court. In addition, Swayne was close to the governor of Ohio, William Dennison, who personally came to Washington to lobby for Swayne. The Ohio congressional delegation also recommended him.

Swayne fulfilled Republican hopes that he would uphold the extraordinary Civil War measures of the national government, and he continued to take a generally nationalist stance in his decisions throughout his years on the court. During his court service, he also lobbied for passage of the 15th Amendment, guaranteeing voting rights for blacks. His own state of Ohio was crucial to the ratification of the

amendment and Swayne used all his influence in his adopted state on behalf of approval.

Twice Swayne maneuvered for the Chief Justiceship — in 1864, when Roger B. Taney died, and again in 1873 when Salmon P. Chase died. But he was disappointed both times. With his mental acuity noticeably declining by 1881, Swayne was persuaded by President Hayes to resign with the promise that his friend and fellow-Ohioan Stanley Matthews would be chosen as his successor.

Samuel Freeman Miller

(1862-1890)

Born: April 5, 1816, Richmond, Ky.

Education: Transylvania University, M.D., 1838; studied law privately, admitted to the bar in 1847.

Official Positions: justice of the peace and member of the Knox County, Ky., court, an administrative body, in the 1840s.

Supreme Court Appointment: nominated associate justice by President Abraham Lincoln July 16, 1862, to replace Justice Peter V. Daniel, who died; confirmed July 16, 1862, by a voice vote; replaced on court by Henry B. Brown, nominated by President Benjamin Harrison.

Family: married, first, Lucy Ballinger, ca. 1839, died ca. 1854, three children; second, Elizabeth Winter Reeves, widow of his law partner, 1857, two children.

Died: Oct. 13, 1890, Washington, D.C.

Personal Background

The son of a Pennsylvania-German father and a mother from North Carolina, both of whom migrated to Kentucky at the turn of the nineteenth century, Miller began his career as a medical doctor. After graduating from the medical department of Transylvania University in 1838, he set up practice in Barboursville in Kentucky's small, mountainous Knox County.

Miller soon developed an interest in legal and political matters. He joined a debating society and studied law on the side, passing his bar exam in 1847. He favored gradual emancipation of slaves, and when the Kentucky constitutional convention of 1849 strengthened the position of slavery in the state, Miller freed his own slaves and moved west to Iowa, a free state.

Public Career

In Iowa, Miller abandoned medicine and set up a prosperous law practice in Keokuk. With political tensions rising in the 1850s, Miller joined the public arena and helped organize the Republican Party in Iowa, serving as chairman of the Keokuk County GOP organization. By 1860 Miller was one of the leading Republican figures in the state and a strong backer of Abraham Lincoln for the party's presidential nomination. In 1861 Miller made a try for the Republican gubernatorial nomination but was defeated by incumbent Gov. Samuel J. Kirkwood.

Miller's appointment to the Supreme Court came despite his lack of judicial experience. With the creation of a new circuit west of the Mississippi, western congressmen and politicians, including a unanimous Iowa delegation, pressed for Miller's appointment. Lincoln's agreement to choose him made Miller the first Supreme Court justice from west of the Mississippi.

Miller was one of the five justices to serve on the electoral commission in 1877 to resolve the disputed presidential election of 1876 between Democrat Samuel J. Tilden and Republican Rutherford B. Hayes. Miller voted down the line with the Republican majority to give the presidency to Hayes.

Twice Miller was considered for Chief Justice — in 1873 and 1888 — but was passed over both times. His name was also mentioned for the presidency in 1880 and 1884, but no significant movement developed. Miller worked on the court almost up to the point of his death on Oct. 13, 1890.

David Davis
(1862-1877)

Born: March 9, 1815, Cecil County, Md.
Education: graduated Kenyon College, 1832; Yale Law School, 1835.
Official Positions: Illinois state representative, 1845-47; member, Illinois constitutional convention, 1847; Illinois state circuit judge, 1848-62.
Supreme Court Appointment: nominated associate justice by President Lincoln Dec. 1, 1862, to replace John A. Campbell, who resigned; confirmed by the Senate Dec. 8, 1862, by a voice vote; replaced on court by John Marshall Harlan, nominated by President Hayes.
Family: married, first, Sarah Woodruff, Oct. 30, 1838, died 1879; second, Adeline Burr, March 14, 1883, two daughters.
Died: June 26, 1886, Bloomington, Ill.

Personal Background

Davis was born in Maryland of Welsh ancestry. After studying law, he sought his fortune in the West.

Settling first in Pekin, Ill., he moved within a year to Bloomington, which became his lifelong home. He was active in Whig politics, running a losing race for the state senate in 1840 but winning a state house seat in 1844. It was during this period that he first became acquainted with Abraham Lincoln, a relationship that deepened over the years and was to have a major effect on Davis' life.

Public Career

After one term in the state house, Davis was chosen a member of the Illinois constitutional convention of 1847. At the convention, he fought for a popularly-elected judiciary, replacing the system of election by the legislature. Davis' position prevailed, and in 1848 he was elected a judge of the eighth state judicial circuit, a position he was re-elected to twice and which he held until his appointment to the Supreme Court.

Among the prominent lawyers who practiced before Judge Davis in Illinois were Abraham Lincoln and Stephen Douglas. Davis became close to Lincoln in the 1850s and joined the new Republican party with him when their Whig party fell apart. Davis became Lincoln's campaign manager in 1860 and was perhaps the most important person in securing Lincoln the Republican presidential nomination that year.

Lincoln appointed Davis to the Supreme Court vacancy created by the resignation of Justice John A. Campbell, an Alabaman who withdrew to join the Confederate effort.

Davis' interest in politics never faded. After Lincoln's death, he became disenchanted with the Republican Party. In 1872 he was nominated for president by the Labor Reform Party, a splinter group. Davis hoped to use this nomination to further his candidacy for the Liberal Republicans, a group of anti-Grant Republicans. But when the Liberals chose Horace Greeley instead, Davis declined the Labor Reform nomination.

Tired of his career on the Supreme Court, Davis accepted his election in 1877 by the Illinois legislature to the U.S. Senate and resigned from the court. The timing was unfortunate, for Davis had been expected to be a key member of the electoral commission set up to decide the disputed presidential election of 1876. Davis' political independence would have made him the swing vote on an otherwise evenly-divided commission. His replacement was a Republican, Justice Joseph P. Bradley, who voted with the Republicans and gave the election to Republican Rutherford B. Hayes. At the time, it was thought that Davis might have voted with the Democrats on at least some of the disputed electoral votes, but he indicated later that he did not disagree with the commission's decisions.

Davis served one term in the Senate (1877-83), voting independently, and then retired. From 1881 to 1883, he was president pro tem of the Senate, which under the succession law then in effect made him next in line for the presidency if anything had happened to President Arthur.

Stephen Johnson Field
(1863-1897)

Born: Nov. 4, 1816, Haddam, Conn.
Education: graduated Williams College, 1837, class valedictorian; studied law in private firms, admitted to the bar in 1841.

Official Positions: Alcalde of Marysville, 1850; California state representative, 1850-51; California supreme court justice, 1857-63.

Supreme Court Appointment: nominated associate justice by President Abraham Lincoln March 6, 1863, for a newly created seat; confirmed by the Senate March 10, 1863, by a voice vote; replaced on court by Joseph McKenna, nominated by President McKinley.

Family: married Virginia Swearingen June 2, 1859; no children.

Died: April 9, 1899, in Washington, D.C.

Personal Background

The son of a New England Congregational clergyman, Field was born into a family which produced several prominent members. His brothers included David Dudley Field, a noted New York lawyer and politician; Cyrus West Field, a promoter of the first Atlantic cable; and Henry Martyn Field, a leading clergyman and author. Field's nephew, David J. Brewer, was himself a Supreme Court justice (1889-1910) and served with Field on the court for the last eight years of Field's service.

Field studied law with his brother Dudley and with John Van Buren, son of President Martin Van Buren. He was admitted to the New York bar in 1841 and for the next seven years practiced in partnership with his brother.

But in 1849, after a trip to Europe, he decided to strike out on his own and moved to California. Settling in Marysville, in the heart of the gold fields, Field lived the rough-and-tumble life of a frontier entrepreneur.

Public Career

Field served in 1850 as Maryville's alcalde (the chief local administrative office under the old Spanish system). He quarreled with a local judge and was twice disbarred and once sent to jail for contempt of court.

Field was elected to the California House in 1850 and during his year of service was the chief drafter of the civil and criminal codes for the new state. After being defeated in a bid for the state senate in 1851, he resumed his legal career for a time and then was elected to the California supreme court as a Democrat in 1857.

In 1863 Congress authorized an additional seat on the U.S. Supreme Court, partly to gain a new justice who would support the Civil War measures of the federal government, and partly because there was a need for a new circuit for the west coast. Many cases concerning land and mineral issues were coming to the court from California, and westerners wanted someone on the court familiar with those issues.

The California and Oregon congressional delegations unanimously recommended Field for the new seat, even though he was a Democrat. He had staunchly supported the Union cause and was an acknowledged expert in land and mining issues. So Lincoln appointed him.

During his service on the court, Field served, in 1877, on the electoral commission which decided the contested presidential election in favor of Republican Rutherford B. Hayes. Field voted on the losing Democratic side on all questions.

Field's name was mentioned for the Democratic presidential nomination in 1880 and 1884, but his candidacy did not advance very far. He aspired to be Chief Justice in 1888, when Waite died, but President Cleveland picked Melville W. Fuller instead.

In the 1890s, Field's mental powers were visibly declining, and he was taking less and less part in court proceedings. Finally, the other justices strongly hinted that he resign. Ironically, Field himself had been part of an effort to persuade aging Justice Robert C. Grier to resign in 1877. Field did finally quit the court in late 1897, but only after passing John Marshall's record of 34 years and five months of service.

Salmon Portland Chase
(1864-1873)

Born: Jan. 13, 1808, Cornish, N.H.
Education: Dartmouth College, 1826.
Official Positions: U.S. Senator from Ohio, 1849-55, 1861; Governor of Ohio, 1856-60; U.S. Secretary of the Treasury, 1861-64.

Supreme Court Appointment: nominated Chief Justice by President Abraham Lincoln, Dec. 6, 1864, to replace Chief Justice Roger B. Taney, who died; confirmed by the Senate Dec. 6, 1864, by a voice vote; replaced on court by Morrison R. Waite, appointed by President Grant.

Family: married, first, Katherine Jane Garniss, March 4, 1834, died Dec. 1, 1835; second, Eliza Ann Smith, Sept. 26, 1839, died Sept. 29, 1845; third, Sara Belle Dunlop Ludlow, Nov. 6, 1846, died Jan. 13, 1852, six daughters, only two of whom lived beyond infancy.

Died: May 7, 1873, New York City.

Personal Background

Chase grew up and made his career in Ohio but was born in New Hampshire of a prominent family that traced its roots in this country back to 1640. An uncle, Dudley Chase, served as a U.S. senator for Vermont (1813-17 and 1825-31), and another uncle, Philander Chase, was the Protestant Episcopal Bishop of Ohio (1818-31). Chase's father was a tavern-keeper who held various local political offices.

Upon his father's death in 1817, Chase went to live with his uncle Philander in Ohio and was brought up under his stern discipline. Throughout his life, Chase retained a strong and righteous religious streak, inculcated in his early years by his uncle.

After graduation from Dartmouth, Chase went to Washington, D.C., opened a private school, and studied law under Attorney General William Wirt. He was admitted to the bar in 1829, then moved west to Cincinnati to begin his distinguished legal career.

Chase became involved early in the anti-slavery movement and took a prominent role in defending runaway slaves, arguing one case up to the Supreme Court. For his activities, he became known as the "attorney general for runaway negroes."

Public Career

Chase's opposition to slavery soon moved him into politics, and he became a leader of the anti-slavery Liberty Party in the 1840s. In 1848 he joined the Free Soilers and helped write part of the party's platform. The following year, when the Free Soilers held the balance of power in the Ohio legislature, they helped the Democrats organize the legislature in return for the Democrats' support in electing Chase to the U.S. Senate.

In the Senate, Chase joined such anti-slavery stalwarts as William Seward and Benjamin Wade. When the old party system broke up, he helped to form the new Republican party.

In 1855 Chase was elected governor of Ohio and re-elected in 1857. He was mentioned for the Republican presidential nomination in both 1856 and 1860, but did not receive many votes. In 1861 he was elected once again to the U.S. Senate, but resigned after only two days to take a seat in President Lincoln's cabinet. As Lincoln's Treasury secretary, Chase was responsible for financing the war, first with large borrowings and then with the issue of paper money. He also devised a new federal banking system which became the cornerstone of American finance for the next half-century.

But Chase was not happy with Lincoln's leadership and allowed himself to become the focus of an anti-Lincoln group within the Republican party, which wanted to dump the president in 1864. Twice that year, efforts were made to substitute Chase for Lincoln, but the efforts of the radicals were not successful. Chase also had a series of running quarrels with Lincoln over other matters and submitted his resignation several times. Lincoln finally accepted it in the summer of 1864.

When Chief Justice Taney died in October, Chase was Lincoln's first choice for the post. Despite their differences, Lincoln had high regard for Chase's abilities. And the Republicans wanted someone on the court who they felt would sustain the extraordinary measures taken by the federal government during the war and others contemplated for the postwar period.

Chase was probably the most politically-involved Chief Justice in American history, both because of his own ambitions and because of the tumultuous state of the country. In the spring of 1865, Chief Justice Chase made a tour of the South to study conditions there and report to President Andrew Johnson. Later, in 1868, Chase presided at the impeachment trial of Johnson and fought with the radical Republicans for his rights as presiding officer of the trial. In both 1868 and 1872, Chase made no secret of his still-burning presidential ambitions and allowed friends to maneuver politically for him. But as in the past, he was disappointed in his hopes for the nation's highest office.

William Strong
(1870-1880)

Born: May 6, 1808, Somers, Conn.
Education: Yale College, B.A., 1828; M.A., 1831.
Official Positions: U.S. Representative, 1847-51; Pennsylvania supreme court justice, 1857-68.
Supreme Court Appointment: nominated associate justice by President Ulysses Grant Feb. 7, 1870, to replace Robert C. Grier, who retired; confirmed by the Senate Feb. 18, 1870, by a voice vote; replaced by William B. Woods, nominated by President Hayes.
Family: married, first, Priscilla Lee Mallery Nov. 28, 1836, died 1844, two daughters, one son; second, Rachel Davis Bull, a widow, Nov. 22, 1849, two daughters, two sons.
Died: Aug. 19, 1895, Lake Minnewassa, N.Y.

Personal Background

Strong was born into an old New England family which traced its ancestry in America back to 1630. He was the eldest of eleven children of a Presbyterian clergyman. After getting an M.A. from Yale in 1831, Strong taught school in Connecticut and New Jersey and studied law briefly at Yale Law School. But he moved to Pennsylvania to begin his legal career and was admitted to the Philadelphia bar in 1832. He then began practice in Reading, a thriving industrial town in the heart of the rich Pennsylvania-Dutch country. Since many of his clients did not speak English, Strong mastered the local German dialect and soon developed a thriving practice.

Public Career

After establishing himself as a member of Reading's elite through his successful law career, Strong was elected to two terms in the U.S. House as an anti-slavery Democrat (1847-51). Then, in 1857, he was elected to a fifteen-year term on the Pennsylvania supreme court. He was elected to the court as a Democrat, but with the coming of the Civil War, Strong joined the Republican party.

In 1864, when Chief Justice Roger B. Taney died, Lincoln considered Strong as a potential replacement, but finally chose Salmon P. Chase instead. Strong resigned from the Pennsylvania court in 1868 to devote himself to making money, but in 1869 his name came up again for a court vacancy, this time as an associate justice. Justice Grier had announced his retirement because of age and infirmity, and President Grant's advisers recommended Strong for the spot. But there was great sentiment in the country and the Congress for Edwin M. Stanton, the former secretary of war. Members of Congress circulated a petition for Stanton which was signed by a large majority of both houses; as a result Grant sent up Stanton's name instead of Strong's. Stanton was confirmed Dec. 20, 1869, but died suddenly four days later, never having had a chance to participate in court proceedings.

With Stanton's death, the way was finally clear for Strong to go onto the court. His selection was clouded by charges that Grant was trying to "pack" the court to reverse a decision unfavorable to the Civil War legal tender acts.

During his court service, he was known for his strong intellect and the forceful and articulate manner in which he presented his arguments. He was appointed a member of the Electoral Commission of 1877 which decided the disputed presidential election of 1876 in favor of Republican Rutherford B. Hayes. Strong supported Hayes on all the votes of the commission.

Strong's court career lasted only 10 years. He retired at the peak of his intellectual abilities.

After his retirement from the court, Strong — then 72 — devoted himself to religious work, something which he had begun while still on the bench. From 1883 to 1895, he was president of the American Sunday School Union; he also served as vice president of the American Bible Society from 1871 to 1895, and was president of the American Tract Society from 1873 to 1895.

Joseph P. Bradley
(1870-1892)

Born: March 14, 1813, Berne, N.Y.

Education: Rutgers University, graduated 1836.

Official Positions: None.

Supreme Court Appointment: nominated associate justice by President Ulysses Grant Feb. 7, 1870, succeeding James Wayne, who died in 1867 and whose seat remained vacant by act of Congress until 1870; confirmed by the Senate March 21, 1870, by a 46-9 vote; replaced on court by George Shiras Jr., nominated by President Benjamin Harrison.

Family: married Mary Hornblower in 1844; seven children.

Died: Jan. 22, 1892, Washington, D.C.

Personal Background

Bradley's life and career exemplify the traditional American "Horatio Alger" success story. The oldest of eleven chidren, Bradley was raised on a small farm in penurious circumstances. But he showed an early aptitude for learning and after going to a country school, began teaching at the age of 16. A local minister took an interest in him and sponsored his entrance to Rutgers University, where he was graduated in 1836.

Bradley then studied law in the office of Archer Gifford, collector of the port of Newark, N.J., and passed the bar in 1839. His assiduous legal work soon paid off in a successful law practice. Specializing in patent, commercial, and corporate law, he became counsel for various railroads, the most important being the powerful Camden and Amboy Railroad. Another fillip to his career came when he married Mary Hornblower in 1844, daughter of the chief justice of the New Jersey supreme court.

Bradley had a lifelong interest in mathematics and geology. He devised a perpetual calendar designed to determine the day of the week any date fell on throughout history. And he researched and wrote a treatise on the origins of the steam engine. Always an avid reader, he had a library numbering 16,000 volumes.

The middle initial "P" did not stand for a middle name, but Bradley adopted its use some time during his early life, perhaps after his father's name, Philo.

Public Career

Bradley was a Whig before the Civil War, and went to Washington, D.C., in the winter of 1860-61 to lobby for a compromise settlement of issues between the North and South. But once the war broke out, he supported the Union cause and the Lincoln administration unreservedly. He ran a losing race for the U.S. House as a unionist in 1862. After the war, he identified with the radical wing of the Republican party and run unsuccessfully as a Grant presidential elector in 1868.

Grant nominated Bradley for a seat on the court in February 1870, the same day he chose William Strong for another court vacancy. (The choices raised a storm later because they made possible the reversal of a crucial court decision, *Hepburn v. Griswold*, involving the validity of the Civil War legal tender acts).

The other major controversy of Bradley's court career came in 1877 when he served on the electoral commission established to determine the outcome of the disputed presidential election of 1876. With the commission divided seven-to-seven along partisan lines, Supreme Court Justice David Davis, an independent, was to have been the fifteenth and deciding member. But Davis withdrew from the commission because the Illinois legislature had chosen him to be a U.S. senator, and Bradley was substituted as the next least partisan justice. But he voted with the Republicans on all the issues, awarding all 20 disputed electoral votes to Republican Rutherford B. Hayes, thus making him president by one vote. Though he was excoriated in the Democratic press, Bradley always contended that he voted on the basis of the legal and constitutional questions and not on a partisan basis.

The rest of Bradley's career on the court was quieter. He was known for careful research and thoughtful analysis. He worked until practically the day of his death, Jan. 22, 1892.

Ward Hunt
(1873-1882)

Born: June 14, 1810, Utica, N.Y.

Education: graduated with honors from Union College, 1828.

Official Positions: New York state assemblyman, 1839; Mayor of Utica, 1844; member, New York state court of appeals, 1866-69; New York state commissioner of appeals, 1869-73.

Supreme Court Appointment: nominated associate justice by President Ulysses Grant Dec. 3, 1872, to replace Samuel Nelson, who retired; confirmed by the Senate Dec. 11, 1872 by a voice vote; took his seat on the court Jan. 9, 1873; replaced by Samuel Blatchford, nominated by President Arthur.

Family: married, first, Mary Ann Savage, 1837, died 1845; second, Marie Taylor, 1853, two children.

Died: March 24, 1886, Washington, D.C.

Personal Background

Hunt was born and made his career in the upstate New York city of Utica. His father was a banker there, and Hunt was descended from early New England settlers. After graduation from Union College, Hunt studied law, first at a private academy in Litchfield, Conn., and then with a local Utica judge, Hiram Denio. After admission to the bar in 1831, he formed a partnership with the judge and built a lucrative practice.

Public Career

While practicing law, Hunt became actively engaged in politics. He was elected to the New York state assembly (lower house) as a Jacksonian Democrat in 1838, and served a one-year term. Later he served a year as mayor of Utica in 1844.

Hunt's ties with the Democratic party began to loosen in the 1840s, when he opposed the annexation of Texas and the expansion of slavery. In 1848 he broke with the party to back Martin Van Buren's presidential bid on the anti-slavery Free Soil ticket.

In 1853 Hunt lost a bid for the state supreme court (the state court of original jurisdiction in New York) as a Democrat, partly because many Democrats refused to back him due to his apostasy in 1848. With the increasing sharpness of the slavery issue thereafter, Hunt finally broke permanently with the Democratic party and helped found the Republican party in New York in 1855-56. During the process, he formed an alliance with fellow Utica native Roscoe Conkling, who was to become the boss of New York Republican politics and to whom Hunt was to owe his appointment to the Supreme Court.

In 1865 Hunt was elected to the New York state court of appeals, the state's highest court, and became its chief judge in 1868. Following a court reorganization in 1869, he became commissioner of appeals, a position he held until his Supreme Court appointment.

Several other more famous names were presented to President Grant for the court vacancy, but Conkling, Grant's close ally, prevailed on the president to choose Hunt.

Hunt's service is considered one of the more inconspicuous in the court's history, and he was responsible for few major opinions.

After only six years service he suffered a paralytic stroke which incapacitated him from further service, but he did not retire from the court for another three years. The law then in effect granted a full pension only to justices who had reached the age of 70 and had served on the court for ten years.

Finally, with the court in danger of becoming bogged down because of Hunt's illness and the increasing age of several other justices, Congress passed a special law exempting Hunt from the terms of the pension law, granting him retirement at full pay if he would resign from the court within thirty days of enactment of the exemption. He resigned the day the law went into effect and died four years later.

Hunt's sponsor, Roscoe Conkling, was nominated by President Arthur to succeed Hunt. But Conkling declined, and the seat went to Samuel Blatchford.

Morrison Remick Waite
(1874-1888)

Born: Nov. 29, 1816, Lyme, Conn.

Education: Graduated from Yale College, 1837.

Official Positions: Ohio state representative, 1850-52; President of the Ohio constitutional convention, 1873-74.

Supreme Court Appointment: nominated Chief Justice by President Ulysses Grant Jan. 19, 1874, to replace Salmon P. Chase, who died; confirmed by the Senate Jan. 21, 1874, by a 63-0 vote; replaced on court by Melville W. Fuller, nominated by President Cleveland.

Family: married his second cousin, Amelia C. Warner, Sept. 21, 1840; five children.

Died: March 23, 1888, Washington, D.C.

Personal Background

Born into an old New England family, Waite counted among his forebears a chief justice of the Connecticut state supreme court, a prominent Connecticut justice of the peace, and a Revolutionary War hero. He attended one of New England's most prestigious institutions of higher learning, Yale College, graduating in the famous class of 1837. (Other members of the class included Samuel J. Tilden, later governor of New York and Democratic presidential nominee in 1876; William Evarts, later secretary of state under President Hayes (1877-81), and Edwards Pierrepont, later attorney general under President Grant (1875-76).

Seeing greater opportunity in the frontier than in Connecticut, Waite moved to northwest Ohio in 1838 and studied law with Samuel D. Young, a prominent attorney in Maumee City. Waite was admitted to the bar in 1839 and practiced in Maumee City until 1850, when he moved to the booming city of Toledo on Lake Erie. There he made a name for himself as a specialist in railroad law and developed a large business clientele.

Public Career

While Waite came to the Supreme Court as one of the least experienced and least known Chief Justices — he had never held a judicial position nor practiced before the Supreme Court before his appointment — he nevertheless had been involved in public affairs on and off for almost thirty years. Twice he ran for Congress from the northwest Ohio district encompassing Toledo, as a Whig in 1846 and as an independent Republican in 1862, but lost both times. He was elected to the state house in 1849, serving one term. Throughout the Civil War, Waite was strongly pro-Union, and by speeches and writing attempted to rally the population to the Union cause.

Waite was offered a seat on the Ohio supreme court in 1863 but declined in favor of an informal advisory role to the governor. The major break which brought Waite to the attention of the national administration headed by President Grant occurred in 1871 when he was appointed a member of the U.S. delegation to the Geneva Arbitration, which was to settle the Alabama claims case. The U.S. was demanding compensation from Great Britain for allowing Confederate vessels to be fitted out in British ports and operate from them during the Civil War. Waite's hard work during the arbitration proceedings and the final award to the United States of $15.5 million dollars brought Waite a measure of national attention and praise.

Upon returning to the United States, Waite was elected to the Ohio constitutional convention in 1873 and was unanimously chosen its president. It was while he was presiding over the convention that he received word that President Grant had nominated him as Chief Justice. The selection came as a complete surprise to both the nation and to Waite. Waite was in effect Grant's fourth choice for the post, with his first choice refusing to accept the job and his next two withdrawing under threat of being rejected by the Senate.

At first, Waite was treated with some condescension by his fellow court members because of his inexperience, but he soon asserted his authority. By the end of his service he received praise for his industriousness if not his boldness or imaginativeness.

Waite also made efforts to protect his post from being involved in national politics, as it had not been under his predecessor, Salmon P. Chase, who had angled for the presidential nomination. Waite refused to allow his name to be considered for the 1876 Republican presidential nomination. And he also declined to make himself available for service on the electoral commission formed in 1877 to determine the outcome of the disputed 1876 presidential contest.

Even while fulfilling his duties on the court, Waite assumed an additional load of civic responsibilities. He served as trustee of the Peabody Education Fund from 1874 to 1888 and was a member of the Yale Corporation from 1882 to 1888.

John Marshall Harlan
(1877-1911)

Born: June 1, 1833, Boyle County, Ky.

Education: Centre College, A.B., 1850; studied law at Transylvania University, 1851-53.

Official Positions: adjutant general of Kentucky, 1851; judge, Franklin County, 1858; state attorney general, 1863-67; member, Louisiana Reconstruction Commission, 1877; member, Bering Sea Tribunal of Arbitration, 1893.

Supreme Court Appointment: nominated associate justice by President Rutherford B. Hayes Oct. 17, 1877, to replace David Davis, who resigned; confirmed by U.S. Senate Nov. 29, 1877, by a voice vote; replaced on court by Mahlon Pitney, nominated by President Taft.

Family: married Malvina F. Shanklin Dec. 23, 1856; six children.

Died: Oct. 14, 1911, Washington, D.C.

Personal Background

Harlan was born into a prominent Kentucky political family, with both ancestors and descendants taking important roles in public life. His father, James Harlan, an admirer of Henry Clay's patriotism and John Marshall's leadership on the court, was a U.S. Representative from Kentucky (1835-39) and also served as attorney general and secretary of state of Kentucky. Justice Harlan's son, John Maynard Harlan (1864-1934), became a prominent Chicago lawyer and was the unsuccessful Republican nominee for mayor of Chicago in 1897 and 1905. And his grandson and namesake John Marshall Harlan (1899-1971) was himself a Supreme Court justice (1955-71).

Young Harlan studied law at Transylvania University, known as the "Harvard of the West," and then completed his legal education in his father's law office. He was admitted to the bar in 1853.

Public Career

Harlan's only judicial experience before his appointment to the Supreme Court was his first office, Franklin County judge, from 1858 to 1859. After that one-year experience on the bench, Harlan turned to politics. He ran for the U.S. House in 1859 as the candidate of a coalition of anti-Democratic groups, including the Whigs and Know-Nothings, but lost by 67 votes.

As a slaveholder and a member of the southern aristocracy, Harlan had difficulty following many of the nation's Whigs into the new Republican party. In the presidential election of 1860, he backed the Constitutional Union party, which stood for a compromise settlement of the increasingly bitter sectional conflict. But when the Civil War came, Harlan chose to stay loyal to the Union and served as an officer in the northern forces.

Upon the death of his father in 1863, Harlan resigned his commission and ran successfully for attorney general of Kentucky on the pro-Union ticket. Although opposed to many policies of the Lincoln administration — he supported Democrat George B. McClellan against Lincoln in 1864 — and believing the postwar constitutional amendments ending slavery and attempting to guarantee the rights of blacks were a mistake, Harlan eventually gravitated into the Republican party and was its nominee for governor of Kentucky in 1875. He was also prominently mentioned as a Republican vice-presidential candidate in 1872. But the major impact Harlan had on the national political scene came in 1876, when he headed the Kentucky delegation to the Republican national convention. At a critical moment during the deadlocked proceedings, Harlan swung the state's votes to Ohio Gov. Rutherford B. Hayes, thus helping start a bandwagon moving in Hayes' direction. Hayes was nominated and elected and acknowledged his debt to Harlan by considering him for appointment as attorney general. Although other political considerations intervened so that no Cabinet post was open for Harlan, Hayes kept him in mind. The new president appointed him to head a commission to settle the rival claims of two factions for control of Louisiana in the spring of 1877. Then, when Supreme Court Justice Davis resigned to enter the U.S. Senate, Hayes nominated Harlan to fill the vacancy.

Harlan's tenure on the court — almost 34 years — was one of the longest in the court's history, being exceeded by only four other justices. During his service on the court, he was called on by President Benjamin Harrison in 1892 to serve as the U.S. representative in the arbitration of the Bering Sea controversy with Great Britain.

He had a lively temperament, often delivering his opinions extemporaneously, in the style of an old-fashioned Kentucky stump speech. His vigorous attacks on several famous majority decisions earned him the title of "great dissenter." He was also one of the "last of the tobacco-spitting judges," a habit that was rapidly disappearing by the time of Harlan's death.

William Burnham Woods

(1880-1887)

Born: Aug. 3, 1824, Newark, Ohio.

Education: attended Western Reserve College for three years; graduated from Yale University, 1845.

Official Positions: mayor of Newark, Ohio, 1856; Ohio state representative, 1858-62, speaker in 1858-60 and minority leader in 1860-62; chancellor, middle chancery district of Alabama, 1868-69; U.S. circuit judge for fifth judicial circuit, 1869-80.

Supreme Court Appointment: nominated associate justice by President Rutherford B. Hayes Dec. 15, 1880, to replace William Strong, who resigned; confirmed by the Senate Dec. 21, 1880, by a 39-8 vote; replaced by Lucius Q. C. Lamar, nominated by President Cleveland.

Family: married Anne E. Warner June 21, 1855; one son and one daughter.

Died: May 14, 1887, Washington, D.C.

Personal Background

Woods was a native Ohioan, born in Newark in the central part of the state. His father, a farmer and merchant, was from Kentucky, while his mother came from New England. Following his education at Western Reserve University and Yale, Woods studied law with S. D. King, a prominent lawyer in his home town of Newark. After passing the bar in 1847, he joined in partnership with his mentor, King, until the Civil War changed the course of his life.

Public Career

Following a rise to local prominence through the practice of law in Newark, the county seat of Licking County, Ohio, Woods was chosen mayor of his native city in 1856. The following year, he was elected to the state legislature, and was chosen speaker. An ardent Democrat, he opposed the rise of the newly established Republican party. When the Democrats lost control of the statehouse in the 1859 elections, Woods became the minority leader.

At first, he opposed the war policy of President Lincoln, but as the conflict continued he became convinced of the necessity of victory over the South. He joined the Union army in 1862, seeing action in the battles of Shiloh and Vicksburg and marching with Sherman through Georgia. He rose to the rank of brigadier general in 1865 and was brevetted a major general just before being mustered out of service in February 1866. His brother, Charles Robert Woods (1827-1885), was a well-known officer in the Union army.

After the war, Woods settled in Alabama, engaging in cotton planting, investing in an iron works, and resuming the practice of law. His decision to reside in the South invited the charge of being a "carpetbagger," but his name was never linked to the corruption and profligacy associated with that term.

By this time, Woods had become a Republican and was elected chancellor of the middle chancery division of Alabama on his new party's ticket in 1868. When President Grant and the national Republican party came to power the next year, Woods received an appointment as a circuit court judge for the fifth circuit (Florida, Georgia, Alabama, Mississippi, Louisiana, and Texas). Despite his northern origins and Union military background, he gained the respect of his southern neighbors and colleagues. Among his efforts to master his job was the necessity of learning the Louisiana law, which was based on the Napoleonic code. In 1877 Woods moved to Atlanta.

In 1880, when President Hayes was looking for a southerner to appoint to the court, he decided on Woods. Hayes made a constant effort throughout his administration to bring southerners back into the federal government. Woods became the first Supreme Court justice appointed from a southern Confederate state since 1853.

Woods served only six and a half years on the court, and was partially incapacitated by illness during the last months. The tradition of a new southern seat on the court was continued when President Cleveland picked as Woods' successor Lucius Q. C. Lamar of Mississippi.

Stanley Matthews

(1881-1889)

Born: July 21, 1824, Cincinnati, Ohio.

Education: Kenyon College, A.B., 1840.

Official Positions: assistant prosecuting attorney, Hamilton County, 1845; clerk, Ohio House of Representatives, 1848-49; judge, court of common pleas, Hamilton Co., 1851-53; member, Ohio Senate, 1855-58; U.S. attorney for southern Ohio, 1858-61; judge, superior court of Cincinnati, 1863-65; counsel, Hayes-Tilden electoral commission, 1877; member, U.S. Senate, R-Ohio, 1877-79.

Supreme Court Appointment: nominated associate justice by President Rutherford B. Hayes Jan. 26, 1881, to replace Noah Swayne, who resigned; no action by Senate; renominated by President Garfield March 14, 1881; confirmed by U.S. Senate May 12, 1881, by a 24-23 vote; replaced by David J. Brewer, nominated by President Benjamin Harrison.

Family: married, first, Mary Ann Black Feb. 1843, died 1885, eight children; second, Mary Theaker, 1887.

Died: March 22, 1889, Washington, D.C.

Personal Background

Thomas Johnson and Isabella Brown Matthews' first child, born in Cincinnati in 1824, was named Thomas Stanley. He preferred to be called Stanley and dropped his first name when he became an adult. His maternal grandfather, Col. William Brown, was an Ohio pioneer who settled in Hamilton County in 1788. His father, a Virginian, served as Morrison professor of mathematics and natural history at Sylvania University in Lexington, Ky., for a number of years before becoming president of Cincinnati's Woodward High School, which his son attended.

Matthews entered Kenyon College as a junior and graduated in 1840. After reading law for two years in Cincinnati, he moved to Maury County, Tenn., where he passed the bar at the age of 18 and began his legal practice and the editorship of the *Tennessee Democrat,* a weekly paper supporting James K. Polk for president.

In 1844 Matthews married Mary Ann Black, the daughter of a prosperous Tennessee farmer. They had eight children. After her death in 1885 he wed Mary Theaker of Washington, D.C.

Public Career

Matthews left Tennessee when he was 20 and returned to Cincinnati. Within a year he was appointed assistant prosecuting attorney for Hamilton County and made editor of the *Cincinnati Morning Herald.* His strong stance against slavery won him election as clerk of the Ohio House of Representatives in 1848. Three years later he was elected one of three judges in the court of common pleas in Hamilton County. Matthews served in the Ohio state senate from 1855-58 and as U.S. attorney for southern Ohio from 1858-61, a post to which he was appointed by President Buchanan. Although personally opposed to slavery, as U.S. attorney Matthews upheld the Fugitive Slave Act and prosecuted W. B. Connelly, a reporter who helped two slaves escape.

An officer in Ohio's 23rd and 51st regiment of volunteers, Matthews resigned his command in 1863 to accept election to Cincinnati's superior court. Two years later he returned to his private practice of railroad and corporate law. During Reconstruction Matthews was active in Republican politics as a presidential elector in 1864 and 1868, temporary chairman of the Liberal Republican convention in 1872 and GOP congressional candidate in 1876. He failed to win a seat in the 45th U.S. Congress in part because of the unpopularity of his prosecution of Connelly before the war.

Matthews campaigned for presidential candidate Rutherford B. Hayes and was one of the principal spokesmen on his behalf at the 1877 electoral commission. When Senator John Sherman of Ohio was appointed secretary of the Treasury in Hayes' cabinet, Matthews was elected by the legislature to fill his Senate seat. In January 1878 he introduced the "Matthews resolution" for the remonetization of silver.

Matthews' nomination to the Supreme Court by President Hayes upon the resignation of Justice Swayne of Ohio was not confirmed by the Senate. The appointment was criticized as merely a reward for Matthews' aid in Hayes' disputed victory over Samuel J. Tilden. The president was accused of cronyism; he and Matthews were fellow students at Kenyon College, lawyers in Cincinnati and officers in the 23rd Ohio infantry.

Matthews was renominated by President Garfield, Hayes' successor, but received continued opposition. Some feared Matthews' defense of large corporations and railroads during his legal practice would hinder his ability to dispense justice impartially on the court. A vote on the nominee was finally taken on May 12, 1881; he was confirmed 24-23.

Matthews died in Washington, D.C., during his eighth year on the court.

Horace Gray
(1881-1902)

Born: March 24, 1828, Boston, Mass.

Education: Harvard College, A.B., 1845; Harvard Law School, 1849.

Official Positions: reporter, Massachusetts supreme judicial court, 1854-64; associate justice, 1864-73, chief justice, 1873-81.

Supreme Court Appointment: nominated associate justice by President Chester Arthur Dec. 19, 1881, to replace Nathan Clifford, who died; confirmed by Senate Dec. 20, 1881, by a 51-5 vote; replaced on court by Oliver Wendell Holmes Jr., nominated by President Theodore Roosevelt.

Family: married Jane Matthews June 4, 1889.

Died: Sept. 15, 1902, Nahant, Mass.

Personal Background

Harriet Upham Gray gave birth to her first child March 24, 1828, and named him Horace after her father, a businessman in the iron industry. His grandfather, Lieutenant-Governor William Gray, was the son of a poor New England shoemaker. He made his fortune as one of the first American merchants and shipowners to trade with Russia, India and China. Horace Gray's uncle, Francies Calley Gray, was a Massachusetts legal historian and his younger half-brother, John Chipman Gray, a renowned professor at Harvard Law School.

Gray graduated from Harvard in 1845 and traveled abroad. Reversals in the family business forced him to return to Boston to choose a business career. Although Gray's chief interest had always been natural history, he chose the legal profession and at Harvard Law School studied industriously. Reading law with Judge John Lowell and clerking in the attorney's offices of Sohier & Welch completed Gray's preparation for the bar, which he passed in 1851. He practiced in Boston for 13 years.

As a young Boston lawyer Gray was a member of the Free Soil Party, which advocated free homesteads and opposed the expansion of slavery into the territories. Late in his life Gray married Jane Matthews, the daughter of Supreme Court Justice Stanley Matthews.

Public Career

Gray's career in the Massachusetts judiciary began in 1854 as a reporter for the state supreme court. After six years as a reporter he ran for state attorney general but failed to obtain the nomination of the Republican party, which he joined soon after its founding. Gov. John A. Andrews promoted Gray to the position of associate justice on August 23, 1864. Gray was 36 years old, the youngest appointee in the history of the supreme court of Massachusetts. The death or resignation of senior justices elevated Gray to the chief justiceship in 1873.

During his 17 years of service on the state court, Gray dissented only once and during his lifetime none of his decisions were overruled. Gray was respected for his careful historical research and knowledge of legal precedent. As chief justice he employed as his law clerk a bright young Harvard student, Louis D. Brandeis.

President James A. Garfield considered nominating Horace Gray to the Supreme Court after the death of Justice Nathan Clifford on July 25, 1881. But Garfield died prior to making the appointment. His successor, Chester Alan Arthur, appointed Gray associate justice on December 19, 1881. The Senate, anxious to fill Clifford's seat, which had been vacant for five months, confirmed Arthur's nominee the following day by a 51-5 vote.

On July 9, 1902, after 20 years of service, the 74-year-old Supreme Court justice informed President Theodore Roosevelt of his resignation. He died in September in Nahant, Mass.

Personal Background

Samuel Blatchford, born in New York City in 1820, was the son of the former Julia Ann Mumford, daughter of a well-known publicist, and Richard M. Blatchford, counsel for the Bank of England and the Bank of the United States and a Whig in the New York legislature. His paternal grandfather, a British clergyman and sire of 17 children, immigrated to Lansingburg, N.Y., in 1795.

At the age of 13, Blatchford entered Columbia College and four years later graduated at the top of his class. From 1837-41 he prepared for the bar as the private secretary of his father's friend, New York Governor William H. Seward. Blatchford passed the bar in 1842, practiced law with his father for three years and joined Seward's law firm in Auburn, N.Y. In 1844 he married Caroline Appleton of Lowell, Mass.

Public Career

After nine years as a partner with Seward & Morgan, Blatchford and Seward's nephew established the New York City firm, Blatchford, Seward & Griswold. He declined a seat on the New York supreme judicial court in 1855 to devote himself to his admiralty and international law practice.

During his legal career Blatchford reported extensively on federal court decisions. *Blatchford's Circuit Court Reports* (1852) included cases from New York's second circuit since 1845 and *Blatchford's and Howland's Reports* (1855) contributed to the extant knowledge of admiralty cases in the southern district. His extensive research into the state's judicial history as well as his expertise in admiralty law qualified Blatchford for the post of district judge for southern New York to which he was appointed in 1867 and for his subsequent appointment to the second circuit court in 1872.

After 15 years in the federal judiciary, Judge Blatchford was nominated to the Supreme Court by President Arthur. Roscoe Conkling, a New York lawyer and politician, was the president's first choice to fill the vacancy on the court created by the retirement of Justice Ward Hunt of New York. Although confirmed by the Senate, Conkling declined the appointment. Arthur's second choice, Sen. George F. Edmunds of Vermont, also declined. Blatchford accepted and the Senate readily confirmed the president's third nominee — Blatchford, a moderate Republican from an influential New York family, a successful lawyer and an experienced district and circuit court judge.

Blatchford served as trustee of Columbia University from 1867 until his death in 1893 in Newport, R.I.

Samuel Blatchford

(1882-1893)

Born: March 9, 1820, New York City.

Education: Columbia College, A.B., 1837.

Official Positions: judge, southern district of New York, 1867-72; judge, second circuit of New York, 1872-82.

Supreme Court Appointment: nominated associate justice by President Chester Arthur March 13, 1882, to replace Ward Hunt, who resigned; confirmed by Senate March 27, 1882, by a voice vote; replaced on court by Edward D. White, nominated by President Cleveland.

Family: married Caroline Appleton Dec. 17, 1844.

Died: July 7, 1893, Newport, R.I.

Lucius Quintus Cincinnatus Lamar

(1888-1893)

Born: Sept. 17, 1825, Eatonton, Ga.

Education: Emory College, A.B., 1845.

Official Positions: member, Georgia House of Representatives, 1853; member, U.S. House of Representatives, 1857-60, 1873-77; member, U.S. Senate, 1877-85; secretary of interior, 1885-88.

Supreme Court Appointment: nominated associate justice by President Grover Cleveland Dec. 6, 1887, to replace William Woods, who died; confirmed by U.S. Senate Jan. 16, 1888, by a 32-28 vote; replaced on court by Howell Edmunds Jackson, nominated by President Benjamin Harrison.

Family: married, first, Virginia Longstreet July 15, 1847, died 1884, one son, three daughters; second, Henrietta Dean Holt Jan. 5, 1887, no children.

Died: Jan. 23, 1893, Vineville, Ga.

Personal Background

Of French Huguenot ancestry, Lamar was born into the landed aristocracy of the prewar South in 1825. The fourth of Lucius Quintus Cincinnatus' and Sarah Bird Lamar's eight children, he attended the Georgia Conference Manual Labor School, an institution that combined farm work with academics. Lamar graduated from Emory College in 1845 and two years later wed its president's daughter, Virginia Longstreet.

Lamar read law in Macon, Ga., passed the bar in 1847 and shortly thereafter followed his father-in-law to Oxford, Miss. The Reverend Augustus B. Longstreet became president of the University of Mississippi and Lamar taught mathematics and practiced law. The two men were devoted to one another. Longstreet had lost his only son; Lamar's own father had committed suicide when Lamar was nine years old.

Public Career

In 1852 Lamar returned to Georgia and established a successful legal practice with a close friend, E. C. Walthall, in Covington. The following year he was elected to the state legislature. The dissolution of his partnership and his failure to obtain the Democratic nomination to Congress prompted Lamar's return to Mississippi in 1855. He settled on a plantation and began practicing law and participating in state politics. A Jefferson Davis supporter and states' rights extremist, Lamar was elected to Congress in 1857 but resigned before his term expired. He personally drafted the state's ordinance of secession at the Mississippi Secession Convention of 1861.

Lamar served the Confederacy as colonel of the 18th Mississippi Regiment until an attack of apoplexy, an ailment since childhood, forced him to retire from active duty in May 1862. As special envoy to Russia he attended diplomatic briefings in Europe in 1863, but because of lack of support for the Confederate cause never went to Russia. He spent the remainder of the war as a judge advocate for the Army of Northern Virginia.

When General Lee surrendered, Lamar was 40 years old. Two of his brothers had died in battle; his friend Jefferson Davis was in prison; he was in debt. Disqualified from public office, he returned to Mississippi to practice law and teach metaphysics at the university.

Although a partisan sectionalist before the war, Lamar publicly advocated reconciliation and cooperation during the difficult days of Reconstruction. Pardoned for his role in the Confederacy, he was re-elected to Congress in 1872. His

eulogy of Massachusetts unionist Charles Sumner, heralded by the Boston *Advertiser* as the most significant and hopeful word from the South since the war, won Lamar national acclaim as the "great pacificator." A representative of the new South, Lamar reached the Senate in 1877. His reputation as a politician guided by more than sectional interests was strengthened by his refusal to follow the directive of the Mississippi legislature to support legislation authorizing the free coinage of silver. Anxious to demonstrate the South's desire to serve the entire nation, Lamar resigned from his second Senate term to accept a cabinet appointment. As Grover Cleveland's secretary of the interior, he directed the reclamation of thousands of acres of public lands and the establishment of a new Indian policy. While in office Lamar married Henrietta Dean Holt.

The death in 1887 of Justice William Woods, a Georgia Republican, created the first vacancy on the Supreme Court in six years. Although Lamar's appointment by President Cleveland was strongly opposed by many Republican senators, supporters Stanford of California and Stewart of Nevada argued persuasively that Lamar's rejection would be interpreted as a ban against all Confederate veterans. The 63-year-old nominee was narrowly confirmed by the Senate, 32-28.

Lamar served on the court for five years. He died from apoplexy in his native Georgia on January 23, 1893. Seventeen years later the Lamar family could boast of another member on the bench — Joseph Rucker Lamar.

Melville Weston Fuller
(1888-1910)

Born: Feb. 11, 1833, Augusta, Maine.

Education: Bowdoin College, A.B., 1853; studied at Harvard Law School and read law, 1853-55.

Official Positions: member, Illinois house of representatives, 1863-1864; member, Venezuela-British Guiana Border Commission, 1899; member, Permanent Court of Arbitration at the Hague, 1900-1910.

Supreme Court Appointment: nominated Chief Justice by President Grover Cleveland April 30, 1888, to replace Morrison R. Waite, who died; confirmed by U.S. Senate July 20, 1888, by a 41-20 vote; replaced as Chief Justice by Edward D. White, nominated by President Taft.

Family: married, first, Calista Ophelia Reynolds June 28, 1858, died 1864, two daughters; second, Mary E. Coolbaugh May 30, 1866, five daughters, one son.

Died: July 4, 1910, Sorrento, Maine.

Personal Background

The second son of Frederick Augustus Fuller and the former Catherine Martin Weston was born in Augusta, Maine, in 1833. When Melville Weston Fuller was two months old, his mother divorced his father on the grounds of adultery and took her son to live with his grandfather, a judge on the Maine supreme court. Although she remarried when Fuller was 11, he continued to live with Judge Weston in Augusta.

Fuller attended Bowdoin College, where he was active in politics and a prolific writer of verse. He graduated Phi Beta Kappa in 1853 and, like both his grandfathers and his own father, chose the legal profession. Fuller read law in Bangor and after six months at Harvard Law School passed the bar. He began to practice in Augusta at the age of 22 and the same year took an editorial position on *The Age,* a local Democratic paper owned by his father's brother. At the age of 24 he was elected president of the common council and appointed city solicitor.

Like many young men in the 1850s, Fuller was lured west by the promise of a better life in the frontier. He settled in the booming railroad town of Chicago and started practicing real estate and commercial law.

Fuller was married twice. His first wife, Calista Ophelia Reynolds, died of tuberculosis six years after they were married. Mary Ellen Coolbaugh, the daughter of the president of Chicago's Union National Bank, and Fuller were wed in 1866. She bore him a son and five daughters. He had two daughters by his previous marriage.

Public Career

In Chicago, Fuller pursued a political as well as a legal career. He managed Stephen Douglas' presidential campaign against Abraham Lincoln in 1858, attended the Illinois Constitutional Convention three years later and served in the Illinois House of Representatives from 1863-64.

Meanwhile Fuller's legal practice and real estate investments on the North Shore prospered; his earnings by the 1880s reached an estimated $30,000 a year. Fuller acted as Chicago's counsel in litigation over the city's rights to Lake Michigan shore property. He also defended — in a nationally publicized case — the Reverend Charles E. Cheney, rector of Christ Church in Chicago, who was accused of canonical disobedience by an ecclesiastical tribunal because of his "low church" practices. A high Episcopalian himself, Fuller opened the way for the founding of the Reformed Protestant Episcopal Church in America.

Grover Cleveland met Melville Fuller during a western presidential tour and was impressed by his "sound money," low-tariff economic philosophy.

Although Fuller had previously declined the positions of civil service chairman and solicitor general in Cleveland's administration, he accepted the appointment of Chief Justice on April 30, 1888. The Republican Senate soon voiced its objections to the Democratic nominee. Midwesterners were wary of his ties with big corporations. Northerners accused him of anti-Union sentiment and circulated the pamphlet "The War Record of Melville Fuller," which was discredited only after Robert T. Lincoln, son of the former president, attested to his loyalty. The Philadelphia *Press* claimed that Cleveland's nominee was the most obscure man ever appointed Chief Justice.

Although Fuller had never held federal office, his professional credentials were sound and his appointment geographically expedient. Since Justice Davis' resignation in 1877, the seventh judicial circuit, comprising Illinois, Indiana and Wisconsin, had been unrepresented on the bench. Fuller was confirmed by the Senate, 41-20, nearly three months after his appointment.

During his court tenure, Fuller served on the Venezuela-British Guiana Border Commission and the Permanent Court of Arbitration in the Hague. An efficient and courteous leader of the court for 22 years, he was well-respected by his colleagues, particularly by Justice Holmes.

When Cleveland returned to the presidency he offered Fuller the position of secretary of state, but Fuller declined, believing his acceptance would lower the dignity of the court in the mind of the public. He died of heart failure at the age of 77 at his summer home in Sorrento, Maine.

David Josiah Brewer
(1890-1910)

Born: Jan. 20, 1837, Smyrna, Asia Minor.

Education: Wesleyan University, 1852-53; Yale University, A.B., 1856; Albany Law School, LL.B., 1858.

Official Positions: commissioner, U.S. circuit court in Leavenworth, Kansas; 1861-62; judge of probate and criminal courts, Leavenworth County, 1863-64; judge, first judicial district of Kansas, 1865-69; Leavenworth city attorney, 1869-70; justice, Kansas supreme court, 1870-84; judge, eighth federal circuit, 1884-89; president, Venezuela-British Guiana Border Commission, 1895.

Supreme Court Appointment: nominated associate justice by President Benjamin Harrison Dec. 4, 1889, to replace Stanley Matthews, who died; confirmed by U.S. Senate Dec. 18, 1889, by a 53-11 vote; replaced on court by Charles Evans Hughes, nominated by President Taft.

Family: married, first, Louise R. Landon Oct. 3, 1861, died 1898; second, Emma Miner Mott June 5, 1901.

Died: March 28, 1910, Washington, D.C.

Personal Background

Brewer was born in 1837 in Smyrna, Asia Minor, now Izmir, Turkey, where his father was a Congregational missionary. With his infant son and wife Emilia (Field), the daughter of a New England clergyman, Reverend Josiah Brewer returned to America to become chaplain of St. Francis Prison, in Wethersfield, Conn. Young Brewer had three notable uncles: David Dudley Field, a jurist; Cyrus W. Field, a financier and promoter of the trans-Atlantic telegraph cable; and Stephen Johnson Field, a Supreme Court justice from California from 1863-97.

Brewer attended Wesleyan University for two years before enrolling in his father's alma mater, Yale University, from which he was graduated with honors in 1856. After reading law for a year in David Field's office, Brewer attended Albany Law School. He passed the New York bar in 1858 and the Kansas bar the following year, having decided to go west as his uncle Stephen had done.

When he was 24 Brewer married Louise R. Landon of Burlington, Vt., who died seven years later. At the age of 64 he wed Emma Miner Mott of Washington, D.C.

Public Career

Brewer's first official position was administrative. He was appointed U.S. commissioner of the circuit court in Leavenworth, Kansas, in 1861. After two years he was nominated judge of probate and criminal courts. From 1865-69 Brewer served as state district attorney and the following year as city attorney for Leavenworth until his election at the age of 33 to the Kansas supreme court. When Kansas passed a prohibition amendment in 1881, Judge Brewer sought to defend the rights of manufacturers against the confiscation of their property without compensation. Brewer's 14 years of service on the state court ended in 1884 when he was appointed to the eighth federal circuit by President Arthur.

When Justice Stanley Matthews died, Republican senators Plumb and Ingalls of Kansas urged President Benjamin Harrison to appoint Brewer to the court. During his consideration of the nomination, the president received a letter from Brewer himself recommending the appointment of Henry Billings Brown, a Michigan district court judge who had been in his class at Yale. Impressed by Brewer's generous comments about his friend, Harrison nominated the circuit court judge from Kansas instead. Although Brewer's appointment was opposed by some prohibitionists, he was confirmed by the Senate by a 53-11 vote.

During his 20 years on the Supreme Court, Brewer spoke out freely on the issues of the day. He advocated independence for the Philippines, suffrage for women and residency rights for Chinese aliens in America. Brewer was one of the original officers in the American Society of International Law and in 1895 presided over the congressional commission to oversee the disputed Venezuela-British Guiana boundary. A lecturer on American citizenship at Yale and corporate law at Columbian University, now George Washington University, Brewer also edited collections of the world's best orations and essays and wrote numerous books and articles. He was a lifelong member of the Congregational Church and active in missionary work.

Brewer died suddenly on March 28, 1910, in Washington, D.C.

Henry Billings Brown
(1891-1906)

Born: March 2, 1836, South Lee, Mass.

Education: Yale University, A.B., 1856; studied briefly at Yale Law School and Harvard Law School.

Official Positions: U.S. deputy marshal, 1861; assistant U.S. attorney, 1863-68; circuit judge, Wayne County, 1868; federal judge, eastern district of Michigan, 1875-90.

Supreme Court Appointment: nominated associate justice by President Benjamin Harrison Dec. 23, 1890, to replace Samuel Miller, who died; confirmed by U.S. Senate Dec. 29, 1890, by a voice vote; replaced on court by William H. Moody, nominated by President Theodore Roosevelt.

Family: married, first, Caroline Pitts July 1864, died 1901; second, Josephine E. Tyler June 25, 1904.

Died: Sept. 4, 1913, New York City.

Personal Background

The son of a prosperous merchant, Brown was born in the small town of South Lee, Mass., and raised in a middle-class Protestant home. His parents, Billings and Mary (Tyler) Brown prepared their son for the legal career they had chosen for him with a private secondary school and Yale University education. A moderately good student, he graduated from Yale in 1856 and went abroad for a year of further study.

Brown began his legal education as a law clerk in Ellington, Conn. After a few months he returned to Yale to attend lectures at the law school. Brown also studied briefly at Harvard Law School.

In 1859 the 23-year-old law student moved to Detroit. Within a year he finished his legal apprenticeship and passed the bar. Wealthy enough to hire a substitute, Brown escaped military service in the Civil War and immediately began his private practice.

Caroline Pitts, a member of a prosperous Detroit family, was Brown's wife for 37 years until her death in 1901. Three years later, at the age of 67, he married Josephine E. Tyler from Crosswicks, N.J., the widow of a lieutenant in the U.S. Navy.

Public Career

In the early days of the Lincoln administration, Brown was appointed deputy U.S. marshal for Detroit, his first official position. After two years he was promoted to assistant U.S. attorney for the eastern district of Michigan. Detroit was a busy Great Lakes port, and Brown became an expert in admiralty law.

Republican Governor Henry H. Crapo appointed Brown interim circuit judge for Wayne County in 1868. Defeated in his bid for election to a full term, Brown returned to private practice and formed a partnership with J. S. Newberry and Ashley Pond that specialized in shipping cases. After an unsuccessful congressional campaign in 1872, he resumed his practice until a welcome appointment three years later by President Grant to the post of district judge of eastern Michigan.

During his 14 years as district judge, Brown won a national reputation as an authority on admiralty law. Howell Edmunds Jackson, a sixth federal circuit court judge, urged President Harrison to appoint Brown to the Supreme Court after the death of Justice Miller. Harrison had served with Jackson in the Senate and followed the advice of his former colleague. Nominated associate justice on December 23, 1890, Brown was confirmed by the Senate within the week. Three years later Justice Brown returned Jackson's favor by recommending his appointment to the court.

Brown is considered to have been a centrist on the court, seldom dissenting and always seeking the middle ground.

Despite an attack of neuritis in 1890 which blinded him in one eye, Brown served on the court for 15 years. At the age of 70, severely handicapped by his impaired vision, he resigned. He lived in semi-retirement in Bronxville, N.Y., until his death on September 4, 1913, at the age of 77.

George Shiras Jr.
(1892-1903)

Born: January 26, 1832, Pittsburgh, Pa.

Education: Ohio University, 1849-51; Yale, B.A., 1853, honorary LL.D., 1883; studied law at Yale and privately, admitted to the bar in 1855.

Supreme Court Appointment: nominated associate justice by President Benjamin Harrison July 19, 1892, to replace Joseph P. Bradley, who died; confirmed by U.S. Senate July 26, 1892, by a voice vote; replaced on court by William R. Day, nominated by President Theodore Roosevelt.

Family: married Lillie E. Kennedy December 31, 1857; two sons.

Died: August 2, 1924, Pittsburgh, Pa.

Personal Background

Shiras was born January 26, 1832, in Pittsburgh, Pa., into a family which had been in America since the 1760s. His father, of Scotch ancestry, married a Presbyterian minister's daughter, Eliza Herron, and was successful enough in the family brewery business to retire in his early thirties to a farm near the Ohio River. Here young Shiras, with his two brothers, spent his early years helping in his father's orchards.

In 1849 he left to attend Ohio University at Athens, Ohio, but after two years transferred to Yale, where he graduated in 1853. He then read law at Yale (without graduating) and in the Pittsburgh law office of Judge Hopewell Hepburn before being admitted to the Allegheny County bar in November 1855. Before settling down in Pittsburgh in 1858 to become Judge Hepburn's law partner, he spent several years practicing law in Dubuque, Iowa, with his brother, Oliver Perry, who later became a federal district judge in northern Iowa.

On December 31, 1857, he married a Pittsburgh manufacturer's daughter, Lillie E. Kennedy, with whom he had two sons. Both offspring followed him into the law profession, and one, George S. III, served as U.S. Representative from Pennsylvania to the 58th Congress from 1903-1905.

Upon the death of Judge Hepburn in 1862, Shiras maintained a successful independent practice until his accession to the Supreme Court in 1892. In more than 30 years of law practice in his native city, Shiras maintained a reputation of absolute integrity, of moderation in politics and manner, of restraint and good judgment, and of dignity and wit. The years Shiras prospered and plied his trade in Pittsburgh were those when the iron and steel, coal, and railroad magnates were amassing their fortunes. Despite his financial success and lucrative practice, Shiras remained modest, unostentatious and respected by his peers. In 1883 he received from Yale an honorary LL.D. degree, the first alumnus to do so.

To the end he preferred quiet living among family and friends and his pursuits as a naturalist rather than seeking the limelight. His moderation seemed to be reflected in both his professional and personal lives.

Public Career

Shiras' life was centered mainly in the private sector and he held no public offices until his Supreme Court appointment. In 1881 he refused the Pennsylvania state legislature's offer of the U.S. Senate nomination. A moderate Republican, he remained aloof from party politics and the state political machine, facts which favored his appointment to the high court. In 1888 he served as a presidential elector.

In July 1892, at the age of 60, he was nominated by President Harrison to be an associate justice of the Supreme Court to replace Joseph P. Bradley of New Jersey, who had died in January. Although Shiras had the support of the Pennsylvania bar, of the iron and steel interests (including Andrew Carnegie's personal support) and of U.S. Representative John Dalzell, the U.S. senators who headed the state Republican machine vigorously opposed his appointment. President Harrison had sent Shiras' name to the Senate without first consulting Senators James Donald Cameron and Matthew S. Quay as senatorial courtesy dictated. However, when the press and prominent persons including former Yale classmates came to his defense and the opposition was shown to be purely political, the matter was resolved and he was confirmed by unanimous consent.

Respected for his analytical powers and as a legal technician, Shiras exhibited a quiet competence and bore his share of the workload during his ten years on the court.

He resigned, as he had earlier resolved to do, at the age of 71, and lived out the years of his retirement in quiet comfort, shuttling between homes in Florida and the Lake Superior region of northern Michigan until his death in 1924 at age 92.

Howell Edmunds Jackson
(1893-1895)

Born: April 8, 1832, Paris, Tenn.

Education: West Tennessee College, A.B., 1849; University of Virginia, 1851-52; Cumberland University, 1856.

Official Positions: custodian of sequestered property for Confederate states, 1861-65; judge, Court of Arbitration for western Tennessee, 1875-79; state legislature, 1880; U.S. Senate, 1881-86; judge, 6th federal circuit court, 1886-91; circuit court of appeals, 1891-1893.

Supreme Court Appointment: nominated associate justice by President Benjamin Harrison Feb. 2, 1893, to replace Lucius Q. C. Lamar, who died; confirmed by U.S. Senate Feb. 18, 1893, by a voice vote; replaced on the court by Rufus W. Peckham, nominated by President Cleveland.

Family: married, first, Sophia Malloy in 1859, died 1873, four children; second, Mary E. Harding in April 1874, three children.

Died: August 8, 1895, West Meade, Tenn.

Personal Background

In 1830 Alexander Jackson left his medical practice in Virginia and moved to Paris, Tenn., with his wife Mary (Hurt) Jackson, the daughter of a Baptist minister. Two years later their eldest son, Howell Edmunds, was born. Howell grew up in Jackson, Tenn., and studied classics at Western Tennessee College, graduating at the age of 18. He continued his education at the University of Virginia from 1851-52. After completing a year in the legal department of Cumberland University in Lebanon, Tenn., Jackson passed the bar and began practicing law in his hometown.

In 1859 Jackson moved to Memphis, formed the partnership, Currin & Jackson, specializing in corporate, railroad and banking cases, and married a local woman, Sophia Malloy. After her death in 1873, Jackson wed Mary E. Harding, the daughter of General W. G. Harding, the owner of a 3,000-acre thoroughbred stock farm near Nashville. The western part of the property, West Meade, became Jackson's home, where he lived with his second wife, their three children and the four children of his previous marriage.

Although opposed to secession, Jackson served the Confederacy as the receiver of confiscated property and after the Civil War was twice appointed to the Court of Arbitration of western Tennessee. His younger brother, William Hicks — the husband of General Harding's daughter Selene, who inherited the Belle Meade plantation — was a famous brigadier general in the Confederate Army, known by his men as the "red fox."

Public Career

In 1881 Jackson, a respected lawyer and anti-repudiation Tennessean during the Reconstruction, was elected to the state house of representatives. Because of factions within the Democratic Party over the state debt, he was elected the following year to the U.S. Senate. A Whig before the war, Jackson had been able to win the needed support of Republicans and "state-credit" Democrats. In the Senate he served on the Post Office, Pensions, Claims, and Judiciary Committees and loyally defended President Grover Cleveland's tariff measures.

At the president's request, Jackson reluctantly resigned before his Senate term expired to fill a vacancy on the sixth judicial federal circuit. When the circuit court of appeals was established in 1891, Jackson became its first presiding judge. During his Senate career, Jackson was seated next to a Republican senator from Indiana, Benjamin Harrison. As president, Harrison remembered his former colleague and friend and nominated him to the Supreme Court on February 2, 1893, to fill the vacancy created by the death of Justice Lucius Q. C. Lamar. Grover Cleveland had been elected to a second term in November, and the lame-duck president realized Senate confirmation of a Republican nominee was unlikely. With the strong backing of Supreme Court Justice Henry Billings Brown, who had known him on the sixth federal circuit, Jackson was confirmed by the Senate Feb. 18, 1893.

One year after his appointment, Justice Jackson contracted a severe case of tuberculosis. Hoping to recuperate in the West, Jackson left Washington in October 1894. In May 1895 a full court was needed to rehear a case on the constitutionality of income taxes, the eight active justices having been evenly divided on the question. Unwell but unwilling to resign, Jackson returned to Washington. Three months after his dissent from the court's decision ruling income taxes unconstitutional, Jackson succumbed to tuberculosis at his home in Nashville.

Edward Douglass White
(1894-1921)

Born: Nov. 3, 1845, Parish of Lafourche, La.

Education: Mount St. Mary's College, Emmitsburg, Md., 1856; Georgetown College, Washington, D.C., 1857-61; studied law under Edward Bermudez, admitted to the bar in 1866.

Official Positions: Louisiana state senator, D, 1874; associate justice, Louisiana Supreme Court, 1878-80; United States Senator, D-La., 1891-94.

Supreme Court Appointment: nominated associate justice by President Grover Cleveland Feb. 19, 1894, to replace Samuel Blatchford, who died; confirmed by the Senate Feb. 19, 1894, by a voice vote.

Nominated Chief Justice of the United States by President Taft Dec. 12, 1910, to replace Melville Fuller, who died; confirmed by the Senate Dec. 12, 1910, by a voice vote; replaced as Chief Justice by ex-president Taft, appointed by President Harding.

Family: married Virginia Montgomery Kent, November 1894.

Died: May 19, 1921, in Washington, D.C.

Personal Background

White was born and raised in the deep South. His Irish-Catholic ancestors originally settled in Pennsylvania, but his peripatetic father moved the family farther into frontier country until they finally reached Louisiana. There the family prospered on a large farm. White's father, a Whig, spent four years as a judge on the New Orleans city court and served five terms in the U.S. House of Representatives (1829-34; 1839-43) and one term as governor of Louisiana (1834-38).

White received his early education at local Jesuit schools. In 1856 he enrolled for one year at Mount St. Mary's College, Emmitsburg, Md., and then entered Georgetown College (now University) in Washington, D.C. His academic career was interrupted by the Civil War; White joined the Confederate Army. He was captured in 1863 and spent the remainder of the war as a prisoner.

Public Career

After the war he began his legal career by reading law under the direction of Edward Bermudez, a successful New Orleans lawyer. Admitted to the Louisiana bar in 1868, White established a lucrative practice in New Orleans and became involved in Democratic politics. He was elected to the state senate in 1874, and his support of Francis T. Nicholls in the 1877 gubernatorial election gained him at age 33 an appointment to the Louisiana supreme court in 1878. Nicholls' successor, however, engineered White's removal from the court in 1880 through the passage of a law setting a minimum age requirement for justices which the youthful White failed to meet. Retribution came in 1888 when Nicholls was again elected governor and the state legislature gave one of Louisiana's U.S. Senate seats to Edward D. White.

White's short Senate career was marked by efforts to restrict the power of the federal government, except in matters protecting sugar farmers in the south from foreign competition. White himself farmed a large sugar-beet plantation. His unexpected appointment to the Supreme Court came in 1894. Beleaguered President Cleveland had sought to replace Justice Samuel Blatchford (who died July 7, 1893) with appointees from New York, Blatchford's home state. On two separate occasions, however, Cleveland's choices were rejected by the Senate in deference to the wishes of New York's senators, who were two of the president's chief detractors. In frustration, Cleveland nominated White, who was approved immediately.

White's appointment to the Chief Justiceship was equally surprising. Chief Justice Melville Fuller died July 4, 1910, and President Taft, on Dec. 12, 1910, elevated White to the post. He was the first associate justice successfully to be elevated to Chief Justice.

Historians tend to explain Taft's selection of White as Chief Justice in one of two ways. One side holds that Taft chose White, a southern Catholic, as a symbol of the president's desire to reduce lingering anti-South and anti-Catholic sentiments and to gain southern and Catholic support in the next election. The other, less sympathetic, view argues that Taft reckoned that he would have a better chance to receive appointment to the Chief Justiceship himself (a lifelong ambition) after he left the White House if he appointed the aging White (65) instead of the other contender for the post, the relatively young (48) Charles Evans Hughes.

White was 75 years old and had been on the Supreme Court for 26 years — and Chief Justice for the last ten years — when Warren G. Harding was elected president in 1920. White was suddenly taken ill May 13, 1921, and died May 19. His replacement on the court was the ever-eager William Howard Taft.

Rufus Wheeler Peckham

(1896-1909)

Born: Nov. 8, 1838, Albany, N.Y.

Education: Albany Boys' Academy; studied privately in Philadelphia.

Official Positions: district attorney, Albany County, 1869-72; corporation counsel, City of Albany, 1881-83; judge, New York supreme court, 1883-86; judge, New York court of appeals, 1886-95.

Supreme Court Appointment: nominated associate justice by President Grover Cleveland Dec. 3, 1895, to replace Howell E. Jackson, who died; confirmed by U.S. Senate Dec. 9, 1895, by a voice vote; replaced on court by Horace Harmon Lurton, nominated by President Taft.

Family: married Harriette M. Arnold, Nov. 14, 1866; two sons.

Died: Oct. 24, 1909, Altamont, N.Y.

Personal Background

Peckham was born in Albany in 1838, the son of Rufus Wheeler and Isabella (Lacey) Peckham, members of an old New York family. His father and his older brother, Wheeler Hazard Peckham, were both prominent lawyers and active in state Democratic politics. As district attorney for Albany County, Peckham Sr. was elected to the U.S. House of Representatives. He also served on the state supreme court and the New York court of appeals. During a vacation in 1873, Judge Peckham was lost at sea.

Rufus Wheeler Peckham the younger was educated at the Albany Boy's Academy and studied privately in Philadelphia. After a year in Europe with his brother, Rufus returned to Albany to read law in his father's firm, Peckham & Tremain. He joined the firm at the age of 27 and in 1866 married Harriette M. Arnold, the daughter of a wealthy New York merchant.

Peckham's elder son, a one-time president of the New York Bar Association, served as special counsel in the prosecution of the Tweed Ring in the city's political corruption trials.

Public Career

Like his father before him, Peckham began his public career as district attorney for Albany County. In this post he gained recognition for his skillful prosecution and conviction of criminals involved in railroad express-car robberies. First as county attorney and then as corporation counsel for the City of Albany from 1881-83, Peckham participated actively in upstate New York politics and became well-acquainted with Governor Grover Cleveland. Peckham's political connections, his legal reputation and his respected name helped win him election to the state supreme court in 1883 and to the New York court of appeals three years later.

After Justice Jackson's death, President Grover Cleveland nominated his friend associate justice of the Supreme Court. Peckham was confirmed without objection although his brother's nomination three months before to fill Justice Blatchford's seat had been rejected due to political infighting. (Senator David B. Hill, D-N.Y., Wheeler's chief opponent, also succeeded in blocking the confirmation of William B. Hornblower, President Cleveland's second choice for the Blatchford seat.)

During his 13 years on the bench, Peckham vigorously upheld the individual's right to contract and favored state regulation only when interstate commerce was directly and substantially affected. He dissented from the court's decision in 1898 to uphold a Utah statute limiting the working day in mines, smelters and oil refineries to eight hours and also questioned the validity of a state law requiring compulsory vaccination.

On the whole, Peckham was considered a conservative justice out of touch with the Industrial Revolution.

Justice Peckham died in Altamont, N.Y., on October 24, 1909, at the age of 71.

Joseph McKenna
(1898-1925)

Born: August 10, 1843, Philadelphia, Pa.

Education: Benicia Collegiate Institute, graduated in 1865; admitted to the bar in 1866.

Official Positions: district attorney, Solano County, Calif., 1866-70; member, California house of representatives, 1875-76; member, U.S. House of Representatives, 1885-92; judge, U.S. ninth judicial circuit, 1892-97; U.S. attorney general, 1897.

Supreme Court Appointment: nominated associate justice by President William McKinley Dec. 16, 1897, to replace Stephen J. Field, who resigned; confirmed by U.S. Senate Jan. 21, 1898, by a voice vote; replaced on court by Harlan F. Stone, nominated by President Coolidge.

Family: married Amanda F. Bornemann June 10, 1869; three daughters.

Died: Nov. 21, 1926, Washington, D.C.

Personal Background

Joseph McKenna, the first child of Irish immigrants John and Mary Ann (Johnson) McKenna, was born in 1843 in the Irish quarter of Philadelphia. The growing popularity in Philadelphia of the staunchly anti-immigrant, anti-Catholic American Party contributed to the failure of John McKenna's bakery business. Hoping for success on the frontier, he took his family west, travelling third class on a Panamanian steamship to Benicia, Calif. In this small coastal town he succeeded in obtaining a better life for his family before his death when Joseph was 15 years old.

Young McKenna attended public schools, graduated from the law department of the Benicia Collegiate Institute in 1865, and the following year was admitted to the California bar. The Republican party was becoming increasingly powerful in California, having elected in 1861 railroad pioneer Leland Stanford as first Republican governor. McKenna switched his membership to the Republican party, became acquainted with Stanford, and participated actively in political affairs. He was elected district attorney for Solano County in 1866 and three years later married Amanda F. Bornemann of San Francisco, his wife for 55 years.

Public Career

After his initial political success, election to the state legislature in 1875, McKenna suffered a string of defeats. He was an unsuccessful candidate for the speakership of the California house of representatives, from which he resigned after one term. Although twice nominated by his party for the U.S. Congress, he suffered two defeats prior to his election in 1885.

During four terms in the House, McKenna won passage of legislation extending railroad land grants, improving port facilities and restricting the freedoms of Chinese workers. Considering his own immigrant parentage, McKenna's support for the latter is surprising, despite its popularity with his constituents.

As a member of the House Ways and Means Committee, McKenna became friends with its chairman, William McKinley. Another political ally in Congress was Senator Leland Stanford. On Stanford's recommendation, President Harrison appointed McKenna to California's ninth judicial circuit. A circuit court judge for five years, McKenna was then promoted to attorney general. Within a year of assuming the post, he was nominated to the Supreme Court. When Justice Field resigned, President McKinley chose McKenna, another Californian and a trusted friend, to fill the vacancy. Over the objections of many to McKenna's ties with Leland Stanford and western railroad interests, the Senate confirmed the appointment.

Realizing his own need for further legal training, McKenna studied for a few months at Columbia University Law School before taking office. Nevertheless, his early years on the bench proved difficult because of his lack of knowledge of the law and his inability to construct an opinion that expressed the convictions of his colleagues.

McKenna served on the court for 26 years. He was 82 years old and in failing health when Chief Justice Taft and the other members of the court finally persuaded him to step down. The following year he died in his sleep at his home in Washington, D.C.

Oliver Wendell Holmes Jr.
(1902-1932)

Born: March 8, 1841, Boston, Mass.

Education: Harvard College, A.B., 1861; LL.B., 1866.

Official Positions: associate justice, Massachusetts supreme court, 1882-99, chief justice, 1899-1902.

Supreme Court Appointment: nominated associate justice by President Theodore Roosevelt Dec. 2, 1902, to replace Horace Gray, who resigned; confirmed by U.S. Senate Dec. 4, 1902, by a voice vote; replaced on court by Benjamin N. Cardozo, nominated by President Hoover.

Family: married Fanny Bowdich Dixwell June 17, 1872; no children.

Died: March 6, 1935; Washington, D.C.

Personal Background

Born in Boston in 1841, Holmes was named after his father, a professor of anatomy at Harvard Medical School as well as a poet, essayist and novelist in the New England literary circle that included Longfellow, Emerson, Lowell and Whittier. Dr. Holmes' wife, Amelia Lee (Jackson) Holmes, was the third daughter of Massachusetts supreme court justice Charles Jackson. Young Holmes attended a private Latin school in Cambridge run by Epes Sargent Dixwell and received his undergraduate education at Harvard, graduating as class poet in 1861 as had his father 32 years before him.

Commissioned after graduation a second lieutenant in the Massachusetts Twentieth Volunteers, known as the Harvard Regiment, Holmes was wounded three times in battle. At the end of his three-year enlistment, he was mustered out a captain in recognition of his bravery and gallant service. After the Civil War, Holmes returned to Harvard to study law despite his father's conviction that "a lawyer can't be a great man."

He was admitted to the Massachusetts bar in 1867, and practiced in Boston for 15 years, beginning with the firm of Chandler, Shattuck & Thayer and later forming with Shattuck his own partnership. In 1872 Holmes married Fanny Bowdich Dixwell, the daughter of his former schoolmaster and a friend since childhood. No children were born during their marriage of 57 years.

During his legal career Holmes taught constitutional law at his alma mater, edited the *American Law Review* and lectured on common law at the Lowell Institute. His 12 lectures were compiled in a volume entitled *The Common Law* and published shortly before his fortieth birthday after more than ten years of work. The London *Spectator* heralded Holmes' treatise as the most original work of legal speculation in decades. *The Common Law* was quickly translated into German, Italian and French.

Public Career

In 1882 Massachusetts' governor appointed Holmes — then a full professor at the Harvard Law School in a chair established by Boston lawyer Louis D. Brandeis — an associate justice of the Massachusetts supreme court. Holmes served on the state court for 20 years, the last three as chief justice, and wrote more than 1,000 opinions, many of them involving labor disputes. Holmes' progressive labor views, criticized by railroad and corporate interests, were favorably considered by President Theodore Roosevelt during his search in 1902 for someone to fill the "Massachusetts seat" on the Supreme Court, vacated by the retirement of 74-year-old Bostonian Horace Gray. Convinced of his compatibility with the administration's national policies, Roosevelt nominated Holmes associate justice December 2, 1902. The 61-year-old judge was confirmed without objection two days later.

Holmes' 29 years of service on the Supreme Court spanned the tenures of Chief Justices Fuller, White, Taft and Hughes and the administrations of Presidents Roosevelt, Taft, Wilson, Harding, Coolidge and Hoover. For 25 years he never missed a session and walked daily the 2-1/2 miles from his home to court. Like Justice Brandeis, Holmes voluntarily paid an income tax despite the majority's ruling which exempted federal judges. Unlike the idealistic and often moralistic Brandeis, with whom he is frequently compared, Holmes was pragmatic, approaching each case on its particular facts.

Although a lifelong Republican, on the court Holmes did not fulfill Roosevelt's expectations as a loyal party man. His dissent shortly after his appointment from the court's decision to break up the railroad trust of the Northern Securities Company surprised the nation and angered the president.

At the suggestion of Chief Justice Hughes and his colleagues on the bench, Holmes resigned on January 12, 1932, at the age of 91. A widower since his wife's death in 1929, he continued to spend his winters in Washington,

D.C., and his summers in Beverly Farms, Mass. He died at his Washington home two days before his 94th birthday.

William Rufus Day
(1903-1922)

Born: April 17, 1849, Ravenna, Ohio.

Education: University of Michigan, A.B., 1870; University of Michigan Law School, 1871-72.

Official Positions: judge, Court of Common Pleas, Canton, Ohio, 1886-90; first assistant U.S. secretary of state, 1897-98; U.S. secretary of state, 1898; member, United States delegation, Paris Peace Conference, 1899-99; judge, sixth circuit, United States Court of Appeals; umpire, Mixed Claims Commission, 1922-23.

Supreme Court Appointment: nominated associate justice by President Theodore Roosevelt Feb. 19, 1903, to replace George Shiras Jr., who resigned; confirmed by the U.S. Senate Feb. 23, 1903, by a voice vote; replaced on court by Pierce Butler, nominated by President Harding.

Family: married Mary Elizabeth Schaefer, 1875; four sons.

Died: July 9, 1923, Mackinac Island, Mich.

Personal Background

William Day was raised in a family with a strong judicial background. His maternal great-grandfather, Zephania Swift, was the chief justice of Connecticut; his grandfather, Rufus Spalding, was a member of the Ohio supreme court; his father, Luther Day, served as chief justice of Ohio. It seemed predetermined, then, that William Day, after receiving his A.B. from the University of Michigan in 1870, should enter the law school at his alma mater. Before starting law school he studied law for one year in his home town of Ravenna, Ohio, and then attended law school for a year at the University of Michigan. He returned home to Ohio in 1872 and set up a law practice in Canton, about 25 miles from Ravenna.

In Canton, Day established a solid reputation and a lucrative law practice. He also became a good friend of another young attorney in Canton, William McKinley. Day and McKinley traveled in the same Republican circles, and McKinley soon came to rely on Day for help and counsel.

While McKinley's political fortunes took him to the U.S. House of Representatives (1877-84; 1885-91) and the governor's mansion (1892-96), Day remained in Canton, married a local woman, and raised a family of four boys.

Public Career

Day's popularity was so great in the Canton area that he was elected in 1886 judge of the Court of Common Pleas after receiving both the Democratic and Republican nominations. Three years later he was appointed to the United States District Court by President Benjamin Harrison.

However, his frail health prevented him from serving in that position.

When his friend McKinley was elected president, Day was named first assistant secretary of state in the administration. His job consisted of assisting the aged and failing secretary of state, John Sherman, in performing the country's diplomatic chores. After the war between Spain and the United States over Cuba officially began April 11, 1898, Sherman was eased out of the State Department and replaced by Day, who had been closely involved in the events leading up to the outbreak of hostilities. Day served as secretary of state only from April 26 to August 26, 1898; during his brief tenure, however, he oversaw the delicate negotiations between the United States and Spain and was able to obtain assurances of neutrality and goodwill from Western European countries.

In August McKinley named Day to the U.S. commission to negotiate the terms of the peace with Spain. Day is credited with the plan to pay Spain $20 million for the Philippines.

His work on the peace commission finished, Day was named by McKinley in 1899 to the sixth circuit, United States Court of Appeals, located in Cincinnati. Day enjoyed his four years on the bench — it was close to home, and his colleagues included future president and Supreme Court Chief Justice William Howard Taft and future Associate Justice Horace H. Lurton.

Day was, of course, deeply shocked by the 1901 assassination of his longtime friend, President McKinley. As a tribute to his friend and patron, Day began to mark each of the late president's birthdays with a memorial service. It was at one of these services in January 1903 in Canton, attended by McKinley's successor, Theodore Roosevelt, that Day first learned of Roosevelt's intention to name him to the Supreme Court. After Day introduced the president to the audience, Roosevelt surprised the crowd by referring to Day as "Mr. Justice Day." His appointment was announced officially Feb. 19, 1903.

Day retired from the court Nov. 13, 1922. He accepted an appointment from President Harding to serve as an umpire on the Mixed Claims Commission, a board established to settle claims remaining from World War I. Day worked on the commission only until May 1923. He died July 9, 1923, at his summer home on Mackinac Island, Michigan.

William Henry Moody

(1906-1910)

Born: Dec. 23, 1853, Newbury, Mass.
Education: Harvard University, A.B., cum laude, 1876; Harvard University Law School, 1876-77.
Official Positions: city solicitor, Haverhill, 1888-90; district attorney, eastern district of Massachusetts, 1890-

95; U.S. House of Representatives, R-Mass., 1895-1902; secretary of the Navy, 1902-04; attorney general of the United States, 1904-06.
Supreme Court Appointment: nominated associate justice by President Theodore Roosevelt Dec. 3, 1906, to replace Henry B. Brown, who retired; confirmed by the U.S. Senate Dec. 12, 1906, by a voice vote; replaced on court by Willis Van Devanter, nominated by Taft.
Family: Unmarried.
Died: July 2, 1917, Haverhill, Mass.

Personal Background

Moody was born in a house in Newbury, Mass., that had been the Moody family home for over 200 years. He was raised in nearby Danvers, Mass., attended Phillips Academy in Andover, Mass., and graduated cum laude from Harvard University in 1876. In the fall of that year he entered the Harvard School of Law but left in January 1877. To prepare for his entry to the bar he began an 18-month course of study in the law offices of Boston lawyer and author Richard Henry Dana. Although three years of study were normally required before an applicant was allowed to take the oral examination, an exception was made in Moody's case, and he passed easily.

Moody left Boston after his admittance to the bar in 1878 and established a private practice in Haverhill, Mass. His clientele soon included most of the industries and manufacturers in the region. As his prestige grew, Moody became involved in Republican politics and in 1888 began his public career as city solicitor for Haverhill.

Public Career

Two years later he was named district attorney for the eastern district of Massachusetts. His most famous case (and the one that spread his name across the country) was the prosecution of Lizzie Borden, the alleged ax murderer of Fall River, Mass. Although Borden was acquitted by a sympathetic jury, Moody's adept handling of the state's case brought him to the attention of state Republican leaders, notably Sen. Henry Cabot Lodge (1893-1924).

In 1895 Moody won a special election to fill the U.S. House seat in Massachusetts' sixth congressional district vacated by the death of Rep. William Cogswell (1887-95). The same year, Moody made the acquaintance of New York Police Commissioner Theodore Roosevelt and the two men became close friends over the next few years.

In the House, Moody was respected for his mastery of details and facts. When Theodore Roosevelt ascended to the presidency after the assassination of President William McKinley, Moody was one of Roosevelt's first choices for his cabinet. As secretary of the Navy, Moody won increased congressional appropriations to enlarge and improve the U.S. fleet. This, of course, met with the hearty approval of President Roosevelt, who said of Moody, "we have never had as good a Secretary of the Navy...."

Moody's next assignment in the Roosevelt administration was to replace Attorney General Philander Knox in 1904 and to continue the administration's prosecution of trusts. A dedicated progressive Republican, Moody personally argued for the government in the successful suit against the beef trust, *Swift and Company v. United States, 196 U.S. 375 (1905)*.

Moody's appointment to the Supreme Court was not without controversy; he was thought to be too radical. Opponents pointed to his eager prosecution of trusts and his enthusiasm for progressive reforms. Criticism notwithstanding, Moody was confirmed by the Senate Dec. 12, 1906, to replace Justice Henry B. Brown.

Moody's Supreme Court career was shortened by the onslaught of a crippling form of arthritis that forced his retirement in 1910. He returned home to Haverhill, where he died July 2, 1917.

Horace Harmon Lurton

(1909-1914)

Born: Feb. 26, 1844, Newport, Ky.

Education: University of Chicago, 1860; Cumberland Law School, L.B., 1867.

Official Positions: chancellor in equity, 1875-78; judge, Tennessee supreme court, 1886-93; judge, Sixth Circuit Court of Appeals, 1893-1909.

Supreme Court Appointment: nominated associate justice by President William Howard Taft Dec. 13, 1909, to replace Rufus W. Peckham, who died; confirmed by U.S. Senate Dec. 20, 1909, by a voice vote; replaced on court by James C. McReynolds, nominated by President Wilson.

Family: married Mary Francis Owen, Sept. 1867; two sons, two daughters.

Died: July 12, 1914, Atlantic City, N.J.

Personal Background

Horace Harmon Lurton was born in Kentucky in 1844, the same year Democrat James Knox Polk defeated Whig Henry Clay for the presidency over the issue of annexation of the Republic of Texas. Lurton left Kentucky as a young boy with his mother, Sarah Ann (Harmon) Lurton, and his father, Dr. Lycurgus Leonidas Lurton, a physician who later became an Episcopal minister, and moved to Clarksville, Tenn., a town of 15,000 on the Cumberland River. At age 16, he went north and attended the University of Chicago until the outbreak of the Civil War.

Lurton served in the Confederate Army in both the Kentucky and Tennessee infantries before his capture during Gen. Grant's siege of Fort Donelson. He escaped from Camp Chase in Columbus, Ohio, and joined General John Hunt Morgan's daredevil marauders, famous throughout the South for their surprise attacks on Union railroads, bridges and telegraph stations. Lurton was captured again in July 1863. During his incarceration in one of the northernmost camps on Lake Erie he contracted tuberculosis. Fearing for her son's life, Sarah Ann Lurton went to Washington and succeeded in persuading President Lincoln to let her son return with her to Clarksville before the end of the war.

After his recuperation at home, Lurton attended Cumberland University Law School in Lebanon, Tenn. He graduated in 1867, married Mary Francis Owen, the daughter of a local physician, and returned to Clarksville to practice law. Through his partner James A. Bailey, who took Andrew Johnson's Senate seat in 1877, Lurton became involved in Democratic politics. He was appointed by the governor to the sixth chancery division of Tennessee, becoming at 31 the youngest chancellor in the state's history.

In 1878 Lurton returned to the practice of law in an eight-year partnership with ex-chancellor Charles G. Smith.

During this period Lurton became a prosperous and well-respected Clarksville citizen as president of the Farmer's and Merchants' National Bank, vestryman of Trinity Episcopal Church and trustee of the University of the South.

Public Career

Lurton was elected to the Tennessee Superior Court in 1886 and served for seven years. Immediately following his promotion to chief justice, he was appointed to the U.S. court of appeals for the sixth circuit by President Grover Cleveland. William Howard Taft was the presiding judge. Lurton succeeded him in office when Taft left the sixth circuit court to become governor general of the Philippines. In addition to his judicial responsibilities Lurton taught constitutional law at Vanderbilt University from 1898-1905 and served as dean the following four years.

Close personal friendship as well as respect for his judicial ability prompted President Taft to make 65-year-old Lurton his first Supreme Court appointment. "There was nothing I had so much at heart in my whole administration," said Taft of his choice.

Lurton took a symbolic train ride northward to assume his new responsibilities. Explaining the personal significance of the trip he stated, "I felt that in appointing me, President Taft, aside from manifestations of his friendship, had a kindly heart for the South; that he wished to draw the South to him with cords of affection. So, being a southerner myself, I determined to go to Washington through the South — every foot of the way."

Lurton served only five years. The 70-year-old justice died of a heart attack July 12, 1914, in Atlantic City, N.J.

Charles Evans Hughes

(1910-1916; 1930-1941)

Born: April 11, 1862, Glens Falls, N.Y.

Education: Colgate University, 1876-78; Brown University, A.B., 1881, A.M., 1884; Columbia Law School, LL.B., 1884.

Official Positions: special counsel, New York state investigating commissions, 1905-06; governor of New York, 1907-10; U.S. secretary of state, 1921-25; U.S. delegate, Washington Armament Conference, 1921; U.S. member,

Permanent Court of Arbitration, 1926-30; judge, Permanent Court of International Justice, 1928-30.

Supreme Court Appointment: nominated associate justice by President William Howard Taft April 25, 1910, to replace David J. Brewer, who died; confirmed by U.S. Senate May 2, 1910, by a voice vote; resigned June 10, 1916, to become Republican presidential candidate; replaced on court by John H. Clarke, nominated by President Wilson; nominated Chief Justice Feb. 3, 1930, by President Hoover, to replace Chief Justice Taft, who resigned; confirmed by U.S. Senate Feb. 13, 1930, by a 52-26 vote; replaced on court by Harlan F. Stone, nominated by Franklin D. Roosevelt.

Family: married Antoinette Carter Dec. 5, 1888; one son, two daughters.

Died: August 27, 1948, Osterville, Mass.

Personal Background

Charles Evans Hughes was born during the Civil War in Glens Falls, N.Y., the only child of David Charles Hughes, an abolitionist minister, and his wife Mary Catherine (Connelly) Hughes. When the Reverend Hughes became secretary of the American Bible Union, the family left the Adirondacks and moved to New York City in 1873. Charles was schooled at home by his parents until age 14 when he enrolled in Madison College (now Colgate University). Before his junior year he transferred to Brown University, chosen because of its Baptist tradition, which appealed to his parents, and its city location, which appealed to him. After graduation Hughes taught Greek, Latin and algebra at the Delaware Academy in Delhi, N.Y., and clerked for the Wall Street firm of Chamberlin, Carter & Hornblower to earn money for law school. He graduated from Columbia in 1884 and passed the bar at age 22 with a nearly perfect score.

Hughes then returned to Chamberlin, Carter & Hornblower and married Antoinette Carter, the daughter of one of the partners. Two years later the firm became Carter, Hughes & Cravath. Hughes' legal practice in New York City continued for 20 years, with an interim of three years teaching law at Cornell University.

Public Career

In 1905 Hughes began investigating illegal rate-making practices and fraudulent insurance activities in New York as special counsel for the Stevens Gas Commission and the Armstrong Insurance Committee, established by the state legislature. His successful exposure of racketeering won him national recognition. Endorsed by President Theodore Roosevelt, Hughes defeated William Randolph Hearst in a 1906 race for governor and was re-elected two years later.

When President William Howard Taft appointed Hughes to the Supreme Court to fill the vacancy left by Justice Brewer's death in 1910, his nomination met with the approval of the court and the press. According to the liberal paper *The World,* "Mr. Taft could not have made a better or more popular selection." Justifying his acceptance of the seat on the Supreme Court to New York Republicans who envisioned for him a great political future, Hughes explained, "I had no right to refuse. A refusal on the ground that some time or other I might be a candidate for the Presidency ... would have been absurd."

After six years on the court, Hughes resigned to run for president, endorsed by both the Republican and Progressive parties. "Wilson with Peace and Honor or Hughes with Roosevelt and War?" was a popular slogan of the Democrats, critical of Hughes' advocacy of military preparedness against Germany. The former Supreme Court justice lost the 1916 election by only 23 electoral votes. After his defeat he returned to the practice of law as senior partner in the New York firm, Hughes, Rounds, Schurman & Dwight.

When Warren G. Harding became president, he appointed Hughes secretary of state, a post which he also held during the Coolidge administration. At the Washington Armament Conference in 1921 Hughes was instrumental in the agreement reached by the major powers to limit the naval race, end the Anglo-Japanese Alliance and recognize China's open door diplomacy.

Unlike the general acclaim which greeted Hughes' Supreme Court appointment in 1910, his nomination as Chief Justice by President Hoover 20 years later met considerable opposition in the Senate. "No man in public life so exemplifies the influence of powerful combinations in the political and financial worlds as does Mr. Hughes," Senator Norris of Nebraska objected. Critics felt Hughes' representation of America's largest corporations after he left the State Department jeopardized his ability to defend the rights of the ordinary citizen on the court. Supporters, on the other hand, pointed to his efforts on behalf of world peace during his legal career as a member of the Permanent Court of Arbitration in the Hague and the Permanent Court of International Justice.

On Feb. 13, 1930, confirmation was reached in the Senate by a 52-26 vote. Hughes' son, Charles Evans Jr., resigned the same day from his position in the Hoover administration as solicitor general.

After 11 years of service as Chief Justice, Hughes informed President Roosevelt of his wish to retire due to "considerations of health and age." This announcement was followed by widespread commendation by his colleagues on the bench. Justice Frankfurter likened Hughes' ability to marshal the court to "Toscanini lead[ing] an orchestra" and Justice Douglas praised his "generosity, kindliness and forbearance."

In 1942, a year after his retirement, Hughes was awarded the American Bar Association medal for conspicuous service to jurisprudence. He died at his summer cottage on Cape Cod at the age of 86.

Willis Van Devanter
(1910-1937)

Born: April 17, 1859, Marion, Ind.

Education: Indiana Asbury University, A.B., 1878; University of Cincinnati Law School, LL.B., 1881.

Official Positions: city attorney, Cheyenne, 1887-88; member, Wyoming territorial legislature, 1888; chief justice, Wyoming Territory supreme court, 1889-90; assistant

U.S. attorney general, 1897-1903; judge, eighth circuit, U.S. Court of Appeals, 1903-10.

Supreme Court Appointment: nominated associate justice by President William Howard Taft Dec. 12, 1910, to replace William H. Moody; confirmed by U.S. Senate Dec. 15, 1910, by a voice vote; replaced on court by Hugo L. Black, nominated by President Franklin D. Roosevelt.

Family: married Dellice Burhans Oct. 10, 1883.

Died: Feb. 8, 1941, in Washington, D.C.

Personal Background

Willis Van Devanter was born April 17, 1859, in Marion, Ind., nine years after his parents had moved west. The oldest of eight children, Van Devanter attended Indiana Asbury (now DePauw) University and the University of Cincinnati Law School.

After receiving his law degree in 1881 he joined his father's law firm in Marion. Three years later, after marrying Dellice Burhans of Michigan, he left the relative security of his native Indiana for Cheyenne in the Wyoming Territory. There he established a thriving practice and became involved in Republican politics through his close friendship with Governor (and later U.S. Senator) Francis E. Warren. Warren became head of the Republican party in Wyoming and remained an influential friend throughout Van Devanter's career.

Public Career

In 1886 Van Devanter worked on a commission that revised the territory's statutes. He served as city attorney in Cheyenne in 1887 and the following year was elected to the territorial legislature. The next year, 1889, when Van Devanter was just 30 years old, President Benjamin Harrison named him chief justice of the Wyoming Territory supreme court. He only served as chief justice for one year before resigning to resume private practice.

Van Devanter enjoyed a thriving practice and remained active in Republican politics, serving as chairman of the Wyoming state committee (1892-94) and as a member of the Republican National Committee (1896-1900). His service to the party was rewarded in 1897 when President William McKinley named him as assistant attorney general assigned to the Interior Department. There he relied on his years of experience in Wyoming to specialize in legal questions regarding public lands and Indian matters. He also found time to lecture at Columbian (now George Washington) University.

In 1903 President Theodore Roosevelt appointed Van Devanter to the eighth circuit, U.S. Court of Appeals. His years on the bench were marked by a concern for jurisdictional questions, land claims, rights of railroads and other complex technical areas.

When Justice Edward D. White was appointed Chief Justice by President Taft on Dec. 12, 1910, Van Devanter was also named to fill the associate-justice vacancy created by the retirement of William H. Moody, who resigned Nov. 20, 1910.

Van Devanter's nomination was strongly opposed by several liberals, particularly William Jennings Bryan, who said that Van Devanter was "the judge that held that two railroads running parallel to each other for two thousand miles were not competing lines, one of the roads being that of Union Pacific," one of Van Devanter's former clients.

He retired from the court June 2, 1937, and died Feb. 8, 1941, in Washington, D.C.

Joseph Rucker Lamar
(1910-1916)

Born: Oct. 14, 1857, Elbert County, Ga.

Education: University of Georgia, 1874-75; Bethany College, A.B., 1877; Washington and Lee University, 1877.

Official Positions: member, Georgia legislature, 1886-89; commissioner to codify Georgia laws, 1893; associate justice, Georgia supreme court, 1903-05; member, mediation conference, Niagara Falls, Canada, 1914.

Supreme Court Appointment: nominated associate justice by President William Howard Taft Dec. 12, 1910, to replace Edward D. White, who became Chief Justice; confirmed by U.S. Senate Dec. 15, 1912, by a voice vote; replaced on court by Louis D. Brandeis, nominated by President Wilson.

Family: married Clarinda Huntington Pendleton Jan. 13, 1879; two sons, one daughter.

Died: Jan. 2, 1916, Washington, D.C.

Personal Background

Joseph Rucker Lamar was named after his maternal grandfather on whose antebellum plantation, Cedar Grove in Ruckersville, Ga., he was born and raised. Both the Ruckers and the Lamars were socially prominent Georgia families. Mary, the youngest daughter of Joseph Rucker, merchant, planter, banker and founder of Ruckersville, married James Sanford Lamar of French Huguenot ancestry.

Other notable relatives were Mirabeau Buonaparte Lamar, president of the Republic of Texas from 1838-1841, and Lucius Quintus Cincinnatus Lamar, associate justice of the Supreme Court from 1888-1893.

After his mother's death when he was eight, Joseph Lamar left Cedar Grove and moved to Augusta, where his father became a minister in the Disciples of Christ church, a new Protestant denomination founded by Alexander Campbell, the president of Bethany College during James Lamar's attendance. Greatly influenced by Campbell, Joseph's father left his legal career to join the ministry. Woodrow Wilson's father was the minister of the leading Presbyterian church in Augusta and the two boys became close friends.

Lamar attended Martin Institute and Richmond Academy in Georgia and the Penn Lucy Academy in Baltimore before enrolling in the University of Georgia. Consenting to his father's wishes, he transferred to Bethany College, from which he graduated in 1877. After reading law at Washington and Lee University and clerking for the well-known Augusta lawyer, Henry Clay Foster, Lamar passed the Georgia bar. He married Clarinda Huntington Pendleton, the daughter of the president of Bethany College, and they lived with her family for one year while he taught Latin at the college.

Public Career

Lamar's legal practice began in 1880 when Henry Clay Foster, for whom he had clerked while a law student, asked him to become a partner. During their joint practice for more than ten years, Lamar served for two terms in the Georgia legislature. As elected representative for Richmond County, he continued studying the state's history of jurisprudence, his special field of interest, and wrote a number of essays. Lamar's research on Georgia's legal history was recognized in 1893 by the governor, who asked him to help rewrite Georgia's law codes.

During his legal practice, Lamar also served on the examining board for applicants to the Georgia bar. This experience helped prepare him for a seat on the Georgia supreme court, which he occupied from 1903-05. Overworked and homesick for Augusta, Lamar resigned before his term expired and returned to private law practice, this time in a partnership specializing in railroad law with E. H. Callaway, a former superior court judge.

President Taft nominated Lamar associate justice of the Supreme Court Dec. 12, 1910, much to the Georgian's surprise. He had become acquainted with the president during two brief vacations in Augusta. Lamar did not expect to be confirmed by the Senate because he was little known outside of the South and was a member of the Democratic party. Rarely had presidents crossed party lines in making Supreme Court appointments. Lamar's fears were allayed; he was confirmed three days after his nomination.

During his last term Justice Lamar overworked himself in the performance of his judicial responsibilities. He suffered a stroke in September 1916 and died three months later at 58 after only five years on the bench. "The whole country has reason to mourn," President Wilson telegraphed Mrs. Lamar. "It has lost an able and noble servant. I have lost in him one of my most loved friends."

Mahlon Pitney
(1912-1922)

Born: Feb. 5, 1858, Morristown, N.J.

Education: College of New Jersey (Princeton), A.B., 1879; A.M., 1882.

Official Positions: U.S. House of Representatives, 1895- 99; member, New Jersey senate, 1899-1901; president, New Jersey senate, 1901; associate justice, New Jersey supreme court, 1901-08; chancellor of New Jersey, 1908-12.

Supreme Court Appointment: nominated associate justice Feb. 19, 1912, by President William H. Taft to replace John M. Harlan, who died; confirmed by the U.S. Senate March 13, 1912, by a 50-26 vote; replaced on court by Edward T. Sanford, nominated by President Harding.

Family: married Florence T. Shelton Nov. 14, 1891; two sons, one daughter.

Died: Dec. 9, 1924, Washington, D.C.

Personal Background

The second son of Henry Cooper Pitney and his wife Sarah Louisa (Halsted) Pitney was born on a farm in Morristown, N.J., on Feb. 5, 1858. He was named Mahlon after his paternal great grandfather, a British descendant who fought for the Americans in the Revolution of 1776. Mahlon Pitney attended the College of New Jersey, now Princeton University, and graduated in 1879; Woodrow Wilson was a classmate.

He received his legal education from his father, "a walking encyclopedia of law," and after passing the New Jersey bar in 1882 practiced for seven years in the industrial iron town of Dover. When his father was appointed vice chancellor of New Jersey in 1889, Pitney moved back to Morristown to take over his legal practice. At the age of 33 he married a local woman, Florence T. Shelton.

Public Career

The popular choice among New Jersey Republicans, Pitney was elected to a Fourth District congressional seat in 1894. As a member of the 54th Congress, he endorsed conservative monetary policies and easily won a second term with the additional support of Democrats who favored gold-backed currency. Pitney resigned Jan. 5, 1899, after his election to the New Jersey state senate.

Party leader William J. Sewall advised Pitney to remain in the legislature for a few years before running for governor, the political office to which he most aspired. When Republicans gained control of the state senate, Pitney was elected its president. Appointment to the New Jersey supreme court by Governor Foster M. Voorhees in 1901 altered his gubernatorial ambitions. For the next 20 years Pitney pursued a judicial career, the culmination of which was the position of chancellor of New Jersey. His father had been vice chancellor 19 years before.

Pitney was greatly surprised when President Taft nominated him associate justice of the Supreme Court Feb. 19, 1912. They had met seven days before at a dinner party in Newark and discussed another associate justice of the New Jersey supreme court, Francis J. Swayze, who was being considered for the bench. After the Pitney nomination, Taft acknowledged, "I did consider with a good deal of care another lawyer from New Jersey."

The Senate confirmed the Pitney nomination within a month although there was some objection on the part of liberal senators and union leaders to Pitney's anti-labor record as a New Jersey judge. After the 50-26 vote in favor of confirmation, Pitney received a congratulatory telegram from New Jersey governor and former Princeton classmate Woodrow Wilson, who assured him "a better choice could not have been made."

"His meticulously detailed opinions," says historian Fred I. Israel, "although often repetitious and quite heavy in style, reveal a troubled man's attempt to deal with complex legal and social problems in what seemed to him a logical and consistent manner."

Mental and physical stress forced the 64-year-old justice to resign after ten years of service. He suffered a stroke in August 1922 and retired in December. Pitney's premature death two years later in Washington, D.C., has been attributed to the strain of overwork while on the court.

James Clark McReynolds
(1914-1941)

Born: Feb. 3, 1862, Elkton, Ky.

Education: Vanderbilt University, B.S., class valedictorian, 1882; University of Virginia, LL.B., 1884.

Official Positions: assistant U.S. attorney, 1903-07; U.S. attorney general, 1913-14.

Supreme Court Appointment: nominated associate justice by President Woodrow Wilson Aug. 19, 1914, to replace Horace H. Lurton, who died; confirmed by the U.S. Senate Aug. 29, 1914, by a 44-6 vote. replaced on the court by Robert H. Jackson, nominated by President Franklin D. Roosevelt.

Family: unmarried.

Died: Aug. 24, 1946, in Washington, D.C.

Personal Background

McReynolds was born in a Kentucky community that exhibited considerable sympathy for the Confederacy during the Civil War. Raised on a plantation, he was the son of highly moral parents who were members of the fundamentalist Campbellite religious sect.

After receiving his B.S. from Vanderbilt University in Nashville, Tenn., McReynolds traveled to Charlottesville to study law at the University of Virginia. He received his LL.B. there in 1884 and returned to Nashville to practice law. His legal business in Nashville went uninterrupted until 1903, except for a short stint as secretary to Sen. Howell Edmunds Jackson (D-Tenn., 1881-86, Supreme Court justice, 1893-95). McReynolds' clients included several companies and corporations in Nashville. In 1900 he took a part-time position teaching law at Vanderbilt University.

Public Career

He ran for Congress in 1896 as a "Gold Democrat" with some Republican support, but his arrogant and standoffish manners while campaigning alienated a majority of the voters. His candidacy, however, provided him with a measure of prominence in the Democratic party.

In 1903 he was appointed an assistant U.S. attorney in the Roosevelt administration. During his four years at the Justice Department, McReynolds handled several antitrust prosecutions, including the court battles with the anthracite coal trust and the tobacco trust. So involved was he in trust-busting that he once referred to the American Tobacco Co. as a group of "commercial wolves and highwaymen."

He resigned from the U.S. attorney's office in 1907 and took up law practice in New York City. He continued, however, to assist the Justice Department with antitrust cases over the next several years. A Wilson supporter in the

election of 1912, he was named U.S. attorney general in the new administration. Although he served as attorney general for little more than a year, McReynolds managed to anger several members of Congress and executive branch officials with his temper and haughtiness. To smooth the waters President Wilson named McReynolds to the Supreme Court Aug. 19, 1914, to replace Justice Horace H. Lurton, who had died in July.

McReynolds retired from the court Feb. 1, 1941. He died Aug. 24, 1946, in Washington, D.C.

Louis Dembitz Brandeis
(1916-1939)

Born: Nov. 13, 1856, Louisville, Ky.

Education: Harvard Law School, LL.B., 1877.

Official Positions: "people's attorney," Public Franchise League and Massachusetts State Board of Trade, 1897-1911; counsel, New England Policyholders' Protective Committee, 1905; special counsel, wage and hour cases in California, Illinois, Ohio and Oregon, 1907-14; counsel, Ballinger-Pinchot investigation, 1910; chairman, arbitration board, New York garment workers' labor disputes, 1910-16.

Supreme Court Appointment: nominated associate justice Jan. 28, 1916, by President Woodrow Wilson, to replace Joseph R. Lamar, who died; confirmed by the U.S. Senate June 1, 1916, by a 47-22 vote; replaced on court by William O. Douglas, nominated by President Franklin D. Roosevelt.

Family: married Alice Goldmark March 23, 1891; two daughters.

Died: Oct. 5, 1941, Washington, D.C.

Personal Background

Louis Dembitz Brandeis was born Nov. 13, 1856, in Louisville, Ky., the son of Adolph and Fredericka Dembitz Brandeis, Jewish emigrants from Bohemia after the unsuccessful democratic revolts of 1848. His father was a prosperous grain merchant who provided his family with comfort, education and culture. Having completed two years of preparatory studies at the Annen-Realschule in Dresden, but without a college degree, Brandeis enrolled at Harvard Law School when he was 18 years of age. He graduated in 1877 with the highest average in the law school's history. After eight months practicing law in St. Louis, Brandeis returned to Cambridge — for him "the world's center" — and with Bostonian Samuel D. Warren Jr., second in their law school class, opened a one-room office downtown.

Warren & Brandeis and the successor firm Brandeis, Dunbar & Nutter handled a variety of cases and were highly successful. By the time he was 35, Brandeis was earning more than $50,000 a year. He and his wife Alice Goldmark of New York preferred to live simply, however, and set a ceiling on their personal expenditures of $10,000 a year. As a young lawyer Brandeis devoted many hours to his alma mater. He helped raise funds for a teaching post for Oliver Wendell Holmes Jr. and was one of the founders of the *Harvard Law Review.*

The turn of the century marked the rapid growth in America of corporate monopolies — the "curse of bigness," as Brandeis described it. He chose to protect the rights not of special interest groups but of the general public, and usually without a fee for his services. Brandeis initiated sliding scale gas rates in Boston that lowered consumer costs while raising corporate dividends and instituted savings bank insurance policies, another reform later implemented in the rest of the country. He defended municipal control of Boston's subway system and opposed the monopolistic practices of the New Haven Railroad. He arbitrated labor disputes in New York's garment industry and established the constitutionality of several state maximum hour and minimum wage statutes. For 37 years Brandeis devoted his time, energy and talents to a host of public causes. He called himself an "attorney for the situation;" the press adopted the popular title "people's attorney."

Public Career

President Wilson respected Brandeis and often sought his opinion. He nominated him associate justice of the Supreme Court Jan. 28, 1916, to fill the vacancy left by Justice Lamar's death. Vicious opposition to his appointment ensued. One particularly vituperative critic described Brandeis as a "business-baiter, stirrer up of strife, litigious lover of hate and unrest, destroyer of confidence, killer of values, commercial coyote, spoiler of pay envelopes."

Factory owners paying higher wages, New Haven Railroad stockholders, moguls in the Boston transit system, insurance and gas industries — in short, all the losers in court — united to voice their objections to the appointment. Among those seeking satisfaction for past injuries was William Howard Taft. His administration had been embarrassed by an investigation led in part by Brandeis of the conservation practices of Secretary of Interior Richard A. Ballinger.

The former president, ambitious for a justiceship himself, described the nomination as "one of the deepest wounds that I have had as an American and a lover of the Constitution" and spoke of the "indelible stain" on the Wilson administration that confirmation would bring.

Another critic, Clarence W. Barron, editor and publisher of the *Wall Street Journal,* also felt the choice was unwise, "There is only one redeeming feature in the nomination and that is that it will assist to bury Mr. Wilson in the next Presidential election."

The president viewed the political climate differently. He believed Brandeis was a smart choice who would attract the needed Progressive vote. A divided Republican party was unlikely to win him the election a second time.

During four months of acrimonious debate over his appointment, Brandeis quietly pursued his legal practice. He went to the office every day and did not resort to personal attacks against his opponents. "Your attitude while the wolves yelp is sublime," his young nephew wrote.

The hearings in the Senate Judiciary Committee turned up no valid grounds for rejection. According to Senator Thomas J. Walsh, Brandeis' only "real crime" was that "he had not stood in awe of the majesty of wealth." One of his supporters from the Harvard Law School, Arthur

Hill, attributed the opposition to the fact that "Mr. Brandeis is an outsider, successful and a Jew."

Brandeis was confirmed by the Senate on June 1, 1916, by a vote of 47-22, thus becoming the first Jew on the Supreme Court.

At 82, Brandeis resigned from the court but not from public service. After 22 years on the bench, he devoted the last two years of his life to the Zionist movement and a boycott of German products. As *The New York Times* noted upon his retirement in 1939, "the storm against him . . . seems almost incredible now."

John Hessin Clarke
(1916-1922)

Born: Sept. 18, 1857, Lisbon, Ohio.

Education: Western Reserve University, A.B., 1877, A.M., 1880; LL.D., 1916.

Official Positions: federal judge, U.S. District Court for Northern District of Ohio, 1914-16.

Supreme Court Appointment: nominated associate justice July 14, 1916, by President Woodrow Wilson, to replace Charles Evans Hughes, who resigned; confirmed by the U.S. Senate July 24, 1916, by a voice vote; replaced on court by George Sutherland, nominated by President Harding.

Family: unmarried.

Died: March 22, 1945, San Diego, Calif.

Personal Background

John Hessin Clarke, the son of Irish Protestants John and Melissa (Hessin) Clarke, was born Sept. 18, 1857, in Lisbon, Ohio. His father had left Ireland in 1830 and settled in Lisbon, the county seat, where he practiced law and participated in liberal Democratic politics. His son graduated Phi Beta Kappa from Western Reserve College in Hudson, Ohio, and returned to Lisbon to study law under his father's tutelage. He passed the bar with honors in 1878 and joined his father's practice.

Public Career

In 1880 Clarke moved to Youngstown where his career in corporate law began. Under his ownership and direction, the town newspaper the *Vindicator* became a strong voice for progressive reform. Clarke, a member of the Youngstown literary society, lectured on Shakespeare and James Russell Lowell. He was an honorary life trustee of the Youngstown Public Library and bequeathed the library $100,000 in his will.

Clarke left Youngstown and his legal practice of 17 years to join the Cleveland firm, William & Cushing, in 1897. As general counsel for the Nickel Plate Railroad he remained true to his liberal politics and advocated antitrust and anti-rebate legislation. A progressive reformer, Clarke supported suffrage for women, mandatory civil service and public disclosure of campaign expenditures.

In 1894 he ran for the U.S. Senate but was defeated by incumbent Calvin S. Brice. Chairman of the Ohio State Democratic Sound Money Convention, Clarke disagreed with William Jennings Bryan's free silver populism and split from the Democrats at the 1896 national convention over that issue. He ran for the Senate a second time in 1914 but withdrew when another Irishman, Timothy Hogan, announced his candidacy.

After more than 35 years in the legal profession and progressive politics, Clarke received his first federal post. In 1914 President Wilson appointed him federal judge for the Northern District of Ohio.

When Charles Evans Hughes resigned from the court to run against Wilson, the president considered nominating Attorney General Tom Gregory or Republican Senator Warren G. Harding to fill the vacancy. He decided instead on Judge Clarke because he wanted a decidedly progressive justice with an antitrust record on Chief Justice White's staid court.

After his nomination, Clarke was described by the *New York World* as "singularly like Brandeis in having been a successful corporation lawyer whose practice served only to quicken his sympathies and activities for the causes of political and social justice." Indeed, President Wilson had hoped that Clarke would join Brandeis "to restrain the court from the extreme reactionary course which it seem[ed] inclined to follow." He was therefore greatly disappointed when Clarke resigned from the court to promote American participation in the League of Nations, even though the League was Wilson's own dream. Clarke informed the president he would "die happier" working for world peace rather than devoting his time "to determining whether a drunken Indian had been deprived of his land before he died or whether the digging of a ditch was constitutional or not."

From 1922-30 Clarke presided over the League of Nations' Non-Partisan Association of the United States and — against the advice of his physician, who was concerned about his heart — spoke on its behalf across the country.

At the age of 80, Clarke emerged unexpectedly from his retirement in San Diego to endorse over nationwide radio President Roosevelt's court-packing plan. He died March 22, 1945, shortly before the convening of the San Francisco Conference that created the United Nations.

William Howard Taft

(1921-1930)

Born: Sept. 15, 1857, Cincinnati, Ohio.

Education: Yale University, A.B., class salutatorian, 1878; Cincinnati Law School, LL.B., 1880.

Official Positions: assistant prosecuting attorney, Hamilton County, Ohio, 1881-83; assistant county solicitor, Hamilton County, 1885-87; Ohio superior court, 1887-90; U.S. solicitor general, 1890-91; federal judge, sixth circuit, 1892-1900; chairman, Philippine Commission, 1900-01; civil governor of the Philippines, 1901-04; secretary of war, 1904-08; president of the United States, 1909-13; joint chairman, National War Labor Board, 1918-19.

Supreme Court Appointment: nominated Chief Justice by President Warren Harding June 30, 1921, to replace Chief Justice Edward D. White, who died; confirmed by the U.S. Senate June 30, 1921, by a voice vote; replaced on court by Chief Justice Charles Evans Hughes, nominated by President Hoover.

Family: married Helen Herron June 19, 1886; two sons, one daughter.

Died: March 8, 1930, in Washington, D.C.

Personal Background

Public service was a tradition in the Taft family; William Howard Taft extended it to its limit during his lifetime. His grandfather, Peter Rawson Taft, was a judge on the probate and county courts in Windham County, Vt.; Alphonso Taft, William Howard's father, served two terms on the Ohio superior court before he was named secretary of war in the last months of the Grant administration. He also briefly served President Grant as attorney general, and later was ambassador to Austria-Hungary and Russia during the Arthur administration. William Howard's brother, Charles Phelps Taft, R-Ohio, served a term in the U.S. House of Representatives, 1895-97.

Born in Cincinnati, Taft received an A.B. in 1878 from Yale University, where he was the salutatorian of his graduating class. He returned to Ohio, entered Cincinnati Law School and took a job as a law reporter for the Cincinnati *Commercial*. He continued to report for the newspaper through 1880, the year in which he received his LL.B. and was admitted to the bar.

In 1886 he married Helen Herron. They raised one daughter and two sons, one of whom, Robert Alphonso Taft, R-Ohio, served in the U.S. Senate, 1939-53. Taft's grandson, Robert Taft Jr., R-Ohio, served in the House of Representatives, 1963-65, 1967-71, and the Senate, 1971-76.

Public Career

In 1881 Taft plunged into Republican politics and gave his support to a candidate for county prosecutor. After his candidate won, Taft was selected to be an assistant county prosecutor. He went back to private practice in 1883.

Taft was named to a two-year term as assistant county solicitor for Hamilton County in 1885 and, in 1887, when he was barely 30 years old, was appointed to the Ohio superior court.

He sat on the superior court bench until President Benjamin Harrison in 1890 named him solicitor general. In 1892, after Congress created additional judgeships for the federal circuit courts, Taft sought and received appointment to the sixth circuit.

Taft remained on the circuit court for eight years. He left reluctantly in 1900 when President McKinley asked him to head a commission established to ensure the smooth transition from military to civilian government in the Philippines in the aftermath of the Spanish-American War. In 1901 he was made civilian governor of the Philippines, a position he held until President Theodore Roosevelt named him secretary of war to replace Elihu Root in 1904.

Once in the cabinet, Taft became one of Roosevelt's closest advisers; the president increasingly relied on Taft to handle important matters for the administration. As secretary of war Taft was in command of the Panama Canal project and made a goodwill tour of the site. He also was dispatched in 1906 to Cuba to investigate for the president reports of revolutionary activity.

As Taft's prestige grew in the administration, so did his influence in the Republican party. With Roosevelt's backing he won the party's nomination for president and the subsequent election in 1908. He was sworn in as the twenty-ninth president of the United States March 4, 1909.

The presidency was a post that Taft did not particularly covet — he would have preferred a seat on the Supreme Court as Chief Justice, but he sought the presidency at the urging of his wife and Republican party regulars. His single term in office was not controversial. It saw the institution of the postal savings system and the Tariff Board, the intervention of American troops in the affairs of the Dominican Republic, the ratification of the Sixteenth Amendment to the Constitution and a continuation of the trust-busting begun under Theodore Roosevelt.

Taft also named six men to the Supreme Court, including a Chief Justice, Edward D. White. The others he named to the court were Horace A. Lurton, Charles Evans Hughes (who resigned from the court to run for president in 1916, lost, and was named Chief Justice in 1930 by President Hoover to replace Taft), Willis Van Devanter, Joseph R. Lamar and Mahlon Pitney. When Taft was named Chief Justice in 1921 only two of his appointees, Van Devanter and Pitney, were still on the bench.

Soon after he was elected president Taft began to fall out of favor with former President Roosevelt. The two men came to represent opposing sides of a division within the Republican party; when Taft was renominated in 1912, Roosevelt ran for president under the banner of his Bull Moose Party and effectively splintered the Republican vote. After the election, which was won by Democrat Woodrow Wilson, Taft described Roosevelt as "the most dangerous man that we have had in the country since its origin."

After leaving the White House, Taft taught constitutional law at Yale University, served a year as president of the American Bar Association, wrote magazine articles and was a frequent participant on the lecture circuit. He was elected president of the League to Enforce Peace in 1915. In 1916 he and four other former presidents of the American Bar Association joined with current president Elihu Root in writing to the U.S. Senate to register their disapproval of President Wilson's nomination of Louis D. Brandeis to the Supreme Court. During this period Taft also continued discreetly to publicize his desire to be named to the high court, especially as Chief Justice.

As Chief Justice, Taft was responsible for the creation of a judicial conference of senior federal judges, and passage of the Judiciary Act of 1925.

Taft served as the joint chairman of the National War Labor Board, 1918-19. An enthusiastic advocate of the League of Nations, he embarked on a 15-state tour in an attempt to rally support for the league. His greatest ambition was achieved when President Harding named him Chief Justice June 30, 1921, to replace Chief Justice Edward D. White. Taft is the only person in U.S. history to hold both the presidency and the Chief Justiceship.

George Sutherland
(1922-1938)

Born: March 25, 1862, Buckinghamshire, England.
Education: Brigham Young Academy, 1878-81; University of Michigan Law School, 1883.
Official Positions: Utah state senator, R, 1896-1900; U.S. House of Representatives, 1901-03; U.S. Senate, 1905-17; chairman, advisory committee to the Washington Conference for the Limitation of Naval Armaments, 1921; U.S. counsel, Norway-United States arbitration, The Hague, 1921-22.
Supreme Court Appointment: nominated associate justice by President Warren Harding Sept. 5, 1922, to replace Justice John H. Clarke, who resigned; confirmed by the Senate Sept. 5, 1922, by a voice vote; replaced on court by Stanley F. Reed, nominated by President Franklin D. Roosevelt.
Family: married Rosamund Lee June 18, 1883; two daughters, one son.
Died: July 18, 1942, Stockbridge, Mass.

Personal Background

Sutherland was brought to the United States in 1863 by his parents. His father, a recent convert to the Church of Jesus Christ of Latter-day Saints, settled his family in Springville in the Utah Territory. The senior Sutherland soon deserted the Mormons, but the family remained in Utah. George Sutherland learned the value of thrift and hard work in his childhood — he left school at age 12 to help support the family. By the time he was 16, however, he had saved enough money to enroll himself at Brigham Young Academy in Provo. After three years at that school, he spent a year working for the company building the Rio Grande Western Railroad and in 1883 entered the University of Michigan Law School. He studied law for only one year before returning to Provo to start his law practice. He also returned to marry Rosamund Lee of Beaver, Utah.

Public Career

After 10 years in Provo, Sutherland in 1893 moved to Salt Lake City. When the territory achieved statehood in 1896, Sutherland, running as a Republican, was elected to the first state senate. In 1900 he was elected to the U.S. House of Representatives. He declined to run for a second term in the House but was elected in 1904 to the U.S. Senate.

During his first term in the Senate, Sutherland endorsed several reform measures, including the Pure Food and Drug Act (1906), the Postal Savings Act (1910) and a compensation bill for workers injured in interstate commerce (1911-12). He also played a major role in the revision and codification of federal criminal statutes. Among legislative programs he opposed were statehood for Arizona and New Mexico (1912), the Federal Reserve Act (1913), the

Sixteenth Amendment (1913), Clayton Antitrust Act (1914), and the Federal Trade Commission Act (1914). He also opposed the nomination of Louis D. Brandeis to the Supreme Court.

In 1916 Sutherland failed in his attempt to be renominated by the Utah Republican party. He stayed in Washington, D.C., practiced law and remained in touch with former Senate colleague Warren G. Harding. Sutherland developed into one of Harding's closest advisers and worked on his successful presidential campaign in 1920. Soon thereafter Sutherland represented the Harding administration as chairman of the advisory committee to the Washington Conference for the Limitation of Naval Armaments in 1921 and as counsel in arbitration between Norway and the United States over matters of shipping.

President Harding named Sutherland to the Supreme Court when Justice John H. Clarke unexpectedly resigned from the court to work for the cause of world peace. He retired from the court Jan. 17, 1938, and died in Stockbridge, Mass., July 18, 1942.

Pierce Butler

(1922-1938)

Born: March 17, 1866, Northfield, Minn.

Education: Carleton College, A.B., B.S., 1887; LL.D., 1923.

Official Positions: assistant county attorney, Ramsey County, Minn., 1891-93; county attorney, 1893-97.

Supreme Court Appointment: nominated associate justice Nov. 23, 1922, by President Warren Harding, to replace William R. Day, who resigned; confirmed by U.S. Senate Dec. 21, 1922, by a 61-8 vote; replaced on court by Frank Murphy, nominated by President Roosevelt.

Family: married Annie M. Cronin Aug. 25, 1891; eight children.

Died: Nov. 16, 1939, Washington, D.C.

Personal Background

Pierce Butler was born in Northfield, Minn., on St. Patrick's Day in 1866, the sixth of Patrick and Mary Gaffrey Butler's eight children. His parents, Roman Catholics, settled on a farm in the Northwest after immigrating from Ireland during the potato famine of the 1840s. With money earned at a nearby dairy, Pierce attended Carleton College in his home town and graduated in 1887 with a bachelor of arts and a bachelor of science degree. He left Northfield to read law with the St. Paul firm of Pinch & Twohy and was admitted to the bar in 1888 at age 22.

Butler began his legal career practicing law with Stan Donnelly, the son of Ignatius Donnelly, a Minnesota congressman and future vice presidential candidate of the People's Party.

Public Career

In 1891 Butler was elected assistant attorney of Ramsey County, which includes St. Paul. While county attorney he formed the firm, How, Butler & Mitchell, and later became senior partner of Butler, Mitchell & Doherty. Attorney General George Wickersham chose Butler to represent the federal government in a number of antitrust cases around 1910. His skillful prosecution won him the attorney general's praise as the "foremost lawyer in his part of the country" and brought him to President Harding's attention.

When Justice Day's resignation in 1922 left a vacancy on the court, Butler was Chief Justice Taft's top choice for the seat. During arbitration in Canada the year before, Taft had been favorably impressed with Butler and recommended him to Harding. There were other reasons for Taft's strong preference, however. He wanted to obtain a conservative majority on the court. Butler's conservative judicial past made Taft confident that if appointed he would align himself with Justices Van Devanter, McReynolds and Sutherland. The president also was reminded by Taft of the political advantages of a Butler appointment: Taft, a Protestant, had replaced Chief Justice White, a Catholic, and another Catholic was needed on the bench.

Although Taft succeeded in convincing President Harding of Butler's merits, Senate liberals were not so easily persuaded. Their primary objection concerned Butler's defense of the Northern Pacific, Great Northern, and Chicago, Burlington and Quincy railroads during his legal practice. In the opinion of Senator-elect Henrik Shipstead of Minnesota, "the appointment of Judge Gary of the United States Steel Corporation would not ... be more unfitting or improper than the appointment of Mr. Butler."

Also criticized were Butler's actions as regent of the University of Minnesota from 1907-24. Faculty members whose economic or political views differed from his own had been dismissed or refused tenure. He was a reactionary with no tolerance for dissent, the liberal academics claimed. Despite the opposition to Butler's appointment, only eight senators voted against his confirmation Dec. 21, 1922.

Butler died in Washington, D.C., during his seventeenth year of service on the court. As anticipated, he was a staunch advocate of the court's *laissez faire* decisions during his tenure.

Edward Terry Sanford

(1923-1930)

Born: July 23, 1865, Knoxville, Tennessee.

Education: University of Tennessee, B.A. and Ph.B., 1883; Harvard, B.A., 1884, M.A., 1889; Harvard Law School, LL.B., 1889; editor of the *Harvard Law Review.*

Official Positions: special assistant to the U.S. attorney general, 1906-1907; assistant U.S. attorney general, 1907-1908; federal judge, U.S. District Court for the middle and eastern districts of Tennessee, 1908-23.

Supreme Court Appointment: nominated associate justice by President Warren Harding Jan. 24, 1923, to replace Mahlon Pitney, who retired; confirmed by the Senate Jan. 29, 1923 by a voice vote; replaced on court by Owen J. Roberts, nominated by President Hoover.

Family: married Lutie Mallory Woodruff Jan. 6, 1891; two daughters.

Died: March 8, 1930, Washington, D.C.

Personal Background

Born in Knoxville on July 23, 1865, three months after the South had surrendered to the Union armies, Sanford grew up in one of the few Republican enclaves in the post-Civil War South. His father, Edward J. Sanford, had come to Tennessee in 1852 from Connecticut where his family had lived since 1634. In Tennessee, he rose from poverty to make a fortune in the lumber and construction business and became a prominent member of the Republican party. Sanford's mother, Emma Chavannes, of Swiss ancestry, educated her son at local private schools.

Following his education at the University of Tennessee and Harvard, Sanford studied in France and Germany for a year, returning to Knoxville, settling into the practice of law, and marrying a local woman.

Public Career

Sanford's first official position came in 1905 at the age of 41 when he accepted the post of special assistant to U.S. Attorney General William H. Moody (later appointed to the Supreme Court). Sanford's task — as one of President Theodore Roosevelt's "trustbusters" — was to prosecute the fertilizer trust under the Sherman Antitrust Act of 1890. In 1907, he became assistant attorney general. A year later, Roosevelt nominated him as federal district judge for the middle and eastern districts of Tennessee, a post Sanford held until his nomination to the Supreme Court in 1923.

After World War I, Sanford worked to mobilize support for the Treaty of Versailles and U.S. membership in the League of Nations. Although the treaty was defeated in the Senate, Sanford's efforts brought him to the attention of Chief Justice Taft — with whom he had become acquainted during his Justice Department service — and to Attorney General Harry M. Daugherty. They suggested his name to President Warren G. Harding when Justice Mahlon Pitney retired on Dec. 31, 1922, giving Harding a fourth vacancy on the court to fill during his term.

Harlan Fiske Stone
(1925-1946)

Born: Oct. 11, 1872, Chesterfield, N.H.

Education: Amherst College, A.B., 1894, M.A., 1897, LL.D., 1913; Columbia University, LL.B., 1898.

Official Positions: attorney general, 1924-25.

Supreme Court Appointment: nominated associate justice by President Calvin Coolidge Jan. 5, 1925, to replace Joseph McKenna, who resigned; confirmed by the U.S. Senate Feb. 5, 1925, by a 71-6 vote; nominated Chief Justice by President Franklin D. Roosevelt June 12, 1941, to replace Chief Justice Hughes, who resigned; confirmed by the U.S. Senate June 27, 1941, by a voice vote; replaced on court by Fred M. Vinson, nominated by President Truman.

Family: married Agnes Harvey Sept. 7, 1899; two sons.

Died: April 22, 1946, Washington, D.C.

Personal Background

Harlan Fiske Stone was born Oct. 11, 1872, in Chesterfield, N.H., the son of Ann Sophia (Butler) and Frederick Lawson Stone, a New England farmer. Phi Beta Kappa and president of his class at Amherst College, Stone graduated with an A.B. in 1894, one year before Calvin Coolidge, and with an M.A. three years later.

A Columbia University law school graduate, Stone was admitted to the New York bar, married Agnes Harvey and began his legal practice with the firm, Sullivan & Cromwell, in 1899. For the next 25 years he divided his time between his Wall Street practice and a career as professor of law and dean at Columbia.

Public Career

In 1924 President Coolidge appointed his fellow Republican and Amherst alumnus to succeed controversial Harry M. Daugherty as attorney general. Stone began a reorganization of the Justice Department and recommended J. Edgar Hoover to head the FBI. The Supreme Court resignation of Justice McKenna in 1925 gave Coolidge the opportunity to promote his old friend to the bench after only a year in his Cabinet. Despite reservations over Stone's moderate conservatism and ties to Wall Street wealth (five years earlier he had been J. P. Morgan's counsel), Stone was confirmed by the Senate Feb. 5, 1925.

A spokesman for judicial restraint on the Taft and Hughes courts, Stone was nominated Chief Justice by President Roosevelt 16 years later.

When the Agricultural Adjustment Act was declared unconstitutional by a 6-3 majority in 1936, Stone had sided with the president, declaring that the court was not "the only agency of government that must be assumed to have the capacity to govern." Stone recognized the danger of the court's becoming a "legislative Constitution-making body," and Roosevelt needed a Chief Justice who would not thwart his programs. Moreover, a Republican appointment, the president felt, would show him to be a non-partisan leader. Favored by the press and bar, Stone's selection as Chief Justice was well received. Archibald MacLeish described the nomination as "the perfect word spoken at the perfect moment."

For Stone, the appointment was not the culmination of a lifelong ambition: "I cannot say I had any thought of being a member of the Supreme Court or any other court," said Stone recalling his ambitions as a 21-year-old college student, "for I believed then, as I do now, that the best insurance of a happy life and reasonable success in it is devotion to one's immediate job and happiness in doing it."

Stone achieved far more than "reasonable success." Progressing from the most junior to senior associate justice and finally to Chief Justice, he occupied consecutively, as none of his predecessors had done, every seat on the bench.

Stone's 21 years of service on the court ended suddenly. On April 22, 1946, while reading a dissent in a naturalization case, he was stricken, dying later in the day.

Owen Josephus Roberts
(1930-1945)

several of whom were convicted but received relatively short prison sentences. He returned to private practice once again in 1930.

In May 1930, after the Senate refused to confirm President Hoover's nomination of North Carolina judge John J. Parker to the Supreme Court because of Parker's rulings upholding "yellow dog" labor contracts and his derogatory comments on blacks, Roberts was named to replace him and was confirmed May 20, 1930.

In addition to his court duties, Roberts oversaw an investigation of the attack on Pearl Harbor and headed the Commission for the Protection and Salvage of Artistic and Historic Monuments in Europe that traced and catalogued art objects stolen or destroyed by the Germans during World War II.

After retiring from the court, he returned to his alma mater and served as dean of the University of Pennsylvania Law School from 1948 to 1951. He was involved in the world federalist movement and served in 1953 as the chairman of the Fund for the Advancement of Education. He died May 17, 1955, in West Vincent Township, Pa.

Born: May 2, 1875, Germantown, Pa.

Education: University of Pennsylvania, A.B., Phi Beta Kappa, 1895; LL.B. cum laude, 1898.

Official Positions: assistant district attorney, 1901-04; special deputy attorney general, eastern district of Pennsylvania, 1918; special United States attorney, 1924-30; chairman, Pearl Harbor Inquiry Board, 1941-42.

Supreme Court Appointment: nominated associate justice by President Herbert Hoover May 9, 1930, to replace Edward Terry Sanford, who died; confirmed by the U.S. Senate May 20, 1930, by a voice vote,; replaced by Harold H. Burton, nominated by President Truman.

Family: married Elizabeth Caldwell Rogers, 1904.

Died: May 17, 1955, West Vincent Township, Pa.

Personal Background

Roberts' ancestors left Wales in 1808 and settled in southeastern Pennsylvania. Roberts was a quiet youngster who displayed a love for books and an aptitude for debating. He attended the University of Pennsylvania, from which he graduated Phi Beta Kappa in 1895. He went on to the University of Pennsylvania Law School where he was the associate editor of the *American Law Register*, 1897-98, and graduated cum laude in 1898. Because of his distinguished academic record, Roberts was named a University Fellow in 1898, a position he held for two years. He continued to teach part-time at the university until 1919.

Public Career

Roberts entered private practice in Philadelphia in 1898. In 1901 he was named assistant district attorney in Philadelphia. Roberts returned to private practice in 1905 and built a prosperous business representing a large clientele, including several corporations.

Appointed a special deputy attorney general in 1918, Roberts prosecuted several cases in the Philadelphia area under the terms of the Espionage Act. In 1924 President Calvin Coolidge named him and former Senator Atlee Pomerene, D-Ohio (1911-23), as special United States attorneys to investigate the scandals of the Harding administration. Through thorough investigative work, Roberts uncovered a network of bribes to administration officials,

Benjamin Nathan Cardozo
(1932-1938)

Born: May 24, 1870, New York, N.Y.

Education: Columbia University, A.B., 1889; A.M., 1890; Columbia Law School, 1891 (no degree).

Official Positions: justice, supreme court of New York, 1914; judge, court of appeals for New York State., 1914-32, chief judge, 1926-32.

Supreme Court Appointment: nominated associate justice Feb. 15, 1932, by President Herbert Hoover, to replace Oliver Wendell Holmes Jr., who resigned; confirmed by the Senate Feb. 24, 1932, by a voice vote; replaced on the court by Felix Frankfurter, nominated by President Franklin D. Roosevelt.

Family: unmarried.

Died: July 9, 1938, Port Chester, N.Y.

Personal Background

The youngest son of Albert and Rebecca Washington Cardozo, Benjamin Nathan Cardozo was born in New York City on May 24, 1870. His parents were descendants of Sephardic Jews who had settled in New York in the mid-eighteenth century, and one of his ancestors authored the words at the base of the Statue of Liberty. Benjamin's childhood was spent in the aftermath of the Boss Tweed scandal, which implicated his father, a Tammany Hall judge, in the political corruption of the city government. Charged with graft, Albert Cardozo resigned rather than face impeachment.

At age 15, Benjamin Cardozo was admitted to Columbia University. He graduated with honors in 1889, completed his master's degree the following year and began to study at the law school. In 1891 he was admitted to the New York bar without a law degree — a not uncommon practice at that time — and began practicing appellate law with his older brother in the city. Cardozo remained a bachelor and had only a few close friends. He was very fond of his older unmarried sister Ellen and lived with her until her death in 1929.

Public Career

After 23 years as a private lawyer, Cardozo ran against Tammany Hall on the fusion ticket in 1914 and was elected by a narrow margin to the New York supreme court, the state's trial bench. Shortly thereafter, Governor Martin A. Glynn appointed him to a temporary position on the New York court of appeals, on which he was to serve for 18 years. Elected to a full term as associate judge in 1917, he became chief judge six years later and won for the court its reputation as the leading state court in the country. Cardozo's early judicial writings were used by lawyers as a handbook, and his lectures at Yale Law School on a number of topics were extended and published as *The Nature of the Judicial Process* in 1921, *The Growth of the Law* in 1924 and *The Paradoxes of Legal Science* four years later.

When 90-year-old Justice Holmes announced his retirement, Senator Robert F. Wagner, D-N.Y., presented Cardozo's name to President Hoover. University faculty, newspapermen, political leaders and members of the bar all voiced their endorsement of the New York judge. Within 10 days of Holmes' resignation, a tally of names received at the White House showed Cardozo a clear favorite. *The New York Times* described the unanimity of support for him as "quite without precedent."

Hoover was unconvinced, however. Two justices from New York, Hughes and Stone, and one Jew, Brandeis, were quite enough, he thought. Only after Stone offered his resignation (which was not accepted) on Cardozo's behalf did Hoover make his decision, appointing him Feb. 15, 1932. Harvard professor Zechariah Chafee Jr. praised the nomination: the president's choice "ignored geography and made history."

Cardozo served on the court for six years until his death in 1938 after a long illness. In *Nine Old Men*, columnists Drew Pearson and Robert S. Allen described the silver-haired justice as "the hermit philosopher." In the 1938 memorial court testimony, "the strangely compelling power of that reticent, sensitive and almost mystical personality" was remembered.

Hugo Lafayette Black
(1937-1971)

Born: Feb. 27, 1886, Harlan, Ala.
Education: Birmingham Medical College, 1903-04; University of Alabama, LL.B., 1906.
Official Positions: police court judge, Birmingham, 1910-11; solicitor, Jefferson County, Ala., 1915-17; United States Senator, D-Ala., 1927-37.
Supreme Court Appointment: nominated associate justice by President Franklin D. Roosevelt Aug. 12, 1937, to replace Willis Van Devanter, who retired; confirmed by the U.S. Senate Aug. 17, 1937, by a 63-16 vote; replaced by Lewis F. Powell Jr., nominated by President Nixon.
Family: married, first, Josephine Foster February 1921, died 1951, two sons, one daughter; second, Elizabeth Seay DeMeritte Sept. 11, 1957.
Died: Sept. 25, 1971, Washington, D.C.

Personal Background

The eighth child of a Baptist storekeeper and farmer, Hugo Black spent the first years of his life in the hill country near Harlan, Ala. When he was still a youngster, his family moved to Ashland, a larger community where his father's business prospered. Black attended the local schools in Ashland and after trying one year at Birmingham Medical College, decided to study law. At 18, he entered the University of Alabama Law School at Tuscaloosa.

Upon receipt of his LL.B., Black returned to Ashland and set up his first law practice. The following year a fire destroyed his office and library; Black left for Birmingham. There he quickly established a relationship with labor by defending the United Mine Workers strikers in 1908. Black also developed an expertise for arguing personal injury cases.

Public Career

He was named a part-time police court judge in Birmingham in 1911 and was elected county solicitor (public prosecutor) for Jefferson County in 1914. As solicitor, he gained a measure of local fame for his investigation of reports of the brutal means the police employed while questioning suspects at the notorious Bessemer jail. When he left the solicitor's post to enter the army in World War I, Black had succeeded in emptying a docket that had once held as many as 3,000 pending cases.

His brief military career kept him within the borders of the United States; he returned to practice in Birmingham in 1918, married a local woman the following year and continued to increase his business, still specializing in labor law and personal injury cases. In 1923 he joined the Ku Klux Klan, but resigned from the organization two years later just before announcing his intention to run for the Democratic nomination for the Senate seat held by Oscar Underwood, D-Ala. (1915-27). Campaigning as the poor man's candidate, Black won the party's endorsement and the subsequent election. He entered the Senate in 1927 and immediately began to study history and the classics at the Library of Congress to compensate for his lack of formal education.

During his two terms in the Senate Black used committee hearings to investigate several areas, including abuses of marine and airline subsidies and the activities of lobbying groups. In 1933 he introduced a bill to create a 30-hour work week. This legislation, after several alterations, was finally passed in 1938 as the Fair Labor Standards Act. One of the Senate's strongest supporters of President Roosevelt, Black spoke out in favor of Roosevelt's 1937 court-packing scheme and other New Deal programs. His support for the administration and his strong liberal instincts led the president to pick Black as his choice to fill the Supreme Court seat vacated by the retirement of Willis Van Devanter.

Black's previous affiliation with the Ku Klux Klan was widely reported in the national news media after his Senate confirmation. The furor quickly quieted, however, when the new justice admitted in a dramatic radio broadcast that he had indeed been a member of the Klan but added that he had resigned many years before and would comment no further. A man who during his court career always carried in his pocket a copy of the United States Constitution, Black retired from the court Sept. 17, 1971, after suffering a stroke. He died eight days later.

Stanley Forman Reed
(1938-1957)

Born: Dec. 31, 1884, Minerva, Ky.

Education: Kentucky Wesleyan University, A.B., 1902; Yale University, A.B., 1906; legal studies, University of Virginia and Columbia University (no degree); graduate studies, University of Paris, 1909-10.

Official Positions: general counsel, Federal Farm Board, 1929-32; general counsel, Reconstruction Finance Corporation, 1932-35; special assistant to attorney general, 1935; solicitor general, 1935-38.

Supreme Court Appointment: nominated associate justice by President Franklin D. Roosevelt Jan. 15, 1938, to replace George Sutherland, who resigned; confirmed by U.S. Senate Jan. 25, 1938, by a voice vote; replaced on court by Charles E. Whittaker, appointed by President Eisenhower.

Family: married Winifred Elgin May 11, 1908; two sons.

Personal Background

Stanley Forman Reed was born Dec. 31, 1884, in tobacco-rich Mason County, Ky. His father, John A. Reed, practiced medicine and his mother, Frances Forman Reed, was active in political and social affairs and served from 1932-35 as registrar general of the National Society of Daughters of the American Revolution (DAR). Stanley received undergraduate degrees from Kentucky Wesleyan and Yale universities and studied law at the University of Virginia and Columbia University. He married Winifred Elgin from his hometown May 11, 1908, and they left the following year for Paris where he took graduate courses in civil and international law at the Sorbonne.

Reed practiced law in Maysville, Ky., population 6,500, with the firm, Browning, Reed & Zeigler, from 1910-1917 and during this period served in the Kentucky General

Assembly for four years. After a brief interim in the U.S. Army as a first lieutenant, he returned to his legal practice. The Chesapeake & Ohio Railroad and the Burley Tobacco Growers Cooperative were two of his clients.

Public Career

In 1929 Reed's experience with Burley Tobacco in market control through group sales became needed in Washington. Following the recommendation of the tobacco cooperative's president, James C. Stone, President Hoover appointed Reed general counsel for the Federal Farm Board, newly established to resell surpluses of American farm commodities abroad. After two years with the board, Reed was promoted to general counsel for the Reconstruction Finance Corporation, Hoover's loan-granting agency in the Depression to help banks, businesses and agricultural enterprises.

One of new President Roosevelt's most controversial economic policies was to raise prices by reducing the gold content of the dollar. He appointed Reed special assistant to the attorney general with the unique task of defending the government's legal right to change the requirement of certain private companies for payment in gold. Reed argued the *Gold Clause Cases* before the Supreme Court in 1935; his success with this assignment made Roosevelt confident that as solicitor general Reed would be able to argue persuasively before the Supreme Court the constitutionality of his New Deal legislation. Despite such defeats as the court's decision to invalidate the Agricultural Adjustment Act in 1936, Solicitor General Reed succeeded in defending the constitutionality of the National Labor Relations Act and other important measures of the Roosevelt era.

When Justice Sutherland retired in 1938, Roosevelt had the opportunity to add to the court the second justice of his choosing. Stanley Forman Reed, whose 10 years of government experience under both Republican and Democratic administrations and 17 years in private practice well qualified him for the bench, was his choice.

From 1939 to 1941 Justice Reed chaired President Roosevelt's Commission on Civil Service Improvement. After his resignation from the court in 1957, he also served as chairman of President Eisenhower's U.S. Civil Rights Commission. Reed soon left the commission because he felt his continued involvement with the federal judiciary disqualified him. Reed argued 35 cases before the Court of Claims and 25 cases before the Court of Appeals in the District of Columbia during his retirement. He maintained an office in the Supreme Court until his move to New York, where he resided in mid-1979.

Felix Frankfurter
(1939-1962)

Born: Nov. 15, 1882, Vienna, Austria.

Education: College of the City of New York, A.B., 1902; Harvard University School of Law, LL.B., 1906.

Official Positions: assistant United States attorney, southern New York district, 1906-09; law officer, Bureau of Insular Affairs, War Department, 1910-14; assistant to the secretary of war, secretary and counsel, President's Mediation Commission, assistant to the secretary of labor, 1917-18; chairman; War Labor Policies Board, 1918.

Supreme Court Appointment: nominated associate justice by President Franklin D. Roosevelt Jan. 5, 1939, to replace Benjamin Cardozo, who died; confirmed by the U.S. Senate Jan. 17, 1939, by a voice vote; replaced on court by Arthur Goldberg, nominated by President Kennedy.

Family: married Marion A. Denman Dec. 20, 1919.

Died: Feb. 22, 1965, Washington, D.C.

Personal Background

An Austrian Jew, Felix Frankfurter came to the United States with his parents in 1894 and was raised amidst the squalor of New York's Lower East Side. He attended City College and, after an impressive three years at Harvard University School of Law, took a job with a New York law firm but was soon recruited away by Henry L. Stimson, the United States attorney for the southern district of New York.

Public Career

Stimson had been appointed by President Theodore Roosevelt. At the end of the Roosevelt administration in 1909, Stimson went into private practice for a short time and brought Frankfurter with him. After an unsuccessful bid for the governorship of New York, Stimson was named secretary of war under President Taft.

Frankfurter accompanied his mentor to Washington, D.C., and was appointed legal officer in the War Department's Bureau of Insular Affairs.

In 1914 Harvard University offered Frankfurter a teaching post in the Law School and he happily returned to his alma mater. In addition to his teaching duties, Frankfurter became involved in the Zionist movement, argued a number of minimum wage and maximum hour cases for the National Consumers League and helped found the *New Republic*.

Frankfurter returned to Washington, D.C., in 1917 as an assistant to Secretary of War Newton D. Baker. That same year, President Wilson named a Mediation Commission to handle the rash of strikes obstructing the defense industry; Frankfurter was named its secretary and counsel. While serving on the commission, Frankfurter investigated the handling of the case of Tom Mooney, the alleged "Preparedness Day Parade Bomber," and the Bisbee (Ariz.) deportation case wherein approximately 1,000 miners were taken roughly from their labor camps in Arizona and dropped in a deserted town in New Mexico. In both instances Frankfurter found grounds to suspect that the rights of the individuals involved had been violated. This, as well as his highly publicized arguments in defense of Sacco and Vanzetti, his work with the National Association for the Advancement of Colored People, and the fact that he was a founding member of the American Civil Liberties Union earned him a reputation as a die-hard liberal that would follow him throughout his career.

He also served as chairman of the War Labor Policies Board. This position first introduced him to Franklin D.

Roosevelt who, as assistant secretary of the Navy, sat on the board.

At war's end, Frankfurter attended the Paris Peace Conference as a representative of the American Zionist Movement and then returned to Cambridge. In 1919, he married Marion A. Denman. The ceremony took place in Judge Learned Hand's chambers and was performed by Judge Benjamin Cardozo of the New York Court of Appeals.

At Harvard, Frankfurter enjoyed a growing reputation as an expert on the Constitution and the Supreme Court. He was offered a seat on the Massachusetts Supreme Judicial Court in 1932, which he declined. His friendship with Franklin Roosevelt grew closer; in 1933 the newly elected president asked him to be solicitor general, another post Frankfurter declined. He remained, however, a close adviser to the president and recommended to him a number of Harvard graduates eager to work in the Roosevelt administration, including Thomas G. Corcoran, one of the most influential New Dealers.

Named to the Supreme Court in 1939 to replace Justice Benjamin Cardozo, he was Roosevelt's third appointment. He continued to advise the president on a number of issues until Roosevelt's death in 1945. Frankfurter remained on the court until he suffered a debilitating stroke in 1962. He died in Washington, D.C., in 1965.

He was the author of *The Case of Sacco and Vanzetti*, 1927; *The Business of the Supreme Court* (with James M. Landis), 1928; *The Labor Injunction* (with Nathan Greene), 1930; *The Public and Its Government*, 1930; *The Commerce Clause Under Marshall, Taney and Waite*, 1937; *Mr. Justice Holmes and the Supreme Court*, 1939; and was the editor of several volumes on various areas of law.

William Orville Douglas
(1939-1975)

Born: Oct. 16, 1898, Maine, Minn.

Education: Whitman Collee, BA., 1920, Phi Beta Kappa; Columbia Law School, LL.B., 1925.

Official Positions: member, Securities and Exchange Commission, 1936-39, chairman, 1937-39.

Supreme Court Appointment: nominated associate justice by President Franklin D. Roosevelt March 20, 1939, to replace Louis D. Brandeis, who retired; confirmed by the Senate April 4, 1939, by a 62-4 vote; replaced on court by John Paul Stevens, nominated by President Ford.

Family: married, first, Mildred Riddle Aug. 16, 1923, divorced 1954, one son, one daughter; second, Mercedes Hester Dec. 14, 1954, divorced 1963; third, Joan Martin, August 1963, divorced 1966; fourth, Cathleen Heffernan, July 1966.

Personal Background

Born into an impoverished farm family in Minnesota shortly before the turn of the 20th century, Douglas spent his early years in Yakima, Washington. A polio attack as a child sparked Douglas' lifelong passion for the outdoors, as he hiked the mountains near his home to build strength in his weakened legs.

After graduating from Whitman College in Walla Walla, Wash., in 1920, Douglas decided to pursue a law career. Despite his lack of funds, he determined to go east to study law at Columbia University Law School. Douglas quickly became one of the school's top students.

Following law school, a two-year stint with a prestigious Wall Street law firm convinced Douglas that representing corporate clients would not be to his liking. After a year back in Yakima, Douglas joined the law faculty at Columbia University. In 1929 he moved to New Haven, Conn., to teach law at Yale.

Public Career

By the time the Depression struck in 1929, Douglas had already developed a reputation as one of the country's foremost financial law experts. So when President Franklin D. Roosevelt needed staff for the newly formed Securities and Exchange Commission (SEC), created in 1934, he called on Douglas, who joined the commission in 1936; he became its chairman in 1937.

Douglas' 1939 Supreme Court nomination sailed through the Senate. Such easy relations with Congress, however, were not to mark Douglas' forthcoming years in Washington. Twice he faced the threat of impeachment, although neither in 1953 nor in 1970 did the move gain any real support.

Douglas' lifestyle and liberal political views — plus conservative resentment at the Senate's rejection of two of President Nixon's Supreme Court nominees — were the main spur behind the 1970 impeachment attempt. The justice's relations with the Parvin Foundation, recipient of considerable income from gambling interests, were held up for scrutiny. Anti-establishment sentiments expressed in one of his many books further fueled the attack. His controversial marital history also raised congressional eyebrows. But a special House Judiciary Subcommittee created to investigate the charges found no grounds for impeachment.

Douglas suffered a paralytic stroke in January 1975. At first, Douglas attempted to continue his work on the court, but in November 1975 he resigned, citing the pain and physical disability resulting from the stroke. At the time of his retirement, he had served 36 years and seven months, longer than any other justice.

Francis William Murphy
(1940-1949)

Born: April 13, 1890, Harbor Beach, Mich.

Education: University of Michigan, A.B., 1912, LL.B., 1914; graduate study, Lincoln's Inn, London, and Trinity College, Dublin.

Official Positions: chief assistant attorney general, eastern district of Michigan, 1919-20; judge, Recorder's Court, Detroit, 1923-30; mayor of Detroit, 1930-33; governor general of Philippine Islands, 1933-35; U.S. high commissioner to Philippines, 1935-36; governor, state of Michigan, 1937-39; attorney general, 1939-40.

Supreme Court Appointment: nominated associate justice by President Franklin D. Roosevelt Jan. 4, 1940, to replace Pierce Butler, who died; confirmed by the U.S. Senate Jan. 15, 1940, by a voice vote; replaced on court by Tom C. Clark, nominated by President Truman.

Family: unmarried.

Died: July 19, 1949, Detroit, Mich.

Personal Background

Frank — christened Francis William — Murphy was born April 13, 1890, in Harbor Beach, Mich., the third child of Irish Catholic parents, John T. Murphy, a country lawyer, and his wife Mary (Brennan) Murphy. As a young boy, Frank promised his mother that he would never smoke or drink and he kept that promise until adulthood. He received his undergraduate and law degrees from the University of Michigan and after his admission to the bar in 1914 clerked for the Detroit firm, Monaghan & Monaghan, for three years, teaching law at night school. During World War I Murphy served with the American Expeditionary Force in France and with the Army of Occupation in Germany. He did not return home immediately after the war but took graduate courses at Lincoln's Inn in London and Trinity College in Dublin.

Public Career

Murphy began his career in Michigan as chief assistant attorney general for the eastern district. After practicing law in Detroit for three years, he became judge for the Recorder's Court, the principal criminal court in Detroit. In the midst of the Depression, Murphy, a pro-Labor Democrat and advocate of federal relief, was elected mayor of Detroit and served from 1930-33.

Franklin Delano Roosevelt was governor of New York during this period. The midwesterner supported Roosevelt's candidacy in 1932 and when he became president endorsed his Works Progress Administration (WPA) wholeheartedly.

In recognition of his support, Roosevelt named Murphy governor general of the Philippine Islands and in 1935, when commonwealth status was won, appointed him U.S. high commissioner. In the Far East as in the midwest, Murphy enacted such New Deal policies as maximum hour and minimum wage laws. Once the independent government was working smoothly, he returned to Michigan, but his high regard for the people of the Philippines continued. The American and Philippine flags hung side by side in his Supreme Court office.

From 1937-39 Murphy served as governor of Michigan. Immediately upon taking office, he was faced with a sit-down strike of 135,000 automotive workers. Murphy's refusal to call out the state troopers earned him many critics and cost him re-election in 1938.

Murphy aspired to be secretary of war in Roosevelt's cabinet. A bit of political juggling landed him the position of attorney general instead. Roosevelt had a lot of people to please. To Solicitor General (later Supreme Court justice) Robert H. Jackson he wrote, "I want you for my attorney general, Bob, but I want to name Murphy immediately to something and since I can't name him to what he himself wants, it is desirable to use the attorney generalship temporarily for that purpose." During his one year in that office, Murphy indicted a number of Democratic political bosses, most notably Tom Pendergast of Kansas City, brought suit against numerous trust companies and established the first civil rights unit in the Justice Department.

When Justice Butler died in 1939, President Roosevelt filled the vacancy in kind by appointing another Democrat and Catholic — Frank Murphy. Murphy did not want the job. To his parish priest he wrote, "I am not too happy about going on the court. A better choice could have been made." So anxious was he for involvement in the war effort that during court recesses Murphy served as an infantry officer in Fort Benning, Ga., much to the dismay of Chief Justice Stone.

On the court, described by Murphy as the "Great Pulpit," he preached civil liberties and his moralizing rhetoric gave birth to the saying "justice tempered with Murphy." Murphy's Catholicism did not influence his decisionmaking even where Jehovah's Witnesses, a strongly anti-Catholic sect, was concerned. He upheld their right to proselytize door to door and in the court's second flag-salute decision voted with the majority to invalidate the salute as a compulsory requirement in schools.

Frank Murphy died July 19, 1949, in Detroit, Mich., at the age of 59. With the sudden deaths that year of Murphy and Wiley B. Rutledge, the court lost two of its most consistently liberal spokesmen.

James Francis Byrnes
(1941-1942)

Born: May 2, 1879, Charleston, S.C.

Education: St. Patrick's Parochial School (never graduated); studied law privately, admitted to the bar in 1903.

Official Positions: court reporter, second circuit, S.C., 1900-08; solicitor, second circuit, S.C., 1908-10; U.S. House of Representatives, D-S.C., 1911-25; U.S. Senate, D-S.C., 1931-41; director, Office of Economic Stabilization, 1942-43; director, Office of War Mobilization and Reconversion, 1943-45; secretary of state, 1945-47; governor of South Carolina, 1951-55.

Supreme Court Appointment: nominated associate justice by President Franklin D. Roosevelt June 12, 1941, to replace James McReynolds, who retired; confirmed by the U.S. Senate June 12, 1941, by a voice vote; replaced on court by Wiley B. Rutledge, appointed by President Roosevelt.

Family: married Maude Busch May 2, 1906; no children.

Died: April 9, 1972, Columbia, S.C.

Personal Background

The son of Irish immigrants, James Francis Byrnes was born May 2, 1879, in the Charleston of the post-Reconstruction South. He was named after his father, who died shortly before his birth. Elisabeth E. McSweeney Byrnes supported the family as a dressmaker. At age 14, James left school to work as a law clerk in a Charleston firm for $2 a week. With his mother's help he learned shorthand and won an exam for a court stenographer's job in Aiken, S.C., where he served as official court reporter for the second circuit for eight years, reading law in his spare time. Byrnes passed the bar in 1903 and the same year bought the Aiken newspaper, *Journal and Review,* and became its editor.

Public Career

As solicitor or district attorney for South Carolina's second circuit, Byrnes unexpectedly won a seat in the U.S. House of Representatives in 1910. "I campaigned on nothing but gall and gall won by 57 votes," he later reminisced. During his second term, he became well acquainted with Franklin Delano Roosevelt, Woodrow Wilson's assistant secretary of the Navy, who often appeared before the House Appropriations Committee on which Byrnes sat.

A speechwriter and political strategist for Roosevelt's campaign in 1932, he continued his loyal support of the administration during his two terms in the Senate despite his objections to certain New Deal labor and welfare policies. The president twice considered his friend as a running mate but decided in favor of Henry Wallace in 1940 and Senator Harry S Truman four years later. Byrnes' failure to obtain the vice presidential nomination was attributable in part to his unpopularity with northern liberals, and anti-Catholic sentiment despite his conversion to the Episcopalian faith.

Roosevelt rewarded Byrnes for his loyalty by nominating him to the Supreme Court June 12, 1941. So valuable was he to the president as a troubleshooter behind the scenes in the Senate that after Justice McReynolds announced his retirement in January, Roosevelt kept him in the Cabinet for six months before announcing him as McReynolds' successor.

Byrnes was restless on the court. "My country's at war and I want to be in it," he wrote. "I don't think I can stand the abstractions of jurisprudence at a time like this." He didn't have to stand it very long and never wrote a single court opinion. After 16 months Roosevelt asked him to resign to handle domestic affairs.

Both as director of the Office of Economic Stabilization from 1942-43 and as director of the Office of War Mobilization the following two years, Byrnes exercised great power in the administration. As the president himself stated when he called Byrnes from the court to the White House, "I want you to act as a judge and I will let it be known that your decision is my decision and that there is no appeal. For all practical purposes, you will be assistant President." In 1945 Byrnes accompanied Roosevelt to the meeting in Yalta with Stalin and Churchill, and as secretary of state in the Truman administration attended the Potsdam Conference.

Critical of the concentration of power in the Fair Deal government and criticized for his firm hand with the

Soviets as secretary of state, Byrnes resigned from Truman's cabinet in 1947. For four years he practiced law in South Carolina and in Washington, D.C., with the firm, Hogan & Hartson. A proponent of states' rights and separate-but-equal schooling for blacks, Byrnes was elected governor of South Carolina in 1950. This was the last public office of his distinguished career. Few justices held so many positions of responsibility after leaving the bench.

Byrnes' autobiography, *All in a Lifetime* (1958), was written during his retirement. His first book, *Speaking Frankly,* published in 1947, described his firsthand experience with postwar diplomacy. Byrnes died of a heart attack April 9, 1972, in Columbia, S.C.

Robert Houghwout Jackson
(1941-1954)

Born: Feb. 13, 1892, Spring Creek, Pa.

Education: local schools in Frewsburg, N.Y.; Albany (N.Y.) Law School, 1912.

Official Positions: general counsel, Internal Revenue Bureau, 1934-36; special counsel, Securities and Exchange Commission, 1935; assistant attorney general, 1936-38; solicitor general, 1938-39; attorney general, 1940-41; chief United States prosecutor, Nuremberg war crimes trial, 1945-46.

Supreme Court Appointment: nominated associate justice by President Franklin D. Roosevelt June 12, 1941, to replace Harlan F. Stone, who was promoted to Chief Justice; confirmed by the Senate July 7, 1941, by a voice vote; replaced on court by John Marshall Harlan, nominated by President Eisenhower.

Family: married Irene Gerhardt April 24, 1916; one daughter, one son.

Died: Oct. 9, 1954, Washington, D.C.

Personal Background

A descendant of eighteenth-century settlers of Warren County, Pa., Jackson grew up across the border near Jamestown, N.Y., and began his law career there at 18 as an apprentice in a local firm. After a year studying law at Albany Law School, he began his career in earnest, laying the foundation for a lucrative general practice.

Public Career

Jackson entered politics at 21 when he was elected a Democratic state committeeman. His term as committeeman, marked by controversy over dispensing patronage posts, convinced Jackson that he preferred law to politics and he refused to run for re-election; he said later that politics had "filled my office with people who came there asking political favors and waging political fights."

His early contact with Roosevelt and his growing reputation as a talented advocate brought Jackson to Washington in 1934 as the counsel to the Internal Revenue Bureau, where he won a much-publicized $750,000 judgment in an income tax suit brought against the fabulously wealthy former Treasury Secretary Andrew W. Mellon. Jackson rose quickly in the Roosevelt administration: he was named assistant attorney general in 1936, solicitor general in 1938 and attorney general in 1940.

During that time, Jackson also became one of Roosevelt's closest advisers and supporters. He campaigned for the president's re-election in 1936 and was a chief assistant at the 1940 Democratic convention, supported the president's court-packing scheme and devised the legal means for Roosevelt in 1940 to give destroyers to Great Britain in exchange for American bases on British territories in the Caribbean, the West Indies and the North Atlantic.

Named to the Supreme Court in July 1941 to the seat vacated after Justice Stone was appointed Chief Justice, Jackson also served as the chief United States prosecutor at the Nuremburg war crimes trial in 1945-46. He originated the concept upon which the successful prosecution of the Nazi leaders was based, i.e., that it is a crime against international society to plan and wage an aggressive war.

While Jackson was in Germany, growing dissension among the Supreme Court justices reached a climax; it was reported that on the death of Chief Justice Harlan F. Stone, two justices had threatened to resign if Jackson was elevated to Chief Justice. Jackson exacerbated the controversy by releasing a letter he had written to President Truman castigating Justice Hugo L. Black for his participation in a case argued by Black's former law partner.

Jackson remained on the court until his death in 1954. He was the author of *The Struggle for Judicial Supremacy,* 1941; *Full Faith and Credit — The Lawyer's Clause of the Constitution,* 1945; *The Case Against the Nazi War Criminals,* 1946; *The Nuremberg Case,* 1947; and *The Supreme Court in the American System of Government,* 1955.

Wiley Blount Rutledge
(1943-1949)

Born: July 20, 1894, Cloverport, Ky.

Education: University of Wisconsin, A.B., 1914; University of Colorado, LL.B. 1922.

Official Positions: judge, Court of Appeals for District of Columbia, 1939-43.

Supreme Court Appointment: nominated associate justice by President Franklin D. Roosevelt Jan. 11, 1943, to replace James F. Byrnes, who resigned; confirmed by the Senate Feb. 8, 1943, by a voice vote; replaced on court by Sherman Minton, nominated by President Truman.

Family: married Annabel Person August 28, 1917; two daughters, one son.

Died: Sept. 10, 1949, York, Maine.

Personal Background

In the small town of Cloverport, Ky., Mary Lou (Wigginton) Rutledge gave birth to her first son July 20, 1894, and named him for his father, Wiley Blount, a backwoods Baptist preacher. His mother's tubercular condition and his father's search for a pastorate caused the Rutledge family to move from Texas to Louisiana to North Carolina, finally settling in Asheville, N.C., where Pastor Rutledge found a position. When Wiley was nine years old, his mother died, whereupon his father took his three children and headed west again. Although raised in the conservative Christian tradition, Wiley Blount Rutledge later adopted the Unitarian faith.

An ancient-languages major and debating team captain, Rutledge transferred his junior year from Marysville College in Tennessee to the University of Wisconsin, from which he was graduated in 1914. Unable to afford legal studies there, he attended instead the University of Indiana law school part-time, supporting himself as a high school teacher in Bloomington.

Law school and teaching responsibilities proved too strenuous for Rutledge's health. He contracted a serious case of tuberculosis and went to recover in the mountains near Asheville. Two years later he married Annabel Person, a classmate at Marysville. They lived in New Mexico and Colorado, where he taught high school and continued to recuperate. He resumed his legal studies full-time at the University of Colorado and graduated in 1922, seven years after receiving his undergraduate degree. For the next two years Rutledge practiced law with the Boulder law firm, Goss, Kimbrough & Hutchinson, before returning to academia as a professor of law, and dean for more than 15 years.

Public Career

Rutledge first came to Franklin Delano Roosevelt's attention because of his outspoken support for the president's court-packing plan as dean of the University of Iowa College of Law from 1935-1939. So unpopular was the proposed judicial reorganization in the midwest that several Iowa state legislators threatened to withhold university salary increases to protest Dean Rutledge's unorthodox liberal stand. In a letter to his friend Irving Brant of the *St. Louis Star-Times* in 1936, Rutledge expressed confidence that Roosevelt would be able to gain control of the court if re-elected: "I feel sure he will have the opportunity to make a sufficient number of liberal appointments to undo the major harm."

Recommended by Justice Frankfurter and Irving Brant, Rutledge himself was appointed to the court seven years later. Although he had four years of federal judicial experience as a Roosevelt appointee to the Court of Appeals for the District of Columbia, some doubted his legal qualifications for the job. During Senate confirmation hearings Senator William Langer challenged "the wisdom of the choice of this inexperienced member of the bar. . . . Second-best generals and admirals will not bring us victory and peace. Second-best justices or legal mediocrities will not insure justice in our land."

Judicial experience, however, was not the president's deciding criterion. As he explained to his eighth and last Supreme Court appointee, "Wiley, we had a number of candidates for the court who were highly qualified, but they didn't have geography — you have that." Rutledge died suddenly September 10, 1949, after six years on the court.

Harold Hitz Burton
(1945-1958)

Born: June 22, 1888, Jamaica Plain, Mass.

Education: Bowdoin College, A.B., 1909; Harvard University LL.B., 1912.

Official Positions: Ohio House of Representatives, 1929; director of law, Cleveland, 1929-1932; acting mayor of Cleveland, Nov. 9, 1931-Feb. 20, 1932; mayor of Cleveland, 1935-40; United States Senate, 1941-45.

Supreme Court Appointment: nominated associate justice by President Harry S Truman Sept. 19, 1945, to replace Owen J. Roberts, who retired; confirmed by the U.S. Senate Sept. 19, 1945, by a voice vote; replaced by Potter Stewart, appointed by President Eisenhower.

Family: married Selma Florence Smith June 15, 1912; two daughters, two sons.

Died: Oct. 28, 1964, Washington, D.C.

Personal Background

Burton grew up in Jamaica Plain, Mass., a suburb of Boston, in a Republican, Unitarian family. He received a B.A. from Bowdoin College, Brunswick, Maine, in 1909, and an LL.B. from Harvard University in 1912. He married a local woman, Selma Florence Smith of West Newton, Mass., and together they headed to Ohio, where Burton believed it would be easier to establish a law practice than in the East.

During the next five years, Burton engaged in private practice in Ohio (1912-14), worked for a Utah public utility (1914-16), and was an attorney for an Idaho public utility (1917). When World War I began, he was assigned to the 361st Infantry, United States Army, where he rose to the rank of captain. After the war, Burton returned to Cleveland and private practice.

Public Career

Burton served a one-year term as a Republican representative to the Ohio State legislature in 1929 and, that same year, was named Cleveland's director of law, a position he held until 1932. After a brief term as acting mayor of Cleveland in 1931-32, he won the 1935 mayoral election running as a reformer who would rid the city of gangsters. Twice re-elected by the largest majorities in the city's history, he was elected to the U.S. Senate in 1941. There he gained a reputation as an internationalist, particularly for his sponsorship of the "B²H²" resolution of 1943 which urged United States participation in a postwar international peace organization. (The resolution was named after its four sponsors, Sens. Burton, Joseph Ball, R-Minn., Carl Hatch, D-N.M., and Joseph Lister Hill, D-Ala.) Burton was also a member of the "Truman Committee" investigating fraudulent war claims against the government.

Justice Owen J. Roberts' retirement from the court July 31, 1945, gave President Truman his first opportunity to appoint a Supreme Court justice. The membership of the "New Deal" court was heavily Democratic, with the single exception of Chief Justice Harlan Fiske Stone, who had been appointed an associate justice by Republican President Calvin Coolidge. He had been named Chief Justice, however, by President Roosevelt. Truman was under considerable pressure to name a Republican to the vacant seat. By naming Burton, the president not only improved his relationship with Republican congressional leaders but also gained a justice who, though he was a member of the opposition, was at least a former colleague.

After 13 years on the bench, Burton, suffering from the debilitating Parkinson's disease, retired Oct. 13, 1958. He died six years later in Washington, D.C.

Frederick Moore Vinson
(1946-1953)

Born: January 22, 1890, Louisa, Ky.
Education: Centre College, A.B., 1909; LL.B., 1911.
Official Positions: commonwealth's attorney, 32nd judicial district, 1921-1924; U.S. House of Representatives, D-Ky., 1924-1929, 1931-1938; judge, Court of Appeals for District of Columbia, 1938-1943; director, Office of Economic Stabilization, 1943-1945; Federal Loan Administrator, 1945; director, Office of War Mobilization and Reconversion, 1945; secretary of the Treasury, 1945-1946.
Supreme Court Appointment: nominated Chief Justice by President Harry S Truman June 6, 1946, to replace Chief Justice Harlan F. Stone, who died; confirmed by the Senate June 20, 1946, by a voice vote; replaced on court by Earl Warren, nominated by President Eisenhower.
Family: married Roberta Dixson, January 24, 1923; two sons.
Died: September 8, 1953, Washington, D.C.

Personal Background

In the small town of Louisa, Ky., on Jan. 22, 1890, Fred M. — christened Frederick Moore — Vinson was born to James Vinson, the county jailer, and his wife, Virginia Ferguson Vinson. He worked his way through school, graduating with an A.B. from Centre College, Ky., in 1909 and from law school two years later. His 17 years of legal practice in the state began in 1911 when he passed the bar at the age of 21.

Public Career

Vinson's first official position came as commonwealth attorney for Kentucky's 32nd judicial district. When a vacancy occurred in Kentucky's 9th district for a U.S.

congressional seat, Vinson, a resident for 33 years and well-known for his grocery, milling and banking enterprises as well as for his legal practice, was elected. He served in the House from 1924-29 and from 1931-38, the intervening years spent practicing law in Ashland, Ky. An influential member of the House Ways and Means Committee, Vinson worked for passage of President Roosevelt's tax and coal programs.

He resigned his seat in 1938 to become judge for the Court of Appeals in the District of Columbia, a position to which he was appointed by Roosevelt in recognition of his New Deal support. After 12 years of legislative experience and five years in the federal judiciary, Vinson began his career in the executive branch as director of the Office of Economic Stabilization in the Roosevelt administration. His knowledge of tax matters and his ties with Congress well qualified him for this position.

Vinson gained further administrative experience as Federal Loan Administrator and director of the Office of War Mobilization and Reconversion, a post previously held by former congressman and Supreme Court Justice James F. Byrnes.

When Harry S Truman became president in 1945, he recognized his need for experienced advisers. Vinson's two years in the previous administration as a political organizer and congressional liaison made him valuable to Truman, who appointed him secretary of the Treasury. In this position Vinson administered the last of the war bond drives and recommended the Revenue Act of 1945 to raise taxes.

After the death of Harlan F. Stone, Vinson was appointed Chief Justice on June 6, 1946. Truman recognized in his friend and adviser someone who realized the need for strong government by the executive. As a congressman, Vinson had endorsed President Roosevelt's court-packing plan and on the court usually supported presidential authority in Truman's controversial decisions involving labor and Cold War-generated national security measures.

Such was the president's esteem for Vinson that he hoped he would succeed him in office. Vinson, however, did not aspire to the presidency.

Vinson died of a heart attack Sept. 8, 1953, ending seven years of service on the court.

Tom Campbell Clark
(1949-1967)

Born: Sept. 23, 1899, Dallas, Texas.
Education: University of Texas, A.B., 1921; L.L.B., 1922.
Official Positions: civil district attorney, Dallas County, Texas, 1927-1932; special assistant, Justice Department, 1937-1943; assistant attorney general, 1943-1945; attorney general, 1945-1949; director, Federal Judicial Cen-

ter, 1968-1970; U.S. Court of Appeals, various circuits, by special arrangement, 1967-1977.

Supreme Court Appointment: nominated associate justice by President Harry S Truman Aug. 2, 1949, to replace Frank Murphy, who died; confirmed by the U.S. Senate Aug. 18, 1949, by a 73-8 vote; replaced on the court by Thurgood Marshall, nominated by President Johnson.

Family: Married Mary Jane Ramsey Nov. 8, 1924; one daughter, two sons.

Died: June 13, 1977, New York, N.Y.

Personal Background

The son of a prominent Dallas lawyer active in Democratic politics in Texas, Tom Clark maintained a close relationship with the Democratic party throughout most of his life. After a brief stint in the infantry that failed to extend beyond training in Texas because the war ended, Clark entered the University of Texas, where he received his A.B. in 1921 and his LL.B. a year later. While a student he met Mary Jane Ramsey, the daughter of a Texas supreme court justice. They were married in 1924.

Public Career

Clark practiced law in his father's firm until his friendship with the Democratic party in general — and Tom Connally, D-Texas (House 1917-29, Senate 1929-53), in particular — resulted in his appointment as Dallas civil district attorney in 1927. He returned to private practice in 1932.

Named a special assistant in the Justice Department in 1937, Clark worked in antitrust matters, was the civilian coordinator of the program to evacuate Japanese-Americans from the West Coast, and prosecuted fraudulent war claims, an activity which brought him into contact with then-Sen. Harry S Truman, D-Mo., head of the Senate War Investigating Committee. Clark was promoted to assistant attorney general in 1943 and the following year cultivated his friendship with Truman by supporting his vice presidential bid at the Democratic convention. When Truman assumed the presidency after the death of Franklin Roosevelt in 1945, he chose Clark as his attorney general. During his four years as the president's lawyer, Clark remained active in antitrust and led the efforts of his department to prosecute the American leaders of the Communist Party and other alleged subversives. The department also drafted the first attorney general's list of dangerous political organizations. Truman relied on the anticommunist zeal of his Justice Department to defend his administration against charges of being "soft" on communism in the 1948 presidential campaign.

Truman, in his third appointment to the Supreme Court, nominated Clark Aug. 2, 1949, to replace Justice Frank Murphy, the only Roman Catholic then on the bench. The president was criticized for his choice of Clark, a Presbyterian, but Truman argued that religious considerations should not apply to the selection of Supreme Court justices.

To avoid any appearance of a conflict of interest, Clark resigned from the court in 1967 when President Johnson named his son, Ramsey Clark, attorney general.

Clark was a founder of the Federal Judicial Center, a unit within the judicial branch that studies ways to improve the administration of the courts, and served as its first director, 1968-1970. Until his death in June 1977, he accepted assignments on various circuits of the United States Court of Appeals to help ease the federal caseload.

Sherman Minton
(1949-1956)

Born: October 20, 1890, Georgetown, Ind.

Education: Indiana University, LL.B., 1915; Yale University, LL.M., 1917.

Official Positions: Indiana public counselor, 1933-1934; U.S. Senate, D-Ind., 1935-1941; administrative assistant to President Franklin Delano Roosevelt, 1941; federal judge, Seventh Circuit Court of Appeals, 1941-1949.

Supreme Court Appointment: nominated associate justice by President Harry S Truman September 15, 1949, to replace Wiley B. Rutledge, who died; confirmed by the U.S. Senate October 4, 1949, by a 48-16 vote; replaced on court by William J. Brennan Jr, nominated by President Eisenhower.

Family: married Gertrude Gurtz August 11, 1917; two sons, one daughter.

Died: April 9, 1965, in New Albany, Ind.

Personal Background

Sherman Minton, the son of John Evan and Emma Lyvers Minton, was born on Oct. 20, 1890, in the village of Georgetown, Ind., eight miles from New Albany, his residence for many years, and was raised in a middle-class midwestern home. Tall and broad-shouldered, Shay, as he was called by his friends, attended Indiana University where he excelled in football and basketball as well as his studies. In 1925 he graduated at the top of his class at the law college; future GOP presidential candidate Wendell L. Willkie and Paul V. McNutt, who later became governor of Indiana, were classmates. After graduation Minton left the state with a $500 scholarship to attend Yale Law School for a year of graduate studies.

Public Career

McNutt appointed his former classmate and fellow liberal Democrat to his first official position, as an Indiana public counselor, in 1933. Two years later Minton successfully ran for the Senate on the New Deal ticket. "Sure I'm a New Dealer. I'd be ashamed to be an old dealer," he once explained. Minton's political career was adversely affected by his other notable classmate, Willkie. Minton lost his bid for Senate re-election in 1940 due to support for the Willkie ticket in their home state of Indiana.

Beginning his third term as president, Franklin Delano Roosevelt remembered Minton's Senate endorsement of his plan to pack the court with justices of his choosing and his support for other New Deal policies. In 1941 the president asked Minton to join his staff as an adviser in charge of coordinating military agencies and later that year appointed him to the Seventh Circuit Court of Appeals. In the White House, Minton backed Harry S Truman's efforts in the Senate to establish a new committee to investigate defense activities. The two men had become good friends in 1935 as freshman senators. "As far as you are concerned I am just as approachable as I was when we sat together in the Senate," President Truman wrote Minton ten years later.

After Wiley B. Rutledge's death it took Truman only five days to name his replacement on the Supreme Court: Sherman Minton, a fellow midwesterner, a political supporter and friend of nearly 15 years. He was appointed to the court September 15, 1949. Although a liberal legislator, Minton proved to be a conservative justice. Most of his decisions favored the restrictive powers of the government over the civil liberties of the individual.

Pernicious anemia forced Minton to resign on Oct. 15, 1956, after seven years of service. His retirement announcement suggests that perhaps his career on the court had not been as influential as he might have hoped: "There will be more interest in who will succeed me than in my passing. I'm an echo."

He spent the last nine years of his life in retirement in his hometown of New Albany, Ind., and died in 1965.

Earl Warren
(1953-1969)

Born: March 19, 1891, Los Angeles, Calif.
Education: University of California, B.L., 1912; J. D., 1914.
Official Positions: deputy city attorney of Oakland, Calif., 1919-20; deputy assistant district attorney, Alameda County, 1920-23; chief deputy district attorney, Alameda County, 1923-25; district attorney, Alameda County, 1925-39; attorney general of California, 1939-43; governor of California, 1943-53.
Supreme Court Appointment: nominated Chief Justice by President Dwight D. Eisenhower Sept. 30, 1953, to replace Chief Justice Fred M. Vinson, who died; confirmed March 1, 1954, by a voice vote; replaced on the court by Warren E. Burger, nominated by President Nixon.
Family: married Nina P. Meyers Oct. 14, 1925; three sons, three daughters.
Died: July 9, 1974, Washington, D.C.

Personal Background

Warren was born in Los Angeles, Calif., the son of Scandanavian immigrant parents. Soon afterwards, the family moved to Bakersfield, where his father worked as a railroad car repairman. In 1938, after Warren had become active in politics, his father was bludgeoned to death in a crime that was never solved.

Warren worked his way through college and law school at the University of California. After graduation, he worked in law offices in San Francisco and Oakland, the only time in his career that he engaged in private practice.

Public Career

From 1920 until his resignation from the Supreme Court in 1969, Warren served without interruption in public office. His first post was deputy city attorney for Oakland. Then Warren was named a deputy district attorney for Alameda County, which embraces the cities of Oakland, Alameda, and Berkeley.

In 1925 Warren was appointed district attorney when the incumbent resigned. He won election to the post in his own right in 1926, 1930, and 1934. During his 14 years as district attorney, Warren developed a reputation as a crime fighter, sending a city manager and several councilmen to jail on graft charges and smashing a crooked deal involving garbage collection.

A Republican, Warren decided in 1938 to run for state attorney general. He cross-filed and won three primaries — his own party's, as well as the Democratic and Progressive Party contests.

In 1942 Warren ran for governor of California. Although he was at first rated an underdog, he wound up defeating incumbent Democratic Governor Culbert Olson by a margin of 342,000, winning 57.1 percent of the total votes cast. He was twice re-elected, winning the Democratic as well as the Republican nomination in 1946 and defeating Democrat James Roosevelt, son of President Franklin D. Roosevelt, by an almost two-to-one margin in 1950.

At first viewed as a conservative governor — he denounced "communistic radicals" and supported the wartime federal order to move all persons of Japanese ancestry away from the West Coast — Warren developed a progressive image after the war. In 1945 he proposed a state program of prepaid medical insurance and later championed liberal pension and welfare benefits.

Warren made two bids for national political office. In 1948 he ran for vice president on the Republican ticket with Gov. Thomas E. Dewey of New York. In 1952 he sought the Republican presidential nomination. But with little chance to win, he threw his support at a crucial moment behind Gen. Dwight D. Eisenhower, helping him win the battle against Sen. Robert A. Taft of Ohio for the nomination.

That support resulted in Eisenhower's political indebtedness to Warren, which the president repaid in 1953, after the death of Chief Justice Fred M. Vinson, by nominating the Californian to replace him. Reflecting on his choice years later in light of the Warren Court's liberal record, Eisenhower called the Warren appointment "the biggest damn-fool mistake I ever made."

In addition to his work on the court, Warren headed the commission which investigated the assassination of President John F. Kennedy. Warren retired in 1969, and died five years later.

John Marshall Harlan
(1955-1971)

Born: May 20, 1899, Chicago, Ill.

Education: Princeton University, B.A., 1920; Rhodes Scholar, Oxford University, Balliol College, B.A. in jurisprudence, 1923; New York Law School, LL.B., 1925.

Official Positions: assistant U.S. attorney, southern district of New York, 1925-27; special assistant attorney general of New York state, 1928-30; chief counsel, New York State Crime Commission, 1951-53; judge, U.S. Court of Appeals for the Second Circuit, 1954-55.

Supreme Court Appointment: nominated associate justice by President Dwight D. Eisenhower Nov. 8, 1954, to replace Robert Jackson, who died; Senate consideration postponed, formally renominated Jan. 10, 1955; confirmed by the U.S. Senate on March 16, 1955, by a 71-11 vote; replaced on the court by William H. Rehnquist, nominated by President Nixon.

Family: married Ethel Andrews Nov. 10, 1928; one daughter.

Died: Dec. 29, 1971, Washington D.C.

Personal Background

The namesake and grandson of Supreme Court Justice (1877-1911) John Marshall Harlan, Harlan was born in Chicago, where his father was a prominent attorney. His father, John Maynard Harlan, was also engaged in politics, running two losing races for mayor of Chicago near the turn of the century.

The younger Harlan attended Princeton University, graduating in 1920. Awarded a Rhodes Scholarship, he spent the next three years studying jurisprudence at Balliol College, Oxford. Returning to the United States, he earned his law degree in 1924 from New York Law School.

Public Career

For the next 25 years Harlan was a member of a prominent Wall Street law firm, but took periodic leaves to serve in various public positions. In 1925 he became an assistant U.S. attorney for the southern district of New York. He returned to private practice but soon left again, this time to serve as one of the special prosecutors in a state investigation of municipal graft.

During World War II, Harlan served as head of the Operational Analysis Section of the Eighth Air Force. After the war he returned to private practice, but was soon called again to public service. From 1951 to 1953 he was chief counsel to the New York State Crime Commission, which Gov. Thomas E. Dewey had appointed to investigate the relationship between organized crime and state government.

During the same period, Harlan also became active in various professional organizations, serving as chairman of the committee on professional ethics of the Association of the Bar of the City of New York and later as chairman of its committee on the judiciary and as vice president of the association.

A lifelong Republican, Harlan was nominated in January 1954 by President Eisenhower to the U.S. court of appeals for the second circuit. Harlan had hardly begun his work there, however, when the president named him in November 1954 to the U.S. Supreme Court. The Senate, then in special session to consider the censure of Sen. Joseph R. McCarthy, postponed consideration of his nomination until the new Congress met in 1955, so Harlan remained on the appeals court until confirmed by the Senate in March 1955.

William Joseph Brennan Jr.
(1956-   )

Born: April 25, 1906, Newark, N.J.

Education: University of Pennsylvania, B.S., 1928; Harvard Law School, LL.B., 1931.

Official Positions: New Jersey superior court judge, 1949-50; appellate division, 1950-52; associate justice, New Jersey supreme court, 1952-56.

Supreme Court Appointment: received a recess appointment as an associate justice by President Dwight D. Eisenhower Oct. 16, 1956, to replace Sherman Minton, who resigned; nominated as an associate justice by President Eisenhower Jan. 14, 1957; confirmed by the U.S. Senate March 19, 1957 by a voice vote.

Family: married Marjorie Leonard May 5, 1928; two sons, one daughter.

Personal Background

Brennan was born in Newark, N.J., the second of eight children of Irish parents who immigrated to the United States in 1890. Brennan displayed impressive academic abilities early in life. He was an outstanding student in high school, an honors student at the University of Pennsylvania's Wharton School of Finance, and graduated in the top 10 percent of his Harvard Law School Class in 1931.

After law school Brennan returned to Newark, where he joined a prominent law firm. After the passage of the Wagner Labor Act in 1935, he began to specialize in labor law.

With the outbreak of World War II, Brennan entered the Army, serving as a manpower troubleshooter on the staff of the undersecretary of war, Robert B. Patterson. At the conclusion of the war, Brennan returned to his old law firm. But as his practice swelled, Brennan, a devoted family man, began to resent the demands which it placed on his time.

Public Career

A desire to temper the pace of his work was one of the reasons Brennan accepted an appointment to the newly created New Jersey superior court in 1949. Brennan had been a leader in the movement to establish the court as part of a large program of judicial reform. Thus it was not surprising when Republican Gov. Alfred E. Driscoll named Brennan, a registered but inactive Democrat, to the court.

During his tenure on the superior court, Brennan's use of pre-trial procedures to speed up the disposition of cases brought him to the attention of New Jersey supreme court justice Arthur T. Vanderbilt. It was reportedly at Vanderbilt's suggestion that Brennan was moved first in 1950 to the appellate division of the superior court and then in 1952 to the state supreme court. Late in 1956, when President

Eisenhower was looking for a justice to replace Sherman Minton, Vanderbilt and others strongly recommended Brennan for the post, and Eisenhower gave him a recess appointment in October. There was some criticism that Eisenhower was playing politics by nominating a Roman Catholic Democrat to the bench so close to the election in order to curry favor with voters. But Brennan's established integrity and non-political background minimized the impact of the charges.

Charles Evans Whittaker
(1957-1962)

Born: February 22, 1901, Troy, Kansas.
Education: University of Kansas City Law School, LL.B., 1924.
Official Positions: federal judge, U.S. District Court for Western District of Missouri, 1954-1956; judge, Eighth Circuit Court of Appeals, 1956-1957.
Supreme Court Appointment: nominated associate justice by President Dwight D. Eisenhower March 2, 1957, to replace Stanley Reed, who resigned; confirmed by the U.S. Senate March 19, 1957, by a voice vote; replaced on court by Byron R. White, nominated by President Kennedy.
Family: married Winifred R. Pugh, July 7, 1928; three sons.
Died: November 26, 1973, Kansas City, Missouri.

Personal Background

Charles Evans Whittaker's beginnings were humble. The son of Charles and Ida Miller Whittaker, he was born in eastern Kansas on February 22, 1901, and raised on his father's farm. After his nomination to the Supreme Court, Whittaker described to the Senate Judiciary Committee his early life: "I went to school in a little white school house on the corner of my father's farm through nine grades and then I went to high school in Troy, Kansas, and rode a pony to school through six miles of mud night and morning for about a year and a half."

Whittaker quit school after his mother died on his sixteenth birthday. Four years later he applied to the University of Kansas City Law School and was accepted only after agreeing to private tutoring in the high school subjects he had missed. His education was financed from the sale of pelts of animals he trapped on the Kansas plains and from part-time work as an office boy in the law firm, Watson, Gage & Ess. In 1923 he passed the Missouri bar exams and a year later graduated from law school.

Whittaker joined the law firm that he had served as office boy and after two years became a senior partner. He represented many corporate clients including Union Pacific and Montgomery Ward.

Public Career

Whittaker served as president of the Missouri Bar Association from 1953-1954. His distinguished legal career in the state included positions on the U.S. District Court for the Western District from 1954 to 1956 and on the U.S. Court of Appeals for the Eighth Circuit in 1956 and 1957.

President Eisenhower considered previous judicial experience one of the most important criteria for a Supreme Court justice. Whittaker's outstanding qualifications as well as his ties to the Republican party made him a likely choice to fill the vacancy left by Stanley Reed's retirement. On March 19, 1957, Charles Whittaker became the first Supreme Court justice born in Kansas and appointed from Missouri.

Physically exhausted from overwork, Whittaker followed his doctor's advice and resigned from the court at the age of 61 after only five years of service.

Following his retirement Whittaker did not return to his former legal practice nor was he active in public life. In 1965 he served on the legal staff of General Motors and the following year was asked by the Senate Committee on Standards and Conduct to help devise a code of senatorial ethics. The spread of civil disobedience in the 1960s particularly disturbed him and he addressed the American Bar Association on various occasions concerning the need for "redress in the courts rather than in the streets."

Potter Stewart
(1958-   )

Born: Jan. 23, 1915, Jackson, Mich.
Education: Yale University, B.A., cum laude, 1937; Yale Law School, LL.B., cum laude, 1941; fellow, Cambridge University, Cambridge, England, 1937-38.
Official Positions: member, Cincinnati, Ohio, city council 1950-53; vice mayor of Cincinnati, 1952-53; judge, U.S. Court of Appeals for the sixth circuit, 1954-58.
Supreme Court Appointment: received recess appointment as associate justice from President Dwight D. Eisenhower Oct. 14, 1958, to replace Harold H. Burton, who resigned; nominated associate justice by President Eisenhower Jan. 17, 1959; confirmed by the U.S. Senate May 5, 1959, by a 70-17 vote.
Family: married Mary Ann Bertles April 24, 1943; two sons, one daughter.

Personal Background

Stewart is the son of an established middle-class Cincinnati family with a strong tradition of public service and a respect for the benefits of a good education. Stewart's father, James Garfield Stewart, was mayor of Cincinnati from 1938 to 1947 and was the Republican nominee for governor of Ohio in 1944. He served on the Ohio supreme court from 1947 until his death in 1959.

After early schooling in Cincinnati, Stewart was sent to two of the most prestigious eastern schools — Hotchkiss preparatory and Yale University, where he received numerous academic honors and graduated Phi Beta Kappa in 1937. After completing his undergraduate work at Yale, he spent a year abroad doing postgraduate work at Cambridge University in England. Returning to the United States in 1938, he began law school at Yale. After graduation in 1941, Stewart moved to New York, where he joined a Wall Street law firm. He had hardly begun work there, however, when World War II broke out and he joined the Navy. Stewart found himself a deck officer aboard oil tankers plying the Atlantic and Mediterranean.

After the war, Stewart at first returned to his New York law practice but soon moved to his home town of Cincinnati, where he joined one of its leading law firms.

Public Career

Once Stewart settled in Cincinnati, he took up the family's tradition of public service. He was twice elected to the city council and served one term as vice mayor. He was also actively involved in the 1948 and 1952 Republican presidential campaigns. In both years, he supported the efforts of his friend Sen. Robert A. Taft to secure the Republican presidential nomination. When Eisenhower won the party's endorsement instead in 1952, Stewart actively supported him in the fall campaign.

Stewart's appointment in 1954 to the U.S. Court of Appeals for the sixth circuit ended his direct participation in politics. He was President Eisenhower's fifth and last appointment to the Supreme Court. He received a recess appointment in 1958, and Eisenhower sent his nomination to the new Congress early in 1959.

Byron Raymond White
(1962-   )

Born: June 8, 1917, Fort Collins, Colo.

Education: University of Colorado, B.A., Phi Beta Kappa, 1938; Rhodes Scholar, Oxford University, 1939; Yale Law School, LL.B., magna cum laude, 1946.

Official Positions: law clerk to Chief Justice Fred M. Vinson, 1946-47; U.S. deputy attorney general, 1961-62.

Supreme Court Appointment: nominated associate justice by President John F. Kennedy March 30, 1962, to replace Charles E. Whittaker, who resigned; confirmed by the U.S. Senate April 11, 1962, by a voice vote.

Family: married Marion Stearns, 1946; one son, one daughter.

Personal Background

White was born in Fort Collins, Colo., but grew up in Wellington, a small town in the sugar beet area of the state.

His father was in the lumber business and served as a Republican mayor of Wellington.

Ranking first in his high school class, White in 1934 won a scholarship to the University of Colorado, where he earned a reputation as an outstanding scholar-athlete. He was first in his class, a member of Phi Beta Kappa and the winner of three varsity letters in football, four in basketball and three in baseball. By the end of his college career in 1938 he had been dubbed "Whizzer" White for his prowess as a football player, a performance which earned him both a national reputation and a one-year contract with the old Pittsburgh Pirates professional football team.

But after a year as a pro football player, White sailed for England to attend Oxford University, where he had received a coveted Rhodes Scholarship. When World War II broke out in September 1939, White returned to the United States and enrolled in Yale Law School, alternating law study with playing professional football for the Detroit Lions.

When the United States entered the war, White served in the Navy in the South Pacific. He returned to Yale after the war, earning his law degree magna cum laude.

Public Career

After graduation from law school, White served as law clerk to the new Chief Justice, Fred M. Vinson. In 1947 he returned to his native Colorado, where for the next 14 years he practiced law with a prominent Denver law firm.

Several times during his adult life, White had crossed paths with the young John F. Kennedy. The two first met when White was studying at Oxford and Kennedy's father, Joseph, was ambassador to the Court of St. James. They met again during White's wartime service in the South Pacific. And when White clerked for Vinson in Washington in 1946-47, he renewed his acquaintance with Kennedy, then a freshman U.S. Representative.

In 1960, when Kennedy decided to run for president, White joined the campaign and headed the pre-convention Kennedy effort in Colorado. After Kennedy's nomination, White became chairman of the National Citizens for Kennedy organization, designed to attract independents and Republicans.

After his election, Kennedy named White to the post of deputy attorney general, a position he held until Kennedy named him to the Supreme Court in 1962.

Arthur Joseph Goldberg
(1962-1965)

Born: Aug. 8, 1908, Chicago, Ill.

Education: Northwestern University, B.S.L., 1929; J.D., summa cum laude, 1930.

Official Positions: Secretary of Labor, 1961-1962; United States Ambassador to the United Nations, 1965-1968.

Supreme Court Appointment: nominated associate justice by President John F. Kennedy Aug. 29, 1962, to replace Felix Frankfurter, who retired; confirmed by the U.S. Senate Sept. 25, 1962, by a voice vote. Appointed U.S. Ambassador to the United Nations July 20, 1965, by President Lyndon B. Johnson; replaced on the court by Abe Fortas, nominated by President Johnson.

Family: married Dorothy Kurgans July 18, 1931; one daughter, one son.

Personal Background

The youngest of 11 children born to Russian Jewish immigrants, Goldberg was admitted to the Illinois bar at age 20. He first gained national attention as counsel to the Chicago Newspaper Guild during its 1938 strike. After serving as a special assistant in the Office of Strategic Services during World War II, Goldberg returned to the practice of labor law, representing both the Congress of Industrial Organizations (CIO) and the United Steelworkers of America. He played a key role in the 1955 merger of the CIO with the American Federation of Labor and worked as a special counsel to the AFL-CIO until 1961.

Public Career

Appointed secretary of labor in the first year of the Kennedy administration, Goldberg's tenure saw the passage of the Area Redevelopment Act of 1961, congressional approval of an increase in the minimum wage and the reorganization of the Office of Manpower Administration (now the Employment and Training Administration).

Goldberg was President Kennedy's second Supreme Court appointment, named Aug. 29, 1962, to replace Felix Frankfurter, who had held the "Jewish seat" since 1939. It had been occupied formerly by Justice Benjamin N. Cardozo, 1932-38.

President Johnson named Goldberg U.S. Ambassador to the United Nations July 20, 1965, to replace Adlai Stevenson, who had died July 14 in London. Goldberg resigned the post in 1968. After an unsuccessful race for governor of New York against Republican incumbent Nelson Rockefeller in 1970, Goldberg returned to Washington, D.C., where he remains in private practice. A frequent guest instructor at universities and colleges, he is the author of *AFL-CIO: Labor United*, 1956; *Defenses of Freedom*, 1966; *Equal Justice: The Warren Era of the Supreme Court*, 1972.

Abe Fortas
(1965-1969)

Born: June 19, 1910, Memphis, Tenn.

Education: Southwestern College, A.B., 1930; Yale Law School, LL.B., 1933.

Official Positions: assistant director, corporate reorganization study, Securities and Exchange Commission, 1934-37; assistant director, public utilities division, Securities and Exchange Commission, 1938-39; general counsel, Public Works Administration, 1939-40, and counsel to the bituminous coal division, 1939-41; director, division of power, Department of the Interior, 1941-42; under secretary of the interior, 1942-46.

Supreme Court Appointment: nominated associate justice by President Lyndon B. Johnson July 28, 1965, to replace Arthur J. Goldberg, who resigned; confirmed by the U.S. Senate Aug. 11, 1965, by a voice vote; replaced on the court by Harry A. Blackmun, nominated by President Nixon.

Family: married Carolyn Eugenia Agger July 9, 1935.

Personal Background

Fortas, the son of an English immigrant cabinetmaker, was born on June 19, 1910, in Memphis, Tenn. After working his way through Southwestern College in Memphis, from which he received a B.A. in 1930, Fortas went north to Yale Law School. He served as editor of the school's law journal and graduated in 1933.

Fortas developed an interest in music and began to play the violin in various string quartets, a practice he has continued throughout his life. In 1935 he married Carolyn Eugenia Agger, who became a renowned tax lawyer in her own right.

Upon graduation, Fortas became an associate professor of law at Yale. But the excitement and activity generated by President Franklin D. Roosevelt's New Deal in Washington soon enticed the young lawyer away from academic pursuits and into public affairs.

Public Career

Throughout the 1930s Fortas held a series of jobs in the Roosevelt administration, mostly involving detailed legal work in such newly created agencies as the Securities and Exchange Commission and the Public Works Administration. In 1942 he was appointed under secretary of the interior, serving under the controversial and irascible Harold L. Ickes.

Following the Second World War, Fortas helped found the law firm of Arnold, Fortas and Porter, which quickly became one of Washington's most prestigious legal institutions. The firm specialized in corporation law, but its members, including Fortas, found time to litigate some important civil and individual rights cases as well.

In 1948 Fortas successfully defended a congressman from Texas — Lyndon B. Johnson — in a challenge to Johnson's election victory in the Texas Democratic senatorial primary. That defense was the basis for an enduring friendship between the two men, and Fortas became one of Johnson's most trusted advisers.

Preferring his role as confidential adviser, Fortas in 1964 declined Johnson's offer to name him attorney general. But when Arthur J. Goldberg resigned from the Supreme Court in 1965, Johnson ignored Fortas' opposition and appointed him to the Supreme Court.

When Chief Justice Earl Warren voiced his intention to resign in 1968, Johnson decided to elevate Fortas to the Chief Justiceship. But amid charges of "cronyism," events began to unfold which ultimately led to Fortas' undoing.

In the face of strong opposition from Republicans and conservative Democrats, Johnson was finally forced to withdraw the nomination, but not before it was revealed that Fortas had received $15,000 to teach a course at a local university.

Then, in May of 1969, *Life* magazine revealed that since becoming a justice Fortas had accepted — and then returned several months later — $20,000 from a charitable foundation controlled by the family of an indicted stock manipulator.

The allegations touched off talk of impeachment proceedings against Fortas. In mid-May, despite his denial of any "wrongdoing on my part," Fortas resigned from the court. He then returned to private law practice in Washington in partnership with another attorney.

Thurgood Marshall
(1967-   )

Born: July 2, 1908, Baltimore, Md.

Education: Lincoln University, A.B., cum laude, 1930; Howard University Law School, LL.B., 1933.

Official Positions: judge, U.S. Court of Appeals for the second circuit, 1961-65; U.S. Solicitor General, 1965-67.

Supreme Court Appointment: nominated associate justice by President Lyndon B. Johnson June 13, 1967, to replace Tom C. Clark, who resigned; confirmed by the U.S. Senate Aug. 30, 1967, by a 69-11 vote.

Family: married Vivian Burey Sept. 4, 1929, died Feb. 1955, two sons; married Cecelia Suryat Dec. 17, 1955.

Personal Background

Marshall was born in Baltimore, Md., the son of a primary school teacher and a club steward. In 1926 he left Baltimore to attend the all-black Lincoln University in Chester, Pa., where he developed a reputation as an outstanding debater. After graduating cum laude in 1930, Marshall decided to study law and entered Howard University in Washington, D.C.

During his law-school years, Marshall began to develop an interest in civil rights. After graduating first in his law school class in 1933, Marshall commenced a long and historic involvement with the National Association for the Advancement of Colored People (NAACP). In 1940 he became the head of the newly formed NAACP Legal Defense and Education Fund, a position he held for more than 20 years.

Over those two decades, Marshall coordinated the fund's attack on segregation in voting, housing, public accommodations and education. The culmination of his career as a civil rights attorney came in 1954 as chief counsel in a series of cases grouped under the title *Brown v. Board of Education*. In that historic case, which Marshall argued before the Supreme Court, civil rights advocates convinced the court to declare that segregation in public schools was unconstitutional.

Public Career

In 1961 Marshall was appointed by President Kennedy to the U.S. Court of Appeals for the second circuit, but because of heated opposition from southern Democratic senators, he was not confirmed until a year later.

Four years after he was named to the circuit court, Marshall was chosen by President Lyndon B. Johnson to be the nation's first black solicitor general. During his years as the government's chief advocate before the Supreme Court, Marshall scored impressive victories in the areas of civil and constitutional rights. He won Supreme Court approval of the 1965 Voting Rights Act, voluntarily informed the court that the government had used electronic eavesdropping devices in two cases, and joined in a suit that successfully overturned a California constitutional amendment that prohibited open housing legislation.

On June 13, 1967, President Johnson chose Marshall to become the first black appointed as a justice of the Supreme Court.

Warren Earl Burger
(1969-   )

Born: Sept. 17, 1907, St. Paul, Minn.

Education: attended the University of Minnesota, 1925-27; St. Paul College of Law (now Mitchell College of Law), LL.B., magna cum laude, 1931.

Official Positions: U.S. assistant attorney general, civil division, Justice Department, 1953-56; judge, U.S. Court of Appeals for the District of Columbia, 1956-69.

Supreme Court Appointment: nominated Chief Justice by President Richard M. Nixon May 21, 1969, to replace Chief Justice Earl Warren, who resigned; confirmed by the U.S. Senate June 9, 1969, by a 74-3 vote.

Family: married Elvera Stromberg Nov. 8, 1933; one son, one daughter.

Personal Background

Burger was born in St. Paul, Minn., the fourth of seven children of Swiss and German parents. Financially unable to attend college full time, Burger spent the years following his 1925 graduation from high school attending college and law school evening classes — two years at the University of Minnesota and four at St. Paul College of Law, now Mitchell College of Law. To support himself, Burger worked during the day selling life insurance.

After graduating with honors from law school in 1931, Burger joined a respected law firm in Minnesota, where he practiced until 1953. He also taught part time at his alma mater, Mitchell College of Law, from 1931 to 1948.

Burger developed a deep interest in art and is himself an accomplished sculptor; as Chief Justice, he became chairman of the board of the National Gallery of Art. He is also an antiques buff, a connoisseur of fine wines, and serves as chancellor of the Smithsonian Institution.

Public Career

Soon after beginning his law career in Minnesota, Burger became involved in state Republican politics. In 1938 he helped in the successful campaign of Harold E. Stassen for governor of Minnesota.

It was during Stassen's unsuccessful bid for the Republican presidential nomination 10 years later that Burger first met a man who was to figure largely in his future — Herbert Brownell, campaign manager for GOP presidential nominee Thomas E. Dewey, then governor of New York and later attorney general in the Eisenhower administration. It was Brownell who would bring Burger to Washington in 1953 to serve as assistant attorney general in charge of the civil division.

Burger's stint as assistant attorney general from 1953 to 1956 was not without controversy. His decision to defend the government's action in the dismissal of John F. Peters, a part-time federal employee, on grounds of disloyalty — after Solicitor General Simon E. Sobeloff had refused to do so on grounds of conscience — won Burger the enmity of many liberals.

But Burger's overall record as assistant attorney general apparently won President Eisenhower's approval, and in 1956 Burger was appointed to the U.S. Court of Appeals for the District of Columbia circuit. As an appeals-court judge, Burger developed a reputation as a conservative, especially in criminal justice cases.

Off the bench, Burger became increasingly outspoken in his support of major administrative reform of the judicial system — a cause he continued to advocate as Chief Justice. Due in large part to Burger's efforts, the American Bar Association and other legal groups established the Institute of Court Management to train court executive officers, bring new management techniques to the courts, and relieve judges of paperwork. During Burger's first years as Chief Justice, Congress also approved a number of measures to streamline and modernize the operations of the federal judiciary.

President Nixon's appointment of Burger as Chief Justice on May 21, 1969, caught most observers by surprise. For despite the white-haired nominee's years of service in the Justice Department and the court of appeals, he was little known outside the legal community. But Nixon apparently was impressed by Burger's consistent argument as an appeals judge that the Constitution should be read narrowly — a belief Nixon had stressed during his 1968 presidential campaign.

Born: Nov. 12, 1908, Nashville, Ill.

Education: Harvard University, B.A., Phi Beta Kappa, summa cum laude in mathematics, 1929; Harvard Law School, LL.B., 1932.

Official Positions: clerk, U.S. Court of Appeals for the Eighth Circuit, 1932-33; judge, U.S. Court of Appeals for the Eighth Circuit, 1959-70.

Supreme Court Appointment: nominated associate justice by President Richard M. Nixon April 14, 1970, to replace Abe Fortas, who resigned; confirmed by the U.S. Senate May 12, 1970, by a 94-0 vote.

Family: married Dorothy E. Clark June 21, 1941; three daughters.

Personal Background

Although born in southern Illinois, Blackmun spent most of his early years in the Minneapolis-St. Paul area, where his father was an official of the Twin Cities Savings and Loan Company. It was in grade school that Blackmun began a lifelong friendship with Warren Burger, with whom he was later to serve on the Supreme Court.

After showing an early aptitude for mathematics, Blackmun went east after high school to attend Harvard University on a scholarship. At Harvard, Blackmun majored in mathematics and thought briefly of becoming a physician.

But Blackmun chose the law instead. After graduating Phi Beta Kappa from Harvard in 1929, Blackmun entered Harvard Law School, from which he graduated in 1932. During his law-school years, Blackmun supported himself with a variety of odd jobs, including tutoring in math and driving the launch for the college crew team.

After law school, Blackmun returned to St. Paul, where he served for a year and a half as a law clerk to United States Circuit Court Judge John B. Sanborn, whom Blackmun was to succeed on the court 26 years later. He left the clerkship in 1933 to teach at the Mitchell College of Law in St. Paul, Chief Justice Burger's alma mater.

After a year of teaching, Blackmun opted for private practice. In 1934 he joined the Minneapolis law firm where he was to remain for 16 years. Then, in 1950, he accepted a post as "house counsel" for the world-famous Mayo Clinic in Rochester, Minn. There, Blackmun quickly developed a reputation among his colleagues as a serious man totally engrossed in his profession.

Public Career

That reputation followed him to the bench of the U.S. Court of Appeals for the eighth circuit, to which Blackmun was appointed by President Eisenhower in 1959. As an appeals court judge, Blackmun became known for his scholarly and thorough opinions.

Blackmun's nomination for the Supreme Court was President Nixon's third try to fill the seat vacated by Justice Abe Fortas' resignation. The Senate had refused to confirm his first two nominees — Clement F. Haynsworth Jr. of South Carolina and G. Harrold Carswell of Florida. Thereupon, Nixon said that he had concluded from the rejection of his first two nominees that the Senate "as it is presently constituted" would not confirm a southern nominee who was also a judicial conservative.

Nixon then turned to Chief Justice Burger's close friend, who was confirmed without opposition. During his first years on the court, Blackmun was frequently described along with Burger as one of the "Minnesota Twins."

Harry Andrew Blackmun
(1970-   )

Lewis Franklin Powell Jr.
(1971-   )

Born: Sept. 19, 1907, Suffolk, Va.

Education: Washington and Lee University, B.S., Phi Beta Kappa, 1929; Washington and Lee University Law School, LL.B., 1931; Harvard Law School, LL.M., 1932.

Official Positions: president of the Richmond School Board, 1952-61; member, 1961-69, and president, 1968-69, Virginia state board of education; president of the American Bar Association, 1964-65; president, American College of Trial Lawyers, 1968-69.

Supreme Court Appointment: nominated associate justice by President Richard M. Nixon Oct. 21, 1971, to replace Hugo L. Black, who resigned; confirmed by the U.S. Senate Dec. 6, 1971, by an 89-1 vote.

Family: married Josephine M. Rucker May 2, 1936; three daughters, one son.

Personal Background

Powell was born in Suffolk, in Tidewater Virginia, but spent most of his life in Richmond. He attended college and law school at Washington and Lee University in Lexington, Va., then Harvard Law School, where he earned a master's degree in 1932.

Following his year at Harvard, Powell returned to Virginia, where he joined one of the state's oldest and most prestigious law firms, located in Richmond. Powell eventually became a senior partner, continuing his association with the firm until his nomination to the Supreme Court.

Over the years, Powell's practice made him no stranger to blue-chip boardrooms. Among the companies represented during Powell's years with the law firm were the Baltimore and Ohio Railroad Co., the Prudential Insurance Company of America and the Virginia Electric and Power Co.

Public Career

Powell's reputation as a moderate stemmed from his work as president from 1952 to 1961 of the Richmond school board, and later as a member and president of the Virginia state board of education. In the face of intense pressure for "massive" resistance to desegregation, Powell consistently advocated keeping the schools open.

A one-year stint from 1964 to 1965 as president of the American Bar Association (ABA) provided Powell with a national platform from which to express his views on a variety of subjects and enhanced his reputation as a moderate. On the liberal side, Powell spoke out against inadequate legal services for the poor and worked to create the legal services program of the Office of Economic Opportunity. A more conservative tone characterized his view of social ills caused by parental permissiveness and his stern denunciations of civil disobedience and other forms of civil demonstrations. And as a member in 1966 of President Lyndon B. Johnson's Crime Commission, Powell participated in a minority statement criticizing Supreme Court rulings upholding the right of criminal suspects to remain silent.

Powell was the only Democrat among President Nixon's Supreme Court appointees.

William Hubbs Rehnquist
(1971-   )

Born: Oct. 1, 1924, Milwaukee, Wis.

Education: Stanford University, B.A., Phi Beta Kappa, "with great distinction" 1948, M.A., 1948; Harvard University, M.A. in political science, 1950; Stanford University Law School, LL.B., 1952.

Official Positions: law clerk to Supreme Court Justice Robert H. Jackson, 1952-53; U.S. assistant attorney general, office of legal counsel, 1969-1971.

Supreme Court Appointment: nominated associate justice by President Richard M. Nixon Oct. 21, 1971, to replace John Marshall Harlan, who resigned; confirmed by the U.S. Senate Dec. 10, 1971, by a 68-26 vote.

Family: married Natalie Cornell Aug. 29, 1953; one son, two daughters.

Personal Background

Rehnquist was born in Milwaukee and grew up there. After World War II service in the Air Force, he entered Stanford University, where he received both a B.A. and an M.A. in 1948. He earned another M.A. in political science at Harvard University (conferred in 1950) before returning to Stanford to attend law school. He graduated first in his class in 1952.

Public Career

After finishing law school, Rehnquist became a law clerk to Supreme Court Justice Robert H. Jackson. In 1952 he wrote a memorandum for Jackson that would later come back to haunt him during his Senate confirmation hearings: The memorandum favored separate but equal schools for blacks and whites. Asked about those views by the Senate Judiciary Committee in 1971, Rehnquist repudiated them, declaring that they were Justice Jackson's, not his own.

Following his clerkship, Rehnquist decided to begin law practice in the economically burgeoning Southwest. In 1953 he moved to Phoenix, Ariz., and immediately became immersed in state Republican politics. From his earliest days in the state, he was associated with the party's most conservative wing. A 1957 speech denouncing the liberalism of the Warren court typified his views at the time.

During the 1964 presidential campaign, Rehnquist campaigned ardently for GOP candidate Barry Goldwater.

It was during the campaign that Rehnquist met and worked with Richard G. Kleindienst, who, as President Nixon's deputy attorney general, would later appoint Rehnquist to head the Justice Department's office of legal counsel as an assistant attorney general.

Rehnquist quickly became one of the Nixon administration's chief spokesmen on Capitol Hill, commenting on issues ranging from wiretapping to rights of the accused. It was Rehnquist's job to review the legality of all presidential executive orders and other constitutional law questions in the executive branch. He frequently testified before congressional committees in support of the administration's policies — most of which matched his own conservative philosophy. So tightly reasoned and articulate was his testimony — backing such controversial matters as government surveillance of American citizens and tighter curbs on obscene materials — that even many liberal members of Congress applauded his ability.

In 1971 the once-obscure Phoenix lawyer was nominated by President Nixon to the Supreme Court and approved by the Senate, 68-26.

John Paul Stevens

(1975-   )

Born: April 20, 1920, Chicago, Ill.

Education: University of Chicago, B.A., Phi Beta Kappa, 1941; Northwestern University School of Law, J. D. magna cum laude, 1947.

Official Positions: law clerk to Supreme Court Justice Wiley B. Rutledge, 1947-48; associate counsel, subcommittee on the study of monopoly power, U.S. House Judiciary Committee, 1951; member, U.S. Attorney General's National Committee to Study the Antitrust Laws, 1953-55; judge, U.S. Court of Appeals for the seventh circuit, 1970-75.

Supreme Court Appointment: nominated associate justice by President Gerald R. Ford Nov. 28, 1975, to replace William O. Douglas, who resigned; confirmed by the U.S. Senate Dec. 17, 1975, by a 98-0 vote.

Family: married Elizabeth Jane Sheeren June 7, 1942; one son, three daughters.

Personal Background

A member of a prominent Chicago family, Stevens graduated Phi Beta Kappa from the University of Chicago in 1941. After a wartime stint in the Navy during which he earned the Bronze Star, he returned to Chicago to enter Northwestern University Law School, graduating in 1947. Stevens then served as a law clerk to Supreme Court Justice Wiley B. Rutledge. He left Washington to join a prominent Chicago law firm which specialized in antitrust law.

Stevens developed a reputation as a pre-eminent antitrust lawyer, and after three years formed his own law firm. He also taught part-time at Northwestern and the University of Chicago law schools until his appointment by President Nixon in 1970 to the U.S. Court of Appeals for the seventh circuit.

An enthusiastic pilot, Stevens flies his own small plane. He underwent open heart surgery in the early 1970s, but fully recovered.

Public Career

Stevens developed a reputation as a political moderate during his undergraduate days at the University of Chicago, then an overwhelmingly liberal campus. But although a registered Republican, he was never active in partisan politics. Nevertheless, Stevens served as Republican counsel in 1951 to a House Judiciary subcommittee's study of monopoly power. He also served from 1953 to 1955, during the Eisenhower administration, as a member of the attorney general's National Committee to Study the Antitrust Laws.

When President Ford nominated Stevens to the Supreme Court seat vacated by veteran liberal William O. Douglas, court-watchers and other observers struggled to pin an ideological label on the new nominee. But on the whole, they decided that he was neither a doctrinaire liberal nor a conservative, but a centrist whose well-crafted, scholarly opinions made him a "judge's judge." He was unanimously confirmed.

PART VII

MAJOR DECISIONS
OF THE COURT

Major Decisions of the Court 1790-1979

Every Supreme Court decision begins with a dispute between persons. The interests they assert and defend may be personal ones, corporate ones, or official ones, but every case begins with a disagreement between individuals.

Early in its history the court made clear that it would not rule on theoretical situations or hypothetical cases. It would only resolve actual "cases and controversies" arising from real collisions of rights and powers. To decide a hypothetical case, said the justices, would be to exceed the function which the Constitution gave the court.

The individuals who bring their complaints before the justices are a varied group. William Marbury wished to secure his appointment as a justice of the peace. Dred Scott sought his freedom. Linda Brown wanted to attend her neighborhood school. Clarence Gideon felt he should have a lawyer to help him defend himself in court. Richard Nixon wanted to keep his White House tapes confidential.

The court resolved each of those cases, and the hundreds more which have appeared on its docket through the years, on the basis of its particular facts.

The immediate impact of each decision was simply to answer the claims of Marbury, Scott, Brown, Gideon and Nixon, settling one particular situation. Many of the court's rulings have no further impact.

But often — as in these cases — the decision has a larger significance, upholding or striking down similar laws or practices or claims, establishing the court's own power in new areas, or finding that some areas lie outside that power.

To the Supreme Court, wrote Richard Kluger in the foreword to his book *Simple Justice,*

> ...the nation has increasingly brought its most vexing social and political problems. They come in the guise of private disputes between only the litigating parties, but everybody understands that this is a legal fiction and merely a convenient political device. American society thus reduces its most troubling controversies to the scope — and translates them into the language — of a lawsuit.

Although the progress of cases to the Supreme Court is slow, the body of issues before the court in a particular period does provide a reflection of the trends of public concern. Most of the major cases decided by the court from 1790 until 1860 dealt with questions of the balance between state and federal power. War issues were reflected in the rulings of the war years; civil rights and state powers questions marked the era of Reconstruction. As the nation's economy flourished and grew, more and more questions of business law — and the power of government over business — came to the court. And in the mid-20th century questions of individual rights and liberties began to dominate.

Following are summary descriptions of the Supreme Court's major rulings from *Chisholm v. Georgia* in 1793, through those issued in the summer of 1979. Arranged in chronological order, the summaries consist of a general subject heading, the case name, its citation, the vote by which it was decided, the date upon which the decision was announced, the name of the justice writing the major court opinion, the names of those in dissent, and a summary statement of the court's holding. (In some early cases, the vote or the exact date of its announcement are unavailable.)

More detailed discussion and analysis of the decisions included here may be located in other parts of the book by using the case index, p. 1009.

Sources for Decisions

The primary source for this section on major decisions was *United States Reports,* the official record of Supreme Court decisions and opinions published by the U.S. Government Printing Office.

This source was supplemented by three unofficial records: *United States Law Week,* published by the Bureau of National Affairs; *Supreme Court Reporter,* published by West Publishing Co.; and *United States Supreme Court Reports, Lawyers' Edition,* published by Lawyers Co-operative Publishing Co.

Where specific dates and votes were not available from these sources, they were occasionally drawn from the following secondary sources:

Paul A. Freund, gen. ed. *History of the Supreme Court of the United States.* New York: Macmillan Publishing Co., 1971, 1974, 1971. Vol. I: *Antecedents and Beginnings to 1801,* by Julius Goebel Jr.; Vol. V: *The Taney Period, 1836-1864,* by Carl B. Swisher; Vol. VI: *Reconstruction and Reunion, 1864-1888, Part One,* by Charles Fairman.

Charles Warren. *The Supreme Court in United States History.* rev. ed. 2 vols. Boston: Little, Brown & Co., 1922, 1926.

1790-1799

Federal Courts

Chisholm v. Georgia (2 Dall. 419), decided by a 4-1 vote, Feb. 18, 1793. Chief Justice Jay wrote the court's major opinion; Iredell dissented.

Citizens of one state have the right — under Article III of the Constitution — to sue another state in federal court, even without the consent of the defendant state.

This ruling was reversed by adoption of the 11th Amendment, forbidding such suits without the consent of the defendant state.

Taxes

Hylton v. United States (3 Dall. 171), decided without dissent in the February 1796 term. All three participating justices — Chase, Paterson and Iredell — submitted opinions; Cushing, Wilson and Ellsworth did not participate; Wilson filed an opinion.

The court upheld a federal tax on carriages, ruling that the only taxes that were direct and therefore required by the Constitution to be apportioned among the states were head taxes and taxes on land.

This definition remained in force until 1895 when the court held that income taxes were also direct and must be apportioned; that decision was overturned by ratification of the 16th Amendment.

Treaties

Ware v. Hylton (3 Dall. 199), decided by a 4-0 vote, March 7, 1796. Chase delivered the major opinion for the court; Iredell did not participate in the decision, but did place an opinion in the record.

The court ruled that treaties made by the United States overrode any conflicting state laws.

The 1783 Treaty of Paris with Britain, ending the Revolutionary War, provided that neither Britain nor the United States would block the efforts of the other nation's citizens to secure repayment of debts in the other country. This provision rendered invalid Virginia's law allowing debts owed by Virginians to British creditors to be "paid off" through payments to the state.

Ex Post Facto Laws

Calder v. Bull (3 Dall. 386), decided by a vote of 4-0, Aug. 8, 1798. Chase wrote the court's opinion. Paterson, Iredell and Cushing also wrote opinions.

The Constitution's ban on *ex post facto* laws does not forbid a state to nullify a man's title to certain property. The court held that this ban applied only to laws making certain actions criminal after they had been committed. The ban was not intended to protect property rights, the court wrote.

1800-1809

Judicial Review

Marbury v. Madison (1 Cr. 137), decided without dissent, Feb. 24, 1803. Chief Justice Marshall wrote the opinion of the court.

Congress may not expand or contract the Supreme Court's original jurisdiction. Thus Congress exceeded its power when in Section 13 of the Judiciary Act of 1789 it authorized the Supreme Court to issue writs of *mandamus*

in original cases ordering federal officials to perform particular acts.

Therefore, the court ruled, although William Marbury had a right to receive his commission as a justice of the peace — already signed and sealed, but not delivered — the Supreme Court lacked the power, under its original jurisdiction, to order its delivery.

The immediate import of the decision was to absolve the Jefferson administration of the duty to install several of President Adams' appointments in such posts. The lasting significance was the establishment of the court's power to review acts of Congress and declare invalid those it found in conflict with the Constitution.

Federal Courts

Bank of the United States v. Deveaux (5 Cr. 61), decided without dissent, March 15, 1809. Chief Justice Marshall wrote the court's opinion; Livingston did not participate in the decision.

The court gave a strict interpretation to the "diversity" requirement in federal cases — the rule that certain cases could be heard in federal, not state, courts simply because the two parties were residents of different states. Cases involving corporations, the court held, could only come into federal courts for this reason if *all* the stockholders of the corporation lived in a state other than that of the opposing party. This strict rule resulted in very little corporate litigation in the federal courts until 1844 when the rule was revised.

1810-1819

Contracts

Fletcher v. Peck (6 Cr. 87), decided without dissent March 16, 1810. Chief Justice Marshall wrote the court's opinion; Johnson filed a separate opinion.

The Constitution forbids a state to impair the obligation of contracts. This prohibition denies a state legislature the power to annul titles to land secured under a land grant approved by a previous session of the legislature.

Judicial Review

Martin v. Hunter's Lessee (1 Wheat. 304), decided without dissent, March 20, 1816. Story wrote the court's opinion; Chief Justice Marshall did not participate in the case.

The court upheld as constitutional Section 25 of the Judiciary Act of 1789, which gave the Supreme Court the power to review, and reverse or affirm, state court rulings rejecting a federally-based challenge to a state law or state action.

Contracts

Dartmouth College v. Woodward (4 Wheat. 519), decided by a 5-1 vote, Feb. 2, 1819. Chief Justice Marshall wrote the court's opinion; Duvall dissented.

The Constitution, by its provision forbidding state action impairing the obligation of contracts, denies a state the power to alter or repeal private corporate charters, such as that between the state of New Hampshire and the trustees of Dartmouth College to establish that institution.

Sturges v. Crowninshield (4 Wheat. 122), decided without dissent, Feb. 17, 1819. Chief Justice Marshall wrote the court's opinion.

The Constitution's grant of power to Congress to enact a uniform bankruptcy law does not deny states the power to pass insolvency statutes, at least until Congress enacts a bankruptcy law.

However, the constitutional ban on state action impairing the obligation of contracts denies a state the power to enact a law freeing debtors from liability for debts contracted *before* the law's passage.

Power of Congress

McCulloch v. Maryland (4 Wheat. 316), decided without dissent, March 6, 1819. Chief Justice Marshall wrote the court's opinion.

In a broad definition of the Constitution's grant to Congress of the power to enact all laws which are "necessary and proper" to execute the responsibilities given the legislative branch by the Constitution, the court ruled that Congress had the authority to charter a national bank in the exercise of its fiscal and monetary powers. The necessary and proper clause empowered Congress to adopt any appropriate and legitimate means for achieving a legislative goal; it was not confined to using only those means that were indispensable to reaching that end.

The court also held that the national bank was immune to state taxation. Observing that the "power to tax involves the power to destroy," the court began to develop the doctrine that one government may not tax certain holdings of another government.

1820-1829

Judicial Review

Cohens v. Virginia (6 Wheat. 264), decided without dissent, March 3, 1821. Chief Justice Marshall delivered the court's opinion.

For the second time, the court reaffirmed the constitutionality of Section 25 of the Judiciary Act of 1789, under which the Supreme Court was empowered to review, and affirm or reverse, the rulings of state courts denying federal claims.

Commerce

Gibbons v. Ogden (9 Wheat. 1), decided without dissent, March 2, 1824. Chief Justice Marshall wrote the court's opinion.

In its first definition of Congress' power to regulate interstate commerce, the court ruled that Congress could regulate all commerce that extends to or affects more than one state. Furthermore, the court defined commerce as intercourse, including navigation and other modes of transportation, as well as commercial transactions. The court also declared that the congressional authority to regulate commerce is superior to state power to regulate the same commerce.

This important decision laid the foundation for the modern interpretation of the power which gives Congress virtually exclusive control over all business, even that which only indirectly affects interstate commerce.

Federal Courts

Osborn v. Bank of the United States (9 Wheat. 738), decided with one dissenting vote, March 18, 1824. Chief Justice Marshall wrote the court's opinion; Johnson dissented.

How To Read A Citation

The official version of Supreme Court decisions and opinions is contained in a series of volumes entitled *United States Reports*, published by the U.S. Government Printing Office.

While there are several unofficial compilations of court opinions, including *United States Law Week* published by the Bureau of National Affairs, *Supreme Court Reporter* published by West Publishing Co., and *United States Supreme Court Reports, Lawyers' Edition* published by Lawyers Co-operative Publishing Co., it is the official record that is generally cited. (An unofficial version or the official slip opinion might be cited if a decision has not yet been officially reported.)

A citation to a case includes, in order, the name of the parties to the case, the volume of *United States Reports* in which the decision appears, the page in the volume that the opinion begins on, the page from which any quoted material is taken and the year the decision was made.

For example, *Colegrove v. Green*, 328 U.S. 549 at 553 (1946) means that the Supreme Court decision and opinion in the case of Colegrove against Green may be found in volume 328 of *United States Reports* beginning on page 549. The specific quotation in question will be found on page 553. The case was decided in 1946.

Reporters of Decisions

Until 1875 the official reports of the court were published under the names of the court reporters and it is their names, or abbreviated versions, which appear in cites for those years. A citation such as *Marbury v. Madison*, 1 Cranch 137 (1803) means that the opinion in the case of Marbury against Madison will be found in the first volume of reporter Cranch beginning on page 137. (Between 1875 and 1883 a court reporter named William T. Otto compiled the decisions and opinions; his name appears on the volumes for those years as well as the *United States Reports* volume number, but Otto is seldom cited.)

The titles of the volumes to 1875, the full names of the reporters and the corresponding *United States Reports* volumes are:

1-4	Dall.	Dallas	1-4 U.S.
1-9	Cranch or Cr.	Cranch	5-13 U.S.
1-12	Wheat.	Wheaton	14-25 U.S.
1-16	Pet.	Peters	26-41 U.S.
1-24	How.	Howard	42-65 U.S.
1-2	Black	Black	66-67 U.S.
1-23	Wall.	Wallace	68-90 U.S.

The court upheld the right of the Bank of the United States to sue state officials in federal court. It held that the 11th Amendment — allowing states to be sued in federal court by citizens of another state only with the consent of the defendant state — did not deny federal courts jurisdiction over a case brought against a state official for actions under an unconstitutional state law or in excess of his legal authority.

Power of Congress

Wayman v. Southard (10 Wheat. 1), decided without dissent, Feb. 12, 15, 1825. Chief Justice Marshall wrote the court's opinion.

In this decision the court for the first time recognized the power of Congress to delegate portions of its legislative authority. In this case the court sanctioned the right of Congress to set an objective and then authorize an administrator to promulgate rules and regulations to achieve that objective. The right to delegate such authority provides the basis for creation of the federal regulatory agencies.

Power of the President

Martin v. Mott (12 Wheat. 19), decided without dissent in the January 1827 term. Story wrote the court's opinion.

The president's decision to call out the militia was not subject to judicial review and was binding on state authorities. As a result of congressional delegation of the power to the president, the decision to call out the militia, the court said, "belongs exclusively to the President, and ... his decision is conclusive upon all other persons."

Contracts

Ogden v. Saunders (12 Wheat. 213), decided by a 4-3 vote, Feb. 18, 1827. Washington wrote the court's major opinion; Chief Justice Marshall, Story and Duvall dissented.

The constitutional ban on state action impairing the obligation of contracts does not deny states the power to enact insolvency statutes which provide for the discharge of debts contracted *after* its passage.

Mason v. Haile (12 Wheat. 370), decided by a 6-1 vote in the January 1827 term. Thompson wrote the court's opinion; Washington dissented.

The Constitution's contract clause does not prevent a state from abolishing imprisonment as a punishment for debtors who fail to pay their obligations. Modifying the remedy for defaulting on a contract does not inevitably impair the obligation incurred under the contract.

Taxes

Brown v. Maryland (12 Wheat. 419), decided by a 6-1 vote, March 12, 1827. Chief Justice Marshall wrote the court's opinion; Thompson dissented.

The court reinforced its broad interpretation of congressional power to regulate interstate commerce, ruling that a state unconstitutionally infringed on that power when it taxed imported goods that were still the property of the importer and in their original package.

Weston v. City Council of Charleston (2 Pet. 449), decided by a 4-2 vote, March 18, 1829. Chief Justice Marshall wrote the court's opinion; Johnson and Thompson dissented.

A city tax on United States stock impermissibly hinders the exercise of the federal power to borrow money.

Commerce

Willson v. Blackbird Creek Marsh Co. (2 Pet. 245), decided without dissent in the January 1829 term. Chief Justice Marshall wrote the court's opinion.

A state may exercise its police power to regulate matters affecting interstate commerce if Congress has not enacted conflicting legislation regulating the same matters.

Federal Courts

Foster v. Neilson (2 Pet. 253), decided without dissent in the January 1829 term. Chief Justice Marshall delivered the court's opinion.

The court refused to rule on a boundary dispute involving territory east of the Mississippi River claimed by both the United States and Spain. Chief Justice Marshall described the matter as a "political question" which it was not the business of the judiciary to resolve.

1830-1839

Bills of Credit

Craig v. Missouri (4 Pet. 410), decided by a 4-3 vote, March 12, 1830. Chief Justice Marshall wrote the court's opinion; Johnson, Thompson and McLean dissented.

The constitutional provision barring states from issuing bills of credit denies a state the power to authorize the issuance of state loan certificates.

State Powers

Worcester v. Georgia (6 Pet. 515), decided without dissent, March 3, 1832. Chief Justice Marshall wrote the court's opinion.

Federal jurisdiction over Indian affairs is exclusive, leaving no room for state authority. States lack any power to pass laws affecting Indians living in Indian territory within their borders. The court thus reversed the conviction, under Georgia law, of two missionaries who had failed to comply with a state law requiring the licensing of all white persons living in Indian territory.

Individual Rights

Barron v. Baltimore (7 Pet. 243), decided without dissent, in the January 1833 term. Chief Justice Marshall wrote the court's opinion.

The Bill of Rights was added to the Constitution to protect persons only against the action of the federal, not the state, government. The court rejected the effort of a wharf owner to invoke the Fifth Amendment to compel the city of Baltimore to compensate him for the value of his wharf, which he claimed had been rendered useless as a result of city action.

Commerce

New York v. Miln (11 Pet. 102), decided by a 6-1 vote, in the January 1837 term. Barbour wrote the court's opinion; Story dissented.

The court sustained a New York statute, which required all ships arriving in New York to report lists of passengers, against a challenge that the statute interfered with federal power to regulate foreign commerce. The state law was a valid exercise of state police power to protect public welfare against an influx of paupers, the majority said.

Bills of Credit

Briscoe v. Bank of the Commonwealth of Kentucky (11 Pet. 257), decided by a vote of 6-1, Feb. 11, 1837. McLean wrote the court's opinion; Story dissented.

The constitutional language forbidding states to issue bills of credit is not violated by a state law authorizing issuance of notes by a state-chartered bank, in which the state owns all the stock.

Contracts

Charles River Bridge v. Warren Bridge (11 Pet. 420), decided by a 4-3 vote, in the January 1837 term. Chief Justice Taney wrote the court's opinion; Story, Thompson and McLean dissented.

Charters granted by the state should never be assumed to limit the state's power of eminent domain. Absent an explicit grant of exclusive privilege, a corporate charter granted by the state should not be interpreted as granting such a privilege and thereby limiting the state's power to charter a competing corporation.

The court rejected the claim of the owners of the Charles River Bridge that their charter implicitly granted them a monopoly of the foot passenger traffic across the river — and was impaired by state action authorizing construction of a second bridge over that same river.

Federal Courts

Kendall v. United States ex rel. Stokes (12 Pet. 524), decided by votes of 9-0 and 6-3, in the January 1838 term. Thompson wrote the court's opinion; Chief Justice Taney, Barbour and Catron dissented in part.

The court held that federal courts — if they have jurisdiction over the controversy involved — have the power to issue a writ of *mandamus* to an executive branch official ordering him to take some ministerial action which he is required by law to perform. The court distinguished between ministerial actions of executive officials, which are prescribed by law or regulation and about which there is little discretion, and policy or political actions of those officials, which are beyond the reach of the courts.

1840-1849

Foreign Affairs

Holmes v. Jennison (14 Pet. 540), decided by a 4-4 vote in the January 1840 term. Chief Justice Taney wrote an opinion for himself, Story, McLean and Wayne; Barbour, Baldwin, Catron and Thompson filed separate opinions; McKinley did not participate.

A fugitive from Canada, detained in Vermont, sought release through a petition for a writ of *habeas corpus*. After the state supreme court denied his petition, he asked the Supreme Court to review that action. The court divided 4-4 over whether it had jurisdiction in the case. Taney, Story, McLean and Wayne held that the court did have jurisdiction; Barbour, Baldwin, Catron and Thompson disagreed.

The 4-4 vote meant that the court dismissed the case for lack of jurisdiction. But the significance of the case came in Taney's declaration that states were forbidden by the Constitution to take any independent role in foreign affairs, and thus a state governor could not surrender a fugitive within his jurisdiction to a foreign country who sought the fugitive's return.

Taxes

Dobbins v. Erie County (16 Pet. 435), decided without dissent in the January 1842 term. Wayne wrote the court's opinion.

Extending the principle adopted in *McCulloch v. Maryland* (1819) that the power to tax involves the power to destroy, the court held that states could not tax the income of federal officials.

This decision, together with that in *Collector v. Day* (11 Wall. 113, 1871), which held that the federal govern-

ment, for the same reason, could not tax the incomes of state officials, led to establishment of numerous intergovernmental tax immunities that were not removed until 1939 when *Dobbins* and *Collector* were overruled.

Slavery

Prigg v. Pennsylvania (16 Pet. 539), decided by votes of 9-0 and 6-3, March 1, 1842. Story wrote the court's opinion; Chief Justice Taney, Thompson and Daniel dissented in part.

The court struck down a Pennsylvania law concerning procedures for the return of fugitive slaves to owners in other states, finding the law in conflict with the federal Fugitive Slave Act. Story declared that federal power over fugitive slaves was exclusive, denying states any power to enact any laws on that subject. On this point the three justices dissented.

Federal Courts

Louisville Railroad Company v. Letson (2 How. 497), decided without dissent, March 15, 1844. Wayne wrote the court's opinion.

Effectively overruling its 1809 decision in *Bank of the United States v. Deveaux*, the court declared that a corporation would be assumed to be a citizen of the state in which it was chartered. This assumed citizenship, for purposes of diversity jurisdiction, facilitated the movement of corporate litigation into federal courts.

Interstate Boundaries

Rhode Island v. Massachusetts (4 How. 591), decided by votes of 8-0 and 7-1 in the January 1846 term. McLean wrote the court's opinion; Chief Justice Taney dissented in part.

This was the first decision of the court resolving an interstate boundary dispute. The court affirmed its jurisdiction over these matters, a point upon which Chief Justice Taney dissented, and then resolved the dispute in favor of Massachusetts, the state which had challenged the court's jurisdiction to hear the case at all.

Commerce

Thurlow v. Massachusetts, Fletcher v. Rhode Island, Peirce v. New Hampshire (The License Cases) (5 How. 504), decided without dissent, March 6, 1847. Chief Justice Taney, McLean, Catron, Daniel, Woodbury and Grier all wrote separate opinions.

The court upheld the right of states to require that all sales of intoxicating liquors within their borders be licensed, including imported liquor. This was viewed as a valid exercise of state police power. But a majority of the justices could not agree on the line of reasoning leading to this decision. Six separate opinions were written.

Federal Courts

Luther v. Borden (7 How. 1), decided by a 5-1 vote, Jan. 3, 1849. Chief Justice Taney delivered the court's opinion; Woodbury dissented; Catron, McKinley and Daniel did not participate.

The guaranty clause of the Constitution — stating that the United States will guarantee to each state a republican form of government — is enforceable only through the political branches, not the judiciary.

The court refused to resolve a dispute between two competing political groups, each of which asserted it was the lawful government of Rhode Island. This was a "political question," held the court, which it would leave to Congress to resolve.

Commerce

Smith v. Turner, Norris v. Boston (The Passenger Cases) (7 How. 283), decided by a 5-4 vote, Feb. 7, 1849. McLean wrote the court's opinion; Chief Justice Taney, Daniel, Nelson and Woodbury dissented.

In apparent contradiction to its decision in *New York v. Miln,* the court struck down state laws that placed a head tax on each passenger brought into a U.S. port. The revenue was intended to support immigrant paupers, but the majority held that such state laws conflicted with federal power to regulate interstate and foreign commerce even though Congress had not acted in this area.

1850-1859

Commerce

Cooley v. Board of Wardens of Port of Philadelphia (12 How. 299), decided by a 7-2 vote in the December 1851 term. Curtis wrote the court's opinion; McLean and Wayne dissented.

Adopting what is called the "selective exclusiveness doctrine," the majority ruled that Congress had exclusive power to regulate commerce that was national in nature and demanded uniform regulation. The states retained the authority to regulate commerce that was local in nature.

Pennsylvania v. Wheeling and Belmont Bridge (13 How. 518), decided by a 7-2 vote, Feb. 6, 1852. McLean wrote the court's opinion; Chief Justice Taney and Daniel dissented.

A bridge built under state direction across the Ohio River was so low that it obstructed interstate commerce, the court ruled, ordering that the bridge either be raised so that ships could pass under it or be taken down.

In its first legislative reversal of a Supreme Court decision, Congress passed a law declaring that the bridge did not interfere with interstate commerce and requiring ships to be refitted so that they could pass under the bridge. The court upheld this statute in 1856.

Due Process

Murray's Lessee v. Hoboken Land and Improvement Co. (18 How. 272), decided by a unanimous vote, Feb. 19, 1856. Curtis wrote the court's opinion.

The court held that the due process clause of the Fifth Amendment was a limitation on the legislature as well as on the executive and the judiciary.

The Fifth Amendment "cannot be construed as to leave Congress free to make any process 'due process of law' by its mere will." In this decision the court began to define due process, stating that any process in conflict with specific constitutional provisions or the "settled modes and usages" of proceedings in English and early American practice was not due process of law.

Contracts

Dodge v. Woolsey (18 How. 331), decided by a 6-3 vote, April 8, 1856. Wayne wrote the majority opinion; Campbell, Catron and Daniel dissented.

A state may not revoke a tax exemption which it has included in a charter, grant or contract. The Constitution's ban on state action impairing the obligation of contracts forbids such revocation.

This ruling declared unconstitutional part of the Ohio constitution, the first time the court had so nullified part of a state's constitution.

Slavery

Scott v. Sandford (19 How. 393), decided by a 7-2 vote, March 6, 1857. Each justice submitted a separate opinion. Chief Justice Taney's is considered the formal opinion of the court; McLean and Curtis dissented.

In what many consider the most ill-considered decision in Supreme Court history, the majority declared unconstitutional the already-repealed Missouri Compromise of 1820. Congress, the court declared, did not have the authority to prohibit slavery in the territories. The majority also held that blacks were not and could not become citizens of the United States and therefore were not entitled to its privileges and immunities. This part of the decision was overturned by ratification of the 14th Amendment in 1868.

Federal Courts

Ableman v. Booth, United States v. Booth (21 How. 506), decided by a unanimous vote, March 7, 1859. Chief Justice Taney wrote the court's opinion.

State courts lack the power to issue writs of *habeas corpus* ordering federal courts or federal officers to justify the detention of a prisoner or release him.

The court overturned the action of state courts in using the writ to order federal officials to release a man convicted in federal court of violating the federal Fugitive Slave Act.

1860-1869

Extradition

Kentucky v. Dennison (24 How. 66), decided by a unanimous vote, March 14, 1861. Chief Justice Taney wrote the opinion.

The constitutional statement that a "person charged in any state with treason, felony or other crime, who shall flee from justice, and be found in another state, shall, on demand of the executive authority of the state from which he fled, be delivered up, to be removed to the state having jurisdiction of the crime" is not enforceable by the federal government. The Constitution imposes a moral obligation upon a governor to surrender a fugitive sought and requested by another governor, but that obligation cannot be enforced in the federal courts.

Power of the President

The Prize Cases (2 Black 635), decided by a 5-4 vote, March 10, 1863. Grier wrote the majority opinion; Chief Justice Taney, Catron, Clifford and Nelson dissented.

These cases involved the capture of four ships seized while trying to run the Union blockade of Confederate ports which Lincoln instituted in April and which Congress sanctioned in July 1861. The court sustained the president's power to proclaim the blockade without a congressional declaration of war. A state of war already existed, the majority said, and the president was obligated "to meet it in the shape it presented itself, without waiting for Congress to baptize it with a name...."

Ex parte Milligan (4 Wall. 2), decided by votes of 9-0 and 5-4, April 3, 1866. Full opinions in the case were not announced until December 17, 1866. Davis wrote the majority opinion; Chief Justice Chase, Miller, Swayne and Wayne dissented in part.

The court held unanimously that the president lacks the power to authorize trial of civilians by military tribunal in wartime in areas where civil courts are still functioning.

Five justices, with Davis as their spokesman, said that even Congress and the president acting together lacked power to authorize military commissions to try civilians in areas out of the actual war zone.

Ex Post Facto Laws

Cummings v. Missouri, Ex parte Garland (4 Wall. 277, 333), decided by votes of 5-4, Jan. 14, 1867. Field wrote the majority opinion; Chief Justice Chase, Swayne, Davis and Miller dissented.

Neither the states nor the federal government may constitutionally require persons who wish to practice certain professions or exercise certain civil rights to take a "test oath" affirming past as well as present loyalty to the United States.

The court held invalid state and federal "test oaths," enacted to exclude persons who had supported the Confederacy from certain offices and certain professions. These requirements, held the court, violated the constitutional prohibitions on *ex post facto* laws and bills of attainder.

Federal Courts

Mississippi v. Johnson (4 Wall. 475), decided by a unanimous vote, April 15, 1867. Chief Justice Chase wrote the opinion.

The Supreme Court lacks jurisdiction over the political acts of the president; it has no power to issue an order directing him to stop enforcing acts of Congress, even if those acts are challenged as unconstitutional.

Ex parte McCardle (7 Wall. 506), decided by a unanimous vote, April 12, 1869. Chief Justice Chase wrote the opinion.

The Constitution authorizes Congress to make exceptions to the appellate jurisdiction of the Supreme Court. That grant includes the power to revoke the court's appellate jurisdiction over cases already argued and awaiting decision before it. Without jurisdiction over a case, the court can do nothing but dismiss it.

Congress had acted to revoke the court's jurisdiction over certain cases in which lower courts denied prisoners' petitions for release through a writ of *habeas corpus.* Congress did so because it feared that in this particular case, where a southern editor held by military authorities for "impeding" the Reconstruction effort sought his release, the court would declare the Reconstruction Acts themselves unconstitutional.

State Powers

Texas v. White (7 Wall. 700), decided by a 6-3 vote, April 12, 1869. Chief Justice Chase wrote the majority opinion. Justices Wayne, Grier and Miller dissented in part.

States lack the power to secede from the Union. From a legal point of view, Texas and the other states which had approved ordinances of secession had never left the Union.

Commerce

Paul v. Virginia (8 Wall. 168), decided by a unanimous vote, Nov. 1, 1869. Field wrote the opinion.

Insurance is a local business, not interstate commerce, the court held. Thus the states, not Congress, were responsible for regulating insurance practices even though insurance transactions crossed state lines. The court reversed this ruling in 1944 but Congress quickly returned authority to regulate insurance to the states.

Taxes

Woodruff v. Parham (8 Wall. 123), decided without dissent, Nov. 8, 1869. Miller wrote the opinion.

States are not constitutionally forbidden to tax goods "imported" from other states. The constitutional language forbidding states to tax imports or exports applies only to goods coming from or going to foreign countries.

States may tax goods from other states, once interstate transportation of those goods has ended, even if they are still in their original packages.

Veazie Bank v. Fenno (8 Wall. 533), decided by a 7-2 vote, Dec. 31, 1869. Chief Justice Chase wrote the majority opinion; Nelson and Davis dissented.

Congress may use its power to tax as a regulatory tool to support or enforce exercise of another constitutional power, even if the tax is designed to eliminate the matter taxed.

In this case, the court sustained a federal statute that placed a 10 percent tax on the circulation of state bank notes in order to give the untaxed national bank notes a competitive edge and drive the state notes out of the market. The court said the tax was a legitimate means through which Congress could exercise its constitutional authority to regulate currency.

1870-1879

Currency

Hepburn v. Griswold (First Legal Tender Case) (8 Wall. 603), decided by a 4-3 vote, Feb. 7, 1870. Chief Justice Chase wrote the majority opinion; Davis, Miller and Swayne dissented.

The court declared unconstitutional acts of Congress that substituted paper money for gold as legal tender for the payment of debts contracted prior to adoption of the first legal tender act in 1862.

The statute had been enacted to help the Union finance the Civil War, but the court held it an improper exercise of Congress' implied powers under the "necessary and proper" clause.

Knox v. Lee, Parker v. Davis (Second Legal Tender Case) (12 Wall. 457), decided by a 5-4 vote, May 1, 1871. Strong wrote the majority opinion; Chief Justice Chase, Nelson, Clifford and Field dissented.

Overturning its 1870 decision in *Hepburn v. Griswold,* the majority held that Congress had exercised its implied powers properly when it made paper money legal tender for the payment of debts. The fact that the two justices appointed to the court since the first decision supported the reversal led to charges that the court had been "packed."

Taxes

Low v. Austin (13 Wall. 29), decided by a unanimous vote, Jan. 29, 1872. Field wrote the opinion.

The constitutional language forbidding states to tax imports or exports prohibits state taxes on goods imported from foreign countries so long as those goods retain their character as imports.

Official Immunity

Bradley v. Fisher (13 Wall. 335), decided by a 7-2 vote, April 8, 1872. Field wrote the majority opinion; Davis and Clifford dissented.

Setting out the doctrine of judicial immunity, the court ruled that judges may not be sued for their official actions, no matter how erroneous or injurious those actions may be.

Privileges and Immunities

The Slaughterhouse Cases: The Butchers' Benevolent Association of New Orleans v. The Crescent City Livestock Landing and Slaughterhouse Co., Esteben v. Louisiana (16 Wall. 36), decided by a 5-4 vote, April 14, 1873. Miller wrote the majority opinion; Chief Justice Chase, Field, Swayne and Bradley dissented.

Louisiana did not violate the 14th Amendment when it granted a monopoly on the slaughterhouse business to one company for all of New Orleans. The right of other butchers to do business is neither a "privilege and immunity" of U.S. citizenship protected by the 14th Amendment nor an aspect of the "property" protected by the amendment's due process guarantee.

Bradwell v. State of Illinois (16 Wall. 130), decided by an 8-1 vote, April 15, 1873. Miller wrote the majority opinion; Chief Justice Chase dissented.

A state does not violate the 14th Amendment's guarantee of the privileges and immunities of U.S. citizenship when it refuses on the grounds of gender to license a woman to practice law in its courts. The right to practice law is not a privilege or immunity of U.S. citizenship.

Minor v. Happersett (21 Wall. 162), decided by a unanimous vote, March 29, 1875. Chief Justice Waite wrote the opinion.

The privileges and immunities clause of the 14th Amendment does not guarantee women the right to vote. A state therefore does not violate that amendment's guarantee when it denies a woman the right to vote. "[T]he Constitution of the United States does not confer the right of suffrage on anyone," the court said.

Commerce

Henderson v. Wickham, Commissioners of Immigration v. The North German Lloyd, Chy Lung v. Freeman (92 U.S. 259, 275), decided without dissent, March 20, 1876. Miller wrote the opinion.

A state may not require shipowners to give bond for each alien their ships bring into its ports. Despite the argument that this requirement would reduce the potential burden which immigrants place upon state finances, this bond requirement impermissibly interferes with the federal power to regulate foreign commerce.

This ruling resulted in the passage in 1882 of the first general federal immigration law in U.S. history.

Jury Trials

Walker v. Sauvinet (92 U.S. 90), decided by a 7-2 vote, April 24, 1876. Chief Justice Waite wrote the majority opinion; Clifford and Field dissented.

The Seventh Amendment, guaranteeing a jury trial in suits at common law involving more than $20, affects only federal, not state, trials. A trial by jury in such cases is not guaranteed in state proceedings by the 14th Amendment.

Voting Rights

United States v. Reese (92 U.S. 214), decided by an 8-1 vote, March 27, 1876. Chief Justice Waite wrote the majority opinion; Hunt dissented.

The 15th Amendment, forbidding states to deny anyone the right to vote because of race, color or previous condition of servitude, did not give anyone the right to vote. It simply guaranteed the right to be free from racial discrimination in the exercise of the right to vote — a right granted under state, not federal, laws. Therefore Congress exceeded its power to enforce the 15th Amendment when it enacted laws which penalized state officials who denied Negroes the right to vote, refused to count votes or obstructed citizens from voting.

United States v. Cruikshank (92 U.S. 542), decided by a unanimous vote, March 27, 1876. Chief Justice Waite wrote the opinion.

The court dismissed indictments brought against Louisiana citizens accused of using violence and fraud to prevent Negroes from voting. Because the indictments did not charge that these actions were motivated by racial discrimination, they were not federal offenses. "We may suspect," Waite wrote, "that race was the cause of the hostility but it is not so averred."

State Powers

Munn v. Illinois (94 U.S. 113), decided by a 7-2 vote, March 1, 1877. Chief Justice Waite wrote the majority opinion; Field and Strong dissented.

The court acknowledged the right of states to regulate private business in the exercise of their police power. The court sustained a state law setting the maximum rate that grain elevator operators could charge for grain storage. The court declared that private property dedicated to public use was subject to government regulation.

Civil Rights

Hall v. DeCuir (95 U.S. 485), decided without dissent, Jan. 14, 1878. Chief Justice Waite wrote the opinion.

A state law forbidding racial discrimination on common carriers operating in the state impermissibly infringes upon the federal power to regulate interstate commerce. Equal access to steamboat accommodations is a matter which requires national, uniform regulation and thus is outside the proper scope of state regulation.

1880-1889

Voting Rights

Ex parte Siebold (100 U.S. 371), decided by a 7-2 vote, March 8, 1880. Bradley wrote the majority opinion; Field and Clifford dissented.

Confirming federal power to protect the electoral process in congressional elections in the states, the court upheld federal laws making it a federal crime for state election officers to neglect their duty in congressional elections. The court upheld the convictions of two state officials tried and convicted for stuffing the ballot box.

Contracts

Stone v. Mississippi (101 U.S. 814), decided without dissent, May 10, 1880. Chief Justice Waite wrote the opinion.

A state may not permanently contract away any portion of its police power, its power to act to protect the general welfare. Thus, held the court, Mississippi did not act in violation of the contract clause when it amended its constitution to ban lotteries. This state action had been challenged as impairing the earlier obligation of another legislature which chartered a state lottery corporation.

Power of Congress

Kilbourn v. Thompson (103 U.S. 168), decided by a unanimous vote, Jan. 24, Feb. 28, 1881. Miller wrote the opinion.

The power of Congress to investigate is not unlimited, nor is its power to punish witnesses who refuse to cooperate with such an investigation. Investigations must be confined to subject areas over which Congress has jurisdiction, their purpose must be enactment of legislation and they may not merely inquire into the private affairs of citizens. Contempt citations issued against witnesses who refuse to cooperate in investigations that do not meet these standards are invalid.

This was the first case in which the Supreme Court asserted its authority to review the propriety of congressional investigations. The court subsequently modified the standards laid out in this case, but its basic limitations on the power of Congress to investigate remain in effect.

Civil Rights

Civil Rights Cases (109 U.S. 3), decided by an 8-1 vote, Oct. 15, 1883. Bradley wrote the court's opinion; Harlan dissented.

Neither the 13th nor the 14th Amendment empowers Congress to enact a law barring discrimination against blacks in privately owned public accommodations. The 14th Amendment prohibits only state-sponsored discrimination, not private discriminatory acts, the court held. Moreover, private discrimination does not violate the 13th Amendment because "such an act of refusal has nothing to do with slavery or involuntary servitude."

The decision effectively blocked further attempts by Congress in the post-Civil War period to end private racial discrimination; not until 1964 did Congress enact and the court sustain a federal law prohibiting discrimination in privately owned public accommodations.

Voting Rights

Ex parte Yarbrough (110 U.S. 651), decided by a unanimous court, March 3, 1884; Miller wrote the opinion.

The court upheld as a valid exercise of congressional power to enforce the 15th Amendment legislation penalizing persons who conspired to stop Negroes from exercising their right to vote. The court upheld the convictions of several members of the Ku Klux Klan for intimidating a black man in order to stop him from voting. In some cases, the court held, the 15th Amendment does confer the right to vote, as well as the right to be free of racial discrimina-

tion in voting, and Congress has the power to enforce that right.

Due Process

Hurtado v. California (110 U.S. 516), decided by a 7-1 vote, March 3, 1884. Mathews wrote the majority opinion; Harlan dissented; Field did not participate.

The due process clause of the 14th Amendment does not require states to use grand jury indictments or presentments in capital offenses.

Taxes

Head Money Cases (112 U.S. 580), decided by a unanimous vote, Dec. 8, 1884. Miller wrote the opinion.

The constitutional requirement that indirect taxes be uniform is met if the tax operates the same upon all subjects being taxed; an indirect tax is not unconstitutional simply because the subject being taxed is not distributed uniformly throughout the United States.

Search and Seizure

Boyd v. United States (116 U.S. 616), decided without dissent, Feb. 1, 1886. Bradley wrote the opinion.

The court held that a revenue statute compelling a defendant to produce in court his private papers was unconstitutional as an unreasonable search and seizure violating the Fourth Amendment and as compelled self-incrimination in violation of the Fifth Amendment.

Equal Protection

Yick Wo v. Hopkins (118 U.S. 356), decided by a unanimous vote, May 10, 1886. Matthews wrote the opinion.

The 14th Amendment protects persons, not just citizens of the United States. Holding that a city's arbitrary enforcement of a fire hazard ordinance had discriminated against Chinese laundry owners in violation of the amendment's equal protection clause, the court said that guarantee applied "to all *persons* within the territorial jurisdiction, without regard to any differences of race, of color, or of nationality...."

Santa Clara County v. Southern Pacific Railroad Co. (118 U.S. 394), decided by a unanimous vote, May 10, 1886. Harlan wrote the opinion; Chief Justice Waite made a preliminary announcement.

Before the court heard arguments in this case, involving a tax dispute between a county, a state, and a railroad, Chief Justice Waite announced that the equal protection clause of the 14th Amendment applied to protect corporations as well as individuals. Corporations were thus established to be "persons" within the meaning of that amendment, and able to invoke its protection.

Commerce

Wabash, St. Louis and Pacific Railway Co. v. Illinois (118 U.S. 557), decided by a 6-3 vote, Oct. 25, 1886. Miller wrote the majority opinion; Chief Justice Waite, Bradley and Gray dissented.

States may not regulate the rates charged by railroads which form part of an interstate network, even if the state regulates only the intrastate portion of a trip. Such state regulation infringes upon the federal power to regulate interstate commerce.

State Powers

Mugler v. Kansas (123 U.S. 623), decided by an 8-1 vote, Dec. 5, 1887. Harlan wrote the majority opinion; Field dissented.

The court upheld a state law which forbade the manufacture and sale of intoxicating liquor in the state. Rejecting a challenge to this law as abridging the privileges and immunities of U.S. citizenship, as well as the due process guarantee of the 14th Amendment, the court held the law a proper exercise of the state police power to safeguard the public health and morals.

Federal Courts

Wisconsin v. Pelican Insurance Company (127 U.S. 265), decided without dissent, May 14, 1888. Gray wrote the opinion.

States may not invoke the original jurisdiction of the Supreme Court to enforce their criminal laws against non-residents. The Supreme Court refused to enforce the order of a Wisconsin court against a Louisiana corporation for failing to comply with Wisconsin laws.

Commerce

Kidd v. Pearson (128 U.S. 1), decided without dissent, Oct. 22, 1888. Lamar wrote the opinion.

The court upheld a state law which forbade the manufacture of liquor in the state — even if it was for sale and consumption outside the state. This law did not infringe federal power to regulate interstate commerce, held the court. Manufacture of goods is not commerce and cannot be regulated as interstate commerce.

Immigration

Chinese Exclusion Cases (Chae Chan Ping v. United States) (130 U.S. 581), decided by a unanimous vote, May 13, 1889. Field wrote the opinion.

The power of Congress over the entry of aliens, derived from the need to preserve the nation's sovereign status, is exclusive and absolute. This decision sustained an act of Congress which barred the entry of Chinese aliens into the country.

1890-1899

Treaties

Geofroy v. Riggs (133 U.S. 258), decided by a unanimous vote, February 3, 1890. Field wrote the opinion.

It is within the scope of the treaty power of the United States to regulate the inheritance by aliens of land and other property in the United States. The court declared that the treaty power was unlimited except by the Constitution. Field observed: "It would not be contended that it extends so far as to authorize what the Constitution forbids. . . ."

Civil Rights

Louisville, New Orleans and Texas Railway Co. v. Mississippi (133 U.S. 587), decided by a 7-2 vote, March 3, 1890. Brewer wrote the majority opinion; Harlan and Bradley dissented.

Mississippi does not infringe on the federal power to regulate interstate commerce when it by law requires railroads doing business in the state to provide separate accommodations for black and white passengers. The state

supreme court found this to apply solely to intrastate railroad operations. The Supreme Court accepted those findings and held the requirement was no burden on interstate commerce.

Federal Courts

United States v. Texas (143 U.S. 621), decided by a 7-2 vote, Feb. 29, 1892. Harlan wrote the majority opinion; Chief Justice Fuller and Lamar dissented.

By joining the Union, states acquiesce in the constitutional provision extending federal judicial power over all cases in which the United States is a party, including those brought by the United States against a state. The court rejected Texas' argument that the court lacked jurisdiction over such a case.

Due Process

Chicago, Milwaukee & St. Paul Railway Co. v. Minnesota (134 U.S. 418), decided by a 6-3 vote, March 24, 1890. Blatchford wrote the majority opinion; Bradley, Gray and Lamar dissented.

If a state deprives a company of the power to charge reasonable rates for the use of its property and provides for no judicial review of those rate limitations, the state is depriving the company of its property without due process of law.

Courts have the power to decide on the reasonableness of rates set by states for companies to charge and due process requires that an opportunity for judicial review of these rates be provided.

Self-Incrimination

Counselman v. Hitchcock (142 U.S. 547), decided by a unanimous vote, Jan. 11, 1892. Blatchford wrote the opinion.

Only a grant of complete and absolute immunity against prosecution for an offense revealed in compelled testimony is sufficient to justify waiver of the Fifth Amendment privilege against compelled self-incrimination.

The court struck down as insufficient under this standard the existing federal immunity statute which protected a witness only against the actual use of his testimony as evidence against him, not against its indirect use to obtain other evidence against him.

Compacts

Virginia v. Tennessee (148 U.S. 503), decided without dissent, April 3, 1893. Field wrote the opinion.

A compact to resolve a boundary dispute between two states need not be approved formally by Congress in order to be permissible. The Constitution does declare that "no state shall, without the consent of Congress, . . . enter into any Agreement or Compact with another state," but this requirement of formal consent applies only to compacts tending to increase the political power of the states at the expense of national authority or the federal government.

Commerce

United States v. E. C. Knight Co. (156 U.S. 1), decided by an 8-1 vote, Jan. 21, 1895. Chief Justice Fuller wrote the majority opinion; Harlan dissented.

In its first interpretation of the Sherman Anti-trust Act, the court ruled that the act did not apply to a trust that refined more than 90 percent of the sugar sold in the country.

Congress had no constitutional power to regulate manufacture, the court stated. The fact that much of the refined sugar was intended for sale in interstate commerce made no difference. Such sales would affect interstate commerce only indirectly. Congressional authority extended only to regulation of matters that directly affected interstate commerce.

This distinction between matters affecting interstate commerce directly or indirectly was a significant modification of the court's 1824 *Gibbons v. Ogden* opinion, in which it held that the Constitution gave Congress authority to regulate intrastate matters that affected other states.

The holding in *Knight* was gradually eroded by later decisions.

Federal Courts

California v. Southern Pacific Co. (157 U.S. 229), decided by a 7-2 vote, March 18, 1895. Chief Justice Fuller wrote the majority opinion; Harlan and Brewer dissented.

The Supreme Court does not have original jurisdiction over cases brought by a state against its own citizens; such suits are generally to be brought in state courts, not federal courts.

Taxes

Pollock v. Farmers' Loan and Trust Co. (158 U.S. 601), decided by a 5-4 vote, May 20, 1895. Chief Justice Fuller wrote the majority opinion; Harlan, Jackson, Brown and White dissented.

Taxes on income derived from real estate and personal property are direct taxes and therefore must be apportioned among the states according to population. With this ruling the court struck down the first general income tax law enacted by Congress and overruled two earlier decisions which defined head taxes and taxes on land as the only two forms of direct taxation.

The decision led to adoption and ratification in 1913 of the 16th Amendment which exempted income taxes from the Constitution's apportionment requirement.

Commerce

In re Debs (158 U.S. 564) decided by a unanimous vote, May 27, 1895. Brewer wrote the court's opinion.

Eugene V. Debs and other leaders of the 1894 Pullman strike challenged their contempt convictions for violating a federal court injunction ordering them to halt the strike. A lower court upheld the validity of the injunction under the authority of the Sherman Anti-trust Act. The Supreme Court affirmed the validity of the injunction — and Debs' conviction — but on the broader grounds of national sovereignty, which the court said gave the federal government authority to remove obstructions to interstate commerce and transportation of the mails.

Civil Rights

Plessy v. Ferguson (163 U.S. 537), decided by an 8-1 vote, May 18, 1896. Brown wrote the majority opinion; Harlan dissented.

A state law requiring trains to provide separate but equal facilities for black and white passengers does not infringe upon federal authority to regulate interstate commerce nor is it in violation of the 13th or 14th Amendments. The train was local; a legal distinction between the two races did not destroy the legal equality of the two races guaranteed by the 13th Amendment, and the 14th Amendment protected only political, not social, equality, the majority said.

In dissent, Justice John Marshall Harlan declared that the "Constitution is color-blind, and neither knows nor tolerates classes among citizens." The "separate but equal" doctrine remained effective until the 1954 *Brown v. Board of Education* decision.

Due Process

Allgeyer v. Louisiana (165 U.S. 578), decided without dissent, March 1, 1897. Peckham wrote the opinion.

The court declared that the liberty protected by the due process clause of the 14th Amendment against denial by the state included the freedom to make a contract. The court struck down a state law which forbade its citizens to obtain insurance from out-of-state companies.

This was the first recognition by the court of the protected "freedom of contract" which the justices would use subsequently to strike down minimum wage and maximum hour laws.

Chicago, Burlington & Quincy Railroad Company v. Chicago (166 U.S. 226), decided by a 7-1 vote, March 1, 1897. Harlan wrote the majority opinion; Brewer dissented; Chief Justice Fuller did not participate.

The 14th Amendment guarantee of due process requires a state, when it takes private property for public use, to provide just compensation to the property owner.

Holden v. Hardy (169 U.S. 366), decided by a 7-2 vote, Feb. 28, 1898. Brown wrote the majority opinion; Brewer and Peckham dissented.

The court upheld, against a due process challenge, Utah's law that limited the number of hours that miners could work in underground mines.

The "freedom of contract" is subject to certain limitations imposed by the state in the exercise of its police power to protect the health of workers in hazardous conditions, the court said.

Smyth v. Ames (169 U.S. 466), decided by a 7-0 vote, March 7, 1898. Harlan wrote the opinion; Chief Justice Fuller and McKenna did not participate in the decision.

Corporations are persons within the protection of the 14th Amendment's guarantee of due process. That guarantee requires states to set railroad rates sufficiently high to ensure the railroad companies a fair return on the value of the investment and just compensation for the use of their property.

To ensure compliance with this standard, federal courts have the power to review the rates.

Citizenship

United States v. Wong Kim Ark (169 U.S. 649) decided by a 6-2 vote, March 28, 1898. Gray wrote the majority opinion; Chief Justice Fuller and Harlan dissented; McKenna did not participate.

Children born in the United States to resident alien parents are citizens of the United States even if their parents are barred from becoming citizens because of their race.

This was the first case in which the court interpreted the clause of the 14th Amendment that defines U.S. citizens as all persons born in the United States and remaining under its jurisdiction.

Voting Rights

Williams v. Mississippi (170 U.S. 213), decided by a unanimous vote, April 25, 1898. McKenna delivered the opinion.

A state does not violate the equal protection clause of the 14th Amendment when it requires eligible voters to be able to read, write, interpret or understand any part of the Constitution.

1900-1905

Privileges and Immunities

Maxwell v. Dow (176 U.S. 581), decided by an 8-1 vote, Feb. 25, 1900. Peckham wrote the majority opinion; Harlan dissented.

The right to be tried by a jury of 12 persons is not one of the privileges and immunities of United States citizenship protected by the 14th Amendment against violation by states.

The court upheld a state court judgment reached by a jury composed of eight persons — instead of 12 as required in federal courts.

Taxes

Knowlton v. Moore (178 U.S. 41), decided by a 5-3 vote, May 14, 1900. White wrote the majority opinion; Brewer dissented in part; Harlan and McKenna dissented; Peckham did not participate.

The constitutional requirement that indirect taxes be uniform does not require that the tax rate be uniform, only that the same rate be applied to the same class in the same manner throughout the United States.

Territories

The Insular Cases, decided May 27, 1901: *DeLima v. Bidwell* (182 U.S. 1), decided by a 5-4 vote; Brown wrote the majority opinion; Gray, McKenna, Shiras and White dissented. *Downes v. Bidwell* (182 U.S. 244), decided by a 5-4 vote; Brown wrote the majority opinion; Chief Justice Fuller, Harlan, Brewster and Peckham dissented.

In these two cases the court ruled that as a result of U.S. annexation of Puerto Rico, the island was no longer a foreign country but neither was it a part of the United States included within the full protection of the Constitution. The Constitution applied automatically only to states, the court held, and it was up to Congress, in the exercise of its power to govern territories, to determine whether the Constitution should apply in particular territories.

In a third case, *Dorr v. United States* (195 U.S. 138, 1904), the court adopted the "incorporation theory," still in effect, under which the Constitution automatically applies in territories that have been formally incorporated into the United States either through ratified treaty or act of Congress, but not to unincorporated territories.

Commerce

Champion v. Ames (188 U.S. 321), decided by a 5-4 vote, Feb. 23, 1903. Harlan wrote the majority opinion; Chief Justice Fuller, Brewer, Peckham and Shiras dissented.

In its first recognition of a federal "police" power, the court sustained a federal law banning the shipment of lottery tickets in interstate commerce. Just as states might regulate intrastate matters in order to protect the health, welfare and morals of their residents, so might Congress exercise its authority to regulate interstate commerce for the same purposes.

Northern Securities Co. v. United States (193 U.S. 197), decided by a 5-4 vote, March 14, 1904. Harlan wrote the majority opinion; Chief Justice Fuller, White, Holmes and Peckham dissented.

A holding company formed solely to eliminate competition between two railroad lines was a combination in restraint of trade and therefore in violation of the federal antitrust act.

This ruling represented a major modification of the *Knight* sugar trust decision in 1895: the majority now held that although the holding company itself was not in interstate commerce, it sufficiently affected that commerce by restraining it and thus came within the scope of the federal antitrust statute.

Taxes

McCray v. United States (195 U.S. 27), decided by a 6-3 vote, May 31, 1904. White wrote the court's opinion; Chief Justice Fuller, Brown and Peckham dissented.

Congress may use its power to tax as a regulatory "police" power. So long as the tax produces some revenue, the court will not examine the motivation for imposing the tax.

Using this reasoning, the court upheld a federal statute which placed a high tax on oleo which was colored yellow to resemble butter. That tax was obviously designed to eliminate the competition to butter, but the court held that the tax was lawful on its face and that the court had no power to "restrain the exercise of a lawful power on the assumption that a wrongful purpose or motive has caused the power to be exerted."

This ruling came little more than a year after the court held that Congress could also use its interstate commerce power as a "police" power; the two decisions substantially increased congressional power to regulate commerce in the United States.

Commerce

Swift and Co. v. United States (196 U.S 375), decided by a unanimous vote, Jan. 30, 1905. Holmes wrote the opinion.

Congress has authority to regulate local commerce that is part of an interstate current of commerce. This was the court's first enunciation of the "stream-of-commerce" doctrine.

Thus, the court held that meatpackers who combined to fix the price of livestock and meat bought and sold in Chicago stockyards were in violation of the federal antitrust act because the meatpacking operation was the middle part of an interstate transaction in which cattle were shipped from out of the state into Chicago for slaughter and packing and then shipped to other states for sale.

Due Process

Lochner v. New York (198 U.S. 45), decided by a 5-4 vote, April 17, 1905. Peckham wrote the majority opinion; Day, Harlan, Holmes and White dissented.

The court struck down a New York law limiting the hours which bakery employees could work. The majority found the law a denial of due process, infringing upon the freedom of contract. Because there was no sufficient health reason for the hours limit, the law was held to be outside the police power of the state.

1906-1910

State Powers

Georgia v. Tennessee Copper Company (206 U.S. 230), decided by a unanimous vote, May 13, 1907. Holmes wrote the opinion.

In one of the first "environmental law" cases to come to the court, the justices declared that a state could come into federal court to obtain an order directing a company in another state to cease polluting the air the two states shared.

Commerce

Adair v. United States (208 U.S. 161), decided by a 6-2 vote, Jan. 27, 1908. Harlan wrote the court's opinion; Holmes and McKenna dissented; Moody did not participate.

A federal statute prohibiting employers from making contracts that required an employee to promise not to join a labor union as a condition of employment exceeds federal authority to regulate interstate commerce. This prohibition also violates the "freedom of contract."

This decision, which was later overruled, placed these so-called "yellow dog" contracts beyond the reach of federal power. It was one of several decisions of the early 20th century in which the court ruled against the interests of the labor movement.

Loewe v. Lawler (Danbury Hatters Case) (208 U.S. 274), decided by a unanimous vote, Feb. 3, 1908. Chief Justice Fuller wrote the opinion.

A union attempting to organize workers in a factory in one state by setting up boycotts of stores in other states that sell the factory's products (secondary boycotts) becomes a combination in restraint of trade and in violation of the federal antitrust law.

This decision led to adoption of provisions in the Clayton Anti-trust Act of 1914 exempting labor unions from actions under the antitrust laws.

State Powers

Muller v. Oregon (208 U.S. 412), decided by a unanimous vote, Feb. 24, 1908. Brewer wrote the opinion.

The court upheld Oregon's law setting maximum hours for women working in laundries. The court relied on the argument that longer working hours might impair the childbearing function of women. State limitation of those hours was therefore justified as a health measure, properly within the state police power.

Federal Courts

Ex parte Young (209 U.S. 123), decided by an 8-1 vote, March 23, 1908. Peckham wrote the majority opinion; Harlan dissented.

Federal judges may properly enjoin, temporarily, the enforcement of a state law challenged as unconstitutional. The injunction may remain in effect until the validity of the law is determined.

Self-Incrimination

Twining v. New Jersey (211 U.S. 78), decided by an 8-1 vote, Nov. 9, 1908. Moody delivered the majority opinion; Harlan dissented.

The 14th Amendment does not automatically extend the Fifth Amendment privilege against compelled self-incrimination — or other provisions of the Bill of Rights — to state defendants. Thus the constitutional rights of state defendants are not impaired when a judge or prosecutor comments adversely upon their failure to testify in their own defense.

Cruel and Unusual Punishment

Weems v. United States (217 U.S. 349), decided by a 4-2 vote, May 2, 1910. McKenna wrote the majority opinion; White and Harlan dissented; Moody and Lurton did not participate.

The court held that a law of the Philippines, a U.S. territory, providing punishment of 12 years at hard labor in chains for falsifying an official document was "cruel and unusual punishment" prohibited by the Eighth Amendment.

1911-1915

Federal Courts

Muskrat v. United States (219 U.S. 346), decided by a unanimous vote, Jan. 23, 1911. Day wrote the opinion.

The court dismissed a case which Congress had authorized certain Indians to bring in order to test the constitutionality of certain laws. There was no actual dispute or conflict of rights and interests here, the court held, and thus there was no "case or controversy" properly within its power to resolve.

Commerce

Standard Oil Co. v. United States (221 U.S. 1), decided by an 8-1 vote, May 15, 1911. Chief Justice White wrote the majority opinion; Harlan dissented in part.

Only unreasonable combinations and undue restraints of trade are illegal under the federal antitrust act. In this decision, which resulted in the break-up of the Standard Oil monopoly, a majority of the court for the first time adopted the so-called "rule of reason;" it is still applied to antitrust cases today. Previously, the court had held that *any* combination which restrained trade, whether "reasonable" or "unreasonable," was a violation of the federal statute.

Contempt

Gompers v. Buck's Stove and Range Co. (221 U.S. 418), decided by a unanimous court, May 15, 1911. Lamar wrote the opinion.

Civil contempt and criminal contempt are distinguished by the character and purpose of the penalty imposed for them. The purpose of a punishment for civil contempt is remedial — to convince a witness to testify, for example — while the purpose of punishment for criminal contempt is clearly punitive, to vindicate the authority of the court. Civil contempt ends whenever the person held in contempt decides to comply with the court; criminal contempt is punished by a fixed sentence.

State Powers

Coyle v. Smith (221 U.S. 559), decided by a 7-2 vote, May 29, 1911. Lurton wrote the court's opinion; McKenna and Holmes dissented.

States are admitted into the Union on an equal footing with all other states; Congress may not place any restrictions on matters wholly under the state's control as a condition of entry. This ruling invalidated a congressional requirement that Oklahoma's state capital remain in Guthrie, Okla., for seven years after statehood was granted.

Search and Seizure

Weeks v. United States (232 U.S. 383), decided by a unanimous vote, Feb. 24, 1914. Day wrote the opinion.

A person whose Fourth Amendment rights to be secure against unreasonable search and seizure are violated by federal agents has the right to require that evidence obtained in the search be excluded from use against him in federal courts.

Commerce

Shreveport Rate Case: Houston, East and West Texas Railway Co. v. United States; Texas and Pacific Railway Co. v. United States (234 U.S. 342), decided by a 7-2 vote, June 8, 1914. Hughes wrote the majority opinion; Lurton and Pitney dissented.

Congress may regulate intrastate rail rates if they are so intertwined with interstate rail rates that it is impossible to regulate the one without regulating the other. This so-called "Shreveport Doctrine" was eventually expanded to allow regulation of other intrastate matters that affected interstate commerce.

Due Process

Frank v. Mangum (237 U.S. 309), decided by a 7-2 vote, April 12, 1915. Pitney wrote the majority opinion; Holmes and Hughes dissented.

The court upheld a state conviction for murder although the trial court atmosphere was dominated by anti-Semitism and hostility. The majority reasoned that review of the conviction by Georgia's highest state court guaranteed the defendant due process.

Interstate Relations

Virginia v. West Virginia (238 U.S. 202), decided by a unanimous vote, June 14, 1915. Hughes wrote the opinion.

In one of the longest-running disputes to come before the court, the justices held in 1915 that West Virginia owed Virginia some $12 million — its share of the pre-Civil War state debts of Virginia, which West Virginia had agreed to assume upon its becoming a separate state.

Voting Rights

Guinn v. United States (238 U.S. 347), decided by an 8-0 vote, June 21, 1915. Chief Justice White wrote the opinion; McReynolds did not participate.

The court declared an Oklahoma "grandfather clause" for voters an unconstitutional evasion of the 15th Amendment guarantee that states would not deny citizens the right to vote because of their race. Oklahoma law imposed a literacy test upon potential voters but exempted all persons whose ancestors voted in 1866. The court said that though race, color or previous servitude were not mentioned in the law, selection of a date prior to adoption of the 15th Amendment was obviously intended to disenfranchise Negroes in "direct and positive disregard" of the amendment.

United States v. Mosley (238 U.S. 383), decided by a 7-1 vote, June 21, 1915. Holmes wrote the opinion; Lamar dissented; McReynolds did not participate.

The court upheld congressional power to regulate elections tainted with fraud and corruption. For the second time the court upheld provisions of the 1870 Enforcement Act implementing the 15th Amendment. In *Ex parte Yarbrough* (1884) the court had sustained congressional power to penalize persons who used violence and intimidation to prevent Negroes from voting.

State Powers

Hadacheck v. Los Angeles (239 U.S. 394), decided by a unanimous vote, Dec. 12, 1915. McKenna wrote the opinion.

The power to pass zoning laws is part of the state police power, enabling the state to control the use to which certain lands are put. A city's use of this power to forbid brickmaking in a certain area is valid, and does not deny due process to a brickmaker, even if it puts him out of business.

1916-1920

Taxes

Brushaber v. Union Pacific Railroad Co. (240 U.S. 1), decided by a 7-2 vote, Jan. 24, 1916. Chief Justice White wrote the majority opinion; McKenna and Pitney dissented.

With two other cases decided the same day, the court in this decision sustained the 1913 general income tax law enacted after ratification of the 16th Amendment. This decision completed the action necessary to nullify the court's 1895 ruling that income taxes were direct taxes that must be apportioned among the states according to population. The 16th Amendment exempted income taxes from the apportionment requirement.

Power of Congress

Clark Distilling Co. v. Western Maryland Railway (242 U.S. 311), decided by a 7-2 vote, Jan. 8, 1917. Chief Justice White wrote the majority opinion; Holmes and Van Devanter dissented.

The court upheld the power of the states under the federal Webb-Kenyon Act of 1913 to forbid the entry of intoxicating liquor into their territory.

The act giving the states that power had been challenged as an unconstitutional delegation of power, but the court held it was permissible because the statute established the precise conditions under which the states might act.

Due Process

Bunting v. Oregon (243 U.S. 426), decided by a 5-3 vote, April 9, 1917. McKenna wrote the majority opinion; Chief Justice White, McReynolds and Van Devanter dissented; Brandeis did not participate.

Extending its 1908 decision in *Muller v. Oregon,* the court upheld an Oregon law setting 10 hours as the maximum permissible workday for all industrial workers.

Buchanan v. Warley (245 U.S. 60), decided by a unanimous vote, Nov. 5, 1917. Day wrote the opinion.

City ordinances that segregate neighborhoods by restricting some blocks to white residents only and other blocks to black residents only violate the 14th Amendment, which forbids states to deprive persons of property rights except by due process of law.

This decision led to the growth of private restrictive covenants under which neighbors would agree to sell or rent their homes only to persons of the same race. The court upheld such private covenants in the 1926 case of *Corrigan v. Buckley.*

Power of Congress

Selective Draft Law Cases (245 U.S. 366), decided by a unanimous vote, Jan. 7, 1918. Chief Justice White wrote the opinion.

Congress is authorized to institute a compulsory draft of persons into the armed forces under its power to raise armies and the "necessary and proper" clause. Moreover, service in the military is one of the duties of a citizen in a "just government." Compulsory conscription is not involuntary servitude in violation of the 13th Amendment.

Commerce

Hammer v. Dagenhart (247 U.S. 251), decided by a 5-4 vote, June 3, 1918. Day wrote the majority opinion; Holmes, McKenna, Brandeis and Clarke dissented.

Narrowing the federal "police" power substantially, the court struck down a federal statute that prohibited the shipment in interstate commerce of any goods produced by child laborers.

Labor was an aspect of manufacture, an intrastate matter not subject to federal control, the majority held. Furthermore, Congress could prohibit shipments in interstate commerce only of goods that were in themselves harmful. Because products made by children were not themselves harmful, Congress had no authority to forbid their shipment.

This decision and a 1922 ruling that Congress had used its taxing power unconstitutionally in a second law intended to bring an end to child labor were overruled in 1941.

Freedom of Expression

Schenck v. United States (249 U.S. 47), decided by a unanimous vote, March 3, 1919. Holmes wrote the opinion.

In its first decision dealing with the extent of protection afforded by the First Amendment, the court sustained the Espionage Act of 1917 against a challenge that it violated the guarantees of freedom of speech and press.

The First Amendment is not an absolute guarantee, the court said. Freedom of speech and press may be constrained if "the words used are used in such circumstances and are of such a nature as to create a clear and present danger that they will bring about the substantive evils that Congress has a right to prevent."

Treaties

Missouri v. Holland (252 U.S. 416), decided by a 7-2 vote, April 19, 1920. Holmes wrote the majority opinion; Van Devanter and Pitney dissented.

In order to implement a treaty, Congress may enact legislation that without a treaty might be an unconstitutional invasion of state sovereignty.

After lower courts ruled an act of Congress protecting migratory birds an unconstitutional invasion of powers reserved to the states, the U.S. government negotiated a treaty with Canada for the protection of the birds. After the Senate ratified it, Congress again enacted protective legislation to fulfill the terms of the treaty. Sustaining this second act, the court wrote: "It is obvious that there may

be matters of the sharpest exigency for the national well-being that an act of Congress could not deal with but that a treaty followed by such an act could. . . ."

1921-1925

Commerce

Duplex Printing Press Co. v. Deering (254 U.S. 443), decided by a 6-3 vote, Jan. 3, 1921. Pitney wrote the majority opinion. Brandeis, Holmes and Clarke dissented.

Reading the Clayton Act narrowly, the majority held that federal courts were prohibited from issuing injunctions only against legal and normal labor union operations. A secondary boycott was a combination in restraint of trade, which was illegal under the federal antitrust law. Courts therefore could use injunctions to stop illegal secondary boycotts.

Power of Congress

Newberry v. United States (256 U.S. 232), decided by a 5-4 vote, May 2, 1921. McReynolds wrote the majority opinion; Chief Justice White, Pitney, Brandeis and Clark dissented in part.

The court reversed the conviction of Truman H. Newberry for violating an act of Congress limiting campaign expenditures in a primary election. The court held that Congress lacked power to regulate primary campaigns because a primary was "in no real sense part of the manner of holding the election."

Dillon v. Gloss (256 U.S. 368), decided by a unanimous vote, May 16, 1921. Van Devanter wrote the opinion.

The power of Congress to designate the manner in which the states shall ratify proposed amendments to the Constitution includes the power to set a "reasonable" time period within which the states must act.

State Powers

Ponzi v. Fessenden (258 U.S. 254), decided by a unanimous vote, March 27, 1922. Chief Justice Taft wrote the opinion.

With the consent of the federal government, a state court may issue a writ of *habeas corpus* to federal officials, directing them to present a federal prisoner to state court for trial there on state charges.

Taxes

Bailey v. Drexel Furniture Co. (259 U.S. 20), decided by an 8-1 vote, May 15, 1922. Chief Justice Taft wrote the majority opinion; Clarke dissented.

In its second decision frustrating congressional efforts to end child labor, the court invalidated a federal law that imposed a 10 percent tax on the net profits of any company that employed children under a certain age. The court said the tax was an impermissible use of Congress' police power because Congress intended it as a penalty rather than a source of revenue. The court overruled this and its 1918 *Hammer v. Dagenhart* decision in 1941.

Double Jeopardy

United States v. Lanza (260 U.S. 377), decided by an 8-0 vote, Dec. 11, 1922. Chief Justice Taft delivered the opinion.

Where both federal and state jurisdictions make the same act a crime the double jeopardy guarantee of the Fifth

Amendment does not prohibit a federal prosecution and a state prosecution of the same defendant for the same crime.

Due Process

Moore v. Dempsey (261 U.S. 86), decided by a 6-2 vote, Feb. 19, 1923. Holmes wrote the majority opinion; McReynolds and Sutherland dissented.

Mob domination of the atmosphere of a trial can deny a defendant his right to a fair trial guaranteed by the Sixth Amendment.

Adkins v. Children's Hospital (261 U.S. 525), decided by a 5-3 vote, April 9, 1923. Sutherland wrote the majority opinion; Chief Justice Taft, Holmes and Sanford dissented; Brandeis did not participate.

The court struck down an act of Congress setting a minimum wage for women and children workers in the District of Columbia. The majority found this law a price-fixing measure, in violation of the freedom of contract protected by the Fifth Amendment against infringement by federal action.

Federal Courts

Massachusetts v. Mellon, Frothingham v. Mellon (262 U.S. 447), decided by a unanimous court, June 4, 1923. Sutherland wrote the opinion.

Rejecting a state and a taxpayer's challenges to a federal grant-in-aid program as unconstitutional, the court held that the taxpayer lacked "standing" to sue, because her share of the federal revenues expended in the challenged program was too minute to constitute the personal interest which one must have in a matter in order to bring a challenge to it in federal court.

Search and Seizure

Carroll v. United States (267 U.S. 132), decided by a 7-2 vote, March 2, 1925. Chief Justice Taft delivered the majority opinion; McReynolds and Sutherland dissented.

The ruling extended the scope of permissible searches which could be conducted without a warrant. Federal agents could make warrantless searches of automobiles where a reasonable suspicion of illegal actions existed.

Personal Liberty

Pierce v. Society of Sisters (286 U.S. 510), decided by a unanimous vote, June 1, 1925. McReynolds wrote the opinion.

A state law which requires all children in the first eight grades to attend public, rather than private or parochial, schools violates the 14th Amendment due process guarantee of "personal liberty." Implicit in this liberty is the right of parents to choose the kind of education they want for their children.

Freedom of Speech

Gitlow v. New York (268 U.S. 652), decided by a 7-2 vote, June 8, 1925. Sanford wrote the majority opinion; Holmes and Brandeis dissented.

The First Amendment prohibition against government abridgment of the freedom of speech applies to the states as well as to the federal government. The freedoms of speech and press "are among the fundamental personal rights and 'liberties' protected by the due process clause of the 14th

Amendment from impairment by the states," the court asserted. This decision was the first of a long line of rulings which held that the 14th Amendment extended the guarantees of the Bill of Rights to state, as well as federal, action.

1926-1930

Civil Rights

Corrigan v. Buckley (271 U.S. 323), decided by a unanimous vote, May 24, 1926. Sanford wrote the opinion.

Civil rights are not protected by the Fifth, 13th or 14th Amendments against the discriminatory actions of private individuals. Therefore there is no constitutional protection for individuals who have been discriminated against as a result of the use of private restrictive covenants, under which residents of one race living in a neighborhood agree among themselves not to sell or rent their homes to members of another race.

Power of the President

Myers v. United States (272 U.S. 52), decided by a 6-3 vote, Oct. 25, 1926. Chief Justice Taft wrote the majority opinion; Holmes, Brandeis and McReynolds dissented.

This decision upheld the president's power to remove certain classes of postmasters from office without congressional consent. The court held that the statute creating the positions — which also provided for removal only with congressional consent — was an unconstitutional incursion upon executive power. The court implied that the president's removal power was virtually unlimited, extending even to members of independent regulatory agencies.

State Powers

Euclid v. Ambler Realty Co. (272 U.S. 365), decided by a 6-3 vote, Nov. 22, 1926. Sutherland wrote the majority opinion; Butler, McReynolds and Van Devanter dissented.

A city's zoning ordinance excluding apartment houses from certain neighborhoods is an appropriate use of the police power and does not violate the due process guarantee in denying an individual the right to use his property as he desires. If the classification of land use in a zoning ordinance is "fairly debatable," it will be upheld.

Due Process

Tumey v. Ohio (273 U.S. 510), decided by a unanimous vote, March 7, 1927. Chief Justice Taft wrote the opinion.

The 14th Amendment guarantee of due process assures a defendant a trial before an impartial judge. A state, therefore, may not allow a city's mayor to serve as judge in cases, when half the fines collected go into the city treasury. A defendant is denied due process when he is tried before a judge with a direct, personal, pecuniary interest in ruling against him.

Voting Rights

Nixon v. Herndon (273 U.S. 536), decided by a unanimous vote, March 7, 1927. Holmes wrote the opinion.

The court invalidated a Texas law that excluded Negroes from voting in primary elections of the Democratic Party. The court declared the Texas "white primary" law unconstitutional as a violation of the equal protection clause of the 14th Amendment.

Due Process

Buck v. Bell (274 U.S. 200), decided by an 8-1 vote, May 2, 1927. Holmes wrote the majority opinion; Butler dissented.

The court held that Virginia did not violate the 14th Amendment's due process guarantee when it sterilized, without her consent, a mentally defective mother.

Freedom of Association

Whitney v. California (274 U.S. 357), decided by a unanimous vote, May 16, 1927. Sanford wrote the opinion.

The court upheld a state law that made it a crime to organize and participate in a group that advocated the overthrow by force of the established political system. The law was challenged as a violation of the First Amendment freedoms of speech and assembly.

Taxes

J. W. Hampton Jr. & Co. v. United States (276 U.S. 394), decided by a unanimous vote, April 9, 1928. Chief Justice Taft wrote the opinion.

Imposition of protective tariffs is a permissible exercise of the power to tax, a power which may be used to regulate as well as to raise revenue.

Search and Seizure

Olmstead v. United States (277 U.S. 438), decided by a 5-4 vote, June 4, 1928. Chief Justice Taft wrote the majority opinion; Brandeis, Holmes, Butler and Stone dissented.

Wiretaps do not violate the Fourth Amendment's prohibition against unreasonable searches and seizures where no entry of private premises occurred.

Jury Trials

Patton v. United States (281 U.S. 276), decided by a 7-0 vote, April 14, 1930. Sutherland wrote the opinion; Chief Justice Hughes did not participate.

The three essential elements of a jury trial required in federal courts by the Sixth Amendment are a panel of 12 jurors, supervision by a judge and a unanimous verdict.

1931-1934

Freedom of Speech

Stromberg v. California (283 U.S. 359), decided by a 7-2 vote, May 18, 1931. Chief Justice Hughes wrote the majority opinion; McReynolds and Butler dissented.

A state violates the First Amendment guarantee of free speech when it penalizes persons who raise a red flag as a symbol of opposition to organized government. The court did not directly address the First Amendment issue in this case but held instead that the language of the statute was impermissibly vague. Although aimed at curbing symbolic speech that advocated the unlawful overthrow of the government, the statute's language conceivably permitted punishment for the flying of any banner symbolizing advocacy of a change in government, even through peaceful means.

Freedom of the Press

Near v. Minnesota (283 U.S. 697), decided by a 5-4 vote, June 1, 1931. Chief Justice Hughes wrote the majority opinion; Butler, Van Devanter, McReynolds and Sutherland dissented.

A state law which bars continued publication of a newspaper that prints malicious or defamatory articles is a prior restraint of the press in violation of the First Amendment. This was the first time that the court specifically enforced the First Amendment's guarantee of freedom of the press against abridgment by a state.

Voting Rights

Nixon v. Condon (286 U.S. 73), decided by a 5-4 vote, May 2, 1932. Cardozo wrote the majority opinion; McReynolds, Butler, Sutherland and Van Devanter dissented.

Exclusion of Negroes from voting in primary elections — as a result of action by the Democratic Party — constituted denial of equal protection of the laws and was impermissible under the 14th Amendment. The political party, the court held, acted as the agent of the state in denying Negroes access to primary elections.

After the court's decision in *Nixon v. Herndon* (1927), the Texas legislature authorized the state party executive committee to set voting qualifications for its primary. The party excluded Negroes. The court held this action unconstitutional, saying that neither the state nor political parties could exclude Negroes from primaries on the basis of race alone.

Wood v. Broom (287 U.S. 1), decided by a 5-4 vote, Oct. 18, 1932. Chief Justice Hughes wrote the majority opinion; Brandeis, Stone, Cardozo and Roberts dissented.

When Congress in the Apportionment Act of 1929 omitted the requirement that electoral districts for congressional elections be contiguous, compact and equal, it effectively repealed similar requirements in previous laws. Thus, federal courts could not act to correct malapportionment in state districts.

Right to Legal Counsel

Powell v. Alabama (287 U.S. 45), decided by a 7-2 vote, Nov. 7, 1932. Sutherland wrote the majority opinion; Butler and McReynolds dissented.

Under the particular circumstances of this — the "First Scottsboro Case" — in which a number of young black men charged with raping two white women were tried in a hostile community atmosphere — the failure of the trial court to provide the defendants the effective aid of an attorney in presenting their defense constituted a denial of due process guaranteed them by the 14th Amendment.

Contracts

Home Building and Loan Assn. v. Blaisdell (290 U.S. 398), decided by a 5-4 vote, Jan. 8, 1934. Chief Justice Hughes wrote the majority opinion; Sutherland, Van Devanter, Butler and McReynolds dissented.

The court upheld an emergency state mortgage moratorium law against the challenge that it violated the constitutional ban on state action impairing the obligation of contracts.

State Powers

Nebbia v. New York (291 U.S. 502), decided by a 5-4 vote, March 5, 1934. Roberts wrote the majority opinion; McReynolds, Butler, Van Devanter and Sutherland dissented.

The court abandoned its "public interest" rationale for determining which areas of business were properly subject to state regulation — a line of cases begun in *Munn v. Illinois* in 1877.

In this case the court upheld a New York law which set an acceptable range of prices to be charged for milk within the state. The majority declared that states could regulate almost any business in the interest of the public good, so long as the regulation was reasonable and effected through appropriate means.

1935

Power of Congress

Panama Refining Co. v. Ryan (293 U.S. 388), decided by an 8-1 vote, Jan. 7, 1935. Chief Justice Hughes wrote the majority opinion; Cardozo dissented.

The court declared invalid a provision of the National Industrial Recovery Act that authorized the president to prohibit from interstate commerce oil produced in violation of state regulations controlling the amount of production. The court said this congressional delegation of power was unconstitutionally broad because it left too much to the discretion of the president. This was the first of the court's rulings striking down New Deal legislation.

Currency

Gold Clause Cases: Norman v. Baltimore and Ohio Railroad Co. (294 U.S. 240), *Nortz v. United States* (294 U.S. 317), *Perry v. United States* (294 U.S. 330), decided by 5-4 votes, Feb. 18, 1935. Chief Justice Hughes wrote the majority opinion; McReynolds, Butler, Sutherland and Van Devanter dissented.

The power of Congress to regulate the value of currency permits it to abrogate clauses in private contracts requiring payment in gold. But the federal power to borrow money "on the credit of the United States" prohibits Congress from abrogating such clauses contained in government bonds and other federal contracts.

Voting Rights

Grovey v. Townsend (295 U.S. 45), decided by a unanimous vote, April 1, 1935. Roberts wrote the opinion.

The court held that the Texas Democratic Party did not violate the 14th Amendment by deciding to confine membership in the party to white citizens. A political party was a private organization, the court ruled, and the 14th Amendment's guarantee did not reach private action.

Jury Trials

Norris v. Alabama (294 U.S. 587), decided by an 8-0 vote, April 1, 1935. Chief Justice Hughes wrote the opinion; McReynolds did not participate.

In the "Second Scottsboro Case," the court set aside the conviction of the Negro defendant because blacks had been consistently barred from service on both the grand jury and trial jury in this case.

Commerce

Railroad Retirement Board v. Alton Railroad Co. (295 U.S. 330), decided by a 5-4 vote, May 6, 1935. Roberts wrote the majority opinion; Chief Justice Hughes, Brandeis, Cardozo and Stone dissented.

Congress exceeded its authority when it enacted the Railroad Retirement Act of 1934, which set up a comprehensive pension system for railroad workers, the court held, invalidating the act. The pension plan was unrelated to

interstate commerce, the majority said, and, in addition, several parts of it violated the guarantee of due process.

Schechter Poultry Corp. v. United States (295 U.S. 495), decided by a unanimous vote, May 27, 1935. Chief Justice Hughes wrote the opinion.

Congress exceeded its authority to delegate legislative powers and to regulate interstate commerce when it enacted the National Industrial Recovery Act. The section of the statute that permitted the president to approve "fair competition" codes under certain conditions left the chief executive with too much discretionary power. Furthermore, the statute regulated matters of intrastate commerce that affected interstate commerce only indirectly and so were not within federal power to regulate.

Power of the President

Humphrey's Executor v. United States (295 U.S. 602), decided by a unanimous vote, May 27, 1935. Sutherland wrote the opinion.

The court denied the president the power to remove members of independent regulatory agencies without the consent of Congress and limited sharply the executive removal power given such broad scope in the 1926 decision in *Myers v. United States.*

1936

The Spending Power

United States v. Butler (297 U.S. 1), decided by a 6-3 vote, Jan. 6, 1936. Roberts wrote the majority opinion; Stone, Brandeis and Cardozo dissented.

In its first interpretation of the power of Congress to spend for the general welfare, the court held that Congress could not combine that power with the power to tax in order to regulate a matter that was outside the scope of federal authority — in this instance, agricultural production.

The ruling declared unconstitutional the Agricultural Adjustment Act of 1933, which sought to regulate agricultural production by taxing processors of basic food commodities and then using the revenue from that tax to pay benefits to farmers who reduced their production of those commodities.

Freedom of the Press

Grosjean v. American Press Co. (297 U.S. 233), decided by a unanimous vote, Feb. 10, 1936. Sutherland wrote the opinion.

A state law that places a 2 percent tax on the gross receipts of certain newspapers, and not others, is a prior restraint on the press in violation of the First Amendment. Although labeled a tax on the privilege of doing business, the law had actually been written so that the tax fell only on those newspapers that opposed the administration of the state governor.

Power of Congress

Ashwander v. Tennessee Valley Authority (297 U.S. 288), decided by votes of 8-1 and 5-4, Feb. 17, 1936. Chief Justice Hughes wrote the majority opinion; McReynolds, Brandeis, Stone, Roberts and Cardozo dissented in part.

The court implicitly upheld the statute authorizing the establishment of the Tennessee Valley Authority when it sustained the authority of the TVA to enter into a contract for the sale of the excess energy generated by a TVA-operated dam. The court observed that construction of the dam was within the federal government's powers to defend the nation and improve navigation and that the Constitution gave the federal government unfettered power to dispose of government property.

This statute was one of only two major early New Deal laws declared valid by the court.

Carter v. Carter Coal Co. (298 U.S. 238), decided by a 6-3 vote, May 18, 1936. Sutherland wrote the majority opinion; Chief Justice Hughes wrote a separate opinion; Cardozo, Brandeis and Stone dissented.

Striking down the Bituminous Coal Conservation Act of 1935, the court found that Congress had unconstitutionally delegated its legislative powers to private parties in that statute when it allowed a majority of coal mine operators to set mandatory wage and hours standards for the entire coal industry.

The court also held unconstitutional the statute's provisions providing collective bargaining rights for miners. Such labor relations were local in nature and not subject to regulation by Congress under its interstate commerce powers.

Due Process

Brown v. Mississippi (297 U.S. 278), decided by a unanimous court, Feb. 17, 1936. Chief Justice Hughes wrote the opinion.

States may not use coerced confessions as evidence at the trial of persons from whom the confessions were obtained by torture. Use of a person's involuntary statements to convict him is a clear denial of due process of law.

Morehead v. New York ex rel. Tipaldo (298 U.S. 587), decided by a 5-4 vote, June 1, 1936. Butler wrote the majority opinion; Chief Justice Hughes, Brandeis, Cardozo and Stone dissented.

The court struck down a New York minimum wage law for women and children workers, declaring all minimum wage laws a violation of due process. The decision was overruled in the 1937 decision of *West Coast Hotel Co. v. Parrish.*

Power of the President

United States v. Curtiss-Wright Export Corp. (299 U.S. 304), decided by a 7-1 vote, Dec. 21, 1936. Sutherland wrote the majority opinion; McReynolds dissented; Stone did not participate.

The court upheld an act of Congress authorizing the president, at his discretion, to embargo arms shipments to foreign belligerents in a South American war.

The plenary nature of the federal government's power over foreign affairs permitted Congress greater latitude in delegating power to the president in international relations than in internal matters. Sutherland described the power of the president in foreign affairs as "plenary and exclusive." The president is "the sole organ of the federal government in . . . international relations."

1937

Freedom of Assembly

DeJonge v. Oregon (299 U.S. 353), decided by an 8-0 vote, Jan. 4, 1937. Chief Justice Hughes wrote the opinion; Stone did not participate.

The First Amendment guarantee of the freedom of peaceable assembly prohibits a state from convicting a person under its criminal syndicalism act for organizing and participating in a meeting at which no illegal action was discussed, even if the meeting was held under the auspices of an association which had as its goal the overthrow by force of the federal government.

This was the first decision in which the court recognized that the right of assembly was on an equal plane with the rights of free speech and free press and that the First Amendment guarantee of freedom of assembly was applicable to the states through the due process clause of the 14th Amendment.

Due Process

West Coast Hotel Co. v. Parrish (300 U.S. 379), decided by a 5-4 vote, March 29, 1937. Chief Justice Hughes wrote the majority opinion; Butler, McReynolds, Sutherland and Van Devanter dissented.

The court upheld Washington state's law setting minimum wages for women and children workers. The court overruled its 1923 decision in *Adkins v. Children's Hospital* in which it had declared minimum wage laws to be price-fixing in violation of freedom of contract and the guarantee of due process, and its 1936 decision in *Morehead v. Tipaldo.*

Palko v. Connecticut (302 U.S. 319), decided by an 8-1 vote, Dec. 6, 1937. Cardozo wrote the majority opinion; Butler dissented.

The due process clause of the 14th Amendment does not require states to observe the double jeopardy guarantee of the Fifth Amendment. The promise that an individual will not be tried twice for the same crime is "not of the very essence of a scheme of ordered liberty" and thus due process does not mandate its application to the states.

Commerce

National Labor Relations Board v. Jones & Laughlin Steel Corp. (301 U.S. 1), decided by a 5-4 vote, April 12, 1937. Chief Justice Hughes wrote the majority opinion; McReynolds, Butler, Sutherland and Van Devanter dissented.

The federal power to regulate interstate commerce permits Congress to regulate intrastate matters that directly burden or obstruct interstate commerce. In this case, the court found that a dispute between management and labor that threatened to close down a Pennsylvania steel factory directly affected interstate commerce because the factory was in a stream of commerce.

This decision, in which the court finally abandoned its narrow view of the federal power to regulate interstate commerce, sustained the constitutionality of the National Labor Relations Act of 1935.

The Spending Power

Steward Machine Co. v. Davis (301 U.S. 548), decided by a 5-4 vote, May 24, 1937. Cardozo wrote the majority opinion; McReynolds, Butler, Sutherland and Van Devanter dissented.

A system to induce employers to participate in the federal unemployment compensation program by taxing them and then giving those who participate a tax credit is a valid exercise of the taxing and spending powers to regulate interstate commerce. While not in commerce, employment affects commerce and therefore falls within the reach of federal regulation.

Helvering v. Davis (301 U.S. 619), decided by a 7-2 vote, May 24, 1937. Cardozo wrote the majority opinion; McReynolds and Butler dissented.

Effectively overturning its 1936 *Butler* ruling, the court sustained the Social Security Act of 1935. This statute placed a tax on employees and employers, the revenue from which was used to pay benefits to retired employees. Such a program was an appropriate combination of the power to tax and the power to spend for the general welfare, the court said.

Voting Rights

Breedlove v. Suttles (302 U.S. 277), decided by a unanimous vote, Dec. 6, 1937. Butler wrote the opinion.

The court upheld a Georgia law that required all inhabitants of the state between the ages of 21 and 60 to pay an annual poll tax of $1.00. Under the state constitution payment of the tax was a prerequisite to voting in any election. The court ruled that the tax did not constitute denial of equal protection in violation of the 14th Amendment nor did it violate the 15th Amendment ban on racial discrimination in voting.

1938

Freedom of the Press

Lovell v. Griffin (303 U.S. 444), decided by an 8-0 vote, March 28, 1938. Chief Justice Hughes wrote the opinion; Cardozo did not participate.

A city ordinance which prohibits circulation on public streets of handbills or literature of any kind without written permission from the city manager is an unconstitutional prior restraint on freedom of the press. (In subsequent cases, the court said that a city could regulate the manner of distributing handbills.)

Right to Legal Counsel

Johnson v. Zerbst (304 U.S. 458), decided by a 6-2 vote, May 23, 1938. Black wrote the majority opinion; McReynolds and Butler dissented; Cardozo did not participate.

The Sixth Amendment guarantee that in "all criminal prosecutions, the accused shall enjoy the right . . . to have the Assistance of Counsel for his defence" means that federal courts may not deprive anyone of liberty or life unless he has been provided the aid of an attorney at his trial or has explicitly waived his right to that aid.

Civil Rights

Missouri ex rel. Gaines v. Canada (305 U.S. 337), decided by a 7-2 vote, Dec. 12, 1938. Chief Justice Hughes wrote the majority opinion; McReynolds and Butler dissented.

A state denies equal protection of the laws to a black student when it refuses him admission to its all-white law school, even though it volunteers to pay his tuition at any law school in an adjacent state. By providing a law school for whites but not for blacks the state has created a privilege which one race can enjoy but the other cannot.

This was the first in a series of decisions which resulted in abandonment of the "separate but equal" doctrine of *Plessy v. Ferguson* (1896).

1939

Taxes

Graves v. New York ex rel. O'Keefe (306 U.S. 466), decided by a 7-2 vote, March 27, 1939. Stone wrote the court's opinion; Butler and McReynolds dissented.

The court specifically overruled two earlier decisions (*Collector v. Day,* 1871, and *Dobbins v. Erie County,* 1842), which had held that the income of state and federal government employees was immune to taxation by the non-employing governing body. The *Graves* decision led to the demise of most intergovernmental tax immunities.

Commerce

Mulford v. Smith (307 U.S. 38), decided by a 7-2 vote, April 17, 1939. Roberts wrote the majority opinion; Butler and McReynolds dissented.

Congress has authority to limit the amount of any commodity to be shipped in interstate commerce, the court said. The imposition of marketing quotas on certain agricultural commodities is therefore valid because such quotas are at the "throat" of interstate commerce.

By this decision the court sustained the validity of the second agricultural adjustment act against a challenge that the marketing quotas actually served to limit production, an area which Congress had no authority to regulate.

Federal Courts

Coleman v. Miller (307 U.S. 433), decided by a 7-2 vote, June 5, 1939. Chief Justice Hughes wrote the majority opinion; Butler and McReynolds dissented.

The question of what constitutes a "reasonable" time period for the ratification by states of proposed constitutional amendments is a political question for Congress, not the court, to resolve.

The question of whether a state which has rejected a constitutional amendment may later reverse itself and ratify the amendment is also a political question which Congress must answer.

Voting Rights

Lane v. Wilson (307 U.S. 268), decided by a 6-2 vote, May 22, 1939. Frankfurter wrote the majority opinion; McReynolds and Butler dissented; Douglas did not participate.

In *Guinn v. United States* (1915), the court held unconstitutional an Oklahoma "grandfather clause" exemption to a literacy test requirement for voters. The state legislature then adopted a second voting registration law which exempted from registration all those who had voted in the 1914 election, conducted while the "grandfather clause" was still in effect. The new law required all other potential voters to register within a two-week period. The court held the second law invalid as a violation of the 15th Amendment ban on racial discrimination in voting.

Freedom of Assembly

Hague v. C.I.O. (307 U.S. 496), decided by a 5-2 vote, June 5, 1939. There was no majority opinion; Roberts, Stone and Chief Justice Hughes wrote separate concurring opinions; McReynolds and Butler dissented; Frankfurter and Douglas did not participate.

The right to speak and assemble peaceably in public may not be arbitrarily prohibited by federal, state or local governments. Three members of the majority found this right to be a privilege and immunity of national citizenship; two justices found it implicit in the personal liberty protected by the 14th Amendment's due process clause. This latter, broader view, which secured the right to all persons, not just citizens, was eventually accepted by a majority of the court's members.

1940

Freedom of Religion

Cantwell v. Connecticut (310 U.S. 296), decided by a unanimous vote, May 20, 1940. Roberts wrote the opinion.

States may limit the free exercise of religion only by statutes which are narrowly drawn and applied in a nondiscriminatory manner. Therefore, a state may not convict a sidewalk preacher for breach of the peace under a general ordinance which sweeps in "a great variety of conduct under a general and indefinite characterization" and leaves too much discretion to the officials applying it. Furthermore, such a person may not be convicted under a general breach of the peace statute if there is no evidence that his speech, although insulting to some religions, caused any disturbance or threatened any "clear and present menace to public peace."

Likewise, a state statute which requires persons who wish to solicit for religious causes to obtain permits, but allows state officials discretion in determining which causes are religious and therefore violates the First Amendment guarantee of the free exercise of religion.

This was the first decision in which the court specifically applied the First Amendment's guarantee of free exercise of religion against state action.

Minersville School District v. Gobitis (310 U.S. 586), decided by an 8-1 vote, June 3, 1940. Frankfurter wrote the majority opinion; Stone dissented.

In this first "flag-salute" case, the court sustained a state law requiring all school children to pledge allegiance to the U.S. flag. The requirement had been challenged because participation in such a pledge conflicted with the religious beliefs of Jehovah's Witnesses. They therefore argued that the compulsory pledge violated the First Amendment's guarantee of free exercise of religion.

Religious liberty must give way to political authority so long as that authority is not used directly to promote or restrict religion, the court said. The "mere possession of religious convictions ... does not relieve the citizen from the discharge of political responsibilities."

In 1943 the court reversed this decision with its ruling in the case of *West Virginia State Board of Education v. Barnette.*

Taxes

Sunshine Anthracite Coal Co. v. Adkins (310 U.S. 381), decided by an 8-1 vote, May 20, 1940. Douglas wrote the majority opinion; McReynolds dissented.

The use of the tax power as a penalty is an appropriate means for Congress to employ in regulating interstate commerce, the court said. The court in this ruling upheld the second coal conservation act, which placed a high tax on coal sold in interstate commerce but exempted from payment those producers who agreed to abide by industry price and competition regulations.

1941

Commerce

United States v. Darby Lumber Co. (312 U.S. 100), decided by a unanimous vote, Feb. 3, 1941. Stone wrote the opinion.

Congress has authority to prohibit the shipment in interstate commerce of any goods manufactured in violation of federally established minimum wage and maximum hours standards. In this decision the court also overruled the 1918 decision in *Hammer v. Dagenhart,* in which it had held that Congress had no power to prohibit the shipment in interstate commerce of goods made by children.

Edwards v. California (314 U.S. 160), decided by a unanimous vote, Nov. 24, 1941. Byrnes wrote the opinion.

A state impermissibly obstructs interstate commerce when it penalizes persons who bring indigent persons into the state to reside there. The court in this ruling struck down California's "anti-Okie" law.

In a concurring opinion, four justices held the right to travel to be one of the privileges and immunities of national citizenship protected by the 14th Amendment from abridgment by the states.

Freedom of Assembly

Cox v. New Hampshire (312 U.S. 569), decided by a unanimous vote, March 31, 1941. Chief Justice Hughes wrote the opinion.

The First Amendment guarantees of free speech and peaceable assembly do not bar states from setting the time, place and manner of parades on public streets in order that they do not interfere unduly with other use of the streets. Such ordinances must be precisely drawn and applied in a non-discriminatory fashion.

Voting Rights

United States v. Classic (313 U.S. 299), decided by a 5-3 vote, May 26, 1941. Stone wrote the majority opinion; Black, Murphy and Douglas dissented. Chief Justice Hughes did not participate.

Congress has the power to regulate primary elections when the primary is an integral part of the process of selecting candidates for federal office.

This decision overruled the 1921 *Newberry* decision holding that Congress could regulate only general elections, not primary elections.

1942

Freedom of Speech

Chaplinsky v. New Hampshire (315 U.S. 568), decided by a unanimous vote, March 9, 1942. Murphy wrote the opinion.

A state does not violate the First Amendment by enacting a precisely drawn and narrowly applied law making it a crime to use, in public, "fighting words" — words so insulting as to provoke violence from the person to whom they are directed. Fighting words, the lewd and obscene, profanity and libelous statements are among the classes of speech that have so little value in advancing thought or ideas that they fall outside the protection of the First Amendment guarantees of freedom of speech and press, the court said.

Right to Legal Counsel

Betts v. Brady (316 U.S. 455), decided by a 6-3 vote, June 1, 1942. Roberts wrote the majority opinion; Black, Douglas and Murphy dissented.

The 14th Amendment's due process clause does not require states to supply defense counsel to defendants too poor to employ their own attorney.

Equal Protection

Skinner v. Oklahoma (316 U.S. 535), decided by a unanimous vote, June 1, 1942. Douglas wrote the opinion.

A state law that provides for involuntary sterilization of certain felons violates the equal protection clause of the 14th Amendment because it does not treat all persons convicted of the same crime in the same manner.

This was the first decision in which the court recognized that individuals have certain constitutionally protected "fundamental interests," in this case, procreation, with which a state may interfere only if it shows a compelling need to do so.

War Powers

Ex parte Quirin (317 U.S. 1), decided by an 8-0 vote, July 31, 1942. Chief Justice Stone wrote the opinion; Murphy did not participate.

The Supreme Court upheld the jurisdiction of a presidentially established military commission, instead of a civilian jury, to try seven Nazi saboteurs. Congress had already provided for the trial of spies by military commission and the acts charged against the saboteurs were acts of war. The guarantee of jury trial under the Sixth Amendment applies to civilian — not military — courts.

This decision firmly established the power of civil courts to review the jurisdiction of presidential military commissions.

Commerce

Wickard v. Filburn (317 U.S. 111), decided by a unanimous vote, Nov. 9, 1942. Jackson wrote the opinion.

The federal power to prevent burdens on interstate commerce permits the federal government to regulate matters that are neither interstate nor commerce. The court made this point in a decision sustaining a penalty levied against a farmer who had produced for his own consumption more wheat than he was allotted under the 1938 Agricultural Adjustment Act. The court held that Congress had the power to prevent home-grown wheat from competing with wheat sold in interstate commerce.

This decision is regarded as the high point in the court's broad interpretation of federal regulatory powers authorized under the interstate commerce clause of the Constitution.

1943

Due Process

McNabb v. United States (318 U.S. 332), decided by a 7-1 vote, March 1, 1943. Frankfurter wrote the majority opinion; Reed dissented; Rutledge did not participate.

The court established the federal rule that a person accused of a federal crime must be taken before a judicial officer for arraignment without delay after arrest.

Freedom of Religion

Murdock v. Pennsylvania (319 U.S. 105), decided by a 5-4 vote, May 3, 1943. Douglas wrote the majority opinion; Reed, Frankfurter, Roberts and Jackson dissented.

A city ordinance which requires all persons taking orders for or delivering goods door-to-door to obtain a license from the city and which places a tax of $1.50 a day on the privilege of door-to-door solicitation is unconstitutional as applied to Jehovah's Witnesses who go from house to house soliciting new members and selling religious literature. "A state may not impose a charge for the enjoyment of a right granted by the federal Constitution," the majority said.

This decision specifically overruled the previous year's decision in *Jones v. Opelika* (316 U.S. 584, 1942) in which the court upheld such license fees as applied to Jehovah's Witnesses on the grounds that these activities were primarily commercial and so fell outside the protection of the First Amendment.

West Virginia State Board of Education v. Barnette (319 U.S. 624), decided by a 6-3 vote, June 14, 1943. Jackson wrote the majority opinion; Roberts, Reed and Frankfurter dissented.

The First Amendment guarantee of the free exercise of religion protects the right of persons to remain silent and forbids the government to compel them to participate in a symbolic display of patriotic unity that conflicts with their religious beliefs.

With this ruling the court upheld the right of Jehovah's Witnesses' children to refuse to participate in compulsory flag salute ceremonies in public schools. The decision overruled the 1940 holding in *Minersville School District v. Gobitis* in which a majority held that religious liberty must give way to political authority so long as that authority was not used directly to promote or restrict religion.

War Powers

Hirabayashi v. United States (320 U.S. 810), decided by a unanimous vote, June 21, 1943. Chief Justice Stone wrote the opinion.

The court upheld the wartime curfew law placed on Japanese-Americans living on the west coast as an appropriate exercise by the president and Congress of the federal war powers.

Nor did the curfew law, by making a classification based solely on race, violate the Fifth Amendment. In this instance, consideration of race was relevant to the national security.

1944

Power of Congress

Yakus v. United States (321 U.S. 414), decided by a 6-3 vote, March 27, 1944. Chief Justice Stone wrote the majority opinion; Roberts, Murphy and Rutledge dissented.

The court sustained portions of the Emergency Price Control Act of 1942 giving the federal price administrator discretionary power to enforce the act, including the maximum prices set under it. The law was challenged as an unconstitutional delegation of legislative power. The court held that the standards for decisions under the law were "sufficiently definite and precise" and said it was "unable to find in them an unauthorized delegation of legislative power."

Voting Rights

Smith v. Allwright (321 U.S. 649), decided by an 8-1 vote, April 3, 1944. Reed wrote the majority opinion; Roberts dissented.

When party primaries are part of the machinery for choosing state and national officials, the action of any political party to exclude Negroes from voting in primaries is "state action" within the prohibitions of the 14th and 15th Amendments. This decision reversed *Grovey v. Townsend* (1935).

Commerce

United States v. South-Eastern Underwriters Assn. (322 U.S. 533), decided by a 4-3 vote, June 5, 1944. Black wrote the majority opinion; Chief Justice Stone and Frankfurter dissented; Jackson dissented in part; Roberts and Reed did not participate.

Insurance transactions are matters in interstate commerce subject to regulation under the federal antitrust act.

This ruling overturned a long line of decisions, beginning in 1869, which held that purely financial and contractual transactions, such as insurance, were not in commerce, even if they involved parties in different states, and were therefore not subject to federal regulation.

Because this decision called into question the validity of all state insurance regulations, Congress quickly passed a statute permitting states to continue to regulate insurance. The court upheld that statute in *Prudential Insurance Co. v. Benjamin* (328 U.S. 408, 1946).

War Powers

Korematsu v. United States (323 U.S. 214), decided by a 6-3 vote, December 18, 1944. Black wrote the majority opinion; Roberts, Murphy and Jackson dissented.

The court upheld the 1942 removal of Japanese-Americans to relocation centers at inland camps away from the west coast. It held that the removal program was within the combined war powers of the president and the Congress.

In this case, for the first time, a majority of the court said it would give classifications by race increased attention to ensure that racial antagonism did not lie at the base of the classification. In this instance, however, the court held that military necessity warranted the racial classification.

1946

Freedom of Religion

Girouard v. United States (328 U.S. 61), decided by a 5-3 vote, April 22, 1946. Douglas wrote the majority opinion; Chief Justice Stone, Reed and Frankfurter dissented; Jackson did not participate.

The oath that persons must swear to become naturalized citizens does not expressly require them to swear to bear arms in defense of the United States. Thus a person who meets all other qualifications for naturalization should not be barred from citizenship because he is unwilling to bear arms, an activity that conflicts with his religious beliefs.

This decision overturned three earlier rulings in which the court had interpreted the naturalization oath to require a willingness to bear arms. The decisions had barred from citizenship two women, who would not have been required to serve in the armed forces in any event, and a 54-year old divinity school professor unlikely to be called for duty because of his age.

Bills of Attainder

United States v. Lovett (328 U.S. 303), decided by a 7-0 vote, June 3, 1946. Black wrote the court's opinion; Jackson did not participate.

The court declared invalid, as an unconstitutional bill of attainder, a section of an appropriations law that prohibited payment of salaries to three specifically named federal employees unless they were re-nominated and reconfirmed to their positions.

Civil Rights

Morgan v. Virginia (328 U.S. 373), decided by a 6-1 vote, June 3, 1946. Reed wrote the court's opinion; Burton dissented; Jackson did not participate.

A state law requiring segregated seating on buses traveling interstate places an unconstitutional burden on interstate commerce. Where interstate commerce is involved, bus seating requires uniform national rules; otherwise the constant shifting of seats and rearrangement demanded by various state laws will burden interstate commerce.

Voting Rights

Colegrove v. Green (328 U.S. 549), decided by a 4-3 vote, June 10, 1946. Frankfurter wrote the majority opinion; Black, Douglas and Murphy dissented; Jackson did not participate.

The court declined to intervene to compel the rural-dominated Illinois legislature to redistrict congressional election districts. The districts had not been redrawn since 1901, creating population disparities of as much as nine to one between rural and urban regions within the state.

The problem presented a political question beyond judicial power to resolve, the court said.

1947

Cruel and Unusual Punishment

Louisiana ex rel. Francis v. Resweber (329 U.S. 459), decided by a 5-4 vote, Jan. 13, 1947. Reed wrote the majority opinion; Burton, Douglas, Murphy and Rutledge dissented.

Assuming without argument that the Eighth Amendment ban on cruel and unusual punishment applied to state as well as federal actions, the court nevertheless held that this ban was not violated by the state's execution of a man whose first execution attempt failed due to a malfunctioning electric chair.

Freedom of Religion

Everson v. Board of Education of Ewing Township (330 U.S. 1), decided by a 5-4 vote, Feb. 10, 1947. Black wrote the majority opinion; Jackson, Frankfurter, Rutledge and Burton dissented.

State reimbursement of parents for the cost of transporting their children to parochial schools does not violate the First Amendment clause barring government establishment of religion. Such reimbursements aid parents and children, not the church-affiliated shools.

This was the first case in which the court specifically held that the First Amendment's establishment clause applied to the states as well as the federal government.

Power of Congress

United Public Workers v. Mitchell (330 U.S. 75), decided by a 4-3 vote, Feb. 10, 1947. Reed wrote the majority opinion; Black, Douglas and Rutledge dissented; Murphy and Jackson did not participate.

The court sustained the 1939 Hatch Act, upholding the power of Congress to impose limitations on the political activity of government employees.

Contempt

United States v. United Mine Workers (330 U.S. 258), decided by a divided court, March 6, 1947. Chief Justice Vinson wrote the majority opinion; Murphy and Rutledge dissented; Black, Frankfurter, Douglas and Jackson dissented in part.

The same action may constitute civil and criminal contempt. The justices upheld the conviction of the United Mine Workers of America and its president, John L. Lewis, for both types of contempt for failure to obey a court order forbidding a strike.

Offshore Lands

United States v. California (332 U.S. 19), decided by a 6-2 vote, June 23, 1947. Black wrote the majority opinion; Frankfurter and Reed dissented; Jackson did not participate.

The federal government, not the states, owns the tidelands immediately adjacent to the states and the oil therein. The court reaffirmed this opinion in two subsequent cases, but then sustained — as an exercise of Congress' unrestricted power to dispose of government property — an act of Congress giving coastal states right to the tidelands oil (*Alabama v. Texas,* 347 U.S. 272, 1954).

Jury Trials

Fay v. New York (332 U.S. 261), decided by a 5-4 vote, June 23, 1947. Jackson wrote the majority opinion; Murphy, Black, Douglas and Rutledge dissented.

The court upheld New York's "blue ribbon" jury system, saying that panels of specially qualified jurors disproportionately representing upper economic and social strata were not deliberately discriminatory and did not violate the Constitution.

1948

Freedom of Religion

Illinois ex rel. McCollum v. Board of Education (333 U.S. 203), decided by an 8-1 vote, March 8, 1948. Black wrote the majority opinion; Reed dissented.

The First Amendment clause barring government establishment of religion is violated by a voluntary "released time" program in which religious instruction is given to public school students in the public school during school time.

The court in 1952 sustained a released time program in which students left the school premises to receive religious instruction (*Zorach v. Clauson,* 343 U.S. 306, 1952).

Equal Protection

Shelley v. Kraemer (334 U.S. 1), decided by a 6-0 vote, May 3, 1948. Chief Justice Vinson wrote the opinion; Reed, Jackson and Rutledge did not participate.

The 14th Amendment does not bar private parties from entering into racially restrictive covenants, which exclude blacks from buying or renting homes in "covenanted" neighborhoods, but it does prohibit state courts from enforcing such covenants. Such enforcement constitutes state action denying equal protection of the laws.

1949

Freedom of Speech

Terminiello v. Chicago (337 U.S. 1), decided by a 5-4 vote, May 16, 1949. Douglas wrote the majority opinion; Chief Justice Vinson, Frankfurter, Jackson and Burton dissented.

The court reversed the conviction, for breach of the peace, of a speaker whose remarks in a meeting hall provoked a near-riot among protesters gathered outside the hall.

Without reaching the issue of whether the First Amendment guarantee of free speech protected such inciteful speech, the majority held that the trial court's definition of breach of the peace was so broad that it included speech that was clearly protected by the First Amendment.

Search and Seizure

Wolf v. Colorado (338 U.S. 25), decided by a 6-3 vote, June 27, 1949. Frankfurter wrote the majority opinion; Douglas, Murphy and Rutledge dissented.

The Fourth Amendment protection of individuals against unreasonable searches and seizures by government agents applies against searches by state, as well as federal, agents.

State judges, however, are not required to exclude from use evidence obtained by searches in violation of this guarantee.

1950

Search and Seizure

United States v. Rabinowitz (339 U.S. 56), decided by a 5-3 vote, Feb. 20, 1950. Minton wrote the majority opinion; Frankfurter, Jackson and Black dissented; Douglas did not participate.

The Fourth Amendment guarantee of security against unreasonable searches is not violated by the warrantless search, incident to a lawful arrest, of the person arrested and the premises on which the arrest takes place if they are subject to the control of the suspect.

Freedom of Association

American Communications Assn. v. Douds (339 U.S. 382), decided by a 5-1 vote, May 8, 1950. Chief Justice Vinson wrote the majority opinion; Black dissented. Douglas, Clark and Minton did not participate.

The court upheld the provision of the Taft-Hartley Act which required each officer of a labor union to file an affidavit swearing that he was not a member of or affiliated with the Communist Party. The court held that Congress could properly impose this requirement as part of its power to prevent political strikes obstructing interstate commerce.

Civil Rights

Sweatt v. Painter (339 U.S. 629), decided by a unanimous vote, June 5, 1950. Chief Justice Vinson wrote the opinion.

A state may not deny admission to a state law school to a black even if there is a "black" law school available to the applicant. The court found the facilities of the "black" school inferior to those provided by the "white" school, and therefore in violation of the "separate but equal" doctrine established by the court in 1896.

McLaurin v. Oklahoma State Regents for Higher Education (339 U.S. 637), decided by a unanimous vote, June 5, 1950. Chief Justice Vinson wrote the opinion.

Going beyond its ruling in *Sweatt v. Painter* and eroding the "separate but equal" doctrine even more, the court ruled that once a black was admitted to a state university, the state could not deny him the right to use all its facilities, including the library, lunchroom and classrooms.

1951

Freedom of Speech

Kunz v. New York (340 U.S. 290), decided by an 8-1 vote, Jan. 15, 1951. Chief Justice Vinson wrote the majority opinion; Jackson dissented.

A New York City ordinance that barred worship services on public streets without a permit is an unconstitutional prior restraint on the exercise of the First Amendment rights of free speech and free exercise of religion.

Feiner v. New York (340 U.S. 315), decided by a 6-3 vote, Jan. 15, 1951. Chief Justice Vinson wrote the majority opinion; Black, Douglas and Minton dissented.

In this case, the court sustained the conviction, for breach of the peace, of a street speaker who refused to stop speaking after police asked him to desist. The majority held that the police had acted not to suppress speech but to preserve public order, a legitimate reason for limiting speech.

This decision, read with the decisions in *Terminiello v. Chicago* (1949) and *Kunz v. New York* (1951) demonstrate the difficulty the court had in defining precisely the circumstances in which a state might properly curtail free speech.

Dennis v. United States (341 U.S. 494), decided by a 6-2 vote, June 4, 1951. Chief Justice Vinson wrote the majority opinion; Black and Douglas dissented; Clark did not participate.

The court upheld convictions under the Smith Act of 1940 for speaking and teaching about communist theory advocating forcible overthrow of the government. Communist Party members challenged these convictions as abridgments of First Amendment rights.

Freedom of Association

Joint Anti-Fascist Refugee Committee v. McGrath (341 U.S. 123), decided by a 5-3 vote, April 30, 1951. Burton wrote the majority opinion; Chief Justice Vinson, Reed and Minton dissented; Clark did not participate.

The court upheld the power of the attorney general to prepare and distribute a list of subversive organizations to aid the work of the federal Loyalty Review Board.

Garner v. Board of Public Works (341 U.S. 716), decided by a 5-4 vote, June 4, 1951. Clark wrote the majority opinion; Burton, Frankfurter, Black and Douglas dissented.

The court upheld a loyalty oath requirement for public employees. Such a requirement was not a denial of due process or invalid as a bill of attainder or an *ex post facto* law.

Excessive Bail

Stack v. Boyle (342 U.S. 1), decided by an 8-0 vote, Nov. 5, 1951. Chief Justice Vinson wrote the opinion; Minton did not participate.

The court held that the amount of bail required of twelve Communist leaders prosecuted under the Smith Act of 1940 was excessive and violated the Eighth Amendment's prohibition of excessive bail.

1952

Search and Seizure

Rochin v. California (342 U.S. 165), decided by an 8-0 vote, Jan. 2, 1952. Frankfurter wrote the opinion; Minton did not participate.

The court held that state police officers who used a stomach pump to obtain evidence of drugs — which a suspect had swallowed in their presence — violated Fourth Amendment prohibitions against unreasonable searches and seizures.

Excessive Bail

Carlson v. Landon (342 U.S. 524), decided by a 5-4 vote, March 10, 1952. Reed wrote the majority opinion; Black, Frankfurter, Burton and Douglas dissented.

The court ruled that five alien members of the Communist Party could be detained without bail pending the outcome of deportation proceedings. Denial of bail was justified because deportation was not a criminal proceeding.

Power of the President

Youngstown Sheet and Tube Co. v. Sawyer (343 U.S. 579), decided by a 6-3 vote, June 2, 1952. Black wrote the majority opinion; Chief Justice Vinson, Reed and Minton dissented.

The court held that President Truman had exceeded his power in seizing the nation's steel mills to prevent a strike. The president had based the seizure order on his general powers as commander in chief and chief executive. But the court held he could not take such action without express authorization from Congress.

1953

Voting Rights

Terry v. Adams (345 U.S. 461), decided by an 8-1 vote, May 4, 1953. Black wrote the majority opinion; Minton dissented.

The court held unconstitutional the all-white Texas Jaybird Party primary — held before the regular Democratic Party primary — whose winners usually then won the Democratic nomination and election to county offices. The court ruled that the Jaybird primary was an integral part of the election process and that the exclusion of blacks from this process violated the 15th Amendment.

War Powers

Rosenberg v. United States (346 U.S. 273), decided by a 6-3 vote, June 19, 1953. Chief Justice Vinson wrote the majority opinion; Frankfurter, Black and Douglas dissented.

The court, after meeting in special session, lifted a stay of execution for Julius and Ethel Rosenberg, convicted of violating the Espionage Act of 1917 and sentenced to death.

Justice Douglas had granted the stay in order that lower courts might consider the argument of the Rosenbergs' attorney that the espionage act had been repealed by subsequent passage of the Atomic Energy Act of 1946. The Rosenbergs were convicted of having conveyed atomic secrets to the Soviet Union. They were executed as soon as the court lifted the stay.

1954

Civil Rights

Brown v. Board of Education of Topeka (347 U.S. 483), decided by a unanimous vote, May 17, 1954. Chief Justice Warren wrote the opinion.

In this historic school desegregation decision, the court declared that separate public schools for black and white students were inherently unequal. State-sanctioned segregation in public schools therefore violated the equal protection guarantee of the 14th Amendment.

In the companion case of *Bolling v. Sharpe* (347 U.S. 497), the court ruled that the congressionally-mandated segregated public school system in the District of Columbia violated the Fifth Amendment's due process guarantee of personal liberty.

In *Brown,* the court specifically overruled the "separate but equal" doctrine first enunciated in *Plessy v. Ferguson* (1896) so far as it applied to public schools. The ruling also led to the abolition of state-sponsored segregation in other public facilities.

1955

Civil Rights

Brown v. Board of Education of Topeka (349 U.S. 294), decided by a unanimous vote, May 31, 1955. Chief Justice Warren wrote the opinion.

In this case, the court laid out guidelines for ending segregation in public schools. The court placed primary responsibility on local school officials, recognizing that local factors would call for different treatment and timing, but admonishing the boards to proceed toward desegregation "with all deliberate speed."

Federal district courts were to retain jurisdiction of school desegregation cases. These courts could grant school districts additional time to complete desegregation once the process was begun, but the school boards were given the burden of justifying such delays.

1956

Self-Incrimination

Ullmann v. United States (350 U.S. 422), decided by a 7-2 vote, March 26, 1956. Frankfurter wrote the majority opinion; Douglas and Black dissented.

The court sustained the Immunity Act of 1950, which provided that witnesses cannot claim their privilege against self-incrimination if the government grants them immunity from prosecution for any crimes revealed in their testimony.

Slochower v. Board of Education of New York City (350 U.S. 551) decided by a 5-4 vote, April 9, 1956. Clark wrote the majority opinion; Reed, Burton, Harlan and Minton dissented.

The court held invalid a provision of the New York City charter which provided for summary dismissal of employees who invoked the Fifth Amendment privilege against self-incrimination. Such a practice violated the due process guarantee of the 14th Amendment, the court said.

State Powers

Pennsylvania v. Nelson (350 U.S. 497), decided by a 6-3 vote, April 2, 1956. Chief Justice Warren wrote the majority opinion; Reed, Minton and Burton dissented.

States may not pass laws punishing persons for seditious activity against the federal government; Congress has pre-empted that field by passing federal legislation on that subject.

1957

Power of Congress

Watkins v. United States (354 U.S. 178), decided by a 6-1 vote, June 17, 1957. Chief Justice Warren wrote the majority opinion; Clark dissented; Burton and Whittaker did not participate.

Declaring that "there is no congressional power to expose for the sake of exposure," the court held that congressional investigations may be undertaken only in aid of the legislative function. House and Senate instructions to their investigating committees must therefore fully spell out the investigating committee's purpose and jurisdiction.

Furthermore, a witness may refuse with impunity to answer questions if they are not pertinent to the investigation. "It is the duty of the investigative body, upon objection of the witness on grounds of pertinency, to state . . . the subject under inquiry at the time and the manner in which the propounded questions are pertinent thereto," the majority said.

This ruling reversed the contempt conviction of a labor union officer who answered questions about his own association with the Communist Party but refused to answer similar questions about other people.

Freedom of Speech

Yates v. United States (354 U.S. 298), decided by votes of 6-1 and 4-3, June 17, 1957. Harlan wrote the majority opinion; Clark dissented; Black and Douglas dissented in part; Brennan and Whittaker did not participate.

The court held that in prosecuting persons for violating the Smith Act by advocating the forcible overthrow of the government the United States must show active engagement on the part of the defendant in such an effort, not simply passive action — overt acts, not just abstract arguments.

The decision made it much more difficult for the government to obtain convictions under the Smith Act.

Due Process

Mallory v. United States (354 U.S. 449), decided by a unanimous vote, June 24, 1957. Frankfurter delivered the opinion.

The court reversed a criminal conviction of a man interrogated by law enforcement officials without being informed of his constitutional rights and held for an unnecessarily long period between his arrest and arraignment. Such practices, held the court, deprived him of his liberty without due process of law.

Obscenity

Roth v. United States, Alberts v. California (354 U.S. 476), decided by votes of 7-1 and 6-3, June 24, 1957. Brennan wrote the majority opinion; Harlan dissented in part; Black and Douglas dissented.

Obscene material is not protected by the First Amendment guarantees of freedom of speech and press. Material is obscene, the court said, if the average person would consider that its dominant theme appealed to prurient interest.

This was the first definition of obscenity offered by the court. It was modified in several subsequent decisions and finally replaced with another standard in the 1973 case of *Miller v. California.*

1958

Cruel and Unusual Punishment

Trop v. Dulles (356 U.S. 86), decided by a 5-4 vote, March 31, 1958. Chief Justice Warren wrote the majority opinion; Frankfurter, Burton, Clark and Harlan dissented.

The Eighth Amendment ban on cruel and unusual punishment prohibits the use of expatriation or denaturalization as punishment for persons found guilty of desertion from the armed forces in wartime.

Personal Liberty

Kent v. Dulles (357 U.S. 117), decided by a 5-4 vote, June 16, 1958. Douglas wrote the majority opinion; Clark, Harlan, Burton and Whittaker dissented.

The freedom to travel is part of the personal liberty protected by the due process guarantee of the Fifth and 14th Amendments.

Congress has not authorized the secretary of State to withhold passports from citizens because of their beliefs or associations.

Power of the President

Wiener v. United States (357 U.S. 349), decided by a unanimous vote, June 30, 1958. Frankfurter wrote the opinion.

This decision reinforced the "nature of the office" approach to the presidential removal power. The court held that where the duties of the office included quasi-judicial functions — and where there was no statutory provision for removal — the president lacked the power to remove an incumbent official from his post simply to replace him with a person of his own choice.

Freedom of Association

NAACP v. Alabama ex rel. Patterson (357 U.S. 449), decided by a unanimous vote, June 30, 1958. Harlan wrote the opinion.

The freedom to associate with others is implicit in the freedoms of speech and assembly guaranteed by the First Amendment. The right to associate carries with it the right of privacy in that association.

A state court order requiring the NAACP to produce its membership lists is therefore an unconstitutional restraint on NAACP members' right of association. The state did not show a sufficient interest in the disclosure of the lists to justify the limitation such disclosure placed on freedom of association.

Civil Rights

Cooper v. Aaron (358 U.S. 1), decided by a unanimous vote, Sept. 12, 1958. Chief Justice Warren wrote the opinion; each justice personally signed it.

Standing firm against defiance of its 1954 and 1955 decisions declaring public school segregation unconstitutional, the court refused a request by Little Rock, Ark., school officials for a delay in desegregation of their public schools. Local school officials had made the request after Gov. Orval Faubus called out the state national guard to block the entrance to a Little Rock high school to prevent entry by black students. Federal troops were eventually sent to the city to restore order and protect the black students, and the school board asked for delay of further desegregation efforts. The court convened a special session in late summer of 1958 to hear the case.

In a sharp rebuke to Faubus and state legislators, the court said that the rights of black children could "neither be nullified openly and directly by state legislators or state executive officials nor nullified indirectly by them by evasive schemes for segregation."

1959

Voting Rights

Lassiter v. Northampton County Board of Elections (360 U.S. 45), decided by a unanimous vote, June 8, 1959. Douglas delivered the opinion.

The court upheld North Carolina's requirement that all persons must be able to read and write a section of the state constitution in English before being allowed to vote. Such a provision, applied in a non-discriminatory way, did not violate the 14th, 15th or 17th Amendments, the court held.

Power of Congress

Barenblatt v. United States (360 U.S. 109), decided by a 5-4 vote, June 8, 1959. Harlan wrote the majority opinion; Chief Justice Warren, Black, Brennan and Douglas dissented.

Retreating from its ruling in the 1957 *Watkins* case, the court held that the First Amendment rights of witnesses appearing before congressional investigating committees may be limited when the public interest outweighs the private interest.

In this case, the federal government's interest in preserving itself against those who advocated the forceful overthrow of that government outweighed the right of the witness, a teacher, to conduct a classroom discussion on the theoretical nature of communism.

1960

Search and Seizure

Elkins v. United States (364 U.S. 206), decided by a 5-4 vote, June 27, 1960. Stewart wrote the majority opinion; Frankfurter, Clark, Harlan and Whittaker dissented.

In this decision the court abandoned the "silver platter" doctrine that permitted use — in federal court — of evidence illegally seized by state authorities and handed over to federal authority. The court held that such a practice violated the Fourth Amendment prohibition against unreasonable search and seizure.

Voting Rights

Gomillion v. Lightfoot (364 U.S. 339), decided by a unanimous vote, Nov. 4, 1960. Frankfurter wrote the opinion.

The court held unconstitutional, as a violation of the 15th Amendment guarantee of the right to vote, a state legislative districting plan that excluded almost all black voters from voting in city elections in Tuskegee, Ala.

1961

Freedom of Association

Communist Party v. Subversive Activities Control Board (367 U.S. 1), decided by a 5-4 vote, June 5, 1961. Harlan wrote the majority opinion; Chief Justice Warren, Black, Douglas and Brennan dissented.

The court upheld provisions of the Subversive Activities Control Act of 1950 requiring the Communist Party to register with the Justice Department, list its officials and file financial statements. The court rejected the party's arguments that the registration provisions were unconstitutional as a bill of attainder and a violation of the First Amendment guarantees of freedom of speech and association.

Scales v. United States, Noto v. United States (367 U.S. 203, 290), decided by 5-4 votes, June 5, 1961. Harlan wrote the majority opinions; Chief Justice Warren, Black, Douglas and Brennan dissented.

The First Amendment freedoms of speech and association are not violated by laws providing penalties for active membership in a group specifically intending to bring about the violent overthrow of the government.

Search and Seizure

Mapp v. Ohio (367 U.S. 643), decided by a 5-4 vote, June 19, 1961. Clark wrote the majority opinion; Stewart, Harlan, Frankfurter and Whittaker dissented.

Evidence obtained in violation of the Fourth Amendment guarantee against unreasonable search and seizure must be excluded from use at state as well as federal trials. The court overruled *Wolf v. Colorado* (1949) on this point.

Equal Protection

Hoyt v. Florida (368 U.S. 57), decided by a unanimous vote, Nov. 20, 1961. Harlan wrote the opinion.

The court sustained, against a challenge that it violated the equal protection guarantee, a state law generally excluding women from jury duty. The exclusion was rational in light of the state's interest in preventing interference with women's traditional functions as wives, homemakers and mothers, the court said.

1962

Voting Rights

Baker v. Carr (369 U.S. 186), decided by a 6-2 vote, March 26, 1962. Brennan wrote the majority opinion;

Frankfurter and Harlan dissented; Whittaker did not participate.

The court for the first time held that constitutional challenges to the maldistribution of voters among legislative districts might properly be resolved by federal courts. The court rejected the doctrine — set out in *Colegrove v. Green* in 1946 — that all such apportionment challenges were "political questions" beyond the proper reach of the federal courts.

Freedom of Religion

Engel v. Vitale (370 U.S. 421), decided by a 6-1 vote, June 25, 1962. Black wrote the majority opinion; Stewart dissented; Frankfurter and White did not participate.

Public school officials may not require pupils to recite a state-composed prayer at the beginning of each school day, even though the prayer is denominationally neutral and pupils who so desire may be excused from reciting it. Official state sanction of religious prayers or utterances constitutes an unconstitutional attempt to establish religion, the majority held.

The court reaffirmed this decision in the 1963 case of *School District of Abington Township v. Schempp* (374 U.S. 203), in which the court held that the state-ordered recitation of the Lord's Prayer and the reading of the Bible in the public school system as part of a devotional exercise also violated the establishment clause.

Cruel and Unusual Punishment

Robinson v. California (370 U.S. 660), decided by a 6-2 vote, June 25, 1962. Stewart wrote the majority opinion; Clark and White dissented; Frankfurter did not participate.

It is a violation of the Eighth Amendment ban on cruel and unusual punishment for a state to make narcotics addiction a criminal offense.

1963

Freedom of Association

NAACP v. Button (371 U.S. 415), decided by a 6-3 vote, Jan. 14, 1963. Brennan wrote the majority opinion; Harlan, Clark and Stewart dissented.

A state law, directed against the NAACP, which forbids solicitation of clients by an agent of an organization that litigates cases in which it is not a party and has no pecuniary interest, impermissibly infringes on the First Amendment right of association. "Abstract discussion is not the only species of communication which the Constitution protects; the First Amendment also protects vigorous advocacy, certainly of lawful ends, against government intrusion," the court wrote.

Freedom of Speech

Edwards v. South Carolina (372 U.S. 229), decided by an 8-1 vote, Feb. 25, 1963. Stewart wrote the majority opinion; Clark dissented.

The court reversed the breach-of-the-peace convictions of student demonstrators who had marched peacefully to protest racial discrimination. The court held that the breach-of-the-peace statute was unconstitutionally broad and had been used in this case to penalize the exercise of free speech, assembly and petition for redress of grievances "in their most pristine and classic form," a clear violation of the First Amendment.

Right to Counsel

Gideon v. Wainwright (372 U.S. 335), decided by a unanimous vote, March 18, 1963. Black delivered the opinion.

The due process clause of the 14th Amendment extends to state as well as federal defendants the Sixth Amendment guarantee that all persons charged with serious crimes will be provided the aid of an attorney. *Betts v. Brady* (1942) is overruled. States are required to appoint counsel for defendants who can not afford to pay their own attorneys' fees.

Federal Courts

Fay v. Noia (372 U.S. 391), decided by a 6-3 vote, March 18, 1963. Brennan wrote the majority opinion; Harlan, Clark and Stewart dissented.

In some circumstances, a state prisoner may challenge his imprisonment through a federal writ of *habeas corpus* even if he has not appealed his conviction through the state court system. The requirement that a state prisoner "exhaust" all state remedies before challenging his conviction in federal courts simply means that a state prisoner must have tried all state remedies still available to him at the time he comes into federal court seeking the writ of *habeas corpus*.

Voting Rights

Gray v. Sanders (372 U.S. 368), decided by an 8-1 vote, March 18, 1963. Douglas wrote the majority opinion; Harlan dissented.

Georgia's "county unit" system of electing officers to state posts violates the equal protection guarantee of the 14th Amendment by giving more weight to the votes of persons in rural, than in urban, counties. The basic idea of political equality, inherent in the American system, held the court, "can mean only one thing — one person, one vote."

Search and Seizure

Ker v. California (374 U.S. 23), decided by a 5-4 vote, June 10, 1963. Clark wrote the majority opinion; Chief Justice Warren, Brennan, Douglas and Goldberg dissented in part.

The same standards apply to determine whether federal and state searches and seizures are reasonable and thus permissible under the Fourth Amendment. (The justices disagreed over whether the warrantless search at issue in this case was reasonable.)

1964

Voting Rights

Wesberry v. Sanders (376 U.S. 1), decided by a 6-3 vote, Feb. 17, 1964. Black wrote the majority opinion; Clark dissented in part; Harlan and Stewart dissented.

Substantial disparity in the population of congressional districts in a state is unconstitutional, violating the provision for election of members of the House of Representatives "by the people of the several states." Congressional voting districts within states must be as nearly equal in population as possible.

Reynolds v. Sims (377 U.S. 533), decided by an 8-1 vote, June 15, 1964. Chief Justice Warren wrote the majority opinion; Harlan dissented.

The equal protection clause of the 14th Amendment requires application of the "one person, one vote" apportionment rule to both houses of a state legislature.

Freedom of the Press

New York Times Co. v. Sullivan (376 U.S. 254), decided by a unanimous vote, March 9, 1964. Brennan wrote the opinion.

The First Amendment guarantee of freedom of the press protects the press from libel suits for defamatory reports on public officials unless the officials prove that the reports were made with actual malice. Actual malice is defined as "with knowledge that it [the defamatory statement] was false or with reckless disregard of whether it was false or not."

Until this decision, libelous statements had not been protected by the First Amendment.

Civil Rights

Griffin v. County School Board of Prince Edward County (377 U.S. 218), decided by a 7-2 vote, May 25, 1964. Black wrote the majority opinion; Clark and Harlan dissented in part.

Finally losing patience with state defiance of its school desegregation decisions, the court declared that there had been "entirely too much deliberation and not enough speed." The court declared unconstitutional, as a violation of the 14th Amendment's equal protection clause, the closing of all the public schools in Prince Edward County, Va., to avoid the impact of desegregation.

Heart of Atlanta Motel v. United States (379 U.S. 241), decided by a unanimous vote, Dec. 14, 1964. Clark wrote the opinion.

Under its authority to regulate interstate commerce, Congress has the power to prohibit racial discrimination in privately owned public accommodations. This ruling, which effectively overturned the court's 1883 decision in the *Civil Rights Cases,* sustained Title II of the Civil Rights Act of 1964. That section prohibited discrimination, on the basis of race, religion or national origin, in accommodations that catered to interstate travelers or that served food or provided entertainment, a substantial portion of which was shipped through interstate commerce.

Self-Incrimination

Malloy v. Hogan (378 U.S. 1), decided by a 5-4 vote, June 15, 1964. Brennan wrote the majority opinion; Harlan, Clark, White and Stewart dissented.

The Fifth Amendment protection against self-incrimination is extended to state defendants through the due process clause of the 14th Amendment.

Murphy v. The Waterfront Commission of New York Harbor (378 U.S. 52), decided by a unanimous vote, June 15, 1964. Goldberg wrote the opinion.

The Fifth Amendment privilege against compelled self-incrimination protects witnesses granted immunity by either state or federal officials from prosecution in either jurisdiction based on their testimony.

Freedom of Association

Aptheker v. Secretary of State (378 U.S. 500), decided by a 7-2 vote, June 22, 1964. Goldberg wrote the majority opinion; Clark and White dissented.

The court declared unconstitutional a section of the Subversive Activities Control Act of 1950 that denied passports — and thus the right to travel — to persons who belonged to organizations listed as subversive by the attorney general. The court found the law too broad because it failed to distinguish between persons who joined such organizations with the full knowledge of their subversive purpose and those persons who were "unknowing." Nor did the law take into account the purpose of the intended travel.

Right to Counsel

Escobedo v. Illinois (378 U.S. 478), decided by a 5-4 vote, June 22, 1964. Goldberg wrote the majority opinion; Harlan, Stewart, White and Clark dissented.

The court expanded a suspect's right to counsel under the Sixth Amendment, holding that confessions obtained by police who had not advised the suspect of his right to counsel — or acceded to his requests for counsel — were inadmissible as evidence in court.

1965

Due Process

Pointer v. Texas (380 U.S. 400), decided by a unanimous vote, April 5, 1965. Black wrote the opinion.

The Sixth Amendment guarantee of the right to confront and cross-examine witnesses is applied to state defendants by the 14th Amendment's due process clause.

Federal Courts

Dombrowski v. Pfister (380 U.S. 479), decided by a 5-2 vote April 26, 1965. Brennan wrote the majority opinion; Harlan and Clark dissented; Black and Stewart did not participate.

Federal courts need not abstain from ordering state officials to halt enforcement of a law justifiably attacked as in violation of the First Amendment, even if the person seeking the order has not yet exhausted all state procedures for challenging that law.

Voting Rights

Harman v. Forssenius (380 U.S. 528), decided by a unanimous vote, April 27, 1965. Chief Justice Warren wrote the opinion.

A Virginia law imposing special registration requirements on persons not paying the state's poll tax violates the 24th Amendment's ban on poll taxes in federal elections.

Self-Incrimination

Griffin v. California (380 U.S. 609), decided by a 7-1 vote, April 28, 1965. Douglas wrote the majority opinion; Stewart dissented; Chief Justice Warren did not participate.

The Fifth Amendment privilege against compelled self-incrimination, as applied to the states through the due process guarantee of the 14th Amendment, is infringed when a judge or prosecutor comments adversely during a trial upon a defendant's failure to testify in his own behalf.

Albertson v. Subversive Activities Control Board (382 U.S. 70), decided by an 8-0 vote, Nov. 15, 1965. Brennan delivered the opinion; White did not participate.

The court overturned convictions of Communist Party members ordered to register personally with the attorney general under provisions of the Subversive Activities Control Act of 1950. The registration orders, the court said, violated the Fifth Amendment privilege against self-incrimination.

Personal Privacy

Griswold v. Connecticut (381 U.S. 479), decided by a 7-2 vote, June 7, 1965. Douglas wrote the majority opinion; Stewart and Black dissented.

A state unconstitutionally interferes with personal privacy in the marriage relationship when it prohibits anyone, including married couples, from using contraceptives. The majority agreed that a right of personal privacy is implicit in the Constitution, but did not concur on the exact source of this right.

1966

Voting Rights

South Carolina v. Katzenbach (383 U.S. 301), decided by an 8-1 vote, March 7, 1966. Chief Justice Warren wrote the majority opinion; Black dissented.

The court upheld provisions of the Voting Rights Act of 1965 as a proper exercise of congressional power to enforce the 15th Amendment ban on racial discrimination in voting.

Harper v. Virginia State Board of Elections (383 U.S. 663), decided by a 7-2 vote, March 24, 1966. Douglas wrote the majority opinion; Black and Harlan dissented.

State laws which make the right to vote contingent upon payment of a tax violate the equal protection clause of the Fourteenth Amendment.

Freedom of Association

Elfbrandt v. Russell (384 U.S. 11), decided by a 5-4 vote, April 18, 1966. Douglas wrote the majority opinion; White, Clark, Harlan and Stewart dissented.

The court declared an Arizona loyalty oath unconstitutional because it violated the First Amendment right of freedom of association by penalizing persons for membership in certain groups whether or not they joined the group with the specific intent of engaging in unlawful acts.

Self-Incrimination

Miranda v. Arizona (384 U.S. 436), decided by a 5-4 vote, June 13, 1966. Chief Justice Warren wrote the majority opinion; Clark, Harlan, Stewart and White dissented.

The guarantee of due process requires that suspects in police custody be informed of their right to remain silent, that anything they say may be used against them, and that they have the right to counsel — before any questioning of the suspect can permissibly take place.

1967

Freedom of Association

Keyishian v. Board of Regents (385 U.S. 589), decided by a 5-4 vote, Jan. 23, 1967. Brennan wrote the majority opinion; Clark, Harlan, Stewart and White dissented.

The court invalidated New York State's teacher loyalty oath requirement holding that the law was too vague and uncertain. Membership in the Communist Party alone was not sufficient grounds to disqualify a teacher from public school employment.

United States v. Robel (389 U.S. 258), decided by a 6-2 vote, Dec. 11, 1967. Chief Justice Warren wrote the majority opinion; White and Harlan dissented; Marshall did not participate.

The court nullified a section of the Subversive Activities Control Act of 1950 which forbade a member of a group listed as subversive by the attorney general to take a job in a defense industry. The court held that the provision violated the individual's First Amendment right of association.

Due Process

Klopfer v. North Carolina (386 U.S. 213), decided by a unanimous vote March 13, 1967. Chief Justice Warren wrote the opinion.

The Sixth Amendment right to a speedy trial applies in state, as well as federal, proceedings.

In re Gault (387 U.S. 1), decided by a 7-2 vote, May 15, 1967. Fortas wrote the majority opinion; Harlan and Stewart dissented.

The court extended some — but not all — due process privileges to juvenile court proceedings. The privilege against self-incrimination and the right to counsel were among the rights extended.

Washington v. Texas (388 U.S. 14), decided by a unanimous vote, June 12, 1967. Chief Justice Warren wrote the opinion.

Compulsory process to obtain witnesses in the defendant's favor is so fundamental to the Sixth Amendment guarantee of a fair trial that it is applicable to state trials through the due process clause of the 14th Amendment.

Search and Seizure

Warden v. Hayden (387 U.S. 294), decided by an 8-1 vote, May 29, 1967 Brennan wrote the majority opinion; Douglas dissented.

The decision upheld as reasonable and constitutional law enforcement searches for mere evidence as well as for implements and products of crime.

Katz v. United States (389 U.S. 347), decided by a 7-1 vote, Dec. 18, 1967. Stewart wrote the majority opinion for the court; Black dissented; Marshall did not participate.

The court abandoned its view, set out in the 1928 decision in *Olmstead v. United States,* that electronic surveillance and wiretapping were not "searches and seizures" within the scope of the Fourth Amendment. The amendment protects people, not places; it protects what an individual seeks to preserve as private, even in a place accessible to the public, held the court.

Civil Rights

Loving v. Virginia (388 U.S. 1), decided by a unanimous vote, June 12, 1967. Chief Justice Warren wrote the opinion.

A state law providing punishment for persons who enter into interracial marriages violates both the equal protection and due process clauses of the 14th Amendment. "Under our Constitution, the freedom to marry or not

marry a person of another race resides with the individual and cannot be infringed by the state," the court declared.

This was the first decision in which the court explicitly stated that classifications by race were "inherently suspect" and therefore justifiable only by compelling reasons.

Right to Counsel

United States v. Wade (388 U.S. 218), decided by a unanimous vote, June 12, 1967. Brennan wrote the opinion.

A police line-up identification of a suspect — made without the suspect's attorney present — is inadmissable as evidence at trial.

1968

Due Process

Duncan v. Louisiana (391 U.S. 145), decided by an 8-1 vote, May 20, 1968. White wrote the majority opinion; Harlan dissented.

The 14th Amendment's guarantee of due process requires states to provide trial by jury to persons accused of serious crimes.

Civil Rights

Green v. County School Board of New Kent County, Va. (391 U.S. 430), decided by a unanimous vote, May 27, 1968. Brennan wrote the opinion.

Local school district officials have an affirmative duty to eliminate segregation "root and branch" from public schools, the court said, striking down a "freedom-of-choice" plan that would have maintained segregated schools in New Kent County, Va. "The burden on a school board today is to come forward with a [desegregation] plan that promises realistically to work and . . . to work *now,*" the court declared.

Jones v. Alfred H. Mayer Co. (392 U.S. 409), decided by a 7-2 vote, June 17, 1968. Stewart wrote the majority opinion; Harlan and White dissented.

The 1866 Civil Rights Act bars private as well as state-backed racial discrimination in the sale and rental of housing. This decision reinterpreted congressional authority to enforce the 13th Amendment adopted to remove "the badges of slavery." In the *Civil Rights Cases* of 1883, the court had held that Congress had no authority to enforce the guarantees of the 13th Amendment against private acts of discrimination.

Search and Seizure

Terry v. Ohio (392 U.S. 1), decided by an 8-1 vote, June 10, 1968. Chief Justice Warren wrote the majority opinion; Douglas dissented.

The court upheld the police practice of "stop and frisk," saying that when a police officer observes unusual conduct and suspects a crime is about to be committed, he may "frisk" a suspect's outer clothing for dangerous weapons. Such searches do not violate the Fourth Amendment's prohibition against unreasonable searches and seizures.

Federal Courts

Flast v. Cohen (392 U.S. 83), decided by an 8-1 vote, June 10, 1968. Chief Justice Warren wrote the majority opinion; Harlan dissented.

Modifying its 1923 ruling in *Frothingham v. Mellon,* the court held that a federal taxpayer may have the requisite standing to bring a federal challenge to federal spending and taxing programs which he charges are unconstitutional.

To prove the necessary personal interest in such programs, the court ruled, the taxpayer must establish a logical connection between his taxpayer status and the claim before the court. This connection or "nexus" must be shown to prevent federal courts from becoming merely forums for the airing of generalized grievances about government programs and policies.

1969

Freedom of Speech

Tinker v. Des Moines Independent Community School District (393 U.S. 503), decided by a 7-2 vote, Feb. 24, 1969. Fortas wrote the majority opinion; Harlan and Black dissented.

Students have the right to engage in peaceful non-disruptive protest, the court said, recognizing that the First Amendment guarantee of freedom of speech protects symbolic as well as oral speech. The wearing of black armbands to protest the Vietnam War was "closely akin" to the "pure speech" protected by the First Amendment, the majority said, and therefore a public school ban on this form of protest, which did not disrupt the school's work or offend the rights of others, violated these students' rights.

Voting Rights

Kirkpatrick v. Preisler (394 U.S. 526), decided by a 6-3 vote, April 7, 1969. Brennan wrote the majority opinion; Harlan, Stewart and White dissented.

Congressional districts with population variances of 3.1 percent from mathematical equality are unconstitutional unless the state can show that such variations are unavoidable.

Gaston County v. United States (395 U.S. 285), decided by a 7-1 vote, June 2, 1969. Harlan wrote the majority opinion; Black dissented.

The court denied a county's request — under provisions of the 1965 Voting Rights Act — to reinstate a literacy test for voters. The combination of such a test, the court ruled, with previous deprivation of educational opportunity for blacks in the county, would abridge the right to vote on account of race.

Personal Liberty

Shapiro v. Thompson, Washington v. Legrant, Reynolds v. Smith (394 U.S. 618), decided by a 6-3 vote, April 21, 1969. Brennan wrote the majority opinion; Chief Justice Warren, Black and Harlan dissented.

The right to travel is constitutionally protected. State or federal requirements that a person reside within a jurisdiction for one year before becoming eligible for welfare assistance violates individual rights to due process and equal protection of the laws; no compelling government interest was presented to justify this infringement on the right to travel.

Power of Congress

Powell v. McCormack (395 U.S. 486), decided by a 7-1 vote, June 16, 1969. Chief Justice Warren wrote the majority opinion; Stewart dissented.

The House of Representatives does not have the authority to exclude from membership a duly elected representative who meets the constitutional qualifications of age, residence and citizenship. The House had acted unconstitutionally when it voted to exclude Rep. Adam Clayton Powell, D-N.Y., for misconduct and misuse of public funds.

The court did not deny the unquestionable interest of Congress in maintaining its own integrity, but said such interest could be maintained by the use of each chamber's power to punish and expel its members. The court did reject the argument that the case presented a "political question," holding that a determination of Powell's right to his seat required only the interpretation of the Constitution, the traditional function of the court.

Due Process

Benton v. Maryland (395 U.S. 784), decided by a 6-2 vote, June 23, 1969. Marshall wrote the opinion; Stewart and Harlan dissented in part.

The court overruled *Palko v. Connecticut* (1937) to declare that the 14th Amendment due process guarantee extends the double jeopardy guarantee of the Fifth Amendment against state, as well as federal, action.

Search and Seizure

Chimel v. California (395 U.S. 752), decided by a 6-2 vote, June 23, 1969. Stewart wrote the opinion; White and Black dissented.

The court narrowed the limits of permissible searches conducted without a warrant incident to lawful arrest. Police may search only the immediate area around the suspect from which he could obtain a weapon or destroy evidence. A person's entire dwelling cannot be searched simply because he is arrested there.

This decision overruled *United States v. Rabinowitz* (1950).

1970

Due Process

In re Winship (397 U.S. 358), decided by a 5-3 vote, March 31, 1970. Brennan wrote the majority opinion; Chief Justice Burger, Black and Stewart dissented.

The 14th Amendment guarantee of due process requires that juveniles, like adult defendants, be found guilty "beyond a reasonable doubt." The court forbade states to use a lesser standard of proof in juvenile proceedings.

Williams v. Florida (399 U.S. 78), decided by a 7-1 vote, June 22, 1970. White wrote the majority opinion; Marshall dissented; Blackmun did not participate.

A six-member jury in non-capital state cases is constitutional. The number twelve is an "historical accident;" a jury can perform as well with six as with twelve members.

Voting Rights

Oregon v. Mitchell, Texas v. Mitchell, U.S. v. Idaho, U.S. v. Arizona (400 U.S. 112), decided by a 5-4 vote on lowered voting age, by an 8-1 vote on residency requirements and by a unanimous vote on literacy test ban, Dec. 21, 1970. Black wrote the opinion; Chief Justice Burger, Harlan, Stewart and Blackmun dissented on the question of age; Harlan dissented on the residency issue.

Congress has the power to lower the voting age for federal — but not for state and local — elections, to restrict state residency requirements to 30 days for voters in presidential elections, and to ban literacy tests as voter qualification devices in any election.

1971

Federal Courts

Younger v. Harris (401 U.S. 37), decided by an 8-1 vote, Feb. 23, 1971. Black wrote the majority opinion; Douglas dissented.

Federal judges should not normally issue orders to state officials to halt enforcement of a state law or ongoing state proceedings — at least without a showing that continued enforcement of the law threatens to do irreparable injury to the person seeking the order.

Self-Incrimination

Harris v. New York (401 U.S. 222), decided by a 5-4 vote, Feb. 24, 1971. Chief Justice Burger wrote the majority opinion; Black, Douglas, Brennan and Marshall dissented.

Voluntary statements made by a defendant not properly warned of his constitutional rights may be used in court to impeach his credibility if he takes the witness stand in his own defense and contradicts the earlier statements.

Civil Rights

Griggs v. Duke Power Co. (401 U.S. 424), decided by an 8-0 vote, March 8, 1971. Chief Justice Burger wrote the opinion; Brennan did not participate.

In its first case implicitly upholding the right of Congress to bar employment discrimination based on race, the court held that the Civil Rights Act of 1964 prohibits employers from requiring a high school diploma or score on a general intelligence test as a condition for employment or promotion if neither test is related to job skills and if both tend to disqualify more black than white applicants.

Swann v. Charlotte-Mecklenburg County Board of Education (402 U.S. 1), decided by a unanimous vote, April 20, 1971. Chief Justice Burger wrote the opinion.

Busing, racial balance ratios and gerrymandered school districts are all permissible interim methods of eliminating the vestiges of state-imposed segregation from southern schools.

There were limits to the remedies which might be used to eliminate the remnants of segregation, the court said, but no fixed guidelines setting such limits could be established. The court acknowledged that there might be valid objections to busing when so much time or distance is involved as to risk the children's health or to impinge significantly on the education process.

Equal Protection

Graham v. Richardson (403 U.S. 365), decided by a unanimous vote, June 14, 1971. Blackmun wrote the opinion.

Extending the protection of the equal protection guarantee to aliens, the court struck down state laws denying welfare benefits to aliens who lived in the United States less than 15 years and denying benefits to all resident aliens. The court held that all classification by alienage was "suspect," requiring an especially close scrutiny by the court to ensure compliance with the equal protection guarantee.

Reed v. Reed (404 U.S. 71), decided by a 7-0 vote, Nov. 22, 1971. Chief Justice Burger wrote the opinion.

The 14th Amendment guarantee of equal protection invalidates a state law which automatically prefers a father over a mother as executor of a son's estate. "To give a mandatory preference to members of either sex over members of the other . . . is to make the very kind of arbitrary legislative choice forbidden by the equal protection clause," the court said in its first opinion declaring a state law unconstitutional on the grounds that it discriminated against women.

Due Process

McKeiver v. Pennsylvania, In re Burrus (403 U.S. 528), decided by votes of 6-3 and 5-4, June 21, 1971. Blackmun wrote the majority opinion; Douglas, Black and Marshall dissented, joined in *Burrus* by Brennan.

The Sixth Amendment right to trial by jury does not extend to juvenile defendants.

Freedom of Religion

Lemon v. Kurtzman (403 U.S. 602), decided by an 8-0 vote, June 28, 1971. Chief Justice Burger wrote the opinion; Marshall did not participate.

In this case, the court established a three-part test to determine whether state aid to parochial schools violated the First Amendment's ban on government action "establishing" religion.

State aid is permissible, the court said, if it is intended to achieve a secular legislative purpose, if its primary effect neither advances nor inhibits religion, and if it does not foster excessive government entanglement with religion.

Applying this test, the court declared invalid a state law authorizing supplemental salary grants to certain parochial school teachers and another state law authorizing reimbursement to parochial schools for teachers' salaries, textbooks and instructional materials; the court found that both laws fostered an excessive entanglement between government and religion.

Freedom of the Press

New York Times Co. v. United States, United States v. The Washington Post (403 U.S. 713), decided by a 6-3 vote, June 30, 1971. The opinion was unsigned; each justice wrote a separate opinion expressing his individual views. Chief Justice Burger, Blackmun and Harlan dissented.

The court in its brief *per curiam* opinion denied the government's request for a court order barring continued publication in *The New York Times* and *The Washington Post* of articles based on classified documents detailing the history of U.S. involvement in Indochina, popularly known as the Pentagon Papers.

Any request for prior restraint of the press bears a "heavy presumption against its constitutional validity," the court said, and the government had failed to show sufficient justification for imposing such restraint.

1972

Self-Incrimination

Kastigar v. United States (406 U.S. 441), decided by a 5-2 vote, May 22, 1972. Powell wrote the opinion; Douglas and Marshall dissented; Rehnquist and Brennan did not participate.

The narrowed witness immunity provisions of the 1970 Organized Crime Control Act do not infringe upon the Fifth Amendment privilege against self-incrimination. In any subsequent prosecution of an immunized witness, the government must demonstrate that the evidence is derived from sources independent of testimony given under a grant of immunity.

Due Process

Johnson v. Louisiana, Apodaca v. Oregon (406 U.S. 356, 404), decided by 5-4 votes, May 22, 1972. White wrote the majority opinion; Douglas, Brennan, Stewart and Marshall dissented.

The constitutional guarantee of a jury trial applied to state courts does not require that the jury's verdict be unanimous. Lack of unanimity on the question of guilt does not constitute evidence of a reasonable doubt of guilt.

Furman v. Georgia, Jackson v. Georgia, Branch v. Texas (408 U.S. 238), decided by a 5-4 vote, June 29, 1972. The court's opinion was unsigned; each justice filed a separate opinion. Chief Justice Burger, Blackmun, Powell and Rehnquist dissented.

The court nullified all death penalty statutes in the United States. It held that the procedures they provided for judges and juries to follow in deciding when and whether to impose a sentence of death upon a defendant left so much discretion to the judge and jury that the result was arbitrary, irrational and deprived defendants of due process of law.

Right to Counsel

Argersinger v. Hamlin (407 U.S. 25), decided by a unanimous vote, June 12, 1972. Douglas wrote the opinion.

The right of counsel applies in trials for all offenses, state and federal, where a jail sentence is a possible penalty.

Official Immunity

United States v. Brewster (408 U.S. 501), decided by a 6-3 vote, June 29, 1972. Chief Justice Burger wrote the opinion; Brennan, Douglas and White dissented.

The constitutional immunity conferred on members of Congress by the "speech or debate clause" does not protect them from prosecution for accepting a bribe in order to vote a certain way on a legislative matter.

The holding cleared the way for prosecution of former Sen. Daniel B. Brewster (D Md. 1963-69), who had been indicted in 1969 on charges of accepting $24,000 in bribes from the mail order firm of Spiegel Inc. to influence his vote on changes in postal rates. Taking a bribe is illegal, the majority wrote, and is no part of the legislative process. It is therefore subject to prosecution and punishment in the nation's courts.

Freedom of the Press

Branzburg v. Hayes, In re Pappas, United States v. Caldwell (408 U.S. 665), decided by a 5-4 vote, June 29, 1972. White wrote the majority opinion; Douglas, Brennan, Stewart and Marshall dissented.

The constitutional guarantee of freedom of the press does not privilege news reporters to refuse — without risking contempt charges — to provide information to grand juries concerning a crime or the sources of evidence concerning a crime.

1973

Personal Privacy

Roe v. Wade (410 U.S. 113), *Doe v. Bolton* (410 U.S. 179), decided by 7-2 votes, Jan. 22, 1973. Blackmun wrote the majority opinions; Rehnquist and White dissented.

The right to privacy, grounded in the 14th Amendment's due process guarantee of personal liberty, encompasses and protects a woman's decision whether or not to bear a child. This right is impermissibly abridged by state laws which make abortion a crime.

During the first trimester of pregnancy, the decision to have an abortion should be left entirely to a woman and her physician. The state can forbid abortions by non-physicians.

During the second trimester, the state may regulate the abortion procedure in ways reasonably related to maternal health. And during the third trimester, the state may, if it wishes, forbid all abortions except those necessary to save the mother's life.

Voting Rights

Mahan v. Howell, City of Virginia Beach v. Howell, Weinberg v. Prichard (410 U.S. 315), decided by a 5-3 vote, February 21, 1973. Rehnquist wrote the opinion; Brennan, Douglas and Marshall dissented; Powell did not participate.

The court's decision in this case relaxed the requirement that state legislative districts be as nearly equal as possible — holding that states may apply more flexible standards in drawing new state legislative districts than in congressional redistricting.

The decision approved a Virginia plan permitting a 16 percent variation between the largest and smallest population districts.

Equal Protection

San Antonio Independent School District v. Rodriguez (411 U.S. 1), decided by a 5-4 vote, March 21, 1973. Powell wrote the majority opinion; Marshall, Douglas, Brennan and White dissented.

The right to an education is not a fundamental right guaranteed by the Constitution. Wealth is not a suspect way of classifying persons.

Therefore, the equal protection guarantee does not require that courts give the strictest scrutiny to a state decision to finance public schools from local property taxes, a decision resulting in wide disparities among districts in the amount spent per pupil.

States do not deny anyone the opportunity for an education by adopting this means of financing public education. Financing public schools from local property taxes rationally furthers a legitimate state purpose and so is upheld.

Due Process

Strunk v. United States (412 U.S. 434), decided by a unanimous vote, June 11, 1973. Chief Justice Burger wrote the opinion.

The court ruled that the only remedy for denial of a defendant's right to a speedy trial is dismissal of the charges against him. The court rejected the attempt of a judge to remedy a 10-month delay in trial by reducing the eventual sentence imposed on the defendant by that length of time.

Civil Rights

Keyes v. Denver School District No. 1 (413 U.S. 189), decided by a 7-1 vote, June 21, 1973. Brennan wrote the majority opinion; Rehnquist dissented; White did not participate.

This was the first time the court had defined the responsibility of school officials, in a district where racial segregation had never been required by law *(de jure)*, to act to desegregate public schools.

The court held that school officials were constitutionally obligated to desegregate a school system if the segregation there had resulted from intentional school board policies. In the case of racially segregated schools within a system, the burden of proof was on the school board to prove such segregation was not a result of intentional board actions.

Obscenity

Miller v. California (413 U.S. 15), decided by a 5-4 vote, June 21, 1973. Chief Justice Burger wrote the majority opinion; Brennan, Stewart, Marshall and Douglas dissented.

States have the power, without violating the First Amendment, to regulate material which is obscene in its depiction or description of sexual conduct. Material is obscene if the average person, applying contemporary local community standards, would find that it appeals to the prurient interest, and if it depicts in a patently offensive way, sexual conduct specifically defined by the applicable state law, and if the work, taken as a whole, lacks serious literary, artistic, political or scientific value.

This was the first definition of obscenity to command the approval of a majority of the justices since 1957; it was less stringent than the prevailing standard and consequently gave the states more control over obscene materials.

1974

Federal Courts

Edelman v. Jordan (415 U.S. 651), decided by a 5-4 vote, March 25, 1974. Rehnquist wrote the majority opinion; Brennan, Douglas, Marshall and Blackmun dissented.

The 11th Amendment immunity of states from federal lawsuits brought by citizens without the state's consent protects a state from a federal court order directing it to spend money to remedy past abuses.

Federal judges may order a state to halt enforcement of a law which violates due process and equal protection but that order may only reach future action — it may not require the state to remedy past damages inflicted under the invalid law.

In 1976 the court substantially modified the reach of this decision, holding unanimously in *Fitzpatrick v. Bitzer, Bitzer v. Matthews* (427 U.S. 445) that federal courts could order states to pay retroactive benefits to persons against whom the state had discriminated in violation of the 14th Amendment.

Equal Protection

Geduldig v. Aiello (417 U.S. 484), decided by a 6-3 vote, June 17, 1974. Stewart wrote the majority opinion; Douglas, Brennan and Marshall dissented.

California did not violate the constitutional guarantee of equal protection by excluding from its disability insurance program women unable to work because of pregnancy-related disabilities.

Women were not denied equal protection by this exclusion because, the majority said, "there is no risk from which men are protected and women are not." The decision to exclude the risk of pregnancy from the risks insured by the state plan was a rational one in light of the state interest in maintaining a low-cost, self-supporting insurance fund.

Power of the President

United States v. Nixon (418 U.S. 683), decided by an 8-0 vote, July 24, 1974. Chief Justice Burger wrote the opinion; Rehnquist did not participate.

Neither the separation of powers nor the need to preserve the confidentiality of presidential communications can alone justify an absolute executive privilege of immunity from judicial demands for evidence to be used in a criminal trial.

The court held that President Richard M. Nixon must comply with a subpoena for tapes of certain White House conversations, sought for use as evidence against White House aides charged with obstruction of justice in regard to the investigation of the break-in at the Democratic National Headquarters in the Watergate Office Building in June 1972.

Civil Rights

Milliken v. Bradley (418 U.S. 717), decided by a 5-4 vote, July 25, 1974. Chief Justice Burger wrote the majority opinion; Douglas, Brennan, Marshall and White dissented.

A multi-district remedy for school segregation, such as busing school children across district lines, can only be ordered by a federal court when there has been a finding that all the districts involved have been responsible for the segregation to be remedied.

The court reversed a lower court's order directing busing across city, county and district lines in order to desegregate the schools of Detroit, Mich. The majority ordered the lower court to devise a remedy that would affect only the city schools.

1975

Jury Trials

Taylor v. Louisiana (419 U.S. 522), decided by an 8-1 vote, Jan. 21, 1975. White wrote the majority opinion; Rehnquist dissented.

State laws generally exempting women from jury duty are unconstitutional because they violate the Sixth Amendment requirement that juries be drawn from a fair cross-section of the community.

The court overruled its 1961 decision in *Hoyt v. Florida,* which upheld this general exclusion of women from jury duty as rational in light of the state's interest in preventing interference with women's traditional functions as wives, homemakers and mothers.

Equal Protection

Weinberger v. Wiesenfeld (420 U.S. 636), decided by an 8-0 vote, March 19, 1975. Brennan wrote the opinion; Douglas did not participate.

Social Security law which pays widows with small children, but not widowers with small children, survivors' benefits violates the guarantee of due process by providing working women with fewer benefits for their Social Security contributions than it provides to working men. "It is no less important for a child to be cared for by its sole surviving parent when that parent is male rather than female," wrote Brennan, pointing out that the intended purpose of this benefit was to allow a mother not to work but to stay home and care for her young children.

Freedom of Speech

Bigelow v. Virginia (421 U.S. 809), decided by a 7-2 vote, June 16, 1975. Blackmun wrote the opinion; Rehnquist and White dissented.

Commercial advertising enjoys some First Amendment protection; *Valentine v. Chrestensen* (1942) held that the manner in which such ads were distributed could be regulated — not that advertising was itself unprotected.

The court reversed the conviction of a newspaper editor in Virginia for violating a state law against "encouraging" abortions by running an advertisement including information on legal abortions available in New York. This law was an improper effort by the state to control what its citizens could hear or read, the court held.

Commerce

Goldfarb v. Virginia State Bar (421 U.S. 773), decided by an 8-0 vote, June 16, 1975. Chief Justice Burger wrote the opinion; Powell did not participate.

Lawyers are not exempt from the provisions of federal antitrust laws. Minimum fee schedules adopted by bar associations and enforced to regulate the prices charged by attorneys for their services constitute price-fixing in violation of the antitrust laws.

Civil Rights

Albemarle Paper Co. v. Moody (422 U.S. 405), decided by a 7-1 vote, June 25, 1975. Stewart wrote the majority opinion; Chief Justice Burger dissented; Powell did not participate.

Back pay awards to victims of employment discrimination are the rule, not the exception, in cases won by employees under Title VII of the 1964 Civil Rights Act. Back pay awards are warranted to carry out the intent of Congress to make persons whole for injuries suffered on account of unlawful discrimination and should not be restricted to cases in which the employer is found to have acted in bad faith.

1976

Taxes

Michelin Tire Corp. v. Wages (423 U.S. 276), decided by an 8-0 vote, Jan. 14, 1976. Brennan wrote the opinion; Stevens did not participate.

The court overruled its 1872 decision in the case of *Low v. Austin,* which forbade states to tax imported goods so long as those goods retained their character as imports.

The court held that the export-import clause of the Constitution did not bar a county from imposing a property tax on imported goods stored prior to sale, so long as the tax does not discriminate against imported goods.

Freedom of Speech

Buckley v. Valeo (424 U.S. 1), decided by votes of 8-0, 7-1, and 6-2, Jan. 31, 1976. The opinion was unsigned; Chief

Justice Burger, Blackmun, Rehnquist, White and Marshall all dissented in part; Stevens did not participate.

The First Amendment guarantee of freedom of expression is impermissibly infringed by the limits placed by the 1974 Federal Election Campaign Act Amendments on the amounts which a candidate for federal office may spend. The vote was 7-1; White dissented. The majority did find the limits permissible for candidates who accepted public financing of their campaigns for the presidency.

The court upheld, 6-2, the limits which the law placed on the amount individuals and political committees could contribute to candidates. This was only a marginal restriction on a contributor's First Amendment freedom, justified by the interest in preventing corruption, the majority said. Burger and Blackmun dissented.

The court upheld, 6-2, the system of public financing set up by the law for presidential campaigns and elections. Burger and Rehnquist dissented. Burger also dissented from the majority's decision to uphold the law's requirements for public disclosure of campaign contributions of more than $100 and campaign expenditures of more than $10.

The court unanimously agreed that the Federal Election Commission, as set up by the 1974 law, was unconstitutional as a violation of the separation of powers.

Civil Rights

Hills v. Gautreaux (425 U.S. 284), decided by an 8-0 vote, April 20, 1976. Stewart wrote the opinion; Stevens did not participate.

Federal courts have the power to order housing officials who have contributed to the racial segregation of public housing in a city to remedy that situation by developing public housing throughout the metropolitan area. The court upheld a federal court order for such an area-wide solution to the segregation of public housing in Chicago, a situation for which federal Housing and Urban Development officials had been found partially responsible.

Washington v. Davis (426 U.S. 229), decided by a 7-2 vote, June 7, 1976. White wrote the majority opinion; Brennan and Marshall dissented.

Job qualification tests are not unconstitutional simply because more black than white job applicants fail them. Some racially discriminatory purpose must be found in order for such a test to be in violation of the constitutional guarantees of due process and equal protection. "Disproportionate impact is not irrelevant, but it is not the sole touchstone of an invidious racial discrimination forbidden by the Constitution."

Runyon v. McCrary, Fairfax-Brewster School, Inc. v. Gonzales, Southern Independent School Association v. McCrary (427 U.S. 160), decided by a 7-2 vote, June 25, 1976. Stewart wrote the majority opinion; White and Rehnquist dissented.

Racially segregated private schools which refuse to admit black students violate the Civil Rights Act of 1866, which gave "all persons within the jurisdiction of the United States the same right . . . to make and enforce contracts . . . as is enjoyed by white citizens."

Pasadena City Board of Education v. Spangler (427 U.S. 424), decided by a 6-2 vote, June 28, 1976. Rehnquist wrote the opinion; Brennan and Marshall dissented; Stevens did not participate.

Once a school board has implemented a racially neutral plan for attendance of students at city schools, it is not constitutionally required to continue juggling student assignments in order to maintain a certain racial balance in the student body of each school.

Commerce

National League of Cities v. Usery, California v. Usery (426 U.S. 833), decided by a 5-4 vote, June 24, 1976. Rehnquist wrote the majority opinion; Brennan, White, Marshall and Stevens dissented.

Congress exceeded its power to regulate interstate commerce when it extended federal minimum wage and overtime standards to cover state and local government employees by its 1974 amendments to the Fair Labor Standards Act. Determination of state government employees' wages and hours is one of the "attributes of sovereignty attaching to every state government, which may not be impaired by Congress."

Freedom of Association

Elrod v. Burns (427 U.S. 347), decided by a 5-3 vote, June 28, 1976. Brennan wrote the majority opinion; Chief Justice Burger, Powell and Rehnquist dissented; Stevens did not participate.

The First Amendment freedom of political association is violated by the practice of patronage firing — the discharge by a new officeholder of those public employees not belonging to his political party.

Freedom of the Press

Nebraska Press Association v. Stuart (427 U.S. 539), decided by a unanimous vote, June 30, 1976. Chief Justice Burger wrote the opinion.

A gag order limiting severely what the press can report about pre-trial proceedings in a mass murder case violates the First Amendment guarantee of a free press.

If ever permissible, this sort of prior restraint of publication can be justified only by the most extreme circumstances. In most situations, judges concerned about preserving a defendant's right to a fair trial by an unbiased jury have many less drastic means of ensuring that potential jurors are not prejudiced by publicity.

Cruel and Unusual Punishment

Gregg v. Georgia (428 U.S. 153), *Proffitt v. Florida* (428 U.S. 242), *Jurek v. Texas* (428 U.S. 262), decided by 7-2 votes, July 2, 1976. Stewart wrote the majority decision in *Gregg;* Stevens wrote the majority decision in *Jurek;* Powell wrote the majority decision in *Proffitt;* Brennan and Marshall dissented.

Death, as a punishment for persons convicted of first degree murder, is not in and of itself cruel and unusual punishment in violation of the Eighth Amendment. That amendment, however, requires that the sentencing judge or jury consider the individual character of the offender and the circumstances of the particular crime before deciding whether or not to impose the death sentence. A two-part proceeding — one for the determination of guilt or innocence and a second for determining the sentence — provides an opportunity for such individualized consideration prior to sentencing.

Woodson v. North Carolina (428 U.S. 280), *Roberts v. Louisiana* (428 U.S. 325), decided by votes of 5-4, July 2,

1976. Stewart wrote the majority opinion in *Woodson;* Stevens wrote the majority opinion in *Roberts;* Chief Justice Burger, White, Rehnquist and Blackmun dissented.

States may not make death the mandatory penalty for first-degree murder. Such mandatory sentences fail to meet the constitutional requirement for consideration of the individual offender and offense prior to the decision to impose the death penalty.

Federal Courts

Stone v. Powell, Wolff v. Rice (428 U.S. 465), decided by a 6-3 vote, July 6, 1976. Powell wrote the majority opinion; Brennan, Marshall and White dissented.

A state prisoner's claim that illegally obtained evidence was used to convict him cannot serve as a basis for a federal court order of his release through a writ of *habeas corpus* — unless the state failed to provide the prisoner an opportunity for full and fair hearing of his challenge to the evidence.

Equal Protection

Craig v. Boren (429 U.S. 190), decided by a 7-2 vote, Dec. 20, 1976. Brennan wrote the majority opinion; Chief Justice Burger and Rehnquist dissented.

A classification based on gender is invalid unless it is substantially related to the achievement of an important governmental objective.

Using this rule, the court declared unconstitutional a state law that permitted the sale of 3.2 beer to women at age 18 but not to men until age 21. The law was not substantially related to the state's expressed goal of promoting traffic safety.

1977

Civil Rights

Village of Arlington Heights v. Metropolitan Housing Development Corporation (429 U.S. 252), decided by a 5-3 vote, Jan. 11, 1977. Powell wrote the majority opinion; Brennan and Marshall dissented in part; White dissented; Stevens did not participate.

Without any showing of discriminatory motive, the refusal of a village to rezone property to permit building of a housing development for low- and moderate-income persons of both races does not violate the 14th Amendment guarantee of equal protection.

Voting Rights

United Jewish Organizations of Williamsburgh v. Carey (430 U.S. 144), decided by a 7-1 vote, March 1, 1977. White wrote the majority opinion; Chief Justice Burger dissented; Marshall did not participate.

The court upheld the use of racial criteria by the state of New York in its 1974 state legislative redistricting plan drawn to comply with the 1965 Voting Rights Act. The court said that even if the result of the redistricting diluted the vote of a white ethnic minority — in this case the Hasidic Jewish community of Brooklyn — the Constitution "does not prevent a state subject to the Voting Rights Act from deliberately creating or preserving black majorities in particular districts in order to ensure that its reapportionment plan" complies with the act.

Taxes

Complete Auto Transit Inc. v. Brady (430 U.S. 274), decided by a unanimous vote, March 8, 1977. Blackmun wrote the opinion.

The commerce clause — granting Congress the power to regulate interstate and foreign commerce — does not forbid a state to tax an interstate enterprise doing business within the state for the "privilege" of doing business there.

Such taxes are permissible so long as the taxed activity has a sufficient nexus with the taxing state; the tax does not discriminate against interstate commerce, is fairly apportioned and is related to services provided by the state.

Cruel and Unusual Punishment

Coker v. Georgia (433 U.S. 584), decided by a 7-2 vote, June 29, 1977. White wrote the majority opinion; Burger and Rehnquist dissented.

The court held that the sentence of death for the crime of rape is an excessive and disproportionate penalty fobidden by the Eighth Amendment ban on cruel and unusual punishments.

1978

Search and Seizure

Marshall v. Barlows, Inc. (436 U.S. 307), decided by a 5-3 vote, May 23, 1978. White wrote the majority opinion; Stevens, Blackmun and Rehnquist dissented; Brennan did not participate.

The court held unconstitutional the provision of the Occupational Safety and Health Act of 1970 which allowed warrantless inspection of covered businesses. Searches of business premises without a warrant and without the owner's consent violate the Fourth Amendment's guarantee against unreasonable searches and seizures. An OSHA inspector must obtain a search warrant when the business-man objects to a warrantless search.

Zurcher v. The Stanford Daily (436 U.S. 547), decided by a 5-3 vote, May 31, 1978. White wrote the majority opinion; Stewart, Marshall and Stevens dissented; Brennan did not participate.

The Fourth Amendment does not preclude or limit the use of search warrants for searches of places owned or occupied by innocent third parties not suspected of any crime.

The First Amendment guarantee of freedom of the press does not require that information concerning a crime which is suspected to be in the possession of a newspaper be sought by a subpoena rather than a search warrant.

Jury Trials

Ballew v. Georgia (435 U.S. 223), decided by a unanimous vote, March 21, 1978. Blackmun wrote the opinion.

In order to fulfill the constitutional guarantee of trial by jury, state juries must be composed of at least six members.

Freedom of Speech

First National Bank of Boston v. Bellotti (435 U.S. 765), decided by a 5-4 vote, April 26, 1978. Powell wrote the majority opinion; White, Brennan, Marshall and Rehnquist dissented.

State law banning corporate expenditures relative to a referendum issue which does not materially affect corporations' business impermissibly abridges political speech protected by the First Amendment. "If the speakers here were not corporations, no one would suggest that the state could silence their proposed speech. It is the type of speech indispensable to decisionmaking in a democracy, and this is no less true because the speech comes from a corporation rather than an individual," the majority said.

Civil Rights

Regents of University of California v. Bakke (438 U.S. 265), decided by votes of 5-4 and 5-4, June 28, 1978. Powell announced the judgment of the court; Stevens and Brennan filed separate opinions; Stevens was joined by Chief Justice Burger, Rehnquist and Stewart; Brennan was joined by Marshall, White and Blackmun.

A special admissions program for a state medical school under which a set number of places were set aside for minority group members — and white applicants were denied the opportunity to compete for those seats — clearly violated Title VI of the 1964 Civil Rights Act which forbids the exclusion of anyone, because of race, from participation in a federally funded program.

Admissions programs which consider race as one of a complex of factors involved in the decision to admit or reject an applicant are not unconstitutional in and of themselves. "Government may take race into account when it acts not to demean or insult any racial group, but to remedy disadvantages cast on minorities by past racial prejudice, at least when appropriate findings have been made by judicial, legislative, or administrative bodies with competence to act in this area."

Federal Courts

Monell v. Department of Social Services, City of New York (436 U.S. 658), decided by a 7-2 vote, June 6, 1978. Brennan wrote the majority opinion; Chief Justice Burger and Rehnquist dissented.

City officials, municipalities and municipal agencies are not immune from civil rights damage suits filed under the Civil Rights Act of 1871. Cities may be held liable for damages if action pursuant to official policy violates someone's constitutional rights. Cities are not liable simply because their employees or agents infringe upon such rights in the course of their duties.

Official Immunity

Butz v. Economou (438 U.S. 478), decided by a 5-4 vote, June 29, 1978. White wrote the majority opinion; Chief Justice Burger, Rehnquist, Stewart and Stevens dissented.

Federal officials are not absolutely immune from damage suits based upon their performance of official duties. Even when carrying out directives from Congress, federal officials are subject to the restraints of the Constitution.

1979

Right to Legal Counsel

Scott v. Illinois, decided by a 5-4 vote, March 5, 1979. Rehnquist wrote the majority opinion; Brennan, Marshall, Stevens and Blackmun dissented.

A state defendant is guaranteed the right to legal counsel, paid by the state if necessary, only in cases that actually lead to imprisonment, not in all cases where imprisonment is a potential penalty.

Equal Protection

Orr v. Orr, decided by a 6-3 vote, March 5, 1979. Brennan wrote the majority opinion; Powell, Rehnquist and Burger dissented.

States violate the 14th Amendment guarantee of equal protection when they allow women, but not men, to receive alimony as part of a divorce settlement.

Jury Trial

Burch v. Louisiana, decided by a unanimous vote, April 17, 1979. Rehnquist wrote the opinion.

A state deprives a defendant of his constitutional right to a jury trial when it allows him to be convicted by the non-unanimous vote of a six-person jury.

Due Process

Davis v. Passman, decided by a 5-4 vote, June 5, 1979. Brennan wrote the majority opinion; Chief Justice Burger, Powell, Rehnquist and Stewart dissented.

An individual who has been denied the rights of due process and equal protection under the Fifth Amendment guarantee against federal action can bring a federal suit for damages based on that amendment.

This decision for the first time provided a constitutional basis for job discrimination charges by congressional employees, who are not protected by the guarantees of the federal civil rights laws.

Official Immunity

United States v. Helstoski, decided by a 5-3 vote, June 18, 1979. Chief Justice Burger wrote the majority opinion, Brennan dissented; Stevens and Stewart dissented in part; Powell did not participate.

The Constitution's provision that members of Congress may not be questioned outside Congress "for any Speech or Debate in either House" forbids the government, in prosecuting a member for accepting a bribe in return for a legislative act, to introduce evidence of the legislative act. The constitutional provision was intended to preclude prosecution of members for legislative acts.

Hutchinson v. Proxmire, decided by a 7-2 vote, June 26, 1979. Chief Justice Burger wrote the majority opinion; Brennan dissented; Stewart dissented in part.

The Constitution's "Speech or Debate clause" does not protect a senator from being sued for libel as a result of statements made in press releases and newsletters.

An individual who does not seek to thrust himself into the public eye or otherwise draw public attention, but who is drawn into public notice by events outside his control, is not a public figure subject to the "actual malice" standard set out by the Supreme Court for libel suits brought by public officials.

Civil Rights

United Steelworkers of America v. Weber, Kaiser Aluminum v. Weber, United States v. Weber, decided by a 5-2 vote, June 27, 1979. Brennan wrote the majority opinion; Chief Justice Burger and Rehnquist dissented; Powell and Stevens did not participate.

Title VII of the 1964 Civil Rights Act — which forbids racial discrimination in employment — does not forbid employers to adopt voluntarily race-conscious affirmative action programs to encourage minority participation in areas of work in which they have traditionally been under-represented.

Columbus Board of Education v. Penick, Dayton Board of Education v. Brinkman, decided by votes of 7-2 and 5-4, July 2, 1979. White wrote the majority opinion in both cases; Rehnquist and Powell dissented in both; Chief Justice Burger and Stewart dissented in the *Dayton* case.

School boards operating segregated school systems at the time of the 1954 decision in *Brown v. Board of Education* are under an affirmative duty to end that segregation — even if it was not imposed as a result of state law. The court upheld system-wide busing orders for Dayton and Columbus, Ohio, where segregated schools had not been required by law since 1888.

Freedom of the Press

Gannett v. DePasquale, decided by a 5-4 vote, July 2, 1979. Stewart wrote the majority opinion; Blackmun, Brennan, White and Marshall dissented in part.

The Constitution's guarantee of the right to a public trial is intended for the benefit of the defendant, not the public.

Members of the public do not have a constitutional right to attend a criminal trial, and thus a judge may constitutionally exclude press and public from a pretrial hearing in order to avoid publicity prejudicial to the defendant and thus protect his right to a fair trial.

APPENDIX

Declaration of Independence 913

Articles of Confederation 914

The Constitution 918

Acts of Congress Held Unconstitutional 926

Rules of the Supreme Court 932

Supreme Court Nominations 946

Judiciary Act of 1789 949

Circuit Court of Appeals Act of 1891 957

Judiciary Act of 1925 960

Roosevelt's 1937 Court Reform Plan 964

Fortas' Letter of Resignation 983

Glossary of Legal Terms 984

Declaration of Independence

In Congress, July 4, 1776,

The Unanimous Declaration of the
Thirteen United States of America,

When in the Course of human events, it becomes necessary for one people to dissolve the political bands which have connected them with another, and to assume among the Powers of the earth, the separate and equal station to which the Laws of Nature and of Nature's God entitle them, a decent respect to the opinions of mankind requires that they should declare the causes which impel them to the separation.

We hold these truths to be self-evident, that all men are created equal, that they are endowed by their Creator with certain unalienable Rights, that among these are Life, Liberty and the pursuit of Happiness. That to secure these rights, Governments are instituted among Men, deriving their just powers from the consent of the governed. That whenever any form of Government becomes destructive of these ends, it is the Right of the People to alter or to abolish it, and to institute new Government, laying its foundation on such principles and organizing its powers in such form, as to them shall seem most likely to effect their Safety and Happiness. Prudence, indeed, will dictate that Government long established should not be changed for light and transient causes; and accordingly all experience hath shown, that mankind are more disposed to suffer, while evils are sufferable, than to right themselves by abolishing the forms to which they are accustomed. But when a long train of abuses and usurpations, pursuing invariably the same Object evinces a design to reduce them under absolute Despotism, it is their right, it is their duty, to throw off such Government, and to provide new Guards for their future security.—Such has been the patient sufferance of these Colonies; and such is now the necessity which constrains them to alter their former Systems of Government. The history of the present King of Great Britain is a history of repeated injuries and usurpations, all having in direct object the establishment of an absolute Tyranny over these States. To prove this, let Facts be submitted to a candid world.

He has refused his Assent to Laws, the most wholesome and necessary for the public good.

He has forbidden his Governors to pass Laws of immediate and pressing importance, unless suspended in their operation till his Assent should be obtained; and when so suspended, he has utterly neglected to attend to them.

He has refused to pass other Laws for the accommodation of large districts of people, unless those people would relinquish the right of Representation in the Legislature, a right inestimable to them and formidable to tyrants only.

He has called together legislative bodies at places unusual, uncomfortable, and distant from the depository of their Public Records, for the sole purpose of fatiguing them into compliance with his measures.

He has dissolved Representative Houses repeatedly, for opposing with manly firmness his invasions on the rights of the people.

He has refused for a long time, after such dissolutions, to cause others to be elected; whereby the Legislative Powers, incapable of Annihilation, have returned to the People at large for their exercise; the State remaining in the mean time exposed to all the dangers of invasion from without, and convulsions within.

He has endeavoured to prevent the population of these States; for that purpose obstructing the Laws of Naturalization of Foreigners; refusing to pass others to encourage their migration hither, and raising the conditions of new Appropriations of Lands.

He has obstructed the Administration of Justice, by refusing his Assent to Laws for establishing Judiciary Powers.

He has made Judges dependent on his Will alone, for the tenure of their offices, and the amount and payment of their salaries.

He has erected a multitude of New Offices, and sent hither swarms of Officers to harass our People, and eat out their substance.

He has kept among us, in times of peace, Standing Armies without the Consent of our legislature.

He has affected to render the Military independent of and superior to the Civil Power.

He has combined with others to subject us to a jurisdiction foreign to our constitution, and unacknowledged by our laws; giving his Assent to their acts of pretended legislation:

For quartering large bodies of armed troops among us:

For protecting them, by a mock Trial, from Punishment for any Murders which they should commit on the Inhabitants of these States:

For cutting off our Trade with all parts of the world:

For imposing taxes on us without our Consent:

For depriving us in many cases, of the benefits of Trial by Jury:

For transporting us beyond Seas to be tried for pretended offences:

For abolishing the free System of English Laws in a neighbouring Province, establishing therein an Arbitrary government, and enlarging its Boundaries so as to render it at once an example and fit instrument for introducing the same absolute rule into these Colonies:

For taking away our Charters, abolishing our most valuable Laws, and altering fundamentally the Forms of our Governments:

For suspending our own Legislature, and declaring themselves invested with Power to legislate for us in all cases whatsoever.

He has abdicated Government here, by declaring us out of his Protection and waging War against us.

He has plundered our seas, ravaged our Coasts, burnt our towns, and destroyed the lives of our people.

He is at this time transporting large armies of foreign mercenaries to compleat the works of death, desolation and tyranny, already begun with circumstances of Cruelty & perfidy scarcely paralleled in the most barbarous ages, and totally unworthy the Head of a civilized nation.

He has constrained our fellow Citizens taken Captive on the high Seas to bear Arms against their Country, to become the executioners of their friends and Brethren, or to fall themselves by their Hands.

He has excited domestic insurrections amongst us, and has endeavoured to bring on the inhabitants of our frontiers, the merciless Indian Savages, whose known rule of warfare, is an undistinguished destruction of all ages, sexes and conditions.

In every stage of these Oppressions We have Petitioned for Redress in the most humble terms: Our repeated Petitions have been answered only by repeated injury. A Prince, whose character is thus marked by every act which may define a Tyrant, is unfit to be the ruler of a free People.

Nor have We been wanting in attention to our Brittish brethren. We have warned them from time to time of attempts by their legislature to extend an unwarrantable jurisdiction over us. We have reminded them of the circumstances of our emigration and settlement here. We have appealed to their native justice and magnanimity, and we have conjured them by the ties of our common kindred to disavow these usurpations, which, would inevitably interrupt our connections and correspondence. They too have been deaf to the voice of justice and of consanguinity. We must, therefore, acquiesce in the necessity, which denounces our Separation, and hold them, as we hold the rest of mankind, Enemies in War, in Peace Friends.

JOHN HANCOCK.

We, therefore, the Representatives of the united States of America, in General Congress, Assembled, appealing to the Supreme Judge of the world for the rectitude of our intentions, do, in the Name, and by Authority of the good People of these Colonies, solemnly publish and declare, That these United Colonies are, and of Right ought to be Free and Independent States; that they are Absolved from all Allegiance to the British Crown, and that all political connection between them and the State of Great Britain, is and ought to be totally dissolved; and that as Free and Independent States, they have full Power to levy War, conclude Peace, contract Alliances, establish Commerce, and to do all other Acts and Things which Independent States may of right do. And for the support of this Declaration, with a firm reliance on the Protection of Divine Providence, we mutually pledge to each other our Lives, our Fortunes and our sacred Honor.

New Hampshire:	Josiah Bartlett, William Whipple, Matthew Thornton.	**Delaware:**	Caesar Rodney, George Read, Thomas McKean.
Massachusetts-Bay:	Samuel Adams, John Adams, Robert Treat Paine, Elbridge Gerry.	**Georgia:**	Button Gwinnett, Lyman Hall, George Walton.
Rhode Island:	Stephen Hopkins, William Ellery.	**Maryland:**	Samuel Chase, William Paca, Thomas Stone, Charles Carroll of Carrollton.
Connecticut:	Roger Sherman, Samuel Huntington, William Williams, Oliver Wolcott.	**Virginia:**	George Wythe, Richard Henry Lee, Thomas Jefferson, Benjamin Harrison, Thomas Nelson Jr., Francis Lightfoot Lee, Carter Braxton.
New York:	William Floyd, Philip Livingston, Francis Lewis, Lewis Morris.	**North Carolina:**	William Hooper, Joseph Hewes, John Penn.
Pennsylvania:	Robert Morris, Benjamin Rush, Benjamin Franklin, John Morton, George Clymer, James Smith, George Taylor, James Wilson, George Ross.	**South Carolina:**	Edward Rutledge, Thomas Heyward Jr., Thomas Lynch Jr., Arthur Middleton.
		New Jersey:	Richard Stockton, John Witherspoon, Francis Hopkinson, John Hart, Abraham Clark.

Articles of Confederation

Agreed to by Congress November 15, 1777; Ratified and in Force, March 1, 1781

To all to whom these Presents shall come, we the undersigned Delegates of the States affixed to our Names send greeting. Whereas the Delegates of the United States of America in Congress assembled did on the fifteenth day of November in the Year of our Lord One Thousand Seven Hundred and Seventy seven, and in the Second Year of the Independence of America agree to certain articles of Confederation and perpetual Union between the States of Newhampshire, Massachusetts-bay, Rhodeisland and Providence Plantations, Connecticut, New York, New Jersey, Pennsylvania, Delaware, Maryland, Virginia, North-Carolina, South-Carolina and Georgia in the Words following, viz. "Articles of Confederation and perpetual Union between the states of Newhampshire, Massachusetts-bay, Rhodeisland and Providence Plantations, Connecticut, New-York, New-Jersey, Pennsylvania, Delaware, Maryland, Virginia, North-Carolina, South-Carolina and Georgia.

Art. I. The Stile of this confederacy shall be "The United States of America."

Art. II. Each state retains its sovereignty, freedom and independence, and every Power, Jurisdiction and right, which is not by this confederation expressly delegated to the United States, in Congress assembled.

Art. III. The said states hereby severally enter into a firm league of friendship with each other, for their common defence, the security of their Liberties, and their mutual and general welfare, binding themselves to assist each other, against all force offered to, or attacks made upon them, or any of them, on account of religion, sovereignty, trade, or any other pretence whatever.

Art. IV. The better to secure and perpetuate mutual friendship and intercourse among the people of the different states in this union, the free inhabitants of each of these states, paupers, vagabonds and fugitives from Justice excepted, shall be entitled to all privileges and immunities of free citizens in the several states; and the people of each state shall have free ingress and regress to and from any other state, and shall enjoy therein all the privileges of trade and commerce, subject to the same duties, impositions and restrictions as the inhabitants thereof respectively, provided that such restriction shall not extend so far as to prevent the removal of property imported into any state, to any other state of which the Owner is an inhabitant; provided also that no imposition, duties or restriction shall be laid by any state, on the property of the united states, or either of them.

If any Person guilty of, or charged with treason, felony, or other high misdemeanor in any state, shall flee from Justice, and be found in any of the united states, he shall upon demand of the Governor or executive power, of the state from which he fled, be delivered up and removed to the state having jurisdiction of his offence.

Full faith and credit shall be given in each of these states to the records, acts and judicial proceedings of the courts and magistrates of every other state.

Art. V. For the more convenient management of the general interests of the united states, delegates shall be annually appointed in such manner as the legislature of each state shall direct, to meet in Congress on the first Monday in November, in every year, with a power reserved to each state, to recal its delegates, or any of them, at any time within the year, and to send others in their stead, for the remainder of the Year.

No state shall be represented in Congress by less than two, nor by more than seven Members; and no person shall be capable of being a delegate for more than three years in any term of six years; nor shall any person, being a delegate, be capable of holding any office under the united states, for which he, or another for his benefit receives any salary, fees or emolument of any kind.

Each state shall maintain its own delegates in a meeting of the states, and while they act as members of the committee of the states.

In determining questions in the united states, in Congress assembled, each state shall have one vote.

Freedom of speech and debate in Congress shall not be impeached or questioned in any Court, or place out of Congress, and the members of congress shall be protected in their persons from arrests and imprisonments, during the time of their going to and from, and attendance on congress, except for treason, felony, or breach of the peace.

Art. VI. No state without the Consent of the united states in congress assembled, shall send any embassy to, or receive any embassy from, or enter into any conference, agreement, or alliance or treaty with any King, prince or state; nor shall any person holding any office of profit or trust under the united states, or any of them, accept of any present, emolument, office or title of any kind whatever from any king, prince or foreign state; nor shall the united states in congress assembled, or any of them, grant any title of nobility.

No two or more states shall enter into any treaty, confederation or alliance whatever between them, without the consent of the united states in congress assembled, specifying accurately the purposes for which the same is to be entered into, and how long it shall continue.

No state shall lay any imposts or duties, which may interfere with any stipulations in treaties, entered into by the united states in congress assembled, with any king, prince or state, in pursuance of any treaties already proposed by congress, to the courts of France and Spain.

No vessels of war shall be kept up in time of peace by any state, except such number only, as shall be deemed necessary by the united states in congress assembled, for the defence of such state, or its trade; nor shall any body of forces be kept up by any state, in time of peace, except such number only, as in the judgment of the united states, in congress assembled, shall be deemed requisite to garrison the forts necessary for the defence of such state; but every state shall always keep up a well regulated and disciplined militia, sufficiently armed and accoutred, and shall provide and constantly have ready for use, in public stores, a due number of field pieces and tents, and a proper quantity of arms, ammunition and camp equipage.

No state shall engage in any war without the consent of the united states in congress assembled, unless such state be actually invaded by enemies, or shall have received certain advice of a resolution being formed by some nation of Indians to invade such state, and the danger is so imminent as not to admit of a delay, till the united states in congress assembled can be consulted: nor shall any state grant commissions to any ships or vessels of war, nor letters of marque or reprisal, except it be after a declaration of war by the united states in congress assembled, and then only against the kingdom or state and the subjects thereof, against which war has been so declared, and under such regulations as shall be established by the united states in congress assembled, unless such state be infested by pirates, in which case vessels of war may be fitted out for that occasion, and kept so long as the danger shall continue, or until the united states in congress assembled shall determine otherwise.

Art. VII. When land-forces are raised by any state for the common defence, all officers of or under the rank of colonel, shall be appointed by the legislature of each state respectively by whom such forces shall be raised, or in such manner as such state shall direct, and all vacancies shall be filled up by the state which first made the appointment.

Art. VIII. All charges of war, and all other expences that shall be incurred for the common defence or general welfare, and allowed by the united states in congress assembled, shall be defrayed out of a common treasury, which whall be supplied by the several states, in proportion to the value of all land within each state, granted to or surveyed for any Person, as such land and the buildings and improvements thereon shall be estimated according to such mode as the united states in congress assembled, shall from time to time direct and appoint. The taxes for paying that proportion shall be laid and levied by the authority and direction of the legislatures of the several states within the time agreed upon by the united states in congress assembled.

Art. IX. The united states in congress assembled, shall have the sole and exclusive right and power of determining on peace and war, except in the cases mentioned in the sixth article—of sending and receiving ambassadors—entering into treaties and alliances, provided that no treaty of commerce shall be made whereby the legislative power of the respective states shall be restrained from imposing such imposts and duties on foreigners, as their own people are subjected to, or from prohibiting the exportation or importation of any species of goods or commodities whatsoever—of establishing rules for deciding in all cases, what captures on land or water shall be legal, and in what manner prizes taken by land or naval forces in the service of the united states shall be divided or appropriated—of granting letters of marque and reprisal in times of peace—appointing courts for the trial of piracies and felonies committed on the high seas and establishing courts for receiving and determining finally appeals in all cases of captures, provided that no member of congress shall be appointed a judge of any of the said courts.

The united states in congress assembled shall also be the last resort on appeal in all disputes and differences now subsisting or that hereafter may arise between two or more states concerning boundary, jurisdiction or any other cause whatever; which authority shall always be exercised in the manner following. Whenever the legislative or executive authority or lawful agent of any state in controversy with another shall present a petition to congress, stating the matter in question and praying for a hearing, notice thereof shall be given by order of congress to the legislative or executive authority of the other state in controversy, and a day assigned for the appearance of the parties by their lawful agents, who shall then be directed to appoint by joint consent, commissioners or judges to constitute a court for hearing and determining the matter in question: but if they cannot agree, congress shall name three persons out of each of the united states, and from the list of such persons each party shall alternately strike out one, the petitioners beginning, until the number shall be reduced to thirteen; and from that number not less than seven, nor more than nine names as congress shall direct, shall in the presence of congress be drawn out by lot, and the persons whose names shall be so drawn or any five of them, shall be commissioners or judges, to hear and finally determine the controversy, so always as a major part of the judges who shall hear the cause shall agree in the determination: and if either party shall neglect to attend at the day appointed, without shewing reasons, which congress shall judge sufficient, or being present shall refuse to strike, the congress shall proceed to nominate three persons out of each state, and the secretary of congress shall strike in behalf of such party absent or refusing; and the judgment and sentence of the court to be appointed, in the manner before prescribed, shall be final and conclusive; and if any of the parties shall refuse to submit to the authority of such court, or to appear to defend their claim or cause, the court shall nevertheless proceed to pronounce sentence, or judgment, which shall in like manner be final and decisive, the judgment or sentence and other proceedings being in either case transmitted to congress, and lodged among the

acts of congress for the security of the parties concerned: provided that every commissioner, before he sits in judgment, shall take an oath to be administered by one of the judges of the supreme or superior court of the state, where the cause shall be tried, "well and truly to hear and determine the matter in question, according to the best of his judgment, without favour, affection or hope of reward:" provided also that no state shall be deprived of territory for the benefit of the united states.

All controversies concerning the private right of soil claimed under different grants of two or more states, whose jurisdictions as they may respect such lands, and the states which passed such grants are adjusted, the said grants or either of them being at the same time claimed to have originated antecedent to such settlement of jurisdiction, shall on the petition of either party to the congress of the united states, be finally determined as near as may be in the same manner as is before prescribed for deciding disputes respecting territorial jurisdiction between different states.

The united states in congress assembled shall also have the sole and exclusive right and power of regulating the alloy and value of coin struck by their own authority, or by that of the respective states—fixing the standard of weights and measures throughout the united states—regulating the trade and managing all affairs with the Indians, not members of any of the states, provided that the legislative right of any state within its own limits be not infringed or violated—establishing and regulating post-offices from one state to another, throughout all the united states, and exacting such postage on the papers passing thro' the same as may be requisite to defray the expences of the said office—appointing all officers of the land forces, in the service of the united states, excepting regimental officers —appointing all the officers of the naval forces, and commissioning all officers whatever in the service of the united states—making rules for the government and regulation of the said land and naval forces, and directing their operations.

The united states in congress assembled shall have authority to appoint a committee, to sit in the recess of congress, to be denominated "A Committee of the States," and to consist of one delegate from each state; and to appoint such other committees and civil officers as may be necessary for managing the general affairs of the united states under their direction—to appoint one of their number to preside, provided that no person be allowed to serve in the office of president more than one year in any term of three years; to ascertain the necessary sums of Money to be raised for the service of the united states, and to appropriate and apply the same for defraying the public expences—to borrow money, or emit bills on the credit of the united states, transmitting every half year to the respective states an account of the sums of money so borrowed or emitted,—to build and equip a navy—to agree upon the number of land forces, and to make requisitions from each state for its quota, in proportion to the number of white inhabitants in such state; which requisition shall be binding, and thereupon the legislature of each state shall appoint the regimental officers, raise the men and cloath, arm and equip them in a soldier like manner, at the expence of the united states, and the officers and men so cloathed, armed and equipped shall march to the place appointed, and within the time agreed on by the united states in congress assembled: But if the united states in congress assembled shall, on consideration of circumstances judge proper that any state should not raise men, or should raise a smaller number than its quota, and that any other state should raise a greater number of men than the quota thereof, such extra number shall be raised, officered, cloathed, armed and equipped in the same manner as the quota of such state, unless the legislature of such state shall judge that such extra number cannot be safely spared out of the same, in which case they shall raise, officer, cloath, arm and equip as many of such extra number as they judge can be safely spared. And the officers and men so cloathed, armed and equipped, shall march to the place appointed, and within the time agreed on by the united states in congress assembled.

The united states in congress assembled shall never engage in a war, nor grant letters of marque and reprisal in time of peace, nor enter into any treaties or alliances, nor coin money, nor regulate the value thereof, nor ascertain the sums and expences necessary for the defence and welfare of the united states, or any of them, nor emit bills, nor borrow money on the credit of the united states, nor appropriate money, nor agree upon the number of vessels of war, to be built or purchased, or the number of land or sea forces to be raised, nor appoint a commander in chief of the army or navy, unless nine states assent to the same: nor shall a question on any other point, except for adjourning from day to day be determined, unless by the votes of a majority of the united states in congress assembled.

The congress of the united states shall have power to adjourn to any time within the year, and to any place within the united states, so that no period of adjournment be for a longer duration than the space of six Months, and shall publish the Journal of their proceedings monthly, except such parts thereof relating to treaties, alliances or military operations as in their judgment require secresy; and the yeas and nays of the delegates of each state on any question shall be entered on the Journal, when it is desired by any delegate; and the delegates of a state, or any of them, at his or their request shall be furnished with a transcript of the said Journal, except such parts as are above excepted, to lay before the legislatures of the several states.

Art. X. The committee of the states, or any nine of them, shall be authorised to execute, in the recess of congress, such of the powers of congress as the united states in congress assembled, by the consent of nine states, shall from time to time think expedient to vest them with; provided that no power be delegated to the said committee, for the exercise of which, by the articles of confederation, the voice of nine states in the congress of the united states assembled is requisite.

Art. XI. Canada acceding to this confederation, and joining in the measures of the united states, shall be admitted into, and entitled to all the advantages of this union: but no other colony shall be admitted into the same, unless such admission be agreed to by nine states.

Art. XII. All bills of credit emitted, monies borrowed and debts contracted by, or under the authority of congress, before the assembling of the united states, in pursuance of the present confederation, shall be deemed and considered as a charge against the united states, for payment and satisfaction whereof the said united states, and the public faith are hereby solemnly pledged.

Art. XIII. Every state shall abide by the determinations of the united states in congress assembled, on all questions which by this confederation are submitted to them. And the Articles of this confederation shall be inviolably observed by every state, and the union shall be perpetual; nor shall any alteration at any time hereafter be made in any of them; unless such alteration be agreed to in a congress of the united states, and be afterwards confirmed by the legislatures of every state.

And Whereas it hath pleased the Great Governor of the World to incline the hearts of the legislatures we respectively represent in congress, to approve of, and to authorize us to ratify the said articles of confederation and perpetual union. Know Ye that we the under-signed delegates, by virtue of the power and authority to us given for that purpose, do by these presents, in the name and in behalf of our respective constituents, fully and entirely ratify and confirm each and every of the said articles of confederation and perpetual union, and all and singular the matters and things therein contained: And we do further solemnly plight and engage the faith of our respective constituents, that they shall abide by the determinations of the united states in congress assembled, on all questions, which by the said confederation are submitted to them. And that the articles thereof shall be inviolably observed by the states we respectively represent, and that the union shall be perpetual. In Witness whereof we have hereunto set our hands in Congress. Done at Philadelphia in the state of Pennsylvania the ninth Day of July in the Year of our Lord one Thousand seven Hundred and Seventy-eight, and in the third year of the independence of America.

New Hampshire:	Josiah Bartlett, John Wentworth Jr.	**New York:**	James Duane, Francis Lewis, William Duer, Gouverneur Morris.	**Virginia:**	Richard Henry Lee, John Banister, Thomas Adams, John Harvie, Francis Lightfoot Lee.
Massachusetts:	John Hancock, Samuel Adams, Elbridge Gerry, Francis Dana, James Lovell, Samuel Holten.	**New Jersey:**	John Witherspoon, Nathaniel Scudder.	**North Carolina:**	John Penn, Cornelius Harnett, John Williams.
		Pennsylvania:	Robert Morris, Daniel Roberdeau, Jonathan Bayard Smith, William Clingan, Joseph Reed.	**South Carolina:**	Henry Laurens, William Henry Drayton, John Mathews, Richard Hutson, Thomas Heyward Jr.
Rhode Island:	William Ellery, Henry Marchant, John Collins.	**Delaware:**	Thomas McKean, John Dickinson, Nicholas Van Dyke.		
Connecticut:	Roger Sherman, Samuel Huntington, Oliver Wolcott, Titus Hosmer, Andrew Adams.	**Maryland:**	John Hanson, Daniel Carroll.	**Georgia:**	John Walton, Edward Telfair, Edward Langworthy.

Constitution of the United States

We the People of the United States, in Order to form a more perfect Union, establish Justice, insure domestic Tranquility, provide for the common defence, promote the general Welfare, and secure the Blessings of Liberty to ourselves and our Posterity, do ordain and establish this Constitution for the United States of America.

Article I

Section 1. All legislative Powers herein granted shall be vested in a Congress of the United States, which shall consist of a Senate and House of Representatives.

Section 2. The House of Representatives shall be composed of Members chosen every second Year by the People of the several States, and the Electors in each State shall have the Qualifications requisite for Electors of the most numerous Branch of the State Legislature.

No Person shall be a Representative who shall not have attained to the age of twenty five Years, and been seven Years a Citizen of the United States, and who shall not, when elected, be an Inhabitant of that State in which he shall be chosen.

[Representatives and direct Taxes shall be apportioned among the several States which may be included within this Union, according to their respective Numbers, which shall be determined by adding to the whole Number of free Persons, including those bound to Service for a Term of Years, and excluding Indians not taxed, three fifths of all other Persons.]¹ The actual Enumeration shall be made within three Years after the first Meeting of the Congress of the United States, and within every subsequent Term of ten Years, in such Manner as they shall by Law direct. The Number of Representatives shall not exceed one for every thirty Thousand, but each State shall have at Least one Representative; and until such enumeration shall be made, the State of New Hampshire shall be entitled to chuse three, Massachusetts eight, Rhode-Island and Providence Plantations one, Connecticut five, New-York six, New Jersey four, Pennsylvania eight, Delaware one, Maryland six, Virginia ten, North Carolina five, South Carolina five, and Georgia three.

When vacancies happen in the Representation from any State, the Executive Authority thereof shall issue Writs of Election to fill such Vacancies.

The House of Representatives shall chuse their Speaker and other Officers; and shall have the sole Power of Impeachment.

Section 3. The Senate of the United States shall be composed of two Senators from each State, [chosen by the Legislature thereof,]² for six Years; and each Senator shall have one Vote.

Immediately after they shall be assembled in Consequence of the first Election, they shall be divided as equally as may be into three Classes. The Seats of the Senators of the first Class shall be vacated at the Expiration of the second Year, of the second Class at the Expiration of the fourth Year, and of the third Class at the Expiration of the sixth Year, so that one third may be chosen every second Year; [and if Vacancies happen by Resignation, or otherwise, during the Recess of the Legislature of any State, the Executive

thereof may make temporary Appointments until the next Meeting of the Legislature, which shall then fill such Vacancies.]³

No Person shall be a Senator who shall not have attained to the Age of thirty Years, and been nine Years a Citizen of the United States, and who shall not, when elected, be an Inhabitant of that State for which he shall be chosen.

The Vice President of the United States shall be President of the Senate, but shall have no Vote, unless they be equally divided.

The Senate shall chuse their other Officers, and also a President pro tempore, in the Absence of the Vice President, or when he shall exercise the Office of President of the United States.

The Senate shall have the sole Power to try all Impeachments. When sitting for that Purpose, they shall be on Oath or Affirmation. When the President of the United States is tried the Chief Justice shall preside: And no Person shall be convicted without the Concurrence of two thirds of the Members present.

Judgment in Cases of Impeachment shall not extend further than to removal from Office, and disqualification to hold and enjoy any Office of honor, Trust or Profit under the United States: but the Party convicted shall nevertheless be liable and subject to Indictment, Trial, Judgment and Punishment, according to Law.

Section 4. The Times, Places and Manner of holding Elections for Senators and Representatives, shall be prescribed in each State by the Legislature thereof; but the Congress may at any time by Law make or alter such Regulations, except as to the Places of chusing Senators.

The Congress shall assemble at least once in every Year, and such Meeting shall [be on the first Monday in December],⁴ unless they shall by Law appoint a different Day.

Section 5. Each House shall be the Judge of the Elections, Returns and Qualifications of its own Members, and a Majority of each shall constitute a Quorum to do Business; but a smaller Number may adjourn from day to day, and may be authorized to compel the Attendance of absent Members, in such Manner, and under such Penalties as each House may provide.

Each House may determine the Rules of its Proceedings, punish its Members for disorderly Behaviour, and, with the Concurrence of two thirds, expel a Member.

Each House shall keep a Journal of its Proceedings, and from time to time publish the same, excepting such Parts as may in their Judgment require Secrecy; and the Yeas and Nays of the Members of either House on any question shall, at the Desire of one fifth of those Present, be entered on the Journal.

Neither House, during the Session of Congress, shall, without the Consent of the other, adjourn for more than three days, nor to any other Place than that in which the two Houses shall be sitting.

Section 6. The Senators and Representatives shall receive a Compensation for their Services, to be ascertained by Law, and paid out of the Treasury of the United States. They shall in all Cases, except Treason, Felony and Breach of the Peace, be privileged from Arrest during their Attendance at the Session of their respective Houses, and in going to and returning from the same; and for any Speech or Debate in either House, they shall not be questioned in any other Place.

No Senator or Representative shall, during the Time for which he was elected, be appointed to any civil Office under the Authority of the United States, which shall have been created, or the Emoluments whereof shall have been encreased during such time; and no Person holding any Office under the United States, shall be a Member of either House during his Continuance in Office.

Section 7. All Bills for raising Revenue shall originate in the House of Representatives; but the Senate may propose or concur with amendments as on other Bills.

Every Bill which shall have passed the House of Representatives and the Senate, shall, before it become a Law, be presented to the President of the United States; If he approve he shall sign it, but if not he shall return it, with his Objections to that House in which it shall have originated, who shall enter the Objections at large on their Journal, and proceed to reconsider it. If after such Reconsideration two thirds of that House shall agree to pass the Bill, it shall be sent, together with the Objections, to the other House, by which it shall likewise be reconsidered, and if approved by two thirds of that House, it shall become a Law. But in all such Cases the Votes of both Houses shall be determined by yeas and Nays, and the Names of the Persons voting for and against the Bill shall be entered on the Journal of each House respectively. If any Bill shall not be returned by the President within ten Days (Sunday excepted) after it shall have been presented to him, the Same shall be a Law, in like Manner as if he had signed it, unless the Congress by their Adjournment prevent its Return, in which Case it shall not be a Law.

Every Order, Resolution, or Vote to which the Concurrence of the Senate and House of Representatives may be necessary (except on a question of Adjournment) shall be presented to the President of the United States; and before the Same shall take Effect, shall be approved by him, or being disapproved by him, shall be repassed by two thirds of the Senate and House of Representatives, according to the Rules and Limitations prescribed in the Case of a Bill.

Section 8. The Congress shall have Power To lay and collect Taxes, Duties, Imposts and Excises, to pay the Debts and provide for the common Defence and general Welfare of the United States; but all Duties, Imposts and Excises shall be uniform throughout the United States;

To borrow Money on the credit of the United States;

To regulate Commerce with foreign Nations, and among the several States, and with the Indian Tribes;

To establish an uniform Rule of Naturalization, and uniform Laws on the subject of Bankruptcies throughout the United States;

To coin Money, regulate the Value thereof, and of foreign Coin, and fix the Standard of Weights and Measures;

To provide for the Punishment of counterfeiting the Securities and current Coin of the United States;

To establish Post Offices and post Roads;

To promote the Progress of Science and useful Arts, by securing for limited Times to Authors and Inventors the ex-

clusive Right to their respective Writings and Discoveries;

To constitute Tribunals inferior to the supreme Court;

To define and punish Piracies and Felonies commited on the high Seas, and Offences against the Law of Nations;

To declare War, grant Letters of Marque and Reprisal, and make Rules concerning Captures on Land and Water;

To raise and support Armies, but no Appropriation of Money to that Use shall be for a longer Term than two Years;

To provide and maintain a Navy;

To make Rules for the Government and Regulation of the land and naval Forces;

To provide for calling forth the Militia to execute the Laws of the Union, suppress Insurrections and repel Invasions;

To provide for organizing, arming, and disciplining, the Militia, and for governing such Part of them as may be employed in the Service of the United States, reserving to the States respectively, the Appointment of the Officers, and the Authority of training the Militia according to the discipline prescribed by Congress;

To exercise exclusive Legislation in all Cases whatsoever, over such District (not exceeding ten Miles square) as may, by Cession of Particular States, and the Acceptance of Congress, become the Seat of the Government of the United States, and to exercise like Authority over all Places purchased by the Consent of the Legislature of the State in which the Same shall be, for the Erection of Forts, Magazines, Arsenals, dock-Yards, and other needful Buildings;—And

To make all Laws which shall be necessary and proper for carrying into Execution the foregoing Powers, and all other Powers vested by this Constitution in the Government of the United States, or in any Department or Officer thereof.

Section 9. The Migration or Importation of such Persons as any of the States now existing shall think proper to admit, shall not be prohibited by the Congress prior to the Year one thousand eight hundred and eight, but a Tax or duty may be imposed on such Importation, not exceeding ten dollars for each Person.

The Privilege of the Writ of Habeas Corpus shall not be suspended, unless when in Cases of Rebellion or Invasion the public Safety may require it.

No Bill of Attainder or ex post facto Law shall be passed.

No Capitation, or other direct, Tax shall be laid, unless in Proportion to the Census of Enumeration herein before directed to be taken.[5]

No Tax or Duty shall be laid on Articles exported from any State.

No Preference shall be given by any Regulation of Commerce or Revenue to the Ports of one State over those of another; nor shall Vessels bound to, or from, one State, be obliged to enter, clear or pay Duties in another.

No Money shall be drawn from the Treasury, but in Consequence of Appropriations made by Law; and a regular Statement and Account of the Receipts and Expenditures of all public Money shall be published from time to time.

No Title of Nobility shall be granted by the United States: And no Person holding any Office of Profit or Trust under them, shall, without the Consent of the Congress, accept of any present, Emolument, Office, or Title, of any kind whatever, from any King, Prince or foreign State.

Section 10. No State shall enter into any Treaty, Alliance, or Confederation; grant Letters of Marque and Reprisal; coin Money; emit Bills of Credit; make any Thing but gold and silver Coin a Tender in Payment of Debts; pass any Bill of Attainder, ex post facto Law, or Law impairing the Obligation of Contracts, or grant any Title of Nobility.

No State shall, without the Consent of the Congress, lay any Imposts or Duties on Imports or Exports, except what may be absolutely necessary for executing it's inspection Laws: and the net Produce of all Duties and Imposts, laid by any State on Imports or Exports, shall be for the Use of the Treasury of the United States; and all such Laws shall be subject to the Revision and Controul of the Congress.

No State shall, without the Consent of Congress, lay any Duty of Tonnage, keep Troops, or Ships of War in time of Peace, enter into any Agreement or Compact with another State, or with a foreign Power, or engage in War, unless actually invaded, or in such imminent Danger as will not admit of delay.

Article II

Section 1. The executive Power shall be vested in a President of the United States of America. He shall hold his Office during the Term of four Years, and, together with the Vice President, chosen for the same Term, be elected, as follows

Each State shall appoint, in such Manner as the Legislature thereof may direct, a Number of Electors, equal to the whole Number of Senators and Representatives to which the State may be entitled in the Congress: but no Senator or Representative, or Person holding an Office of Trust or Profit under the United States, shall be appointed an Elector.

[The Electors shall meet in their respective States, and vote by Ballot for two Persons, of whom one at least shall not be an Inhabitant of the same State with themselves. And they shall make a List of all the Persons voted for, and of the Number of Votes for each; which List they shall sign and certify, and transmit sealed to the Seat of the Government of the United States, directed to the President of the Senate. The President of the Senate shall, in the Presence of the Senate and House of Representatives, open all the Certificates, and the Votes shall then be counted. The Person having the greatest Number of Votes shall be the President, if such Number be a Majority of the whole Number of Electors appointed; and if there be more than one who have such Majority, and have an equal Number of Votes, then the House of Representatives shall immediately chuse by Ballot one of them for President; and if no Person have a Majority, then from the five highest on the list the said House shall in like Manner chuse the President. But in chusing the President, the Votes shall be taken by States, the Representation from each State having one Vote; a quorum for this Purpose shall consist of a Member or Members from two thirds of the States, and a Majority of all the States shall be necessary to a Choice. In every Case, after the Choice of the President, the Person having the greatest Number of Votes of the Electors shall be the Vice President. But if there should remain two or more who have equal Votes, the **Senate shall chuse from them by Ballot the Vice President.**][6]

The Congress may determine the Time of chusing the Electors, and the Day on which they shall give their Votes; which Day shall be the same throughout the United States.

No Person except a natural born Citizen, or a Citizen of the United States, at the time of the Adoption of this Constitution, shall be eligible to the Office of President; neither shall any Person be eligible to that Office who shall not have attained to the Age of thirty five Years, and been fourteen Years a Resident within the United States.

In Case of the Removal of the President from Office, or of his Death, Resignation, or Inability to discharge the Powers and Duties of the said Office,[7] the Same shall devolve on the Vice President, and the Congress may by Law provide for the Case of Removal, Death, Resignation or Inability, both of the President and Vice President, declaring what Officer shall then act as President, and such Officer shall act accordingly, until the Disability be removed, or a President shall be elected.

The President shall, at stated Times, receive for his Services, a Compensation, which shall neither be encreased nor dimished during the Period for which he shall have been elected, and he shall not receive within that Period any other Emolument from the United States, or any of them.

Before he enter on the Execution of his Office, he shall take the following Oath or Affirmation: —"I do solemnly swear (or affirm) that I will faithfully execute the Office of President of the United States, and will to the best of my Ability, preserve, protect and defend the Constitution of the United States."

Section 2. The President shall be Commander in Chief of the Army and Navy of the United States, and of the Militia of the several States, when called into the actual Service of the United States; he may require the Opinion, in writing, of the principal Officer in each of the executive Departments, upon any Subject relating to the Duties of their respective Offices, and he shall have Power to grant Reprieves and Pardons for Offenses against the United States, except in Cases of Impeachment.

He shall have Power, by and with the Advice and Consent of the Senate, to make Treaties, provided two thirds of the Senators present concur; and he shall nominate, and by and with the Advice and Consent of the Senate, shall appoint Ambassadors, other public Ministers and Consuls, Judges of the supreme Court, and all other Officers of the United States, whose Appointments are not herein otherwise provided for, and which shall be established by Law: but the Congress may by Law vest the Appointment of such inferior Officers, as they think proper, in the President alone, in the Courts of Law, or in the Heads of Departments.

The President shall have Power to fill up all Vacancies that may happen during the Recess of the Senate, by granting Commissions which shall expire at the End of their next Session.

Section 3. He shall from time to time give to the Congress Information of the State of the Union, and recommend to their Consideration such Measures as he shall judge necessary and expedient; he may, on extraordinary Occasions, convene both Houses, or either of them, and in Case of Disagreement between them, with Respect to the Time of Adjournment, he may adjourn them to such Time as he shall think proper; he shall receive Ambassadors and other public Ministers; he shall take Care that the Laws be faithfully executed, and shall Commission all the Officers of the United States.

Section 4. The President, Vice President and all Civil Officers of the United States, shall be removed from office on Impeachment for, and Conviction of, Treason, Bribery, or other high Crimes and Misdemeanors.

Article III

Section 1. The judicial Power of the United States, shall be vested in one supreme Court, and in such inferior Courts as the Congress may from time to time ordain and establish. The Judges, both of the supreme and inferior Courts, shall hold their Offices during good Behaviour, and shall, at stated Times, receive for their Services, a Compensation, which shall not be diminished during their Continuance in Office.

Section 2. The judicial Power shall extend to all Cases, in Law and Equity, arising under this Constitution, the Laws of the United States, and Treaties made, or which shall be made, under their Authority;—to all Cases affecting Ambassadors, other public Ministers and Consuls;—to all Cases of admiralty and maritime Jurisdiction;—to Controversies to which the United States shall be a Party;—to Controversies between two or more States;—between a State and Citizens of another State[8];—between Citizens of different States;—between Citizens of the same State claiming Lands under Grants of different States, and between a State, or the Citizens thereof, and foreign States, Citizens or Subjects.[8]

In all Cases affecting Ambassadors, other public Ministers and Consuls, and those in which a State shall be Party, the supreme Court shall have original Jurisdiction. In all the other Cases before mentioned, the supreme Court shall have appellate Jurisdiction, both as to Law and Fact, with such Exceptions, and under such Regulations as the Congress shall make.

The Trial of all Crimes, except in cases of Impeachment, shall be by Jury; and such Trial shall be held in the State where the said Crimes shall have been committed; but when not committed within any State, the Trial shall be at such Place or Places as the Congress may by Law have directed.

Section 3. Treason against the United States, shall consist only in levying War against them, or in adhering to their Enemies, giving them Aid and Comfort. No Person shall be convicted of Treason unless on the Testimony of two Witnesses to the same overt Act, or on Confession in open Court.

The Congress shall have Power to declare the Punishment of Treason, but no Attainder of Treason shall work Corruption of Blood, or Forfeiture except during the Life of the Person attainted.

Article IV

Section 1. Full Faith and Credit shall be given in each State to the public Acts, Records, and judicial Proceedings of every other State. And the Congress may by general Laws prescribe the Manner in which such Acts, Records and Proceedings shall be proved, and the Effect thereof.

Section 2. The Citizens of each State shall be entitled to all Privileges and Immunities of Citizens in the several States.

A Person charged in any State with Treason, Felony, or other Crime, who shall flee from Justice, and be found in another State, shall on Demand of the executive Authority of the State from which he fled, be delivered up, to be removed to the State having Jurisdiction of the Crime.

[No Person held to Service or Labour in one State, under the Laws thereof, escaping into another, shall, in Consequence of any Law or Regulation therein, be discharged from such Service or Labour, but shall be delivered up on Claim of the Party to whom such Service or Labour may be due.][9]

Section 3. New States may be admitted by the Congress into this Union; but no new State shall be formed or erected within the Jurisdiction of any other State; nor any State be formed by the Junction of two or more States, or Parts of States, without the Consent of the Legislatures of the States concerned as well as of the Congress.

The Congress shall have Power to dispose of and make all needful Rules and Regulations respecting the Territory or other Property belonging to the United States; and nothing in this Constitution shall be so construed as to Prejudice any Claims of the United States, or of any particular State.

Section 4. The United States shall guarantee to every State in this Union a Republican Form of Government, and shall protect each of them against Invasion; and on Application of the Legislature, or of the Executive (when the Legislature cannot be convened) against domestic Violence.

Article V

The Congress, whenever two thirds of both Houses shall deem it necessary, shall propose Amendments to this Constitution, or, on the Application of the Legislatures of two thirds of the several States, shall call a Convention for proposing Amendments, which, in either Case, shall be valid to all Intents and Purposes, as Part of this Constitution, when ratified by the Legislatures of three fourths of the several States, or by Conventions in three fourths thereof, as the one or the other Mode of Ratification may be proposed by the Congress; Provided [that no Amendment which may be made prior to the Year One thousand eight hundred and eight shall in any Manner affect the first and fourth Clauses in the Ninth Section of the first Article; and][10] that no State, without its Consent, shall be deprived of its equal Suffrage in the Senate.

Article VI

All Debts contracted and Engagements entered into, before the Adoption of this Constitution, shall be as valid against the United States under this Constitution, as under the Confederation.

This Constitution, and the Laws of the United States which shall be made in Pursuance thereof; and all Treaties made, or which shall be made, under the Authority of the United States, shall be the supreme Law of the Land; and the Judges in every State shall be bound thereby, any Thing in the Constitution or Laws of any State to the Contrary notwithstanding.

The Senators and Representatives before mentioned, and the Members of the several State Legislatures, and all executive and judicial Officers, both of the United States and of the several States, shall be bound by Oath or Affirmation, to support this Constitution; but no religious Test shall ever be required as a Qualification to any Office or public Trust under the United States.

Article VII

The Ratification of the Conventions of nine States, shall be sufficient for the Establishment of this Constitution between the States so ratifying the Same. Done in Convention by the Unanimous Consent of the States present the Seventeenth Day of September in the Year of our Lord one thousand seven hundred and Eighty seven and of the Independence of the United States of America the Twelfth In witness whereof We have hereunto subscribed our Names, George Washington, President and deputy from Virginia.

New Hampshire:	John Langdon, Nicholas Gilman.
Massachusetts:	Nathaniel Gorham, Rufus King.
Connecticut:	William Samuel Johnson, Roger Sherman.
New York:	Alexander Hamilton.
New Jersey:	William Livingston, David Brearley, William Paterson, Jonathan Dayton.
Pennsylvania:	Benjamin Franklin, Thomas Mifflin, Robert Morris, George Clymer, Thomas FitzSimons, Jared Ingersoll, James Wilson, Gouverneur Morris.
Delaware:	George Read, Gunning Bedford Jr., John Dickinson, Richard Bassett, Jacob Broom.
Maryland:	James McHenry, Daniel of St. Thomas Jenifer, Daniel Carroll.
Virginia:	John Blair, James Madison Jr.
North Carolina:	William Blount, Richard Dobbs Spaight, Hugh Williamson.
South Carolina:	John Rutledge, Charles Cotesworth Pinckney, Charles Pinckney, Pierce Butler.
Georgia:	William Few, Abraham Baldwin.

[The language of the original Constitution, not including the Amendments, was adopted by a convention of the states on Sept. 17, 1787, and was subsequently ratified by the states on the following dates: Delaware, Dec. 7, 1787; Pennsylvania, Dec. 12, 1787; New Jersey, Dec. 18, 1787; Georgia, Jan. 2, 1788; Connecticut, Jan. 9, 1788; Massachusetts, Feb. 6, 1788; Maryland, April 28, 1788; South Carolina, May 23, 1788; New Hampshire, June 21, 1788.

Ratification was completed on June 21, 1788.

The Constitution subsequently was ratified by Virginia, June 25, 1788; New York, July 26, 1788; North Carolina, Nov. 21, 1789; Rhode Island, May 29, 1790; and Vermont, Jan. 10, 1791.]

Amendments

Amendment I

(First ten amendments ratified Dec. 15, 1791.)

Congress shall make no law respecting an establishment of religion, or prohibiting the free exercise thereof; or abridging the freedom of speech, or of the press; or the right of the people peaceably to assemble, and to petition the Government for a redress of grievances.

Amendment II

A well regulated Militia, being necessary to the security of a free State, the right of the people to keep and bear Arms, shall not be infringed.

Amendment III

No Soldier shall, in time of peace be quartered in any house, without the consent of the Owner, nor in time of war, but in a manner to be prescribed by law.

Amendment IV

The right of the people to be secure in their persons, houses, papers, and effects, against unreasonable searches and seizures, shall not be violated, and no Warrants shall issue, but upon probable cause, supported by Oath or affirmation, and particularly describing the place to be searched, and the persons or things to be seized.

Amendment V

No person shall be held to answer for a capital, or otherwise infamous crime, unless on a presentment or indictment of a Grand Jury, except in cases arising in the land or naval forces, or in the Militia, when in actual service in time of War or public danger; nor shall any person be subject for the same offence to be twice put in jeopardy of life or limb; nor shall be compelled in any criminal case to be a witness against himself, nor be deprived of life, liberty, or property, without due process of law; nor shall private property be taken for public use, without just compensation.

Amendment VI

In all criminal prosecutions, the accused shall enjoy the right to a speedy and public trial, by an impartial jury of the State and district wherein the crime shall have been committed, which district shall have been previously ascertained by law, and to be informed of the nature and cause of the accusation; to be confronted with the witnesses against him; to have compulsory process for obtaining witnesses in his favor, and to have the Assistance of Counsel for his defence.

Amendment VII

In Suits at common law, where the value in controversy shall exceed twenty dollars, the right of trial by jury shall be preserved, and no fact tried by a jury, shall be otherwise re-examined in any Court of the United States, than according to the rules of the common law.

Amendment VIII

Excessive bail shall not be required, nor excessive fines imposed, nor cruel and unusual punishments inflicted.

Amendment IX

The enumeration in the Constitution, of certain rights, shall not be construed to deny or disparage others retained by the people.

Amendment X

The powers not delegated to the United States by the Constitution, nor prohibited by it to the States, are reserved to the States respectively, or to the people.

Amendment XI *(Ratified Feb. 7, 1795)*

The Judicial power of the United States shall not be construed to extend to any suit in law or equity, commenced or prosecuted against one of the United States by Citizens of another State, or by Citizens or Subjects of any Foreign State.

Amendment XII *(Ratified June 15, 1804)*

The Electors shall meet in their respective states and vote by ballot for President and Vice-President, one of whom, at least, shall not be an inhabitant of the same state with themselves; they shall name in their ballots the person voted for as President, and in distinct ballots the person voted for as Vice-President, and they shall make distinct lists of all persons voted for as President, and of all persons voted for as Vice-President, and of the number of votes for each, which lists they shall sign and certify, and transmit sealed to the seat of the government of the United States, directed to the President of the Senate;—The President of the Senate shall, in the presence of the Senate and House of Representatives, open all the certificates and the votes shall then be counted;—The person having the greatest number of votes for President, shall be the President, if such number be a majority of the whole number of Electors appointed; and if no person have such majority, then from the persons having the highest numbers not exceeding three on the list of those voted for as President, the House of Representatives shall choose immediately, by ballot, the President. But in choosing the President, the votes shall be taken by states, the representation from each state having one vote; a quorum for this purpose shall consist of a member or members from two-thirds of the states, and a majority of all the states shall be necessary to a choice. [And if the House of Representatives shall not choose a President whenever the right of choice shall devolve upon them, before the fourth day of March next following, then the Vice-President shall act as President, as in the case of the death or other constitutional disability of the President—][11]The person having the greatest number of votes as Vice-President, shall be the Vice-President, if such number be a majority of the whole number of Electors appointed, and if no person have a majority, then from the two highest numbers on the list, the Senate shall choose the Vice-President; a quorum for the purpose shall consist of two-thirds of the whole number of Senators, and a majority of the whole number shall be necessary to a choice. But no person constitutionally ineligible to the office of President shall be eligible to that of Vice-President of the United States.

Amendment XIII *(Ratified Dec. 6, 1865)*

Section 1. Neither slavery nor involuntary servitude, except as a punishment for crime whereof the party shall have been duly convicted, shall exist within the United States, or any place subject to their jurisdiction.

Section 2. Congress shall have power to enforce this article by appropriate legislation.

Amendment XIV *(Ratified July 9, 1868)*

Section 1. All persons born or naturalized in the United States and subject to the jurisdiction thereof, are citizens of the United States and of the State wherein they reside. No State shall make or enforce any law which shall abridge the privileges or immunities of citizens of the United States; nor shall any State deprive any person of life, liberty, or property, without due process of law; nor deny to any person within its jurisdiction the equal protection of the laws.

Section 2. Representatives shall be apportioned among the several States according to their respective numbers, counting the whole number of persons in each State, excluding Indians not taxed. But when the right to vote at any election for the choice of electors for President and Vice President of the United States, Representatives in Congress, the Executive and Judicial officers of a State, or the members of the Legislature thereof, is denied to any of the male inhabitants of such State, being twenty-one years of age,[12] and citizens of the United States, or in any way abridged, except for participation in rebellion, or other crime, the basis of representation therein shall be reduced in the proportion which the number of such male citizens shall bear to the whole number of male citizens twenty-one years of age in such State.

Section 3. No person shall be a Senator or Representative in Congress, or elector of President and Vice President, or hold any office, civil or military, under the United States, or under any State, who, having previously taken an oath, as a member of Congress, or as an officer of the United States, or as a member of any State legislature, or as an executive or judicial officer of any State, to support the Constitution of the United States, shall have engaged in insurrection or rebellion against the same, or given aid or comfort to the enemies thereof. But Congress may by a vote of two-thirds of each House, remove such disability.

Section 4. The validity of the public debt of the United States, authorized by law, including debts incurred for payment of pensions and bounties for services in suppressing insurrection or rebellion, shall not be questioned. But neither the United States nor any State shall assume or pay any debt or obligation incurred in aid of insurrection or rebellion against the United States, or any claim for the loss or emancipation of any slave; but all such debts, obligations and claims shall be held illegal and void.

Section 5. The Congress shall have power to enforce, by appropriate legislation, the provisions of this article.

Amendment XV *(Ratified Feb. 3, 1870)*

Section 1. The right of citizens of the United States to vote shall not be denied or abridged by the United States or by any State on account of race, color, or previous condition of servitude.

Section 2. The Congress shall have power to enforce this article by appropriate legislation.

Amendment XVI *(Ratified Feb. 3, 1913)*

The Congress shall have power to lay and collect taxes on incomes, from whatever source derived, without apportionment among the several States, and without regard to any census or enumeration.

Amendment XVII *(Ratified Apr. 8, 1913)*

The Senate of the United States shall be composed of two Senators from each State, elected by the people thereof, for six years; and each Senator shall have one vote. The electors in each State shall have the qualifications requisite for electors of the most numerous branch of the State legislatures.

When vacancies happen in the representation of any State in the Senate, the executive authority of such State shall issue writs of election to fill such vacancies: *Provided,* That the legislature of any State may empower the executive thereof to make temporary appointments until the people fill the vacancies by election as the legislature may direct.

This amendment shall not be so construed as to affect the election or term of any Senator chosen before it becomes valid as part of the Constitution.

[Amendment XVIII *(Ratified Jan. 16, 1919)*

Section 1. After one year from the ratification of this article the manufacture, sale, or transportation of intoxicating liquors within, the importation thereof into, or the exportation thereof from the United States and all territory subject to the jurisdiction thereof for beverage purposes is hereby prohibited.

Section 2. The Congress and the several States shall have concurrent power to enforce this article by appropriate legislation.

Section 3. This article shall be inoperative unless it shall have been ratified as an amendment to the Constitution by the legislatures of the several States, as provided in the Constitution, within seven years from the date of the submission hereof to the States by the Congress.]¹³

Amendment XIX *(Ratified Aug. 18, 1920)*

The right of citizens of the United States to vote shall not be denied or abridged by the United States or by any State on account of sex.

Congress shall have power to enforce this article by appropriate legislation.

Amendment XX *(Ratified Jan. 23, 1933)*

Section 1. The terms of the President and Vice President shall end at noon on the 20th day of January, and the terms of Senators and Representatives at noon on the 3d day of January, of the years in which such terms would have ended if this article had not been ratified; and the terms of their successors shall then begin.

Section 2. The Congress shall assemble at least once in every year, and such meeting shall begin at noon on the 3d day of January, unless they shall by law appoint a different day.

Section 3.¹⁴ If, at the time fixed for the beginning of the term of the President, the President elect shall have died, the Vice President elect shall become President. If a President shall not have been chosen before the time fixed for the beginning of his term, or if the President elect shall have failed to qualify, then the Vice President elect shall act as President until a President shall have qualified; and the Congress may by law provide for the case wherein neither a President elect nor a Vice President elect shall have qualified, declaring who shall then act as President, or the manner in which one who is to act shall be selected, and

such person shall act accordingly until a President or Vice President shall have qualified.

Section 4. The Congress may by law provide for the case of the death of any of the persons from whom the House of Representatives may choose a President whenever the right of choice shall have devolved upon them, and for the case of the death of any of the persons from whom the Senate may choose a Vice President whenever the right of choice shall have devolved upon them.

Section 5. Sections 1 and 2 shall take effect on the 15th day of October following the ratification of this article.

Section 6. This article shall be inoperative unless it shall have been ratified as an amendment to the Constitution by the legislatures of three-fourths of the several States within seven years from the date of its submission.

Amendment XXI *(Ratified Dec. 5, 1933)*

Section 1. The eighteenth article of amendment to the Constitution of the United States is hereby repealed.

Section 2. The transportation or importation into any State, Territory or possession of the United States for delivery or use therein of intoxicating liquors, in violation of the laws thereof, is hereby prohibited.

Section 3. This article shall be inoperative unless it shall have been ratified as an amendment to the Constitution by conventions in the several States, as provided in the Constitution, within seven years from the date of the submission hereof to the States by the Congress.

Amendment XXII *(Ratified Feb. 27, 1951)*

Section 1. No person shall be elected to the office of the President more than twice, and no person who has held the office of President, or acted as President, for more than two years of a term to which some other person was elected President shall be elected to the office of the President more than once. But this Article shall not apply to any person holding the office of President when this Article was proposed by the Congress, and shall not prevent any person who may be holding the office of President, or acting as President, during the term within which this Article becomes operative from holding the office of President or acting as President during the remainder of such term.

Section 2. This Article shall be inoperative unless it shall have been ratified as an amendment to the Constitution by the legislatures of three-fourths of the several States within seven years from the date of its submission to the States by the Congress.

Amendment XXIII *(Ratified March 29, 1961)*

Section 1. The District constituting the seat of Government of the United States shall appoint in such manner as the Congress may direct:

A number of electors of President and Vice President equal to the whole number of Senators and Representatives in Congress to which the District would be entitled if it were a State, but in no event more than the least populous State; they shall be in addition to those appointed by the States, but they shall be considered, for the purposes of the election of President and Vice President, to be electors appointed by a State; and they shall meet in the District and perform such duties as provided by the twelfth article of amendment.

Section 2. The Congress shall have power to enforce this article by appropriate legislation.

Amendment XXIV *(Ratified Jan. 23, 1964)*

Section 1. The right of citizens of the United States to vote in any primary or other election for President or Vice President, for electors for President or Vice President, or for Senator or Representative in Congress, shall not be denied or abridged by the United States or any State by reason of failure to pay any poll tax or other tax.

Section 2. The Congress shall have power to enforce this article by appropriate legislation.

Amendment XXV *(Ratified Feb. 10, 1967)*

Section 1. In case of the removal of the President from office or of his death or resignation, the Vice President shall become President.

Section 2. Whenever there is a vacancy in the office of the Vice President, the President shall nominate a Vice President who shall take office upon confirmation by a majority vote of both Houses of Congress.

Section 3. Whenever the President transmits to the President pro tempore of the Senate and the Speaker of the House of Representatives his written declaration that he is unable to discharge the powers and duties of his office, and until he transmits to them a written declaration to the contrary, such powers and duties shall be discharged by the Vice President as Acting President.

Section 4. Whenever the Vice President and a majority of either the principal officers of the executive departments or of such other body as Congress may by law provide, transmit to the President pro tempore of the Senate and the Speaker of the House of Representatives their written declaration that the President is unable to discharge the powers and duties of his office, the Vice President shall immediately assume the powers and duties of the office as Acting President.

Thereafter, when the President transmits to the President pro tempore of the Senate and the Speaker of the House of Representatives his written declaration that no inability exists, he shall resume the powers and duties of his office unless the Vice President and a majority of either the principal officers of the executive department or of such other body as Congress may by law provide, transmit within four days to the President pro tempore of the Senate and the Speaker of the House of Representatives their written declaration that the President is unable to discharge the powers and duties of his office. Thereupon Congress shall decide the issue, assembling within forty-eight hours for that purpose if not in session. If the Congress, within twenty-one days after receipt of the latter written declaration, or, if Congress is not in session, within twenty-one days after Congress is required to assemble, determines by two-thirds vote of both houses that the President is unable to discharge the powers and duties of his office, the Vice President shall continue to discharge the same as Acting President; otherwise, the President shall resume the powers and duties of his office.

Amendment XXVI *(Ratified July 1, 1971)*

Section 1. The right of citizens of the United States, who are eighteen years of age or older, to vote shall not be denied or abridged by the United States or by any State on account of age.

Section 2. The Congress shall have power to enforce this article by appropriate legislation.

Footnotes

1. The part in brackets was changed by section 2 of the Fourteenth Amendment.

2. The part in brackets was changed by section 1 of the Seventeenth Amendment.

3. The part in brackets was changed by the second paragraph of the Seventeenth Amendment.

4. The part in brackets was changed by section 2 of the Twentieth Amendment.

5. The Sixteenth Amendment gave Congress the power to tax incomes.

6. The material in brackets has been superseded by the Twelfth Amendment.

7. This provision has been affected by the Twenty-fifth Amendment.

8. These clauses were affected by the Eleventh Amendment.

9. This paragraph has been superseded by the Thirteenth Amendment.

10. Obsolete.

11. The part in brackets has been superseded by section 3 of the Twentieth Amendment.

12. See the Twenty-sixth Amendment.

13. This Amendment was repealed by section 1 of the Twenty-first Amendment.

14. See the Twenty-fifth Amendment.

Source: U.S. Congress, House, Committee on the Judiciary, *The Constitution of the United States of America, As Amended Through July 1971*, H. Doc. 93-215, 93rd Cong., 2nd sess., 1974.

Acts of Congress Held Unconstitutional in Whole or in Part by the Supreme Court

Sources: compiled from Library of Congress, *The Constitution of the United States of America; Analysis and Interpretation*, S. Doc., 92-82, 92d Cong., 2d sess., 1973; 1976 Supplement, S. Doc. 94-200, 94th Cong. 2d sess., 1976; Library of Congress, Congressional Research Service.

1. Act of September 24, 1789 (1 Stat. 81, § 13, in part).
   Provision that "...[the Supreme Court] shall have power to issue...writs of mandamus, in cases warranted by the principles and usages of law, to any...persons holding office, under authority of the United States" as applied to the issue of mandamus to the Secretary of State requiring him to deliver to plaintiff a commission (duly signed by the President) as justice of the peace in the District of Columbia, *held* an attempt to enlarge the original jurisdiction of the Supreme Court, fixed by Article III, § 2.
   Marbury v. *Madison*, 1 Cr. (5 U.S.) 137 (1803).

2. Act of February 20, 1812 (2 Stat. 677).
   Provisions establishing board of revision to annul titles conferred many years previously by governors of the Northwest Territory were *held* violative of the due process clause of the Fifth Amendment.
   Reichart v. *Felps*, 6 Wall. (73 U.S.) 160 (1868).

3. Act of March 6, 1820 (3 Stat. 548, § 8, proviso).
   The Missouri Compromise, prohibiting slavery within the Louisiana Territory north of 36° 30', except Missouri, *held* not warranted as a regulation of Territory belonging to the United States under Article IV, § 3, clause 2 (and *see* Fifth Amendment).
   Scott v. *Sandford*, 19 How. (60 U.S.) 393 (1857).

4. Act of February 25, 1862 (12 Stat. 345, § 1); July 11, 1862 (12 Stat. 532, § 1); March 3, 1863 (12 Stat. 711, § 3), each in part only.
   "Legal tender clauses," making noninterest-bearing United States notes legal tender in payment of "all debts, public and private," so far as applied to debts contracted before passage of the act, *held* not within express or implied powers of Congress under Article I, § 8, and inconsistent with Article I, § 10, and Fifth Amendment.
   Hepburn v. *Griswold*, 8 Wall. (75 U.S.) 603 (1870); overruled in *Knox* v. *Lee (Legal Tender Cases)*, 12 Wall. (79 U.S.) 457 (1871).

5. Act of March 3, 1863 (12 Stat. 756, § 5).
   "So much of the fifth section...as provides for the removal of a judgment in a State court, and in which the cause was tried by a jury to the circuit court of the United States for a retrial on the facts and law, is not in pursuance of the Constitution, and is void" under the Seventh Amendment.
   The Justices v. *Murray*, 9 Wall. (76 U.S.) 274 (1870).

6. Act of March 3, 1863 (12 Stat. 766, § 5).
   Provision for an appeal from the Court of Claims to the Supreme Court—there being, at the time, a further provision (§ 14) requiring an estimate by the Secretary of the Treasury before payment of final judgments, *held* to contravene the judicial finality intended by the Constitution, Article III.
   Gordon v. *United States*, 2 Wall. (69 U.S.) 561 (1865). (Case was dismissed without opinion; the grounds upon which this decision was made were stated in a posthumous opinion by Chief Justice Taney printed in the appendix to volume 117 U.S. 697.)

7. Act of June 30, 1864 (13 Stat. 311, § 13).
   Provision that "any prize cause now pending in any circuit court shall, on the application of all parties in interest...be transferred by that court to the Supreme Court...," as applied to a case where no action had been taken in the Circuit Court on the appeal from the district court, *held* to propose an appeal procedure not within Article III, § 2.
   The Alicia, 7 Wall. (74 U.S.) 571 (1869).

8. Act of January 24, 1865 (13 Stat. 424).
   Requirement of a test oath (disavowing actions in hostility to the United States) before admission to appear as attorney in a federal court by virtue of any previous admission, *held* invalid as applied to an attorney who had been pardoned by the President for all offenses during the Rebellion—as *ex post facto* (Article I, § 9, clause 3) and an interference with the pardoning power (Article II, § 2, clause 1).
   Ex parte Garland, 4 Wall. (71 U.S.) 333 (1867).

9. Act of March 2, 1867 (14 Stat. 484, § 29).
   General prohibition on sale of naphtha, etc., for illuminating purposes, if inflammable at less temperature than 110° F., *held* invalid "except so far as the section named operates within the United States, but without the limits of any State," as being a mere police regulation.
   United States v. *Dewitt*, 9 Wall. (76 U.S.) 41 (1870).

10. Act of May 31, 1870 (16 Stat. 140, §§ 3, 4).
    Provisions penalizing (1) refusal of local election officials to permit voting by persons offering to qualify under State laws, applicable to any citizens; and (2) hindering of any person from qualifying or voting, *held* invalid under Fifteenth Amendment.
    United States v. *Reese*, 92 U.S. 214 (1876).

11. Act of July 12, 1870 (16 Stat. 235).
    Provision making Presidential pardons inadmissible in evidence in Court of Claims, prohibiting their use by that court in deciding claims or appeals, and requiring dismissal of appeals by the Supreme Court in cases where proof of loyalty had been made otherwise than as prescribed by law, *held* an interference with judicial power under Article III, § 1, and with the pardoning power under Article II, § 2, clause 1.
    United States v. *Klein*, 13 Wall. (80 U.S.) 128 (1872).

12. Act of June 22, 1874 (18 Stat. 1878, § 4).
    Provision authorizing federal courts, in suits for forfeitures under revenue and custom laws, to require production of documents, with allegations expected to be proved therein to be taken as proved on failure to produce such documents, was *held* violative of the search and seizure provision of the Fourth Amendment and the self-incrimination clause of the Fifth Amendment.
    Boyd v. *United States*, 116 U.S. 616 (1886).

13. Revised Statutes 1977 (Act of May 31, 1870, 16 Stat. 144).
    Provision that "all persons within the jurisdiction of the United States shall have the same right in every State and Territory to make and enforce contracts...as is enjoyed by white citizens...," *held* invalid under the Thirteenth Amendment.
    Hodges v. *United States*, 203 U.S. 1 (1906).

14. Revised Statutes 4937-4947 (Act of July 8, 1870, 16 Stat. 210), and Act of August 14, 1876 (19 Stat. 141).
    Original trademark law, applying to marks "for exclusive use within the United States," and a penal act designed solely for the protection of rights defined in the earlier measure, *held* not supportable by Article I, § 8, clause 8 (copyright clause), nor Article I, § 8, clause 3, by reason of its application to intrastate as well as interstate commerce.
    Trade-Mark Cases, 100 U.S. 82 (1879).

15. Revised Statutes 5132, subdivision 9 (Act of March 2, 1867, 14 Stat. 539).
    Provision penalizing "any person respecting whom bankruptcy proceedings are commenced...who, within 3 months before the commencement of proceedings in bankruptcy, under the false color and pretense of carrying on business and dealing in the ordinary course of trade, obtains on credit from any person any goods or chattels with intent to defraud...," *held* a police regulation not within the bankruptcy power (Article I, § 4, clause 4).
    United States v. *Fox*, 95 U.S. 670 (1878).

16. Revised Statutes 5507 (Act of May 31, 1870, 16 Stat. 141, § 4).
    Provision penalizing "every person who prevents, hinders, controls, or intimidates another from exercising...the right of suffrage, to whom that right is guaranteed by the Fifteenth Amendment to the Constitution of the United States, by means of bribery...," *held* not authorized by the Fifteenth Amendment.
    James v. *Bowman*, 190 U.S. 127 (1903).

17. Revised Statutes 5519 (Act of April 20, 1871, 17 Stat. 13, § 2).
    Section providing punishment in case "two or more persons in any State...conspire...for the purpose of depriving...any person...of the equal protection of the laws...or for the purpose of preventing or hindering the constituted authorities of any State...from giving or securing to all persons within such State...the equal protection of the laws...," *held* invalid as not being directed at state action proscribed by the Fourteenth Amendment.
    United States v. *Harris*, 106 U.S. 629 (1883).
    In *Baldwin* v. *Franks*, 120 U.S. 678 (1887), an attempt was made to distinguish the *Harris* case and to apply the statute to a con-

spiracy directed at aliens within a State, but the provision was *held* not enforceable in such limited manner.

18. Revised Statutes of the District of Columbia, § 1064 (Act of June 17, 1870, 16 Stat. 154, § 3).

Provision that "prosecutions in the police court [of the District of Columbia] shall be by information under oath, without indictment by grand jury or trial by petit jury," as applied to punishment for conspiracy held to contravene Article III, § 2, clause 3, requiring jury trial of all crimes.

Callan v. *Wilson,* 127 U.S. 540 (1888).

19. Act of March 1, 1875 (18 Stat. 336, §§ 1, 2).

Provision "That all persons within the jurisdiction of the United States shall be entitled to the full and equal enjoyment of the accommodations...of inns, public conveyances on land or water, theaters, and other places of public amusement; subject only to the conditions and limitations established by law, and applicable alike to citizens of every race and color, regardless of any previous condition of servitude"—subject to penalty, *held* not to be supported by the Thirteenth or Fourteenth Amendments.

Civil Rights Cases, 109 U.S. 3 (1883), as to operation within States.

20. Act of March 3, 1875 (18 Stat. 479, § 2).

Provision that "if the party [i.e., a person stealing property from the United States] has been convicted, then the judgment against him shall be conclusive evidence in the prosecution against [the] receiver that the property of the United States therein described has been embezzled, stolen, or purloined," *held* to contravene the Sixth Amendment.

Kirby v. *United States,* 174 U.S. 47 (1899).

21. Act of July 12, 1876 (19 Stat. 80, sec. 6, in part).

Provision that "postmasters of the first, second, and third classes...may be removed by the President by and with the advice and consent of the Senate," *held* to infringe the executive power under Article II, § 1, clause 1.

Myers v. *United States,* 272 U.S. 52 (1926).

22. Act of August 14, 1876 (19 Stat. 141, Trademark Act). *See* Revised Statutes 4937, above, No. 14.

23. Act of August 11, 1888 (25 Stat. 411).

Clause, in a provision for the purchase or condemnation of a certain lock and dam in the Monongahela River, that "...in estimating the sums to be paid by the United States, the franchise of said corporation to collect tolls shall not be considered or estimated...," *held* to contravene the Fifth Amendment.

Monongahela Navigation Co. v. *United States,* 148 U.S. 312 (1893).

24. Act of May 5, 1892 (27 Stat. 25, § 4).

Provision of a Chinese exclusion act, that Chinese persons "convicted and adjudged to be not lawfully entitled to be or remain in the United States shall be imprisoned at hard labor for a period not exceeding 1 year and thereafter removed from the United States...(such conviction and judgment being had before a justice, judge, or commissioner upon a summary hearing), *held* to contravene the Fifth and Sixth Amendments.

Wong Wing v. *United States,* 163 U.S. 228 (1896).

25. Joint Resolution of August 4, 1894 (28 Stat. 1018, No. 41).

Provision authorizing the Secretary of the Interior to approve a second lease of certain land by an Indian chief in Minnesota (granted to lessor's ancestor by art. 9 of a treaty with the Chippewa Indians), *held* an interference with judicial interpretation of treaties under Article III, § 2, clause 1 (and repugnant to the Fifth Amendment).

Jones v. *Meehan,* 175 U.S. 1 (1899).

26. Act of August 27, 1894 (28 Stat. 553-560, §§ 27-37).

Income tax provisions of the tariff act of 1894. "The tax imposed by §§ 27 and 37, inclusive...so far as it falls on the income of real estate and of personal property, being a direct tax within the meaning of the Constitution, and, therefore, unconstitutional and void because not apportioned according to representation [Article I, § 2, clause 3], all those sections, constituting one entire scheme of taxation, are necessarily invalid" (158 U.S. 601, 637).

Pollock v. *Farmers' Loan & Trust Co.,* 157 U.S. 429 (1895), and rehearing, 158 U.S. 601 (1895).

27. Act of January 30, 1897 (29 Stat. 506).

Prohibition on sale of liquor "...to any Indian to whom allotment of land has been made while the title to the same shall be held in trust by the Government...," *held* a police regulation infringing state powers, and not warranted by the commerce clause, Article I, § 8, clause 3.

Matter of Heff, 197 U.S. 488 (1905), overruled in *United States* v. *Nice,* 241 U.S. 591 (1916).

28. Act of June 1, 1898 (30 Stat. 428).

Section 10, penalizing "any employer subject to the provisions of this act" who should "threaten any employee with loss of employment...because of his membership in...a labor corporation, association, or organization" (the act being applicable "to any common carrier...engaged in the transportation of passengers or property...from one State...to another State...," etc.), *held* an infringement of the Fifth Amendment and not supported by the commerce clause.

Adair v. *United States,* 208 U.S. 161 (1908).

29. Act of June 13, 1898 (30 Stat. 451, 459).

Stamp tax on foreign bills of lading, *held* a tax on exports in violation of Article I, § 9.

Fairbank v. *United States,* 181 U.S. 283 (1901).

30. Same (30 Stat. 451, 460).

Tax on charter parties, as applied to shipments exclusively from ports in United States to foreign ports, *held* a tax on exports in violation of Article I, § 9.

United States v. *Hvoslef,* 237 U.S. 1 (1915).

31. Act of June 6, 1900 (31 Stat. 359, § 171).

Section of the Alaska Code providing for a six-person jury in trials for misdemeanors, *held* repugnant to the Sixth Amendment, requiring "jury" trial of crimes.

Rassmussen v. *United States,* 197 U.S. 516 (1905).

32. Act of March 3, 1901 (31 Stat. 1341, § 935).

Section of the District of Columbia Code granting the same right of appeal, in criminal cases, to the United States or the District of Columbia as to the defendant, but providing that a verdict was not to be set aside for error bound in rulings during trial, *held* an attempt to take an advisory opinion, contrary to Article III, § 2.

United States v. *Evans,* 213 U.S. 297 (1909).

33. Act of June 11, 1906 (34 Stat. 232).

Act providing that "every common carrier engaged in trade or commerce in the District of Columbia...or between the several States...shall be liable to any of its employees...for all damages which may result from the negligence of any of its officers...or by reason of any defect...due to its negligence in its cars, engines...roadbed," etc., *held* not supportable under Article I, § 8, clause 3 because it extended to intrastate as well as interstate commercial activities.

The Employers' Liability Cases, 207 U.S. 463 (1908). (The act was upheld as to the District of Columbia in *Hyde* v. *Southern R. Co.,* 31 App. D.C. 466 (1908); and as to the Territories, in *El Paso & N.E. Ry.* v. *Gutierrez,* 215 U.S. 87 (1909).)

34. Act of June 16, 1906 (34 Stat. 269, § 2).

Provision of Oklahoma Enabling Act restricting relocation of the State capital prior to 1913, *held* not supportable by Article IV, § 3, authorizing admission of new States.

Coyle v. *Smith,* 221 U.S. 559 (1911).

35. Act of February 20, 1907 (34 Stat. 889, § 3).

Provision in the Immigration Act of 1907 penalizing "whoever...shall keep, maintain, control, support, or harbor in any house or other place, for the purpose of prostitution...any alien woman or girl, within 3 years after she shall have entered the United States," *held* an exercise of police power not within the control of Congress over immigration (whether drawn from the commerce clause or based on inherent sovereignty).

Keller v. *United States,* 213 U.S. 138 (1909).

36. Act of March 1, 1907 (34 Stat. 1028).

Provisions authorizing certain Indians "to institute their suits in the Court of Claims to determine the validity of any acts of Congress passed since...1902, insofar as said acts...attempt to increase or extend the restrictions upon alienation...of allotments of lands of Cherokee citizens...," and giving a right of appeal to the Supreme Court, *held* an attempt to enlarge the judicial power restricted by Article III, § 2, to cases and controversies.

Muskrat v. *United States,* 219 U.S. 346 (1911).

37. Act of May 27, 1908 (35 Stat. 313, § 4).

Provision making locally taxable "all land [of Indians of the Five Civilized Tribes] from which restrictions have been or shall be removed," *held* a violation of the Fifth Amendment, in view of the Atoka Agreement, embodied in the Curtis Act of June 28, 1898, providing tax-exemption for allotted lands while title in original allottee, not exceeding 21 years.

Choate v. *Trapp,* 224 U.S. 665 (1912).

38. Act of February 9, 1909, § 2, 35 Stat. 614, as amended.

Provision of Narcotic Drugs Import and Export Act creating a presumption that possessor of cocaine knew of its illegal importation into the United States *held,* in light of the fact that more cocaine is produced domestically than is brought into the country and in absence of any showing that defendant could have known his cocaine was imported, if it was, inapplicable to support conviction from mere possession of cocaine.

Turner v. *United States,* 396 U.S. 398 (1970).

39. Act of August 19, 1911 (37 Stat. 28).

A proviso in § 8 of the Federal Corrupt Practices Act fixing a maximum authorized expenditure by a candidate for Senator "in any campaign for his nomination and election," as applied to a primary election, *held* not supported by Article I, § 4, giving Congress power to regulate the manner of holding elections for Senators and Representatives.

Newberry v. *United States*, 256 U.S. 232 (1921), overruled in *United States* v. *Classic*, 313 U.S. 299 (1941).

40. Act of June 18, 1912 (37 Stat. 136, § 8).

Part of § 8 giving the Juvenile Court of the District of Columbia (proceeding upon information) concurrent jurisdiction of desertion cases (which were, by law, punishable by fine or imprisonment in the workhouse at hard labor for 1 year), *held* invalid under the Fifth Amendment, which gives right to presentment by a grand jury in case of infamous crimes.

United States v. *Moreland*, 258 U.S. 433 (1922).

41. Act of March 4, 1913 (37 Stat. 988, part of par. 64).

Provision of the District of Columbia Public Utility Commission Act authorizing appeal to the United States Supreme Court from decrees of the District of Columbia Court of Appeals modifying valuation decisions of the Utilities Commission, *held* an attempt to extend the appellate jurisdiction of the Supreme Court to cases not strictly judicial within the meaning of Article III, § 2.

Keller v. *Potomac Elec. Co.*, 261 U.S. 428 (1923).

42. Act of September 1, 1916 (39 Stat. 675).

The original Child Labor Law, providing "that no producer...shall ship...in interstate commerce...any article or commodity the product of any mill...in which within 30 days prior to the removal of such product therefrom children under the age of 14 years have been employed or permitted to work more than 8 hours in any day or more than 6 days in any week...," *held* not within the commerce power of Congress.

Hammer v. *Dagenhart*, 247 U.S. 251 (1918).

43. Act of September 8, 1916 (39 Stat. 757, § 2(a), in part).

Provision of the income tax law of 1916, that a "stock dividend shall be considered income," to the amount of its cash value," *held* invalid (in spite of the Sixteenth Amendment) as an attempt to tax something not actually income, without regard to apportionment under Article I, § 2, clause 3.

Eisner v. *Macomber*, 252 U.S. 189 (1920).

44. Act of October 6, 1917 (40 Stat. 395).

The amendment of §§ 24 and 256 of the Judicial Code (which prescribe the jurisdiction of district courts) "saving...to claimants the rights and remedies under the workmen's compensation law of any State," *held* an attempt to transfer federal legislative powers to the States—the Constitution, by Article III, § 2, and Article I, § 8, having adopted rules of general maritime law.

Knickerbocker Ice Co. v. *Stewart*, 253 U.S. 149 (1920).

45. Act of September 19, 1918 (40 Stat. 960).

Specifically, that part of the Minimum Wage Law of the District of Columbia which authorized the Wage Board "to ascertain and declare...(a) Standards of minimum wages for women in any occupation within the District of Columbia, and what wages are inadequate to supply the necessary cost of living to any such women workers to maintain them in good health and to protect their morals...," *held* to interfere with freedom of contract under the Fifth Amendment.

Adkins v. *Children's Hospital*, 261 U.S. 525 (1923), overruled in *West Coast Hotel Co.* v. *Parrish*, 300 U.S. 379 (1937).

46. Act of February 24, 1919 (40 Stat. 1065, § 213, in part).

That part of § 213 of the Revenue Act of 1918 which provided that "...for the purposes of this title...the term 'gross income'...includes gains, profits, and income derived from salaries, wages, or compensation for personal service (including in the case of...judges of the Supreme and inferior courts of the United States...the compensation received as such)..." as applied to a judge in office when the act was passed, *held* a violation of the guaranty of judges' salaries, in Article III, § 1.

Evans v. *Gore*, 253 U.S. 245 (1920).

Miles v. *Graham*, 268 U.S. 501 (1925), held it invalid as applied to a judge taking office subsequent to the date of the act.

47. Act of February 24, 1919 (40 Stat. 1097, § 402(c)).

That part of the estate tax law providing that "gross estate" of a decedent should include value of all property "to the extent of any interest therein of which the decedent has at any time made a transfer or with respect to which he had at any time created a trust, in contemplation of or intended to take effect in possession or enjoyment at or after his death (whether such transfer or trust is made or created before or after the passage of this act), except in case of a *bona fide* sale..." as applied to a transfer of property made prior to the act and intended to take effect "in possession or enjoyment" at death of grantor, but not in fact testamentary or designed to evade taxation, *held* confiscatory, contrary to Fifth Amendment.

Nicholds v. *Coolidge*, 274 U.S. 531 (1927).

48. Act of February 24, 1919, title XII (40 Stat. 1138, entire title).

The Child Labor Tax Act, providing that "every person...operating...any...factory...in which children under the age of 14 years have been employed or permitted to work...shall pay...in addition to all other taxes imposed by law, an excise tax equivalent to 10 percent of the entire net profits received...for such year from the sale...of the product of such...factory...," *held* beyond the taxing power under Article I, § 8, clause 1, and an infringement of state authority.

Bailey v. *Drexel Furniture Co. (Child Labor Tax Case)*, 259 U.S. 20 (1922).

49. An Act of October 22, 1919 (41 Stat. 298, § 2), amending Act of August 10, 1917 (40 Stat. 277, § 4).

(a) § 4 of the Lever Act, providing in part "that it is hereby made unlawful for any person willfully...to make any unjust or unreasonable rate or charge in handling or dealing in or with any necessaries..." and fixing a penalty, *held* invalid to support an indictment for charging an unreasonable price on sale—as not setting up an ascertainable standard of guilt within the requirement of the Sixth Amendment.

United States v. *Cohen Grocery Co.*, 255 U.S. 81 (1921).

(b) That provision of § 4 making it unlawful "to conspire, combine, agree, or arrange with any other person to...exact excessive prices for any necessaries" and fixing a penalty, *held* invalid to support an indictment, on the reasoning of the *Cohen Grocery* case.

Weeds, Inc. v. *United States*, 255 U.S. 109 (1921).

50. Act of August 24, 1921 (42 Stat. 187, Future Trading Act).

(a) § 4 (and interwoven regulations) providing a "tax of 20 cents a bushel on every bushel involved therein, upon each contract of sale of grain for future delivery, except...where such contracts are made by or through a member of a board of trade which has been designated by the Secretary of Agriculture as a 'contract market'...," *held* not within the taxing power under Article I, § 8.

Hill v. *Wallace*, 259 U.S. 44 (1922).

(b) § 3, providing "That in addition to the taxes now imposed by law there is hereby levied a tax amounting to 20 cents per bushel on each bushel involved therein, whether the actual commodity is intended to be delivered or only nominally referred to, upon each...option for a contract either of purchase or sale of grain...," *held* invalid on the same reasoning.

Trusler v. *Crooks*, 269 U.S. 475 (1926).

51. Act of November 23, 1921 (42 Stat. 261, § 245, in part).

Provision of Revenue Act of 1921 abating the deduction (4 percent of mean reserves) allowed from taxable income of life insurance companies in general by the amount of interest on their tax-exempts, and so according no relative advantage to the owners of the tax-exempt securities, *held* to destroy a guaranteed exemption.

National Life Ins. v. *United States*, 277 U.S. 508 (1928).

52. Act of June 10, 1922 (42 Stat. 634).

A second attempt to amend §§ 24 and 256 of the Judicial Code, relating to jurisdiction of district courts, by saving "to claimants for compensation for injuries to or death of persons other than the master or members of the crew of a vessel, their rights and remedies under the workmen's compensation law of any State..." *held* invalid on authority of *Knickerbocker Ice Co.* v. *Stewart*.

Washington v. *Dawson & Co.*, 264 U.S. 219 (1924).

53. Act of June 2, 1924 (43 Stat. 313).

The gift tax provisions of the Revenue Act of 1924, applicable to gifts made during the calendar year, were *held* invalid under the Fifth Amendment insofar as they applied to gifts made before passage of the act.

Untermeyer v. *Anderson*, 276 U.S. 440 (1928).

54. Act of February 26, 1926 (44 Stat. 70, § 302, in part).

Stipulation creating a conclusive presumption that gifts made within two years prior to the death of the donor were made in contemplation of death of donor and requiring the value thereof to be included in computing the death transfer tax on decedent's estate was *held* to effect an invalid deprivation of property without due process.

Heiner v. *Donnan*, 285 U.S. 312 (1932).

55. Act of February 26, 1926 (44 Stat. 95, § 701).

Provision imposing a special excise tax of $1,000 on liquor dealers operating in States where such business is illegal, was *held* a penalty, without constitutional support following repeal of the Eighteenth Amendment.

United States v. *Constantine*, 296 U.S. 287 (1935).

56. Act of March 20, 1933 (48 Stat. 11, § 17, in part).

Clause in the Economy Act of 1933 providing "...all laws granting or pertaining to yearly renewable term war risk insurance are hereby repealed," *held* invalid to abrogate an outstanding contract of insurance, which is a vested right protected by the Fifth Amendment.

Lynch v. *United States*, 292 U.S. 571 (1934).

57. Act of May 12, 1933 (48 Stat. 31).

Agricultural Adjustment Act providing for processing taxes on agricultural commodities and benefit payments therefrom to farmers, *held* not within the taxing power under Article I, § 8, clause 1.

United States v. *Butler,* 297 U.S. 1 (1936).

58. Joint Resolution of June 5, 1933 (48 Stat. 113, § 1).

Abrogation of gold clause in Government obligations, *held* a repudiation of the pledge implicit in the power to borrow money (Article I, § 8, clause 2), and within the prohibition of the Fourteenth Amendment, against questioning the validity of the public debt. (The majority of the Court, however, held plaintiff not entitled to recover under the circumstances.)

Perry v. *United States,* 294 U.S. 330 (1935).

59. Act of June 16, 1933 (48 Stat. 195, the National Industrial Recovery Act).

(a) Title I, except § 9.

Provisions relating to codes of fair competition, authorized to be approved by the President in his discretion "to effectuate the policy" of the act, *held* invalid as a delegation of legislative power (Article I, § 1) and not within the commerce power (Article I, § 8, clause 3).

Schechter Corp. v. *United States,* 295 U.S. 495 (1935).

(b) § 9(c).

Clause of the oil regulation section authorizing the President "to prohibit the transportation in interstate...commerce of petroleum...produced or withdrawn from storage in excess of the amount permitted...by any State law..." and prescribing a penalty for violation of orders issued thereunder, *held* invalid as a delegation of legislative power.

Panama Refining Co. v. *Ryan,* 293 U.S. 388 (1935).

60. Act of June 16, 1933 (48 Stat. 307, § 13).

Temporary reduction of 15 percent in retired pay of judges, retired from service but subject to performance of judicial duties under the Act March 1, 1929 (45 Stat. 1422), was *held* a violation of the guaranty of judges' salaries in Article III, § 1.

Booth v. *United States,* 291 U.S. 339 (1934).

61. Act of April 27, 1934 (48 Stat. 646, § 6), amending § 5(i) of Home Owners' Loan Act of 1933.

Provision for conversion of state building and loan associations into federal associations, upon vote of 51 percent of the votes cast at a meeting of stockholders called to consider such action, *held* an encroachment on reserved powers of State.

Hopkins Savings Assn. v. *Cleary,* 296 U.S. 315 (1935).

62. Act of May 24, 1934 (48 Stat. 798).

Provision for readjustment of municipal indebtedness, though "adequately related" to the bankruptcy power, was *held* invalid as an interference with state sovereignty.

Ashton v. *Cameron County Dist.,* 298 U.S. 513 (1936).

63. Act of June 27, 1934 (48 Stat. 1283).

The Railroad Retirement Act, establishing a detailed compulsory retirement system for employees of carriers subject to the Interstate Commerce Act, *held* not a regulation of commerce within the meaning of Article I, § 8, clause 3, and violative of the due process clause (Fifth Amendment).

Railroad Retirement Board v. *Alton R. Co.,* 295 U.S. 330 (1935).

64. Act of June 28, 1934 (48 Stat. 1289, ch. 869).

The Frazier-Lemke Act, adding subsection (s) to § 75 of the Bankruptcy Act, designed to preserve to mortgagors the ownership and enjoyment of their farm property and providing specifically, in paragraph 7, that a bankrupt left in possession has the option at any time within 5 years of buying at the appraised value—subject meanwhile to no monetary obligation other than payment of reasonable rental, *held* a violation of property rights, under the Fifth Amendment.

Louisville Bank v. *Radford,* 295 U.S. 555 (1935).

65. Act of August 24, 1935 (49 Stat. 750).

Amendments of Agricultural Adjustment Act *held* not within the taxing power.

Rickert Rice Mills v. *Fontenot,* 297 U.S. 110 (1936).

66. Act of August 30, 1935 (49 Stat. 991).

Bituminous Coal Conservation Act of 1935, *held* to impose, not a tax within Article I, § 8, but a penalty not sustained by the commerce clause (Article I, § 8, clause 3).

Carter v. *Carter Coal Co.,* 298 U.S. 238 (1936).

67. Act of June 25, 1938 (52 Stat. 1040).

Federal Food, Drug, and Cosmetic Act of 1938, § 301(f), prohibiting the refusal to permit entry or inspection of premises by federal officers *held* void for vagueness and as violative of the due process clause of the Fifth Amendment.

United States v. *Cardiff,* 344 U.S. 174 (1952).

68. Act of June 30, 1938 (52 Stat. 1251).

Federal Firearms Act, § 2(f), establishing a presumption of guilt based on a prior conviction and present possession of a firearm, *held* to violate the test of due process under the Fifth Amendment.

Tot v. *United States,* 319 U.S. 463 (1943).

69. Act of October 14, 1940 (54 Stat. 1169, § 401(g)); as amended by Act of January 20, 1944 (58 Stat. 4, § 1).

Provision of Aliens and Nationality Code (8 U.S.C. § 1481(a) (8)), derived from the Nationality Act of 1940, as amended, that citizenship shall be lost upon conviction by court martial and dishonorable discharge for deserting the armed services in time of war, *held* invalid as imposing a cruel and unusual punishment barred by the Eighth Amendment and not authorized by the war powers conferred by Article I, § 8, clauses 11 to 14.

Trop v. *Dulles,* 356 U.S. 86 (1958).

70. Act of November 15, 1943 (57 Stat. 450).

Urgent Deficiency Appropriation Act of 1943, § 304, providing that no salary should be paid to certain named federal employees out of moneys appropriated, *held* to violate Article I, § 9, clause 3, forbidding enactment of bill of attainder or *ex post facto* law.

United States v. *Lovett,* 328 U.S. 303 (1946).

71. Act of September 27, 1944 (58 Stat. 746, § 401 (J)); and Act of June 27, 1952 (66 Stat. 163, 267-268, § 349(a) (10)).

§ 401 (J) of Immigration and Nationality Act of 1940, added in 1944, and § 49(a) (10) of the Immigration and Nationality Act of 1952 depriving one of citizenship, without the procedural safeguards guaranteed by the Fifth and Sixth Amendments, for the offense of leaving or remaining outside the country, in time of war or national emergency, to evade military service *held* invalid.

Kennedy v. *Mendoza-Martinez,* 372 U.S. 144 (1963).

72. Act of July 31, 1946 (ch. 707, § 7, 60 Stat. 719).

District court decision holding invalid under First and Fifth Amendments statute prohibiting parades or assemblages on United States Capitol grounds is summarily affirmed.

Chief of Capitol Police v. *Jeanette Rankin Brigade,* 409 U.S. (1972).

73. Act of June 25, 1948 (62 Stat. 760).

Provision of Lindbergh Kidnapping Act which provided for the imposition of the death penalty only if recommended by the jury *held* unconstitutional inasmuch as it penalized the assertion of a defendant's assertion of his Sixth Amendment right to a jury trial.

United States v. *Jackson,* 390 U.S. 570 (1968).

74. Act of May 5, 1950 (64 Stat. 107).

Article 3(a) of the Uniform Code of Military Justice subjecting civilian ex-servicemen to court martial for crime committed while in military service *held* to violate Article III, § 2, and the Fifth and Sixth Amendments.

Toth v. *Quarles,* 350 U.S. 11 (1955).

75. Act of May 5, 1950 (64 Stat. 107).

Insofar as Article 2(11) of the Uniform Code of Military Justice subjects civilian dependents accompanying members of the armed forces overseas in time of peace to trial, in capital cases, by court martial, it is violative of Article III, § 2, and the Fifth and Sixth Amendments.

Reid v. *Covert,* 354 U.S. 1 (1957).

Insofar as the aforementioned provision is invoked in time of peace for the trial of noncapital offenses committed on land bases overseas by employees of the armed forces who have not been inducted or who have not voluntarily enlisted therein, it is violative of the Sixth Amendment.

McElroy v. *United States,* 361 U.S. 281 (1960).

Insofar as the aforementioned provision is invoked in time of peace for the trial of noncapital offenses committed by civilian dependents accompanying members of the armed forces overseas, it is violative of Article III, § 2, and the Fifth and Sixth Amendments.

Kinsella v. *United States,* 361 U.S. 234 (1960).

Insofar as the aforementioned provision is invoked in time of peace for the trial of a capital offense committed by a civilian employee of the armed forces overseas, it is violative of Article III, § 2, and the Fifth and Sixth Amendments.

Grisham v. *Hagan,* 361 U.S. 278 (1960).

76. Act of August 16, 1950 (64 Stat. 451, as amended).

Statutory scheme authorizing the Postmaster General to close the mails to distributors of obscene materials *held* unconstitutional in the absence of procedural provisions which would assure prompt judicial determination that protected materials were not being restrained.

Blount v. *Rizzi,* 400 U.S. 410 (1971).

77. Act of August 28, 1950 (§ 202(f)(1)(E), 64 Stat. 485, 42 U.S.C. § 402(f)(1)(D)).

Social Security Act provision awarding survivors' benefits based on the earnings of a deceased wife to widower only if he was receiving at least half of his support from her at the time of her death, whereas widow receives benefits regardless of dependency violates equal protection element of Fifth Amendment's due process clause because of its impermissible gender classification.

Califano v. *Goldfarb,* 430 U.S. 199 (1977).

78. Act of September 23, 1950 (Title I, § 5, 64 Stat. 992).

Provision of Subversive Activities Control Act making it unlawful for member of Communist front organization to work in a defense plant *held* to be an overbroad infringement of the right of association protected by the First Amendment.

United States v. *Robel,* 389 U.S. 258 (1967).

79. Act of September 23, 1950 (64 Stat. 993, § 6).

Subversive Activities Control Act of 1950, § 6, providing that any member of a Communist organization, which has registered or has been ordered to register, commits a crime if he attempts to obtain or use a passport, *held* violative of due process under the Fifth Amendment.

Aptheker v. *Secretary of State,* 378 U.S. 500 (1964).

80. Act of September 23, 1950 (Title I, §§ 7, 8, 64 Stat. 993).

Provisions of Subversive Activities Control Act of 1950 requiring in lieu of registration by the Communist Party registration by Party members may not be applied to compel registration of or to prosecute for refusal to register, alleged members who have asserted their privilege against self-incrimination inasmuch as registration would expose such persons to criminal prosecution under other laws.

Albertson v. *Subversive Activities Control Board,* 382 U.S. 70 (1965).

81. Act of October 30, 1951 (§ 5(f)(ii), 65 Stat. 683, 45 U.S.C. §231a(c)(3)(ii)).

Provision of Railroad Retirement Act similar to section voided in *Goldfarb.*

Railroad Retirement Board v. *Kalina* 431 U.S. 909 (1977).

82. Act of June 27, 1952 (Title III, § 349, 66 Stat. 267).

Provision of Immigration and Nationality Act of 1952 providing for revocation of United States citizenship of one who votes in a foreign election *held* unconstitutional under § 1 of the Fourteenth Amendment.

Afroyim v. *Rusk,* 387 U.S. 253 (1967).

83. Act of June 27, 1952 (66 Stat. 163, 269, § 352(a) (1)).

§ 352(a) (1) of the Immigration and Nationality Act of 1952 depriving a naturalized person of citizenship for "having a continuous residence for three years" in state of his birth or prior nationality *held* violative of the due process clause of the Fifth Amendment.

Schneider v. *Rusk,* 377 U.S. 163 (1964).

84. Act of August 26, 1954 (68A Stat. 525, Int. Rev. Code of 1954, §§ 4401-4423).

Provisions of tax laws requiring gamblers to pay occupational and excise taxes may not be used over an assertion of one's privilege against self-incrimination either to compel extensive reporting of activities, leaving the registrant subject to prosecution under the laws of all the States with the possible exception of Nevada, or to prosecute for failure to register and report, because the scheme abridged the Fifth Amendment privilege.

Marchetti v. *United States,* 390 U.S. 39 (1968), and *Grosso* v. *United States,* 390 U.S. 62 (1968).

85. Act of August 16, 1954 (68A Stat. 560, Marijuana Tax Act, §§ 4741, 4744, 4751, 4753).

Provisions of tax laws requiring possessors of marijuana to register and to pay a transfer tax may not be used over an assertion of the privilege against self-incrimination to compel registration or to prosecute for failure to register.

Leary v. *United States,* 395 U.S. 6 (1969).

86. Act of August 16, 1954 (68A Stat. 728, Int. Rev. Code of 1954, §§ 5841, 5851).

Provisions of tax laws requiring the possessor of certain firearms, which it is made illegal to receive or to possess, to register with the Treasury Department may not be used over an assertion of the privilege against self-incrimination to prosecute one for failure to register or for possession of an unregistered firearm since the statutory scheme abridges the Fifth Amendment privilege.

Haynes v. *United States,* 390 U.S. 85 (1968).

87. Act of August 16, 1954 (68A Stat. 867, Int. Rev. Code of 1954, § 7302).

Provisions of tax laws providing for forfeiture of property used in violating internal revenue laws may not be constitutionally used in face of invocation of privilege against self-incrimination to condemn money in possession of gambler who had failed to comply with the registration and reporting scheme held void in *Marchetti* v. *United States,* 390 U.S. 39 (1968).

United States v. *United States Coin & Currency,* 401 U.S. 715 (1971).

88. Act of July 18, 1956 (§ 106, Stat. 570).

Provision of Narcotic Drugs Import and Export Act creating a presumption that possessor of marijuana knew of its illegal importation into the United States *held,* in absence of showing that all marijuana in United States was of foreign origin and that domestic users could know that their marijuana was more likely than not of foreign

origin, unconstitutional under the due process clause of the Fifth Amendment.

Leary v. *United States,* 395 U.S. 6 (1969).

89. Act of August 10, 1956 (70A Stat. 65, Uniform Code of Military Justice, Articles 80, 130, 134).

Servicemen may not be charged under the Act and tried in military courts because of the commission of non-service connected crimes committed off-post and off-duty which are subject to civilian court jurisdiction where the guarantees of the Bill of Rights are applicable.

O'Callahan v. *Parker,* 395 U.S. 258 (1969).

90. Act of August 10, 1956 (70A Stat. 35, § 772(f)).

Provision of statute permitting the wearing of United States military apparel in theatrical productions only if the portrayal does not tend to discredit the armed force imposes an unconstitutional restraint upon First Amendment freedoms and precludes a prosecution under 18 U.S.C. § 702 for unauthorized wearing of uniform in a street skit disrespectful of the military.

Schacht v. *United States,* 398 U.S. 58 (1970).

91. Act of September 2, 1958 (§ 5601(b) (1), 72 Stat. 1399).

Provision of Internal Revenue Code creating a presumption that one's presence at the site of an unregistered still shall be sufficient for conviction under a statute punishing possession, custody, or control of an unregistered still unless defendant otherwise explained his presence at the site to the jury is unconstitutional because the presumption is not a legitimate, rational, or reasonable inference that defendant was engaged in one of the specialized functions prescribed by the statute.

United States v. *Romano,* 382 U.S. 136 (1965).

92. Act of September 2, 1958 (§ 1(25)(b), 72 Stat. 1446), and Act of September 7, 1962 (§ 401, 76 Stat. 469).

Federal statutes providing that spouses of female members of the Armed Forces must be dependent in fact in order to qualify for certain dependent's benefits, whereas spouses of male members are statutorily deemed dependent and automatically qualified for allowances, whatever their actual status, is an invalid gender classification under the equal protection principles of the Fifth Amendment's due process Clause.

Frontiero v. *Richardson,* 411 U.S. 677 (1973).

93. Act of September 14, 1959 (§ 504, 73 Stat. 536).

Provision of Labor-Management Reporting and Disclosure Act of 1959 making it a crime for a member of the Communist Party to serve as an officer or, with the exception of clerical or custodial positions, as an employee of a labor union *held* to be a bill of attainder and unconstitutional.

United States v. *Brown,* 381 U.S. 437 (1965).

94. Act of October 11, 1962 (§ 305, 76 Stat. 840).

Provision of Postal Services and Federal Employees Salary Act of 1962 authorizing Post Office Department to detain material determined to be "communist political propaganda" and to forward it to the addressee only if he requested it after notification by the Department, the material to be destroyed otherwise, *held* to impose on the addressee an affirmative obligation which amounted to an abridgment of First Amendment rights.

Lamont v. *Postmaster General,* 381 U.S. 301 (1965).

95. Act of October 15, 1962 (76 Stat. 914).

Provision of District of Columbia laws requiring that a person to be eligible to receive welfare assistance must have resided in the District for at least one year impermissibly classified persons on the basis of an assertion of the right to travel interstate and therefore *held* to violate the due process clause of the Fifth Amendment.

Shapiro v. *Thompson,* 394 U.S. 618 (1969).

96. Act of December 16, 1963 (77 Stat. 378, 20 U.S.C. § 754).

Provision of Higher Education Facilities Act of 1963 which in effect removed restriction against religious use of facilities constructed with federal funds after 20 years *held* to violate the establishment clause of the First Amendment inasmuch as the property will still be of considerable value at the end of the period and removal of the restriction would constitute a substantial governmental contribution to religion.

Tilton v. *Richardson,* 403 U.S. 672 (1971).

97. Act of July 20, 1965 (§ 339, 79 Stat. 409).

Section of Social Security Act qualifying certain illegitimate children for disability insurance benefits by presuming dependence but disqualifying other illegitimate children, regardless of dependency, if the disabled wage earner parent did not contribute to the child's support before the onset of the disability or if the child did not live with the parent before the onset of disability denies latter class of children equal protection as guaranteed by the due process clause of the Fifth Amendment.

—*Jiminez* v. *Weinberger,* 417 U.S. 628 (1974).

98. Act of September 3, 1966 (§ 102(b), 80 Stat. 831), and Act of April 8, 1974 (§§ 6(a)(1) (amending § 3(d) of Act), 6(a)(2) (amending 3(e)(2)(C), 6(a)(5) (amending § (s)(5), and 6(a)(6) (amending § 3(x)).

Those sections of the Fair Labor Standards Act extending wage and hour coverage to the employees of state and local governments are invalid because Congress lacks the authority under the commerce clause to regulate employee activities in areas of traditional governmental functions of the States.

—*National League of Cities* v. *Usery,* 426 U.S. 833 (1976).

99. Act of January 2, 1968 (§ 163(a)(2), 81 Stat. 872).

District court decisions holding unconstitutional under Fifth Amendment's due process clause section of Social Security Act that reduced, perhaps to zero, benefits coming to illegitimate children upon death of parent in order to satisfy the maximum payment due the wife and legitimate children are summarily affirmed.

—*Richardson* v. *Davis,* 409 U.S. 1069 (1972).

Richardson v. *Griffin,* 409 U.S. 1069 (1972).

100. Act of January 2, 1968 (§ 407, 81 Stat. 882, 42 U.S.C. § 607).

Provision of Social Security Act awarding benefits to families when dependent children have been deprived of parental support because of the unemployment of the father violates the equal protection principle of the Fifth Amendment due process clause because of the impermissible gender classification.

Califano v. *Westcott* (June 25, 1979).

101. Act of June 22, 1970 (ch. III, 84 Stat. 318).

Provision of Voting Rights Act Amendments of 1970 which set a minimum voting age qualification of 18 in state and local elections *held* to be unconstitutional because beyond the powers of Congress to legislate.

Oregon v. *Mitchell,* 400 U.S. 223 (1970).

102. Act of December 29, 1970 (§ 8(a), 84 Stat. 1598, 29 U.S.C. § 657 (a)).

Provision of Occupational Safety and Health Act authorizing inspections of covered work places in industry without warrant violates Fourth Amendment.

Marshall v. *Barlow's, Inc.,* 436 U.S. 307 (1978).

103. Act of January 11, 1971 (§ 2, 84 Stat. 2048).

Provision of Food Stamp Act disqualifying from participation in program any household containing an individual unrelated by birth, marriage, or adoption to any other member of the household violates the due process clause of the Fifth Amendment.

Department of Agriculture v. *Moreno,* 413 U.S. 528 (1973).

104. Act of January 11, 1971 (§ 4, 84 Stat. 2049).

Provision of Food Stamp Act disqualifying from participation in program any household containing a person 18 years or older who had been claimed as a dependent child for income tax purposes in the present or preceding tax year by a taxpayer not a member of the household violates the due process clause of the Fifth Amendment.

Dept. of Agriculture v. *Murry,* 413 U.S. 508 (1973).

105. Federal Election Campaign Act of February 7, 1972 (86 Stat. 3), as amended by the Federal Election Campaign Act Amendments of 1974 (88 Stat. 1263), adding or amending 18 U.S.C. §§ 608(a), 608(e), and 2 U.S.C. § 437c.

Provisions of election law that forbid a candidate or the members of his immediate family from expending personal funds in excess of specified amounts, that limit to $1,000 the independent expenditures of any person relative to an identified candidate, and that forbid expenditures by candidates for federal office in excess of specified amounts violate the First Amendment speech guarantees; provisions of the law creating a commission to oversee enforcement of the Act are an invalid infringement of constitutional separation of powers in that they devolve responsibilities upon a commission four of whose six members are appointed by Congress and all six of whom are confirmed by the House of Representatives as well as by the Senate, not in compliance with the appointments clause.

Buckley v. *Valeo,* 424 U.S. 1 (1976).

Rules of the Supreme Court
of the United States

Source: CLB's Law Printing Company, Washington, D.C.

PART I. THE COURT.

1.

Clerk.

1. The clerk of this court shall reside and keep the office at the seat of the National Government, and he shall not practice as attorney or counsellor in any court, while he continues in office.

2. The clerk shall not permit any original or certified record or paper to be taken from the office, except temporarily for purposes of printing, and except, on proper application from counsel or from the clerk or the presiding judge of a court below whose judgment is sought to be reviewed, for return to such court, after the conclusion of the proceedings in this court. Original or file copies of pleadings, papers, or briefs may not be withdrawn by litigants.

3. The clerk's office will be open from 9:00 A.M. to 5:00 P.M. Mondays through Fridays, and from 9:00 A.M. to noon on Saturdays, legal holidays excepted.

2.

Library.

1. The library for the bar shall be open to members of the bar of this court, to members of Congress, and to law officers of the executive or other departments of the Government.

2. The library shall be open during such times as the reasonable needs of the bar require and shall be governed by the regulations made by the librarian with the approval of the chief justice.

3. Books may not be removed from the building.

3.

Term.

1. The court will hold an annual term commencing on the first Monday in October of each year and may hold such adjourned or special terms as may be necessary.

2. The court will at every term announce the date after which no case will be called for argument, or be submitted for decision at that term, unless otherwise ordered for special cause shown.

3. At the end of each term, all cases on the docket shall be continued to the next term.

4.

Sessions, Quorum, and Adjournments.

1. Open sessions of the court will be held at ten a.m. on the first Monday in October of each year, and thereafter as announced by the court. Unless otherwise ordered, the court sits to hear arguments from ten until noon, recesses until one, and adjourns for the day at three.

2. Unless otherwise ordered the court will not schedule arguments on Fridays or Saturdays.

3. In the absence of a quorum, on any day appointed for holding a session of the court, the justices attending (or, if no justice is present, the clerk or a deputy clerk) may adjourn the court until there is a quorum.

4. The court may, in appropriate instances, direct the clerk or the marshal to announce recesses and adjournments.

PART II. ATTORNEYS AND COUNSELLORS.

5.*

Admission to the Bar.

1. It shall be requisite to the admission of attorneys or counsellors to practice in this court, that they shall have been such for three years past in the highest court of a State, Territory, District, Commonwealth, or Possession, and that their private and professional characters shall appear to be good.

2. Each applicant shall file with the clerk (1) a certificate from the presiding judge or clerk of the proper court evidencing his admission to practice there and that he is presently in good standing, and (2) his personal statement, on the form approved by the court and furnished by the clerk, which shall be endorsed by two members of the bar of this court who are not related to the applicant.

3. If the documents submitted by the applicant demonstrate that he possesses the necessary qualifications, the clerk shall so notify the applicant and he may be admitted without appearing in court. Upon the applicant's signing the oath or affirmation and paying the fee required under Rule 52(d), the clerk shall issue a certificate of admission to the applicant. However, if the applicant so elects he may be admitted on oral motion by a member of the bar in open court, provided the applicant has satisfied the requirements for admission.

4. Each applicant shall take or subscribe the following oath or affirmation, viz:

I, ..., do solemnly swear (or affirm) as an attorney and as a counsellor of this court I will conduct myself uprightly, and according to law, and that I will support the Constitution of the United States.

See Rule 52(d) for fee required.

6.

Admission of Foreign Counsel.

An attorney, barrister, or advocate who is qualified to practice in the courts of any foreign state may be specially admitted to the bar of this court for purposes limited to a particular case. He shall not, however, be authorized to act as attorney of record. In the case of such applicants, the oath shall not be required and there shall be no fee. Such admissions shall be only on motion of a member of the bar of this court, notice of which signed by such member and reciting all relevant facts shall be filed with the clerk at least three days prior to the motion.

7.

Clerks To Justices Not To Practice.

No one serving as a law clerk or secretary to a justice of this court shall practice as an attorney or counsellor in any court or before any agency of government while continuing in that position; nor shall he after separating from that position practice as an attorney or counsellor in this court until two years have elapsed after such separation; nor shall he ever participate, by way of any form of professional consultation and assistance, in any case that was pending in this court during the period that he held such position.

---

* Revised on October 12, 1970.

8.

Disbarment.

Where it is shown to the court that any member of its bar has been disbarred from practice in any State, Territory, District, Commonwealth, or Possession, or has been guilty of conduct unbecoming a member of the bar of this court, he will be forthwith suspended from practice before this court. He will thereupon be afforded the opportunity to show good cause, within forty days, why he should not be disbarred. Upon his response to the rule to show cause, or upon the expiration of the forty days if no response is made, the court will enter an appropriate order; but no order of disbarment will be entered except with the concurrence of a majority of the justices participating.

PART III. ORIGINAL JURISDICTION.

9.

Procedure in Original Actions.

1. This rule applies only to actions within the original jurisdiction of the court under the Constitution. Original applications for writs in aid of the court's appellate jurisdiction are governed by Part VII of these rules.

2. The form of pleadings and motions in original actions shall be governed, so far as may be, by the Federal Rules of Civil Procedure, and in other respects those rules, where their application is appropriate, may be taken as a guide to procedure in original actions in this court.

3. The initial pleading in any original action shall be prefaced by a motion for leave to file such pleading, and both shall be printed in conformity with Rule 39. A brief in support of the motion for leave to file, which shall comply with Rule 39, may be filed with the motion and pleading. Sixty copies of each document, with proof of service as prescribed by Rule 33, are required, except that, where the adverse party is a State, service shall be made on the governor and attorney general of such State.

4. The case will be placed upon the original docket when the motion for leave to file is filed with the clerk. The docket fee must be paid at that time, and the appearance of counsel for the plaintiff entered.

5. The adverse party or parties may, within sixty days after receipt of the motion for leave to file and allied documents, file sixty printed copies of a brief or briefs in opposition to such motion, which shall conform to Rule 39. When such brief or briefs in opposition have been filed, or the time within which they may be filed has expired, the motion, pleading and briefs shall be distributed to the court by the clerk. The court may thereafter grant or deny the motion or set it down for argument.

6. Additional pleadings may be filed, and subsequent proceedings had, as the court shall direct.

7. Any process against a State issued from the court in an original action shall be served on the governor and attorney general of such State.

8. A summons issuing out of this court in any original action shall be served on the defendant sixty days before the return day set out therein; and if the defendant, on such service of the summons, shall not respond by the return day, the plaintiff shall be at liberty to proceed *ex parte*.

PART IV. JURISDICTION ON APPEAL.

10.

Appeal — How Taken — Parties.

1. An appeal permitted by law to this court shall be taken by filing a notice of appeal, in the form and at the place prescribed by this rule, and shall be perfected by docketing the case in this court as provided in Rule 13.

2. The notice of appeal shall specify the parties taking the appeal, shall designate the judgment or part thereof appealed from, giving the time of its entry, and shall specify the statute or statutes under which the appeal to this court is taken. A copy of the notice of appeal shall be served on all parties to the proceeding in the court where the judgment appealed from was issued, in the manner prescribed by Rule 33, and proof of such service shall be filed with the notice of appeal.

3. If the appeal is taken from a federal court, the notice of appeal shall be filed with the clerk of such court. If the appeal is taken from a state court, the notice of appeal shall be filed with the clerk of the court possessed of the record.

4. All parties to the proceeding in the court from whose judgment the appeal is being taken shall be deemed parties in this court, unless the appellant shall notify the clerk of this court in writing of his belief that one or more of the parties below have no interest in the outcome of the appeal. A copy of such notice shall be served on all parties to the proceeding below and a party noted as no longer interested may remain a party here by notifying the clerk, with service on the other parties, that he has an interest in the appeal. All parties other than the appellant shall be appellees, but appellees who support the position of the appellant shall meet the time schedule for filing papers which is provided for the appellant, except that any response by such appellees to a jurisdictional statement shall be filed as promptly as possible after receipt of the jurisdictional statement.

11.

Appeal — Time for Taking and Docketing.

1. An appeal to review the judgment of a state court of last resort in a criminal case shall be deemed in time when the notice of appeal prescribed by Rule 10 is filed with the clerk of the court possessed of the record within ninety days after the entry of such judgment and the case is docketed within the time provided in Rule 13.

2. An appeal permitted by law from a district court to this court in a criminal case shall be in time when the notice of appeal prescribed by Rule 10 is filed with the clerk of the district court within thirty days after entry of the judgment or order appealed from and the case is docketed within the time provided in Rule 13.

3. An appeal in all other cases shall be in time when the notice of appeal prescribed by Rule 10 is filed with the clerk of the appropriate court within the time allowed by law for taking such appeal and the case is docketed within the time provided in Rule 13.

12.

Certification of Record.

1. A party intending to appeal may, prior to filing the notice of appeal or at any time thereafter prior to action by this court on the appeal, request the clerk of the court possessed of the record to certify it, or any part of it, and to provide for its transmission to this court, but the filing of the record in this court is not required for docketing an appeal. If the appellant has not done so, the appellee may request such clerk to certify and transmit the record or any part of it. Thereafter, the clerk of this court or any party to the appeal may request that additional parts of the record be certified and transmitted to this court. A copy of all requests for certification and transmission shall be sent to all parties to the proceeding.

2. When requested to certify and transmit the record, or any part of it, the clerk of the court possessed of the record shall number the documents to be certified comprising the record and shall transmit with them a numbered list of the documents, identifying each with reasonable definiteness.

3. Whenever it shall be necessary or proper, in the opinion of the presiding judge of the court from which the appeal is taken, that original papers of any kind should be inspected in this court in lieu of copies, such presiding judge may make such rule or order for the safekeeping, transporting, and return of such original papers as

to him may seem proper. If the record has been printed for the use of the court below, such printed record plus the proceedings in the court below may be certified as the record unless one of the parties or the clerk of this court otherwise requests.

4. When more than one appeal is taken to this court from the same judgment, it shall be sufficient to prepare a single record containing all the matter designated or agreed upon by the parties, without duplication.

13.

Docketing Cases.

1. Not more than ninety days after the entry of the judgment appealed from it shall be the duty of the appellant to docket the case in the manner set forth in paragraph 2 of this rule, except that in the case of appeals pursuant to Section 1252, 1253, or 2282 of Title 28 of the United States Code the time limit for docketing shall be sixty days from the filing of the notice of appeal. For good cause shown, a justice of this court may extend the time for docketing a case for a period not exceeding sixty days. Where application under this rule is made, paragraph 2 of Rule 34 governs timeliness. Such applications are not favored.

2. Counsel for the appellant shall enter his appearance, pay the docket fee, and file, with proof of service as prescribed by Rule 33, forty copies of a printed statement as to jurisdiction, which shall comply in all respects with Rule 15. The case will then be placed on the docket.

3. It shall be the duty of the appellant to notify all appellees on a form supplied by the clerk of the date of docketing and of the docket number of the case.

14.

Dismissing Appeals for Non-Prosecution.

1. After a notice of appeal has been filed, but before the case has been docketed in this court, the parties may at any time dismiss the appeal by stipulation filed in the court possessed of the record, or that court may dismiss the appeal upon motion and notice by the appellant. For dismissal after the case has been docketed, see Rule 60.

2. If a notice of appeal has been filed but the case has not been docketed in this court within the time for docketing, plus any enlargement thereof duly granted, the court possessed of the record may dismiss the appeal upon motion of the appellee and notice to the appellant, and may make such orders thereon with respect to costs as may be just.

3. If a notice of appeal has been filed but the case has not been docketed in this court within the time for docketing, plus any enlargement thereof duly granted, and the court possessed of the record has for any reason denied an appellee's motion, made as provided in the foregoing paragraph, to dismiss the appeal, the appellee may have the cause docketed and the appeal dismissed in this court, by producing a certificate, whether in term or vacation, from the clerk of the court possessed of the record, establishing the foregoing facts, and by filing a motion to dismiss, which shall conform to Rule 35 and be accompanied by proof of service as prescribed by Rule 33. The clerk's certificate shall be attached to the motion, but it shall not be necessary for the appellee to file the record. In the event that the appeal is thereafter dismissed, the court will give judgment against the appellant and in favor of appellee for costs. In no case shall the appellant be entitled to docket the cause after the appeal shall have been dismissed under this paragraph, unless by special leave of court.

15.

Jurisdictional Statement.

1. The jurisdictional statement required by paragraph 2 of Rule 13 shall contain in the order here indicated —

(a) A reference to the official and unofficial reports of the opinions delivered in the courts below, if any, and if reported.

Any such opinions shall be appended as provided in subparagraph (h) hereof.

(b) A concise statement of the grounds on which the jurisdiction of this court is invoked, showing:

(i) The nature of the proceeding and the statute pursuant to which it is brought;

(ii) The date of the judgment or decree sought to be reviewed and the time of its entry, the date of any order respecting a rehearing, the date the notice of appeal was filed, and the court in which it was filed;

(iii) The statutory provision believed to confer on this court jurisdiction of the appeal;

(iv) Cases believed to sustain the jurisdiction.

(v) If the validity of the statute of a state, or statute or treaty of the United States is involved, its text shall be set out verbatim, citing the volume and page where it may be found in the official edition. If the statutory or treaty provisions that are involved are lengthy, the citation alone will suffice at this point, and their pertinent text shall be set forth in an appendix.

A copy of the judgment or decree, of any order on rehearing, and of the notice of appeal shall be appended as provided in subparagraphs (i) and (j) hereof.

(c) The questions presented by the appeal, expressed in the terms and circumstances of the case but without unnecessary detail. The statement of the questions should be short and concise and should not be repetitious. The statement of a question presented will be deemed to include every subsidiary question fairly comprised therein. Only the questions set forth in the jurisdictional statement or fairly comprised therein will be considered by the court.

(d) A concise statement of the case containing the facts material to the consideration of the questions presented. If the appeal is from a state court, the statement of the case shall also specify the stage in the proceedings in the court of first instance, and in the appellate court, at which, and the manner in which, the federal questions sought to be reviewed were raised; the method of raising them (e.g., by a pleading, by request to charge and exceptions, by assignment of error); and the way in which they were passed upon by the court; with such pertinent quotations of specific portions of the record, or summary thereof, with specific reference to the places in the record where the matter appears (e.g., ruling on exception, portion of the court's charge and exception thereto, assignment of error) as will support the assertion that the rulings of the court were of a nature to bring the case within the statutory provision believed to confer jurisdiction on this court.

(e) If the appeal is from a state court, there shall be included a presentation of the grounds upon which it is contended that the federal questions are substantial (*Zucht* v. *King*, 260 U.S. 174, 176, 177), which shall show that the nature of the case and of the rulings of the court was such as to bring the case within the jurisdictional provisions relied on and the cases cited to sustain the jurisdiction (subparagraph (b) (iv) hereof), and shall include the reasons why the questions presented are so substantial as to require plenary consideration, with briefs on the merits and oral argument, for their resolution.

(f) If the appeal is from a federal court, there shall similarly be included a statement of the reasons why the questions presented are so substantial as to require plenary consideration, with briefs on the merits and oral argument, for their resolution.

(g) If the appeal is from a decree of a district court granting or denying an interlocutory injunction, the statement must also include a showing of the matters in which it is contended that the court has abused its discretion by such action. See *United States* v. *Corrick*, 298 U.S. 435; *Mayo* v. *Lakeland Highlands Canning Co.*, 309 U.S. 310.

(h) There shall be appended to the statement a copy of any opinions delivered upon the rendering of the judgment or decree sought to be reviewed, including, if not reported, earlier opinions in the same case, or opinions in companion cases, reference to which may be necessary to ascertain the grounds of the judgment or decree; and, if the appeal is from a federal court, there shall similarly be appended the court's findings of fact and conclusions of law, if any were separately made.

(i) There shall be appended to the statement a copy of the judgment or decree and of any order on rehearing, including in each the caption showing the name of the court issuing it, the title and number of the case, and the date of entry of the judgment or decree, and of any order on rehearing.

(j) There shall be appended to the statement a copy of the notice of appeal showing the date it was filed and the name of the court where it was filed.

2. The jurisdictional statement shall be printed in conformity with Rule 39.

3. Where several cases are appealed from the same court that involve identical or closely related questions, it shall suffice to file a single jurisdictional statement covering all the cases.

16*

Motion to Dismiss or Affirm.

1. Within thirty days after receipt of the jurisdictional statement, unless the time is enlarged by the court or a justice thereof, or by the clerk under the provisions of paragraph 5 of Rule 34, the appellee may file a printed motion to dismiss, or motion to affirm. In cases where the United States or any agency, officer or employee thereof is the appellee, the appellee shall have an additional twenty days to file said motions. Where appropriate, a motion to affirm may be united in the alternative with a motion to dismiss.

(a) The court will receive a motion to dismiss any appeal on the ground that the appeal is not within the jurisdiction of this court, because not taken in conformity to statute or to these rules.

(b) The court will receive a motion to dismiss an appeal from a state court on the ground that it does not present a substantial federal question; or that the federal question sought to be reviewed was not timely or properly raised, or expressly passed on; or that the judgment rests on an adequate non-federal basis.

(c) The court will receive a motion to affirm the judgment sought to be reviewed on appeal from a federal court on the ground that it is manifest that the questions on which the decision of the cause depends are so unsubstantial as not to need further argument.

(d) The court will receive a motion to dismiss or affirm on any other grounds which the appellee wishes to present as reasons why the court should not set the case for argument.

2. The motion to dismiss or affirm shall be printed in conformity with Rules 35 and 39, and forty copies, with proof of service as prescribed by Rule 33, shall be filed with the clerk.

3. Upon the filing of such motion, or the expiration of the time allowed therefor, or express waiver of the right to file, the jurisdictional statement and the motion, if any, shall be distributed by the clerk to the court for its consideration.

4. Briefs opposing motions to dismiss or affirm may be filed, but distribution of the jurisdictional statement and consideration thereof by this court will not be delayed pending the filing of such briefs. Forty copies of such briefs prepared in accordance with Rule 39 and served as prescribed by Rule 33 shall be filed.

5. Any party may file a supplemental brief at any time while a jurisdictional statement is pending calling attention to new cases or legislation or other intervening matter not available at the time of his last filing.

6. After consideration of the papers distributed pursuant to this rule, the court will enter an appropriate order. If such order notes probable jurisdiction, or postpones consideration of the

---

* Revised on November 22, 1971.

question of jurisdiction to the hearing of the case on the merits, the case shall stand for argument. If the record has not previously been filed, the clerk of this court shall certify it and transmit it to this court. If consideration of the question of jurisdiction is postponed, counsel should address themselves, at the outset of their briefs and oral argument, to the question of jurisdiction.

17.

Use of Single Appendix.

After the court has noted or postponed jurisdiction any portion of the record to which the parties wish to direct the court's particular attention shall be printed in a single appendix prepared by the appellant under the procedures provided in Rule 36, but the fact that any part of the record has not been printed shall not prevent the parties or the court from relying on it.

18.

Supersedeas on Appeal.

1. Whenever an appellant entitled thereto desires a stay on appeal, he may present for approval to a judge of the court whose decision is sought to be reviewed, or to such court when action by that court is required by law, or, subject to paragraph 2 hereof, to a justice of this court, a motion to stay the enforcement of the judgment appealed from, with which, if the stay is to act as a supersedeas, shall be tendered a supersedeas bond which shall have such surety or sureties as said judge, court, or justice may require. The bond shall be conditioned for the satisfaction of the judgment in full together with costs, interest, and damages for delay, if for any reason the appeal is dismissed or if the judgment is affirmed, and to satisfy in full such modification of the judgment and such costs, interest, and damages as this court may adjudge and award. When the judgment is for the recovery of money not otherwise secured, the amount of the bond shall be fixed at such sum as will cover the whole amount of the judgment remaining unsatisfied, costs on the appeal, interest, and damages for delay, unless the judge, court, or justice after notice and hearing and for good cause shown fixes a different amount or orders security other than the bond. When the judgment determines the disposition of the property in controversy as in real actions, replevin, and actions to foreclose mortgages or when such property is in the custody of the marshal or when the proceeds of such property or a bond for its value is in the custody or control of any court wherein were had the proceedings appealed from, the amount of the supersedeas bond shall be fixed at such sum only as will secure the amount recovered for the use and detention of the property, the costs of the action, costs on appeal, interest, and damages for delay.

2. Application hereunder to a justice of this court will normally not be entertained unless application therefor has first been made to a judge of the court rendering the decision appealed from, or to such court, or unless the security offered below has been disapproved by such judge or court. All such applications are governed by Rules 50 and 51.

PART V. JURISDICTION ON WRIT OF CERTIORARI.

19.

Considerations Governing Review on Certiorari.

1. A review on writ of certiorari is not a matter of right, but of sound judicial discretion, and will be granted only where there are special and important reasons therefor. The following, while neither controlling nor fully measuring the court's discretion, indicate the character of reasons which will be considered:

(a) Where a state court has decided a federal question of substance not theretofore determined by this court, or has decided it in a way probably not in accord with applicable decisions of this court.

(b) Where a court of appeals has rendered a decision in conflict with the decision of another court of appeals on the same matter; or has decided an important state or territorial question in a way in conflict with applicable state of territorial law; or has decided an important question of federal law which has not been, but should be, settled by this court; or has decided a federal question in a way in conflict with applicable decisions of this court; or has so far departed from the accepted and usual course of judicial proceedings, or so far sanctioned such a departure by a lower court, as to call for an exercise of this court's power of supervision.

2. The same general considerations outlined above will control in respect of petitions for writs of certiorari to review judgments of the Court of Claims, of the Court of Customs and Patent Appeals, or of any other court whose determinations are by law reviewable on writ of certiorari.

20.

Certiorari to a Court of Appeals Before Judgment.

A writ of certiorari to review a case pending in a court of appeals, before judgment is given in such court, will be granted only upon a showing that the case is of such imperative public importance as to justify the deviation from normal appellate processes and to require immediate settlement in this court. *See United States* v. *Bankers Trust Co.*, 294 U.S. 240; *Railroad Retirement Board* v. *Alton R. Co.*, 295 U.S. 330; *Rickert Rice Mills* v. *Fontenot*, 297 U.S. 110; *Carter v. Carter Coal Co.*, 298 U.S. 238; *Ex parte Quirin*, 317 U.S. 1; *United States* v. *United Mine Workers*, 330 U.S. 258; *Youngstown Co.* v. *Sawyer*, 343 U.S. 579.

21.

Review on Certiorari — How Sought — Parties.

1. A party intending to file a petition for certiorari may, prior to filing the case in this court or at any time thereafter prior to action by this court on the petition, request the clerk of the court possessed of the record to certify it, or any part of it and to provide for its transmission to this court, but the filing of the record in this court is not a requisite for docketing the petition. If the petitioner has not done so, the respondent may request such clerk to certify and transmit the record or any part of it. Thereafter, the clerk of this court or any party to the case may request that additional parts of the record be certified and transmitted to this court. A copy of all requests for certification and transmission shall be sent to all parties to the proceeding.

2. When requested to certify and transmit the record, or any part of it, the clerk of the court possessed of the record shall number the documents to be certified and shall transmit with the record a numbered list of the documents, identifying each with reasonable definiteness. If the record has been printed for the use of the court below, such printed record plus the proceedings in the court below may be certified as the record unless one of the parties or the clerk of this court otherwise requests. The provisions of Rule 12(3) with respect to original papers shall apply to all cases sought to be reviewed on writ of certiorari.

3. Counsel for the petitioner shall file with the clerk of this court, with proof of service as provided by Rule 33, forty copies of a petition which shall comply in all respects with Rule 23 and shall enter his appearance and pay the docket fee. The case will then be placed on the docket. It shall be the duty of counsel for the petitioner to notify all respondents, on a form supplied by the clerk, of the date of filing and of the docket number of the case. Such notice shall be served as required by Rule 33.

4. All parties to the proceeding in the court whose judgment is sought to be reviewed shall be deemed parties in this court, unless the petitioner shall notify the clerk of this court in writing of his belief that one or more of the parties below have no interest in the outcome of the petition. A copy of such notice shall be served on all parties to the proceeding below and a party noted as no longer interested may remain a party here by notifying the clerk, with service on the other parties, that he has an interest in the petition. All parties other than the petitioner shall be respondents, but respondents who support the position of the petitioner shall meet the time schedule for filing papers which is provided for the petitioner, except that any response by such respondents to the petition shall be filed as promptly as possible after receipt of the petition.

22.

Review on Certiorari — Time for Petitioning.

1. A petition for writ of certiorari to review the judgment of a state court of last resort in a criminal case shall be deemed in time when it is filed with the clerk within ninety days after the entry of such judgment. A justice of this court, for good cause shown, may extend the time for applying for a writ of certiorari in such cases for a period not exceeding sixty days.

2. A petition for writ of certiorari to review the judgment of a court of appeals in a criminal case shall be deemed in time when it is filed with the clerk within thirty days after the entry of such judgment. A justice of this court, for good cause shown, may extend the time for applying for a writ of certiorari in such cases for a period not exceeding thirty days. If the original judgment in such a case was entered in a district court in Alaska, Guam, Hawaii, Puerto Rico, the Virgin Islands, or the Canal Zone, the petition shall be deemed filed in time if mailed by air-mail under a postmark dated within the thirty-day period or due extension thereof.

3. A petition for writ of certiorari in all other cases shall be deemed in time when it is filed with the clerk within the time prescribed by law.

4. An application for extension of time within which to file a petition for writ of certiorari must set out, as in a petition for certiorari (see Rule 23(1), subparagraphs (b) and (f)), the grounds on which the jurisdiction of this court is invoked, must identify the judgment sought to be reviewed and have appended thereto a copy of the opinion, and must set forth with specificity the reasons why the granting of an extension of time is deemed justified. For the time and manner of presenting an application for extension of time within which to file a petition for writ of certiorari, see Rules 34, 35(2), and 50. Such applications are not favored.

23.

The Petition for Certiorari.

1. The petition for writ of certiorari shall contain in the order here indicated —

(a) A reference to the official and unofficial reports of the opinions delivered in the courts below, if any, and if reported. Any such opinions shall be appended as provided in subparagraph (i) hereof.

(b) A concise statement of the grounds on which the jurisdiction of this court is invoked, showing:

(i) The date of the judgment or decree sought to be reviewed, and the time of its entry;

(ii) The date of any order respecting a rehearing, and the date and terms of any order granting an extension of time within which to petition for certiorari; and

(iii) The statutory provision believed to confer on this court jurisdiction to review the judgment or decree in question by writ of certiorari.

(c) The questions presented for review, expressed in the terms and circumstances of the case but without unnecessary detail. The statement of a question presented will be deemed to include every subsidiary question fairly comprised therein.

Only the questions set forth in the petition or fairly comprised therein will be considered by the court.

(d) The constitutional provisions, treaties, statutes, ordinances, or regulations which the case involves, setting them out verbatim, and citing the volume and page where they may be found in the official edition. If the provisions involved are lengthy, their citation alone will suffice at this point, and their pertinent text shall be set forth in an appendix.

(e) A concise statement of the case containing the facts material to the consideration of the questions presented.

(f) If review of the judgment of a state court is sought, the statement of the case shall also specify the stage in the proceedings in the court of first instance and in the appellate court, at which, and the manner in which, the federal questions sought to be reviewed were raised; the method of raising them (e.g., by a pleading, by request to charge and exceptions, by assignment of error); and the way in which they were passed upon by the court; such pertinent quotations of specific portions of the record, or summary thereof, with specific reference to the places in the record where the matter appears (e.g., ruling on exception, portion of the court's charge and exception thereto, assignment of errors) as will show that the federal question was timely and properly raised so as to give this court jurisdiction to review the judgment on writ of certiorari.

Where the portions of the record relied upon under this subparagraph are voluminous, then they shall be included in an appendix to the petition, which may, if more convenient, be separately presented.

(g) If review of the judgment of a federal court is sought, the statement of the case shall also show the basis for federal jurisdiction in the court of first instance.

(h) A direct and concise argument amplifying the reasons relied on for the allowance of the writ. See Rule 19.

(i) There shall be appended to the petition a copy of any opinions delivered upon the rendering of the judgment or decree sought to be reviewed, including all opinions of courts on administrative agencies in the case, and, if reference thereto is necessary to ascertain the grounds of the judgment or decree, opinions in companion cases. The opinions shall include the caption showing the name of the court or agency issuing the same and the title and numbers of the case and the date of their entry. If whatever is required by this paragraph to be appended to the petition is voluminous, it may, if more convenient, be separately presented.

(j) If review of the judgment or decree of a state court is sought, there shall also be appended to the petition a copy of the judgment or decree in question and any order on rehearing; and, if review of the judgment or decree of a federal court is sought, there shall similarly be appended a copy of such judgment or decree and any order on rehearing, which may however be limited to the portions thereof sought to be reviewed. The judgments, decrees, or orders on rehearing shall include the caption showing the name of the court issuing the same, the title and number of the case, and the date of entry of such judgment, decree and order.

2. The petition for writ of certiorari shall be printed in conformity with Rule 39.

3. All contentions in support of a petition for writ of certiorari shall be set forth in the body of the petition, as provided in subparagraph (h) of paragraph 1 of this rule. No separate brief in support of a petition for writ of certiorari will be received, and the clerk will refuse to file any petition for writ of certiorari to which is annexed or appended any supporting brief.

4. The failure of a petitioner to present with accuracy, brevity, and clearness whatever is essential to a ready and adequate understanding of the points requiring consideration will be a sufficient reason for denying his petition.

5. Where several cases are sought to be reviewed on certiorari to the same court that involve identical or closely related questions, it shall suffice to file a single petition for writ of certiorari covering all the cases.

24*

Brief in Opposition — Reply — Supplemental Briefs.

1. Counsel for the respondent shall have thirty days (unless enlarged by the court or a justice thereof, or by the clerk under the provisions of paragraph 5 of Rule 34), after receipt of a petition, within which to file forty printed copies of an opposing brief disclosing any matter or ground why the cause should not be reviewed by this court. See Rule 19. Such brief in opposition shall comply with Rule 39 and with the requirements of Rule 40 governing a respondent's brief, and shall be served as prescribed by Rule 33. In cases where the United States or any agency, officer or employee thereof is the respondent, the respondent shall have an additional twenty days to file the said opposing brief.

2. No motion by a respondent to dismiss a petition for writ of certiorari will be received. Objections to the jurisdiction of the court to grant writs of certiorari may be included in briefs in opposition to petitions therefor.

3. Upon the expiration of the period for filing the respondent's brief, or upon an express waiver of the right to file, or upon the actual filing of such brief in a shorter time, the petition and brief, if any, shall be distributed by the clerk to the court for its consideration.

4. Reply briefs addressed to arguments first raised in the briefs in opposition may be filed, but distribution under paragraph 3 hereof will not be delayed pending the filing of such briefs.

5. Any party may file a supplemental brief at any time while a petition for a writ of certiorari is pending calling attention to new cases or legislation or other intervening matter not available at the time of his last filing.

25.

Order Granting or Denying Certiorari.

1. Whenever a petition for writ of certiorari to review a decision of any court is granted, the clerk shall enter an order to that effect, and shall forthwith notify the court below and counsel of record of the granting of the petition. If the record has not previously been filed, the clerk of this court shall request the clerk of the court possessed of the record to certify it and transmit it to this court. A formal writ shall not issue unless specially directed.

2. Whenever application for a writ of certiorari to review a decision of any court is denied, the clerk shall enter an order to that effect, and shall forthwith notify the court below and counsel of record. The order of denial will not be suspended pending disposition of a petition for rehearing except by order of the court or of a justice thereof.

26.

Use of Single Appendix.

After certiorari has been granted any portion of the record to which the parties wish to direct the court's particular attention shall be printed in a single appendix prepared by the petitioner under the procedures provided in Rule 36, but the fact that any part of the record has not been printed shall not prevent the parties or the court from relying on it.

27.

Stay Pending Review on Certiorari.

Applications pursuant to 28 U.S.C. § 2101(f) to a justice of this court will normally not be entertained unless application for a stay has first been made to a judge of the court rendering the decision sought to be reviewed, or to such court, or unless the security offered below has been disapproved by such judge or court. All such applications are governed by Rules 50 and 51.

---

* Revised on November 22, 1971

PART VI. JURISDICTION OF CERTIFIED QUESTIONS.

28.

Questions Certified by a Court of Appeals or by the Court of Claims.

1. Where a court of appeals or the Court of Claims shall certify to this court a question or proposition of law, concerning which it desires instruction for the proper decision of a cause, the certificate shall contain a statement of the nature of the cause and of the facts on which such question or proposition of law arises. Questions of fact cannot be certified. Only questions or propositions of law may be certified, and they must be distinct and definite.

2. If in a cause certified by a court of appeals it appears that there is special reason therefor, this court may on application, or on its own motion, require that the entire record be sent up, so that it may consider and decide the entire matter in controversy.

29.

Procedure in Certified Cases.

1. When a case is certified, the certificate itself constitutes the record. The clerk will upon receipt thereof from the court below notify the appellant in the court of appeals, or the plaintiff in the Court of Claims, who shall thereupon pay the docket fee, after which the case will be placed on the docket. If the appellant or plaintiff fails to pay the fee, the appellee or defendant may do so. The appearance of counsel for the party paying the fee shall be entered at the time of payment.

2. After docketing, the certificate shall be submitted to the court for a preliminary examination to determine whether the case shall be set for argument or whether the certificate will be dismissed.

3. Any portion of the record to which the parties wish to direct the court's particular attention shall be printed in a single appendix prepared by the appellant or plaintiff in the court below under the procedures provided in Rule 36, but the fact that any part of the record has not been printed shall not prevent the parties or the court from relying on it.

4. Briefs on the merits in cases on certificates shall comply with Rules 39, 40 and 41, except that the brief of the party who was appellant or plaintiff below shall be filed within forty-five days of the order setting the case down for argument.

PART VII. JURISDICTION TO ISSUE EXTRAORDINARY WRITS

30.

Considerations Governing Issuance of Extraordinary Writs.

The issuance by the court of any writ authorized by 28 U.S.C. § 1651(a) is not a matter of right but of sound discretion sparingly exercised. See the following cases, which are cited by way of illustration only: *Ex parte Bollman and Swartwout,* 4 Cranch 75; *Ex parte Peru,* 318 U.S. 578; *Ex parte Abernathy,* 320 U.S. 219; *Ex parte Hawk,* 321 U.S. 114; *House* v. *Mayo,* 324 U.S. 42; *U.S. Alkali Export Assn.* v. *United States,* 325 U.S. 196; *DeBeers Consol. Mines* v. *United States,* 325 U.S. 212; *Ex parte Betz,* 329 U.S. 672; *Ex parte Fahey,* 332 U.S. 258.

31.

Procedure on Applications for Extraordinary Writs.

1. The petition in any proceeding seeking the issuance of a writ by this court authorized by 28 U.S.C. § 1651(a) or 28 U.S.C. § 2241 shall be prefaced by a motion for leave to file such petition, and both shall be printed. All contentions in support of the petition shall be included in the petition. The case will be placed upon the docket when forty copies of the printed papers, with proof of service as prescribed by Rule 33 (subject to paragraph 5 of this rule), are filed with the clerk and the docket fee is paid. The appearance of counsel for the petitioner must be entered at this time.

2. If the petition seeks issuance of a common law writ of certiorari under 28 U.S.C. § 1651(a), there may also be filed, at the time of docketing, a certified copy of the record, including all proceedings in the court to which the writ is sought to be directed. However, the filing of such record is not required. The petition shall, except for the addition of the motion for leave to file, follow as far as may be the form for a petition for certiorari prescribed by Rule 23, and shall set forth with particularity why the relief sought is not available in any other court, or cannot be had through other appellate processes. The respondent may, within thirty days after receipt of the motion and petition, file forty printed copies of a brief in opposition, as provided in Rule 24.

3. If the petition seeks issuance of a writ of prohibition, a writ of mandamus, or both in the alternative, it shall set forth with particularity why the relief sought is not available in any other court, and there shall be appended to such petition a copy of the judgment or order in respect of which the writ is sought, including a copy of any opinion rendered in that connection, and such other papers as may be essential to an understanding of the petition. The petition shall follow, insofar as applicable, the form for the petition for writ of certiorari prescribed by Rule 23. The motion and petition shall be served on the judge or judges to whom the writ is sought to be directed, and shall also be served on every other party to the proceeding in respect of which relief is desired. The judge or judges, and the other parties, may, within thirty days after receipt of the motion and petition, file forty printed copies of a brief or briefs in opposition thereto, with proof of service. If the judge or judges concerned do not desire to contest the motion and petition, they may so advise the clerk and all parties by letter. All parties, other than the judge or judges, who are served pursuant to this paragraph, shall also be deemed to be respondents for all purposes in the proceeding in this court.

4. When briefs in opposition under paragraphs 2 and 3 of this rule have been filed, or when the time within which they may be filed has expired, or upon an express waiver of the right to file, the motion, petition, and briefs shall be distributed to the court by the clerk.

5. If the petition seeks issuance of an original writ of habeas corpus, it shall comply with the requirements of 28 U.S.C. § 2242, and in particular with the last paragraph thereof; and, if the relief sought is from the judgment of a state court, shall specifically set forth how and wherein the petitioner has exhausted his remedies in the state courts. See *Ex parte Abernathy,* 320 U.S. 219; *Ex parte Hawk,* 321 U.S. 114. Proceedings under this paragraph will be *ex parte,* unless the court requires the respondent to show cause why leave to file the petition for a writ of habeas corpus should not be granted. Neither refusal of leave to file, without more, nor an order of transfer under authority of 28 U.S.C. § 2241(b), is an adjudication on the merits, and the former action is to be taken as without prejudice to a further application to any other court for the relief sought.

6. If the court orders the cause set down for argument, the clerk will notify the parties whether additional briefs are required, when they must be filed, how much time has been allotted for oral argument, and, if the case involves a petition for common law certiorari, that the parties shall proceed to print an appendix pursuant to Rule 36.

32.

Certiorari to Correct Diminution of Record Abolished.

The writ of certiorari to correct diminution of the record is abolished.

PART VIII. PRACTICE.

33.

Service and Special Rule Where Constitutionality of Act of Congress in Issue.

1. Whenever any pleading, motion, notice, brief or other document is required by these rules to be served, such service may be made personally or by mail on each adverse party. If the document to be served is printed, three copies shall be served on each other party separately represented in the proceeding. If the document is not printed, service of a single copy on each other party separately represented shall suffice. If personal, service shall consist of delivery, at the office of counsel of record, to counsel or a clerk therein. If by mail, it shall consist of depositing the same in a United States post office or mail box, with first class postage prepaid, addressed to counsel of record at his post office address. Where the person on whom service is to be made resides 500 miles or more from the person effecting service, such mailing must be made with air mail postage prepaid.

2. (a) If the United States or an officer or agency thereof is a party, service of all briefs, pleadings, notices and papers shall, notwithstanding the foregoing paragraph, be made upon the Solicitor General, Department of Justice, Washington, D.C. 20530. Where an agency of the United States authorized by law to appear in its own behalf is a party in addition to the United States, such agency shall also be served, in addition to the Solicitor General, in every case.

(b) In any proceeding in whatever court arising wherein the constitutionality of any Act of Congress affecting the public interest is drawn in question and the United States or any agency, officer or employee thereof is not a party, all initial pleadings, motions or papers in this court shall recite that 28 U.S.C. § 2403 may be applicable and shall be served upon the Solicitor General, Department of Justice, Washington, D.C. 20530. In proceedings from any court of the United States as defined by 28 U.S.C. § 451, such initial pleading, motion or paper shall state whether or not any such court has, pursuant to 28 U.S.C. § 2403, certified to the Attorney General the fact that the constitutionality of such Act of Congress was drawn in question.

3. Whenever proof of service is required by these rules, it must be stated that all parties required to be served have been served and such service may be shown, either by indorsement on the document served or by separate instrument, by any one of the methods set forth below; and it is not necessary that service on each party required to be served be effected in the same manner or evidenced by the same proof:

(a) By an acknowledgment of service of the document in question, signed by counsel of record for the party served.

(b) By a certificate of service of the document in question, reciting the fact and circumstances of service in compliance with the appropriate paragraph of this rule, such certificate to be signed by a member of the bar of this court representing the party in behalf of whom such service has been effected. If counsel certifying to such service has not up to that time entered his appearance in this court in respect of the cause in which such service is made, his appearance shall accompany the certificate of service if the same is to be filed in this court.

(c) By an affidavit of service of the document in question, reciting the fact and circumstances of service in compliance with the appropriate paragraph of this rule, whenever such service is effected by any person not a member of the bar of this court.

4. Whenever proof of service is required by these rules, it must accompany or be indorsed upon the document in question at the time such document is presented to the clerk for filing. Any document filed with the clerk by or on behalf of counsel of record whose appearance has not previously been entered must be accompanied by an entry of appearance.

34.

Computation and Enlargement of Time.

1. In computing any period of time prescribed or allowed by these rules, by order of court, or by any applicable statute, the day of the act, event, or default after which the designated period of time begins to run is not to be included. The last day of the period so computed is to be included, unless it is a Sunday or a legal holiday, in which event the period runs until the end of the next day which is neither a Sunday nor a holiday. A half holiday shall be considered as other days and not as a holiday.

2. Whenever any justice of this court or the clerk is empowered by law or under any provision of these rules to extend the time within which a party may petition for a writ of certiorari or docket an appeal or file any brief or paper, an application seeking such extension must be presented to the clerk within the period sought to be extended. Applications for extension of time to file petitions for certiorari or to docket appeals shall be submitted at least ten days before the expiration of the period sought to be extended and will not be granted except in the most extraordinary circumstances if filed during the last ten days of such period.

3. All applications seeking an extension of time within which a party may petition for a writ of certiorari or docket an appeal or file any brief or paper must be presented and served upon all other parties as provided in Rule 50, but such applications for extension of time, if once denied, may not be renewed before another justice after expiration of the period sought to be extended.

4. Whenever a justice or the clerk has granted an extension of time within which a party may petition for a writ of certiorari or docket an appeal or file any brief or paper it shall be the duty of the party to whom such extension is granted to give all other parties to the proceeding prompt notice thereof.

5. All applications for extensions of time to file briefs, motions, appendices or other papers, to designate parts of records for printing in appendices, or otherwise to comply with time limits provided by these rules, except applications for extensions of time to file petitions for certiorari, to docket appeals, to petition for rehearings or to issue mandates shall in the first instance be acted upon by the clerk, whether addressed to him, to the court or to a justice. Any party aggrieved by the clerk's action on such application may request that it be submitted to a justice or to the court.

35.

Motions.

1. Every motion to the court shall state clearly its object and the facts on which it is based. A brief in support of the motion (other than motions under Rule 31) may be filed therewith.

2. Motions and applications addressed to a single justice need not be printed, and only a typewritten original need be filed. Motions in actions within the court's original jurisdiction shall be printed, and sixty copies shall be filed. Motions to dismiss or affirm made under Rule 16, motions to bring up the entire record under Rule 28(2), motions for permission to file a brief *amicus curiae*, any motions the granting of which would be dispositive of the entire case or would affect the final judgment to be entered (other than a motion to docket or dismiss under Rule 14, or a motion for voluntary dismissal under Rule 60), and any motions to the court accompanied by a supporting brief, shall likewise be printed, and forty copies of the motion and of the brief, if any, shall be filed. All other motions to the court need not be printed, and it shall be sufficient to file a typewritten original and nine legible typewritten copies; but the court may by subsequent order require any such motion to be printed by the moving party.

3. Motions to the court shall be filed with the clerk, with proof of service unless *ex parte* in nature. For applications and motions addressed to a single justice, see Rule 50. No motion shall be presented in open court, other than a motion for admission to the bar, except when the proceeding to which it refers is being argued. Oral argument will not be heard on any motion unless the court specially assigns it therefor.

4. Action by the court or a justice on contested motions will ordinarily, but not always, be withheld to permit responses by opposing parties, but such responses shall be made as promptly as possible considering the nature of the relief asked and any asserted need for emergency action, and, in any event, shall be made within ten days unless otherwise ordered by the court or a justice, or by the clerk under the provisions of paragraph 5 of Rule 34. Responses to printed motions shall be printed if time permits.

5. Printed motions must comply with Rule 39 with respect to format, signatures, and index. Typewritten motions must similarly comply with Rule 47.

36.

Printing of Appendices.

1. In the absence of a stipulation pursuant to paragraph 4 below, the appellant or petitioner shall, within forty-five days after the order noting or postponing jurisdiction or of the order granting the writ of certiorari, prepare and file forty copies of an appendix to the briefs which shall contain: (1) the relevant docket entries in the proceeding below; (2) any relevant pleading, charge, finding or opinion; (3) the judgment, order or decision in question; and (4) any other parts of the record to which the parties wish to direct the court's particular attention. At the same time or promptly thereafter the appellant or petitioner shall file with the clerk a statement of the costs of preparing the appendix. The appellant or petitioner shall serve at least three copies of the appendix and a copy of the statement of costs on each of the other parties to the proceeding.

2. The parties are encouraged to agree as to the contents of the appendix. In the absence of agreement, not later than ten days after the order noting or postponing jurisdiction or of the order granting the writ of certiorari, the appellant or petitioner shall serve on the appellee or respondent a designation of the parts of the record which he intends to include in the appendix and a statement of the issues which he intends to present for review. If in the judgment of the appellee or respondent the parts of the record designated by the appellant or petitioner are not sufficient, the appellee or respondent shall, within ten days after receipt of the designation, serve upon the appellant or petitioner a designation of additional parts to be included in the appendix. The appellant or petitioner shall include the parts thus designated in the appendix. In designating parts of the record for inclusion in the appendix, the parties shall have regard for the fact that the record on file with the clerk is always available to the court for reference and examination and shall not engage in unnecessary designation.

3. Unless the parties otherwise agree, the cost of producing the appendix shall initially be paid by the appellant or petitioner, but if the appellant or petitioner considers that parts of the record designated by the appellee or respondent for inclusion are unnecessary for the determination of the issues presented he may so advise the appellee or respondent and the appellee or respondent shall advance the cost of including such parts unless the court or a justice by appropriate order fixes the initial allocation of the expense of printing the appendix. The cost of producing the appendix shall be taxed as costs in the case, but if either party shall cause matter to be included in the appendix unnecessarily the court may impose the cost of producing such parts on the party.

4. If the parties shall so stipulate, or the court shall so order, preparation of the appendix may be deferred until after the briefs have been filed, and the appendix may be filed fourteen days after service of the brief of the appellee or respondent, or at least twenty days before the case is set for argument, whichever is later. If the preparation and filing of the appendix are thus deferred, the provisions of paragraph 1, 2, and 3 of this rule shall apply, except that the designations referred to therein shall be made by each party at the time his brief is served, and a statement of the issues presented shall be unnecessary.

5. If the deferred appendix authorized by paragraph 4 of this rule is employed, references in the briefs to the record may be to the pages of the parts of the record involved, in which event the original paging of each part of the record shall be indicated in the appendix by placing in brackets the number of each page at the place in the appendix where that page begins. Or if a party desires to refer in his brief directly to pages of the appendix, he may serve and file typewritten or page proof copies of his brief within the time required by Rule 41 with appropriate references to the pages of the parts of the record involved. In that event, within ten days after the appendix is filed he shall serve and file copies of the brief in the form prescribed by Rule 39 containing references to the pages of the appendix in place of or in addition to the initial references to the pages of the parts of the record involved. No other changes may be made in the brief as initially served and filed, except that typographical errors may be corrected.

6. At the beginning of the appendix there shall be inserted a list of the parts of the record which it contains in the order in which the parts are set out therein, with references to the pages of the appendix at which each part begins. The relevant docket entries shall be set out following the list of contents. Thereafter, other parts of the record shall be set out in chronological order. When matter contained in the reporter's transcript of proceedings is set out in the appendix, the page of the transcript at which such matter may be found shall be indicated in brackets immediately before the matter which is set out. Omissions in the text of papers or of the transcript must be indicated by asterisks. Immaterial formal matters (captions, subscriptions, acknowledgments, etc.) shall be omitted. A question and its answer may be contained in a single paragraph.

7. Exhibits designated for inclusion in the appendix may be contained in a separate volume, or volumes, suitably indexed. The transcript of a proceeding before an administrative agency, board, commission or officer used in an action in the district court shall be regarded as an exhibit for the purpose of this paragraph.

8. The court may by order dispense with the requirement of an appendix and may permit cases to be heard on the original record, with such copies of the record, or relevant parts thereof, as the court may require.

9. For good cause shown the time limits specified in this rule may be shortened or enlarged by the court, by a justice thereof, or by the clerk under the provisions of paragraph 5 of Rule 34.

37.

Translations.

Whenever any record transmitted to this court shall contain any document, paper, testimony, or other proceedings in a foreign language, without a translation of such document, paper, testimony, or other proceedings, made under the authority of the lower court, or admitted to be correct, the case shall be reported by the clerk, to the end that this court may order that a translation be supplied and, if necessary, printed as a part of the appendix.

38.

Models, Diagrams, and Exhibits of Material.

1. Models, diagrams, and exhibits of material forming part of the evidence taken in a case, and brought up to this court for its inspection, shall be placed in the custody of the clerk at least one week before the case is heard or submitted.

2. All such models, diagrams, and exhibits of material placed in the custody of the clerk must be taken away by the parties within forty days after the case is decided. When this is not done, it shall be the duty of the clerk to notify counsel to remove the articles forthwith; and if they are not removed within a reasonable time after such notice, the clerk shall destroy them, or make such other disposition of them as to him may seem best.

39.

Form of Appendices, Petitions, Briefs, Etc.

1. All appendices, petitions, motions and briefs, printed for the use of the court must be in such form and size that they can be conveniently bound together, so as to make an ordinary octavo

volume, having pages 6-1/8 by 9-1/4 inches and type matter 4-1/6 by 7-1/6 inches, except that appendices in patent cases may be printed in such size as is necessary to utilize copies of patent documents. They and all quotations contained therein, and the matter appearing on the covers, must be printed in clear type (never smaller than 11-point type) adequately leaded; and the paper must be opaque and unglazed. If footnotes are included, they may not be printed in type smaller than 9-point.

2. All printed documents presented to the court, other than appendices, must bear on the cover the name and post office address of the member of the bar of this court who is counsel of record for the party concerned, and upon whom service is to be made. The individual names of other counsel and, if desired, their post office addresses, may be added. The body of the document shall at its close bear the printed names of counsel of record and of such other individual counsel as may be desired. One copy of every printed motion filed with the clerk (other than a motion to dismiss or affirm under Rule 16) must in addition bear, at the appropriate place in the body thereof, the manuscript signature of counsel of record.

3. All printed documents presented to the court other than appendices, which in this respect are governed by Rule 36, shall, unless they are less than ten pages in length, be preceded by a subject index of the matter contained therein, with page references, and a table of the cases (alphabetically arranged), text books and statutes cited, with references to the pages where they are cited.

4. Printing, as the term is used in these rules, shall include any process capable of producing a clear black image on white paper but shall not include ordinary carbon copies. If papers are filed in a form which is not clearly legible, the clerk will require that new copies be substituted, but the filing shall not thereby be deemed untimely.

40.

Briefs — In General.

1. Briefs of an appellant or petitioner on the merits shall be printed as prescribed in Rule 39, and shall contain in the order here indicated —

(a) A reference to the official and unofficial reports of the opinions delivered in the courts below, if there were such and they have been reported.

(b) A concise statement of the grounds on which the jurisdiction of this court is invoked, with citation to the statutory provision and to the time factors upon which such jurisdiction rests.

(c) The constitutional provisions, treaties, statutes, ordinances and regulations which the case involves, setting them out verbatim, and citing the volume and page where they may be found in the official edition. If the provisions involved are lengthy, their citation alone will suffice at this point, and their pertinent text shall be set forth in an appendix.

(d)(1) The questions presented for review, expressed in the terms and circumstances of the cases but without unnecessary detail. The statement of a question presented will be deemed to include every subsidiary question fairly comprised therein.

(2) The phrasing of the questions presented need not be identical with that set forth in the jurisdictional statement or the petition for certiorari, but the brief may not raise additional questions or change the substance of the questions already presented in those documents. Questions not presented according to this paragraph will be disregarded, save as the court, at its option, may notice a plain error not presented.

(e) A concise statement of the case containing all that is material to the consideration of the questions presented, with appropriate references to the appendix, e.g., (A. 12) or to the record, e.g., (R. 12).

(f) In briefs on the merits, or in any briefs wherein the argument portion extends beyond twenty printed pages, a summary of argument, suitably paragraphed, which should be a succinct, but accurate and clear, condensation of the argument actually made in the body of the brief. It should not be a mere repetition of the headings under which the argument is arranged.

(g) The argument, exhibiting clearly the points of fact and of law being presented, citing the authorities and statutes relied upon.

(h) A conclusion, specifying with particularity the relief to which the party believes himself entitled.

2. Whenever, in the brief of any party, a reference is made to the appendix or the record, it must be accompanied by the appropriate page number. When the reference is to a part of the evidence, the page citation must be specific. If the reference is to an exhibit, both the page number at which the exhibit appears and at which it was offered in evidence must be indicated, e.g., (Pl. Ex. 14; R. 199, 2134).

3. The brief filed by an appellee or respondent shall conform to the foregoing requirements, except that no statement of the case need be made beyond what may be deemed necessary in correcting any inaccuracy or omission in the statement of the other side, and except that items (a), (b), (c) and (d) need not be included unless the appellee or respondent is dissatisfied with their presentation by the other side.

4. Reply briefs shall conform to such portions of this rule as are applicable to the briefs of an appellee or respondent, but need not contain a summary of argument, regardless of their length, if appropriately divided by topical headings.

5. Briefs must be compact, logically arranged with proper headings, concise, and free from burdensome, irrelevant, immaterial, and scandalous matter. Briefs not complying with this paragraph may be disregarded and stricken by the court.

41.

Briefs on the Merits — Time for Filing.

1. Counsel for the appellant or petitioner shall file with the clerk forty copies of his printed brief on the merits, within forty-five days of the order noting or postponing probable jurisdiction or of the order granting the writ of certiorari.

2. Forty printed copies of the brief of the appellee or respondent shall be filed with the clerk within thirty days after the receipt by him of the brief filed by the appellant or petitioner.

3. Reply briefs will be received up to three days before the case is called for hearing; but, since later filing may delay consideration of the case, only by leave of court thereafter.

4. The periods of time stated in paragraphs 1 and 2 of this rule may be enlarged as provided in Rule 34, upon motion duly made; or, if a case is advanced for hearing, the time for filing briefs may be abridged as circumstances shall require, pursuant to order of the court on its own or a party's motion.

5. Whenever a party desires to present late authorities, newly enacted legislation, or other intervening matters that were not available in time to have been included in his brief in chief, he may file forty printed copies of a supplemental brief, restricted to such new matter and otherwise in conformity with these rules, up to the time the case is called for hearing, or, by leave of court, thereafter.

6. No brief will be received through the clerk or otherwise after a case has been argued or submitted, except upon special leave.

7. No brief will be received by the clerk unless the same shall be accompanied by proof of service as required by Rule 33.

42.

Briefs of an Amicus Curiae.

1. A brief of an *amicus curiae* prior to consideration of the jurisdictional statement or of the petition for writ of certiorari, filed with the consent of the parties, or a motion for leave to file when consent is refused, may be filed only if submitted a reasonable time prior to the consideration of the jurisdictional statement or of the

petition for writ of certiorari. Such motions are not favored. Distribution to the court under the applicable rules of the jurisdictional statement or of the petition for writ of certiorari, and its consideration thereof, will not be delayed pending the receipt of such brief or the filing of such motion.

2. A brief of an *amicus curiae* in cases before the court on the merits may be filed only after order of the court or when accompanied by written consent of all parties to the case and presented within the time allowed for the filing of the brief of the party supported.

3. When consent to the filing of a brief of an *amicus curiae* is refused by a party to the case, a motion for leave to file may timely be presented to the court. It shall concisely state the nature of the applicant's interest, set forth facts or questions of law that have not been, or reasons for believing that they will not adequately be, presented by the parties, and their relevancy to the disposition of the case; and it shall in no event exceed five printed pages in length. A party served with such motion may seasonably file an objection concisely stating the reasons for withholding consent.

4. Consent to the filing of a brief of an *amicus curiae* need not be had when the brief is presented for the United States sponsored by the Solicitor General; for any agency of the United States authorized by law to appear in its own behalf, sponsored by its appropriate legal representative; for a State, Territory, or Commonwealth sponsored by its attorney general; or for a political subdivision of a State, Territory, or Commonwealth sponsored by the authorized law officer thereof.

5. All briefs, motions, and responses filed under this rule shall be printed; shall comply with the applicable provisions of Rules 35, 39, and 40 (except that it shall be sufficient to set forth the interest of the *amicus curiae,* the argument, the summary of argument if required by Rule 40(1)(f) and the conclusion); and shall be accompanied by proof of service as required by Rule 33.

43.

Call and Order of the Calendar.

1. The clerk shall, at the commencement of each term, prepare a calendar, consisting of the cases that have become or will be available for argument, which shall be arranged in the first instance in the order in which they are ordered set down for argument, and which shall indicate the time allotted to each. The arrangement of cases on the calendar shall be subject to modification in the light of availability of appendices, extensions of time to file briefs, and of orders granting motions to advance or postpone or specially setting particular cases for argument. Cases will be calendared so that they will not normally be called for argument less than two weeks after the brief of the appellee or respondent has been filed. The clerk shall keep the calendar current throughout the term, adding cases as they are set down for argument, and making rearrangements as required. He shall periodically publish hearing lists in advance of each argument session, for the convenience of counsel and the information of the public.

2. Unless otherwise ordered, the court, on the second Monday of each term, will commence calling cases for argument in the order in which they stand on the calendar, and proceed from day to day during the term in the same order, except as hereinafter provided.

3. Cases will not be called until they are actually reached for argument. The clerk will seasonably advise counsel when they are required to be present in court.

4. Cases may be advanced or postponed by order of the court, upon motion duly made showing good cause therefor.

5. Two or more cases, involving the same question, may, on the court's own motion or by special permission on the motion or stipulation of the parties, be argued together as one case, or on such terms as may be prescribed.

44.

Oral Argument.

1. Oral argument should undertake to emphasize and clarify the written argument appearing in the briefs theretofore filed. The court looks with disfavor on any oral argument that is read from a prepared text.

2. The appellant or petitioner shall be entitled to open and conclude the argument. But when there are cross-appeals or cross-writs of certiorari they shall be argued together as one case and in the time of one case, and the court will, by order seasonably made, advise the parties which one is to open and close.

3. Unless otherwise directed, one half hour on each side will be allowed for argument. Any request for additional time shall be presented not later than fifteen days after service of the petitioner's, or appellant's, brief on the merits by letter addressed to the clerk (copy to be sent opposing counsel), and shall set forth with specificity and conciseness why the case cannot be presented within the half hour limitation.

4. Unless additional time has been granted, one counsel only will be heard for each side, except by special permission when there are several parties on the same side. Divided arguments are not favored by the court.

5. In any case, and regardless of the number of counsel participating, a fair opening of the case shall be made by the party having the opening and closing.

6. Oral argument will not be heard on behalf of any party for whom no brief has been filed.

7. Counsel for an *amicus curiae* whose brief has been duly filed pursuant to Rule 42 may, with the consent of a party, argue orally on the side of such party, provided that neither the time nor the number of counsel permitted for oral argument on behalf of that party under the preceding paragraphs of this rule will thereby be exceeded. In the absence of such consent, argument by counsel for an *amicus curiae* may be made only by special leave of court, on motion particularly setting forth why such argument is thought to provide assistance to the court not otherwise available. Such motions, unless made on behalf of the United States or of a State, Territory, Commonwealth, or Possession, are not favored.

45.

Submission on Briefs by One or Both Parties Without Oral Argument.

1. The court looks with disfavor on the submission of cases on briefs, without oral argument, and therefore may, notwithstanding such submission, require oral argument by the parties.

2. When a case is called and no counsel appear to present argument, but briefs have been filed, the case will be treated as having been submitted.

3. When a case is called, if a brief has been filed for only one of the parties and no counsel appears to present oral argument for either party, the case will be regarded as submitted on that brief.

46.

Joint or Several Appeals or Petitions for Writs of Certiorari; Summons and Severance Abolished.

Parties interested jointly, severally, or otherwise in a judgment may join in an appeal or a petition for writ of certiorari therefrom; or, without summons and severance, any one or more of them may appeal or petition separately or any two or more of them may join in an appeal or petition.

47.

Form of Typewritten Papers.

1. All papers specifically permitted by these rules to be presented to the court without being printed shall, subject to Rule 53(1), be typewritten or otherwise duplicated upon opaque, unglazed paper, 8-1/2 by 13 inches in size (legal cap), and shall be stapled or bound at the upper left-hand corner. The typed matter, except quotations, must be doublespaced. When more than one original is required by any rule, the copies must be legible.

2. The original copy of all typewritten motions and applications must be signed in manuscript by the party or by counsel, but,

in a cause not yet docketed, such counsel need not be a member of the bar of this court.

48.

Death, Substitution, and Revivor — Public Officers, Substitution and Descriptions.

1. Whenever either party shall die after filing notice of appeal to this court or filing of petition for writ of certiorari in this court, the proper representative of the deceased may appear and, upon motion, be substituted as a party to the proceeding. If such representative shall not voluntarily become a party, the other party may suggest the death on the record, and on motion obtain an order that, unless such representative shall become a party within a designated time, the party moving for such an order, if appellee or respondent, shall be entitled to have the appeal or petition for or writ of certiorari dismissed or the judgment vacated for mootness, as may be appropriate; and, if the party so moving be appellant or petitioner, shall be entitled to proceed as in other cases of nonappearance by appellee or respondent. Such substitution, or, in default thereof, such suggestions, must be made within six months after the death of the party, else the case shall abate.

2. Whenever, in the case of a suggestion made as provided in paragraph 1 of this rule, the case cannot be revived in the court whose judgment is sought to be reviewed because the deceased party has no proper representative within the jurisdiction of that court, but does have a proper representative elsewhere, proceedings shall then be had as this court may direct.

3. When a public officer is a party to a proceeding here in his official capacity and during its pendency dies, resigns, or otherwise ceases to hold office, the action does not abate and his successor is automatically substituted as a party. Proceedings following the substitution shall be in the name of the substituted party, but any misnomer not affecting the substantial rights of the parties shall be disregarded. An order of substitution may be entered at any time, but the omission to enter such an order shall not affect the substitution.

4. When a public officer is a party in a proceeding here in his official capacity, he may be described as a party by his official title rather than by name; but the court may require his name to be added.

49.

Custody of Prisoners in Habeas Corpus Proceedings.

1. Pending review of a decision in a habeas corpus proceeding commenced before a court, justice or judge of the United States for the release of a prisoner, a person having custody of the prisoner shall not transfer custody to another unless such transfer is directed in accordance with the provisions of this rule. Upon application of a custodian showing a need therefor, the court, justice or judge rendering the decision may make an order authorizing transfer and providing for the substitution of the successor custodian as a party.

2. Pending review of a decision failing or refusing to release a prisoner in such a proceeding, the prisoner may be detained in the custody from which release is sought, or in other appropriate custody, or may be enlarged upon his recognizance, with or without surety, as may appear fitting to the court or justice or judge rendering the decision, or to the court of appeals or to this court, or to a judge or justice of either court.

3. Pending review of a decision ordering the release of a prisoner in such a proceeding, the prisoner shall be enlarged upon his recognizance, with or without surety, unless the court or justice or judge rendering the decision, or the court of appeals or this court, or a judge or justice of either court, shall otherwise order.

4. An initial order respecting the custody or enlargement of the prisoner, and any recognizance or surety taken, shall govern review in the court of appeals and in this court unless for special reasons shown to the court of appeals or to this court, or to a judge

or justice of either court, the order shall be modified or an independent order respecting custody, enlargement or surety shall be made.

50.

Applications to Individual Justices; Practice in Chambers.

1. All motions and applications addressed to individual justices shall normally be submitted to the clerk, who will promptly transmit them to the justice concerned. If oral argument on the application is desired, request therefor shall accompany the application.

2. All motions and applications addressed to individual justices shall be accompanied by proof of service on all other parties. In urgent cases, proof of telegraphic dispatch to such parties of notice that the motion, application, or request is being made will suffice.

3. The clerk will in due course advise all counsel concerned, by means as speedy as may be appropriate, of the time and place of the hearing, if any, or, if no hearing is requested or granted, of the disposition made of the motion or application.

4. During the term, applications will be addressed to the justice duly allotted to the circuit within which the case arises. The court or the chief justice will seasonably instruct the clerk as to the distribution of applications during vacation, and whenever a circuit justice is temporarily absent or disabled.

5. A justice denying an application made to him will note his denial thereon. Thereafter, unless action on such application is by law restricted to the circuit justice, or is out of time under Rule 34(3), the party making the application may renew the same to any other justice, subject to the provisions of this rule. Except where the denial has been without prejudice, such renewed applications are not favored.

6. Any justice to whom an application for a stay or for bail is submitted may refer the same to the court for determination.

51.

Stays.

1. Stays may be granted by a justice of this court as permitted by law; and writs of injunction may be granted by any justice in cases where they might be granted by the court. For supersedeas on appeal, see Rule 18; for stay pending review on certiorari, see Rule 27.

2. All applications for stays or injunctions made pursuant to this or any other rule must show whether application for the relief sought has first been made to the appropriate court or courts below, or to a judge or judges thereof, and shall be submitted as provided in Rule 50. See Rules 18(2) and 27.

3. If an application for a stay addressed to the court is received in vacation, the clerk will refer it pursuant to Rule 50(4).

52.

Fees.

In pursuance of 28 U.S.C. § 1911, the fees to be charged by the clerk of this court are fixed as follows:

(a) For docketing a case on appeal (except a motion to docket and dismiss under Rule 14(3), wherein the fee is $25.00) or on petition for writ of certiorari or docketing any other proceeding, $100.00, to be increased to $150.00 in a case on appeal or writ of certiorari when oral argument is permitted.

(b) For making a copy (except a photographic reproduction) of any record or paper, and comparison thereof, 40 cents per page of 250 words or fraction thereof; for comparing for certification a copy (except a photographic reproduction) of any record or paper when such copy is furnished by the person requesting its certification, 10 cents for each page of 250 words or fraction thereof.

For a photographic reproduction and certification of any record or paper, 50 cents per page; and for comparing with the original thereof any photographic reproduction of any record or paper, when furnished by the person requesting its certification, 5 cents for each page, and 50 cents for each certificate.

(c) For a certificate and seal, $3.00.

(d) For an admission to the Bar and certificate under seal, $25.00.

(e) For a duplicate certificate of an admission to the Bar under seal, $10.00.

PART IX. SPECIAL PROCEEDINGS.

53.

Proceedings in Forma Pauperis.

1. A party desiring to proceed in this court *in forma pauperis* shall file a motion for leave so to proceed, together with his affidavit setting forth facts showing that he comes within the statutory requirements. See 28 U.S.C. § 1915; *Adkins* v. *Dupont Co.,* 335 U.S. 331. One copy of each will suffice. Papers in cases presented under this rule should, whenever possible, comply with Rule 47.

2. With the motion and affidavit there shall be filed the appropriate substantive document — statement as to jurisdiction, petition for writ of certiorari, or motion for leave to file, as the case may be — which shall comply in all respects with the rules governing the same, except that it shall be sufficient to file a single copy thereof.

3. When the papers required by paragraphs 1 and 2 of this rule are presented to the clerk, accompanied by proof of service as prescribed by Rule 33, he will, without payment of any docket or other fees, file them, and place the case on the docket.

4. The appellee or respondent in a case *in forma pauperis* may respond in the same manner and within the same time as in any other case of the same nature, except that the filing of a single response, typewritten or otherwise duplicated, with proof of service as required by Rule 33, will suffice whenever petitioner or appellant has filed unprinted papers.

5. While making due allowance for cases presented under this rule by persons appearing *pro se,* the clerk will refuse to receive any motion for leave to proceed *in forma pauperis* when it and the papers submitted therewith do not comply with the substance of this court's rules, or when it appears that the accompanying papers are obviously out of time.

6. If, in a case presented under this rule, the court enters an order noting or postponing probable jurisdiction, or granting a writ of certiorari, and the case is set down for argument, the court will make such order respecting the furnishing of a record and the printing of an appendix as may be appropriate. The court may, in any case presented under this rule, require the furnishing of the record prior to its consideration of the motion papers.

7. Whenever the court appoints a member of the bar to serve as counsel for an indigent party, the briefs prepared by such counsel will, unless he requests otherwise, be printed under the supervision of the clerk; and the clerk will in any event reimburse such counsel for necessary travel expenses including first-class transportation from his home to Washington, D.C., and return in connection with the argument of the cause.

8. In any case arising on direct review of a judgment in a criminal case originating in a federal court where this court has granted certiorari or noted or postponed jurisdiction and where the defendant in the original proceeding is financially unable to obtain adequate representation or to meet the necessary expenses in this court, the court will appoint counsel who may be compensated, and whose necessary expenses may be repaid, to the extent provided by the Criminal Justice Act of 1964 (78 Stat. 552; 18 U.S.C. § 3006A).

54.

Veterans' and Seamen's Cases.

1. A veteran suing to establish reemployment rights under the provisions of Section 9(d) of the Universal Military Training and Service Act, as amended (50 U.S.C. App. § 459(d)), or under similar provisions of law exempting veterans from the payment of fees or court costs, may proceed upon typewritten papers as under Rule 53, except that the motion shall ask leave to proceed as a veteran, the affidavit shall set forth the moving party's status as a veteran, and the case will be placed on the docket.

2. A seaman suing pursuant to 28 U.S.C. § 1916 may proceed without prepayment of fees or costs or furnishing security therefor, but he is not relieved of printing costs nor entitled to proceed on typewritten papers except by separate motion, or unless, by motion and affidavit, he brings himself within Rule 53.

PART X. DISPOSITION OF CAUSES.

55.

Opinions of the Court.

1. All opinions of the court shall be handed to the clerk immediately upon the delivery thereof. He shall cause the same to be printed and shall deliver a copy to the reporter of decisions.

2. The original opinions shall be filed by the clerk for preservation.

3. Opinions printed under the supervision of the justices delivering the same need not be copied by the clerk into a book of records; but at the end of each term he shall cause them to be bound in a substantial manner, and when so bound they shall be deemed to have been recorded.

56.

Interest and Damages.

1. Where judgments for the payment of money are affirmed, and interest is properly allowable, it shall be calculated from the date of the entry of the judgment below until the same is paid, at the same rate that similar judgments bear interest in the courts of the state where such judgment was rendered.

2. In all cases where an appeal delays proceedings on the judgment of the lower court, and appears to have been sued out merely for delay, damages at a rate not exceeding 10 percent, in addition to interest, may be awarded upon the amount of the judgment.

3. In cases in admiralty, damages and interest may be allowed only if specially directed by the court.

4. Where a petition for writ of certiorari has been filed, and there appears to be no ground for granting such a writ, the court may, in appropriate cases, adjudge to the respondent reasonable damages for his delay.

57.

Costs.

1. In all cases of affirmance of any judgment or decree by this court, costs shall be paid by appellant or petitioner unless otherwise ordered by the court.

2. In cases of reversal or vacating of any judgment or decree by this court, costs shall be allowed to the appellant or petitioner, unless otherwise ordered by the court. The cost of the transcript of record from the court below shall be a part of such costs, and be taxable in that court as costs in the case.

3. The cost of printing the appendix in this court is a taxable item. The cost of printing briefs, motions, petitions, and jurisdictional statements is not a taxable item.

4. In cases where questions have been certified, including such cases where the certificate is dismissed, costs shall be equally divided unless otherwise ordered by the court; but where the entire record has been sent up (Rule 28, par. 2), and a decision is rendered on the whole matter in controversy, costs shall be allowed as provided in paragraphs 1 and 2 of this rule.

5. In all actions commenced prior to July 18, 1966, no costs shall be allowed in this court either for or against the United States or an officer or agency thereof, except where specially authorized by statute and directed by the court. In all other actions, costs as provided in this rule shall be allowed for or against the United States or an officer or agent thereof (unless expressly waived or otherwise ordered by the court) except that no such costs shall be allowed in criminal cases.

6. When costs are allowed in this court, it shall be the duty of the clerk to insert the amount thereof in the body of the mandate, or other proper process, sent to the court below, and annex to the same the bill of items taxed in detail. The prevailing side in such a case is not to submit to the clerk any bill of costs.

7. In appropriate instances, the court may adjudge double costs.

58.

Rehearings.

1. A petition for rehearing of judgments or decisions other than those denying or granting certiorari, may be filed with the clerk in term time or in vacation, within twenty-five days after judgment or decision, unless the time is shortened or enlarged by the court or a justice thereof. Such petition must briefly and distinctly state its grounds; it must be supported by a certificate of counsel to the effect that it is presented in good faith and not for delay; it must be printed in conformity with Rule 39; and forty copies, one of which shall bear the manuscript signature of counsel to the certificate, must be filed, accompanied by proof of service as prescribed by Rule 33. A petition for rehearing is not subject to oral argument, and will not be granted, except at the instance of a justice who concurred in the judgment or decision and with the concurrence of a majority of the court.

2. A petition for rehearing of orders on petitions for writs of certiorari may be filed with the clerk in term time or vacation, subject to the requirements respecting time, printing, number of copies furnished, manuscript signature to certificate, and service, as provided in paragraph 1 of this rule. Any petition filed under this paragraph must briefly and distinctly state grounds which are confined to intervening circumstances of substantial or controlling effect (e.g., *Sanitary Refrigerator Co.* v. *Winters,* 280 U.S. 30, 34, footnote 1; *Massey* v. *United States,* 291 U.S. 608), or to other substantial grounds available to petitioner although not previously presented (e.g., *Scribner-Schroth Co.* v. *Cleveland Trust Co.,* 305 U.S. 47, 50). Such petition is not subject to oral argument. A petition for rehearing filed under this paragraph must be supported by a certificate of counsel to the effect that it is presented in good faith and not for delay, and counsel must also certify that the petition is restricted to the grounds above specified.

3. No reply to a petition for rehearing will be received unless requested by the court. No petition for rehearing will be granted in the absence of such a request and an opportunity to submit a reply in response thereto.

4. Consecutive petitions for rehearings, and petitions for rehearing that are out of time under this rule, will not be received.

59.

Process; Mandates.

1. All process of this court shall be in the name of the President of the United States, and shall contain the given names, as well as the surnames, of the parties.

2. Subject to paragraph 3 of this rule, mandates shall issue as of course after the expiration of twenty-five days from the day the judgment is entered, unless the time is shortened or enlarged by an order of the court or of a justice thereof, or unless the parties stipulate that it be issued sooner. The filing of a petition for rehearing will, unless otherwise ordered, stay the mandate until disposition of such petition, and if the petition is then denied, the mandate shall issue forthwith. When, however, a petition for rehearing is not acted upon prior to adjournment or is filed after the court adjourns, the judgment or mandate of the court will not be stayed unless specifically so ordered by the court or a justice thereof.

3. In cases coming from federal courts, a formal mandate shall not issue unless specially directed. In the absence of such direction, it shall suffice for the clerk to send to the proper court, within the time and under the conditions set out in paragraph 2 of this rule, a copy of the opinion or order of this court, and a certified copy of the judgment of this court, which in cases under this paragraph shall include provisions for the recovery of costs if any are awarded.

60.

Dismissing Causes.

1. Whenever the parties thereto shall, by their attorneys of record, file with the clerk an agreement in writing that an appeal, petition for or writ of certiorari, or motion for leave to file or petition for an extraordinary writ be dismissed, specifying the terms as respects costs, and shall pay to the clerk any fees that may be due him, the clerk shall, without further reference to the court, enter an order of dismissal.

2. Whenever an appellant or petitioner in this court shall, by his attorney of record, file with the clerk a motion to dismiss a proceeding to which he is a party, with proof of service as prescribed by Rule 33, and shall tender to the clerk any fees and costs that may be due, the adverse party may within fifteen days after service thereof file an objection, limited to the quantum of damages and costs in this court alleged to be payable, or, in a proper case, to a showing that the moving party does not represent all appellants or petitioners if there are more than one. The clerk will refuse to receive any objection not so limited.

3. Where the objection goes to the standing of the moving party to represent the entire side, the party moving for dismissal may within ten days thereafter file a reply, after which time the matter shall be laid before the court for its determination.

4. If no objection is filed, or if upon objection going only to the quantum of damages and costs in this court, the party moving for dismissal shall within ten days thereafter tender the whole of such additional damages and costs demanded, the clerk shall, without further reference to the court, enter an order of dismissal. If, after objection as to quantum of damages and costs in this court, the moving party does not respond with such a tender, then the clerk shall report the matter to the court for its determination.

5. No mandate or other process shall issue on a dismissal under this rule without an order of the court.

PART XI. APPLICATION OF TERMS.

61.

Term "State Court" Includes Supreme Court of Puerto Rico.

The term "state court" when used in these rules includes the Supreme Court of the Commonwealth of Puerto Rico, and references in these rules to the law and statutes of a state include the law and statutes of the Commonwealth of Puerto Rico.

PART XII. EFFECTIVE DATE.

62.

Effective Date of Amendments.

The amendments to these rules adopted June 15, 1970, shall become effective July 1, 1970.

Supreme Court Nominations, 1789-1979

Name	State	Date of Birth	Nominated by	To Replace	Date of Appointment	Confirmation or Other Action*		Date Resigned	Date of Death	Years Service
John Jay	N.Y.	12/12/1745	Washington		9/24/1789	9/26/1789		6/29/1795	5/17/1829	6
John Rutledge	S.C.	1739	Washington		9/24/1789	9/26/1789		3/5/1791	6/21/1800	1
William Cushing	Mass.	3/1/1732	Washington		9/24/1789	9/26/1789			9/13/1810	21
Robert H. Harrison	Md.	1745	Washington		9/24/1789	9/26/1789	(D)		4/20/1790	
James Wilson	Pa.	9/14/1742	Washington		9/24/1789	9/26/1789			8/21/1798	9
John Blair	Va.	1732	Washington		9/24/1789	9/26/1789		1/27/1796	8/31/1800	6
James Iredell	N.C.	10/5/1751	Washington	Harrison	2/8/1790	2/10/1790			10/20/1799	9
Thomas Johnson	Md.	11/4/1732	Washington	Rutledge	11/1/1791	11/7/1791		3/4/1793	10/26/1819	1
William Paterson	N.J.	12/24/1745	Washington	Johnson	2/27/1793	2/28/1793	(W)			
William Paterson†			Washington	Johnson	3/4/1793	3/4/1793			9/9/1806	13
John Rutledge#			Washington	Jay	7/1/1795	12/15/1795	(R, 10-14)			
William Cushing#			Washington	Jay	1/26/1796	1/27/1796	(D)			
Samuel Chase	Md.	4/17/1741	Washington	Blair	1/26/1796	1/27/1796			6/19/1811	15
Oliver Ellsworth	Conn.	4/29/1745	Washington	Jay	3/3/1796	3/4/1796	(21-1)	9/30/1800	11/26/1807	4
Bushrod Washington	Va.	6/5/1762	Adams	Wilson	12/19/1798	12/20/1798			11/26/1829	31
Alfred Moore	N.C.	5/21/1755	Adams	Iredell	12/6/1799	12/10/1799		1/26/1804	10/15/1810	4
John Jay#			Adams	Ellsworth	12/18/1800	12/19/1800	(D)			
John Marshall	Va.	9/24/1755	Adams	Ellsworth	1/20/1801	1/27/1801			7/6/1835	34
William Johnson	S.C.	12/27/1771	Jefferson	Moore	3/22/1804	3/24/1804			8/4/1834	30
H. Brockholst Livingston	N.Y.	11/25/1757	Jefferson	Paterson	12/13/1806	12/17/1806			3/18/1823	16
Thomas Todd	Ky.	1/23/1765	Jefferson	New Seat	2/28/1807	3/3/1807			2/7/1826	19
Levi Lincoln	Mass.	5/15/1749	Madison	Cushing	1/2/1811	1/3/1811	(D)		4/14/1820	
Alexander Wolcott	Conn.	9/15/1758	Madison	Cushing	2/4/1811	2/13/1811	(R, 9-24)		6/26/1828	
John Quincy Adams	Mass.	7/11/1767	Madison	Cushing	2/21/1811	2/22/1811	(D)		2/23/1848	
Joseph Story	Mass.	9/18/1779	Madison	Cushing	11/15/1811	11/18/1811			9/10/1845	34
Gabriel Duvall	Md.	12/6/1752	Madison	Chase	11/15/1811	11/18/1811		1/10/1835	3/6/1844	23
Smith Thompson	N.Y.	1/17/1768	Monroe	Livingston	12/8/1823	12/19/1823			12/18/1843	20
Robert Trimble	Ky.	11/17/1776	J. Q. Adams	Todd	4/11/1826	5/9/1826	(27-5)		8/25/1828	2
John J. Crittenden	Ky.	9/10/1787	J. Q. Adams	Trimble	12/17/1828	2/12/1829	(P)		7/26/1863	
John McLean	Ohio	3/11/1785	Jackson	Trimble	3/6/1829	3/7/1829			4/4/1861	32
Henry Baldwin	Pa.	1/14/1780	Jackson	Washington	1/4/1830	1/6/1830	(41-2)		4/21/1844	14
James M. Wayne	Ga.	1790	Jackson	Johnson	1/7/1835	1/9/1835			7/5/1867	32
Roger B. Taney	Md.	3/17/1777	Jackson	Duvall	1/15/1835	3/3/1835	(P)			
Roger B. Taney†			Jackson	Marshall	12/28/1835	3/15/1836	(29-15)		10/12/1864	28
Philip P. Barbour	Va.	5/25/1783	Jackson	Duvall	12/28/1835	3/15/1836	(30-11)		2/25/1841	5
William Smith	Ala.	1762	Jackson	New Seat	3/3/1837	3/8/1837	(23-18) (D)		6/10/1840	
John Catron	Tenn.	1786	Jackson	New Seat	3/3/1837	3/8/1837	(28-15)		5/30/1865	28
John McKinley	Ala.	5/1/1780	Van Buren	New Seat	9/18/1837	9/25/1837			7/19/1852	15
Peter V. Daniel	Va.	4/24/1784	Van Buren	Barbour	2/26/1841	3/2/1841	(22-5)		5/31/1860	19
John C. Spencer	N.Y.	1/8/1788	Tyler	Thompson	1/9/1844	1/31/1844	(R, 21-26)		5/18/1855	
Reuben H. Walworth	N.Y.	10/26/1788	Tyler	Thompson	3/13/1844	6/17/1844	(W)		11/27/1867	
Edward King	Pa.	1/31/1794	Tyler	Baldwin	6/5/1844	6/15/1844	(P)			
Edward King†			Tyler	Baldwin	12/4/1844	2/7/1845	(W)		5/8/1873	
Samuel Nelson	N.Y.	11/10/1792	Tyler	Thompson	2/4/1845	2/14/1845		11/28/1872	12/13/1873	27
John M. Read	Pa.	2/21/1797	Tyler	Baldwin	2/7/1845	No action			11/29/1874	
George W. Woodward	Pa.	3/26/1809	Polk	Baldwin	12/23/1845	1/22/1846	(R, 20-29)		5/10/1875	
Levi Woodbury	N.H.	12/22/1789	Polk	Story	12/23/1845	1/3/1846			9/4/1851	5
Robert C. Grier	Pa.	3/5/1794	Polk	Baldwin	8/3/1846	8/4/1846		1/31/1870	9/26/1870	23
Benjamin R. Curtis	Mass.	11/4/1809	Fillmore	Woodbury	12/11/1851	12/29/1851		9/30/1857	9/15/1874	5
Edward A. Bradford	La.	9/27/1813	Fillmore	McKinley	8/16/1852	No action			11/22/1872	
George E. Badger	N.C.	4/13/1795	Fillmore	McKinley	1/10/1853	2/11/1853	(P)		5/11/1866	
William C. Micou	La.	1806	Fillmore	McKinley	2/24/1853	No action			4/16/1854	
John A. Campbell	Ala.	6/24/1811	Pierce	McKinley	3/22/1853	3/25/1853		4/26/1861	3/13/1889	8

Boldface - Chief Justice
Italics - Did not serve
Earlier court service. See above.
† Earlier nomination not confirmed. See above.
D Declined

W Withdrawn
P Postponed
R Rejected
* Where no vote is listed, confirmation was by voice vote or otherwise unrecorded.

Name	State	Date of Birth	Nomi-nated by	To Replace	Date of Ap-pointment	Confirmation or Other Action*		Date Resigned	Date of Death	Years Service
Nathan Clifford	Maine	8/18/1803	Buchanan	Curtis	12/9/1857	1/12/1858	(26-23)		7/25/1881	23
Jeremiah S. Black	Pa.	1/10/1810	Buchanan	Daniel	2/5/1861	2/21/1861	(R, 25-26)		8/19/1883	
Noah H. Swayne	Ohio	12/7/1804	Lincoln	McLean	1/21/1862	1/24/1862	(38-1)	1/24/1881	6/8/1884	19
Samuel F. Miller	Iowa	4/5/1816	Lincoln	Daniel	7/16/1862	7/16/1862			10/13/1890	28
David Davis	Ill.	3/9/1815	Lincoln	Campbell	12/1/1862	12/8/1862		3/7/1877	6/26/1886	14
Stephen J. Field	Calif.	11/4/1816	Lincoln	New Seat	3/6/1863	3/10/1863		12/1/1897	4/9/1899	34
Salmon P. Chase	Ohio	1/13/1808	Lincoln	Taney	12/6/1864	12/6/1864			5/7/1873	8
Henry Stanbery	Ohio	2/20/1803	Johnson	Catron	4/16/1866	No action			6/26/1881	
Ebenezer R. Hoar	Mass.	2/21/1816	Grant	New Seat	12/15/1869	2/3/1870	(R, 24-33)		1/31/1895	
Edwin M. Stanton	Pa.	12/19/1814	Grant	Grier	12/20/1869	12/20/1869	(46-11)		12/24/1869	
William Strong	Pa.	5/6/1808	Grant	Grier	2/7/1870	2/18/1870		12/14/1880	8/19/1895	10
Joseph P. Bradley	N.J.	3/14/1813	Grant	New Seat	2/7/1870	3/21/1870	(46-9)		1/22/1892	21
Ward Hunt	N.Y.	6/14/1810	Grant	Nelson	12/3/1872	12/11/1872		1/7/1882	3/24/1886	9
George H. Williams	Ore.	3/23/1823	Grant	Chase	12/1/1873	1/8/1874	(W)		4/4/1910	
Caleb Cushing	Mass.	1/17/1800	Grant	Chase	1/9/1874	1/13/1874	(W)		1/2/1879	
Morrison R. Waite	Ohio	11/29/1816	Grant	Chase	1/19/1874	1/21/1874	(63-0)		3/23/1888	14
John M. Harlan	Ky.	6/1/1833	Hayes	Davis	10/17/1877	11/29/1877			10/14/1911	34
William B. Woods	Ga.	8/3/1824	Hayes	Strong	12/15/1880	12/21/1880	(39-8)		5/14/1887	6
Stanley Matthews	Ohio	7/21/1824	Hayes	Swayne	1/26/1881	No action				
Stanley Matthews†			Garfield	Swayne	3/14/1881	5/12/1881	(24-23)		3/22/1889	7
Horace Gray	Mass.	3/24/1828	Arthur	Clifford	12/19/1881	12/20/1881	(51-5)	7/9/1902	9/15/1902	20
Roscoe Conkling	N.Y.	10/30/1829	Arthur	Hunt	2/24/1882	3/2/1882	(39-12) (D)		4/18/1888	
Samuel Blatchford	N.Y.	3/9/1820	Arthur	Hunt	3/13/1882	3/27/1882			7/7/1893	11
Lucius Q. C. Lamar	Miss.	9/17/1825	Cleveland	Woods	12/6/1887	1/16/1888	(32-28)		1/23/1893	5
Melville W. Fuller†	Ill.	2/11/1833	Cleveland	Waite	4/30/1888	7/20/1888	(41-20)		7/4/1910	22
David J. Brewer	Kan.	1/20/1837	Harrison	Matthews	12/4/1889	12/18/1889	(53-11)		3/28/1910	20
Henry B. Brown	Mich.	3/2/1836	Harrison	Miller	12/23/1890	12/29/1890		5/28/1906	9/4/1913	15
George Shiras Jr.	Pa.	1/26/1832	Harrison	Bradley	7/19/1892	7/26/1892		2/23/1903	8/2/1924	10
Howell E. Jackson	Tenn.	4/8/1832	Harrison	Lamar	2/2/1893	2/18/1893			8/8/1895	2
William B. Hornblower	N.Y.	5/13/1851	Cleveland	Blatchford	9/19/1893	1/15/1894	(R, 24-30)		6/16/1914	
Wheeler H. Peckham	N.Y.	1/1/1833	Cleveland	Blatchford	1/22/1894	2/16/1894	(R, 32-41)		9/27/1905	
Edward D. White	La.	11/3/1845	Cleveland	Blatchford	2/19/1894	2/19/1894			5/19/1921	17
Rufus W. Peckham	N.Y.	11/8/1838	Cleveland	Jackson	12/3/1895	12/9/1895			10/24/1909	13
Joseph McKenna	Calif.	8/10/1843	McKinley	Field	12/16/1897	1/21/1898		1/5/1925	11/21/1926	26
Oliver W. Holmes	Mass.	3/8/1841	Roosevelt	Gray	12/2/1902	12/4/1902		1/12/1932	3/6/1935	29
William R. Day	Ohio	4/17/1849	Roosevelt	Shiras	2/19/1903	2/23/1903		11/13/1922	7/9/1923	19
William H. Moody	Mass.	12/23/1853	Roosevelt	Brown	12/3/1906	12/12/1906		11/20/1910	7/2/1917	3
Horace H. Lurton	Tenn.	2/26/1844	Taft	Peckham	12/13/1909	12/20/1909			7/12/1914	4
Edward D. White#			Taft	Fuller	12/12/1910	12/12/1910				10#
Charles E. Hughes	N.Y.	4/11/1862	Taft	Brewer	4/25/1910	5/2/1910		6/10/1916	8/27/1948	6
Willis Van Devanter	Wyo.	4/17/1859	Taft	Moody	12/12/1910	12/15/1910		6/2/1937	2/8/1941	26
Joseph R. Lamar	Ga.	10/14/1857	Taft	White	12/12/1910	12/15/1910			1/2/1916	5
Mahlon Pitney	N.J.	2/5/1858	Taft	Harlan	2/19/1912	3/13/1912	(50-26)	12/31/1922	12/9/1924	10
James C. McReynolds	Tenn.	2/3/1862	Wilson	Lurton	8/19/1914	8/29/1914	(44-6)	1/31/1941	8/24/1946	26
Louis D. Brandeis	Mass.	11/13/1856	Wilson	Lamar	1/28/1916	6/1/1916	(47-22)	2/13/1939	10/5/1941	22
John H. Clarke	Ohio	9/18/1857	Wilson	Hughes	7/14/1916	7/24/1916		7/18/1922	3/22/1945	6
William H. Taft	Ohio	9/15/1857	Harding	White	6/30/1921	6/30/1921		2/3/1930	3/8/1930	8
George Sutherland	Utah	3/25/1862	Harding	Clarke	9/5/1922	9/5/1922		1/17/1938	7/18/1942	15
Pierce Butler	Minn.	3/17/1866	Harding	Day	11/23/1922	12/21/1922	(61-8)		11/16/1939	17
Edward T. Sanford	Tenn.	7/23/1865	Harding	Pitney	1/24/1923	1/29/1923			3/8/1930	7
Harlan F. Stone	N.Y.	10/11/1872	Coolidge	McKenna	1/5/1925	2/5/1925	(71-6)		4/22/1946	16
Charles E. Hughes#			Hoover	Taft	2/3/1930	2/13/1930	(52-26)	7/1/1941		11#
John J. Parker	N.C.	11/20/1885	Hoover	Sanford	3/21/1930	5/7/1930	(R, 39-41)		3/17/1958	
Owen J. Roberts	Pa.	5/2/1875	Hoover	Sanford	5/9/1930	5/20/1930		7/31/1945	5/17/1955	15
Benjamin N. Cardozo	N.Y.	5/24/1870	Hoover	Holmes	2/15/1932	2/24/1932			7/9/1938	6
Hugo L. Black	Ala.	2/27/1886	Roosevelt	Van Devanter	8/12/1937	8/17/1937	(63-16)	9/17/1971	10/25/1971	34
Stanley F. Reed	Ky.	12/31/1884	Roosevelt	Sutherland	1/15/1938	1/25/1938		2/26/1957		19
Felix Frankfurter	Mass.	11/15/1882	Roosevelt	Cardozo	1/5/1939	1/17/1939		8/28/1962	2/22/1965	23

Name	State	Date of Birth	Nomi-nated by	To Replace	Date of Ap-pointment	Confirmation or Other Action*		Date Resigned	Date of Death	Years Service
William O. Douglas	Conn.	10/16/1898	Roosevelt	Brandeis	3/20/1939	4/4/1939	(62-4)	11/12/1975		36
Frank Murphy	Mich.	4/13/1890	Roosevelt	Butler	1/4/1940	1/15/1940			7/19/1949	9
Harlan F. Stone#			Roosevelt	Hughes	6/12/1941	6/27/1941				5#
James F. Byrnes	S.C.	5/2/1879	Roosevelt	McReynolds	6/12/1941	6/12/1941		10/3/1942	4/9/1972	1
Robert H. Jackson	N.Y.	2/13/1892	Roosevelt	Stone	6/12/1941	7/7/1941			10/9/1954	13
Wiley B. Rutledge	Iowa	7/20/1894	Roosevelt	Byrnes	1/11/1943	2/8/1943			9/10/1949	6
Harold H. Burton	Ohio	6/22/1888	Truman	Roberts	9/19/1945	9/19/1945		10/13/1958	10/28/1964	13
Fred M. Vinson	Ky.	1/22/1890	Truman	Stone	6/6/1946	6/20/1946			9/8/1953	7
Tom C. Clark	Texas	9/23/1899	Truman	Murphy	8/2/1949	8/18/1949	(73-8)	6/12/1967	6/13/1977	18
Sherman Minton	Ind.	10/20/1890	Truman	Rutledge	9/15/1949	10/4/1949	(48-16)	10/15/1956	4/9/1965	7
Earl Warren	Calif.	3/19/1891	Eisenhower	Vinson	9/30/1953	3/1/1954		6/23/1969	6/9/1974	15
John M. Harlan	N.Y.	5/20/1899	Eisenhower	Jackson	1/10/1955	3/16/1955	(71-11)	9/23/1971	12/29/1971	16
William J. Brennan Jr.	N.J.	4/25/1906	Eisenhower	Minton	1/14/1957	3/19/1957				
Charles E. Whittaker	Mo.	2/22/1901	Eisenhower	Reed	3/2/1957	3/19/1957		4/1/1962	11/26/73	5
Potter Stewart	Ohio	1/23/1915	Eisenhower	Burton	1/17/1959	5/5/1959	(70-17)			
Byron R. White	Colo.	6/8/1917	Kennedy	Whittaker	3/30/1962	4/11/1962				
Arthur J. Goldberg	Ill.	8/8/1908	Kennedy	Frankfurter	8/29/1962	9/25/1962		7/25/1965		3
Abe Fortas	Tenn.	6/19/1910	Johnson	Goldberg	7/28/1965	8/11/1965		5/14/1969		4
Thurgood Marshall	N.Y.	6/2/1908	Johnson	Clark	6/13/1967	8/30/1967	(69-11)			
Abe Fortas#			Johnson	Warren	6/26/1968	10/4/1968	(W)			
Homer Thornberry	Texas	1/9/1909	Johnson	Fortas	6/26/1968	No action				
Warren E. Burger	Minn.	9/17/1907	Nixon	Warren	5/21/1969	6/9/1969	(74-3)			
Clement Haynsworth Jr.	S.C.	10/30/1912	Nixon	Fortas	8/18/1969	11/21/1969	(R, 45-55)			
G. Harrold Carswell	Fla.	12/22/1919	Nixon	Fortas	1/19/1970	4/8/1970	(R, 45-51)			
Harry A. Blackmun	Minn.	11/12/1908	Nixon	Fortas	4/14/1970	5/12/1970	(94-0)			
Lewis F. Powell Jr.	Va.	9/19/1907	Nixon	Black	10/21/1971	12/6/1971	(89-1)			
William H. Rehnquist	Ariz.	10/1/1924	Nixon	Harlan	10/21/1971	12/10/1971	(68-26)			
John Paul Stevens	Ill.	4/20/1920	Ford	Douglas	11/28/75	12/17/1975	(98-0)			

Sources: Leon Friedman and Fred L. Israel, eds., *The Justices of the United States Supreme Court, 1789-1969;* Executive Journal of the U.S. Senate, 1789-1975; Congressional Quarterly, 1971 and 1975 Almanacs.

Judiciary Act of 1789

Source: Public Statutes at Large of the United States of America. Vol. I. Boston: Charles C. Little & James Brown, 1845. Footnotes have been deleted.

STATUTE I
Sept. 24, 1789.

An Act to establish the Judicial Courts of the United States.

SECTION I. *Be it enacted by the Senate and House of Representatives of the United States of America in Congress assembled,* That the supreme court of the United States shall consist of a chief justice and five associate justices, any four of whom shall be a quorum, and shall hold annually at the seat of government two sessions, the one commencing the first Monday of February, and the other the first Monday of August. That the associate justices shall have precedence according to the data of their commissions, or when the commissions of two or more of them bear date on the same day, according to the respective ages.

Supreme court to consist of a chief justice, and five associates. Two sessions annually. Precedence.

SEC. 2. *And be it further enacted,* That the United States shall be, and they hereby are divided into thirteen districts, to be limited and called as follows, to wit: one to consist of that part of the State of Massachusetts which lies easterly of the State of New Hampshire, and to be called Maine District; one to consist of the State of New Hampshire, and to be called New Hampshire District; one to consist of the remaining part of the State of Massachusetts, and to be called Massachusetts district; one to consist of the State of Connecticut, and to be called Connecticut District; one to consist of the State of New York, and to be called New York District; one to consist of the State of New Jersey, and to be called New Jersey District; one to consist of the State of Pennsylvania, and to be called Pennsylvania District; one to consist of the State of Delaware, and to be called Delaware District; one to consist of the State of Maryland, and to be called Maryland District; one to consist of the State of Virginia, except that part called the Distict of Kentucky, and to be called Virginia District; one to consist of the remaining part of the State of Virginia, and to be called Kentucky District; one to consist of the State of South Carolina, and to be called South Carolina District; and one to consist of the State of Georgia, and to be called Georgia District.

Thirteen districts.

Maine.
N. Hampshire.

Massachusetts.

Connecticut.
New York.

New Jersey.

Pennsylvania.
Delaware.

Maryland.

Virginia.

Kentucky.

South Carolina.
Georgia.

SEC. 3. *And be it further enacted,* That there be a court called a District Court, in each of the afore mentioned districts, to consist of one judge, who shall reside in the district for which he is appointed, and shall be called a District Judge, and shall hold annually four sessions, the first of which to commence as follows, to wit: in the districts of New York and of New Jersey on the first, in the district of Pennsylvania on the second, in the district of Connecticut on the third, and in the district of Delaware on the fourth, Tuesdays of November next; in the districts of Massachusetts, of Maine, and of Maryland, on the first, in the district of Georgia on the second, and in the districts of New Hampshire, of Virginia, and of Kentucky, on the third Tuesdays of December next; and the other three sessions progressively in

A district court in each district.

Four sessions annually in a district; and when held.

the respective districts on the like Tuesdays of every third calendar month afterwards, and in the district of South Carolina, on the third Monday in March and September, the first Monday in July, and the second Monday in December of each and every year, commencing in December next; and that the District Judge shall have power to hold special courts at his discretion. That the stated District Court shall be held at the places following, to wit: in the district of Maine, at Portland and Pownalsborough alternately, beginning at the first; in the district of New Hampshire, at Exeter and Portsmouth alternately, beginning at the first; in the district of Massachusetts, at Boston and Salem alternately, beginning at the first; in the district of Connecticut, alternately at Hartford and New Haven, beginning at the first; in the district of New York, at New York; in the district of New Jersey, alternately at New Brunswick and Burlington, beginning at the first; in the district of Pennsylvania, at Philadelphia and York Town alternately, beginning at the first; in the district of Delaware, alternately at Newcastle and Dover, beginning at the first; in the district of Maryland, alternately at Baltimore and Easton, beginning at the first; in the district of Virginia, alternately at Richmond and Williamsburgh, beginning at the first; in the district of Kentucky, at Harrodsburgh; in the district of South Carolina, at Charleston; and in the district of Georgia, alternately at Savannah and Augusta, beginning at the first; and that the special courts shall be held at the same place in each district as the stated courts, or in districts that have two, at either of them, in the discretion of the judge, or at such other place in the district, as the nature of the business and his discretion shall direct. And that in the districts that have but one place for holding the District Court, the records thereof shall be kept at that place; and in districts that have two, at that place in each district which the judge shall appoint.

Special district courts.
Stated district courts; when holden.

Special courts, where held.

Where records kept.

SEC. 4. *And be it further enacted,* That the before mentioned districts, except those of Maine and Kentucky, shall be divided into three circuits, and be called the eastern, the middle, and the southern circuit. That the eastern circuit shall consist of the districts of New Hampshire, Massachusetts, Connecticut and New York; that the middle circuit shall consist of the districts of New Jersey, Pennsylvania, Delaware, Maryland and Virginia; and that the southern circuit shall consist of the districts of South Carolina and Georgia, and that there shall be held annually in each district of said circuits, two courts, which shall be called Circuit Courts, and shall consist of any two justices of the Supreme Court, and the district judge of such districts, any two of whom shall constitute a quorum: *Provided,* That no district judge shall give a vote in any case of appeal or error from his own decision; but may assign the reasons of such his decision.

Three circuits, and how divided.

First session
of the circuit
courts; when
holden.

SEC. 5. *And be it further enacted,* That the first session of the said circuit court in the several districts shall commence at the times following, to wit: in New Jersey on the second, in New York on the fourth, in Pennsylvania on the eleventh, in Connecticut on the twenty-second, and in Delaware on the twenty-seventh, days of April next; in Massachusetts on the third, in Maryland on the seventh, in South Carolina on the twelfth, in New Hampshire on the twentieth, in Virginia on the twenty-second, and in Georgia on the twenty-eighth, days of May next, and the subsequent sessions in the respective districts on the like days of every sixth calendar month afterwards, except in South Carolina, where the session of the said court shall commence on the first, and in Georgia where it shall commence on the seventeenth day of October, and except when any of those days shall happen on a Sunday, and then the session shall commence on the next day following. And

Where holden.

the sessions of the said circuit court shall be held in the district of New Hampshire, at Portsmouth and Exeter alternately, beginning at the first; in the district of Massachusetts, at Boston; in the district of Connecticut, alternately at Hartford and New Haven, beginning at the last; in the district of New York, alternately at New York and Albany, beginning at the first; in the district of New Jersey, at Trenton; in the district of Pennsylvania, alternately at Philadelphia and Yorktown, beginning at the first; in the district of Delaware, alternately at New Castle and Dover, beginning at the first; in the district of Maryland, alternately at Annapolis and Easton, beginning at the first; in the district of Virginia, alternately at Charlottesville and Williamsburgh, beginning at the first; in the district of South Carolina, alternately at Columbia and Charleston, beginning at the first; and in the district of Georgia, alternately at Savannah and Augusta, beginning at the first. And the

Circuit courts.
Special sessions.

circuit courts shall have power to hold special sessions for the trial of criminal causes at any other time at their discretion, or at the discretion of the Supreme Court.

Supreme court
adjourned by
one or more
justices; cir-
cuit courts
adjourned.

SEC. 6. *And be it further enacted,* That the Supreme Court may, by any one or more of its justices being present, be adjourned from day to day until a quorum be convened; and that a circuit court may also be adjourned from day to day by any one of its judges, or if none are present, by the marshal of the district until a quorum be convened; and that a district court, in case of the inability of the judge to attend at the commencement of a session, may by virtue of a written order from the said judge, directed to the marshal of the district, be adjourned by the said marshal to such

District courts
adjourned.

day, antecedent to the next stated session of the said court, as in the said order shall be appointed; and in case of the death of the said judge, and his vacancy not being supplied, all process, pleadings and proceedings of what nature soever, pending before the said court, shall be continued of course until the next stated session after the appointment and acceptance of the office by his successor.

The courts
have power to
appoint clerks.

SEC. 7. *And be it [further] enacted,* That the Supreme Court, and the district courts shall have power to appoint clerks for their repetive courts, and that the clerk for each district court shall be clerk also of the circuit court in such district, and

Their oath or
affirmation.

each of the said clerks shall, before he enters upon the execution of his office, take the following oath or affirmation, to wit: "I, A. B., being appointed clerk of   , do solemnly swear, or affirm, that I will truly and faithfully enter and record all the orders, decrees, judgments and proceedings of the said court, and that I will faithfully and impartially discharge and perform all the duties of my said office, according to the best of my abilities and understanding. So help me God." Which words, so help me God, shall be omitted in all cases where an affirmation is admitted instead of an oath. And the said clerks shall also severally give bond, with sufficient sureties, (to be approved of by the Supreme and district courts respectively) to the United States, in the sum of two thousand dollars, faithfully to discharge the duties of his office, and seasonably to record the decrees, judgments and determinations of the court of which he is clerk.

Oath of jus-
tices of supreme
court and judges
of the district
court.

SEC. 8. *And be it further enacted,* That the justices of the Supreme Court, and the district judges, before they proceed to execute the duties of their respective offices, shall take the following oath or affirmation, to wit: "I, A. B., do solemnly swear or affirm, that I will administer justice without respect to persons, and do equal right to the poor and to the rich, and that I will faithfully and impartially discharge and perform all the duties incumbent on me as   , according to the best of my abilities and understanding, agreeably to the constitution and laws of the United States. So help me God."

District courts
exclusive juris-
diction.

SEC. 9. *And be it further enacted,* That the district courts shall have, exclusively of the courts of the several States, cognizance of all crimes and offences that shall be cognizable under the authority of the United States, committed within their respective districts, or upon the high seas; where no other punishment than whipping, not exceeding thirty stripes, a fine not exceeding one hundred dollars, or a term of imprisonment not exceeding six months, is to be inflicted; and shall

Original cog-
nizance in mari-
time causes and
of seizure under
the laws of the
United States.

also have exclusive original cognizance of all civil causes of admiralty and maritime jurisdiction, including all seizures under laws of impost, navigation or trade of the United States, where the seizures are made, on waters which are navigable from the sea by vessels of ten or more tons burthen, within their respective districts as well as upon the high seas; saving to suitors, in all cases, the right of a common law remedy, where the common law is competent to give it; and shall also have exclusive original cognizance of all seizures on land, or other waters than as aforesaid, made, and of all suits for penalties and forfeitures incurred, under the laws of the United States. And shall also have cognizance, concurrent with the courts of the several States, or the circuit courts, as the case may be, of all causes where an alien sues for a tort only in violation of the law of nations or a treaty of the United States. And shall also have cognizance, concurrent as last men-

Concurrent
jurisdiction.

tioned, of all suits at common law where the United States sue, and the matter in dispute amounts, exclusive of costs, to the sum or value of one hundred dollars. And shall also have jurisdiction exclusively of the courts of the several States, of all suits against consuls or vice-consuls, except for offences above the description aforesaid. And

Trial of fact by jury.

the trial of issues in fact, in the district courts, in all causes except civil causes of admiralty and maritime jurisdiction, shall be by jury.

Kentucky district court.

SEC. 10. *And be it further enacted,* That the district court in Kentucky district shall, besides the jurisdiction aforesaid, have jurisdiction of all other causes, except of appeals and writs of error, herinafter made cognizable in a circuit court, and shall proceed therein in the same manner as a circuit court, and writs of error and appeals shall lie from decisions therein to the Supreme Court in the same causes, as from a circuit court to the Supreme Court, and under the same regulations.

Maine district court.

And the district court in Maine district shall, besides the jurisdiction herein before granted, have jurisdiction of all causes, except of appeals and writs of error herein after made cognizable in a circuit court, and shall proceed therein in the same manner as a circuit court: And writs of error shall lie from decisions therein to the circuit court in the district of Massachusetts in the same manner as from other district courts to their respective circuit courts.

Circuit courts original cognizance where the matter in dispute exceeds five hundred dollars.

SEC. 11. *And be it further enacted,* That the circuit courts shall have original cognizance, concurrent with the courts of the several States, of all suits of a civil nature at common law or in equity, where the matter in dispute exceeds, exclusive of costs, the sum or value of five hundred dollars, and the United States are plaintiffs, or petitioners; or an alien is a party, or the suit is between a citizen of the State where the suit is brought, and a citizen of another State. And shall have exclu-

Exclusive cognisance of crimes and offences cognizable under the laws of the United States.

sive cognizance of all crimes and offences cognizable under the authority of the United States, except where this act otherwise provides, or the laws of the United State shall otherwise direct, and concurrent jurisdiction with the district courts of the crimes and offences cognizable

No person to be arrested in one district for trial in another on any civil suit.

therein. But no person shall be arrested in one district for trial in another, in any civil action before a circuit or district court. And no civil suit shall be brought before either of said courts

Limitation as to civil suits.

against an inhabitant of the United States, by any original process in any other district than that whereof he is an inhabitant, or in which he shall be found at the time of serving the writ, nor shall

Actions on promissory notes.

any district or circuit court have cognizance of any suit to recover the contents of any promissory note or other chose in action in favour of an assignee, unless a suit might have been prosecuted in such court to recover the said contents if no assignment had been made, except in cases of foreign bills of exchange. And the circuit courts shall also have

Circuit courts shall also have appellate jurisdiction.

appellate jurisdiction from the district courts under the regulations and restrictions herein after provided.

Matter in dispute above 500 dollars.

Removal of causes from state courts.

SEC. 12. *And be it further enacted,* That if a suit be commenced in any state court against an alien, or by a citizen of the state in which the suit is brought against a citizen of another state, and the matter in dispute exceeds the aforesaid sum or value of five hundred dollars, exclusive of costs, to be made to appear to the satisfaction of the court; and the defendant shall, at the time of entering his appearance in such state court, file a petition for the removal of the cause for trial into the next circuit court, to be held in the district where the suit is pending, or if in the district of Maine to the district court next to be holden therein, or if in

Special bail.

Kentucky district to the district court next to be holden therein, and offer good and sufficient surety for his entering in such court, on the first day of its session, copies of said process against him, and also for his there appearing and entering special bail in the cause, if special bail was originally requisite therein, it shall then be the duty of the state court to accept the surety, and proceed no further in the cause, and any bail that may have been originally taken shall be discharged and the said copies being entered as aforesaid, in such court of the United States, the cause shall there proceed in the same manner as if it had been brought there by original process. And

Attachment of goods holden to final judgment.

any attachment of the goods or estate of the defendant by the original process, shall hold the goods or estate so attached, to answer the final judgment in the same manner as by the laws of such state they would have been holden to answer final judgment, had it been rendered by the court in which the suit commenced. And if in any action

Title of land where value exceeds 500 dollars.

commenced in a state court, the title of land be concerned, and the parties are citizens of the same state, and the matter in dispute exceeds the sum or value of five hundred dollars, exclusive of costs, the sum or value being made to appear to the satisfaction of the court, either party, before the trial, shall state to the court and make affidavit if they require it, that he claims and shall rely upon a right or title to the land, under a grant from a state other than that in which the suit is pending, and produce the original grant or an exemplification of it, except where the loss of public records shall put it out of his power, and shall move that the adverse party inform the court, whether he claims a right or title to the land under a grant from the state in which the suit is pending; the said adverse [party] shall give such information, or otherwise not be allowed to plead such grant, or give it in evidence upon the trial, and if he informs that he does claim under such grant, the party claiming under the grant first mentioned may then, on motion, remove the cause for trial to the next circuit court to be holden in such district, or

If in Maine and Kentucky, where causes are removable.

if in the district of Maine, to the court next to be holden therein; or if in Kentucky district, to the district court next to be holden therein; but if he is the defendant, shall do it under the same regulations as in the beforementioned case of the removal of a cause into such court by an alien; and neither party removing the cause, shall be allowed to plead or give evidence of any other title than that by him stated as aforesaid, as the

Issues in fact by jury.

ground of his claim; and the trial of issues in fact in the circuit courts shall, in all suits, except those of equity, and of admiralty, and maritime jurisdiction, be by jury.

Supreme court exclusive jurisdiction.

SEC. 13. *And be it further enacted,* That the Supreme Court shall have exclusive jurisdiction of all controversies of a civil nature, where a state is a party, except between a state and its citizens; and except also between a state and citizens of other states, or aliens, in which latter case it shall have original but not exclusive jurisdiction. And shall have exclusively all such jurisdiction of suits

Proceedings against public ministers.

or proceedings against ambassadors, or other public ministers, or their domestics, or domestic servants, as a court of law can have or exercise consistently with the law of nations; and original, but not exclusive jurisdiction of all suits brought by ambassadors, or other public ministers, or in which a consul, or vice consul, shall be a party.

And the trial of issues in fact in the Supreme Court, in all actions at law against citizens of the United States, shall be by jury. The Supreme Court shall also have appellate jurisdiction from the circuit courts and courts of the several states, in the cases herein after specially provided for; and shall have power to issue writs of prohibition to the district courts, when proceeding as courts of admiralty and maritime jurisdiction, and writs of *mandamus*, in cases warranted by the principles and usages of law, to any courts appointed, or persons holding office, under the authority of the United States.

SEC. 14. *And be it further enacted*, That all the before-mentioned courts of the United States, shall have power to issue writs of *scire facias*, *habeas corpus*, and all other writs not specially provided for by statute, which may be necessary for the exercise of their respective jurisdictions, and agreeable to the principles and usages of law. And that either of the justices of the supreme court, as well as judges of the district courts, shall have power to grant writs of *habeas corpus* for the purpose of an inquiry into the cause of commitment — *Provided*, That writs of *habeas corpus* shall in no case extend to prisoners in gaol, unless where they are in custody, under or by colour of the authority of the United States, or are committed for trial before some court of the same, or are necessary to be brought into court to testify.

SEC. 15. *And be it further enacted*, That all the said courts of the United States, shall have power in the trial of actions at law, on motion and due notice thereof being given, to require the parties to produce books or writings in their possession or power, which contain evidence pertinent to the issue, in cases and under circumstances where they might be compelled to produce the same by the ordinary rules of proceeding in chancery; and if a plaintiff shall fail to comply with such order, to produce books or writings, it shall be lawful for the courts respectively, on motion, to give the like judgment for the defendant as in cases of nonsuit; and if a defendant shall fail to comply with such order, to produce books or writings, it shall be lawful for the courts respectively on motion as aforesaid, to give judgment against him or her by default.

SEC. 16. *And be it further enacted*, That suits in equity shall not be sustained in either of the courts of the United States, in any case where plain, adequate and complete remedy may be had at law.

SEC. 17. *And be it futher enacted*, That all the said courts of the United States shall have power to grant new trials, in cases where there has been a trial by jury for reasons for which new trials have usually been granted in the courts of law; and shall have power to impose and administer all necessary oaths or affirmations, and to punish by fine or imprisonment, at the discretion of said courts, all contempts of authority in any cause or hearing before the same; and to make and establish all necessary rules for the orderly conducting business in the said courts, provided such rules are not repugnant to the laws of the United States.

SEC. 18. *And be it further enacted*, That when in a circuit court, judgment upon a verdict in a civil action shall be entered, execution may on motion of either party, at the discretion of the court, and on such conditions for the security of the adverse party as they may judge proper, be stayed forty-two days from the time of entering judgment, to give time to file in the clerk's office of said court, a petition for a new trial. And if such petition be there filed within said term of forty-two days, with a certificate thereon from either of the judges of such court, that he allows the same to be filed, which certificate he may make or refuse at his discretion, execution shall of course be further stayed to the next session of said court. And if a new trial be granted, the former judgment shall be thereby rendered void.

SEC. 19. *And be it further enacted*, That it shall be the duty of circuit courts, in causes in equity and of admiralty and maritime jurisdiction, to cause the facts on which they found their sentence or decree, fully to appear upon the record of either from the pleadings and decree itself, or a state of the case agreed by the parties, or their counsel, or if they disagree by a stating of the case by the court.

SEC. 20. *And be it further enacted*, That where in a circuit court, a plaintiff in an action, originally brought there, or a petitioner in equity, other than the United States, recovers less than the sum or value of five hundred dollars, or a libellant, upon his own appeal, less than the sum or value of three hundred dollars, he shall not be allowed, but at the discretion of the court, may be adjudged to pay costs.

SEC. 21. *And be it further enacted*, That from final decrees in a district court in causes of admiralty and maritime jurisdiction, where the matter in dispute exceeds the sum or value of three hundred dollars, exclusive of costs, an appeal shall be allowed to the next circuit court, to be held in such district. *Provided nevertheless*, That all such appeals from final decrees as aforesaid, from the district court of Maine, shall be made to the circuit court, next to be holden after each appeal in the district of Massachusetts.

SEC. 22. *And be it further enacted*, That final decrees and judgments in civil actions in a district court, where the matter in dispute exceeds the sum or value of fifty dollars, exclusive of costs, may be re-examined, and reversed or affirmed in a circuit court, holden in the same distict, upon a writ of error, whereto shall be annexed and returned therewith at the day and place therein mentioned, an authenticated transcript of the record, an assignment of errors, and prayer for reversal, with a citation to the adverse party, signed by the judge of such district court, or a justice of the Supreme Court, the adverse party having at least twenty days' notice. And upon a like process, may final judgments and decrees in civil actions, and suits in equity in a circuit court, brought there by original process, or removed there from courts of the several States, or removed there by appeal from a district court where the matter in dispute exceeds the sum or value of two thousand dollars, exclusive of costs, be re-exam-

Marginal notes:

Sup. Court appellate jurisdiction.

Writs of Prohibition.

Of Mandamus.

Courts may issue writs scire facias, habeas corpus, &c.

Limitation of writs of habeas corpus.

Parties shall produce books and writings.

Suits in equity limited.

Courts may grant new trials.

Execution may be stayed on conditions.

Facts to appear on record.

Costs not allowed unless 500 dollars recovered.

Appeals from the district to the circuit court where matter in dispute exceeds 300 dolls.

Final decrees re-examined above 50 dollars.
Altered by the 2d section of the act of March 3, 1803, chap. 40.

And suits in equity, exceeding 2000 dollars in value.

ined and reversed or affirmed in the Supreme Court, the citation being in such case signed by a judge of such circuit court, or justice of the Supreme Court, and the adverse party having at least thirty days' notice. But there shall be no

Writs of error limited. reversal in either court on such writ of error for error in ruling any plea in abatement, other than a plea to the jurisdiction of the court, or such plea to a petition or bill in equity, as is in the nature of a demurrer, or for any error in fact. And writs of error shall not be brought but within five years after rendering or passing the judgment or decree complained of, or in case the person entitled to such writ of error be an infant, *feme covert, non compos mentis,* or imprisoned, then within five years as aforesaid, exclusive of the time of such disability. And every justice or judge signing a citation on any writ of error as aforesaid, shall

Plaintiff to give security. take good and sufficient security, that the plaintiff in error shall prosecute his writ to effect, and answer all damages and costs if he fail to make his plea good.

Writ of error a supersedeas. SEC. 23. *And be it further enacted,* That a writ of error as aforesaid shall be a supersedeas and stay execution in cases only where the writ of error is served, by a copy thereof being lodged for the adverse party in the clerk's office where the record remains, within ten days, Sundays exclusive, after rendering the judgment or passing the decree complained of. Until the expiration of which term of ten days, executions shall not issue in any case where a writ of error may be a supersedeas; and whereupon such writ of error the Supreme or a circuit court shall affirm a judgment or decree, they shall adjudge or decree to the respondent in error just damages for his delay, and single or double costs at their discretion.

Judgment or decree reversed. SEC. 24. *And be it further enacted,* That when a judgment or decree shall be reversed in a circuit court, such court shall proceed to render such judgment or pass such decree as the district court should have rendered or passed; and the Supreme Court shall do the same on reversals therein, except where the reversal is in favor of the plaintiff, or petitioner in the original suit, and the damages to be assessed, or matter to be decreed, are uncertain, in which case they shall remand the cause for a final decision. And the Supreme Court

Supreme court not to issue execution but mandate. shall not issue execution in causes that are removed before them by writs of error, but shall send a special mandate to the circuit court to award execution thereupon.

Cases in which judgment and decrees of the highest court of a state may be examined by the supreme court, on writ of error. SEC. 25. *And be it further enacted,* That a final judgment or decree in any suit, in the highest court of law or equity of a State in which a decision in the suit could be had, where is drawn in question the validity of a treaty or statute of, or an authority exercised under the United States, and the decision is against their validity; or where is drawn in question the validity of a statute of, or an authority exercised under any State, on the ground of their being repugnant to the constitution, treaties or laws of the United States, and the decision is in favour of such their validity, or where is drawn in question the construction of any clause of the constitution, or of a treaty, or statute of, or commission held under the United States, and the decision is against the title, right, privilege or exemption specially set up or claimed by either party, under such clause of the said Consti-

tution, treaty, statute or commission, may be re-examined and reversed or affirmed in the Supreme Court of the United States upon a writ of error, the citation being signed by the chief justice, or judge or chancellor of the court rendering or passing the judgment or decree complained of, or by a justice of the Supreme Court of the United States, in the same manner and under the same

Proceedings on reversal. regulations, and the writ shall have the same effect, as if the judgment or decree complained of had been rendered or passed in a circuit court, and the proceeding upon the reversal shall also be the same, except that the Supreme Court, instead of remanding the cause for a final decision as before provided, may at their discretion, if the cause shall have been once remanded before, proceed to a final decision of the same, and award

No writs of error but as above mentioned. execution. But no other error shall be assigned or regarded as a ground of reversal in any such case as aforesaid, than such as appears on the face of the record, and immediately respects the before mentioned questions of validity or construction of the said constitution, treaties, statutes, commissions, or authorities in dispute.

In cases of forfeiture the courts may give judgment according to equity. SEC. 26. *And be it further enacted,* That in all causes brought before either of the courts of the United States to recover the forfeiture annexed to any articles of agreement, covenant, bond, or other speciality, where the forfeiture, breach or non-performance shall appear, by the default or confession of the defendant, or upon demurrer, the court before whom the action is, shall render judgment therein for the plaintiff to recover so much as is due according to equity. And when the

Jury to assess damages when the sum is uncertain. sum for which judgment should be rendered is uncertain, the same shall, if either of the parties request it, be assessed by a jury.

Marshal to be appointed. Duration of office. SEC. 27. *And be it further enacted,* That a marshal shall be appointed in and for each district for the term of four years, but shall be removable from office at pleasure, whose duty it shall be to attend the district and circuit courts when sitting therein, and also the Supreme Court in the district in which that court shall sit. And to execute throughout the district, all lawful precepts directed to him, and issued under the authority of the United States, and he shall have power to command all necessary assistance in the execution of his duty, and to appoint as there shall be occasion, one or more deputies, who shall be

Deputies removable by the district and circuit courts. removable from office by the judge of the district court, or the circuit court sitting within the district, at the pleasure of either; and before he enters on the duties of his office, he shall become bound for the faithful performance of the same, by himself and by his deputies before the judge of the district court to the United States, jointly and severally, with two good and sufficient sureties,

Sureties. inhabitants and freeholders of such district, to be approved by the district judge, in the sum of twenty thousand dollars, and shall take before said judge, as shall also his deputies, before they enter on the duties of their appointment, the

Oath of marshal, and of his deputies. following oath of office: "I, A. B., do solemnly swear or affirm, that I will faithfully execute all lawful precepts directed to the marshal of the district of   under the authority of the United States, and true returns make, and in all things well and truly, and without malice or partiality, perform the duties of the office of marshal (or marshal's deputy, as the case may be) of the district of　　　　, during my continuance in said office, and take only my lawful fees. So help me God."

If marshal, or his deputy, a party to a suit, process to be directed to a person selected by the court.

Deputies to continue in office on the death of the marshal.

Defaults of deputies.

Powers of the executor or administrator of deceased marshals.

Marshal's power after removal.

SEC. 28. *And be it further enacted,* That in all causes wherein the marshal or his deputy shall be a party, the writs and precepts therein shall be directed to such disinterested person as the court, or any justice or judge therof may appoint, and the person so appointed, is hereby authorized to execute and return the same. And in case of the death of any marshal, his deputy or deputies shall continue in office, unless otherwise specially removed; and shall execute the same in the name of the deceased, until another marshal shall be appointed and sworn: And the defaults or misfeasances in office of such deputy or deputies in the mean time, as well as before, shall be adjudged a breach of the condition of the bond given, as before directed, by the marshal who appointed them; and the executor or administrator of the deceased marshal shall have like remedy for the defaults and misfeasances in office of such deputy or deputies during such interval, as they would be entitled to if the marshal had continued in life and in the exercise of his said office, until his successor was appointed, and sworn or affirmed: And every marshal or his deputy when removed from office, or when the term for which the marshal is appointed shall expire, shall have power notwithstanding to execute all such precepts as may be in their hands respectively at the time of such removal or expiration of office; and the marshal shall be held answerable for the delivery to his successor of all prisoners which may be in his custody at the time of his removal, or when the term for which he is appointed shall expire, and for that purpose may retain such prisoners in his custody until his successor shall be appointed and qualified as the law directs.

Trial of cases punishable with death to be had in county.

Jurors by lot.

Writs of venire facias from clerk's office.

SEC. 29. *And be it further enacted,* That in cases punishable with death, the trial shall be had in the county where the offence was committed, or where that cannot be done without great inconvenience, twelve petit jurors at least shall be summoned from thence. And jurors in all cases to serve in the courts of the United States shall be designated by lot or otherwise in each State respectively according to the mode of forming juries therein now practised, so far as the laws of the same shall render such designation practicable by the courts or marshals of the United States; and the jurors shall have the same qualifications as are requisite for jurors by the laws of the State of which they are citizens, to serve in the highest courts of law of such State, and shall be returned as there shall be occasion for them, from such parts of the district from time to time as the court shall direct, so as shall be most favourable to an impartial trial, and so as not to incur an unnecessary expense, or unduly to burthen the citizens of any part of the district with such services. And writs of *venire farias* when directed by the court shall issue from the clerk's office, and shall be served and returned by the marshal in his proper person, or by his deputy, or in case the marshal or his deputy is not an indifferent person, or is interested in the event of the cause, by such fit person as the court shall specially appoint for that purpose, to whom they shall administer an oath or affirmation that he will truly and impartially serve and return such writ. And when from chal-

Juries de talibus, &c.

Mode of proof.

Depositions de bene esse.

Adverse party to be notified.

Notice in admiralty and maritime causes.

Agent notified.

Depositions retained.

Persons may be compelled to appear and testify.

Appeal allowed.

lenges or otherwise there shall not be a jury to determine any civil or criminal cause, the marshal or his deputy shall, by order of the court where such defect of jurors shall happen, return jurymen *de talibus circumstantibus* sufficient to complete the pannel; and when the marshal or his deputy are disqualified as aforesaid, jurors may be returned by such disinterested person as the court shall appoint.

SEC. 30. *And be it further enacted,* That the mode of proof by oral testimony and examination of witnesses in open court shall be the same in all the courts of the United States, as well in the trial of causes in equity and of admiralty and maritime jurisdiction, as of actions at common law. And when the testimony of any person shall be necessary in any civil cause depending in any district in any court of the United States, who shall live at a greater distance from the place of trial than one hundred miles, or is bound on a voyage to sea, or is about to go out of the United States, or out of such district, and to a greater distance from the place of trial than as aforesaid, before the time of trial, or is ancient or very infirm, the deposition of such person may be taken *de bene esse* before any justice or judge of any of the courts of the United States, or before any chancellor, justice or judge of a supreme or superior court, mayor or chief magistrate of a city, or judge of a county court or court of common pleas of any of the United States, not being of counsel or attorney to either of the parties, or interested in the event of the cause, provided that a notification from the magistrate before whom the deposition is to be taken to the adverse party, to be present at the taking of the same, and to put interrogatories, if he think fit, be first made out and served on the adverse party or his attorney as either may be nearest, if either is within one hundred miles of the place of such caption, allowing time for their attendance after notified, not less than at the rate of one day, Sundays exclusive, for every twenty miles travel. And in causes of admiralty and maritime jurisdiction, or other cases of seizure when a libel shall be filed, in which an adverse party is not named, and depositions of persons circumstanced as aforesaid shall be taken before a claim be put in, the like notification as aforesaid shall be given to the person having the agency or possession of the property libelled at the time of the capture or seizure of the same, if known to the libellant. And every person deposing as aforesaid shall be carefully examined and cautioned, and sworn or affirmed to testify the whole truth, and shall subscribe the testimony by him or her given after the same shall be reduced to writing, which shall be done only by the magistrate taking the deposition, or by the deponent in his presence. And the depositions so taken shall be retained by such magistrate until he deliver the same with his own hand into the court for which they are taken, or shall, together with a certificate of the reasons as aforesaid of their being taken, and of the notice if any given to the adverse party, be by him the said magistrate sealed up and directed to such court, and remain under his seal until opened in court. And any person may be compelled to appear and depose as aforesaid in the same manner as to appear and testify in court. And in the trial of any cause of admiralty or maritime jurisdiction in a district court, the decree in which may be appealed from, if either party shall suggest to and satisfy the court that probably it will not be in his power to produce the witnesses there testifying before the circuit court should an appeal be had, and shall move that their testimony be taken down in writing, it shall be so done by the clerk of the court. And if an appeal be had, such testimony may be used on the trial of the same if it shall appear to the satisfaction of the court which shall try the appeal, that the witnesses are then dead or gone out of the United States, or to a greater distance than as aforesaid from the place where the court is sitting, or that by reason of age, sickness, bodily infirmity or imprisonment, they are unable to travel and appear at court, but not otherwise. And unless the same shall be made to appear on the trial of any cause, with respect to witnesses whose depositions may have been taken therein, such depositions shall not be admitted or used in the cause. *Provided,* That nothing herein shall be construed to prevent any court of the United States from granting a *dedimus potestatem* to take depositions according to common usage, when it may be necessary to prevent a failure or delay of justice, which power they shall severally possess, nor to extend to depositions taken in *perpetuam rei memoriam,* which if they relate to matters that may be cognizable in any court of the United States, a circuit court on application thereto made as a court of equity, may, according to the usages in chancery direct to be taken.

Depositions used in case of sickness, death, &c.

Dedimus potestatem as usual.

SEC. 31. *And be it [further] enacted,* That where any suit shall be depending in any court of the United States, and either of the parties shall die before final judgment, the executor or administrator of such deceased party who was plaintiff, petitioner, or defendant, in case the cause of action doth by law survive, shall have full power to prosecute or defend any such suit or action until final judgment; and the defendant or defendants are hereby obliged to answer thereto accordingly; and the court before whom such cause may be depending, is hereby empowered and directed to hear and determine the same, and to render judgment for or against the executor or administrator, as the case may require. And if such executor or administrator having been duly served with a *scire facias* from the office of the clerk of the court where such suit is depending, twenty days beforehand, shall neglect or refuse to become a party to the suit, the court may render judgment against the estate of the deceased party, in the same manner as if the executor or administrator had voluntarily made himself a party to the suit. And the executor or administrator who shall become a party as aforesaid, shall, upon motion to the court where the suit is depending, be entitled to a continuance of the same until the next term of the said court. And if there be two or more plaintiffs or defendants, and one or more of them shall die, if the cause of action shall survive to the surviving plaintiff or plaintiffs, or against the surviving defendant or defendants, the writ or action shall not be thereby abated; but such death being suggested upon the record, the action shall proceed at the suit of the surviving plaintiff or plaintiffs against the surviving defendant or defendants.

Executor or administrator may prosecute and defend.

Neglect of executor or administrator to become a party to the suit, judgment to be rendered. Executor and administrator may have continuance.

Two plaintiffs. Surviving plaintiff may continue suit.

SEC. 32. *And be it further enacted,* That no summons, writ, declaration, return, process, judgment, or other proceedings in civil causes in any of the courts of the United States, shall be abated, arrested, quashed or reversed, for any defect or want of form, but the said courts respectively shall proceed and give judgment according as the right of the cause and matter in law shall appear unto them, without regarding any imperfections, defects, or want of form in such writ, declaration, or other pleading, return, process, judgment, or course of proceeding whatsoever, except those only in cases of demurrer, which the party demurring shall specially sit down and express together with his demurrer as the cause thereof. And the said courts respectively shall and may, by virtue of this act, from time to time, amend all and every such imperfections, defects and wants of form, other than those only which the party demurring shall express as aforesaid, and may at any time permit either of the parties to amend any defect in the process or pleadings, upon such conditions as the said courts respectively shall in their discretion, and by their rules prescribe.

Writs shall not abate for defect of form.

Exceptions.

Courts may amend imperfections.

SEC. 33. *And be it further enacted,* That for any crime or offence against the United States, the offender may, by any justice or judge of the United States, or by any justice of the peace, or other magistrate of any of the United States where he may be found agreeably to the usual mode of process against offenders in such state, and at the expense of the United States, be arrested, and imprisoned or bailed, as the case may be, for trial before such court of the United States as by this act has cognizance of the offence. And copies of the process shall be returned as speedily as may be into the clerk's office of such court, together with the recognizances of the witnesses for their appearance to testify in the case; which recognizances the magistrate before whom the examination shall be, may require on pain of imprisonment. And if such commitment of the offender, or the witnesses shall be in a district other than that in which the offence is to be tried, it shall be the duty of the judge of that district where the delinquent is imprisoned, seasonably to issue, and of the marshal of the same district to execute, a warrant for the removal of the offender, and the witnesses, or either of them, as the case may be, to the district in which the trial is to be had. And upon all arrests in criminal cases, bail shall be admitted, except where the punishment may be death, in which cases it shall not be admitted but by the supreme or a circuit court, or by a justice of the supreme court, or a judge of a district court, who shall exercise their discretion therein, regarding the nature and circumstances of the offence, and of the evidence, and the usages of law. And if a person committed by a justice of the supreme or a judge of a district court for an offence not punishable with death, shall afterwards procure bail, and there be no judge of the United States in the district to take the same, it may be taken by any judge of the supreme or superior court of law of such state.

Criminals against U.S. arrested by any justice of the peace.

Recognizance to be returned to the clerk's office.

Offender may be removed by warrant.

Bail admitted.

Bail, how taken.

SEC. 34. *And be it further enacted,* That the laws of the several states, except where the constitution, treaties or statutes of the United States shall otherwise require or provide, shall be regarded as rules of decision in trials at common law in the courts of the United States in cases where they apply.

Laws of States rules of decision.

SEC. 35. *And be it further enacted,* That in all the courts of the United States, the parties may plead and manage their own causes personally or by the assistance of such counsel or attorneys at law as by the rules of the said courts respectively shall be permitted to manage and conduct causes therein. And there shall be appointed in each district a meet person learned in the law to act as attorney for the United States in such district, who shall be sworn or affirmed to the faithful execution of his office, whose duty it shall be to prosecute in such district all delinquents for crimes and offences, cognizable under the authority of the United States, and all civil actions in which the United States shall be concerned, except before the supreme court in the district in which that court shall be holden. And he shall

receive as a compensation for his services such fees as shall be taxed therefor in the respective courts before which the suits or prosecutions shall be. And there shall also be appointed a meet person, learned in the law, to act as attorney-general for the United States, who shall be sworn or affirmed to a faithful execution of his office; whose duty it shall be to prosecute and conduct all suits in the Supreme Court in which the United States shall be concerned, and to give his advice and opinion upon questions of law when required by the President of the United States, or when requested by the heads of any of the departments, touching any matters that may concern their departments, and shall receive such compensation for his services as shall by law be provided.

APPROVED, September 24, 1789.

Circuit Court of Appeals Act of 1891

Source: Public Statutes at Large of the United States of America. Vol. XXVI. Washington,
D.C.: U.S. Government Printing Office, 1891.

March 3, 1891

An act to establish circuit courts of appeals and to define and regulate in certain cases the jurisdiction of the courts of the United States, and for other purposes.

United States courts. Additional circuit judges to be appointed. Qualifications, etc.

Be it enacted by the Senate and House of Representatives of the United States of America in Congress assembled, That there shall be appointed by the President of the United States, by and with the advice and consent of the Senate, in each circuit an additional circuit judge, who shall have the same qualifications, and shall have the same power and jurisdiction therein that the circuit judges of the United States, within their respective circuits, now have under existing laws, and who shall be entitled to the same compensation as the circuit judges of the United States in their respective circuits now have.

Circuit court of appeals created. Composition.

General powers.

SEC. 2. That there is hereby created in each circuit a circuit court of appeals, which shall consist of three judges, of whom two shall constitute a quorum, and which shall be a court of record with appellate jurisdiction, as is hereafter limited and established. Such court shall prescribe the form and style of its seal and the form of writs and other process and procedure as may be conformable to the exercise of its jurisdiction as shall be conferred by law. It shall have the ap-

Marshal.

pointment of the marshal of the court with the same duties and powers under the regulations of the court as are now provided for the marshal of the Supreme Court of the United States, so far as the same may be applicable. The court shall also

Clerk.

appoint a clerk, who shall perform and exercise the same duties and powers in regard to all matters within its jurisdiction as are now exercised and performed by the clerk of the Supreme Court of the United States, so far as the same may

Salaries.

be applicable. The salary of the marshal of the court shall be twenty-five hundred dollars a year, and the salary of the clerk of the court shall be three thousand dollars a year, to be paid in equal proportions quarterly. The costs and fees in the

Costs, etc.

Supreme Court now provided for by law shall be costs and fees in the circuit courts of appeals; and the same shall be expended, accounted for, and paid for, and paid over to the Treasury Department of the United States in the same manner as is provided in respect of the costs and fees in the Supreme Court.

Rules, etc.

The court shall have power to establish all rules and regulations for the conduct of the business of the court within its jurisdiction as conferred by law.

Constitution of court.

SEC. 3. That the Chief-Justice and the associate justices of the Supreme Court assigned to each circuit, and the circuit judges within each circuit, and the several district judges within each circuit, shall be competent to sit as judges of the circuit court of appeals within their respective circuits in the manner hereinafter provided. In

Precedence.

case the Chief-Justice or an associate justice of the Supreme Court should attend at any session of the circuit court of appeals he shall preside, and the circuit judges in attendance upon the court in

the absence of the Chief-Justice or associate justice of the Supreme Court shall preside in the order of the seniority of their repective commissions.

Service of district judges

In case the full court at any time shall not be made up by the attendance of the Chief-Justice or an associate justice of the Supreme Court and circuit judges, one or more district judges within the circuit shall be competent to sit in the court according to such order or provision among the district judges as either by general or particular

Proviso

No judge to sit on appeal from his court.

assignment shall be designated by the court: *Provided,* That no justice or judge before whom a cause or question may have been tried or heard in a district court, or existing circuit court, shall sit on the trial or hearing of such cause or question in

Terms.

the circuit court of appeals. A term shall be held annually by the circuit court of appeals in the

Regular.

several judicial circuits at the following places: In the first circuit, in the city of Boston; in the second circuit, in the city of New York; in the third circuit, in the city of Philadelphia; in the fourth circuit, in the city of Richmond; in the fifth circuit, in the city of New Orleans; in the sixth circuit, in the city of Cincinnati; in the seventh circuit, in the city of Chicago; in the eighth circuit, in the city of Saint Louis; in the ninth circuit in the city of San Francisco; and in such

Additional.

First term.

other places in each of the above circuits as said court may from time to time designate. The first terms of said courts shall be held on the second

Post, p. 1115.

Monday in January, eighteen hundred and ninety-one, and thereafter at such times as may be fixed by said courts.

No appeal allowed from district to circuit courts.

SEC. 4. That no appeal, whether by writ of error or otherwise, shall hereafter be taken or allowed from the district court to the existing circuit courts, and no appellate jurisdiction shall hereafter be exercised or allowed by said existing circuit courts, but all appeals by writ of error

Appeals, etc., from circuit court.

otherwise, from said district courts shall only be subject to review in the Supreme Court of the United States or in the circuit court of appeals hereby established, as is hereinafter provided, and the review, by appeal, by writ of error, or otherwise, from the existing circuit courts shall be had only in the Supreme Court of the United States or in the circuit courts of appeals hereby established according to the provisions of this act regulating the same.

Appeals allowed direct to Supreme Court.

SEC. 5. That appeals or writs of error may be taken from the district courts or from the existing circuit courts direct to the Supreme Court in the following cases:

Jurisdiction questions.

In any case in which the jurisdiction of the court is in issue; in such cases the question of jurisdiction alone shall be certified to the Supreme Court from the court below for decision.

Prizes.

From the final sentences and decrees in prize causes.

Capital crimes.

In cases of conviction of a capital or otherwise infamous crime.

Constitutional questions.

In any case that involves the construction or application of the Constitution of the United States.

Construction of law, treaty, etc.

In any case in which the constitutionality of any law of the United States, or the validity or construction of any treaty made under its authority, is drawn in question.

Conflict of laws.

In any case in which the constitution or law of a State is claimed to be in contravention of the Constitution of the United States.

Appeals from highest State court.

Nothing in this act shall affect the jurisdiction of the Supreme Court in cases appealed from the highest court of a State, nor the construction of the statute providing for review of such cases.

Jurisdiction of court of appeals.

SEC. 6. That the circuit courts of appeals established by this act shall exercise appellate jurisdiction to review by appeal or by writ of error final decision in the district court and the existing circuit courts in all cases other than those provided for in the preceding section of this act, unless otherwise provided by law, and the judg-

Judgments final.

ments or decrees of the circuit courts of appeals shall be final in all cases in which the jurisdiction is dependent entirely upon the opposite parties to the suit or controversy, being aliens and citizens of the United States or citizens of different States; also in all cases arising under the patent laws, under the revenue laws, and under the criminal laws and in admiralty cases, excepting that in every such subject within its appellate jurisdiction

Certificate for instruction.

the circuit court of appeals at any time may certify to the Supreme Court of the United States any questions or propositions of law concerning

Proceedings in Supreme Court.

which it desires the instruction of that court for its proper decision. And thereupon the Supreme Court may either give its instruction on the questions and propositions certified to it, which shall be binding upon the circuit courts of appeals in such case, or it may require that the whole record and cause may be sent up to it for its consideration, and thereupon shall decide the whole matter in controversy in the same manner as if it had been brought there for review by writ of error or appeal.

Certiorari to Supreme Court.

And excepting also that in any such case as is hereinbefore made final in the circuit court of appeals it shall be competent for the Supreme Court to require, by certiorari or otherwise, any such case to be certified to the Supreme Court for its review and determination with the same power and authority in the case as if it had been carried by appeal or writ of error to the Supreme Court.

Appeals and writs of error.

In all cases not hereinbefore, in this section, made final there shall be of right an appeal or writ of error or review of the case by the Supreme Court of the United States where the matter in controversy shall exceed one thousand dollars besides costs. But no such appeal shall be taken or writ of error sued out unless within one year after

Limitation.

the entry of the order, judgment, or decree sought to be reviewed.

Appeal in equity causes.

SEC. 7. That where, upon a hearing in equity in a district court, or in an existing circuit court, an injunction shall be granted or continued by an interlocutory order or decree, in a cause in which an appeal from a final decree may be taken under the provisions of this act to the circuit court of appeals, an appeal may be taken from such interlocutory order or decree granting or continuing such injunction to the circuit court of appeals:

Proviso.

To be taken in 30 days.

Provided, That the appeal must be taken within thirty days from the entry of such order or decree, and it shall take precedence in the appellate court; and the proceedings in other respects in the court below shall not be stayed unless otherwise ordered by that court during the pendency of such appeal.

Expenses of attending judges.

SEC. 8. That any justice or judge, who, in pursuance of the provisions of this act, shall attend the circuit court of appeals held at any place other than where he resides shall, upon his written certificate, be paid by the marshal of the district in which the court shall be held his reasonable expenses for travel and attendance, not to exceed ten dollars per day, and such payments shall be allowed the marshal in the settlement of his accounts with the United States.

Court rooms in public buildings.

SEC. 9. That the marshals of the several districts in which said circuit court of appeals may be held shall, under the direction of the Attorney-General of the United States, and with his approval, provide such rooms in the public buildings of the United States as may be necessary, and pay

Expenses.

Proviso.

Rent.

all incidental expenses of said court, including criers, bailiffs, and messengers: Provided, however, That in case proper rooms can not be provided in such buildings, then the said marshals, with the approval of the Attorney-General of the United States, may, from time to time, lease such rooms as may be necessary for such courts. That

Compensation to officers.

the marshals, criers, clerks, bailiffs, and messengers shall be allowed the same compensation for their respective services as are allowed for similar services in the existing circuit courts.

Remanding causes reviewed by Supreme Court.

SEC. 10. That whenever an appeal or writ of error or otherwise a case coming directly from the district court or existing circuit court shall be reviewed and determined in the Supreme Court the cause shall be remanded to the proper district or circuit court for further proceedings to be taken in pursuance of such determination. And when-

From circuit courts of appeal.

ever on appeal or writ of error or otherwise a case coming from a circuit court of appeals shall be reviewed and determined in the Supreme Court the cause shall be remanded by the Supreme Court to the proper district or circuit court for further proceedings in pursuance of such determi-

Review in circuit court of appeals.

nation. Whenever on appeal or writ or error or otherwise a case coming from a district or circuit court shall be reviewed and determined in the circuit court of appeals in a case in which the decision in the circuit court of appeals is final such cause shall be remanded to the said district or circuit court for further proceedings to be there taken in pursuance of such determination.

Appeals, etc., to be brought in six months.

SEC. 11. That no appeal or writ of error by which any order, judgment, or decree may be reviewed in the circuit courts of appeals under the provisions of this act shall be taken or sued out except within six months after the entry of the order, judgment, or decree sought to be reviewed:

Proviso.

Less time in certain cases.

Provided however, That in all cases in which a lesser time is now by law limited for appeals or writs of error such limits of time shall apply to appeals or writs of error in such cases taken to or sued out from the circuit courts of appeals. And

Rules and regulations, etc.

all provisions of law now in force regulating the methods and system of review, through appeals or writs of error, shall regulate the methods and system of appeals and writs of error provided for in this act in respect of the circuit courts of appeals, including all provisions for bonds or other securities to be required and taken on such appeals, in respect of cases brought or to be brought to that court, shall have the same powers and duties as to the allowance of appeals or writs of error, and the conditions of such allowance, as now by law belong to the justices or judges in respect of the existing courts of the United States respectively.

Issue of writs.

R.S., sec. 716, p. 136.

SEC. 12. That the circuit court of appeals shall have the powers specified in section seven hundred and sixteen of the Revised Statutes of the United States.

Appeals, etc., from Indian Territory Court.

SEC. 13. Appeals and writs of error may be taken and prosecuted from the decisions of the United States court in the Indian Territory to the Supreme Court of the United States, or to the circuit court of appeals in the eighth circuit, in the same manner and under the same regulations as from the circuit or district courts of the United States, under this act.

Appeals to Supreme Court.

SEC. 14. That section six hundred and ninety-one of the Revised Statutes of the United States

R.S., sec. 691, p. 128, repealed.

Vol. 18, p. 316, repealed.

Inconsistent laws repealed.

Jurisdiction in cases from Territorial supreme courts.

and section three of an act entitled "An act to facilitate the disposition of cases in the Supreme Court, and for other purposes," approved February sixteenth, eighteen hundred and seventy-five, be, and the same are hereby repealed. And all acts and parts of acts relating to appeals or writs of error inconsistent with the provisions for review by appeals or writs of error in the preceding sections five and six of this act are hereby repealed.

SEC. 15. That the circuit court of appeal in cases in which the judgments of the circuit courts of appeal are made final by this act shall have the same appellate jurisdiction, by writ of error or appeal, to review the judgments, orders, and decrees of the supreme courts of the several Territories as by this act they may have to review the judgments, orders, and decrees of the district court and circuit courts; and for that purpose the several Territories shall, by orders of the Supreme court, to be made from time to time, be assigned to particular circuits.

Approved, March 3, 1891.

Judiciary Act of 1925

Source: Public Statutes at Large of the United States of America. Vol. XLIII, Part 1.
Washington, D.C.: U.S. Government Printing Office, 1925.

February 13,
1925. [H.R. 8206.]
[Public, No. 415.]

Judicial Code.

Circuit Courts
of Appeals.
Appeals or writs
of error to.
Vol. 38, p. 803,
amended.
In district courts.
Exception.
Hawaii and Porto
Rico district
courts.
Alaska and
Virgin Islands.
Cases
reviewable.

Canal Zone.
Vol. 42, p. 1006.

Hawaii and Porto
Rico Supreme
Courts.
Cases
reviewable.

United States
Court for China.
Other appellate
jurisdiction.

Specified orders,
etc., of district
courts.

Awards of rail-
way employees'
controversies.
Vol. 38, p. 107.

Bankruptcy
cases.
Vol. 30, p. 553.

In Alaska and
Hawaii.
In Porto Rico.

Distribution
to circuits.

Further speci-
fied authority.
Federal Trade
Commission
orders.
Vol. 38, p. 720.

Orders of Inter-
state Commerce
Commission,
etc.,
under Clayton
Act.
Vol. 38, p. 735.

Appeals allowed
from injunctions
and interlocu-
tory orders of
district courts.
Cases specified.
Vol. 36, p. 1157,
amended.

Authority of
Supreme Court.

Provisos.
Precedence
given.

Additional bond
discretionary.

Supreme Court.
Writ of error
allowed from
decision of
State court
against validity

An Act To amend the Judicial Code, and to further define the jurisdiction of the circuit courts of appeals and of the Supreme Court, and for other purposes.

Be it enacted by the Senate and House of Representatives of the United States of America in Congress assembled, That sections 128, 129, 237, 238, 239, and 240 of the Judicial Code as now existing be, and they are severally, amended and reenacted to read as follows:

SEC. 128. (a) The circuit courts of appeal shall have appellate jurisdiction to review by appeal or writ of error final decisions —

"First. In the district courts, in all cases save where a direct review of the decision may be had in the Supreme Court under section 238.

"Second. In the United States district courts for Hawaii and for Porto Rico in all cases.

"Third. In the district courts for Alaska or any division thereof, and for the Virgin Islands, in all cases, civil and criminal, wherein the Constitution or a statute or treaty of the United States or any authority exercised thereunder is involved; in all other civil cases wherein the value in controversy, exclusive of interest and costs, exceeds $1,000; in all other criminal cases where the offense charged is punishable by imprisonment for a term exceeding one year or by death, and in all habeas corpus proceedings; and in the district court for the Canal Zone in the cases and mode prescribed in the Act approved September 21, 1922, amending prior laws relating to the Canal Zone.

"Fourth. In the Supreme Courts of the Territory of Hawaii and of Porto Rico, in all civil cases, civil or criminal, wherein the Constitution or a statute or treaty of the United States or any authority exercised thereunder is involved; in all other civil cases wherein the value in controversy, exclusive of interest and costs, exceeds $5,000, and in all habeas corpus proceedings.

"Fifth. In the United States Court for China, in all cases.

"(b) The circuit court of appeals shall also have appellate jurisdiction—

"First. To review the interlocutory orders or decrees of the district courts which are specified in section 129.

"Second. To review decisions of the district courts sustaining or overruling exceptions to awards in arbitrations, as provided in section 8 of an Act entitled 'An Act providing for mediation, conciliation, and arbitration in controversies between certain employers and their employees,' approved July 15, 1913.

"(c) The circuit courts of appeal shall also have an appellate and supervisory jurisdiction under sections 24 and 25 of the Bankruptcy Act of July 1, 1898, over all proceedings, controversies, and cases had or brought in the district courts under that Act or any of its amendments, and shall exercise the same in the manner prescribed in those sections; and the jurisdiction of the Circuit Court of Appeals for the Ninth Circuit in this

regard shall cover the courts of bankruptcy in Alaska and Hawaii, and that of the Circuit Court of Appeals for the First Circuit shall cover the court of bankruptcy in Porto Rico.

"(d) The review under this section shall be in the following circuit courts of appeal: The decisions of a district court of the United State within a State in the circuit court of appeals for the circuit embracing such State; those of the District Court of Alaska or any division thereof, the United States district court, and the Supreme Court of Hawaii, and the United States Court for China, in the Circuit Court of Appeals for the Ninth Circuit; those of the United States district court and the Supreme Court of Porto Rico in the Circuit Court of Appeals for the First Circuit; those of the District Court of the Virgin Islands in the Circuit Court of Appeals for the Third Circuit; and those of the District Court of the Canal Zone in the Circuit Court of Appeals for the Fifth Circuit.

"(e) The circuit courts of appeal are further empowered to enforce, set aside, or modify orders of the Federal Trade Commission, as provided in section 5 of 'An Act to create a Federal Trade Commission, to define its powers and duties, and for other purposes,' approved September 26, 1914; and orders of the Interstate Commerce Commission, the Federal Reserve Board, and the Federal Trade Commission, as provided in section 11 of 'An Act to supplement existing laws against unlawful restraints and monopolies, and for other purposes,' approved October 15, 1914.

"SEC. 129. Where, upon a hearing in a district court, or by a judge thereof in vacation, an injunction is granted, continued, modified, refused, or dissolved by an interlocutory order or decree, or an application to dissolve or modify an injunction is refused, or an interlocutory order or decree is made appointing a receiver, or refusing an order to wind up a pending receivership or to take the appropriate steps to accomplish the purposes thereof, such as directing a sale or other disposal of property held thereunder, an appeal may be taken from such interlocutory order or decree to the circuit court of appeals; and sections 239 and 240 shall apply to such cases in the circuit courts of appeals as to other cases therein; *Provided,* That the appeal to the circuit court of appeal must be applied for within thirty days from the entry of such order or decree, and shall take precedence in the appellate court; and the proceedings in other respects in the district court shall not be stayed during the pendency of such appeal unless otherwise ordered by the court, or the appellate court, or a judge thereof: *Provided, however,* That the distict court may, in its discretion, require an additional bond as a condition of the appeal."

SEC. 237. (a) A final judgment or decree in any suit in the highest court of a State in which a decision in the suit could be had, where is drawn in question the validity of a treaty or statute of the United States, and the decision is against its

of treaty or statute of United States. If validity of State statute drawn in question as repugnant to Constitution, etc. Vol. 39, p. 726, amended. Authority of Supreme Court.

validity; or where is drawn, in question the validity of a statute of any State, on the ground of its being repugnant to the Constitution, treaties, or laws of the United States, and the decision is in favor of its validity, may be reviewed by the Supreme Court upon a writ of error. The writ shall have the same effect as if the judgment or decree had been rendered or passed in a court of the United States. The Supreme Court may reverse, modify, or affirm the judgment or decree of such State court, and may, in its discretion, award execution or remand the cause to the court from which it was removed by the writ.

Certiorari to State court where validity of United States treaty or statute drawn in question.

"(b) It shall be competent for the Supreme Court, by certiorari, to require that there be certified to it for review and determination, with the same power and authority and with like effect as if brought up by writ of error, any cause wherein a final judgment or decree has been rendered or passed by the highest court of a State in which a decision could be had where is drawn in question the validity of a treaty or statute of the United States; or where is drawn in question the validity of a statute of any State on the ground of its being repugnant to the Constitution, treaties, or laws of the United States; or where any title, right, privilege, or immunity is specially set up or claimed by either party under the Constitution, or any treaty or statute of, or commission held or authority exercised under, the United States; and the power to review under this paragraph may be exercised as well where the Federal claim is sustained as where it is denied. Nothing in this paragraph shall be construed to limit or detract from the right to a review on a writ of error in a case where such a right is conferred by the preceding paragraph; nor shall the fact that a review on a writ of error might be obtained under the preceding paragraph be an obstacle to granting a review on certiorari under this paragraph.

State law as repugnant to the Constitution, etc. Title, etc., set up under United States authority.

Use of writ of error not hereby limited.

Writ of error not dismissed if certiorari proper mode of review, etc.

"(c) If a writ of error be improvidently sought and allowed under this section in a case where the proper mode of invoking a review is by a petition for certiorari, this alone shall not be a ground for dismissal; but the papers whereon the writ of error was allowed shall be regarded and acted on as a petition for certiorari and as if duly presented to the Supreme Court at the time they were presented to the court or judge by whom the writ of error was allowed: *Provided,* That where in such a case there appears to be no reasonable ground for granting a petition for certiorari it shall be competent for the Supreme Court to adjudge to the respondent reasonable damages for his delay, and single or double costs, as provided in section 1010 of the Revised Statutes."

Proviso. Damages, etc., if no reasonable ground for certiorari.

R.S., sec. 1010, p. 189.

Direct review of action of district courts in specified Acts limited. Vol. 38, p. 804, amended. Expediting antitrust, etc., cases. Vol. 32, p. 823.

"SEC. 238. A direct review by the Supreme Court of an interlocutory or final judgment or decree of a district court may be had where it is so provided in the following Acts or parts of Acts, and not otherwise:

"(1) Section 2 of the Act of February 11, 1903, 'to expedite the hearing and determination' of certain suits brought by the United States under the antitrust or interstate commerce laws, and so forth.

Adverse decisions in criminal cases. Vol. 34, p. 1246.

"(2) The Act of March 2, 1907, 'providing for writs of error in certain instances in criminal cases' where the decision of the district court is adverse to the United States.

Restricting interlocutory

"(3) An Act restricting the issuance of interlocutory injunctions to suspend the enforcement of

injunctions against State laws, etc. Vol. 37, p. 1013, amended.

the statute of a State or of an order made by an administrative board or commission created by and acting under the statute of a State, approved March 4, 1913, which Act is hereby amended by adding at the end thereof, 'The requirement respecting the presence of three judges shall also apply to the final hearing in such suit in the district court; and a direct appeal to the Supreme Court may be taken from a final decree granting or denying a permanent injunction in such suit.'

Requirement for presence of three judges, etc.

Judgments, etc., on Interstate Commerce Commission orders. Vol. 38, p. 220.

"(4) So much of 'An Act making appropriations to supply urgent deficiencies in appropriations for the fiscal year 1913, and for other purposes,' approved October 22, 1913, as relates to the review of interlocutory and final judgments and decrees in suits to enforce, suspend, or set aside orders of the Interstate Commerce Commission other than for the payment of money.

Orders by Interstate Commerce Commission as to livestock, poultry, etc. Vol. 42, p. 168.

"(5) Section 316 of 'An Act to regulate interstate and foreign commerce in livestock, livestock products, dairy products, poultry, poultry products, and eggs, and for other purposes' approved August 15, 1921."

Questions certified for instructions by courts of appeals. Vol. 36, p. 1157, amended.

Authority of court.

"SEC. 239. In any case, civil or criminal, in a circuit court of appeals, or in the Court of Appeals of the District of Columbia, the court at any time may certify to the Supreme Court of the United States any questions or propositions of law concerning which instructions are desired for the proper decision of the cause; and thereupon the Supreme Court may either give binding instructions on the questions and propositions certified or may require that the entire record in the cause be sent up for its consideration, and thereupon shall decide the whole matter in controversy in the same manner as if it had been brought there by writ of error or appeal."

Allowance of certiorari to courts of appeals on petition of either party. Vol. 36, p. 1157, amended.

SEC 240. (a) In any case, civil or criminal, in a circuit court of appeals, or in the Court of Appeals of the District of Columbia, it shall be competent for the Supreme Court of the United States, upon the petition of any party thereto, whether Government or other litigant, to require by certiorari, either before or after a judgment or decree by such lower court, that the cause be certified to the Supreme Court for determination by it with the same power and authority, and with like effect, as if the cause had been brought there by unrestricted writ of error or appeal.

Writ of error or appeal allowed, where decision against validity of State law as repugnant to United States Constitution, etc.

Limitation.

(b) Any case in a circuit court of appeals where is drawn in question the validity of a statute of any State, on the ground of its being repugnant to the Constitution, treaties, or laws of the United States, and the decision is against its validity, may, at the election of the party relying on such State statute, be taken to the Supreme Court for review on writ of error or appeal; but in that event a review on certiorari shall not be allowed at the instance of such party, and the review on such writ of error or appeal shall be restricted to an examination and decision of the Federal questions presented in the case.

No other review by Supreme Court.

"(c) No judgment or decree of a circuit court of appeals or of the Court of Appeals of the District of Columbia shall be subject to review by the Supreme Court otherwise than as provided in this section."

Certiorari, etc., allowed. Railway employees

SEC. 2. That cases in a circuit court of appeals under section 8 of "An Act providing for mediation, conciliation, and arbitration in controversies

arbitrations.
Vol. 38, p. 107.
Trade Commission orders.
Vol. 38, p. 720.

Clayton Act enforcement.
Vol. 38, p. 735.

between certain employers and their employees," approved July 15, 1913; under section 5 of "An Act to create a Federal Trade Commission, to define its powers and duties, and for other purposes," approved September 26, 1914; and under section 11 of "An Act to supplement existing laws against unlawful restraints and monopolies, and for other purposes," approved October 15, 1914, are included among the cases to which sections 239 and 240 of the Judicial Code shall apply.

Court of Claims.
May certify to Supreme Court questions of law for instruction.

SEC. 3. (a) That in any case in the court of Claims, including those begun under section 180 of the Judicial Code, that court at any time may certify to the Supreme Court any definite and distinct questions of law concerning which instructions are desired for the proper disposition of the cause; and thereupon the Supreme Court may give appropriate instructions on the questions certified and transmit the same to the Court of Claims for its guidance in the further progress of the cause.

Certiorari by either party of any cause for review and determination.

(b) In any case in the Court of Claims, including those begun under section 180 of the Judicial Code, it shall be competent for the Supreme Court, upon the petition of either party, whether Government or claimant, to require, by certiorari, that the cause, including the findings of fact and the judgment or decree, but omitting the evidence, be certified to it for review and determination with the same power and authority, and with like effect, as if the cause had been brought there by appeal.

No other review of judgments.

(c) All judgments and decrees of the Court of Claims shall be subject to review by the Supreme Court as provided in this section, and not otherwise.

Claims cases in district courts subject to like review as other judgments.
Ante, p. 938.

SEC. 4. That in cases in the district courts wherein they exercise concurrent jurisdiction with the Court of Claims or adjudicate claims against the United States the judgments shall be subject to review in the circuit courts of appeals like other judgments of the district courts; and sections 239 and 240 of the Judicial Code shall apply to such cases in the circuit courts of appeals as to other cases therein.

District of Columbia Court of Appeals. Jurisdiction of, like circuit court of appeals.

SEC. 5. That the Court of Appeals of the District of Columbia shall have the same appellate and supervisory jurisdiction over proceedings, controversies, and cases in bankruptcy in the District of Columbia that a circuit court of appeals has over such proceedings, controversies, and cases within its circuit, and shall exercise that jurisdiction in the same manner as a circuit court of appeals is required to exercise it.

Habeas corpus.
Circuit courts of appeals to review final orders for.

SEC. 6. (a) In a proceeding in habeas corpus in a district court, or before a district judge or a circuit judge, the final order shall be subject to review, on appeal, by the circuit court of appeals of the circuit wherein the proceeding is had. A circuit judge shall have the same power to grant writs of habeas corpus within his circuit that a district judge has within his district; and the order of the circuit judge shall be entered in the records of the district court of the district wherein the restraint complained of is had.

By District of Columbia Court of Appeals.

(b) In such a proceeding in the Supreme Court of the District of Columbia, or before a justice thereof, the final order shall be subject to review, on appeal, by the Court of Appeals of that District.

Authority of Supreme Court.
Ante, p. 938.

(c) Sections 239 and 240 of the Judicial Code shall apply to habeas corpus cases in the circuit courts of appeals and in the Court of Appeals of the District of Columbia as to other cases therein.

Circuit courts of appeals jurisdiction in State court cases.
R.S., secs. 765, 766, p. 144.
Vol. 35, p. 40.

(d) The provisions of sections 765 and 766 of the Revised Statutes, and the provisions of an Act entitled "An Act restricting in certain cases the right of appeal to the Supreme Court in habeas corpus proceedings," approved March 10, 1908, shall apply to appellate proceedings under this section as they heretofore have applied to direct appeals to the Supreme Court.

Philippine Islands.
Cases where certiorari from Supreme Court allowed.

Vol. 36, p. 1158.

No other appellate review allowed.

SEC. 7. That in any case in the Supreme Court of the Philippine Islands wherein the Constitution, or any statute or treaty of the United States is involved, or wherein the value in controversy exceeds $25,000, or wherein the title or possession of real estate exceeding in value the sum of $25,000 is involved or brought in question, it shall be competent for the Supreme Court of the United States, upon the petition of a party aggrieved by the final judgment or decree, to require, by certiorari, that the cause be certified to it for review and determination with the same power and authority, and with like effect, as if the cause had been brought before it on writ of error or appeal; and, except as provided in this section, the judgments and decrees of the Supreme Court of the Philippine Islands shall not be subject to appellate review.

Time limit for bringing judgments to Supreme Court for review.

SEC. 8 (a) That no writ of error, appeal, or writ of certiorari, intended to bring any judgment or decree before the Supreme Court for reivew shall be allowed or entertained unless application therefor be duly made within three months after the entry of such judgment or decree, excepting that writs of certiorari to the Supreme Court of the Philippine Islands may be granted where application therefor is made within six months:

Proviso.
Extension for cause.

Provided, That for good cause shown either of such periods for applying for a writ of certiorari may be extended not exceeding sixty days by a justice of the Supreme Court.

Certiorari allowed prior to hearing in courts of appeals.

(b) Where an application for a writ of certiori is made with the purpose of securing a removal of the case to the Supreme Court from a circuit court of appeals or the Court of Appeals of the District of Columbia before the court wherein the same is pending has given a judgment or decree the application may be made at any time prior to the hearing and submission in that court.

Time limit to apply for review by circuit courts of appeals.

(c) No writ of error or appeal intended to bring any judgment or decree before a circuit court of appeals for review shall be allowed unless application therefor be duly made within three months after the entry of such judgment or decree.

Judgments may be stayed in cases subject to certiorari from Supreme Court.

Surety to be given, etc.

(d) In any case in which the final judgment or decree of any court is subject to review by the Supreme Court on writ of certiorari, the execution and enforcement of such judgment or decree may be stayed for a reasonable time to enable the party aggrieved to apply for and to obtain a writ of certiorari from the Supreme Court. The stay may be granted by a judge of the court rendering the judgment or decree or by a justice of the Supreme Court, and may be conditioned on the giving of good and sufficient security, to be approved by such judge or justice, that if the aggrieved party fails to make application for such writ within the period allotted therefor, or fails to obtain an order granting his application, or fails to make his plea good in the Supreme Court, he shall answer for all damage and costs which the other party may sustain by reason of the stay.

Ascertainment of value not disclosed upon record, if jurisdiction depends on amount thereof.

SEC. 9. That in any case where the power to review, whether in the circuit courts of appeals or in the Supreme Court, depends upon the amount or value in controversy, such amount or value, if not otherwise satisfactorily disclosed upon the record, may be shown and ascertained by the oath of a party to the cause or by other competent evidence.

Appellate courts. No case dismissed, solely for mistake of procedure. Vol. 39, p. 727.

SEC. 10. That no court having power to review a judgment or decree of another shall dismiss a writ of error solely because an appeal should have been taken, or dismiss an appeal solely because a writ of error should have been sued out; but where such error occurs the same shall be disregarded and the court shall proceed as if in that regard its power to review were properly invoked.

Action if Federal, etc., officer dies while suit pending.

SEC. 11. (a) That where, during the pendency of an action, suit, or other proceeding brought by or against an officer of the United States, or of the District of Columbia, or the Canal Zone, or of a county, city, or other governmental agency of such Territory or insular possession, and relating to the present or future discharge of his official duties, such officer dies, resigns, or otherwise ceases to hold such office, it shall be competent for the court wherein the action, suit, or proceeding is pending, whether the court be one of first instance or an appellate tribunal, to permit the cause to be continued and maintained by or against the successor in office of such officer, if within six months after his death or separation from the office it be satisfactorily shown to the court that there is a substantial need for so continuing and maintaining the cause and obtaining an adjudication of the questions involved.

Cause continued, and successor substituted if substantial need thereof.

Similar action as to State, etc., officer.

(b) Similar proceedings may be had and taken where an action, suit, or proceeding brought by or against an officer of a State, or of a county, city, or other governmental agency of a State, is pending in a court of the United States at the time of the officer's death or separation from the office.

Notice of proposed substitution to be given.

(c) Before a substitution under this section is made, the party or officer to be affected, unless expressly consenting thereto, must be given reasonable notice of the application therefor and accorded an opportunity to present any objection which he may have.

Federal incorporation not a ground for action in district courts. *Proviso.* Except if Government principal owner of stock.

SEC. 12. That no district court shall have jurisdiction of any action or suit by or against any corporation upon the ground that it was incorporated by or under and Act of Congress: *Provided,* That this section shall not apply to any suit, action, or proceeding brought by or against a corporation incorporated by or under an Act of Congress wherein the Government of the United States is the owner of more than one-half of its capital stock.

Laws repealed.

Judicial Code sections.

SEC. 13. That the following statutes and parts of statutes be, and they are, repealed:

Sections 130, 131, 133, 134, 181, 182, 236, 241,

Appellate jurisdiction, court of appeals to Supreme Court. Vol. 38, pp. 803, 804 Writs of error to Supreme Court. Vol. 39, p. 726.

Judgments of Philippine Supreme Court. Vol. 39, p. 555.

Review by Supreme Court of suits against the United States. Vol. 24, pp. 506, 507.

Direct appeal in habeas corpus. Vol. 35, p. 40.

Review of bankruptcy cases. Vol. 30, p. 553.

Porto Rico courts. Vol. 39, p. 966.

Hawaii courts. Vol. 42, p. 120.

Canal Zone district courts. Vol. 37, p. 566.

Bankruptcy appeals. R.S., secs. 763, 764, p. 143. Vol. 23, p. 437. Actions against Federal officers. Vol. 30, p. 822. Contracts repugnant to the Constitution. Vol. 42, p. 366. Transfers of appeals and writs of error. Vol. 42, p. 837. All other inconsistent Acts, etc.

Effective in three months. Pending cases in Supreme Court, etc., not affected.

242, 243, 244, 245, 246, 247, 248, 249, 250, 251, and 252 of the Judicial Code.

Sections 2, 4, and 5 of "An Act to amend an Act entitled 'An Act to codify, revise, and amend the laws relating to the judiciary,' approved March 3, 1911," approved January 28, 1915.

Sections 2, 3, 4, 5, and 6 of "An Act to amend the Judicial Code, to fix the time when the annual term of the Supreme Court shall commence, and further to define the jurisdiction of that court," approved September 6, 1916.

Section 27 of "An Act to declare the purpose of the people of the United States as to the future political status of the people of the Philippine Islands, and to provide a more autonomous government for those islands," approved August 29, 1916.

So much of sections 4, 9, and 10 of "An Act to provide for the bringing of suits against the Government of the United States," approved March 3, 1887, as provides for a review by the Supreme Court on writ of error or appeal in the cases therein named.

So much of "An Act restricting in certain cases the right of appeal to the Supreme Court in habeas corpus proceedings," approved March 10, 1908, as permits a direct appeal to the Supreme Court.

So much of sections 24 and 25 of the Bankruptcy Act of July 1, 1898, as regulates the mode of review by the Supreme Court in the proceedings, controversies, and cases therin named.

So much of "An Act to provide a civil government for Porto Rico, and for other purposes," approved March 2, 1917, as permits a direct review by the Supreme Court of cases in the courts of Porto Rico.

So much of the Hawaiian Organic Act, as amended by the Act of July 9, 1921, as permits a direct review by the Supreme Court of cases in the courts in Hawaii.

So much of section 9 of the Act of August 24, 1912, relating to the government of the Canal Zone as designates the cases in which, and the courts by which, the judgments and decrees of the district court of the Canal Zone may be reviewed.

Sections 763 and 764 of the Revised Statutes.

An Act entitled "An Act amending section 764 of the Revised Statutes," approved March 3, 1885.

An Act entitled "An Act to prevent the abatement of certain actions," approved February 8, 1899.

An Act entitled "An Act to amend section 237 of the Judicial Code," approved February 17, 1922.

An Act entitled "An Act to amend the Judicial Code in reference to appeals and writs of error," approved September 14, 1922.

All other Acts and parts of Acts in so far as they are embraced within and superseded by this Act or are inconsistent therewith.

SEC. 14. That this Act shall take effect three months after its approval; but it shall not affect cases then pending in the Supreme Court, nor shall it affect the right to a review, or the mode or time for exercising the same, as respects any judgment or decree entered prior to the date when it takes effect.

Approved, February 13, 1925.

Roosevelt's 1937 Court Reform Proposal

Source: U.S. Congress, Senate, Committee on the Judiciary, Reorganization of the
Federal Judiciary, S Rept. 711, 75th Congress, 1st session, 1937.

Letter of Attorney General

February 2

The President,
The White House.

MY DEAR MR. PRESIDENT: Delay in the administration of justice is the outstanding defect of our Federal judicial system. It has been a cause of concern to practically every one of my predecessors in office. It has exasperated the bench, the bar, the business community, and the public.

The litigant conceives the judge as one promoting justice through the mechanism of the courts. He assumes that the directing power of the judge is exercised over its officers from the time a case is filed with the clerk of the court. He is entitled to assume that the judge is pressing forward litigation in the full recognition of the principle that "justice delayed is justice denied." It is a mockery of justice to say to a person when he files suit that he may receive a decision years later. Under a properly ordered system rights should be determined promptly. The course of litigation should be measured in months and not in years.

Yet in some jurisdictions the delays in the administration of justice are so interminable that to institute suit is to embark on a life-long adventure. Many persons submit to acts of injustice rather than resort to the courts. Inability to secure a prompt judicial adjudication leads to improvident and unjust settlements. Moreover, the time factor is an open invitation to those who are disposed to institute unwarranted litigation or interpose unfounded defenses in the hope of forcing an adjustment which could not be secured upon the merits. This situation frequently results in extreme hardships. The small businessman or the litigant of limited means labors under a grave and constantly increasing disadvantage because of his inability to pay the price of justice.

Statistical data indicate that in many districts a disheartening and unavoidable interval must elapse between the date that issue is joined in a pending case and the time when it can be reached for trial in due course. These computations do not take into account the delays that occur in the preliminary stages of litigation or the postponements after a case might normally be expected to be heard.

The evil is a growing one. The business of the courts is continually increasing in volume, importance, and complexity. The average case load borne by each judge has grown nearly 50 percent since 1913, when the district courts were first organized on their present basis. When the courts are working under such pressure it is inevitable that the character of their work must suffer.

The number of new cases offset those that are disposed of, so that the courts are unable to decrease the enormous backlog of undigested matters. More than 50,000 pending cases, exclusive of bankruptcy proceedings, overhang the Federal dockets — a constant menace to the orderly processes of justice. Whenever a single case requires a protracted trial the routine business of the court is further neglected. It is an intolerable situation and we should make shift to amend it.

Efforts have been made from time to time to alleviate some of the conditions that contribute to the slow rate of speed with which cases move through the courts. The Congress has recently conferred on the Supreme Court the authority to prescribe rules of procedure after verdict in criminal cases and the power to adopt and promulgate uniform rules of practice for civil actions at law in the district courts. It has provided terms of court in certain places at which Federal courts had not previously convened. A small number of judges have been added from time to time.

Despite these commendable accomplishments sufficient progress has not been made. Much remains to be done in developing procedure and administration, but this alone will not meet modern needs. The problem must be approached in a more comprehensive fashion if the United States is to have a judicial system worthy of the Nation. Reason and necessity require the appointment of a sufficient number of judges to handle the business of the Federal courts. These additional judges should be of a type and age which would warrant us in believing that they would vigorously attack their dockets rather than permit their dockets to overwhelm them.

The cost of additional personnel should not deter us. It must be borne in mind that the expense of maintaining the judicial system constitutes hardly three-tenths of 1 percent of the cost of maintaining the Federal establishment. While the estimates for the current fiscal year aggregate over $23,000,000 for the maintenance of the legislative branch of the Government, and over $2,100,000,000 for the permanent agencies of the executive branch, the estimated cost of maintaining the judiciary is only about $6,500,000. An increase in the judicial personnel, which I earnestly recommend, would result in a hardly perceptible percentage of increase in the total annual Budget.

This result should not be achieved, however, merely by creating new judicial positions in specific circuits or districts. The reform should be effectuated on the basis of a consistent system which would revitalize our whole judicial structure and assure the activity of judges at places where the accumulation of business is greatest. As congestion is a varying factor and cannot be foreseen, the system should be flexible and should permit the temporary assignment of judges to points where they appear to be most needed. The newly created personnel should constitute a mobile force, available for service in any part of the country at the assignment and direction of the Chief Justice. A functionary might well be created to be known as proctor, or by some other suitable title, to be appointed by the Supreme Court and to act under its direction, charged with the duty of continuously keeping informed as to the state of Federal judicial business throughout the United States and of assisting the Chief Justice in assigning judges to pressure areas.

I append hereto certain statistical information, which will give point to the suggestions I have made.

These suggestions are designed to carry forward the program for improving the processes of justice which we have discussed and worked upon since the beginning of your first administration.

The time has come when further legislation is essential.

To speed justice, to bring it within the reach of every citizen, to free it of unnecessary entanglements and delays are primary obligations of our Government.

Respectfully submitted.

HOMER CUMMINGS,
Attorney General.

Roosevelt's Message to Congress

February 5

February 5, 1937. — Referred to the Committee on the Judiciary and ordered to be printed.

THE WHITE HOUSE, *February 5, 1937*
TO THE CONGRESS OF THE UNITED STATES:

I have recently called the attention of the Congress to the clear need for a comprehensive program to reorganize the administrative machinery of the executive branch of our Government. I now make a similar recommendation to the Congress in regard to the judicial branch of the Government, in order that it also may function in accord with modern necessities.

The Constitution provides that the President "shall from time to time give to the Congress information of the state of the Union, and recommend to their consideration such measures as he shall judge necessary and expedient." No one else is given a similar mandate. It is therefore the duty of the President to advise the Congress in regard to the judiciary whenever he deems such information or recommendation necessary.

I address you for the further reason that the Constitution vests in the Congress direct responsibility in the creation of courts and judicial offices and in the formulation of rules of practice and procedure. It is, therefore, one of the definite duties of the Congress constantly to maintain the effective functioning of the Federal judiciary.

The judiciary has often found itself handicapped by insufficient personnel with which to meet a growing and more complex business. It is true that the physical facilities of conducting the business of the courts have been greatly improved, in recent years, through the erection of suitable quarters, the provision of adequate libraries, and the addition of subordinate court officers. But in many ways these are merely the trappings of judicial office. They play a minor part in the processes of justice.

Since the earliest days of the Republic, the problem of the personnel of the courts has needed the attention of the Congress. For example, from the beginning, over repeated protests to President Washington, the Justices of the Supreme Court were required to "ride circuit" and, as circuit justices, to hold trials throughout the length and breadth of the land — a practice which endured over a century.

In almost every decade since 1789 changes have been made by the Congress whereby the numbers of judges and the duties of judges in Federal courts have been altered in one way or another. The Supreme Court was established with 6 members in 1789; it was reduced to 5 in 1801; it was increased to 7 in 1807; it was increased to 9 in 1837; it was increased to 10 in 1863; it was reduced to 7 in 1866; it was increased to 9 in 1869.

The simple fact is that today a new need for legislative action arises because the personnel of the Federal judiciary is insufficient to meet the business before them. A growing body of our citizens complain of the complexities, the delays, and the expense of litigation in United States courts.

A letter from the Attorney General, which I submit herewith, justifies by reasoning and statistics the common impression created by our overcrowded Federal dockets — and it proves the need for additional judges.

Delay in any court results in injustice.

It makes lawsuits a luxury available only to the few who can afford them or who have property interests to protect which are sufficiently large to repay the cost. Poorer litigants are compelled to abandon valuable rights or to accept inadequate or unjust settlements because of sheer inability to finance or to await the end of a long litigation. Only by speeding up the processes of the law and thereby reducing their cost, can we eradicate the growing impression that the courts are chiefly a haven for the well-to-do.

Delays in the determination of appeals have the same effect. Moreover, if trials of original actions are expedited and existing accumulations of cases are reduced, the volume of work imposed on the circuit courts of appeals will further increase.

The attainment of speedier justice in the courts below will enlarge the task of the Supreme Court itself. And still more work would be added by the recommendation which I make later in this message for the quicker determination of constitutional questions by the highest court.

Even at the present time the Supreme Court is laboring under a heavy burden. Its difficulties in this respect were superficially lightened some years ago by authorizing the Court, in its discretion, to refuse to hear appeals in many classes of cases. This discretion was so freely exercised that in the last fiscal year, although 867 petitions for review were presented to the Supreme Court, it declined to hear 717 cases. If petitions in behalf of the Government are excluded, it appears that the Court permitted private litigants to prosecute appeals in only 108 cases out of 803 applications. Many of the refusals were doubtless warranted. But can it be said that full justice is achieved when a court is forced by the sheer necessity of keeping up with its business to decline, without even an explanation, to hear 87 percent of the cases presented to it by private litigants?

It seems clear, therefore, that the necessity of relieving present congestion extends to the enlargement of the capacity of all the Federal courts.

A part of the problem of obtaining a sufficient number of judges to dispose of cases is the capacity of the judges themselves. This brings forward the question of aged or infirm judges — a subject of delicacy and yet one which requires frank discussion.

In the Federal courts there are in all 237 life tenure permanent judgeships. Twenty-five of them are now held by judges over 70 years of age and eligible to leave the bench on full pay. Originally no pension or retirement allowance was provided by the Congress. When after 80 years of our national history the Congress made provision for pensions, it found a well-entrenched tradition among judges to cling to their posts, in many instances far beyond their years of physical or mental capacity. Their salaries were small. As with other men, responsibilities and obligations accumulated. No alternative had been open to them except to attempt to perform the duties of their offices to the very edge of the grave.

In exceptional cases, of course, judges, like other men, retain to an advanced age full mental and physical vigor. Those not so fortunate are often unable to perceive their own infirmities. "They seem to be tenacious of the appearance of adequacy." The voluntary retirement law of 1869 provided, therefore, only a partial solution. That law, still in force, has not proved effective in inducing aged judges to retire on a pension.

This result had been foreseen in the debates when the measure was being considered. It was then proposed that when a judge refused to retire upon reaching the age of 70, an additional judge should be appointed to assist in the work of the court. The proposal passed the House but was eliminated in the Senate.

With the opening of the twentieth century, and the great increase of population and commerce, and the growth of a more complex type of litigation, similar proposals were introduced in the Congress. To meet the situation, in 1913, 1914, 1915, and 1916, the Attorneys General then in office recommended to the Congress that when a district or a circuit judge failed to retire at the age of 70, an additional judge be appointed in order that the affairs of the court might be promptly and adequately discharged.

In 1919 a law was finally passed providing that the President "may" appoint additional district and circuit judges, but only upon a finding that the incumbent judge over 70 "is unable to discharge efficiently all the duties of his office by reason of mental or physical disability of permanent character." The discretionary and indefinite nature of this legislation has rendered it ineffective. No President should be asked to determine the ability or disability of any particular judge.

The duty of a judge involves more than presiding or listening to testimony or arguments. It is well to remember that the mass of details involved in the average of law cases today is vastly greater and more complicated than even 20 years ago. Records and briefs must be read; statutes, decisions, and extensive material of a technical, scientific, statistical, and economic nature must be searched and studied; opinions must be formulated and written. The modern tasks of judges call for the use of full energies.

Modern complexities call also for a constant infusion of new blood in the courts, just as it is needed in executive functions of the Government and in private business. A lowered mental or physical vigor leads men to avoid an examination of complicated and changed conditions. Little by little, new facts become blurred through old glasses fitted, as it were, for the needs of another generation; older men, assuming that the scene is the same as it was in the past, cease to explore or inquire into the present or the future.

We have recognized this truth in the civil service of the Nation and of many States by compelling retirement on pay at the age of 70. We have recognized it in the Army and Navy by retiring officers at the age of 64. A number of States have recognized it by providing in their constitutions for compulsory retirement of aged judges.

Life tenure of judges, assured by the Constitution, was designed to place the courts beyond temptations or influences which might impair their judgments; it was not intended to create a static judiciary. A constant and systematic addition of younger blood will vitalize the courts and better equip them to recognize and apply the essential concepts of justice in the light of the needs and the facts of an ever changing world.

It is obvious, therefore, from both reason and experience, that some provision must be adopted which will operate automatically to supplement the work of older judges and accelerate the work of the court.

I, therefore, earnestly recommend that the necessity of an increase in the number of judges be supplied by legislation providing for the appointment of additional judges in all Federal courts, without exception, where there are incumbent judges of retirement age who do not choose to retire or to resign. If an elder judge is not in fact incapacitated, only good can come from the presence of an additional judge in the crowded state of the dockets; if the capacity of an elder judge is in fact impaired, the appointment of an additional judge is indispensable. This seems to be a truth which cannot be contradicted.

I also recommend that the Congress provide machinery for taking care of sudden or long-standing congestion in the lower courts. The Supreme Court should be given power to appoint an administrative assistant who may be called a proctor. He would be charged with the duty of watching the calendars and the business of all the courts in the Federal system. The Chief Justice thereupon should be authorized to make a temporary assignment of any circuit or district judge hereafter appointed in order that he may serve as long as needed in any circuit or district where the courts are in arrears.

I attach a carefully considered draft of a proposed bill, which, if enacted, would, I am confident, afford substantial relief. The proposed measure also contains a limit on the total number of judges who might thus be appointed and also a limit on the potential size of any one of our Federal courts.

These proposals do not raise any issue of constitutional law. They do not suggest any form of compulsory retirement for incumbent judges. Indeed, those who have reached the retirement age, but desire to continue their judicial work, would be able to do so under less physical and mental strain and would be able to play a useful part in relieving the growing congestion in the business of our courts. Among them are men of eminence and great ability whose services the Government would be loath to lose. If, on the other hand, any judge eligible for retirement should feel that his court would suffer because of an increase in its membership, he may retire or resign under already existing provisions of law if he wishes so to do. In this connection let me say that the pending proposal to extend to the Justices of the Supreme Court the same retirement privileges now available to other Federal judges, has my entire approval.

One further matter requires immediate attention. We have witnessed the spectacle of conflicting decisions in both trial and appellate courts on the constitutionality of every form of important legislation. Such a welter of uncomposed differences of judicial opinion has brought the law, the courts, and, indeed, the entire administration of justice dangerously near to disrepute.

A Federal statute is held legal by one judge in one district; it is simultaneously held illegal by another judge in another district. An act valid in one judicial circuit is invalid in another judicial circuit. Thus rights fully accorded to one group of citizens may be denied to others. As a practical matter this means that for periods running as long as 1 year or 2 years or 3 years — until final determination can be made by the Supreme Court — the law loses its most indispensable element — equality.

Moreover, during the long processes of preliminary motions, original trials, petitions for rehearings, appeals, reversals on technical grounds requiring retrials, motions before the Supreme Court, and the final hearing by the highest tribunal — during all this time labor, industry, agriculture, commerce, and the Government itself go through an unconscionable period of uncertainty and embarrassment. And it is well to remember that during these long processes the normal operations of society and government are handicapped in many cases by differing and divided opinions in the lower courts and by the lack of any clear guide for the dispatch of business. Thereby our legal system is fast losing another essential of justice — certainty.

Finally, we find the processes of government itself brought to a complete stop from time to time by injunctions issued almost automatically, sometimes even without notice to the Government, and not infrequently in clear violation of the principle of equity that injunctions should be granted only in those rare cases of manifest illegality and irreparable damage against which the ordinary course of the law offers no protection. Statutes which the Congress enacts are set aside or suspended for long periods of time, even in cases to which the Government is not a party.

In the uncertain state of the law, it is not difficult for the ingenious to devise novel reasons for attacking the validity of new legislation or its application. While these questions are laboriously brought to issue and debated through a series of courts, the Government must stand aside. It matters not that the Congress has enacted the law, that the Executive has signed it, and that the administrative machinery is waiting to function. Government by injunction lays a heavy hand upon normal processes; and no important statute can take effect — against any individual or organization with the means to employ lawyers and engaged in wide-flung litigation — until it has passed through the whole hierarchy of the courts. Thus the judiciary, by postponing the effective date of acts of the Congress, is assuming an additional function and is coming more and more to constitute a scattered, loosely organized, and slowly operating third house of the National Legislature.

This state of affairs has come upon the Nation gradually over a period of decades. In my annual message to this Congress I expressed some views and some hopes.

Now, as an immediate step, I recommend that the Congress provide that no decision, injunction, judgment, or decree on any constitutional question be promulgated by any Federal court without previous and ample notice to the Attorney General and an opportunity for the United States to present evidence and be heard. This is to prevent court action on the constitutionality of acts of the Congress in suits between private individuals, where the Government is not a party to the suit, without giving opportunity to the Government of the United States to defend the law of the land.

I also earnestly recommend that, in cases in which any court of first instance determines a question of constitutionality, the Congress provide that there shall be a direct and immediate appeal to the Supreme Court and that such cases take precedence over all other matters pending in that court. Such legislation will, I am convinced, go far to alleviate the inequality, uncertainty, and delay in the disposition of vital questions of constitutionality arising under our fundamental law.

My desire is to strengthen the administration of justice and to make it a more effective servant of public need. In the American ideal of government the courts find an essential and constitutional place. In striving to fulfill that ideal, not only the judges but the Congress and the Executive as well, must do all in their power to bring the judicial organization and personnel to the high standards of usefulness which sound and efficient government and modern conditions require.

This message has dealt with four present needs:

First, to eliminate congestion of calendars and to make the judiciary as a whole less static by the constant and systematic addition of new blood to its personnel; second, to make the judiciary more elastic by providing for temporary transfers of circuit and district judges to those places where Federal courts are most in arrears; third, to furnish the Supreme Court practical assistance in supervising the conduct of business in the lower courts; fourth, to eliminate inequality, uncertainty, and delay now existing in the determination of constitutional questions involving Federal statutes.

If we increase the personnel of the Federal courts so that cases may be promptly decided in the first instance, and may be given adequate and prompt hearing on all appeals; if we invigorate all the courts by the persistent infusion of new blood; if we grant to the Supreme Court further power and responsibility in maintaining the efficiency of the entire Federal judiciary; and if we assure Government participation in the speedier consideration and final determination of all constitutional questions, we shall go a long way toward our high objectives. If these measures achieve their aim, we may be relieved of the necessity of considering any fundamental changes in the powers of the courts or the Constitution of our Government — changes which involve consequences so far reaching as to cause uncertainty as to the wisdom of such course.

FRANKLIN D. ROOSEVELT

White House Broadcast

March 9, 1937

Last Thursday I described in detail certain economic problems which everyone admits now face the Nation. For the many messages which have come to me after that speech, and which it is physically impossible to answer individually, I take this means of saying "thank you."

Tonight, sitting at my desk in the White House, I make my first radio report to the people in my second term of office.

I am reminded of that evening in March, four years ago, when I made my first radio report to you. We were then in the midst of the great banking crisis.

Soon after, with the authority of the Congress, we asked the Nation to turn over all of its privately held gold, dollar for dollar, to the Government of the United States.

Today's recovery proves how right that policy was.

But when, almost two years later, it came before the Supreme Court its constitutionality was upheld only by a five-to-four vote. The change of one vote would have thrown all the affairs of this great Nation back into hopeless chaos. In effect, four Justices ruled that the right under a private contract to exact a pound of flesh was more sacred than the main objectives of the Constitution to establish an enduring Nation.

In 1933 you and I knew that we must never let our economic system get completely out of joint again — that we could not afford to take the risk of another great depression.

We also became convinced that the only way to avoid a repetition of those dark days was to have a government with power to prevent and to cure the abuses and the inequalities which had thrown that system out of joint.

We then began a program of remedying those abuses and inequalities — to give balance and stability to our economic system — to make it bomb-proof against the causes of 1929.

Today we are only part-way through that program — and recovery is speeding up to a point where the dangers of 1929 are again becoming possible, not this week or month perhaps, but within a year or two.

National laws are needed to complete that program. Individual or local or state effort alone cannot protect us in 1937 any better than ten years ago.

It will take time — and plenty of time — to work out our remedies administratively even after legislation is passed. To complete our program of protection in time, therefore, we cannot delay one moment in making certain that our National Government has power to carry through.

Four years ago action did not come until the eleventh hour. It was almost too late.

If we learned anything from the depression we will not allow ourselves to run around in new circles of futile discussion and debate, always postponing the day of decision.

The American people have learned from the depression. For in the last three national elections an overwhelming majority of them voted a mandate that the Congress and the President begin the task of providing that protection — not after long years of debate, but now.

The Courts, however, have cast doubts on the ability of the elected Congress to protect us against catastrophe by meeting squarely our modern social and economic conditions.

We are at a crisis in our ability to proceed with that protection. It is a quiet crisis. There are no lines of depositors outside closed banks. But to the far-sighted it is far-reaching in its possibilities of injury to America.

I want to talk with you very simply about the need for present action in this crisis — the need to meet the unanswered challenge of one-third of a Nation ill-nourished, ill-clad, ill-housed.

Last Thursday I described the American form of Government as a three horse team provided by the Constitution to the American people so that their field might be plowed. The three horses are, of course, the three branches of government — the Congress, the Executive and the Courts. Two of the horses are pulling in unison today; the third is not. Those who have intimated that the President of the United States is trying to drive that team, overlook the simple fact that the President, as Chief Executive, is himself one of the three horses.

It is the American people themselves who are in the driver's seat.

It is the American people themselves who want the furrow plowed.

It is the American people themselves who expect the third horse to pull in unison with the other two.

I hope that you have re-read the Constitution of the United States. Like the Bible, it ought to be read again and again.

It is an easy document to understand when you remember that it was called into being because the Articles of Confederation under which the original thirteen States tried to operate after the Revolution showed the need of a National Government with power enough to handle national problems. In its Preamble, the Constitution states that it was intended to form a more perfect Union and promote the general welfare; and the powers given to the Congress to carry out those purposes can be best described by saying that they were all the powers needed to meet each and every problem which then had a national character and which could not be met by merely local action.

But the framers went further. Having in mind that in succeeding generations many other problems then undreamed of would become national problems, they gave to the Congress the ample broad powers "to levy taxes * * * and provide for the common defense and general welfare of the United States."

That, my friends, is what I honestly believe to have been the clear and underlying purpose of the patriots who wrote a Federal Constitution to create a National Government with national power, intended as they said, "to form a more perfect union * * * for ourselves and our posterity."

For nearly twenty years there was no conflict between the Congress and the Court. Then, in 1803, Congress passed a statute which the Court said violated an express provision of the Constitution. The Court claimed the power to declare it unconstitutional and did so declare it. But a little later the Court itself admitted that it was an extraordinary power to exercise and through Mr. Justice Washington laid down this limitation upon it: "It is but a decent respect due to the wisdom, the integrity and the patriotism of the Legislative body, by which any law is passed, to presume in favor of its validity until its violation of the Constitution is proved beyond all reasonable doubt."

But since the rise of the modern movement for social and economic progress through legislation, the Court has more and more often and more and more boldly asserted a power to veto laws passed by the Congress and State Legislatures in complete disregard of this original limitation.

In the last four years the sound rule of giving statutes the benefit of all reasonable doubt has been cast aside. The Court has been acting not as a judicial body, but as a policy-making body.

When the Congress has sought to stabilize national agriculture, to improve the conditions of labor, to safeguard business against unfair competition, to protect our national resources, and in many other ways, to serve our clearly national needs, the majority of the Court has been assuming the power to pass on the wisdom of these Acts of the Congress — and to approve or disapprove the public policy written into these laws.

That is not only my accusation. It is the accusation of most distinguished Justices of the present Supreme Court. I have not the time to quote to you all the language used by dissenting Justices in many of these cases. But in the case holding the Railroad Retirement Act unconstitutional, for instance, Chief Justice Hughes said in a dissenting opinion that the majority opinion was "a departure from sound principles," and placed "an unwarranted limitation upon the commerce clause." And three other Justices agreed with him.

In the case holding the A.A.A. unconstitutional, Justice Stone said of the majority opinion that it was a "tortured construction of the Constitution." And two other Justices agreed with him.

In the case holding the New York Minimum Wage Law unconstitutional, Justice Stone said that the majority were actually reading into the Constitution their own "personal economic predilections," and that if the legislative power is not left free to choose the methods of solving the problems of poverty, subsistence and health of large numbers in the community, then "government is to be rendered impotent." And two other Justices agreed with him.

In the face of these dissenting opinions, there is no basis for the claim made by some members of the Court that something in the Constitution has compelled them regretfully to thwart the will of the people.

In the face of such dissenting opinions, it is perfectly clear, that as Chief Justice Hughes has said: "We are under a Constitution but the Constitution is what the Judges say it is."

The Court in addition to the proper use of its judicial functions has improperly set itself up as a third House of the Congress — a super-legislature, as one of the Justices has called it — reading into the Constitution words and implications which are not there, and which were never intended to be there.

We have, therefore, reached the point as a Nation where we must take action to save the Constitution from the Court and the Court from itself. We must find a way to take an appeal from the Supreme Court to the Constitution itself. We want a Supreme Court which will do justice under the Constitution — not over it. In our Courts we want a government of laws and not of men.

I want — as all Americans want — an independent judiciary as proposed by the framers of the Constitution. That means a Supreme Court that will enforce the Constitution as written — that will refuse to amend the Constitution by the arbitrary exercise of judicial power — amendment by judicial say-so. It does not mean a judiciary so independent that it can deny the existence of facts universally recognized.

How then could we proceed to perform the mandate given us? It was said in last year's Democratic platform "If these problems cannot be effectively solved within the Constitution, we shall seek such clarifying amendment as will assure the power to enact those laws, adequately to regulate commerce, protect public health and safety, and safeguard economic security." In other words, we said we would seek an amendment only if every other possible means by legislation were to fail.

When I commenced to review the situation with the problem squarely before me, I came by a process of elimination to the conclusion that short of amendments the only method which was clearly constitutional, and would at the same time carry out other much needed reforms, was to infuse new blood into all our Courts. We must have men worthy and equipped to carry out impartial justice. But, at the same time, we must have Judges who will bring to the Courts a present-day sense of the Constitution — Judges who will retain in the Courts the judicial functions of a court, and reject the legislative powers which the Courts have today assumed.

In forty-five out of the forty-eight States of the Union, Judges are chosen not for life but for a period of years. In many States Judges must retire at the age of seventy. Congress has provided financial security by offering life pensions at full pay for Federal Judges on all Courts who are willing to retire at seventy. In the case of Supreme Court Justices, that pension is $20,000 a year. But all Federal Judges, once appointed, can, if they choose, hold office for life, no matter how old they may get to be.

What is my proposal? It is simply this: whenever a Judge or Justice of any Federal Court has reached the age of seventy and does not avail himself of the opportunity to retire on a pension, a new member shall be appointed by the President then in office, with the approval, as required by the Constitution, of the Senate of the United States.

That plan has two chief purposes. By bringing into the Judicial system a steady and continuing stream of new and younger blood, I hope, first, to make the administration of all Federal justice speedier and, therefore, less costly; secondly, to bring to the decision of social and economic problems younger men who have had personal experience and contact with modern facts and circumstances under which average men have to live and work. This plan will save our national Constitution from hardening of the judicial arteries.

The number of Judges to be appointed would depend wholly on the decision of present Judges now over seventy, or those who would subsequently reach the age of seventy.

If, for instance, any one of the six Justices of the Supreme Court now over the age of seventy should retire as provided under the plan, no additional place would be created. Consequently, although there never can be more than fifteen, there may be only fourteen, or thirteen, or twelve. And there may be only nine.

There is nothing novel or radical about this idea. It seeks to maintain the Federal bench in full vigor. It has been discussed and approved by many persons of high authority ever since a similar proposal passed the House of Representatives in 1869.

Why was the age fixed at seventy? Because the laws of many States, the practice of the Civil Service, the regulations of the Army and Navy, and the rules of many of our Universities and of almost every great private business enterprise, commonly fix the retirement age at seventy years or less.

The statute would apply to all the Courts in the Federal system. There is general approval so far as the lower Federal courts are concerned. The plan has met opposition only so far as the Supreme Court of the United States itself is concerned. If such a plan is good for the lower courts it certainly ought to be equally good for the highest Court from which there is no appeal.

Those opposing this plan have sought to arouse prejudice and fear by crying that I am seeking to "pack" the Supreme Court and that a baneful precedent will be established.

What do they mean by the words "packing the Court"?

Let me answer this question with a bluntness that will end all *honest* misunderstanding of my purposes.

If by that phrase "packing the Court" it is charged that I wish to place on the bench spineless puppets who would disregard the law and would decide specific cases as I wished them to be decided, I make this answer — that no President fit for his office would appoint, and no Senate of honorable men fit for their office would confirm, that kind of appointees to the Supreme Court.

But if by that phrase the charge is made that I would appoint and the Senate would confirm Justices worthy to sit beside present members of the Court who understand those modern conditions — that I will appoint Justices who will not undertake to override the judgment of the Congress on legislative policy — that I will appoint Justices who will act as Justices and not as legislators — if the appointment of such Justices can be called "packing the Courts," then I say that I and with me the vast majority of the American people favor doing just that thing — now.

Is it a dangerous precedent for the Congress to change the number of the Justices? The Congress has always had, and will have, that power. The number of Justices has been changed several times before — in the Administrations of John Adams and Thomas Jefferson, — both signers of the Declaration of Independence — Andrew Jackson, Abraham Lincoln and Ulysses S. Grant.

I suggest only the addition of Justices to the bench in accordance with a clearly defined principle relating to a clearly defined age limit. Fundamentally, if in the future, America cannot trust the Congress it elects to refrain from abuse of our Constitutional usages, democracy will have failed far beyond the importance to it of any kind of precedent concerning the Judiciary.

We think it so much in the public interest to maintain a vigorous judiciary that we encourage the retirement of elderly Judges by offering them a life pension at full salary. Why then should we leave the fulfillment of this public policy to chance or make it dependent upon the desire or prejudice of any individual Justice?

It is the clear intention of our public policy to provide for a constant flow of new and younger blood into the Judiciary. Normally every President appoints a large number of District and Circuit Judges and a few members of the Supreme Court. Until my first term practically every President of the United States had appointed at least one member of the Supreme Court. President Taft appointed five members and named a Chief Justice — President Wilson three — President Harding four including a Chief Justice — President Coolidge one — President Hoover three including a Chief Justice.

Such a succession of appointments should have provided a Court well-balanced as to age. But chance and the disinclination of individuals to leave the Supreme bench have now given us a Court in which five Justices will be over seventy-five years of age before next June and one over seventy. Thus a sound public policy has been defeated.

I now propose that we establish by law an assurance against any such ill-balanced Court in the future. I propose that hereafter, when a Judge reaches the age of seventy, a new and younger Judge shall be added to the Court automatically. In this way I propose to enforce a sound public policy by law instead of leaving the composition of our Federal Courts, including the highest, to be determined by chance or the personal decision of individuals.

If such a law as I propose is regarded as establishing a new precedent — is it not a most desirable precedent?

Like all lawyers, like all Americans, I regret the necessity of this controversy. But the welfare of the United States, and indeed of the Constitution itself, is what we all must think about first. Our difficulty with the Court today rises not from the Court as an institution but from human beings within it. But we cannot yield our constitutional destiny to the personal judgment of a few men who, being fearful of the future, would deny us the necessary means of dealing with the present.

This plan of mine is no attack on the Court; it seeks to restore the Court to its rightful and historic place in our system of Constitutional Government and to have it resume its high task of building anew on the Constitution "a system of living law."

I have thus explained to you the reasons that lie behind our efforts to secure results by legislation within the Constitution. I hope that thereby the difficult process of constitutional amendment may be rendered unnecessary. But let us examine that process.

There are many types of amendment proposed. Each one is radically different from the other. There is no substantial group within the Congress or outside it who are agreed on any single amendment.

It would take months or years to get substantial agreement upon the type and language of an amendment. It would take months and years thereafter to get a two-thirds majority in favor of that amendment in *both* Houses of the Congress.

Then would come the long course of ratification by three-fourths of the States. No amendment which any powerful economic interests or the leaders of any powerful political party have had reason to oppose has ever been ratified within anything like a reasonable time. And thirteen States which contain only five percent of the voting population can block ratification even though the thirty-five States with ninety-five percent of the population are in favor of it.

A very large percentage of newspaper publishers, Chambers of Commerce, Bar Associations, Manufacturers' Associations, who are trying to give the impression that they really do want a constitutional amendment would be the first to exclaim as soon as an amendment was proposed "Oh! I was for an amendment all right, but this amendment that you have proposed is not the kind of an amendment that I was thinking about. I am, therefore, going to spend my time, my efforts and my money to block that amendment, although I would be awfully glad to help get some other kind of amendment ratified."

Two groups oppose my plan on the ground that they favor a constitutional amendment. The first includes those who fundamentally object to social and economic legislation along modern lines. This is the same group who during the campaign last Fall tried to block the mandate of the people.

Now they are making a last stand. And the strategy of that last stand is to suggest the time-consuming process of amendment in order to kill off by delay the legislation demanded by the mandate.

To them I say — I do not think you will be able long to fool the American people as to your purposes.

The other group is composed of those who honestly believe the amendment process is the best and who would be willing to support a reasonable amendment if they could agree on one.

To them I say — we cannot rely on an amendment as the immediate or only answer to our present difficulties. When the time comes for action, you will find that many of those who pretend to support you will sabotage any constructive amendment which is proposed. Look at these strange bed-fellows of yours. When before have you found them really at your side in your fights for progress?

And remember one thing more. Even if an amendment were passed, and even if in the years to come it were to be ratified, its meaning would depend upon the kind of Justices who would be sitting on the Supreme Court bench. An amendment like the rest of the Constitution is what the Justices say it is rather than what its framers or you might hope it is.

This proposal of mine will not infringe in the slightest upon the civil or religious liberties so dear to every American.

My record as Governor and as President proves my devotion to those liberties. You who know me can have no fear that I would tolerate the destruction by any branch of government of any part of our heritage of freedom.

The present attempt by those opposed to progress to play upon the fears of danger to personal liberty brings again to mind that crude and cruel strategy tried by the same opposition to frighten the workers of America in a pay-envelope propaganda against the Social Security Law. The workers were not fooled by that propaganda then. The people of America will not be fooled by such propaganda now.

I am in favor of action through legislation:

First, because I believe that it can be passed at this session of the Congress.

Second, because it will provide a reinvigorated, liberal-minded Judiciary necessary to furnish quicker and cheaper justice from bottom to top.

Third, because it will provide a series of Federal Courts willing to enforce the Constitution as written, and unwilling to assert legislative powers by writing into it their own political and economic policies.

During the past half century the balance of power between the three great branches of the Federal Government, has been tipped out of balance by the Courts in direct contradiction of the high purposes of the framers of the Constitution. It is my purpose to restore that balance. You who know me will accept my solemn assurance that in a world in which democracy is under attack, I seek to make American democracy succeed.

Letter of Chief Justice Hughes

March 21

SUPREME COURT OF THE UNITED STATES
Washington, D.C., March 21, 1937.

HON. BURTON K. WHEELER,
United States Senate, Washington, D.C.

MY DEAR SENATOR WHEELER: In response to your inquiries, I have the honor to present the following statement with respect to the work of the Supreme Court:

1. The Supreme Court is fully abreast of its work. When we rose on March 15 (for the present recess) we had heard argument in cases in which certiorari had been granted only 4 weeks before — February 15.

During the current term, which began last October and which we call "October term, 1936", we have heard argument on the merits in 150 cases (180 numbers) and we have 28 cases (30 numbers) awaiting argument. We shall be able to hear all these cases, and such others as may come up for argument, before our adjournment for the term. There is no congestion of cases upon our calendar.

This gratifying condition has obtained for several years. We have been able for several terms to adjourn after disposing of all cases which are ready to be heard.

2. The cases on our docket are classified as original and appellate. Our original jurisdiction is defined by the Constitution and embraces cases to which States are parties. There are not many of these. At the present time they number 13 and are in various stages of progress to submission for determination.

Our appellate jurisdiction covers those cases in which appeal is allowed by statute as a matter of right and cases which come to us on writs of certiorari.

The following is a comparative statement of the cases on the dockets for the six terms preceding the current term:

For terms 1930-32

	1930	1931	1932
Total cases on dockets	1,039	1,023	1,037
Disposed of during term	900	884	910
Cases remaining on dockets	139	139	127
Distribution of cases:			
Cases disposed of:			
Original cases	8	1	4
Appellate, on merits	326	282	257
Petitions for certiorari	566	601	649
Remaining on dockets:			
Original cases	16	19	17
Appellate, on merits	76	60	56
Petitions for certiorari	47	60	54

For terms 1933-35

	1933	1934	1935
Total cases on dockets	1,132	1,040	1,092
Disposed of during term	1,029	931	990
Cases remaining on docket	103	109	102
Distribution of cases:			
Cases disposed of:			
Original cases	4	5	4
Appellate, on merits	293	256	269
Petitions for certiorari	732	670	717
Remaining on dockets:			
Original cases	15	13	12
Appellate, on merits	43	51	56
Petitions for certiorari	45	45	34

Further statistics for these terms, and those for earlier terms, are available if you desire them.

During the present term we have thus far disposed of 666 cases which include petitions for certiorari and cases which have been argued on the merits and already decided.

3. The statute relating to our appellate jurisdiction is the act of February 13, 1925 (43 Stat. 936). That act limits to certain cases the appeals which come to the Supreme Court as a matter of right. Review in other cases is made to depend upon the allowance by the Supreme Court of a writ of certiorari.

Where the appeal purports to lie as a matter of right, the rules of the Supreme Court (rule 12) require the appellant to submit a jurisdictional statement showing that the case falls within that class of appeals and that a substantial question is involved. We examine that statement, and the supporting and opposing briefs, and decide whether the Court had jurisdiction. As a result, many frivolous appeals are forthwith dismissed and the way is open for appeals which disclose substantial questions.

4. The act of 1925, limiting appeals as a matter of right and enlarging the provisions for review only through certiorari was most carefully considered by Congress. I call attention to the reports of the Judiciary Committees of the Senate and House of Representatives (68th Cong., 1st sess.). That legislation was deemed to be essential to enable the Supreme Court to perform its proper function. No single court of last resort, whatever the number of judges, could dispose of all the cases which arise in this vast country and which litigants would seek to bring up if the right of appeal were unrestricted. Hosts of litigants will take appeals so long as there is a tribunal accessible. In protracted litigation, the advantage is with those who command a long purse. Unmeritorious appeals cause intolerable delays. Such appeals clog the calendar and get in the way of those that have merit.

Under our Federal system, when litigants have had their cases heard in the courts of first instance, and the trier of the facts, jury or judge, as the case may require, has spoken and the case on the facts and law has been decided, and when the dissatisfied party has been accorded an appeal to the circuit court of appeals, the litigants, so far as mere private interests are concerned, have had their day in court. If further review is to be had by the Supreme Court it must be because of the public interest in the questions involved. That review, for example, should be for the purpose of resolving conflicts in judicial decisions between different circuit courts of appeals or between circuit courts of appeals and State courts where the question is one of State law; or for the purpose of determining constitutional questions or settling the interpretation of statutes; or because of the importance of the questions of law that are involved. Review by the Supreme Court is thus in the interest of the law, its appropriate exposition and enforcement, not in the mere interest of the litigants.

It is obvious that if appeal as a matter of right is restricted to certain described cases, the question whether review should be allowed in other cases must necessarily be confided to some tribunal for determination, and, of course, with respect to review by the Supreme Court, that Court should decide.

5. Granting certiorari is not a matter of favor but of sound judicial discretion. It is not the importance of the parties or the amount of money involved that is in any sense controlling. The action of the Court is governed by its rules from which I quote the following (rule 38, par. 5):

"5. A review on writ of certiorari is not a matter of right, but of sound judicial discretion, and will be granted only where there are special and important reasons therefor. The following, while neither controlling nor full measuring the Court's discretion, indicate the character of reason which will be considered:

"(*a*) Where a State court has decided a Federal question of substance not therefore determined by this Court, or has decided it in a way probably not in accord with applicable decisions of this Court.

"(*b*) Where a circuit court of appeals has rendered a decision in conflict with the decision of another circuit court of appeals on the same matter; or has decided an important question of local law in a way probably in conflict with applicable local decisions; or has decided an important question of general law in a way probably untenable or in conflict with the weight of authority; or has decided an important question of Federal law which has not been, but should be, settled by this Court; or has decided a Federal question in a way probably in conflict with applicable decisions of this Court; or has so far departed from the accepted and usual course of judicial proceedings, or so far sanctions such a departure by a lower court, as to call for an exercise of this Court's power of supervision.

"(*c*) Where the United States Court of Appeals for the District of Columbia has decided a question of general importance, or a question of substance relating to the construction or application of the Constitution, or a treaty or statute, of the United States, which has not been, but should be, settled by this Court; or where that court has not given proper effect to an applicable decision of this Court."

These rules are impartially applied, as it is most important that they should be.

I should add that petitions of certiorari are not apportioned among the Justices. In all matters before the Court, except in the more routine of administration, all the Justices — unless for some reason a Justice is disqualified or unable to act in a particular case — participate in the decision. This applies to the grant or refusal of petitions for certiorari. Furthermore, petitions for certiorari are granted if four Justices think they should be. A vote by a majority is not required in such cases. Even if two or three of the Justices are strongly of the opinion that certiorari should be allowed, frequently the other Justices will acquiesce in their view, but the petition is always granted if four so vote.

6. The work of passing upon these applications for certiorari is laborious but the Court is able to perform it adequately. Observations have been made as to the vast number of pages of records and briefs that are submitted in the course of a term. The total is imposing but the suggested conclusion is hasty and rests on an illusory basis. Records are replete with testimony and evidence of facts. But the questions on certiorari are questions of law. So many cases turn on the facts, principles of law not being in controversy. It is only when the facts are interwoven with the questions of law which we should review that the evidence must be examined and then only to the extent that it is necessary to decide the questions of law.

This at once disposes of a vast number of factual controversies where the parties have been fully heard in the courts below and have no right to burden the Supreme Court with the dispute which interests no one but themselves.

This is also true of controversies over contracts and documents of all sorts which involve only questions of concern to the immediate parties. The applicant for certiorari is required to state in his petition the grounds for his application and in a host of cases that disclosure itself disposes of his request. So that the number of pages of records and briefs afford no satisfactory criterion of the actual work involved. It must also be remembered that Justices who have been dealing with such matters for years have the aid of a long and varied experience in separating the chaff from the wheat.

I think that it is safe to say that about 60 percent of the applications for certiorari are wholly without merit and ought never to have been made. There are probably about 20 percent or so in addition which have a fair degree of plausibility but which fail to survive critical examination. The remainder, falling short, I believe, of 20 percent, show substantial grounds and are granted. I think that it is the view of the members of the Court that if any error is made in dealing with these applications it is on the side of liberality.

7. An increase in the number of Justices of the Supreme Court, apart from any question of policy, which I do not discuss, would not promote the efficiency of the Court. It is believed that it would impair that efficiency so long as the Court acts as a unit. There would be more judges to hear, more judges to confer, more judges to discuss, more judges to be convinced and to decide. The present number of Justices is thought to be large enough so far as the prompt, adequate, and efficient conduct of the work of the Court is concerned. As I have said, I do not speak of any other considerations in view of the appropriate attitude of the Court in relation to questions of policy.

I understand that it has been suggested that with more Justices the Court could hear cases in divisions. It is believed that such a plan would be impracticable. A large proportion of the cases we hear are important and a decision by a part of the Court would be unsatisfactory.

I may also call attention to the provisions of article III, section 1, of the Constitution that the judicial power of the United States shall be vested "in one Supreme Court" and in such inferior courts as the Congress may from time to time ordain and establish. The Constitution does not appear to authorize two or more Supreme Courts or two or more parts of a supreme court functioning in effect as separate courts.

On account of the shortness of time I have not been able to consult with the members of the Court generally with respect to the foregoing statement, but I am confident that it is in accord with the views of the Justices. I should say, however, that I have been able to consult with Mr. Justice Van Devanter and Mr. Justice Brandeis, and I am at liberty to say that the statement is approved by them.

I have the honor to remain,
Respectfully yours,
CHARLES E. HUGHES,
Chief Justice of the United States.

HON. BURTON K. WHEELER,
United States Senate, Washington, D.C.

Senate Judiciary Committee Report

June 7

June 7 (calendar day, June 14), 1937.—Ordered to be printed

MR. McCARRAN (for MR. KING), from the Committee on the Judiciary, submitted the following

ADVERSE REPORT
[To accompany S. 1392]

The Committee on the Judiciary, to whom was referred the bill (S. 1392) to reorganize the judicial branch of the Government, after full consideration, having unanimously amended the measure, hereby report the bill adversely with the recommendation that it do not pass.

The amendment agreed to by unanimous consent, is as follows:

Page 3, lines 5, 8, and 9, strike out the words "hereafter appointed."

Summary of Proposed Measure

The bill, as thus amended, may be summarized in the following manner:

By section 1 (a) the President is directed to appoint an additional judge to any court of the United States when and only when three contingencies arise:

(*a*) That a sitting judge shall have attained the age of 70 years;

(*b*) That he shall have held a Federal judge's commission for at least 10 years;

(*c*) That he has neither resigned nor retired within 6 months after the happening of the two contingencies first named.

The happening of the three contingencies would not, however, necessarily result in requiring an appointment, for section 1 also contains a specific defeasance clause to the effect that no nomination shall be made in the case of a judge, although he is 70 years of age, has served at least 10 years and has neither resigned nor retired within 6 months after the happening of the first two contingencies, if, before the actual nomination of an additional judge, he dies, resigns, or retires. Moreover, section 6 of the bill provides that "it shall take effect on the 30th day after the date of its enactment."

Thus the bill does not with certainty provide for the expansion of any court or the appointment of any additional judges, for it will not come into operation with respect to any judge in whose case the described contingencies have happened, if such judge dies, resigns, or retires within 30 days after the enactment of the bill or before the President shall have had opportunity to send a nomination to the Senate.

By section 1 (b) it is provided that in event of the appointment of judges under the provisions of section 1 (a), then the size of the court to which such appointments are made is "permanently" increased by that number. But the number of appointments to be made is definitely limited by this paragraph. Regardless of the age or service of the members of the Federal judiciary, no more than 50 judges may be appointed in all; the Supreme Court may not be increased beyond 15 members; no circuit court of appeals, nor the Court of Claims, nor the Court of Customs and Patent Appeals, nor the Customs Court may be increased by more than 2 members; and finally, in the case of district courts, the number of judges now authorized to be appointed for any district or group of districts may not be more than doubled.

Section 1 (c) fixes the quorum of the Supreme Court, the Court of Appeals for the District of Columbia, the Court of Claims, and the Court of Customs and Patent Appeals.

Section 1 (d) provides that an additional judge shall not be appointed in the case of a judge whose office has been abolished by Congress.

Section 2 provides for the designation and assignment of judges to courts other than those in which they hold their commissions. As introduced, it applied only to judges to be appointed after the enactment of the bill. As amended, it applies to all judges regardless of the date of their appointment, but it still alters the present system in a striking manner, as will be more fully indicated later.

Circuit judges may be assigned by the Chief Justice for service in any circuit court of appeals. District judges may be similarly assigned by the Chief Justice to any district court, or by the senior circuit judge of his circuit (but subject to the authority of the Chief Justice) to any district court within the circuit.

After the assignment of a judge by the Chief Justice, the senior circuit judge of the district in which he is commissioned may certify to the Chief Justice any reason deemed sufficient by him to warrant the revocation or termination of the assignment, but the Chief Justice has full discretion whether or not to act upon any such certification. The senior circuit judge of the district to which such assignment will be made is not given similar authority to show why the assignment should not be made effective.

Section 3 gives the Supreme Court power to appoint a Proctor to investigate the volume, character, and status of litigation in the circuit and district courts, to recommend the assignment of judges authorized by section 2, and to make suggestions for expediting the disposition of pending cases. The salary of the Proctor is fixed at $10,000 per year and provision is made for the functions of the office.

Section 4 authorizes an appopriation of $100,000 for the purposes of the act.

Section 5 contains certain definitions.

Section 6, the last section, makes the act effective 30 days after enactment.

The Argument

The committee recommends that the measure be rejected for the following primary reasons:

I. The Bill does not accomplish any one of the objectives for which it was originally offered.

II. It applies force to the judiciary and in its initial and ultimate effect would undermine the independence of the courts.

III. It violates all precedents in the history of our Government and would in itself be a dangerous precedent for the future.

IV. The theory of the bill is in direct violation of the spirit of the American Constitution and its employment would permit alteration of the Constitution without the people's consent or approval; it undermines the protection our constitutional system gives to minorities and is subversive of the rights of individuals.

V. It tends to centralize the Federal district judiciary by the power of assigning judges from one district to another at will.

VI. It tends to expand political control over the judicial department by adding to the powers of the legislative and executive departments respecting the judiciary.

Bill Does Not Deal With Injunctions

This measure was sent to the Congress by the President on February 5, 1937, with a message . . . setting forth the objectives sought to be attained.

It should be pointed out here that a substantial portion of the message was devoted to a discussion of the evils of conflicting decisions by inferior courts on constitutional questions and to the alleged abuse of the power of injunction by some of the Federal courts. These matters, however, have no bearing on the bill before us, for it contains neither a line nor a sentence dealing with either of those problems.

Nothing in this measure attempts to control, regulate, or prohibit the power of any Federal court to pass upon the constitutionality of any law — State or National.

Nothing in this measure attempts to control, regulate, or prohibit the issuance of injunctions by any court, in any case, whether or not the Government is a party to it.

If it were to be conceded that there is need of reform in these respects, it must be understood that this bill does not deal with these problems.

Objectives as Originally Stated

As offered to the Congress, this bill was designed to effectuate only three objectives, described as follows in the President's message:

1. To increase the personnel of the Federal courts "so that cases may be promptly decided in the first instance, and may be given adequate and prompt hearing on all appeals";

2. To "invigorate all the courts by the permanent infusion of new blood";

3. To "grant to the Supreme Court further power and responsibility in maintaining the efficiency of the entire Federal judiciary."

The third of these purposes was to be accomplished by the provisions creating the office of the Proctor and dealing with the assignment of judges to courts other than those to which commissioned.

The first two objectives were to be attained by the provisions authorizing the appointment of not to exceed 50 additional judges when sitting judges of retirement age, as defined in the bill, failed to retire or resign. How totally inadequate the measure is to achieve either of the named objectives, the most cursory examination of the facts reveals.

Bill Fails of Its Purpose

In the first place, as already pointed out, the bill does not provide for any increase of personnel unless judges of retirement age fail to resign or retire. Whether or not there is to be an increase of the number of judges, and the extent of the increase if there is to be one, is dependent wholly upon the judges themselves and not at all upon the accumulation of litigation in any court. To state it another way the increase of the number of judges is to be provided, not in relation to the increase of work in any district or circuit, but in relation to the age of the judges and their unwillingness to retire.

In the second place, as pointed out in the President's message, only 25 of the 237 judges serving in the Federal courts on February 5, 1937, were over 70 years of age. Six of these were members of the Supreme Court at the time the bill was introduced. At the present time there are 24 judges 70 years of age or over distributed among the 10 circuit courts, the 84 district courts, and the 4 courts in the District of Columbia and that dealing with customs cases in New York. Of the 24, only 10 are serving in the 84 district courts, so that the remaining 14 are to be found in 5 special courts and in the 10 circuit courts. . . . Moreover, the facts indicate that the courts with the oldest judges have the best records in the disposition of business. It follows, therefore, that since there are comparatively few aged justices in service and these are among the most efficient on the bench, the age of sitting judges does not make necessary an increase of personnel to handle the business of the courts.

There was submitted with the President's message a report from the Attorney General to the effect that in recent years the number of cases has greatly increased and that delay in the administration of justice is interminable. It is manifest, however, that this condition cannot be remedied by the contingent appointment of new judges to sit beside the judges over 70 years of age, most of whom are either altogether equal to their duties or are commissioned in courts in which congestion of business does not exist. It must be obvious that the way to attack congestion and delay in the courts is directly by legislation which will increase the number of judges in those districts where the accumulation exists, not indirectly by the contingent appointment of new judges to courts where the need does not exist, but where it may happen that the sitting judge is over 70 years of age.

Local Justice Centrally Administered

Perhaps, it was the recognition of this fact that prompted the authors of the bill to draft section 2 providing for the assignment of judges "hereafter appointed" to districts other than those to which commissioned. Such a plan, it will not be overlooked, contemplates the appointment of a judge to the district of his residence and his assignment to duty in an altogether different jurisdiction. It thus creates a flying squadron of itinerant judges appointed for districts and circuits where they are not needed to be transferred to other parts of the country for judicial service. It may be doubted whether such a plan would be effective. Certainly it would be a violation of the salutary American custom that all public officials should be citizens of the jurisdiction in which they serve or which they represent.

Though this plan for the assignment of new judges to the trial of cases in any part of the country at the will of the Chief Justice was in all probability intended for no other purpose than to make it possible to send the new judges into districts where actual congestion exists, it should not be overlooked that most of the plan involves a possibility of a real danger.

To a greater and a greater degree, under modern conditions, the Government is involved in civil litigation with its citizens. Are we then through the system devised in this bill to make possible the selection of particular judges to try particular cases?

Under the present system (U.S.C., title 28, sec. 17) the assignment of judges within the circuit is made by the senior circuit judge, or, in his absence, the circuit justice. An assignment of a judge from outside the district may be made only when the senior circuit judge or the circuit justice makes certificate of the need of the district to the Chief Justice. Thus is the principle of local self-government preserved by the present system.

This principle is destroyed by this bill which allows the Chief Justice, at the recommendation of the Proctor, to make assignments anywhere regardless of the needs of any district. Thus is the administration of justice to be centralized by the proposed system.

Measure Would Prolong Litigation

It has been urged that the plan would correct the law's delay, and the President's message contains the statement that "poorer litigants are compelled to abandon valuable rights or to accept inadequate or unjust settlements because of sheer inability to finance or to await the end of long litigation." Complaint is then made that the Supreme Court during the last fiscal year "permitted private litigants to prosecute appeals in only 108 cases out of 803 applications."

It can scarcely be contended that the consideration of 695 more cases in the Supreme Court would have contributed in any degree to curtailing the law's delay or to reducing the expense of litigation. If it be true that the postponement of final decision in cases is a burden on poorer litigants as the President's message contends, then it must be equally true that any change of the present system which would enable wealthy litigants to pursue

their cases in the Supreme Court would result only in an added burden on the "poorer litigants" whose "sheer inability to finance or to await the end of long litigation" compels them "to abandon valuable rights or to accept inadequate or unjust settlements."

Of course, there is nothing in this bill to alter the provisions of the act of 1925 by which the Supreme Court was authorized "in its discretion to refuse to hear appeals in many classes of cases." The President has not recommended any change of that law, and the only amendment providing an alteration of the law that was presented to the committee was, on roll call, unanimously rejected by the committee. It is appropriate, however, to point out here that one of the principal considerations for the enactment of the certiorari law was the belief of Congress that the interests of the poorer litigant would be served and the law's delay reduced if the Supreme Court were authorized to reject frivolous appeals. Congress recognized the fact that wealthy clients and powerful corporations were in a position to wear out poor litigants under the old law. Congress was convinced that, in a great majority of cases, a trial in a nisi prius court and a rehearing in a court of appeals would be ample to do substantial justice. Accordingly, it provided in effect that litigation should end with the court of appeals unless an appellant could show the Supreme Court on certiorari that a question of such importance was involved as to warrant another hearing by the Supreme Court. Few litigated cases were ever decided in which the defeated party thought that justice had been done and in which he would not have appealed from the Supreme Court to Heaven itself, if he thought that by doing so he would wear down his opponent.

The Constitution provides for one Supreme Court (sec. 1, art. III) and authorizes Congress to make such exceptions as it deems desirable to the appellate jurisdiction of the Supreme Court (sec. 2, art. III). One obvious purpose of this provision was to permit Congress to put an end to litigation in the lower courts except in cases of greatest importance, and, also, in the interest of the poorer citizen, to make it less easy for wealthy litigants to invoke delay to defeat justice.

No alteration of this law is suggested by the proponents of this measure, but the implication is made that the Supreme Court has improvidently refused to hear some cases. There is no evidence to maintain this contention. The Attorney General in his statement to the committee presented a mathematical calculation to show how much time would be consumed by the Justices in reading the entire record in each case presented on appeal. The members of the committee and, of course the Attorney General, are well aware of the fact that attorneys are officers of the Court, that it is their duty to summarize the records and the points of appeal, and that the full record is needed only when, after having examined the summary of the attorneys, the court is satisfied there should be a hearing on the merits.

The Chief Justice, in a letter presented to this committee ... made it clear that "even if two or three of the Justices are strongly of the opinion that certiorari should be allowed, frequently the other judges will acquiesce in their view, but the petition is always granted if four so vote."

It thus appears from the bill itself, from the message of the President, the statement of the Attorney General, and the letter of the Chief Justice that nothing of advantage to litigants is to be derived from this measure in the reduction of the law's delay.

Question of Age Not Solved

The next question is to determine to what extent "the persistent infusion of new blood" may be expected from this bill.

It will be observed that the bill before us does not and cannot compel the retirement of any judge, whether on the Supreme Court or any other court, when he becomes 70 years of age. It will be remembered that the mere attainment of three score and ten by a particular judge does not, under this bill, require the appointment of another. The man on the bench may be 80 years of age, but this bill will not authorize the President to appoint a new judge to sit beside him unless he has served as a judge for 10 years. In other words, age itself is not penalized; the penalty falls only when age is attended with experience.

No one should overlook the fact that under this bill the President, whoever he may be and whether or not he believes in the constant infusion of young blood in the courts, may nominate a man 69 years and 11 months of age to the Supreme Court, or to any court, and, if confirmed, such nominee, if he never had served as a judge, would continue to sit upon the bench unmolested by this law until he had attained the ripe age of 79 years and 11 months.

We are told that "modern complexities call also for a constant infusion of new blood in the courts, just as it is needed in executive functions of the Government and in private business." Does this bill provide for such? The answer is obviously no. As has been just demonstrated, the introduction of old and inexperienced blood into the courts is not prevented by this bill.

More than that, the measure, by its own terms, makes impossible the "constant" or "persistent" infusion of new blood. It is to be observed that the word is "new", not "young."

The Supreme Court may not be expanded to more than 15 members. No more than two additional members may be appointed to any circuit court of appeals, to the Court of Claims, to the Court of Customs and Patent Appeals, or to the Customs Court, and the number of judges now serving in any district or group of districts may not be more than doubled. There is, therefore, a specific limitation of appointment regardless of age. That is to say, this bill, ostensibly designed to provide for the infusion of new blood, sets up insuperable obstacles to the "constant" or "persistent" operation of that principle.

Take the Supreme Court as an example. As constituted at the time this bill was presented to the Congress, there were six members of that tribunal over 70 years of age. If all six failed to resign or retire within 30 days after the enactment of this bill, and none of the members died, resigned, or retired before the President had made a nomination, then the Supreme Court would consist of 15 members. These 15 would then serve, regardless of age, at their own will, during good behavior, in other words, for life. Though as a result we had a court of 15 members 70 years of age or over, nothing could be done about it under this bill, and there would be no way to infuse "new" blood or "young" blood except by a new law further expanding the Court, unless, indeed, Congress and the Executive should be willing to follow the course defined by the framers of the Constitution for such a contingency and submit to the people a constitutional amendment limiting the terms of Justices or making mandatory their retirement at a given age.

It thus appears that the bill before us does not with certainty provide for increasing the personnel of the Federal judiciary, does not remedy the law's delay, does not serve the interest of the "poorer litigant" and does not provide for the "constant" or "persistent infusion of new blood" into the judiciary. What, then, does it do?

The Bill Applies Force to the Judiciary

The answer is clear. It applies force to the judiciary. It is an attempt to impose upon the courts a course of action, a line of decision which, without that force, without that imposition, the judiciary might not adopt.

Can there be any doubt that this is the purpose of the bill? Increasing the personnel is not the object of this measure; infusing young blood is not the object; for if either one of these purposes had been in the minds of the proponents, the drafters would not have written the following clause to be found on page 2, lines 1 to 4, inclusive:

Provided, That no additional judge shall be appointed hereunder if the judge who is of retirement age dies, resigns, or retires prior to the nomination of such additional judge.

Let it also be borne in mind that the President's message submitting this measure contains the following sentence:

If, on the other hand, any judge eligible for retirement should feel that his Court would suffer because of an increase of its membership, he may retire or resign under already existing provisions of law if he wishes to do so.

Moreover, the Attorney General in testifying before the committee (hearings, pt. 1, p. 33) said:

If the Supreme Court feels that the addition of six judges would be harmful to that Court, it can avoid that result by resigning.

Three invitations to the members of the Supreme Court over 70 years of age to get out despite all the talk about increasing personnel to expedite the disposition of cases and remedy the law's delay. One by the bill. One by the President's message. One by the Attorney General.

Can reasonable men by any possibility differ about the constitutional impropriety of such a course?

Those of us who hold office in this Government, however humble or exalted it may be, are creatures of the Constitution. To it we owe all the power and authority we possess. Outside of it we have none. We are bound by it in every official act.

We know that this instrument, without which we would not be able to call ourselves presidents, judges, or legislators, was carefully planned and deliberately framed to establish three coordinate branches of government, every one of them to be independent of the others. For the protection of the people, for the preservation of the rights of the individual, for the maintenance of the liberties of minorities, for maintaining the checks and balances of our dual system, the three branches of the Government were so constituted that the independent expression of honest difference of opinion could never be restrained in the people's servants and no one branch could overawe or subjugate the others. That is the American system. It is immeasurably more important, immeasurably more sacred to the people of America, indeed, to the people of all the world than the immediate adoption of any legislation however beneficial.

That judges should hold office during good behavior is the prescription. It is founded upon historic experience of the utmost significance. Compensation at stated times, which compensation was not to be diminished during their tenure, was also ordained. Those comprehensible terms were the outgrowths of experience which was deepseated. Of the 55 men in the Constitutional Convention, nearly one-half had actually fought in the War for Independence. Eight of the men present had signed the Declaration of Independence, in which, giving their reasons for the act, they had said of their king: "He has made judges dependent upon his will alone for their tenure of office and the amount and payment of their salaries." They sought to correct an abuse and to prevent its recurrence. When these men wrote the Constitution of their new Government, they still sought to avoid such an abuse as had led to such a bloody war as the one through which they had just passed. So they created a judicial branch of government consisting of courts not conditionally but absolutely independent in the discharge of their functions, and they intended that entire and impartial independence should prevail. Interference with this independence was prohibited, not partially but totally. Behavior other than good was the sole and only cause for interference. This judicial system is the priceless heritage of every American.

By this bill another and wholly different cause is proposed for the intervention of executive influence, namely, age. Age and behavior have no connection; they are unrelated subjects. By this bill, judges who have reached 70 years of age may remain on the bench and have their judgment augmented if they agree with the new appointee, or vetoed if they disagree. This is far from the independence intended for the courts by the framers of the Constitution. This is an unwarranted influence accorded the appointing agency, contrary to the spirit of the Constitution. The bill sets up a plan which has as its stability the changing will or inclination of an agency not a part of the judicial system. Constitutionally, the bill can have no sanction. The effect of the bill, as stated by the Attorney General to the committee, and indeed by the President in both his message and speech, is in violation of the organic law.

Object of Plan Acknowledged

No amount of sophistry can cover up this fact. The effect of this bill is not to provide for an increase in the number of Justices composing the Supreme Court. The effect is to provide a forced retirement or, failing in this, to take from the Justices affected a free exercise of their independent judgment.

The President tells us in his address to the Nation of March 9 . . . Congressional Record, March 10, page 2650:

> When the Congress has sought to stabilize national agriculture, to improve the conditions of labor, to safeguard business against unfair competition, to protect our national resources, and in many other ways, to serve our clearly national needs, the majority of the Court has been assuming the power to pass on the wisdom of these acts of the Congress and to approve or disapprove the public policy written into these laws * * *. We have, therefore, reached the point as a nation where we must take action to save the Constitution from the Court and the Court from itself. We must find a way to take an appeal from the Supreme Court to the Constitution itself. We want a Supreme Court which will do justice under the Constitution — not over it. In our courts we want a government of laws and not of men.

These words constitute a charge that the Supreme Court has exceeded the boundaries of its jurisdiction and invaded the field reserved by the Constitution to the legislative branch of the Government. At best the accusation is opinion only. It is not the conclusion of judicial process.

Here is the frank acknowledgement that neither speed nor "new blood" in the judiciary is the object of this legislation, but a change in the decisions of the Court — a subordination of the views of the judges to the views of the executive and legislative, a change to be brought about by forcing certain judges off the bench or increasing their number.

Let us, for the purpose of the argument, grant that the Court has been wrong, wrong not only in that it has rendered mistaken opinions but wrong in the far more serious sense that it has substituted its will for the congressional will in the matter of legislation. May we nevertheless safely punish the Court?

Today it may be the Court which is charged with forgetting its constitutional duties. Tomorrow it may be the Congress. The next day it may be the Executive. If we yield to temptation now to lay the lash upon the Court, we are only teaching others how to apply it to ourselves and to the people when the occasion seems to warrant. Manifestly, if we may force the hand of the Court to secure our interpretation of the Constitution, then some succeeding Congress may repeat the process to secure another and a different interpretation and one which may not sound so pleasant in our ears as that for which we now contend.

There is a remedy for usurpation or other judicial wrongdoing. If this bill be supported by the toilers of this country upon the ground that they want a Court which will sustain legislation limiting hours and providing minimum wages, they must remember that the procedure employed in the bill could be used in another administration to lengthen hours and to decrease wages. If farmers want agricultural relief and favor this bill upon the ground that it gives them a Court which will sustain legislation in their favor, they must remember that the procedure employed might some day be used to deprive them of every vestige of a farm relief.

When members of the Court usurp legislative powers or attempt to exercise political power, they lay themselves open to the charge of having lapsed from that "good behavior" which determines the period of their official life. But, if you say, the process of impeachment is difficult and uncertain, the answer is, the people made it so when they framed the Constitution. It is not for us, the servants of the people, the instruments of the Constitution, to find a more easy way to do that which our masters made difficult.

But, if the fault of the judges is not so grievous as to warrant impeachment, if their offense is merely that they have grown old, and we feel, therefore, that there should be a "constant infusion of new blood", then obviously the way to achieve that result is by constitutional amendment fixing definite terms for the members of the judiciary or making mandatory their retirement at a given age. Such a provision would indeed provide for the constant infusion of new blood, not only now but at all times in the future. The plan before us is but a temporary expedient which operates once and then never again, leaving the Court as permanently expanded to become once more a court of old men, gradually year by year falling behind the times.

What Size the Supreme Court?

How much better to proceed according to the rule laid down by the Constitution itself than by indirection to achieve our purposes. The futility and absurdity of the devious rather than the direct method is illustrated by the effect upon the problem of the retirement of Justice Van Devanter.

According to the terms of the bill, it does not become effective until 30 days after enactment, so the number of new judges to be appointed depends not upon the bill itself, not upon the conditions as they exist now or as they might exist when the bill is enacted, but upon conditions as they exist 30 days thereafter. Because Justice Van Devanter's retirement was effective as of June 2, there were on that date only five rather than six Justices on the Supreme Court of retirement age. The maximum number of appointments, therefore, is now 5 rather than 6 and the size of the Court 14 rather than 15. Now, indeed, we have put an end to 5-to-4 decisions and we shall not be harassed by 8-to-7 decisions. Now instead of making one man on the Court all-powerful, we have rendered the whole Court impotent when it divides 7 to 7 and we have provided a system approving the lower court by default.

But we may have another vacancy, and then the expanded court will be 13 rather than 14. A court of 13 with decisions by a vote of 7 to 6 and the all-powerful one returned to his position of judicial majesty. Meanwhile, the passage of years carries the younger members onward to the age of retirement when, if they should not retire, additional appointments could be made until the final maximum of 15 was reached.

The membership of the Court, between 9 and 15, would not be fixed by the Congress nor would it be fixed by the President. It would not even be fixed by the Court as a court, but would be determined by the caprice or convenience of the Justices over 70 years of age. The size of the Court would be determined by the personal desires of the Justices, and if there be any public advantage in having a court of any certain size, that public advantage in the people's interest would be wholly lost. Is it of any importance to the country that the size of the Court should be definitely fixed? Or are we to shut our eyes to that factor just because we have determined to punish the Justices whose opinions we resent?

But, if you say the process of reform by amendment is difficult and uncertain, the answer is, the people made it so when they framed the Constitution, and it is not for us, the servants of the people, by indirection to evade their will, or by devious methods to secure reforms upon which they only in their popular capacity have the right to pass.

A Measure Without Precedent

This bill is an invasion of judicial power such as has never before been attempted in this country. It is true that in the closing days of the administration of John Adams, a bill was passed creating 16 new circuit judges while reducing by one the number of places on the Supreme Court. It was charged that this was a bill to use the judiciary for a political purpose by providing official positions for members of a defeated party. The repeal of that law was the first task of the Jefferson administration.

Neither the original act nor the repealer was an attempt to change the course of judicial decision. And never in the history of the country has there been such an act. The present bill comes to us, therefore, wholly without precedent.

It is true that the size of the Supreme Court has been changed from time to time, but in every instance after the Adams administration, save one, the changes were made for purely administrative purposes in aid of the Court, not to control it.

Because the argument has been offered that these changes justify the present proposal, it is important to review all of the instances.

They were seven in number.

The first was by the act of 1801 reducing the number of members from six, as originally constituted, to five. Under the Judiciary Act of 1789 the circuit courts were trial courts and the Justices of the Supreme Court sat in them. That onerous duty was removed by the act of 1801 which created new judgeships for the purpose of relieving the members of the Supreme Court of this task. Since the work of the Justices was thereby reduced, it was provided that the next vacancy should not be filled. Jeffersonians explained the provision by saying that it was intended merely to prevent Jefferson from making an appointment of a successor to Justice Cushing whose death was expected.

The next change was in 1802 when the Jefferson administration restored the membership to six.

In neither of these cases was the purpose to influence decisions.

The third change was in 1807 under Jefferson when, three new States having been admitted to the Union, a new judicial circuit had to be created, and since it would be impossible for any of the six sitting Justices of the Supreme Court to undertake the trial work in the new circuit (Ohio, Kentucky, and Tennessee), a seventh Justice was added because of the expansion of the country. Had Jefferson wanted to subjugate John Marshall this was his opportunity to multiply members of the Court and overwhelm him, but he did not do it. We have no precedent here.

Thirty years elapsed before the next change. The country had continued to expand. New States were coming in and the same considerations which caused the increase of 1807 moved the representatives of the new West in Congress to demand another expansion. In 1826 a bill adding three justices passed both Houses but did not survive the conference. Andrew Jackson, who was familiar with the needs of the new frontier States, several times urged the legislation. Finally, it was achieved in 1837 and the Court was increased from 7 to 9 members.

Here again the sole reason for the change was the need of a growing country for a larger Court. We are still without a precedent.

Changes During the Reconstruction Period

In 1863 the western frontiers had reached the Pacific. California had been a State since 1850 without representation on the Supreme Court. The exigencies of the war and the development of the coast region finally brought the fifth change when by the act of 1863 a Pacific circuit was created and consequently a tenth member of the High Court.

The course of judicial opinion had not the slightest bearing upon the change.

Seventy-five years of constitutional history and still no precedent for a legislative attack upon the judicial power.

Now we come to the dark days of the reconstruction era for the sixth and seventh alterations of the number of justices.

The congressional majority in Andrew Johnson's administration had slight regard for the rights of minorities and no confidence in the President. Accordingly, a law was passed in 1866, providing that no appointments should be made to the Court until its membership had been reduced from 10 to 7. Doubtless, Thaddeus Stevens feared that the appointees of President Johnson might not agree with reconstruction policies and, if a constitutional question should arise, might vote to hold unconstitutional an act of Congress. But whatever the motive, a reduction of members at the instance of the bitterest majority that ever held sway in Congress to prevent a President from influencing the Court is scarcely a precedent for the expansion of the Court now.

By the time General Grant had become President in March 1869 the Court had been reduced to 8 members by the operation of the law of 1866. Presidential appointments were no longer resented, so Congress passed a new law, this time fixing the membership at 9. This law was passed in April 1869, an important date to remember, for the *Legal Tender* decision had not yet been rendered. Grant was authorized to make the additional appointment in December. Before he could make it however, Justice Grier resigned, and there were thus two vacancies.

The charge has been made that by the appointment to fill these vacancies Grant packed the Court to affect its decision in the *Legal Tender case*. Now whatever Grant's purpose may have been in making the particular appointments, it is obvious that Congress did not create the vacancies for the purpose of affecting any decision, because the law was passed long before the Court had acted in *Hepburn v. Griswold* and Congress made only one vacancy, but two appointments were necessary to change the opinion.

It was on February 7, 1870, that the court handed down its judgment holding the Legal Tender Act invalid, a decision very much deplored by the administration. It was on the same date that Grant sent down the nomination of the two justices whose votes, on a reconsideration of the issue, caused a reversal of the decision. As it happens, Grant had made two other nominations first, that of his Attorney General, Ebenezer Hoar, who was rejected by the Senate, and Edwin Stanton, who died 4 days after having been confirmed. These appointments were made in December 1869, 2 months before the decision, and Stanton was named, according to Charles Warren, historian of the Supreme Court, not because Grant wanted him but because a large majority of the members of the Senate and the House urged it. So Grant must be acquitted of having packed the Court and Congress is still without a precedent for any act that will tend to impair the independence of the Court.

A Precedent of Loyalty to the Constitution

Shall we now, after 150 years of loyalty to the constitutional ideal of an untrammeled judiciary, duty bound to protect the constitutional rights of the humblest citizen even against the Government itself, create the vicious precedent which must necessarily undermine our system? The only argument for the increase which survives analysis is that Congress should enlarge the Court so as to make the policies of this administration effective.

We are told that a reactionary oligarchy defies the will of the majority, that this is a bill to "unpack" the Court and give effect to the desires of the majority; that is to say, a bill to increase the number of Justices for the express purpose of neutralizing the views of some of the present members. In justification we are told, but without authority, by those who would rationalize this program, that Congress was given the power to determine the size of the Court so that the legislative branch would be able to impose its will upon the judiciary. This amounts to nothing more than the declaration that when the Court stands in the way of a legislative enactment, the Congress may reverse the ruling by enlarging the Court. When such a principle is adopted, our constitutional system is overthrown!

This, then, is the dangerous precedent we are asked to establish. When proponents of the bill assert, as they have done, that Congress in the past has altered the number of Justices upon the Supreme Court and that this is reason enough for our doing it now, they show how important precedents are and prove that we should now refrain from any action that would seem to establish one which could be followed hereafter whenever a Congress and an executive should become dissatisfied with the decisions of the Supreme Court.

This is the first time in the history of our country that a proposal to alter the decisions of the court by enlarging its personnel has been so boldly made. Let us meet it. Let us now set a salutary precedent that will never be violated. Let us, of the Seventy-fifth Congress, in words that will never be disregarded by any succeeding Congress, declare that we would rather have an independent Court, a fearless Court, a Court that will dare to announce its honest opinions in what it believes to be the defense of the liberties of the people, than a Court that, out of fear or sense of obligation to the appointing power, or factional passion, approves any measure we may enact. We are not the judges of the judges. We are not above the Constitution.

Even if every charge brought against the so-called "reactionary" members of this Court be true, it is far better that we await orderly but inevitable change of personnel than that we impatiently overwhelm them with new members. Exhibiting this restraint, thus demonstrating our faith in the American system, we shall set an example that will protect the independent American judiciary from attack as long as this Government stands.

An Independent Judiciary Essential

It is essential to the continuance of our constitutional democracy that the judiciary be completely independent of both the executive and legislative branches of the Government, and we assert that independent courts are the last safeguard of the citizen, where his rights, reserved to him by the express and implied provisions of the Constitution, come in conflict with the power of governmental agencies. We assert that the language of John Marshall, then in his 76th year, in the Virginia Convention (1829-31), was and is prophetic:

> Advert, sir, to the duties of a judge. He has to pass between the Government and the man whom the Government is prosecuting; between the most powerful individual in the community and the poorest and most unpopular. It is of the last importance that in the exercise of these duties he should observe the utmost fairness. Need I express the necessity of this? Does not every man feel that his own personal security and the security of his property depends on that fairness? The judicial department comes home in its effect to every man's fireside; it passes on his property, his reputation, his life, his all. Is it not, to the last degree, important that he should be rendered perfectly and completely independent, with nothing to influence or control him but God and his conscience?

The condition of the world abroad must of necessity cause us to hesitate at this time and to refuse to enact any law that would impair the independence of or destroy the people's confidence in an independent judicial branch of our Government. We unhesitatingly assert that any effort looking to the impairment of an independent judiciary of necessity operates toward centralization of power in the other branches of a tripartite form of government. We declare for the continuance and perpetuation of government and rule by law, as distinguished from government and rule by men, and in this we are but reasserting the principles basic to the Constitution of the United States. The converse of this would lead to and in fact accomplish the destruction of our form of government, where the written Constitution with its history, its spirit, and its long line of judicial interpretation and construction, is looked to and relied upon by millions of our people. Reduction of the degree of the supremacy of law means an increasing enlargement of the degree of personal government.

Personal government, or government by an individual, means autocratic dominance, by whatever name it may be designated. Autocratic dominance was the very thing against which the American Colonies revolted, and to prevent which the Constitution was in every particular framed.

Courts and the judges thereof should be free from a subservient attitude of mind, and this must be true whether a question of constitutional construction or one of popular activity is involved. If the court of last resort is to be made to respond to a prevalent sentiment of a current hour, politically imposed, that Court must ultimately become subservient to the pressure of public opinion of the hour, which might at the moment embrace mob passion abhorrent to a more calm, lasting consideration.

True it is, that courts like Congresses, should take account of the advancing strides of civilization. True it is that the law, being a progressive science, must be pronounced progressively and liberally; but the milestones of liberal progress are made to be noted and counted with caution rather than merely to be encountered and passed. Progress is not a mad mob march; rather, it is a steady, invincible stride. There is ever-impelling truth in the lines of the great liberal jurist, Mr. Justice Holmes, in *Northern Securities v. The United States*, wherein he says:

> Great cases like hard cases make bad law. For great cases are called great, not by reason of their real importance in shaping the law of the future, but because of some accident of immediate overwhelming interest which appeals to the feel-

ings and distorts the judgment. These immediate interests exercise a kind of hydraulic pressure which makes what previously was clear, seem doubtful, and before which even well settled principles of law will bend.

If, under the "hydraulic pressure" of our present need for economic justice, we destroy the system under which our people have progressed to a higher degree of justice and prosperity than that ever enjoyed by any other people in all the history of the human race, then we shall destroy not only all opportunity for further advance but everything we have thus far achieved.

The whole bill prophesies and permits executive and legislative interferences with the independence of the Court, a prophecy and a permission which constitute an affront to the spirit of the Constitution.

> The complete independence of the courts of justice is peculiarly essential in a limited Constitution. By a limited Constitution, I understand one which contains certain specified exceptions to the legislative authority; such, for instance, as that it shall pass no bills of attainder, no ex-post-facto laws, and the like. Limitations of this kind can be preserved in practice no other way than through the medium of courts of justice, whose duty it must be to declare all acts contrary to the manifest tenor of the Constitution void. Without this, all the reservations of particular rights or privileges would amount to nothing (The Federalist, vol. 2, p. 100, no. 78).

The spirit of the Constitution emphasizing the establishment of an independent judicial branch was reenunciated by Madison in Nos. 47 and 48 (The Federalist, vol. 1, pp. 329, 339) and by John Adams (Adams' Works, vol. 1, p. 186).

If interference with the judgment of an independent judiciary is to be countenanced in any degree, then it is permitted and sanctioned in all degrees. There is no constituted power to say where the degree ends or begins, and the political administration of the hour may apply the essential "concepts of justice" by equipping the courts with one strain of "new blood", while the political administration of another day may use a different light and a different blood test. Thus would influence run riot. Thus perpetuity, independence, and stability belonging to the judicial arm of the Government and relied on by lawyers and laity, are lost. Thus is confidence extinguished.

The President Gives Us Example

From the very beginning of our Government to this hour, the fundamental necessity of maintaining inviolate the independence of the three coordinate branches of government has been recognized by legislators, jurists, and presidents. James Wilson, one of the framers of the Constitution who later became a Justice of the Supreme Court, declared that the independence of each department recognizes that its proceedings "shall be free from the remotest influence, direct or indirect, of either of the other two branches." Thus it was at the beginning. Thus it is now. Thus it was recognized by the men who framed the Constitution and administered the Government under it. Thus it was declared and recognized by the present President of the United States who, on the 19th day of May 1937, in signing a veto message to the Congress of the United States of a measure which would have created a special commission to represent the Federal Government at the World's Fair in New York City in 1939, withheld his approval because he felt that the provision by which it gave certain administrative duties to certain Members of Congress amounted to a legislative interference with executive functions. In vetoing the bill, President Roosevelt submitted with approval the statement of the present Attorney General that:

> In my opinion those provisions of the joint resolution establishing a commission composed largely of Members of the Congress and authorizing them to appoint a United States commissioner general and two assistant commissioners for the New York World's Fair, and also providing for the expenditure of the appropriation made by the resolution, and for the

administration of the resolution generally, amount to an unconstitutional invasion of the province of the Executive.

The solicitude of the President to maintain the independence of the executive arm of the Government against invasion by the legislative authority should be an example to us in solicitude to preserve the independence of the judiciary from any danger of invasion by the legislative and executive branches combined.

Extent of the Judicial Power

The assertion has been indiscriminately made that the Court has arrogated to itself the right to declare acts of Congress invalid. The contention will not stand against investigation or reason.

Article III of the Federal Constitution provides that the judicial power "shall extend to all cases in law and equity arising under this Constitution, the laws of the United States and treaties made under their authority."

The words "under this Constitution" were inserted on the floor of the Constitutional Convention in circumstances that leave no doubt of their meaning. It is true that the Convention had refused to give the Supreme Court the power to sit as a council of revision over the acts of Congress or the power to veto such acts. That action, however, was merely the refusal to give the Court any legislative power. It was a decision wholly in harmony with the purpose of keeping the judiciary independent. But, while carefully refraining from giving the Court power to share in making laws, the Convention did give it judicial power to construe the Constitution in litigated cases.

After the various forms and powers of the new Government had been determined in principle, the Convention referred the whole matter to the Committee on Detail, the duty of which was to draft a tentative instrument. The report of this committee was then taken up section by section on the floor, debated and perfected, whereupon the instrument was referred to the Committee on Style which wrote the final draft.

When the Committee on Detail reported the provision defining the judicial power, it read as follows:

> The jurisdiction of the Supreme Court shall extend to all cases arising under laws passed by the Legislature of the United States, etc. (Elliot's Debates, vol. 5, p. 380).

On August 27, 1787, when this sentence was under consideration of the full Convention, it was changed to read as follows on motion of Dr. Johnson:

> The jurisdiction of the Supreme Court shall extend to all cases arising under this Constitution and the laws passed by the Legislature of the United States.

Madison in his notes (Elliot's Debates, vol. 5, p. 483) reports the incident in this language:

> Dr. Johnson moved to insert the words, "this Constitution and the" before the word "laws."
>
> Mr. Madison doubted whether it was not going too far, to extend the jurisdiction of the Court generally to cases arising under the Constitution, and whether it ought not to be limited to cases of a judiciary nature. The right of expounding the Constitution, in cases not of this nature, ought not to be given to that department.
>
> The motion of Dr. Johnson was agreed to, nem. con., it being generally supposed that the jurisdiction given was constructively limited to cases of a judiciary nature.

In other words, the framers of the Constitution were not satisfied to give the Court power to pass only on cases arising under the laws but insisted on making it quite clear that the power extends to cases arising "under the Constitution." Moreover, Article VI of the Constitution, clause 2, provides:

> This Constitution and the laws of the United States which shall be made in pursuance thereof * * * shall be the supreme law of the land * * *.

Language was never more clear. No doubt can remain. A pretended law which is not "in pursuance" of the Constitution is no law at all.

A citizen has the right to appeal to the Constitution from such a statute. He has the right to demand that Congress shall not pass any act in violation of that instrument, and, if Congress does pass such an act, he has the right to seek refuge in the courts and to expect the Supreme Court to strike down the act if it does in fact violate the Constitution. A written constitution would be valueless if it were otherwise.

The right and duty of the Court to construe the Constitution is thus made clear. The question may, however, be propounded whether in construing that instrument the Court has undertaken to "override the judgment of the Congress on legislative policy." It is not necessary for this committee to defend the Court from such a charge. An invasion of the legislative power by the judiciary would not, as has already been indicated, justify the invasion of judicial authority by the legislative power. The proper remedy against such an invasion is provided in the Constitution.

Very Few Laws Held Unconstitutional

We may, however, point out that neither in this administration nor in any previous administration has the Supreme Court held unconstitutional more than a minor fraction of the laws which have been enacted. In 148 years, from 1789 to 1937, only 64 acts of Congress have been declared unconstitutional — 64 acts out of a total of approximately 58,000.

These 64 acts were held invalid in 76 cases, 30 of which were decided by the unanimous vote of all the justices, 9 by the agreement of all but one of the justices, 14 by the agreement of all but two, another 12 by agreement of all but three. In 11 cases only were there as many as four dissenting votes when the laws were struck down.

Only four statutes enacted by the present administration have been declared unconstitutional with three or more dissenting votes. And only 11 statutes, or parts thereof, bearing the approval of the present Chief Executive out of 2,699 signed by him during his first administration, have been invalidated. Of the 11, three — the Municipal Bankruptcy Act, the Farm Mortgage Act, and the Railroad Pension Act — were not what have been commonly denominated administration measures. When he attached his signature to the Railroad Pension Act, the President was quoted as having expressed his personal doubt as to the constitutionality of the measure. The Farm Mortgage Act, was later rewritten by the Congress, reenacted, and in its new form sustained by the court which had previously held it void. Both the Farm Mortgage Act in its original form and the National Recovery Administration Act were held to be unconstitutional by a unanimous vote of all the justices. With this record of fact, it can scarcely be said with accuracy that the legislative power has suffered seriously at the hands of the Court.

But even if the case were far worse than it is alleged to be, it would still be no argument in favor of this bill to say that the courts and some judges have abused their power. The courts are not perfect, nor are the judges. The Congress is not perfect, nor are Senators and Representatives. The Executive is not perfect. These branches of government and the office under them are filled by human beings who for the most part strive to live up to the dignity and idealism of a system that was designed to achieve the greatest possible measure of justice and freedom for all the people. We shall destroy the system when we reduce it to the imperfect standards of the men who operate it. We shall strengthen it and ourselves, we shall make justice and liberty for all men more certain when, by patience and self-restraint, we maintain it on the high plane on which it was conceived.

Inconvenience and even delay in the enactment of legislation is not a heavy price to pay for our system. Constitutional democracy moves forward with certainty rather than with speed. The safety and the permanence of the progressive march of our civilization are far more important to us and to those who are to come after us than the enactment now of any particular law. The

Constitution of the United States provides ample opportunity for the expression of popular will to bring about such reforms and changes as the people may deem essential to their present and future welfare. It is the people's charter of the powers granted those who govern them.

Guaranties of Individual Liberty Threatened

Let it be recognized that not only is the commerce clause of the Constitution and the clauses having to do with due process and general welfare involved in the consideration of this bill, but every line of the Constitution from the preamble to the last amendment is affected. Every declarative statement in those clauses which we choose to call the Bill of Rights is involved. Guaranties of individual human liberty and the limitation of the governing powers and processes are all reviewable.

During the period in which the writing and the adoption of the Constitution was being considered, it was Patrick Henry who said:

The Judiciary are the sole protection against a tyrannical execution of the laws. They (Congress) cannot depart from the Contitution; and their laws in opposition would be void.

Later, during the discussion of the Bill of Rights, James Madison declared:

If they (the rights specified in the Bill of Rights) were incorporated into the Constitution, independent tribunals of justice will consider themselves in a peculiar manner the guardians of those rights; they will be an impenetrable bulwark against every assumption of power in the legislative or Executive; they will be naturally led to resist every encroachment upon rights stipulated in the Constitution by the Declaration of Rights.

These leaders, who were most deeply imbued with the duty of safeguarding human rights and who were most concerned to preserve the liberty lately won, never wavered in their belief that an independent judiciary and a Constitution defining with clarity the rights of the people, were the only safeguards of the citizen. Familiar with English history and the long struggle for human liberty, they held it to be an axiom of free government that there could be no security for the people against the encroachment of political power save a written Constitution and an uncontrolled judiciary.

This has now been demonstrated by 150 years of progressive American history. As a people, Americans love liberty. It may be with truth and pride also said that we have a sensitive regard for human rights. Notwithstanding these facts, during 150 years the citizen over and over again has been compelled to contend for the plain rights guaranteed in the Constitution. Free speech, a free press, the right of assemblage, the right of a trial by jury, freedom from arbitrary arrest, religious freedom — these are among the great underlying principles upon which our democracy rests. But for all these, there have been occasions when the citizen has had to appeal to the courts for protection as against those who would take them away. And the only place the citizen has been able to go in any of these instances, for protection against the abridgment of his rights, has been to an independent and uncontrolled and incorruptible judiciary. Our law reports are filled with decisions scattered throughout these long years, reassuring the citizen of his constitutional rights, restraining States, restraining the Congress, restraining the Executive, restraining majorities, and preserving the noblest in rights of individuals.

Minority political groups, no less than religious and racial groups, have never failed, when forced to appeal to the Supreme Court of the United States, to find in its opinions the reassurance and protection of their constitutional rights. No finer or more durable philosophy of free government is to be found in all the writings and practices of great statesmen than may be found in the decisions of the Supreme Court when dealing with great problems of free government touching human rights. This would not have been possible without an independent judiciary.

Court Has Protected Human Rights

No finer illustration of the vigilance of the Court in protecting human rights can be found than in a decision wherein was involved the rights of a Chinese person, wherein the Court said:

When we consider the nature and the theory of our institutions of government, the principles upon which they are supposed to rest, and review the history of their development, we are constrained to conclude that they do not mean to leave room for the play and action of purely personal and arbitrary power. * * * The fundamental rights to life, liberty, and the pursuit of happiness considered as individual possessions are secured by those maxims of constitutional law which are the monuments showing the victorious progress of the race in securing to men the blessings of civilization under the reign of just and equal laws, so that in the famous language of the Massachusetts Bill of Rights, the government of the Commonwealth "may be a government of laws and not of men." For the very idea that one man may be compelled to hold his life or the means of living or any material right essential to the enjoyment of life, at the mere will of another, seems to be intolerable in any country where freedom prevails, as being the essence of slavery itself. *(Yick Wo v. Hopkins,* 118 U.S. 356.)

In the case involving the title to the great Arlington estate of Lee, the Court said:

No man in this country is so high that he is above the law. No officer of the law may set that law at defiance, with impunity. All the officers of the Government, from the highest to the lowest, are creatures of the law and are bound to obey it. *(U.S. v. Lee,* 106 U.S. 196.)

In a noted case where several Negroes had been convicted of the crime of murder, the trial being held in the atmosphere of mob dominance, the Court set aside the conviction, saying:

The State is free to regulate the procedure of its courts in accordance with its own conceptions of policy, unless in so doing it "offends some principle of justice so rooted in the traditions and conscience of our people as to be ranked as fundamental." *(Snyder v. Mass.; Rogers v. Peck,* 199 U.S. 425, 434.)

The State may abolish trial by jury. It may dispense with indictment by a grand jury and substitute complaint or information. *(Walker v. Sauvinet,* 92 U.S. 90; *Hurtado v. California,* 110 U.S. 516; *Snyder v. Mass.,* supra.) But the freedom of the State in establishing its policy is the freedom of constitutional government and is limited by the requirement of due process of law. Because a State may dispense with a jury trial, it does not follow that it may substitute trial by ordeal. The rack and torture chamber may not be substituted for the witness stand. The State may not permit an accused to be hurried to conviction under mob domination — where the whole proceeding is but a mask — without supplying corrective process * * *.

Under a law enacted by a State legislature, it was made possible to censor and control the press through the power of injunction on the charge that the publication of malicious, scandalous, and defamatory matters against officials constituted a nuisance. The Supreme Court, holding the law void, said:

The administration of government has become more complex, the opportunities for malfeasance and corruption have multiplied, crime has grown to most serious proportions, and the danger of its protection by unfaithful officials and of the impairment of the fundamental security of life and property by criminal alliances and official neglect, emphasizes the primary need of a vigilant and courageous press, especially in great cities. The fact that the liberty of the press may be abused by miscreant purveyors of scandal does not make less necessary the immunity of the press from previous restraint in dealing with official misconduct.

Speaking of the rights of labor, the Supreme Court has said:

Labor unions are recognized by the Clayton Act as legal when instituted for mutual help and lawfully carrying out their legitimate objects. They have long been thus recognized by the courts. They were organized out of the necessities of the situation. A single employee was helpless in dealing with an employer. He was dependent ordinarily on his daily wage for the maintenance of himself and family. If the employer refused to pay him the wages that he thought fair, he was nevertheless unable to leave the employ and to resist arbitrary and unfair treatment. Union was essential to give laborers opportunity to deal on equality with their employer. They united to exert influence upon him and to leave him in a body in order by this inconvenience to induce him to make better terms with them. They were withholding their labor of economic value to make him pay what they thought it was worth. The right to combine for such a lawful purpose has in many years not been denied by any court. The strike became a lawful instrument in a lawful economic struggle or competition between employer and employees as to the share or division between them of the joint product of labor and capital *(American Foundries v. Tri City Council,* 257 U.S. 184).

In another instance where the rights of labor were involved, the Court said:

The legality of collective action on the part of employees in order to safeguard their property interests is not to be disputed. It has long been recognized that employees are entitled to organize for the purpose of securing the redress of grievances and to promote agreements with employers relating to rates of pay and conditions of work. Congress * * * could safeguard it and seek to make their appropriate collective action an instrument of peace rather than of strife. Such collective action would be a mockery if representation were made futile by interference with freedom of choice. Thus the prohibition by Congress of interference with the selection of representatives for the purpose of negotiation and conference between employers and employees, instead of being an invasion of the constitutional rights of either, was based on the recognition of the rights of both *(Texas & New Orleans Railway Co. v. Brotherhood of Railway & Steamship Clerks,* 281 U.S. 548).

By the philosophy behind the pending measure it is declared that the Bill of Rights would never be violated, that freedom of speech, freedom of assemblage, freedom of the press, security in life, liberty, and property would never be challenged. Law takes its greatest force and its most secure foundation when it rests on the forum of experience. And how has our court of last resort in the past been called upon to contribute to that great fortification of the law?

In *Cummings v. Missouri* the rights of the lowly citizen were protected in the spirit of the Constitution by declaring that "no State shall pass any bill of attender or ex post fact in law." In the *Milligan case,* in the midst of the frenzied wake of the Civil War, it was the Supreme Court which sustained a citizen against an act of Congress, suspending the right of trial by jury.

In the case of *Pierce v. The Society of Sisters,* it was the Supreme Court that pronounced the inalienable right of the fathers and mothers of America to guide the destiny of their own children, when that power was challenged by an unconstitutional act of a sovereign State.

Only a few months ago in the Scottsboro cases the rights of a Negro to have counsel were upheld by this Court under the due process clause of the Constitution. On March 26 of this year, in the *Herndon case,* the rights of freedom of speech and freedom of assembly were reenunciated. Only a few weeks ago the Supreme Court construed the Constitution to uphold the Wagner Labor Act.

It would extend this report beyond proper limits to pursue this subject and trace out the holdings of the Court on the many different phases of human rights upon which it has had to pass; but the record of the Court discloses, beyond peradventure of doubt, that in preserving and maintaining the rights of American citizens under the Constitution, it has been vigilant, able, and faithful.

If, at the time all these decisions were made, their making had been even remotely infuenced by the possibility that such pronouncement would entail the appointment of a co-judge or co-judges to "apply the essential concepts of justice" in the light of what the then prevailing appointing power might believe to be the "needs of an ever-changing world" these landmarks of liberty of the lowly and humble might not today exist; nor would they exist tomorrow. However great the need for human progress and social uplift, their essentials are so interwoven and involved with the individual as to be inseparable.

The Constitution of the United States, courageously construed and upheld through 150 years of history, has been the bulwark of human liberty. It was bequeathed to us in a great hour of human destiny by one of the greatest characters civilization has produced — George Washington. It is in our hands now to preserve or to destroy. If ever there was a time when the people of Ameica should heed the words of the Father of Their Country this is the hour. Listen to his solemn warning from the Farewell Address:

It is important, likewise, that the habits of thinking, in a free country, should inspire caution in those intrusted with its administration, to confine themselves within their respective constitutional spheres, avoiding, in the exercises of the powers of one department, to encroach upon another. The spirit of encroachment tends to consolidate the powers of all the departments in one, and thus to create, whatever the form of government, a real despotism. A first estimate of that love of power, and proneness to abuse it, which predominates in the human heart, is sufficient to satisfy us of the truth of this position. The necessity of reciprocal checks in the exercise of political power, by dividing and distributing it into different depositories, and constituting each the guardian of the public weal, against invasions by the others, has been evinced by experiment, ancient and modern; some of them in our own country, and under our own eyes. To preserve them must be as necessary as to institute them. If, in the opinion of the people, the distribution or modification of the constitutional powers be, in any particular, wrong, let it be corrected by an amendment in the way which the Constitution designates. But let there be no change by usurpation; for though this, in one instance, may be the instrument of good, it is the customary weapon by which free governments are destroyed. The precedent must always greatly overbalance, in permanent evil, any partial or transient benefit which the use can, at any time, yield.

Summary

We recommend the rejection of this bill as a needless, futile, and utterly dangerous abandonment of constitutional principle.

It was presented to the Congress in a most intricate form and for reasons that obscured its real purpose.

It would not banish age from the bench nor abolish divided decisions.

It would not affect the power of any court to hold laws unconstitutional nor withdraw from any judge the authority to issue injunctions.

It would not reduce the expense of litigation nor speed the decision of cases.

It is a proposal without precedent and without justification.

It would subjugate the courts to the will of Congress and the President and thereby destroy the independence of the judiciary, the only certain shield of individual rights.

It contains the germ of a system of centralized administration of law that would enable an executive so minded to send his judges into every judicial district in the land to sit in judgment on controversies between the Government and the citizen.

It points the way to the evasion of the Constitution and establishes the method whereby the people may be deprived of their right to pass upon all amendments of the fundamental law.

It stands now before the country, acknowledged by its proponents as a plan to force judicial interpretation of the Constitution, a proposal that violates every sacred tradition of American democracy.

Under the form of the Constitution it seeks to do that which is unconstitutional.

Its ultimate operation would be to make this Government one of men rather than one of law, and its practical operation would be to make the Constitution what the executive or legislative branches of the Government choose to say it is — an interpretation to be changed with each change of administration.

It is a measure which should be so emphatically rejected that its parallel will never again be presented to the free representatives of the free people of America.

WILLIAM H. KING.
FREDERICK VAN NUYS.
PATRICK McCARRAN.
CARL A. HATCH.
EDWARD R. BURKE.
TOM CONNALLY.
JOSEPH C. O'MAHONEY.
WILLIAM E. BORAH.
WARREN R. AUSTIN.
FREDERICK STEIWER.

Individual Views of Mr. Hatch

In filing this separate brief statement on S. 1392 it is not intended to depart in any degree from the recommendation of the majority report for the committee to the effect that S. 1392 should not pass. In that recommendation I join.

It should be noted that the recommendation and the arguments advanced by the majority are directed against the bill in its present form. It has been my thought that the principal objections set forth in the majority report can be met by proper amendments to the bill; that with sufficient safeguards, it can be made a constructive piece of legislation, not designed for the immediate present, but to provide a permanent plan for the gradual and orderly infusion of new blood into the courts. Such a plan, intended to aid in the better administration of justice and to enable the courts to discharge their judicial function more efficiently, but so safeguarded that it cannot be used to change or control judicial opinions, is within both the spirit and the letter of the constitution.

Intending to offer amendments which it is believed will accomplish this purpose, I desire to make this additional statement to accompany the majority report.

CARL A. HATCH.

Proposed Bill

June 7

Be it enacted by the Senate and the House of Representatives of the United States of America in Congress assembled, That —

(a) When any judge of a court of the United States, appointed to hold his office during good behavior, has heretofore or hereafter attained the age of seventy years and has held a commission or commissions as judge of any such court or courts at least ten years, continuously or otherwise, and within six months thereafter has neither resigned nor retired, the President, for each such judge who has not so resigned or retired, shall nominate, and by and with the advice and consent of the Senate, shall appoint one additional judge to the court to which the former is commissioned: *Provided,* That no additional judge shall be appointed hereunder if the judge who is of retirement age dies, resigns, or retires prior to the nomination of such additional judge.

(b) The number of judges of any court shall be permanently increased by the number appointed thereto under the provisions of subsection (a) of this section. No more than fifty judges shall be appointed thereunder, nor shall any judge be so appointed if such appointment would result in (1) more than fifteen members of the Supreme Court of the United States, (2) more than two additional members so appointed to a circuit court of appeals, the Court of Claims, the United States Court of Customs and Patent Appeals, or the Customs Court, or (3) more than twice the number of judges now authorized to be appointed for any district or, in the case of judges appointed for more than one district, for any such group of districts.

(c) That number of judges which is at least two-thirds of the number of which the Supreme Court of the United States consists, or three-fifths of the number of which the United States Court of Appeals for the District of Columbia, the Court of Claims, or the United States Court of Customs and Patent Appeals consists, shall constitute a quorum of such court.

(d) An additional judge shall not be appointed under the provisions of this section when the judge who is of retirement age is commissioned to an office as to which Congress has provided that a vacancy shall not be filled.

Sec. 2 (a) Any circuit judge hereafter appointed may be designated and assigned from time to time by the Chief Justice of the United States for service in the circuit court of appeals for any circuit. Any district judge hereafter appointed may be designated and assigned from time to time by the Chief Justice of the United States for service in any district court, or, subject to the authority of the Chief Justice, by the senior circuit judge of his circuit for service in any district court within the circuit. A district judge designated and assigned to another district hereunder may hold court separately and at the same time as the district judge in such district. All designations and assignments made hereunder shall be filed in the office of the clerk and entered on the minutes of both the court from and to which a judge is designated and assigned, and thereafter the judge so designated and assigned shall be authorized to discharge all the judicial duties (except the power of appointment to a statutory position or of permanent designation of a newspaper or depository of funds) of a judge of the court to which he is designated and assigned. The designation and assignment of a judge shall not impair his authority to perform such judicial duties of the court to which he was commissioned as may be necessary or appropriate. The designation and assignment of any judge may be terminated at any time by order of the Chief Justice or the senior circuit judge, as the case may be.

(b) After the designation and assignment of a judge by the Chief Justice, the senior circuit judge of the circuit in which such judge is commissioned may certify to the Chief Justice any consideration which such senior circuit judge believes to make advisable that the designated judge remain in or return for service in the court to which he was commissioned. If the Chief Justice deems the reasons sufficient he shall revoke or designate the time of termination of such designation and assignment.

(c) In case a trial or hearing has been entered upon but has not been concluded before the expiration of the period of service of a district judge designated and assigned hereunder, the period of service shall, unless terminated under the provisions of subsection (a) of this section, be deemed to be extended until the trial or hearing has been concluded. Any designated and assigned district judge who has held court in another district than his own shall have power, notwithstanding his absence from such district and the expiration of any time limit in his designation, to decide all matters which have been submitted to him within such district, to decide motions for new trials, settle bills of exceptions, certify or authenticate narratives of testimony, or perform any other act required by law or the rules to be performed in order to prepare any case so tried by him for review in an appellate court; and his action thereon in writing filed with the clerk of the court where the trial or hearing was had shall be as valid as if such action had been taken by him within that district and within the period of his designation. Any designated and assigned circuit judge who has sat on another court than his own shall have power, notwithstanding the expiration of any time limit in his designation, to participate in the decision of all matters submitted to the court while he was sitting and to perform or participate in any act appropriate to the disposition or review of matters submitted while he was sitting on such court, and his action thereon shall be as valid as if it had been taken while sitting on such court and within the period of his designation.

Sec. 3. (a) The Supreme Court shall have power to appoint a proctor. It shall be his duty (1) to obtain and, if deemed by the Court to be desirable, to publish information as to the volume, character, and status of litigation in the district courts and circuit courts of appeals, and such other information as the Supreme Court may from time to time require by order, and it shall be the duty of any judge, clerk, or marshal of any court of the United States promptly to furnish such information as may be required by the proctor; (2) to investigate the need of assigning district and circuit judges to other courts and to make recommendations thereon to the Chief Justice; (3) to recommend, with the approval of the Chief Justice, to any court of the United States methods for expediting cases pending on its dockets; and (4) to perform such other duties consistent with his office as the Court shall direct.

(b) The proctor shall, by requisition upon the Public Printer, have any necessary printing and binding done at the Government Printing Office and authority is conferred upon the Public Printer to do such printing and binding.

(c) The salary of the proctor shall be $10,000 per annum, payable out of the Treasury in monthly installments, which shall be in full compensation for the services required by law. He shall also be allowed, in the discretion of the Chief Justice, stationery, supplies, travel expenses, equipment, necessary professional and clerical assistance, and miscellaneous expenses appropriate for performing the duties imposed by this section. The expenses in connection with the maintenance of his office shall be paid from the appropiation of the Supreme Court of the United States.

Sec. 4. There is hereby authorized to be appropriated, out of any money in the Treasury not otherwise appropriated, the sum of $100,000 for the salaries of additional judges and the other purposes of this Act during the fiscal year 1937.

Sec. 5. When used in this Act—

(a) The term "judge of retirement age" means a judge of a court of the United States, appointed to hold his office during good behavior, who has attained the age of seventy years and has held a commission or commissions as judge of any such court or courts at least ten years, continuously or otherwise, and within six months thereafter, whether or not he is eligible for retirement, has neither resigned nor retired.

(b) The term "circuit court of appeals" includes the United States Court of Appeals for the District of Columbia; the term "senior circuit judge" includes the Chief Justice of the United States Court of Appeals for the District of Columbia; and the term "circuit" includes the District of Columbia.

(c) The term "district court" includes the District Court of the District of Columbia but does not include the district court in any territory or insular possession.

(d) The term "judge" includes justice.

Sec. 6. This Act shall take effect on the thirtieth day after the date of its enactment.

Fortas Letter Explaining Resignation

The text of the May 14, 1969, letter of resignation from Justice Abe Fortas to Chief Justice Earl Warren:

My dear Chief Justice:

I am filing with you this memorandum with respect to my association with the Wolfson Family Foundation, and a statement of the reasons which in my judgment indicate that I should resign in order that the Court may not continue to be subjected to extraneous stress which may adversely affect the performance of its important functions.

As you know, I have delayed issuing a detailed report or announcing my decision until it could first be communicated to the members of the Court. In my judgment, this was the only proper course open to me as an Associate Justice of this Court, because of the Court's position as a separate and independent branch of the government under the Constitution. Because of the Court's recess, this report was not possible until yesterday.

In the spring or summer of 1965, before I was nominated as Associate Justice of the Supreme Court, my law firm represented New York Shipbuilding Corporation, a company controlled by Mr. Louis E. Wolfson, with respect to various civil claims. Later in the summer of 1965, and also before my nomination, my firm was retained in connection with some securities problems of Merritt-Chapman and Scott Corporation, of which Mr. Wolfson was Chairman of the Board.

I became acquainted with Mr. Wolfson and he told me about the Wolfson Family Foundation and his hopes and plans for it. He knew that its program — the improvement of community relations and the promotion of racial and religious cooperation — concerned matters to which I had devoted much time and attention.

Mr. Wolfson stated that he intended to increase the Foundation's resources, and he hoped that the Foundation might expand its work so as to make unique and basic contributions in its field. As we proceeded in our discussions, Mr. Wolfson suggested that he would like me to participate in and help shape the Foundation's program and activities. I told him I was interested in these objectives and that I hoped we would continue our discussions.

I became a member of the Court in October 1965. Shortly thereafter, Mr. Wolfson was in Washington and again conferred with me about the Foundation's work and my possible association with it. I again indicated my interest in the Foundation's program and in expanding its scope, and we discussed the possibility of my participating in the project on a long-term basis. Because of the nature of the work, there was no conflict between it and my judicial duties. It was then my opinion that the work of the Court would leave me adequate time for the Foundation assignments.

The Board of the Foundation met in December 1965, and approved, by resolution, an agreement under which I was to perform services for the Foundation. It was understood between us that the program in question was a long-range one and that my association would be meaningful only if it were on a long-term basis. The agreement, therefore, contemplated that I would perform continuing services, and, instead of fixing variable compensation from time to time for work done, it provided that I would receive Twenty Thousand Dollars per year for my life with arrangements for payments to Mrs. Fortas in the event of my death.

In January 1966, I received a check for Twenty Thousand Dollars under the agreement, and began my association with the Foundation. In June of that year I attended and participated in a meeting of the Trustees of the Foundation at Jacksonville, Florida.

It is my recollection that Mr. Wolfson did not attend the meeting. I went from Jacksonville to his farm at Ocala where I had an overnight visit, as I recall, with him and his family.

Later, in June 1966, I reached the decision that the continuing role in the Foundation's work which our agreement contemplated should be terminated. There were two reasons for this decision: My work for the Court was much heavier than I had anticipated and my idea of the amount of time I would have free for non-judicial work had been a substantial over-estimate. I had also learned shortly before informing the Foundation of my decision to terminate the arrangement, that the SEC had referred Mr. Wolfson's file to the Department of Justice for consideration as to criminal prosecution.

I therefore wrote a letter to the Foundation, addressed to its General Counsel, dated June 21, 1966, cancelling the agreement we had entered into, subject to completing the projects for the year. I recited as my reason only the burden of Court work.

In September and October of 1966, Mr. Louis E. Wolfson was indicted on separate charges stemming from stock transactions, and in December 1966, I returned to the Foundation, in its entirety, the sum of Twenty Thousand Dollars previously paid to me. I concluded that, because of the developments which had taken place, the services which I had performed should be treated as a contribution to the Foundation.

Since becoming a member of the Court, I have not, at any time, directly or indirectly, received any compensation from Mr. Wolfson or members of his family or any of his associates for advice, assistance or any reason whatever, except the Foundation fee which was returned.

Since I became a member of the Court, Mr. Wolfson on occasion would send me material relating to his problems, just as I think he did to many other people, and on several occasions he mentioned them to me, but I have not interceded or taken part in any legal, administrative or judicial matter affecting Mr. Wolfson or anyone associated with him.

It is my opinion, however, that the public controversy relating to my association with the Foundation is likely to continue and adversely affect the work and position of the Court, absent my resignation. In these circumstances, it seems clear to me that it is not my duty to remain on the Court, but rather to resign in the hope that this will enable the Court to proceed with its vital work free from extraneous stress.

There has been no wrongdoing on my part. There has been no default in the performance of my judicial duties in accordance with the high standards of the office I hold. So far as I am concerned, the welfare and maximum effectiveness of the Court to perform its critical role in our system of government are factors that are paramount to all others. It is this consideration that prompts my resignation which, I hope, by terminating the public controversy, will permit the Court to proceed with its work without the harassment of debate concerning one of its members.

I have written a letter asking President Nixon to accept my resignation, effective as of this date.

I leave the Court with the greatest respect and affection for you and my colleagues, and my thanks to all of you and to the staff of the Court for your unfailing helpfulness and friendship. I hope that as I return to private life, I shall find opportunities to continue to serve the Nation and the cause of justice which this Court so ably represents.

Sincerely,

ABE FORTAS

Glossary of Common Legal Terms

Accessory. In criminal law, a person not present at the commission of an offense who commands, advises, instigates or conceals the offense.

Acquittal. Discharge of a person from a charge of guilt. A person is acquitted when a jury returns a verdict of not guilty. A person may also be acquitted when a judge determines that there is insufficient evidence to convict him or that a violation of due process precludes a fair trial.

Adjudicate. To determine finally by the exercise of judicial authority, to decide a case.

Affidavit. A voluntary written statement of facts or charges affirmed under oath.

A fortiori. With stronger force, with more reason.

Amicus curiae. A friend of the court, a person not a party to litigation, who volunteers or is invited by the court to give his views on a case.

Appeal. To take a case to a higher court for review. Generally, a party losing in a trial court may appeal once to an appellate court as a matter of right. If he loses in the appellate court, appeal to a higher court is within the discretion of the higher court. Most appeals to the U.S. Supreme Court are within the court's discretion.

However, when the highest court in a state rules that a U.S. statute is unconstitutional or upholds a state statute against the claim that it is unconstitutional, appeal to the Supreme Court is a matter of right.

Appellant. The party that appeals a lower court decision to a higher court.

Appellee. One who has an interest in upholding the decision of a lower court and is compelled to respond when the case is appealed to a higher court by the appellant.

Arraignment. The formal process of charging a person with a crime, reading him the charge, asking whether he pleads guilty or not guilty, and entering his plea.

Attainder, Bill of. A legislative act pronouncing a particular individual guilty of a crime without trial or conviction and imposing a sentence upon him.

Bail. The security, usually money, given as assurance of a prisoner's due appearance at a designated time and place (as in court) in order to procure in the interim his release from jail.

Bailiff. A minor officer of a court usually serving as an usher or a messenger.

Brief. A document prepared by counsel to serve as the basis for an argument in court, setting out the facts of and the legal arguments in support of his case.

Burden of proof. The need or duty of affirmatively proving a fact or facts which are disputed.

Case Law. The law as defined by previously decided cases, distinct from statutes and other sources of law.

Cause. A case, suit, litigation or action, civil or criminal.

Certiorari, Writ of. A writ issued from the Supreme Court, at its discretion, to order a lower court to prepare the record of a case and send it to the Supreme Court for review.

Civil law. Body of law dealing with the private rights of individuals, as distinguished from criminal law.

Class action. A lawsuit brought by one person or group on behalf of all persons similarly situated.

Code. A collection of laws, arranged systematically.

Comity. Courtesy, respect; usually used in the legal sense to refer to the proper relationship between state and federal courts.

Common law. Collection of principles and rules of action, particularly from unwritten English law, which derive their authority from longstanding usage and custom or from courts recognizing and enforcing these customs. Sometimes used synonymously with case law.

Consent decree. A court-sanctioned agreement settling a legal dispute and entered into by the consent of the parties.

Contempt (civil and criminal). Civil contempt consists in the failure to do something which the party is ordered by the court to do for the benefit of another party. Criminal contempt occurs when a person willfully exhibits disrespect for the court or obstructs the administration of justice.

Conviction. Final judgment or sentence that the defendant is guilty as charged.

Criminal law. That branch of law which deals with the enforcement of laws and the punishment of persons who, by breaking laws, commit crimes.

Declaratory judgment. A court pronouncement declaring a legal right or interpretation but not ordering a specific action.

De facto. In fact, in reality.

Defendant. In a civil action, the party denying or defending itself against charges brought by a plaintiff. In a criminal action, the person indicted for commission of an offense.

De jure. As a result of law, as a result of official action.

Deposition. Oral testimony from a witness taken out of court in response to written or oral questions, committed to writing, and intended to be used in the preparation of a case.

Dicta. See Obiter dictum.

Dismissal. Order disposing of a case without a trial.

Docket. See Trial docket.

Due process. Fair and regular procedure. The Fifth and 14th Amendments guarantee persons that they will not be deprived of life, liberty or property by the government until fair and usual procedures have been followed.

Error, Writ of. A writ issued from an appeals court to a lower court requiring it to send to the appeals court the record of a case in which it has entered a final judgment and which the appeals court will now review for error.

Ex parte. Only from, or on, one side. Application to a court for some ruling or action on behalf of only one party.

Ex post facto. After the fact; an *ex post facto* law makes an action a crime after it has already been committed, or otherwise changes the legal consequences of some past action.

Ex rel. Upon information from; usually used to describe legal proceedings begun by an official in the name of the state, but at the instigation of, and with information from, a private individual interested in the matter.

Grand jury. Group of 12 to 23 persons impanelled to hear in private evidence presented by the state against persons accused of crime and to issue indictments when a majority of the jurors find probable cause to believe that the accused has committed a crime. Called a "grand" jury because it comprises a greater number of persons than a "petit jury."

Grand jury report. A public report released by a grand jury after an investigation into activities of public officials that fall short of criminal actions. Grand jury reports are often called "presentments."

Guilty. A word used by a defendant in entering a plea or by a jury in returning a verdict, indicating that the defendant is legally responsible as charged for a crime or other wrongdoing.

Habeas corpus. Literally, "you have the body"; a writ issued to inquire whether a person is lawfully imprisoned or detained. The writ demands that the persons holding the prisoner justify his detention or release him.

Immunity. A grant of exemption from prosecution in return for evidence or testimony.

In camera. "In chambers." Refers to court hearings in private without spectators.

In forma pauperis. In the manner of a pauper, without liability for court costs.

In personam. Done or directed against a particular person.

In re. In the affair of, concerning. Frequent title of judicial proceedings in which there are no adversaries, but rather where the matter itself — as a bankrupt's estate — requires judicial action.

In rem. Done or directed against the thing, not the person.

Indictment. A formal written statement based on evidence presented by the prosecutor from a grand jury decided by a majority vote, charging one or more persons with specified offenses.

Information. A written set of accusations, similar to an indictment, but filed directly by a prosecutor.

Injunction. A court order prohibiting the person to whom it is directed from performing a particular act.

Interlocutory decree. A provisional decision of the court which temporarily settles an intervening matter before completion of a legal action.

Judgment. Official decision of a court based on the rights and claims of the parties to a case which was submitted for determination.

Jurisdiction. The power of a court to hear a case in question, which exists when the proper parties are present, and when the point to be decided is within the issues authorized to be handled by the particular court.

Juries. See grand jury and petit jury.

Magistrate. A judicial officer having jurisdiction to try minor criminal cases and conduct preliminary examinations of persons charged with serious crimes.

Mandamus. "We command." An order issued from a superior court directing a lower court or other authority to perform a particular act.

Moot. Unsettled, undecided. A moot question is also one which is no longer material; a moot case is one which has become hypothetical.

Motion. Written or oral application to a court or a judge to obtain a rule or an order.

Nolo contendere. "I will not contest it." A plea entered by a defendant at the discretion of the judge with the same legal effect as a plea of guilty, but it may not be cited in other proceedings as an admission of guilt.

Obiter dictum. Statements by a judge or justice expressing an opinion and included with, but not essential to, an opinion resolving a case before the court. Dicta are not necessarily binding in future cases.

Parole. A conditional release from imprisonment under conditions that if the prisoner abides by the law and other restrictions that may be placed upon him, he will not have to serve the remainder of his sentence. But if he does not abide by specified rules, he will be returned to prison.

Per curiam. "By the court." An unsigned opinion of the court, or an opinion written by the whole court.

Petit jury. A trial jury, originally a panel of 12 persons who tried to reach a unanimous verdict on questions of fact in criminal and civil proceedings. Since 1970, the Supreme Court has upheld the legality of state juries with fewer than 12 persons. Because it comprises fewer persons than a "grand jury," it is called a "petit" jury.

Petitioner. One who files a petition with a court seeking action or relief, including a plaintiff or an appellant. But a petitioner is also a person who files for other court action where charges are not necessarily made; for example, a party may petition the court for an order requiring another person or party to produce documents. The opposite party is called the respondent.

When a writ of certiorari is granted by the Supreme Court, the parties to the case are called petitioner and respondent in contrast to the appellant and appellee terms used in an appeal.

Plaintiff. A party who brings a civil action or sues to obtain a remedy for injury to his rights. The party against whom action is brought is termed the defendant.

Plea Bargaining. Negotiations between prosecutors and the defendant aimed at exchanging a plea of guilty from the defendant for concessions by the prosecutors, such as reduction of charges or a request for leniency.

Pleas. See Guilty and Nolo contendere.

Presentment. See Grand jury report.

Prima facie. At first sight; referring to a fact or other evidence presumably sufficient to establish a defense or a claim unless otherwise contradicted.

Probation. Process under which a person convicted of an offense, usually a first offense, receives a suspended sentence and is given his freedom, usually under the guardianship of a probation officer.

Quash. To overthrow, annul or vacate; as to quash a subpoena.

Recognizance. An obligation entered into before a court or magistrate requiring the performance of a specified act — usually to appear in court at a later date. It is an alternative to bail for pre-trial release.

Remand. To send back. In the event of a decision being remanded, it is sent back by a higher court to the court from which it came for further action.

Respondent. One who is compelled to answer the claims or questions posed in court by a petitioner. A defendant and an appellee may be called respondents, but the term also includes those parties who answer in court during actions where charges are not necessarily brought or where the Supreme Court has granted a writ of certiorari.

Seriatim. Separately, individually, one by one.

Stare Decisis. "Let the decision stand." The principle of adherence to settled cases, the doctrine that principles of law established in earlier judicial decisions should be accepted as authoritative in similar subsequent cases.

Statute. A written law enacted by a legislature. A collection of statutes for a particular governmental division is called a code.

Stay. To halt or suspend further judicial proceedings.

Subpoena. An order to present one's self before a grand jury, court or legislative hearing.

Subpoena duces tecum. An order to produce specified documents or papers.

Tort. An injury or wrong to the person or property of another.

Transactional immunity. Protects a witness from prosecution for any offense mentioned in or related to his testimony, regardless of independent evidence against him.

Trial docket. A calendar prepared by the clerks of the court listing the cases set to be tried.

Use immunity. Protects a witness against the use of his own testimony against him in prosecution.

Vacate. To make void, annul or rescind.

Writ. A written court order commanding the designated recipient to perform or not perform acts specified in the order.

SUBJECT AND CASE INDEXES

Subject Index

A

Abortion - 645, 677
Adams, John
  Appointments - 748, 752
  Conflicts with Jeffersonians - 235-237, 654, 658, 664, 665, 698, 707, 753
  Judicial power, review - 69-71, 270
  Origins and development of Court - 10-12
  Presidential pressure on the Court - 687, 688, 692
Adams, John Quincy
  Court nominations - 657
  Court operations - 753
  Court size - 664
  Origins and development of Court - 14, 16, 786
  Presidential pressure on the Court - 691
Adams, Samuel - 83
Administrative Office of the U.S. Courts - 751, 767, 773
Advertising (See Speech, Freedom of)
Agreements (See Treaties and Agreements)
Agricultural Adjustment Act of 1933 - 43, 102, 103, 109, 117, 121, 240, 242, 244, 321, 355, 677, 702, 888
Agricultural Marketing Act - 102
Agriculture
  Congressional commerce power - 102, 103
  New Deal legislation - 240, 242
Air Quality Act of 1967 - 105
Alexandria Advertiser - 706
Alien Acts - 235, 299, 374, 394, 499, 501, 503, 698
Aliens (See also Immigration and Naturalization)
  Congressional powers - 142-147, 880
  Discrimination, equal rights - 349, 584, 625-629, 903
  Political association - 503
  State powers - 349
Altgeld, John P. - 218
Ambassadors - 260, 262
Amendments (See Constitution; individual amendments)

B

Badger, George E. - 21, 656, 657, 691, 713, 788
Bail Reform Act of 1966 - 577
Baldwin, Henry
  Biography - 784, 810, 811
  Origins and development of Court - 16, 18, 20
  Presidential pressure on the Court - 691
Baltimore Sun - 710
Bankruptcy
  Congressional powers - 155
  Equal rights - 642
  State powers - 312
Barbour, Philip P.
  Biography - 786, 787, 812, 813
  Origins and development of Court - 18, 20
  Presidential pressure on the Court - 688
  State powers - 306, 323, 358
Bell, Griffin - 721
Bill of Rights (See also individual amendments)

American Law Review - 712, 714
Amicus Curiae - 693, 737, 984
Anti-Injunction Act of 1793 - 275, 277
Antitrust
  Congressional powers - 90-95, 676, 882
  Labor and antitrust - 38, 93, 676
  Lawyers, fees - 906
  Rule of reason - 36, 92, 93, 883
Appropriations
  Congressional powers - 116-118
Armed Services (See Military Affairs)
Arthur, Chester A.
  Supreme Court appointments - 29, 786
Articles of Confederation - 6, 914
Associated Press - 721
Atlanta Constitution - 718
Atomic Energy Act of 1946 - 896
Attorneys
  Bar membership - 283, 631
  Supreme Court bar - 763, 764
Auroa - 709, 710

First amendment rights - 390, 391, 402, 441, 458, 461
Fourteenth amendment, and - 378, 383, 384, 523-525, 528, 529, 565, 572
States, and - 17, 30, 33, 34, 36, 44, 45, 49, 52, 53, 301, 337-339, 343-347, 353, 388
Bills of Attainder - 76, 77, 337, 338, 893
Bingham, John A. - 139, 375, 378, 674
Bituminous Coal Act of 1937 - 112
Bituminous Coal Conservation Act of 1935 (Guffey Act) - 43, 78, 82, 98, 113, 115, 121, 242, 355, 677, 889
Black, Hugo L.
  Bills of attainder - 77
  Biography - 787, 788, 790, 849
  Comity - 295
  Congressional Powers
    Citizenship - 157
    Commerce - 104, 105
    Investigations - 160, 162, 164
    Lobby regulation - 174
    New states - 134
  Court operations, traditions - 740, 742, 745, 746, 750, 757, 766
  Individual Rights
    Aliens - 627
    Due process - 527, 528, 532, 533, 546, 552, 556, 559, 563, 566, 567, 577
    Freedom of expression - 390, 391, 409, 410, 415, 416, 418, 420, 426, 430-435, 438-441, 457-460, 463-467
    Personal privacy - 645
    Political association - 503-517
    Poverty groups - 641
    Racial equality - 610, 613, 615, 618, 619
    Right to travel - 104
    Voting rights - 480, 482, 483, 486, 490, 492
  Judicial power - 278, 279
  Origins and development of Court - 44-55
  Presidential Powers
    Inherent powers, limits - 217
    Treaties - 204
    Truman administration - 244
    Wartime - 194
  Presidential pressure on the Court - 687, 689, 690, 693

Roosevelt appointee, as - 44, 244, 657, 702
State Powers
Commerce - 319, 320
Restraints - 362, 363
State-Federal supremacy - 302
Black, Jeremiah S. - 23, 656, 657, 667, 668, 691, 713, 764, 784
Blackmun, Harry A.
Biography - 785, 788, 864
Congressional Powers
Citizenship - 146, 147
State sovereignty - 106
Court operations - 740
Individual Rights
Due process - 531, 540, 551, 561, 578, 579
Freedom of expression - 432, 438, 439, 445
Personal privacy - 343, 645
Political association - 515
Racial equality - 603, 605
Sex discrimination - 633
Voting rights - 497
Judicial restraint - 289
Nixon appointee, as - 55, 245
Pressures on the Court
Presidential - 687, 693
Press - 719
State taxation power - 332
Blair, John
Biography - 783, 786, 787, 797
Origins and development of Court - 8-10
Presidential pressure on the Court - 688
Blatchford, Samuel
Biography - 786, 828
Due process - 556
Origins and development of Court - 29, 32
Boston Courier - 709
Boston Daily Advertiser - 708
Boston Gazette - 706
Boston Herald - 715
Bradford, Edward A. - 21, 656
Bradley, Joseph P.
Biography - 791, 792, 823
Due process - 31, 541
Extra-judicial activities - 757
Maritime law - 86
Nomination, confirmation - 26, 120, 664
Origins and development of Court - 26-32
Presidential pressure on the Court - 686, 689
Sex discrimination - 631
State Powers
Individual rights - 338-340
Taxation - 332, 333
Brandeis, Louis D.
Biography - 785, 788, 790, 842, 843
"Brandeis brief" - 35, 36
Congressional Powers
Commerce - 93, 99, 100
Taxation - 115

Court operations, traditions - 740, 742, 745, 746, 766
Individual Rights
Freedom of expression - 387, 388, 396, 398, 400, 401, 404, 405, 417, 462
Political association - 499, 500
Wiretapping - 551
Judicial power - 268, 282
Judicial restraint, Brandeis rules - 287, 288, 294
Nomination - 657, 658, 788
Origins and development of Court - 35-37, 43, 45
Presidential Powers
Power of removal - 213, 214
Roosevelt administration - 241-244
Pressures on the Court
Congressional - 657, 658
Presidential - 683, 684, 687
Press - 722
Public opinion - 702
Separability clauses - 113
State powers - 326, 327
Brennan, William J. Jr.
Biography - 785, 788, 859, 860
Congressional Powers
Commerce - 105
Congressional immunity - 168, 170
Expatriation - 145
Investigations - 162, 163
Court operations - 737, 738
Individual Rights
Due process - 529, 541-544, 557, 563, 568, 576, 578, 579
Freedom of expression - 380, 403, 417, 428, 429, 432, 434, 436-439, 444-448, 460, 461, 470
Personal privacy - 645
Political association - 504-506, 508, 514-518
Poverty groups and equal protection - 642, 646
Racial equality - 598-600, 605-607, 621
Sex discrimination - 633-638
Voting rights - 491, 494-496
Judicial power - 274, 277, 279
Judicial restraint - 293
Origins and development of Court - 51, 53
Presidential Powers
Executive privilege - 234
Foreign affairs - 200, 201
Nixon, Watergate - 247
Pardons - 228
Presidential pressure on the Court - 684, 685, 687
State Powers
Individual rights - 348
Taxation - 330
Brewer, David J.
Biography - 789, 830, 831
Court traditions - 745
House, Senate rules - 175

Judicial restraint - 289, 291
Origins and development of Court - 31, 33, 35, 36
Presidential emergency powers - 219
Presidential pressure on the Court - 686, 691
Brown, Henry B.
Biography - 831
Congressional Powers
Commerce - 87
Police power - 35
Taxation - 32
Territories - 139, 140, 142
Individual Rights
Due process - 556
Equal rights - 341, 342, 382, 608, 609
Nomination - 31
Origins and development of Court - 31-35
Presidential pressure on the Court - 686
Bryan, William Jennings - 692, 693
Buchanan, James
Origins and development of Court - 22, 23
Pressures on the Court
Congressional - 657, 667
Presidential - 137, 691
Press - 710, 712, 713
Relationship with Grier - 183
Supreme Court appointments - 784, 786, 788, 791
Budget and Accounting Act of 1921 - 212
Burger, Warren E.
Biography - 863, 864
Chief Justice, as - 751, 752
Congressional Powers
Congressional immunity - 170
Members of Congress, qualifications - 166
War power - 127
Court operations, traditions - 663, 678, 731, 736, 740, 745, 747, 758, 768
Individual Rights
Aliens - 628
Due process - 529, 536, 548, 549, 561-563, 578, 579
Freedom of expression - 391, 427, 429, 432, 438, 439, 444, 446, 451, 460-462, 468, 469
Political association - 515, 518
Poverty groups - 642
Racial equality - 589, 590, 600-606, 619
Sex discrimination - 632, 633, 635, 638
Voting rights - 494
Judicial power - 281
Judicial restraint - 292
Nixon appointee, as - 54, 182, 245
Presidential Powers
Executive privilege - 232-234
Nixon, Watergate - 55, 247, 740
Pardons - 227

Pressures on the Court
  Congressional - 655, 663, 678
  Presidential - 690, 693
  Press - 717-724
State Powers
  Commerce - 320
  Individual rights - 350
  National supremacy - 302
Burr, Aaron - 11, 13, 231, 237, 660
Burton, Harold H.
  Biography - 785, 787, 855, 856
  Congressional war powers - 129
  Court operations - 742, 750
  Individual Rights
    Due process - 576, 577
    Freedom of expression - 409
    Political association - 502, 507, 509, 512-514
    Voting rights - 489
  Jurisdiction - 670
  Origins and development of Court - 48, 49, 51
  Presidential powers - 244
  Presidential pressure on the Court - 683, 684
Business and Industry
  Antitrust (See Antitrust)
  Commerce (See Commerce)
  Racial discrimination - 610, 611
Busing - 601-607, 677, 903, 909 (See also Education; Equal Rights)
Butler, Pierce
  Biography - 785, 788, 846
  Individual Rights
    Due process - 41
    Freedom of expression - 41, 425
    Voting rights - 483
  Nomination - 39
  Origins and development of Court - 39, 41-45
  Presidential powers - 241
  Pressures on the Court
    Presidential - 684, 686, 689
    Public - 701
  State powers - 42, 44, 327
Byrnes, James F.
  Biography - 787, 790, 844, 853
  Freedom of religion - 456
  Nomination, resignation - 47, 790
  Presidential pressure on the Court - 683

C

Campaign Financing - 172, 173, 420 (See also Elections)
Campbell, John A.
  Biography - 785, 790, 817, 818
  Nomination - 21, 713
  Origins and development of Court - 21, 23, 27, 29
  Presidential pressure on the Court - 686
  Privileges and immunities, citizens - 27, 339

Resignation - 23, 755
Territories, slavery - 138
Capital Punishment - 575-579, 904, 907, 908
Cardozo, Benjamin N.
  Biography - 785-788, 848, 849
  Congressional Powers
    Commerce - 67, 78, 97-100
    Taxation - 118
  Court operations, traditions - 742, 746, 749, 750
  Individual Rights
    Due process - 346, 528, 548, 572
    Freedom of expression - 391
    Voting rights - 481
  Judicial review - 269
  Origins and development of Court - 37, 41, 43-45
  Presidential powers - 241, 242, 244
  Pressures on the Court
    Presidential - 684, 686, 687
    Public - 702
  State Powers
    Individual rights - 346
    Police power - 327
    Reserved powers - 354
    Taxation - 333
Carswell, G. Harrold - 55, 656, 662, 687, 693, 717, 719, 720, 753, 756, 785
Carter, Jimmy - 784
Case or Controversy Doctrine - 287
Catron, John
  Appointment - 664
  Biography - 784, 791, 813
  Congressional powers, territories - 137, 138
  Origins and development of Court - 19, 23-25
  Presidential war powers - 188
  Pressures on the Court
    Presidential - 686
    Press - 711
Censorship (See Press, Freedom of)
Certiorari, Writ of - 128, 264, 265, 271-273, 734
Charleston Courier - 708, 709
Chase, Salmon P.
  Biography - 790, 791, 821, 822
  Chief Justice, as - 751, 756, 757
  Congressional currency powers - 26, 119, 121, 182
  Johnson impeachment - 749
  Judicial power - 276
  Jurisdiction - 256, 263, 264, 668
  Origins and development of Court - 23, 25-28
  Presidential privileges and immunities - 229, 230
  Pressures on the Court
    Presidential - 688, 689
    Press - 710, 714
  Relationship with Lincoln - 25, 240
  State powers - 300, 339
Chase, Samuel
  Biography - 783, 786, 800, 801
  Congressional war powers - 126
  Constitutional amendments - 150

Court salaries - 663
Extra-judicial activities - 756
Impeachment - 12, 71, 236, 237, 653, 654, 658-660, 698, 706, 709, 710, 756, 791
Jurisdiction - 257
Origins and development of Court - 10-14
Presidential pressure on the Court - 692
Presidential treaty powers - 200
State powers - 337
Unanimous decisions - 741
Chattanooga Times - 715, 716
Chicago Republican - 712
Chicago Tribune - 713, 718
Child Labor Act of 1916 - 72, 355
Child Labor Tax Act of 1919 - 38, 355
Children
  Child labor - 38, 72, 96, 97, 114, 115, 121, 321, 322, 354, 355, 454, 675, 885
  Illegitimacy - 585, 634
Choate, Joseph H. - 110
Cincinnati Gazette - 711
Circuit Court of Appeals Act of 1891 - 31, 32, 265, 753, 754, 957 (text)
Citizenship (See also Immigration and Naturalization)
  Congressional powers - 68, 142-147
  14th amendment protection, rights - 475, 477, 489, 590, 610, 613, 615-618, 881 (See also Fourteenth Amendment)
Citizenship Act of 1907 - 145
Civil Rights (See Equal Rights)
Civil Rights Act of 1866 - 53, 139, 258, 382, 590, 603, 607, 613, 614, 616, 621, 674, 901, 906
Civil Rights Act of 1871 - 908
Civil Rights Act of 1875 - 30, 103, 120, 151, 340, 355, 608, 676
Civil Rights Act of 1957 - 484
Civil Rights Act of 1964 - 53, 104, 152, 259, 382, 484, 584, 589, 590, 604, 607, 612, 616, 619-621, 632, 636-638, 676, 899, 903, 906, 908, 909
Civil Rights Act of 1968 - 615
Civil Rights Commission - 484, 588
Civil Service Act of 1883 - 211, 517
Civil Service Commission - 210, 628
Clark, Tom C.
  Biography - 788, 789, 856, 857
  Congressional Powers
    Commerce - 104
    Congressional witnesses - 161
  Court jurisdiction - 670
  Court operations - 739
  Individual Rights
    Due process - 52, 53, 346, 549, 557, 560, 561, 576
    Equal rights - 611, 612, 750
    Freedom of expression - 415, 436, 438, 440, 442, 466
    Political association - 502-516
    Voting rights - 490, 491
  Judicial power - 283

Origins and development of Court - 49, 52-54
Presidential pressure on the Court - 683, 684
Presidential seizure power - 49, 244
Relationship with Truman - 182
Resignation - 54, 755
State powers - 331, 346
Clarke, John H.
Biography - 843, 844
Freedom of expression - 398, 399
Origins and development of Court - 37-39
Search and seizure - 542
Clay, Henry - 18, 748, 764, 784
Clayton Antitrust Act of 1914 - 38, 93, 95, 276, 676, 883, 885
Clerks of the Court - 759-761
Cleveland, Grover
Presidential Powers
Emergencies - 217-219
Vetoes - 222
Presidential pressure on the Court - 686
Supreme Court nominations - 30, 33, 657, 747, 786-788
Clifford, Nathan
Biography - 786, 788, 790, 792, 818
Buchanan appointee, as - 22, 712
Court traditions, operations - 745, 762
Extra-judicial activities - 757
Origins and development of Court - 22, 24, 26, 28, 29
Presidential war powers - 24, 188
Coastal Licensing Act of 1793 - 83-85
Columbian Centinel - 707, 708
Comity - 294, 295
Commerce
Congressional Powers
Agriculture - 102, 103
Antitrust law - 90-95
Chronology of Supreme Court decisions - 94
Civil rights - 103-105
Foreign commerce - 100 (See also *Foreign Trade*)
Insurance - 105 (See also *Insurance*)
Labor (See *Labor, Labor Unions*)
Modern commerce power - 103-106
Navigation - 83-86
New Deal legislation - 98-103
Origins and development - 15, 16
Police power - 95-97
Railroads - 87-90
Major Supreme Court decisions - 873-893, 906, 907
Original package doctrine - 100, 329-331
Racial discrimination - 316, 321, 608-613
Shreveport doctrine - 88, 884
State Powers
Control of commerce - 315-322
Police power - 322-328

Taxation of commerce - 328-334
Stream of commerce doctrine - 85, 91-93, 882
Communications Act of 1934 - 447
Communications and Telecommunications
Broadcasting, free expression - 447
Congressional commerce power - 101
Free press (See *Press, Freedom of*)
Communist Control Act of 1954 - 501, 513
Congress (See also *House of Representatives; Senate*)
Acts declared unconstitutional - 120, 121, 926
Bankruptcy powers - 155
Citizenship, naturalization powers - 142-147
Commerce Powers
Agriculture - 102, 103
Antitrust law - 90-95
Chronology of Supreme Court decisions - 94
Civil rights - 103-105
Early history - 15, 16, 34, 35, 82-85
Environmental law - 105
Insurance - 105
Labor standards - 98-102
Major Supreme Court decisions - 873, 874, 878, 879, 882, 884, 885, 888-890, 907
Modern commerce power - 103-106
Navigation - 83-86
New Deal legislation - 98-103
Police power - 95-97, 882, 885
Railroads - 87-90
Congressional witnesses - 158-164, 879
Constitution, amendment powers - 149-153
Delegation of powers - 75, 78, 874, 884, 888, 889, 892
District of Columbia powers - 155
Due process - 524
Eminent domain - 141
Federal property, power over (box) - 140
Fiscal and Monetary Powers
Borrowing - 117
Currency - 118-122, 877, 888
Spending - 116-118, 889, 890
Taxation - 76, 109-116, 873, 877, 882, 890, 891
Foreign Affairs Powers
Foreign aid - 132
Treaties - 130, 131, 885
War - 125-130, 892, 893, 896
Immigration - 628, 880
Impeachment, presidents - 229
Implied powers - 73, 157
Inherent powers - 74, 141
Internal Affairs Powers
Elections regulation - 171-174, 884, 885, 891
Immunity - 167-170, 904

Lobby regulation - 174
Punishment - 166, 167, 902
Qualifications - 165, 166
Rules - 175
Investigation powers - 157-164, 879, 896, 897
Judicial review and legislative power - 7, 8, 69-80, 270
Legislation (See *Legislation*)
Limits on Congressional powers (box) - 76, 77
Miscellaneous powers - 155
Patent and copyright powers - 155
Postal powers - 155
Powers, major Supreme Court decisions - 873, 874, 877-880, 882-885, 888-894, 896, 897, 902
Pressures on the Court
Individual pressures - 655-664
Institutional and procedural pressures - 664-672
Periods of confrontation - 653-655
Reversals of rulings - 672-680
Statehood powers - 133, 134, 883
Territories - 135-142, 882
Conkling, Roscoe - 29, 692
Connecticut Courant - 707, 710
Conscientious Objectors - 143, 457
Constitution
Amendments (See also *individual amendments*)
Amending power - 149, 150
Enforcement power - 151, 152
Ratification procedures - 150, 151, 885, 890
Reversals of rulings through amendments - 653, 673-676
Citizenship references (box) - 144
Commerce clause (See *Commerce*)
Contract clause - 309-315
General welfare clause - 117
Necessary and proper clause - 15, 73, 74, 116, 119, 125, 128, 131
Speech or debate clause - 166-170, 904, 909
Supremacy clause - 69, 204, 267
Text - 918
Consumer Credit Protection Act of 1968 - 97
Contempt
Judicial power - 279-285, 440, 441
Major Supreme Court decisions - 879, 883, 894
Contract, Freedom of - 33-40, 44, 45, 326-328, 343, 526, 527, 881-883, 886, 889
Contract, Obligation of - 309-315, 872, 874-876, 879, 887
Coolidge, Calvin
Pocket veto - 222
Presidential pressure on the Court - 685, 693
Supreme Court appointments - 39, 42, 788
Corrupt Practices Act - 420
Counterfeiting - 155

Courts (See Federal Courts)
Cox, Archibald - 247
Cranch, William - 12-14, 706, 762
Crime Control and Safe Streets Act of 1968 - 552, 559, 561, 568
Criminal Appeals Act of 1907 - 265
Criminal Law
  Congressional reversals of Court decisions - 677, 679, 680
  Due Process
    Confessions - 558-564, 889
    Cruel and unusual punishment - 52, 346, 575-580, 883, 893, 897, 898, 907, 908
    Double jeopardy - 571-573, 885, 889, 902
    Exclusionary rule - 37, 539, 541, 547-549
    Fair trial - 53, 344, 345, 440-443, 529-537, 886-888, 894, 901, 904, 907-909
    Juveniles - 346, 531, 901-903
    Legal counsel - 48, 565-569, 887, 890, 892, 899-901, 904, 908, 909
    Plea bargaining - 562, 563
    Right to bail - 577
    Search and seizure - 39, 49, 52, 346, 539-553, 879, 884, 886, 887, 894, 895, 897-899, 901, 902, 908
    Self-incrimination - 53, 345, 346, 524, 525, 528, 552-564, 880, 883, 896, 899, 900, 903
    Silver platter doctrine - 548, 549, 898
  Extradition - 876
  Major Supreme Court decisions - 876-909
  Press coverage - 440-444, 718
  State powers - 344-347
Criminal Syndicalism Acts - 404, 406, 513
Crittenden, John J. - 16, 656, 691
Cruel and Unusual Punishment (See Criminal Law)
Currency
  Congressional powers - 118-122, 128, 129, 155
  Major Supreme Court decisions - 877, 888
Curtis, Benjamin R.
  Biography - 786, 787, 790, 816, 817
  Congressional Powers
    Commerce - 85
    Territories - 137, 138
  Court operations, traditions - 742, 746
  Due process - 524, 525
  Origins and development of Court - 21, 22, 26
  Pressures on the Court
    Congressional - 668
    Presidential - 686
    Press - 712
  Resignation - 26, 662, 755
  State commerce powers - 318, 322
Cushing, Caleb - 28, 656, 657, 714
Cushing, William

Adams' administration, conflicts - 235, 664
  Biography - 783, 786, 795, 796
  Chief Justiceship, and - 748
  Origins and development of Court - 8-14
  State powers, judicial review - 304

D

Daily Union - 711
Dallas, Alexander J. - 12, 762
Daniel, Peter V.
  Biography - 784, 786, 787, 814, 815
  Congressional powers, territories - 138
  Court operations - 762
  Origins and development of Court - 20, 23
  Presidential pressure on the Court - 691
  State powers, eminent domain - 313
Davis, David
  Biography - 792, 820
  Court traditions, operations - 745, 756, 757
  Origins and development of Court - 23-28
  Presidential pressure on the Court - 689
  Presidential war powers - 188-190
Davis, Jefferson - 688, 714
Davis, John W. - 593, 594
Day, William R.
  Biography - 836, 837
  Congressional Powers
    Commerce - 96, 97
    Taxation - 114
  Individual Rights
    Equal rights - 613
    Search and seizure - 541
  Judicial restraint - 288
  Origins and development of Court - 34-39
  State commerce power - 322
Death Penalty - 575-579, 904, 907, 908
Declaration of Independence - 913
Declaratory Judgments - 278, 279
Defense and National Security
  Supreme Court jurisdiction - 670, 671
  Wartime powers - 79, 125-130, 191
Denver Post - 715
Des Moines Register - 716
Dies, Martin - 76, 160
Discrimination (See Equal Rights)
District of Columbia
  Congressional powers - 156
  Voting rights - 156
Double Jeopardy (See Criminal Law)
Douglas, Stephen A. - 136, 692, 713, 784
Douglas, William O.
  Biography - 790, 791, 851, 852

Congressional Powers
  Citizenship, naturalization - 144, 145
  Congressional immunity - 168, 169
  Congressional investigations, witnesses - 160, 162, 164
  Lobby regulation - 174
  New states - 134
  Taxation - 114
  War power - 126-128, 130
Court operations, traditions - 732, 735-742, 746, 750, 757, 767
Impeachment attempts - 653, 658, 660-663, 756
Individual Rights
  Due process - 523, 528, 533, 541, 543, 551, 556-558, 563, 567, 568, 576-578
  Freedom of expression - 408-410, 415, 418, 419, 432, 434-439, 446, 448, 453-459, 462, 463, 467, 470
  Personal privacy - 343, 644
  Political association - 501-517
  Poverty groups - 642, 646
  Racial equality - 598, 615
  Sex discrimination - 350
  Voting rights - 348, 480, 483, 490-492, 496
Judicial power - 278
Jurisdiction - 666
Origins and development of Court - 45, 47-49, 52, 55
Presidential Powers
  Foreign affairs - 200, 206
  Pardons and reprieves - 228
  War - 191, 192
Pressures on the Court
  Congressional - 653, 658, 660-663, 666
  Presidential - 683
  Press - 721, 722
Roosevelt appointee, as - 244
Stare decisis - 294
State Powers
  Individual rights - 343, 348, 350
  Police power - 359
Truman administration - 244

Draft Evasion - 145

Dual Federalism Doctrine - 200, 319, 322-324, 354

Due Process (See also Fifth Amendment; Fourteenth Amendment)
  Aliens - 628
  Background - 375-378, 382-384, 523-528
  Contempt proceedings - 284, 285
  Criminal Law (See Criminal Law)
  Freedom of contract (See Contract, Freedom of)
  Major Supreme Court decisions - 876, 879-884, 886, 887, 889, 892, 896, 897, 899-904, 909
  Personal privacy - 343, 644, 645
  Political association - 516
  Poverty groups - 641-643

Property - 31-34, 141, 314, 526-527
Racial discrimination - 103, 139, 585, 588, 593, 595, 614, 619, 620
Sex discrimination - 633, 635
State powers - 342-347
Duvall, Gabriel
Biography - 786, 790, 807, 808
Origins and development of Court - 14, 16, 17
Presidential pressure on the Court - 688
Resignation - 17, 755
State powers, contract clause - 312

E

Eastland, James O. - 168, 169, 594, 658
Education
Equal Rights
Admissions - 604, 908
Poverty groups - 643-646
Private schools - 602, 603
School busing - 601-607, 677, 903, 909
Segregation, desegregation - 49-53, 348, 590-607, 717, 718, 896, 897, 899, 901, 905-907, 909
Sex discrimination - 632
Flag salute - 47, 411, 457-459, 716, 891
Freedom of religion - 53, 457-460, 462-470, 675, 898
Parochial schools - 466-470
Eighteenth Amendment
Enforcement - 115, 151
Ratification - 149, 150
Eighth Amendment *(See also Bill of Rights)*
Cruel and unusual punishment - 52, 346, 374, 575-580, 897, 898, 907, 908 *(See also Criminal Law)*
Expatriation - 145
Major Supreme Court decisions - 883, 893, 895, 897, 898, 907, 908
Eisenhower, Dwight D.
Individual Rights
Equal rights - 597, 699
Political rights - 507-510
Presidential Powers
Emergencies - 217
Executive privilege - 232
Impoundment of funds - 246
Pardons, reprieves, commutations - 227
Removal power - 215
War powers - 194
Presidential pressure on the Court - 683-685
Supreme Court appointments - 50, 51, 747, 751, 784, 785, 788
Elections
Congressional investigations, regulations - 164, 171-174, 878, 884, 885, 891
Districts, Apportionment
Congressional - 52, 293, 347, 356, 494, 899, 902, 904

State legislative - 52, 293, 347, 356, 495-497, 675, 904, 907
Freedom of expression - 420, 431
Racial gerrymander - 483
Voting rights *(See Political Rights)*
Electronic Surveillance *(See Wiretapping)*
Elementary and Secondary Education Act of 1965 - 291, 469
Eleventh Amendment
Citizens, federal court suits - 9, 16, 111, 144, 152, 260, 304, 307, 353-356, 698, 905
Constitutional challenge - 149
Jurisdiction - 673
Sex discrimination - 638
Ellsworth, Oliver
Biography - 783, 801, 802
Chief Justice, as - 235, 748, 752
Judicial review - 69, 70
Judiciary Act of 1789 - 257, 267
Origins and development of Court - 9-11
Presidential pressure on the Court - 692
Emancipation Proclamation - 189
Emergency Banking Act of 1933 - 240
Emergency Price Control Act of 1942 - 129, 130, 191, 892
Eminent Domain - 141, 312-314, 875
Employers' Liability Act - 88
Employment *(See also Labor, Labor Unions)*
Equal Rights
Aliens - 625-628
Racial equality - 584, 605, 618-621, 903, 909
Sex discrimination - 427, 631-638
Endangered Species Act of 1973 - 677
Enforcement Act of 1870 - 171, 172, 479
Environment
Congressional powers - 105
State powers - 358, 883
Equal Employment Opportunities Commission - 619
Equal Footing Doctrine - 133, 134
Equal Pay Act of 1963 - 584, 632, 637, 638
Equal Protection *(See also Equal Rights; Fourteenth Amendment)*
Aliens - 349, 625-629
Background - 381, 382
Major Supreme Court decisions - 879, 892, 894, 896, 898-901, 903-905, 907, 909
Poverty groups - 349, 641-646
Segregation - 348, 349, 587-621
Voting rights *(See Political Rights)*
Women - 349, 350, 631-639
Equal Rights
Aliens - 349, 584, 625-629, 903
Congressional powers - 103-105, 120
Congressional witnesses - 160-164
Constitutional amendments - 151
Fundamental interest doctrine -

585, 586, 643, 892
Illegitimate children - 634
Legislative reversals of Court rulings - 676
Major Supreme Court decisions - 874-876, 878-881, 886, 890, 893, 895-897, 899, 901, 903-909
Poverty groups - 349, 641-646
Racial Equality
Education - 348, 590-607, 896, 897, 899, 901, 903-909
Employment - 584, 618-621, 903, 906, 909
Housing - 348, 613-618, 901, 906, 907
Juries - 532
Press coverage - 717, 718
Public pressure on Court - 699-701
Separate but equal doctrine - 31, 33, 348, 349, 382, 587-591, 595, 596, 610, 700, 881, 890, 895, 896
Travel, accommodations - 585, 607-613, 897, 899, 902
Reverse discrimination - 56, 604, 605
Sex discrimination - 349, 350, 427, 532, 584, 631-639, 905, 907, 909
State powers - 338-351
Voting *(See Political Rights)*
Equal Rights Amendment - 149, 150, 632
Erdman Act of 1898 - 120, 121
Error, Writ of - 271
Espionage Act of 1917 - 49, 396, 397, 400, 499, 885, 896
Ex Post Facto **Laws** - 76, 77, 337, 338, 872, 877
Exclusionary Rule - 37, 539, 541, 547-549
Executive Agreements - 204-206 *(See also Treaties and Agreements)*
Executive Privilege - 230-234, 718, 719
Extradition - 876

F

Fair Housing *(See Housing)*
Fair Housing Act of 1968 - 53, 382, 617, 618
Fair Labor Standards Act of 1938 - 45, 78, 101, 244, 322, 328, 354, 355, 907
Fair Trial *(See Criminal Law)*
Fairness Doctrine - 446
Faubus, Orval - 50, 597, 733
Federal Assimilative Crimes Act of 1948 - 79
Federal Communications Act - 551, 552
Federal Corrupt Practices Act of 1911 - 38, 172, 174, 355
Federal Courts
Judicial immunity (box) - 290
Judicial Power
Contempt power - 279-285, 440, 441

Declaratory judgments - 278, 279
Habeas corpus - 76, 128, 187, 189, 239, 271-274, 899, 907
Injunctions - 275-278
Judicial review - 69-73, 158-160, 267-271, 303-308
Mandamus - 70-72, 270, 274, 275
Judicial Restraint
Advisory opinions - 287-289
Cases and controversies - 287, 289
Comity - 294, 295
Friendly suits, test cases - 289-291
Mootness - 289
Political questions - 292, 293
Precedent - 294
Rules of restraint (box) - 288
Standing to sue - 291, 292, 886
Jurisdiction - 256-266
Major Supreme Court decisions - 872-877, 880, 881, 883, 886, 890, 899-903, 905, 907, 908

Federal Declaratory Judgment Act of 1934 - 278

Federal Election Campaign Act of 1974 - 56, 420, 906

Federal Election Commission - 173

Federal Employers' Liability Act - 355

Federal Farm Bankruptcy Act - 43, 44

Federal Judicial Center - 751, 767, 768

Federal Jury Selection and Service Act of 1968 - 532

Federal Power Commission - 86, 90

Federal Rules of Civil Procedure - 282

Federal Rules of Criminal Procedure - 283, 542, 559, 577

Federal Tort Claims Act - 261

Federal Trade Commission Act - 240

Federalist Papers - 6-8, 65, 69-71, 115, 117, 165, 224, 255, 267, 315, 353

Field, Stephen J.
Appointment - 664
Bills of attainder - 76
Biography - 785, 788, 790, 792, 820, 821
Congressional taxation powers - 110
Extra-judicial activities - 756, 757
Freedom of expression - 404, 452
Judicial immunity - 290
Judicial power - 283
Jurisdiction - 668
Justices, protection of - 216
Origins and development of Court - 23, 25-28, 31-33
Presidential pardon powers - 225
Pressures on the Court
Congressional - 664, 668
Presidential - 684
Resignation - 33, 755
State Powers
Commerce - 330, 332
Individual rights - 338-340
Interstate relations - 366

Fifteenth Amendment
Enforcement - 28, 151, 152, 171, 375
Major Supreme Court decisions -

878, 879, 884, 890, 893, 895, 897, 898, 900
Political rights - 68, 139, 144, 338, 341, 342, 475-490, 631

Fifth Amendment *(See also Bill of Rights; Criminal Law; Due Process)*
Access to justice - 642
Bankruptcy and due process - 155
Civil rights and commerce - 104
Congressional witnesses - 163, 164
Draft evasion - 145
Eminent domain - 141, 338
Expatriation - 145
Labor disputes - 89, 121
Major Supreme Court decisions - 876, 879, 880, 885, 886, 896, 899, 900, 902, 904, 909
Military justice - 128
Personal privacy - 644
Political association - 506-514
Racial discrimination - 585, 593, 595, 611-614, 620
Search and seizure *(See Criminal Law)*
Self-incrimination *(See Criminal Law)*
Sex discrimination - 633, 635
Territories, slavery - 135, 138, 140, 142
Wartime legislation - 129
"Yellow-dog" contracts - 120, 121

Fillmore, Millard
Presidential commutation power - 226
Pressures on the Court
Presidential - 691
Press - 710, 713
Supreme Court nominations - 21, 657, 786, 788

First Amendment *(See also Bill of Rights)*
Freedom of assembly - 412-419, 887, 889, 891
Freedom of association - 402, 403, 887, 897-901, 907
Freedom of expression - 387-394
Freedom of press - 423-449 *(See also Press, Freedom of)*
Freedom of religion - 451-470 *(See also Religion, Freedom of)*
Freedom of speech - 395-422 *(See also Speech, Freedom of)*
Injunctions, and - 277-279, 430
Major Supreme Court decisions - 885-908
Political rights - 476, 499-520
Privacy - 343, 344, 644, 722
Racial discrimination - 611, 612

Footnote Four - 378, 379

Foraker Act of 1900 - 140

Ford, Gerald
Aliens - 628
Douglas (William O.) impeachment attempts - 791
Nixon pardon - 224, 225

Relationship with Court - 747, 756, 758
Supreme Court appointment - 55

Fordney-McComber Act - 75

Foreign Affairs
Congressional powers - 125-132
Court's role - 200, 260, 293
Presidential Powers
Ambassadors - 199, 205, 209
Recognition of foreign governments - 205
Treaties and agreements - 199-207
War powers - 187-198
Senate's role - 201
States' role - 200, 362, 875

Foreign Service Act of 1946 - 210

Foreign Trade
Congressional powers - 100
Export duties - 77

Fortas, Abe
Biography - 862, 863
Congressional witnesses - 162
Individual Rights
Due process - 543, 567, 576
Freedom of expression - 438, 467
Voting rights - 494
Nomination for Chief Justice - 54, 656
Presidential pressure on the Court - 683, 684, 690, 691, 693
Relationship with Johnson (Lyndon) - 54, 183, 684, 690, 758
Resignation - 653, 656, 658, 660-662, 691, 693, 719, 723, 755, 788, 791, 983

Fourteenth Amendment *(See also Due Process; Equal Protection; Equal Rights; Privileges and Immunities)*
Adoption, effect - 139, 151, 375
Citizenship - 27, 28, 68, 71, 111, 120, 139, 142-147, 338-341
Congressional pressure on Court - 673, 674
Enforcement - 106, 151, 152
Equal protection - 347-350, 583-647 *(See also Equal Protection)*
Freedom of contract - 33-43, 44, 45, 326-328, 343, 526, 527, 881-883, 886, 889
Freedom of expression - 388, 389, 401-403, 406, 408, 411-417, 425, 434, 436-438, 444, 452, 455, 458, 466
Freedom of political association - 500, 516, 518
Major Supreme Court decisions - 878-909
Property rights - 30, 141
Racial discrimination - 29, 33, 103, 338-342
Right to travel - 104
Voting rights - 475-496

Fourth Amendment *(See also Bill of Rights; Criminal Law)*
Exclusionary rule - 37, 539, 541, 547-549

Major Supreme Court decisions - 879, 884, 886, 887, 894, 895, 898, 899, 901, 908
Personal privacy - 644
Search and seizure *(See Search and Seizure)*
Warrants - 539-545, 550
White House tapes (Nixon) - 245-247
Wiretapping - 53, 245, 547, 550-553

Frankfurter, Felix
Biography - 786, 788, 789, 850, 851
Congressional Powers
Commerce - 84
Congressional immunity - 168
Expatriation - 145
Investigations - 160, 161, 164
Court operations, traditions - 739-747, 757, 758
Individual Rights
Due process - 383, 539, 544, 548, 549, 556, 558, 559, 577
Freedom of expression - 386, 391, 394, 409, 418, 419, 435, 441, 453, 457-459, 463
Political association - 506, 509-514
Poverty groups - 641
Voting rights - 480, 483, 489-492, 502
Judicial power - 271, 281, 282, 284
Judicial restraint - 287, 293
Jurisdiction - 255, 257, 260, 261, 264, 666
Origins and development of Court - 45, 47, 48, 52
Presidential Powers
Removal power - 211, 215
Roosevelt administration - 243, 244
Truman administration - 244
Presidential pressure on the Court - 683-685, 690
Relationship with Roosevelt - 45, 183
Relationship with Warren (Earl) - 750-752, 757
State Powers
Commerce - 309, 315, 316, 328
Individual rights - 347
Taxation - 330
Wages - 327

Frazier-Lemke Farm Mortgage Act of 1934 - 677
Freedmen's Bureau Act - 139
Freedom of Contract *(See Contract, Freedom of)*
Freedom of Information Act of 1966 - 242
Freedom of Press *(See Press, Freedom of)*
Freedom of Religion *(See Religion, Freedom of)*
Freedom of Speech *(See Speech, Freedom of)*
Fugitive Slave Act - 20, 22, 136, 217, 273, 307, 361, 875, 876
Full Faith and Credit - 365

Fuller, Melville W.
Biography - 829, 830
Congressional Powers
Commerce - 87, 91, 93
Taxation - 110, 115, 674
Territories - 142
Court operations, traditions - 739, 740, 745, 751
Origins and development of Court - 30-32, 35, 36, 38
Presidential pressure on the Court - 691
State commerce powers - 320, 325
Fundamental Fairness *(See Due Process)*
Fundamental Interest Doctrine - 585, 586, 643, 892
Futures Trading Act of 1921 - 114, 355

G

Garfield, James A.
Presidential pressure on the Court - 691
Presidential veto power - 221
Supreme Court appointment - 29
Garland, Augustus H. - 25, 225, 245, 246, 747, 761, 762, 764
General Advertiser - 708, 709
Georgia Journal - 709
Georgia Republican - 706
Gerrymandering - 342, 356, 483, 601
Gold Reserve Act of 1934 - 240
Goldberg, Arthur J.
Appointment - 52, 492
Biography - 788, 861; 862
Individual Rights
Due process - 558, 560
Freedom of expression - 403, 434
Personal privacy - 645
Political association - 503, 507
Presidential pressure on the Court - 683, 684, 690
Resignation - 54, 755
Grain Futures Act of 1922 - 92, 115
Grandfather Clauses - 37, 342, 480, 593, 884, 890
Grant, Ulysses S.
Presidential Powers
Executive immunity - 230
Impoundment of funds - 246
Removal power - 211
Pressures on the Court
Congressional - 655-657, 664, 665
Presidential - 689
Press - 712-714
Supreme Court nominations - 26-28, 67, 119, 120, 655-657, 664, 665, 712-714, 784, 790, 791
Grants-in-Aid Programs - 116
Gray, Horace
Biography - 786, 827, 828
Court operations - 740, 766
Due process - 577

Jurisdiction - 263
Nomination, resignation - 29, 34
Tariffs - 112
Grier, Robert C.
Biography - 784, 790, 791, 816
Congressional powers, territories - 137, 138
Jurisdiction - 668
Origins and development of Court - 20, 24, 26
Presidential war powers - 126, 188, 189
Pressures on the Court
Congressional - 655, 664, 668
Presidential - 686, 689, 691
Relationship with Buchanan - 183
Retirement - 26, 119, 655, 664, 755, 774
Guffey Act *(See Bituminous Coal Conservation Act of 1935)*

H

Habeas Corpus Act of 1867 - 263, 264, 272
Habeas Corpus, **Writ of**
Judicial power - 271-274, 362
Jurisdiction - 263, 654, 666-669
Major Supreme Court decisions - 876, 877, 885, 899
Military justice - 128
Wartime suspension of - 24, 76, 187, 189, 239
Hamilton, Alexander
Conflicts, Supreme Court and Presidents - 235, 237
Congressional investigations - 157
Court role, function - 6-10
General welfare clause - 117
Implied powers of Congress - 73, 74
Judges, taxation immunity - 115
Judicial review - 65, 69-71
Jurisdiction, federal courts - 255
Members of Congress, qualifications - 165
Presidential pardon power - 224
State commerce power - 315
Treaties - 199
Vetoes - 221
War powers - 125, 185
Hand, Augustus - 428, 453
Hand, Learned - 502, 686, 740
Harding, Warren G.
Executive powers, privilege - 212, 231
Presidential pressure on the Court - 684, 686, 691
Supreme Court appointments - 38, 39, 42, 785, 788, 789
Harlan, John Marshall (1877-1911)
Biography - 790, 825, 826
Congressional Powers
Citizenship - 146
Commerce - 88, 91, 92, 95, 96
Taxation - 110

Territories - 140
Court operations, traditions - 739, 740, 742, 745, 755
Individual Rights
  Due process - 525, 526, 528
  Equal rights - 341, 700, 713
Judicial power - 268
Origins and development of Court - 28, 31-36
State Powers
  Commerce - 321
  Individual rights - 341
  Police power - 324, 325, 360
Harlan, John Marshall (1955-1971)
  Biography - 858, 859
  Congressional immunity - 169, 170
  Congressional witnesses - 161, 162
  Individual Rights
    Due process - 549, 557-561, 572, 576
    Freedom of expression - 402, 407, 411, 428, 429, 432, 436, 438, 439, 460
    Fundamental interest doctrine - 586
    Personal privacy - 645
    Political association - 504-516
    Poverty groups - 642
    Racial equality - 591, 609, 615, 616
    Sex discrimination - 534, 637
    Voting rights - 481, 483, 486, 491-495
  Judicial power - 269
  Jurisdiction - 670
  Origins and development of Court - 51-55
  Presidential pressure on the Court - 687, 693
Harper's Weekly - 711-714
Harrison Anti-Narcotics Act of 1914 - 114
Harrison, Benjamin
  Presidential pressure on the Court - 684
  Supreme Court appointments - 31, 32, 785, 789
Harrison, Robert H. - 8
Harrison, William Henry - 784
Hartford Courant - 716
Hastie, William H. - 482
Hatch Act of 1939 - 117, 211, 517, 518, 894
Hayes, Rutherford B.
  Court nominations - 28, 29, 657, 787, 790
  Presidential pressure on the Court - 691
Haynsworth, Clement Jr. - 54, 656, 662, 683, 687, 693, 717-720, 753, 785
Health, Health Care
  Aliens - 628
  Inspections, warrants - 550
  Insurance *(See Insurance)*
  State police powers - 324-326, 358, 360
Henry, Patrick - 83
Hepburn Act of 1906 - 87, 676

Higher Education Facilities Act of 1963 - 469
Hill, David B. - 32, 657, 686, 786, 788
Hoar, Ebenezer R. - 26, 119, 655-657, 689, 713
Holmes, Oliver Wendell Jr.
  Biography - 786, 790, 835, 836
  Congressional Powers
    Commerce - 82, 88, 90, 91, 97
    Taxation - 114, 115
    Treaty powers - 203
  Court operations - 739-742
  Hughes as Chief Justice - 750
  Individual Rights
    Aliens - 626
    Due process - 529, 548, 550, 552
    Freedom of expression - 389, 390, 392, 396-401, 404, 406, 440, 499, 500, 505
    Voting rights - 481
  Judicial power - 268, 273
  Judicial review - 303
  Origins and development of Court - 34-41, 50
  Presidential Powers
    Pardons - 224, 227
    Removal power - 213, 214
  Presidential pressure on the Court - 685, 686
  Resignation - 41, 661, 755
  State Powers
    Commerce - 322, 327
    Police power - 358, 360
    Taxation - 357
Home Owners' Loan Act - 355
Hoover, Herbert
  Presidential Powers
    Appointments - 210, 657
    Depression era - 240
    Power to sign bills - 223
    Recognition of foreign governments - 205
  Pressures on the Court
    Presidential - 684, 686, 687, 691
    Press - 714
    Public opinion - 701
  Supreme Court appointments - 41, 42, 785, 786, 788
Hornblower, William B. - 32, 656, 657, 686
House of Representatives *(See also Congress)*
  Internal Affairs, Membership
    Elections regulation - 171-174
    Immunity - 167-170
    Lobby regulation - 174
    Punishment - 166, 167
    Qualifications - 165, 166, 902
    Rules - 175
Housing
  Equal rights - 348, 613-618, 901, 906, 907
  Inspections, warrants - 550
Houston Chronicle - 718
Howard, Benjamin - 20, 21, 23, 710, 711
Hughes, Charles Evans

Biography - 789, 790, 838, 839
Chief Justice, as - 749-751, 755, 766, 771
Congressional Powers
  Commerce - 88, 89, 98-100
  Delegation of powers - 78
  Elections regulation - 172
  Fiscal and monetary powers - 121, 122
  Judicial review - 71
Court operations - 737-743
Individual Rights
  Aliens - 625
  Due process - 344, 523, 532, 559
  Freedom of expression - 379, 425-427, 437, 453
  Political association - 500
  Racial equality - 591, 609
  Right of assembly - 389, 405, 411, 413
Judicial power - 270, 271, 278
Judicial restraint - 287
Nomination - 36, 657, 658
Origins and development of Court - 26, 36-38, 41-47
Presidential powers - 241-243
Pressures on the Court
  Presidential - 686, 689-691
  Public - 701, 702
State Powers
  Contracts - 314
  Individual rights - 344, 348
  Police - 327, 328
Hunt, Ward
  Biography - 823, 824
  Nomination - 27
  Resignation - 29, 790

I

Immigration Act of 1907 - 355
Immigration and Nationality Act of 1952 - 143, 145, 146, 503
Immigration and Naturalization *(See also Aliens)*
  Border searches - 546
  Congressional powers - 142-147, 880
  Equal rights, aliens - 625-629
  State powers - 318, 324
Immunity *(See Self-Incrimination, Criminal Law)*
Immunity Act of 1950 - 896
Immunity Act of 1954 - 163, 556
Impeachment
  Judiciary - 236, 237, 658-663
  Presidents - 229
In Forma Pauperis - 734, 735, 738, 985
Injunctions - 93, 96, 275-278, 362, 430
Insurance
  Regulation of - 105, 319, 320, 677, 877, 893
  Sex discrimination - 635-637
Internal Revenue Act of 1867 - 355

Internal Security Act of 1950 - 146, 169, 501, 503, 505-508, 577
Interstate Commerce Act of 1887 - 81, 87, 90, 103, 104, 319, 556, 609, 610
Interstate Commerce Commission (ICC) - 82, 87, 103, 129, 318, 319, 321, 676
Iredell, James
  Biography - 783, 789, 790, 797-799
  Origins and development of Court - 8-10
  Presidential powers, foreign affairs - 200
  State rulings, judicial review - 303

J

Jackson, Andrew
  Conflict with Supreme Court - 17, 182, 238, 239, 307
  Presidential Powers
    Executive privilege - 231
    Removal power - 211
    Vetoes - 221
  Pressures on the Court
    Congressional - 657, 664
    Presidential - 683, 688, 691
    Press - 707, 709
  Supreme Court appointments - 16-19, 657, 664, 755, 783, 788
Jackson, Howell E.
  Biography - 785, 832, 833
  Congressional taxation power - 110, 115
  Origins and development of Court - 32, 33
  Presidential pressure on the Court - 684, 686
Jackson (Miss.) Clarion-Ledger - 718
Jackson, Robert H.
  Biography - 788, 854
  Congressional Powers
    Commerce - 103, 104
    Lobby regulation - 174
    War power - 125, 126, 130
  Court function, role - 6
  Court operations, traditions - 738, 742, 745, 746, 766
  Extra-judicial activities - 757
  Individual Rights
    Due process - 344, 524, 533, 539, 544
    Equal rights - 595, 750
    Freedom of expression - 378, 379, 390, 409-411, 454, 458, 459, 463
    Freedom of political association - 502, 503, 509, 511, 513, 517
    Voting rights - 482, 489
  Judicial power - 267, 284
  Origins and development of Court - 6, 47, 48, 51
  Presidential Powers
    Commander in Chief - 185, 194, 196
    Executive privilege - 231

  General responsibilities - 181
  Inherent powers, limits - 217
  Presidential pressure on the Court - 683, 689, 690
  Roosevelt administration - 243
  Solicitor General, as - 759
  State Powers
    Commerce - 321
    Individual rights - 344
    Judicial review - 308
Jaworski, Leon - 232, 247
Jay, John
  Adams' administration - 235
  Biography - 783, 790, 793, 794
  Chief Justice, as - 663, 748, 752, 755, 757, 758
  Court operations - 733
  Judicial review - 303, 304
  Origins and development of Court - 8-11
  Pressures on the Court
    Congressional - 663
    Presidential - 687, 692
    Press - 707
Jefferson, Thomas
  Congressional Powers
    Commerce - 84
    Implied powers of Congress - 73
    Judicial review - 69-71
  Court operations - 748, 753, 756
  Freedom of expression - 394, 396, 423, 461
  Judicial power - 270
  Presidential Powers
    Emergencies - 217
    Executive privilege - 231
    Foreign affairs - 199
    Impoundment of funds - 246
  Pressures on the Court
    Presidential - 683, 685, 688, 692
    Press - 707, 709
    Public opinion - 698
  Relationship with Court - 10-12, 15, 182, 235-237, 654, 658-660, 741
  State powers - 299-301
  Supreme Court appointments - 13, 14, 786
Johnson, Andrew
  Congressional powers - 119, 139
  Federal court jurisdiction - 263
  Impeachment - 25, 263, 749
  Judicial power - 276
  Presidential Powers
    Commander in Chief - 189
    Immunity - 229
    Pardons - 224, 226
    Removal power - 211
    Vetoes - 221
  Pressures on the Court
    Congressional - 654, 657, 664, 668
    Presidential - 688
    Press - 713
  Supreme Court appointment conflicts - 25, 654, 657, 664, 753, 784
Johnson, Lyndon B.
  Boykin pardon - 169
  Douglas (William O.), and - 662

  Presidential Powers
    Commander in Chief - 194-196
    Executive privilege - 232
  Pressures on the Court
    Congressional - 657, 660, 662, 671, 679, 680
    Presidential - 683, 684, 690
    Press - 715, 719
  Relationship with Fortas - 183, 758
  Supreme Court jurisdiction - 671
  Supreme Court nominations - 54, 657, 660, 788, 791
  Voting rights - 484
  Warren court - 747, 758
Johnson, Thomas
  Biography - 783, 790, 799
  Origins and development of Court - 8, 9
Johnson, William
  Biography - 790, 804, 805
  Congressional commerce power - 84
  Court operations - 741, 742
  Jefferson appointee, as - 748
  Judicial review - 305
  Origins and development of Court - 13, 17
Judicial Conference of the United States - 748, 751, 758, 767, 773
Judicial Power *(See Federal Courts)*
Judicial Review *(See also Federal Courts)*
  Congressional investigations - 158-160
  Congressional legislation - 7, 8, 69-73, 268-270
  Jurisdiction *(See Federal Courts; Supreme Court)*
  Major Supreme Court decisions - 872, 873
  States - 267, 270, 303-308
Judiciary Act of 1789
  Court schedule - 732
  Court size - 664, 748, 753
  Court workload - 678
  Judicial power - 267-282, 307, 362
  Judicial review - 7, 69, 303, 305
  Jurisdiction - 71, 257-266, 666, 669
  Major Supreme Court decisions - 872, 873
  Origins and development of Court - 7-12, 15, 785
  Text - 949
Judiciary Act of 1801 - 9, 11, 12, 236, 665, 692, 698, 732, 753
Judiciary Act of 1802 - 732
Judiciary Act of 1807 - 753
Judiciary Act of 1817 - 762
Judiciary Act of 1837 - 664
Judiciary Act of 1863 - 664, 753
Judiciary Act of 1867 - 761
Judiciary Act of 1869 - 753, 755, 774
Judiciary Act of 1925 - 38, 265, 266, 678, 734, 736, 960 (text)
Juries
  Fair Trial
    Free press and impartial jury - 440

Jury selection, size - 529-534
Major Supreme Court decisions -
878, 887, 888, 898, 902, 904, 905,
908, 909
Women on juries - 534, 637, 898, 905

K

Kansas City Star - 715, 716
Kennedy, John Fitzgerald
Equal rights - 589
Presidential powers - 194, 232, 246
Presidential pressure on the Court -
683, 684
Supreme Court appointments - 52
Warren Commission - 752, 757, 758
Warren Court - 747
Kentucky Resolutions - 299
King, Edward - 20, 656, 784
King, Rev. Martin Luther Jr. - 414, 433,
434, 484, 589, 679
Knowland, William F. - 685

L

Labor, Labor Unions
Antitrust law - 38, 93, 676, 883
Child labor - 38, 72, 89, 96, 97, 114,
115, 121, 321, 322, 354, 454, 675, 885
Discrimination - 618-621
Freedom of contract (See Contract,
Freedom of)
Injunctions - 93, 96, 276
Loyalty oaths, political association -
77, 510, 511
New Deal legislation - 98-102, 240
Picketing - 396, 416-419
Railway labor - 88, 120, 121
Wage and hour standards - 33-39,
43, 89, 98-102, 105, 106, 121, 244,
326-328, 526, 527, 883, 884, 889, 891,
907
"Yellow-dog contracts" - 35, 82, 88,
120, 883
Labor Management and Reporting
Act of 1959 - 77
Labor-Management Relations (Taft-
Hartley) Act - 49, 77, 217, 244, 276,
510, 894
LaFollette, Robert M. - 175, 693
Lamar, Joseph R.
Biography - 785, 840
Executive discretion - 216
Extra-judicial activities - 757
Judicial power - 281
Origins and development of Court
- 36, 37
Presidential pressure on the Court -
684
Lamar, Lucius Q.C.
Biography - 689, 690, 787

Origins and development of Court
- 30, 32
State commerce powers - 320
Legal Tender Acts - 26, 120, 128, 129,
182, 240, 294, 712, 877
Legislation
Acts held unconstitutional - 120,
121, 926
Acts infringing on state powers
(box) - 355
Congressional powers - 65-79 (See
also Congress)
Judicial review, restraint - 65, 66, 69-
72, 267-270, 293
Presidential power to sign bills - 223
Reversal of rulings through legisla-
tion - 653, 676, 677
Separability clauses - 113
Substantive due process - 31, 343,
524, 526, 527
Wartime - 128-130
Lend-Lease Act of 1941 - 129, 204
Lever Food Control Act of 1917 - 129,
190
Libel - 54, 424, 433-440, 899, 909
Life Magazine - 437, 660, 661, 719, 755,
758
Lincoln, Abraham
Conflict with Supreme Court - 238-
240
Congressional war powers - 126
Habeas corpus, writ of - 76, 239, 699
Presidential Powers
Emergencies - 24, 217
Pardons, reprieves, commuta-
tions - 226
War powers - 185-190, 195
Presidential pressure on the Court -
683, 684, 688, 692
Relationship with Chase - 25, 119,
182
Supreme Court appointments - 23-
25, 33, 655, 657, 664, 667, 783-786
Lincoln, Levi - 14, 786
Lincoln (Nebr.) State Journal - 716
Literacy Tests - 342, 347, 479-481, 890,
902
Livingston, Henry Brockholst
Biography - 786, 805, 806
Origins and development of Court
- 13, 15
Lobbies, Lobbying
Regulation - 174, 175
Los Angeles Times - 440, 441, 715, 716,
721
Louisville Courier-Journal - 445, 713,
718
Loyalty Oaths, Programs - 25, 338, 508-
518, 877, 895, 900
Lurton, Horace H.
Biography - 785, 790, 838
Congressional powers, new states -
133
Origins and development of Court
- 36, 37
Presidential pressure on the Court -
684

M

Madison, James
Bill of Rights - 374, 378
Congressional Powers
Commerce - 83
Fiscal and monetary powers - 117
Judicial review - 69-71
Freedom of religion - 461, 464
Judicial power - 267, 270, 274
Origins and development of Court
- 8, 11, 13
Presidential Powers
Appointments, removal - 210, 213
Foreign affairs - 199
Pressures on the Court
Presidential - 685
Press - 707, 708
Sedition Acts - 235
State Powers
Judicial review - 305
State sovereignty
- 305, 353
Wolcott nomination - 707, 786
Management Reporting and Disclo-
sure Act of 1959 - 511
Mandamus, Writ of - 70-72, 270, 274,
275, 875, 985
Mann Act - 95, 96
Maritime Affairs
Congressional powers - 86
Federal courts, jurisdiction - 257,
258
Marshall, John
Biography - 787, 790, 803, 804
Chief Justice, as - 11, 12, 235, 696,
698, 699, 748, 751, 753-755
Congressional Powers
Citizenship, naturalization - 143,
144
Commerce power - 66, 81, 83, 84,
91, 100, 102
Delegation of powers - 75
Implied powers - 73, 74
Inherent powers - 75
Judicial review - 7, 65, 69-72
Taxation - 116
Territories - 135
Treaty powers - 131
War power - 125
Court operations - 741, 742
Due process - 524
Judicial power - 267, 270, 275
Judicial restraint - 292, 294, 698
Jurisdiction - 261, 262, 265
Origins and development of Court
- 5, 7, 9-19, 46
Presidential Powers
Appointments - 210
Foreign affairs - 199-202
Immunity - 230
Jackson administration - 238, 239
Jefferson administration, conflicts
- 182, 235-237
Pardons - 224
Privilege - 231

Pressures on the Court
  Congressional - 658-660, 665, 666
  Presidential - 685, 687, 688, 692
  Press - 706, 707, 709, 714
  Public opinion - 696, 698, 699
Slavery - 376
Sovereign immunity - 261
State Powers
  Commerce - 315, 316, 322, 323
  Contracts - 309-313
  Ex post facto laws - 337
  Individual rights - 338, 375
  Interstate relations - 366
  National supremacy - 299-307
  Police power - 324, 325
  Reserved powers - 353
  Taxation - 328-330, 357
Marshall, Thurgood
Biography - 863
Congressional Powers
  Campaign finance - 173
  Congressional immunity - 168
  Subpoenas (box) - 163
  War power - 127
Court operations - 738
Individual Rights
  Due process - 529, 534, 535, 541, 544, 557, 563, 572, 576, 578
  Freedom of expression - 416, 417, 432, 438, 439, 445-448, 461
  Freedom of political association - 517
  Poverty groups - 646
  Racial equality - 592-595, 605-607, 615, 621
  Sex discrimination - 637, 638
  Voting rights - 482, 496
Nomination - 54, 657, 658
Presidential pardon power - 228
Pressures on the Court
  Congressional - 657, 658
  Presidential - 684
Solicitor General, as - 759
Marshals of the Court - 761, 762
Matthews, Stanley
Biography - 790, 826, 827
Due process - 525
Nomination - 28, 656, 657
Origins and development of Court - 28, 29, 31
Pressures on the Court
  Congressional - 656, 657
  Presidential - 691
McCarran Act of 1950 - 105, 501, 505-508, 513
McKenna, Joseph
Biography - 788, 790, 835
Congressional Powers
  Commerce - 95
  Elections regulation - 172
  Territories - 140
Individual Rights
  Freedom of expression - 399
  Voting rights - 479
Origins and development of Court - 33-39
Presidential pardon power - 224

Presidential pressure on the Court - 684
McKinley, John
Biography - 787, 813, 814
Origins and development of Court - 19, 21
McKinley, William
Presidential powers - 187, 205
Supreme Court appointments - 33, 788
McLean, John
Biography - 790, 791, 809, 810
Congressional Powers
  Commerce - 84
  Territories - 137, 138
Court operations - 753
Extra-judicial activities - 756, 757
Origins and development of Court - 16, 18, 19, 22, 23
Pressures on the Court
  Presidential - 688
  Press - 710, 711
State Powers
  Coins, currency - 333
  Commerce - 317, 318
  Police power - 324
  Taxation - 311
McReynolds, James C.
Biography - 788, 842
Congressional Powers
  Commerce - 101
  Fiscal and monetary - 122
Court operations, traditions - 743, 746
Origins and development of Court - 37, 41-47
Presidential Powers
  Foreign affairs - 201
  Power of removal - 213
  Roosevelt administration - 241, 242
Pressures on the Court
  Presidential - 685, 689
  Public - 701
Meat Inspection Act of 1906 - 97
Micou, William C. - 21, 656, 691
Military Affairs
Congressional Powers
  Conscientious objectors - 134, 457
  Desertion - 145
  Draft, draft evasion - 145, 885
  War powers - 125-130
Presidential Powers
  Military trials - 192, 892
  War powers - 187-198
Miller, Samuel F.
Biography - 784-786, 792, 819, 820
Court traditions - 745
Extra-judicial activities - 757
Individual Rights
  Due process - 525
  Equal protection - 381
  Sex discrimination - 631
  Voting rights - 342, 478, 479
Judicial power - 267, 280
Origins and development of Court

- 5, 23-28, 31
Presidential Powers
  Executive discretion - 216
  Pardons - 225
  Treaties - 202
  War - 188
Presidential pressure on the Court - 686, 689
Sovereign immunity - 261
State Powers
  Commerce - 319
  Immigration - 318, 319
  Individual rights - 339, 340, 342, 365, 366
  Police power - 358
  Taxation - 330, 357
Minimum Wages - 33-36, 43, 89, 98-102, 105, 106, 121, 244, 326-328, 526, 527, 883, 884, 889, 891, 907
Minorities *(See also Equal Rights)*
Racial Equality
  Education - 348, 590-607
  Employment - 584, 618-621
  Housing - 348, 613-618
  Juries - 532
  Press coverage - 717, 718
  Travel, accommodations - 585, 607-613
Minton, Sherman
Biography - 788, 857, 858
Individual Rights
  Due process - 546
  Equal rights - 750
  Freedom of expression - 410
  Freedom of political association - 502, 509, 511-514
Origins and development of Court - 49, 51
Presidential Powers
  Postwar emergency powers - 194, 244
  Relationship with Truman - 182
Missouri Compromise - 22, 120, 135, 136, 138, 876
Mitchell, John N. - 245, 247, 553, 687
Monroe, James
Court size - 664
Foreign affairs - 205
Supreme Court nominations - 15, 786
Moody, William H.
Biography - 788, 837, 838
Due process - 528
Presidential pressure on the Court - 684
Relationship with Roosevelt - 35, 183
Resignation - 36
Moore, Alfred
Biography - 790, 803
Nomination - 10
Municipal Bankruptcy Act of 1934 - 43, 242, 355, 677
Murphy, Frank
Biography - 787, 788, 790, 852, 853
Citizenship, naturalization - 144
Court operations - 742, 766

Individual Rights
    Due process - 528, 533, 534, 544, 545, 567, 576
    Freedom of expression - 418, 458, 459
    Freedom of political association - 517
    Voting rights - 482, 489
Origins and development of Court - 45, 47-49
Presidential pressure on the Court - 684

N

Natchez Press - 709
Nation - 712-714
National Court of Appeals - 736, 768
National Firearms Act of 1934 - 115
National Gazette - 709
National Industrial Recovery Act (NIRA) - 43, 78, 82, 98, 121, 240-242, 677, 702, 888
National Intelligencer - 15, 708, 709
National Labor Relations Act of 1935 (NLRA) - 44, 99-102, 243, 321, 393, 417, 426, 665, 677, 889
National Labor Relations Board - 100, 101, 510
Naturalization (See *Immigration and Naturalization*)
Necessary and Proper Clause (See *Constitution*)
Nelson, Samuel
    Biography - 785, 786, 790, 815
    Court operations - 774
    Nomination - 20, 657
    Origins and development of Court - 20, 22, 24, 26, 27
    Presidential pressure on the Court - 684
    Presidential war powers - 188, 189
    Slavery - 137, 138
Neutrality Acts of 1935-1937 - 191
Neutrality Proclamation - 199
New Deal - 42-44, 97-103, 117, 240-244, 268, 269, 354, 355, 654, 665, 677, 689, 702, 714-717
New Hampshire Gazette - 708
New Orleans Times-Picayune - 717
New York Commercial Advertiser - 709
New York Courier - 711
New York Daily Advertiser - 709
New York Evening Post - 707, 709, 711
New York Herald - 711, 713
New York Herald-Tribune - 715, 716
New York Independent - 711
New York Statesman - 709
New York Times
    Commercial speech - 421
    Confidentiality - 445
    Court coverage - 712, 713, 715-721, 724, 743, 751

Libel - 433-436, 438-440
    Pentagon Papers - 245, 431-433, 903
New York Tribune - 710-714
Newark Daily Advertiser - 710
Newspapers (See *Press Coverage; individual newspapers*)
Niles Register - 706, 708, 709
Nineteenth Amendment
    Citizens' rights - 144
    Constitutional challenge - 149, 150
    Enforcement - 151
    Voting rights - 477, 631
Ninth Amendment - 343, 644, 645
Nixon, Richard M.
    Conflicts with Supreme Court - 245-248
    Criminal rights - 679
    Executive privilege - 232, 733, 740
    Foreign affairs - 195, 196, 205, 206
    Freedom of expression - 423
    Pardon - 224, 225
    Presidential immunity - 231
    Presidential veto power - 223
    Pressures on the Court
        Presidential - 683-685, 687, 690, 692, 693
        Press - 717-720, 724
    "Saturday Night Massacre" - 759
    Supreme Court appointments - 54, 55, 182, 561, 578, 656, 661, 747, 753, 756, 783, 785, 788, 791
    Voting age - 674
    White House tapes, papers - 55, 232-234, 247, 338, 718, 719, 740, 905
    Wiretaps - 552
Non-Intercourse Act of 1809 - 75
Norris-LaGuardia Act of 1932 - 93, 276, 618, 676
North American Review - 711
Northwest Ordinance of 1787 - 133, 135

O

Obscenity - 428-431, 897, 905
Occupational Safety and Health Act of 1970 - 908
Office of Price Administration (OPA) - 191, 276
Oklahoma Enabling Act - 355
Omnibus Crime Control and Safe Streets Act of 1968 - 245, 679
Organized Crime Control Act of 1970 - 557, 904
Original Package Doctrine - 100, 329-331

P

Packers and Stockyards Act of 1921 - 92
Pardons - 221, 224-228

Parker, John J. - 41, 656, 657
Passport Act of 1926 - 215
Passports - 507
Patents and Copyrights - 155
Paterson, William
    Adams' administration, conflicts - 235
    Biography - 783, 789, 799, 800
    Origins and development of Court - 9-13
    Presidential foreign affairs powers - 200, 201
    Presidential pressure on the Court - 687
Peckham, Rufus W.
    Antitrust - 91, 92
    Biography - 834
    Freedom of contract - 326, 343
    Origins and development of Court - 33-36
Peckham, Wheeler H. - 32, 656, 657, 686
Pennsylvanian - 711
Pensions and Retirement
    Sex discrimination - 638
    Supreme Court justices - 243, 661, 755, 756, 774
Pentagon Papers - 55, 245, 380, 431-433, 733, 903
Peters, Richard Jr. - 16, 21, 762
Pickering, John - 236, 659, 660
Pierce, Franklin
    Executive privilege - 231
    Presidential emergency powers - 217
    Pressures on the Court
        Presidential - 686, 691
        Press - 713
    Supreme Court nominations - 21, 657, 785, 788
Pitney, Mahlon
    Biography - 841
    Elections regulation - 172
    Freedom of expression - 400
    Judicial power - 273
    Origins and development of Court - 36, 37, 39
    Presidential pressure on the Court - 686
Political Question Doctrine - 20, 48, 49, 200, 292, 293, 348, 356, 491, 898
Political Rights (See also *Elections*)
    Districts, apportionment - 52, 380, 381, 489-497, 718
    Free expression - 165, 172, 173
    Major Supreme Court decisions - 878, 879, 882, 884, 886-888, 890, 891, 893, 895, 897-900, 902, 904, 907
    Political association, freedom of - 380, 381, 476, 499-520
    Poverty groups - 643
    Sex discrimination - 631, 637
    Voting rights - 48, 52, 149-152, 156, 341, 342, 347, 348, 380, 475-497, 585, 718
Polk, James K.
    Presidential Powers

Executive privilege - 231
War - 186
Presidential pressure on the Court - 686, 691
Supreme Court nominations - 20, 657, 784, 786
Poll Taxes - 342, 347, 482, 643
Pornography - 359, 428-431
Postal Services
Congressional powers - 155
Presidential powers - 212-214
Poverty Groups
Equal protection - 349, 585, 641-646
Powell, Adam Clayton Jr. - 165-167, 902
Powell, Lewis F. Jr.
Biography - 785, 865
Court operations - 738, 754
Individual Rights
Due process - 535, 540, 546, 555, 557, 561, 578, 579
Freedom of expression - 417, 420, 423, 439, 444, 445, 468
Political association - 518
Poverty groups - 349, 644-646
Racial equality - 598, 604-606, 617, 621
Sex discrimination - 633, 637
Voting rights - 494, 495
Judicial restraint - 292
Jurisdiction - 255
Nixon administration - 245, 246
Nomination - 55
Presidential pressure on the Court - 684, 687, 693
State police power - 359
President (*See also individual presidents*)
Commander-in-Chief Powers
China, Cuba, Vietnam - 194
Conduct of war - 24, 195, 876, 892, 893
Control of property - 195
Field decisions - 195
Lincoln - 187
Military justice, trials - 192, 195
Postwar - 193
Roosevelt - 190
Undeclared wars (box) - 186
Wartime seizure power - 193
Wilson - 190
Confrontations with Supreme Court - 235-250
Executive immunity - 229, 230, 905
Executive Powers
Appointments - 209-211, 655, 798
Delegation of power - 216
Emergencies - 217-219
Executive discretion - 216
Removal - 41, 211-216, 886, 888, 897
Executive privilege - 230-234
Foreign policy powers - 43, 44, 199-207, 889
Pardons and reprieves - 224-228
Powers, major Supreme Court decisions - 874, 876, 886, 888, 889, 892,

893, 895, 897, 905
Pressures on the Court - 683-694
Vetoes - 221-223
Presidential Recordings and Materials Preservation Act - 247
Press Coverage (*See also Press, Freedom of; individual newspapers*)
Pressures on the Court - 705-725
Supreme Court press officer - 764
Press, Freedom of (*See also First Amendment; Speech, Freedom of*)
Access and confidentiality - 443-449
Background - 378-380
Broadcasting - 446, 447
Fair trial - 440-443
Major Supreme Court decisions - 885, 887, 888, 890, 897, 899, 903-905, 907, 909
Obscenity - 428-431
Prior restraint - 423-433
Subsequent punishment, libel - 424, 433-440
Pressures on the Court
Congressional
Individual pressure - 655-664
Institutional and procedural pressure - 664-672
Periods of confrontation - 653-655
Reversals of rulings - 672-680
Presidential - 683-694
Press - 705-725
Public opinion - 695-703
Workload - 678, 736
Privacy
Burger and media - 722
Right to privacy - 343, 437, 539-553, 644, 645, 900, 904
Privileges and Immunities (*See also Fourteenth Amendment*)
Citizenship - 28, 339-341, 375, 477, 587, 878, 882
Congressional witnesses - 163
Due process (*See Due Process*)
Federal officials - 908
Judiciary - 290, 878
Major Supreme Court decisions - 878, 882
Members of Congress - 167-170, 904, 909
President - 229-234, 905
Racial discrimination - 139
Right to travel - 105, 585
Sovereign immunity (box) - 261
States - 357, 361, 365
Voting rights - 475, 477
Prohibition - 149 (*See also Eighteenth Amendment*)
Property Rights
Eminent domain - 141, 312-314, 875
State powers - 30, 32, 301, 309-334
Wartime powers - 195
Prostitution - 95
Public Utility Holding Company Act - 156
Pure Food and Drug Act of 1906 - 36, 96

R

Racial Discrimination (*See Equal Rights*)
Railroad Retirement Act of 1934 - 89, 113, 241, 677, 888
Railroads
Commerce - 87-90, 318
Labor - 88, 120, 121, 618
Pensions - 89, 241
Safety - 89
Segregation - 607-610, 618
Shreveport doctrine - 88, 884
Railway Labor Act of 1930 - 44, 89, 618
Railway Labor Board - 89
Raleigh News and Observer - 718
Randolph, John - 659, 660, 697, 698
Read, John M. - 20, 656, 691, 784
Reapportionment
Congressional districts - 494
Equal protection - 347, 348
Political question doctrine - 293, 356
State legislative districts - 495-497, 675
State sovereignty - 356
Reconstruction Acts - 25, 263, 272, 276, 480, 667
Reed, Stanley F.
Biography - 787, 850
Court operations - 742
Individual Rights
Due process - 575, 577
Equal rights - 750
Freedom of expression - 408, 409, 420, 459
Freedom of political association - 502, 509, 513, 514, 517
Voting rights - 482, 489
Judicial precedent - 294
Origins and development of Court - 45, 47, 48, 51
Presidential Powers
Commander in Chief - 194
Executive privilege - 231
Truman administration - 244
Presidential pressure on the Court - 683
Roosevelt appointee, as - 45, 244
Solicitor General, as - 759
Regulatory Agencies
Congress, delegation of powers - 75, 874
Presidential appointments and removal - 211-216, 888
Rehnquist, William H.
Biography - 865, 866
Court traditions - 746, 766
Executive privilege - 234
Individual Rights
Due process - 544, 547, 561, 563, 578, 579
Freedom of expression - 412, 420, 439, 468
Freedom of political association - 518

Fundamental interest doctrine - 586

Racial equality - 603-607

Sex discrimination - 633, 635, 636

Voting rights - 494-496

Nixon appointee, as - 55, 245

Nixon, Watergate - 247

Presidential pressure on the Court - 683, 687, 693

State Powers

Commerce - 56, 320

Electoral districts - 356

State sovereignty - 105, 106, 356, 362, 363

Religion, Freedom of

Background - 378-380

Education - 47, 53, 462-470, 675

Establishment of religion - 461-470

Flag salute - 47, 457-459, 716, 717

Free exercise of religion - 452-461

Major Supreme Court decisions - 891-895, 898, 903

State powers - 344

Renegotiation Act - 129, 130

Reporters of Decisions - 762, 763

Richmond Enquirer - 709

Richmond Times - 713

Roane, Spencer - 305

Roberts, Owen J.

Biography - 848

Congressional Powers

Commerce - 89, 99, 100, 102

Taxation - 117, 118

Court traditions, operations - 747, 756, 757

Hughes as Chief Justice - 749

Individual Rights

Due process - 566, 567

Freedom of expression - 405, 407, 408, 410, 430, 459

Voting rights - 482

Judicial power - 268, 276

Jurisdiction - 666

Nomination - 41, 657

Origins and development of Court - 41-44, 47, 48

Presidential Powers

Delegated powers - 191

New Deal legislation - 241-243

Pressures on the Court

Presidential - 689, 690

Public opinion - 702

State Powers

Minimum wages, hours - 327

Public interest regulation - 325

Reserved powers - 354

Robinson, Joseph T. - 788

Roosevelt, Franklin D.

Bills of attainder - 76

Black support - 588

Chief Justiceship, extra-judicial activities - 752

Conflicts with Supreme Court - 240-244, 654

Court-packing plan - 44, 242-244, 588, 654, 661, 664, 665, 689, 702, 716, 753, 964 (text)

Douglas (William O.), and - 757

New Deal legislation - 97-103, 117, 121, 240, 241, 677, 702

Origins and development of Court - 42-47

Presidential Powers

Commander in Chief - 182, 185, 190-193, 195

Foreign policy - 201, 204-206

Impoundment of funds - 246

Power of removal - 214, 215

Vetoes - 221-223

Pressures on the Court

Presidential - 683, 686, 689, 690, 692

Press - 714-716

Public opinion - 701

Relationship with Frankfurter - 183, 758

Supreme Court appointments - 44, 45, 47, 783, 785, 788, 789

Roosevelt, Theodore

Presidential Powers

Antitrust - 91

Executive agreements - 205

Foreign wars - 187

Stewardship theory - 182

Presidential pressure on the Court - 684, 685

Relationship with Moody - 183

Supreme Court appointments - 34, 35, 786, 788

Rule of Four - 264

Rutledge, John

Biography - 783, 787, 794, 795

Court traditions, operations - 748, 766

Nomination for Chief Justice - 656

Origins and development of Court - 8, 9

Pressures on the Court

Congressional - 657

Press - 707

Rutledge, Wiley B.

Biography - 854, 855

Congressional Powers

Citizenship, naturalization - 144

Commerce - 91

Court operations - 742

Individual Rights

Due process - 383, 528, 533, 544, 576

Freedom of expression - 379, 391, 410, 456, 458, 467

Freedom of political association - 517

Voting rights - 490

Origins and development of Court - 47-49

S

St. Louis Evening News - 711

St. Louis Post Dispatch - 716

St. Paul Pioneer Press - 716

San Francisco Chronicle - 716

Sanford, Edward T.

Biography - 846, 847

Due process - 344

Freedom of expression - 401, 404

Origins and development of Court - 39, 41

Presidential pressure on the Court - 686

Presidential veto power - 222

Saturday Evening Post - 436, 438

Sawyer, Charles - 244

Schools (See Education)

Search and Seizure (See also Fourth Amendment)

Due Process

Administrative inspections - 550, 551

Arrests - 544-547

Automobile searches - 39, 547

Exclusionary rule - 541, 548, 549

Individual rights - 539-553

Wiretaps - 39, 547, 550-553

Free press - 448

Major Supreme Court decisions - 879, 884, 886, 887, 894, 895, 897-899, 901, 902, 908

State courts - 49, 52, 346

Second Amendment - 374 (See also Bill of Rights)

Second War Powers Act of 1942 - 129

Securities and Exchange Commission - 156

Sedition Acts - 12, 235, 237, 374, 388, 394, 396, 433, 499, 501, 698

Segregation - 49-53, 583-621, 699, 700, 717, 718 (See also Equal Rights)

Selective Service Acts - 37, 128, 129, 193

Self-Incrimination (See Criminal Law)

Senate (See also Congress)

Court confirmations, rejections - 655-658, 686, 795

Internal Affairs, Membership

Elections regulation - 171-174

Immunity - 167-170

Lobby regulation - 174

Punishment - 166, 167

Qualifications - 165, 166

Rules - 175

Presidential appointments - 209-211, 655-658, 686

Treaty powers - 130, 131, 199, 201

Separability Clause - 113

Separate but Equal Doctrine

Background - 31, 33, 46, 49, 50

Individual rights - 382, 587-591, 595, 596, 610

Major Supreme Court decisions - 881, 890, 895

Public pressure on Court - 700

State powers - 348, 349

Seventeenth Amendment - 897

Seventh Amendment - 374, 529, 530, 878 (See also Bill of Rights)

Sex Discrimination (See Equal Rights)

Shaw, Lemuel - 590, 591
Sheppard-Towner Act - 116
Sherman Antitrust Act of 1890 - 32, 35-37, 81, 88, 90-96, 105, 319, 320, 361, 426, 880, 881
Shiras, George Jr.
　Biography - 787, 832
　Congressional powers - 87, 140
　Origins and development of Court - 32, 34, 35
Silver Platter Doctrine - 548, 549, 898
Sirica, John - 234, 247
Sixteenth Amendment
　Congressional tax power - 109, 112, 120, 884
　Judges and taxes - 115
　Proposal, adoption - 111, 674
Sixth Amendment *(See also Bill of Rights; Criminal Rights)*
　Contempt proceedings - 284, 285
　Expatriation - 145
　Jury trials, due process - 345, 440-443, 529-534, 562
　Major Supreme Court decisions - 886, 887, 892, 899-901, 903, 905
　Military justice - 128
　Right to counsel - 560, 565-569, 679, 899, 900
　Sex discrimination - 637
　Territories, rights - 140, 142
　Wartime legislation - 129
Slavery *(See Equal Rights; Thirteenth Amendment)*
Smith Act of 1940 - 49, 51, 281, 284, 362, 400, 433, 501-505, 513, 577, 669, 671, 895, 896
Smith, William - 19, 664
Social Security Act - 44, 67, 118, 243, 633, 634, 890
Solicitors General - 759, 760
Sovereign Immunity - 261
Speech, Freedom of *(See also First Amendment; Press, Freedom of)*
　Advertising - 421, 906
　Background - 378-380
　Campaign financing - 165, 172, 173, 420
　Congressional immunity - 169
　Congressional witnesses - 160-164
　Lobby regulation - 174
　Major Supreme Court decisions - 885-887, 891, 894-898, 902, 906, 908
　Obscenity - 428-431, 897, 905
　Political association - 499-520
　Postal powers - 156
　Public speech, public safety - 406-422
　Seditious speech, safety of state - 396-406
　State powers - 344
　White House tapes (Nixon) - 247
　Wiretapping - 245, 246
Speech or Debate Clause - 166-170, 904, 909 *(See also Congress; Constitution)*
Speedy Trial Act of 1974 - 535, 678
Spencer, John C. - 20, 656

Springfield Republican - 712
Stanbery, Henry - 26, 656, 657, 664, 668, 784
Stanford Daily - 448
Stanton, Edwin M. - 26, 655, 688, 689, 714, 746, 790
Stare Decisis - 287, 294, 705, 747, 985
States
　Bills of credit - 874
　Compacts - 880
　Congressional delegation of powers - 79
　Congressional districts - 494
　Eminent domain - 312-314, 875
　Federal-state tax immunities - 116
　Foreign policy role - 200
　Grants-in-aid programs - 116
　Interstate boundaries - 875
　Interstate relations - 365-367, 884
　Judicial restraint - 293, 698
　Judicial review - 303-308, 698
　Legislative districts - 495-497
　Liability - 354-357
　Loyalty oaths - 512-517
　Militias - 125
　New states, admission of - 133, 134
　Powers
　　Commerce - 315-322, 876
　　Contracts, obligation of - 309-315, 872, 874-876, 879, 887
　　Individual rights - 337-350
　　Judicial - 360, 361
　　Major Supreme Court decisions - 874, 877, 878, 880, 883-887, 896
　　Police - 28, 40, 314, 322-328, 358-360, 875, 878-880, 884, 886
　　Reserved - 353, 354
　　Taxation - 310, 311, 328-333, 357-360, 875, 877, 878
　Secession - 877
　Sedition statutes - 400-406, 513
　Slavery - 16, 18-23, 338, 375-378, 587, 588 *(See also Equal Rights)*
　State as sovereign - 353-364
　Voting requirements (box) - 485
Stevens, John Paul
　Biography - 866
　Court operations, traditions - 735, 746, 747, 766
　Individual Rights
　　Death penalty - 579
　　Freedom of expression - 444-448
　　Racial equality - 604, 605
　　Search and seizure - 543, 544
　　Sex discrimination - 633, 635, 637, 638
　Origins and development of Court - 55, 56
　State sovereignty - 105, 356, 363
Stewart, Potter
　Biography - 860, 861
　Congressional Powers
　　Congressional immunity - 168
　　Investigations - 161, 163
　　Members of Congress, qualifications - 166
　　War power - 126

Individual Rights
　Due process - 529, 536, 540, 546, 549, 552, 557, 560, 561, 563, 568, 572, 576, 578, 579
　Freedom of expression - 403, 414, 415, 432, 436, 438, 439, 444-448, 461, 464
　Personal privacy - 645
　Political association - 506, 511, 514-517
　Poverty groups - 642
　Racial equality - 603, 604, 616, 617, 620
　Sex discrimination - 633, 635
　Voting rights - 483, 491, 494, 495
　Jurisdiction - 259
　Origins and development of Court - 51-53
　State Powers
　　Commerce - 320
　　Contract clause - 315
Stone, Harlan Fiske
　Biography - 783, 785, 788, 790, 847, 848
　Chief Justice, as - 750-752, 757
　Congressional Powers
　　Commerce - 98-102
　　Elections regulation - 172
　　Fiscal and monetary powers - 118
　Court traditions, operations - 742, 745, 766, 772
　Individual Rights
　　"Footnote 4" - 378, 379
　　Freedom of expression - 391, 408, 454, 458
　　Racial equality - 588
　　Voting rights - 482, 489
　Judicial power - 269
　Nomination - 39, 657, 658
　Origins and development of Court - 39, 41, 43, 45, 47, 48
　Presidential Powers
　　Commander in Chief - 192
　　Foreign policy - 201
　　Roosevelt administration - 241-243
　Pressures on the Court
　　Presidential - 683, 685, 686, 689, 690
　　Public - 702
　Relationship with Roosevelt - 758
　State Powers
　　Commerce - 322
　　Police power - 327
　　State sovereignty - 354, 357, 361
Story, Joseph
　Biography - 786, 790, 806, 807
　Congress, inherent powers - 74
　Court operations - 753, 773, 774
　Court size - 665
　Freedom of religion - 451
　Judicial power - 267
　Jurisdiction - 666
　Origins and development of Court - 13-20
　Presidential emergency and war powers - 186, 217

Presidential pressure on the Court - 685, 688
State Powers
Contracts - 310, 312
Judicial review - 305-307
Stream of Commerce Doctrine - 85, 91-93, 882
Strong, William
Biography - 791, 792, 822, 823
Congressional powers - 121
Extra-judicial activities - 757
Jurisdiction - 258
Nomination, confirmation - 120, 664
Origins and development of Court - 26, 28, 29
Presidential pressure on the Court - 686, 689
State taxation power - 331
Submerged Lands Act - 134, 677
Subpoenas
Congressional investigations - 163
Due process - 534, 541
Subversive Activities Control Act of 1950 - 53, 513, 898, 900, 901
Subversive Activities Control Board - 506, 508
Summary Suspension Act of 1950 - 669
Supremacy Clause - 69, 204, 267, 304, 305
Supreme Court (*See also Federal Courts; names of individual members*)
Appointments
Controversial justices - 791
Foreign-born justices - 789
Geographical factors, regional seats - 785-787
Justices from the Cabinet (box) - 246
Justices who served in Congress (box) - 171
Longest vacancies - 784
Longevity - 790
Nominations, rejections, confirmations - 653, 655-658, 795, 946 (list)
Presidential appointments - 209, 683, 783-785, 798
Qualifications, experience - 683, 787-790
Relatives on Court - 791
Religious background - 788
Chief Justice
Administrative assistant - 752
Biographies - 783-866
Burger - 751
Hughes - 749, 750
Marshall - 748
Perquisites, salary - 115, 663, 752, 774
Roles, duties - 748-752
Stone - 750
Taft - 748, 749
Warren - 750, 751
Cost of the Court - 773, 774
Extraordinary majority - 665

Housing the Court - 769-772
Judicial immunity - 290
Judicial restraint - 287-295
Jurisdiction - 260-266, 666-672, 877, 881
Justices
Biographies - 783-866
Court operations - 753, 754
Extra-judicial activities - 756-758
Impeachment - 658-663, 756
Perquisites - 758
Removal from office - 658-663
Retirement - 661, 755, 756
Salaries - 115, 653, 663, 758, 774
Terms - 665
Major decisions - 871-909
Operations of the Court
Arguments - 735
Conferences - 739
Opinions - 739
Reporting of decisions - 743
Review process - 734
"Rule of four" - 264
Schedule - 732
Workload (box) - 678, 736
Powers - 5-58, 267-285
Press access to Court building (box) - 723
Press coverage - 705-725
Pressures (*See Pressures on Court*)
Reversal of rulings, Congressional - 653, 672-680
Rules (text) - 932
Size of the Court - 653, 664, 665
Supporting Personnel
Administrative assistant - 752
Administrative Office - 751, 767
Clerk - 759-761
Curator - 764
Federal Judicial Center - 751, 767
Historical Society - 768
Law clerks - 765, 766
Legal officers - 764
Librarian - 764, 765
Marshal - 761, 762
Messengers - 766, 767
Press officer - 764
Reporter of decisions - 762, 763
Solicitor general - 759, 760
Supreme Court Bar - 763, 764
U.S. Judicial Conference - 748, 751, 767
Traditions of the Court - 744-747
Supreme Court Retirement Act of 1937 - 44, 243, 661
Sutherland, George
Biography - 789, 845, 846
Congressional Powers
Commerce - 98-100
Delegation of powers - 79
Election investigations, regulation - 164, 172
Fiscal and monetary powers - 116, 117
Inherent powers - 75
War power - 125
Individual Rights

Due process - 345, 527, 565, 566
Freedom of expression - 426
Judicial restraint - 291
Origins and development of Court - 39, 41-45
Presidential Powers
Foreign policy - 182, 201, 202, 206
Power of removal - 214
Roosevelt administration - 241, 242, 244
Pressures on the Court
Presidential - 686, 689
Public - 701
Separability clauses - 113
State Powers
Criminal rights, due process - 345
Police power - 327, 359
Supreme Court pensions - 661
Swayne, Noah H.
Biography - 790, 818, 819
Court traditions, operations - 745, 762
Origins and development of Court - 23-29
Presidential pressure on the Court - 686, 688, 689, 691
Presidential war powers - 188
State Powers
Commerce - 332
Privileges and immunities, citizens - 339
Syndicalism Act of 1919 (California) - 500

T

Taft-Hartley Act of 1947 - 49, 77, 217, 244, 276, 510, 894
Taft, William Howard
Biography - 787, 844, 845
Chief Justice, as - 748, 749, 751
Congressional Powers
Commerce - 88, 92
Delegation of powers - 75
Taxation - 111, 112, 114
Court operations, traditions - 745, 759, 766, 767, 771
Due process - 345, 523, 529, 547, 550, 571
Judicial power - 268, 284
Jurisdiction - 265, 266
Origins and development of Court - 36-43
Presidential Powers
Executive powers - 209, 211-214, 216
Extent of powers - 182
Pardons - 227
Pressures on the Court
Congressional - 661, 674
Presidential - 684, 686, 691
State Powers
Contracts - 327
Due process - 345
Taxation - 322
Supreme Court appointments - 783, 785, 788, 789

Taney, Roger B.
Biography - 790, 811, 812
Chief Justice, as - 18-23, 748, 751, 755, 788
Congressional Powers
Citizenship - 142
Commerce - 84, 104
Slavery - 120, 136-138, 142
Court operations, traditions - 741, 746
Habeas corpus - 76
Jackson appointee, as - 755
Judicial power - 283
Judicial restraint - 289, 293, 294
Nomination - 17, 656, 657, 707
Origins and development of Court - 16-25
Presidential Powers
Emergencies - 217
Foreign affairs - 200
Lincoln administration, conflicts - 238-240
War - 186, 188, 189
Pressures on the Court
Presidential - 684, 688
Press - 710-712, 721
Public opinion - 699
State Powers
Contracts - 313
Judicial power - 361
National supremacy - 299, 301, 302, 354
Police power - 316, 317, 323, 324
Taxation - 328, 329
Taxes, Taxation
Church exemptions - 461, 462
Congressional powers, limits - 76, 109-116, 873, 877, 882, 887, 908
Federal
Direct - 109, 872, 884
Immunity - 115, 116
Income - 32, 37, 109-112, 120, 875, 881, 884, 890
Indirect - 879, 881, 882
Police, regulatory power - 112-116
Uniformity - 112
Major Supreme Court decisions - 872-875, 877-879, 881, 882, 884, 885, 887, 890, 891, 902, 906, 908
Poll taxes - 342, 347, 482, 643
Standing to sue - 291, 886, 902
State
Commerce - 331-333, 877, 878
Exemptions - 310, 311, 461, 462, 875
Limitations - 328-333
Taylor, Zachary - 784
Teapot Dome Scandal - 159, 231
Tennessee Valley Authority (TVA) - 43, 86, 240, 241, 677, 888
Tenth Amendment
Commerce - 102, 322
Foreign relations - 200
State as sovereign - 353, 354
Taxation - 322
Treaties - 203, 204

Tenure of Office Act of 1867 - 211
Territories
Congressional powers - 135-142, 882
Incorporation doctrine - 142, 882
Third Amendment - 374, 644 (See also *Bill of Rights*)
Thirteenth Amendment
Enforcement - 28, 151, 152, 375
Major Supreme Court decisions - 879, 881, 885, 901
Political rights - 68
Racial equality - 120, 139, 338, 339, 608, 612-614, 616, 673
Selective Service - 128
Thompson, Smith
Biography - 786, 808, 809
Extra-judicial activities - 756, 757
Origins and development of Court - 15, 20
Presidential immunity - 230
Thornberry, Homer - 54, 656, 684
Tillman Act - 172
Time **Magazine** - 439, 724
Todd, Thomas
Appointment - 13, 664
Biography - 806
Origins and development of Court - 13, 16
Trademarks - 155, 355
Transportation (See also *Travel, Accommodations*)
Commerce - 83-90, 95-97
Railroads (See *Railroads*)
Transportation Act of 1920 - 88, 89
Travel, Accommodations
Major Supreme Court decisions - 897, 899, 902
Right to travel - 104, 507, 607-613, 642, 643
Treason - 398
Treaties and Agreements
Congressional powers - 130-132, 201, 885
Major Supreme Court decisions - 872, 880, 885
Panama Canal (box) - 131
Presidential powers - 202-207
Trimble, Robert
Biography - 787, 809
Nomination - 16
Truman, Harry S
Conflicts with Supreme Court - 244, 245
Douglas (William O.), and - 757
Political association, freedom of - 506, 508
Presidential Powers
Impoundment of funds - 246
Power to sign bills - 223
War - 185, 193, 195, 217
Presidential pressure on the Court - 683-686, 690
Supreme Court appointments - 48-50, 182, 785, 788
Tidelands oil - 677

Vinson nomination - 745
Tucker Act of 1887 - 261
Twenty-Fifth Amendment - 151
Twenty-First Amendment - 115, 325
Twenty-Fourth Amendment
Citizens' rights - 144
Enforcement - 151
Voting rights - 347, 477, 483, 900
Twenty-Sixth Amendment
Congressional pressure on Court - 674
Enforcement - 151
Voting rights - 144, 477
Twenty-Third Amendment
Enforcement - 151
Voting rights - 156, 477
Tyler, John
Executive privilege - 231
Presidential pressure on the Court - 684, 686, 691
Supreme Court nominations - 20, 656, 657, 784-786

U

United Nations Participation Act of 1945 - 204
United Press International - 721
United States Telegraph - 709

V

Van Buren, Martin
Foreign affairs - 205
Origins and development of Court - 19, 20, 786
Van Devanter, Willis
Biography - 839, 840
Hughes as Chief Justice - 750
New Deal - 241, 244, 701, 702
Origins and development of Court - 36, 37, 41-45
Presidential pressure on the Court - 689
Retirement - 661
Vetoes - 221-223
Vinson, Fred M.
Biography - 856
Court traditions, operations - 742, 745, 746, 751, 757, 766
Individual Rights
Due process - 577
Equal rights - 592, 593, 614
Freedom of expression - 392, 408-410
Freedom of political association - 502, 504, 509-511
Search and seizure - 544
Judicial power - 282
Origins and development of Court - 48-50

Presidential Powers
Executive privilege - 232
Truman administration - 244, 245
War - 193, 194
Presidential pressure on the Court - 690
Virginia Argus - 707
Virginian-Pilot - 441
Voting *(See Political Rights)*
Voting Rights Act Amendments of 1970 - 355
Voting Rights Act of 1965 - 53, 151, 152, 347, 357, 380, 475, 480, 481, 485-488, 584, 589, 674, 900, 902, 907

W

Wagner Act - 716
Waite, Morrison R.
Biography - 824, 825
Chief Justice, as - 751
Congress and official conduct - 211
Court traditions - 745
Jurisdiction - 262
Origins and development of Court - 28-30
Presidential pressure on the Court - 686
State Powers
Commerce - 318, 319, 321
Individual rights - 341, 342, 345
Police power - 314, 325
Voting rights - 341, 342, 345, 478
Wall Street Journal - 716, 718, 719, 721
Wallace, John William - 23, 30, 762
Walworth, Reuben H. - 20, 656, 686, 784
War Claims Act of 1948 - 215
War Labor Disputes Act of 1943 - 129, 193
War Powers
Congress - 125-130
Major Supreme Court decisions - 892, 893
President - 187-198
War Powers Act of 1973 - 196
War Relocation Authority - 192
Warrants - 539-545, 550 *(See also Fourth Amendment; Search and Seizure)*
Warren, Earl
Bills of attainder - 77
Biography - 787, 789, 858
Chief Justice, as - 654, 655, 660, 661, 750-752, 756-758, 766
Citizenship, expatriation - 142, 145
Congressional investigations - 157, 160-163
Court traditions - 744, 747
Individual Rights
Bill of Rights - 374
Due process - 383, 535, 543, 545, 560, 561, 568, 575, 578
Freedom of expression - 430, 438

Personal privacy - 645
Political association - 501, 505-514
Racial equality - 589, 593-596, 600, 700
Right to travel - 104
Voting rights - 481, 486, 493
Judicial power - 269
Judicial restraint - 287, 289, 291, 292
Members of Congress, qualifications - 166
Origins and development of Court - 50-54
Pressures on the Court
Congressional - 654, 655, 660, 661, 669, 679
Presidential - 683, 685, 690
Press - 705, 717, 718, 721, 722
State powers - 302, 347
Washington, Bushrod
Biography - 790, 802, 803
Extra-judicial activities - 756
Origins and development of Court - 10-13, 16
State powers - 312
Washington Federalist - 708
Washington, George
Implied powers of Congress - 73
Origins and development of Court - 8, 9, 18
Presidential Powers
Appointments - 210
Executive privilege - 231
Foreign policy - 199
Pardons, reprieves - 224
Presidential pressure on the Court - 687, 692
Supreme Court appointments - 657, 707, 748, 783, 785-787, 789
Supreme Court, role - 752
Washington Post - 245, 431-433, 444, 713, 716-721, 903
Washington Star - 715-720
Washington Union - 711
Water Pollution Control Act of 1972 - 247
Water Quality Improvement Act of 1970 - 105
Wayne, James M.
Biography - 784, 787, 790, 811
Origins and development of Court - 17, 18, 23-25
Presidential war power - 188
Pressures on the Court
Congressional - 664
Presidential - 688
State contracts - 311
Webb-Kenyon Act of 1913 - 79, 325, 884.
Webster, Daniel
Candidate for Supreme Court, as - 688
Congressional powers - 15, 16, 83, 84, 315
Court presence, style - 708, 764
State powers - 15, 311, 315
Taney nomination - 18
Wheaton, Henry - 14, 762

White, Byron R.
Biography - 861
Campaign finance - 173
Congressional immunity - 168-170
Court traditions, operations - 745, 766
Individual Rights
Due process - 530, 531, 534, 543-547, 557, 560-562, 576-579
Freedom of expression - 420, 432, 435-439, 445, 446, 448, 460, 461, 467, 468
Personal privacy - 645
Political association - 381, 507, 508, 511, 515-517
Poverty groups - 646
Racial equality - 603, 605, 610, 614, 616, 617, 620
Voting rights - 488, 492, 494-496
Judicial power - 285
Origins and development of Court - 52, 53, 55
Presidential impoundment of funds - 247
Presidential pressure on the Court - 683, 684
State taxation power - 328, 333
White, Edward D.
Biography - 785-788, 833, 834
Chief Justice, as - 749, 751
Congressional Powers
Commerce - 92
Delegation of power - 75
Taxation - 114
Territories - 140, 142
War power - 128
Judicial power - 281
Nomination - 32, 657
Origins and development of Court - 32, 35-38
Presidential pressure on the Court - 684, 686, 691
Voting rights - 480
Whittaker, Charles E.
Biography - 860
Congressional witnesses - 161
Individual Rights
Due process - 549
Political association - 504, 506, 507, 510, 514
Voting rights - 484, 491, 492
Origins and development of Court - 51, 52
Williams, George H. - 28, 656, 714
Wilmington (Del.) Morning News - 718
Wilson Act of 1890 - 325
Wilson, James
Biography - 783, 789, 796, 797
Origins and development of Court - 8-10
Wilson, Woodrow
Black support - 588
Congressional investigations - 157
Minimum wages - 89
Presidential Powers
Executive powers - 211, 212

Foreign affairs - 205
Pardons - 224
Power to sign bills - 223
Wartime - 185, 190, 193, 195
Presidential pressure on the Court - 684, 685
Supreme Court appointments - 37, 42, 746, 788
Wiretapping - 39, 53, 245, 547, 550-553, 887, 901 *(See also Fourth Amendment)*
Witnesses

Congressional - 160-164
Defendant's right to subpoena, confront - 534-536
Wolcott, Alexander - 14, 656, 657, 707, 786
Women
Juries, on - 534, 637, 898, 905
Sex discrimination - 349, 350, 532, 534, 631-639 *(See also Equal Rights)*
Voting rights *(See Political Rights)*
Woodbury, Levi
Biography - 786, 787, 790, 815, 816

Origins and development of Court - 20, 21
Woods, William B.
Biography - 787, 826
Origins and development of Court - 29, 30
Presidential pressure on the Court - 686
Woodward, George W. - 20, 656, 657, 686, 784
Writs *(See individual writs)*

Case Index

A

Abby Dodge, The, 223 U.S. 167 (1912) - 100

Abel v. United States, 362 U.S. 217 (1960) - 146

Ableman v. Booth, 21 How. 506 (1859) - 22, 273, 360, 362, 377, 710, 876

Abrams v. United States, 250 U.S. 616 (1919) - 390, 398

Abrams v. Van Schaick, 293 U.S. 188 (1934) - 288

Adair v. United States, 208 U.S. 162 (1908) - 88, 94, 121, 883, 927

Adams v. Williams, 407 U.S. 144 (1972) - 545

Adamson v. California, 332 U.S. 46 (1947) - 528, 557, 558

Adderly v. Florida, 385 U.S. 39 (1966) - 415

Addy v. United States, 264 U.S. 239 (1947) - 195

Adkins v. Children's Hospital, 261 U.S. 525 (1923) - 39, 40, 44, 327, 527, 886, 889, 928

Adler v. Board of Education, City of New York, 342 U.S. 485 (1952) - 512-514

Afroyim v. Rusk, 387 U.S. 253 (1967) -146, 930

Agnello v. United States, 269 U.S. 20 (1925) - 544

Alabama v. Texas, 347 U.S. 272 (1954) - 134, 894

Alabama Power Co. v. Ickes, 302 U.S. 464 (1938) - 292

Albemarle Paper Co. v. Moody, 422 U.S. 405 (1975) - 620, 906

Alberts v. California, 354 U.S. 476 (1957) - 428, 897

Albertson v. Subversive Activities Control Board, 382 U.S. 70 (1965) - 53, 508, 555, 900, 930

Alderman v. United States, 394 U.S. 166 (1969) - 552

Alexander v. Holmes Board of Education, 396 U.S. 19 (1969) - 600

Alicia, The, 7 Wall. 571 (1869) - 926

Allgeyer v. Louisiana, 166 U.S. 578 (1897) - 33, 343, 526, 881

Almeida-Sanchez v. United States, 413 U.S. 266 (1973) - 546

Almy v. California, 24 How. 170 (1861) - 328

Amalgamated Food Employees Union Local 590 v. Logan Valley Plaza, 391 U.S. 308 (1968) - 417

American Communications Assn. v. Douds, 339 U.S. 382 (1950) - 49, 77, 510, 894

American Federation of Labor v. Swing, 312 U.S. 321 (1941) - 417

American Party of Texas v. White, 415 U.S. 767 (1974) - 487

American Steel Foundries v. Tri-City Central Trades Council, 257 U.S. 184 (1921) - 38, 276, 980

Anastaplo, In re, 348 U.S. 946 (1955) - 515

Anderson v. Dunn, 6 Wheat. 204 (1821) - 158

Andresen v. Maryland, 427 U.S 463 (1976) - 543

Apodaca v. Oregon, 406 U.S. 404 (1972) - 531, 904

Aptheker v. Secretary of State, 378 U.S. 500 (1964) - 507, 514, 899, 900, 930

Argersinger v. Hamlin, 407 U.S. 25 (1972) - 568, 904

Ashton v. Cameron County District, 298 U.S. 513 (1936) - 242, 355, 677, 929

Ashton v. Kentucky, 384 U.S. 195 (1966) - 435

Ashwander v. Tennessee Valley Authority, 297 U.S. 288 (1936) - 86, 140, 287, 288, 888

Associated Enterprises Inc. v. Toltec Watershed Improvement District, 410 U.S. 743 (1973) - 496

Associated Press v. National Labor Relations Board, 301 U.S. 186 (1937) - 426

Associated Press v. United States, 326 U.S. 1 (1945) - 426

Associated Press v. Walker, 388 U.S. 131 (1967) - 436

Austin v. Tennessee, 179 U.S. 343 (1900) - 527

Austin Independent School Board v. United States, 429 U.S. 190 (1976) - 598, 620

Avent v. North Carolina, 373 U.S. 375 (1963) - 611

Avery v. Georgia, 345 U.S. 559 (1952) - 532

Avery v. Midland County, 390 U.S. 474 (1968) - 496

B

Bailey v. Drexel Furniture Co., 259 U.S. 20 (1922) - 38, 72, 94, 113, 114, 115, 121, 355, 675, 885, 928

Baird v. State Bar of Arizona, 401 U.S. 23 (1971) - 515

Baker v. Carr, 369 U.S. 186 (1962) - 52, 72, 73, 200, 292, 293, 348, 356, 381, 489-492, 494, 495, 675, 898

Bakery and Pastry Drivers v. Wohl, 315 U.S. 769 (1942) - 418

Bakke Case. See University of California Regents v. Bakke.

Baldwin v. Franks, 120 U.S. 678 (1887) - 926

Baldwin v. New York, 399 U.S. 66 (1970) - 531

Ballew v. Georgia, 435 U.S. 223 (1978) - 908

Bank of Augusta v. Earle, 13 Pet. 519 (1839) - 324

Bank of the United States v. Deveaux, 5 Cr. 61 (1809) - 872, 875

Barenblatt v. United States, 360 U.S. 109 (1959) - 161, 162, 897

Barker v. Wingo, 407 U.S. 514 (1972) - 535

Barron v. Baltimore, 7 Pet. 243 (1833) - 17, 30, 141, 374, 375, 378, 383, 388, 524, 525, 674, 874

Barrows v. Jackson, 346 U.S. 249 (1953) - 614, 615

Barry v. United States ex rel. Cunningham, 279 U.S. 597 (1929) - 164, 173

Bates v. City of Little Rock, 361 U.S. 516 (1960) - 403

Bauman v. Ross, 168 U.S. 548 (1897) - 141

Beauharnais v. Illinois, 343 U.S. 250 (1952) - 435

Beer v. United States, 425 U.S. 131 (1976) - 487

Beilan v. Board of Public Education, School District of Philadelphia, 357 U.S. 399 (1958) - 514

Bell v. Ohio, 438 U.S. 637 (1978) - 579

Bell v. School, City of Gary, 377 U.S. 924 (1964) - 598

Benton v. Maryland, 395 U.S. 784 (1969) - 346, 571, 572, 902

Berea College v. Kentucky, 211 U.S. 45 (1908) - 288

Berman v. Parker, 348 U.S. 26 (1954) - 141

Betts v. Brady, 316 U.S. 455 (1942) - 48, 52, 345, 566, 892, 899

Bibb v. Navajo Freight Lines, 359 U.S. 520 (1959) - 317
Biddle v. Perovich, 274 U.S. 480 (1927) - 227
Bigelow v. Virginia, 421 U.S. 809 (1975) - 421, 906
Bitzer v. Matthews, 427 U.S. 445 (1976) - 905
Bivens v. Six Unknown Named Agents, 403 U.S. 388 (1971) - 549
Blackledge v. Allison, 431 U.S. 63 (1977) - 563
Blount v. Rizzi, 400 U.S. 410 (1971) - 929
Board of Education of Central School District No. 1 v. Allen, 392 U.S. 236 (1968) - 467
Board of Education of Netcong, N.J. v. State Board of Education, 401 U.S. 1013 (1971) - 465
Board of Trade of Chicago v. Olsen, 262 U.S. 1 (1923) - 92, 115
Board of Trustees v. United States, 289 U.S. 48 (1933) - 100
Bolling v. Sharpe, 347 U.S. 497 (1954) - 585, 593, 896
Boom Co. v. Patterson, 98 U.S. 403 (1879) - 141
Booth v. United States, 291 U.S. 339 (1934) - 929
Bordenkircher v. Hayes, 434 U.S. 357 (1978) - 563
Boyce v. Anderson, 2 Pet. 151 (1829) - 17, 377
Boyce Motor Lines Inc. v. United States, 342 U.S. 337 (1952) - 533
Boyd v. United States, 116 U.S. 616 (1886) - 30, 31, 541, 543, 879, 926
Boynton v. Virginia, 364 U.S. 464 (1960) - 610, 611
Braden v. United States, 365 U.S. 431 (1961) - 162
Bradley v. Fisher, 13 Wall. 335 (1872) - 290, 878
Bradley v. School Board of City of Richmond, 382 U.S. 103 (1965) - 599
Bradwell v. State of Illinois, 16 Wall. 131 (1873) - 631, 878
Brady v. United States, 397 U.S. 742 (1970) - 562
Branch v. Texas, 408 U.S. 238 (1972) - 576, 904
Brandenburg v. Ohio, 395 U.S. 444 (1969) - 406, 513
Branzburg v. Hayes, 408 U.S. 665 (1972) - 445, 904
Braunfeld v. Brown, 366 U.S. 599 (1961) - 459, 460
Breed v. Jones, 421 U.S. 519 (1975) - 531
Breedlove v. Suttles, 302 U.S. 277 (1937) - 483, 643, 890
Breithaupt v. Abrams, 352 U.S. 432 (1957) - 549, 552
Briscoe v. Bank of Kentucky, 11 Pet. 257 (1837) - 17-19, 333, 874
Briscoe v. Bell, 432 U.S. 404 (1977) - 487
Bridges v. California, 314 U.S. 252 (1941) - 440
Briggs v. Elliott, 347 U.S. 483 (1954) - 592, 593
Brinegar v. United States, 338 U.S. 161 (1949) - 547
Broadrick v. Oklahoma State Personnel Board, 413 U.S. 548 (1973) - 517
Brotherhood of Trainmen v. Howard, 343 U.S. 768 (1951) - 618
Brown v. Board of Education of Topeka, 347 U.S. 483 (1954); 349 U.S. 294 (1955) - 50, 52, 349, 382, 589, 592, 594-600, 602, 684, 699, 700, 747, 750, 751, 881, 896, 909
Brown v. Houston, 114 U.S. 622 (1885) - 330
Brown v. Louisiana, 383 U.S. 132 (1966) - 415
Brown v. Maryland, 12 Wheat. 419 (1827) - 16, 84, 100, 325, 328-330, 874
Brown v. Mississippi, 297 U.S. 278 (1935) - 43, 559, 889
Brown v. South Carolina Board of Education, 393 U.S. 222 (1968) - 602
Brown v. Walker, 162 U.S. 591 (1896) - 556
Brushaber v. Union Pacific Railroad Co., 240 U.S. 1 (1916) - 37, 884
Bryant v. Zimmerman, 278 U.S. 63 (1928) - 403
Buchanan v. Warley, 245 U.S. 60 (1917) - 613, 884
Buck v. Bell, 274 U.S. 200 (1927) - 40, 887
Buckley v. Valeo, 424 U.S. 1 (1976) - 56, 172, 173, 420, 487, 585, 906, 931

Bullock v. Carter, 405 U.S. 135 (1972) - 487, 643
Bunting v. Oregon, 243 U.S. 426 (1917) - 37, 326, 327, 527, 884
Burch v. Louisiana (1979) - 531, 909
Burdeau v. McDowell, 256 U.S. 465 (1921) - 540
Burdick v. United States, 236 U.S. 79 (1915) - 224
Burns v. Fortson, 410 U.S. 686 (1973) - 485
Burns Baking Co. v. Bryan, 264 U.S. 504 (1924) - 269, 527
Burroughs and Cannon v. United States, 290 U.S. 534 (1934) - 172
Burrus, In re, 403 U.S. 528 (1971) - 531, 903
Burton v. United States, 196 U.S. 283 (1905) - 288
Burton v. Wilmington Parking Authority, 365 U.S. 715 (1961) - 611
Butchers' Benevolent Assn. of New Orleans v. Crescent City Livestock Landing and Slaughterhouse Co. See Slaughterhouse Cases.
Butenko v. United States, 394 U.S. 166 (1969) - 552
Butler v. Boston & S. Steamship Co., 131 U.S. 527 (1889) - 86
Buttfield v. Stranahan, 192 U.S. 470 (1904) - 100
Butz v. Economou, 438 U.S. 478 (1978) - 261, 908

C

Caban v. Mohammed (1979) - 634
Calder v. Bull, 3 Dall. 386 (1798) - 77, 872
Califano v. Goldfarb, 430 U.S. 199 (1977) - 633, 929
Califano v. Westcott (1979) - 931
California v. Southern Pacific Co., 157 U.S. 229 (1895) - 881
California v. Usery, 426 U.S. 833 (1976) - 907
Callan v. Wilson, 127 U.S. 540 (1888) - 927
Camara v. Municipal Court, 387 U.S. 523 (1967) - 550
Caminetti v. United States, 242 U.S. 470 (1917) - 95
Campagnie Francaise De Navigation a Vapeur v. Louisiana State Board of Health, 186 U.S. 380 (1902) - 100
Cantwell v. Connecticut, 310 U.S. 296 (1940) - 389, 408, 414, 419, 453, 454, 891
Cantrell v. Forest City Publishing Co., 419 U.S. 245 (1974) - 437
Carlson v. Landon, 342 U.S. 524 (1952) - 146, 577, 895
Carpenters and Joiners Union v. Ritter's Cafe, 315 U.S. 722 (1942) - 418
Carrington v. Rash, 380 U.S. 89 (1965) - 485
Carroll v. United States, 267 U.S. 133 (1925) - 39, 547, 886
Carter v. Carter Coal Co., 298 U.S. 238 (1936) - 43, 67, 72, 98, 99, 101, 113, 115, 242, 291, 355, 677, 889, 929
Central Union Trust v. Garvan, 254 U.S. 554 (1921) - 195
Chae Chan Ping v. United States, 131 U.S. 581 (1889) - 146, 880
Chambers v. Florida, 309 U.S. 227 (1940) - 559
Champion v. Ames, 188 U.S. 321 (1903) - 35, 94, 95, 882
Chaplinsky v. New Hampshire, 315 U.S. 568 (1942) - 407, 429, 433, 891
Chapman, In re, 167 U.S. 661 (1897) - 159
Chapman v. Meier, 420 U.S. 1 (1975) - 497
Charles River Bridge v. Warren Bridge, 11 Pet. 420 (1837) - 17, 18, 313, 314, 323, 875
Cheff v. Schnackenberg, 384 U.S. 373 (1966) - 282
Cherokee Nation v. Georgia, 5 Pet. 1 (1831) - 17, 238, 307, 666, 709
Chicago Board of Trade v. United States, 246 U.S. 231 (1918) - 93
Chicago, Burlington & Quincy Railroad Co. v. City of Chicago, 167 U.S. 226 (1897). See Granger Cases.
Chicago & Grand Trunk Railway v. Wellman, 144 U.S. 339 (1892) - 288

Chicago, Milwaukee & St. Paul Railway Co. v. Ackley, 94 U.S. 179 (1877). *See* Granger Cases.

Chicago, Milwaukee & St. Paul Railway Co. v. Minnesota, 135 U.S. 418 (1890) - 31, 526, 880

Chimel v. California, 395 U.S. 752 (1969) - 546, 902

Child Labor Tax Case. *See* Bailey v. Drexel Furniture Co.

Chinese Exclusion Case. *See* Chae Chan Ping v. United States.

Chisholm v. Georgia, 2 Dall. 419 (1793) - 111, 259, 303-305, 354, 673, 697, 698, 871, 872

Choate v. Trapp, 224 U.S. 665 (1912) - 927

Chief of Capitol Police v. Jeanette Rankin Brigade, 409 U.S. 971 (1972) - 929

Christoffel v. United States, 338 U.S. 84 (1949) - 175

Chy Lung v. Freeman, 92 U.S. 275 (1876) - 319, 878

Cipriano v. City of Houma, 395 U.S. 701 (1969) - 485

City of Greenwood, Miss. v. Peacock, 384 U.S. 808 (1966) - 259

City of Lafayette, La. v. Louisiana Power & Light Co., 435 U.S. 389 (1978) - 361

City of Virginia Beach v. Howell, 410 U.S. 315 (1973) - 904

Civil Rights Cases, 109 U.S. 3 (1883) - 30, 103, 120, 338-341, 348, 355, 608, 609, 612, 613, 700, 710, 713, 879, 927

Civil Service Commission v. Letter Carriers, 413 U.S. 548 (1973) - 517, 518

Clark v. Uebersee-Finanz-Korp., 332 U.S. 480 (1947) - 195

Clark Distilling Co. v. Western Maryland Railway, 242 U.S. 311 - 884

Clarke v. Deckebach, 274 U.S. 392 (1927) - 626, 627

Cleveland Board of Education v. LeFleur, 414 U.S. 632 (1974) - 635

Cochran v. Louisiana Board of Education, 281 U.S. 370 (1930) - 466

Coffin v. Coffin, 4 Mass. 1 (1808) - 169

Cohen v. California, 403 U.S. 15 (1971) - 407, 429

Cohen v. Chesterfield County School Board, 414 U.S. 632 (1974) - 635

Cohens v. Virginia, 6 Wheat. 264 (1821) - 15, 265, 266, 307, 360, 666, 873

Coker v. Georgia, 433 U.S. 583 (1977) - 579, 908

Cole v. Young, 351 U.S. 536 (1956) - 669, 671

Colegrove v. Green, 328 U.S. 549 (1946) - 49, 52, 347, 483, 489-491, 893, 898

Coleman v. MacLennan, 98 P. 281 (1908) - 434

Coleman v. Miller, 307 U.S. 433 (1939) - 150, 151, 890

Collector v. Day, 11 Wall. 113 (1871) - 355, 357, 875, 890

Colonnade Catering Corp. v. United States, 397 U.S. 72 (1970) - 551

Colorado Anti-Discrimination Commission v. Continental Airlines, 372 U.S. 714 (1963) - 619

Columbia Broadcasting System Inc. v. Democratic National Committee, 412 U.S. 94 (1973) - 446

Columbus Board of Education v. Penick (1979) - 909

Columbus & Greenville Railway v. Miller, 283 U.S. 96 (1931) - 288

Commissioner of Internal Revenue v. Sullivan, 356 U.S. 27 (1958) - 114

Commissioners of Immigration v. The North German Lloyd, 92 U.S. 259 (1876) - 878

Committee for Public Education and Religious Liberty v. Nyquist, 413 U.S. 756 (1973) - 468

Communist Party v. Subversive Activities Control Board, 367 U.S. 87 (1961) - 53, 506, 898

Communist Party of Indiana v. Whitcomb, 414 U.S. 441 (1974) - 516

Complete Auto Transit Inc. v. Brady, 430 U.S. 274 (1977) - 332, 908

Connally v. General Construction Co., 269 U.S. 385 (1926) - 533

Connor v. Finch, 431 U.S. 407 (1977) - 497

Consolidated Edison v. National Labor Relations Board, 305 U.S. 197 (1938) - 101

Cooke v. United States, 267 U.S. 517 (1925) - 284

Cooley v. Board of Wardens of the Port of Philadelphia, 12 How. 299 (1852) - 21, 81, 84, 94, 103, 317, 318, 321, 876

Coolidge v. New Hampshire, 403 U.S. 443 (1971) - 540, 547

Cooper v. Aaron, 358 U.S. 1 (1958) - 50, 52, 599, 733, 897

Corfield v. Coryell, 6 Fed. Cases 3230 (1823) - 366

Corrigan v. Buckley, 271 U.S. 323 (1926) - 40, 613, 886

Cornell v. Coyne, 192 U.S. 418 (1904) - 77

Corning Glass Works v. Brennan, 417 U.S. 188 (1974) - 637

Cotting v. Godard, 183 U.S. 79 (1901) - 527

Counselman v. Hitchcock, 143 U.S. 547 (1892) - 31, 32, 556, 880

Cousins v. Wigoda, 419 U.S. 477 (1975) - 518

Cox v. New Hampshire, 312 U.S. 569 (1941) - 408, 409, 413, 454, 891

Cox Broadcasting Corp. v. Cohn, 420 U.S. 469 (1975) - 437, 439

Coyle v. Smith, 221 U.S. 559 (1911) - 133, 355, 883, 927

Craig v. Boren, 429 U.S. 190 (1975) - 635, 907

Craig v. Harney, 331 U.S. 367 (1947) - 441

Craig v. Missouri, 4 Pet. 410 (1830) - 17, 19, 333, 666, 874

Cramer v. United States, 325 U.S. 1 (1945) - 398

Cramp v. Board of Public Instruction, Orange County, Fla., 368 U.S. 278 (1961) - 514

Cross v. Harrison, 16 How. 165 (1853) - 139

Crowell v. Benson, 285 U.S. 22 (1932) - 288

Cummings v. Missouri, 4 Wall. 277 (1867) - 25, 76, 338, 877, 980

Cumming v. Richmond (Ga.) County Board of Education, 175 U.S. 528 (1899) - 591

Cupp v. Murphy, 412 U.S. 291 (1973) - 552

Curtis Publishing Co. v. Butts, 388 U.S. 131 (1967) - 436, 438

Curtiss, Ex parte, 106 U.S. 371 (1882) - 211

D

Dalia v. United States (1979) - 553

Danbury Hatters Case, The (Loewe v. Lawlor), 208 U.S. 274 - 35, 88, 93, 94, 883

Dandridge v. Williams, 397 U.S. 471 (1970) - 643

Daniel v. Paul, 395 U.S. 298 (1969) - 105, 613

Daniel Ball, The, 10 Wall. 557 (1871) - 94

Dartmouth College v. Woodward, 4 Wheat. 519 (1819) - 14, 309, 311, 312, 708, 872

Davidson v. City of New Orleans, 96 U.S. 97 (1878) - 141

Davis v. Newton Coal Co., 267 U.S. 292 (1925) - 195

Davis v. Beason, 134 U.S. 333 (1890) - 452, 453

Davis v. Board of School Commissioners of Mobile County, Ala., 402 U.S. 33 (1971) - 602

Davis v. County School Board of Prince Edward County, Va., 347 U.S. 483 (1954) - 592

Davis v. Passman (1979) - 909

Day-Brite Lighting Inc. v. Missouri, 342 U.S. 421 (1952) - 527

Dayton (Ohio) Board of Education v. Brinkman, 433 U.S. 406 (1977) - 598, 606; (1979), 909

Debs v. United States, 249 U.S. 211 (1919) - 397

Debs, In re, 159 U.S. 564 (1895) - 32, 33, 219, 276, 284, 881

DeFunis v. Odegaard, 416 U.S. 312 (1974) - 605

DeJonge v. Oregon, 299 U.S. 353 (1937) - 389, 402, 403, 405, 413, 889

DeKalb County Community School District v. DeSpain, 390 U.S. 906 (1968) - 465

DeLima v. Bidwell (Insular Cases), 182 U.S. 1 (1901) - 139, 882

Delaware v. Prouse (1979) - 547

Dennis v. United States, 341 U.S. 494 (1951) - 49, 51, 387, 392, 502-505, 895

Dept. of Agriculture v. Moreno, 413 U.S. 528 (1973) - 931

Dept. of Agriculture v. Murry, 413 U.S. 508 (1973) - 931

Deutsch v. United States, 367 U.S. 456 (1961) - 162

Dillon v. Gloss, 256 U.S. 368 (1921) - 150, 885

Dobbins v. Erie County, 16 Pet. 435 (1842) - 357, 875, 890

Dodge v. Woolsey, 18 How. 331 (1856) - 311, 876

Doe v. Bolton, 410 U.S. 113 (1973) - 55, 289, 343, 904

Doe v. McMillen, 412 U.S. 306 (1973) - 168

Dombrowski v. Eastland, 387 U.S. 82 (1967) - 168, 169

Dombrowski v. Pfister, 380 U.S. 479 (1965) - 54, 277, 278, 362, 513, 900

Dooley v. United States, 182 U.S. 222 (1901) - 195

Dorchy v. Kansas, 264 U.S. 286 (1924) - 113

Dorr v. United States, 195 U.S. 139 (1904) - 141, 882

Dothard v. Rawlinson, 433 U.S. 321 (1977) - 637

Douglas v. California, 372 U.S. 353 (1963) - 642

Douglas v. City of Jeannette, 319 U.S. 158 (1943) - 455

Douglas v. Seacoast Products Inc., 431 U.S. 265 (1977) - 85

Downes v. Bidwell (Insular Cases), 182 U.S. 244 (1901) - 140, 141, 882

Dred Scott Case. See Scott v. Sandford.

Duncan v. Louisiana, 391 U.S. 146 (1968) - 345, 530, 532, 901

Dunn v. Blumstein, 405 U.S. 330 (1972) - 485

Duplex Printing Press Co. v. Deering, 254 U.S. 443 (1921) - 38, 93, 94, 276, 885

E

Eakin v. Raub, 12 Sergeant and Rawle 330 Pa. (1825) - 72

Eastland v. United States Servicemen's Fund, 421 U.S. 491 (1975) - 163

Edelman v. Jordan, 415 U.S. 651 (1974) - 905

Edwards v. California, 314 U.S. 161 (1941) - 104, 891

Edwards v. South Carolina, 372 U.S. 229 (1963) - 415, 898

Edwards v. United States, 236 U.S. 482 (1932) - 223

Eisenstadt v. Baird, 405 U.S. 438 (1972) - 645

Eisner v. Macomber, 252 U.S. 189 (1920) - 112, 928

Elfbrandt v. Russell, 384 U.S. 17 (1966) - 514, 900

Elkins v. United States, 364 U.S. 206 (1960) - 549, 897

El Paso & N.E. Railway v. Gutierrez, 215 U.S. 87 (1909) - 927

Elrod v. Burns, 427 U.S. 347 (1976) - 518, 907

Emblem v. Lincoln Land Co., 184 U.S. 660 (1902) - 140

Employers' Liability Cases, 207 U.S. 463 (1908) - 94, 355, 927; 223 U.S. 1 (1912) - 94, 355

Emspak v. United States, 349 U.S. 190 (1955) - 163

Engel v. Vitale, 370 U.S. 421 (1962) - 54, 464, 898

Epperson v. Arkansas, 393 U.S. 97 (1968) - 463

Erie Railroad Co. v. Tompkins, 304 U.S. 64 (1938) - 262

Escobedo v. Illinois, 378 U.S. 478 (1964) - 53, 346, 560, 561, 567, 568, 900

Esteben v. Louisiana. See Slaughterhouse Cases.

Euclid v. Ambler Realty Co., 272 U.S. 365 (1926) - 40, 359, 527, 886

Evans v. Abney, 396 U.S. 435 (1970) - 610

Evans v. Cornman, 398 U.S. 419 (1970) - 485

Evans v. Gore, 253 U.S. 245 (1920) - 115, 290, 928

Evans v. Newton, 382 U.S. 296 (1966) - 610

Everson v. Board of Education of Ewing Township, 330 U.S. 1 (1947) - 389, 466, 467, 893

F

Fairbanks v. United States, 181 U.S. 283 (1901) - 77, 927

Fairchild v. Hughes, 258 U.S. 127 (1922) - 288

Fairfax's Devisee v. Hunter's Lessee, 7 Cr. 602 (1813) - 305

Fairfax-Brewster School v. Gonzalez, 427 U.S. 161 (1970) - 603, 906

Faretta v. California, 422 U.S. 806 (1975) - 568

Fay v. New York, 332 U.S. 261 (1947) - 532, 894

Fay v. Noia, 372 U.S. 391 (1963) - 274, 899

Federal Communications Commission v. Pacifica Foundation, 438 U.S. 726 (1978) - 407, 447

Federal Communications Commission v. National Citizens Committee for Broadcasting, 436 U.S. 775 (1978) - 447

Federal Power Commission v. Hope Natural Gas, 320 U.S. 591 (1944) - 527

Feiner v. New York, 340 U.S. 315 (1951) - 410, 895

Feres v. United States, 340 U.S. 136 (1950) - 261

Field v. Clark, 144 U.S. 649 (1892) - 100, 216

First Legal Tender Case. See Hepburn v. Griswold.

First Scottsboro Case. See Powell v. Alabama.

First National Bank of Boston v. Bellotti, 435 U.S. 765 (1978) - 420, 908

Fiske v. Kansas, 274 U.S. 380 (1927) - 404, 405

Fitzpatrick v. Bitzer, 427 U.S. 445 (1976) - 152, 620, 638, 905

Flast v. Cohen, 392 U.S. 83 (1968) - 54, 289, 291, 292, 469, 901, 902

Fleming v. Page, 9 How. 603 (1850) - 195

Fletcher v. Peck, 6 Cr. 87 (1810) - 13, 14, 291, 309-311, 698, 872

Fletcher v. Rhode Island (The License Cases), 5 How. 504 (1847) - 875

Florida ex rel. Hawkins v. Board of Control, 350 U.S. 413 (1956) - 597

Ford v. United States, 264 U.S. 239 (1947) - 195

Fortson v. Dorsey, 379 U.S. 433 (1965) - 495

Foster v. Neilson, 2 Pet. 253 (1829) - 20, 67, 874

Fowler v. Rhode Island, 345 U.S. 67 (1953) - 453, 456

Frank v. Mangum, 237 U.S. 309 (1915) - 272, 529, 884

Frank v. Maryland, 359 U.S. 360 (1959) - 550

Franks v. Bowman Transportation Co. Inc., 424 U.S. 747 (1976) - 621

Franks v. Delaware, 438 U.S. 155 (1978) - 540

Freedman v. Maryland, 380 U.S. 51 (1965) - 430

Frohwerk v. United States, 249 U.S. 204 (1919) - 397, 398

Frontiero v. Richardson, 411 U.S. 677 (1973) - 633, 930

Frothingham v. Mellon, 262 U.S. 447 (1923) - 291, 886, 902

Fuentes v. Shevin, 407 U.S. 67 (1972) - 533

Furman v. Georgia, 408 U.S. 238 (1972) - 576, 578, 579, 904

G

Gaffney v. Cummings, 412 U.S. 736 (1973) - 496, 497

Galvan v. Press, 347 U.S. 522 (1954) - 503

Gannett Co. v. DePasquale (1979) - 536, 909

Garland, Ex parte, 4 Wall. 333 (1867) - 25, 76, 77, 120, 224-226, 283, 877, 926

Garner v. Board of Public Works of the City of Los Angeles, 341 U.S. 716 (1951) - 512-514, 516, 895

Garner v. Louisiana, 368 U.S. 158 (1961) - 411

Garnett, In re, 142 U.S. 1 (1891) - 86

Garrison v. Louisiana, 379 U.S. 64 (1964) - 435

Gastelum-Quinones v. Kennedy, 374 U.S. 469 (1963) - 503

Gaston County v. United States, 395 U.S. 285 (1969) - 481, 486, 902

Gault, In re, 387 U.S. 1 (1967) - 531, 901
Gebhart v. Belton, 347 U.S. 483 (1954) - 593
Geduldig v. Aiello, 417 U.S. 484 (1974) - 635, 905
General Electric Co. v. Gilbert, 429 U.S. 126 (1976) - 636
Georgia v. Brailsford, 2 Dall. 402 (1792) - 9, 741
Georgia v. Rachel, 384 U.S. 780 (1880) - 259
Geofrey v. Riggs, 133 U.S. 258 (1890) - 880
Georgia v. Tennessee Copper Co., 206 U.S. 230 (1907) - 883
Gerende v. Board of Supervisors of Elections, 341 U.S. 56 (1951) - 512, 514, 516
German Alliance Insurance Co. v. Lewis, 233 U.S. 389 (1914) - 527
Gertz v. Robert Welch Inc., 418 U.S. 323 (1974) - 438, 439
Gibbons v. Ogden, 9 Wheat. 1 (1824) - 15, 16, 66, 81, 83-85, 84, 100, 315, 316, 322-324, 328, 330, 709, 873, 881
Giboney v. Empire Storage and Ice Co., 336 U.S. 490 (1949) - 418
Gibson v. Chouteau, 13 Wall. 92 (1872) - 140
Gibson v. Florida Legislative Investigating Committee, 372 U.S. 539 (1963) - 403
Gideon v. Wainwright, 372 U.S. 335 (1963) - 52, 54, 55, 345, 346, 560, 567, 568, 642, 899
Gilbert v. California, 388 U.S. 263 (1967) - 552, 568
Gilbert v. Minnesota, 254 U.S. 325 (1920) - 362, 388
Gillette v. United States, 401 U.S. 437 (1971) - 457
Gilmore v. City of Montgomery, 417 U.S. 556 (1974) - 603
Ginzburg v. United States, 383 U.S. 463 (1966) - 429
Girouard v. United States, 328 U.S. 61 (1946) - 48, 143, 461, 893
Gitlow v. New York, 268 U.S. 652 (1925) - 39, 45, 344, 378, 388, 401, 405, 500, 886
Glasser v. United States, 315 U.S. 60 (1942) - 569
Glona v. American Guarantee and Liability Insurance Co., 391 U.S. 73 (1968) - 634
Gober v. City of Birmingham, 373 U.S. 374 (1963) - 611
Goesaert v. Cleary, 335 U.S. 464 (1948) - 631
Gold Clause Cases, 294 U.S. 240 (1935) - 43, 117, 122, 888
Goldberg v. Kelly, 397 U.S. 254 (1970) - 533
Goldblatt v. Town of Hempstead, 369 U.S. 590 (1962) - 141
Goldfarb v. Virginia State Bar, 421 U.S. 773 (1975) - 906
Goldman v. United States, 316 U.S. 130 (1942) - 552
Goldstein v. United States, 316 U.S. 114 (1942) - 552
Gomez v. Prez, 409 U.S. 535 (1973) - 634
Gomillion v. Lightfoot, 364 U.S. 339 (1960) - 52, 483, 487, 490, 898
Gompers v. Buck's Stove & Range Co., 221 U.S. 418 (1911) - 276, 281, 883
Gong Lum v. Rice, 275 U.S. 78 (1927) - 591
Gonzalez v. Archbishop, 280 U.S. 1 (1929) - 462
Gooding v. Wilson, 405 U.S. 518 (1972) - 407
Gordon v. United States, 2 Wall. 561 (1865) - 926
Goss v. Board of Education of Knoxville, 373 U.S. 683 (1963) - 599
Goss v. Lopez, 419 U.S. 565 (1975) - 533
Gouled v. United States, 255 U.S. 298 (1921) - 542, 543
Graham v. Richardson, 403 U.S. 365 (1971) - 627, 903
Granger Cases, The, 94 U.S. 113 (1877) - 28-31, 33, 42, 141, 318, 319, 325, 526, 878, 881, 888
Gravel v. United States, 408 U.S. 606 (1972) - 168
Graves v. New York ex rel. O'Keefe, 306 U.S. 466 (1939) - 357, 890
Gray v. Sanders, 372 U.S. 368 (1963) - 52, 54, 348, 492, 899
Great Falls Manufacturing Co. v. Attorney General, 125 U.S. 581 (1888) - 288
Green v. County School Board of New Kent County, Va., 391 U.S. 430 (1968) - 53, 599, 901

Green v. New York City Board of Elections, 389 U.S. 1048 (1968) - 485
Green v. United States, 355 U.S. 184 (1957) - 571
Greene v. McElroy, 360 U.S. 474 (1959) - 510
Gregg v. Georgia, 428 U.S. 153 (1976) - 578, 579, 907
Gregory v. City of Chicago, 394 U.S. 111 (1969) - 416
Griffin v. California, 380 U.S. 609 (1965) - 53, 558, 900
Griffin v. County School Board of Prince Edward County, Va., 377 U.S. 218 (1964) - 53, 599, 899
Griffin v. Illinois, 351 U.S. 12 (1956) - 51, 641
Griffiths, In re, 413 U.S. 717 (1973) - 283
Grisham v. Hagan, 361 U.S. 278 (1960) - 929
Griggs v. Duke Power Co., 401 U.S. 424 (1971) - 619, 903
Griswold v. Connecticut, 381 U.S. 479 (1965) - 53, 343, 527, 644, 900
Grosjean v. American Press Co., 297 U.S. 233 (1936) - 426, 888
Grosso v. United States, 390 U.S. 62 (1968) - 930
Groves v. Slaughter, 15 Pet. 449 (1841) - 19, 324, 377
Grovey v. Townsend, 295 U.S. 45 (1935) - 41, 42, 347, 481, 482, 888
Guinn v. United States, 238 U.S. 347 (1915) - 37, 480, 884, 890
Gustafson v. Florida, 414 U.S. 260 (1973) - 547

H

Hadacheck v. Los Angeles, 239 U.S. 394 (1915) - 884
Hadley v. Junior College District of Metropolitan Kansas City, Mo., 397 U.S. 50 (1970) - 496
Hague v. Committee for Industrial Organization (CIO), 307 U.S. 496 (1939) - 46, 407, 408, 890
Hainsworth v. White, 415 U.S. 767 (1974) - 487
Hall v. DeCuir, 95 U.S. 485 (1878) - 29, 103, 321, 608, 878
Hamilton v. Alabama, 368 U.S. 52 (1961) - 568
Hamilton v. Dillon, 21 Wall. 73 (1875) - 195
Hammer v. Dagenhart, 247 U.S. 251 (1918) - 37, 45, 72, 82, 94, 96, 97, 101, 102, 114, 121, 321, 322, 355, 675, 885, 928
Hampton v. Mow Sun Wong, 426 U.S. 88 (1976) - 585, 628
Hampton, J.W. Jr. & Co. v. United States, 276 U.S. 394 (1928) - 41, 100, 887
Hannegan v. Esquire, 327 U.S. 146 (1946) - 431
Harman v. Forssenius, 380 U.S. 528 (1965) - 483, 900
Harper v. Virginia State Board of Elections, 383 U.S. 663 (1966) - 483, 643, 900
Harris v. New York, 401 U.S. 222 (1971) - 55, 562, 564, 903
Harris v. United States, 382 U.S. 146 (1947) - 281, 544, 546
Hartzel v. United States, 322 U.S. 680 (1944) - 400
Harisiades v. Shaughnessy, 342 U.S. 580 (1952) - 503
Haupt v. United States, 330 U.S. 631 (1947) - 398
Haver v. Yaker, 9 Wall. 32 (1869) - 195
Haynes v. United States, 390 U.S. 85 (1968) - 930
Head Money Cases, 112 U.S. 580 (1884) - 112, 131, 202, 879
Healy v. James, 408 U.S. 170 (1972) - 517
Heart of Atlanta Motel v. United States, 379 U.S. 241 (1964) - 53, 94, 104, 611, 899
Heiner v. Donnan, 285 U.S. 312 (1932) - 928
Helvering v. Davis, 301 U.S. 619 (1937) - 44, 94, 118, 121, 890
Helvering v. Gerhardt, 304 U.S. 414 (1938) - 357
Henderson v. Morgan, 426 U.S. 637 (1978) - 563
Henderson v. Wickham, 92 U.S. 259 (1876) - 878
Hendrick v. Maryland, 235 U.S. 610 (1915) - 288
Henneford v. Silas Mason Co., 300 U.S. 577 (1937) - 333
Hepburn v. Griswold (First Legal Tender Case), 8 Wall. 603 (1870) - 26, 71, 119-121, 182, 664, 689, 712, 877, 926
Herbert v. Lando (1979) - 435

Hernandez v. Texas, 347 U.S. 475 (1954) - 532
Herndon v. Lowry, 301 U.S. 242 (1937) - 405, 406
Hill v. Stone, 421 U.S. 289 (1975) - 485
Hill v. Wallace, 259 U.S. 44 (1922) - 355, 928
Hills v. Gautreaux, 424 U.S. 284 (1976) - 616, 906
Hirabayashi v. United States, 320 U.S. 81 (1943) - 192, 892
Hodges v. United States, 203 U.S. 1 (1906) - 926
Hoke v. United States, 227 U.S. 308 (1913) - 95
Holden v. Hardy, 170 U.S. 366 (1898) - 34, 326, 526, 881
Hollingsworth v. Virginia, 3 Dall. 378 (1798) - 149, 673
Holloway v. Arkansas, 435 U.S. 475 (1978) - 569
Holmes v. Jennison, 14 Pet. 540 (1840) - 19, 362, 875
Holt v. United States, 218 U.S. 245 (1910) - 552
Holtzman v. Schlesinger, 414 U.S. 1314 (1973) - 127
Home Building & Loan Assn. v. Blaisdell, 290 U.S. 398 (1934) - 314, 315, 701, 887
Hopkins Savings Assn. v. Cleary, 296 U.S. 315 (1935) - 355, 929
Hot Oil Case. *See* Panama Refining Co. v. Ryan.
Houchins v. KQED Inc., 438 U.S. 1 (1978) - 444
Houston, East and West Texas Railway Co. v. United States. *See* Shreveport Rate Cases.
Hoyt v. Florida, 368 U.S. 57 (1961) - 534, 637, 898
Hudgens v. National Labor Relations Board, 424 U.S. 507 (1976) - 417
Hudgings, Ex parte, 249 U.S. 378 (1919) - 281
Hudson v. Parker, 157 U.S. 277 (1895) - 577
Hudson and Smith v. Guestier, 6 Cr. 281 (1810) - 294
Hughes v. Superior Court of California, 339 U.S. 460 (1950) - 419
Huidekoper's Lessee v. Douglass, 3 Cr. 1 (1805) - 741
Humphrey's Executor v. United States, 295 U.S. 602 (1935) - 214-216, 888
Hunter v. Erickson, 393 U.S. 385 (1969) - 615
Hunter v. Fairfax's Devisee, 3 Dall. 305 (1796) - 305
Hurd v. Hodge, 334 U.S. 24 (1948) - 614
Hurtado v. California, 110 U.S. 516 (1884) - 30, 525, 533, 879
Hutchinson v. Proxmire (1979) - 909
Hyde v. Southern Railroad Co., 31 App. D.C. 466 (1908) - 927
Hylton v. United States, 3 Dall. 172 (1796) - 9, 291, 872
Hynes v. Oradell, 425 U.S. 610 (1976) - 420

I

Illinois ex rel. McCollum v. Board of Education, 333 U.S. 203 (1948) - 462, 894
Income Tax Case. *See* Pollock v. Farmers' Loan & Trust Co.
Insular Cases, 182 U.S. 1 (1901) - 34, 139-141, 187, 882
International Brotherhood of Teamsters, Local 695 v. Vogt, 354 U.S. 284 (1957) - 419
International Paper Co. v. United States, 282 U.S. 399 (1931) - 195
Irvin v. Dowd, 366 U.S. 717 (1961) - 441
Irvine v. California, 347 U.S. 129 (1954) - 549
Irvine v. Marshall, 20 How. 558 (1858) - 140
Ivanov v. United States, 394 U.S. 166 (1969) - 552

J

Jacobellis v. Ohio, 378 U.S. 184 (1964) - 429
Jacobson v. Massachusetts, 197 U.S. 11 (1905) - 456, 527
Jackson v. Georgia, 408 U.S. 238 (1972) - 576, 904
Jackson, Ex parte, 96 U.S. 727 (1878) - 156, 431
James v. Bowman, 190 U.S. 127 (1903) - 927
James v. Valtierra, 402 U.S. 138 (1971) - 615

Jencks v. United States, 353 U.S. 657 (1957) - 670
Jenkins v. Georgia, 418 U.S. 153 (1974) - 429
Jiminez v. Weinberger, 417 U.S. 628 (1974) - 634, 930
Johannessen v. United States, 225 U.S. 227 (1912) - 77
Johnson v. Louisiana, 406 U.S. 356 (1972) - 531, 904
Johnson v. Robinson, 415 U.S. 361 (1974) - 457
Johnson v. Zerbst, 304 U.S. 458 (1938) - 46, 566, 567, 890
Joint Anti-Fascist Refugee Committee v. McGrath, 341 U.S. 123 (1951) - 509, 895
Jones v. Alfred H. Mayer Co., 392 U.S. 409 (1968) - 47, 152, 603, 616, 901
Jones v. Meehan, 175 U.S. 1 (1899) - 927
Jones v. Opelika, 316 U.S. 584 (1942) - 47, 391, 455, 456, 458, 892
Jones v. Van Zandt, 5 How. 215 (1848) - 377
Jurek v. Texas, 428 U.S. 262 (1976) - 578, 579, 907
Justices, The v. Murray, 9 Wall. 274 (1870) - 926

K

Kahn v. Shevin, 416 U.S. 351 (1974) - 632
Kaiser Aluminum & Chemical Corp. v. Weber (1979) - 606, 909
Kastigar v. United States, 406 U.S. 441 (1972) - 556, 903
Katz v. United States, 389 U.S. 247 (1967) - 552, 901
Katzenbach v. McClung, 379 U.S. 294 (1964) - 105, 612
Katzenbach v. Morgan, 384 U.S. 641 (1966) - 486
Kawakita v. United States, 343 U.S. 717 (1952) - 398
Kedroff v. St. Nicholas Cathedral of Russian Orthodox Church, 363 U.S. 190 (1960) - 462
Keller v. Potomac Electric Co., 261 U.S. 428 (1923) - 928
Keller v. United States, 213 U.S. 139 (1909) - 95, 355, 927
Kendall v. United States ex rel. Stokes, 12 Pet. 524 (1838) - 19, 230, 276, 875
Kennedy v. Mendoza-Martinez, 372 U.S. 145 (1963) - 145, 929
Kent v. Dulles, 357 U.S. 116 (1958) - 507, 670, 897
Kentucky v. Dennison, 24 How. 66 (1861) - 366, 876
Ker v. California, 374 U.S. 23 (1963) - 539, 547, 899
Keyes v. Denver School District No. 1, 413 U.S. 189 (1973) - 598, 905
Keyishian v. Board of Regents of the University of the State of New York, 385 U.S. 589 (1967) - 516, 518, 900
Kidd v. Pearson, 129 U.S. 1 (1888) - 90, 94, 880
Kilbourn v. Thompson, 103 U.S. 169 (1881) - 158, 159, 167, 168, 879
Kimm v. Rosenberg, 363 U.S. 405 (1960) - 146
Kingsley Books v. Brown, 354 U.S. 436 (1957) - 430
Kinsella v. United States, 361 U.S. 234 (1960) - 929
Kirby v. Illinois, 406 U.S. 682 (1972) - 568
Kirby v. United States, 174 U.S. 47 (1899) - 927
Kirkpatrick v. Preisler, 385 U.S. 450 (1967) - 52, 494-496, 902
Klopfer v. North Carolina, 386 U.S. 213 (1967) - 535, 901
Knauer v. United States, 328 U.S. 654 (1946) - 143-145
Knickerbocker Ice Co. v. Stewart, 253 U.S. 150 (1920) - 355, 928
Knowlton v. Moore, 178 U.S. 41 (1900) - 76, 882
Knox v. Lee (Second Legal Tender Case), 12 Wall. 457 (1871) - 26, 120-122, 689, 877, 926
Konigsberg v. State Bar of California, 366 U.S. 36 (1961) - 283, 515, 669
Korematsu v. United States, 323 U.S. 214 (1944) - 47, 192, 382, 584, 893
Kovacs v. Cooper, 336 U.S. 77 (1949) - 409
Kramer v. Union Free School District No. 15, 395 U.S. 818 (1969) - 485

Kunz v. New York, 340 U.S. 290 (1951) - 410, 414, 452, 454, 895

L

Labine v. Vincent, 401 U.S. 532 (1971) - 634

Lalli v. Lalli, 439 U.S. 259 (1978) - 634

Lamont v. Postmaster General, 381 U.S. 301 (1965) - 431, 930

Landmark Communications Inc. v. Virginia, 435 U.S. 829 (1978) - 441

Lane v. Wilson, 307 U.S. 268 (1939) - 37, 890

Larson v. Domestic & Foreign Corp., 337 U.S. 682 (1949) - 261

Lassiter v. Northampton County Board of Elections, 360 U.S. 45 (1959) - 480, 485, 897

Lau v. Nichols, 414 U.S. 563 (1974) - 607

Lauf v. E.G. Shinner & Co., 303 U.S. 315 (1938) - 93, 276

Law Students Civil Rights Research Council v. Wadmond, 401 U.S. 155 (1971) - 515

Leary v. United States, 395 U.S. 6 (1969) - 930

Legal Tender Cases, 12 Wall. 457 (1871) - 22, 26, 27, 71, 129, 182, 240, 688, 689, 710, 712, 877, 926

Leisy v. Hardin, 136 U.S. 100 (1890) - 323

Lemke v. Farmers Grain Co., 258 U.S. 50 (1922) - 92

Lemon v. Kurtzman, 403 U.S. 602 (1971) - 467, 903

Lerner v. Casey, 357 U.S. 468 (1958) - 514

Levy v. Louisiana, 391 U.S. 68 (1968) - 634

License Cases, 5 How. 504 (1847) - 316, 875

Lichter v. United States, 334 U.S. 742 (1948) - 130

Light v. United States, 220 U.S. 523 (1911) - 288

Linkletter v. Walker, 381 U.S. 618 (1965) - 549

Liverpool, N.Y. & Philadelphia Steamship Co. v. Emigration Commissioners, 113 U.S. 33 (1885) - 288

Lloyd Corporation Ltd. v. Tanner, 407 U.S. 551 (1972) - 417

Loan Assn. v. Topeka, 20 Wall. 655 (1875) - 357

Local Plumbers Union #10 v. Graham, 345 U.S. 192 (1953) - 419

Lochner v. New York, 198 U.S. 45 (1905) - 35-39, 44, 269, 326-328, 343, 526, 527, 882

Lockett v. Ohio, 438 U.S. 586 (1978) - 579

Loewe v. Lawlor (The Danbury Hatters Case), 208 U.S. 274 (1908) - 35, 88, 93, 94, 883

Lombard v. Louisiana, 373 U.S. 267 (1963) - 611

Los Angeles v. Manhart, 435 U.S. 702 (1978) - 638

Los Angeles Times Case. *See* Times-Mirror Co. v. Superior Court of California.

Lottawanna, The, 21 Wall. 558 (1875) - 86

Lottery Case, The. *See* Champion v. Ames.

Louisiana ex rel. Francis v. Resweber, 329 U.S. 459 (1947) - 575, 893

Louisville Bank v. Radford, 295 U.S. 555 (1935) - 929

Louisville Joint Stock Land Bank v. Radford, 295 U.S. 555 (1935) - 677

Louisville, New Orleans & Texas Railway v. Mississippi, 134 U.S. 587 (1890) - 31, 608, 880

Louisville Railroad Co. v. Letson, 2 How. 497 (1844) - 875

Lovell v. Griffin, 303 U.S. 444 (1938) - 47, 427, 452, 455, 890

Loving v. Virginia, 388 U.S. 1 (1967) - 53, 644, 901

Low v. Austin, 13 Wall. 29 (1872) - 878, 906

Lubin v. Panish, 415 U.S. 709 (1974) - 487, 643

Luria v. United States, 231 U.S. 9 (1913) - 143

Luther v. Borden, 7 How. 1 (1849) - 20, 217, 293, 356, 875

Lynch v. United States, 292 U.S. 571 (1934) - 928

M

MacDougall v. Green, 335 U.S. 281 (1948) - 487, 488

Madsen v. Kinsella, 343 U.S. 341 (1952) - 195

Mahan v. Howell, 410 U.S. 315 (1973) - 495, 904

Mahler v. Eby, 264 U.S. 32 (1924) - 77

Mallory v. United States, 354 U.S. 449 (1957) - 52, 559, 561, 679, 896, 897

Malloy v. Hogan, 378 U.S. 1 (1964) - 53, 345, 346, 557, 558, 560, 899

Manual Enterprises v. Day, 370 U.S. 478 (1962) - 429

Mapp v. Ohio, 367 U.S. 643 (1961) - 52, 346, 539, 547, 549, 898

Marbury v. Madison, 1 Cr. 138 (1803) - 5, 7, 11-13, 26, 65, 69-72, 74, 210, 229, 231, 236, 270, 271, 274-276, 292, 303, 654, 658, 659, 696, 698, 706-708, 872, 926

Marcello v. Bonds, 349 U.S. 302 (1955) - 146

Marchetti v. United States, 390 U.S. 39 (1968) - 930

Marsh v. Alabama, 326 U.S. 501 (1946) - 416, 417

Marshall v. Barlow's Inc., 436 U.S. 307 (1978) - 550, 908, 931

Marshall v. Gordon, 243 U.S. 521 (1917) - 159

Marston v. Lewis, 410 U.S. 679 (1973) - 485

Martin v. City of Struthers, 319 U.S. 142 (1943) - 420, 453

Martin v. Hunter's Lessee, 1 Wheat. 304 (1816) - 14, 15, 267, 306, 360, 361, 742, 872

Martin v. Mott, 12 Wheat. 19 (1827) - 186, 217, 874

Maryland v. Wirtz, 392 U.S. 183 (1968) - 105, 328

Mason v. Haile, 12 Wheat. 370 (1827) - 16, 874

Massachusetts v. Mellon, 262 U.S. 447 (1923) - 292, 886

Massiah v. United States, 377 U.S. 201 (1964) - 560

Mathews v. deCastro, 429 U.S. 181 (1976) - 632

Mathews v. Diaz, 426 U.S. 67 (1976) - 628

Mathews v. Lucas, 427 U.S. 495 (1976) - 634

Matter of Heff, 197 U.S. 488 (1905) - 927

Mattox v. United States , 157 U.S. 237 (1895) - 535, 536

Maxwell v. Dow, 176 U.S. 581 (1900) - 34, 36, 525, 882

Mayer v. Chicago, 404 U.S. 189 (1971) - 641

Mayor of New York v. Miln. *See* New York v. Miln.

McCabe v. Atchison, Topeka & Santa Fe Railroad, 235 U.S. 152 (1914) - 609

McCardle, Ex parte, 7 Wall. 506 (1869) - 25, 263, 264, 272, 667, 668, 877

McCray v. United States, 195 U.S. 27 (1904) - 38, 94, 113, 114, 882

McCready v. Virginia, 94 U.S. 391 (1877) - 626

McCulloch v. Maryland, 4 Wheat. 316 (1819) - 11, 14-16, 73, 74, 125, 329, 357, 708, 873, 875

McDaniel v. Barresi, 402 U.S. 39 (1971) - 603

McDaniel v. Paty, 435 U.S. 618 (1978) - 461

McDonald v. Santa Fe Trail Transportation Co., 427 U.S. 273 (1976) - 621

McDonald v. United States, 335 U.S. 451 (1948) - 545

McDonnell Douglas Corp. v. Green. 411 U.S. 807 (1973) - 620

McElroy v. United States, 361 U.S. 281 (1960) - 929

McGautha v. California, 402 U.S. 183 (1971) - 576, 578

McGhee v. Sipes, 334 U.S. 1 (1948) - 614

McGrain v. Daugherty, 273 U.S. 136 (1927) - 159, 160, 163, 175, 231

McGrath v. National Assn. of Manufacturers, 344 U.S. 804 (1952) - 174

McKane v. Durston, 153 U.S. 684 (1894) - 577

McKeiver v. Pennsylvania, 403 U.S. 528 (1971) - 531, 903

McLaurin v. Oklahoma State Regents for Higher Education, 339 U.S. 637 (1950) - 49, 592, 895

McMann v. Richardson, 397 U.S. 759 (1970) - 563
McNabb v. United States, 318 U.S. 322 (1943) - 283, 558, 679, 892
Meek v. Pittinger, 421 U.S. 349 (1975) - 469
Merryman, Ex parte, 17 Fed. Cases 9487 (1861) - 25, 76, 189, 239, 240
Metropolitan Housing Development Corporation v. Village of Arlington Heights, 558 F. 2d 1293 (1977) - 617
Meyer v. Nebraska, 262 U.S. 390 (1923) - 388, 644
Miami Herald Publishing Co. v. Tornillo, 418 U.S. 241 (1974) - 427
Michelin Tire Corp. v. Wages, 423 U.S. 276 (1976) - 906
Michigan v. Mosley, 423 U.S. 96 (1975) - 564
Michigan v. Tucker, 417 U.S. 433 (1974) - 563
Michigan v. Tyler, 426 U.S. 499 (1978) - 551
Miles v. Graham, 268 U.S. 501 (1925) - 115, 290, 928
Milk Wagon Drivers Union v. Meadowmoor Dairies Inc., 312 U.S. 287 (1941) - 418
Miller v. California, 413 U.S. 15 (1973) - 429, 897, 905
Milligan, Ex parte, 4 Wall. 2 (1866) - 25, 76, 189, 190, 229, 240, 667, 688, 876, 877
Milliken v. Bradley, 418 U.S. 717 (1974) - 606, 616, 617, 905
Mills v. Alabama, 384 U.S. 214 (1966) - 431
Minersville School District v. Gobitis, 310 U.S. 586 (1940) - 47, 344, 411, 455, 457, 458, 891, 892
Minnesota Rate Cases, 230 U.S. 252 (1913) - 88, 89
Minor v. Happersett, 21 Wall. 163 (1875) - 477, 479, 631, 878
Miranda v. Arizona, 384 U.S. 436 (1966) - 53, 55, 346, 560-563, 567, 568, 679, 900
Mississippi v. Johnson, 4 Wall. 475 (1867) - 25, 276, 667, 877
Missouri v. Holland, 252 U.S. 416 (1920) - 131, 358, 362, 202, 203, 204, 885
Missouri ex rel. Gaines v. Canada, 305 U.S. 337 (1938) - 46, 348, 591, 890
Mitchell v. Harmony, 13 How. 115 (1852) - 195
Monongahela Navigation Co. v. United States, 148 U.S. 312 (1893) - 927
Monell v. Dept. of Social Services, City of New York, 436 U.S. 658 (1978) - 908
Montgomery Ward & Co. v. United States, 326 U.S. 690 (1944) - 193
Moore v. Dempsey, 261 U.S. 86 (1923) - 39, 273, 528, 529, 886
Moore v. Ogilvie, 394 U.S. 814 (1969) - 487
Moose Lodge 107 v. Irvis, 407 U.S. 164 (1972) - 612
Mora v. McNamara, 389 U.S. 934 (1967) - 126
Morehead v. New York ex rel. Tipaldo, 298 U.S. 587 (1936) - 43, 44, 527, 889
Morgan v. Virginia, 328 U.S. 373 (1946) - 49, 104, 609, 893
Morris v. Gressette, 432 U.S. 491 (1977) - 487
Mugler v. Kansas, 123 U.S. 623 (1887) - 526, 880
Muir v. Louisville Park Theatrical Assn., 347 U.S. 971 (1954) - 597, 610
Mulford v. Smith, 307 U.S. 38 (1939) - 94, 121, 244, 677, 672
Mullan v. United States, 141 U.S. 240 (1891) - 195
Muller v. Oregon, 208 U.S. 412 (1908) - 36, 326, 327, 527, 632, 883, 884
Munn v. Illinois (Granger Cases), 94 U.S. 113 (1877) - 28, 30, 31, 42, 318, 325, 526, 878, 888
Murdock v. Memphis, 20 Wall. 590 (1874) - 667
Murdock v. Pennsylvania, 319 U.S. 105 (1943) - 47, 391, 455, 456, 892
Murphy v. Ramsey, 114 U.S. 15 (1885) - 77
Murphy v. The Waterfront Commission of New York Harbor, 378 U.S. 52 (1964) - 558, 899
Murray v. Curlett, 374 U.S. 203 (1963) - 464-466

Murray's Lessee v. Hoboken Land & Improvement Co., 18 How. 272 (1856) - 21, 524, 525, 876
Muskrat v. United States, 219 U.S. 346 (1911) - 287, 291, 883, 927
Myers v. United States, 272 U.S. 52 (1926) - 41, 212-215, 886, 888, 927

N

NAACP v. Alabama ex rel. Patterson, 357 U.S. 449 (1958) - 403, 514, 403, 897
NAACP v. Button, 371 U.S. 415 (1963) - 403, 898
Nardone v. United States, 302 U.S. 379 (1937) - 551
Nashville v. Cooper, 6 Wall. 247 (1868) - 259
Nashville Gas Co. v. Satty, 434 U.S. 137 (1977) - 636
National Assn. of Manufacturers v. McGrath, 103 F. Supp. 510 (D.C. 1952) - 174
National Board of YMCA v. United States, 395 U.S. 85 (1969) - 141
National Broadcasting Co. v. United States, 319 U.S. 190 (1943) - 447
National Labor Relations Board v. Fainblatt, 306 U.S. 601 (1939) - 101
National Labor Relations Board v. Jones & Laughlin Steel Corp., 301 U.S. 1 (1937) - 94, 100, 101, 121, 677, 889
National League of Cities v. Usery, 426 U.S. 833 (1976) - 56, 94, 105, 106, 355, 907
Nathanson v. United States, 290 U.S. 41 (1933) - 540
National Life Insurance Co. v. United States, 277 U.S. 508 (1928) - 928
National Paper Co. v. Bowers, 266 U.S. 373 (1924) - 77
Neagle, In re, 136 U.S. 1 (1890) - 32, 216, 280
Near v. Minnesota, 283 U.S. 697 (1931) - 41, 425, 887
Nebbia v. New York, 291 U.S. 502 (1934) - 42, 527, 701, 887
Nebraska Press Assn. v. Stuart, 427 U.S. 539 (1976) - 443, 907
New Jersey v. Wilson, 7 Cr. 165 (1812) - 310
New York v. Miln, 11 Pet. 102 (1837) - 17-19, 316, 318, 323, 324, 665, 874, 876
New York Times Co. v. Sullivan, 376 U.S. 254 (1964) - 54, 421, 433-435, 437, 899
New York Times Co. v. United States, 403 U.S. 713 (1971) - 245, 431, 432, 733, 903
Newberry v. United States, 256 U.S. 232 (1921) - 38, 46, 171, 172, 355, 481, 482, 885, 891, 928
Niemotko v. Maryland, 340 U.S. 268 (1951) - 413, 454
Nicholds v. Coolidge, 274 U.S. 531 (1927) - 928
Nix v. Hedden, 150 U.S. 305 (1893) - 112
Nixon v. Administrator, General Services Administration, 433 U.S. 425 (1977) - 233, 234, 247
Nixon v. Condon, 286 U.S. 73 (1932) - 41, 481, 887
Nixon v. Herndon, 273 U.S. 536 (1927) - 40, 126, 481, 886
Nixon v. United States. *See* United States v. Nixon.
Norman v. Baltimore and Ohio Railroad Co. (Gold Clause Case), 294 U.S. 240 (1935) - 43, 888
Norris v. Alabama (Second Scottsboro Case), 294 U.S. 587 (1935) - 41, 532, 888
Norris v. Boston (Passenger Cases), 7 How. 283 (1849) - 876
North v. Russell, 427 U.S. 328 (1976) - 529
North Carolina v. Pearce, 395 U.S. 711 (1969) - 572
North Carolina State Board of Education v. Swann, 402 U.S. 43 (1971) - 602

Northern Securities Co. v. United States, 193 U.S. 197 (1904) - 35, 36, 91, 685, 882

Nortz v. United States (Gold Clause Case), 294 U.S. 317 (1935) - 888

Norwood v. Harrison, 413 U.S. 455 (1973) - 602

Noto v. United States, 367 U.S. 290 (1961) - 505, 898

Nye v. United States, 313 U.S. 33 (1941) - 280

O

O'Brien v. Brown, 409 U.S. 1 (1972) - 733

O'Callahan v. Parker, 395 U.S. 258 (1969) - 128, 930

Offutt v. United States, 348 U.S. 11 (1954) - 284

Ogden v. Saunders, 12 Wheat. 213 (1827) - 16, 312, 874

Okanogan Indians et al v. United States (Pocket Veto Case) - 222, 223

Oklahoma Press Publishing Co. v. Walling, 327 U.S. 186 (1946) - 426

Olmstead v. United States, 277 U.S. 438 (1928) - 39, 550, 552, 887, 901

Olsen v. Nebraska, 313 U.S. 236 (1941) - 527

O'Malley v. Woodrough, 307 U.S. 277 (1939) - 115, 290

Oregon v. Hass, 420 U.S. 714 (1975) - 564

Oregon v. Mitchell, 400 U.S. 112 (1970) - 355, 481, 485, 902, 931

Organization for a Better Austin v. Keefe, 402 U.S. 415 (1971) - 430

Orr v. Orr (1979) - 909

Osborn v. Bank of the United States, 9 Wheat. 738 (1824) - 16, 354, 873

Oyama v. California, 332 U.S. 633 (1948) - 626

P

Packer Corp. v. Utah, 285 U.S. 105 (1932) - 527

Palko v. Connecticut, 302 U.S. 319 (1937) - 44, 346, 391, 528, 572, 644, 889, 902

Palmer v. Thompson, 403 U.S. 217 (1971) - 610

Panama Refining Co. v. Ryan, 293 U.S. 388 (1935) - 43, 121, 241, 677, 888, 929

Pappas, In re, 408 U.S. 665 (1972) - 445, 904

Parham v. Hughes (1979) - 634

Parker v. Brown, 317 U.S. 341 (1943) - 361

Parker v. Davis (Second Legal Tender Case), 12 Wall. 457 (1871) - 877

Pasadena City Board of Education v. Spangler, 427 U.S. 424 (1976) - 607, 906

Passenger Cases, 7 How. 283 (1849) - 20, 104, 317, 318, 324, 876

Passman v. Davis (1979) - 585

Patton v. Mississippi, 332 U.S. 463 (1947) - 532

Patton v. United States, 281 U.S. 276 (1930) - 530, 887

Paul v. Virginia, 8 Wall. 169 (1869) - 105, 319, 331, 332, 877

Peck & Co. v. Lowe, 247 U.S. 166 (1918) - 77

Peik v. Chicago & Northwestern Railway Co., 94 U.S. 165 (1877). See Granger Cases.

Peirce v. New Hampshire (The License Cases), 5 How. 504 (1847) - 875

Pell v. Procunier, 417 U.S. 817 (1974) - 444

Pennekamp v. Florida, 328 U.S. 331 (1946) - 441

Pennsylvania v. Board of Directors of City Trusts of Philadelphia, 353 U.S. 230 (1957) - 610

Pennsylvania v. Nelson, 350 U.S. 497 (1956) - 50, 362, 513, 669, 671, 896

Pennsylvania v. Wheeling and Belmont Bridge Co., 13 How 518 (1852); 18 How. 421 (1856) - 21, 85, 676, 714, 876

Pensacola Telegraph Co. v. Western Union Telegraph Co., 96 U.S. 1 (1878) - 324

Perez v. Brownell, 356 U.S. 44 (1958) - 145, 146

Perez v. Ledesma, 401 U.S. 82 (1971) - 279

Perry v. Sinderman, 408 U.S. 593 (1972) - 533

Perry v. United States (Gold Clause Case), 294 U.S. 330 (1935) - 117, 888, 929

Peterson v. City of Greenville, 373 U.S. 244 (1963) - 611

Peterson, Ex parte, 253 U.S. 300 (1920) - 283

Philadelphia v. New Jersey, 437 U.S. 617 (1978) - 320

Phillips v. Martin Marietta Corp., 400 U.S. 542 (1971) - 637

Phoenix v. Kolodzieski, 399 U.S. 204 (1970) - 485

Pierce v. Society of Sisters, 268 U.S. 510 (1925) - 40, 389, 456, 602, 644, 886, 980

Pierce v. United States, 252 U.S. 239 (1929) - 399

Pierson v. Ray, 386 U.S. 547 (1967) - 290

Pipe Line Cases, 234 U.S. 548 (1914) - 90

Pipefitters v. United States, 407 U.S. 385 (1972) - 420

Pittsburgh Press Co. v. Pittsburgh Commission on Human Relations, 413 U.S. 376 (1973) - 427

Planned Parenthood of Central Missouri v. Danforth, 428 U.S. 52 (1976) - 645

Plessy v. Ferguson, 164 U.S. 537 (1896) - 31, 33, 49, 50, 103, 294, 321, 341, 342, 348, 349, 381, 382, 587, 589-591, 595, 608, 700, 710, 713, 742, 881, 890, 896

Plumley v. Massachusetts, 156 U.S. 461 (1894) - 323

Pocket Veto Case (Okanogan Indians et al. v. United States), 279 U.S. 655 (1929) - 222, 223

Poindexter v. Louisiana Finance Commission, 389 U.S. 571 (1968) - 602

Pointer v. Texas, 380 U.S. 400 (1965) - 536, 900

Pollock v. Farmers' Loan & Trust Co., 157 U.S. 429 (1895); and 158 U.S. 601 (1895) - 32, 71, 76, 110-113, 120, 269, 275, 276, 291, 357, 674, 692, 881, 927

Pollard v. Hagan, 3 How. 212 (1845) - 133

Ponzi v. Fessenden, 258 U.S. 254 (1922) - 273, 885

Pope v. Williams, 193 U.S. 621 (1903) - 485

Poulos v. New Hampshire, 345 U.S. 395 (1953) - 414

Powell v. Alabama (First Scottsboro Case), 287 U.S. 45 (1932) - 41, 345, 528, 565-568, 887

Powell v. McCormack, 395 U.S. 486 (1969) - 165, 166, 167, 902

Powell v. Pennsylvania, 128 U.S. 678 (1888) - 323, 527

Powell v. Texas, 392 U.S. 514 (1968) - 576

Presbyterian Church in the United States v. Mary Elizabeth Blue Hull Memorial Presbyterian Church, 393 U.S. 440 (1969) - 462

Prigg v. Pennsylvania, 16 Pet. 539 (1842) - 19, 377, 875

Primus, In re, 436 U.S. 412 (1978) - 403

Prince v. Massachusetts, 321 U.S. 159 (1944) - 454

Prize Cases, 2 Black 635 (1863) - 24, 126, 187-189, 664, 876

Procunier v. Hillery, 417 U.S. 817 (1974) - 444

Procunier v. Martinez, 416 U.S. 396 (1974) - 444

Proffitt v. Florida, 428 U.S. 325 (1976) - 578, 579, 907

Providence Bank v. Billings, 4 Pet. 514 (1830) - 16, 310, 311, 313

Prudential Insurance Co. v. Benjamin, 328 U.S. 408 (1946) - 893

Public Utilities Commission of the District of Columbia v. Pollack, 343 U.S. 451 (1952) - 409

Q

Quilloin v. Walcott, 434 U.S. 246 (1978) - 634
Quinn v. United States, 349 U.S. 156 (1955) - 163
Quirin, Ex parte, 317 U.S. 1 (1942) - 47, 192, 195, 732, 892

R

Railroad Retirement Board v. Alton Railroad Co., 295 U.S. 330 (1935) - 43, 94, 113, 677, 888, 929
Railroad Retirement Board v. Kalina, 431 U.S. 909 (1977) - 930
Rakas v. Illinois, 439 U.S. 129 (1978) - 547
Rassmussen v. United States, 197 U.S. 516 (1905) - 927
Ray v. Atlantic Richfield Co., 435 U.S. 152 (1978) - 85
Raymond Motor Transportation Inc. v. Rice, 434 U.S. 429 (1978) - 317
Red Lion Broadcasting Co. v. Federal Communications Commission, 395 U.S. 367 (1969) - 446
Redrup v. New York, 386 U.S. 767 (1967) - 429
Reed v. County Commissioners of Delaware County, Pa., 277 U.S. 376 (1928) - 164
Reed v. Reed, 404 U.S. 71 (1971) - 632, 903
Regina v. Hicklin, L.R. 3 Q.B. 360 (1868) - 428
Regents of University of California v. Bakke, 438 U.S. 265 (1978) - 56, 605, 606, 908
Reichart v. Felps, 6 Wall. 160 (1868) - 926
Reid v. Covert, 354 U.S. 1 (1957) - 204, 929
Reitman v. Mulkey, 387 U.S. 369 (1967) - 614
Reynolds v. Sims, 377 U.S. 533 (1964) - 52, 53, 149, 269, 488, 492, 493, 495, 496, 585, 675, 899
Reynolds v. Smith, 394 U.S. 618 (1969) - 902
Reynolds v. United States, 98 U.S. 146 (1879) - 452
Rhode Island v. Massachusetts, 4 How. 591 (1846) - 875
Ribnik v. McBride, 277 U.S. 350 (1928) - 527
Richardson v. Davis, 409 U.S. 1069 (1972) - 931
Richardson v. Griffin, 409 U.S. 1069 (1972) - 931
Richardson v. Ramirez, 418 U.S. 24 (1974) - 485
Richmond v. United States, 422 U.S. 358 (1975) - 487, 504
Richmond School Board v. Virginia State Board of Education, 412 U.S. 92 (1973) - 603
Rickert Rice Mills v. Fontenot, 297 U.S. 110 (1936) - 929
Rideau v. Louisiana, 373 U.S. 723 (1963) - 442
Robbins v. Shelby County Taxing District, 120 U.S. 489 (1887) - 332, 333
Roberts v. City of Boston, 59 Mass. 198 (1849) - 590, 591
Roberts v. Louisiana, 428 U.S. 325 (1976) - 907
Robinson v. California, 370 U.S. 660 (1962) - 52, 576, 898
Robinson v. Memphis and Charleston Railroad Co. See Civil Rights Cases.
Robinson, Ex parte, 19 Wall. 505 (1874) - 279
Rochin v. California, 342 U.S. 166 (1952) - 548, 552, 895
Roe v. Wade, 410 U.S. 113 (1973) - 55, 289, 343, 904
Rogers v. Bellei, 401 U.S. 815 (1971) - 146
Rogers v. Paul, 382 U.S. 198 (1965) - 599
Rogers v. Richmond, 365 U.S. 534 (1961) - 559
Rogers v. United States, 340 U.S. 367 (1951) - 163
Roosevelt v. Meyer, 1 Wall. 512 (1863) - 119
Rosenberg v. United States, 346 U.S. 273 (1953) - 732, 896
Rosenblatt v. Baer, 383 U.S. 75 (1966) - 435
Rosenbloom v. Metromedia Inc., 403 U.S. 29 (1971) - 438, 439
Ross v. Moffit, 417 U.S. 600 (1974) - 569
Roth v. United States, 354 U.S. 476 (1957) - 52, 428, 431, 897
Roudebush v. Hartke, 405 U.S. 15 (1972) - 173
Rowan v. Post Office Dept., 397 U.S. 728 (1970) - 431
Rowoldt v. Perfetto, 355 U.S. 115 (1957) - 503
Runyon v. McCrary, 426 U.S. 161 (1976) - 603, 906
Russell v. United States, 369 U.S. 749 (1962) - 162

S

Saia v. New York, 334 U.S. 558 (1948) - 409
Sailors v. Board of Education, 387 U.S. 105 (1967) - 496
St. Louis Malleable Casting Co. v. Prendergast Construction Co., 260 U.S. 469 (1923) - 288
Salyer Land Co. v. Tulare Water District, 410 U.S. 743 (1973) - 496
San Antonio School District v. Rodriguez, 411 U.S. 1 (1973) - 643, 904
Santa Clara County v. Southern Pacific Railroad Co., 118 U.S. 394 (1886) - 879
Santa Cruz Fruit Packing Co. v. National Labor Relations Board, 303 U.S. 453 (1938) - 101
Santiago v. Nogueras, 214 U.S. 260 (1909) - 195
Santobello v. New York, 404 U.S. 257 (1971) - 563
Saturday Evening Post Case. See Curtis Publishing Co. v. Butts.
Saxbe v. Washington Post, 417 U.S. 843 (1974) - 444
Scales v. United States, 367 U.S. 203 (1961) - 505, 898
Schacht v. United States, 398 U.S. 58 (1970) - 412, 930
Schaefer v. United States, 251 U.S. 466 (1920) - 399
Schechter Poultry Corp. v. United States, 295 U.S. 495 (1935) - 43, 94, 98, 99, 101, 121, 241, 242, 677, 702, 888, 929
Schenck v. United States, 249 U.S. 47 (1919) - 37, 38, 392, 397, 398, 499, 885
Schick v. Reed, 419 U.S. 256 (1974) - 227
Schlesinger v. Ballard, 419 U.S. 498 (1975) - 632
Schmerber v. California, 384 U.S. 757 (1966) - 552
Schneckloth v. Bustamonte, 412 U.S. 218 (1973) - 540
Schneider v. Irvington, 308 U.S. 148 (1939) - 421, 427
Schneider v. Rusk, 377 U.S. 164 (1964) - 144, 145, 930
Schneiderman v. United States, 320 U.S. 118 (1943) - 143, 503, 504
School District of Abington Township v. Schempp, 374 U.S. 203 (1963) - 464, 898
Schware v. New Mexico Board of Bar Examiners, 353 U.S. 232 (1957) - 515
Scopes v. State, 155 Tenn. 105 (1927) - 463
Scott v. Illinois (1979) - 908
Scott v. Sandford, 19 How. 393 (1857) - 16, 21-23, 26, 33, 68, 71, 72, 111, 120, 135-139, 142, 238, 271, 291, 301, 339, 376, 377, 674, 692, 699, 702, 710-712, 714, 742, 755, 791, 876, 926
Scottsboro Cases. See Powell v. Alabama; Norris v. Alabama.
Seaboard Air Line Co. v. Blackwell, 244 U.S. 310 (1917) - 317
Seacombe, Ex parte, 19 How. 9 (1857) - 283
Second Legal Tender Cases. See Knox v. Lee; Parker v. Davis.
Second Scottsboro Case. See Norris v. Alabama.
See v. City of Seattle, 387 U.S. 541 (1967) - 550
Selective Draft Law Cases, 245 U.S. 366 (1918) - 37, 128, 885
Senn v. Tile Layers Union, 301 U.S. 468 (1937) - 417
Shapiro v. Thompson, 394 U.S. 618 (1969) - 104, 643, 902, 930
Shelley v. Kraemer, 334 U.S. 1 (1948) - 49, 613, 614, 894
Shelton v. Tucker, 364 U.S. 479 (1964) - 403, 514
Sheppard v. Maxwell, 384 U.S. 333 (1966) - 442, 443
Sherbert v. Verner, 374 U.S. 398 (1963) - 460, 461

Shreveport Rate Cases, 234 U.S. 342 (1914) - 36, 88, 89, 94, 99, 884

Shuttlesworth v. Birmingham, 373 U.S. 262 (1963) - 611

Shuttlesworth v. City of Birmingham, 394 U.S. 148 (1969) - 414

Sibron v. New York, 392 U.S. 40 (1968) - 545

Siebold, Ex parte, 100 U.S. 371 (1880) - 171, 478, 878

Sifuentes v. United States, 428 U.S. 543 (1976) - 546

Siler v. Louisville & Nashville R. Co., 213 U.S. 175 (1909) - 288

Silesian American Corp. v. Clark, 332 U.S. 469 (1947) - 195

Silverman v. United States, 365 U.S. 505 (1961) - 552

Silverthorne Lumber Co. v. United States, 251 U.S. 385 (1921) - 548

Sinclair v. United States, 279 U.S. 263 (1929) - 160, 161

Sipuel v. Board of Regents of the University of Oklahoma, 332 U.S. 631 (1948) - 592

Skinner v. Oklahoma ex rel. Williamson, 316 U.S. 535 (1942) - 527, 585, 644, 892

Slaughterhouse Cases, 16 Wall. 36 (1873) - 26-29, 31, 301, 339, 340, 358, 478, 526, 587, 688, 878

Slochower v. Board of Higher Education of New York City, 350 U.S. 551 (1956) - 51, 514, 669, 896

Smith v. Allwright, 321 U.S. 649 (1944) - 48, 347, 482, 893

Smith v. Daily Mail (1979) - 437

Smith v. Goguen, 415 U.S. 566 (1974) - 412

Smith v. Hooey, 393 U.S. 374 (1969) - 273

Smith v. Turner (Passenger Cases), 7 How. 283 (1849) - 876

Smyth v. Ames, 170 U.S. 466 (1898) - 34, 527, 881

Sniadach v. Family Finance Corp. et al., 395 U.S. 337 (1969) - 533

South Carolina v. Katzenbach, 383 U.S. 301 (1966) - 53, 152, 480, 481, 486, 900

South Carolina Highway Dept. v. Barnwell Brothers, 303 U.S. 177 (1938) - 317

Southern Independent School Assn. v. McCrary, 426 U.S. 160 (1976) - 906

Southern Pacific Co. v. Arizona, 325 U.S. 761 (1945) - 317

Southern Railway Co. v. King, 217 U.S. 524 (1910) - 317

Southern Railway Co. v. United States, 222 U.S. 20 (1911) - 89

Spence v. Washington, 418 U.S. 405 (1974) - 412

Stack v. Boyle, 342 U.S. 1 (1951) - 577, 895

Stafford v. Wallace, 258 U.S. 495 (1922) - 92, 94

Standard Oil Co. v. United States, 221 U.S. 1 (1911) - 94, 883

Stanley v. Georgia, 394 U.S. 557 (1969) - 343

Stanley v. Illinois, 405 U.S. 645 (1972) - 634

Starr v. Campbell, 208 U.S. 527 (1908) - 195

Stanton v. Stanton, 421 U.S. 7 (1975) - 632

Steel Seizure Case. See Youngstown Sheet and Tube Co. v. Sawyer.

Steele v. Louisville and Nashville Railroad Co., 323 U.S. 192 (1944) - 618

Steffel v. Thompson, 415 U.S. 495 (1974) - 279

Stein v. Oshinsky, 382 U.S. 957 (1965) - 465

Steward Machine Co. v. Davis, 301 U.S. 548 (1937) - 44, 94, 118, 121, 889

Stolar, In re, 401 U.S. 23 (1971) - 515

Stone v. Mississippi, 101 U.S. 814 (1880) - 28, 314, 879

Stone v. Powell, 428 U.S. 465 (1976) - 549, 907

Stone v. Wisconsin, 94 U.S. 181 (1877). See Granger Cases.

Strader v. Graham, 10 How. 82 (1850) - 21, 22, 136, 138, 377

Strauder v. West Virginia, 100 U.S. 303 (1880) - 259, 587, 637

Street v. New York, 394 U.S. 576 (1969) - 412

Stroble v. California, 343 U.S. 181 (1951) - 441

Stromberg v. California, 283 U.S. 259 (1931) - 41, 344, 887

Strunk v. United States, 412 U.S. 434 (1973) - 904

Stuart v. Laird, 1 Cr. 299 (1803) - 665

Stump v. Sparkman, 435 U.S. 349 (1978) - 290

Sturges v. Crowininshield, 4 Wheat. 122 (1819) - 14-16, 706, 872

Sugar Trust Case. See United States v. E.C. Knight Co.

Summers, In re, 325 U.S. 651 (1945) - 283

Sunshine Anthracite Coal Co. v. Adkins, 310 U.S. 381 (1940) - 121, 677, 891

Swaim v. United States, 166 U.S. 553 (1897) - 195

Swann v. Adams, 385 U.S. 440 (1967) - 495

Swann v. Charlotte-Mecklenburg County Board of Education, 402 U.S. 1 (1971) - 55, 601, 603, 607, 903

Sweatt v. Painter, 339 U.S. 629 (1950) - 49, 349, 592, 595, 895

Swift v. Tyson, 16 Pet. 1 (1842) - 262

Swift & Co. v. United States, 196 U.S. 375 (1905) - 35, 91, 92, 94, 882

T

Takahashi v. Fish and Game Commission, 334 U.S. 410 (1948) - 627

Talley v. California, 362 U.S. 60 (1950) - 430

Taylor v. Louisiana, 419 U.S. 522 (1975) - 534, 637, 905

Teamsters v. United States, 431 U.S. 324 (1977) - 621

Tennessee v. Davis, 100 U.S. 257 (1880) - 259

Tenney v. Brandhove, 341 U.S. 367 (1951) - 168

Terminiello v. Chicago, 337 U.S. 1 (1940) - 408, 415, 894, 895

Terrace v. Thompson, 263 U.S. 197 (1923) - 626

Terry v. Adams, 345 U.S. 461 (1953) - 482, 895

Terry v. Ohio, 392 U.S. 1 (1968) - 545, 901

Test Oath Cases. See Garland, Ex parte; Cummings v. Missouri.

Texas v. Mitchell, 400 U.S. 112 (1970) - 485, 902

Texas v. White, 7 Wall. 700 (1869) - 26, 300, 877

Texas and New Orleans Railway Co. v. Brotherhood of Railway and Steamship Clerks, 281 U.S. 548 (1930) - 980

Texas and Pacific Railway Co. v. United States. See Shreveport Rate Cases.

Thomas v. Collins, 323 U.S. 516 (1945) - 391, 410, 420

Thornhill v. Alabama, 310 U.S. 88 (1940) - 47, 418, 419

Thurlow v. Massachusetts (License Cases), 5 How. 504 (1847) - 875

Tillman v. Wheaton-Haven Recreation Assn. Inc., 410 U.S. 431 (1973) - 612, 616

Tilton v. Richardson, 403 U.S. 672 (1971) - 469, 470, 930

T.I.M.E. v. United States, 431 U.S. 324 (1977) - 621

Time Inc. v. Hill, 385 U.S. 374 (1967) - 437

Time v. Firestone, 424 U.S. 448 (1976) - 439

Times Film Corp. v. City of Chicago, 364 U.S. 43 (1961) - 430

Times-Mirror Co. v. Superior Court of California, 314 U.S. 252 (1941) - 440, 441

Tinker v. Des Moines School District, 393 U.S. 503 (1969) - 412, 902

Toledo Newspaper Co. v. United States, 247 U.S. 402 (1918) - 280

Tollett v. Henderson, 411 U.S. 258 (1973) - 563

Torasco v. Watkins, 367 U.S. 488 (1961) - 453, 460, 461

Tot v. United States, 319 U.S. 463 (1943) - 929

Toth v. Quarles, 350 U.S. 11 (1955) - 929

Totten v. United States, 92 U.S. 105 (1876) - 195

Townsend v. Sain, 372 U.S. 293 (1963) - 273

Trade-Mark Cases, 100 U.S. 82 (1879) - 355, 926

Trafficante v. Metropolitan Life Insurance Co., 409 U.S. 205 (1972) - 615

Trimble v. Gordon, 430 U.S. 762 (1976) - 634
Trop v. Dulles, 356 U.S. 86 (1958) - 145, 575, 897, 929
Truax v. Raich, 239 U.S. 33 (1915) - 625
Trupiano v. United States, 334 U.S. 699 (1948) - 545
Trusler v. Crooks, 269 U.S. 475 (1926) - 928
Tumey v. Ohio, 273 U.S. 510 (1927) - 39, 529, 886
Turner v. United States, 396 U.S. 398 (1970) - 927
Turpin v. Burgess, 117 U.S. 504 (1886) - 77
Twining v. New Jersey, 211 U.S. 78 (1908) - 36, 53, 528, 557-559, 565, 883
Tyler v. The Judges, 179 U.S. 405 (1900) - 288
Tyson & Brother v. Banton, 273 U.S. 418 (1927) - 527

U

Ullmann v. United States, 350 U.S. 422 (1956) - 163, 556, 896
United Jewish Organizations of Williamsburgh v. Carey, 430 U.S. 145 (1977) - 487, 907
United Public Workers v. Mitchell, 330 U.S. 75 (1947) - 517, 518, 211, 894
United States v. Appalachian Electric Power Co., 311 U.S. 377 (1940) - 86
v. Arizona, 400 U.S. 112 (1970) - 485, 902
v. Ballard, 322 U.S. 78 (1944) - 453, 454
v. Ballin, 145 U.S. 1 (1892) - 175
v. Bekins, 304 U.S. 27 (1938) - 677
v. Belmont, 301 U.S. 324 (1936) - 206
v. Biswell, 406 U.S. 311 (1972) - 551
v. Booth, 21 How. 506 (1859) - 360, 876
v. Brewster, 408 U.S. 501 (1972) - 170, 904
v. Brignoni-Ponce, 422 U.S. 873 (1975) - 546
v. Brown, 381 U.S. 437 (1965) - 77, 511, 930
v. Burr, 25 Fed. Cas. 55 (1807) - 237
v. Butler, 297 U.S. 1 (1936) - 43, 94, 102, 115, 117, 118, 242, 244, 269, 355, 677, 888, 890, 929
v. Committee for Industrial Organization, 335 U.S. 106 (1948) - 420
v. California, 332 U.S. 19 (1947) - 134
v. Calandra, 414 U.S. 338 (1974) - 549
v. Caldwell, 408 U.S. 665 (1972) - 445, 904
v. California, 332 U.S. 19 (1932) - 677, 894
v. CalTech Philippines Inc., 344 U.S. 150 (1952) - 195
v. Caltex, 344 U.S. 150 (1952) - 141
v. Carolene Products Co., 304 U.S. 145 (1938) - 45, 378, 379, 391
v. Cardiff, 344 U.S. 174 (1952) - 929
v. Chandler-Dunbar Water Co., 229 U.S. 53 (1913) - 140
v. Clarke, 8 Pet. 436 (1934) - 261
v. Classic, 313 U.S. 299 (1941) - 46, 48, 172, 482, 891, 928
v. Cohen Grocery Co., 255 U.S. 81 (1921) - 928
v. Constantine, 296 U.S. 287 (1935) - 928
v. Cruikshank, 92 U.S. 542 (1876) - 342, 345, 412, 478, 878
v. Curtiss-Wright Export Corp., 299 U.S. 304 (1936) - 44, 125, 200-202, 206, 889
v. Darby Lumber Co., 312 U.S. 100 (1941) - 45, 94, 101, 244, 322, 328, 354, 527, 675, 891
v. DeWitt, 9 Wall. 41 (1870) - 355, 926
v. Dickinson, 331 U.S. 745 (1947) - 141
v. Dionisio, 410 U.S. 1 (1973) - 552
v. Doremus, 249 U.S. 86 (1919) - 114
v. Dowdy, 414 U.S. 823 (1973) - 170
v. E.C. Knight Co., 157 U.S. 1 (1888) - 32, 90, 94, 320, 880, 881
v. Eureka Mining Co., 357 U.S. 156 (1958) - 141
v. Evans, 213 U.S. 297 (1909) - 927

v. Fox, 95 U.S. 670 (1878) - 926
v. Gratiot, 14 Pet. 526 (1840) - 140
v. Harris, 106 U.S. 629 (1883) - 926
v. Harriss, 347 U.S. 612 (1954) - 174, 175, 413
v. Helstoski (1979) - 909
v. Hudson and Goodwin, 7 Cr. 32 (1812) - 14
v. Hvoslef, 237 U.S. 1 (1915) - 77, 927
v. Idaho, 400 U.S. 112 (1970) - 485, 902
v. Jackson, 390 U.S. 570 (1968) - 562, 929
v. Janis, 428 U.S. 433 (1976) - 549
v. Jenkins, 420 U.S. 358 (1975) - 573
v. Johnson, 383 U.S. 170 (1966) - 169, 170
v. Judge Peters, 5 Cr. 115 (1809) - 304, 305
v. Kauten, 134 F. 2d 703 (1943) - 453
v. Klein, 13 Wall. 128 (1872) - 226, 926
v. Kras, 409 U.S. 434 (1973) - 642
v. Lanza, 260 U.S. 377 (1922) - 571, 885
v. Laub, 385 U.S. 475 (1967) - 507
v. Lee, 106 U.S. 196 (1882) - 261, 979
v. Louisiana, 339 U.S. 699 (1950) - 134
v. Lovasco, 431 U.S. 783 (1977) - 534
v. Lovett, 328 U.S. 303 (1946) - 76, 893, 929
v. MacCollum, 426 U.S. 317 (1976) - 641
v. Macintosh, 283 U.S. 605 (1931) - 453
v. Mandujano, 425 U.S. 564 (1976) - 564
v. Mara, 410 U.S. 19 (1973) - 552
v. Martinez-Fuerte, 428 U.S. 543 (1976) - 546
v. Matlock, 415 U.S. 165 (1974) - 541
v. Midwest Oil Co., 236 U.S. 459 (1915) - 216
v. Miller, 317 U.S. 369 (1943) - 141
v. Miller, 425 U.S. 435 (1976) - 543
v. Moreland, 258 U.S. 433 (1922) - 928
v. Mosely, 238 U.S. 383 (1915) - 480, 884
v. Nice, 241 U.S. 591 (1916) - 927
v. Nichols. *See* Civil Rights Cases.
v. Nixon, 418 U.S. 683 (1974) - 55, 231-233, 733, 740, 905
v. O'Brien, 391 U.S. 367 (1968) - 412
v. One Book Entitled "Ulysses", 72 F. 2d 705 (1934) - 429
v. Orito, 413 U.S. 140 (1973) - 431
v. Ortiz, 422 U.S. 891 (1975) - 546
v. Provoo, 350 U.S. 857 (1955) - 534
v. Rabinowitz, 339 U.S. 56 (1950) - 545, 546, 894
v. Railroad Co., 17 Wall. 322 (1873) - 355
v. Reese, 92 U.S. 214 (1876) - 151, 341, 342, 478, 878, 926
v. Reynolds, 345 U.S. 1 (1953) - 231
v. Richardson, 418 U.S 167 (1974) - 292
v. Robel, 389 U.S. 258 (1967) - 508, 514, 901, 930
v. Robinson, 414 U.S. 218 (1973) - 547
v. Romano, 382 U.S. 136 (1965) - 930
v. Rumely, 345 U.S. 41 (1953) - 160
v. Russell, 13 Wall. 623 (1869) - 195
v. Ryan. *See* Civil Rights Cases.
v. Santana, 427 U.S. 38 (1976) - 544
v. Schwimmer, 279 U.S. 644 (1929) - 461
v. Scotland Neck Board of Education, 407 U.S. 484 (1972) - 600
v. Scott, 437 U.S. 82 (1978) - 573
v. Seeger, 380 U.S. 164 (1965) - 453, 457
v. Shaw, 309 U.S. 495 (1940) - 261
v. Shipp, 203 U.S. 563 (1906) - 280
v. Singleton. *See* Civil Rights Cases.
v. Smith, 286 U.S. 6 (1932) - 175
v. South-Eastern Underwriters Assn., 322 U.S. 533 (1944) - 893
v. Standard Brewery Co., 251 U.S. 210 (1920) - 195
v. Stanley. *See* Civil Rights Cases.

v. Steffens, 100 U.S. 82 (1879) - 355
v. Sullivan, 274 U.S. 259 (1927) - 114
v. Texas, 144 U.S. 621 (1892) - 880
v. Texas, 339 U.S. 707 (1950) - 134
v. Thirty-seven Photographs, 402 U.S. 363 (1971) - 431
v. Trans-Missouri Freight Assn., 167 U.S. 290 (1897) - 92
v. Twelve 200-Ft. Reels of Super 8 MM Film, 413 U.S. 123 (1973) - 431
v. United Auto Workers, 352 U.S. 567 (1957) - 420
v. United Mine Workers, 330 U.S. 258 (1947) - 276, 742, 894
v. United States Coin & Currency, 401 U.S. 715 (1971) - 930
v. Wade, 388 U.S. 218 (1967) - 552, 568, 679, 901
v. The Washington Post, 403 U.S. 713 (1971) - 245, 733, 903
v. Watson, 423 U.S. 411 (1976) - 544
v. Weber (1979) - 606, 909
v. Wheeler, 435 U.S. 313 (1978) - 571
v. Wilson, 7 Pet. 151 (1833) - 224
v. Wilson, 421 U.S. 309 (1975) - 281
v. Wilson, 420 U.S. 332 (1975) - 573
v. Wong Kim Ark, 170 U.S. 649 (1898) - 142, 143, 881
v. Wrightwood Dairy Co., 315 U.S. 110 (1942) - 102
United States ex rel. Milwaukee Social Democratic Publishing Co. v. Burleson, 255 U.S. 407 (1921) - 431
United States ex rel. Tennessee Valley Authority v. Welch, 327 U.S. 546 (1946) - 141
United Steelworkers of America v. United States, 361 U.S. 39 (1959) - 276
United Steelworkers of America v. Weber (1979) - 56, 606, 909
University of California Regents v. Bakke, 438 U.S. 265 (1978) - 56, 605, 606, 908
Untermeyer v. Anderson, 276 U.S. 440 (1928) - 928
Urciola v. Hodge, 334 U.S. 24 (1948) - 614

V

Vale v. Louisiana, 399 U.S. 30 (1969) - 547
Valentine v. Chrestensen, 316 U.S. 52 (1942) - 421, 906
Van Brocklin v. Tennessee, 117 U.S. 152 (1886) - 140
Veazie v. Moor, 14 How. 568 (1852) - 85, 90
Veazie Bank v. Fenno, 8 Wall. 533 (1869) - 112, 333, 877
Village of Arlington Heights v. Metropolitan Housing Development Corp., 429 U.S. 252 (1977) - 617, 618, 620, 907
Village of Belle Terre v. Boraas, 416 U.S. 1 (1974) - 359, 617
Virginia v. Rives, 100 U.S. 313 (1880) - 259
Virginia v. Tennessee, 149 U.S. 503 (1893) - 880
Virginia v. West Virginia, 238 U.S. 202 (1915) - 884
Virginia State Board of Pharmacy v. Virginia Citizens Consumer Council, Inc., 425 U.S. 748 (1976) - 421

W

Wabash, St. Louis & Pacific Railway Co. v. Illinois, 118 U.S. 557 (1886) - 30, 87, 879
Wade v. United States, 426 F. 2d 64 (1970) - 37
Walker v. City of Birmingham, 388 U.S. 307 (1967) - 414
Walker v. Sauvinet, 92 U.S. 90 (1876) - 530, 878
Wall v. Parrot Silver & Copper Co., 244 U.S. 407 (1917) - 288
Walz v. Tax Commission, 397 U.S. 694 (1970) - 461, 468

Ware v. Hylton, 3 Dall. 199 (1796) - 9, 16, 200, 206, 304, 305, 362, 872
Warden v. Hayden, 387 U.S. 294 (1967) - 542, 543, 901
Warth v. Seldin, 422 U.S. 490 (1975) - 615
Washington v. Davis, 426 U.S. 229 (1976) - 598, 617, 620, 906
Washington v. Dawson & Co., 264 U.S. 219 (1924) - 355, 928
Washington v. Legrant, 394 U.S. 618 (1969) - 902
Washington v. Texas, 388 U.S. 14 (1967) - 534, 901
Watkins v. United States, 354 U.S. 178 (1957) - 51, 157, 160, 161, 669, 671, 896, 897
Watson v. Jones, 13 Wall. 679 (1872) - 462
Watson v. Memphis, 373 U.S. 526 (1962) - 610
Wayman v. Southard, 10 Wheat. 1 (1825) - 283, 874
Weber v. Aetna Casualty & Surety Co., 406 U.S. 165 (1972) - 634
Weber v. Freed, 239 U.S. 325 (1915) - 100
Weber Case (1979). See Kaiser Aluminum & Chemical Corp. v. Weber; United Steelworkers of America v. Weber; United States v. Weber.
Weeds Inc. v. United States, 255 U.S. 109 (1921) - 928
Weeks v. United States, 232 U.S. 383 (1914) - 541, 542, 548, 884
Weems v. United States, 217 U.S. 349 (1910) - 575, 883
Weiman v. Updegraff, 344 U.S. 183 (1952) - 513
Weinberg v. Prichard, 410 U.S. 315 (1973) - 904
Weinberger v. Salfi, 422 U.S. 749 (1975) - 632
Weinberger v. Wiesenfeld, 420 U.S. 636 (1975) - 585, 633, 905
Wells v. Rockefeller, 394 U.S. 542 (1969) - 494-496
Welsh v. United States, 398 U.S. 333 (1970) - 453, 457
Welton v. Missouri, 91 U.S. 275 (1876) - 332, 333
Wesberry v. Sanders, 376 U.S. 1 (1964) - 52, 492, 494, 496, 899
West Coast Hotel Co. v. Parrish, 300 U.S. 379 (1937) - 44, 243, 327, 527, 889, 928
West River Bridge v. Dix, 6 How. 530 (1848) - 314
West Virginia State Board of Education v. Barnette, 319 U.S. 624 (1943) - 47, 344, 390, 411, 453, 455, 458, 459, 891, 892
Weston v. City Council of Charleston, 2 Pet. 449 (1829) - 16, 117, 874
Wheeler v. Barrera, 417 U.S. 402 (1974) - 469
White v. Regester, 412 U.S. 755 (1973) - 497
White v. Weiser, 412 U.S. 783 (1973) - 494
Whitney v. California, 274 U.S. 357 (1927) - 388, 403-406, 500, 513, 887
Whitus v. Georgia, 385 U.S. 545 (1967) - 532
Wickard v. Filburn, 317 U.S. 111 (1942) - 94, 103, 892
Wiener v. United States, 357 U.S. 349 (1958) - 215, 897
Wilcox v. McConnel, 13 Pet. 498 (1839) - 209
Wilkinson v. United States, 365 U.S. 399 (1961) - 162
Williams v. Florida, 399 U.S. 78 (1970) - 530, 531, 902
Williams v. Illinois, 399 U.S. 235 (1970) - 642
Williams v. Mississippi, 171 U.S. 213 (1898) - 34, 479, 882
Williams v. Rhodes, 393 U.S. 23 (1968) - 487
Williams v. Standard Oil Co. of Louisiana, 278 U.S. 235 (1929) - 113
Williams v. Suffolk Insurance Co., 13 Pet. 414 (1839) - 205
Willson v. Blackbird Creek Marsh Co., 2 Pet. 245 (1829) - 17, 84, 85, 316, 323, 874
Wilshire Oil Co. v. United States, 295 U.S. 100 (1935) - 288
Wilson v. Girard, 354 U.S. 524 (1957) - 733
Wilson v. New, 243 U.S. 332 (1917) - 37, 89, 94
Winona & St. Peter Railroad Co. v. Blake, 94 U.S. 180 (1877). See Granger Cases.
Winship, In re, 397 U.S. 358 (1970) - 531, 902

Wisconsin v. Pelican Insurance Co., 128 U.S. 265 (1888) - 880

Wisconsin v. Yoder, 406 U.S. 205 (1972) - 460

Witherspoon v. Illinois, 391 U.S. 510 (1968) - 576

Wolf v. Colorado, 338 U.S. 25 (1949) - 49, 539, 548, 549, 894, 898

Wolff v. Rice, 428 U.S. 465 (1976) - 549, 907

Wolff Packing Co. v. Court of Industrial Relations, 262 U.S. 522 (1923) - 527

Wolman v. Walter, 433 U.S. 229 (1977) - 469

Wong Wing v. United States, 163 U.S. 228 (1896) - 927

Wong Yang Sung v. McGrath, 339 U.S. 33 (1950) - 146

Wood v. Broom, 287 U.S. 1 (1932) - 489, 887

Wood v. Georgia, 370 U.S. 375 (1962) - 441

Woodruff v. Parham, 8 Wall. 123 (1869) - 330, 877

Woods v. Miller Co., 333 U.S. 139 (1948) - 130

Woodson v. North Carolina, 428 U.S. 280 (1976) - 907

Wooley v. Maynard, 430 U.S. 705 (1977) - 411

Worcester v. Georgia, 6 Pet. 515 (1832) - 874

Wright v. Emporia City Council, 407 U.S. 451 (1972) - 600

Wright v. United States, 302 U.S. 583 (1938) - 223

Wright v. Vinson Branch, 300 U.S. 440 (1937) - 677

Wyman v. James, 400 U.S. 309 (1971) - 551

XYZ

Yakus v. United States, 321 U.S. 414 (1944) - 129, 191, 192, 892

Yarbrough, Ex parte, 110 U.S. 651 (1884) - 342, 478, 879, 884

Yates v. United States, 356 U.S. 363 (1958) - 51, 283, 393, 504, 505, 669-671, 896

Yerger, Ex parte, 8 Wall. 85 (1869) - 272, 668, 669

Yick Wo v. Hopkins, 118 U.S. 356 (1886) - 349, 625, 879, 979

Young, Ex parte, 209 U.S. 123 (1908) - 277, 356, 362, 883

Younger v. Harris, 401 U.S. 37 (1971) - 55, 278, 279, 903

Youngstown Sheet and Tube Co. v. Sawyer (Steel Seizure Case), 343 U.S. 579 (1952) - 49, 181, 182, 185, 193, 194, 196, 244, 245, 685, 895

Zacchini v. Scripps-Howard Broadcasting Co., 433 U.S. 562 (1977) - 436

Zemel v. Rusk, 381 U.S. 1 (1965) - 507

Zorach v. Clausen, 343 U.S. 306 (1952) - 463, 894

Zurcher v. The Stanford Daily, 436 U.S. 547 (1978) - 449, 543, 908

Zwickler v. Koota, 389 U.S. 241 (1967) - 279